ALSO BY ROBERT M. PARKER, JR.

The World's Greatest Wine Estates

Parker's Wine Buyer's Guide (Editions 1–6)

Bordeaux: A Consumer's Guide to the World's Finest Wines

Wines of the Rhône Valley

Burgundy:
A Comprehensive Guide to the Producers, Appellations, and Wines

*The Complete,
Easy-to-Use
Reference
on Recent Vintages,
Prices, and Ratings
for More than 8,000
Wines from All the
Major Wine Regions*

ROBERT M. PARKER, JR.

PARKER'S WINE BUYER'S GUIDE

Seventh Edition

VOLUME 1 FRANCE

A Dorling Kindersley Book

Dorling Kindersley
LONDON, NEW YORK, MUNICH, MELBOURNE, and DELHI

Seventh edition published in Great Britain in 2008 by
Dorling Kindersley Limited
80 Strand, London WC2R 0RL

A Penguin Company

Designed by Suet Y. Chong

Manufactured in the United States of America

A complete CIP catalogue record for this book is available from the British Library.

Parker, Robert M.
   [Wine buyer's guide]
   Parker's wine buyer's guide.—7th ed. / Robert M. Parker, Jr.
      p. cm.
   Includes bibliographical references and index.
   1. Wine and winemaking.   I. Title.

ISBN-13: 978-1-4053-2639-1

Printed and bound in China by CTPS Ltd

Portions of this book were previously published in Robert Parker's bimonthly newsletter
The Wine Advocate.

Portions of the preface were originally published in the September 2008 issue of *Food & Wine.*

Discover more at **www.dk.com**

For Pat and Maia

and

To all those passionate men and women who understand the land, respect their craft, and admire the intricacies of nature, and all those artisans who coax from their soils the purest and most noble expression of agriculture—an unmanipulated, natural, honest, and expressive beverage that transcends time and place yet never fails to tantalize us, fire our passions, and profoundly touch our lives, we salute and honor you.

CONTENTS

THE WINES OF WESTERN EUROPE: PART I

FRANCE

VOLUME 2

THE WINES OF WESTERN EUROPE: PART II

ACKNOWLEDGMENTS

First and foremost, to my team of contributors, who have added their areas of expertise, which has benefited the book enormously: David Schildknecht, Antonio Galloni, Dr. Jay Miller, Mark Squires, and Neal Martin, my profound thanks for your exceptional efforts.

To the tiny staff at *The Wine Advocate,* who were heavily involved in gathering information and putting it into some sort of sensible arrangement, I owe a great deal of thanks. Despite Joan Passman's officially retiring at the end of 2006, her heartfelt loyalty and concern for my mental well-being has her still working several days a week and has helped expedite the book's completion. Her full-time replacement, Annette Piatek, did as much as anybody, and I can't thank her enough for her hardworking and conscientious efforts in gathering information, sorting through it, and trying to make some sort of sense of everything all of us have written. She was assisted very capably by the other *Wine Advocate* staffer, Betsy Sobolewski.

At the professional publishing level, my editor, Amanda Murray, deserves an enormous amount of credit for making sense of our verbose commentary, cleaning it up, and assisting all of us in making certain ideas clearer. In short, her enormous efforts have made the book significantly better, and we all deeply appreciate it. I would also like to thank the rest of the Simon & Schuster crew, including Kate Ankofski, Anne Cherry, Suet Chong, Linda Dingler, Nancy Inglis, and John Wahler.

Every author requires plenty of psychological support, and I suspect I receive more than most. The love of my life, my beautiful wife, Patricia, always provides wisdom and counsel, and is an encouraging voice when things seem gloomiest. I must not forget my wonderful daughter, Maia. Now that she is in college, I actually see less of her these days than of my two furry companions, Buddy, a three-year-old English bulldog, and Hoover, his favorite friend (and mine too, for that matter), who at ten years old still has remarkable vigor and youthfulness.

I also want to acknowledge a longtime friend, bon vivant, and exceptionally wise man by the name of Dr. Park B. Smith, a spiritual elder brother whose love of wine and laserlike thinking have provided enormous wisdom to me over many years.

Finally, to the following friends, supporters, and advisers, a heartfelt "million thanks"—
all of you have taught me valuable lessons about wine and, more important, about life: Jim
Arseneault, Anthony Barton, Ruth Bassin and the late Bruce and Addy Bassin, Hervé Ber-
laud, Bill Blatch, Thomas B. Böhrer, Barry Bondroff, Daniel Boulud, Rowena and Mark
Braunstein, Christopher Cannan, Dick Carretta, Jean-Michel Cazes, Corinne Cesano, Jean-
Marie Chadronnier, M. and Mme Jean-Louis Charmolue, Charles Chevalier, Bob Cline, Jef-
frey Davies, Hubert de Boüard, Jean and Annie Delmas, Jean-Hubert Delon and the late
Michel Delon, Dr. Albert H. Dudley III, Barbara Edelman, Fédéric Engérer, Michael Etzel,
Paul Evans, Terry Faughey, the legendary Fitzcarraldo—my emotional and quasi-fictional
soulmate—Joel Fleischman, Mme Capbern Gasqueton, Dan Green, Josué Harari, Alexandra
Harding, Dr. David Hutcheon, Barbara G. and Steve R. R. Jacoby, Joanne and Joe James,
Jean-Paul Jauffret, Daniel Johnnes; Nathaniel, Archie, and Denis Johnston; Ed Jonna, Elaine
and Manfred Krankl, Robert Lescher, Bernard Magrez, Adam Montefiore of Carmel Winery, Patrick Maroteaux, Pat and Victor Hugo Morgenroth; Christian, Jean-François, and the
late Jean-Pierre Moueix; Bernard Nicolas, Jill Norman, Les Oenarchs (Bordeaux), Les Oenarchs (Baltimore), François Pinault, Frank Polk, Paul Pontallier, Bruno Prats, Jean-Guillaume
Prats, Judy Pruce, Dr. Alain Raynaud, Martha Reddington, Dominique Renard, Michel
Richard, Alan Richman, Dany and Michel Rolland; Pierre Rovani and his father, Yves Rovani; Robert Roy, Carlo Russo, Ed Sands, Erik Samazeuilh, Bob Schindler, Ernie Singer, El-
liott Staren, Daniel Tastet-Lawton, Lettie Teague, Alain Vauthier, the late Steven Verlin,
Peter Vezan, Robert Vifian, Sonia Vogel, Jeanyee Wong, and Gérard Yvernault.

THE LAST THIRTY YEARS

FROM "MEDIEVAL TIMES" TO THE GOLDEN AGE OF WINE

Looking back 30 years, it's nearly impossible to comprehend how provincial the wine world was circa 1978, the year I launched my journal, *The Wine Advocate*. With virtually no wine-by-the-glass programs in restaurants, the U.S. was not yet importing a number of the wines recognized as the greatest of their countries, including Vega Sicilia in Spain and Penfolds Grange in Australia. There were no selections from New Zealand, virtually nothing from Australia, and only a handful of Riojas from Spain. Italy was represented largely by Chiantis, a few generic wines from the north, and an ocean of industrial jug wine from Bardolino and Valpolicello. California was largely a nonentity: none of the so-called cult wines existed, and the state's best wines rarely received any press. Nor were there any stirrings of the Golden State's revolution in quality that was about to be unleashed. Even La Belle France, the reference point for so many of the world's greatest wines, was a perennial underachiever: only a handful of Bordeaux's most famous classified growths—those châteaux recognized more than 160 years ago as making the best wines in Bordeaux—actually produced wines that were palatable. Appellations renowned today, such as Pomerol and St.-Émilion, were considered the refuge of ignorant peasants, and the quality of their wines usually reflected these sentiments. South America was another nonfactor, Malbec was an unknown grape, and Argentina was equally unknown as a wine-producing region. Next door, the proliferation of value wines from Chile was a decade away.

Yet dramatic changes were about to begin. In the U.S., which has become the largest fine-wine market in the world with the Far East nipping at our heels, the post–World War II baby boomers were coming of age and earning decent money. Many had traveled abroad, developing the more refined lifestyle of good wine and cuisine they had witnessed in western Europe.

In trying to make sense of everything that has happened in the last three decades, I have broken down these years into what I consider the most significant developments impacting the higher quality and exceptional diversity of the wines we enjoy today—not so much in order of importance but rather in the chronological order these events occurred.

PROFESSIONAL OENOLOGISTS AND WINEMAKING CONSULTANTS

Bordeaux is irrefutably the epicenter for high wine quality and wine education. Setting the precedent for great professors of oenology was the late Professor Émile Peynaud, who reigned over Bordeaux throughout the 1950s, '60s, and '70s. Peynaud was ahead of his time, advocating later harvests to capture fully ripened fruit, labor-intensive, radical viticulture (technical stuff like shoot positioning, leaf pulling, and crop thinning), and smaller crop yields. His strong belief in picking ripe fruit and selecting only the best lots for the top wines would eventually have its day, but not until long after he had retired. Peynaud's most influential successor was one of his students, Michel Rolland, born in the backwaters of Pomerol. Rolland, arguably the person who has had the most profound effect on wine quality, has become the world's leading wine consultant. Virtually every estate he has touched has resulted in finer wines. A believer in naturally low yields, the harvest of ripe fruit, and a draconian selection process to put the very best product together as a blend, Rolland has literally reshaped modern winemaking. The wines produced under his direction are more concentrated than in the past, made from cleaner, riper fruit, and have the tannin, structure, and intrinsic material to drink well younger but last longer than the legends of the past. With his influence spreading to a young group of winemaking consultants such as Stéphane Derenoncourt, Rolland shares the spotlight increasingly with other great oenologists of Bordeaux such as Denis Dubourdieu.

While Rolland has fixed his famous name to some extraordinary projects in the New World, particularly in California, the appearance of brilliant winemaking consultants in the Golden State has also resulted in higher-quality wines. The first, and still among the greatest of all, was Helen Turley, who essentially put cult wines on the map with the work she did at wineries such as Pahlmeyer Winery, Bryant Family Vineyard, Colgin Cellars, and Blankiet Estate. Her enormous influence has fostered even more talented consultants emerging from California: Mark Aubert (Aubert; Bryant Family Vineyard), Paul Hobbs (Paul Hobbs Winery; Viña Cobos, Argentina), Bob Foley (Robert Foley Vineyards; formerly of Pride Mountain, Switchback Ridge, Corté Riva Vineyards), Andy Erickson (Screaming Eagle), Martha McClellan (Levy & McClellan; Sloan; Blankiet Estate), Mark Herold (Merus; Hestan Vineyards; Kaymen; Kobalt Wines), Heidi Barrett (La Sirena), Thomas Brown (Maybach Family Vineyards; Schrader Cellars; formerly at Turley Wine Cellars), and Philippe Melka (Melka Wines; Gemstone Vineyard; Hundred Acre; Lail Vineyards; Marston Family Vineyard; Pre-Vail; Roy Estate; Seavey Vineyard; Vineyard 29; et al) are some of the finest, sharing in common the fervent beliefs that 1) 90% of the quality emerges from a vineyard's *terroir* and site, 2) vineyards have to be meticulously managed and respected, 3) no great wines can be produced from less than fully ripened fruit, 4) grapes have to be handled gently, and 5) every act in both the vineyard and winery has to be aimed at producing the unmanipulated, uncompromising essence of a vineyard, a varietal, and a vintage.

The superstar consultant-oenologist has also encouraged a group of serious viticultural managers to take over a vineyard and manage it impeccably for their clients. The best of these is the guru for the great vineyards of northern California, David Abreu, and in California's Central Coast region, Jeff Newton. When a top vineyard manager who knows how to control yields, manage crop yields, prune, and—in California—when and how much to irrigate, combines with uncompromising winemaking, the formula is struck for compelling world-class wines.

The most fallacious argument about the globe-trotting winemaking fashionistas implies that their wines all taste the same. Nothing could be further from the truth. Each has a unique philosophy and different means to an end, but essentially they all share the basics: a healthy respect for the vineyard, a minimalist approach in the winery (unless something goes wrong, of course), and the belief that what is in the bottle should reflect the uncompromised, unmanipulated purity of the fruit that was harvested.

THE WINE PRESS AND CRITIC

Wine writers have been around nearly as long as wine, but in general, until the last three decades, writing was uncritical and emphasized wine as a romantic as well as historic beverage. Viable criticism or comparative tastings offered as guidelines to the wine buyer were eschewed for fear of offending the wine trade, which most writers depended on to survive. In 1978, I was certainly not the first to launch a private journal that would accept no advertising; several were already in existence, most notably Robert Finigan's *Private Guide to Wine* and the *Underground Wine Newsletter*. In addition, 30 years ago, *The Wine Spectator* was a superficial tabloid newspaper before Marvin Shankin acquired and transformed it into a worldwide brand and powerhouse. Both Finigan's newsletter and the *Underground Wine Journal* ceased publication long ago, but there is no question they have been replaced by the work of hundreds, if not thousands, of wine writers throughout the world.

This is no more apparent than when tasting the newest vintage of Bordeaux, which is traditionally sold as wine futures two years before the wines are bottled. When I first started going to Bordeaux as a professional taster in 1979, there were only a handful of writers who would come in the spring to taste the wines, mostly now deceased or retired British writers, such as the late Edmund Penning-Rowsell and Harry Waugh, and several still alive, most notably David Peppercorn and his wife, Serena Sutcliffe. By 1989, the number of wine writers descending on Bordeaux to taste the newest vintage had grown to 500 or more. Today, well over 2,000 writers, critics, and journalists from all parts of the world—Europe, China, Japan, Scandinavia, the U.S., of course, South America, and Central America—descend on this hallowed region. Just name any country where a wine shop exists, and there will be some member of the wine press from that region.

Of course, this has all led to an extraordinary amount of wine information available to the consumer, which cuts both ways, good and bad. The best critics are serious about their responsibilities and accountable to their readers. They put in the work, time, and discipline required for tasting professionally, and offer unbiased as well as comprehensive reports. The rest are simply there for a free ride—free wine samples, free travel, free lodging—and the resultant writing is, as one might expect, unreliable. Nevertheless, wine has become so pervasive in so many cultures and the price of top wines so expensive that, combined with the rarity of many top wines, consumers do need respectable sources of information. As a result the strategic importance of an independent wine press continues to have a growing and dramatic role. I see no softening or dilution of that influence, even with the advent of many free Internet wine blogs, which usually do little more than raise the level of useless white noise to a deafening and confusing level of nonsense.

THE CULINARY REVOLUTION

There has undeniably been a revolution in wine quality that has touched every part of the world where grapes can grow in temperate climates. This has coincided with an extraordinary revolution in professional kitchens, most notably in the U.S., but also in such far-flung places as New Zealand, Australia, and Spain. While France and Italy clearly dominated culinary circles 30 years ago, today the finest restaurants are located in such unlikely places as Las

Vegas, Nevada, Tokyo, Japan, and San Sebastian, Spain. The demand for high-quality, creative, and naturally farmed organic food has been accompanied by an insatiable thirst for higher-quality, more diverse wine.

When I first started, there may have been five or six top-notch restaurants in Washington, D.C. and virtually none in my hometown of Baltimore. Today Washington, D.C., must have 30 to 40 top eating establishments, with more opening every year. Even blue-collar Baltimore has awakened, so that now there are at least a dozen. New York City, one of the world's meccas for fine dining, has become equaled in this country—surreally, I might add—only by Las Vegas, Nevada. (Who could have predicted that?) Yet, most important, the wine consumer has enthusiastically supported the culinary revolution and, in turn, served as a catalyst for a dizzying array of wines.

DIVERSITY IN WINE

The largest myth in the wine world, constructed on half truths, inaccurate observations, and shrewd journalistic manipulation, purports that the wine market has become so globalized that international companies are producing monochromatic wines from a limited number of grape varieties, resulting in bland, standardized wine quality and causing all wines to taste the same. This is appallingly untrue. Moreover, it cannot be backed by any specific evidence and generally makes headlines without any serious discussion.

Truth be known, wine quality is not only significantly superior to what it was a mere 10 years ago—much less 30—but there is substantial evidence that the diversity of wine styles is many times greater than it was 10 or 20 years ago. When I started, and even for many years after, it was impossible to find wine from some of Italy's indigenous varieties, such as Aglianico, Nero d'Avola, or Piedirosso. Today many of these wonderful grapes produce world-class wines, and the areas of Italy that gave birth to them are enjoying a renaissance. One sees the same thing in Spain, with grapes such as Tempranillo, Mourvèdre, Grenache (Garnacha), Carignan (Cariñena), and even a long-forgotten grape called Mencía.

Around the world regions exist that were virtually unknown a decade back and were not even in a wine atlas when I started. Japan's Koshu, a grape planted more than 1,000 years ago near Mt. Fuji, is making a dramatic comeback. In Italy alone, the number of wines emerging from the south has skyrocketed, whether from Sicily, Corsica, or the boot of Italy. Wines from Campania, Aglianico del Vulture, Molise, Salice Salentino, and Primitivo di Manduria are commonly encountered at top wine shops. In Spain, sensational wines are emerging now from long-forgotten areas such as Priorato, Toro, Jumilla, Bierzo, Navarra, Sotomano, and Catalunya. There wasn't a wine to be found from any of these areas 30 or even 15 years ago, yet today any self-respecting importer of Spanish or Italian wine would be embarrassed not to have a stylistically diverse selection from these emerging areas.

In France, the ascendancy of the southern Rhône, the explosion of quality in Languedoc-Roussillon, and even the very conservative, traditional Bordeaux, have hundreds of young men and women producing splendid wine from unheralded vineyards, forgotten appellations, and reborn sites. Who had heard of Fronsac or the Côtes du Castillon a decade ago? Today both of these "satellites" of Bordeaux are esteemed for their top-quality and reasonably priced wines. I could go on and discuss the extraordinary boutique wines coming from artisanal producers in Australia, New Zealand, and, more recently, eastern Europe. There are more styles of wine, more wines from indigenous varieties, and more distinctive and original wines from unknown viticultural areas than have ever previously existed in the world, with most of this development occurring in the last 10 to 15 years.

Take the U.S., for example. Could anyone have predicted the explosive quality and diversity of Pinot Noirs from Oregon, California's Russian River, the Sonoma Coast, or Santa Rita Hills northwest of Santa Barbara? The dramatic increase in quality here has been matched by similar trends in Washington State, Oregon, and New York. The overwhelming evidence is that globalization, or standardization, is largely a fabricated falsehood with no credible supporting evidence. It does remain appealing to reactionary romantics and their ilk who fear any change, but it is unlikely ever to become an accepted truism given the diversity and quality of wines today.

THE SOFT TOUCH PHILOSOPHY OF WINEMAKING

The revolution in wine quality has its epicenter in both the vineyard and the wine cellar. Back in the 1960s, progressive changes occurred rather slowly, and were derailed by the international oil crisis and economic slump of the '70s. But they hit full gear in the mid- to late '80s, and are now in evidence in every conscientious wine cellar in the world.

When I first started making vineyard visits professionally, it was hard to find satisfactory sanitation in wineries and modern, temperature-controlled wood, steel, or cement fermentors. Many cellars were incredibly musty, with aromas of locker room, stale mushroom, and rotting garbage intertwined with the smell of wine. The famed first growths of Haut-Brion and Latour were two of the first estates to invest in temperature-controlled stainless steel fermentors, allowing them to pick the fruit later, ferment it under rigid temperature control, and avoid the problems that plagued many ripe vintages of the past.

Today virtually every serious estate in the world has some degree of temperature control, and the sanitary conditions under which the wines are made are far more meticulous. This alone has been a remarkable technological advancement in wine quality, resulting in significantly better wines with fewer defects, sweeter fruit, riper tannins, and generally lower acidity. In addition, most serious estates now do an extraordinary triage as the grapes come into the cellar. The so-called sorting table, which was originally used just as a quick system of transportation to the fermentation tanks or vats, is now often manned by as many as 50 to 60 people sorting out leaves and rotten, unripe, or blemished fruit. It is not surprising that the producers who perform the most severe triage at the sorting tables often produce the finest wines. (And keep in mind, most of these producers have also done a very rigorous triage in the vineyard before the grapes even get to the winery.)

Along with all the investments, the general philosophy of vinifying wine has been to treat it ever more gently, avoiding any kind of bruising. Fashionable methods came from traditional winemaking in Burgundy and include prefermentation cold soaks designed to intensify the aromatic character of the wines, cooler, more gentle macerations, and moving the wine without pumping. All have been designed to produce cleaner, fresher, more complex wines.

This is a far cry from the seat-of-your-pants fermentations of the past that were often troubled, causing the development of unwanted organisms and volatile components. Of course, one can read articles about technology gone amok and the rampant use of reverse osmosis machines to remove alcohol or water, and the same thing with entropy, which is the removal of water under a vacuum system to concentrate the grape must. Many top estates do have such machines, but their application is often limited to rainy years or to small component parts as opposed to the entire crop. It is true that the danger of using a concentration machine is that in concentrating the wine, you also concentrate the wine's defects. Such practices, which need to be approached with caution and by a skilled operator, can improve the wine, and, when practiced carefully, it is virtually impossible to tell that these methods have ever been utilized. The doom-and-gloom skeptics, who first pointed the finger at such high-tech machines when employed at Léoville–Las Cases in the mid-1980s, are hard pressed to find out if and how they have damaged the wine in any way, since virtually every vintage of Las Cases made with reverse osmosis is still a young wine 20 years after the fact.

The soft approach to winemaking, initiated by Peynaud and another of his protégés, Dr. Pascal Ribeau-Guyon, shortened the time wines spent in barrel, preserving the integrity of the fruit and vintage character. Their belief was that the wines should age in the bottle rather than in the barrel, from which they often emerge not only aged but tired. The shortening of the barrel-aging period, the improved sanitation, and the fact that the wine produced from the fruit is so much purer and nuanced, has given us wines far greater in character, *terroir* characteristics, and vintage personality.

Likewise, the French process of racking the wine, a traditional practice of brutally moving wines from one barrel to the next, has been curtailed dramatically. Producers have become increasingly concerned with accelerating development and desiccating the wine's fruit with this process. Today, top wines are frequently moved by gravity or under a blanket of neutral gases. The result is far younger-tasting, more natural wines than in the past.

Finally, the decision at bottling to move away from an eviscerating and industrial-styled fining and filtration has only helped to keep aromatics, texture, and fruit concentration in the wine. This is not a black-and-white issue, and cloudy wines should certainly be filtered, but by and large, there has been a dramatic lessening of the fining and filtration process, producing wines with increased *terroir* character in addition to intensified flavors, texture, and aromatics.

IMPROVED VINEYARD HEALTH

With the soft winemaking approach resulting in more texture, nuance, and complexity, many of the finest producers have recognized that the vineyard does not respond well when overfertilized. More and more vineyards have dramatically improved their health through the so-called green movement, moving toward quasi-organic farming, out-and-out organic framing, or to the most extreme style, biodynamic farming.

Certainly, no one should argue that organic or biodynamic wines are intrinsically superior to those that are not. But it is a healthy movement and an accelerating one, thanks to increasing acceptance of techniques that do not rely on chemicals. When combined with the improved natural health of the vineyards today compared to 30 years ago, as well as the increased knowledge of viticulture, vinification, and the more natural winemaking styles of today, there is no question that the result is better fruit and, as a consequence, better wines.

THE DRINK OF CHOICE

I never thought I would see the day when wine would outpoll beer as the favorite beverage of Americans. First and foremost, there was once an overbearing, snobbish approach to wine consumption that trickled down primarily from European wine elitists. However, cigarettes have been replaced by glasses of red wine in virtually all of Hollywood's blockbuster movies, and reservatrol, that wonderful component found in red wine's antioxidant tannin, is getting more and more play in medical circles as a valuable asset for good health. Though I'm no doctor, just the idea of drinking wine over a leisurely meal has a positive effect by virtue of the fact that it is elegant, relaxing, and fun.

WORLDWIDE INTEREST AND STRATOSPHERIC PRICES

For the world's finest wines, the increased popularity has put a strain on pricing. What many consumers fail to recognize is that the top vineyards are limited in size, both by geography and the laws of a particular country. Production, in most cases, will vary up or down depending on what Mother Nature provides. The actual acreage under vine in any famous appellation for most famous estates is fixed, and their production set without varying dramatically. Take, for example, the famed first-growth estate in Bordeaux, Château Latour. In a high-quality year, when the crop size is small, they are lucky to produce 10,000 cases of Latour. Even in an abundant year, rarely do they exceed 12,000 to 13,000 cases, no different than the production of Latour 50 or 100 years ago. And it won't be any different 100 years from now.

When I first started writing about wine, the principal markets for Latour were a handful of luxury hotels and restaurants in western Europe, England, and the U.S. Today the marketplace is all of Europe, wealthy parts of South and Central America, and, of course, the emerging giants in the fine-wine market: China, Japan, Korea, and Southeast Asia. It doesn't take much increased demand to recognize that the allocations for a property that only produces 10,000 to 13,000 cases of wine will be sorely strained. This applies even more so to smaller estates in Burgundy or the Rhône Valley as well as tiny boutique operations in the New World. The supply is limited, yet the demand continues to grow, seemingly resistant to economic downturns.

In short, there is simply too much discretionary wealth in the world, and too much demand for the world's finest wines, to cause prices for the finest and most prestigious wines to drop. In 1995, I predicted that first-growth Bordeaux would hit $10,000 per case in ten years; well, they have done that and then some, and in a much shorter period. This trend will only continue.

Unfortunately, many of these wines will become nothing more than museum pieces to be talked about and traded but rarely drunk. This is a sad aspect of the otherwise extraordinary enthusiasm that has taken place throughout the civilized world.

CONCLUSION

Three decades ago, I never would have imagined the enormous progress in wine quality, nor could I have anticipated the staggering number of fine wines from such untraditional areas as South America, Australia, southern France, southern Italy, and, of course, California, Oregon, and Washington State.

Thirty years have passed all too quickly, but there is no question that I have been fortunate. In my personal quest for the vinous equivalent of the Holy Grail, I have had the opportunity to see, taste, and consume a dramatically superior array of wines, with greater personality, expression, and individuality in all price ranges than has ever existed in the past. After 30 years, my glass is not only half full, it runneth over.

—ROBERT PARKER

HOW TO USE THIS GUIDE

This book is both an educational manual and a buying guide; it is not an encyclopedic listing of wine producers and growers. It is intended to make you a more formidable, more confident wine buyer by providing you with sufficient insider's information to permit the wisest possible choice when you make a wine-buying decision. The finest producers as well as the best known (not necessarily a guarantee of quality) from the world's greatest viticultural regions are evaluated, as well as many of the current and upcoming releases available in the marketplace. If readers cannot find a specific vintage of a highly regarded wine, they still have at their fingertips a wealth of information and evaluations concerning the best producers for each viticultural area. Readers should be confident in knowing that they will rarely make a mistake (unless, of course, the vintage is absolutely dreadful) with a producer rated "outstanding" or "excellent" in this buyer's guide. These producers are the finest and most consistent in the world. Taste is obviously subjective, but we have done our best to provide an impartial and comprehensive consumer's guide, whose heart, soul, and value are the evaluations (star ratings) of the world's finest producers.

Note: Readers should recognize that I am fully responsible for the chapters on Bordeaux, Provence, the Rhône Valley, and California. My colleagues, who work full-time for me, are responsible for the following chapters: David Schildknecht covers Alsace, Austria, Burgundy, Central Europe, Champagne, East of the West Coast, France's Southwest, Germany, the Jura and Savoie, the Languedoc and Roussillon, and the Loire Valley. Dr. Jay Miller is responsible for Argentina, Australia, Chile, Oregon, Spain, Washington State, and the section on Port. Antonio Galloni has written all the chapters on Italy; Mark Squires covers Israel and Portugal; and my British counterpart, Neal Martin, is responsible for the chapters on New Zealand and South Africa.

ORGANIZATION

Each section on a specific viticultural region covered in this manual is generally organized as follows:

1. An overview of the viticultural region
2. A buying strategy
3. A summary of the quality of recent vintages for the area
4. A quick-reference list to that area's best producers/growers
5. For upcoming, current, and very recent releases, a specific numerical rating and antici-pated maturity curve have been provided. We have added an estimated price range for a 750-ml bottle of wine. As most American consumers know, with our 50 states and Byzan-tine system of local liquor laws, prices vary dramatically from state to state, city to city, and even from wine shop to wine shop. The new *Parker's Wine Buyer's Guide* essentially focuses on wines that are available in the marketplace now as well as those coming into the market over the next 24 months. The specific tasting commentaries, which I included in previous editions, have gotten so comprehensive, we would have had to sacrifice coverage of some areas in order to incorporate them. We decided that the tasting notes would be eliminated since, in the introductory section, the general profiles of the wines from that area are amply covered.

VITICULTURAL AREAS COVERED

This guide cannot cover every viticultural area in the world, but the world's most significant areas are well represented. In western Europe, France, Italy, Germany, Austria, Spain, and Portugal are profiled in detail. In North America, California continues to receive significant coverage, reflecting its dominance in the marketplace, but Washington State and Oregon have far greater coverage than they have had in the past. Also from the New World, so to speak, the increased importance of the wines of Australia, New Zealand, Argentina, Chile, and, to a lesser extent, South Africa, have dictated dramatically more coverage for those re-gions than in previous editions.

RATING THE PRODUCERS AND GROWERS

Who's who in the world of wine becomes readily apparent after years of tasting the wines, visiting the vineyards, and touring the wine cellars of the world's producers and growers. Great producers are, unfortunately, still quite rare, but certainly more growers and producers today are making better wine, with better technology and more knowledge. Just before the producer profiles and wine ratings that come at the end of each section are lists that rate the best producers on a five-star system: five stars and an "outstanding" to producers deemed to be the very best; four stars to producers who are "excellent," three stars to "good" producers, and two stars to producers rated "average." Since the aim of this book is to provide you with the names of the very best producers, its overall content is dominated by the top producers rather than the less successful ones.

Those few growers/producers who have received five-star ratings are those who make the world's finest wines, and they have been selected for this rating for two reasons: first, because they make the greatest wine of their particular viticultural region, and second, because they are remarkably consistent and reliable even in mediocre and poor vintages. Ratings, whether numerical ratings of individual wines or classifications of growers, are always likely to create controversy among not only the growers but wine tasters themselves. But if done impartially, with a global viewpoint and firsthand, on-the-premises (*sur place*) knowledge of the wines, the producers, and the type and quality of the winemaking, such ratings can be reliable and powerfully informative. The important thing for readers to remember is that those growers/ producers who received either a four-star or five-star rating are producers worth searching out; I suspect few consumers will ever be disappointed with one of their wines. The three-star growers/producers are less consistent but can be expected to make average to above-average wines in the very good to excellent vintages. Their weaknesses can be either from the fact that their vineyards are not as strategically placed, or because for financial or other reasons they are unable to make the severe selections necessary for the finest-quality wine.

The rating of the growers/producers of the world's major viticultural regions is perhaps the most important point of this book. Years of wine tasting have taught me many things, but the more one tastes and assimilates the knowledge of the world's regions, the more one begins to isolate the handful of truly world-class growers and producers who seem to rise above the crowd in great as well as mediocre vintages. I always admonish consumers against blind faith in one grower or producer, or in one specific vintage. But the producers and growers rated "outstanding" and "excellent" are as close to a guarantee of high quality as you are likely to find.

VINTAGE SUMMARIES

Although wine advertisements proclaiming "a great vintage" abound, I have never known more than several viticultural areas of the world to have a great vintage in the same year. The chances of a uniformly great vintage are extremely remote, simply because of significantly different microclimates, soils, and so on in every wine-producing region. It is easy to fall into the trap of thinking that because Bordeaux had great vintages in 1982, 1990, and 2000, every place else in Europe did, too. Certainly, in both 1982 and 2000, nothing could be further from the truth. Nevertheless, a Bordeaux vintage's reputation unfortunately seems to dictate what the world thinks about many other wine-producing areas. This obviously creates many problems, since in poor Bordeaux vintages the Rhône or Alsace or Champagne could have an excellent year, and in great Bordeaux vintages those same areas could have bad years because of poor climate conditions. For California, many casual observers seem to think every year is a top year, and this image is, of course, promoted by that state's publicity-conscious Wine Institute. It may be true that California rarely has a disastrous vintage, but tasting certainly proves that 1988, 1989, and 1998 are different in style and more irregular in quality than 1994 or 1995, or for that matter, more recent years such as 2004 or 2005. Yet it is true that no other viticultural area in the world has enjoyed as many consecutive great vintages as California since 1990. With the exception of 1998, California has had a bevy of very good to terrific years. In this guide, there are vintage summaries for each viticultural area because the vintages are so very different in both quantity and quality. Never make the mistake of assuming that one particular year is great everywhere or poor everywhere. For example, 2005 was an absolutely sensational vintage in California for varietals such as Cabernet Sauvignon, Chardonnay, Pinot Noir, Syrah, and Sauvignon Blanc, but it was a terrible year for Zinfandel.

TASTING NOTES AND RATINGS

When possible, most of my tastings are done under peer-group, single-blind conditions; in other words, the same types of wines are tasted against each other, and the producers' names are not known. The ratings reflect an independent, critical look at the wines. Neither price nor the reputation of the grower/producer affects the rating in any manner. I spend three months of every year tasting in vineyards. During the other nine months of the year, I devote six- and sometimes seven-day workweeks to tasting and writing. I do not participate in wine judgings or trade tastings for many reasons, but principal among these are: 1) I prefer to taste from an entire bottle of wine; 2) I find it essential to have professional tasting glasses, properly sized and cleaned; 3) the temperatures of the wines must be correct; and 4) I prefer to determine the allocation of time for the number of wines I will critique.

The numerical ratings are a guide to what I think of the wine vis-à-vis its peer group: Wines rated above 85 are good to excellent, and any wine rated 90 or above will be outstanding for its particular type. While some would suggest that scoring is not well suited to a beverage that has been romantically extolled for centuries, wine is no different from any other consumer product. There are specific standards of quality that full-time wine professionals recognize, and there are benchmark wines against which all others can be judged. I know of no one with three or four different glasses of wine in front of him or her, regardless of how good or bad the wines might be, who cannot say, "I prefer this one to that one." Scoring wines is simply taking a professional's opinion and applying a numerical system to it on a consistent basis. Moreover, scoring permits rapid communication of information to expert and novice alike.

The score given for a specific wine reflects the quality of the wine at its best. I often tell people that evaluating a wine and assigning a score to a beverage that will change and evolve for up to a decade or more is analogous to taking a photograph of a marathon runner. Much can be ascertained, but, as with a moving object, the wine will evolve and change. I try to retaste wines from obviously badly corked or defective bottles, since a wine from a single bad bottle does not indicate an entirely spoiled batch. If retasting is not possible, I will reserve judgment. Many of the wines reviewed have been tasted several times, and the score represents a cumulative average of the wine's performance in tastings to date.

Here, then, is a general guide to interpreting my numerical rating system:

90–100 Equivalent to an A and given for an outstanding or special effort. Wines in this category are the very best produced for their type. Though there is a big difference between a 90 and a 99, both are top marks. Few wines actually make it into this top category, simply because there are not that many truly profound wines.

80–89 Equivalent to a B, and such a wine, particularly in the 85–89 range, is very good. Many of the wines that fall into this range are often great values as well. I have many of these wines in my personal cellar.

70–79 Represents a C, or an average mark, but obviously 79 is a much more desirable rating than 70. Wines that receive scores of 75–79 are generally pleasant, straightforward wines that lack complexity, character, or depth. If inexpensive, they may be ideal for uncritical quaffing.

Below 70 A score of D or F, depending on where you went to school, is a sign of an unbalanced, flawed, or terribly dull or diluted wine that is of little interest to the discriminating consumer.

Note: A point score with spreads signifies an evaluation made before the wine was bottled.

My scoring system starts with a potential of 50 points. The wine's general color and appearance can earn up to 5 points. Since most wines today are well made, thanks to modern technology and the increased use of professional oenologists, most tend to receive at least 4, and often 5, points. Aroma and bouquet can earn up to 15 points, depending on the intensity level and dimension of the aroma and bouquet, as well as the wine's cleanliness. The flavor and finish can earn up to 20 points, and again, intensity of flavor, balance, cleanliness, and depth and length on the palate are all important considerations. Finally, the overall quality level or potential for further evolution and improvement—aging—can earn up to 10 points.

Scores are important for the reader to gauge a professional critic's overall qualitative placement of a wine among its peers. However, it is also vital to consider the description of the wine's style, personality, and potential. No scoring system is perfect, but a system that provides for flexibility in scores, if applied by the same experienced taster without prejudice, can quantify levels of wine quality and can be a responsible, reliable, uncensored, and highly informative account that provides the reader with one professional's judgment. However, there can never be any substitute for your own palate nor any better education than tasting the wine yourself.

QUOTED PRICES

For a number of reasons, no one suggested retail price for a particular wine is valid through-out the country. Take Bordeaux as an example. Bordeaux is often sold as "wine futures" two full years before the wine is bottled and shipped to America. This opening or base price can often be the lowest price one will encounter for a Bordeaux, particularly if there is a great demand for the wines because the vintage is reputed to be excellent or outstanding. As for other imported wines, prices will always vary for Bordeaux according to the quality of the vintage, the exchange rate of the dollar against foreign currencies, and the time of purchase by the retailer, wholesaler, or importer—was the wine purchased at a low futures price in the spring following the vintage, or when it had peaked in price and was very expensive?

Another consideration in pricing is that in many states wine retailers can directly import the wines they sell and can thereby bypass middlemen, such as wholesalers, who usually tack on their own 25% markup. The bottom line in all of this is that in any given vintage for Bordeaux, or for any imported wine, there is no standard suggested retail price. Prices can differ by as much as 50% for the same wine in the same city. However, in cities where there is tremendous competition among wine shops, the markup for wines can be as low as 10% or even 5%, significantly less than the normal 50% to 55% markup for full retail price in cities where there is little competition. I always recommend that consumers pay close attention to the wine shop advertisements in major newspapers and wine publications. For example, *The New York Times* Living Section and *The Wine Spectator* are filled with wine advertisements that are a barometer for the market price of a given wine. Readers should remember, however, that prices differ considerably, not only within the same state but within the same city. The approximate price range reflects the suggested retail price that includes a 40% to 60% markup by the retailer in most major metropolitan areas. Therefore, the price may be higher in many states in the Midwest and in other less-populated areas, where there is little competition among wine merchants. In major competitive marketplaces where there are frequent discount wars, such as Washington, D.C., New York, San Francisco, Boston, Los Angeles, Chicago, and Dallas, prices are often lower. The key for you as a reader and consumer is to follow the advertisements in a major newspaper and to shop around. Most major wine retailers feature sales in the fall and spring; summer is the slow season and generally the most expensive time to buy wine.

THE ROLE OF A WINE CRITIC

"A man must serve his time to every trade save censure—critics all are ready made." Thus wrote Lord Byron. It has been said often enough that anyone with a pen, notebook, and a few bottles of wine can become a wine critic. And that is exactly the way I started when, in late summer 1978, I sent out a complimentary issue of what was then called the *Baltimore/ Washington Wine Advocate*.

There were two principal forces that shaped my view of a wine critic's responsibilities. I was then, and remain today, significantly influenced by the independent philosophy of consumer advocate Ralph Nader. Moreover, I was marked by the indelible impression left by my law school professors, who in the post-Watergate era pounded into their students' heads a broad definition of conflict of interest. These two forces have governed the purpose and soul of *The Wine Advocate* and of my books.

In short, the role of the critic is to render judgments that are reliable. They should be based on extensive experience and on a trained sensibility for whatever is being reviewed. In practical terms, this means the critic should be blessed with the following attributes:

Independence It is imperative for a wine critic to pay his own way. Gratuitous hospitality in the form of airline tickets, hotel rooms, guest houses, etc., should never be accepted either abroad or in this country. And what about wine samples? I purchase more than 75% of the wines I taste, and though I have never requested samples, I do not feel it is unethical to accept unsolicited samples that are shipped to my office. Many wine writers claim that these favors do not influence their opinions. Yet how many people in any profession are prepared to bite the hand that feeds them? Irrefutably, the target audience is the wine consumer, not the wine trade. While it is important to maintain a professional relationship with the trade, I believe the independent stance required of a consumer advocate often, not surprisingly, results in an adversarial relationship with the wine trade. It can be no other way. In order to pursue independence effectively, it is imperative to keep one's distance from the trade. While this attitude may be misinterpreted as aloofness, such independence guarantees hard-hitting, candid, and uninfluenced commentary.

Courage Courage manifests itself in what I call "democratic tasting." Judgments ought to be made solely on the basis of the product in the bottle, not the pedigree, the price, the rarity, or one's like or dislike of the producer. The wine critic who is totally candid may be considered dangerous by the trade, but an uncensored, independent point of view is of paramount importance to the consumer. A judgment of wine quality must be based on what is in the bottle. This is wine criticism at its purest, most meaningful. In a tasting, a $10 bottle of Petit Château Pauillac should have as much of a chance as a $200 bottle of Lafite-Rothschild or Latour. Overachievers should be spotted and praised and their names highlighted and shared with the consuming public. Underachievers should be singled out for criticism and called to account for their mediocrities. Outspoken and irreverent commentary is unlikely to win many friends in the commerce of wine, but wine buyers are entitled to such information. When a critic bases his or her judgment on what others think, or on the wine's pedigree, price, or perceived potential, then wine criticism is nothing more than a sham.

Experience It is essential to taste extensively across the field of play to identify the benchmark reference points and to learn winemaking standards throughout the world. This is the most time-consuming and expensive aspect of wine criticism, as well as the most fulfilling for the critic; yet it is rarely practiced. Lamentably, what often transpires is that a tasting of 10 or 12 wines from a specific region or vintage will be held, and the writer then issues a definitive judgment on the vintage based on a microscopic proportion of the wines. This is irresponsible—and appalling. It is essential for a wine critic to taste as comprehensibly as is physically possible, which means tasting every significant wine produced in a region or vintage before reaching qualitative conclusions. Wine criticism, if it is ever to be regarded as a serious profession, must be a full-time endeavor, not the pursuit of part-timers dabbling in a field that is so complex and requires such time commitment. Wine and vintages, like everything important in life, cannot be reduced to black-and-white answers.

It is also essential to establish memory reference points for the world's greatest wines. There is such a diversity of wine and multitude of styles that this may seem impossible. But tasting as many wines as one possibly can in each vintage, and from all of the classic wine regions, helps one memorize benchmark characteristics that form the basis for making comparative judgments between vintages, wine producers, and wine regions.

Individual accountability Though I have never found anyone's wine-tasting notes compelling reading, notes issued by consensus of a committee are even more insipid and often misleading. Judgments by committees supposedly sum up a group's personal preferences—but how do they take into consideration the possibility that each individual may have reached his or her decision using totally different criteria? Did one judge adore the wine because of its typicity while another decried it for the same reason, or was the wine's individuality given greater merit? It is impossible to know. That is never in doubt when an individual authors a tasting critique.

Committees rarely recognize wines of great individuality. A look at the results of tasting competitions reveals that well-made mediocrities garner the top prizes, and thus, sadly, blandness is elevated to a virtue. A wine with great individuality and character will never win a committee tasting because at least one taster will find something objectionable about it.

I have always sensed that individual tasters, because they are unable to hide behind the collective voice of a committee, hold themselves to a greater degree of accountability. The opinion of a reasonably informed and comprehensive individual taster, despite the taster's prejudices and predilections, is always a far better guide to the ultimate quality of a wine than the consensus of a committee. At least the reader knows where the individual stands, whereas with a committee, one is never quite sure.

Emphasis on pleasure and value Too much wine writing focuses on glamour French wine regions such as Burgundy, Bordeaux, and on California Cabernet Sauvignon and Chardonnay. These are important, and they make up the backbone of most serious wine enthusiasts' cellars. But value and diversity in wine types must always be stressed. Wines that taste great young, such as Chenin Blanc, Dolcetto, Beaujolais, Côtes du Rhône, Merlot, and Zinfandel, are no less serious or compelling because they must be drunk within a few years rather than be cellared for a decade or more before consumption. Wine is, in the final analysis, a beverage of pleasure, and intelligent wine criticism should be a blend of both hedonistic and analytical schools of thought—to the exclusion of neither.

The focus on qualitative issues It is an inescapable fact that too many of the world's renowned growers and producers have intentionally permitted production levels to soar to such extraordinary heights that many wines' personalities, concentrations, and characters are in jeopardy. While there remain a handful of fanatics who continue, at some financial sacrifice, to reject significant proportions of their harvest to ensure that only the finest-quality wine is sold under their name, they are dwindling in number. For much of the last decade, production yields throughout the world have broken records with almost every new vintage. The results are wines that increasingly lack character, concentration, and staying power. The argument that more carefully and competently managed vineyards result in larger crops is nonsense.

In addition to high yields, advances in technology have provided the savoir faire to produce more correct wines, but the abuse of practices such as acidification and excessive fining and filtration have compromised the final product. (For more on these and other techniques, see pages 18–21.) These problems are rarely and inadequately addressed by the wine-writing community. Wine prices have never been higher, but is the consumer always getting a better wine? The wine writer has the responsibility to give broad qualitative issues high priority.

Candor No one argues with the incontestable fact that tasting is a subjective endeavor. The measure of an effective wine critic should be his or her timely and useful rendering of an intelligent laundry list of good examples of different styles of winemaking in various price categories. Articulating in an understandable fashion why the critic finds the wines enthralling or objectionable is manifestly important to both the reader and the producer. The critic must always seek to educate and to provide meaningful guidelines, never failing to emphasize that there is no substitute for the consumer's palate, nor any better education than the reader's own tasting of the wine. Having the advantage of access to the world's wine production, the critic must try to minimize bias yet also should share with readers the reasoning behind bad reviews. For example, I will never be able to overcome my dislike for vegetal-tasting New World Cabernets, overtly herbaceous red Loire Valley wines, or excessively acidified New World whites.

My ultimate goal in writing about wines is to seek out the world's greatest wines and greatest wine values. But I feel that, in the process of ferreting out such wines, the critic should never shy away from criticizing producers whose wines are found lacking. Given that the consumer is the true taster of record, the "taste no evil" approach to wine writing serves no one but the wine trade. Constructive and competent criticism has proven that it can benefit producers as well as consumers, since it forces underachievers to improve the quality of their fare and, by lauding overachievers, encourages them to maintain high standards, to the benefit of all who enjoy and appreciate good wine.

[about wine]

HOW TO BUY WINE

If you have made your choices in advance, buying wine seems simple enough—you go to your favorite wine merchant and purchase a few bottles. However, there are some subtleties to buying wine that one must be aware of in order to ensure that the wine is in healthy condition and is unspoiled.

To begin with, take a look at the bottle of wine you are about to buy. Wine abuse is revealed by the condition of the bottle in your hand. First of all, if the cork has popped above the rim of the bottle and is pushed out on the lead or plastic capsule that covers the top of the bottle, look for another bottle to buy. Wines that have been exposed to very high temperatures expand in the bottle, putting pressure on the cork and pushing it upward against the capsule. And the highest-quality wines, those that have not been overly filtered or pasteurized, are the most vulnerable to the ill effects of abusive transportation or storage. A wine that has been frozen in transit or storage will likewise push the cork out, and though freezing a wine is less damaging than heating it, both are hazardous to its health. Any cork that is protruding above the rim of the bottle is a bad sign. The bottle should be returned to the shelf and never, ever purchased.

Finally, there is a sign indicating poor storage conditions that can generally be determined only after the wine has been decanted, though sometimes it can be spotted in the neck of the bottle. Wines that have been exposed to very high temperatures, particularly deep, rich, intense red wines, often form a heavy coat or film of coloring material on the inside of the glass. With a Bordeaux less than three years old, a coating such as this generally indicates that the wine has been subjected to very high temperatures and has undoubtedly been damaged. However, one must be careful here, because this type of sediment does not always indicate a poor bottle of wine; vintage Port regularly throws it, and so do huge, rich Rhône and Piedmontese wines.

On the other hand, there are two conditions consumers frequently think are signs of a flawed wine when nothing could be further from the truth. Some uninformed consumers return bottles of wine for the very worst reason—because of a small deposit of sediment in the bottom of the bottle. In fact, for most wines, this is the healthiest sign one could find. The tiny particles of sandlike sediment that precipitate to the bottom of a bottle simply indicate that the wine has been naturally made and has not been subjected to a traumatic flavor- and character-eviscerating filtration. Such wine is truly alive and is usually full of all its natural flavors. However, keep in mind that white wines rarely throw a deposit, and it is rare to see a deposit in young wines less than two or three years of age.

Another reason that wine consumers erroneously return bottles to retailers is the presence of small crystals called tartrate precipitates. These crystals are found in all types of wines but most commonly in white wines from Germany and Alsace. They often shine and resemble little slivers of cut glass. They simply mean that somewhere along its journey a wine was exposed to temperatures below 40° F in shipment, and the cold has caused some tartaric crystals to precipitate. These are harmless, tasteless, and totally natural in many bottles of wine. They have no effect on the quality and normally signify that the wine has not been subjected by the winery to an abusive, sometimes damaging, cold-stabilization treatment for cosmetic purposes only.

Fortunately, most of the better wine merchants, wholesalers, and importers are more cognizant today of the damage that can be done by shipping wine in unrefrigerated containers, especially in the middle of summer. Tragically, far too many wines are still damaged by poor transportation and storage, and it is the consumer who suffers. A general rule is that heat is much more damaging to fine wines than cold. Remember, there are still plenty of wine merchants, wholesalers, and importers who treat wine no differently than they treat beer or liquor, and the wine buyer must therefore be armed with a bit of knowledge.

HOW TO STORE WINE

Wine has to be stored properly if it is to be served in a healthy condition. All wine enthusiasts know that subterranean wine cellars that are vibration free, dark, damp, and kept at a constant 55° F are considered perfect for wine. However, few of us have such perfect accommodations for our beloved wines—and, though these conditions are ideal, most wines will thrive and develop well under other circumstances. I have tasted many old Bordeaux wines from closets and basements that have reached 65° to 70° F in summer, and the wines have been perfect. In cellaring wine, keep the following rules in mind and you will not be disappointed with a wine that has gone over the hill prematurely.

First of all, in order to cellar wines safely for 10 years or more, keep them around 65° F, perhaps 68° F, but no higher. If the temperature rises to 70° F, be prepared to drink your red wines within 10 years. Under no circumstances should you store and cellar white wines more than 1 to 2 years at temperatures above 70° F. Wines kept at temperatures above 65° F will age faster, but unless the temperature exceeds 70° F, they will not age badly. If you can somehow get the temperature down to 65° F or below, you will never have to worry about the condition of your wines. At 55° F, the ideal temperature according to the textbooks, the wines actually evolve so slowly that your grandchildren are likely to benefit from the wines more than you. Constancy in temperature is most essential, and any changes in temperature should occur slowly. White wines are much more fragile and much more sensitive to temperature changes and higher temperatures than red wines. Therefore, if you do not have ideal storage conditions, buy only enough white wine to drink over a one- to two-year period.

Second, be sure that your storage area is odor free, vibration free, and dark. A humidity level above 50% is essential; 70% to 75% is ideal. With a humidity level over 75%, the labels become moldy and deteriorate. A humidity level below 40% will keep the labels in great shape but cause the corks to become very dry, possibly shortening the potential life expectancy of your wine. Low humidity is believed to be nearly as great a threat to a wine's health as high temperature. There has been no research to prove this, and limited studies I have done are far from conclusive.

Third, always bear in mind that wines from vintages that have produced powerful, rich, concentrated, full-bodied wines travel and age significantly better than wines from vintages that have produced lighter-weight wines. Transatlantic or cross-country transport is often traumatic for a fragile, lighter-styled wine from either Europe or California, whereas the richer, more intense, bigger wines from the better vintages seem much less travel-worn after their journey.

Fourth, I always recommend buying a wine as soon as it appears on the market, assuming of course that you have tasted the wine and like it. The reason for this is that there are still too many American wine merchants, importers, wholesalers, and distributors who are indifferent to the way wine is stored. This attitude still persists, though with dramatic improvement over the last decade. The important thing for you as a consumer to remember, after you have inspected the bottle to make sure it appears healthy, is that you should stock up on wines as quickly as they come on the market and approach older vintages with a great deal of caution and hesitation unless you have absolute faith in the merchant from whom you bought the wine. Furthermore, you should be confident that your merchant will stand behind the wine if it is flawed from poor storage.

THE QUESTION OF HOW MUCH AGING

The majority of wines taste best when they are just released or consumed within one to two years of the vintage. Many wines are drinkable at five, ten, or even 15 years of age, but based on my experience only a small percentage are more interesting and more enjoyable after extended cellaring than they were when originally released.

It is important to have a working definition of what the aging of wine actually means. I define the process as nothing more than the ability of a wine, over time, 1) to develop more pleasurable nuances, 2) to expand and soften in texture and, for red wines, to exhibit an additional melting away of tannins, and 3) to reveal a more compelling aromatic and flavor profile. In short, the wine must deliver additional complexity, increased pleasure, and more interest as an older wine than it did when released. Only such a performance can justify the purchase of a wine in its youth for the purpose of cellaring it for future drinking. Unfortunately, only a tiny percentage of the world's wines fall within this definition of ageworthiness.

It is fundamentally false to believe that a wine cannot be serious or profound if it is drunk young. In France, the finest Bordeaux, the northern Rhône Valley wines (particularly l'Hermitage and Côte Rôtie), a few red Burgundies, some Châteauneuf-du-Papes, and, surprisingly, many of the sweet white Alsace and sweet Loire Valley wines do indeed age well and are frequently much more enjoyable and complex when drunk five, ten, or even 15 years after the vintage. But virtually all other French wines—from Champagne to Côtes du Rhône, from Beaujolais to the petits châteaux of Bordeaux, and the vast majority of red and white Burgundies—are better in their youth.

The French have long adhered to the wine-drinking strategy that younger is better. Centuries of wine consumption, not to mention gastronomic indulgence, have taught the French something that Americans and Englishmen have failed to grasp: Most wines are more pleasurable and friendly when young.

The French know that the aging and cellaring of wines, even those of high pedigree, are often fraught with more disappointments than successes. Nowhere is this more in evidence than in French restaurants, especially in Bordeaux, the region that boasts what the world considers the longest-lived dry red wines. A top vintage of Bordeaux can last 20 to 30 years, sometimes 40 or more, but look at the wine lists of Bordeaux's best restaurants. The great 1990s have long disappeared down the throats of Frenchmen and -women. Even the tannic, young, yet potentially very promising 1996s, which Americans have squirreled away for drinking later this century, are now hard to find. Why? Because they have already been consumed. Many of the deluxe restaurants, particularly in Paris, have wine lists of historic vintages, but these are largely for rich tourists.

This phenomenon is not limited to France. Similar drinking habits prevail in the restaurants of Florence, Rome, Madrid, and Barcelona. Italians and Spaniards also enjoy their wines young. This is not to suggest that Italy does not make some wines that improve in the bottle. In Tuscany, for example, a handful of Chiantis and some of the finest new-breed Tuscan red wines (e.g., the famed Cabernet Sauvignon called Sassicaia) will handsomely repay extended cellaring, but most never get the opportunity. In the Piedmont section of northern Italy, no one will deny that a fine Barbaresco or Barolo improves after a decade in the bottle, but, by and large, all of Italy's other wines are meant to be drunk young, a fact that Italians have long known and that you should observe as well.

With respect to Spain, it is the same story, although a Spaniard's tastes differ considerably from those of the average Italian or Frenchman. In Spain, the intense smoky vanilla aroma of new oak (particularly American) is prized. As a result, the top Spanish wine producers from the most renowned wine region, Rioja, and other viticultural regions as well tend to age their wines in oak barrels so that they can develop this particular aroma. In addition, unlike French and Italian wine producers, or even their New World counterparts, Spanish wineries are reluctant to release their wines until they are fully mature. As a result, most Spanish wines are smooth and mellow when they arrive on the market. They may keep for five to ten years, but they generally do not improve. This is especially true with Spain's most expensive wines, the Reservas and Gran Reservas from Rioja, which are usually not released until five to eight years after the vintage. The one exception may be the wine long considered Spain's greatest red, the Vega Sicilia Unico. This powerful wine, frequently released when it is already 10 or 20 years old (the immortal 1970 was released in 1995), does appear capable of lasting for 20 to 35 years after its release. Yet I wonder how much it improves.

What does all this mean to you? Unlike any other wine consumers in the world, most American and English wine enthusiasts fret over the perfect moment to drink a wine. There is none. Almost all modern-day vintages, even ageworthy Bordeaux or Rhône Valley wines, can be drunk when released. Some of them will improve, but many will not. If you enjoy drinking a 1989 Bordeaux now, who could be so foolish as to suggest that you are making an error because the wine will be appreciably better in five to ten years?

In America and Australia, winemaking is much more dominated by technology. Though a handful of producers still adhere to the artisanal, traditional way of making wine as done in Europe, most treat the vineyard as a factory and winemaking as a manufacturing process. As a result, such techniques as excessive acidification, brutally traumatic centrifugation, and eviscerating sterile filtration are routinely utilized to produce squeaky-clean, simplistic, sediment-free, spit-polished, totally stable yet innocuous wines with statistical profiles that fit neatly within strict technical parameters. Yet these techniques denude wines of their flavors, aromas, and pleasure-giving qualities. Moreover, they reveal a profound lack of respect for the vineyard, the grape variety, the vintage, and the wine consumer, who, after all, is seeking pleasure, not blandness.

In both Australia and California, the alarming tendency of most Sauvignon Blancs and Chardonnays to collapse in the bottle and to drop their fruit within two to three years of the vintage has been well documented. Yet some of California's and Australia's most vocal advocates continue to advise wine consumers to cellar and invest (a deplorable word when it comes to wine) in Chardonnays and Sauvignon Blancs. It is a stupid policy. If the aging of wine is indeed the ability of a wine to become more interesting and pleasurable with time, then the rule of thumb to be applied to American and Australian Sauvignon Blancs and Chardonnays is that they must be drunk within 12 months of their release unless the consumer has an eccentric fetish for fruitless wines with blistering acidity and scorching alcohol levels. Examples can be found of producers whose Chardonnays and Sauvignon Blancs can last for five to ten years and improve during that period, but they are distressingly few.

With respect to red wines, a slightly different picture emerges. Take, for example, the increasingly fashionable wines made from the Pinot Noir grape. No one doubts the immense progress made in both California and Oregon in turning out fragrant, supple Pinot Noirs that are delicious upon release. But I do not know of any American producer who is making Pinot Noir that can actually improve beyond 10 or 12 years in the bottle. And this is not in any way a criticism.

Even in Burgundy there are probably no more than a dozen producers who make their wines in such a manner that they improve and last for more than a decade. Many of these wines can withstand the test of time in the sense of being survivors, but they are far less interesting and pleasurable at age ten than when they were two or three years old. Of course, the producers and retailers who specialize in these wines will argue otherwise, but they are in the business of selling. Do not be bamboozled by the public relations arm of the wine industry or the fallacious notion that red wines all improve with age. If you enjoy them young, and most likely you will, then buy only the quantities needed for near-term consumption.

America's most famous dry red wine, however, is not Pinot Noir but Cabernet Sauvignon, particularly from California and, to a lesser extent, from Washington State. The idea that most California Cabernet Sauvignons improve in the bottle is a myth. And the belief that all California Cabernet Sauvignons are incapable of lasting in the bottle is equally unfounded. Today no one would be foolish enough to argue that the best California Cabernets cannot tolerate 15 or 20, even 25 or 30 years of cellaring.

I frequently have the opportunity to taste 20- to 30-year-old California Cabernet Sauvignons, and they are delicious. But have they significantly improved because of the aging process? A few of them have, though most still tend to be relatively grapy, somewhat monolithic, earthy, and tannic at age 20. Has the consumer's patience in cellaring these wines for all those years justified the expense and the wait? Lamentably, the answer will usually be no. Most of these wines are no more complex or mellow than they were when young.

Because these wines will not crack up and fall apart, there is little risk associated with stashing the best of them away, but I am afraid the consumer who patiently waits for the proverbial "miracle in the bottle" will find that wine cellaring can all too frequently be an expensive exercise in futility.

If you think it over, the most important issue is why so many of today's wines exhibit scant improvement in the aging process. Though most have always been meant to be drunk when young, I am convinced that much of the current winemaking philosophy has led to numerous compromises in the winemaking process. The advent of micropore sterile filters, so much in evidence at every modern winery, may admirably stabilize a wine, but, regrettably, these filters also destroy the potential of a wine to develop a complex aromatic profile. When they are utilized by wine producers who routinely fertilize their vineyards excessively, thus overcropping, the results are wines that reveal an appalling lack of bouquet and flavor.

The prevailing winemaking obsession is to stabilize wine so it can be shipped to the far corners of the world 12 months a year, stand upright in overheated stores indefinitely, and never change or spoil if exposed to extremes of heat and cold, or unfriendly storage conditions. For all intents and purposes, the wine is no longer alive. This is acceptable, even desirable, for inexpensive jug wines, but for the fine-wine market, where consumers are asked to pay $20 or more per bottle, it is a winemaking tragedy. These stabilization and production techniques thus affect the aging of wine because they preclude the development of the wine's ability to evolve and to become a more complex, tasty, profound, and enjoyable beverage.

HOW TO SERVE WINE

There are really no secrets for proper wine service—all one needs is a good corkscrew; clean, odor-free glasses; and a sense of the order of how wines should be served and of whether a wine needs to be aired or allowed to breathe. The major mistakes that most Americans, as well as most restaurants, make are: 1) fine white wines are served entirely too cold; 2) fine red wines are served entirely too warm; and 3) too little attention is given to the glass into which the wine is poured. (It might contain a soapy residue or stale aromas picked up in a closed china closet or cardboard box.) All of these things can do much more to damage the impact of a fine wine and its subtle aromas than you might imagine. Most people tend to think that the wine must be opened and allowed to "breathe" well in advance of serving. Some even think a wine must be decanted, a rather elaborate procedure, but not essential unless sediment is present in the bottle and the wine needs to be poured carefully off. With respect to breathing or airing wine, I am not sure anyone has all the answers. Certainly, no white wine requires any advance opening and pouring. Red wines can be enjoyed within 15 to 30 minutes of being opened and poured into a clean, odor- and soap-free wine decanter. There are of course examples that can always be cited where the wine improves for seven to eight hours, but these are quite rare. Although these topics seem to dominate much of the discussion in wine circles, a much more critical aspect for me is the appropriate temperature of the wine and of the glass in which it is to be served. The temperature of red wines is very important, and in America's generously heated dining rooms, temperatures are often 75° to 80° F, higher than is good for fine red wine. A red wine served at such a temperature will taste flat and flabby, with its bouquet diffuse and unfocused. The alcohol content will also seem higher than it should be. The ideal temperature for most red wines is 62° to 67° F; light red wine such as Beaujolais should be chilled to 55° F. For white wines, 55° to 60° F is perfect, since most will show all their complexity and intensity at this temperature, whereas if they are chilled to below 45° F it will be difficult to tell, for instance, whether the wine is a Riesling or a Chardonnay.

In addition, there is the important issue of wineglasses. An all-purpose, tulip-shaped glass of 8 to 12 ounces is a good start for just about any type of wine, but think the subject over carefully. If you go to the trouble and expense of finding and storing wine properly, shouldn't you treat the wine to a good glass? The finest glasses for both technical and hedonistic purposes are those made by the Riedel Company of Austria. I have to admit that I was at first skeptical about these glasses. George Riedel, the head of his family's crystal business, claims to have created these glasses specifically to guide (by specially designed rims) the wine to a designated section of the palate. These rims, combined with the general shape of the glass, emphasize and promote the different flavors and aromas of a given varietal.

All of this may sound absurdly highbrow or esoteric, but the effect of these glasses on fine wine is profound. I cannot emphasize enough what a difference they make. If the Sommelier Series is too expensive, Riedel does make less expensive lines that are machine-made rather than hand-blown. The most popular are the Vinum glasses, which sell for about $20 per glass. The Bordeaux Vinum glass is a personal favorite as well as a spectacular glass, not only for Bordeaux but for Rhône wines and white Burgundies. There are also numerous other glasses designed for Nebbiolo-based wines, rosé wines, old white wines, and Port wines, as well as a specially designed glass for sweet Sauternes-type wines.

And, last but not least, remember: No matter how clean the glass appears to be, be sure to rinse the glass or decanter with unchlorinated well or mineral water just before it is used. A decanter or wineglass left sitting for any time is a wonderful trap for room and kitchen odors that are undetectable until the wine is poured and they yield their off-putting smells. This phenomenon and soapy residues left in the glasses have ruined more wines than any defective cork or, I suspect, poor storage from an importer, wholesaler, or retailer. I myself put considerable strain on one friendship simply because I continued to complain at every dinner party about the soapy glasses that interfered with the enjoyment of the wonderful Bordeaux wines being served.

FOOD AND WINE MATCHUPS

The art of serving the right bottle of wine with a specific course or type of food has become terribly overlegislated, to the detriment of the enjoyment of both wine and food. Newspaper and magazine columns, even books, are filled with precise rules that seemingly make it a sin not to have chosen the perfect wine to accompany the meal. The results have been predictable. Instead of enjoying a dining experience, most hosts and hostesses fret, usually needlessly, over their choice of which wine to serve with the meal.

The basic rules of the wine-food matchup game are not difficult to master. These are the tried-and-true, allegedly cardinal principles such as young wines before old wines, dry wines before sweet wines, white wines before red wines, red wines with meat, and white wines with fish. However, these general principles are riddled with exceptions, and your choices are a great deal broader than you have been led to expect. One of France's greatest restaurant proprietors once told me that if people would simply pick their favorite wines to go along with their favorite dishes, they would be a great deal happier. Furthermore, he would be pleased not to have to witness so much nervous anxiety and apprehension on their faces. I'm not sure I can go that far, but since my gut feeling is that there are more combinations of wine and food that work reasonably well than do not, let me share some of my basic observations about this whole field. There are several important questions you should consider:

Does the food offer simple or complex flavors? America's—and I suppose the wine world's—two favorite grapes, Chardonnay and Cabernet Sauvignon, can produce majestic wines of exceptional complexity and flavor depth. However, as food wines they are remarkably one-dimensional and work well only with dishes that have relatively straightforward and simple flavors. Cabernet Sauvignon marries beautifully with basic meat-and-potato dishes, filet mignon, lamb chops, steaks, etc. Furthermore, as Cabernet Sauvignon– and Merlot-based wines get older and more complex, they require simpler and simpler dishes to complement their complex flavors. Chardonnay goes beautifully with most fish courses, but when one adds different aromas and scents to a straightforward fish dish—by grilling, or by adding ingredients in an accompanying sauce—Chardonnays are often competitive rather than complementary wines to serve. The basic rule, then, is simple, uncomplex wines with complex dishes, and complex wines with simple dishes.

What are the primary flavors in both the wine and food? A complementary wine choice can often be made if one knows what to expect from the primary flavors in the food to be eaten. The reason that creamy and buttery sauces with fish, lobster, even chicken or veal, work well with Chardonnay or white Burgundies is because of the buttery, vanilla aromas in the fuller, richer, lustier styles of Chardonnay. On the other hand, a mixed salad with an herb dressing and pieces of grilled fish or shellfish beg for an herbaceous, smoky Sauvignon Blanc or French Sancerre or Pouilly Fumé from the Loire Valley. For the same reason, a steak au poivre in a creamy brown sauce, with its intense, pungent aromas and complex flavors, calls for a big, rich, peppery Rhône wine such as a Châteauneuf-du-Pape or Gigondas.

Are the texture and flavor intensity of the wine proportional to the texture and flavor intensity of the food? Did you ever wonder why fresh, briny, sea-scented oysters that are light and zesty taste so good with a Muscadet from France or a lighter-styled California Sauvignon Blanc or Italian Pinot Grigio? It is because these wines have the same weight and light texture as the oysters. Why is it that the smoky, sweet, oaky, tangy flavors of a grilled steak or loin of lamb work best with a Zinfandel or Rhône Valley red wine? First, the full-bodied, supple, chewy flavors of these wines complement a steak or loin of lamb cooked over a wood fire. Sauté the same steak or lamb in butter or bake it in the oven and the flavors are less complex; then a well-aged Cabernet Sauvignon– or Merlot-based wine from California, Bordeaux, or Australia is called for.

Another telling example of the importance of matching the texture and flavor intensity of the wine with the food is the type of fish you have chosen to eat. Salmon, lobster, shad, and bluefish have intense flavors and a fatty texture, and therefore require a similarly styled, lusty, oaky, buttery Chardonnay to complement them. On the other hand, trout, sole, turbot, and shrimp are leaner, more delicately flavored fish and therefore mandate lighter, less intense wines such as nonoaked examples of Chardonnay from France's Mâconnais region, or Italy's Friuli-Venezia Giulia area. In addition, a lighter-styled Champagne or German Riesling (ideally a dry Kabinett) goes extremely well with trout, sole, or turbot, but falls on its face when matched against salmon, shad, or lobster. One further example of a texture and flavor matchup is the classic example of a heavy, unctuous, rich, sweet Sauternes with foie gras. The extravagantly rich and flavorful foie gras cannot be served with any other type of wine, as it would overpower a dry red or white wine. The fact that both the Sauternes and the foie gras have intense, concentrated flavors and similar textures is the exact reason why this combination is so decadently delicious.

What is the style of wine produced in the vintage that you have chosen? Several of France's greatest chefs have told me they prefer off years of Bordeaux and Burgundy to great years, and have instructed their sommeliers to buy the wines for the restaurant accordingly. How can this be? From the chef's perspective, the food, not the wine, should be the focal point of the meal. They fear that a great vintage of Burgundy or Bordeaux, with wines that are exceptionally rich, powerful, and concentrated, not only takes attention away from their cuisine but makes matching a wine with the food much more troublesome. Thus, chefs prefer a 2004 Bordeaux on the table with their food as opposed to a superconcentrated 2005 or 2000. The great vintages, though marvelous wines, are not always the best vintages to choose for the ultimate matchup with food. Lighter-weight yet tasty wines from so-so years can complement delicate and understated cuisine considerably better than the great vintages, which should be reserved for very simple courses of food.

Is the food to be served in a sauce? Years ago, at Michel Guérard's restaurant in Eugénie-les-Bains, I ordered fish served in a red wine sauce. Guérard recommended a red Graves wine from Bordeaux, since the sauce was made from a reduction of fish stock and a red Graves. The combination was successful and opened my eyes for the first time to the possibilities of fish with red wine. Since then I have had tuna with a green peppercorn sauce accompanied by a California Cabernet Sauvignon (a great matchup) and salmon sautéed in a red wine sauce happily married to a young vintage of red Bordeaux. A white wine with any of these courses would not have worked. Another great match was veal in a creamy morel sauce with a Tokaj from Alsace.

A corollary to this principle of letting the sauce dictate the type of wine you order is when the actual food is prepared with a specific type of wine. For example, coq au vin, an exquisite peasant dish, can be cooked and served in either a white wine or red wine sauce. I have found when I had coq au vin au Riesling, a dry Alsace Riesling with it is simply extraordinary. In Burgundy I have often had coq au vin in a red wine sauce consisting of a reduced Burgundy wine, and the choice of a red Burgundy makes the dish even more special.

When you travel, do you drink locally produced wines with the local cuisine? It is no coincidence that the regional cuisines of Bordeaux, Burgundy, Provence, and Alsace in France, and Tuscany and Piedmont in Italy, seem to enhance and complement the local wines. In fact, most restaurants in these areas rarely offer wines from outside the local region. One always wonders what came first, the cuisine or the wine? Certainly, America is beginning to develop its own regional cuisine, but except for California and the Pacific Northwest, few areas promote the local wines as appropriate matchups with the local cuisine. For example, in my backyard a number of small wineries make an excellent white wine called Seyval Blanc, which is the perfect foil for both the oysters and blue channel crabs from the Chesapeake Bay. Yet few restaurants in the Baltimore–Washington area promote these local wines, which is a shame. Regional wines with regional foods should be a top priority not only when traveling in Europe but also in America's viticultural areas.

Have you learned the best and worst wine and food matchups? If this entire area of wine and food combinations still seems too cumbersome, then your best strategy is simply to learn some of the greatest and worst combinations. I can also add a few pointers I have learned through my own experiences, usually bad ones. Certain wine and food relationships of contrasting flavors can be sublime. Perhaps the best example is a sweet, creamy-textured Sauternes with a salty, aged Stilton or Roquefort cheese. The combination of two opposite sets of flavors and textures is sensational in this particular instance. Another great combination is Alsace Gewurztraminer or Riesling with ethnic cuisine such as Indian and Chinese. The sweet-and-sour combinations and spiciness of the cuisines seem to work beautifully with these two wines from Alsace.

One of the great myths about wine and food matchups is that red wines work well with cheese. The truth of the matter is that they rarely work well with cheese. Most cheeses, especially favorite wine cheeses such as Brie and double and triple creams, have a very high fat content, and most red wines suffer enormously when drunk with them. If you want to shock your guests but also enjoy wine with cheese, serve a white wine made from the Sauvignon Blanc grape such as a Sancerre or Pouilly Fumé from France. The dynamic personalities of these two wines and their tangy, zesty acidity stand up well to virtually all types of cheese, especially with fresh goat cheeses.

Another myth is that dessert wines go best with desserts. Most people seem to like Champagne or a sweet Riesling, sweet Chenin Blanc, or a Sauternes with dessert. Putting aside that chocolate-based desserts are always in conflict with any type of wine, I find that dessert wines are best served as the dessert or after the dessert. Whether it be cake, fruit tarts, ice cream, or candy, I've always enjoyed dessert wines more when they are the centerpiece of attention than when they are accompanying a sweet dessert.

If wine and food matchups still seem too complicated for you, remember that in the final analysis, a good wine served with a good dish to good company is always in good taste. *À votre santé.*

WHAT'S BEEN ADDED TO YOUR WINE?

Over the last decade, people have become much more sensitive to what they put in their bodies. The hazards of smoking, excessive fat consumption, and high blood pressure are taken seriously by increasing numbers of people, not just in America but in Europe as well. While this movement is to be applauded, an extremist group, labeled by observers as "neoprohibitionists" or "new drys," has tried to exploit the individual's interest in good health by promoting the idea that the consumption of any alcoholic beverage is inherently dangerous, an abuse that undermines society and family. These extremists do not care about moderation; they want the total elimination of wine (one of alcohol's "evil spirits") from the marketplace. In the process, they have misrepresented wine and consistently ignored specific data demonstrating that moderate wine drinking is more beneficial than harmful to individuals. Unfortunately, the law prohibits the wine industry from promoting the proven health benefits of wine.

Wine is one of the most natural of all beverages, but it is true that additives can be included in a wine (the neoprohibitionists are taking aim at these as being potentially lethal). Following are those items that can be added to wine.

Acids Most cool-climate vineyards never have the need to add acidity to wine, but in California and Australia, acidity is often added to give balance to the wines, as grapes from these hot-climate areas often lack sufficient natural acidity. Most serious wineries add tartaric acidity, a type found naturally in wine. Wineries that are less quality oriented dump in pure citric acid, which results in wine that tastes like a lemon-lime sorbet.

Clarification agents A list of items that are dumped into wine to cause suspended particles to coagulate (known as "fining") includes morbid names such as dried ox blood, isinglass, casein (milk powder), kaolin (clay), bentonite (powdered clay), and the traditional egg white. These fining agents are designed to make the wine brilliant and particle free; they are harmless, but top wineries either don't use them or use them minimally.

Oak Many top-quality red and white wines spend most of their lives aging in oak barrels. It is expected that wine stored in wood will take on some of the toasty, smoky, vanilla flavors of wood. These aromas and flavors, if not overdone, add flavor complexity to a wine. Cheap wine can also be marginally enhanced by the addition of oak chips, which provide a more aggressive, raw flavor of wood. But remember, oak works only with certain types of wine, and its usage is analogous to a chef's use of salt, pepper, or garlic. In excessive amounts or with the wrong dish, the results are ghastly.

Sugar In most of the viticultural regions of Europe—except for southern France, Portugal, and Spain—the law permits the addition of sugar to the fermenting grape juice in order to raise alcohol levels. This practice, called *chaptalization,* is performed in cool years when the grapes do not attain sufficient ripeness. It is never done in the hot climate of California or in most of Australia, where low natural acidity, not low sugars, is the problem. Judicious chaptalization raises the alcohol level by 1% to 2%.

Sulfites All wines must now carry a label indicating that the wine contains sulfites. Sulfite (also referred to as SO_2 or sulfur dioxide) is a preservative used to kill bacteria and microorganisms. It is sprayed on virtually all fresh vegetables and fruits, but a tiny percentage of the population, especially asthmatics, are allergic to SO_2. The fermentation of wine produces some sulfur dioxide naturally, but it is also added to oak barrels by burning a sulfur stick inside the barrel in order to kill any bacteria; it is added again at bottling to prevent the wine from oxidizing. Quality wines should never smell of sulfur (a burning-match smell) because serious winemakers keep the sulfur level very low. Some wineries do not employ sulfites. When used properly, sulfites impart no smell or taste to the wine, and except for those who have a known allergy to them, are harmless to the general population. Used excessively, sulfites impart the aforementioned unpleasant smell and a prickly taste sensation. Obviously, people who are allergic to sulfites should not drink wine, just as people who are allergic to fish roe should not eat caviar.

Tannin Tannin occurs naturally in the skins and stems of grapes, and the content from the crushing of the grape skins and subsequent maceration of the skins and juice is usually more than adequate to provide sufficient natural tannin. Tannin gives a red wine grip and backbone, and also acts as a preservative. However, on rare occasions tannin is added to a spineless wine.

Yeasts Though many winemakers rely on the indigenous wild yeasts in the vineyard to start the fermentation, it is becoming more common to employ cultured yeasts for this procedure. There is no health hazard here, but the increasing reliance on the same type of yeast in winemaking all over the world leads to wines with similar bouquets and flavors.

ORGANIC WINES

Organic wines are produced without fungicides, pesticides, or chemical fertilizers, with no additives or preservatives. They continue to gain considerable consumer support. In principle, organic wines should be as excellent as nonorganic, but no one should assume that, because a wine is not organic, it suffers in comparison with those that are. One can argue that most organic wine producers tend to do less manipulation and processing of their wines, and therefore the consumer receives a product that is far more natural than wines that have been manufactured and processed to death. However, many nonorganic wines are great wines, and making arbitrary black-and-white judgments about quality based on whether a wine is organic or not is foolhardy.

There is tremendous potential for production of huge quantities of organic wines, particularly from viticultural areas that enjoy copious quantities of sunshine and wind, the so-called Mediterranean climate. In France, the Languedoc-Roussillon region, Provence, and the Rhône Valley have the potential to produce organic wines if their proprietors desire. Southern Italy, much of Spain, and much of California has this potential as well, and southern Australia seems to have weather conditions that would encourage the possibility of developing organic vineyards. Certainly, more and more viticulturalists and wine estates are moving in an organic direction.

The most extreme form of organic farming, called biodynamic farming, is an entire subject unto itself. There are some fabulous winemakers in the world who have followed biodynamic principles with great success (Michel Chapoutier and the Domaine Leroy in Burgundy are two who stand out), but again, one should not make an assumption that, because a wine is biodynamic, it is intrinsically superior to a wine that is organic or nonorganic.

[the dark side of wine]

THE GROWING INTERNATIONAL STANDARDIZATION OF WINE STYLES

Although technology allows winemakers to produce wine of increasingly better quality, the continuing obsession with technically perfect wines is unfortunately stripping wines of their identifiable and distinctive character. Whether it is the excessive filtration of wines or insufficiently critical emulation of winemaking styles, the downside of modern winemaking is that it is now increasingly difficult to tell an Italian Chardonnay from one made in France or California or Australia. When the corporate winemakers of the world begin to make wines all in the same way, designing them to offend the least number of people, wine will no doubt lose its fascinating appeal and individualism and become no better than most brands of whiskey, gin, Scotch, or vodka. One must not forget that the great appeal of wine is that it is a unique, distinctive, fascinating beverage and different every time one drinks it. Winemakers and the owners of wineries, particularly in America, must learn to take more risks so as to preserve the individual character of their wines, even at the risk that some consumers may find them bizarre or unusual. It is this distinctive quality of wine that will ensure its future.

DESTROYING THE JOY OF WINE BY EXCESSIVE ACIDIFICATION, OVERZEALOUS FINING, AND ABRASIVE FILTRATION

Since the beginning of my career as a professional wine critic, I have tried to present a strong case against the excessive manipulation of wine. One look at the producers of the world's greatest wines will reveal irrefutably that the following characteristics are shared by all of them—whether they be from California, France, Italy, Spain, or Germany: 1) They are driven to preserve the integrity of the vineyard's character, the grape variety's identity, and the vintage's personality; 2) They believe in low crop yields; 3) Weather permitting, they harvest only physiologically mature (versus analytically ripe) fruit; 4) They use simplistic winemaking and cellaring techniques, in the sense that they are minimal interventionists, preferring to permit the wine to make itself; 5) Though they are not opposed to fining or filtration if the wine is unstable or unclear, if the wine is made from healthy, ripe grapes and is stable and clear, they will absolutely refuse to strip it by excessive fining and filtration at bottling.

Producers who care only about making wine as fast as possible and collecting their accounts receivable also have many things in common. They turn out neutral, vapid, mediocre wines, and they are believers in huge crop yields, with considerable fertilization to promote massive crops, as large as the vineyard can render (six or more tons per acre, compared to modest yields of three tons per acre). Their philosophy is that the vineyard is a manufacturing plant, and cost efficiency dictates that production be maximized. They rush their wine into bottle as quickly as possible in order to get paid. They believe in *processing* wine, which usually involves centrifuging it initially, then practicing multiple fining and filtration procedures, particularly a denuding sterile filtration. This guarantees that the wine is lifeless but stable, so the wine's being able to withstand temperature extremes and stand upright on a grocery store's shelf has priority over giving the consumer true pleasure. These wineries harvest earlier than anybody else because they are unwilling to take any risk, delegating all questions regarding wine to their oenologists, who, they know, have as their objectives security and stability, which is in conflict with the consumer's goal of finding joy in wine.

The effect of excessive manipulation of wine, particularly aggressive fining and filtration, is dramatic. It destroys a wine's bouquet as well as its ability to express its *terroir* and varietal character. It also mutes the vintage's character. Fining and filtration can be done lightly, causing only minor damage, but most wines produced in the New World (California, Australia, and South America, in particular) and most bulk wines produced in Europe are sterile-filtered. This procedure requires numerous prefiltrations to get the wines clean enough to pass through a micropore membrane filter. This system of wine stability and clarification strips, eviscerates, and denudes a wine of much of its character.

Some wines can suffer such abuse with less damage. Thick, tannic, concentrated Syrah- and Cabernet Sauvignon–based wines may even survive these wine lobotomies—diminished in aromatic and flavor dimension but still live. Wines such as Pinot Noir and Chardonnay are destroyed in the process.

Thanks to a new generation of producers, particularly in France, aided by a number of specialist importers from America, there has been a movement against unnecessary fining and filtration. One has only to look at the extraordinary success enjoyed by such American importers as Kermit Lynch, Weygandt-Metzler, North Berkeley Imports, and Robert Kacher to realize how much consumer demand exists for a natural, unfiltered, uncompromised wine that is a faithful representation of its vineyard and vintage. Most serious wine consumers do not mind not being able to drink the last half ounce of wines because of sediment. They know this sediment means they are getting a flavorful, authentic, unprocessed wine that is much more representative than one that has been stripped at bottling.

Other small importers who have followed the leads of Lynch and Kacher include Peter Weygandt of Weygandt-Metzler, Unionville, Penn.; Neal Rosenthal Select Vineyards, New York, N.Y.; Eric Solomon of European Cellars, New York, N.Y.; Don Quattlebaum of New Castle Imports, Myrtle Beach, S.C.; Fran Kysela of Kysela Père et Fils of Winchester, Va.; Martine Saunier of Martine's Wines, San Rafael, Calif.; North Berkeley Imports, Berkeley, Calif.; Jorge Ordoñez, Dedham, Mass.; Leonardo LoCascio, Ho-Ho-Kus, N.J.; Dan Philips, Oxnard, Calif.; John Larchet, Australia; Jeffrey Davies, West Nyack, N.Y.; Alain Junguenet, Watchung, N.J.; Rare Wine Company, Sonoma, Calif.; Patrick Mata, New Rochelle, N.Y.; Aurelio Cabestrero, Grapes of Spain, Lorton, Va.; TGIC Wine Importers, Woodland Hills, Calif.; Vine Connections, Sausalito, Calif.; the portfolio of Marc de Grazia Selections represented by various American importers; Vin Divino, Chicago, Ill.; Robert Chadderdon Selections, New York, N.Y.; and David Shiverick, Los Angeles, Calif., to name some of the best known. They often insist that their producers not filter wines shipped to the U.S., resulting in a richer, more ageworthy wine being sold in America than elsewhere in the world. Even some of this country's largest importers, most notably Kobrand Corporation, in New York City, are encouraging producers to move toward more gentle and natural bottling techniques.

I am certain there would be an even more powerful movement to bottle wines naturally with minimal clarification if the world's wine press were to examine the effect of excessive fining and filtration. I find it difficult to criticize many American wine writers, because the vast majority of them are part-timers. Few have the time or resources to taste the same wines before and after bottling. Yet I remain disappointed that many of our most influential writers and publications have remained strangely silent, particularly in view of the profound negative impact filtration can have on the quality of fine wine. The English wine-writing corps, which includes many veteran, full-time wine writers, has an appalling record on this issue, especially in view of the fact that many of them make it a practice to taste before and after bottling. For those who care about the quality of wine, and the preservation of the character of the vineyard, vintage, and grape variety, the reluctance of so many writers to criticize the wine industry undermines the entire notion of wine appreciation.

Even a wine writer of the stature of Hugh Johnson comes out strongly on the side of processed, neutral wines that can be safely shipped 12 months of the year. Readers may want to consider Johnson's, and his co-author, James Halliday's, comments in their book *The Vintner's Art—How Great Wines Are Made.* Halliday is an Australian wine writer and winery owner, and Hugh Johnson may be this century's most widely read wine author. In their book they chastise the American importer Kermit Lynch for his "romantic ideals," which they describe as "increasingly impractical." Johnson and Halliday assert, "The truth is that a good fifty percent of those artisan Burgundies and Rhônes are bacterial time bombs." Their plea for compromised and standardized wines is supported by the following observation: "The hard reality is that many restaurants and many consumers simply will not accept sediment." This may have been partially true in America 20 years ago, but today the consumer not only wants but demands a natural wine. Moreover, the savvy wine consumer understands that sediment in a bottle of fine wine is a healthy sign. The position, which both writers defend—that modern-day winemaking and commercial necessity require that wines be shipped 12 months a year and be durable enough to withstand months on retailers' shelves in both cold and hot temperature conditions—is highly debatable. America now has increasing numbers of responsible merchants, importers, and restaurant sommeliers who go to great lengths to guarantee the client a healthy bottle of wine that has not been abused. Astonishingly, Johnson and Halliday conclude that consumers cannot tell the difference between a filtered and an unfiltered wine! In summarizing their position, they state, "but leave the wine for 1, 2, or 3 months (one cannot tell how long the recovery process will take), and it is usually impossible to tell the filtered from the nonfiltered wine, provided the filtration at bottling was skillfully carried out." After nearly 30 years of conducting such tastings, I find this statement not only unbelievable, but not supported by any tasting. Am I to conclude that all of the wonderful wines I have tasted from cask that were subsequently damaged by vigorous fining and filtration were bottled by incompetent people who did not know how to filter? Am I to think that the results of the extensive comparative tastings (usually blind) that I have done of the same wine, filtered versus unfiltered, were bogus? Are the enormous aromatic, flavor, textural, and qualitative differences that result from vigorous clarification figments of my imagination? Astoundingly, the wine industry's reluctance to accept responsibility for preserving all that the best vineyards and vintages can achieve is excused rather than condemned.

If excessive fining and filtration are not bad enough, consider the overzealous additions of citric and tartaric acids employed by Australian and California oenologists to perk up their wines. You know the feeling—you open a bottle of Australian or California Chardonnay and not only is there no bouquet (because it was sterile-filtered), but tasting the wine is like biting into a fresh lemon or lime. It is not enjoyable. What you are experiencing is the result of the misguided philosophy among New World winemakers to add too much acidity as a cheap life insurance policy for their wines. This "life insurance" is in fact a death certificate. Because these producers are unwilling to reduce their yields and unwilling to assume any risk, and because they see winemaking as nothing more than a processing technique, they generously add acidity. It does serve as an antibacterial, antioxidizing agent, thus helping to keep the wine fresh. But those who acidify the most are usually those who harvest appallingly high crop yields, so there is little flavor to protect! After 6 to 12 months of bottle age, what little fruit is present fades, and the consumer is left with a skeleton of sharp, shrill acid levels, alcohol, wood (if utilized), and no fruit—an utterly reprehensible way to make wine.

I do not object to the use of these techniques for bulk and jug wines that the consumer is buying for value, or because of brand-name recognition. But for any producer to sell a wine as a handcrafted, artisan product at $20 or more a bottle, these practices are shameful. Anyone who tells you that excessive acidification, fining, and filtration do not damage a wine is either a fool or a liar.

THE INFLATED WINE PRICING OF RESTAURANTS

Given the vast sums of American discretionary income spent in restaurants, a strong argument could be made that the cornerstone in increased wine consumption and awareness must be restaurants. However, most restaurants treat wine as a luxury item, marking it up an exorbitant 200% to 500%, thus effectively discouraging the consumption of wine. This practice of offering wines at huge markups also serves to reinforce the mistaken notion that wine is only for the elite and the superrich.

The wine industry does little about this practice, being content merely to see its wines placed on a restaurant's list. But the consumer should rebel and avoid restaurants that charge exorbitant wine prices, no matter how sublime the cuisine. This is nothing more or less than a legitimized mugging.

Fortunately, things are slightly better today than they were a decade ago, as some restaurant owners are now regarding wine as an integral part of the meal and not merely as a device to increase the bill.

COLLECTORS VERSUS CONSUMERS

I have reluctantly come to believe that many of France's greatest wine treasures—the first growths of Bordeaux, including the famous sweet nectar made at Château d'Yquem, Burgundy's most profound red wines from the Domaine de la Romanée-Conti, and virtually all of the wines from the tiny white wine appellation of Montrachet—are never drunk or, should I say, swallowed. Most of us who purchase or cellar wine do so on the theory that eventually every one of our splendid bottles will be swirled, sloshed, sniffed, sipped, and, yes, guzzled, with friends. That, of course, is one of the joys of wine, and those of you who partake of this pleasure are true wine lovers. There are, however, other types of wine collectors—the collector-investor, the collector-spitter, and even the nondrinking collector.

Several years ago I remember being deluged with telephone calls from a man wanting me to have dinner with him and tour his private cellar. After several months of resisting, I finally succumbed. This very prominent businessman had constructed an impressive cellar beneath his sprawling home. It was enormous and immaculately kept, with state-of-the-art humidity and temperature controls. I suspect it contained in excess of 10,000 bottles. There were cases of such thoroughbreds as Pétrus, Lafite-Rothschild, Mouton-Rothschild, and rare vintages of the great red Burgundies such as Romanée-Conti and La Tâche, and to my astonishment there were also hundreds of cases of 10- and 15-year-old Beaujolais, Pouilly-Fuissé, Dolcetto, and California Chardonnays—all wines that should have been drunk during their first four or five years. I diplomatically suggested that he should inventory his cellar, as there seemed to be a number of wines that mandated immediate consumption.

About the time I spotted the fifth or sixth case of what was undoubtedly ten-year-old Beaujolais vinegar, I began to doubt the sincerity of my host's enthusiasm for wine. These unthinkable doubts (I was much more naive then than I am now) were amplified at dinner. As we entered the sprawling kitchen and dining room complex, he proudly announced that neither he nor his wife actually drank wine, and then asked if I would care for a glass of mineral water, iced tea—or, if I preferred, a bottle of wine. During my sorrowful drive home that evening, I lamented that I had not opted for the mineral water. For when I made the mistake of requesting wine, my host proceeded to grab a bottle of wine that one of his friends suggested should be consumed immediately. It was a brown, utterly repugnant, senile Bordeaux from 1969, perhaps the worst vintage in the last 25 years. Furthermore, the château was a notorious underachiever from the famous commune of Pauillac. The wine he chose does not normally merit buying in a good vintage, much less a pathetic one. I shall never forget my host opening the bottle and saying, "Well, Bob, this wine sure smells good."

Regrettably, this nondrinking collector continues to buy large quantities of wine, not for investment, and obviously not for drinking. The local wine merchants tell me his type is not rare. To him, a collection of wine is like a collection of crystal, art, sculpture, or china— something to be admired, to be shown off, but never, ever to be consumed.

More ostentatious by far is the collector-spitter, who thrives on gigantic tastings where 50, 60, sometimes even 70 or 80 vintages of great wines, often from the same châteaux, can be "tasted." Important members of the wine press are invited (no charge, of course) in the hope that this wine happening will receive a major article in the *New York* or *Los Angeles Times,* and the collector's name will become recognized and revered in the land of winedom. These collector-spitters relish rubbing elbows with famous proprietors and telling their friends, "Oh, I'll be at Château Lafite-Rothschild next week to taste all of the château's wines between 1870 and 1987. Sorry you can't be there." I have, I confess, participated in several of these events and have learned from the exercise of trying to understand them that their primary purpose is to feed the sponsor's enormous ego, and often the château's ego as well.

I am not against academic tastings where a limited number of serious wine enthusiasts sit down to taste 20 or 30 different wines (usually young ones), because that is a manageable number that both neophytes and connoisseurs can generally grasp. But to taste 60 or more rare and monumental vintages at a tasting marathon is excessive. To put it simply, what happens at these tastings is that much of the world's greatest, rarest, and most expensive wines are spit out. No wine taster I have ever met could conceivably remain sober, even if only the greatest wines were swallowed, but I can assure you, there is only remorse in spitting out 1929 or 1945 Mouton-Rothschild.

Recollections of these events have long troubled me. I vividly remember one tasting held at a very famous restaurant in Los Angeles where a number of compelling bottles from one of France's greatest estates were opened. Many of the wines were exhilarating. Yet, whether it was the otherworldly 1961 or the opulent 1947, the reactions I saw on the faces of those 40 or so people, each of whom had paid several thousand dollars to attend, made me wonder whether we were tasting 50 different vintages of France's greatest wines or 50 bottles of Pepto-Bismol. Fortunately, the organizer did appear to enjoy the gathering and appreciate the wines, but among the guests I never once saw a smile or any enthusiasm or happiness in the course of this extraordinary 12-hour tasting.

I remember another marathon tasting held in France by one of Europe's leading collector-spitters, which lasted all day and much of the night. There were more than 90 legendary wines served, and midway through the afternoon I was reasonably certain there was not a sober individual remaining except for the chef and his staff. By the time the magnum of 1929 Mouton-Rothschild was served (one of the century's greatest wines), I do not think there was a guest left, myself included, who was competent enough to know whether he was drinking claret or Beaujolais.

I have also noticed at these tastings that many collector-spitters did not even know when a bottle was corked (it would have the smell of moldy cardboard and taste as bad), or when a bottle was oxidized and undrinkable, proving the old saying that money does not always buy good taste. Of course, most of these tastings are media happenings designed to stroke the host's vanity. All too frequently they undermine the principle that wine is a beverage of pleasure, and that is my basic regret.

The third type of collector, the investor, is motivated by the possibility of reselling the wines for profit. Eventually, most or all of these wines return to the marketplace, and much of it wends its way into the hands of serious consumers who share it with their spouses or good friends. Of course, they often must pay dearly for the privilege, but wine is not the only product that falls prey to such manipulation. I hate to think of wine being thought of primarily as an investment, but the world's finest wines do appreciate significantly in value, and it would be foolish to ignore the fact that more and more shrewd investors are looking at wine as a way of making money.

UNSPEAKABLE PRACTICES

It is a frightening thought, but I have no doubt that a sizable percentage (between 10% and 25%) of the wines sold in America have been damaged because of exposure to extremes of heat. Smart consumers have long been aware of the signs of poor storage. They have only to look at the bottle. As discussed earlier in the How to Buy Wine section (see page 8), the first sign that a bottle has been poorly stored is when a cork is popped above the rim and is pushed out against the lead or plastic capsule that covers the top of the bottle.

Another sign that the wine has been poorly stored is seepage, known as legs, down the rim of the bottle. This is the sometimes sticky, dry residue of a wine that has expanded, seeped around the cork, and dripped onto the rim, almost always due to excessively high temperatures in transit or storage. Few merchants take the trouble to wipe the legs off, and they can often be spotted on wines shipped during the heat of the summer or brought into the U.S. through the Panama Canal in unair-conditioned containers. Consumers should avoid buying wines that show dried seepage legs originating under the capsule and trickling down the side of the bottle.

Also be alert for young wines (those less than four years old) that have more than one-half inch of air space, or ullage, between the cork and the liquid level in the bottle. Modern bottling operations generally fill bottles within one-eighth inch of the cork, and more than one-half inch of air space should arouse your suspicion.

The problem, of course, is that too few people in the wine trade take the necessary steps to ensure that the wine is not ruined in shipment or storage. The wine business has become so commercial that wines, whether from California, Italy, or France, are shipped year-round, regardless of weather conditions. Traditionally, wines from Europe were shipped only in the spring or fall, when the temperatures encountered in shipment would be moderate, assuming they were not shipped by way of the Panama Canal. The cost of renting an air-conditioned or heated container for shipping wines adds anywhere from 20 to 40 cents to the wholesale cost of the bottle, but when buying wines that cost more than $200 a case, I doubt the purchaser would mind paying the extra premium knowing that the wine will not smell or taste cooked when opened.

Many importers claim to ship in reefers (the trade jargon for temperature-controlled containers), but only a handful actually do. America's largest importer of high-quality Bordeaux wine rarely, if ever, uses reefers, and claims to have had no problems with its shipments. Perhaps they would change their minds if they had witnessed the cases of 1986 Rausan-Ségla, 1986 Talbot, 1986 Gruaud-Larose, and 1986 Château Margaux that arrived in the Maryland–Washington, D.C., market with stained labels and pushed-out corks. Somewhere between Bordeaux and Washington, D.C., these wines had been exposed to torrid temperatures. It may not have been the fault of the importer, as the wine passed through a number of intermediaries before reaching its final destination. But pity the poor consumers who buy these wines, put them in their cellars, and open them 10 or 15 years in the future. Who will grieve for them?

The problem with temperature extremes is that the naturally made, minimally processed, hand-produced wines are the most vulnerable to this kind of abuse. Therefore, many importers, not wanting to assume any risks, have gone back to their suppliers and demanded "more stable" wines. Translated into real terms, this means the wine trade prefers to ship vapid, denuded wines that have been "stabilized," subjected to a manufacturing process, and either pasteurized or sterile-filtered so they can be shipped 12 months a year. Though their corks may still pop out if subjected to enough heat, their taste will not change, because for all intents and purposes these wines are already dead when they are put in the bottle. Unfortunately, only a small segment of the wine trade seems to care.

There are some wine merchants, wholesalers, and importers who are cognizant of the damage that can be done when wines are not protected, and who take great pride in representing hand-made, quality products, but the majority of the wine trade continues to ignore the risks. They would prefer that the wine be denuded by pasteurization, cold stabilization, or a sterile filtration. Only then can they be shipped safely under any weather conditions.

WINE PRODUCERS' GREED

Are today's wine consumers being hoodwinked by the world's wine producers? Most growers and/or producers have intentionally permitted production yields to soar to such extraordinary levels that the concentration and character of their wines are in jeopardy. There remain a handful of fanatics who continue, at some financial sacrifice, to reject a significant proportion of their harvest in order to ensure that only the finest-quality wine is sold under their name. However, they are dwindling in number. Fewer producers are prepared to go into the vineyard and cut bunches of grapes to reduce the yields. Fewer still are willing to cut back prudently on fertilizers. For much of the last decade, production yields throughout the world continued to break records with each new vintage. The results are wines that increasingly lack character, concentration, and staying power. In Europe, the most flagrant abuses of overproduction occur in Germany and Burgundy, where yields today are three to almost five times what they were in the 1950s. The argument that the vineyards are more carefully and competently managed, and that this results in larger crops, is misleading. Off the record, many a seriously committed wine producer will tell you, "The smaller the yield, the better the wine."

If one wonders why the Domaine Leroy's Burgundies taste richer than those from other domaines, it is due not only to quality winemaking but also to the fact that their yields are one-third those of other Burgundy producers. If one asks why the best Châteauneuf-du-Papes are generally Rayas, Pégaü, Bonneau, and Beaucastel, it is because their yields are one-half those of other producers of the appellation. The same assertion applies to J. J. Prüm and Müller-Cattoir in Germany. Not surprisingly, they have conservative crop yields and produce one-third the amount of wine their neighbors produce.

Though I do not want to suggest that there are no longer any great wines, and that most of the wines now produced are no better than the plonk peasants drank in the 19th century, the point is that overfertilization, modern sprays that prevent rot, the development of highly prolific clonal selections, and the failure to keep production levels modest have all resulted in yields that may well be combining to destroy the reputations of many of the most famous wine regions of the world. Trying to find a flavorful Chardonnay from California today is not much easier than finding a concentrated red Burgundy that can age gracefully beyond 10 years. The production yields of Chardonnay in California have often resulted in wines that have only a faint character of the grape and seem almost entirely dominated by acidity and/or the smell of oak barrels. What is appalling is that there is so little intrinsic flavor. Yet Chardonnays remain the most popular white wine in this country, so what incentive is there to lower yields?

Of course, if the public, encouraged by a noncritical, indifferent wine media, is willing to pay top dollar for mediocrity, then little is likely to change. On the other hand, if consumers start insisting that $15 or $20 should at the very minimum fetch a wine that provides genuine pleasure, perhaps that message will gradually work its way back to the producers.

WINE WRITERS' ETHICS AND COMPETENCE

The problems just described have only occasionally been acknowledged by the wine media, which generally has a collective mind-set of never having met a wine it doesn't like.

Wine writing in America has rarely been a profitable or promising full-time occupation. Historically, the most interesting work was always done by the people who sold the wine. There's no doubting the influence or importance of the books written by Alexis Lichine and Frank Schoonmaker. But both men made their fortunes by selling rather than writing about wine, and both managed to write about wine objectively, despite their ties to the trade.

There are probably not more than a dozen or so independent wine experts in this country who support themselves entirely by writing. Great Britain has long championed the cause of wine writers and looked upon them as true professionals. But even there, with all their experience and access to the finest European vineyards, most of the successful wine writers have been involved in the sale and distribution of wine. Can anyone name an English wine writer who criticized the performance of Lafite-Rothschild between 1961 and 1974, or Margaux between 1964 and 1977? Meanwhile, the consumer was getting screwed.

It is probably unrealistic to expect writers to develop a professional expertise with wine without access and support from the trade, but such support can compromise their findings. If they are beholden to wine producers for the wines they taste, they are not likely to fault them. If their trips to vineyards are the result of the winemaker's largesse, they are unlikely to criticize what they have seen. If they are lodged at the châteaux and their trunks are filled with cases of wine (as, sadly, is often the case), can a consumer expect them to be critical, or even objective?

Putting aside this ethical dilemma, many wine writers are lacking the global experience to evaluate wine properly. What has emerged from such inexperience is a school of wine writing that is primarily trained to look at the wine's structure and acid levels, and this philosophy is too frequently in evidence when judging wines. The level of pleasure that a wine provides, or is capable of providing in the future, would appear to be irrelevant. The results are wine evaluations that read as though one were measuring the industrial strength of different grades of cardboard rather than a beverage that many consider nature's greatest gift to mankind. Balance is everything in wine, and wines that taste too tart or tannic rarely ever age into flavorful, distinctive, charming beverages. While winemaking and wine technology are indeed better, and some of the most compelling wines ever made are being produced today, there are far too many mediocre wines sitting on the shelves that hardly deserve their high praise.

There are, however, some interesting trends. The growth of *The Wine Spectator,* with its staff of full-time writers obligated to follow a strict code of non–conflict of interest, has resulted in better and more professional journalism. It also cannot be discounted that this flashy magazine appears twice a month. This is good news for the wine industry, frequently under siege by the antialcohol extremists. Finally, to *The Wine Spectator*'s credit, more of their tasting reports are authored by one or two people, not an anonymous, secretive committee. I have already aired my criticism of wine magazines and tastings whose evaluations are the result of a committee's vote.

Given the vitality of our nation's best wine guides, it is unlikely that wine writers will have less influence in the future. The thousands and thousands of wines that come on the market, many of them overpriced and vapid, require consumer-oriented reviews from the wine-writing community. But until a greater degree of professionalism is attained, until more experience is evidenced by wine writers, until their misplaced and misinformed emphasis on high acidity and structure is forever discredited, until most of the British wine media begin to understand and adhere to the basic rules of conflict of interest, until we all remember that this is only a beverage of pleasure, to be seriously consumed but not taken too seriously, then and only then will the quality of wine writing and the wines we drink improve. Will all of this happen, or will we be reminded of the words of Marcel Proust: "We do not succeed in changing things according to our desire, but gradually our desire changes. The situation that we hope to change because it was intolerable becomes unimportant. We have not managed to surmount the obstacle as we were absolutely determined to do, but life has taken us around it, led us past it, and then if we turn around to gaze at the remote past, we can barely catch sight of it, so imperceptible has it become."

IN VINO VERITAS?

Virtually everything that follows came from an essay I wrote in the mid-1990s, which then provoked an interview with several FBI agents conducting an ongoing investigation regarding fraudulent wine. More recently this has come full circle, with a major lawsuit by one of the most famous wine collectors in the United States, Bill Koch, against a rather mysterious rare wine purveyor living in Munich named Hardy Rodenstock. The lawsuit was based on what was allegedly a fraudulent bottle sold at Christie's and verified by Michael Broadbent as coming from the personal cellar of Thomas Jefferson. The lawsuit is still pending as lawyers fight over jurisdictional issues, but it has also spawned a book called *The Billionaire's Vinegar* by Benjamin Wallace, a compelling read about fraudulent wines and all the shenanigans that seem to surround this rarefied topic, where corruption, greed, and perhaps even outright criminality walk hand in hand with aristocratic auctioneers and famous collectors.

There is no doubt that the overwhelming majority of rare and fine wine sold today, either at retail or through one of the numerous wine auctions, involves legitimate bottles. Yet over the last six months I have accumulated enough evidence to suggest that some warning flags need to be raised before this insidious disease becomes a vinous ebola. Shrewd buyers, reputable merchants, and auction companies that specialize in top vintages take measures to authenticate bottles of wine that may cost thousands of dollars. The top auction houses, aware of the growing evidence of phony bottles, are going to great lengths to authenticate the legitimacy of each wine they sell. Nevertheless, a con artist can easily reproduce a bottle (even the finest Bordeaux châteaux use glass bottles that are among the cheapest and easiest to obtain in the world), a label, a cork, and a capsule, deceiving even the most astute purchaser. Think it over—high-quality, limited-production, rare wine may be the only luxury-priced commodity in the world that does not come with a guarantee of authenticity, save for the label and cork, and the former can be easily duplicated, particularly with one of today's high-tech scanners.

The wine marketplace has witnessed obscene speculation for such modern-day vintages as 1990, certain 1989s, and, of course, 1982. The appearance of dishonest segments of society with only one objective, to take full advantage of the enormous opportunity that exists to make a quick buck by selling bogus wines, is not that shocking. This has always been a problem, but, based on the number of letters and telephone calls I have received from victims who have been the recipients of suspiciously labeled wines with even more doubtful contents, it is a subject that needs to be addressed.

It was nearly 20 years ago that I saw my first fraudulent bottles of fine wine. Cases of 1975 Mouton-Rothschild were being sold in New York for below market value. The wine was packed in shabby cardboard cases with washed-out labels. In addition to those warning signs, the bottles had the words "Made in Canada" on the bottom, and the capsules did not have the characteristic Mouton-embossed printing. Blatant recklessness and slipshod work by the criminal made the fraud easy to detect.

Many producers of these limited-production, rare wines are aware of the frauds perpetrated with their products, but they have chosen to maintain a low profile for fear that widespread dissemination of potentially inflammatory information will unsettle (to put it mildly) the fine-wine marketplace. No doubt the news that 100 or so phony cases of Château ABC are floating around in the world marketplace would suppress the value of the wine. The estates that make the world's most cherished wines (and we all know who they are) need to develop a better system for guaranteeing the authenticity of their product, but, lamentably, few have been so inclined. Four of the elite Bordeaux châteaux do make it more difficult for counterfeiting pirates. Pétrus has, since the 1988 vintage, utilized a special label that when viewed under a specific type of light reveals a code not apparent under normal lighting conditions. In 1996, Pétrus went further, instituting an engraved bottle with the word "Pétrus" etched in the glass. Château d'Yquem incorporates a watermark in their label to discourage imitators. Haut-Brion was among the first to utilize a custom-embossed bottle, in 1957. In 1996, Lafite-Rothschild also launched an antifraud-engraved bottle. More recently, Château Margaux has inserted a special code in the print of each bottle. Whether by creating more sophisticated labels that are not as easy to reproduce (with serial numbers, watermarks, etc.), or by employing a fraud squad devoted to tracking down the provenance of these phony bottles, something must be done.

Space does not permit me to discuss all the shocking frauds I have learned of or have been called in to help prove. I myself have seen phony bottles of Domaine Leflaive Montrachet, Château Rayas, Cheval Blanc, Vieux Château Certan, and Château Le Pin. Reports of phony bottles come in with surprising frequency and have been confirmed in conversations with retailers, both in this country and in England. They have told me of fraudulent cases of 1989 and 1982 Le Pin, 1982 Pétrus, 1982 and 1975 Lafleur, 1947 Cheval Blanc, 1928 Latour, and 1900 Margaux, with nonbranded blank corks and photocopied labels! With respect to the 1928 Latour, the merchant, suspecting he had been duped, opened it and told me he was sure it was a young California Pinot Noir. One major American merchant, outraged at being sold phony wine, attempted to contact the European seller, only to find out he had moved, with no forwarding address, from his office in Paris. The seller has never been found.

A wine buyer from one of this country's most prominent restaurants recently told me about problems he had encountered when opening expensive bottles for his clients. All of these wines had been purchased from a reputable merchant who had bought the wine from a gray marketeer selling private cellars in Europe. Corks of 1961 Haut-Brion and 1970 Latour were either illegible or intentionally had the vintage scratched off. Since this buyer had vast tasting experience with these wines, detection of the fraud was relatively easy. He was convinced that the 1961 Haut-Brion was fraudulent, as it tasted like a much lighter vintage of Haut-Brion (he suspected it was 1967). With the "1970," the cork had been altered, but closer inspection revealed it to be the 1978 Latour.

What is so surprising is that most fraudulent efforts to date appear to be the work of kindergarten criminals using washed-out, photocopied labels, and unconvincing corks or capsules. However, with the technology available today, authentic-looking bottles, capsules, corks, and labels can be easily duplicated, and for these counterfeits, only a person who knows the taste of the wine could tell if the contents were bogus.

For the record, I wrote up in *The Wine Advocate* that I went to only one tasting of rare wines hosted by Rodenstock, in Munich in the mid-1990s. These were annual events that I had intentionally avoided, but I felt almost embarrassingly stupid for not taking part, as virtually every other major wine writer had, passing up an opportunity to taste some of the rarest and greatest wines ever made. If Rodenstock is ever proven to be a master blender, he is a gifted one, because what I tasted at that event, aside from several bad bottles, were absolutely extraordinary wines in great condition that actually did resemble the châteaux that were on the labels. However, since few people get the chance to taste ancient magnums from the 1920s or earlier of Pétrus and other wines from Bordeaux, one would never really know what a pristine bottle would taste like, so one can only extrapolate from what modern-day vintages taste like and judge whether the wines have much of the character of current-day, authentic bottles from great years. In this respect, everything I tasted seemed quite consistent with the château's *terroir* and the character of the vintage, but again, as I have stated to several people, whether the wines were legitimate or fake, they were undeniably great wines.

SAFETY GUIDELINES

Dealing with the gray market To date, almost all the fraudulent bottles have come from wines purchased in the so-called gray market. This means the wines have not gone through normal distribution channels, where a contractual relationship exists between the producer and the vendor. Bottles of French wines with the green French tax stamps on the top of the capsule have obviously been purchased in France and then resold to gray-market operators. I do not want to denigrate the best of the gray-market operators, because I am a frequent purchaser from these sources, and those that I know are legitimate, serious, and professional about what they buy. Nevertheless, it is irrefutable that most of the suspicious wine showing up is from rogue gray-market operators.

Label awareness Wine bottles that have easily removable neck labels to indicate the vintage are especially prone to tampering. It is easy to transfer a neck label from a poor vintage to one with a great reputation. Sadly, almost all Burgundies fall into this category, as well as some Rhône Valley wines. Many of the top Burgundy producers have begun to brand the cork with the appropriate vintage and vineyard, particularly if it is a premier or grand cru. However, this is a relatively recent practice, largely implemented in the late 1980s by top estates and *négociants*. The only way a buyer can make sure the cork matches the neck and bottle labels is to remove the capsule. Any purchaser who is the least bit uneasy about the provenance of a wine should not hesitate to pull off the capsule. Irregular, asymmetrical labels with tears and smears of glue are a sign that someone may have tampered with the bottle. Perhaps the trend (now widely employed by California wineries such as Robert Mondavi and Kendall-Jackson) to discontinue the use of capsules should be considered by top estates in France, Italy, and Spain. An alternative would be to design a capsule with a window slot, permitting the purchaser to have a view of the cork's vintage and vineyard name. A more practical as well as inexpensive alternative would be to print the name of the vineyard and vintage on the capsule, in addition to the cork.

Badly faded, washed-out labels (or photocopied labels) should be viewed with sheer horror! However, readers should realize that moldy or deteriorated labels from a damp, cold cellar are not signs of fraudulent wines but, rather, of superb cellaring conditions. I have had great success at auctions buying old vintages that have moldy, tattered labels. Most speculators shy away from such wines because their priority is investing, not consumption.

Know the market value Most purchasers of expensive rare wines are extremely knowledgeable about the market value of these wines. If the wine is being offered at a significantly lower price than fair market value, it would seem incumbent on the purchaser to ask why he or she is the beneficiary of such a great deal. Remember, if it sounds too good to be true, it probably is.

Origin verification For both rare old vintages and young wines, demanding a guarantee as to the provenance of the wine being purchased is prudent. As a corollary, it is imperative that readers deal with reputable merchants who will stand behind the products they sell. If a merchant refuses to provide details of the origin of where the wine was purchased, take your business elsewhere, even if it means laying out more money for the same wine.

Lot numbers Because of some tainted Perrier water a few years ago, the European Community now requires most potable beverages to carry a lot number (but only on those sold in member nations, thus excluding the U.S.). This is usually a tiny number located somewhere on the label that begins with the letter *L*, followed by a serial number, which can range from several digits to as many as eight or more. Most producers use the vintage as part of the lot number. In the case of Domaine Leflaive, the vintage year is indicated by the last two digits of the lot number. However, in some instances (e.g., Comtes Lafon), the first two numbers provide the vintage year. For Lynch-Bages or Pichon–Longueville Baron, the vintage appears in the middle of the lot number. But be advised, many tiny growers do not use lot numbers on wines sold to non-EC countries (the U.S., for example). Virtually all the Bordeaux châteaux have used lot numbers since the 1989 vintage.

No sediment in older wines Wines more than 10 to 15 years old, with no sediment and/or with fill levels that reach the bottom of the cork, should always be viewed with suspicion. Several Burgundian *négociants* sell "reconditioned" bottles of ancient vintages that have fills to the cork and lack sediment. I have always been skeptical of this practice, but those *négociants* claim they have a special process for siphoning off the sediment. Certainly no Bordeaux château utilizes such an unusual and debatable method. Wines that have been recorked at a Bordeaux château will say so, either on the cork or on both the label and the cork, and the year in which it was recorked will usually be indicated. Among the most illustrious estates of Bordeaux, only Pétrus refuses to recork bottles, because so many suspicious bottles have been brought to them for recorking. Both Cheval Blanc and Latour indicate both on the cork and the label the date and year of recorking. In these cases, the authentic bottles will have very good fills as the wine has been topped off, but older vintages still display considerable sediment.

Unmarked cardboard cases Wines that have been packaged in unlabeled cardboard boxes are always suspect, because every Burgundy domaine uses its own customized cardboard box with the name of the estate as well as the importer's name printed on the box, and almost all the prominent Bordeaux châteaux use wooden boxes with the name of the château as well as the vintage branded into the wood. However, to complicate matters, readers should realize that wines from private cellars consigned to auction houses usually must be repackaged in unmarked cardboard boxes, since they had been stored in bins in a private cellar.

Rare, mature vintages in large formats Great wines from ancient rare vintages such as 1900, 1921, 1926, 1928, 1929, 1945, 1947, 1949, and 1950 (especially the Pomerols) that are offered in large formats, particularly double magnums, jeroboams, imperials, and the extremely rare Marie-Jeanne (a three-bottle size), should be scrutinized with the utmost care. Christian Moueix told me that a European vendor had offered rare vintages of Pétrus in Marie-Jeanne formats. To the best of Moueix's knowledge, Pétrus never used Marie-Jeanne bottles! Large formats of rare old vintages were used very sparingly at most top châteaux, so if anyone is contemplating purchasing an imperial of 1900 Margaux, be sure to verify the wine's authenticity. What some of the skeptics of these old bottles, including Moueix, don't acknowledge is that until the last three decades of the 20th century, many châteaux, and especially the lesser-known properties in St.-Émilion and Pomerol, often sold full barrels of wine (the equivalent of 300 bottles) to wealthy families in Belgium, Holland, and other countries. Many of these families bottled the wines as they saw fit, including magnums, double magnums, and even imperials. This would explain how some of these could eventually show up in the marketplace, but I still believe it is better to be safe than sorry when contemplating buying a rare vintage in large formats, especially from a highly regarded estate.

Common sense The need to develop a relationship with experienced and reputable merchants is obvious, but too often consumers are seduced by the lowest price. If it is an $8 Corbières, that's fine, but a prized vintage of a first-growth Bordeaux is not likely to be sold cheaply.

I hope the industry will address these issues in a more forthright manner and begin to take more action designed to protect its members, as well as consumers. Additionally, I urge the renowned estates that benefit from glowing reviews to recognize that it is only in their long-term interest to relentlessly seek a solution to this problem, and combine their efforts and resources to track down those who are responsible for fabricating fraudulent bottles of expensive wine. Surely the time has come for more sophisticated labels (with serial numbers and watermarks), designer bottles that are less easy to replicate, and capsules with vintages and vineyard names. An open avenue of communication with the wine buyer, where these frauds can be identified and confirmed and the commercial and consumer marketplace can be fully apprised of the problem, is essential to preserve the authenticity of the world's finest wines, as well as the integrity and security of purchasing fine wine.

[what constitutes a great wine?]

What is a great wine? This is one of the most controversial subjects of the vinous world. Isn't greatness in wine, much like a profound expression of art or music, something very personal and subjective? As much as I agree that the appreciation and enjoyment of art, music, or wine is indeed personal, high quality in wine, as in art and music, does tend to be subject to widespread agreement. Except for the occasional contrarian, greatness in art, music, or wine, though difficult to define precisely, enjoys a broad consensus.

Many of the most legendary wines of this century—1945 Mouton-Rothschild, 1945 Haut-Brion, 1947 Cheval Blanc, 1947 Pétrus, 1961 Latour, 1982 Mouton-Rothschild, 1982 Le Pin, 1982 Léoville–Las Cases, 1989 Haut-Brion, 1990 Margaux, and 1990 Pétrus, to name some of the most renowned red Bordeaux—are profound and riveting wines, even though an occasional discordant view about them may surface. Tasting is indeed subjective, but like most of the finest things in life, though there is considerable agreement as to what represents high quality, no one should feel forced to feign fondness for a work of Picasso or Beethoven, much less a bottle of 1961 Latour.

One issue about the world's finest wines that is subject to little controversy relates to how such wines originate. Frankly, there are no secrets about the origin and production of the world's finest wines. Great wines emanate from well-placed vineyards with microclimates favorable to the specific types of grapes grown. Profound wines, whether from France, Italy, Spain, California, or Australia, are also the product of conservative viticultural practices that emphasize low yields and physiologically rather than analytically ripe fruit. After 24 years spent tasting more than 200,000 wines, I have never tasted a superb wine that was made from underripe fruit. Does anyone enjoy the flavors present when biting into an underripe orange, peach, apricot, or cherry? Low yields and ripe fruit are essential for the production of extraordinary wines, yet it is amazing how many wineries seem not to understand this fundamental principle.

In addition to the commonsense approach of harvesting mature (ripe) fruit and discouraging, in a viticultural sense, the vine from overproducing, the philosophy employed by a winery in making wine is of paramount importance. Exceptional wines (whether red, white, or sparkling) emerge from a similar philosophy, which includes the following: 1) permit the vineyard's *terroir* (soil, microclimate, distinctiveness) to express itself; 2) allow the purity and characteristics of the grape variety or blend to be represented faithfully in the wine; and 3) follow an uncompromising, noninterventionalistic winemaking philosophy that eschews the food-processing, industrial mind-set of high-tech winemaking—in short, give the wine a chance to make itself naturally without the human element attempting to sculpt or alter the wine's intrinsic character, so that what is placed in the bottle represents as natural an expression of the vineyard, variety, and vintage as is possible. In keeping with this overall philosophy, winemakers who attempt to reduce traumatic clarification procedures such as fining and filtration, while also lowering sulfur levels (which can dry out a wine's fruit, bleach color from a wine, and exacerbate the tannin's sharpness) produce wines with far more aromatics and flavors, as well as more enthralling textures. These are wines that offer consumers their most compelling and rewarding drinking experiences.

Assuming there is a relatively broad consensus as to how the world's finest wines originate, what follows is my working definition of an exceptional wine. In short, what are the characteristics of a great wine?

The Ability to Please Both the Palate and the Intellect Great wines offer satisfaction on a hedonistic level and also challenge and satiate the intellect. The world offers many delicious wines that appeal to the senses but are not complex. The ability to satisfy the intellect is a more subjective issue. Wines that experts call "complex" are those that offer multiple dimensions in both their aromatic and flavor profiles, and have more going for them than simply ripe fruit and a satisfying, pleasurable, yet one-dimensional quality.

The Ability to Hold the Taster's Interest I have often remarked that the greatest wines I've ever tasted could easily be recognized by bouquet alone. These profound wines could never be called monochromatic or simple. They hold the taster's interest, not only providing the initial tantalizing tease but possessing a magnetic attraction because of their aromatic intensity and nuance-filled layers of flavors.

The Ability of a Wine to Offer Intense Aromas and Flavors Without Heaviness An analogy can be made to eating in the finest restaurants. Extraordinary cooking is characterized by its purity, intensity, balance, texture, and compelling aromas and flavors. What separates exceptional cuisine from merely good cooking, and great wines from good wines, is their ability to offer extraordinary intensity of flavor without heaviness. It has been easy in the New World (especially in Australia and California) to produce wines that are oversized, bold, big, rich, but heavy. Europe's finest wineries, with many centuries more experience, have mastered the ability to obtain intense flavors without heaviness. However, New World viticultural areas (particularly in California) are quickly catching up, as evidenced by the succession of remarkable wines produced in Napa, Sonoma, and elsewhere in the Golden State during the 1990s. Many of California's greatest wines of the 1990s have sacrificed none of their power and richness but no longer possess the rustic tannin and oafish feel on the palate that characterized so many of their predecessors of 10 and 20 years ago.

The Ability of a Wine to Taste Better with Each Sip Most of the finest wines I have ever drunk were better with the last sip than the first, revealing more nuances and more complex aromas and flavors as the wine unfolded in the glass. Do readers ever wonder why the most interesting and satisfying glass of wine is often the last one in the bottle?

The Ability of a Wine to Improve with Age This is, for better or worse, an indisputable characteristic of great wines. One of the unhealthy legacies of the European wine writers (who dominated wine writing until the last decade) is the belief that in order for a wine to be exceptional when mature, it had to be nasty when young. My experience has revealed just the opposite—wines that are acidic, astringent, and generally fruitless and charmless when young become even nastier and less drinkable when old. That being said, it is true that new vintages of top wines are often unformed and in need of 10 to 12 years of cellaring (for top California Cabernets, Bordeaux, and Rhônes), but those wines should always possess a certain accessibility so that even inexperienced wine tasters can tell the wine is—at minimum—made from very ripe fruit. If a wine does not exhibit ripeness and richness of fruit when young, it will not develop nuances with aging. Great wines unquestionably improve with age. I define "improvement" as the ability of a wine to become significantly more enjoyable and interesting in the bottle, offering more pleasure when old than when it was young. Many wineries (especially in the New World) produce wines they claim "will age," but this is nothing more than a public relations ploy. What they should really say is that they "will survive." They can endure 10 to 20 years of bottle age, but they were more enjoyable in their exuberant youthfulness.

The Ability of a Wine to Offer a Singular Personality Their singular personalities set the greatest wines apart from all others. It is the same with the greatest vintages. Descriptions such as "classic vintage" have become nothing more than a reference to what a viticultural region does in a typical (normal) year. Exceptional wines from exceptional vintages stand far above the norm, and they can always be defined by their singular qualities—both aromatically and in their flavors and textures. The opulent, sumptuous qualities of the 1982 and 1990 red Bordeaux; the rugged tannin and immense ageability of the 1986 red Bordeaux; the seamless, perfectly balanced 1994 Napa and Sonoma Cabernet Sauvignons and proprietary blends; and the plush, sweet fruit, high alcohol and glycerin of the 1990 Barolos and Barbarescos—all are examples of vintage individuality.

MAKING SENSE OF *TERROIR*

An Asian proverb says, "Knowing in part may make a fine tale, but wisdom comes from seeing the whole." And so it is with the concept of *terroir,* that hazy, intellectually appealing notion that a plot of soil plays the determining factor in a wine's character. The French are the world's most obsessive people regarding the issue of *terroir*. And why not? Many of that country's most renowned vineyards are part of an elaborate hierarchy of quality based on their soil and exposition. The French would have everyone believe that no one on planet Earth can equal the quality of their Pinot Noir, Chardonnay, Cabernet, Syrah, etc., because their privileged *terroir* is unequaled. One of France's most celebrated wine regions, Burgundy, is often cited as the best place to search for the fullest expression of *terroir*. Proponents of *terroir* (the *terroiristes*) argue that a particular piece of ground and its contribution to what is grown there give its product a character that can be distinguished from that same product grown on different soils and slopes. Burgundy, with its classifications of grand cru and premier cru vineyards, *village* vineyards, and generic viticultural areas, is the *terroiristes'* raison d'être.

Lamentably, *terroir* has become such a politically correct buzzword that in some circles it is an egregious error not to utter some profound comments about finding "a sense of somewhereness" when tasting a Vosne-Romanée Les Malconsorts or a Latricières-Chambertin. Leading *terroiristes* such as wine producer Lalou Bize-Leroy, Burgundy wine broker Becky Wasserman, and author Matt Kramer make a persuasive and often eloquent case about the necessity of finding, as Kramer puts it, "the true voice of the land" in order for a wine to be legitimized.

Yet, as with so many things about wine, especially tasting it, there is no scientific basis for anything Bize, Wasserman, or Kramer propose. What they argue is what most Burgundians and owners of France's finest vineyards give lip service to—that for a wine to be authentic and noble it must speak of its *terroir*.

On the other side of this issue are the "realists," or should I call them modernists? They suggest that *terroir* is merely one of many factors that influence the style of a wine. The realists argue that a multitude of factors determine a wine's style, quality, and character. Soil, exposition, and microclimate (*terroir*) most certainly impart an influence, but so do the following:

Rootstock Is it designed to produce prolific or small crop levels?

Yeasts Does the winemaker use the vineyard's wild yeasts or are commercial yeasts employed? Every yeast, wild or commercial, will give a wine a different set of aromatics, flavor, and texture.

Yields and vine age High yields from perennial overcroppers result in diluted wine. Low yields, usually less than 2 tons per acre or 35 to 40 hectoliters per hectare, result in wines with much more concentration and personality. Additionally, young vines have a tendency to overproduce, whereas old vines produce small berries and less wine. Crop thinning is often employed with younger vineyards to increase the level of concentration.

Harvest philosophy Is the fruit picked underripe to preserve more acidity, or is it allowed to ripen fully to emphasize the lushness and opulence of a given variety?

Vinification techniques and equipment There are an amazing number of techniques that can change the wine's aromas and flavors. Moreover, equipment choice (different presses, destemmers, etc.) can have a profound influence on the final wine.

Élevage (the wine's upbringing) Is the wine brought up in oak barrels, concrete vats, stainless steel, or large oak vats (which the French call *foudres*)? What is the percentage of new oak? What is the type of oak (French, Russian, American, etc.)? All of these elements exert a strong influence on the wine's character. Additionally, transferring wine (racking) from one container to another has an immense impact on a wine's bouquet and flavor. Is the wine allowed to remain in long contact with its lees (believed to give the wine more aromatic complexity and fullness)? Or is it racked frequently for fear of picking up an undesirable lees smell?

Fining and filtration Even the most concentrated and profound wines that *terroiristes* consider quintessential examples of the soil can be eviscerated and stripped of their personality and richness by excessive fining and filtering. Does the winemaker treat the wine with kid gloves, or is the winemaker a manufacturer-processor bent on sculpting the wine?

Bottling date Does the winemaker bottle early to preserve as much fruit as possible, or does he bottle later to give the wine a more mellow, aged character? Undoubtedly, the philosophy of when to bottle can radically alter the character of a wine.

Cellar temperature and sanitary conditions Some wine cellars are cold and others are warm. Different wines emerge from cold cellars (where development is slower and the wines are less prone to oxidation) than from warm cellars (where the maturation of aromas and flavors is more rapid and the wines are quicker to oxidize). Additionally, are the wine cellars clean or dirty?

These are just a handful of factors that can have extraordinary impact on the style, quality, and personality of a wine. As the modernists claim, the choices that man himself makes, even when they are unquestionably in pursuit of the highest quality, can contribute far more to a wine's character than the vineyard's *terroir*.

If one listens to Robert Kacher, a realist, or to Matt Kramer, a *terroiriste*, it is easy to conclude they inhabit different worlds. But the irony is that usually they tend to agree as to the producers making the finest wines.

If you are wondering where I stand on *terroir*, I do believe it is an important component in the production of fine wine. If one is going to argue *terroir*, the wine has to be made from exceptionally low yields, fermented with only the wild yeasts that inhabit the vineyard, brought up in a neutral medium, such as old barrels, cement tanks, or stainless steel, given minimal cellar treatment, and bottled with little or no fining or filtration. However, I would argue that the most persuasive examples of *terroir* arise not from Burgundy but, rather, from Alsace or Austria.

For example, if I were to take up the cause of the *terroiristes*, I would use one of Alsace's greatest domaines, that of Leonard and Olivier Humbrecht, to make a modest case for *terroir*. The Humbrechts do everything to emphasize the differences in their vineyard holdings. Yet why is it so easy to identify the wines of Zind-Humbrecht in a blind tasting? Certainly their Hengst-Riesling tastes different from their Riesling and from their Clos St.-Urbain. The question is, is one tasting the *terroir* or the winemaker's signature? Zind-Humbrecht's wines, when matched against other Alsatian wines, are more powerful, richer, and intense. Zind-Humbrecht's yields are lower and they do not filter the wine at bottling. These wines possess not only an identifiable winemaker's signature but also a distinctive vineyard character.

Terroir, as used by many of its proponents, is often a convenient excuse for upholding the status quo. If one accepts the fact that *terroir* is everything and is essential to legitimize a wine, how should consumers evaluate the wines from Burgundy's most famous grand cru vineyard, Chambertin? This 32-acre vineyard boasts 23 different proprietors. But only a handful of them appear committed to producing an extraordinary wine. Everyone agrees this is a hallowed piece of ground, but I can think of only a few—Domaine Leroy, Domaine Ponsot, Domaine Rousseau, and Trapet—that produce wines that merit the stratospheric reputation of this vineyard. Yet the Chambertins of these producers are completely different in style. The Trapet wine is the most elegant, supple, and round, Leroy's is the most tannic, backward, concentrated, and meaty, and Rousseau's is the darkest-colored, most dominated by new oak, and most modern in style, taste, and texture. Among the other 18 or 20 producers (and I am not even thinking about the various *négociant* offerings), what Burgundy wine enthusiasts are likely to encounter on retailers' shelves ranges from mediocre to appallingly thin and insipid. What wine, may I ask, speaks for the soil of Chambertin? Is it the wine of Leroy, the wine of Trapet, or the wine of Rousseau? Arguments such as this can be made with virtually any significant Bordeaux or Burgundy vineyard. Which has that notion of "somewhereness" that is raised by the *terroiristes* to validate the quality of a vineyard?

Are *terroiristes* kindergarten intellectuals who should be doing more tasting and less talking? Of course not. But they can be accused of naively swallowing the tallest tale in Burgundy. On the other hand, the realists should recognize that no matter how intense and concentrated a wine can be from a modest vineyard in Givry, it will never have the sheer complexity and class of a Vosne-Romanée grand cru from a conscientious producer.

In conclusion, think of *terroir* as you do salt, pepper, and garlic. In many dishes they can represent an invaluable component, imparting wonderful aromas and flavors, yet alone, they do not make the dish. Moreover, all the hyperventilation over *terroir* obscures the most important issue of all—identifying and discovering the producers who make wines that are worth drinking and savoring!

RECOMMENDED READING

Following is a personal list of publications and books I have found to offer interesting and often authoritative information on the world's wines.

JOURNALS AND MAGAZINES

La Revue du Vin de France, 38–48 Rue Victor-Hugo, 92532 Levallios-Perret, France; fax 011 33 1 41 40 23 09. This remains France's leading wine magazine and is available only in French. However, the sale of the magazine and the departure of Europe's finest taster, Michel Bettane, seriously damaged the magazine. Bettane and his partner, Thierry Desseauve, have their own website, which is one of the few places to find their highly regarded commentary. As for the *Revue du Vin de France,* it is still worth reading, especially if you are fluent in French, but it is no longer the brilliant journal on French viticulture that it once was.

International Wine Cellar, PO Box 20021, Cherokee Station, New York, NY 10021; telephone 1-800-WINE-505. $54.00 for six bimonthly issues, written by Stephen Tanzer and others. For more than two decades Stephen Tanzer has published *International Wine Cellar*. Tanzer is a fine taster and a good writer, and his publication, which accepts no advertising, is extremely reliable for both European and American wines. He has begun adding new people into the mix but with no falloff in quality. If you are seriously interested in the upscale wine market, this is an essential publication.

Robert Parker's *Wine Advocate,* PO Box 311, Monkton, MD 21111; telephone 410-329-6477. $75 for six bimonthly issues. For more than a quarter of a century, this was written by a guy named Robert M. Parker, Jr. As the wine world grew and I got older, I realized I needed help and I have now assembled some of the world's finest palates and writers to cover areas that I was never able to review to the extent that I wanted. While I still cover Bordeaux, California, and the Rhône Valley, this book reflects the efforts of my new team, which I think offers the most comprehensive and finest articles and tasting notes on wine in the world, and without pictures or any advertising.

Decanter, Broadway House, 1st Floor, 2–6 Fulham Broadway, London, SW6 5UE, UK; fax 011 44 20 7381 5282. England's dominant wine publication, *Decanter* gives readers a British point of view. The quality of the writing, the superficiality of the tastings, and the decidedly anti-American point of view encouraged by the editors are lamentable. This used to be a great magazine, but now it reads more like a sordid anti-American editorial, with the entire writing staff regurgitating the same articles again and again as to why the world no longer pays attention to the British point of view. Yet because of this rather 19th-century British viewpoint, the magazine offers a different point of view and should be read.

The Wine Spectator (subscriptions), P.O. Box 37367, Boone, IA 50037-0367; telephone 1-800-752-7799. $50 per year. The world's most widely read wine magazine. Publisher Marvin Shanken continues to fine-tune and improve an already strong magazine devoted to covering the wines of the world. No one does a better job of keeping its readers abreast of current events in the wine world. Mixing restaurant pieces with extensive wine ratings, as well as highly laudable articles on traveling in various wine regions, food and wine matchups, interesting recipes, and profiles of leading wine personalities, Shanken has built this one-time obscure newsletter into a serious publication read around the world. This magazine is required reading for wine enthusiasts. It does accept advertising, but contrary to all the cynics, I don't think there's a connection between good scores and advertising revenue.

The World of Fine Wine (subscriptions), Dovetail Services UK Ltd., 800 Guillat Avenue, Kent Science Park, Sittingbourne, Kent, ME9 8GU, UK; quarterly; $169 (USD) per year. This highbrow magazine, with artistic photography and a bevy of important correspondents, is absurdly overpriced but does offer well-thought-out articles, beautiful pictures (far superior to those in *The Wine Spectator* or other American picture magazines) and some thought-provoking commentary. Overly ambitious, one hopes *The World of Fine Wine* will succeed, but the outrageously high price asked for it seems to guarantee that it will reach only a fragment of the audience that it should.

Burghound.com, $190 in print or $125 online. Allen Meadows has quickly become the guru for diehard Burgundy lovers, offering a quarterly Internet newsletter with a breadth and depth of coverage on Burgundy that is unprecedented. Anyone spending the huge dollars necessary to play in this minefield should seriously consider a subscription to Meadows's guide. He does seem to have swallowed the entire Burgundy philosophy hook, line, and sinker, meaning that for him a grand cru will always produce better wines than a premier cru, and it is doubtful he has ever met a Burgundy he didn't like. Burgundy needs a spokesperson, though, and he is a hardworking one who clearly loves these wines, perhaps more than most normal people would. He seems to be realizing that there is only a limited number of subscribers at this price point and for these rare and notoriously unreliable wines, so he is branching out into domestic Pinot Noirs, a good move in my opinion.

Jancisrobinson.com, $139 for a 12-month online subscription. Jancis Robinson has emerged as England's finest wine writer. Gifted with her prose, thorough in her analytical skills, and always looking for a good story, her opinion should be considered seriously, and anyone interested in fine wine ought to subscribe to her valuable tasting research and commentaries. Of course, she's also a highly successful editor. (See the next section of recommended books.)

BOOKS

Burton Anderson, *Vino* (New York: Alfred Knopf) and *The Wine Atlas of Italy* (New York: Simon & Schuster). *Vino* was a breakthrough book on the importance and potential of Italian wine. *The Wine Atlas of Italy* is a very good reference book for the wine regions of that beautiful country.

Alexis Bespaloff, *Frank Schoonmaker's Encyclopedia* (New York: William Morrow). This dry but well-researched reference should be a part of every wine enthusiast's library.

Michel Bettane and Thierry Desseauve. *Le Classement 2007* (Luxembourg: Wine and Food Data International). This is a Michelin Guide–styled book that rates those French wine producers whom Bettane and Desseauve consider the finest. It is based on a one- to three-star system and includes a short synopsis on each estate. Tasting notes are nonexistent.

Michael Broadbent, *The Great Vintage Wine Book,* editions I and II (London: Mitchell Beazley). Broadbent was among the first to make an art out of exceptionally descriptive and meaningful tasting notes. Moreover, he is a gifted taster whose experience in classic, older Bordeaux vintages is unmatched.

Stephen Brook, *Bordeaux, The People, Power, and Politics* (London: Mitchell Beazley) and *Wine People* (New York: Vendange Press). Excellent looks at the world of Bordeaux through the eyes of one of the most talented British wine writers, Brook's candid analysis of Bordeaux is top-flight. *Wine People* consists of mini profiles and biographies of people whom Brook considers the who's who of wine. A stylish, handsome book with major omissions as well as some dubious entries, but nevertheless beautifully done and a worthy addition to wine literature.

Oz Clarke, *Essential Wine Book, Annual Wine Guide*, and *Regional Wine Guides* (New York: Simon & Schuster). These lively, informative, well-written books from this multitalented English wine writer offer a candor and lively prose more typical of the American wine-writing style than that of an Englishman. The witty Clarke is also a terrific taster.

James M. Gabler, *Wine into Words—A History and Bibliography of Wine Books in the English Language* (Baltimore: Bacchus Press). This superbly organized, comprehensive book needs to be updated, but it is an essential contribution to the history of wine writing, as well as a much-needed reference work.

Rosemary George, *The Wines of the South of France* (London: Faber & Faber). The first book dedicated to extensive coverage of France's Languedoc-Roussillon region. It is an exceptionally well written book from one of Britain's least known but most professional as well as respected Masters of Wine.

James Halliday, *The Wine Atlas of Australia and New Zealand* and *The Wine Atlas of California* (New York: Viking Press). These two extraordinary classic guides on two important wine regions are unequaled in their scope and quality. While Halliday's work on Australia and New Zealand is impressive, his tome on California is a tour de force, offering the finest perspective of California wine yet authored. It is destined to be a reference for years to come.

Hugh Johnson, *Modern Encyclopedia of Wine, The History of Wine,* and *The World Atlas of Wine* (New York: Simon & Schuster). These classic reference books written by the world's best-selling wine writer should be part of every wine lover's library. In 2007, the *Atlas* was again brilliantly updated and enlarged with significant contributions by English prima donna Jancis Robinson. *The World Atlas of Wine* may well be the finest wine book in existence.

Matt Kramer, *Making Sense of Wine, Making Sense of California,* and *Making Sense of Burgundy* (New York: William Morrow). Whether you agree or disagree with winedom's most articulate *terroiriste,* Kramer's provocative books offer aggravating as well as controversial insights and perspectives that are required reading. It is of little importance to Kramer that he is incapable of proving much of what he postulates, but the ride he gives readers is well worth the price of admission.

John Livingstone-Learmonth, *The Wines of the Rhône Valley* (London: Faber & Faber). One of the finest books on the great wines of the Rhône Valley, this reliable guide is a must-purchase for partisans of the wines from this great winemaking region.

Jay McInerney, *Bacchus and Me: Adventures in the Wine Cellar* (New York: Lyons Press). The famous novelist known for *Bright Lights, Big City* turns his irreverent pen and palate to wine. The result is a splendid wine adventure that showcases his immense writing skills and surprisingly gifted palate.

Robert M. Parker, Jr., *Bordeaux, Burgundy,* and *The Wines of the Rhône Valley and Provence* (New York: Simon & Schuster). All three books are comprehensive consumer guides offering passionate but critical, independent, and uncensored views of three important winemaking regions.

Edmund Penning-Rowsell, *The Wines of Bordeaux* (London: Penguin Books). A classic reference for the history of Bordeaux and its most renowned proprietors and their châteaux.

Jancis Robinson, *Vines, Grapes, and Wines* (New York: Alfred Knopf), *Vintage Time Charts* (London: Weidenfeld & Nicholson), and *The Oxford Companion to Wine* (New York: Oxford University Press). These three classics by Robinson, a gifted wine writer, are authoritative evidence of this woman's seemingly infinite ability to fashion informative, accurate books that are essential reading. *The Oxford Companion* is a must.

Andrew Sharp, *Wine Taster's Secrets—A Step by Step Guide to the Art of Wine Tasting* (Toronto: Warwick). An extremely well written book with the most informative and perceptive chapters on wine tasting I have read. This is the finest book for both beginners and serious wine collectors about the actual tasting process—lively, definitive, and candid.

Steven Spurrier and Michel Dovaz, *Académie du Vin Introductory Course to Wine* (London: Willow Books). Along with Kevin Zraly's classic, this is one of the finest guides to winedom for beginners.

Tom Stevenson, *The Wines of Alsace* (London: Faber & Faber). The definitive work on the underrated wines of Alsace. Extremely thorough, accurate, and erudite, this is a must for enthusiasts of these wines.

James Suckling, *Vintage Port* (New York: Wine Spectator Press). This is the only reliable, comprehensive consumer's guide to vintage Port. Suckling's exceptionally well-done book merits considerable attention from Port enthusiasts.

Harry Waugh, *Harry Waugh's Diaries* (publisher unknown). In late November 2001, at age 97, Harry Waugh died. One of the greatest gentlemen to ever inhabit the wine world, Waugh was an extraordinary ambassador for the joys of wine connoisseurship. I recall fondly his lectures stateside when he toured on behalf of Les Amis du Vin. I remember even better a blind tasting of 1975 Bordeaux in London in the mid-1980s. Waugh, who had lost his sense of smell because of an automobile accident, correctly identified more of the 1975s than any others among the distinguished group of participants, which included Michael Broadbent, the late Edmund Penning-Rowsell, Clive Coates, and me. About one wine he said, "I'm sad I can't smell it because the weight and texture suggest it must be the 1975 Latour." Of course he was right. His multiple-volume series *Harry Waugh's Diaries* were written records of his tastings—candid, refreshing, and always informative. I'm sure they can still be found on websites dedicated to purchasing books.

Alan Young, *Making Sense of Wine Tasting* (Sydney: Lennard). An underrated book from an Australian who has clearly given an exceptional amount of thought to the process of tasting wine, this classic has remained undiscovered by much of the world's wine press.

Kevin Zraly, *Windows on the World Wine Course* (New York: Sterling Publishing). This is the finest introductory guide to wine. I highly recommend it to readers who are trying to get a handle on the complicated world of vino. A fun and very informed read. Connoisseurs who think they already know it all will learn something from Zraly's classic.

THE TONGUE-IN-CHEEK GUIDE TO WINE

THE WINE WORLD'S BIGGEST LIES

15. The reason the price is so high is because the wine is rare and great.
14. You probably had a "corked" bottle.
13. It is going through a dumb period.
12. We ship and store all our wines in temperature-controlled containers.
11. You didn't let it breathe long enough.
10. You let it breathe too long.
9. Sediment is a sign of a badly made wine.
8. Boy, are you lucky . . . this is my last bottle/case.
7. Just give it a few years.
6. We picked before the rains.
5. The rain was highly localized; we were lucky it missed our vineyard.
4. There's a lot more to the wine business than just moving boxes.
3. Robert Parker's *Wine Advocate* (or *The Wine Spectator*) is going to give it a 94 in the next issue.
2. This is the greatest wine we have ever made, and, coincidentally, it is the only wine we now have to sell.
1. It's supposed to smell and taste like that.

THE LANGUAGE OF THE WINEMAKER

What They Say in the Vineyard/Winery	*What They Really Mean—* *The Plain English Guide*
This is a classic vintage for cellaring!	The wine is excessively tannic, and it will undoubtedly lose most of its fruit long before the tannin melts away.
This is a supple, fruity wine that is very commercial.	This is a thin, diluted, watery wine made from a vineyard that was atrociously overcropped. It should have a shelf life of one to four years.
One can sense the nobility of *terroir* in the aromas and taste of this wine.	The weather during the growing season and harvest was so cold and wet that the grapes never matured—some even rotted—and the wine tastes only of acidity, tannin, wood, alcohol, and copious quantities of damp earth—hence, *terroir* triumphs again.
We were fortunate enough to harvest before the rain.	We harvested before the last deluge (forgetting of course to inform you that prior to the last inundation it had rained heavily for the previous 5 to 10 days).
This is a classic vintage in the style of the great traditional years of the region.	Once again we did not have enough sunshine and heat to ripen the grapes, thus we produced wines that are hard, acidic, angular, compact, and tannic from underripe fruit. Sadly, they are filled with more acidity and tannin than sugar and fruit. Only a fool would buy this.

Do you want to taste my wines?	I have one or two barrels of exquisite Cuvée Vieilles Vignes set aside, made from exceptionally ripe fruit, which I serve to all my importers, clients, and those nosy, obtrusive wine writers in order to give them an impression of what I am capable of achieving.
Those people who follow organic or biodynamic farming in the vineyard are phony, pseudoviticulturists.	We use every chemical treatment known to man—insecticides, herbicides, tons of nitrogen and other fertilizers, including Miracle-Gro—in an effort to kill everything in the vineyard, except, of course, the vine!
Mr. Parker (or any other wine critic/writer) knows nothing.	We cannot influence him, nor can we bribe him. A shameful man, he doesn't even write in his publication what we tell him to. Why can't we go back to the old days when we could stuff a trunkful of samples into a wine critic's car and get the reviews we desire?
This is the greatest wine I have ever made in my life.	This is the only wine we have to sell.
This wine is closed and needs time because it has just been recently bottled.	Anybody who bottles naturally, with very low SO$_2$ and no fining or filtering, knows perfectly well that the wine tastes just as good in the bottle as it did in the cask. However, we are modern-day industrialists or, as we say, "wine processors." We use the *maladie à la mise* ("malady of the bottling") excuse to justify the poor performance of our wines. If the truth be known, our wines have been stripped, nuked, and denuded, and they are incapable of improvement in the future. Amazingly, writers and buyers have been swallowing this BS for at least four decades!
Parker (or any other wine critic/writer) never tasted my wine!	I did not get a 90-point score.
Parker (or any other wine critic/writer) only likes heavily oaked, internationally styled fruit bombs.	I did not get a 90-point score.

WESTERN EUROPE
PART I

[alsace]

PERPLEXING IDENTITY AND RICH REWARDS

This heartbreakingly beautiful, frequently fought over region between the Vosges Mountains and the Rhine—home to many of the world's great wines—can hardly any longer be called "undiscovered." Yet, the same apparent cliché that was applied to the wines of Alsace in American markets a quarter century ago still has a core of truth: that a sprinkling of German elements in these French libations and doubts as to whether what's in the bottle will taste dry or sweet give the consumer pause. Alsace's tall fluted bottles, regional grapes, and Germanic place-names are all shared with other parts of the Rhine basin, and during two extended and calamitous periods in its recent history this region was part of Germany. In their predilections, though—from conceptions of cuisine to those of personal liberty—the citizens of Alsace have long been very French.

During the dark period of viticultural colonization by the German Reich, this region's vignerons were discouraged from striving for high quality, lest their wines compete with those across the Rhine and to the north. In 1945, some of the most savage and devastating warfare ever unleashed on a region all too familiar with savagery and war ushered in a remarkably abrupt period of rebirth and reinvention. The fateful decision was taken—then practically without precedent—to promote, as Alsace's wine elite, bottlings composed of and named for single grape varieties. In replanting ravaged and neglected vineyards, emphasis was placed on entire parcels dedicated to the noble Riesling and distinctive Gewurztraminer.

The wines of Alsace with their striking personalities, simple labeling, and (for France) distinctively tall and fluted bottles, enjoyed tremendous success at home, making their way to Charles de Gaulle's Élysée Palace and Paris's elite restaurants, as well as to the tables of countless wine-loving French of modest means, at a time when within France, wines other than Bordeaux seldom traveled far outside their local regions. Markets in Belgium, the Netherlands, and Germany were reestablished during the boom times of the 1960s and 1970s; in the 1980s the wines of Alsace set out to conquer the U.S. In some respects, the markets have not changed radically in the quarter century since. While total exports to America continue slowly to rise, Alsace still ships around three times as much (in both volume and value) to its leading export market—the Benelux—as it does to the U.S., which jostles for position with Germany and Denmark. And one hears both frustrated growers and American merchants bemoaning the sluggish pace at which even—or perhaps in view of today's prices, especially—wines from many top growers turn. To be sure, back in the 1980s when Robert Parker's *Wine Advocate* took the lead in championing the distinctiveness and exceptional quality potential of Alsace wine, competition in the U.S. markets from the white wines of Austria and Italy, or from dry-tasting German Riesling, was not nearly so keen as is the case today. Still, Alsace producers should ask themselves to what extent they bear responsibility for the lack of progress in capturing the hearts, imaginations, and palates of American wine lovers.

The marketing advantages these wines gained through being clearly labeled with the names of grapes should have been multiplied many times over when California, followed by much of the rest of the New World, adopted that same approach. But clarity too often gave way to consumer confusion over whether a wine would taste dry or distinctly sweet. In the 1980s, growers and critics could simply seek to reassure Americans with the slogan "Alsace wine tastes dry." The categories known as *vendange tardive* ("late harvest") and *sélection de grains nobles* ("selected ennobled berries") applied to either subtly or nobly sweet wines, but those designations and the scarcity and high prices of the wines so labeled rendered confusion less likely. Today, the picture is very different. A considerable share of Alsace wine—and, for wines from certain grape varieties, a majority—now tastes distinctly sweet, and consumers again despair (this time with very good reason) of knowing what they will uncork. Zind-Humbrecht introduced a five-point numerical scale to designate perceived sweetness. But such scales are almost certainly destined to remain winery internal.

Residual sugar in wine need not equate to "sweet tasting," nor need it (widespread prejudice to the contrary notwithstanding) vitiate the versatility of a wine at table. Riesling from the Mosel, Rheingau, or Nahe, for example, displays an amazing capacity for harmony and a dry taste impression at modest levels of residual sugar. But the Riesling of Alsace, benefiting from its relatively warm, dry weather, displays a very different structure, lower acidity, and a distinctly diminished capacity for canceling out sugar. And when it comes to Alsace's other frequently inherently low-acid, grape varieties, it's not clear that they retain their versatility, or are in any sense improved under the influence of residual sugar.

No amount of frustration or market confusion, however, can obscure the fact that Alsace's top growers continue to render from their numerous grapes and geologically multifarious sites some of the world's most profound and potentially long-lived as well as varietally and stylistically diverse white wines. Furthermore, there is the same youthful energy and keen ambition among her growers that one senses today in so many other regions of Europe. The nearly 90 Alsace vignerons practicing organic viticulture (one-third of these following a biodynamic regimen that even its detractors will admit is hugely demanding), and farming around 6% of total Alsace acreage—a figure that may be without precedent—certainly bespeaks a willingness both literally and figuratively to plow a hard row in the quest for quality.

It is high time for consumers to rediscover Alsace wine by rediscovering its best and best-known practitioners, as well as a new generation of talents. Those whose interest has been piqued by the recently ascendant Rieslings of Germany and Austria should reexperience why those of Alsace are classics every bit as steeped in the lore of exceptionally diverse *terroir* and even more so in the lure of cuisine both haute and humble. (It's hard to comprehend why some vintners in Alsace still profess horror that tall fluted bottles leave them prone to misunderstanding and prejudice. Riesling has cachet today, and its international outward symbol, whether dry or sweet, is precisely that striking, graceful bottle shape, one that is exclusively protected within France for Alsace.) As for the best among Alsace's Pinot Gris, dry Muscat, or

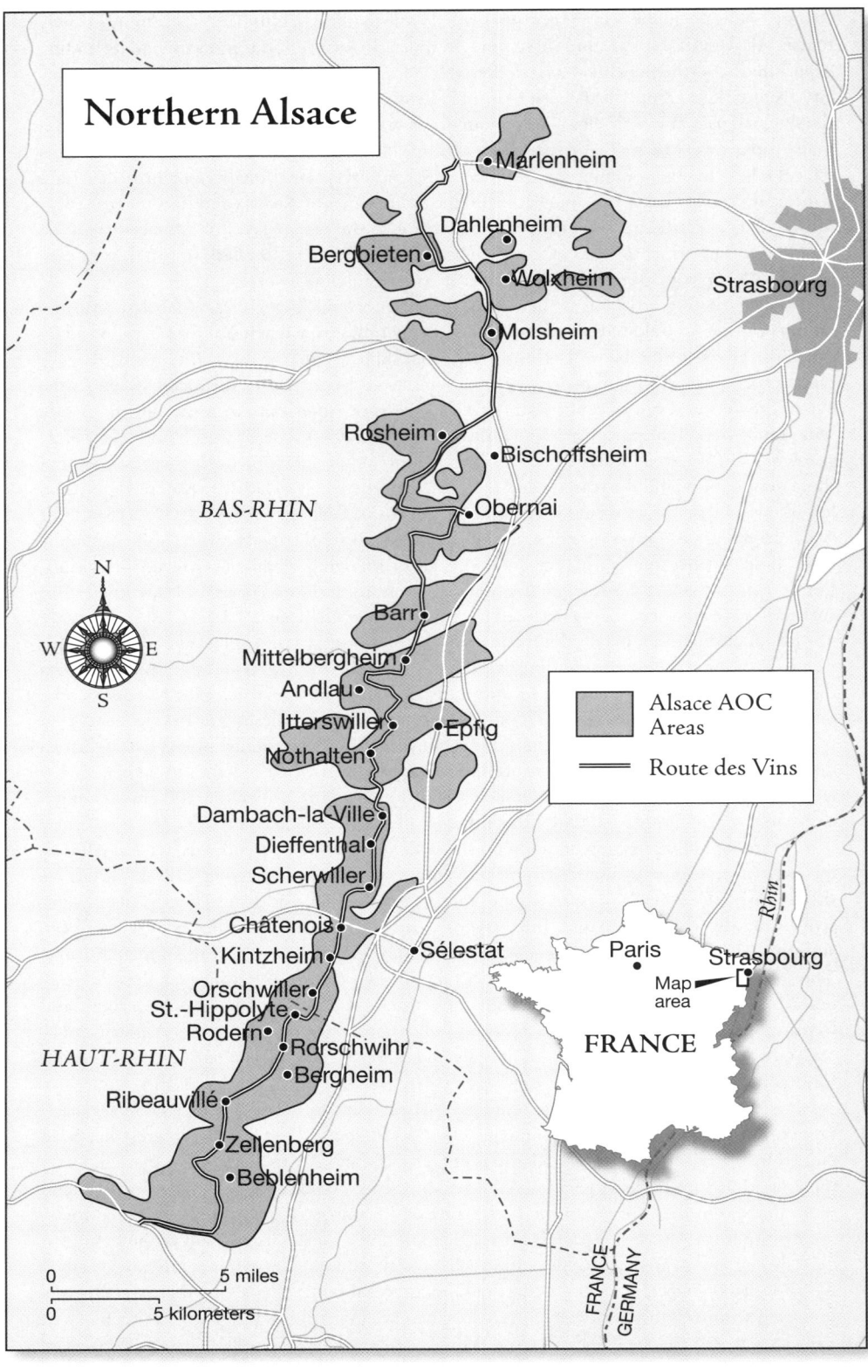

Northern Alsace

BAS-RHIN

HAUT-RHIN

- Marlenheim
- Dahlenheim
- Bergbieten
- Wolxheim
- Strasbourg
- Molsheim
- Rosheim
- Bischoffsheim
- Obernai
- Barr
- Mittelbergheim
- Andlau
- Itterswiller
- Epfig
- Nothalten
- Dambach-la-Ville
- Dieffenthal
- Scherwiller
- Châtenois
- Kintzheim
- Sélestat
- Orschwiller
- St.-Hippolyte
- Rodern
- Rorschwihr
- Bergheim
- Ribeauvillé
- Zellenberg
- Beblenheim

	Alsace AOC Areas
	Route des Vins

Paris

Strasbourg

Map area

FRANCE

Rhin

FRANCE
GERMANY

0   5 miles
0   5 kilometers

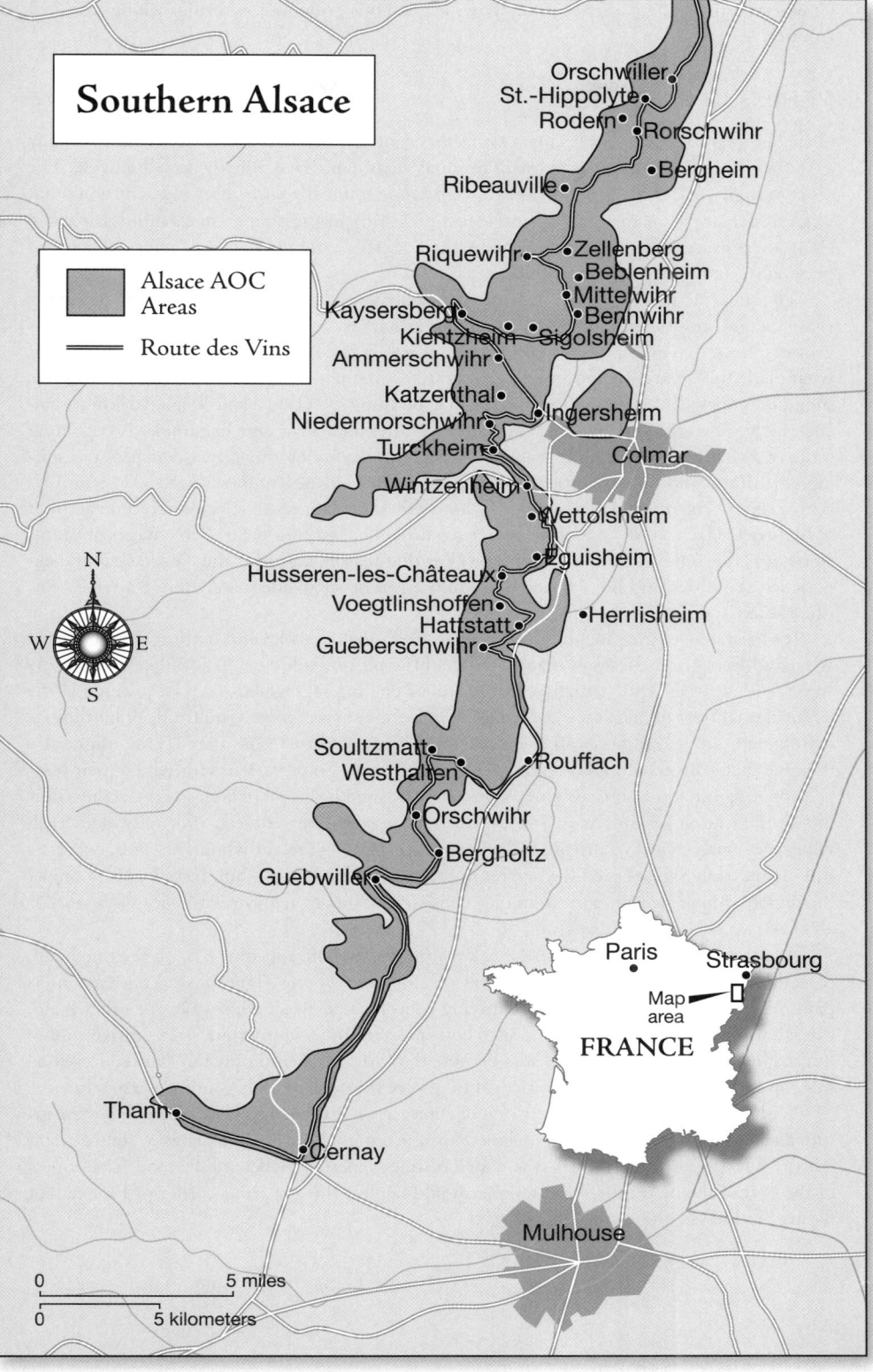

Southern Alsace

Alsace AOC Areas

Route des Vins

Orschwiller
St.-Hippolyte
Rodern
Rorschwihr
Bergheim
Ribeauville
Riquewihr
Zellenberg
Beblenheim
Mittelwihr
Kaysersberg
Bennwihr
Kientzheim
Sigolsheim
Ammerschwihr
Katzenthal
Niedermorschwihr
Ingersheim
Turckheim
Colmar
Wintzenheim
Wettolsheim
Eguisheim
Husseren-les-Châteaux
Voegtlinshoffen
Herrlisheim
Hattstatt
Gueberschwihr
Soultzmatt
Rouffach
Westhalten
Orschwihr
Bergholtz
Guebwiller

Paris
Strasbourg
Map area
FRANCE

Thann
Cernay

Mulhouse

N
W E
S

0   5 miles
0   5 kilometers

Gewurztraminer, these have as yet no peers beyond this province's notoriously long-disputed frontier.

PERILS IN PARADISE

Once one gets past the grower elite, two factors contribute to the mediocrity of far too many of today's Alsace wines. One is rampant residual sugar, which has already been discussed. The other is high yields. Or, if not yields, how else to account for wine after pleasant wine that lacks sufficient personality or grip and leaves no lasting impression on one's mind or palate? Consumers must be admonished to choose their sources carefully to ensure wines of genuine personality and satisfying concentration.

To some extent, admittedly, sweetness is simply a result of high grape sugar. Increasingly ripe vintages, combined with more selectivity at harvest among the most quality-conscious growers, keep driving up the levels of sugar at which the fruit is harvested. It's almost as if what made this a paradise for grape growing in the first place—warmth, sunshine, and steep, sheltered slopes—is becoming too much of a good thing. Steering a course and striking a balance between sugar and alcohol (and potential attendant heat and harshness) is becoming more of a challenge (often exacerbated by precarious acidity); ultimately it demands rethinking viticultural and cellaring practices, so as to promote ripeness of flavor with less accumulation of sugar. Too many Alsace growers whose wines display deficiencies in extract on account of high yields lack a critical tool for buffering alcohol or burying sugar. Percentages or grams alone, it's true, tell little; however, precisely for that reason, a grower must have skill and experience as a taster and hone his or her intuitions in order to adequately judge a wine's finished balance.

It's hard, too, to imagine that the sheer proliferation of cuvées and bottlings at the typical Alsace address—sometimes as many as three different lines of wine, in addition to the nobly sweet, and at times with virtually every parcel or picking segregated—can be justified in the name of quality or of marketplace demand. Often, one suspects that a multitude of bottlings is maintained out of tradition and sheer inertia. This should be reconsidered. One might also imagine that growers would become specialized in those grape varieties for which their temperament, family traditions, or vineyards were best suited. But there are no signs of any coming simplification or limitations on production or consumer choices. Not only does each winery jealously guard its private and commercial clients—each of whom, it seems, expects a full menu, from Sylvaner to Gewurztraminer, from each address—but, frankly, every one of the region's top growers has in common a consistent ability to achieve excellence with most or all of Alsace's classic seven *cépages*.

As for *vendange tardive* and *sélection de grains nobles* bottlings, there is, on the one hand, something heartening about the numbers of ambitious young vignerons taking enormous pains in laboriously harvesting and vinifying concentrated sweet elixirs. On the other hand, this is a source of frustration because such bottlings are now so numerous, so expensive, and so limited in their usefulness at table, and because they are too often simply imbalanced in sweetness, and may demand years in bottle just to resolve the issue of their genuine personalities.

Without question, then, sheer surfeit of choice as well as label confusion inevitably constitute a challenge for wine writers no less than consumers in their approaches to the wines of Alsace. But the potential rewards, the wines' distinctiveness, variety, and the food-friendliness of the best of them, are such that no one should neglect this gorgeous corner of France that nature has blessed and history so scourged.

[the grapes]

Given the dominance in Alsace of wines labeled with the name of their grape variety, and given the sheer number of varieties with which this region succeeds along its entire length, it is appropriate to give extended consideration to this cast of characters. Growers traditionally refer to their region's seven varieties—Sylvaner, Pinot Blanc, Riesling, Muscat, Pinot Gris, Gewurztraminer, and Pinot Noir—but, as we shall see, there are really a dozen distinct *cépages* worthy of note.

At the humblest extreme of Alsace's wide grape spectrum lie Chasselas and Sylvaner. Given this region's former emphasis on cheap and plentiful wines, it is not surprising that several thousand acres of mostly very old vines of the traditionally lowly Sylvaner remain here, along with sporadic stands of Chasselas, which is also sold as a table grape. But one has only to consider Franconia in German Bavaria, or the Vaud around Lake Geneva in Switzerland, to realize that even those dog grapes Sylvaner and Chasselas can have their day, or rather, their *terroir*. While most of the wines grown from these varieties in Alsace are undistinguished—Sylvaner, frequently coarse and flabby; Chasselas, grassy and thin—low yields, in certain sites, can deliver engaging personality and gustatory versatility. Mittelbergheim in northern Alsace, following years of intense lobbying by Albert Seltz and other local growers, was recently granted "grand cru" status for its Sylvaner. (Ostertag's Sylvaner from nearby is a gem, if one can beat the annual rush to buy it.) Dirler-Cadé and Rolly-Gassmann are among growers in the south lavishing care on that variety, while Boxler, Kientzler, and Schoffit have long delivered improbably rich and flavorful Chasselas.

"Pinot Blanc" or "Pinot d'Alsace" is in fact typically a blend, often consisting in large measure of the gentle, low-acid Auxerrois, together with a member of the Pinot family to which Alsace growers usually refer as "true Pinot," or by the traditionally less specific name of "Klevner." Pinot Gris may also be included in so-called "Pinot Blanc," and some of the big-berried, high-yielding of that clan fully justify its ending up in nondescript blends. At their best, though, Pinot Blanc blends from Alsace can be a versatile delight. Apple, citrus fruit, and floral character and juicy, straightforward appeal are their strengths. Pure Auxerrois—a grape that arrived from Luxembourg and has no known connections with the Auxerre—may be labeled as such. It can exert a special appeal of its own, as proven by the luscious and at times even ageworthy results from Auxerrois champions Josmeyer, Albert Mann, and Rolly-Gassmann. Particularly in less ripe years (although these have lately been few), the tangerine, lemon, and herbal notes of this variety can give it a faux Riesling or Muscat character; in riper years, it can be lush without heaviness. Examples of pure "true Pinot" (very occasionally labeled "Klevner") seem to have become rare in recent years. (Boxler's "Reserve Pinot Blanc" is one.) That is sad, because pure "true Pinot" can offer a fascinating combination of flowers and pit fruits with meaty, mineral depth. The overwhelming majority of wine labeled Alsace Pinot Blanc or Pinot d'Alsace is vinified in tank, but most of the best of them are rendered in the traditional, large, oval, old-oak *Fuder* of the region, a characteristic shared by many, though certainly by no means all, of the top wines from "noble" grapes as well. A significant percentage of Alsace Pinot Blanc and Auxerrois goes into the production of sparkling Crémant d'Alsace, which can range in quality from dull (at the industrial level) to delightful (in the case of Albert Mann and Muré).

When Auxerrois was registered—initially only as an "experimental variety"—after World War II, another transplant was simultaneously tested for use in Pinot blends, a grape by the name of Chardonnay. A few growers even bottled it pure, and the results could be interesting. The authorities decided eventually that Auxerrois, not Chardonnay, would be vested with citizen's rights, and the planting of Chardonnay was officially curtailed. (During the heyday of Chardonnay in the world's wine markets, there must have been some Alsace bureaucrats who regretted that decision.) It was only around a decade ago that Chardonnay, no matter what age a grower's vines or where they stood, was ruled no longer welcome in Alsace's Pinot Blanc. The most famous Chardonnay in the region—Zind-Humbrecht's in their great Clos Windsbuhl (along with roughly one-third Auxerrois)—now informs a fascinating, *barrique*-aged wine that they call simply "Zind." Chardonnay remains here and there, but in most instances you won't get the grower to divulge this.

Riesling in Alsace is capable of some of its most complex, long-lived expressions, and most experienced observers, asked to name the most profound and ageworthy wines in Alsace, would place the region's best Rieslings at the head of their lists. Among those who hold to the importance of *terroir,* Riesling is generally credited with the greatest sensitivity in its geological underpinnings (see below) and the greatest ability to channel a place. Such formidable Riesling houses as Beyer, Hugel, and Trimbach generally do not even put their top Riesling bottlings on the market for several years, and one can expect top dry Alsace Riesling from good vintages to mature satisfyingly in bottle for anywhere between one and two decades, and the best *vendange tardive* renditions for even longer. In addition to the diverse floral, citric, pit-fruited, herbal, spicy, and mineral characteristics for which Riesling from Germany or Austria, too, is known, examples of Riesling from Alsace sometimes take on a hint of fuel oil, generally referred to as a "petrol" note—particularly if they came from certain chalky soils, and increasingly as they mature.

Just as with wines labeled Pinot Blanc or Pinot d'Alsace, those labeled Muscat d'Alsace generally represent a blend of two distinct grapes: Muscat à Petit Grains and Muscat Ottonel. The latter variety, bred roughly 150 years ago, probably with a table grape (Chasselas?) as one parent, is the more common in two senses, both more widely grown and generally less distinctive in aroma. Pungent notes of sage, citrus zest, and apricot are typical. But, though there are a few 100% Ottonel exceptions, it generally takes the addition of the small-berried, temperamental "Petit Grains" Muscat (the same grape that is responsible for the best sweet Muscats of southern France) to deliver a diversity of floral and spice character, mineral nuances, and a wine that—although nearly always drunk young—can mature fascinatingly for up to a decade. There are scarcely any pure examples of this nobler Muscat in Alsace today. In fact, one has to make an effort to locate any of the shrinking number of exciting Muscats d'Alsace, not to mention those that are finished dry since, in the local Alsace market, consumers' conceptions of this category (like those of Pinot Gris and Gewurztraminer) have undergone a radical shift over the past two decades, and sweetness is now expected. The result is that one of Alsace's most distinctive and versatile wines which was never well known outside its home, due to a finicky, frost- and insect-sensitive vine and consequently ever-diminishing acreage, has been further marginalized; it is drunk, if at all, as a mere apéritif. Consumers are strongly recommended to seek out the inimitable experience offered by the dry Muscat d'Alsace of Boxler, Dirler-Cadé, or Zind-Humbrecht.

With the notoriously opulent Pinot Gris (as with Gewurztraminer), the temptation to residual sugar has been especially great, despite this variety's low acidity, because potential alcohol of 15% was not uncommon even 20 years ago, and sugar levels at harvest have increased notably and steadily over the past two decades. Telltale signs of this variety include a distinctly pungent smokiness, flavors of peaches and toasted nuts, and often a Burgundian "animality," amplitude, and creaminess of texture. There is a legend that this grape was brought to Alsace from Hungary, and in consequence of further embellishment of the tale it became known as "Tokay d'Alsace." Until 2007, both that name and "Pinot Gris" appeared on labels. In deference to Hungarian Tokaji, this is no longer permitted. With its compact bunches, Pinot Gris easily traps moisture and is therefore prone to botrytis, that sometimes miracle fungus that inhibits fermentation while also concentrating grape sugar. Pinot Gris is thus, along with Gewurztraminer, the grape that informs Alsace's most richly textured, high-alcohol, and flamboyant wines, as well as a sizable share of *vendanges tardives* and *sélections de grains nobles.*

Is there a more distinctive or unforgettably intense aromatic wine profile than the rose petal, lychee, bacon fat, baking spice, and sweet pea scents of ripe Gewurztraminer? Here, too, a once astonishing range of food pairings (don't scoff, for example, at traditional, high-alcohol, dry Gewurztraminer with raw oysters, unless you've tried it!) has been greatly reduced by wines of seemingly knee-jerk, superficial sweetness. (This is also an ideal picnic wine, as even the stiffest breeze won't blow its scents away. The most profound wines of which this variety is capable (and perhaps, too, the very best of its fellow bronze- and purple-colored grape Pinot Gris) may well lie in the realm of selective picking, *vendange tardive,* and residual sweetness. But such a conclusion by no means warrants sweetness throughout a grower's range. No wine lover should consider him- or herself wise to the potential of Gewurztraminer until he or she has tasted a dry, full-bodied example from the likes of Beyer, Hugel, or Trimbach (or one of the Zind-Humbrecht Gewurztraminer, whose coding informs you that it will taste dry). The Savignin grape, an exotically floral and pungent member of the Traminer family, best known for its dominant role in the oxidative wines of the Jura, also persists in Alsace in a few places, and is even legally honored as Klevener de Heiligenstein, for its performance in a cluster of northern Alsace villages.

Until the past decade, Pinot Noir was of serious interest to only a handful of Alsace growers—Deiss, Hugel, Muré—and even fewer consumers. Today, though, there is an array of distinctive examples, some from stands of remaining old vines, but many recently planted. The most common failing is not a lack of ripeness. Even 20 years ago, the aforementioned practitioners of the black Pinot art were routinely achieving alcohol levels over 12.5% without tricks or chaptalization. Rather, the frequent problem is too aggressive a use of new barrels or regimen of extraction. Still, there is a lot of promise and personality among Pinots of the Côte des Vosges, and anybody who overlooks Alsace or counts this region out of contention in the world Pinot Noir sweepstakes is making a mistake.

ONCE AND FUTURE BLENDS

The postwar ascendancy of single-variety bottling and labeling did not completely sweep away Alsace's earlier tradition of blends. These persisted at the low end of the price spectrum, generally under the name Edelzwicker, although seldom appearing in American markets. Hugel revived and trademarked the term "Gentil" for its widely distributed entry-level wine, a more euphonious and less misleading term for blends—*Edel* means "noble," which is explicably what such wines were *not*—and later agreed to its use by other growers. With the steady erosion of the U.S. dollar's value against the euro in the early years of this century, more low-end blends have been exported, and much can be said in their favor, in particular for the ability to utilize Gewurztraminer (occasionally even Muscat) as a sort of spicy seasoning to more neutral base wines such as the still common Sylvaner, with the addition of Riesling to lend pep and brightness to a blend that would otherwise be low in acidity.

One man, however, has single-mindedly pursued a course of blending that goes far beyond the mere exploration of synergies in the cellar. Jean-Michel Deiss of Bergheim—already by the mid-1980s considered one of the foremost vintners of Alsace—conceived a plan to turn back his viticultural clock to an early 20th or even late 19th century time zone, in the process giving new meaning to the notions of cru and *terroir.* He replanted nearly all of his vineyards in field blends of multiple grape varieties. This daring move—even given Deiss's prominence, well-known intellectualism, and charisma—would not merit extended consideration if the results two decades later were not among the most extraordinary wines of the region, and now beginning to find their imitators.

Deiss's theory is that multiple *cépages* are needed to express a site's *terroir,* much in the way that a rich vocabulary—or, in the case of music, multiple registers or instruments—is needed to articulate an idea. The mixture in any given site is influenced by historical precedent and by Deiss's intuitions and experience of the needs of each *cépage,* and also by his holistic, biodynamic world view. He insists—supplementing his presentation with the evidence of harvest records and photographs—that given cohabitation in a suitable *terroir,* grape varieties will ripen concurrently that would ordinarily mature weeks apart. Whether in response to his metaphysics, to the profound complexity of his wines in the glass, or simply to his stubbornness and influence, the authorities in 2007 acceded to grand cru status for blends from sites so rated. Many younger growers are just beginning to experiment with high-end blends, whether in their cellars or in what is planted, and it is safe to predict, in view of Deiss's success and influence, that the numbers of such proprietary and single-vineyard blends will increase.

A TOUR OF ALSACE *TERROIR*

A CROSS-SECTION OF ALSACE

The drainage, exposure, geological composition, and, not least, the relatively rain-free environment enjoyed by the best Alsace vineyards depends on their location in the foothills of the Vosges Mountains and along a few small rivers that cut through on their way to the Rhine. The villages of the region, too, took what shelter they could from the cruel buffeting of historical forces in the foothills of the Vosges. Much of the production of wine in Alsace, however, comes from the plain that stretches 10 to 15 miles east to the mighty Rhine. Here, this region's arguably too-high crop levels can, if not restrained by law, reach an industrial scale, and grapes are routinely harvested by machine. Little wonder, then, that a great deal of Alsace wine sadly lacks distinction. Most of it is destined for her traditionally largest markets in Germany and the Benelux, rather than for the U.S. This west–east cross-sectional perspective also reveals the notable fact that—just as is the case in the German Pfalz to the north, whose high Haardt Hills are really an extension of the Vosges, and in conspicuous contrast with their Riesling-bearing cousins in the Rheingau or the Mosel—the vineyards of Alsace and their wines simply are not influenced by the great body of water that flows nearby.

Another type of cross-section of Alsace's vineyards reveals a striking fact about this region that virtually none of its vintners and few experienced outside observers doubt is intimately connected with the quality of its wines: namely, a complex array of often fundamentally, sometimes dramatically, different rock structures. Pick by name, chemical composition, or geological era practically any important wine-growing soil of France or Germany, from the alternating schist, gneiss, and granite of Roussillon to the distinctive, pebbly, chalk-clay soils of Burgundy's Côte d'Or, from the red sandstone of Nierstein on the Rhine to the signature mussel-fossil chalk of Franconia on the Main, and chances are you'll find that very same stuff somewhere in the huge, stone-studded geological layer cake that is Alsace. It doesn't take much imagination to conceive—and, more important, you'll conclude that this is not just your imagination—that a virtually continuous strip of vineyards stretching for nearly 70 miles, growing seven major grapes on the greatest diversity of soils and rocks in any wine-growing region of the world, and subject to the cultural poles of France and Germany, will produce dizzyingly complex wines.

GRAND CRUS AND TERROIR

Since the first so-called grand cru sites of Alsace were officially declared, nearly a quarter of a century has passed, and 51 different vineyard areas have been so designated. The choice and delimitation of such sites has predictably generated, and continues to generate, many heated disputes. Some of the influential vintners who first envisioned a system of Alsace crus—most conspicuously, Jean "Johnny" Hugel—became disenchanted with the idea, as well as with the messy political realities of wine legislation. Subsequent developments certainly have borne out many of the critics' predictions. It seemed as if every village of any viticultural importance was determined to secure its own grand cru, whose boundaries were then stretched so as not to leave too many local vintners bereft—even if this was done at the price of historical accuracy, geological homogeneity, or any reasonable sense of what constitutes an ideal exposure. In several instances, just as is true of entire small appellations in the south of France, production of a given cru is virtually monopolized by the local *cave coopérative*. Significantly, none of the three most important grower-*négociants* of Alsace—Beyer, Hugel, or Trimbach—has chosen to utilize on their labels the names of those grand crus in which nearly all of their best wines originate.

During these past 25 years, the few Alsace vineyard names to have imprinted themselves on the collective memory of wine lovers—whether official grand crus (such as Brand), parts of crus (like Trimbach's Clos Ste.-Hune, home to Alsace's most renowned Riesling), or neither (such as Zind-Humbrecht's by now justly famed Clos Windsbuhl)—have predictably done so thanks to the quality achieved by a single grower or a very few growers who bottle outstanding wines that were so designated, not because of any law. The classification of Burgundy harbors perpetual, Europe-wide allure thanks to the attendant reputation of its wines. But it preserves its measure of authority and cachet by virtue of long-standing tradition. Any attempt today to create such a hierarchy *ab initio* is probably doomed, and to generate such a hierarchy in hopes of creating cachet is to put the cart before the horse. Even in Burgundy, the quality established by a few growers and marketed under a vineyard name takes precedence over established classification; otherwise Cros Parantoux, Les Amoureuses, or Clos St.-Jacques would not be more prestigious than many a grand cru. In listing the wines rated in this chapter, no notice is taken of whether or not their sites of origin are official Alsace grand crus.

Skepticism about the project of delimiting Alsace grand crus is, however, by no means the same as skepticism about the very concept of *terroir* so beloved of French vintners and modern-day marketers alike. If one wishes to explore the degree (if any) to which the singular geological diversity (and, naturally, other microclimatic aspects as well) of Alsace's vineyards may result in tasteably distinctive characteristics and family resemblances, then one needs to be aware of their vineyards of origin. Since the overwhelming majority of Alsace producers bottle multiple pickings or cuvées from each of their many grape varieties, then label these with the names of the sites in which they grew, one is tempted to suggest they would be engaging in an enormous self-deception—a swindle of the wine-drinking public, even—if a wine's vineyard of origin had no gustatory significance. Even inexperienced tasters will have little difficulty perceiving the often striking and systematic differences in character from one bottling to another in a given winery, whether or not the taster believes that these differences are indeed due to site.

Since the official grand crus of Alsace are generally (whether for sufficient reason) so rated for all four of the grape varieties characteristically designated as "noble"—Riesling, Gewurztraminer, Pinot Gris, and Muscat—it is interesting to try to discern possible nuances of flavor or structural characteristics in common among different varieties grown on the same site. Another fascinating and deliciously instructive exercise is to compare renditions of the same variety and site at different winemaking addresses. If there is anything to the notion of *terroir*—and the vast majority of tasters experienced in Alsace's wine, particularly Riesling, do not doubt this—then this exercise serves to focus tasters' attention on the differences in house style. We shall embark now on a brief excursion to a series of sites and growers where such comparisons are possible. Other important vineyards, including numerous important monopoles, will be discussed in the sketches supplied below each of the most important producers.

SOME IMPORTANT VINEYARDS WITH MULTIPLE HIGH-PERFORMANCE OWNERS

The Altenberg de Bergbieten—a fossil-rich chalk-clay and gypsum site in the hills of northern Alsace, immediately west of Strasbourg—has proven capable of sustaining long-lived Riesling and Gewurztraminer, as well as striking Muscat, all with an unusual brightness and underlying leanness that may owe something to the soil. Compare the wines of Frédéric Mochel (nearly all of whose acreage is in this site) with those of the widow and sons of the late Roland Schmitt.

The Altenberg de Bergheim is one of Alsace's most renowned wine villages, located midway between the cities of Sélestat and Colmar; its soil is composed of fossil-rich chalk and clay. Useful comparisons can be made between the wines of Charles Koehly and Gustave Lorenz, but the grower who did more than any other to make this site famous in modern times, Jean-Michel Deiss, vinifies a unique field blend of all of Alsace's grape varieties from this site. (See notes on blends above and the sketch of the Marcel Deiss winery below.)

The granite-over-limestone Brand vineyard in Turckheim (its name deriving from the legend that a dragon vented his wrath by scorching this hillside bare) is the source of some of the finest and most distinctive wines in Alsace, generally possessing exuberant floral perfume and inner-mouth intricacy of flavor. Among the outstanding sources are Boxler, Josmeyer, and (growing only Riesling here) Zind-Humbrecht. Brand bottlings from Philippe Ehrhart and Pierre Sparr (in both instances, their Pinot Gris in particular) are also worth comparing.

The steep Furstentum cru just northwest of Colmar is shared by the communities of Sigolsheim and Kientzheim but is also adjacent to Kaysersberg. This steep, complexly stony, magnesium-rich site, facing south across a sheltering valley, is home to exceptional Pinot Gris and Gewurztraminer from the star-studded cast of Paul Blanck (the estate that pushed for official recognition of this site before others "discovered" it), Bott-Geyl, Albert Mann, and Domaine Weinbach.

The deep, chalky soils, high elevation, and easterly exposure of the Goldert in Gueberschwihr (a few miles south of Colmar) have long been known for their ability to render complex, surprisingly acid-rich and strikingly ageworthy Gewurztraminer, Pinot Gris, and Muscat. Compare the wines of Ernst Burn (a domaine consisting almost entirely of Goldert holdings) and Zind-Humbrecht. Both wineries also render Riesling from these soils and exposure that strongly suggest how *terroir* can "bend" a grape variety, in this case into a rather extreme shape!

The chalky Hengst vineyard in Wintzenheim, just west of Colmar, is another site that seems to leave a heavy footprint and is farmed by a cast of viticultural stars, notably Barmès-Buecher, Josmeyer, Albert Mann, and Zind-Humbrecht.

The Herrenweg, situated between Wintzenheim and Turckheim, is rather undistinguished-looking in its relative flatness; it was certainly never anyone's candidate for grand cru status. But the especially friable, alluvial soils here, formed by eroded rock from the surrounding hills, have demonstrated an ability to render distinctive wine from most of Alsace's grapes and are shared by so many growers—foremost among these Josmeyer, Schleret, and Zind-Humbrecht—that consumers beginning to explore Alsace are apt to encounter this site by name.

The Kitterlé vineyard in the south of Alsace is one of the region's many geological layer cakes featuring sandstone, mica, greywacke, and schist. This is not, incidentally, the only Alsace grand cru to have acquired its original reputation with a grape—Pinot Blanc, in this instance—that is not even permitted to call itself grand cru when grown there today. One can compare the Gewurztraminer from Schlumberger—far and away the largest local landholder—with one from the exceptional section of this site that Dirler-Cadé now owns.

The Mambourg, a warm, south-facing, marl and Oligocene limestone site overlooking Sigolsheim (the site of a ferociously deadly German-American tank battle in 1945), will reveal its particular aptitude, especially with Gewurztraminer, in a comparison of wines from Michel Fonné, Pierre Sparr, Marc Tempé, and its newest shareholder, Domaine Weinbach. (As this same hill turns to face east, becoming the Marckrain, one can compare the Gewurztraminer of Fonné and Weinbach, who now have holdings in a site once virtually monopolized by the growers' cooperative of Bennwihr.)

From the limestone and marl Pfersigberg just south of Colmar, try comparing the Gewurztraminer of Barmès-Buecher and Kuentz-Bas or the Rieslings of Scherer and Beyer (the latter bottled as Cuvée les Écaillers and also, in nearly if not 100% single-vineyard form, as Comtes d'Eguisheim).

The Rangen, situated in Thann along the river Thur (not far from the mountainous Vosges sources of both the Mosel and the Saar) in the extreme south of Alsace, is the site of an ancient volcano. The soil here is so acidic that parts of it were deemed by agronomists unsuitable for viticulture of any sort. But a couple of hardy souls and their vines persisted, and from those pioneers the site's two principal current owners, Schoffit and Zind-Humbrecht, acquired their initial acreage. Léonard Humbrecht proved not only this location's potential for greatness, but demonstrated how extensive an area here could successfully support both Riesling and Pinot Gris. Few wines in Alsace are as dramatically distinctive as those from the Rangen, and tasters will be left wondering where their charlike smokiness and pungency come from, if not from the site itself.

Kaysersberg's Schlossberg—a mélange of diverse minerals over a steep bed of granite—is home to some of Alsace's most distinctively delicious Rieslings, notably those of Paul Blanck, Albert Mann (whose share adjoins Blanck's and came via marriage into the Blanck clan), and Domaine Weinbach.

The Sommerberg in Niedermorschwihr, directly west of Colmar, is weathered granite and mica that under the farming of Albert Boxler, has long birthed some of the world's greatest Riesling. Now that Bernard Schoffit has acquired acreage here as well, it is possible to compare his results.

The comically named sandstone Zinnkoepfle (literally "tin head") vineyard, situated in Soultzmatt, midway between Colmar and Mulhouse, nowadays has a couple of dynamic new shareholders. One should compare renditions of Gewurztraminer from Agathé Bursin, Paul Kubler, and veteran René Muré.

[recent vintages]

2007
The 2007 vintage, with its early flowering (as elsewhere in western Europe), moderate summer temperatures, and long, clear window for harvesting (still early by long-term averages, finishing by mid-October at most estates) looks to most growers to have been a great success, particularly for Riesling.

2006
2006 is what is known (euphemistically) as a "wine grower's vintage," which is to say that only those who rigorously controlled yield and vigilantly manicured their vines stood a chance of making outstanding wine. The source of difficulty in this case was warm, humid weather, heavy mid-September rains, and premature rot. Quality to a significant extent also came down to the size, skill, flexibility, and motivation of the picking crews at a domaine's disposal. Establishments habituated to picking by a predetermined schedule or with machines were simply unable to achieve excellence. The challenges were not categorically different (only in

degree) from those of the two previous vintages, or of several other recent ripe, but problematic, years.

2005

"It used to be you could almost assign a color to a vintage," says André Ostertag, "and then you understood" what to expect. "Okay, it was a cool vintage, so you had more acid and less sugar. It's a warm vintage? Then you have more alcohol. But that isn't possible anymore because you have in the same vintage everything [in the] extreme. And this makes understanding a vintage very difficult for wine growers, because you can no longer project." No vintages better prove Ostertag's point than the pair under consideration at the time he spoke, 2004 and 2005. But these years also prove a simpler adage offered by Olivier Humbrecht: "As long as one of the two—August or September—is warm and dry, you can have a successful vintage. And if I had to choose between them, I would much prefer a nice September." Vintage 2005 was characterized by a summer that veered from vicious heat spikes in July to a much cooler than normal August (a pattern from 2004 through 2007), followed by a warm September. Late September and early October rains pumped grapes up to proportions that risked rupture and precocious rot, but thereafter the growers received a reprieve. Sunshine returned, although occasional light rain as well as regular fog encouraged botrytis (in the best instances, noble) and growers picked, over an extended period, grapes in highly variable states of maturity and health. The cool August and lack of drought stress conduced to preservation of acids and extract. The best wines tend either to have been picked early (especially Pinot Gris and Gewurztraminer, with unusual acid retention) or else late, under the influence of noble rot, concentrated by steady shrinking of the grapes, which naturally depressed yields. By no means all growers had achieved phenolic maturity (i.e., ripe skins), particularly with Riesling, when they felt encroaching rot compelled them to harvest.

2004

Pressure to harvest ahead of rot was even greater during the inordinately rainy October of vintage 2004, which capped a generally cool and sporadically rainy summer. Just as virtually everywhere in western Europe, the vines had generated many fruitful buds and consequently many bunches of grapes in compensation for the penury of 2003 so that, following an unusually cool August, it was clear that only those who rigorously controlled nature's bounty and optimized the energy of their vines would achieve outstanding results. But September proved a boon with almost unremitting warmth and sunshine. In the end, sugar levels were seldom a problem—indeed, the problem was sometimes too high potential alcohol, not to mention encroaching rot, by the time skins had truly ripened. Welcome, in short, to the increasingly unpredictable, confounded ripening conditions of the early 21st century! Cooler weather as October advanced proved a boon for those who had been able to delay harvest, putting the brakes on rampant spread of rot, very little of it noble. In the final analysis, though, an amazing number of top Alsace growers fielded 2004s that could hold their own vis-à-vis 2005 (although seldom in the nobly sweet categories), a tribute to the sensitive but, when necessary, ruthless viticultural and harvest practices prevailing among this elite group.

2003

As elsewhere in western Europe, 2003 was characterized in Alsace by such extreme heat and drought that many wines suffered deficiency of acidity or extract. Still, in their rather outsized way, there are many impressive successes, opulent whites as well as some of the richest, not to mention the earliest harvested Pinot Noirs in the history of this region. The numerous *vendange tardive* and *sélection de grains nobles* bottlings often taste more of sheer desiccation than of noble rot. This is a vintage every wine lover will want to experience from bottle, but it ought to be approached with caution because only the greatest successes are likely to stand the test of time. All of the wines have unusual personalities, including (even in their youths) tendencies toward jammy and caramelized fruit.

2002

A cool and rainy August and early September followed by warmer but still humid conditions during harvest made for a tricky 2002, another vintage that required low yields and vigilance in the vineyards if there was to be success. The late-ripening and resilient Riesling is the clear star. 2001 benefited from a warm and sunny October and, despite not entirely noble botrytis, the overall quality was excellent. It is nothing short of remarkable that so many excellent vintage 2000 wines were recorded in Alsace, since just north in Germany's Pfalz, the heat and rain of August almost completely compromised the Riesling harvest. Still, the best Alsace wines from this year are those where the rot was noble (which it wasn't always), so those seeking wines of honeyed richness, in Riesling as well as in Gewurztraminer and Pinot Gris, will be especially rewarded. It was harder to escape the deleterious effects of warmth and rain in the mildew- and rot-plagued late summer of 1999. Nevertheless, the best growers managed to turn in some outstanding results, at the price of stringent selection, and hence low yields.

Among earlier vintages, the high-acid, botrytis-tinged 1998s and 1996s, copious 1997s, and late-ripening 1995s have all proven relatively variable in ageability, but the best dry wines from these vintages are very much worth enjoying now, and nobly sweet wines worth holding. The best 1994s display a remarkable combination of sheer density with ennobled richness, and the *vendanges tardives* will prove to be especially long keepers, whereas the wines of 1993 for the most part should have been consumed already. 1992 and 1991 form an interesting contrast, the former virtually vitiated by the huge size of the crop, the latter by summer drought and torrential late September rains. Yet at a few outstanding domaines, such as Boxler and Zind-Humbrecht, the 1992s are classic dry wines from healthy fruit and the 1991s exotic from their brush with botrytis, yet also intensely mineral and full of fruit. As in Germany and on the Loire, the trio of vintages 1988, 1989, and 1990 represented at the time a nearly unprecedented streak of ripeness. Stylish, elegant 1988s contrast with the combination of structure with botrytis-tinged richness that characterizes the 1990s, or in the enveloping opulence of 1989. Other outstanding Alsace vintages of recent times include 1985, 1983, 1971, 1964, 1959, and 1953. And, in their almost freakishly ripe and botryitzed ways, those 1976s and 1967s that neither toppled over on account of alcohol nor succumbed to bitterness may still be intensely memorable in an outsized way.

—DAVID SCHILDKNECHT

[the ratings]

ALSACE'S BEST PRODUCERS

★ ★ ★ ★ ★ (OUTSTANDING)

Léon Beyer (Eguisheim)*	Dirler-Cadé (Bergholtz)
Albert Boxler (Niedermorschwihr)	Hugel & Fils (Riquewihr)*
Marcel Deiss (Bergheim)	Marc Kreydenweiss (Andlau)

---

*The relatively high-volume basic (or, as they would express it, "classic") bottlings from Beyer, Hugel, and Trimbach—those in which the name of the grape variety is not allied to any other quality distinction on the label—are uniformly good. The same can be said for most wines bottled under the Muré label. However, it is the reserve-level and estate wines from top sites that entitle these producers to their high ratings.

Domaine Albert Mann (Wettolsheim)   Domaine Weinbach (Kaysersberg)
F. E. Trimbach (Ribeauvillé)*   Domaine Zind-Humbrecht (Turckheim)

* * * * (EXCELLENT)

Bott-Geyl (Niedermorschwihr)   André Ostertag (Epfig)
Josmeyer (Wintzenheim)   Rolly-Gassmann (Rorschwihr)
René Muré–Clos St.-Landelin (Rouffach)*   Bernard Schoffit (Colmar)

* * * (VERY GOOD)

Barmès-Buecher (Wettolsheim)   Paul Kubler (Soultzmatt)
Paul Blanck (Kientzheim)   Kuentz-Bas (Husseren-les-Châteaux)
Léon Boesch (Westhalten)   Meyer-Fonné (Katzenthal)
Ernst Burn (Gueberschwihr)   Frédéric Mochel (Traenheim)
Agathe Bursin (Westhalten)   André Pfister (Dahlenheim)
Michel Fonné (Bennwihr)   Martin Schaetzel (Ammerschwihr)
Pierre Frick (Pfaffenheim)   Charles Schleret (Turckheim)
André Kientzler (Ribeauvillé)   Marc Tempé (Zellenberg)

* * (GOOD)

J. B. Adam (Ammerschwihr)   André Scherer (Eguisheim)
Lucien Albrecht (Orschwihr)   J.-P. Schmitt (Scherwiller)
Laurent Barth (Westhalten)   Roland Schmitt (Bergbieten)
Bernhard & Reibel (Chântenois)   Gérard Schueller (Husseren-les-Châteaux)
Joseph & Christian Binner (Ammerschwihr)   Albert Seltz (Mittelbergheim)
Cave de Bibeauville   Sick-Dreyer (Ammerschwihr)
Philippe Ehrhart—Domaine St.-Rémy   Jean Sipp (Ribeauvillé)
  (Wettolsheim)   Sipp-Mack (Hunawihr)
Jean-Marie Haag (Soultzmatt)   Pierre Sparr (Sigolsheim)
Clement Klur (Katzenthal)   Sylvie Spielman (Bergheim)
Charles Koehly (Bergheim)   Martine & Vincent Stoeffler (Barr)
Gustave Lorentz (Bergheim)   Gérard Weinzorn (Niedermorschwihr)
Frédéric Mallo & Fils (Hunawihr)   Ziegler-Mauler (Mittelwihr)
Julien Meyer (Nothalten)   Valentin Zusslin (Orschwihr)
Mittnacht-Klack (Riquewihr)

[tasting commentaries]

BARMÈS-BUECHER   * * *
WETTOLSHEIM $15.00–$50.00

The affable François Barmès vocally advocates biodynamic viticulture and earlier harvesting to achieve balanced wines of juicy fruit and digestibility. That said, more than a few of his wines are relatively big-bodied and occasionally betray their alcohol in harshness or heat. While the lineup here is typically (for Alsace) gargantuan, one has to say that most of the single-site bottlings do evince distinctive personalities.

2004 Pinot Auxerrois	87	now
2005 Pinot Blanc Rosenberg	87	now
2000 Riesling Tradition	88	now
2000 Riesling Herrenweg	92	now–2015
2005 Riesling Rosenberg	87	now–2011

2000 Riesling Rosenberg	91	now–2014
2005 Riesling Clos Sand	87	now–2011
2004 Riesling Clos Sand	87	now–2010
2000 Riesling Kruett	89	now–2010
1998 Riesling Liementhal	93	now–2012
2005 Riesling Steingrübler	88	now–2014
2004 Riesling Steingrübler	88	now–2012
2000 Riesling Steingrübler	89	now–2014
2005 Riesling Hengst	91	now–2014
2004 Riesling Hengst	87	now–2014
2000 Riesling Hengst	92	now–2016
1999 Riesling Hengst	88	now
1998 Riesling Hengst	92	now–2012
2005 Pinot Gris Rosenberg Calcarius	87	2009–2012
2004 Pinot Gris Rosenberg Calcarius	87	now–2010
2000 Pinot Gris Rosenberg Bas de Coteau	89	now–2010
2004 Pinot Gris Rosenberg Silicis	88	now
2000 Pinot Gris Rosenberg Haut de Coteau	88	now–2010
1998 Pinot Gris Rosenberg H	89	now–2011
1998 Pinot Gris Rosenberg Vieilles Vignes	90	now–2012
1998 Pinot Gris Rosenberg Vendange Tardive	94	now–2015
1999 Pinot Gris Wintzenheim Sélection de Grains Nobles	88	now–2010
2000 Gewurztraminer Wintzenheim	89	now
2005 Gewurztraminer Herrenweg	87	now–2011
2000 Gewurztraminer Herrenweg	91	now–2010
2005 Gewurztraminer Rosenberg	91	now–2014
2004 Gewurztraminer Rosenberg	89	now–2012
2005 Gewurztraminer Pfersigberg	89	now–2012
2004 Gewurztraminer Pfersigberg	88	now–2012
2005 Gewurztraminer Steingrübler	88	now–2013
2004 Gewurztraminer Steingrübler	90	now–2017
2000 Gewurztraminer Steingrübler	89	now–2010
2005 Gewurztraminer Hengst	91	now–2015
2004 Gewurztraminer Hengst	89	now–2015
2000 Gewurztraminer Hengst	94	now–2012
1998 Gewurztraminer Hengst Vendange Tardive	93	now–2012
2005 Pinot Noir Vieilles Vignes	88	now–2011
2000 Pinot Noir Vieilles Vignes	90	now

LÉON BEYER ★★★★★
EGUISHEIM $14.00–$150.00

Marc Beyer continues to uphold traditions of dry-tasting wine and late release. Even the very occasional Vendange Tardive bottling here is generally only subtly sweet. This is not an Alsace address that seems to have received much fanfare in the English-language press in recent years, but the wines have been constant in their quality for close to a quarter century at least. What one observer would describe as "classic," another might call "retro," but from the sleek, vibrant, chalky Riesling Écaillers (grown in the Pfersigberg) to the powerfully rich, full, and adamantly dry Gewurztraminer Comtes d'Eguisheim, each Beyer cuvée has its decisively distinctive profile.

2005 Pinot Blanc	87	now
2005 Riesling	87	now–2010
2005 Riesling Les Écaillers	88	2009–2017
2004 Riesling Les Écaillers	90	now–2020
2003 Riesling Les Écaillers	87	now–2012
2002 Riesling Les Écaillers	92	now–2020
2001 Riesling Les Écaillers	90	now–2016
2005 Riesling Comtes d'Eguisheim	89	2010–2015
2004 Riesling Comtes d'Eguisheim	91	now–2020
2003 Riesling Comtes d'Eguisheim	88	now–2011+?
2002 Riesling Comtes d'Eguisheim	90	now–2013
2001 Riesling Comtes d'Eguisheim	89	now–2011
2005 Riesling R de Beyer	89	now–2013
2004 Riesling R de Beyer	92	now–2020
2002 Riesling R de Beyer	91	now–2018
2005 Muscat d'Alsace Réserve	89	now–2013
2005 Pinot Gris Réserve	89	now–2015
2004 Pinot Gris Réserve	90	now–2018
2005 Pinot Gris Comtes d'Eguisheim	91	now–2018
2005 Gewurztraminer	88	now–2010
2005 Gewurztraminer Comtes d'Eguisheim	93	now–2028+
2003 Gewurztraminer Comtes d'Eguisheim	90	now–2028+
2001 Gewurztraminer Comtes d'Eguisheim	94	now–2028+
1998 Gewurztraminer Sélection de Grains Nobles	94	now–2035+
1998 Gewurztraminer Sélection de Grains Nobles Quintessence	95	now–2040+

PAUL BLANCK ★ ★ ★
KIENTZHEIM $25.00–$100.00

Frédéric and Philippe Blanck are among the most determined late-releasers, with top wines often appearing only after three or four years in bottle. Frédéric Blanck is eloquent in his expressions of traditionalism and viticultural idealism and renders a number of classically dry yet elegant and even delicate Rieslings. (He says he cannot sell a truly dry Pinot Gris in France nowadays.) Sometimes the vinous concentration on exhibit here fails, however, to accord with Blanck's idealism.

2005 Pinot Auxerrois	87	now
2004 Riesling Rosenbourg	87	now–2010
2005 Riesling Furstentum	89	now–2014
1998 Riesling Furstentum Vieilles Vignes	89	now–2010
2004 Riesling Schlossberg	88	now–2012
2003 Riesling Schlossberg	90	now–2011
1998 Riesling Schlossberg	87	now
1998 Riesling Sommerberg	88	now
2004 Gewurztraminer Mambourg	87	now–2011

LÉON BOESCH ★ ★ ★
WESTHALTEN $20.00

Seldom seen in the U.S. market until now, this winery is an excellent source of traditional dry Riesling and Gewurztraminer. Farming on biodynamic principles, Gérard and Mathieu Boesch have major holdings in the great Zinnkoepflé cru.

BOTT-GEYL ★ ★ ★ ★
NIEDERMORSCHWIHR $20.00–$150.00

Young, articulate Jean-Christophe Bott is passionate about quality and unafraid of making sacrifices on its behalf, and this will probably be one of the more talked-about Alsace domaines in the coming decade. Bott has adopted a biodynamic regimen in the vineyards and is now holding most of his wines 6 to 24 months in bottle before release. Clarity and cleanliness run through all of these, and it is encouraging to taste so many uncompromisingly dry Rieslings, although occasionally bitterness or alcohol intrude. Bott feels capable of encouraging dryness in various ways in the vineyard and the cellar without ever intervening in or attempting to restart sluggish fermentations. Many of the Pinot Gris and Gewurzrtraminer wines represent, by his own admission, "a compromise . . . between good complexity [and ripeness] and not having too much sugar," and the late-harvested examples, in particular, sometimes need to shed a boatload of sweetness before their personalities can come into focus.

2004 Riesling Grafenreben	88	now–2012
2000 Riesling Grafenreben	88	now
1998 Riesling Grafenreben	89	now–2010
2004 Riesling Kronenbourg	87	now–2010+?
2000 Riesling Mandelberg	90	now–2014
1999 Riesling Mandelberg	90	now–2010
1998 Riesling Mandelberg	90	now–2012
2005 Riesling Schoenenbourg	87	2010–2015+?
2004 Riesling Schoenenbourg	88	2009–2012+?
2000 Riesling Schoenenbourg	89	now–2012
1999 Riesling Schoenenbourg	90	now
1998 Riesling Schoenenbourg	90	now–2012
2000 Riesling Grafenreben Vendange Tardive Cuvée Pierre-Antoine	91	now–2014
2000 Pinot Gris Beblenheim	89	now–2013
2000 Pinot Gris Schloesselreben	91	now–2010
2005 Pinot Gris Furstentum	88	2010–2015
2004 Pinot Gris Furstentum	89	2009–2013+?
2000 Pinot Gris Furstentum	90	now–2013
1999 Pinot Gris Furstentum	88	now
1998 Pinot Gris Furstentum	92	now
2005 Pinot Gris Sonnenglanz	87	2010–2015+?
2004 Pinot Gris Sonnenglanz	88	2010–2014
2000 Pinot Gris Sonnenglanz	92	now–2014
1998 Pinot Gris Sonnenglanz	93	now–2012
2005 Pinot Gris Sonnenglanz Vendange Tardive	89	2010–2017+?
2000 Pinot Gris Sonnenglanz Vendange Tardive	96	now–2020
2000 Pinot Gris Sonnenglanz Vendange Tardive	98	now–2030
1999 Pinot Gris Sonnenglanz Vendange Tardive	91	now–2015
1999 Pinot Gris Sélection de Grains Nobles	92	now–2019
2004 Gewurzrtraminer Les Éléments	87	now–2010
2000 Gewurzrtraminer Beblenheim	90	now–2011
2005 Gewurztraminer Furstentum	89	2009–2018
2004 Gewurztraminer Furstentum	90	now–2015
2000 Gewurztraminer Furstentum	94	now–2022
1999 Gewurztraminer Furstentum	91	now
2005 Gewurztraminer Sonnenglanz	90	now–2020

2004 Gewurztraminer Sonnenglanz	90	2010–2015+?
2000 Gewurztraminer Sonnenglanz	93	now–2012
1999 Gewurztraminer Sonnenglanz	90	now
1998 Gewurztraminer Sonnenglanz Vieilles Vignes	94	now–2010
2000 Gewurztraminer Schloesselreben	89	now–2010
2005 Gewurztraminer Schloesselreben Botrytis L'Exception	88	2010–2016+?
2005 Gewurztraminer Sonnenglanz Vendange Tardive	88	2011–2016+?
2000 Gewurztraminer Sonnenglanz Vendange Tardive	95	now–2017
2000 Gewurztraminer Furstentum Vendange Tardive	95	now–2018
1998 Gewurztraminer Furstentum Vendange Tardive	94	now–2012
2005 Pinot Gris Sonnenglanz Sélection de Grains Nobles	90	2012–2020+?
2000 Pinot Gris Sonnenglanz Sélection de Grains Nobles	96	now–2022+?
2005 Gewurztraminer Sonnenglanz Sélection de Grains Nobles	90	2011–2038+
2002 Gewurztraminer Sonnenglanz Sélection de Grains Nobles	92	2018–2025+?
1998 Gewurztraminer Sonnenglanz Sélection de Grains Nobles	96	now–2015
2005 Pinot Noir	87–88	now–2012

ALBERT BOXLER ★ ★ ★ ★ ★
NIEDERMORSCHWIHR $25.00–$125.00

The domaine of Albert Boxler, where young Jean Boxler began calling the shots several years ago, has long exhibited a consistency and quality that very few other wineries in France—much less Alsace—can equal. This is demonstrated not just by their superb results with "noble" varieties in less than easy vintages, but is already evident at the ostensibly "low end" of the varietal spectrum, where one can only wish more estates were rendering wines of such delicious distinction. In Boxler's case, even Chasselas and Sylvaner are included. The bottling of so many different Riesling and Pinot Gris wines by parcel and picking is justified by their glorious quality and individuality. (Boxler often designates diverse parcels and pickings by means of discreet lot numbers on their labels.)

2005 Sylvaner	88	now–2010
2005 Pinot Blanc	89	now–2010
2004 Pinot Blanc Réserve	90	now–2011
2000 Riesling	89	now
2005 Riesling Réserve	91	now–2016
2004 Riesling Réserve	90	2009–2015
2005 Riesling Brand	93	now–2020
2004 Riesling Brand	91	2010–2018
2004 Riesling Brand K	91	2011–2018
2005 Riesling Sommerberg	92	now–2020
2004 Riesling Sommerberg	92	now–2016
2005 Riesling Sommerberg E	94	now–2020
2004 Riesling Sommerberg E	93	2009–2018
2000 Riesling Sommerberg L31	92	2009–2012
2000 Riesling Sommerberg L31E	92	2009–2012
2000 Riesling Sommerberg L31D	96	2009–2020

2005 Riesling Sommerberg D Vendange Tardive	95	now–2022
2004 Riesling Sommerberg D Vendange Tardive	94	2011–2022
2005 Riesling Sommerberg E Vendange Tardive	93	2010–2022
2004 Riesling Sommerberg Vendange Tardive		
Cuvée Zacharie	93	2009–2020
2000 Pinot Gris	88	now
2005 Pinot Gris Vieilles Vignes	91	now–2014
2004 Pinot Gris Sommerberg	90	now–2016
2005 Pinot Gris Brand	91	2010–2016
2004 Pinot Gris Brand	90	now–2016
1999 Pinot Gris Brand	90	now–2010
2004 Pinot Gris Brand S	92	2010–2018
1999 Pinot Gris Brand Vendange Tardive	92	now–2014
2005 Pinot Gris Sommerberg Vendange Tardive "#1"*	93	now–2022
2005 Pinot Gris Sommerberg Vendange Tardive "#2"*	92	now–2022
2005 Pinot Gris Brand Sélection de Grains Nobles	93	2010–2028
2005 Gewurztraminer Réserve	89	now–2015
2004 Gewurztraminer Brand	91	now–2016
2000 Gewurztraminer Brand	88	now
2000 Gewurztraminer Sélection de Grains Nobles	94	now–2025

ERNST BURN   ★ ★ ★
GUEBERSCHWIHR $25.00–$125.00

Francis Burn enthusiastically and unapologetically embraces late-harvest, botrytis, and residual sugar in his finished wines. This is a far cry from his father's style, whose Riesling (through 1990) from Geuberschwihr's very chalky, relatively water-retentive soils could admittedly be quite austere in its youth. But then, Muscat and Gewurztraminer were always the strongest suits in these sites. Embracing botrytis has in one sense not been difficult in recent years, for there has been so much of it. Keeping the wines from veering into bitterness, heat, and/or excessive sweetness is another matter. Burn insists that his wines generally need a few years in bottle to work off some of that sweetness, but his pattern of release is so slow that several 2005s had not yet been bottled in spring 2007.

2004 Sylvaner	88	now
2004 Pinot Blanc	87	now
2005 Riesling	88	now–2010
2005 Pinot Gris	87–88	now–2010
2005 Riesling Goldert Clos St.-Imer Cuvée		
de la Chapelle	89	now–2015
2004 Riesling Goldert Clos St.-Imer Cuvée		
de la Chapelle	88	2009–2012+
2000 Riesling Goldert Clos St.-Imer Cuvée		
de la Chapelle	86–88	now
2005 Pinot Gris Goldert Clos St.-Imer Cuvée		
de la Chapelle	89–90	now–2016
2004 Pinot Gris Goldert Clos St.-Imer Cuvée		
de la Chapelle	87	now–2010
2000 Pinot Gris Goldert Clos St.-Imer Cuvée		
de la Chapelle	92–94	now–2012

Note: As of publication, no decision had been made about how to label these two as yet unreleased *vendange tardive* bottlings, so they are arbitrarily referred to by number.

1998 Pinot Gris Goldert Clos St.-Imer Cuvée de la Chapelle	92	now–2012
2005 Gewurztraminer Goldert Clos St.-Imer Cuvée de la Chapelle	88–89	now–2014+
2004 Gewurztraminer Goldert Clos St.-Imer Cuvée de la Chapelle	88	2009–2012
2005 Gewurztraminer Goldert Clos St.-Imer Cuvée de la Chapelle Vendange Tardive	91	now–2020
1998 Gewurztraminer Goldert Clos St.-Imer Cuvée de la Chapelle Vendange Tardive	92	now–2011
2005 Pinot Gris Goldert Clos St.-Imer Cuvée de la Chapelle Vendange Tardive	92	now–2028
2005 Muscat Goldert Clos St.-Imer Cuvée de la Chapelle	88	now–2010
2005 Muscat Goldert Clos St.-Imer Cuvée de la Chapelle Vendange Tardive	89	now–2012

AGATHE BURSIN ★ ★ ★
WESTHALTEN $17.00–$50.00

Agathe Bursin—whose inaugural vintage was 2000, prior to which her family sold their grapes to the local co-op—is one of Alsace's major emerging talents. Although this widely traveled young *viticultrice* (her preferred title) farms fewer than 10 acres and is already chronically sold out, she says she does not intend to increase production by more than another third, and then only over the long run.

2005 Sylvaner	87	now
2004 Sylvaner	87	now
2005 Sylvaner Eminence	88	now
2005 Riesling	87	now–2012
2004 Riesling	88	now–2012
2005 Riesling Zinnkoepflé	90	now–2015
2004 Riesling Zinnkoepflé	89	now–2015
2005 Pinot Gris Zinnkoepflé	90	now–2013
2004 Pinot Gris Zinnkoepflé	90	now–2014
2005 Gewurztraminer Zinnkoepflé	89	now–2012
2004 Gewurztraminer Zinnkoepflé	91	now–2014
2000 Gewurztraminer Zinnkoepflé	89	now
2005 Pinot Noir	88–89	2009–2012+?

MARCEL DEISS ★ ★ ★ ★ ★
BERGHEIM $24.00–$150.00

Jean-Michel Deiss has been growing some of the finest wines in Alsace for more than a quarter of a century and with them—as well as with his passionately articulate discourse—has captured the imagination and affection of wine enthusiasts worldwide. But the bearded sage of Bergheim is never satisfied; beginning in the late 1980s, he began to completely rethink his wines. The result, beginning a decade ago, was new acquisitions and plantings to achieve single-vineyard, multivariety, barrel-fermented bottlings the likes of which had scarcely been seen in Alsace for the better part of a century, and which Deiss considers ideal vehicles for expressing *terroir*. But even the remaining *monocépage* wines here are brilliantly expressive. (It's too soon for many of these blends to have acquired a track record for ageability.)

2005 Pinot Blanc	91	now
2004 Pinot Blanc	90	now
2005 Riesling	90	now–2012
2004 Riesling Beblenheim	88	now–2012
2000 Riesling St.-Hippolyte	89	now–2010
1998 Riesling Engleberg	89	now–2010
1998 Riesling Grasberg	89	now–2010
2000 Riesling Altenberg de Bergheim	94	now–2016
1998 Riesling Altenberg de Bergheim	91	now–2012
1998 Riesling Schoenenbourg	92	now–2012
2005 Pinot Gris Beblenheim	90	now–2013
2004 Pinot Gris Beblenheim	89	now–2011
2000 Pinot Gris Beblenheim	91	now–2012
2005 Pinot Gris Bergheim	90	2010–2015
2000 Pinot Gris Bergheim	93	2010–2015
2000 Pinot Gris Altenberg de Bergheim	94	now–2020
1998 Pinot Gris Altenberg de Bergheim	94	now–2012
2000 Pinot Gris Huebel Vendange Tardive	94	now–2020
2005 Gewurztraminer St.-Hippolyte	90	2010–2016
2004 Gewurztraminer St.-Hippolyte	91	2009–2016
2005 Gewurztraminer Bergheim	90	2009–2016
2004 Gewurztraminer Bergheim	92	now–2017
2000 Gewurztraminer Altenberg de Bergheim	96	now–2014
2005 Langenberg	92	now–2015+
2004 Langenberg	92	now–2014+
2005 Engelgarten	91	now–2015+
2004 Engelgarten	90	now–2014+
2004 Engelgarten	93	now–2014
2005 Rotenberg	90	now–2015+
2004 Rotenberg	93	now–2015+
2000 Rotenberg	94	now–2014
2005 Schoffweg	93	now–2018+
2004 Schoffweg	91	now–2016+
2005 Grasberg	92	now–2016+
2004 Grasberg	94	now–2018+
2000 Grasberg	94	now–2016
2005 Burg	91	now–2016+
2004 Burg	93	now–2018+
2000 Burg	93	now–2016
2005 Gruenspiel	91	now–2016+
2004 Gruenspiel	90	2009–2019+
2000 Gruenspiel	92	2009–2012
2005 Heubuhl	92	now–2015+
2004 Heubuhl	90	now–2013+
2005 Mambourg	90	2010–2018+
2004 Mambourg	89	2010–2017+
2005 Altenberg de Bergheim	95	now–2020
2004 Altenberg de Bergheim	94	now–2018
2000 Altenberg de Bergheim	98	now–2025
1998 Altenberg de Bergheim	94	now–2015
2005 Schoenenbourg	95	now–2025

2004 Schoenenbourg	96	now–2025
2000 Schoenenbourg	96	now–2018
2005 Muscat d'Alsace	92	now–2012
2004 Muscat d'Alsace	90	now–2012
2004 Burlenberg red	89	now–2015
2003 Burlenberg red	91	2011–2018
2000 Burlenberg red	89–90	now–2012

DIRLER-CADÉ ★ ★ ★ ★ ★
BERGHOLZ $20.00–$70.00

This consistently exceptional estate in the south of Alsace has been enhanced by the involvement of the new generation—Jean Dirler and his wife, Ludivine (née Cadé). The entire domaine has been farmed biodynamically since 1998 (parts of the Kessler and Kitterle with horse), a factor the family thinks especially beneficial, given the climatic extremes that have prevailed in recent years. Riesling and Pinot Gris are generally fermented in large, older barrels here, and other whites usually in tank.

2004 Sylvaner Vieilles Vignes	90	now–2011
2005 Pinot [white from Pinot Noir]	87	now
2005 Pinot Cuvée Vieilles Vignes	88	now
2000 Riesling Réserve	88	now
2005 Riesling Bollenberg	89	2009–2013
2005 Riesling Belzbrunnen	88	2010–2015
2005 Riesling Saering	90	2011–2018
2004 Riesling Saering	92	now–2018
2000 Riesling Saering	89	now–2012
2005 Riesling Spiegel	92	now–2024
2004 Riesling Spiegel	89	now–2013
2000 Riesling Spiegel	90	now–2014
2005 Riesling Kessler	94	now–2022
2000 Riesling Kessler	91	now–2015
2005 Riesling Kessler Heisse Wanne	94	now–2028
2004 Riesling Kessler Cuvée Cecile	91	now–2023
2004 Riesling Kessler Vendange Tardive	90	2010–2015+
2000 Riesling Saering Vendange Tardive	92	2010–2014
2005 Pinot Gris Réserve	90	now–2012
2004 Pinot Gris Réserve	88	now–2010
2005 Pinot Gris Kessler	91	now–2020
2004 Pinot Gris Schwarzberg	87	2009–2012
2004 Pinot Gris Schimberg	90	now–2013
2000 Pinot Gris Saering	89	now–2010
2000 Pinot Gris Schwarzberg Vendange Tardive	92	2010–2016
2000 Pinot Gris Kessler Sélection de Grains Nobles	94	2010–2020
2005 Gewurztraminer	88	now–2011
2005 Gewurztraminer Kessler	90	now–2015
2004 Gewurztraminer Kessler	91	now–2015
2000 Gewurztraminer Kessler	92	now–2012
2005 Gewurztraminer Kitterle	91	now–2018
2000 Gewurztraminer Kitterle	90	now–2010
2005 Gewurztraminer Saering	93	now–2023
2004 Gewurztraminer Spiegel	93	now–2020

2005 Muscat d'Alsace Saering	91	now–2015
2004 Muscat d'Alsace Saering	89	now–2012
2005 Muscat d'Alsace Spiegel	89	2009–2015
2004 Muscat d'Alsace Spiegel	88	2009–2012

MICHEL FONNÉ ★ ★ ★
BENNWIHR $13.00–$30.00

A considerable quantity of the wine Michel Fonné crafts is bottled from the properties and under the name of his septuagenarian uncle, René Barth. The acreage Fonné inherited from his father became completely free of commitments to the local co-op only in 2002, which means more in the near future of that scarce commodity, distinctively delicious yet modestly priced Alsace wine. Vinification here is, with few exceptions, in stainless steel; bottling is completed by September, but release often comes only after a year or two in bottle.

2005 Pinot Blanc Vignoble de Bennwihr	87	now
2004 Pinot Blanc Vignoble de Bennwihr	88	now
2005 Riesling Vignoble de Bennwihr	87	now–2010
2004 Riesling Vignoble de Bennwihr	87	now
2004 Riesling Rebgarten Vieilles Vignes	88	now–2011
2005 Riesling Mambourg	87	now–2012
2004 Riesling Mambourg	90	now–2012
2005 Pinot Gris Roemerberg	87	now–2011
2005 Pinot Gris Roemerberg Vieilles Vignes	88	2009–2012
2004 Pinot Gris Marckrain	89	now–2011+
2005 Gewurztraminer Marckrain	90	now–2012+
2004 Gewurztraminer Marckrain	91	now–2012+
2005 Muscat d'Alsace Marckrain	90	now–2011
2004 Muscat d'Alsace	88	now

PIERRE FRICK ★ ★ ★
PFAFFENHEIM $20.00–$70.00

Alsace's pioneer in biodynamic viticulture, and something of a stylistic maverick as well, Pierre Frick is not afraid to take chances in the cellar. His best wines are dry-finishing, imposingly rich, and long-lived. The Riesling Steinert is routinely full of mineral concentration. Since levels of sulfur are routinely low, these wines need ideal conditions if they are to be cellared but then can age impressively.

2000 Riesling Rot-Murlé	88	now–2012
2000 Riesling Steinert	90	now–2014
2000 Riesling Cuvée Précieuse	90	now–2012
2000 Riesling Vorbourg Vendange Tardive	92	now–2015
2000 Pinot Gris Rot-Murlé	90	now–2015
2000 Pinot Gris Cuvée Précieuse	90	now–2012
2000 Gewurztraminer Steinert	92	now–2012
2000 Gewurztraminer Vorbourg	92	now–2012
2000 Pinot Noir Rot-Murlé	89	now–2010

HUGEL & FILS ★ ★ ★ ★ ★
RIQUEWIHR $15.00–$250.00

The Hugels, like the Beyers and Trimbachs, are true to tradition in their emphasis on dry-tasting wines across the varietal spectrum and in release of their best wines only after a year or, usually, more of bottle age. What international attention was paid to Alsace wine in the 1970s and early 1980s was in no small part due to Jean "Johnny" Hugel, whose nephews Marc (the cellarmaster) and Étienne Hugel were among the pioneers in late-harvested and nobly sweet wines, in serious Alsace Pinot Noir, and (although they seldom labeled any wines by site) in the explication of Alsace *terroir*. Their Jubilee bottlings are from the Schoenenbourg (Riesling) and Sporen (Gewurztraminer). Hugel's Gentil blend is very satisfying if consumed within two years of harvest. Their basic varietal line of wines (from purchased fruit) is reliable, but wines labeled Tradition that incorporate estate-grown fruit (the more so in more difficult vintages) are always far more interesting—although, unfortunately, seldom seen in the U.S.

2004 Riesling Tradition	91	now–2015
2005 Riesling Jubilee	92	now–2020
2004 Riesling Jubilee	90	now–2015
2000 Riesling Jubilee	88–89	now
1998 Riesling Jubilee	88	now–2012
1998 Riesling Homage à Jean Hugel	89	now–2015
2001 Riesling Vendange Tardive	94	now–2020+
1998 Riesling Vendange Tardive	92	now–2016
2000 Riesling Sélection de Grains Nobles S	97	now–2025+
1998 Riesling Sélection de Grains Nobles S	96	now–2020
2005 Pinot Gris Tradition	90	now–2015
2004 Pinot Gris Tradition	87	now–2012+?
2005 Pinot Gris Jubilee	89	2010–2015+?
2000 Pinot Gris Jubilee	87–88	now–2010
1998 Pinot Gris Homage à Jean Hugel	90	now–2012
2001 Pinot Gris Vendange Tardive	92	now–2020
2001 Pinot Gris Sélection de Grains Nobles	93	2012–2022
1998 Pinot Gris Sélection de Grains Nobles	94	now–2015
2005 Gewurztraminer	87	now
2005 Gewurztraminer Tradition	88	now–2012
2005 Gewurztraminer Jubilee	90	now–2018
2004 Gewurztraminer Jubilee	87	2009–2012+?
1998 Gewurztraminer Homage à Jean Hugel	89	now
2001 Gewurztraminer Vendange Tardive	91	now–2020
1998 Gewurztraminer Vendange Tardive	93	now–2012
2005 Gewurztraminer Sélection de Grains Nobles	97	2012–2028
2002 Gewurztraminer Sélection de Grains Nobles	92	now–2028
2001 Gewurztraminer Sélection de Grains Nobles	93	now–2030+?
1998 Gewurztraminer Sélection de Grains Nobles	94	now–2015
2005 Pinot Noir Jubilée	89	now–2014
2003 Pinot Noir Les Neveux	92	2010–2018

JOSMEYER ★ ★ ★ ★
WINTZENHEIM $25.00–$120.00

Under the viticultural direction of Jean Meyer's son-in-law Christopher Ehrhart, this domaine has embraced biodynamic methods. Stylistic sensitivity and restraint; concern for cuisine compatibility; a special fondness for that underdog variety Auxerrois; and staggered release of wines continue to distinguish this fine estate, which in recent years has curtailed its *négociant* activities.

2005 Pinot Blanc Mise du Printemps	87	now
2004 Pinot Blanc Les Lutins	88	now–2010

2005 Pinot Auxerrois H Vieilles Vignes	88	2009–2013
2004 Pinot Auxerrois H Vieilles Vignes	89	now–2012
2005 Riesling Les Pierrets	89	2009–2014
2004 Riesling Le Kottabe	88	now
2004 Riesling Le Dragon	90	now–2012
2004 Riesling Brand	90	now–2015
2005 Riesling Hengst	90	now–2020
2004 Riesling Hengst	91	now–2018
2004 Pinot Gris Le Fromenteau	88	now
2004 Pinot Gris Fondation 1854	89	now–2012+
2005 Pinot Gris Brand	88	now–2018
2004 Pinot Gris Brand	92	now–2015
2000 Pinot Gris Brand	89	now–2010
2005 Pinot Gris Hengst	88	now–2013
2005 Gewurztraminer Les Folastries	88	now
2005 Gewurztraminer Hengst	90	now–2016
2004 Gewurztraminer Brand	91	now–2016
2004 Pinot Noir Tête de Cuvée	88	now–2012+

ANDRÉ KIENTZLER ⋆ ⋆ ⋆
RIBEAUVILLÉ $20.00–$100.00

André Kientzler's wines are seldom seen in the U.S. He excels even with "minor" varieties—notably Auxerrois and Chasselas—as well as with "noble" grapes (above all, Riesling) in the great crus of Geisberg and Osterberg.

MARC KREYDENWEISS ⋆ ⋆ ⋆ ⋆
ANDLAU $19.00–$150.00

Marc Kreydenweiss might seem like less of an Alsace maverick now that so many of his fellow vignerons have joined him in embracing biodynamic methods, but his wines still possess a style of their own, dry and influenced by malolactic fermentation and long lees contact. Kreydenweiss's labels all feature artistic works commissioned for the purpose, and he somehow conjures correspondingly distinctive and memorable sensations out of his vineyards and into the glass. The Kritt Pinot Blanc–Auxerrois blend represents one of the best wine values in Alsace.

2005 Pinot Blanc Kritt	90	now–2012
2004 Pinot Blanc Kritt	89	now–2010
2000 Riesling Andlau	90	now–2010
2005 Riesling Clos Rebberg	90	now–2015
2000 Riesling Clos Rebberg	95	now–2018
2005 Riesling Wiebelsberg	92	now–2016
2004 Riesling Wiebelsberg	91	now–2015
2000 Riesling Wiebelsberg	91	now–2016
1998 Riesling Wiebelsberg	89	now–2010
2005 Riesling Kastelberg	90	now–2018
2004 Riesling Kastelberg	88	now–2014+?
2000 Riesling Kastelberg	94	now–2018
1998 Riesling Kastelberg	92	now–2012
2000 Riesling Clos Rebberg Sélection de Grains Nobles	93	now–2022
2005 Clos du Val d'Éléon Riesling-Pinot Gris	89	now–2013+?

2000 Clos du Val d'Éléon Riesling-Pinot Gris	89	now–2010
2005 Pinot Gris Lerchenberg	89	2009–2012+?
2004 Pinot Gris Moenchberg	91	now–2014+?
2000 Pinot Gris Moenchberg	91	now–2014
1998 Pinot Gris Moenchberg	91	now–2010
2000 Pinot Gris Clos Rebberg	95	now–2018
1998 Pinot Gris Clos Rebberg	89	now–2010
2005 Pinot Gris Clos Rebberg Vendange de Noël	94	now–2020+?
2005 Pinot Gris Moenchberg Vendange Tardive	90	now–2018
2005 Pinot Gris Clos Rebberg Sélection de Grains Nobles	93	now–2028
2000 Pinot Gris Clos Rebberg Sélection de Grains Nobles	93	now–2020
2005 Gewurztraminer Kritt	89	now–2015
2005 Gewurztraminer Kritt Vendange de Noël	91	now–2012

PAUL KUBLER ⋆⋆⋆
SOULTZMATT $18.00–$60.00

After earning his oenology degree from Bordeaux, and a stage at Cloudy Bay, young Philippe Kubler took over at his family's domaine beginning with the 2004 vintage. He is a talented vigneron, one to watch.

2005 Riesling Breitenberg	89	now–2012+
2005 Pinot Gris K	88	now–2011+?
2005 Gewurztraminer Zinnkoepflé	91	now–2015+?

KUENTZ-BAS ⋆⋆⋆
HUSSEREN-LES-CHÂTEAUX $18.00–$120.00

Since 2004, the Kuentz-Bas domaine—which had in 2001 been somewhat reduced in size by a split between its then managing partners—has belonged to the large Ammerschwihr winery J. B. Adam, and young Samuel Tottoli has been in charge. His obvious enthusiasm and detail-consciousness (as well as, he maintains, a biodynamic viticultural turn) are having salutary results. One aspect of house style here probably could not be changed, even if desired: Malolactic bacteria clearly have the run of the place. Wines sold under the Tradition label are serviceable, but real interest begins with those labeled Collection and Collection Rare.

2005 Auxerrois Collection	88	now
2004 Riesling Collection	87	now–2010
2005 Riesling Collection Rare	88	now–2012
2004 Riesling Collection Rare	89	now–2013
2005 Riesling Pfersigberg	90	now–2016
2004 Riesling Pfersigberg	89	now–2015
2004 Riesling Sélection de Grains Nobles Cuvée Jérémy	93	2009–2023
2005 Pinot Gris Collection	87	now–2010
2004 Pinot Gris Collection	88	now–2010
2005 Pinot Gris Collection Rare	89	now–2012
2004 Pinot Gris Collection Rare	90	now–2011
2005 Pinot Gris Eichberg	89	2009–2013
2005 Pinot Gris Sélection de Grains Nobles Cuvée Jérémy	89	2012–2020+?
2005 Gewurztraminer Collection	87	now–2010

2004 Gewurztraminer Collection	87	now
2004 Gewurztraminer Eichberg	87	now–2011+
2005 Gewurztraminer Pfersigberg	91	now–2016
2004 Gewurztraminer Pfersigberg	90	now–2015
2005 Gewurztraminer Vendange Tardive Cuvée Caroline	90	2010–2017+?

ALBERT MANN ✶ ✶ ✶ ✶ ✶
WETTOLSHEIM $15.00–$150.00

In the nearly two decades since this domaine was consolidated, the Barthelmé brothers, Jacky and Maurice, have maintained their position near the forefront of Alsace viticulture, farming a range of relatively far-flung and outstanding vineyards, as well as offering excellent value virtually throughout their range, anchored by routinely outstanding Pinot Blanc and Auxerrois. The brothers are very conscious of the need to promote ripeness while inhibiting sugar retention, and hard at work experimenting with ways (including certain biodynamic practices) to accomplish this.

2005 Pinot Blanc	87	now
2004 Pinot Blanc	90	now
2005 Auxerrois Vieilles Vignes	89	now
2004 Auxerrois Vieilles Vignes	90	now–2011
2000 Riesling	88	now
2005 Riesling Cuvée Albert	87	now
2004 Riesling Cuvée Albert	89	now–2011
2000 Riesling Cuvée Albert	89	now–2010
2005 Riesling Schlossberg	90	now–2016
2004 Riesling Schlossberg	93	now–2020
2000 Riesling Schlossberg	91	now–2012
1999 Riesling Schlossberg	89	now
2005 Riesling Furstentum	91	now–2018
2004 Riesling Furstentum	91	now–2016+
2000 Riesling Furstentum	93	now–2014
1999 Riesling Furstentum	91	now–2010
1998 Riesling Pfleck Vendange Tardive	92	now–2012
2004 Riesling Altenbourg Vendange Tardive	91	now–2020
2000 Riesling Altenbourg Sélection de Grains Nobles	95	now–2030
2005 Pinot Gris Cuvée Albert	88	now–2010
2004 Pinot Gris Cuvée Albert	88	now–2011
2000 Pinot Gris Vieilles Vignes	89	now–2011
2000 Pinot Gris Pfersigberg	92	2010–2014
2005 Pinot Gris Furstentum	88	2010–2014
2004 Pinot Gris Furstentum	89	2010–2013+?
2000 Pinot Gris Furstentum	92	now–2014
1999 Pinot Gris Furstentum	92	now–2012
1998 Pinot Gris Furstentum	89	now
2005 Pinot Gris Hengst	90	now–2017
2004 Pinot Gris Hengst	91	now–2017
2000 Pinot Gris Hengst	91	now–2016
2004 Pinot Gris Altenbourg Vendange Tardive	90	now–2018
2000 Pinot Gris Altenbourg Vendange Tardive	94	now–2016
1999 Pinot Gris Altenbourg Vendange Tardive	92	now–2020

2000 Pinot Gris Altenbourg Sélection de Grains Nobles	93	now–2030
1999 Pinot Gris Altenbourg Sélection de Grains Nobles	94	now–2025
1998 Pinot Gris Altenbourg Sélection de Grains Nobles	95	now–2025
2000 Pinot Gris Altenbourg Sélection de Grains Nobles Le Tri	97	now–2030+?
1998 Pinot Gris Altenbourg Sélection de Grains Nobles Le Tri	97	now–2025+?
2000 Pinot Gris Hengst Sélection de Grains Nobles	93	now–2030
2005 Gewurztraminer	87	now
2004 Gewurztraminer	89	now–2011
2000 Gewurztraminer	89	now
2000 Gewurztraminer Altenbourg	91	now–2010
2005 Gewurztraminer Steingrubler	91	now–2018
2004 Gewurztraminer Steingrubler	92	now–2018
2000 Gewurztraminer Steingrubler	94	now–2015
1999 Gewurztraminer Steingrubler	90	now
2005 Gewurztraminer Furstentum Vieilles Vignes	92	2010–2020
2004 Gewurztraminer Furstentum Vieilles Vignes	92	now–2018
2000 Gewurztraminer Furstentum Vieilles Vignes	95	now–2015
1999 Gewurztraminer Furstentum Vieilles Vignes	91	now
2005 Gewurztraminer Altenbourg Vendange Tardive	92	now–2027
2000 Gewurztraminer Altenbourg Vendange Tardive	93	now–2016
1999 Gewurztraminer Furstentum Vendange Tardive	91	now–2018
2005 Gewurztraminer Furstentum Sélection de Grains Nobles	93	now–2033
2000 Gewurztraminer Furstentum Sélection de Grains Nobles	95	now–2025
1998 Gewurztraminer Furstentum Sélection de Grains Nobles	96	now–2020
2005 Muscat Altenbourg Vendange Tardive	90	now–2017
2005 Muscat Altenbourg Sélection de Grains Nobles	94	now–2030
2005 Pinot Noir Grand Hengst	89	now–2012+

MEYER-FONNÉ ★ ★ ★
KATZENTHAL $16.00–$150.00

Felix Meyer is one of the more ambitious and successful young vignerons of Alsace, and is in the process of expanding his already large holdings, extending over a considerable range of *villages,* to include additional top crus. Furthermore, his prices are very reasonable. Many of the young wines, however—particularly the Gewurztraminer—are rather superficially sweet.

2005 Gentil d'Alsace	87	now
2005 Pinot d'Alsace	87	now
2004 Pinot Blanc Vieilles Vignes	87	now
2005 Riesling Vignobles de Katzenthal	87	now–2010
2004 Riesling Vignobles de Katzenthal	88	now–2011
2004 Riesling Pfoeller	88	now–2017
2005 Riesling Wineck-Schlossberg	87	now–2012+

2004 Riesling Wineck-Schlossberg	89	now–2015
2005 Riesling Kaefferkopf	88	now–2012
2004 Riesling Kaefferkopf	87	now–2013+
2004 Riesling Wineck-Schlossberg Sélection de Grains Nobles	91	now–2028
2005 Pinot Gris Hinterburg de Katzenthal	89	now–2013
2004 Pinot Gris Hinterburg de Katzenthal Cuvée Éloi	88	now–2012
2005 Pinot Gris Hinterburg de Katzenthal Vendange Tardive	92	now–2020
2005 Pinot Gris Hinterburg de Katzenthal Sélection de Grains Nobles	93	now–2028
2005 Gewurztraminer Réserve Particulière	87	now–2011
2005 Gewurztraminer Kaefferkopf	88	2009–2013
2005 Gewurztraminer Wineck-Schlossberg	90	2010–2015
2004 Gewurztraminer Wineck-Schlossberg	87	2010–2012+
2005 Gewurztraminer Wineck-Schlossberg Vendange Tardive	91	now–2018
2004 Gewurztraminer Wineck-Schlossberg Vendange Tardive	87	2011–2015
2005 Gewurztraminer Dorfburg Vieilles Vignes Sélection de Grains Nobles	92	now–2028

FRÉDÉRIC MOCHEL ✱ ✱ ✱
TRAENHEIM $15.00–$75.00

Frédéric and son Guillaume Mochel clearly work as an excellent team, farming almost exclusively acreage in the steep chalky slopes of Bergbieten's Altenberg, but bottling only their top cuvées as vineyard-designated grands crus. The best Muscat and Gewurztraminer here sometimes offer almost Riesling-like clarity and refreshment.

2005 Sylvaner	87	now
2005 Riesling Altenberg de Bergbieten	89	now–2014
2004 Riesling Altenberg de Bergbieten	90	now–2015
2005 Riesling Altenberg de Bergbieten Cuvée Henriette	91	2011–2018
2004 Riesling Altenberg de Bergbieten Cuvée Henriette	90	now–2016
2001 Riesling Altenberg de Bergbieten Cuvée Henriette	89	now–2010
2005 Muscat d'Alsace Altenberg de Bergbieten	87	now–2011+
2004 Muscat d'Alsace Altenberg de Bergbieten	88	now–2012
2005 Pinot Gris	88	now–2010
2001 Gewurztraminer	88	now
2004 Gewurztraminer Altenberg de Bergbieten	88	now–2012
2005 Gewurztraminer Vendange Tardive	88	2010–2015

RENÉ MURÉ–CLOS ST.-LANDELIN ✱ ✱ ✱ ✱
ROUFFACH $40.00–$110.00

René Muré has been practicing organic viticulture for a decade, and is now experimenting with biodynamics and extensive replanting with old selections and tight spacing—trying, as he says, to take things in the vineyards back to his grandfather's days. In these warm sites, he produces relatively broad wines; he is particularly concerned with developing methods to brake sugar accumulation and retain acidity. But, as if hedging his bets, Muré has also sought permission from the authorities to plant a small block of Syrah! (This estate has been serious about Pinot Noir for more than a quarter century.) Wines denoted as Côte de Rouffach or simply René Muré (which include some grand cru Vorbourg and Zinnkoepflé bottlings) are from purchased fruit, whereas estate wines are labeled Clos St.-Landelin.

2005 Riesling Clos St.-Landelin Vorbourg	88–89	2010–2013+
2004 Riesling Clos St.-Landelin Vorbourg	90	now–2015
2000 Riesling Clos St.-Landelin Vorbourg	92	now–2012
1999 Riesling Clos St.-Landelin Vorbourg	92	now–2012
1998 Riesling Clos St.-Landelin Vorbourg	91	now–2012
2000 Riesling Zinnkoepflé	92	now–2012
1999 Riesling Zinnkoepflé	89	now–2010
2005 Riesling Zinnkoepflé Vendanges Tardives	89	now–2017
2001 Riesling Clos St.-Landelin Vorbourg		
Vendange Tardive	90	now–2016
2004 Pinot Gris Lutzetal	88	now
1999 Pinot Gris Lutzetal	90	now
2004 Pinot Gris Clos St.-Landelin Vorbourg	87	now–2011
2000 Pinot Gris Clos St.-Landelin Vorbourg	92	now–2014
1999 Pinot Gris Clos St.-Landelin Vorbourg	90	now
2005 Pinot Gris Clos St.-Landelin Vorbourg		
Vendange Tardive	89	now–2017
2002 Pinot Gris Clos St.-Landelin Vorbourg		
Sélection de Grains Nobles	92	now–2038
2000 Pinot Gris Clos St.-Landelin Vorbourg		
Sélection de Grains Nobles	98	now–2040
2005 Gewurztraminer Zinnkoepflé Vendange Tardive	90	now–2017
2004 Gewurztraminer Zinnkoepflé Vendange Tardive	89	now–2016
2000 Gewurztraminer Clos St.-Landelin Vorbourg	93	now–2012
1999 Gewurztraminer Clos St.-Landelin Vorbourg	90	now
2005 Gewurztraminer Clos St.-Landelin Vorbourg		
Vendange Tardive	90–91	now–2028
2004 Gewurztraminer Clos St.-Landelin Vorbourg		
Vendange Tardive	89	now–2018+
2001 Gewurztraminer Clos St.-Landelin Vorbourg		
Vendange Tardive	92	now–2018
2000 Gewurztraminer Clos St.-Landelin Vorbourg		
Vendange Tardive	95	now–2020
1998 Gewurztraminer Clos St.-Landelin Vorbourg		
Vendange Tardive	92	now–2012
2002 Gewurztraminer Clos St.-Landelin Vorbourg		
Sélection de Grains Nobles	93	now–2033
2004 Muscat d'Alsace Clos St.-Landelin Vorbourg		
Vendange Tardive	88	2010–2014
1999 Muscat d'Alsace Clos St.-Landelin Vorbourg		
Vendange Tardive	92	now
2001 Muscat d'Alsace Clos St.-Landelin Vorbourg		
Sélection de Grains Nobles	90	now–2033
2005 Pinot Noir Clos St.-Landelin	87	2010–2013
2000 Pinot Noir Clos St.-Landelin	87	now–2010

ANDRÉ OSTERTAG * * * *
EPFIG $20.00–$150.00

André Ostertag continues to render some of the most distinctively delicious and thought-provoking wines in Alsace. He now has 120 parcels among his 35 acres (all farmed biodynamically), and few if any growers give more thought than does Ostertag to aesthetic and stylistic considerations when it comes to vinifying and assembling (as well as labeling) his many lots. His single-vineyard Riesling and small-barrel-fermented Pinot Gris are fascinating to compare; his Sylvaner and Muscat are among Alsace's most consistently fine; and he shoots for the (botrytis-dusted) moon with his tiny crop of Gewurztraminer, and frequently hits.

2005 Sylvaner Vieilles Vignes	89	now
2005 Muscat d'Alsace Fronholz	88	now–2011
2005 Riesling Clos Mathis	88	2010–2013+
2004 Riesling Clos Mathis	89	now–2014
2005 Riesling Heissenberg	89	now–2016
2004 Riesling Heissenberg	90	now–2016
2000 Riesling Heissenberg	89	now–2012
1998 Riesling Heissenberg	91	now–2012
2005 Riesling Fronholz	91	now–2018
2004 Riesling Fronholz	90	now–2017
2000 Riesling Fronholz	89	now–2011
2005 Riesling Muenchberg	93	now–2020
2004 Riesling Muenchberg	91	2010–2020
2000 Riesling Muenchberg	92	now–2016
1999 Riesling Muenchberg	92	now–2010
1998 Riesling Muenchberg	94	now–2014
2004 Riesling Muenchberg Vendange Tardive	94	now–2028
2000 Riesling Muenchberg Vendange Tardive	92	now–2018
2005 Pinot Gris	88	now–2012
2004 Pinot Gris	89	now–2012
2005 Pinot Gris Fronholz	90	2010–2014
2004 Pinot Gris Fronholz	89	now–2013
2000 Pinot Gris Fronholz	89	now–2012
2005 Pinot Gris Zellberg	89	now–2014
2004 Pinot Gris Zellberg	88	2009–2013
2000 Pinot Gris Zellberg	89	now–2012
1999 Pinot Gris Zellberg	91	now
2005 Pinot Gris A360P [Muenchberg]	90–91	2009–2018
2004 Pinot Gris A360P [Muenchberg]	91	now–2018
2000 Pinot Gris Muenchberg	91	now–2014
1999 Pinot Gris Muenchberg	92	now–2012
1998 Pinot Gris Muenchberg	90	now
2005 Gewurztraminer Fronholz Vendange Tardive	90	2012–2018+
2004 Gewurztraminer Fronholz Vendange Tardive	91	2012–2022
2000 Gewurztraminer Fronholz Vendange Tardive	93	now–2016
1998 Gewurztraminer Fronholz Vendange Tardive	93	now–2012
2005 Gewurztraminer Fronholz Sélection de Grains Nobles	95	now–2035
1998 Gewurztraminer Fronholz Sélection de Grains Nobles	93	now–2012+

ANDRÉ PFISTER ✴ ✴ ✴
DAHLENHEIM $17.00–$100.00

Young Melanie Pfister put in time at Méo-Camuzet, Zind-Humbrecht, and Cheval Blanc before recently officially joining her father André at the family's 22-acre estate a dozen miles west of Strasbourg. Riesling is the dominant variety here in acreage, as well as in degree of vinous concentration and rate of success, although the debut of Cuvée 8 (a blend of Riesling, Pinot Gris, Gewurztraminer, and Muscat) was auspicious.

2005 Pinot Blanc	88	now
2005 Riesling Engelberg	91	now–2018
2004 Riesling Engelberg	89	now–2014
2005 Riesling Silberberg	88	now–2012
2005 Cuvée 8	91	now–2012+
2005 Gewurztraminer Engelberg	87	now–2011
2004 Gewurztraminer Engelberg	88	now–2012

ROLLY-GASSMANN ✴ ✴ ✴ ✴
RORSCHWIHR $25.00–$125.00

Pierre Gassmann prides himself on following the family tradition of late picking, generally waiting, as he puts it, "until the berries turn blue" to rescue them from the vine. A tasting of young wines chez Rolly-Gassmann is akin to an athletic event, given the sheer number of them and their generally high levels of residual sugar. (Even Auxerrois and Sylvaner are generally noticeably sweet here.) The best Rolly-Gassmann wines manage that sugar without obscuring vineyard-specific characteristics or fatiguing the palate; the estate typically releases its wines after anywhere between 2 and 10 years in bottle.

2005 Sylvaner Réserve Millésime	87	now–2010
2005 Sylvaner Weingarten	88	now–2012
2005 Pinot Blanc	88	now
2004 Pinot Blanc	88	now
2005 Auxerrois Rotleibel	87	now–2011
2005 Auxerrois Rotleibel	88	now–2012
2005 Auxerrois Moechreben	88	now–2012
2004 Auxerrois Moenchreben	89	now–2013
2000 Auxerrois Moenchreben	88	now–2010
2004 Riesling	87	now–2012
2004 Riesling Réserve Millésime	88	now–2014
2004 Riesling Kappelweg	88	now–2014
2004 Riesling Pflaenzerreben	88	now–2015
2000 Riesling Pflaenzerreben	88	now–2011
2004 Riesling Vendange Tardive	88	2012–2020
2005 Riesling Silberberg Vendange Tardive	87	now–2015+
2005 Riesling Pflaenzerreben Vendange Tardive	90	2012–2025
2005 Riesling Vendange Tardive Cuvée Yves	90	now–2028
2005 Riesling Kappelweg Vendange Tardive	91	2012–2030
2004 Pinot Gris Brandhurst	87	now–2011
2004 Pinot Gris Rotleibel	90	now–2015
2000 Pinot Gris Rotleibel	89	now
2004 Pinot Gris Réserve Rolly-Gassmann	90	now–2017
2005 Pinot Gris Vendange Tardive	92	now–2028
2000 Pinot Gris Vendange Tardive	90	now–2020
2005 Pinot Gris Rotleibel Vendange Tardive	91	now–2025

2005 Pinot Gris Sélection de Grains Nobles	94	now–2035
2004 Gewurztraminer	88	now–2011
2004 Gewurztraminer Oberer Weingarten	91	now–2018
2000 Gewurztraminer Oberer Weingarten	90	now–2012
2004 Gewurztraminer Stegreben	91	now–2018
2004 Gewurztraminer Kappelweg	92	now–2020
2005 Gewurztraminer Brandhurst Vendange Tardive	91	now–2022
2004 Gewurztraminer Brandhurst Vendange Tardive	94	now–2028
2000 Gewurztraminer Brandhurst Vendange Tardive	90	now–2017
2005 Gewurztraminer Oberer Weingarten Vendange Tardive	90	now–2022
2005 Gewurztraminer Kappelweg Vendange Tardive	91	now–2022
2000 Gewurztraminer Kappelweg Vendange Tardive	90	now–2015
2005 Gewurztraminer Haguenau Vendange Tardive	90	2011–2025
2000 Gewurztraminer Haguenau Vendange Tardive	92	2011–2020
2005 Gewurztraminer Stegreben Vendange Tardive	91	now–2022
2004 Muscat d'Alsace	88	now–2011
2005 Muscat d'Alsace Moenchreben	89	now–2014
2004 Muscat d'Alsace Moenchreben	90	now–2014

MARTIN SCHAETZEL ✳ ✳ ✳
AMMERSCHWIHR $18.00–$70.00

Here is another one of the region's pioneers in biodynamic viticulture (and as a professor of oenology, Schaetzel presumably understands the modern scientific aspects of viticulture equally well). This is a source that demonstrates the true cru potential of some parts of the large and geologically diverse vineyard area demarcated as Kaefferkopf, and farms the far-flung crus of Schlossberg and Rangen as well.

2000 Riesling Cuvée Réserve	89	now
2000 Riesling Kaefferkopf Granit	92	now–2014
2000 Riesling Kaefferkopf Cuvée Nicolas	92	now–2012
2000 Riesling Schlossberg	91	now–2012
2000 Riesling Rangen	93	now–2014
2000 Pinot Gris Cuvée Réserve	88	now–2010
2000 Pinot Gris Rosenbourg	89	now–2012
2000 Pinot Gris Marckrain	91	now–2014
2000 Gewurztraminer Kaefferkopf	91	now–2010
2000 Gewurztraminer Cuvée Isabelle	90	now–2010
2000 Gewurztraminer Cuvée Catherine	91	now–2012
2000 Gewurztraminer Cuvée Réserve	89	now

CHARLES SCHLERET ✳ ✳ ✳
TURCKHEIM $20.00–$120.00

Charles Schleret (who founded his small, eponymous domaine in 1950) may be signaling that he is near retirement. Still, his enthusiasm; the simple hierarchy of his wines; their leisurely pace of release; the rarity of VT or SGN bottlings; the large apron Schleret wears over his jacket and tie; and, above all, his style, are constants. It is hard not to succumb to nostalgia here, and to become just a little peeved in recognition of how rare Alsace wines with such versatility, modesty, simple labeling, and effortless grace have become nowadays.

2005 Pinot Blanc	89	now
2005 Riesling Herrenweg	87	now
2005 Muscat d'Alsace	90	now–2012
2005 Pinot Gris Herrenweg	88	now–2011
1998 Pinot Gris Herrenweg	87	now
2000 Pinot Gris Sélection de Grains Nobles	92	now–2020
2005 Gewurztraminer Herrenweg	87	now–2010
2000 Gewurztraminer Sélection de Grains Nobles	93	now–2022

BERNARD SCHOFFIT ★★★★
COLMAR $20.00–$200.00

Schoffit generates opulent, rich, generally low-acid wines from the Harth, just outside Colmar—a phenomenon perfectly illustrated by his "low-end" wines, including a Pinot Gris–like Chasselas—as well as often flamboyant and dramatic wines from the Rangen de Thann, where he goes beyond *sélection de grains nobles* and has bottled some phenomenally high-sugar and low-alcohol essences he calls Larmes de Lave ("tears of lava"). As the list below demonstrates, Schoffit is enamored of Pinot Gris.

2005 Pinot Blanc Auxerrois Vieilles Vignes	88	now–2010
2005 Chasselas Vieilles Vignes	89	now–2013
2004 Riesling Harth Tradition	87	now–2012
2004 Riesling Harth Cuvée Alexandre Vieilles Vignes	87	now–2013+
1999 Riesling Harth Cuvée Caroline	89	now–2011
2005 Riesling Sommerberg	87	2009–2013+
1999 Riesling Sommerberg	89	now–2010
2005 Riesling Rangen de Thann Clos St.-Théobald	89	2010–2014
2000 Riesling Rangen de Thann Clos St.-Théobald	93	now–2015
1999 Riesling Rangen de Thann Clos St.-Théobald	93	now–2015
1999 Riesling Rangen de Thann Clos St.-Théobald Vendange Tardive	94	now–2020
1998 Riesling Rangen de Thann Clos St.-Théobald Sélection de Grains Nobles	96	now–2020+
2005 Pinot Gris Cuvée Alexandre	88	now–2014
2000 Pinot Gris Vieilles Vignes Cuvée Alexandre	91	now–2012
1999 Pinot Gris Vieilles Vignes Cuvée Alexandre	89	now–2010
1998 Pinot Gris Vieilles Vignes Sigillé de Qualité de la Confrèrie de St.-Étienne	92	now–2012
2005 Pinot Gris Rangen de Thann Clos St.-Théobald	89	2009–2014
2004 Pinot Gris Rangen de Thann Clos St.-Théobald	87	now–2013+
2000 Pinot Gris Rangen de Thann Clos St.-Théobald	96	now–2017
1999 Pinot Gris Rangen de Thann Clos St.-Théobald	94	now–2018
2005 Pinot Gris Rangen de Thann Clos St.-Théobald Vendange Tardive	91	2010–2023
2005 Pinot Gris Rangen de Thann Clos St.-Théobald Vendange Tardive Lot 2	92	now–2025
2002 Pinot Gris Rangen de Thann Clos St.-Théobald Vendange Tardive	94	now–2023
2000 Pinot Gris Rangen de Thann Clos St.-Théobald Vendange Tardive	94	now–2020
1999 Pinot Gris Rangen de Thann Clos St.-Théobald Vendange Tardive	94	now–2020

1998 Pinot Gris Rangen de Thann Clos St.-Théobald Vendange Tardive	95	now–2020
2002 Pinot Gris Rangen de Thann Clos St.-Théobald Sélection de Grains Nobles	94	now–2033
2001 Pinot Gris Rangen de Thann Clos St.-Théobald Sélection de Grains Nobles	92	2010–2022
2000 Pinot Gris Rangen de Thann Clos St.-Théobald Sélection de Grains Nobles	93	now–2030
1999 Pinot Gris Rangen de Thann Clos St.-Théobald Sélection de Grains Nobles	96	now–2035
1998 Pinot Gris Rangen de Thann Clos St.-Théobald Sélection de Grains Nobles Lot 1	97	now–2025
1998 Pinot Gris Rangen de Thann Clos St.-Théobald Sélection de Grains Nobles Lot 2	98	now–2025
2000 Pinot Gris Rangen de Thann Clos St.-Théobald Sélection de Grains Nobles Tri	93	now–2030
2005 Pinot Gris Rangen de Thann Clos St.-Théobald Larmes de Lave	94	2010–2035+
2001 Pinot Gris Rangen de Thann Clos St.-Théobald Larmes de Lave	93	2012–2030+
2005 Gewurztraminer Harth Cuvée Caroline	87	now–2011+
2000 Gewurztraminer Harth Cuvée Alexandre	90	now
1999 Gewurztraminer Harth Cuvée Alexandre	89	now
2000 Gewurztraminer Harth Vieilles Vignes Cuvée Alexandre	92	now–2012
2005 Gewurztraminer Rangen de Thann Clos St.-Théobald	90	now–2016
2000 Gewurztraminer Rangen de Thann Clos St.-Théobald	94	now–2014
1999 Gewurztraminer Rangen de Thann Clos St.-Théobald	93	now–2011
2000 Gewurztraminer Vendange Tardive	90	now–2012
1998 Gewurztraminer Rangen de Thann Clos St.-Théobald Sélection de Grains Nobles	95	now–2015
2005 Muscat d'Alsace Tradition	90	now–2011
1998 Muscat d'Alsace Sélection de Grains Nobles	92	now–2012

MARC TEMPÉ ★ ★ ★
ZELLENBERG $22.00–$140.00

Some critics call vinous adventurer Marc Tempé an iconoclast; others call him a reactionary. Tempé bottled his first wines in 1995 and has been working biodynamically for a decade. His wines ferment longer and reside in cask longer (generally two to three years) than any others in Alsace today. Malolactic fermentation generally takes place (although he doesn't force it), and he welcomes botrytis for the complexity it adds even to dry wines. Add to all of these considerations a penchant for minimal doses of sulfur, and you often have wines that, while in some sense "slow moving," are not easy targets to capture in a momentary, youthful tasting note. They can also be among the most rewarding, not just intriguing, wines in Alsace.

2005 Pinot Blanc Zellenberg	86–88	now–2010
2005 Pinot Blanc Priegel	88–90	2009–2013+

2005 Auxerrois Vieilles Vignes	88–90	now–2012
2005 Riesling St.-Hippolyte	87–89	now–2012+
2000 Riesling St.-Hippolyte	89	now
1998 Riesling St.-Hippolyte	88–89	now
2004 Riesling Zellenberg	89	now–2012
2004 Riesling Burgreben	88	now–2011
2003 Riesling Burgreben	90	now–2012+
1998 Riesling Burgreben	90	now
2003 Riesling Grafenreben	87	2009–2011+
2005 Pinot Gris Zellenberg	88–90	now–2014
2004 Pinot Gris Zellenberg	89	2009–2012
2000 Pinot Gris Rodelsberg	89	now–2010
2004 Gewurztraminer Zellenberg	87	now–2011+
2000 Gewurztraminer Zellenberg	89	now
2003 Gewurztraminer Mambourg	91	now–2015
2002 Gewurztraminer Mambourg S Sélection de Grains Nobles	92–94	now–2022+

F. E. TRIMBACH ★ ★ ★ ★ ★
RIBEAUVILLÉ $15.00–$200.00

The Trimbach family continues to render some of the world's finest and most refined Riesling; to uphold the principle that wine of Alsace (unless VT) should not taste sweet; to release wines only when they believe those wines say "it's time" (generally six or more years for the top cuvées); and to ship 40,000 cases (or 40% of their production) to the United States. Notable recent developments include the enhanced quality of their réserve-level wines as well as outstanding performances with Pinot Gris. A measure of the extent to which Riesling has "arrived" as an international star is that Trimbach's Clos Ste.-Hune—until recently an affordable splurge for wine lovers of modest means, and often to be had in older vintages—has fallen prey to soaring after-market prices.

2005 Riesling Réserve	91	now–2015
2004 Riesling Réserve	88	now–2013+
2002 Riesling Frédéric Émile	92	2009–2018
2001 Riesling Cuvée Frédéric Émile 375th Anniversary	93	2010–2025
2005 Riesling Cuvée Frédéric Émile	93	2010–2025
2004 Riesling Cuvée Frédéric Émile	92	2009–2024
2000 Riesling Cuvée Frédéric Émile	91	now–2015
1999 Riesling Cuvée Frédéric Émile	88	now–2010
1998 Riesling Cuvée Frédéric Émile	91	now–2012
2005 Riesling Clos Ste.-Hune	94	2012–2030
2004 Riesling Clos Ste.-Hune	94	2011–2029
2002 Riesling Clos Ste.-Hune	93	2010–2024
2000 Riesling Clos Ste.-Hune	94	now–2022
1998 Riesling Clos Ste.-Hune	95	now–2018
2002 Riesling Vendange Tardive	92	now–2022
2000 Riesling Frédéric Émile Vendange Tardive	92	now–2015
1998 Riesling Frédéric Émile Vendange Tardive	95	now–2016
2001 Riesling Frédéric Émile Sélection de Grains Nobles	94	2012–2030+
2000 Riesling Frédéric Émile Sélection de Grains Nobles	94	now–2020

2005 Pinot Gris Réserve	89	now–2013
2000 Pinot Gris Réserve	89	now–2011
2005 Pinot Gris Réserve Personnelle	93	2010–2022
2004 Pinot Gris Réserve Personnelle	90	2009–2018
2002 Pinot Gris Réserve Personnelle	90	now–2015+
2000 Pinot Gris Réserve Personnelle	90	now–2014
1999 Pinot Gris Réserve Personnelle	87	now
2005 Pinot Gris Extra	92	2012–2024
2002 Pinot Gris Extra	94	now–2020
2000 Pinot Gris Hommage à Jeanne	93	now–2018
2000 Pinot Gris Vendange Tardive	92	now–2015
2005 Pinot Gris Sélection de Grains Nobles	95	now–2030
2000 Pinot Gris Sélection de Grains Nobles Hors Choix	96	now–2030
2005 Gewurztraminer	87	now
2005 Gewurztraminer Réserve	90	2009–2015
2004 Gewurztraminer Réserve	87	2009–2013
2005 Gewurztraminer Seigneurs de Ribeaupierre	92	2010–2022
2004 Gewurztraminer Seigneurs de Ribeaupierre	90	2009–2018
2000 Gewurztraminer Seigneurs de Ribeaupierre	92	now–2012
1999 Gewurztraminer Seigneurs de Ribeaupierre	88	now
2005 Gewurztraminer Vendange Tardive	91	2012–2022+
2002 Gewurztraminer Vendange Tardive	92	now–2018
2000 Gewurztraminer Vendange Tardive	93	now–2016
1999 Gewurztraminer Vendange Tardive	89	now–2011
1998 Gewurztraminer Vendange Tardive	93	now–2014
2000 Gewurztraminer Sélection de Grains Nobles Hors Choix	97	now–2025

DOMAINE WEINBACH ★★★★★
KAYSERSBERG $22.00–$500.00

The dynamic trio of Fallers—Colette and her daughters, Catherine and Laurence—continues to bottle some of France's—not just Alsace's—richest and most flamboyant wines. Beginning with 2005, all of their vineyards, which have recently been extended, are being biodynamically farmed. One has to scrutinize each Weinbach label carefully, so numerous (perhaps *too* numerous for consumers as well as journalists) are the cuvées. Réserve-designated wines (including Cuvée Théo, named for Colette Faller's late husband and son of the estate's founders) originate in the Clos des Capucins, the grounds of the original monastery, along the little river Weiss. Vineyard-designated bottlings are further distinguished according to age of vines, position ("Catherine" generally mid-slope, "Laurence" lower elevation), or condition ("l'Inédit" is botrytis-influenced).

2005 Sylvaner Réserve	87	now
2004 Sylvaner Réserve	87	now
2004 Pinot Blanc Réserve	88	now
2005 Riesling Réserve Personnelle	90	now–2010
2001 Riesling Réserve Personnelle	88	now
2000 Riesling Réserve Personnelle	88	now
2005 Riesling Réserve Cuvée Théo	90	now–2013
2004 Riesling Réserve Cuvée Théo	88	now–2011
2001 Riesling Réserve Cuvée Théo	89	now–2010
2000 Riesling Réserve Cuvée Théo	90	now–2012

1998 Riesling Réserve Cuvée Théo	89	now
2005 Riesling Schlossberg	91	now–2017
2004 Riesling Schlossberg	88	now–2010
2001 Riesling Schlossberg	91	now–2012
2000 Riesling Schlossberg	90	now–2012
1999 Riesling Schlossberg	89	now–2010
2005 Riesling Cuvée Ste.-Catherine	90	now–2018
2004 Riesling Cuvée Ste.-Catherine	88	now–2011
2001 Riesling Cuvée Ste.-Catherine	93	now–2015
2000 Riesling Cuvée Ste.-Catherine	91	now–2015
1999 Riesling Cuvée Ste.-Catherine	90	now–2010
1998 Riesling Cuvée Ste.-Catherine	91	now–2012
2005 Riesling Schlossberg Cuvée Ste.-Catherine	93	now–2022
2004 Riesling Schlossberg Cuvée Ste.-Catherine	89	now–2012
2001 Riesling Schlossberg Cuvée Ste.-Catherine	95	now–2016
2000 Riesling Schlossberg Cuvée Ste.-Catherine	93	now–2016
1999 Riesling Schlossberg Cuvée Ste.-Catherine	91	now–2012
1998 Riesling Schlossberg Cuvée Ste.-Catherine	92	now–2012
2005 Riesling Schlossberg Cuvée Ste.-Catherine l'Inédit	93	now–2027
2004 Riesling Schlossberg Cuvée Ste.-Catherine l'Inédit	91	now–2014
2001 Riesling Schlossberg Cuvée Ste.-Catherine l'Inédit	96	now–2018
2000 Riesling Schlossberg Cuvée Ste.-Catherine l'Inédit	95	now–2016
1999 Riesling Schlossberg Cuvée Ste.-Catherine l'Inédit	93	now–2015
1998 Riesling Schlossberg Cuvée Ste.-Catherine l'Inédit	93	now–2015
1999 Riesling Vendange Tardive	90	now–2012
1998 Riesling Vendange Tardive	90	now–2010
2005 Riesling Schlossberg Vendange Tardive	93	now–2024
2004 Riesling Schlossberg Vendange Tardive	92	now–2022
2001 Riesling Schlossberg Vendange Tardive	91	now–2014
2000 Riesling Schlossberg Vendange Tardive	90	now–2014
1998 Riesling Schlossberg Vendange Tardive	93	now–2016
2004 Riesling Schlossberg Vendange Tardive Trie Spéciale	94	now–2027
2004 Riesling Schlossberg Sélection de Grains Nobles	96	now–2032
2000 Riesling Schlossberg Sélection de Grains Nobles	94	now–2020
1998 Riesling Schlossberg Sélection de Grains Nobles	95	now–2020
2004 Riesling Schlossberg Quintessence de Grains Nobles	94	now–2037
2001 Riesling Schlossberg Quintessence de Grains Nobles	97	now–2025+
2005 Pinot Gris Cuvée Ste.-Catherine	90	now–2012
2004 Pinot Gris Cuvée Ste.-Catherine	87	now
2001 Pinot Gris Cuvée Ste.-Catherine	89	now–2011
2000 Pinot Gris Cuvée Ste.-Catherine	88	now
1998 Pinot Gris Cuvée Ste.-Catherine	89	now

2005 Pinot Gris Cuvée Laurence	91	now–2015
2004 Pinot Gris Cuvée Laurence	88	now–2012
2001 Pinot Gris Cuvée Laurence	93	now–2015
2000 Pinot Gris Cuvée Laurence	91	now–2012
1998 Pinot Gris Cuvée Laurence	92	now–2012
2005 Pinot Gris Altenbourg Cuvée Laurence	92	now–2016
2004 Pinot Gris Altenbourg Cuvée Laurence	91	now–2015
2001 Pinot Gris Altenbourg Cuvée Laurence	92	now–2013
1999 Pinot Gris Altenbourg Cuvée Laurence	92	now–2015
1998 Pinot Gris Altenbourg Cuvée Laurence	94	now–2015
2005 Pinot Gris Altenbourg Vendange Tardive	90	now–2014
2004 Pinot Gris Altenbourg Vendange Tardive	91	now–2012
2001 Pinot Gris Altenbourg Vendange Tardive	94	now–2018
2000 Pinot Gris Altenbourg Vendange Tardive	92	now–2016
1999 Pinot Gris Altenbourg Vendange Tardive	94	now–2016
1999 Pinot Gris Sélection de Grains Nobles	95	now–2022
1998 Pinot Gris Sélection de Grains Nobles	95	now–2020
2002 Pinot Gris Altenbourg Sélection de Grains Nobles	95	now–2030
2005 Pinot Gris Altenbourg Sélection de Grains Nobles	94	now–2037
2000 Pinot Gris Altenbourg Sélection de Grains Nobles	96	now–2025+
1998 Pinot Gris Altenbourg Sélection de Grains Nobles	99	now–2025+
2005 Pinot Gris Altenbourg Quintessence de Grains Nobles	95	now–2032
2001 Pinot Gris Altenbourg Quintessence de Grains Nobles	99	now–2020+
1999 Pinot Gris Altenbourg Quintessence de Grains Nobles	97	now–2025
2005 Gewurztraminer Réserve Personnelle	89	now–2010
2001 Gewurztraminer Réserve Personnelle	90	now
2000 Gewurztraminer Réserve Personnelle	90	now
2005 Gewurztraminer Cuvée Théo	89	now–2010+
2004 Gewurztraminer Cuvée Théo	88	now–2010
2001 Gewurztraminer Cuvée Théo	88	now
2000 Gewurztraminer Cuvée Théo	90	now
2005 Gewurztraminer Cuvée Laurence	92	now–2019
2004 Gewurztraminer Cuvée Laurence	90	now–2014
2001 Gewurztraminer Cuvée Laurence	92	now–2012
2000 Gewurztraminer Cuvée Laurence	93	now–2011
1999 Gewurztraminer Cuvée Laurence	90	now
1998 Gewurztraminer Cuvée Laurence	90	now–2010
2005 Gewurztraminer Altenbourg Cuvée Laurence	94	now–2025
2004 Gewurztraminer Altenbourg Cuvée Laurence	93	now–2022
2001 Gewurztraminer Altenbourg Cuvée Laurence	92	now–2011
2000 Gewurztraminer Altenbourg Cuvée Laurence	95	now–2014
1999 Gewurztraminer Altenbourg Cuvée Laurence	92	now–2012
1998 Gewurztraminer Altenbourg Cuvée Laurence	93	now–2010
2004 Gewurztraminer Mambourg Cuvée Laurence	92	now–2024
2004 Gewurztraminer Furstentum Cuvée Laurence	91	now–2022
1999 Gewurztraminer Furstentum Cuvée Laurence	92	now–2012
2004 Gewurztraminer Vendange Tardive	91	now–2019
2005 Gewurztraminer Altenbourg Vendange Tardive	91	2010–2015+

2001 Gewurztraminer Altenbourg Vendange Tardive	91	now–2014
1999 Gewurztraminer Altenbourg Vendange Tardive	94	now–2014
2005 Gewurztraminer Furstentum Vendange Tardive	93	now–2020+
2004 Gewurztraminer Furstentum Vendange Tardive	90	2012–2015+
2001 Gewurztraminer Furstentum Vendange Tardive	94	now–2019
2000 Gewurztraminer Furstentum Vendange Tardive	92	now–2012
1998 Gewurztraminer Furstentum Vendange Tardive	93	now–2012
2005 Gewurztraminer Markrain Vendange Tardive	91	now–2014+
2001 Gewurztraminer Mambourg Vendange Tardive	92	now–2014
2000 Gewurztraminer Mambourg Vendange Tardive	93	now–2014
2005 Gewurztraminer Altenbourg Sélection de Grains Nobles	92	2012–2027
1998 Gewurztraminer Furstentum Sélection de Grains Nobles	94	2012–2020
2005 Gewurztraminer Mambourg Sélection de Grains Nobles	93	2012–2027+
2005 Gewurztraminer Mambourg Quintessence de Grains Nobles	95	now–2037
2002 Gewurztraminer Furstentum Quintessence de Grains Nobles	94	now–2035
2001 Gewurztraminer Furstentum Quintessence de Grains Nobles	100	now–2030+
2005 Gewurztraminer Altenbourg Quintessence de Grains Nobles	97	now–2030
1998 Gewurztraminer Altenbourg Quintessence de Grains Nobles	97	now–2020+
2004 Muscat d'Alsace Réserve	89	now
2004 Pinot Noir Réserve	87	now

DOMAINE ZIND-HUMBRECHT ✶ ✶ ✶ ✶ ✶
TURCKHEIM $20.00–$300.00

Few if any French wine estates have enjoyed a more prominent rise to fame than the one formed when Léonard Humbrecht of Gueberschwihr married Geneviève Zind of Wintzenheim in 1959. In the decade that followed, Léonard Humbrecht purchased and reclaimed vineyard land from Hunawihr down to the forgotten southwestern extreme of Alsace at Thann. The result was a family domaine whose scope eclipsed that of others and whose exceptional quality advanced to the forefront of the region when son Olivier Humbrecht took its reins in the late 1980s. Low yields, late picking, a biodynamic viticultural regimen, and vinification in large, old, temperature-controlled casks are characteristic of this estate. Generally, a high percentage of the wines are bottled with significant residual sugar, but this depends on the vintage, and Humbrecht is not afraid to bottle dry wines of 15% to 16% alcohol, if he thinks it is nature's will. These wines vividly reflect some of the oldest vines and best sites as well as the most conscientious winegrowing and winemaking practices in Alsace.

2005 Zind	89–90	now–2012+
2004 Zind	89	now–2011+
2001 Zind	89	now
2005 Pinot d'Alsace	88–89	now–2010
2005 Riesling	87	now–2011
2004 Riesling	87	now–2010
2005 Riesling Gueberschwihr	90	now–2017

2004 Riesling Gueberschwihr	90	now–2017
2001 Riesling Gueberschwihr	90	now–2013
2000 Riesling Gueberschwihr	89	now
2001 Riesling Thann	90	now–2012
2005 Riesling Turckheim	87	now–2010+
2004 Riesling Turckheim	88	now–2012
2001 Riesling Turckheim	89	now–2011
2000 Riesling Turckheim	91	now–2012
2005 Riesling Herrenweg Lot 144	89	now–2011
2005 Riesling Herrenweg Lot 148	88	2009–2012
2004 Riesling Herrenweg	88	now–2014
2001 Riesling Herrenweg	91	now–2011
2000 Riesling Herrenweg	92	now–2012
1999 Riesling Herrenweg	90	now–2010
2005 Riesling Clos Häuserer	92	now–2022
2004 Riesling Clos Häuserer	87	2010–2015+
2001 Riesling Clos Häuserer	93	now–2014
2000 Riesling Clos Häuserer	92	now–2014
1999 Riesling Clos Häuserer	90	now–2012
1998 Riesling Clos Häuserer	90	now–2010
2005 Riesling Brand	89	now–2012+
2001 Riesling Brand	98	now–2022
2000 Riesling Brand	97	now–2020
1999 Riesling Brand	92	now–2012
1998 Riesling Brand	93	now–2014
2005 Riesling Rangen Clos St.-Urbain	91	2011–2018+
2004 Riesling Rangen Clos St.-Urbain	91	2010–2017
2001 Riesling Rangen Clos St.-Urbain	96	now–2020
2000 Riesling Rangen Clos St.-Urbain	96	now–2018
1999 Riesling Rangen Clos St.-Urbain	91	now–2015
1998 Riesling Rangen Clos St.-Urbain	94	now–2016
2005 Riesling Heimbourg	91	now–2014
2004 Riesling Heimbourg	90	now–2014+
2001 Riesling Heimbourg	92	now–2013
2000 Riesling Heimbourg	89	now
1999 Riesling Heimbourg	91	now–2012
1998 Riesling Heimbourg	90	now–2012
2005 Riesling Clos Windsbuhl	90	2010–2018
2001 Riesling Clos Windsbuhl	94	now–2015
1999 Riesling Clos Windsbuhl	90	now–2012
2004 Riesling Brand Vendange Tardive	97	now–2032
2000 Riesling Brand Vendange Tardive	98	now–2025
2004 Riesling Clos Windsbuhl Vendange Tardive	94	2012–2027
2000 Riesling Clos Windsbuhl Vendange Tardive	97	2012–2020
1998 Riesling Clos Windsbuhl Vendange Tardive	94	now–2015
1998 Riesling Rangen Clos de Thann St.-Urbain Sélection de Grains Nobles	96	now–2025
2005 Pinot Gris	87	now–2010
2004 Pinot Gris Lot 150	89	now–2011
2005 Pinot Gris Vieilles Vignes	90	now–2020
2000 Pinot Gris Vieilles Vignes	91	now–2015

1999 Pinot Gris Vieilles Vignes	91	now–2012
1998 Pinot Gris Vieilles Vignes	90	now
2005 Pinot Gris Herrenweg	90	2010–2018+
2004 Pinot Gris Herrenweg	90	now–2012+
2001 Pinot Gris Herrenweg	90	now–2011
1999 Pinot Gris Herrenweg	89	now
2005 Pinot Gris Rotenberg	92	now–2022
2004 Pinot Gris Rotenberg	91	now–2011+
2001 Pinot Gris Rotenberg	95	now–2018
2000 Pinot Gris Rotenberg	90	now–2012
2005 Pinot Gris Heimbourg	90	now–2020
1999 Pinot Gris Heimbourg	91	now–2012
1998 Pinot Gris Heimbourg	92	now–2012
2001 Pinot Gris Clos Jebsal	94	now–2020
2005 Pinot Gris Rangen de Thann Clos St.-Urbain	92	now–2027
2004 Pinot Gris Rangen de Thann Clos St.-Urbain	???	2010
2001 Pinot Gris Rangen de Thann Clos St.-Urbain	94	now–2020
2000 Pinot Gris Rangen de Thann Clos St.-Urbain	97	now–2025
2004 Pinot Gris Clos Windsbuhl	92	now–2019
2001 Pinot Gris Clos Windsbuhl	96	now–2025
2000 Pinot Gris Clos Windsbuhl	95	now–2020
1999 Pinot Gris Clos Windsbuhl	93	now–2015
1998 Pinot Gris Clos Windsbuhl	93	now–2012
2000 Pinot Gris Herrenweg Vendange Tardive	93	now–2020
1998 Pinot Gris Rotenberg Vendange Tardive	92	now–2015
2005 Pinot Gris Clos Windsbuhl Vendange Tardive	93	now–2028+
2000 Pinot Gris Clos Windsbuhl Vendange Tardive	93	now–2030
1998 Pinot Gris Rangen de Thann Clos St.-Urbain Vendange Tardive	96	now–2025
2005 Pinot Gris Clos Jebsal Vendange Tardive	92	2012–2027
2004 Pinot Gris Clos Jebsal Vendange Tardive	95	now–2027
2000 Pinot Gris Clos Jebsal Vendange Tardive	94	now–2025
1999 Pinot Gris Clos Jebsal Vendange Tardive	92	now–2015
1998 Pinot Gris Clos Jebsal Vendange Tardive	93	now–2015
2005 Pinot Gris Clos Jebsal Sélection de Grains Nobles	95	2022–2040+
2000 Pinot Gris Clos Jebsal Sélection de Grains Nobles	98	now–2040
1999 Pinot Gris Clos Jebsal Sélection de Grains Nobles	93	now–2020+
1998 Pinot Gris Clos Jebsal Sélection de Grains Nobles	98	now–2030+
2005 Pinot Gris Heimbourg Sélection de Grains Nobles	97	now–2037
2001 Pinot Gris Heimbourg Sélection de Grains Nobles	98	now–2040
2005 Pinot Gris Rotenberg Sélection de Grains Nobles	96–97	2020–2035+
2001 Pinot Gris Rotenberg Sélection de Grains Nobles	97	now–2030+

1998 Pinot Gris Rangen de Thann Clos St.-Urbain		
Sélection de Grains Nobles	98	now–2030
2005 Pinot Gris Clos Windsbuhl Sélection de Grains		
Nobles Trie Spéciale	96–98	2025–2045+
2005 Gewurztraminer	87	now–2010
2004 Gewurztraminer	88	now–2011
2000 Gewurztraminer	89	now
2000 Gewurztraminer Turckheim	88	now
2005 Gewurztraminer Wintzenheim	88	now–2011
2004 Gewurztraminer Wintzenheim	89	now–2014
2001 Gewurztraminer Wintzenheim	89	now
2000 Gewurztraminer Wintzenheim	91	now–2010
2005 Gewurztraminer Gueberschwihr	90	now–2012
2004 Gewurztraminer Gueberschwihr	90	now–2014
2001 Gewurztraminer Gueberschwihr	89	now
2005 Gewurztraminer Herrenweg	89	now–2018
2004 Gewurztraminer Herrenweg	90	now–2014+
2001 Gewurztraminer Herrenweg	90	now–2010
2000 Gewurztraminer Herrenweg	91	now–2012
1999 Gewurztraminer Herrenweg	90	now
2005 Gewurztraminer Heimbourg	91	now–2020
2004 Gewurztraminer Heimbourg	92	now–2020
2001 Gewurztraminer Heimbourg	92	now–2010
2000 Gewurztraminer Heimbourg	94	now–2013
1999 Gewurztraminer Heimbourg	91	now
1998 Gewurztraminer Heimbourg	90	now
2005 Gewurztraminer Hengst	92	now–2022
2004 Gewurztraminer Hengst	88	now–2020
2001 Gewurztraminer Hengst	91	now–2010
2000 Gewurztraminer Hengst	93	now–2013
1999 Gewurztraminer Hengst	92	now
1998 Gewurztraminer Hengst	94	now–2012
2005 Gewurztraminer Rangen de Thann Clos		
St.-Urbain	92	now–2020
2004 Gewurztraminer Rangen de Thann Clos		
St.-Urbain	???	now–2015+
1999 Gewurztraminer Rangen de Thann Clos		
St.-Urbain	91	now
2004 Gewurztraminer Clos Windsbuhl	94	now–2022+
2001 Gewurztraminer Clos Windsbuhl	91	now–2012
2000 Gewurztraminer Clos Windsbuhl	91	now–2012
1999 Gewurztraminer Clos Windsbuhl	91	now
1998 Gewurztraminer Clos Windsbuhl	92	now–2012
2004 Gewurztraminer Goldert	91	now–2020
2001 Gewurztraminer Goldert	92	now–2010
1999 Gewurztraminer Goldert	91	now
2005 Gewurztraminer Goldert Vendange Tardive	91	now–2028
2000 Gewurztraminer Goldert Vendange Tardive	94	now–2024
1998 Gewurztraminer Goldert Vendange Tardive	94	now–2020
1999 Gewurztraminer Heimbourg Vendange Tardive	92	now–2012
1998 Gewurztraminer Heimbourg Vendange Tardive	93	now–2012

2005 Gewurztraminer Clos Windsbuhl Vendange Tardive	94	now–2030
2001 Gewurztraminer Clos Windsbuhl Vendange Tardive	95	now–2020
2001 Gewurztraminer Rangen de Thann Clos St.-Urbain Vendange Tardive	93	now–2018
2000 Gewurztraminer Rangen de Thann Clos St.-Urbain Vendange Tardive	98	now–2020
1998 Gewurztraminer Rangen de Thann Clos St.-Urbain Vendange Tardive	97	now–2018
2005 Gewurztraminer Heimbourg Sélection de Grains Nobles	94	2014–2030
2005 Muscat d'Alsace Herrenweg	88	now–2014
2004 Muscat d'Alsace Herrenweg	89	now–2014
2005 Muscat d'Alsace Goldert	91	now–2017
2004 Muscat d'Alsace Goldert	92	now–2020
2001 Muscat d'Alsace Goldert	94	now–2011

[bordeaux]

The Bordeaux region is the world's largest supplier of high-quality, ageworthy, powerful, yet elegant table wine. The production of the Bordeaux châteaux is enormous, but most consumers are largely interested in the top 1% of the output that represents the truly great wines.

RED WINE Much of Bordeaux's fame rests on its production of dry red table wine, yet only a tiny percentage of Bordeaux's most prestigious wine comes from famous appellations such as Margaux, St.-Julien, Pauillac, and St.-Estèphe, all located in an area called the Médoc, and Graves, Pomerol, and St.-Émilion. From these areas the wine is expensive yet consistently high in quality.

WHITE WINE Bordeaux produces sweet, rich, honeyed wines from two famous areas, Sauternes and Barsac. An ocean of dry white wine is made, much of it insipid and neutral in character, except for the excellent dry white wines made in the Graves area and its subappellation, Pessac-Léognan.

[grape varieties]

Following are the most important types of grapes used in the red and white wines of Bordeaux.

REDS

For red wines, three major grape varieties are planted in Bordeaux—Cabernet Sauvignon, Cabernet Franc, and Merlot—as well as two minor varieties, Petit Verdot and Malbec. The type of grape used has a profound influence on the style of wine that is ultimately produced.

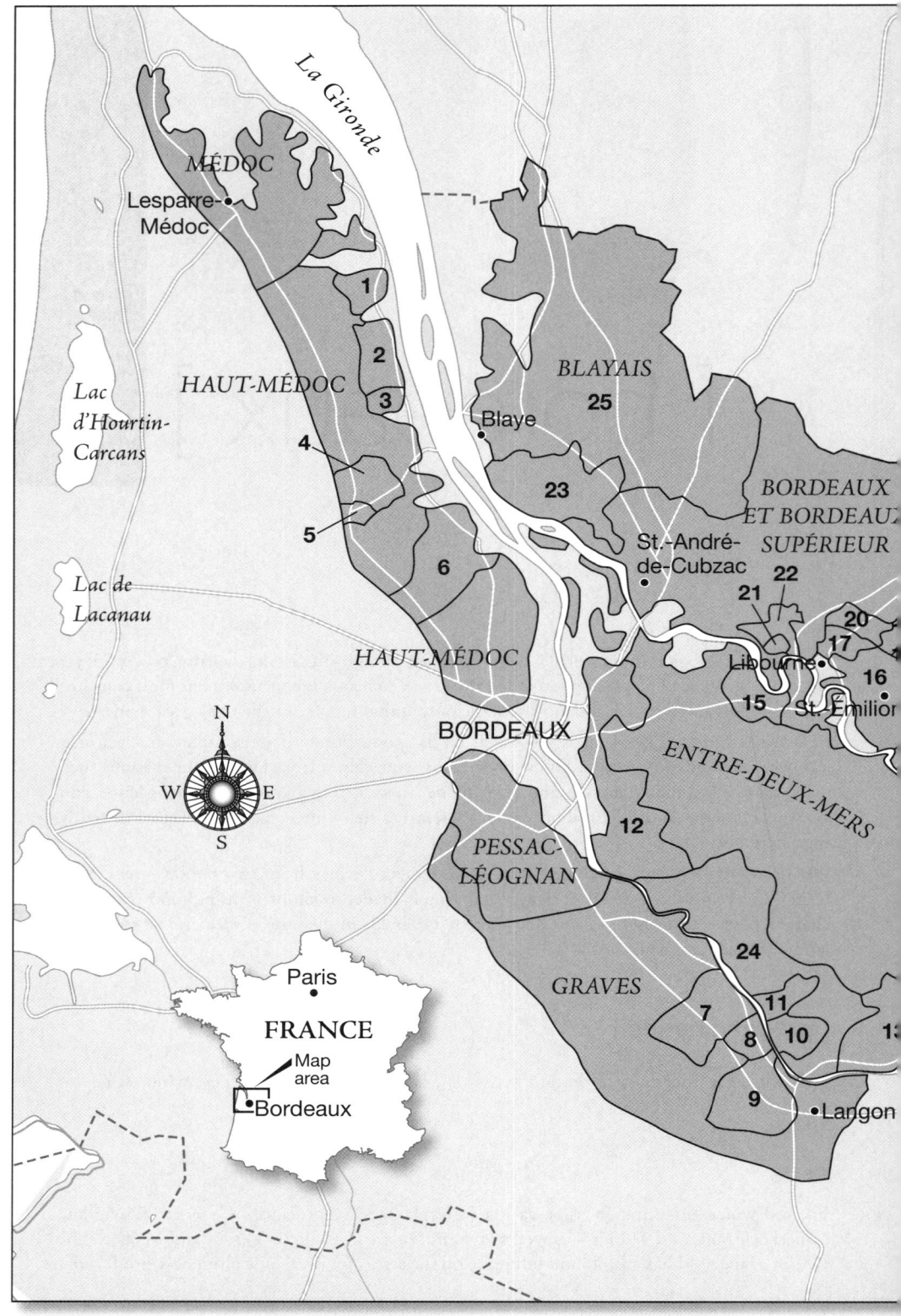

La Gironde

MÉDOC

Lesparre-Médoc

1

HAUT-MÉDOC

2

3

4

Lac
d'Hourtin-
Carcans

5

6

BLAYAIS

25

23

Blaye

St.-André-
de-Cubzac

22

21

20

17

16

Libourne

15

St.-Émilion

BORDEAUX
ET BORDEAUX
SUPÉRIEUR

Lac de
Lacanau

HAUT-MÉDOC

ENTRE-DEUX-MERS

N

W   E

S

BORDEAUX

12

PESSAC-
LÉOGNAN

24

Paris

FRANCE

Map
area

Bordeaux

GRAVES

7

11

8

10

13

9

Langon

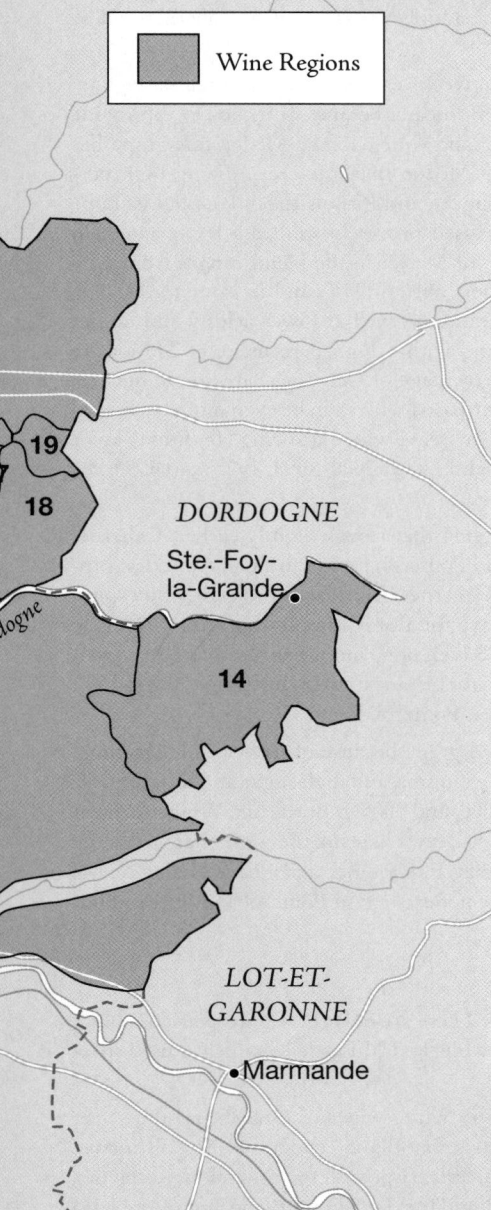

The Bordeaux Appellations

Wine Regions

1 St.-Estèphe
2 Pauillac
3 St.-Julien
4 Listrac
5 Moulis
6 Margaux
7 Cérons
8 Barsac
9 Sauternes
10 Ste.-Croix-du-Mont
11 Loupiac
12 Premières Côtes de Bordeaux
13 Côtes de Bordeaux St.-Macaire
14 Ste.-Foy-Bordeaux
15 Graves de Vayres
16 St.-Émilion
17 Lussac St.-Émilion
   Montagne-St.-Émilion
   St.-Georges-St.-Émilion
   Puisseguin-St.-Émilion
18 Côtes de Castillon
19 Côtes de Francs
20 Lalande de Pomerol
21 Pomerol
22 Fronsac
23 Côtes de Bourg
24 Cadillac
25 Blayais

DORDOGNE

Ste.-Foy-
la-Grande

*LOT-ET-
GARONNE*

•Marmande

```
0        5        10 miles
0    5        10 kilometers
```

CABERNET SAUVIGNON This grape is highly pigmented, very astringent, and tannic, providing the framework, strength, dark color, character, and longevity for the wines in a majority of the vineyards in the Médoc. It ripens late, is resistant to rot because of its thick skin, and has a pronounced black currant aroma, sometimes intermingled with subtle herbaceous scents that take on the overtones of cedarwood and tobacco with aging. Aside from such prestigious appellations as Pomerol and St.-Émilion, virtually all Bordeaux châteaux use primarily Cabernet Sauvignon blended with other red grape varieties. In the Médoc, the average percentage of Cabernet Sauvignon in the blend ranges from 40% to 85%; in Graves, 40% to 60%; in St.-Émilion, 10% to 20%; and in Pomerol it is virtually nonexistent. Furthermore, the blends change according to the vintage. For example, when climatic conditions favor Cabernet Sauvignon (2002, 1996, and 1986 are the most obvious), a higher percentage of Cabernet will be utilized in the final blend.

MERLOT Merlot ripens, on an average, one to two weeks earlier than Cabernet Sauvignon, and is utilized by virtually every wine château in Bordeaux because of its ability to provide softness and round, generous, fleshy, supple, alcoholic wines. In the Médoc this grape has enjoyed increased presence in the blends—several Médoc châteaux are utilizing high percentages of it (Palmer, Cos d'Estournel, Haut-Marbuzet, and Pichon-Lalande)—but its fame is in the wines it renders in Pomerol, where it is used profusely, and to a lesser extent in St.-Émilion. In the Médoc the average percentage of Merlot in the blend ranges from 15% to 50%; in Graves, from 20% to 50%; in St.-Émilion, 35% to 95%; and in Pomerol, 50% to 100%. Merlot produces wines with less color saturation as well as lower acidity and tannin than Cabernet Sauvignon. As a general rule, wines with a high percentage of Merlot are drinkable much earlier than wines with a high percentage of Cabernet Sauvignon, but frequently they age just as well. However, some Merlot-based wines can be even more backward than a Cabernet Sauvignon (Pétrus, for example). In years where growing conditions favor Merlot, a higher percentage is often used in the blend (2001, 2000, 1998, 1995, and 1994, for example).

CABERNET FRANC A relative of Cabernet Sauvignon that ripens slightly earlier, Cabernet Franc (sometimes called Bouchet in St.-Émilion and Pomerol) is used in small to modest proportions in order to add complexity and bouquet. Cabernet Franc has a pungent, often spicy, sometimes weedy, olive-like aroma. It does not have the fleshy, supple character of Merlot, nor the astringency, power, and color of Cabernet Sauvignon, and it has recently fallen from favor in the Médoc. The average percentage of Cabernet Franc used in the blend is 0% to 15%; in Graves, 5% to 35%; in St.-Émilion, 25% to 66%; in Pomerol, 5% to 35%.

PETIT VERDOT A useful but generally difficult red grape because of its very late ripening. Petit Verdot provides intense color, mouth-gripping tannins, and high sugar and thus high alcohol when it ripens fully, as it did in 1982, 1996, 2000, and 2005 in Bordeaux. When unripe it provides a nasty, sharp, acidic character. In the Médoc, few châteaux use more than 5% in the blend, and those that do are generally properties that, like Palmer and Pichon-Lalande, use high percentages of Merlot. Petit Verdot is virtually nonexistent in Pomerol and St.-Émilion.

WHITES

Bordeaux produces both dry and sweet white wine. There are only three grape varieties used: Sauvignon Blanc and Sémillon, for dry and sweet wine, and Muscadelle, which is used sparingly.

SAUVIGNON BLANC Used for making both the dry white wines of Graves and the sweet white wines of the Barsac/Sauternes region, Sauvignon Blanc renders a very distinctive wine with a pungent, somewhat herbaceous aroma, and crisp, austere, mineral-laced flavors. Among the dry white Graves, a few châteaux employ 100% Sauvignon Blanc, but most blend it with Sémillon. Less Sauvignon Blanc is used in the winemaking blends in the Sauternes region than in Graves.

SÉMILLON Very susceptible to the famous noble rot called botrytis, which is essential to the production of excellent sweet wines, Sémillon is used to provide a fat, rich, creamy, intense texture to both the dry wines of Graves and the rich, sweet wines of Sauternes. Sémillon is quite fruity when young, and wines with a high percentage of Sémillon seem to take on weight and viscosity as they age. For these reasons, higher percentages of Sémillon are used in making the sweet wines of the Barsac/Sauternes region than in the white wines of Graves.

MUSCADELLE The rarest of the white wine grapes planted in Bordeaux, Muscadelle is a fragile grape that is susceptible to disease but, when healthy and mature, produces a wine with an intense, flowery, perfumed character. It is used only in tiny proportions by châteaux in the Barsac/Sauternes region and is increasingly being used by some white wine producers of Graves to add exotic tropical-fruit nuances.

[the wines]

Following are the general flavor characteristics of Bordeaux's most notable types of wines.

ST.-ESTÈPHE This appellation has more Merlot planted than elsewhere in the Médoc, but the wines of St.-Estèphe have been traditionally known for their hardness because of the heavier, thicker clay soils in the area. Although generalizations can be dangerous, most St.-Estèphe wines possess less expressive and flattering bouquets, have a tougher character, and are more stern, tannic wines than those found elsewhere in the Médoc. They are usually full-bodied, with considerable aging potential.

PAUILLAC A classic Pauillac seems to be what most people think of as a Bordeaux—a rich black currant, cedary bouquet, followed by medium- to full-bodied flavors with a great deal of richness and tannin. The fame of this area translates into high prices.

ST.-JULIEN St.-Juliens are frequently indistinguishable from the wines of Pauillac. The wines of St.-Julien are filled with rich, curranty fruit and smell of cedar and spices. The overall quality of this appellation's winemaking is superb, so consumers take note!

MARGAUX Margaux are the lightest wines of the Médoc (the gravelly soils are partially responsible), but in great vintages they are perhaps the most seductive. Until the late 1990s, the overall quality of the winemaking in this appellation was appallingly lower than in any other appellation in the Médoc, but yesterday's underperformers have largely disappeared. In a top vintage a great Margaux has an undeniable floral, berry-scented bouquet backed up by the smell of oak, licorice, and earth. In body and tannin, Margaux wines, despite elevated percentages of Cabernet Sauvignon, tend to mature more quickly than a St.-Julien, Pauillac, or St.-Estèphe. For bouquet lovers, the best wines of Margaux can be compelling.

GRAVES AND PESSAC-LÉOGNAN RED These are the easiest of all Bordeaux wines to pick out in blind tastings, as they have a distinctive mineral smell as well as the scent and taste of tobacco, cedar, and scorched earth, similar to volcanic rocks. Graves are generally the lightest wines made in Bordeaux, but they are intensely flavorful and savory.

ST.-ÉMILION It is difficult to generalize about the taste of St.-Émilions, given the divergent styles, but most St.-Émilions tend to be softer and fleshier wines than Médocs. Increasingly, the top wines are as succulent and lush as Pomerols. Because of the elevated percentages of Cabernet Franc planted in this appellation, St.-Émilions can have a distinctive herbaceous, cedary bouquet, but Merlot continues to take a bigger and bigger share of the final blend. Since the early 1990s, this appellation has exploded with new producers as well as wines of increasingly higher quality. Moreover, the so-called "garage wine" movement started in St.-Émilion in the early 1990s continues to flourish as young, highly motivated producers compete for attention with their distinctive wines, made from tiny yields and ripe fruit. For quality and diversity, this is the most exciting appellation of Bordeaux.

POMEROL Pomerols are often called the Burgundies of Bordeaux because of their rich, supple, more fruit forward and accessible personalities. However, they age extremely well and are undeniable choices for hedonists who want oodles of rich black currant, black cherry, sometimes blackberry fruit. In the great vintages one can find an exquisite opulence in these wines, but other than the top two dozen estates, quality is irregular.

GRAVES AND PESSAC-LÉOGNAN WHITE The top-notch whites are aged in oak and made from the Sauvignon Blanc and Sémillon grapes. Often they start off excessively oaky, but they fill out beautifully with age and develop creamy, rich flavors that marry beautifully with the oak. The finest examples easily last 20 to 25 years.

BARSAC/SAUTERNES Depending on the vintage and the degree of the noble rot (botrytis) that affects the grapes, the wines can taste either fat, ripe, and characterless (in years when there is little botrytis) or wonderfully exotic, with a bouquet of honeyed tropical fruits, buttered nuts, and crème brûlée (in the great vintages, when there is plenty).

SATELLITE APPELLATIONS There are very large quantities of wine produced in a bevy of other, lesser-known, appellations of Bordeaux. Most of these wines are widely commercialized in many markets, but have met with only moderate success in America because of this country's obsession with luxury names and prestigious appellations. For the true connoisseur, the wines of Bordeaux's satellite appellations can in fact represent outstanding bargains, particularly in top vintages, such as 1982, 1990, 2000, 2003, and 2005, where excellent climatic conditions and the improved use of modern technology by many of these estates resulted in a vast selection of fine wines at modest prices.

MOST IMPORTANT SATELLITE APPELLATIONS

Fronsac and Canon-Fronsac In the 18th and 19th centuries the vineyards sprinkled over the hillsides and hollows of Fronsac and Canon-Fronsac—only a few miles west of Libourne—were better known than the wines of Pomerol and sold for higher prices than the wines of St.-Émilion. But because access to Pomerol was easier and because most of the brokers had their offices in Libourne, the vineyards of Pomerol and St.-Émilion were exploited more effectively than those of Fronsac and Canon-Fronsac. Consequently, this area fell into a long period of obscurity from which it has just recently begun to rebound.

Lalande de Pomerol Lalande de Pomerol is a satellite commune of nearly 2,250 acres of vineyards located just north of Pomerol and Néac. The vineyards, which produce only red wine, are planted on relatively light, gravelly, sandy soils with the meandering river Barbanne as the appellation's northern boundary. The top level of good Lalande de Pomerol is easily the equivalent of a midlevel Pomerol. The only downside to the wines of Lalande de Pomerol is that they generally need to be consumed within five to six years of the vintage.

Côtes de Bourg The Côtes de Bourg, a surprisingly vast appellation of nearly 10,000 acres, is located on the right bank of the Gironde River, just a five-minute boat ride from the more famous appellation of Margaux. The vineyards here are actually older than those in the Médoc, as this attractively hilly area was once the center of the strategic forts built during the Plantagenet period of France's history. The views from the hillside vineyards adjacent to the river are magnificent. The local chamber of commerce has attempted to draw the public's attention to this area by calling Bourg "the Switzerland of the Gironde." They should instead stress the appeal of the best wines from the Côtes de Bourg, which are made in an uncomplicated but fruity, round, appealing style, and talk up the lovely port village of the area, the ancient hillside town of Bourg-sur-Gironde.

Blaye There are just over 6,700 acres of vines in the Blaye region, located directly north of Bourg. The best vineyard areas are entitled to the appellation called Premières Côtes de Blaye. While there are quantities of white wine produced in the Blaye region, most of the Premières Côtes de Blaye are dedicated to the production of red wine, which is very similar to the red wine of Bourg. At its best it is forward, round, richly fruity, soft, and immensely satisfying in a low-key manner.

Loupiac and Ste.-Croix-de-Mont With the wine prices of Barsac and Sauternes soaring, these two appellations should play a more important role for the producers of the sweet white wines of Loupiac and Ste.-Croix-du-Mont. These two appellations, 24 miles south of Bordeaux on the right bank of the Garonne, facing Barsac and Sauternes across the river, have an ideal southern exposure. These areas received appellation status in 1930, and many observers believe the excellent exposure of the top vineyards and the clay/limestone soil base is favorable for producing sweet wines, particularly in view of the fact that the morning mists so essential for the formation of botrytis are a common occurrence in this area. The entire appellation of Loupiac consists of 1,359 acres. Although the sweet wines are receiving increasing attention from wine lovers, dry white wines, as well as a moderate quantity of dry red wines, are also produced.

AGING POTENTIAL OF RECENT TOP VINTAGES FOR THE FINEST WINES
St.-Estèphe: 8–35 years; 2005, 2003, 2000, 1996, 1995, 1990, 1986, 1982
Pauillac: 8–40 years; 2005, 2003, 2000, 1996, 1995, 1990, 1986, 1982
St.-Julien: 8–35 years; 2005, 2003, 2000, 1996, 1995, 1990, 1986, 1982
Margaux: 8–30 years; 2005, 2004, 2003, 2000, 1999, 1996, 1995, 1990, 1986, 1983
Pessac-Léognan Red: 8–30 years; 2005, 2003, 2001, 2000, 1998, 1995, 1990, 1989, 1988, 1982
Pessac-Léognan White: 5–20 years; 2006, 2005, 2004, 2001, 2000, 1998, 1997, 1995, 1994, 1989, 1988, 1983
St.-Émilion: 8–25 years; 2005, 2003, 2001, 2000, 1998, 1995, 1990, 1989, 1988, 1982
Pomerol: 5–30 years; 2006, 2005, 2001, 2000, 1998, 1995, 1990, 1989, 1988, 1982
Barsac/Sauternes: 10–50 years; 2005, 2003, 2001, 1998, 1990, 1989, 1988, 1986, 1983, 1976, 1975
Fronsac/Canon-Fronsac: 5–20 years; 2005, 2003, 2000, 1998
Lalande de Pomerol: 3–6 years; 2005, 2000, 1998
Bourg: 3–10 years; 2005, 2000, 1998
Blaye: 2–4 years; 2005, 2000
Loupiac: 5–15 years; 2005, 2001, 1998, 1997, 1996, 1990, 1989, 1988
Ste.-Croix-de-Mont: 4–12 years; 2005, 2001, 1998, 1997, 1996, 1990, 1989, 1988

OVERALL QUALITY LEVEL

Of the world's greatest viticultural regions, Bordeaux consistently produces wine of the highest level of quality. Although an ocean of one-dimensional, innocuous wines is common, bad wine is rare. For the world's top producers of Cabernet Sauvignon, Merlot, and Cabernet Franc, Bordeaux remains the point of reference.

IMPORTANT INFORMATION

For the wine consumer trying to develop a degree of expertise when buying the wines of Bordeaux, the most important information to learn is which wine-producing estates (châteaux) are producing the best wines today. A review of the top categories of châteaux in Bordeaux is a quick way to learn of producers with high commitments to quality. However, consumers should also familiarize themselves generally with the styles of the wines from the different appellations. Some tasters will prefer the austere, sterner style of Bordeaux represented by St.-Estèphe or Pauillac, whereas others will love the lavish lushness and opulence of a Pomerol or St.-Émilion. It has been my experience that the Graves wines, with their distinctive mineral scent and tobacco bouquet, are often least favored among neophytes, but as consumers gain experience, the Graves character becomes one that is admired. As far as the famous official 1855 classifications of wine quality in Bordeaux, they are all out of date and are merely of academic interest to the consumer. These historic classifications were employed both to promote more wines and to establish well-delineated benchmarks of wine quality. But because of negligence, incompetence, or just plain greed, some of the highly ranked châteaux produce mediocre and poor wines that hardly reflect their placement in these classifications. A more valid guideline to the quality of Bordeaux wines is the rating of producers starting on page 107; these ratings reflect the overall quality of the wines produced rather than their historical pedigree.

BORDEAUX VINTAGE SUMMARIES 1945–2006

This is a general assessment and profile of the Bordeaux vintages 1945 through 2006. While the top wines for each acceptable vintage are itemized, the perception of a vintage is a general view of that particular viticultural region. For wine consumers, a vintage summary is important as a general guide to the level of potential excellence that could have been attained in a particular year by a conscientious grower or producer of wine. But thin, diluted, characterless wines can be made by incompetent and greedy producers in good and even great years. And in mediocre and poor vintages, good wines can be made by skillful vintners willing to make a careful selection of only the best grapes and the best cuvées.

2006—A Quick Study

St.-Estèphe ★★★	Graves red ★★★★
Pauillac ★★★	Graves white ★★★★
St.-Julien ★★★	Pomerol ★★★★
Margaux ★★★	St.-Émilion ★★★★
Médoc, Haut-Médoc cru bourgeois ★★★	Barsac/Sauternes★★

Size A very large crop, but after severe selections, the amount of wine produced by the top estates was relatively modest.

Important information A surprisingly good year for the top properties, as the futures campaign opened with prices far disproportionate to quality of the vintage. The wines are overpriced, despite the exceptionally high quality of the Pomerols, which are not far off the pace of the 2005s.

Maturity 2006 is a tannic, structured vintage that will require considerable aging.

Prices Prices are entirely too high, especially for Americans with weak dollars vis-à-vis the euro.

I did not think the highlights of 2006 had the promise they have since fulfilled. There wasn't much talk about the vintage following the harvest, and after the wine press and the proprietors exhausted themselves with their praise of the 2005s, there was little need to start additional speculative fires. However, the 2006 vintage has produced many fine wines, and overall it is superior to 2004. The weather was hot in June and July, but August was cool and rainy. The first two weeks of September were again torrid and hot, setting the stage for what many believed would be a vintage to rival and possibly eclipse 2005. However, substantial rain fell across the region before the end of September. Overall, the entire viticultural season, from April's flowering to autumn's harvest, was much drier and warmer than normal. In Pomerol, the Merlot harvest began for a handful of estates before the first heavy rains hit. The Cabernet Franc was generally picked during the last 10 days of September, and the Cabernet Sauvignon was harvested from the end of September through the first two weeks of October.

Consider the following statistics for the critical growing season—the seven months from April through October. During these months, it was hotter than normal every month except August, which was only 1.6 degrees C below normal (35 degrees F). June, July, September, and October were all at least 3 degrees C above normal (37 degrees F). Precipitation figures are equally revealing. The average rainfall for these seven months is typically 979 millimeters (about 37.5 inches). In 2006, it was 901 millimeters (36 inches), a drier than average year. All of this explains why the 2006 crop had lower acids and yields than 2004 and 2005 as well as alcohols that are less than in 2005 but higher than in 2004.

It is an exciting vintage for the dry whites, largely because the grapes were harvested between the end of August and before the first rains began. This no doubt explains their super-concentration, wonderful minerality, and zesty freshness.

The sweet wines of Barsac and Sauternes experienced problems with rot in September, and unless estates were willing to do a draconian triage, it was a challenging vintage. My first tasting trip was too early to sample these offerings, but I did taste the 2006 Château d'Yquem, which the estate believes will be one of their greatest efforts. According to estate manager Pierre Lurton, it will be the finest they have yet made under the new ownership. The vintage is certainly impressive and appears to be nearly as promising as the 2001, which I thought was perfect.

As for the red wines, the finest *terroirs* excelled with the style of the Médocs. Why? Only well-financed top *terroirs* were in a position to do deleafings as well as crop thinnings once or twice during the summer months and to make a severe selection once the wines were fermented. It was not unusual for a Médoc classified growth to eliminate 40% to 65% of their production. 2006 appears to be a repeat of 1996 or 1986, two vintages that produced wines with high percentages of Cabernet Sauvignon in their blends, strong tannins, and, in the best cases, impressive concentration. However, outside the top *terroirs* and the most famous names, the vintage becomes dramatically more mixed and problematic. As one might suspect, the estates that could not afford to do deleafings, crop thinnings, or severe selections have produced dry, hard, angular, generally charmless wines. In Graves and Pessac-Léognan, in addition to the brilliant whites, there are also some top-notch reds. No doubt the reasonably early Merlot harvest explains brilliant efforts such as La Mission Haut-Brion.

Unlike 1986 and 1996, which did not favor the right-bank wines of Pomerol and St.-Émilion, 2006 presents a totally different scenario. The Pomerols are excellent across the board, including the satellite appellation of Lalande de Pomerol. These wines taste as if they are from a completely different vintage than the Médocs. They possess sweet tannin, low acidity, ripe fruit, and loads of flesh and charm. In many ways, they remind me of the vastly underrated 2001 Pomerols. The 2006 Pomerols will be gorgeous wines to drink young, but the best of them will age well. Moreover, a handful of true blockbusters were produced from vineyards where much of the harvest took place before the heavy rains arrived in mid-September. St.-Émilion appears to be the wild card in this vintage, with quality all over the board. Unlike 2005, a monumental vintage for all of St.-Émilion, 2006 includes some truly classic, great wines as well as some disappointments. Overall, it is good to very good, but this vast appellation, with its enormous diversity of *terroirs,* is more irregular than any other major appellation.

As for longevity, the 2006 Médocs should enjoy 20 to 35 years of life, but they will be more approachable in their youth than the 1986s or 1996s. The wines of Graves and Pomerol should be drinkable at reasonably young ages (much like the 2001s), but they should keep for two decades or more. Because of the diversity of the St.-Émilions, it is impossible to generalize. Some can be drunk young, whereas others have high tannin levels that may or may not be resolved with barrel and bottle aging.

THE BEST WINES OF 2006

St.-Estèphe: Calon-Ségur, Cos d'Estournel, Montrose

Pauillac: Batailley, Clerc Milon, Duhart-Milon, Grand-Puy-Lacoste, Haut-Bages-Libéral, Lafite-Rothschild, Latour, Lynch-Bages, Mouton-Rothschild, Pichon-Baron, Pichon-Lalande, Pontet-Canet

St.-Julien: Beychevelle, Branaire-Ducru, Lagrange, Léoville-Barton, Léoville–Las Cases, Léoville-Poyferré, St. Pierre

Margaux: d'Angludet, Boyd-Cantenac, Brane-Cantenac, Giscours, d'Issan, Kirwan, Lascombes, Malescot–St.-Exupéry, Château Margaux, Marojallia, Château Palmer, Rauzan-Ségla, Du Tertre

Pessac-Léognan Red: Branon, Carbonnieux, Haut-Bailly, Haut-Brion, La Mission–Haut-Brion, Pape Clément, Smith–Haut-Lafitte

Pomerol: Le Bon Pasteur, Certan de May, Clos l'Église, La Croix St.-Georges, La Conseillante, L'Église Clinet, L'Évangile, Feytit-Clinet, Le Gay, Gazin, Hosanna, Lafleur, Pétrus, Le Pin, Trotanoy, La Violette

Lalande de Pomerol, Fronsac, Canon-Fronsac: Jean de Gué, Le Plus de la Fleur Boüard, Moulin Haut-Laroque, Haut-Carles, De Chamfrou, Grand-Ormeau-Madeleine

St.-Émilion: Angélus, l'Arrosée, Les Asteries, Ausone, Barde-Haut, Beau-Séjour Bécot, Beauséjour-Duffau, Bellevue, Bellevue Mondotte, Canon–La Gaffelière, Cheval Blanc, Clos St.-Martin, Clos de l'Oratoire, Clos de Sarpe, La Confession, Croix de Labrie, Le Dôme, Fleur-Cardinale, Fonplégade, La Gomerie, Gracia, Grand Corbin-Despagne, Larcis Ducasse, Lucia, Pierre de Lune, Magrez Fombrauge, Monbousquet, Pavie, Pavie-Decesse, Pavie-Macquin, Quinault L'Enclos

Barsac/Sauternes: d'Yquem

2005—A Quick Study

St.-Estèphe ****	Graves red *****
Pauillac *****	Graves white *****
St.-Julien ****	Pomerol *****
Margaux ****	St.-Émilion *****
Médoc, Haut-Médoc cru bourgeois ****	Barsac/Sauternes *****

Size A moderately large crop; by no means the biggest but not small.

Important information An extremely dry year with nearly perfect conditions, although the lack of heat spells may have produced less than ideal ripening in the northern Médoc's Cabernet Sauvignon vineyards. Because of the drought, the vintage produced concentrated wines high in alcohol, with higher acidity than usual.

Maturity The wines possess extremely high tannin and will require many years to reach drinkability. The safest bets for drinking in seven to ten years are the Margaux, Graves, Pomerols, and St.-Émilions. The northern Médocs will not be approachable for 10 to 15 years.

Prices Future prices are relatively high, largely because of the weak U.S. dollar. If buyers are not seeking the most prestigious/glamorous names, there are some great bargains to be had.

After 28 years of tasting Bordeaux wines every March, I can safely state that 2005 cannot be compared to any previous vintage in my experience. Why? One can safely generalize that many 2005 red Bordeaux possess (1) the highest tannin levels ever measured, (2) the highest dry extracts and concentration ever measured, (3) the highest natural alcohol levels ever measured, and (4) an anomaly—surprisingly fresh, lively acid levels and reasonably modest pHs. What does all this mean, and how did it happen?

The short answer is that the growing season was extraordinarily dry. It was also warm, but unlike most summers, scorching heat waves never occurred. Consequently, the vineyards, if slightly stressed from the droughtlike conditions, were never brutalized by torrid heat. There was some rain in August: about an inch in Pomerol, St.-Émilion, and Graves on August 17, and light rainfall in the Médoc on August 25. September was not quite as perfect as the pundits claimed, but it was close to ideal and, by Bordeaux standards, very dry. Some showers arrived on September 8, and heavier rain moved through the region on the 25th. Following that date there was a window of extraordinary weather that lasted until October 12. Even after that date, the weather remained balmy and reasonably dry. All of this meant no one was in a hurry to harvest. The cool nights and warm days preserved unprecedented levels of acidity in the finest wines of the vintage, which are characterized by massive richness and structure.

During my March 2006 tasting trip, there were days when I had the same excitement/jubilation that I remember experiencing when I tasted the 1982s in March 1983. On other days, notably when I was tasting the northern Médocs, I was less enthusiastic and wondered if 2005 was even the equal of 2003 or 2000. Of course, this vintage is completely different in style from 1982, perhaps less so on the right bank, where so many incredibly sumptuous, ripe, intense, heady wines were produced. And in 1982, the Médoc's weakness was the appellation of Margaux, which, ironically, is one of the greatest strengths of 2005. In fact, I have never tasted better Margauxs than the 2005s. Overall, 2005 is unquestionably a remarkable as well as consistent vintage.

However, there are several sobering issues with some 2005s. The incredibly high tannin levels, especially noticeable in the northern Médoc communes of St.-Julien, Pauillac, and St.-Estèphe, appear to be adequately balanced by massive concentration and fruit. That's a good sign. But I remain convinced that the northern Médocs will shut down after bottling, and will require many years of cellaring until everything comes back into focus and harmony. Though these wines will possess 30 to 50 years of longevity, they will not have the early appeal possessed by the 1982s and 1990s. Do not let anyone suggest that many of the renowned northern Médoc classified growths will be drinkable in the next decade, unless you are a masochist with an addiction to tannin. I prefer the 2003 northern Médocs over their 2005 counterparts. And of course, let's not forget the brilliance of 2000 in the northern Médoc or, for that matter, 1996. Elsewhere, the sweetness of the tannins counterbalanced by the fruit's extraordinary opulence and richness will make the wines more accessible, and their evolution should follow a faster timetable than the northern Médocs will. In short, for Margaux, Graves, Pomerol, and St.-Émilion, this is a singular vintage of compelling greatness.

It is no easy task to give readers a point of reference for this vintage. To reiterate, I have never tasted so many extraordinarily rich, concentrated, massive wines so high in tannin and extract yet with such precision, definition, and freshness. It is clearly a singular vintage that should evolve into one of the great vintages of Bordeaux. However, it seems premature and risky to conclude so soon that the finest wines of 2005 are superior to the best of 2003, especially the northern Médocs, or the best wines of 2000, 1998 (for Pomerol and St.-Émilion), 1990, or the most profound 1989s and 1982s. Only time will prove the true quality of 2005, but it is beginning life as an extraordinary as well as remarkably consistent vintage. If there is any year even remotely similar, it is 2000 because of the overall consistency, the high number of superb offerings, and the fact that there are so many good minor wines. I suspect the greatest

2005s of Pomerol, St.-Émilion, Graves, and Margaux are marginally superior to 2000, yet I am cautious about the northern Médocs, which should turn out beautifully and be very long-lived, but require enormous patience.

Astonishingly, 2005 is also a terrific vintage for Bordeaux's dry whites. They are powerful, with good acidity as well as superb concentration and depth. My limited tastings of the Barsac/Sauternes indicate that those regions have enjoyed another extraordinary vintage. The wines I tasted were not far off the magical 2001s.

Given the unprecedented degree of hype surrounding 2005, everyone is concerned about prices. It is safe to assume that the first growths, super-seconds, and a few other limited-production cuvées that are in great demand will be priced in the stratosphere, yet as Bordeaux history has demonstrated, those prices will seem inexpensive 10 to 20 years from now. However, there is so much good wine in 2005, even from less than prestigious châteaux that are not exactly the darlings of speculators, that there will be an ocean of very high quality wine available at reasonable prices. As long as readers/consumers do not chase the points or labels, they will have plenty of impeccably high-quality wine to drink from this vintage.

Despite the doom-and-gloom cynics who would like to see Bordeaux prices return to those of the late 1960s, the world has changed, and Bordeaux remains the most cherished and respected wine in the world for longevity and elegance. This is not the worst of all times to buy Bordeaux—quite the contrary—it is the best of times to be purchasing Bordeaux and to be a wine lover.

The malolactic fermentations for some of the St.-Émilions were relatively late, and some of those wines were just at the end of them when I tasted them. Given how well they performed, that is a positive sign since I would expect the wines to flesh out even more after the completion of their malolactic fermentations.

THE BEST WINES OF 2005

St.-Estèphe: Calon-Ségur, Cos d'Estournel, Lafon-Rochet, Montrose

Pauillac: d'Armailhac, Clerc Milon, Duhart-Milon, Grand-Puy-Lacoste, Lafite-Rothschild, Lynch-Bages, Mouton-Rothschild, Pichon-Longueville-Baron, Pontet-Canet

St.-Julien: Beychevelle, Branaire-Ducru, Ducru-Beaucaillou, Lagrange, Léoville-Barton, Léoville–Las Cases, Léoville-Poyferré, St.-Pierre

Margaux: Boyd-Cantenac, Brane-Cantenac, Giscours, d'Issan, Kirwan, Lascombes, Malescot-St.-Exupéry, Château Margaux, Marojallia, Palmer, Prieuré-Lichine, Rauzan-Ségla, Du Tertre

Pessac-Léognan/Graves Red: Branon, Carbonnieux, Domaine de Chevalier, Haut-Bailly, Haut-Bergey, Haut-Brion, La Mission–Haut-Brion, Pape Clément, Smith–Haut-Lafitte, La Tour–Haut-Brion

Pomerol: Le Bon Pasteur, Certan de May, La Clémence, Clinet, Clos du Clocher, Clos l'Église, La Conseillante, L'Église Clinet, L'Évangile, Feytit-Clinet, La Fleur de Gay, La Fleur-Pétrus, Le Gay, Gazin, Hosanna, Lafleur, Le Moulin, Pétrus, Le Pin, Rouget, Trotanoy, Vieux-Château-Certan, Vray-Croix-de-Gay

Lalande de Pomerol, Fronsac, Canon-Fronsac: Fontenil, Grand Ormeau, Le Plus de la Fleur de Boüard, La Vieille Cure

St.-Émilion: L'Angélus, l'Arrosée, Ausone, Barde-Haut, Beau-Séjour-Bécot, Beauséjour-Duffau, Bellevue, Bellevue-Mondotte, Canon, Canon–La Gaffelière, Chauvin, Cheval Blanc, Clos Fourtet, Clos St.-Martin, Clos de Sarpe, La Clotte, La Confession, Croix de Labrie, Le Dôme, Faugères Cuvée Spéciale Péby, Figeac, Fleur-Cardinale, Fombrauge, La Gaffelière, La Gomerie, Gracia, Grand-Mayne, Grand-Pontet, Grandes Murailles, l'Hermitage, Larcis Ducasse, Pierre de Lune, Lynsolence, Magdelaine, Magrez Fombrauge, Monbousquet, La Mondotte, Moulin–St. Georges, Pavie, Pavie-Decesse,

Pavie-Macquin, Quinault l'Enclos, Rol Valentin, Sanctus, Troplong-Mondot, Valandraud

Others: Cantemerle (Haut-Médoc), Clos Les Lunelles (Côtes de Castillon), Fougas Maldoror (Côtes de Bourg), Haut-Condissas (Médoc), Joanin Bécot (Côtes de Castillon), La Lagune (southern Médoc), Sociando-Mallet (Haut-Médoc)

Barsac/Sauternes: Climens, Coutet, Guiraud, De Malle, Rieussec, La Tour Blanche, d'Yquem

2004—A Quick Study

St.-Estèphe ***	Graves red ***
Pauillac ***	Graves white **
St.-Julien ***	Pomerol ***
Margaux ***	St.-Émilion ***
Médoc, Haut-Médoc crus bourgeois **	Barsac/Sauternes ***

Size The largest crop in the history of Bordeaux.

Important information A very late harvest, saved by a beautiful September and early October, produced classic wines with fresh acidity and fragrant aromatics. Only châteaux that severely crop-thinned and made a strict selection produced very good wines.

Maturity The wines have extremely high tannins but are generally not astringent. They will mature gracefully for 15 to 20 years.

Price The 2004 futures campaign was a disaster. Prices never took off, largely because of the huge harvest and a good rather than exciting vintage.

The weather that shaped 2004 developed in three stages: 1) A perfect early season and flowering produced the largest Bordeaux harvest in history. The flowering was quick and even, and the resulting enormous crop required serious thinning in order to obtain any quality. 2) The summer was largely a nonevent in Bordeaux. Though there were reasonable amounts of sunshine and cooler than usual temperatures in July, August was miserable, with considerable rainfall and low temperatures (the latter was actually a blessing, as it prevented the spread of rot). 3) As in 2002, 1996, and 1986, September brought unseasonably high temperatures as well as plenty of sunshine. The Indian summer and generally dry, sunny conditions continued into early October before everything deteriorated in the middle of the month. The results were a late as well as huge harvest, even after crop thinning and vineyard selections, with wines very high in tannin content.

Unlike some vintages, in which it is clear that the Médoc and its late-ripening Cabernet Sauvignon are superior to the right bank's earlier-ripening Merlot and Cabernet Franc, 2004 does not favor one appellation over another. Success was earned by producers who practiced careful and diligent work in the vineyard, kept their crop size moderate, had the patience to harvest only the ripest fruit, and implemented a severe triage, both for the grapes coming into the cellars and for selection after the wine was made. There are good wines in every major appellation, but the following comments express the vintage's positive and negative features.

POSITIVES

1. At the level of the classified and more famous estates, 2004 is a uniform vintage whose consistency surpasses that of 2003 or 2002.
2. The wines possess excellent color as well as loads of fruit, with considerable elegance and finesse.
3. The finest wines are pure and aromatically expressive.

4. Vibrancy, freshness, good acidity, and a relatively classic style seem to have emerged, without the telltale austerity exhibited by classic vintages of the past.
5. The wines appear to be ageworthy and gracious, reminiscent of improved versions of 1999, or riper versions of 1966 or 1988.

NEGATIVES

1. This is a difficult vintage below the famed estates and classified-growth level. Yields were too high and the selection process too costly for the smaller châteaux and crus bourgeois to produce impressive wines. The quality is decidedly mediocre, with only a few exceptions.
2. While the finest wines possess relatively ripe, sweet tannin, the high level of tannin can lead to borderline austerity and potential hardness. I have a few reservations about the ageability of the wines once the fruit and baby fat fall away.
3. One of the vintage's obvious defects is a lack of texture, density, depth, and fat. Rarely does one find a 2004 that is full-bodied, concentrated, and dense, which are always signs of the greatest vintages.
4. Though some producers believe that in the Médoc, 2004 is comparable to 1996, or not far off the quality of 2000, that seems overly optimistic, if not wishful, thinking. This is a good to very good vintage at the top end, but it's irregular. In fact, there is a deficiency of truly prodigious wines, and I do not envision more than two or three wines ever meriting ratings in the elite 95 to 100-point range. But don't lose perspective . . . how many times do any of us actually consume such rare and compelling elixirs?

THE BEST WINES OF 2004

St.-Estèphe: Calon-Ségur, Cos d'Estournel, Montrose
Pauillac: Les Forts de Latour, Lafite-Rothschild, Latour, Mouton-Rothschild, Pichon-Longueville-Baron, Pichon-Longueville Comtesse de Lalande, Pontet-Canet
St.-Julien: Branaire Ducru, Ducru Beaucaillou, Léoville-Barton, Léoville–Las Cases, Léoville-Poyferré
Margaux: Brane-Cantenac, Giscours, Lascombes, Malescot St.-Exupéry, Château Margaux, Marojallia, Palmer, Du Tertre
Pessac-Léognan/Graves Red: Branon, Haut-Bailly, Haut-Brion, Malartic-Lagravière, La Mission–Haut-Brion, Pape Clément, Smith–Haut-Lafitte
Pessac-Léognan/Graves White: Domaine de Chevalier, Haut-Brion, Pape Clément
Pomerol: Le Bon Pasteur, Clos L'Église, L'Église-Clinet, L'Évangile, La Fleur de Gay, Le Gay, Hosanna, Lafleur, Le Moulin, Pétrus, Le Pin, Trotanoy, Vieux-Château-Certan
St.-Émilion: L'Angélus, Ausone, Barde-Haut, Beau-Séjour Bécot, Bellefont-Belcier, Bellevue, Bellevue Mondotte, Canon–La Gaffelière, Cheval Blanc, Clos de Dubreuil, Clos Fourtet, Clos de Sarpe, La Clotte, Fleur-Cardinale, La Gomerie, Grand-Pontet, Larcis Ducasse, Lessègue, Lucia, Magrez Fombrauge, Monbousquet, La Mondotte, Pavie-Decesse, Pavie-Macquin, Quinault l'Enclos, La Tour Figeac, Troplong Mondot, Trotte Vieille
Barsac/Sauternes: Raymond-Lafon, Rieussec, d'Yquem

2003—A Quick Study

St.-Estèphe *****	Graves red ***
Pauillac *****	Graves white *****
St.-Julien *****	Pomerol **
Margaux ****	St.-Émilion ****
Médoc, Haut-Médoc crus bourgeois **	Barsac/Sauternes ****

Size A reasonably sized crop, but after the selections were made, a much smaller amount of high-quality wine was produced than for any vintage between 1994 and 2002.

Important information: A historic, unprecedented summer of heat and drought broke all records in Bordeaux. It is one of the most irregular Bordeaux vintages I have ever experienced. There are several dozen remarkably great wines that will be considered legendary for the next 50 to 60 years, but inconsistency is the rule. Sauternes enjoyed another fine vintage, although it is slightly below the quality of the monumental 2001s.

Maturity The best wines are both very opulent, deep, as well as tannic. I suspect the vintage will always have a precocious charm, but the most concentrated wines will behave like the top 1982s or 1959s and be very long-lived. The less successful wines, many Pomerol, need to be consumed in their first 10 to 15 years.

Price Prices will be absurdly high for the top wines, especially for those purchased with currency other than euros.

First and foremost some of the specific weather information that follows was taken from the extensive report authored by Bill Blatch, the *négociant* and proprietor of Vintex in Bordeaux. No one keeps better weather-related records, and I thank him for that. I have added my observations since I was in Bordeaux from late August, through the first several weeks of September 2003.

The prominent weather characteristics of 2003 were heat and drought However, the drought was less extreme in Bordeaux than elsewhere in France. I am sure what explains the character and success of the top 2003s is the fact that in spite of the torrid heat in June and August, Bordeaux enjoyed some welcome showers in August, followed by light rain in September, all of which helped refresh the vineyards. Many of the northern Médoc producers felt that the light showers they received over the weekend of September 6–7, and again on September 9, were key to saving their Cabernet Sauvignon. Where the vines were still healthy, the August and September rains reenergized the vines, many of which had shut down, and allowed those proprietors to wait for full phenolic maturity. Sadly, this situation was much worse in other parts of France, particularly Burgundy, where numerous producers were forced to harvest before the beginning of September because of fears of low acids and over-ripeness.

Looking back over the growing season, spring was largely uneventful, and the flowering occurred with only a few problems. However, summer arrived early, and nearly record heat afflicted Bordeaux during its famous Vin Expo week. Obviously, by the end of July it had been a hot summer, but not one for the record books. August proved to be a record setter for Bordeaux, with an average temperature of 90°F versus the record of 85° set in 1991. The single-day temperature of 105°F battered that of 102° set in 1998. More important was the number of days over 86°F. The highest previously recorded was in 1990 (15 days), but in 2003 the number was 20. Unlike 1990, the August nights remained very hot, not allowing the vines time to recover from the Sahara-like conditions of the days.

More important, and one of the keys to understanding the 2003 vintage in Bordeaux, is that there were showers the weekend of August 16–17, August 19, and light rain on both August 24 and August 30 (and I do mean relatively insignificant rain because I was there during that latter period). September cooled down to normal temperatures (save for very warm weather during the third week), and was dry except for light rain on September 6, 7, and 9 and virtually insignificant amounts on September 21, 27, and 30.

The 2003 Bordeaux harvest was divided into two separate chapters. First were those who harvested extremely early. This was mandated for the white grapes of Pessac-Léognan, when Haut-Brion and some of its neighbors began bringing in Sauvignon Blanc and Sémillon as early as the end of the second week of August—a new record. The red wine harvest was essentially forced on producers in early September, particularly in some of the plateau vineyards of Pomerol, where there was nothing more to be gained as the grapes were desiccated and the foliage on the vines was beginning to fall. The Pétrus vineyard, the most notable early harvester, had completed its harvest by the end of the first week of September, but, unlike its neighbors, it sits on a buttonhole of clay. It is probably safe to say that half of the Bordeaux vineyards were harvested by September 15. By this time, some of Bordeaux's more conservative oenologists were advocating significant acidifications because the grapes were high in sugar but extremely low in acidity. Producers who allowed the oenologists to take control of the fermentations and adjust the acidity made a catastrophic error. Producers who did not manipulate their cuvées (the great majority of the Bordeaux châteaux, contrary to what the rumormongers reported), ended up producing wines that have acid and pH parameters comparable to those from hot years such as 1990, 1982, and 1959. Months after the wines had been vinified, several oenologists admitted to adjusting the acidity too much based on preharvest grape analyses, rather than doing the analyses from readings taken in the must.

The second part of the harvest consisted of producers (mostly in the Médoc and on the clay and limestone plateau hillsides of St.-Émilion called *argile-calcaire*) who had more water-retentive soils and realized that despite high sugar readings and falling acid levels their grape skins and tannins were not fully mature. They delayed their harvests until the last two weeks of September. Bad weather never materialized, and those who waited were usually rewarded with the finest wines of the vintage.

Most Bordeaux old-timers have had a great deal of fun trying to compare 2003 with famous hot-year vintages of the past. After my eight-day immersion course in trying to understand the results of this very complicated year, I reluctantly came to the conclusion that I was tasting six different vintages. Hopefully, my tasting notes will make this clear, but at this time 2003 could be called a mélange of 1975 (15%), 1982 (20%), 1989 (25%), 1990 (20%), 1991 (15%), and 5% something so sublime and fascinating that there is no vintage in my oenological reference library that offers a legitimate comparison.

THE BEST WINES OF 2003

St.-Estèphe: Calon-Ségur, Cos d'Estournel, Montrose
Pauillac: Grand-Puy-Lacoste, Lafite-Rothschild, Latour, Mouton-Rothschild, Pichon-
    Longueville-Baron, Pichon-Longueville–Comtesse de Lalande, Pontet-Canet
St.-Julien: Branaire Ducru, Ducru-Beaucaillou, Léoville-Barton, Léoville–Las Cases,
    Léoville-Poyferré
Margaux: Giscours, Château Margaux, Marojallia
Pessac-Léognan/Graves Red: Haut-Brion, La Mission–Haut-Brion, Pape Clément, Smith–
    Haut-Lafitte
Pessac-Léognan/Graves White: Domaine de Chevalier, de Fieuzal, Haut-Brion-Blanc,
    Laville Haut-Brion, Pape Clément Blanc
Pomerol: Hosanna, Lafleur, Pétrus, Trotanoy
St.-Émilion: L'Angélus, Ausone, Bellevue, Bellevue-Mondotte, Cheval Blanc, Clos Fourtet,
    Clos de Sarpe, Fombrauge, Gracia, l'Hermitage, Lynsolence, Magrez Fombrauge,
    La Mondotte, Pavie, Pavie-Decesse, Pavie-Macquin, Péby-Faugères, Rol Valentin,
    Valandraud
Barsac/Sauternes: Climens, Coutet, Raymond-Lafon, Rieussec, Suduiraut, La Tour Blanche

2002—A Quick Study

St.-Estèphe ∗∗∗	Graves red ∗∗∗
Pauillac ∗∗∗	Graves white ∗∗∗
St.-Julien ∗∗∗	Pomerol ∗∗

Margaux ★★★   St.-Émilion ★★★
Médoc, Haut-Médoc crus bourgeois ★★★   Barsac/Sauternes ★★★★

Size Compared to 2000 and 2001, 2002 was a smaller crop, largely because of difficulty with the Merlot as well as modest production levels of the Cabernet Sauvignon and Cabernet Franc.

Important information In August 2002, most Bordeaux producers feared the vintage would be a disaster. Flowering had been irregular, and the summer was virtually nonexistent. However, a high-pressure area settled in and the entire month of September was extremely dry, allowing late pickers to harvest fully ripe Cabernet Sauvignon.

Maturity status This vintage is high in tannin and structure as well as above-average acidity levels for Bordeaux. The 2002s are likely to close down and need a number of years to reopen. It is not a vintage for hedonists or those seeking early enjoyment. Patience is the operative word for this vintage.

Price The outbreak of the United States involvement in Iraq, combined with the dramatically impaired U.S. dollar vis-à-vis the euro, resulted in little interest in the 2002 vintage from the American marketplace. Sales in Europe were stronger because of the attractively low 2002 prices and the strength of the euro. These wines are likely to remain reasonably priced as this is a somewhat forgotten vintage.

Lamentably, 2002 is in danger of being forgotten, for many reasons. First, it was an irregular year. Merlot had problems on the right bank, but the Cabernet Sauvignon performed well, even, in a few examples in the Médoc, brilliantly. The Graves wines are very good, as are the sweeties from Barsac and Sauternes. Yet even the dramatic deflationary spiral of 2002 Bordeaux pricing was not sufficient to stir much interest. Certain Europeans and a few American customers bought some of the classic Médocs as futures, but by and large there was little excitement. It does not appear prices will move upward, with the possible exception of a half dozen or so wines. With the prospect of compelling wines in 2003, 2002 will largely be lost in the shadows of its successor as well as the two vintages that preceded it—the very good to excellent 2001s (which are far more consistent, accessible, and charming than most 2002s), and the profound 2000s (which may one day have competition from some 2003s). The prospect of two "vintages of the century" in the last four years is unnerving and strains one's credulity, but as I note elsewhere in this book, there has been a profound winemaking revolution in Bordeaux over the last 25 years.

In late August 2002, my sources in Bordeaux forewarned that the vintage appeared to be a disaster. Flowering had been irregular earlier in the year. There had been a poor crop set because of cold and wet weather in late May, which seemed to have affected the Merlot more than the Cabernet vineyards (although some of those were also affected). According to Bill Blatch in his exceptionally detailed and thorough vintage report, the early damage assessment was that 60% to 70% of the right-bank Merlot crop was affected by *coulure* and *millerandage* (essentially, a lack of grapes due to inadequate pollination). Additionally, the warm weather Bordeaux normally enjoys June through August never materialized. It was relatively cool, but not particularly wet, even though the summer was reputed to be damp. As Bill Blatch stated, the summer was cooler than normal, and basically overcast, with many dull, drizzly days, which seemed to have the effect of "demoralizing growers."

The French—as well as most other viticultural growers in western Europe—maintain, June makes the quantity and September makes the quality. Some will say August makes the style. September 2002 was reminiscent of September 1978, a year that the late English gentleman and taster Harry Waugh called a miracle vintage. While the first eight days of September were nothing to get excited about, fine, cool, dry weather moved in during the week of September 9 and remained largely uninterrupted except for a storm on September 20 and some rain in early October. In short, it was the Indian summer that saved the vintage, particularly for the late-harvested Cabernet Sauvignon in the Médoc, which is clearly the strong point of the 2002 vintage.

THE BEST WINES OF 2002

St.-Estèphe: Cos d'Estournel
Pauillac: d'Armailhac, Clerc Milon, Les Forts de Latour, Lafite-Rothschild, Latour, Lynch-Bages, Mouton-Rothschild, Pichon-Longueville–Comtesse de Lalande, Pontet-Canet
St.-Julien: Branaire Ducru, Léoville-Barton, Léoville–Las Cases, Léoville-Poyferré
Margaux: Giscours, Malescot St.-Exupéry, Château Margaux, Marojallia, Palmer
Pessac-Léognan/Graves Red: Haut-Brion, Pape Clément, Smith–Haut-Lafitte
Pessac-Léognan/Graves White: Domaine de Chevalier, Fieuzal, Haut-Brion-Blanc, Laville-Haut-Brion, Malartic-Lagravière, Smith–Haut-Lafitte
Pomerol: Clos l'Église, La Croix St.-Georges, L'Église-Clinet, l'Évangile, Le Gay, Lafleur, Pétrus
St.-Émilion: L'Angélus, Ausone, Bellevue-Mondotte, Canon–La Gaffelière, Clos Fourtet, Clos de Sarpe, Fombrauge, Gracia, Magrez Fombrauge, Monbousquet, Pavie, Pavie-Decesse, Quinault l'Enclos, Troplong Mondot, Valandraud
Barsac/Sauternes: Climens, De Fargues, Guiraud, Lafaurie-Péyraguey, de Malle, Raymond-Lafon, Rieussec, Suduiraut, La Tour Blanche

2001—A Quick Study

St.-Estèphe ★★★	Graves Red ★★★★
Pauillac ★★★	Graves White ★★★★★
St.-Julien ★★★	Pomerol ★★★★
Margaux ★★★	St.-Émilion ★★★★
Médoc, Haut-Médoc crus bourgeois ★★	Barsac/Sauternes ★★★★★

Size Another large crop, but after the selections, fewer *grands vins* from the top estates were produced than in 2000.

Important information An extremely cold (but also dry) September has given the wines fresh acidity and a more tangy, elegant, medium-bodied style than some of the bigger vintages. These wines are consistently excellent in Pomerol, St.-Émilion, and Graves, but less consistent in the Médoc. It is a profound/great vintage in Sauternes.

Maturity This vintage will probably be relatively slow to evolve given the good acid levels and tannins most wines possess. None of them has the size of the 2000s or the best 1998s, but they are certainly not wimpy wines.

Price The Bordelais, recognizing a market saturated with not only their wine but wine from throughout the world, dropped prices significantly in an effort to move these wines through the marketplace.

Statistically, the winter of 2000 was wet and warm. The following spring was largely uneventful save for some frost alerts in an unusually cool, overcast April. By the end of May 2001, temperatures were high. In fact, according to Bill Blatch at Vintex, in his annual weather report, it was an "unusually violent heat wave." High temperatures occurred again in late June and early July, but then summer disappeared, as anyone who was vacationing in Europe can attest. Cloudy skies, cold temperatures, and a freakish succession of drizzly days made for an unusually cool, uncomfortable July, creating concerns about when the 2001 harvest might take place. August was irregular, experiencing periods of both high heat and below normal temperatures. When September arrived, it appeared that the harvest would occur during the last week of the month for Merlot, and the beginning of October for the Cabernets.

I was in the Rhône Valley during the first two weeks of September 2001, and even there it was cold, with 14 straight days of intense mistral winds howling through the valley from the north. In Bordeaux, temperatures were 5° below normal, a significant trend that lasted the entire month. However, Bordeaux was also extremely dry during this period. According to the statistics, rainfall in September was off by 66%, always a positive sign. The only rain was on September 22 and 23.

Pomerol and St.-Émilion's Merlot harvest did not begin in earnest until the end of September, and it continued through the first week of October. In the Médoc, the Merlot harvest lasted October 1–10. Cabernet Franc throughout Bordeaux was harvested during the same period. The Cabernet Sauvignon was picked unusually late, most coming in October 7–12. A handful of estates waited even longer. Rainfall in October was more problematic, with showers occurring on October 2, 3, 6, 7, and 8, but no inundations.

Production was enormous, although slightly below 2000. Vinifications were tricky, with malolactics far slower than in previous years.

To no one's surprise, most claim this vintage is qualitatively superior to 1999, but in a classic style with fresh acidity, a cooler-climate taste, and more noticeable tannin. Comparisons along the lines of so-called "classic" vintages such as 1955, 1979, 1981, and 1988 are commonly heard, yet the vintage, overall, is superior to all of these years. Much has changed in terms of lower crop yields, different vinification techniques, and more severe selections in both the vineyard and the cellars. For those reasons, older vintages are generally useless for comparison purposes. The Médoc appears to be more uneven than expected, particularly one of my favorite appellations, St.-Julien.

2001 has produced wines that are denser than the 1999s (more concentrated), but also with higher levels of tannin. The 2001s possess plenty of structure and tannin, as well as charm and succulence. Undeniably, the style of the vintage is lighter, less impressive, and less concentrated than 2000, with some notable exceptions, especially in St.-Émilion and Pomerol. For the red wines, one can safely say it is a good, sometimes excellent, yet irregular vintage.

With respect to Bordeaux's sweet white wines, the onset of botrytis was ideal, and the higher than normal acidity (because of the cool temperatures) resulted in a sensational vintage for many Sauternes and Barsac producers. Clearly, 2001 is the finest year for this region since the outstanding trio of 1988, 1989, and 1990.

—ROBERT PARKER

THE BEST WINES OF 2001

St.-Estèphe: Calon-Ségur, Cos d'Estournel, Montrose

Pauillac: Clerc Milon, Grand-Puy-Lacoste, Lafite-Rothschild, Latour, Mouton-Rothschild, Pichon-Longueville–Comtesse de Lalande

St.-Julien: Branaire, Ducru-Beaucaillou, Léoville-Barton, Léoville–Las Cases, Léoville-Poyferré

Margaux: Brane-Cantenac, Clos du Jaugueyron, d'Issan, Lascombes, Château Margaux, Marojallia, Palmer

Pessac-Léognan/Graves Red: Branon, Haut-Bergey, Haut-Brion, Larrivet Haut-Brion, La Mission–Haut-Brion, Pape Clément, Smith–Haut-Lafitte

Pessac-Léognan/Graves White: Carbonnieux, De Fieuzal, La Louvière, Haut-Brion-Blanc, Laville-Haut-Brion, Malartic-Lagravière, Pape Clément Blanc

Pomerol: Le Bon Pasteur, Clos L'Église, La Croix St.-Georges, L'Église-Clinet, L'Évangile, La Fleur de Gay, Gazin, Hosanna, Lafleur, Pétrus, Le Pin, Vieux-Château-Certan

St.-Émilion: L'Angélus, Ausone, Beau-Séjour Bécot, Beauséjour-Duffau, Bellevue-
Mondotte, Canon–La Gaffelière, Cheval Blanc, Clos St.-Martin, Clos de Sarpe, La
Clusière, La Confession, La Couspaude, Ferrand Lartigue, La Fleur Morange,
Fombrauge, Gracia, Grand-Pontet, Les Grandes Murailles, l'Hermitage, Magrez
Fombrauge, Monbousquet, La Mondotte, Pavie, Pavie-Decesse, Péby-Faugères, Quinault
L'Enclos Rol Valentin, Troplong Mondot, Valandraud
Barsac/Sauternes: Climens, Clos Haut-Peyraguey, Coutet, Doisy-Daëne L'Extravagant,
Doisy-Védrines, Guiraud, Lafaurie-Peyraguey, De Maille, Raymond-Lafon, Rieussec,
Sigalas-Ribaud, Suduiraut, La Tour Blanche

[the ratings]

BORDEAUX'S BEST PRODUCERS OF DRY RED WINE:

Note: Where a producer has been assigned a range of stars, ∗∗∗/∗∗∗∗ for example, the lower
rating has been used for placement in this hierarchy.

∗ ∗ ∗ ∗ ∗ (OUTSTANDING)

L'Angélus (St.-Émilion)
Ausone (St.-Émilion)
Bellevue-Mondotte (St.-Émilion)
Canon-La Gaffelière (St.-Émilion)
Cheval Blanc (St.-Émilion)
Clos L'Église (Pomerol) (since 1998)
Cos d'Estournel (St.-Estèphe)
La Conseillante (Pomerol)
Ducru-Beaucaillou (St.-Julien)
L'Église Clinet (Pomerol)
L'Évangile (Pomerol)
La Fleur-Pétrus (Pomerol) (since 1995)
La Gomerie (St.-Émilion)
Grand-Puy-Lacoste (Pauillac)
Haut-Brion (Graves)
Lafite-Rothschild (Pauillac)
Lafleur (Pomerol)
Latour (Pauillac)
Léoville-Barton (St. Julien)
Léoville–Las Cases (St.-Julien)
Léoville-Poyferré (St.-Julien)
Lynch-Bages (Pauillac)
Magrez Fombrauge (St.-Émilion)
Château Margaux (Margaux)

Marojallia (Margaux)
La Mission–Haut-Brion (Graves)
Monbousquet (St.-Émilion)
La Mondotte (St.-Émilion)
Montrose (St.-Estèphe)
Mouton-Rothschild (Pauillac)
Palmer (Margaux)
Pape Clément (Graves)
Pavie (St.-Émilion)
Pavie-Decesse (St.-Émilion) (since 1998)
Pavie-Macquin (St.-Émilion)
Péby-Faugères (St.-Émilion)
Pétrus (Pomerol)
Pichon-Longueville-Baron (Pauillac)
Pichon-Longueville–Comtesse de Lalande
(Pauillac)
Le Pin (Pomerol)
Pontet-Canet (Pomerol)
Smith–Haut-Lafitte (Pessac-Léognan)
Le Tertre-Rôteboeuf (St.-Émilion)
Troplong-Mondot (St.-Émilion)
Trotanoy (Pomerol)
Valandraud (St.-Émilion)
Vieux-Château-Certan (Pomerol)

∗ ∗ ∗ ∗ (EXCELLENT)

Domaine de l'A (Côtes de Castillon)
D'Aiguihle (Côtes de Castillon)
L'Arrosée (St.-Émilion)
Barde-Haut (St.-Émilion)
Balthus (Bordeaux)
Beau Séjour-Bécot (St.-Émilion)
Beauséjour-Duffau (St.-Émilion)

Bellevue (St.-Émilion)
Bolaire (Bordeaux)
Le Bon Pasteur (Pomerol)
Bouscat Les Portes de L'Âme (Bordeaux)
Branaire-Ducru (St.-Julien)
Brane-Cantenac (Margaux) (since 1998)
Branon (Pessac-Léognan)

Calon-Ségur (St.-Estèphe)
Les Carmes–Haut-Brion (Graves)
Certan de May (Pomerol)
De Chambrun (Lalande de Pomerol)
Domaine de Chevalier (Graves)
Certan-Marzelle (Pomerol)
Charmail (Haut-Médoc)
Chauvin (St.-Émilion)
Clerc Milon (Pauillac)
Clinet (Pomerol)
Clos Dubreuil (St.-Émilion)
Clos Fourtet (St.-Émilion)
Clos St.-Julien (St.-Émilion)
Clos des Lunelles (Côtes de Castillon)
Clos de L'Oratoire (St.-Émilion)
Clos St.-Martin (St.-Émilion)
Clos de Sarpe (St.-Émilion)
La Clotte (St.-Émilion)
La Clusière (St.-Émilion)
Côte de Baleau (St.-Émilion)
La Confession (St.-Émilion)
La Couspaude (St.-Émilion)
Croix de Labrie (St.-Émilion)
La Dominique (St.-Émilion)
Duhart-Milon (Pauillac)
Faugères (St.-Émilion)
Ferrand Lartigue (St.-Émilion)
La Fleur de Gay (Pomerol)
Le Fleur de Jaugue (St.-Émilion)
Les Forts de Latour (Pauillac)
Le Gay (Pomerol)
Gazin (Pomerol)
Girolate (Bordeaux)
Giscours (Margaux)
Gracia (St.-Émilion)
Grand-Mayne (St.-Émilion)
Grand Ormeau Madeleine (Lalande de
    Pomerol)
Les Grands Chênes (Médoc)
Les Grands Maréchaux
Grandes-Murailles (St.-Émilion)
Haut-Bailly (Graves)

Haut-Bergey (Graves) (since 1998)
Haut-Carles (Fronsac)
Les Grands Maréchaux
Haut-Condissas (Medoc)
Haut-Marbuzet (St.-Estèphe)
Hosanna (Pomerol)
d'Issan (Margaux)
Jean de Gué (Lalande de Pomerol)
Joanin Bécot (Côtes de Castillon)
Kirwan (Margaux)
Lafon-Rochet (St.-Estèphe)
Lagrange (St.-Julien)
La Lagune (Ludon)
Larcis Ducasse (St.-Émilion) (since 2003)
Larmande (St.-Émilion)
Lascombes (Margaux)
La Louvière (Graves)
Malartic-Lagravière (Graves)
Malescot St.-Exupéry (Margaux)
Le Moulin (Pomerol)
Moulin–Haut-Laroque (Fronsac)
Moulin–St.-Georges (St.-Émilion)
Nénin (Pomerol) (since 1998)
Pipeau (St.-Émilion)
Le Plus de La Fleur Boüard (Lalande
    de Pomerol)
Pontet-Canet (Pauillac)
Poujeaux (Moulis)
La Prade (Côtes de Francs)
Quinault L'Enclos (St.-Émilion)
Rauzan-Ségla (Margaux)
Rollan de By (Médoc)
Rol Valentin (St.-Émilion)
St.-Pierre (St.-Julien)
La Serénité (Pessac-Léognan)
La Servitude Volontaire (Haut-Médoc)
Sociando-Mallet (Haut-Médoc)
Talbot (St.-Julien)
La Tour Carnet (Haut-Médoc)
Valmengaux (Bordeaux)
La Vieille Cure (Fronsac)

∗ ∗ ∗ (GOOD PRODUCERS)

D'Angludet (Margaux)
D'Armailhac (Pauillac)
Bahans Haut-Brion (Graves)
Balestard–La-Tonnelle (St.-Émilion)
Batailley (Pauillac)
Beauregard (Pomerol)
Bel-Air (Lalande de Pomerol)

Bellegrave (Pomerol)
Belles-Graves (Lalande de Pomerol)
Bertineau St.-Vincent (Lalande de Pomerol)
Beychevelle (St.-Julien)
Bonalgue (Pomerol)
Le Boscq (Médoc)
Bourgneuf (Pomerol)

Cadet-Piola (St.-Émilion)
Canon (Canon-Fronsac)
Canon (St.-Émilion)
Cantemerle (Macau)
Cantenac-Brown (Margaux)
Cap de Mourlin (St.-Émilion)
Carbonnieux (Graves)
de Carles (Fronsac)
Carruades de Lafite-Rothschild (Pauillac)
Cassagne–Haut-Canon–La Truffière
    (Canon-Fronsac)
Certan-Giraud (Pomerol)
Chantegrive (Graves)
La Chapelle de la Mission (Graves)
Chasse-Spleen (Moulis)
Chauvin (St.-Émilion)
Citran (Haut-Médoc)
Clos du Clocher (Pomerol)
Clos des Jacobins (St.-Émilion)
Clos du Marquis (St.-Julien)
Clos René (Pomerol)
La Clotte (St.-Émilion)
La Conseiller (Bordeaux Supérieur)
Corbin (St.-Émilion)
Corbin-Michotte (St.-Émilion)
Cormeil-Figeac (St.-Émilion)
Cos Labory (St.-Estèphe)
Coufran (Haut-Médoc)
Coutelin-Merville (St.-Estèphe)
Couvent des Jacobins (St.-Émilion)
La Croix du Casse (Pomerol)
La Croix de Gay (Pomerol)
Croizet-Bages (Pauillac)
Croque Michotte (St.-Émilion)
Dalem (Fronsac)
La Dame de Montrose (St.-Estèphe)
Dassault (St.-Émilion)
Daugay (St.-Émilion)
La Dauphine (Fronsac)
Dauzac (Margaux)
Destieux (St.-Émilion)
Domaine de L'Église (Pomerol)
Feytit-Clinet (Pomerol)
Figeac (St.-Émilion)
De Fieuzal (Graves)
La Fleur (St.-Émilion)
Fonbel (St.-Émilion)
Fonplégade (St.-Émilion)
Fonroque (St.-Émilion)
Fontenil (Fronsac)
Fourcas-Loubaney (Listrac)

Franc-Mayne (St.-Émilion)
La Gaffelière (St.-Émilion)
La Garde Réserve du Château (Graves)
Gigault-Cuvée Viva (Premières Côtes
    de Blaye)
Gironville (Haut-Médoc)
Gloria (St.-Julien)
Grand Corbin (St.-Émilion)
Grand-Pontet (St.-Émilion)
Grand-Puy–Ducasse (Pauillac)
Grée Laroque (Bordeaux Supérieur)
Gruaud-Larose (St.-Julien)
Guerry (Côtes de Bourg)
Guillot-Clauzel (Pomerol)
La Gurgue (Margaux)
Haut-Beyzac (Haut-Médoc)
Haut-Batailley (Pauillac)
Haut-Corbin (St.-Émilion)
Haut-Faugères (St.-Émilion)
Haut-Sociando (Blaye)
L'Hermitage (St.-Émilion)
Hortevie (St.-Julien)
Château Hostens-Picant (Ste.-Foy)
Jonqueyrès (Bordeaux Supérieur)
Labégorce-Zédé (Margaux)
Lalande-Borie (St.-Julien)
Lanessan (Haut-Médoc)
Langoa Barton (St.-Julien)
Laplagnotte-Bellevue (St.-Émilion)
Larrivet–Haut-Brion (Graves)
Lucie (St.-Émilion)
Latour à Pomerol (Pomerol)
Lusseau (St.-Émilion)
Lynch-Moussas (Pauillac)
Magdelaine (St.-Émilion)
Magneau (Graves)
Marjosse (Bordeaux)
Marquis de Terme (Margaux)
Maucaillou (Moulis)
Mazeris (Canon-Fronsac)
Meyney (St.-Estèphe)
Monbrison (Margaux)
Moulin Pey-Labrie (Canon-Fronsac)
Moulin Rouge (Haut-Médoc)
Olivier (Graves)
Les Ormes de Pez (St.-Estèphe)
Les Ormes-Sorbet (Médoc)
Parenchère (Bordeaux Supérieur)
Patache d'Aux (Médoc)
du Pavillon (Canon-Fronsac)

Pavillon Rouge de Margaux
(Margaux)
Les Pensées de Lafleur (Pomerol)
Petit-Village (Pomerol)
Peyredon Lagravette (Listrac)
de Pez (St.-Estèphe)
Phélan-Ségur (St.-Estèphe)
Pibran (Pauillac)
Picque-Caillou (Graves)
De Pitray (Côtes de Castillon)
Plaisance (Premières Côtes de
Bordeaux)
Potensac (Médoc)
Poujeaux (Moulis)
Prieuré-Lichine (Margaux)
Réserve de la Comtesse (Pauillac)
Roc des Cambes (Côtes de Bourg)
Rolland-Maillet (St.-Émilion)
De Sales (Pomerol)
Seguin (Pessac-Léognan)
La Serre (St.-Émilion)

Siran (Margaux)
Soudars (Haut-Médoc)
Soutard (St.-Émilion)
Tayac (Côtes de Bourg)
Tertre Daugay (St.-Émilion)
La Tonnelle (Blaye)
La Tour de By (Médoc)
La Tour Figeac (St.-Émilion)
La Tour–Haut-Brion (Graves)
Tour Haut-Caussan (Médoc)
Tour du Haut-Moulin (Haut-Médoc)
La Tour–St.-Bonnet (Médoc)
La Tour Séguy (Bourg)
Les Tourelles de Longueville
(Pauillac)
Trianon (St.-Émilion)
Trotte Vieille (St.-Émilion)
Veyry (Côtes de Castillon)
Vieux Fortin (St.-Émilion)
La Violette (Pomerol)

* * (AVERAGE)

Beaumont (Haut-Médoc)
Belair (St.-Émilion)
Belgrave (Haut-Médoc)
La Cabanne (Pomerol)
Chambert-Marbuzet (St.-Estèphe)
Clarke (Listrac)
Clos La Madeleine (St.-Émilion)
Cordeillan-Bages (Pauillac)
La Croix (Pomerol)
Durfort-Vivens (Margaux)
L'Enclos (Pomerol)
Faurie de Souchard (St.-Émilion)
Ferrière (Margaux)
La Fleur Gazin (Pomerol)
La Fleur-Pourret (St.-Émilion)
Fonbadet (Pauillac)
Fonréaud (Listrac)
Fourcas-Dupré (Listrac)
Fourcas-Hosten (Listrac)
de France (Graves)
Château Gassies (Premières Côtes
de Bordeaux)
Gombaude-Guillot (Pomerol)
Gressier–Grand Poujeaux (Moulis)
Haut Sarpe (St.-Émilion)
Le Jurat (St.-Émilion)
Lagrange (Pomerol)

Lamarque (Haut-Médoc)
Larose-Trintaudon (Haut-Médoc)
Laroze (St.-Émilion)
Latour-Martillac (Graves)
Liversan (Haut-Médoc)
Malescasse (Haut-Médoc)
Marbuzet (St.-Estèphe)
Martinens (Margaux)
Mazeyres (Pomerol)
Montviel (Pomerol)
Moulin du Cadet (St.-Émilion)
Pédésclaux (Pauillac)
Petit Faurie-Soutard (St.-Émilion)
Petit-Figeac (St.-Émilion)
Plince (Pomerol)
Pouget (Margaux)
Puy-Blanquet (St.-Émilion)
Rahoul (Graves)
Rauzan-Gassies (Margaux)
Rochebelle (St.-Émilion)
Rocher Bellevue Figeac (St.-Émilion)
Rouet (Fronsac)
Taillefer (Pomerol)
La Tour de Mons (Margaux)
Vieux Clos St.-Émilion
(St.-Émilion)
Villemaurine (St.-Émilion)

BORDEAUX'S BEST PRODUCERS OF DRY WHITE WINES

★ ★ ★ ★ ★ (OUTSTANDING)

Domaine de Chevalier (Pessac-Léognan)
De Fieuzal (Pessac-Léognan)
Haut-Brion (Pessac-Léognan)

Laville–Haut-Brion (Pessac-Léognan)
Pape Clément (Pessac-Léognan)
Smith–Haut-Lafitte (Pessac-Léognan)

★ ★ ★ ★ (EXCELLENT)

Aile d'Argent (Bordeaux)
Carbonnieux (Pessac-Léognan)
Clos Floridene (Pessac-Léognan)
Couhins-Lurton (Pessac-Léognan)

La Louvière (Pessac-Léognan)
Latour-Martillac (Pessac-Léognan)
Malartic-Lagravière (Pessac-Léognan)
Pavillon Blanc du Château Margaux
    (Bordeaux)

★ ★ ★ (GOOD)

d'Archambeau (Graves)
Bauduc Les Trois Hectares (Bordeaux)
Blanc de Lynch-Bages (Pauillac)
Bouscaut (Pessac-Léognan)
Caillou Blanc de Talbot (Bordeaux)
Carsin (Bordeaux)
Domaine Challon (Bordeaux)
Chantegrive (Graves)
La Closière (Bordeaux)
La Grande Clotte (Bordeaux)
Château Coucheroy (Pessac-Léognan)
Doisy-Daëne (Bordeaux)
Château Ferbos (Graves)
Ferrande (Graves)
G de Château Guiraud (Bordeaux)
La Garde-Réserve du Château (Graves)

Château Graville-Lacoste (Graves)
Haut-Gardère (Graves)
Loudenne (Bordeaux)
Château de Malle (Graves)
Château Millet (Graves)
Pirou (Graves)
Plaisance (Bordeaux)
Pontac Monplaisir (Graves)
R de Rieussec (Bordeaux)
Rahoul (Graves)
Respide Médeville (Graves)
Reynon (Bordeaux)
Château de Rochemorin
    (Pessac-Léognan)
Roquefort (Bordeaux)
Thieuley (Bordeaux)

★ ★ (AVERAGE)

De France (Graves)

Olivier (Graves)

BORDEAUX'S BEST PRODUCERS OF BARSAC/SAUTERNES

★ ★ ★ ★ ★ (OUTSTANDING)

Climens (Barsac)
Coutet Cuvée Madame (Barsac)
Doisy-Daëne l'Extravagant (Barsac)

Lafaurie-Peyraguey (Sauternes)
Rieussec (Sauternes)
d'Yquem (Sauternes)

★ ★ ★ ★ (EXCELLENT)

D'Arche-Pugneau (Sauternes)
Coutet (regular cuvée) (Barsac)
Doisy-Dubroca (Barsac)
de Fargues (Sauternes)
Gilette (Sauternes)

Guiraud (Sauternes)
Rabaud-Promis (Sauternes)
Raymond-Lafon (Sauternes)
Suduiraut (Sauternes)★★★★/★★★★★
La Tour Blanche (Sauternes)

d'Arche (Sauternes)	Lamothe-Despujols (Sauternes)
Bastor-Lamontagne (Sauternes)	Lamothe-Guignard (Sauternes)★★★/★★★★
Broustet (Barsac)	Liot (Sauternes)
Caillou (Barsac)	de Malle (Sauternes)
Clos Haut-Peyraguey (Sauternes)	Nairac (Barsac)
Doisy-Daëne (Barsac)	Piada (Barsac)
Doisy-Dubroca (Barsac)	Rabaud-Promis (Sauternes)
Doisy-Védrines (Barsac)	Rayne-Vigneau (Sauternes)
Filhot (Sauternes)	Romer du Hayot (Sauternes)
Haut-Claverie (Sauternes)	Roûmieu-Lacoste (Barsac)
Les Justices (Sauternes)	Sigalas-Rabaud (Sauternes)
Lamothe (Sauternes)	

★ ★ (AVERAGE)

Myrat (Sauternes)	Suau (Barsac)

GETTING A HANDLE ON SECONDARY LABELS

Secondary wines with secondary labels (known as *marques*) are not a recent development. Léoville–Las Cases first made a second wine (Clos du Marquis) in 1904, and in 1908 Château Margaux produced its first Le Pavillon Rouge du Château Margaux. Yet two decades ago, about the only second labels most Bordeaux wine enthusiasts encountered were those from Latour (Les Forts de Latour), Margaux (Le Pavillon Rouge du Château Margaux), and perhaps that of Lafite-Rothschild (Moulin des Carruades). Today, virtually every classified growth, as well as many crus bourgeois and numerous estates in Pomerol and St.-Émilion, has second labels for their batches of wine deemed not sufficiently rich, concentrated, or complete enough to go into their top wine, or *grand vin*. This was one of the major developments of the 1980s, fostered no doubt by the enormous crop sizes in most of the vintages. A handful of cynics have claimed that secondary labels are created largely to keep prices high, but such charges are nonsense. The result has generally been far higher quality for a château's best wine. It simply allows a château to declassify the production from young vines, from vines that overproduce, and from parcels harvested too soon or too late, into a second, or perhaps even a third, wine that still has some of the quality and character of the château's *grand vin*.

The gentleman who encouraged most châteaux to develop second wines was the famed oenologist Professor Émile Peynaud. Over the last decade, the number of second wines has increased more than tenfold. Some properties, such as Léoville–Las Cases, have even begun to utilize a third label for wines deemed not good enough for the second label! Of course, all this complicates buying decisions for consumers. The wine trade has exacerbated matters by seizing on the opportunity to advertise wine that "tastes like the *grand vin*" for one-half to one-third the price. In most cases, there is little truth to such proclamations. I find that most second wines have only a vague resemblance to their more esteemed siblings. Most are the product of throwing everything that would normally have been discarded into another label for commercial purposes. Some second wines, such as those of the first growths, particularly Les Forts de Latour and Bahans Haut-Brion, are indeed excellent, occasionally outstanding (taste the 1982 Les Forts de Latour or 1989 Bahans-Haut-Brion), and can even resemble the style and character of the *grand vin*. But the words "caveat emptor" should be etched deep in the minds of consumers who routinely purchase the second labels of Bordeaux châteaux thinking they are getting something reminiscent of the property's top wine. In an effort to clarify the situation of second labels, the following chart rates the secondary wines on a one- to five-star basis.

While I think it is important to underscore the significance that the stricter the selection, the better the top wine, it is also important to remember that most second wines are rarely worth the price asked.

Note: Where a second wine merits purchasing, the vintage is listed.

EXPLANATION OF THE STARS

***** The finest second wines
**** Very good second wines
*** Pleasant second wines
** Average-quality second wines
* Of little interest

SECONDARY LABELS

GRAND VIN	SECOND VIN
Andron-Blanquet	St.-Roch**
L'Angélus	Carillon de L'Angélus**
D'Angludet	Domaine Baury**
D'Arche	D'Arche-Lafaurie**
L'Arrosée	Les Côteaux du Château L'Arrosée**
Balestard–La-Tonnelle	Les Tourelles de Balestard**
Bastor-Lamontagne	Les Remparts de Bastor**
Beau-Séjour Bécot	Tournelle des Moines**
Beaumont	Moulin d'Arvigny*
Beauséjour-Duffau	La Croix de Mazerat**
Belair	Roc-Blanquant*
Beychevelle	Amiral de Beychevelle***
	Réserve de L'Amiral***
Bonalgue	Burgrave*
Bouscaut	Valoux**
Branaire-Ducru	Duluc**
Brane-Cantenac	Château Notton**
	Domaine de Fontarney**
Broustet	Château de Ségur**
La Cabanne	Compostelle**
Cadet-Piola	Chevaliers de Malta**
Caillou	Petit-Mayne*
Calon-Ségur	Marquis de Ségur**
Canon	Clos J. Kanon**
Canon–La Gaffelière	Côte Migon-La Gaffelière**
Cantemerle	Villeneuve de Cantemerle**
Cantenac-Brown	Canuet**
	Lamartine**
Carbonnieux	La Tour-Léognan**
Certan-Giraud	Clos du Roy**
Chambert-Marbuzet	MacCarthy**
Chasse-Spleen	L'Ermitage de Chasse-Spleen**
Chauvin	Chauvin Variation*
Cheval Blanc	Le Petit Cheval***

Climens	Les Cyprès de Climens**
Clos Fourtet	Domaine de Martialis**
Clos Haut-Peyraguey	Haut-Bommes**
Clos René	Moulinet-Lasserre**
Colombier-Monpelou	Grand Canyon**
Corbin-Michotte	Les Abeilles**
Cos d'Estournel	Pagodes de Cos****
Couvent des Jacobins	Beau-Mayne
La Croix	Le Gabachot**
Croizet-Bages	Enclos de Moncabon*
Dauzac	Laborde**
Doisy-Védrines	La Tour-Védrines**
La Dominique	St.-Paul de la Dominique**
Ducru-Beaucaillou	La Croix****
Duhart-Milon-Rothschild	Moulin de Duhart**
Durfort-Vivens	Domaine de Curé-Bourse*
L'Église-Clinet	La Petite L'Église***
de Fieuzal	L'Abeille de Fieuzal**
Figeac	Grangeneuve**
Fonplégade	Château Côtes Trois Moulins**
La Gaffelière	Clos La Gaffelière**
	Château de Roquefort**
Giscours	Cantelaude**
Gloria	Haut-Beychevelle Gloria**
	Peymartin**
Grand-Mayne	Les Plantes du Mayne**
Grand-Puy-Ducasse	Artigues-Arnaud**
Grand-Puy-Lacoste	Lacoste-Borie**
Gruaud-Larose	Sarget de Gruaud-Larose**
Guiraud	Le Dauphin**
Haut-Bailly	La Parde de Haut-Bailly***
Haut-Batailley	La Tour d'Aspic**
Haut-Brion	Bahans Haut-Brion***** (2005, 2003, 2001, 2000, 1998, 1995, 1990, 1989, 1988, 1987)
Haut-Marbuzet	Tour de Marbuzet**
d'Issan	Candel**
Labegorcé-Zédé	Château de l'Amiral**
Lafite-Rothschild	Carruades de Lafite**** (2005, 2003, 2002, 2001, 2000, 1998, 1996, 1995, 1990, 1989)
Lafleur	Les Pensées de Lafleur***** (2006, 2005, 2004, 2003, 2000, 1990, 1989, 1988)
Lafon-Rochet	Le Numéro 2 de Lafon-Rochet***
Lagrange	Les Fiefs de Lagrange***
La Lagune	Ludon-Pomiès-Agassac**
Lanessan	Domaine de Ste.-Gemme**
Larmande	Château des Templiers**
Lascombes	Segonnes**
	La Gombaude**
Latour	Les Forts de Latour***** (2006, 2005, 2004, 2003, 2002, 2001, 2000, 1999, 1996, 1995, 1990, 1989, 1982, 1978)

Léoville-Barton	Lady Langoa★★★★ (1989)
Léoville–Las Cases	Clos du Marquis★★★★★ (2006, 2005, 2002, 2000, 1996, 1995, 1994, 1990, 1989, 1988, 1986, 1982)
	Grand Parc★★★
Léoville-Poyferré	Moulin-Riche★★
La Louvière	L de la Louvière★★★★
	Coucheray★★
	Clos du Roi★★
Lynch-Bages	Haut-Bages–Averous★★★★
Malescot St.-Exupéry	de Loyac★
	Domaine du Balardin★
de Malle	Château de Ste.-Hélène★★
Château Margaux	Pavillon Rouge du Château Margaux★★★★★ (2005, 2003, 2002, 2001, 2000, 1999, 1996, 1995, 1990)
Marquis de Terme	Domaine des Gondats
Maucaillou	Cap de Haut
	Franc-Caillou
Meyney	Prieuré de Meyney
Monbrison	Cordat
Montrose	La Dame de Montrose★★★★ (2006, 2005, 2003, 2000, 1999, 1996, 1991, 1990)
Mouton-Rothschild	Le Petit Mouton★★★ (2005, 2000, 1999)
Palmer	Alter Ego de Palmer★★★★ (2005, 2001, 2000, 1999)
Pape Clément	Le Clémentin du Pape Clément★★★
Phélan-Ségur	Franck Phélan
Pichon-Longueville-Baron	Les Tourelles de Pichon★★★
Pichon-Longueville–Comtesse de Lalande	Réserve de la Comtesse★★★★ (2003, 2002, 2000, 1997, 1996, 1995)
Pontet-Canet	Les Hauts de Pontet★★
Potensac	Gallais-Bellevue★★
	Lassalle★★
	Goudy-la-Cardonne★★
Poujeaux	La Salle de Poujeaux★★
Le Prieuré	Château l'Olivier★★
Prieuré-Lichine	Clairefont★★
Rabaud-Promis	Domaine de L'Estremade★★
Rahoul	Petit Rahoul★★
Rauzan-Ségla	Lamouroux★★
Rieussec	Clos Labère★★★
St.-Pierre	Clos d'Uza★★
	St.-Louis le Bosq★★
de Sales	Chantalouette★★
Siran	Bellegarde★★
	St.-Jacques★★
Smith–Haut-Lafitte	Les Hauts de Smith–Haut-Lafitte★★★
Sociando-Mallet	Lartigue-de-Brochon★★
Soutard	Clos de la Tonnelle★★
Talbot	Connétable de Talbot

Tertre Daugay	Château de Roquefort***
La Tour Blanche	Mademoiselle de St.-Marc**=
La Tour de By	Moulin de la Roque*
	La Roque de By*
Tour Haut-Caussan	La Landotte**
La Tour-Martillac	La Grave-Martillac**
Troplong-Mondot	Mondot***
Valandraud	Virginie de Valandraud***
Vieux-Château-Certan	Clos de la Gravette***

THE BEST WINE VALUES IN BORDEAUX

HIGH-QUALITY ESTATES FOR UNDER $20 A BOTTLE

St.-Estèphe: Tronquoy-Lalande, Le Boscq

Pauillac: none

St.-Julien: Glana, Hortevie, Lalande-Borie

Margaux and the southern Médoc: d'Arsac

Pessac-Léognan/Graves: none

Moulis and Listrac: Clarke

Médoc and Haut-Médoc: d'Aurilhac, Bellevue, Cambon La Pelouse, Camensac, Charmail, d'Escurac, La Goulée, Les Grands Chênes, Greysac, Haut-Condissas, Rollan de By, Sénéjac, Tour de Haut-Moulin, La Tour Séran

Pomerol: none

St.-Émilion: none

Lalande de Pomerol: Bertineau St.-Vincent, De Chambrun, La Fleur-Boüard, Grand-Ormeau, Jean de Gué Cuvée Prestige, Haut-Chaigneau, Le Sergue

Côtes de Bourg: Fougas Maldoror, Roc de Cambes, Guerry

Côtes de Blaye: Bel-Air La Royère, Clos Lascombes, Garreau, Gigault Cuvée Viva, Les Grands Maréchaux, Haut-Colombier, Peyraud, Roland La Garde, Ségonzac Vieilles Vignes

Côtes de Francs: Marsau, La Prade, Puygueraud

Bordeaux—generic, Premières Côtes, and Supérieur: Beaulieu, Bel-Air Grande Cuvée, Bolaire, Bois Pertuis, Bonnet, Bouscat, Brondeau, Caris, Carsin Black Label, Clos Chaumont, Conseiller, La Cour d'Argent, Domaine de Courteillac, Croix-Mouton, La Croix de Roche, Le Doyenne, De La Garde, Grée Laroque, Marjosse, Parenchère Cuvée Raphaël, Le Pin Beausoleil, Plaisance Tradition, Rauzan-Despagne, Reignac, Reignon, Thébot, Thieuley, Tour de Mirambeau

Côtes de Castillon: Domaine de l'A, d'Aiguilhe, d'Aiguilhe Querre, Brisson, Cap de Faugères, Clos Louie, Clos Puy Arnaud, Côte Montpezat, Dubois-Grimon, Joanin Bécot, Le Pin de Belcier, Veyry, Vieux Champ de Mars, 20 Mille

Fronsac/Canon-Fronsac: Fontenil, Haut-Carles, Moulin–Haut Laroque, La Vieille Cure, Vrai Canon Bouché

Barsac/Sauternes: none

St.-Georges–St.-Émilion: none

Puisseguin-St.-Émilion: Branda, La Mauriane

Entre-Deux-Mers (dry white wines): none

Bordeaux Premières Côtes and generic Bordeaux (dry white wines): none

THE PITFALLS AND PLEASURES

The purchase of wine, already fraught with plenty of pitfalls for consumers, becomes immensely more complex and risky when one enters the wine futures sweepstakes.

On the surface, buying wine futures is nothing more than investing money in a case or cases of wine at a predetermined "future price" long before the wine is bottled and shipped to this country. For years, future offerings have been largely limited to Bordeaux wines, although they are seen occasionally from other regions. You invest in wine futures on the assumption that the wine will appreciate significantly in price between the time you purchase the future and the time the wine has been bottled and imported. Purchasing the right wine, from the right vintage, in the right international financial climate, can represent significant savings. On the other hand, it can be quite disappointing to invest heavily in a wine future only to witness the wine's arrival 12 to 18 months later at a price equal to or below the future price and to discover that the wine is inferior in quality as well.

In Bordeaux, during the spring following the harvest, the estates or châteaux offer for sale a portion of their crops. The first offering, or *première tranche,* usually offers a good indication of the trade's enthusiasm for the new wine, the prevailing market conditions, and the ultimate price the public will have to spend. Brokers and *négociants* who take an early position on a vintage frequently offer portions of their purchases to importers/wholesalers/retailers to make available publicly as a "wine future." These offerings are usually made to the retail shopper during the first spring after the vintage. For example, the 2000 Bordeaux vintage was being offered for sale as a wine future in June 2001, and the hugely applauded 2005s in late spring 2006.

Purchasing wine at this time is not without numerous risks. Though 90% of the quality of the wine and the style of the vintage can be ascertained by professionals tasting the wine in its infancy, the increased interest in buying Bordeaux wine futures has led to a soaring number of journalists—some qualified, some not—to try their hands at judging young Bordeaux wines. The results have been predictable. Many writers serve no purpose other than to hype the vintage as great and, in their effort to sell articles, write more glowing accounts of a vintage than the publicity firms doing promotion for the Bordeaux wine industry. Consumers should read numerous points of view from trusted professionals and ask the following questions: 1) Is the professional taster experienced in tasting young as well as old Bordeaux vintages? 2) How much time does the taster actually spend tasting Bordeaux during the year, visiting the properties, and thinking about the vintage? 3) Does the professional taster express his or her viewpoint in an independent, unbiased form, free of trade advertising? 4) Has the professional looked deeply at the weather conditions, harvesting conditions, grape-variety-ripening profiles, and soil types that respond differently depending on the weather scenario? And, most important, 5) Does the taster/critic follow up the barrel tasting by purchasing most of the finest wines in bottle from retailers in the U.S.? Writers must be prepared to invest in the bottled wine to guarantee that what they taste from barrel is the same as what has been bottled. For more than 25 years I have heard rumors of "writer's cuvées," special juiced-up samples that are not representative of the true blend at the château, designed to impress tasters. This is largely a myth as disproved by the tastings I have done from bottled vintages. In most cases, the bottled wines are better than when tasted from cask, at least in the case of classified-growth Bordeaux. Nevertheless, the professional critic must always be on guard against being set up.

When wine futures are offered for sale there is generally a great deal of enthusiasm for the newest vintage from both the proprietors and the wine trade. Many wine producers and merchants live by the saying in France that "the greatest wines ever made are the ones that are available for sale." The business of the wine trade is to sell wine, and consumers should be aware that they will no doubt be inundated with claims of "great wines from a great vintage at great prices." This has been used time and time again for good vintages and, in essence, has undermined the credibility of many otherwise responsible retailers, as well as a number of journalists. In contrast, writers who fail to admit or to recognize greatness where warranted are no less inept and irresponsible.

In short, there are only four valid reasons to buy Bordeaux wine futures.

1. Are you buying top-quality, preferably superb wine from an excellent, or better yet, a great vintage?

No vintage can be reviewed in black-and-white terms. Even in the greatest vintages there are disappointing appellations, as well as mediocre wines. At the same time, vintages that are merely good to very good can produce some superb wines. Knowing who are the underachievers and overachievers is paramount in making a good buying decision. There is no reason to buy wines as futures except for the top performers in a given vintage, because prices generally will not appreciate in the period between the release of the future prices and when the wines are bottled. The exceptions are always the same—top wines and great vintages. If the financial climate is such that the wine will not be at least 25% to 30% more expensive when it arrives in the marketplace, then most purchasers are better off investing their money elsewhere.

2. Do the prices you must pay look good enough that you will ultimately save money by paying less for the wine as a future than for the wine when it is released in two to three years?

Many factors must be taken into consideration to make this determination. In certain years, Bordeaux may release its wines at lower prices than it did the previous year (the most recent examples are 1986, 1990, 2002, and 2004). There is also the question of the international marketplace. In 2002 the U.S. dollar was still relatively strong, but the unsettling events of September 2001, the war in Iraq, the unpopularity of the U.S. government, the potential nuclear showdown in Iran, and general global negativism caused a profound slippage in the dollar's value. Thus it made sense to purchase the 2000s, but 2002s less so, and the hugely hyped 2005s come out at very high prices at a time when the dollar appears to have hit rock bottom. Buying large quantities of 2005s may prove more dangerous than most observers believe. The 2006 futures prices, at least for Americans buying them in dollars, were priced entirely too high for the quality of the vintage. The Bordelais had a worldwide market in 2006 and decided that the American market was not as significant a factor. The international marketplace conditions, the perceived reputation of a given vintage, and the rarity of a particular estate all must be considered in determining whether the wine will become much more expensive when released than its price when offered as a wine future.

3. Do you want to be guaranteed of getting top, hard-to-find wine from a producer with a great reputation who makes only small quantities of wine?

Even if the vintage is not irrefutably great, or you cannot be assured that prices will increase, there are always a handful of small estates, particularly in Pomerol and St.-Émilion, that produce such limited quantities of wine, and who have worldwide followers, that their wines warrant buying as a future if only to reserve your case from an estate whose wines have pleased you in the past. In Pomerol, limited-production wines such as Le Pin, Clinet, La Conseillante, L'Évangile, Le Fleur de Gay, Lafleur, and Bon Pasteur have produced many popular wines during the decades of the 1980s and 1990s, yet are very hard to find in the marketplace. In St.-Émilion, some of the less renowned, modestly sized estates such as L'Angélus, L'Arrosée, Grand-Mayne, Pavie-Macquin, La Dominique, Tertre Rôteboeuf, and Troplong Mondot produce wines that are not easy to find after bottling. There is also a burgeoning number of St.-Émilion "garage wines" that are high in quality but made in limited quantities of 500 to 1,000 cases. Consequently, their admirers throughout the world frequently reserve and pay for these wines as futures. Limited-production wines from high-quality estates merit buying futures even in good to very good years.

4. Do you want to buy wine in half bottles, magnums, double magnums, jeroboams, or imperials?

Frequently overlooked as one of the advantages of buying wine futures is that you can request that your merchant have the wines bottled to your specifications. There is always a surcharge for such bottlings, but if you have children born in a certain year, or you want the luxury of buying half bottles (a size that makes sense for daily drinking), the only time to do this is when buying the wine as a future.

Finally, should you decide to enter the futures market, be sure you know the other risks involved. The merchant you deal with could go bankrupt, and your unsecured sales slip would make you one of probably hundreds of unsecured creditors of the bankrupt wine merchant hoping for a few cents on your investment. Another risk is that the supplier the merchant deals with could go bankrupt or be fraudulent. You may get a refund from the wine merchant, but you will not get your wine. Therefore, be sure to deal only with a wine merchant who has dealt in selling wine futures before and one who is financially solvent. And buy wine futures only from a wine merchant who has received confirmed commitments as to the quantities of wine he or she will receive. Some merchants sell Bordeaux futures to consumers before they have received commitments from suppliers. Be sure to ask for proof of the merchant's allocations. If you do not, then the words "caveat emptor" could have special significance to you.

For many Bordeaux wine enthusiasts, buying wine futures of the right wine, in the right vintage, at the right time guarantees that they have liquid gems worth four or five times the price they paid for the wine.

[tasting commentaries]

DOMAINE DE L'A ★ ★ ★
CÔTES DE CASTILLON $18.00–$32.00

From a biodynamic home property of Stéphane Derenoncourt, this offering is usually an impeccably made sleeper of the vintage that is given the "full Monty" treatment of malolactic fermentation in barrel, aging on its lees, and no fining or filtration at bottling. In most vintages the blend is about two-thirds Merlot, 20% to 25% Cabernet Franc, and the rest Cabernet Sauvignon. Sadly, production is less than 1,000 cases. However, this is a promising estate still selling at a fair price.

2005	91	now–2020		2001	89	now–2011
2004	90	now–2019		2000	88	now–2012
2003	89	now–2013		1999	89	now–2014
2002	87	now–2011				

ACAPPELLA ★ ★ ★
MONTAGNE–ST.-ÉMILION $25.00–$28.00

It is too soon to know if this is going to be an up-and-coming estate from Montagne–St.-Émilion, but the first signs are very positive. Acappella has produced modern-style wines meant to be drunk young but capable of lasting seven to eight years.

2005	87	now–2015		2003	90	now–2014

D'AGASSAC ★ ★ ★
HAUT-MÉDOC $15.00–$16.00

A slumbering property that is just beginning to awaken, d'Agassac has considerable potential given its location.

2004	78	now–2010	2001	87	now–2012
2003	83	now–2011	2000	86	now
2002	81	now–2012			

D'AIGUILHE ★ ★ ★ ★
CÔTES DE CASTILLON $20.00–$30.00

One of the many up-and-coming estates from the Côtes de Castillon, this large property is owned by Stephan von Neipperg, who makes the wine with the assistance of hot-shot wine-making guru Stéphane Derenencourt. This is the latest property acquired by von Neipperg, the owner of Canon-La Gaffelière, Clos de l'Oratoire, and La Mondotte. 2000 was the first vintage in which he controlled the viticulture as well as the vinification and, as one can well imagine, the result was simply exceptional! Reasonably priced. Smart Bordeaux enthusiasts should be purchasing this wine at the earliest opportunity.

2005	92	now–2017	2001	89	now–2014
2004	89	now–2014	2000	90	now–2015
2003	90	now–2018	1999	87	now–2014
2002	87	now–2011	1998	87	now

D'AIGUILHE QUERRE ★ ★ ★
CÔTES DE CASTILLON $25.00–$30.00

The winemaking consultant for this *garagiste* operation is Jean-Michel Fernandez. The six-acre vineyard, planted with Merlot and Cabernet Franc, is making better wines but not yet in the top echelon of the Côtes de Castillon.

2005	91	now–2016	2002	86–87	now
2004	87	now–2012	2001	88	now
2003	85	now–2012	2000	88	now–2012

AMPELIA ★ ★ ★
CÔTES DE CASTILLON $20.00

An estate owned by the same proprietors as Grand Corbin-Despagne in St.-Émilion and a seemingly up-and-coming estate like so many of these avant-garde estates in the Côtes de Castillon. These are big, deep, beefy, good-colored wines in a very modern style.

| 2005 | 88 | now–2015 | 2001 | 89 | now–2012 |

L'ANCIEN ★ ★
POMEROL $20.00

Pleasant, one-dimensional wines emerge from this relatively obscure estate.

| 2005 | | | | 85 | now–2011 |

ANDREAS ★ ★ ★
ST.-ÉMILION $22.00–$40.00

A wine produced under the consultation of Jean-Luc Thunevin, Andreas is a solidly made, somewhat monolithic wine that is meant to be drunk in its first seven to ten years.

| 2001 | 86–87 | now–2011 | 1999 | 84 | now |
| 2000 | 87 | now–2011 | 1998 | 86 | now |

LES ANGELOTS DE GRACIA ★★★★
ST.-ÉMILION $75.00–$90.00

From the idiosyncratic proprietor and stonemason Michel Gracia, this tiny *garagiste* operation fashions provocative wines from incredibly tiny yields of 21 hectoliters per hectare (225 U.S. gallons per acre) made from 80% Merlot and 20% Cabernet Franc with above 13% alcohol. Very rich, very pure, and very impressive.

2005		90+	now–2026+

L'ANGÉLUS ★★★★★
ST.-ÉMILION $80.00–$200.00

Prior to the late 1980s, L'Angélus was a mediocre St.-Émilion. However, it quickly became the poster child and catalyst for the qualitative revolution in St.-Émilion and since 1988 there has been not a hiccup. Hubert de Boüard, the manager of L'Angélus, has had enormous influence on the higher overall quality level of many St.-Émilions. It is only testimony to his talent that L'Angélus was elevated to premier grand cru status in 1996's reclassification. This is one of the great, shining success stories and superstar estates of St.-Émilion and all of Bordeaux. Fabulous wines.

2006	92–95	now–2027+	2000	96	now–2030
2005	98	2012–2042+	1999	88	now–2017
2004	95	2009–2022	1998	93	now–2020
2003	93	now–2023	1997	89	now–2012
2002	91	now–2020	1996	91+	now–2025
2001	93	now–2017	1995	95	now–2025

Past Glories 1994 (92), 1993 (92), 1990 (96), 1989 (96), 1988 (91)

D'ANGLUDET ★★★
MARGAUX $20.00–$42.00

Through hard work and talent, the late Peter Sichel took this château from virtual post–World War II obscurity to international prominence. Year after year, the wines qualify as sleepers of the vintage, but prices remain modest.

2005	90	now–2022	1999	87	now–2012
2004	89	now–2022	1998	86	now–2010
2003	89	now–2018	1997	78–80	now–2012
2002	89	now–2015	1996	88	now–2015
2001	88	now–2015	1995	88	now–2010
2000	88	now–2017			

DES ANNEREAUX ★★
LALANDE DE POMEROL $20.00

Des Annereaux is a small-scale wine from Lalande de Pomerol that is always pleasant but frequently lacking depth and intensity.

2000	86–87	now	1996	81–84	now

L'ARCHANGE ★★★
ST.-ÉMILION $25.00–$45.00

A relatively new entry from St.-Émilion, this wine is produced by highly respected oenologist Pascal Chatonnet. It is a good, solid, modern-style St.-Émilion that lacks power and richness, but it's well-made, reasonably priced, and worth a try.

2005	88	now–2017	2001	86–88	now–2012
2004	89	now–2016	2000	89	now–2014
2003	86–88	now–2012			

ARIA DU CHÂTEAU DE LA RIVIÈRE ★ ★ ★
FRONSAC $20.00–$30.00

Aria is the luxury cuvée from the vast estate of La Rivière.

| 2005 | | 89 | now–2015 |

D'ARMAILHAC ★ ★ ★ ★
PAUILLAC $25.00–$65.00

D'Armailhac, another up-and-coming Pauillac estate, remains, to the consuming public, the least well known of the three Pauillac properties of the late Baron Philippe de Rothschild (the others are Mouton-Rothschild and Clerc Milon), and prices remain realistic. My tastings indicate that the Rothschild brain trust is clearly bent on improving the lot of d'Armailhac and intend for it to compete year in and year out with some of the best wines of Pauillac. This is a property to follow closely as prices have tended to fall below its quality level.

2006	88–90+	now–2022	2000	91	now–2020
2005	90+	2011–2031+	1999	89	now–2017
2004	89	now–2022	1998	89	now–2016
2003	90	now–2019	1997	87	now
2002	89+	now–2019	1996	87	now–2018
2001	89	now–2017	1995	89	now–2012

ARMENS ★ ★ ★
ST.-ÉMILION $25.00

Comte Léo de Malet, proprietor of La Gaffelière, is also the owner of this estate of St.-Émilion. His son, Alexandre de Malet, is responsible for the vinifications. To date, the wines have been largely uninspiring and overoaked, but there is talent in the cellars.

| 2001 | 87–88 | now–2013 | 2000 | 88 | now–2016 |

ARNAULD ★ ★
HAUT-MÉDOC $15.00

North on the famous Médoc Route de Vin (D2), just past the village of Arcins, is Château Arnauld. This property is owned by the Theil-Roggy family, who long ago established the reputation of Château Poujeaux in nearby Moulis for one of the most distinctive wines of the Médoc. Arnauld is good and solid, but never inspiring.

| 2000 | | 87 | now |

L'ARROSÉE ★ ★ ★ ★
ST.-ÉMILION $28.00–$58.00

This estate's new owner is clearly on the right path to restoring this impeccable *terroir* to its former glory. Top-flight oenologist Gilles Pouquet is overseeing the vinification, and the result is a wine that combines the best of Burgundy and Bordeaux. Old-timers will no doubt remember the brilliant 1986, 1985, 1982, and 1961 . . . all of which remain in fine form. This great *terroir* has unlimited potential and some of the finest wines of St.-Émilion should emerge over the next decade. Pure elegance allied to power.

2006	92–94	2010–2030	2000	89	now–2018
2005	93	2011–2026	1999	86	now
2004	90	now–2021	1998	86	now–2015
2003	91	now–2021	1997	86	now
2002	88	now–2013	1996	87+?	now–2016
2001	86	now–2012	1995	90	now–2012

Past Glories 1990 (93), 1986 (92), 1985 (93), 1982 (93), 1961 (94)

LES ASTERIES ★ ★ ★ ★
ST.-ÉMILION $75.00–$90.00

This 100% new oak–aged cuvée, a blend of 85% Merlot (from 70-year-old vines) and 15% Cabernet Franc, emerges from the visionary self-styled revolutionary Jonathan Malthus, who is better known for the wines he fashions at Le Dôme.

| 2006 | 89–91 | now–2018 | 2005 | 95 | now–2021 |

AURÉLIUS ★ ★ ★
ST.-ÉMILION $25.00

This 4,000-case cuvée of 85% Merlot and 15% Cabernet Franc is the product of the large St.-Émilion cooperative. For a wine produced by a cooperative, Aurélius is well made and worthy of interest. In short, this is a monolithic wine that is not bad but hardly ever inspiring.

2004	75	now	2001	84	now
2003	79	now	2000	87–88	now–2011
2002	78	now			

D'AURILHAC ★ ★ ★
HAUT-MÉDOC $15.00–$25.00

Year in and year out, this is a best buy pick from one of the best-run properties in Haut-Médoc, and well worth its price. Vintages drink well young yet can keep for ten or more years.

| 2005 | 87 | now–2015 | 2003 | 87–88 | now–2014 |
| 2004 | 87 | now–2011 | 2000 | 88 | now–2013 |

AUSONE ★ ★ ★ ★ ★
ST.-ÉMILION
AUSONE $200.00–$750.00; CHAPELLE D'AUSONE $80.00–$100.00

What can be said further about the perfectionist proprietor Alain Vauthier? Here is a man who sees the future. He has taken one of the most hallowed *terroirs* of Bordeaux and pushed it to even higher levels of quality, working like a zealot in the vineyard, making draconian selections in the cellar, thereby reducing what was already a tiny production to produce only the quintessence of this gorgeous old-vine vineyard on the limestone hillsides of St.-Émilion. He has made one of the finest wines of the vintage for the last decade or so, and the accolades he has received worldwide seem only to propel him to greater heights.

The stricter selection process at the estate has resulted in the production of a small quantity of second wine. Readers should not hesitate to check out La Chapelle d'Ausone.

2006 Ausone	95–97	2016–2060
2005 Ausone	100	2020–2100
2004 Ausone	94+	2015–2047
2003 Ausone	100	2020–2090
2002 Ausone	95	2011–2035
2001 Ausone	98	2012–2050+
2000 Ausone	100	2020–2075
1999 Ausone	95	2015–2050
1998 Ausone	94+	2010–2050
1997 Ausone	91	now–2020
1996 Ausone	93+	now–2040
1995 Ausone	93	now–2045
2006 Chapelle d'Ausone	91–93	now–2031+
2005 Chapelle d'Ausone	94	2010–2025
2004 Chapelle d'Ausone	90	now–2026+
2003 Chapelle d'Ausone	93	now–2021+
2002 Chapelle d'Ausone	90	now–2020
2001 Chapelle d'Ausone	90	now–2017
2000 Chapelle d'Ausone	90	now–2025
1999 Chapelle d'Ausone	90	now–2020

Past Glories 1990 (92+), 1988 (91), 1983 (94), 1982 (95+), 1929 (96), 1921 (92), 1900 (94), 1874 (96)

BALESTARD ★★★
BORDEAUX $18.00–$23.00

Vinified under the auspices of Jean-Luc Thunevin of Valandraud fame, Jean-Charles Castex's Balestard is one of the finest generic Bordeaux that money can buy. This wine can compete with many more expensive wines, and thus represents a very good value.

2000	88–89	now		1998	87	now
1999	87	now		1997	87	now

BALESTARD–LA-TONNELLE ★★/★★★
ST.-ÉMILION $25.00–$35.00

I have always regarded Balestard–La-Tonelle as a downsized Lynch-Bages of St.-Émilion. This property, owned by the Capdemourlin family, produces a densely colored, big, deep, rich, and chewy style of wine. The property takes its name from the writings of the 15th-century poet François Villon, who wrote about "drinking this divine nectar which carries the name of Balestard."

2004	84	now–2012		1999	85	now–2012
2003	85	now–2013		1998	86	now–2010
2002	83	now–2011		1997	78	now
2001	86	now–2014		1996	83	now
2000	87	now–2015		1995	86	now

BALTHUS ★★★★
BORDEAUX SUPÉRIEUR $30.00–$35.00

The new baby of proprietor Yves Vatelot, this tiny 7.5-acre vineyard (100% Merlot) is situated near his home estate, Reignac. Planted on gravel, clay, and limestone soils, the wine is put through an experimental vinification program, with the alcoholic and malolactic fermentations taking place in small barrels, aging on lees, and bottling without fining or filtration after

23 months. The winemaking consultant is Michel Rolland. This is very expensive but impeccably made wine that is in the modern style but very impressive.

2005	92–94	now–2023		2003	92	now–2016
2004	90	now–2018		2002	90	now–2013

BARDE-HAUT ★★★★
ST.-ÉMILION $30.00–$40.00

A seriously run estate owned by the Garcin-Cathiard family, with winemaking genius Dr. Alain Raynaud doing the consulting. This overachieving estate is making modern-style, rich St.-Émilions from ripe Merlot and handled with minimal intervention. It is an estate to keep an eye on and offers good value.

2005	93	2010–2030		2000	91	now–2016
2004	89	now–2023		1999	89+	now–2012
2003	88	now–2016		1998	90	now–2018
2002	87	now–2014		1997	90	now–2014
2001	88?	now–2014				

BARET ★★
PESSAC-LÉOGNAN $15.00–$25.00

This is a rather modest Pessac-Léognan estate turning out easygoing wines that are largely uninspiring.

2004	85	now–2011		2000	82–84	now
2003	83	now		1999	86	now–2011
2002	79	now		1998	86	now
2001	81	now				

BARRABAQUE ★★★
CANON-FRONSAC $18.00–$22.00

Château Barrabaque, established in 1747, makes good wine with an occasional exciting performance such as the one in 2005.

2005	88	2011–2020		2000	87	now–2013
2003	86	now–2014		1999	85–86	now
2002	86–88	now		1998	86–87	now–2012
2001	86–87	now–2012				

BATAILLEY ★★★★
PAUILLAC $18.00–$40.00

Batailley, a traditionally styled Pauillac, is often difficult to assess in its youth. It never performs as well young as it does at 10 to 12 years of age. Shrewd buyers should know that the quality of Batailley's wines have improved greatly and that the prices remain reasonable. The wines never seem to hit the majestic heights of the top half dozen Pauillacs, but they age exceptionally well. Recent vintages have shown even greater strength and style.

2005	91	2013–2038+		1999	86	now–2012
2004	90	2009–2025		1998	87	now–2017
2003	88	2009–2025		1997	84	now–2012
2002	86+	now–2013		1996	87	now–2020
2001	87	now–2014		1995	87	now–2015
2000	86?	now–2020				

BEAU-SÉJOUR BÉCOT ★ ★ ★ ★
ST.-ÉMILION $40.00–$65.00

This modern-style St.-Émilion estate, situated on the plateau adjacent to the walled village of St.-Émilion, has performed admirably over the last decade or more. Prior to that, the wines were vegetal, thin, and poorly made, but that has all changed as the dynamic Bécot family has ratcheted up quality by inaugurating a strict selection process and treating the wine like a spoiled child. This is a modern-style, delicous St.-Émilion that, in top vintages, can be enjoyed during its first 10–15 years.

2007	86–88	now–2017	2003	93	now–2015
2006	90–92	2010–2022	2002	88	now–2014
2005	94	2010–2025	2001	90	now–2017
2004	91	now–2018	2000	93	2010–2023

BEAU-SITE ★ ★
ST.-ESTÈPHE $15.00

Owned by the well-known Bordeaux family of Pierre Castéja, these wines are generally pleasant but uninspiring. They are distributed exclusively through the *négociant* firm of Borie-Manoux.

2003	87	now–2014	2000	85	now–2010

BEAULIEU COMTES DE TASTES ★ ★ ★ ★
BORDEAUX SUPÉRIEUR $15.00–$25.00

This estate makes a handsome claret, an insider's wine that is well balanced, with ripe tannins, good, sweet fruit, and well above its humble pedigree and modest pricing. This is an estate for people who want to drink fine Bordeaux at a realistic price.

2005	89	now–2012	2002	87	now
2004	87	now	2001	87	now
2003	89	now–2013	2000	88	now

BEAUMONT ★ ★/★ ★
HAUT-MÉDOC $15.00

This very large property seems to have improved somewhat in quality, but it is still a largely uninspiring cru bourgeois in the Médoc.

2004	86	now–2012	2000	87	now–2010
2001	86–87	now			

BEAUREGARD ★ ★ ★
POMEROL $28.00–$48.00

Though the Beauregard wines remain precocious, they are more seductive and more consistent lately, with more flesh and power than before. The 2005 is a candidate for the finest wine produced at this château. These wines are fairly priced for a Pomerol appellation.

2005	90	now–2021	1999	88	now–2014
2004	88	now–2019	1998	88	now–2016
2003	86	now–2012	1997	87	now
2002	87–88	now–2012	1996	87	now
2001	87	now–2013	1995	87	now–2010
2000	88	now–2016			

BEAUSÉJOUR-DUFFAU ★★★★
ST.-ÉMILION $45.00–$85.00

At each tasting of the prodigious 1990, one of the greatest wines ever made, I ask myself why this estate cannot come close to achieving that level of quality in other top vintages. Regardless, Beauséjour-Duffau is known for its very high quality wines, especially since the mid-1980s. They remain some of the most complex, ethereal St.-Émilions, generally dense and powerful but reserved and austere, with a mineral character. They are not for those unable to defer gratification, as they usually require a decade of cellaring before their tannins begin to melt. The 2005 is unquestionably the most compelling wine made at this estate since their perfect 1990.

2005	91	2015–2030+	1999	87	now–2018
2004	90	2009–2023	1998	89	now–2016
2003	89	now–2020	1997	85	now
2002	88	now–2015	1996	87?	now–2015
2001	90	now–2019	1995	88	now–2025
2000	92	2013–2025+			

Past Glories 1990 (100)

BEAU SOLEIL ★★/★★★
POMEROL $25.00–$50.00

The 2000 Beau Soleil was the last vintage produced by Jean-Michel Arcaute before his tragic drowning in 2001. Located off the coast of Arcachon, the estate today produces soundly made Pomerols that are rich and fruity but not terribly complex.

2001	89	now–2014	1997	85	now
2000	88	now–2016	1996	85–86	now
1999	87	now–2010	1995	87	now
1998	87	now–2011			

BEL-AIR ★★/★★★
LALANDE DE POMEROL $15.00–$22.00

This is a traditional style of Lalande de Pomerol that seems to be largely admired by old-timers and reactionary wine writers who tend to favor very austere, excessively tannic wine.

2000	84–86	now	1998	87	now
1999	76–79	now			

BEL-AIR GRANDE CUVÉE ★★★
BORDEAUX SUPÉRIEUR $10.00–$15.00

Bel-Air Grand Cuvée is one of the best of the Bordeaux Supérieurs. The estate is run by the Despagne family, who are among the most innovative and visionary families of Bordeaux, turning out a bevy of inexpensive but impeccably made wines. A joy for frugal consumers.

2005	87	now–2011	2000	87–88	now

BEL-AIR LA ROYÈRE ★★★
PREMIÈRES CÔTES DE BLAYE $18.00

This is a serious "little" wine made with the consulting assistance of Valandraud's Jean-Luc Thunevin.

2005	87	now–2010	2000	85–86	now
2003	87–89	now–2010	1999	82–85	now
2001	85–86	now	1997	85–86	now

BELAIR * *
ST.-ÉMILION $35.00–$45.00

The tiny vineyard of Belair is jointly owned by Pascal Delbeck and Christian Moueix. Delbeck used to make the wines of Ausone. His approach is to make mineral-laced wines that are relatively light, restrained, and subtle. He is very outspoken about Bordeaux wines with too much concentration and power, so this is an intelligent choice for readers looking for lighter-style wines from famous properties that underperform. That said, look for the Moueix influence to bulk up the wines with more body and flavor. This is a great, great *terroir* that remains a conspicuous underachiever.

2005	87	2012–2022	2001	86	now–2014
2004	78	now–2017	2000	87	now–2020
2003	88	now–2016	1997	86	now–2010
2002	84	now–2020	1996	86	now–2012

BELGRAVE * * *
HAUT-MÉDOC $20.00–$35.00

After a long period in the qualitative doldrums, Belgrave is producing much better wines. The proprietor, the Dourthe firm, has been making slow but persistent progress in upgrading the quality of this estate.

2005	89	2012–2020	2000	88	now–2014
2004	88	now–2017	1999	86	now–2010
2003	89	now–2020	1998	87	now–2015
2002	87–88	now–2013	1997	81–84	now
2001	87	now–2014			

BELLE-VUE * * * *
HAUT-MÉDOC $14.00–$19.00

This is another of the overachieving estates in Haut-Médoc that is not a classified growth and does not have much of a reputation, but insiders are flocking to buy this wine, an extremely well made blend of Cabernet Sauvignon, Merlot, and Petit Verdot. It is a delicious wine to drink young yet seems to have the ability to age for five to eight or more years in the top vintages.

2005	88	now–2016	2000	89	now
2004	88	now–2013	1999	87	now
2003	88	now–2014	1998	87	now
2002	88	now–2015	1997	85	now
2001	87–91	now–2012			

BELLEFONT-BELCIER * * * *
ST.-ÉMILION $20.00–$45.00

Bellefont-Belcier is another St.-Émilion estate that long made mediocre wines and now seems to have improved dramatically in quality. It is never going to be one of the best estates of the region, but the wines today show good, spicy, cedary notes with ripe fruit and silky tannins, and the prices remain reasonable. The 2005 is a revelation.

2006	89–91	2010–2020	2000	90	now–2016
2005	94	2012–2042	1999	87?	now–2011
2004	88	now–2019	1998	87	now–2010
2003	88–90	now–2015	1997	84	now
2002	85	now–2011	1996	87	now
2001	88	now–2012	1995	87	now

BELLEGRAVE ★ ★ ★
POMEROL $23.00–$28.00

Jean-Marie Bouldy's wines are generally soft and easy to drink and understand, with seductive fruit. They are meant to be consumed in their youth. Prices are reasonable for the appellation.

2005	89	now–2022	1998	86	now
2001	86	now–2012	1997	87	now
2000	88	now–2015	1996	84	now

BELLEVUE ★ ★ ★ ★/★ ★ ★ ★ ★
ST.-ÉMILION $30.00–$75.00

An up-and-coming potential superstar, this south-facing vineyard of 15+ acres (40-year-old vines) planted on pure limestone (near Beau-Séjour Bécot and Beauséjour-Duffau) is impeccably run and farmed biodynamically by St.-Émilion's and Pomerol's highly sought after wunderkinder Nicolas Thienpont and Stéphane Derenoncourt. Their debut vintage was the brilliant 2000. A château to follow closely! The estate was sold to Angélus in 2008.

2006	92–94	2012–2025	2002	87	now–2017
2005	94+	2012–2028+	2001	88	now–2014
2004	88?	2011–2027	2000	95	now–2020
2003	93+	2011–2025+			

BELLEVUE MONDOTTE ★ ★ ★ ★ ★
ST.-ÉMILION $150.00–$175.00

The quintessential *garage* wine, Bellevue Mondotte emerges from a five-acre vineyard acquired by Chantal and Gérard Perse in 2002. Situated on pure limestone above the Perses' two other vineyards, Pavie and Pavie-Decesse, the average age of the vines is 45 years, and the blend tends to be dominated by Merlot (90%) with tiny dollops of Cabernet Franc and Cabernet Sauvignon. A prodigious wine of extraordinary intensity, it differs from Pavie in that it is more open-knit, expansive, and ripe, and not as strikingly intense in minerality. This wine is difficult to find but is spectacular in its richness and drama, certainly since its acquisition by the Perse family. It is one of Bordeaux's greatest wines.

2006	96–100	2012–2042+	2003	98	2009–2036
2005	99	2017–2057	2002	91	now–2017+
2004	95	2010–2032	2001	94+	now–2022

BELLEVUE DE TAYAC ★ ★ ★
MARGAUX $20.00–$30.00

I know little about this property except that they produced an impressive 2005 that sells for a song. It appears to be an estate to watch.

2005				89	now–2021

BELLISLE-MONDOT ★★★
ST.-ÉMILION $15.00–$25.00

Not to be confused with Bellevue-Mondotte (the luxury estate of Gérard Perse), the Bellisle-Mondotte vineyard sits on the other side of the Mondotte *terroir,* with a cool, windswept, north-facing exposition. This well-placed property is to be taken seriously. Vinification is supervised by St.-Émilion's leading revolutionary, Jean-Luc Thunevin.

2005	90	now–2021		1999	88	now–2012
2002	88	now–2015		1998	82	now–2010
2001	85	now–2011		1997	85	now
2000	90+	now–2017				

BEL ORME TRONQUOY DE LALANDE ★★
HAUT-MÉDOC $15.00–$20.00

I remember a profound 1945 Bel Orme Tronquoy de Lalande drunk on New Year's Day 1985. I also have good notes on the 1982, 1989, and 1990. But generally, my experience with this property, located in the very northern part of the Médoc, has been uninspiring. Hopefully, the changing ownership in 2006, when it was purchased along with nearby Château Montrose, will signal increased quality. The 2006 looked good.

2006	85–87	now–2015		2000	87	now–2013
2005	85	now–2016				

BERLIQUET ★★★
ST.-ÉMILION $25.00–$50.00

This is another St.-Émilion estate that has improved considerably over recent years. The property has a good exposition, and the wines represent a synthesis of traditional and modern winemaking. In most vintages, Berliquet can age nicely for 10 to 15 years.

2005	89	now–2021		2000	90	now–2020
2004	85	now–2012		1999	88	now–2013
2003	88	now–2014		1998	89	now–2016
2002	87	now–2015		1997	88	now–2012
2001	89	now–2012				

BERNADOTTE ★★★
HAUT-MÉDOC $12.00–$20.00

This up-and-coming estate is making better and better wines and merits attention, although its affiliation with the owners of Pichon-Lalande will ensure that it always sells for a relatively hefty price.

2004	86–88	now–2014		1999	86	now–2012
2003	90	now–2016		1998	87	now–2011
2002	85	now–2011		1997	85–87	now
2001	87–88	now–2012		1996	85?	now
2000	89	now–2011				

BERTINEAU ST.-VINCENT ★★★
LALANDE DE POMEROL $15.00–$25.00

This property owned by Dany and Michel Rolland consistently produces one of the finest values in Lalande de Pomerol.

2005	88	now–2012		2000	88	now–2010
2004	87	now–2011		1999	87	now
2003	87	now		1998	87	now
2002	86–88	now		1997	85	now
2001	87–88	now–2010				

BEYCHEVELLE ★ ★ ★
ST.-JULIEN $25.00–$55.00

Although the last several vintages exhibit considerable promise, Beychevelle remains the most conspicuous underachiever in the otherwise brilliant appellation of St.-Julien. The wines of Beychevelle are generally soft and smooth, and accessible in their youth. The most recent vintages have shown improvement and, though they are fully mature by 10 years of age, they have the requisite stuffing to withstand 15 or more years of cellaring. Shrewd consumers should note that Beychevelle is not one of St.-Julien's most expensive crus classés.

2006	90–92	2011–2028		2000	91	now–2020
2005	90	2014–2025		1999	86	now–2012
2004	89	now–2022		1998	87	now–2016
2003	90	2009–2022		1997	78	now
2002	86	now–2013		1996	86	now–2012
2001	88	now–2013		1995	85	now–2012

Past Glories 1986 (92), 1982 (91), 1953 (92), 1928 (97)

LA BIENFAISANCE ★ ★ ★ ★
ST.-ÉMILION $35.00–$55.00

This is an up-and-coming estate, thanks to the efforts of proprietor Patrick Baseden and his winemaking guru-consultant, Stéphane Derenoncourt.

2005	92	now–2022+		2003	90	now–2018+
2004	89	now–2019		2001	87	now–2014

BOLAIRE ★ ★ ★ ★
BORDEAUX SUPÉRIEUR $25.00–$28.00

Although 2003 is Bolaire's debut vintage, it appears this will be a serious estate that consumers should keep an eye on. Moreover, it will be an original one, given the incredibly high percentage of Petit Verdot (39%) planted in the vineyard. The remaining vines include Merlot and Cabernet Sauvignon.

2005	89	now–2014		2003	85	now–2013
2004	88	now–2017				

LE BON PASTEUR ★ ★ ★ ★
POMEROL $45.00–$60.00

Le Bon Pasteur is the home estate of Dany and Michel Rolland, both brilliant oenologists. This is not one of the finest *terroirs* of Pomerol, but because of the talent of the proprietors, the wines overachieve in just about every vintage, and there have been some years, such as 1982, 1990, 2000, and 2005, when they actually surpass some of the greatest wines of Pomerol. The wines are usually drinkable within three to four years of the vintage but capable of lasting two decades.

2006	90–92	now–2023+		2000	94	now–2017
2005	94	2012–2037+		1999	90+	now–2016
2004	90	now–2023		1998	91	now–2016
2003	89	now–2020		1997	88	now–2010
2002	88	now–2013		1996	88	now–2011
2001	92	now–2017		1995	89	now–2012

Past Glories 1990 (91), 1989 (90), 1982 (96)

BONALGUE ★ ★ ★
POMEROL $16.00–$24.00

Bonalgue, a small, impressively run estate, is consistently one of the better values in Pomerol, an appellation that has become frightfully expensive. This is a classic Pomerol, fruity, savory, and mouth-filling.

2005	88	now–2018		1998	87	now–2011
2004	87	now–2014		1997	86	now
2001	87–89	now–2015		1996	86	now
2000	89	now–2012		1995	86	now
1999	87	now				

BONNET ★ ★/★ ★
BORDEAUX $15.00–$25.00

Bonnet is the home estate of André Lurton, one of the most influential wine personalities of Bordeaux. This property makes a very good value, both white and red Bordeaux that sell for a song, and because of its affiliation with Lurton it is always a wine of quality and character even though the price remains humble.

2004	83	now
2003	85	now
2001	86	now
2000	85	now
2005 Divinus	89	now–2015
2000 Divinus de Bonnet	87	now–2011
2005 Réserve	87	now–2010
2000 Réserve	86–87	now
1998 Réserve	83–85	now
1997 Réserve	84	now

LE BOSCQ ★ ★ ★
ST.-ESTÈPHE $32.00

Le Boscq is an attractive, solid performer making chunky yet fruit-driven wines that represent good value.

2005	87	2009–2015		2003	87	now–2012
2004	84–86	now				

BOURGNEUF-VAYRON ★ ★ ★
POMEROL $30.00–$55.00

Bourgneuf-Vayron seems to be exploiting the full potential of its vineyard, so consumers better watch out. They should know, however, that some vintages have exhibited a green pepper character that may not appeal to everyone. In general, this is a relatively rustic style of Pomerol that is powerful, muscular, and masculine. Certainly recent vintages demonstrate more charm and ripeness.

2005	84	2011–2026	1998	89+?	now–2020
2004	87?	2010–2018	1997	87?	now–2012
2001	90	now–2015	1996	87+?	now–2012
2000	89+	now–2018	1995	89	now–2014
1999	87?	now–2014+			

BOUSCAT ★ ★ ★
BORDEAUX SUPÉRIEUR $18.00–$32.00

This terrific Bordeaux Supérieur, which behaves like a grand cru classé, is made from Merlot, Cabernet Franc, Cabernet Sauvignon, and surprisingly, some Malbec. The consulting oenologist is the well-known Claude Gros, one of the most talented men in France. Sadly, production is small, but for consumers lucky enough to find a bottle, it is a knockout value.

2005 Cuvée La Gargone	89	now–2012
2004 Cuvée La Gargone	87	now–2013
2003 Cuvée La Gargone	90	now–2013
2002 Cuvée La Gargone	88	now–2013
2001 Cuvée La Gargone	87	now
2000 Cuvée La Gargone	88	now
2005 Les Portes de l'Âme	92	now–2017
2004 Les Portes de l'Âme	89+	now–2011
2003 Les Portes de l'Âme	91	now–2016

BOUSCAUT ★ ★
PESSAC-LÉOGNAN $20.00–$45.00

This property, one of the few among all the classified growths of Graves, remains content to turn out unexciting white and red wines. As a younger generation of the Lurton family have taken over Bouscaut, the quality has inched up a bit, but this is still one of the most dramatic underachievers in all of Bordeaux.

2004	86	now–2014	2006 Blanc	86–88	now–2015
2003	85	now–2012	2005 Blanc	87	now–2018
2001	88	now–2018	2003 Blanc	85	now–2010
2000	86	now–2015	2002 Blanc	84	now–2012
1999	82	now–2012	2001 Blanc	86	now–2013
1998	75	now–2012	2000 Blanc	84	now–2011

BOUTISSE ★ ★ ★
ST.-ÉMILION $35.00–$42.00

This is one of the properties of proprietor Christian Dauriac that is making monolithic, corpulent, chunky, but flavorful wines.

2003	87–89+	now–2014+	1998	85–86	now
2002	87–89	now–2013	1997	84	now
1999	82–84	now			

BOYD-CANTENAC ★★★★
MARGAUX $25.00–$50.00

This estate has enjoyed a renaissance. The best wines I have tasted from Boyd-Cantenac have been since 2000, but the wines remain excellent values, since the new level of quality has not yet been perceived worldwide.

2006	88–90	2012–2024	2000	88+	now–2018
2005	92	2015–2030+	1999	86	now–2012
2004	91	2009–2022	1998	86	now–2011
2003	89+	2011–2026	1997	78	now
2002	90	2010–2020+	1996	88	2010–2020
2001	90	now–2017	1995	87	now–2018

BRANAIRE-DUCRU ★★★★
ST.-JULIEN $25.00–$50.00

Branaire-Ducru's offerings are always distinctive, fragrant St.-Juliens. The wines produced in the 1980s were inconsistent, but the construction of a new cellar as well as the introduction of a new winemaking team and a second label have resulted in strong efforts since the mid-'90s. One cannot underestimate Patrick Maroteaux, the energetic administrator, who is past president of Bordeaux's Union des Grands Crus. I thought the 2003 and 2005 Branaire-Ducru were among the finest wines ever made at this estate.

2006	92–94	2012–2025	2000	93	now–2025
2005	95	2013–2030+	1999	89	now–2017
2004	90	now–2023	1998	89	now–2016
2003	95	2009–2026	1997	87	now
2002	90	now–2020+	1996	89	now–2018
2001	91	now–2015	1995	90	now–2018

Past Glories 1989 (92), 1982 (90), 1975 (91)

BRANDA ★★/★★★
PUISSÉGUIN-ST.-ÉMILION $15.00–$18.00

Branda is a reliable wine from this largely forgotten satellite appellation. Made with the assistance of St.-Émilion's superstar winemaking guru Jean-Luc Thunevin, this wine usually represents good value.

2005	87	now–2013	2000	88	now–2011
2003	87–89	now–2013	1999	87	now
2001	87	now–2009	1998	88	now

BRANE-CANTENAC ★★★★
MARGAUX $30.00–$50.00

Henri Lurton has resurrected this estate over recent vintages, particularly since 1998, with the 2000 and 2005 being its greatest successes since 1961. This is another example of a Margaux estate that is making better and better wines because of more intense work in the vineyard, stricter selection both in the vineyard and in the cellars, and a meticulous vinification. These are now gloriously perfumed wines of brilliant finesse and elegance.

2005	94	2010–2035	1999	89+	now–2016
2004	90	2009–2022+	1998	88	now–2017
2003	91	now–2024	1997	84	now
2002	89	now–2016	1996	88	now–2016

| 2001 | 89 | now–2014 | | 1995 | 86 | now–2012 |
| 2000 | 92 | now–2020+ | | | | |

BRANON ★★★★/★★★★★
PESSAC-LÉOGNAN $65.00–$135.00

Perhaps the first garage wine from the Graves region, the production of this Merlot–Cabernet Franc blend averages 500 cases. The wine for Branon is produced from a special parcel of vines that were originally part of the Haut-Bergey estate. Alain Raynaud is now the wine-making consultant for all of the Garcin family's wines (Haut-Bergey and Clos l'Église in Pomerol, Barde-Haut in St.-Émilion, and Branon in Pessac-Léognan). The 2005 is the finest effort from Branon since 2000.

2006	90–94	now–2028+		2002	88	now–2012
2005	96	2012–2042		2001	91	now–2017
2004	91	2009–2020+		2000	96	2009–2025
2003	88?	now–2014				

BRILLETTE ★★★
MOULIS $18.00

The wines from this vast 374-acre estate are not yet well known, but the quality of the wine-making is high. This is a wine for those who admire a hefty dose of oak in their wines. It is best drunk within a decade of the vintage.

| 2001 | 86 | now | | 2000 | 87 | now–2012 |

BRISSON ★★★
CÔTES DE CASTILLON $10.00–$20.00

Brisson, an exuberant, fruity, velvety-textured wine, is consistently one of my favorite sleepers of the vintage and a candidate for the best value in terms of pennies for points.

2005	88	now–2014		1998	88	now
2003	87	now–2011		1997	87	now
2001	85–86	now		1996	85–87	now
2000	87	now		1995	87	now
1999	87	now				

BROWN ★★★
PESSAC-LÉOGNAN $22.00–$28.00

Brown is an underrated estate that can produce strong efforts in both red and white wines. Readers should take more note of this estate, making elegant yet very flavorful wines from Pessac-Léognan.

2001	88–90	now–2012		1998	87	now
2000	89	now–2015		2001 Blanc	89	now–2011
1999	87	now				

LA CABANNE ★★
POMEROL $15.00–$20.00

La Cabanne is run by the Estager family. The vineyard is highly morcellated (multiple parcels), but the château itself is situated in the heart of Pomerol, not far from the famed Château Trotanoy. The quality is at best average.

2000	83–86?	now–2011		1996	81–83	now
1999	83–85	now		1995	86	now
1998	84–87	now				

CADET-BON ★ ★
ST.-ÉMILION $25.00

This estate is finally making a qualitative comeback now that Stéphane Derenoncourt is consulting. Beware of anything older than 2005.

2005	90	2011–2020+

CADET PIOLA ★ ★ ★
ST.-ÉMILION $20.00–$35.00

After decades of rather burly, tannic, hard wines, Cadet Piola seems to be building more charm, finesse, and suppleness into their efforts. The wines never short-change consumers on flavor and are certainly quite ageworthy.

2005	89	now–2021		2000	86	now–2013
2004	82	now–2015		1996	83	now
2003	88?	now–2017		1995	85	now–2012
2001	86–87	now–2013				

CALON-SÉGUR ★ ★ ★ ★
ST.-ESTÈPHE $28.00–$105.00

This estate, which possesses one of the greatest *terroirs* of Bordeaux, is faring particularly well under the administration of Madame Gasqueton. Vintages since the mid-1990s have been exceptionally high in quality, especially the very top vintages. Moreover, prices at Calon-Ségur are extremely reasonable, particularly when compared to its nearby competitors, Montrose and Cos d'Estournel. Despite the relatively high percentage of Merlot (usually around 40% or more), these wines are very slow to evolve and blossom but are candidates for aging for 30+ years.

2006	90–93	2012–2025		2000	94	2012–2040
2005	92+	2015–2045		1999	87	now–2012
2004	89	now–2018		1998	89+	now–2030
2003	94	2009–2030		1997	80	now
2002	89	now–2017		1996	92	2009–2028
2001	90	now–2019		1995	92+	now–2035

Past Glories 1990 (90), 1988 (91), 1982 (94)

CAMBON LA PELOUSE ★ ★ ★/★ ★ ★ ★
HAUT-MÉDOC $12.00–$17.00

This large, 150-acre vineyard in Macau, not far from the well-known classified-growth vineyards of Cantemerle and Giscours, has come of age lately, producing fine wines that tend to be a blend of 60% Merlot, 30% Cabernet Sauvignon, and 10% Cabernet Franc. Part of the high-quality Haut-Médoc group of châteaux called Biturica, it is one of the best values in Bordeaux today.

2005	89	now–2014		2001	89	now–2012
2004	86	now–2013		2000	88	now
2003	87	now–2012		1999	86	now
2002	86	now–2010				

CAMENSAC ★★★
HAUT-MÉDOC $18.00–$24.00

Camensac is among the least known of the 1855 classified growths. No doubt its location, well inland and west of St.-Julien in the commune of St.-Laurent, partly explains the relative obscurity, and the wines from this estate were largely mediocre until the Forner brothers purchased it in 1965 and set about the expensive task of replanting the vineyards and renovating the *chai* and winemaking facilities. The wines of Camensac possess good concentration and a straightforward, foursquare style.

2004	87–89	now–2021	1999	87	now–2015
2003	89	now–2016	1998	86	now–2010
2002	86	now–2013	1997	86	now
2001	86	now–2012	1996	85	now
2000	89	now–2015			

CANON ★★★/★★★★
ST.-ÉMILION $45.00–$60.00

This famous property on the hillsides outside medieval St.-Émilion has rebounded after a series of miserable performances in the mid-1990s. Though the wines are not of the quality one would expect from a premier cru of St.-Émilion, they have started to improve, especially since 1998. The 2005 is the finest Canon produced under the Chanel ownership.

2006	89–92	2010–2024	2000	89	now–2020
2005	91	2012–2025	1999	87	now–2013
2004	88	now–2019	1998	88	now–2015
2003	89	now–2018	1997	82	now
2002	89	now–2020	1996	80	now–2015
2001	88+	now–2014	1995	74	now

Past Glories 1989 (92), 1982 (94), 1959 (95)

CANON DE BREM ★★★
CANON-FRONSAC $14.00–$28.00

This 18-acre vineyard was purchased in 2000 from the Moueix family by Jean Halley (founder of the Promodès supermarket chain) along with the slightly larger Fronsac estate of La Dauphine. Since then, the wines have completely changed in quality. In 2006 this estate became extinct, and production was merged into La Dauphine.

2005	89	now–2016	1999	87	now–2012+
2004	86–87	2009–2021	1998	88	now–2015
2003	87	now–2022	1997	86	now
2002	80	now	1996	78	now
2001	88+	now–2019	1995	86	now–2010
2000	87	now–2011			

CANON–LA GAFFELIÈRE ★★★★
ST.-ÉMILION $45.00–$115.00

Since being brought back to life in the late 1980s by the talented Stephan von Neipperg, this estate has enjoyed an unparalleled succession of terrific vintages. This exuberant wine is made in a forward, opulent, sumptuous style and is meant to be drunk in its first 15 or so years. It is a very rich, spicy, lush, and savory wine that shows very well when young.

2006	91–94	2011–2024	2000	95	now–2022
2005	94	2010–2030	1999	92	now–2016
2004	91	now–2023	1998	93	now–2022
2003	89	now–2016	1997	90	now–2015
2002	88	now–2013	1996	90	now–2020
2001	92	now–2013	1995	91+	now–2020

Past Glories 1994 (90), 1990 (92)

CANTEMERLE ★★★
HAUT-MÉDOC $20.00–$38.00

Although quality here has been decidedly mixed over recent vintages, this property deserves a higher ranking than its 1855 classification. Cantemerle exhibits a lighter style, with rich, supple fruitiness and an intensely fragrant bouquet. The resurrection in quality started with the 2005, after some listless performances.

2006	90–92	2009–2020+	2000	88	now–2014
2005	90	2011–2022	1999	79	now–2012
2004	87	now–2017	1998	84	now–2011
2003	85	now–2016	1997	85–86	now
2002	81	now–2010	1996	87	now–2015
2001	87	now–2016	1995	86	now–2010

Past Glories 1989 (91), 1983 (91), 1961 (92), 1953 (94)

CANTENAC-BROWN ★★★
MARGAUX $25.00–$46.00

If the 2006 is any indication, the new ownership might well get this property back to form. The wines are always good in color, muscular, tannic, big, and rich, but they lack charm, complexity, and allure. There is certainly no shortage of material in the wine, but some finesse and elegance are desired. Hopefully the uninspiring past performances are just that.

2006	90–92	2015–2030	2000	90	now–2018
2005	87+?	2012–2027	1999	89	now–2014
2004	86	now–2014	1998	88	now–2016
2003	87	now–2017	1997	85	now–2014
2002	86	now–2015	1996	86	now–2015
2001	88	now–2014	1995	80	now–2010

CAP DE FAUGÈRES ★★★★
CÔTES DE CASTILLON $13.00–$18.00

This is one of the outstanding estates in the increasingly fashionable region of the Côtes de Castillon, just to the east of St.-Émilion. Adjacent to the Faugères vineyard, which is also making super St.-Émilion, Cap de Faugères has produced delicious wines over recent years. Michel Rolland is the consulting oenologist.

2005	89	now–2016	2001	89	now–2011
2004	88	now–2012	2000	89	now–2015
2003	90–92	now–2015	1999	87	now
2002	87	now–2011	1998	88	now–2011

CAP DE MOURLIN ★★/★★★
ST.-ÉMILION $20.00–$24.00

The Capdemourlin family have been property owners in St.-Émilion for more than five centuries. Until 1983 there were two grand cru St.-Émilions with the name Cap de Mourlin, one owned by Jean Capdemourlin and one by Jacques Capdemourlin. These two estates have been united since 1983, ending the confusion for consumers. This is a chunky, rustic, fruity wine.

2001	86–87	now–2012	1999	84	now
2000	87	now–2014	1998	84	now

CARBONNIEUX ★★★★
PESSAC-LÉOGNAN $18.00–$38.00

This Pessac-Léognan property has come on strongly over recent vintages. Although Carbonnieux's white wines have always been among Bordeaux's finest, the reds have taken on more weight and richness, particularly since 2003. For some reason, the top vintages of red wine at Carbonnieux remind me of grand cru reds from the Côte de Beaune in Burgundy. This is Bordeaux with a seductive and sensual personality.

2006	90–92	2010–2025+	1996	86	now–2009
2005	91	2013–2026	1995	87	now–2011
2004	90	now–2022	2006 Blanc	86–88	now–2016
2003	89	now–2021	2005 Blanc	93	now–2025
2002	86	now–2013	2003 Blanc	91	now–2012
2001	89	now–2014	2001 Blanc	91	now–2018+
2000	89	now–2018	2000 Blanc	87	now–2015
1999	86	now–2010	1999 Blanc	87–88	now–2010
1998	87	now–2013	1998 Blanc	90	now–2016
1997	81	now	1997 Blanc	86	now

LES CARMES HAUT-BRION ★★★★
PESSAC-LÉOGNAN $30.00–$75.00

Readers looking for Bordeaux at its most elegant with a strong Cabernet Franc personality, à la Cheval Blanc, should check out the finesse-filled, delicate offerings from Les Carmes Haut-Brion, a little treasure tucked beside Château Haut-Brion in the Bordeaux suburb known as Pessac. These wines are often difficult to judge in their first decade, as they appear light in their youth but tend to put on weight with *élevage* and bottle age.

2006	88–90	2011–2022	2000	94	now–2020
2005	92	2010–2025	1999	89	now–2012
2004	89+	now–2021	1998	90	now–2020
2003	89	now–2017	1997	87	now
2002	90	now–2015	1996	87	now
2001	89	now–2016	1995	87	now

Past Glories 1959 (93)

LE CARRÉ
★★★ / ST.-ÉMILION $50.00

The 2005 is the debut offering of this *garagiste* wine from a vineyard next to Clos Fourtet. A modern-style wine with no shortage of personality, it is a noteworthy new addition to the ever-expanding portfolio of Château Teyssier's Jonathan Malthus.

2006	90–92	2009–2019+	2005	92	2009–2020

CARSIN ★★/★★★
PREMIÈRES CÔTES $12.00–$16.00

This is a straightforward, fruity, almost Beaujolais-style Bordeaux that is always well made and ideal for drinking in its first three to four years.

2005	87	now

CASSAGNE HAUT-CANON ★★
CANON-FRONSAC $14.00–$25.00

This estate is something of a one-hit wonder, having produced a marvelous 1989 but nothing before or since that ever reached the level of that particular vintage. The lackluster performance is hard to understand, because the property is well located with ideal soils and a good south-southeast exposition.

2005	84–85	now–2012	1996	76–78	now
2000	87–88	now–2014	1995	85–87	now
1997	81–83	now			

DU CAUZE ★★★
ST.-EMILION $18.00–$25.00

These are solid, somewhat monolithic, but well-oaked and concentrated wines with good muscle and St.-Émilion character. Proprietor Bruno Laporte produces this wine from a clay, limestone, and gravel vineyard and sells it at realistic prices.

2003	88–90	now–2014	1998	87–88	now–2011
2001	87	now–2014	1997	82	now
2000	88	now–2012	1995	85	now
1999	86	now			

CERTAN-GIRAUD ★★★
POMEROL $30.00–$40.00

Certan-Giraud is a now defunct property that has been split into two estates owned by Christian Moueix. (See Certan-Marzelle and Hosanna.) This entry is for historical purposes only. The older vintages that may show up at auction under this label are probably a risky purchase because of the irregular quality.

1998	85	now	1996	84	now
1997	86	now	1995	87	now

CERTAN-MARZELLE ★★★★
POMEROL $55.00–$75.00

This is an eight-acre parcel of what was formerly known as Certan-Giraud that proprietor Christian Moueix divided into two parcels, with the oldest vines and better parcels becoming Hosanna and the balance Certan-Marzelle. The latter part of the vineyard produces a 100% Merlot cuvée meant to be open-knit, seductive, and ideal for drinking early on.

2006	91–93	now–2027	2002	87	now–2010
2005	89	now–2019	2001	92	now–2014
2004	90	now–2017	2000	90	now–2014
2003	89	now–2014			

CERTAN DE MAY ★★★★
POMEROL $65.00–$125.00

After producing some exceptional wines in the 1980s (1988, 1987, 1986, 1985, and 1982), this property went through an irregular period, but it appears to be making a comeback since Michel Rolland was brought in as a consultant in 2004. Rolland had full responsibility for the 2004 vintage, but 2005 marks a return to the glory years of the 1980s. This property, sandwiched between Pétrus, Vieux-Château-Certan, and Lafleur, has an exquisite *terroir* and unlimited potential.

2006	91–94	2010–2030	2000	91	now–2018
2005	92	2010–2025	1999	87	now–2012
2004	89+	2010–2022	1998	86?	now–2010
2003	88	now–2018	1997	86	now
2002	85	now–2012	1996	87?	now–2015
2001	87?	now–2014	1995	90+	now–2020

Past Glories 1990 (91), 1988 (92+), 1986 (90), 1985 (94), 1982 (96+), 1981 (90), 1979 (93), 1945 (96)

DE CHAMBRUN ★★★★
LALANDE DE POMEROL $25.00–$38.00

Along with La Fleur de Boüard, de Chambrun is the most impressive wine currently being produced in Lalande de Pomerol. However, unlike La Fleur de Boüard, Chambrun's production is minuscule—only 3.5 acres of vines. Under the inspired leadership of Jean-Philippe Janoueix, this estate is emerging as one of the superstars of this bucolic appellation, a source of up-front, delicious, Pomerol-styled wines that sell for reasonable prices.

2005	89	2015–2020	1999	88	now–2012
2004	88–90	now–2020	1998	90	now–2012
2003	89	now–2016	1997	88	now–2010
2001	89	now–2015	1996	87	now–2010
2000	90–92	now–2017			

CHANTEGRIVE ★★/★★★
GRAVES $15.00–$19.00

Among lower-priced Graves, Chantegrive usually represents a very good value in both white and red wines.

2004	83	now–2011
2001	87	now–2012
2000	88	now–2012
1999	85–86	now
1998	86–87	now
2005 Cuvée Caroline (blanc)	85–87	now
2001 Cuvée Caroline (blanc)	89	now
1999 Cuvée Caroline (blanc)	86–87	now

CHARMAIL ★★★★
HAUT-MÉDOC $16.00–$42.00

Along with Sociando-Mallet, this property has emerged as one of the superstars in the Haut-Médoc firmament. The 72-acre vineyard is planted on clay and gravelly soils, not far from the Gironde. What makes Charmail so interesting is the 15-day cold maceration at an incredibly low 5°C, followed by four-week maceration, aging on the lees, and natural bottling. The wine is always one of the blackest in the Médoc, an intriguing blend of 40% to 50% Merlot, 25% to 30% Cabernet Sauvignon, hefty doses of Cabernet Franc, and a dollop of Petit Verdot.

2005	90	now–2018	1999	88	now–2012
2004	89	now–2017	1998	88	now–2013
2003	88–90	now–2015	1997	88	now
2002	88	now–2012	1996	89	now–2010
2001	87	now–2011	1995	88	now
2000	93	now–2014			

LES CHARMES-GODARD ★ ★ ★
CÔTES DE FRANCS $20.00–$25.00

A well-run, little-known estate making competent reds as well as charming whites, this small property is located in the obscure but up-and-coming satellite appellation of Côtes de Francs.

2005 Blanc	87	now–2012

CHASSE-SPLEEN ★ ★ ★/★ ★ ★ ★
MOULIS $18.00–$35.00

One of the two finest estates of Moulis (the other being Poujeaux), Chasse-Spleen's large vineyard is planted with 70% Cabernet Sauvignon, 25% Merlot, and 5% Petit Verdot. During the 1970s and '80s, Chasse-Spleen often produced wines that were as good as a third growth, and prices jumped as consumers began to realize that the wine was undervalued. However, the wines have been inconsistent since the early 1990s.

2005	88	2013–2030	1999	81–84	now–2012
2004	88	now–2017	1998	87	now
2003	86	now–2013	1997	84	now
2001	88	now–2016	1996	86?	now–2017
2000	88–89	now–2020	1995	86	now

Past Glories 1989 (91), 1986 (90), 1985 (90), 1975 (90), 1970 (90), 1949 (94)

CHAUVIN ★ ★ ★ ★
ST.-ÉMILION $30.00–$55.00

Under the inspired leadership of Béatrice Ondet and Marie-France Février, this property is fashioning better and better wines. Moreover, prices remain reasonable. Until 1999, the estate produced a luxury microcuvée called Vieux Château Chauvin. This truly spectacular St.-Émilion came from a small vineyard that is now included in the standard Château Chauvin.

2005	91	2009–2021+
2004	89+	now–2022
2003	89	now–2016
2002	87	now–2013
2001	90	now–2016
2000	92	now–2018
1999	89	now–2014
1998	89+	now–2015
1997	88	now
1996	88	now–2011
1995	87	now–2009
1998 Vieux Château Chauvin	91	now–2022

CHEVAL BLANC ✦ ✦ ✦ ✦ ✦
ST.-ÉMILION CHEVAL BLANC $250.00–$400.00; LE PETIT CHEVAL $65.00–$75.00

One of the most elegant and noble wines in all of Bordeaux, made in a distinctive lighter, more delicate style because of the high percentage of Cabernet Franc in the final blend (usually between 40% and 55%), Cheval Blanc produces aromatic, long-lived wines that represent the quintessential, complex style of Bordeaux. It is never a powerful wine but is consistently well made, and even more consistent since Pierre Lurton began managing it. This property is now owned by the Moët-Hennessey luxury empire of Bernard Arnault. In addition, Albert Frères, one of Belgium's most successful businessmen (and a noted gourmet), has an important stake in the estate.

2006 Cheval Blanc	92–95	2012–2028
2005 Cheval Blanc	96	2014–2030+
2004 Cheval Blanc	90	2010–2022
2003 Cheval Blanc	89	now–2020
2002 Cheval Blanc	90	now–2018
2001 Cheval Blanc	93	now–2018
2000 Cheval Blanc	100	2010–2030+
1999 Cheval Blanc	93	now–2022
1998 Cheval Blanc	96+	2009–2030
1997 Cheval Blanc	88	now
1996 Cheval Blanc	90	now–2015
1995 Cheval Blanc	92	now–2020
2005 Le Petit Cheval	89	2013–2048+
2004 Le Petit Cheval	87	now–2017
2003 Le Petit Cheval	87	now–2013
2001 Le Petit Cheval	87–89	now–2011
2000 Le Petit Cheval	90	now–2012

Past Glories 1990 (100), 1986 (92), 1985 (93), 1983 (95), 1982 (100), 1981 (90), 1975 (90), 1964 (95), 1961 (93), 1959 (92), 1955 (90), 1953 (95), 1949 (96), 1948 (96), 1947 (100), 1921 (98)

DOMAINE DE CHEVALIER ✦ ✦ ✦ ✦
PESSAC-LÉOGNAN $30.00–$50.00

Stéphane Derenoncourt was brought in as the lead consultant at this noble estate in Pessac-Léognan. As a result, the tannins are sweeter, the oak is more subtle and better integrated, and the wine is more textured and complex, particularly since 1998. The white wines are among the longest-lived dry whites of France and worth the lofty price of admission.

2006	90–92	2009–2029
2005	92	2012–2037
2004	90	2009–2022+
2003	90	now–2019
2002	88	now–2015
2001	90	now–2016
2000	90	now–2025
1999	88	now–2014
1998	87	now–2015
1997	85	now
1996	88	now–2016
1995	80?	now–2015
2006 Blanc	92–94	2010–2030

2005 Blanc			95	2010–2040		
2004 Blanc			94	2009–2035		
2003 Blanc			95	now–2030		
2002 Blanc			89	now–2022		
2001 Blanc			95	2010–2040		
2000 Blanc			90	now–2023		
1999 Blanc			87	now–2015		
1998 Blanc			88	now–2020		
1997 Blanc			84	now		
1996 Blanc			78	now–2015		
1995 Blanc			85	now–2015		

CITRAN ★ ★ ★
HAUT-MÉDOC $15.00–$28.00

The wines of Citran have been consistent over past years. If there is any criticism, it would be that the use of new oak gives them a dramatic, even charred, character that may not please those who prefer more delicate and subtle clarets. They usually can keep for at least a decade. Prices have gone up slightly over recent years.

2003	86	now–2013	1998	86	now
2002	88	now–2015	1997	86	now
2001	85	now–2010	1996	87	now–2015
2000	88+	now–2015	1995	86	now
1999	86	now			

CLARKE ★ ★ ★
LISTRAC $15.00–$35.00

Owned by the Rothschild family in Europe, Clarke has had a very successful early decade of the 21st century and has emerged as one of the best estates in Listrac. The wines are dark, tannic, rich, and concentrated, and there is even a rabbi-approved kosher cuvée available.

2004	87	now–2022	2000	87	now–2014
2003	87	now–2016	1999	85	now–2010
2002	89	now–2020	1998	87	now–2015
2001	86	now–2011			

LA CLÉMENCE ★ ★ ★/★ ★ ★ ★
POMEROL $65.00–$112.00

This relatively new, blue-chip, 7.5-acre estate is owned by Christian Dauriac, who has done such a great job at his nearby St.-Émilion estate, Destieux. Although part of this small vineyard sits on some of Pomerol's famous blue clay, there is also some gravel and sand in the soil. The proprietor uses Burgundian fermentation techniques to produce a powerful, oaky mouthstaining wine.

2005	92	2010–2030+	2002	88	now–2015
2004	89+?	2009–2018	2001	90	now–2016
2003	87	now–2013	2000	91	now–2018

CLERC MILON ★ ★ ★ ★
PAUILLAC $28.00–$50.00

Until 1985, the wines of Clerc Milon were frequently light and undistinguished, but vintages over the last 10 to 15 years display a lush fruity quality; greater depth, flavor, and dimension;

and lavish quantities of toasty new oak. Given their quality, these wines, which are made by the same staff that makes Mouton-Rothschild, are somewhat undervalued.

2006	91–93	2013–2025	2000	91	now–2020
2005	92	2012–2025+	1999	90	now–2018
2004	90	2012–2025	1998	91	now–2025
2003	91+	2010–2026	1997	87	now–2010
2002	90	2011–2020+	1996	90	now–2018
2001	88?	now–2019	1995	89	now–2015

CLINET ★ ★ ★ ★
POMEROL $55.00–$110.00

This property hit its apogee in 1989 and 1990 and then seemed to become increasingly irregular. The proprietors died tragically in 2001, and the property was eventually sold. The new owner has been on a frustratingly slow learning curve but seems to have gotten more consistent over recent vintages. This can be one of the better Pomerols, full-bodied, dense, powerful, rich, and long-lived but with supple tannins.

2006	90–92	2009–2027	2000	92	now–2020+
2005	92	2010–2036	1999	88	now–2015
2004	90	now–2022	1998	90?	now–2020
2003	86	now–2014	1997	89	now–2012+
2002	88	now–2015	1996	91+?	now–2020
2001	89+	now–2014	1995	96	now–2025

Past Glories 1990 (96), 1989 (100)

CLOS BADON ★ ★ ★/★ ★ ★
ST.-ÉMILION $18.00–$40.00

This small vineyard (just under 20 acres), situated near La Gaffelière, has always held promise. The owner is St.-Émilion's omnipresent Jean-Luc Thunevin, and his debut vintage was 1998. The wines are generally rich, opulently textured, and made from extremely ripe fruit.

2005	90	now–2021	2000	89	now–2015
2003	87–89	now–2012	1999	88	now–2012
2002	87	now–2012	1998	90	now
2001	87–88	now–2013			

CLOS CHAUMONT ★ ★ ★
PREMIÈRES CÔTES DE BORDEAUX $14.00–$16.00

This is one of the finest wines of the Premières Côtes de Bordeaux, based on about two-thirds Merlot and the rest mostly Cabernet Sauvignon with a bit of Cabernet Franc. Every good-vintage Clos Chaumont offers reasonably good value and high-quality wine. Shrewd consumers have been checking this property out for years, so look for these wines to become increasingly scarce and their prices to inch up.

2005	89	now–2014	1999	88	now
2001	85–87	now	1998	88	now
2000	88	now			

CLOS DU CLOCHER ★ ★ ★
POMEROL $30.00–$55.00

In the best vintages, the wines of Clos du Clocher are generously flavored, full-bodied, and attractive despite their lack of polish and finesse. Unfortunately, prices are rather high because of the small production that is gobbled up by fans from the Benelux countries.

2005	89	now–2019		1999	87	now–2014
2004	87	now–2015		1998	88	now–2015
2003	86–88	now–2012		1997	86?	now
2002	87–88	now–2013		1996	86	now
2001	88	now–2014		1995	87	now
2000	90	now–2020				

CLOS DUBREUIL ★ ★ ★ ★/★ ★ ★ ★ ★
ST.-ÉMILION $45.00–$110.00

A quintessential St.-Émilion *vin de garage,* this 3-acre, 300-case winery is managed by Louis Mitjavile, the son of François Mitjavile (of Le Tertre Rôteboeuf fame), who fashions wines in the same ripe and sensual style favored by his father. One of Bordeaux's sexiest wines, Clos Dubreuil is a blend of 95% Merlot and 5% Cabernet Franc. The vineyard is planted in clay and limestone soils, and the fruit is harvested very ripe.

2005	92	now–2015		2000	91	now–2020
2004	91	now–2020		1999	90	now–2014
2003	92	now–2015		1998	92	now–2017
2002	90	now–2011		1997	89	now
2001	91	now–2016				

CLOS L'ÉGLISE ★ ★ ★
CÔTES DE CASTILLON $19.00–$28.00

Now owned by Gérard Perse, this estate makes attractive, elegant wines based mostly on Merlot with a touch of the two Cabernets. As one might expect from a Perse-owned property, the vineyard is impeccably managed and the wine cleanly made. Clos l'Église is clearly the softest and earliest drinker among all the Perse estates.

2005	89	now–2016		2000	90	now–2015
2002	88–90	now		1999	88	now
2001	89	now–2012				

CLOS L'ÉGLISE ★ ★ ★ ★ ★
POMEROL $75.00–$175.00

Since its acquisition in 1997 by the Garcin-Cathiard family, Clos l'Église has risen to be one of the finest Pomerols. Michel Rolland was brought in as a consultant but was later replaced by Dr. Alain Raynaud. Both men were charged with overseeing wines that were once appallingly mediocre, vegetal, and uninspiring but are now simply fabulous. Vintages post-1997 have been a succession of gorgeous wines. This is now routinely one of the top seven or eight wines of Pomerol in addition to being one of the richest and most complex wines of Bordeaux. The Garcin-Cathiards also own Château Haut-Bergey in Pessac-Léognan and Barde-Haut in St.-Émilion.

2006	92–94	now–2022		2001	95	now–2014
2005	96	2011–2030		2000	96	2010–2030
2004	91	now–2021		1999	93	now–2016+

2003	89	now–2016	1998	96	now–2018
2002	92	now–2015	1997	90	now–2015

CLOS FOURTET ★ ★ ★ ★
ST.-ÉMILION $30.00–$110.00

New owner Philippe Cuvelier has resurrected this once famous estate, which had languished in the doldrums for many decades. Since 2000, this has been one of the best premiers grands crus classés of St.-Émilion, with striking richness, color, intensity, and minerality.

2006	90–93	now–2016	2000	90+	2010–2022
2005	98	2012–2030+	1999	88	now–2014
2004	90	now–2019	1998	90	now–2016
2003	94	now–2026+	1997	87	now
2002	90	now–2016	1996	89	now–2018
2001	91	now–2018	1995	88	now–2018

CLOS DES JACOBINS ★ ★ ★
ST.-ÉMILION $25.00–$35.00

In 2001 Hubert de Boüard of L'Angélus fame was brought in to make the wine here. Because of that, the wines of Clos des Jacobins have been consistent since 2001—deeply colored, rich, round, creamy, and plummy, often with an opulence of ripe fruit. There is an absence of astringent, aggressive tannins, making Clos des Jacobins a wine that requires consumption within its first 10 to 12 years.

2005	91	now–2022	2001	89	now–2011
2004	89	now–2019	1999	82	now
2003	86	now–2014	1997	85	now
2002	87–89	now–2012	1996	82	now

CLOS DU JAUGUEYRON ★ ★ ★ ★
MARGAUX/HAUT-MÉDOC $20.00–$125.00

This is a microscopic estate producing two wines of the same name, one brilliant and of very limited production under the Margaux appellation. The other, in slightly larger quantities, is an Haut-Médoc. The latter is the ultimate Médoc garage wine—rich, concentrated, perfumed, and impeccably well made. If you can find it, it is well worth buying.

2005 Haut-Médoc	88	now–2014
1999 Haut-Médoc	87	now
1998 Haut-Médoc	87	now
2005 Margaux	90	now–2021+
2004 Margaux	91–93	now–2026
2003 Margaux	87	now–2014
2002 Margaux	88–90	now–2012
2001 Margaux	91	now–2019
2000 Margaux	92	now–2022
1999 Margaux	91	now–2015
1998 Margaux	89	now–2012

CLOS LOUIE ★★★★
CÔTES DE CASTILLON $35.00

In this tiny *garagiste* operation in the Côtes de Castillon making very concentrated wines, the quality is very high but the production limited. One of the oldest parcels of Merlot vines (140+ years of age) is one of Clos Louie's important component parts.

2005	92	2009–2016+		2003	90	now–2014
2004	88	now–2019				

CLOS LES LUNELLES ★★★★/★★★★★
CÔTES DE CASTILLON $30.00–$45.00

Purchased by Gérard and Chantal Perse in 2001, Clos Les Lunelles is the leading estate of the Côtes de Castillon and a blockbuster wine made with impeccable viticultural and winemaking techniques. For value, the wine offers significant quality and is also potentially the longest-lived wine of the Côtes de Castillon region. It is mostly Merlot with a tiny bit of Cabernet Sauvignon and Cabernet Franc.

2006	92–94	now–2018		2003	92	now–2021
2005	94	2010–2020+		2002	90	now–2013
2004	92	now–2014		2001	92	now–2016

CLOS MANOU ★★★★
MÉDOC $25.00–$35.00

Another tiny microcuvée from a *garagiste* property in the Médoc, Clos Manou is well made and worth considering if you can find it.

2005	90	now–2016		2001	88	now–2011
2004	89	now–2022		2000	88	now–2010
2003	93	now–2021				

CLOS MARSALETTE ★★★★
PESSAC-LÉOGNAN $25.00–$35.00

A property worth taking a look at now that it is owned by the brilliant Stephan von Neipperg. Clos Marsalette is a small vineyard producing just over 1,200 cases, but the wine has been beautifully made over recent vintages, thanks to the work of Neipperg and his wunderkind guru-consultant Stéphane Derenoncourt. A very soft, elegant, aromatic style of wine, it is designed for consumption within a decade of the vintage.

2005	92	now–2016		2003	87–88	now–2012
2004	87	now–2013				

CLOS DE L'ORATOIRE ★★★★
ST.-ÉMILION $35.00–$54.00

A well-placed property that was acquired by Stephan von Neipperg in the 1990s, this estate has produced fleshy, full-bodied, rich, flamboyant and concentrated wines capable of aging 15 or so years.

2006	90–93	now–2021		2000	94	now–2020
2005	93	now–2022+		1999	91	now–2015
2004	90?	now–2021		1998	92	now–2020
2003	88	now–2014		1997	89	now–2013+
2002	89	now–2013		1996	90	now–2017
2001	90	now–2016		1995	89	now–2015

CLOS PUY-ARNAUD ★★★★
CÔTES DE CASTILLON $20.00–$30.00

Clos Puy-Arnaud is a seriously run property that consistently produces one of the top two or three wines of the Côtes de Castillon. This estate of 20+ acres sits on clay and limestone soils and is run with considerable attention to detail by Thierry Valette. It has been very strong in recent vintages.

2005	88+	now–2021+		2002	88	now–2011
2004	88	now–2014		2001	87–88	now–2013
2003	90	now–2014		2000	87	now–2011

CLOS RENÉ ★★★/★★★★
POMEROL $18.00–$50.00

There is no doubt that some recent vintages have produced the best wines from Clos René in recent memory. Perhaps the counseling of Michel Rolland, the highly respected Libourne oenologist and proprietor of Le Bon Pasteur, has made the difference. Because it is not one of the best-known Pomerols, Clos René remains reasonably priced.

2005	89	now–2022		2000	88+	now–2017
2003	84–87	now–2011		1999	87	now–2011
2001	86–88	now–2010		1998	86	now–2009

Past Glories 1947 (95)

CLOS ST.-JULIEN ★★★
ST.-ÉMILION $20.00–$45.00

Proprietor Cathérine Papon-Nouvel runs this tiny vineyard, situated behind Château Soutard and planted on pure limestone with equal parts Merlot and Cabernet Franc. Malolactic fermentation takes place in new oak, and the wine is aged 18 months prior to bottling. This is a solidly constructed wine that has plenty of muscle but often lacks charm.

2005	94	2015–2045		2001	91	now–2019
2004	90	2010–2020+		2000	90	now–2020
2003	89–91+	now–2017		1999	89	now–2010

CLOS ST.-MARTIN ★★★★★
ST.-ÉMILION $33.00–$60.00

This can be a prodigious wine (as it was in 1998, 2000, 2001, and 2005). It is a tiny estate, the smallest in St.-Émilion, and incidentally adjacent to the town's cemetery. Michel Rolland is the consulting winemaker, and the quality of the winemaking and its noble *terroir* make this estate highly desired by those in the know. The proprietors, the Reiffers family, also own up-and-coming estates such as Les Grandes Murailles and Côte de Baleau. This is a compelling wine.

2006	92–94	2015–2025		2001	93+	2010–2025
2005	98	2012–2035		2000	96	2010–2030
2004	90+	2010–2020		1999	86	now–2012
2003	88?	2012–2025		1998	91	now–2020
2002	88	now–2014		1997	86	now

CLOS DE SARPE ★★★★
ST.-ÉMILION $40.00–$70.00

Production is less than 1,000 cases at this 9-acre *garagiste* estate whose consultant is Michel Rolland's foremost assistant, Jean-Philippe Fort. Situated on St.-Émilion's limestone plateau, the vineyard is planted with 85% Merlot and 15% Cabernet Franc. This offering is meant for those with 19th-century tastes, as the proprietor believes in full extraction and huge tannin. These massive, even monster wines are meant to be drunk decades after their release. Most vintages experience 40- to 50-day macerations, and tiny yields of 13 to 25 hectoliters per hectare (between 140 and 265 U.S. gallons per acre) result in extremely concentrated wines. Only for the patient!

2006	92–95+	2016–2040+	2001	95+	2010–2025
2005	95+	2015–2065	2000	95+	2010–2035
2004	90+	2017–2035+	1999	90	now–2018
2003	88+?	now–2021	1998	90+?	now–2015
2002	89+?	2015–2030+			

LA CLOTTE ★★★★
ST.-ÉMILION $25.00–$45.00

I adore the wonderfully charming, sensual wines produced from this 9.8-acre vineyard, planted on a mixture of soils including sand, clay, and limestone. It is a blend of 80% Merlot and the rest primarily Cabernet Franc with a touch of Cabernet Sauvignon from vines averaging 40 years of age. This wine has taken off in quality over the last several years, revealing a deeper richness and broader texture. La Clotte is under most consumers' radar, and the tiny production of 1,200-plus cases makes it difficult to find. The top-notch 2005 was made under the guidance of Michel Rolland's top employee, Jean-Philippe Fort. The only downside: the name is unappealing to English speakers.

2005	93	now–2022	2001	88	now–2012
2004	90	now–2021	2000	91	now–2016
2003	90	now–2016	1999	87	now–2010
2002	88	now–2013	1998	89	now–2011

LA CLUSIÈRE ★★★★★
ST.-ÉMILION $95.00–$165.00

These notes are now of only historical interest, since this tiny vineyard, which only produced a few hundred cases, now has been incorporated into the larger vineyard of Favie, a famed St.-Émilion. The 2001 was the last vintage of La Clusière, which in 2000 and 2001 made remarkable wines with Gérard Perse at the helm. Its final two vintages should ensure this will be one of the darlings of speculators and wine historians for many years.

2001	95	now–2020	1999	93	now–2020
2000	100	now–2035	1998	90+	now–2020

COLOMBIER-MONPELOU ★★
PAUILLAC $20.00

Colombier-Monpelou is one of the least impressive wines of Pauillac, although it has shown a few small signs of life over recent vintages. Most of the wines I have tasted from this estate are light and lacking concentration and distinction. Nevertheless, the wine finds a rather buoyant marketplace in France, no doubt because of its appellation and lowly price for a Pauillac.

2000	86	now–2013

LA COMMANDERIE ★ ★/★ ★ ★
ST.-ÉMILION $23.00

This property should be producing better and better wines now that the talented Hubert de Boüard is La Commanderie's consultant.

2005	87	now–2015		2002	86–88	now–2011
2003	88	now–2016		2001	88	now–2016

LA CONFESSION ★ ★ ★ ★
ST.-ÉMILION $25.00–$60.00

One of the most impressive winemakers and proprietors of the right bank (Pomerol and St.-Émilion), Jean-Philippe Janoueix, who is also the creative force behind the wines of Chambrun in Lalande de Pomerol and La Croix St.-Georges in Pomerol, burst on the scene with some very impressive wines from this St.-Émilion estate. This wine is given all the Burgundian treatments of malolactic fermentation in barrel, extended lees contact, and no fining or filtration. It is a serious wine with a blend almost identical to that of Cheval Blanc. A name to watch as well as to buy.

2006	91–93+	2012–2025		2003	90	now–2020+
2005	95	2013–2030+		2002	90	now–2017
2004	91	now–2022		2001	93+	now–2015

LA CONSEILLANTE ★ ★ ★ ★/★ ★ ★ ★ ★
POMEROL $60.00–$155.00

When it is good, La Conseillante is one of Bordeaux's quintessential examples of elegance, finesse, and suppleness. If there is a criticism to address, it would be a slight lack of concentration and selection in certain vintages, which prevents the wine from competing with its nearest neighbors, L'Évangile, Cheval Blanc, and Pétrus. Highly prized, La Conseillante is generally expensive. The *terroir* is spectacular, so there can never be any excuses for mediocrity.

2006	92–95	now–2026		2000	96	now–2030
2005	96	2012–2032+		1999	89	now–2012
2004	89	now–2022		1998	90	now–2016
2003	89	now–2016		1997	88	now–2012
2002	82	now–2011		1996	88	now–2014
2001	89+?	now–2016		1995	89	now–2014

Past Glories 1990 (98), 1989 (97), 1986 (89), 1985 (94), 1983 (88), 1982 (95), 1981 (91), 1970 (92), 1959 (95), 1953 (90), 1949 (97), 1947 (91)

LA CONSEILLER ★ ★ ★/★ ★ ★ ★
BORDEAUX SUPÉRIEUR $22.00

Shrewd insiders and bargain hunters have been stocking up on this brilliant wine from Jean-Philippe Janoueix despite its humble appellation. This is quite a tasty, full-throttle wine regardless of its lowly pedigree.

2005	91	now–2015		2003	90	now–2014
2004	89	now–2014		2002	87–89	now

CORBIN ★ ★/★ ★ ★
ST.-ÉMILION $18.00–$38.00

Annabelle Bardinet, the proprietor, seems to be making better wine at Corbin, but this estate seems to be going through a period of irregularity.

2005	88	now–2021		1999	85	now
2003	88–90	now–2020		1998	88	now–2012
2002	87	now–2013		1997	85	now
2001	88	now–2010		1996	80?	now
2000	88	now–2012		1995	86	now

CORBIN-MICHOTTE * */* * *
ST.-ÉMILION $25.00

Corbin-Michotte is one of five châteaux that sit along the Pomerol border with Corbin in their name. One single parcel (rare in Bordeaux), it has the potential to be one of the best wines of this particular microclimate of St.-Émilion but rarely is. Much of Corbin-Michotte is sold directly to clients in Europe, particularly Switzerland.

2000	88	now–2011		1996	86	now
1998	87	now		1995	89	now
1997	86	now				

CORDEILLAN-BAGES* * *
PAUILLAC $25.00–$28.00

Cordeillan-Bages comes from a vineyard adjacent to the luxury hotel-restaurant of the same name just south of the town of Pauillac owned by Jean-Michel Cazes, the proprietor of Lynch-Bages. This wine is often lacking a bit in breadth, nuance, and expansiveness, but it is certainly well made.

2004	86	now–2016		2001	88	now–2014
2003	86–88	now–2015		2000	90	now–2020
2002	87–88	now–2023		1999	87	now–2014

CORMEIL-FIGEAC * *
ST.-ÉMILION $20.00–$28.00

The wines from Cormeil-Figeac are easygoing, attractive, fruit-driven efforts. If wines such as this were inexpensive, they would be ideal choices for restaurants.

1998	86	now–2012		1997	85	now

COS D'ESTOURNEL * * * * *
ST.-ESTÈPHE
COS D'ESTOURNEL $125.00–$175.00; LES PAGODES DE COS $25.00–$35.00

Cos d'Estournel, after having played runner-up to Montrose in the 1950s and 1960s, emerged in the 1980s, 1990s, and early 21st century as a noteworthy rival of Montrose and even some of the nearby first growths in Pauillac. The estate is owned by the Swiss pork entrepreneur Michel Reybier, who has given carte blanche authority to Jean-Guillaume Prats to make the wine. This is a modern-style wine with a hefty respect for tradition, but the owner and winemaker are two of the leading visionaries in Bordeaux, and the wine reflects their brilliance and liberalism. This is certainly a wine of first-growth quality and, if you have the money, a wine to buy.

2006	92–94	2014–2044
2005	98	2013–2025+
2004	92	2009–2020+
2003	98	now–2036+
2002	93+	now–2020
2001	93	now–2019

2000	92+	2010–2022
1999	88	now–2018
1998	88	now–2018
1997	87	now
1996	93+	now–2030
1995	95	now–2025
2005 Les Pagodes de Cos	90	now–2018
2004 Les Pagodes de Cos	86–88	now–2016
2003 Les Pagodes de Cos	88	now–2017
2002 Les Pagodes de Cos	89	now–2017
2000 Les Pagodes de Cos	89	now–2018

Past Glories 1994 (91), 1990 (95), 1986 (95), 1985 (93), 1982 (96), 1961 (92), 1959 (92), 1953 (93)

COS LABORY ★ ★ ★
ST.-ESTÈPHE $28.00–$42.00

For decades one of the most disappointing of all classified growths, Cos Labory has emerged over the last ten years as a better wine but one that still tends to perform below its official pedigree. However, prices do remain reasonable.

2005	89+	2013–2023	1999	87	now–2012
2004	89	now–2019	1998	86	now
2003	87	now–2016	1997	86	now
2002	83	now–2020	1996	88	now–2018
2001	78	now–2012	1995	88+?	now–2015
2000	88	now–2016			

CÔTE DE BALEAU ★ ★ ★/★ ★ ★ ★
ST.-ÉMILION $30.00–$35.00

An up-and-coming St.-Émilion estate owned by the Reiffers family, also the proprietors of Clos St.-Martin and Les Grandes Murailles. Production is just under 3,000 cases. The omnipresent Michel Rolland looks after the vinification.

2005	87	now–2019	2000	90	now–2018
2004	87	now–2019	1999	87?	now–2009
2003	87–90	now–2017	1998	90	now–2020
2002	87	now–2014	1997	85	now
2001	90	now–2021			

CÔTE MONTPEZAT CUVÉE COMPOSTELLE ★ ★ ★
CÔTES DE CASTILLON $15.00–$20.00

Recent vintages have held high promise, which, combined with fair prices, are a consumer's dream.

2005	86	now–2014

CÔTE LA PRADE ★ ★ ★
CÔTES DE FRANCS $15.00–$20.00

Owned by Thierry Valette and Nicolas Thienpont, this ten-acre property is situated on a limestone and clay plateau as well as hillsides. The vineyard is planted with 80% Merlot and 20% Cabernet Franc. Cool years tend to be very challenging for this *terroir*.

2005	88	now–2015	2004	84–85	now–2012

COUFRAN ★★★
HAUT-MÉDOC $15.00–$30.00

Owned by the Miailhe family, this estate generally produces well-made and pleasant wines that also represent fairly good values. As a general rule, they must be drunk within six to eight years after the vintage. For a wine from the Médoc, Coufran utilizes a very high percentage of Merlot in the blend, usually 75% or more.

2004	87–89	now–2016	1999	82–85	now
2003	89	now–2014	1998	86–87	now
2002	87	now–2012	1997	84	now
2001	85–87	now–2009	1996	86	now
2000	88	now–2013	1995	85	now

COUHINS-LURTON ★★★★
PESSAC-LÉOGNAN $25.00–$35.00

André Lurton, another member of the ubiquitous Lurton family, enthusiastically runs this small gem of a property. For many years they produced only a white wine, one of the best of the region, made from 100% Sauvignon Blanc, fermented in new oak, and aged for nearly ten months prior to bottling. Now they have added to their portfolio a red wine, which is very Burgundian in style.

2005 Rouge	89	now–2021
2005 Blanc	92	now–2020
2001 Blanc	91	now–2015
1998 Blanc	92	now–2012
1995 Blanc	87	now

LA COUR D'ARGENT ★★★
BORDEAUX $10.00–$15.00

This estate produces top-notch values in low-prestige, generic Bordeaux that provide plenty of character at bargain-basement prices.

2005	86	now–2010	2000	87	now
2003	85–87	now			

DOMAINE DE COURTEILLAC ★★★/★★★★
BORDEAUX SUPÉRIEUR $10.00–$12.00

Another sleeper selection that consistently makes wines well above its humble pedigree, this is a fleshy, well-made, richly fruity, solidly constructed wine that drinks well for five to six years.

2005	87	now–2010	2000	87–88	now
2001	86–88	now	1999	84	now

LA COUSPAUDE ★★★★
ST.-ÉMILION $35.00–$55.00

Another garage wine from St.-Émilion, this well-made, modern-style wine is usually a blend of 70% Merlot, with the rest Cabernet Franc and sometimes some Cabernet Sauvignon. There are about 3,000 cases, a relatively large amount for a *vin de garage*. This is another in the exotic Le Pin school of St.-Émilions, made from extremely ripe fruit and bottled without filtration. The upbringing at La Couspaude is far from traditional, as the wines enjoy significant new-oak aging. The talented Michel Rolland oversees the vinifications at the estate.

2005	91	now–2021	1999	87	now
2003	89	now–2013	1998	92	now–2015
2002	87	now–2011	1997	88	now–2010
2001	89	now–2012	1996	88	now
2000	92	now–2016+	1995	90	now–2015

COUVENT DES JACOBINS   ★ ★ ★
ST.-ÉMILION $20.00–$36.00

Couvent des Jacobins, named after the 13th-century Dominican monastery that once existed on this site, is meticulously run by the Joinaud-Borde family, who have owned the property since 1902. I suspect this estate could produce even better wines than it does, but there is no denying their charming, open-knit style.

2001	87–88	now–2013	1998	86	now–2012
2000	88	now–2015	1997	86	now
1999	85	now	1995	86–88	now

LE CROCK   ★ ★ ★
ST.-ESTÈPHE $18.00–$25.00

Le Crock is a beautiful château situated to the south of Montrose and just north of Cos d'Estournel. In this Walt Disney–like setting, river swans are often seen bathing themselves below the hillside château. Le Crock is owned by the proprietors of Léoville-Poyferré, the Cuveliers and, after a long period of mediocrity, has just begun to ratchet up the level of quality, starting with the strong 2003.

2003				87–89	now–2016

LA CROIX DU CASSE   ★ ★/★ ★ ★
POMEROL $25.00–$35.00

The late Jean-Michel Arcaute, the manager who took Château Clinet from mediocrity to superstardom, passed away in a tragic drowning accident in 2001, and his untimely death left a void at this estate. Located south of the village of Catusseau, on a terrace of sandy and gravel-based soils, this tiny Pomerol estate is not as renowned or as well placed as many other Pomerols, but the quality can be a good surprise, even though the wine is expensive.

2003	85	now–2012	1998	90	now–2016
2001	87	now–2015	1997	88	now
2000	88+?	now–2018?	1996	88	now–2011
1999	89	now–2015	1995	90	now–2015

LA CROIX L'ESPERANCE CUVÉE D'EXCEPTION   ★ ★ ★ ★
LUSSAC–ST.-ÉMILION $35.00

Part of Bernard Magrez's Cuvée d'Exception marketing approach has been to carve out small parcels of established vineyards, exploit them to their full potential, and treat each of the estate's wines as if it were a renowned first growth in vinification and upbringing. The 2005 is about as serious, concentrated, and full-bodied as a wine from this satellite appellation can be. This 500-case, 100% Merlot cuvée represents something new . . . something exciting.

2005	90	2009–2022	2003	89	now–2014
2004	85–87	now			

LA CROIX DE GAY ★ ★ ★/★ ★ ★ ★
POMEROL $22.00–$50.00

Owned by the Raynaud and Lebreton families, Dr. Raynaud's sister, Chantal Lebreton, assumed control of this estate in the mid-1990s. The property is known for producing delicate, understated, restrained Pomerols in a medium-weight, fruit-forward style.

2005	89	now–2021	1999	88	now–2012
2004	87	now–2015	1998	87	now–2013
2003	85	now–2011	1997	86	now
2002	86–87	now–2011	1996	85	now
2001	89	now–2016	1995	87	now
2000	89+	now–2016			

Past Glories 1964 (90), 1947 (92)

CROIX DE LABRIE ★ ★ ★ ★ ★
ST.-ÉMILION $70.00–$175.00

Owner Michel Puzio has expanded production to a whopping 750 cases—great news, as this has been one of St.-Émilion's most dazzling garage wines over the last decade (made with the consultation of Jean-Luc Thunevin of Valandraud fame). This is a wine of dramatic intensity and flamboyant aromas in a decidedly modern style. A hedonistic and intellectual tour de force.

2006	92–94	now–2021	2001	91	now–2014
2005	94	2011–2025+	2000	95	now–2020
2004	89	now–2015	1999	93	now–2012
2003	93	now–2016	1998	93	now–2014
2002	88	now–2012			

CROIX MOUTON ★ ★ ★ ★
BORDEAUX SUPÉRIEUR $20.00

Formerly known as Mouton (the name had to be changed because of a lawsuit by Mouton Rothschild), this is another impressive small estate represented by the immensely talented Jean-Philippe Janoueix. The wines are well above their pedigree and well worth seeking out by lovers of Bordeaux. This wine emerges from a 50-acre vineyard planted with 80% Merlot and the rest Cabernet Franc and Petit Verdot.

2005 Croix Mouton	89	now–2016
2003 Mouton	87–89	now–2012

LA CROIX DE PERENNE CUVÉE D'EXCEPTION ★ ★ ★ ★
PREMIÈRES CÔTES DE BLAYE $35.00

This is part of Bernard Magrez's special artisanal wine portfolio. It is a fleshy, fast-forward, limited-quantity wine.

2005	90	now–2015

LA CROIX DE PRIEURE ★ ★ ★ ★
PREMIÈRES CÔTES DE BLAYE $30.00

La Croix de Prieure is part of the Cuvée d'Exception series of hand-crafted, artisanal wines from special parcels of established vineyards created by Bernard Magrez to showcase the extraordinary potential of some forgotten appellations, in this case the Premières Côtes de Blaye.

2004	89–91	now–2011	2003	90	now–2012

LA CROIX DE ROCHE ✦ ✦ ✦
BORDEAUX SUPÉRIEUR $10.00–$14.00

Readers looking for a Bordeaux that resembles a premier cru red Burgundy should check out the wines of La Croix de Roche. This is a bargain-priced wine ready to drink in its first two to three years.

2000	87	now	1999	87	now

LA CROIX ST.-GEORGES ✦ ✦ ✦ ✦
POMEROL $40.00–$55.00

This small vineyard near the famed Château Le Pin in Pomerol is run by the Jean-Philippe Janoueix family, whose youngest members are extremely serious about quality. The production is small at this true *garagiste* operation, and the best vintage to date is clearly 2000 (a magnificent wine), but subsequent vintages have also turned out well.

2006	94–96	2010–2025	2002	89+	now–2013
2005	95	2011–2032	2001	90	now–2016
2004	88+	2009–2022	2000	95	now–2020+
2003	88	now–2014	1999	93	now–2020

CROIZET-BAGES ✦ ✦/✦ ✦
PAUILLAC $20.00–$35.00

Croizet-Bages is owned and managed by the Quié family, who also are proprietors of the well-known Margaux estate, Rauzan-Gaussies. This wine has been a consistent underachiever for many decades but seems to be improving—ever so slightly. Still, there is nothing of classified-growth quality at Croizet-Bages except its historic pedigree. Caveat emptor!

2005	86	now–2019	1999	78	now–2012
2004	86	now–2015	1998	81	now
2003	85	now–2014	1997	81	now–2010
2002	74	now–2010	1996	87	now–2014
2001	78	now–2012	1995	85	now
2000	86	now–2013			

CROQUE-MICHOTTE ✦ ✦ ✦
ST.-ÉMILION $28.00–$32.00

The vineyard of Croque-Michotte is well situated in the Graves section of the St.-Émilion appellation, adjacent to the Pomerol border, close to the better-known estates of Cheval Blanc and La Dominique. The wine produced here is usually ready to drink within the first five or six years of a vintage, and it rarely improves beyond a decade.

1999	86	now–2010	1998	87	now–2011

CROS FIGEAC ✦ ✦
ST.-ÉMILION $20.00–$30.00

Cros Figeac is a middling St.-Émilion with a good *terroir* that is rarely exploited.

2001	87	now–2014	1999	87	now
2000	88	now–2015	1998	87	now–2011

CRU MONPLAISIR ★ ★/★ ★ ★
BORDEAUX SUPÉRIEUR $10.00–$15.00

Situated close to the town of Margaux, this 12.5-acre estate is owned by the Grangerou family, a name known by longtime followers of Château Margaux as the family that produced numerous cellarmasters for many decades. A blend of Merlot and Cabernet Sauvignon, these are solid if uninspiring efforts.

2005	88	now–2012	2001	85	now
2003	86–88	now–2011	2000	87	now
2002	86	now			

CHÂTEAU DE CRUZEAU ★ ★ ★
PESSAC-LÉOGNAN $22.00

This underrated property produces savory and immediately drinkable wine, both white and red, and certainly represents good value.

2001	85–87	now	1999	85–86	now
2000	89	now–2013+	1998	85–86	now

LES CRUZELLES ★ ★ ★/★ ★ ★ ★
LALANDE DE POMEROL $18.00–$38.00

This 25-acre vineyard, planted in clay and gravelly soils not totally dissimilar from those of Denis Durantou's renowned vineyard L'Église Clinet, is planted with 30-year-old vines consisting of 60% Merlot and 40% Cabernet Franc. The wine is the result of a classic vinification, much like what Durantou employs at L'Église Clinet. It is undoubtedly a property that needs to be taken seriously.

2006	89–91	now–2014	2002	88	now–2011
2005	90	???	2001	86–88	now–2011
2004	85	now–2013	2000	90	now–2015
2003	84–86	now–2011			

D'ARSAC ★ ★ ★
MARGAUX $20.00

This large estate has gotten very serious about quality, but consumers should stick to vintages since 2005.

2005				90	now–2019

DALEM ★ ★ ★
FRONSAC $12.00–23.00

A consistently well made, attractive, fruit-forward, consumer-friendly wine from Fronsac, Dalem's offerings remain bargain priced.

2005	89	now–2014	1999	86	now
2004	85–87	now–2012	1998	86	now
2003	87	now–2016	1997	85	now
2001	87	now–2009	1996	82	now
2000	87	now–2010	1995	85	now

DASSAULT ★★★/★★★★
ST.-ÉMILION $18.00–$32.00

In the early and mid-1990s, Dassault clearly had a problem with too many musty bottles. That problem has been completely alleviated, and Dassault has made dramatic improvements over recent years. Readers seeking immediately drinkable, soft, savory clarets with character should take note. This is obviously a property on the upswing and merits more and more attention, as its prices remain reasonable.

2006	89–90	now–2018	2000	88	now–2014
2005	90	now–2022	1999	87	now
2004	89	now–2017	1998	87	now–2011
2003	88	now–2012	1997	86	now
2002	87	now–2010	1996	76?	now
2001	85	now–2013	1995	85	now

DAUGAY ★★★
ST.-ÉMILION $16.00–$28.00

Readers should be taking more interest in this reasonably priced, well-made St.-Émilion made by the brother of the owner of the renowned Château L'Angélus. A solidly made, realistically priced St.-Émilion.

2005	88	now–2013	1998	87	now
2001	87–88	now–2011	1997	84	now
2000	87	now–2012	1996	85	now
1999	86	now	1995	85	now

LA DAUPHINE
FRONSAC $16.00–$25.00

This 25-acre vineyard was acquired by Jean Halley in 2000, and since then the wine quality has soared. La Dauphine remains a blend of 85% Merlot and 15% Cabernet Franc but now possesses more ripeness and texture than previous vintages.

2005	90	now–2015	1999	86	now
2004	87	now–2013	1998	87	now
2003	88	now–2014	1997	86	now
2002	81	now–2010	1996	86	now
2001	88	now–2010	1995	87	now
2000	87	now–2011			

DAUZAC ★★★/★★★★
MARGAUX $22.00–$32.00

Noteworthy improvement in the wines of Dauzac has occurred, particularly since the mid-1990s. André Lurton, the well-known proprietor of numerous Bordeaux châteaux, particularly in Pessac-Léognan, is in full administrative control, and recent vintages have exhibited more promise and character.

2005	91	2014–2030	1999	88	now–2016
2004	87?	now–2017	1998	87	now–2017
2003	87	now–2018	1997	78	now
2002	87	now–2013	1996	86	now–2015
2001	88?	now–2016	1995	86?	now–2015
2000	89	now–2016			

GÉRARD DEPARDIEU   * * * *
BORDEAUX $N/A

The famous French actor Gérard Depardieu has joined forces with one of Bordeaux's leading visionaries and revolutionaries, Bernard Magrez, the proprietor of Pape Clément. Together they purchase small parcels of vines and collaborate with Magrez's wine-making team (led by Michel Rolland and Jean Cordeau) to produce luxury, limited-production cuvées (about 500 cases each) of at least a dozen wines. Two of those efforts emerge from Bordeaux, but I should point out that he also produces extraordinary wines made from Syrah, Carignan, and Grenache from Morocco (called Lumière), and two spectacular Algerian red wine cuvées from a similar blend (called Domaine St.-Augustin). These amazing offerings are the finest wines I have ever tasted from Algeria and Morocco. In 2003, Depardieu, who often seems even more passionate about wine and food than acting, also released cuvées from the Languedoc-Roussillon, Priorato, and Toro in Spain. In particular, the 2000 Toro sample I tasted with him was extraordinary. The following are some of the Bordeaux wines Depardieu is associated with, and readers should remember that the brilliant winemaking consultant Michel Rolland plays a part in the winemaking and blending. These wines are all distributed by Bernard Magrez.

2005 Confiance Cuvée d'Exception	Côtes de Blaye	88–91	now–2014
2004 Confiance Cuvée d'Exception	Côtes de Blaye	90	now–2014
2003 Confiance	Côtes de Blaye	90	now–2013
2002 Confiance	Côtes de Blaye	90	now–2014
2005 La Croix de Peyrolie		93	now–2021
2004 La Croix de Peyrolie		90–92	now–2016
2003 La Croix de Peyrolie		90	now–2016
2002 La Croix de Peyrolie		89	now–2010
2005 Ma Vérité Cuvée d'Exception	Haut-Médoc	92	now–2014
2004 Ma Vérité	Haut-Médoc	87–88	now–2016
2003 Ma Vérité	Haut-Médoc	88+	now–2021
2002 Ma Vérité	Haut-Médoc	88	now–2013

VINS DESPAGNE   * * * *
BORDEAUX $12.00–$25.00

One of the most admirable operations in Bordeaux is that of the Despagne family, which produces extraordinary wines from such humble appellations as Bordeaux Supérieur and Premières Côtes de Bordeaux. Along with their oenologist, Michel Rolland, they are visionaries and revolutionaries making wines that can compete with some of Bordeaux's most renowned estates, at least during their first decade of life. They have proven that with modern winemaking techniques as well as less manipulation, ripe fruit, and low yields, astonishing results can be produced from unheralded *terroirs*. How they will age remains to be seen, but these offerings will be delicious during their first five to ten years of life. Critics may deem them too internationally styled, but they represent a tour de force in wine making.

Consumers and critics often focus on the great Bordeaux estates that sell for the highest prices, but Bordeaux desperately needs more producers like the Despagnes to produce wines such as this, since more than 90% of the entire viticultural area is generic appellations such as Bordeaux and Bordeaux Supérieur. Bravo!

Here are the properties commercialized under the Despagne name, all of which represent fabulous value and are wonderful wines to drink in their first five to seven years.

2003 Bel Air	90	ncw–2010
2003 Bel Air La Perponcher	90	ncw–2014

2001 Bel Air La Perponcher	87	now
2003 Bel Air La Perponcher Blanc	90	now
2001 Bel Air La Perponcher Blanc	89	now–2013
2005 Girolate	90	now–2016
2003 Girolate	91	now–2014
2002 Girolate	89	now
2001 Girolate	91	now–2015
2003 Mont-Pérat	87	now
2002 Mont-Pérat	87	now
2001 Mont-Pérat	87	now
2000 Mont-Pérat	89	now–2012
2003 Rauzan Despagne	89	now–2011
2002 Rauzan Despagne	87	now
2001 Rauzan Despagne	88	now
2000 Rauzan Despagne	88	now–2012
2003 Rauzan Despagne Blanc	91	now
2001 Rauzan Despagne Blanc	90	now
2000 Rauzan Despagne Blanc	90	now
2002 Rauzan Despagne Grand Réserve	89	now
2001 Rauzan Despagne Grand Réserve	88	now–2018
2000 Rauzan Despagne Grand Réserve	89	now–2011
2003 Tour de Mirambeau Cuvée Passion	89	now–2011
2002 Tour de Mirambeau Cuvée Passion	90	now
2001 Tour de Mirambeau Cuvée Passion	89	now
2000 Tour de Mirambeau Cuvée Passion	89	now–2011
1998 Tour de Mirambeau Cuvée Passion	87	now
2003 Tour de Mirambeau Cuvée Passion Blanc	90	now

DESTIEUX ★★★★
ST.-ÉMILION $30.00–$45.00

For years proprietor Christian Dauriac produced earthy, powerful, somewhat rustic, but personality filled wines. They also represented very good values. However, from 2003 on, he began to ratchet up the level of quality, introducing more complexity, charm, and finesse without sacrificing the power and muscle of these corpulent, concentrated St.-Émilions.

2005	93	2012–2022	1999	87	now–2015
2004	89+	2010–2020+	1998	87	now–2015
2003	92	now–2021+	1997	86	now
2002	88	now–2013	1996	86	now–2012
2001	90	now–2018	1995	85	now–2010
2000	89+	now–2018			

LE DÔME ★★★★
ST.-ÉMILION $75.00–$125.00

This 1,000-case blend of Cabernet Franc and Merlot is fashioned by Jonathan Malthus. Most of the Cabernet Franc emerges from a vineyard near L'Angélus. This is a fashionable wine made in the spirit of the famed Cheval Blanc with no compromises by a very passionate uncompromising proprietor.

2006	92–94	2010–2022+	2003	93	now–2021
2005	96	2010–2020	2001	92+	now–2019
2004	90–92	now–2022			

LA DOMINIQUE ★★★/★★★★
ST.-ÉMILION $32.00–$50.00

This has always been one of my favorite St.-Émilion estates for both quality and value. Although recent efforts have been largely uninspiring, I doubt that's a reason to abandon this wonderfully placed estate, just across the border from Pomerol's famed duo of L'Évangile and Cheval Blanc. There have been many terrific wines from La Dominique, although it is worrisome that some of the vintages of the early 21st century were disjointed and lacking personality.

2005	90	now–2022	1999	88	now
2004	76–78	now	1998	90	now–2015
2003	82?	now–2011	1997	86	now
2002	86	now–2014	1996	88	now–2012
2001	87	now–2012	1995	89	now–2015
2000	91	now–2017			

Past Glories 1990 (93), 1989 (93), 1982 (91)

LA DOYENNE ★★★
PREMIÈRES CÔTES DE BORDEAUX $10.00–$19.00

Value hunters should check out this wine, a sleeper pick in several vintages. From modest yields of 45 hectoliters per hectare (480 U.S. gallons per acre), this blend of 70% Merlot, 20% Cabernet Sauvignon, and 10% Cabernet Franc is bottled unfiltered. It can compete with wines costing five times as much.

2005	88	now–2012	1999	88	now
2001	87	now	1998	89	now
2000	88	now			

DUBOIS-GRIMON ★★★
CÔTES DE CASTILLON $15.00–$22.00

This is one of the little-known, new-wave, luxury Côtes de Castillons that offers stunningly high quality.

2005	88	now–2012	2000	88	now–2013
2003	87–89	now–2012	1999	87–89	now–2010
2002	87–89	now	1998	89+	now–2012
2001	85–87	now–2010			

DUBRAUD ★★★
BLAYE $15.00

Located in the new, higher appellation simply called Blaye, Dubraud produces solidly made wines.

2003	85–87	now	2000	88	now
2001	85	now			

DUCLUZEAU ★★★
LISTRAC $30.00

This is the estate of Monique Borie, the mother of the proprietors of Ducru-Beaucaillou and Grand-Puy-Lacoste. Ducluzeau incorporates one of the highest Merlot percentages of any Bordeaux and as a result is a fruity, very soft, tasty wine for early drinking.

2004	85–87	now–2014	2003	88	now–2013

DUCRU-BEAUCAILLOU ★★★★★
ST.-JULIEN
DUCRU-BEAUCAILLOU $100.00–$120.00;
LA CROIX DE BEAUCAILLOU $20.00

This estate is now being run by Bruno Borie, the eldest son of the late Jean-Eugène Borie. He replaced his younger brother, Xavier Borie, who remains fully responsible for Grand-Puy-Lacoste and Haut-Batailley. I affectionately call Ducru-Beaucaillou the Lafite-Rothschild of St.-Julien. Under Bruno Borie, the already extremely high quality of the wines has been pushed to new heights, and this is clearly a wine of first-growth quality, especially since 2003.

2005 La Croix de Beaucaillou	91	now–2020
2004 La Croix de Beaucaillou	88	now–2012
2000 La Croix de Beaucaillou	87	now–2014
1999 La Croix de Beaucaillou	89	now–2010
2006 Ducru-Beaucaillou	94–96	2017–2035
2005 Ducru-Beaucaillou	97	2015–2050
2004 Ducru-Beaucaillou	93	2009–2032
2003 Ducru-Beaucaillou	96	2010–2025+
2002 Ducru-Beaucaillou	89	now–2020
2001 Ducru-Beaucaillou	89	now–2016
2000 Ducru-Beaucaillou	94+	2010–2035
1999 Ducru-Beaucaillou	91	now–2018
1998 Ducru-Beaucaillou	91+	now–2025
1997 Ducru-Beaucaillou	87	now–2015+
1996 Ducru-Beaucaillou	96	now–2035
1995 Ducru-Beaucaillou	94	now–2025

Past Glories 1994 (90), 1986 (92), 1985 (92), 1982 (94), 1978 (90), 1970 (92), 1961 (96), 1959 (90), 1953 (93), 1947 (93)

DUHART-MILON ★★★★
PAUILLAC $36.00–$50.00

Duhart is a château to watch as the Rothschilds (of Lafite) are making serious investments and pushing full throttle to upgrade the quality and image of this estate.

2006	91–93	2012–2025	2000	90	now–2019
2005	94	2011–2026	1999	88	now–2011
2004	91	2010–2022	1998	89+	now–2020
2003	92+	2010–2030	1997	87	now–2010
2002	89	now–2020	1996	90	now–2020
2001	89	now–2017	1995	87	now–2014

Past Glories 1982 (93)

DOMAINE DE L'ÉGLISE ★★★/★★★★
POMEROL $45.00–$55.00

Another property owned by Philippe Castéja. There is no question that this beautifully situated estate on the Pomerol plateau could produce better wines. However, recent vintages are promising, and the 2005 is the finest wine to date.

2006	88–91	now–2018	2000	89+	now–2020
2005	92	2011–2026	1999	88	now–2014
2003	87–89	now–2012	1998	87	now–2012

2002	86–88	now–2011		1997	85	now
2001	89	now–2016		1995	87	now–2016

Past Glories 1989 (90)

L'ÉGLISE CLINET ★ ★ ★ ★ ★
POMEROL $105.00–$225.00

Under the inspired leadership of Denis Durantou, this wine is frequently one of Bordeaux's superstars, particularly when Pomerol experiences a ripe, excellent vintage. In fact, L'Église Clinet has been so impressive over the last decade that it can now be said to rival Pétrus. For purists and traditionalists of Bordeaux, this is possibly their favorite wine of the right bank and a wine of incredible longevity.

2006	96–98+	2009–2039+		2000	96	2010–2035+
2005	100	2015–2035+		1999	92	now–2025
2004	93	2011–2025		1998	94+	now–2035
2003	88	now–2016		1997	91	now–2015+
2002	86	now		1996	93	now–2020
2001	94	now–2020		1995	96	2010–2030

Past Glories 1994 (90), 1990 (92), 1989 (90?), 1986 (92), 1985 (95), 1975 (92), 1971 (92), 1961 (92), 1959 (96), 1950 (95), 1949 (99), 1947 (100), 1945 (98), 1921 (100)

L'ENCLOS ★ ★
POMEROL $18.00–$20.00

This vineyard, situated in one of Pomerol's less prestigious areas, has not performed up to its capabilities for a number of years. There is nothing wrong with their wines, but the recent vintages are light and lack the concentration and density of their older siblings of the 1980s.

2005	85	now–2019		1998	85–86	now
2001	84–85	now–2011		1997	85–86	now
2000	85	now		1996	77–80	now
1999	80–82	now		1995	86	now

EPICUREA (CHÂTEAU MARTINAT) ★ ★ ★
CÔTES DE BOURG $20.00–$28.00

A special cuvée produced from Château Martinat's oldest vines, this 90% Merlot/10% Malbec blend is aged in 100% new French oak and bottled unfined as well as unfiltered.

2005	90	now–2021		2001	88	now
2003	85–87	now		2000	89	now–2010
2002	87	now				

D'ESCURAC ★ ★ ★ ★
MÉDOC $13.00–$24.00

A terrific value, d'Escurac is one of the Médoc's bright, shining success stories and worth serious consideration. It is a wine that competes favorably with its much more expensive neighbors. Moreover, it is drinkable upon release.

2005	89	now–2015		2001	87–88	now–2010
2004	86	now–2011		2000	88	now–2013
2003	89	now–2012		1999	85–86	now
2002	86	now–2012				

L'ESSENCE DES VIGNOBLES DOURTHE ★★★★
BORDEAUX $25.00–$40.00

The showcase offering from the large *négociant* firm of Dourthe, this wine, which represents a blend of the finest materials they possess, is treated like a luxury cuvée. Michel Rolland is the consulting oenologist, and the wine is the personal project of Jean-Marie Chadronnier, Dourthe's visionary CEO. For a generic Bordeaux it is a concentrated, flamboyant effort that is, qualitatively, closer to a top-classified growth.

2003	89	now–2016		2001	87–88	now–2011
2002	88–90	now		2000	89	now–2013

L'ÉVANGILE ★★★★★
POMEROL $50.00–$250.00

Now that the Rothschilds (of Lafite-Rothschild fame) are the sole owners of this estate, major investments and extraordinary efforts in both the vineyard and cellar are being made. L'Évangile already rivals Pétrus and Lafleur as one of the finest wines of the appellation. The estate has also introduced a second wine called Blason, which permits them to cull out lots not good enough for the grand vin. This is irrefutably one of the great wines of Bordeaux and set for glory under the Rothschild administration.

2006	92–94	2009–2034
2005	95	2010–2030
2004	90	2009–2021+
2003	88	now–2016
2002	90	now–2017
2001	91	now–2017
2000	96+	2010–2035
1999	89	now–2015
1998	95+	2009–2035
1997	89	now–2012
1996	90?	now–2016
1995	92	now–2020
2005 Blason de L'Évangile	86	now–2015

Past Glories 1994 (92), 1990 (96), 1989 (90), 1985 (95), 1983 (90), 1982 (96), 1975 (96), 1961 (99), 1947 (97)

EXCELLENCE DE BOIS PERTUIS ★★★★
BORDEAUX $35.00–$45.00

A project of Bernard Magrez, which he terms Cuvée d'Exception, this 100% Merlot is fashioned from a five-acre parcel cropped at very low yields. Readers will have to look long and hard to find a better generic Bordeaux. A credit to Magrez and his consulting oenologist, Michel Rolland, these wines admirably demonstrate what can be achieved from these humble appellations.

2005	89	now–2021		2002	89	now–2010
2004	90	now–2015		2001	90	now–2010
2003	90	now–2011				

FAIZEAU VIEILLES VIGNES ★★★/★★★★
MONTAGNE–ST.-ÉMILION $22.00–$28.00

This estate's wines are made by the sister of Dr. Alain Raynaud, of Quinault L'Enclos fame (so there is plenty of genetic talent for making fine wine). Produced from 100% old vine, hillside-grown Merlot, they are bottled after spending 16 to 18 months in a combination of new and old oak, with neither fining nor filtration. Perhaps it is just the *terroir,* but they are somewhat one-dimensional, straightforward efforts, which, if they sold for a lower price, would be decent values.

2005	90	now–2021	1999	86–87	now–2012
2004	87	now–2015	1998	86	now–2010
2003	89	now–2014	1997	85–86	now
2002	87	now	1996	82	now
2001	88	now–2012	1995	85–86	now
2000	90	now–2013			

FAUGÈRES ★ ★ ★ ★
ST.-ÉMILION
FAUGÈRES $20.00–$35.00; PÉBY $66.00–$135.00

This estate offers some of the best values of St.-Émilion. It changed ownership several years ago, but the quality has remained high. The superb garage wine, originally called Péby-Faugères after the former proprietor's late husband, is something serious and intense. It is a 500- to 600-case lot of concentrated, dramatic, intense wine meant for 20 or more years of aging. Produced from a south-facing parcel—considered the best one—of the Faugères vineyard in St.-Émilion, this remarkable wine competes with the best wines of Bordeaux. The new owners decided to change the name of the luxury cuvée from Péby-Faugères to Cuvée Spéciale Péby. Michel Rolland remains the consulting oenologist for this estate.

2006 Cuvée Spéciale Péby	90–92+	now–2023
2005 Cuvée Spéciale Péby	95+	2012–2025
2006 Faugères	89–91	now–2018
2005 Faugères	91	2010–2020
2004 Faugères	90	now–2022
2003 Faugères	89	now–2018
2002 Faugères	89	now–2013
2001 Faugères	90	now–2014
2000 Faugères	91	now–2018
1999 Faugères	88	now–2012
1998 Faugères	90	now–2015
1997 Faugères	87	now–2010
1996 Faugères	87	now–2012
1995 Faugères	87	now
2004 Péby-Faugères	92+	now–2027
2003 Péby-Faugères	93	now–2020+
2002 Péby-Faugères	87	now–2017
2001 Péby-Faugères	94	now–2020
2000 Péby-Faugères	96	now–2020
1999 Péby-Faugères	94	now–2018
1998 Péby-Faugères	95	now–2018+

FAURIE DE SOUCHARD ★ ★/★ ★
ST.-ÉMILION $20.00–$26.00

Faurie de Souchard, one of the oldest properties in St.-Émilion, has been owned by the Jabiol family since 1933. Unlike many St.-Émilions that are made to be drunk within their first five to six years, most vintages of Faurie de Souchard can last 10 to 15 years. If the wines are to be criticized at all, it is because their tannins often exceed extraction levels of fruit.

| 2000 | 87 | now–2014 | 1998 | 87 | now |
| 1999 | 86 | now–2015 | | | |

FERET-LAMBERT ★ ★ ★
BORDEAUX SUPÉRIEUR $15.00

Feret-Lambert tends to produce good values from less prestigious Bordeaux soils. An insider's value wine.

| 2005 | 89+ | now–2013 | 2001 | 87 | now |

FERRAND-LARTIGUE ★ ★ ★ ★
ST.-ÉMILION $25.00–$45.00

The owner of this tiny gem of a property does everything possible to produce the finest wines. Even though it is not a premier grand cru or even grand cru classé, Ferrand-Lartigue is superior to many wines with those higher pedigrees. Quantities are very limited and the wine popular among consumers because of the succulent, flamboyant, sometimes even ostentatious show of fruit and wood this wine exhibits in its youth.

2005	90	now–2022	1999	89	now–2012
2004	86+	now–2013	1998	90	now–2015
2003	88	now–2014	1997	88	now
2002	87	now–2011	1996	90	now–2013
2001	90	now–2014	1995	89	now
2000	91	now–2015			

FERRIÈRE ★ ★
MARGAUX $25.00–$35.00

Named a third growth in the 1855 classification, Ferrière has been a perennial underachiever. The estate is owned by Claire Villars-Lurton. The wine has recently shown signs of improvement, but Ferrière is not among the more interesting wines of Margaux.

2000	88	now–2015	1996	86	now–2014
1998	85	now–2012	1995	87	now–2015
1997	84	now			

FEYTIT-CLINET ★ ★ ★ ★
POMEROL $28.00–$50.00

This property is on the rebound since the owners, the Chasseuil family, took over the winemaking. The 17.3-acre vineyard, ideally situated between Trotanoy and Latour à Pomerol, is planted in sandy/gravel soils with 85% Merlot and 15% Cabernet Franc. This is clearly an estate to keep a close eye on, as the quality has soared since its escape from a long-term lease with the firm of Jean-Pierre Moueix.

2006	90–93	now–2021	2002	87–89	now–2011
2005	93	2011–2025	2001	89	now–2016
2004	89	now–2021+	2000	87	now–2014
2003	87	now–2014	1998	88+	now–2016

DE FIEUZAL ★ ★ ★/★ ★ ★ ★
PESSAC-LÉOGNAN $28.00–$45.00

Once one of the least-known Graves properties, de Fieuzal's obscurity seems to have ended during the mid-1980s, when its wines became noticeably richer and more complex. While the estate does not rival such stars of the appellation as Haut-Brion or La Mission Haut-Brion, its wines are among some of the more dazzling in Graves, with the 2000 being the strongest success in nearly a decade. Amazingly, the high quality has not been accompanied by soaring prices, and de Fieuzal represents one of the best quality-to-price ratios in the entire Graves region. I still have a slight preference for the white wines of de Fieuzal over the reds, but both are worthy of attention.

2005	90	2010–2025
2004	89+	2009–2022
2003	88	now–2021
2002	87	now–2015
2001	89	now–2019
2000	90+	now–2022
1999	87	now
1998	86	now–2015
1997	86	now–2012
1996	88+	now–2020
1995	90	now–2020
2006 Blanc	88–90	now–2020
2005 Blanc	92	now–2020
2003 Blanc	91	now–2015
2002 Blanc	87	now–2010
2001 Blanc	93	now–2020
2000 Blanc	86	now–2010
1999 Blanc	75	now
1998 Blanc	78	now
1996 Blanc	88	now–2012
1995 Blanc	88	now–2010

FIGEAC   * * */* * * *
ST.-ÉMILION $50.00–$75.00

I know the proprietors of this estate think I have been unduly tough on their wines, but I am in fact a fan of Figeac's finest vintages. Though always a wine of finesse, a sense of dilution can sometimes underwhelm tasters, but this is not the case with the 2000 or 2005, an impressive duo for this estate. In the great vintages this traditionally made St.-Émilion clearly lives up to its splendid *terroir,* which many observers feel actually eclipses that of its nearby neighbor Cheval Blanc. Yet my instincts suggest that this estate still underachieves far too frequently.

2005	90	2009–2020		1999	89	now–2014
2004	86?	now–2016		1998	90	now–2016
2003	88	now–2018		1997	76	now
2002	88	now–2015		1996	82	now
2001	89	now–2020		1995	90	now–2012
2000	93	now–2018				

Past Glories 1990 (94), 1982 (93), 1970 (90), 1964 (94), 1961 (94?), 1959 (91), 1955 (95), 1953 (93), 1949 (94)

LA FLEUR   * * *
ST.-ÉMILION $21.00–$32.00

Over recent years, the style of La Fleur has offered straightforward, open-knit, ripe fruit presented in an easy-to-understand manner. Readers looking for in-your-face, deliciously fruity, seductive St.-Émilion should check out this value-priced wine.

2006	89–91	now–2016	1999	85	now
2005	90	now–2019	1998	89	now
2004	89	now–2019	1997	87	now
2003	88	now–2013	1996	86	now
2002	87	now	1995	87	now

LA FLEUR D'ARTHUS ★★/★★★
ST.-ÉMILION $25.00–$30.00

This solidly made offering originates from an unheralded *terroir*. The wine has begun to exhibit fine charm and finesse, but it is still too rustic.

2005	88	now–2017+

FLEUR DE BARBEYRON ★★★
ST.-ÉMILION $20.00

This ten-acre estate is owned by the proprietor of the St.-Émilion fruit bomb Pipeau.

2005	91	now–2021

LA FLEUR DE BOÜARD ★★★★/★★★★★
LE PLUS DE LA FLEUR DE BOÜARD;
LALANDE DE POMEROL; LA FLEUR DE BOÜARD $25.00–$30.00;
LE PLUS DE LA FLEUR DE BOÜARD $90.00

It is difficult to find a more dedicated winemaking couple than Corinne and Hubert de Boüard. They also co-own L'Angélus with other family members, but they are the sole proprietors of this property, a 40-acre estate planted with 80% Merlot and 20% Cabernet Franc and Cabernet Sauvignon. In addition to the grand vin, they also produce a luxury cuvée, Le Plus de La Fleur de Boüard. The latter wine is culled from specific parcels and vinified in tiny, squat stainless-steel and oak fermentors. It receives the full Burgundy treatment of malolactic fermentation in barrel and aging on lees. It is also bottled (unfined and unfiltered) much later than La Fleur de Boüard (usually 33 months following the vintage). Production for the luxury wine is tiny, 250 cases versus nearly 6,000 cases of La Fleur.

2006 La Fleur de Boüard	90–93	now–2016
2005 La Fleur de Boüard	89	now–2014
2004 La Fleur de Boüard	90	now–2017
2003 La Fleur de Boüard	89+	now–2016
2002 La Fleur de Boüard	88	now–2015
2001 La Fleur de Boüard	88	now–2019
2000 La Fleur de Boüard	91	now–2018
1999 La Fleur de Boüard	88	now–2012
1998 La Fleur de Boüard	89	now–2013
2005 Le Plus de la Fleur de Boüard	93–95	now–2025
2004 Le Plus de la Fleur de Boüard	92	now–2022
2003 Le Plus de la Fleur de Boüard	90+	now–2023
2002 Le Plus de la Fleur de Boüard	88	now–2020
2001 Le Plus de la Fleur de Boüard	91	now–2014
2000 Le Plus de la Fleur de Boüard	95	now–2016

FLEUR-CARDINALE ★★★★
ST.-ÉMILION $35.00

Fleur-Cardinale's new owners, Dominique Decosters and his beautiful wife, Florence, of Haviland porcelain fame, assisted admirably by the top oenologist in Michel Rolland's laboratory, Jean-Philippe Fort, have turned this 40-plus-acre vineyard into one of St.-Émilion's bright shining stars. The vineyard consists of 45 acres planted (in rich clay-limestone soils) with 70% Merlot, 15% Cabernet Sauvignon, and 15% Cabernet Franc. From 2003 onward, this has been a stunningly made St.-Émilion that remains underpriced for its spectacular level of quality.

2006	91–93	now–2021	2000	87	now–2009
2005	95	2012–2022+	1999	85	now
2004	91	now–2022	1998	87	now
2003	91	now–2021	1997	86	now
2002	87	now–2015	1996	84	now
2001	88	now–2012	1995	86	now

LA FLEUR DU CHÂTEAU BOUQUEYRAN ★★★
MOULIS $28.00–$35.00

This is a small estate run by Monsieur Porcheron, who made a name for himself with Marojallia, his garage wine effort in the appellation of Margaux.

2001	87	now–2014	2000	87	now–2011

FLEUR DE ROSE STE.-CROIX ★★★
LISTRAC $25.00

This limited-production cuvée (600+ cases) is a blend of Cabernet Sauvignon and Merlot from another vineyard owned by Monsieur Porcheron, the proprietor of Marojallia.

2001	88–90	now–2015	2000	90	now–2016

LA FLEUR DE GAY ★★★★/★★★★★
POMEROL $75.00–$125.00

La Fleur de Gay, the luxury cuvée of La Croix de Gay, was launched by Dr. Alain Raynaud in 1982. This estate represents a parcel of 7.5 acres culled from the large La Croix de Gay vineyard. The wine, a 100% Merlot fashioned from minuscule yields of 20 to 35 hectoliters per hectare (374 U.S. gallons per acre), is made by Dr. Raynaud's sister, Chantal Lebreton. The wine is vinified in the manner of a great Burgundy, with malolactic fermentation in barrel, aging on lees, and no filtration at bottling.

2006	91–94	2009–2029	2000	94	now–2018
2005	92	2012–2037+	1999	90	now–2016
2004	91	2009–2022	1998	90	now–2016
2003	88	now–2018	1997	87	now
2002	86	now–2013	1996	85	now–2010
2001	90	now–2016	1995	88+?	now–2015

Past Glories 1990 (92), 1989 (94+), 1988 (93), 1987 (90)

LA FLEUR DE JAUGUE ★★★/★★★★
ST.-ÉMILION $20.00–$32.00

This impeccably run estate deserves more attention. Proprietor Georges Bigaud is not a household name in either Bordeaux or the export markets, but he is a serious producer of quality wine. His small, 15,000-bottle production is a perennial best-value entry. Moreover, this consistently well made, delicious St.-Émilion, capable of lasting a decade or more, still sells for a song. What is so impressive about La Fleur de Jaugue is its purity, symmetry, and elegance. The 2000 appears to be the finest wine yet produced at the estate. The second wine, Jaugue Blanc, is also worthy of attention.

2006	89–91	now–2018	1999	87	now
2005	90	now–2018	1998	90	now–2012
2004	89	now–2014	1997	87	now
2002	87	now	1996	87	now
2001	87	now–2011	1995	89	now
2000	90	now–2014			

LA FLEUR MONGIRON ★★★/★★★★
BORDEAUX $14.00–$25.00

One of the most serious generic Bordeaux made, La Fleur Mongiron enjoys micro-oxygenation, aging on its lees, and bottling without fining or filtration. It is a very fine wine for the price.

2003	87	now–2011	2000	89	now–2010
2002	87	now	1999	87	now
2001	88	now–2010			

LA FLEUR MORANGE ★★★★
ST.-ÉMILION $45.00–$84.00

Claude Gros, the brilliant oenologist responsible for some of the greatest wines of the Languedoc-Roussillon (e.g., Château de La Négly), oversees the winemaking at La Fleur Morange. This 70% Merlot and 30% Cabernet Franc garage wine, made from a five-acre parcel of 70-year-old vines, has been aged in 100% new oak, and subjected to such creative qualitative treatments as extensive crop thinning, *microbullage, pigeage,* and aging on lees. The result is impressive and 2005 may be the finest vintage in this estate's relatively short history. Readers should pay close attention to La Fleur Morange.

2005 La Fleur Morange	96	2009–2025
2004 La Fleur Morange	88	now–2019
2003 La Fleur Morange	88	now–2014
2001 La Fleur Morange	92	now–2020
2000 La Fleur Morange	91+	now–2020+
2005 La Fleur Morange Mathilde	93	2012–2030+

LA FLEUR-PÉTRUS ★★★★
POMEROL $45.00–$75.00

This is the quintessentially elegant style of Pomerol favored by Christian Moueix and his winemaking team. Moueix is trying to push this estate's quality level to greater heights, as evidenced by recent vintages. He acquired a parcel of old vines from Château Le Gay and has instituted a more rigorous selection in both the vineyard and cellars. The winery itself has also been renovated. Some of La Fleur-Pétrus's finest wines are being produced now, which means that prices can only escalate.

2006	94–96+	2010–2030+	1999	89	now–2015
2005	93	2012–2037	1998	95	now–2020
2004	90	now–2019	1997	87	now–2012
2003	89	now–2018+	1996	89	now–2015
2002	88	now–2017	1995	91+	now–2025

2001	90	now–2016	2005 Blanc	90	now–2012
2000	95	now–2025			

FOMBRAUGE ★★★★
ST.-ÉMILION $25.00–$28.00

Another of the Bernard Magrez properties that has exploded in recent vintages with remarkably high quality, Fombrauge is the largest vineyard in St.-Émilion, and Magrez is finally exploiting its full potential. Since the late 1990s, this estate has been a consistent sleeper of the vintage.

Magrez is also fashioning limited quantities of an Appellation Bordeaux Controllée white from Fombrauge's vineyard, as well as a special project called Le Sublime du Fombrauge from a one-hectare (2.47-acre) parcel. The first few vintages of this dry white have been splendid.

2006	88–90	now–2018
2005	90	2012–2034
2004	89	now–2019
2003	89	now–2014
2002	90	now–2017
2001	90	now–2016
2000	90	now–2015
1999	88	now–2010
1998	86	now
2006 Blanc	89–91	now–2013
2005 Blanc	90	now–2012
2004 Blanc	87	now
2004 Le Sublime du Fombrauge (white)	90	now–2016+

FONBADET ★★/★★★
PAUILLAC $18.00

Fonbadet has traditionally been a well-vinified wine that, in some vintages in the 1980s, could surpass several of the classified growths of Pauillac. However, recently the wine has been somewhat off form, although certainly drinkable and pleasant, but not nearly as impressive as it was 10 or 15 years ago.

2001	85–86	now–2010	1997	79	now
2000	87	now–2012	1995	83	now
1998	82–84	now			

FONBEL ★★★/★★★★
ST.-ÉMILION $35.00

Alain Vauthier, who owns this small estate, has been ratcheting up the level of quality at Fonbel just as he has at his more well-known properties, Ausone and Moulin St.-Georges.

2005	90	now–2022	2003	89	now–2016
2004	90	now–2015			

FONPLÉGADE ★★★
ST.-ÉMILION $22.00–$25.00

This estate has underperformed for many years despite its privileged *terroir*. However, the wines have greatly improved recently as a new owner, an American, has taken over the viticulture and winemaking, so better wines are likely to emerge in the 21st century.

2006	90–92	now–2023	2000	89+	now–2018
2005	92	2012–2025	1998	72–76	now
2004	89	2009–2022	1996	76–78	now
2001	86–88	now–2013	1995	86	now–2012

FONROQUE ★ ★ ★
ST.-ÉMILION $20.00–$24.00

Fonroque is situated in an isolated location north and west of St.-Émilion. In style it tends to be of the robust, rich, tannic, medium-bodied school of St.-Émilions. It can take aging well and in good vintages actually needs cellaring of at least two to three years before being consumed. Recent vintages have demonstrated more suppleness and charm, but this remains a muscular, very virile style of St.-Émilion.

2005	90	2012–2032	1998	81	now
2003	86	now–2011	1997	78	now
2001	88	now–2015	1996	76	now
2000	86	now	1995	87	now–2012

FONTENIL ★ ★ ★ ★
FRONSAC $15.00–$30.00

Fontenil, the home estate of Dany and Michel Rolland, is currently among the finest estates in Fronsac, producing wines that are consistently excellent values. The 2000, 2003, and 2005 are the finest wines yet produced at the estate. In 2000, Michel Rolland utilized plastic sheathing on part of his vineyard as a precaution against heavy rains (that never materialized). Though this was only an experimental practice, appellation authorities would not allow that parcel to be entitled to appellation status, or to be vintage dated; hence the special cuvée of nonvintage Le Défi de Fontenil.

2006	90–92	now–2021	2000	91	now–2015
2005	90	2009–2025	1999	88	now–2012
2004	88	now–2019	1998	88	now–2014
2003	90	now–2022	1997	86	now
2002	88	now–2013	1996	85	now
2001	91	now–2016	1995	87	now

FOUGAS MALDOROR ★ ★ ★ ★
CÔTES DE BOURG $17.00–$20.00

This terrific Côtes de Bourg, along with the famed Roc de Cambes, represents the benchmark for this appellation's greatest wines. Jean-Yves Béchet, the proprietor, spares no expense and makes no compromise to turn out this sumptuous blend of 50% Merlot, 25% Cabernet Sauvignon, and 25% Cabernet Franc. The 1998, 1999, and 2000 are certainly sleepers of their respective vintages as well as fabulous values for their exceptional quality. Moreover, the vineyard is more than 25 acres in size, so good quantities are available. Thrifty readers should squirrel these wines away by the case.

2005	87	now–2016	2001	90	now–2010
2004	87–88	now–2012	2000	89	now–2015
2003	88	now–2012	1999	87	now
2002	87	now	1998	90	now–2011

FOURCAS-DUPRÉ ★★★
LISTRAC $18.00

This is a somewhat hard, austere style of wine, yet very typical of Listrac. Several recent vintages have suggested that more charm and finesse is emerging, but fruit lovers need to steer clear of this estate.

2005	83	now–2015	1997	85–86	now
2003	87	now–2014	1996	84–86	now
2000	87	now	1995	84	now
1999	83	now			

FOURCAS-LOUBANEY ★★★
LISTRAC $20.00–$25.00

This is one of the best wines of the Listrac appellation. Unfortunately, the modest production is rarely seen except by a small group of avid Bordeaux aficionados. Although I have not tasted a fully mature vintage of Fourcas-Loubaney, many vintages have been impressive in their youth.

2000	86	now	1997	86	now
1999	83	now	1995	87	now
1998	85	now			

FRANC MAILLET ★★★
POMEROL $18.00–$45.00

St.-Émilion's "bad boy," Jean-Luc Thunevin, is behind the vinification and upbringing of this small Pomerol estate. The *garagiste extraordinaire* of St.-Émilion has produced an even more impressive wine in the limited-production Cuvée Jean-Baptiste.

2004	88	now–2017
2001	88–90	now–2016
2000	89	now–2014
1999	88	now–2014
1998	87	now–2009
2005 Cuvée Jean-Baptiste	91+	now–2018
2003 Cuvée Jean-Baptiste	90	now–2014
2001 Cuvée Jean-Baptiste	92	now–2015
2000 Cuvée Jean-Baptiste	92	now–2020
1999 Cuvée Jean-Baptiste	90	now–2020
1998 Cuvée Jean-Baptiste	87	now–2009
2005 Tête de Cuvée	88–90	now–2021

FRANC MAYNE ★★★
ST.-ÉMILION $22.00–$32.00

This property, which has changed owners several times, has never been one of my favorite St.-Émilions, always possessing a vegetal streak in its flavors. The last few vintages have been slightly better, but to date this is not a terribly interesting wine.

2005	91	2012–2025	2000	88	now–2018
2004	88	now–2017	1999	87	now–2017
2003	88	now–2016	1998	88	now–2015
2002	86	now–2014	1997	76	now
2001	85	now–2014	1996	84	now

DE FRANCE ★★
PESSAC-LÉOGNAN $15.00–$20.00

Virtually the entire vineyard of this property, which is a neighbor of the more renowned Château de Fieuzal, has been replanted since 1971. The proprietor, an industrialist, has spared little expense in renovating the property and building a new winery with state-of-the-art stainless-steel fermentation tanks. The results to date have not been nearly as impressive as one might have hoped.

2005	86	now–2016	2002 Blanc	88	now
2004	84	now–2012	2001 Blanc	87	now
2003	78	now–2011	2000 Blanc	82	now
2000	84	now–2011	1999 Blanc	87	now
1999	83	now	1998 Blanc	87	now
1998	74	now	1997 Blanc	87	now
2003 Blanc	87	now			

DE FRANCS LES CÉRISIERS ★★★
CÔTES DE FRANCS $15.00–$20.00

This wine is the result of a partnership between the Boüard and Hébrard families. The 2000 is the finest example I have tasted since they began producing it more than a decade ago.

2001	86	now	2000	88	now–2013

GABY ★★★
CANON-FRONSAC $22.00–$25.00

Gaby is a straightforward, rather austere style of Canon-Fronsac with notes of minerals and berry fruit but dusty tannins.

2005	86	now–2015	2002	78	now–2011
2003	88	now–2020	2001	87	now–2010

LA GAFFELIÈRE ★★★★
ST.-ÉMILION $35.00–$85.00

Always one of the more elegant, restrained, graceful St.-Émilions, the wines of La Gaffelière have been showing more stuffing in their mid-palate, as well as greater sweetness and concentration over the recent vintages. The owner, Comte de Malet-Roquefort, is also the proprietor of the St.-Émilion property Tertre Daugay.

2006	89–91	2009–2018	2000	90	now–2019
2005	96	2014–2030	1999	89	now–2015
2004	92	2010–2022	1998	89	now–2015
2003	92	2011–2025+	1997	85	now
2002	89	now–2015	1996	87	now–2012
2001	90	now–2018	1995	87	now–2010

MAISON GALHAUD CUVÉE LYON ★★★
BORDEAUX $17.00

These inexpensive Bordeaux are well worth searching for in the marketplace.

2004	87	now–2011	2003	89	now

LA GARDE ★ ★ ★
PESSAC-LÉOGNAN $18.00–$30.00

An impressive-looking estate sitting on gravel outcroppings south of the village of Martillac, this ancient property has made an important rebound and the wines are generally solidly made, represent good value, and are worth consumers' attention.

2005 La Garde	87	now–2015
2004 La Garde	84	now
2003 La Garde	87	now–2013
2001 Réserve du Château	87	now–2013
2000 Réserve du Château	89	now–2017
1999 Réserve du Château	87	now
1998 Réserve du Château	87	now
1997 Réserve du Château	85	now
1996 Réserve du Château	78	now
1995 Réserve du Château	88	now
1998 Réserve du Château Blanc	89	now

GARREAU ★ ★/★ ★
CÔTES DE BLAYE $20.00–$27.00

This good estate, one of the Côtes de Blaye's qualitative leaders, fashions very fine wines that value-conscious readers should seek out. The blend is generally 75% Cabernet Sauvignon and 25% Merlot.

2001 Côtes de Bourg	86	now
2000 Côtes de Bourg	89	now–2013
2000 Cuvée Armande	87	now–2010
2000 Premières Côtes de Blaye	87	now
1998 Premières Côtes de Blaye	87	now

LE GAY ★ ★ ★ ★
POMEROL $32.00–$75.00

An estate on the rise, Le Gay deserves a serious look now that perfectionist proprietress Cathérine Péré-Vergé is running the show. The 2004 vintage was the first in which she came close to having the raw materials necessary to produce a top-flight wine, and she and her consulting oenologist, Michel Rolland, hit a home run in 2005. Much like L'Évangile, owned by the Rothschilds, this is an estate on a meteoric rise to fame and fortune in Pomerol.

2006	93–95	2011–2030	2000	90	now–2020
2005	95	2017–2035+	1999	87	now–2014
2004	93	2011–2027	1998	89	now–2016
2003	90	2010–2020+	1997	86	now
2002	89	2010–2020	1996	74	now
2001	88	now–2017	1995	82	now–2015

Past Glories 1989 (90), 1950 (98), 1949 (96), 1947 (100), 1945 (94)

GAZIN ★ ★ ★ ★
POMEROL $40.00–$65.00

This superbly situated vineyard, adjacent to Pétrus and just down the road from l'Évangile and La Conseillante, has made an impressive rebound and has been producing higher and higher quality wines for over a decade. Gazin is now one of the most impressive Pomerols, which is good news for consumers as it is one of Pomerol's largest properties, with the potential to produce 10,000 cases. The wines are full-bodied and exhibit abundant depth and power, as well as noticeable toasty new oak. However, there is sometimes a tendency to utilize too much new oak.

2006	90–92+	2012–2025		2000	90	now–2020
2005	94	2013–2025		1999	89	now–2014
2004	90	2009–2022		1998	91	now–2020
2003	89	now–2021		1997	87?	now–2009
2002	87	now–2015		1996	89	now–2018
2001	94	2009–2020		1995	90+	now–2018

Past Glories 1994 (90), 1990 (93), 1961 (93)

GIGAULT CUVÉE VIVA ★ ★ ★/★ ★ ★ ★
PREMIÈRES CÔTES DE BLAYE $14.00–$18.00

This 33-acre vineyard, one of the best run in the Côtes de Blaye, has been consistently excellent over the last decade. One of the co-owners is the fashionable consultant-guru Stéphane Derenoncourt. This wine offers superb value and is consistently well made.

2005	89	now–2010		2002	85	now
2004	87	now–2014		2001	86	now
2003	90	now–2012		2000	89	now–2010

GISCOURS ★ ★ ★ ★
MARGAUX $45.00–$50.00

This was one of the best wines of the Margaux appellation in the 1960s and 1970s and then fell on hard times. However, it has rebounded impressively, thanks to the extraordinary work of Eric Albada Jelgensma. The wines have been consistently excellent over recent vintages and are still fairly priced, so shrewd consumers, take notice.

2006	89–91	now–2021		2000	92	now–2020
2005	91	2011–2025		1999	89	now–2017
2004	91	now–2021		1998	87	now–2014
2003	90	now–2021		1997	85	now
2002	90	now–2021		1996	83	now
2001	90	now–2015		1995	85	now–2010

Past Glories 1978 (90), 1975 (92)

GLORIA ★ ★ ★ ★
ST.-JULIEN $25.00–$30.00

Gloria has always been an example of why the 1855 classification of the Médoc wines is so outdated. Gloria makes wine from vineyards purchased from neighboring classified châteaux and, during the last 25 years, in top vintages they are certainly as good as many of the wines produced in classified growths. Shrewd merchants and consumers have long known Gloria's quality, and the wine has been widely merchandised in America and abroad. Moreover, recent vintages may be better than ever.

2006	89–91	now–2021+		2000	89	now–2015
2005	90	now–2023		1998	85	now
2004	89	now–2017		1997	87	now
2003	90	now–2016		1996	88	now–2013
2002	89	now–2015		1995	88	now–2013
2001	88	now–2014				

GOMBAUDE GUILLOT ★★
POMEROL $20.00–$40.00

This has become an intriguing property to follow. I remember tasting years ago a range of vintages from the 1970s and being unimpressed. But a vertical tasting between 1998 back through 1982 left me with the conclusion that in certain years Gombaude Guillot can produce a Pomerol of stunning quality. However, recent vintages have left me unimpressed and the quality has rarely been sufficient even to include in *The Wine Advocate*.

2000	75	now		1996	78	now

LA GOMERIE ★★★★★
ST.-ÉMILION $65.00–$110.00

This 6.2-acre vineyard planted with 30-year-old 100% Merlot vines can produce some of Bordeaux's sexiest, most voluptuous wines. Given the heavy, sandy soils atop the famed Crasse de Fer, I am surprised it did so well in 2003. The vinification is impeccable: this wine receives *garagiste*/Burgundian techniques such as malolactic fermentation in barrel, aging on lees, and no filtration at bottling. Oddly enough, when such ancient Burgundy winemaking techniques are used outside France's Côte d'Or, they are called "international, modern-style winemaking"—try to figure that out.

2006	90–93	now–2021		2000	96	now–2016
2005	95	now–2022+		1999	86	now–2012
2004	91	now–2021		1998	94	now–2014
2003	94	now–2016		1997	89	now–2010
2002	88	now–2013		1996	92	now–2018
2001	92	now–2014		1995	93	now–2012

LA GOULÉE ★★★★
MÉDOC $30.00

An innovative effort from Cos d'Estournel's Jean-Guillaume Prats and Michel Reydier, this complex, rich, opulently styled wine is perfect for readers looking for a modern style of Bordeaux to drink during its first 10 to 12 years. It is a beautiful wine that should have huge crowd appeal and satisfy on both hedonistic and intellectual levels. Bordeaux could certainly use more wines like this to reenergize the marketplace.

2005	89	now–2019		2003	90	now–2014
2004	87	now–2013				

GRACIA ★★★★★
ST.-ÉMILION $75.00–$99.00

The quintessential garage wine, Gracia is made from a 4.5-acre parcel, hand destemmed as well as hand harvested, fermented, given a long maceration, and bottled unfined and unfiltered. The 250- to 275-case production disappears quickly, given the insatiable demand for this blend of primarily Merlot and the rest Cabernet Franc with a touch of Cabernet Sauvignon. The 2005 is one of the finest wines yet made by Gracia's proprietor, who receives consulting advice from the brilliant winemaker Alain Vauthier of Ausone as well as Michel Rolland.

2006	93–95	now–2031		2001	91	now–2014
2005	96	2015–2040+		2000	93	now–2018
2004	93+	2012–2030		1999	91	now–2020
2003	90?	now–2020		1998	92	now–2016
2002	89	now–2016		1997	89	now–2012

GRAND CORBIN ★ ★ ★
ST.-ÉMILION $20.00–$25.00

The Girauds, an ancient family originally from Pomerol, own Grand Corbin and, like their nearby neighbor Figeac, employ a relatively high percentage of Cabernet Franc in the blend. This works well when the Cabernet ripens fully, but in years that it does not, Grand Corbin tends to come across as too herbaceous, even vegetal.

2002	86	now	1999	70?	now
2001	85	now–2011	1996	86	now–2018+
2000	87	now–2011			

GRAND CORBIN-DESPAGNE ★ ★ ★ ★
ST.-ÉMILION $15.00–$32.00

Grand Corbin-Despagne is an up-and-coming St.-Émilion estate fashioning muscular, powerful wines that require cellaring. 1998 is the breakthrough vintage for this property, which is located on the gravelly plateau of St.-Émilion, not far from Cheval Blanc and La Conseillante. The 1999s and 2000s are top-flight.

2006	90–91	2010–2020+	2001	88	now–2013
2005	90+	2012–2022	2000	90	now–2018
2004	90	2009–2022	1999	88	now–2013
2003	88	now–2016	1998	88+	now–2016
2002	87	now–2018			

GRAND-DESTIEU ★ ★ ★/★ ★ ★ ★
ST.-ÉMILION $50.00–$75.00

This impressive wine from Jonathan Malthus, the proprietor of Château Teyssier, needs a few years to settle down, but it reveals beautiful potential.

2006	91–93	2010–2020	2005	91	2011–2020+

GRAND-MAYNE ★ ★ ★ ★
ST.-ÉMILION $38.00–$50.00

The late Baron Philippe de Rothschild, after tasting the 1955 Grand -Mayne at a restaurant in Belgium, immediately placed an order for several cases, offering to replace the Grand-Mayne with a similar number of bottles of the Mouton-Rothschild! This is one of my favorite St.-Émilion estates as well. Neither the 2002 nor 2003 will make consumers forget any of the top-notch efforts Grand-Mayne produced since the late 1990s, but the 2005 is the best Grand-Mayne since the blockbuster 1998.

2005	93	2013–2025	1999	90	now–2013
2004	89	2009–2017	1998	93	now–2020
2003	90	now–2013	1997	87	now
2002	87	now–2012	1996	88	now–2014
2001	89	now–2020	1995	90	now–2015
2000	92	now–2018			

Past Glories 1990 (90), 1989 (92)

GRAND ORMEAU ★★★★
LALANDE DE POMEROL $15.00–$25.00

Run by J. C. Beton, this property, one of the finest in Lalande de Pomerol, is very consistent in good vintages. The Cuvée de Madeleine, a *tête de cuvée* (selection of the finest barrels), is also noteworthy.

2005 Cuvée de Madeleine	90+	now–2015
2003 Cuvée de Madeleine	88	now–2011
2000 Cuvée de Madeleine	90	now–2009
2005 Grand Ormeau	91	now–2015
2004 Grand Ormeau	88	now–2014
2003 Grand Ormeau	87	now–2011
2001 Grand Ormeau	88	now–2010
2000 Grand Ormeau	86	now
1999 Grand Ormeau	85	now
1998 Grand Ormeau	89	now
1997 Grand Ormeau	86	now
1996 Grand Ormeau	85	now
1995 Grand Ormeau	86	now

AU GRAND PARIS ★★/★★★
BORDEAUX SUPÉRIEUR $8.00

The world needs more of this type of inexpensive Bordeaux. This tasty effort is fashioned from a small vineyard planted on clay and limestone soils.

2005	84	now		2000	86	now
2003	86–87	now				

GRAND-PONTET ★★★★
ST.-ÉMILION $25.00–$40.00

Another up-and-coming St.-Émilion estate, Grand-Pontet is run by Sophie Pocquet, the sister of Gérard and Dominique Bécot of Beau-Séjour Bécot. Produced from a 35-acre vineyard, the wine is a traditional blend of 70% Merlot, with the rest equal parts Cabernet Franc and Cabernet Sauvignon. This estate has been quite good over the last few vintages, but the quality exploded in 2000, offering an extra dimension in both aromas and flavors. Grand-Pontet is undervalued in today's wine market, a rarity for Bordeaux. Value-conscious consumers, take note.

2005	93	2012–2042		1999	85	now–2010
2004	88	now–2017		1998	90	now–2018
2003	89+	now–2022		1997	87	now
2002	87	now–2013		1996	89	now–2010
2001	90	now–2014		1995	88	now
2000	92	now–2015				

GRAND-PUY-DUCASSE ★★★
PAUILLAC $24.00–$35.00

This estate finally seems to be getting more serious about quality, as recent vintages seem to be on an upward trajectory. A fifth-growth Pauillac, Grand-Puy-Ducasse has been largely ignored by consumers and the wine press. Unquestionably, the current prices for its vintages are below those of most other Pauillacs, making it a notable value, given the fine quality that now routinely emerges from the modern cellars located not in the middle of a beautiful vineyard but in downtown Pauillac.

2005	91	now–2022+		1999	86	now–2009
2004	90	now–2021		1998	87	now–2013
2003	90	now–2021		1997	85	now
2002	88	now–2013		1996	87	now–2015
2001	87	now–2011		1995	87	now–2010
2000	88	now–2012				

GRAND-PUY-LACOSTE ★ ★ ★ ★
PAUILLAC $28.00–$50.00

A classic, workmanlike effort that consistently results in outstanding wines seems to be the modus operandi of Xavier Borie's Grand-Puy-Lacoste. Even in less than thrilling vintages, this estate produces a chewy, robust Pauillac offering sumptuous cassis fruit. Grand-Puy-Lacoste has become one of the most popular wines in Bordeaux, largely because of its un-abashed, exuberant, blackberry/cassis fruit character and full-bodied, hedonistic appeal. I pulled all the Grand-Puy-Lacoste vintages from my cellar for a dinner party, and my favorite for current consumption remains the blockbuster 1982, followed by the fleshy 1990. There is significant optimism for both the brawny, dense, formidably endowed 1995 and 1996, while the 1998 and 2000 are unquestionably fine successes.

2006	90–92	2010–2025		2000	92	now–2025
2005	95	2014–2030		1999	89	now–2018+
2004	89	now–2022		1998	90	now–2016
2003	88	now–2018		1997	87	now–2009
2002	86	now–2012		1996	93+	now–2030
2001	88	now–2014		1995	95	2010–2025

Past Glories 1994 (90), 1990 (95), 1986 (91), 1982 (95), 1970 (91), 1961 (93?), 1959 (92), 1949 (96), 1947 (94)

GRAND VILLAGE ★ ★ ★ ★
BORDEAUX SUPÉRIEUR $20.00–$25.00

This is the home property of the Guinaudeau family, owners of Château Lafleur in Pomerol. This is a very reasonably priced, elegant wine.

2004	84	now		2003	87	now–2010

GRANDES MURAILLES ★ ★ ★ ★
ST.-ÉMILION $28.00–$36.00

The Reiffers family owns three small, very impressive (since the late 1990s) St.-Émilion es-tates. In addition to Grandes Murailles, they own the small estate of Côte de Baleau and Clos St.-Martin. Since 1998, this trio has been extremely close in quality, but in 2000 I had a mar-ginal preference for Grandes Murailles. Usually the darkest (almost black) of the three Reiffers offerings, it also has the sweetest fruit and tannin. The blend is generally 90% Merlot and 10% Cabernet Franc. The wines have greatly improved since Michel Rolland was brought in as a consultant. Annual production averages 700 cases.

2005	91	2012–2025		2000	93	now–2016
2004	90	now–2019		1999	87	now
2003	88+?	2010–2018?		1998	90	now–2016
2002	88	now–2017		1997	87	now–2009
2001	93	now–2017		1996	77–81	now

LES GRANDS CHÊNES ★★★★
MÉDOC $14.00–$29.00

A sleeper wine, Les Grands Chênes is one of the estates owned by a Bordeaux visionary, Bernard Magrez, who has transformed Pape Clément in Pessac-Léognan and Fombrauge in St.-Émilion into two brilliant wine-producing estates. This is one of his cru bourgeois estates that represents fine value in the marketplace and consistently performs well above its pedigree in blind tastings. A wine for bargain-conscious consumers to seek out.

2006 Les Grands Chênes	87–89	2009–2016
2005 Les Grands Chênes	91	2009–2024
2004 Les Grands Chênes	88	now–2013
2003 Les Grands Chênes	88	now–2012
2002 Les Grands Chênes	88	now–2013
2001 Les Grands Chênes	86	now
2000 Les Grands Chênes	86	now
1999 Les Grands Chênes	85	now
1996 Les Grands Chênes	86	now
1995 Les Grands Chênes	86	now
2001 Cuvée Prestige	89	now–2013
2000 Cuvée Prestige	88	now–2011
1999 Cuvée Prestige	85	now
1996 Cuvée Prestige	87	now–2010
1995 Cuvée Prestige	86	now

LES GRANDS MARÉCHAUX ★★★/★★★★
PREMIÈRES CÔTES DE BLAYE $12.00–$18.00

One of Bordeaux's finest values, the impeccably made, Merlot-dominated Les Grands Maréchaux is well worth seeking out. Most vintages are meant to be consumed during their first five to six years. Fortunately, approximately 7,000 cases are produced.

2005	90	now–2011		2001	85	now
2004	87–88	now–2010		2000	87	now
2003	90	now–2011		1999	85	now
2002	86	now		1998	86	now

LA GRANGÈRE ★★
ST.-ÉMILION $20.00

The debut release from Nadia and Pierre Durand (horse buffs may remember him as France's gold medal winner in the equestrian championships held in South Korea) was the 2000 La Grangère, made with the assistance of oenologist Denis Dubourdieu. This wine has generally not lived up to the potential that one would imagine with Dubourdieu behind it.

2002	86	now–2011		2000	89	now–2015
2001	87	now–2011				

LA GRAVE À POMEROL ★★★
POMEROL $23.00–$36.00

This estate, previously called La Grave Trigant de Boisset, has been owned by Christian Moueix since 1971, and there is no question he has been upgrading the quality over recent years. Though not among the most expensive Pomerols, neither is it among the finest values of the appellation. However, the high level of quality of recent vintages (the gorgeous 1998 being their finest wine to date) makes this estate's wines worthy of attention. La Grave à

Pomerol exhibits a character similar to Pétrus, although never the mass, concentration, or power of that great estate. One of my friends once referred to it, accurately, as "Pétrus for the poor."

2005	88	now–2022	1999	87	now
2004	84	now–2015	1998	90	now–2016
2003	87	now–2013	1997	86	now
2002	85	now–2011	1996	86	now
2001	89	now–2011	1995	88	now–2009
2000	88	now–2017			

LA GRAVIÈRE ★★★
LALANDE DE POMEROL $23.00

La Gravière is another estate run by Madame Péré-Vergé (also the proprietor of Montviel and Le Gay). Her ownership alone guarantees a good level of quality and increasing promise.

| 2005 | 89 | 2010–2022+ | 2001 | 87 | now–2010 |
| 2003 | 88–90 | now–2012 | | | |

LES GRAVIÈRES ★★★★
ST.-ÉMILION $25.00–$52.00

From a tiny vineyard on extremely gravelly, sandy soils in St.-Sulpice, this is one of the few St.-Émilions made from 100% Merlot. Early vintages have all been impressive. The proprietor is Denis Baraud.

2005	91	now–2021+	2000	89	now–2012
2004	87–89	now–2018	1999	87	now
2003	91	now–2018	1998	88	now–2011
2001	90	now–2012			

GRÉE-LAROQUE ★★★
BORDEAUX SUPÉRIEUR $15.00–$24.00

This garage wine is from a 3.5-acre vineyard in an area known as St.-Ciers d'Abzac (north of Fronsac). The vineyard is planted with 75% Merlot, 20% Cabernet Franc, and 5% Cabernet Sauvignon. The wine is aged on its lees with the famed micro-oxygenation and looked after by the hotshot wine guru from the right bank, Stéphane Derenoncourt. This is also a noteworthy value.

2005	88	now–2012	2002	87	now
2004	87	now–2011	2001	87	now
2003	89	now–2011	2000	89	now

GREYSAC ★★★
MÉDOC $10.00–$20.00

Greysac fulfilled many of my wine needs when I used to buy it regularly in the mid- to late 1970s, but during the 1980s and 1990s it never appeared to be as impressive. However, that seemed to change with the 2003, a tasty Medoc with fleshy texture, medium body, and classic flavors.

2004	84–86	now–2010	2000	86–87	now–2012
2003	88	now–2014	1999	85	now
2002	86	now	1995	78–80	now

GRUAUD LAROSE ★★★
ST.-JULIEN $35.00–$75.00

For decades, Gruaud Larose produced St.-Julien's most massive and backward wine. The estate was purchased in 1997 by Jacques Merlaut, the well-known proprietor of many other châteaux, including Chasse-Spleen. Under the new ownership, there has been a trend to produce a more refined, less rustic and massive style of Gruaud, and I expect this winemaking direction to continue as it is also reflected in the style of Merlaut's other estates. The production is large and the quality consistently good; however, since 2000 there seems to be more than a little something missing in Gruaud Larose and the wine no longer reaches the level of the greatness it exhibited in the past. The previous regime turned out many first-growth-quality wines, in vintages such as 1982, 1985, 1986, and 1990.

2005	89?	2012–2025	1999	89	now–2015
2004	86	now–2016	1998	88	now–2016
2003	88	now–2021	1997	86	now–2010
2002	88	now–2018	1996	89	now–2018
2001	90	now–2018	1995	89	now–2020
2000	94+	2015–2030+			

Past Glories 1990 (95), 1986 (94+), 1985 (90), 1983 (90), 1982 (96), 1961 (96), 1953 (93), 1945 (96+), 1928 (97)

JEAN DE GUÉ ★★★★
LALANDE DE POMEROL $16.00–$29.00

This is an up-and-coming Lalande de Pomerol estate owned by the Aubert family. Readers should seek out this wine for its lavish richness and flamboyant personality.

2005 Jean de Gué	90	now–2015
2003 Jean de Gué	87–88	now–2011
2002 Jean de Gué	88	now–2011
2001 Jean de Gué	86	now
2000 Jean de Gué	90	now–2012
1999 Jean de Gué	87	now
1998 Jean de Gué	88	now
2002 Jean de Gué Cuvée Prestige	87	now
1999 Jean de Gué Cuvée Prestige	87	now
1998 Jean de Gué Cuvée Prestige	88	now
1997 Jean de Gué Cuvée Prestige	85	now

GUIBOT LA FOURVIEILLE ★★★
PUISSEGUIN–ST.-ÉMILION $14.00–$17.00

This property offers a pleasant, value-priced, 100% Merlot cuvée from one of St.-Émilion's satellite appellations. The wine spends 12 months in oak.

2005	87	now–2010	2000	87	now–2010
2001	88	now–2010	1999	86	now

LA GURGUE ★★
MARGAUX $18.00

This property is owned by Claire Villars Lurton, who also owns Ferrière. The quality of the wine is largely mediocre.

2000	87	now–2010	1996	84	now
1998	78	now	1995	82	now
1997	76	now			

HAUT-BAGES LIBÉRAL ★ ★ ★/★ ★ ★ ★
PAUILLAC $25.00–$32.00

This estate belongs to the Merlaut family, who also own, among other properties, the famed Gruaud Larose of St.-Julien. Since the mid-1970s, the wines have been well made and are characterized by their power and richness, as well as cassis-dominated aromas (no doubt due to the high percentage of Cabernet Sauvignon in the blend). Because the wines of Haut-Bages Libéral are undervalued in view of their quality, they can still be purchased at reasonable prices.

2006	89–91	now–2021+	1998	86	now–2014
2005	90	2011–2031	1997	79	now
2004	90	now–2022	1996	87+	now–2017
2003	87?	now–2016	1995	85?	now–2012
2000	89	now–2018			

Past Glories 1986 (90), 1982 (91)

HAUT-BAILLY ★ ★ ★ ★/★ ★ ★ ★ ★
PESSAC-LÉOGNAN $28.00–$50.00

This property is making impressive wines under the new administration of American Robert Wilmers and by his wine-making team, led by Véronique Sanders. I have had a tendency to consistently underrate the wines young, since they are relatively delicate, and that style hasn't changed, but there does seem to be more midpalate and intensity than in the past. This is the quintessential Graves, a blend of power, finesse, elegance, complexity, and longevity, and the new proprietor seems to be exploiting this estate to its full potential. A property on the rise!

2006	91–94	2012–2030	2000	91	now–2025
2005	95	2013–2030+	1999	88	now–2017
2004	93	2010–2024	1998	93	now–2010
2003	90	now–2020+	1997	86	now
2002	90	now–2016	1996	87	now–2015
2001	90	now–2018	1995	90	now–2018

Past Glories 1990 (92), 1961 (93), 1928 (90)

HAUT-BATAILLEY ★ ★ ★
PAUILLAC $22.00–$35.00

This estate produces good but rarely inspiring wines. Proprietor Xavier Borie is attempting to upgrade the quality, but more often it has more in common with a midweight St.-Julien than a Pauillac.

2006	89–91	2012–2020	2000	90+	now–2015
2005	89	2010–2024	1999	87	now
2004	88	now–2019	1998	86	now–2014
2003	87	now–2016	1997	85	now
2002	87	now–2015	1996	90	now–2015
2001	87	now–2012	1995	89	now–2010

HAUT-BERGEY
PESSAC-LÉOGNAN $20.00–$42.00

This property has been consistently fine since it was taken over by the Garcin-Cathiard family (who also own the Pomerol estate of Clos l'Église) in the late 1990s. The owners enlist the services of Dr. Alain Raynaud, who has replaced Michel Rolland and Jean-Luc Thunevin, so there has been no shortage of serious consultants at this estate.

2006	90–92	now–2021
2005	92	2011–2025
2004	90	now–2015
2003	86	now–2013
2002	87	now–2012
2001	90	now–2015
2000	94	now–2020
1999	90	now
1998	87	now
2006 Blanc	90–92	now–2016
2005 Blanc	91	now–2016
2003 Blanc	89	now
2002 Blanc	87	now
2001 Blanc	90	now–2014
2000 Blanc	87	now–2011
1999 Blanc	87	now

HAUT-BEYZAC ★ ★ ★/★ ★ ★ ★
HAUT-MÉDOC $15.00–$30.00

Situated in the northern sector of the Médoc, this U.S.-owned estate merits serious consideration. At the bottom of its three-tiered hierarchy are the Haut-Beyzac cuvées, followed by the Haut-Beyzac I Second wines, and the top offerings, the so-called Château Haut-Beyzac Grand Vin (which represents only 10% of the production).

2004	87	now–2012
2003	87	now–2009
2004 I Second	89	now–2017
2003 I Second	89	now–2014
2004 Château Haut-Beyzac Grand Vin	89+	2009–2016
2003 Château Haut-Beyzac Grand Vin	91	now–2018

HAUT-BRION ★ ★ ★ ★ ★
PESSAC-LÉOGNAN HAUT-BRION $100.00–$325.00;
BAHANS HAUT-BRION $25.00–$40.00

All things considered—viticultural management, winemaking, *élevage,* and overall attention to detail—there are probably no more experienced and talented Bordeaux wine deities than the Delmas family (grandfather, father, and now, son) who have been making Haut-Brion since the 1920s. Jean-Bernard Delmas, who started in 1961 and retired following the 2003 vintage, has been replaced by his son Jean-Philippe, who immediately proved himself with an absolutely magnificent 2005, one of the great Haut-Brions of the last 25 years. As an American who has witnessed some of the brilliant efforts by other Bordelais winemakers in California, I lament the fact that Jean Delmas has not had the opportunity to provide consultation for the production of California Cabernet Sauvignon.

Although it is officially in a suburb, Haut-Brion is situated essentially within the city of Bordeaux. This gives it one of the area's warmest and most precocious *terroirs,* a fact that has favored it in numerous vintages. The estate is undoubtedly making wine that merits its first-growth status. In fact, the vintages from 1978 onward have always proven to be among the finest wines produced in Bordeaux, as well as personal favorites.

There are only 500 to 800 cases of the Haut-Brion Blanc, a blend of Sémillon and Sauvignon, but year in and year out it is often the single greatest dry white wine made in Bordeaux, yet it is not one of the classified properties in all the different hierarchies imposed on Bordeaux.

Bahans Haut-Brion, the second wine of the famous Château Haut-Brion, is consistently one of the best second wines produced in Bordeaux and also one of my favorites.

2006 Haut-Brion	92–94+	2015–2030+
2005 Haut-Brion	98	2012–2040+
2004 Haut-Brion	92	now–2032
2003 Haut-Brion	95	2009–2036
2002 Haut-Brion	89	2010–2020
2001 Haut-Brion	94	2009–2020
2000 Haut-Brion	98+	2012–2040
1999 Haut-Brion	93	now–2025
1998 Haut-Brion	96+	now–2035
1997 Haut-Brion	89	now–2014
1996 Haut-Brion	95	now–2035
1995 Haut-Brion	96	now–2035
2005 Bahans Haut-Brion	89	2015–2040+
2004 Bahans Haut-Brion	88	now–2017
2003 Bahans Haut-Brion	89	now–2014
2002 Bahans Haut-Brion	87	now–2010
2001 Bahans Haut-Brion	88	now–2012
2000 Bahans Haut-Brion	90	now–2016
1999 Bahans Haut-Brion	88	now–2015
1998 Bahans Haut-Brion	88	now–2016
1997 Bahans Haut-Brion	85	now
1996 Bahans Haut-Brion	87	now–2012
1995 Bahans Haut-Brion	89	now
2006 Haut-Brion Blanc	94–97	now–2026
2005 Haut-Brion Blanc	95+	now–2030
2004 Haut-Brion Blanc	91	now–2035
2003 Haut-Brion Blanc	97	now–2036+
2001 Haut-Brion Blanc	93+	now–2030
2000 Haut-Brion Blanc	90	now–2015
1999 Haut-Brion Blanc	92	now–2020
1998 Haut-Brion Blanc	96	now–2035
1997 Haut-Brion Blanc	96	now–2022
1996 Haut-Brion Blanc	92	2010–2025
1995 Haut-Brion Blanc	92	now–2025
2004 Les Plantiers de Haut-Brion Blanc	93	now–2016
2003 Les Plantiers de Haut-Brion Blanc	90	now

Past Glories 1994 (93), 1993 (92), 1992 (90), 1990 (96), 1989 (100), 1988 (91), 1986 (96), 1985 (94), 1982 (94), 1979 (93), 1978 (90?), 1975 (93+), 1964 (90), 1961 (100), 1959 (100), 1957 (90), 1955 (97), 1953 (95), 1949 (91), 1945 (100), 1928 (97), 1926 (97)

Past Glories 1989 (90)

HAUT-BRISSON ★★★
ST.-ÉMILION $16.00–$18.00

One of St.-Émilion's most attractive overperformers, Haut-Brisson is generally available for a realistic price. This wine deserves greater attention from consumers seeking good value.

2001	88	now–2011		1999	87	now
2000	88	now–2010				

HAUT-CARLES ★★★★
FRONSAC $17.00–$25.00

Another consistently high-quality producer, this top-notch Fronsac estate ranks with Fontenil, La Vieille Cure, and Moulin-Haut-Laroque as one of the four best properties of the appellation.

2006	89–91	now–2021+
2005	89+	2009–2021+
2004	90	now–2022
2003	89	now–2018+
2002	88	now–2015
2001	89	now–2013
2000	89	now–2015
NV La Preuve par Carles	90–92	now–2019

HAUT-CHAIGNEAU ★★★
LALANDE DE POMEROL $16.00–$22.00

Oenologist Pascal Chatonnet, the man responsible for discovering the causes behind the choranisol contamination that plagued a bevy of Bordeaux properties in the early 1990s, produces fine Lalande de Pomerols at Haut-Chaigneau.

2001	85–87	now
2000	88	now–2010
1999	85–87	now
1998	86	now
1998 Cuvée Prestige	88	now
1997 Cuvée Prestige	85	now

HAUT-CONDISSAS PRESTIGE ★★★★
HAUT-MÉDOC $20.00–$25.00

Haut-Condissas, the luxury cuvée of Rollan de By, is one of the finest Haut-Médoc wines made and can often compete with some of the classified growths in quality.

2005	90	now–2022		2000	88	now–2012
2004	90	now–2022		1999	87	now–2010
2003	90	now–2016		1998	88	now–2014
2001	89	now–2012				

HAUT-GRAVET ★★★/★★★★
ST.-ÉMILION $30.00–$35.00

The owners of Haut-Gravet, the Aubert family, also produce La Couspaude and Jean de Gué, a St.-Émilion and a Lalande de Pomerol. This is a modern-style, noticeably oaky, full-bodied, dramatic St.-Émilion that may lack finesse and subtlety but makes up for it in a forceful display of fruit, muscle, and new oak.

2005	89	2012–2023+	2000	90	now–2020
2003	88	now–2018	1999	86	now
2001	89	now–2014	1998	87	now–2010

HAUT-MAILLET ★★
POMEROL $22.00–$26.00

This 12.4-acre estate is owned by the Estager family. This is a wine that has never impressed me in any of my tastings.

1998	78	now	1996	80	now
1997	75	now	1995	82–85	now

HAUT-MARBUZET ★★★/★★★★
ST.-ESTÈPHE $30.00–$38.00

Haut-Marbuzet is one of the oldest estates in St.-Estèphe, but its fame can be traced only to 1952, when it was purchased by the father of the current proprietor, Henri Duboscq. Duboscq, a flamboyant personality who tends to describe his wines by making analogies to the body parts of prominent female movie stars, has created one of the most immensely popular wines of Bordeaux, particularly in France, Belgium, Holland, and England. Some critics have charged that his winemaking style borders on vulgarity, and others have suggested that Haut-Marbuzet fails to age gracefully. While the wine is usually delicious when released, my tastings of old vintages back through 1961 have generally indicated that Haut-Marbuzet is best when drunk within its first 10 to 13 years.

2005	85?	now–2019	1999	88	now–2012
2004	88	now–2015	1998	87	now–2011
2003	88	now–2014	1997	85	now
2002	87	now	1996	87	now
2001	89	now–2012	1995	87	now
2000	87	now			

Past Glories 1990 (93), 1986 (90), 1982 (94), 1975 (90), 1970 (90), 1961 (90)

HAUT-MAZERIS ★★★/★★★★
FRONSAC–CANON-FRONSAC $26.00–$34.00

This is a wine to take seriously. The breakthrough vintage was the 2003, followed up by a solid 2005, so this may be an up-and-coming estate well worth considering.

2005 Canon-Fronsac	89+	now–2018
2003 Canon-Fronsac	91	now–2021
2002 Canon-Fronsac	81	now–2011
2005 Fronsac	90	now–2018
2003 Fronsac	87	now–2012

HAUT-NADEAU ★★/★★★
BORDEAUX SUPÉRIEUR $15.00–$16.00

A solidly made Bordeaux Supérieur that represents good value, Haut-Nadeau is best drunk in its first two to four years.

2001	87	now
2000	86	now
2003 Cuvée Prestige	85	now–2010
2000 Cuvée Prestige	87	now
2000 Réserve	87	now

HAUT-SOCIANDO ★★/★★★
CÔTES DE BLAYE $8.00–$15.00

A fruity, soft, easygoing style of Côtes de Blaye that is well made and inexpensive, Haut-Sociando warrants consumption within two to three years of the vintage.

2003	85	now	1996	80	now
2001	84	now			

HAUT-VILLET ★★★
ST.-ÉMILION $28.00–$55.00

I often have difficulty assessing these wines, largely because I have never tasted a mature Haut-Villet, so I do not know if they are capable of absorbing all their tannin and wood. They are concentrated, full-bodied, aggressive St.-Émilions. Haut-Villet tends to be extremely muscular, with heavy, almost excessive new oak and a tannic, powerful style that suggests significant cellaring is possible, but I wonder if wines like this ever really come into balance.

2003 Haut-Villet	87	now–2016
2000 Haut-Villet	87	now–2014
1999 Haut-Villet	86	now–2012
1998 Haut-Villet	87	now–2016
1997 Haut-Villet	80	now
2000 Haut-Villet Cuvée Pomone	90	now–2020
1999 Haut-Villet Cuvée Pomone	88	now–2014
1998 Haut-Villet Cuvée Pomone	89+?	now–2020

LES HAUTS-CONSEILLANTS ★★★
LALANDE DE POMEROL $16.00

This is a solid, reliable wine from Lalande de Pomerol that offers good, sweet cherry fruit, often with a touch of underbrush and herbs.

2001	86	now–2009	1997	84	now
2000	87	now–2010	1996	72	now
1998	86	now			

L'HERMITAGE
ST.-ÉMILION $45.00–$80.00

A top-notch *garagiste* estate, this 7.5-acre vineyard sandwiched between L'Angélus and Beauséjour-Duffau is planted with Merlot and Cabernet Franc. Virtually every radical new-wave technique designed to enhance color, fruit, *terroir*, texture, and longevity is employed at L'Hermitage. This is usually a top-echelon wine of superb richness, purity, and texture with 15 or so years of aging potential.

2005	92	2009–2029	2000	91	now–2018
2004	88	now–2015	1999	88	now–2010
2003	90	now–2016	1998	89+	now–2016
2002	89	now–2013	1997	88	now
2001	92	now–2014			

HORTEVIE ★ ★ ★
ST.-JULIEN $15.00–$28.00

This is a reliable, richly fruity, medium-bodied St.-Julien that is not often seen but represents very good value as well as a classic taste of St.-Julien. It is best drunk in its first decade of life.

2005	88	now–2022	1999	86	now
2004	87	now–2014	1998	84	now
2003	88	now–2018	1997	86	now
2001	85	now–2011	1996	87	now–2012
2000	87	now–2013	1995	87	now–2012

HOSANNA ★ ★ ★ ★/★ ★ ★ ★ ★
POMEROL $75.00–$100.00

This estate, superbly situated on the plateau of Pomerol, was formerly known as Château Certan-Giraud. The finest parcels were renamed Hosanna in 1999 after acquisition by the Moueix family. Christian Moueix merits praise for bringing its quality to a splendid new level. The property has been reduced to the tenderloin section of what was Certan-Giraud and is now a ten-acre vineyard planted with 70% Merlot and 30% Cabernet Franc. Readers should think of this wine as Pomerol's version of Cheval Blanc, as that seems to be the intention of the new owners. Hosanna is on the upswing, so prices will only increase. About 1,500 cases are now produced annually.

2006	95–97	2010–2020+
2005	95	2012–2025+
2004	90+?	now–2022
2003	90	now–2021+
2001	93	now–2014
2000	96	now–2020
1999	90	now–2016
1996 Certan-Giraud	84	now
1995 Certan-Giraud	87	now–2009

HOSTENS-PICANT ★ ★/★ ★ ★
STE.-FOY $8.00–$16.00

Because of low yields and its cold, clay *terroir,* Hostens-Picant produces atypically big wines from this obscure appellation. Though they may never be complex, they are savory, mouth filling, and full-bodied, with sweet tannin as well as loads of glycerin and concentration.

2003	88	now–2013
2002	86	now
2001	86	now
2000	85	now
1998	84	now
1996	84	now
1995	85	now
2003 Cuvée d'Exception	88	now–2013

| 2001 Cuvée d'Exception | 87 | now |
| 2000 Cuvée Luculus | 86 | now–2010 |

D'ISSAN ★ ★ ★ ★
MARGAUX $25.00–$45.00

One of the more beautiful properties of the Médoc—it features a moated castle, for example—this Margaux estate has made impressive qualitative progress over the last decade and is now a quintessentially elegant wine with intense flavors, wonderful finesse, and an almost surreal lightness and perfume. Almost all of its progress should be attributed to the enthusiastic and passionate young proprietor, Emmanuel Cruse.

2006	90–93	now–2021	2000	93	now–2020
2005	95	2009–2025+	1999	89+	now–2016
2004	91	2009–2020+	1998	87	now–2014
2003	90	now–2021	1997	86	now
2002	89	now–2017	1996	88	now–2020
2001	89	now–2018	1995	87	now–2014

JOANIN BÉCOT ★ ★ ★ ★
CÔTES DE CASTILLON $20.00–$28.00

This is an excellent as well as fashionable estate in Côtes de Castillon, where a lot of over-achievers perform at impressive levels. These are rich, concentrated wines that are modern in style but loaded with flavor. An intelligent buy.

2005	90	now–2021	2002	87	now–2011
2004	89	now–2015	2001	90	now–2012
2003	90	now–2014			

LES JONQUEYRÈS ★ ★/★ ★ ★
BORDEAUX $15.00

Les Jonqueyrès is generally a very reliable, inexpensive wine from a humble appellation that offers good value.

2005 Jonqueyrès Cuvée Dorothea	86	now–2011
2003 Les Jonqueyrès	86	now–2011
1995 Les Jonqueyrès	85	now

KIRWAN ★ ★ ★ ★
MARGAUX $26.00–$55.00

This once moribund estate has totally reversed itself after a long period of mediocrity. Under the inspired leadership of Marie-Louise Schyler, over the last decade and a half it has produced wines that are the best I have tasted since some of the monumental Kirwans of the mid-1900s. The wines are powerful, rich, concentrated, but lacking none of their Margaux typicity. Schyler's commitment to excellence, a draconian selection process for the top wine, and the ability to take risks in order to produce only the best has made for a total turnaround in quality. Kirwan still represents very good value for a well-known classified growth in the Médoc.

2006	88–91	2013–2023+	2000	90+	2010–2023
2005	92+	2015–2030+	1999	89+	now–2015
2004	90	2012–2025	1998	90	now–2025
2003	93	2009–2022+	1997	87	now–2010

| 2002 | 88 | now–2025 | 1996 | 88 | now–2025 |
| 2001 | 90 | now–2019 | 1995 | 85 | now–2018 |

LABÉGORCE ★ ★
MARGAUX $18.00–$20.00

This is the less heralded and less impressive sister château of Labégorce Zédé, which sits nearby. Labégorce tends to be easygoing, fruity, but relatively light and undistinguished.

2004	80?	now	1999	85	now
2001	85	now–2009	1998	81	now
2000	87	now–2013	1997	78	now

LABÉGORCE ZÉDÉ ★ ★ ★
MARGAUX $20.00–$22.00

Labégorce Zédé is a well-made wine that shows good, solid fruit and plenty of new oak in many vintages, and it is certainly a good bet in top vintages for the appellation of Margaux. It is best drunk in its first 10 to 12 years.

2005	87	now–2016+	1997	86	now
2004	85	now–2013	1996	85	now–2013
2000	87	now–2013	1995	85	now
1999	85	now			

LAFITE-ROTHSCHILD ★ ★ ★ ★ ★
PAUILLAC LAFITE ROTHSCHILD $125.00–$450.00;
CARRUADES DE LAFITE $29.00–$56.00

The competition that now exists between the famous first growths of the Médoc is something to behold. They are all pushing the envelope of quality, but certainly none more than Charles Chevalier at Lafite-Rothschild. Administrator Chevalier has accomplished brilliant work since he took charge of Lafite-Rothschild's winemaking in 1994. This estate is now unquestionably the star among the Médoc's first growths, producing riveting wines in every vintage since Chevalier's ascension to power. The 1996 was the wine of the vintage, and the 1997 was unquestionably the finest first growth of the year. Furthermore, even though 1998 favored the Merlot-based wines of St.-Émilion, Pomerol, and to a lesser extent Graves, Lafite-Rothschild again produced a strong candidate for wine of the vintage. The 1999 and 2000 are also fine successes. The 2003 is immortal and probably a modern-day clone of the 1959. A true first-growth château embodying elegance, nobility, and beautiful concentrated fruit, Lafite-Rothschild is clearly living up to its immortal reputation. Only a tiny percentage of the harvest is included in the final blend, and there is little room for compromise. Since 1998, the winery has used a new engraved bottle designed to prevent fraudulent imitations.

The second wine of Lafite-Rothschild, Carruades de Lafite, has become one of the finest second wines produced. The 2003 is absolutely stunning. The wine shares much of the same character as its more famous sibling—just the tannins are lighter and the wine is made in a style that gives it immediate accessibility—but the Lafite mystique and personality can be detected.

2006			91–94+	2014–2054
2005			96+	2015–2050+
2004			95	2011–2037
2003			100	2010–2050
2002			94	now–2025
2001			94	now–2020

2000	100	2010–2050
1999	95	now–2030
1998	98	now–2035
1997	92	now–2015+
1996	100	2012–2050
1995	95	now–2028
2005 Carruades de Lafite	89	now–2022
2004 Carruades de Lafite	88	now–2020
2003 Carruades de Lafite	93	now–2021+
2002 Carruades de Lafite	87	now–2015
2001 Carruades de Lafite	87	now–2014
2000 Carruades de Lafite	90	now–2018
1999 Carruades de Lafite	89	now–2015
1998 Carruades de Lafite	90	now–2015
1997 Carruades de Lafite	88	now
1996 Carruades de Lafite	89	now–2020+
1995 Carruades de Lafite	87	now

Past Glories 1994 (90+?), 1990 (92+), 1989 (90+), 1988 (94), 1986 (100), 1983 (93), 1982 (100), 1976 (93), 1975 (92?), 1959 (99), 1934 (90), 1921 (93), 1870 (96), 1864 (92), 1848 (96)

LAFLEUR　★★★★★
POMEROL $50.00–$350.00

Lafleur is a tiny treasure of a vineyard that has always been one of my all-time favorite Bordeaux wines. Year in and year out it is right at the same level as Pétrus, in some years even eclipsing Pétrus. The wines are noteworthy because of the extraordinary density of fragrance and flavor that the Cabernet Franc seems to achieve on these high-plateau vineyards in Pomerol. Of course, that represents only about 30% of the final blend in most vintages, but the Merlot achieves a nobility and complexity at Lafleur equaled by only a handful of estates in Pomerol. This is one of the world's majestic wines, one of the greatest of all of the Bordeaux estates, and its price reflects truly first-growth quality.

2006	93–95+	2016–2056
2005	95+	2017–2067
2004	94	2012–2032+
2003	95	now–2025
2002	89	now–2016
2001	92	2009–2019
2000	100	2012–2040+
1999	93	2010–2025
1998	94	2010–2040+
1997	88?	now–2015
1996	92+	2012–2030+
1995	93+	2020–2050
2004 Les Pensées de Lafleur	87	now–2022
2003 Les Pensées de Lafleur	86	now–2015
2002 Les Pensées de Lafleur	84	now
2000 Les Pensées de Lafleur	90	now–2017
1999 Les Pensées de Lafleur	88	now–2014

Past Glories 1994 (93+), 1993 (90), 1992 (88), 1990 (97), 1989 (95+), 1988 (94), 1986 (91+), 1985 (96), 1983 (93), 1982 (100), 1979 (98+), 1978 (93), 1975 (100), 1966 (96), 1962 (91), 1961 (98), 1955 (92), 1950 (100), 1949 (96+), 1947 (100), 1945 (100)

LAFLEUR-GAZIN ★★★
POMEROL $27.00–$42.00

For decades, the vineyard was farmed and the wines, made by the firm of Jean-Pierre Moueix, were mediocre. Then the lease arrangement expired and all of a sudden this estate, which has beautifully situated vineyards between Gazin and Lafleur, began making seriously endowed, complex, complete wines. This is definitely an up-and-coming estate to keep a watchful eye on.

2005	85	now–2019	1999	87	now–2011
2004	86	now–2015	1998	89	now–2016
2001	89	now–2016	1997	85	now
2000	87	now–2014	1996	86	now–2009

LA FLEUR DE PLINCE ★★
POMEROL $25.00–$30.00

La Fleur de Plince is a straightforward, somewhat monolithic style of Pomerol that is serviceable but never inspiring.

2000	87	now–2015

LAFON-ROCHET ★★★★
ST.-ESTÈPHE $26.00–$42.00

The Tesseron family, who have done so much to propel Pontet-Canet into the limelight, continue to upgrade the quality of Lafon-Rochet. This is another Bordeaux estate performing well above its classification. To date, prices have not caught up with the quality that has emerged over recent years.

2006	89–90	now–2024	1999	87	now–2012
2005	90	2013–2033	1998	88	now–2016
2004	90	now–2022	1997	86	now
2003	90+	2010–2025	1996	90	now–2020
2001	87	now–2015	1995	89	now–2018
2000	90	now–2016			

LAFORGE ★★★
ST.-ÉMILION $25.00–$50.00

This 2,000-case blend of primarily Merlot and small quantities of Cabernet Franc is made by Jonathan Malthus. It is a low-key, medium-weight St.-Émilion for drinking during its first decade.

2005	95	now–2022	2001	88	now–2016
2003	90	now–2016			

LAGRANGE ★★/★★★
POMEROL $25.00–$38.00

One rarely sees the wine of Lagrange. Well situated near the plateau of Pomerol, the vineyard is planted with 95% Merlot and 5% Cabernet Franc. The wine tends to be rather brawny, densely colored Pomerol with significant power and tannins but not much complexity. Older vintages such as 1978, 1975, and 1970 have all proven to be stubbornly big, brooding, coarse wines that have been slow to develop. This is not a style of wine that I find attractive.

2006	91–94	2012–2027	1999	86	now
2005	89	now–2022	1998	86	now–2015

2004	87	now–2018	1997	85	now
2001	88	now–2014	1996	76	now
2000	87?	now–2020?	1995	86	now–2011

LAGRANGE ★ ★ ★ ★
ST.-JULIEN $25.00–$50.00

When the huge Japanese company Suntory purchased Lagrange in 1983, they began a complete renovation not only of the château and of the cellars but of the vineyards as well. No expense has been spared, and the wines have gone from distressingly irregular to stunning in an amazingly short period of time. Vintages from 1985 onward have shown impressive depth of flavor welded to plenty of tannin and toasty new oak and a savory and lush style. Moreover, Lagrange remains currently underpriced, given its present level of quality.

2005	91?	2015–2030	1999	86	now–2012
2004	89+	2011–2025	1998	88	now–2015
2003	91	now–2024	1997	85	now
2002	89	2009–2020	1996	92	now–2022
2001	90	now–2018	1995	90	now–2020
2000	93	now–2025			

Past Glories 1990 (93), 1989 (90), 1986 (92)

LA LAGUNE ★ ★ ★ ★
HAUT-MÉDOC $22.00–$38.00

The most southern of the famous estates in the Médoc, La Lagune has benefited from considerable investment in its state-of-the-art, space-age winery and in the 21st century has begun to make wines that rival the marvelous efforts produced here in the 1970s and 1980s. This remains a wine that has virtually a grand cru Burgundian complexity and savory character, and it is often a great value among the famous names of Bordeaux.

2006	92–94	2009–2029	2000	86	now–2014
2005	95	2012–2037+	1999	85	now–2010
2004	90	now–2021	1998	82	now
2003	90	now–2021+	1997	86	now
2002	87	now–2013	1996	86	now–2018
2001	87	now–2011	1995	88	now–2018

Past Glories 1990 (90), 1989 (90), 1982 (92), 1978 (88), 1976 (89), 1970 (89)

LAMARQUE ★ ★/★ ★ ★
MÉDOC $15.00–$20.00

Lamarque is a typically good, middle-weight, central Médoc wine. It seems to have a touch of the St.-Julien elegance, mixed with round, supple, soft, ripe fruity flavors. The owners, the Gromand family, make the wine with great care. Lamarque should be consumed within seven to eight years of the vintage. Prices remain among the more reasonable for a cru bourgeois.

2000	87–88	now–2012	1997	79	now
1999	86	now	1996	78–80	now
1998	85–86	now	1995	84–86	now

LANESSAN ★★*/★★★★
MÉDOC $24.00–$27.00

An insider's wine. Lanessan often makes wines of classified-growth quality that can keep for decades. Readers should consider them hypothetical crosses between a St.-Julien and a Pauillac. This underrated Médoc consistently produces wines of fifth-growth quality.

2005	90	2010–2027	1998	86–87	now–2015
2004	87	now–2013	1997	87	now–2012
2001	87–89	now–2017	1996	88	now–2016
2000	89	now–2015	1995	87	now
1999	86	now			

LANGOA BARTON ★★★★
ST.-JULIEN $43.00–$55.00

This is often referred to as the second wine of Léoville-Barton, but it is actually a separate estate, producing wines that are slightly softer than the more formidably endowed and broodingly backward Léoville-Bartons. Proprietor Anthony Barton deserves credit for keeping Langoa Barton's prices realistic and at the same time producing some of St.-Julien's finest wines. This property does not always receive the respect it merits, but its wines, especially the most recent vintages, are extremely strong.

2006	90–92	2013–2030	2000	91+	2010–2035
2005	90?	2015–2040	1999	87?	now–2015
2004	90	2013–2025+	1998	89+	now–2025
2003	90	now–2026	1997	84	now
2002	90	2012–2022	1996	86+?	now–2020
2001	88	now–2016	1995	86+?	now–2016

Past Glories 1959 (90), 1953 (90), 1948 (93)

LANIOTE ★★*/★★★
ST.-ÉMILION $20.00–$28.00

A historic property that has remained in the same family for centuries, this ancient estate comes complete with chapel and extensive catacombs, making a visit mandatory. I have had limited experience with the wines from this tiny vineyard. The property, located northwest of the town of St.-Émilion, sits on rich clay, limestone, and iron-enriched soils.

2004	81?	now–2013	1999	80	now
2001	86–88	now–2014?	1998	88	now–2014
2000	86	now–2012	1997	86	now

LAPLAGNOTTE-BELLEVUE ★★★/★★★★
ST.-ÉMILION $22.00

This estate is owned by Claude de Labarre, one of the former coproprietors of Cheval Blanc. The vineyard is planted with 70% Cabernet Sauvignon, 20% Cabernet Franc, and 10% Merlot. The wines of Laplagnotte-Bellevue are generally elegant, fruity, straightforward, and savory, and are reasonably priced. The estate debuted a microcuvée called Laplagnotte in 1999.

2001	88	now–2012
2000	89	now–2015
1999	88	now
1998	85–87	now
1997	86	now

1996			86	now		
1995			86	now		
2003 Laplagnotte			89–91	now–2015		
2001 Laplagnotte			90	now–2014		
2000 Laplagnotte			91	now–2015		
1999 Laplagnotte			88	now–2010		

LARCIS DUCASSE ＊＊＊＊
ST.-ÉMILION $25.00–$55.00

This 26.7-acre vineyard merits serious consideration. For more than five decades, its fabulous *terroir* (just down the street from Pavie), with a brilliant south-facing exposition on pure clay and limestone soils, with vines averaging 40 years of age, made one mediocre vintage after another. All that changed after the outstanding duo of Nicolas Thienpont and Stéphane Derenoncourt arrived as consultants in 2002. The 2005 Larcis Ducasse will go down as the most profound wine made at this estate since their monumental 1945. Time to catch this locomotive before the world jumps on.

2006	91–94	now–2021+		2000	87	now–2017
2005	98	2011–2030		1999	82	now
2004	92	now–2022		1998	85	now–2011
2003	90	now–2016		1997	84	now
2002	90	now–2012		1996	81	now
2001	86	now–2009				

Past Glories 1945 (90)

LARMANDE ＊＊/＊＊＊
ST.-ÉMILION $28.00–$35.00

This estate has generally produced very good to excellent wines until several recent vintages, which seemed disjointed and unusually vegetal. Certainly there is a good track record here, so perhaps this is just a temporary hiccup, as this has always been a *terroir* with fine potential.

2005	87	now–2020		1999	86	now
2004	87	now–2015		1998	87	now–2015
2003	77	now–2013		1997	86	now
2002	87	now–2012		1996	88	now–2010
2001	92	now–2019		1995	88	now
2000	88	now–2014				

Past Glories 1988 (90)

LAROSE-TRINTAUDON ＊＊＊
HAUT-MÉDOC $16.00

For years, the largest vineyard in the Médoc produced a straightforward, supple, correct wine of no great distinction, but since the late 1990s the wines have become richer and more interesting. The second wine here is Larose-Perganson.

2001 Larose-Trintaudon		85–86	now
2000 Larose-Trintaudon		85–86	now
1998 Larose-Trintaudon		83	now
1997 Larose-Trintaudon		85	now
1996 Larose-Trintaudon		86	now
2000 Larose-Perganson		85	now
1999 Larose-Perganson		85	now

1998 Larose-Perganson	85	now
1997 Larose-Perganson	86	now
1996 Larose-Perganson	86	now

LAROZE ★ ★
ST.-ÉMILION $20.00–$26.00

This property has rebounded nicely, producing over recent years a succession of overtly fruity, soft, open-knit, user-friendly wines. However, the vineyards, planted in light sandy soil, do not represent one of St.-Émilion's better *terroirs*. The wines are vinified in a modern, up-to-date facility.

2005	89	now–2022	1999	84	now
2001	86	now–2011	1998	87	now
2000	88	now–2011			

LARRIVET HAUT-BRION ★ ★ ★/★ ★ ★ ★
PESSAC-LÉOGNAN $24.00–$35.00

Christine (a dead ringer for the young Michelle Phillips) and Philippe Gervoson have greatly increased the quality of the wine from this splendidly situated estate in Pessac-Léognan. Improvements began in 1996, and the estate has hit peaks in both 1998 and 2000, although 1999 and 1997 are also fine wines. Michel Rolland is the consulting oenologist.

2005	90	now–2022
2004	89	now–2022
2003	86	now–2016
2002	87	now–2018
2001	90	now–2018
2000	90	now–2020
1999	89	now–2015
1998	90	now–2018
1997	86	now
1996	87	now–2009
2006 Blanc	88–90	now–2016
2005 Blanc	90	now–2016
2002 Blanc	85	now–2014
2001 Blanc	90	now–2012
2000 Blanc	87	now–2013
1999 Blanc	87	now
1998 Blanc	89	now
1997 Blanc	86	now
1996 Blanc	74	now–2010
1995 Blanc	76	now–2017

LASCOMBES ★ ★ ★ ★
MARGAUX $24.00–$52.00

This property has exploded in quality since it was acquired by the U.S. company Colony Capital. Château Reignac's Yves Vatelot was brought in to oversee the wine making, and everything was revolutionized with the assistance of Dr. Alain Raynaud and Michel Rolland. This has now become one of Margaux's top wines, challenging even Château Palmer and Château Margaux.

2006	90–93	now–2021	2000	90	now–2016
2005	95	2012–2035	1999	77	now
2004	93	2010–2025	1998	83	now–2013
2003	92	now–2021+	1997	76	now
2002	93	now–2020	1996	80	now
2001	92	now–2016	1995	79	now

Past Glories 1959 (90)

LASSÈGUE ★ ★ ★
ST.-ÉMILION $45.00–$50.00

With American Jess Jackson's first venture into Bordeaux he has shown that, along with his top-flight French winemaker, Pierre Seillan (of Vérité fame), he is capable of achieving immediate success. The vineyard is well situated on both limestone and sand, several miles from Pavie and Larcis Ducasse, and enjoys a relatively hot microclimate. The 2003 was a good beginning, and the 2004 and 2005 Lassègues are meant for patient connoisseurs.

| 2006 | 89–91 | 2014–2025 | 2004 | 90–91 | 2010–2020 |
| 2005 | 91 | 2014–2030 | 2003 | 87–89 | now–2016 |

LATOUR ★ ★ ★ ★ ★
PAUILLAC
LATOUR $125.00–$550.00; LES FORTS DE LATOUR $36.00–$55.00;
PAUILLAC $35.00

This estate was bought in 1994 by Paris businessman François Pinault, largely because it was his favorite wine from Bordeaux. Under his ownership, the winery and cellars have undergone major renovations; enormous improvements in both the *cuverie* and cellars have taken place; and there is, of course, the wine. Pinault has pushed Latour to even greater heights, and in recent vintages Latour has often produced the wine of the vintage, as it did in 1999, 2001, 2002, 2003 (along with Lafite and Ausone), and 2005. This is a first growth operating on all cylinders, producing absolutely riveting wines of great richness and intensity, which are increasingly selling at the level of famous works of art.

The character of Forts de Latour (their second wine) is astonishingly similar to Latour itself, only lighter and quicker to mature. Les Forts de Latour is certainly the finest of the second labels produced by the well-known châteaux in Bordeaux. This second wine has quickly emerged as one of the two or three best second wines in all of Bordeaux, especially since 2000.

There is not much made, but the Pauillac (their third wine) makes a mockery of most generic AOC offerings. For shrewd consumers looking for the taste of Latour at a fraction of the price, this is a wine to seek out.

2006 Latour	93–96	2015–2040
2005 Latour	96+	2015–2050+
2004 Latour	95	2012–2037
2003 Latour	100	2010–2040+
2002 Latour	96	2012–2045
2001 Latour	95	now–2025
2000 Latour	98+	2012–2050
1999 Latour	93	now–2032
1998 Latour	90	2009–2030
1997 Latour	86	now–2014
1996 Latour	99	2015–2050
1995 Latour	96+	2012–2050

2006 Les Forts de Latour	89	now–2026
2005 Les Forts de Latour	92	now–2026
2004 Les Forts de Latour	90	now–2022
2003 Les Forts de Latour	92	now–2021+
2002 Les Forts de Latour	92	now–2020
2001 Les Forts de Latour	90	now–2016
2000 Les Forts de Latour	90	now–2025
1999 Les Forts de Latour	90	now–2017+
1998 Les Forts de Latour	88	now–2020
1997 Les Forts de Latour	87	now
1996 Les Forts de Latour	90	now–2018
1995 Les Forts de Latour	89+	now–2015
2005 Pauillac	89	2020–2060
2004 Pauillac	87	now–2016
2003 Pauillac	91	now–2016
2002 Pauillac	88	now–2017
2001 Pauillac	86–87	now–2013
2000 Pauillac	89	now–2013
1996 Pauillac	86–88	now

Past Glories 1994 (92?), 1993 (89), 1990 (98+), 1986 (90), 1982 (100), 1978 (94), 1975 (93+), 1971 (93), 1970 (98+), 1966 (96), 1964 (90), 1962 (94), 1961 (100), 1959 (98+), 1949 (100), 1948 (94), 1945 (96), 1928 (100), 1926 (93), 1924 (94), 1921 (90)

Past Glories 1990 (90), 1982 (92)

LATOUR À POMEROL * * *
POMEROL $50.00–$65.00

From the late 1940s through the 1961 vintage, there was probably no greater wine made in Bordeaux than vintages such as 1945, 1947, 1948, 1949, 1950, 1959, and 1961 at Latour à Pomerol, produced by the Libourne firm of Jean-Pierre Moueix. Since then, though quite good and classically Pomerol, the wine has never reached such levels of majesty and intensity. Nevertheless, for anyone lucky enough to come across some of those ancient vintages, this can be an extraordinary wine.

2006	90–92	2010–2030	2000	91+	now–2019
2005	90	2009–2029	1999	88	now–2015
2004	89+	2011–2020+	1998	90	now–2020
2003	86?	now–2014	1997	88	now
2002	85	now–2012	1996	88	now–2014
2001	88	now–2015	1995	89+	now–2020

Past Glories 1982 (93), 1970 (94), 1961 (100), 1959 (98), 1950 (99), 1948 (98), 1947 (100), 1945 (100)

LATOUR-MARTILLAC * * *
PESSAC-LÉOGNAN $22.00–$36.00

By the standards of other Graves properties, Latour-Martillac is not an old estate, as the history of the vineyard traces only to the mid-19th century. However, it has been owned by one of Bordeaux's most famous families, the Kressmanns, since 1930. Though the white wines of this estate have improved considerably since 1987 and have become fine examples of white Graves, the reds remain somewhat monolithic, rich in fruit, and powerful, but rather straightforward.

2005	89	2009–2029
2004	85	now–2019
2003	86	now–2016
2001	87	now–2013
2000	89	now–2016
1999	86	now–2012
1998	87	now–2016
1997	86	now–2011
1996	83	now
1995	86	now
2003 Blanc	87	now
2002 Blanc	85	now
2001 Blanc	89	now–2018
2000 Blanc	85	now–2011
1999 Blanc	87	now
1998 Blanc	87	now

LAUSSAC ★ ★/★ ★ ★
CÔTES DE CASTILLON $18.00–$22.00

Laussac remains a pleasant, elegant style of wine. It is best drunk during its first four to five years.

2003	87	now–2012	2001	87	now–2012
2002	86	now			

LAVILLE HAUT-BRION ★ ★ ★ ★ ★
PESSAC-LÉOGNAN $85.00–$125.00

The question of which vineyard in Bordeaux produces the most profound dry white Bordeaux is sometimes a toss-up between Domaine de Chevalier, Haut-Brion, and Laville Haut-Brion. Of course, the latter two are made by the same winemaking team, and Laville Haut-Brion's tiny vineyard, which sits near La Mission Haut-Brion, produces one of the most remarkably long-lived white wines of France. Production is under 1,000 cases, and it is always a blend of Sauvignon and Sémillon fermented and aged in new oak. It takes on a waxy richness with aging but evolves for 40 to 50 years, which is rather amazing.

2006 Blanc	92–94	2012–2040
2005 Blanc	94+	2010–2050
2004 Blanc	91	now–2031
2003 Blanc	96	now–2031+
2001 Blanc	91+	2010–2025
2000 Blanc	89	now–2015
1999 Blanc	91	now–2017
1998 Blanc	95	2010–2030
1997 Blanc	88	now
1996 Blanc	90	now–2018+
1995 Blanc	88	now–2010

LÉOVILLE-BARTON ★ ★ ★ ★ ★
ST.-JULIEN $35.00–$100.00

One of the classic wines of Bordeaux and still realistically priced, Léoville-Barton is becoming increasingly popular because of its extraordinary quality-to-price ratio. Proprietor Anthony Barton continues to fashion beautifully elegant yet powerful, masculine, virile wines meant for long-term aging. In addition, his pricing exhibits a humility that is both refreshing and noteworthy. This is uncompromising, classic Bordeaux meant for those who have the patience to wait at least a decade or more and expect the wine to last for 50 or more years.

2006	92–94	2016–2035	2000	96+	2015–2040
2005	94?	2020–2060+	1999	88+?	now–2022
2004	92+	2015–2030+	1998	91	now–2035
2003	95+	2012–2030+	1997	86	now–2010
2002	92	2012–2028	1996	92+	now–2030
2001	92	now–2020	1995	91	now–2025

Past Glories 1994 (90+), 1990 (94+), 1989 (90), 1986 (92), 1985 (92), 1982 (93+), 1975 (90), 1961 (92), 1959 (94), 1953 (95), 1949 (95), 1948 (96), 1945 (98)

LÉOVILLE–LAS CASES ★ ★ ★ ★ ★
ST.-JULIEN
LÉOVILLE–LAS CASES $75.00–$215.00;
CLOS DU MARQUIS $25.00–$43.00

Léoville–Las Cases is unquestionably one of the great names and wines of Bordeaux. Since 1982, it has consistently been of first-growth quality, with some vintages superior to several first growths. The wines are generally deeply colored, tannic, big, and concentrated, and potentially long-lived. Over recent years, they have also exhibited both power and elegance in a harmonious style. These traditional St.-Juliens require patience, as they are ready to drink only after 10 to 15 years' aging. If the 1855 classification were revised, Léoville–Las Cases would surely be a serious candidate for first-growth status.

Clos du Marquis, the second wine of Léoville–Las Cases, is frequently as good as or better than many Médoc classified growths. One of the best second wines of the region, it is very much in the style of its bigger sibling, but with softer tannins and greater accessibility.

2006 Léoville–Las Cases	93–95+	2011–2041
2005 Léoville–Las Cases	98	2018–2050+
2004 Léoville–Las Cases	93	2012–2028
2003 Léoville–Las Cases	93+	2012–2023
2002 Léoville–Las Cases	95	2012–2030
2001 Léoville–Las Cases	93	2011–2030
2000 Léoville–Las Cases	100	2015–2040
1999 Léoville–Las Cases	93	now–2022
1998 Léoville–Las Cases	93	now–2025
1997 Léoville–Las Cases	89	now–2016
1996 Léoville–Las Cases	98+	2010–2040
1995 Léoville–Las Cases	95	now–2025
2005 Clos du Marquis	91	2015–2035
2004 Clos du Marquis	88	now–2021
2003 Clos du Marquis	90	now–2021
2002 Clos du Marquis	89	now–2013
2001 Clos du Marquis	89+	now–2018
2000 Clos du Marquis	92	now–2020+
1999 Clos du Marquis	86	now–2012
1998 Clos du Marquis	90	now–2014
1997 Clos du Marquis	86	now–2012
1996 Clos du Marquis	90	now–2018
1995 Clos du Marquis	90	now–2013

Past Glories 1994 (93), 1993 (90), 1992 (90), 1990 (96), 1989 (91), 1988 (92), 1986 (98+), 1985 (93), 1983 (91), 1982 (100), 1978 (90), 1975 (92+)

LÉOVILLE-POYFERRÉ ✶ ✶ ✶ ✶ ✶
ST.-JULIEN $36.00–$70.00

Of all three Léovilles of St.-Julien, Poyferré is the least well known and the most undervalued, most certainly because of its irregular track record since 1961. However, things have changed over recent years, with the modernization of the cellars, the making of a second wine, and the use of more new oak for the *élevage,* as well as the increasingly attentive watch of coproprietor Didier Cuvelier, who brought in Michel Rolland as a consultant. All these elements combined have finally pushed this estate into the elite of the appellation. Though Léoville-Poyferré does not enjoy the reputation of its two more prestigious neighbors, it is now a wine well worth consumers' attention. The 2003 was prodigious and should ensure that more and more attention will be given to this particular Léoville.

2006	91–93+	2011–2028		2000	95	now–2025
2005	93	2015–2030+		1999	89	now–2016
2004	93	2009–2027		1998	88	now–2014
2003	98	2009–2030		1997	87	now
2002	90	2011–2020		1996	93	now–2028
2001	90	now–2016		1995	90+	now–2030

LILIAN-LADOUYS ✶ ✶
ST.-ESTÈPHE $18.00–$20.00

This is one St.-Estèphe that is hard for me to recommend, given the number of corked bottles I have had, although some of the older vintages were actually quite tasty. Caveat emptor.

1999	65–69	now		1996	85–86	now–2012
1998	82–83	now		1995	81	now
1997	78	now				

LIVERSAN ✶ ✶
HAUT-MÉDOC $18.00

Liversan aims for wines with a deep color, fine extract, soft tannins, and grip, concentration, and length.

2000	87	now–2010		1997	85	
1998	82	now		1996	86	now

LOUDENNE ✶ ✶ ✶
MÉDOC $18.00

Though I have enjoyed the fruity, straightforward white wines from Loudenne, I have generally found the red wine from this estate to be extremely light. Although it is correctly made, it lacks complexity, richness, and staying power. However, 2003 was a breakthrough effort and sleeper selection for Loudenne—the finest effort produced in many years.

2003	87	now–2013		1999	78	now
2002	82	now		1997	85	now
2001	85	now		1995	78	now

CHÂTEAU LOUIS ★★★
ST.-ÉMILION $40.00–$50.00

A new proprietor, Thierry de la Brosse (also the principal owner of the famed Paris bistro l'Ami Louis), purchased a St.-Émilion property called Rol de Fombrauge and renamed it after his restaurant. This tiny, 7.5-acre estate is planted with 90% Merlot and 10% Cabernet Franc, and Stéphane Derenoncourt has been brought in to oversee the winemaking. The debut, 2006, is impressive.

2006	88–90	now–2021+

LA LOUVIÈRE ★★★
PESSAC-LÉOGNAN $18.50–$32.00

This estate owned by André Lurton produces one of the most consistently well made wines of Pessac-Léognan, as well as one of the better values of this appellation, in both red and white. Though unclassified, La Louvière is superior to many of the crus classés. In particular, recent vintages have been on a quality level equivalent to a Médoc fourth growth.

2005	87	now–2022
2004	88	now–2017
2003	85	now–2016
2001	88	now–2014
2000	90	now–2015
1999	85	now
1998	88	now–2014
1996	87	now–2015
1995	87	now–2011
2006 Blanc	88–90	now–2014
2005 Blanc	89	now
2003 Blanc	90	now
2002 Blanc	88	now
2001 Blanc	90	now–2013
2000 Blanc	87	now
1999 Blanc	88	now
1998 Blanc	90	now

LUCHEY-HALDE ★★★
PESSAC-LÉOGNAN $30.00–$32.00

I believe 2003 is the first vintage I tasted from this estate, which is owned by a school for agricultural engineers. One of the few remaining vineyards within the city limits of Mérignac (home to Bordeaux's burgeoning airport), the wine is a blend of primarily Cabernet Sauvignon and Merlot and a touch of Cabernet Franc and Petit Verdot (a variety rarely seen in Pessac-Léognan).

2005	88–90	now–2012	2003	89	now–2014
2004	84	now–2016	2005 Blanc	89	now–2015

LUCIA ★★★★
ST.-ÉMILION $32.00–$55.00

This garage wine emerges from an 11.5-acre vineyard next to Clos Fourtet. A blend of mostly Merlot with the rest Cabernet Franc (the property also includes some old-vine Malbec), consultant Stéphane Derenoncourt practices all the Burgundian winemaking techniques in its upbringing. This is a dramatic St.-Émilion, known for its flashy display of fruit, oak, and concentration. It should age nicely for 10 to 15 years.

2006	90–93	now–2021	2003	89	now–2013
2005	95	now–2027+	2002	89	now–2013
2004	91	now–2020	2001	90	now–2014

LUSSEAU ★ ★ ★/★ ★ ★ ★
ST.-ÉMILION $31.00–$45.00

The *régisseur* of all the Gérard Perse estates in St.-Émilion, Laurent Lusseau, owns this microscopic one-acre property planted with 43-year-old vines (80% Merlot and 20% Cabernet Franc). This style of wine is soft, opulent, and meant to be drunk in its first ten years.

2006	90–92	now–2016	1999	89	now
2005	90	now–2017+	1998	89	now
2004	89	now–2013	1997	87	now
2003	89	now–2012	1996	86	now
2001	89	now–2010	1995	86	now
2000	90	now–2011			

LYNCH-BAGES ★ ★ ★ ★
PAUILLAC $35.00–$85.00

After a slump between 1971 and 1979, Lynch-Bages has produced an uninterrupted series of fine wines, largely because of the immense work accomplished by Jean-Michel Cazes. Today nobody would argue that this wine's present quality is akin to that of a second growth. Lynch-Bages is generally a robust, rich, and opulent Pauillac, combining the character and class of the top efforts of this appellation. After 2000, a succession of good wines were produced but nothing superb, which does raise my eyebrows, but both 2005 and 2006 look like a return to form, in a softer, slightly lighter style.

2006	91–93	2011–2031
2005	91	2010–2025
2004	89	now–2021
2003	89	now–2020
2002	88	now–2017
2001	89	now–2018
2000	95+	now–2025
1999	90	now–2017+
1998	89	now–2016
1997	86	now
1996	91+	now–2025
1995	90	now–2015
2003 Blanc de Lynch-Bages	87	now
2001 Blanc de Lynch-Bages	90	now
2000 Blanc de Lynch-Bages	86	now

LYNCH-MOUSSAS ★ ★/★ ★ ★
PAUILLAC $24.00–$35.00

Lynch-Moussas is a long-forgotten, underperforming Pauillac that seems to be making a few noises about improving its reputation among consumers. The estate is owned and controlled by the Castéja family, who operate the well-known Bordeaux *négociant* business Borie-Manoux. Despite the good situation of the vineyards (near Grand-Puy-Lacoste), in the past

the wines of this estate were generally light and simple. However, ever since 2000 the quality
has turned around and vintages from 2000 onward have shown a bit more intensity and character than in the past.

2005	88	2011–2018	1999	85	now
2004	88	now–2017	1998	87	now–2015
2003	88	now–2018	1997	78–80	now
2002	81	now–2011	1996	86	now–2012
2001	83	now–2010	1995	86	now–2016
2000	88	now–2015			

LYNSOLENCE ★★★★
ST.-ÉMILION $37.00–$55.00

A brilliantly run *garagiste* property, this 6.5-acre estate in St.-Sulpice (the neighbor of Monbousquet and Valandraud) is one of the finest garage wines of St.-Émilion. Generally 100%
Merlot from vines more than 40 years old planted in different types of soil, the yields are low,
the winemaking impeccable, and the wine dramatic and noteworthy. It is certainly capable of
lasting 10 to 15 years.

2006	91–94	2010–2030	2001	89	now–2012
2005	91+	2012–2025+	2000	90	now–2015
2004	90	now–2022	1999	87	now–2010
2003	92	now–2020	1998	89	now–2013
2002	88	now–2012			

MAGDELAINE ★★★/★★★★
ST.-ÉMILION $45.00–$75.00

This is one of the more delicate, finesse-styled wines of St.-Émilion, reflecting the traditional
winemaking philosophy of Christian Moueix.

2006	89–91	2009–2018	2000	92+	now–2020
2005	90	2012–2025	1999	88	now–2015
2004	88	now–2017	1998	92	now–2020
2003	90	now–2016	1997	87	now
2002	87	now–2015	1996	87	now–2012
2001	89	now–2013	1995	90	now–2012

Past Glories 1990 (92), 1989 (90), 1961 (92), 1959 (90)

MAGREZ FOMBRAUGE ★★★★/★★★★★
ST.-ÉMILION $125.00–$180.00

Magrez Fombrauge is culled from the very best parcel of the larger Fombrauge and cosseted
with Burgundian winemaking techniques. A blend of approximately 80% Merlot and the rest
Cabernet Franc, this Bordeaux has a most dramatic and flamboyant modern style—very hedonistic and unforgettable.

2006	89–92	2011–2027
2005	95	2012–2025
2004	91	now–2022+
2003	94	now–2021+
2002	90	now–2015
2001	94	now–2016
2000	98	now–2020
2006 white	90–92	now–2014

MAGREZ-TIVOLI ★★★★
MÉDOC $35.00

One of the tiny Cuvées d'Exception of revolutionary proprietor Bernard Magrez, this wine is composed of 64% Merlot and 36% Cabernet Sauvignon and emerges from a 6-acre, 40-year-old vineyard, planted in the Médoc's gravelly soils. Magrez and his winemaking team, led by Michel Rolland, are the visionaries behind these wines, which must be tasted to be believed.

2006 Cuvée d'Exception	90–92	2009–2023
2005 Cuvée d'Exception	92	now–2022
2004	90	now–2015
2003	90	now–2022
2002	91	now–2014

MALARTIC-LAGRAVIÈRE ★★★★
PESSAC-LÉOGNAN $24.00–$45.00

This is another estate that continues to make better and better wines that are exceptionally elegant but flavorful as well as ageworthy. Malartic-Lagravière remains under the radar for many wine consumers, given several decades of mediocre performances by the previous proprietor. However, all that has changed, and dramatically so. Under the inspired leadership of Alfred-Alexandre Bonnie and his wife, Michelle, who bought Malartic-Lagravière in 1997, this estate is now making some of the finest wines of Pessac-Léognan. A complete makeover of the château, *cuverie,* and aging cellars has resulted in a space-age winemaking facility that started producing with strong efforts in 1998. The red wine is still elegant but much more concentrated than in the past, and the white wines are wonderfully delicate but intense. This is certainly an undervalued estate making top-notch wines that merit serious consideration.

2006	89–91	now–2022+
2005	92	2011–2036+
2004	89	now–2025
2003	89	now–2018
2002	90	now–2020
2001	90	now–2018
2000	90	now–2020
1999	90	now–2014
1998	89	now–2015
1997	88	now
1996	76	now–2010
1995	76	now
2006 Blanc	88–90	now–2018
2003 Blanc	91	now
2005 Blanc	92	now–2022
2002 Blanc	87	now
2001 Blanc	90	now–2015
2000 Blanc	85	now–2011
1999 Blanc	86	now–2011
1998 Blanc	89	now–2015
1997 Blanc	87	now
1996 Blanc	79	now
1995 Blanc	86	now

MALESCASSE ★★
HAUT-MÉDOC $28.00

This property tends to produce solid, tannic, charmless wines.

2001	85	now	1997	84	now
2000	87	now–2010	1996	82	now
1999	82	now	1995	85	now
1998	84	now			

MALESCOT ST.-EXUPÉRY ★★★★
MARGAUX $27.00–$50.00

A brilliantly run estate that somehow seems to remain under the radar of many serious wine consumers. Since 1990, the estate has made a succession of beautifully elegant yet powerfully concentrated wines with 15 to 25 years of aging potential. Despite these consecutive top-flight efforts, the wine remains modestly priced and needs to be sought out by serious consumers. This is a great Margaux and a fabulous property.

2006	92–94	2010–2025	2000	92+	now–2020
2005	97	2011–2030	1999	90	now–2012
2004	90	now–2027	1998	90	now–2017
2003	92	now–2021+	1997	85	now–2010
2002	92	now–2022	1996	91	now–2025
2001	88	now–2015	1995	90	now–2018

Past Glories 1990 (90), 1961 (92), 1959 (90)

MARBUZET ★★/★★★
ST.-ESTÈPHE $20.00–$25.00

If I had to pick one of the most beautiful and romantically situated properties in the Médoc, it would be this gloriously situated château with its superb terrace and wonderful gardens. In fact, the château (still owned by the Prats family, even though the vineyards were sold), which faces the Gironde River, bears a remarkable resemblance to the Blanc House in Washington, D.C. These are solid, fruity, simple wines.

2004	86	now–2016	1998	82	now
2003	89	now–2014	1997	85	now
2002	85	now–2012			

CHÂTEAU MARGAUX ★★★★★
MARGAUX
CHÂTEAU MARGAUX $125.00–$425.00;
PAVILLON BLANC $55.00–$75.00; PAVILLON ROUGE $29.00–$55.00

After a distressing period of mediocrity in the 1960s and 1970s, this property has returned to form under the auspices of the Mentzelopoulos family, who bought it in 1977. It took the new owners only one vintage to produce a wine worthy of this estate's premier grand cru status. Today, Margaux is consistently top-flight and generally one of the finest first growths of Bordeaux. The style of Margaux is one of opulent richness, with a deep, complex bouquet of ripe black currants, spicy vanilla, and violets. Today the estate is owned jointly by the Mentzelopoulos and Agnelli families, and managed by the brilliant Paul Pontallier. What is probably less well known is that their white wine, 100% Sauvignon Blanc, is one of the finest dry whites of Bordeaux and has been especially strong since the late 1990s, although one can argue that there's nothing at all wrong with the vintages prior to that. Their second wine, which easily represents 30% to 50% of the declassified Château Margaux, is Pavillon Rouge, which also has come on strong lately with some beautiful efforts in the 21st century.

2006 Château Margaux	93–95	2017–2050+
2005 Château Margaux	98+	2015–2060+
2004 Château Margaux	93	now–2027
2003 Château Margaux	99	2011–2035
2002 Château Margaux	93	2010–2030
2001 Château Margaux	93	now–2024
2000 Château Margaux	100	2010–2050
1999 Château Margaux	94	now–2017
1998 Château Margaux	91+	now–2030
1997 Château Margaux	90	now–2015
1996 Château Margaux	99	2010–2045
1995 Château Margaux	95	2010–2040
2006 Pavillon Blanc du Château Margaux	94	now–2030
2005 Pavillon Blanc du Château Margaux	93	now–2020
2004 Pavillon Blanc du Château Margaux	93	now–2026
2003 Pavillon Blanc du Château Margaux	87	now
2002 Pavillon Blanc du Château Margaux	91	now
2001 Pavillon Blanc du Château Margaux	94	now–2020
2000 Pavillon Blanc du Château Margaux	89	now–2015
1999 Pavillon Blanc du Château Margaux	94	now–2020
1998 Pavillon Blanc du Château Margaux	91	now–2010
1996 Pavillon Blanc du Château Margaux	90	now
2005 Pavillon Rouge du Château Margaux	91	now–2022
2004 Pavillon Rouge du Château Margaux	89	now–2022
2003 Pavillon Rouge du Château Margaux	92	now–2021+
2002 Pavillon Rouge du Château Margaux	87	2010–2015
2001 Pavillon Rouge du Château Margaux	87	now–2012
2000 Pavillon Rouge du Château Margaux	89	now–2018
1999 Pavillon Rouge du Château Margaux	87	now–2012
1997 Pavillon Rouge du Château Margaux	86	now–2010

Past Glories 1994 (92), 1990 (100), 1986 (96+), 1985 (94), 1983 (96), 1982 (98+), 1981 (91), 1979 (93), 1978 (92), 1961 (93), 1953 (98), 1947 (92), 1928 (98), 1900 (100)

MARJOSSE ★★/★★★
BORDEAUX $8.00–$10.00

This estate is owned by Pierre Lurton, the manager of Cheval Blanc. The wines—whether red or white—are always a reliable value. Ths is a wine to drink in its first four to five years.

2005	86	now–2012	1998	85	now
2001	85	now	1997	85	now
2000	88	now	1996	86	now
1999	81	now	1995 Blanc	86	now

MAROJALLIA ★★★★/★★★★★★
MARGAUX $65.00–$175.00

A *garagiste* operation in Margaux, Marojallia continues to be one of the finest wines of the appellation. It is owned by the Porcheron family, but this 7.5-acre vineyard in Margaux's Arsac is run by St.-Émilion's revolutionary and highly influential winemaker Jean-Luc Thunevin and his partner, Murielle Andraud. She is the primary winemaker here. Consumers should also keep an eye on Marojallia's second wine, Clos Margalène, a very good value.

2006	92–95	2009–2029	2002	90	2010–2020
2005	95	2012–2025	2001	91	now–2016
2004	90	now–2022	2000	93+	now–2020
2003	90	2009–2020+	1999	91	now–2018

MARQUIS D'ALESME BECKER ★ ★
MARGAUX $22.00–$25.00

This estate tends to produce mediocre, lightweight wines.

2005	85	now–2014	2000	81	now–2012
2001	78	now–2012			

MARQUIS DE TERME ★ ★ ★
MARGAUX $25.00–$35.00

One of the least known and most disappointing classified growths of Margaux, Marquis de Terme has had an infusion of much-needed money to modernize the cellars and purchase at least 30% to 33% new oak casks for each vintage. The owners have also instituted a stricter selection policy with the introduction of a second wine.

2005	88	2012–2025	1999	81	now
2004	88	now–2019	1998	82	now
2003	87	now–2016	1997	79	now
2002	83	now–2011	1996	89+?	2009–2025
2001	86	now–2011	1995	87	now–2018
2000	87	now–2015			

MARSAU ★ ★ ★/★ ★ ★ ★
CÔTES DE FRANCS $12.00–$25.00

From his estate in Côtes de Francs proprietor Jean-Marie Chadronnier produces 100% Merlot wines that consistently qualify as sleepers of their vintages. These Pomerol look-alikes sell for reasonable prices. Unfortunately, available quantities are small.

2005	87	now–2015	1999	87	now
2004	87	now–2013	1998	87	now–2011
2003	89	now–2014	1997	85	now
2002	87	now–2011	1996	86	now
2001	90	now–2012	1995	87	now
2000	90	now–2013			

MARTINENS ★ ★
MARGAUX $20.00

This cru bourgeois is consistently one of the most disappointing wines produced in the Médoc. This wine is largely insipid and well behind most of the other estates in the Margaux appellation.

2000	86	now–2012	1996	73	now
1997	81	now			

MAUCAILLOU ★ ★ ★
MOULIS $18.00–$30.00

Maucaillou has consistently represented one of the best wine values in the Médoc. The wine is impeccably made in a rather robust, tannic, concentrated style but with a certain silkiness in the top vintages.

2004	86	now–2014	1999	87	now
2003	87	now–2013	1998	84	now
2002	87	now–2012	1997	86	now
2001	87	now–2012	1996	84	now
2000	86	now–2011	1995	82	now

MAUGEY ★ ★ ★
BORDEAUX $25.00–$30.00

This is something of an insider's wine, largely applauded and praised in Europe for its rugged consistency but somehow not finding favor in American wine circles. The wine is well made, medium-bodied, and better than American wine drinkers think but not nearly as profound as Europeans tend to believe.

2005	88+	2012–2018	2003	87	now–2014

LA MAURIANE ★ ★/★ ★ ★
PUISSEGUIN–ST.-ÉMILION $18.00–$24.00

This wine is made with the consulting assistance of St.-Émilion's ubiquitous Jean-Luc Thunevin. It is pleasant but somewhat one-dimensional.

2002	86–88	now	1999	89	now–2012
2001	88	now–2011	1998	87	now
2000	88–90	now	1997	85	now

MAZERIS ★ ★ ★ ★
CANON-FRONSAC $20.00

The wines of Mazeris usually present aromas of black raspberry and mineral, are backward with considerable structure, and are meant for moderate aging.

1999	83	now	1996	84	now
1998	86	now	1995	85	now
1997	85	now			

MAZEYRES ★ ★/★ ★ ★
POMEROL $30.00–$35.00

This up-and-coming estate is in the capable hands of Alain Moueix. Prices are realistic for such a limited-production Pomerol.

2004	87	now–2017	1998	88	now–2013
2003	87	now–2015	1997	74	now
2002	88	now–2015	1996	74	now
1999	85	now	1995	79	now

MÉJEAN ★★★
GRAVES $28.00–$32.00

This six-acre *garagiste*-like property in Graves appears to be serious about wine quality, as evidenced by recent vintages. Atypical for this appellation, the blend is high in Merlot (80%) with the rest Cabernet Sauvignon.

2005	91	now–2014		2003	90	now–2014
2004	87	now–2014				

MESSILE-AUBERT ★★★
MONTAGNE ST.-ÉMILION $25.00

This up-and-coming property is in the satellite appellation of Montagne St.-Émilion and owned by Jean-Claude Aubert, one of St.-Émilion's movers and shakers.

2005	88	now–2021
2004	87	now–2013
2003 Cuvée Prestige	87	now–2012
2002	87	now
2001	88	now–2012

MEYNEY ★★/★★★
ST.-ESTÈPHE $18.00–$20.00

What has happened to this estate? One of the great overachievers of the 1970s and 1980s (the 1975, 1982, 1986, and 1989 are superb), Meyney seems to have hit hard times. At best, Meyney has a fairly big style, with good fruit and excellent aging potential. Vinification and upbringing are controlled by one of Bordeaux's most respected oenologists, Georges Pauli.

2005	86	2017		1998	82	now
2004	84	now–2017		1997	78	now
2001	80	now		1996	85	now
2000	82	now–2014		1995	89	now–2011

Past Glories 1989 (90), 1986 (90), 1982 (90), 1975 (90)

MILENS ★★★
ST.-ÉMILION $25.00–$30.00

St.-Émilion's well-known revolutionary, Jean-Luc Thunevin, oversees the vinification of Milens, a wine well worth checking out.

2001	87–88	now–2013		1999	87	now–2010
2000	89	now–2018		1998	88	now

MILLE ROSES ★★★
HAUT-MÉDOC $17.00–$28.00

Another member of the high-quality Biturica group of cru bourgeois estates in the southern Médoc, Mille Roses is produced from a vineyard of 21+ acres near Giscours. The blend is generally two-thirds Merlot and one-third Cabernet Sauvignon. Located not far from Cambon La Pelouse, one of my favorite sleeper estates, Mille Roses merits a look by serious consumers.

2005	87	now–2013		2002	86	now–2011
2004	87	now–2012		2001	89	now–2012
2003	86	now–2010		2000	89	now–2010

LA MISSION HAUT-BRION * * * * *
PESSAC-LÉOGNAN
LA MISSION $78.00–$250.00;
LA CHAPELLE $23.00–$42.00

One of the great names of Bordeaux, with a historic track record of fabulous vintages through-out the 20th century, La Mission Haut-Brion has been owned by the Dillon family, Ameri-cans, since 1983. The estate went through a slight period of transition but since 1989 has produced a string of consistently great wines that rank among the finest of Bordeaux. The style is more opulent, fleshy, and dramatic compared to the restrained glory and nobility of its neighboring rival, Haut-Brion. La Mission Haut-Brion is certainly a wine of first-growth quality, brilliantly made and extremely long-lived. (Usually 30 to 50 years is possible with the best vintages.)

Readers looking for an excellent value should seek out the limited-production second wine of La Mission Haut-Brion, La Chapelle. It can be very fine and certainly ranks as one of the best second wines in all of Bordeaux.

2006 La Mission Haut-Brion	96–98	2012–2035+
2005 La Mission Haut-Brion	97	2013–2051
2004 La Mission Haut-Brion	90	now–2022
2003 La Mission Haut-Brion	94	now–2026
2002 La Mission Haut-Brion	89	now–2020
2001 La Mission Haut-Brion	91	2010–2020
2000 La Mission Haut-Brion	100	2011–2045
1999 La Mission Haut-Brion	91	now–2018
1998 La Mission Haut-Brion	94	now–2030
1997 La Mission Haut-Brion	87	now–2012
1996 La Mission Haut-Brion	90	now–2025
1995 La Mission Haut-Brion	94	2010–2030
2005 La Chapelle	91	now–2016
2004 La Chapelle	89	now–2015
2003 La Chapelle	89	now–2012
2002 La Chapelle	86	now–2013
2001 La Chapelle	88	now–2009
2000 La Chapelle	89	now–2018
1999 La Chapelle	88	now–2010
1998 La Chapelle	89	now–2011
1997 La Chapelle	83	now
1996 La Chapelle	86	now
1995 La Chapelle	90	now

Past Glories 1994 (91), 1993 (90), 1990 (95), 1989 (100), 1988 (90), 1986 (91), 1985 (92), 1982 (100), 1981 (90), 1979 (91), 1978 (96), 1975 (98), 1964 (91), 1961 (100), 1959 (100), 1955 (100), 1953 (93), 1952 (93), 1950 (95), 1949 (100), 1948 (93), 1947 (95), 1945 (94), 1929 (97)

MONBOUSQUET * * * *
ST.-ÉMILION $40.00–$115.00

Gérard Perse, the proprietor, deserves congratulations and accolades for the immense work he has accomplished. This estate, formerly known for producing soft, Beaujolais-style wines, was turned around in 1994 and has since produced a string of phenomenal efforts. One of the most profound changes noticeable in Bordeaux is that even those jealous and critical of the outspoken Perse have finally come to the conclusion (based on so many blind tastings by Eu-ropean critics) that no one in Bordeaux, or perhaps France, is more committed to quality wine. Monbousquet has never had a distinguished *terroir,* according to the soil academics, but the wines Perse has made since the mid-1990s transcend their origins. Readers should realize that Monbousquet is not meant to be cellared for 20 to 30 years, it is meant to be consumed during its first seven to eight years. It is a beautifully made wine that has performed well in every blind tasting I have conducted, often outscoring far more hallowed as well as expensive wines.

Readers should also take a look at the white wine of Monbousquet, which is certainly the best white wine made on the right bank and capable of challenging the dry white wines of Pessac-Léognan.

2006	92–94	now–2021
2005	95	2011–2031+
2004	90	now–2021
2003	93	now–2016
2002	90	now–2017
2001	91	now–2016
2000	95	now–2018
1999	94	now–2017
1998	94	now–2020
1997	90	now–2010
1996	90	now–2017
1995	92	now–2020
2006 Blanc	90–92	now–2014
2005 Blanc	92	now–2012
2004 Blanc	93	now
2003 Blanc	90	now
2001 Blanc	90	now
1998 Blanc	91	now

Past Glories 1994 (90)

MONBRISON ★★/★★★
MARGAUX $20.00–$30.00

This estate made some wonderful wines in the early 1980s and then seemed to succumb to a period of irregularity. Recent vintages have taken on more quality and Margaux classicism.

2004	84	now–2015	1999	85	now
2002	85	now–2010	1998	87	now–2011
2003	86	now–2014	1997	76	now
2001	87	now–2010	1996	85	now–2012
2000	88	now–2014	1995	85	now

LA MONDOTTE ★★★★★
ST.-ÉMILION $85.00–$375.00

The ultimate garage wine, La Mondotte is frightfully expensive yet worth every cent. Among the most concentrated wines of Bordeaux, La Mondotte is not an overly extracted aberration that is all muscle, flesh, extract, and new wood. This wine possesses elegance, complexity, and, with time, a distinctive *terroir* character. This amazing microcuvée emerges from a 30-year-old parcel of Merlot planted on a hillside near Tertre Rôteboeuf and Canon–La Gaffelière. Annual production averages 800 cases.

2006	93–96	2012–2030	2000	98+	now–2030
2005	99	2015–2040+	1999	94	now–2020

2004	93+	2011–2032	1998	96+	now–2030
2003	95	now–2026	1997	94	now–2015
2002	88	now–2020	1996	97	now–2025
2001	94	now–2017			

MONTLISSE ★ ★ ★
ST.-ÉMILION $20.00–$25.00

Montlisse is owned by Christian Dauriac, whose home estate is Destieux. The vineyards of this property are planted in clay and limestone soils and tend to produce a reasonably priced but somewhat monolithic and chunky style of St.-Émilion.

2003	88–90	now–2014	2000	90	now–2020
2001	87–88	now–2015	1999	88	now–2014

MONTROSE ★ ★ ★ ★ ★
ST.-ESTÈPHE
MONTROSE $150.00–$200.00;
LA DAME DE MONTROSE $18.00–$37.00

The big news in Bordeaux in the spring of 2006 was the sale of Château Montrose. Visitors to St.-Estèphe will find the modest château situated on high ground with a magnificent view of the Gironde River. The property was owned by the Charmolüe family from 1896 until 2006 and then sold to a huge telecommunications giant. This property has made magnificent wines with many old vintages that have stood 50 or more years of cellaring. Since 1989, I think this property has hit new heights, often producing a wine of first-growth quality, especially 1989, 1990, 1996, 2000, 2003, and 2005. The second wine, La Dame de Montrose, is also one of the better second wines in all of Bordeaux.

2006 Montrose	92–95	now–2036+
2005 Montrose	95	2015–2035
2004 Montrose	91	now–2022
2003 Montrose	97+	2010–2035
2002 Montrose	90	now–2016
2001 Montrose	91	2009–2020
2000 Montrose	97	now–2040
1999 Montrose	90	now–2025
1998 Montrose	90+	now–2030
1997 Montrose	87	now
1996 Montrose	91+	2009–2025
1995 Montrose	93	now–2028
2005 La Dame de Montrose	88	now–2022
2004 La Dame de Montrose	88	now–2016
2003 La Dame de Montrose	89	now–2018
2002 La Dame de Montrose	87	now–2013
2000 La Dame de Montrose	89	now–2013
1999 La Dame de Montrose	87	now

Past Glories 1994 (91), 1990 (100), 1989 (96), 1986 (91), 1982 (91), 1970 (92+), 1964 (92), 1961 (95), 1959 (95), 1955 (94), 1953 (96)

MONTVIEL ★ ★
POMEROL $25.00–$29.00

An up-and-coming Pomerol owned by Madame Péré-Vergé. The 2001 and 2003 were the finest Montviels I have ever tasted from this estate.

2005	87	now–2015		1998	85–86	now–2010
2004	86	now–2013		1997	84	now
2003	87–90	now–2016		1996	81–83	now
2001	89	now–2014		1995	75–77	now
1999	82	now				

LE MOULIN ★★★★
POMEROL $34.00–$65.00

This tiny estate, which burst on the scene with a sumptuous 1998, continues to offer wines that have more in common with Le Pin in flavor and exoticism than price. Made in a similar style, with extravagant, toasty new oak and ripe Merlot fruit, they display flamboyant notes of caramel, mocha, and jammy berry/cherry fruit. Readers should take note.

2006	90–92	now–2021		2001	92	now–2016
2005	91	2010–2030		2000	92	now–2016
2004	87–89	now–2019		1999	89	now–2014
2003	88	now–2013		1998	90	now–2013
2002	88	now–2013		1997	86	now

MOULIN DU CADET ★★
ST.-ÉMILION $25.00

Moulin du Cadet is a microestate of 12 acres located on the plateau north of St.-Émilion. It tends to produce rather fragrant, lighter-styled wines that lack depth but display attractive bouquets.

2000	79	now		1995	85	now
1998	86	now–2011				

MOULIN HAUT-LAROQUE ★★★★
FRONSAC $18.00–$25.00

One of the four best wines of Fronsac (the others being La Vieille Cure, Fontenil, and Haut-Carles), this is an impeccably run estate producing wines based on Merlot and Cabernet Franc that can easily withstand 20 or more years of aging. The wines are reasonably priced, given that they compete with some of the best wines in Pomerol and St.-Émilion.

2006	89–91	now–2016		1999	85	now
2005	92	2009–2025		1998	85	now
2004	90	now–2022		1997	85	now
2003	90+	now–2019		1996	76	now
2001	87	now–2016		1995	84	now
2000	90	now–2020				

MOULIN PEY-LABRIE ★★★
CANON-FRONSAC $18.00–$28.00

This has always been a serious Canon-Fronsac estate, and recent vintages continue to support its position as one of the stars of that bucolic and potentially promising appellation.

2005	90	now–2015+		1999	85	now
2004	85	now–2018		1998	87	now–2015
2003	90	now–2021+		1997	87	now
2002	87	now–2012		1996	81	now
2001	86–87	now–2010		1995	85	now
2000	87	now–2012				

MOULIN-ROUGE ★★★
HAUT-MÉDOC $12.00–$15.00

Moulin-Rouge is always a consistent offering as well as a noteworthy value. The highly morcellated vineyard (there must be at least six separate parcels) is located north of the village of Cussac-Fort-Médoc, just south of the appellation of St.-Julien. Not surprisingly, the wine often has the character of a good St.-Julien, somewhat reminiscent of such wines as Hortevie and Terrey-Gros-Cailloux but significantly less expensive. The wines are workmanlike efforts.

2000	87	now–2010		1997	85	now
1999	83	now		1996	85	now
1998	86	now		1995	85	now

MOULIN ST.-GEORGES ★★★★
ST.-ÉMILION $22.00–$32.00

This estate is owned by Alain Vauthier, a gentleman best known for having resurrected the quality of Ausone over the last decade. Readers should think of Moulin St.-Georges as a more forward, earlier-drinking, inexpensive alternative to Ausone. Those who can neither afford nor invest the requisite patience in Ausone should seek out its smaller sibling.

2005	90	2011–2025		1999	90	now–2016
2004	89	now–2017		1998	89	now–2016
2003	91	2009–2026		1997	87	now
2002	88	now–2015		1996	88	now–2015
2001	90	now–2016		1995	90	now–2016
2000	91	now–2018				

MOULINET ★★
POMEROL $25.00

This has always been an uninspiring Pomerol property making rather innocuous, boring wines, and I don't see anything really changing despite rumors to the contrary.

2000	82	now–2012		1996	83	now
1998	84	now		1995	83	now
1997	84	now				

MOUTON-ROTHSCHILD ★★★★★
PAUILLAC
MOUTON-ROTHSCHILD $125.00–$325.00; LE PETIT MOUTON $28.00–$50.00

Mouton-Rothschild is the place and wine that the late Baron Philippe de Rothschild singularly created. In 1973, Mouton was reclassified as a "first growth." Through the production of an opulently rich and remarkably deep, exotic style of Pauillac, the baron has been the only person able to effect a change in the 1855 Médoc classification. There is no question that several vintages of this wine qualify as some of the finest Bordeaux I have ever tasted (1929, 1945, 1947, 1953, 1955, 1959, 1982, 1986, and 2006). However, I have also encountered numerous mediocre bottles, which is rather embarrassing for a château of this status and a great disappointment for the consumer (1964, 1967, 1973, 1974, 1976, 1977, 1978, 1979, 1980, and 1990). However, recent vintages have been top-flight, especially from 1995 onward, evidence that Mouton remains faithful to its classification and reputation under the auspices of Philippine de Rothschild.

Readers are starting to see more and more of the second wine, Le Petit Mouton, but to date it has been a relatively uninspiring effort, which is somewhat surprising. One wine well worth considering is their white wine, Aile d'Argent, which is entitled only to a Bordeaux appellation, but it is increasingly well made and well worth buying for drinking during its first four to five years.

2006	96–98+	2018–2050
2005	96	2015–2055
2004	92+	2020–2035
2003	95+	2012–2040+
2002	93	2015–2030
2001	89	2013–2025+
2000	97+	2012–2050+
1999	93	now–2030
1998	96	2012–2050
1997	90	now–2015+
1996	94+	now–2030
1995	95+	2010–2030
2006 Aile d'Argent Blanc	91–93	now–2012
2005 Aile d'Argent Blanc	91	now
2004 Aile d'Argent Blanc	89	now–2010
2003 Aile d'Argent Blanc	89	now
2005 Le Petit Mouton	88	now–2020+
2004 Le Petit Mouton	87	???
2001 Le Petit Mouton	84	now–2010
2000 Le Petit Mouton	89	now–2015
1999 Le Petit Mouton	88	now–2017
1998 Le Petit Mouton	88	now–2012

Past Glories 1994 (91+), 1989 (90), 1986 (100), 1985 (90), 1983 (90), 1982 (100), 1970 (93?), 1966 (90), 1962 (92), 1961 (98?), 1959 (100), 1955 (97), 1953 (95), 1949 (94), 1947 (97), 1945 (100)

NENIN ★ ★ ★
POMEROL $45.00–$70.00

There have been major investments and improvements implemented at this estate by the Delon family, owners of the great Médoc estate Léoville–Las Cases. The best vintages to date of Nenin, which was acquired in the 1990s by the late Michel Delon and his son Jean-Hubert Delon, has been the 2000, although the 1998 is not far off. However, whatever the reason might be, these wines have still not lived up to the potential one might expect from the powers who run Nenin.

2005	90	2011–2036
2004	89	now–2021
2003	87	now–2021
2002	86	now
2001	88	now–2015
2000	93	2009–2025
1999	88	now–2018
1998	90	now–2025
1997	87	now–2010
1996	85	now
1995	86	now
2004 Fugue de Nenin	86	now

2000 Fugue de Nenin	88	now–2010
1997 Fugue de Nenin	85	now

CHÂTEAU OLIVIER ★★/★★★
PESSAC-LÉOGNAN $16.00–$32.00

After years of uninspiring performances, Olivier's vineyards, crowned by one of the region's most gorgeous medieval moated châteaux, is beginning to fashion elegant, stylish, richly fruity wines. This onetime underachiever is beginning to exploit the full potential of the vineyards, and recent vintages have been the finest I've tasted. Nevertheless, this property still ranks well behind the leaders of the appellation.

2005	87	now–2021
2004	85	now–2012
2001	85	now
2000	87	now–2013
1999	86	now–2011
1998	88	now–2016
1997	86	now–2010
1996	86	now–2012
1995	84	now
2005 Blanc	88	now–2020
2003 Blanc	84	now
2002 Blanc	74	now
2001 Blanc	87	now–2013
2000 Blanc	88	now–2010
1999 Blanc	87	now
1998 Blanc	88	now

LES ORMES DE PEZ ★★★
ST.-ESTÈPHE $18.00–$24.00

Les Ormes de Pez is a popular wine, in large part because of its generously flavored, sometimes sweet and plump personality, and also thanks to the promotional efforts of the owner, Jean-Michel Cazes. This is a cru bourgeois to which consumers looking for high quality at modest prices should always give serious consideration.

2005	86	now–2015	1999	86	now
2004	85	now–2012	1998	87	now–2011
2003	86	now–2013	1997	81	now
2002	86	now–2010	1996	86	now–2014
2001	86	now	1995	86	now
2000	89	now–2015			

LES ORMES SORBET ★★★
MÉDOC $15.00–$35.00

A perennial overachiever, this well-run property turns out stylish, attractive, medium-weight wines that represent good value. Since the mid-1980s the proprietor has produced one of the best wines in the northern Médoc. The style that has emerged at Les Ormes Sorbet is one of deep color and a pronounced toasty vanilla oakiness. These wines have the potential for a decade of longevity.

2000	88	now–2011	1996	86	now
1999	81	now	1995	85	now

CHÂTEAU PALMER ★★★★★
MARGAUX
PALMER $65.00–$115.00; ALTER EGO DE PALMER $35.00

Palmer can be as profound as many first growths, and in vintages such as 1961, 1966, 1967, 1970, 1975, 1983, 1989, 1995, 2001, 2004, and 2005 it can be better than many of them. The style of Palmer is one of sensational fragrance and bouquet, so much so that great vintages can be identified in blind tastings by their smell alone. The wine's texture is rich, often supple and lush, and the flavor is always deeply fruity and concentrated. Recent vintages have been formidable efforts. Recently, coproprietor Frank Mahler-Besse and manager Thomas Duroux have also started producing a very good second wine called Alter Ego de Palmer, which will, no doubt, help to further increase the quality of the grand vin.

2006	91–94	2011–2041
2005	97	2015–2050+
2004	94	2011–2025+
2003	89	2010–2020
2002	94	2012–2028
2001	90	2010–2022
2000	95+	2010–2035
1999	95	now–2025
1998	91	now–2028
1997	87	now
1996	91+	now–2028
1995	90	now–2020
2005 Alter Ego de Palmer	90	now–2022
2004 Alter Ego de Palmer	88	now–2016
2003 Alter Ego de Palmer	87	now–2016

Past Glories 1990 (90), 1989 (95), 1983 (98), 1978 (90), 1975 (90), 1970 (95+), 1966 (96), 1962 (91), 1961 (99), 1945 (97), 1928 (96), 1900 (96)

PAPE CLÉMENT ★★★★★
PESSAC-LÉOGNAN $25.00–$90.00

Recent vintages have indicated that the unbridled dynamism of Bernard Magrez, the proprietor, has clearly pushed this property into first-growth quality levels. The enormous efforts made in the vineyards and the draconian selection process for the top wine have produced wine that now rivals those of its nearby neighbors, Haut-Brion and La Mission Haut-Brion, located a few miles from Pape Clément. No one in Bordeaux is pushing the envelope of quality as hard and as enthusiastically as Magrez, with perhaps the sole exception being Gérard and Chantal Perse at Pavie and Pavie-Decesse. While he continues to fashion one of Pessac-Léognan's most impeccably made wines, Magrez's second wine, Le Clémentin, is also a noteworthy effort, and of course there is the white Pape Clément, which is made in very limited quantities but is superb.

2006	92–94+	2012–2030
2005	98	2012–2042
2004	91	now–2022
2003	94	now–2026+
2002	93	now–2023
2001	95	now–2020
2000	95	now–2025
1999	91	now–2018

1998		93	now–2025
1997		87	now–2011
1996		94	now–2020
1995		89	now–2016
2006 Blanc		93	now–2025
2005 Blanc		96	now–2020
2004 Blanc		94	now–2026
2003 Blanc		93	now–2012
2002 Blanc		91	now–2010
2001 Blanc		91	now–2015
2000 Blanc		90	now–2011
1999 Blanc		90	now
2005 Le Clémentin Pape Clément		90	now–2015

Past Glories 1990 (93), 1988 (92), 1986 (92), 1961 (92)

PAS DE L'ANE ★★/★★★
ST.-ÉMILION $45.00

The vineyards at Pas de l'Ane are planted with 50% Cabernet Franc and 50% Merlot. This is a pleasant but one-dimensional wine.

2003	87–90	now–2016		1999	88–90	now
2001	85	now				

PATACHE D'AUX ★★/★★★
MÉDOC $12.00–$15.00

One of my favorite petits châteaux of Bordeaux, this is a reliable cru bourgeois usually dominated by Cabernet Sauvignon. If you are looking for a well-made, reasonably priced cru bourgeois that does not require deferred gratification, this is a worthy choice.

2000	87	now–2013		1996	86	now
1999	85	now		1995	84	now

PAVIE ★★★★★
ST.-ÉMILION $150.00–$255.00

Since purchasing this property and gaining total control over the viticulture, vinification, and *élevage* in 1998, proprietor Gérard Perse has fashioned some of the greatest Pavies of the last 100 years (1998, 1999, 2000, 2003, and 2005). Working with the renowned Michel Rolland, his oenologist, and Dr. Alain Raynaud of Château Quinault l'Enclos, Perse has done significant vineyard replanting, reduced yields to a lowly 30 hectoliters (792 gallons) per hectare (2.47 acres), built a new *cuverie* and cellar, and instituted a draconian selection process to produce the finest wine money can provide. If wine is to be judged by what is in the bottle, Pavie has become a fabulous first-growth-quality estate, offering extraordinary elegance married to awesome levels of richness. After Ausone, Pavie may well have the greatest *terroir* of St.-Émilion, and now the wines reflect that.

2006	96–98	2012–2030+		2000	100	2012–2050
2005	98+	2017–2050+		1999	95	now–2030
2004	95+	2009–2025+		1998	95+	now–2045
2003	98+	2010–2050		1997	86	now
2002	94	now–2025		1996	84	now–2012
2001	96	now–2024		1995	78	now–2010

Past Glories 1990 (90), 1986 (90), 1961 (90)

PAVIE-DECESSE ★ ★ ★ ★ ★
ST.-ÉMILION $109.00–$150.00

This is another estate that has been resurrected under the inspired leadership of Gérard Perse, who has done so much at Monbousquet and Pavie. Since a large portion of this vineyard was incorporated into Pavie in 2002, Pavie-Decesse is now a small, nine-acre site planted on pure limestone above that of Pavie. Pavie-Decesse has never produced better wines than those fashioned under the helmsmanship of Perse and his consultant oenologist, Michel Rolland. The vineyard, which benefits from a noble *terroir,* produces sweeter, more approachable wines than its bigger, more famous sibling, Pavie.

2006	94–96	2012–2030	2000	96	now–2030
2005	96+	2017–2040+	1999	93	now–2025
2004	94	2012–2025	1998	91+	now–2025
2003	96	now–2026+	1997	89	now–2014
2002	93	now–2020	1996	77?	now
2001	95	now–2018	1995	82?	now–2010

Past Glories 1990 (90)

PAVIE-MACQUIN ★ ★ ★ ★ ★
ST.-ÉMILION $35.00–$90.00

The property, which is farmed biodynamically, has a high percentage of extremely old vines and is run by one of the Thienpont family members. Pavie-Macquin has been producing brilliant wines for most of the last decade and continues to behave as if it were the Lafleur of St.-Émilion. The old-vine intensity and backstrapping, superconcentrated, highly extracted style, with an abundance of fruit, body, and tannin, combine to produce a noteworthy candidate for extended cellaring. Production from the estate's 36 acres (planted with 70% Merlot, 25% Cabernet Franc, and 5% Cabernet Sauvignon) averages 4,000 cases.

2006	92–95	2013–2030	2000	95	2010–2025
2005	98+	2017–2052+	1999	90	now–2020
2004	93	2012–2028	1998	95	now–2030
2003	95	2009–2034	1997	90	now–2015+
2002	89	2009–2016	1996	89	2010–2020
2001	89	now–2017	1995	89	now–2025

Past Glories 1990 (91), 1989 (90)

PÉDÉSCLAUX ★ ★
PAUILLAC $20.00

In a time when it is virtually impossible to find a classified-growth Bordeaux not living up to its pedigree, Pédésclaux continues to meander along, making indifferent albeit solid, cleanly made wines that lack distinction.

2005	82	now–2014	2000	86	now–2014

PETIT BOCQ ★ ★ ★
ST.-ESTÈPHE $14.00–$18.00

The unpretentious Petit Bocq is a consistently well made, flavorful St.-Estèphe whose high Merlot content provides an up-front succulence as well as a delicious, fruit-driven style. This small estate of 17+ acres planted with 70% Merlot, 25% Cabernet Sauvignon, and 5% Cabernet Franc produces wines that generally merit interest, particularly for those seeking value in Bordeaux.

2003	87	now–2014	1998	85	now
2001	87	now	1996	86	now
2000	88	now–2012	1995	86	now
1999	87	now			

PETIT GRAVET AINE ★★★
ST.-ESTÈPHE $50.00

Another *garagiste* estate composed of nearly seven acres, the wines are solid, rich, and tannic.

2005			89+	now–2022

PETIT VILLAGE ★★★
POMEROL $32.00–$55.00

A relatively large estate in Pomerol that has lacked some direction despite its excellent owner-ship; recent vintages have been good to very good but rarely inspiring. One would expect more from Petit Village, but the best recent vintage I can remember tasting was the extraordinary 1982.

2005	87	now–2019	1999	88	now–2012
2004	87	now–2017	1998	89	now–2016
2003	86	now–2012	1997	81	now
2002	85	now	1996	86	now
2001	88	now–2013	1995	86	now
2000	90	now–2016			

Past Glories 1990 (90), 1988 (92), 1982 (93)

PÉTRUS ★★★★★
POMEROL $800.00–$1,000.00

Pétrus, the undisputed king of Pomerol and probably the most famous red wine in the world, was an inconsistent performer between 1976 and 1988, but since 1989 there have been few Bordeaux wines that match this property for its extraordinary combination of power, rich-ness, complexity, and elegance. These wines are all noteworthy efforts, but they fetch a king's ransom, as this is the single most expensive dry red wine of Bordeaux and indeed one of the most expensive red wines in the world.

2006	94–96	2020–2050+	2000	100	2013–2050
2005	96+	2018–2050+	1999	94	now–2030
2004	93	2017–2035	1998	100	2010–2040
2003	95+	now–2036	1997	91	now–2025
2002	90	2009–2020	1996	92	2010–2035
2001	95	now–2027	1995	95+	2012–2050

Past Glories 1994 (93+), 1993 (92+), 1992 (90+), 1990 (100), 1989 (100), 1988 (91), 1982 (98?), 1975 (98+), 1971 (95), 1970 (98+), 1967 (92), 1964 (97), 1962 (91), 1961 (100), 1959 (93), 1950 (99), 1949 (95), 1948 (95), 1947 (100), 1945 (98+), 1929 (100), 1921 (100), 1900 (89)

PEY LA TOUR ★★★
BORDEAUX SUPÉRIEUR $10.00–$20.00

A wonderful value that tends to fall off most consumers' radar screens largely because it is owned by the major *négociant* firm Dourthe. The winemaking is impressive and the wine very inexpensive. This is one of the better wines carrying this humble appellation.

2003		86–88	now
2001		86–87	now
2000		87	now
2003 Réserve		87	now
2001 Réserve		87	now

PEYROU ★★
CÔTES DE CASTILLON $11.00–$18.00

Peyrou is a solidly made, chunky, fleshy wine with good character and aging potential of up to a decade.

2005 unfiltered				85	now–2011
2003 unfiltered	85	now–2012			
2000 unfiltered				87–88	now
1999 unfiltered				86–87	now
1998 unfiltered				87	now
1995 unfiltered				85	now

DE PEZ ★★
ST.-ESTÈPHE $22.00–$26.00

I have been waiting for this property to reassert itself since being taken over by the Roederer Champagne firm in the mid-1990s. So far the early efforts have been good but relatively uninspiring.

2003	87	now–2015	1998	74	now
2002	85	now–2010	1997	84	now
2001	85	now–2012	1996	84	now–2012
2000	87	now–2020	1995	86	now

PHÉLAN-SÉGUR ★★★
ST.-ESTÈPHE $18.00–$26.00

Despite the efforts of the Gardinier family, who bought this estate in the 1980s, Phélan-Ségur has not performed as well as expected over recent years, and most vintages of the 1990s were rather disappointing. However, while not truly exceptional, the 2000, 2003, and 2005 are fine efforts. Prices are fairly high relative to the quality.

2005	89	now–2022	1999	82	now
2004	87	now–2015	1998	85	now
2003	88	now–2016	1997	82	now
2002	86	now–2011	1996	86	now
2001	87	now–2011	1995	84	now
2000	87	now			

PIBRAN ★★★
PAUILLAC $22.00–$28.00

Pibran comes from a vineyard situated on the high plateau of Pauillac, near both Pontet-Canet and Mouton-Rothschild. Given the moderate price, it offers consumers a good introduction to the wines of Pauillac. Since Jean-Michel Cazes took over responsibility for the making of Pibran, the wine has become more noticeably fruity, plump, and tasty.

2003	89	now–2016	1998	87	now–2015
2001	84	now–2010	1997	74	now

2000	87	now–2017	1996	89	now–2016
1999	86	now–2015	1995	85	now

PICHON-LONGUEVILLE-BARON * * * * *
PAUILLAC $42.00–$85.00

This noble-looking château opposite Pichon-Longueville–Comtesse de Lalande and Latour was sold in the late 1980s by its owners—the Bouteiller family—to the insurance conglomerate known as AXA. To the company's credit, they hired Jean-Michel Cazes of Château Lynch-Bages to oversee the vineyard and winemaking. The Cazes touch, which included later picking dates, a stricter selection, the introduction of a second wine, and the utilization of a higher percentage of new oak casks, made for a dramatic turnaround in quality. As a consequence, Pichon-Longueville-Baron, frequently called Pichon-Baron, now merits its prestigious second-growth status. With Cazes taking a well-deserved retirement in 2000, highly respected Christian Seely is the administrator and the high quality has continued unabated.

2006	92–94	2012–2025+	2000	96	now–2028
2005	94	2013–2043	1999	89	now–2014
2004	93	2009–2022	1998	90	now–2020
2003	94+	now–2025	1997	86	now
2002	89	now–2016	1996	91	now–2028
2001	93	now–2019	1995	90	now–2016

PICHON-LONGUEVILLE–COMTESSE DE LALANDE * * * * *
PAUILLAC PICHON-LALANDE $55.00–$125.00; RÉSERVE DE LA COMTESSE $32.00

At present, Pichon-Longueville–Comtesse de Lalande (Pichon-Lalande) is unquestionably the most popular and, since 1978, one of Pauillac's most consistently brilliant wines. It can rival the three famous first growths of this commune. The wines of Pichon-Lalande have been very successful since 1961, but there is no question that in the late 1970s and early 1980s, under the energetic helm of Madame de Lancquesaing (affectionately called La Générale by her peers), the quality rose dramatically. Additionally, one can't say enough about the brilliant work being done by manager Thomas Do-Chi-Nam, who started at Pichon-Lalande in 1992. Pichon-Lalande was sold in 2006 to the Roederer Champagne firm. The only perplexing aspect is the estate's propensity to underperform in some truly great vintages, for example 1990 and 2005.

2006		94–96	2015–2030+
2005		86	2012–2025
2004		92	now–2027
2003		95	now–2026+
2002		94	2010–2025
2001		93	now–2018
2000		97	now–2025
1999		87	now–2012
1998		87	now–2015
1997		89	now–2010
1996		96	now–2025
1995		95	now–2020
2004 Réserve de la Comtesse		88–90	now–2016
2003 Réserve de la Comtesse		88	now–2016

Past Glories 1994 (91), 1989 (92), 1988 (90), 1986 (94), 1985 (90), 1983 (94), 1982 (99), 1979 (90), 1978 (92), 1975 (90), 1961 (95), 1945 (96)

PICQUE CAILLOU ★ ★ ★
PESSAC-LÉOGNAN $15.00–$24.00

Picque Caillou is among the last surviving vineyards of the commune of Mérignac, now better known as the location of Bordeaux's ever-expanding international airport. The soil is not unlike the terrain of the famous Pessac châteaux of Haut-Brion and Pape Clément—not surprising, since they are neighbors. Judging by recent vintages, this estate is currently on the rebound.

2004	85	now–2013
2003	87	now–2012
2001	86	now
2000	88	now
1999	85	now
1998	85	now
2001 Blanc	86	now
2000 Blanc	78	now

PIERRE DE LUNE ★ ★ ★ ★
ST.-ÉMILION $42.00–$60.00

Pierre de Lune is one of the garage wines made by the *maître de chai* of Clos Fourtet. This is an opulent, fleshy wine, individualistic and of impeccably high quality, but somehow it seems to get lost in the proliferation of *garagiste* wines of St.-Émilion, which is a shame.

2006	90–92	now–2018	2001	90	now–2013
2005	95	now–2027	2000	90	now–2012
2003	92	now–2016	1999	88	now–2015

LE PIN ★ ★ ★ ★ ★
POMEROL $1,000.00

When the Thienpont family bought this tiny vineyard, it was, by their own admission, to fashion a Pétrus-like wine of great richness and majesty. The first vintages were superb, and Le Pin quickly became not only one of the greatest Pomerols but also Bordeaux's most exotic and luxurious, not to mention most expensive, wine. The estate now has to face considerable competition from all the new St.-Émilion upstarts, wines that often match Le Pin while selling for more reasonable prices.

P.S. The 2003 was completely declassified.

2006	93–96	now–2031	1999	93	now–2015
2005	93	2011–2025	1998	95	now–2018
2004	95	now–2027	1997	86?	now
2002	93	now–2020	1996	92	now–2020
2001	98	now–2024	1995	94	now–2025
2000	98+	now–2025			

Past Glories 1994 (91+), 1993 (90), 1990 (98), 1989 (96), 1988 (92), 1986 (91), 1985 (93), 1983 (98), 1982 (100)

LE PIN BEAUSOLEIL ★ ★ ★
BORDEAUX SUPÉRIEUR $18.00

This seriously run 12.5-acre property produces attractive wines that are meant to be drunk within seven to eight years. Highly respected winemaking consultant Stéphane Derenoncourt fashions this blend of 60% Merlot and the rest Cabernet Sauvignon, Cabernet Franc, and a touch of Malbec.

| 2005 | 90 | now–2012 | 2001 | 86 | now |
| 2003 | 87 | now | 2000 | 88 | now |

LE PIN DE BELCIER ★ ★ ★
CÔTES DE CASTILLON $14.00–$16.00

Le Pin de Belcier is a reliable Côtes de Castillon property.

2005	87	now–2011	2000	89	now–2015
2003	88	now–2014	1999	86	now
2002	87	now	1998	86	now
2001	86	now–2012			

PINDEFLEUR ★ ★ ★
ST.-ÉMILION $20.00–$30.00

Since purchasing this property, Dominique Mestrequilhem has been attempting to produce a wine in the image of his other estate, the wonderfully exuberant, fruity Pipeau.

| 2006 | | | 88–90 | now–2016 |

PIPEAU
ST.-ÉMILION $22.00–$28.00

One of my favorite St.-Émilions because of its sexy, exuberant, hedonistic style, Pipeau is the type of wine I would love to find more frequently at restaurants. In vintages such as 2000, 2003, and 2005, this unpretentious effort becomes bigger, more structured, and more muscular than it is in near-term drinking years such as 2001. Pipeau is also one of the best values to emerge from St.-Émilion in many years.

2006	90–91	now–2020	2001	89	now–2013
2005	90	2009–2024+	2000	90	now–2018
2004	90	now–2017	1999	89	now–2010
2003	88	now–2016	1998	88	now

PLINCE ★ ★
POMEROL $28.00–$30.00

Plince is a solid Pomerol, fairly rich, hefty, spicy, deep, and rarely complex, but usually satisfying. The Moreau family owns this property, but the commercialization is controlled by the Libourne firm of Jean-Pierre Moueix.

| 1999 | 85 | now | 1996 | 84 | now |
| 1998 | 85 | now | | | |

LA POINTE ★ ★ ★
POMEROL $20.00–$42.00

La Pointe has been an irregular performer, but this generally underachieving estate turned in some competent efforts in recent good vintages in Pomerol such as 2005, 2001, and 2000.

2005	86	now–2019	2000	88	now–2012
2004	87	now–2015	1999	87	now–2012
2003	86	now–2013	1998	84	now
2002	86	now–2013	1996	82	now
2001	88	now–2012	1995	83	now

POMEAUX ★★/★★★
POMEROL $35.00

The 2005 Pomeaux is the finest effort I have ever tasted from this small, American-owned Pomerol estate. Displaying copious quantities of red and black fruits in a juicy, crunchy format, it possesses medium to full body, adequate acidity, and ripe, silky tannin. Enjoy this plump, pure, nuanced, tasty 2005 during its first 12 to 15 years.

2005	88	now–2020		2004	83	now–2013

PONTET-CANET
PAUILLAC $25.00–$55.00

As most well-informed insiders in Bordeaux know, proprietor Alfred Tesseron has been doing everything right since 1994 in order to fully develop the enormous potential of this vineyard adjacent to Mouton-Rothschild. Some serious work is done in the vineyard, including debudding, deleafing, and crop thinning. Yields have dropped dramatically. The harvest usually takes place in several stages in an attempt to maximize ripeness, and there are two separate sorting tables, and of course a severe selection. Moreover, enormous investments have modernized the winery Pontet-Canet's recent efforts, especially the 2000, 2003, and 2005, have been wines that show that its nearby first-growth neighbor, Mouton-Rothschild, has some serious competition.

2006	93–95+	2016–2040+		2000	92+	2010–2030+
2005	96+	2015–2035+		1999	88+	now–2016
2004	90+	2014–2025+		1998	86	now–2012
2003	95	2010–2035		1997	85?	now–2010
2002	88	2011–2020		1996	92+	2010–2035
2001	89	now–2017		1995	92	now–2025

Past Glories 1994 (93), 1961 (94?), 1945 (93), 1929 (90)

POTENSAC ★★★
MÉDOC $16.00–$20.00

Owned by the Delon family of Léoville–Las Cases, Potensac has been a noteworthy offering for more than two decades. This large vineyard, situated near St.-Yzans, produces wine so far above the level of quality found in this region of the Médoc that they are a tribute to the efforts of the Delons and the *maître de chai,* Michel Rolland. Any serious Bordeaux enthusiast should search out this wine.

2004	84	now–2011		1999	86	now–2010
2003	89	now–2013		1998	87	now
2002	85	now		1997	85	now
2001	87	now–2012		1996	89	now–2014
2000	89	now–2011		1995	87	now

POUJEAUX ★★★/★★★★
MOULIS $18.00–$32.00

The star of Moulis, as well as a perennial sleeper and best-buy qualitative pick in the Médoc, this estate continues to turn out excellent wines. Poujeaux is clearly a wine that deserves to be ranked as a fifth growth in any new classification of the Bordeaux hierarchy. Poujeaux produced superb wines in 2003, 2001, and 2000 and one of the best wines of the vintage in 1997.

2005	89	2010–2025		1999	88	now–2013
2004	90	now–2022		1998	88	now–2016

2003	88	now–2018	1997	89	now–2015
2002	87	now–2017	1996	86	now–2015
2001	89	now–2012	1995	87	now–2015
2000	88	now–2016+			

LA PRADE ★ ★ ★
CÔTES DE FRANCS $20.00

One of the Côtes de Francs's finest estates, La Prade often produces soft, opulent, fleshy wines that can be consumed during their first six to eight years of life.

2005	91	now–2015	2004	89	now–2015

LE PRIEURE ★ ★ ★
ST.-ÉMILION $30.00–$34.00

This promising 15-acre estate, owned by Olivier Guichard, has potential, given its vineyard location between Troplong-Mondot and Trottevielle.

2005	86	now–2022	2003	87	now–2012
2004	84	now–2012			

PRIEURE-LICHINE ★ ★ ★ ★
MARGAUX $20.00–$38.00

Once owned by one of the great men of wine, Russian immigrant Alexis Lichine, Prieure-Lichine was sold when he passed away. There have been significant changes made at this well-known estate. The wine remains primarily a blend of nearly equal parts Cabernet Sauvignon and Merlot, with a tiny dose of Petit Verdot and even less Cabernet Franc. Yields have been cut significantly to under 35 hectoliters per hectare (375 U.S. gallons per acre), and of course much more work is now being done in the vineyard than ever before. While the wines had declined significantly under the administration of Lichine and his son, Prieure-Lichine is now one of the more exciting up-and-coming properties of the Margaux appellation.

2005	92	now–2022	1999	85	now–2010
2004	90	now–2022	1998	87	now
2003	90	now–2020	1997	79	now
2002	89	now–2017	1996	86	now
2001	89	now–2014	1995	84	now
2000	88	now–2012			

PRIEURE MALESAN ★ ★ ★
PREMIÈRES CÔTES DE BLAYE $15.00

Emerging as the maker of the most consistent as well as delicious Côtes de Blaye, this estate, owned by Pape Clément's proprietor, Bernard Magrez, produces a blend of Merlot and Cabernet Sauvignon.

2002	87	now
2001	87	now
2000	86	now
2002 Hommage de Malesan	87	now
2001 Hommage de Malesan	90	now–2012
2003 Passion de Prieure Malesan	87	now
2002 Passion de Prieure Malesan	89	now–2013
2001 Passion de Prieure Malesan	88–90	now–2013

LA PROVIDENCE ★★★/★★★★
POMEROL $15.00–$75.00

This is an estate to watch now that Pomerol kingpin Christian Moueix has purchased the property. The vineyard is well situated and one would anticipate exciting wines to emerge.

2006	94–96	now–2026+		2005	90	2012–2032+

PUYGUERAUD ★★★
CÔTES DE FRANCS $25.00–$32.00

The cool climate of Côtes de Francs (or, as the French refer to it, the Côtes de Froid) causes difficulties in vintages such as 2004, but in hot years (such as 2003), the wines excel. Stéphane Derenoncourt is the consultant at this estate, which is owned by the Thienpont family. Cuvée Georges is a second label, which includes a healthy percentage of Malbec.

2005	89	2010–2018
2004	87	now–2015
2003	89	now–2016+
2004 Cuvée Georges	88	now–2015
2003 Cuvée Georges	87	now–2014

QUINAULT L'ENCLOS ★★★
ST.-ÉMILION $38.00–$84.00

This is an emerging St.-Émilion estate run by Dr. Alain and Françoise Raynaud. Situated within the Libourne city limits on gravelly soils, Quinault could be called the Haut-Brion of St.-Émilion, given the facts that it (1) is totally surrounded by a *clos* (wall enclosure), (2) is within the city limits, and (3) possesses stony topsoils. Since their first vintage in 1997, the Raynauds have taken this 37-acre vineyard to new heights. They continue to experiment with concentration techniques, but the blend of 80% Merlot, 10% Cabernet Sauvignon, and 10% Cabernet Franc ultimately results in a wine that is beautifully pure and elegant, with considerable aging potential. In 2005, the Raynauds introduced a kosher cuvée, the Quinault Lafleur Kasher.

2006	92–94	2009–2024
2005	94	2012–2025
2004	91	now–2022
2003	89	now–2020
2002	90	now–2020
2001	92	now–2019
2000	94	now–2018
1999	91	now–2015
1998	94	now–2020
1997	88	now–2011+
2005 Quinault Lafleur Kasher	88	now–2019

RAHOUL ★★
GRAVES $18.00–$24.00

This property is located near the village of Portets. The wine has been decidedly mediocre. Every once in a while a good white or red emerges, but generally I find this wine charmless.

2001	85	now
2000	86	now–2012
1999	75	now

1998	84	now
1997	70	now
1996	78	now
1995	83	now
2000 Blanc	86	now
1999 Blanc	87	now
1998 Blanc	85	now

RAUZAN-GASSIES ★ ★ ★
MARGAUX $24.00–$38.00

The *terroir* of Rauzan-Gassies has unlimited potential, but the will to excel seems to have been absent in recent vintages. In style, Rauzan-Gassies tends toward heaviness and corpulence for a Margaux, without the fragrance or finesse normally associated with the better wines of this commune. However, the estate has the ability to produce fairly concentrated, powerful wines. In most vintages, the wines of Rauzan-Gassies have reached maturity surprisingly quickly for a classified growth, usually within seven to eight years of the vintage, but in 2005 Rauzan-Gassies produced its finest and potentially longest-lived wine ever.

2005	92	2015–2045+	1999	87	now–2012
2004	87	now–2017	1998	85	now
2003	89	now–2021	1997	83	now
2002	87	now–2013	1996	75	now
2001	88	now–2014	1995	86	now–2012
2000	90	now–2022			

RAUZAN-SÉGLA ★ ★ ★/★ ★ ★ ★
MARGAUX $36.00–$55.00

Now under the ownership of Chanel, the house of haute couture and perfume, enormous amounts of money have been invested in the vineyards and winery. Things didn't improve as quickly as I would have expected, but 2005 looked to be inspiring, so perhaps Rauzan-Ségla is back in top form.

2006	90–93	2010–2035	2000	90+	now–2020
2005	94+	2015–2030+	1999	88	now–2017+
2004	89	2009–2022	1998	89	now–2018
2003	88	now–2023	1997	79	now
2002	90	2009–2022	1996	88	2010–2025
2001	89	now–2015	1995	90	2010–2025

REIGNAC ★ ★ ★/★ ★ ★ ★
BORDEAUX SUPÉRIEUR $19.00–$45.00

These wines are well worth buying. In fact, Reignac is the reference point for what can be achieved in Bordeaux's less prestigious appellations; a rich, supple wine.

2005	92	now–2017
2004	86	now–2012
2003	89	now–2014
2002	87	now–2011
2001	90	now–2012
2000	92	now–2013
1999	89	now–2010
1998	88	now

2006 Blanc	90–92	now–2010
2005 Blanc	91	now
2004 Blanc	90	now
2003 Blanc	90	now
2001 Blanc	90–91	now

RIOU DE THAILLAS ★★★★
ST.-ÉMILION $25.00–$35.00

This small, quasi-garage wine is made by Jean-Yves Béchet, the owner of the stunning Côtes de Bourg estate called Fougas-Maldoror. Unfortunately, there is not much of it, as the vineyard, located on the Pomerol border, is just over six acres in size.

2001	88	now–2012	1999	87	now
2000	89	now–2014	1998	87	now–2011

RIPEAU ★★
ST.-ÉMILION $21.00–$29.00

I had high hopes that this underachieving estate was emerging from a long period of mediocrity, but I am still not convinced that this producer can make high-quality wine. Time will tell.

2001	85	now	1999	87	now–2010
2000	87	now–2013	1998	85?	now

ROC DE CAMBES ★★★★
CÔTES DE BOURG $20.00–$42.00

One of the undisputed leaders of the Côtes de Bourg appellation, this estate, owned by François Mitjavile (the proprietor of Tertre Rôteboeuf) continues to turn out delicious, chocolate-scented and -flavored wines. If wine is a beverage of pleasure, Roc de Cambes satisfies that requirement impeccably.

2005	90	now–2016	1999	88	now
2004	86	now–2015	1998	91	now
2003	87	now–2010	1997	86	now
2001	90	now–2010	1996	88	now
2000	90	now–2015	1995	90	now

Past Glories 1990 (90)

ROCHEBELLE ★★★
ST.-ÉMILION $24.00–$36.00

This well-placed property, situated next to Troplong-Mondot and close to La Mondotte, produces fine wines that remain reasonably priced for their quality level.

2003	86	now–2014	1998	88	now–2016
2001	86	now–2010	1997	87	now
2000	89	now–2017	1996	87	now–2010
1999	87	now–2011			

ROCHER BELLEVUE FIGEAC ★★★
ST.-ÉMILION $16.00–$26.00

This vineyard, situated on the plateau near both Figeac and the border of Pomerol, is planted with an extremely high percentage of Merlot. The result is a juicy, almost succulently fruity, round wine that makes for delicious drinking early and is best within seven to eight years. I would be cautious about buying anything older.

2005	89	now–2019	1998	88	now–2011
2002	87	now–2015	1997	85	now
2001	90	now–2016	1996	85	now
2000	88	now–2015	1995	85	now
1999	87	now			

ROL VALENTIN ★ ★ ★ ★
ST.-ÉMILION $45.00–$100.00

Although proprietor Eric Prissette's first vintage was only 1995, Rol Valentin has quickly become one of the leading garage wines of St.-Émilion. The 11.4-acre vineyard, situated on two sectors (two-thirds on sandy soils not far from Cheval Blanc and La Dominique and one-third on clay and limestone just north of La Gomerie), is planted with 85% Merlot 8% Cabernet Sauvignon, and 7% Cabernet Franc. Eric Prisette's consultant is the wunderkind Stéphane Derenoncourt. By any standard this is superb wine, capable of aging 15 or more years.

2005	93+	2012–2020+	1999	89	now–2013
2004	88	2010–2018	1998	90	now–2014
2003	90	now–2016	1997	88	now
2002	89	now–2016	1996	90	now–2014
2001	90	now–2015	1995	90	now–2013
2000	93	now–2018			

ROLLAN DE BY ★ ★ ★ ★
HAUT-MÉDOC $15.00–$20.00

Under the auspices of Jean and Catherine Guyon, Rollan de By has become one of the finest Haut-Médoc cru bourgeois estates.

2006	88–90	now–2021	2000	88	now–2013
2005	90	now–2022	1999	86	now
2004	89	now–2017	1998	86	now
2003	88	now–2014	1997	84	now
2001	86	now–2011			

ROLLAND-MAILLET ★ ★/★ ★ ★
ST.-ÉMILION $14.00–$16.00

Bordeaux insiders often look for this well-made St.-Émilion owned and vinified by the famous Libourne oenologist Michel Rolland. The vineyard sits facing Pomerol, across the road from Rolland's beloved estate of Bon Pasteur. Rolland-Maillet tends to be a chunky, deeply concentrated, opaquely colored St.-Émilion that can age for up to a decade. What it lacks in finesse and elegance it often makes up for with pure power and robustness.

2004	87	now–2014	1999	85	now
2003	86	now–2014	1998	85	now
2002	86	now	1996	85	now
2001	87	now–2011	1995	85	now
2000	88	now–2013			

ROUET ⋆⋆
FRONSAC $16.00

In the early 1980s I had some good vintages of Rouet, but everything since has been diluted, high in acidity, and vegetal, so this is a wine that I can never recommend.

2005	82	now		1995	85	now
2000	84	now				

ROUGET ⋆⋆⋆⋆
POMEROL $27.00–$40.00

Rouget's story is typical in modern-day Bordeaux—new money, a new owner, more attention to detail, and a stricter selection process result in a vastly superior wine. This property has clearly rebounded from a prolonged period of mediocrity, as evidenced by what they have achieved with recent vintages (in particular from 1997 onward), producing the finest Rouget since their glory years of the 1940s, 1950s, and early 1960s.

2005	90	now–2021		2000	90	now–2020
2004	89	now–2017		1999	89	now–2012
2003	88	now–2012		1998	89	now–2015
2002	87	now–2012		1997	86	now
2001	90	now–2012				

ST.-DOMINGUE ⋆⋆⋆/⋆⋆⋆⋆
ST.-ÉMILION $40.00–$65.00

When Clément Fayat was denied the right to annex a neighboring parcel of vines to the vineyard of La Dominique, he decided he would produce a microcuvée called St.-Domingue. These wines are generally exotic, opulent, and ripe, with aromas of toasty new oak. The debut vintage of this operation was 1998.

2001	90	now–2012		1999	88?	now–2012
2000	92	now–2017		1998	88	now–2010

ST.-PIERRE ⋆⋆⋆⋆
ST.-JULIEN $42.00–$50.00

This estate continues to languish in the shadows cast by the glamorous superstars of the St.-Julien appellation. Given the usually realistic price, consumers should put this lack of recognition to good use.

2006	92–94	now–2026+		2004	92	2012–2025
2005	93	2015–2045		2003	93+	2010–2030

DE SALES ⋆⋆⋆
POMEROL $20.00–$25.00

After a period of mediocrity, de Sales is on a comeback trail, which is good news for consumers looking for a more reasonably priced Pomerol. This large estate has begun to reassert its position as one of the better values in high-quality wine from this tiny, bucolic appellation. This is one of the lightest wines of Pomerol but nicely made and not dissimilar from a midweight red Burgundy.

2001	87	now–2012		1997	82	now
2000	89	now–2015		1996	79	now
1999	88	now–2012		1995	87	now
1998	88	now–2010				

SANCTUS ★ ★ ★ ★
ST.-ÉMILION $33.00–$65.00

Sanctus is the luxury cuvée of Château La Bienfaisance. A nine-acre garage operation, Sanctus has boasted Stéphane Derenoncourt as its consultant since 2001 (when the quality began to soar). The vineyard is planted with 70% Merlot and 30% Cabernet Franc.

2005	93	now–2022+	2001	90	now–2021
2004	90	now–2019	2000	90+	now–2018
2003	92	now–2021+	1999	78	now–2012
2002	88	now–2014	1998	80?	now

SANSONNET ★ ★/★ ★ ★
ST.-ÉMILION $22.00–$30.00

Because of a series of poor performances, this estate was relegated to grand cru status at the 1996 St.-Émilion reclassification. Since then it has been bought by the d'Aulan family, and under the auspices of the young and talented Patrick d'Aulan it has rebounded over recent vintages.

2004	87	now–2013	2000	88	now–2016
2003	87–90	now–2014	1999	86	now–2010
2001	85–86	now–2013			

SÉNÉJAC ★ ★ ★
HAUT-MÉDOC $16.00–$20.00

A marvelously photogenic estate (poplar-lined roads and ponds), Sénéjac is located in the southern part of the Médoc, west of the town of Parempuyre and just south of the village Arsac. Since this estate was acquired by Thierry Rustmann, manager of the St.-Julien classified growth Talbot, the quality of Sénéjac has soared.

2005	88	now–2019	2000	87	now–2010
2004	88	now–2016	1999	80	now
2003	89	now–2014	1998	86	now
2002	86	now–2012	1997	80	now
2001	85	now	1996	85	now

LA SÉRÉNITE (POUMEY) CUVÉE D'EXCEPTION ★ ★ ★ ★
PESSAC-LÉOGNAN $25.00

La Sérénite, the luxury cuvée created from the Pessac-Léognan property Château Poumey, is part of the Cuvée d'Exception series of wines from Bernard Magrez. This five-acre parcel, planted with equal parts Cabernet Sauvignon and Merlot, is treated like a first growth in terms of vinification, upbringing, and marketing.

2006	90–92	now–2016	2004	90	now–2015
2005	91	now–2022	2003	90	now–2014

LA SERGUE ★ ★ ★
LALANDE DE POMEROL $18.00–$25.00

Pascal Chatonnet, one of Bordeaux's most respected oenologists, owns this small gem in Lalande de Pomerol, producing very elegant wines with early appeal.

2005	90	now–2012
2002	86	now
2001	87	now–2010

2000	88	now
1999	86	now
1998	87	now
1997	86	now
2001 La Pignère de la Sergue	88	now–2010

LA SERVITUDE VOLONTAIRE CUVÉE D'EXCEPTION * * * *
HAUT-MÉDOC $35.00

This 100% Merlot cuvée is another limited-production *garagiste,* an artisanal offering from Bordeaux visionary Bernard Magrez.

2006	90–92	now–2016	2004	90	now–2015
2005	93	now–2022	2003	90	now–2014

SIRAN * * *
MARGAUX $20.00–$42.00

This property in Labarde in the southern part of the Margaux appellation is making consistently delicious, fragrant, deeply colored wines that are frequently on a quality level with a Médoc fifth growth. The estate is owned and managed by William Alain B. Miailhe, a meticulous grower, who produces in an average year 12,000 cases of rich, flavorful, polished wine that admirably reflects the Margaux appellation. The wine is also distinguished by a Mouton-Rothschild–like label that boasts a different artist's painting each year.

2005	89	now–2018	1999	87	now–2010
2004	89	now–2022+	1998	87	now–2020
2003	87+?	now–2018	1997	78	now
2002	87	now–2017	1996	83	now–2012
2001	86	now–2014	1995	87	now–2014
2000	88+	now–2020			

SMITH–HAUT-LAFITTE * * * */* * * * *
PESSAC-LÉOGNAN $32.00–$55.00

Kudos to the Cathiard family, who acquired this once underperforming estate in 1990. They have spared no expense or effort in producing wines (both red and white) that are among the finest in Bordeaux in virtually every vintage. Since its acquisition by the Cathiards, this property has become one of Bordeaux's success stories, producing elegant, flavorful, complex, very complete wines. Some of the recent vintages, such as the 2000, 2001, and 2005, both in red and white, have been exquisite wines, and this is now one of the reigning reference points of Pessac-Léognan and a wine to seek out for its nobility, complexity, and longevity.

2006	91–93	2012–2025
2005	95	2012–2042+
2004	93	2009–2022
2003	92	now–2021+
2002	90	now–2019
2001	92	now–2022
2000	94	now–2025
1999	90	now–2015
1998	90	now–2018
1997	87	now–2011
1996	90	now–2016
1995	90	now–2018

2006 Blanc		93–95	now–2022
2005 Blanc		95+	now–2028
2003 Blanc		93	now–2016
2002 Blanc		90	now
2001 Blanc		92	now–2018
2000 Blanc		87	now–2011
1999 Blanc		89	now

SOCIANDO-MALLET ★ ★ ★ ★
HAUT-MÉDOC $25.00–$45.00

One of the cru bourgeois estates that always performs at classified-growth quality levels, for 20 years Sociando-Mallet has been the insider's choice for top-quality wine that will easily withstand two decades of cellaring. This great estate, with a subsoil nearly identical to that of Pauillac, fashions structured and massive wines that often require eight to ten years of aging. Bottles of the 1970, 1975, and 1982 from my cellar are still youthful and evolving!

2006	90–92	2013–2033	2000	92+	2012–2030+
2005	91+	2015–2035+	1999	89+	now–2018
2004	90	2012–2027	1998	88	now–2018
2003	94	2012–2036+	1997	90	now–2014
2002	89	2013–2025	1996	90	2009–2025
2001	93	now–2020	1995	90	now–2025

Past Glories 1990 (92), 1989 (90), 1986 (90), 1985 (90), 1982 (92)

TAILLEFER ★ ★
POMEROL $23.00–$26.00

This wine has never impressed me and continues to be solidly made, pleasant, but generally uninspiring—a Pomerol that lacks the lustiness, exuberance, and concentration of the best efforts of the appellation.

2005	86	now–2015	1999	85	now
2004	84	now–2010	1998	85	now–2010
2001	85	now	1997	82	now
2000	87	now–2016	1995	84	now

TALBOT ★ ★ ★ ★
ST.-JULIEN $24.00–$55.00

This may be the largest vineyard in the Médoc, with nearly 300 acres under vine. There was a period in the 1990s when Talbot seemed to be a bit off form, but quality over recent vintages has displayed more promise. This estate is capable of producing very special wines, as anyone who has tasted their 1982 or 1986 can easily attest. Even with recent improvements, nothing today matches the exquisite quality of those two wines.

2006	89–91	2010–2030	2000	90	now–2020
2005	90	now–2027	1999	88	now–2012
2004	88	now–2019	1998	88	now–2016
2003	90	now–2020	1997	85	now
2002	78	now–2013	1996	89	now–2017
2001	89	now–2020	1995	88	now–2012

Past Glories 1986 (96), 1983 (91), 1982 (96), 1953 (90), 1945 (94)

TERTRE DAUGAY ★ ★
ST.-ÉMILION $20.00–$28.00

This was a property that, because of sloppy winemaking and lack of effective management, completely lost credibility during the 1960s and 1970s. In 1978 the proprietor of La Gaffelière, Comte Léo de Malet-Roquefort, purchased the property and has made significant improvements both to the vineyards and the wine cellars. It has taken some time for the vineyard to rebound, but recent years have been more promising, particularly after such a prolonged period of mediocrity.

2005	85	2010–2018	1999	86	now–2011
2003	88	now–2015	1998	87	now–2011
2002	86	now–2011	1997	86	now
2001	86	now–2011	1996	80	now
2000	86	now–2012	1995	82	now

DU TERTRE ★ ★ ★ ★
MARGAUX $20.00–$36.00

Proprietor Eric Albada Jelgersma is doing a splendid job rebuilding this estate and producing wines of higher and higher quality. The finest du Tertre in many years was the 2005, and the 2000 and 2001 are close behind in quality. This once perennial underachiever is a property that shrewd consumers would be well advised to keep an eye on. Du Tertre is a stylish, full-flavored, somewhat exotic Margaux with good aging potential. Moreover, it remains reasonably priced.

2005	90	2010–2025	1999	87	now–2014
2004	88	now–2019	1998	88+	now–2015
2003	90	now–2020	1997	85	now
2002	89	now–2019	1996	90	now–2018
2001	90	now–2014	1995	86	now–2015
2000	91	now–2018			

TERTRE RÔTEBOEUF ★ ★ ★ ★
ST.-ÉMILION $64.00–$160.00

Tertre Rôteboeuf (the "hill of the belching beef") is a 14.7-acre vineyard planted with 85% Merlot and 15% Cabernet Franc. Since the early 1980s, under the auspices of the talented François Mitjavile, this has been one of the most distinctive, exotic, compelling wines made in St.-Émilion. It is gorgeous to drink young, yet promises to age well for 15+ years in the finest vintages.

2005	98	2014–2028	1999	91	now–2017
2004	89	now–2022	1998	96	now–2018+
2003	89	now–2016	1997	87	now
2002	86	now–2011	1996	89	now–2012
2001	90	now–2014	1995	94+	now–2020
2000	96	now–2025			

Past Glories 1994 (90), 1990 (98), 1989 (95), 1988 (91), 1986 (91), 1985 (90)

LA TOUR CARNET ★ ★ ★ ★
HAUT-MÉDOC $18.00–$32.00

La Tour Carnet has been completely resurrected under the dynamic leadership of its proprietor, Bernard Magrez, who brought in famed oenologist Michel Rolland to oversee the vinification. Under the new ownership, the wines have dramatically improved, signaling a return of form to this long-forgotten classified growth. Prices have not yet caught up with the exciting new level of quality of La Tour Carnet, so consumers who are wine drinkers rather than speculators, take notice.

2006	91–93	2012–2030
2005	91	2012–2042
2004	90	2011–2024
2003	90	now–2016
2002	89	now–2017
2001	91	now–2016
2000	89	now–2016
1999	86	now–2010
1998	83	now
1997	78	now
1996	86	now
1995	78	now
2006 Blanc	90	now–2012
2005 Blanc	90	now–2010

LA TOUR–FIGEAC ★★★/★★★★
ST.-ÉMILION $25.00–$32.00

Once a part of the original Figeac vineyard, this has always been a property with enormous potential. The 36-acre vineyard is well situated between Cheval Blanc and Figeac, with Pomerol looming on its western border. The wife of Stéphane Derenoncourt, Christine, is now making the wines, which are given Burgundian treatments such as malolactic fermentation in barrel and aging on lees. The blend is 70% Merlot and 30% Cabernet Franc.

2005	91	2011–2024		2000	91	now–2015
2004	85	now–2015		1999	86	now
2003	89	now–2017		1998	90	now–2015
2002	88	now–2016		1996	85	now–2012
2001	90	now–2017				

LA TOUR HAUT-BRION ★★★
PESSAC-LÉOGNAN $36.00–$47.00

Prior to 1983, this was the second wine of La Mission Haut-Brion. Since the Dillon family and Jean Delmas assumed control of the winemaking, the style of La Tour Haut-Brion has changed considerably. Administrator Delmas has chosen to make La Tour Haut-Brion in a more refined style. The result has been a less imposing, more supple wine, yet I would love to see a return to the great classics of the past such as the 1982, 1975, 1961, 1959, and 1949. But that will never happen, as the proprietors decided in 2006 to blend the entire production with the second wine of La Mission Haut-Brion Chapelle, ending this château's tenure as a separate wine.

2005	89	2015–2025		1999	90	now–2017
2004	88	now–2022		1998	89	now–2018
2003	88?	now–2020		1997	86	now
2002	88	now–2015		1996	87	now
2001	89	now–2013		1995	88	now–2015
2000	92	now–2020				

Past Glories 1982 (98), 1978 (95), 1975 (96), 1961 (95), 1959 (92), 1955 (94), 1947 (95)

TOUR MAILLET ★★
POMEROL $25.00

Tour Maillet is a rather one-dimensional, straightforward Pomerol that offers some charm and pleasure but little else.

2005	87	now–2017		2000	87	now–2016
2001	85	now				

TOUR SERAN ★★★
MÉDOC $20.00

This 24.7-acre vineyard in Bégadan is owned by Jean Guyon and produces very good fruit-driven wines that represent excellent value.

2005	90	now–2018		2004	88	now–2013

LES TROIS CROIX ★★/★★★
FRONSAC $15.00–$18.00

This property is owned by Patrick Léon, the former manager at Mouton-Rothschild and Napa Valley's Opus One. The wine has generally been a nice, commercial, midstream style of Fronsac but nothing more. Rather surprising in view of the ownership.

2005	87	now–2016		1998	85	now
2001	84	now		1997	86	now
2000	87	now–2011				

TRONQUOY-LALANDE ★★★
ST.-ÉMILION $25.00–$28.00

Now under the same ownership as Montrose, this property's 2005 is the first vintage where crop thinning and a selection took place for the top wine. An estate on the move upward.

2005	89	2010–2015		2004	85	now–2017

TROPLONG MONDOT ★★★★★
ST.-ÉMILION $32.00–$79.00

I am a huge fan of this property run by Christine Valette, who has been producing great St.-Émilions since the late 1980s, and I have been an avid purchaser of many of her wines. This estate continues to merit substantial praise. These are classic, very long-lived, powerful, concentrated wines designed for serious aging.

2006	91–94+	2012–2030		2000	96	2009–2026
2005	99	2015–2040		1999	89	now–2018
2004	89+	2009–2025		1998	93	now–2025
2003	92+	2012–2025+		1997	89	now–2010
2002	88	now–2016		1996	88+?	now–2018
2001	93	now–2017		1995	92	now–2020

Past Glories 1994 (90), 1990 (98), 1989 (96)

TROTANOY ★★★★★
POMEROL $60.00–$125.00

After continuously expressing my disappointment with the wines produced at Trotanoy between 1983 and 1989, I am thrilled with what has been taking place since the 1990 vintage. One of my favorite estates has returned to the form displayed during their glory years in the 1960s and early 1970s. Recent vintages, especially the 1998, are profound.

2006	90–92	2011–2031	2000	92	2009–2030
2005	95	2015–2030+	1999	89	now–2014
2004	89+	2012–2025	1998	95	now–2030
2003	90+	2009–2020	1997	89	now–2015
2002	89	now–2016	1996	89	now–2017
2001	90	now–2019	1995	93	now–2025

Past Glories 1990 (91), 1982 (94), 1975 (95), 1971 (93), 1970 (96), 1967 (91), 1964 (90), 1961 (98)

TROTTEVIEILLE * * */* * * *
ST.-ÉMILION $35.00–$55.00

In an effort to improve the quality at this up-and-coming estate, proprietor Philippe Castéja has instituted a more severe selection process in the vineyard as well as the cellars. These wines are well worth seeking in view of their reasonable price and high level of quality.

2006	89–91	now–2021	2000	89	now–2019
2005	92	2011–2031+	1999	89	now–2016
2004	89	now–2022	1998	86	now–2015
2003	90+	2010–2023	1997	86	now
2002	88	now–2015	1996	87	now–2012
2001	89+	now–2019	1995	87?	now–2016

Past Glories 1989 (90)

CHÂTEAU DE VALANDRAUD * * * */* * * * *
ST.-ÉMILION $125.00–$400.00

Proprietor Jean-Luc Thunevin and his partner, Murielle Andraud, are the de facto leaders of the St.-Émilion *vin de garage* effort. If that is not unsettling enough to the Médoc aristocracy, they have also started up garage operations in Margaux (Marojallia) and in Graves (Branon). There has been an explosion of interest in these microcuvées, most of which offer impressive quality. Jean-Luc and Murielle's aim at de Valandraud is to produce an enormously rich, concentrated, and beautifully delineated St.-Émilion with minimal handling and to bottle it without fining or filtration. They have succeeded in positioning their wine as a microtreasure that is sought by billionaire collectors throughout the world. However, even though I am a great admirer of Château de Valandraud, I still cannot comprehend the extremely high price it fetches.

2006	90–93+	2012–2025+
2005	95	2010–2025+
2004	91+	2012–2025
2003	93	now–2020
2002	93	now–2026+
2001	94	now–2020
2000	93	now–2019
1999	90	now–2015
1998	93	now–2020
1997	89	now–2010
1996	91	now–2018
1995	95	now–2020
2003 Blanc	90	now
2005 Kosher Cuvée	91	2012–2030
2003 Kosher Cuvée	89+	now–2026
2002 Kosher Cuvée	89	now–2012

Past Glories 1994 (94+), 1993 (93)

VALMENGAUX ★★★/★★★★
BORDEAUX $15.00–$18.00

This seriously run property, located on a plateau not far from Fronsac, is planted with 83% Merlot, 12% Cabernet Sauvignon, and 5% Cabernet Franc. The 7.5-acre vineyard is run by Vincent and Béatrice Rapin, whose father owns Ferrand-Lartigue. The wine is sold for a song.

2005	90	now–2013		2002	85	now
2004	88	now–2013		2001	89	now
2003	89	now–2012		2000	88	now

VEYRY ★★★
CÔTES DE CASTILLON $16.00–$21.00

This is another star from the up-and-coming appellation of Côtes de Castillon, situated adjacent to St.-Émilion. The wines, made under the auspices of Jean-Luc Thunevin, usually qualify as sleepers of the vintage and are very fairly priced.

2005	87			2000	87	now–2010
2003	88	now–2012		1999	87	now
2002	88	now		1998	87	now
2001	86	now		1997	86	now

LA VIEILLE CURE ★★★★
FRONSAC $18.00–$27.00

This estate, owned by a U.S. consortium, has been doing spectacular work over the last half dozen or so vintages. The wine is primarily Merlot that has been picked ripe and vinified impeccably. Over recent years, La Vieille Cure has become one of the leading estates of Fronsac. Its style is one of opulence, complexity, and sexy, up-front fruit, but with enough tannin and structure to age for a decade.

2006	89–91	2010–2020		2000	90	now–2013
2005	93	now–2028		1999	87	now–2010
2004	88–90	now–2021		1998	87	now
2003	92	now–2018+		1997	86	now
2002	87	now–2015		1996	86	now–2010
2001	90	now–2014		1995	87	now

VIEUX CHAMPS DE MARS ★★★/★★★★
CÔTES DE CASTILLON $14.00–$23.00

This is another up-and-coming estate from the Côtes de Castillon. The 42-acre vineyard produces blends of 80% Merlot, 10% Cabernet Sauvignon, and 10% Cabernet Franc. In 1999, Vieux Champs de Mars introduced a special blend of about 80% old-vine Merlot (planted in 1904) and 20% Cabernet Franc called Cuvée Johanna which, as one might expect, just has more depth. Both wines are put through a cold premaceration before fermentation, and then punched down in small oak fermentors, à la red Burgundy. They experience malolactic fermentation in barrel, and represent the more creative side of St.-Émilion winemaking. Neither is fined nor filtered. These are great picks for consumers seeking high-quality wines to drink over the next decade that won't break the bank.

2006	93–96	2010–2030
2005	87–88	now–2012
2003	88	now–2010

2001		85–87	now
2000		86	now
1999		86	now
1998		87	now
1995		86	now
2005 Cuvée Johanna		90–92	now–2016
2003 Cuvée Johanna		90	now–2012
2001 Cuvée Johanna		88	now
2000 Cuvée Johanna		89	now
1999 Cuvée Johanna		86	now

VIEUX-CHÂTEAU-CERTAN ★★★★★
POMEROL $68.00–$150.00

A visit to the *chai* of Vieux-Château-Certan reveals a healthy respect for tradition. For most of the post–World War II era, Vieux Château Certan was made by Léon Thienpont, but since his death in 1985 the property has been managed by his son, Alexandre, who apprenticed as the *régisseur* at the St.-Émilion château La Gaffelière. When the young, shy Thienpont took over the estate, old-timers scoffed at his lack of experience, but he asserted himself immediately, introducing crop-thinning techniques and malolactic fermentation in barrel for the Merlot.

Vieux Château Certan bases its style and complexity on a high percentage of Cabernet Franc. The wine that emerges from the vineyard never has the strength of a Pétrus or other Merlot-dominated wines of the plateau, but it often has a perfume and elegance that recalls a top wine from the Médoc. Because of its historic reputation for excellence, Vieux Château Certan is expensive.

2005	95	2016–2030+	1999	91	now–2018
2004	93+	2012–2025	1998	94+	now–2030
2003	93	now–2020	1997	85	now
2002	93	now–2018	1996	87	now–2016
2001	93	now–2022	1995	88?	now–2020
2000	94+	2010–2030			

Past Glories 1990 (93), 1988 (91), 1986 (90), 1975 (90), 1964 (90), 1952 (94), 1950 (97), 1948 (98), 1947 (97), 1945 (98–100), 1928 (96)

VIEUX FORTIN ★★★
ST.-ÉMILION $20.00–$22.00

This consistently well made St.-Émilion emerges from a vineyard that is not far from Figeac and Cheval Blanc. It usually represents a very good value.

1999	85–87	now	1996	85–87	now
1998	87–89	now	1995	86	now
1997	83–85	now			

VILLA BEL-AIR ★★
GRAVES $16.00–$22.00

This estate is owned by Jean-Michel Cazes, the renowned proprietor of the Pauillac estate Lynch-Bages. Surprisingly, the quality is pleasant rather than inspired.

2005		85	now–2012
2003		80	now
2002		83	now

2001			88	now–2012
2000			88	now–2010
1999			86	now
2001 Blanc			90	now–2010
2000 Blanc			87	now
1999 Blanc			89	now

VRAY-CROIX-DE-GAY ★★★
POMEROL $35.00–$45.00

Pomerol lovers should be taking note of Vray-Croix-de-Gay, which is beginning to fashion some serious wines—not surprising, since it is a beautifully located *terroir* on what is usually called the sweet spot of Pomerol—the plateau.

2005	88	2012–2032	2000	89	now–2014
2004	86	now–2022	1999	76	now
2003	89+?	now–2014	1998	86	now–2017
2002	88	now–2017	1997	85	now
2001	90	now–2016			

YON-FIGEAC ★★
ST.-ÉMILION $22.00–$30.00

Yon-Figeac is a beautifully turreted château, with vineyards located northwest of the town of St.-Émilion on shallow, sandy soil. The vineyard is relatively large, with 62 acres planted with 80% Merlot and 20% Cabernet Franc. The style of wine produced tends to be round and silky, with a good deal of red- and black-fruit character.

| 2001 | 86 | now–2011 | 1999 | 87 | now–2010 |
| 2000 | 88 | now–2015 | | | |

[burgundy]

WINES OF SEDUCTIVE MYSTERY

The simplest thing about Burgundy—many fans as well as detractors would say "the only thing simple"—is that for all intents and purposes it is made from just two grapes: Pinot Noir for red and Chardonnay for white. Stylistically, too, most vintners and observers can agree on certain ideals for Burgundy wine, both red and white: clarity of flavor; striking perfume; a balance of caressing textural richness with vivacity and refreshment (even in reds); the capacity to express the distinctiveness of a particular site; and along with all of these traits, a measure of genuine mystery. Many of Burgundy's names have long been famous, and people will pay to have those names on the label of the wine they are drinking even if—thanks to lax viticulture and wine making—the taste is neither distinguished nor distinctive. But, ultimately, these prices are paid because at least a certain amount of Burgundy delivers characteristics only Burgundy can offer, sometimes including aromas that make you wonder that such a thing could come from grapes. Fruits and berries often, yes, but animal (bloody, smoky, musky, gamey, even fecal), fungal, floral, spicy, and—for lack of any more appropriate word—mineral characteristics one often must struggle to describe; textural nuances not available from any other of the world's grapes; a colloquy of flavors and a seductive sensuality that can leave the taster both profoundly satisfied and scratching his or her head in wonder—all that is Burgundy at its best.

If you ask the denizens of this region and its wine's most fervent followers how to account for such remarkable traits in wine, most will tell you bluntly "it's the *terroir* [stupid]!" By this is meant the unique microclimates of these vineyards, and above all their underlying soil and

[245]

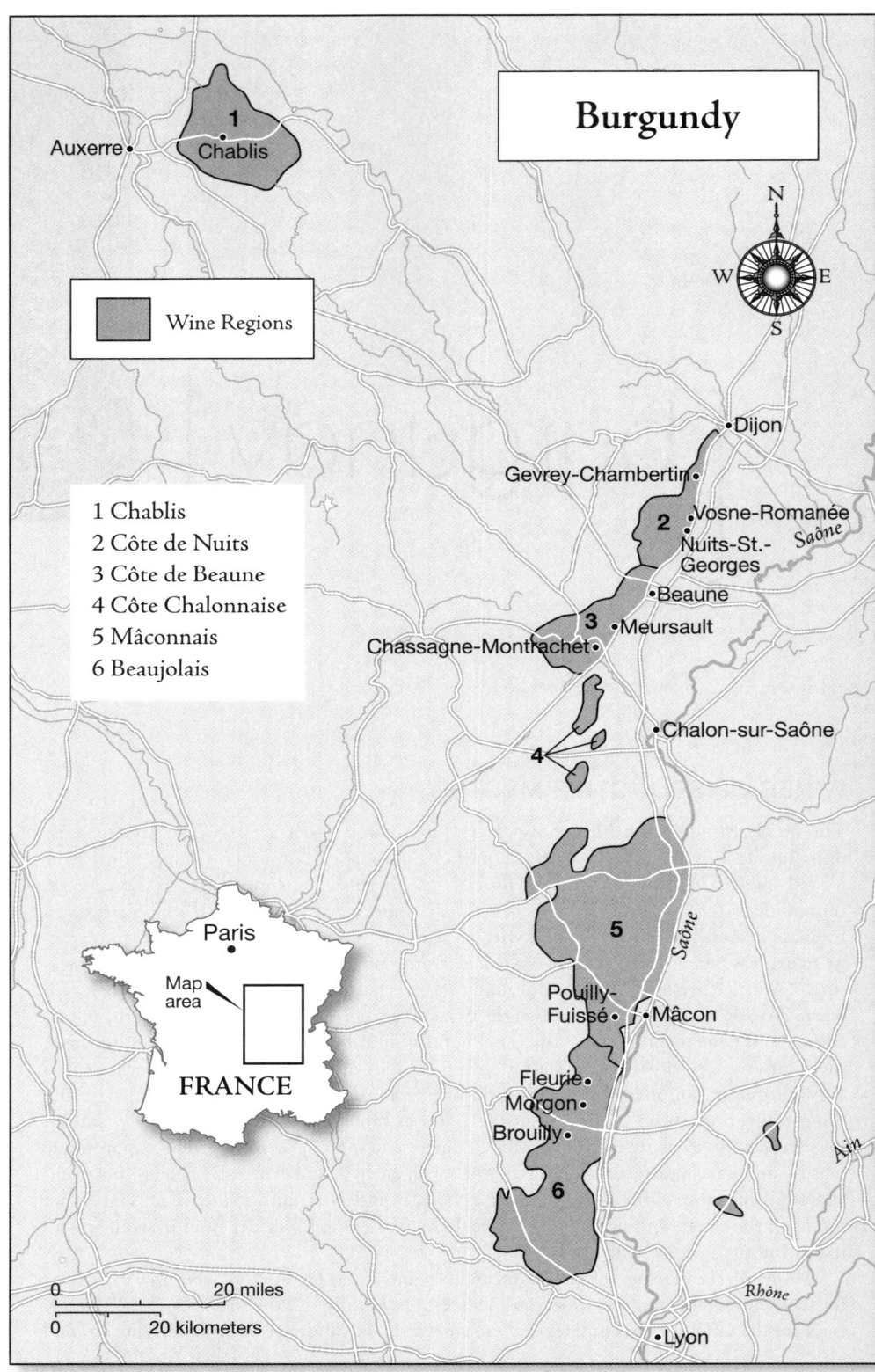

Burgundy

N
W · E
S

Auxerre

1
Chablis

Wine Regions

1 Chablis
2 Côte de Nuits
3 Côte de Beaune
4 Côte Chalonnaise
5 Mâconnais
6 Beaujolais

Dijon

Gevrey-Chambertin

2 Vosne-Romanée
Nuits-St.-
Georges

Saône

Beaune

3 Meursault

Chassagne-Montrachet

Chalon-sur-Saône

4

5

Saône

Pouilly-
Fuissé Mâcon

Fleurie
Morgon
Brouilly

6

Ain

Paris

Map
area

FRANCE

Rhône

0 ____ 20 miles
0 ____ 20 kilometers

Lyon

rock structure. Most of those who devote considerable time to tasting these wines come away convinced that differences in character between the wines of different sites—particularly as noted at one and the same cellar—can in part be accounted for by features of those sites. This is not the place to try to make that case in any detail, or to refute it. But bearing in mind the possibility of doing either will pique a wine enthusiast's interest and appetite for the often inexplicable taste of Burgundy. A very basic orientation in geology is necessary at least to set the stage. "Burgundy" is in fact regularly used in two quite different senses. The more inclusive of these encompasses five subregions. The Côte d'Or or "golden slope" (which may have been named for its exposure, its vast and brilliant fields of flowering mustard, or for some other thing, but probably not its vines) runs south from Burgundy's ancient capital, Dijon, parallels the river Saône, and terminates less than a dozen miles after having passed the region's wine capital of Beaune. The Côte d'Or is itself divided into northern and southern halves, the Côte de Nuits and Côte de Beaune. A very few miles farther south, near the small city of Chalon-sur-Saône commences a string of hillsides less dominated by the vine, but still important for their wine, and known collectively as the Côtes Chalonnaise. Continuing south, we enter the high hills and dramatically diverse exposures of the Mâcon. And at the southern edge of the Mâcon begins Beaujolais, which terminates slightly north of the city of Lyon. Halfway between Paris and the Côte d'Or—in short, well north and west of any of the rest of Burgundy—is Chablis (sometimes known, together with its related vineyards, as the Auxerre or Yonne). The more restricted sense of "Burgundy" excludes Chablis and Beaujolais, and, not coincidentally, those regions are geologically quite distinct, as we shall explain in further detail later on.

Attending to the virtually continuous stretch of vineyards that begins at Dijon and ends at the northern edge of Beaujolais, we can say very simply that it is composed of limestone rock of Jurassic origin. The most important geological features of any given site in which Burgundy's vines are planted will be its ratio of sticky clay or marl to that of stones or pebbles, and the fractures, layering, or displacement of rock strata that occur beneath the surface. Even those many scientists who voice a measure of skepticism about the notion of "terroir" will grant the critical importance of drainage and moisture retention in a plant's metabolism, which in turn forces one to consider the medium in which the vine's roots burrow (or—as it often seems—drill) and how far they get. In addition to their diverse structural characteristics, different soils and sites also display chemical variations, for instance the presence of more iron, which turns certain sites rosy pink or rusty red, and most Burgundian vintners will tell you, too, of how these influence the plant and thus the wine. Less controversial—indeed, unassailable—is the importance of such factors as exposure to sun and wind, heat retention (itself a function not just of sun and wind, but also of rock content), and elevation (since, other things being equal, every step up is a step down in cumulative heat). The Burgundian Côtes, in particular the Côte d'Or, are periodically bisected by *combes,* where streams flow through. These can leave mere fissures, virtual canyons, or broader side valleys, and their slopes add to the diversity of Burgundy's vineyards. For true Burgundian believers in *terroir,* to map these sites is in effect to show a blueprint of the wines, and to impeccably grow and vinify the grapes is to construct another sort of representation—in a most delicious medium—of the sites. Not, of course, that the growers deny the element of self-expression, nor the countless other factors that will influence how any wine tastes. But location and, in particular, exposure, soil, and underlying rock are held to be so important that they form the basis for a complex classification of vineyards to which we shall turn in further detail shortly.

WINES WITH A LONG HISTORY

Wines from the Dijon area were being praised as early as the sixth century, and the Benedictine monks of Cluny in the Mâcon acquired and developed vineyard land in the Côte d'Or from at least the 12th century, around the same time Cistercians purchased major vineyard tracts in Chablis and in the Côte d'Or at Vougeot, which in 1336 they walled in to create the famous Clos de Vougeot. These monastic connections would not be worth mentioning in our context if they did not help to explain how Burgundy wine evolved and what it is today. The monks pursued two sorts of selection in the interest of wine quality: selection of site and of vine. They had the patience and the institutional structure to painstakingly locate by trial and error the best spots for planting the vine, and the individual vines most capable of producing tasty, well-concentrated fruit, then propagate and protect them. The genetic perfection of vines for wine was a labor not just of generations but of centuries. Burgundy first gained international notoriety during the period of the Avignon popes in the 14th century, and in the wake of that newfound status, the first Valois duke of Burgundy, Philip the Bold, intervened on behalf of wine quality by banishing the "disloyal grape" known as Gamay from the region and inisting that only the "noble Pinot" (Noir) be grown. Today, Gamay persists in a few places in the Côte d'Or, but it seldom conduces to wine of any distinction, and in bottle—if blended with Pinot—it must take the appellation Passetoutgrains to warn of its identity. From Philips's time, the rise of Burgundy's reputation proved unstoppable. But Gamay retreated to the granite hills of Beaujolais, where it has proven itself capable of singular excellence if not loyalty. With white wines, incidentally, the picture is more clouded. But until the 20th century, Chardonnay was not that widely planted in the Côte d'Or, and it shared acreage with Aligoté— wines from which are nowadays labeled Bourgogne Aligoté—and with white and "gris" variations on (or mutations of) Pinot, which are nowadays few and far between in Burgundy.

The secularization of vineyard land following the French Revolution and under Napoleon is the next historic watershed of relevance to Burgundy today. Fragmentation of vineyards into small family properties was compounded by the Napoleonic code of law and the equal division of inheritance among siblings. With few exceptions, Burgundy has remained a patchwork of small landholdings ever since. At 32 acres, the famous cru of Chambertin, for instance, is only three acres larger than Château Pétrus, Bordeaux's iconic "small château." Pétrus has only one owner bottling a single wine each vintage, whereas Chambertin is in the hands of some 30 growers. With allowances for how their crop is bottled, bought, and sold in any given 21st-century year, three dozen different wines are likely to be labeled as Chambertin. All of the crus in the Côte de Nuits are equivalent in acreage to Château Margaux plus one other large property in the Margaux commune (take your pick). This fragmentation into small plots explains not only why the same family name and vineyard name may appear on a Burgundy label with numerous different first names, but also why the parents and children, siblings, or cousins in question may or may not collaborate in working their vines and making wine. Typical holdings are so tiny that extreme strategies are sometimes employed in order to hold an estate functionally together across generations, not to mention in order to raise sufficient cash to pay crippling inheritance taxes on land whose value is nowadays astronomical. Where family collaboration succeeds, it helps insure that the quantity of wine from any given named site or cru is large enough to market. Sometimes it is a case of having enough rows of vines to fill a single, standard 225-liter (roughly 300-bottle) barrel. But even if there is a common effort, the finished product (whether in bottle or in barrel) must be sold proportionally under the names of its different owners. More important, the morselization of Burgundy's vineyards explains the evolution of its modern mercantile system. A complex web of rental and sharecropping models evolved to mitigate the effects of relentless fragmentation. And the most important and recognizable entity in the business of Burgundy wine came to be the *négociant,* a firm that would purchase grapes or wines from growers, then vinify, blend, and market them.

Négociants dominated the sale of Burgundy past the mid-20th century. But in the late 1920s, Jacques d'Angerville, Armand Rousseau, and Henri Gouges became the first Burgundy growers to bottle their own wine at their domaines and sell directly to private customers, restaurateurs, and very soon to importers as well. They took this action not because they were brave visionaries—although they were that—but because it was forced on them when they were blacklisted for decrying the penchant of *négociants* for blending their local Pinots with wines from other regions of France and of passing off as crus wines of mediocre quality and nonnoble lineage. The birth of estate bottling was soon to revolutionize the way the world saw Burgundy, but this would not have happened had not the early proponents been growers of exceptional caliber, and had not several other visionaries emerged. A man named Raymond Baudouin, who founded the magazine *Revue du Vin de France* (aimed at winegrowers and connoisseurs alike), championed the movement and introduced American writer Frank Schoonmaker to Burgundy's fledgling estate bottlers. After prohibition was repealed in the United States—and at a time when France was still in economic doldrums—Schoonmaker began importing and advocating the wines of Burgundy estates and hired the young Russian Alexis Lichine as his right-hand man. At the same time, American wine connoisseur Frederick Wildman started an import company and signed on Rousseau. After World War II, these men educated Americans not just to Burgundy wine itself, but to the very traditional Burgundian notion that the highest quality resides in the identity of individual sites and parcels, and to the (for Burgundy, revolutionary) notion that quality was a product of personal integrity and individualism, a theme that could hardly fail to resonate in the U.S.

THE MODERN RENAISSANCE OF BURGUNDY

The domaine-bottling movement rapidly gained momentum in the 1970s and early 1980s thanks in no small part to the evolution of the American wine market, as a wave of importers and agents established portfolios that remain today, beginning with Robert Haas (who founded his Vineyard Brands in 1973), then Becky Wassermann, Kermit Lynch, and Martine Saunier. A crisis of oversupply throughout France had left growers and merchants there holding enormous quantities of wine, particularly from vintage 1972, which counted widely as unsellable. But unlike in Bordeaux, 1972 was an outstanding vintage in Burgundy. And unlike in Bordeaux, an estate's entire production in Burgundy might fit in a single truck. It was in part through importers like these that such iconic and profoundly influential vignerons as Henri Jayer (whose agent Alexis Lichine passed him on to Martine Saunier) and Hubert de Montille (who opened Kermit Lynch's eyes to Burgundy) first came to international prominence after selling their 1972s in the U.S. Soon after (moving into the 1980s) came among others Robert Chadderdon, Robert Kacher, Neal Rosenthal, Peter Vezan, and Peter Weygandt. A number of American agents became involved in a crusade for quality that transcended Burgundy and transformed the business of wine, introducing refrigerated shipping (here Lynch was the prime mover) and becoming actively involved in many wine-making decisions, such as paying premiums for unfiltered bottlings or barrel selections. So prominent had the American proponents of Burgundy become and so successful the best-known estate bottlers, that the *négociants* were widely proclaimed to be on the way out. The sinking economic fortunes and lackluster wines bottled by so many of them fueled this speculation. But rumors of that venerable institution's demise were premature, as we shall see.

The collaboration of the early estate bottlers had been a notable departure from prevailing norms. Traditionally, growers in Burgundy had been insulated from one another by social reticence, by their dependence on the *négociant,* and by the anonymity to which the purchase in barrel consigned their wines. Many had little idea the sort of wine their neighbors had in barrel, much less growers a town or two distant, or those in other parts of France. But in the late 20th century, many factors contributed to change, catalyzed in part by the cross-pollinating effects of the independent breed of import agents that seem to be a specialty of English-speaking countries. As more and more was written in English about Burgundy—English merchant Anthony Hanson's seminal *Burgundy* of 1982, for instance—wine collectors and New World winemakers began visiting growers' cellars with increasing frequency, visits that were eventually reciprocated by a new generation of Burgundians. Owners of domaines from outside Burgundy were the rare exception for most of the 20th century, and the idea of a local native whose family was unconnected with wine (Burgundy, after all, required certain other professions to function!) was even stranger. Yet when ophthalmologist Dr. George Mugneret (in the late 1930s) and lawyer Hubert de Montille (in the late 1940s) founded domaines for love of wine and ran them as passionate hobbies, they unknowingly set a pattern for the future. When outsiders Gérard Potel and Jacques Seysses arrived in the 1960s—the former purchasing Domaine Pousse d'Or and the latter with seemingly quixotic zeal founding his own Domaine Dujac (after briefly working for Potel)—new gusts of openness and innovation blew through once staid and insular Burgundy. Young vintners began discussing wine with one another, not to mention with their importers and with winegrowers from elsewhere. Questions such as "Why do we do what we do?" and "How can we make our wines better?" no longer remained the prerogative of just a few fervent mavericks. The price of Burgundy wine afforded its growers not just the luxury of posing such questions—whether with scientific rigor or simply as soul-searching, mind-expanding exercises—but also the means to act on their hypotheses and hopes.

The dedication, rigor, imagination, and exchange of ideas that have come to characterize Burgundy during the past quarter century are nowhere more in evidence than in the growers' comportment to their vines and soil, and in their consciences as farmers. Another outsider (his name notwithstanding), soil specialist Claude Bourguignon, shocked the growers of the Côte d'Or with his substantiated claims that overdependence on machines and chemical crutches for cultivation had left less microbial life in their precious soils than in the Sahara. And he demonstrated in theory why this mattered to the plants' metabolism and ultimately to flavor, a case that dozens of Burgundy's most ambitious idealists then tried to make in the glass. The most radical recent extension of this concern with the health of soil and vine is the widespread adoption by Burgundy growers of so-called biodynamic methods, as originally advocated by Austrian theosophist Rudolf Steiner in the 1920s. This is not the place to delve into the methods and mantras of a self-styled holism that incorporates preparations of homeopathic proportions, an emphasis on the lunar and stellar calendar, and other rituals that have not been subjected to rigorous scientific study, and which most modern scientists would reject outright. The point is that these methods—which demand (but go beyond) a pesticide- and herbicide-free regimen and the tilling of the soil (sometimes by hand or hoof)—represent an extreme discipline on the part of both true believers and those who practice them simply to see whether they "might work." Here, too, the growers of Burgundy can afford such labor-intensive methods of cultivation and can pass the costs on to their customers. (Although it must be pointed out that biodynamics is the rage in other parts of France as well.) The roster of biodynamic practitioners is swelling year by year, and includes many of Burgundy's foremost growers. The number of growers who make and bottle their own production increases steadily, too.

But the *négociant* concept—not to mention its embodiments—was not dead. Many once venerable institutions, it is true, fell prey to an increasing insistence by consumers on the imprimatur of *mis en bouteille au domaine* (estate bottling) and to loss of contracts as talented growers were tempted to try their hands as vintners and bottle merchants. But the fit *négociants* survived, eventually becoming stronger. From the moment that Jacques Lardière was appointed commercial director of Maison Louis Jadot in 1980 (he had already worked there for a decade), he set an unprecedented example of what a *négociant* could be. The sale of Jadot in 1985 to its longtime, family-owned importer Kobrand ushered in a decade during which Jadot set new standards of rigor for the purchase of grapes and wine, while systematically buying more and more land, becoming in effect a super estate bottler. It was a path that other leading *négociants*—notably Bouchard Père et Fils and Joseph Drouhin—also followed. Meanwhile, a new breed of nimble, risk-taking *négociants* emerged. Belgian Jean-Marie Guffens moved to the Mâcon and became a winemaking celebrity. In 1990 he founded a completely new *négociant* firm (Verget), contracting with his grower-suppliers on the basis of a complex formula that reflected the grapes' quality and subsequent market trends (not merely appellation), and becoming actively—even invasively—involved in their decision making and harvesting. His actions were considered rash if not downright revolutionary, which pleased the outspoken, iconoclastic, and left-leaning Guffens no end. Before long, tremors from Verget were felt in other parts of Burgundy. Today, there exists a host of such hands-on *négociants,* often happy to work with units as small as a barrel or two of any given wine, and passionately involved in viticultural minutiae. Dominique Laurent, Lucien le Moine, Philippe Pacalet, and Nicolas Potel are among the most reliable sources of great Burgundy today. Agent Becky Wassermann and fellow American and "cult" Napa estate owner Ann Colgin teamed up to purchase and rejuvenate the small *négociant* house Camille Giroud. Meanwhile, more and more of the top domaines have sprouted their own grape-buying *négociant* branches and have not been satisfied with less than the same high standards they set for their domaine wines. The upshot of all this is an unprecedented boon to the consumer, and greatly diminished chances that fruit from old vines in special places will any longer suffer the indignity of being tossed anonymously into a huge blend.

GETTING THE GRAPES RIPE, AND RIGHT

One of the most intriguing things about enjoying Burgundy wine is precisely the opportunity to test, to have confirmed, or have demolished (if one's mind and palate remain open) the hunches, hypotheses, or prejudices that we form. Growers are far from immune to speculations of the same sort, and this was true of them long before the advent of Burgundian self-criticism and professional training for so many young growers. Sometimes a grower's musings, hunches, or theories are informed by viticultural and oenological study, sometimes not. The famous 19th-century philosopher F. H. Bradley once wrote that "metaphysics is the finding of bad reasons for what we believe on instinct." By that definition, the ranks of winegrowers are replete with consummate metaphysicians, and none more so than those of Burgundy. Few vintners will rest content to tell a visiting taster what it is they do without offering their reasons for so doing and frequently purporting to demonstrate why alternative methods must fail. Yet experienced tasters are usually well aware of counterexamples to such claims of exclusivity, often lurking just behind a neighboring vintner's cellar door. In humble recognition of that circumstance—and since a detailed look at pros and cons of myriad methods is beyond the scope of this book—we shall now merely glance at some of the innumerable issues and alternatives that conscientious Burgundy growers face, beginning with their soil and vines.

In its pickiness as to location—and, many would add, in its capacity to evoke a site—Pinot Noir is second to no other grape. Its vulnerability (and to an only slightly lesser extent that of Chardonnay) to frost, rot, viruses, and mildew can be crippling. Moreover, getting the fruit ripe—not that this suffices to make great wine—is far from a foregone conclusion. For centuries (with at most, perhaps, occasional exceptional departures from this norm) Burgundy's grapes more years than not failed to fully ripen even in the sense of amassing sufficient sugar (potential alcohol) to give a stable, mouth-filling wine. If grapes reached 9% or 10% potential alcohol, beet sugar was added to bring this up a point or two. (We shall discuss this procedure—chaptalization—further when we tackle winemaking issues.) In recent years, ironically, Burgundy has gotten a taste of "New World" problems, with grapes reaching elevated potential alcohol, but not tasting ripe or full of flavor. The site and how it is farmed are highly relevant to ripeness, and how the soil is worked or chemically treated ultimately affects taste. The use of hand-guided, lightweight machines or (in extreme but increasingly frequent instances) horses who tread the rows like equine dancers, avoids compaction of the soil that would hinder plant metabolism, while plowing deep and tight against the vine. This severs the surface roots that vines constantly send out in an effort to enjoy the easy life, but which would render grapes instantly vulnerable to heavy rain and lacking in the intensity or flavor depth conveyed by deep root structures. (This is one reason why, other things being equal, old vines are superior.) Increasingly, one finds the best growers fertilizing at most with only occasional applications of manure, and the choice and management of cover crops for mulching between rows has taken on huge significance. Gradually, ever more of Burgundy's growers are swearing off herbicides and making a conscious effort to rebuild their soils, returning the wealth of living organisms that several postwar generations inadvertently destroyed, and redressing inadvertent imbalances. The use of nitrogen fertilizers, for instance, had left growers with grapes deficient in acidity (prompting knee-jerk acidification, although it was illegal) and exacerbated the effects of overcropping (leading to yet more chaptalization, and hollow-tasting wine).

The choice of vine is also hugely important. Another major reason why old vines have such importance (and, like Grenache, Riesling, or Zinfandel, to name some others, Pinot Noir and Chardonnay can outlive any human) is genetic superiority and diversity. In their small but critical way, they form a link to the great work of selection and propagation carried on by monks for centuries. When growers speak today of *pinot fin,* they mean a plant with tiny berries in small, conical bunches of the sort that probably gave this grape its name (for being pinecone-like). But the dominant strains of Pinot after the mid-20th century did not look at all this way, and their wine could not have the same perfume or concentration. An old vineyard of *pinot fin* or similar ancient variants of Chardonnay is a repository through selection of the wisdom and good taste of generations of growers. At the same time, such vineyards display tremendous genetic diversity, each vine a unique person, as it were. Nature and natural selection abhor uniformity, as many a vintner who had come to rely on inferior nursery stock or a poorly chosen clone discovered (in the glass, not just the vineyard) with dismay. The clonal invasion that started in the 1970s did not bring solely misfortune, since such clones, too, were the fruits of ambitious viticultural projects, begun in this case after World War II. But that meant early clones were also the product of a much less quality- and more yield-conscious time, not to mention one with different weather patterns. Growers discovered they must shop with care from a menu that eventually became extensive, and many of them believe that only a cocktail of different clones can mimic or substitute for selection and natural diversity. At the dawn of a new century, significant numbers of growers began working together or with plant specialists to systematize the traditional *sélection massale,* the selection and propagation of cuttings from old vines. To find vines not afflicted with viruses represents a huge part of this task. Disastrous choices of plant material can be made from one year to the next, but it takes more than one human generation to recreate by mass selection a vineyard with mature vines, the sort of vineyard from which most great Burgundies originate even today.

The number one culprit when Burgundy disappoints is high yields (especially with Pinot Noir). Even if fruit technically ripens, too-high yields will typically eviscerate the wine of flavor personality and texture. The official measure of yields is hectoliters per hectare—i.e., volume of juice per surface area—and the law stipulates maximums for each class of Burgundy. In practice, these legal limits are set too high to really conduce to excellent quality in all but ideal weather conditions. But on top of that, a so-called PLC (Plafond Limite de Classement) is routinely stipulated, namely the amount by which growers are permitted in light of nature's vicissitudes (or their collective pleas and excuses) to exceed the technical limit of their appellation. Certainly, yield reduction can be taken to extremes and result in imbalanced wine. But so far, serious examples of this in Burgundy have yet to be discovered, and some iconic Burgundy growers like Dugat-Py and Leroy routinely make wine (naturally for a price!) at a crop level not even half what is permitted. In fact, hectoliters per hectare is not really a very meaningful measure of what counts for quality in wine. More important—not just for ripening but for resistance to rot, mildew, and pests—is the number of bunches (imagine them as mouths to feed) a vine is asked to ripen, together with the size of berries and clusters, their looseness or compactness, and other factors that translate to concentration in the eventual wine. The issue of planting density has become increasingly important to Burgundy growers, although theories vary about how it affects ripeness or health when plants compete in a small space. And all of these aspects of fruit, of course, are tied to clonal or mass selection and the genetic profile of the vine. We have not even delved into the subject of rootstock. (Remember that specialized rootstock with exclusively American ancestry is needed to protect vines from the dreaded root louse phylloxera that devastated the Northern Hemisphere a century and more ago.) "Matching," as it is optimistically called, one's vine and soil to one's rootstock is a mixture of science, art, and intuition. And productivity is also directly related to the choice of rootstock to which vines are grafted.

So many considerations and decisions . . . and we have not yet touched on actual cultivation. The training of vines and strategy for pruning and selecting buds have complicated and far-reaching implications for the ripening of grapes. As usual, there are more ancient and newer models and strategies, and many of the best winegrowers find themselves striking a balance between the embrace of innovation and evidence from controlled experiments on the one hand and an inclination to rediscover elements of tradition on the other. What modern New World growers would call "canopy management"—that is to say, the manicure of the vines' foliage—is critical to bottled outcomes, since leaves are the worker bees in the vine's photosynthetic campaign. When and how vines flower and set fruit will be determined by the weather, site, and many other factors. A poor flowering from an evolutionary standpoint (or from that of crop size) is not always a bad thing for quality. *Millerandage,* or "hens and chicks," where tiny sometimes pipless berries (or none at all) develop alongside more normal ones, leaving gaps in between, is practically a necessary condition for a truly great Pinot Noir vintage in Burgundy. (More will be said about that in our discussion of the 2005 vintage.) Once grapes emerge, decisions in the vineyard take on immediate relevance. The choice and timing of sprays against disease greatly influence how fruit evolves. Timely spraying might prevent an uncontainable outbreak of mildew or rot. (Even biodynamic growers treat their vines, not just with homeopathic preparations but with traditional copper sulfate.) But fungicides can retard the fruit's evolution.

A very hot topic nowadays throughout the world of viticulture, but especially in Burgundy, is *vendange verte* or "green harvest." This is the removal of less-developed or otherwise imperfect fruit during the summer; it theoretically lightens the vines' load, permitting the remaining grapes to ripen more successfully. But there is plenty of room for controversy and head scratching over how, when, or whether. Sometimes, for instance, the vine reacts by pumping up the remaining berries, perhaps even to the bursting point. Some growers maintain that the most important work of yield reduction must come at pruning, not after fruit has set, because imbalances of the sort that prompt green harvest should be avoided in the first place. But how does one divine the course of future weather at the time of pruning?

In often rainy Burgundy and with such thin-skinned grapes (literally and figuratively) as Pinot Noir and Chardonnay, a grower has more than sufficient cause to fret. And with increasingly early harvests in recent years, even France's usually sacrosanct August holiday sometimes must be sacrificed. The moment chosen to harvest grapes and choice of strategy are frequently as headache inducing as the work is backbreaking, given that one is dealing with grapes as sensitive as Burgundy's and with so much money at stake. With few exceptions, good (let alone better) Burgundy demands hand harvesting. That means the size, motivation, stamina, instincts, eye-nose coordination, and many other aspects of one's picking crew are critical to success. Many of the best domaines are able to rely on a crack collection of experienced pickers from the neighborhood or family, seasoned with students and enthusiastic wine freaks who out of love volunteer to travel from distant places. But many growers—especially those with larger estates—must secure crews of foreign laborers. There are many aspects of grapes' maturation that can be measured, such as sugar, acidity, berry size, and even such sophisticated factors as fluid pressure on the wall of the grape. But ultimately, past experience, taste, and intuition must be a grower's guides.

GUIDING THE FRUIT FROM VINE TO BOTTLE

The sensitivity of Burgundy's grapes, particularly Pinot Noir, really becomes evident once one picks them. The smaller the container into which the fruit is picked, the less chance skins will rupture or be damaged, and the most quality-conscious growers utilize small, shallow plastic boxes. If the weather is warm, dry ice may be used to keep the freshly picked fruit from harm. Rarely are the bunches and berries uniformly ripe and healthy, so depending on the rigor of the grower and the degree of deviance from his or her ideal, some degree of sorting or bunch selection will take place. The first line of defense, of course, is a trained picker. But nowadays, the better Burgundy establishments (who, once again, can best afford this) employ a *table de tri,* or "sorting table." This might be merely a perforated steel sheet, but often it is a conveyor belt permitting inspection of the fruit and picking out of damaged, rotten, under-ripe, or otherwise imperfect berries, not to mention anything other than grapes and stems. Vibrators or fans may be installed to aid the process. A classic Burgundy cellar has three levels, so fruit drops into fermentors, presses, and eventually barrels all by gravity. Grapes and young wine do not appreciate being nudged, let alone prodded, shoveled, or pumped, and the best handling, particularly with Pinot, is the least. In less traditional facilities or shallow cellars, you'll see conveyor belts and forklifts among other tools used to guarantee that the movement of grapes, juice, and wine is as unencumbered as possible.

With Pinot Noir, an issue immediately arises whether to remove the stems and crush the grapes. (Today there are sophisticated "stemmer-crushers" that will destem but not crush, if you desire.) In few places in the world is this still a "hot" issue, because the stems are nearly always cast aside. But several of the most prestigious Burgundy estates—Dujac and Domaine de la Romanée-Conti, for instance—persisted in the very traditional practice called *vendange entière,* in which the stems, along with a large percentage of intact berries, go into the fermentor. One has to have not just ripe, healthy fruit but also lignified ("woodened") stems to get away with this procedure, otherwise green wood flavors ensue. Why do it? Proponents offer many arguments and are now winning new adherents to this old approach. It's said the floral and spice nuances are enhanced, but most of all—as we shall shortly see—it makes a difference to the course of fermentation.

Another much-disputed topic is the cold soak. It was among the critical observations of the late, great Henri Jayer that color, perfume, and vividness of Pinot fruit could be enhanced if the grapes and juice sat several days before the onset of fermentation. Like many seemingly novel ideas, it may have had its origins in necessity, since during chilly harvests like the spectacularly successful one of 2005, it can take four or five days for fermentation to kick in without one's doing anything to retard it. If you want to ensure that fermentation is delayed, chilling and/or the addition of sulfur are essential. For Chardonnay, if there is to be prefermentative contact between skins and juice, this usually takes place in the press, which is where white grapes go after sorting. The natural settling—or in some cases centrifuging or other rigorous separating—of the Chardonnay juice from its *bourbes,* or solid matter, is critical to the progress of fermentation for white Burgundy, which usually takes place in barrel but may take place (or at least get started) in tank. Whether to add commercial strains of yeast or to permit wild yeasts to ferment the grapes they rode in on is yet another topic that—regardless of whether the wine is red or white—can raise the temperature of growers and oenologists higher than that of the most turbulent fermentation. On the one side seems to lie control and on the other anarchy. Most of Burgundy's best growers file briefs supporting anarchy, claiming that ambient yeasts (which might just as easily originate in the cellar as the vineyard) conduce to more felicitous fermentations and complex results in bottle. The issues here are as diverse as the paths yeasts themselves take in multiplying, so we cannot risk exposing ourselves to them in any detail here. Speaking of which, traditionally Burgundy growers use open-topped fermentors for Pinot Noir—usually stainless steel but sometimes wood or concrete—although closed tanks of various sorts are also sometimes employed.

The issues of whether to add sugar (chaptalize) or acid (which is illegal except in instances of special dispensation) to one's juice loom prominently on the Burgundian horizon. In theory, a properly managed vineyard in a good site should not need any adjustment. And in fact, in recent years, most growers easily achieve 12% to 14% natural potential alcohol in their grapes. Yet "acid adjustment" (as it's euphemistically known) is still widespread, not only because of growers who don't trust their grapes and talents to deliver a balanced wine, but also because high pH leaves wines vulnerable to bacteriological spoilage, and adding tartaric acid is the chosen corrective. Chaptalization, too, is widely practiced, but in a fashion that—though technically illegal (since sugar is supposed to be added only once and to unfermented juice)—seems only to benefit quality. Very small amounts of sugar—a small fraction of a percent of total alcohol—are added over time to extend the process of fermentation, and hence the quality of flavors extracted from the skins. Some growers claim a similar effect can be achieved with *vendange entière* as unruptured berries release their sugar late in the fermentative process.

Regardless of whether stems or unruptured berries are included, three basic strategies for extracting flavor from the skins apply to Pinot Noir fermentation in open vessels. The first and best known (because colorful) is *pigeage*. The modern English equivalent is "punch-down," because the cap of skins is plunged into the fermenting mass below. But traditionally this is a "foot treading" of the cap, which in large vessels means clinging to the edge of the fermentor for dear life (one slip could mean suffocation in the rising column of CO_2) and dog paddling. This work is still done by scantily clad vintners, but nowadays long, handheld plungers or mechanical paddles that run along a track over the fermentors usually do the job. The second extraction method is *remontage,* essentially the technique of percolation as in brewing coffee, with small amounts of juice pumped gently over the cap. The third is *délestage*—"rack-and-return" in Californese—whereby all of the juice is gently siphoned from the fermentor and then returned to mingle with the cap. A few growers submerge the cap for an extended period beneath a lattice, a method more common in Beaujolais. Each technique has its benefits and its liabilities, and a savvy grower will modify his or her regimen according to the material nature has delivered. Just as fermentation commences, some growers will perform a *saignée,* that is, bleed the vat of some of its juice so as to enhance the skin-to-juice ratio of what is left behind. It's possible to make some lovely rosé wines from what is bled away (most Burgundy growers do not bother, though), but it is also possible to create a tannin imbalance in eventual red wine if one is not careful. Just as prefermentative maceration is a topic of great interest to growers, so, too, the length of any postfermentative extraction comes in for scrutiny. The total period of extraction in Pinot Noir can vary radically, from one to three weeks, and during the active period of fermentation one or another means may be employed to lower the temperature if the grower believes this conducive to a better balanced or more flavorful wine. Here, too, there is seldom consensus.

The choice of barrels is a touchstone of style or quality and a hot-button topic for far too many growers, importers, and consumers. Barrels, after all, are only a tool and can be used poorly or well. There are important benefits from small barrel maturation (notably controlled intake of oxygen and clarification), and some prefer new wood above all for its cleanliness. If the wine itself is concentrated enough and protected by its lees (dead yeasts and particulate matter), you may not notice new barrels in tasting the wine, yet their absence might make the tasting experience less pleasurable for many. In that sense, no wine is "overoaked," but only "underwined." Still, the arguments about new barrels (including not just whether they conduce to good taste but also whether their use is "traditional") flare without any sign of resolution. The standard size (a *pièce* or *barrique*) is 225 liters (25 standard cases), but larger volumes are sometimes employed, which give less taste of wood in their new state due to smaller surface-to-volume ratio. Both red and white Burgundy wines normally go through so-called malolactic fermentation, really a transformation by bacteria of malic (green apple) acid to lactic (milk) acid, with a corresponding shift in the wine's flavors and texture. This can happen in tank before they go to barrel but more normally happens in barrel (where, as mentioned, most whites undergo their primary, alcohol, fermentation). Occasionally, this malolactic transformation fails to take place (or at least, to any significant degree) because ripeness is so advanced that there is virtually no malic acid present but, rather, overwhelming tartaric acid. And with whites, sometimes a wine or a portion thereof is "blocked" (by chilling and sulfuring) from undergoing the malolactic transformation, because the winemaker wants to enhance its acid impression. The malolactic transformation usually takes place in Burgundy cellars as it warms up in spring following the alcoholic fermentation. But occasionally "malo" finishes before alcoholic fermentation or (as in 2005) it can take a year or more to finish. As long as a wine is "in malo," the CO_2 it traps helps to protect it from oxidation. Even so, most growers add some sulfur to a wine during what's known as its *élevage* ("upbringing") in the cellar. So when and under what circumstances a wine "does its malo," in what size and age of barrel (and from what forest and cooper) it matures, when and to what degree it is sulfured (too much and it can "harden" to wine, too little and it can tip over literally to the dark side), and countless other factors influence the finished taste.

Length of *élevage* is also hugely variable. Most growers bottle whites before reds, but not always. Red wines are typically bottled after anywhere from 12 to 24 months and whites after 9 to 18 months, but some will fall outside those parameters. With whites especially, but sometimes with reds as well, the handling of the lees is of great importance. If they are "healthy" (i.e., the skins are rot and blemish free) then it is generally thought beneficial to leave the wine in contact with them, as they guard against oxidation and enhance texture and flavor. Actively stirring them up from the bottom of the barrel—called *bâtonnage*—may enhance their virtues or, if some growers are to be believed, can tire the wines or promote superficial "fattiness" of an ephemeral or downright unsightly sort. Discussions of these issues with vintners often quickly leave the realms of science and enter those of metaphysics or personal taste, where they are argued with great passion. Some growers make a principle of handling the young wine's lees a certain way, while most adapt their methods to the vintage, but they often do not agree with one another about what the vintage demands. After the barrels of wine from a given site or picking have finished their malolactic fermentations, they are generally "racked" off their lees, given a dose of sulfur, and returned to (another) barrel—but not always. Some vintners in some years will try not to move the wine at all until the barrels are finally "assembled" together in a tank and then bottled, either immediately or after an interim period in tank or back in barrel. So here, too, there is a multitude of options, any of which can have enormous impact on the wine's eventual taste. A few growers follow the old-fashioned practice of bottling each barrel separately. In that case, even if the wine was assembled before its return to barrel, and especially if it was never moved, bottles with identical labels might be from different barrels, and thus in essence different wines.

Having a limpid, even brilliant gold or ruby glinting in one's glass has long been taken as a mark of quality in itself, and to clarify Burgundy, it is often fined with egg white, bentonite (a clay), skimmed milk, isinglass (from fish bladders), or other proteins that gradually settle out and pull particulate matter with them. Even more frequently, wine is filtered. And around this topic have accumulated innumerable controversies and tales. Some vintners favor filtration as insurance, lest the wine become bacteriologically active in bottle. Some frown on filtering, though the reasons given vary. It "strips out" something from the wine, it's sometimes said. Certainly a wine's high-pressure passage through a filter means pumping and thus trauma. And if we're talking Pinot, this is a wine that sometimes goes into a pout as if from some imaginary slight—that is to say, for no apparent reason, let alone when it's under the pressure of a pump. It might be that, absent pump or filter, the most important advantage of unfiltered bottling is that it forces one to bottle when the wine "falls bright," or settles quietly in the barrel on its own, and that this moment somehow is the best for capturing aroma, flavor, and texture. It was no less a luminary than Henri Jayer, not some American importer or promoter, who first affixed to bottles a strip label reading: "This wine has not been filtered." There are those vintners who say "some years and wines I filter, and some not," and who run conscientious "filter trials" in order to decide the issue. It's hard to argue with that. A couple of things can, however, be said with certainty from experience with fractional bottlings of "the same" wine from tank. An unfiltered wine often has a richer mouth feel than its filtered counterpart, whatever other advantages (or handicaps) one might claim for it, whether in youth or maturity. And a filtered and an unfiltered wine are really never "the same" wine even if they came from the same assemblage in tank and were bottled at the same time. The taste and aroma as well as texture are different from the moment of bottling and generally deviate further over time. To put this in perspective, one has to bear in mind that Burgundy Pinot Noir and Chardonnay have proven especially subject to bottle variation from one cellar to another simply because they are so sensitive to movement and to differences in temperature.

Apropos bottle variation, even if every bottle of a given wine is given the same dose of sulfur and identical corks, variation in one and the same cellar could still occur. The basic chemistry of wine maturation is not yet well understood, and even so seemingly fundamental a concept as oxygen ingress through the cork is controversial. In the real world of TCA-tainted corks ("corked bottles"), many growers utilize several different types of corks for each bottling lot, to minimize their risk. In that case, each bottle is different, and not always subtly. In fact, experiences with white Burgundies of the mid-1990s in particular (discussed further under Buying and Cellaring Burgundy) have made this distressingly evident. To date, only Laroche in Chablis and Mâcon-based Verget have converted significant portions of their production to screw-cap closures. That both of these firms deal exclusively in white wines of which the majority is exported has no doubt made their markets more receptive to this transition.

The use of sulfur throughout *élevage* and especially its addition at the time of bottling has become another much-discussed topic. Particularly among growers who practice organic (including biodynamic) farming methods (or *négociants* who encourage them), there has been a marked tendency to diminish levels of sulfur. These vintners may be acting partly on aesthetic principles. A low-sulfur wine can sometimes initially taste dull or flat if one has become accustomed to wines with higher sulfur levels. (The effect of sulfur on flavor is a bit like that of monosodium glutamate in food.) But there is no question that the combination of nonfiltration with a low level of sulfur can enhance the textural richness of a wine and shade the flavors in ways that many tasters find alluring. That said, three other motivations appear to be stronger than aesthetics. There is a widespread sense among many (especially French) consumers that lower-sulfur wine is healthier. There is an almost metaphysical presumption among some growers that "doping" their vinous children with more sulfur than is absolutely necessary distorts the wines' "true nature." Finally, an attitude is operative here much like that which has led so many Champagne estate bottlers to lower to imperceptible levels their wines' residual sugar (eliminating any dosage). It is a statement by the vintner about what he or she can get away with: "My grapes and *élevage* are so impeccably clean and healthy that the wine does not need more than an absolute minimum of sulfur." As a preservative, sulfur naturally relates to issues of longevity. Several of the finest small *négociants* in Burgundy—Pacalet, Potel, and (in the Mâcon) Jean Rijckaert—make a point of using very little sulfur. How will this influence the way their wines mature in bottle? The truth is no one knows, as it is relatively early days yet for these firms. Domaine Ponsot's Pinots receive no sulfur in their *élevage* and age magnificently. On the other hand, they are extremely concentrated by nature and receive injections of inert gases at bottling. It surely is no crime if one's Burgundy "peaks" a bit sooner rather than later. In reality, though, small differences in sulfur can almost certainly lead to large differences in the way, not just how quickly, a wine evolves. Lest we should appear to be placing unnecessary emphasis on this one element, bear in mind: Much of what we taste in wine—including characteristics most often associated with the influence of *terroir* and the identification of site by taste—originates in various sulfur-containing compounds. We're left with lots of mysteries . . . but then, that perfectly fits our subject, Burgundy.

THE COMPLICATIONS OF CLASSIFICATION

The principle of Burgundian vineyard classification is a pyramid of quality, with generic Burgundy (Bourgogne) as its base, then wines of so-called *villages* stature, then premier cru, and at the apex grand cru. Even the basic Bourgogne level is not entirely simple. As we have already had occasion to note, wines made from the Aligoté grape are labeled Bourgogne Aligoté and blends containing Gamay as Bourgogne Passetoutgrains. Wines grown in the hills above the Côte d'Or (generally from relatively gentle slopes) are Bourgogne Hautes-Côtes de Nuits or Bourgogne Hautes-Côtes de Beaune, depending on their location. Most but not all villages have certain vineyards designated as premier cru, and there are more than 400 such crus. One of the annoyances of Burgundy labeling is that the same vineyard name can sometimes have multiple (at times quite different) spellings. And when it comes to a name like Perrières ("stones"), there will be many different vineyards of that name (though only one per village or commune). Even if a site does not have premier cru status, provided it is an official communal place name (*lieu-dit*) it can appear on the label. The names of *villages* wines as well as premier crus can thus take the form [village + site]; however, if the wine has only communal status the vineyard name must be separated from that of the village and in smaller print. The words "Premier Cru" (or "1er Cru") might not be very prominent on the label, since for example if it proclaims in large, bold letters on a single line "Meursault Perrières," it is already true by labeling law and convention that the wine in question must be premier cru. A wine representing a blend from more than one premier cru is normally bottled simply as "premier cru," although occasionally a pair of vineyards will be cited on a label. Grand crus are to be recognized for their being labeled with only the name of the site (e.g., Musigny), very occasionally with a *lieu-dit* subheading. "Great," you may be saying, "I've got this nailed, so let's get on to something a bit more interesting than nomenclature, shall we?" But not so fast! There is a further complication (this being Burgundy), but at least it makes an entertaining tale.

Crusaders for honesty in wine marketing complained for centuries about the unscrupulous sale of inferior wine under the names of famous vineyards, but France did not begin to codify its current system of *appellation contrôlée* until the 1930s. Prior to that there was a constant battle between those (including legal authorities) attempting to protect the identities of great wine and those who wanted to use the luster of great names to sell whatever wine it was they had. In the most infamous Burgundy instance, with Montrachet widely touted as the world's finest white wine yet growing in only one small vineyard, the temptation was constant to sell other white wines from nearby under that great name. In fact, the vineyards immediately adjacent were given hyphenated names like Bâtard-("bastard") Montrachet. One momentous day in 1879, it dawned on the mayor of Puligny—one of the two towns Le Montrachet straddles—that no matter what any wine law might say, there was a simple and unassailable way to co-opt Montrachet for every wine grown in his village. So, on November 27 of that year, the commune of Puligny officially became Puligny-Montrachet. His neighbors in Chassagne scarcely waited until the ink dried on that proclamation to officially rename their own village Chassagne-Montrachet. The town of Gevrey had appended Chambertin to its name already in 1847, and Aloxe-Corton had followed suit. This caught on with a vengeance after 1879, and almost before cartographers could keep up the names of most of Burgundy's best-known winegrowing villages had changed. In the end, the vineyards chosen by certain towns (Nuits-*St.-Georges*, Pernand-*Vergelesses*) were only accorded premier cru status under *appellation contrôlée* legislation, and certain villages with no single preeminent vineyard on which burghers could agree (Volnay, Meursault, or Pommard, for example) resisted the renaming trend. Still, one now knows why a village wine may have within it the name of a grand cru (Gevrey-*Chambertin*, Chambolle-*Musigny*, Morey-*St.-Denis*, etc.). It was, dear wine lover, not for your instruction, but rather to *mislead*—and a good job has been done of that over the past dozen decades.

An easy and relatively accurate way to envision Burgundy's classificatory hierarchy (at least, as it applies to the Côte d'Or) is as a cross-section running east to west. At the relatively level edge of the Saône plain east of a typical wine village, the appellation is generally just Bourgogne, and sometimes that humble classification reaches into or around the village itself. Ordinarily, though, vineyards in the immediate vicinity of a village are classified as *villages* wines, and they represent slightly better drainage and exposure than accrued to the town's Bourgogne-rated sites. With premier cru, we are ordinarily talking about a significant degree of slope, with excellent drainage and exposure, climbing the gentle slopes or hills west of a village. If there are grand cru–rated vineyards in a commune (again, with some exceptions) these occupy what locals sometimes call "the kidney of the slope," that is, the place that is best drained, most sheltered, and best focuses the sun's rays. "Best drained" here does not mean the spot from which moisture most quickly disappears, but rather the place where the balance of moisture-retentive clay and heat-retentive, drainage-facilitating stones is ideal. Above the grand crus on a given stretch of hillside frequently lies another, narrower band of *villages*-classified vineyard, where soil is often lighter and rockier, and temperatures cooler. And above that (sometimes contiguous or in immediate proximity) are vineyards classified as Bourgogne Hautes-Côtes. In some places (such as at celebrated Vosne-Romanée) there are premier crus above the grand crus as well, so that one can imagine a curve along which lie symmetrical bands (from east to west): Bourgogne—*villages*—premier cru—grand cru—premier cru—*villages*—Bourgogne (Hautes-Côtes). Things are seldom this neat, and there are many exceptions, but as a template for understanding Burgundy, this regularly repeated pattern suffices.

As has been noted, geological variations in Jurassic limestone, its retention and conduction of heat and water, and a vineyard's exposure, elevation, and positioning along the *côte* are all factors of great importance in the Burgundian mind. On these factors rest in large part not just the level of classification of a given piece of land but the very notion of vineyard-specific wine character or *terroir*. In Burgundian theory, each place exhibits its specific *terroir* character. Even if one learns the names and rankings of all of Burgundy's vineyards, any sense that these convey about the flavor of the wines is subject to a host of qualifications, and is above all influenced by the weather in a given year ("the vintage") and by the hand of man. Classification is in short anything but a safe guide to Burgundy quality. In theory, a wine must at least pass muster with a tasting panel to be permitted to sell under its appellation. In practice, the process is perfunctory. *Terroir*-dependent flavor characteristics—whose very existence many skeptics would deny—are only likely to be revealed under the same circumstances where learning the names begins to play a useful role for the consumer, namely when sampling wines of multiple crus or villages from a single grower. And this must be a grower with low enough yields and clean enough working habits to give his or her Pinot Noir or Chardonnay grapes—let alone the *terroir*—a chance to express themselves. Only then is it worth seeking to recognize whatever traits, if any, accrue to wines of certain sites from year to year at this address. If a grower's Nuits-St.-Georges tastes pretty much like his or her *villages* Vosne Romanée, which in turn tastes scarcely distinguishable from a premier cru, we would feel dissatisfied (not to mention cheated to pay the price of the cru). Wines of distinction will be distinctive. And if a mere Bourgogne is distinctive—even if not distinguished—that is a good sign of an excellent grower. Few growers, though, give all of their wines the same *élevage,* so you may be left wondering whether any systematic differences in flavor you perceive can really be laid at the stone portals of *terroir*. Over time, though, a sense of site-specific character may emerge, just as does one of vintage character. To your nose and palate, the wines of vintage *x* from Mr. A may much more closely resemble those of vintage *y* or *z* from Mr. A than they do wines of vintage *x* from Mr. B. And this could well repeat itself many times. But that does not mean that there is no such thing as vintage character or characteristics that are vintage dependent. And, over time, the face of the vintage may emerge. The same is true—or so it can be argued—of character conferred on wine by a particular site.

Terroir has for centuries been Burgundy's most notorious sales tool. (And lately it is being much used in the New World, too.) What is notorious is straying from mystery into mystification, selling wine only on its famous name, crying "typicity" when in honesty what is meant is mediocrity, and calling stinks or flaws marks of *terroir*. An honest, reflective, self-respecting grower has no need to deceive himself or the consumer in these ways. For such a grower, *terroir* will not serve as a crutch or an excuse to silence critical discussion, but as a touchstone for judging workmanship. You can measure the quality of a vintner's product—like those of a carpenter or a chef—based on what he or she makes of the naturally given, provided, that is, you have some sense of that given, in this case the grape, the vintage, and the site. But you cannot appreciate the potential of the naturally given except insofar as human hands and minds have made something out of it. And so, vintner and *terroir* test one another's quality. A grower should be chided who renders mediocre wine from a site known to be capable of distinction. On the other hand, a grower who renders deliciously distinctive wine from a humble appellation deserves special praise. This, then, is why Burgundy's classification matters. Although really codified only in the 1930s, it nevertheless incorporates centuries of experience with where one can achieve the best fruit and the most distinguished wine. It gives us a fixed point of reference for comparing the styles, the quality-consciousness, and the abilities of different vintners. It gives us a sense of where they may be falling short of their potential and where overachieving. Over the years, some premier cru–rated sites have consistently performed like grand crus, both in the glass and in the marketplace, and a very few have been upgraded. But a grand cru performance can never happen unless the grower is talented. Conversely, there are many grand crus—more frequently, portions of grand crus—that do not achieve distinction even in known good hands. One look at the position of the Clos Vougeot or at Charmes-Chambertin compels us to ask why a grand cru incorporates land so low and flat. The answer is, it shouldn't, but it does for reasons of history and politics. Occasionally the institution entrusted with regulating *appellation contrôlée* (INAO) revises some part of Burgundy's classification, but downright declassifications are infrequent, and one can be sure no part of the Clos Vougeot—however deserving—will ever suffer such a fate. Eventually, regardless of classification, the market punishes overrated terroirs and vintners alike, which is why many a premier cru sells for more than any given grand cru.

BUYING AND CELLARING BURGUNDY: CHALLENGES AND STRATEGIES

Traditionally, Burgundy has traded by appellation. This has meant lots of mediocre wine for whose names hapless consumers (or satisfied snobs) pay high prices. But it also meant that one generally paid the same or little more for excellent wine of appellation *x* from a go-getter than one did from a grower more interested in taking long vacations than in tending to the vines. There is still some relative value to be found in Burgundy based on unjust neglect accorded certain villages (and we shall discuss examples below) and on cru-snobbism. Since the mid-'90s, though, Burgundy has slowly been adopting a paradigm that seems only common sense to those of us who take our bearings from the "New World": It is becoming a meritocracy. One well-reputed grower's bottle from a modest appellation now often sells at a price higher than another grower's bottle from a well-known cru. In the transactions of *négociants* with growers, pricing by appellation dies a harder death, but here, too, change is coming. It's really amazing how long Burgundy's middlemen and retail merchants abroad, too, seemed to resist—and some still do—the supposedly inexorable forces of an open market, but that was bound to change. Growers in Burgundy always raised or lowered prices incrementally, and most still do. But whereas for decades prices went up in response to a short or occasionally an outstanding harvest, and then came down again, the trend has been inexorably up in recent years. Furthermore, winery price adjustments have become both bolder and more calculated, and reactions by merchants to supply and demand have become volatile or even violent to a degree once reserved for classified Bordeaux.

Take the great 2005 vintage red Burgundies, for example, and their predecessor. The crop size in 2005 was normal at most domaines—it just didn't seem that way due to demand. Increases ex-cellar were generally in the zero (yes, there were some of those!) to 15% range vis-à-vis the extremely scarce and for that reason unprecedentedly high-priced 2003s, which is to say roughly 10% to 25% vis-à-vis 2004. But the later a grower released his wines, the greater the increases, in response to gathering excitement about the vintage. Americans had to add a premium for the deterioration of the dollar. Then there were increased markups by brokers, courtiers, importers, distributors, and retailers trying to capitalize on an excellent vintage and/ or to make up for losses being incurred in seeking a ready market for 2004s (in a climate where "gouge or dump" bipolar disorder afflicts far too many merchants). Thus, one arrived at what were widely and understandably viewed as shockingly steep increases in price, often 50% to 100% over what had been asked in 2004. And prices on many 2004s continued to drop as merchants panicked lest they be unable to sell them. This offered an excellent opportunity for consumers enamored of a fresh-fruited style of red Burgundy and willing to search out the exceptions in a difficult vintage, but it also seemed to confirm the cynical adage of a schizoid era that "there are only two ways for consumers to buy Burgundy: 'on future' or on closeout." It's easy, though, to imagine a scenario far worse than this—and to pray it isn't realized! Suppose one took the prices of 2005 vintage cru classé Bordeaux—produced in the tens of thousands of cases per château—as a baseline, and then tried to factor in the relative scarcity of Burgundy wines frequently produced in quantities of 250 cases or fewer (often as few as one or two barrels, i.e., 25 to 50 cases). An argument could thus be made that Burgundy lovers are still being spared the sort of market forces that normally apply, and certainly apply in Bordeaux, where a critical mass and market mechanisms permit specific wines to trade as commodities. One reason is that small Burgundy growers still think in terms of taking care of their customers' needs year in, year out. And within each vintage, they typically offer each customer (particularly those in the trade) a set proportion of production across the board. Outstanding vintages or sites are in effect leveraged to sell those of lesser reputation. Once the wine leaves the grower's hand, though, the strategies by which it's sold can, as we just saw, vary greatly.

Merchants virtually never actually own Burgundy *en primeur*—at best they have allocations or promissory notes. So when you place an advance order—as in excellent vintages you will be advised to do—you're really buying such a note passed down from the grower, often through several further sets of hands, to the merchant who has promised it to you. Because the quantities produced are often tiny, small errors, miscalculations, wines an estate diverts to its own cellars, or damaged goods can spell the difference between whether or not the customer gets what he or she was promised or has come to expect. (There is always wine from classified Bordeaux châteaux in the marketplace with which to make up for shortages, albeit at a price; not so with Burgundy.) Burgundian Pinot Noir and Chardonnay are extremely sensitive to travel and temperature variation, so make sure you know how your purchases will be or have been shipped (refrigerated and insulated, never allowed to warm beyond a cool room temperature for even a short period, and never rattled around on railroad cars).

The most powerful factor in the consumer's favor—vastly improving the odds of scoring Burgundy gems—is that there have never before been so many different outstanding Burgundies in the marketplace. The sources of new quality are diverse. More and more small domaines have been incorporated over the past decade from family holdings, and more and more well-established domaines become seriously quality conscious, whether out of inspiration or survival instinct. The new breed of *négociants* and the many who have added *négociant* bottlings parallel to their estate lineups are seeking out and winning the trust of small growers whose fruit may previously have been anonymously blended away. Inspired or goaded by the competition, more and more long-established *négociants* are achieving new standards of attention to detail and increasingly effective PR, i.e., Producing Results. There is also a significant amount of barrel selection taking place in Burgundian cellars at the behest of American importers or agents, not only the best known of them—many of whom have adopted an active roll in supporting and sharing the risks of unfiltered bottling or longer *élevage*—but also smaller merchants who service localized markets or agents who work with only a few such merchants as well. Values notwithstanding, good Burgundy will not come cheap. But there have never before been so many growers or merchants concerned to offer the best possible quality.

It is often said that there are no Burgundy values. Aside from the genuine bargains in Mâcon and (that very different land of Gamay) Beaujolais—both of which we shall consider separately below—and the occasional merchant's closeout of good wine from an unfashionable vintage, is this claim really true? Not at all, if you seek wines possessing distinctively delicious character of a sort only possible in Burgundy, that sell for under $35. But finding such wines will generally take some effort, no less than finding more expensive Burgundy of high quality. When one considers the price that must be paid for really good Pinot Noir from California, Oregon, Australia, New Zealand, or elsewhere in the "Old World" such as Austria or Germany, the best values from this grape's homeland actually look unbeatable. Since the standards of the grower are of paramount importance, it's best to concentrate on the top performers and look for less expensive appellations on their price lists. Most growers, even the elite, in famous villages of the Côte d'Or make at least some wine of simple Bourgogne appellation, because they have inherited property of such humble standing and find it useful to offer their customers something less expensive. Often the vines from which such wines are made are very old, since if prestigious growers consider investing the time and money necessary to replant—because vines are diseased or yields impractically low—they will think twice when it comes to a wine whose importance to the bottom line is negligible, and simply leave old vines lie. Frequently, appellation Bourgogne is rendered in small quantities at such estates, but not always. In Vosne-Romanée, for example, the tiny amount of Bourgogne Rouge from Mugneret-Gibourg has a customer base as covetous as that for their crus. But next door at Domaine Anne Gros, there is red and white Bourgogne (including Hautes Côtes de Nuits) of excellent quality in relative profusion (certainly relative to her quantity of grand cru). Beyond the Bourgogne of prestigious growers, certain villages offer quite consistent value. Marsannay in the northern Côte de Nuits is one such place, its wines frequently less expensive than Côte de Nuits-Villages from farther south. Chorey-les-Beaune just north of Beaune is another. And even if wines from its hilly neighbor Savigny-les-Beaune are nowadays generally over $35 U.S., they offer great value relative to more expensive *villages* wines from Volnay or Pommard. The reds and whites of Monthélie above Volnay fall into a similar category, as do the whites of Auxey-Duresses immediately west of Monthélie. Working one's way yet farther west along the same *combe,* one comes to St.-Romain. The whites from its extremely elevated and stony sites not long ago had a reputation for hardness, lack of generosity, and shrill acids, but the combined effects of Mother Nature and such ambitious vintners as Frédéric Cossard and Emmanuel Giboulet are showing a different and delicious face of St.-Romain, tasting like the Chablis of the Côte d'Or. Simple appellation Chablis, when it is from a good site, properly rendered, can be a genuine bargain. For other values in Burgundy Pinot Noir and Chardonnay, one must look south.

Santenay, near the terminus of the Côte d'Or, is another of those places whose wines might cost Americans closer to $40, but at its best—in red and occasionally white—can represent good value. Perhaps the most commercially accessible source of value is the Côte Chalonnaise, whose villages—Bouzeron, Givry, Mercurey, Rully, and Montagy—beckon with whites and reds of cru-, *villages-,* and simple Bourgogne appellation. The number of good, reliable estates there has increased dramatically in recent years, as has vineyard acreage.

Finally, some words on cellaring and aging potential. No wines on Earth are more profoundly satisfying than the finest aged red or white Burgundy. But of all the world's great, ageworthy wines, Burgundy's profundity is the most elusive and its pursuit most fraught with peril and uncertainty. The sensitivity, caprice, and moodiness of Pinot Noir in the grower's cellar, as well as its vulnerability (along with Chardonnay's) to travel have already been discussed. These traits will follow them to your cellar, too. Furthermore, precisely on account of the experimentation, innovation, and (some growers hope, at any rate) return to tradition that has gone hand in hand with today's quality renaissance, track records set at an estate by earlier generations—whether remarkable or dismal—should neither reassure nor deter us from cellaring today's wines. We simply have to acknowledge that prognostications are more speculative the more things change, even if for the better.

What should the wine lover do? First of all, relish the wines of Burgundy for one of their great virtues: anthropomorphically put, their seductive youthful beauty. Few of the world's great wines are so often capable of offering so much pleasure and intrigue in their youth as those of Burgundy, and it is really the exception (as in 2005 for reds or 2004 for whites) when a truly outstanding vintage honestly seems a shame to drink young. Those anxious to test the ability of their bottles of Burgundy to go some unspecified distance should bear in mind that for all the profundity that a great old bottle can reveal, a lot more sorrow and regret has entered the world on account of corks pulled too late rather than too soon. Be prepared to monitor the condition of your maturing Burgundies at least every couple of years.

So much has been written recently about the premature oxidation and demise of white Burgundy, especially wines of the 1995 and 1996 vintages—both of which were widely pronounced great in their youth, and the latter pronounced in need of lengthy cellaring—that to confine this subject to a few sentences is difficult. Here are some points to bear in mind. No one theory has gained acceptance as to what happened, but it seems likely that the widespread use of peroxide wash (as a substitute for chlorine) on corks and possibly also of silicone coating (instead of less slippery paraffin) played roles. A desire to use less sulfur at bottling, combined with certain other aspects of *élevage,* seems to have left many wines precariously close to a tipping point, where perhaps small differences in air intake or other factors sent certain bottles tumbling into oxidative oblivion, while other bottles of the same wine in the same cellar (often with different corks) remained fresh. Suffice it to say that recent experience has frightened many collectors from holding white Burgundy, and the growers are testing a multitude of theories, or at least acting on their best hunches, and making changes they hope will alleviate the problem. Time will tell. Other sorts of wine from this period have shown some similar tendencies, but none to anywhere near the same degree as white Burgundy. Again, the good news is that these wines can be relished in their youth, and the manifestly excellent but tightly strung 2004 whites—which were as a group fresh and impressive and beginning to blossom in late 2007—should probably be revisited in 2009 to monitor their freshness and evolution.

RED BURGUNDY—A TOUR OF ITS TERRITORY

The northern limits of the Côte d'Or are all now suburbs of the city of Dijon, and many once important vineyards have succumbed to sprawl, while a few are ripe for rediscovery. The first significant wine village is Marsannay, home to a remarkable number of good Pinot Noir values, not just from the producers whom the rankings later in this chapter reveal as being located in this town but also from vintners based in Marsannay's famous neighbor to the south, Gevrey-Chambertin. (The Domaine Roty has made something of a specialty of excellent Marsannay.) There are no premier crus in Marsannay, but most of the better wines are labeled with the name of a *lieu-dit,* and several excellent sites in slightly less flat Couchey to the south are also labeled as Marsannay. (Marsannay is also the sole Burgundy village with its own appellation for rosé wine, and not many decades ago the town could sell little else.) Next comes Fixin, a town whose reputation was once much greater than it is today, and whose several premier crus are practically unknown. Pinot Noir from here tends toward considerable density of tannin, darkness of berry and forest floor flavors, and an almost overtly stony impression. The best wines can develop very impressively over time, but the classic Pinot traits of elegance, textural allure, and overall sex appeal are seldom to be found in Fixin. Just south of Fixin is the tiny village of Brochon, whose name cannot be found on any labels, but whose top sites are entitled to call themselves Gevrey-Chambertin, while others inform excellent wines of Côte de Nuits-Villages appellation.

Gevrey-Chambertin produces the largest volume of any Côte d'Or appellation, and many would say that the number of serious bottling growers here is the largest as well (so large that mention of specific estates in connection with the survey that follows would take up too much space). Nine of the Côte de Nuits's grand cru vineyards are here (even if not quite all of their acreage is on the level that suggests), plus at least one premier cru that most observers would place near the head of the list, should any premier crus ever be upgraded. And due to the diligence of so many vintners—if not also to the inherent quality potential of these hillsides—there are few communes in Burgundy from which you will encounter more wines labeled with the names of sites not rated as premier cru. Amid all this wealth, we can offer only a small amount of orientation and guidance. First off—and this is probably another reason one so often sees wines labeled by *lieu-dit*—there is an unprecedented amount of acreage rated as *villages* Gevrey that's situated east of the *route nationale* and uninspiring in its flatness. (There was once more of it, but a much-needed if still too sparing cutback was undertaken in the 1990s.) Those who farm vines on steep hillsides or in other excellent locations not accorded premier cru status understandably hope that you as a consumer might gradually associate those spots as well as their farmers with higher quality. Second, one needs to note that an entire group of steep vineyards to the north and west of town follow the curvature of the Combe de Lavaux back into the mountains. The wines of this self-contained group display some of the most distinctive expressions of meat, mineral, spices, and flowers anywhere in the Côte d'Or, as well as superb ageability. The Clos St.-Jacques (with only five owners, each possessed of a top-to-bottom strip, and some of whom also sell to top *négociants*) is grand cru in all but official name, and the superb, steep premier crus arrayed on either side of it—best known among them Lavaux St.-Jacques, Poissenot, Cazetiers, Combe aux Moine, and Champaux—are places to remember.

The other celebrated sites of Gevrey, including all nine official grand crus, are strung out to the south of town. First come two especially fine premier crus, Corbeaux and Fonteny. (Seek out Clair, Roty, or Serafin to experience Fonteny.) The three grand crus nearest the village—Ruchottes-Chambertin (tiny, and nearly all in the hands of Mugneret, Rousseau, and Trapet), Mazis-Chambertin, and Clos de Bèze—are uniformly superbly situated. First among equals is Clos de Bèze, as demonstrated by the fact that wine grown here can be labeled simply "Chambertin" (the name of the next site south), but the converse is not permitted. Alluring scents of rose petal and licorice over a base of deep black cherry are typical manifestations of these great sites. Just below the Clos de Bèze are the justly celebrated small grand crus of Chapelle-Chambertin and Griotte-Chambertin, and south of the Clos along a ridge that runs into Morey-St.-Denis are the grand cru Latricières-Chambertin and premier cru Combottes.

Below Chambertin and Latricières-Chambertin are the slightly controversial grand crus Charmes-Chambertin and Mazoyères-Chambertin, which commence with excellent drainage and exposure, but as they slope down toward the *route nationale* are somewhat inferior. Adding confusion, wine from the Mazoyères can be—and usually is—labeled with the more euphonious and marketable name Charmes, while the converse does not hold. Only experience or expert advice will tell you where the really good Charmes is grown and bottled, though as a rule only quality-conscious growers who own excellent parcels in Mazoyères even attempt to market wine under that name, so it becomes a mark of likely excellence. Where comparison is possible at a single address between "real" Charmes and Mazoyères, one more often than not can figure out which is which, as the former displays more pure cherry fruit and refinement while the latter generally more gamey, smoked, or roasted meat character, sometimes chocolate, and a hint of herbal bitterness, all of these characteristics often encountered in the next commune south, Morey-St.-Denis.

Morey-St.-Denis continues the line of grand crus, but returns to higher elevation and more overtly rocky terrain, as is suggested by the first name we come to, Clos de la Roche. This is one of the largest grand crus yet one of the consistently best. The smaller Clos St.-Denis is also uniformly superbly situated, but bottles are hard to locate (Dujac being the best known landholder). The next two grand crus south are *monopoles,* Clos des Lambrays (all vinified by the eponymous estate) and Clos de Tart (owned by the *négociant* Mommessin). A sliver of the next grand cru south, Bonnes Mares, also belongs to Morey-St.-Denis, but we shall consider it below in our account of Chambolle. The sites just mentioned cover virtually all of the vineyard land above the town of Morey-St.-Denis itself. A corresponding string of premier crus is located immediately below town, most of them in strips with similar exposures and comparable quality potential, even if some are little known. The best known are Clos des Ormes, Les Millandes, Les Blanchards, and Clos Sorbè. South of town and up against the Chambolle border are the excellent, tiny Les Ruchots just below Clos de Tart (look for Arlaud) and La Bussière (owned by Roumier).

The wines of Chambolle include some of Burgundy's most celebrated. As a rule, one encounters here some of the most vividly bright, berrylike fruit characteristics of any Pinots, but also effusively and exotically floral, illusively carnal, and distinctly stony dimensions. The grand cru Bonnes Mares, typically yielding one of Burgundy's most intensively and pungently fruited wines, occupies a high ridge north of the town, its southern extension trailing off into two excellent but tiny premier crus, Les Cras (look for Roumier) and Les Fuées. A veritable carpet of premier crus is spread out below Bonnes Mares and extending south past the eastern edge of the village, among the best and best known being (north to south) Les Sentiers, Les Baudes, Gruenchers, Beaux Bruns, Les Chatelots, Les Feusselottes, Les Charmes, Les Chabiots, Les Borniques, Les Hauts Doix, and Les Amoureuses. The last named, with relatively few owners, consistently yields one of Burgundy's most seductively perfumed Pinots, and rightly sells for a grand cru price. Immediately uphill and arching over the top of the Clos Vougeot is the great Le Musigny, a site that would probably vie with Romanée-Conti and Clos de Bèze in any "best of Burgundy" competition that the region's growers or the world's self-proclaimed connoisseurs might envision. There is an awful lot of *villages*-rated acreage in both Morey and Chambolle, most of it relatively level and east of the premier cru belt but some—a good bit more interesting—in the hills above the grand crus. In one peculiar instance, the Combe d'Orveaux high above Clos Vougeot virtually interpenetrates Musigny, but it is not premier cru–rated. The commune of Vougeot itself is utterly dominated by the vast clos that bears its name. But speaking of ratings, while it is understandable why this great architectural and cultural artifact bequeathed the world by the monks of Cîteaux seven centuries ago is treated as a unit, and while the best portions of the clos (in essence, the closer one comes to Musigny) are superb and can render wine of mysteriously meaty depth, much of the *terroir* here is low-lying and scarcely of premier cru quality. Vougeot actually has three premier crus, all west of the town and north of the Clos Vougeot, and as one goes from Les Cras, to Vigne Blanche, and further uphill to Les Petits Vougeots, which borders Le Musigny and Les Amoureuses, the quality potential not surprisingly increases.

As a group, the 8 grand crus and 15 premier crus of Vosne-Romanée are the most written about and coveted red Burgundies. Few if any Pinots in the world offer more intriguing spice, berry fruit, decadent floral and carnal elements, or sheer mystery than do the best wines of Vosne-Romanée. These can run the gamut from powerful and gripping to almost ethereally perfumed and delicate depending on the site and on the vintner's style. Immediately south of Le Musigny and the upper half of Clos Vougeot come two appellations—Echézeaux and Grands Echézeaux—that technically belong to the commune of Flagey-Echézeaux, which lies more than a mile east on the plain. Grands Echézeaux is much the smaller and is consistently high in quality potential, being tucked against an excellent portion of the Clos Vougeot. Echézeaux borders it to the west and south, and takes up an area almost as large as that of the Clos Vougeot and almost as variable in quality. As with Clos Vougeot, you will sometimes see growers adding the name of a *lieu-dit* to Echézeaux on their label in an attempt to call attention to their parcel's excellent situation. (The best are Echézeaux du Dessus, bordering Grands Echézeaux, and Echézeaux en Orveaux, bordering Le Musigny.) South of Echézeaux are (from highest to lowest) the premier crus Les Beaux Monts, Les Brulées, and Les Suchots, all of their names more consistently reliable indicators of quality than is Echézeaux. A narrow *combe* splits the commune, and on the other side lie the grand crus of Richebourg and Romanée St.-Vivant, followed by La Romanée, Romanée-Conti, La Grande Rue, and La Tâche. A very few owners carve up all of this fabled grand cru ground. The Domaine de la Romanée-Conti owns not only all of the eponymous vineyard but also of La Tâche, and the majority of Romanée St.-Vivant. La Grande Rue is the *monopole* of Domaine Lamarche and the tiny La Romanée of Liger-Belair, while most of Richebourg is in the hands of half a dozen owners, including three branches of the Gros family. On the high hillsides above this bevy of grand crus lie the premier crus Cros Parantoux (made famous by Henri Jayer, who bought it and brought it back to life), Les Petits Monts, and Aux Reignots, all of which sell at elevated prices and are capable of striking excellence. Yet one does not even have to travel halfway back in time to World War II to find vineyard maps in which these crus are scarcely noted and large portions of them shown unplanted. Nowadays, there is a major thrust up into these high hillsides above Vosne-Romanée, and some outstanding wines are also coming from Les Barreaux and Champs-Perdrix, even though neither of them has premier cru status. South of La Tâche and with a similar exposure lie Les Gaudichots (what little there is of it—most was elevated in 1932 to become the major part of La Tâche) and Aux Malconsorts. Two slightly less remarkable premier crus are situated lower down, Les Chaumes and Clos des Réas. One can peruse the many geological maps and cross-sections that have been used to illustrate why Vosne-Romanée's hillside is so remarkable, but no one has penetrated the mysteries surrounding how it is these features can alter *flavor,* or why the personalities of each cru are so distinct. Much of what passes for *villages* appellation in Vosne, though, is low-lying land and very variable in quality.

The huge expanse that is appellation Nuits-St.-Georges can be divided into three sectors. North of the town itself lie a series of premier cru sites that are essentially a continuation of Vosne-Romanée's crus: high up (from north to south) Les Damodes, Aux Chaignots, and Aux Torey and below them (again north to south) Aux Boudots, Au Cras, La Richemoné, Aux Murgers, Aux Vignerondes, Aux Bousselots, and Aux Argillas. Farther downhill lies a great expanse of *villages*-rated vineyard land of largely lackluster potential, the northern sections—clearly because of politics, not *terroir*—belonging to Vosne-Romanée. South of the town of Nuits-St.-Georges, the premier crus are too numerous to list in total, but include the well-known (and, in good winemaking hands, excellent) Rue de Chaux, Les Procès, Les Pruliers,

Roncière, Les Poirets, Les Perrières, Les Cailles, Les Vaucrains, and Les St.-Georges, of which the three last named are generally considered the greatest. Farther south, now officially in the commune of Premeaux-Prissey but still labeled as Nuits-St.-Georges, are among other premier crus Les Forêts and Les Argillières, and, last, two large crus that are *monopoles:* Clos de l'Arlot (of the eponymous domaine) and Clos de la Maréchale (of Jacques-Frédéric Mugnier). It is scarcely possible to dissect the geological structure of flavors of Nuits-St.-Georges, as the 40 premier crus spread along this expanse are so varied and their ownership so diverse. But the fact that an estate with property only in Nuits-St.-Georges—that of Robert Chevillon— would make virtually any informed observer's cut for the top two dozen red wine domaines in all of Burgundy, and that the wines of another excellent estate entirely situated in this commune—that of Henri Gouges—were among the first Burgundies ever estate-bottled and among Burgundy's first ambassadors to the U.S., speak volumes for the quality potential of these appellations. Because this territory is so large, though, there is also much mediocrity, and it has to be said that in Nuits-St.-Georges, simple *villages* appellation means very little by way of recommendation. There are a few notable non–premier cru *lieux-dits* such as the Aux St.-Julien of Daniel Bocquenet, but that is very much an exception. Beyond the great stone quarries of Comblanchien and the Clos de la Maréchale, at the southern edge of the Côte de Nuits, much of the acreage bears the appellation Côte de Nuits-Villages. Interestingly, some of the most promising sites in the Hautes-Côtes de Nuits lie just a little way into the hills around Magny-les-Villers.

The Côte de Beaune commences with Burgundy's largest grand cru, Corton. Because of its size, many of its wines are bottled with the names of their individual *lieux-dits* appended. Around this huge hill lie the communes of Ladoix (immediately to the north), Aloxe-Corton (at the southern edge of the grand cru), and Pernand-Vergelesses (to the west, and incorporating the original white wine sector of the grand cru, which will be discussed in our tour of Chardonnay-growing Burgundy). Corton is capable of meaty, mineral mysteries, sometimes of great structural density and sometimes of great elegance. But it must be said that unfortunately the average quality of wine produced here reflects this site's huge size more than it does its grand cru stature. Of the surrounding communes, Aloxe offers the best opportunities for Pinot—its premier cru Les Chaillots occasionally turning in a distinguished performance— and Pernand-Vergelesses from the premier cru Les Vergelesses can be rewarding. The Vergelesses vineyard is shared with Savigny-les-Beaune, a town set well back into the hills that offers two enticing menus of vineyards, one running east and north toward Pernand-Vergelesses, which in addition to the Vergelesses itself includes such excellent premier crus as Aux Serpentières, Aux Gravains, and Aux Guettes. On the other side of town, running back out toward Beaune, are such distinguished premier crus as Les Jarrons (aka La Dominode), Les Narbantons, Les Peuillets, and (segueing into the Beaune cru of the same name) Les Marconnets. The reds of Savigny, while a highly diverse group, tend generally to lead with meaty (often smoked meat), mineral, and forest floor rather than overtly red- or black-fruited notes, and are characterized by excellent stamina. It doesn't hurt that this village has long been home to numerous overachieving vintners. The premier crus of Beaune are so diverse as to defy generalization, and so numerous as to defy an anywhere-near-complete listing on this occasion. There are probably just too many of them, period. And many of them are too large. This commune has scarcely any *villages*-rated wine! But then, one has to consider that it is the region's capital of wine commerce, and when the Côte d'Or was finally officially classified, *négociants* with Beaune addresses had the political clout to get their way. (It's said, though, that fear of infighting and of higher taxes kept the town fathers from applying for any grand crus!) All of the vineyards are located west of the city. Important premier crus include (from north to south): Marconnets, Cent-Vignes, Bressandes, Grèves (incorporating Bouchard Père et Fils's famous Vigne de l'Enfant Jésus), Teurons, Cras, Vignes-Franches (incorporating

Jadot's justly celebrated Clos des Ursules), Boucherottes, Clos des Mouches, and Les Epenottes. For all of its surplus of crus, make no mistake that the best Beaune Pinots are exceptionally complex and long-lived.

The village of Pommard presents a contrast with Beaune in numerous respects. There is a great deal of *villages*-rated land as well as Bourgogne lying "on the flats," most of it not especially distinguished. The best premier crus, though, can be outstanding and long-lived, and there are a considerable number of steep, high sites above the premier crus that lately have been showing their potential. Also in contrast with Beaune, most Pommard has a close family resemblance, with relatively firm tannins, black-fruit and roasted-meat character, at its best complex, but more powerful than refined. The common denominator for most of this commune is reddish, iron-rich chalk-clay, which naturally leads anyone who takes the principle of *terroir* at all seriously to see it starkly illustrated here. Nearest to Beaune, we have the Clos des Épenots (*monopole* of the eponymous estate) and Grands Épenots, which give outstanding, long-lived Pinots even though the exposition here is nearly flat. Above them are, among other premier crus, the Pézerolles and Charmots, and tucked high up against the walls of an intersecting *combe,* Les Arvelets. South of town, among the numerous premier crus are Rugiens (quite steep, and arguably Pommard's best location), Fremiers, and Jarollières. Here we pass into Volnay, but those inclined to seek *terroir* will once again find it here, because two Volnay premier crus along the Pommard line share some of its iron—Frémiets and Les Brouillards—and are frequently mistaken in the glass for Pommard. The "real" Volnay character tends to favor flowers, brown spices, red fruits, and intricacy of flavor, along with refinement of tannins and texture that no Pommard has ever imitated. A cluster of small premier crus are grouped immediately around and in the village itself: Clos des Ducs (a d'Angerville *monopole*), Clos du Château des Ducs (a *monopole* of Lafarge), Clos de la Bousse d'Or and Clos d'Audignac (both *monopoles* of the Domaine de la Pousse d'Or). All of these, like the village itself, are effectively hillside sites despite their "urban" setting. East of town are premier crus Mitans and l'Ormeaux, and south of town, four of this commune's best: Clos des Chênes (look particularly for Lafarge), Taillepieds, Champan, and Caillerets (the last named including Pousse d'Or's *monopole* Clos des 60 Ouvrées). The premier cru vineyards of Santenots (entitled to labeling by subappellation) extend deep into Meursault, and much of their surface is planted with Chardonnay and labeled Meursault. The powerful presence and qualitative example set by d'Angerville, Lafarge, Lafon, de Montille, and the Domaine de la Pousse d'Or is one reason seasoned Burgundy lovers are so often enamoured of Volnay's wines, and if any grand crus for red wine were ever to join Corton along the Côte de Beaune, they would certainly include one or more of Volnay's top sites, many of whose wines already sell for more than Corton. Although its several premier crus are little known, the hill town of Monthélie, immediately southwest of Volnay, can give some lovely and affordable facsimiles of its more famous neighbor's spicy, refined Pinot. It shares the excellent premier cru Les Duresses with Auxey-Duresses, along a *combe* farther into the hills.

There is not a lot of Pinot Noir left in Meursault or in Puligny-Montrachet, but Chassagne-Montrachet is another matter. These reds are often rather rustic in tannin but can be interesting and delicious, provided one happens on an estate (such as Château de la Maltroye) whose skills with Pinot approach those with Chardonnay. Below Chassagne, we are in Santenay, whose vineyards stretch for a considerable distance south and west, including a bevy of premier crus about most of which few people have ever heard. The best wines from Clos Tavennes and Les Gravières—meaty, mineral, and sturdy—suggest that much more could be made of Santenay's *terroir*. As its slope turns west we arrive at a trio of tiny villages whose vineyards have for twenty years had their own appellation—Maranges—and attendant (but thus far obscure) premier crus. More time may tell a different story, but at present, Maranges's wines have not proven to be worth a detour on one's way to the Côte Chalonnaise (which commences a mere two miles southeast of Santenay), where some of Burgundy's best values can be found. The villages of Rully, Mercurey, and Givry are this subregion's Pinot Noir centers. Their more than 70 collective "premier crus" are almost an affront to that term just for being so numerous. But at the best addresses—Besson, Dureuil, Joblot, Lumpp, Racquillet, de Villaine—the differences from one site to another become apparent, and the amount of excellent wine bodes well for some of these sites' genuinely meriting their official status. It is not a slight to these villages and growers to say that their best wines to date seem to offer a transition from the character of Côte d'Or Pinots to those of the New World. The flamboyant personalities that many of them exhibit and their purity and intensity of sheer red fruits may represent a dominance of winemaking over *terroir,* or then again may be an expression of *terroir*. It is too early to say, really. Twenty years ago, the concentration not to mention prices of Jean-Marc Joblot's Givrys led locals to scorn their lack of *typicité* and made him seem like a complete maverick. It was apparently shocking for wines like this to be crafted in the Côte Chalonnaise. But no more: The same intelligent and passionate advocacy can now be found at many addresses, their numbers swelling year by year. If there are any "frontiers" left in Burgundy, this is surely one, and you can entertain your taste buds and indulge your pinotphilia at a very fair price.

[recent vintages]

RED BURGUNDY

In an effort to flesh out the account of viticultural and wine-making issues offered above, our survey of vintages begins with a more detailed look at three recent, dramatically different vintages for red Burgundy and at how vintners and their grapes reacted to the weather.

2005

This is one of Burgundy's great red wine vintages. (It was also a fine year for Gamay in the very different soils of Beaujolais, which will be taken up separately.) What explains the quality? As Étienne Grivot put it, 2005 demonstrated that luminosity, not heat, is what Pinot Noir craves, and that gradual ripening is the ideal. Whereas extremely dry vintages (such as 1976 or 2003) are usually also hot, in 2005 a pattern of balmy summer days with cool nights provided for full ripeness of flavor without excessive potential alcohol and with excellent retention of ripe acidity. Rain arrived briefly and sporadically the first week in September—just enough, in fact, to give the parched vines one last push. Growers could harvest late and leisurely, but many were ready to begin picking as soon as the official gun was sounded in mid-September, if not before. This sunshine and leisure combined to optimize ripeness and flavor in every single parcel, even simple appellation Bourgogne. The rigorous triage that has become so important a guarantor of quality and a badge of honor among Burgundian vignerons in the past 15 years would have been overkill in 2005. As Grivot also put it, "You could fall asleep at the sorting table this year watching the grapes go by." There was a lot of *millerandage* in 2005, imperfections in pollination from an evolutionary standpoint but fantastic for a winemaker, and nearly always a feature of great vintages. First, significant numbers of the tiny "shot" berries add to the space available in the cluster for air circulation and sun penetration, keeping the fruit dry and optimizing conditions for ripening. Second, the berries are little bundles of flavor concentration, whose high sugar is released late in fermentation and in 2005 rendered unnecessary the sort of fractional chaptalization in which most vintners otherwise engage so as to prolong alcoholic extraction. Faced with thick-skinned fruit of perfect ripeness, free of rot and full of tiny concentrated berries, a majority of growers backed off on extraction, some even approaching the virtual absence of punch-down that characterized their approach to the nearly raisined fruit of 2003. (Though a few growers took the opposite approach, vowing that it would be a shame not to extract the maximum from grapes this good.) Fermentations started slowly due to cool weather, so most wines effectively experienced four or five days of cold soak—during which color and perfume are extracted in the absence of alcohol—without the need for dry ice or sulfur. Malolactic fermentation took place at most estates with unprecedented lateness and protraction, so much so that many wines finished only late in 2006. (Yet, a few cellars experienced "normal" onset and progression of malolactic fermentation in the spring of 2005—why?)

The personality of wines from this luminous, gloriously healthy, and ripe vintage is positively kinetic, but decidedly on the dark side of the flavor spectrum, with fresh, sometimes faintly tart black fruits, overt and at times almost austerely mineral flavors, and mysterious, even brooding forest-floor complexities. Many of the best Pinots of 2005 push the limit of ripeness consistent with freshness, and the limit of sheer density consistent with elegance. Firm, fine tannins are never far from the surface, even where these Pinots' youthful textures are already silken or creamy. These wines will need time in the bottle to show their true colors, and most of them should be expected to shut down for an extended period soon after bottling.

2003 and 2004

2004 will be remembered as an enormous vintage, the vines having (as throughout Europe) set large crops in a natural evolutionary reaction to the penury of 2003. It will also be remembered for relatively tart, fresh-fruited wines that often lacked richness. By contrast, 2003—the earliest red Burgundy harvest in nearly a century and the warmest summer on record—will further be remembered for its paucity of wine (thanks to widespread frost in spring and desiccation of berries in late summer) and for Pinots of enormous richness and fat that sometimes suffered from too little freshness. And yet these vintages, in some ways diametrically opposed, have certain common aspects because of changing weather and ripening patterns in Burgundy in recent years. 2004 is not your classic, long-term, below-average Burgundy vintage in which chaptalization was needed to bring wines up to a decent standard of body. True, given the huge crop, a damp midsummer, and a freakishly cool August, growers were panicked going into the stretch. But not only did a warm September rescue what might well have been a disaster, many growers were amazed (as in fact they had been in several recent years) to find themselves harvesting fruit of high potential alcohol. Indeed, roughly half of the bottled 2004 reds from top addresses are higher in alcohol than their 2005 counterparts. The really striking and revelatory thing about 2004 is the extent to which it shares the problem so starkly confronted by most Burgundian growers in 2003: what freakish heat and drought in August 2003 accomplished by means of shutting down the vines' metabolic activity, the combination of an unseasonably cool August and warm September achieved in 2004: grapes high in sugar but often (literally) green and underripe at the center. The chocolate-covered pickles familiar from many arid new-world regions were legion among 2003 red Burgundies (indeed, how widespread is becoming evident only as these wines develop), and the most familiar downside of 2004 is Pinots that are alcoholically bloated yet skinny in fruit.

No one should push the analogy between 2003 and 2004 past a certain point. Many 2003s display jammy or raisined character (though often alongside green elements), and most are possessed of tough underlying tannins. (Some are even great wines, with the sumptuous folds of fruit necessary to cover the tannins and the sheer density to remain vivid and stable in bottle, as did the best 1959s.) Furthermore, while total acidity was low, tartaric acid was so high that it was often hard to tell when or even whether certain 2003s underwent malolactic fermentation. In 2004, by contrast, the cool summer locked in a very crisp, fresh-fruited personality, not to mention high levels of malic (green apple) acid. Malolactic fermentations were thus profound in effect, giving many 2004s a surprisingly gentle midpalate impression despite their aromatic suggestions of tart, brisk fruit. But no one will try to argue that this is a formula for harmony. The best 2004s should be enjoyed for their tension. Only a very few 2004s possess the requisite concentration or structure for significant aging, even in instances where the flavors are of a sort one would want to revisit years from now.

Both of these vintages also vividly demonstrate the need for growers to rethink traditional assumptions. It could be said of 2003 that whoever applied "normal" methods produced results in bottle as freakish as the weather, whereas to nurse Pinot Noir through that summer and into the bottle with any of its classic virtues intact demanded that one take abnormal action. With potential alcohol pushing 15% in mid-August and fruit dehydrating, many growers were worried the yeasts would have trouble even finishing the fermentations and that to allow the fruit to hang much longer would court disaster, so they picked. Those who had somehow managed their vines to obtain truly ripe rather than merely superficially sweet fruit could succeed. And in the last week of that month, the weather broke, and sporadic showers, cooler temperatures, and morning dew literally revived the grapes, lowering sugar, raising acidity, and above all allowing the berries to ripen down to their pips. So those who waited to pick had better odds of success. As for extraction, practically anything a vintner did to encourage it might be too much. Some of the best 2003s received no punch-downs or scarcely any, and the wines obtained deep colors, rich fruit, and formidable tannins. Some growers added acid—it was permitted this year—and some did not, with no clear pattern so far as to which approach produced better wine.

A SURVEY OF OTHER VINTAGES

Traditionally, the vicissitudes of weather have dictated that about a third of the time, Pinot Noir simply fails to ripen sufficiently to have satisfying body without chaptalization or to have sweet primary fruit flavors, let alone to reflect *terroir*. The success or failure of a vintage still often hangs in the balance right up until picking. We can, however, forget about that traditionally high rate of failure when considering the past two decades, during which—thanks to generally warm weather—chaptalization has been minimal and ripe fruit the norm. (And that is even before factoring in today's higher standards of fruit selection.) Yet, for all of the advantages of elevated temperatures in getting Pinot Noir ripe (or at least high in sugar at harvest), warmer weather has also increased vine stress during the frequent and protracted periods of drought and promoted rot in vintages when inopportune rain fell in late summer or at harvest. The superficial differences yet similar underlying pitfalls of 2004 and 2003 put these problems in perspective. 2005 reminds us that slow but steady, luminous but moderate wins the race to achieve great Burgundy. But if recent developments set the trend, vintages of this sort may be at least as rare in the future as they were back in the days when Burgundian vignerons cherished every hour of genuine heat and were happy to have reached 12% natural alcohol by October!

Over the past decade, vintages 2005, 2002, and 1999 have proven the most consistently excellent for red Burgundy. Yet only 2005—and to a slightly lesser extent 1999—appears to have produced a majority of rich, ripe long-keepers, wines that can be enjoyed with 10 to 25 years in bottle. The 2002s have been delicious early, and whether more than a decade's maturation will be merited seems doubtful. (Nor was there anything foolish about savoring their youthful pleasures—quite the contrary.) From vintages 2007, 2006, 2004, 2003, 2001, and 1998, one must contend with highly variable quality even among the best domaines, depending on local weather, on all the strategic considerations in the vineyard and cellar that have been described, and, of course—as always with nature—on a stubborn, irreducible remnant of luck. Yet several of these tricky vintages—2003, 2001, and 1998—will have resulted in a significant minority of wines worth cellaring; indeed, the best 2003s are not only impressive in a larger-than-life way, they may prove practically ageless.

The best 2006s will offer much more charm because of their very ripe flavors than the

2004s (which for the most part should be drunk before 2010). Alcoholic heat, overripe spoiled-fruit flavors, and hints of rot drag down the quality of some wines. That said, 2006 has turned out far better (particularly in the Côte de Nuits) than any growers anticipated early on in the wines' evolution. 2002 offered a cool summer but September heat and wind not only ripened the crop, they also surprised many growers with its high sugar, and thus alcohol. It might then seem as though 2002 offered a foretaste of 2004, and there are certainly similarities. Fresh berry flavors and a note of tartness in wines that underwent long and profound malolactic fermentations certainly characterize 2002, but there is clarity, invigorating vivacity, and above all textural nuance and a seamless sweetness of fresh fruit that are largely lacking in 2004. Vintage 2001 was characterized by high levels of malic acid retention and come-from-behind ripeness in a harvest that commenced relatively late. August hail in the Côte de Beaune and enhanced September rain there vis-à-vis the Côte de Nuits made for two very different qualities of wine. Advocates (or apologists) for 2001 call it a "classic" vintage. At least in the Côte de Nuits, the best wines display the Burgundian virtues of brightness, meat and mineral flavors, and mystery. But the wines have remained relatively reticent, and the biggest mystery is whether they will retain a certain prickliness of exterior and hardness at the core. They are worth revisiting at 8 to 12 years of age. 2000, by contrast, is less worth remembering. Thin grape skins were susceptible to summer humidity and consequent mildew and rot. And just when the official harvest was announced (not that most grapes were ripe yet), it commenced to rain. Thanks to the quality consciousness and rigorous selection at so many of today's estates, a surprising number of enjoyable Pinots were produced, but the time to have enjoyed most of them is past.

1999 is a vintage with rich, ripe fruit and flattering perfume. The crop was very large, yet berry size generally small and grape skins thick and robust, in dramatic contrast with 2000, so that while late-summer rain reenergized the vines, it did not jeopardize the fruit. Most of 1999's beautifully balanced reds will enjoy a second decade of satisfying evolution, but they are nearly all delicious now. In complete contrast, the 1998 vintage brought a difficult combination of protracted fungal pressure, heat, and shutdown in late summer, followed by rain and consequent rot at harvest time. The wonder is how interesting, even impressive, some of the best wines are. But they flunked charm school, and a certain ornery astringency is to be expected even as they enter their second decade in bottle. This is a controversial vintage, with many growers insisting they will yet have their day and some critics insisting that they are only dogs. Do not avoid opportunities to sample them (they are frequently distinctive), but do not put money on any you have not sampled recently. In a near-rehearsal for the more extreme 2003 vintage, 1997 brought 50-year-record sugar levels at harvest, very ripe, occasionally cooked fruit flavors, and a complete absence of rot. And yet few wines showed genuine concentration or distinctive personalities. The best were soft and generous; some are still lovely, but most (with 10 years in the bottle) are at or past their prime.

The 1996 vintage is known across northern Europe for its combination of high sugar and high acidity in the grapes and the resultant Pinots remain remarkably fresh and invigoratingly intense even today, no doubt too much so for certain tasters. By contrast, the 1995s are more obvious in their expression of ripe fruit flavors but less active and less refined in tannins. The best wines of either vintage, especially the 1996s, are well worth revisiting. A similar recommendation must count as controversial for the intensely tannic but at times profound 1993s. Some would say it's still too early to enjoy them, and others that they were too lacking in sensual sweetness all along to make satisfyingly meaty old bones. The best wines of this vintage have an athletic leanness and stamina, and they will have fascinating stories to tell at the finish line. The ingratiating 1992s are now well past their prime. 1991 displays much virtue, even now, after having spent its life in the shadow of 1990. This was a very tiny crop (hailed on in many sectors) that nevertheless needed a long season to ripen, and then demanded selectivity at harvest lest underripe or rot-tinged fruit enter the press. But the successful wines—many more in the Côte de Nuits than in Côte de Beaune—have lovely richness, underlying firmness even today, and fascinating depth.

The 1990 vintage was the most widely praised in recent times (until 2005). Homogeneous high ripeness, sweetly rich fruit, and sumptuous textures were this vintage's calling card from the barrel and have proven to constitute whatever claim to greatness it retains. As they have aged, ripe, sweet, and sometimes jamlike fruit continues to mark the best wines, but further complexities are often lacking, some wines are fading, and few if any appear likely to improve. The 1990s are still worth seeking out simply in order to gain an impression or appreciation of one of the most talked-about vintages of recent times. Among other favorable red Burgundy vintages of recent decades (and from which the very best wines are still worth revisiting) are 1988, 1985, 1978, 1972, and 1971. Glorious vintages from the more distant past include 1969, 1961, 1959, 1953, 1949, 1947, and 1945.

—DAVID SCHILDKNECHT

[the ratings]

BURGUNDY'S PRODUCERS OF PINOT NOIR

Note: Many of these producers are rated for their white wine in a separate list below. Beaujolais producers are rated in a separate list elsewhere in this chapter.

★ ★ ★ ★ ★ (OUTSTANDING)

Robert Chevillon (Nuits-St.-Georges)*
Domaine du Clos de Tart (Morey-St.-Denis)
Dugat-Py—Bernard Dugat
  (Gevrey-Chambertin)
Domaine Dujac (Morey-St.-Denis)*
Domaine Jean Grivot (Vosne-Romanée)
Maison Louis Jadot (*négociant,* Beaune)
Dominique Laurent (*négociant,* Nuits-
  St.-Georges)
Domaine Leroy (Vosne-Romanée)
Hubert Lignier (Morey-St.-Denis)

Perrot-Minot (Morey-St.-Denis)
Lucien Le Moine (*négociant,* Beaune)
Domaine Georges Mugneret-Gibourg
  (Vosne-Romanée)
Domaine Ponsot (Morey-St.-Denis)*
Domaine de la Romanée-Conti
  (Vosne-Romanée)*
Georges Roumier—Christophe Roumier
  (Chambolle-Musigny)*
Domaine Comte Georges de Vogüé
  (Chambolle-Musigny)*

★ ★ ★ ★ (EXCELLENT)

Bertrand Ambroise (Premeaux-Prissey)*
Domaine Marquis d'Angerville (Volnay)
Domaine Comte Armand—Domaine des
  Epeneaux (Pommard)*
Domaine Robert Arnoux—Pascal Lachaux
  (Vosne-Romanée)
Denis Bachelet (Gevrey-Chambertin)
Ghislaine Barthod (Chambolle-
  Musigny)
Jean Boillot (Volnay)

Lucien Boillot Père et Fils (Gevrey-
  Chambertin)*
Bruno Clair (Marsannay)*
Maison Joseph Drouhin (*négociant,* Beaune)
Claude Dugat (Gevrey-Chambertin)
Sylvie Esmonin (Gevrey-Chambertin)
Forey Père et Fils (Vosne-Romanée)
Domaine Fourrier (Gevrey-Chambertin)
Domaine Germain Père et Fils—Château
  de Chorey (Chorey-les-Beaune)*

---

*From the very tiny proportion of their vineyards planted with white grapes (Chardonnay, Pinot Blanc, or Aligoté), these estates bottle one to three wines of quality comparable to that of their reds. Details can be found in the grower profiles elsewhere in this chapter. These estates are not listed a second time below under the heading Burgundy's Producers of White Wine.

Geantet-Pansiot (Gevrey-Chambertin)

Domaine Henri Gouges
  (Nuits-St.-Georges)*

Robert Groffier (Morey-St.-Denis)

Anne Gros (Vosne-Romanée)*

Jayer-Gilles (Magny-les-Villers)*

Michel Lafarge (Volnay)*

Domaine des Comtes Lafon (Meursault)

Domaine Fernand Lecheneaut & Fils
  (Nuits-St.-Georges)

Domaine du Vicomte Liger-Belair
  (Vosne-Romanée)

Maison Frédéric Magnien (négociant,
  Morey-St.-Denis)

Michel Magnien (Morey-St.-Denis)

Méo-Camuzet (Vosne-Romanée)

Domaine de Montille (Volnay)*

Denis Mortet (Gevrey-Chambertin)

Jacques-Frédéric Mugnier—Château de
  Chambolle-Musigny

Philippe Pacalet (négociant, Beaune)

Maison Nicolas Potel (négociant, Nuits-
  St.-Georges)

Domaine Jacques Prieur (Meursault)

Domaine Roblet-Monnot (Bligny-les-
  Beaune—Volnay)

Joseph Roty (Gevrey-Chambertin)

Emmanuel Rouget (Flagey-Echézeaux)

Armand Rousseau (Gevrey-Chambertin)

Christian Serafin (Gevrey-Chambertin)

Domaine Thibault Liger-Belair
  (Vosne-Romanée)

Cécile Tremblay (Bligny-les-Beaune—Vosne)

Jacky Truchot (Morey-St.-Denis)

* * * (VERY GOOD)

Domaine Amiot-Servelle
  (Chambolle-Musigny)

Arlaud Père et Fils (Morey-St.-Denis)

Domaine de l'Arlot (Premeaux-Prissey)*

Pierre Bertheau (Chambolle-Musigny)

Domaine Bitouzet-Prieur (Volnay)

Domaine Simon Bize
  (Savigny-les-Beaune)*

Jean-Yves Bizot (Vosne-Romanée)*

Daniel Bocquenet (Nuits-St.-Georges)

Maison Henri Boillot—Jean Boillot
  (Meursault)

Jean Boillot (Volnay)

Domaine Jean-Marc Boillot (Pommard)

Louis Boillot et Fils (Chambolle-Musigny)

Domaine Bonneau du Martray
  (Pernand-Vergelesses)

Bouchard Père et Fils (négociant, Beaune)

Sylvain Cathiard (Vosne-Romanée)

Philippe Charlopin (Gevrey-Chambertin)

Hubert Chauvenet-Chopin
  (Premeaux-Prissey)

Domaine du Clos des Lambrays
  (Morey-St.-Denis)

Philippe Collotte (Marsannay)

Domaine Confuron-Cotetidot
  (Vosne-Romanée)

Domaine du Courcel (Pommard)

Domaine des Croix (Beaune)*

Domaine Dublère—Blair Pethel
  (Savigny-les-Beaune)

Vincent Dureuil (Rully)

Maurice Ecard (until 2006)
  (Savigny-les-Beaune)*

Alex Gambal (négociant, Beaune)

Vincent Girardin (Chassagne-Montrachet)

Maison Camille Giroud (négociant, Beaune)

Jean-Marc Joblot (Givry)

Lignier-Michelot—Virgile Lignier
  (Morey-St.-Denis)

Château de la Maltroye
  (Chassagne-Montrachet)

Domaine Maume (Gevrey-Chambertin)

Xavier Monnot (Meursault)

Jean-Marc Pavelot (Savigny-les-Beaune)*

Domaine des Perdrix (Nuits-St.-Georges)

Domaine de la Pousse d'Or (Volnay)*

Gérard Raphet (Morey-St.-Denis)

Michèl et Patrice Rion
  (Nuits-St.-Georges)*

Nicolas Rossignol (Volnay)

Domaine Anne et Hervé Sigaut
  (Chambolle-Musigny)

Domaine Tollot-Beaut et Fils
  (Chorey-les-Beaune)*

Domaine Trapet Père et Fils
  (Gevrey-Chambertin)

Joseph Voillot (Volnay)*

Pierre Amiot (Morey-St.-Denis)

Domaine Bertagna (Vougeot)*

G. & X. Besson (Givry)*

Albert Bichot (*négociant,* Beaune)

Pascal Bouley (Volnay)

Régis Bouvier (Marsannay)

Alain Burguet (Gevrey-Chambertin)

Carré-Courbin (Beaune)

Chandon de Briailles (Savigny-les-Beaune)*

Chanson Père et Fils (*négociant,* Beaune)

Maurice Chapuis (Aloxe-Corton)*

Jérôme Chezeaux (Premeaux-Prissey)

David Clark (Morey-St.-Denis)

Domaine du Clos Frantin—Albert Bichot
  (Vosne-Romanée)

Domaine Colinot (Irancy/Yonne)

Edmond Cornu (Ladoix)

Jean-Luc Dubois (Chorey-les-Beaune)

Michel et Joanna Ecard
  (Savigny-les-Beaune)

Jean Fournier (Marsannay)

Jean Garaudet (Pommard)*

Anne-François Gros (Pommard)

Michel Guillard (Gevrey-Chambertin)

Domaine Pierre Guillemot
  (Savigny-les-Beaune)

Domaine Huber-Verdereau (Volnay)*

Maison Louis Latour (*négociant,* Beaune)

François Lumpp (Givry)

Château de la Maltroye
  (Chassagne-Montrachet)

Catherine et Claude Maréchal
  (Bligny-les-Beaune)

Domaine Monthélie-Douhairet-Porcheret
  (Monthélie)*

Domaine Albert Morot (Beaune)

Thierry Mortet (Gevrey-Chambertin)

Lucien Muzard et Fils (Santenay)

Sylvain Pataille (Marsannay)

François Raquillet (Mercurey)

Gilles Remoriquet (Nuits-St.-Georges)

Domaine Daniel Rion (Premeaux-Prissey)

Domaine Rossignol-Trapet
  (Gevrey-Chambertin)

A. & P. de Villaine (Bouzeron)

Domaine de la Vougeraie
  (Premeaux-Prissey)

WHITE BURGUNDY: A TOUR OF ITS TERRITORY

Leaving aside the Mâcon and Chablis (which we shall cover shortly), our survey of Burgundy's white wines begins just outside Dijon as it did for reds, because the town of Marsannay grows some interesting Chardonnay. In upper elevations and very chalky sites along the Côte de Nuits, white grapes—above all Aligoté, but Chardonnay and probably Pinot Blanc as well—were once common. But by the mid-20th century, acreage of whites here was no longer large. Still, that does not mean that wine lovers should ignore it—*au contraire*. The roster of distinguished growers who vinify a few barrels of exceptional white grown in famed Côte de Nuits towns is quite impressive, most notably (running from north to south) Domaine Ponsot (Morey-St.-Denis, mainly from Aligoté); Comte de Vogüé (in Musigny); Henri Gouges (Nuits-St.-Georges from a white mutation of Pinot Noir discovered at this domaine); Robert Chevillon (Nuits-St.-Georges blanc, Bourgogne, and Aligoté); and Domaine de l'Arlot (Nuits-St.-Georges blanc). The problem will be latching on to a few bottles of any of these. (And, by the way, all of the aforementioned have excellent potential in the cellar.) The overwhelming majority of white wine from the Côte d'Or, however, comes from the Côte de Beaune.

For all the fame and the high prices associated with white Burgundies of the Côte de Beaune, the historical primacy of Pinot Noir even in this sector is pointed up by its classification. There are only six grand cru appellations for Chardonnay, and these are concentrated in only two locations. The first is at the Côte de Beaune's northern tier. Between the towns of Aloxe-Corton and Pernand-Vergelesses rises the enormous, butte-like hill of Corton, whose whites are grand cru Corton-Charlemagne—the west-facing edge of this huge hill (an exposure unprecedented in the Côte d'Or) consists of sections known as En Charlemagne and Le Charlemagne. Nowadays white is grown in many other of the hill's sections, but here it is not permitted to carry their *lieux-dits,* only the name Corton-Charlemagne. No white Burgundy is firmer or more often calls forth the word "mineral," and also none is any more finely delineated in flavor or longer-lived than the best Corton-Charlemagne. The Vergelesses vineyard of Pernand is home to numerous interesting, if often somewhat austere, whites and like the much less common whites from west of there and back into the high hills above Savigny-les-Blanc, they have scored more satisfying successes in recent warm vintages. Although Burgundy's wine capital of Beaune is primarily known for its reds, close to 7% of the communal acreage is white, including some fascinating and ageworthy wines, notably that of Drouhin from the Clos des Mouches; the Clos de la Figuine *monopole* and Champs Pimont of Jacques Prieure; and the Sur les Grèves bottlings of Jadot and of Bouchard (who also bottle, as Clos du Château, a blend of several Beaune crus planted with Chardonnay). White Beaune tends to lean toward pithy, nutty, stony, and youthfully austere flavors but is well worth seeking out. South of Beaune—past the vineyards of Pommard and Volnay—the Côte splits, with one branch bending west around Monthélie, past Auxey Duresses, and eventually into St.-Romain, high in the hills and arguably more a part of the Hautes-Côtes than the Côte d'Or. All three of these villages have interesting whites (and St.-Romain is dominated by Chardonnay) about which more can be read above in the section Buying and Cellaring Burgundy in its paragraph on finding values.

The southernmost vineyard in Volnay is Santenots and is prefaced by the name Meursault on the label if the wine is Chardonnay, which much of this vineyard is. One often encounters the nowadays excellent rendition by Bouchard. Several much less frequently seen premier crus of Meursault are adjacent to Santenots on the north side of town. The wines of this sector can often manage to be quite rich and spicy but with an underlying stoniness. Three premier crus immediately south of Meursault the village are somewhat unjustly in the shadow of the great trio of Meursault vineyards that lie farther south, toward Puligny. This first group is made up of the Gouttes d'Or, Poruzots, and Bouchères vineyards. The Poruzots from the François and Remi Jobard domaines and the renditions of the other two sites from Buisson-Charles are among those to look for. Then comes the mighty trio of Charmes, Genevrières, and Perrières. The last of these—and the stoniest, as its name suggests—gives without question Meursault's finest wine; indeed, it is generally thought of as the grand cru of the village. A great many both celebrated and less well-known growers own shares in all three or two of three, so consumers with the requisite disposable income or the luck of attending some well-organized tastings can satisfy themselves as to whatever recognizable identity accrues to each of these vineyards. Perrières is usually clearly the deepest, longest, and most complex wine of the three. The aromas and flavors of Meursault often include toasted grain and nuts, as well as saline, stony, or other notes that practically demand the use of "mineral" vocabulary. Some frequently seen and often superb sites that are not premier cru include Narvaux and Les Tillets, high in the hills above the Goutte d'Or and Genevrières respectively.

Meursault-Perrières segues into the Champ Canet, Combottes, and Les Referts vineyards of Puligny-Montrachet. Seemingly subtle changes in the soil and the nature of the fossil limestone are generally held responsible for the changes in scent and flavor, which by the time one gets deeper into the commune of Puligny—to such premier crus as Les Folatières and Clavaillon—are unmistakable, the wines being dominated by pit fruits and sometimes the pithy bitterness of the pits themselves, succulent yet very refined. Anyone who gets a chance to taste the Domaine Leflaive or Sauzet renditions of these sites is lucky, but there are many other excellent and more frequently encountered examples such as those of *négociants* Henri (Jean) Boillot, Bouchard, and Jadot. An interesting cluster of crus above Folatières and around the tiny hamlet of Blagny can display great intricacy with generally ligher frames and pronounced acidity as befits their higher elevation. These include among others the tiny and superb La Truffière (with just a few owners, including Bruno Colin and Bernard Morey), Blagny itself as premier cru, Chalumeaux, and Champ-Gain. As we approach the grand crus and the border with Chassagne-Montrachet, three Puligny premier crus of almost equal stature stand out: Les Pucelles, Les Cailleret, and minuscule Les Demoiselles. The last-named site is in two sets of hands (Amiot and Colin-Deleger), and Pucelles is best sought out at Jean Boillot or Leflaive. An important share of Cailleret was sold off in the late 1980s, so there are now more owners of that superb neighbor of the grand crus Chevalier-Montrachet and Le Montrachet. Chevalier-Montrachet often possesses more refinement and scarcely less mystery than Le Montrachet, but the latter boasts at its best unsurpassed depth, density, and persistence. Compared with these two titans, the three grand crus just down the slope— Bâtard-Montrachet, the smaller Bienvenues-Bâtard-Montrachet, and the tiny Criots-Bâtard-Montrachet—might not be quite so grand, but they can certainly be magnificent. The top *négociants* are the most frequently encountered sources of these grand crus, but with prices putting them beyond the reach of all but so few consumers, we won't linger over further recommended sources. Wines from the small Les Enseignières—just below Bâtard-Montrachet but not classified premier cru—can be good values, but the problem is finding any bottles. The best premier cru vineyards of St.-Aubin—Les Murgers-des-Dents-de-Chiens and En Remilly—are steep, stony, and high above the grand crus. Until recent decades, much of this land was not even planted, but that has changed, and recent warm ripening seasons are making these crus—which sell for well less than a *villages* Puligny-Montrachet—increasingly worth seeking out from the likes of Colin-Morey and the Colins, to name just two.

The commune of Chassagne-Montrachet shares Le Montrachet and Bâtard-Montrachet with Puligny but incorporates all of the Criots-Bâtard-Montrachet. There is then a significant drop-off immediately south of the grand crus, both in elevation and reputation. The premier crus of Chassagne are located on higher slopes to the west and southwest of the grand crus. Three of the better known of those immediately west of the grand crus and north of the town of Chassagne itself are Les Chaumées, Les Vergers, and Chenevottes. As one penetrates Chassagne, juicy citrus, flowers, and red berries regularly appear in the glass. The cast of premier crus around the town itself and strung out to the south en route to Santenay is so large that we cannot stop to mention the majority of them, and some rarely appear in the market under their own names. Among the best known are (from north to south) Clos St.-Jean, Maltroie, Champs Gain, En Cailleret, La Romanée, Morgeot (by far the largest), Francemont, and Clos Pitois. The rating and descriptions of growers that follow in this chapter will offer some excellent starting places to search for these wines. Among *négociants,* Jadot is notable for their huge array of Chassagne-Montrachet crus, much of that acreage coming from the Duc de Magenta estate, which they acquired in the 1980s. Just as a large part of Chassagne's acreage was first planted with Chardonnay only in the second half of the 20th century, so too, significant acreage across the line in Santenay (southwest of Chassagne) is now planted in Chardonnay and sometimes generates relatively good value.

But the top values are to be found farther south in the Côte Chalonnaise. The northernmost town, Bouzeron, has *appellation contrôlée* status only for Aligoté, but the best of these (most famously that of De Villaine) offer terrific personality and value, and there is excellent Chardonnay from that neighborhood, bottled simply as Bourgogne Blanc. Immediately south is Rully, then Mercurey, and then Givry. All three are better known for their Pinot Noir, but one taste of the white Rully of Deux Montille or Dureuil will instantly convince you how seriously one must take this subregion, and what good value it can offer in white wine. The top vintners in Mercurey and Givry (see the grower ratings) are also bottling some whites. As a rule, these wines—from a chalk-clay mixture millions of years away from that of the Côte d'Or—have their own style, with citrus, flowers, pit fruits, and mineral aspects that sometimes put one in mind of Riesling. Some five miles south of Givry and near the terminus of the Chalonnaise comes its one appellation dedicated solely to Chardonnay, that of Montagny. The well-known and widely distributed version from Louis Latour is excellent, and nowadays one meets with others such as Deux Montille. As previously noted, each of the Chalonnaise *vil-*

lages save for Bouzeron has a wealth of—indeed, almost certainly too many—premier crus, into the details of which we shall not delve.

[recent vintages]

WHITE BURGUNDY

2004–2006

A closer look at these three excellent vintages should offer insights as well as leave behind questions that will serve wine lovers well when they approach future harvest reports and vintage assessments. (Chablis and the Mâcon will be dealt with separately thereafter.) The complications and contrasts that apply to growing and winemaking decisions in Burgundy will be on prominent display in the account that follows. Almost throughout Europe, 2006 was another precocious vintage. A rainy mid-August followed a high summer of extreme heat, and in Burgundy's Côte d'Or, the pattern was repeated with warm early September temperatures and then rain. At that point, the pressures of rot became more than most vines or vintners could withstand, and when the official harvest was declared—in fact, before that for many who sought dispensation—most growers immediately began to pick. They were, however, faced with two potentially incompatible demands. The presence of rot demanded careful selection. But rot—or at least its precursors, with Chardonnay turning violet or bluish—was spreading at a rate that seemed to demand rapid harvest. Fortunately, many of the top Burgundy domaines are able to muster a large number of skilled pickers quickly, and this was critical to success. Yet, some growers thought their fruit could and should be riper, and they did not begin until a week or ten days later. One can usually tell the wines of early harvesters from those of late pickers, with the latter being softer, more exotic in aroma, and higher in alcohol—but, interestingly, not always. Which wines one prefers will have more to do with a taster's stylistic preferences than with any other factor, because in the final analysis, even Chardonnays harvested from what their growers admitted were "blue grapes" seldom betray (at least in their youth) any telltale negative signs of rot. For all of their richness, few of the wines tasted downright deficient in freshness in their youth, but measurable levels of acidity varied widely. When it came to *élevage,* approaches and rationales were also dramatically diverse. Many growers pulled their 2006 vintage wines from barrel early and minimized lees contact, in the interest (they insisted) of preserving fruit and freshness. Some bottled as early as they ever have, while others moved the wines from barrel early, then let them sit in tank. A vocal minority of vintners, though, insisted that in this of all vintages the young wines needed 18 months or more in barrel and on their lees to express their personalities, gain structure, and be proofed against an early decline in bottle. (Other measures taken in an effort to ward off premature oxidation were too numerous to be canvassed here.) Only time will tell what approach to harvest and *élevage* was best, if in fact a consensus is ever achieved. Meanwhile, we have a diverse group of largely very fine young wines.

2005

White Burgundy's growing season in 2005 was warm and relatively dry, so much so that the official date of harvest was nearly a week earlier than in 2006. Yet few of the best growers started picking then, because most thought the flavors were not ripe. One does not always achieve lower acidity as the grapes hang longer, but certainly in this year that was the case. The resultant wines are generally rich and full, but in their youth they lacked the nooks and crannies and the diversity of fruit flavors that make the latter vintage especially lovely. If asked to make comparison with 2004, most growers say that they prefer it to 2005. Yet, on the surface, conditions would appear not to have been at all propitious. Just as with Pinot Noir, a large crop appeared likely never to fully ripen, but did so when sun and warmth arrived in September. And also as with Pinot, growers who waited until late in that month to pick were astonished to find levels of sugar sometimes as high as those of hot, dry 2003. Acids were high, too—especially malic acid, so the malolactic transformation was profound. Yet the tension in the finished wines is seldom discordant as so often in the vintage's reds. Opinions on retaining or stirring of the lees varied as widely as they did in 2006. Enormously aromatic, bright and refreshing, yet with a sense of density belying the generous yields, the better young 2004s stimulate taste buds, appetite, and intellect. Those who much prefer white Burgundy in a plush, overtly rich format, though, will always prefer 2006 or 2005.

OTHER WHITE BURGUNDY VINTAGES

Particularly in white Burgundy, early official first days of harvest have become the new norm, and increasingly quality-conscious, crop-chopping growers are successfully appealing—as was the case for many in 2006—for permission to harvest earlier than the official first day, lest rot or overripeness compromise excellent potential quality. So (just as in many other white wine regions of northern Europe) deficiency of ripeness—or at least sugar—is less and less often the source of a vintage's weakness. But this does not mean recent vintages have been without perils of their own. As verteran and virtual icon Jean-François Coche of Meursault puts it, "our flowers come earlier than ever and the weather is so good that our vines—which need to suffer to make great wine—are too happy."

The extreme heat and drought of 2003 saw vintners interrupting their holidays in mid-August and rushing home to round up crews of pickers. Yet, even with potential alcohol levels threatening to set records to match a record early harvest, the truth is that just as with much Pinot Noir, some of the Chardonnay fruit was not really ripe in flavor. It was virtually impossible to delay picking until month's end, if not on account of potentially excessive sugar, then on account of the press of Pinot Noir that would soon require picking. So, white wines could not benefit from the break in the weather that took place in the last days of August 2003. Besides high potential alcohol, growers had to deal with low acidity and excessively high pH, and most acidified their musts, with varying degrees of success. Since virtually all of the malic acid had been baked from the grapes, there was little malolactic transformation, and what there was took place early. This circumstance, together with the fat and opulence displayed by the young wines, led many growers to move them off of their lees, out of barrel, and into bottle early. But a vocal minority of growers appears likely to have the last word and to have rendered 2003s with more flavor interest, more representative of their sites, less marked by the desiccation and heat of the vintage, and more apt to improve in bottle. This minority argued that precisely because of the amorphous character of the young white 2003s, they needed long stays on their lees to firm-up and gain structure and personality. Levels of malic acid were low in 2002 as well, but there any comparison with 2003 ends! Precisely their high acidity (which, because it was tartaric, did not diminish through malolactic conversion) marks the wines of 2002, occasionally to excess. A relatively cool, long growing season and wines with considerable elegance and intricacy of flavor—long on floral and mineral dimensions—characterize this lovely vintage. An even longer growing season made 2001 the closest that the Côte d'Or has come in recent years to a vintage typical of long-term averages. One had to wait until late September for stubborn malic acidity to recede and sugars and flavors to achieve ripeness, and then the window was narrow before the onset of early October rain. Yet, the 2001s turned out surprisingly impressive as a group, overtly dense, if less refined than their immediate predecessors or successors. In the best instances, whites from both 2002 and 2001 can benefit from further cellaring, but as had already been noted, there are too few "best instances" and far too many incidents of premature oxidation in recent white Burgundies for even expert observers to hazard generalizations (sometimes not even among the wines of a single domaine) or for consumers to hazard wholesale collecting.

The weakness of both 2000 and 1999 lay in copious flowering and a natural tendency toward overproduction. In 2000, this meant that when the official harvest date was announced grapes were seldom ripe. Immediately thereafter, heavy rain fell in the Côte de Beaune. When it was over, many growers panicked in fear of rot and began picking, but those who waited achieved some lovely if not always terribly concentrated successes best drunk within their first decade. In 1999 there was ample ripeness and concentration despite a very large crop, but many wines lack a bit of personality. The authorities certainly share some culpability in this and other vintages for raising the allowable yields beyond an already too lenient norm. These wines were easy to drink in their youth, but only the best of them have proven worth cellaring past six or eight years. The 1998 crop suffered from irregular budding and ripening potential due to widespread frost, and massive outbreaks of the fungus known as oidium. In August the weather turned so hot that Burgundy experienced—what was then a rarity—a shutdown of the vines and sunburned fruit, after which the heavens opened and rain brought massive rot. Time has not been kind to the astringent, naturally high-alcohol, yet not entirely ripe-tasting wines that resulted. On the whole, the full-bodied 1997s displayed more personality than the 1999s, but they often failed to deliver complete ripeness or concentration despite their high natural alcohol (a harbinger of several subsequent vintages to come), and nearly all were best enjoyed within a decade.

At this point in our brief survey, one might well ask "why proceed?" since the premature oxidation that has afflicted so many white Burgundies from the mid-'90s has already been discussed above (not to mention well publicized), and how many white Burgundies are now being crafted for aging longer than 12 or 15 years in bottle? These are fair questions. The sagas of 1994 and 1993 can safely be forgotten. Indeed, there was no need for holding on to any, quite apart from issues of premature aging. The 1992s were generous, rich, and satisfying but are also now largely past their prime. Two vintages, though, remain worthy of our further consideration. Where wines of the unusual 1996 vintage have escaped the rather capricious onset of premature demise, they remain fascinatingly concentrated and invigorating. This was a vintage with a strong transregional character. From the Loire (with Chenin and Sauvignon) through Burgundy to the Riesling of Alsace and Germany, there was exceptionally high acidity and extract combined with high grape sugars and a touch of (largely noble) rot that gives some wines a haunting white truffle cast. Cool summer nights caused the grapes to stubbornly retain their acidity, and at the point when acids would normally have begun to diminish in September, subtle dehydration of the fruit due to wind kept compensating, resulting in the extreme sense of concentration and high acidity that so many of these wines possess. The oily-rich, opulent 1995s were very impressive as young wines, and some of them have kept faith with that promise. Two of the most outstanding vintages for white Burgundy of recent decades are 1986 and 1979, and wines from the handful of top estates can still be riveting, leading one to wistfully wonder (indeed worry) whether for all of the improved batting averages of recent years, with respect to quality and longevity, perhaps "they don't make them like that anymore."

THE MÂCON: HOME OF CHARDONNAY AND ITS BEST VALUES

In truth, nobody knows whether the town of Chardonnay gave its name to that ubiquitous white wine grape or vice versa. But all signs point toward the dramatic limestone hills of the Mâcon in southern Burgundy as Chardonnay's birthplace. What's certain is that until the mid-20th century, not only was acreage of Chardonnay virtually nonexistent outside Burgundy, Champagne, and the Jura, but most of it was concentrated in Chablis, the Mâcon, and a very few locations on the Côte d'Or (today's grand crus and the top sites in Meursault). The Mâcon has always been a source of volume white wine, but it never enjoyed the renown and high prices that even Beaujolais benefited from a century ago, and which accrue to Chablis or the Côte d'Or. That Pouilly-Fuissé was the source of Chardonnay's first mass invasion of American markets did nothing in the long run for its quality reputation, since most of this wine was simply overpriced Mâcon, and tended to come from co-ops or *négociants*. But since the early 1990s, the Mâcon has spawned or attracted many quality-conscious not to say fanatic vintners, and today one can without equivocation state that this is where the greatest Chardonnay values of the world—not just of Burgundy—reside. "Readers who continue to be label-conscious shoppers, ignoring the finest Mâconnaise producers, need a wake-up call," wrote Robert Parker in a 1993 issue of *The Wine Advocate*. "There are at least a half dozen superb Mâconnaise estates making wines that rival and often surpass many Côte d'Or premier and grand crus. . . . These wines sell for one-sixth to one-tenth the price of a Bâtard-Montrachet. . . . Is anyone listening?" Judging from the fact that prices of famous Côte d'Or crus have rocketed out of range of most wine lovers' discretionary income while the best Mâconnaise elite generally sell for under 50 dollars a bottle and many for half that, one could argue that only a few consumers must have been listening. So much the better, then, for those who did! The quality of Mâconnais wine at many addresses has risen recently, as the region's new elite are setting benchmarks and inspiring younger growers.

The vast majority of wine here is simply labeled Mâcon or—if coming from legally favored sectors, as does most of what is exported—Mâcon-Village. Numerous villages are permitted to append their individual names to "Mâcon" so that we have such wines as Mâcon-Viré or Mâcon-Vegisson, or even a Mâcon-Fuissé for portions of that village which are not—along with wines from three other villages at the Mâcon's southern edge—accorded the grander appellation Pouilly-Fuissé. The names Pouilly-Loché and Pouilly-Vinzelles accrue to wine grown next-door in two towns that inexplicably did not join Chaintre, Fuissé, Solutré, and Vergisson, but were later rewarded (for their intransigence?) with tiny appellations of their own. Scattered outside Pouilly-Fuissé and slightly overlapping Beaujolais is the appellation Saint-Véran, whose wines are nearly always priced midway between those of Mâcon-Village and Pouilly-Fuissé. In 1998, a new appellation was created in the middle Mâcon, named for its principal villages Viré-Clessé. Even Pouilly-Fuissé is normally thought of as a wine for early drinking, but there have always been exceptions and the sort of quality that Barraud, Cordier, Guffens, Jean Thevenet, and a few others have been rendering in the past dozen or so years shows every indication of holding its own in bottle against Côte d'Or premier crus. Relative to its better-known neighbors to the north, the Mâcon struggled more with rain and rot in 2006, but there are still many lovely wines, and healthy, ripe fruit in 2005 made for terrific successes. Both 2004 and 2002 were also excellent, and arguably in both 2001 and 2000—certainly in 1999—the Mâcon outperformed the Côte d'Or thanks to its generally warmer weather and earlier ripening, among other factors. That said, the quality of average Mâcon is all too often marked by the effects of overcropping, machine harvesting, and a preference for "safe rather than full of flavor" picking.

CHABLIS: CHARDONNAY'S MAGIC CHALKBOARD

Situated halfway between Beaune and Paris, Chablis sits on a band of fossil-laden white Kimmeridgean chalk, which runs through southern Champagne, the eastern Loire, and across the English Channel. Its best-known physical manifestation is Dover's white cliffs. Its best-known vinous manifestation is surely this wine with its world-renowned name. Yet confusion followed Chablis wherever its famous name went, precisely because it went so many places. This was, for instance, the name used for generic "jug" whites in the U.S.

for decades, disappearing only in the 1980s. Its fame and the killing frosts that sometimes wiped out an entire crop became excuses for a high-yield mind-set. Yet with a climate that rendered inherently precarious full ripeness, enormous crops invited mean, green flavors. Propensity for rain and rot—while grapes hung later than elsewhere in Burgundy—led to a widespread tendency to sulfur with a heavy hand. And that only accentuated high acidity or unripe flavors. One has to say that for much of the late 20th century, the difference in quality between a very few standard-bearers and all other producers of Chablis was depressingly dramatic.

Like all of Burgundy, Chablis suffered from poor choices of clones, overproduction, and chemical treatments to the soil. It also suffers from widespread machine harvesting, which includes the vast majority of basic appellation Chablis. And there is still much knee-jerk sulfuring. How many French, one wonders—confronted with any wine oversulfured—wrinkle their noses and smilingly say *"goût de Chablis."* New-world winemakers routinely refer to any Chardonnay that is high in acid, is stainless steel–fermented, and/or has not been through malolactic fermentation as "Chablis style," as if Chablis consisted in a style. A higher acidity than Chardonnay from the Cote d'Or can be expected, but it must be ripe. And if it's ripe, the effects of malolactic fermentation will be subtle and enrich the wine. And while some growers—notably Louis Michel—render Chablis brilliantly in stainless steel, much of this region's best wine spends time in wood. Change is coming more slowly here, but there are brilliant stars like René Dauvissat and François Raveneau for idealistic vintners (including of course their own sons, Vincent and Bernard) to follow. Iconoclastic outsiders like Bordelais Didier Séguier, director of William Fèvre and—ever a thorn in the side of the Chablisiens—Jean-Marie Guffens of Mâcon-based Verget have been important agents of change. Neither ripeness nor cleanliness—let alone profundity—can yet be assumed, but they are a lot more likely today than at any other time in Chablis history. Burgundy's renaissance did not, it seems, pass over this region, but merely showed up late. There has never been a better time to discover these remarkably distinctive wines.

The greatest compliment paid Chablis by first-time tasters lucky enough to be presented with a good one is "I much prefer this to a Chardonnay." But, you say, "it *is* Chardonnay." Perhaps, but it does not taste much like any other. What strikes one especially is its table manners. If you set out to find harmonious and interesting marriages of good Chablis with meals, you'll find it follows the lead of Sauvignon from the Loire, or of Champagne, and seldom if ever can be found at home where Chardonnay from the Côte d'Or, the Mâcon, or anywhere else on earth fits in at table. This seems a perfect lesson in *terroir:* Chablis aligning itself with its Kimmeridgean brethren. Andrew Jefford once memorably wrote of Chablis that "its little basket of orchard fruits is often hidden beneath a pile of white stones." But what is most striking is the degree to which even in youth—and even more so than young red or white wine from the Côte d'Or—Chablis is not primarily about fruits and berries. No wine on earth save Mosel Riesling gives greater appearance of actually smelling and tasting like the rocks from which it grows. If you have a chance to visit, break up a piece of its distinctive fossiliferous chalk and smell. Could be that it's the power of suggestion or the product of an overly fertile imagination, but if so, then this is either an astonishing coincidence or an astonishingly prevalent deception! Moreover, Chablis can offer one of the most strikingly carnal manifestations of grapes, with flavors and aromas often vividly resembling rich, herb-laced chicken stock.

THE VINEYARDS AND APPELLATIONS OF CHABLIS

The classification of vineyards in this subregion is a thing unto itself. Even the apparent familiarity from the Côte d'Or of the terms *"villages,"* "premier cru," and "grand cru" proves to be an illusion. There are numerous villages with their own sometimes less than subtle microclimatic and geological characteristics, but the law recognizes just one mega-village: Chablis.

(Some cooler spots and those with less pervious limestone cap rock are classified Petit Chablis.) Not only are villages not credited (although Verget has taken to—and thus far gotten away with!—noting "*terroir de*____," filling in a village name on its labels), but it is also illegal in Chablis to mention a vineyard unless it is an official cru. (In other words, it is impermissible to label with the name of a *lieu-dit*.) This is a system that seems to offer owners of village property little incentive to craft something distinctive, although thank goodness so many do. And it is a system especially unfortunate in the light of history. There are slightly fewer than 10,000 acres in this entire region, but by the middle of the last century, that had dipped to barely over 7,000 acres, and when its crus were delimited, much top-quality land went unclassified because untended or unplanted. With the classification of Chablis premier crus, something verging on the deceptive was achieved. While there are only 7 grand crus, there are no fewer than 79 premier crus. But fewer than a dozen of their names regularly appear on labels, and then frequently do not refer to the specific vineyard of that name but rather to wine from any number of other nearby crus or a blend of these. Take, for example, "Premier Cru Vaillons." In addition to naming a specific site, these words may also be used—and usually are—to refer to wine from seven other sites in Vaillon's vicinity. Among the most frequently encountered premier crus are Mont de Milieu, Montée de Tonnerre, Fourchaume, Vaillons, Montmains (including its subcrus Les Forêts and Butteaux), Côte de Léchet, and Beauroy. Some growers and observers try to make a distinction of character between sites on the right bank of the Serein (including the first three on the list just offered) and those opposite. But the truth is that the many premier crus offer a virtual crazy quilt of exposures, defying any coherent geographical narrative unless one has an accurate vineyard map and considerable time, which we shall not take here. The grand crus, by contrast, are contiguous, sitting directly on the right bank of the Serein, looking south over the town of Chablis itself. These are (from west to east): Bougros, Les Preuses, Vaudésir, Grenouilles, Valmur, Les Clos, and Blanchot. Given their heat-trapping microclimates, they often result in wines of much more fat and richness, wines of a dramatically different character from—rather than being a quality extension of—premier cru Chablis. In cool, lean vintages of a sort very familiar from the '80s and before, when the Chardonnay struggles to ripen, successful grand cru wines sometimes taste as if they came from an entirely different vintage. Over the past 10 or 12 generally warm years, increasingly many Chablis lovers and even some growers have been heard to say that the grand crus are practically not producing Chablis any longer but some unfamiliar if distinctively delicious expression of the Chardonnay grape. (The greatest sign of indignation one hears is "Why . . . it tastes like a Côte de Beaune!")

No account of the greater Chablis area can be complete without a mention of St.-Bris, a relatively recent appellation that applies to an old tradition of growing Sauvignon Blanc in certain sites near the Yonne River, between Auxerre and the limits of Chablis No one who savors these distinctly delicious wines will fail to find the family resemblance to Chablis, which growers and *terroiristes* naturally chalk up to the chalk. Some excellent Chardonnay from this neighborhood is bottled as Bourgogne Côtes d'Auxerre or Bourgogne Chitry, and there is even the Pinot Noir appellation of Irancy, from which increasingly many interesting even though relatively lightweight wines have been emerging. Here and there at considerable distance from Chablis and Auxerre are patches of Chardonnay (less often, Pinot) to remind us that at one time the greater area of the Yonne—with its then uniquely rapid access to Paris by boat—was practically one vast vineyard. The largest and most interesting such distant outpost is at Vézelay, two dozen miles south of Chablis, where both a local grower co-op and several individual vintners are building a reputation for Bourgogne Vézelay as refreshing, interesting, and offering outstanding value.

CELLARING CHABLIS, AND RECENT VINTAGES

Although Chablis has a reputation for long aging, that has only applied—in our time, anyway—to the very best growers, whose wines are clean, concentrated, and distinctive enough to hold a taster's interest. In such instances, even humble basic-appellation Chablis has been known to taste lovely at eight or ten years of age, and the better premier cru and grand cru bottlings can easily improve for a dozen or more years, a better track record in the cellar than that of most white wines classified premier cru in the Côte d'Or.

2006

Given Chablis's location and the nature of its classification, it will come as no surprise that vintages do not consistently track with those in the Côte d'Or, and that a good vintage at one level of classification might not be equally good at another—and 2006 illustrates this nicely. For the first time on record, Chablis began picking before the harvest of Chardonnay in the Côte d'Or. There was less rain and fungal pressure, but few growers were taking chances and most picked in the days immediately following the official harvest or—by appealing to the authorities for permission—two or three days before. The result is wines with opulence and richness such as was once almost unimaginable in this region, yet the best of these are not without a depth of flavors that, for lack of any other more suitable word, must surely be called "mineral." (What one does not so often encounter is noticeable acidity nor much of the overtly crushed-stone notes that generally have typified Chablis.) Without question, well-situated and well-tended vines in simple appellation Chablis were able to achieve in 2006 an unprecedented balance of richness and vivacity, and even Petite Chablis had a chance to shine. Among the premier crus, one notes a tendency for higher elevations and less sunny exposures to be favored. And when it comes to grand crus, while the best wines are profound, many tasters will feel that they are often overripe and lacking in cut, freshness, or finesse.

2005

In 2005, circumstances were reversed, with Chablis receiving more rain than the Côte d'Or, and some wineries finding themselves trapped between not entirely ripe flavors on the one hand, and elevated potential alcohol and botrytis on the other. Heady alcohol and exotic aromas abound in most of the finished wines. How will Chablis with the richness and relative softness of the 2006s and 2005s mature? The most honest answer is that such vintages are unprecedented, and we shall see. But botrytis is likely to overtake many of the 2005s, leading to bitterness, whereas the best 2006 premier crus should age well for at least a decade.

2004

Given that 2004 is a vintage of taut, energetic, and mineral wines on the Côte d'Or, it isn't surprising that with similar weather that year, the wines of Chablis have those same characteristics in spades. But the vintage is marginally less successful here than in the Côte d'Or, because in a more "normal" vintage of this sort—in other words, one in which grapes must struggle and remain hanging longer to get ripe—high yields (a given in 2004) are more of a handicap. In fact, it looked as Chablis approached the late innings of the game with Nature as though there would be a shutout. But September and October warmth and sunshine largely saved the day. Even so, there was a lot of malic acid in the finished grapes, and after often protracted malolactic conversions the wines frequently lacked the mouthwatering sort of acidity or orchard-fruit notes that riper Chablis can give.

2003

The Chablis of hot, dry 2003 are very worth tasting if for no other reason than to gain perspective on the possible, and to enjoy some very rich and opulent wines. But they are certainly freaks of nature, generally lacking in the refreshment that Chablis can normally be counted on to deliver. Frost was (typically) even more destructive here than farther south in Burgundy, but lightening the crop load in the end benefited the vines, and at least when the harvest started— although it was the earliest on record, a week later than on the Côte d'Or—temperatures had moderated.

2002

In 2002, Chablis was blessed with exceptional conditions, very much like those of its Kimmeridgean neighbors on the Loire. Dry autumn winds helped concentrate the fruit and keep it healthy, and growers could take their time and pick at optimal ripeness while retaining lovely acidity. The only problem one encounters at some excellent addresses is traceable to 2003. Wines of 2002 not protected by deep cellars or temperature-controlled storage tanks underwent an exceptionally warm *élevage,* and some of them lost a bit of freshness and probably a few years of aging potential during the searing summer of 2003. Still, this is the recent vintage to seek out for a taste of what classic Chablis is and can become with bottle age.

2001

There was a certain tendency to leanness in the high-malic, unevenly ripened wines of 2001, which growers were afraid to try to moderate through long contact with the lees unless their grape skins were in rude good health at harvest, which was too often not the case. Still, there are successes from the top addresses well worth revisiting at age six or eight.

2000

Vintage 2000 was capable here of outperforming the Côte d'Or. Even if high yields in most instances undercut the possibility of real profundity, there are many wonderful wines appropriate to enjoying at ten or a dozen years' age.

Earlier Vintages

Wine lovers should approach with caution Chablis of the freakishly concentrated, high-acid, erratically performing 1996s, but wines from the very best growers can be quite exciting. The best wines of 1990 are also most impressive, striking an excellent balance between ripeness and acid and mineral impressions.

[the ratings]

BURGUNDY'S PRODUCERS OF WHITE WINE (INCLUDING THOSE OF CHABLIS AND THE MÂCON)

* * * * * (OUTSTANDING)

Domaine d'Auvenay—Leroy (St.-Romain)
Domaine Bonneau du Martray
  (Pernand-Vergelesses)
Jean-François Coche-Dury (Meursault)
René et Vincent Dauvissat (Chablis)
Domaine William Fèvre (Chablis)

Domaine Guffens-Heynen
  (Vergisson/Mâcon)
Domaine des Comtes Lafon (Meursault)
Domaine Leflaive (Puligny-Montrachet)
François Raveneau (Chablis)

* * * * (EXCELLENT)

Daniel Barraud (Vergisson/Mâcon)
Jean Boillot (Volnay)

Maison Henri Boillot—Jean Boillot
  (*négociant,* Meursault)

Domaine Jean-Marc Boillot (Pommard)

Domaine de Bongran—Jean Thevenet
(Quintaine/Mâcon)

Bouchard Père et Fils (*négociant*, Beaune)

Jean-Marc Brocard (Chablis)

Domaine Buisson-Charles—Michel Buisson
(Meursault)

Michel Colin-Deleger (Chassagne-
Montrachet)

Domaine Comtesse Bernard de Cherisey—
Martelet de Cherisey (Blagny)

Domaine Cordier Père et Fils / Maison
Christophe Cordier (Fuissé/Mâcon)

Jean-Paul et Benoît Droin (Chablis)

Domaine Dublère—Blair Pethel
(*négociant*, Savigny-les-Beaune)

Domaine Arnaud Ente (Meursault)

Domaine Jean-Philippe Fichet (Meursault)

Albert Grivault (Meursault)

Patrick Javillier (Meursault)

François Jobard (Meursault)

Domaine Laroche (Chablis)

Château de la Maltroye
(Chassagne-Montrachet)

Lucien Le Moine (*négociant*, Beaune)

Philippe Pacalet (*négociant*, Beaune)

Paul Pernot (Puligny-Montrachet)

Jean-Marc Pillot (Chassagne-Montrachet)

Château de Puligny-Montrachet
(Puligny-Montrachet)

Domaine Ramonet (Chassagne-
Montrachet)

Domaine Roulot (Meursault)

Étienne Sauzet (Puligny-Montrachet)

Verget—Jean-Marie Guffens
(*négociant*, Sologny/Mâcon)

★ ★ ★ (VERY GOOD)

Guy Amiot et Fils (Chassagne-Montrachet)

Hervé Azo (Chablis)

Domaine Bitouzet-Prieur (Volnay)

Domaine Billaud-Simon (Chablis)

Bret Brothers / La Soufrandière
(Vinzelles/Mâcon)

Domaine de la Cadette (Vézelay/Yonne)

Domaine Louis Carillon (Puligny-
Montrachet)

Bruno Colin (Chassagne-Montrachet)

Philippe Colin (Chassagne-Montrachet)

Marc Colin et Fils (Chassagne-
Montrachet)

Pierre-Yves Colin-Morey
(Chassagne-Montrachet)

Jean et Sebastien Dauvissat (Chablis)

Maison Deux Montille (*négociant*, Meursault)

Maison Joseph Drouhin (*négociant*, Beaune)

Domaine Dublère—Blair Pethel
(Savigny-les-Beaune)

Vincent Dureuil (Rully)

Benoit Ente (Puligny-Montrachet)

Château de Fuissé—J. J. Vincent
(Fuissé/Mâcon)

Jean-Noël Gagnard
(Chassagne-Montrachet)

Vincent Girardin (Chassagne-Montrachet)

Emmanuel Giboulet (Combertault)

Maison Camille Giroud (*négociant*, Beaune)

Domaine G. & J.-H. Goisot—Corps de
Garde (St.-Bris-le-Vineux/Yonne)

Corinne et Jean-Pierre Grossot
(Chablis)

Domaine Guillemot-Michel
(Quintaine/Mâcon)

Domaine Les Hertiers du Comte Lafon
(Milly/Mâcon)

Domaine Remi Jobard (Meursault)

Maison Louis Latour (*négociant*, Beaune)

Domaine Latour-Giraud (Meursault)

Domaine Long-Depaquit—
Albert Bichot (Chablis)

Château de la Maltroye (Chassagne-
Montrachet)

Domaine Joseph Matrot—Thierry Matrot
(Meursault)

Domaine Mestre-Michelot (Meursault)

Louis Michel (Chablis)

Domaine Michelot (Meursault)

François Mikulski (Meursault)

Xavier Monnot (Meursault)

Alice et Olivier de Moor (Chablis)

Bernard Morey et Fils
(Chassagne-Montrachet)

Marc Morey (Chassagne-Montrachet)

Domaine Pierre Morey (Meursault)

Maison Morey-Blanc—Pierre Morey
(Meursault)

Michel Niellon (Chassagne-Montrachet)

Gilbert Picq et Ses Fils (Chablis)

Maison Nicolas Potel
(*négociant*, Nuits-St.-Georges)

Domaine Jacques Prieur (Meursault)
Jean Rijckaert (*négociant*, Leynes/Mâcon)
Domaine Robert-Denogent (Fuissé)

Domaine Servin (Chablis)
Laurent Tribut (Chablis)
A. & P. de Villaine (Bouzeron)

* * (GOOD)

Domaine Boyer-Martenot (Meursault)
Domaine du Chalet Pouilly—Agnès et
  Bernard Léger-Plumet (Solutré/Mâcon)
Domaine de la Chapelle—Catherine &
  Pascal Rollet (Pouilly/Mâcon)
Chartron & Trebuchet
  (*négociant*, Puligny-Montrachet)
Domaine Chassorney—Frédéric Cossard
  (St.-Romain)
Michel Coutoux (*négociant*,
  Chassagne-Montrachet)
Maria Cuny (Vézelay)
Vincent Dancer (Chassagne-Montrachet)
Domaine des Deux Roches
  (Davayé/Mâcon)
Georges Duboeuf (*négociant*, Mâconnaise)
Domaine Dupont-Fahn (Meursault)
Domaine J. A. Ferret (Fuissé)
Alex Gambal (*négociant*, Beaune)
Domaine des Gerbeaux (Mâconnaise)
Domaine Emilian Gillet—Jean Thevenet
  (Quintaine/Mâcon)
Frédéric Gueguen—Domaine des
  Chenevières (Chablis)
Jean-Marc Joblot (Givry)

Vincent et François Jouard
  (Chassagne-Montrachet)
Roger Lassarat (Vergisson/Mâcon)
Domaine Lavantureux (Chablis)
Olivier Leflaive (*négociant*,
  Puligny-Montrachet)
François Lumpp (Givry)
Olivier Merlin—Domaine du Vieux
  St.-Sorlin (La Roche Vineuse/Mâcon)
Christian Moreau Père et Fils (Chablis)
Henri Perrusset (Farges/Mâcon)
Isabelle & Denis Pommier (Chablis)
François Raquillet (Mercurey)
Domaine de Roally—Gauthier Thévenet
  (Viré/Mâcon)
Jacques et Nathalie Saumaize
  (Vergisson/Mâcon)
Domaine Saumize-Michelin
  (Vergisson/Mâcon)
Francine et Olivier Savary (Maligny-Chablis)
Domaine des Temps Perdu—Clothilde
  Davenne (Chablis)
Éric Texier (*négociant*, Mâcon)
Domaine Valette (Chaintré)
Cave Henry de Vézelay (Vézelay)

BEAUJOLAIS—GAMAY'S STRONGHOLD

Philip the Bold, Duke of Burgundy, may have succeeded in banishing the "disloyal grape" Gamay from the Côte d'Or more than six centuries ago, but it found a home in the high, granite Beaujeu Hills and made a name for itself that is now known around the world. That said, Beaujolais's notoriety has worked against it recently. For more than four decades, America's shores were annually lapped by a frothy, purple ocean of "Nouveau" and growers were happy to have a ready market for wine that could bring a cash return before most of France's vintners had even done their first racking. Sadly, much of this wine that passed for Beaujolais was crafted in a formulaic mold, resulting in a tutti-frutti, banana bubble gum–scented, heady, sometimes headache-inducing beverage that had little to do with this region's potential. It had a great run, but Beaujolais nouveau and its ilk have fallen from fashion and are unlikely to bounce back. To the extent that Beaujolais becomes more serious but without losing its vivacity and immediate sensual appeal, it may simply be exploring its roots. A century ago, the best wines of Fleurie, Moulin-à-Vent, Morgon, and others of what are today Beaujolais's crus went head to head in price and reputation with many a Pinot from the Côte d'Or. Today, the value of vineyard acreage in this region has dropped alarmingly as nowhere else in France, and growers are in a crisis. Before it is over, many of these steep hillsides with their thick-necked, head-pruned old vines hugging the stones may be lost to viticulture. But the seeds and sprouts of a revival are still present.

Clean, well-concentrated Gamay from this region is a delight to drink in its youth, and even what is sold simply as appellation Beaujolais or (more frequently) Beaujolais-Villages need not suffer for lack of personality. The massive and diverse output of *négociant* Georges Duboeuf, together with the virtually omnipresent Beaujolais-Villages of *négociant* Louis Jadot guarantee that there would be no shortage of delicious Beaujolais abroad even if it came from only these two sources. But Beaujolais has long been home to dedicated estate bottlers of a renegade stripe, guaranteeing that there is also highly distinctive—at times even quirky—artisanal Beaujolais to be had, fit to fascinate even the most jaded palate. In fact, many of the world's most jaded palates have no idea what they are missing. The most obvious distinction between the sort of Beaujolais crafted by a minority of mavericks and visionaries and the rest can be found in the method of production. Commonly, Beaujolais is vinified by what is known as carbonic maceration (or, more properly, semicarbonic maceration). This involves sealing whole clusters of fruit into a covered tank. Once fermentation commences as the weight of berries causes some of them to bleed and fall prey to yeasts, pressure from the resulting carbon dioxide takes care of the rest, with much of the fruit literally fermenting from the inside of the berry out. The chemical details need not detain us. Suffice it to say that the results are always vividly redolent of fruits and berries, but tend to lack textural nuance, and—as was intended—tannin. A minority of growers vinify their wine along lines more recognizable from Burgundy: cold soak followed by fermentation in open-top containers, sometimes with punch-downs, often with a lattice used to keep the cap of skins submerged beneath the surface of the fermenting juice. This minority usually matures their young wines in larger, older, oval oak casks, but occasionally also in Burgundy-size *barriques*. The result is Beaujolais with more tannic structure, often with intriguing complexity, yet still full of fruit and easy to enjoy young. Ironically, the father of modern Beaujolais and of the technique of carbonic maceration—Jules Chauvet (who died in 1989)—was also the inspiration for many of the region's present-day mavericks in their insistence on organic viticulture, no chaptalization, and minimal use of sulfur in the cellar. Chauvet disciple Marcel Lapierre founded his domaine in the early 1970s and became the inspiration for what is often called the Gang of Four in the commune of Morgon, which in the guerrilla war against the manufacturers of cookie-cutter Beaujolais became a sort of headquarters. They found an early American champion in importer Kermit Lynch.

Today a bevy of growers and specialty *négociants* are pushing the envelope and exploring what is possible with Gamay. It's not, however, as though only small estates are interested in employing more "Burgundian" methods. Jacques Lardière of Louis Jadot and his Beaujolais-based counterpart Guillaume de Castelnau have adopted a model at the Château des Jacques (Moulin-à-Vent) and Château des Lumières (Morgon) that calls for extracting flavors and tannin from Gamay with abandon (highly controlled!) and aging the wines up to a year in *barriques*. Like many smaller growers, Lardière claims the mantle of tradition for his methods. If nothing else, the ancient rows of stone slabs on the floor of the Château des Jacques were clearly designed for supporting hundreds of small barrels. But "tradition" is a notoriously slippery and elastic concept. The important thing to recognize is that there are numerous ways to render enticing and even exciting wines in Beaujolais, and then to taste them for oneself.

Having repeatedly mentioned Burgundy—which is quite understandable in any discussion of Beaujolais, since technically it is a subregion—it will be useful to address a notion that has become widely accepted but on closer inspection may be myth. It's often said that really good Beaujolais can age, and as it does it "pinots." One hears this from vintners of the Côte d'Or and Beaujolais alike. Ultimately it is an issue for wine lovers to decide for themselves. But the smoky scents and the peculiar balance of fruity and gamey elements in many older cru Beaujolais really more resemble a northern Rhône Syrah—not to mention their conspicuous absence of the silken or otherwise refined texture that accrues to the best Pinots. A family resemblance to wines of Côte Rôtie and St.-Joseph would at least have a basis in granitic (and schistic and related volcanic) soils. As to how the notion or myth that Beaujolais "Pinots" got started, that is easy enough to comprehend. A comparison with Burgundy or Pinot represented the highest form of flattery that a denizen of the Côte d'Or could bestow on anyone else's wine. And a grower in Beaujolais was happy to be flattered, and taken seriously.

Though one commonly speaks of "granite hills," the soils of Beaujolais are actually quite diverse. Not only is there schist as well—most notably the iron-rich form found in parts of Morgon—but there are also basalt (including Morgon's most famous section, the Côte du Py) and other igneous outcroppings. The presence of various minerals tints the granite different hues which—to a true *terroiriste*, at least—correspond to the wines' flavor shadings. (Or is this sometimes power of suggestion? The bluish soils of Côte de Brouilly are absolutely prone to vivid blueberry fruit.) More fundamentally, the degree to which these volcanic and metamorphic rocks are weathered to a consistency of small rocks, gravel, or sand and the amount of moisture-retentive clay that is present clearly affect the plants' metabolism. The most commonly encountered appellation (at least in export markets)—Beaujolais-Villages—applies to granitic hills in the northern half of Beaujolais, in and around the various crus. At the northern edge of Beaujolais, bordering the appellation Saint-Véran, the town of Leynes is entitled to is own Beaujolais-Leynes appellation, in essence a way station on the road to cru status, which it has never been awarded. But with this exception, the Beaujolais-Villages appellation does not function in the manner of the corresponding Mâcon-Villages, in that there are no other villages permitted to insert their names into it. The simple Beaujolais appellation applies to a band of lower elevation vineyards on alluvial soils nearer the Saône, but principally to the entire, widely spread out southern half of Beaujolais, where there is as much chalk and clay as there is granite. To an extent, one has to give Philip the Bold credit and admit that on chalk-clay soils, Gamay simply does not exhibit the perfume and forward fruit that it acquires in granitic and other volcanic sites. Still, these wines from the south can sometimes be delightful and interesting, with a cherry-pit bitterness more pronounced than in the north, and a couple of the most inspiring and influential growers in all of Beaujolais—Jean-Paul Brun and Pierre Chermette—have their home acreage in the chalk belt here. Not coincidentally, they also bottle excellent Beaujolais Blanc from Chardonnay.

The crus of Beaujolais—which extend in a roughly five- to six-mile-wide band of hills covering around 15 miles north to south, or slightly less than half of the region's total length—are of varying ages and pedigrees. Régnié, for instance, was created only in 1988, and in the current local economic climate is lucky to achieve a price significantly higher than that of a Beaujolais-Villages, whereas the reputation of Moulin-à-Vent dates back to the 19th century and even today it is usually able to command a slightly higher price than that of any other cru. The Beaujolais cru begin at the edge of the St.-Véran appellation of the Mâcon, immediately adjacent to which is St.-Amour. Along with Chénas, this is the tiniest Beaujolais cru, with a mixture of sand and clay that makes for effusively fruity, immediately appealing wine. Juliénas introduces an element of schist and stonier granite, but similar clay content, here generally giving a richer wine. Chénas—dominated by weathered granite and sand, is a highly peculiar appellation in that it sits between Juliénas and Moulin-à-Vent and in places interpenetrates the latter, but the acreage immediately adjacent to the town of Chénas itself belongs to the more highly reputed Moulin-à-Vent appellation. Why this territory was not originally or subsequently incorporated into Moulin-à-Vent is hard to fathom, but the best wines exhibit similar complexity and ageworthiness. Moulin-à-Vent itself lays claim to particularly manganese-rich, reddish granite, and perhaps that is what conduces to the sort of structure and complexity exhibited by the best wines from this appellation, which reaches up to the edges of the unofficial capital of Beaujolais, Romanèche-Thorins. (There is no village of Moulin-à-Vent, only the old windmill that gives it that name.) South and west of Moulin-à-Vent, Fleurie—with its pure granite—can offer the florality its name promises, yet also some of the structure and ageworthiness of Moulin-à-Vent. The highest-elevation cru, composed of granite and porphyry reduced to sand, Chiroubles generally yields the most delicate and among the most perfumed wines of Beaujolais. Morgon, with its variations on weathered schist, granite, and basalt, is a fascinatingly heterogeneous appellation and source of Beaujolais with more overtly animal elements than any other, capable of serious development in bottle. Régnié—on sandy, rose-colored, weathered granite and porphyry—is another relatively high-altitude cru, often highly perfumed but usually forward. The large cru of Brouilly incorporates several villages (all with variations on sandy granite) and tends toward blueberry, blackberry, and licorice in flatteringly intense form, sometimes with overtly stony notes, which are even more prominent in Côte de Brouilly whose "blue" granite hillside is essentially the cone of the ancient volcano that is now Mont-Brouilly. Both Brouilly and Côte de Brouilly have been known to age formidably.

Having mentioned the potential for certain crus of Beaujolais to age well, it must be emphasized that this applies nowadays only to the wines of a few top growers in those crus, and even so, their best wines are practically irresistible after a few months or a year in bottle. Cellaring Beaujolais is something to try out with a few bottles from the best address in Fleurie, Moulin-à-Vent, Morgon, or Côte de Brouilly and see how you like the results. But we shall not engage in a long litany of vintage assessments here. Tasters lucky enough to unearth and sample the occasional remaining wine from a good *négociant* of the early 20th century will find out that Beaujolais can be profoundly rewarding even at 80 or more years of age. Of recent harvests, that of 2005 was especially successful, but 2006 has plenty of charm if a bit less sheer density, and the early harvest of 2007 offered ample ripeness. The 2003s were unusually fat, rich, outsize Beaujolais, and some of them might make old bones. Certainly these are interesting to sample if one happens upon one, simply (as so often with this extreme vintage) to gain a sense of what is possible. In 2003, even the many leading growers in Beaujolais who eschew chaptalization bottled wines with 13.5% to 14.5% alcohol, or two full percentage points above their norm, so naturally the wines could never offer the same refreshment as is typical for this region. Since even the best Beaujolais seldom exceeds $25 retail, happy are those wine lovers who find that they have a particular affection for it.

—DAVID SCHILDKNECHT

[the ratings]

THE PRODUCERS OF BEAUJOLAIS

✶ ✶ ✶ ✶ ✶ (OUTSTANDING)

Jean-Marc Burgaud (Villié-Morgon)
Clos de la Roilette (Fleurie)
Bernard Diochon (Romanèche-Thorins)
Jean Foillard (Villié-Morgon)
Jean-Claude Lapalu (St.-Étienne-la-
    Varenne/Brouilly)

Marcel Lapierre (Villié-Morgon)
Yvon Métras (Fleurie)
Domaine du Vissoux—Pierre Chermette
    (St.-Véran)*

✶ ✶ ✶ ✶ (EXCELLENT)

Nicole Chanrion—Domaine de la Voute
    des Croze (Cercié/Côte de Brouilly)
Domaine Cheysson (Chiroubles)

Michel Chignard (Fleurie)
Louis-Claude Desvignes
    (Villié-Morgon)

*These estates also bottle excellent and distinctive Beaujolais Blanc or Bourgogne Blanc from the southern portion of this region.

Georges Duboeuf (*négociant*, Romanèche-Thorins)*

Château des Jacques—Louis Jadot (Romanèche-Thorins)

Eric Janin (Romanèche-Thorins)

Château des Lumières—Louis Jadot (Villié-Morgon)

Potel-Aviron—Nicolas Potel (*négociant*, Chapelle de Guinchay)

Domaine des Terres Dorées—Jean-Paul Brun (Charnay)*

Michel Tête—Domaine de Clos du Fief (Juliénas)

Château Thivin (Odenas/Brcuilly)

* * * (VERY GOOD)

Daniel Bouland (Villié-Morgon)

Guy Breton (Villié-Morgon)

Domaine des Champs-Grillés (St.-Amour)

Hubert Lapierre (La Chapelle-de-Guinchay/Chénas)

Pavillon de Chavannes—Paul Jambon (Quincie/Brouilly)

Dominique Piron (Villié-Morgon)

Jean-Paul Thevenet (Villié-Morgon)

M. J. Vincent et Fils—Château de Fuissé (Mâcon)

* * (GOOD)

Bertrand et Anke de Boissieu—Château de Lavernette

Jean-Marie Burgaud (Régnié)

Domaine Calot (Villié-Morgon)

Damien Dupeuble (Le Breuil)

Domaine du Granit—Gino Bertolla (Romanèche-Thorins)

Domaine de la Madone (Le Perreon)

Laurent Martray (Odenas/Brcuilly)

Olivier Merlin—Domaine du Vieux St.-Sorlin (La Roche Vineuse/Mâcon)

Alain Michaud (Saint-Lager/Brouilly)

Domaine Joel Rochette (Régnié)

Jean-Paul Ruet (Cercié/Côte de Brouilly)

Georges Viornery (Odenas/Brouilly)

Note: In the grower profiles that follow, Beaujolais growers have been omitted for reasons of space.

[tasting commentaries]

BERTRAND AMBROISE * * * *
PRÉMEAUX-PRISSE $25.00–150.00

Bertrand Ambroise farms a wide, impressive range of appellations and vinifies with a fanatic dedication to low yields and the preservation of fruit quality, but also with no concessions to the faint of heart. His wines strike some tasters as hyperconcentrated and flirting with overextraction, whereas others enthusiastically adopt them as a benchmark. Ambroise works largely with 400-liter (106-gallon) barrels rather than standard 225-liter (60-gallon) *barriques*, diminishing the surface-to-volume ratio in an effort to moderate the flavoring effects of new oak, but the wines still tend to taste robustly woody. This address delivers impressive concentration even at the low end of its lineup.

2003 St.-Romain Blanc	89	now
2003 Ladoix Blanc Le Grechon	92	now–2012
2002 Ladoix Blanc Le Grechon	90	now–2013
2000 Ladoix Blanc Le Grechon	90–91	now
2003 Corton-Charlemagne	92	now–2012
2002 Corton-Charlemagne	93–95	now–2016
2001 Corton-Charlemagne	94	now–2011
2000 Corton-Charlemagne	92–94	now–2012

1999 Corton-Charlemagne	90–91	now–2012
2005 Bourgogne	88	now–2010
2005 Bourgogne Vieilles Vignes	88–89	now–2012
2003 Bourgogne Vieilles Vignes	88–90	now–2010
2003 St.-Romain Rouge	88–89	now–2010
2001 Pommard Les Saussilles	88–89	now
2005 Beaune Perrières	90–91	2010–2015
2003 Beaune Perrières	90–92	now–2013
2002 Beaune Perrières	90	now–2011
2001 Beaune Perrières	90	now
2005 Côtes de Nuits-Villages	87–88	2010–2015
2003 Côtes de Nuits-Villages	87–89	now–2010
2002 Côtes de Nuits-Villages	89	now–2011
2002 Vougeot Les Crâs	90–92	now–2014
1999 Vougeot Les Crâs	90–93	now–2011
2005 Nuits-St.-Georges	88–89	2010–2015+?
2003 Nuits-St.-Georges	89–90	now–2013
2002 Nuits-St.-Georges	88–89	now–2010
2005 Nuits-St.-Georges Cuvée Vieilles Vignes	91–92	2012–2018+?
2003 Nuits-St.-Georges Cuvée Vieilles Vignes	90–92	now–2014
2002 Nuits-St.-Georges Cuvée Vieilles Vignes	89–90	now–2012
2001 Nuits-St.-Georges Cuvée Vieilles Vignes	88–90	now
2000 Nuits-St.-Georges Cuvée Vieilles Vignes	88	now
2005 Nuits-St.-Georges En Rue de Chaux	88–90	2012–2018+?
2003 Nuits-St.-Georges En Rue de Chaux	89–90	now–2013
1999 Nuits-St.-Georges En Rue de Chaux	89–90	now–2010
2005 Nuits-St.-Georges Clos des Argillières	92–93	2012–2020
2003 Nuits-St.-Georges Clos des Argillières	92–93	now–2014
2002 Nuits-St.-Georges Clos des Argillières	89–90	now–2012
1999 Nuits-St.-Georges Clos des Argillières	89–90	now
2005 Nuits-St.-Georges Aux Cras	90–91	2012–2020+?
2005 Nuits-St.-Georges Les Vaucrains	91–92	2012–2022+?
2003 Nuits-St.-Georges Les Vaucrains	90–92	now–2015
2002 Nuits-St.-Georges Les Vaucrains	90–92	now–2015
2001 Nuits-St.-Georges Les Vaucrains	90–91	now–2011
2000 Nuits-St.-Georges Les Vaucrains	89	now–2011
1999 Nuits-St.-Georges Les Vaucrains	91–93	now–2012
2003 Corton Le Rognet	91–93	2010–2018
2002 Corton Le Rognet	94–96	2009–2022
2001 Corton Le Rognet	88–91	now–2012
2000 Corton Le Rognet	93	now–2014
1999 Corton Le Rognet	94–97	now–2015
1996 Corton Le Rognet	93–95	now
2005 Clos de Vougeot	92–93	2012–2020+?
2003 Clos de Vougeot	93–94	now–2017
2002 Clos de Vougeot	91–92	now–2019
2001 Clos de Vougeot	86–89	now
2000 Clos de Vougeot	90	now–2011

GUY AMIOT ET FILS ★★★
CHASSAGNE-MONTRACHET $40.00–$1,500.00

Guy Amiot produces generally opulent, generous, rich wines from a remarkable collection of vines, although this is not the address at which to seek particular refinement or exceptional clarity. The red Chassagnes here are usually meaty and full of fruit but often a bit hard and rustic. Amiot is one of two owners of the remarkable premier cru Les Demoiselles, neighbor to Le Montrachet and Chevalier-Montrachet.

2002 St.-Aubin En Remilly	88	now
2002 Chassagne-Montrachet Clos St.-Jean	88	now
2000 Chassagne-Montrachet Clos St.-Jean	89–91	now–2010
2002 Chassagne-Montrachet Les Macherelles	89	now–2010
2002 Chassagne-Montrachet Les Champs Gains	89	now–2010
2002 Chassagne-Montrachet Les Vergers	91	now–2011
2000 Chassagne-Montrachet Les Vergers	88–89	now
1999 Chassagne-Montrachet Les Vergers	90	now
2002 Chassagne-Montrachet Les Caillerets	93	now–2014
2000 Chassagne-Montrachet Les Caillerets	89–91	now–2012
1999 Chassagne-Montrachet Les Caillerets	91	now–2010
2002 Chassagne-Montrachet Les Demoiselles	92	now–2013
1999 Chassagne-Montrachet Les Demoiselles	89	now
2002 Montrachet	94	now–2017
2000 Montrachet	90–92	now–2014
1999 Montrachet	94	now–2012

DOMAINE AMIOT-SERVELLE ★★★
CHAMBOLLE-MUSIGNY $60.00–$200.00

Christian Amiot crafts refined, texturally nuanced Pinots from Chambolle vineyards, including the premier crus Les Charmes, Les Amoureuses, and the seldom seen Derrière-la-Grange.

DOMAINE MARQUIS D'ANGERVILLE ★★★★
VOLNAY $35.00–$150.00

The late Jacques d'Angerville was one of Burgundy's pioneers in estate bottling, a tireless crusader for quality control, and a winegrower who bottled consistently refined, perfumed, texturally subtle, dramatically distinctive Pinot Noir from some of the best sites in Volnay, including his *monopole* Clos des Ducs. Jacques's son Guillaume and longtime wine-making collaborator and brother-in-law Renaud de Villette offered an apt tribute to the legacy of the recently deceased marquis not just with their outstanding 2005 collection but with their deliciously odds-beating 2004, when on top of the universal difficulties of that vintage they had to deal with the ravages of hail on Volnay. The Volnay labeled 1er Cru here is sourced from Mitans, Pitures, Les Anges, and young vines in the Clos des Ducs—in short, from both high-elevation and high-rent districts—and it tastes it.

2005 Bourgogne	87–88	now–2011
2005 Volnay	88–89	2010–2015
2005 Volnay Frémiets	88–89	2010–2015+?
2005 Volnay 1er Cru	91–92	now–2018
2005 Volnay Caillerets	92–93	2013–2022
2005 Volnay Champans	91–93	2013–2020+?
2003 Volnay Champans	89–90	now–2015

2002 Volnay Champans		87–89	now–2014
1999 Volnay Champans		88–90	now–2012
2005 Volnay Clos des Ducs		94–95	2013–2025
2003 Volnay Clos des Ducs		89–92	2011–2020
2002 Volnay Clos des Ducs		89–91	now–2018
2000 Volnay Clos des Ducs		89	now–2011
1999 Volnay Clos des Ducs		91–94	now–2012
1996 Volnay Clos des Ducs		92–94	now
2005 Volnay Taillepieds		93–94	2012–2022+?
2003 Volnay Taillepieds		91–93	2010–2020
2002 Volnay Taillepieds		90–91	now–2017
2000 Volnay Taillepieds		91	now
1999 Volnay Taillepieds		91–93	now–2012+?

ARLAUD PÈRE ET FILS ★★★
MOREY-ST.-DENIS $25.00–$250.00

The Arlauds seem wisely concerned to begin backing off on extraction and new wood, while not sacrificing the concentration that is generally a common denominator among their wines. The domaine has added numerous crus, though not huge total acreage, and built an impressive winery in the past several years. Cyprien Arlaud, who half a dozen years ago took the lead in vinification from his father, Hervé, has recently been joined by his younger brother Roman. Morey-St.-Denis Les Ruchots, just beneath the Grand Cru Clos de Tart, and ancient vines in Gevrey-Chambertin Les Combottes give two of the Arlauds' most consistently excellent wines. Would that there were more than a mere three barrels (ca. 75 cases) of their consistently standout Clos St.-Denis, which is plowed with a horse by Hervé's daughter, Bertille. At the opposite end of the scale in price and availability, their Bourgogne Roncevie, from old vines growing across the road from Champs-Chenys and the Grand Cru Mazoyères, is one of the world's consistently best Pinot Noir values.

2005 Bourgogne Roncevie	89	now–2012
2005 Chambolle-Musigny	89	now–2014
2005 Chambolle-Musigny Les Noirons	88–89	2010–2016
2005 Chambolle-Musigny Les Sentiers	89–90	now–2016
2005 Chambolle-Musigny Les Chatelots	91	now–2018+?
2005 Gevrey-Chambertin	89	now–2015
2005 Gevrey-Chambertin Les Combottes	91–92	2012–2020
2005 Morey–St.-Denis Cheseaux	88	now–2015+?
2005 Morey–St.-Denis Les Blanchards	89–90	now–2016
2005 Morey–St.-Denis Les Millandes	90	now–2016
2005 Morey–St.-Denis Les Ruchots	90–91	now–2018
2005 Charmes Chambertin	89–90	2010–2018+?
2005 Bonnes Mares	88–89	2012–2018+?
2005 Clos de la Roche	91–92	2012–2020
2005 Clos St.-Denis	92–93	2012–2022

DOMAINE DE L'ARLOT ★★★
PRÉMEAUX-PRISSE $30.00–$300.00

Jean-Pierre de Smet managed this estate from its 1987 purchase by the French insurance group AXA, then turned over the reins in 2006 to his young technical director, Olivier Leriche. The vineyard practices here are biodynamic and vinification often includes the stems, with a generally leisurely pace to the bottling. The best of these wines possess considerable depth but are never showy. The *monopole* Clos de l'Arlot is typically rather refined and floral for Nuits-St.-Georges, the Clos des Forêts St.-Georges (also a *monopole*) being meatier and larger framed. (Petit Arlot and Petit Plets are the second wines of these respective crus.) The white Clos de l'Arlot is florally and minerally complex and texturally nuanced. (Fruit from young vines is bottled as *villages* Nuits-St.-Georges Blanc.)

2002 Nuits-St.-Georges Blanc	87	now
2002 Nuits-St.-Georges Clos de l'Arlot Blanc	90	now–2013
2001 Nuits-St.-Georges Clos de l'Arlot Blanc	90	now
2005 Côte de Nuits Villages Clos du Chapeau	87	now–2012
2002 Côte de Nuits Villages Clos du Chapeau	88	now
2005 Nuits-St.-Georges Petit Arlot	87	now–2011
2005 Nuits-St.-Georges Petit Plets	86–88	now–2012
2005 Nuits-St.-Georges Clos de l'Arlot	89–90	now–2015
2002 Nuits-St.-Georges Clos de l'Arlot	90	now–2011
2001 Nuits-St.-Georges Clos de l'Arlot	89	now
2005 Nuits-St.-Georges Clos des Forêts St.-Georges	90–92	2012–2018
2002 Nuits-St.-Georges Clos des Forêts St.-Georges	91	now–2012
1999 Nuits-St.-Georges Clos des Forêts St.-Georges	89–92	now–2010
2005 Vosne-Romanée Les Suchots	90–92	now–2017
2002 Vosne-Romanée Les Suchots	90	now–2012+?
2000 Vosne-Romanée Les Suchots	89	now
2005 Romanée St.-Vivant	92–94	2010–2018+?
2003 Romanée St.-Vivant	92	now–2014
2002 Romanée St.-Vivant	91	now–2011
2000 Romanée St.-Vivant	93	now–2010
1999 Romanée St.-Vivant	89–91	now–2011

DOMAINE COMTE ARMAND—DOMAINE DES EPENEAUX ★★★★
POMMARD $40.00–$120.00

Young Benjamin Leroux took over in 1999 from Pascal Marchand, who made this estate's modern reputation, and the wines have never tasted better, nor been more ageworthy. The domaine, farmed biodynamically, has also continued to grow, through purchase and rental, beyond their famous 13-acre core property, the Clos des Epeneaux. The bottling labeled 1er Cru is effectively the second wine of the Clos des Epeneaux.

2005 Auxey-Duresses 1er Cru	89–91	2010–2014
2005 Volnay	89–91	2010–2015
2003 Volnay	87–89	now–2014
2005 Volnay Frémiets	90–92	2012–2018
2003 Volnay Frémiets	90–91	now–2016
2005 Pommard 1er Cru	89–91	now–2020
2005 Pommard Clos des Epeneaux	94–96	2012–2025
2003 Pommard Clos des Epeneaux	93–95	2010–2020
2001 Pommard Clos des Epeneaux	89–91	now
2000 Pommard Clos des Epeneaux	91	now–2012
1999 Pommard Clos des Epeneaux	89–91	now–2015
1996 Pommard Clos des Epeneaux	92	now–2010

DOMAINE ROBERT ARNOUX—PASCAL LACHAUX * * * *
VOSNE-ROMANÉE $30.00–$750.00

Pascal Lachaux, the late Robert Arnoux's son-in-law and a trained pharmacist, has been in charge here now for nearly two decades. He maintains low-yielding, impeccably manicured vines and crafts wines of great refinement, polish, and at times understatement. The family's Les Suchots and Romanée-St.-Vivant have long been icons, but the entire array of Nuits-St.-Georges and Vosne-Romanée vineyards here is formidable. Lachaux's 2006s are stunningly successful for the vintage.

2005 Chambolle-Musigny	89	now–2014
2002 Chambolle-Musigny	89	now–2012
2005 Nuits-St.-Georges	87	now–2012
2002 Nuits-St.-Georges	88	now–2011
2005 Nuits-St.-Georges Les Poisets	89	now–2015+?
2002 Nuits-St.-Georges Les Poisets	88–90	now–2012
1999 Nuits-St.-Georges Les Poisets	89	now
2005 Nuits-St.-Georges Les Procès	89	now–2015+?
2005 Nuits-St.-Georges Clos Des Corvées Pagets	90	now–2017
2002 Nuits-St.-Georges Clos Des Corvées Pagets	91	now–2015
2001 Nuits-St.-Georges Clos Des Corvées Pagets	90–93	now–2013
2000 Nuits-St.-Georges Clos Des Corvées Pagets	88	now
1999 Nuits-St.-Georges Clos Des Corvées Pagets	89	now–2010
2005 Vosne-Romanée	88	now–2013
2002 Vosne-Romanée	88	now–2011
2001 Vosne-Romanée	87–89	now
2005 Vosne-Romanée Les Hautes Maizières	89	now–2015
2002 Vosne-Romanée Les Hautes Maizières	89	now–2012
1999 Vosne-Romanée Les Hautes Maizières	89	now
2005 Vosne-Romanée Les Chaumes	90	now–2017
2003 Vosne-Romanée Les Chaumes	90	now–2015
2002 Vosne-Romanée Les Chaumes	90–92	now–2014
2001 Vosne-Romanée Les Chaumes	89–90	now–2010
2000 Vosne-Romanée Les Chaumes	89	now
1999 Vosne-Romanée Les Chaumes	90	now–2012
2005 Vosne-Romanée Aux Reignots	90	now–2018
2002 Vosne-Romanée Aux Reignots	94	now–2011
2001 Vosne-Romanée Aux Reignots	89–91	now–2018
2000 Vosne-Romanée Aux Reignots	92	now
1999 Vosne-Romanée Aux Reignots	92	now–2012
1998 Vosne-Romanée Aux Reignots	90	now
2005 Vosne-Romanée Les Suchots	92	now–2022
2003 Vosne-Romanée Les Suchots	93	now–2020
2002 Vosne-Romanée Les Suchots	94	now–2017
2001 Vosne-Romanée Les Suchots	89–91	now–2012
2000 Vosne-Romanée Les Suchots	90	now–2011
1999 Vosne-Romanée Les Suchots	93	now–2015
1996 Vosne-Romanée Les Suchots	91–93	now–2010
2005 Clos de Vougeot	89	2012–2020+?
2003 Clos de Vougeot	95	now–2020
2002 Clos de Vougeot	95	now–2020
2001 Clos de Vougeot	86–88	now–2020

1999 Clos de Vougeot	94	now–2020
1998 Clos de Vougeot	91	now–2020
2005 Echézeaux	91	20⁻3–2020
2002 Echézeaux	94	now–2017
2000 Echézeaux	91	now–2012
1999 Echézeaux	91	now–2015
1996 Echézeaux	90–92	now
2005 Romanée St.-Vivant	94	now–2025
2002 Romanée St.-Vivant	95	now–2018
2001 Romanée St.-Vivant	90–93	now–2015
2000 Romanée St.-Vivant	93	now–2010
1999 Romanée St.-Vivant	91	now–2015
1998 Romanée St.-Vivant	93	now–2010
1996 Romanée St.-Vivant	93–96	now–2012
1993 Romanée St.-Vivant	94	now–2010

DOMAINE D'AUVENAY-LEROY * * * * *
ST.-ROMAIN $100.00–$2,500.00+

This private domaine of Madame Lalou Bize-Leroy is run by her along the same rigorous, meticulous lines as Domaine Leroy: biodynamic viticulture, very low yields, a risk-taking harvest strategy, and cautious, thoughtful vinification. The results include some of the richest, most complex, most ageworthy of the white Burgundies. They can also, as in 2006, be supremely elegant.

2003 Auxey-Duresses Blanc	91	now–2013
2002 Auxey-Duresses Blanc	94	now–2015
2001 Auxey-Duresses Blanc	91	now–2010
2002 Auxey-Duresses Blanc Les Boutonniers	93	now–2019
2001 Auxey-Duresses Blanc Les Boutonniers	92	now–2010
2000 Meursault Chaumes des Perrières	89–90	now
2000 Meursault Pré de Manche	89–90	now
2003 Meursault Les Narvaux	91	now–2012
2002 Meursault Les Narvaux	93	now–2014
2001 Meursault Les Narvaux	93	now–2012
2000 Meursault Les Narvaux	90–92	now–2012
1999 Meursault Les Narvaux	90	now
1997 Meursault Les Narvaux	92	now
1996 Meursault Les Narvaux	96	now–2015+?
2003 Meursault Les Gouttes d'Or	91	now–2014
2002 Meursault Les Gouttes d'Or	91	now–2016
2001 Meursault Les Gouttes d'Or	91	now–2010
2000 Meursault Les Gouttes d'Or	92–93	now–2013
1999 Meursault Les Gouttes d'Or	91	now–2010
1997 Meursault Les Gouttes d'Or	93	now
1996 Meursault Les Gouttes d'Or	94	now–2014
2003 Puligny-Montrachet La Richarde	93	now–2014
2002 Puligny-Montrachet La Richarde	90	now–2014
2001 Puligny-Montrachet La Richarde	89	now
2000 Puligny-Montrachet La Richarde	90–92	now–2011
1999 Puligny-Montrachet La Richarde	89	now
2003 Puligny-Montrachet Les Folatières	89	now–2013

2002 Puligny-Montrachet Les Folatières	91	now–2014
2001 Puligny-Montrachet Les Folatières	92	now–2010
2000 Puligny-Montrachet Les Folatières	90–91	now–2011
1999 Puligny-Montrachet Les Folatières	90	now
1996 Puligny-Montrachet Les Folatières	95	now–2015
2003 Criots-Bâtard-Montrachet	88	now–2012
2002 Criots-Bâtard-Montrachet	95	now–2018
2001 Criots-Bâtard-Montrachet	96	now–2014
2000 Criots-Bâtard-Montrachet	92–94	now–2012
1999 Criots-Bâtard-Montrachet	93	now–2011
2003 Chevalier-Montrachet	94	now–2015
2002 Chevalier-Montrachet	99	now–2020
2001 Chevalier-Montrachet	93	now–2014
2000 Chevalier-Montrachet	91–92	now–2014
1999 Chevalier-Montrachet	93	now–2014
1996 Chevalier-Montrachet	98	now–2018
2003 Bonnes Mares	93	now–2015
2002 Bonnes Mares	93	now–2016
1999 Bonnes Mares	93	now–2015
1997 Bonnes Mares	94	now–2011
1996 Bonnes Mares	95	now–2015
2003 Mazis-Chambertin	92	now–2017
2002 Mazis-Chambertin	99	now–2020
1999 Mazis-Chambertin	95	now–2018
1997 Mazis-Chambertin	95	now–2014
1996 Mazis-Chambertin	97	now–2020

HERVÉ AZO * * *
CHABLIS $20.00–$40.00

The appellation Chablis and a small amount of premier cru Chablis of Brittany-born Hervé Azo were absorbed into Jean-Marc Brocard's huge company in 2005 but continue to be vinified so as to preserve their own identity, and offer excellent value and ageworthiness.

DENIS BACHELET * * * *
GEVREY-CHAMBERTIN $30.00–$175.00

Denis Bachelet was a very young man fresh from viticultural school when in 1982 he took control of the small inheritance around which his domaine subsequently took shape. The estate is still tiny (e.g., only 200 cases of Charmes) and Bachelet has remained focused on purity of fruit and restrained fermentation and *élevage,* resulting in some of the silkiest, most perfumed, most elegant renditions of Pinot from Gevrey *terroir.*

2005 Bourgogne	88	now–2012
2005 Côtes de Nuits-Villages	89–90	now–2015
2005 Gevrey-Chambertin Vieilles Vignes	91–92	2013–2020
2005 Gevrey-Chambertin Les Corbeaux	91–92	2012–2018
2005 Charmes-Chambertin Vieilles Vignes	96–97	2015–2025

DANIEL BARRAUD * * * *
VERGISSON/MÂCON $20.00–$40.00

Daniel and Martine Barraud bottle with striking consistency some of the finest wines in the Mâcon. Their meticulous diligence at every level, from the scrutiny of ripening grapes and strategizing of (generally late) harvest to slow, watchful maturation in small (largely new) barrels, makes this domaine exemplary. Old vines in great locations naturally also contribute to the level of quality here. Son Julien began with vintage 2006 vinifying a Mâcon-Chaintré of his own, which will supplement the estate's otherwise very small amount of acreage outside the Pouilly-Fuissé appellation. The Pouilly-Fuissé here is segregated by parcel, other than two complimentary sites blended as Alliance de Vergisson. Any suspicions that there must be a trade-off between lush, ripe fruit and clarity or minerality will be banished by those who taste at this address.

2002 Mâcon-Vergisson La Roche	91	now–2010
2002 St.-Véran En Crêches	91	now–2010
2001 St.-Véran En Crêches	90	now
2004 St.-Véran Les Pommards	87	now
2002 St.-Véran Les Pommards	87	now–2010
2001 St.-Véran Les Pommards	91	now
2000 St.-Véran Les Pommards	89–90	now
2004 Pouilly-Fuissé Alliance de Vergisson	88	now–2010
2003 Pouilly-Fuissé Alliance de Vergisson	88	now
2002 Pouilly-Fuissé Alliance de Vergisson	92	now–2011
2001 Pouilly-Fuissé Alliance de Vergisson	90	now
2004 Pouilly-Fuissé En France	89	now–2011
2002 Pouilly-Fuissé En France	92	now–2011
2004 Pouilly-Fuissé La Verchère Vieilles Vignes	87	now
2003 Pouilly-Fuissé La Verchère Vieilles Vignes	89	now
2002 Pouilly-Fuissé La Verchère Vieilles Vignes	93	now–2010
2001 Pouilly-Fuissé La Verchère Vieilles Vignes	92	now
2004 Pouilly-Fuissé La Roche	92	now–2013
2002 Pouilly-Fuissé La Roche	92	now–2012
2001 Pouilly-Fuissé La Roche	91	now
2000 Pouilly-Fuissé La Roche	90	now–2012
2004 Pouilly-Fuissé En Bulands Vieilles Vignes	90	now–2012
2003 Pouilly-Fuissé En Bulands Vieilles Vignes	89	now
2002 Pouilly-Fuissé En Bulands Vieilles Vignes	94	now–2014
2001 Pouilly-Fuissé En Bulands Vieilles Vignes	92	now–2012
2000 Pouilly-Fuissé En Bulands Vieilles Vignes	92–94	now–2014
2004 Pouilly-Fuissé Les Crays Vieilles Vignes	89	now–2011
2002 Pouilly-Fuissé Les Crays Vieilles Vignes	93	now–2011
2001 Pouilly-Fuissé Les Crays Vieilles Vignes	93	now–2013
2000 Pouilly-Fuissé Les Crays Vieilles Vignes	92	now–2012
1999 Pouilly-Fuissé Les Crays Vieilles Vignes	91	now

GHISLAINE BARTHOD * * * *
CHAMBOLLE-MUSIGNY $35.00–$150.00

Sharing expanded wine-making facilities with her husband, Louis Boillot, Ghislaine Barthod continues to render some of the purest, most expressively fruity and consistently excellent as well as ageworthy Pinots in Burgundy. She farms exclusively Chambolle *terroir*.

2005 Bourgogne	88–89	now–2010
2005 Chambolle-Musigny	90–91	now–2014
2003 Chambolle-Musigny	89	now–2010
2002 Chambolle-Musigny	88–89	now–2011
2005 Chambolle-Musigny Aux Combottes	90–91	now–2014

2005 Chambolle-Musigny Les Chatelots	92–93	now–2016
2003 Chambolle-Musigny Les Chatelots	88	now–2012
2002 Chambolle-Musigny Les Chatelots	89–91	now–2011
2001 Chambolle-Musigny Les Chatelots	87–89	now
1999 Chambolle-Musigny Les Chatelots	88–90	now
2005 Chambolle-Musigny Les Baudes	91–92	now–2015
2003 Chambolle-Musigny Les Baudes	90	now–2015
2002 Chambolle-Musigny Les Baudes	90–92	now–2015
2001 Chambolle-Musigny Les Baudes	87–88	now
1999 Chambolle-Musigny Les Baudes	89–90	now–2010
2005 Chambolle-Musigny Aux Beaux Bruns	89–90	now–2015
2003 Chambolle-Musigny Aux Beaux Bruns	89	now–2014
2002 Chambolle-Musigny Aux Beaux Bruns	92–94	now–2016
2001 Chambolle-Musigny Aux Beaux Bruns	90–92	now–2013
1999 Chambolle-Musigny Aux Beaux Bruns	90–92	now–2012
2005 Chambolle-Musigny Les Charmes	93–94	now–2018
2002 Chambolle-Musigny Les Charmes	93–95	now–2017
2001 Chambolle-Musigny Les Charmes	89–91	now
1999 Chambolle-Musigny Les Charmes	93–95	now–2014
2005 Chambolle-Musigny Les Fuées	93–94	2010–2019
2003 Chambolle-Musigny Les Fuées	88	2010–2013
2002 Chambolle-Musigny Les Fuées	91–93	2010–2016
2005 Chambolle-Musigny Les Véroilles	94–95	2010–2020
2003 Chambolle-Musigny Les Véroilles	90	2010–2016
2002 Chambolle-Musigny Les Véroilles	91–93	2010–2018
1999 Chambolle-Musigny Les Véroilles	88–90	2010–2012
2005 Chambolle-Musigny Les Cras	94–95	now–2020
2002 Chambolle-Musigny Les Cras	92–94	now–2018
1999 Chambolle-Musigny Les Cras	89–90	now–2010

PIERRE BERTHEAU * * *
CHAMBOLLE-MUSIGNY $70.00–$200.00

Pierre and François Bertheau render textbook Chambolle, not necessarily for pinotphiles who crave extroverted richness and certainly not for those seeking flamboyant use of wood. Their Chambolle-Musigny and Chambolle-Musigny 1er Cru are rotated between largely used *barriques* and large traditional *Fuder*. It is hard to imagine a clearer, more distinct set of personalities and Chambolle-typical elegance, florality, spice, sheer brightness, carnal mystery, and mineral depth than one encounters in the best wines at this address. If their 2005s are indicative of things to come, the Bertheaus' surprisingly little-recognized domaine will move up in this guide's ratings.

2005 Chambolle-Musigny	92	now–2015
2005 Chambolle-Musigny 1er Cru	94	now–2018
2005 Chambolle-Musigny Les Amoureuses	95	2012–2020
2005 Chambolle-Musigny Les Charmes	93	2010–2018
2005 Bonnes Mares	94	2010–2018+?

DOMAINE BILLAUD-SIMON ★★★
CHABLIS $22.00–$100.00

Samuel Billaud is crafting very precise, intense representations of some of the best sites in Chablis, improving in recent vintages by moving away from machine harvesting and giving the young wines the benefit of longer lees contact.

DOMAINE BITOUZET-PRIEUR ★★★
VOLNAY $40.00–$100.00

Vincent Bitouzet farms an enviable and probably unprecedented array of the best premier crus in both Volnay and Meursault. Fortunately, he does them justice. An unhurried *élevage,* with reds often not bottled for two years, no doubt plays a role in the richness, polish, and satisfying aging that characterize Bitouzet's wines.

DOMAINE SIMON BIZE ★★★
SAVIGNY-LES-BEAUNE $30.00–$250.00

Wines from this address seldom make concessions to early drinkability or cheap thrills, but for those who enjoy Pinot with an athletic leanness, layered complexity, and abundance of animal and mineral nuances, this is a great place. The few Bize whites are also full of stamina and interest, including a consistently striking Bourgogne Les Perrières from high above Savigny.

2005 Bourgogne Les Perrières	89	now–2011
2005 Savigny-les-Beaune Les Bourgeots	89	now–2014
2005 Savigny-les-Beaune Les Grands Liards	88	now–2014
2005 Aloxe-Corton Le Suchot	87	now–2012
2005 Savigny-les-Beaune Aux Serpentières	91	2010–2016
2005 Savigny-les-Beaune Les Marconnets	90	2012–2018
2005 Savigny-les-Beaune Les Fourneaux	88	now–2014+?
2005 Savigny-les-Beaune Aux Guettes	92	now–2016
2005 Savigny-les-Beaune Aux Vergelesses	93	2012–2018
2005 Latricières-Chambertin	91	2010–2018+?

JEAN-YVES BIZOT ★★★
VOSNE-ROMANÉE $80.00–$300.00

Jean-Yves Bizot, who was mentored by his famous neighbor Henri Jayer, emphasizes the tender, perfumed, gentle side of Pinot, occasionally perhaps too much so for the 100% new-oak regimen he employs. The wines are all hand-bottled, barrel by barrel (i.e., without assemblage), so be aware that each, including those rated below, represents a unique but not otherwise identified ca. 300-bottle lot. This gentle, old-fashioned approach to bottling conserves, among other elements, CO_2, permitting the use of only minimal amounts of sulfur. The wine bottled here each vintage simply as Vosne-Romanée 1er Cru is Echézeaux from parcels Bizot considers less desirable and so declassifies.

2005 Vosne-Romanée	88	now–2010+?
2005 Vosne-Romanée Vieilles Vignes	89	now–2012
2005 Vosne-Romanée Les Jachées	91	2010–2014+?
2005 Vosne-Romanée Les Réas	90	2010–2016
2005 Vosne-Romanée 1er Cru	92	2011–2018
2005 Echézeaux	93	2012–2018+?

DANIEL BOCQUENET   ★★★
NUITS-ST.-GEORGES $40.00–$150.00

Daniel Bocquenet is one of the Côte d'Or's free spirits, cultivating his sense of quality and personal integrity as carefully as his wicked sense of humor. All of his generally excellent basic Nuits-St.-Georges is sold off under a private label, leaving him to lavish low yields, lengthy fermentation, and 100% new wood on only three wines, each consistently rich and flamboyant even in difficult vintages. Bocquenet assembles his wines in the Bordeaux manner, culling out barrels he deems inferior, then blending the remainder in one large tank and bottling without filtration at whatever point (over a wide range in time) the wine manages to more or less clarify itself. His wines continue to offer consistent quality and value.

2005 Nuits-St.-Georges Aux St.-Julien	89–91	now–2015
2003 Nuits-St.-Georges Aux St.-Julien	90–92	now–2014
2002 Nuits-St.-Georges Aux St.-Julien	90–92	now–2014
1999 Nuits-St.-Georges Aux St.-Julien	88–90	now
2005 Vosne-Romanée La Croix Blanche	90–92	2010–2016
2003 Vosne-Romanée La Croix Blanche	90–92	now–2014
2002 Vosne-Romanée La Croix Blanche	87–88	now–2011
2005 Echézeaux	91–93	2011–2018+?
2003 Echézeaux	92–95	2012–2020
2002 Echézeaux	92–94	now–2016

MAISON HENRI BOILLOT—JEAN BOILLOT   ★★★★
MEURSAULT $40.00–$1,000.00+

In his capacity as *négociant* specializing in the whites of the Côte d'Or, Jean Boillot has quickly established a superb reputation. In the last several years he has added to this by securing contracts on fruit from a remarkable number of the most prestigious sites.

2002 Meursault	89	now
2001 Meursault	90	now
2003 Meursault Les Bouchères	87	now
2002 Meursault Les Bouchères	90	now
2001 Meursault Les Bouchères	91	now–2010
2002 Meursault Les Cras	92	now–2012
2001 Meursault Les Cras	92	now–2011
2000 Meursault Les Cras	93	now–2010
2002 Meursault Les Gouttes d'Or	91	now–2010
2001 Meursault Les Gouttes d'Or	91	now
2002 Meursault Poruzots	88	now
2001 Meursault Poruzots	92	now
2000 Meursault Poruzots	89	now
2003 Meursault Charmes	86	now
2002 Meursault Charmes	91–93	now–2011
2001 Meursault Charmes	94	now–2010
2000 Meursault Charmes	92	now–2012
2003 Meursault Les Genevrières	89	now–2011
2002 Meursault Les Genevrières	89	now
2001 Meursault Les Genevrières	90	now
2000 Meursault Les Genevrières	88–89	now
1999 Meursault Les Genevrières	90	now
1996 Meursault Les Genevrières	92	now
2002 Meursault Les Perrières	89–91	now–2010

2001 Meursault Les Perrières	94	now–2011
2000 Meursault Les Perrières	90–92	now–2012
2003 Puligny-Montrachet	88	now
2002 Puligny-Montrachet	89	now
2003 Puligny-Montrachet Les Folatières	89	now
2002 Puligny-Montrachet Les Folatières	92–93	now–2012
2001 Puligny-Montrachet Les Folatières	89	now
2000 Puligny-Montrachet Les Folatières	91–93	now–2012
1999 Puligny-Montrachet Les Folatières	91	now–2011
2003 Puligny-Montrachet Les Caillerets	87	now
2002 Puligny-Montrachet Les Caillerets	90–92	now–2012
2003 Chassagne-Montrachet	88	now
2002 Chassagne-Montrachet	88	now
2003 Chassagne-Montrachet Chenevottes	89	now
2001 Chassagne-Montrachet Clos St.-Jean	91	now
2003 Chassagne-Montrachet Les Chaumes	90	now
2002 Chassagne-Montrachet Les Chaumes	89	now
2001 Chassagne-Montrachet Les Chaumes	91	now–2010
2000 Chassagne-Montrachet Les Chaumes	90	now
2003 Chassagne-Montrachet Les Embrazées	90	now–2010
2002 Chassagne-Montrachet Les Embrazées	89	now
2001 Chassagne-Montrachet Les Embrazées	90	now
2003 Chassagne-Montrachet Les Macherelles	90	now–2011
2003 Chassagne-Montrachet Les Vergers	87	now
2003 Bienvenue Bâtard-Montrachet	89–90	now–2011
2001 Bienvenue Bâtard-Montrachet	95	now–2011
2003 Criots Bâtard-Montrachet	90–92	now–2013
2001 Criots Bâtard-Montrachet	89	now–2010
2003 Bâtard-Montrachet	90–92	now–2013
2002 Bâtard-Montrachet	94–95	now–2014
2001 Bâtard-Montrachet	93	now–2010
2000 Bâtard-Montrachet	93–95	now
2003 Chevalier-Montrachet	91–93	now–2014
2002 Chevalier-Montrachet	94–96	now–2016
2001 Chevalier-Montrachet	94	now–2014
2000 Chevalier-Montrachet	95–97	now–2016
1999 Chevalier-Montrachet	93	now–2012
1996 Chevalier-Montrachet	94	now–2010
2003 Montrachet	92–93	now–2015
2002 Montrachet	92–94	now–2014
2001 Montrachet	96	now–2016
2000 Montrachet	92–93	now–2013
1999 Montrachet	95	now–2014
2003 Corton-Charlemagne	91–93	now–2015
2002 Corton-Charlemagne	92–95	now–2015
2001 Corton-Charlemagne	96	now–2015
2000 Corton-Charlemagne	91–93	now–2012
1999 Corton-Charlemagne	91	now–2010

JEAN BOILLOT
★★★ (RED) ★★★★ (WHITE) VOLNAY $50.00–$150.00

Henri Boillot's meticulous, indeed fanatic, pursuit of quality both at his family domaine and in his work as a *négociant* of the new breed has already brought him to within hailing distance of the Côte d'Or's best producers. Boillot has been an enthusiastic supporter of a slightly larger than *barrique* barrel size, which he believes helps him work with a high percentage of new wood while avoiding an obvious oakiness of flavor and conserving freshness. His recent whites in fact always retain lift and liveliness, no matter how richly textured and layered.

2003 Savigny-les-Beaune Blanc Les Vergelesses	89	now–2010
2002 Meursault Les Genevrières	90–93	now–2011
2002 Puligny-Montrachet	89	now
2003 Puligny-Montrachet Clos de la Mouchère	87	now
2002 Puligny-Montrachet Clos de la Mouchère	91–94	now–2014
2001 Puligny-Montrachet Clos de la Mouchère	93	now–2010
2000 Puligny-Montrachet Clos de la Mouchère	94	now–2010+?
1996 Puligny-Montrachet Clos de la Mouchère	93	now–2010
2003 Puligny-Montrachet Les Perrières	88	now–2010
2002 Puligny-Montrachet Les Perrières	90–93	now–2013
2001 Puligny-Montrachet Les Perrières	91	now–2010
2000 Puligny-Montrachet Les Perrières	93	now–2012+?
1999 Puligny-Montrachet Les Perrières	92	now–2012
2003 Puligny-Montrachet Les Pucelles	90	now–2010
2002 Puligny-Montrachet Les Pucelles	89–91	now–2012
2001 Puligny-Montrachet Les Pucelles	93	now–2010
2000 Puligny-Montrachet Les Pucelles	92–95	now–2012+?
1999 Puligny-Montrachet Les Pucelles	91	now–2010
2002 Savigny-les-Beaune Les Lavières	87–89	now–2010
2002 Beaune Clos du Roi	86–88	now–2010
2003 Beaune Les Epenottes	89–90	now–2011
2002 Beaune Les Epenottes	87–88	now–2010
1999 Beaune Les Epenottes	91	now
2002 Volnay Les Chevrets	89–90	now–2011
2000 Volnay Les Chevrets	90	now
1999 Volnay Les Chevrets	90	now–2012
2002 Volnay Les Fremiets	90–92	now–2012
1999 Volnay Les Fremiets	93	now–2011
2003 Volnay Les Caillerets	88–90	now–2017
2002 Volnay Les Caillerets	92–95	now–2018
2001 Volnay Les Caillerets	88	now–2010
2000 Volnay Les Caillerets	94	now–2010+?
1999 Volnay Les Caillerets	92	now–2012

JEAN-MARC BOILLOT
★★★ (RED) ★★★★ (WHITE) POMMARD $50.00–$500.00

Jean-Marc Boillot, brother of Henri Boillot, excels with both Chardonnay and Pinot Noir. The core of his estate is a share of the superb Sauzet holdings, inherited through his mother, which he supplements by acting as a *négociant*, buying grapes from additional top-flight crus. Boillot believes in active lees contact for his whites, yet also favors Riesling-like transparency and mineral nuance. The result is often the best of two worlds.

2002 Meursault	89	now
2002 Puligny-Montrachet	90	now
2003 Puligny-Montrachet Champ Canet	89	now–2011
2002 Puligny-Montrachet Champ Canet	94	now–2013
2000 Puligny-Montrachet Champ Canet	89	now–2010
2002 Puligny-Montrachet La Garenne	91	now–2010
2000 Puligny-Montrachet La Garenne	91	now
2003 Puligny-Montrachet La Truffière	88	now–2010
2002 Puligny-Montrachet La Truffière	95	now–2016
2000 Puligny-Montrachet La Truffière	89	now–2011
1996 Puligny-Montrachet La Truffière	92	now
2002 Puligny-Montrachet Les Referts	92	now–2012
2000 Puligny-Montrachet Les Pucelles	91	now–2010
2003 Puligny-Montrachet Les Combettes	90	now–2011
2002 Puligny-Montrachet Les Combettes	95	now–2015
2000 Puligny-Montrachet Les Combettes	91	now–2011
1999 Puligny-Montrachet Les Combettes	90	now
1996 Puligny-Montrachet Les Combettes	93	now
2002 Bâtard-Montrachet	96	now–2015
1999 Volnay Clos Carelle Sous La Chapelle	87–89	now
1999 Volnay Ronceret	88–90	now–2011
2003 Pommard Jarollières	89–91	now–2018
1999 Pommard Jarollières	89–91	now–2011
1999 Pommard Rugiens	93–95	now–2012
1996 Pommard Rugiens	93–95	now

LOUIS BOILLOT ET FILS ∗ ∗ ∗
CHAMBOLLE-MUSIGNY $40.00–$150.00

Working from a facility adjacent to that of his wife, Ghislaine Barthod, Louis Boillot fields a large, geographically diverse, distinctively delicious range of pure-fruited Pinots.

2005 Bourgogne	89–90	now–2010
2005 Côtes de Nuits-Villages	89–90	now–2010
2005 Beaune Les Epenotes	89–91	now–2012+?
2005 Pommard	88–90	now–2012+?
2005 Volnay	90–92	now–2011+?
2005 Chambolle-Musigny Les Beaux Bruns	88–90	now–2013
2005 Gevrey-Chambertin	88–90	now–2012
2005 Volnay Les Anges	89–91	now–2015
2005 Volnay Les Brouillards	87–89	now–2012+?
2005 Volnay Les Caillerets	90–92	now–2015
2005 Pommard Fremiers	91–93	now–2015
2005 Pommard Les Croix Noires	90–92	now–2015
2005 Gevrey-Chambertin Les Champonnet	89–91	now–2014
2005 Gevrey-Chambertin Les Cherbaudes	92–94	now–2017+?
2005 Gevrey-Chambertin Les Evocelles	91–93	now–2017
2005 Nuits-St.-Georges Les Pruliers	92–94	now–2017+?

LUCIEN BOILLOT ET FILS ★ ★ ★ ★
GEVREY-CHAMBERTIN $35.00–$140.00

Lucien Boillot inherited an impressive set of vineyards, to which he added before passing the baton to his meticulous and ambitious son, Pierre. Among the standouts in the collection of nuanced and complex wines at this address—many from vines of 60–100 years' age—are Gevrey-Chambertin Les Cherbaudes, Nuits-St.-Georges Les Prûliers, Pommard Les Croix Noires, Volnay Caillerets, and the sole white, Puligny-Montrachet Les Perrières.

DOMAINE DE BONGRAN—JEAN THÉVENET ★ ★ ★ ★
QUINTAINE/MÂCON $30.00–$100.00

Prior to the labors of Jean Thévenet, both the styles and the sheer quality of Mâcon that he bottles were unimaginable. Late harvests from low-yielding vines make for Chardonnay fruit from the vineyards of Clessé that displays opulence, high natural sugar, and unique spiciness. Subjecting such rich raw materials to unhurried fermentations with ambient yeasts, Thévenet was frequently left with a hint of residual sugar, on account of which his wines were sometimes declassified by the legal authorities. Moreover, he welcomed botrytis and began vinifying extraordinary nobly sweet cuvées as well. All of this, Thévenet insists, is traditional—but a tradition that had long been forgotten. When the appellation Viré-Clessé was minted in 1997, Thévenet's wines, far and away the finest ever produced in this sector, were explicitly excluded, so he began selling them merely as Mâcon-Villages. (A decade later, the legal watchdogs rescinded their decision.) The Cuvée Tradition bottling from this domaine is released only three years after the vintage, the nobly sweet wines (in years when one of two cuvées is essayed) even later. Jean's son Gautier is now active here and at the sister estate, Domaine Emilian Gillet in Viré, and has in addition taken over the nearby Domaine de Roally in Viré, crafting there distinctive wines that offer good value.

2004 Mâcon-Villages Cuvée Tradition	89–91	now–2012
2003 Mâcon-Villages Cuvée Tradition	91–93	now–2014
2002 Mâcon-Villages Cuvée Tradition	91	now–2012
2001 Mâcon-Villages Cuvée Tradition	91	now
2000 Mâcon-Villages Cuvée Tradition	92	now–2010
2003 Mâcon-Villages Cuvée Botrytis	93	now–2019
1999 Mâcon-Villages Cuvée Levroutée	91–93	now–2012

DOMAINE BONNEAU DU MARTRAY
★ ★ ★ (RED) ★ ★ ★ ★ ★ (WHITE) PERNAND-VERGELESSES $75.00–$175.00

This exceptional domaine run since 1994 by Jean-Charles Le Bault de la Morinière consists of a single large west-facing expanse of the grand cru–rated hill of Corton, mostly Chardonnay with a small block of Pinot. His ideal is long-keeping wines of great clarity and precision. In numerous respects de la Morinière has further refined the already striking style and superb quality of the wines bottled under his father, Jean. No detail is too small to be taken on faith or escape scrutiny at this address, whether it is an exploration of differences in *terroir* and genetic heritage between parcels or the precise timing of interventions in the evolution of young wines. The white spends at most one year in barrels (only a modest share of them new), then continues its evolution (still on its fine lees) in stainless steel. As impressive as is young Bonneau du Martray Corton-Charlemagne, it is only with bottle age that these wines reveal their full depth of flavor.

2003 Corton-Charlemagne	90–93	now–2014
2002 Corton-Charlemagne	92	now–2016
2001 Corton-Charlemagne	91	now–2014

2000 Corton-Charlemagne	94	now–2016
1999 Corton-Charlemagne	91–92	now–2012
1998 Corton-Charlemagne	91	now–2010
1997 Corton-Charlemagne	89	now
1996 Corton-Charlemagne	92	now–2012
1995 Corton-Charlemagne	93	now–2010
2003 Corton	90–92	now–2016
2001 Corton	90	now–2014
2000 Corton	88	now–2012
1999 Corton	87–89	now–2012

BOUCHARD PÈRE ET FILS
* * * (RED) * * * * (WHITE) *NÉGOCIANT*, BEAUNE $20.00–$1,000.00+

Since the purchase of this venerable Beaune institution by Henriot in 1995, Bouchard Père et Fils (not to be confused with the *négociant* house Bouchard Aîné et Fils) is being pulled to the forefront of Burgundy quality by director Stéphane Follin-Arbelet (before him, Bernard Hervet) and winemaker Philippe Prost. A gargantuan new gravity-fed winemaking facility is capable of handling the fruits of Bouchard's equally awe-inspiring 130 hectares (320 acres) of vines (Burgundy's largest estate, with 84 hectares, or 210 acres, in premier and grand crus alone), not to mention the enormous range of wine from purchased fruit or wines. Their building must house the world's largest collection of simultaneous vinifications and single-vineyard cuvées, if not also the largest sheer number of *barriques*. Fully 40% of the reds are vinified in open-top fermentors with manual punch-downs (the balance in a battery of rotofermentors), and the system of traffic control alone that must be in place during the crush is hard to imagine. Highlights of Bouchard's vineyards and bottlings include their flagship Beaune Grèves Vigne de l'Enfant Jésus; their *monopole* Beaune Clos de la Mousse; their extended acreage of white Beaune; their outstanding parcels in Volnay, Vosne-Romanée, and Gevrey-Chambertin; and their exceptional holdings in Meursault, Puligny, and Chassagne, including enough Chevalier-Montrachet to justify two separate bottlings. (Until 2002, Bouchard vinified the Liger-Belair *monopole* Grand Cru La Romanée, whose vinification has since reverted to that family.)

2003 Aloxe Corton	88	now–2012
2002 Savigny-les-Beaune Les Lavières	88–89	now–2011
2005 Beaune Les Teurons	88	now–2013
2005 Beaune Clos de la Mousse	87	now–2012
2002 Beaune Les Marconnets	89–91	now–2011
2005 Beaune Grèves Vigne de l'Enfant Jésus	90	now–2016
2002 Beaune Grèves Vigne de l'Enfant Jésus	86–88	now–2011
2005 Volnay Caillerets Ancienne Cuvée Carnot	89	now–2015
2005 Volnay Clos des Chenes	90	now–2016
2002 Volnay Clos des Chenes	86–88	now–2014
2002 Volnay Frémiets	89–90	now–2011
2002 Pommard	87–88	now
2005 Pommard Pézerolles	87–89	now–2015
2002 Pommard Pézerolles	90–92	now–2014
2005 Pommard Rugiens	88–90	now–2017
2002 Pommard Rugiens	90–92	now–2016
2005 Corton	87–89	now–2014+?
2002 Corton	90–93	now–2015
2002 Chambolle-Musigny	87–88	now–2011

2002 Chambolle-Musigny—Domaine Bouchard	88–90	now–2011
2005 Nuits-St.-Georges Domaine du Clos St.-Marc	87	now–2012+?
2005 Nuits-St.-Georges Les Cailles	89	now–2017
2002 Nuits-St.-Georges Les Cailles	88	now–2013
2002 Nuits-St.-Georges Les Porrets St.-Georges	89	now–2014
2005 Gevrey-Chambertin Les Cazetiers	89	now–2016+?
2002 Gevrey-Chambertin Les Cazetiers	90	now–2014
1999 Gevrey-Chambertin Les Cazetiers	90	now
2005 Vosne-Romanée Les Suchots	91	now–2018
2005 Vosne-Romanée Les Malconsorts	90	now–2016+?
2002 Vosne-Romanée Aux Reignots	94	now–2018
2005 Echézeaux	88	now–2016+?
2002 Echézeaux	89	now–2014
2000 Echézeaux	88	now
2005 Clos Vougeot	89–91	now–2015+?
2005 Clos Vougeot—Domaine Bouchard	90–92	now–2018
2002 Clos Vougeot—Domaine Bouchard	89	now–2015
2002 La Romanée	97	now–2020
2000 La Romanée	90	now–2012
1999 La Romanée	92	now–2012
1997 La Romanée	94–96	now–2010
2005 Bonnes Mares	90–92	now–2020
2005 Chapelle-Chambertin	90–92	now–2018
2002 Charmes-Chambertin	92	now–2015
2005 Chambertin Clos de Bèze	92–94	now–2020
2002 Chambertin Clos de Bèze	94	now–2018
1999 Chambertin Clos de Bèze	92	now–2012
1997 Chambertin Clos de Bèze	93–95	now–2010
2002 Beaune du Château Blanc	87–88	now
2003 Meursault Les Clous	87	now
2002 Meursault Les Charmes	87–89	now–2010
2002 Meursault Genevrières	86–88	now
1997 Meursault Les Perrières	91–92	now
2003 Puligny-Montrachet	89	now
2002 Puligny-Montrachet Les Chalumeaux	89–91	now–2010
2002 Puligny-Montrachet Champ Gains	87–88	now
2002 Puligny-Montrachet Les Folatières	88–90	now–2011
2000 Puligny-Montrachet Les Pucelles	87–89	now
2002 Bâtard-Montrachet	92–94	now–2012
2001 Bâtard-Montrachet	87–88	now
2003 Chevalier-Montrachet	87	now–2010
2002 Chevalier-Montrachet	88–90	now–2012
2001 Chevalier-Montrachet	88–89	now
2000 Chevalier-Montrachet	87–89	now
1999 Chevalier-Montrachet	90–92	now–2010
1996 Chevalier-Montrachet	92–94	now–2010
2003 Chevalier-Montrachet La Cabotte	91	now–2015
2002 Chevalier-Montrachet La Cabotte	93–94	now–2015
2001 Chevalier-Montrachet La Cabotte	88–90	now–2010
2000 Chevalier-Montrachet La Cabotte	91–93	now–2012
1999 Chevalier-Montrachet La Cabotte	91–94	now–2012

1998 Chevalier-Montrachet La Cabotte	90–93	now–2010
1997 Chevalier-Montrachet La Cabotte	93–95	now
2003 Montrachet	90	now–2014
2002 Montrachet	92–94	now–2015
2001 Montrachet	89–91	now–2012
2000 Montrachet	91–92	now–2012
1999 Montrachet	91–93	now–2013
1998 Montrachet	90–93	now–2010
1997 Montrachet	94–96	now–2012
1996 Montrachet	92–95	now–2012

BRET BROTHERS/LA SOUFRANDIÈRE ✶ ✶ ✶
VINZELLES/MÂCON $20.00–$50.00

Bottling both as *négociants* and under their estate name La Soufrandière. young Jean-Guillaume and Jean-Philippe Bret are partisans of low yields and biodynamic cultivation who craft from an outstanding collection of largely old vines some of the more delicious and interesting wines in the Mâcon. The best is surely yet to come from this disciplined, dynamic, risk-friendly duo.

JEAN-MARC BROCARD ✶ ✶ ✶ ✶
CHABLIS $20.00–$100.00

Jean-Marc Brocard built up his domaine, and later his *négociant* business, beginning in the mid-1970s until they became the largest as well as among the best in Chablis. His son Julien and young, opinionated Québécois cellarmaster Patrick Piuze are promising to push the envelope on quality, which, along with a sheer detail-consciousness at every level, is already remarkably high for such a staggeringly large range of wines, including labels from various family estates that have either been absorbed into Domaine Brocard or whose wines are vinified under the supervision of the Brocard team. Purity of fruit and immediate appeal (not that these wines cannot age well) are among the stated goals. Vinification is in stainless steel.

DOMAINE BUISSON-CHARLES—MICHEL BUISSON ✶ ✶ ✶ ✶
MEURSAULT $40.00–$70.00

The estate of Michel Buisson, whose son-in-law Patrick Essa now takes the lead, has to be one of the finest domaines in Burgundy that few wine lovers have ever heard of. These are white Burgundies for the Riesling or Chenin lover, offering clarity, refreshment, and minerality yet not stinting on richness or structure, and whose track record in the cellar is among the best of any Chardonnay-based wines in the world. Largely old barrels, passive lees contact (i.e., no stirring), and unhurried bottling figure in the Buisson regimen. Although production—particularly of the single-vineyard Meursaults Tesson, Charmes, Les Bouchères, and Gouttes d'Or—is very small, some new acreage will come online (along with a completely renovated cellar) beginning in 2008.

DOMAINE DE LA CADETTE ✶ ✶ ✶
VÉZELAY/YONNE $15.00–$20.00

Jean Montanet is one of several growers whose ambitions and talents were incubated in the grower cooperative Henry de Vézelay (in fact, he was among its founding members) and who then struck out on his own. He is now well ahead of the pack in Vézelay, bottling Chablis-like Chardonnay that demonstrates why the slopes around this town were once so famous for their wine. The Pinot here shows promise as well. The vineyards are farmed along biodynamic principles, complemented by "back to the future" vinification. The estate's two whites (the lesser of which is bottled merely as Bourgogne rather than Bourgogne Vézelay) represent two of the very best values in all Burgundy.

DOMAINE LOUIS CARILLON   ✴ ✴ ✴
PULIGNY-MONTRACHET $50.00–$200.00

Jacques Carillon has been turning out reliably rich representations of his appellations for more than 20 years.

2003 Puligny-Montrachet	86–88	now
2003 Puligny-Montrachet	86–87	now
2003 Puligny-Montrachet Champs Canet	87–89	now–2010
2002 Puligny-Montrachet Champs Canet	87–88	now
2003 Puligny-Montrachet Les Perrières	88–89	now–2010
2003 Puligny-Montrachet Les Perrières	88–89	now–2011
2003 Puligny-Montrachet Les Referts	90–91	now–2011
2002 Puligny-Montrachet Les Referts	88–89	now–2012
2001 Puligny-Montrachet Les Referts	90–92	now
2000 Puligny-Montrachet Les Referts	89–90	now–2010
1999 Puligny-Montrachet Les Referts	89–91	now
2003 Puligny-Montrachet Les Combettes	88–90	now–2010
2001 Puligny-Montrachet Les Combettes	87–88	now
2003 Bienvenues-Bâtard Montrachet	89–91	now–2012
2002 Bienvenues-Bâtard Montrachet	90–92	now–2011
2001 Bienvenues-Bâtard Montrachet	91–92	now–2012
2000 Bienvenues-Bâtard Montrachet	91–93	now–2010

SYLVAIN CATHIARD   ✴ ✴ ✴
VOSNE-ROMANÉE $45.00–$550.00

Sylvain Cathiard emerged in the late 1980s as an estate bottler, notably of wine from the crus of Orveaux, Reignots, and Malconsorts. He has significantly expanded his acreage over the last decade while continuing to render wines of consistent clarity and fascination.

2005 Chambolle-Musigny Les Clos de l'Orme	90–91	now–2012
2005 Nuits St.-Georges Aux Murgers	92–93	now–2018
2005 Vosne-Romanée	89–90	now–2010
2005 Vosne-Romanée Aux Malconsorts	92–93	now–2016
2005 Vosne-Romanée En Orveaux	89–90	now–2018
2005 Vosne-Romanée Aux Reignots	90–91	now–2018
2005 Vosne-Romanée Les Suchots	91–92	now–2018
2005 Romanée-St.-Vivant	93–94	now–2022

PHILIPPE CHARLOPIN—CHARLOPIN-PARIZOT   ✴ ✴ ✴
GEVREY-CHAMBERTIN $50.00–$500.00

A proponent of late harvesting, early bottling, and preservation of sweet fruit and velvety texture, Philippe Charlopin built up his domaine of more than two dozen appellations over the past two decades in a bootstrapping manner that would be difficult to emulate in Burgundy at today's land prices. He recently began vinifying a range of Chablis.

2003 Bourgogne Cuvée Prestige	88	now–2010
2003 Fixin Clos de Fixey	88	now–2010
2003 Vosne-Romanée	88	now–2011
2003 Gevrey-Chambertin Clos de la Justice	91	now–2010

2003 Charmes-Chambertin	95	ncw–2014
1999 Charmes-Chambertin	93–95	ncw–2014
2003 Chambertin	91	2009–2018
1999 Chambertin	93–95	now–2015
1999 Echézeaux	91–92	now–2012
1999 Clos St.-Denis	92–94	now–2015
2003 Bonnes Mares	93	now–2017

HUBERT CHAUVENET–CHOPIN ★ ★ ★
PRÉMEAUX-PRISSEY $30.00–$175.00

Daniel Chopin was long the source of a tiny but outstanding trickle of Pinot. Hubert Chauvenet upholds his father-in-law's high standards, including the absence of pretension or vinous cosmetics. Even in difficult years like 2004, the Chaignots and Clos Vougeot here can be superb.

2005 Bourgogne	88	now–2011
2005 Côte de Nuits-Villages	88	now–2011
2005 Chambolle-Musigny	89–90	now–2012
2005 Nuits-St.-Georges	88–90	now–2012
2005 Nuits-St.-Georges Les Argillas	91–93	now–2018
2005 Nuits-St.-Georges Les Chaignots	92–94	now–2020
2005 Nuits-St.-Georges Les Murgers	90–92	now–2015
2005 Nuits-St.-Georges Aux Thorey	89–91	now–2014
1999 Nuits-St.-Georges Aux Thorey	89–91	now
2005 Clos Vougeot	91–93	now–2018
1999 Clos Vougeot	89–91	now–2010

DOMAINE COMTESSE BERNARD DE CHERISEY—
MARTELET DE CHERISEY ★ ★ ★ ★
BLAGNY $70.00–$100.00

Laurent and Hélène Martelet temporarily work, with genuinely ancient methods, out of a rudimentary cellar on the property of his aunt, one of the few residents of the hillside hamlet of Blagny. The two Puligny premier crus and Meursault-Blagny at this address are truly lacy in their intricacy of flavor, impossible to describe without resort to the word "mineral." The distinctive Blagny rouge is superb as well. This recently constituted tiny estate will not remain little known for long.

ROBERT CHEVILLON ★ ★ ★ ★ ★
NUITS-ST.-GEORGES $40.00–$150.00

Robert Chevillon and his sons Bertrand and Denis are in a class by themselves among the major Nuits-St.-Georges landholders for the diligence and determination with which they work their vineyards and the consistently excellent, ageworthy results they deliver, each cru retaining its distinct personality. Long fermentations and leisurely barrel evolution are de rigueur. Chevillon has never been one to follow fad or fashion. New wood is only sparingly employed, and not only are these wines routinely given a light filtration but one has the impression that the family has never seriously entertained the alternative, despite having long had Kermit Lynch, one of the world's strongest proponents of nonfiltration, as their importer. The rare trio of whites here (from three grapes, culminating in a Nuits-St.-Georges from mutant Pinot Noir) is also worth trying to track down.

| 2005 Nuits-St.-Georges Vieilles Vignes | 89–90 | now–2014 |
| 2005 Nuits-St.-Georges Les Chaignots | 92–93 | now–2018 |

2003 Nuits-St.-Georges Les Chaignots	89–90	now–2010
2002 Nuits-St.-Georges Les Chaignots	88–90	now–2012
1999 Nuits-St.-Georges Les Chaignots	89–91	now
2005 Nuits-St.-Georges Les Bousselots	91–92	2010–2018
2002 Nuits-St.-Georges Les Bousselots	88–90	2010–2013
1999 Nuits-St.-Georges Les Bousselots	89–90	now–2011
2003 Nuits-St.-Georges Les Perrières	93–95	now–2015
2002 Nuits-St.-Georges Les Perrières	91–93	now–2018
2001 Nuits-St.-Georges Les Perrières	87–88	now
1999 Nuits-St.-Georges Les Perrières	91–94	now–2012
2005 Nuits-St.-Georges Les Roncières	91–92	2010–2018
2002 Nuits-St.-Georges Les Roncières	90–92	now–2018
1999 Nuits-St.-Georges Les Roncières	88–90	now–2012
2005 Nuits-St.-Georges Les Pruliers	92–93	2010–2020
2002 Nuits-St.-Georges Les Pruliers	91–93	now–2018
2001 Nuits-St.-Georges Les Pruliers	88–90	now
1999 Nuits-St.-Georges Les Pruliers	90–93	now–2012
1996 Nuits-St.-Georges Les Pruliers	90–92	now
2005 Nuits-St.-Georges Les Cailles	93–94	2010–2022
2003 Nuits-St.-Georges Les Cailles	89–91	now–2014
2002 Nuits-St.-Georges Les Cailles	92–94	now–2019
2001 Nuits-St.-Georges Les Cailles	88–90	now
1999 Nuits-St.-Georges Les Cailles	92–95	now–2014
1996 Nuits-St.-Georges Les Cailles	91–94	now–2010
2005 Nuits-St.-Georges Les St.-Georges	95–96	2012–2025
2002 Nuits-St.-Georges Les St.-Georges	93–95	now–2022
2001 Nuits-St.-Georges Les St.-Georges	89–91	now
1999 Nuits-St.-Georges Les St.-Georges	90–92	now–2011
1996 Nuits-St.-Georges Les St.-Georges	92–94	now–2010
2005 Nuits-St.-Georges Les Vaucrains	94–95	2012–2025
2003 Nuits-St.-Georges Les Vaucrains	91–93	now–2015
2002 Nuits-St.-Georges Les Vaucrains	92–94	now–2020
2001 Nuits-St.-Georges Les Vaucrains	90–91	now–2010
2000 Nuits-St.-Georges Les Vaucrains	93	now
1999 Nuits-St.-Georges Les Vaucrains	91–93	now–2015
1996 Nuits-St.-Georges Les Vaucrains	91–94	now–2012

BRUNO CLAIR ★ ★ ★ ★
MARSANNAY $30.00–$275.00

Bruno Clair and his longtime cellarmaster Philippe Brun persist in rendering Pinots of uncompromising structure and acid retention that can often be short on youthful charm, a temporary deficiency accentuated by the particularly stony, high-elevation locations of some of his parcels in Gevrey, Chambolle, Vosne, and Morey. The core of this domaine consists of properties inherited through the former Clair-Dau estate, the balance of which was sold to Louis Jadot. The ancient vines in Savigny Dominode are among Burgundy's oldest. The resultant wine, like those Clair bottles from exceptional parcels in Gevrey-Chambertin, is characteristically profound and long-lived.

2001 Corton-Charlemagne	93–95	now–2010
2005 Savigny-les-Beaune La Dominode	91–93	2012–2022
2003 Savigny-les-Beaune La Dominode	88	now–2011

2001 Savigny-les-Beaune La Dominode	89–91	now–2011
2000 Savigny-les-Beaune La Dominode	89	now
1999 Savigny-les-Beaune La Dominode	89–91	now–2010
2005 Marsannay Les Longeroies	87–89	now–2010
2005 Chambolle-Musigny Les Véroilles	89–91	2010–2015
2005 Morey-St.-Denis En la Rue de Vergy	89–91	now–2015
2001 Morey-St.-Denis En la Rue de Vergy	90–91	now–2012
2005 Vosne-Romanée Les Champs Perdrix	90–92	2012–2018
2005 Gevrey-Chambertin	86–88	now–2012
2005 Gevrey-Chambertin Petite Chapelle	90–92	now–2018
2001 Gevrey-Chambertin Petite Chapelle	89–91	now–2011
1999 Gevrey-Chambertin Petite Chapelle	89–91	now
2005 Gevrey-Chambertin Clos du Fonteny	91–93	now–2018
2005 Gevrey-Chambertin Les Cazetiers	91–93	2012–2020
2003 Gevrey-Chambertin Les Cazetiers	89	now–2010
1999 Gevrey-Chambertin Les Cazetiers	87–88	now
2005 Gevrey-Chambertin Clos St.-Jacques	93–95	2012–2024+?
2003 Gevrey-Chambertin Clos St.-Jacques	89	now–2011
2001 Gevrey-Chambertin Clos St.-Jacques	88–90	now–2010
2000 Gevrey-Chambertin Clos St.-Jacques	92	now–2010
2005 Chambertin Clos de Bèze	94–96	2012–2024+?
2003 Chambertin Clos de Bèze	91	now–2013
2001 Chambertin Clos de Bèze	92	now–2012
1996 Chambertin Clos de Bèze	92–95	now

DOMAINE DU CLOS DE TART * * * * *
MOREY-ST.-DENIS $300.00

For more than a decade, this *monopole* of the *négociant* house Mommessin has delivered consistently grand as well as flamboyantly oaky results under the care of Sylvain Pithiot, also the man behind an exceptional series of topographical maps indispensable to serious students of Burgundy.

2005 Clos de Tart	94	now–2025
2003 Clos de Tart	94	2010–2025
2002 Clos de Tart	94–96	now–2018
2000 Clos de Tart	90	now
1999 Clos de Tart	93–95	now–2012
1996 Clos de Tart	91–94	now

DOMAINE DU CLOS DES LAMBRAY * * *
MOREY-ST.-DENIS $70.00–$200.00

Director Thierry Brouin is a partisan of fermenting *vendange entière* (with whole clusters and stems) and fearlessly extracts during fermentation to achieve Pinot of structure and longevity even if at the expense of early charm. Until 2006 (a year in which Brouin had exceptional success), Morey-St.-Denis Les Loups functioned in effect as the second wine of the estate, incorporating young vines and lesser lots of the Clos des Lambray, plus the fruit of two other small parcels.

2005 Morey-St.-Denis Les Loups	88–90	now–2014
2005 Clos de Lambray	91–93	2013–2020+?
2003 Clos de Lambray	92	2009–2020
2002 Clos de Lambray	90–92	now–2014

1999 Clos de Lambray	89–91	now–2013
1996 Clos de Lambray	92	now–2012

JEAN-FRANÇOIS COCHE-DURY ★ ★ ★ ★ ★
MEURSAULT $40.00–$3,000.00

Jean-François Coche-Dury has long been known as one of the handful of finest white wine growers on the planet. From this estate, even a wine of simple appellation Bourgogne (there happen to be one each from Pinot, Chardonnay, and Aligoté) reflects sensitive, meticulous work at all levels. The wines are never filtered. The top wines are frequently firm at first and mature magnificently. For 20 years, fellow winegrowers as well as wine professionals of every sort have craved Coche's audience and in return for their patience been educated and inspired.

2002 Bourgogne Blanc	89–90	now
2002 Meursault Clos de la Barre	89–91	now–2011
2002 Meursault Les Chaumes	89–91	now
2003 Meursault Les Narvaux	89–90	now–2012
2002 Meursault Les Narvaux	92–94	now–2012
2001 Meursault Les Narvaux	91–93	now–2012
2000 Meursault Les Narvaux	90–92	now
1999 Meursault Les Narvaux	88–90	now
2003 Meursault Vireuils Dessous	89–90	now–2010
2002 Meursault Vireuils Dessous	89–91	now–2011
2001 Meursault Vireuils Dessous	90–92	now–2011
2000 Meursault Vireuils Dessous	89–90	now–2011
2003 Meursault Caillerets	89–91	now–2012
2002 Meursault Caillerets	92–94	now–2014
2001 Meursault Caillerets	92–94	now–2013
2000 Meursault Caillerets	91–93	now–2011
2003 Meursault Genevrières	86–88	now
2002 Meursault Genevrières	90–92	now–2011
2001 Meursault Genevrières	92–94	now–2013
2000 Meursault Genevrières	92–93	now–2011
2003 Meursault Perrières	88–91	now–2014
2002 Meursault Perrières	95–97	now–2016
2001 Meursault Perrières	98–100	now–2017
2000 Meursault Perrières	95–97	now–2015
1999 Meursault Perrières	90–91	now
1996 Meursault Perrières	99	now–2010
2003 Puligny-Montrachet Les Enseignières	88–90	now–2010
2002 Puligny-Montrachet Les Enseignières	90–92	now–2012
2001 Puligny-Montrachet Les Enseignières	90–92	now
2000 Puligny-Montrachet Les Enseignières	90–92	now
2003 Corton Charlemagne	91–93	now–2015
2002 Corton Charlemagne	95–97	now–2016
2001 Corton Charlemagne	98–100	now–2015
2000 Corton Charlemagne	94–95	now–2015
1999 Corton Charlemagne	92–93	now–2012
1996 Corton Charlemagne	96–99	now–2010

BRUNO COLIN ★ ★ ★
CHASSAGNE-MONTRACHET $18–$70.00

The estate of Michel Colin was largely divided up between his sons in 2004 Bruno farms a bevy of excellent Chassagne premier crus as well as the family's precious morsel of Puligny La Truffière and will be supplementing his production with some purchased fruit. The early results are very satisfying.

DOMAINE MARC COLIN ET FILS ★ ★ ★
CHASSAGNE-MONTRACHET $40.00–$1,000.00+

Pierre-Yves Colin made the wines at this consistently fine address from 2001 until 2005. Marc Colin's three other children will now coordinate operations.

2003 St.-Aubin Le Charmois	88	now–2010
2002 St.-Aubin Le Charmois	89	now
2001 St.-Aubin Le Charmois	88	now
2002 St.-Aubin La Chatenière	91	now–2010
2001 St.-Aubin Les Combes	89	now
2003 St.-Aubin En Monceau	88	now
2002 St.-Aubin En Monceau	89	now
2003 St.-Aubin En Remilly	89	now–2011
2002 St.-Aubin En Remilly	90	now
2002 St.-Aubin Les Murgers des Dents de Chien	91	now–2010
2002 St.-Aubin Sentier du Clos	88	now
2002 St.-Aubin Sur Gamay	89	now
2002 Puligny-Montrachet Les Enseignières	89	now
2003 Puligny-Montrachet La Garenne	87	now
2002 Puligny-Montrachet La Garenne	90	now–2010
2001 Puligny-Montrachet La Garenne	88	now
2002 Puligny-Montrachet Le Trézin	88	now
2003 Chassagne-Montrachet Les Chenevottes	88	now
2002 Chassagne-Montrachet Les Enseignières	89	now
2002 Chassagne-Montrachet Vide-Bourses	90	now–2010
2001 Chassagne-Montrachet Vide-Bourses	91	now
2003 Chassagne-Montrachet Les Champs-Gain	89	now–2011
2002 Chassagne-Montrachet Les Champs-Gain	91	now–2011
2001 Chassagne-Montrachet Les Champs-Gain	90	now
2003 Chassagne-Montrachet Les Caillerets	86	now
2002 Chassagne-Montrachet Les Caillerets	92	now–2011
2001 Chassagne-Montrachet Les Caillerets	90	now
2000 Chassagne-Montrachet Les Caillerets	90	now
1999 Chassagne-Montrachet Les Caillerets	90	now
2003 Bâtard-Montrachet	89–90	now–2013
2002 Bâtard-Montrachet	92	now–2012
2001 Bâtard-Montrachet	91	now–2010
2003 Montrachet	89–90	now–2000
2002 Montrachet	93	now–2014
2001 Montrachet	93	now–2017
2000 Montrachet	92	now–2016
1999 Montrachet	92	now–2012
1998 Montrachet	93	now–2012
1996 Montrachet	93	now–2015

PHILIPPE COLIN ★ ★ ★
CHASSAGNE-MONTRACHET $25.00–$2,000.00

The share of property which Philippe Colin inherited from his father, Michel, includes a portion of Chevalier-Montrachet plus well-situated crus in Chassagne and St.-Aubin. Like his brother Bruno, Philippe will supplement his production by purchasing fruit, and his first vintages have displayed fine quality.

MICHEL COLIN–DELÉGER ★ ★ ★ ★
CHASSAGNE-MONTRACHET $70.00–$250.00

In his semiretirement beginning in 2004 Michel Colin has retained three precious crus: Chassagne En Remilly, Puligny Les Demoiselles (neighbor to Le Montrachet and Chevalier-Montrachet), and Chevalier-Montrachet. There being only the trio of wines here from extraordinary sites naturally raises his ranking in this guide, but the quantities are minuscule.

2003 Chassagne-Montrachet	89	now
2003 Chassagne-Montrachet En Remilly	88	now
2002 Chassagne-Montrachet En Remilly	92	now–2010
2001 Chassagne-Montrachet En Remilly	89	now
2003 Chassagne-Montrachet La Maltroie	87	now
2002 Chassagne-Montrachet La Maltroie	89	now–2010
2003 Chassagne-Montrachet Les Chaumes	88	now
2001 Chassagne-Montrachet Les Chaumes	88	now
2003 Chassagne-Montrachet Les Chenevottes	88	now
2002 Chassagne-Montrachet Les Chenevottes	89	now
2000 Chassagne-Montrachet Les Chenevottes	87	now
2003 Chassagne-Montrachet Les Vergers	89	now
2002 Chassagne-Montrachet Les Vergers	93	now–2012
2001 Chassagne-Montrachet Les Vergers	91	now–2012
2003 Chassagne-Montrachet Morgeot	91	now–2010
2002 Chassagne-Montrachet Morgeot	89	now
2003 Puligny-Montrachet Les Demoiselles	92	now–2012
2002 Puligny-Montrachet Les Demoiselles	92	now–2015
2001 Puligny-Montrachet Les Demoiselles	92	now–2012
1999 Puligny-Montrachet Les Demoiselles	92	now
2003 Chevalier-Montrachet	91	now–2012
2002 Chevalier-Montrachet	93	now–2012
2001 Chevalier-Montrachet	91	now–2012
1999 Chevalier-Montrachet	91	now–2011

PIERRE-YVES COLIN–MOREY ★ ★ ★
CHASSAGNE-MONTRACHET $40.00–$400.00

When Marc Colin divided his estate among his four children, Pierre-Yves, who had been making the Marc Colin wines for several vintages, struck off on his own. The early results, from meticulously chosen fruit from top parcels ranging up to grand cru, are impressive, reflecting Pierre-Yves's desire to emulate some of the transparency, minerality, and intricacy of the greatest Rieslings. His collection includes several St.-Aubins of outstanding potential, from among the many sites in that commune that were part of the Domaine Marc Colin.

PHILIPPE COLLOTTE ✱✱✱
MARSANNAY $30.00–$80.00

Collotte's Pinots from Marsannay and Chambolle have only recently shown up in the U.S. market, but it is clear that we shall be hearing a lot about this talented young winemaker in coming years. His small production is especially worth a search for as long as the wines remain underpriced.

2005 Marsannay Cuvée Vieilles Vignes	90	now–2011

DOMAINE CONFURON-COTETIDOT ✱✱✱
VOSNE-ROMANÉE $35.00–$200.00

Yves Confuron, who also makes the wines at Domaine du Courcel in Pommard, follows an intensive viticultural regimen, including plowing and the propagation of his own vine selections. Vinification is of whole clusters, with stems, which makes for wines that generally are relatively slow to evolve.

1999 Echézeaux	88–90	now–2010
1999 Mazis-Chambertin	90–92	now

DOMAINE CORDIER PÈRE ET FILS/MAISON
CHRISTOPHE CORDIER ✱✱✱✱
FUISSÉ/MÂCON $20.00–$75.00

Christophe Cordier appears to have boundless energy and ambition. In addition to his own domaine, among the finest in the Mâcon, he buys fruit for a wide array of other Mâconnaise bottlings under his *négociant* label, which has been expanded to include Beaujolais and the Côte de Beaune. Flamboyant fruit and high levels of new oak are part of the routine here, yet the wines are anything but superficial, seldom lacking in subtleties of perfume or deep mineral dimensions.

2004 Mâcon Aux Bois d'Allier	88	now
2004 Mâcon-Fuissé Vieilles Vignes	89	now
2004 Mâcon-Milly-Lamartine Vieilles Vignes	89	now
2004 St.-Véran En Faux	91	now–2010
2002 St.-Véran En Faux	91	now
2004 St.-Véran Clos à la Côte	90	now
2002 Pouilly-Fuissé Fine Josephine	93	now–2010
2002 Pouilly-Fuissé Fût XII	92	now–2010
2002 Pouilly-Fuissé Fût XIV	92	now–2011
2001 Pouilly-Fuissé Fût XV	90	now
2001 Pouilly-Fuissé Fût XVI	92	now–2010
2001 Pouilly-Fuissé Fût XVII	90	now
2001 Pouilly-Fuissé Fût XXIV	92	now–2011
2000 Pouilly-Fuissé La Grande Botrytis	91	now–2015
2002 Pouilly-Fuissé Jean Gustave	93	now–2010
2001 Pouilly-Fuissé Jean Gustave	91	now–2010
2003 Pouilly-Fuissé Juliette la Grande	94	now–2016
2002 Pouilly-Fuissé Juliette la Grande	92–94	now–2015
2000 Pouilly-Fuissé Juliette la Grande	90	now–2014
2000 Pouilly-Fuissé Les Schistes Vieilles Vignes	88–90	now–2010
2004 Pouilly-Fuissé Terroirs Rares	90	now–2011
2004 Pouilly-Fuissé Vers Cras	92	now–2010
2002 Pouilly-Fuissé Vers Cras	91	now–2010

2000 Pouilly-Fuissé Vers Cras	92–94	now–2012
1999 Pouilly-Fuissé Vers Cras	94	now–2011
2004 Pouilly-Fuissé Vers Pouilly	91	now–2011
2002 Pouilly-Fuissé Vers Pouilly	92	now–2010
2001 Pouilly-Fuissé Vers Pouilly	91	now–2011
2000 Pouilly-Fuissé Vers Pouilly	92–94	now–2010
2004 Pouilly-Fuissé Vieilles Vignes	91	now–2011
2004 Pouilly-Fuissé Vieilles Vignes	90	now–2012
2001 Pouilly-Fuissé Vieilles Vignes	90	now
2000 Pouilly-Fuissé Vieilles Vignes	92–93	now–2010
2004 Pouilly-Fuissé Les Vignes Blanches	90	now–2011
2002 Pouilly-Fuissé Les Vignes Blanches	92	now–2012
2001 Pouilly-Fuissé Les Vignes Blanches	89	now
2000 Pouilly-Fuissé Les Vignes Blanches	90–91	now–2011
1999 Pouilly-Fuissé Les Vignes Blanches	92–93	now–2011

DOMAINE DE COURCEL ★ ★ ★
POMMARD $30.00–$100.00

Yves Confuron, who has been making the wine here for a decade, believes in prolonged, whole-cluster fermentation to bring out the floral and other subtle dimensions inherent in the fruit of old vines. These are not wines for the impatient, but highly reward the time one gives them both in the glass and in the bottle.

2005 Bourgogne	89–90	now–2012
2005 Pommard Vaumuriens	90–91	now–2016
2005 Pommard Croix Noires	87–88	now–2014
2005 Pommard Les Fremiers	89–90	now–2016
2005 Pommard Grand Clos des Épenots	91–92	now–2020
1999 Pommard Grand Clos des Épenots	87–89	now–2010
2005 Pommard Rugiens	93–94	now–2022
1999 Pommard Rugiens	89–90	now–2012

DOMAINE DES CROIX ★ ★ ★
BEAUNE $50.00–$200.00

In 2005, David Croix acquired the excellent parcels and old vines of the former Domaine Duchet in Beaune. Early results display the same sensitivity and refinement that characterize Croix's winemaking at Maison Camille Giroud. From 2006, the Beaune Pertuisots is especially fascinating, and there is a sensational Corton Charlemagne.

JEAN ET SEBASTIEN DAUVISSAT ★ ★ ★
CHABLIS $25.00–$100.00

This father-son team displays an experimental spirit in vinification and achieves distinctive, ageworthy results, particularly with their very old vines in Vaillons.

RENÉ ET VINCENT DAUVISSAT ★ ★ ★ ★ ★
CHABLIS $40.00–$250.00

Impeccable care of the vines, low yields, and slow evolution in small barrels of mixed age are among the practices at this extraordinary domaine, whose wines age magnificently. Even the small amount of basic appellation Chablis here can be intensely interesting. Expect to find both the face of the vineyard and the vintage prominently reflected in a glass of Dauvissat wines. There is nothing formulaic, cosmetic, or routine about the way this father-son team approaches their work. Several of the identical wines are bottled under the Dauvissat-Camus label.

2004 Chablis	88	now
2002 Chablis	89	now
2004 Chablis La Forest	91	now–2012
2002 Chablis La Forest	91	now–2011
2004 Chablis Séchet	89	now–2011
2002 Chablis Séchet	89	now–2010
2004 Chablis Vaillons	91	now–2011
2004 Chablis Vaillons	91	now–2010
2004 Chablis Les Clos	94	now–2014
2002 Chablis Les Clos	95	now–2018
2004 Chablis Les Preuses	91	now–2012
2002 Chablis Les Preuses	93	now–2016

MAISON DEUX MONTILLE SOEUR ET FRÈRE   ✶ ✶ ✶
NÉGOCIANT, MEURSAULT $25.00–$250.00

In 2003, Alixe de Montille and her brother Étienne, director of the Château de Puligny and Domaine de Montille, formed a small *négociant* business specializing in whites. Her approach, influenced by that of her husband, Jean-Marc Roulot, displays the wines in a delightful transparency and interplay of flavors. Beginning with the first Deux Montille vintage, the Rully and the Montagny have already numbered themselves among the handful of the finest whites of the Côte Chalonnaise. The lineup includes some excellent values from the high hills of the Côte de Beaune in places such as Auxey-Duresses and Pernand-Vergelesses, as well as a wide range of Pulignys and Meursaults. While the sources are impeccably chosen, the range of wines on offer has differed significantly from year to year. Although the total production is expected to remain modest, the number of individual bottlings has been increasing, working up to Chevalier-Montrachet.

JEAN-PAUL ET BENOIT DROIN   ✶ ✶ ✶ ✶
CHABLIS $25.00–$100.00

Benoit Droin took over responsibility for his father's cellar in 1999 and has since been relentlessly pushing the envelope on quality across a range of more than a dozen bottlings, including a quintet of grand crus. Look for dramatically different personalities from each one. You will not have a dull moment in either Droin's company or that of his wines.

MAISON JOSEPH DROUHIN
✶ ✶ ✶ ✶ (RED) ✶ ✶ ✶ (WHITE)   NÉGOCIANT, BEAUNE $20.00–$1,000.00+

The enormous Maison Drouhin operation is nevertheless still very much a family operation. Robert Drouhin's daughter Véronique, who also looks after the vinification at Domaine Drouhin Oregon, and sons Frédéric and Philippe were long supported by the oenologist Laurence Jobard, whom Jérôme Faure-Brac replaced in 2007. The range includes Chablis as well as the Côte d'Or. Fruit from a great many properties owned or accessed by Drouhin is declassified and blended, leaving only selected *terroirs* as the subjects of single-site bottlings. The Bourgogne Véro, a brand launched several years ago in both red and white, represents a blend of *villages* wines and even some premier cru–classified sites intended, as Véronique puts it, "to present a picture of Burgundy Pinot" and sell for a Bourgogne price. Even Drouhin's ubiquitous, 25,000-case generic Laforet displays a nuance and textural allure, and the Chorey-les-Beaune offers exceptional value. The Drouhin wines, never showy, manage to combine restraint and polish with an abundance of flavor interest. The Beaune Clos des Mouches is something of a company calling card. The size and benchmark quality of their holdings in the commune of Chambolle climax in an often awesome Musigny.

2003 Meursault Perrières	87–89	now
2002 Meursault Perrières	90–91	now
2002 Chassagne-Montrachet Marquis de Laguiche	90	now
2002 Puligny-Montrachet Les Folatières	89–91	now–2010
2002 Puligny-Montrachet Les Pucelles	89–91	now–2010
2003 Montrachet	89–91	now–2014
2002 Montrachet	92–93	now–2015
2001 Montrachet	88–91	now–2012
2000 Montrachet	90–92	now–2014
1999 Montrachet	89–91	now–2010
1998 Montrachet	90	now
2004 Chablis Domaine de Vaudon	89	now–2010
2002 Chablis Domaine de Vaudon	89	now
2002 Chablis Vaillons	89	now
2003 Chablis Vaudesir	88	now–2013
2002 Chablis Vaudesir	90	now
2004 Chablis Les Clos	93	now–2014
2003 Chablis Les Clos	89	now–2011
2000 Chablis Les Clos	90	now
2002 Bâtard-Montrachet	92–93	now–2013
2005 Bourgogne Véro	89	now
2005 Chorey-les-Beaune	90	now–2010
2005 Beaune Grèves	91	2010–2015
2005 Beaune Clos des Mouches	92	2010–2015
2003 Beaune Clos des Mouches	89	now–2012
2003 Beaune Clos des Mouches Blanc	88	now–2010
2002 Beaune Clos des Mouches Blanc	89–90	now–2010
2003 Nuits-St.-Georges Les Procès	87	now–2011
2005 Chambolle-Musigny	89	now–2012
2002 Chambolle-Musigny	87–89	now–2010
2005 Chambolle-Musigny 1er Cru	91	now–2015
2005 Chambolle-Musigny Les Baudes	91	now–2015
2005 Chambolle-Musigny Les Amoureuses	94	2012–2022
2000 Chambolle-Musigny Les Amoureuses	90	now–2010
2005 Gevrey-Chambertin	88	2009–2013
2005 Vosne-Romanée Les Petits Monts	95	now–2017
2003 Vosne-Romanée Les Petits Monts	88	now–2013
1999 Corton	91–93	now–2011
2005 Corton Bressandes	91	now–2017
2005 Charmes-Chambertin	90	now–2017
2005 Griotte-Chambertin	93	2010–2020
2002 Griotte-Chambertin	92–94	now–2016
1999 Griotte-Chambertin	90–92	now–2010
1999 Chambertin	89–91	now
2005 Chambertin Clos de Bèze	96	2012–2024
2002 Chambertin Clos de Bèze	91–93	now–2018
2001 Chambertin Clos de Bèze	89–91	now–2012
2005 Clos Vougeot	92	2010–2020

2005 Grands-Echézeaux	93	now–2022
2005 Bonnes Mares	92	2012–2022
2002 Bonnes Mares	91–93	now–2016
2001 Bonnes Mares	90–92	2011–2012
1999 Bonnes Mares	90–91	now–2012
2005 Musigny	97	now–2027
2000 Musigny	90	now–2012

DOMAINE DUBLÈRE—BLAIR PETHEL ★ ★ ★
SAVIGNY-LES-BEAUNE $40.00–$200.00

North Carolina native Blair Pethel has parlayed his love of Burgundy into a small domaine with serious ambitions. Beginning with a piece of Corton-Charlemagne, he has expanded in his first three vintages to incorporate a range of reds as well as whites. Pethel talks of emphasizing purity, clarity, and minerality, even when the raw material is very ripe, but has already proven that he can walk the walk.

CLAUDE DUGAT ★ ★ ★ ★
GEVREY-CHAMBERTIN $30.00–$300.00

Claude Dugat has displayed his talents as a carpenter and stonemason in restoring a 13th-century ecclesiastical building to house his winery. His Pinot Noirs display an even higher level of artistry with similar substantiality. These are wines of tremendous fruit concentration framed by new wood, frequently culminating in Charmes-Chambertin and Griotte-Chambertin of monumental proportions and with a cult reputation. Tiny-berried vines selected by Dugat's horticulturist grandfather are permitted to ripen only ten or a dozen small clusters. "I don't like to say that I make my vines suffer," Dugat remarks, "because I love them. I prefer to say that I make them work hard for me."

2005 Bourgogne	87	2010–2012
2005 Gevrey-Chambertin	89	now–2017
2005 Gevrey-Chambertin 1er Cru	91	2012–2020
2003 Gevrey-Chambertin 1er Cru	92	now–2012
2002 Gevrey-Chambertin 1er Cru	92–94	now
1999 Gevrey-Chambertin 1er Cru	90–92	now
2005 Gevrey-Chambertin Lavaux St.-Jacques	94	2014–2024
2002 Gevrey-Chambertin Lavaux St.-Jacques	93–95	now–2013
2001 Gevrey-Chambertin Lavaux St.-Jacques	89–91	now
2000 Gevrey-Chambertin Lavaux St.-Jacques	93	now
1999 Gevrey-Chambertin Lavaux St.-Jacques	90	now–2010
2005 Charmes-Chambertin	93	2012–2022
2002 Charmes-Chambertin	96–97	now–2015
2001 Charmes-Chambertin	90–92	now–2012
2000 Charmes-Chambertin	94	now–2011
1999 Charmes-Chambertin	96	now–2012
1997 Charmes-Chambertin	93–95	now
2005 Griotte-Chambertin	95	2015–2028
2003 Griotte-Chambertin	96	2015–2024
2002 Griotte-Chambertin	97–98	now–2016
2001 Griotte-Chambertin	90–93	now–2012
2000 Griotte-Chambertin	94	now–2014
1999 Griotte-Chambertin	93–96	now–2012
1997 Griotte-Chambertin	93–95	now–2012

1996 Griotte-Chambertin	98–100	now
2005 Chapelle-Chambertin	93	2013–2022+?
2003 Chapelle-Chambertin	93	now–2014
2002 Chapelle-Chambertin	97–98	now–2017
2001 Chapelle-Chambertin	91–93	now–2013

DUGAT-PY—BERNARD DUGAT *****
GEVREY-CHAMBERTIN $40.00–$1,000.00

From a domaine that in the early '90s incorporated only three appellations—Bourgogne, Gevrey *villages,* and Charmes-Chambertin—Bernard Dugat and his wife, Jocelyne (née Py) have built an enviable collection of crus and honed quality to an exceptional degree. Experimenting with traditional whole-cluster fermentation and backing off on extraction, Dugat still produces from his low-yielding, organically farmed, largely very old vines wines so concentrated that one hears them accused of being "unnaturally" sweetly fruited and concentrated. In a search for "unnatural" practices one might cite the deep plough furrows that at all times distinguish Dugat's generally tiny parcels from those of his neighbors, or a harvest (with permission) ahead of the legally official starting date, because his vines are given so little fruit to ripen. If more growers walked Dugat's walk, there would be less talk, and more great Burgundy. But this level of concentration, allied to elegance, clarity, freshness, and refinement, does not come cheaply, and Dugat's high prices are another cause of envy and resentment among some neighbors.

2005 Gevrey-Chambertin Vieilles Vignes	91	now–2017
2002 Gevrey-Chambertin Vieilles Vignes	89–90	now–2012
2005 Gevrey-Chambertin Les Evocelles	92–93	now–2017
2002 Gevrey-Chambertin Les Evocelles	90–92	now–2015
2001 Gevrey-Chambertin Les Evocelles	90–92	now–2012
2005 Vosne-Romanée Vieilles Vignes	93–94	now–2019
2003 Vosne-Romanée Vieilles Vignes	88	now–2012
2002 Vosne-Romanée Vieilles Vignes	90–92	now–2016
2001 Vosne-Romanée Vieilles Vignes	89–90	now–2010
1999 Vosne-Romanée Vieilles Vignes	88–90	now–2010
2005 Gevrey-Chambertin Coeur du Roi	91–92	2010–2017
2003 Gevrey-Chambertin Coeur du Roi	90	now–2013
2002 Gevrey-Chambertin Coeur du Roi	90–92	now–2015
2001 Gevrey-Chambertin Coeur du Roi	91–93	now–2014
2000 Gevrey-Chambertin Coeur du Roi	91	now–2012
2005 Gevrey-Chambertin 1er Cru	93–94	2010–2022
2003 Gevrey-Chambertin 1er Cru	92	now–2014
2002 Gevrey-Chambertin 1er Cru	92–94	now–2017
2001 Gevrey-Chambertin 1er Cru	92–95	now–2014
1999 Gevrey-Chambertin 1er Cru	89–90	now–2010
1998 Gevrey-Chambertin 1er Cru	92–94	now–2010
1997 Gevrey-Chambertin 1er Cru	89–92	now
2005 Gevrey-Chambertin Petite Chapelle	92–93	2012–2020
2003 Gevrey-Chambertin Petite Chapelle	91	now–2014
2002 Gevrey-Chambertin Petite Chapelle	93–96	now–2018
2001 Gevrey-Chambertin Petite Chapelle	90–93	now–2012
2000 Gevrey-Chambertin Petite Chapelle	95	now–2015
2005 Gevrey-Chambertin Lavaux-St.-Jacques	95–96	now–2027
2003 Gevrey-Chambertin Lavaux-St.-Jacques	92	now–2015

2002 Gevrey-Chambertin Lavaux-St.-Jacques	93–96	ncw–2018
2001 Gevrey-Chambertin Lavaux-St.-Jacques	92–95	ncw–2014
1999 Gevrey-Chambertin Lavaux-St.-Jacques	91–92	ncw–2011
2005 Gevrey-Chambertin Les Champeaux	94–95	2012–2027
2005 Charmes-Chambertin	96–97	2012–2030
2003 Charmes-Chambertin	95	now–2015
2002 Charmes-Chambertin	95–98	now–2017
2001 Charmes-Chambertin	95–97	now–2015
2000 Charmes-Chambertin	96	now–2018
1999 Charmes-Chambertin	92–94	now–2012
1998 Charmes-Chambertin	93–95	now
1997 Charmes-Chambertin	92–95	now
2005 Mazoyères-Chambertin	95–96	2014–2030
2005 Mazis-Chambertin	98–99	2014–2032
2003 Mazis-Chambertin	96	now–2019
2002 Mazis-Chambertin	96–98	now–2025
2001 Mazis-Chambertin	93–96	now–2017
2000 Mazis-Chambertin	97	now–2020
1999 Mazis-Chambertin	94–95	now–2015
1997 Mazis-Chambertin	93–95	now–2012
2005 Chambertin	97–98	2015–2032
2003 Chambertin	98	now–2022
2002 Chambertin	97–100	2012–2030
2001 Chambertin	97–100	now–2020
1999 Chambertin	96–98	2011–2031
1997 Chambertin	95–96	now

DOMAINE DUJAC * * * * *
MOREY-ST.-DENIS $70.00–$700.00

After two years as an intern with Gérard Potel at the Domaine de la Pousse d'Or, the Parisian Jacques Seysses founded his domaine in 1968. Little by little his acreage and skills grew, until Seysses's keenly experimental mind, coupled with a receptiveness to tradition, led him to a style and quality of Pinot Noir that achieved international fame by the estate's second decade. The already rich array of crus at Domaine Dujac has recently been augmented by the purchase (along with de Montille) of the Société Civile du Clos de Thorey from Thomas-Moillard, bringing a raft of choice parcels, including three new grand cru holdings, for a staggering total of eight. To supplement in particular the volume of *villages*-level wine, the Seysses's *négociant* line, labeled Dujac Fils & Père, has been enhanced. Even with the California-trained oenologist Diana Seysses (née Snowden) joining her husband, Jeremy, and in-laws Jacques and Alec, and with a new winery at the old address, one wonders how this family is able to keep up with their responsibilities. Yet the results are consistently outstanding, and at times astounding. A generous application of new wood and the fermentation of whole clusters with stems are among the features of the Dujac regimen that many observers find surprising, given the refinement and sheer sensual appeal of these wines, usually even in their youth.

2005 Gevrey-Chambertin (Dujac Fils & Père)	90	now–2013
2003 Gevrey-Chambertin (Dujac Fils & Père)	88	now–2010
2005 Morey-St.-Denis (Dujac Fils & Père)	91	2010–2013
2002 Morey-St.-Denis (Dujac Fils & Père)	89	now
2005 Chambolle-Musigny (Dujac Fils & Père)	89	now–2012
2005 Chambolle-Musigny	89	2010–2013

2002 Chambolle-Musigny	89	now–2010
2005 Morey-St.-Denis	92	now–2015
2005 Morey-St.-Denis 1er Cru	92	2012–2018
2003 Morey-St.-Denis 1er Cru	90	now–2013
2002 Morey-St.-Denis 1er Cru	88	now–2012
2005 Nuits-St.-Georges Clos Thorey	91	2010–2015+?
2005 Chambolle-Musigny Les Gruenchers	91	now–2016
2002 Chambolle-Musigny Les Gruenchers	89	now–2013
2005 Gevrey-Chambertin Les Combottes	90	2010–2016
1999 Gevrey-Chambertin Les Combottes	89–91	now–2012
2005 Vosne-Romanée Les Malconsorts	93	2012–2020+?
2005 Vosne-Romanée Les Beaux Monts	94	2012–2020+?
2005 Charmes-Chambertin	92	now–2020
2002 Charmes-Chambertin	93	now–2014
2005 Bonnes Mares	94	2010–2024
2002 Bonnes Mares	94	now–2016
1999 Bonnes Mares	92–94	now–2012
1997 Bonnes Mares	94	now
2005 Chambertin	96	2010–2024
2005 Clos de la Roche	96	2010–2022
2002 Clos de la Roche	93	now–2016
2001 Clos de la Roche	89–91	now–2012
1999 Clos de la Roche	90–92	now–2012
1997 Clos de la Roche	93	now
2005 Clos St.-Denis	95	2010–2022
2003 Clos St.-Denis	92	now–2017
2002 Clos St.-Denis	90	now–2011
1999 Clos St.-Denis	89–91	now–2011
1997 Clos St.-Denis	92	now
2005 Echézeaux	93	2010–2020
2002 Echézeaux	92	now–2013
2001 Echézeaux	89–91	now–2010
1999 Echézeaux	91–92	now–2010
2005 Romanée-St.-Vivant	97	2010–2024

VINCENT DUREUIL ∗ ∗ ∗
RULLY $20.00–$90.00

Young Vincent Dureuil must rate as one of Burgundy's great overachievers, demonstrating the quality that is possible in the Côte Chalonnaise and offering a lesson in passionate ambition by having built his own estate prior to inheriting that of his father. Since 1997 he has had the opportunity to farm one piece of property in the high-rent districts of the Côte de Nuits (the Clos des Argillières), so wine lovers now have a new standard by which to measure Dureuil as a vintner. Whether in red or white, even the humblest appellations bottled here display concentration and class.

2003 Rully Blanc Chapitre	88–89	now
2003 Rully Blanc Maizières	89–91	now–2011
2005 Bourgogne Passetoutgrain	88	now
2005 Rully Vieilles Vignes	89	2009–2013
2005 Rully En Rosey	89	now–2011
2002 Rully En Rosey	88	now–2010

2005 Rully En Guesnes	90	now–2013
2002 Rully En Guesnes	90	now–2011
2005 Rully Maizières	91	2010–2015
2003 Rully Maizières	88–89	now–2011
2002 Rully Maizières	91	now–2012
2001 Rully Les Margotes Vieilles Vignes	91	now
2005 Rully 1er Cru	91	now–2015
2002 Rully 1er Cru	91–92	now–2015
2005 Rully Clos de Chapitre	92	now–2014
2005 Mercurey Le Bois de Lalier Vieilles Vignes	90	now–2012
2005 Nuits-St.-Georges Clos des Argillières	94	2012–2017
2002 Nuits-St.-Georges Clos des Argillières	92–94	now–2017
2001 Nuits-St.-Georges Clos des Argillières	89	now

MAURICE ECARD ★ ★ ★
SAVIGNY-LES-BEAUNE $40.00–$50.00

Maurice Ecard's wines have long been among the most ageworthy of Savigny and among Burgundy's best values. As a result of his ill health and family disagreements, Maurice transferred his estate to Vincent Sauvestre, who trades as a Burgundy *négociant* under the name Béjot. That firm plans to vinify the wines of Domaine Ecard separately in future years, but the 2005s will be the last wines to come directly from Ecard's hand.

2005 Savigny-les-Beaune Les Jarrons	90	2010–2019
2002 Savigny-les-Beaune Les Jarrons	91–93	now–2015
1999 Savigny-les-Beaune Les Jarrons	90	now–2011
2005 Savigny-les-Beaune Les Narbantons	88	2010–2016
2002 Savigny-les-Beaune Les Narbantons	90–92	now–2014
1999 Savigny-les-Beaune Les Narbantons	90	now–2011
2005 Savigny-les-Beaune Les Peuillets	87	now–2014
2002 Savigny-les-Beaune Les Peuillets	87–89	now–2012
1999 Savigny-les-Beaune Les Peuillets	91	now–2010
2005 Savigny-les-Beaune Les Serpentières	87	now–2012
2002 Savigny-les-Beaune Les Serpentières	87–89	now–2012
1999 Savigny-les-Beaune Les Serpentières	90	now–2010

DOMAINE ARNAUD ENTE ★ ★ ★ ★
MEURSAULT $25.00–$150.00

Arnaud Ente's Chardonnays (indeed, even his Aligoté) display concentration yet refinement and an almost lacy detail, along with nearly perfect pitch when it comes to balance and the judicious use of new wood and lees. Farming organically and bottling unfiltered and at a leisurely pace, Ente has taken his wines from their first estate-bottling in 1994 to international note at the onset of the new century, and it is clear that he has no intention of resting on his laurels. From centarian vines in the Ormeaux vineyard he crafts a remarkable Meursault labeled La Sève du Clos (formerly known simply as Vieilles Vignes).

2003 Meursault	89	now–2010
2002 Meursault	89–91	now–2010
2001 Meursault	91	now–2010
2003 Meursault Clos des Ambres	90	now–2011
2002 Meursault Clos des Ambres	90–92	now–2010
2003 Meursault Goutte d'Or	90	now–2011
2002 Meursault Goutte d'Or	90–92	now–2011

2001 Meursault Goutte d'Or	93	now–2011
2000 Meursault Goutte d'Or	88–90	now–2010
2003 Meursault La Sève du Clos	89	now–2011
2002 Meursault La Sève du Clos	92–94	now–2012
2001 Meursault La Sève du Clos	94	now–2011
2000 Meursault Vieilles Vignes	89–91	now–2010
1999 Meursault Vieilles Vignes	91–92	now–2010
2003 Puligny-Montrachet Les Referts	89	now–2011
2002 Puligny-Montrachet Les Referts	94–95	now–2013
2001 Puligny-Montrachet Les Referts	91	now–2011
2003 Volnay Santenots	89	now–2011

BENOIT ENTE ★ ★ ★
PULIGNY-MONTRACHET $25.00–$100.00

Benoit Ente is an as yet underappreciated grower of great sensitivity and openness to experimentation. He once preferred a fatter, flashier style, but in recent years his wines have displayed outstanding clarity and mineral depth as well as offering unusual value. Everything from Bourgogne Aligoté to his premier cru Puligny-Montrachet bottlings can be highly recommended.

SYLVIE ESMONIN ★ ★ ★ ★
GEVREY-CHAMBERTIN $30.00–$175.00

Sylvie Esmonin is a staunch believer in the use of whole clusters with stems ("the method of my grandfather's day") to enhance florality, fruit, and structure, all of which she thinks presupposes a late harvest. But Esmonin claims that her methods of vinification, which also encompass late bottling, help moderate the efficiency of alcoholic conversion. The results, from an extraordinary Clos St.-Jacques through two cuvées of Gevrey *villages* to an exceptional value Côte de Nuits-Villages from Brochon and Bourgogne from old vines below the village of Gevrey, speak loudly in her favor. Even the wines of lesser appellations from this address deserve bottle aging, their consistently low levels of sulfur notwithstanding.

2005 Bourgogne	89–90	now–2011
2005 Côte de Nuits-Villages	91–92	now–2014
2005 Gevrey-Chambertin	90–91	now–2014
2005 Gevrey-Chambertin Vieilles Vignes	93–94	2012–2018
2005 Gevrey-Chambertin Clos St.-Jacques	96–97	now–2022

DOMAINE WILLIAM FÈVRE ★ ★ ★ ★ ★
CHABLIS $20.00–$150.00

Since Joseph Henriot assumed control of this vast domaine, with its attendant *négociant* business, Didier Séguier and his team have brought quality to the forefront of the region. The sensitive application of wood of varying sizes and ages and the balance achieved at this address between richness and clarity, the complex layering of flavors, and the sheer sensual appeal are exemplary. The extent of Fèvre's holdings encourages them to bottle more than one rendition of certain crus. Whether a generic appellation Chablis or a grand cru, consumers are virtually assured of an outstanding wine that unmistakably reflects its origins.

2004 Chablis	89	now–2010
2004 Chablis Chablis Fourchaume Vignoble de Vaulorent	94	now–2014
2002 Chablis Chablis Fourchaume Vignoble de Vaulorent	90	now–2012
2004 Chablis Montée de Tonerre	92	now–2012
2002 Chablis Montée de Tonerre	92	now–2013

2004 Chablis Montmains	89	now–2011
2002 Chablis Montmains	89	now
2004 Chablis Vaillons	92	now–2013
2002 Chablis Vaillons	89	now–2011
2004 Chablis Bougros Côte de Bouguerots	95	now–2016
2002 Chablis Bougros Côte de Bouguerots	93	now–2017
2000 Chablis Bougros Côte de Bouguerots	92	now–2012
2004 Chablis Les Clos	96	now–2017
2002 Chablis Les Clos	94	now–2018
2000 Chablis Les Clos	91	now–2015
2004 Chablis Les Preuses	94	now–2013
2002 Chablis Les Preuses	93	now–2014
2004 Chablis Valmur	94	now–2015
2002 Chablis Valmur	91	now–2012
2000 Chablis Valmur	91	now–2010
2004 Chablis Vaudesir	93	now–2015
2002 Chablis Vaudesir	91	now–2014

DOMAINE JEAN-PHILIPPE FICHET ★★★★
MEURSAULT $30.00–$120.00

Following a path reminiscent of one of his mentors, the equally underappreciated Michel Buisson, Jean-Philippe Fichet eschews an active working of the lees or the extensive use of new wood and aims successfully at executing wines of clarity, precision, purity, and tensile strength. Though the results will not please tasters seeking plushness or unctuousness, the track record of these wines in bottle is formidable. One can only wonder at what Fichet might achieve if he owned more celebrated vineyards, but each of his nonpremier cru single-vineyard Meursault bottlings dramatically expresses its own personality and origins, and even his generic cuvées are worth cellaring for a few years.

FOREY PÈRE ET FILS ★★★★
VOSNE-ROMANÉE $50.00–$200.00

Regis Forey is known as one of the few owners of Vosne-Romanée Les Gaudichots, but while that rare bottling is frequently the high point of his collection, there is consistent quality throughout this cellar, from generic Bourgogne through a range of premier crus in three *villages* to grand crus Echézeaux and Clos Vougeot. Forey has been experimenting lately with a significant number of 500-liter, 133-gallon (double *barrique*) barrels to diminish the stave surface-to-wine-volume ratio and enhance freshness, without sacrificing richness. Though seldom showy, these are profoundly satisfying, ageworthy wines, bottled unfiltered, with very low levels of sulfur.

2005 Bourgogne	87	now–2010
2005 Morey-St.-Denis	89–90	now–2012
2005 Nuits-St.-Georges	89	now–2012
2005 Vosne-Romanée	91	now–2014
2005 Morey-St.-Denis 1er Cru	91	now–2014
2005 Nuits-St.-Georges Les Perrières	92	now–2016
2005 Nuits-St.-Georges Les St.-Georges	93	now–2017
2005 Vosne-Romanée Les Petits Monts	92	2010–2017
2005 Vosne-Romanée Les Gaudichots	94	2012–2020
2005 Echézeaux	92	2012–2020
2005 Clos Vougeot	92	2012–2020

DOMAINE FOURRIER ★★★★
GEVREY-CHAMBERTIN $40.00–$350.00

The articulate, opinionated Jean-Marie Fourrier staunchly believes in the inclusion of un-crushed fruit, leaving the young wines on their lees with attendant high CO_2 retention for 18 months before bottling, employing a mere 20% of new barrels for all his wines, and applying only minimal sulfur. That the property from which he sources is all owned outright and is largely in vines of over 50 years' age planted by his father or grandfather before the days of clones helps explain the consistently excellent quality at this address. Prices here have risen steeply recently, particularly for their rare Clos St.-Jacques and Griotte-Chambertin, but their range of bottlings from Vougeot, Chambolle, Morey, and above all Gevrey all merit their prices and the interest of pinotphiles.

2005 Vougeot Les Petits Vougeots	90–91	now–2017
2005 Chambolle-Musigny	90–91	now–2017
2005 Chambolle-Musigny Les Gruenchers	91–92	now–2019
2005 Morey-St.-Denis Clos Solon	88–89	now–2017+?
2005 Morey-St.-Denis Clos Sorbé	91–92	now–2019
2005 Gevrey-Chambertin Aux Echézeaux	89–90	now–2017
2005 Gevrey-Chambertin Champs-Perrières	88–90	now–2017
2005 Gevrey-Chambertin Cherbaudes	91–92	now–2019
2005 Gevrey-Chambertin Les Goulots	89–91	now–2019
2005 Gevrey-Chambertin Les Champeaux	90–91	now–2019
2005 Gevrey-Chambertin Combe aux Moines	92–93	2010–2022
2005 Gevrey-Chambertin Clos St.-Jacques	94–95	2015–2027
2005 Griottes-Chambertin	93–94	now–2024+?

CHÂTEAU FUISSÉ—J. J. VINCENT ★★★
FUISSÉ/MÂCON $25.00–$60.00

The Vincent family bottles numerous formidable cuvées from their extensive holdings in the Pouilly-Fuissé appellation. The aim is concentration and ageworthiness. No fear of new wood is exhibited in these wines, which can sometimes exhibit a bit of stiffness in their youth.

JEAN-NOËL GAGNARD ★★★
CHASSAGNE-MONTRACHET $30.00–$250.00

Jean-Noël Gagnard's daughter Caroline Lestimé has taken this estate to a new level of quality since assuming control a decade ago. Expect rich yet well-focused wines, from *villages*-level Chassagne all the way up to Bâtard-Montrachet.

2002 Chassagne-Montrachet Les Blanchots Dessus	88–90	now–2010
2001 Chassagne-Montrachet Les Blanchots Dessus	92–93	now–2011
2000 Chassagne-Montrachet Les Blanchots Dessus	90–92	now–2010
2002 Chassagne-Montrachet Les Chaumées	87–88	now–2011
2001 Chassagne-Montrachet Les Chaumées	89–91	now–2010
2002 Chassagne-Montrachet Les Chenevottes	88–90	now–2010
2002 Chassagne-Montrachet Le Champ Gain	89–90	now–2011
2001 Chassagne-Montrachet Le Champ Gain	90–92	now–2010
2002 Chassagne-Montrachet Clos de la Maltroye	90–91	now–2012
2001 Chassagne-Montrachet Clos de la Maltroye	89–91	now–2010
2002 Chassagne-Montrachet La Maltroye	89–91	now–2010
2002 Chassagne-Montrachet Morgeot	91–92	now–2012
2001 Chassagne-Montrachet Morgeot	91–93	now–2011

2000 Chassagne-Montrachet Morgeot	88–89	now
2002 Bâtard-Montrachet	91–94	now–2015
2001 Bâtard-Montrachet	89–91	now–2011
2000 Bâtard-Montrachet	89–92	now–2012
1999 Bâtard-Montrachet	91–92	now–2011

ALEX GAMBAL ★ ★ ★
NÉGOCIANT, BEAUNE $25.00–$175.00

Alex Gambal went from trading in Washington, D.C., real estate to trading in Burgundy wine by way of stints working with broker Becky Wassermann and studying at the Lycée Viticole in Beaune at the improbable age of 39. It has been almost a decade now since Gambal began his *négociant* business. With a sophisticated, huge, gravity-fed, historic facility in the center of Beaune; increasingly high-quality long-term grape contracts; a gradual accumulation of his own vine acreage; and clearly adept assistance from winemaker Fabrice Laronze, Gambal is demonstrating impressive results with his 4,000 to 5,000 cases annually, 60% of which are Chardonnay.

2003 Chassagne-Montrachet	88	now
2003 Chassagne-Montrachet Clos St.-Jean	89–90	now
2002 Chassagne-Montrachet Maltroie	90–92	now–2013
2003 Meursault Clos du Cromin	89	now–2010
2002 Meursault Clos du Cromin	90	now
2003 St.-Aubin Murgers des Dents de Chiens	90	now
2002 St.-Aubin Murgers des Dents de Chiens	90–92	now
2005 Bourgogne Cuvée Les Deux Papis	87	now
2005 Savigny-les-Beaune	89	now–2012
2005 Volnay-Santenots Vieilles Vignes	90–91	2010–2014
2002 Vosne-Romanée	87–88	now–2010
2005 Vosne-Romanée Vieilles Vignes	91–92	2010–2015
2002 Vosne-Romanée Vieilles Vignes	89	now–2012
1999 Vosne-Romanée Vieilles Vignes	90–91	now–2010
2005 Chambolle-Musigny	90	now–2012
2005 Chambolle-Musigny Les Charmes	91–92	now–2014
2005 Chambolle-Musigny Les Amoureuses	89–90	2010–2014+?
2005 Echézeaux	93	2010–2017
2002 Echézeaux	91	now–2016
1999 Echézeaux	90–93	now–2010
2005 Clos Vougeot	91–92	2012–2017+?
2003 Clos Vougeot	91	now–2018
2002 Clos Vougeot	94–96	now–2020
1999 Clos Vougeot	91–93	now–2012

GEANTET-PANSIOT ★ ★ ★ ★
GEVREY-CHAMBERTIN $30.00–$175.00

Unusually, Vincent Geantet bottles all his wines at one time, observing a barrel regimen that is the same regardless of appellation: one-third each of new, one-year, and two-year wood. Extended prefermentative maceration helps enhance the brightness of fruit exhibited by Pinots, many from very old vines. Actively stirring the lees promotes richness. His wines tend to be delightful even in their youth, regardless of appellation, and his Gevrey premier cru Le Poissenot and Charmes-Chambertin are profoundly delicious and excellent keepers.

2005 Bourgogne Pinot Fin	87	now
2005 Marsannay Champ-Perdrix	88	now–2010
2005 Chambolle-Musigny Vieilles Vignes	91	now–2014
2002 Chambolle-Musigny Vieilles Vignes	90	now–2012
2002 Chambolle-Musigny 1er Cru	91	now–2012
2005 Chambolle-Musigny Les Baudes	91	2010–2014
2005 Chambolle-Musigny Les Feusselottes	92	2010–2015
2005 Gevrey-Chambertin Les Jeunes Rois	89	now–2011
2002 Gevrey-Chambertin Les Jeunes Rois	89	now–2010
2005 Gevrey-Chambertin Vieilles Vignes	89	now–2012
2005 Gevrey-Chambertin En Champs	90	now–2013
2002 Gevrey-Chambertin En Champs	90	now–2012
2005 Gevrey-Chambertin Le Poissenot	95	now–2017
2002 Gevrey-Chambertin Le Poissenot	93	now–2012
1999 Gevrey-Chambertin Le Poissenot	90	now–2010
2005 Charmes-Chambertin	94	now–2017
2002 Charmes-Chambertin	93	now–2012
1999 Charmes-Chambertin	93	now–2013

DOMAINE GERMAIN PÈRE ET FILS—CHÂTEAU DE CHOREY   ★★★★
CHOREY-LES-BEAUNE $30.00–$100.00

Benoit Germain has been at pains to retain the distinctive personalities and transparency to *terroir* as well as ageability that wines of the Château de Chorey routinely displayed under the regime of his father, François. At the same time, through varied, sensitive fermentative techniques, the younger Germain promotes more flattering primary fruit and a refined tannic structure, rendering the wines more approachable in their youth. Germain is also beginning to incorporate elements of biodynamics. His Beaune premier crus Cras, Teurons, and Vignes Franches are the long-term standouts, but the value offered by Germain's Chorey-les-Beaune and white Pernand-Vergelesses can generally be appreciated at any time within one to five years of bottling.

2005 Chorey-les-Beaune Vieilles Vignes	90–91	now–2012
2005 Beaune 1er Cru Domaine de Saux	91–92	now–2013
2005 Beaune Teurons	91–92	2010–2017
2005 Beaune Vignes Franches Vieilles Vignes	92–93	2011–2020
2005 Beaune Les Cras Vieilles Vignes	93–94	2012–2022
2005 Beaune 1er Cru Tante Berthe	90–92	2012–2017+?

EMMANUEL GIBOULET   ★★★
COMBERTAULT $25.00–$70.00

From largely unheralded *terroir* in the Côte de Beaune, Hautes-Côtes de Nuits, and St.-Romain, Emmanuel Giboulet is achieving unexpectedly excellent, distinctive results in both red and white.

VINCENT GIRARDIN   ★★★
CHASSAGNE-MONTRACHET $35.00–$450.00

Vincent Girardin manages a Santenay-based domaine as well as an enormous *négociant* business, some of whose wines are bottled under the Baron de la Charrière label. Top honors, unsurprisingly, go to his white premier crus and small volumes of grand cru.

2003 Chassagne-Montrachet Clos de la Truffière	89	now–2010
2003 Chassagne-Montrachet Morgeot Vieilles Vignes	87	now–2010

2002 Chassagne-Montrachet Morgeot Vieilles Vignes	90–91	now–2012
2003 Meursault Narvaux	89	now–2010
2002 Meursault Narvaux	89–91	now–2010
2003 Meursault-Charmes Des Dessus	88	now–2010
2002 Meursault-Charmes	90–92	now–2011
2001 Meursault-Charmes	91	now
2000 Meursault-Charmes	89	now
1999 Meursault-Charmes	92	now
2003 Meursault Genevrières	88	now–2010
2001 Meursault Perrières	91	now–2010
2001 Meursault Le Poruzot-Dessus Vieilles Vignes	90	now
2001 Puligny-Montrachet Caillerets	91	now–2010
2003 Puligny-Montrachet Les Combottes	91	now–2011
2002 Puligny-Montrachet Les Combottes	91–93	now–2012
2001 Puligny-Montrachet Les Combottes	90	now
2003 Puligny-Montrachet Les Folatières	89	now–2010
2002 Puligny-Montrachet Les Folatières	89–91	now–2012
2000 Puligny-Montrachet Les Folatières	90	now
2003 Puligny-Montrachet Les Pucelles	90	now–2011
2001 Puligny-Montrachet Les Pucelles	94	now–2011
2000 Puligny-Montrachet Les Pucelles	89	now
2003 Puligny-Montrachet Les Referts	87	now
2002 Puligny-Montrachet Les Referts	91–92	now–2012
2003 Bâtard-Montrachet	89	now–2013
2002 Bâtard-Montrachet	94–96	now–2015
2001 Bâtard-Montrachet	91	now–2010
2000 Bâtard-Montrachet	90–92	now–2011
2003 Bienvenue-Bâtard-Montrachet	92	now–2014
2002 Bienvenue-Bâtard-Montrachet	93–94	now–2016
2000 Bienvenue-Bâtard-Montrachet	93	now–2010
2003 Chevalier-Montrachet	92	now–2014
2002 Chevalier-Montrachet	93–94	now–2016
2001 Chevalier-Montrachet	90	now–2011
2000 Chevalier-Montrachet	90	now–2011
2000 Montrachet	91–93	now–2013
1999 Montrachet	89–91	now–2010
2003 Corton-Charlemagne	88	now–2011
2002 Corton-Charlemagne	93–94	now–2016
2001 Corton-Charlemagne	90	now–2011
2003 Quintessence de Corton-Charlemagne	90	now–2014
2002 Pommard Les Épenots	91–93	now–2014
1999 Pommard Grands Épenots	92–93	now–2011
2000 Pommard Grands Épenots Vieilles Vignes	89	now
2002 Pommard Rugiens	88–90	now–2014
2000 Pommard Rugiens	89	now–2012
1999 Pommard Rugiens	90–92	now–2011
2003 Santenay Les Gravières	89	now–2010
1999 Volnay Clos des Chênes	90–92	now–2010
2003 Volnay Santenots	89	now–2010
2002 Volnay Santenots	89–90	now–2012
2002 Corton-Bressandes	90–92	now–2014

2000 Corton-Bressandes	89	now	
1999 Corton-Perrières	92–94	now–2012	
2002 Corton-Renardes	90–91	now–2011	
2001 Corton-Renardes	89	now	
1999 Corton-Renardes	93–95	now–2014	
2003 Corton Vieilles Vignes	93	now–2015	
2002 Gevrey-Chambertin	91	now–2015	
2003 Charmes-Chambertin	95	now–2015	
2002 Charmes-Chambertin	92–94	now–2015	
1999 Charmes-Chambertin	93–95	now–2013	
2003 Clos de la Roche	92	now–2015	
2002 Clos de la Roche	89–91	now–2014	
1999 Clos de la Roche	90–91	now–2010	
2000 Clos St.-Denis	92	now–2012	
1999 Clos Vougeot	91–92	now–2012	
2002 Echézeaux	91–93	now–2017	
1999 Romanée-St.-Vivant	89–90	now	

MAISON CAMILLE GIROUD * * *
NÉGOCIANT, BEAUNE $30.00–$200.00

This small family-owned *négociant* was for years an inside tip among pinotphiles, distinguished by an amazing price list of old wines. The business was purchased in 2002 by a group of U.S. investors led by Napa vintner Ann Colgin in a deal brokered by Beaune-based U.S.-born import agent Becky Wassermann, who assumed the role of director until 2008. At only 4,500 cases or so, vintage 2005 represented the largest production in the firm's history. The young, manifestly talented winemaker David Croix intends to keep the number of wines small enough to continue working intensively in the vineyard with most of his suppliers. A portion of Côte de Nuits grand cru represents purchased wine; all other purchases are of grapes. (Three properties, including a parcel of old vines in the Cras, still belong to the Giroud family.) Croix ages the wines largely in newly purchased once-used barrels, with an emphasis on youthful restraint and long aging potential of the sort for which Camille Giroud has long been known. One major change is that today's wines will all be sold young—indeed, they sell out immediately on release, as do those of most of Burgundy's top domaines.

2005 Hautes-Côtes de Beaune Au Cretot	87–88	now–2000	
2003 Aloxe-Corton	90	now–2012	
2003 Aloxe-Corton Les Guerets	92	now–2016	
2003 Santenay	90	now–2010	
2005 Beaune Cent Vignes	88–90	now–2000	
2005 Beaune Les Avaux	87–89	2010–2018	
2005 Beaune Les Cras	90–92	2012–2025	
2003 Beaune Les Cras	87	now–2010	
2005 Pommard Épenots	88–90	2010–2020	
2003 Pommard Épenots	91	now–2016	
2005 Volnay Taillepieds	89–91	2010–2020	
2005 Corton Les Chaumes	91–93	now–2016+?	
2003 Corton Les Chaumes	93	now–2017	
2005 Corton Rognets	88–90	2010–2018	
2005 Corton Clos Du Roi	89–91	2012–2022	
2005 Vosne-Romanée	89–91	now–2018	
2005 Vosne-Romanée	88	now–2012	

2005 Nuits-St.-Georges Les Vaucrains	90–92	now–2025
2003 Nuits-St.-Georges Les Vaucrains	91	now–2016
2005 Chapelle-Chambertin	89–91	2010–2020
2005 Latricières-Chambertin	93–94	2012–2028
2005 Chambertin	92–94	2010–2026
2003 Clos Vougeot	94	now–2020

DOMAINE G. & J.-H. GOISOT—CORPS DE GARDE ★ ★ ★
ST.-BRIS-LE-VINEUX/YONNE $20.00–$50.00

Ghislaine and Jean-Hugues Goisot's estate is singularly suited to demonstrating the power of Auxerre *terroir*. From Bourgogne Aligoté through Chardonnay-based Bourgogne Côtes d'Auxerre (including, in recent vintages, impressive single-vineyard bottlings) to St.-Bris (one bottling each from Sauvignon Blanc and the rare Sauvignon Gris), all of the white wines at this address, regardless of grape variety, display an unmistakable family resemblance of *terroir* and style, as well as consistently high quality.

DOMAINE HENRI GOUGES ★ ★ ★ ★
NUITS-ST.-GEORGES $35.00–$170.00

Henri Gouges was a pioneer in estate-bottling and the drafting of Burgundy's *appellation contrôlée* legislation. At this domaine Christian Gouges and his cousin Pierre perpetuate a tradition of Nuits-St.-Georges premier crus that successfully strive for balance as opposed to power, and aging potential at the expense of an easy sensuality. No more than 20% new wood is employed on any of their crus. The estate's two rare whites, from a mutation of Pinot Noir first isolated by Henri Gouges, follow the same pattern of achieving depth and ageworthiness, even if for the first year or two they may be more formidable than lovable.

2005 Bourgogne	87	now
2005 Nuits-St.-Georges	88	now–2012
2003 Nuits-St.-Georges	88–90	now–2012
2002 Nuits-St.-Georges	89	now–2012
1999 Nuits-St.-Georges Blanc Les Perrières	92	now–2011
2005 Nuits-St.-Georges Les Chaignots	90	2010–2015
2003 Nuits-St.-Georges Les Chaignots	89–90	now–2013
2002 Nuits-St.-Georges Les Chaignots	90	now–2013
2005 Nuits-St.-Georges Les Chênes Carteaux	89	2010–2014
2002 Nuits-St.-Georges Les Chênes Carteaux	90	now–2013
2005 Nuits-St.-Georges Clos des Porrets St.-Georges	89	2010–2014
2003 Nuits-St.-Georges Clos des Porrets St.-Georges	90–92	now–2015
2002 Nuits-St.-Georges Clos des Porrets St.-Georges	92–93	now–2016
2000 Nuits-St.-Georges Clos des Porrets St.-Georges	90	now
2005 Nuits-St.-Georges Les Pruliers	90–92	now–2020
2003 Nuits-St.-Georges Les Pruliers	91–93	2010–2020
2002 Nuits-St.-Georges Les Pruliers	93–95	now–2020
2000 Nuits-St.-Georges Les Pruliers	90	now–2010
2005 Nuits-St.-Georges Les St.-Georges	92–94	2014–2026
2003 Nuits-St.-Georges Les St.-Georges	91–94	2015–2025+?
2002 Nuits-St.-Georges Les St.-Georges	93–95	now–2020
2000 Nuits-St.-Georges Les St.-Georges	92	now–2012
1999 Nuits-St.-Georges Les St.-Georges	89–91	now–2012
1997 Nuits-St.-Georges Les St.-Georges	91–93	now–2010
1996 Nuits-St.-Georges Les St.-Georges	93	now–2012

2005 Nuits-St.-Georges Les Vaucrains	91–93	2012–2022
2003 Nuits-St.-Georges Les Vaucrains	92–94	2010–2020
2002 Nuits-St.-Georges Les Vaucrains	94–96	now–2022
2000 Nuits-St.-Georges Les Vaucrains	90	now–2012
1999 Nuits-St.-Georges Les Vaucrains	89–92	now–2012
1997 Nuits-St.-Georges Les Vaucrains	91–93	now–2010
1996 Nuits-St.-Georges Les Vaucrains	90–92	now

DOMAINE ALBERT GRIVAULT ★ ★ ★
MEURSAULT $70.00–$150.00

A new generation completely replanted this family's *monopole* Meursault Perrières Clos des Perrières in 1985, with the result that they are again beginning to produce wines possessed of the richness, complexity, and ageability that made this domaine a beacon of white Burgundy quality in the 1970s and early '80s.

DOMAINE JEAN GRIVOT ★ ★ ★ ★
VOSNE-ROMANÉE $50.00–$900.00

After years of experimentation and evolution, Étienne Grivot has achieved a style that combines firm underlying structure with a succulence and freshness of fruit, as well as a subtlety of perfume and texture that does full justice to this estate's extraordinary collection of nearly two dozen appellations. These include a range of Nuits-St.-Georges and Vosne-Romanée premier crus as well as prime parcels in Clos Vougeot, Echézeaux, and Richebourg. Luminosity, not heat, suggests Grivot, is what Pinot Noir craves, and the same (metaphorically speaking) could be said about the ideals embodied in his wines.

2005 Vosne-Romanée	89–90	now–2012
2002 Vosne-Romanée	87–89	now
2005 Nuits-St.-Georges Les Charmois	87–88	now–2012
2003 Nuits-St.-Georges Les Charmois	89	now–2012
2002 Nuits-St.-Georges Les Charmois	88–89	now–2010
2005 Nuits-St.-Georges Les Roncières	90–91	now–2014
2005 Nuits-St.-Georges Les Roncières	88–90	now–2012
2005 Nuits-St.-Georges Les Boudots	91–92	2010–2016
2002 Nuits-St.-Georges Les Boudots	90–92	2010–2014
1999 Nuits-St.-Georges Les Boudots	89–91	now
2005 Vosne-Romanée Les Beaumonts	92–93	now–2018
2003 Vosne-Romanée Les Beaumonts	95	2010–2019
2005 Vosne-Romanée Les Beaumonts	91–93	now–2014
2005 Vosne-Romanée Les Brulées	92–93	now–2016+?
2005 Vosne-Romanée Aux Reignots	94–95	now–2022
2005 Vosne-Romanée Les Suchots	93–94	now–2020
2002 Vosne-Romanée Les Suchots	92–94	now–2016
2005 Clos Vougeot	90–91	2012–2020
2002 Clos Vougeot	92–95	now–2020
2000 Clos Vougeot	90	now–2010
1999 Clos Vougeot	89–91	now–2010
2005 Echézeaux	93–94	now–2022
2003 Echézeaux	96	now–2020
2002 Echézeaux	93–95	now–2018
2001 Echézeaux	89–91	now–2012
2000 Echézeaux	91	now–2010

1999 Echézeaux	92–94	now–2013
2005 Richebourg	96–97	2014–2026
2003 Richebourg	95	now–2020
2002 Richebourg	94–97	now–2024
2001 Richebourg	89–91	now–2012
2000 Richebourg	91	now–2010
1999 Richebourg	95–97	now–2012
1997 Richebourg	92–95	now
1996 Richebourg	94–97	now–2010

ROBERT GROFFIER ★ ★ ★ ★
MOREY-ST.-DENIS $35.00–$700.00

Three generations of Groffiers—Robert, Serge, and Nicolas—now work full-time at this domaine, whose always low yields make for formidable ripeness and intensity even in difficult vintages like 2004. The Groffiers have backed off a bit on the use of new oak in recent vintages, but with no loss of richness. Even the Bourgogne Passetoutgrains at this address is a serious proposition, paradoxically representing the family's only acreage in their home commune of Morey-St.-Denis. They own far and away the largest single share of three Chambolle premier crus: the Amoureuses, its neighbor Hauts Doix, and Sentiers, as well as superb pieces of Bonnes Mares and Chambertin Clos de Bèze.

2005 Bourgogne Passetoutgrains	89	now
2005 Bourgogne	87–88	now
2005 Gevrey-Chambertin	90	now–2010
2003 Gevrey-Chambertin	87	now–2010+?
2002 Gevrey-Chambertin	89	now
2005 Chambolle-Musigny Les Hauts Doix	92	2010–2016
2002 Chambolle-Musigny Les Hauts Doix	91	now–2011
1999 Chambolle-Musigny Les Hauts Doix	89	now
2005 Chambolle-Musigny Les Sentiers	91	2011–2014+?
2002 Chambolle-Musigny Les Sentiers	92	now–2011
2001 Chambolle-Musigny Les Sentiers	91	now–2011
2000 Chambolle-Musigny Les Sentiers	90	now–2010
1999 Chambolle-Musigny Les Sentiers	89–90	now
2005 Chambolle-Musigny Les Amoureuses	93	now–2018
2002 Chambolle-Musigny Les Amoureuses	94	now–2014
2001 Chambolle-Musigny Les Amoureuses	90	now–2010
2000 Chambolle-Musigny Les Amoureuses	92	now–2010
1999 Chambolle-Musigny Les Amoureuses	92	now–2010
1997 Chambolle-Musigny Les Amoureuses	92	now
1996 Chambolle-Musigny Les Amoureuses	93	now–2010
2005 Bonnes Mares	94	now–2018
2003 Bonnes Mares	93	now–2014
2002 Bonnes Mares	93	now–2014
2001 Bonnes Mares	89	now–2010
1999 Bonnes Mares	93	now–2012
1996 Bonnes Mares	95	now–2012
2005 Chambertin Clos de Bèze	95	2012–2020
2002 Chambertin Clos de Bèze	96	now–2017
2001 Chambertin Clos de Bèze	88	now
1999 Chambertin Clos de Bèze	95	now–2014

1998 Chambertin Clos de Bèze	93	now
1997 Chambertin Clos de Bèze	95	now
1996 Chambertin Clos de Bèze	95	now–2014

ANNE GROS ★ ★ ★ ★
VOSNE-ROMANÉE $30.00–$700.00

Anne Gros's generally light touch with extraction leads her to capture an element of delicacy in even the ripest vintages. Over the past decade, hers have proven to be the most consistently interesting, excellent wines from the tripartite Gros inheritance. (The two other estates of this extended family are Domain Jean Gros and Gros Frère et Soeur.) Her largest acreage is in the Combe d'Orveau, high above Clos Vougeot and Echézeaux, but the Vosne-Romanée from the similarly high-elevation Les Barreaux vineyard; Clos Vougeot (labeled to reflect its location in the Grand Maupertui sector); and Richebourg are the stars in this cellar. In recent years, Gros has become serious about Chardonnay, which she has planted in the Hautes-Côtes de Nuits and in the appellation Bourgogne below Vosne-Romanée. Wines from these vines offer considerable refinement and depth at a modest price.

2005 Chambolle-Musigny La Combe d'Orveau	90	now–2012
2002 Chambolle-Musigny La Combe d'Orveau	88	now–2011
2005 Vosne-Romanée Les Barreaux	90	2010–2014+?
2002 Vosne-Romanée Les Barreaux	88	now
2005 Clos Vougeot Le Grand Maupertui	92	2012–2022
2003 Clos Vougeot Le Grand Maupertui	92	2010–2020
2002 Clos Vougeot Le Grand Maupertui	92	now–2014
1999 Clos Vougeot Le Grand Maupertui	92–94	now–2015
2005 Richebourg	95	2012–2024
2003 Richebourg	96	now–2022
1999 Richebourg	94–97	now–2017
1998 Richebourg	93	now–2010
1997 Richebourg	94	now
1996 Richebourg	93	now–2012

CORINNE ET JEAN-PIERRE GROSSOT ★ ★ ★
CHABLIS $22–$50.00

This large family domaine renders delicious, site-typical Chablis and Chablis premier cru, with a particular emphasis on the vineyards of Les Fourneaux, which lie at their doorstep in the tiny village of Fleys. The use of new wood on their top cuvées does not obscure the site-specific perfume or minerality.

DOMAINE GUFFENS-HEYNEN ★ ★ ★ ★ ★
VERGISSON/MÂCON $40.00–$100.00

Jean-Marie Guffens and his wife, Maine, wandered into France from Belgium more than a quarter century ago with no specific plan, just loving the country. Catching the "wine infection," they settled in the Mâcon, bought property, and began vinifying. Within a decade, this tiny domaine that follows almost primitively traditional practices had acquired an international reputation. Guffens's fanatic pursuit of quality found a very different outlet when he established the *négociant* firm Verget in 1990, but few white Burgundies from any appellation or vintner surpass in complexity or ageability the top Pouilly-Fuissé bottlings from this estate. In keeping with the scrupulousness with which Guffens segregates the fruit from multiple sites and even more numerous pickings as well as selective use of lees, the number and names of different bottlings vary from year to year. Only in exceptional vintages does Guffens bottle separately the fruit of the high-elevation Clos des Petits Croux. Mâcon-Pierreclos bottlings from Guffens-Heynen can be as inspiring as Pouilly-Fuissé from any other address. Recently, Guffens has acquired some new parcels, so the tiny level of production here will increase slightly.

2002 Mâcon-Pierreclos	89	now
2001 Mâcon-Pierreclos	89	now
2000 Mâcon-Pierreclos	89–91	now–2010
2004 Mâcon-Pierreclos Le Chavigné	90	now–2011
2002 Mâcon-Pierreclos Le Chavigné	90	now–2011
2001 Mâcon-Pierreclos Le Chavigné	93	now–2013
2000 Mâcon-Pierreclos Le Chavigné	94–96	now–2012
2004 Mâcon-Pierreclos Tri de Chavigné	91	now–2014
2002 Mâcon-Pierreclos Tri de Chavigné	93	now–2012
2004 Pouilly-Fuissé	87	now–2012
2003 Pouilly-Fuissé	87	now
2001 Pouilly-Fuissé	91	now–2011
2002 Pouilly-Fuissé La Côte	89	now–2010
2004 Pouilly-Fuissé La Roche	95	now–2015
2002 Pouilly-Fuissé La Roche	94	now–2014
2000 Pouilly-Fuissé Les Croux	91–93	now–2012
2003 Pouilly-Fuissé Premier Jus des Hauts de Vignes	88	now–2010
2000 Pouilly-Fuissé Les Hauts de Vignes	94–96	now–2015
2002 Pouilly-Fuissé Tri de Hauts de Vignes	94	now–2015
2001 Pouilly-Fuissé Tri de Levroutes	92	now–2013
2002 Pouilly-Fuissé Clos des Petits Croux	93	now–2015
2001 Pouilly-Fuissé Clos des Petits Croux	92	now–2010

DOMAINE GUILLEMOT-MICHEL ✳ ✳ ✳
QUINTAINE/MÂCON $40.00–$100.00

Marc and Pierrette Guillemot, cousins to and neighbors of Jean Thévenet, craft similarly opulent exemplars of Quintaine *terroir,* including amazing late-harvested and botrytis-affected elixirs. The Guillemots are among Burgundy's early, unabashed proponents of biodynamic viticulture.

2004 Mâcon-Villages	90	now
2003 Mâcon-Villages	92	now–2011
2002 Mâcon-Villages	91	now
2001 Mâcon-Villages Sélection de Grains Cendrées	91	now–2013

MAISON LOUIS JADOT ✳ ✳ ✳ ✳ ✳
NÉGOCIANT, BEAUNE $25.00–$500.00

Jacques Lardière annually presides over a collection of red and white Burgundies unprecedented in its combination of breadth and high quality. Jadot wines of either color are seldom intended to flatter in their youth but rather to achieve an eventual balance of fruit acidity with structure. Chardonnay from even the most celebrated sites seldom undergoes more than a partial malolactic fermentation, and postfermentative extraction promotes formidably tannic reds, which Lardière is seldom in a hurry to bottle. One can be almost certain that a Jadot Burgundy, from whatever part of their enormous spectrum of wines, including those of *villages* level, will possess clarity of flavor and a site-specific distinction. Jadot is owned by the same family that owns this *négociant*'s longtime distributor, Kobrand, freeing manager Pierre-Henry Gagey and Lardière to pursue large-scale excellence. Major shares of the firm's fruit come from the Gagey family domaines; the once-famous estates of Duc de Magenta in Chassagne-Montrachet and the Marsannay-based Clair-Däu; and an extended range of vineyards (above all Beaune premier crus) that have been part of Jadot since its mid-19th-century founding. It is hard to single out individual stars in the illustrious Jadot nebula, but their long-keeping Pinot Noir from the *monopole* Beaune Clos des Ursules (part of the Vignes Franches premier cru) is something of a flagship, and their Musigny and Chevalier-Montrachet Les Demoiselles frequently represent the summits of Jadot artistry.

2003 Beaune Grèves Blanc	88–89	now–2015
2003 Santenay Blanc Clos de Malte	88	now–2011
2002 Santenay Blanc Clos de Malte	87–89	now–2010
2002 Savigny-les-Beaune Blanc	88–89	now–2010
2003 Savigny-les-Beaune Blanc Les Guettes	88	now
2002 Savigny-les-Beaune Blanc Les Guettes	88–90	now–2010
1999 Chassagne-Montrachet Caillerets	89–90	now–2010
2003 Chassagne-Montrachet Morgeot	87–88	now–2011
2002 Chassagne-Montrachet Morgeot	89–91	now–2015
2003 Chassagne-Montrachet Morgeot Duc de Magenta	90	now–2012
2002 Chassagne-Montrachet Morgeot Duc de Magenta	89–91	now–2015
2000 Chassagne-Montrachet Morgeot Duc de Magenta	88–90	now–2011
2003 Meursault	88–89	now–2010
2002 Meursault	89–90	now–2011
2002 Meursault Blagny	90–92	now–2015
2000 Meursault Charmes	87–89	now–2011
2003 Meursault Genevrières	89–90	now–2014
2002 Meursault Genevrières	91–93	now–2015
2000 Meursault Genevrières	88–89	now–2011
2002 Meursault Goutte d'Or	89–90	now–2013
2002 Meursault Perrières	89–92	now–2015
2000 Meursault Perrières	90–91	now–2012
2003 Puligny-Montrachet	87–89	now–2012
2002 Puligny-Montrachet	88–89	now–2011
2002 Puligny-Montrachet Champ-Gain	88–90	now–2015
2000 Puligny-Montrachet Les Combettes	88–89	now–2012
2002 Puligny-Montrachet Clos de la Garenne Duc de Magenta	92–95	now–2016
2000 Puligny-Montrachet Clos de la Garenne Duc de Magenta	91–92	now–2012
2003 Puligny-Montrachet Les Folatières	87–88	now–2015
2002 Puligny-Montrachet Les Folatières	91–93	now–2015
2000 Puligny-Montrachet Les Folatières	89–91	now–2012
1999 Puligny-Montrachet Les Folatières	89–91	now–2011
2002 Puligny-Montrachet Les Referts	88–90	now–2012
2000 Puligny-Montrachet Les Referts	89–91	now
2002 Puligny-Montrachet Perrières	91–93	now–2014
2000 Puligny-Montrachet Perrières	91–92	now–2012
2001 Bienvenue-Bâtard-Montrachet	87–89	now
1999 Bienvenue-Bâtard-Montrachet	88–90	now–2010
2003 Bâtard-Montrachet	90–92	now–2016
2002 Bâtard-Montrachet	94–97	now–2019
2000 Bâtard-Montrachet	90–91	now–2012

1999 Bâtard-Montrachet	89–91	now–2010
1998 Bâtard-Montrachet	88–91	now–2010
2001 Chevalier-Montrachet	89–91	now–2016
1999 Chevalier-Montrachet	90–92	now–2010
1996 Chevalier-Montrachet	92–95	now–2012
1999 Chevalier-Montrachet Les Demoiselles	91–92	now–2012
1996 Chevalier-Montrachet Les Demoiselles	94–97	now–2015
2003 Corton-Charlemagne	90–92	now–2016
2002 Corton-Charlemagne	94–97	now–2019
2001 Corton-Charlemagne	88–90	now–2012
2000 Corton-Charlemagne	90–92	now–2012
1999 Corton-Charlemagne	88–89	now–2010
2003 Montrachet	95	now–2017
2002 Montrachet	95	now–2020
2001 Montrachet	88–89	now–2012
2000 Montrachet	91–92	now–2012
1999 Montrachet	93–95	now–2014
1998 Montrachet	91–94	now–2012
1996 Montrachet	95–97	now–2015
2005 Pernand-Vergelesses Clos de la Croix Pierre	86–88	now–2012
2003 Pernand-Vergelesses Clos de la Croix Pierre	88–90	now–2013
2002 Santenay Clos de Malte	87–88	now
2005 Savigny-les-Beaune Les Dominodes	88–90	2010–2016
2003 Beaune Les Avaux	87–89	now–2015
2002 Beaune Les Avaux	87–89	now–2013
2005 Beaune Boucherottes	88–90	2010–2015
2002 Beaune Boucherottes	87–88	now–2013
2002 Beaune Bressandes	89–91	now–2012
2002 Beaune Chouacheux	89–90	now–2011
2005 Beaune Clos des Couchereaux	87–89	now–2013
2002 Beaune Clos des Couchereaux	88–89	now–2013
2005 Beaune Theurons	89–91	now–2016
2002 Beaune Theurons	89–90	now–2013
2005 Beaune Vignes Franches Clos des Ursules	89–91	2010–2017
2002 Beaune Vignes Franches Clos des Ursules	90–91	now–2015
2000 Beaune Vignes Franches Clos des Ursules	89	now–2010
2002 Pommard	88–90	now–2010
2005 Pommard Clos de la Commaraine	86–88	2010–2013+?
2002 Pommard Clos de la Poutre	89–90	now–2011
2005 Pommard Grands Épenots	86–88	2010–2014
2005 Pommard Rugiens	88–90	2010–2015
2003 Pommard Rugiens	91–92	now–2017
2002 Pommard Rugiens	88–90	now–2012
1999 Pommard Rugiens	89–90	now
2005 Volnay Clos de la Barre	87–89	2010–2013
2002 Volnay Clos de la Barre	89–91	now–2013
1999 Volnay Clos de la Barre	88–90	now–2010
2005 Volnay Clos des Chènes	87–89	2010–2015
2003 Volnay Clos des Chènes	89–91	now–2015
2002 Volnay Clos des Chènes	87–89	now
2003 Corton-Grèves	90–92	now–2020

2005 Corton-Pougets	90–92	2012–2022
2002 Corton-Pougets	88–89	now–2019
1999 Corton-Pougets	89–92	now–2012
1997 Corton-Pougets	89–91	now–2010
2005 Vosne-Romanée	88–90	now–2012
2002 Vosne-Romanée	87–89	now–2010
2005 Gevrey-Chambertin	87–89	now–2012
2005 Nuits-St.-Georges Les Boudots	87–89	2010–2015
2003 Nuits-St.-Georges Les Boudots	89	2010–2018
2002 Nuits-St.-Georges Les Boudots	88–90	2010–2012
1999 Nuits-St.-Georges Les Boudots	90–91	now–2010
2002 Chambolle-Musigny	89–90	now–2012
2005 Chambolle-Musigny Les Baudes	89–91	now–2016
2002 Chambolle-Musigny Les Baudes	89–90	now–2014
2005 Chambolle-Musigny Les Fuées	87–89	2010–2016
2003 Chambolle-Musigny Les Fuées	88	now–2015
2002 Chambolle-Musigny Les Fuées	89–91	now–2015
1999 Chambolle-Musigny Les Fuées	90–92	now–2011
2002 Chambolle-Musigny Les Sentiers	89–91	now–2014
2005 Chambolle-Musigny Les Amoureuses	91–93	2010–2020
2002 Chambolle-Musigny Les Amoureuses	89–91	now–2017
1999 Chambolle-Musigny Les Amoureuses	87–89	now–2011
1997 Chambolle-Musigny Les Amoureuses	90–93	now
1996 Chambolle-Musigny Les Amoureuses	91–93	now
2002 Gevrey-Chambertin Les Cazetières	91–93	now–2016
2005 Gevrey-Chambertin Les Estournelles St.-Jacques	91–93	2010–2020
2003 Gevrey-Chambertin Les Estournelles St.-Jacques	88	now–2019
2002 Gevrey-Chambertin Les Estournelles St.-Jacques	88–90	now–2016
2002 Gevrey-Chambertin Combes aux Moines	90–92	now–2015
2002 Gevrey-Chambertin La Petite Chapelle	90–92	now–2016
2002 Gevrey-Chambertin Lavaux St.-Jacques	90–91	now–2015
2005 Gevrey-Chambertin Clos St.-Jacques	92–94	2012–2022
2003 Gevrey-Chambertin Clos St.-Jacques	92	2010–2020
2002 Gevrey-Chambertin Clos St.-Jacques	92–94	now–2018
1999 Gevrey-Chambertin Clos St.-Jacques	91–93	now–2012
1997 Gevrey-Chambertin Clos St.-Jacques	92–94	now
1996 Gevrey-Chambertin Clos St.-Jacques	91–93	now–2010
2005 Vosne-Romanée Les Beaux Monts	92–94	2012–2022
2002 Vosne-Romanée Les Beaux Monts	91–93	now–2018
1999 Vosne-Romanée Les Beaux Monts	91–93	now–2012
2005 Vosne-Romanée Les Suchots	90–92	2012–2020
2003 Vosne-Romanée Les Suchots	90	now–2016
2002 Vosne-Romanée Les Suchots	89–91	now–2018
2005 Clos de la Roche	91–93	now–2020
1999 Clos de la Roche	89–90	now–2011
1997 Clos de la Roche	89–92	now
2005 Clos St.-Denis	92–94	2012–2022
2002 Clos St.-Denis	92–94	now–2018
1999 Clos St.-Denis	89–91	now–2011
1997 Clos St.-Denis	90–93	now
2005 Clos Vougeot	93–95	2012–2024

2003 Clos Vougeot	95	now–2020
2002 Clos Vougeot	92–94	now–2017
1999 Clos Vougeot	92–95	now–2012
1997 Clos Vougeot	90–94	now
1996 Clos Vougeot	93–95	now–2014
2005 Echézeaux	91–93	2012–2020
2002 Echézeaux	91–93	now–2017
2000 Echézeaux	91	now–2010
1999 Echézeaux	90–93	now–2013
2005 Grands-Echézeaux	91–93	2012–2020
2003 Grands-Echézeaux	94	now–2020
2005 Chapelle-Chambertin	92–94	2012–2022
2003 Chapelle-Chambertin	96	2012–2022
2002 Chapelle-Chambertin	97–99	now–2020
1999 Chapelle-Chambertin	92–95	now–2014
1997 Chapelle-Chambertin	91–93	now
1996 Chapelle-Chambertin	92–94	now–2010
2005 Charmes-Chambertin	89–91	2012–2018
2002 Charmes-Chambertin	89–91	now–2015
1997 Grands-Echézeaux	90–93	now
1996 Grands-Echézeaux	91–93	now
2005 Latricières-Chambertin	91–93	2012–2020
2003 Latricières-Chambertin	92	2011–2020
2002 Latricières-Chambertin	93–95	now–2019
2002 Mazis-Chambertin	89–91	now–2018
1997 Mazis-Chambertin	90–93	now–2010
1996 Mazis-Chambertin	90–93	now–2012
1996 Ruchottes-Chambertin	91–93	now–2012
2005 Chambertin Clos de Bèze	93–95	2013–2026
2003 Chambertin Clos de Bèze	95	2012–2022
2002 Chambertin Clos de Bèze	95–98	2010–2024
1999 Chambertin Clos de Bèze	88–91	now–2012
1997 Chambertin Clos de Bèze	94–96	now–2015
1996 Chambertin Clos de Bèze	92–95	now–2014
1996 Romanée-St.-Vivant	91–93	now
2005 Bonnes Mares	93–95	2013–2024
2003 Bonnes Mares	98	now–2022
2002 Bonnes Mares	97–99	now–2020
2001 Bonnes Mares	89–92	now–2012
1997 Bonnes Mares	93–95	now
1996 Bonnes Mares	94–96	now–2010
2005 Musigny	95–97	2010–2028+?
2003 Musigny	97	2012–2025
2002 Musigny	94–97	2010–2024
2001 Musigny	89–92	now–2012
1999 Musigny	90–92	now–2012
1997 Musigny	93–95	now
1996 Musigny	93–95	now–2010

PATRICK JAVILLIER ★ ★ ★ ★
MEURSAULT $30.00–$200.00

Patrick Javillier is one of Burgundy's tireless experimenters, which has paid off in whites of increasing refinement and complexity. The Javillier method relies heavily on carefully timed rackings and the creative use of the lees. The aim is to vinify three and if possible four different lots for each eventual bottling, one to emphasize structure, one for fruit, one for fat or texture, and one for minerality. Javillier's Corton-Charlemagne and Meursault-Charmes represent relatively recent, very tiny acquisitions. He has convincingly built his reputation with non–premier cru sites, two of which he has combined to create the benchmark cuvée Meursault Tête de Murger. Javillier's limited bottling of Bourgogne labeled for its geological origins as Oligocène and his white Savigny-les-Beaune from the quarrylike Montchenevoy high above that village can be among the most distinctive wines of their respective appellations. For many years, Javillier labeled as *cuvée spéciale* any batches bottled late and unfiltered, which included the majority of those imported to the U.S., but nowadays all his whites fit that description.

2002 Bourgogne Cuvée des Forgets	88–90	now
2003 Bourgogne Cuvée Oligocène Cuvée Spéciale	88–90	now–2011
2002 Bourgogne Cuvée Oligocène Cuvée Spéciale	90–91	now–2012
2003 Meursault Clos du Cromin Cuvée Spéciale	88–89	now–2011
2002 Meursault Clos du Cromin	89	now
2003 Meursault Les Clous Cuvée Spéciale	89–90	now–2010
2002 Meursault Les Clous Cuvée Spéciale	88–89	now–2010
2001 Meursault Les Clous Cuvée Spéciale	90–91	now
2001 Meursault Les Narvaux	89	now
2003 Meursault Tête de Murger Cuvée Spéciale	90–92	now–2012
2002 Meursault Tête de Murger Cuvée Spéciale	91–92	now–2012
2001 Meursault Tête de Murger Cuvée Spéciale	90–91	now
2000 Meursault Tête de Murger Cuvée Spéciale	88–91	now
2003 Meursault Les Tillets Cuvée Spéciale	88–90	now–2010
2002 Meursault Les Tillets Cuvée Spéciale	90–92	now–2010
2003 Meursault Charmes Cuvée Spéciale	88–89	now–2012
2002 Meursault Charmes Cuvée Spéciale	92–94	now–2013
2001 Meursault Charmes Cuvée Spéciale	89–91	now–2010
2000 Meursault Charmes Cuvée Spéciale	89–91	now–2010
2003 Puligny-Montrachet Les Levrons Cuvée Spéciale	88–89	now–2010
2002 Puligny-Montrachet Les Levrons Cuvée Spéciale	88–90	now–2010
2003 Corton-Charlemagne Cuvée Spéciale	92–94	now–2020
2002 Corton-Charlemagne Cuvée Spéciale	92–94	now–2018
2001 Corton-Charlemagne Cuvée Spéciale	91–93	now–2010

JAYER-GILLES ★ ★ ★ ★
MAGNY-LES-VILLERS $55.00–$300.00

Gilles Jayer-Gilles vinifies some of the most concentrated, compromise-free wines in Burgundy. He spares neither pains in keeping down yields nor costs in buying new barrels. Those looking for gently caressing Pinots or being averse to new wood should seek satisfaction elsewhere. The combination of power and clarion complexity in the best wines at this address, culminating in the Echézeaux du Dessus, can be riveting as well as long-lasting on the palate, in the glass, and in the cellar. But even Jayer-Gilles's Hautes-Côtes de Beaune and Hautes-Côtes de Nuits (in white as well as red) run very much in the same stylistic vein as bottlings from appellations of higher pedigree.

2003 Bourgogne Aligoté	89	now
2003 Bourgogne Blanc Hautes-Côtes de Beaune	90	now–2011
2002 Bourgogne Blanc Hautes-Côtes de Beaune	89	now
2003 Bourgogne Blanc Hautes-Côtes de Nuits	90	now–2012
2002 Bourgogne Blanc Hautes-Côtes de Nuits	90	now–2010
2005 Bourgogne Hautes-Côtes de Beaune	86–88	now–2011
2003 Bourgogne Hautes-Côtes de Beaune	88–90	now–2012
2005 Bourgogne Hautes-Côtes de Nuits	87–89	now–2012
2003 Bourgogne Hautes-Côtes de Nuits	88–90	now–2013
2002 Bourgogne Hautes-Côtes de Nuits	89–90	now
2005 Côte de Nuits-Villages	89–91	2010–2014
2003 Côte de Nuits-Villages	89–90	now–2014
2002 Côte de Nuits-Villages	87–89	now–2010
2005 Nuits-St.-Georges Les Hauts Poirets	90–92	2010–2017
2003 Nuits-St.-Georges Les Hauts Poirets	86–88	now–2012+?
2002 Nuits-St.-Georges Les Hauts Poirets	90–92	now–2012
2005 Nuits-St.-Georges Les Damodes	92–94	2011–2019
2003 Nuits-St.-Georges Les Damodes	92–94	now–2016
2001 Nuits-St.-Georges Les Damodes	88–90	now–2010
1999 Nuits-St.-Georges Les Damodes	88–90	now
2005 Echézeaux du Dessus	94–95	2012–2022
2003 Echézeaux du Dessus	91–94	now–2018
2001 Echézeaux du Dessus	91–93	now–2013
1999 Echézeaux du Dessus	90–92	now–2012
1997 Echézeaux du Dessus	92	now
1996 Echézeaux du Dessus	93–95	now–2012

FRANÇOIS JOBARD * * * *
MEURSAULT $30.00–$130.00

François Jobard has long been known for crafting clear, complex, ageworthy Meursault free of what he would deem the cosmetic influence of new wood, or *bâtonnage*. Given time in the cellar, these wines blossom to their own distinctive sort of richness, always underlain by seemingly mineral notes, precisely hewn in flavor, and never forgetting wine's primary duty to refresh. His son Antoine is thoughtfully and creatively following his father's path. The family's major shares of Meursault Genevrières and Poruzots are the top performers in this cellar.

2003 Meursault	88–89	now
2003 Meursault Blagny	88–89	now–2012
2002 Meursault Blagny	90–91	now–2011
2002 Meursault En la Barre	88–90	now
2003 Meursault Charmes	90–92	now–2012
2002 Meursault Charmes	91–93	now–2015
2000 Meursault Charmes	88–90	now
2003 Meursault Genevrières	92–93	now–2014
2002 Meursault Genevrières	91–92	now–2015
2003 Meursault Poruzots	90–91	now–2013
2002 Meursault Poruzots	90–92	now–2015
2000 Meursault Poruzots	88–90	now–2010
2003 Puligny Montrachet le Trezin	89–90	now
2002 Puligny Montrachet le Trezin	89–90	now–2010

DOMAINE RÉMI JOBARD ★ ★ ★
MEURSAULT $25.00–$90.00

Rémi Jobard, a nephew of François Jobard, is dedicated to an organic regimen in his vineyards and slow, attentive vinification. The results are impressive all the way from his appellation Bourgogne to his four Meursault premier crus.

2002 Chassagne-Montrachet Les Chaumes	89–90	now
2003 Chassagne-Montrachet Chevalière	88–89	now
2002 Chassagne-Montrachet Chevalière	89–90	now–2010
2001 Chassagne-Montrachet Chevalière	89–91	now
2002 Meursault En Luraule	89–90	now
2001 Meursault En Luraule	88–90	now
2003 Meursault Sous la Velle	86–88	now
2002 Meursault Sous la Velle	89–90	now
2003 Meursault Charmes	90–91	now–2012
2002 Meursault Charmes	91–94	now–2013
2001 Meursault Charmes	93–95	now–2011
2000 Meursault Charmes	90–92	now–2011
2003 Meursault Genevrières	91–92	now–2012
2002 Meursault Genevrières	90–92	now–2012
2001 Meursault Genevrières	89–92	now
2003 Meursault Poruzots	89–90	now–2011
2002 Meursault Poruzots	91–93	now–2012
2001 Meursault Poruzots	90–92	now–2010
2000 Meursault Poruzots	89–90	now

JEAN-MARC JOBLOT ★ ★ ★
GIVRY $40.00–$50.00

Jean-Marc Joblot relies on rotofermentors for thorough extraction and is unafraid of new wood, but his Pinots are not just well concentrated. They are well balanced and possessed of considerable refinement, once again proving that the best reds of the Côte Chalonnaise deserve more serious attention than most accord them. (The whites here can be impressive as well.)

2005 Givry Pied de Chaume	89	now–2011
2002 Givry Pied de Chaume	88	now
1999 Givry Pied de Chaume	90	now
2005 Givry Clos des Bois Cheveaux	90	now–2014
2002 Givry Clos des Bois Cheveaux	89	now–2012
2005 Givry Clos du Cellier aux Moines	89	2010–2015
2003 Givry Clos du Cellier aux Moines	91–93	now–2014
2002 Givry Clos du Cellier aux Moines	91–92	now–2016
2001 Givry Clos du Cellier aux Moines	88–89	now–2011
1999 Givry Clos du Cellier aux Moines	89	now–2013
2005 Givry Clos de la Servoisine	90	2010–2016
2003 Givry Clos de la Servoisine	90–92	now–2014
2002 Givry Clos de la Servoisine	91–92	now–2015
2001 Givry Clos de la Servoisine	88–89	now–2011
1999 Givry Clos de la Servoisine	93	now–2012

Michel Lafarge has been a master for three decades of unshowy yet consistently delicious, profound Volnay, and the collaboration of his son Frédéric Lafarge has only enhanced the quality on offer at this address. Is there another domaine that has three generic reds routinely worthy of attention even by those with the disposable income to afford premier crus? Among Volnays here, the premier crus Clos des Chênes and *monopole* Clos du Château des Ducs are still the top performers, but a recently segregated bottling from Mitan and one from a newly acquired parcel in Caillerets may well be future stars. Any of the Volnays here can in a given year be seriously challenged by the estate's Beaune Grèves and Pommard Pézerolles. And, whether it is Bourgogne Aligoté or Meursault, a Lafarge white should not be overlooked.

2005 Bourgogne Passetoutgrain	88–89	now
2005 Bourgogne Passetoutgrain l'Exception	89–90	now–2012
2005 Bourgogne	88–89	now–2010
2005 Côte de Beaune-Villages	87–88	now–2010
2005 Beaune Les Aigrots	87–88	2010–2013+?
2005 Beaune Grèves	90–91	2011–2015
2002 Beaune Grèves	87–89	now–2014
2005 Pommard Pézerolles	89–90	2011–2016+?
2003 Pommard Pézerolles	91–93	2010–2020
2002 Pommard Pézerolles	88–91	now–2018
2001 Pommard Pézerolles	90–92	now–2011
2000 Pommard Pézerolles	91	now–2012
1999 Pommard Pézerolles	87–89	now–2012
2005 Volnay	90–91	now–2014
2002 Volnay	87–88	now–2010
2005 Volnay Vendanges Sélectionnées	90–91	2010–2013+?
2002 Volnay Vendanges Sélectionnées	88–90	now–2012
2005 Volnay 1er Cru	91–92	2011–2015
2003 Volnay 1er Cru	87–89	now–2013+?
2002 Volnay 1er Cru	87–89	now–2014
2005 Volnay Mitans	91–92	now–2015
2005 Volnay Caillerets	91–92	now–2016+?
2003 Volnay Caillerets	89–91	now–2016+?
2001 Volnay Caillerets	88–90	now
2002 Volnay Caillerets	92–94	now–2017
2005 Volnay Clos du Château des Ducs	93–94	now–2018
2003 Volnay Clos du Château des Ducs	88–90	2010–2018
2002 Volnay Clos du Château des Ducs	89–92	now–2017
2000 Volnay Clos du Château des Ducs	90	now–2010
1999 Volnay Clos du Château des Ducs	89–92	now–2018
2005 Volnay Clos des Chênes	93–94	2010–2020
2003 Volnay Clos des Chênes	90–92	2010–2020
2002 Volnay Clos des Chênes	91–93	now–2018
2000 Volnay Clos des Chênes	91	now–2010
1999 Volnay Clos des Chênes	88–90	now–2012
1996 Volnay Clos des Chênes	92–94	now–2014

DOMAINE DES COMTES LAFON
★★★★(RED) ★★★★★(WHITE) MEURSAULT $50.00–$1,000.00

Rather than work beside his father, Dominique Lafon chose to garner experience in the trade and abroad until in 1987 the time came for control of the family estate to pass to him. Through conscientious viticulture and ever-increasing concern for the health of his soils, as well as via relentless experimentation in his vineyards and cellar, Lafon has kept ratcheting up quality, arriving in recent vintages at an exemplary balance of richness with clarity and refinement. The four Meursault premier crus and, of course, the Montrachet are consistently memorable, but ostensibly lesser whites, including the *monopole* Meursault Clos de la Barre, can all be recommended and are all in great demand. The Volnay-Santenots du Milieu and smaller lots of Volnay Clos des Chênes and Volnay Champans combine polish and richness with precision and finesse. The Monthélie from the Duresses premier cru should also not be missed. Under Dominique Lafon's regime, the estate has grown by taking back portions of vineyards that had previously been sharecropped, but it is not as though this growth comes even remotely close to satisfying demand.

2003 Meursault	89–90	now
2002 Meursault	89–91	now
2003 Meursault Désirée	90–92	now–2010
2002 Meursault Désirée	89–91	now
2003 Meursault Clos de la Barre	90–92	now–2011
2002 Meursault Clos de la Barre	91–93	now–2014
2001 Meursault Clos de la Barre	88–89	now
2000 Meursault Clos de la Barre	89–91	now
2003 Meursault Charmes	91–93	now–2012
2002 Meursault Charmes	94–95	now–2013
2001 Meursault Charmes	93–95	now–2011
2000 Meursault Charmes	92–94	now–2011
1999 Meursault Charmes	90–92	now–2010
2003 Meursault Genevrières	89–91	now–2011
2002 Meursault Genevrières	91–93	now–2012
2001 Meursault Genevrières	90–92	now
2000 Meursault Genevrières	92–94	now–2010
2003 Meursault Goutte d'Or	91–93	now–2013
2002 Meursault Goutte d'Or	91–93	now–2012
2000 Meursault Goutte d'Or	90–92	now–2010
2003 Meursault Perrières	88–90	now–2013
2002 Meursault Perrières	94–96	now–2014
2001 Meursault Perrières	90–92	now–2010
2000 Meursault Perrières	93–96	now–2010
2003 Puligny-Montrachet Champ-Gain	90–91	now–2011
2002 Puligny-Montrachet Champ-Gain	90–92	now–2011
2001 Puligny-Montrachet Champ-Gain	91–93	now
2000 Puligny-Montrachet Champ-Gain	89–91	now–2010
2003 Montrachet	94–96	now–2018
2002 Montrachet	98–100	now–2017
2001 Montrachet	95–97	now–2015
2000 Montrachet	93–95	now–2013
1999 Montrachet	93–95	now–2012
1997 Montrachet	95–97	now–2010
1996 Montrachet	96–99	now–2012

2005 Monthélie Les Duresses	90–91	now–2014
2002 Monthélie Les Duresses	89–91	now–2011
2005 Volnay	88	now–2013
2002 Volnay	88–89	now–2010
2005 Volnay Champans	92–93	now–2018
2003 Volnay Champans	90–92	now–2014
2002 Volnay Champans	90–93	now–2017
1999 Volnay Champans	88–91	now–2012
2005 Volnay Clos des Chênes	91–92	now–2017
2003 Volnay Clos des Chênes	90–91	now–2013
2002 Volnay Clos des Chênes	89–92	now–2016
1999 Volnay Clos des Chênes	88–91	now–2010
2005 Volnay Santenots du Milieu	92–93	now–2020
2002 Volnay Santenots du Milieu	93–95	now–2019
2001 Volnay Santenots du Milieu	88–89	now
1999 Volnay Santenots du Milieu	91–93	now

DOMAINE LES HERTIERS DU COMTE LAFON ⋆ ⋆ ⋆
MILLY/MÂCON $20.00–$40.00

In time for the new millennium, Dominique Lafon founded this winery, where together with a team independent of his Meursault estate he is turning out rich, expressive *villages*-designated Mâcons. Improved viticulture, more stringent selection, and more experience in the region can all be expected to pay further dividends in coming years.

2004 Mâcon-Chardonnay Clos de la Crochette	89	now
2004 Mâcon-Milly-Lamartine	88	now
2004 Mâcon-Milly-Lamartine Clos du Four	90	now–2010
2002 Mâcon-Milly-Lamartine Clos du Four	90	now
2004 Mâcon-Uchizy Les Maranches	88	now

DOMAINE LAROCHE ⋆ ⋆ ⋆ ⋆
CHABLIS $20.00–$175.00

A tireless, ambitious promoter of his native region, Michel Laroche has amassed a vast estate, supplemented by work as a *négociant* and complemented by programs in the Languedoc, Chile, and South Africa. A French pioneer in the use of screw cap closures, Laroche is in general unafraid to experiment. Chablis here achieves an unusual measure of richness as well as, in the top echelons, an unabashed oakiness, yet the wines remain very recognizably of their distinctive sites and in no way lacking in finesse. From basic appellation Chablis to exceptional grand cru bottlings, these are wines that will win new friends for their region from among Chardonnay and white Burgundy lovers worldwide.

MAISON LOUIS LATOUR ⋆ ⋆ ⋆
NÉGOCIANT, BEAUNE $20.00–$400.00

Louis-Fabrice Latour and oenologist Jean-Charles Thomas garner frequent praise for their white wines but have drawn some criticism, particularly directed at their practice of flash pasteurization, for their Pinots. Some of their reds even in excellent vintages lack the requisite clarity or concentration to be distinctive. This house enjoys a relatively strong level of control over many small, often semiretired landholders in certain communes such as Chambolle, and selectively pays top dollar for wines in barrel from a range of prestigious appellations. But the best Latour wines are generally their whites, and among the reds those from their own domaine holdings in several Beaune premier crus: Aloxe-Corton Les Chaillots, Corton (sold as Château Corton Grancey), Chambertin, and Romanée St.-Vivant (the portion known and labeled as Les 4 Journaux). The Corton-Charlemagne and Chevalier-Montrachet Les Demoiselles are routinely outstanding. Latour was a pioneer in quality Chardonnay from Montagny and continues to set an especially high standard for value in that Côte Chalonnaise appellation.

2003 Chassagne-Montrachet Les Chenevottes	88	now
2002 Chassagne-Montrachet Les Chenevottes	89–91	now–2010
2003 Chassagne-Montrachet Les Caillerets	89	now–2010
2002 Chassagne-Montrachet Les Caillerets	93–94	now–2015
2002 Chassagne-Montrachet Morgeots	90–91	now–2011
2003 Meursault Blagny	88	now
2003 Meursault Charmes	90	now
2003 Meursault Goutte d'Or	89	now
2002 Meursault Goutte d'Or	89–91	now–2010
2002 Meursault Genevrières	90–93	now–2012
2003 Meursault Perrières	91–93	now–2012
2002 Meursault Perrières	90–92	now
2003 Meursault Poruzots	87	now
2002 Puligny-Montrachet Les Folatières	89–91	now–2011
2001 Puligny-Montrachet Les Folatières	90–92	now–2010
2002 Puligny-Montrachet Les Referts	91–92	now–2011
2001 Puligny-Montrachet Les Referts	89–91	now–2010
2002 Puligny-Montrachet Les Truffières	91–93	now–2011
2003 Corton-Charlemagne	89	now–2011+?
2002 Corton-Charlemagne	91–93	now–2012
2001 Corton-Charlemagne	91–94	now–2012
1999 Corton-Charlemagne	90–91	now
2003 Bâtard-Montrachet	90	now–2011
2002 Bâtard-Montrachet	92–94	now–2015
2001 Bâtard-Montrachet	89–92	now–2010
2000 Bâtard-Montrachet	90–92	now–2013
2003 Bienvenue-Bâtard-Montrachet	88	now–2014
2002 Bienvenue-Bâtard-Montrachet	91–93	now–2014
2001 Bienvenue-Bâtard-Montrachet	89–90	now–2010
2002 Criots-Bâtard-Montrachet	92–94	now–2014
2000 Criots-Bâtard-Montrachet	90–92	now–2013
2003 Chevalier-Montrachet Les Demoiselles	90	now–2014
2002 Chevalier-Montrachet Les Demoiselles	91–94	now–2015
2003 Montrachet	89	now–2014
2002 Montrachet	95–97	now–2016
2001 Montrachet	92–95	now–2013
2000 Montrachet	90–92	now–2012
1999 Montrachet	90–92	now
2005 Beaune Les Vignes Franches	89	now–2012
2005 Corton Grancey	87–89	now–2015
2005 Clos de la Roche	90	now–2014
2005 Chambertin	90	now–2017
2003 Chambertin	91	now–2015
2005 Romanée-St.-Vivant Les 4 Journaux	90	now–2014+?

DOMAINE LATOUR-GIRAUD ★ ★ ★
MEURSAULT $30.00–$90.00

Jean-Pierre Latour vinifies a significant portion of his whites in tank, then moves them to barrel for malolactic fermentation and further maturation. The best Meursault from this address, particularly from their substantial holdings in the premier cru Genevrières (subject to two different bottlings), displays an admirable mix of brightness and energy with richness of fruit.

2003 Meursault Cuvée Charles Maxime	88–89	now–2010
2003 Meursault Le Limozin	88–90	now–2010
2002 Meursault Le Limozin	88–89	now
2003 Meursault Les Narvaux	87–88	now–2010
2002 Meursault Les Narvaux	87–89	now
2003 Meursault Les Bouchères	86–88	now
2002 Meursault Les Bouchères	89–91	now–2012
2002 Meursault Charmes	91–93	now–2010
2000 Meursault Charmes	90–91	now
2002 Meursault-Genevrières	92–94	now–2011
2000 Meursault-Genevrières	90–91	now–2011
2003 Meursault-Genevrières Cuvée des Pierres	90–91	now–2011
2002 Meursault-Genevrières Cuvée des Pierres	93–95	now–2013
2000 Meursault-Genevrières Cuvée des Pierres	91–93	now–2012
2002 Meursault Perrières	91–92	now–2012
2002 Meursault Poruzots	88–90	now
2003 Puligny-Montrachet Champs Canet	88–89	now–2010
2002 Puligny-Montrachet Champs Canet	90–92	now–2010

DOMINIQUE LAURENT ★ ★ ★ ★ ★
NÉGOCIANT, NUITS-ST.-GEORGES $30.00–$80.00

Laurent buys wine, not grapes. He distinguishes between those of his wines he calls "naive" or "peasant," by which essentially he means those whose fruit was destemmed and has undergone variations on gentle extraction, and those that are vinified with whole clusters and stems in what he considers an approximation to ancient method such as in his opinion "only two or three [other] people truly practice." The latter clearly are the wines that define his mission and in which he takes an active role in fermentation, but quality is outstanding here across the board, with the best wines setting extraordinary standards of richness, refinement, and complexity. Laurent is at pains to put to rest persistent rumors that his wines are bottled barrel by barrel or in batches over time. Since the 1999 vintage, the totality of each wine (which typically amounts to fewer than 100 cases) has in fact been assembled in tank and bottled from there, without filtration or pumping. Since 1999, too, there has been no sulfur added during the *élevage*, and only a low dosage at bottling. And while the expression "200% new oak" (often spoken derogatorily) originated with this cellar, Laurent nowadays utilizes new customized barrels with restraint, ascending to 100% only with certain crus. Laurent sells a line labeled Cuvée Tradition largely inside France and Cuvées Vieilles Vignes worldwide. Laurent's small production of white wine, which includes dramatically distinctive Chablis and Meursault, is little known in the U.S., nor has the recent inauguration of a "Domaine Laurent"— initially with only a few appellations—been attended by the fanfare that such exciting news deserves.

2005 Chorey-les-Beaune Vieilles Vignes	87–89	now–2011
2005 Aloxe-Corton Vieilles Vignes	88–90	now–2013

2005 Santenay Vieilles Vignes	89–91	now–2015
2005 Beaune Vieilles Vignes	90–92	now–2015
2005 Pommard Vieilles Vignes	88–90	2010–2015
2005 Pommard 1er Cru Vieilles Vignes	89–91	2010–2017
2005 Volnay Vieilles Vignes	86–88	now–2013+?
2005 Volnay Santenots Vieilles Vignes	90–92	now–2022
2005 Volnay Clos des Chênes Vieilles Vignes	93–95	2010–2025
2005 Beaune Grèves Vieilles Vignes	87–89	2010–2015+?
2005 Beaune 1er Cru Vieilles Vignes	90–92	now–2015
2005 Pommard Les Charmots Vieilles Vignes	92–94	now–2020
2005 Pommard Les Épenots Vieilles Vignes	91–93	now–2020
2005 Pommard Rugiens Vieilles Vignes	91–93	2010–2022
2005 Corton Vieilles Vignes	89–91	2010–2017+?
2005 Fixin Hervelets Vieilles Vignes	89–91	now–2015
2005 Chambolle-Musigny Derrière la Grange Vieilles Vignes	89–91	now–2015
2005 Chambolle-Musigny Charmes Vieilles Vignes	87–89	now–2012+?
2005 Vosne-Romanée Les Beaux Monts Vieilles Vignes	93–95	2010–2022
2005 Vosne-Romanée Les Suchots Vieilles Vignes	93–95	now–2022
2005 Gevrey-Chambertin Les Cazetiers Vieilles Vignes	90–92	2012–2018
2005 Gevrey-Chambertin Estournelles St.-Jacques Vieilles Vignes	89–91	2010–2016+?
2005 Gevrey-Chambertin Lavaux St.-Jacques Vieilles Vignes	93–95	2010–2024
2005 Gevrey-Chambertin Clos St.-Jacques Vieilles Vignes	96–98	2010–2027
2005 Gevrey-Chambertin Combottes Vieilles Vignes	94–96	now–2024
2005 Nuits-St.-Georges Les Vaucrains Vieilles Vignes	93–95	2010–2020
2005 Nuits-St.-Georges Les St.-Georges Vieilles Vignes	90–92	2010–2018+?
2005 Charmes-Chambertin Vieilles Vignes	92–94	now–2020
2005 Mazis-Chambertin Vieilles Vignes	93–95	2010–2022
1997 Mazis-Chambertin Vieilles Vignes	90–92	now–2010
2005 Latricières-Chambertin Vieilles Vignes	93–95	2012–2025
2005 Clos St.-Denis Vieilles Vignes	93–95	2012–2022
2005 Clos de la Roche Vieilles Vignes	92–94	2012–2020+?
2005 Echézeaux Vieilles Vignes	93–95	now–2020+?
2005 Grands Echézeaux Vieilles Vignes	92–94	now–2020
2005 Clos Vougeot Vieilles Vignes	93–95	2012–2022
2005 Chambertin Vieilles Vignes	96–98	2014–2030
2005 Chambertin Clos de Bèze Vieilles Vignes	95–97	2014–2028
1997 Chambertin Clos de Bèze	93–95	now–2012
2005 Bonnes Mares Vieilles Vignes	94–96	now–2022

DOMAINE FERNAND LECHENEAUT ET FILS * * * *
NUITS-ST.-GEORGES $30.00–$300.00

The Lecheneaut brothers Vincent and Philippe produce sumptuous, rich reds with the requisite concentration to resist any obvious marking by their 50% to 100% of new oak. These are
generally forward, early flattering, often positively flamboyant wines, even in a usually structured vintage like 2005. Excellent *villages* wines from five prestigious communes, outstanding
premier crus from Chambolle and Nuits-St.-Georges, and a tiny quantity of exceptional Clos

de la Roche are not the entire story here. Chorey-les-Beaune and Marsannay offer plenty of appeal for consumers who have less than $50 to spend on a serious bottle of Pinot Noir.

2005 Marsannay	88–89	now–2010
2005 Chambolle-Musigny	91–92	now–2012
2002 Chambolle-Musigny	89–90	now–2010
2005 Gevrey-Chambertin	90–91	now–2014
2002 Gevrey-Chambertin	89–91	now–2011
2002 Nuits-St.-Georges	87–88	now–2011
2005 Morey-St.-Denis	89–90	now–2012
2002 Morey-St.-Denis	88–89	now–2010
2005 Vosne-Romanée	90–91	now–2012
2002 Vosne-Romanée	89–91	now–2010
2005 Chambolle-Musigny 1er Cru	92–93	now–2015
2002 Chambolle-Musigny 1er Cru	92–94	now–2013
2001 Chambolle-Musigny 1er Cru	89–91	now
2005 Morey-St.-Denis Clos des Ormes	92–93	now–2015
1999 Nuits-St.-Georges Les Cailles	90–93	now–2012
2005 Nuits-St.-Georges Les Damodes	93–94	2010–2018
2002 Nuits-St.-Georges Les Damodes	92–94	now–2015
2001 Nuits-St.-Georges Les Damodes	90–92	now–2010
2000 Nuits-St.-Georges Les Damodes	92	now
2005 Nuits-St.-Georges Les Pruliers	91–92	now–2016
2002 Nuits-St.-Georges Les Pruliers	94–96	now–2018
2005 Clos de la Roche	92–93	2010–2018
2002 Clos de la Roche	98–100	now–2018
2001 Clos de la Roche	91–93	now–2010
2000 Clos de la Roche	90	now–2018
1997 Clos de la Roche	92–94	now
1996 Clos de la Roche	96–98	now–2012

DOMAINE LEFLAIVE * * * * *
PULIGNY-MONTRACHET $30.00–$1,000.00+

Director Anne-Claude Leflaive and winemaker Pierre Morey (who retired in 2007 to concentrate on his own domaine) have combined to set standards for white Burgundy that few other estates can approach. Their Puligny premier crus and grand crus combine richness and polish with depth and at times almost a lacy intricacy of flavor that can take a taster's breath away. No one should pass up a chance to purchase *villages* Puligny or generic Bourgogne from this estate either, and even those are worth cellaring. Leflaive has been farming biodynamically since taking control of her family's domaine in 1990 and has taken a leading role in promoting such farming practices since converting her entire estate to them a decade ago.

2000 Puligny-Montrachet Clavaillon	89–91	now
2000 Puligny-Montrachet Les Combettes	90–92	now–2014
2000 Puligny-Montrachet Les Folatières	89–91	now–2012
2000 Puligny-Montrachet Les Pucelles	91–93	now–2014
1999 Puligny-Montrachet Les Pucelles	89–91	now
2000 Bâtard-Montrachet	90–92	now–2011
1999 Bâtard-Montrachet	90–91	now–2010
2000 Bienvenue-Bâtard-Montrachet	92–93	now–2010
2000 Chevalier-Montrachet	91–93	now–2013
1999 Chevalier-Montrachet	90–92	now–2011

1997 Chevalier-Montrachet	92–94	now–2010
1996 Chevalier-Montrachet	96	now–2012
2000 Montrachet	92–94	now–2014
1999 Montrachet	91–93	now–2012
1997 Montrachet	94–96	now–2012
1996 Montrachet	97–99	now–2015

DOMAINE LEROY ★ ★ ★ ★ ★
VOSNE-ROMANÉE $120.00–$2,000.00+

Together with her St.-Romain-based Domaine d'Auvenay, Lalou Bize-Leroy (once joint manager and still part owner of the Domaine de la Romanée-Conti) runs this estate with something bordering on fanaticism. Whether the topic is her biodynamic beliefs and practices, minuscule yields, or astronomical prices, the common theme is one of extremism in the pursuit of quality. Leroy's whites are plush and sumptuous yet dense to the point of implosion, and her reds offer the most viscous, rich fruit possessed by any Pinot Noirs on the planet, although their sheer concentration (not to mention new oak) generally lends them formidable tannic structure. Leroy characteristically bottles all her wines at around 14 months. In 2004 she declassified the production from her many celebrated crus to *villages*-level wines, albeit ones priced in excess of $200 a bottle. Even if it is "just" her appellation Bourgogne, Burgundy lovers owe it to themselves to sample the craft and artistry of Leroy.

2002 Corton-Charlemagne	95	now–2018+?
2001 Corton-Charlemagne	97	now–2018
2000 Corton-Charlemagne	95	now–2018
1999 Corton-Charlemagne	90	now–2014
1997 Corton-Charlemagne	93	now–2011
2005 Pommard Les Vignots	91	now–2014
2003 Pommard Les Vignots	92	now–2012
2002 Pommard Les Vignots	92	now–2015
2002 Nuits-St.-Georges	91	now–2011
2005 Nuits-St.-Georges Aux Lavières	90	now–2012
2005 Nuits-St.-Georges Aux Allots	89	now–2012
1999 Nuits-St.-Georges Aux Allots	90	now–2010
2005 Nuits-St.-Georges Bas de Combe	92	now–2014
2005 Vosne-Romanée Aux Genaivrières	93	now–2015
2003 Vosne-Romanée Aux Genaivrières	91	now–2012
2002 Vosne-Romanée Aux Genaivrières	89	now–2011
1999 Vosne-Romanée Aux Genaivrières	90	now–2010
2005 Chambolle-Musigny Les Fremières	93	now–2015
2003 Chambolle-Musigny Les Fremières	92	now–2013
2002 Chambolle-Musigny Les Fremières	91	now–2012
2005 Savigny-les-Beaune Les Narbantons	92	now–2014
2002 Savigny-les-Beaune Les Narbantons	91	now–2011
2001 Savigny-les-Beaune Les Narbantons	90	now
1999 Savigny-les-Beaune Les Narbantons	93	now–2015
2005 Volnay Santenots du Milieu	93	now–2015
2003 Volnay Santenots du Milieu	94	now–2015
2002 Volnay Santenots du Milieu	91	now–2012
2005 Nuits-St.-Georges Aux Vignerondes	94	now–2015
2002 Nuits-St.-Georges Aux Vignerondes	92	now–2012
1999 Nuits-St.-Georges Aux Vignerondes	91	now–2015

1997 Nuits-St.-Georges Aux Vignerondes	91	now–2010
1996 Nuits-St.-Georges Aux Vignerondes	95	now–2012
2005 Nuits-St.-Georges Les Boudots	94	now–2015
2003 Nuits-St.-Georges Les Boudots	95	now–2015
2002 Nuits-St.-Georges Les Boudots	93	now–2014
2001 Nuits-St.-Georges Les Boudots	90	now–2010
2000 Nuits-St.-Georges Les Boudots	94	now–2012
1999 Nuits-St.-Georges Les Boudots	94	now–2015
1998 Nuits-St.-Georges Les Boudots	94	now
1997 Nuits-St.-Georges Les Boudots	93	now–2010
1996 Nuits-St.-Georges Les Boudots	96	now–2012
2005 Vosne-Romanée Les Brulées	94	now–2017
2003 Vosne-Romanée Les Brulées	92	now–2012
2002 Vosne-Romanée Les Brulées	94	now–2015
1999 Vosne-Romanée Les Brulées	88	now–2010
1997 Vosne-Romanée Les Brulées	93	now–2010
1996 Vosne-Romanée Les Brulées	93	now–2012
2005 Vosne-Romanée Les Beaux Monts	94	now–2017
2002 Vosne-Romanée Les Beaux Monts	94	now–2015
1999 Vosne-Romanée Les Beaux Monts	93	now–2015
1997 Vosne-Romanée Les Beaux Monts	93	now–2010
1996 Vosne-Romanée Les Beaux Monts	96	now–2012
2005 Chambolle-Musigny Les Charmes	95	now–2017
2003 Chambolle-Musigny Les Charmes	95	now–2015
2002 Chambolle-Musigny Les Charmes	95	now–2014
1999 Chambolle-Musigny Les Charmes	92	now–2015
1997 Chambolle-Musigny Les Charmes	93	now–2010
1996 Chambolle-Musigny Les Charmes	95	now–2012
2005 Gevrey-Chambertin Les Combottes	93	now–2017
2003 Gevrey-Chambertin Les Combottes	96	now–2017
2002 Gevrey-Chambertin Les Combottes	94	now–2015
2001 Gevrey-Chambertin Les Combottes	90	now–2010
2000 Gevrey-Chambertin Les Combottes	93	now–2012
1999 Gevrey-Chambertin Les Combottes	92	now–2015
1998 Gevrey-Chambertin Les Combottes	92	now
1997 Gevrey-Chambertin Les Combottes	94	now
1996 Gevrey-Chambertin Les Combottes	93	now–2010
2005 Corton-Renardes	95	now–2016
2002 Corton-Renardes	95	now–2015
1999 Corton-Renardes	97	now–2018
1998 Corton-Renardes	95	now–2012
1997 Corton-Renardes	96	now–2012
1996 Corton-Renardes	94	now–2012
2005 Romanée-St.-Vivant	97	2012–2018+?
2003 Romanée-St.-Vivant	94	now–2015
2002 Romanée-St.-Vivant	96	now–2016
2001 Romanée-St.-Vivant	91	now–2010
2000 Romanée-St.-Vivant	92	now–2010
1998 Romanée-St.-Vivant	93	now
1997 Romanée-St.-Vivant	95	now–2010
1996 Romanée-St.-Vivant	97	now–2012

2005 Richebourg	95	2012–2018+?
2003 Richebourg	96	now–2017
2002 Richebourg	97	now–2018
2001 Richebourg	92	now–2012
2000 Richebourg	94	now–2012
1999 Richebourg	95	now–2018
1998 Richebourg	95	now
1997 Richebourg	98	now–2012
1996 Richebourg	97	now–2015
2005 Clos Vougeot	94	2010–2020+?
2003 Clos Vougeot	97	now–2019
2002 Clos Vougeot	96	now–2018
2001 Clos Vougeot	90	now
2000 Clos Vougeot	92	now–2011
1999 Clos Vougeot	93	now–2018
1997 Clos Vougeot	96	now–2010
1996 Clos Vougeot	95	now–2012
2005 Musigny	98	now–2025+?
2003 Musigny	93	now–2015
2002 Musigny	98	now–2020
1999 Musigny	94	now–2018
1998 Musigny	96	now
1997 Musigny	95	now–2012
1996 Musigny	96	now–2016
2005 Clos de la Roche	96	now–2025
2003 Clos de la Roche	98	now–2020
2002 Clos de la Roche	96	now–2020
2001 Clos de la Roche	93	now–2013
1999 Clos de la Roche	96	now–2018
1998 Clos de la Roche	96	now–2014+?
1997 Clos de la Roche	98	now–2014
1996 Clos de la Roche	99	now–2015
2005 Latricières-Chambertin	96	2012–2020+?
2003 Latricières-Chambertin	95	now–2017
2002 Latricières-Chambertin	96	now–2019
1999 Latricières-Chambertin	94	now–2018
1998 Latricières-Chambertin	95	now
1997 Latricières-Chambertin	94	now
1996 Latricières-Chambertin	97	now–2012
2005 Chambertin	98	2014–2028+?
2003 Chambertin	96	now–2012
2002 Chambertin	98	2014–2025
2001 Chambertin	91	now–2010
2000 Chambertin	95	now–2014
1999 Chambertin	95	now–2018
1998 Chambertin	94	now–2010
1997 Chambertin	97	now–2012

DOMAINE DU COMTE LIGER-BELAIR ★ ★ ★ ★
VOSNE-ROMANÉE $80.00–$1200.00

Young Louis-Michel Liger-Belair, who considers himself to have been a student of the late, great Henri Jayer, has ambitious plans and soon will vinify more of his family's property, over which he only recently began assuming control. He has also rented a superb set of Vosne vineyards from a domaine that formerly sold its grapes. "I try to avoid much extraction," says Liger-Belair, but he has no compunction about a ten-day cold soak nor about the lavish (100%) application of new barrels, which can sometimes threaten to overwhelm these relatively delicately styled Pinots. As home to the grand cru La Romanée and prime acreage in the neighboring Vosne-Romanée premier cru Aux Reignots, not to mention as a place simmering with ideas, ambition, and ideals, this domaine is bound to be much scrutinized by lovers of Burgundy over the coming decade.

2005 Vosne-Romanée La Colombière	90	now–2012
2003 Vosne-Romanée La Colombière	92	now–2012
2005 Vosne-Romanée Clos du Château	88	now–2010+?
2003 Vosne-Romanée Les Chaumes	94	now–2014
2005 Vosne-Romanée Aux Reignots	91	2010–2014+?
2003 Vosne-Romanée Aux Reignots	96	now–2018
2005 La Romanée	93	2010–2018+?
2003 La Romanée	97	now–2020

DOMAINE THIBAULT LIGER-BELAIR ★ ★ ★ ★
VOSNE-ROMANÉE $30.00–$500.00

Like his cousin at Comte Liger-Belair in Vosne-Romanée, Thibault Liger-Belair is young, ambitious in the pursuit of quality, well traveled, and currently in the process of taking back family property from rental and *négociant* contracts. His barrels are in an ancient, inhospitably cold cellar in the center of Nuits-St.-Georges. Liger-Belair has begun pursuing a biodynamic regimen and has inaugurated a rigorously controlled *négociant* arm, its wines labeled Thibault Liger-Belair Successeurs. Low sulfur and a significant inclusion of whole clusters, depending on the circumstances and site, are among other prominent features of his approach. In 2005 the results included some very powerful, formidably structured wines, and he certainly beat the odds in 2004 as well. Liger-Belair professes caution lest his wines sacrifice polish and finesse to the overextraction of tannins, and so far he has trod that fine line. While the battery of grand crus here is impressive, the lowest rungs on the price list are overachievers, notably the striking Hautes-Côtes de Nuits Clos de Prieuré from a cool, breezy, late-ripening, south-facing wall of Marne clay high above the town of Arcenant.

2005 Bourgogne Grands Chaillots	88	now
2005 Bourgogne Hautes-Côtes de Nuits Clos de Prieuré	91	now–2011
2005 Vosne Romanée Aux Réas	89–91	2010–2013
2005 Chambolle Les Gruenchers	89–91	now–2013
2005 Corton Les Rognets	90–92	now–2015+?
2005 Corton-Renardes	89–91	now–2014+?
2005 Clos Vougeot	92–94	2012–2018+?
2003 Clos Vougeot	94	2010–2020
2005 Nuits-St.-Georges La Charmotte	88–90	now–2012+?
2002 Nuits-St.-Georges La Charmotte	88–89	now–2010
2005 Nuits-St.-Georges Les St.-Georges	91–93	2010–2017+?
2003 Nuits-St.-Georges Les St.-Georges	92	2010–2018+?
2002 Nuits-St.-Georges Les St.-Georges	90–93	now–2016
2005 Richebourg	92–94	2014–2020+?

HUBERT LIGNIER ★ ★ ★ ★ ★
MOREY-ST.-DENIS $50.00–$500.00

For more than two decades, Hubert Lignier turned out exceptionally deep, complex, intriguingly perfumed ageworthy renditions of Clos de la Roche, Charmes-Chambertin, and premier crus in Chambolle, Morey-St.-Denis, and Gevrey-Chambertin. His wines first gained serious attention among Burgundy lovers in the U.S. In the late 1990s, Hubert's son Romain gradually took the reins, upholding the estate's extraordinary standards. After Romain's untimely death, his American widow, Kellen Lignier, and the rest of the Lignier family were unable to agree on pooling their resources. The result is that, beginning with vintage 2006, septuagenarian Hubert Lignier and his younger son Laurent have begun making wine from one-third of their previous acreage, and the remaining crop is being vinified independently at a new estate named for Romain's children, Domaine Lucie et Auguste Lignier.

2005 Chambolle-Musigny	88–90	now–2012
2002 Chambolle-Musigny	89–90	now
2005 Morey-St.-Denis Vieilles Vignes	88–90	now–2014
2005 Gevrey-Chambertin	87–89	now–2010
2002 Gevrey-Chambertin	89–91	now
2005 Chambolle-Musigny Les Baudes	92–94	2012–2022
2003 Chambolle-Musigny Les Baudes	91	now–2014
2002 Chambolle-Musigny Les Baudes	92–94	now–2015
2001 Chambolle-Musigny Les Baudes	88–90	now–2010
1999 Chambolle-Musigny Les Baudes	89–90	now–2010
1996 Chambolle-Musigny Les Baudes	90–93	now–2010
2005 Gevrey-Chambertin Les Combottes	91–93	now–2020
2003 Gevrey-Chambertin Les Combottes	90	now–2014
2002 Gevrey-Chambertin Les Combottes	90–92	now–2013
1999 Gevrey-Chambertin Les Combottes	92–94	now–2012+?
1996 Gevrey-Chambertin Les Combottes	92–94	now–2010
2005 Morey-St.-Denis Les Chaffots	89–91	now–2014
2003 Morey-St.-Denis Les Chaffots	91	now–2013
2005 Morey-St.-Denis La Riotte	90–92	now–2017
2005 Morey-St.-Denis 1er Cru Vieilles Vignes	92–94	2012–2025
2003 Morey-St.-Denis 1er Cru Vieilles Vignes	89	now–2014
2002 Morey-St.-Denis 1er Cru Vieilles Vignes	91–93	now–2016
1999 Morey-St.-Denis 1er Cru Vieilles Vignes	92–94	now–2011
2005 Charmes-Chambertin	92–94	now–2022
2003 Charmes-Chambertin	89	now–2015
2002 Charmes-Chambertin	91–93	now–2014
2001 Charmes-Chambertin	89–90	now–2010
1999 Charmes-Chambertin	92–94	now
1996 Charmes-Chambertin	90–93	now–2010
2005 Clos de la Roche	94–96	2012–2030
2003 Clos de la Roche	94	now–2017+?
2002 Clos de la Roche	93–95	now–2020
2001 Clos de la Roche	89–91	now–2010
1999 Clos de la Roche	94–96	now–2020
1997 Clos de la Roche	94	now–2020
1996 Clos de la Roche	94–96	now–2018

LIGNIER-MICHELOT—VIRGILE LIGNIER ✳✳✳
MOREY-ST.-DENIS $50.00–$200.00

Young Virgile Lignier, at most a distant relative of the much better known Hubert Lignier, is crafting Pinots with considerable care and sensitivity. His excellent collection in a vintage as challenging as 2004 demonstrates that Burgundy lovers should be paying more attention to this address.

2005 Chambolle-Musigny Vieilles Vignes	87	now–2011
2005 Morey-St.-Denis En la Rue de Vergy	88	now–2011
2005 Morey-St.-Denis Vieilles Vignes	89	now–2012
2005 Morey-St.-Denis Aux Charmes	90	now–2014
2005 Morey-St.-Denis Les Cheneverys	89	now–2013+?
2005 Morey-St.-Denis Les Faconnières	91	2010–2015
2005 Clos de la Roche	90	now–2015+?

DOMAINE LONG-DEPAQUIT—ALBERT BICHOT ✳✳✳
CHABLIS $20.00–$100.00

This huge venerable estate now under the control of Beaune-based *négociant* Bichot manages nearly 10% of total Chablis grand cru acreage, including the *monopole* La Moutonne, between Vaudésir, of which it is officially a part, and Les Preuses. The 2005 and 2006 collections here were formidable, very much in keeping with Albéric Bichot's intentions to bottle ageworthy wines that reflect strong individuality and vineyard identity as well as live up to the great reputation this domaine once enjoyed. Early in 2007, a new team was put in place, triggered by the departure of Jean Didier-Basch, who had been responsible for making the wines of the two previous vintages.

MAISON FRÉDÉRIC MAGNIEN ✳✳✳✳
NÉGOCIANT, MOREY-ST.-DENIS $30.00–$300.00

The enormous range of wines that Frédéric Magnien vinifies under his own name as a *négociant* offers striking richness and a price-to-quality balance even in its lower echelons. His lengthy lineup of celebrated crus includes many utterly flamboyant wines, with a tendency throughout the Magnien portfolio toward what some tasters may interpret as extraneous, toasted-oak sweetness and a flirtation with overripeness. But readers craving extroverted sweetly rich Pinot are going to be thrilled. What's more, Maison Magnien has scored consistent successes even in difficult vintages such as 2004. Frédéric Magnien typifies the new style *négociant* in ferreting out fruit from exceptional parcels that would previously have suffered less than scrupulous winemaking or an anonymous if not ignominious amalgamation into blends in large Burgundy houses. He does not quibble with growers about price, but insists on an active role in the vineyards and control of the harvest, then lavishes attention on their fruit, with the result that literally dozens of outstanding red Burgundies that until only a few years ago did not exist now enter the marketplace through this address.

2003 Pommard Grands Épenots	94	2010–2020
2002 Chambolle-Musigny Vieilles Vignes	89–90	now–2011
2003 Gevrey-Chambertin Clos de la Justice	87	now–2012
2002 Gevrey-Chambertin Clos de la Justice	87	now–2010
2003 Gevrey-Chambertin Les Jeunes Rois	89	now–2014
2002 Gevrey-Chambertin Les Jeunes Rois	88	now–2010
2003 Gevrey-Chambertin La Perrière	91–93	now–2015
2002 Gevrey-Chambertin Les Seurvrées	88	now
2002 Gevrey-Chambertin Vieilles Vignes	86–87	now–2010

2003 Vosne-Romanée Au Dessus de la Rivière	90	now–2011
2002 Vosne-Romanée Au Dessus de la Rivière	87–88	now–2010
2002 Chambolle-Musigny 1er Cru	86–88	now–2012
2002 Chambolle-Musigny Les Baudes	91–92	now–2014
2002 Chambolle-Musigny Charmes Vieilles Vignes	93–94	now–2015
2003 Chambolle-Musigny Les Feuselottes	92	now–2016
2002 Chambolle-Musigny Les Feuselottes	91–93	now–2012
2002 Chambolle-Musigny Les Hauts-Doix	90	now–2012
2003 Chambolle-Musigny Les Amoureuses	93	2010–2020
2002 Chambolle-Musigny Les Amoureuses	93–94	now–2015
2001 Chambolle-Musigny Les Amoureuses	91	now–2010
1999 Chambolle-Musigny Les Amoureuses	94	now–2010
2003 Gevery-Chambertin Les Cazetiers	90	now–2014
2002 Morey-St.-Denis Clos Baulet	91–92	now–2014
2003 Morey-St.-Denis Les Blanchards	89	now–2012
2003 Morey-St.-Denis Les Ruchots	91	now–2015
2002 Morey-St.-Denis Les Ruchots	91–92	now–2014
2000 Morey-St.-Denis Les Ruchots	89	now
1999 Morey-St.-Denis Les Ruchots	90	now
2003 Morey-St.-Denis Clos Sorbé	89	now–2011
2002 Morey-St.-Denis Clos Sorbé	88	now–2010
2002 Nuits-St.-Georges Les Bousselots	87	now–2010
2003 Nuits-St.-Georges Les Longecourts	90	now–2011
2002 Nuits-St.-Georges Les Pruliers	91–93	now–2015
2003 Nuits-St.-Georges Les St.-Georges	93	now–2017
2002 Nuits-St.-Georges Les St.-Georges	93–95	now–2015
2001 Nuits-St.-Georges Les St.-Georges	90	now–2011
2000 Nuits-St.-Georges Les St.-Georges	90	now
2003 Nuits-St.-Georges Aux Thorey	90	now–2013
2003 Vosne-Romanée Les Suchots	89	now–2015
2002 Vosne-Romanée Les Suchots	89–91	now–2015
1999 Vosne-Romanée Les Suchots	91	now–2010
2003 Echézeaux	91	now–2014
1999 Bonnes Mares	95	now–2015
2003 Chambertin Clos de Bèze	93	2010–2020
2002 Chambertin Clos de Bèze	94–96	now–2016
1999 Chambertin Clos de Bèze	93	now–2013
1999 Chapelle-Chambertin	90	now–2010
2002 Charmes-Chambertin	94–96	now–2016
2001 Charmes-Chambertin	93	now–2012
1999 Charmes-Chambertin	92	now–2010

MICHEL MAGNIEN ★★★★
MOREY-ST.-DENIS $60.00–$300.00

The wines Frédéric Magnien makes at his family estate seem to exhibit slightly less flamboyance than many of those he vinifies as a *négociant*, but certainly they are formidably palate staining, with abundant underlying tannins and in most instances the lavish sweet spiciness of oak.

2005 Bourgogne	88	now
2003 Gevrey-Chambertin Les Goulets	91	now–2013

2003 Gevrey-Chambertin Les Goulets	90–91	now–2015
2005 Gevrey-Chambertin Les Seurvrées Vieilles Vignes	88	now–2013
2002 Gevrey-Chambertin Les Seurvrées Vieilles Vignes	89–90	now–2011
2005 Chambolle-Musigny Les Fremières	87	now–2012
2003 Chambolle-Musigny Les Sentiers	92	now–2013
2002 Chambolle-Musigny Les Sentiers	92–94	now–2014
2005 Gevrey-Chambertin Aux Echézeaux	90	20¯0–2014
2003 Gevrey-Chambertin Aux Echézeaux	88	now–2011
2002 Gevrey-Chambertin Aux Echézeaux	89–91	now–2014
2005 Gevrey-Chambertin Les Cazetiers	91	2010–2016+?
2003 Gevrey-Chambertin Les Cazetiers	92	now–2014
2003 Gevrey-Chambertin Les Cazetiers	92–93	now–2012
1999 Gevrey-Chambertin Les Cazetiers	92	now–2010
2003 Morey-St.-Denis Les Chaffots	92	now–2013
2002 Morey-St.-Denis Les Chaffots	91–93	now–2012
2001 Morey-St.-Denis Les Chaffots	90–92	now–2011
2000 Morey-St.-Denis Les Chaffots	92	now–2011
1999 Morey-St.-Denis Les Chaffots	92	now–2012
2005 Morey-St.-Denis Les Millandes	89	now–2013
2003 Morey-St.-Denis Les Millandes	92	now–2013
2002 Morey-St.-Denis Les Millandes	90–92	now–2012
2000 Morey-St.-Denis Les Millandes	90	now
2003 Morey-St.-Denis Mont Luisants	92	now–2012
2002 Morey-St.-Denis Mont Luisants	88–90	now–2010
2005 Morey-St.-Denis	88	now–2011
2005 Morey-St.-Denis Trés Girard	87	now–2012
2002 Morey-St.-Denis Trés Girard	87–89	now–2010
2003 Charmes Chambertin	94	now–2015
2002 Charmes Chambertin	93–94	now–2015
2001 Charmes Chambertin	92	now–2010
2005 Clos de la Roche	93	now–2018
2003 Clos de la Roche	96	now–2018
2002 Clos de la Roche	91–93	now–2012
2001 Clos de la Roche	94	now–2013
2000 Clos de la Roche	93	now–2012
1999 Clos de la Roche	93	now–2012
2003 Clos St.-Denis	96	now–2010
2002 Clos St.-Denis	95–97	now–2015
2001 Clos St.-Denis	92–94	now–2014
2000 Clos St.-Denis	90	now–2012

CHÂTEAU DE LA MALTROYE
(RED)*(WHITE) CHASSAGNE-MONTRACHET $50.00–$350.00

Jean-Pierre Cournut presides over an outstanding assortment of Chassagne-Montrachet premier crus, including the *monopole* Château de la Maltroye, not to mention this domaine's tiny morsel of Bâtard-Montrachet. He achieves a balance of richness with a clarity and refinement that are exemplary. This is also one of the few estates in Chassagne, nearly all of which possess extensive acreage of Pinot Noir in premier cru vineyards, to produce some truly distinguished reds.

DOMAINE JOSEPH ET PIERRE MATROT—THIERRY MATROT ★ ★ ★
MEURSAULT $50.00–$150.00

Director and winemaker Thierry Matrot believes in late harvest and capturing the richness of fruit in his Meursault and Puligny-Montrachet premier crus, but he is stoutly against the use of new oak, which he considers a cosmetic.

2003 Meursault Blagny	88	now–2010
2003 Meursault Chevalières	87	now
2002 Meursault Charmes	91	now–2012
2000 Meursault Charmes	88–91	now
2002 Meursault Perrières	91	now–2014
2003 Meursault Perrières	87	now–2010
2001 Meursault Perrières	90	now–2012
2000 Meursault Perrières	88–91	now–2012
1999 Meursault Perrières	91	now
2003 Puligny-Montrachet Les Chalumeaux	89	now–2010
2002 Puligny-Montrachet Les Chalumeaux	91	now–2012
2000 Puligny-Montrachet Les Chalumeaux	91–92	now–2010
2001 Puligny-Montrachet Les Combottes	90	now–2012
2003 Puligny-Montrachet Les Combottes	89	now–2012
2002 Puligny-Montrachet Les Combottes	91–92	now–2013
2000 Puligny-Montrachet Les Combottes	91–92	now–2011

DOMAINE MAUME ★ ★ ★
GEVREY-CHAMBERTIN $30.00–$175.00

Bertrand Maume has taken the reins from his father, Bernard, a biochemistry professor at Dijon University who built his family domaine's excellent reputation and added to its enviable collection of crus beginning in the late 1950s. The best wines from this address have always been uncompromisingly structured and highly distinctive in personality. Despite what Maume Père's profession might suggest, the goal was never squeaky-clean vinification. This estate was both one of the last to still use an ancient wooden press and one of the first in the postwar era to bottle without filtration.

2005 Gevrey-Chambertin Les Champeaux	86–88	now–2012+?
2005 Gevrey-Chambertin Lavaux St.-Jacques	87–89	now–2013+?
2005 Charmes-Chambertin	89–91	now–2015+?
2005 Mazis-Chambertin	90–92	2010–2016+?

MÉO-CAMUZET ★ ★ ★ ★
VOSNE-ROMANÉE $30.00–$1,200.00

The Camuzet family's properties achieved notoriety when Étienne Camuzet rented a portion of his exceptional holdings to the young Henri Jayer, who singlehandedly made the reputation of the Cros Parantoux vineyard and later went on to vinify wines at the Domaine Méo-Camuzet as well. In 1988 Jayer retired, at which time the portion of Camuzet property he had farmed reverted to the family domaine. The internationally trained Jean-Nicolas Méo, a grand-nephew of Étienne Camuzet, then took control of Méo-Camuzet and has since proven more than equal to the task. These are sumptuous, rich, concentrated Pinots that do not, however, lack refinement or intricacy. Those who will never be able to taste the more celebrated crus from Méo-Camuzet can rest assured that everything from their very affordable appellation Bourgogne on up reflects the same high standards and attention to detail. Production has been boosted in recent vintages by an extensive range of *négociant* wines under the label Méo-Camuzet Frère et Soeur.

2001 Corton	89–91	now–2012
1999 Corton	93–95	now–2015
1996 Corton	91–93	now–2010
2005 Corton Clos Rognets	91–92	2010–2016
2005 Bourgogne	89	now
2005 Marsannay	87	now–2010
2005 Fixin	88	now–2011
2005 Fixin Clos du Chapitre	88	2010–2012
2005 Nuits-St.-Georges	89	now–2012
2005 Chambolle-Musigny Les Feusselottes	91	now–2015
2003 Chambolle-Musigny Les Feusselottes	90	now–2013
2005 Nuits-St.-Georges Les Argillats	90	now–2015
2003 Nuits-St.-Georges Les Argillats	92	now–2014
2005 Nuits-St.-Georges Aux Boudots	92	now–2015+?
2005 Nuits-St.-Georges Aux Murgers	92–93	2010–2018
2001 Nuits-St.-Georges Aux Murgers	88–89	now
2000 Nuits-St.-Georges Aux Murgers	91	now
2005 Vosne-Romanée Les Chaumes	92–93	now–2016
2005 Vosne-Romanée Cros Parantoux	94–95	2010–2022+?
2001 Vosne-Romanée Cros Parantoux	87–88	now
1999 Vosne-Romanée Cros Parantoux	90–93	now–2012
2005 Vosne-Romanée Les Brulées	95–96	now–2022
2001 Vosne-Romanée Les Brulées	90–91	now–2011
1999 Vosne-Romanée Les Brulées	88–90	now
2005 Echézeaux	90–91	now–2016
2003 Echézeaux	95	2010–2020
2001 Echézeaux	90–92	now–2013
1999 Echézeaux	90–91	now–2011
2005 Clos Vougeot	93–94	2012–2018
2001 Clos Vougeot	91–93	now–2012
2005 Richebourg	94–95	2012–2025
2003 Richebourg	96	now–2020
2001 Richebourg	91–94	now–2015
2000 Richebourg	94	now–2012
1999 Richebourg	91–93	now–2013
1996 Richebourg	93–95	now–2012

DOMAINE MESTRE-MICHELOT ★ ★ ★
MEURSAULT $30.00–$120.00

Jean-François Mestre makes the wines here as well as at his father-in-law's neighboring Domaine Michelot. With shares in all three of Meursault's most prestigious premier crus—Charmes, Genevrières, and Perrières—as well as a choice portion of the underrated non–premier cru Narvaux vineyard, Mestre turns out richly satisfying, distinctive whites.

LOUIS MICHEL ★ ★ ★
CHABLIS $25.00–$100.00

Other than for the outstanding quality of his wines, Louis Michel is best known for his vocal advocacy of a stainless-steel regimen of vinification and maturation. These are wines which even at the grand cru level (which represents only a tiny fraction of the estate's production) never forget their first duty to refresh. Vibrant, firmly etched personalities are the rule throughout Michel's extensive lineup, whose best wines exhibit a riveting complexity and formidable aging potential.

DOMAINE MICHELOT ★★★
MEURSAULT $30.00–$120.00

This domaine formerly run by and named for Bernard Michelot is now under the direction of son-in-law Jean-François Mestre, who also makes the wines at the neighboring Domaine Mestre-Michelot. The wines here sometimes seem to benefit from an extra measure of richness than those at Mestre-Michelot, but with slightly less precision.

FRANÇOIS MIKULSKI ★★★
MEURSAULT $30.00–$120.00

In 1991, François Mikulski rented a portion of certain outstanding vineyards from his uncle Pierre Boillot, with whom he had worked in the 1980s. His regimen has evolved toward organic viticulture and a laissez-faire approach in the cellar. The wines—from a range of premier crus, although Mikulski says he wishes these included Perrières—are rich yet full of nooks and crannies of flavor that make for striking personalities. Even the generic whites are well worth exploring here, and Mikulski is serious about his several reds. The Mikulski "package"—not really a label but rather fired-on ink designed to resemble the chalk markings by which bottles are normally identified in Burgundy cellars—is to say the least dramatically unorthodox.

2003 Volnay Santenots du Milieu	89	now–2011
2003 Meursault Charmes	92	now–2012
2003 Meursault Genevrières	93	now–2014
2001 Meursault Genevrières	92	now–2010
2003 Meursault Goutte d'Or	91	now–2013
2001 Meursault Poruzots	91	now

LUCIEN LE MOINE
★★★★★(RED)★★★★(WHITE) *NÉGOCIANT*, BEAUNE $70.00–$600.00

As a *négociant*, Mounir Saouma is unique, and so are both the rapidity and height of Lucien Le Moine's rise. ("Le Moine" stems from Saouma's stay in the 1980s at a Trappist monastery in Jerusalem, which ultimately conferred a winemaking vocation on this would-be journalist.) In business only since 2000, he and his wife, Rotem Brakir, working alone, purchase tiny batches of juice (in the case of whites) and young wine (immediately following primary fermentation) from manifestly exceptional, strictly premier and grand cru sites, raising them in the grower's cellar for the first three to four months in custom-constructed new barrels of oak from the Jupilles forests in western France. (Saouma champions its use on account of its tightness of grain and relative flavor neutrality.) Saouma and Brakir put great stock in phenolic maturation and acid-retention in the fruit, employment of whole clusters, retention and absorption of lees in the young wines (especially in tannic vintages like 2005 or 2003), cold temperatures, low sulfur, late malolactic fermentation, one sole gravity racking, late bottling, and in general methods as close as possible to approximating the way they imagine vinification proceeded prior to World War II. Their mere 2,000 total cases are often spread over 50 or more lots, as Saouma puts it, "focusing on their individuality." The array of crus represented in this tiny cellar and the richness and the complexity of their vinous representations are stunning.

2002 Chassagne-Montrachet Les Cenevottes	88–89	now–2010
2003 Chassagne-Montrachet Morgeot	88–90	now–2010
2002 Chassagne-Montrachet Morgeot	89–91	now–2012
2003 Meursault Genevrières	88–90	now–2011
2002 Meursault Genevrières	88–90	now–2010
2003 Meursault Perrières	88–90	now–2011
2002 Meursault Perrières	90–92	now–2012
2003 Puligny-Montrachet Les Folatières	89–90	now–2010
2002 Puligny-Montrachet Les Folatières	90–92	now–2011
2000 Puligny-Montrachet Les Folatières	90–92	now–2010
1999 Puligny-Montrachet Les Folatières	92	now
2003 Corton-Charlemagne	88–90	now–2011
2002 Corton-Charlemagne	90–93	now–2016
2001 Corton-Charlemagne	89	now–2011
2002 Montrachet	94–97	now–2018
2000 Montrachet	87–90	now–2010
1999 Montrachet	93	now–2013
2005 Volnay Caillerets	95	now–2018
2002 Volnay Caillerets	89–91	now–2014
1999 Volnay Caillerets	91	now
2005 Pommard Épenots	91–93	now–2016
2002 Pommard Épenots	92–94	now–2018
2005 Pommard Grands Épenots	91–93	2010–16
2002 Pommard Les Rugiens	92–93	now–2014
1999 Pommard Les Rugiens	90	now
2005 Chambolle-Musigny Les Amoureuses	95	now–2018
2002 Chambolle-Musigny Les Amoureuses	92–95	now–2017
2000 Chambolle-Musigny Les Amoureuses	92	now–2010
1999 Chambolle-Musigny Les Amoureuses	93	now–2012
2005 Chambolle-Musigny Les Charmes	92	now–2016
2002 Chambolle-Musigny Les Charmes	92–94	now–2016
2005 Gevrey-Chambertin Les Cazetiers	94	now–2020
2003 Gevrey-Chambertin Les Cazetiers	91	now–2012
2002 Gevrey-Chambertin Les Cazetiers	92	now–2014
2002 Gevrey-Chambertin Lavaux-St.-Jacques	90–92	now–2017
2000 Gevrey-Chambertin Lavaux-St.-Jacques	92	now–2015
2005 Nuits-St.-Georges Les Vaucrains	92–94	now–2018
2002 Nuits-St.-Georges Les Vaucrains	92	now–2015
2005 Nuits-St.-Georges Les St.-Georges	90–92	2010–2018
1999 Nuits-St.-Georges Les St.-Georges	90	now
2005 Nuits-St.-Georges Les Cailles	94–96	2010–2020
2005 Vosne-Romanée Les Malconsorts	91–93	now–2018
2005 Vosne-Romanée Les Suchots	95–97	now–2020
2002 Vosne-Romanée Les Suchots	91–93	now–2016
2005 Bonnes Mares	94–96	2010–2022
2003 Bonnes Mares	95–97	now–2019
2002 Bonnes Mares	95–97	now–2022
1999 Bonnes Mares	92	now–2012
2005 Chambertin Clos de Bèze	96–98	2012–2025
2003 Chambertin Clos de Bèze	93–94	now–2018
2002 Chambertin Clos de Bèze	90–93	now–2020

2000 Chambertin Clos de Bèze	91	now–2010
2005 Charmes-Chambertin	91–93	now–2020
2000 Charmes-Chambertin	90	now
1999 Charmes-Chambertin	90	now–2011
2005 Clos St.-Denis	92–94	now–2022
2003 Clos St.-Denis	93	now–2018
2002 Clos St.-Denis	90–93	now–2018
2005 Clos de la Roche	94–96	now–2022
2003 Clos de la Roche	95	now–2017
2002 Clos de la Roche	91–93	now–2013
1999 Clos de la Roche	93	now–2012
2002 Clos Vougeot	94–96	now–2020
2005 Grands Echézeaux	92–94	2010–2020
2003 Echézeaux	94	now–2017
2002 Echézeaux	89–91	now–2018
2001 Echézeaux	90–91	now–2011
1999 Echézeaux	93	now–2016
2005 Mazis-Chambertin	95–97	2012–2025
2003 Mazis-Chambertin	95	now–2019
2002 Mazis-Chambertin	93–95	now–2020
2001 Mazis-Chambertin	91–93	now–2012
2000 Mazis-Chambertin	92	now–2011
2005 Richebourg	95–97	2014–2025+?
2005 Romanée-St.-Vivant	97–99	2012–2025

XAVIER MONNOT ★ ★ ★
MEURSAULT $40.00–$150.00

Xavier Monnot recently began bottling wine from his grandfather René Monnier's acreage under his own label. This is a young man full of ideas, whom we shall be hearing much about. His Pinots are marked by a cold soak and 30% to 40% new wood to give a brashly fruity, attention-grabbing first impression, but there are depth and density of fruit and minerals as well, clearly originating from well-controlled yields. The impressive whites (including premier crus in Puligny-Montrachet as well as Meursault) are also unapologetically oaky but bursting at their tightly stitched seams with fruit and mineral abundance.

2005 Beaune Cent Vignes	90	now–2013+?
2005 Volnay Clos des Chênes	91	2010–2015+?

DOMAINE DE MONTILLE ★ ★ ★ ★
VOLNAY $35.00–$250.00

Étienne de Montille, now operating out of spacious, newly restored cellars in Meursault, has confidently taken his wines in a more approachable, fruit-forward direction as well as one of greater consistency than prevailed during his father and domaine founder Hubert's regime, yet without sacrificing the brightness, minerality, and mystery that typified those wines at their best. In 2005 de Montille retained whole clusters for nearly all his vinifications, a practice he is convinced promotes floral and fruit expression as well as adding another layer of tannin structure from stems. The core of the estate, a bevy of premier crus in Volnay and Pommard, was repeatedly supplemented over the past decade, but then came what de Montille calls a once-in-a-lifetime opportunity of acquiring (with Domaine Dujac) the choice holdings of the Société Civile du Clos de Thorey from Thomas-Moillard. Domaine De Montille has thereby achieved a singular place among Burgundy domaines with a range of great sites from Volnay to Vosne to which, on the strength of the 2005 vintage, they are more than merely doing justice. De Montille also finds time to manage the Château de Puligny-Montrachet.

2005 Bourgogne	90	now–2010
2005 Beaune Les Sizies	90–91	now–2012
2005 Beaune Les Perrières	89–90	now–2011
2005 Beaune Les Grèves	91–92	now–2015
2005 Volnay La Carelle Sous la Chapelle	90–91	2010–2014
2005 Volnay Les Brouillards	88	now–2011+?
2005 Volnay Les Mitans	89–90	2010–2014+?
2005 Volnay Les Champans	91–92	now–2015
2005 Volnay Les Taillepieds	94–95	2010–2018+?
2005 Pommard Les Grands Épenots	92–93	now–2016
2005 Pommard Pezerolles	92–93	now–2016
2005 Pommard Les Rugiens	93–94	now–2020+?
2005 Corton Clos du Roi	91–92	2010–2016+?
2005 Nuits-St.-Georges Clos des Grandes Vignes	90–91	now–2012+?
2005 Nuits-St.-Georges Les Thorey	91–92	2010–2015+?
2005 Vosne-Romanée Les Malconsorts	94–95	2010–2018
2005 Vosne-Romanée Les Malconsorts—Christianne	96–97	2012–2020+?
2005 Clos Vougeot	91–92	

ALICE ET OLIVIER DE MOOR * * *
CHABLIS $20.00–$50.00

In out-of-the-way Courgis, the de Moors make a specialty of unfashionable but delicious wines, such as their unmistakably Chablis-like Bourgogne Aligoté, Bourgogne-Chitry, and St.-Bris. They also make fascinating Chablis—considerably more of it in the last several years in their expanded cellar. The approach in the cellar is always experimental and risk-taking, with some wines rendered in barrel and some in tank.

2002 Bourgogne Aligoté	90	now
2002 St.-Bris	89	now
2004 Chablis Bel Air et Clardy	89	now
2002 Chablis Bel Air et Clardy	90	now–2010
2000 Chablis Bel Air	92	now
2004 Chablis La Rosette	90	now–2010
2002 Chablis La Rosette	92	now–2011
2000 Chablis La Rosette	93	now

BERNARD MOREY ET FILS * * *
CHASSAGNE-MONTRACHET $30.00–$300.00

The wealth of winemaking Moreys in Chassagne and Meursault is bound to cause confusion. Bernard Morey routinely renders well-concentrated, distinctive wines from a wide array of premier crus in St.-Aubin, Chassagne, and Puligny, supplementing family holdings with wines from purchased fruit. Beginning in 2007, Bernard's sons Thomas and Vincent each took their share of this domaine and began a new estate.

2002 St.-Aubin Les Charmois	89	now
2003 Chassagne-Montrachet Caillerets	92	now–2011
2002 Chassagne-Montrachet Caillerets	94	now–2012
2000 Chassagne-Montrachet Caillerets	93	now
2003 Chassagne-Montrachet Les Chenevottes	90	now–2010

2002 Chassagne-Montrachet Les Chenevottes	90	now–2012
2003 Chassagne-Montrachet Clos St.-Jean	89	now–2010
2002 Chassagne-Montrachet Clos St.-Jean	90	now–2010
2003 Chassagne-Montrachet Les Embrazées	88	now–2010
2002 Chassagne-Montrachet Les Embrazées	90	now–2010
2000 Chassagne-Montrachet Les Embrazées	92	now
2003 Chassagne-Montrachet Morgeot	89	now–2010
2002 Chassagne-Montrachet Morgeot	93	now–2010
2001 Chassagne-Montrachet Morgeot	91	now
2000 Chassagne-Montrachet Morgeot	90	now
2003 Puligny-Montrachet La Truffière	92	now–2013
2002 Puligny-Montrachet La Truffière	92	now–2013
2001 Puligny-Montrachet La Truffière	92	now–2010
2000 Puligny-Montrachet La Truffière	92	now–2012
1999 Puligny-Montrachet La Truffière	92	now
1996 Puligny-Montrachet La Truffière	94	now
2003 Bâtard-Montrachet	91	now–2012
2002 Bâtard-Montrachet	93	now–2012
2001 Bâtard-Montrachet	93	now
2000 Bâtard-Montrachet	92	now–2013
1999 Bâtard-Montrachet	90	now–2010
1996 Bâtard-Montrachet	95	now–2010

MARC MOREY ★★★
CHASSAGNE-MONTRACHET $30.00–$300.00

The wines of Marc Morey, made by his son-in-law, Bernard Mollard, offer consistently opulent renditions of Chassagne premier crus as well as Bâtard- and Chevalier-Montrachet.

2002 Chassagne-Montrachet Les Caillerets	91	now–2011
2001 Chassagne-Montrachet Les Caillerets	93	now–2012
2002 Chassagne-Montrachet Les Chenevottes	90	now–2010
2001 Chassagne-Montrachet Les Chenevottes	90	now–2010
2002 Chassagne-Montrachet Morgeot	92	now–2011
2001 Chassagne-Montrachet Morgeot	92	now–2012
2003 Chassagne-Montrachet Les Vergers	88	now
2002 Chassagne-Montrachet Les Vergers	89	now–2011
2001 Chassagne-Montrachet Les Vergers	93	now–2012
2003 Chassagne-Montrachet Les Virondots	91	now–2011
2002 Chassagne-Montrachet Les Virondots	92	now–2012
2001 Chassagne-Montrachet Les Virondots	91	now–2012
2003 Bâtard-Montrachet	89	now–2010
2002 Bâtard-Montrachet	93	now–2012
2001 Bâtard-Montrachet	90	now–2010
1996 Bâtard-Montrachet	94	now
2003 Chevalier-Montrachet	92	now–2014
2002 Chevalier-Montrachet	90	now–2010
2001 Chevalier-Montrachet	92	now–2014

DOMAINE PIERRE MOREY AND MAISON MOREY-BLANC—
PIERRE MOREY ★ ★ ★
MEURSAULT $30.00–$300.00

Pierre Morey, who until retirement in 2007 had long made the wines at Domaine Leflaive, follows biodynamic principles at his own estate as well. Until the 1990s he was farming and bottling wine from some of Lafon's most celebrated vineyards. Under the Morey-Blanc label (Blanc being his wife's maiden name), Morey acts as a *négociant,* purchasing small amounts of fruit, often from prestigious vineyards. Quality here is very good and the distinctiveness of individual vineyards well preserved, though the overall results cannot be compared with those at Domaine Leflaive.

2003 Meursault Les Tessons	87–88	now–2010
2003 Meursault Les Genevrières	89	now–2011
2003 Meursault Les Perrières	89–91	now–2013
2000 Meursault Les Perrières	87–89	now
2003 Bâtard-Montrachet	89–90	now–2014
2000 Bâtard-Montrachet	90–92	now–2012
2003 Corton-Charlemagne (Morey-Blanc)	89	now–2015
2003 Montrachet	90	now–2015

DENIS MORTET ★ ★ ★ ★
GEVREY-CHAMBERTIN $50.00–$350.00

Through the 1990s, Denis Mortet increased the size and stature of his domaine, becoming known as one of the most meticulous, relentlessly perfectionist growers in Burgundy. Taking over this domaine in his midtwenties after his father's death, Arnaud Mortet bottled a superb collection from his father's final, 2005 harvest. The young Mortet emphasizes that he will continue a search for elegance and refinement begun by his father in recent years, with a lighter touch during fermentation, and at least for vintage 2006 the employment of some previously used barrels to somewhat deemphasize wood at the modest end of the price spectrum. Even lesser appellations here excel, notably the Marsannay Les Longerois and Bourgogne sourced from vines in pebbly soil at Daix, a northwestern suburb of Dijon once renowned for its Pinot but today obscure. Mortet excellence has its high bottle price.

2005 Bourgogne Cuvée de Noble Souche	90–91	now–2011+?
2003 Bourgogne Cuvée de Noble Souche	89	now–2010
2002 Bourgogne Cuvée de Noble Souche	88–89	now
2005 Marsannay Les Longeroies	87–89	now–2010
2005 Fixin	87–88	now–2011
2003 Gevrey-Chambertin	89	now–2010
2002 Gevrey-Chambertin	88–90	now
2003 Gevrey-Chambertin Combe du Dessus	90	now–2012
2002 Gevrey-Chambertin Combe du Dessus	90–91	now–2011
2001 Gevrey-Chambertin Combe du Dessus	89–90	now–2010
2002 Gevrey-Chambertin En Derée	89–90	now–2012
2005 Gevrey-Chambertin Mes Cinq Terroirs	91–92	now–2013
2003 Gevrey-Chambertin En Motrot	90	now–2011
2002 Gevrey-Chambertin En Motrot	89–90	now–2011
2001 Gevrey-Chambertin En Motrot	89–90	now–2010
2003 Gevrey-Chambertin Aux Velle	92	now–2013
2002 Gevrey-Chambertin Aux Velle	90–91	now–2011
2005 Chambolle-Musigny Aux Beaux Bruns	88–90	now–2012+?

2003 Chambolle-Musigny Aux Beaux Bruns	92	now–2012
2002 Chambolle-Musigny Aux Beaux Bruns	92–94	now–2015
2001 Chambolle-Musigny Aux Beaux Bruns	91–93	now–2012
2005 Gevrey-Chambertin 1er Cru	92–93	now–2014
2003 Gevrey-Chambertin 1er Cru	91	now–2013
2002 Gevrey-Chambertin 1er Cru	92–93	now–2015
2001 Gevrey-Chambertin 1er Cru	89–90	now–2012
2005 Gevrey-Chambertin Les Champeaux	93–94	now–2020
2003 Gevrey-Chambertin Les Champeaux	93	now–2015
2002 Gevrey-Chambertin Les Champeaux	92–94	now–2016
2001 Gevrey-Chambertin Les Champeaux	89–91	now–2012
2005 Gevrey-Chambertin Lavaux St.-Jacques	95–96	now–2024
2003 Gevrey-Chambertin Lavaux St.-Jacques	93	now–2016
2002 Gevrey-Chambertin Lavaux St.-Jacques	93–95	now–2017
2005 Chambertin	95–96	now–2024
2003 Chambertin	94	now–2016
2002 Chambertin	97–99	now–2020
2001 Chambertin	94–95	now–2016
1997 Chambertin	92–95	now–2010
1996 Chambertin	92–95	now–2012
2005 Clos Vougeot	89–90	now–2015+?
2003 Clos Vougeot	93	now–2014
2002 Clos Vougeot	94–96	now–2018
2001 Clos Vougeot	89–91	now–2012

DOMAINE GEORGES MUGNERET-GIBOURG * * * * *
VOSNE-ROMANÉE $30.00–$300.00

Dr. Georges Mugneret, an ophthalmologist, operated his domaine out of love, which showed in some of the most fascinating, consistently excellent Pinot Noirs in Burgundy. His widow and two daughters, Marie-Andrée and Marie-Christine, have been running the estate since his death in 1988. They have progressively enhanced their attention to all manner of detail and further refined the style of the wines, all the while taking back control over vineyards that had been sharecropped by others. Everything from the Mugnerets' tiny amount of Bourgogne to their similarly fractional amount of Ruchottes-Chambertin from old vines (wine from the young vines is bottled as Gevrey-Chambertin) can be enthusiastically recommended for finely chiseled fruit and mineral character as well as for the textural nuance and mysterious carnality that makes red Burgundy singular.

2002 Bourgogne	88–90	now–2010
2005 Gevrey-Chambertin	88–89	now–2012
2002 Gevrey-Chambertin	89–91	now
2005 Vosne-Romanée	90–91	now–2016
2002 Vosne-Romanée	89–91	now–2012
2005 Nuits-St.-Georges Les Chaignots	91–92	now–2020
2002 Nuits-St.-Georges Les Chaignots	90–92	now–2016
2001 Nuits-St.-Georges Les Chaignots	88	now–2010
2003 Nuits-St.-Georges Vignes Rondes	93	now–2020
2005 Chambolle-Musigny Les Feusselottes	93–94	now–2016
2002 Chambolle-Musigny Les Feusselottes	91–93	now–2014
2001 Chambolle-Musigny Les Feusselottes	90	now–2012
2005 Clos Vougeot	95–96	2012–2028

2003 Clos Vougeot	95–98	now–2018+?
2001 Clos Vougeot	91	now–2014
2005 Echézeaux	91–92	now–2020
2002 Echézeaux	92–94	now–2018
2001 Echézeaux	92	now–2012
2005 Ruchottes-Chambertin	93–94	2012–2026
2003 Ruchottes-Chambertin	88	now–2020+?
2002 Ruchottes-Chambertin	93–95	now–2020
2001 Ruchottes-Chambertin	91	now–2016

JACQUES-FRÉDÉRIC MUGNIER—
CHÂTEAU DE CHAMBOLLE-MUSIGNY * * * *
CHAMBOLLE-MUSIGNY $70.00–$400.00

Frédéric Mugnier has made some of the most delicious, intriguing Pinot Noirs in Burgundy since the mid-1980s, for much of which time he continued to work as an airline pilot. The 2004 return of the Mugnier family's 24-acre *monopole* Nuits-St.-Georges Clos de la Maréchale (managed and vinified for decades by Faiveley) presented Mugnier with significant challenges in vinification and logistics, but he has expanded and modernized his cellar to accommodate a greatly enhanced volume of wine while permitting greater attention to detail in all bottlings. Mugnier advocates unusually late but limited *pigeage*. "After all," he notes, "we take great care not to crush the berries, so it doesn't make sense to do an early *pigeage* and break them," and a late punch-down further extends the fermentation. His aim is to achieve refinement of flavor and texture. One taste of Mugnier's 2004s or 2006s confirms that he can succeed brilliantly in this aim even when nature does not make it easy. And with nature's full cooperation, Mugnier rendered an extraordinary 2005 collection, culminating in a silken-textured, explosively aromatic, impulsively intense, seemingly weightless Musigny.

2005 Nuits-St.-Georges Clos de la Maréchale	89–91	now–2012+?
2005 Chambolle-Musigny	90–92	now–2014
2003 Chambolle-Musigny	90	now–2011
2002 Chambolle-Musigny	88–89	now–2011
2005 Chambolle-Musigny Les Fuées	91–93	now–2018
2003 Chambolle-Musigny Les Fuées	91	now–2013
2002 Chambolle-Musigny Les Fuées	89–91	now–2012
2005 Chambolle-Musigny Les Amoureuses	93–95	now–2020
2003 Chambolle-Musigny Les Amoureuses	95	now–2015
2002 Chambolle-Musigny Les Amoureuses	90–92	now–2015
2001 Chambolle-Musigny Les Amoureuses	91–93	now–2012
1999 Chambolle-Musigny Les Amoureuses	91–93	now–2010
2005 Bonnes Mares	90–92	2010–2018+?
2003 Bonnes Mares	93	now–2015
2002 Bonnes Mares	90–92	now–2016
2005 Musigny	96–98	2010–2025+?
2003 Musigny	92	now–2015
2002 Musigny	91–93	now–2015
2001 Musigny	91–93	now–2012
2000 Musigny	91	now–2011
1999 Musigny	90–93	now–2013
1997 Musigny	93	now–2012

MICHEL NIELLON ★ ★ ★
CHASSAGNE-MONTRACHET $40.00–$300.00

Michel Niellon, who nowadays works with his two sons-in-law, has achieved an excellent reputation, above all for his Bâtard- and Chevalier-Montrachet. The wines at this address are consistently ripe and rich, if not always the last word in subtlety or finesse.

2002 Chassagne-Montrachet Champ-Gain	90	now–2010
2002 Chassagne-Montrachet Chaumées	89	now
2003 Chassagne-Montrachet Clos St.-Jean	88	now–2010
2002 Chassagne-Montrachet Clos St.-Jean	89	now
2001 Chassagne-Montrachet Clos St.-Jean	91	now
2003 Chassagne-Montrachet La Maltroie	87	now
2002 Chassagne-Montrachet La Maltroie	91	now–2010
2001 Chassagne-Montrachet La Maltroie	90	now–2010
1999 Chassagne-Montrachet La Maltroie	91	now
2003 Bâtard-Montrachet	88	now–2010
2002 Bâtard-Montrachet	94	now–2012
2001 Bâtard-Montrachet	94	now–2013
2000 Bâtard-Montrachet	94	now–2012
1999 Bâtard-Montrachet	91	now–2011
1996 Bâtard-Montrachet	99	now–2012
2003 Chevalier-Montrachet	89	now–2011
2002 Chevalier-Montrachet	92	now–2012
2001 Chevalier-Montrachet	95	now–2013
2000 Chevalier-Montrachet	92	now–2013
1999 Chevalier-Montrachet	92	now–2012
1996 Chevalier-Montrachet	99	now–2012

PHILIPPE PACALET ★ ★ ★ ★
NÉGOCIANT, BEAUNE $50.00–$200.00

It is hardly sufficient to refer to the colorful, articulate Philippe Pacalet—a Ph.D. in biochemistry who commenced his operation seven years ago after making wine at the Domaine Prieuré-Roch—as simply another of Burgundy's new breed of *négociants*. Working out of de Montille's former cellar, this nephew of Beaujolais's Maurice Lapierre employs whole clusters, gentle extraction, low sulfur, very little new oak (he prefers to buy once-used barrels), and bottles his generally small lots by hand. Interestingly, he rolls all of his barrels once, in summer, to disburse the lees. Pacalet specializes in locating sources of old *pinot fin* selections ("real Pinot, like pinecones") and will purchase and then sell off significant amounts of fruit to gain access to a grower's single, tiny parcel of old vines. Whether working with Pinot Noir or Chardonnay, he achieves generous perfume, flavor, and texture, in a key very much marked by these wines' low sulfur levels, which also dictate that they should be cellared only under ideal conditions. These wines are scarce and expensive, but to taste them is a revelation. No one seriously interested in Burgundy should neglect this experience.

2005 Pommard	90	now–2012+?
2005 Pommard Chanlains	91	now–2014+?
2005 Gevrey-Chambertin	92	now–2013+?
2005 Gevrey-Chambertin Perrières	92	now–2013+?
2005 Gevrey-Chambertin Lavaux St.-Jacques	96	now–2018+?
2005 Nuits-St.-Georges	93	now–2013+?
2005 Chambolle-Musigny 1er Cru	94	now–2015+?
2005 Charmes-Chambertin	94	now–2018+?

JEAN-MARC PAVELOT ★ ★ ★
SAVIGNY-LES-BEAUNE $30.00–$50.00

Jean-Marc Pavelot, recently joined by his son Hugues, has for more than two decades been a source for fascinating, affordable, ageworthy reds of Savigny premier cru appellation. These wines are not about gloss or surface polish, but rather the sometimes head-scratching mysteries of Pinot Noir and Burgundy *terroir*.

2005 Beaune Bressandes	87–89	now–2012+?
2005 Pernand-Vergelesses Les Vergelesses	86–88	2010–2014
2005 Savigny-les-Beaune	89	now–2012
2005 Savigny-les-Beaune La Dominode	89–91	2012–2018
2005 Savigny-les-Beaune Les Gravains	89–91	2010–2017
2005 Savigny-les-Beaune Les Guettes	88–90	2010–2015
2005 Savigny-les-Beaune Les Narbantons	89–91	2010–2017
2005 Savigny-les-Beaune Les Peuillets	88–90	2010–2015

DOMAINE DES PERDRIX ★ ★ ★
NUITS-ST.-GEORGES $70.00–$200.00

Owned by Maison Antonin Rodet, this domaine is producing sumptuous Pinots, notably from the *monopole* Nuits-St.-Georges Aux Perdrix and from well-situated Echézeaux.

2003 Nuits-St.-Georges	89	now–2012
2002 Nuits-St.-Georges	89–90	now–2013
2003 Nuits-St.-Georges Aux Perdrix	90	now–2014
2002 Nuits-St.-Georges Aux Perdrix	91–93	now–2016
2002 Vosne-Romanée	89–90	now–2012
2002 Echézeaux	94–96	now–2018

PAUL PERNOT ★ ★ ★ ★
PULIGNY-MONTRACHET $35.00–$175.00

A significant percentage of what Paul Pernot and his sons Michel and Paul vinify is sold to the *négociant* Drouhin. What is bottled at the domaine is of outstanding quality, ranging from not-so-simple appellation Bourgogne through a range of rich, expressive *villages*-level and premier cru wines (including Puligny-Montrachet Folatières, of which they own by far the largest share) to Bienvenue-Bâtard-Montrachet and Bâtard-Montrachet, which those lucky enough to compare will find endlessly intriguing and seductive.

PERROT-MINOT ★ ★ ★ ★ ★
MOREY-ST.-DENIS $40.00–$350.00

Christophe Perrot-Minot is fanatically dedicated to the pursuit of old-vine parcels with preclonal genetic diversity and minuscule yields, as well as to uncompromisingly sensitive vinification, aiming to achieve "a good balance of fineness and elegance with concentration . . . and a certain density from low yields but no artificial concentration from *pigeage*." The wines are racked only when they are assembled for bottling (by gravity, and unfiltered), thus remaining for the longest possible time under a protective blanket of lees and CO_2. Perrot-Minot offers a staggering range of appellations and stunningly high-quality Pinots, which for all their sheer intensity and impeccable surface polish display a subtlety and intrigue of the sort that only this grape, grown in Burgundy, can deliver. In the lineup here, a taster is apt to discover vineyards and corners of the Côte d'Or that he or she has never before encountered and experience a richness, complexity, and length that proclaim "grand cru" long before arriving at the half dozen wines that are actually so classified. Certain of these wines are bottled under the name Henri Perrot-Minot.

2005 Chambolle-Musigny Vieilles Vignes	92–93	now–2015
2005 Vosne-Romanée	92	now–2015
2005 Gevrey-Chambertin Les Perrières Vieilles Vignes	92–93	now–2015+?
2005 Morey-St.-Denis En la Rue de Vergy	91	now–2014
2005 Morey-St.-Denis La Riotte Vieilles Vignes	94–95	now–2017
1999 Morey-St.-Denis La Riotte Vieilles Vignes	88–90	now
2005 Chambolle Musigny La Combe d'Orveau Vieilles Vignes	96	now–2020
1999 Chambolle Musigny La Combe d'Orveau Vieilles Vignes	89–91	now–2010
2005 Vosne-Romanée Champs Perdrix Vieilles Vignes	94	2010–2017
2005 Vosne-Romanée Les Beaux-Monts Vieilles Vignes	93–94	now–2018
2005 Nuits-St.-Georges La Richemone Vieilles Vignes	94–95	now–2018
2005 Nuits-St.-Georges La Richemone Vieilles Vignes Ultra	95–96	now–2020
2005 Clos Vougeot Vieilles Vignes	96–97	2010–2025
2005 Chapelle-Chambertin Vieilles Vignes	95–96	2014–2025
2005 Charmes-Chambertin Vieilles Vignes	94–95	2014–2025+?
1999 Charmes-Chambertin Vieilles Vignes	92	now–2016
1996 Charmes-Chambertin Vieilles Vignes	92–94	now
2005 Mazoyères-Chambertin Vieilles Vignes	96–97	2014–2027
1999 Mazoyères-Chambertin Vieilles Vignes	90–92	now–2015
1996 Mazoyères-Chambertin Vieilles Vignes	91–93	now
2005 Chambertin Clos de Bèze Vieilles Vignes	99–100	2012–2030
2005 Chambertin Vieilles Vignes	95–96	2012–2025+?

GILBERT PICQ ET SES FILS ★ ★ ★
CHABLIS $20.00–$40.00

Didier Picq, whose brother Pascal manages the vineyards, believes in unhurried, unfussy vinification solely in tank, and his wines offer decisive personalities, strong on characteristics one can only describe as mineral, well worth chewing over or cellaring for a few years even if they are not notably polished or refined. The Picqs have no grand cru holdings, and their flagship is the little-known premier cru Vosgros, located on a hillside near their hamlet of Chichée, quite apart from the other classified vineyards of Chablis.

JEAN-MARC PILLOT ★ ★ ★ ★
CHASSAGNE-MONTRACHET $30.00–$300.00

Jean-Marc Pillot recently took over from his father, Jean, whose name still appears on the estate labels. J.-M. produces a range of Chassagne crus, including some from purchased fruit, of clarion purity and intensity. But the sheer concentration and surface polish achieved by this trained oenologist by no means preclude wines that reflect their individual vineyard origins and offer thought-provoking complexity. Pillot's lineup culminates in an exceptional Chevalier-Montrachet. He intends all his crus to be worth cellaring; it will be most interesting to track their evolution.

DOMAINE PONSOT
MOREY-ST.-DENIS $50.00–$350.00

Laurent Ponsot vinifies to the beat of a different drummer, as did his father, Jean-Marie, before him, whether in his employment of a basket press from 1945, his reliance on exclusively truly old barrels, his aggressive *pigeage,* or his virtual refusal since 1988 to sulfur the wines (nitrogen and CO_2 are administered at bottling). The results are as distinctive as the methods, but also profoundly impressive and proven to age magnificently. Certainly one has to adjust to a background level of chocolate flavor and the lack of a certain pep that is otherwise conveyed, MSG-wise, to wines that receive a strong dose of sulfur during their *élevage.* These are perhaps the most powerful wines in Burgundy, but even when their alcohols reach as high as 15% you do not notice. It is not unusual for the wines from Ponsot's wide assortment of grand crus (Clos de la Roche making up most of their volume) to stay in barrel for two years. The white Morey-St.-Denis Mont Luisants here, which has at various times incorporated Pinot Blanc and Chardonnay, has since 2006 been 100% Aligoté, and a revelation of the depth and complexity to which that grape can aspire in an unexpected place.

2005 Bourgogne Cuvée Pinson	88–89	now–2010
2005 Chambolle-Musigny Cuvée des Cigales	90–92	now–2014
2005 Gevrey-Chambertin Cuvée de l'Abeille	90–92	now–2015
2005 Chambolle-Musigny Les Charmes	90–92	now–2013
2005 Morey-St.-Denis Cuvée des Grives	89–91	now–2013
2005 Morey-St.-Denis 1er Cru Cuvée des Alouettes	90–92	now–2016
2005 Charmes-Chambertin	90–92	now–2016
2005 Griottes-Chambertin	92–94	2010–2018
2005 Chapelle-Chambertin	93–95	now–2018
2005 Chambertin	93–95	2010–2020+?
2005 Clos St.-Denis Cuvée du Centenaire	95–97	now–2025+?
2005 Clos de la Roche Cuvée Vieilles Vignes	96–98	now–2027+?

MAISON NICOLAS POTEL
**** (RED) *** (WHITE) *NÉGOCIANT,* NUITS-ST.-GEORGES $25.00–$700.00

Nicolas Potel, son of the late Gérard Potel of the Domaine de la Pousse d'Or in Volnay, is a noted exemplar of the new breed of hands-on micro-*négociants.* Some might even argue that he is the reductio ad absurdum of the micro approach, on the basis of his seemingly unmanageable number of tiny lots (typically three to five but sometimes only one or two barrels). But one only has to consider his uniformly superlative results. There is no question that Potel taps both the goodwill of prestigious growers and some extraordinary sources never subjected to individual bottlings before he arrived on the scene. Vinification, over which he has control in the vast majority of cases, is scrupulously low sulfur and in 2007 virtually entirely with whole clusters. A significant percentage of the acreage from which Potel sources—all planted to *sélections massales*—is farmed organically and in many cases biodynamically, a trend he vocally supports. For 2007 a Domaine Potel will officially debut, with wines from holdings in Savigny and Beaune. Potel also operates the Potel-Aviron partnership, a fastidious Beaujolais *négociant* operation.

2005 Santenay Clos Tavannes	91	now–2015
2005 Savigny-les-Beaune Les Peuillets	91	now–2015
2005 Savigny-les-Beaune Hauts Jarrons	90	now–2014
2005 Beaune Montée Rouge	90	now–2013
2005 Beaune Clos des Vignes Franches	89	now–2014+?
2005 Beaune Teurons	92	now–2017
2005 Beaune Grèves	92	now–2017
2005 Volnay Clos des Chênes	90	now–2016
2005 Volnay Santenots	91	now–2016
1999 Volnay Santenots	88–89	now–2011
2005 Volnay Vieilles Vignes	88	now–2012

2005 Volnay Champans	91	2010–2016
2005 Vosne-Romanée Vieilles Vignes	89	2010–2013
2005 Chambolle-Musigny Aux Échanges	91	2010–2015
2005 Nuits-St.-Georges	90	now–2013
2005 Nuits-St.-Georges Les Damodes	91	2010–2015
2005 Nuits-St.-Georges Les Murgers	93	now–2016
2005 Nuits-St.-Georges Les Pruliers	92	now–2014
2005 Nuits-St.-Georges Les Boudots	91	now–2015
2005 Vosne-Romanée Les Petits Monts	91–92	now–2015
2005 Vosne-Romanée Les Beaux Monts	93–94	now–2016
2005 Vosne-Romanée Les Brulées	91–92	now–2015
2005 Vosne-Romanée Les Suchots	92–93	now–2016
1999 Vosne-Romanée Les Suchots	90–92	now–2010
2005 Vosne-Romanée Les Gaudichots	93–94	now–2018
2005 Gevrey-Chambertin Le Petite Chapelle	93–94	now–2017
2005 Gevrey-Chambertin Lavaux St.-Jacques	94–95	2010–2019
2005 Charmes-Chambertin	92–93	now–2017
1999 Charmes-Chambertin	91–93	now–2011
2005 Latricières-Chambertin	94–95	2010–2019
2005 Chambertin	97–98	2010–2023
2005 Chambertin Clos de Bèze	94–95	2010–2023
2005 Clos St.-Denis	94–95	2010–2023
1999 Clos St.-Denis	92–93	now–2012
2005 Clos de la Roche	95–96	2010–2023
2005 Echézeaux	94–95	now–2019
1999 Echézeaux	89–91	now
2005 Grands-Echézeaux	91–92	2010–2016+?
2005 Bonnes Mares	94–95	2010–2020
1999 Bonnes Mares	91–93	now–2012
2005 Romanée-St.-Vivant	97–98	2010–2026

DOMAINE DE LA POUSSE D'OR ★ ★ ★
VOLNAY $40.00–$150.00

Outsider Gérard Potel took over this domaine (historically linked with the holdings of today's Domaine de la Romanée-Conti) in 1964 and brought it to considerable renown. He died in 1997 virtually at the moment of signing over the property to his then partners. Soon after, another outsider, the ambitious and conscientious Patrick Landanger, purchased Pousse d'Or. Landanger has expanded the holdings to include parcels in Corton and Puligny Caillerets (with further additions unquestionably to come) and made huge investments in the vineyards and cellar that have been reflected in the quality of recent vintages. Pousse d'Or incorporates no fewer than three Volnay *monopoles:* the contiguous Clos d'Audignac and Clos de la Bousse d'Or adjoining the estate just below the town, and the Clos des 60 Ouvrées within the Cailleret. The Santenays here can offer excellent value, and like the Volnays—at least based on the track record under the former regimen—ageworthiness.

2005 Santenay Les Gravières	88	now–2012
2002 Santenay Les Gravières	89–90	now–2011
2005 Santenay Clos Tavennes	91	now–2016
2002 Santenay Clos Tavennes	90–92	now–2012
2005 Volnay Clos de la Bousse d'Or	92	now–2022
2002 Volnay Clos de la Bousse d'Or	92–93	now–2018

2002 Volnay Caillerets	89–91	now–2017
2005 Volnay Caillerets Clos des 60 Ouvrées	94	2010–2025
2002 Volnay Caillerets Clos des 60 Ouvrées	92–94	now–2019
2005 Volnay Clos d'Audignac	88	now–2014+?
2002 Volnay Clos d'Audignac	89–91	now–2017
2005 Pommard Jarollières	91	2010–2015
2002 Pommard Jarollières	87–89	now–2014
2005 Corton Bressandes	89	2010–2014+?
2002 Corton Bressandes	91–94	now–2019
2005 Corton Clos du Roi	93	2012–2022
2003 Corton Clos du Roi	88–90	now–2015
2002 Corton Clos du Roi	90–93	now–2018

DOMAINE JACQUES PRIEUR
★★★★(RED)★★★(WHITE) MEURSAULT $50.00–$1,000.00

This domaine has been on an upward path since an influx of capital from Maison Rodet in the early 1990s. Martin Prieur and the Rodet oenologist Nadin Gublin strive to capture purity of fruit in their Pinot Noir through gentle extraction, although their young wines can tend to taste confectionery due to the influence of toasty new wood and a sheer sweetness of ripe raw material. New wood is also lavished on the whites, yet these by no means lack precision, clarity, or focus. The collection of parcels here is extraordinary, encompassing five grand crus in red (including Chambertin and Musigny) and three in white, including Le Montrachet.

2003 Meursault Perrières	86–87	now
2002 Meursault Perrières	92–95	now–2014
2000 Meursault Perrières	89–90	now
2005 Meursault Rouge Clos de Mazeray	89	now–2012
2003 Puligny-Montrachet Les Combettes	86–87	now
2002 Puligny-Montrachet Les Combettes	92–94	now–2011
2002 Chevalier-Montrachet	90–93	now–2015
2000 Chevalier-Montrachet	91–93	now–2012
2005 Corton Bressandes	92–93	now–2018
2002 Corton Bressandes	92–94	now–2015
1999 Corton Bressandes	91–93	now–2012
2000 Corton-Charlemagne	89–90	now–2012
1999 Corton-Charlemagne	89–91	now–2011
1997 Corton-Charlemagne	91–93	now
1996 Corton-Charlemagne	93–95	now–2010
2002 Montrachet	92–95	now–2017
2000 Montrachet	93–94	now–2014
1999 Montrachet	92–94	now–2012
1998 Montrachet	90–94	now–2010
1997 Montrachet	93–95	now
1996 Montrachet	93–96	now–2012
2005 Beaune Clos de la Figuine	90	now–2012
2002 Beaune Clos de la Figuine	89–91	now–2012
2005 Beaune Grèves	91	now–2014
2005 Beaune Champs Pimont	87–89	now–2012+?
2002 Beaune Champs Pimont	89–91	now–2012
2005 Volnay Champans	91–92	now–2016
2003 Volnay Champans	90–92	now–2014

1999 Volnay Champans	91–92	now–2012
2005 Volnay Santenots	90	now–2014+?
2005 Volnay Clos des Santenots	91–92	now–2016
2003 Volnay Clos des Santenots	89–90	now–2012
2002 Volnay Clos des Santenots	90–92	now–2014
2005 Clos Vougeot	91–92	2010–2018
2003 Clos Vougeot	95	now–2020
2002 Clos Vougeot	96–99	now–2024
2000 Clos Vougeot	90	now–2010
2005 Echézeaux	92–93	2010–2018
2003 Echézeaux	91	now–2016
2002 Echézeaux	93–95	now–2018
2005 Chambertin	92–93	2012–2020
2003 Chambertin	92	2012–2016
2002 Chambertin	94–96	2012–2020
2005 Musigny	94–95	now–2022
2003 Musigny	93	now–2019
2002 Musigny	94–97	now–2022
2000 Musigny	92	now–2010
1999 Musigny	91–93	now–2012
1997 Musigny	93–95	now–2010
1996 Musigny	94–96	now

CHÂTEAU DE PULIGNY-MONTRACHET * * * *
PULIGNY-MONTRACHET $40.00–$1,000.00

The team of Étienne de Montille and Jacques Montagon has in only a few years brought the exceptional collection of vineyards at this domaine (owned by Crédit Foncier de France) to full expression of their potential. Restraint in vinification rather than an attempt to make a flashy statement results in Chardonnays of exceptional purity, refinement, and intricacy.

DOMAINE RAMONET * * * *
CHASSAGNE-MONTRACHET $30.00–$1,000.00

This domaine was hugely significant in the recent history of Burgundy, having been "discovered" by the U.S. importer Frank Schoonmaker shortly before World War II, not very long after its founding by Pierre Ramonet. Grandsons Noël and Jean-Claude Ramonet today uphold the family tradition, unafraid to let the wines "make themselves" to a degree that many other vintners only talk about. Each wine from among the many outstanding crus in the Ramonet arsenal (culminating in three grand crus) comes off as something of a force of nature, and those seeking designer refinement may find some of these powerful wines unnecessarily brusque. The Ramonets are serious about their several red Chassagnes as well.

2001 Chassagne-Montrachet Boudriottes	89	now
2001 Chassagne-Montrachet Caillerets	87	now–2010
2001 Chassagne-Montrachet Les Ruchottes	89	now–2010
2000 Chassagne-Montrachet Les Ruchottes	90–92	now–2010
2001 Puligny-Montrachet Champs Canet	89	now
2001 Chevalier-Montrachet	92–94	now–2012
2001 Montrachet	91–94	now–2014
2000 Montrachet	91–93	now–2015
1999 Montrachet	90–92	now–2014
1998 Montrachet	91–94	now–2010

GÉRARD RAPHET ★★★
MOREY-ST.-DENIS $30.00–$250.00

Jean Raphet officially retired and passed on his domaine to his son Gérard with the 2002 vintage, but the latter had been responsible for the vineyards for many years. It would be hard to find an estate where to a greater degree winemaking is virtually over once the grapes are picked. Despite the family's major holdings in Clos Vougeot and Charmes-Chambertin, the consistent stars in this cellar have long been the Gevrey-Chambertin Lavaux St.-Jacques and Chambertin Clos de Bèze (each representing just 75 to 100 cases from old vines), followed by the Morey-St.-Denis Les Millandes and Clos de la Roche. But beginning in 2002, Gérard Raphet decided to set aside the fruit of his oldest, best-situated vines in the Clos Vougeot to produce 50 to 100 cases of a cuvée Vieilles Vignes to compete with his other best wines.

2005 Chambolle-Musigny	90	now–2012
2005 Gevrey-Chambertin Lavaux St.-Jacques	94	now–2018
2001 Charmes-Chambertin	90	now
2000 Charmes-Chambertin	92	now
2005 Chambertin Clos de Bèze	96	2010–2026
2003 Chambertin Clos de Bèze	98	now–2020
2002 Chambertin Clos de Bèze	94	now–2015
1999 Clos de la Roche	92	now–2011
2001 Clos Vougeot	90	now
2005 Clos Vougeot Vieilles Vignes	93	2010–2020
2003 Clos Vougeot Vieilles Vignes	97	now–2020

FRANÇOIS RAVENEAU ★★★★★
CHABLIS $80.00–$7,000.00

During the 1970s and early '80s, François Raveneau built a reputation as an uncompromising adherent to the methods and yields of a bygone era and a singular beacon of Chablis quality. Even in vintages (then not infrequent) when other vintners struggled to get their grapes ripe, one could rest virtually assured of magic in the wines of Raveneau. Since his son Jean-Marie took control in the mid-'80s, these have become cult wines to an extent not conceived of in wine lovers' dreams a quarter century ago, but the domaine's acreage has not grown to meet demand. These are wines (numbering five premier and three grand crus) of tremendous concentration and energy that can stand up to the significant percentage of new barrels employed, but that demand time in the cellars of those lucky enough to acquire any.

2004 Chablis Chapelot	86–88	now–2010
2004 Chablis Fôrets	90	now–2011
2004 Chablis Blanchots	90–92	now–2012
2002 Chablis Blanchots	93–95	now–2018
1996 Chablis Blanchots	93–95	now–2010
2004 Chablis Les Butteaux	89–90	now–2011
2002 Chablis Les Butteaux	91–92	now–2012
2004 Chablis Montée de Tonerre	90–91	now–2012
2002 Chablis Montée de Tonerre	90–91	now–2010
2004 Chablis Montmain	90	now–2011
2002 Chablis Montmain	89–90	now–2010
2004 Chablis Les Clos	92–94	now–2013
2002 Chablis Les Clos	98–100	now–2020
1997 Chablis Les Clos	93–95	now
1996 Chablis Les Clos	94–96	now–2012

2004 Chablis Valmur	91–94	now–2014
2002 Chablis Valmur	96–98	now–2020
1997 Chablis Valmur	90–93	now
1996 Chablis Valmur	94	now–2012

JEAN RIJCKAERT ★ ★ ★
NÉGOCIANT, LEYNES/MÂCON $25.00–$90.00

Originally Jean-Marie Guffens's partner in Verget, Jean Rijckaert subsequently established his own small, hands-on *négociant* firm specializing in wines of the Mâcon and Jura. (He also owns considerable vineyard acreage.) Unhurried vinification with minimal intervention and low sulfur characterize Rijckaert's approach, which has recently been extended to encompass several choice parcels in the Côte de Beaune.

2002 Viré-Clessé Thurissey (Rijckaert)	91	now
2002 Pouilly-Fuissé En Bulands Vieilles Vignes (Claude Loup)	90–92	now–2010
2003 Pouilly-Fuissé En Bulands La Roche (Mme. Gerin)	88	now
2004 Pouilly-Fuissé Vers Chanes (Serge Mornand)	90	now–2010
2002 Pouilly-Fuissé Vers Chanes (Serge Mornand)	92–94	now
2004 St.-Véran En Faux (J. P. Volluet)	91	now
2004 St.-Véran En Faux Vieilles Vignes (J. P. Volluet)	90	now–2010
2002 St.-Véran En Avonne (Rijckaert)	90	now
2004 Meursault Les Vireuils Vieilles Vignes	90	now–2011
2001 Bâtard-Montrachet	92–94	now
2003 Corton-Charlemagne	89–91	now–2012
2002 Corton-Charlemagne	93–94	now–2014
2001 Corton-Charlemagne	90–91	now

DOMAINE MICHÈLE ET PATRICE RION ★ ★ ★
NUITS-ST.-GEORGES $30.00–$300.00

For more than two decades, Patrice Rion vinified generous and richly satisfying wines at the Domaine Daniel Rion. At the beginning of the new century, he and his wife established their own estate, incorporating an enormous range of vineyard holdings all the way up to grand cru Bonnes Mares.

2002 Chambolle-Musigny Les Charmes	90–92	now–2015
2002 Chambolle-Musigny Les Cras	88–89	now–2010
2003 Nuits-St.-Georges Clos des Argillières	90–91	now–2013
2002 Nuits-St.-Georges Clos des Argillières	91–94	now–2014

DOMAINE ROBERT-DENOGENT ★ ★ ★
FUISSÉ $25.00–$50.00

Jean-Jacques Robert is one of the most ambitious growers in the Pouilly-Fuissé appellation. His wines, on which he is unafraid to lavish new wood and extended lees contact, are rich, big boned, yet sharply focused and full of flavor detail.

2000 Pouilly-Fuissé Cuvée Claude Denogent Vieilles Vignes	91	now
2000 Pouilly-Fuissé La Croix Vieilles Vignes	89	now
2000 Pouilly-Fuissé Les Reisses Vieilles Vignes	89	now

DOMAINE ROBLET-MONNOT   ＊ ＊ ＊ ＊
BLIGNY-LES-BEAUNE—VOLNAY $30.00–$130.00

Operating out of his family's fourth-generation press house in Volnay and a newly renovated but modest facility in Bligny that he shares with his wife and Vosne viticulturist, Cécile Tremblay, Pascal Roblet is turning out some of the most promising new wines of the Côte de Beaune. The regimen here recently turned biodynamic, and the approach in the cellar is restrained in extraction (generally including whole clusters) and in its use of new wood, very much oriented toward finesse rather than overt fruitiness or power. Given its tiny size—only 15 acres—this domaine's superb wines are bound to become difficult to acquire. Amazingly, Roblet says not one of his rich, ripe 2005s reached even 13% natural alcohol.

2005 Bourgogne	88–89	now–2010
2005 Auxey-Duresses Le Val	89–90	now–2011
2005 Volnay St.-François	92–93	now–2014
2005 Volnay Santenots	91	now–2014
2005 Volnay Brouillards	92	2010–2015
2005 Pommard Arvelets	92–93	2010–2017
2005 Volnay Pitures	94	2010–2018
2005 Volnay Taillepieds	95	2010–2020

DOMAINE DE LA ROMANÉE-CONTI   ＊ ＊ ＊ ＊ ＊
VOSNE-ROMANÉE $500.00–$10,000.00

This domaine under the direction of Aubert de Villaine, composed of holdings in seven grand crus (two of them *monopoles*), is the most renowned in Burgundy. The estate owns a barrel's worth of one additional grand cru, Bâtard-Montrachet, which is served strictly in-house, and the fruits of their considerable, superbly situated premier cru acreage in Vosne-Romanée are sold to *négociants*. The viticultural practice here is organic and will soon be biodynamic for the entire estate. Yields are extremely low, and de Villaine has taken the leadership regionally in repropagating ancient, genetically diverse vine selections. He was also a pioneer in the rigorous sorting of fruit after picking. Fermentation here includes whole clusters and stems. The wines are moved almost entirely by gravity and generally bottled in five-barrel batches. Overall, de Villaine's aim is to recapture methods of viticulture and vinification that might have prevailed a century ago. The reputation of the Domaine de la Romanée-Conti and the quality of its wines has approached the level achieved today in no small part thanks to de Villaine's tireless, quality-conscious labors. The domaine's wines are as profound, complex, and ageworthy as any from the appellations that it shares with other growers. And the Pinot Noir from their two *monopoles*—the typically tensile, intense La Tâche and the startlingly perfumed, kaleidoscopically complex, supremely elegant Romanée-Conti—truly exhibit a categorical difference from any other wines on earth.

2003 Montrachet	97	now–2015
2002 Montrachet	94	now–2018
2001 Montrachet	92–94	now–2013
2000 Montrachet	95	now–2010
1999 Montrachet	93	now–2011
1997 Montrachet	94	now
1996 Montrachet	96	now–2016
2005 Echézeaux	94–95	now–2020
2003 Echézeaux	95	now–2019
2002 Echézeaux	89	now–2014
1999 Echézeaux	91–93	now–2013

1996 Echézeaux	90–92	now
2005 Grands-Echézeaux	95–96	2012–2025
2003 Grands-Echézeaux	96	2010–2020
2002 Grands-Echézeaux	89	now–2018
2001 Grands-Echézeaux	89–90	now–2014
1999 Grands-Echézeaux	90–93	now–2014
1996 Grands-Echézeaux	91–93	now–2012
2005 Richebourg	94–95	2012–2026+?
2003 Richebourg	97	2013–2025
2001 Richebourg	90–92	now–2015
1999 Richebourg	94–97	now–2018
1997 Richebourg	93	now
1996 Richebourg	93–96	now–2018
2005 La Tâche	98–99	2016–2035
2003 La Tâche	99	2013–2030
2002 La Tâche	93	now–2019
2001 La Tâche	90–93	now–2014
1999 La Tâche	93–96	now–2018
1997 La Tâche	93	now–2012
1996 La Tâche	94–97	now–2020
2005 Romanée-Conti	99–100	2016–2030
2003 Romanée-Conti	95	2014–2030
2002 Romanée-Conti	90	now–2022
2001 Romanée-Conti	91–93	now–2016
1999 Romanée-Conti	95–99	now–2020
1997 Romanée-Conti	95	now–2012
1996 Romanée-Conti	96–98	now–2020
2005 Romanée-St.-Vivant	96–97	2014–2028
2003 Romanée-St.-Vivant	95	2010–2018
2002 Romanée-St.-Vivant	90	now–2016
2001 Romanée-St.-Vivant	88–89	now–2014
1999 Romanée-St.-Vivant	88–91	now–2014
1996 Romanée-St.-Vivant	91–93	now–2012

NICOLAS ROSSIGNOL * * *
VOLNAY $35.00–$120.00

A bewilderingly large number of Rossignols inhabit Volnay, and the wines of young Nicolas Rossignol (who took over his domaine in 1996 after a few years of an itinerant apprenticeship) reside behind more than one door bearing that family name. This Rossignol offers an enormous range of Pinots (eight Volnays, four wines each from Beaune and Pommard, plus myriad other appellations) aged in multiple cellars and possessed of consistent excellence, not to mention prices well below those commanded by Volnay's most celebrated vignerons. Rossignol employs whole clusters in certain cuvées ("I'm using a little more each year since 2003," he explains, "insofar as the vintage permits"), is cautious in fermentative extraction from his already concentrated raw material, and indulges in a "very attentive" postalcoholic maceration insofar as the quality of fruit in a given vintage permits. The use of new wood here is judicious (none was introduced in 2004, for example; "a former importer pushed me to use more new wood," he relates, "but those cuvées didn't hold up"); and Rossignol attempts to match the character of his different crus to barrels from different *tonneliers*.

2005 Bourgogne L'Hertière	88	now
2005 Beaune	90	now–2012
2005 Pommard Chanlins	91	2010–2015+?
2005 Savigny-les-Beaune	89	now–2012
2005 Savigny-les-Beaune Les Forneaux	90	2010–2015
2005 Volnay	92	2010–2015
2005 Volnay Caillerets	94	2010–2018
2005 Volnay Chevret	92	2010–2016
1999 Volnay Chevret	90	now–2010
2005 Volnay Frémiets	92	2011–2016+?
1999 Volnay Frémiets	88	now
1999 Volnay Santenots	90	now–2010

JOSEPH ROTY ★ ★ ★ ★
GEVREY-CHAMBERTIN $40.00–$750.00

The garrulous, opinionated, sometimes secretive Joseph "Jo" Roty has become a legend in his time. More importantly, his wines have themselves taken on legendary status. How does he manage to achieve such shockingly deep colors, such concentration, and such seamless integration of fruit and new wood? At least partial explanations can be found in his use of an extended period of cold soak, followed by long, leisurely fermentation; *élevage* in *barriques* whose wood Roty (having at one time built his own) says is guaranteed to have been air dried for three years; and very late bottling. Certainly, Roty's enviable, almost incredible collection of ancient vines in Gevrey's most celebrated grand cru vineyards has contributed to his fame. But in fact his bottlings from nonpremier cru vineyards in Gevrey and (increasingly in recent years, under his son Philippe's name) from Marsannay demonstrate more vividly than those of virtually any other estate the potential for rendering outstanding Burgundy from ostensibly lesser sites. Roty's two sons have managed a smooth assumption of responsibilities from their father, and the quality at this address has never been more impressive.

2005 Bourgogne Grand Ordinaire	87–88	now
2005 Bourgogne Cuvée de Pressonnier	88–89	now–2010
2005 Côte de Nuits Villages	89–90	now–2014
2005 Marsannay Quartier	89–90	now–2013
2005 Marsannay Champs St.-Étienne	89–90	now–2014
2005 Marsannay En Ouzelois	88–89	2010–2015
2005 Marsannay Boivin	89–90	now–2013
2005 Marsannay Clos de Jeu	91–92	now–2016
2005 Gevrey-Chambertin Champs-Chenys	89–90	now–2015
2005 Gevrey-Chambertin Champs-Chenys Vieilles Vignes	92–93	2010–2017
2005 Gevrey-Chambertin Clos Prieur	89–90	2010–2017
2005 Gevrey-Chambertin La Brunelle	89–91	2010–2017
2005 Gevrey-Chambertin Les Fontenys	94–95	2012–2022
1999 Gevrey-Chambertin Les Fontenys	89–91	now–2010
1996 Gevrey-Chambertin Les Fontenys	89–92	now–2010
2005 Mazis-Chambertin	95–96	2010–2025
2005 Griottes-Chambertin	94–96	2010–2025
1999 Griottes-Chambertin	95–98	2010–2016
1996 Griottes-Chambertin	92–94	2010–2012
2005 Charmes-Chambertin Très Vieilles Vignes	97–98	2012–2028

1999 Charmes-Chambertin Très Vieilles Vignes	95–97	now–2016
1996 Charmes-Chambertin Très Vieilles Vignes	92–95	now–2015

EMMANUEL ROUGET ★ ★ ★ ★
FLAGEY-ECHÉZEAUX $50.00–$500.00

As nephew, apprentice, confidant, and eventual heir to the great Henri Jayer, Emmanuel Rouget counted as an important Burgundy vintner from the moment he began making wine under his own label in 1985. Fortunately, the quality of his product lived up to his advance billing, his uncle's confidence, and the potential of the superb sites he collected through various sharecropping arrangements as well as his eventual inheritance. Recent expansion has given the blunt yet passionate former mechanic a facility that suits his talents, to supplement the cramped cellar underneath his house in out-of-the-way Flagey. A seductive perfume, silken texture, and harmonious colloquy of new wood and sumptuous fruit typify Rouget's Pinots, which culminate in the Jayer signature cru, Cros Parantoux. While these wines are scarce and high in price for their appellations, Rouget routinely bottles outstanding generic cuvées and a Savigny-les-Beaune that will fall within the special-occasion budgets of most wine lovers, if only they can latch on to a bottle or two.

2005 Savigny-les-Beaune	88–90	now–2010
2005 Vosne-Romanée	91–93	now–2016
2005 Vosne-Romanée Les Beaumonts	92–94	2012–2022
1996 Vosne-Romanée Les Beaumonts	90–92	now
2005 Vosne-Romanée Cros Parantoux	93–95	2012–2027
1997 Vosne-Romanée Cros Parantoux	94	now
1996 Vosne-Romanée Cros Parantoux	93–95	now–2012
2005 Echézeaux	91–93	now–2020
1996 Echézeaux	92–94	now–2010

DOMAINE JEAN-MARC ROULOT ★ ★ ★ ★
MEURSAULT $60.00–$100.00

The thoughtful, articulate Jean-Marc Roulot, whose domaine until recently still bore the name of his father, Guy, divides his time between the stage and the cellar. Roulot crafts the most elegant, transparent, intricate, and refined Meursaults. While he owns small portions of the great Charmes and Perrières vineyards, the bulk of his production is in single-vineyard Meursault from sites not classified premier cru but which he demonstrates can each eloquently testify in the glass to the uniqueness of their soils and microclimates. This was nowhere more in evidence than in Roulot's nascent 2006s.

2003 Meursault Les Bouchères	87–88	now–2010
2002 Meursault Les Bouchères	91	now–2010
2003 Meursault Les Luchets	90–91	now–2010
2003 Meursault Meix Chavaux	89–90	now–2010
2002 Meursault Meix Chavaux	89–90	now–2010
2003 Meursault Les Tessons	87–88	now
2002 Meursault Les Tessons	89–91	now–2011
2001 Meursault Les Tessons	89–91	now
2000 Meursault Les Tessons	88–90	now–2010
2003 Meursault Les Tillets	90–91	now–2011
2002 Meursault Les Tillets	91–93	now–2012
2000 Meursault Les Tillets	89–91	now–2010
2003 Meursault Les Vireuils	88–89	now
2002 Meursault Les Vireuils	88–89	now–2010

2003 Meursault Charmes	89–90	now–2011
2002 Meursault Charmes	89–90	now–2011
2001 Meursault Charmes	91–93	now–2013
2000 Meursault Charmes	89–91	now–2012
2003 Meursault Perrières	89–90	now–2012
2002 Meursault Perrières	90–92	now–2012
2001 Meursault Perrières	92–94	now–2012
2000 Meursault Perrières	91–93	now–2012
2003 Meursault Porusot	89–90	now–2010

GEORGES ROUMIER—CHRISTOPHE ROUMIER ★ ★ ★ ★ ★
CHAMBOLLE-MUSIGNY $50.00–$1,000.00

Christophe Roumier has brought his family's already famous domaine to a singular level of excellence through an exemplary application of intelligence, sensitivity, and hard work. His Pinots, as well as his rare Corton Charlemagne, combine lushness and sensuality with a mysterious resonance and fascinating detail of flavor. His family's stellar collection of crus (including Les Amoureuses, Clos Vougeot, Musigny, and Bonnes Mares) is supplemented by leases on properties ranging from *villages* level to grand cru (Charmes- and Ruchottes-Chambertin). This is one of those worrisomely numerous Burgundy domaines where, given the fate of its exceptional 2005 vintage wines in the marketplace, one hesitates before attempting to indicate an upper bound for prices. Thankfully, though, the volumes of Roumier appellation Bourgogne, *villages* Chambolle, and Morey-St.-Denis Clos de la Bussière (a *monopole*) are significant, and their quality-to-price ratio is still excellent.

2003 Corton-Charlemagne	94	now–2012
2002 Corton-Charlemagne	88	now–2012
2001 Corton-Charlemagne	90–91	now–2012
2000 Corton-Charlemagne	91	now–2012
1997 Corton-Charlemagne	93	now
1996 Corton-Charlemagne	91–93	now–2010
2005 Bourgogne	89	now–2010
2005 Morey-St.-Denis Clos de la Bussière	90–91	now–2014
2003 Morey-St.-Denis Clos de la Bussière	90	now–2012
2002 Morey-St.-Denis Clos de la Bussière	88–89	now–2012
2005 Chambolle-Musigny	89	now–2012
2003 Chambolle-Musigny	89	now–2010+?
2002 Chambolle-Musigny	89	now–2011
2005 Chambolle-Musigny Les Combottes	89–90	now–2012+?
2005 Chambolle-Musigny Les Cras	93–94	now–2018
2002 Chambolle-Musigny Les Cras	89–90	now–2012
2001 Chambolle-Musigny Les Cras	89–91	now
2005 Chambolle-Musigny Les Amoureuses	93–94	2012–2020
2003 Chambolle-Musigny Les Amoureuses	95	now–2017
2002 Chambolle-Musigny Les Amoureuses	93	now–2015
1999 Chambolle-Musigny Les Amoureuses	92–94	now–2012
1997 Chambolle-Musigny Les Amoureuses	92	now
1996 Chambolle-Musigny Les Amoureuses	91–93	now–2011
2005 Charmes-Chambertin	91–92	2010–2018
2003 Charmes-Chambertin	92	now–2014
2002 Charmes-Chambertin	89–91	now–2013
2000 Charmes-Chambertin	90	now–2010

2005 Ruchottes-Chambertin	94–95	2010–2022
2002 Ruchottes-Chambertin	90–93	now–2015
1999 Ruchottes-Chambertin	88–90	now–2012
1997 Ruchottes-Chambertin	92	now
1996 Ruchottes-Chambertin	92–94	now–2010
2005 Bonnes Mares	96–97	2010–2025
2003 Bonnes Mares	93	now–2019
2002 Bonnes Mares	94–97	now–2017
2001 Bonnes Mares	89–91	now–2010
2000 Bonnes Mares	91	now–2011
1999 Bonnes Mares	92–94	now–2014
1997 Bonnes Mares	93	now–2010
1996 Bonnes Mares	93–95	now–2017
2005 Musigny	97–98	2010–2028
2001 Musigny	90–92	now–2012
2000 Musigny	90	now–2012
1999 Musigny	90–92	now–2014
1997 Musigny	92	now
1996 Musigny	94–97	now–2018

ARMAND ROUSSEAU ★★★★
GEVREY-CHAMBERTIN $50.00–$500.00

Armand Rousseau assembled a remarkable collection of vineyards in the first quarter of the last century and was a pioneer in estate-bottling. With Eric Rousseau taking over increasingly from his oenologist father Charles (the face of the domaine since 1959; indeed, for many wine lovers virtually the face of Gevrey), the bottling may end up being slightly earlier than in the past. But such routine features as triage occurring exclusively in the vineyards (not the press house); the inclusion of whole clusters and stems; precocious malolactic fermentation; a reliance on older barrels; and an eventual light plaque filtration for all wines remain as before. Given the long-running success of these Pinots in subtly yet insistently conveying the distinct personalities of their great sites and standing the test of time, some might well ask, "Why change the recipe?" whereas others will wonder whether the wines could be made even better. This much is sure: The best among six grand crus and three premier crus chez Rousseau (meaning above all their Chambertin, Chambertin Clos de Bèze, Gevrey-Chambertin Clos St.-Jacques, Ruchottes-Chambertin, and Clos de la Roche) are icons of Burgundy *terroir*.

2005 Charmes-Chambertin	88–90	now–2015
2002 Charmes-Chambertin	88–89	now–2011
2005 Mazis-Chambertin	89–91	2010–2016+?
2003 Mazis-Chambertin	89–91	now–2016
2002 Mazis-Chambertin	87–89	now–2015
1999 Mazis-Chambertin	88–90	now–2010
2005 Clos de la Roche	92–94	2010–2024
2002 Clos de la Roche	90–92	now–2016
1999 Clos de la Roche	87–89	now–2010
2005 Ruchottes-Chambertin Clos des Ruchottes	93–95	2014–2025
2002 Ruchottes-Chambertin Clos des Ruchottes	89–92	now–2016
1999 Ruchottes-Chambertin Clos des Ruchottes	88–90	now–2012
1997 Ruchottes-Chambertin Clos des Ruchottes	89–92	now
1996 Ruchottes-Chambertin Clos des Ruchottes	89–92	now–2010
2005 Gevrey-Chambertin	88–90	now–2013

2005 Gevrey-Chambertin Lavaux St.-Jacques	91–93	now–2016
2005 Gevrey-Chambertin Les Cazetiers	89–91	2010–2015
2002 Gevrey-Chambertin Les Cazetiers	86–88	now
2005 Gevrey-Chambertin Clos St.-Jacques	94–96	2010–2027
2003 Gevrey-Chambertin Clos St.-Jacques	91	now–2018
2002 Gevrey-Chambertin Clos St.-Jacques	92–94	now–2020
1999 Gevrey-Chambertin Clos St.-Jacques	90–92	now–2016
1997 Gevrey-Chambertin Clos St.-Jacques	90–93	now
1996 Gevrey-Chambertin Clos St.-Jacques	92–94	now–2010
2005 Chambertin Clos des Bèze	96–98	2014–2030
2003 Chambertin Clos des Bèze	93	2012–2020+?
2002 Chambertin Clos des Bèze	94–96	now–2024
1999 Chambertin Clos des Bèze	92–95	now–2018
1997 Chambertin Clos des Bèze	91–94	now–2010
1996 Chambertin Clos des Bèze	92–94	now–2016
2005 Chambertin	96–98	2014–2035
2003 Chambertin	92	2012–2020+?
2002 Chambertin	94–96	now–2024
1999 Chambertin	90–93	now–2018
1997 Chambertin	91–93	now–2010
1996 Chambertin	94–96	now–2020

ÉTIENNE SAUZET ★★★★
PULIGNY-MONTRACHET $35.00–$1,000.00

By the time inheritance split up his domaine in 1990, Sauzet proprietor Gérard Boudot had already achieved a reputation as one of Burgundy's foremost Chardonnay vintners. He then became a pioneer in the art of managing a domaine and functioning as a specialized *négociant* under a single roof with a single brand identity, an approach forced on him if he was to make up for the third of his estate that had passed to his brother-in-law Jean-Marc Boillot. The array of celebrated premier cru and grand cru appellations here is awesome, as can also be said for the sheer intensity, polish, and craftsmanship reflected in Boudot's wines. At times those very characteristics can lead to wines more formidable than lovable, but there is little doubt that those able to pay the price of a Sauzet wine will enjoy a dazzling performance. For the less well off, the generic Bourgogne here surpasses most of what passes for Puligny-Montrachet *villages*.

2003 Chassagne-Montrachet	88	now
2002 Puligny-Montrachet Champ Canet	92–94	now–2012
2001 Puligny-Montrachet Champ Canet	90	now
2000 Puligny-Montrachet Champ Canet	89–91	now–2011
1999 Puligny-Montrachet Champ Canet	92	now
2003 Puligny-Montrachet Les Combettes	90–92	now–2013
2002 Puligny-Montrachet Les Combettes	90–92	now–2011
2001 Puligny-Montrachet Les Combettes	91	now
2000 Puligny-Montrachet Les Combettes	90–94	now–2010
1999 Puligny-Montrachet Les Combettes	94	now–2014
1998 Puligny-Montrachet Les Combettes	90–92	now–2010
1996 Puligny-Montrachet Les Combettes	94	now
2002 Puligny-Montrachet Les Folatières	88–90	now–2010
2001 Puligny-Montrachet Les Combettes	89	now
2000 Puligny-Montrachet Les Combettes	89	now

1999 Puligny-Montrachet Les Combettes	90	now
2003 Puligny-Montrachet La Garenne	90	now–2011
2003 Puligny-Montrachet La Garenne	90	now
2003 Puligny-Montrachet Les Perrières	89	now–2010
2002 Puligny-Montrachet Les Perrières	91–92	now–2011
2000 Puligny-Montrachet Les Perrières	89	now
1999 Puligny-Montrachet Les Perrières	89	now
2003 Puligny-Montrachet Les Referts	89	now–2011
2002 Puligny-Montrachet Les Referts	89–91	now–2010
2001 Puligny-Montrachet Les Referts	90	now
2000 Puligny-Montrachet Les Referts	89	now
2003 Bâtard-Montrachet	89–91	now–2012
2002 Bâtard-Montrachet	93–96	now–2012
2001 Bâtard-Montrachet	91	now–2010
2000 Bâtard-Montrachet	93–94	now–2013
1999 Bâtard-Montrachet	93	now–2013
1998 Bâtard-Montrachet	95	now–2010
1996 Bâtard-Montrachet	92	now
2003 Bienvenue-Bâtard-Montrachet	90–91	now–2013
2002 Bienvenue-Bâtard-Montrachet	92–94	now–2014
2001 Bienvenue-Bâtard-Montrachet	92	now–2012
2000 Bienvenue-Bâtard-Montrachet	91–92	now–2012
1999 Bienvenue-Bâtard-Montrachet	92	now–2012
1996 Bienvenue-Bâtard-Montrachet	93	now
2003 Chevalier-Montrachet	86–88	now–2011
2002 Chevalier-Montrachet	91–93	now–2013
2001 Chevalier-Montrachet	92	now–2012
2000 Chevalier-Montrachet	92–93	now–2015
1999 Chevalier-Montrachet	92	now–2012
1998 Chevalier-Montrachet	92	now
1996 Chevalier-Montrachet	92	now
2003 Montrachet	90–92	now–2015
2002 Montrachet	93–96	now–2015
2001 Montrachet	94	now–2011
2000 Montrachet	93–94	now–2015
1999 Montrachet	93	now–2012
1998 Montrachet	94	now
1996 Montrachet	96	now–2010

CHRISTIAN SERAFIN * * * *
GEVREY-CHAMBERTIN $35.00–$375.00

It seems fitting that the wines of Serafin, who trained as a carpenter, would be surrounded by new wood. For all their typically intense, sweet fruit (heightened by extended cold soaking), there is a certain stylistic stiffness which, particularly in vintages of natural concentration and structure, demands that one wait six or eight years before pulling any corks. A preponderance of old vines contributes significantly to the impressive quality at this estate.

2005 Chambolle-Musigny Les Baudes	89–90	now–2013
2003 Chambolle-Musigny Les Baudes	90	now–2015
2002 Chambolle-Musigny Les Baudes	89–90	now–2012
1999 Chambolle-Musigny Les Baudes	90	now–2010

2005 Morey-St.-Denis Les Millandes	92–93	2010–2015
2002 Morey-St.-Denis Les Millandes	88–89	now–2012
2001 Gevrey-Chambertin Vieilles Vignes	89–91	now–2012
1999 Gevrey-Chambertin Vieilles Vignes	90	now
2001 Gevrey-Chambertin Vieilles Vignes	88–89	now–2010
2005 Gevrey-Chambertin Les Corbeaux	89–90	2010–2013+?
2003 Gevrey-Chambertin Les Corbeaux	88	now–2014
2002 Gevrey-Chambertin Les Corbeaux	87–88	now–2011
2005 Gevrey-Chambertin Fonteny	92–93	2010–2016
2002 Gevrey-Chambertin Fonteny	87–89	now–2012
2001 Gevrey-Chambertin Fonteny	87–89	now–2011
1999 Gevrey-Chambertin Fonteny	87–89	now–2011
1996 Gevrey-Chambertin Fonteny	87–89	now
2005 Gevrey-Chambertin Les Cazetiers	94–95	2010–2018
2003 Gevrey-Chambertin Les Cazetiers	94	now–2019
2002 Gevrey-Chambertin Les Cazetiers	89–91	now–2014
2001 Gevrey-Chambertin Les Cazetiers	89–91	now–2012
1999 Gevrey-Chambertin Les Cazetiers	90–92	now–2012
1996 Gevrey-Chambertin Les Cazetiers	91–93	now
2005 Charmes-Chambertin	94–95	now–2018
2002 Charmes-Chambertin	90–92	now–2013
2001 Charmes-Chambertin	93–95	now–2012
1999 Charmes-Chambertin	97	now–2012
1996 Charmes-Chambertin	93–95	now–2010

DOMAINE SERVIN ***
CHABLIS $25.00–$80.00

François Servin's acreage includes no less than four grand crus and three premier crus. Since the arrival of the young Australian vintner Marc Cameron and the involvement of the importer Peter Weygandt, Servin has begun experimenting with hand-harvested, more leisurely fermented and matured, as well as unfiltered bottlings. These include one from Les Pargues, a site not rated as premier cru but possessed of distinctive personality and, at this address, memorable quality.

DOMAINE ANNE ET HERVÉ SIGAUT ***
CHAMBOLLE-MUSIGNY $50.00–$100.00

Anne and Hervé Sigaut deserve to be much better known as a source for the Chambolle virtues of florality, spice, high-toned fruit, and finesse. They offer excellent value *villages* wine and three prime premier crus.

DOMAINE TOLLOT-BEAUT ET FILS ***
CHOREY-LES-BEAUNE $40.00–$150.00

The large Tollot family runs a domaine with a corresponding wealth of appellations, each of which is characteristically rendered with mouthwatering richness and plenty of personality. More than half their acreage is appellation Chorey-les-Beaune that offers consistent value. There are premier cru holdings in Aloxe-Corton, Savigny-les-Beaune (including the *mono-pole* Champ Chevrey), and Beaune. The apex of complexity and ageworthiness is reached with two Cortons and a Corton-Charlemagne.

2002 Corton	89–91	now–2014
2003 Corton-Charlemagne	90–92	now–2013

1999 Corton-Charlemagne	89–91	now–2011
1998 Corton-Charlemagne	92	now
1996 Corton-Charlemagne	91–94	now–2010
2003 Corton-Bressandes	88–90	now–2014
2002 Corton-Bressandes	89–92	now–2015
1999 Corton-Bressandes	89–91	now–2012
2003 Beaune Clos du Roi	89–91	now–2013
2002 Savigny-les-Beaune Les Lavières	86–88	now–2010

DOMAINE TRAPET PÈRE ET FILS   ✴ ✴ ✴
GEVREY-CHAMBERTIN $30.00–$300.00

Young Jean-Louis Trapet evinces an inspiring degree of sincerity and that rarest of human virtues, "humbition." Clearly determined to return his family's estate to the celebrated place it occupied on the international stage for much of the late 20th century, Trapet thinks a critical tool is the practice of biodynamics, in which the domaine was recently officially certified. The wines, including an enviable trio of grand crus, are not sulfured at all during their *élevage,* and only minimally so at bottling, demanding that the typical taster recalibrate his or her palate accordingly.

2003 Gevrey-Chambertin	88	now–2011
2005 Gevrey-Chambertin Ostrea	88	2010–2013
2005 Gevrey-Chambertin La Petite Chapelle	89	2010–2013
2002 Gevrey-Chambertin La Petite Chapelle	90	now–2011
2005 Gevrey-Chambertin Clos Prieur	89	2010–2013
2002 Gevrey-Chambertin Clos Prieur	90	now–2010
2005 Gevrey-Chambertin 1er Cru	90	2010–2014
2005 Chapelle-Chambertin	92	now–2017
2002 Chapelle-Chambertin	91	now–2011
1997 Chapelle-Chambertin	91–94	now
1996 Chapelle-Chambertin	91–93	now–2010
2005 Latricière-Chambertin	91	2011–2016
2002 Latricière-Chambertin	93	now–2013
1997 Latricière-Chambertin	91–93	now
1996 Latricière-Chambertin	90–92	now
2005 Chambertin	93	2012–2017
2003 Chambertin	92	now–2015
2002 Chambertin	94	now–2014
1997 Chambertin	93–95	now
1996 Chambertin	92–94	now

CÉCILE TREMBLAY   ✴ ✴ ✴ ✴
BLIGNY-LES-BEAUNE—VOSNE $30.00–$200.00

Cécile Tremblay shares a winemaking facility with her husband, Pascal Roblet, in out-of-the-way Bligny. Whether or not one puts credence in the practices of biodynamics, it is evident that the "conversion" at this address is for Tremblay and Roblet an extension of their pains-taking, labor-intensive attention to vineyard details and sensitivity to the vine's environment, which goes so far as to include plowing certain parcels by horse. This grandniece of Henri Jayer is rendering from her choice but fewer than eight acres (including two premier and two grand crus) some of the most exciting new wines in the Côte de Nuits, pure and full of finesse. This domaine is bound to become one of Burgundy's elite, but sadly, almost as surely (given the price of land today) to remain tiny.

2005 Chambolle-Musigny Les Feusselottes	94	now–2018
2005 Morey-St.-Denis Les Tres Girard	91	now–2013
2005 Nuits-St.-Georges	89	2010–2013
2005 Vosne-Romanée Vieilles Vignes	92	now–2015
2005 Vosne-Romanée Les Beaumonts	94–95	2010–2020
2005 Chapelle-Chambertin	94	now–2018
2005 Echézeaux	93	now–2018

LAURENT TRIBUT ⋆ ⋆ ⋆
CHABLIS $25.00–$50.00

Laurent Tribut is Vincent Dauvissat's brother-in-law. The two domaines collaborate on harvest and apply comparable methods, so it is not surprising that the much less known Tribut, with his modest acreage and two premier crus, is a source for some wines full of personality as well as offering excellent value.

JACKY TRUCHOT ⋆ ⋆ ⋆ ⋆
MOREY-ST.-DENIS $35.00–$100.00

After 26 vintages (22 of them having been sold in the U.S., which became his largest market), and no heirs, 68-year-old Jacky Truchot retired after bottling his superb 2005 collection. He will continue to vinify only the small portion of Clos Sorbé behind the hulking family manor (familiar to Burgundy lovers from the old photograph on his label), and even that is for sale along with the house. Truchot's Pinots could rightly be called old-fashioned, which made them all the more exceptional and coveted in recent years. The expression "grown, not made" has never been truer than of these wines of a farmer bonded with his vines, all of them offering consistently excellent value, not least the Charmes-Chambertin from vines planted in 1920.

2005 Morey-St.-Denis	88	now–2014
2005 Morey-St.-Denis Clos Sorbé Vieilles Vignes	90	now–2022
2005 Chambolle-Musigny Les Sentiers	91	now–2022
2005 Morey-St.-Denis Les Blanchards	91	now–2022
2005 Charmes-Chambertin Vieilles Vignes	95	2010–2028
2005 Clos de la Roche Vieilles Vignes	94	now–2026

VERGET—JEAN-MARIE GUFFENS ⋆ ⋆ ⋆ ⋆
NÉGOCIANT, SOLOGNY/MÂCON $20.00–$300.00

When Belgian Jean-Marie Guffens founded Verget in 1990, the notions that a négociant would play a hands-on role in cultivation and harvest or pay growers by a complex formula that guaranteed a return superior to whatever his competitors might end up paying were radical. Novel too was Guffens's varied regimen of vinification (with many sorts of vessels) and sophisticated selection and utilization of the lees. The result was wines whose alliance of ripe yet precise fruit, mineral focus, and textural richness set a distinctive new standard that within five years made Verget one of Burgundy's most talked-about sources of white Burgundy. Guffens had assiduously studied the vineyards, proprietors, and commerce of the Côte d'Or, picking a moment to inaugurate his venture when the large Beaune-based négociants were vulnerable. But over the years his emphasis leaned toward other areas. Showcasing individual villages, vineyards, and terroirs of the Mâcon (home to his own Domaine Guffens-Heynen)— part of the initial Verget plan—took on greater significance in the new millennium. Guffens has carried on an occasionally interrupted love–hate relationship with Chablis, where for a time he had a press house; as with Mâcon his aim is to reveal the untapped, too little realized potential of an entire region. In 1997, Guffens purchased Château des Tourettes in the Luberon and nowadays he vinifies a wide range of both reds and whites from that property, under the label Verget du Sud. Guffens prides himself on his image as a maverick who suffers no fools gladly, but it is his inventiveness, idealism, and integrity—all evident in the wines—that will leave a lasting mark on Burgundy's commerce and wine culture.

2003 Mâcon-Burgy Les Prusettes Caniculus	88	now
2002 Mâcon-Bussières Vieilles Vignes du Clos	91	now
2003 Mâcon-Bussières Vieilles Vignes du Clos Caniculus	90	now
2004 Mâcon-La Roche Vineuse Vieilles Vignes de Somère	89	now
2004 Mâcon-Charnay Le Clos de St.-Pierre	89	now
2002 Mâcon-Bussières Vieilles Vignes du Clos	91	now
2003 Mâcon-Uchizy Vigne de la Martine Caniculus	89	now
2002 Mâcon-Vergisson La Roche	90	now
2000 Pouilly-Fuissé Cuvée des 10 Ans	91–93	now–2012
2004 Pouilly-Fuissé Les Combes Vieilles Vignes Terroir de Pouilly	92	now–2012
2002 Pouilly-Fuissé Terroirs de Vergisson	90	now–2010
2004 Pouilly-Fuissé Terroirs de Vergisson La Roche	91	now–2011
2002 Pouilly-Fuissé Terroirs de Vergisson La Roche	92	now–2011
2002 Pouilly-Fuissé Terroirs de Vergisson Vignes du Sessus	91	now–2010
2002 St.-Véran Le Clos	90	now
2003 St.-Véran Les Cras Caniculus	90	now–2010
2004 St.-Véran Mise Tardive	87	now
2002 St.-Véran Terres Noires	91	now
2000 St.-Véran Terres Noires	90	now
2002 St.-Véran Vignes de St.-Claude	90	now
2003 Viré-Clessé Vieilles Vignes de Roally Caniculus	89	now
2004 Chablis Cuvée de la Butte	91	now–2010
2002 Chablis Cuvée de la Butte	91	now–2012
2000 Chablis Cuvée des 10 Ans	89	now–2011
2004 Chablis Grande Élevage	90	now–2010
2003 Chablis Terroir de Chablis	88	now
2002 Chablis Terroir de Chablis	89	now
2003 Chablis Terroir de Fleys	90	now
2002 Chablis Terroir de Fleys	89	now
2002 Chablis Terroir de Poinchy	89	now
2004 Chablis Les Fôrets	92	now–2011
2002 Chablis Les Fôrets	91	now–2015
2000 Chablis Les Fôrets	89	now–2011
2003 Chablis Fourchaume	89	now–2011
2002 Chablis Fourchaume	91	now–2016
1996 Chablis Fourchaume Vieilles Vignes	93–96	now
2004 Chablis Fourchaume Vieilles Vignes de Vaulorens	92	now–2012
2002 Chablis Fourneaux	91	now–2013
2004 Chablis Mont de Milieu	90	now–2010
2002 Chablis Mont de Milieu	93	now–2016
2002 Chablis Montée de Tonerre	92	now–2015

2000 Chablis Montée de Tonerre	90–92	now–2010
1996 Chablis Montée de Tonerre	92	now
2004 Chablis Vaillons	90	now–2011
2003 Chablis Vaillons	90	now–2012
2002 Chablis Vaillons	91	now–2014
2000 Chablis Vaillons	91	now–2011
2004 Chablis Vaillons Vieilles Vignes des Minots	89	now–2010
2002 Chablis Vaillons Vieilles Vignes des Minots	96	now–2016
2004 Chablis Vaillons Vignes des Épinottes	92	now–2012
2004 Chablis Bougros	93	now–2013
2004 Chablis Bougros Côte de Bougueraud	94	now–2013
2003 Chablis Bougros Côte de Bougueraud	88	now–2010
2002 Chablis Bougros Côte de Bougueraud	91	now–2011
2000 Chablis Bougros Côte de Bougueraud	90–91	now–2012
1996 Chablis Valmur	93–96	now
1996 Chablis Vaudesir	91–93	now
2004 Bourgogne Grande Élevage	88	now
2002 Chassagne-Montrachet Les Chaumées	89	now
2004 Chassagne-Montrachet Les Chenevottes	91	now–2011
2003 Chassagne-Montrachet Les Chenevottes Caniculus	90	now
2000 Chassagne-Montrachet Franchemont	91–93	now–2010
1996 Chassagne-Montrachet La Maltroye Vieilles Vignes	91–94	now
1996 Chassagne-Montrachet Morgeot Vieilles Vignes	92–95	now–2010
2004 Chassagne-Montrachet Pimont	87	now
1996 Chassagne-Montrachet La Romanée	94–97	now–2010
1996 Chassagne-Montrachet En Remilly	93–96	now–2010
2004 Meursault	88	now–2010
1996 Meursault Charmes Vieilles Vignes	94–97	now–2010
2002 Meursault Les Tillets	92	now–2014
2000 Meursault Les Tillets	91–93	now–2011
2003 Meursault Les Tillets Caniculus	90	now–2011
2002 Meursault Rougets	88	now–2012
2002 Puligny-Montrachet Les Enseignères	90	now
2004 Puligny-Montrachet Sous les Puits	87	now
2002 Puligny-Montrachet Sous les Puits	88	now–2011
2004 Bâtard-Montrachet	92	now–2012
2002 Bâtard-Montrachet	95	now–2016
2001 Bâtard-Montrachet	93	now–2010
2000 Bâtard-Montrachet	91–93	now–2013
1996 Bâtard-Montrachet	98–100	now–2012+?
2004 Corton-Charlemagne	93	now–2014
2003 Corton-Charlemagne	89	now–2012
2002 Corton-Charlemagne	94	now–2016
2001 Corton-Charlemagne	92	now–2011
1996 Corton-Charlemagne	95–98	now–2012
2004 Corton-Charlemagne Vieilles Vignes Canicule	92	now–2013

A. & P. DE VILLAINE ★ ★ ★
BOUZERON $30.00–$45.00

Over more than 30 years, even as he helped restore the quality and reputation of the Domaine de la Romanée Conti, Aubert de Villaine refined the quality of wine at the domaine he and his American wife, Pamela, founded, bringing well-deserved attention to the Côte Chalonnaise. In particular, de Villaine championed the Aligoté of Bouzeron, which received its own appellation in 1979 and of which his remains the outstanding example. The winemaking direction is now passing from de Villaine to the manifestly able hands of his nephew Pierre Benoit, and this domaine remains an excellent source of red as well as white Burgundy value.

2005 Bourgogne Rouge La Digoine	87	now
2005 Bourgogne Rouge La Fortune	88	now
2005 Mercurey Les Montots	88	now–2010

DOMAINE COMTE GEORGES DE VOGÜÉ ★ ★ ★ ★ ★
CHAMBOLLE-MUSIGNY $100.00–$1,000.00

Among the oldest estate bottlers in Burgundy and owners of 70% of the grand cru Musigny, the Domaine Comte Georges de Vogüé is the source of many legendary libations. But when oenologist François Millet and commercial director Jean-Luc Pepin were hired in 1986, both the quality and reputation of the wines were due for a comeback, which is what this team delivered. Devoting meticulous attention to virtually every possible detail of viticulture, vinification, and *élevage,* the intellectually intense Millet scarcely spared expenses. No fewer than three reds now come from the estate's holdings in Musigny. Old vines from the choicest portions continue to be bottled as Musigny Vieilles Vignes, a wine whose complexity only a tiny handful of Burgundies can equal. The fruit of young vines is declassified and sold as Chambolle-Musigny. And a Chambolle 1er Cru bottling plays a role not unlike that of second wine to the Vieilles Vignes, incorporating fruit from vines of varying ages. Musigny Blanc exists as a grand cru appellation solely due to the small Chardonnay acreage of this domaine. But bottlings subsequent to the replanting of those vines in 1993 have been labeled Bourgogne (there being no legal provision for white wine of Chambolle-Musigny appellation), with the bottle price being raised as the vines mature. The almost savagely intense, berry-concentrated Bonnes Mares and the seductively perfumed, mysteriously carnal Chambolle-Musigny Les Amoureuses complete the portfolio of this prestigious estate.

2005 Chambolle-Musigny	90–91	2010–2015
2003 Chambolle-Musigny	88	now–2014
2002 Chambolle-Musigny	90–91	now–2011
2001 Chambolle-Musigny	89–91	now–2011
2000 Chambolle-Musigny	89	now
2003 Chambolle-Musigny 1er Cru	93	now–2015
2005 Chambolle-Musigny Les Amoureuses	94–95	now–2018
2002 Chambolle-Musigny Les Amoureuses	92–93	now–2016
2001 Chambolle-Musigny Les Amoureuses	92–94	now–2012
1999 Chambolle-Musigny Les Amoureuses	88–90	now
2005 Bonnes Mares	93–94	2010–2022
2003 Bonnes Mares	94	now–2020
2002 Bonnes Mares	92–94	2010–2017
2001 Bonnes Mares	89–90	now–2010
2000 Bonnes Mares	91	now–2012
1999 Bonnes Mares	89–90	now
1997 Bonnes Mares	91–93	now

1996 Bonnes Mares	92–95	now–2010
2005 Musigny Vieilles Vignes	96–98	2010–2025
2003 Musigny Vieilles Vignes	98	2010–2025
2002 Musigny Vieilles Vignes	97–99	now–2018
2001 Musigny Vieilles Vignes	94–96	now–2015
2000 Musigny Vieilles Vignes	93	now–2012
1999 Musigny Vieilles Vignes	90–92	now
1997 Musigny Vieilles Vignes	93–95	now–2012
1996 Musigny Vieilles Vignes	94–97	now–2014

JOSEPH VOILLOT ★ ★ ★
VOLNAY $35.00–$100.00

Jean-Pierre Charlot promotes a brisk, athletically lean, often downright rapier style, on which opinions are bound to diverge. If it sets you salivating to imagine the brightness, transparency, and cut of a Riesling in the medium of Pinot Noir—characteristics perhaps more appropriate to the estate's Volnays than its Pommards—then do not miss this address. The most recent Meursaults here have been revealing Charlot's talent for Chardonnay as well.

2002 Meursault Chevaliers	89	now
2003 Meursault Les Cras	87	now–2010
2003 Beaune Coucherais	87–88	now–2013
2002 Volnay	87–89	now–2011
2005 Volnay Vieilles Vignes	88	now–2013
2003 Volnay Vieilles Vignes	88–90	now–2013
2005 Volnay Les Brouillards	90–91	now–2015
2002 Volnay Les Brouillards	89–91	now–2015
2000 Volnay Les Brouillards	90	now
2005 Volnay Champans	89–90	now–2015
2002 Volnay Champans	90–92	now–2016
2005 Volnay Caillerets	87–88	now–2014
2005 Volnay Les Fremiets	88–89	now–2014
2003 Volnay Les Fremiets	88–90	now–2014
2002 Volnay Les Fremiets	88–89	now–2010
2002 Pommard	87–88	now–2011
2003 Pommard Clos Micault	89–90	now–2014
2001 Pommard Clos Micault	88–90	now
2003 Pommard Vieilles Vignes	87–88	now–2013
2003 Pommard Les Épenots	91–93	now–2019
2002 Pommard Les Épenots	91–93	now–2018
2001 Pommard Les Épenots	88–90	now–2010
2005 Pommard Les Petits Épenots	89–90	now–2016
2005 Pommard Pezerolles	88–89	now–2014
2003 Pommard Pezerolles	91–92	now–2016
2002 Pommard Pezerolles	91–93	now–2016
2000 Pommard Pezerolles	90	now
2005 Pommard Rugiens	91–92	now–2020
2003 Pommard Rugiens	87–89	now–2018
2002 Pommard Rugiens	92–94	now–2018
2000 Pommard Rugiens	90	now

[champagne]

FRANCE'S FAMOUS YET LITTLE-KNOWN APPELLATION

Champagne is betrayed by its very success. Not that this will cause any sleepless nights or soul searching on the part of the region's powerful merchants, who face demand so strong that there is serious talk of expanding the boundaries of what is already a mega-appellation. Champagne is ill served by the widespread failure to appreciate it *as wine,* with all of the attention to *terroir,* the grower's craft, and pairing it with cuisine (not to mention such mundane and potentially unpleasant matters as yields, additives, and labeling) that are practically taken for granted anywhere else in the world of wine. Champagne is first and foremost a commodity, a celebratory beverage, a status symbol. And given that its brands are among the most spectacularly successful, lucrative, and long-lived in the history of human commerce, who among the interested parties would want to rock that mighty luxury vessel? It is impossible to overlook the fact that Champagne's commodity value is based on what consumers want to be seen drinking, not the quality of what is in the glass.

The history of Champagne and its almost unparalleled marketing success is, up to a point, not unlike that of other regions of northern France. Proximity to Paris and navigable waterways were important advantages, but no doubt there was indeed something special about the synergy of Pinot Noir and certain sites, because even in the Middle Ages, some of the towns today most closely associated with that grape had already achieved renown. However, the huge area that is today called Champagne did not have any single identity as a growing region. That seems to have come in the 17th century, at around the same time that the legendary monk Dom Pérignon was introducing rigorous vineyard and cellar practices in the neighborhood of Épernay, and that an appreciation developed for the then minority of local wine that serendipitously sparkled as a result of refermenting in the bottle. From the beginning of the 19th century, Champagne was harnessed to invention, technique, and mechanization, and its reputation and market reach (rather than its bottles) exploded. Stronger glass and tight-fitting yet elastic corks were introduced, and it was discovered how to mathematically express the relationship between residual sugar and the postfermentative pressure of carbon dioxide.

Combining these innovations meant that one could safely and practically bottle sparking wine. From the cellars of the famous Widow Clicquot emerged the wooden racks and the technique to isolate the yeast deposit at the mouth of the bottle, whence it could more easily be removed: *remuage* (or riddling)—literally a slight shaking—was periodically administered to the bottle as it was moved ever closer to an upside-down position. A means of disgorgement was later perfected whereby the yeast deposit was frozen into a shallow plug, to be blown out by the pressure of the gas. In the late 20th century, the work of riddling for the most part passed to huge mechanical gyro-palates. Disgorgement, too, was largely mechanized, and synthetic, algae-based beads have recently been developed, caged within which yeasts can still perform their fermentative function. Before the decade is out, this latest innovation may render disgorgement as it has been known obsolete.

Ever since Champagne's rise to prominence as a sparkling beverage, it has not wanted for imitators or competitors. Nowadays, a significant number of wines around the world are fashioned by what was—until the recent advent of enhanced trademark restrictions—referred to as *méthode champenoise* ("Champagne method") of second fermentation in the bottle. Many of these wines utilize the same grape varieties as Champagne. Some of these Champagne imposters are serious, complex, and food-friendly, not to mention suitable for all manner of celebrations. What, if anything, makes a bottle of Champagne worth more than any other sparkling wine? The answers will reveal again the dichotomy at the heart of this appellation. If there are good gustatory reasons to prefer Champagne, one can expect the Champenois in predictably French fashion to chalk this up to—in a word to "chalk" itself, or speaking more broadly, to *terroir* and microclimate. But there is no overlooking the fact that the historical name—in effect the one big brand that is Champagne—is quite sufficient (practically by definition) to account for the premium price people will pay. And that price is very often paid for truly undistinguished—even mediocre—wine, vinified and blended on an industrial scale that would not in any other region of the world be associated with the wine market's "premium sector," and purchased in the same grocery or liquor stores as its inexpensive international, industrial kin. To talk of *terroir* is infinitely more appealing, but talk is cheap, whereas the laws and practices that have characterized Champagne for the past century—blending of base wines over a vast and geologically heterogeneous region; classification of crus by postal code rather than microclimate; vinification as a sort of secret house recipe—have marginalized any possible influence of *terroir*.

Yet, however we choose to account for what Champagne means on a commercial level, and however much disappointing wine is bottled under its name, the best of it is truly as distinctive and diverse as wine from any of France's appellations. There is unique excitement to be had not just in uncorking a bottle of Champagne but also in savoring its contents. This revelation is increasingly dawning on wine lovers the world over.

The past dozen years have arguably witnessed Champagne being at last pulled into the orbit of fine wine. The impetus for this has been the "discovery" that beyond the roughly 200 *négociants* of Champagne—ranging from the well-known "grandes marques" (some producing tens of millions of bottles annually) to the obscure (some so small as to produce only a few hundred thousand bottles)—lie more than ten times that many bottling growers, at least a few dozen of whom are skilled artisans offering a profoundly delicious finished product. Champagne vinified and bottled by its grower is fascinating for the same reasons as an estate-bottled wine from anywhere else. It offers clearer insights into the heart and mind of a particular person, and into a place. The unique savor of Champagne is indeed bound up with the peculiar ripening conditions, microclimate, and soils of this vast region, and in a grower's Champagne, one characteristically encounters the specificity (of village or even site) that in every other growing region of France is taken as the basis on which to judge a wine's pedigree. Nobody is in a position to know his or her vines and fruit more intimately than the grower, and no one can react more swiftly or decisively to the needs of vines that are practically under his

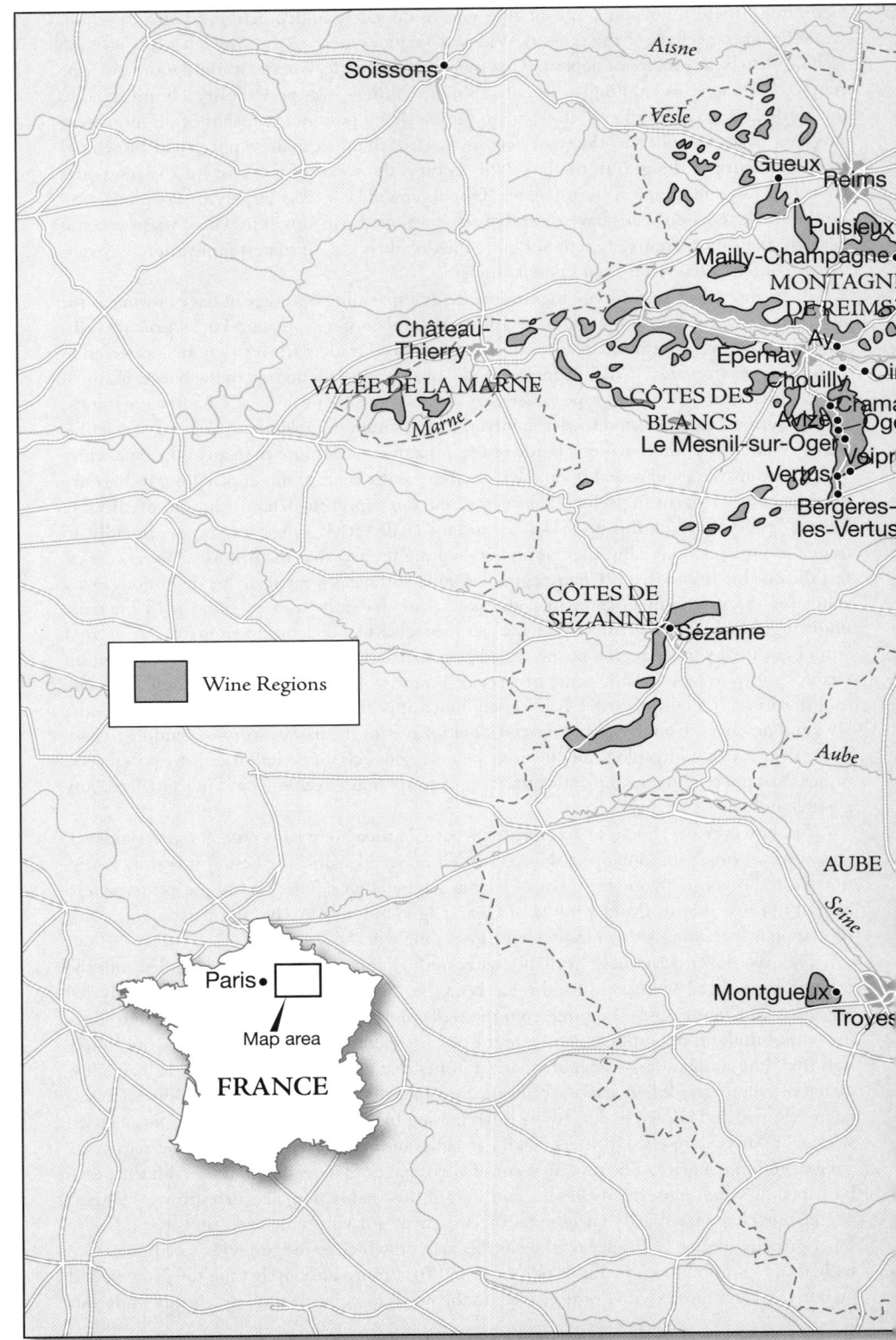

Soissons

Aisne

Vesle

Gueux

Reims

Puisieux

Mailly-Champagne

MONTAGNE
DE REIMS

Ay

Château-
Thierry

Épernay

Chouilly

Oi

VALÉE DE LA MARNE

CÔTES DES
BLANCS

Crama

Avize

Og

Marne

Le Mesnil-sur-Oger

Voipr

Vertus

Bergères-
les-Vertus

CÔTES DE
SÉZANNE

Sézanne

Aube

Wine Regions

AUBE

Seine

Paris

Map area

FRANCE

Montgueux

Troyes

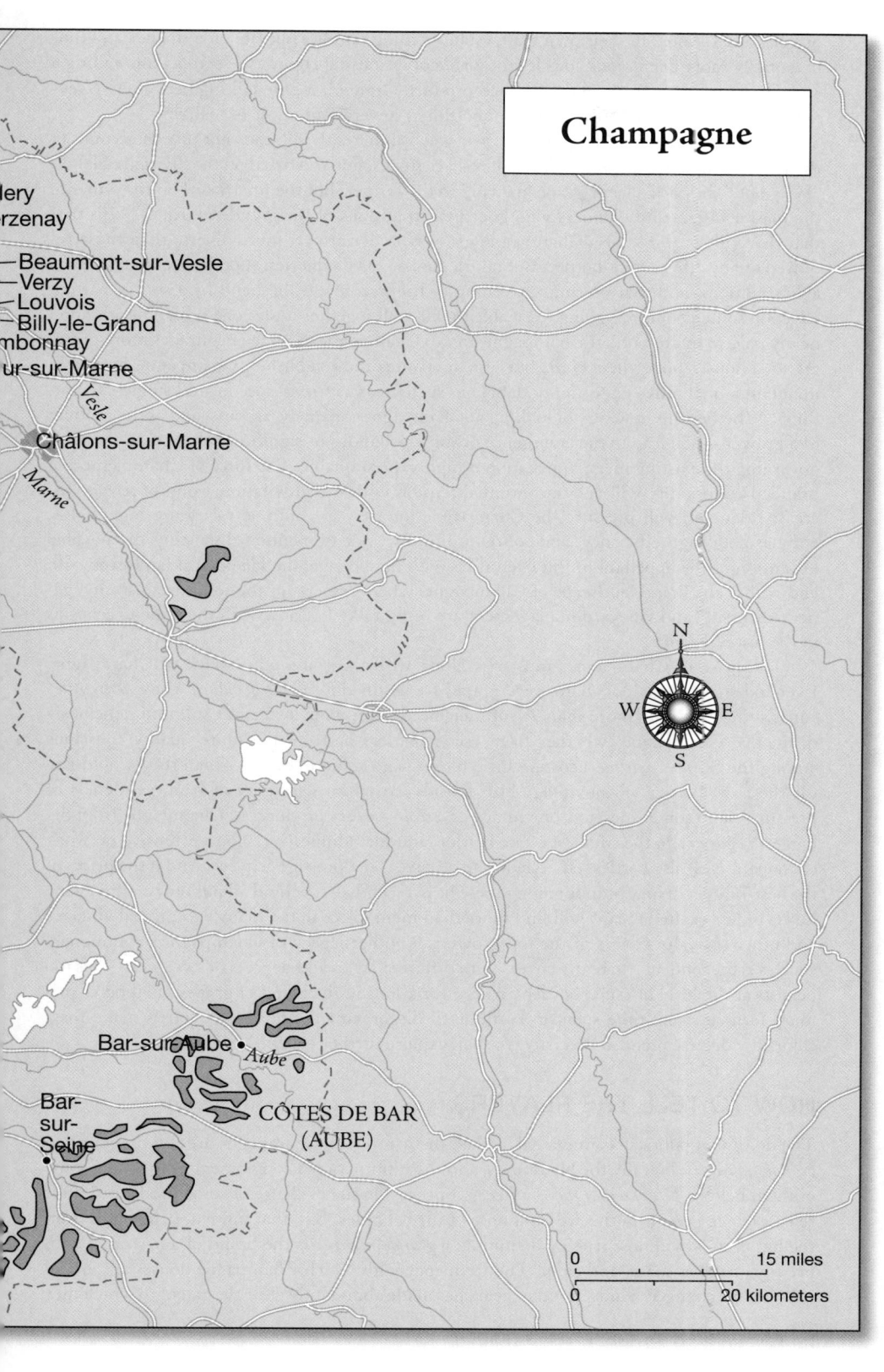

Champagne

ery
rzenay

—Beaumont-sur-Vesle
—Verzy
—Louvois
—Billy-le-Grand
mbonnay
ur-sur-Marne

Vesle

Châlons-sur-Marne

Marne

Bar-sur-Aube • *Aube*

Bar-
sur-
Seine

CÔTES DE BAR
(AUBE)

N
W   E
S

0   15 miles
0   20 kilometers

or her nose. Limited to their own fruit, estate-bottling families operate on a smaller and thus potentially more detail-conscious level capable of exercising rigorous selectivity and taking a craftsman's personal pride in the finished product. Granted, we are talking here about *potential* that as yet only a small percentage of bottling growers come close to realizing.

Many *négociants* would argue that their way is inherently superior not just on account of their wide-ranging sources and depth of reserve stocks, but also based on the division of labor. "Why not," they ask, "leave grape growing to the farmer, but the final word on the wines to the master tasters and blenders who guard the traditions of the grande marques?" It's true that the skills required of a Champagne grower-bottler are yet more diverse than those required of any other estate-bottler. But take a pool of 2,000 wineries, superb *terroir,* and venerable traditions, add that precious leavening of fire in a few bellies, and by a sort of natural selection some people are going to be able to put it all together under one roof. The attention newly paid to estate-bottled Champagne and to Champagne as wine encourages more growers to seriously hone their craft, but also motivates the established Champagne houses to maintain a qualitative edge and to dabble in such areas as *terroir*-specific and single-site bottlings. Whether this new way of looking at Champagne—namely, as wine, and as the product of a grower—will lead to the emergence of subappellations or significant changes in the rules governing the existing mega-appellation is highly questionable. The force of Champagne as a branded commodity will create continued tension with the gravitational pull of *terroir.* Increased demand will pressure the Champagne industry to continue tolerating high yields, emphasizing high efficiency, and sourcing liberally, not to mention discussing the possible expansion of the appellation. But even if laws do not change, the ideological landscape will, and with it the literal landscape of Champagne, where respect for the soil, sustainability, genetic diversity, and vineyard management are being talked of now with the same urgency as in the rest of France.

The price of Champagnes must rise along with the commodity value of Champagne. Even today, nearly half of all growers' grapes are destined for the *négociants,* whose own vineyards suffice for little more than 9% of their needs. But wine lovers can still find deliciously distinctive Champagne (whether from estate bottlers or from the more quality conscious among the *grandes marques*) costing little more—and sometimes less—than they would pay for the most boring of nonvintage brut brands. Based on selectivity of fruit, gentleness of pressing—and sometimes, too, on vintage or *terroir*—every producer of Champagne from the biggest *négociant* to the smallest estate bottler (and including this region's extensive network of cooperatives) also bottles self-styled "tête de cuvée" or "prestige" cuvées. And if the prices of the best-known luxury brands among these have recently left behind all but the wealthy, wine lovers of less exalted means will find more than mere solace in the many exceptional vintages and other specialty cuvées of the top growers. Another legacy of Champagne's commercial success is the tendency to bottle cuvées with different styles and degrees of sweetness. This too persists at the level of estate bottlers, where variations in the blend of grapes, method of primary fermentation, time spent in bottle until disgorgement, and dosage, often make for a colorfully diverse menu, a diversity we shall explore further below.

HOW TO TELL THE PLAYERS

The dominant political, commercial, and aesthetic forces in Champagne are still the so-called *grandes marques*, literally the big brands, and the multinational conglomerates to whom some of them belong. *Grande marque* is a fuzzy concept. On the evidence of some producers' press releases, being one is in the eyes and nose of the beholder. But, that influence emanates from the big brands is almost true by definition: a *grande marque* is the brand of a *négociant* with prestige, market share, and clout. The frequency with which Champagne houses and brand names have changed hands in recent years has made abundantly clear the extent to which they are indeed houses and brands. Many a name has been separated from whatever vineyard land once informed production, sometimes even from its cellars and old stock, and many a style has been dramatically altered, so that in truth an impressive stone edifice and a label are the only remaining constants. Even where the integrity of a great Champagne name remains secure—as is, for instance, almost certainly true of Moët & Chandon, Krug, Ruinart, and Veuve-Clicquot—changes in corporate ownership can scarcely fail to leave indelible marks in the market, if not the wines themselves. And it is astonishing to realize that the aforementioned quartet of *grandes marques* all belong to a single conglomerate, and together account for 20% of total Champagne sales. Collectively, the roughly 200 *négociants* account for 60% of Champagne sales, a somewhat lower percentage within France and concomitantly higher abroad.

The code letters NM (*négociant manipulant*) appear in small print on the label of any *négociant* Champagne. However, as mentioned previously, the term "*négociant*" can apply to a wide range of different establishments. A separate code, MA (for "*marque d'acheteur*" or "buyer's brand"), signifies any of the hundreds of private labels in circulation, but in fact the vast number of defunct *négociants* that live on as labels can easily cause confusion. (And, as also already mentioned, even some "live" Champagne houses are only one step away from being mere labels.) The capital letters RN (for "*récoltant manipulant*," literally meaning "crop manipulator") signify a bottling grower. But the line is less clearcut than these abbreviations suggest, because just as in the rest of France, many quality-conscious growers are officially becoming *négociants* in order to reap both the crops of some of their neighbors and certain tax advantages that paradoxically accrue if one sells grapes to oneself. The Domaine Jean Milan, for example, is normally treated as a grower—in fact it is part of an increasingly well-known, extremely quality-oriented, and ideologically militant portfolio of what its agent (-provocateur) Terry Theise calls "farmer fizz"—but since Milan recently began purchasing more than 5% of their grapes, they are officially NM.

The code CM refers to a grower cooperative. Several of the excellent local cooperatives of Champagne deserve to be better known—and in fact some already are well known, but under their brand names rather than as cooperatives per se. (The well-known Nicolas Feuillatte brand represents the production of the huge central cooperative of Champagne in Chouilly.) The cooperatives are yet another source of potential label confusion, and many of what appear to be grower-bottled wines in fact constitute grapes sent to the local co-op and returned in bottles with the grower's name on them. Only a small percentage of Champagne sold in American markets—other than wine from cooperatives—is grower-bottled. But a decade ago, the percentage was practically nil.

A telling indication of the degree to which commercial interests dominate in Champagne law and practice is that to be a *négociant manipulant* permits one to purchase not just grapes or young, still wines, but even bottled wine which one can then disgorge and label with one's name. It is a point of controversy and an unpopular subject with many Champagne *négociants* to what degree this option of purchasing bottles sur-lattes is utilized. For many wine lovers, it will be sufficiently shocking simply to recognize the laxity of a law that permits *négociants* to buy from growers, co-ops, or one another and to in essence put their label on any bottle that they purchase. In this sense, to be a *négociant* in Champagne is indeed to be a brand. But such laxity is by no means peculiar to Champagne. In most of the world's sparkling wine–producing countries, the bubbly commodity is considered under the aspect of manufacturing and governed by laws very different from those drawn up to regulate the growing and vinification of still wine. So, for example, German law until the very late 20th century permitted sparkling wine to be labeled as Deutscher Sekt that contained wine from almost anywhere in Europe *but* Germany.

READING A CHAMPAGNE LABEL

A host of specialized terminology applies to Champagne, only a small portion of which—emphasizing terms that routinely occur on labels—will be considered on this occasion. Virtually all Champagne is made from some combinations of three grapes: Chardonnay, Pinot Meunier, and Pinot Noir (the latter pair commonly referred to simply as Meunier and Pinot respectively). These grape names seldom appear on a label, but Champagne made exclusively from the Chardonnay grape is labeled as *blanc de blancs*; any made exclusively from black grapes may be labeled *blanc de noirs*. In practice, few Champagnes carry the latter designation, because the blend is nearly always improved by the presence of at least some Chardonnay, and unless a wine is sourced exclusively from Pinot Noir grown in one of the villages best known for that variety, there is seldom any wish to advertise that a Champagne is produced from all-black grapes, which could include the much- (if unjustly) maligned Pinot Meunier. By contrast, many villages and two entire subregions of Champagne—notably the famous Côte des Blancs, whose name would seem to be a giveaway—are utterly dominated by Chardonnay. And the gustatory and marketing allure of the best *blanc de blancs* from the aforementioned Côte has inspired many growers even in primarily Pinot villages to craft small lots of *blanc de blancs* as well. A pair of "forgotten grapes" of Champagne—Arbanne and Petit Meslier—as well as Pinot Blanc and Pinot Gris (here known as Fromenteau), remain legally approved and have not entirely disappeared. In fact, L. Aubry Fils and Moutard Père et Fils feature precisely these grapes in highly interesting special cuvées.

Champagne is made either through brief skin contact during fermentation or—far more frequently—by adding a bit of still red wine just prior to bottling, as a result of which one encounters delicious rosé Champagne in the Côte des Blancs that is, for all intents and purposes, pink Chardonnay. Under the description Coteaux Champenois, a small amount of still wine—both red and (less often) white—is bottled, the best of which can be intriguing and delicious, so technically it is wrong to say of this region that it consists solely in one mega-appellation. Still wines fetch remarkably high prices from certain villages where Pinot Noir characteristically ripens best. In at least one such village, Bouzy, the traditional base wine had as a matter of course considerable color from the skins of Pinot Noir. Despite the high reputation and price of Bouzy's wines, growers found it necessary for much of the 20th century to charcoal-filter it, blend it with Chardonnay, or take prophylactic measures in the cellar in order to render it suitably blond or golden, and thus acceptable to the *négociants*. Today, some sparkling wines that flaunt their Pinot origins have prompted a revival of the color and cuvée designation Oeil de Perdrix ("partridge eye").

In order to add complexity and sweetness to the finished product, Champagne is traditionally finished—after disgorgement and just before final corking—with the addition of a *dosage* or *liqueur de dosage,* consisting of some combination of older wine, cane or beet sugar, and concentrated grape must. An array of terminology arose in the 19th century to characterize the level of residual sugar and the degre of sweetness exhibited by any given Champagne. "Extra dry" actually refers to Champagne with notable sweetness (having at least 15 grams of residual sugar, but generally significantly more) and applies in practice to very few of today's wines. This seems peculiar until one reflects that in the 19th and for much of the 20th century, Champagne was essentially a sweet libation, and bottles labeled "extra dry" came almost as close to dry-tasting as one could get. The driest category was known as "brut," and today the vast majority of Champagne is so labeled and can legally contain up to 15 grams of residual sugar. This leeway in permissible sugar level—together with acidity, dry extract, alcohol, and other quantifiable factors that effect the perception of sweetness—makes for the very broad gustatory range and conceptual fuzziness of "brut."

In the best instances, the residual sugar in Champagne functions much as it does in German Riesling, enhancing a wine's array of flavors and aromas while balancing the sharpness of naturally high acidity associated with a relatively cool growing region. (For further consideration of this topic, consult the discussion of dosage below, and that of balance in the chapter devoted to wines of Germany.) And, just as in Germany, it has become fashionable among some growers to play "how low can you go?" on the principle that the better one's wine, the less in need it is of any confectionary cosmetic. Increasingly, one sees wines labeled extra brut (under 6 grams residual sugar) or even non-dosé or brut natur to signify the absence of any dosage and fewer than 3 grams of residual sugar. But what makes sense in principle—or makes for good promotional copy—often violates the commonsense concept of balance and the sensory dictates of the human palate. Many a serious taster will aver that the "sweet spot"—the perfect point of balance, that is, not the point at which sweetness becomes obvious—is generally between 6 and 10 grams. There is, however, no way to tell from the designation brut whether or not you will perceive distinct sweetness, or possibly even severe dryness. Genuinely sweet Champagne—suitable even for service with dessert (although in fact many great French restaurants perpetuate the oddity if not travesty of serving brut Champagne with sweets)—is known as demi-sec. But of this (like extra dry), relatively little is produced.

CHAMPAGNE'S CRUS

One will also encounter—particularly in the echelons of growers—wines labeled grand cru or premier cru. These have a technical meaning in Champagne more than a little at odds with their use anywhere else in France, in that they refer not to particular sites, but rather to *villages*. But like so much about this region that appears to us as if seen through the proverbial looking glass, if seen through a Champagne flute and from the perspective of a *négociant,* this postal code characterization of crus has its own logic. The *négociant* or agent would traditionally come to town to purchase grapes. The growers would traditionally not have differentiated the fruit of different parcels. What interested both the *négociant* and the grower was the likelihood that the grapes on sale in this particular village would exhibit the requisite ripeness, robustness, and flavor intensity that constitute good raw material for a Champagne that will eventually be blended from a wide range of villages and subregions. For that purpose, a scale was created, originally ranging from 50 to 100, but for almost the past quarter of a century defined as 80% to 100% of the maximum price that would be paid for grapes. (This was, until recently, also the highest price that *could* be paid. Today, prices are no longer fixed by law, but the table of crus remains unchanged.) Villages for whose Chardonnay or Pinot Noir grapes the highest price was paid were designated grand cru. Those achieving 90%–98% of the maximum price were considered premier cru.

There are 17 grand crus, two of which are so rated for one grape variety only:

Ambonnay
Avize
Aÿ
Beaumont-sur-Vesle
Bouzy
Chouilly (for Chardonnay only)
Cramant
Le Mesnil-sur-Oger
Louvois
Mailly-Champagne
Oger
Oîry
Puisieulx
Sillery

Tour-sur-Marne (for Pinot Noir only)
Verzenay
Verzy

There are 38 other villages rated premier cru, plus Chouilly and Tour-sur-Marne have that status for the portion of their crops not from Chardonnay or Pinot Noir respectively. The premier crus are: Avenay-Val-d'Or; Bergères-les-Vertus; Bezannes; Billy-le-Grand; Bisseuil; Chamery; Champillon; Chigny-les-Roses; Chouilly (for Pinot only); Coligny (Chardonnay only); Cormontreuil; Cuis; Cumières; Dizy; Ecueil; Etréchy (Chardonnay only); Grauves; Hautvillers; Jouy-les-Reims; Les Mesneux; Ludes; Mareuil-sur-Aÿ; Montbré; Mutigny; Pargny-les-Reims; Pierry; Rilly-la-Montagne; Sacy; Taissy; Tauxières-Mutry; Tour-sur-Marne (Chardonnay only); Trépail; Trois-Puits; Vaudemanges; Vertus; Ville-Dommange; Villeneuve-Renneville; Villers-Allerand; Villers-aux-Noeuds; Voipreux.

What does it really tell you about a Champagne that it is designated grand cru or premier cru? First, it is essential to bear in mind that since the vast majority of *négociant* Champagnes (and many grower Champagnes) are blended between villages, they do not qualify for labeling as crus. Second, given that entire villages rather than specific sites or sorts of soil and microclimate are rated, the best sites in a premier cru–rated village are likely inherently better than the lesser sites in a grand cru village. Still, these designations do offer some indication of the potential quality of fruit that informs a wine so labeled, and they tell us that the grapes came from a particular neighborhood. Furthermore, certain characteristics really can be found to distinguish the flavor of Chardonnay or Pinot Noir from individual towns. The special prestige of a few towns such as Mesnil-sur-Oger in the Côtes des Blancs or Ambonnay in the Montagne de Reims subregion really is merited not just because their grapes ripen more fully or frequently, but because of certain aromatic, flavor, and structural characteristics inherent in base wines vinified from their fruit. The classification of Champagne crus does not incorporate any villages outside of the two aforementioned subregions plus a third, the Vallée de la Marne. However, there are a few traditionally well-reputed villages outside those subregions that exhibit excellent potential. (For further geographical details, see A Tour of Champagne below.) For the most part, any attempt to label a Champagne with the name of a particular vineyard will be thwarted by the law, although here and there exceptions appear to have been tolerated or producers have flirted on their labels with allusions to site.

WHAT INFLUENCES CHAMPAGNE FLAVOR?
THE CONSEQUENCES OF BLENDING

Naturally, factors influencing the flavor of Champagne include all of those applicable to other wines. But various familiar considerations acquire distinctive significance here, and a number of factors unique to Champagne production must be considered as well. We have already touched on the issues of *terroir* and of site- or village-specific character. Champagne encompasses a large range, from a small minority grown in their own particular vineyard to those sourced from towns lying as much as 100 miles distant from one another, producing some of the largest volumes of blended wine in the world. The ratio of the three major grape varieties may remain relatively constant in a Champagne bottled under a specific label, or it might change from one year or batch to the next, reflecting the attempt to achieve a relatively unchanging flavor profile; the success, failure, abundance, or scarcity of fruit from a given variety in a given vintage; or simply the creative whim of the producer. A minority of Champagne is vintage dated. Those that are so dated generally lay claim to a more rarefied status—and always to a higher price—though whether or not the claim or price is justified is another matter. Bottling growers generally have far fewer stocks of older Champagne held in reserve with which to blend, so their nonvintage blends frequently come close to being single-vintage—certainly close enough to distinctly reflect the flavor profile of the dominant vintage.

With so much Champagne being nonvintage, and with there being so many variables in the blend, one needs to ask, "How can you tell that two Champagnes are the same? What exactly counts as 'the same'?" The answer to the second question could take us deep into semantic and metaphysical realms. And at least a partial answer to the first is that very often, you can't. Let's postulate that "the same Champagne" means one and the same blended *assemblage*, cuvée, or batch, disgorged on the same day or adjacent days. Some producers—particularly among estate bottlers—will put a lot number in tiny letters on their label. Sometimes, although the lot is in some way designated, unless you know precisely where to look (which might well involve peering through the bottle at the back side of the label or neck label) and what to look for, you'll be clueless. A less inscrutable method that is fortunately becoming more common among growers is to indicate the disgorgement date (usually with the word "degorgé" preceding the date). Too often, though—especially among *négociants*—you will search in vain for any identifying clue, although the producer may take pains to assure you that part of the point of blending is to achieve homogeneity of flavor.

TIME ON THE LEES, DISGORGEMENT DATE, AND CELLARING

Champagne is required to spend 12 months in bottle prior to disgorgement, but in practice few will achieve any significant complexity, harmony, or textural allure until they have spent twice that long. This time, during which bottles rest on their sides (*sur lattes*) in a cellar, is critical to the wine's flavor, above all for enriching and facilitating the complex chemical interactions between dead yeasts and young wine. Even six months in the life of a young Champagne can make a major flavor difference, so if (let's say) a grower blends what he intends to be a year's worth of nonvintage Champagne based largely on his or her 2004 vintage, and disgorges half of it in May 2007 and the rest after the harvest and just in time for the holidays, the former wine will probably taste noticeably brighter in fruit and the latter significantly richer and more complex. Furthermore, a comparison in November of the recently disgorged batch with a bottle of that disgorged in April—the same blend and age, in other words, but having spent the previous six months in a different state—will again reveal significant differences, since Champagne ages differently (and generally more rapidly) once it has been disgorged than it does while still resting on (and—as vintners often say—"nourished by") the moribund yeasts. These phenomena are the reason why it isn't merely convenient to use disgorgement date as a means of indicating a nonvintage blend and its relative freshness—although these are the most important practical benefits—and why in fact it makes profound sense to treat as "the same Champagne" only two identical blends that have been disgorged at the same time. Often, a producer's finest cuvées—even though these will generally be vintage dated—are subject to multiple disgorgements over a period of several years. In such a case, two bottles of vintage Champagne with the same label may in important senses be far from "the same wine," and only a disgorgement date will serve to disambiguate the reference to producer and vintage. (For more words on freshness, see Important Information, below.)

An entire class of Champagne could be described as *récemment dégorgé* or R.D. ("recently disgorged"), a term and abbreviation that originated with and are legally protected for labeling purposes by the venerable house of Bollinger. This is vintage-dated Champagne that is disgorged only after a lengthy stay on the dead yeasts left from second fermentation. Champagne can remain remarkably free of oxidation and gain enormous complexity for many years on its lees. By contrast, after its disgorgement and release, consumers are commonly advised that there is considerable risk in cellaring Champagne—even under ideal temperature and humidity. The habit of doing so continues to flourish in the U.K. but is practiced much less in other countries. Yet, even if the risks of excessive oxidation or loss of pressure exist, they should not be exaggerated. Five to ten years in the cellar for really well-concentrated and well-balanced Champagne from a grower or *négociant* with a track record for consistent quality is not an unreasonable expectation and can be highly rewarding. Krug—arguably Champagne's foremost *négociant*—regularly releases older vintages of extraordinary quality that were disgorged many years ago.

YIELDS, PRESSES, AND VESSELS

The law permits yields in Champagne (as measured in volume of juice per surface area) to reach two to three times that which we associate with top-quality wines from other famous French appellations. Excessive yields can definitely be implicated in the boredom that many Champagnes—despite their effervescence—engender. That said, the sort of ripeness required for properly balanced Champagne is not the same as that which we associate with still wine appellations governing Chardonnay or Pinot Noir. The aim is not to make Burgundy, a grower is sure to tell you (possibly with some indignation), but Champagne. To concentrate on the most obvious difference, harvesting Chardonnay or Pinot Noir at levels of sugar above 12% potential alcohol is apt to result in flavors ill suited to the vivacity, the edge of acidity, and the "minerality" that characterize Champagne at its best. Rather, a conscientious grower will typically pick at 9%–10% potential alcohol and add sugar (chaptalize) so as to achieve a base wine around 11% or 11.5%.

Champagne producers intent on achieving high quality walk a fine line. Harvest late and at too high a potential alcohol and the resultant wine will be clumsy; too early, and it is liable to taste green and unpleasantly underripe. The sad truth is that most growers and *négociants* sin on the side of safety in this relatively cool and often rain-plagued region, picking underripe grapes safe in the assumption that after chaptalization, blending, second fermentation, lees maturation, and liberal dosage have played their parts, the resultant wine will not taste obviously unripe (and will in any case sell well enough given its appellation). Grounds for cynicism abound. The highest possible yields inevitably result in lower sugar in the grapes at harvest. But the more a grower makes up this deficit through the addition of sugar in the press house, the more he or she—with perfect legality—adds to the total volume of wine produced over and beyond the maximum yield per acre, and thus to his or her bottom line. As long as these reciprocal incentives to overcrop and overchaptalize remain in place, Champagne as a region cannot fulfill its quality potential.

The "transparency" of flavor exhibited by fine Champagne—and this admittedly insufficient metaphor points to the genre's relatively low alcohol level (generally around 12% after second fermentation and dosage), high acidity, and stark yet often delicately etched flavor profile—renders it sensitive to any number of winemaking procedures, yet few wines are subjected to so much handling and treatment as the typical nonvintage Champagne. Sensitivity begins on the vine, but the moment and method by which the grapes are pressed has traditionally been considered of special importance for Champagne. This is the sole region where the traditional, vertical basket presses (now undergoing a revival worldwide) never went out of fashion. (They operate slowly and give low yields, but can produce an initial run of juice that possesses exceptional clarity.) Traditionally, Champagne must is graded according to the degree to which the grapes were pressed. "Free run" juice is best, and each successive degree of pressure adds bitterness and coarseness to the base material.

Most Champagne initially ferments and ages in tank, but a few of the best Champagnes ferment and/or are aged in barrels, ranging from traditional ovals of more than 1,000-liter capacity down to that international standard 225-liter denomination, the *barrique* (and, of course, varying in age as well). The trick is to benefit from the barrel's potential to subtly enhance the oxidative development of the young wine as well as to promote its clarification prior to bottling and the onset of the second fermentation. A few intrepid growers are refraining from pumping and filtering in the hope of preserving dimensions of aroma, flavor, and texture that might otherwise be lost or disturbed, and such an approach virtually demands that one work in barrel. Another significant factor in determining flavor is whether a grower permits the young wines to undergo malolactic conversion—the transformation of malic (green apple) acid, generally abundant in Champagne grapes, to lactic acid. Some do so routinely. Some intentionally inhibit that transformation. Some fit their approach to the vintage or the individual cuvée. And some appear content to let nature decide.

"DOSING" AND DESCRIBING THE FINISHED WINE

Much has already been said about dosage and residual sugar (in the section Reading a Champagne Label). But the influence on flavor of precisely what is added to top off the bottle after disgorgement can be profound. In the limiting case—usually labeled "non-dosé," "brut zéro," or "brut natur"—the bottle is topped off with more of the same, bone-dry wine. The use of even small amounts of older wines as part of the dosage can have significant effects because mature wines of this sort frequently display emphatic and distinctive flavors. The issue of residual sugar in relation to balance has already been discussed, but the decision whether to utilize cane or beet sugar, or instead concentrated grape must, is of separate significance. There is no question in growers' minds that the results will differ, but whereas many believe that concentrated must is superior—and less "foreign" to wine—these concentrates originate in the south of France, which puts them far away from Chardonnay, Pinot, or Meunier, not to mention Champagne. Furthermore, tales abound concerning the (legal) addition of brandy, but Champagne houses resolutely refuse to divulge such "secrets" of their recipe. The degree of suspicion is probably in itself sufficient to explain why the very concept of dosage leaves a bad taste in the mouths of many young, quality-conscious growers, who in consequence avoid any added residual sugar even if the balance of their wines would benefit from it.

A really thorough account of any given Champagne should reflect most of the factors we have just reviewed. Thus, a given batch of brut nonvintage might be described as

70% Pinot Noir, 20% Pinot Meunier, 10% Chardonnay
70% vintage 2004, 20% reserve wine from 2003, and 10% from 2002
Fermented in tank, except for half of the Pinot Noir fermented in older, 500-liter barrels
Permitted to undergo full malolactic conversion
Disgorged November 2007, after 28 months on its lees
Given a dosage of old bottled stock from vintage 1979, together with cane sugar sufficient for
    10 grams per liter

To such a description could also be added the village or villages of origin. Perhaps it is only the die-hard wine enthusiast who will find this much detail of interest. (But then, their numbers probably include many who have read this far.) Above all, it is fascinating and comforting to peruse an extended description. For the wines of many growers, given a lot number or disgorgement date, it is possible to obtain information with this degree of specificity and completeness. When it comes to *négociant* Champagnes—particularly those blended on an industrial scale—it would be hard to imagine (and probably harder yet to obtain) such a thorough accounting.

IMPORTANT INFORMATION

By now, the litany of common causes of disappointing Champagne hardly requires extensive elaboration. Overcropping, overchaptalization, overprocessing, underripe fruit, excessive acidity, obtrusive sweetness, too little sweetness, too short a time on the lees . . . these are a few of the major culprits. The problem is that nothing on the label will alert you to the likelihood of disappointment save for the name of the producer, and even that may not be terribly reliable. The range of quality within many larger Champagne houses or estates can be extremely wide. If residual sugar is applied with too little sensitivity to taste, one batch of nonvintage brut might taste well balanced, and another—with the same measurable grams per liter— might not. (And incidentally, many *négociants* and some growers will vary the dosage according to their perception of market preferences, or according to their importers' preferences.) All producers of Champagne strive to avoid disappointing their customers, and while a small, quality-conscious Champagne grower with a devout following may post a "sorry, temporarily sold out" note on the cellar door, few estates and no *négociants* will risk this. It is thus all too common to encounter otherwise excellent wine from generally reliable sources whose awkwardness and "greenness" can be laid at the door of too early disgorgement and a rush to market. Around the turn of the most recent millennium, this problem was widely in evidence. And so was another, far more insidious source of disappointing Champagne.

In an earlier era, when critical awareness of Champagne as an appellation and of industry practice was far less developed than it is today, wine lovers would frequently be amazed to fall in love with a certain Champagne when tasted in the region, only to discover that wine with the same label tasted at home did not remotely measure up to their recollections. The floral bloom, the delicate perfume, the textural nuances . . . all had wilted, replaced by flavors of burnt pie dough, stale biscuits, and dead leaves. Who stole the soul of these wines? Careless or irresponsible merchants, unrefrigerated shipping containers, and warm warehouses—that's who! The situation has improved only a little in recent times. Champagne is inherently unforgiving of mistreatment, which comes as no surprise given the sensitivity to travel and poor storage of Pinot Noir and Chardonnay from Burgundy. But that accounts for only part of the quality problem. Precisely because Champagne is traded as a commodity—the vast majority of it without a vintage date—it is too often thoughtlessly handled. Sadly, most folks are buying bubbly for the label, which can be stored indefinitely at any temperature. But every subpar bottle opened some New Year's Eve or at any other time represents a senseless waste of opportunity to spark the interest of a consumer in one of the world's great wines.

What is the solution? Some specialist French wine importers take pains to ensure that their product is properly shipped and is distributed with care. And one of the finest *négociants*—Bollinger—significantly altered their marketing strategy in the 1990s in an effort to guard against quality-control problems in the import, distribution, and retail sectors. Those producers who label their wines with the disgorgement date perform a major service. But there is no guarantee that a bottle of Champagne has not been exposed to damaging heat or vibration even if it was recently disgorged and, conversely, a quality-conscious retail merchant or restaurateur might be offering you an opportunity to purchase an impeccably stored wine long since disgorged and unavailable from the winery or the importer. In the end, unless you know the chain of custody for the bottle and have justified confidence in your merchant or sommelier, you will forever be taking a risk. But most serious wine consumers will conclude that the rewards of a good bottle are worth it. Meanwhile, they should be on the lookout for and vociferously protest the first signs of abuse.

A TOUR OF CHAMPAGNE

There are a number of good reasons, aside from the reader's patience, for restricting our tour of Champagne to a brief overview. While 55 villages count as either grand or premier crus, the names of many smaller crus will seldom be found on any label. As yet, the number of conscientious growers in any given town may be quite small. As already noted, only a modest percentage of the best Champagne is labeled with village or cru, and the number of individual vineyards whose names have thus far found their way past the authorities and onto a label is minuscule. Furthermore, awareness of Champagne *terroir* and of the potential and characteristics of different towns and sites is relatively new and rudimentary, often even among growers themselves. We are at the threshold of an age of self-consciousness, exploration, and experimentation. A decade from now—and possibly sooner—the viticultural map of Champagne will have been transformed by the work of this appellation's best practitioners and import agents. There will be enough of them, with experience and experiments under their belts, to begin connecting the dots. Details and places will emerge that are known today to only a few intrepid veteran growers and young prodigies, or to history—or not yet known at all.

There are officially four major subregions of Champagne: the Vallée de la Marne, the Montagne de Reims, the Côte des Blancs (whose rather distant southern extension is the Côte de Sézanne), and the Côte des Bar. This last—formerly (and often still) referred to as the Aube—is something of a stepchild. Its incorporation into the Champagne-growing region in 1911 touched off genuine warfare among the authorities, the army, and the populace of the "classic" Champagne districts to the north (who, admittedly, had other grievances too). Closer to Chablis than to Reims or Épernay—which are more than 100 miles distant from the greatest concentration of southern vineyards—the Côte des Bar shares with Chablis (and the eastern Loire) its distinctive, fossil-rich Kimmeridgean limestone. Vineyards stretch along the Seine and Aube rivers (the principal towns being Bar-sur-Seine and Bar-sur-Aube) but also in between them and well away from their microclimatic influence. Oddly, given the nature of the soil here, Pinot Noir is dominant, which must have cultural or historical reasons. Where there is Chardonnay, it can taste strikingly Chablis-like and quite remarkable. Just outside the city of Troyes and about midway down the Seine between Bar and the Côte de Sézanne lies the singularly high hill town of Montgeux, surrounded by Chardonnay vines. This site has always been a valued source for top *négociants*, and only recently, estate-bottled wines from Jacques Lassaigne have permitted wine lovers to experience the meaty, mysterious depth of which it is capable. No fewer than half a dozen other isolated outposts of viticulture north and west of the Côte des Bar are part of official Champagne, and who knows what treasures they might one day reveal?

The Côte de Sézanne represents a narrow and repeatedly interrupted strip of Chardonnay vineyards stretching from just north of the Seine to the edge of its larger and far more prestigious sister the Côte des Blancs, which in turn reminds one of Burgundy's Côte d'Or with its continuous string of east-facing slopes. That there are excellent vineyards in the Sézanne can be inferred from the number of top-flight producers (Alain Robert of Mesnil, for one) who place significant importance on them. No doubt in time—if this has not already happened—some bottling growers from the region will offer us delicious and more direct evidence of that excellence. The vineyards of Bergères-les-Vertus and Vertus at the southern end of the Côte des Blancs are rated only premier cru. Then follows a string of grand cru villages: Le Mesnil-sur-Oger, Oger, Avize, Cramant, and not far south from the Marne, Chouilly. Northwest of Cramant lies Cuis, whose premier cru fruit—if one believes its foremost grower, Pierre Gimonnet—can enhance the complexity and ageworthiness of wine from its two grand cru neighbors. Chardonnay from this subregion tends toward strikingly floral top notes and a savory depth that positively dares you to avoid the word "mineral." (In Avize, for instance, growers speak of a characteristic "graphite" note.) If there is a first among the grand crus of the Côte des Blancs, it is Mesnil. Krug's Clos de Mesnil is the most expensive and celebrated Chardonnay cuvée in Champagne, and arguably no fewer than half a dozen of the top 20 Champagne producers are based here (see The Best Producers of Champagne).

"Valée de la Marne" is perfectly intelligible as a description; however, the winding course of the Marne from Montreuil-aux-Lions (less than 20 miles from the Disneyland Park of Paris) and Château Thierry upstream as far as Tour-sur-Marne incorporates distinctly different subsoils and microclimates. For most of this stretch—featuring south-facing sites overlooking the river—Pinot Meunier dominates over Champagne's pair of more famous grapes, and the wines tend (provided the Meunier is genuinely ripe) toward fruit-filled generosity. This is true of Hautvillers, Cumières, Dizy, and Épernay. Only as we pass north of the Côte des Blancs and west into the so-called Grande Vallée de Marne with its grand cru villages of Aÿ and Tour-sur-Marne (and, in between, premier crus Mareuil-sur-Aÿ and Bisseuil) does the best of the region's chalk become exposed, and Pinot Noir overwhelmingly asserts its importance. The Pinot Noir of Aÿ is generally considered among Champagne's best, and thanks to the presence of several excellent bottling growers as well as the predominance of this village's fruit in the wines of Bollinger and Gosset (two fine *négociants* based there), one can actually get a handle on its typical character. In youth, its Pinot can exhibit expressive orchard and blue fruit notes and fine floral notes. As it matures, smoky, maltlike pungency becomes a village signature.

The Montagne de Reims incorporates some of Champagne's finest vineyards but also a great diversity of microclimates and exposures. Imagine this subregion as a fish hook. The barb of the hook commences northeast of Aÿ. North of Tour-sur-Marne come the grand cru villages Bouzy and Ambonnay, both with reputations for Pinot Noir extending back to the Middle Ages, and still sources for serious still red wine as well as Champagne. Pinot in Bouzy tends to emphasize red and black fruits, often with a decidedly charlike, smoky overtone. Ambonnay can deliver subtle red fruits but is more about the meaty, forest-floor mystery, and at its best the "I-can't-believe-it's-from-grapes" experience that Pinot alone can deliver. North of Ambonnay, in the crook of the hook, lie premier crus Trépail and Villers-Marmery, the latter an outpost of Chardonnay in this territory otherwise colonized by Pinot Noir. As the hills bend westward, they overlook the river Vesle and the Aisne-Marne canal at Verzy and Verzenay, whose contiguous vineyards yield yet more Pinot with a fine veil of berry fruit that is frequently ripped apart with wild, animal intensity. Next door, the vineyards of grand cru villages Sillery and Puisieulx have a reputation for a somewhat tamer expression of Pinot meatiness, although as in so many instances it is hard to tell, due to a relative paucity of growers showcasing these sites. Immediately west of Verzenay lies Mailly-Champagne, whose production is dominated by a very good local co-op; then come Ludes, Chigny-les-Roses, and Rilly-la-Montagne (where Villemart et Cie is showcasing deeply savory and saline mineral potential for Chardonnay-dominated cuvées that remind one in some ways of grand cru Chablis).

Continuing up the long side of the hook, the Petite Montagne de Reims passes southwest of Reims. As one heads west, the inclination of the slopes diminishes and the soil becomes sandier and lighter, but the potential for Pinot Meunier–dominated—indeed, often 100% Meunier—wines of refinement, generosity, and complexity is being demonstrated in neighboring villages by Aubry (at Jouy-les-Reims); Roger Coulon and Egly-Ouriet (from very old vines in Vrigny); and Jérôme Prévost (at Gueux). North of Gueux, across the river Vesle, lies what could be called the "Côte de Vesle," better known by the name of the nearby Massif de St.-Thierry. South and west of the Petite Montagne, more than two dozen little-known villages stretch along the Valée de l'Ardre, where Pinot Meunier again predominates. But the best wines of the Petite Montagne demonstrate that any prejudice against Meunier as a variety is misplaced, and here and there, growers and wines are emerging to suggest just how many as yet obscure subregions may be capable of distinctively delicious results.

—DAVID SCHILDKNECHT

[the ratings]

The following list does not attempt to distinguish between *négociants* and grower-bottlers, since—as explained above—the lines are often blurred: *négociants* vary enormously in size and extent of landholdings, and some growers supplement their acreage by becoming *négociants*. The towns where these producers are based are noted, which in the case of most estates also reflects the location of their principal acreage. But readers should draw no automatic conclusion from the address to the source of fruit. (Reims, for example, is not itself a wine-growing village, and the producers with that address listed below are all *négociants*). Because any thorough list of Champagne producers is inherently heterogeneous, and because the range of cuvées—especially from large *négociants*—can vary dramatically in quality, no attempt has been made to distinguish more than two broad categories.

THE BEST PRODUCERS OF CHAMPAGNE

★ ★ ★ ★ ★ (OUTSTANDING)

Bollinger (Aÿ)

Egly-Ouriet (Ambonnay)

Pierre Gimonnet et Fils (Cuis)

Gosset (Aÿ)

Jacquesson (Dizy)

Krug (Reims)

Jean Lallement et Fils (Verzenay)

Larmandier-Bernier (Vertus)

Pierre Moncuit (Le Mesnil-sur-Oger)

Pierre Peters (Le Mesnil-sur-Oger)

Alain Robert (Le Mesnil-sur-Oger)

Louis Roederer (Reims)

Salon (Le Mesnil-sur-Oger)

Jacques Selosse (Avize)

Vilmart et Cie (Rilly-la-Montagne)

★ ★ ★ / ★ ★ ★ ★ (VERY GOOD-EXCELLENT)

Agrapart et Fils (Avize)

Pierre Arnould (Verzenay)

L. Aubry Fils (Jouy-les-Reims)

Paul Bara (Bouzy)

Edmond Barnaut (Bouzy)

Françoise Bedel (Crouttes-sur-Marne)

Benoît-Lahaye (Bouzy)

Bérèche et Fils (Ludes)

Billecart-Salmon (Mareuil-sur-Aÿ)

Henri Billiot Fils (Ambonnay)

Bonnaire (Cramant)

Cédric Bouchard (Celles-sur-Ources)

Bernard Brémont (Ambonnay)

Canard-Duchêne (Ludes)

Cattier (Chigny-les-Roses)

Chartogne-Taillet (Merfy)

Guy de Chassey (Louvois)

Gaston Chiquet (Dizy)

Collard-Chardelle
    (Villers-sous-Châtillon)

Roger Coulon (Vrigny)

Delamotte (Le Mesnil-sur-Oger)

Delavenne Père et Fils (Bouzy)

Deutz (Aÿ)

José Dhondt (Oger)

Diebolt-Vallois (Cramant)

Pascal Doquet (Le Mesnil-sur-Oger)

Duval-Leroy (Vertus)

Nicolas Feuillatte (Chouilly-Épernay)

Fleury Père et Fils (Courteron)

Veuve Fourny et Fils (Vertus)

Georges Gardet (Chigny-les-Roses)

Gatinois (Aÿ)

Claude Genet (Chouilly)

René Geoffroy (Cumières)

Bernard Girardin (Mancy)

Gosset-Brabant (Aÿ)

Henri Goutorbe (Aÿ)

Marc Hebrart (Mareuil-sur-Aÿ)

Charles Heidsieck (Épernay)

Henriot (Reims)

Laherte Frères (Chavot)

Lamiable (Tours-sur-Marne)

P. Lancelot-Royer (Cramant)

Guy Larmandier (Vertus)

Jacques Lassaigne—Champagne Alexandre
    (Montgueux)

J. Lassalle (Chigny-les-Roses)

Jean Laurent (Celles-sur-Ources)

Laurent-Perrier (Tour-sur-Marne)

David Leclapart (Trépail-Marne)

R. & L. Legras (Chouilly)

A. R. Lenoble (Damery)

Lilbert-Fils (Cramant)

Mailly Grand Cru (Mailly-Champagne)

A. Margaine (Villers-Marmery)

José Michel et Fils (Moussy)

Jean Milan (Oger)

Moët & Chandon (Épernay)

Moutard Père et Fils (Buxeuil)

G. H. Mumm (Reims)

Bruno Paillard (Reims)

Palmer & Co. (Reims)
Pehu-Simonet (Verzenay)
Joseph Perrier (Châlons-en-Champagne)
Perrier-Jouët (Épernay)
Philipponnat (Mareuil-sur-Aÿ)
Ployez-Jacquemart (Ludes)
Roger Pouillon et Fils (Mareuil-sur-Aÿ)
Jérôme Prévost (Gueux)
Pol Roger (Épernay)
Ruinart (Reims)
Camille Savès (Bouzy)

François Secondé (Sillery)
De Sousa & Fils (Avize)
A. Soutiran (Ambonnay)
Taittinger (Reims)
Tarlant (Oeuilly)
Trouillard (Épernay)
Varnier-Fannière (Avize)
Vazart-Coquart et Fils (Chouilly)
De Venoge (Épernay)
Jean Vesselle (Bouzy)
Veuve Clicquot (Reims)

Note: Very brief profiles are supplied below only for the producers rated "outstanding," plus a selection from among those producers rated "very good to excellent" (favoring those whose wines are in the U.S. market). The difficulty of disambiguating descriptions of nonvintage wines; the risks of purchasing Champagne that has been in the commercial pipeline for any length of time (both topics amply discussed above); and the infrequency (for now, at least) with which consumers cellar Champagne all argued against listing and rating specific wines. Due to the recent and in some cases shockingly rapid rise in prices for well-known prestige cuvées, as well as the volatility of the Champagne market in general, no price ranges are indicated. As a rule of thumb, excellent basic nonvintage brut bottlings from Champagne growers or those of the top *négociants,* when on sale, are apt to sell for U.S. $35.00–$45.00 retail.

[tasting commentaries]

L. AUBRY FILS ★★★/★★★★
JOUY-LES-REIMS

The Aubry brothers render an excellent Meunier-based basic brut, and among other things a fascinating series of cuvées labeled La Nombre d'Or that resurrect the "forgotten" grapes of Champagne, Petit Meslier, Arbanne, and Fromenteau (aka Pinot Gris). They stopped selling to *négociants* in 2001 and are militant in their advocacy of estate bottling. The sources of fruit are all from neighboring villages at the western edge of the Petite Montagne de Reims.

PAUL BARA ★★★/★★★★
BOUZY

Bara is in effect "Mr. Bouzy," a reliable local institution and international calling card. Look for honest value and true representation of this celebrated cru's Pinot Noir–driven personality.

EDMOND BARNAUT ★★★/★★★★
BOUZY

Oenologist Philippe Secondé offers elegant, refined variations on Bouzy terroir, augmented with fruit from near Château Thierry, at the western end of the Marne Valley.

FRANÇOISE BEDEL ★★★/★★★★
CROUTTES-SUR-MARNE

This is an up-and-coming source for Meunier-based cuvées from the westernmost edge of the Vallée de la Marne; indeed, her location not many minutes distant from the traffic snarls of Paris may help Bedel build her reputation.

BENOÎT-LAHAYE ★ ★ ★/★ ★ ★ ★
BOUZY

This small grower is an insider tip in the relatively crowded field of Bouzy estate bottlers.

BILLECART-SALMON ★ ★ ★/★ ★ ★ ★
MAREUIL-SUR-AŸ

A modest-sized *négociant* that has long enjoyed a large reputation as a "small" Champagne house, Billecart's Meunier-heavy basic brut is unexciting, but their special cuvées combine generosity and roundness with finesse. Clos St.-Hillaire is, as its name suggests, the product of a single vineyard, planted in Pinot Noir. Billecart's fruit-forward rosé has long enjoyed an especially strong American following.

HENRI BILLIOT FILS ★ ★ ★/★ ★ ★ ★
AMBONNAY

Offering excellent, elegant expressions of Ambonnay's inherent complexity, Billiot's lineup includes two *tête de cuvée* bottlings.

BOLLINGER ★ ★ ★ ★ ★
AŸ

Among the most consistent in quality of the prominent *négociants*—as well as one of the few to offer an outstanding basic cuvée (here dubbed "Special")—Bollinger leans heavily on its own and neighbors' Pinot Noir vineyards so that a sense of Aÿ typicity emerges from the glass. The R.D. late disgorgements here have almost legendary status, surpassed only by the rare Vieilles Vignes Françaises from two parcels of Pinot that for unknown, seemingly miraculous reasons survived the phylloxera epidemic and have been propagated and flourishing on their own roots (i.e., ungrafted) ever since.

CÉDRIC BOUCHARD ★ ★ ★/★ ★ ★ ★
CELLES-SUR-OURCES

A young, idealistic, biodynamic grower in a Côte des Bar town that is intriguingly full of estate bottlers, Bouchard offers striking *blanc de noirs* and *blanc de blancs*.

CATTIER ★ ★ ★/★ ★ ★ ★
CHIGNY-LES-ROSES

The Cattier brothers' claim to fame is roughly a thousand cases annually of superb Clos du Moulin, a prestige cuvée inaugurated soon after World War II and consisting of roughly equal parts of Chardonnay and Pinot Noir from three vintages.

CHARTOGNE-TAILLET ★ ★ ★/★ ★ ★ ★
MERFY

Despite the lack of notoriety for their village and its neighbors along the river Vesle, Elisabeth and Philippe Chartognes offer Champagne of richness, refinement, and great flavor interest at reasonable prices.

GASTON CHIQUET ★ ★ ★/★ ★ ★ ★
DIZY

The Chiquet family lays claim to having become the first estate bottlers in Champagne, in 1919. Young Nicolas Chiquet is today delivering cuvées of impressive refinement, including a Meunier-dominated brut Tradition and a rare *blanc de blancs* from Aÿ.

COLLARD-CHARDELLE ★★★/★★★★
VILLERS-SOUS-CHÂTILLON

With the retirement of René Collard in the mid-1990s after more than half a century of bottling Meunier-based, cask-matured Champagne of often startling complexity and longevity—truly Champagne *as wine*—it might seem as if an era of ancient methods had ended. But not only is Olivier Collard carrying on his grandfather's winemaking traditions, releases here are so leisurely that it is far from being too late to purchase and sample bottles of René's own profoundly delicious handiwork.

ROGER COULON ★★★/★★★★
VRIGNY

Among several sources for fascinating Champagne from the "Meunier belt" of the Petite Montagne de Reims, Coulon's top cuvées are barrel fermented and include one that showcases Meunier from ancient, ungrafted vines.

DELAMOTTE ★★★/★★★★
LES MESNIL-SUR-OGER

Delamotte is affiliated with Salon, and in addition to their own impressive Côte des Blancs holdings and Pinot Noir from Ambonnay and Bouzy, they inherit any young wines that Salon elects not to bottle under that enormously prestigious label. (In some years, this can amount to the entire production, as Salon does not by any means "declare" every vintage.)

DEUTZ ★★★/★★★★
AŸ

Long possessed of a stolid reputation, Deutz was purchased by Roederer in 1996, and the low-toned richness for which the best Deutz Champagne was known seems to have been augmented by finer nuances. Furthermore, the basic brut nonvintage (borrowing a leaf from the parent company) is more than merely reliable.

EGLY-OURIET ★★★★★
AMBONNAY

Building on his father's already excellent work, Francis Egly has come to epitomize the strivings of estate bottlers to render Champagne that will be judged as wine and reflect its *terroir*. (Consistent with those ideals, Egly has developed what is almost certainly Champagne's most ambitious project with still Pinot Noir—all, incidentally, raised in new barrels.) An increasing percentage of cask maturation, unfiltered base wine, and a minimum of three years on the lees are among this estate's features. The Brut Tradition, Vignes de Vrigny (from Meunier), Blanc de Noirs Vieille Vignes (with the depth of the finest Burgundy), and vintage cuvée are consistently striking, but all of this grower's bottlings can be heartily recommended.

FLEURY PÈRE ET FILS ★★★/★★★★
COURTERON

This estate is located so far up the Seine it nearly ends up in the Côte d'Or. But it is very much on French wine enthusiasts' radar screens thanks to its prominently biodynamic methods and its fascinating if at times quirky wines. The basic brut nonvintage Carte Rouge is pure Pinot Noir, deliciously redolent of orchard fruits and berries.

GATINOIS ★ ★ ★/★ ★ ★ ★
AŸ

Gatinois is so serious about reflecting the *terroir* of Bouzy in his wines that he relies almost entirely on Pinot Noir from the town's best slopes; he also displays serious intentions with still red wine.

RENÉ GEOFFROY ★ ★ ★/★ ★ ★ ★
CUMIÈRES

Jean-Baptiste Geoffroy has a reputation for viticultural rigor, and it certainly shows through in wines of impressively consistent clarity and complexity. The "basic" brut is far from basic, and the barrel-fermented, vintage-dated Cuvée René Geoffroy can be meaty and mightily impressive.

PIERRE GIMONNET ET FILS ★ ★ ★ ★ ★
CUIS

Gimmonet is a poster child for the Côte des Blancs and an advocate of purity, sharp relief, and pronounced minerality combined with near weightlessness, a set of virtues probably uniquely possible in the best sites of this celebrated Champagne subregion. That said, as part of his perpetual striving for excellence and distinctive expressions of Champagne, in 2002 Gimmonet acquired parcels of Pinot Noir in Aŷ and Mareuil-sur-Aŷ, which now inform a new half-and-half cuvée called Paradoxe.

GOSSET ★ ★ ★ ★ ★
AŸ

Cointreau purchased this venerable Aŷ house from the Gosset family in 1994 and has continued the tradition of outstanding quality, although one has always needed to "trade up" to their Grande Réserve bottling in order to experience the complexity and textual polish that make Gosset a name with which to reckon. The Grande Millésime and Célebris generally reveal profound complexity and ageability.

GOSSET-BRABANT ★ ★ ★/★ ★ ★ ★
AŸ

Michel and Christian Gosset's grandfather Gabriel parted ways with his family's famous house, appending his wife's name to that of their small domaine. The floral, citrus, and pit fruit–dominated Brut Tradition is very white wine–like (despite being Pinot Noir) and consistently delicious. The domaine's grand cru bottlings exhibit excellent depth and Aŷ-typical pungency reminiscent of buckwheat or peat.

CHARLES HEIDSIECK ★ ★ ★/★ ★ ★ ★
ÉPERNAY

Generally considered the flagship of Rémy Martin's Champagne holdings, Charles Heidsieck is known as a source for rich, supple, forward Champagne, culminating in both a prestige *blanc de blancs* and *blanc de noirs* (the latter called Champagne Charlie). Cellarmaster Daniel Thibault, who died in 2002, is credited with having made the modern reputation of this house.

HENRIOT ★ ★ ★/★ ★ ★ ★
REIMS

Joseph Henriot recently bought back his family's Champagne house, although he is better known for—and has achieved more striking results from—his purchases of Bouchard Père et

Fils in Beaune and William Fèvre in Chablis. But advances in quality in Champagne cannot be achieved simply from one vintage to the next. This is an address to investigate in the coming years.

JACQUESSON ★ ★ ★ ★ ★
DIZY

Jacquesson has the reputation of being a *négociant* who acts like the most meticulous grower. Fermentation is largely in traditional old ovals (*foudres*). Each batch of excellent nonvintage brut is coded to identify its origins, and the code explained on the label—a welcome and almost unprecedented degree of commercial disclosure and clarity. Premier cru–labeled bottlings are often riveting in their complexity and the grand cru cuvées, including their vintage Signature, can be sublime. The Jacquesson brothers are even managing to get away with a couple of vineyard-designated bottlings—and frankly, these are two Champagne vignerons who should simply be left to "do their (beautiful) thing."

KRUG ★ ★ ★ ★ ★
REIMS

Barrel fermentation, intricate blending across a wide range of *terroirs,* exceptional depth of vintages, and long lees aging are just a few factors one could point to in an effort to explain the quality and mystique of this family-run (but conglomerate-owned) *grande marque*. Krug's "entry level" is an aptly named Grande Cuvée of often stunning richness and complexity, very much in keeping with a price comparable to that of other houses' prestige cuvées. Vintage Krug can be counted on for profundity; the single-vineyard Clos de Mesnil (inaugurated with vintage 1979, which was not released until 1986) is the most multidimensional Chardonnay cuvée imaginable; and a pure Pinot counterpart, the Clos d'Ambonnay, was unveiled in 2008. These wines are characteristically released at a slow pace—occasionally well after they have been disgorged—and have a fine track record for aging, provided one has a sufficiently high discretionary income and low cellar temperature.

JEAN LALLEMENT ET FILS ★ ★ ★ ★ ★
VERZENAY

Both the Lallements' astonishingly concentrated, multifaceted, even mysterious, and anything but basic nonvintage brut and their Brut Réserve distill the essence of Verzenay Pinot Noir (hewing consistently to a blend with 20% Chardonnay). Prices are amazingly reasonable given the quality at this address.

LARMANDIER-BERNIER ★ ★ ★ ★ ★
VERTUS

Pierre Larmandier passionately believes in old, genetically diverse vines; works his vineyards biodynamically; vinifies in traditional casks with ambient yeasts; and routinely bottles his wines with low or no dosage, in theory projecting the nakedness of *terroir*. And it doesn't work only in theory. The richness of flavor and texture exhibited by these wines carries them, and the Vertus- and Cramant-specific bottlings in particular—like Larmandier's verbal explications—fervently express the belief that Champagne can and should be a vehicle for expressing *terroir*.

JACQUES LASSAIGNE—CHAMPAGNE ALEXANDRE ★ ★ ★/★ ★ ★ ★
MONTGUEUX

Jacques Lassaigne decided to single-handedly demonstrate the quality of Montgueux's historic *terroir* (see A Tour of Champagne, above) by becoming its sole estate bottler. He acquired an old facility (Champagne Alexandre, whose name he soon dropped in deference to his own) where he is exploring the potential of his vineyards and experimenting in the cellar. From the very first disgorgements, Lassaigne's wines have displayed a uniquely robust, meaty, deeply mineral-rich expression of Chardonnay that it is hard to resist the temptation of referring to as "Montgueux *terroir*."

J. LASSALLE ✱✱✱/✱✱✱✱
CHIGNY-LES-ROSES

This family estate has long been a source for consistently excellent Champagne, including their basic Préférence bottling, and has been well-represented in the U.S. Delicacy and subtlety are hallmarks of the Lassalle style, very much including the vintage-dated *blanc de blancs* and the Cuvée Angeline.

JEAN LAURENT ✱✱✱/✱✱✱✱
CELLES-SUR-OURCES

Laurent is one of the more rigorous growers in the Côte des Bar. His wines are *monocépage*, the basic nonvintage brut and rosé being 100% Pinot Noir, and supplemented by a *blanc de blancs*. The excellent vintage bottlings are not released before 8 to 10 years, and small reserves of much older vintages are sometimes disgorged to order.

LAURENT-PERRIER ✱✱✱/✱✱✱✱
TOUR-SUR-MARNE

The basic bottling from this huge house has not proven particularly interesting, but rosé and ultra brut cuvées as well as the Grand Siècle *tête de cuvée* frequently distinguish themselves.

DAVID LECLAPART ✱✱✱/✱✱✱✱
TRÉPAIL-MARNE

Leclapart has attracted attention for his biodynamic farming, spontaneous fermentation in barrel, and bottling without filtration and can be expected to deliver wines with strong, individual personalities.

R. & L. LEGRAS ✱✱✱/✱✱✱✱
CHOUILLY

Given the consistent excellence of Legras Champagne, it is surprising this house is not better known. The firmly chiseled mineral style of their *blanc de blancs* is formidable, and their Cuvée Saint Vincent, rendered only in top vintages, is memorably complex.

LILBERT-FILS ✱✱✱/✱✱✱✱
CRAMANT

Georges and Bertrand Lilbert render dynamic, high-tension, ultra-clear expressions of Cramant that deserve to be better known in the U.S.

A. MARGAINE ✱✱✱/✱✱✱✱
VILLERS-MARMERY

Margaine offers consistently excellent expressions of Villers-Marmery Chardonnay (his basic brut has less than 10% Pinot Noir) with a Riesling-like exchange of vivid, luscious fruit with stony, saline minerality.

JOSÉ MICHEL ET FILS ✱✱✱/✱✱✱✱
MOUSSY

This Meunier-dominated house offers an enticing, fruit-forward brut nonvintage and a satisfying array of other cuvées, including older vintages, all at attractive prices.

JEAN MILAN ★★★/★★★★
OGER

The Milans recently—and no doubt wisely—elected to supplement their less than 14 acres with fruit purchased under careful supervision from neighbors. The offerings here culminate in a single-vineyard *blanc de blancs* from 50-year-old vines called Terres de Noël that rivals the best of this genre in its provocative and intriguing complexity.

MOËT & CHANDON ★★★/★★★★
ÉPERNAY

Champagne's best-known behemoth demonstrates that excellence can be achieved even in enormous (if in fact unknown) volume with their Dom Pérignon cuvée, which does not so much reveal the limits of luxury-brand potential in Champagne as suggest that there might not be any. With considerable fanfare, Moët released in 2001 three nonvintage grand cru wines, each entirely from a single grape variety, which helped break the ice among *négociants* with regard to talking and tasting *terroir*.

PIERRE MONCUIT ★★★★★
LE MESNIL-SUR-OGER

This family estate is one of the prime sources for great Champagne illustrative of the best *terroir* in the Côte des Blancs, combining clarity, refreshment, and palpable extract with at times head-scratching, oceanic depth of flavors that resist any adjective other than "mineral." Uniquely, Moncuit cuvées are all single vintage, but are only labeled with the vintage in top years.

G. H. MUMM ★★★/★★★★
REIMS

This well-known establishment has been through considerable change in recent decades (culminating in its sale in 2001 to the gargantuan Allied Domecq) but is generally thought to be on a qualitative rebound. The grand cru *blanc de blancs* Mumm de Cramant has long been the most distinguished wine from this house, but over the last decade a new luxury cuvée dubbed Cuvée R Lalou and coming from carefully selected parcels in eight grand cru villages shows promise.

BRUNO PAILLARD ★★★/★★★★
REIMS

This Champagne house was founded by Bruno Paillard only a quarter of a century ago. A wide range of successful cuvées is essayed in various styles, and disgorgement date is practically least among the many details included on what are surely the most informative back labels in the region.

JOSEPH PERRIER ★★★/★★★★
CHÂLONS-EN-CHAMPAGNE

A small *négociant* in out-of-the-way Châlons, Joseph Perrier produces Champagne that tends toward richness and low-toned depth. Their more than respectable basic bottling is known as Cuvée Royale, in honor of having supplied the British royals in the Victorian and Edwardian eras.

PERRIER-JOUËT ★★★/★★★★
ÉPERNAY

This is another huge Champagne house now owned by Allied Domecq and widely predicted to begin moving up in the qualitative sweepstakes. The style—up to and including their prestige cuvée in its well-known flower bottle—is light and on the sweet side.

PIERRE PETERS ★★★★★
LE MESNIL-SUR-OGER

This family estate produces a highly expressive and refined range that showcases the exceptional potential of Mesnil's vineyards. Their Cuvée Spéciale is from a single parcel of ancient vines and offers formidable complexity and ageability.

PHILIPPONNAT ★★★/★★★★
MAREUIL-SUR-AŸ

The one wine from this historically important Champagne house that continues to make it worth talking about is the profound and notoriously ageworthy Clos des Goisses, a blend of Chardonnay and Pinot Noir from a dramatically steep site along the Aisne-Marne Canal.

PLOYEZ-JACQUEMART ★★★/★★★★
LUDES

This small house is young by Champagne standards (founded in 1930), but they augment their acreage in Ludes and Mailly with obviously well-chosen fruit from an array of grand crus, and the whole range here including basic nonvintage brut reflects an attention to detail. A portion of the wine is barrel fermented and hand riddled.

JÉRÔME PRÉVOST ★★★/★★★★
GUEUX

A recent feature in one of Europe's most prestigious wine publications ran under the headline "Garage Wines in Champagne? No, it's not going to come to that." Obviously, the author has never visited the tiny structure in the back of Jérôme Prévost's house in what amounts to suburban Reims. Primary fermentation takes place in a tiny, unlit World War II bomb shelter under the street. The sole wine, La Closerie Les Béguines, comes from the nearby plot that Prévost inherited from his grandmother, and is 100% Meunier. It is also startlingly unique and delicious. An adjacent plot has been planted with the entire catalog of Champagne *cépage* (including "the forgotten" varieties) for a future cuvée. In the vinosity and singularity of his wines and their preindustrial vinification, Prévost puts one just a bit in mind of Alain Robert (see below).

ALAIN ROBERT ★★★★★
LE MESNIL-SUR-OGER

No other Champagne establishment is at all like that of Alain Robert, both in the striking personalities of its wines and in the degree to which both their *élevage* and the reception accorded visitors (by appointment only) are consciously premodern. For the trade, wine is disgorged strictly to order, and the menu of cuvées available for disgorgement at any given time is generally kept very short. These are *blanc de blancs* designed to showcase the character of Mesnil (although Robert's now infrequent lower-echelon bottlings benefit from his holdings in Oger and the Côte de Sézanne). Barrel-fermented, never filtered, never released with fewer than six years on the lees (and nowadays generally many more), they are the ultimate instances of Champagne-as-wine—indeed, their relatively low pressure and considerable oxidative development on release (both factors designed to enhance their marriage with cuisine) put off some tasters. Robert's vintage-dated Tradition is—along with Krug's Clos de Mesnil and Salon—one of the great white peaks of the Champagne range.

LOUIS ROEDERER ★ ★ ★ ★ ★
REIMS

This exemplary large house delivers consistent quality from their nonvintage Brut Premier up to their celebrated *tête de cuvée* Cristal. The latter, it must be said, is a source of unhappiness among wine lovers because here is a celebrated luxury brand that especially deserves to be treated as one of the world's great wines, yet it also trades at the highest possible prices as one of the world's most coveted status symbols, putting it virtually out of reach to all but the wealthy. Not just the cellar work or blending expertise at this establishment explains its high quality, but above all the facts that its own vineyards supply much of its needs, and purchased fruit is subject to unusual scrutiny.

POL ROGER ★ ★ ★/★ ★ ★
ÉPERNAY

Pol Roger is a family-owned Champagne house and its own vineyards supply a significant percentage of its needs. The vintage *blanc de blancs* cuvée here is known as Brut Chardonnay and is pretty consistently impressive and cellarworthy, and the *tête de cuvée* Winston Churchill (in existence for less than a quarter-century and named for the person whose preference was most responsible for publicizing this house) cries out for cellaring.

RUINART ★ ★ ★/★ ★ ★
REIMS

This house is all about *blanc de blancs* (even their rosé is essentially Pinot-tinted Chardonnay) and the quality is quite fine, particularly considering the large-scale production. Ruinart's vast, ancient cellars are renowned even in this region that is riddled with cellars.

SALON ★ ★ ★ ★ ★
LE MESNIL-SUR-OGER

Since its inception nearly a century ago, Salon has always been a one-wine establishment. Its eponymous cuvée—entirely from vines in Mesnil—is only essayed in the best vintages and seldom disgorged or released with fewer than 10 years of bottle age. Caressing in texture and spellbinding in complexity, Salon displays remarkable postdisgorgement stamina. A range of vintages is normally kept on offer, and from the 1990s, five of these were declared—a near record at this address.

FRANÇOIS SECONDÉ ★ ★ ★/★ ★ ★
SILLERY

Secondé's wines offer a rare glimpse of the *terroir* of grand cru Sillery and tend toward formidable complexity, density, acidity, and ageworthiness.

JACQUES SELOSSE ★ ★ ★ ★ ★
AVIZE

It's quite possible that no Champagne grower since Dom Pérignon has been more written about or more influential than Anselm Selosse. Fanatic in his pursuit of biodynamic methods, of Champagne-as-wine, and above all of integrity and truth in *terroir*, Selosse eschews chaptalization, cultured yeasts, filtration, and all manner of other (in his view) modern ills. Risk taking is pursued here to the point where every one of many cuvées offers the vigneron and the taster a wild ride all its own, and that is just how Selosse wants it. Wines are bottled and released in answer to an inner voice and not the dictates of the market. (Selosse bottled all of his production from the 1997 vintage in magnum, just as Burgundy's Hubert de Montille notoriously had his entire 1983 crop.) The influence of wood and frequently advanced oxidative evolution in some cuvées can be divisive but there is no arguing about the greatness of the best of them, and with so many of the younger generation queuing up to do internships here, Selosse's continued influence on the course of Champagne (and indeed of French wine in general) is assured.

DE SOUSA & FILS ★ ★ ★/★ ★ ★ ★
AVIZE

This is another grower who deserves to be better known. Methods in the vineyards are biodynamic, and in the cellar, too, de Sousa is not afraid to do things the hard way. The barrel-fermented Cuvée des Caudalies is a standout.

TAITTINGER ★ ★ ★/★ ★ ★ ★
REIMS

This large and venerable house changed hands twice in the past several years, but there is now a substantial share of family ownership. The prestige Comtes de Champagne is one of the region's outstanding *blanc de blancs* and often worth cellaring.

VARNIER-FANNIÈRE ★ ★ ★/★ ★ ★ ★
AVIZE

Denis Varnier is another true grower-artisan. His single-vineyard, old-vine Cuvée St.-Denis begs to be cellared, and all of his wines deserve to be enjoyed at the table.

JEAN VESSELLE ★ ★ ★/★ ★ ★ ★
BOUZY

The most interesting wine from grower Delphine Vesselle is her Oeil de Perdrix *blanc de noirs,* faintly toasty, always very dry, yet deliciously full of red fruits.

VEUVE CLICQUOT ★ ★ ★/★ ★ ★ ★
REIMS

This vast house is known worldwide for their "yellow label" nonvintage brut as well as for their *tête de cuvée* La Grande Dame—full, rich Champagne that in many ways resembles the grand old lady on its label and certainly does her historical reputation no discredit.

VILMART ET CIE ★ ★ ★ ★ ★
RILLY-LA-MONTAGNE

Laurent Champs works entirely in cask or *barrique,* with meticulously and organically farmed fruit from Rilly-la-Montagne and its immediate neighborhood. The estate's geographical location makes the predominance of Chardonnay here unusual. The best Vilmart cuvées are among the most complex, powerful, and structured wines in Champagne.

[france's southwest]

FOREVER FORGOTTEN?

"Southwest of France"—at least when it comes to wine—is shorthand for "everything in this quarter of France that is *not* Bordeaux." It may be unfair to such a vast, diverse, and culturally disparate collection of growing areas to be known by what they're *not*, but the practice merely reflects their luckless fate for most of the past millennium. The many major rivers watering this region all converge on the port of Bordeaux, which as a result has had the upper hand commercially and politically during centuries of contentious and often bellicose coexistence with its winegrowing neighbors to the east, southeast, and south. Even the best known winegrowing area of the southwest, Cahors, owes its place in wine history and in large part its reputation today to the almost legendary "black wine"—a sort of cooked wine concentrate—once routinely used to add body and flavor to wines that were then marketed as Bordeaux. Better known than Cahors is Armagnac, but that famous brandy has fallen from popularity in modern times, so much so that cheap and cheerful Côtes de Gascogne from white grapes that never make it into a barrel, much less a still, is now the commercial mainstay of the Armagnac-producing region.

After the ravages of phylloxera, much of the southwest never recovered, and the late-20th-century revival of Madiran, despite its having retained many ancient vines, has been headlined as a "return from the dead." Cahors was sooner to experience a revival of sorts, after World War II. But the devastating frost of 1956 crippled this area even more than it did Bordeaux, and when Cahors achieved *appellation contrôlée* status in 1971, the late Jean Jouffreau was one of the only distinguished growers, and the only one with any old vines of the traditional Auxerrois (aka Malbec). Today the acreage of Cahors is only around 15 percent of what it was before phylloxera. But the qualitative revival in these two potentially (once again) important red wine regions is symptomatic of the promise and reawakening that characterize much of the great Southwest.

A TOUR OF THE TERRITORY

We begin our tour in what can unapologetically be called "Bordeaux's backyard." Unlike most of the southwest of France, the grape varieties and styles of wine that characterize Bergerac and Monbazillac; the less-well-known Montravel, Pécharmant, and Saussignac; as well as several even more obscure associated subappellations, are those familiar from immediately west in Bordeaux, as is the river that runs through them, the Dordogne. Traditionally this area concentrated on the production of nobly sweet wine from Sémillon, Sauvignon, and Muscatelle, and today it is far too little known or noted that the top growers of Monbazillac— Domaine de la Borie Blanche, Grande Maison, and Tirecul la Gravière—can compete with the elite of Barsac and Sauternes. This unjust neglect is certainly due in large part to the simple, sad fact that sweet wines are underappreciated. Dry whites bottled by growers of Monbazillac take the name Bergerac (although there can also be sweet wines with the latter appellation). The appellation of Montravel, spread out along the southern shore of the Dordogne, has understandably chosen to focus increasingly on dry wines, and the best of these are more interesting than a great deal of white from Bordeaux. For fascinating and affordable examples, consumers should make room on their shopping lists for such stylistically diverse wines as the Bergerac of Luc Conti's Tour des Gendres and of Thierry Després at Grande Maison, or the Montravel of Guy-Jean Kreusch known as K de Krevel. Pécharmant, just northeast of the town of Bergerac, is devoted to growing Merlot and the Cabernets. But a newfound interest in reds is spreading throughout the environs of Bergerac, with some bottled as Bergerac, some as Côtes de Bergerac, and some (since 2003) as Montravel. Given the rising prices and quality of so many satellite appellations of Bordeaux—not to mention the wealth of oenological talent and just plain wealth that emanates from Bordeaux and Libourne—it is practically inevitable that serious reds from the "Far East" will become increasingly important on the international stage.

To the south of Bergerac, Côtes de Duras features a similar mix of grapes and styles. But immediately to its south, on either side of the Garonne, is a region that introduces us to some uniquely local varieties. Côtes du Marmandais is as diverse in its *cépages* as in its geological underpinnings, with Abouriou, Fer Servadou, and Côt (aka Malbec) joining the familiar Bordelais cast. (Syrah, too, is permitted.) Élian da Ros, a veteran of Alsace's great Domaine Zind-Humbrecht, is demonstrating that world-class red is possible from this still obscure region. Upstream and south of the Garonne, wine from Buzet has yet to show similar potential.

Well to the east of the above-mentioned appellations, almost due north of Toulouse and spread far inland from either shore of the river Lot, is Cahors. This region traditionally featured the Malbec (known locally as Auxerre), and that grape's revival has gone hand-in-hand with the revival of the region. The principal blending varieties here are Merlot and Tannat (a star in its own right in Madiran in the deep southwest), which function almost as softening and firming agents, respectively. Malbec itself in these parts delivers somewhat less exuberant black fruits than those associated with wines of Mendoza (in sweet, jamlike form) or of the Loire (where they tend toward tartness) but offers distinctive scents of cardamom and white pepper and can take on striking subtlety and complexity. Vines are grown in gravel soils— traditionally terraced—along the river and in the adamant limestone plateau above. Though the rather unfashionably traditional and anything but flamboyant wines of the Jouffreaus' Clos de Gamot and the rich, thoroughly modern reds of ambitious outsiders Jean-Marie Verhaeghe's Domaine du Cèdre and Alain-Dominique Perrin's Château Lagrazette are so far the only Cahors that remotely challenge any of the world's great reds, this region is generating an increasingly broad and delicious stream of affordable, characterful, and easy to enjoy wines deserving of more consumer attention.

Immediately north of Toulouse and south of the Tarn River lies Fronton (or Côtes du Frontonnais), where Frédéric Ribes of the Domaine Le Roc has demonstrated the uncanny synergy of Negrette and Syrah in a dramatically distinctive cuvée called Don Quichotte that for maximum impact should be tasted blind. More than one other Frontonnais grower is following similar intuitions, and this region's long-standing association solely with forgettable quaffing wine may soon come to an end.

Northeast of Toulouse, between the Aveyron and Tarn rivers, lies the enormous but little-known region of Gaillac. Here a host of largely indigenous and otherwise obscure grape varieties come into their own—Duras, Fer, Len de l'El, Mauzac, Ondenc—although such better-known *cépages* as Gamay, Muscadelle, Sauvignon, and Syrah can also be found. White, pink, and red; dry and sweet; sparkling and still: Gaillac offers from its colorful cast of grapes a vast array of wines that, in the hands of a few of its more colorful winemaking characters, can be memorable.

The territory we have covered in our brief tour represents the northeastern third of France's southwest. South of Buzet and west of Toulouse and the Frontonnais lies the extensive area entitled to bottle wine as Côtes de Gascogne, including the classic districts of Armagnac. As already mentioned, there is an immense amount of sometimes delicious dry (and occasionally sweet) whites generated here from Ugni Blanc, Colombard, Gros Manseng, and Sauvignon—so much of it in fact that these wines serve as most Americans' somewhat misleading (because atypical and easily forgettable) vinous calling card of the southwest.

Just south of the Bas Armagnac region lies Madiran. To its west is the multipartite but thus far undistinguished appellation of Béarn, and north of that the Côte St.-Mont, whose model cooperative Producteurs Plaimont offers some excellent values both red and white. White wines—dry, off-dry, or sweet—grown in and around Madiran carry the odd-sounding appellation of Pacherenc du Vic-Bilh (originating in a name for the pole-training of the local vines). The ferocious potential flavor and tannic intensity of the local Tannat grape can be mitigated to some extent by the practice of softening it through the addition of no less formidable a variety than Cabernet Sauvignon, as well as Cabernet Franc. In fact, if one imagines the black fruits, smoked walnuts, and iron filings that can characterize Franc magnified into an almost hulking form, one has some notion of Tannat. That said, even pure Tannat wines crafted in tanks or old barrels in the 1970s by such domaines as Laplace (today Château d'Aydie) and Pichard softened and became memorably complex with a few years in bottle. (And they were then notably long-lived.) It is no coincidence that the technique known as *microbullage,* or micro-oxygenation, which has become a prevalent tool for taming tannins both in Europe and the New World, originated here (with oenologist Patrick Ducournau of Chapelle l'Enclos and Domaine Mouréou). But the hero of Madiran's modern resurgence is the cantankerous and workaholic Alain Brumont (no friend, as it happens, of "micro-ox"), who demonstrated in the late '80s at his Château Montus that Madiran could compete for richness, complexity, and ageworthiness with the world's other great, new *barrique*-raised reds. Brumont offers richly rewarding wines full of character under the Bouscassé and Meinjarre labels, as well. It's not just the distinctive qualities of the Tannat grape and the local *terroirs* or the stylistic versatility and vision of its front-running vintners that commend Madiran to our attention: this is also one of the last outposts in France for vines that survived phylloxera. (Denis Capmartin claims that some of those at his excellent Domaine Barréjat are pushing two centuries.) This region has potential and justification for generating much more international excitement than it has so far.

The whites of Pacherenc should not be overlooked, but in their style and principal grape varieties—the Gros Manseng and Petit Manseng—they point toward the appellation of Jurançon in the Pyrenean foothills to the south. This is unique among the world's great growing regions for sweet, nonfortified wine in not depending on (and in fact relatively infrequently benefiting from) botrytis. Instead, the grapes normally concentrate simply through long hang time; slow, spontaneous dehydration; and occasionally frost. This manner of concentration—in conjunction with the musky, carnal, pungently citric and zesty character of the two sorts of Manseng grapes themselves—can result in long-lived wines of haunting, mysterious complexity, amazing transparency, and remarkable delicacy. The dry whites of Jurançon tend, in a way that resembles those of Hungary's Tokaj region and its Furmint grape, to be a work in progress, rendered challenging by the grapes' natural tendency to bitterness and brusqueness when harvested before overripeness has set in. That said, dry wines from Jurançon's foremost growers—notably Henri Ramonteu of Domaine Cauhapé—can be both invigorating and intriguing.

Deeper into the mountains, east of Jurançon and southeast of Bayonne and Biarritz, lies Irouléguy, France's one quintessentially Basque wine region (as becomes immediately evident from the unpronounceable names on its labels). The principal grapes, however, are those of Madiran and Jurançon. It appears to require a certain restraint and a clear stylistic vision to tame the inherent savagery of red Irouléguy, but the Domaines Arretxea, Etxegaraya, and Illaria have been notably successful in achieving that goal, and their wines are well worth experiencing.

—DAVID SCHILDKNECHT

[the ratings]

THE SOUTHWEST OF FRANCE'S BEST PRODUCERS

***** (OUTSTANDING)

Domaine Cauhapé (Jurançon)
Grande Maison (Monbazillac, Bergerac)

Château Montus—Domaines Brumont (Madiran, Pacherenc)
Tirecul la Gravière (Monbazillac)

**** (EXCELLENT)

Château d'Aydie—Laplace (Madiran, Pacherenc)
Domaine de la Borie Blanche (Monbazillac, Bergerac)
Domaine Bru-Baché (Jurançon)
Château Le Cèdre (Cahors)

Clos de Gamot, Château de Cayrou—Jouffreau (Cahors)
Château Lagrézette (Cahors)
Élian da Ros (Côtes du Marmandais)
Tour des Gendres—Moulin des Dames (Bergerac)

*** (VERY GOOD)

Domaine Arretxea (Irouléguy)
Château de Bachen (Tursan)
Domaine Barréjat—Capmartin (Madiran)
Domaine Bellegarde (Jurançon)
Domaine Berthoumieu (Madiran, Pacherenc)
Clos la Coutale (Cahors)
Clos Lapeyre (Jurançon)
Clos de Triguedina (Cahors)
Clos Uroulat (Jurançon)

Puy de Grave—K de Krevel (Montravel, Pécharmant)
Domaine Etxegaraya (Irouléguy)
Château Grinou (Bergerac, Saussignac)
Domaine Guirouilh (Jurançon)
Domaine Haut-Monplaisir (Cahors)
Domaine Illarria (Irouléguy)
Château de la Jaubertie (Bergerac)
Lafitte-Teston (Madiran, Pacherenc)

Domaine Mouréou—Chapelle l'Enclos (Madiran)
Château de Panisseau (Bergerac)
Domaine Pichard (Madiran)

Domaine Le Roc (Fronton)
Domaine des Verdots (Bergerac, Monbazillac)
Domaine de Viella (Madiran, Pacherenc)

* * (GOOD)

Domaine de l'Ancienne Cure (Bergerac, Pécharmant, Monbazillac)
Château de Bélingard (Bergerac, Monbazillac)
Domaine Causse Marines (Gaillac)
Château Champerel (Pécharmant)
Château La Colline (Bergerac)
Château Court-les-Mûts (Bergerac)
Domaine du Haut-Pécharmant (Pécharmant)
Château de Haute-Serre (Cahors)
Domaine du Have (Côtes de Gascogne)
Domaine de Ménard (Côtes de Gascogne)
Château Monestier La Tour (Bergerac, Saussignac)

Château Moulin Caresse (Bergerac, Montravel)
Château du Perron (Madiran)
Château Pineraie (Cahors)
R. et B. Plageoles (Gaillac)
Château Plaisance (Fronton)
Domaine de Pouy (Côtes de Gascogne)
Producteurs Plaimont (Côte St.-Mont, Côtes de Gascogne, Madiran, Pécharmant)
Château Le Reyssac (Bergerac)
Domaine de Rieux (Côtes de Gascogne)
Domaine des Savarines (Cahors)
Domaine du Tariquet (Côtes de Gascogne)
Domaine Theulet (Bergerac, Monbazillac)
Château de Tiregand (Pécharmant)

[the jura and the savoie]

MOUNTAINS AND MYSTERIES

Looking east across the basin of the Saône River from Burgundy's Côte d'Or, one sees the geological twin of that "golden slope," the mountains of the Jura. On an exceptionally clear day, one can even make out Mont Blanc and the Alps in the Savoie to the southeast. These mountains that parallel the Côte d'Or, the Mâcon, and Beaujolais at a distance of roughly 50 to 80 miles are home to diverse vines, microclimates, and wine-growing traditions, most of them little appreciated even inside France, let alone abroad. The total theoretical vineyard acreage of the Savoie (including, as is common practice, the equally sprawling and fragmented, primarily sparkling wine–producing region of Bugey to its west) is a mere 20% of that encompassed by either of the next-largest French growing regions, Alsace and the Southwest. And the Jura is only two-thirds as large a growing area as the Savoie. It has been said—probably with only slight hyperbole—that in years when the winter Olympic games have been held in the Savoie, the visitors left behind a local populace that had to "import" wine from elsewhere in France in order to slake their thirst until the next harvest! Nevertheless, an experience with these minor global wine players of the Jura and Savoie can be richly rewarding, not just on account of their delicious diversity, but precisely because one has to make an effort to obtain them. Happily, over the past decade their availability in the U.S. has grown from nearly nil to more than respectable.

To generalize very crudely—and for those who might not read beyond this paragraph—one can say about the Jura that its classic wines will strike most tasters as among the strangest (weirdest, even) and most out of step with modern fashion of any in the world. So if intrigue and mind expansion are part of what motivates you, then you absolutely must take at least a few sips and sniffs, even if it is in the end simply to wrinkle your nose and say "no thanks!" There are a few lovely wines from Chardonnay (a grape that may have originated here) and Pinot Noir, particularly sparkling cuvées, that one might compare with wines from elsewhere in France and that can be said to represent good value. But the vast majority of Jura wine, and the wines most typical of this region, actually represent a collaboration of man and vine, not just with the usual fermentative yeasts, but with a variety of other "microflora." The resultant wines have an oxidative as well as "flor" character (think of Sherry, although very few of the Jura's wines are fortified) and generally do not come cheap.

The Savoie represents such a crazy quilt of vine varieties, sites, and styles as to make it hard to generalize. But this much is for sure: Among other things, this region (more specifically one sector and grape) renders some of the best values in crisp, refreshing, delicate, low-alcohol white wine in the world, and therefore represents a treasure trove of bargains (with certain qualifications, as we shall see). Beyond that, there are Savoie reds from Syrah's close relative (in fact an ancestor) Mondeuse that range from simple and light to concentrated and tannic, and a constellation of wines from the indigenous Altesse grape (aka Roussette de Savoie) that are endlessly fascinating but—like white Hermitage or St. Joseph from the Rhône—tend to become interesting only with a few years in the cellar, in the course of which they undergo decidedly oxidative development on which lovers of fresh fruit may frown.

THE JURA AND ITS GRAPES

There are only four significant appellations in the Jura, which comprises a 50-mile-long north-south strip. Côtes du Jura covers virtually the entire region like an umbrella. Near the Jura's northern fringe, an especially intensively planted area incorporating nearly a dozen villages goes under the appellation Arbois (with a subappellation for the village of Pupillin). Near the center of the Côtes du Jura, two individual villages are singled out as appellations in their own right: Château-Chalon and l'Étoile. The soil throughout the Jura represents slight (if significant) variants of Marne clay, limestone, and marl. So far, you may say, so good . . . and unusually simple for France! But you're in for a surprise: In a sort of inverse of Burgundy, the complexities in the Jura arise from its plethora of grape varieties and winemaking styles.

Chardonnay is one of the dominant white Jura grapes, and in fact if it did not originate in the Mâcon then it probably did here. It is the basis for a wide range of wines including the prestigious l'Étoile. Pinot Noir, too, plays a significant role. Then the cast turns local. The white grape Savignin forms the basis for the region's most prestigious oxidized wines, including Château-Chalon. (It can also be a component in l'Étoile.) This variety appears to be an antecedent of Gewurztraminer, and is the same as what is known in Alsace as Klevener de Heiligenstein. Two unusual reds are of great importance: the pale but highly perfumed Poulsard, and the ruddier Trousseau (which, oddly, is also grown in Australia, whence it came via Portugal and was thus misnamed Touriga). The Poulsard figures especially in Arbois, and the Trousseau most notably in sweet wines from throughout the Jura.

Fresh-fruited Jura wines, particularly from Chardonnay, can resemble those of the Mâcon. And, with or without Pinot, fresh-fruited Chardonnay sometimes forms the basis for excellent and affordable Crémant du Jura—American consumers would be wise to sample them. (The outstanding brut bubblies from Clavelin and Tissot are widely available.) But more often, exposure in the cellar to ambient microorganisms quickly renders even tank-raised and relatively early-bottled Jura wines (not to mention those matured in cask) *typé,* as locals term it, which is to say lightly oxidized and having taken on nutty, pungent piquancy. What both fresh-fruited and *typé* Jura wine have in common (at their best) is clarity of flavors; a lean, spare structure; relatively high acidity; and enormous aromatic and palate penetration. The principal difference in taste is that the *typé* wines are much more complex than their fresh-fruited cousins. In that respect, one could think of a Jura wine's evolution as akin to that of many cheeses, which start out lacking distinctive aroma, flavor, texture, or punch, but acquire them (sometimes in spades!) as they ripen.

The greatest of the dry Jura wines—including Château-Chalon and l'Étoile—are examples of *vins jaunes*. These are produced by permitting the wine a lengthy stay in barrel, during which some of it evaporates, and—as the barrels are not topped off—the contents oxidize and grow a flavor-sponsoring film of specialized yeasts. A *vin jaune* may not by law be bottled for at least six years after harvest, and normally spends the entire intervening period in cask. A squat, antique shape of bottle of 620-milliliter capacity known as a *clavelin* is the official vessel (for which reason many such wines that come to the States are specially bottled in internationally recognized 375-milliliter format). The Jura is also one of the world's few centers for *vin de paille*, an off-dry or decidedly sweet elixir obtained by drying the grapes—literally on a straw mat, but in Jura practice in well-ventilated trays—before pressing. These must achieve at least 18% potential and 14.5% actual alcohol and be cask-aged for at least three years. Whether *vin jaune* or *vin de paille,* a top Jura wine can often develop positively for hours or even days after opening, and for decades in bottle. Finally, there is a heady and often impressive local variation on sweet fortified wine known as *macvin du Jura*. (This centuries-old wine in fact officially has its own appellation, awarded, incidentally, only in 1991, long after the prefix "Mac" had come to acquire a derogatory connotation in certain French circles.)

THE SAVOIE AND ITS GRAPES

The Savoie consists of many isolated subregions and patches of vines ranging all the way from the southern shores of Lake Geneva (just north of the Swiss city of the same name) to the valley of the Isère between the city of Chambéry and the skiing center of Albertville, west of Mont Blanc. Steep slopes are nearly universal here, and narrow valleys or lakes figure in many appellations as well. Because of such heat-retentive features and the often luminous blue Alpine skies, these wines (grown so close to snow-capped peaks that flatlanders often find their concentration on them hijacked by the scenery) benefit from higher total annual heat accumulation than those of Alsace or Champagne.

Aside from Gamay, Pinot Noir, and a little Chardonnay, Chasselas, and (in Bugey) Poulsard, the grapes of the Savoie appear to have originated in and are largely confined to their region. The Mondeuse produces tannic reds with the peppery pungency and sometimes the gamey complexity of Syrah, which its egg-shaped berries resemble. (Even in the Savoie there are only 500 acres of Mondeuse, but it turns out to have been renamed Refosco when it crossed the Alps into Italy, and from there it occasionally made the journey to northern California, where Mike Officer of Carlisle located and now bottles the fruit of one tiny, ancient patch). Recently, it was genetically proven that the much less common white variant Mondeuse Blanche is one of the parents of Syrah, which must in consequence have followed the Rhône south from here. The other most distinctive Savoie grapes are white. Altesse—otherwise known as Roussette de Savoie (which doubles as the official appellation for most of the wines produced from it)—can produce wines of riveting complexity after they ripen in bottle, normally taking on an oxidative patina in the process. Long thought (although, it has recently been demonstrated, erroneously) to have been related to the Furmint of Tokaj, it shares with that variety floral, honeyed, pungent aromas and youthful sharpness. Bergeron is a local variant of Roussanne (another grape that may have migrated from here downstream along the Rhône). Both piquant and opulent, its Savoie incarnations can be hauntingly complex and long-lived (though not as long-lived as a great Altesse). The other distinctive Savoie white—and this region's most widely planted variety—is the Jacquère, which lends itself to refreshing, early-drinking, delicately floral, herbal, and "mineral" wines with low alcohol, moderate acidity, and at their best outstanding price-to-quality rapport. Around the Jura town of Ayze, a local variant of the Jura's Savignin—if not the identical grape—is called Gringet. And a white called Molette figures prominently in the sparkling wines of Seyssel and Bugey.

The appellation system of Savoie suggests that the authorities must have come under the influence less of the local wines than of some powerful hallucinogen. The overarching "vin de Savoie" can be combined with the names of grape varieties, certain towns, or even a combination of the two, and to comprehend the Savoie's nesting of subappellations might require the application of set theory. Better to simply give you a superficial tour, highlighting a few names of particular interest. At the northern edge of the region, along Lake Geneva, the dominant vine is Chasselas. That, along with location, makes for wines somewhat resembling their far more numerous Swiss cousins. South of the city of Geneva, along the upper reaches of the Rhône, we come to Seyssel, known for its sparkling wine. Part of the personality of Seyssel comes from the (minimum 10%) Altesse that must be blended with Molette to produce it, and still wines from this neighborhood—one of the two most densely planted in the entire region—are bottled as Roussette de Savoie or (in one village) under the subappellation Frangy. A little farther down the Rhône and paralleling the elongated Lac de Bourget are grown two of the most striking crus rendered from Altesse, Jongieux and Marestel, the latter from some of the most amazing cliff-hanging terraces to be found anywhere in the world of wine.

On the south side of Chambéry—which itself lies just south of the Lac de Bourget—we encounter the one other densely planted sector of the Savoie. Here the dominant grape is Jacquère, which takes the appellations (depending on village of origin) Abymes, Apremont, Arbin, Chignin, Cruet, and Montmélian. Not all of the sites are steep, and there is plenty of potential to overcrop Jacquère so as to achieve slightly grassy, herbaceous results, which are too often covered over with cosmetic residual sugar. But when this grape is properly ripened in chalky, steep slopes and vinified with care, the results are little icons of vinous refreshment, evoking in a glass of the Savoie's mountain air, flower-covered meadows, and cold, milky glacial flour coursing through turbulent streams. Jean Masson is this grape's consummate *terroiriste* as well as its boldest experimenter, multiplying distinct microclimates by distinctive vinifications for a gallery of memorable Apremonts. Amazingly, the *terroir* of Abymes and parts of Apremont are among the world's youngest, consisting in large part of the rubble deposited by a megaavalanche when Mont Granier collapsed in 1248, burying the then-existing villages. Today the butte-like rump of the mountain forms the area's signature skyline and a mute monument to a legendary disaster.

In Chignin grows the Savoie's potentially great Bergeron (i.e., Roussanne), with its own appellation. Chignin-Bergeron is also sadly subject to abuse, and too often underripe wine, when subjected to malolactic fermentation, tastes more of dairy products and popcorn than of Bergeron or Chignin. But when gotten right—as in the best examples from André et Michel Quénard—Chignin-Bergeron is stunning in its combination of richness and refinement. There is a considerable amount of good red wine produced from Mondeuse in the Jacquère- and Bergeron-growing districts of the Savoie. But when one follows the southwest-facing slopes around Chignin as far as the river Isère and turns 90 degrees, a range of slopes facing the river offers new opportunities—including Kimmeridgean and Oxfordian chalk like that of Sancerre or Chablis—not only for diverse whites, but for the most complex and ageworthy Mondeuse reds thus far produced, notably those of Michel Grisard at his Prieuré St.-Christophe.

—DAVID SCHILDKNECHT

[the ratings]

THE BEST PRODUCERS OF THE JURA

* * * * (EXCELLENT)

Jean et Laurent Macle (Château-Chalon)
Jacques Puffeney (Arbois)

André et Mireille (Stéphane) Tissot (Arbois, Côtes du Jura)

* * * (VERY GOOD)

Lucien Aviet (Arbois)
Jean-Marc Brignot (Arbois)
Domaine Ganevat (Côtes du Jura)
Domaine Alain Labet (Côtes du Jura)
Domaine Ligier Père et Fils (Arbois)
Frédéric Lornet (Arbois)

Domaine de Montbourgeau—Nicole Dériaux (l'Étoile)
Pierre Overnoy et Emmanuel Houillon (Arbois)
Jean Rijckaert—*négociant* (Arbois, Côtes du Jura)

* * (GOOD)

Domaine Berthet-Bondet (Château-Chalon, Côtes du Jura)
Philippe Butin (Château-Chalon, Côtes du Jura)
Hubert Clavelin (Château-Chalon, Côtes du Jura)

Henri Maire—*négociant* (Arbois, Côtes du Jura, Château-Chalon)
Domaine Pignier (Côtes du Jura)
Domaine de la Pinte (Arbois)
Domaine Rolet (Arbois)

THE BEST PRODUCERS OF THE SAVOIE

* * * * (EXCELLENT)

Domaine Dupasquier (Roussette de Savoie, Marestel)
Michel Grisard—Prieuré St.-Christophe (Mondeuse, Roussette de Savoie)

Jean Masson (Apremont)
André & Michel Quénard (Chignin, Chignin-Bergeron)

* * * (VERY GOOD)

Domaine Belluard (Haute Savoie—*cépage* Gringet)
Gilles Berlioz (Chignin, Chignin-Bergeron, Mondeuse)
Pierre Boniface—*négociant* (Apremont)
Patrick Bottex (Bugey-Cerdon)
Jean-Pierre et Jean-François Grisard (Mondeuse, Roussette de Savoie)
Domaine Labbé—Pont Royal (Abymes)

Louis Magnin (Arbin-Mondeuse, Altesse, Chignin-Bergeron)
Maison Mollex (Seyssel)
Franck Peillot (Bugey-Montagrieu)
Pascal et Annick Quénard (Chignin, Chignin-Bergeron)
Raymond Quénard (Chignin, Chignin-Bergeron)

Cave de Chautagne (Chautagne, Roussette de Savoie)

Domaine de l'Idylle—Philippe et François Trollier (Cruet, Arbin-Mondeuse)

Edmond Jacquin (Marestel)

Château de Lucey (Roussette de Savoie, Mondeuse)

Bruno Lupin (Roussette de Savoie—Frangy)

Yves-Girard Madoux (Chignin, Chignin-Bergeron, Mondeuse)

Domaine Renardat-Fâche (Bugey-Cerdon)

Domaine Saint-Germain (Mondeuse, Roussette de Savoie)

Chantal et Guy Tournoud (Abymes, Apremont)

Château de la Violette (Abymes, Roussette de Savoie)

Jean Vullien (Rousette de Savoie)

[the languedoc] [and roussillon]

GREAT BARGAINS AND GREAT AMBITIONS

Say "Languedoc" to most wine enthusiasts—including those in France—and the name evokes a sense of the place that would not have registered two decades ago, when any notion that consumers had of "the Midi" was geographically amorphous and qualitatively dubious. What brought to modern prominence France's oldest wine-growing region—one whose fortunes seemed to have suffered steady decline since the Middle Ages—was qualitative innovation and the search for bargains, each reinforcing the other. Robert Parker's first full-scale report on this region in his *Wine Advocate* in June 1991 was subtitled "great wine values for tough economic times." He added that this area "has undergone an amazing transformation since the mid-eighties," and that "some of America's most innovative importers are flocking to the region in search of delicious, bargain-priced wines." An economic recession is hardly needed to justify consumers setting their sights on the Languedoc and Roussillon, its smaller, southern neighbor. It's never a bad season for bargain hunting, and with prices of France's most famous crus at all-time highs (in euros, not to mention dollars!), the hunt for affordable quality has taken on new fervor.

Another part of what Robert Parker wrote nearly two decades ago remains in force as well. Nearly all of the eight American importers he singled out then as "hav[ing] the most at stake in this up-and-coming viticultural region"—including Christopher Cannan, Robert Kacher, Dan Kravitz, Kermit Lynch, Jack Siler, and Eric Solomon—are still ambitiously engaged in the Languedoc and Roussillon. Meanwhile, a cadre of other importers and agents—Jeffrey Davies, Peter Vezan, and Peter Weygandt among the most prominent—have added their discoveries and projects, and at the same time more and more talented and ambitious growers from across Europe are descending on the latest, if not indeed the last, French wine

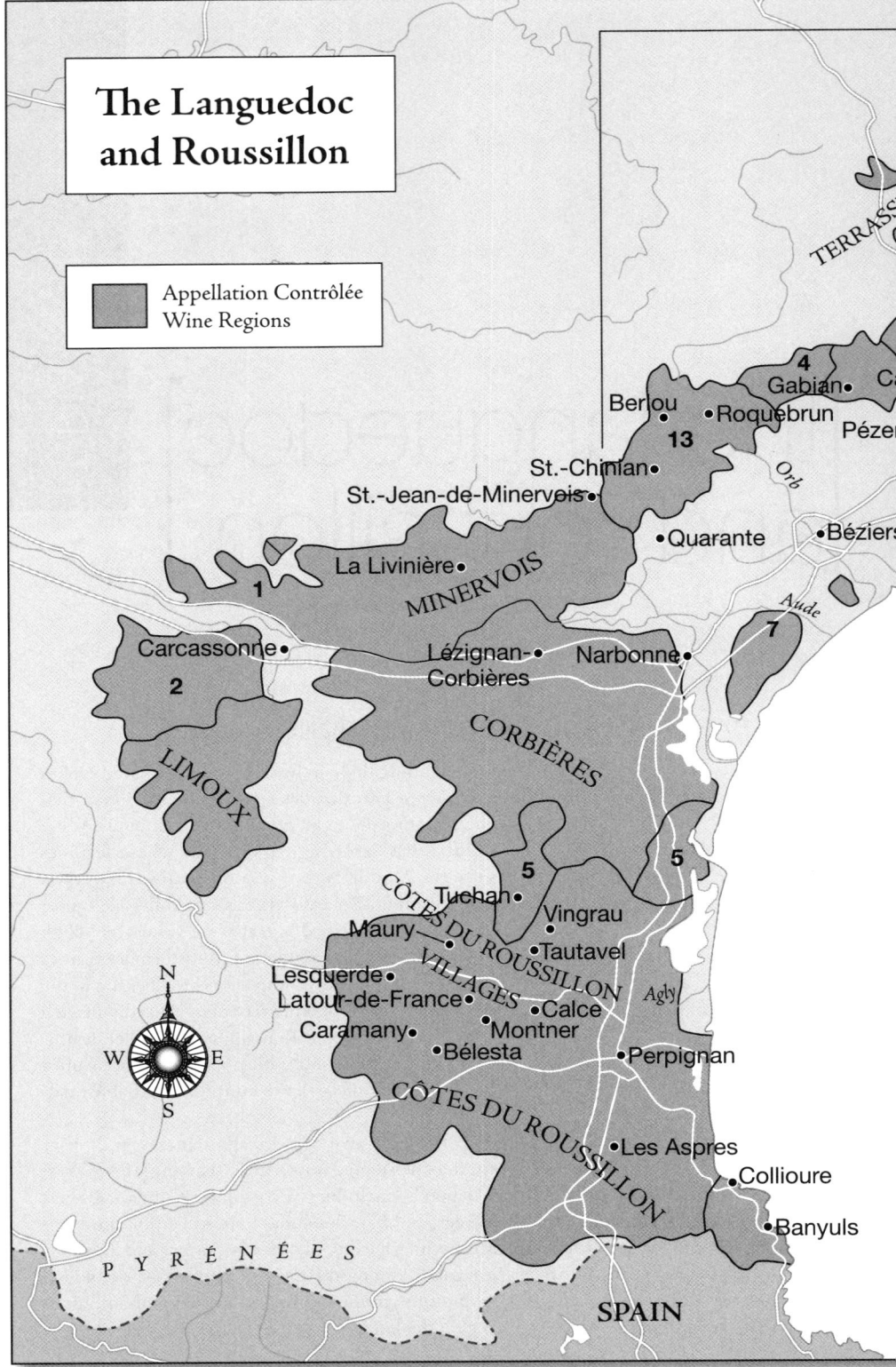

The Languedoc and Roussillon

Appellation Contrôlée Wine Regions

TERRASS

4

Gabian

Berlou • Roquébrun

Péze

Ca

13

St.-Chinian

St.-Jean-de-Minervois

Quarante

Béziers

La Livinière

Orb

1

MINERVOIS

Aude

Carcassonne

Lézignan-Corbières

Narbonne

7

2

CORBIÈRES

LIMOUX

5

5

CÔTES DU ROUSSILLON

Tuchan

Vingrau

Maury

Tautavel

VILLAGES

Lesquerde

Latour-de-France

Calce

Agly

Caramany

Montner

Bélesta

Perpignan

CÔTES DU ROUSSILLON

N

W E

S

Les Aspres

Collioure

Banyuls

P Y R É N É E S

SPAIN

COTEAUX DU LANGUEDOC

Claret
Lauret • •Sauturargues
•Fontanès
Pic-St.-Loup▲
ntpeyroux
14
•Les Matelles
•Aniane •Castries
6
8 9
Montpellier
Pargoire
12
10
•Sète

Nîmes

COSTIÈRES DE NÎMES

Hérault
Rhône
Rhône

MEDITERRANEAN SEA

1 Cabardès
2 Clairette du Languedoc
3 Côtes de la Malepère
4 Faugères
5 Fitou
6 Grès de Montpellier
7 La Clape
8 La Méjanelle
9 Muscat de Frontignan
10 Muscat de Lunel
11 Muscat de Mireval
12 Picpoul de Pinet
13 St.-Chinian
14 St.-Saturnin

•Paris

FRANCE

Map area

0   30 miles
0   30 kilometers

frontier. The sheer number of ambitious wineries with U.S. agents is staggering. It is in short the best of times for discovering the Languedoc and its wines.

And yet it is the worst of times as well. For all its promise, much of the Languedoc is in crisis, trapped in a downward spiral of ever-higher yields chasing ever-lower prices, to the point of fomenting grower riots. As French politicians and EU technocrats grapple to arrest this descent and assuage the fear and anger of frustrated vignerons, they will be looking to reduce significantly the accumulated "wine lake" and vast vine acreage, to ease many growers into early retirement or alternative livelihoods, and to address the cycle of subsidy and surplus. Growers who cannot break free of that less-than-merry-go-round are farming on borrowed time. The Languedoc and Roussillon have slaked Gallic thirst with inexpensive reds ever since railroads drastically reduced the cost of shipping in the 1860s. A century later—as France gave up Algeria—this region redoubled that role. But French thirst is not what it once was. And other lands, including neighboring Spain and the New World, can render deeply colored, even powerful wines at bargain prices and with greater uniformity. The French are realizing with consternation that they have fallen behind in the marketplace for inexpensive wine, and they ought not to assume that clever marketing and industrial efficiencies of scale provide the answer.

The viticultural goal of the Languedoc and Roussillon, like that of France herself, must lie in offering wines of distinctiveness and distinction, among them bargains, to be sure, but of high quality and not easily replicated. A quarter of all French wine is still being grown here. But for the sake of the region's own economic health, not to mention that of France and the EU, there must be both less and better-quality wine in future. Given the microclimatic, geological, and cultural diversity of this vast Mediterranean arc that runs from the Rhône to the Pyrenees, the diversity of its vines (many of them also having arrived recently from elsewhere), and the ambitions of so many growers, the Languedoc and Roussillon are singularly situated to realize this goal, and that is the 21st-century good news for wine lovers the world over.

A CROSS-SECTION OF FRANCE'S FERTILE (BUT DRY) CRESCENT

The Languedoc and Roussillon encompass more than 500,000 acres of vineyards; this area has been significantly reduced in recent years but is still immense by any standard. Prior to canvassing this productive crescent from tip to tip and appellation by appellation, it is critical to consider a typical cross-section as it relates to climate. Annual rainfall in some parts of the Languedoc and Roussillon is as little as 15 inches, and in years of drought (whose frequency has of late increased) it may fall to less than half of that amount. Drought is enhanced by one of Europe's most notorious, nearly omnipresent winds, the tramontane. Summer temperatures can exceed 100°F. Under such circumstances, high grape sugars and low acidity are the norm. This makes the region seem a paradise for growers who have traditionally struggled to get sufficient sugar in their grapes.

But sugar cannot compensate if flavors are unripe, and drought- and heat-stressed vines cannot complete their photosynthetic labors. Rich flavors are commendable, but if a wine lacks lift or liveliness, it can be simply leaden. And so the game with nature in the Languedoc and Roussillon takes on its own distinctive rules and challenges. Soils that can conserve sufficient water must be sought. Cooler locations must be found where ripening time will be extended into autumn, the effects of drought are not compounded, and the results are balanced and ripe-tasting. Often this means north-facing slopes. The two most ready sources of air conditioning—sea and mountains—are present in abundance. Quality wine growing therefore usually hugs the coast or heads into the hills. In a few locations, high hillsides meet the shore, but generally a cross-section reveals warmer stretches in between that tend to promote alcohol rather than character in their wines.

Along the coast, sandy and pebbly soils can—when vines are properly managed—help regulate yields and promote character. Flat terrain permits machine harvesting, critical to survival nowadays for many growers in an area where the average price of grapes is low. But most old vines throughout the Languedoc and Roussillon (especially the traditionally dominant Grenache and Carignan) are head-pruned or bushlike, crouching low against the wind, their thick arms radiating from a heavy trunk. And vines like these, as opposed to those trained high or onto wires, tend to resist harvesting by machine.

As one heads toward France's Massif Centrale, the mountains are dominated by volcanic and metamorphic families of stone—granite, gneiss, and above all massive, crumbling seams of schist—or else by sedimentary variations on chalk and clay. The particular sensitivity of the Languedoc to water deficit, combined with its wide range of grape varieties and often rugged terrain, exacerbates the significance of yields and selectivity, as well as *terroir*. High yields pose an almost impossible burden on vines to ripen fruit properly. And on steep sites machine harvesting—always questionable if high quality is one's aim—becomes nearly impossible. Truly quality-conscious hand-harvesters must be prepared to laboriously select, so as to by-pass stricken vines or shriveled berries. But time and skilled hands are expensive.

One often hears it said that warmer climes and vintages are less reflective of *terroir*. But in the most obvious of ways in which wine reflects rocks and soil—accepted even by those skeptical of any chemical connections—vines' underlying geology is a critical factor in retention of and accessibility to water. To take but one example, the massive dark striations of ancient schist on which so many wines of the Languedoc and Roussillon are grown create veritable vine superhighways to tap underlying moisture and promote persistent plant metabolism even amid scorching heat, drought, and the relentless howling of the mistral. Nor, incidentally, are tasteable distinctions of *terroir* here merely subtle, let alone imaginary. Even if any "taste of 'minerals' " is only in one's mind (as may well be the case), the fundamental character of fruit and tannin—especially in extreme weather conditions—is marked by how availability of water and/or drainage determine the ripening trajectory of the grapes and the window for harvesting.

As extreme as was 2003 from an historical perspective, there is reason for concern that extended drought and excessive heat may in coming decades more frequently plague the Languedoc. French authorities have recently legalized irrigation (permitted on an emergency basis virtually throughout Europe in 2003—however, most water was rationed). But they have done so with what can only be termed ineptitude and lack of insight. Growers are permitted to spray or flood their vineyards, greatly enhancing the likelihood of pumped-up, diluted fruit, superficial root structures, and long-term vine dependency, while guaranteeing that most of that precious resource, whose scarcity spurred legislative action in the first place, evaporates. However, any permanent installation—such as drip lines, a technology without which both the quality and quantity of today's Austrian, Australian, Californian, and Washingtonian wines would be almost unthinkable—is thus far expressly forbidden

[grape varieties]

The same three red grapes are of greatest importance here as in the southern Rhône, namely Grenache, Syrah, and Mourvèdre. As in that region, too, Counoise is a minority but interesting partner in certain wines, and the generally suavely textured but relatively demure Cinsault is widely featured in blends, particularly for rosé. In the Languedoc, however, there is much more acreage of Carignan than in the southern Rhône. As a rule, most Carignan and

Cinsault is from old, stocky, head-pruned vines. There is much old acreage of Grenache as well, along with younger plantings, whereas Syrah and Mourvèdre vines of over 25 years in age are the exception; and these varieties are generally trained to wires. The relative advantages and disadvantages of older vine material or newer clones as well as of head pruning versus wire training are subjects of intense debate, so readers will be spared an account of these other than in certain specific instances as we tour the appellations and their principal growers below.

Among whites, Bourboulenc, Clairette, Roussanne, Marsanne, Viognier, Grenache Blanc, and Muscat (the last generally for sweet wine) are shared with the Rhône. But two varieties—Rolle (aka Vermentino) and Picpoul—less often encountered in the Rhône (even though the latter is among those officially permitted in Châteauneuf-du-Pape) play significant roles in parts of the Languedoc. The prestigious northern Rhône white trio of Roussanne, Marsanne, and Viognier are largely newcomers here, represented by young vines and youthful, experimental styles.

When some coastal areas of the Languedoc briefly boomed in the latter decades of the last century, it was by producing wines from young vines of the "international" varieties: Chardonnay, Merlot, Cabernet Sauvignon, and Sauvignon Blanc. But the demand for such wines never flourished within France, and to the extent that so-called "fighting varietals" fought it out for market share in English-speaking countries, California, and Australia soon put Languedoc vignerons on the ropes. International varieties continue to be cultivated, and there are certainly some surprises and good values among them, as well as a few vintners who are genuinely serious about their quality potential (and a pair of western Languedoc appellations in which they figure). But it is doubtful that any of these represent the destiny of Languedoc viticulture.

[winegrowing and winemaking]

PRACTICES AND PITFALLS

Given the sunshine and warmth that prevail in Mediterranean France, it might seem paradoxical, but the most common flaw in wines grown here—just as in so-called cool climate regions—is underripeness. The difference is that in the south, grape sugar generally arrives in abundance, guaranteeing ample if not downright high alcohol, whereas achieving phenolic ripeness—i.e., tasty as opposed to vegetal or "green" flavors in the skins, and the absence of astringency in the pits—is more problematic. Excessive yields, mechanized picking, and premature harvesting all contribute to deficiently ripe fruit among the far too many Languedoc growers whose attention is largely consumed by trying to hold a precarious bottom line. But the Languedoc and Roussillon also share with other warm climes the risk that vines will simply "shut down" in response to heat and drought, thus marking time in their phenolic evolution. Meantime, clusters of grapes no longer sustained by active metabolism may fall prey to raisining, exacerbating the surge of sugars. The vinous results of such circumstances are like chocolate-covered pickles: superficial, gummy sweetness wrapped around green astringency, precisely mirroring the condition of the grapes themselves.

When the phenols or tannins are ripe in these warm regions, they are nevertheless abundant. Another pitfall for Languedoc and Roussillon proprietors, even when they have managed to get their fruit expressively ripe, is overextraction of tannin. A frequent antidote to this—and a practice still employed with easily 90% of Carignan—is carbonic maceration, the anaerobic whole-berry fermentation technique commercialized in Beaujolais. But barring significant modifications, this method can render superficially fruity and facile-textured wines. Quality of extraction, though, is an area in which increasing sophistication has been achieved in the past decade. Not only are oenologists more aware of how to capture color and aroma without bringing along hard tannins, but also fewer estate owners are fixated on the notion that "bigger is better." Lessons from places as far away (and different from one another) as Burgundy and Australia are being tested in the Languedoc today, and never has such a range of textures and flavor personalities been offered by wines of this region, once thought of as a monolithic source of powerful but rustic black wine.

Sheer excess of alcohol can certainly sometimes be a problem in the south of France. But percentage points on labels can't signify whether your palate will suffer from alcoholic heat or astringency. Languedoc and Roussillon wines of silken texture and irresistible richness that do not betray levels of alcohol well in excess of 15% are legion. No doubt some vintners and some EU bureaucrats have cast a jealous eye on California where, in the language of dealcoholization guru Clark Smith, winemakers can "dial in their sweet spot" on the alcoholic spectrum. For now, though, France continues to play by different rules in the game with nature, and lowering a wine's alcohol is forbidden.

Of the four principal red grapes grown in the Languedoc and Roussillon, three—Syrah, Mourvèdre, and Carignan—exhibit an inherent proclivity for reduction (hydrogen bonding) which, in the relatively anaerobic environment of stainless steel so frequently favored for less expensive Languedoc wines, can lead to youthful muteness or even acrid, gamey, or rotten-egg stench from hydrogen sulfide, a risk sometimes further exacerbated by well-meaning attempts to conserve flavor and enhance texture through minimal handling or unpumped, unfiltered bottling. (In questionable instances, try decanting before crying "flawed!") On the other hand, the Languedoc's ostensibly top cuvées have generally been treated to a stay in *barriques,* an expense that does much to explain the often wide gulf in retail prices within a given domaine. Yet anyone with extensive experience in this part of the world must occasionally wonder, if not about the compatibility of these grapes, *terroirs,* and tannins with new oak, then about the quality of wood that many growers are getting for their 500 or more euros per *barrique.* Too many of their results are extraneously woody. And among wines aged in used *barriques,* excessive brett (a bacteriological infection that is an inherent danger in such relatively low-pH wines unless one acidifies or works with compulsive cleanliness) is all too familiar.

Taking a lead from Châteauneuf-du-Pape in the use of large oaken *foudres* is not easy without access to wood that has been kept clean and in continuous contact with wine for years, if not generations. Recently, many of the world's top *tonneliers* (barrel makers) have returned to building 1,000- to 3,000-liter ovals for the first time in half a century, but those do not come cheap. And purchasing new midsize barrels represents no less of an investment than that in 225-liter *barriques.* Still, these are among the promising routes that more and more quality-conscious vignerons in the Languedoc and Roussillon are taking, some patronizing *tonneliers* as far away as Austria. A veritable renaissance of concrete, with smaller, more sophisticatedly sealed and creatively molded vessels, is opening additional vinificatory vistas. Micro-oxygenation (percolating air through wines at highly controlled rates) is another technique that appears to work for many growers in warding off reduction and building harmonious, handsome tannins.

A TOUR OF THE MAJOR LANGUEDOC GROWING AREAS

RESERVATIONS ABOUT APPELLATION

Most of the Languedoc and Roussillon appellations have been established only in the past quarter century, and official classification of these wine regions is—more than with any others in France—a work in progress. Furthermore, it is a work primarily of bureaucrats, so the word "progress" merits skepticism. A taste of the increasingly improving wines from many appellations—and sometimes, merely a glance at the map!— can leave one puzzled as to why lines were drawn where they were. On the one hand, appellations have been created whose names one sees as yet on very few high-quality wines. On the other hand, the quality of wine in certain growing sectors has far outstripped the bureaucrats' ability to recognize it, assuming the growers in those sectors have the political clout to receive full legal consideration, or that they even care. Due to the commendably free-wheeling and experimental approach taken by so many of the most talented vintners of the Languedoc and Roussillon, many of the best wines lack *appellation contrôlée* not on account of where they were grown, but on account of what was grown and how the grapes were blended. And the use of as yet obscure subappellations on their labels strikes many vintners as a marketing handicap. Since the significance of France's various *vins de pays* with their often long and only occasionally euphonious names, routinely referenced on labels in minuscule fonts, is nearly nugatory as an indication of style and only slightly more so of *terroir,* in the tour that follows (and in the subsequent ranking of producers) reference is only occasionally made by name to *vins de pays*.

COSTIÈRES DE NÎMES The Costières de Nîmes represents the transition in soils, climate, and tradition between the southern Rhône and the Languedoc. In fact, one would have difficulty arguing against considering this 22-year-old appellation east of the once celebrated Roman city of Nîmes—its northern edge touching the Rhône—as part of the southern Rhône, and it has in fact been bounced back and forth. Heavy pebbles (*gallets*) and sand, both generally underlain by vital, water-retentive seams of clay, alternate here just as they do in Châteauneuf, and they support the same grape varieties. And here, too, red wine is overwhelmingly dominant, yet there are more promising whites with each passing year. But in a typical sign of transition to the Languedoc, Costières de Nîmes reds are permitted up to 40% Carignan (which, admittedly, the authorities have been whittling away). The climate here is affected by its immediate proximity to the Mediterranean. And there is another reason for wine lovers to envision this appellation as part of the Languedoc, namely the freewheeling style in which so many of the top bottling growers are expressing themselves. (For a ranking of Languedoc and Roussillon producers, please consult the list below.)

There are a number of top Costières de Nîmes one might mistake for excellent (inevitably more expensive) Châteauneuf-du-Pape, but many of the best exhibit a liberty in blending and a flamboyance of sweet fruit and new wood that make the wines of Châteauneuf seem restrained (if more complex and elegant) by comparison. Perhaps on account of this, Costières de Nîmes seems to be more highly reputed in the U.S. than in France. But it is hard to say which came first—style or American reputation—since among the import agents actively involved in promoting the growers of this region there are some, such as Robert Kacher, who collaborate with them on special *cuvées américaines*. Indications are that some of the better reds of the Costières de Nîmes can evolve interestingly in bottle, but it is too early to assess the full potential of this talent-filled region, just as of so many others in the south of France.

COTEAUX DU LANGUEDOC—THE MONTPELLIER SECTOR Created nearly a quarter century ago, the now vast Coteaux du Languedoc is an umbrella appellation, straddling three French departments and a vast range of soils and microclimates, which—at least in theory—covers a significant percentage of the Languedoc's finest wines. In keeping with the best viticultural opportunities afforded in the south of France (see A Cross-Section of France's Fertile [but Dry] Crescent, above), this appellation includes both coastal and hilly or mountainous landscapes, although the latter predominate.

Coastal viticulture around Montpellier has historical priority due to the importance of sweet wines from the Muscat Blanc à Petits Grains. The wines of Frontignan were already famous when Thomas Jefferson visited and lauded them in the outgoing 18th century, and Muscat de Frontignan has been an official appellation since the 1930s. (In a more modern example of what it takes to get an appellation, two neighboring ones—Muscat de Mireval and Muscat de Lunel, the former immediately adjacent to Frontignan and the latter on the edge of the Costières de Nîmes—are almost entirely controlled by those towns' local co-ops, so if there even is a distinctive *terroir* character, it would be very hard to distinguish it from house style.) Immediately inland from Frontignan is another of the Coteaux du Languedoc subappellations uniquely associated with (and named for) a white grape: Picpoul de Pinet. The citric, saline, light, and refreshing wine of the Picpoul grape has—superficially, at least— surprisingly much (despite its Mediterranean origins) in common with Loire Muscadet, and there are both an excellent co-op and a bevy of talented grower-bottlers on hand to supply ever more quality conscious renditions of this inexpensive libation.

Several other coastal and foothill subappellations around Montpellier are dominated by their respective cooperatives and by growers—as in the nearby delta of the Rhône—who dabble extensively in "international" grapes to render inexpensive, varietally labeled wines. And, to make matters more confusing, these coastal subappellations fall under a new Grès de Montpellier appellation that creates its own umbrella under an umbrella, incorporating more than one-quarter of all of the winegrowing villages in the entire Coteaux du Languedoc! *La Méjanelle,* immediately east of Montpellier, is much tinier than other local subappellations but so far, more significant. The potential of its soils—similar to those of the Costières de Nîmes, but only three miles from the water—was already deliciously demonstrated two decades ago by Languedoc pioneer Jean Clavel. And, at St.-Pargoire in the rocky limestone hills a dozen miles north of Pinet (of Picpoul fame), real estate agent-turned-vigneron Marlene Soria crafts the remarkable, ageworthy Coteaux du Languedoc of her Domaine Peyre Rose, and American *agent-viticulteur* Jeffrey Davies (with the team from Château de la Négly) crafts his Clos des Truffiers from Syrah vines that the town's mayor had the foresight to plant four decades ago. That what may well be the two greatest Languedoc wines yet to emerge did so outside an obscure village until recently not even covered by an appellation testifies to the newness and excitement of this region.

In the mountains some dozen miles north of Montpellier—all within sight of the massive peak from which this appellation takes its name—are the 12 villages that make up Pic St.-Loup. This area has been an exciting proving ground for the potential of Syrah, Grenache, and Mourvèdre in a sector that was anonymous less than 20 years ago, and since its official naming in 1994 has become associated with some of the most expressive and complex as well as most expensive wines in the Languedoc. Only a fraction of the acreage of this appellation has so far been planted, yet villages immediately outside it have also demonstrated their outstanding potential.

At the edge of the vast wilderness known as the Cévennes, 20 and more miles west of Montpellier, lie two more exciting subappellations and frontiers of viticultural quality: Montpeyroux and St.-Saturnin. The pioneering work of Aimé Comeyras at his Domaine l' Aiguelière demonstrated already a quarter century ago the great potential of Syrah in Montpeyroux. Yet the dramatic, chalky hills above this town—as opposed to the relatively flat terrain he farmed—are only now being reestablished, in places where vestiges of terraces remain from earlier centuries. St.-Saturnin is home to one of the Languedoc's foremost vintners, Olivier Jullien, who prefers to sell his wine as Coteaux du Languedoc without appending that town name. Here, too, a "subumbrella" appellation has just been created, known as Terrasses du Larzac. The two most famous estates in this area are those of early Languedoc prophet of quality Aimé Guibert (Mas Duamas Gassac) and of Laurent Vaillé (Granges des Pères), both in the same small village of Aniane, only three miles downhill and across the Hérault River from Montpeyroux. But, having established their reputations at a time when this wild territory had not yet been carved into appellations, it is likely that both of these strong-willed gentlemen will continue to label their wines as Vin de Pays de l'Hérault.

NORTH AND WEST OF BÉZIERS Beginning again on the coast, several Coteaux du Languedoc subappellations can be found south of Béziers and on the outskirts of Narbonne, one—La Clape—of considerable significance. Beginning with the pioneering efforts of the late Jean

Demolombe at his Domaine Pech-Redon, it was clear that this spot where mountains meet the sea had special potential for rich yet refined reds, redolent of berries and herbs. Today the wines that Château de la Négly is bottling here would in and of themselves suffice to put La Clape on the world's wine map.

A massive arc of hilly and mountainous vineyards begins northeast of Béziers and extends to the north of Narbonne and La Clape. Across the Hérault and a few miles south of St.-Pargoire lie Pézenas, Caux, and Gabian—among several significant Coteaux du Languedoc wine towns—with distinctively complex, pebbly, and evidently vine-root-friendly soils. In 1975 (around the same time as Aimé Guibert began Mas Daumas Gassac) pioneer Alain Roux established the vineyards of Prieuré de St.-Jean de Bébian, just outside Pézenas. Under its subsequent owners this remains one of the Languedoc's leading addresses and a beacon for the quality potential of this area's gentle slopes. Between Pézenas and Béziers, the often excellent and widely marketed red wines retain a *vin de pays* rather than *appellation contrôlée* status, as Côtes de Thongue, whereas immediately north of Pézenas is another Languedoc appellation named for its white wine grape, Clairette du Languedoc, that covers a large area but whose wines are seldom seen abroad.

West of Pézenas, the terrain becomes ever steeper, and we reach two major, self-standing appellations: Faugères and its larger, western neighbor, St.-Chinian. Without question, a significant percentage of the best wines in the Languedoc are issuing from these districts. Such growers as Gilbert Alquier, Frédéric Albaret (Domaine St.-Antonin), and Isabelle Champart have demonstrated the potential for ageworthy reds that combine concentration with elegance and complexity. And Hildegard Horat (La Grange de Quatre Sous)—contributing her contrarian "four cents worth"—has demonstrated the striking potential of Cabernet Franc and Malbec, grapes not even authorized for these appellations. The boundaries here were rather oddly drawn, since roughly half of Appellation St.-Chinian, nearest Faugères, shares with it a mountainous terrain of schistic stone, whereas the balance of the appellation is limestone-based, with much of its terrain dropping away into gentle hills and plain. In tasting at wineries where grapes are grown on both of these soil types, the particularly intense smoky pungency and "wet stone" finishing character in the wines of schistic origin is generally evident. Since 2005, Faugères has also been recognized for white wines, whereas St.-Chinian has not.

ALONG THE AUDE As the mountains at the southwestern edge of St.-Chinian drop to hills and approach the river Aude, one reaches Minervois, the third largest of the Languedoc's appellations (the largest being that "umbrella" known as Coteaux du Languedoc). An appellation for almost 25 years and extending nearly as many miles inland along the Aude to the edge of the famous walled city of Carcassonne, Minervois incorporates two subappellations: Muscat de St.-Jean de Minervois (along the border with St.-Chinian and near the ancient town of Minerve itself) for sweet Muscat, and centrally located La Livinière for chalky hills that have demonstrated vinous distinction. A sizable band of the Languedoc's most innovative and successful growers are located around La Livinière, where, as in so much of the Languedoc, the relative potential and roles of Grenache, Syrah, and Carignan (and to a lesser extent Mourvèdre) are far from predetermined.

On the far side of Carcassonne from Minervois lies the small appellation of Cabardes, forming in all respects a transition from the Mediterranean Languedoc to the continental growing regions of France's southwest. Just as in certain parts of Provence (but otherwise nowhere else in France) the classic Bordeaux grapes (two Cabernets and a Merlot) may here be blended with those classics of the south, Grenache and Syrah, within an official *appellation contrôlée*. Wines from this appellation are not yet widespread, but those from a couple of estates suggest that they can be as intriguing as their pivotal location and mixture of varieties suggests. Directly south of Carcassonne comes another obscure transitional district, the Côtes de la Malpère, which lacks full-fledged *appellation contrôlée* status and in which Merlot and the Cabernets play an even more prominent role. There are a couple of serious strivers here as well.

South along the Aude from the Côtes de la Malpère comes the singular appellation of Limoux, devoted in large part to sparkling wine. Improbably, in this sector, with its vistas south to the high Pyrenees and numerous cool microclimates, the obscure Mauzac of Gaillac, the Chenin Blanc of the Loire, and the Chardonnay of Burgundy grow cheek by jowl. The ambitious Toques & Clochers bottlings of Chardonnay from the Vignerons du Sieur d'Arques co-op supply a taste of Limoux's sparkling potential for nonsparkling wine. and even modestly priced Chardonnay from the Languedoc that originates in this sector (e.g., the Les Jamelles brand) distinguishes itself from most Chardonnay grown along the Mediterranean coast for relative brightness, balance, and flavor interest.

CORBIÈRES AND FITOU To the south of Minervois, across the Aude and extending back to the Mediterranean coast, lies the Languedoc's vast, generally mountainous, and geologically complex second-largest appellation, Corbières. This lovely, largely unspoiled area with its numerous stands of ancient Grenache and Carignan vines has been a magnet for both established and would-be wine growers from throughout France and beyond, although it must be said that only a few wines manage to transcend the rather rustic, foursquare, forward, and full style of reds that generally prevails here. White wines are permitted too, and although they represent a small minority, some—such as a Roussanne-Viognier Corbières *blanc* from the Domaine du Grand Crès of former Domaine de la Romanée-Conti manager Hervé Leferrer—point the way toward a potentially bright future.

The appellation Fitou is really two distinct sectors lying 10 miles apart and bordered by (at places interspersed with) patches of appellation Corbières. Half of Fitou is located on windswept, pebbly, chalk-clay soils rising immediately from the Mediterranean. The other half is mountainous and schistic. Alone among France's appellations, Fitou mandates the presence of (30% to 70%) Carignan. Back in 1948 when this appellation was created, Syrah and Mourvèdre had scarcely penetrated Fitou's acreage (then as now dominated by two co-ops), and its gerrymandered boundaries evidently conformed to local political will or whim. But this curious and long-derided appellation may have the last laugh, as—particularly from its mountainous interior—have issued increasingly many memorably rich and complex red wines. And, just as in parts of St.-Chinian and in the Côtes du Roussillon's best sectors, which abut Fitou to the south—not to mention in Spain's supernova Priorat—the synergistic combination of schist and that former "trash grape" Carignan is being revealed, and property values in a former "low rent" district are on the rise.

ROUSSILLON: FRANCE'S NEWEST (PERHAPS LAST) FRONTIER

The name "Roussillon" was until recently known to wine lovers—if at all—through the conjunction "Languedoc-Roussillon." Any division of neighboring regions is bound to incorporate an element of arbitrariness, and important common factors unite these two areas; grapes from either or both can now be bottled as "Languedoc." Nevertheless, there are good reasons to treat separately the fewer than 100,000 variously appellated acres tucked up against the Spanish border and looking out over the ocean and/or the Pyrenees. This is northern Catalonia, a region once dominated by another monarch and tongue than those of France or the Languedoc. Its geological complexity of schist, gneiss, granite, and limestone and its microclimate are distinct. What's more, the vintners beg of us the favor of referring to their region on its own, and given the amount of excitement they are generating in the glass and the extraordinary values represented by so many of their wines, this is a courtesy they deserve and we can well afford.

Until a dozen years ago—and to some extent still today—Roussillon represented one of the few spots in France where ancient vines and terrific *terroir* were within the financial means of young, aspiring, and independent winegrowers, and a small but precious stream of pioneers (beginning with Gérard Gauby in the mid-'80s) trickled into this region until then dominated by the venerable Mas Blanc and Mas Amiel along with a few (albeit occasionally worthy) cooperatives. But the rock bottom price of land did not last. Priorat's unprecedented rocket flight from obscurity to celebrity was witnessed worldwide, not to mention immediately across the border. It was only a matter of time before Roussillon's vignerons and outsiders eyeing its *terroir* would ask themselves: "Are not these the same ancient vines of Grenache and Carignan (that former trash grape, now informing $100+ bottles)? Does our schist not smell as sweet?" And so it was, that on the heels of early pioneers—following the pattern set in Priorat—Roussillon was overrun by newcomers, some flush with venture capital, some famous as winemakers elsewhere in the world, all lured by the smell of schistic seams of black gold. So far, their bets seem to be paying off, because while bargains are legion, the top wines are selling for Côte Rôtie or cru classé rather than Châteauneuf or cru bourgeois prices.

A NOTE ON ROUSSILLON GRAPES

The most significant difference among black grapes in Roussillon relative to the Languedoc is a heavier reliance on Carignan. Nor should this by any means be taken as a drawback. The quality of most of Roussillon's best reds is in fact inseparable from this once-despised *cépage,* and Marjorie Gallet at Le Roc des Anges has even demonstrated that an unblended parcel of ancient Carignan vines is capable of offering more complexity and elegance than does any attempt at blending it with other grapes. Young plantings of Syrah and Mourvèdre in this region will need time to show their mettle, but every indication is that these will play an ever-increasing if still supplementary role in rendering reds of increasing depth and complexity. Whether it made sense to legally mandate a measure of Syrah or Mourvèdre for reds of Côtes du Roussillon-Villages is another matter, considering how many of this region's best wines are essentially blends of only Grenache and Carignan.

Among white wine grapes, a noteworthy Roussillon specialty is Grenache Gris. The best examples are already proving themselves to be among the most intriguingly distinctive and ageworthy whites of southern France. In addition to the entire Rhône and Languedoc cast of white wine characters, one also encounters in Roussillon considerable acreage of Macabeu (Macabeo) as well as such oddities as Tourbat (like Vermentino, better known from Sardinia) and Carignan Blanc.

Roussillon is also home to a tradition of *vins doux naturels,* fortified sweet wines that include some of the best of the south's ubiquitous Muscat, but most notably the Grenache-based elixirs of coastal Banyuls and mountainous Maury (excellent-value alternatives to vintage or wooded Ports, with a chocolate compatibility all their own), and these are canvassed below as well. All things considered, this border region is among today's most colorful as well as exciting vinous frontiers.

ROUSSILLON'S EVOLVING APPELLATIONS

Côtes de Roussillon and Côtes de Roussillon-Villages are the geographically dominant Roussillon appellations. But many talented growers have turned their backs on the latter, in particular. As already mentioned, one reason is that the Villages appellation for reds inexplicably requires the inclusion of Syrah and/or Mourvèdre (to a recently raised, whopping minimum of 30%), as well as the use of at least three different grapes, whereas virtually all of the best, old-vines raw material is either Carignan or Grenache, and in consequence many of the most successful wines rely entirely on these two. For whites, the Villages appellation fails to recognize what may be the most interesting local variety, Grenache Gris. And an arbitrary if not unrealistically low 15% alcohol limit further handicaps this appellation. The upshot is that a significant amount of the most interesting wine of Roussillon is labeled as Vin de Pays des Côtes Catalanes or Vin de Pays des Pyrénées-Orientales (either of which at least have the advantage of alluding to more familiar indicators of the geographical location of this as yet underappreciated corner of France). Several recently established or discussed designations will be mentioned at the appropriate stops along the brief tour of the region that follows.

For fortified sweet wines, or *vins doux naturels,* as they are known here, two broad appellations apply: Muscat de Rivesaltes and—for a wide range of blends, but generally Grenache-based—Rivesaltes. The undistinguished-looking town of Rivesaltes—located along the Agly River just north of Roussillon's only city, Perpignan—is itself vine-free. But these two appellations to which its name accrues are so enormous that they take in part of the adjacent Languedoc as well. Muscat de Rivesaltes is typically bottled and sold young, while Rivesaltes is generally left in cask—often for many years—before being bottled. Quality of wine within these categories varies dramatically, but there are some sweet Muscats here (such as at Mas Amiel) that number among the world's best, and even a few distinguished wines (such as at Domaine de Rancy) to save the obscure and generally low reputation of appellation Rivesaltes.

A BRIEF TOUR OF ROUSSILLON

If one travels south through the mountainous, inland sector of Fitou, one crosses into Roussillon amid some of its most ruggedly craggy landscape and most important vineyards—alternating schist and limestone—around the towns of Vingrau and Tautavel. (The former is now an official—but so far little-used—subappellation, Côtes du Roussillon-Villages.) One of the region's most talented vintners, Hervé Bizeul (Clos des Fées), has only got half his tongue in cheek when he calls wines from ancient Grenache vines in one of the highest and most exposed passes in these mountains "La Petite Sibérie."

Immediately to the west lies Maury, with its own appellation for fortified red or white Grenache-based wines. These are traditionally cask conditioned, but increasingly bottled young as "vintage" Maury, too. Mas Amiel—the best-known Maury estate—adopted the remarkable practice of storing its sweet wine in glass demijohns and exposing them outdoors to the severity of the elements for a year before returning them to barrel. Reds from the schistic Maury sector are also impressive. Farther west—in fact, as far west as vines penetrate Roussillon, amid more rocky hills—come the promising vineyards of an area that was to have received its own vin de pays designation as Coteaux Fenouillèdes, a proposal which somehow ran afoul of the bureaucracy, but which would have made sense, because several of the region's most impressive new projects—most notably that of Bordeaux *garagiste* Jean-Luc Thunevin (Calvet-Thunevin)—are located there.

South of Maury, along the twisting river Agly—in an only slightly gentler landscape where granite and gneiss alternate with schist—grow many of Roussillon's notable reds and dry whites. Three towns—Caramany, Lesquerde, and Latour de France—have been granted their own subappellations, although production in the first of these is dominated by a single cooperative, and only the last named of the trio has acquired any reputation, as home to among others Jean-Louis Tribouley, who nonetheless eschews mention of this subappellation on his labels. A few miles south of the Agly (from west to east), Bélesta, Montner, and Calce are all home to outstanding estates, in the case of Calce one of the first if not also foremost of Roussillon's late-20th-century pioneers, Gérard Gauby.

Dozens of winegrowing villages stretch south of Perpignan all the way to the edge of the high Pyrenees. So far, none of them has achieved much notoriety, but that could quickly change. Around Les Aspres, Jean-Marc Lafage is growing some strikingly successful (and inexpensive) whites as part of his extensive domaine. And the promising Domaine Les Foulards Rouges of Rhône transplant Jean-François Nicq features highly distinctive Grenache and Syrah almost on the Spanish frontier.

Directly fronting the seacoast just north of the Spanish border is Banyuls, home of Roussillon's other great fortified wine (and hence, along with Maury, the only other wine of this region known by name to wine lovers 20 years ago). This wine must be at least half Grenache, but in practice all of the best are dominated by that grape. Just as Mas Amiel was largely responsible for the reputation of Maury in a period when most Roussillon wine was anonymous, in Banyuls it was the great name of Dr. Parcé that assured this chocolate-loving wine a place in the great restaurants and private cellars of France. Just north of Banyuls is another gorgeous wine and fishing village, Collioure, with vineyards of Grenache, Mourvèdre, and Syrah (and to a lesser extent Carignan and Cinsault) on rugged slopes, some perched directly over the sea. Here the wine is dry, the producers are the same talented bunch who farm Banyuls, and the results can be profound as well as ageworthy.

[recent vintages]

In an area ranging from the basin of the Rhône to the fringes of the Pyrenees, from seacoast to high interior mountains, generalizations about vintage character are difficult, indeed dangerous. The year 2001 can definitely be called a classic throughout the region, having delivered wines with richness yet freshness. But 2002 and 2003 did their devilish best to land growers in all sectors a one-two punch and left many only one more such harvest away from bankruptcy. 2002 was the year of biblical late August rain in the southern Rhône. Heavy rains extended through much of the Languedoc as well, in many places compromising the crop of Grenache. And only at low yields could Syrah—let alone the notoriously sun-loving, late-ripening Mourvèdre and Carignan—perform satisfactorily. In the end, there were numerous lovely if by Mediterranean standards relatively light and supple reds, but always in small volume. There followed the hottest and driest year in more than a century, wreaking havoc with normal viticultural routines. Even in those (not infrequent) instances of reds with formidable ripeness and concentration, the grapes of 2003 were few, and drastically short of juice. (With hindsight, vintages 1998 and 1999 appear to have been less extreme rehearsals for 2003 and 2002, respectively.)

Growers were treated to less freakish weather and a mild summer in 2004 (after a well-watered winter), from which a bumper crop was harvested, the best wines of which manage to avoid betraying high yields. (This is weather of the sort that used to prevail on a regular basis, remarks Laurent Vaillé of Grange des Pères.) The dangerously dry yet temperate summer of 2005—a vintage like 2003 exhibiting a strong transregional character across much of Europe—presented renewed challenges to ripeness and success. For some sectors, growers, and grapes, the drought was broken inopportunely close to harvest; for others, apparently, just in time to restart the process of assimilation and phenolic maturation. The advantages or disadvantages of sporadic rain and a relatively cool August in 2006 were also very much a function of differences in microclimate and methods of crop management, whereas the extraordinarily protracted growing season of 2007—with its record early-flowering, cool late summer and balmy autumn—had growers smiling broadly.

—DAVID SCHILDKNECHT

[the ratings]

THE LANGUEDOC'S BEST PRODUCERS

(C.d.L. = Coteaux du Languedoc; V.d.P. = Vin de Pays. The names of subappellations are appended only in instances where those names are intimately associated with the producer in question or appear on his or her labels.)

* * * * * (OUTSTANDING)

Mas Champart (St.-Chinian)
Clos Marie (C.d.L. Pic St.-Loup)
Clos des Truffiers (C.d.L.)
Domaine de Courbissac (Minervois)
Domaine Foulaquier (C.d.L. Pic St.-Loup)
Domaine de la Grange des Pères
    (V.d.P. de l'Hérault)

Mas Jullien (C.d.L.)
Mas Lumen (C.d.L.)
Château de la Négly (C.d.L. La Clape)
L'Oustal Blanc (Minervois)
Domaine Peyre Rose (C.d.L.)
Yannick Pelletier (St.-Chinian)
Domaine St.-Antonin (Faugères)

* * * * (EXCELLENT)

Gilbert Alquier et Fils (Faugères)
Domaine d'Aupilhac (C.d.L. Montpeyroux)
Domaine Les Aurelles (C.d.L.)
Mas d'Auzières (C.d.L.)
Mas de la Barben (C.d.L.)
Bertrand-Bergé (C.d.L., Fitou)
Domaine de Boede (C.d.L. La Clape)
Domaine Borie de Maurel (Minervois)
Domaine Canet-Valette (St.-Chinian)
Domaine Pierre Clavel
    (C.d.L. La Méjanelle)
La Croix de St.-Jean (Minervois)
Domaine Pierre Cros (Minervois)
Mas de Daumas Gassac (V.d.P. de l'Hérault)
Château l'Euzière (C.d.L. Pic St.-Loup)
Domaine Gaujal St.-Bon (C.d.L. Picpoul
    de Pinet)

Château Grès St.-Paul (C.d.L.)
Hecht & Bannier (*négociant*)
Domaine Hegarty-Chamans (Minervois)
Domaine de l'Hortus (C.d.L. Pic St.-Loup)
Château de Lancyre (C.d.L. Pic St.-Loup)
Domaine Maris (Minervois)
Domaine Mortiès (C.d.L. Pic St.-Loup)
Mourgues du Grès (Costières de Nîmes)
Château d'Or et de Gueules
    (Costières de Nîmes)
La Péira en Damaisèla (C.d.L. Terrasses
    du Larzac)
Prieuré de St.-Jean-de-Bébian (C.d.L.)
Domaine Puech Chaud/Puech Noble
    (C.d.L.)
Domaine La Sauvageonne (C.d.L.)

* * * (VERY GOOD)

Domaine de l'Aiguelière
    (C.d.L. Montpeyroux)
Domaines des Aires Hautes (Minervois)
Mourrel Azurat (Fitou)
Clos Bagatelle (St.-Chinian)
Domaine Baptiste-Boutes (Minervois)
Domaine Léon Barral (Faugères)
Domaine de Baubiac (C.d.L.)
Château de Belles Eaux (C.d.L.)
Borie la Vitarelle (St.-Chinian)
Lo Bosc (V.d.P.)
Mas des Bressades (Costières
    de Nîmes)
Château de Cabriac (Corbières)

Domaine Camp Galhan (Costières
    de Nîmes)
Domaine des Cantarelles (Costières
    de Nîmes)
Château de Capitoul (C.d.L. La Clape)
Mas Carlot (Costières de Nîmes)
Champ des Soeurs (Fitou)
Clos de la Causse—Domaine la Combe
    Blanche (Minervois)
Col des Vents (Corbières)
Domaine La Colombette (V.d.P. Coteaux
    du Libron)
Domaine La Combe Blanche (Minervois)
Château Coupe-Roses (Minervois)

Château Creyssels (C.d.L. Picpoul de Pinet)

Domaine la Croix Belle (V.d.P. Côtes de Thongue)

Domaine Donjon (Minervois)

Château des Erles (Corbières, Fitou)

Domaine de l'Ermitage du Pic St.-Loup

Château des Estanilles (Faugères)

Étang des Colombes (Corbières)

Domaine Faurmarie (C.d.L. Grès de Montpellier)

Domaine Maria Fita (Fitou)

Domaine de Fontsainte (Corbières)

Château Grande Cassagne (Costières de Nîmes)

Domaine du Grand Crès (Corbières)

La Grange de Quatre Sous (St.-Chinian)

Mas de Guiot (Costières de Nimes)

Domaine Lacroix-Vanel (C.d.L.)

Domaine Massamier (Minervois)

Château de Mattes-Sabran (Corbières)

Domaine Moulinier (St.-Chinian)

Mourrel Azurat (Fitou)

Château de Nages (Costières de Nîmes)

Domaine Navarre (St.-Chinian)

Plan de l'Om (C.d.L.)

Château d'Oupia (Minervois)

Domaine Pech-Redon (C.d.L. La Clape)

Domaine des Perrières—Marc Kreydenweiss (Costières de Nimes)

Château de la Peyrade (Muscat de Frontignan)

Domaine Prieuré St.-Martin de Laure (Minervois)

Puech Auriol (V.d.P.)

Domaine Puech-Haut (C.d.L.)

Domaine Rimbert (St.-Chinian)

Château La Roque (C.d.L. Pic St.-Loup)

Domaine St.-Martin de la Garrigue (C.d.L.)

Domaine Terre Inconnue

Domaines des Terres Falmet (St.-Chinian)

Château Tour Boisée (Minervois)

Domaine de la Tour Penedesses (C.d.L.)

Château de Valcombe (Costières de Nîmes)

Château de Valflaunès (C.d.L. Pic St.-Loup)

* * (GOOD)

Abbaye de Valmagne (C.d.L.)

Clos de l'Anhel (Corbières)

Domaine de l'Arjolle (V.d.P. Côtes de Thongue)

Château Auzias (Cabardès)

Domaine de Barroubio (Minervois)

Gérard Bertrand (various appellations)

Mas des Brunes (V.d.P. Côtes de Thongue)

Château Cascadais (Corbières)

Mas Cal Demoura (C.d.L.)

Château de Campuget (Costières de Nîmes)

Château Capion (C.d.L.)

Cave de Pomerols-Hugues Beaulieu (C.d.L. Picpoul de Pinet)

Domaine Alain Chabanon (C.d.L. Montpeyroux)

Domaine Coston (C.d.L. Terrasses du Larzac)

La Font de l'Olivier (V.d.P. Côtes de Thongue)

Domaine de Fontenelles (Corbières)

Mas Gabinele (Faugères)

Domaine Gautier (Fitou)

Château Gibalaux Bonnet (Minervois)

Domaine de Gourgazaud (Minervois)

Domaine de Gournier (Costières de Nîmes)

Domaine du Grand Arc (Corbières)

Clos du Gravillas (Minervois)

Château Guilhem (Côtes de la Malpère)

Les Jamelles (V.d.P. varietals)

Château Jouclary (Cabardès)

Khalkhal-Pamies (Minervois)

Château Laborie-Fouisseau (Faugères)

Château Lascaux (C.d.L. Pic St.-Loup)

Château Lavabre (C.d.L. Pic St.-Loup)

Domaine de la Louvière (Côtes de la Malpère)

Domaine Magellan (V.d.P. Côtes de Thongue)

Maxime Magnon (Fitou)

Château Mansenoble (Corbières)

Château de Montpezat (C.d.L.)

Domaine de Moulines (V.d.P. de l'Hérault)

Château Mas Neuf (Costières de Nîmes)

Domaine la Noble (V.d.P.)

Moulin de Ciffre (Faugères, St.-Chinian, C.d.L.)

Domaine du Poujol (C.d.L.)

Château de Rieux (Minervois)

Château St.-Eulalie (Minervois)

Château St.-Germain (C.d.L.)

Vignerons du Sieur d'Árques—"Toques &
Clochers" (Limoux)
Domaine Stella Nova (C.d.L.)

Domaine Tabatu (St.-Chinian)
Domaine Zelige-Caravent
(C.d.L. Pic St.-Loup)

ROUSSILLON'S BEST PRODUCERS

(C.d.R.= Growers in regions covered by the Côtes du Roussillon or Côtes du Roussillon-Villages appellations, although those names are not always featured on their labels.)

★ ★ ★ ★ ★ (OUTSTANDING)

Domaine de Bila Haut–Chapoutier (C.d.R.)
Domaine du Mas Blanc (Banyuls, Collioure)
Domaine Calvet-Thunevin (C.d.R.)
Domaine du Clos des Fées (C.d.R.)

Domaine de l'Edre (C.d.R.)
Domaine Gauby (C.d.R.)
Domaine Jean-Louis Tribouley (C.d.R.)

★ ★ ★ ★ (EXCELLENT)

Domaine Mas Amiel (C.d.R., Maury)
Domaine La Casenove (C.d.R.)
Les Clos des Paulilles (Banyuls, Collioure)
Clot de l'Oum (C.d.R.)
Coume del Mas (Banyuls, Collioure)
Mas de la Devèze (C.d.R.)

Hecht & Bannier (*négociant*)
Domaine Lafage (C.d.R.)
Le Roc des Anges (C.d.R.)
Domaine de la Tour Vieille
(Banyuls, Collioure)

★ ★ ★ (VERY GOOD)

Cave de l'Abbé Rous (Banyuls,
Collioure)
Agly Brothers (C.d.R.)
Château de Caladroy (C.d.R.)
Domaine Ferrer Ribière (C.d.R.)
Domaine de Força Réal (C.d.R.)
Domaine Les Foulards Rouges (C.d.R.)
Domaine Gardiés (C.d.R.)
Mas Janeil (C.d.R.)
Domaine Madeloc (Banyuls, Collioure)
Domaine Matassa (C.d.R.)

Peña—Les Vignerons de Cases de
Pène (C.d.R.)
Domaine Picquemal (C.d.R.)
Domaine Olivier Pithon (C.d.R.)
Préceptorie de Centernach (C.d.R., Maury)
Domaine de Rancy (Rivesaltes)
Domaine de la Rectorie
(Banyuls, Collioure)
Domaine Sarda Mallet (C.d.R.)
Domaine des Soulanes (C.d.R.)
Walden (C.d.R.)

★ ★ (GOOD)

Domaine Cazes (Rivesaltes)
Mas Cristine (Rivesaltes)
Domaine Fontanel (C.d.R.)

Château de Jau (C.d.R.)
Domaine Puig Parahy (C.d.R.)

[tasting commentaries]

CAVE DE L'ABBÉ ROUS ★ ★ ★
BANYULS, COLLIOURE $20.00–$65.00

Under the direction of Alain Raynaud, the Cave de l'Abbé Rous co-op in Banyuls turns out some excellent wines, notably their flagship Banyuls Helyos.

2002 Banyuls Helyos   91   now–2015

DOMAINE DES AIRES HAUTES ★★★
MINERVOIS $9.00–$30.00

Among the best known and best producers among numerous talented growers around the town of La Livinière, the Chabert brothers also render an extraordinary value Sauvignon Blanc, which, however, needs to be drunk young.

2005 Malbec	87	now
2004 Minervois les Combelles	86	now
2004 Minervois la Livinières	90	now–2010
2003 Minervois Clos de l'Escandil	91	now–2012

DOMAINE GILBERT ALQUIER ★★★★
FAUGÈRES $18.00–$30.00

Gilbert Alquier demonstrated in the 1980s that wines from the schistic soils of Faugères could display a refinement, a mysterious marriage of fruit, herb, meat and mineral flavors, and an ageability of which at the time few people suspected any Languedoc wine capable. His sons now run the estate and continue to pursue a policy of leisurely release.

1998 Faugères	88	now

MAS AMIEL ★★★★
CÔTES DU ROUSSILLON-VILLAGES, MAURY $15.00–$55.00

Since the acquisition by Olivier Decelle of Maury's (if not Roussillon's) best-known estate and his instatement of young Stéphane Gallet as winemaker, quality at vast Mas Amiel has gone from strength to strength, benefiting inter alia from a new facility, more stringent selection at every level, and more imagination. They bottle an enormous range of wines from dry white, rosé, and red through a variety of sweet fortified and Maury in both "vintage" and cask matured (i.e., "tawny") style, the latter featuring a year spent outdoors in glass demijohn, which has a long tradition here. (Blends of this latter sort will change every year or two.) But there are also some wonderful experiments, such as the Privilège, made from desiccated fruit and vinified in small, new, upright barrels which are then closed up and turned on their sides for aging the young wine.

2005 Côtes du Roussillon-Villages Le Plaisir	87	now
2005 Côtes du Roussillon-Villages Notre Terre	89	now–2010
2005 Côtes du Roussillon-Villages Carerades	90–91	2009–2013
2004 Côtes du Roussillon-Villages Carerades	90	now–2011
2003 Maury Vintage Blanc	91	now
2005 Muscat de Rivesaltes	88	now
2004 Muscat de Rivesaltes Collection	90	now
2004 Maury Vintage	90	now–2010
2000 Maury Vintage	91	now
2004 Maury Vintage Réserve	91	now–2012
2004 Maury Vintage Privilège	92	now–2014
2003 Maury Vintage Privilège	90	now
2004 Maury Vintage Charles Dupuy	93	2010–2018
2000 Maury Vintage Charles Dupuy	91	now–2010
Maury 10 Ans d'Age	88	now–2010
Maury 15 Ans d'Age	90	now–2012

DOMAINE D'AUPILHAC ★★★★
COTEAUX DU LANGUEDOC MONTPEYROUX $12.00–$35.00

Sylvain Fadat's nowadays huge Montpeyroux domaine routinely turns out excellent values as well as some ambitiously concentrated old-vine Carignan and blends. And the excitement has probably only begun, as Fadat is one of the pioneers in rebuilding and planting ancient terraces in the rocky slopes above Montpeyroux.

1999 Coteaux du Languedoc Montpeyroux	88	now
2005 Coteaux du Languedoc Montpeyroux Les Cocalières	87	2010–2015
2004 Coteaux du Languedoc Montpeyroux Lou Maset	87	now
2005 Le Carignan	90	2009–2014
2004 Le Carignan	89	now–2011

MAS D'AUZIÈRES ★★★★
COTEAUX DU LANGUEDOC $23.00–$35.00

Irène Tolleret and her oenologist husband have begun an exciting project with the classic Rhône varieties planted in "shards" (les Éclats) of limestone near Pic St.-Loup. Pure, creamy-rich, though occasionally (at least in their youth) superficially oaky character has marked their early releases.

2005 Coteaux du Languedoc Les Éclats	89	now
2005 Coteaux du Languedoc Les Éclats	90	now–2010
2004 Coteaux du Languedoc Le Bois de Périé	88	2009–2012

DOMAINE BAPTISTE-BOUTES ★★★
MINERVOIS $12.00–$14.00

From the crack team at Château de la Négly, the Baptiste-Boutes Minervois is a consistent value and a generous expression of Minervois fruit.

2005 Minervois	88	now–2010

MAS DE LA BARBEN ★★★★
COTEAUX DU LANGUEDOC $20.00–$50.00

This is the Languedoc outpost of Chapoutier. Michel Chapoutier's biodynamically farmed vineyards, tiny yields, extended fermentations, indigenous yeasts, lack of fining or filtration—in short, his complete refusal to compromise—earns him jealousy in many quarters, but the result is exceptional, ageworthy wines.

2006 Coteaux du Languedoc Les Lauzières	86	now–2011
2004 Coteaux du Languedoc Les Lauzières	87–90	now
2006 Coteaux du Languedoc Les Sabines	89	now–2011
2004 Coteaux du Languedoc Les Sabines	89–92	now–2011
2003 Coteaux du Languedoc Les Sabines	90	now–2011
2006 Coteaux du Languedoc Calice	92–94	now–2017
2005 Coteaux du Languedoc Calice	90	now–2019
2004 Coteaux du Languedoc Calice	91–93	now–2018
2003 Coteaux du Languedoc Calice	92	now–2018
2003 Coteaux du Languedoc Barben	90–92	now–2012

LÉON BARRAL ★ ★ ★ ★
FAUGÈRES $20.00–$50.00

Didier Barral crafts a range of serious cuvées from Faugères utilizing organic farming methods and an ancient-style basket press.

1998 Faugères Cuvée Tradition	90	now
1998 Faugères Cuvée Jadis	90	now–2010

DOMAINE DE BAUBIAC ★ ★ ★
COTEAUX DU LANGUEDOC $19.00–$21.00

On complex soils just outside the Pic St.-Loup appellation, the Philip brothers craft a rich, plush red with an unusually high percentage of Mourvèdre and corresponding scents and flavors of among others red meat, bay, and fennel.

2003 Coteaux du Languedoc	88	now

DOMAINE BERTRAND-BERGE ★ ★ ★ ★
COTEAUX DU LANGUEDOC, FITOU $20.00–$90.00

In the hills where the Fitou appellation abuts Roussillon, the Bertrands craft a straightforwardly delicious blend of Grenache, Carignan, and Syrah. But their hugely imposing and outrageously rich (almost like a dessert wine) Cuvée Jean Sirven betrays their ambitions.

2004 Fitou Cuvée Ancestrale	89	now
2004 Coteaux du Languedoc Cuvée Jean Sirven	91	now–?

DOMAINE DE BILA HAUT ★ ★ ★ ★
CÔTES DU ROUSSILLON $15.00–$40.00

Michel Chapoutier's outpost in Roussillon—with the aid of exceptionally talented winemaker Gilles Troullier—is sparing no pains to turn out wines of exceptional concentration, complexity, and ageworthiness from minuscule yields on old vines.

2006 Côtes du Roussillon Villages V.I.T.	93–95	now–2017
2006 Côtes du Roussillon Villages Occultum Lapidem	91–93	now–2017
2005 Côtes du Roussillon Villages Occultum Lapidem	90	now–2015
2004 Côtes du Roussillon Villages Occultum Lapidem	90–92	now–2014
2003 Côtes du Roussillon Villages Occultum Lapidem	90	now–2016
2005 Vignes de Bila Haut	89	now–2013

DOMAINE DU MAS BLANC ★ ★ ★ ★ ★
BANYULS, COLLIOURE $30.00–$70.00

The often amazingly complex and always amazingly chocolate-friendly fortified Grenache-based wines of Banyuls (or their dry counterparts from neighboring Collioure) would have remained little known to Americans had it not been for the Domaine du Mas Blanc of Dr. Parcé, where quality has not dipped over at least the past quarter century. No wine lover should die without having experienced these uniquely complex, ageworthy, yet remarkably affordable wines. Rimage signifies early-bottled wines intended to mature somewhat like vintage Port.

2004 Collioure Cosprons Levants	89	2009–2016
2000 Collioure Cosprons Levants	94	now–2014
1994 Collioure Cosprons Levants	89	now
2004 Collioure Clos du Moulin	90	2009–2016
2000 Collioure Clos du Moulin	92	now–2012

1997 Collioure Clos du Moulin	93	now–2010
1994 Collioure Clos du Moulin	95	now
2004 Collioure les Junquets	91	2009–2015
2000 Collioure les Junquets	91	now–2015
2005 Banyuls Rimage	92	2010–2020
2001 Banyuls Rimage	90	now–2016
2000 Banyuls Rimage	90	now–2015
1998 Banyuls Rimage	89	now–2013
1997 Banyuls Rimage	90	now–2011
2005 Banyuls Rimage La Coume	91	2010–2020
2004 Banyuls Rimage La Coume	91	now–2020
2003 Banyuls Rimage La Coume	94	now–2025
2000 Banyuls Rimage La Coume	94	now–2022
1998 Banyuls Rimage La Coume	94	now–2020
1996 Banyuls Rimage La Coume	94	now–2018
1994 Banyuls Rimage La Coume	94	now–2016
1989 Banyuls Rimage La Coume	94	now–2014
1996 Banyuls Vieilles Vignes	91	now–2011

DOMAINE DE BOEDE ★ ★ ★ ★
COTEAUX DU LANGUEDOC LA CLAPE $28.00–$30.00

From the Château de la Négly team of Jean Paux-Rosset and oenologist Claude Gros, the Boede wines are great examples of flamboyance and superripeness free of heat or extraneous oakiness and inviting the next sip.

2003 Coteaux du Languedoc La Clape Les Grès	91	now–2011

BORIE LA VITARELLE ★ ★ ★
ST.-CHINIAN $18.00–$30.00

The affable Jean-François Izarn crafts a wide range of cuvées from the diverse sites and soils (either chalk-based, as the name "Terres Blanches" suggests, or schistic). At their best, these can exhibit polished textures and plenty of personality.

2003 St.-Chinian Les Terres Blanches	88	now–2010

MAS DE BRESSADES ★ ★ ★
COSTIÈRES DE NÎMES $12.00–$20.00

Young Cyril Mares crafts some well-concentrated bargains both red and white and an ambitious, flamboyant, but modestly priced Cabernet-Syrah blend.

2003 Cabernet-Syrah	90	now–2011

CHÂTEAU CABRIAC ★ ★ ★
CORBIÈRES $15.00–$25.00

Jean de Cibeins renders numerous cuvées of Corbières that display a brightness and refinement not often found in this appellation.

2004 Corbières Marquise de Puivert	88	now–2010

CHÂTEAU DE CALADROY ★★★
CÔTES DU ROUSSILLON $14.00–$20.00

The basic bottling of this estate makes an outstanding-value introduction to the genre of Carignan, Grenache, and Syrah on local schist. Cellarmaster Jean-Philippe Agen's more expensive Cuvée St.-Michel is a very ripe Mourvèdre marked by new wood.

2004 Côtes du Roussillon Villages les Schistes	88	now
2003 Côtes du Roussillon Villages les Schistes	89	now–2010
2001 Côtes du Roussillon Villages Cuvée St.-Michel	91	now–2012

CALVET-THUNEVIN ★★★★★
CÔTES DU ROUSSILLON $15.00–$200.00

The five-year-old collaboration of Roussillon native Jean-Roger Calvet and notorious right-bank *garagiste* Jean-Luc Thunevin with ancient vines on apparently rather rare veins of black schist around Maury has predictably resulted in some of the richest, most flamboyant and powerful wines in southern France. They are assuredly susceptible to partisan appraisals and not for the faint of heart—the 2004 Hugo is thickly rich, sweet, liqueurlike, and no doubt over-the-top for many tasters. The Constance cuvée represents an excellent-value introduction to this formidable estate.

2005 Constance	90	now–2011
2004 Côtes du Roussillon-Villages Les Dentelles	91	2009–2014
2004 Côtes du Roussillon-Villages Hugo	????	now–2014+?
2004 Côtes du Roussillon-Villages Les Trois Marie	94	2010–2015+?

DOMAINE CAMP GALHAN ★★★
COSTIÈRES DE NÎMES $12.00–$22.00

On mostly cobbled "soil" northwest of Nîmes, Lionel and Alain Pourquier defy their entitlement to only a *vin de pays* appellation (rather than Costières de Nîmes) with wines of extraordinary value. Look for their Sauvignon Blanc and for Amanlie, their Viognier-Roussanne blend, but drink them within a year and a half. Their reds often feature the sandalwood, deep berry fruit, game, and Provençal herb notes familiar from Châteauneuf-du-Pape but for less than half the price.

2005 Les Grès	90	now–2012
2005 Les Perassières	88	now–2010
2004 Les Perassières	89	now–2010

MAS CARLOT ★★★
COSTIÈRES DE NÎMES $14.00–$16.00

A special, wooded 50-50 cuvée of Mourvèdre and Syrah first made in 2003 in collaboration with importer Robert Kacher, Mas Carlot's Les Enfants Terribles unites sweet plum and blueberry preserves with classic blood-in-a-bottle raw-meat Mourvèdre character for an unforgettable aromatic juxtaposition and amazing value.

2005 Costières de Nîmes Les Enfants Terribles	91	now–2011
2004 Costières de Nîmes Les Enfants Terribles	88	now–2010

DOMAINE LA CASENOVE ★★★★
CÔTES DU ROUSILLON $13.00–$75.00

Former photojournalist Étienne Montes has instituted an "intro level" Catalan red, La Colomina, that represents outstanding value, and he continues to adopt a no-expenses-or-labor-spared approach throughout his range, bottling and releasing a Pla del Rey only when he thinks it appropriate.

2005 La Colomina	89	now–2010
2004 La Garrigue	88	now
2003 La Garrigue	90	now
2000 Côtes du Roussillon-Villages Pla del Rey	93	now–2013

MAS CHAMPART ★★★★★
ST.-CHINIAN $14.00–$30.00

Isabelle Champart has been crafting some of the cleanest, most elegant, yet most soulful wines in the Languedoc for more than a decade. Furthermore, they continue to offer outstanding value. The sumptuous Simonette cuvée—densely packed with animal, herbal, and mineral layers, silky in texture, yet refined—is the best advertisement one could imagine for either the St.-Chinian appellation or the Mourvèdre grape.

2004 St.-Chinian Causse de Bousquet	90	now–2011
2004 St.-Chinian Clos de la Simonette	92	2010–2014

CHAMPS DES SOEURS ★★★
FITOU $17.00–$19.00

The tank-raised Champs des Soeurs delivers all the black fruits, roasted meats, and wild herbs one could ask for at the price, as well as mysteriously stony, iodinelike notes that seem to transport you to the stony Mediterranean shore at the little port of Fitou.

2005 Fitou Bel Amant	88	now–2011

PIERRE CLAVEL ★★★★
COTEAUX DU LANGUEDOC LA MÉJANELLE $12.00–$50.00

Among the Languedoc's best-known and longest-running quality-conscious vintners, Pierre Clavel (who farms along the coast, east of Montpellier) has never stopped innovating, and several of his cuvées are unconventionally fermented in upended *barriques*.

2005 Coteaux du Languedoc Les Garrigues	89	now
2004 Coteaux du Languedoc La Copa Santa	89	now–2011
2003 Coteaux du Languedoc Des Clous	91	now–2013

DOMAINE DU CLOS DES FÉES ★★★★★
CÔTES DU ROUSSILLON $20.00–$250.00

Sommelier, restaurateur, and journalist-turned-winemaker Hervé Bizeul's idealism and ambition created a stir soon after he set up his *garagiste* facility nearly a decade ago, and his subsequent success as well as the flamboyant, nearly hyperconcentrated style of his wines have inspired envy, admiration, and controversy. Tasters who place great value on sheer polish and confectionary sweetness, and who are wholly unperturbed by lavish and conspicuous use of new wood will be the greatest fans of these wines. A high mountain pass above Vingrau (with ancient Grenache vines) gives his most expensive and rare cuvée its name, "Little Siberia."

2005 Côtes du Roussillon Les Sorcières	89	now–2011
2004 Côtes du Roussillon Villages Vieilles Vignes	91	now–2012
2004 Côtes du Roussillon Villages Le Clos de Fées	93	2011–2014+?
2004 Côtes du Roussillon Villages La Petite Sibérie	91	2012–2015+?

CLOS MARIE ✴✴✴✴✴
COTEAUX DU LANGUEDOC PIC ST.-LOUP $25.00–$75.00

The Clos Marie of Christophe Peyrus and François Julien is a superstar in the Languedoc firmament, and no opportunity should be missed to sample their complex results, which go a long way toward accounting for all of the attention that the Pic St.-Loup subappellation itself has garnered over the past dozen years.

2004 Coteaux du Languedoc Pic St.-Loup Métairies du Clos Vieilles Vignes	93	now–2014
2004 Coteaux du Languedoc Pic St.-Loup Simon	92	now–2014
1998 Coteaux du Languedoc Pic St.-Loup Simon	91	now
2004 Coteaux du Languedoc Pic St.-Loup Les Glorieuses	95	2010–2020
1998 Coteaux du Languedoc Pic St.-Loup Les Glorieuses	91	now–2012

LE CLOS DES PAULILLES ✴✴✴✴
BANYULS, COLLIOURE $30.00–$50.00

The huge holdings of Le Clos des Paulilles are part of a vast Roussillon acreage of the Château de Jau and Bernard Dauré has scored numerous recent successes, particularly with his Banyuls.

1999 Collioure	91	now–2012
2000 Banyuls Rimage	92	now–2017
1998 Banyuls Rimage Mise Tardive	92	now–2015
1998 Banyuls Cap Bear	93	now–2022

CLOS DES TRUFFIERS ✴✴✴✴✴
COTEAUX DU LANGUEDOC $150.00–$175.00

From a tiny parcel of nearly 40-year-old Syrah vines outside St. Pargoire (near the source of two of the Languedoc's other most profound—though stylistically very different—Syrahs, those of Marlene Soria's Domaine Peyre Rose), the Clos des Truffiers—owned by importer Jeffrey Davies and managed and vinified by the team from Château de la Négly—is based on exceptionally low yields subjected to extraordinarily rigorous sorting, long maceration, and 26 months' aging in new barrels. Any opportunity to taste it should not be missed, even though the price of admission is steep.

2003 Coteaux du Languedoc Clos des Truffiers	95	2012–2018
2003 Coteaux du Languedoc Clos des Truffiers	92–95	now–2012

CLOT DE L'OUM ✴✴✴✴
CÔTES DU ROUSSILLON $22.00–$50.00

Transplanted engineer Eric Monné assembled and painstakingly restored or replanted many geologically diverse parcels throughout the 1990s, and from them crafts three cuvées (all raised in *barriques,* but of differing ages). They tend to be rather firm in their youth but can blossom to amazing complexity. This is also a great place to test one's conception of (or disbelief in the efficacy of) *terroir* at the barrel, as parcels are by turns gneiss, schist, or granite.

2005 Côtes du Roussillon-Villages Compagnie des Papillons	90	now–2010
2004 Côtes du Roussillon-Villages Compagnie des Papillons	90	now
2005 Côtes du Roussillon-Villages St.-Bart Vieilles Vignes	88	2010–2013

2004 Côtes du Roussillon-Villages Numero Uno	91	2010–2015+?
2002 Côtes du Roussillon Villages Numero Uno	92	now–2012

COUME DEL MAS ★ ★ ★ ★
BANYULS, COLLIOURE $25.00–$45.00

From Philippe and Nathalie Gard's Collioure schistic seaside terraces come some terrific and quite refined dry reds, excellent Banyuls, and an attractive white blend called Folio, which smells of the ocean and scrub.

2006 Folio [white]	88	now
2005 Collioure Schistes	91	now–2011
2005 Collioure Quadratur	91	20⁻0–2013

CHÂTEAU COUPE ROSES ★ ★ ★
MINERVOIS $12.00–$30.00

Pascal Frissant and François Le Calvez offer some gorgeous wine at the low end of their price spectrum, and their ambitious Cuvée Granaxa and Cuvée Orience, though a bit overly tannic and marked by stewed fruit in the searing 2003 vintage, are well worth investigating.

2004 Minervois La Bastide	88	now
2003 Minervois Cuvée Granaxa	88	now–2011
2001 Minervois Cuvée Granaxa	90	now
2004 Minervois Cuvée Vignals	89	now–2010
2000 Minervois Cuvée Vignals	89	now

DOMAINE DE COURBISSAC ★ ★ ★ ★ ★
MINERVOIS $12.00–$30.00

Biodynamic and stylistically maverick Alsace vintner Marc Tempé joined with film producer and wine enthusiast Reinhard Brundig in 2002 to found the Domaine de Courbissac. Tempé is certainly a man of talent. Ironically, his low-sulfur, long-*élevage* wines from Minervois do not seem so unusual amid those of fellow vintners as do his Alsace wines.

2005 Eos	88	now
2004 Minervois	91	now–2012
2003 Minervois	90	now–2012
2004 Minervois La Livinière Pandora	93	now–2015
2003 Minervois La Livinière Pandora	90	now–2015

CHÂTEAU CREYSSELS ★ ★ ★
COTEAUX DU LANGUEDOC PICPOUL DE PINET $12.00–$13.00

Julie Beau is one of the new breed of owners of independent domaines springing up to produce Picpoul with personality at a bargain price. Drink the youngest vintage available and never more than 18 months from the harvest.

LA CROIX DE ST.-JEAN ★ ★ ★ ★
MINERVOIS $22.00–$40.00

A new collaboration between photographer Fabrice Leseigneur and Minervois area grower Michel Fabre, La Croix de St.-Jean is—from the initial taste of it—going to be grabbing future headlines. (Their labels are certainly head turners.)

2005 Lo Mainatge	89	now–2010
2004 Lo Paire	91	2009–2012+?

MAS DE LA DEVEZE ★ ★ ★ ★
CÔTES DU ROUSSILLON $21.00–$90.00

A multitalented outsider, Olivier Bernstein crushed his first fruit in 2003. His "second wine"—a tank-vinified blend of old-vine Grenache and Carignan with some Syrah—is named for the number of the French département Pyrénées-Orientales (66) and designed to provide instant gratification. It functions as it was designed. His "grand vin" and experiments in ultraconcentrated Grenache (Pandora) and Syrah (Astrée) all display great promise and ambition.

2005 Côtes du Roussillon-Villages 66	90	now
2004 Côtes du Roussillon-Villages 66	89	now
2005 Côtes du Roussillon-Villages	90	2010–2013+?
2004 Côtes du Roussillon-Villages	91	2009–2012
2005 Pandora	92	2012–2015+?
2005 Astrée	91	2012–2014+?

DOMAINE DONJON ★ ★ ★
MINERVOIS $10.00–$20.00

Jean Panis not only renders authoritative and excellent value Minervois (from barrel-aged Syrah and Grenache), he also bottles astonishingly inexpensive and vivid Merlot and Cabernet Sauvignon, which should, however, be enjoyed within two years of their harvest.

2003 Minervois Grande Tradition	88	now–2010
2004 Minervois Prestige	90	now–2011
2001 Minervois Prestige	89	now

DOMAINE DE L'EDRE ★ ★ ★ ★ ★
CÔTES DU ROUSSILLON $30.00–$50.00

Jacques Castany and Pascal Dieunidou are two wine freaks out to turn their hobby into a livelihood as they each inherit old vines around Vingrau. Technique and yields are reported to be minimal. The early results are nothing short of phenomenal.

2005 Côtes du Roussillon-Villages	94	now–2015+?
2004 Côtes du Roussillon-Villages L'Aïbre	92	now–2012+?
2005 Côtes du Roussillon-Villages L'Edre	95	now–2017+?

DOMAINE DE L'ERMITAGE DU PIC ST.-LOUP ★ ★ ★
COTEAUX DU LANGUEDOC PIC ST.-LOUP $15.00–$30.00

The Ravaille brothers craft generally restrained but satisfying and affordable Pic St.-Loup.

2005 Coteaux du Languedoc Pic St.-Loup	87	now–2010
2005 Coteaux du Languedoc Pic St.-Loup Cuvée St.-Agnès	88	now–2011

CHÂTEAU DES ERLES ★ ★ ★
CORBIÈRES, FITOU $20.00–$40.00

A J. F. Lurton family property, Château des Erles is turning out at their top end (albeit at relatively hefty prices for these appellations) impressive wines from old Grenache and Carignan with Syrah.

2004 Corbières La Reaoufa	89	now–2010
2003 Fitou	88	now–2011

CHÂTEAU DES ESTANILLES ★★★★
FAUGÈRES $18.00–$30.00

Another "outsider" for whom this is a second career, Loire native Michel Louison has been setting high standards in Faugères for more than a quarter century and is still expanding his domaine. Fermentations are long and the new barrels lavished on the top cuvées.

2001 Faugères Tradition	87	now
2000 Faugères Cuvée Prestige	88	now

ÉTANG DES COLOMBES ★★★
CORBIÈRES $12.00–$25.00

The Gualco family's forthright reds represent just as consistently excellent values today as they did in the early 1980s, when they were among the first ambassadors for Corbières in the U.S. (and sold for only a few dollars). Rich and generous, these wines avoid the clunky earthiness, gaminess, and excessive fat that too often come with the Corbières territory. Their Viognier is worth drinking as well, but only within 18 months of harvest.

2004 Corbières Tradition	88	now
2004 Corbières Vieilles Vignes Cuvée Bicentenaire		now–2011
2004 Corbières Bois Dames		now–2018

CHÂTEAU L'EUZIÈRE ★★★★
COTEAUX DU LANGUEDOC PIC ST.-LOUP $14.00–$22.00

Among the leaders in Pic St.-Loup, Marcelle and Michel Causse are also rendering some of the overwhelmingly best price/quality rapport in an appellation not always distinguished by value. A warning, though: These are the least cuddly sort of Languedoc reds imaginable—intense, bright, saline, invigorating, and intriguing—and will shake one's preconceptions about their genre.

2004 Coteaux du Languedoc Pic St.-Loup Almandin	88	now–2012
1999 Coteaux du Languedoc Pic St.-Loup Almandin	87	now
2004 Coteaux du Languedoc Pic St.-Loup Escarboucles	91	now–2015

DOMAINE FAURMARIE ★★★
COTEAUX DU LANGUEDOC GRÈS DE MONTPELLIER $18.00–$25.00

There was only one cooperative bottling any wine in St.-Bauzille-de-Montmel when the appellation of Pic St.-Loup was created, else the town probably would—and based on the gustatory evidence found at Domaine Faurmarie's should—have been included.

2004 Coteaux du Languedoc Grès de Montpellier L'Écrit Vin	90	now–2011

MARIA FITA ★★★
FITOU $35.00–$50.00

Based in the mountainous interior of the Fitou appellation, this young estate and dream of Alsace-born restaurateur-entrepreneur Jean-Michel Schmitt enjoyed the talents and idealism of winemaker Maxime Magnon (since left to found his own estate) in its first years. Wines never moved from their lees, with low or no added sulfur and a regimen that could have come from the 19th century are all strikingly evident in these unusual and promising wines.

2002 Fitou	88	now
2001 Fitou	91	now

DOMAINE DE FONTSAINTE ∗ ∗ ∗
CORBIÈRES $11.00–$25.00

Long a refuge for American wine lovers on a budget, Bruno Laboucarié's Domaine de Font-sainte continues to offer terrific value. The Demoiselle comes from 100-year-old Carignan vines.

2005 Corbières	88	now
2005 Corbières Réserve La Demoiselle	89	now–2012

DOMAINE FOULAQUIER ∗ ∗ ∗ ∗ ∗
COTEAUX DU LANGUEDOC PIC ST.-LOUP $19.00–$27.00

Swiss architect Pierre Jequier founded his domaine—another one in Pic St.-Loup that looks headed for stardom—in 1999. The vines are in a bowllike sun trap but do not betray their alcohol as heat. Plenty of chances are taken in harvest and vinification and the payoff in complexity as well as sensuality is obvious. Thus far, the prices have remained blessedly low. (The cuvées, incidentally, are named for local bird species.)

2005 Coteaux du Languedoc Pic St.-Loup L'Orphée	89	now–2011
1999 Coteaux du Languedoc Pic St.-Loup L'Orphée	90	now
2004 Coteaux du Languedoc Pic St.-Loup Le Rollier	90	now–2012
2001 Coteaux du Languedoc Pic St.-Loup Le Rollier	89	now
2000 Coteaux du Languedoc Pic St.-Loup Le Rollier	91	now–2010
2004 Coteaux du Languedoc Pic St.-Loup Les Calades	92	2009–2015

DOMAINE GARDIÉS ∗ ∗ ∗
CÔTES DU ROUSSILLON $23.00–$45.00

Jean Gardiés recently took over his family's Roussillon domaine, with holdings in Vingrau and Espira de l'Agly. His best wines demonstrate that Roussillon natives, not just outsiders, are continuing to make waves here.

2005 Côtes du Roussillon-Villages Tautavel Vieilles Vignes	87	now–2010
2005 Côtes du Roussillon-Villages La Torre	88	2009–2012
2003 Côtes du Roussillon-Villages La Torre	90	now–2011+?
2000 Côtes du Roussillon-Villages Les Millères	88	now

DOMAINE GAUBY ∗ ∗ ∗ ∗ ∗
CÔTES DU ROUSSILLON $25.00–$125.00

Gérard Gauby is practicing a rigorous (increasingly biodynamic) viticultural regimen in an attempt to achieve wines of lower alcohol and more finesse. His wines from 2003 and previously are the most impressive dry wines so far to come out of Roussillon, but he is now moving in a distinctively different and still fascinating direction. Gauby is the elder statesman of Roussillon not only on account of his leading qualitative position but also because so many of the young idealists who arrived here late in the last century worked with him or sought his guidance. Any of the wines Gauby made until recently (including profound white blends) have an excellent track record for aging. Whether his more recent wines will age as well or even, as he believes, more successfully, time alone can tell.

2006 Côtes du Roussillon Blanc Les Calcinaire	92	now–2014
2005 Côtes du Roussillon Blanc Les Calcinaire	90	now–2012
2004 Vieilles Vignes Blanc	92	now–2012+?
2004 Côtes du Roussillon-Villages Les Calcinaire	90	2009–2013
2005 Côtes du Roussillon-Villages Les Calcinaire	91	2010–2014
2003 Côtes du Roussillon-Villages Vieilles Vignes	93	2009–2016
2004 Côtes du Roussillon-Villages Vieilles Vignes	90	2009–2013

| 2003 Côtes du Roussillon-Villages Muntada | 95 | 2010–2020 |
| 2004 Côtes du Roussillon-Villages Muntada | 93 | 2010–2017+? |

GAUJAL ST.-BON ★★★★
COTEAUX DU LANGUEDOC PICPOUL DE PINET $10.00–$12.00

Talk about sensational value! The Gaujals know how to get the most out of the Picpoul and its little seaside appellation. They limit their yields and bottle their wine only after seven to eight months *sur lie,* twice as long as most others in this co-op–dominated region. Still, it is best to plan on drinking their gorgeous, refreshing white within three years of the vintage.

| 2005 Picpoul de Pinet | 90 | now |

CHÂTEAU GRANDE CASSAGNE ★★★
COSTIÈRES DE NÎMES $14.00–$16.00

The Dardé brothers render reds that are flamboyant and sumptuous but not without underlying gaminess and stoniness. The cuvée named for their grandfather Hippolyte represents an amazing value.

2001 Costières de Nîmes	88	now–2010
2004 Costières de Nîmes Hippolyte	90	now–2011+?
2003 Costières de Nîmes Hippolyte	90	now–2011
2001 Costières de Nîmes Hippolyte	89	now–2010

DOMAINE DU GRAND CRÈS ★★★
CORBIÈRES $19.00–$28.00

Onetime Domaine de la Romanée-Conti *régisseur* Hervé Leferrer established his Corbières domaine in 1988, with the aim of demonstrating that wines of this appellation can be mineral, graceful, and elegant. He has proved his point, but sometimes the wines lack enough richness and stuffing to completely convince. His white is especially striking.

| 2005 Corbières Blanc | 88 | now |
| 2005 Corbières Majeure | 87 | now–2010 |

LA GRANGE DES PÈRES ★★★★★
HÉRAULT $60.00–$85.00

When Laurent Vaillé (previously engaged in the practice of physical therapy) burst onto the wine scene in the early '90s, he was not afraid to charge a then almost unheard of price, and quickly went to the top of many observers' Best of the Languedoc lists. These reds from very low yielding vines remain impeccably crafted, striking and distinctive. The 2004 exhibits a brightness and savory intensity reminiscent of a cross between Zinfandel and Côte Rôtie. Vaillé's opulent white (from Roussanne and Chardonnay) is more of an acquired taste. Like his mentor and next-door neighbor Aimé Guibert, Vaillé bottles his wines simply as *vins de pays.*

2004 La Grange des Pères	92	now–2014+?
2001 La Grange des Pères	90	now–2012
2000 La Grange des Pères	94	now–2014
1998 La Grange des Pères	93	now
2001 La Grange des Pères Blancs	92	now–2010
2000 La Grange des Pères Blancs	93	now–2010

LA GRANGE DE QUATRE SOUS ★ ★ ★
ST.-CHINIAN $20.00–$30.00

Swiss Hildegard Horat has her idiosyncratic ways and her wines their undeniable wiles. None bears the local St.-Chinian appellation, due to their unorthodox grape varieties, notably Cabernet Franc, Malbec, and Cabernet Sauvignon, along with Syrah. These wines are never showy, but taking time for them is a satisfying and mind-expanding exercise.

2005 Lo Molin	89	2009–2014
2004 Lo Molin	88	2009–2015
2004 Les Serottes	87	2009–2014
2004 La Grange de Quatre Sous	89	2010–2015

HECHT & BANNIER ★ ★ ★ ★
(négociant) $12.00–$50.00

Gregory Hecht and François Bannier's young *négociant* operation promises to be an outstanding source for polished, concentrated wines of the Languedoc and Roussillon and great values.

2004 Minervois	89	now–2010
2003 Côtes du Roussillon Villages	91	now–2011
2003 St.-Chinian	92	now–2014

DOMAINE HEGARTY-CHAMANS ★ ★ ★ ★
MINERVOIS $15.00–$30.00

John Hegarty and Philippa Crane made their fortunes in advertising and now advertise their unorthodox approaches to winemaking with the black sheep on their label. The approach here is no labor spared and it shows from their first vintage, 2003. Along with amazing sheer richness and opulence, there is striking purity of fruit here and enough freshness to keep these wines from becoming the sort of cloying, jam-on-toast caricature that can sometimes ensue when new-world idealists try to pull out all the stops.

2003 No. 3	87	now
2003 Minervois No. 2	90	now–2012?
2003 Minervois No. 1	92	now–2015?

DOMAINE DE L'HORTUS ★ ★ ★ ★
COTEAUX DU LANGUEDOC PIC ST.-LOUP $18.00–$35.00

A Languedoc veteran and formative force of the Pic St.-Loup subappellation, Jean Orliac has clearly not been satisfied to rest on his reputation, but continues to impress with wines as intriguing as they are sensually satisfying. His blended white called Bergerie Classique is also well worth savoring, but preferably within two years of harvest.

2005 Coteaux du Languedoc Pic St.-Loup Bergerie Classique	89	now–2010
2005 Coteaux du Languedoc Clos du Prieur	90	now–2011
2004 Coteaux du Languedoc Pic St.-Loup Grande Cuvée	92	2009–2013

MAS JANEIL ★ ★ ★
CÔTES DU ROUSSILLON $30.00–$35.00

One of the J. F. Lurton family properties in southern France, Mas Janeil is rendering a fascinating Le Tiradou from ancient Grenache vines.

2004 Côtes du Roussillon Villages Le Tiradou	89	now–2011+?

MAS JULLIEN *****
COTEAUX DU LANGUEDOC $26.00–$40.00

Olivier Jullien years ago became one of the most respected vintners in the Languedoc, but he has never rested on his laurels and is constantly searching and changing aspects of his approach, always with an eye toward achieving a refinement and subtlety that are still relatively rare among Languedoc wines. With Jullien, you get poetry on the label and in the bottle. You'd never guess from tasting it that his Les États d'Âme (registering his "state of mind") functions as a "second wine" to his estate red. His white can be interesting and delicious, too, as well as aging nicely for a few years in bottle.

2004 Coteaux du Languedoc Les États d'Âme	90	now–2010
2003 Coteaux du Languedoc Mas Jullien	92	now–2012

DOMAINE LACROIX-VANEL ***
COTEAUX DU LANGUEDOC $18.00–$35.00

If one had to pick one person to epitomize the idealism of the Languedoc's many fools for wine, it could be Jean-Pierre Vanel. Starting out with a dream and a small acreage of vines on pebbly, complex *terroir* inherited from his grandmother and struggling all the way, he has already crafted some of the region's most supple and sophisticated wines with a primitive basement facility and an assortment of small tanks.

2004 Coteaux du Languedoc Fine Amor	89	now
2004 Coteaux du Languedoc Mélanie	90	now–2012
2000 Coteaux du Languedoc Mélanie	90	now

DOMAINE LAFAGE ****
CÔTES DU ROUSSILLON $10.00–$50.00

Jean-Marc Lafage has assembled extensive acreage ranging from the Mediterranean coast into the foothills of the Pyrenees. Much in demand as a consultant outside of France as well, Lafage and his importer Eric Solomon are rendering a huge service to consumers with several cuvées—Novellum Chardonnay; a white blend, Côte d'Est; and a red Côte Sud—that represent incredible values. (The two whites should be enjoyed in their first year in bottle.) Lafage's 2004 Le Vignon exhibits a combination of clarity and plush texture that eludes all but a few Languedoc or Roussillon reds, and if it is typical of what is to come from this estate in the future, it will take its place as one of this region's elite.

2006 Cuvée Centenaire white	87	now
2005 Côte Sud	90	now
2003 Côtes du Roussillon Cuvée Lea	91	now–2012
2004 Côtes du Roussillon Le Vignon	93	now–2014+?

DOMAINE LANCYRE ****
COTEAUX DU LANGUEDOC PIC ST.-LOUP $14.00–$25.00

The team of Bernard Durand and Regis Valentin is talented with more than just the classic red blends of Pic St.-Loup, which in their case offer outstanding value. From 2006, they began labeling their white "Roussanne" to call attention to its distinctiveness and perhaps make it seem more familiar to Americans. They also craft one of the finest rosés on the planet, suitable for reflection as well as reflexively drinking, but always in its first two years.

2006 Roussanne	88	now
2002 Coteaux du Languedoc Pic St.-Loup	88	now
2005 Coteaux du Languedoc Pic St.-Loup Vieilles Vignes	91	now–2011
2002 Coteaux du Languedoc Pic St.-Loup Grande Cuvée	90	now

CHÂTEAU LASCAUX ★★★
COTEAUX DU LANGUEDOC PIC ST.-LOUP $14.00–$28.00

Jean-Benoît Cavalier's domaine routinely turns out excellent values in a ripe, soft style that will please new-world palates as well as fans of Languedoc *terroir*. Only at the top end of his range does new wood sometimes threaten to become obtrusive.

2005 Coteaux du Languedoc	88	now–2010
2004 Coteaux du Languedoc	87	now
2004 Coteaux du Languedoc Pic St.-Loup	89	now–2011

MAS LUMEN ★★★★★
COTEAUX DU LANGUEDOC $22.00–$40.00

Begun in 2001, and farming a complex array of soils in Gabian (whose growers rejected a 1982 invitation to join the then-new appellation of Faugères), Pascal Perret's Mas Lumen has set impeccable standards—albeit at the price of minuscule yields and to the tune of a mere 800–900 cases annually. These are well worth the search it will take to locate some bottles. The blends vary from year to year, and Prélude is raised in a mixture of barrels and tank, while La Sylve is rendered in newer barrels.

2003 Coteaux du Languedoc Prélude	88	now–2010
2002 Coteaux du Languedoc Prélude	90	now–2010
2001 Coteaux du Languedoc Prélude	92	now–2012
2002 Coteaux du Languedoc La Sylve	91	now–2011
2001 Coteaux du Languedoc La Sylve	92	now–2014

DOMAINE MADELOC ★★★
BANYULS, COLLIOURE $30.00–$60.00

Well-known northern Rhône vintner Pierre Gaillard and Jean and Mathieu Baills have shown some very fine results already at this four-year-old winery, the most notable of these being among their dry red Collioures.

2004 Collioure Crestall	89	2010–2012+?
2004 Collioure Magenca	90	now–2011+?

DOMAINE MARIS ★★★★
MINERVOIS $15.00–$50.00

Since Robert Eden took over Domaine Maris in La Livinière (then just granted its own Minervois subappellation) just over a decade ago, he has made it the base for an ambitious *négociant* project and developed a wide range of biodynamically farmed estate wines of which the top, barrel-aged exemplars—while sourced entirely from La Livinière—are declassified, because they are *mono-cépage* (as well as being labeled largely in English).

2004 Syrah La Touge	90	now
2004 Syrah Old Vine	89	now
2004 Grenache Old Vine	92	now–2010+?

DOMAINE MASSAMIER LA MIGNARDE ★★★
MINERVOIS $9.00–$25.00

One wonders how Frantz Venes turns out something as good as his Cuvée des Oliviers *blanc* (Sauvignon with a soupçon of Viognier) for around $10 U.S. retail. (But drink it within two years of harvest.) His reds are not especially refined, but they are as frequently delicious as his methods are unorthodox. The top cuvées begin fermenting by *macération carbonique* (see section on Beaujolais), then moving the juice to new, upended barrels to complete fermentation, and bottling early.

2005 Minervois Cuvée Aubin	87	now–2010
2005 Carignan Expression	89	now–2011
2001 Carignan Expression	90	now
2003 Cinsault Expression	87	now
2004 Tenement de Garouilhas	88	now–2011?
2001 Tenement de Garouilhas	92	now–2014

CHÂTEAU DE MATTES-SABRAN ★ ★ ★
CORBIÈRES $13.00–$18.00

Jean-Luc Brouillat's domaine has turned out some impressive bargains over the years, more than making up in richness for anything they might lack in refinement. His sumptuous late-bottled Syrah Clos du Redon is definitely winter-weight wine.

2004 Corbières Le Viala	87	now
2005 Corbières Clos du Redon	90	now–2012

MAS MORTIES ★ ★ ★ ★
COTEAUX DU LANGUEDOC $40.00–$60.00

After nearly 15 years at Mas Morties, Rémy Duchemin and Michel Jorcin must be considered among the veterans of their appellation. In his review of the inaugural 1993 vintage, Robert Parker wrote enthusiastically that Mas Morties "tastes like it should cost $45"—more than four times its retail price then. Today, the wines indeed cost between $40 and $50, but they justify it. "Jamais Content" sums up their tireless commitment to ever better quality, and the wine of that name could be taken for top-notch Côte Rôtie.

2004 Coteaux du Languedoc Pic St.-Loup	90	now–2010
2004 Coteaux du Languedoc Pic St.-Loup		
Jamais Content	91	2009–2014
2001 Que Sera Sera	91–92	now–2010

DOMAINE MOULINIER ★ ★ ★
ST.-CHINIAN $15.00–$25.00

With chalk, sand, and schist soils, the team at Domaine Moulinier has a wide scope for playing with the Rhône family or reds, but their most impressive wine is Syrah from—as its name indicates—the "grilled terraces" of schist, matured in new wood.

2004 St.-Chinian Les Terrasses Grillée	87	now

MOURREL AZURAT ★ ★ ★
FITOU $10.00–$12.00

Mourrel Azurat is actually a separate label for Fitou produced by Massamier la Mignarde, and the inaugural wine offers mind-boggling value and a complex set of flavors that will transport there anyone who has braved the winds of Fitou's cobbled, scrubby, seaside vineyards.

2005 Fitou	88	now

CHÂTEAU DE NAGES ★ ★ ★
COSTIÈRES DE NÎMES $13.00–$25.00

Given that Michel Gassier divides his time between growing wine to bottle under several labels and running one of the region's largest fruit orchards, he doesn't seem to have had to compromise on quality, and his most recent releases suggest he is moving his way up in the pecking order of this appellation full of overachievers. The whites here, though, are not nearly as flashy or luscious as the reds.

2005 Costières de Nîmes Réserve	89	now–2010
2004 Costières de Nîmes Réserve	87	now
2004 Costières de Nîmes Cuvée Joseph Torres	90	now–2012
2003 Costières de Nîmes Vieilles Vignes	88	now

DOMAINE NAVARRE ★ ★ ★
ST.-CHINIAN $15.00–$25.00

Thierry Navarre—based in tiny Roquebrun, in a dramatic gorge of the river Orb—farms chalky as well as schistic soils and the results are excellent values.

2000 St.-Chinian Laouzil	89	now
2000 St.-Chinian Cuvée Olivier	90	now–2010

CHÂTEAU DE LA NÉGLY ★ ★ ★ ★ ★
COTEAUX DU LANGUEDOC LA CLAPE $18.00–$150.00

Through ruthless control of yields, meticulous selectivity, and a relentlessly envelope-pushing approach to ripening their fruit and extracting its flavors, Jean Paux-Rosset and his oenologist Claude Gros have over the past decade set new standards for the entire Languedoc, not just their La Clape neighborhood. Plush, polished, and often heady—the product of low yields and cru classé winemaking—these wines make voluminous statements. The Port du Ciel goes beyond enveloping to almost suffocating richness.

2005 Coteaux du Languedoc La Clape La Côte	87	now
2005 Coteaux du Languedoc La Clape La Falaise	92	now–2010
2005 Coteaux du Languedoc La Clape l'Ancély	91	now–2016+?
1998 Coteaux du Languedoc La Clape l'Ancély	95	now–2014
2003 Coteaux du Languedoc La Clape La Port du Ciel	94	now–2018+?
1999 Coteaux du Languedoc La Clape La Port du Ciel	96	now–2017
1998 Coteaux du Languedoc La Clape La Port du Ciel	94	now–2012

CHÂTEAU D'OR ET DE GUEULES ★ ★ ★ ★
COSTIÈRES DE NÎMES $13.00–$30.00

Diane de Puymorin purchased (and renamed) this property in 1998 and is generating wines of amazing richness and complexity for a relative pittance. Her La Bolida is a virtual essence of Mourvèdre. It will be most fun to track the evolution of her early releases in bottle.

2003 Costières de Nîmes	91	now–2010+?
2003 Costières de Nîmes La Bolida	93	now–2012+?

CHÂTEAU D'OUPIA ★ ★ ★
MINERVOIS $13.00–$25.00

From centenarian Carignan vines, with some Syrah and Grenache, André Iché crafts an excellent value Minervois Tradition that is rather Cornas-like in its scents of ripe cherries and chopped liver. He also matures a couple of cuvées in new wood.

2005 Minervois Tradition	88	now

L'OUSTAL BLANC ★★★★★
MINERVOIS $30.00–$45.00

Claude Fonquerle and his oenologist Philippe Cambie earned their stripes in Châteauneuf-du-Pape and in 2002 began to vinify in Minervois. They rely on extremely low yields (in part from centenarian Carignan vines) and rigorously sort the fruit, and some of the fermentation is in small, upended barrels. The wines—like their labels—are flamboyant, almost over-the-top, and utterly striking.

2005 Naick 5	92	now–2010+?
2004 Minervois	93	now–2012+?
2004 Minervois La Livinière	91	2010–2015+?

DOMAINE PECH-REDON ★★★
COTEAUX DU LANGUEDOC LA CLAPE $15.00–$28.00

Proprietor Jean-Claude Bousquet (vice-president of France's wine regulatory agency, the INAO), follows Pech-Redon's late founder Jean Demolombe in crafting distinctive reds from this coastal area. Nowadays the wines have more polish than in Demolombe's day, but they still hint at simmering wild herb and wild animal intensity and are still excellent values.

2005 Coteaux du Languedoc La Clape Les Cades	89	now–2010
2004 Coteaux du Languedoc La Clape l'Epervier	90	2009–2012

LA PÈIRA EN DAMAISÊLA ★★★★
COTEAUX DU LANGUEDOC $N/A

New neighbors to Grange de la Père and Mas Daumas Gassac, La Pèira en Damaisela is the property of composer Robert Dougan, surrounded by young talent working under the guidance of oenologist Claude Gros (of Château de la Négly fame). From barrel, the 2005s were too impressive not to include in this guide, even though the first wines have yet to be marketed. That the estate's "second wine" outshone its "grand vin" prior to bottling is no doubt connected with its being near-100% Syrah, whereas Las Flors is more than half Grenache and Mourvèdre. Be on the lookout for these wines.

2005 Coteaux du Languedoc Orbriers de la Pèira	89–90	2009–2010+?
2005 Coteaux du Languedoc Las Flors de la Pèira	91–92	2009–2012+?
2005 Coteaux du Languedoc La Pèira	90–91	2011–2015+?

YANNICK PELLETIER ★★★★★
ST.-CHINIAN $20.00–$37.00

Yannick Pelletier is meticulously farming 21 mostly schistic acres at the northern edge of St.-Chinian, and the result is a bevy of as yet little-known wines at the apex of their appellation. Plenty of intrigue and enjoyment await any readers who can corner a few bottles of these and chart their evolution over the next several years. Production of all Pelletier wines is tiny—surely in large part due to his draconian yields—so stake your claim to a share before his star rises prominently above the horizon.

2005 St.-Chinian l'Oiselet	87	now
2005 St.-Chinian l'Engoulevent	91	now–2011+?
2004 St.-Chinian l'Engoulevent	90	now–2010
2005 St.-Chinian Coccigrues	92	now–2013+?
2004 St.-Chinian Coccigrues	92	now–2012+?

PEÑA LES VIGNERONS DE CASES PÈNE * * *
CÔTES DU ROUSSILLON $9.00–$22.00

For purposes of U.S. labeling at least, the remarkably quality-conscious grower cooperative in tiny Pène is known simply as Peña. Landholder-president Jean-Christophe Bourquin and longtime oenologist Joseph Gonzales continue a streak of incredible values in collaboration with their long-time importer Dan Kravitz, notably the irresistible Ninet de Peña Rosé and Viognier and their Cuvée de Peña red. There are also some powerful if as yet relatively rustic "reserve" wines.

2005 Cuvée de Peña	88	now

DOMAINE PEYRE ROSE * * * * *
COTEAUX DU LANGUEDOC $75.00–$100.00

During a lull in the economy, ex–real estate agent Marlene Soria decided to try her hand at making wine on two small, adjacent plots covered with suffering Syrah vines and fist- and head-sized limestone. Since the vines could give only one or two bunches, and the untrained Soria was determined to let the wine make itself as much as possible (it was years before the "winery" even got electricity, much less lived up to that name) the results were a revelation. Today some large wooden ovals alternate with tank. The wines are not bottled before three years, nor released until Soria feels they are ready. They are reminiscent of a cross between Hermitage and pre-1982 Bordeaux.

1998 Clos des Cistes	93	now–2012
1998 Clos Syrah Léone	91	now–2010

OLIVIER PITHON * * *
CÔTES DU ROUSSILLON $15.00–$35.00

Olivier Pithon (whose older brother Jo's domaine in the Loire is better known) has been crafting serious and refined whites as well as reds since 2001, practicing intensive, low-tech viticulture, including horse plowing.

2003 Côtes du Roussillon-Villages Saturne	88	now–2011+?

PLAN DE L'OM * * *
COTEAUX DU LANGUEDOC $18.00–$25.00

Joël Faucou left the co-op of St.-Jean de la Blaquière and set up his own domaine in 2001. He is full of interesting ideas and experimental in a positive way, his wines show promise, and the most successful of them—such as his Carignan-based Paysage—have palate-staining presence.

2005 Coteaux du Languedoc Paysage	88	now–2011
2003 Coteaux du Languedoc Miejour	87	now–2010

PRIEURÉ DE ST.-JEAN-DE-BÉBIAN * * * *
COTEAUX DU LANGUEDOC $30.00–$45.00

Languedoc pioneer Alain Roux already brought this property just outside Pézenas (purchased by his grandfather) to prominence in the 1970s. In 1994 Jean-Claude Le Brun and Chantal Lecouty purchased the property and have been trying to bring more refinement to the wines without losing the richness that has characterized them from the beginning.

1999 Coteaux du Languedoc	88	now–2010
1998 Coteaux du Languedoc	91	now–2012

DOMAINE PUECH NOBLE/PUECH CHAUD ★ ★ ★ ★
COTEAUX DU LANGUEDOC $28.00–$33.00

René Rostaing of Côte Rôtie crafts refined, complex Syrah-based Languedoc that (perhaps not surprisingly) reminds one of the northern Rhône. His white—an original blend of Grenache Blanc, Roussanne, and Vermentino (aka Rolle)—is luscious and exotic, yet refreshing. Beginning with the release of the 2005 red, the domaine name has changed from Puech Chaud to Puech Noble.

2005 Coteaux du Languedoc	89	2C09–2013
2004 Coteaux du Languedoc	89	2C10–2013
2003 Coteaux du Languedoc	89	ncw–2010
1999 Coteaux du Languedoc	91	ncw–2012
2005 Coteaux du Languedoc Blanc	90	ncw

DOMAINE PUECH-HAUT ★ ★ ★
COTEAUX DU LANGUEDOC $28.00–$100.00

Gérard Bru employs both Claude Gros and the famous Michel Rolland as consultants, which might strike most proprietors as overkill. His property in St.-Drézéry is just outside the city of Montpellier, and his Syrah-dominated top wine—though no one could call it "good value"— represents a concentrated, peaty, tobacco-tinged and unabashedly powerful exhibition of Pic St.-Loup's potential.

2003 Coteaux du Languedoc St.-Drézéry	88	2009–2013
2003 Coteaux du Languedoc Pic St.-Loup	89	now
2003 Coteaux du Languedoc Pic St.-Loup Clos du Pic	91	now–2013

DOMAINE DE RANCY ★ ★ ★
RIVESALTES $20.00–$100.00

Jean-Hubert Verdaguer sells off most of his crop to the local cooperative so that he can follow a family tradition (once widespread in Roussillon) of devoting his attention to oxidized, "rancio"-styled wines, aged for many years in an assortment of old barrels, and in his case entirely from Maccabeu vines. Wines back to 1950 are currently on offer and imported (so if you are looking to match a birth year, this is a place to remember).

1990 Rivesaltes Ambré	90	now–2015+

DOMAINE DE LA RECTORIE ★ ★ ★
BANYULS, COLLIOURE $20.00–$45.00

Thierry and Marc Parcé are among the more established (yet iconoclastic) Roussillon growers, and in recent years they also make Maury and a range of distinctive dry reds at the Préceptorie de Centernach.

2005 Banyuls Cuvée Léon Parcé	90	now–2012

DOMAINE RIMBERT ★ ★ ★
ST.-CHINIAN $14.00–$50.00

Jean-Marie Rimbert is among the Languedoc's most jocular and imaginative vignerons—and in this colorful territory, that's saying something. Every cuvée name is a play on words and lately there are new cuvées wherever one turns. (If, as Rimbert implicitly maintains, you have to be a "mas-au-schiste" to farm these stony mountains, the same might apply to citing varieties by percentage and "explaining" all of his labels.) The common themes are schist and Carignan (in conjunction with the usual collaborative *cépages*). His most powerful wine (formerly called Le Carignator) is a multivintage, *solera*-style blend; a new top cuvée is named simply for his appellation and town.

2005 St.-Chinian Les Travers de Marceau	87	now
1999 St.-Chinian Mas au Schiste	89	now
2005 Chant de Marjolaine	88	now–2011
2001 Chant de Marjolaine	89	now
2004 St.-Chinian Berlou	89	2009–2012+?
(NV) El Carignator II	90	now–2010

LE ROC DES ANGES ★ ★ ★ ★
CÔTES DU ROUSSILLON $22.00–$50.00

At age 26, and at the start of a new century northern Rhône native Marjorie Gallet founded her Rock of Angels estate on schist and old vines around the village of Montner. The fruit from one parcel of Carignan planted in 1903 has proven both multifaceted and resistant to felicitous cohabitation with her other lots.

2004 Côtes du Roussillon-Villages Vieilles Vignes	90	2009–2012
2003 Côtes du Roussillon-Villages Vieilles Vignes	88	now–2011
2002 Côtes du Roussillon-Villages Vieilles Vignes	89	now
2001 Côtes du Roussillon-Villages Vieilles Vignes	89	now–2010
2003 Carignan 1903	91	2010–2016+?
2002 Carignan 1903	89	2009–2014+?
2001 Carignan 1903	94	now–2018

CHÂTEAU LA ROQUE ★ ★ ★
COTEAUX DU LANGUEDOC PIC ST.-LOUP $15.00–$25.00

Jack Boutin's reds have long been known for their fleshy, fruit-filled, often downright flamboyant ways. Cupa Numismaë is a serious, prominently oaked, Syrah-based flagship cuvée.

DOMAINE ST.-ANTONIN ★ ★ ★ ★ ★
FAUGÈRES $12.00–$25.00

After years spent breaking schistic stones by hand and apparently living like a hermit, Frédéric Albaret has some of the finest wines in all of southern France and some of the most amazing values in the world of wine to show for it. Interestingly, Albaret utilizes a rotation of 600-liter barrels (with part of his Tradition left in tank), and neither fines nor filters. The *terroir* and barrels seem to break the tannins the way Albaret would crush rocks—or is it also a question of gentle extraction?

2003 Faugères Tradition	91	now–2011
2004 Faugères Magnoux	94	now–2015
2003 Faugères Magnoux	92	now–2013

DOMAINE ST. MARTIN DE LA GARRIGUE ★ ★ ★
COTEAUX DU LANGUEDOC $11.00–$30.00

In the 15 years since this huge property acquired new owners (and more recently a new winemaker), it and they have turned out an exceptional number of excellent values. Both their Picpoul de Pinet and Coteaux du Languedoc white blend also offer excellent value but should be enjoyed within two years of the harvest.

2005 Coteaux du Languedoc Tradition	88	now
2005 Coteaux du Languedoc Grès de Montpellier	87	now

DOMAINE LA SAUVAGEONNE ★★★★
COTEAUX DU LANGUEDOC $12.00–$32.00

Impressively perched on a schistic hill above St.-Jean-de-la-Blaquière in the Terrasses du Larzac, Domaine La Sauvageonne often bottled distinctive wines under its former owners, but when young Englishman Gavin Crisfield "discovered" it in 2001 and persuaded an investor to purchase the property and install him as winemaking director, quality really took off. A wine bearing only the estate's name is a blend of Cabernet Sauvignon and Merlot, and one with the Languedoc-Gaelic hybrid name Puech de Glen is pure Syrah from the highest point on the estate. Neither is bottled every year.

2005 Coteaux du Languedoc Les Ruffes	88	now
2004 Coteaux du Languedoc Pica Broca	87	now
2004 Coteaux du Languedoc Puech de Glen	90	now–2013
2001 Coteaux du Languedoc Puech de Glen	91	now–2012
2004 La Sauvageonne	90	now–2010

DOMAINE SARDA-MALET ★★★
CÔTES DU ROUSSILLON $15.00–$40.00

Jérôme Malet seems to be successfully pushing the envelope on quality of late at this well-established domaine. His Le Sarda cuvée offers outstanding value.

2005 Côtes du Roussillon Le Sarda	90	now–2010
2004 Côtes du Roussillon Réserve	89	now–2012
2004 Côtes du Roussillon Terroir Mailloles	89	2009–2011

DOMAINE DES SOULANES ★★★
CÔTES DU ROUSSILLON, MAURY $17.00–$25.00

Daniel Lafitte's estate near Maury has shown considerable promise, particularly with its dry reds, most of them from blends that preclude the Côtes du Roussillon appellations.

2005 Cuvée Jean Pull	88	2009–2011+?
2004 Cuvée Jean Pull	89	now–2011
2003 Cuvée Jean Pull	89	now
2003 Côtes du Roussillon-Villages Sarrat del Mas	88	now–2011
2002 Bastoul Lafitte	91	now–2010

DOMAINE DES TERRES FALMET ★★★
ST.-CHINIAN $13.00–$17.00

Internationally experienced Yves Falmet farms 60 steep, contiguous acres on which he grows notable wine values. Perhaps his top wine does not yet quite live up to its name ("Intoxication of the Summit"), but he is on the way up.

2004 Carignan	87	now
2003 St.-Chinian l'Ivresses des Cimes	88	now–2010

TERRE INCONNUE ★★★
COTEAUX DU LANGUEDOC $N/A

Robert Creus puts his passion into a rather ambitious hobby, vinifying Syrah, Grenache, Carignan, and even Tempranillo northeast of Montpellier. Each variety has its own cuvée, and they are not *appellation contrôlée*. Rich and distinctive, even "idiosyncratic," his wines deserve to be better known and available in the U.S.

DOMAINE LA TOUR BOISÉE ★ ★ ★
MINERVOIS $12.00–$30.00

Jean-Louis Poudou has shown great imagination and quality consciousness with wines ranging from amazingly inexpensive to both tank- and new-wood-rendered upper-echelon cuvées
from the classic Rhône red varieties. His whites are also very worth investigating, provided
one drinks them within two years of harvest.

2004 Minervois	87	now

DOMAINE DE LA TOUR PENEDESSES ★ ★ ★
COTEAUX DU LANGUEDOC $12.00–$60.00

Alexandre Fouque offers a bewilderingly long list of bottlings involving no fewer than 15
grape varieties. His top-end (barrel-aged) releases revealed a trademark seamless, sweet richness, though often his wines are opaque in more than one sense: dark, dense, and at times a bit
impenetrable.

2004 Coteaux du Languedoc Cuvée Antique	90	now–2012
2004 Coteaux du Languedoc Montée Volcanique	88	now–2010
2004 Coteaux du Languedoc Clos de Magrignan Montée des Schistes	89	now–2010

DOMAINE DE LA TOUR VIEILLE ★ ★ ★ ★
BANYULS, COLLIOURE $20.00–$50.00

Over the past quarter-century, Christine Campadieu and Vincent Cantié have built up an
impressive reputation, and their most recent releases demonstrate that they are among the
elite estates of Roussillon, excelling in the dry reds of their hometown Collioure (where some
of their many parcels directly overlook the ocean) and almost as much so in the fortified sweet
wines of neighboring Banyuls.

2005 Collioure Puig Oriole	93	2009–2015+?
2004 Collioure Puig Oriole	92	now–2014
2004 Collioure Puig Ambeille	91	now–2014+?
2004 Collioure La Pinede	90	now–2011
2005 Banyuls Vendanges	90	now–2020
2004 Banyuls Vendanges	89	now–2018
2000 Banyuls Vendanges	91	now–2017

JEAN-LOUIS TRIBOULEY ★ ★ ★ ★ ★
CÔTES DU ROUSSILLON $16.00–$20.00

Tribouley is a protégé of Gérard Gauby, who started on his own in 2002 and farms two of his
parcels of old-vine Grenache in the Coume du Roy biodynamically and with a mule. These
rich, superripe, yet complex and not at all heavy wines are a revelation and among the most
extraordinary wine values to be found anywhere.

2005 Les Bacs Vieilles Vignes	93	now–2012+?
2004 Serrat den Franc	93	now–2012+?
2005 Orchis	92	now–2012+?

[the loire valley]

THE BARGAIN GARDEN OF FRANCE

Admittedly, it is stretching things to treat the Loire as just one region. This river flows almost 700 miles while draining nearly one-quarter of France, and wine issues from a wide range of grapes and environments along nearly its entire arc, from the rugged hills of the Auvergne (not far west of the northern Rhône's vineyards) to the gusty shores of the Atlantic in Brittany. But the French themselves make a whole of the region when they refer to this entire produce-wealthy area as the Garden of France. It is high time wine lovers recognize it as the bargain garden of French wines. From few if any other places on Earth can one still harvest such affordable yet distinctively delicious wines, a vast stylistic and varietal range. The Loire's wines generally offer forthright, generous vinous personalities and food compatibility while frequently harboring a depth that reflects their historically and geologically layered origins. Even top crus from this region's leaders—including those of global wine-growing champions—remain remarkably modest in price. To the extent that the Loire harbors any "cult" wines—and there are several for which even local wine geeks often search in vain—these generally still top out at well under three figures in U.S. dollars.

There are also copious quantities of lackluster or flawed wines from each of the Loire's more than 60 appellations. In this respect, U.S. consumers have an advantage over their French counterparts in the enormous range of quality Loire growers whose wines have been winnowed out for representation by dozens of specialty French wine importers. Many of the most notable agents active in the U.S. markets—Joe Dressner, Kermit Lynch, Robert Kacher, Peter Vezan, and Peter Weygandt, to name only a few—made Loire wines a cornerstone of

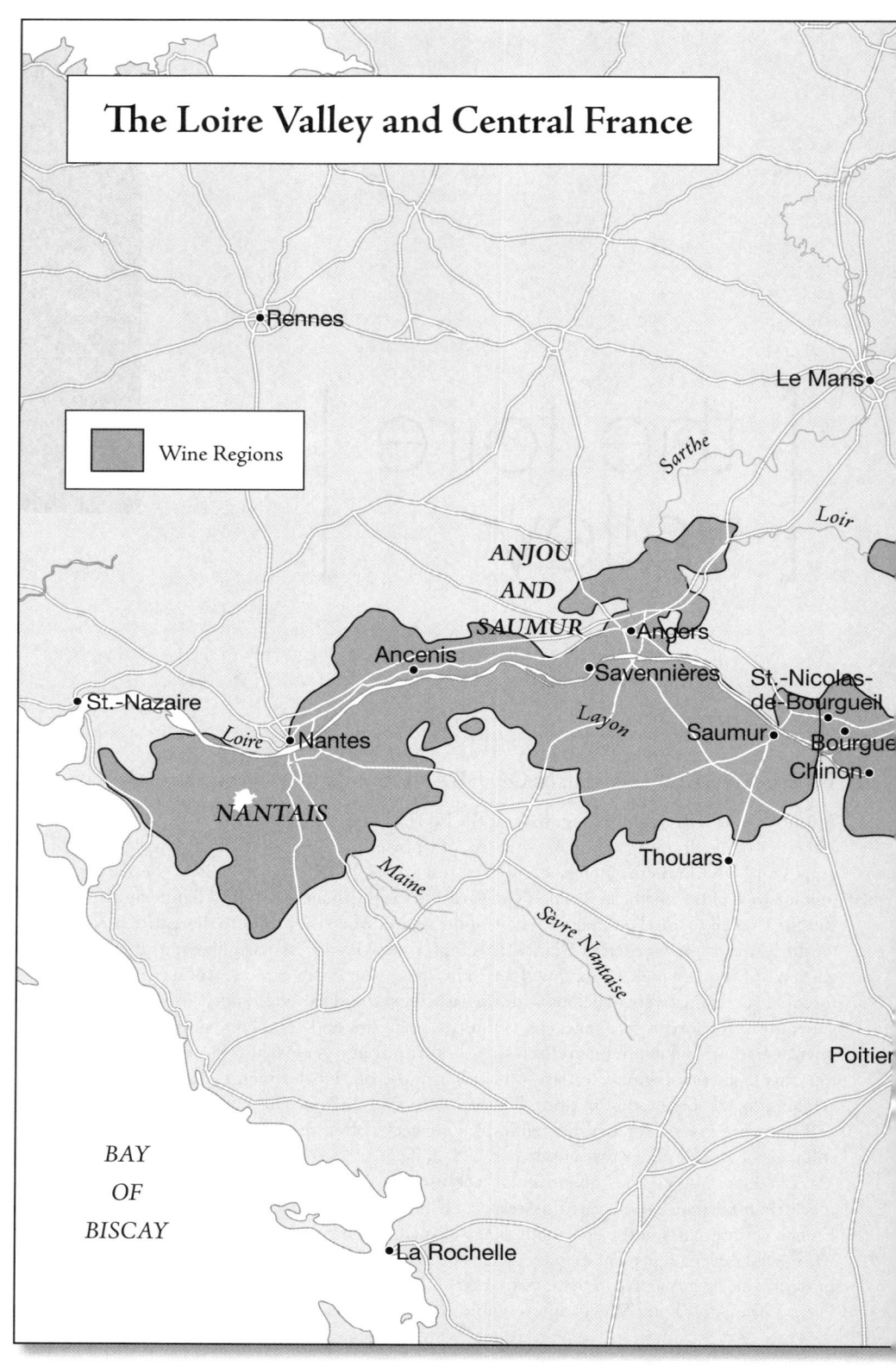

The Loire Valley and Central France

Wine Regions

Rennes

Le Mans

Sarthe

Loir

ANJOU
AND
SAUMUR

Ancenis

Angers

Savennières

St.-Nicolas-
de-Bourgueil

St.-Nazaire

Loire

Nantes

Layon

Saumur

Bourgue

Chinon

NANTAIS

Maine

Sèvre Nantaise

Thouars

Poitier

BAY
OF
BISCAY

La Rochelle

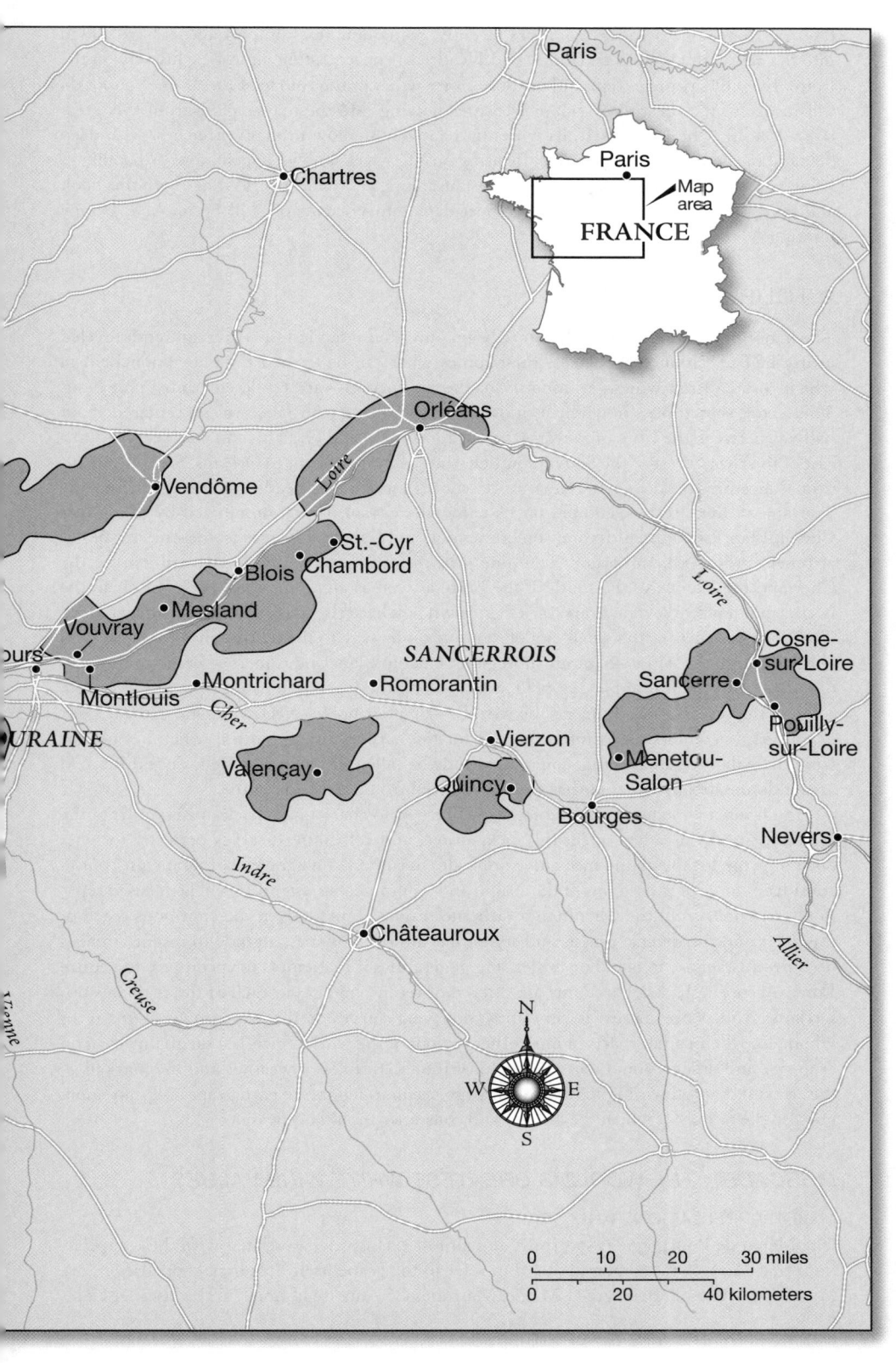

their portfolios two decades ago. More recently, many new small import agents have gotten into the act, with at least one (Jon-David Headrick) concentrating almost exclusively on the Loire. Even by tasting a thousand or more Loire wines in the course of a year one cannot do full justice to the breadth of vinous treasures flowing into the marketplace from this great river. Yet, like the Loire itself, its wines lie relatively shallow in many stretches, with deep demand in export markets generally focusing on a few well-known appellations or pooling in a few metropolitan markets. Merchants, restaurateurs, and wine lovers who—with this book and corkscrew in hand—take even a short exploratory excursion will be hooked. Happy hunting!

A TOUR OF THE LOIRE

The major production areas of the Loire begin only after it has left the Auvergne and traveled nearly half its distance to the sea. First comes what can be termed the Sauvignon Belt, in which rosé and red wines—a minority of the production—are rendered from Pinot Noir. This sector, sometimes known by its most famous locality as the Sancerrois, is centered about halfway between the cities of Nevers (famous for its oak) and Orléans, and cuts deeply south-east of the river. West of the Sauvignon Belt, the river bows north to Orléans. Serious viticultural concentration does not return to its shores until it has headed south again into the Touraine, a huge sector centered on its namesake city of Tours, dominated by the grapes Chenin Blanc (sometimes dry but sometimes not) and Cabernet France (sometimes frivolous, at others profound). Important Touraine growing areas stretch along two tributaries, the Cher and the Vienne to the south of the Loire as well as along the tiny (no "e") Loir to the north, and in places several grape varieties grown nowhere else make fascinating appearances. The Loire next passes the small city of Saumur on its way to the metropolis of Angers, and hence through the Anjou–Saumur subregions. Chenin Blanc and Cabernet Franc continue to dominate the viticultural playing field. South, along the fog-prone banks of the little Layon, some of the region's—and indeed the world's—greatest nobly sweet wines are grown. West of Angers, one enters the Nantais (named for the harbor city of Nantes, which lies not far from the Atlantic), an area that could most aptly be called the Muscadet Belt, since this broad area is dominated by wines of that name, produced from the Melon grape.

In taking a wine tour of the Loire, it will be best to chart a path back upstream from the Nantais, since Muscadet—plentiful, inexpensive, and refreshing—serves perfectly to whet one's appetite for the abundance and complexity to come. As we travel east, branching out to consider a range of subregions of the Anjou and Touraine, our attention will be focused separately on wines from the Chenin and Cabernet Franc grapes. Given the enormous reach of this river and the diverse grapes and styles that inform its wines, a guide to recent vintages becomes an exercise in bland or misleading generalities if it attempts to encompass the entire Loire. Accordingly, brief accounts are offered of recent vintages in each of the regional subsections. And, since nature is constantly throwing curves at the winegrowers—many of whom, like their counterparts in most other regions of the world, focus less on quality than on crop size and on ensuring themselves against the vicissitudes of weather and the markets—the account that follows highlights not only the peculiar delights of each grape and subregion, but also the pitfalls of which the grower and consumer should be aware.

MUSCADET: THE WORLD'S GREATEST WHITE WINE VALUE?

MAJOR APPELLATIONS AND GRAPES

The Melon de Bourgogne is so firmly, and almost exclusively, associated with these appellations that Muscadet is sometimes used to refer to the grape itself. Its official appellations are Muscadet, Muscadet de Sèvre et Maine, Muscadet Coteaux de la Loire, and Muscadet Côtes de Grandlieu. Generally thin, astringent reds and whites are also produced from the Gamay and Folle Blanche (aka Gros Plant) grapes respectively, in the respective Coteaux d'Ancenis and Gros Plant appellations at the edge of Muscadet territory. Some 30 miles south of Nantes, for the most part directly along the windswept Atlantic coast, are the intriguing vineyards of the Fiefs Vendéens, featuring at times promising Chardonnay, Pinot Noir, and Gamay, as well as Cabernets.

WHAT TO EXPECT

If there is a growing region other than Muscadet offering such distinctively delicious wines possessed of complexity as well as culinary diversity, rendered by impassioned, conscientious growers, and routinely retailing for between U.S. $12 and $15, one can only hope that it too will soon be discovered! Wines from the westernmost stretch of the Loire have become so intimately associated the world over with bivalve mollusks of the nearby Atlantic that it is practically necessary to adopt a new slogan: "Muscadet: It's not just for oysters!" Muscadet is versatility incarnate. Few other wines of the world can taste entirely satisfying and ripe at 12% or less alcohol. As a result, few are better suited to drinking outdoors during the summertime. Furthermore, low-alcohol dry whites insinuate themselves onto the dinner table with an ease that is hardly accidental. They're inherently combinative. Few wines are more refreshing or more dominated by flavor characteristics that we call "mineral." These are the traits that literally keep one's digestive juices flowing, stimulating thirst and appetite. Its high CO_2 level and low price make Muscadet the ideal wine to keep open in the refrigerator from day to day without risking rapid quality deterioration, and to reach for whenever a recipe calls.

While Muscadet is normally thought suitable for drinking only in its raw youth, the best growers and their wines will eagerly contradict this myth. A majority of the Muscadet should be drunk within its first three years while the fresh fruit acids are still elevated and CO_2 (enhanced by bottling *sur-lie,* or directly off the sediment of dead yeasts and other particulate matter) is palpably present. But the exceptions to this generalization include many of the very best wines of the Muscadet appellations, particularly the special cuvées from the top growers. Furthermore, in many of the weathered schist and gneiss soils of this region, the phylloxera—the vicious root louse notorious for having devastated Europe's vineyards a century and more ago—could not survive, so there are wines today that draw some of their gustatory nuance and structural strength from ungrafted, centenarian, genetically diverse heirloom vines.

RECENT VINTAGES

While it was almost impossible to render classic Muscadet in the heat of 2003, both 2004 and 2005 are excellent vintages, the latter generally (but not at all addresses) marginally superior, and 2006 and 2007—despite rain—have proven successful, at least for hand-harvesters. Here, just as nearly everywhere in the Loire that white grapes are grown, 2002 was exceptional for its combination of ripeness and richness with clarity and structure. (Yes, richness and structure are possible in Muscadet!) Many special bottlings from this superb vintage were released by growers only after several years of bottle age, so the odds are not entirely against scoring a few examples. Don't hesitate to sample even a well-stored, upper-echelon cuvée from one of the top growers in a ripe, concentrated vintage such as 1996 or 1990, as you may discover a wine that is enjoying a remarkably vivacious "old age."

IMPORTANT INFORMATION

Reasonable crop levels and hand-harvesting, or extremely adept machine-harvesting, are required if Muscadet is to be properly ripe and capable of expressing the floral, fruit, and mineral nuances that can truly distinguish it. This is a depressed economic region. While it is hard to believe how many vignerons idealistically continue to strive for excellence when the prices their wines command are so pitifully low, there are also many too many growers being sucked down in the vicious spiral of ever higher yields and efficiency with ever lower prices and quality. Muscadet can be vapid and screechy at the same time. Think of it as the naked wine. Without alcohol, residual sugar, oak, body, or high fructose and fruit esters, it had better be naturally well-built and blemish-free if it is going to entice us without benefit of clothing or makeup. Stick to the growers listed below and you will be rewarded, but if you make a mistake you won't be out a lot of dough.

ANJOU AND SAUMUR: NOBLY SWEET AND NOBLY DRY

MAJOR APPELLATIONS AND GRAPES

ANJOU Designates dry (occasionally off-dry) whites from Chenin Blanc (also traditionally known as Pineau de la Loire, but usually referred to simply as Chenin) and reds and rosés generally from Cabernet Franc, but sometimes also from Cabernet Sauvignon, Gamay, or the native Grolleau. Occasionally, one encounters some Chardonnay or even Sauvignon Blanc, either of which may be blended into Chenin in small amounts. The designation Anjou-Villages applies to certain of this area's ostensibly more serious reds.

COTEAUX DU LAYON From Chenin grown along the Layon, just south of the Loire—is dedicated to nobly sweet wines, those from theoretically superior sites being entitled to affix the name of certain villages (as, for instance, Coteaux du Layon St.-Aubin) and the scarcest and most celebrated being entitled to their own appellations, Quarts de Chaume and Bonnezeaux. (The latter legally requires an improbable 230 grams of residual sugar!) North of the Layon stretches the Coteaux de l'Aubance, home to other lusciously sweet wines from Chenin. (Recently, reds from the l'Aubance village of Brissac were even given their own Anjou subappellation.)

SAUMUR Designates dry (occasionally off-dry) whites from Chenin and reds from Cabernet Franc, in rare instances blended with Cabernet Sauvignon or Pineau d'Aunis (about which see more under Touraine below). Much of the Chenin production of Saumur goes into sparkling wine. The best soils and microclimates are theoretically those designated Saumur-Champigny, and indeed some of the most impressive and ageworthy Loire Cabernet Francs originate in that all-red appellation. A seldom-encountered off-dry category of Chenin is known as Coteaux de Saumur.

SAVENNIÈRES Designates dry (and on rare occasions off-dry) whites from Chenin, grown west of the city of Angers. The historically best locations overlooking the river have their own very small subappellations of Roche aux Moines and Coulée de Serrant, the latter a *monopole* of the Joly family.

WHAT TO EXPECT

Just east of Angers grow some of the Loire's historically most celebrated whites: on the north side of the river, on schist, the dry Chenin of Savennières, and to the south—along a tributary, the little Layon, also from Chenin, and on schist or chalky clay, depending on the village— some of the world's greatest nobly sweet wines. The presence of two such dramatically different soils presents an interesting opportunity to taste the French concept of *terroir* in action. Leaving aside the contentious claim that one can somehow "taste the schist" or slate in wines grown on those rocky soils, the very different ways in which schist and chalk-clay soils store water and convey it to the vine make for often dramatic differences in wine character. Thus, for instance, in a hot, dry year the Loire chalk acts like a sponge, whereas vines on schist suffer and may "shut down" (i.e., stop metabolizing). In wet summers or autumns, by contrast, schist has an advantage in shedding rain. Curiously, this region's sweet wine tradition owes its existence to a 17th- and 18th-century appetite in Holland and to the powerful interests of Dutch traders in the duchy of Anjou.

Even the dry variations on Chenin grown in the Anjou regions are among the world's potentially most profound and ageworthy wines, managing a trick virtually unique to their *cépage:* being voluminous and palpably dense while offering lively, mouthwatering acidity. It is this combination that makes Savennières and its cousins so desirable at table: They can meet the richness of a cuisine like-on-like, then in the same sip cut the creaminess or opulence of the dish and leave the palate refreshed. While Saumur is best known for its Cabernet Franc–based reds (of which more below, where the reds of Touraine are discussed) and its multitudes of generally lackluster sparkling wines, there are increasingly many important outposts and inspired growers of (generally dry) Chenin here as well. Aromas of quince, chamomile, bergamot, honeysuckle, snuffed candlewick, and white truffle are among those tasters will encounter with this Chenin in its native Loire habitats.

The nobly sweet wines of the Coteaux du Layon are among the most ageworthy on earth, as well as some of the world's great bargains. (Like any wines that depend on the felicitous action of botrytis, though, they can never enjoy consistent success. See more under Important Information below.) The primary problem for producers of these often exquisite elixirs redolent of honey, flowers, citrus, and pit fruits is that most of us too seldom drink nobly sweet wine of any sort. It's not just for dessert, but it must be imaginatively employed at table. And when savored alone, these "slow wines" make that least reasonable of demands on us: our time. If we are going to savor such wines so seldom, then why open something less than magical? Yes, the rarity of great botrytis has its price. But the amazing thing is that a great nobly sweet Coteaux du Layon can still be purchased for as little as $15 to $25 a half bottle, at most one-quarter of what one would expect to pay for a comparable Sauternes, Tokay, or nobly sweet German Riesling.

RECENT VINTAGES

2002 is the classic among recent years in Anjou, the Coteaux du Layon, and Saumur, balancing freshness and minerality with voluminous richness and capped by lovely botrytis along the Layon. In 2003, and often as well in 2005, there was too much heat and too little water. The dry wines can be top-heavy and tipsy from alcohol, the sweet wines generally less the product of botrytis than of sheer desiccation—not in itself a negative, but too often in this pair of recent vintages accompanied by a crude dried fruit or raisin character and a lack of freshness. There is a lot to like here in 2004, a vintage that presented almost insurmountable challenges for Chenin grown only a little farther east in the Touraine. Certainly, high yields and cool, rainy periods posed challenges in the Anjou, too. But then, in recent years wines from Savennières (along with those of so many other wine regions) seem to benefit from any factors that will promote a slower accumulation of sugar and a longer hang time. As for botrytis, there was plenty in 2004—a great deal of it noble indeed, which will less often be the case in 2006. (For a consideration of recent vintages of reds from the Anjou, see the discussion of Touraine reds below.)

1995 and 1996 as well as the trio of 1988–1990 represent memorable successes. 1996 was a year with a long, luminous, but relatively cool growing season, resulting in wines that combined high ripeness with almost freakishly high acidity and extract. Botrytis came to grapes already concentrated by wind and long exposure. The best dry Chenin of this vintage, not to mention the sweet, are still youthful. (But note that there are also numerous and not entirely explicable instances of premature aging of 1996 and 1995 Loire whites, analogous to—though much less widespread than—those that plague white Burgundy, as discussed in the section devoted to that category.) 1995 also resulted in high ripeness, concentration, and much noble rot. For sweet wines the pair 1989 and 1990 represent a contrast between a vintage in which the fruit concentrated by shriveling with botrytis was almost an afterthought (1989) and one in which the botrytis came early and beneficently (1990). And 1988 represents (much as it happens to for German Riesling) a model of balance and, with the sweet wines, of restrained nobility. No one should hesitate to seek out Chenin of the top producers from any of the afore-mentioned vintages, and in the case of the great sweet wines these are treasures one can still safely cellar. Wines of certain extraordinary older vintages—others from the second half of the 20th century include 1976, 1971, 1969, 1964, 1959, 1953, 1949, 1947, and 1945—turn up more frequently than one might imagine, due to producers like Huët, Moulin Touchais, or the Domaine Aux Moines, who regularly offer cellar treasures on their price lists.

IMPORTANT INFORMATION

In dry wines there is, as previously noted, an increasing tendency—whether one ascribes it to climatic aberration, global warming, growing practices, fashion, or a combination of factors—for sugars to outrun the ripening of the skins, with alcoholically top-heavy or harsh results. Furthermore, there is no question that Chenin has a natural proclivity for reduction (chemi-cally speaking, for hydrogen bonding), which can result in dominant aromas of wet wool. Chenin is also prone to bitterness (of which more under Central Loire below) that high alco-hol can only accentuate. Add to this the chalky or wet-stone mineral sensations that so often figure in the finish of these wines and one has a singular potential for youthful austerity.

Beware as well the penchant for taking Chenin from these climes through malolactic fermentation in small barrels. The results of working the lees in new or newish barrels can be fascinating, but the wines can also easily lose that counterpoint of density and natural richness with minerality and cut which makes the best of them so distinctive. And seldom do labels or back labels reveal the wines that turn out to taste more like would-be white Burgundies. (Nor for that matter is it always evident whether a wine is dry or sweet; see further discussion of this topic under Touraine below.) With nobly sweet wines, one must beware precisely as in any other botrytis region. We are, after all, talking about rot, a dangerous, seldom entirely beneficent creature. That the Coteaux du Layon and its subappellations feature the lowest yields mandated in all of France is not in itself a guarantee of quality. Rare are the wines to which botrytis comes with delicacy and in the bloom of the berries' already perfect ripeness, stealthily working its honey-inducing magic without leaving behind smudgy, fungal finger-prints.

TOURAINE: QUEEN CHENIN AND HER COURT

MAJOR APPELLATIONS

Vouvray and Montlouis—each consisting of several villages, including the ones with those names, and located respectively north and south of the Loire—are home to Chenin Blanc ranging from dry (generally labeled *sec*) through off-dry (*demi-sec*) to nobly sweet (here known by the almost untranslatable term *moelleux*—with the same root as "marrow") and from still through lightly effervescent (*pétillant*) to high-pressure sparkling. The soils here, and in much of the central Loire, are a variety of limestone known as *tuffeau,* superb in its balance of drain-age and moisture retention, with a penetrability that can be strikingly observed in the region's troglodytic villages built into the sides of cliffs.

Coteaux de Loir (with no "e") refers to wines from a small stretch of the river Loir once renowned for its Chenin (in as many basic variations as that of Vouvray or Montlouis) and now reviving that tradition. The reputation of this sector was made by sites clustered near the hamlet of Jasnières, which gives its name to dry or nobly sweet Chenin with the potential to rival any from the Loire. The Coteaux de Loir is also the epicenter for production (albeit mi-nuscule) of rosé and red wine from the Pineau d'Aunis, sometimes known as Chenin Rouge.

WHAT TO EXPECT

Few names are better known to wine lovers than Vouvray, yet some remarkable facts about this appellation are easily overlooked. Its top practitioners—most notably Foreau and Huët, but Fouquet and others follow close behind—are among the preeminent white wine growers in the world, yet few wine lovers have ever drunk a really good, much less great, Vouvray. There is an ocean of Appellation Vouvray, but sad to say much of it is awful. Across the river Loire, and along its tributary the Cher, the small appellation of Montlouis has been home to one of the most amazing and exciting wine revivals of modern France. At least three Montlouis growers—Jacky Blot, François Chidaine, and Xavier Weisskopf (of Rocher des Violettes)—are challenging the local qualitative preeminence of Vouvray. The dry and off-dry wines from these appellations can mature magnificently for decades in bottle, the nobly sweet for even longer. Any wine lover who has tasted a 50-year-old Vouvray from a great vintage of Foreau or Huët will never forget its flavors or amazingly youthful stamina.

Another of the Loire's exciting revivals is taking place some thirty miles north, along the shores of the bucolic little Loir, site of vineyards once as celebrated as those of Vouvray, Savennières, or the Coteaux du Layon but largely abandoned after phylloxera, war, and depression. The wines of Jasnières, like those of Savennières, commanded prices a century ago that rivaled those of any whites in France, including Le Montrachet. Already, one grower, Eric Nicolas of Domaine Bellivière, has once again achieved supreme quality in this still-obscure corner of the Loire, while also proving that the local Pineau d'Aunis can render serious reds.

It's a remarkable fact: Nowhere else in France, and scarcely anywhere else at all outside Germany's Riesling regions, does one encounter wines sparkling and still, dry and sweet (and in between) made from the same grape and soil under the same appellation, as is the case in Vouvray, Montlouis, and the Coteaux de Loir. Talk about one-stop shopping! But there is an annoying factor that consumers cannot avoid. The use of the terms *sec, demi-sec,* and *moelleux* (or *liquoureux*) to designate the degree of sweetness is by no means universal, and in fact there is an increasing tendency for growers to simply bottle wines of a given style under a given name of their choice. The consequent proliferation of winery-internal terminology might be easy for these growers' private, cellar-door customers to learn, but it is frustrating for consumers like those in the United States who have the good fortune to be able to choose from among the wines of dozens of outstanding growers. There is thus no substitute—if the degree of dryness is not mentioned on the label—for consulting a reliable merchant or review.

RECENT VINTAGES

Without question, the 2002 vintage is sensational for Central Loire Chenin. But at the absolute extreme of ripeness—even if the wines are more marked by desiccation than by botrytis—there are some stupendous and probably ageless 2003s as well. 2004 here starkly displays one of wine's most often overlooked surprises: If you don't like the weather, try a few towns over. This is a vintage that growers of Vouvray and Montlouis are happy to forget, when the two major categories of grapes at triage were sparkling base wine and mulch. Yet only a short distance away, in the absence of the heavy rains that fell along the Loire, the little Loir rendered glorious results. You will hear no complaints about the 2005s anywhere in these parts. The grandchildren of today's growers will be relishing comparisons between them and the 2002s. While less awful and very different in character than 2004, 2006 was plagued by rain and (especially in Vouvray) by premature, less-than-noble botrytis, and even the successful wines are apt to be relatively fragile. Early indications are that in 2007 the grapes and their growers will have beaten the odds despite inopportune autumn rain. (For a consideration of some vintages prior to 2002, please consult the discussion above of vintages in Anjou and Saumur, which usually—2004 being a notable exception—track closely those of Vouvray and Montlouis.)

Tendencies toward reduction and bitterness in Chenin were mentioned already (see Anjou and Saumur above), as were the pitfalls of rot. But all of these concerns have special meaning in Vouvray. Given the huge size of this appellation and the plateaulike situation of most of its vineyards, high up behind the bluffs of the Loire, the majority of the harvest is done by machine. There can be amazingly successful machine-harvested wines, but these are the exceptions, and there are precious few such exceptions with Chenin. Anything short of gentle handling only increases the risk of bitterness. And without triage, uniformly ripe and rot free (to say nothing of truly nobly rotten) fruit is almost impossible to achieve in most years. Add high doses of sulfur (as do many growers) to prevent damaged fruit and botrytis infection from leading to wine spoilage, and you have an invitation to sulfurous reduction (H_2S = rotten eggs).

When buying wines from this sector, the situation resembles that in most of Germany's Riesling belt: Stick with the elite practitioners, because the median wine will not reflect these appellations' great potential. The huge difference with most of the world's other great growing regions is the price advantage of the Loire. A glorious Vouvray demi-sec from even the two regional leaders, Foreau or Huët, can be had for $30 to $40, those of the close competition for somewhat less. Compare that with today's prices for a Dönnhoff Riesling Spätlese, a Jobard Meursault, a Peter Michael Chardonnay, or a Hirtzberger Grüner Veltliner Smaragd!

TOURAINE: KING CABERNET, THE FRANC

MAJOR APPELLATIONS

Chinon, the best-known and historically most important of the Loire's red wines, is grown along the Vienne, as well as one tiny stretch of the Loire where the Vienne runs into it from the South. Alongside Chinon's Cabernet Franc (generally referred to here simply as Cabernet or Breton), a small amount of Chenin Blanc is grown and also entitled to the appellation, the best of which can merit tasting.

Bourgueil, unlike Chinon, is an appellation only a small portion of which is actually grown within sight of the Loire. All of the important acreage lies two or three miles north of the river, immediately upstream from where it is intersected by the Vienne. A small percentage of Cabernet Sauvignon is permitted here, but in practice all of the better wines are 100% Cabernet Franc, just like their Chinon counterparts. Immediately west of Bourgueil lies the less important appellation of St.-Nicolas-de-Bourgueil, the historical and geological reasons for whose separate existence need scarcely trouble the minds of wine lovers.

WHAT TO EXPECT

It's time for some straight talk about Cabernet Franc. Yes, this Cabernet so attractive historically for its frost-hardiness can taste like yesterday's plate of green beans or asparagus if it is not ripe. And yes, traditionally the fruit got really ripe along the Loire at most one year in five. But also traditionally, three of five years in the greatest Riesling-growing vineyards of the world were Kabinett vintages, and in one of five the fruit was harvested completely sour. So forget "traditionally": Welcome to the brave, new, warmer world of Loire Valley Cabernet Franc! What will it get you?

At its best, Loire Franc delivers a sweet, ethereal, floral perfume, a silken texture, a piquant nuttiness and spice, with a combination of rich-black fruitedness and refreshment that are matchless. Get it right (and ripe), furthermore, and it ages. Any number of bottles from the stupendous (but at the time much more exceptional than it would seem today) 1989 vintage are still profoundly rich and ready to rack up a third decade. Cathérine and Pierre Bréton's 1906 Bourgueil grown by Pierre's grandfather was hauntingly fruit-filled (but fleshly, not ghostly) and neither madeirized nor acetified at age 100. The fact that a bottle of Clos

Rougeard Saumur-Champigny from the Foucault brothers can set you back as much as a bottle of Trimbach Clos St.-Hune, Pichler Unendlich, or Lafon Meursault Perrières—and is harder to find—should suggest something about what the future might bring. For now, though, the Foucaults are the singular superstars (ironically, in the Saumur rather than the Touraine) and the best of all the rest are still underpriced.

The Cabernet Franc–based wines of Chinon and Bourgueil offer further interesting opportunities to taste in action the concept of *terroir*. Lighter wines are generally grown on sandier or gravelly soil (in Chinon these are the sites nearer the river) while wines with more structure and depth are grown in chalk and clay sites, such as those featured in the hillsides of Chinon along the Vienne. Once again, even if one sidesteps arguments as to the possible flavor signature of certain soils or sites, the promotion of certain sorts of root structures and the manner in which these are supplied with water clearly goes far to explain why certain sites conduce to fruitier, lighter, more forthcoming Franc-based reds and others to *vins de garde*. As more and more separate bottlings appear from individual sites and pickings, it begins to be possible to make comparisons of some of the same or adjacent vineyards as "interpreted" by different growers. One more advantage to Cabernet Franc to which the wider world has already begun to attend: Whether in lighter years, or as a result of "bleeding" the fermentation vat to concentrate the subsequent reds, it makes wickedly good rosé.

RECENT VINTAGES

2005 is a glorious vintage in which to discover the charms of Loire Cabernet Franc. Amazingly, though, underripeness and rot by no means vitiated the 2004 vintage (nor that of 2006) to the extent that it did the Chenin harvest in nearby Vouvray and Montlouis And the ways of the Franc are such that even 2003 could not entirely bake the liveliness out of it. There are many successful, if somewhat outsized, wines that may well mature at what one used to be able to call a glacial pace. Among earlier vintages, 1997, 1995, and 1990, are noteworthy for their quotient of ripe fruit and successful wines, while the 1989, as mentioned, is already almost legendary. To taste Pierre-Jacques Druet's Vaumoreau or Grand Mont bottlings of Bourgueil from that year is to be convinced forever of the profundity and aging potential inherent in Cabernet Franc from these climes and soils. Château de Villeneuve produced a remarkable Saumur Champigny in 1999—generally considered a very challenging vintage—proving that consumers may pay a price for being blinded by vintage. And, as noted, there is no question that Cabernet Franc is ripening fully with increasing frequency on the Loire, the greater challenge (as in so many other northern European growing regions nowadays) being posed not by deficient ripeness but by rot, as in 2006 and 2007.

IMPORTANT INFORMATION

The biggest downside remains that of green, herbaceous flavors or harshly unripe tannins if the fruit is not properly ripe, which can still happen nowadays even when the sugars are high, particularly if drought causes the vines to periodically "shut down." But more and more growers seem to be working around these problems, with substantial cooperation from recent weather patterns.

CENTRAL LOIRE: BARGAINS OF TOURAINE

MAJOR APPELLATIONS AND GRAPES

As an appellation, Touraine signifies whites from Sauvignon or Chenin Blanc, although in practice most of the important ones are Sauvignon. A small percentage of Chardonnay may be blended in but is really significant only in Cheverny (see immediately below). Cabernet Franc, Pinot Noir, Gamay, Côt (aka Malbec), and Cabernet Sauvignon are featured in the Appellation Touraine reds, old Malbec vines presenting especially intriguing vinous opportunities.

The indigenous Pineau d'Aunis and Grolleau—as well as Pinot Meunier and Pinot Gris—are also permitted in wines of this broad appellation. Four subappellations of Touraine have so far been created, but until these are more frequently seen on labels and demonstrate distinctiveness, they are scarcely worth noting. That many of the reds of Touraine appellation—even deeply colored examples of Malbec—are light in body ought not to be held against them. On the contrary, their white-wine-like refreshment value can be best appreciated if they are slightly chilled. (The same can be said for many of the less-ambitious reds of Bourgueil and Chinon.)

Cheverny and Cour-Cheverny are confined to a few villages on the left bank of the Loire around the city of Blois, midway between Orléans and Tours. These are in several respects curious appellations. For Cheverny, the Sauvignon *must* by recent law be blended with 20% or more Chardonnay, although it should be noted that only certain of the wines seem to have benefited recognizably from this. (The reds blend from the full Touraine menu of *cépages*.) Cour-Cheverny—produced by less than a score of vintners (how did they get an appellation to themselves?)—has been around only since 1993 but is a vehicle for the distinctive and ancient white grape Romorantin, generally vinified dry but occasionally with some sweetness.

Valençay and the Coteaux du Vendômois are two Sauvignon-dominated appellations, the former along the Cher extending east toward the Loire's main Sauvignon belt, the latter upstream from the Coteaux de Loir.

WHAT TO EXPECT

As one moves east across the Touraine, Sauvignon grows almost weedlike—in frequency and (alas!) at times in flavor, too. But make no mistake: The best wines from this vast acreage, with its often pebbly, flinty, riverside soils, are among the Loire's greatest bargains. Twenty years ago, only the Barbou family (Domaine des Corbillières) was shipping high-quality Appellation Touraine Sauvignon to the United States, and they had little qualitative company even at home. But the past decade has witnessed a mushrooming of small domaines with ambitious vignerons out to prove that world-class Sauvignon can be grown in favored but not yet famous spots along the banks of the Loire and Cher. A few individual appellations are also gaining recognition, notably Cheverny. The handful of really successful Touraine Sauvignons are more delicious and interesting than 75% or more of what's grown in Sancerre but cost half as much (and they can chase the growers of South Styria, Austria, or Marlborough, New Zealand, around the globe as well).

Cheek by jowl with these Sauvignons grow reds—frequently from ancient vines of the first postphylloxera wave—that consumers also ought not to ignore. Gamay and Malbec—not just Cabernet Franc—can exert considerable and distinctive gustatory attraction, often in vividly fresh-fruited forms. The Malbec from young Mikaël Bouges, for instance, is like a vinous cross-dresser: nearly opaque in the glass yet white-wine-like in its juicy, tart-berry refreshment of the palate. And the unorthodox red blends of Jean-Marie and Thierry Puzelat at Le Clos du Tue-Boeuf—such as their Pinot-Gamay blend, Rouillon—can be fascinating. Cour-Cheverny yields sometimes haunting, pungently floral results with its strange local grape Romorantin.

Some 50 miles south-southwest of Tour and just north of Poitiers, but best mentioned here due to its similar diversity of grapes (most prominently Sauvignon), lies the growing area known as Haut Poitou. During the 1980s, these vineyards experienced a boom in acreage fueled by a short-lived market—both on U.S. retail shelves and those of French supermarkets—for "fighting varietals": inexpensive renditions of the internationally best-known grapes. Today, at least one Haut Poitou grower, Frédéric Brochet (better known for his research on wine perception at the University of Bordeaux), is rendering serious Sauvignon, Pinot Noir, and Cabernet under his Apelidae label. Who knows what the future could bring?

RECENT VINTAGES

Recent vintages are indeed virtually all one need attend to, since wines of the Appellation Touraine are nearly all best drunk within two or three years of bottling. 2005 was quite exceptional in this region and possibly worth savoring for an extra year or two, whereas due to less than perfect weather, wines from 2006 and 2007 will need to be assessed or a case-by-case basis. The one exception to ageworthiness is Cour-Cheverny, as the Romorantin grape has proven capable—both in dry and off-dry versions—of taking on a marvelous, if slightly oxidized, patina after several years and of aging interestingly for a decade or more.

IMPORTANT INFORMATION

Underripeness and machine harvest–induced dullness are the major culprits here, but as with Muscadet, if you take a flying leap on an unknown label, given the prices, you don't have far to fall. 2005 is a perfect vintage from which to discover the myriad wiles of the Touraine, whereas wines from 2004 or 2006 need to be approached somewhat more cautiously, as some will display underripeness and impurity.

SANCERRE, POUILLY & COMPANY

MAJOR APPELLATIONS AND GRAPES

Pouilly-Fumé (on the right bank of the Loire) and Sancerre (just across the river)—the two best-known ambassadors for the Loire worldwide—are dominated by Sauvignon Blanc, exclusively in the case of Pouilly-Fumé, and cohabitating with modest acreage of Pinot Noir in the case of Sancerre. Sancerre extends several miles inland from the river, at which point commences the appellation of Menetou-Salon, sharing the same two grapes and similar soils. A considerable amount of Chasselas is planted in and around Pouilly-Fumé and bottled under the town name Pouilly-sur-Loire, but it rarely travels outside France.

Three small outposts of Sauvignon whose wines can offer excellent value are found well southwest of this stretch of the Loire: Quincy, Reuilly, and the Coteaux du Giennois. The latter two appellations also permit Pinot Noir; distinctive, "partridge eye"–colored Reuilly labeled as *vin gris* issues from Pinot Gris.

WHAT TO EXPECT

The eastern Loire is overwhelmingly dominated by the Sauvignon Blanc grape, although here, as in Touraine, it was not nearly so widespread prior to phylloxera; in fact, Marlborough, New Zealand, has now been growing Sauvignon for more than half as long as anyone was serious about that grape in Sancerre. Pouilly-Fumé, next door, was serious about Sauvignon for longer, but it has been eclipsed in the international markets by the sheer volume of Sancerre. With high volume and demand goes a temptation to stretch yields and court underripeness that is especially deleterious for the Sauvignon grape (about which more below, under Important Information). When Sancerre or Pouilly-Fumé are properly ripe—taking on scents of hedge flowers, citrus, pit fruits, melons, black currants, resinous herbs, and toasted nuts (not to mention that pungent namesake smokiness in the case of the Pouilly-Fumé)—they can exhibit dramatic and consistent differences from one soil type to another. In particular, Sauvignon grown on flint-rich soil (silex) exhibit a wonderful aromatic generosity and openness when compared with the initially more restrained and more tightly stitched examples from the classic white Kimmeridgean chalk (just like the white cliffs of Dover) for which these two great appellations are also well known. Given such striking differences, and the volume of wine that the appellation generates, a good case could be made for Sancerre subappellations.

Menetou-Salon and the isolated outposts of Reuilly and Quincy are increasingly proving their merits in the marketplace, despite a long-standing joke among English-speaking merchants that one "Quincy the point of" the latter appellation. In fact, the beauty and generosity of the best Sauvignons being grown today in these hinterlands should put disbelievers to shame. Pinot Noir is a part of the Sancerre tradition, approved in several neighboring appellations as well. Nowadays one encounters numerous pretentiously extracted and *barrique*-aged examples, but only a few convince. The rosés—having no such duty of seriousness imposed on them—can often be delightful.

RECENT VINTAGES

Really well-made Sancerre (and occasionally also Pouilly-Fumé) from a top site is capable of one or more decades of glorious bottle aging, as wines like those from the Cotats, Edmond Vatan, and de Ladoucette attest. But such Sauvignons are the exceptions, so one ought in general to enjoy these wines within five years of bottling. 2002 is the great recent classic here as well. The 2003s usually lack refreshment; the 2004s are often lacking in ripeness and generosity, but the best are worthy of attention; and the 2005s are generally rich and delicious, a bit too rounded on the whole for classic character but luscious to drink in their youth. The 2006 and 2007 crops—at least where hand-harvested by experts—look early on to have yielded satisfying if probably not exceptional results. Among vintages in the previous decade—for those examples that are truly built to age—1990, 1995–1997, and 1999 were all excellent, with the 1996s possessed of pronounced minerality, citricity, and an aura of white truffle in common with the great Loire Chenins of that vintage.

IMPORTANT INFORMATION

A background of high yields and widespread machine harvesting drags down the quality of many Sauvignons from the eastern Loire, and thin or underripe wines are turned out routinely even in balmy years. In Pouilly-Fumé in particular, lesser wines may exhibit an unpleasantly hard-edged combination of marginally ripe fruit, high acidity, and austere minerality. One might think that as strong aromas of gooseberry, passion fruit, and grassy meadows cross the line into asparagus, grass clippings, boxwood, and cat pee (as routinely happens in Sauvignons of borderline ripeness) such wines would condemn themselves to rejection in the marketplace. But this doesn't seem to be the case. As a sage grower once replied when asked about the agricultural origins of high yields and unripe Sauvignons, "It's not the fertilizer (*l'engrais*), it's the English (*les Anglais*)!" And not just the English: French bistros too serve oceans of underripe Sancerre, and U.S. importers still ship some, so there must be a market. As mentioned, truly ripe, well-concentrated wines—while they may retain notes of gooseberry, hay, or passion fruit—will transport tasters into a much more colorful and delightful range of flavors and aromas, while seldom leaving behind those elements which, for lack of a better expression, are regularly referred to as minerality.

Beware, too, the many special bottlings—frequently in heavy, deeply punted, mysteriously dark glass. There is a penchant, particularly among Sancerrois, to "treat" the fruit of their oldest Sauvignon vines to a stay in small, young barrels, but at most one in five of these cuvées seems to reveal any synergy, and many are just downright annoying in the degree to which wood infiltrates the Sauvignon and destroys the memorable, winsome combination of bright freshness, minerality, and luscious richness that can render Sancerre or Pouilly-Fumé special. (A major exception must be made for Didier Dagueneau, a master in the use of wood.)

—DAVID SCHILDKNECHT

[the ratings]

THE LOIRE'S BEST PRODUCERS

* * * * * (OUTSTANDING)

Domaine des Aubuisières—Bernard
  Fouquet (Vouvray)
Domaine des Baumards (Anjou, Coteaux
  du Layon, Savennières, Quarts de
  Chaume)
Domaine de Bellivière—Eric Nicolas
  (Coteaux du Loir, Jasnières)
Château de Casseloir—Chéreau-Carré
  (Muscadet)
François Chidaine (Montlouis, Vouvray)
Le Clos du Château l'Oiselinière—Chéreau-
  Carré (Muscadet)

Clos Rougeard—Foucault Frères (Saumur,
  Saumur-Champigny)
François Cotat (Sancerre)
Pascal Cotat (Sancerre)
Didier Dagueneau (Pouilly-Fumé)
Philippe Foreau—Domaine du Clos Naudin
  (Vouvray)
Domaine Huët (Vouvray)
Domaine Luneau-Papin (Muscadet)
Domaine de la Taille aux Loups—Jacky
  Blot (Montlouis, Vouvray)
Edmond Vatan (Sancerre)

* * * * (EXCELLENT)

Philippe Alliet (Chinon)
Yannick Amirault (Bourgueil)
Domaine Aux Moines (Savennières)
Bernard Baudry (Chinon)
Francis Blanchet (Pouilly-Fumé)
Gérard Boulay (Sancerre)
Claude Branger (Muscadet)
Catherine et Pierre Bréton (Bourgueil)
François Cazin—Le Petit Chambord
  (Cheverny, Cour-Cheverny)
Didier et Catherine Champalou (Vouvray)
Château de la Chesnaire—Chéreau-Carré
  (Muscadet)
Lucien Crochet (Sancerre)
Serge Dagueneau (Pouilly-Fumé)
Domaine Delesvaux (Coteaux du Layon)
Domaine des Dorices (Muscadet)
Domaine de l'Écu—Guy Bossard
  (Muscadet)
Domaine des Forges (Coteaux du Layon)
Domaine de la Garrelière—François
  Plouzeau (Touraine)
Baron de Ladoucette (Pouilly-Fumé,
  Sancerre)

Damien Laureau (Savennières)
Richard Leroy (Anjou, Coteaux du Layon)
Domaine de la Louvetrie—Joseph Landron
  (Muscadet)
Henry Marionnet—Domaine de la
  Charmoise (Touraine)
Alphonse Mellot (Sancerre)
Thierry Merlin-Cherrier (Sancerre)
Gérard et Pierre Morin (Sancerre)
Domaine de la Pépière—Mark Ollivier
  (Muscadet)
Château Pierre-Bise (Anjou, Coteaux du
  Layon, Savennières, Quarts de Chaume)
Jo Pithon (Anjou, Coteaux du Layon)
Château de la Roche Aux Moines—Nicolas
  Joly (Savennières)
Le Rocher des Violettes (Montlouis)
Hervé Seguin (Pouilly-Fumé)
Château Soucherie—Pierre-Yves Tijou
  (Anjou, Coteaux du Layon, Savennières)
Lucien Thomas et Fils (Sancerre)
Domaine Thomas-Labaille (Sancerre)

* * * (VERY GOOD)

Domaine Allias (Vouvray)
Ampelidae (Haut Poitou)
Mark Angeli—La Ferme de la Sansonnière
  (Anjou, Bonnezeaux)

Michel Bailly (Pouilly-Fumé)
Serge Batard—Domaine les Hautes Noëlles
  (Muscadet)
Pascal Bellier (Cheverny, Cour-Cheverny)

Domaine de la Bergerie (Anjou, Coteaux du Layon, Quarts de Chaume, Savennières)

Henri Bourgeois (Sancerre)

André-Michel Brégeon (Muscadet)

Domaine de la Butte—Jacky Blot (Bourgueil)

Domaine Cady (Coteaux du Layon)

Domaine Cailbourdin (Pouilly-Fumé)

Jacques Carroy (Pouilly-Fumé)

Domaine de la Chanteleuserie (Bourgueil)

Gilbert Chon et Fils (Muscadet)

Daniel Chotard (Sancerre)

Clos Roche Blanche (Touraine)

Domaine du Closel—Château des Vaults (Savennières)

Domaine du Collier (Saumur, Saumur-Champigny)

Domaine des Corbillières—Barbou (Touraine)

Château de Coulaine (Chinon)

Couly-Dutheil (Bourgueil, Chinon, Saumur-Champigny)

Jean Dabin et Fils (Muscadet)

Vincent Delaporte (Sancerre)

Domaine Deletang (Montlouis)

Marc Deschamps (Pouilly-Fumé)

Pierre-Jacques Druet (Bourgueil)

Château d'Epiré (Savennières)

Château de la Fessardière (Muscadet)

Domaine Filliatreau (Saumur, Saumur-Champigny)

Domaine Fouassier Père et Fils (Sancerre)

Philippe Gilbert (Menetou-Salon)

Bertrand Graillot (Coteaux du Giennois)

Domaine des Grandes Vignes (Anjou, Bonnezeaux)

Domaine Guiberteau (Saumur)

Jacques Guindon (Muscadet)

Domaine des Herbauges (Muscadet)

Domaine Denis Jamain (Reuilly)

Charles Joguet (Chinon)

Domaine Mardon (Quincy)

Eric Morgat (Savennières)

Moulin Touchais (Coteaux du Layon)

Henry Natter (Sancerre)

André Neveu (Sancerre)

Domaine de Noiré (Chinon)

Domaine Vincent Ogereau (Anjou, Coteaux du Layon)

Domaine de Pallus (Chinon)

Henry Pellé (Menetou-Salon, Sancerre)

Domaine des Petits Quarts—Godineau Père et Fils (Bonnezeaux)

Vincent Pinard (Sancerre)

François Pinon (Vouvray)

Jacky Preys et Fils (Valençay)

Thierry Puzelat (Touraine)

Domaine de la Quilla (Muscadet)

Jean-Maurice Raffault (Chinon)

Château de la Ragotière (Muscadet)

Hippolyte Reverdy (Sancerre)

Pascal et Nicolas Reverdy (Sancerre)

Domaine Richou (Anjou, Coteaux de l'Aubance)

Domaine des Roches Neuves (Saumur-Champigny)

Jean-Max Roger (Sancerre, Menetou-Salon)

Jean-Claude Roux (Quincy)

Bénédicte de Rycke (Coteaux du Loir, Jasnières)

Domaine des Sablonettes—Joël Ménard (Anjou, Coteaux du Layon)

Silice de Quincy—Jacques Sallé (Quincy)

Château de Suronde (Quarts de Chaunne)

F. Tinel-Blondelet (Pouilly-Fumé)

Moulin Touchais (Coteaux du Layon)

Château de Tracy (Pouilly-Fumé)

Domaine Vacheron (Sancerre)

André Vatan (Sancerre)

Château de Villeneuve (Saumur, Saumur-Champigny)

* * (GOOD)

Domaine du Balbut (Anjou, Coteaux de l'Aubance)

Domaine de Beauregard (Muscadet)

Château de la Bonnelière (Chinon)

Mikäel Bouges (Touraine)

Château de la Bourdinière (Muscadet)

Domaine Bourillon-d'Orleans (Vouvray)

Célestin Blondeau (Sancerre)

Domaine Le Briseau (Coteaux du Loir, Jasnieres)

Michel Brock (Sancerre)

Domaine du Carrou—Dominique Roger (Sancerre)

Domaine des Champs Fleuris (Saumur)

Jean-Claude Chatelain (Pouilly-Fumé, Sancerre)
Laurent Chatenay (Montlouis)
Domaine de la Chauvinière (Muscadet)
Domaine Pierre Cherrier et Fils (Sancerre)
Éric Chevalier (Touraine)
Château du Cleray—Sauvion (Muscadet)
Clos de Cordeliers—Ratron Frères (Saumur-Champigny)
Clos du Tue-Boeuf (Cheverny, Touraine)
Stéphane Coassais (Montlouis)
Château de la Commanderie (Quincy)
Régis Cruchet (Vouvray)
Domaine Joël Delaunay (Touraine)
Domaine du Fontenay (Côte Roannaise)
Domaine du Four à Chaux (Coteaux du Vendômois)
Fournier Pere et Fils (Sancerre)
Château Gaillard (Saumur)
Pierre et Rodolphe Gautier—Domaine du Bel Air (Bourgueil)
Gitton Père (Sancerre)
Domaine La Grange Tiphaine—Damien Delecheneau (Montlouis, Touraine)
Château de la Grille (Chinon)
Domaine des Huards—Michel Gendrier (Cheverny, Cour-Cheverny)
Pascal Jolivet (Pouilly-Fumé, Sancerre)
Claude Lafond (Reuilly)
Béatrice et Pascal Lambert (Chinon)
Langlois-Château (sparkling Saumur)
Noël Legrand (Saumur, Saumur-Champigny)

Domaine Les Loges de la Folie (Montlouis)
Frédéric Mabileau (Bourgueil)
Manoir de la Tête Rouge (Saumur)
Jocelyn Massicot (Pouilly-Fumé)
Régis Minet (Pouilly-Fumé)
Alexandre Monmousseau—Château Gaudrelle (Vouvray)
Agnes et René Mosse (Anjou)
Thierry Nérisson (Bourgueil, Saumur-Champigny, Vouvray)
Domaine de la Perrière (Chinon)
Domaine de la Petite Mairie (Bourgueil)
Philippe Pichard—Domaine de la Chapelle (Chinon)
Philippe Portier (Quincy)
Château de la Presle (Touraine)
Vincent Raimbault (Vouvray)
Jean Reverdy (Sancerre)
Vincent Richard (Touraine)
Matthias Roblin (Sancerre)
Domaine des Rochelles—J.-Y. A. Lebreton (Anjou)
Domaine St.-Nicolas (Fiefs Vendéens)
Domaine du Salvard (Cheverny)
Château de Targé (Saumur-Champigny)
Domaine Philippe Tessier (Cheverny, Cour-Cheverny)
Domaine Michel Thomas et Fils (Sancerre)
La Tour St.-Martin (Menetou-Salon, Valençay)
Domaine des Vieux Pruniers (Sancerre)
Domaine de Villargeau (Coteaux du Giennois)

[tasting commentaries]

DOMAINE ALLIAS ★ ★ ★
VOUVRAY $16.00–$30.00

From an organically farmed five-acre site known as the Clos du Petit Mont, Dominique Allias's superb-value Vouvrays are apt to soon start turning heads internationally.

2005 Vouvray Demi Sec	90	now–2012+?

PHILIPPE ALLIET ★ ★ ★ ★
CHINON $25.00–$40.00

It has been nearly a quarter-century since Philippe Alliet consolidated his family's properties, during which time he has built one of the region's finest reputations while personally remaining remarkably reclusive. Meticulous care in the vineyards, at the press, and in the barrel cellar are assured at this address.

2005 Chinon Vieilles Vignes	88	2009–2012
2004 Chinon Vieilles Vignes	87	now
2005 Chinon L'Huisserie	88–90	2009–2014
2004 Chinon L'Huisserie	87	now
2005 Chinon Coteau de Noiré	89–91	2010–2015
2004 Chinon Coteau de Noiré	88	now–2010

YANNICK AMIRAULT ★★★★
BOURGUEIL $24.00–$40.00

Yannick Amirault has been in charge here for more than 30 years, in which time he has brought his family's *domaine* to the forefront of its appellation. Most fermentation is in mid-sized barrels, and cuvées are segregated by site, with the old vines La Petite Cave bottling definitely intended for cellaring.

2005 Bourgueil La Coudraye	89	now–2010
2005 Bourgueil La Petite Cave	88	2010–2018
2005 Bourgueil Les Quartiers	91	now–2016
2004 Bourgueil Les Quartiers	89	now
2005 St.-Nicolas de Bourgueil Les Malgagnes	90	now–2014+?

MARK ANGELI ★★★
ANJOU $25.00–$50.00

Self-styled (as per his label) *paysan solidaire* and metaphysically, biodynamically inclined vintner Mark Angeli no longer (or at least seldom) chooses to produce nobly sweet Bonnezeaux from his estate, also known as La Ferme de la Sansonnière. Instead he vinifies the fruit of this noble *terroir* to near dryness in barrel and bottles it under the humble Anjou appellation. Somehow it seems as if his rich, expansive Anjou La Lune wants to be a Bonnezeau.

2005 Anjou La Lune	88	now–2010+?

DOMAINE DES AUBUISIÈRES ★★★★
VOUVRAY $17.00–$65.00

For some time now, Bernard Fouquet has been moving the quality of his distinctive, largely stainless-steel-rendered Vouvrays into the exalted echelons of Foreau and Huët, which is to say challenging the world's finest practitioners of white wine, and at an absolutely spectacular price to quality ratio. His latest results all but confirm his arrival.

2005 Vouvray Cuvée de Silex	93	now–2014
2002 Vouvray Cuvée de Silex	91	now–2010
1997 Vouvray Cuvée Alexandre	93	now–2020
2005 Vouvray Demi-Sec Cuvée Les Girardières	90	now–2012
2003 Vouvray Le Marigny 1er Trie	95	now–2025

DOMAINE AUX MOINES ★★★★★
SAVENNIÈRES $22.00–$35.00

The mother–daughter team of Monique and Teresa Laroche keep to a time-honored (and until the last 10 to 15 years still widespread) Loire tradition of releasing wines only after some bottle age, as well as of offering selected older vintages, at unbelievably reasonable prices. If you want to plumb the mysteries of which Chenin Blanc and Loire *terroir* are capable, these wines are a must. The 1994 was spectacular at a dozen years' age.

2004 Savennières—Roche Aux Moines	90	now–2017
2002 Savennières—Roche Aux Moines	93	now–2020

MICHEL BAILLY ★★★
POUILLY-FUMÉ $19.00–$25.00

Michel Bailly crafts an especially lithe, transparent, pure though understated Pouilly-Fumé.

2005 Pouilly-Fumé Les Loges	89	now–2010

SERGE BATARD ★★★
MUSCADET $11.00–$15.00

Serge Batard's Muscadet Les Hautes Noëlles from the Côtes de Grandlieu subappellation is a perennial value, to be enjoyed within two years after its harvest.

BERNARD BAUDRY ★★★★
CHINON $18.00–$35.00

Bernard Baudry—who vinifies in wooden uprights and cement tank rather than stainless steel, insisting that temperatures largely control themselves in the former vessels—is now joined by his son Mathieu in crafting some of Chinon's finest wines, which were seldom if ever finer, he claims, than in 2005. Baudry says he once tried planting some Bordeaux clones of Cabernet Franc but is convinced that painstaking *sélection massale* from his old vines is the only route to top quality. His cuvées are segregated by exposure and soil, whether riverside sand and gravel, clay plateau, or chalky slopes.

2005 Chinon Les Granges	87	now–2010
2005 Chinon Le Domaine	88–89	now–2012
2005 Chinon Les Grézeaux	90–91	2010–2017
2004 Chinon Les Grézeaux	88	now–2010
2005 Chinon Clos Guillot	91–92	now–2014+?
2004 Chinon Clos Guillot	87	now
2005 Chinon La Croix Boissée	90–91	2010–2020
2004 Chinon La Croix Boissée	89	now–2014+?

DOMAINE DES BAUMARD ★★★★★
COTEAUX DU LAYON, QUARTS DE CHAUME, SAVENNIÈRES $20.00–$75.00

The wines from Florent Baumard's vast domaine have become the world's best-known ambassadors for their respective appellations. A remarkable depth of vintages is on offer at any given time, and the pattern of release is late (the nobly sweet 2005s having only hit the market in the autumn of 2007 and their dry counterparts in 2008). No trees are killed in the production of these wines, and at their best they exhibit superb purity of fruit. Even their "regular" bottling of Savennières is from the Clos St.-Yves vineyard, superbly situated between the Clos du Papillon and Roche Aux Moines. Their range of nobly sweet wines from the Coteaux du Layon is too gloriously diverse for us to delve into detail here. Nearly all of Baumard's bottlings have an impressive history of bottle evolution, even though they are nearly always delicious on release.

2004 Savennières	89	now–2015
2003 Savennières	88	now–2017
2002 Savennières	91	now–2019
1997 Savennières	91	now
1996 Savennières	92	now–2015
2004 Savennières Clos du Papillon	91	now–2020

2003 Savennières Clos du Papillon	90	now–2017
2002 Savennières Clos du Papillon	94	now–2014
1997 Savennières Clos du Papillon	92	now–2010
1996 Savennières Clos du Papillon	94	now–2020
2005 Coteaux du Layon Carte d'Or	89	now–2014
2004 Coteaux du Layon Carte d'Or	90	now–2017
2005 Coteaux du Layon Clos de Ste.-Catherine	91	2010–2017
2004 Coteaux du Layon Clos de Ste.-Catherine	93	now–2025
1997 Coteaux du Layon Clos de Ste.-Catherine	93	now–2015
1996 Coteaux du Layon Clos de Ste.-Catherine	94	now–2025
2005 Coteaux du Layon Cuvée Le Paon	90	now–2018
2004 Coteaux du Layon Cuvée Le Paon	92	now–2020
1997 Coteaux du Layon Cuvée Le Paon	91	now–2014
2005 Quarts de Chaume	92	now–2028
2004 Quarts de Chaume	95	now–2033
1997 Quarts de Chaume	94	now–2020
1996 Quarts de Chaume	96	now–2030

PASCAL BELLIER ★★★
CHEVERNY, COUR-CHEVERNY $14.00–$20.00

Pascal Bellier crafts consistently clear, refreshing, fascinatingly floral, musky, and mineral Cheverny.

2005 Cheverny	89	now

DOMAINE DE BELLIVIÈRE ★★★★★
COTEAUX DU LOIR, JASNIÈRES $20.00–$100.00

Christine and Eric Nicolas are not only the poster children for the renaissance of viticulture along the little Loir, whence they came a mere dozen years ago. But they have risen to the ranks of the Loire's (and thus the world's) elite white-wine practitioners, a tribute to their insight and determination as well as to the inherent potential of this once renowned but for half a century moribund region. Furthermore, they have proven the Pineau d'Aunis (Chenin Rouge) capable of profundity and ageworthiness as well. Vinification here is in *demi-muids* and *barriques*, typically around one-quarter new. Many of the whites finish with some residual sugar, especially in a ripe vintage like 2005, but the proprietors rely only on winery-internal cues and labeling conventions to signal this fact to consumers.

2005 Jasnières Calligramme	91–93	now 2018
2005 Jasnières Elixir de Tuf	94	now–2025
2005 Jasnières Les Rosiers	90	now–2014
2004 Jasnières les Rosiers	93	now–2018
2005 Aurore d'Automne [late-harvested rosé]	93	now–?
2005 Coteaux du Loire L'Effraie	90	now–2012
2004 Coteaux du Loire L'Effraie	91	now–2016
2005 Coteaux du Loir Haut-Rasné	95	now–2020+?
2005 Coteaux du Loir Vieilles Vignes Éparses	89–91	now–2015
2004 Coteaux du Loir Vieilles Vignes Éparses	92	now–2016
2005 Coteaux du Loir Hommage à Louis Derré [red]	90	2009–2012+?
2004 Coteaux du Loir Hommage à Louis Derré [red]	91	2009–2012+?
2005 Coteaux du Loir Le Rouge Gorge [red]	92	now–2011+?
2004 Coteaux du Loir Le Rouge Gorge [red]	91	2009–2012+?

FRANCIS BLANCHET ★★★★
POUILLY-FUMÉ $22.00–$28.00

Francis Blanchet's Pouilly-Fumés are consistently modest in price, yet few in the appellation consistently bottle better or more ageworthy wine. His Vieilles Vignes is from classic chalk soil and the Silice from flint. They are grown and vinified in the same way other than an often slightly later bottling for the Silice, but their flavor profiles differ dramatically and systematically.

2005 Pouilly-Fumé Vieilles Vignes	88	now–2012
2002 Pouilly-Fumé Vieilles Vignes	89	now
2005 Pouilly-Fumé Silice	90	now–2012
2003 Pouilly-Fumé Silice	92	now
2002 Pouilly-Fumé Silice	92	now

GÉRARD BOULAY ★★★★
SANCERRE $23.00–$55.00

A conscientious grower with a growing collection of old vines, Gérard Boulay crafts wines which, while delicious in youth, can often be riveting after 7 to 12 years. He recently acquired a parcel in the steep, stony Mont Damnés, from whose oldest vines he has begun bottling a separate Comtesse cuvée. With expanded acreage and a younger generation coming on, this estate might soon be joining the roster of Loire elite.

2005 Sancerre	88	now
2005 Sancerre Clos de Beaujeu	91	now–2014
2004 Sancerre Clos de Beaujeu	89	now–2010
2002 Sancerre Clos de Beaujeu	92	now–2014
2005 Sancerre Mont Damnés	91	now–2014
2005 Sancerre Comtesse	93	now–2018+?
2005 Sancerre Rosé	88	now

CLAUDE BRANGER ★★★★
MUSCADET $11.00–$15.00

Do you think you should avoid "old" Muscadet? Then avoid Claude Branger's late-released Muscadet de Sèvre et Maine Sur Lie Le Fils Les Gras Moutons at your own risk of sensory impoverishment! The 2004 was at its peak in 2007. His "regular" bottling represents good, if less spectacular, value.

ANDRÉ-MICHEL BRÉGEON ★★★
MUSCADET $13.00–$14.00

Brégeon is a perpetual source of Muscadet de Sèvre et Maine Sur Lie with character and a modest price.

CATHERINE ET PIERRE BRÉTON ★★★★
BOURGUEIL $20.00–$40.00

The Brétons have become icons among France's sustainable-viticulture set, advocates of low-sulfur wine (meaning you should lay away bottles only at genuine cellar temperature), and friends of Cabernet Franc. Pierre Bréton tailors his vinifications with impressive sensitivity and adaptation to a diversity of *terroirs* and styles. He has a family reputation to uphold, as one can taste century-old Bourgueil from his grandfather that is still hauntingly lovely, neither acetified nor oxidized.

2005 Bourgueil Trinch!	88	now
2005 Bourgueil Clos Sénéchal	89–91	2010–2018+?
2004 Bourgueil Clos Sénéchal	90	now–2014
2005 Bourgueil Les Galichets	89	now
2005 Bourgueil Nuits d'Ivresse	89–90	2010–2015
2004 Bourgueil Nuits d'Ivresse	88	2009–2011
2005 Bourgueil Les Perrières	90–92	2010–2022
2004 Bourgueil Les Perrières	88–89	2009–2015

DOMAINE DE LA BUTTE ★★★
BOURGUEIL $18.00–$40.00

Jacky Blot of the Domaine de la Taille Aux Loups in Montlouis has operated the Domaine de la Butte in Bourgueil since 2002, quickly vindicating his choice of location as well as his red-wine-making talents. In all likelihood he will be near the forefront of his appellation within only a few more years. His cuvées follow a classic French progression: Le Pied from the lighter soils near the base of the Butte, Les Perrières from the "kidney" of the slope, and Le Haut from the rocky top. Mi-Pente comes from a single parcel of old vines.

2005 Bourgueil Le Pied de la Butte	87	now
2005 Bourgueil Le Haut de la Butte	88	now–2011+?
2005 Bourgueil Mi-Pente	91–92	2010–2018+?
2005 Bourgueil Les Perrières	90	now–2014+?

DOMAINE CADY ★★★
COTEAUX DU LAYON $30.00–$120.00

Philippe Cady is an excellent source for Coteaux du Layon values vinified entirely in tank, and generally available in a range of vintages, in some of which his Les Varennes (from schist) excels and in some his Chaumes, from chalk-clay soil.

2005 Coteaux du Layon St.-Aubin Les Varennes	89	now–2013
2004 Coteaux du Layon St.-Aubin Les Varennes	88	now–2012
2005 Cuvée Volupté Sélection de Grains Nobles	90–92	now–2025
2004 Cuvée Volupté Sélection de Grains Nobles	90	now–2020

A. CAILBOURDIN ★★★
POUILLY–FUMÉ $21.00–$26.00

Alain Cailbourdin remains a consistently reliable source of Pouilly-Fumé, although his Les Cris can make a pungently emphatic but rather austere statement. The Boisfleury reflects its flint in a more generous, floral, lushly fruited character.

2005 Pouilly-Fumé Les Cris	87	2009–2011
2005 Pouilly-Fumé Cuvée de Boisfleury	88	now–2010

JACQUES CARROY ★★★
POUILLY–FUMÉ $18.00–$20.00

Jacques Carroy appears to have stayed under the proverbial radar screen until now, but his blazingly intense, fantastically clinging 2005 effort was just all in a year's work for him. This grower seems destined to be a future star of his appellation.

2005 Pouilly-Fumé	91	now–2012+?

FRANÇOIS CAZIN–LE PETIT CHAMBORD ★ ★ ★ ★
CHEVERNY, COUR-CHEVERNY $15.00–$38.00

François Cazin crafts wines that serve as benchmarks for his appellations as well as providing truly amazing value. He boasts a high average age of vines, bottles by gravity, and obviously is unafraid and able to harvest very ripe, yet with superb acid retention even in an inherently soft vintage like 2005. His Cheverny should be enjoyed within three to four years of the vintage, but his rich, off-dry Cour-Cheverny might age in bottle for more than a decade.

2005 Cheverny	91	now
2004 Cour-Cheverny Cuvée Renaissance	93	now–2014+?

CHÉREAU-CARRÉ ★ ★ ★ ★ ★
MUSCADET $13.00–$35.00

Each wine from the large Chéreau-Carré family of Muscadet is named for its particular property or cuvée. Their Château de la Chesnaire Muscadet de Sèvre et Maine Sur Lie, which is meant to be enjoyed young, is so invigorating and refreshing that if you don't find yourself going back for the next sip, somebody should check your pulse. The Château de Chasseloir Comte Leloup de Chasseloir Muscadet de Sèvre et Maine Sur Lie Cuvée des Ceps Centenaires is distinguished by having one of the longest names in wine-labeling history; coming from 100-and-more-year-old vines in a phylloxera-proof limestone-rich *terroir* unusual for Muscadet; never being released with fewer than three years in bottle; being able to age fascinatingly for more than a decade in good vintages; and representing one of the most remarkable wine values on the planet. Le Clos du Château l'Oiselinière Muscadet de Sèvre et Maine Sur Lie— grown in a sheltered, riverside site of eroded orthogneiss and schist—is as complex as Muscadet can get (which is very!).

2002 Château de Chasseloir Comte Leloup de Chasseloir Muscadet de Sèvre et Maine Sur Lie Cuvée des Ceps Centenaires	92	now–2010
2002 Le Clos du Château l'Oiselinière Muscadet de Sèvre et Maine Sur Lie	93	now–2010

DIDIER ET CATHERINE CHAMPALOU ★ ★ ★ ★
VOUVRAY $15.00–$40.00

The Champalou's dry and off-dry Vouvrays have become among the most frequently seen on U.S. restaurant lists and no wonder, given both their phenomenal quality-to-price rapport and their style. Their basic bottling is what is called in Vouvray *sec tendre,* barely off-dry. *Fondraux* is effectively *demi-sec,* and Le Portail dry and matured in new barrels. However, no one save for a private customer or others very familiar with them could be expected to recognize these winery-internal conventions.

2005 Vouvray	90	now–2011
2005 Vouvray Cuvée des Fondraux	92	now–2014
2005 Vouvray Le Clos du Portail	87	now

DOMAINE DE LA CHANTELEUSERIE ★ ★ ★
BOURGUEIL $15.00–$25.00

Thierry Boucard's Bourgueils from the Domaine de la Chanteleuserie and the downright ridiculous value they offer should win many new converts to the cause of Loire Cabernet Franc. These are very fruit-forward wines. Boucard's only 2005 cuvée about which I had slight reservations was that done in barrel.

2005 Bourgueil Cuvée Alouettes	89	now–2010
2005 Bourgueil Cuvée Vieilles Vignes	89	now–2012+?

FRANÇOIS CHIDAINE ★★★★★
MONTLOUIS, VOUVRAY $27.00–$80.00

Chidaine senior had already made some of the best wines in the Montlouis appellation, but from the time in the mid-'90s that his son began to care for a portion of his family's estate François Chidaine has pushed the envelope on quality to world class. In the process he has adopted biodynamic methods (though preferring to soft-pedal this topic), dropping his yields on dry wines to levels normally associated only with nobly sweet Chenin Blanc, and practicing successive passes over nearly every parcel. In 2002, Chidaine ambitiously took control (via rental) of the estate of Prince Poniatowski in Vouvray, doing glorious justice to twice the acreage and nearly twice the number of individual cuvées that he had previously. The wines are fermented in 600-liter (about 160 gallons) *demi-muids* of varying but youthful ages and linger through spring on their lees. They are never labeled with the traditional designations *sec, demi-sec,* or *moelleux,* but instead certain styles are associated with the same sites or cuvées every year (and nobly sweet *moelleux* is rarely essayed). Les Tuffeaux, Clos Habert, and Le Bouchet are in varying degrees sweet.

2005 Montlouis Clos du Breuil	90	now–2014
2005 Montlouis Les Bournais	91	now–2015
2005 Montlouis Les Tuffeaux	94	now–2018
2002 Montlouis Les Tuffeaux	90	now–2012
2005 Montlouis Clos Habert	93	2010–2020
2005 Vouvray Clos Baudoin	90	now–2013
2005 Vouvray Les Argiles	92	now–2017
2005 Vouvray Le Bouchet	91	2010–2018+?

GILBERT CHON ★★★
MUSCADET $12.00–$14.00

Chon's flowery, almost Riesling-like Château de la Salminière and Clos de la Chapelle from the Sèvre et Maine represent yet more remarkable Muscadet values.

2005 Clos de la Chapelle Muscadet de Sèvre et Maine Sur Lie	90	now

DANIEL CHOTARD ★★★
SANCERRE $22.00–$24.00

Jazz musician and former teacher Daniel Chotard appears to have a fine nose for Sauvignon and Sancerre if his long, clear, nuanced 2005 is to be trusted. This is a name to watch.

2005 Sancerre	89	now–2012+?

DOMAINE DU CLOSEL—CHÂTEAU DES VAULTS ★★★
SAVENNIÈRES $25.00–$40.00

The domaine of the de Jessey family has been the source for some remarkable Savennières, but these have generally not been easy wines to approach, much less cuddle up to, in their youth. A generational change seems likely to bring a slightly more approachable style. (The name of the domaine, too, is changing to that of the family château.) Occasionally there is an off-dry bottling.

2005 Savennières Clos du Papillon	87	2010–2014
2005 Savennières La Jalousie	88	now–2010

CLOS ROCHE BLANCHE ✱✱✱
TOURAINE $12.00–$14.00

Self-taught vintners Catherine Roussel and Didier Barrouillet are particularly well known among French advocates of sustainable viticulture. Their inexpensive Sauvignon and Cabernet Franc prove to be brimming with fascinating aromas and flavors while never forgetting their primary duty to quench thirst.

2005 Touraine Sauvignon	88	now
2005 Touraine Cabernet	87	now

CLOS ROUGEARD ✱✱✱✱✱
SAUMUR, SAUMUR-CHAMPIGNY $50.00–$125.00

Over the past several decades, as the Foucault brothers Nadi and Charlie became cult figures on the French wine scene—replete with an unmarked winery, customer waiting lists, and high prices—their remarkable Saumur-Champigny went relatively unnoticed (and of course virtually unavailable, that being the case at home already) in the United States. Their remarkable wines indeed demonstrate the heights of vinous complexity and ageability to which Cabernet Franc and its growers can aspire along the Loire, and a level which the Foucaults clearly hope and expect that some of their neighbors too will one day reach. The methods in the Foucaults' frigid cellars are much as they would have been two generations ago, little augmented by technology, with long fermentations and wines bottled after only two years in small barrels of mixed ages, typically possessed of almost powdery fine, though abundant, tannins. A Le Clos bottling is assembled from several small parcels and is lower priced than their other offerings. The Foucaults generally bottle only one white, which completely transcends the other wines of the Saumur appellation. Occasionally, in years of truly widespread and noble rot, there is a sweet Coteaux Saumur from this small parcel instead.

2005 Saumur Brézé	92–93	2009–2015
2003 Saumur Brézé	89	now–2010
2002 Saumur Brézé	94	now–2014
2005 Saumur-Champigny Les Poyeux	91–92	2010–2017
2003 Saumur-Champigny Les Poyeux	90	2012–2015+?
2002 Saumur-Champigny Les Poyeux	90	now–2014
2005 Saumur-Champigny Le Bourg	94–95	2010–2025
2003 Saumur-Champigny Le Bourg	91	2014–2017+?
2002 Saumur-Champigny Le Bourg	92	now–2017

DOMAINE DES CORBILLIÈRES ✱✱✱
TOURAINE $12.00–$15.00

The pioneers with Sauvignon in Touraine, the Barbou family—now growing that grape for a fourth generation and having supplied the U.S. for more than a quarter-century—are responsible for the Sauvignon with virtually the finest price-to-quality rapport on the planet. Their Cabernet Franc is archetypal for this variety in its notes of blackberries, machine oil, toasted walnut, and licorice.

2005 Touraine Cabernet	89	now–2010
2005 Touraine Sauvignon	90	now

FRANÇOIS COTAT ✱✱✱✱✱
SANCERRE $35.00–$55.00

Working from the same facility shared for decades by his uncle and father Francis and Paul Cotat, François Cotat has replaced some of their ancient barrels, but in the main he follows the ultratraditional practices of the previous generation, presumably thereby preserving the legendary richness, complexity, and ageability of his Cotat Sancerres from the slopes of Chavignol. (Even the Pinot rosé from here can safely age for a few years.) From time to time the government wine watchdogs find some reason (such as low-level residual sugar) to refuse Cotat the right to label his wines as *appellation contrôlée*, so occasionally you may see vintages with the vineyard designations but not the appellation Sancerre on the label. From time to time, too, there are late-harvested *cuvées speciales*.

2005 Sancerre Les Monts Damnés	91	now–2015
2004 Sancerre Les Monts Damnés	89	now–2014
2002 Sancerre Les Monts Damnés	90	now–2012
2005 Sancerre Culs de Beaujeu	92	now–2018
2004 Sancerre Culs de Beaujeu	90	now–2016
2002 Sancerre Culs de Beaujeu	93	now–2011
2005 Sancerre La Grande Côte	93	now–2018
2004 Sancerre La Grande Côte	89	now–2014
2002 Sancerre La Grande Côte	95	now–2014
2005 Sancerre Rosé	88	now–2011

PASCAL COTAT ★ ★ ★ ★ ★
SANCERRE $38.00–$50.00

Less than two years after Francis and Paul Cotat separated their wine-making activities and Paul's son François took over his share of that domaine, Francis's son Pascal elected to cut back on his work as an automotive plastic surgeon and begin making the wine for the other half of the Cotat clan. In 1999, a facility was set up on the property of the family's Fiat dealership and garage in Sancerre. Each year, Pascal Cotat's wines have displayed increasing authority. Some of the same considerations apply to these wines as to those of François: Should you find a wine labeled *vin de table* rather than Sancerre, do not fret. Do not ignore the rosé, and keep your eye out for the occasional *cuvée speciale*.

2005 Sancerre Les Monts Damnés	93	now–2017
2004 Sancerre Les Monts Damnés	90	now–2014
2003 Sancerre Les Monts Damnés	92	now
2002 Sancerre Les Monts Damnés	92	now–2012
2005 Sancerre La Grande Côte	92	now–2017
2003 Sancerre La Grande Côte	90	now
2002 Sancerre La Grande Côte	95	now–2014

CHÂTEAU DU COULAINE ★ ★ ★
CHINON $17.00–$50.00

The 2005 intro-level wine from Étienne and Pascale de Bonnaventure was long on charm, but this estate gets very serious in the upper echelons of its range, with wines that in strong vintages need time in the cellar.

2005 Chinon	89	now–2010

LUCIEN CROCHET ★ ★ ★ ★
SANCERRE $24.00–$85.00

Lucien Crochet crafts one of the finest and most diverse collections of wine from Sancerre, including one of the most (few!) successful *barrique*-aged versions (LC) and a late-picked cuvée.

2005 Sancerre	89	now–2010
2005 Sancerre La Croix du Roy	91	now–2012
2005 Sancerre Le Chêne	92	now–2014
2002 Sancerre Cuvée LC	90	now
2002 Sancerre Vendange du 19 Octobre	91	now–2012

JEAN DABIN ET FILS ★ ★ ★
MUSCADET $11.00–$13.00

Dabin's Muscadets from the Domaine Gilarderie and Domaine Gras-Moutons can be Chablis-like in their suggestions of minerals and their depth. They represent fabulous values to enjoy within two to three years after the harvest.

2005 Domaine Gras-Moutons Muscadet de Sèvre et Maine Sur Lie	90	now

DIDIER DAGUENEAU ★ ★ ★ ★ ★
POUILLY-FUMÉ $45.00–$100.00

Undoubtedly the Loire's most flamboyant vigneron and wines inhabit this address. Dague-neau's use of new wood with Sauvignon is the most adept anywhere in the world. In addition to four levels of Pouilly-Fumé (the Buisson Rénard is from an especially distinctive single site), Dagueneau occasionally crafts a late-harvested cuvée and is now beginning to farm land on the Mont Damnés in Sancerre.

2005 Blanc Fumé de Pouilly	91	now–2011
2004 Blanc Fumé de Pouilly	90	now
2005 Blanc Fumé de Pouilly Buisson Renard	90	2009–2013
2005 Blanc Fumé de Pouilly Pur Sang	92	now–2015
2005 Blanc Fumé de Pouilly Silex	94	now–2018
2004 Blanc Fumé de Pouilly Silex	91	now–2012

SERGE DAGUENEAU ★ ★ ★ ★
POUILLY-FUMÉ $22.00–$25.00

The domaine of the famous Didier Dagueneau's uncle turns out a rich, lush, consistently ex-cellent Pouilly-Fumé. Serge's two daughters have put in time in California, but the approach here does not involve new wood.

2005 Pouilly-Fumé Les Pentes	91	now–2012

VINCENT DELAPORTE ★ ★ ★
SANCERRE $24.00–$45.00

Delaporte's Sancerres have long been among the most dependable and widely distributed in the U.S. His Cuvée Maxime is generally one of the more successful barrel-fermented efforts from this appellation, preserving its distinctive citric, herbal, and mineral characteristics.

2005 Sancerre	88	now
2004 Sancerre Cuvée Maxime	87	now

DOMAINE DELETANG ★ ★ ★
MONTLOUIS $20.00–$50.00

There was some rearrangement of the Deletang family holdings in recent years, with a slight dip in quality at what was long Montlouis's premier address, but the signs are that Olivier Deletang will bring the quality back to its former level.

2005 Montlouis Demi-Sec Les Batisses	87	2009–2012

MARC DESCHAMPS * * *
POUILLY-FUMÉ $20.00–$40.00

Marc Deschamps turns out a range of bottlings, of which that from the Champs de Cri vineyard is the most promising.

2005 Pouilly-Fumé Les Vignes de Berge	87	now
2005 Pouilly-Fumé Les Champs de Cri	88	now–2011

DOMAINE DES DORICES * * * *
MUSCADET $11.00–$18.00

The Boullaut family are among those who stand the conventional wisdom about Muscadet on its head. They call one cuvée Grande Garde and do not even release it before four or five years of bottle age, at which point you do not have to rush to drink it! Anything that this cuvée lacks in primary fruit it more than makes up with an impression not unlike that of many a mature Grüner Veltliner. Their Hermine d'Or cuvée is almost Sancerre- or Pouilly-Fumé-like in its aromatics and its salty, stony suggestions, and their Cuvée Choisie is a lovely old-vine selection for enjoying within three years of harvest.

2005 Muscadet de Sèvre et Maine Sur Lie Hermine d'Or	90	now
2000 Muscadet de Sèvre et Maine Sur Lie Grande Garde	92	now

PIERRE-JACQUES DRUET * * *
BOURGUEIL $20.00–$80.00

Druet was once the reference point for his appellation—any who have tasted his 1989s will have experienced all that Cabernet Franc can attain in these soils. Quality has been less sure in recent vintages, and one hopes that the highly vocal and opinionated Druet will once again deliver promising messages in the bottle. Druet releases his wines only after bottle maturation. His better 2005s had not yet been tasted in time for this edition.

DOMAINE DE L'ÉCU * * * *
MUSCADET $16.00–$18.00

The consistently masterful Guy Bossard is dedicated heart and soul to the proposition that wines of distinction will be those most distinctively marked by their *terroir*. Each label depicts the soil in question with photographic clarity. That Bossard isn't wasting his time and each wine indeed has its own personality should go without saying. Granite how few wine lovers are willing to take Muscadet seriously, it would be gneiss to see consumers buy the entire set of these and taste them for themselves. (There's no schist here: This well-known component of much Muscadet is apparently missing from Bossard's properties, or else is thought too prosaic to mention.) Enjoy these wines within three to four years of harvest.

2005 Muscadet de Sèvre et Maine Sur Lie Expression de Granite	90	now
2005 Muscadet de Sèvre et Maine Sur Lie Expression d'Orthogneiss	89	now
2005 Muscadet de Sèvre et Maine Sur Lie Expression de Gneiss	90	now

CHÂTEAU D'EPIRÉ ★★★
SAVENNIÈRES $20.00–$30.00

The tank-rendered Savennières of Château d'Epiré can be quite elegant and refreshing for their appellation, although the wines from some concentrated vintages are inaccessible in their youth. Occasionally a special off-dry or sweet cuvée is rendered.

2004 Savennières Cuvée Speciale	89	now–2012

CHÂTEAU DE LA FESSARDIÈRE ★★★
MUSCADET $13.00–$14.00

Working outside any of Muscadet's subregions and in a combination of concrete vat and Fuder, Alexis Sauvion crafts a distinctively and infectiously delicious Muscadet.

2005 Muscadet	90	now

PHILIPPE FOREAU DOMAINE DU CLOS NAUDIN ★=★★★
VOUVRAY $25.00–$100.00

Philippe Foreau is one of the most scrupulous growers and *vinificateurs* as well as one of the most adept tasters in all of France. Vinification here is entirely in small older barrels (save for the base wine for his consistently superb sparkling Brut), and the wines—often riveting even in "lesser" (sec-only) years such as 2004 and 2006—age phenomenally well. The wines of Philippe's grandfather from the 1940s are still fresh today, and unspeakably beautiful.

2005 Vouvray Sec	89	now–2012
2005 Vouvray Demi-Sec	93	now–2020
1997 Vouvray Demi-Sec	92	now–2014
2005 Vouvray Moelleux	91	now–2025
1997 Vouvray Moelleux	91	now–2020
1995 Vouvray Moelleux	91	now–2012
2005 Vouvray Moelleux Réserve	96	now–2035
1997 Vouvray Moelleux Réserve	95	now–2029
1995 Vouvray Moelleux Réserve	97	now–2022

DOMAINE FOUASSIER PÈRE ET FILS ★★★
SANCERRE $20.00–$40.00

Fouassier turns out no fewer than six different cuvées of Sancerre, most reflecting distinctive sites and soils. Clos Paradis, for example, is from classic chalk, while Les Romains designates a flint-dominated site.

2005 Sancerre Les Grands Groux	87	now
2005 Sancerre Clos Paradis	89	now
2005 Sancerre Les Romains	90	now

DOMAINE DE LA GARRELIÈRE ★★★
TOURAINE, CHINON $13.00–$25.00

On the roster of astonishing Loire overachievers can be placed near its head the names of François and Pascale Plouzeau, whose unexpectedly lush, luscious, and positively dense yet floral and refreshing Sauvignon is a revelation. Their Cendrillon adds 15% barrel-fermented Chardonnay and (depending on vintage) some Chenin for an effect slightly reminiscent of very good Austrian Grüner Veltliner. The Plouzeaus also craft Chinon at the Château de la Bonnelière.

2005 Touraine Sauvignon	90	now
2005 Touraine Cendrillon	90	now–2010

PHILIPPE GILBERT ★ ★ ★
MENETOU-SALON $22.00–$35.00

That Philippe Gilbert is clearly one of if not the most talented vintner in his appellation is proven by his complex, rich, silken textured, yet persistently juicy and invigorating "regular" 2005 bottling. And there will also have been a special cuvée from that vintage.

2005 Menetou-Salon	90	now

BERTRAND GRAILLOT ★ ★ ★
COTEAUX DU GIÉNNOIS $12.00–$15.00

Graillot is a young grower outside Sancerre who at least so far has bottled Sauvignon only from vines across the river and north of Pouilly-Fumé. The results are highly appetizing and intriguing, rich, palate coating, and lees-inflected.

2005 Coteaux du Giennois	89	now

JACQUES GUINDON ★ ★ ★
MUSCADET $11.00–$13.00

The preeminent grower in the Coteaux de la Loire (east of Savenièrres and the sole Muscadet appellation along the river Loire itself), Jacques Guindon achieves consistently excellent (and remarkably ageworthy) results from the fruits of his oldest vines, bottled under the name Prestige.

2005 Muscadet des Coteaux de la Loire Sur Lie Prestige	90	now–2010

DOMAINE DES HERBAUGES ★ ★ ★
MUSCADET $10.00–$13.00

Jérôme and Luc Choblet's succulent and refreshing Muscadet from the Côtes de Grandlieu subappellation comes in a ridiculously inexpensive Clos de la Fine version and an only slightly more expensive Clos de la Sénaigerie, grown on mica-schist, that tastes like it was crossed with dry Mosel Riesling and Chablis.

2005 Muscadet Côtes de Grandlieu Clos de la Sénaigerie	90	now

DOMAINE HUËT ★ ★ ★ ★ ★
VOUVRAY $27.00–$180.00

Noël Pinguet, son-in-law of the late, much-lamented Gaston Huët, continues to direct operations at this venerable estate in which an American, Anthony Hwang, now owns the controlling interest. There is no indication that quality has skipped a beat, with the domaine having made the best (strictly for early drinking) of difficult vintages in 2004 and 2006 (when much was left unpicked) and fielded an outstanding collection of ageworthy 2005s that approaches the quality of 2002. The practice here of offering a wide range of vintages also continues. Like so many proponents of biodynamic viticulture, Pinguet asserts that it has made a qualitative difference and rendered wines more distinctly reflective of their *terroir,* while at the same time professing ignorance as to why it works. Even the sparkling wines here are outstanding and ageworthy. Each site here has its distinct geology, microclimate, and personality. Wines from the great vintages of the '40s and '50s are profound and still fresh, so the prognoses noted below may well prove conservative. The estate's legendary Cuvée Constance represents a berry-by-berry selection.

2005 Vouvray Sec Le Haut-Lieu	89	2009–2014
2002 Vouvray Sec Le Haut-Lieu	91	now–2012
2005 Vouvray Sec Le Mont	90	2009–2014
2005 Vouvray Sec Clos du Bourg	90	2010–2018
2005 Vouvray Demi-Sec Le Mont	90	2010–2022
2002 Vouvray Demi-Sec Le Mont	93	now–2020
2005 Vouvray Demi-Sec Clos du Bourg	92	now–2022
2005 Vouvray Moelleux Le Haut Lieu	92	2012–2025
1997 Vouvray Moelleux Le Haut-Lieu 1ère Trie	94	now–2020
2005 Vouvray Moelleux Le Mont	91	now–2025
1997 Vouvray Moelleux Le Mont	90	now–2014
2005 Vouvray Moelleux Le Mont 1ère Trie	90	2012–2027+?
1997 Vouvray Moelleux Le Mont 1ère Trie	96	now–2025
2005 Vouvray Moelleux Clos du Bourg Moelleux 1ère Trie	94	2014–2030
1997 Vouvray Moelleux Clos du Bourg 1ère Trie	95	now–2025
2005 Vouvray Cuvée Constance	96	2016–2050
1999 Vouvray Cuvée Constance	99	now–2045

DOMAINE DENIS JAMAIN ★ ★ ★
REUILLY $17.00–$20.00

Denis Jamain's Pinot Noir is excellent, his Pinot Gris fascinating, and his Sauvignon sets new standards for the always very affordable wines of this appellation.

2005 Reuilly Les Pierre Plates	90	now

CHARLES JOGUET ★ ★ ★
CHINON $19.00–$50.00

Charles Joguet personally retired from winemaking nearly a decade ago. In 2005, his longtime righthand, Michel Pinard, turned over the vineyard and cellar direction to seven-year veteran François-Xavier Barc. The best of the current crops here are highly satisfying and Barc is clearly quality conscious, harboring impressive intentions for the future evolution of this traditionally benchmark estate. Several fruitier reds from alluvial and gravel soils are raised in tank, and those from better sites undergo malolactic fermentation and maturation in barrels of assorted age. Joguet was once the reference point for Chinon, and the vineyard holdings remain superb. Franc de Pied refers to ungrafted vines. The estate's oldest, most-famous vines are in the Clos de la Dioterie.

2005 Chinon Les Petites Roches	87	now
2005 Chinon Cuvée de la Cure	87	now
2005 Chinon Les Varennes du Grand Clos	88–89	2010–2014
2005 Chinon Les Varennes du Grand Clos		
Franc de Pied	90	2011–2017
2005 Chinon Clos du Chêne Vert	87–89	2010–2015
1995 Chinon Clos du Chêne Vert	89	now
2003 Chinon Clos de la Dioterie	90	2009–2015+?
1995 Chinon Clos de la Dioterie Vieilles Vignes	90	now–2012

NICOLAS JOLY—CHÂTEAU DE LA ROCHE AUX MOINES ★ ★ ★ ★
SAVENNIÈRES $35.00–$100.00

The high priest of biodynamics, or at least certainly today's best-known spokesperson for this viticultural movement, Nicolas Joly's moral and metaphysical fervor can leave one wondering whether taste might not be beside the point, but his wines are full of intense, complex flavors.

They can sometimes, as with the 2004s, darken and take on an apparently oxidized character as they stand open for a few hours, although they remain fascinating and traditionally reward cellaring. To beware is the tendency displayed in some recent vintages—notably 2005—to show every bit of their 14.5% to 15% alcohol, which one worries may never integrate. The Coulée de Serrant is a Joly *monopole* that, along with its neighboring subappellation Roche aux Moines, has historically been treated as a Loire grand cru.

2004 Savennières Les Clos Sacrés	91	now–2010+?
2004 Savennières—Roche aux Moines Clos de la Bergerie	92	2010–2013+?
1992 Savennières—Roche aux Moines Clos de la Bergerie	90	now
2004 Savennières—Coulée de Serrant	92	2009–2014+?

BARON PATRICK DE LADOUCETTE ★★★★
POUILLY-FUMÉ, SANCERRE $16.00–$40.00

Long the best known and one of the biggest producers of Pouilly-Fumé, Ladoucette continues to impress with its flagship wine of richness, depth, and ageability. The corresponding Sancerre Comte Lafond, assembled from four villages, has always been impressive as well, and La Poussie—from a uniquely 360-degree amphitheatrical, geologically diverse site in Bué—is formidably concentrated and needs time. The basic, nonappellation Sauvignon Blanc from Ladoucette is good value but should be drunk within two years of its harvest.

2005 Sancerre La Poussie	88	now–2012
2005 Sancerre Comte Lafond	89	now–2010
2005 Pouilly-Fumé	91	2009–2015

JOSEPH LANDRON—DOMAINE DE LA LOUVETRIE ★★★★
MUSCADET $11.00–$25.00

Jo Landron, a walking encyclopedia of Muscadet, farms a diverse range of *terroirs,* showcasing them in bottlings of consistently high quality too numerous to detail here, the best of which deserve to be savored not just in their youth but over several years. Special highlights include his Hermine d'Or, from 40+-year-old vines in gneiss, sand, and chalk; Le Fief du Breil, from a quartz- and flint-rich site that Landron calls "a hill by local standards"; and a barrel-fermented, lees-stirred, late-bottled cuvée grown on quartz-rich orthogneiss soil he calls Haute Tradition.

2005 Muscadet de Sèvre et Maine Sur Lie Hermine d'Or	89	now
2005 Muscadet de Sèvre et Maine Le Fief du Breil	90	now
2004 Muscadet de Sèvre et Maine Le Fief du Breil	91	now
2004 Muscadet de Sèvre et Maine Haute Tradition	89	now

DAMIEN LAUREAU ★★★★
SAVENNIÈRES $24.00–$36.00

Damien Laureau is one of several new talents to emerge in Savennières, and a quite exciting one. Laureau's vines grow in some of the highest vineyards in that appellation, on schist and a rare black metamorphic rock called phanite. His Bel Ouvrage cuvée is selectively harvested and matured in barrel. Laureau's wines avoid the youthful austerity of many Savennières. Only time and a track record in bottle can really tell how they will age.

2005 Savennières Les Genêts	89	now–2011+?
2004 Savennières Les Genêts	88	now–2011+?
2005 Savennières Le Bel Ouvrage	91	now–2014+?
2004 Savennières Le Bel Ouvrage	91	now–2014+?

RICHARD LEROY ★ ★ ★ ★
ANJOU, COTEAUX DU LAYON $35.00–$100.00

A Paris banker-turned-winegrower, Richard Leroy is turning heads in France for both his dry wines and his Coteaux du Layon. Adept use of older barrels and long lees contact do not in any way interfere with the expression in Leroy's two 2005 Anjou bottlings of what one would be hard pressed to avoid calling the expression of fruits and flowers set off by schistic *terroir*.

2005 Anjou Sec Le Clos des Rouliers	91	now–2012+?
2005 Anjou Sec Les Noëls de Montbenault	92	now–2012+?

DOMAINE LUNEAU-PAPIN ★ ★ ★ ★ ★
MUSCADET $14.00–$26.00

Pierre and Monique Luneau-Papin are among those Muscadet vignerons offering a range of different bottles from individual microclimates too numerous to mention all of them here. They also release their wines at a leisurely pace, considering the freshness and complexity of one four-year-old release from these cellars it is no wonder. Cast aside any preconceptions and wallow in the refreshing satisfaction and wonder that these wines instill.

2005 Muscadet de Sèvre et Maine Sur Lie Clos des Allées	90	now–2010
2005 Muscadet de Sèvre et Maine Sur Lie le L d'Or	90	now–2011
2004 Muscadet de Sèvre et Maine Sur Lie le L d'Or	91	now
2002 Muscadet de Sèvre et Maine Clos des Noëlles (Semper Excelsior)	92	now

DOMAINE MARDON ★ ★ ★
QUINCY $14.00–$18.00

Domaine Mardon has long been recognized as a leader in tiny Quincy, and its top bottling, the Cuvée Tres Vieilles Vignes, is quite lush and refined by appellation standards.

2005 Quincy Cuvée Très Vieilles Vignes	89	now

HENRY MARIONNET ★ ★ ★ ★
TOURAINE $14.00–$80.00

Henry Marionnet, who is gradually handing his domaine off to his son Jean-Sébastien, bottles among others a consistently delicious Sauvignon from pebbly, flint-rich *perruche* soil. Occasionally there is a Sauvignon M, a long-keeping, late-harvested elixir from old vines. From among if not the oldest wine-bearing vines on the planet—verified to have been planted (ungrafted, of course) in 1850—Marionnet crafts a tiny amount of remarkable wine of *cépage* Romorantin called Provignage.

2005 Domaine de la Charmoise Touraine Sauvignon	89	now
1997 Touraine Sauvignon M	89	now
2005 Provignage	92	now–2017+?
2000 Provignage	91	now–2014+?

ALPHONSE MELLOT ★ ★ ★ ★
SANCERRE $15.00–$65.00

Alphonse Mellot has been running the domaine of his eponymous father and grandfather for 17 years, since he was 20. In addition to concentrated, barrel-rendered whites, he gives an amazing demonstration of what is possible with Pinot Noir in the Sancerre appellation, although the results are less convincing in the dimensions of textural nuance or mystery than in terms of sheer fruit and tannin extraction and expert use of new wood. Edmond is released only after several years in bottle, at which point it displays admirable polish, richness, and depth.

2005 Sancerre Generation XIX	89	now–2012
2005 Sancerre Rouge La Moussière	89	now–2010?
2005 Sancerre Rouge Generation XIX	89	now–2012?
2005 Sancerre Rouge Grands Champs	88	now–2012+?
2002 Sancerre Edmond	90	now–2010

THIERRY MERLIN-CHERRIER ★ ★ ★ ★
SANCERRE $22.00–$32.00

Based on his results in 2005 and in the challenging 2004 vintage, to say that Thierry Merlin is one of the unsung stars of Bué would be an understatement. Few have better rendered the inherent richness and complexity of the great Chêne Marchand vineyard. Merlin planted cover crops for a decade on his small parcel of this site to bring health and balance to vines planted by his predecessor in the early 1990s. It obviously worked!

2005 Sancerre	90	now–2010
2002 Sancerre	90	now
2005 Sancerre Le Chêne Marchand	91–92	now–2014+?
2004 Sancerre Le Chêne Marchand	92	now–2012+?

ERIC MORGAT ★ ★ ★
SAVENNIÈRES $32.00–$35.00

Eric Morgat is another one of his region's new potential stars, crafting gripping, mouth-filling, and almost certainly highly ageworthy Savennières from holdings near Roche aux Moines.

2004 Savennières	90	2009–2014+?

GÉRARD ET PIERRE MORIN ★ ★ ★ ★
SANCERRE $22.00–$30.00

Pierre Morin is taking over from his father, and to say that quality isn't suffering would be gross understatement. For the first time chez Morin (encouraged by their importer, Peter Weygandt) there was in 2005 a separate, unfiltered cuvée from their old vines in Bué's most famous vineyard, the Chêne Marchand, to go with the Vieilles Vignes cuvée on which they had already been collaborating. (These are the cuvées rated below.) The Ovide is named for the previous owner of one plot of very old vines. Morin is serious about Pinot Noir, too.

2005 Sancerre Vieilles Vignes	90	now–2012
2005 Sancerre Chêne Marchand	93	now–2015+?
2005 Sancerre Cuvée Ovide	91	2009–2013+?
2004 Sancerre Rouge	87	now

MOULIN TOUCHAIS ★ ★ ★
COTEAUX DU LAYON $35.00–$100.00

An iconic Loire estate, Moulin Touchais ferments in stainless and bottles after only six to eight months, then holds the wine back for at least a decade. These may not count among the elite of their appellation in any given vintage, but the opportunity to benefit from maturation, at reasonable prices, should not be missed.

1989 Coteaux du Layon	91	now–2010
1985 Coteaux du Layon	90	now

HENRY NATTER ✳✳✳
SANCERRE $22.00–$30.00

Fermented spontaneously in older barrels but then moved to tank, Henry Natter's basic bottling of Sancerre is highly impressive. His top bottling comes from the Chêne Marchand.

2005 Sancerre	91	now–2011
2002 Sancerre François de la Grange	89	now

ANDRÉ NEVEU ✳✳✳
SANCERRE $22.00–$28.00

André Neveu is a grower in Chavignol whose routinely generous and fruit-filled yet distinctly site-specific bottlings deserve more attention than they seem to receive in the international press. In addition to the cuvées assessed below, there is also a generally excellent bottling called Les Longues Fins.

2005 Sancerre Le Grand Fricambault	89	now–2010
2005 Sancerre Le Manoir Vieilles Vignes	88	now–2010
2005 Sancerre Les Monts Damnés	91	now–2012

DOMAINE DE NOIRÉ ✳✳✳
CHINON $18.00–$35.00

As president of the Chinon growers' syndicate and *régisseur* at next-door Château de la Grille, Jean-Max Manceau was already a very busy man. But now he has begun to build his own small Domaine de Noiré into one of the region's finest. Manceau has a knack for getting Franc really ripe, yet burying the resultant alcohol. (Even his rosé can well exceed 14%, yet be no less infectiously juicy for it.) The Élégance is from gravel soils and raised in tank, the Caractère from chalk-clay parcels higher up, matured in *barriques* of mixed ages. Look for Manceau to rise in the local pecking order.

2005 Chinon Cuvée Élégance	89	now
2005 Chinon Caractère	89–91	2010–2014

DOMAINE DE PALLUS ✳✳✳
CHINON $25.00–$27.00

Young Bertrand Sourdais is best known as the winemaker at the Ribera del Duero's Dominio de Atauta, a job he landed right out of oenology school in Bordeaux and whence he commutes from the Loire. In 2003, Sourdais decided to take over his family's domaine and begin estate-bottling their Chinon. In his second commercial vintage, the 2005, he scored a stunning success. In local theory his sites are not top-grade *terroir*—too close to the river—but he appears able to transcend that limitation.

2005 Chinon Les Pensées de Pallus	90	now–2011+?

HENRY PELLÉ ✳✳✳
MENETOU-SALON, SANCERRE $17.00–$30.00

Henry Pellé has been the prime mover in the Menetou-Salon appellation almost since its inception, bottles numerous cuvées (including a Sancerre), the best of which are his Clos des Blanchais and Clos de Ratier from the town of Morogues (of which he was long mayor, and which is entitled to append its name to the Menetou-Salon appellation).

2005 Menetou-Salon	87	now

DOMAINE DE LA PEPIÈRE ★★★★
MUSCADET $11.00–$20.00

Mark Ollivier is one of the leaders in his appellation, working with all preclonal vines and never rushing his young wines off their lees. His old-vine Granite de Clisson and Cuvée Eden bottlings join his established ancient vines Clos des Briords, and this trio looks set to propel him into the elite echelon of Loire growers. (But his basic bottling is also a delight.)

2005 Muscadet de Sèvre et Maine Sur Lie Clos des Briords	91	now–2010+?
2005 Muscadet de Sèvre et Maine Sur Lie Granite de Clisson	92	now–2012+?

VINCENT PINARD ★★★
SANCERRE $24.00–$35.00

Vincent Pinard offers a range of Sancerre showcasing the best sites around Bué. His Cuvée Flores comes from the renowned Chêne Marchand vineyard.

2005 Sancerre Cuvée Florès	89	now–2012

JO PITHON ★★★★
ANJOU, COTEAUX DU LAYON $15.00–$140.00

Jo Pithon, one of the outspoken advocates of biodynamic viticulture, puts his wines—both dry and nobly sweet—through extended time in *barriques*. The results can include pronounced notes from the lees, of malolatic, and of new wood. About the concentration and seriousness of his wines there is no doubt.

2005 Anjou Les Treilles	87	now
2003 Coteaux du Layon Les 4 Villages	89	now–2011
2003 Coteaux du Layon–Ambroise	92	now–2018
2003 Quarts de Chaume	91	2010–2025+?
1996 Coteaux du Layon-Beaulieu	95–97	now–2020
1996 Coteaux du Layon-Beaulieu Clos des Ortinières	96–98	now–2020
1996 Coteaux du Layon–St.-Lambert	94–97	now–2018
2003 Coteaux du Layon–St.-Lambert Les Bonnes Blanches	90	now–2014

JACKY PREYS ET FILS ★★★
TOURAINE $12.00–$20.00

The wines of Jacky Preys's large domaine are a familiar feature on French wine lists, if less so stateside. His 2005 Fié Gris, from ancient vines of a progenitor of Sauvignon, is consistently the standout of his collection.

2005 Fié Gris	90	now

THIERRY PUZELAT ★★★
TOURAINE $15.00–$25.00

Operating as a *négociant* for organic and biodynamic Touraine growers, Thierry Puzelat (proprietor of Clos du Tue-Boeuf) has come up with sometimes strange and sometimes wonderful discoveries, like a Pineau d'Aunis from a property next to the Clos Roche Blanche.

2005 Touraine Pineau d'Aunis	90	now

DOMAINE DE LA QUILLA ✳ ✳ ✳
MUSCADET $11.00–$12.00

Daniel and Gérard Vinet have been sending consistently high-quality Muscadet to the United States for a quarter-century. Their Muscadet de Sèvre et Maine Sur Lie offers an almost Chablis-like brothy suffusion of mineral suggestions and amazing refreshment in its first two years after harvest, even when it reaches what is for a Muscadet an almost unheard of 13% alcohol.

JEAN-MAURICE RAFFAULT ✳ ✳ ✳
CHINON $16.00–$30.00

From Jean-Maurice Raffault's extensive property and three cellars emerge a wide range of bottlings, segregated by site and soil type, from alluvial through gravel to chalk and clay, and from the riverside up through the slopes to the plateau.

2005 Chinon	89	now–2010
2005 Chinon Les Galluches	88	now–2010+?
2005 Chinon Les Picasses	87	2009–2011+?
2005 Chinon Clos d'Isoré	90	now–2014
2005 Chinon Clos des Capucins	89	2010–2013+?

CHÂTEAU DE LA RAGOTIÈRE ✳ ✳ ✳
MUSCADET $11.00–$15.00

Ragotière has long been a very reliable source for refreshing and engaging Muscadet de Sèvre et Maine Sur Lie, generally to be enjoyed within two or three years of harvest but sometimes still excellent for longer.

HIPPOLYTE REVERDY ✳ ✳ ✳
SANCERRE $22.00–$25.00

The Domaine Hippolyte Reverdy appears—on the strength of their superb, energetic 2005—to be one that has unjustly stayed off the radar screens of most observers. Thanks to importer Kermit Lynch, these wines have come to the U.S. and should be followed.

2005 Sancerre	92	now–2011+?

PASCAL ET NICOLAS REVERDY ✳ ✳ ✳
SANCERRE $24.00–$35.00

Pascal and Nicolas Reverdy have rendered high-tension, high-acid, youthfully austere renditions of Sancerre that lovers of dry (*trocken*) German Riesling as well as those with a bit of patience will especially enjoy. Their Vieilles Vignes cuvée is from 70- to 80-year-old vines fermented in barrel. Tragically, Nicolas was killed in an accident in late 2007.

2005 Sancerre Cuvée Les Coûtes	89	now–2012
2004 Sancerre Vieilles Vignes	90	now–2014

DOMAINE DES ROCHES NEUVES ✳ ✳ ✳
SAUMUR, SAUMUR-CHAMPIGNY $30.00–$50.00

Thierry Germain has gained an enthusiastic following in France. After recently visiting the Wachau, Germain decided he should largely swear off the use of new *barriques*; the effect on his 2004 and 2005 reds seems to have been salutary.

2005 Saumur-Champigny Terres Chaudes	88	now–2010
2004 Saumur-Champigny La Marginale	89	now–2011

LE ROCHER DES VIOLETTES   ★ ★ ★ ★
MONTLOUIS $19.00–$30.00

Xavier Weisskopf not long ago moved from the Rhône to fulfill his vision of a wine domaine in a place where land prices were not yet exorbitant and vinous greatness seemed possible. Man and *terroir* have found their match here. Weisskopf is sure to be recognized within a few years as one of the Loire's elite vignerons. Vinification is largely in barrel with some tank, with the results that are already gorgeously pure, rich, and complex.

2005 Montlouis Sec Cuvée Touche-Mitaine	90	now–2010
2005 Montlouis Cuvée La Negrette	92	now–2012+?
2005 Montlouis Demi-Sec	91	now–2014+?

JEAN-MAX ROGER   ★ ★ ★
MENETOU-SALON, SANCERRE $22.00–$35.00

Grower-*négociant* Jean-Max Roger has been a solid, widely distributed source for open, engaging Sancerre since at least the early 1980s.

2005 Menetou-Salon Morogues Le Petit Clos	87	now
2005 Sancerre Les Caillottes	88	now
2005 Sancerre Vieilles Vignes	87	now–2010

JEAN-CLAUDE ROUX   ★ ★ ★
QUINCY $19.00–$21.00

The many critics who had mean-spirited things to say about this appellation ("Quincy the point of it" and the like) can cover their heads in shame when they taste Jean-Claude Roux's 2005 bottling, a wine of Chablis-like complexity. Hopefully, subsequent vintages will confirm Roux as a rising star.

2005 Quincy	90	now

DOMAINE RICHOU   ★ ★ ★
ANJOU, COTEAUX DE L'AUBANCE $14.00–$55.00

The leading estate in the l'Aubance sector, Richou is serious about its dry whites, reds, and nobly sweet wines, which can have the ageworthiness of their neighbors in the Coteaux du Layon. Their basic Anjou sec is generally lovely to drink within two or three years of harvest, and the Rogeries version is late picked, barrel fermented, and said to reflect the area's distinctive *terroir*.

2005 Anjou Sec Les Rogeries	88	now
2005 Coteaux de l'Aubance La Grande Séléction	89	now–2011
2005 Coteaux de l'Aubance Les 3 Demoiselles	91	2010–2017

BÉNÉDICTE DE RYCKE   ★ ★ ★
COTEAUX DU LOIR, JASNIÈRES $17.00–$30.00

Bénédict de Rycke started out vinifying with her former husband Jean-Michel Aubert at his (unfortunately now defunct) domaine and is now crafting distinctively delicious wines from along the little Loir.

2005 Coteaux du Loir Tradition	88	now–2010
2004 Jasnières Louise	90	now–2016

HERVÉ SEGUIN ★★★★
POUILLY-FUMÉ $23.00–$25.00

Seguin's Pouilly-Fumé is sourced from three of the appellation's top communes, with a preponderance of flint-rich soils suggested by explosively floral aromas and lush fruit, yet no lack of head-scratching nuances that leave the taster reaching for the term "mineral."

2005 Pouilly-Fumé	92	now–2012

CHÂTEAU SOUCHÈRIE ★★★★
ANJOU, COTEAUX DU LAYON, SAVENNIÈRES $18.00–$50.00

Pierre-Yves Tijou and his sons offer a wide array of wines—and from numerous vintages simultaneously—including many user-friendly (which does not preclude profound) and well-priced dry and sweet Chenins often of exemplary elegance, most being vinified in tank but some (such as their Cuvée Anaïs or S) in barrel.

2005 Savennières Clos des Perrières	90	now–2015
2004 Savennières Clos des Perrières Alix	88	now–2010+?
2003 Savennières Cuvée Anaïs	87	now–2010+?
2004 Coteaux du Layon	92	now–2015
2002 Coteaux du Layon Cuvée S	91	now–2012
2002 Coteaux du Layon Vieilles Vignes	92	now–2017
2005 Coteaux du Layon Chaume	90	now–2019
2004 Coteaux du Layon Chaume	89	2009–2015+?
2003 Coteaux du Layon Chaume	92	now–2017
1996 Coteaux du Layon-Beaulieu Cuvée de la Tour	93	now–2025
1995 Coteaux du Layon-Beaulieu Cuvée de la Tour	97	now–2030

DOMAINE DE LA TAILLE AUX LOUPS ★★★★
MONTLOUIS, VOUVRAY $24.00–$130.00

Jacky Blot's *barrique*-vinified, lees-rich Chenins are among the Loire's best and most distinctive. (Since 2002 he has operated the Domaine de la Butte in Bourgueil as well, see above.) What Blot calls "the incredible treasure trove of old vines around Montlouis"—part of what attracted him here nearly twenty years ago, and from which he has developed his own *sélection massale*—certainly contributes to the quality and consistency of his wines, which in recent vintages (witness the normally difficult 2004) has pushed him closer toward elite stature. Incidentally, his numerous sparkling cuvées—especially his cuvée "triple zéro" (with no sugar added at any point)—are excellent.

2005 Montlouis Cuvée des Loups	91	now–2020
2005 Montlouis Demi-Sec	90	now–2015
2005 Montlouis Rémus	91	2010–2020
2005 Montlouis Sec Les Dix Arpents	91	now–2014
2005 Montlouis Sec Rémus Plus	92–93	2010–2018
2005 Montlouis Sec Rémus	89	now–2012+?
2005 Vouvray Sec Les Caburoches	88	now–2012
2005 Vouvray Clos de la Bretonnière	90	2009–2016
2005 Vouvray Moelleux	90	now–2022
2005 Vouvray Clos de Venise	93	now–2020
2004 Vouvray Sec Clos de Venise	93	now–2015+?

DOMAINE THOMAS ET FILS ★★★★
SANCERRE $25.00–$40.00

Jean Thomas ships two-thirds of his 1,800 cases of 2005 Sancerre Clos de la Crèle to the U.S. and a substantial portion of the remainder to the U.K., so it's no wonder he is well known in the English-speaking markets. His Clos de la Crèle is nearly always generously perfumed and lush, though anything but simple. Chaille names an unorthodox cuvée from flint soils that receives a full year of lees enrichment, and Ultimus designates the fruit of old vines, vinified half in *barriques* for one to two years and half in tank. The results here for 2005 reflect not just the usual care but also a new gravity-fed cellar.

2005 Sancerre Clos de la Crèle	91	now–2012
2005 Sancerre Grand Chaille	92	2009–2013
2004 Sancerre Grand Chaille	89	now–2011
2005 Sancerre Ultimus	93	now–2017
2004 Sancerre Ultimus	90	now–2014

DOMAINE THOMAS-LABAILLE ★★★★
SANCERRE $25.00–$35.00

Jean-Paul Labaille apparently inherited many of the old methods from his father-in-law, Claude Thomas. As has happened more recently in the Cotats' cellars, aged barrels were replaced, but low yields and full ripeness in the vineyard, along with hand work and slow maturation in the cellar, are still the norms, resulting in wonderfully pure, classic reflections of the great Mont Damnés site. The Cuvée Buster represents a barrel selection for Labaille's importer, Joe Dressner, which was named for Dressner's bulldog.

2005 Sancerre Les Monts Damnés	90	now–2013+?
2005 Sancerre Les Monts Damnés Cuvée Buster	92	now–2015+?

F. TINEL-BLONDELET ★★★
POUILLY-FUMÉ $22.00–$25.00

Named for a sign once at this domaine that urged travelers to stop and have a bite to eat, Annick Tinel's 2005 Pouilly-Fumé L'Arret Buffatte displays admirable perfume, clarity, cut, and brightness. Genetin refers to an old name for Sauvignon (Muscat Genetin) and to a highly aromatic, elegant cuvée designed for immediate enjoyment.

2005 Pouilly-Fumé L'Arret Buffatte	88	now
2005 Pouilly-Fumé Genetin	89	now

CHÂTEAU DE TRACY ★★★
POUILLY-FUMÉ $25.00–$100.00

There have been significant improvements at Château de Tracy of late. But one must be aware that its wines are the antithesis of the lush, flamboyant examples of Pouilly-Fumé from Seguin or the Dagueneaus. These can offer a lot of finesse, but their chalky underpinnings seem to be reflected in a certain underlying austerity. The Haute Densité in particular lives up to its name.

2005 Pouilly-Fumé	89	now–2011
2005 Pouilly-Fumé Mademoiselle de T	88	now–2010
2005 Pouilly-Fumé Haute Densité	90	2010–2014+?

DOMAINE VACHERON ★ ★ ★
SANCERRE $25.00–$45.00

Jean-Dominique and Jean-Laurent Vacheron are two of the most ambitious growers in Sancerre—ambitious not just for themselves but for their appellation. They employ a labor-intensive, biodynamic regimen on their entire large property, which is divided between classic chalk and flint *terroirs*. Would that more wooded Sancerre were as successful as their Les Romains, where the oak component goes largely unnoticed, save for its subtle influences via the lees and oxidation. The Vacherons are particularly proud of their Pinot Noir, which so far is impressively dense, if somewhat lacking in generosity of fruit or tenderness.

2005 Vacheron Sancerre	89	now–2010
2005 Sancerre Les Romains	90	now–2012

EDMOND VATAN ★ ★ ★ ★ ★
SANCERRE $50.00–$60.00

Edmond Vatan—along with the Cotats, one of the few archtraditionalists remaining in Sancerre—retired in 2003 and his heirs will not (at least for now) bottle wine from his Chavignol vines. But he intends to continue bottling small amounts of wine, which continue to be imported into the United States. The best Sauvignons from this cellar are breathtaking at even 15 to 20 years of age.

2005 Sancerre Clos La Néore	92	now–2018
2004 Sancerre Clos La Néore	91	now–2016
2003 Sancerre Rouge	89	now–2010

CHÂTEAU DE VILLENEUVE ★ ★ ★
SAUMUR, SAUMUR-CHAMPIGNY $17.00–$40.00

Since his youthful days working at Cheval Blanc, Jean-Pierre Chevalier has been determined to craft great Cabernet Franc. With his 1999 Grand Clos he achieved that goal, and his 2005s are his best reds since then. From one small parcel of old Chenin Blanc vines, the domaine bottles two Saumurs, of which the less oaked is more stylish.

2005 Saumur	87	now
2002 Saumur	90	now
2005 Saumur-Champigny	89	now
2005 Saumur-Champigny Vieilles Vignes	89–90	2009–2013+?

[provence]

It is easy to regard Provence as just a dramatic playground for the world's rich and famous; few wine lovers realize that this vast viticultural region in southern France is at least 2,600 years old. For centuries, tourists traveling through Provence have been seduced by the aromatic, flavorful thirst-quenching rosés that complement the distinctive cuisine of the region so well. Today, Provence is an exciting, diverse viticultural region that is turning out not only extremely satisfying rosés but immensely promising red wines and a few encouraging whites. However, it remains largely uncharted territory for wine consumers.

Provence is a mammoth region with seven specific viticultural areas. The best way to approach the subject is to learn what each area has to offer and which properties constitute the leading wine-producing estates. While Provence is blessed with ideal weather for grape growing, not all its vintages are of equal merit. Certainly, of the white and rosé wines of Provence, which require consumption in their youth, only the 2007s ought to be drunk today. The super vintages for all of Provence are those of 2000, 2001, 2005, and 2007. As a general rule, the top red wines of Provence can handle aging for up to a decade in the aforementioned vintages. Following is a brief synopsis of the seven major wine-producing areas in Provence, along with a list of the top wines from each area that merit trying. While the wines of Provence are not overpriced, the collapse of the U.S. dollar against the euro has made these wines less attractively priced to American buyers.

[the region]

BANDOL

In France, Bandol is often called the most privileged appellation of the entire country. Clearly, the scenic beauty of this storybook area offers unsurpassed views of the azure Mediterranean, and the vineyards are spread out on the hillsides overlooking the water. Bandol produces red, rosé, and white wines. It is most famous for its rosé wines, which some consider the best made in France, and its long-lived, intense, tannic red wine, unique in France because it is made from at least 50% of the little-known Mourvèdre grape. If anyone has any doubts about the quality of Mourvèdre, proof can be found in the Château Pradeaux's 1989 and 1990 Mourvèdre Vieilles Vignes. Prices for Bandol have never been cheap, largely because of the never-ending flow of tourists to the area, who buy most of the wine made by the local producers.

There is consensus among connoisseurs that the best red wines come from such producers as the Domaine Pradeaux, Domaine Tempier, Domaine de Pibarnon, and Ott's Château Romassan. While most of these producers also make a white wine, I cannot recommend than with a great deal of enthusiasm, as they always seem to taste dull and heavy. However, the red wines as well as the fresh, personality-filled rosés from these estates are well worth seeking out, expensive though they are. Prices for the rosés now average $25 to $35. While I have had the good fortune to taste red wines of Bandol that have been as old as 15 to 20 years, most of the wines seem to hit their peak after 6 to 10 years in the bottle. Bandol, one of the most strictly regulated appellations in all of France, is certainly the leading candidate of all the Provence appellations for producer of the longest-lived, best-known red wines.

BELLET

Like all of the Provence appellations, the tiny appellation of Bellet, tucked into the hillside behind Nice, produces red, white, and rosé wines. The history of Bellet is rich, as its vineyards were originally cultivated by Phoenician Greeks in 500 B.C. But unless one actually spends time on the Riviera, one is unlikely ever to know how a fine Bellet tastes. Most of the wine produced in this microappellation of only 100-plus acres never makes it outside France, as the local restaurant demand is insatiable. There are only a handful of producers making wine here, the very best being the Château de Crémat, owned by the Bagnis family, a splendid estate of 50 acres that produces nearly 6,000 cases of wine annually. It is rarely seen in the U.S., and its high price of $35 to $45 a bottle has ensured that few consumers know how it really tastes. The Château de Crémat is a unique estate in Provence in that its white wine is of extremely high quality, with the local connoisseurs claiming that the rosé and red wines are the best made in this part of the French Riviera. However, the wines of Bellet remain esoteric, enjoyed by only a handful of people, with prices that seem steep for the quality.

CASSIS

The tiny village of Cassis, located on the western end of France's famous Côte d'Azur, is one of the most charming fishing villages on the Riviera, located on a secluded bay and dwarfed by surrounding steep limestone cliffs. The hordes of tourists who frequent the area ensure that most of the wine made here is consumed at the local bistros, along with the area's ubiquitous *soupe de poisson*. While this appellation makes red and rosé wines, it is the white wine that has made Cassis famous. Its red wine tends to be heavy and uninteresting, and while the rosé can be good, it never seems to approach the quality level of its neighbor Bandol. The white wine, which is often a blend of little-known grapes such as Ugni Blanc, Clairette, and Bourboulenc, is a spicy, fleshy wine with a distinct character that often seems unattractive by itself, but when served with the rich, aromatic seafood dishes of the region takes on a character of its own. The estates of Cassis producing the best white wines include the Clos Ste.-Magdeleine, La Ferme Blanche, and the Domaine du Bagnol. Prices average $25 or more for these white wines, not a good value.

CORSICA

Though Corsica is still a backwater area of France, the Corsicans continue to have such an independent spirit that it's hard to tell whether they have more allegiance to Italy, France, or their own unique brand of liberty and independence. One thing is for certain—vineyards have sprouted up all over this gorgeous mountainous island known as l'Île de Beauté. Given

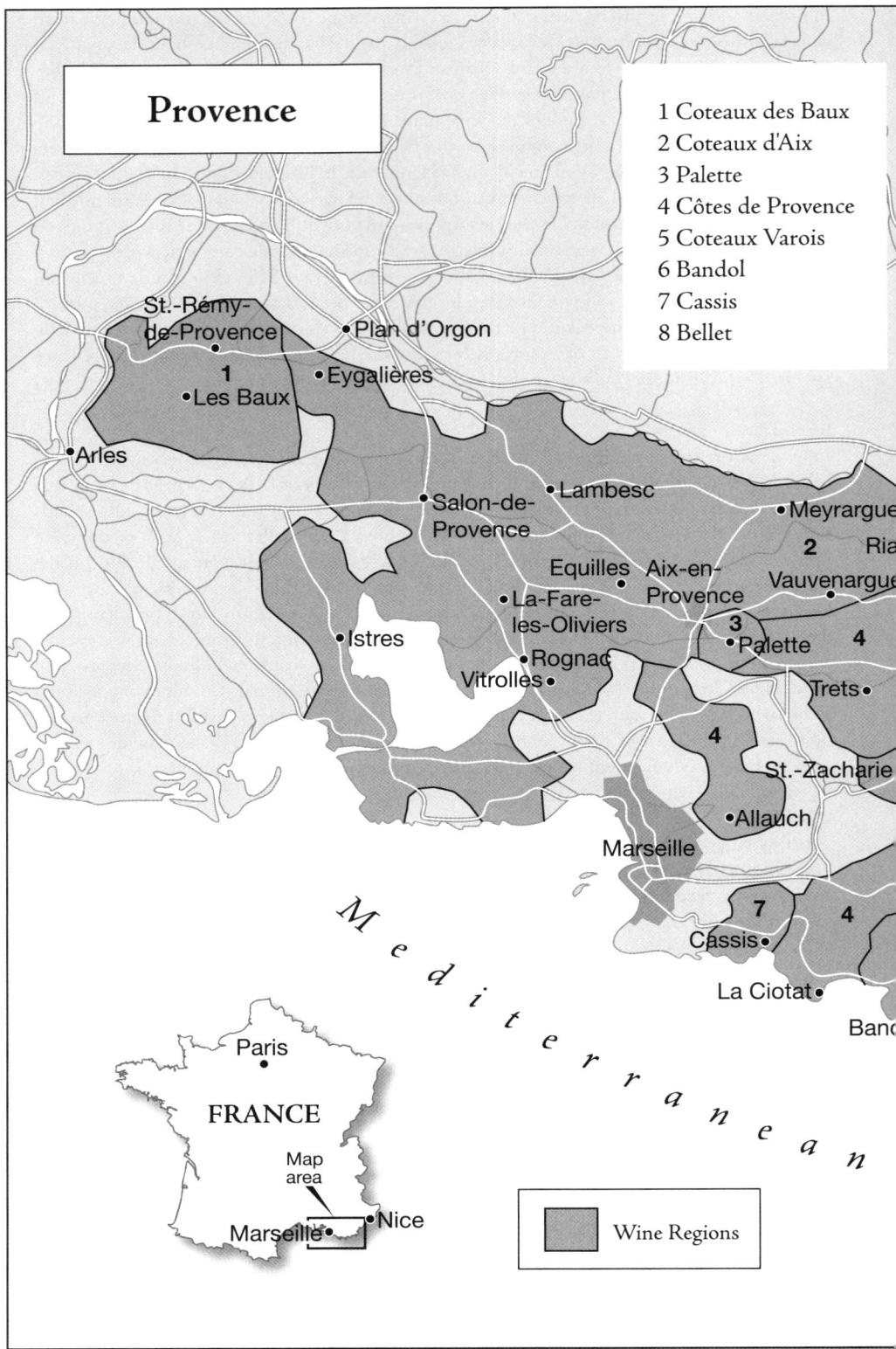

Provence

1 Coteaux des Baux
2 Coteaux d'Aix
3 Palette
4 Côtes de Provence
5 Coteaux Varois
6 Bandol
7 Cassis
8 Bellet

St.-Rémy-de-Provence
• Plan d'Orgon
1
• Les Baux
• Eygalières
• Arles
• Lambesc
Salon-de-Provence
• Meyrargue
2
Ria
Equilles
Aix-en-Provence
Vauvenargue
• La-Fare-les-Oliviers
3
• Istres
• Palette
4
• Rognac
Vitrolles •
Trets •
4
St.-Zacharie
• Allauch
Marseille
7
4
Cassis •
La Ciotat •
Band

Mediterranean

FRANCE
Paris •
Map area
Marseille • • Nice

Wine Regions

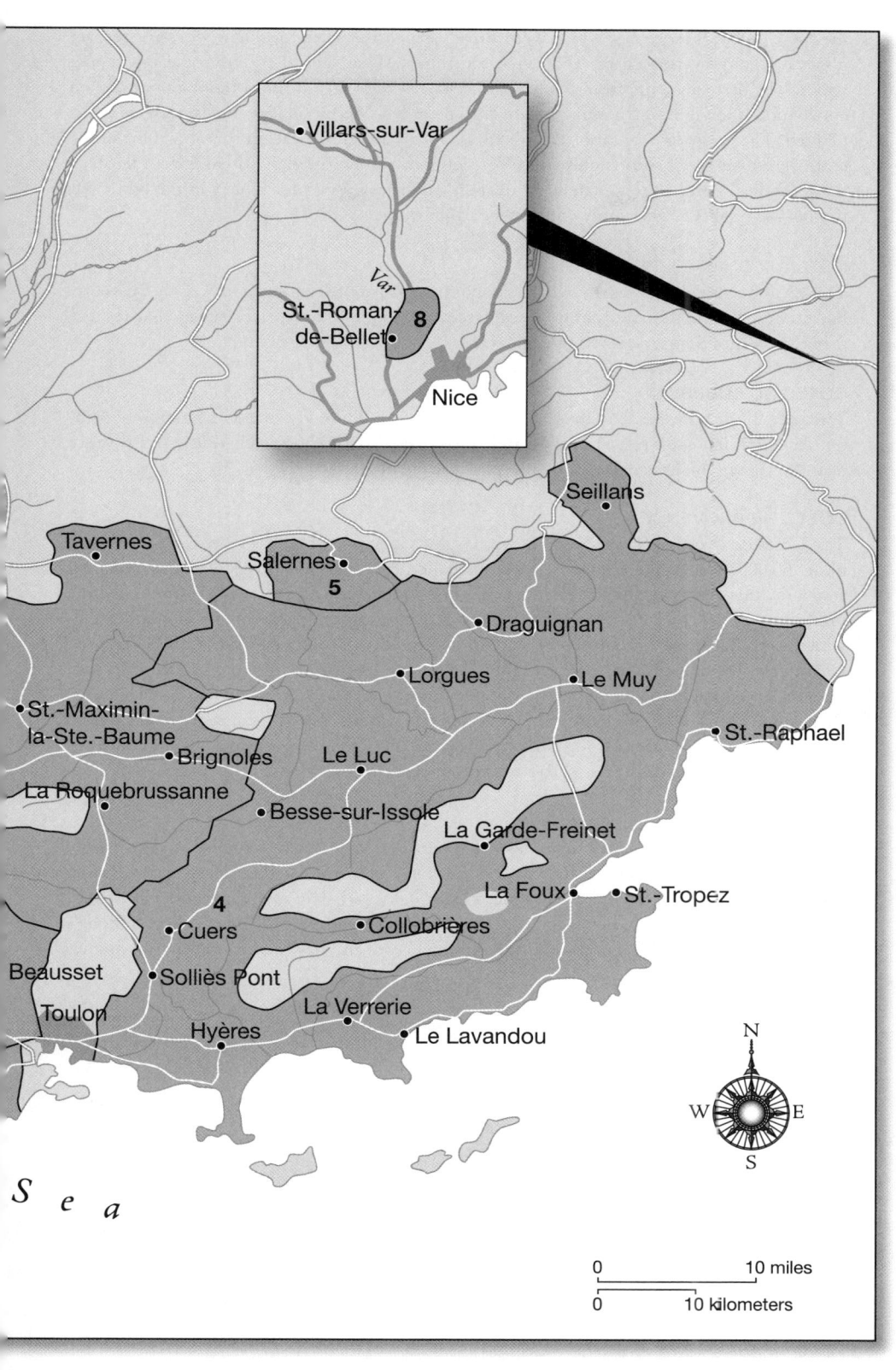

Villars-sur-Var

Var

St.-Roman-
de-Bellet

8

Nice

Seillans

Tavernes

Salernes

5

Draguignan

Lorgues

Le Muy

St.-Maximin-
la-Ste.-Baume

St.-Raphael

Brignoles

Le Luc

La Roquebrussanne

Besse-sur-Issole

La Garde-Freinet

La Foux

St.-Tropez

4

Collobrières

Cuers

Beausset

Solliès Pont

Toulon

La Verrerie

Hyères

Le Lavandou

S e a

N

W   E

S

0   10 miles

0   10 kilometers

the weak dollar, these wines, which were already expensive when the dollar was stronger, are now essentially overpriced for U.S. wine consumers. That said, there are some interesting wines. The best can come from the limestone soils at the very northern tip of Corsica, in an appellation known as Patrimonio, where a grape called Nielluccio (essentially Sangiovese) is planted. They also do a sensational job with relatively sweet Muscats in this area. One of the best dry whites of Corsica comes from Vermentino, another grape with an Italian heritage that does well here. Unfortunately, all of these are pricey wines for what's in the bottle, although the quality has certainly gotten better and better.

COTEAUX D'AIX-EN-PROVENCE
This gigantic viticultural region, which extends primarily north and west of Aix-en-Provence, has numerous small estates making acceptable but generally overpriced wines that require drinking within their first seven to eight years.

CÔTES DU LUBERON
Virtually all the wine made in the Côtes du Luberon is produced by one of the many cooperatives that dominate this region's production. However, this area, located in northern Provence near the villages of Apt and Pertuis, has immense potential.

CÔTES DE PROVENCE
The Côtes de Provence is the best-known, largest viticultural region of Provence, with just under 50,000 acres planted in vines. This appellation is famous for its oceans of dry, flavorful rosé wine that tourists gulp down with great thirst-quenching pleasure. There are many fine producers of Côtes de Provence wines, the best including the very famous Domaines Ott, which is available on virtually every restaurant wine list in southern France, the Domaines Gavoty, the Domaine Richeaume, and the Domaine St.-André de Figuière. All these estates, with the exception of the Domaine Richeaume, produce outstanding rosé wine. The Domaine Richeaume specializes in intense, rich, complex red wines. The Ott wines, no doubt due to their fame within France, sell for fairly hefty prices, but I have never heard anyone complain regarding the quality of their superb rosés and underrated red wines.

PALETTE
Palette is a tiny appellation just to the east of Aix-en-Provence that in actuality consists of only one serious winemaking estate, the Château Simone. This tiny estate of 37 acres produces a surprisingly long-lived, complex red wine; a fairly oaky, old-style rosé wine; and a muscular, full-bodied white wine that behaves as if it were from the northern Rhône Valley. Simone's wines are not inexpensive, but they do age extremely well and have always had a loyal following in France.

[the wines]

A huge quantity of bone-dry, fragrant, crisp rosés is made, as well as rather neutral but fleshy white wines, and higher- and higher-quality red wines.

GRAPE VARIETIES

For red wines, the traditional grape varieties have always been Grenache, Carignan, Syrah, Mourvèdre, and Cinsault. However, a great deal of Cabernet Sauvignon has been planted in the Côtes de Provence and Coteaux d'Aix-en-Provence. The most interesting red wines are generally those with elevated levels of either Syrah, Mourvèdre, or Cabernet Sauvignon. For white wines, Ugni Blanc, Clairette, Marsanne, Bourboulenc, and to a lesser extent Sémillon, Sauvignon Blanc, and Chardonnay are used.

FLAVORS

There is immense variation, due to the number of microclimates and different grapes used. Most red wines have vivid red fruit bouquets that are more intense in the Coteaux des Baux than elsewhere. In Bandol the smells of tree bark, leather, and currants dominate. The white wines seem neutral and clumsy when served without food, but when drunk with the spicy Provençal cuisine they take on life.

AGING POTENTIAL

Rosés: 1–3 years.

White wines: 1–3 years, except for that of the Château Simone, which can last 5–10 years.

Red wines: 5–12 years, often longer for the red wines of Bandol and specific wines such as Pradeaux and Tempier, two Bandol estates with superb track records for long-aged wines.

OVERALL QUALITY LEVEL

The quality level has increased and in general is well above average, but consumers must remember to buy and drink rosé and white wines only when they are less than three years old.

IMPORTANT INFORMATION

Master the types of wine of each appellation of Provence, as well as the names of the top producers.

BUYING STRATEGY

The vintages of choice for the wines of this region are 2007 for the rosés and whites and 2001, 2005, and 2007 for the reds. However, for Americans this buying strategy is somewhat moot unless you are an enthusiast of these wines, given the weak dollar and the relatively pricey nature of everything from Provence.

—ROBERT PARKER

[the ratings]

PROVENCE'S BEST PRODUCERS

* * * * * (OUTSTANDING)

Château Pradeaux Mourvèdre Vieilles
  Vignes (Bandol)
Domaine Tempier Cabassaou (Bandol)

Domaine Tempier La Migoua (Bandol)
Domaine Tempier La Tourtine (Bandol)

* * * * (EXCELLENT)

Antoine Arena Patrimonio
  (Corsica)
Domaine des Béates Terra d'Or (Coteaux
  d'Aix-en Provence)

Commanderie de Peyrassol (Côtes de
  Provence)
Mas de la Dame (Coteaux d'Aix-en-
  Provence-Les Baux)

Mas de Gourgonnier (Coteaux d'Aix-en-Provence-Les Baux)

Domaine Hauvette (Coteaux des Baux)

Luigi-Clos Nicrosi (Corsica)

Domaines Ott—all cuvées (Bandol and Côtes de Provence)

Domaine de Pibarnon (Bandol)

Château Pradeaux (Bandol)

Revelette (Coteaux d'Aix-en-Provence)

Domaine Richeaume (Côtes de Provence)

Tardieu-Laurent—Domaine Bastide de Rhodares (Côtes du Lubéron)

Domaine Tempier Cuvée Spéciale

Domaine Tempier Rosé (Bandol)

Château Vannières (Bandol)

★ ★ ★ (VERY GOOD)

Domaine du Bagnol (Cassis)

Château Barbeyrolles (Côtes de Provence)

Château Bas (Coteaux d'Aix-en-Provence)

La Bastide Blanche (Bandol)

Domaine des Béates (Coteaux d'Aix-en Provence)

Domaine de Beaupré (Coteaux d'Aix-en-Provence)

Domaine La Bernarde (Côtes de Provence)

Mas de Cadenet (Côtes de Provence)

Domaine Caguelouf (Bandol)

Château de Calissanne (Coteaux d'Aix-en-Provence)

Château la Canorgue (Côtes du Lubéron)

Domaine de Catarelli Patrimonio (Corsica)

Castel Roubine (Côtes de Provence)

Cave Cooperative d'Aleria Réserve du Président (Corsica)

Domaine Champagna (Côtes du Ventoux)

Chapoutier Matines Beats (Coteaux d'Aix-en-Provence)

Clos Canaredi (Corsica)

Clos Capitoro (Corsica)

Clos Culombu (Corsica)

Clos Ste.-Magdeleine (Cassis)

Château de Crémat (Bellet)

Domaine de Curebeasse (Côtes de Provence)

Domaine des Feraud (Côtes de Provence)

Château Ferry Lacombe (Côtes de Provence)

Domaine Fiumicicoli (Corsica)

Château de Fonscolombe (Coteaux d'Aix-en-Provence)

Domaine de Fontenille (Côtes du Lubéron)

Domaine de Frégate (Bandol)

Domaine Le Galantin (Bandol)

Domaine de la Garnaude Cuvée Santane (Côtes de Provence)

Château Jean-Pierre Gaussen (Bandol)

Domaine Gavoty (Côtes de Provence)

Domaine Gentile, Patrimonio (Corsica)

Hervé Goudard (Côtes de Provence)

Domaine du Gros Noré (Bandol)

Domaine de l'Hermitage (Bandol)

Château de l'Isolette (Côtes du Lubéron)

Domaine de Lafran-Veyrolles (Bandol)

Domaine de la Laidière (Bandol)

Domaine Leccia Patrimonio (Corsica)

Domaine du Loou (Coteaux Varois)

Château de Maravenne (Côtes de Provence)

Mas Ste.-Berthe (Coteaux d'Aix-en-Provence)

Château de Mille (Côtes du Lubéron)

Domaine Moulin des Costes (Bandol)

Domaine de la Noblesse (Bandol)

Domaine Orenga (Corsica)

Domaine du Paradis (Coteaux d'Aix-en-Provence)

Domaine Comte Peraldi, Ajaccio (Corsica)

Château Rasque (Côtes de Provence)

Domaine Ray-Jane (Bandol)

Château Real-Martin (Côtes de Provence)

Domaine de Rimauresq (Côtes de Provence)

Château Romanin (Coteaux d'Aix-en-Provence-Les Baux)

Mas de la Rouvière (Bandol)

Domaine St.-André de Figuière (Côtes de Provence)

Château St.-Estève (Côtes de Provence)

Château St.-Jean Cuvée Natasha (Côtes de Provence)

Domaine St.-Jean de Villecroze (Coteaux Varois)

Château Ste.-Anne (Bandol)

Château Ste.-Roseline (Côtes de Provence)

Château Salettes (Bandol)

Domaine de la Sanglière (Côtes de
  Provence)
Château Simone (Palette)
Domaine de Terrebrune (Bandol)
Domaine La Torraccia (Corsica)
Domaine de la Tour du Bon (Bandol)
Toussaint Luigi-Muscatella (Corsica)

Château Trevallon (Coteaux d'Aix-en-
  Provence-Les Baux)
Château de Vallongue (Coteaux des Baux)
La Vieille Ferme (Côtes du Lubéron)
Château Vignelaure (Coteaux d'Aix-en-
  Provence-Les Baux)

[the rhône] valley

[the wines]

RED GRAPE VARIETIES

CINSAULT Some growers use a small amount of Cinsault. It ripens very early, gives good yields, and produces wines that offer a great deal of fruit. It seems to offset the high alcohol of the Grenache and the tannins of the Syrah and Mourvèdre. Despite its value, Cinsault seems to have lost some appeal in favor of Syrah or Mourvèdre, but it is a valuable asset to the blend of a southern R hône wine. It is an important component in two of the region's finest Côtes du Rhônes, Fonsalette and Tardieu-Laurent.

COUNOISE Little of this grape exists in the south because of its capricious growing habits. However, I have tasted it separately at Beaucastel and Clos des Papes in Châteauneuf-du-Pape, where its use has been augmented. It lacks weight and fat but possesses finesse and seems to provide richly fruity flavors and a complex perfume of smoked meat, flowers, and berry fruit. Counoise has as much antioxidative potential as Mourvèdre, a high-quality ingredient in the Beaucastel and Clos des Papes blends.

GRENACHE A classic hot-climate grape variety, Grenache is the dominant grape of the southern Rhône. The quality of the wines it produces ranges from hot, alcoholic, unbalanced, coarse wines to rich, majestic, very long-lived, sumptuous wines. The differences are largely caused by the yield of juice per vine. Where Grenache is pruned back and not overly fertilized it can do wondrous things. Many of the finest Châteauneuf-du-Papes remain poignant examples of what majestic heights Grenache can achieve. At its best, it offers aromas of kirsch, black currants, pepper, licorice, and occasionally roasted peanuts.

MOURVÈDRE Everyone seems to agree on the virtues of Mourvèdre, but few want to take the risk and grow it. It flourishes in the Mediterranean appellation of Bandol, but only a handful of Châteauneuf-du-Pape estates have made it an important part (one-third or more) of their blend (Beaucastel and La Nerthe's Cuvée des Cadettes being the exceptions). When fully mature Mourvèdre is harvested, it provides a deep color, a complex, woodsy, leathery aroma, superb structure, and is resistant to oxidation. However, it ripens very late, and unlike other grape varieties has little value until it is perfectly mature. When it lacks maturity, growers say it gives them nothing, for it is colorless, acidic, and bitterly tannic. Given the eccentricities of this grape, it is unlikely that anyone other than the adventurous or passionately obsessed grower will make use of this grape. Its telltale aromas are those of leather, truffles, fresh mushrooms, and tree bark.

MUSCARDIN More common than Terret Noir, Muscardin provides perfume as well as a solid measure of alcohol and strength. Beaucastel uses Muscardin, but by far the most important plantings of Muscardin at a serious winemaking estate are at Chante Perdrix in Châteauneuf-du-Pape. The Nicolet family uses up to 20% in their excellent Châteauneuf-du-Pape.

SYRAH Syrah, the only game in town in the northern Rhône, is relegated to an accessory role in the south. However, its role in providing needed color saturation, structure, backbone, and tannin to the fleshy Grenache is incontestable. Some growers believe it ripens too fast in the hotter south, but in my opinion it is a strong addition to many southern Rhône wines. More and more of the Côtes du Rhône estates are producing special bottlings of 100% Syrah wines that show very good potential. The finest Syrahs made in the southern Rhône are the cuvées of Syrah from the Château de Fonsalette and Domaine Gramenon. Both wines can last and evolve for 15 to 25 years. Their aromas are those of berry fruit, coffee, smoky tar, and hickory wood.

TERRET NOIR Little of this grape is now found in the southern Rhône, although it remains one of the permitted varieties. It was used to give acidity to a wine and to mollify the strong character provided by the Grenache and Syrah. None of the best estates care to employ it anymore.

VACCARESE It was again at Beaucastel where I tasted the wine produced from this grape, which the Perrins vinify separately. Not as powerful and deep as Syrah, nor as alcoholic as Grenache, it has its own unique character giving aromas of pepper, hot tar, tobacco, and licorice.

WHITE GRAPE VARIETIES

BOURBOULENC This grape offers plenty of body. The local cognoscenti also attribute the scent of roses to Bourboulenc, although I cannot as yet claim the same experience.

CLAIRETTE BLANC Until the advent of cold fermentations and modern equipment to minimize the risk of oxidation, Clairette produced heavy, alcoholic, often deep yellow-colored wines that were thick and ponderous. Given the benefit of state-of-the-art technology, it produces soft, floral, fruity wine that must be drunk young. The excellent white Châteauneuf-du-Pape of Vieux Télégraphe has considerable Clairette in it.

GRENACHE BLANC Deeply fruity, highly alcoholic yet low-acid wines are produced from Grenache blanc. When fermented at cool temperatures and when the malolactic fermentation is blocked, it can be a vibrant, delicious wine capable of providing near-term pleasure. The exquisite white Châteauneuf-du-Pape from Henri Brunier, Vieux Télégraphe, contains 25% Grenache Blanc; that of the Gonnet Brothers' Font de Michelle, 50%. In a few examples such as this I find the floral scent of paperwhite narcissus and a character vaguely resembling that of Condrieu.

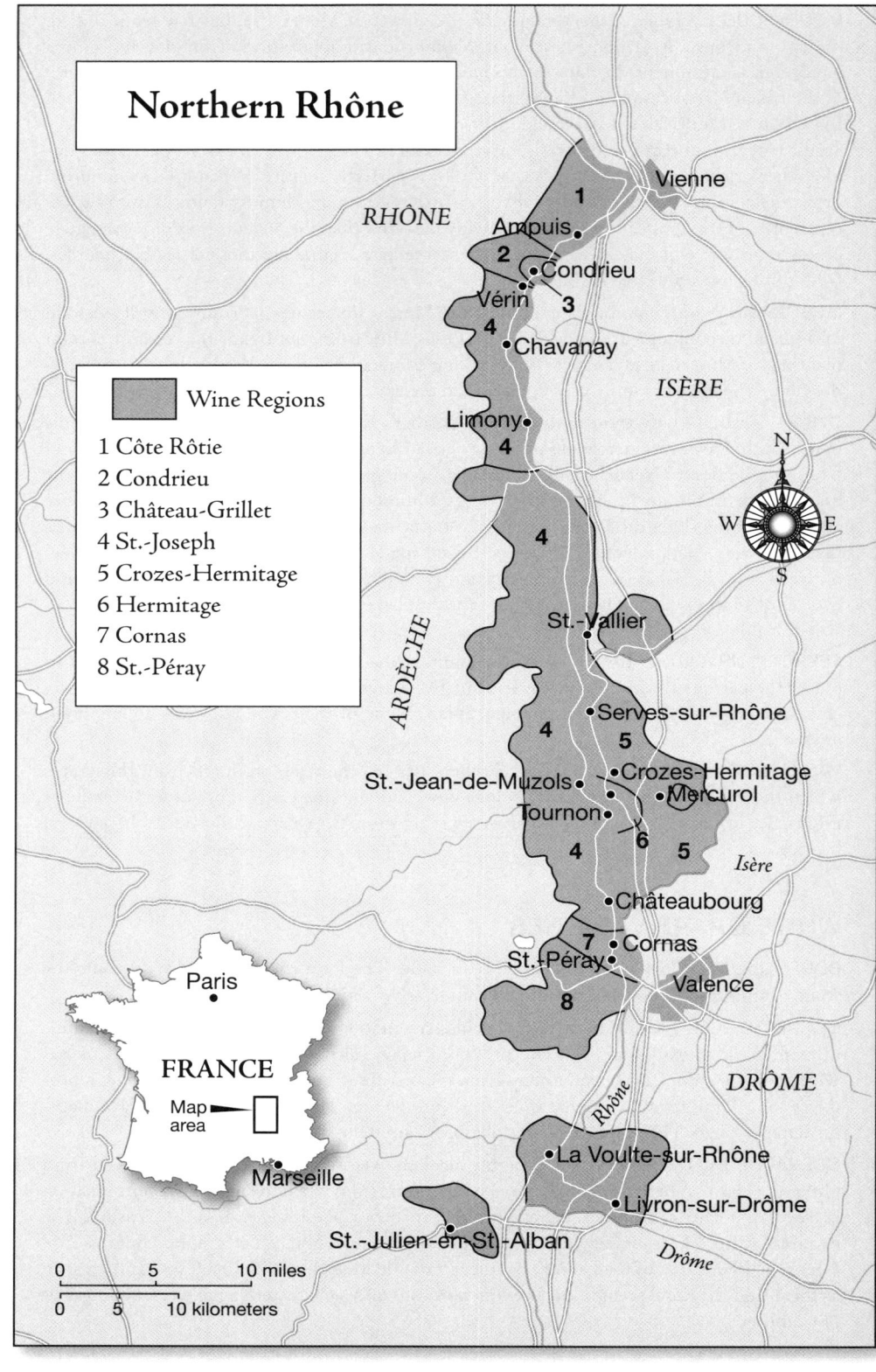

Northern Rhône

RHÔNE

Vienne
Ampuis
Condrieu
Vérin
Chavanay

ISÈRE

Limony

Wine Regions

1 Côte Rôtie
2 Condrieu
3 Château-Grillet
4 St.-Joseph
5 Crozes-Hermitage
6 Hermitage
7 Cornas
8 St.-Péray

St.-Vallier

ARDÈCHE

Serves-sur-Rhône

St.-Jean-de-Muzols
Crozes-Hermitage
Mercurol
Tournon

Isère

Châteaubourg

Cornas
St.-Péray
Valence

DRÔME

Rhône

Paris

FRANCE

Map area

Marseille

La Voulte-sur-Rhône

Livron-sur-Drôme

St.-Julien-en-St.-Alban

Drôme

0   5   10 miles

0   5   10 kilometers

Southern Rhône

FRANCE

Paris

Map area

Marseille

ARDÈCHE

Montélimar

DRÔME *Eygues*

6

•Donzère

6

•Grignan

Ardèche

8

Clansayes

Valréas

1

•Nyons

Rhône

Vinsobres

•Bollène

•St.-Maurice-sur-Eygues

Pont-St.-Esprit•

1 •Rasteau

•Vaison-la-Romaine

Argues

7

St.-Gervais•

•Gigondas

•Malaucène

Bagnols-sur-Cèze•

1

5

St.-Marcel•

Chusclan•

•Orange

•Beaumes-de-Venise

de-Careiret

Lauden•

Châteauneuf-

•Mormoiron

3

du-Pape

Roquemaure•

•Carpentras 7

Lirac•

2

•Bédarrides

Tavel•

4

•Vénasque

GARD

1

Villeneuve-les-Avignon

Châteauneuf-

VAUCLUSE

Domazan•

1

Avignon 1

de-Gadagne

7

•Gordes

Rhône

Coulon

•Apt

Nîmes•

•Cavaillon

•Bonnieux

Tarascon•

BOUCHES-

9

DU-RHÔNE

Mérindol•

Durance

•Cadenet

Wine Regions

1 Côtes du Rhône-Villages
2 Lirac
3 Tavel
4 Châteauneuf-du-Pape
5 Gigondas
6 Coteaux du Tricastin
7 Côtes du Ventoux
8 Côtes du Vivarais
9 Côtes du Luberon

N
W E
S

0   10 miles
0   10 kilometers

MARSANNE The Marsanne planted in the south produces rather chunky wines that must receive help from other varieties because they cannot stand alone. British author Jancis Robinson often claims it smells "not unpleasantly reminiscent of glue." More often than not, I find it resembles a high-class Fino Sherry with a nutty character.

PICARDIN This grape has fallen out of favor, largely because the growers felt it added nothing to their blends. Apparently, its neutral character was its undoing. Yet the Jaboulet firm has made several fine white Châteauneuf-du-Papes with high proportions of Picardin.

PICPOUL Frankly, I have no idea what this grape tastes like. I have never seen it isolated or represented in such a hefty percentage as to be identifiable. Today it is rarely seen in the southern Rhône.

ROUSSANNE For centuries, this grape was the essence of white Hermitage in the northern Rhône, but its small yields and proclivity to disease saw it largely replaced by Marsanne. Making a comeback in the southern Rhône, it has the most character of any of the white wine varietals—aromas of honey, coffee, flowers, and nuts—and produces a wine that can be very long-lived, an anomaly for a white wine in the southern Rhône. The famous Châteauneuf-du-Pape estate Beaucastel uses mostly Roussanne in their white wine, which, not surprisingly, is the longest-lived white wine of the appellation. Since 1986 they have also produced a 100% old-vine Roussanne that can be profound. Grand Veneur, Janasse, and La Nerthe also utilize considerable Roussanne. Because of its oxidative tendencies, vinification is tricky.

VIOGNIER Viognier produces a distinctive white wine that is synonymous with Condrieu and Château Grillet, both in the northern Rhône. In the south, especially in the Côtes du Rhône, there are extensive new plantings. The finest example in the southern Rhône is the Domaine Ste.-Anne in the Côtes du Rhône village of St.-Gervais. Château St.-Estève is another domaine in the Côtes du Rhône that produces a good Viognier. Beaucastel began to utilize it in their white Coudoulet in 1991. Unfortunately, Viognier is not a permitted variety in Châteauneuf-du-Pape, where it could immensely enhance the neutral character of so many of that village's white wines. It is an increasingly important component of white Côtes du Rhône and, in large measure, the most significant reason why these wines have risen in quality.

[appellations]

NORTHERN RHÔNE

CONDRIEU This exotic, often overwhelmingly fragrant wine is low in acidity and must be drunk young but offers hedonistic aromas and flavors of peaches, apricots, and honey, and an unbelievably decadent, opulent finish.

CORNAS The impenetrable black/ruby color, the brutal, even savage tannins in its youth, the massive structure, and the muddy sediment in the bottle are all characteristics of a wine that tastes as if it were made in the nineteenth century. But Cornas wines are among the most virile, robust wines in the world, with a powerful aroma of cassis and raspberries that develops into chestnuts, truffles, licorice, and black currants as it ages. These wines are among the most underrated reds of the world, but patience as well as a fondness for rustic wine is essential if they are to be appreciated.

CÔTE RÔTIE This is an immense, fleshy, rich, fragrant, smoky, medium- to full-bodied, stunning wine with gobs of cassis fruit frequently intertwined with the smell of frying bacon, tapenade, and smoke. One of France's greatest wines, it can last for up to 25 years when well stored.

CROZES-HERMITAGE Despite this appellation's proximity to the more famous appellation of Hermitage, the red wines tend to be soft, spicy, fruity, chunky, vegetal, and rather one-dimensional instead of distinguished. The white wines vary enormously in quality and can be pleasant but are often neutral and acidic.

HERMITAGE At its best, Hermitage is a rich, almost Port-like, viscous, very full-bodied, tannic red wine that can seemingly last forever. It is characterized by intense, even pungent smells of pepper and cassis, intertwined at times with aromas of licorice, melted asphalt, and truffles. The white Hermitage can be neutral, but the finest examples display a bouquet of herbs, minerals, nuts, fino Sherry, acacia flowers, peaches, and a stony, wet-slate-like component. The rare sweet *vin de paille* offers an intoxicating smell of truffles at 8 to 10 years of age.

ST.-JOSEPH This is the northern Rhône's most underrated appellation for red and white wine. The reds and whites are juicy and best drunk young, preferably within 10 years of the vintage. No northern appellation has made as much qualitative progress as St.-Joseph. Moreover, these wines are fairly priced.

ST.-PÉRAY Tiny quantities of still and sparkling white wines are made from this forgotten appellation of the Rhône Valley. Increasingly, the wines merit consumer interest, as producers appear to be getting more minerality and flavors in the wines. Moreover, some producers, most notably Clape and Voge of Cornas, are producing very promising white wines, the Chablis of the Rhône Valley.

SOUTHERN RHÔNE

CHÂTEAUNEUF-DU-PAPE There is an enormous diversity in the styles of Châteauneuf-du-Pape produced. It can be made to resemble a Beaujolais, in which case it offers jammy, soft, fruity flavors and must be drunk quite young. If the wine is vinified in a classic manner, it can be very dense in color, sumptuously rich and full bodied, and can last 15 to 25 years. It is often characterized by the smell of saddle leather, fennel, licorice, black truffles, pepper, nutmeg, and smoked meats. Wines made by both these methods and then blended together, and dominated by the Grenache grape, often smell of roasted peanuts and overripe Bing cherries. While white Châteauneuf-du-Papes were once neutral and uninteresting, significant progress has been made, and many examples now possess floral- and tropical fruit–scented bouquets. However, they must be drunk extremely young.

CÔTES DU RHÔNE The best Côtes du Rhônes offer uncomplicated but deliciously succulent, crunchy, peppery, blackberry and raspberry fruit presented in a supple, full-bodied style that is meant to be consumed within five to six years of the vintage. A handful can improve for 10 to 15 years. The finest Côtes du Rhône and Côtes du Rhône Villages offer some of the greatest red wine values in the world.

CÔTES DU RHÔNE VILLAGES This is another appellation requiring closer study, given the increasing number of high-quality estates. The most exciting *villages* include Cairanne, Rasteau, Sablet, Séguret, St.-Gervais, Beaumes de Venise, Lirac, and Tavel (which produces France's most famous rosé).

GIGONDAS Gigondas offers up a robust, chewy, medium-bodied, rich, generous red wine that has a heady bouquet and supple, rich, spicy flavors. A tiny quantity of a very underrated rosé wine is often made, which should be tried by consumers looking for something special. The Gigondas area is a cooler climate region than either of its nearby neighbors, Vacqueyras and Châteauneuf-du-Pape. Harvest can often be two to three weeks later than in Châteauneuf-du-Pape, and this often challenges growers to harvest ripe fruit before the onset of the October rains.

MUSCAT DE BEAUMES DE VENISE This sweet, alcoholic, but extraordinarily perfumed exotic wine offers up smells of peaches, apricots, coconut, and lychee nuts. It must be drunk in its youth to be fully appreciated.

VACQUEYRAS Given its own appellation designation in 1990, Vacqueyras is an exciting hot-bed of activity. The wines are increasingly sought out by shrewd value-conscious buyers looking for Châteauneuf-du-Pape look-alikes selling for one-half the price. Overall, the number of top estates in Vacqueyras surpasses its better-known next-door rival, Gigondas.

AGING POTENTIAL

NORTHERN RHÔNE, SOUTHERN RHÔNE

Châteauneuf-du-Pape (red): 5–25 years
Châteauneuf-du-Pape (white): 1–2 years, with a few notable exceptions
Condrieu: 2–5 years
Cornas: 5–15 years
Côtes du Rhône: 4–8 years
Côtes du Rhône Villages: 4–8 years
Côte Rôtie: 5–25 years
Crozes-Hermitage: 3–10 years
Gigondas: 5–15 years
Château Grillet: 5–15 years
Hermitage (red): 5–30 years
Hermitage (white): 3–25 years
Muscat de Beaumes de Venise: 1–3 years
St.-Joseph: 3–6 years
Tavel: 1–2 years

OVERALL QUALITY LEVEL

In the northern Rhône appellations of Côte Rôtie, Hermitage, Condrieu, and Cornas, the general level of winemaking is excellent. In the other appellations, it is irregular. In the southern Rhône, Châteauneuf-du-Pape has the broadest range in quality, from thrilling, world-class, sumptuous wines to thin, industrial, diluted ones. However, Châteauneuf-du-Pape is one of France's most exciting regions, because of the young generation of winemakers who are fashioning greater and greater wines. Behind Châteauneuf-du-Pape are Vacqueyras, Rasteau, and Gigondas.

NORTHERN RHÔNE

CÔTE RÔTIE AT A GLANCE

Appellation creation October 18, 1940.

Type of wine produced Red wine only.

Grape varieties planted Syrah and Viognier (up to 20% can be added, but as a rule, few producers utilize more than 5% in their wines; Guigal's famed La Mouline boasts 11% in most vintages).

Acres currently under vine 500.

Quality level At least good, the best exceptional, among the finest red wines in the world.

Aging potential The finest age 5 to 30 years.

General characteristics Fleshy, rich, very fragrant, smoky, full-bodied, stunning wines.

Greatest recent vintages 2007, 2005, 2003, 2001, 1999, 1998, 1997, 1995, 1991, 1990, 1989, 1988, 1985, 1983, 1978, 1976, 1969.

Price range $50–$75, except for Guigal's and Chapoutier's single vineyard and/or luxury cuvées, which cost $150 or more.

Aromatic profile These intensely fragrant wines offer compelling bouquets showcasing scents and flavors of cassis, black raspberries, smoke, bacon fat, violets, olives, and grilled meats. Aromas of vanilla and toast were also evident in the wines that spent a lot of time in new oak casks.

Textural profile These are elegant yet authoritatively powerful wines that are often chewy and deep. They are usually medium- to full-bodied, with surprisingly good acid levels for such ripeness and power. Tannin levels are generally moderate.

THE CÔTE RÔTIE APPELLATION'S MOST PROFOUND WINES

Patrick et Christophe Bonnefond Les Rochains
Chapoutier La Mordorée
Clusel-Roch Les Grandes Places
Delas Frères La Landonne (since 1997)
Delas Frères Seigneur de Maugiron (since 1997)
Pierre Gaillard Côte Rozier
J. M. Gérin Les Grandes Places
J. M. Gérin La Landonne
Guigal Château d'Ampuis
Guigal La Landonne
Guigal La Mouline
Guigal La Turque
Jasmin (since 1999)
Domaine de Monteillet Les Grandes Places
Michel Ogier (since 1991)
Michel Ogier Belle-Hélène
René Rostaing Côte Blonde
René Rostaing Côte Brune La Landonne

[the ratings]

THE CÔTE RÔTIE PRODUCERS

* * * * * (OUTSTANDING)

Chapoutier La Mordorée
Clusel-Roch Les Grandes Places
Delas Frères La Landonne
Pierre Gaillard Côte Rozier—
    La Rose Pourpre
Jean-Michel Gérin Les Grandes Places
Jean-Michel Gérin La Landonne
Guigal Château d'Ampuis

Guigal La Landonne
Guigal La Mouline
Guigal La Turque
Jean-Paul et Jean-Luc Jamet
Michel Ogier
Michel Ogier Belle-Hélène
René Rostaing Côte Blonde
René Rostaing Côte Brune La Landonne

* * * * (EXCELLENT)

Patrick et Christophe Bonnefond
Patrick et Christophe Bonnefond Les
    Rochains
Bernard Burgaud

Domaine Clusel-Roch (other cuvées)
Yves Cuilleron Bassenon
Yves Cuilleron Terres Sombres
Delas Frères Seigneurs de Maugiron

Edmond et David Duclaux
Duclaux La Germine
Duclaux Maison Rouge
Pierre Gaillard
Henri Gallet
Yves Gangloff
Jean-Michel Gérin Champin Le Seigneur
Guigal Côtes Brune et Blonde
Jasmin

Laffoy et Gasse
Laffoy et Gasse Vieilles Vignes
Domaine de Monteillet Les Grande Places
Stéphane Robert
René Rostaing (regular cuvée)
René Rostaing Côte Brune
Tardieu-Laurent
Vidal-Fleury Côtes Brune et Blonde
Vidal-Fleury La Chatillonne

* * * (GOOD)

Gilles Barge Côte Brune
Gilles Barge Cuvée du Plessy
Guy et Frédéric Bernard
De Boisseyt Côte Blonde
Domaine de Bonserine Côte Brune
Domaine de Bonserine La Garde
Domaine de Bonserine La Sarrasine
Domaine de Bonserine Les Moutonnes
Emile Champet
Joel Champet La Viaillère
Michel Chapoutier (regular cuvée)
Domaine Clusel-Roch (regular cuvée)
Lurette & Martin Daubrée

Albert Dervieux-Thaize*
Philippe Faury
André François
Domaine Garon
Stéphane Pichat
Christophe Pichon
J. Michel-Stephan
J. Michel-Stephan Vieilles Vignes
  en Coteaux
Château de Montlys
Mouton Père et Fils
Eric Texier
Daniel Vernay

CONDRIEU AT A GLANCE

Appellation creation April 27, 1940.

Type of wine produced White wine only.

Grape varieties authorized Viognier.

Acres currently under vine Condrieu, 250; Château Grillet, 7.6.

Quality level The top wines are exceptional, as this is one of the rarest and most unique wines in the world, but quality is increasingly irregular.

Aging potential 1–4 years; Château Grillet will keep 5–15 years.

General characteristics An exotic, often overwhelming apricot/peach/honeysuckle fragrance is followed by low-acid, very rich wines that are usually short-lived; ironically, the less successful vintages with higher acidity age longer.

Greatest recent vintages 2007, 2006.

Price range $55–$125.

Aromatic profile Honeysuckle, peaches, apricots, and candied tropical fruit aromas should soar from a glass of a top Condrieu.

Textural profile In ripe vintages, Condrieu tends to be low in acidity but not flabby. Fleshy, decadent, dry, and gloriously fruity and layered flavors should be intense but not heavy. In most vintages a tiny quantity of late-harvested Viognier is produced. It is usually very sweet and somewhat cloying.

---

*Dervieux-Thaize, retired since 1991, leases his vineyards to René Rostaing.

THE CONDRIEU APPELLATION'S MOST PROFOUND WINES

Yves Cuilleron Les Chaillets Vieilles Vignes
Delas Frères Clos Boucher
Yves Gangloff
Guigal La Doriane
Domaine du Monteillet (Antoine Montez)
André Perret Coteau du Chéry
René Rostaing
Georges Vernay Les Chaillées de l'Enfer
Georges Vernay Coteaux du Vernon
François Villard DePoncins

[the ratings]

THE CONDRIEU PRODUCERS

★ ★ ★ ★ ★ (OUTSTANDING)

Yves Cuilleron Les Chaillets Vieilles Vignes
Yves Gangloff
Guigal La Doriane
Guigal (*négociant* bottling)

Domaine du Monteillet (Antoine Montez)
André Perret Clos Chanson
André Perret Coteau du Chéry

★ ★ ★ ★ (EXCELLENT)

Patrick et Christophe Bonnefond
   Côte Chatillon
Chapoutier
Yves Cuilleron (regular cuvée)
Delas Frères Clos Boucher

Philippe et Christophe Pichon
Hervé Richard
René Rostaing
Georges Vernay
François Villard (various cuvées)

★ ★ ★ (GOOD)

Gilles Barge
Domaine du Chên—Marc Rouvière
Domaine Louis Chèze
Delas Frères La Galopine
Domaine Farjon

Philippe Faury
Philippe Faury La Berne
Château Grillet*
Vidal-Fleury

HERMITAGE AT A GLANCE

Appellation creation March 4, 1937.

Type of wine produced Red, white, and *vin de paille,* a dessert-style white wine.

Grape varieties planted Syrah for the red wine; primarily Marsanne and some Roussanne for the white; up to 15% white wine grapes can be blended with the red wine, but as a practical matter this is widely eschewed.

Acres currently under vine 325.

---

*Prior to 1979, five stars; since 1979, three stars. Château Grillet is entitled to its own appellation, a
  very unusual situation in France.

Quality level Prodigious for the finest red wines, good to exceptional for the whites.

Aging potential Red wine, 5–40 plus years; white wine, 3–25 years.

General characteristics Rich, viscous, very full-bodied, tannic red wines. Full-bodied white wines with a unique scent of herbs, minerals, nuts, peaches, and, on occasion, top-rated Fino Sherry.

Greatest recent vintages 2007, 2005, 2003, 1999, 1998, 1995, 1991, 1990, 1989, 1979, 1978, 1972, 1970, 1966, 1961, 1959.

Price range $75–$125 will purchase any wine except for single-parcel wines such as Chapoutier's L'Orée, L'Ermite, Le Méal, and Le Pavillon or Chave's Cuvée Cathelin, which can cost $250 a bottle or more.

Aromatic profile *Red*—Cassis, black pepper, tar, and very ripe red and black fruits characterize a fine young vintage of red Hermitage. With a decade of bottle age, cedar, spice, and cassis can (and often do) resemble a first-growth Pauillac. *White*—Pineapple aromas intertwine with acacia flowers, peach, and honey scents. With extended age (15 or more years), scents of smoked nuts, fino Sherry, and honey can be overpowering.

Textural profile *Red*—Unusually full-bodied, powerful, and tannic, as well as resistant to oxidation, a wine that ages at a glacial pace. *White*—Fruity, full-bodied, and fragrant when young, white Hermitage closes down after four to five years of bottle age, only to reemerge 15–25 years later as an unctuous, dry, thick white wine.

THE HERMITAGE APPELLATION'S MOST PROFOUND WINES

Chapoutier Cuvée l'Orée (white)
Chapoutier Ermitage l'Ermite (red and white)
Chapoutier Le Méal (red and white)
Chapoutier Le Pavillon (red)
J. L. Chave (red)
J. L. Chave (white)
J. L. Chave Cuvée Cathelin (red)
Delas Frères Les Béssards (red)
Bernard Faurie Le Méal (red)
Paul Jaboulet-Aîné Hermitage La Chapelle (red)*
Domaine des Rémizières Cuvée Emilie (red and white)
Marc Sorrel Hermitage Le Gréal (red)

[the ratings]

THE RED HERMITAGE PRODUCERS

* * * * * (OUTSTANDING)

Chapoutier Ermitage l'Ermite
Chapoutier Le Méal
Chapoutier Le Pavillon
J. L. Chave Cuvée Cathelin

J. L. Chave (regular cuvée)
Delas Frères Les Béssards (since 1997)
Domaine des Rémizières Cuvée Emilie

*Before 1991.

* * * * (EXCELLENT)

Albert Belle

Chapoutier Hermitage La Sizeranne
(since 1989)

Domaine du Colombier

Delas Frères Les Béssards

Bernard Faurie (regular cuvée)

Bernard Faurie Le Méal

Paul Jaboulet-Aîné La Chapelle
(prior to 1991, five stars)

Marc Sorrel Cuvée Classique

Marc Sorrel Le Gréal

* * * (GOOD)

Bernard Chave

Delas Frères Marquise de la Tourette

Domaine Fayolle

Ferraton Père et Fils Les Dionnières

Ferraton Père et Fils Le Méal

Alain Graillot

Guigal

Paul Jaboulet-Aîné Hermitage Pied
de la Côte

Jean-Michel Sorrel

Vidal-Fleury

THE WHITE HERMITAGE PRODUCERS

* * * * * (OUTSTANDING)

Chapoutier Cuvée l'Ermite

Chapoutier Cuvée de l'Orée

J. L. Chave

Domaine des Rémizières Cuvée Emilie

* * * * (EXCELLENT)

Chapoutier Cuvée Le Méal

J. L. Grippat

Guigal

Paul Jaboulet-Aîné Chevalier de Sterimberg
(since 1989)

Marc Sorrel Les Rocoules

CROZES-HERMITAGE AT A GLANCE

Appellation creation March 3, 1937.

Type of wine produced Red and white wine.

Grape varieties planted Marsanne and Roussanne for the white wine; Syrah for the red wine, which represents 90% of the appellation's production.

Acres currently under vine 2,550.

Quality level Mediocre to good, occasionally excellent; a few wines are superb.

Aging potential White wine, 1–4 years, red wine, 3–10 years.

General characteristics Tremendous variability in the red wines; the white wines are fleshy, chunky, solid, and rather undistinguished.

Greatest recent vintages 2007, 2005, 2003, 1999, 1998, 1997, 1995, 1991, 1990, 1989, 1988, 1978.

Price range $25–$35.

Aromatic profile It is not dissimilar to Hermitage, but less intense and often with more Provençal herb and olive scents. The Crozes-Hermitage *terroirs* are variable, and the Syrah does not achieve the exceptional ripeness found in Hermitage. The top wines are medium-bodied, with attractive, smoky, peppery, cassis scents and flavors that can resemble a downsized Hermitage. The hillside sites in Larnage tend to offer greater ripeness, the valley floor sites more olive/tapenade nuances.

Textural profile In addition to its deep ruby/purple color, this wine generally possesses medium to full body, moderate tannin, and fine depth in the best examples. It rarely rewards cellaring for more than a decade, except in vintages such as 1978, 1990, and 2007.

THE CROZES-HERMITAGE APPELLATION'S MOST PROFOUND WINES

Albert Belle Cuvée Louis Belle
Chapoutier Les Varonnières
Laurent Combier Clos des Grives
Delas Frères Clos St.-Georges
Delas Frères Tour d'Albon
Ferraton Le Grand Courtil
Alain Graillot Les Guiraudes
Paul Jaboulet-Aîné Domaine Raymond Roure
Paul Jaboulet-Aîné Domaine de Thalabert
Domaine du Pavillon Vieilles Vignes (Stephan Cornu)
Domaine Rémizières Cuvée Christophe (red and white)

[the ratings]

THE CROZE-HERMITAGE PRODUCERS

★ ★ ★ ★ (EXCELLENT)

Albert Belle Cuvée Louis Belle
Chapoutier Les Varonnières
Domaine du Colombier Cuvée Gaby
Domaine du Combier Clos des Grives
Delas Frères Clos St.-Georges
Delas Frères Tour d'Albon

Alain Graillot Cuvée La Guiraude
Paul Jaboulet-Aîné Domaine de Thalabert
Domaine du Pavillon (Stephen Cornu)
   Cuvée Vieilles Vignes
Domaine Rémizières Cuvée Christophe

★ ★ ★ (GOOD)

Albert Belle Cuvée Les Pierrelles
Chapoutier Les Meysonnières
Chapoutier Petite Ruche
Bernard Chave
Domaine de la Collonge
Dard et Ribo Domaine Blanche Laine
Domaine des Entrefaux Le Dessus
   des Entrefaux
Domaine Fayolle La Grande Séguine
Domaine Fayolle Les Voussères

Michel Ferraton Le Grand Courtil
Alain Graillot Cuvée Classique
Guigal
Domaines Pochon/Château de Curson
Domaine Jacques et Jean-Louis Pradelle
   Les Hirondelles
Raymond Roure (acquired by Paul
   Jaboulet-Aîné in 1996)
Vidal-Fleury

ST.-JOSEPH AT A GLANCE

Appellation creation June 15, 1956.

Type of wine produced Red and white wine.

Grape varieties planted Marsanne and Roussanne for white wine; Syrah for red wine.

Acres currently under vine 1,729.

Quality level Average to excellent.

Aging potential White wine, 1–5 years; red wine, 3–8 years.

General characteristics The red wines are the lightest, fruitiest, and most feminine of the northern Rhône. The white wines are perfumed and fleshy with scents of apricots and pears.

Greatest recent vintages 2007, 2005, 2003, 1999.

Price range $25–$50; several old-vine cuvées cost $75 or more.

Aromatic profile *White*—At the top level, the finest white wines are medium-bodied, refreshing, peach/apricot, sometimes pear-scented wines with good citrusy acidity that are delightful to drink within their first two to three years of life. Unfortunately, only a small percentage of dry whites meet these criteria. The majority of white St.-Joseph tend to be neutral, monolithic wines lacking charm and personality. *Red*—Syrah can be at its fruitiest, lightest, and most charming in this appellation. A good St.-Joseph red should display a Burgundian-like black-cherry, raspberry, and occasionally cassis-scented nose with medium body, light tannin, and zingy acidity. These, the Rhône Valley's lightest reds, are best drunk in their first five to six years.

Textural profile *White*—Light to medium body is the prevailing rule, with not much weight. Good freshness, crisp acidity, and an uncomplicated fruit give these wines an appealing lightweight character. *Red*—Good fruit presented in a medium-bodied, zesty format is the hallmark of fine St.-Joseph reds. They should not possess tannin for support but, rather, crisp acidity.

THE ST.-JOSEPH APPELLATION'S MOST PROFOUND WINES

F. Boissonnet Cuvée de la Bélive
Chapoutier Les Granits (red and white)
J. L. Chave
Domaine du Chêne Cuvée Anaïs
Domaine Louis Chèze Cuvée des Anges
Domaine Chèze Cuvée Prestige de Caroline
Domaine Courbis Les Royes
Pierre Coursodon Le Paradis St.-Pierre
Pierre Coursodon La Sensonne
Yves Cuilleron Coteau St.-Pierre (white)
Yves Cuilleron Lyseras (white)
Yves Cuilleron Prestige l'Amarybelle
Yves Cuilleron Cuvée Prestige Le Bois Lombard (white)
Yves Cuilleron Les Serines
Delas Frères François de Touron
Delas Frères Ste.-Epine
Paul Jaboulet-Aîné Le Grand Pompée
Pierre Gaillard Clos de Cuminaille
Guigal Vignes de l'Hospice
Guigal (white)
Domaine du Monteillet (Antoine Montez) Cuvée de Papy
Alain Paret 420 Nuits (red)
Alain Paret Rochecourbe (red)
André Perret (white)
André Perret Les Grisières
Tardieu-Laurent Les Ruches (red)
Raymond Trollat
François Villard Côtes de Mairlant (red and white)
François Villard Réflet

[the ratings]

THE ST.-JOSEPH PRODUCERS

★ ★ ★ ★ ★ (OUTSTANDING)

Chapoutier Les Granits (red)
Domaine Louis Chèze Cuvée des
    Anges (red)
Domaine Louis Chèze Cuvée Prestige
    de Caroline (red)

Coursodon Le Paradis St.-Pierre (red)
Coursodon La Sensonne (red)
Guigal Vignes de l'Hospice (red)
Pascal Perrier Domaine de Gachon (red)

★ ★ ★ ★ (EXCELLENT)

Chapoutier Les Granits (white)
J. L. Chave (red)
Domaine du Chêne Cuvée Anaïs (red)
Domaine Courbis Les Royes (red)
Yves Cuilleron (white)
Yves Cuilleron Cuvée Prestige Le Bois
    Lombard (white)
Bernard Faurie (red)

Alain Graillot (red)
Guigal Lieu Dit St.-Joseph (red)
Paul Jaboulet-Aîné Le Grand Pompée (red)
Domaine du Monteillet (Antoine Montez)
    Cuvée de Papy (red)
André Perret (white)
André Perret Les Grisières (red)
Pascal Perrier Cuvée de Collonjon (red)

★ ★ ★ (GOOD)

Clos de l'Arbalestrier (red)
Roger Blachon (red)
Chapoutier Les Deschants (red and white)
Domaine du Chêne (red)
Domaine Louis Chèze (red)
Domaine Collonge (red)
Courbis (regular cuvée)
Pierre Coursodon l'Olivaie (red)
Yves Cuilleron (red)
Yves Cuilleron Cuvée Prestige (red)
Bernard Faurie (white)
Philippe Faury (red)
Bernard Grippa (red)

Bernard Grippa Cuvée Le Berceau
    (white and red)
Paul Jaboulet-Aîné (white)
Domaine du Monteillet (Antoine Montez)
    (red)
Alain Paret Chais St.-Pierre l'Arm de
    Père (red)
Alain Paret Chais St.-Pierre Domaine de la
    Couthiat (red)
André Perret (red)
St.-Désirat Cave Coopérative
    (red and white)
Vidal-Fleury (red)

CORNAS AT A GLANCE

Appellation creation August 5, 1938.

Type of wine produced Red wine only.

Grape varieties planted Syrah only.

Acres currently under vine 220.

Quality level Good to exceptional.

Aging potential 5–20 years.

General characteristics Black/ruby in color, very tannic, full-bodied, virile, robust wines with powerful aromas and rustic personalities.

Greatest recent vintages 2007, 2005, 2003, 2001, 1999, 1998, 1997, 1991, 1990, 1989, 1985, 1979, 1978, 1976, 1969.

Price range $40–$75.

Aromatic profile Black fruit, earth, minerals, occasionally truffles, smoked herbs, and meats are common.

Textural profile Massive, tannic, nearly coarse flavors have full body, intensity, length, and grip, but are often too savage and uncivilized for many tasters.

THE CORNAS APPELLATION'S MOST PROFOUND WINES

Auguste Clape
Jean-Luc Colombo La Louvée
Domaine Courbis Cornas Les Eygats
Domaine Courbis Cornas La Sabarotte
Vincent Paris Granit 60 Vieilles Vignes
Tardieu-Laurent Vieilles Vignes
Alain Voge Les Vieilles Fontaines
Alain Voge Vieilles Vignes

[the ratings]

THE CORNAS PRODUCERS

* * * * * (OUTSTANDING)

Auguste Clape
Jean-Luc Colombo La Louvée

Alain Voge Les Vieilles Fontaines
Alain Voge Vieilles Vignes

* * * * (EXCELLENT)

Thierry Allemand Cuvée Les Chaillots
Thierry Allemand Cuvée Reynard
Jean-Luc Colombo Les Ruchets
Domaine du Coulet
L. et D. Courbis-Domaine (Champelrose des Royes La Sabarotte)
Dumien-Serette Patou

Eric et Joël Durand Empreintes
Johan Michel Cuvée Jana
Vincent Paris
Tardieu-Laurent Coteaux
Domaine du Tunnel
Domaine du Tunnel Cuvée Prestige

* * * (GOOD)

René Balthazar
Cave Coopérative de Tain l'Hermitage
Chapoutier
Jean-Luc Colombo Terres Brûlées
L. et D. Courbis (regular cuvée)
Delas Frères Cuvée Chante-Perdrix
Charles Despesse Les Côtes
Domaine de Fauterie (Sylvain Bernard)

Paul Jaboulet-Aîné (*négociant* bottling)
Paul Jaboulet-Aîné Domaine de St.-Pierre
Jacques Lemencier
Jean Lionnet Cuvée Rochepertuis
Robert Michel Cuvée des Côteaux
Robert Michel Cuvée le Pied du Coteau
Robert Michel La Geynale
J.-L. Thiers

ST.-PÉRAY AT A GLANCE

Appellation creation December 8, 1936.

Type of wine produced Still and sparkling white wines, the latter representing 60% of the production.

Grape varieties planted Marsanne and Roussanne.

Acres currently under vine 160.

Quality level Below average to average.

Aging potential 2–4 years.

General characteristics Historically, dull, somewhat odd, uninteresting, heavy and diffuse wines emerged from this appellation. However, in the 21st century, producers such as Clape, Voge, and Chaboud began fashioning Chablis-like, dry, mineral-laced wines.

Greatest recent vintages None.

Price range $25–$30.

Aromatic profile The acceptable examples—sadly, there are too few—offer a vague lemony/peachlike smell, with neutral fruit flavors. The majority of the wines are acidic, heavy, and lacking fruit.

Textural profile The sparkling wines are crisp and at times refreshing, but in a low-brow sense. The still wines can be flabby, full-bodied, chewy wines with no real vibrancy. There are only a few interesting St.-Péray wines, but quality is moving upward.

[the ratings]

THE ST.-PÉRAY WINE PRODUCERS

* * * * (EXCELLENT)

Stéphane Chaboud
Stéphane Chaboud Cuvée Arnaud
  (sparkling)

Domaine du Tunnel
Voge Fleur de Crussol

* * * (GOOD)

Auguste Clape

SOUTHERN RHÔNE

CÔTES DU RHÔNE AT A GLANCE

Appellation creation November 19, 1937.

Type of wine produced Red, white, and rosé, although over 95% of the production is red wine.

Grape varieties planted 24 grapes are authorized, 14 designated as primary varieties and 10 as accessory, but for all practical purposes the predominant red wine grape is Grenache, followed by Syrah, Mourvèdre, and Cinsault. For the white wines, Grenache Blanc, Clairette, Bourboulenc, and increasingly Viognier and Roussanne are the principal grapes.

Acres currently under vine 110,495.

Quality level At the cooperative level, which accounts for 75%–80% of the entire generic Côtes du Rhône production, quality ranges from insipid and sterile to very good to excellent; at the estate-bottled level, the quality ranges from below average to exceptional in the case of a half dozen or so overachievers.

Aging potential Over 95% of every bottle of generic Côtes du Rhône, whether red, white, or rosé, should be drunk early; the whites and rosés within two years of the vintage and the reds within two to four years of the vintage. However, some of the seriously endowed wines from the top estates can age for 20-plus years.

General characteristics At the top levels, the white wines have made tremendous progress in quality as a result of modern cold fermentation and the introduction of Viognier and Roussanne in the blend. Even with these improvements, these are wines that are fresh, lively, and meant to be drunk quickly. The red wines vary enormously. A well-made Côtes du Rhône should be bursting with red and black fruits, have a peppery, Provençal herb-scented nose, a supple, velvety texture, and a heady, lusty, spicy finish.

Greatest recent vintages 2007, 2005, 2001, 2000, 1999, 1998, 1995.

Price range $10–$25, except for the single-vineyard and old-vine cuvées of a handful of estates. The best of these wines (i.e., the four- and five-star producers that follow) irrefutably represent many of the greatest red wine values in the world, particularly in vintages such as 2007, 2005, and 2001, 2000.

[the ratings]

THE CÔTES DU RHÔNE AND CÔTES DU RHÔNE-VILLAGES PRODUCERS

***** (OUTSTANDING)

Daniel et Denis Alary La Font d'Estévanas Cairanne
Daniel et Denis Alary La Jean de Verde Cairanne
Domaine des Aphillanthes Cuvée des Galets
Domaine des Aphillanthes Cuvée du Gros
Domaine des Aphillanthes Trois Cépages
André Brunel Cuvée Sommelongue
Robert Charvin Côteaux des Travers Cairanne
Charvin
Coudoulet de Beaucastel
Clos du Caillou Bouquet des Garrigues
Clos du Caillou Très Vieilles Vignes

Château de Fonsalette
Château de Fonsalette Cuvée Syrah
Domaine Gramenon Ceps Centenaire
Domaine de la Janasse Les Garrigues
Mordorée—Reine des Bois Lirac
Domaine de L'Oratoire St.-Martin
Domaine La Réméjeanne Les Eglantiers
Domaine La Réméjeanne Les Genevrières
A. Romero Cuvée Confiance Rasteau
A. Romero Cuvée Prestige Rasteau
A. Romero Fleur de Confiance Rasteau
St.-Cosme Les Deux Albion
Tardieu-Laurent Cuvée Guy Louis

**** (EXCELLENT)

Daniel et Denis Alary (regular cuvée)
Domaine de l'Ameillaud
Domaine d'Andézon
Domaine des Anges
Max Aubert (various cuvées)
Max Aubert Galifay
Domaine de la Bécassonne
Bressy-Masson Rasteau
Domaine de Cabasse
La Canorgue
Jean-Luc Colombo Les Abeilles
Domaine le Couroulu
Cros de la Mure
Domaine de Ferraud
Domaine de Ferraud Cuvée des Demoiselles
Domaine Gramenon (various cuvées)

Domaine des Grands Devers
Château du Grand Moulas
Château du Grand Prébois
Domaine Les Grands Bois Cuvée Eloise Cairanne
Domaine Les Grands Bois Cuvée Gabrielle Cairanne
Domaine Les Grands Bois Cuvée Maximillian Cairanne
Domaine Les Grands Bois Cuvée Mireille Cairanne
Domaine de la Guichard
Guigal
Patrick Lesec (various cuvées)
Jean-Marie Lombard
Domaine Pélaquié

Domaine de la Réméjeanne Les Arbousiers

Domaine de la Réméjeanne Les
  Chevrefeuilles

Domaine des Richaud l'Ebrescade Cairanne

Domaine des Richaud Les Garrigues
  Rabasse-Charavin

Domaine St.-Apollinaire

Domaine Santa Duc

Château de Ségriès

Domaine de la Solitude

Château des Tours

Domaine des Treilles

Vidal-Fleury

La Vieille Ferme (Perrin Réserve de
  Vieilles Vignes)

Domaine du Vieux Chêne (various cuvées)

★ ★ ★ (GOOD)

Domaine des Aires Vielles

Daniel Combe

Château de Domazan

Domaine de l'Espigouette

Domaine les Goubert

Domaine du Grand Prieur

Domaine la Millière

Domaine Mireille et Vincent

Domaine Mitan

Domaine de Mont Redon

Domaine des Moulins

Mourre du Tendre

Domaines Mousset

Domaine de la Renjarde

Château St.-Estève d'Uchaux

Château de Trignon (various cuvées)

La Vieille Ferme (other cuvées)

CHÂTEAUNEUF-DU-PAPE AT A GLANCE

Appellation creation May 15, 1936.

Type of wine produced Red, 93%; white, 7%.

Grape varieties planted 13 (actually 14 if the white clone of Grenache is counted) varieties are permitted; for red wines, Grenache, Syrah, Mourvèdre, Cinsault, Muscardin, Counoise, Vaccarèse, and Terret Noir; for white wines, Grenache Blanc, Clairette, Bourboulenc, Roussanne, Picpoul, and Picardin.

Acres currently under vine 8,100.

Quality level *Red wine*—at the estate-bottled level, very good to exceptional; at the *négociant* level, mediocre to very good. *White wine*—mediocre to exceptional.

Aging potential *Red*—depending on the style, 5–20 years. *White*—1–3 years, except longer for Beaucastel and La Nerthe's Beauvenir.

General characteristics *Red wine*—considerable diversity in stylistic approach can result in full-bodied, generous, rich, round, alcoholic, and long-lived wines to soft, fruity wines that could be called the Beaujolais of Provence. *White wine*—floral, fruity, straightforward, and fresh if drunk within two years of the vintage.

Greatest recent vintages 2007, 2006, 2005, 2003, 2001, 1998, 1995, 1990, 1989, 1981.

Price range $40–$75, with special old vine and/or single vineyard cuvées costing considerably more; $75–$225 is not an unusual price for such rarities.

Aromatic profile *Red*—Given the enormous diversity of winemaking styles in this appellation, the following is a simplified view. Producers who turn out carbonic maceration wines are aiming for early bottling and easy to understand red/black fruit aromas that are appealingly jammy. The producers aiming for fuller-bodied, classically made Châteauneuf-du-Pape produce wines with a vast array of aromatics, ranging from black cherries/currants and blueberries to roasted herbs, the noted Provençal *garrigue* smell (an earthy, *herbes de Provence* aromatic concoction), to overripe peaches and raspberry jam. *White*—The great majority of Châteauneuf-du-Pape white wines have their malolactic fermentation blocked and are made in a style that sees no oak and very early bottling (usually within three to four months of the vintage). These wines are meant to be consumed within one to two years. They offer floral, tropical fruit aromas in a pleasing but uncomplicated bouquet.

Textural profile *Red*—The lighter-styled red wines that have seen partial or full carbonic vinifications can be full-bodied but tend to be soft and fruity, with the appellation's lusty alcohol present, but not the weight and layered, multidimensional personality. More classical offerings vary from muscular, full-bodied, concentrated wines to some with immense proportions that are chewy and thick, with high glycerin and alcohol. They saturate the palate and fall just short of staining the teeth. *White*—The modern style, nonmalolactic, early bottled whites are surprisingly full-bodied and alcoholic, as well as plump and mouthfilling. Their size suggests longevity, but they are meant to be consumed quickly. The few producers who practice full malolactic fermentation and later bottling produce honeyed, unctuously textured thick, juicy wines that can be special if they are bottled without oxidizing.

THE CHÂTEAUNEUF-DU-PAPE APPELLATION'S MOST PROFOUND WINES

WHITE WINES
Château de Beaucastel Cuvée Classique
Château de Beaucastel Roussanne Vieilles Vignes
Les Cailloux
Clos des Papes
Font de Michelle
Grand Veneur La Fontaine
Domaine de la Janasse Cuvée Prestige
Domaine de Marcoux
Domaine de Nalys
Château la Nerthe Cuvée Beauvenir
Château Rayas
Domaine du Vieux-Télégraphe

RED WINES
Paul Autard La Côte Ronde
Domaine La Barroche Pure
Château Beaucastel Cuvée Classique
Château Beaucastel Hommage à Jacques Perrin
Domaine de Beaurenard Cuvée Boisrenard
Bois de Boursan Cuvée des Felix
Henri Bonneau Réserve des Célestins
Bosquet des Papes Cuvée Chante Le Merle
Du Caillou Réserve Le Clos du Caillou
Du Caillou Cuvée Unique (also called Tradition)
Les Cailloux
Les Cailloux Cuvée Centenaire
Chapoutier Barbe Rac
Chapoutier Croix de Bois
Domaine de la Charbonnière Mourre des Perdrix
Domaine de la Charbonnière Cuvée Vieilles Vignes
Charvin
Clos du Mont-Olivet Cuvée du Papet
Clos des Papes

Clos St.-Jean La Combe des Fous
Clos St.-Jean Deus Ex Machina
Clos St.-Michel Cuvée Réservée Grand Clos
Domaine de Cristia Rénaissance
Cristia Vieilles Vignes
Domaine de Ferrand
Font de Michelle Cuvée Étienne Gonnet
Les Galets Blonds (Séléctions Patrick Lesec)
Château de la Gardine Cuvée des Générations
Domaine du Grand Tinel Cuvée Alexis Establet
Domaine du Grand Veneur Cuvée Les Origines
Domaine de la Janasse Cuvée Chaupin
Domaine de la Janasse Cuvée Vieilles Vignes
Domaine de Marcoux Vieilles Vignes
Domaine de la Mordorée Cuvée la Reine des Bois
Château La Nerthe Cuvée des Cadettes
Domaine du Pégaü Cuvée da Capo
Domaine du Pégaü Cuvée Laurence
Domaine Du Pégaü Cuvée Réservée
Domaine du Père Pape La Crau de Ma Mère
Domaine Roger Perrin Réserve des Vieilles Vignes
Château Rayas
Domaine Roger Sabon Cuvée Prestige
Domaine Roger Sabon Secret des Sabon
Domaine Solitude Secrèt
Pierre Usseglio Cuvée de Mon Aïeul
Pierre Usseglio Réserve des Deux Frères
Raymond Usseglio Cuvée Impériale
Cuvée du Vatican Sixtine Réserve
Domaine de la Vieille Julienne Cuvée Réservée
Domaine de la Vieille Julienne Vieilles Vignes
Le Vieux Donjon
Domaine de Vieux Télégraphe

[the ratings]

THE RED CHÂTEAUNEUF-DU-PAPE PRODUCERS

* * * * * (OUTSTANDING)

La Barroche Fiancée
La Barroche Pure
Château de Beaucastel
Château Beaucastel Hommage à Jacques
  Perrin
Domaine de Beaurenard Cuvée Boisrenard
Domaine Henri Bonneau Réserve
  des Céléstins
Bois de Boursan Cuvée des Félix
Le Bosquet des Papes Cuvée Chante
  Le Merle

Les Cailloux Cuvée Centenaire
Chapoutier Barbe Rac
Chapoutier Croix de Bois
Charbonnière Les Hautes Brusquières
Charbonnière Vieilles Vignes
Gérard Charvin
Clos du Mont Olivet Cuvée du Papet
Clos des Papes
Clos St.-Jean La Combe des Fous
Clos St.-Jean Deus Ex Machina
Domaine de Cristia Rénaissance

Cristia Vieilles Vignes
Font de Michelle Cuvée Étienne Gonnet
Château de la Gardine Cuvée
　des Générations
Domaine Grand Veneur Vieilles Vignes
Domaine de la Janasse Cuvée Chaupin
Domaine de la Janasse Cuvée Vieilles
　Vignes
Domaine de Marcoux Cuvée Vieilles
　Vignes
Domaine de la Mordorée Cuvée la Reine
　des Bois
Château La Nerthe Cuvée des Cadettes
Domaine du Pégaü Cuvée da Capo

Domaine du Pégaü Cuvée Réservée
Domaine Roger Perrin Réserve des Vieilles
　Vignes
Château Rayas
Domaine Roger Sabon Cuvée Prestige
Domaine Roger Sabon Secret des Sabon
Domaine Solitude Secrète
Pierre Usseglio Cuvée de Mon Aïeul
Pierre Usseglio Réserve des Deux Frères
Raymond Usseglio Cuvée Impériale
Domaine de Vieille Julienne Cuvée Réservée
Le Vieux Donjon
Domaine du Vieux Télégraphe

* * * * (EXCELLENT)

Pierre André
Paul Autard Cuvée La Côte Ronde
Paul Autard Cuvée Mireille
Lucien Barrot
Domaine de Beaurenard Cuvée Classique
Domaine Bois de Boursan
Henri Bonneau Cuvée Marie Beurrier
Le Bosquet des Papes Cuvée Classique
Château Cabrières Cuvée Prestige
Les Cailloux
Domaine de Chante-Perdrix
Domaine de la Charbonnière Mourre
　du Tendre
Domaine Les Clefs d'Or
Domaine Clos du Caillou
Clos du Mont-Olivet Cuvée Classique
Clos St.-Michel
Domaine de la Côte de l'Ange
Henriet Crouzet-Féraud
Cuvée de Boisdauphin
Cuvée du Vatican
Domaine de Ferrand
Font du Loup Le Puy Rolland
Font de Michelle Cuvée Classique
Domaine de Fontavin
Château Fortia (since 1994)
Domaine du Galet des Papes
Château de la Gardine
Grand Veneur Les Origines

Domaine du Haut des Terres Blanches
Domaine de la Janasse Cuvée Classique
Domaine de Marcoux Cuvée Classique
Mas de Bois Lauzon
Patrick Lesec Selections
Domaine de Montpertuis Cuvée Tradition
Domaine de la Mordorée Cuvée Classique
Moulin-Tacussel
Château du Mourre du Tendre
Domaine de Nalys
Château la Nerthe Cuvée Classique
Domaine du Pégaü Cuvée Laurence
Domaine du Père Caboche Cuvée Elisabeth
　Chambellan
Domaine du Père Pape
Domaine de la Présidente
Domaine La Roquette
Domaine Roger Sabon Cuvée Réservée
Domaine St.-Benoît Grande Garde
Domaine St.-Benoît La Truffière
Domaine de St.-Siffrein
Tardieu-Laurent Cuvée Classique
Tardieu-Laurent Vieilles Vignes
Pierre Usseglio Cuvée Classique
Raymond Usseglio Cuvée Classique
Domaine de la Vieille Julienne Cuvée
　Classique
Domaine de Villeneuve

* * * (GOOD)

Paul Autard
Jean Avril
Domaine de Boisauphin
Domaine des Chanssaud

Domaine Chantadu
Domaine Chante Cigale
Chapoutier La Bernadine
Clos de l'Oratoire des Papes

Clos St.-Jean
Domaine Durieu
Château des Fines Roches
Domaine Lou Frejau
Domaine du Grand Tinel
Domaine Grand Veneur
Guigal
Domaine Haut des Terres Blanches
Paul Jaboulet-Aîné Les Cèdres
   (***** prior to 1970)
Domaine de la Jaufrette
Domaine Mathieu
Château Maucoil
Château Mongin
Domaine de Mont-Redon
Domaine de Montpertuis Cuvée Tradition
Domaine de Palestor
Père Anselme

Père Caboche Cuvée Classique
Domaine Roger Perrin
Domaine de la Pinède
Domaine Pontifical
Domaine des Relagnes
Domaine Riche
Domaine Roger Sabon Les Olivets
St.-Benoît Cuvée Elise
Domaine St.-Benoît Soleil et Festins
Domaine des Sénéchaux
Château Simian
Domaine de la Solitude
Domaine Terre Ferme
Domaine Trintignant
Jean-Pierre Usseglio
Château de Vaudieu
Vidal-Fleury

THE WHITE CHÂTEAUNEUF-DU-PAPE PRODUCERS

* * * * * (OUTSTANDING)

Château Beaucastel Roussanne Vieilles
   Vignes
Grand Veneur La Fontaine

Domaine de la Janasse Cuvée Prestige
Château La Nerthe Cuvée Beauvenir

* * * * (EXCELLENT)

Château Beaucastel Cuvée Classique
Domaine de Beaurenard
Domaine du Caillou
Clos des Papes
Font de Michelle
Domaine de la Janasse

Domaine de Marcoux
Domaine de Nalys
Domaine Roger Perrin
Château Rayas
Domaine du Vieux Télégraphe

* * * (GOOD)

Château de la Gardine
Domaine de Mont-Redon
Château la Nerthe

Domaine du Père Caboche
Domaine de la Roquette
Domaine Trintignant La Reviscoulado

GIGONDAS AT A GLANCE

Appellation creation January 6, 1971.

Type of wine produced Red: 97%; the only other wine permitted is rosé.

Grape varieties planted Grenache, Syrah, Mourvèdre, and Cinsault are the dominant varieties.

Acres currently under vine 2,569.

Quality level Average to exceptional.

Aging potential 5–15 years.

General characteristics A robust, chewy, full-bodied, rich, generous red wine; light, vibrant, fresh, underrated rosé.

Greatest recent vintages 2007, 2005, 2001, 1999, 1998, 1995, 1990, 1989, 1985, 1979, 1978.

Price range $25–$50, with old vine/luxury cuvées $55–$65.

Aromatic profile Earth, *garrigue* (that earthy, Provençal herb mélange), pepper, sweet black cherry, blueberry, and cassis fruit are evident in top examples of Gigondas.

Textural profile Light, fruity, soft, commercially styled wines are produced, but classic Gigondas possesses a medium-bodied, muscular, unbridled power that is fine-tuned in the best examples but rustic to the point of being savage in the more uncivilized styles.

THE GIGONDAS APPELLATION'S MOST PROFOUND WINES

Domaine des Bosquets
Domaine La Bouissière Cuvée Prestige Le Font de Tonin
Domaine La Bouissière Cuvée Tradition
Domaine du Cayron
Clos du Joncuas
Domaine des Espiers Cuvée des Blanches
Domaine Les Gouberts Cuvée Florence
Les Hauts de Montmirail (Daniel Brussat)
Moulin de la Gardette Cuvée Spéciale
Château de St.-Cosme Cuvée Tradition
Château de St.-Cosme Cuvée Valbelle
Domaine Santa Duc Cuvée des Hautes Garrigues
Domaine Santa Duc Cuvée Tradition
Tardieu-Laurent Cuvée Vieilles Vignes
Domaine de la Tourade Font des Aieux

[the ratings]

THE GIGONDAS PRODUCERS

* * * * * (OUTSTANDING)

Domaine La Bouissière Prestige La Font de Tonin
Les Hauts Montmirail (Daniel Brusset)
Château de St.-Cosme Cuvée Valbelle

Château de St.-Cosme Hominis Fides
Domaine Santa Duc Cuvée des Hautes Garrigues

* * * * (EXCELLENT)

Domaine des Bosquets Préférence
Domaine La Bouissière Cuvée Tradition
Clos du Joncuas
Clos du Joncuas Cuvée Esprit de Grenache
Cros de la Mure
Domaine de la Garrigue
Domaine Les Goubert
Patrick Lesec Selections
Domaine de Longue-Toque
Montirius

Moulin de la Gardette
Moulin de la Gardette Cuvée Ventabren
Domaine Les Pallieroudas (Edmonde Burle)
Domaine de Piauger
Domaine Raspail (Ay)
Château Redortier
Château de St.-Cosme Cuvée Classique
Domaine St.-Gayan
Tardieu-Laurent Vieilles Vignes
Domaine du Terme

La Bastide St.-Vincent	L'Oustau Fouquet
Domaine des Bosquets Cuvée Tradition	Domaine Les Pallières
Domaine de Cassan	Domaine du Pesquier
Caves des Vignerons de Gigondas	Château Raspail (Meffre family)
Domaine le Clos des Cazaux	Domaine Romane-Machotte
Domaine des Espiers	Domaine Le Roucas de St.-Pierre
Domaine de Font-Sane	Domaine Ste.-Anne
Domaine de Font-Sane Cuvée Futée	La Soumade
Domaine du Gour de Chaule	Domaine Les Teyssonières
Domaine Grand-Romane	Domaine Les Teyssonières Cuvée
Domaine du Grapillon d'Or	Alexandre
Guigal	Domaine de la Tourade
Domaine de la Mavette	Domaine des Tourelles
Château de Montmirail	Château du Trignon
Notre Dame Les Pallières	Vidal-Fleury

MUSCAT DE BEAUMES DE VENISE AT A GLANCE

Appellation creation 1945.

Type of wine produced The appellation is most famous for its sweet *vins doux naturels,* which are essentially fortified sweet wines made from the Muscat grape. But dry red, white, and rosé are also produced, some of it excellent.

Grape varieties planted All permitted southern Rhône varieties, as well as the only legal plantations of Muscat à Petits Grains in the Rhône Valley (both the white and black variety).

Acres currently under vine 1,087.

Quality level Good to exceptional.

Aging potential 2–4 years.

General characteristics The Muscat is a sweet, alcoholic, extraordinarily perfumed and exotic, rich, decadent dessert wine. The best examples of red wine are classic Côtes du Rhône-Villages with plenty of red and black cherry fruit, peppery, Provençal-herb-scented noses, and gutsy, lusty flavors.

Greatest recent vintages 2006, 2005.

Price range (Muscat de Beaumes de Venise) $20–$30, (Côtes du Rhône-Villages Beaumes de Venise red) $16–$22.

The village's best-kept secret The excellent dry red wines produced by Domaine de Fenouillet, Domaine les Goubert, and Château Redortier.

[the ratings]

THE MUSCAT BEAUMES DE VENISE PRODUCERS

★ ★ ★ ★ ★ (OUTSTANDING)

Domaine de Beaumalric
Domaine de Durban

Paul Jaboulet-Aîné

* * * * (EXCELLENT)

Domaine des Bernardins
Chapoutier
Domaine de Coyeux

Domaine de Fenouillet
Domaine St.-Sauveur
Vidal-Fleury

* * * (GOOD)

Cave des Vignerons de Vacqueyras

Vignerons de Beaumes de Venise

VACQUEYRAS AT A GLANCE

Appellation creation August 9, 1990.

Type of wine produced Red wine represents 95% of the production, with 4% rosé and 1% white.

Grape varieties planted Grenache, Syrah, Mourvèdre, and Cinsault for the red and rosé wines, and Grenache Blanc, Clairette, and Bourboulenc for the white wines.

Acres currently under vine 3,211.

Quality level Very good, and increasingly an appellation that is beginning to explode in quality.

Aging potential 4–12 years.

General characteristics Powerful, rustic, full-bodied red wines that increasingly compete favorably with Châteauneuf-du-Pape and usually surpass much of neighboring Gigondas.

Greatest recent vintages 2007, 2006, 2005, 2001, 2000, 1999, 1998.

Price range $20–$25.

Aromatic profile A classic Provençal/Mediterranean nose of *herbes de Provence, garrigue,* red and black fruits, earth, and olives.

Textural profile Unbridled power along with a fleshy mouth-feel make for a substantial and mouth-filling glass of wine.

RATING THE VACQUEYRAS PRODUCERS

* * * * * (OUTSTANDING)

Domaine des Amouriers Les Genestes
Domaine de la Charbonnière
Domaine Le Couroulu Vacqueyras Vieilles
   Vignes
Domaine Le Sang des Cailloux

Domaine Le Sang des Cailloux Cuvée
   Doucinello
Domaine Le Sang des Cailloux Cuvée Lopy
Tardieu-Laurent Vieilles Vignes

* * * * (EXCELLENT)

Domaine Bouletin Sélection Michel
Domaine de Clos des Cazaux
Domaine Le Couroulu Cuvée Classique
Féraud-Brunel Vacqueyras
La Font de Papier
Domaine La Fourmone
Domaine La Garrigue Cuvée de
   l'Hostellerie
Domaine La Garrigue Cuvée Traditionnelle

Patrick Lesec Selections
La Monardière Réserve des 2 Monades
   Vieilles Vignes
Domaine de la Tourade
Château des Tours
Vidal-Fleury
Les Vins du Troubadour (various cuvées)
Les Vins de Vienne La Sillote

★ ★ ★ (GOOD)

La Bastide St.-Vincent

Domaine de Boissan

Domaine Chamfort

Domaine le Clos des Cazaux

Paul Jaboulet-Aîné

Domaine des Lambertins

Château de Montmirail

Domaine de Montvac

Château de Roques

Domaine de Verquière

TAVEL AT A GLANCE

Appellation creation May 15, 1936.

Type of wine produced Dry rosé only—the sole appellation in France to recognize rosé as the only authorized wine.

Grape varieties planted Grenache and Cinsault dominate the nine authorized varieties, followed by Clairette, Syrah, Bourboulenc, Mourvèdre, Picpoul, Carignan, and Calitor.

Acres currently under vine 2,340.

Quality level Average to very good rosé wines.

Aging potential 1–3 years.

General characteristics The finest Tavels are dry, full-bodied, and boldly flavored.

Greatest recent vintage 2007.

Price range $20–$25.

Aromatic profile Strawberries, cherries, and a vague scent of Provençal *garrigue*.

Textural profile Dry, sometimes austere, full-bodied wines can taste surprisingly rugged and shocking to those weaned on semisweet, soft, flabby, new-world rosés. There are no profound Tavel wines.

[the ratings]

THE TAVEL PRODUCERS

★ ★ ★ ★ ★ (OUTSTANDING)

Domaine de la Mordorée

★ ★ ★ ★ (EXCELLENT)

Domaine de Lafon Roc-Epine

★ ★ ★ (GOOD)

Château d'Aquéria

Domaine Canto-Perdrix

Domaine Corne Loup

Domaine de la Forcardière

Domaine de la Genestière

Guigal

Domaine Méjan-Taulier

Château de Trinquevedel

LIRAC AT A GLANCE

Appellation creation October 14, 1947.

Type of wine produced Red, rosé, and white wines, of which 75% of the production is red, 20% rosé, and 5% white.

Grape varieties planted (red) Grenache Noir, Syrah, Mourvèdre, Cinsault, and Carignan (white) Grenache Blanc, Clairette, Bourboulenc, Ugni Blanc, Picpoul, Marsanne, Roussanne, and Viognier.

Acres currently under vine 1,037.

Quality level Mediocre to good, but improving.

Aging potential 2–8 years.

General characteristics Soft, very fruity, medium-bodied red wines; neutral white wines; exuberantly fresh, fruity rosés (the frugal consumer's Tavel).

Greatest recent vintages 2007, 2005, 2001.

Price range $22–$30.

Aromatic profile Similar to a Côtes du Rhône, with scents of red fruits, spices, and *herbes de Provence*.

Textural profile Soft, fruity, generally medium-bodied red wines and relatively innocuous, one-dimensional white wines. The rosés can be excellent, not dissimilar from a top Tavel.

The Lirac appellation's most profound wine Domaine de la Mordorée.

[the ratings]

THE LIRAC PRODUCERS

* * * * * (OUTSTANDING)
Domaine de la Mordorée La Reine des Bois

* * * * (EXCELLENT)
Château de Cantegril	Château St.-Roch
Domaine Roger Sabon	Domaine de Ségriès

* * * (GOOD)
Château Boucarut	Domaine de la Forcardière
Domaine Canto-Perdrix	Domaine des Garrigues
Domaine des Causses et de St.-Eymes	Domaine Jean Marchand
Domaine des Costes	Domaine de Lafon Roc-Epine

[recent vintages]

2007
At least excellent, but great potential is suggested for 2007, because the Rhône Valley enjoyed the most favored climate in France. Ideal maturity, abundant yields, and generally superb harvest conditions should produce a great classic vintage in both the north and the south.

2006
This is a superb vintage for the northern Rhône's white wines and a very good one for the region's reds. The southern Rhône produced a generous crop of richly fruity, soft, charming wines that will provide delicious near-term drinking. The bigger, denser wines of the south will last for 12 to 15-plus years. This is a vintage of charm, which is welcome following the tannic 2005s.

2005

In the northern Rhône, 2005 is a vintage of very structured, masculine wines with high acidity, much like those of 2004, but also much higher levels of tannin. Because of drought and generally superior weather conditions that existed in 2005 vis-à-vis 2004, the 2005s also possess higher levels of concentration, but these are wines that have a tendency to be austere and monolithic and will require considerable patience. As in every vintage, there are exceptions. The top producers who kept their crops low, waited for full phenolic maturity from the tannins, and realized that acids were excessively high produced some stunning wines that will be exceptionally long-lived. If there are any other vintages to which to compare 2005, they would be 1998 or 1995, two other tannic, backward years that required patience. This is not a blockbuster, profoundly great vintage in the northern Rhône. Of course, writers who parrot back to their readers exactly what the producers tell them will indeed be extolling the vintage, because the producers love it. More importantly, it is the vintage they are presently selling. All 2005s were easy to vinify; there was little or no rot. From the producers' perspective, it was a classic problem-free year. But if you know the best producers—and they are always the ones to follow, whether it is a great vintage or not—your chances of being rewarded are much more in your favor than simply buying blindly in a vintage that has already received excessive accolades.

In the southern Rhône, 2005 was a below-average-sized crop, because of continuing drought and the fact that there are so many old vineyards where low yields are the rule of thumb even in an abundant year. While 2005 is truly an excellent vintage in the south, I do not believe it is a compellingly great vintage, because it has more in common with a beefed up, improved version of 1995 than with what I consider an irrefutably great Châteauneuf-du-Pape vintage like 1998, 2001, or even 2000. Certainly the wines have plenty of structure and possess fresher, more vibrant acidities than most years provide. The top wines also display impressive levels of concentration. However, all the 2005s tend to reveal a certain firmness, and if the grapes were picked too soon, or the vinification/upbringing were not carefully handled, there is a toughness and austerity to the tannins that ultimately will prove to be problematic.

Nevertheless, there is an ocean of top wines. This is partly due to the fact that, as in many other areas of the wine world, the southern Rhône Valley is enjoying a renaissance, thanks to a younger generation of men and women who have taken certain appellations, particularly Châteauneuf-du-Pape and Vacqueyras, to a higher and higher level of quality. When I first began making my yearly tours of the southern Rhône in 1978, there were no more than 10 or 12 Châteauneuf-du-Pape producers making world-class wine, and only 3 or 4 in Vacqueyras. Today in Châteauneuf-du-Pape there are 60 to 75 and in Vacqueyras at least 2 to 3 dozen. The only major southern appellation that seems to lag behind is Gigondas, which for many reasons can boast only 3 or 4 top producers (Santa Duc and St.-Cosme being in a class of their own). This is evidenced by the fact that many top brokers and négociants can make a better blended Gigondas than the estates can.

Another recently emerging appellation that appears to possess unlimited potential is Rasteau, a long-ignored area with a high percentage of old vines as well as fabulous *terroirs*. We should expect more and more top-quality wines to emerge from Rasteau.

In any event, consumers will have plenty of choices to salivate on when the 2005 southern Rhônes hit retailers' shelves. Keep in mind that the bigger wines will require some bottle age (much like the 2001s and 1995s, the two vintages that most closely resemble 2005). If the 2005s' elevated tannins melt completely into the wines' personalities over the next decade, this vintage could turn out to be even superior to my lofty accolades.

2004

With the exception of the white wines—and 2004 is an excellent to outstanding vintage for the dry whites of Hermitage, St.-Joseph, Crozes-Hermitage, and St.-Péray—this is an average to above-average-quality vintage in the northern Rhône. The extraordinarily high yields (50–85 hectoliters, or 1,320–2,245 gallons, per hectare in many vineyards) in addition to less than ideal weather were both problematic. Rain and insufficient sunshine resulted in the potential for many vegetal and herbaceous wines with very high acids as well as meager flesh and concentration. The top producers—people like the Chaves, the Clapes, the Chapoutiers, and the Guigals—did draconian crop thinning and produced successful wine. However, this is a vintage that apologists will describe as elegant, structured, and classic when, in fact, most of the wines lack concentration and depth. Last year I equated it to 1996, which remains a realistic comparison. The top wines are certainly worth buying, but be careful, as there are many disappointments and deceptions in the vintage. However, that said, the whites are beautiful, ripe, and concentrated, with good underlying acidity. They are beauties. I have never felt that the northern Rhône whites were terribly popular with most wine consumers, but hopefully that will change. Certainly they merit attention.

With respect to the 2004 southern Rhône, this was a year where there was just enough sunshine to achieve good rather than great ripeness. However, relatively low yields (caused by droughtlike conditions) produced wines with surprisingly high alcohols that often approached what was achieved in 2003, a rather bizarre year of extreme temperatures, except for the month of September, when the harvest took place. The most appropriate comparison for the 2004 southern Rhônes is to 1999, another vintage that produced very good, elegantly styled efforts. The 2004s possess more fruit as well as alcohol than that vintage, but their evolutions will have much in common with those of the 1999s. The 2004s possess a more restrained style with finesse, very good to excellent concentration, fine balance, and ripe tannin. Moreover, they are consistent in all appellations. Most 2004s will drink well young. The top Châteauneuf-du-Papes and Vacqueyras as well as a handful of the Côtes du Rhônes are best consumed during their first 15 or so years of life, although a few will last longer.

The one worrisome appellation in 2004 was Gigondas, where distressingly mediocre wines were produced. It is hard to understand why since Vacqueyras, which is only a few miles down the road, as well as many of the Côtes du Rhône vineyards abutting Gigondas, performed so well. I am inclined to believe it is due to the growers and winemakers in Gigondas having a tendency to harvest too soon.

2003

In the northern Rhône, wines of extraordinary concentration, high alcohol, elevated tannin, and unctuous textures are the rule of thumb in Côte Rôtie. Production is extremely small, with the finest wines being from producers who did not panic and add excessive acids to their fermentation vats, a practice that turned out to be a major blunder by many estates. While the 2003s may not be as classic as the 1999 Côte Rôties, they are even more concentrated, unctuously textured, and extreme. Given their viscosity, low acidity, and high glycerin, they should be drinkable at a young age. However, there are a number of tart, acidified cuvées. Fat, high alcohol, fleshy, occasionally flabby Condrieus were produced in 2003. A handful possess this tiny appellation's classic minerality and delineation, but they were exceptionally fragile and should have been consumed before the end of 2005. Hermitage was one of the Rhône Valley's epicenters for greatness in 2003. Alcohol levels came in between 14% and 17%. Even though analytically the wines possess little acidity, they are fresh and vigorous, with unprecedented concentration. The color is black to plum, the acidity low or nonexistent, the tannin high but sweet, and the levels of extraction and concentration are beyond anything I have ever before tasted. The white Hermitage offerings will be tricky to follow over the course of their evolution. While they are undeniably fat and tasty, it is questionable whether they will fall apart quickly or age gracefully. In short, 2003 is a very great vintage for the reds, fascinating yet fragile for the whites.

If you think Cornas always produces animalistic, highly tannic wines lacking charm and seductiveness, taste the 2003s! They are enormous reds possessing extraordinary blackberry and crème de cassis flavors, amazing levels of glycerin, and, surprise, surprise, high but sweet, well-integrated tannin. I have never tasted so many massive yet potentially superb Cornas that transcend the appellation's reputation for rustic, virile reds. They should be long-lived despite their lack of acidity, because the yields were low. Both Crozes-Hermitage and St.-Joseph possess so many different *terroirs* spread over such large areas that it is nearly impossible to offer an intelligent, generalized statement about these two appellations as a whole. However, the finest wines of both appellations are more like Hermitages than usual. Because St.-Joseph's finest *terroirs* are on steep hillsides, the wines tend to possess more minerality, but the 2003 vintage produced atypically powerful, freakishly ripe, rich wines with high alcohol as well as tannin. The same can be said for Crozes-Hermitage, although it is always a more variable appellation, because many of these vineyards are on flatlands that tend to overproduce. That was not the case in 2003, however, so the typical Crozes-Hermitage frequently has more fruit, body, glycerin, and alcohol than normal.

St.-Péray, the long-forgotten microsize white wine appellation south of Cornas, enjoyed an amazing year in 2003. While these offerings will never be confused with the Rhône's top white wine cuvées from Hermitage and Châteauneuf-du-Pape, the Marsanne and Roussanne grown in St.-Péray achieved record levels of ripeness in 2003, resulting in tasty, heady, full-bodied, surprisingly good whites. I would not suggest aging them, but there are some good values available for immediate drinkability.

In the southern Rhône, most Châteauneuf-du-Pape producers began their harvest early but finished during the month of September, two to three weeks later than their colleagues in the north. These vineyards are used to more heat and drought, and therefore, the vintage was not as freakish as it was in the north. Moreover, September was a relatively normal month temperaturewise, so once the summer drought and heat subsided at the end of August (when the northern Rhône was largely finished harvesting), Châteauneuf-du-Pape benefited from an average September. The 2003s exhibit plush, hedonistic styles similar to the 2000s, although the alcohols are higher, the acidity lower, and the wines even more forward and heady. Clearly the most successful appellation of the southern Rhône, Châteauneuf-du-Pape produced outstanding efforts. Vineyards from the cooler climate *terroirs* of Gigondas suffered from a maturity blockage, to the degree that this appellation reveals the most irregularity of the top villages. While slightly more consistent, Vacqueyras suffered similar problems with tannin maturity as well as irregularity in quality. Neither appellation attained anywhere near the quality achieved in Châteauneuf-du-Pape, and 2003 falls well behind the quartet of 1998, 1999, 2000, and 2001.

In the Côtes du Rhône villages, the quality largely depends on the age of the vines (older vines did better in the drought) and the type of soil: vineyards planted on limestone and clay soils did better than those planted in sandy, shallow soils. Overall, there are some very fine cuvées of Côtes du Rhône, but this region is irregular in quality and not nearly as consistent as vintages like 1998, 2000, and 2001.

2002

The northern Rhône experienced a mediocre vintage in 2002, as the wines were affected by inclement weather patterns throughout the summer and the fall harvest. While the historic flooding that occurred in the south, especially in Châteauneuf-du-Pape, was not a problem in the north, the vineyards still had to deal with abundant rot, resulting in many diluted and vegetal efforts. Some good wines were produced, but overall this is a vintage to steer clear of unless the wines are discounted dramatically.

In the south, the devastating apocalyptic deluge of September 8–9, which dropped nearly 600 mm (23-plus inches) of rain on sectors of Châteauneuf-du-Pape and some of its neighbors in the Vaucluse and Gard, had a deleterious impact on quality, and only a handful of wine can be recommended. By the way, I was at the epicenter of this historic storm, having my rental car washed off the road (with me in it) in one of the Châteauneuf-du-Pape floods.

Some of the top producers declassified their entire harvest, refusing to declare a wine under the estate name. Most other estates produced only small quantities of modest, superficial wines that revealed modest ripeness but were undeniably diluted. The villages that seem to have fared better include Vacqueyras and Rasteau, as well as some of the more northern Côtes du Rhône-Villages appellations. Nevertheless, even those wines barely surpass a mid-80 point rating.

2001

Although 2001 was stunningly successful in the southern Rhône, particularly for the large appellation of Châteauneuf-du-Pape as well as the hallowed vineyards of rivals Gigondas and Vacqueyras, in the north the vintage was totally different. It's always the same story: Producers who work their vineyards, practice healthy viticulture, keep yields at modest to low levels, and are patient and reflective during complicated harvests always seem to make the best wines. Twenty-five years of wine tastings and extensive travel to the vineyards have demonstrated this conclusively.

Overall, 2001 was a cool year with undesirable harvest conditions. However, the top wines that follow are proportional to vignerons that had low crop levels and were patient during the harvest. Even though the 2001s are more backward and stubbornly constructed, they are undoubtedly better than the 2000s. It appears 2001 had the potential to produce higher peaks of quality, which some producers were able to exploit. However, the wines will need time in the bottle to round into form.

A surprise is the brilliant quality of the white wines. Cold weather late in the 2001 growing season appears to have enhanced the aromatics and definition of the northern Rhône's dry whites. Also surprising is the number of high-quality wines that emerged from Cornas in 2001. In short, selection and confidence in the top vignerons/producers are necessary in order to navigate the tricky 2001 northern Rhône vintage.

In Châteauneuf-du-Pape, 2001 is consistently excellent to outstanding. This area produced full-bodied, dense ruby/purple-colored, powerful, tannic, chewy, pure wines. Ideal weather from early summer through the third week of September was dry and windy. A tiny crop with thick skins resulted in big, burly wines that may not have the succulence or accessibility of the 2000s but possess more concentration, power, and tannin. This is a very promising, ageworthy vintage.

Outside Châteauneuf-du-Pape, the 2001s are at least very good but seem less magical. In depth, the wines of Vacqueyras, Gigondas, Beaumes de Venise, and Cairanne, while very good, are not superior to the quality of 1998, 1999, and 2000. It is hard to know why, but the cool harvest conditions of September seem to have given these wines a certain austerity not noticeable in the Châteauneuf-du-Papes. In any event, there are many successful efforts from the Côtes du Rhône villages.

An insider secret about 2001 is that the 2001 white Châteauneufs may be the finest I have ever tasted. By and large, these wines should have been drunk by 2008.

2000

This is a year of considerable contrast between the south and the north. There was no problem with ripeness in either region, but in the north, high yields and growers' inattention to crop thinning resulted in a ripe but superficially styled vintage. From Côte Rôtie through Cornas the wines are attractive, with saturated colors, low acidity, and sweet fruit. But as the famous advertisement from a few years ago asked, "Where's the beef?" Although there are a few noteworthy exceptions (e.g., the wines of Gérard and Jean-Louis Chave, and Guigal's single-vineyard Côte Rôties), overall the wines lack fat, concentration, and depth. Except for the bigger wines of Hermitage, the 2000 northern Rhônes will be drinkable early and should last for 10 to 15 years.

In the south, Châteauneuf-du-Pape, Gigondas, Vacqueyras, and the surrounding villages of the Côtes du Rhône enjoyed a splendid vintage of great ripeness and concentration in 2000. Unlike their siblings to the north, there is no problem with depth or richness in the finest 2000 southern Rhônes. Stylistically they are similar to 1998, with high alcohol, low acidity, and concentrated, ripe, fleshy, sumptuous personalities. It is the third consecutive impressive vintage for this sector. Consumers will love these wines, which, though different in style, will rival the prodigious 1998s. Most 2000s have been drinkable since their release in 2002, and the top Châteauneuf-du-Papes and the most concentrated old-vine cuvées of Côtes du Rhône, Gigondas, and Vacqueyras will age well for 15 years.

1999

Until 2003, this was the finest Côte Rôtie vintage I had seen. Admittedly, a young generation of growers is pushing quality higher and higher, so that finding disappointing wines is not as easy as it was a decade ago, but for pure opulence, concentration, and extraordinarily high levels of glycerin and extract the 1999 Côte Rôties are exceptional. They are easily the finest vintage for this region since 1978. Oddly, 1999 offered both abundant yields and spectacular quality. In the other appellations, it is unquestionably a top vintage, but perhaps less consistent than in Côte Rôtie. The 1999 Hermitages possess sweet tannin, great ripeness, and opulent, voluptuous textures with plenty of underlying structure. In Crozes-Hermitage, St.-Joseph, and Cornas, quality is generally high, with St.-Joseph being the most consistent. The most inconsistent are Cornas and Condrieu, where yields were high. The white wines of Condrieu lack the concentration of the 1998s. While there are some impressive efforts from Cornas, these wines generally reveal less concentration, more acidity, and a frustrating inconsistency.

In the south, 1999 will largely be ignored as the increasing throngs of southern Rhône wine enthusiasts drink up their 1998s and flock to buy the 2000 and 2001 vintages, all undeniably great years for the southern Rhône. This excellent vintage will simply be overshadowed by those that surround it. Fine ripeness was achieved in all varietals, with Mourvèdre and Syrah performing better in 1999 than in 1998. While very good, Grenache was slightly less successful, without the saturated fatness, flesh, and complexity of 1998 and 2000. Nevertheless, this is a very fine vintage in Châteauneuf-du-Pape, Gigondas, Vacqueyras, and the villages of Côtes du Rhône. Occasionally, producers tending to use higher percentages of Mourvèdre and Syrah made better wines than they did in 1998. Elegance and balance are the operative words to describe the southern Rhône's 1999s, a vintage that will garner better and better press as it evolves. For now, however, it is a forgotten year, given the hype over the surrounding vintages.

1998

In the northern Rhône, a late spring frost severely curtailed yields, particularly on the Côte Rôtie plateau as well as in certain sectors of Condrieu, St.-Joseph, Hermitage, and Crozes-Hermitage. Now that the wines are in the bottle, the vintage is excellent, with all the top domaines producing concentrated, ripe, structured, but tannic, closed wines that come closest in style to those of 1995. There is plenty of character and high quality out of the finest estates, but the bottled wines have now shut down, requiring at least five years (a decade or more for Hermitage) of cellaring to reveal their character. The tannin is high, but so is the concentration. This is a vintage for patient connoisseurs with proper storage facilities. While the 1998 Côte Rôties, Hermitages, Crozes-Hermitages, St.-Josephs, and Cornas are very good, they are less successful than their 1999 counterparts. Condrieu enjoyed a fabulous vintage, but those wines should have been consumed before the end of 2002.

In the southern Rhône, 1998 was a great vintage that continues to build in stature and majesty. It is a benchmark vintage for Châteauneuf-du-Pape. When first reporting on these wines in my journal *The Wine Advocate* (12 months after the vintage), I indicated that it was the finest vintage since 1990. However, it is even better than 1990, producing wines with extraordinary balance. Moreover, the 1998 vintage was produced in part by a younger generation of winemakers dedicated to producing world-class wines. Great wines that did not exist in 1990 have emerged from young hotshots such as Sophie and Catherine Armenier (Domaine de Marcoux's Châteauneuf-du-Pape), Vincent Avril (Clos des Papes's Châteauneuf-du-Pape), Louis Barruol (St.-Cosme's Gigondas), Nicolas Boiron (Bosquet des Papes's Châteauneuf-du-Pape), Philippe Bravay (Domaine de Ferrand's Châteauneuf-du-Pape), André Brunel (Les Cailloux's Châteauneuf-du-Pape), Daniel Brunier (Vieux-Télégraphe's Châteauneuf-du-Pape), Gérard Charvin (Charvin's Châteauneuf-du-Pape), Frédéric and Daniel Coulon (Beaurenard's Châteauneuf-du-Pape), Christopher Délorme (La Mordorée's Châteauneuf-du-Pape and Lirac), Jean-Marc Diffonty (Cuvée du Vatican's Châteauneuf-du-Pape), Laurence Féraud (Pégaü's Châteauneuf-du-Pape), Pierre Perrin (Domaine Perrin's Châteauneuf-du-Pape), Christophe Sabon (La Janasse's Châteauneuf-du-Pape), Michel Tardieu (a *négociant* producing wines from all the southern and northern Rhône appellations), Thierry and Jean-Pierre Usseglio (Pierre Usseglio's Châteauneuf-du-Pape), and Jean-Paul Versino (Bois de Boursan's Châteauneuf-du-Pape). Multiple tastings of the 1998 Châteauneuf-du-Papes out of bottle (I bought as much as I could afford) have proven that these wines have gained amazing weight and richness, surpassing even their pre-bottling conditions. This is a profound, possibly once-in-a-lifetime vintage to buy in quantity. Moreover, these wines will drink well young or can be cellared for 15 to 20-plus years. As great a vintage as it was for Châteauneuf-du-Pape, the surrounding areas of Gigondas, Vacqueyras, and Côtes du Rhône produced excellent, often outstanding wines, but with much more variation in quality.

1997

This vintage is excellent in the north, with wines of low acidity, outstanding ripeness, concentrated styles, and considerable accessibility. It is undoubtedly a superior vintage in the north.

In the southern Rhône, I would presently place the 1997 vintage slightly behind that of 1996, but this is a difficult judgment to make until the 1997s are in bottle. The 1997s may be slightly more irregular, given the difficult harvest conditions, but the wines are ripe, low in acidity, and somewhat diluted. They possess many of the characteristics of the 1996s, being forward, fruity, and charming, but they are not intensely concentrated or capable of significant longevity.

1996

I am pleased with the way the 1996 southern Rhônes have turned out in bottle. They are richly fruity, soft, and not terribly concentrated but are user-friendly, low in acidity, and nicely textured, easy to drink wines that will be ideal for consumption over the next two to four years.

In the north, 1996 produced wines with higher than normal acidity (much as in Burgundy), deep color saturation, a compressed style, and a lean, firm, tannic backbone. This is not a style of wine that excites me, but I realize that some prefer higher acid and firmer, more compressed wines. Nevertheless, where producers in Côte Rôtie, Hermitage, Cornas, and other appellations had low yields and made concentrated wines, some exceptional wines were produced that will be inaccessible while young but long-lived and potentially profound. However, this vintage needs to be approached with caution, as the cooler climate vineyards and vignerons who did not keep their crop yields down produced wines with intensely herbaceous characteristics that are a defect, particularly when allied with higher than normal acidity.

1995

For a handful of producers in Côte Rôtie (Guigal, Chapoutier, Jamet, and René Rostaing), 1995 turned out to be an exceptional vintage. Much like 1994, the summer was warm, even hot at times, with just barely enough rain. Like 1991, 1992, 1993, and 1994, September began on a positive note, but on the ninth the rains began. Intermittently showery weather followed for 10 consecutive days. The producers who felt that 1995 was shaping up to be a replay of 1994, when the rains continued throughout the entire month of September, tended to harvest too soon, picking Syrah that was not physiologically ripe. Those who did not destem in 1995 only exacerbated the impression of greenness and tart acidity, given this grape's naturally high acidity. Producers who took the risk and delayed their harvests were rewarded with superb weather after September 20.

On paper, the 1995 Châteauneuf-du-Pape vintage is an irrefutably promising year. In large part a replay of 1994, 1995 enjoyed a summer that was hot if less torrid than 1994. At the beginning of September, as in 1994, there was widespread optimism for a great vintage if the September weather was good. Lightning can, nevertheless, strike twice in the same place, and on nearly the same date as in 1994 the heavens opened, dumping two weeks of heavy showers on the Rhône Valley between September 7 and September 20. But there was one significant difference. In 1994, the early harvesters usually had more success, because the grape maturity was so advanced by the time of the rains. Delaying the harvest meant potential rot. In 1995, the grapes were one to two weeks behind the maturity curve of the 1994s; thus, the rain was less of a reason to harvest early. Moreover, there was significantly less rain in September 1995 than in the previous September. Unlike 1994, the rain was finished by the end of the third week of September, after which several weeks of clear, dry, warm, windy weather followed, allowing late harvesters to bring in very ripe, healthy fruit that, surprisingly, possessed a high degree of acidity for the degree of physiological ripeness the grapes possessed. While the 1995 vintage can clearly be called excellent in the south, it is not as profound as those of 1989 or 1990 or the ones from 1998, 2000, 2001, 2003, 2005, and 2007 that succeeded it.

1994

Much like all the Rhône Valley vintages following the great one of 1990, 1994 is another complicated year. The torridly hot, sunny summer offered the potential for another 1990 or 1989, but the fall rains caught most northern producers with unharvested grapes. Nevertheless, the better producers who had low crop yields are pleased with the quality, claiming that the 1994s from Côte Rôtie, Hermitage, and Cornas are superior to 1992 and 1993 and possibly as fine as 1985 or 1991.

In the southern Rhône, many producers were able to harvest a significant portion of their vineyards before the heavy rains began. Early assessments of the 1994 vintage suggest that Châteauneuf-du-Pape, followed by Gigondas and several of the Côtes du Rhône villages, have produced their richest, most complete cuvées since the great 1990 vintage. Quantities are small, however, so look for prices to rise if the quality turns out to be as fine as believed.

1993

1993 is both a confusing and an irregular year. The vintage's failures are concentrated in the northern Rhône, especially in Côte Rôtie and Hermitage. Rain and high humidity caused serious problems with mildew and rot in the northern Rhône vineyards, devastating producers who had been on the verge of having a high-quality vintage. It is possible that an event of historic proportions has emerged from the disastrous 1993 vintage in the northern Rhône. Michel Chapoutier, whose faith in the principles of biodynamic organic farming created much controversy among his peers, produced brilliant wines in this dreadful year, offering, in the brash Chapoutier's view, uncontroverted evidence of the merits of this philosophy of vineyard farming.

In contrast, the southern Rhône fared well in 1993. Why? Approximately 50% to 75% of the crop was harvested before any damaging rain. The 1993 vintage poignantly illustrates how different the microclimates are in the northern and southern Rhône, not to mention the *terroirs* and grape varieties. If the northern Rhône's 1993 vintage looks to be the worst that this sector of the Rhône has experienced since 1975, 1977, or 1984, the southern Rhône may yet turn out a vintage that is capable of rivaling that of 1988 and perhaps even 1985.

As the tasting notes that follow evidence, plenty of fine wines have emerged from the last three vintages. Selection is always critical, but Rhône wines, particularly the reds, remain France's least known great wines. While the limited-production great red wines of the northern Rhône, especially Côte Rôtie and Hermitage, are rare and expensive, the southern Rhône red wines, such as Châteauneuf-du-Pape, Gigondas, Vacqueyras, and the top Côtes du Rhones, continue to offer fabulous quality and price rapport.

1992

This year is mediocre in quality, with a number of failures in the Côtes du Rhone villages. Additionally, Gigondas is below average in quality, but Châteauneuf-du-Pape is surprisingly good, although the wines are lighter and significantly less concentrated than such great years as 1989 and 1990.

In the northern Rhône, the vintage has turned out to be of average quality, with the most meticulous producers fashioning surprisingly good, ripe, soft wines that required early consumption. Chapoutier's 1992s are brilliant wines, but they need to be drunk up.

1991

Côte Rôtie enjoyed exceptional success in 1991, and other northern Rhône appellations unquestionably produced very good wines in this vintage. For Côte Rôtie, 1991 has proven to be an exceptional vintage, superior as well as more consistent than 1990. Other northern Rhône appellations that enjoyed success included Cornas, Hermitage, St.-Joseph, and Crozes-Hermitage.

The southern Rhône appellations were devastated by torrential rains in 1991. The quality of virtually every Gigondas and Châteauneuf-du-Pape is suspect, although a few worthy wines have emerged.

1990

This is a superlative vintage throughout the Rhône Valley. In the south, the torridly hot, dry summer resulted in superripe grapes packed with sugar. At the top levels the wines are deeply colored and exceptionally powerful, with high levels of soft tannins and alcohol of 14%–15%-plus. The wines have a more roasted, extreme style than the more classic 1989s but are sumptuous, as well as loaded with concentrated fruit. This year is unquestionably a great vintage in Châteauneuf-du-Pape, an excellent one in Gigondas, and a top-flight year in most of the Côtes du Rhone-Villages. The red wines from both Gigondas and Châteauneuf-du-Pape, despite higher alcohol than the 1989s, will probably mature more quickly than the 1989s, because their acidity levels are lower and these wines are so opulent and precocious. Nevertheless, the top cuvées of Châteauneuf-du-Pape should easily last for another five to ten years.

If you are a lover of Hermitage and Crozes-Hermitage, grab your wallet! In Hermitage, 1990 looks to be even better than the great 1978 vintage. Gérard Chave, Michel Chapoutier, and Gérald Jaboulet all believe it is the finest year for this renowned appellation since 1961. These massive wines are almost black in color, with an extraordinary extraction of fruit, high tannins, and a textural sweetness and succulence. Jaboulet's La Chapelle, Chave's Hermitage, and Chapoutier's luxury cuvée, Le Pavillon, are likely candidates for perfection, provided those who can both find and afford them wait the 15 or more years they will need to attain maturity. Even the wines of Crozes-Hermitage are superconcentrated. Those from Alain Graillot and Paul Jaboulet-Aîné are especially exciting. Côte Rôtie is a mixed bag, with the top cuvées of Chapoutier, Guigal, and a handful of others looking excellent and sometimes extraordinary. Other wines are merely above average in quality. St.-Joseph and Cornas are at least good.

This is unquestionably a great vintage for Châteauneuf-du-Pape, getting my nod as the finest vintage for that appellation since 1978. In fact, it is 1978 that comes to mind when looking for a vintage of similar characteristics. The hot, dry weather produced small grapes with more noticeable tannins than the 1990s. However, when analyzed, most 1990s have the same level of tannins as the 1989s, but the latter taste more structured and are more classically rendered. Given their stunning ripeness and reasonable yields, the 1989 Châteauneuf-du-Papes are nearly as powerful as the 1990s. They have low acidity, spectacular levels of fruit extraction, and a full-bodied, potentially long-lived style. It is a matter of personal taste whether one prefers the 1990s or the 1989s, but both are dazzling vintages. One really has to look to the individual domaine to judge who fared better in one vintage or the other. In Gigondas, 1989 is a more consistent vintage, and again that appellation's best overall year since 1978. For Rhône wine enthusiasts, these two years offer the best opportunities to replenish cellars since 1978 and 1979.

Less massive, more supple opulent wines were produced throughout the northern Rhône. The most successful appellations were Hermitage and Côte Rôtie, the least, Cornas. While the Côte Rôtie producers were ecstatic after the vintage, only the best cuvées of Guigal and a few other wines have the requisite concentration and grip to live up to the initial hyperbole. While these wines are flattering and will make delicious drinking over the next 10 to 15 years, this is an excellent rather than a great vintage. In Hermitage it would be considered a great vintage except for the fact that 1990 succeeded it. The top cuvées are rich and full-bodied, with 20 or more years of longevity. They also have a softness and are less massive on the palate, particularly when tasted next to the 1990s. The vintage is irregular in Cornas. The heat and drought appear to have caused problems for many vineyards in that appellation. As in Hermitage, Crozes-Hermitage enjoyed an excellent year.

—ROBERT PARKER

[tasting commentaries]

DANIEL ET DENIS ALAR ★★★/★★★★
CAIRANNE $12.00–$28.00

One of the reference points for proving how good Côtes du Rhône-Villages Cairanne can be is the family estate of Daniel and Denis Alary. This is always a winning portfolio in both the qualitative and value sweepstakes.

2005 Côtes du Rhône	87	now
2005 Côtes du Rhône-Villages Cairanne	89	now–2010
2005 Côtes du Rhône-Villages Cairanne La Brunote	89	now
2005 Côtes du Rhône-Villages Cairanne La Jean de Verde	90	now
2005 Côtes du Rhône-Villages Cairanne Réserve du Vigneron	88	now
2006 Côtes du Rhône-Villages La Font d'Estévenas Blanc	91	now
2003 Vin de Pays La Grange Daniel	87	now
2005 Vin de Pays La Grange Daniel Blanc	90	now

THIERRY ALLEMONDE ***
CORNAS $35.00–$50.00

While this is somewhat of an insider's favorite among Cornas producers, I have found the wines of Thierry Allemonde to be notoriously irregular. The finest bottles are complex, character-filled wines offering plenty of beefy Syrah fruit.

PIERRE AMADIEU **/***
GIGONDAS $25.00–$35.00

Reasonably good wines have emerged from this large southern Rhône *négociant.*

2004 Gigondas Cuvée Grande Réserve	88	now–2012
2003 Gigondas Cuvée Grande Réserve	88	now–2012
2004 Gigondas Domaine Grande Romane	87	now–2012
2003 Gigondas Domaine Grande Romane	89	now–2012
2004 Gigondas Romane Machotte	89	now–2014
2003 Gigondas Romane Machotte	87	now

DOMAINE DE L'AMEILLAUD ****
CÔTES DU RHÔNE $12.00–$15.00

Domaine de l'Ameillaud is a consistent producer of satisfying wines that represent good values.

2005 Côtes du Rhône	86	now
2005 Côtes du Rhône Petit Chapeau	89	now
2005 Côtes du Rhône-Villages Cairanne	89	now
2000 Côtes du Rhône-Villages Cairanne	88	now
2000 Vin de Pays de Vaucluse	85	now

DOMAINE DES AMOURIERS ****
VACQUEYRAS $18.00–$38.00

One of the stars of the Vacqueyras appellation, this estate consistently produces one of the finest wines of the vintage. Their top cuvée of Vacqueyras, Les Genêstes, is usually a blend of 60% Grenache and 40% Syrah. Readers should never pass up their limited cuvée called Hautes Terrasses, actually a *vin de pays,* since it is made from 100% Syrah.

2005 Vacqueyras Les Genêstes	90	now–2017
2004 Vacqueyras Les Genêstes	89	now–2013
2003 Vacqueyras Les Genêstes	89	now–2015
2001 Vacqueyras Les Genêstes	91	now–2012
2000 Vacqueyras Les Genêstes	90	now–2011
2005 Vin de Pays Les Hautes Terrasses	88	now–2015
2004 Vin de Pays Les Hautes Terrasses	87	now–2012

DOMAINE D'ANDEZON ***
CÔTES DU RHÔNE $10.00–$12.00

These terrific values are custom cuvées selected by importer Eric Solomon exclusively for the U.S. marketplace.

2005 Côtes du Rhône	88	now–2010
2004 Côtes du Rhône	89	now
2004 Côtes du Rhône-Villages	89	now–2011
2005 Côtes du Rhône-Villages La Garnache	90	now–2012

PIERRE ANDRÉ ✷✷✷
CHÂTEAUNEUF-DU-PAPE $30.00–$48.00

Very good, forward, classic Provençal-styled wines emerge from this estate of just under 40 acres. Unlike many domaines, no special cuvées are produced.

2005 Châteauneuf-du-Pape	89	now–2017
2004 Châteauneuf-du-Pape	88	now–2013
2003 Châteauneuf-du-Pape	89	now–2012

LES APHILLANTHES ✷✷✷
CÔTES DU RHÔNE $15.00–$85.00

Les Aphillanthes's 2003s are hard, tannic, and austere, surprising in view of the brilliance of their 1999s, 2000s, and 2001s. The 2006s are much better. Daniel Boulle is the proprietor.

2003 Côtes du Rhône Caésar	85+?	now–2010
2004 Côtes du Rhône Mourvèdre	85	now–2010
2001 Côtes du Rhône-Villages (100% Mourvèdre)	89	now–2018
2004 Côtes du Rhône-Villages Cairanne	85	now–2010
2001 Côtes du Rhône-Villages Cuvée Actium	90	now–2015
2001 Côtes du Rhône-Villages Cuvée Caésar	89	now–2014
2004 Côtes du Rhône-Villages Cuvée du Cros	87	now–2010
2003 Côtes du Rhône-Villages Cuvée du Cros	87	now
2001 Côtes du Rhône-Villages Cuvée du Cros	89	now–2011
2000 Côtes du Rhône-Villages Cuvée du Cros	92	now–2017+
2000 Côtes du Rhône-Villages Cuvée R & R	88	now
2004 Côtes du Rhône-Villages des Galets	87	now
2003 Côtes du Rhône-Villages des Galets	87	now
2001 Côtes du Rhône-Villages des Galets	91	now–2011
2000 Côtes du Rhône-Villages des Galets	90	now–2012
2004 Côtes du Rhône-Villages 3 Cépages	89	now–2014
2003 Côtes du Rhône-Villages 3 Cépages	84	now
2001 Côtes du Rhône-Villages 3 Cépages	91	now–2012+
2000 Côtes du Rhône-Villages 3 Cépages	92	now–2012+
2004 Côtes du Rhône-Villages Vieilles Vignes	87	now–2012
2003 Côtes du Rhône-Villages Vieilles Vignes	85	now
2001 Côtes du Rhône-Villages Vieilles Vignes	91	now–2018+
2000 Côtes du Rhône-Villages Vieilles Vignes	91	now–2012

MAISON ARNOUX ✷✷✷
VACQUEYRAS $19.00–$25.00

Maison Arnoux, an estate situated in the heart of Vacqueyras, produces solidly made tasty Provençal wines.

2004 Vacqueyras Cuvée 1717	87	now–2013
2003 Vacqueyras Cuvée 1717	88	now
2004 Vacqueyras Cuvée Classique	88	now–2013
2004 Vacqueyras Cuvée Jean-Marie Arnoux	90	now–2013
2004 Vacqueyras Cuvée du Seigneur de Lauris	88	now–2013
2003 Vacqueyras Cuvée du Seigneur de Lauris	87	now–2012
2001 Vacqueyras Cuvée du Seigneur de Lauris	88	now–2014
2004 Vacqueyras Cuvée Vieux Clocher	89	now
2001 Vacqueyras Cuvée Vieux Clocher	88+	now–2012

PAUL AUTARD ***/****
CHÂTEAUNEUF-DU-PAPE $15.00–$60.00

Autard's approach to winemaking is modern. He produces a luxury cuvée, La Côte Ronde, that is aged partially in small oak barrels. The basic cuvée of Châteauneuf-du-Pape sees mostly old oak, along with a touch of new. These are good examples of a progressive style of Châteauneuf-du-Pape winemaking, capable of lasting 10 to 15 years. An excellent producer.

2006 Châteauneuf-du-Pape	88	now–2017
2005 Châteauneuf-du-Pape	90	now–2017
2004 Châteauneuf-du-Pape	88	now–2013
2003 Châteauneuf-du-Pape	88	now–2013
2001 Châteauneuf-du-Pape	90	now–2012
2000 Châteauneuf-du-Pape	88	now–2011
1999 Châteauneuf-du-Pape	87	now–2010
2005 Châteauneuf-du-Pape Blanc	86	now
2006 Châteauneuf-du-Pape La Côte Ronde	92	now–2022
2005 Châteauneuf-du-Pape La Côte Ronde	94	2009–2017
2004 Châteauneuf-du-Pape La Côte Ronde	90	now–2017
2003 Châteauneuf-du-Pape La Côte Ronde	91	now–2016+
2001 Châteauneuf-du-Pape La Côte Ronde	91+	now–2013
2000 Châteauneuf-du-Pape La Côte Ronde	91	now–2015
1999 Châteauneuf-du-Pape La Côte Ronde	90	now–2016
1998 Châteauneuf-du-Pape La Côte Ronde	95	now–2021
2006 Châteauneuf-du-Pape Cuvée Julien	93	2013–2038
2005 Côtes du Rhône	85	now–2010
2004 Côtes du Rhône	85	now

JULIETTE AVRIL **
CHÂTEAUNEUF-DU-PAPE $25.00–$35.00

The wines I have tasted from this estate have been competently made, modern-style, fruity, processed Châteauneuf-du-Papes meant to be sold and drunk quickly.

2003 Châteauneuf-du-Pape	87	now–2011

FRANCK BALTHAZAR **
CORNAS $35.00–$45.00

This small, artisanal estate continues to move forward, producing attractive wines from Cornas.

2004 Cornas	87	now–2013
2003 Cornas	89	now–2014

RENÉ BALTHAZAR **
CORNAS $35.00–$42.00

René Balthazar is one of the old-time traditionalists in Cornas, producing tiny quantities of wine from five acres of very old vines.

2001 Cornas	88	now–2013
2000 Cornas	87	now–2011
1999 Cornas	81	now–2012

GILLES BARGE ★ ★
CÔTE RÔTIE $35.00–$47.00

Gilles Barge, the president of the Côte Rôtie syndicate, remains a staunch protector of this appellation's long-standing winemaking style. His traditionally made Côte Rôties are to be admired. One of the few growers to continue producing wines with a substantial percentage of stems included, he appears to utilize more *barriques* for his Côte Brune bottling as opposed to the lighter Cuvée du Plessy. This latter wine (made primarily from Côte Blonde fruit, with some Viognier in the blend) is unquestionably one of the more elegant, aromatic expressions of the appellation. Barge calls it his *cuvée du plaisir*. Not only do some buyers prefer this style, it is important that Côte Rôtie's vignerons offer a diversity of tastes to the public.

2005 Côte Rôtie Côte Brune	85	now–2016
2004 Côte Rôtie Côte Brune	86	now–2012
2003 Côte Rôtie Côte Brune	91	now–2020
2001 Côte Rôtie Côte Brune	85	now
2000 Côte Rôtie Côte Brune	85	now
1999 Côte Rôtie Côte Brune	89	now–2012
2005 Côte Rôtie Cuvée du Plessy	82	now–2012
2004 Côte Rôtie Cuvée du Plessy	82	now
2001 Côte Rôtie Cuvée du Plessy	81	now
2000 Côte Rôtie Cuvée du Plessy	82	now
1999 Côte Rôtie Cuvée du Plessy	85	now

LA BARROCHE ★ ★ ★ ★/★ ★ ★ ★ ★
CHÂTEAUNEUF-DU-PAPE $55.00–$65.00

Proprietors Christian and Julian Barrot of this new estate come from a well-known winemaking family. Their first widely commercialized vintage, 2004, was impressive, and the 2005s were brilliant. There are three cuvées. The Réserve is made from 70- to 80-year-old Grenache vines blended with 50% Syrah, making it a rather modern take on Châteauneuf-du-Pape. The Fiancée is a broad, expansive style of wine with more nuances and complexity. The Pure is 100% Grenache from vines older than 100 years, all grown in sandy soil much like that of the renowned Rayas vineyard. These stunning wines deserve serious attention.

2006 Châteauneuf-du-Pape Fiancée	92	now–2022+
2005 Châteauneuf-du-Pape Fiancée	91+	2012–2032
2006 Châteauneuf-du-Pape Pure	92	now–2022
2005 Châteauneuf-du-Pape Pure	100	now–2027
2006 Châteauneuf-du-Pape Réserve	89	now–2017
2005 Châteauneuf-du-Pape Réserve	89	now–2017

LUCIEN BARROT ★ ★ ★
CHÂTEAUNEUF-DU-PAPE $28.00–$55.00

The Barrot family has been residing in Châteauneuf-du-Pape since the 14th century. However, it is only recently that they have been estate-bottling their wine. Lucien Barrot, one of the members of the small group of artisanal producers called Prestige et Tradition, fashions delicious, textbook Châteauneuf-du-Papes that have given me immense pleasure over the years.

2005 Châteauneuf-du-Pape	89	now–2015
2003 Châteauneuf-du-Pape	87	now–2011
2001 Châteauneuf-du-Pape	89	now–2014
2000 Châteauneuf-du-Pape	88	now
1999 Châteauneuf-du-Pape	87	now

DOMAINE BARVILLE ★ ★ ★
CHÂTEAUNEUF-DU-PAPE $35.00–$55.00

Domaine Barville, which is owned by *négociant* Charles Brotte, produces very reliable as well as ageworthy wines. (See also Brotte.)

2005 Châteauneuf-du-Pape	88	now–2016
2003 Châteauneuf-du-Pape	87	now–2010
2001 Châteauneuf-du-Pape	87	now–2012
2003 Châteauneuf-du-Pape Vieilles Vignes	88	now–2017

LA BASTIDE ST.-DOMINIQUE ★ ★ ★/★ ★ ★ ★
CHÂTEAUNEUF-DU-PAPE $19.00–$50.00

Readers should be on the lookout for these wines, from an up-and-coming estate run by young proprietor Eric Bonnet.

2006 Châteauneuf-du-Pape	85	now–2011
2005 Châteauneuf-du-Pape	85	now–2012
2004 Châteauneuf-du-Pape	88	now–2014
2003 Châteauneuf-du-Pape	87	now–2012
2001 Châteauneuf-du-Pape	89	now–2012
2001 Châteauneuf-du-Pape Secrets de Pignan	93	now–2013
2006 Châteauneuf-du-Pape Secrets de Pignan Vieilles Vignes	89	now–2017
2005 Châteauneuf-du-Pape Secrets de Pignan Vieilles Vignes	91	now–2019
2004 Châteauneuf-du-Pape Secrets de Pignan Vieilles Vignes	90	now–2018
2003 Châteauneuf-du-Pape Secrets de Pignan Vieilles Vignes	90	now–2014
2003 Côtes du Rhône-Villages	87	now–2010
2004 Côtes du Rhône-Villages Cuvée Jules Rochebonne	87	now–2010
2003 Côtes du Rhône-Villages Cuvée Jules Rochebonne	89	now–2010

BASTIDE ST.-VINCENT ★ ★ ★
GIGONDAS $22.00–$32.00

Proprietor Guy Daniel has a small estate located on both the terraces and the plateau of Gigondas. Until a few years ago, this was a relatively inconsistent producer, but things have improved significantly, so that today it is producing one of the finest Vacqueyras of that appellation.

2000 Gigondas	87	now–2010
2003 Gigondas Cuvée Costevieille	91	now–2014
2000 Gigondas Cuvée Costevieille	88+?	now–2010
2003 Gigondas Cuvée Traditionelle	87	now–2013
2001 Vacqueyras Cuvée Pavane	88	now

BEAU MISTRAL ★ ★ ★
RASTEAU $20.00–$23.00

This is a reliable estate making full-bodied, somewhat rustic yet flavorful wines.

2005 Côtes du Rhône-Villages Rasteau	90	now–2017
2004 Côtes du Rhône-Villages Rasteau	88	now–2013

2001 Côtes du Rhône-Villages Rasteau	87	now
2004 Côtes du Rhône-Villages Rasteau Cuvée Florinaelle	87	now–2011

CHÂTEAU DE BEAUCASTEL ✳ ✳ ✳ ✳ ✳
CHÂTEAUNEUF-DU-PAPE
BEAUCASTEL $25.00–$350.00 / PERRINFI $10.00–$13.00 /
LA VIEILLE FERME $8.00–$10.00

One of the great estates of France, this bastion of traditionalism in the southern Rhône relies on a hefty dose of Mourvèdre in their red Châteauneuf-du-Pape as well as considerable amounts of Roussanne in their white Châteauneuf-du-Pape. Located in the northeastern part of the appellation, Beaucastel has for decades consistently produced superlative wines. One could argue that even though Grenache plays second fiddle in an atypical style of Châteauneuf-du-Pape, Beaucastel has been the most consistently great producer of Châteauneuf-du-Pape over the last three decades or more. Much of the credit for this goes to François and Jean-Pierre Perrin, who are now being succeeded by a younger generation. While demand for the estate wines is nearly impossible to satisfy, their *négociant* brand, run by Jean-Pierre's son, Pierre, continues to make better and better wines, developing long-term contracts with growers and branching out in nearly every southern Rhône appellation. Everything here is worth trying, as most of the wines are of top quality.

CHÂTEAU DE BEAUCASTEL

2006 Châteauneuf-du-Pape	93	2013–2040
2005 Châteauneuf-du-Pape	94+	2011–2027+
2004 Châteauneuf-du-Pape	93+	2012–2032+
2003 Châteauneuf-du-Pape	92+	2009–2031
2001 Châteauneuf-du-Pape	96	now–2025
2000 Châteauneuf-du-Pape	94	now–2025
1999 Châteauneuf-du-Pape	91+	now–2025
1998 Châteauneuf-du-Pape	95+	now–2031
2005 Châteauneuf-du-Pape Blanc	90	now–2015
2004 Châteauneuf-du-Pape Blanc	94	now–2017+
2003 Châteauneuf-du-Pape Blanc	92	now
2001 Châteauneuf-du-Pape Blanc	87	now
2000 Châteauneuf-du-Pape Blanc	95	now–2015
1999 Châteauneuf-du-Pape Blanc	95	now–2016
2005 Châteauneuf-du-Pape Hommage à Jacques Perrin	98+	2015–2057+
2004 Châteauneuf-du-Pape Hommage à Jacques Perrin	96	2016–2047+
2003 Châteauneuf-du-Pape Hommage à Jacques Perrin	95	2011–2049+
2001 Châteauneuf-du-Pape Hommage à Jacques Perrin	99+	2012–2040
2000 Châteauneuf-du-Pape Hommage à Jacques Perrin	97+	2010–2040
1999 Châteauneuf-du-Pape Hommage à Jacques Perrin	96	2010–2035
1998 Châteauneuf-du-Pape Hommage à Jacques Perrin	100	now–2031+
2005 Châteauneuf-du-Pape Roussanne Vieilles Vignes (white)	96	now–2011

2004 Châteauneuf-du-Pape Roussanne Vieilles Vignes (white)	96	now–2027
2003 Châteauneuf-du-Pape Roussanne Vieilles Vignes (white)	94	now
2001 Châteauneuf-du-Pape Roussanne Vieilles Vignes (white)	90	now
2000 Châteauneuf-du-Pape Roussanne Vieilles Vignes (white)	99	now–2010
1999 Châteauneuf-du-Pape Roussanne Vieilles Vignes (white)	97	now–2016
2005 Côtes du Rhône Coudoulet	90	now–2022
2004 Côtes du Rhône Coudoulet	90	now–2012
2003 Côtes du Rhône Coudoulet	89	now–2017
2001 Côtes du Rhône Coudoulet	91	now–2019
2000 Côtes du Rhône Coudoulet	88	now–2015
1999 Côtes du Rhône Coudoulet	90	now–2016
2005 Côtes du Rhône Coudoulet Blanc	88	???
2004 Côtes du Rhône Coudoulet Blanc	90	now–2010
2003 Côtes du Rhône Coudoulet Blanc	88	now
2001 Côtes du Rhône Coudoulet Blanc	90	now
2000 Côtes du Rhône Coudoulet Blanc	89	now

PERRIN ET FILS

2006 Châteauneuf-du-Pape Les Sinards	89	now–2022
2005 Châteauneuf-du-Pape Les Sinards	91	now–2019
2004 Châteauneuf-du-Pape Les Sinards	87?	now–2012
2003 Châteauneuf-du-Pape Les Sinards	86?	now–2017
2003 Côtes du Rhône	85	now
2005 Côtes du Rhône Réserve	86	now
2005 Côtes du Rhône Réserve Blanc	88	now
2005 Côtes du Rhône-Villages Vinsobres Les Cornuds	88	now–2012
2004 Côtes du Rhône-Villages Vinsobres Les Cornuds	88	now–2010
2005 Côtes du Rhône-Villages Vinsobres Vieilles Vignes Les Hauts de Julien	91	now–2017
2004 Côtes du Rhône-Villages Vinsobres Vieilles Vignes Les Hauts de Julien	90	now–2017
2003 Côtes du Rhône-Villages Vinsobres Vieilles Vignes Les Hauts de Julien	92	now–2016
2005 Gigondas La Gille	88	now–2014
2004 Gigondas La Gille	89	now–2013
2005 Gigondas Vieilles Vignes	90	now–2016
2005 Vacqueyras Les Christins Vieilles Vignes	89	now–2015

LA VIEILLE FERME

2005 Côtes du Luberon Blanc	86	now
2005 Côtes du Ventoux	85	now

DOMAINE DE BEAURENARD ★★★★/★★★★★
★★★★ / CHÂTEAUNEUF-DU-PAPE $21.00–$85.00

One of the old, classic estates of Châteauneuf-du-Pape, Beaurenard has been estate-bottling for more than 50 years. Their two offerings include the dark-colored regular cuvée and the *barrique*-aged Cuvée Boisrenard (which, despite the wood aging, never loses its Provençal typicality). Both are top-flight Châteauneuf-du-Papes based on 75% to 85% Grenache blended with Mourvèdre, Syrah, and Cinsault. Two cuvées of very fine Rasteau are good selections from the bargain bin.

2006 Châteauneuf-du-Pape	87	now–2011
2005 Châteauneuf-du-Pape	90	now–2022
2004 Châteauneuf-du-Pape	87	now–2013
2003 Châteauneuf-du-Pape	91	now–2016
2001 Châteauneuf-du-Pape	91	now–2014
2000 Châteauneuf-du-Pape	90	now–2018
1999 Châteauneuf-du-Pape	89	now–2011
2006 Châteauneuf-du-Pape Cuvée Boisrenard	90	now–2022
2005 Châteauneuf-du-Pape Cuvée Boisrenard	92+	2011–2025
2004 Châteauneuf-du-Pape Cuvée Boisrenard	90	now–2017
2003 Châteauneuf-du-Pape Cuvée Boisrenard	94	now–2018
2002 Châteauneuf-du-Pape Cuvée Boisrenard	86	now
2001 Châteauneuf-du-Pape Cuvée Boisrenard	97	now–2022
2000 Châteauneuf-du-Pape Cuvée Boisrenard	95	now–2020

ALBERT BELLE ✶✶✶
CROZES-HERMITAGE $23.00–$80.00

Albert Belle and his son are leading producers of very fine red and white Crozes-Hermitage, especially their Cuvée Louis Belle. They also produce a small amount of good Hermitage. Belle's wines continue to exhibit improvement, taking on more complexity and richness with each high-quality vintage. Given their prices, they represent super bargains.

2005 Crozes-Hermitage Blanc	87	now
2004 Crozes-Hermitage Blanc	87	now
2005 Crozes-Hermitage Cuvée Louis Belle	88	now–2011
2004 Crozes-Hermitage Cuvée Louis Belle	88	now–2012
2005 Crozes-Hermitage Les Pierrelles	87	now–2010
2004 Crozes-Hermitage Les Pierrelles	87	now–2011
2005 Hermitage	90	now–2014
2005 Hermitage Blanc	92	now–2018

DOMAINE DE BERANE ✶✶✶
CÔTES DU VENTOUX $15.00–$20.00

A nice discovery in the Côtes du Ventoux, this estate in the village of Mormoiron has 69 acres of vines.

2003 Côtes du Ventoux l'Agapes	88	now
2003 Côtes du Ventoux Les Blaques	89	now–2010

GUY ET FRÉDÉRIC BERNARD ✶✶
CÔTE RÔTIE $38.00–$55.00

Traditional Côte Rôties that are often vegetal as well as irregular in quality seem to be the rule of thumb from this small producer making less than 20,000 bottles of Côte Rôtie.

2005 Côte Rôtie	85	now–2015
2004 Côte Rôtie	82	now–2013
2003 Côte Rôtie	87	now–2012

DOMAINE BERTHET-RAYNE ✶✶✶
CHÂTEAUNEUF-DU-PAPE $28.00–$47.00

Berthet-Rayne appears to be producing better and better wines. This estate tends to be one of the more innovative in the appellation, trying different methods to produce more modern-style, solid, forward Châteauneuf-du-Papes meant to be drunk during their first decade.

2005 Châteauneuf-du-Pape	88	now–2017
2004 Châteauneuf-du-Pape	90	now–2014
2003 Châteauneuf-du-Pape	83?	now
2005 Châteauneuf-du-Pape Cuvée Cadiac	90	2010–2020
2004 Châteauneuf-du-Pape Cuvée Cadiac	90+	now–2019
2003 Châteauneuf-du-Pape Cuvée Cadiac	87?	now–2011

DOMAINE BOIS DE BOURSAN ✶✶✶✶
CHÂTEAUNEUF-DU-PAPE $30.00–$85.00

The Versino brothers run this outstanding estate that produces very Provençal-style Châteauneuf-du-Papes. The basic cuvée smells and tastes like the essence of a Provençal open-air market. The luxury cuvée, Cuvée des Felix, is more concentrated, revealing evidence of wood again.

2006 Châteauneuf-du-Pape	93	now–2016
2005 Châteauneuf-du-Pape	88	now–2019
2004 Châteauneuf-du-Pape	90	now–2015
2003 Châteauneuf-du-Pape	87	now–2015
2001 Châteauneuf-du-Pape	90	now–2016+
2000 Châteauneuf-du-Pape	91	now–2019
1999 Châteauneuf-du-Pape	89	now–2013
2003 Châteauneuf-du-Pape Les Baud	91	now–2022
2006 Châteauneuf-du-Pape Cuvée des Félix	93	2010–2025
2005 Châteauneuf-du-Pape Cuvée des Félix	93	2009–2022
2004 Châteauneuf-du-Pape Cuvée des Félix	91	now–2019
2003 Châteauneuf-du-Pape Cuvée des Félix	92	now–2021
2001 Châteauneuf-du-Pape Cuvée des Félix	95	now–2018
2000 Châteauneuf-du-Pape Cuvée des Félix	96	now–2020
1999 Châteauneuf-du-Pape Cuvée des Félix	93	now–2020
1998 Châteauneuf-du-Pape Cuvée des Félix	97	now–2021

DOMAINE DE BOIS DAUPHIN ✶✶✶
CHÂTEAUNEUF-DU-PAPE $25.00–$55.00

Forward, fruit-driven Châteauneuf-du-Papes are the rule of thumb from Jean Marchand's Bois Dauphin. The Clos des Pontifes is a modern, progressive-styled offering that spends time in new oak.

2003 Châteauneuf-du-Pape	86	now–2010
2001 Châteauneuf-du-Pape	89	now–2011
2000 Châteauneuf-du-Pape	86	now
2003 Châteauneuf-du-Pape Clos des Pontifes	88	now–2016
2001 Châteauneuf-du-Pape Clos des Pontifes	92	now–2014
2000 Châteauneuf-du-Pape Clos des Pontifes	88	now–2013

CUVÉE DE BOISDAUPHIN ★ ★ ★
CHÂTEAUNEUF-DU-PAPE $32.00–$35.00

Not to be confused with Jean Marchand's Bois Dauphin estate, Cuvée de Boisdauphin, owned by the Jacumin family, fashions classic, traditional, old-style Châteauneuf-du-Pape meant for long-term aging, the antithesis of Marchand's Châteauneufs.

2000 Châteauneuf-du-Pape	86	now–2010
1999 Châteauneuf-du-Pape	86	now

DOMAINE DU BOIS DES MÈGES ★ ★ ★
GIGONDAS $20.00–$32.00

A new producer for me in 2004, this was one of the top performers in my tastings of 2003 Gigondas, a variable vintage in this appellation, with few outstanding performers.

2004 Gigondas	90	now–2016
2003 Gigondas	89	now–2017

DOMAINE DU BOIS DE ST.-JEAN ★ ★
VACQUEYRAS $15.00–$25.00

This traditional estate ages its wines in tank prior to bottling. Vincent and Xavier Angles are the proprietors.

2005 Vacqueyras	88	now–2012

DE BOISSEYT-CHOL ★ ★
CÔTE RÔTIE $55.00–$60.00

Relatively light, sometimes herbal, but soft, pleasant Côte Rôties are made at this estate.

2005 Côte Rôtie Côte Blonde	87	now–2015
2004 Côte Rôtie Côte Blonde	86	now–2014

DOMAINE BOISSON ★ ★ ★
CÔTES DU RHÔNE $15.00–$25.00

While under most consumers' radar, this estate is very reliable and produces a tasty group of wines.

2003 Côtes du Rhône	86	now
2003 Côtes du Rhône-Villages Cairanne	87	now–2010
2003 Côtes du Rhône-Villages Cairanne Domaine Cros de Romet	88	now–2010
2003 Côtes du Rhône-Villages Cairanne l'Escigenée	87	now–2010

HENRI BONNEAU ★ ★ ★ ★ ★
CHÂTEAUNEUF-DU-PAPE $50.00–$290.00

One of the legendary and most idiosyncratic producers of Châteauneuf-du-Pape, Henri Bonneau has a patient winemaking process that usually means no Châteauneuf-du-Pape is released for at least five to six years after the vintage. Then when he does declare it his top cuvée, the Réserve des Céléstins, is majestic, tasting more like concentrated beef blood than anything from Bonneau's old Grenache vines. His other cuvée, Marie Beurrier, is nearly as good, but significantly less expensive. This is classic, old-style Châteauneuf-du-Pape made as it was several hundred years ago.

2006 Châteauneuf-du-Pape Cuvée Marie Beurrier		
(probably)	90–93	now–2020
2005 Châteauneuf-du-Pape Cuvée Marie Beurrier	93–95	2018–2025
2004 Châteauneuf-du-Pape Cuvée Marie Beurrier	91–93	now–2020
2003 Châteauneuf-du-Pape Cuvée Marie Beurrier	90	now–2018
2001 Châteauneuf-du-Pape Cuvée Marie Beurrier	90	now–2020
2000 Châteauneuf-du-Pape Cuvée Marie Beurrier	91	now–2017
1999 Châteauneuf-du-Pape Cuvée Marie Beurrier	89	now–2020
1998 Châteauneuf-du-Pape Cuvée Marie Beurrier	90	now–2015
2006 Châteauneuf-du-Pape Réserve des Céléstins		
(probably)	92–95+	now–2022
2005 Châteauneuf-du-Pape Réserve des Céléstins	94–96	2017–2060
2003 Châteauneuf-du-Pape Réserve des Céléstins	91	now–2015
2001 Châteauneuf-du-Pape Réserve des Céléstins	97	now–2030
2000 Châteauneuf-du-Pape Réserve des Céléstins	94	now–2027
1999 Châteauneuf-du-Pape Réserve des Céléstins	94	now–2028
1998 Châteauneuf-du-Pape Réserve des Céléstins	98	2010–2040

PATRICK ET CHRISTOPHE BONNEFOND * * * *
CÔTE RÔTIE $35.00–$76.00

This up-and-coming Côte Rôtie producer works with 18 acres, practices 100% destemming, and produces elegant, quasimodern-styled cuvées. The two finest wines include the relatively limited production Côte Rôtie Les Rochains from the Côte Blonde and the Côte Rôtie Côte Rozier from the Côte Brune.

2006 Condrieu Côtes Chatillon (white)	92	now–2010
2005 Condrieu Côtes Chatillon (white)	93	now
2006 Côte Rôtie	86	now–2013
2005 Côte Rôtie	90	2009–2022
2004 Côte Rôtie	88	now–2013
2003 Côte Rôtie	90	now–2021
2006 Côte Rôtie Côte Rozier	92	now–2016
2005 Côte Rôtie Côte Rozier	92	2012–2022
2004 Côte Rôtie Côte Rozier	89	now–2014
2003 Côte Rôtie Côte Rozier	96	2011–2036
2006 Côte Rôtie Les Rochains	93	now–2015
2005 Côte Rôtie Les Rochains	94	2010–2022
2004 Côte Rôtie Les Rochains	88	now–2013
2003 Côte Rôtie Les Rochains	96	now–2028
2001 Côte Rôtie Les Rochains	92	now–2015
2000 Côte Rôtie Les Rochains	88	now–2010
1999 Côte Rôtie Les Rochains	93	now–2015

DOMAINE DE BONSERINE * * *
CÔTE RÔTIE $39.00–$60.00

This relatively good-sized estate (by Côte Rôtie standards) of just under 30 acres produces a number of good rather than exceptional cuvées. New *barriques* are utilized in the upbringing of these modern-styled wines. Domaine de Bonserine's offerings include one from the Côte Blonde (La Garde) and three from the Côte Brune: Côte Brune, Les Moutonnes, and La Sarrasine.

1999 Côte Rôtie Côte Brune	87+?	now–2017
2006 Côte Rôtie La Garde	87	now–2020

2005 Côte Rôtie La Garde	89	2012–2020
2004 Côte Rôtie La Garde	87	now–2015
2003 Côte Rôtie La Garde	91	now–2016
2000 Côte Rôtie La Garde	87	now–2014
2000 Côte Rôtie Les Moutonnes	85	now–2014
2006 Côte Rôtie La Sarrasine	88	now–2018
2005 Côte Rôtie La Sarrasine	85	???
2004 Côte Rôtie La Sarrasine	86	now–2011
2003 Côte Rôtie La Sarrasine	84	now–2012
2006 Côte Rôtie La Vallière	90	2011–2021
2005 Côte Rôtie La Vallière	90	2014–2022
2003 Côte Rôtie La Vallière	92	now–2023

BOSQUET DES PAPES ★ ★ ★ ★
CHÂTEAUNEUF-DU-PAPE $29.00–$63.00

This is another traditionally run estate that has been making consistently high-quality wines since the late 1970s. The Boiron family makes four distinctive cuvées—the traditional Châteauneuf-du-Pape followed by a cuvée of old vines they call Chante Le Merle, their 100% old-vine Grenache cuvée, and the Gloire de Mon Grand-Père. All are impressive wines with wonderful perfumes, impeccable purity, plenty of flavor, and savory textures.

2006 Châteauneuf-du-Pape	89	now–2015
2005 Châteauneuf-du-Pape	88	now–2022
2004 Châteauneuf-du-Pape	89	now–2015
2003 Châteauneuf-du-Pape	89	now–2016
2001 Châteauneuf-du-Pape	90	now–2019
2000 Châteauneuf-du-Pape	90	now–2018
2006 Châteauneuf-du-Pape Chante Le Merle Vieilles Vignes	90	2009–2020
2005 Châteauneuf-du-Pape Chante Le Merle Vieilles Vignes	92	2011–2022
2004 Châteauneuf-du-Pape Chante Le Merle Vieilles Vignes	91	now–2017
2003 Châteauneuf-du-Pape Chante Le Merle Vieilles Vignes	89+	now–2020
2001 Châteauneuf-du-Pape Chante Le Merle Vieilles Vignes	92+	now–2015
2000 Châteauneuf-du-Pape Chante Le Merle Vieilles Vignes	91	now–2016
2001 Châteauneuf-du-Pape Cuvée Grenache	89	now–2013
2000 Châteauneuf-du-Pape Cuvée Grenache	89	now–2011
2006 Châteauneuf-du-Pape à la Gloire de Mon Grand-Père	90	now–2019
2005 Châteauneuf-du-Pape à la Gloire de Mon Grand-Père	90	2009–2028
2004 Châteauneuf-du-Pape à la Gloire de Mon Grand-Père	91	now–2014
2003 Châteauneuf-du-Pape à la Gloire de Mon Grand-Père	90	now–2015
2001 Châteauneuf-du-Pape à la Gloire de Mon Grand-Père	90	now–2011

DOMAINE DES BOSQUETS * * *
GIGONDAS $22.00

This estate tends to produce old-style Gigondas without the requisite backbone of concentration and intensity to support the long cask aging. Domaine des Bosquets's vineyards possess various expositions, but they are primarily located on the clay and limestone soils of the plain and terraces.

2005 Gigondas	91	2010–2019
2004 Gigondas	88	now–2015
2003 Gigondas	90	now–2012
2001 Gigondas	87	now–2011
2001 Gigondas Préférence	90	now–2014

DOMAINE LA BOUISSIÈRE * * * *
GIGONDAS $25.00–$42.00

This estate's name is a Provençal word for the groves of trees that were cut down in order to plant the vines on the terraces at the foot of the Dentelles de Montmirail. Proprietors Thierry and Gilles Faravel produce two wines—their regular cuvée, a rustic Gigondas, and their cuvée spéciale, La Font de Tonin, made from older vines with no Mourvèdre in the blend. Both wines are bottled without fining or filtration.

2004 Gigondas Cuvée Prestige Le Font de Tonin	88	now–2016
2003 Gigondas Cuvée Prestige Le Font de Tonin	89	now–2013
2001 Gigondas Cuvée Prestige Le Font de Tonin	89	now–2016
2000 Gigondas Cuvée Prestige Le Font de Tonin	90+	now–2018
1999 Gigondas Cuvée Prestige Le Font de Tonin	89	now–2012
2004 Gigondas Cuvée Traditionelle	87	now–2014
2003 Gigondas Cuvée Traditionelle	87	now–2011
2001 Gigondas Cuvée Traditionelle	88	now–2014
2000 Gigondas Cuvée Traditionelle	90	now–2012
1999 Gigondas Cuvée Traditionelle	88	now–2011
2003 Vacqueyras	87	now
2003 Vacqueyras La Ponche	89	now–2010

BOUVACHON-NOMINE * *
CÔTES DU RHÔNE $15.00–$25.00

I taste this estate's wines every year but rarely am able to recommend them.

2004 Châteauneuf-du-Pape	85	now–2010
2003 Châteauneuf-du-Pape	86	now–2011
2005 Côtes du Rhône	84	now
2004 Côtes du Rhône-Villages La Patrasse	86	now

BRESSY-MASSON * * * *
RASTEAU $28.00

These are rustic yet enormously flavorful and substantial offerings from one of the warmest appellations in the Côtes du Rhône-Villages, Rasteau. Consumers looking for wines with a terrific Provençal personality need to check out this estate.

2005 Côtes du Rhône-Villages Rasteau	88	now–2014
2004 Côtes du Rhône-Villages Rasteau	87	now–2011
2000 Côtes du Rhône-Villages Rasteau	88	now

2005 Côtes du Rhône-Villages Rasteau Cuvée Paul-Émile	90	now–2012
2004 Côtes du Rhône-Villages Rasteau Cuvée Paul-Émile	90	now–2017
2003 Côtes du Rhône-Villages Rasteau Cuvée Paul-Émile	90	now–2016
2004 Côtes du Rhône-Villages Rasteau À la Gloire de Mon Père	88	now–2014
2003 Côtes du Rhône-Villages Rasteau À la Gloire de Mon Père	91	now–2015

BROTTE ★ ★ ★
CHÂTEAUNEUF-DU-PAPE $45.00–$55.00

This old-line *négociant* firm is owned by Alain Brotte.

2006 Châteauneuf-du-Pape Père Anselme Fiole Réserve	85	now–2014
2005 Châteauneuf-du-Pape Père Anselme Fiole Réserve	87	2010–2022
2006 Châteauneuf-du-Pape Vieilles Vignes	89	now–2022
2005 Châteauneuf-du-Pape Vieilles Vignes	90	now–2022

LA BRUNELY ★ ★ ★
VACQUEYRAS $25.00

The Brunely estate, situated on the plateau of Sarrians (one of the most renowned sectors of Vacqueyras), can trace its Italian origins back to the fifteenth century. The proprietors are Anne and Charles Carichon. The wines are above average in quality.

2005 Vacqueyras	89	now–2015

DOMAINE BRUSSET ★ ★ ★/★ ★ ★ ★
GIGONDAS $22.00–$42.00

Daniel Brusset is best known for his lavishly wooded Gigondas, but his home cellars are in the village of Cairanne. The bulk of Domaine Brusset's production is in Côtes du Rhône and Côtes du Rhône-Villages Cairanne. These are rich, well-made wines with plenty of flavor. The modern-styled Gigondas relies heavily on new oak, which tends to be relatively pronounced in the wine's youth.

2005 Côteaux des Travers Cairanne	87	now–2011
2004 Côteaux des Travers Cairanne	84	now
2003 Côteaux des Travers Cairanne	86	now
2005 Côtes du Rhône	88	now
2004 Côtes du Rhône	85	now
2003 Côtes du Rhône-Villages Cairanne	85	now
2004 Côtes du Rhône-Villages Cairanne Vendange Chabrille	86	now
2003 Côtes du Rhône-Villages Cairanne Vendange Chabrille	88	now
2003 Gigondas	87	now–2010
2005 Gigondas Domaine Le Grand Montmirail	90–92	now–2019
2000 Gigondas Domaine Le Grand Montmirail	89	now
2005 Gigondas Les Hauts de Montmirail	90–92	now–2022
2003 Gigondas Les Hauts de Montmirail	88	now–2012
2001 Gigondas Les Hauts de Montmirail	88	now–2012

BERNARD BURGAUD ★★★
CÔTE RÔTIE $35.00–$59.00

Burgaud's rustic, traditional Côte Rôties can be very leathery and, as the French say, "smell of animals." These damp old cellars of this small domaine (just over 10 acres) overlook the steep slopes of Côte Rôtie. Burgaud is a generally reliable producer, but the vintages since 2003 have been disappointing.

2005 Côte Rôtie	83	2010–2015
2004 Côte Rôtie	75	now–2013
2003 Côte Rôtie	84?	now
2000 Côte Rôtie	87	now–2014
1999 Côte Rôtie	91+	now–2016

CHÂTEAU CABRIÈRES ★★★
CHÂTEAUNEUF-DU-PAPE $30.00–$75.00

One of Châteauneuf-du-Pape's finest vineyards, located on the stony, high plateau behind the village Cabrières, which made brilliant wines in the late 1950s and 1960s, has recently emerged from a period of producing mainstream, commercial reds that were often excessively fined as well as filtered. This new quality level, obvious since 1998, has resulted in some fruit-forward, commercial Châteauneuf-du-Papes that have their place in the market but do not compare with the great classic vintages of the past (e. g., 1961, 1966, 1967).

2001 Châteauneuf-du-Pape	86	now
2000 Châteauneuf-du-Pape	87	now–2011
2001 Châteauneuf-du-Pape La Centenaire	88	now–2012
2001 Châteauneuf-du-Pape Cuvée Prestige Tête de Cru	90	now–2015
2000 Châteauneuf-du-Pape Cuvée Prestige Tête de Cru	91	now–2018
2001 Châteauneuf-du-Pape La Lettre à Louis Arnaud	93	now–2020
2000 Châteauneuf-du-Pape La Lettre à Louis Arnaud	93+	now–2020

DOMAINE DU CAILLOU ★★★★★
CHÂTEAUNEUF-DU-PAPE $15.00–$250.00

This fabulous estate was resurrected by the late Jean-Denis Vacheron, who accomplished much here between 1998 and 2001. Tragically, Vacheron was killed in an auto accident, but his widow, Sylvie, assisted by winemaker Bruno Gaspard, consultant Philippe Cambie, and nearby friends Jean-Paul Daumen and Laurent Charvin, has taken over the winemaking and continues to turn out fabulous Châteauneuf-du-Papes, including their top wines, the Réserve, Les Quartz, and a bevy of sensational Côtes du Rhônes that are as good as many producers' Châteauneuf-du-Papes. Domaine du Caillou utilizes significant amounts of Mourvèdre and Syrah in their Châteauneuf-du-Pape blends. Bargain hunters should stockpile these superb Côtes du Rhônes.

2005 Châteauneuf-du-Pape	91	now–2021
2004 Châteauneuf-du-Pape	90	now–2016
2003 Châteauneuf-du-Pape	90	now–2013
2001 Châteauneuf-du-Pape	92	now–2016
2000 Châteauneuf-du-Pape	90	now–2015
1999 Châteauneuf-du-Pape	90	now
2006 Châteauneuf-du-Pape Les Clos du Caillou Réserve	92	now–2022+
2005 Châteauneuf-du-Pape Les Clos du Caillou Réserve	95	2011–2025

2004 Châteauneuf-du-Pape Les Clos du Caillou Réserve	93	now–2021
2001 Châteauneuf-du-Pape Les Clos du Caillou Réserve	100	now–2022
2000 Châteauneuf-du-Pape Les Clos du Caillou Réserve	99	now–2020+
1999 Châteauneuf-du-Pape Les Clos du Caillou Réserve	94	now–2018
1998 Châteauneuf-du-Pape Les Clos du Caillou Réserve	99+	now–2026
2003 Châteauneuf-du-Pape Cuvée Unique	88	now–2013
2006 Châteauneuf-du-Pape Les Quartz	91	now–2022
2005 Châteauneuf-du-Pape Les Quartz	93	2010–2022
2004 Châteauneuf-du-Pape Les Quartz	92	now–2019
2003 Châteauneuf-du-Pape Les Quartz	90+	now–2021
2001 Châteauneuf-du-Pape Les Quartz	96	now–2016
2000 Châteauneuf-du-Pape Les Quartz	94	now–2016
2006 Châteauneuf-du-Pape Les Safres	89	now–2017
2005 Côtes du Rhône Bouquet des Garrigues	90	now
2004 Côtes du Rhône Bouquet des Garrigues	87	now
2004 Côtes du Rhône Réserve	90	now–2013
2004 Côtes du Rhône-Villages	87	now–2009
2005 Côtes du Rhône-Villages Les Quartz	91	now–2012
2004 Côtes du Rhône-Villages Les Quartz	87	now–2012

LES CAILLOUX ★ ★ ★ /★ ★ ★ ★ ★
CHÂTEAUNEUF-DU-PAPE $28.00–$250.00

One of the most intelligent and global-thinking proprietors of Châteauneuf-du-Pape is André Brunel. From his 50 acres of vineyards he produces fabulous Châteauneuf-du-Pape as well as 500 cases of his Cuvée Centenaire, which comes primarily from Grenache vines planted in 1889. Small barrels are used for Syrah and Mourvèdre; the Grenache is kept in larger, older wood. The results are some of the best wines of the appellation. Brunel's white wines also have gone from strength to strength.

LES CAILLOUX

2006 Châteauneuf-du-Pape	89	now–2017
2005 Châteauneuf-du-Pape	90	now–2022
2004 Châteauneuf-du-Pape	90	now–2016
2003 Châteauneuf-du-Pape	92	now–2016
2001 Châteauneuf-du-Pape	91	now–2014
2000 Châteauneuf-du-Pape	91	now–2015
1999 Châteauneuf-du-Pape	90	now–2015
2005 Châteauneuf-du-Pape Blanc	92	now
2004 Châteauneuf-du-Pape Blanc	89	now
2003 Châteauneuf-du-Pape Blanc	89	now
2006 Châteauneuf-du-Pape Cuvée Centenaire	94	now–2022
2005 Châteauneuf-du-Pape Cuvée Centenaire	95	2010–2025
2003 Châteauneuf-du-Pape Cuvée Centenaire	96	2009–2020+
2001 Châteauneuf-du-Pape Cuvée Centenaire	96	now–2020
2000 Châteauneuf-du-Pape Cuvée Centenaire	96	now–2018
1998 Châteauneuf-du-Pape Cuvée Centenaire	100	now–2025

ANDRÉ BRUNEL:

2005 Côtes du Rhône Cuvée Sommelongue	87	now–2012
2003 Côtes du Rhône Cuvée Sommelongue	88	now

LE CALICE DE ST.-PIERRE ★ ★ ★
CHÂTEAUNEUF-DU-PAPE $32.00–$40.00

This emerging estate seems to be making better wines than in the past.

2005 Châteauneuf-du-Pape	88	now–2017
2004 Châteauneuf-du-Pape	87	now–2011
2003 Châteauneuf-du-Pape	88	now–2011
2001 Châteauneuf-du-Pape	87	now–2013
2000 Châteauneuf-du-Pape	88	now–2010
2005 Châteauneuf-du-Pape Héritage	90	now–2022
2004 Châteauneuf-du-Pape Héritage	88	now–2015

DOMAINE DES CANTARELLES ★ ★ ★
COSTIÈRES DE NÎMES $18.00–$20.00

This is a fine source for value-priced wines from Provence.

2005 Cabernet Sauvignon-Syrah VDP du Gard Costières de Nîmes	88	now–2011
2004 Cabernet Sauvignon-Syrah VDP du Gard Costières de Nîmes	87	now–2011
2002 Cabernet Sauvignon-Syrah VDP du Gard Costières de Nîmes	87	now
2005 Syrah de Fayel VDP	85	now
2004 Syrah Vielles Vignes	89	now–2015
2005 Viognier VDP	87	now
2002 Viognier VDP du Gard Costières de Nîmes	88	now

DOMAINE DE CASSAN ★ ★/★ ★ ★
GIGONDAS $25.00–$32.00

The wines I have tasted from Domaine de Cassan are competent, traditionally styled Gigondas that are supple enough to be drunk when released, yet capable of lasting for seven to eight years. The 2000 Gigondas is the finest offering I have tasted from this small, 18-acre estate run by the Croset family.

2005 Gigondas	88	now–2016
2004 Gigondas	87	now

CAVE ST.-PIERRE ★ ★/★ ★ ★
CHÂTEAUNEUF-DU-PAPE $15.00–$25.00

This huge *négociant* offers a diverse array of wines, including southern Rhône vintages, wines from Provence, and miscellaneous Languedoc-Roussillon offerings entitled to only a *vin de pays* designation. They produce a competent, medium- to full-bodied chunky Châteauneuf-du-Pape. It is neither insipid nor compelling. It is easy to criticize vast, commercial concerns such as Cave St.-Pierre, but the bottom line is that the quality of the wines is at least acceptable, and occasionally above average.

DOMAINE DU CAYRON ★★★
GIGONDAS $25.00–$32.00

The Faraud family has been making one wine, an extremely concentrated, intense Gigondas, for more than 150 years. Georges and Michel Faraud's wines are such forceful examples of Gigondas that they, more than any other wine of this appellation, require rich stews, cassoulets, and game to absorb their strong personalities. Properly served and matched up with the right culinary offering, they are memorable wines that can take one on a pleasant trip to the 19th century.

2005 Gigondas	89	now–2015
2001 Gigondas	87	now–2011
2000 Gigondas	90	now–2011
1999 Gigondas	92	now–2013

CELLIER DES PRINCES ★★
CHÂTEAUNEUF-DU-PAPE $25.00

The Cellier des Princes, founded in 1924, is the only cooperative in Châteauneuf-du-Pape. Competently made, fruity, and soft, this is not an exciting wine and requires drinking during its first five to six years of life. If tasters concentrate very hard, they will find aromas of *garrigue, herbes de Provence,* and pepper.

2005 Châteauneuf-du-Pape Les Hauts des Côteaux	84	now
2000 Châteauneuf-du-Pape Les Hauts des Côteaux	85	now

STÉPHAN CHABOUD ★★★
ST.-PÉRAY $20.00–$30.00

Young Stéphan Chaboud is trying singlehandedly to resurrect the image of sparkling wines from St.-Péray. He is producing a top-notch still wine as well as a fine sparkler, usually made from Marsanne and a dollop of Roussanne.

2003 Cornas Reserve	89	now–2014
N. V. Cuvée Louis Alexandre	90	now
N. V. St.-Péray Cuvée Arnaud	89	now

JOEL ET ROMAN CHAMPET ★★★
CÔTE RÔTIE $45.00–$60.00

A younger generation has taken charge at this property, which produces two Côte Rôties, a basic blend from different sections of the appellation, and a single vineyard effort called La Viallière, which comes from the Côte Brune. These wines have grown significantly better over the last decade.

CHANABAS ★★★
CHÂTEAUNEUF-DU-PAPE $29.00–$32.00

An American importer needs to take a look at the excellent wines being produced at the Domaine de Chanabas by proprietor Robert Champ, whose cellars are in Piolenc, a small town north of Châteauneuf-du-Pape known as the garlic capital of France.

2001 Châteauneuf-du-Pape	88	now–2012
2000 Châteauneuf-du-Pape	87	now
1999 Châteauneuf-du-Pape	88	now–2011

DOMAINE DES CHANSSAUD ***
CHÂTEAUNEUF-DU-PAPE $28.00–$50.00

Proprietor Patrick Jaume produces good, if unspectacular, Châteauneuf-du-Papes.

2005 Châteauneuf-du-Pape	88	now–2013
2004 Châteauneuf-du-Pape	86	now–2012
2003 Châteauneuf-du-Pape	87	now–2010
2005 Châteauneuf-du-Pape Chanssaud d'Antan	90	now–2017
2004 Châteauneuf-du-Pape Chanssaud d'Antan	88	now–2015
2003 Châteauneuf-du-Pape Chanssaud d'Antan	89	now–2019
2004 Châteauneuf-du-Pape Tour de L'Isle	88	now–2017

CHANTE CIGALE ****
CHÂTEAUNEUF-DU-PAPE $20.00–$55.00

Traditionally made Châteauneuf-du-Papes, primarily Grenache with some Syrah, Mourvèdre, and Cinsault included in the blend, emerge from this estate. Both cuvées are outstanding, but the Vieilles Vignes is top-notch. Both tend to age well.

2005 Châteauneuf-du-Pape	90	now–2020
2004 Châteauneuf-du-Pape	89	now–2017
2003 Châteauneuf-du-Pape	92	now–2016
2005 Châteauneuf-du-Pape Vieilles Vignes	93	2011–2026+
2003 Châteauneuf-du-Pape Vieilles Vignes	94	now–2021
2001 Châteauneuf-du-Pape Vieilles Vignes	91	now–2016

DOMAINE CHANTE-PERDRIX ***/****
CHÂTEAUNEUF-DU-PAPE $30.00–$47.00

The Nicolet family makes a fragrant, exotic style of Châteauneuf-du-Pape with stunning aromatics, sweet tannin, and usually no shortage of seductive powers. This is a Châteauneuf-du-Pape for hedonists who love a Provençal-perfumed style of wine.

2005 Châteauneuf-du-Pape	89	now–2016
2004 Châteauneuf-du-Pape	87	now–2012
2003 Châteauneuf-du-Pape	89	now–2013
2001 Châteauneuf-du-Pape	90	now–2014
2000 Châteauneuf-du-Pape	88	now–2010
1999 Châteauneuf-du-Pape	89	now–2010

CHAPOUTIER ****/*****
NORTHERN RHÔNE $12.00–$285.00

There is no question that Michel Chapoutier remains one of the most compelling wine personalities of the world, and his obsession with *terroir*-based wines is largely unequaled by any other vigneron on the planet. His desire to, as he says, "Make a photograph of the *terroir* and the vintage," is what has led him to biodynamic farming for all of the estate's vineyards and begin to put under contract vineyards that are under farming leases to be at least organic, if not biodynamic. He remains adamantly opposed to any manipulation in the winery, makes no acid adjustments, and allows no fining or filtration, as he believes that each wine—especially his single-vineyard cuvées—should represent the essence of the vintage and the *terroir*. This admirable rhetoric is backed up by the wines that emerge in the bottle. One has to look at the Chapoutier portfolio as different hierarchies, with the lower-level wines offering immediate drinkability and the top, single-vineyard cuvées meant to be aged for decades. Chapoutier's finest efforts are wines of singular greatness and character with extraordinary longevity. For example, his red Hermitages from the first vintages he made (1989 and 1990) after taking over this firm from his father remain very young wines at ages 19 and 18 respectively.

A new project by the Pic family (which owns the famous Valence restaurant) and Chapoutier is the resurrection of the St.-Péray vineyards, the Gamme Pic and Chapoutier St.-Péray (100% Marsanne). Other new undertakings involve vineyards in Côteaux Montélimar (well-known for the ominous nuclear power plant that dominates the landscape 48 miles north of Avignon), the Languedoc, and Roussillon.

RED WINES

2004 Domaine de Bila-Haut Occultum Lapiderm	91	now–2016
2003 Domaine de Bila-Haut Occultum Lapiderm	90	now–2016
2006 Châteauneuf-du-Pape Barbe Rac	93	now–2022+
2005 Châteauneuf-du-Pape Barbe Rac	96	now–2022
2004 Châteauneuf-du-Pape Barbe Rac	93	now–2022
2003 Châteauneuf-du-Pape Barbe Rac	95+	2009–2026
2001 Châteauneuf-du-Pape Barbe Rac	95	now–2024
2000 Châteauneuf-du-Pape Barbe Rac	95	now–2023
2006 Châteauneuf-du-Pape La Bernardine	89	now–2015
2005 Châteauneuf-du-Pape La Bernardine	89	now–2019
2004 Châteauneuf-du-Pape La Bernardine	87	now–2015
2003 Châteauneuf-du-Pape La Bernardine	87	now–2010
2001 Châteauneuf-du-Pape La Bernardine	87	now–2014
2006 Châteauneuf-du-Pape Croix de Bois	92	now–2022
2005 Châteauneuf-du-Pape Croix de Bois	95	2009–2022
2004 Châteauneuf-du-Pape Croix de Bois	93	now–2019
2003 Châteauneuf-du-Pape Croix de Bois	93	now–2021+
2001 Châteauneuf-du-Pape Croix de Bois	94	now–2024
2000 Châteauneuf-du-Pape Croix de Bois	94	now–2023
1999 Châteauneuf-du-Pape Croix de Bois	91	now–2016
2005 Côte Rôtie La Mordorée	94+	2014–2028
2004 Côte Rôtie La Mordorée	90	now–2016
2003 Côte Rôtie La Mordorée	96+	now–2026+
2001 Côte Rôtie La Mordorée	91	now–2014
2000 Côte Rôtie La Mordorée	90	now–2012
2003 Côteaux de Languedoc Mas de la Barben Barben	91	now–2013
2004 Côteaux de Languedoc Mas de la Barben Calice	92	now–2018
2004 Côteaux de Languedoc Mas de la Barben Les Lauzières	88	now–2011
2004 Côteaux de Languedoc Mas de la Barben Les Sabines	90	now–2012
2005 Côtes du Rhône Belleruche	86	now
2004 Côtes du Rhône Belleruche	87	now
2005 Côtes du Rhône-Villages Rasteau	89	now–2022
2005 Crozes-Hermitage Les Meysonnières	87	now
2004 Crozes-Hermitage Les Meysonnières	84	now
2005 Crozes-Hermitage La Petite Ruche	87	now
2005 Crozes-Hermitage Les Varonnières	92	now–2022
2004 Crozes-Hermitage Les Varonnières	91	now–2018
2003 Crozes-Hermitage Les Varonnières	93	now–2021+
2005 Ermitage l'Ermite	98+	2025–2050
2004 Ermitage l'Ermite	93	now–2021+

2003 Ermitage l'Ermite	100	now–2056
2001 Ermitage l'Ermite	99	2012–2040
2000 Ermitage l'Ermite	99+	2009–2035
2005 Ermitage Les Greffieux Vieilles Vignes	94	now–2025
2004 Ermitage Les Greffieux Vieilles Vignes	89	now–2021
2003 Ermitage Les Greffieux Vieilles Vignes	96	2012–2030
2001 Ermitage Les Greffieux Vieilles Vignes	93	now–2020
2005 Ermitage Le Méal	96+	2016–2040
2004 Ermitage Le Méal	90+	now–2018
2003 Ermitage Le Méal	99	2011–2046
2001 Ermitage Le Méal	94	now–2030
2000 Ermitage Le Méal	95	now–2025
2005 Ermitage Le Pavillon	98+	2025–2055
2004 Ermitage Le Pavillon	92	now–2021
2003 Ermitage Le Pavillon	100	now–2056+
2001 Ermitage Le Pavillon	94+	2010–2030
2000 Ermitage Le Pavillon	98+	now–2040
2005 Ermitage La Sizeranne	90	2011–2020
2004 Ermitage La Sizeranne	88	now–2017
2005 St.-Joseph Deschants	87	now
2004 St.-Joseph Deschants	85	now
2005 St.-Joseph Les Granits	93	now–2022
2004 St.-Joseph Les Granits	90	now–2016

WHITE WINES

2005 Ermitage Chante-Alouette	95	now–2025
2004 Ermitage Chante-Alouette	94	now–2010
2003 Ermitage Chante-Alouette	93	now–2011
2005 Ermitage l'Ermite Blanc	98	now–2035
2004 Ermitage l'Ermite Blanc	100	now–2035?
2003 Ermitage l'Ermite Blanc	100	now–2050
2005 Ermitage Le Méal Blanc	98	now–2040
2004 Ermitage Le Méal Blanc	99	now–2040
2003 Ermitage Le Méal Blanc	98+	now–2035?
2005 Ermitage l'Orée	98	now–2050
2004 Ermitage l'Orée	97	now–2025
2003 Ermitage l'Orée	99	now–2055
2001 Ermitage l'Orée	94	2016–2033+

DOMAINE DE LA CHARBONNIÈRE * * * *
CHÂTEAUNEUF-DU-PAPE $16.00–$55.00

Rhône wine enthusiasts need to jump on the bandwagon before the Domaine de la Charbonnière becomes better known. Proprietor Michel Maret is doing everything right, producing wines with terrific individual character from low yields and, over several years, bottling without filtration. This is one of the most serious Châteauneuf-du-Pape estates, which fortunately has good representation in the United States. The Domaine de la Charbonnière's best value, and one of the better wines of the appellation, is their Vacqueyras.

2006 Châteauneuf-du-Pape	89	now–2017
2005 Châteauneuf-du-Pape	90	now–2019
2004 Châteauneuf-du-Pape	89	now–2014

2003 Châteauneuf-du-Pape	88	now–2012
2002 Châteauneuf-du-Pape	85	now
2001 Châteauneuf-du-Pape	88	now–2012
2000 Châteauneuf-du-Pape	89	now–2012
2001 Châteauneuf-du-Pape Blanc	87	now
2006 Châteauneuf-du-Pape Les Hautes Brusquières Cuvée Spéciale	90	2011–2026+
2005 Châteauneuf-du-Pape Les Hautes Brusquières Cuvée Spéciale	91+	now–2022
2004 Châteauneuf-du-Pape Les Hautes Brusquières Cuvée Spéciale	91	now–2019
2003 Châteauneuf-du-Pape Les Hautes Brusquières Cuvée Spéciale	90	now–2016
2001 Châteauneuf-du-Pape Les Hautes Brusquières Cuvée Spéciale	95	now–2017
2000 Châteauneuf-du-Pape Les Hautes Brusquières Cuvée Spéciale	94	now–2016
2006 Châteauneuf-du-Pape Mourre des Perdrix	91	now–2022+
2005 Châteauneuf-du-Pape Mourre des Perdrix	92	now–2022
2004 Châteauneuf-du-Pape Mourre des Perdrix	90	now–2017
2003 Châteauneuf-du-Pape Mourre des Perdrix	89+?	now–2016
2001 Châteauneuf-du-Pape Mourre des Perdrix	92	now–2018
2000 Châteauneuf-du-Pape Mourre des Perdrix	91	now–2014
2006 Châteauneuf-du-Pape Cuvée Vieilles Vignes	91	2011–2026+
2005 Châteauneuf-du-Pape Cuvée Vieilles Vignes	92+	now–2022
2004 Châteauneuf-du-Pape Cuvée Vieilles Vignes	90	now–2018
2003 Châteauneuf-du-Pape Cuvée Vieilles Vignes	91	now–2018
2001 Châteauneuf-du-Pape Cuvée Vieilles Vignes	92+	now–2019
2000 Châteauneuf-du-Pape Cuvée Vieilles Vignes	94	now–2018
2005 Vacqueyras	89	now–2017
2004 Vacqueyras	87	now–2011

DOMAINE G. A. E. C. CHARVIN ★ ★ ★ ★
CHÂTEAUNEUF-DU-PAPE $15.00–$75.00

Gérard Charvin's young son Laurent now runs this 20-acre estate. The Châteauneuf-du-Papes he produces are pure elegance, maybe as close to a grand cru red Burgundy as one will find in this village. Primarily old-vine Grenache with small quantities of Mourvèdre and Vaccarèse, these finesse-styled Châteauneuf-du-Papes boast pure black raspberry fruit, deep medium- to full-bodied textures, and impressive purity. They come close to mimicking the great Château Rayas.

2006 Châteauneuf-du-Pape	94	now–2023
2005 Châteauneuf-du-Pape	93	now–2019
2004 Châteauneuf-du-Pape	90	now–2019
2003 Châteauneuf-du-Pape	93	now–2018
2001 Châteauneuf-du-Pape	95	now–2016
2000 Châteauneuf-du-Pape	95	now–2018
1999 Châteauneuf-du-Pape	92	now–2016
1998 Châteauneuf-du-Pape	96	now–2021
2005 Côtes du Rhône Le Poutet	88	now–2013
2004 Côtes du Rhône Le Poutet	90	now–2011

BERNARD AND YANN CHAVE ★ ★ ★
HERMITAGE $32.00–$76.00

The "other" Chaves, Bernard and Yann, have cellars on the auto route south of Hermitage. These wines are good, but they never hit the heights of those produced by Gérard and Jean-Louis Chave.

2003 Crozes-Hermitage	87	now–2011
2003 Crozes-Hermitage Tête de Cuvée	89	now–2012
2003 Hermitage	90	now–2024

J. L. CHAVE ★ ★ ★ ★ ★
HERMITAGE $75.00–$175.00

This is the model estate for a family-owned vineyard—a great family, a great domaine, a great *terroir,* and great wines. While the father and son, as well as the other 500 years or so of Chaves who have made wines from the hallowed hills of Hermitage, may be world-class tasters, superb chefs, and gifted storytellers, the fact remains that Gérard Chave and, increasingly, his talented young son, Jean-Louis, are among the staunchest guardians of *terroir* and artisanal/artistic winemaking in France. The humility with which they go about their business (mere custodians of privileged spots on Earth is how they look at it) is refreshing, particularly in a world dominated by greed and an industrial wine culture. They make exquisite red and white Hermitage as well as small amounts of St.-Joseph. In the finest vintages, Chave produces tiny amounts of a superexpensive luxury cuvée called Cathelin.

2005 Hermitage	96	2018–2050
2004 Hermitage	94	2011–2032
2003 Hermitage	100	now–2046+
2002 Hermitage	92	now–2015
2001 Hermitage	93	now–2028
2000 Hermitage	96	now–2035
1999 Hermitage	96	2009–2052
2005 Hermitage Blanc	95	now–2030
2004 Hermitage Blanc	95	now–2031
2003 Hermitage Blanc	96	now–2030?
2001 Hermitage Blanc	93	now–2025
2000 Hermitage Blanc	95	now–2023
1999 Hermitage Blanc	94	now–2022+
2003 Hermitage Cuvée Cathelin	100	2015–2060+
2000 Hermitage Cuvée Cathelin	96+	2010–2040
1996 Hermitage Vin de Paille (white dessert)	99	now–2103
2005 St.-Joseph	89	now–2018
2004 St.-Joseph	88	now–2012
2003 St.-Joseph	93	now–2021
2001 St.-Joseph	88	now–2010
2000 St.-Joseph	88	now

DOMAINE DU CHÊNE ★ ★ ★
ST.-JOSEPH $45.00–$55.00

The Rouvier family continues to turn out fine wines from this estate, which have not yet received the accolades they merit. Readers should take note, as prices remain reasonable. The white wines have gone from strength to strength over recent vintages.

2006 Condrieu (white)	92	now
2005 Condrieu (white)	90	now
2005 St.-Joseph Cuvée Anaïs	90	now–2012
2004 St.-Joseph Cuvée Anaïs	89	now–2013

LOUIS CHÈZE ★ ★ ★
ST.-JOSEPH $38.00–$50.00

Having founded this estate only in 1978, Louis Chèze decided that his father's practice of selling the production to *négociants* should be discontinued. This is yet another estate producing better and better wines, in which the young Chèze has invested in both his vineyards and cellars.

2000 St.-Joseph Cuvée des Anges	85	now
2000 St.-Joseph Cuvée Prestige de Caroline	85	now

DOMAINE LA CITADELLE ★ ★ ★
CÔTES DU LUBERON $15.00–$25.00

Domaine La Citadelle is one of the finest estates in Luberon.

2005 Côtes du Luberon Les Artemes	89	now–2012
2005 Côtes du Luberon Le Chataignier	86	now–2011
2005 Côtes du Luberon Gouverneur St.-Auban	90	now–2013

AUGUSTE CLAPE ★ ★ ★ ★ ★
CORNAS $18.00–$88.00

Over the last quarter century, Auguste Clape has been the spiritual and qualitative leader of Cornas. More than any other single person, the gentlemanly, articulate Clape has been responsible for the renewed interest in the wines of Cornas. His son, Pierre-Marie, is now in charge of the winemaking at this benchmark estate. These passionate guardians of traditional Cornas produce magnificent, long-lived, dense, rich wines redolent with notes of blackberries, truffles, licorice, and spring flowers. Their wines represent Cornas at its finest.

2006 Cornas	91	2014–2024
2005 Cornas	91+	2015–2025
2004 Cornas	92	now–2021
2003 Cornas	93	now–2021
2001 Cornas	92	now–2022
2000 Cornas	91	now–2018
2006 Cornas Renaissance	89	now–2020
2005 Cornas Renaissance	91+	2010–2020
2004 Cornas Renaissance	90	now–2016
2003 Cornas Renaissance	89	now–2014
2001 Cornas Renaissance	90	now–2018
2000 Cornas Renaissance	89	now–2012
2005 Côtes du Rhone	85	now
2005 St.-Péray (white)	88	now
2005 Le Vin des Amis Vin de Table	87	now

LES CLEFS D'OR ★ ★ ★
CHÂTEAUNEUF-DU-PAPE $35.00–$42.00

A large estate of nearly 60 acres, Les Clefs d'Or produces classic Châteauneuf-du-Papes redolent with aromas and flavors of blueberries, raspberries, and cherries. Over recent years the style has become noticeably lighter.

2005 Châteauneuf-du-Pape	85	now
2004 Châteauneuf-du-Pape	86	now
2003 Châteauneuf-du-Pape	90	now–2015
2001 Châteauneuf-du-Pape	89	now–2013
2000 Châteauneuf-du-Pape	90	now–2018

CLOS DES BRUSQUIÈRES ★★★
CHÂTEAUNEUF-DU-PAPE $33.00–$35.00

These traditionally made old-style wines came to my attention through a recommendation from the reclusive Henri Bonneau.

2005 Châteauneuf-du-Pape	88	now–2017
2004 Châteauneuf-du-Pape	87	now–2011
2003 Châteauneuf-du-Pape	90	now–2011

LE CLOS DES CAZAUX ★★★
VACQUEYRAS $20.00–$25.00

Traditionally made, full-bodied, peppery, spicy Vacqueyras emerge from this estate. Its cuvées are more similar than dissimilar, and all are noteworthy efforts worth a search of the marketplace.

2003 Vacqueyras	88	now–2010
2003 Vacqueyras Lao Muse	89	now–2012
2004 Vacqueyras Cuvée Prestige	90	now–2015
2003 Vacqueyras Cuvée Prestige	90	now–2011
2001 Vacqueyras Cuvée Prestige	87?	now
2000 Vacqueyras Cuvée Prestige	88	now–2011
2001 Vacqueyras Cuvée Réserve	87?	now
2004 Vacqueyras Cuvée St.-Roche	89	now–2011
2004 Vacqueyras Cuvée des Templiers	88	now
2003 Vacqueyras Cuvée des Templiers	89	now
2001 Vacqueyras Cuvée des Templiers	89	now–2012
2000 Vacqueyras Cuvée des Templiers	86	now

CLOS DU JONCUAS ★★★★
GIGONDAS $28.00–$35.00

This first-rate estate with relatively old vines (averaging 45 years) produces uncompromisingly intense, traditionally styled Gigondas that are aged in *foudre* for one year prior to bottling. The blend tends to be 80 to 85% Grenache and the rest Mourvèdre, with a dollop of Syrah.

2005 Gigondas	90	now–2015
2004 Gigondas	88	now–2012
2003 Gigondas	88	now–2014
2001 Gigondas	90	now–2011
2003 Vacqueyras La Font de Papier	89	now–2012

CLOS DU MONT OLIVET ★★★★★
CHÂTEAUNEUF-DU-PAPE $29.00–$95.00

One of the largest and most important families of Châteauneuf-du-Pape, the Sabons, produce two cuvées of traditionally made, ageworthy Châteauneuf-du-Pape. Both can last easily for 15 to 20 years, but the more limited offering, the spectacular Cuvée du Papet, is one of the most outrageously decadent and complex Châteauneuf-du-Papes of the village. It is worth a special effort to find.

2006 Châteauneuf-du-Pape La Cuvée du Papet	90	2010–2020
2005 Châteauneuf-du-Pape La Cuvée du Papet	92	2010–2025
2004 Châteauneuf-du-Pape La Cuvée du Papet	92	now–2020
2003 Châteauneuf-du-Pape La Cuvée du Papet	92	now–2021
2000 Châteauneuf-du-Pape La Cuvée du Papet	92+	now–2020
1998 Châteauneuf-du-Pape La Cuvée du Papet	96	now–2018
2006 Châteauneuf-du-Pape Cuvée Tradition	87	now–2015
2005 Châteauneuf-du-Pape Cuvée Tradition	90	now–2022
2004 Châteauneuf-du-Pape Cuvée Tradition	87	now–2015
2003 Châteauneuf-du-Pape Cuvée Tradition	89	now–2018
2001 Châteauneuf-du-Pape Cuvée Tradition	87	now–2012
2000 Châteauneuf-du-Pape Cuvée Tradition	90	now–2015
1999 Châteauneuf-du-Pape Cuvée Tradition	89	now–2013

CLOS MONTIRIUS ★ ★ ★ ★
VACQUEYRAS $26.00–$35.00

Proprietors Eric and Christine Saurel have been doing impressive work at this 22-acre estate.

2005 Montirius	90	2010–2016
2004 Montirius	90	now–2012
2005 Vacqueyras	89	2009–2019
2004 Vacqueyras	86	now–2010
2003 Vacqueyras	88	now
2005 Vacqueyras Confidentiel	91	2010–2025

CLOS DE L'ORATOIRE ★ ★ ★
CHÂTEAUNEUF-DU-PAPE $34.00–$38.00

This historic estate has been in existence since the 18th century. In the mid to late 20th century it began flirting with one-dimensional commercial fruity wines. However, Clos de l'Oratoire has rebounded handsomely over the last few vintages and is again fashioning more intense wines with impressive density, richness, and aging ability.

2005 Châteauneuf-du-Pape	90	now–2017
2003 Châteauneuf-du-Pape	90	now–2015
2001 Châteauneuf-du-Pape	88	now–2014
2000 Châteauneuf-du-Pape	89	now–2015
2005 Châteauneuf-du-Pape Les Choregies	92	now–2022
2003 Châteauneuf-du-Pape Les Choregies	93	now–2017
2001 Châteauneuf-du-Pape Les Choregies	91	now–2023
2000 Châteauneuf-du-Pape Les Choregies	92	now–2018

CLOS DES PAPES ★ ★ ★ ★ ★
CHÂTEAUNEUF-DU-PAPE $12.00–$120.00

With 80-plus acres under vine, this extraordinary estate is enjoying an even higher level of quality now that proprietor Paul Avril has the full-time assistance of his son Vincent. The Avrils have a well-deserved reputation for producing wines that evolve and last for 20 to 30 or more years. This is one of the sure bets in both red and white Châteauneuf-du-Pape.

2006 Châteauneuf-du-Pape	97	2010–2035+
2005 Châteauneuf-du-Pape	95	2012–2032

2004 Châteauneuf-du-Pape	95	now–2027
2003 Châteauneuf-du-Pape	97	now–2025
2002 Châteauneuf-du-Pape	88	now–2012
2001 Châteauneuf-du-Pape	95	2009–2020+
2000 Châteauneuf-du-Pape	95	now–2025
1999 Châteauneuf-du-Pape	91	now–2021
2005 Châteauneuf-du-Pape Blanc	93	now–2015
2004 Châteauneuf-du-Pape Blanc	89	now–2011
2003 Châteauneuf-du-Pape Blanc	90	now–2025

CLOS ST.-JEAN * * * * *
SINCE 2003 CHÂTEAUNEUF-DU-PAPE $39.00–$100.00

This was the quintessentially old, rustic style of Châteauneuf-du-Pape. Clos St.-Jean possesses some great vineyards, but the wines were aged entirely too long in old-wood casks. However, the young Vincent Maurel recently took control and, along with the assistance of the brilliant southern Rhône Valley oenologist Philippe Cambie turned things around in one vintage, 2003. Maurel and Cambie have admirably demonstrated what can be accomplished with these superb vineyards. Brilliant wines are now being made, including the top cuvée, the Deus Ex Machina, the Combe des Fous, and the traditional cuvée.

2006 Châteauneuf-du-Pape	92	now–2019
2005 Châteauneuf-du-Pape	93	now–2022
2004 Châteauneuf-du-Pape	91	now–2017
2003 Châteauneuf-du-Pape	90	now–2016
2005 Châteauneuf-du-Pape Blanc	86	now–2010
2004 Châteauneuf-du-Pape Blanc	91	now
2006 Châteauneuf-du-Pape La Combe des Fous	95	2010–2030
2005 Châteauneuf-du-Pape La Combe des Fous	98+	2010–2030
2004 Châteauneuf-du-Pape La Combe des Fous	93	now–2022
2003 Châteauneuf-du-Pape La Combe des Fous	95	now–2020
2006 Châteauneuf-du-Pape Deus Ex Machina	95	now–2027
2005 Châteauneuf-du-Pape Deus Ex Machina	100	2010–2030
2004 Châteauneuf-du-Pape Deus Ex Machina	95	now–2023
2003 Châteauneuf-du-Pape Deus Ex Machina	100	now–2021+
2006 Châteauneuf-du-Pape Vieilles Vignes	92	now–2019
2005 Châteauneuf-du-Pape Vieilles Vignes	93	now–2022

CLOS ST.-MICHEL * * */* * * *
CHÂTEAUNEUF-DU-PAPE $25.00–$55.00

A new generation of Moussets has taken over this estate, and the result is better wines than ever before. The portfolio includes a bevy of value-priced Côtes du Rhônes as well as their top wines, a basic Châteauneuf-du-Pape, the Cuvée Réservée, and the rare, 100% Mourvèdre offering, the Grand Clos.

2006 Châteauneuf-du-Pape	91	2010–2025
2005 Châteauneuf-du-Pape	90	2010–2025
2004 Châteauneuf-du-Pape	88	now–2015
2003 Châteauneuf-du-Pape	87?	now–2017
2001 Châteauneuf-du-Pape	86	now–2010
2000 Châteauneuf-du-Pape	86	now–2010
2006 Châteauneuf-du-Pape Cuvée Réservée	91	2010–2020+
2005 Châteauneuf-du-Pape Cuvée Réservée	93	2010–2025

2004 Châteauneuf-du-Pape Cuvée Réservée	90	now–2019
2003 Châteauneuf-du-Pape Cuvée Réservée	88?	now–2020
2001 Châteauneuf-du-Pape Cuvée Réservée	90	now–2016
2000 Châteauneuf-du-Pape Cuvée Réservée	90+	now–2016
2004 Châteauneuf-du-Pape Grand Clos	93	2010–2030
2001 Châteauneuf-du-Pape Grand Clos	93	now–2019
2000 Châteauneuf-du-Pape Grand Clos	92	now–2017

DOMAINE GUY MOUSSET

2005 Côtes du Rhône	85	now
2005 Côtes du Rhône-Villages Les Garrigues	89	now–2012
2004 Côtes du Rhône-Villages Les Garrigues	88	now

DOMAINE CLUSEL-ROCH ★ ★ ★ ★
CÔTE RÔTIE $42.00–$100.00

Limited production and impeccably high-quality offerings are the rule from the small cellars of Clusel-Roch. Located at the northern end of the Côte Rôtie, in the hamlet called Vérenay, almost all of their vineyards are in the northern Côte Brune, with their most important holdings in Viaillière and Les Grandes Places. The special cuvée Les Grands Places is a 100% Syrah aged in barrel with 50% new oak.

2005 Côte Rôtie	89+	2013–2022
2004 Côte Rôtie	81	now–2018
2003 Côte Rôtie	90	now–2014
2000 Côte Rôtie	87	now
1999 Côte Rôtie	92	now–2017
2005 Côte Rôtie Les Grandes Places	93+	2015–2025
2003 Côte Rôtie Les Grandes Places	94	now–2024
2000 Côte Rôtie Les Grandes Places	88	now–2011

DOMAINE DES COCCINELLES ★ ★ ★
CÔTES DU RHÔNE $15.00–$20.00

In English the name of this biodynamically farmed vineyard means ladybug.

2005 Côtes du Rhône	88	now–2010

COLLECTION ALAIN CORCIA ★ ★ ★
CHÂTEAUNEUF-DU-PAPE $12.00–$75.00

These *négociant* offerings are put together by the Burgundy wine broker Alain Corcia, who is currently doing some of his best work in the Rhône.

2006 Châteauneuf-du-Pape Crème de la Crème	92	now–2017
2006 Châteauneuf-du-Pape Cuvée André Eléazar	91	now–2019
2005 Châteauneuf-du-Pape Cuvée André Eléazar	90	2010–2022
2004 Châteauneuf-du-Pape Cuvée André Eléazar	90	now–2022
2003 Châteauneuf-du-Pape Cuvée André Eléazar	90	now–2014
2006 Châteauneuf-du-Pape Cuvée Hervé	87	now–2015
2005 Châteauneuf-du-Pape Cuvée Hervé	87+?	now–2022
2004 Châteauneuf-du-Pape Cuvée Hervé	90	now–2017
2003 Châteauneuf-du-Pape Cuvée Hervé	91–93	now–2020
2006 Châteauneuf-du-Pape Cuvée Julie	88	now–2022
2005 Châteauneuf-du-Pape Cuvée Julie	88+?	2009–2024
2004 Châteauneuf-du-Pape Cuvée Julie	88–91	now–2015

2003 Châteauneuf-du-Pape Cuvée Julie	90–93	now–2017
2006 Châteauneuf-du-Pape Cuvée Patricia	89	now–2018
2005 Châteauneuf-du-Pape Cuvée Patricia	89	now–2019
2004 Châteauneuf-du-Pape Cuvée Patricia	89	now–2013
2003 Châteauneuf-du-Pape Cuvée Patricia	89	now–2011
2004 Châteauneuf-du-Pape Cuvée Raphael	87–89	now–2012
2003 Châteauneuf-du-Pape Cuvée Raphael	89–91	now–2017
2006 Châteauneuf-du-Pape Tradition	86	now–2012
2005 Châteauneuf-du-Pape Tradition	87	now–2015
2005 Châteauneuf-du-Pape Vieilles Vignes	89–91	now–2019
2005 Côtes du Rhône La Bérardière Très Vieilles Vignes	89	now–2012
2004 Côtes du Rhône La Bérardière Très Vieilles Vignes	87	now
2005 Côtes du Rhône-Villages Cairanne	88–90	now–2013

COLOMBIER ★ ★ ★
CROZES-HERMITAGE $25.00–$30.00

Winemaker Florent Viale first came to my attention because of the very fine 1993s he produced, a vintage in which most of the best northern Rhône producers experienced difficulties. Viale produces two cuvées of red wine, both very good. The Cuvée Gaby, aged for 12 months in 100% new oak casks, appears to possess the concentration and depth to support such an upbringing. The regular red wine cuvée is aged both in cask and in stainless steel.

2004 Crozes-Hermitage Cuvée Gaby	91	now–2016

JEAN-LUC COLOMBO ★ ★ ★/★ ★ ★ ★
CORNAS $12.00–$75.00

Jean-Luc Colombo has become one of the stars of Cornas. Well-known as an oenologist for dozens of Rhône Valley clients, Colombo has had a positive influence in the Rhône, undoubtedly improving the quality of many estates' wines. He is producing some of the finest Cornas produced. His wines, made in a completely different style than those of such superstars as Auguste Clape, are an intelligent blend of *barrique* and concentrated Syrah from this appellation's sun-baked hillsides. A very talented winemaker who has expanded his operation to include many *négociant* wines, Colombo is to be admired for his top-notch Cornas, which are made in a very modern style.

2005 Condrieu Amour de Dieu (white)	93	now
2005 Cornas Force One	90	now–2018
2005 Cornas La Louvée	90+	2012–2025
2004 Cornas La Louvée	89+	now–2018
2003 Cornas La Louvée	93	now–2021+
2005 Cornas Les Ruchets	90	now–2020
2004 Cornas Les Ruchets	90+	now–2014
2003 Cornas Les Ruchets	91	now–2018
2001 Cornas Les Ruchets	91–93	now–2014
2005 Cornas Terres Brûlées	90	now–2015
2004 Cornas Terres Brûlées	90	now–2010

LES COMBES D'ARNEVAL ★ ★ ★
CHÂTEAUNEUF-DU-PAPE $35.00–$40.00

This single vineyard offering is named after a parcel of vines (*lieu-dit*) owned by Jérôme Quiot, better known as the proprietor of Vieux Lazaret and Duclaux. The vines are located at the western edge of the appellation, northwest of the village, near the huge plateau of Mont Redon.

2005 Châteauneuf-du-Pape		87	now–2012
2004 Châteauneuf-du-Pape		87	now–2015
2003 Châteauneuf-du-Pape		87	now–2010

DOMAINE DE LA CÔTE DE L'ANGE ★ ★ ★
CHÂTEAUNEUF-DU-PAPE $26.00–$55.00

The Côte de l'Ange fashions rustic, spicy, meaty Châteauneuf-du-Papes that tend to be short on sweet fruit. However, they are distinctive, and consumers who like the southern Rhône's roasted herb, leather, and sausage-like rather gamey characteristics will enjoy them. They are all traditionally made wines that actually have the endorsement of the reclusive renowned traditionalist Henri Bonneau.

2006 Châteauneuf-du-Pape	88	now–2017
2005 Châteauneuf-du-Pape	88	now–2018
2004 Châteauneuf-du-Pape	88	now–2013
2003 Châteauneuf-du-Pape	89	now–2016
2001 Châteauneuf-du-Pape	87	now–2016
2006 Châteauneuf-du-Pape Cuvée Vieilles Vignes	90	now–2024
2005 Châteauneuf-du-Pape Cuvée Vieilles Vignes	90	2010–2022
2004 Châteauneuf-du-Pape Cuvée Vieilles Vignes	89+	now–2017
2003 Châteauneuf-du-Pape Cuvée Vieilles Vignes	90+	now–2022
2001 Châteauneuf-du-Pape Cuvée Vieilles Vignes	89	now–2014
2000 Châteauneuf-du-Pape Cuvée Vieilles Vignes	90+	now–2020

DOMAINE CÔTEAUX DES TRAVERS ★ ★ ★/★ ★ ★ ★
RASTEAU $12.00–$35.00

This is a well-run estate that has provided me with reliable drinking over many years. Proprietor Robert Charavin owns 20 acres, from which he produces 3,200 cases of sturdy, husky—or as the French say, *solide*—red wine.

2005 Côtes du Rhône-Villages Cairanne Cuvée Séléction	89	now–2017
2004 Côtes du Rhône-Villages Rasteau Cuvée Paul	89	now–2016
2005 Côtes du Rhône-Villages Rasteau Cuvée Prestige	90	now–2017
2004 Côtes du Rhône-Villages Rasteau Cuvée Prestige	90	now–2013

DOMAINE DU COULET ★ ★ ★
CORNAS $45.00–$65.00

A relatively new producer, this estate turns out modern-style wines (some new oak is utilized) with silky tannins and generous, fruit-laden personalities.

2005 Cornas Billes Noires	90	2010–2020
2004 Cornas Billes Noires	88	now–2014
2005 Cornas Les Terrasses du Serre	90+	2012–2020
2004 Cornas Les Terrasses du Serre	88	now–2016
2003 Cornas Les Terrasses du Serre	92	now–2016

DOMAINE COURBIS ★ ★ ★
CORNAS $20.00–$75.00

Courbis is one of the undisputed stars of Cornas. These wines represent a combination of modern-style winemaking and a respect for ancient tradition. The Cornas cuvées are all *barrique*-aged, dense, and powerful, with 10 to 15 years of aging potential. This producer also fashions two spectacular St.-Joseph cuvées.

2006 Cornas Champelrose	89	2012–2020
2005 Cornas Champelrose	91+	2011–2020
2004 Cornas Champelrose	89	now–2018
2003 Cornas Champelrose	92	now–2021
2001 Cornas Champelrose	91	now–2015
2000 Cornas Champelrose	90	now–2013
2006 Cornas Les Eygats	87	2012–2020
2005 Cornas Les Eygats	90+	2011–2020
2004 Cornas Les Eygats	88	now–2014
2003 Cornas Les Eygats	89+	now–2018
2001 Cornas Les Eygats	92	now–2018
2006 Cornas La Saborotte	90	2012–2020
2005 Cornas La Saborotte	92+	2014–2025+
2004 Cornas La Saborotte	90	now–2021
2003 Cornas La Saborotte	93+	now–2026+
2001 Cornas La Saborotte	91	now–2017
2000 Cornas La Saborotte	91	now–2013
2005 St.-Joseph	88+	now–2015
2003 St.-Joseph	90	now–2016
2005 St.-Joseph Les Royes	90	2010–2016
2003 St.-Joseph Les Royes	92	now–2018+

DOMAINE LE COUROULU ＊ ＊ ＊ ＊
VACQUEYRAS $18.00–$28.00

Proprietor Guy Ricard makes rich, flavorful, savory Vacqueyras as well as delicious Côtes du Rhônes. These are satisfying wines full of Provençal sunshine and character.

2005 Vacqueyras Cuvée Classique	89	2009–2019
2004 Vacqueyras Cuvée Classique	89	now–2017
2003 Vacqueyras Cuvée Classique	88	now–2010
2005 Vacqueyras Vieilles Vignes	90	2009–2019
2004 Vacqueyras Vieilles Vignes	89+	now–2017
2003 Vacqueyras Vieilles Vignes	89	now

DOMAINE PIERRE COURSODON ＊ ＊ ＊ ＊
ST.-JOSEPH $25.00–$60.00

The committed young grower who runs this estate has fashioned pleasant, fruity whites and seriously endowed reds over recent vintages. Coursodon's 2003s are the finest wines Jérôme Coursodon has yet produced. Consistency is a virtue here.

2005 St.-Joseph	89	now–2014
2004 St.-Joseph	86	now–2010
2003 St.-Joseph	88	now–2012
2004 St.-Joseph Blanc	85	now–2010
2006 St.-Joseph l'Olivaie	90	now–2020
2005 St.-Joseph l'Olivaie	90	now–2018
2004 St.-Joseph l'Olivaie	88	now–2012
2003 St.-Joseph l'Olivaie	90	now–2016
2006 St.-Joseph Le Paradis St.-Pierre	91	now–2020
2005 St.-Joseph Le Paradis St.-Pierre	91+	2010–2020
2004 St.-Joseph Le Paradis St.-Pierre	89	now–2013
2003 St.-Joseph Le Paradis St.-Pierre	92	now–2021+

2006 St.-Joseph La Sensonne	92	now–2020
2005 St.-Joseph La Sensonne	91+	2010–2020
2003 St.-Joseph La Sensonne	94	now–2026

DOMAINE DE CRISTIA ★★★★/★★★★★
CHÂTEAUNEUF-DU-PAPE $16.00–$75.00

Cristia is an estate on the upswing due to the dedicated efforts of proprietors Alain and Baptiste Grangeon. The style is a synthesis between old-line tradition, with its emphasis on ancient Grenache vines, and a healthy respect for modernist techniques utilizing newer, small oak barrels for aging the Mourvèdre and Syrah.

2006 Châteauneuf-du-Pape	91	now–2022
2005 Châteauneuf-du-Pape	90	now–2019
2004 Châteauneuf-du-Pape	90	now–2022
2003 Châteauneuf-du-Pape	88	now–2016
2001 Châteauneuf-du-Pape	90	now–2019
2005 Châteauneuf-du-Pape Cuvée Renaissance	95+	2012–2035
2004 Châteauneuf-du-Pape Cuvée Renaissance	93	2010–2025
2003 Châteauneuf-du-Pape Cuvée Renaissance	94+	now–2021+
2001 Châteauneuf-du-Pape Cuvée Renaissance	95	now–2017
2000 Châteauneuf-du-Pape Cuvée Renaissance	93+	now–2018
2006 Châteauneuf-du-Pape Vieilles Vignes	94	now–2022
2005 Châteauneuf-du-Pape Vieilles Vignes	96	2011–2035
2004 Châteauneuf-du-Pape Vieilles Vignes	94	now–2026

CROS DE LA MÛRE ★★★★
CHÂTEAUNEUF-DU-PAPE $18.00–$40.00

This estate, located in the village of Mondragon (home to the famous Provençal bistro La Beaugravière), is run by the Michel family. Terrific Côtes du Rhônes, now entitled to the new appellation Massif d'Uchaux, emerge from this top-notch estate as well as small amounts of outstanding Châteauneuf-du-Pape and Gigondas.

2006 Châteauneuf-du-Pape	89	now–2017
2005 Châteauneuf-du-Pape	91	now–2022
2004 Châteauneuf-du-Pape	90	now–2018
2003 Châteauneuf-du-Pape	90	now–2016
2005 Côtes du Rhône Massif d'Uchaux	87	now–2011

OLIVIER CUILLERAS ★★★/★★★★
CÔTES DU RHÔNE $12.00–$25.00

A discovery by the renowned French wine importer Robert Kacher, Olivier Cuilleras appears to be going from strength to strength. Olivier Cuilleras's Côtes du Rhônes emerge from the village of Visan, located in the northern area of the southern Rhône. The Visan and Domaine La Guintrandy are aged completely in tank prior to being bottled without filtration. The Cuvée Louise spends eight months in *barrique*, a small percentage of which is new.

2000 Côtes du Rhône Domaine La Guintrandy	87	now
2000 Côtes du Rhône Cuvée Louise	87	now
2001 Côtes du Rhône Cuvée Louise-Amélie	91	now–2013
2001 Côtes du Rhône-Villages Visan Vieilles Vignes	91	now

YVES CUILLERON ★★★★
CÔTE RÔTIE $27.00–$100.00

Yves Cuilleron, one of the northern Rhône's most brilliant white-wine makers, seems to be capturing some of his white-wine magic with his newest red wine cuvées, particularly those from St.-Joseph. His gorgeous whites from St.-Joseph are essentially from the Marsanne grape, although the Côteau St.-Pierre cuvée is 100% Roussanne. However, the Côte Rôtie still lags behind the quality of the other wines. The top cuvée is called Côteau de Bassenon.

2005 Condrieu Les Chaillets Vieilles Vignes (white)	91	now
2004 Condrieu Les Chaillets Vieilles Vignes (white)	89	now
2003 Côte Rôtie Bassenon	86+?	now
2005 Côte Rôtie Terres Sombres	89	2012–2018
2004 Côte Rôtie Terres Sombres	85?	2009–2015
2003 Côte Rôtie Terres Sombres	89	now–2018
2005 St.-Joseph Les Serines	90	2010–2020

DELAS FRÈRES ★★★★/★★★★★
HERMITAGE $8.00–$200.00

Founded in 1836, Delas Frères has historically produced good wines, but thanks to the deep pockets and financial backing of the huge Deutz-Louis Roederer Champagne firms, and to Burgundian Jacques Granges being given carte blanche to turn this once moribund *négociant* around, Delas Frères has produced top-notch wines over the last decade. Their finest offerings remain their fabulous cuvées of Hermitage, Côte Rôtie, St.-Joseph, Crozes-Hermitage, and Cornas. While their southern Rhône selections are not at the same level of quality, this is one of the bright, shining operations of the northern Rhône.

RED WINES

2005 Châteauneuf-du-Pape Haute Pierre	91	now–2022
2004 Châteauneuf-du-Pape Haute Pierre	89	now–2013
2003 Châteauneuf-du-Pape Haute Pierre	90	now–2018
2005 Cornas Chante Perdrix	89–91+	2010–2020
2004 Cornas Chante Perdrix	90	now–2014
2003 Cornas Chante Perdrix	90	now–2016
2005 Côte Rôtie La Landonne	96	2015–2030
2004 Côte Rôtie La Landonne	94	2010–2022
2003 Côte Rôtie La Landonne	96	2010–2026
2001 Côte Rôtie La Landonne	91+	2009–2020
2000 Côte Rôtie La Landonne	88	now–2014
2005 Côte Rôtie Seigneur de Maugiron	89+	2012–2025
2004 Côte Rôtie Seigneur de Maugiron	88	now–2015
2003 Côte Rôtie Seigneur de Maugiron	93	now–2019
2001 Côte Rôtie Seigneur de Maugiron	89	now–2014
2005 Crozes-Hermitage Le Clos	90+	2012–2020
2004 Crozes-Hermitage Le Clos	88+	now
2003 Crozes-Hermitage Le Clos	92	now–2024
2005 Crozes-Hermitage Les Launes	87	now–2012
2003 Crozes-Hermitage Les Launes	87	now–2010
2005 Crozes-Hermitage Cuvée Tour d'Albon	88	2010–2016
2004 Crozes-Hermitage Cuvée Tour d'Albon	84	now
2003 Crozes-Hermitage Cuvée Tour d'Albon	87	now–2018
2005 Gigondas	89+	now–2015

2005 Hermitage Les Bessards	96	2016–2035
2004 Hermitage Les Bessards	94	2010–2024
2003 Hermitage Les Bessards	96+	2011–2036+
2001 Hermitage Les Bessards	91	2010–2035
2000 Hermitage Les Bessards	92	now–2025
2005 Hermitage Marquis de la Tourette	93+	2015–2030
2004 Hermitage Marquis de la Tourette	91	2009–2022
2003 Hermitage Marquis de la Tourette	95	now–2026+
2004 St.-Joseph Les Challeys	85	now
2004 St.-Joseph François de Tournon	88	now–2016
2003 St.-Joseph François de Tournon	91	now–2021
2004 St.-Joseph Ste.-Épine	89	now–2016
2003 St.-Joseph Ste.-Épine	93+	now–2021+

WHITE WINES

2006 Condrieu Clos Boucher	92	now
2006 Condrieu La Galopine	88	now
2005 Crozes-Hermitage Les Launes Blanc	89	now
2005 Hermitage Marquis de la Tourette Blanc	92	now–2020
2005 St.-Joseph Ste.-Épine	91	2009–2019
2004 St.-Joseph Ste.-Épine	90	now–2016
2005 St.-Joseph Ste.-Épine Blanc	91	now

ALBERT DERVIEUX-THAIZE ★ ★ ★ ★
CÔTE RÔTIE $55.00–$75.00

A name from the past, Albert Dervieux-Thaize has retired and given all his vineyards to René Rostaing, his son-in-law, who has farmed them since 1990. However, older vintages of Dervieux-Thaize sometimes appear in the marketplace, and when they do they can be fabulous wines, as he was a traditional as well as skilled winemaker.

LOUIS DREVON ★ ★
CÔTE RÔTIE $50.00–$52.00

Drevon's estate-bottled wines have never been impressive. They are commercial, loosely knit wines that lack concentration. All things considered, this is an average-quality Côte Rôtie producer.

2000 Côte Rôtie Domaine des Rosièrs	82	now
1999 Côte Rôtie Domaine des Rosièrs	84	now–2010

DOMAINE DUCLAUX ★ ★ ★/★ ★ ★ ★
CHÂTEAUNEUF-DU-PAPE $28.00–$32.00

Owned by Jérôme Quiot, one of France's most powerful men, Domaine Duclaux has been making fine wines over the last several vintages.

2006 Châteauneuf-du-Pape	91	now–2017
2005 Châteauneuf-du-Pape	91	now–2012
2003 Châteauneuf-du-Pape	89	now–2013
2001 Châteauneuf-du-Pape	89	now–2014

BENJAMIN ET DAVID DUCLAUX ＊＊＊＊
CÔTE RÔTIE $50.00–$60.00

An up-and-coming estate, that of brothers Benjamin and David Duclaux (who took over from their father, Edmond) is approximately 13 acres of vines in the Côte Blonde sector of the appellation, near Tupin. They utilize about 20% new oak as well as 100% destemming, and approximately 5% Viognier is cofermented with the Syrah. They produce delicate, finesse-styled Côte Rôties.

2005 Cote Rotie	89+	2010–2024
2004 Côte Rôtie	87	now–2015
2003 Côte Rôtie	93	now–2020
2001 Côte Rôtie	87	now–2015

PIERRE DUMAZET ＊＊＊＊
CONDRIEU $55.00–$70.00

This estate is best known for its tiny production of exotic, extravagantly rich Condrieu. In most vintages, it is one of the most profound wines of the appellation. Some of the finest 2000 Condrieus I tasted were made by Madame Dumazet.

2005 Condrieu Côteau Fournet Blanc	90	now

DUMIEN-SERETTE ＊＊＊
CORNAS $42.00

This solid but irregular producer can turn out fine wines, but consistency is a problem.

2005 Cornas Vieilles Vignes	88+	now–2012
2004 Cornas Vieilles Vignes	87	now–2014

ERIC ET JOËL DURAND ＊＊＊＊
CORNAS $31.00–$49.00

The proprietors of this up-and-coming estate, the Durands, exhibit good winemaking skills, with one foot in the future and one in the past, always a good sign. They have turned in very strong efforts from Cornas since the 2003 vintage. They also produce two impressive offerings from St.-Joseph.

2005 Cornas Confidence	90	2012–2020
2004 Cornas Confidence	89+	now–2014
2004 Cornas Cuvée Classique	87	now–2014
2003 Cornas Cuvée Classique	89	now–2016
2001 Cornas Cuvée Classique	88	now–2013
2000 Cornas Cuvée Classique	89	now
2000 Cornas Les Côteaux	88	now
2005 Cornas Empreintes	89+	2014–2022
2004 Cornas Empreintes	88	now–2018
2000 Cornas Empreintes	88	now–2014
2003 St.-Joseph	88	now–2015
2005 St.-Joseph Les Côteaux	90	now–2015
2003 St.-Joseph Les Côteaux	90	now–2018
2001 St.-Joseph Les Côteaux	87	now
2000 St.-Joseph Les Côteaux	86	now
2005 St.-Joseph Cuvée Lautaret	90+	2011–2018
2003 St.-Joseph Cuvée Lautaret	95	now–2021+

DOMAINE DE DURBAN ★★★★
BEAUMES DE VENISE $18.00–$20.00

The 62-acre Muscat vineyard of Domaine de Durban produces what many observers feel is the finest Muscat Beaumes de Venise of the appellation. If anyone doubts the popularity of Beaumes de Venise, try buying a bottle of Domaine de Durban three or four months after the wine has been released—it rapidly disappears from the marketplace.

2006 Beaumes de Venise (white dessert)	93	now

DOMAINE DURIEU ★★★/★★★★
CHÂTEAUNEUF-DU-PAPE $30.00–$45.00

Irregular quality was the rule of thumb at Domaine Durieu throughout the '70s, '80s, and most of the '90s. However, over recent vintages the quality has been more consistent. This is a relatively large estate with more than 50 acres of well-placed vineyards.

2006 Châteauneuf-du-Pape	88	now–2015
2005 Châteauneuf-du-Pape	90	2010–2025
2004 Châteauneuf-du-Pape	87	now–2013
2001 Châteauneuf-du-Pape	86	now
2000 Châteauneuf-du-Pape	87	now–2013
2006 Châteauneuf-du-Pape Réserve Lucille Avril	90	now–2022
2005 Châteauneuf-du-Pape Réserve Lucille Avril	92+	2010–2030
2004 Châteauneuf-du-Pape Réserve Lucille Avril	90	now–2020
1999 Châteauneuf-du-Pape Réserve Lucille Avril	89	now–2016

DOMAINE DES ENTREFAUX ★★★
CROZES-HERMITAGE $19.00

Increasingly in the Rhône Valley, as well as elsewhere, it is not uncommon for long-term members of cooperatives to decide that it is more challenging, as well as potentially more financially rewarding, to begin to estate-bottle their production, rather than have it commingled in a co-op. Charles Tardy and his partner, Bernard Ange, began bottling their own wines in 1980 and have never looked back. I have generally found the regular cuvées of white and red wine to be midlevel in quality. They are pleasant but undistinguished.

2003 Crozes-Hermitage	92	now–2018

DOMAINE DES ESCARAVAILLES ★★★★
RASTEU $20.00–$27.00

This is an up-and-coming estate with the wines now being made by the renowned, talented oenologist Philippe Cambie. From 160 acres spread throughout Cairanne, Rasteau, and Roaix, strong wines have been produced in 2004 and 2005.

2005 Côtes du Rhône Les Antimagnes	88	now–2015
2004 Côtes du Rhône Les Antimagnes	88	now
2003 Côtes du Rhône Les Antimagnes	87	now
2005 Côtes du Rhône-Villages Cairanne Le Boutine	89	now–2015
2005 Côtes du Rhône-Villages Cairanne Le Ventabren	85	now
2004 Côtes du Rhône-Villages Cairanne Le Ventabren	87	now
2003 Côtes du Rhône-Villages Cairanne Le Ventabren	87	now
2005 Côtes du Rhône-Villages Rasteau Heritage	91	2011–2025
2004 Côtes du Rhône-Villages Rasteau Heritage	89	now–2013
2005 Côtes du Rhône-Villages Rasteau La Ponce	88+	now–2012

2004 Côtes du Rhône-Villages Rasteau La Ponce	90	now
2003 Côtes du Rhône-Villages Rasteau La Ponce	90	now–2011
2005 Côtes du Rhône-Villages Roaix Les Hautes Granges	91	now–2022
2004 Côtes du Rhône-Villages Roaix Les Hautes Granges	90	now–2017

DOMAINE DES ESPIERS ✶✶✶
GIGONDAS $35.00–$37.00

The wine from this tiny five-acre domaine in Gigondas is made primarily from Grenache, with a small quantity of Syrah added for structure and complexity. Proprietor Philippe Cartoux has talent as well as well-placed vineyards.

2004 Gigondas Cuvée Tradition	88+	now–2016
2003 Gigondas Cuvée Tradition	89	now–2015
2000 Gigondas Cuvée Tradition	88	now
2003 Gigondas Cuvée des Blaches	90	now–2013
2000 Gigondas Cuvée des Blaches	91	now–2014

DOMAINE DE L'ESPIGOUETTE ✶✶✶
VACQUEYRAS $18.00

This 52-acre estate is run by the warm, inviting, open Edmonde Latour. The bulk of the estate is located on the mistral-swept part of the Vaucluse known as the Plan de Dieu, which has a particularly hot climate and a precocious *terroir*. The wines of Domaine de l'Espigouette have been estate-bottled for three decades and have shown increasing quality with every good vintage. There are multiple cuvées, all of which are rustic, peppery, flavorful, robust, mouth-filling, textbook Côtes du Rhônes. I generally find the Côtes du Rhône Plan de Dieu slightly richer and more intense than the regular Côtes du Rhône. The best value is often the low-priced, chunky, fleshy Vin de Pays Vaucluse.

2005 Vacqueyras	88	now–2015
2004 Vacqueyras	86	now
2000 Vacqueyras	87	now

BERNARD FAURIE ✶✶✶✶
HERMITAGE $50.00

Faurie is a somewhat underrated traditional producer of very fine red and white Hermitages. Occasionally a single vineyard cuvée from Le Méal is offered. Bernard Faurie's winemaking style comes closest to that of Gérard Chave. While his wines are full-flavored, they retain an elegance and finesse and, like those of Chave, start life very slowly. Faurie produces only 500 cases of red Hermitage and a scant 66 cases of white annually. He also produces 200 to 250 cases of St.-Joseph.

2000 Hermitage	88	now–2012
1999 Hermitage	89	now–2018

PHILIPPE FAURY ✶✶✶
CONDRIEU $42.00–$66.00

Faury is best known for his outstanding Condrieu cuvées (he was president of the Condrieu syndicate for a number of years), which typically taste like honeysuckle and peaches. He also produces straightforward Côte Rôties and St.-Josephs.

2006 Condrieu	90	now
2005 Condrieu	88	now
2006 Condrieu La Berne	91	now

2005 Condrieu La Berne	89	now
2005 Côte Rôtie	88	2009–2019
2004 Côte Rôtie	75	now
2003 Côte Rôtie	88	now–2014
2005 St.-Joseph	85	now
2005 St.-Joseph Vielles Vignes	88	now–2015

EDDIE FERAUD ★ ★ ★
CHÂTEAUNEUF-DU-PAPE $28.00–$52.00

Traditionally made artisanal wines are the rule of thumb for Eddie Feraud.

2005 Châteauneuf-du-Pape	89	2010–2025
2004 Châteauneuf-du-Pape	89	now–2015
2003 Châteauneuf-du-Pape	90	now–2022
2001 Châteauneuf-du-Pape	88	now–2012
2000 Châteauneuf-du-Pape	89	now–2013
1999 Châteauneuf-du-Pape	85	now

FÉRAUD-BRUNEL ★ ★ ★
CHÂTEAUNEUF-DU-PAPE $15.00–$27.00

These *négociant* offerings are of considerable interest, since two of Châteauneuf-du-Pape's most talented wine producers, Laurence Féraud (Domaine Pégaü) and André Brunel (Domaine Les Cailloux), are involved in their creation.

1999 Châteauneuf-du-Pape	89	now–2015
2005 Côtes du Rhône-Villages	88	now–2012
2001 Côtes du Rhône-Villages Cairanne	88	now
2003 Côtes du Rhône-Villages Rasteau	88	now–2015
2001 Côtes du Rhône-Villages Rasteau	89	now–2015
2003 Gigondas	88	now–2013

DOMAINE DE FERRAND ★ ★ ★ ★
CHÂTEAUNEUF-DU-PAPE $12.00–$45.00

Philippe Ferrand, who came to my attention a number of years ago, is one of the most serious of the young generation of vignerons in Châteauneuf-du-Pape. His Côtes du Rhônes are real sleeper selections and not that far off the mark of his brilliant Châteauneuf-du-Papes.

2006 Châteauneuf-du-Pape	93	2010–2030
2005 Châteauneuf-du-Pape	93	now–2022
2004 Châteauneuf-du-Pape	91	2009–2021
2003 Châteauneuf-du-Pape	92	now–2021
2001 Châteauneuf-du-Pape	88	now–2020
2000 Châteauneuf-du-Pape	92	now–2015
1999 Châteauneuf-du-Pape	90	now–2016
2005 Côtes du Rhône Cuvée Antique	87	now–2012
2004 Côtes du Rhône Cuvée Antique Vieilles Vignes	87	now–2011
2003 Côtes du Rhône Cuvée Antique Vieilles Vignes	89	now

DOMAINE ISABEL FERRANDO ★ ★ ★ ★
CHÂTEAUNEUF-DU-PAPE $55.00

This is the home estate of the highly respected Isabel Ferrando, who is better known for making the wines and overseeing the rebound of Domaine St.-Préfert.

2006 Châteauneuf-du-Pape	92	now–2022
2005 Châteauneuf-du-Pape	92	2009–2020
2004 Châteauneuf-du-Pape	91	now–2019

FERRATON PÈRE ET FILS * */* * *
HERMITAGE $12.00–$132.00

Everything at Ferraton is now completely controlled by Michel Chapoutier. Similar to the hierarchy at Chapoutier, there are *négociant* cuvées as well as single-vineyard estate offerings. Now that Chapoutier's winemaking team is overseeing the production, Ferraton's wines have gone from strength to strength. The 2005s and 2006s are the finest wines this estate has yet produced.

2005 Côtes du Rhône Samorens	85	now
2005 Côtes du Rhône Samorens Blanc	89	now
2005 Crozes-Hermitage Le Grand Courtil	88+	2010–2015
2004 Crozes-Hermitage Le Grand Courtil	87+	now–2014
2005 Crozes-Hermitage La Matinière	85+	now
2005 Hermitage Les Dionnières	90	2010–2020
2004 Hermitage Les Dionnières	90	now–2016
2005 Hermitage Le Méal	91	now–2020
2004 Hermitage Le Méal	91	2010–2016
2005 Hermitage Les Miaux	88	2009–2015
2004 Hermitage Les Miaux	87	now–2014
2005 Hermitage Le Reverdy Blanc	92	now
2005 St.-Joseph Les Oliviers Blanc	90	now
2003 St.-Joseph Les Oliviers Blanc	89	now
2005 St.-Joseph La Source	87	now

DOMAINE DES FILLES DURMA * */* * *
VINSOBRES $12.00–$14.00

A newly emerging estate in Vinsobres run by two sisters, the Domaine de Filles Durma's first vintage was 1999.

CHÂTEAU DES FINES ROCHES * * *
CHÂTEAUNEUF-DU-PAPE $40.00–$55.00

Both a winery and a top-notch hotel, which resembles a smaller version of the Excalibur Hotel on Las Vegas's famous strip, just outside the village of Châteauneuf-du-Pape, this estate had long been content to produce fruity, easy, one-dimensional wines. However, all this appears to have changed over the last few years. There are two cuvées of traditional Châteauneuf-du-Pape produced, the white label offering more intensity, richness, and longevity. This large domaine possesses more than 100 acres of vines.

2006 Châteauneuf-du-Pape	86	now–2012
2005 Châteauneuf-du-Pape	88	now–2015
2004 Châteauneuf-du-Pape	85	now–2011
2003 Châteauneuf-du-Pape	87	now–2012
2006 Châteauneuf-du-Pape (white label)	89	now–2019
2005 Châteauneuf-du-Pape (white label)	89	now–2017
2004 Châteauneuf-du-Pape (white label)	89	now–2014
2003 Châteauneuf-du-Pape (white label)	90	now

DOMAINE DE FONDRÈCHE ★ ★ ★ ★
CÔTES DU VENTOUX $11.00–$30.00

The Domaine de Fondrèche has become the superstar of the Côtes du Ventoux, producing remarkably reliable top-notch wines that far exceed their modest prices, whether they are white or red.

One should note that the *négociant* operation from purchased wine or fruit is sold under the Mas Fondrèche label, but all the other wines are from the biodynamically farmed 105 acres of vines. For bargain hunters, this estate is a treasure trove.

2005 Côtes du Ventoux L'éclat Blanc	87	now–2010
2005 Côtes du Ventoux Fayard	88	now–2012
2004 Côtes du Ventoux Fayard	89	now
2003 Côtes du Ventoux Fayard	89	now
2005 Côtes du Ventoux Nadal	90	now–2013
2004 Côtes du Ventoux Nadal	90	now–2012
2003 Côtes du Ventoux Nadal	89	now–2012
2005 Côtes du Ventoux Persia	91	now–2018
2004 Côtes du Ventoux Persia	92	now–2017
2003 Côtes du Ventoux Persia	89+?	now–2014
2005 Côtes du Ventoux Persia Blanc	90	now–2010
2005 Côtes du Ventoux Une Fois	92	now–2017
2005 Mas Fondrèche Côtes du Ventoux O'Sud	85	now
2004 Mas Fondrèche Côtes du Ventoux O'Sud	88	now

CHÂTEAU DE FONTAVIN ★ ★ ★
CHÂTEAUNEUF-DU-PAPE $28.00–$32.00

Fontavin is a sleeper estate emerging as a good source for Châteauneuf-du-Pape.

2003 Châteauneuf-du-Pape	88	now–2013
2001 Châteauneuf-du-Pape	88	now–2011
2000 Châteauneuf-du-Pape	87	now
1999 Châteauneuf-du-Pape	87	now

CHÂTEAU DE LA FONT DU LOUP ★ ★ ★
CHÂTEAUNEUF-DU-PAPE $30.00–$42.00

Multiple cuvées emerge from this 55-acre estate. These stylish, elegant Châteauneuf-du-Papes possess brightness, vibrancy, and Burgundy-like floral-infused sweet cherry fruit. Fashioned by proprietor Charles Mélia, these are not blockbuster, heavy-duty Châteauneuf-du-Papes but rather graceful, restrained efforts.

2000 Châteauneuf-du-Pape	87	now–2011
2000 Châteauneuf-du-Pape La Comtesse	88	now–2014
2000 Châteauneuf-du-Pape Les Fondateurs	87	now–2012
2000 Châteauneuf-du-Pape Le Puy Rolland	89	now–2016
1999 Châteauneuf-du-Pape Le Puy Rolland	88	now–2012

FONT DE MICHELLE ★ ★ ★ ★
CHÂTEAUNEUF-DU-PAPE $28.00–$71.00

One of the most reliable estates of the appellation, the gregarious, outgoing Gonnet brothers have consistently been making high-quality wine since the late 1980s. They aim for a forward style of Châteauneuf-du-Pape that is much more accessible and easy to drink than that of their next-door neighbor, Vieux Télégraphe. However, Font de Michelle's top cuvée, the

Étienne Gonnet, is a knockout wine of richness and modest longevity. They also produce attractive Côtes du Rhônes as well as one of the better white Châteauneuf-du-Papes.

2006 Châteauneuf-du-Pape	87	now–2013
2005 Châteauneuf-du-Pape	87	now–2014
2004 Châteauneuf-du-Pape	87	now–2011
2003 Châteauneuf-du-Pape	89	now–2013
2001 Châteauneuf-du-Pape	90	now–2012
2000 Châteauneuf-du-Pape	89	now–2017
2003 Châteauneuf-du-Pape Blanc	88	now
2006 Châteauneuf-du-Pape Cuvée Étienne Gonnet	89	now–2017
2005 Châteauneuf-du-Pape Cuvée Étienne Gonnet	90	now–2019
2004 Châteauneuf-du-Pape Cuvée Étienne Gonnet	92	now–2014
2003 Châteauneuf-du-Pape Cuvée Étienne Gonnet	93	now–2021
2001 Châteauneuf-du-Pape Cuvée Étienne Gonnet	93	now–2018
2000 Châteauneuf-du-Pape Cuvée Étienne Gonnet	91	now–2016

DOMAINE DE FONT-SANE * * *
GIGONDAS $25.00–$35.00

Since the mid-1980s, the Domaine de Font-Sane has emerged as one of the more reliable producers of Gigondas, a frustratingly irregular appellation. This 35-acre estate has long been owned by the Peysson family. The name Font-Sane comes from a local source for water. The moderately sized vineyard has its best parcels of Grenache in the terraces at the foot of the Dentelles range (limestone and clay soils) and on the flat plateau that extends away from the Dentelles, where the microclimate is much hotter and the gravelly soil includes more sand.

2005 Gigondas	87	now–2014
2003 Gigondas	87	now–2012

DOMAINE DE FONT SARADE * * *
VACQUEYRAS $25.00–$28.00

These are serious offerings from proprietor Bernard Burle.

2004 Vacqueyras	88	now–2010
2003 Vacqueyras	89	now
2004 Vacqueyras Cuvée Prestige	88	now–2010

CHÂTEAU FORTIA * * *
CHÂTEAUNEUF-DU-PAPE $30.00–$55.00

Fortia is the historic estate run by Baron Le Roy, whose grandfather was the creator of the appellation laws in France. While this estate has benefited from more attention to detail, it has not yet returned to its 1970s form, a decade when it often produced one of the top half-dozen Châteauneuf-du-Papes of each vintage. I have had some stunning bottles of the 2003 Châteauneuf-du-Pape Cuvée du Baron, but at other times these bottles have seemed to be slightly less concentrated and more diffuse. I don't know whether there are different bottlings. The finest bottles (and they are superb) may well be the best wines Fortia has made in more than 20 years.

2006 Châteauneuf-du-Pape Cuvée du Baron	88	now–2017
2005 Châteauneuf-du-Pape Cuvée du Baron	88	now–2017
2004 Châteauneuf-du-Pape Cuvée du Baron	87	now–2013
2003 Châteauneuf-du-Pape Cuvée du Baron	92?	now–2018

2001 Châteauneuf-du-Pape Renaissance	92	now–2015
2006 Châteauneuf-du-Pape Réserve	86	now–2017
2006 Châteauneuf-du-Pape Tradition	84	now–2012
2005 Châteauneuf-du-Pape Tradition	85	now–2015
2004 Châteauneuf-du-Pape Tradition	86	now–2011
2003 Châteauneuf-du-Pape Tradition	89	now–2012
2001 Châteauneuf-du-Pape Tradition	88	now–2014

DOMAINE LA FOURMONE L'OUSTEAU-FAUQUET * * *
VACQUEYRAS $18.00–$27.00

Roger Combe's reliable Vacqueyras rarely merit outstanding scores, but they are to be appreciated for their unadulterated, rich, concentrated fruit as well as up-front personalities. They are seductive reds for drinking during their first three to four years of life. As many as four separate cuvées can be produced, but the finest are usually the Sélection Maître de Chai, Trésor du Poète, and Les Ceps d'Or.

2000 Gigondas	87	now
2001 Vacqueyras Les Ceps d'Or	86	now
2004 Vacqueyras Séléction Maître de Chai	87	now–2012
2003 Vacqueyras Séléction Maître de Chai	88	now
2001 Vacqueyras Séléction Maître de Chai	88	now
2004 Vacqueyras Trésor du Poète	88	now–2012
2003 Vacqueyras Trésor du Poète	85	now

ANDRÉ FRANÇOIS * *
CÔTE RÔTIE $32.00–$35.00

Relatively dilute and herbaceous wines are the rule of thumb here.

2005 Côte Rôtie	81	now
2003 Côte Rôtie	78	now
2000 Côte Rotie	75	now
1999 Côte Rôtie	86	now

DOMAINE LOU FRÉJAU * * *
CHÂTEAUNEUF-DU-PAPE $35.00–$45.00

The Chastans, who run the Lou Frejau estate, are one of the better-known families of Châteauneuf-du-Pape. Their origins are in the northern part of the appellation, just south of Orange. This estate makes a fresh, one-dimensional white wine and a medium-bodied, spicy, rustic red.

2005 Châteauneuf-du-Pape	88	now–2014
2004 Châteauneuf-du-Pape	87	now–2011
2001 Châteauneuf-du-Pape	87	now–2012
2000 Châteauneuf-du-Pape	87	now

PIERRE GAILLARD * * * *
CÔTE RÔTIE $28.00–$110.00

Pierre Gaillard has always been a vigneron with considerable promise. For a number of years, Gaillard's wines were mixed in quality, with good wines followed by irregular, uninteresting offerings. However, over the last decade Gaillard has begun to fulfill his potential. Traditionalists will not appreciate Gaillard's reliance on new-oak aging for his Côte Rôties.

2006 Côte Rôtie	87	row–2017
2005 Côte Rôtie	90	2010–2017
2004 Côte Rôtie	87	row–2016
2003 Côte Rôtie	90	row–2016
2000 Côte Rôtie	87	now
2000 Côte Rôtie Côte Rozier Réserve	87	now–2012
2000 Côte Rôtie Les Viallières Réserve	87	now–2012
2006 Côte Rôtie Rose Pourpre	91	2011–2020
2005 Côte Rôtie Rose Pourpre	91+	2011–2018
2004 Côte Rôtie Rose Pourpre	88	now–2018
2003 Côte Rôtie Rose Pourpre	94+	now–2023
2000 Côte Rôtie Rose Pourpre	89	now–2013
2005 St.-Joseph Clos de Cuminaille	89+	2009–2014

DOMAINE DU GALETS DES PAPES ∗ ∗ ∗
CHÂTEAUNEUF-DU-PAPE $27.00–$45.00

Jean-Luc Mayard runs one of the finest estates in Châteauneuf-du-Pape. From a modestly sized property of just over 31 acres, the wines are a synthesis in style between the old, traditionally made examples, and the more modern fruit-driven Châteauneufs. Galets des Papes always seems to produce Châteauneuf-du-Papes with a distinctive resiny component and high levels of spice, pepper, and herbs. They are very Provençal and, when the texture and depth of fruit are there, can be a fine choice.

2005 Châteauneuf-du-Pape	88	now–2017
2004 Châteauneuf-du-Pape	87	now–2012
2003 Châteauneuf-du-Pape	88	now–2010
2001 Châteauneuf-du-Pape	87	now–2012
2000 Châteauneuf-du-Pape	89	now–2010
2005 Châteauneuf-du-Pape Vieilles Vignes	90	2009–2021
2004 Châteauneuf-du-Pape Vieilles Vignes	87+?	now–2015
2003 Châteauneuf-du-Pape Vieilles Vignes	89+?	now–2021
2001 Châteauneuf-du-Pape Vieilles Vignes	90	now–2017
2000 Châteauneuf-du-Pape Vieilles Vignes	90	now–2015

DOMAINE HENRI ET PHILIPPE GALLET ∗ ∗ ∗
CÔTE RÔTIE $50.00–$65.00

This almost nine-acre estate is run by Henri Gallet and his son, Philippe. The winemaking is primarily traditional, although there have been some modern concessions, such as decisions in 1999 to destem the fruit and to age 25% of the crop in small oak and the remainder in moderately sized *foudres* and a handful of *demimuids*. All the wine is bottled unfiltered, and there are two to three bottlings. To my taste, the first bottling is always fresher, with more lively fruit. While the Gallet wines can be slightly vegetal, they tend to hit the high points in top vintages.

2005 Côte Rôtie	88	2010–2026
2004 Côte Rôtie	83	now–2013
2003 Côte Rôtie	88	now–2015
2000 Côte Rôtie	87	now–2012
1999 Côte Rôtie	89+	now–2017

YVES GANGLOFF ★★★
CONDRIEU $50.00

Only a minuscule 200 cases of Condrieu are bottled at this estate, the balance being sold to Marcel Guigal. Not many Condrieu can handle the eight months of wood aging received by Gangloff's wines, but his powerful style holds up well. Some good, but uninspiring, Côte Rôties are also produced.

2005 Condrieu	89	now

CHÂTEAU DE LA GARDINE ★★★★
CHÂTEAUNEUF-DU-PAPE $32.00–$75.00

The Brunel family, which has more than 150 acres dedicated to red wine production, exhibits a decidedly modern view of what Châteauneuf-du-Pape should be. That said, their wines are built for long-term aging and their vintages usually need 12 to 15 years of cellaring until they start to round into form. One could say they want their Châteauneufs to age like Bordeaux. There are now four cuvées produced, the most recent addition being the Peure Bleu, which is made without any sulfur dioxide. Consequently, I suspect this wine is best purchased and drunk close to its origin, given this risky treatment. All things considered, this is a top-flight domaine that has been making long-lived wines for many decades.

2006 Châteauneuf-du-Pape	89	now–2016
2005 Châteauneuf-du-Pape	89+	2010–2025
2004 Châteauneuf-du-Pape	89	now–2018
2003 Châteauneuf-du-Pape	89+	now–2016
2001 Châteauneuf-du-Pape	88	now–2019
2000 Châteauneuf-du-Pape	90	now–2015
2006 Châteauneuf-du-Pape Cuvée des Générations	91	2011–2025
2005 Châteauneuf-du-Pape Cuvée des Générations	93+	2012–2025+
2004 Châteauneuf-du-Pape Cuvée des Générations	91+	2014–2030
2003 Châteauneuf-du-Pape Cuvée des Générations	93	2009–2020+
2001 Châteauneuf-du-Pape Cuvée des Générations	92+	2012–2022
2000 Châteauneuf-du-Pape Cuvée des Générations	94+	now–2025
1998 Châteauneuf-du-Pape Cuvée des Générations	94+	now–2025
2006 Châteauneuf-du-Pape Cuvée l'Immortelle	92	2010–2030
2005 Châteauneuf-du-Pape Cuvée l'Immortelle	91+	2011–2016
2001 Châteauneuf-du-Pape Cuvée l'Immortelle	92	now–2017
2000 Châteauneuf-du-Pape Cuvée l'Immortelle	91	now–2014

DOMAINE GARON ★★★
CÔTE RÔTIE $27.00–$50.00

The 2003 and 2005 from this domaine are the finest vintages I have yet tasted from Jean-François and Carmen Garon.

2004 Côte Rôtie	88	now–2012
2003 Côte Rôtie	92	now–2018
2006 Côte Rôtie Les Triotes	88	now–2017
2005 Côte Rôtie Les Triotes	90	now–2015
2006 Côte Rôtie Les Rochains	90	2011–2017
2005 Côte Rôtie Les Rochains	92	2010–2020
2004 Côte Rôtie Les Rochains	87	now–2019
2003 Côte Rôtie Les Rochains	91+	now–2018

DOMAINE "LA GARRIGUE" ★ ★ ★ ★
VACQUEYRAS $12.00–$40.00

This is one of the largest properties in Vacqueyras. The Bernards (also the proprietors of the excellent restaurant Les Florets in Gigondas) produce a serious, tannic, spicy Vacqueyras that has a penchant for being excessively astringent and coarse. At best, this is a rustic example of the appellation. A small quantity of dry rosé is also produced in addition to an excellent Côtes du Rhône. The two top cuvées are the Vacqueyras Cantarelle and Côtes du Rhône Cuvée Romaine, the latter wine a fabulous bargain.

Readers need to be careful buying these wines, as there are multiple cuvées and significant differences in the quality. The best cuvées are all made by the famed southern Rhône oenologist Philippe Cambie and are represented in the United States by the importer European Selections (Eric Solomon). These wines are custom cuvées bottled much earlier as well as unfined and unfiltered for Solomon. They are different from bottlings sold elsewhere in the world.

2005 Côtes du Rhône Cuvée Romaine	91	now–2017
2004 Côtes du Rhône Cuvée Romaine	90	now
2001 Côtes du Rhône Cuvée Romaine	91	now–2013
2005 Vacqueyras	89+	now–2014
2004 Vacqueyras	91	now–2012
2005 Vacqueyras Cantarelle	92	now–2017
2004 Vacqueyras Cantarelle	91+	now–2014

VINCENT GASSE ★ ★ ★
CÔTE RÔTIE $45.00–$55.00

Intriguing, old-style Côte Rôties that age well emerge from this estate. Vincent Gasse's wines tend to be very strong in top vintages, but miss at least a beat or two in challenging years.

2000 Côte Rôtie	87	now
2000 Côte Rôtie Vieilles Vignes	87	now
1999 Côte Rôtie Vieilles Vignes	90	now

JEAN-MICHEL GÉRIN ★ ★ ★ ★/★ ★ ★ ★ ★
CÔTE RÔTIE $40.00–$150.00

A former president of the Côte Rôtie Syndicate, Jean-Michel Gérin is an ambitious, aggressive producer who is turning out some of the finest wines of the appellation. He believes in employing abundant amounts of new oak, but he never lets the wood overwhelm the wines' fruit and character. His three Côte Rôtie offerings (in ascending order of quality and price) are Champin Le Seigneur, Les Grandes Places, and La Landonne.

2006 Condrieu Côteau de la Loye	91	now
2006 Côte Rôtie Champin Le Seigneur	89	now–2016
2005 Côte Rôtie Champin Le Seigneur	90	2009–2015
2004 Côte Rôtie Champin Le Seigneur	89	now–2012
2003 Côte Rôtie Champin Le Seigneur	91	now–2016
2001 Côte Rôtie Champin Le Seigneur	89	now–2011
2000 Côte Rôtie Champin Le Seigneur	88	now–2010
2006 Côte Rôtie Les Grandes Places	92+	2015–2025
2005 Côte Rôtie Les Grandes Places	92+	2012–2025
2004 Côte Rôtie Les Grandes Places	90	now–2014
2003 Côte Rôtie Les Grandes Places	95+	now–2021+
2001 Côte Rôtie Les Grandes Places	90	now–2016
2000 Côte Rôtie Les Grandes Places	90	now–2015

2006 Côte Rôtie La Landonne	91	now–2025
2005 Côte Rôtie La Landonne	93	2010–2025
2004 Côte Rôtie La Landonne	90	now–2014
2003 Côte Rôtie La Landonne	94+	now–2021
2001 Côte Rôtie La Landonne	90	now–2018
2000 Côte Rôtie La Landonne	91	now–2015

CHÂTEAU GIGOGNAN ★ ★ ★
CHÂTEAUNEUF-DU-PAPE $25.00–$35.00

There is an obvious commercialism in the wines produced by Château Gigognan, but they are fruity and soundly made.

2005 Châteauneuf-du-Pape Clos du Roi	87	now–2015
2003 Châteauneuf-du-Pape Clos du Roi	89	now–2015
2003 Châteauneuf-du-Pape Clos du Roi Blanc	87	now

DOMAINE GIRAUD ★ ★ ★ ★
CHÂTEAUNEUF-DU-PAPE $30.00–$45.00

Former rugby player Pierre Giraud, with the assistance of the brilliant oenologist Philippe Cambie, has dramatically improved this estate's quality. A touch of new oak is used for the Syrah and Mourvèdre, but the Grenache is kept in large *foudres* and tanks.

2006 Châteauneuf-du-Pape	91	now–2017
2005 Châteauneuf-du-Pape	89	2009–2024
2004 Châteauneuf-du-Pape	88	now–2013
2003 Châteauneuf-du-Pape	87	now–2012
2001 Châteauneuf-du-Pape	90	now–2012
2000 Châteauneuf-du-Pape	88	now–2015
2006 Châteauneuf-du-Pape Cuvée Les Gallimardes	92	now–2019
2005 Châteauneuf-du-Pape Cuvée Les Gallimardes	91	2010–2025
2004 Châteauneuf-du-Pape Cuvée Les Gallimardes	90	now–2019
2003 Châteauneuf-du-Pape Cuvée Les Gallimardes	89	now–2020
2001 Châteauneuf-du-Pape Cuvée Les Gallimardes	93	now–2022
2000 Châteauneuf-du-Pape Cuvée Les Gallimardes	89	now–2015
2006 Châteauneuf-du-Pape Cuvée Les Grenaches de Pierre	95	now–2022
2005 Châteauneuf-du-Pape Cuvée Les Grenaches de Pierre	94	2009–2020
2001 Châteauneuf-du-Pape Cuvée Les Grenaches de Pierre	92	now–2014

DOMAINE LES GOUBERTS ★ ★ ★ ★
GIGONDAS $30.00–$35.00

One of the first Gigondas estates to experiment with small *barriques,* Les Gouberts began utilizing these in the early 1980s for aging their top cuvée, Cuvée Florence (named after proprietor Jean-Pierre Cartier's red-haired daughter). These are typically elegant, stylish, sensual/voluptuous efforts. The estate also produces several delicious white and red Côtes du Rhônes, in particular a top-notch white Sablet.

2005 Gigondas	87	now–2013
2003 Gigondas	88	now–2012
2000 Gigondas	87	now–2010

2006 Gigondas Cuvée Florence	91	now–2015
2005 Gigondas Cuvée Florence	90	now–2017
2004 Gigondas Cuvée Florence	87	now–2013
2003 Gigondas Cuvée Florence	87	now–2015
2000 Gigondas Cuvée Florence	90+	now–2018
1999 Gigondas Cuvée Florence	89	now–2011

GOURT DE MAUTENS ★ ★ ★ ★
RASTEAU $30.00–$35.00

Proprietor Jérôme Bressy, a very accomplished producer, exploits this modest-sized estate (30 acres) with vines averaging 50 years in age. Grenache is king here.

2005 Côtes du Rhône-Villages Rasteau	92	2009–2016
2004 Côtes du Rhône-Villages Rasteau	90	now–2013
2003 Côtes du Rhône-Villages Rasteau	90	now–2012
2001 Côtes du Rhône-Villages Rasteau	92	now–2014
2000 Côtes du Rhône-Villages Rasteau	92	now–2013

ALAIN GRAILLOT ★ ★ ★ ★
CROZES-HERMITAGE $25.00–$47.00

One of the reference points for top-flight Crozes-Hermitage, as well as a small amount of St.-Joseph, these wines are all aged in small oak. They represent exceptional bargains in top vintages. Cooler years seem to challenge the phenolic maturity of Graillot's vineyards, which are situated largely on flat plains north of Valence. His top cuvée, La Guiraude, is a superb Crozes-Hermitage that can age well past a decade.

2005 Crozes-Hermitage	87	2012–2018
2004 Crozes-Hermitage	86	now–2010
2003 Crozes-Hermitage	91	now–2024
2001 Crozes-Hermitage	87	now–2013+
2000 Crozes-Hermitage	83	now
2004 Crozes-Hermitage Blanc	89	now
2005 Crozes-Hermitage La Guiraude	89+	2009–2016
2004 Crozes-Hermitage La Guiraude	89	now–2015
2003 Crozes-Hermitage La Guiraude	93	now–2015
2004 Crozes-Hermitage Maxime	88	now–2012
2005 St.-Joseph	86	now–2012
2003 St.-Joseph	92	now–2016
2001 St.-Joseph	87	now

DOMAINE GRAMENON ★ ★ ★ ★
CÔTES DU RHÔNE $20.00–$25.00

Despite the death of proprietor Philippe Laurent many years ago, his wife, Michelle, continues the success he began. This is one of the top Côtes du Rhône estates in the northern Drôme (probably more famous for black truffles than wine). Gramenon's multiple cuvées are all based on old-bush Grenache and are usually bottled with neither fining nor filtration. They represent the essence of their vineyard sites, reeking of *herbes de Provence,* lavender, cherries, and pepper. The finest cuvées are La Sagesse, Sierra du Sud, and Les Hautes de Gramenon, the two top wines Hommage à Pascal and Ceps Centenaires, the latter made from Grenache vines that exceed 100 years of age.

2005 Côtes du Rhône Ceps Centenaires	90	now–2014
2004 Côtes du Rhône Ceps Centenaires	89	now–2012
2004 Côtes du Rhône Ceps Centenaires La Mémé	89	now
2004 Côtes du Rhône Hommage à Pascal	88	now
2005 Côtes du Rhône La Sagesse	89+	now–2015
2004 Côtes du Rhône La Sagesse	87	now–2010
2005 Côtes du Rhône Sierra du Sud	88	now
2004 Côtes du Rhône Sierra du Sud	87	now
2004 Côtes du Rhône-Villages Vinsobres	87	now
2005 Côtes du Rhône-Villages Vinsobres Les Hautes de Gramenon	89	now–2014
2004 Côtes du Rhône-Villages Vinsobres Les Hautes de Gramenon	87	now–2010

GRAND MONTMIRAIL ✶ ✶ ✶
GIGONDAS $25.00–$35.00

This 50-acre domaine produced four noteworthy efforts in 2000.

2003 Gigondas Vieilles Vignes	88	now–2013
2000 Gigondas Vieilles Vignes	90	now–2013
2000 Gigondas Vieilles Vignes Fût de Chêne	90	now–2014
2003 Vacqueyras	88	now–2011
2000 Vacqueyras	88	now
2000 Vacqueyras Fût de Chêne	90	now–2012

DOMAINE GRAND NICOLET ✶ ✶ ✶
RASTEAU $20.00

A promising, emerging estate in Rasteau, Grand Nicolet produces high-quality wines under the guidance of the talented southern Rhône oenologist Philippe Cambie.

2005 Côtes du Rhône	85	now–2011
2005 Côtes du Rhône—Villages Rasteau	86	now–2012
2004 Côtes du Rhône—Villages Rasteau	91	now–2014
2000 Côtes du Rhône—Villages Rasteau	88	now

DOMAINE GRAND-ROMANE ✶ ✶ ✶
GIGONDAS $25.00–$35.00

The Domaine Grand-Romane, part of the Jean-Pierre Amadieu empire, is a sizable domaine planted primarily with Grenache, as well as important percentages of Syrah and, surprisingly, Counoise, a grape variety rarely seen except in Châteauneuf-du-Pape, and then only at top domaines such as Beaucastel and Mont Redon. These are rustic, muscular wines that can age well for 10 to 12 years.

2005 Gigondas	89	2009–2015
2003 Gigondas	88	now–2012

DOMAINE DU GRAND TINEL ✶ ✶ ✶ ✶
CHÂTEAUNEUF-DU-PAPE $32.00–$55.00

Traditionally made Châteauneuf-du-Papes are the rule of thumb from proprietor Elie Jeune, who farms more than 140 acres. His wines, which represent the essence of Provence, reveal plenty of high-quality savory fruit. Grand Tinel's special cuvée, Alexis Establet, is a bulked up, bolder, deeper version of the traditional offering.

2006 Châteauneuf-du-Pape	86	now–2013
2005 Châteauneuf-du-Pape	87	now–2016
2004 Châteauneuf-du-Pape	88	now–2012
2003 Châteauneuf-du-Pape	90	now–2014
2001 Châteauneuf-du-Pape	90	now–2016
2000 Châteauneuf-du-Pape	89	now–2013
2006 Châteauneuf-du-Pape Cuvée Alexis Establet	89	now–2017
2005 Châteauneuf-du-Pape Cuvée Alexis Establet	90	now–2020
2004 Châteauneuf-du-Pape Cuvée Alexis Establet	90	now–2018
2003 Châteauneuf-du-Pape Cuvée Alexis Establet	90	now–2018
2001 Châteauneuf-du-Pape Cuvée Alexis Establet	91+	now–2015
2000 Châteauneuf-du-Pape Cuvée Alexis Establet	92	now–2016

DOMAINE GRAND VENEUR ★ ★ ★ ★ ★
CHÂTEAUNEUF-DU-PAPE $9.00–$56.00

This has been one of the best-run estates in Châteauneuf-du-Pape over the last decade. Alain Jaume and his two capable sons, Sebastien and Christophe, have propelled the Domaine Grand Veneur into the upper echelons of quality. They also offer an impressively well-made *négociant* line of wines that are sold under the name Alain Jaume. The hallmarks of the Grand Veneur wines include their extraordinary purity of flavor and impeccable balance. Moreover, the Jaumes have kept prices remarkably fair. Consumers should not miss the estate's white wines, which are among the finest of the southern Rhône.

RED WINES

2006 Châteauneuf-du-Pape	91	now–2020
2005 Châteauneuf-du-Pape	93	2009–2024
2004 Châteauneuf-du-Pape	91	now–2019
2003 Châteauneuf-du-Pape	93	now–2016+
2001 Châteauneuf-du-Pape	90	now–2016
2000 Châteauneuf-du-Pape	90	now–2011
2006 Châteauneuf-du-Pape Cuvée Les Origines Estate	94	now–2022
2005 Châteauneuf-du-Pape Cuvée Les Origines Estate	95	2011–2026
2004 Châteauneuf-du-Pape Cuvée Les Origines Estate	92	now–2022
2003 Châteauneuf-du-Pape Cuvée Les Origines Estate	95	now–2020
2001 Châteauneuf-du-Pape Cuvée Les Origines Estate	94	now–2016
2000 Châteauneuf-du-Pape Cuvée Les Origines Estate	93	now–2017
2006 Châteauneuf-du-Pape Vieilles Vignes	96	2014–2030+
2005 Côtes du Rhône Réserve	88	now–2010
2005 Côtes du Rhône-Villages Les Champauvins	90	now–2012

WHITE WINES

2005 Châteauneuf-du-Pape Blanc	89	now–2010
2005 Châteauneuf-du-Pape La Fontaine Blanc	92	now–2012

DOMAINE LES GRANDS BOIS ★ ★ ★
CAIRANNE $15.00–$17.00

This reliable producer from the Côtes du Rhône village of Cairanne produces unfiltered cuvées that represent outstanding value.

2005 Côtes du Rhône Cuvée Les Trois Soeurs	87	now–2010
2005 Côtes du Rhône-Villages Cairanne Cuvée Gabrielle	88	now–2011

GRAPILLON D'OR ★★★
GIGONDAS $30.00-$35.00

This is a traditional Gigondas made from a multitude of parcels owned by proprietor Bernard Chauvet, the former president of the syndicate of Gigondas. If the wine tends toward a certain rusticity, it is because everything is done the same way it was a century ago. Chauvet, assisted by his son, makes Gigondas the way it was in the old days, and most top vintages can easily handle 10 to 12 years of cellaring.

2005 Gigondas	88	now–2016

CHÂTEAU GRILLET ★★★
GRILLET $75.00-$125.00

A legendary single wine–single appellation carved from just under ten acres on the steep hill-side, 500 feet above the Rhône River with a perfect amphitheater exposure, Grillet produced great wines in the '50s, '60s, and '70s that added to its mythical reputation. However, since that time few vintages have been of stellar quality. A tendency to pick entirely too soon compromises the wines' fundamental ripeness and character. Nevertheless, I noted encouraging progress with the 2004 and 2005 vintages.

BERNARD GRIPA ★★★
ST.-JOSEPH $25.00

The finest cuvée of Bernard Gripa, a longtime traditional St.-Joseph producer, is Le Berceau. Prices for these wines are exceptionally fair.

J. L. GRIPPAT ★★★
ST.-JOSEPH $25.00-$35.00

This well-known estate, with some superb vineyards in St.-Joseph and Hermitage, was purchased by Marcel Guigal, who has incorporated these sites into the Guigal firmament.

GUIGAL ★★★★★
CÔTE RÔTIE $12.00-$500.00

There is much to admire about Marcel Guigal, but most significant is that he has been a qualitative locomotive that has brought attention to the Rhône Valley, raising the quality bar for the entire region. More importantly, he realizes that most consumers will have access only to his least expensive wines from the Côtes du Rhône, so he has made every effort to continue to increase the quality of both his white and red Côtes du Rhônes. The largest producer of Côte Rôtie, he has largely defined that appellation with his three spectacular single-vineyard offerings: La Landonne, La Mouline, and La Turque. These immortal wines sell for a king's ransom, but they are as good as anything produced anywhere in the world, and they age magnificently. One would think that spending 42 months in 100% new-oak barrels would make them modern-style and oaky, but they are not. The Côte Rôtie for consumers without a millionaire's checking account is the Brune et Blonde and the Château d'Ampuis, which was first introduced in 1995. It is one of the finest five or six Côte Rôties of the appellation but is not at the level of the three single-vineyard cuvées.

RED WINES

2006 Châteauneuf-du-Pape	92	now–2020
2005 Châteauneuf-du-Pape	94	now–2022
2004 Châteauneuf-du-Pape	88	now–2017
2003 Châteauneuf-du-Pape	90	now–2016
2005 Côte Rôtie Brune et Blonde	92	2010–2020

2004 Côte Rôtie Brune et Blonde	88	now
2003 Côte Rôtie Brune et Blonde	93	now–2016
2002 Côte Rôtie Brune et Blonde	82	now
2005 Côte Rôtie Château d'Ampuis	93–95	2012–2025
2004 Côte Rôtie Château d'Ampuis	89	now–2015
2003 Côte Rôtie Château d'Ampuis	96+	now–2026
2002 Côte Rôtie Château d'Ampuis	86	now–2012
2001 Côte Rôtie Château d'Ampuis	92	now–2020
2005 Côte Rôtie La Landonne	96–99	2012–2030
2004 Côte Rôtie La Landonne	92	now–2024+
2003 Côte Rôtie La Landonne	100	2010–2046
2002 Côte Rôtie La Landonne	90	now–2021
2001 Côte Rôtie La Landonne	94	2011–2030
2005 Côte Rôtie La Mouline	96–98	2010–2025
2004 Côte Rôtie La Mouline	91	now–2018
2003 Côte Rôtie La Mouline	100	now–2026
2002 Côte Rôtie La Mouline	90	now–2016
2001 Côte Rôtie La Mouline	95	now–2016
2000 Côte Rôtie La Mouline	91	now–2019
2005 Côte Rôtie La Turque	94–98	2012–2030
2004 Côte Rôtie La Turque	91	now–2021
2003 Côte Rôtie La Turque	100	2010–2040+
2002 Côte Rôtie La Turque	91	now–2018
2001 Côte Rôtie La Turque	96+	2010–2038
2005 Côtes du Rhône	89	now–2011
2004 Côtes du Rhône	87	now–2011
2005 Crozes-Hermitage	90	now–2015
2005 Gigondas	90	now–2016
2005 Hermitage	91	2015–2030
2003 Hermitage Ex-Voto	100	2011–2056+
2001 Hermitage Ex-Voto	95	2015–2040
2005 St.-Joseph	89	now–2015
2005 St.-Joseph Lieu-Dit St.-Joseph	93	now–2018
2005 St.-Joseph Vignes de l'Hospice	95	now–2020
2004 St.-Joseph Vignes de l'Hospice	92	now–2016
2003 St.-Joseph Vignes de l'Hospice	96	now–2026+

WHITE WINES

2006 Condrieu	91	now
2006 Condrieu La Doriane	96	now
2005 Hermitage Blanc	91	now–2016
2005 Hermitage Ex-Voto Blanc	97	now–2025
2003 Hermitage Ex-Voto Blanc	96+	now–2015
2005 St.-Joseph Blanc	88	now
2005 St.-Joseph Lieu-Dit St.-Joseph Blanc	91	now

CHÂTEAU GUIOT ✶✶✶
COSTIÈRES DE NÎMES $10.00–$20.00

This Costières de Nîmes superstar estate is well worth checking out, even in the deplorable 2002 vintage. A large property of 150 acres, Guiot produces delicious wines, including a top-notch rosé, that tend to be fairly priced sleeper selections for those in the know.

CHÂTEAU GUIOT

2005 Cabernet/Syrah VDP	88–90	now–2012
2002 Costières de Nîmes	89	now
2005 Costières de Nîmes Alex	88	now–2012
2004 Costières de Nîmes Alex	87	now–2011
2005 Costières de Nîmes Numa	88	now–2012
2004 Costières de Nîmes Numa	90	now–2012

MAS DE GUIOT

2002 Vin de Pays Gard Cabernet/Syrah	87	now
2001 Vin de Pays Gard Cabernet/Syrah	91	now
2000 Vin de Pays Gard Cabernet/Syrah	89+	now–2010
2004 Vin de Pays Gard Grenache/Syrah	86	now
2003 Vin de Pays Gard Grenache/Syrah	87	now

DOMAINE DU HAUT DES TERRES BLANCHES ★ ★ ★
CHÂTEAUNEUF-DU-PAPE $35.00–$45.00

A member of the Diffonty family runs this estate that makes traditional Châteauneuf-du-Pape aged in vat and old-oak *foudres*. There are numerous bottlings at this property, but the earlier tend to be fresher, with more charm and character. Unfortunately, there is no way for purchasers to ascertain which bottling they are purchasing.

2005 Châteauneuf-du-Pape	88+	now–2016
2003 Châteauneuf-du-Pape	89	now–2015

DOMAINE OLIVIER HILLAIRE ★ ★ ★ ★
CHÂTEAUNEUF-DU-PAPE $45.00–$85.00

When Olivier Hillaire dissolved his partnership with the Domaine des Rélanges, he took one of their top vineyard parcels, Les Petits Pieds d'Armand, with him. Hillaire is a multitalented gentleman, as not only is he a skilled winemaker, but he also owns the finest bakery in the village of Châteauneuf-du-Pape.

2006 Châteauneuf-du-Pape	88	now–2017
2005 Châteauneuf-du-Pape	88	now–2015
2006 Châteauneuf-du-Pape Les Petits Pieds d'Armand	91	2010–2025
2005 Châteauneuf-du-Pape Les Petits Pieds d'Armand	92	2011–2030
2004 Châteauneuf-du-Pape Les Petits Pieds d'Armand	90	now–2022

PAUL JABOULET-AÎNE ★ ★ ★
TAIN L'HERMITAGE $15.00–$198.00

This huge family *négociant* firm, founded in the early 1800s, was sold in 2005 to the Frey family, major investors in the Billecart-Salmon Champagne house as well as the proprietors of Bordeaux's Château La Lagune. They are in the process of rebuilding the credibility that was lost after some less than successful vintages in the late 1990s and early 21st century, precipitated no doubt by the death in 1997 of the firm's inspirational leader, Gérard Jaboulet.

2004 Cornas Les Grandes Terrasses	78	now
2003 Cornas Les Grandes Terrasses	87	now
2005 Cornas Domaine de St.-Pierre	88	2009–2015
2004 Cornas Domaine de St.-Pierre	88	now–2014
2003 Cornas Domaine de St.-Pierre	92	now–2024
2005 Côte Rôtie Les Jumelles	87	now–2012

2005 Côtes du Rhône-Villages		85	now–2010
2005 Côtes du Rhône-Villages Beaumes de Venise			
de Paradou		87	now–2011
2005 Crozes-Hermitage Les Jalets		86	now
2005 Crozes-Hermitage La Mule Blanche (white)		85	now
2005 Crozes-Hermitage Raymond Roure		86	2010–2016
2003 Crozes-Hermitage Raymond Roure		92	now–2026
2005 Crozes-Hermitage Raymond Roure Blanc		89	now
2005 Crozes-Hermitage Domaine de Thalabert		88	now–2015
2004 Crozes-Hermitage Domaine de Thalabert		78	now
2005 Gigondas Pierre Aiguille		88	now–2012
2005 Hermitage La Chapelle		90	now–2022
2003 Hermitage La Chapelle		95+	2011–2039
2001 Hermitage La Chapelle		89+	2010–2020
2006 Hermitage Le Chevalier de Sterimberg (white)		92	now–2020
2006 Muscat Beaumes de Venise (sweet white)		90	now
2005 St.-Joseph Le Grand Pompée		86	now

JEAN-PAUL ET JEAN-LUC JAMET ★ ★ ★ ★
CÔTE RÔTIE $57.00–$69.00

This estate has been one of the most consistent small producers of Côte Rôtie over the last decade. Traditional, rustic, but enormously satisfying Côte Rôties emerge from the Jamet brothers, whose cellars are at the top of the plateau overlooking the village. Production is small, as the estate owns fewer than 16 acres of vines.

2005 Côte Rôtie	88+?	2011–2017
2004 Côte Rôtie	88	now–2013
2003 Côte Rôtie	86	now–2024
2001 Côte Rôtie	92	now–2015
2000 Côte Rôtie	90	now–2018
1999 Côte Rôtie	96	now–2020

DOMAINE DE LA JANASSE ★ ★ ★ ★ ★
CHÂTEAUNEUF-DU-PAPE $10.00–$100.00

This is one of the Rhône Valley's finest-run estates, the credit being due to the dedicated, talented Christophe Sabon, who has taken a very good property and raised it to world-class preeminence. The winemaking style is a blend of arch-conservative, traditional practices combined with some modernist techniques. This large estate produces sensational cuvées of bargain-priced Côtes du Rhônes, one of the finest white Châteauneuf-du-Papes of the appellation, and three stunning red Châteauneufs, including the old-vine Grenache offering called Chaupin and the magnificent, long-lived Vieilles Vignes, which is also dominated by Grenache.

2006 Châteauneuf-du-Pape	92	2010–2025+
2005 Châteauneuf-du-Pape	92	2013–2028
2004 Châteauneuf-du-Pape	92	now–2019
2003 Châteauneuf-du-Pape	90+	now–2021
2001 Châteauneuf-du-Pape	91	now–2014
2000 Châteauneuf-du-Pape	90	now–2013
2006 Châteauneuf-du-Pape Cuvée Chaupin	94	2010–2025+
2005 Châteauneuf-du-Pape Cuvée Chaupin	94	2012–2037
2004 Châteauneuf-du-Pape Cuvée Chaupin	93	2009–2021+

2003 Châteauneuf-du-Pape Cuvée Chaupin	95	now–2021+
2001 Châteauneuf-du-Pape Cuvée Chaupin	95	now–2015
2000 Châteauneuf-du-Pape Cuvée Chaupin	94	now–2018
2005 Châteauneuf-du-Pape Cuvée Prestige Blanc	91	now
2006 Châteauneuf-du-Pape Vieilles Vignes	95	2012–2037
2005 Châteauneuf-du-Pape Vieilles Vignes	98	2015–2040
2004 Châteauneuf-du-Pape Vieilles Vignes	93+	2010–2030
2003 Châteauneuf-du-Pape Vieilles Vignes	97+	2010–2030
2001 Châteauneuf-du-Pape Vieilles Vignes	98	2010–2030
2000 Châteauneuf-du-Pape Vieilles Vignes	96	now–2023
2005 Côtes du Rhône Les Garrigues	92	now
2005 Côtes du Rhône-Villages Terre d'Argile	89	now–2018

PATRICK JASMIN ★ ★ ★
CÔTE RÔTIE $36.00–$42.00

The son of the late Robert Jasmin, Patrick continues to demonstrate a fine touch with his elegant, finesse-styled Côte Rôties, which emerge from three hillside vineyards above the village of Ampuis.

2005 Côte Rôtie	87	now–2016
2004 Côte Rôtie	84	now–2014
2003 Côte Rôtie	87	now–2013
2001 Côte Rôtie	90	now–2012
2000 Côte Rôtie	87	now–2010
1999 Côte Rôtie	90	now–2016

DOMAINE LAFOND ★ ★ ★ ★
LIRAC/CHÂTEAUNEUF-DU-PAPE $8.00–$40.00

An up-and-coming estate that also makes delicious Tavel rosés, Lafond is a trustworthy source for modern-styled, richly fruity, pure wines that are meant to be drunk young. However, their top Châteauneuf-du-Pape has the stuffing to age for ten or more years. For value, check out their Côtes du Rhône and Liracs.

2006 Châteauneuf-du-Pape Roc-Épine	91	now–2019
2005 Châteauneuf-du-Pape Roc-Épine	90	now–2017
2004 Châteauneuf-du-Pape Roc-Épine	89	now–2015
2003 Châteauneuf-du-Pape Roc-Épine	90	now–2016
2001 Châteauneuf-du-Pape Roc-Épine	91	now–2014
2005 Côtes du Rhône Roc-Épine	87	now–2010
2005 Lirac Roc-Épine	90	now–2012
2005 Lirac Roc-Épine Blanc	87	now

MARIE-CLAUDE LAFOY ET VINCENT GASSE ★ ★ ★
CÔTE RÔTIE $40.00–$75.00

Vincent Gasse, an intelligent, articulate, wiry, bald man with a humongous black beard, is one of the few outsiders who has become a success in Côte Rôtie. Born in the famed Loire Valley village of Vouvray, Gasse moved to Ampuis in 1980, establishing a home and cellars on the Route Nationale just across the road from the entrance to Vidal-Fleury. All of his wine is estate-bottled from five parcels of vines on the slopes of Côte Rôtie. An introspective man who farms his vineyards in the biodynamic fashion, Gasse has demonstrated the ability to make fabulous Côte Rôtie in such top vintages as 1990 and 1991, as well as good wines in such less successful vintages as 1992 and 1993.

| 2005 Côte Rôtie | 89 | now–2014 |
| 2005 Côte Rôtie Vieilles Vignes | 90 | now–2020 |

COMTE DE LAUZE ★★/★★★
CHÂTEAUNEUF-DU-PAPE $30.00–$45.00

Straightforward Châteauneuf-du-Papes made in an oxidated style and meant for immediate drinking are produced at this estate. To my taste they are overprocessed and too light.

JACQUES LEMENCIER ★★★
CORNAS $40.00–$45.00

Jacques Lemencier, who apprenticed under Robert Michel before starting his own operation, believes in complete destemming and bottles his wines after nearly a year in barrel. Like most Cornas producers, he never filters his wines. However, after several good vintages I have experienced too many off bottles.

2005 Cornas	88	now–2016
2004 Cornas	87	now–2013
2003 Cornas	89	now–2013

PATRICK LESEC SELECTIONS ★★★★
CHÂTEAUNEUF-DU-PAPE $8.50–$55.00

Patrick Lesec has an impressive, wide-ranging *négociant* portfolio of Rhône wines, with his strengths being his Côtes du Rhône, Gigondas, Vacqueyras, and Châteauneuf-du-Pape selections. In fact, the latter category is outstanding and merits considerable interest. For value seekers, the Côtes du Rhônes offer plenty of character and typicity. These are high-quality wines made with no fining or filtration. Obviously, Lesec has a talent for securing high-quality wine and treating it carefully, with minimal manipulation.

2006 Châteauneuf-du-Pape Bargeton	92	2011–2030
2005 Châteauneuf-du-Pape Bargeton	94+	2011–2036
2004 Châteauneuf-du-Pape Bargeton	93	now–2022
2003 Châteauneuf-du-Pape Bargeton	94	now–2018
2004 Châteauneuf-du-Pape Chasse-Temps	90	now–2018
2003 Châteauneuf-du-Pape Chasse-Temps	91	now–2022
2006 Châteauneuf-du-Pape Les Galets Blonds	93	2011–2030
2005 Châteauneuf-du-Pape Les Galets Blonds	94	2010–2025
2004 Châteauneuf-du-Pape Les Galets Blonds	92	2009–2024
2003 Châteauneuf-du-Pape Les Galets Blonds	95	now–2021+
2005 Châteauneuf-du-Pape Marquis	91	now–2022
2004 Châteauneuf-du-Pape Marquis	89	now–2015
2003 Châteauneuf-du-Pape Marquis	89+	now–2016
2006 Châteauneuf-du-Pape Pierres Dorées	92	2010–2020
2005 Châteauneuf-du-Pape Pierres Dorées	92+	2010–2017
2004 Châteauneuf-du-Pape Pierres Dorées	90+	now–2019
2003 Châteauneuf-du-Pape Pierres Dorées	93	now–2021
2006 Châteauneuf-du-Pape Rubis	90	now–2020
2005 Châteauneuf-du-Pape Rubis	89	now–2017
2005 Rasteau Vieilles Vignes	91	2011–2026
2005 Gigondas Les Espalines Cuvée Romaine	89+	2011–2016
2004 Gigondas Les Espalines Cuvée Romaine	87	now
2005 Gigondas Domaine La Roubine	90	now–2022
2005 Vacqueyras Vieilles Vignes	90	2009–2015

BERNARD LEVET ★★
CÔTE RÔTIE $45.00–$65.00

Vegetal, mediocre Côte Rôties emerge from Levet's cellars, which are located in the tiny, one-horse village of Ampuis.

2005 Côte Rôtie	76	2010–2015
2004 Côte Rôtie	72	now–2014

DOMAINE DE LONGUE TOQUE ★★★
GIGONDAS $28.00–$44.00

This 50-acre estate changed hands several years ago and is now owned by the large Meffre *négociant* firm. The estate had an impressive résumé based on the wines it produced in the late 1970s and 1980s, after which it went through a period of decline. The 2005 offers hope of a renewal.

2005 Gigondas	90	now–2017
2003 Gigondas	86	now
2000 Gigondas	88	now–2013
2003 Gigondas Hommage à Gabriel Meffre	88	now–2014

MACOVILLA ★★★
CHÂTEAUNEUF-DU-PAPE $15.00–$50.00

The following well-endowed impressive wines are the debut releases from one of the southern Rhône's up-and-coming oenologists, Pierre Pervoyrie.

2006 Châteauneuf-du-Pape Pontificale	90	now–2018
2005 Châteauneuf-du-Pape Pontifical	90	now–2016
2006 Châteauneuf-du-Pape Réserve Omega	89	now–2018
2005 Châteauneuf-du-Pape Réserve Omega	90+	2010–2022
2006 Châteauneuf-du-Pape Réserve Ultraranium	89	now–2017
2005 Châteauneuf-du-Pape Réserve Ultraranium	90	2012–2025
2006 Châteauneuf-du-Pape Tradition	86	now–2011
2005 Côtes du Rhône	87	now

JEAN MARCHAND ★★★
CHÂTEAUNEUF-DU-PAPE $29.00–$32.00

Proprietor Jean Marchand turns out distinctively modern-styled Châteauneuf-du-Papes that reveal some evidence of *barrique* as well as less Provençal typicity than many of the appellation's finest wines. Nevertheless, they are deeply fruited, attractive, and ideal for drinking during their first 8 to 12 years of life.

2000 Châteauneuf-du-Pape Clos des Pontifes	89	now–2012
1999 Châteauneuf-du-Pape Clos des Pontifes	87	now

DOMAINE DE MARCOUX ★★★★★
CHÂTEAUNEUF-DU-PAPE $18.00–$250.00

A reference-point estate for Châteauneuf-du-Pape, this biodynamically farmed vineyard, owned by the sisters Sophie and Catherine Armenier, produces wonderful white Châteauneuf-du-Pape, a competent Côtes du Rhône, and two magnificent cuvées of traditionally made red Châteauneuf (no new oak is utilized). These terrific wines age beautifully for 15 to 20 or more years.

2006 Châteauneuf-du-Pape	92	now–2022+
2005 Châteauneuf-du-Pape	93	now–2019
2004 Châteauneuf-du-Pape	91	now–2016+
2003 Châteauneuf-du-Pape	94	now–2023
2001 Châteauneuf-du-Pape	90	now–2016
2000 Châteauneuf-du-Pape	92	now–2018
2006 Châteauneuf-du-Pape Vieilles Vignes	94	2010–2030
2005 Châteauneuf-du-Pape Vieilles Vignes	97	now–2022
2004 Châteauneuf-du-Pape Vieilles Vignes	93	2011–2026
2003 Châteauneuf-du-Pape Vieilles Vignes	87	now–2028
2001 Châteauneuf-du-Pape Vieilles Vignes	96	now–2025
2000 Châteauneuf-du-Pape Vieilles Vignes	96	now–2019

MAS DE BOISLAUZON ★★★★
CHÂTEAUNEUF-DU-PAPE $15.00–$65.00

From a domaine in Châteauneuf-du-Pape impeccably run by the Chaussy family, these wines are extremely elegant, pure, and seem almost like a synthesis in style between a grand cru Burgundy from the Côtes de Nuits and a Châteauneuf-du-Pape.

2006 Châteauneuf-du-Pape	91	now–2022
2005 Châteauneuf-du-Pape	90	now–2019
2004 Châteauneuf-du-Pape	89+	now–2018
2003 Châteauneuf-du-Pape	88	now–2015
2001 Châteauneuf-du-Pape	90	now–2018
2000 Châteauneuf-du-Pape	89	now–2015
2006 Châteauneuf-du-Pape Cuvée du Quet	93	now–2027
2005 Châteauneuf-du-Pape Cuvée du Quet	93+	now–2022
2004 Châteauneuf-du-Pape Cuvée du Quet	91	now–2021+
2003 Châteauneuf-du-Pape Cuvée du Quet	93	now–2024
2001 Châteauneuf-du-Pape Cuvée du Quet	91+	now–2016
2000 Châteauneuf-du-Pape Cuvée du Quet	92	now–2017
2006 Châteauneuf-du-Pape Le Tintot	93	now–2027+
2005 Côtes du Rhône-Villages	88	now–2012

MAS DES BRESSADES ★★★
COSTIÈRES DE NÎMES $15.00–$18.00

Mas des Bressades is another reliable estate in the Costières de Nîmes. Most of the production here is marketed under a *vin de pays* designation, since their white is a Roussanne-Viognier blend and their red a Cabernet Sauvignon–Syrah blend. However, they do produce a small quantity of excellent wine under the appellation of Costières de Nîmes.

2003 Costières de Nîmes Cuvée d'Excellence	87	now
2003 Costières de Nîmes Cuvée d'Excellence Blanc	90	now
2004 Costières de Nîmes Cuvée Tradition (red)	85	now
2003 Costières de Nîmes Cuvée Tradition (red)	89	now
2004 Costières de Nîmes Cuvée Tradition (rosé)	87	now
2004 Vin de Pays Gard Cabernet/Syrah	90	now–2010

MAS CARLOT ★★★
COSTIÈRES DE NÎMES $10.00–$14.00

A reliable and reputable producer, especially for consumers looking for good wine values, these are all fruit forward, cleanly made wines that offer immediate gratification.

2005 Costières de Nîmes Les Enfants Terribles	88	now–2010
2003 Costières de Nîmes Les Enfants Terribles	88	now–2011
2004 Vin de Pays d'Oc Cabernet/Syrah	89	now–2010
2004 Vin de Pays d'Oc Cuvée Tradition	87	now–2010
2004 Vin de Pays d'Oc Cuvée Tradition Blanc	87	now
2003 Vin de Pays d'Oc Cuvée Tradition Blanc	90	now

CHÂTEAU MAS NEUF ★★★
COSTIÈRES DE NÎMES $9.00–$30.00

Run by proprietor Luc Baudet since 2000, this large (153-acre) estate fashions an assortment of good reds and whites. Their less expensive cuvées offer the most in terms of quality and price rapport.

2005 Costières de Nîmes	87	now
2004 Costières de Nîmes	89	now
2005 Costières de Nîmes Blanc	87	now
2005 Costières de Nîmes d'Ou Armonió	88	now–2012
2005 Costières de Nîmes Compostelle	90	now
2003 Costières de Nîmes La Mourvache	86	now–2010

DOMAINE MATHIEU ★★★
CHÂTEAUNEUF-DU-PAPE $26.00–$50.00

Recent efforts from this estate have been more promising than those produced a decade ago. The offerings include a soft, light basic cuvée, a 100% old-vine Grenache wine called Marquis Anselme Mathieu Vignes Centenaire, and a luxury cuvée, Vin di Félibre. All of these wines represent the essence of Provence. They are elegant efforts that are ideal for drinking during their first 10 to 15 years of life.

2006 Châteauneuf-du-Pape	84	now–2011
2005 Châteauneuf-du-Pape	86	now–2012
2004 Châteauneuf-du-Pape	88	now–2011
2003 Châteauneuf-du-Pape	87	now–2013
2001 Châteauneuf-du-Pape	88	now–2014
2001 Châteauneuf-du-Pape Gaussin d'Armandy	89	now–2016
2001 Châteauneuf-du-Pape Marquis Anselme Mathieu	91	now–2019
2006 Châteauneuf-du-Pape Marquis Anselme Mathieu Vignes Centenaire	87	now–2014
2005 Châteauneuf-du-Pape Marquis Anselme Mathieu Vignes Centenaire	88	now–2014
2004 Châteauneuf-du-Pape Marquis Anselme Mathieu Vignes Centenaire	89	now–2014
2003 Châteauneuf-du-Pape Marquis Anselme Mathieu Vignes Centenaire	89+	now–2013
2006 Châteauneuf-du-Pape Vin di Félibre	89	now–2020
2005 Châteauneuf-du-Pape Vin di Félibre	89	2009–2015
2004 Châteauneuf-du-Pape Vin di Félibre	87	now–2023
2003 Châteauneuf-du-Pape Vin di Félibre	89	now–2014

CHÂTEAU MAUCOIL ★★★
CHÂTEAUNEUF-DU-PAPE $10.00–$60.00

Château Maucoil, which owns superb vineyards on the high plateau of Châteauneuf-du-Pape, north of the village, continues to increase the quality of its wines.

2005 Châteauneuf-du-Pape	87	now–2015
2004 Châteauneuf-du-Pape	85	now–2013
2003 Châteauneuf-du-Pape	88	now–2015
2001 Châteauneuf-du-Pape	87	now–2011
2000 Châteauneuf-du-Pape	88	now–2010
2001 Châteauneuf-du-Pape Esprit de Maucoil	90	now–2016
2003 Châteauneuf-du-Pape Lea Conti	91	now–2020
2001 Châteauneuf-du-Pape Lea Conti	91	now–2016
2005 Châteauneuf-du-Pape Privilège	89+	2011–2018
2004 Châteauneuf-du-Pape Privilège	86	now–2013
2003 Châteauneuf-du-Pape Privilège	89	now–2011
2001 Châteauneuf-du-Pape Privilège	90+	now–2014
2000 Châteauneuf-du-Pape Privilège	91	now–2018+

GABRIEL MEFFRE * */* * *
GIGONDAS $9.00–$35.00

There has been a significant jump in quality with the wines from this large *négociant*, located in the village of Gigondas. All of these offerings reveal their individual appellation characteristics.

2003 Châteauneuf-du-Pape	87	now–2011
2003 Châteauneuf-du-Pape Laurus	88	now–2015
2001 Châteauneuf-du-Pape Laurus	87	now
2003 Costières de Nîmes Laurus	86	now
2003 Côtes du Rhône La Chasse du Pape Prestige	87	now
2003 Côtes du Rhône Laurus	86	now–2011
2003 Crozes-Hermitage Laurus	83	now
2003 Gigondas Domaine de Longue Toque	87	now–2013
2001 Gigondas Domaine de Longue Toque Hommage à Gabriel Meffre	91	now–2014
2003 Gigondas Hommage à Gabriel Meffre	88	now–2015
2003 Hermitage Laurus	89+	now–2020
2003 St.-Joseph Laurus	87	now–2012
2003 Vacqueyras Laurus	86	now

ROBERT MICHEL * *
CORNAS $40.00–$58.00

A rustic, old-style red is produced from Michel's superb vineyards high on the steep granite terraces of Cornas. The wines, which are often excruciatingly tannic, are meant for those with primordial taste buds. This winery would benefit from a touch of modernization.

DOMAINE LA MILLIÈRE * * * *
CHÂTEAUNEUF-DU-PAPE $25.00–$45.00

This estate is an up-and-coming newcomer under the capable administration of Aimé and Michel Arnaud. Their 90-year-old vineyard is composed of 70% Grenache and 30% Cinsault, Mourvèdre, and Syrah. Stylish and seductive Châteauneuf-du-Papes are produced, along with an excellent, value-priced Côtes du Rhône.

2006 Châteauneuf-du-Pape Vieilles Vignes	91	now–2020
2005 Châteauneuf-du-Pape Vieilles Vignes	92	now–2017
2004 Châteauneuf-du-Pape Vieilles Vignes	89	now–2013

2003 Châteauneuf-du-Pape Vieilles Vignes	91	now–2014
2005 Côtes du Rhône-Villages Vieilles Vignes	88	now–2012

LA MONARDIÈRE ★ ★ ★ ★
VACQUEYRAS $22.00–$37.00

An important, relatively new name, La Monardière, owned by Christian Vache, is one of Vacqueyras's top estates. The wines tend to be made in a style that falls somewhere between traditional and modern.

2005 Vacqueyras des Deux Monardes	90+	now–2014
2004 Vacqueyras des Deux Monardes	90	now–2012
2003 Vacqueyras des Deux Monardes	87	now–2012
2001 Vacqueyras des Deux Monardes	87	now–2010
2000 Vacqueyras des Deux Monardes	85	now
2005 Vacqueyras Vieilles Vignes	91	now–2016
2004 Vacqueyras Vieilles Vignes	90	now–2013
2003 Vacqueyras Vieilles Vignes	90	now
2001 Vacqueyras Vieilles Vignes	90	now–2014
2000 Vacqueyras Vieilles Vignes	90	now–2015

CHÂTEAU MONGIN ★ ★/★ ★ ★
CHÂTEAUNEUF-DU-PAPE $25.00

This wine is made by students at the Lycée Viticole in the northern sector of Châteauneuf-du-Pape known as Grès. In the process of getting their degrees in oenology they do vineyard work and produce this reliable, fruit-driven, modern-styled Châteauneuf-du-Pape.

2005 Châteauneuf-du-Pape	87	now–2010

CHÂTEAU MONT REDON
CHÂTEAUNEUF-DU-PAPE $15.00–$30.00

The story of this vineyard is a somewhat sad one, as some of the greatest Châteauneuf-du-Papes of the '40s, '50s, and '60s were produced at this fabulously situated estate on the high plateau of Châteauneuf-du-Pape. In the '80s, the wines took on a Beaujolais-like style: fruity, soft, pure, and superficial. It is ironic that in an appellation where many producers are making better and better wines, Mont Redon seems content to live off its reputation.

2005 Châteauneuf-du-Pape	86	now–2013
2004 Châteauneuf-du-Pape	84	now–2011
2006 Châteauneuf-du-Pape Blanc	89	now

CHÂTEAU MONT THABOR ★ ★ ★
CHÂTEAUNEUF-DU-PAPE $32.00–$36.00

Proprietor Daniel Stehelin is worth watching, based on recent vintages. These are traditionally made, gutsy, old-styled offerings produced from a 7.5-acre, 80-year-old vineyard planted with 70% Grenache, 25% Syrah, and 5% miscellaneous varieties.

2006 Châteauneuf-du-Pape	88	now–2014
2005 Châteauneuf-du-Pape	90	2010–2025
2004 Châteauneuf-du-Pape	90	now–2015
2003 Châteauneuf-du-Pape	91	now–2018
2001 Châteauneuf-du-Pape	88	now–2012

DOMAINE DE MONTEILLET ★★★★
NORTHERN RHÔNE $25.00–$90.00

Proprietor Stéphane Montez produces wines under two labels. His estate wines are labeled Domaine de Monteillet, and the others are Vignobles de Monteillet. Antoine and Stéphane Montez are serious vignerons and winemakers.

2006 Condrieu	91	ncw
2006 Condrieu Les Grandes Chaillées	92	ncw
2005 Côte Rôtie Fortis	88+	2010–2018
2003 Côte Rôtie Fortis	90	ncw–2024
2005 Côte Rôtie Les Grandes Places	91+	2010–2026
2004 Côte Rôtie Les Grandes Places	90+	ncw–2016
2003 Côte Rôtie Les Grandes Places	92+	ncw–2021+
2005 St.-Joseph Cuvée de Papy	89+	???

MONTIRIUS ★★★/★★★★
VACQUEYRAS $18.00–$32.00

Christine and Eric Saurel have been making very fine wines over recent vintages, exploiting 60 acres of well-placed vineyards, primarily in Vacqueyras. The average age of Montirius's vines is 40 years. These are relatively modern-styled wines, but they still retain plenty of Provençal character.

2005 Gigondas	88	now
2004 Gigondas	88	now–2010
2005 Vacqueyras	89	now–2010
2004 Vacqueyras	88+	now–2012
2004 Vacqueyras Clos Montirius	87	now–2014

CHÂTEAU DE MONTLYS ★★
CÔTE RÔTIE $55.00–$75.00

An emerging, serious producer situated at the northern end of the Côte Rôtie appellation, just south of the old Roman town of Vienne, Château de Montlys produces two cuvées, the good but straightforward regular bottling and a luxury offering called Côte Rôtie La Fleur de Montlys. The latter effort displays more depth, but the overall style is one of elegance.

2005 Côte Rôtie	84	2010–2015
2004 Côte Rôtie	86	now–2012
2003 Côte Rôtie	87	now–2012
2005 Côte Rôtie La Fleur de Montlys	87+?	2011–2020
2004 Côte Rôtie La Fleur de Montlys	88	now–2014

CHÂTEAU DE MONTMIRAIL ★★★
VACQUEYRAS $22.00

This moderate-sized estate has its cellars in the quaint Côtes du Rhône-Villages Vacqueyras and is run with obvious enthusiasm by Maurice Archimbaud, a somewhat legendary figure in Vacqueyras with a bigger than life personality, and his son-in-law, Jacques Bouteiller.

2005 Gigondas Cuvée de Beauchamp	88	now–2017
2005 Vacqueyras Cuvée de l'Ermite	88	now–2012
2003 Vacqueyras Cuvée de l'Ermite	90	now–2012

DOMAINE MONTPERTUIS ★★★/★★★★
CHÂTEAUNEUF-DU-PAPE $36.00

Monpertuis's talented owner, Paul Jeune, is known for producing traditional Châteauneuf-du-Papes that often need four to five years of cellaring to reveal their potential. This estate of 40+ acres produces two wines, a regular cuvée that is meant to be drunk during its first 10 to 15 years of life and, in top vintages, a Cuvée Tradition that is mostly Grenache and is meant to age for two decades or more.

2003 Châteauneuf-du-Pape	89	now–2018
2001 Châteauneuf-du-Pape	88	now–2015
2001 Châteauneuf-du-Pape Cuvée Tradition	88+	now–2022
1999 Châteauneuf-du-Pape Cuvée Tradition	89	now–2013+
2001 Châteauneuf-du-Pape Cuvée Tradition Vieilles Vignes	91	now–2018

CHÂTEAU CÔTE MONTPEZAT ★★★
COSTIÈRES DE NÎMES $14.00–$16.00

This is another reliable estate in the Costières de Nîmes, but they often use the appellation Vin de Pays, since they tend to put the name of the varietals on the label. When that is done, under French appellation laws, the name of the appellation cannot be utilized.

2004 Palombières	90	now–2010
2003 Palombières	88	now
2004 Vin de Pays d'Oc Cuvée Prestige	88	now–2010
2003 Vin de Pays d'Oc Cuvée Prestige	87	now
2004 Vin de Pays d'Oc Les Enclos	87	now

DOMAINE DE MONTVAC ★★★
VACQUEYRAS $28.00

This estate, run by Monique and Jean Dusserre, is one of the most serious and ambitious in Vacqueyras. These are impeccably made (Jean Dusserre is an oenologist), deeply colored wines that represent a blend of the more rustic, traditional style of Vacqueyras with the modern, rich, fruity, pure examples.

2005 Vacqueyras Cuvée Variation	90	now

DOMAINE DE LA MORDORÉE ★★★★★
CHÂTEAUNEUF-DU-PAPE $12.00–$300.00

It is unlikely anyone could find a better-run estate than Domaine de La Mordorée. With its 135 acres spread out through some of the most impressive appellations of the southern Rhône, biodynamic farming, and a serious commitment to excellence, Christophe Delorme and his team continue to produce extraordinary wines whether whites, rosés, or their portfolio of serious red wines. Anything labeled "Cuvée La Reine des Bois" is a must purchase. Furthermore, Mordorée's assortments of rosés and Côtes du Rhônes are out of this world. This is also a superb source of both white and rosé wines.

2006 Châteauneuf-du-Pape Cuvée La Reine des Bois	94	2009–2023
2005 Châteauneuf-du-Pape Cuvée La Reine des Bois	95	2013–2025+
2004 Châteauneuf-du-Pape Cuvée La Reine des Bois	94	now–2020+
2003 Châteauneuf-du-Pape Cuvée La Reine des Bois	96	now–2021+
2001 Châteauneuf-du-Pape Cuvée La Reine des Bois	100	now–2024
2000 Châteauneuf-du-Pape Cuvée La Reine des Bois	97	now–2020

1999 Châteauneuf-du-Pape Cuvée La Reine des Bois	94	now–2018
1998 Châteauneuf-du-Pape Cuvée La Reine des Bois	99+	now–2035
2005 Châteauneuf-du-Pape La Plume du Peintre	98+	2015–2035
2003 Châteauneuf-du-Pape La Plume du Peintre	99	2010–2040+
2005 Côtes du Rhône La Dame Rousse	87	now–2011
2005 Lirac	87	2009–2019
2005 Lirac Cuvée La Reine des Bois	91	2010–2025
2004 Lirac Cuvée La Reine des Bois	89	now–2013
2003 Lirac Cuvée La Reine des Bois	93	now–2014
2006 Lirac Cuvée La Reine des Bois Blanc	90	now–2010
2005 Lirac Cuvée La Reine des Bois Blanc	88	now

MOULIN DE LA GARDETTE ★★★/★★★★
GIGONDAS $28.00–$32.00

Moulin de la Gardette is one of Gigondas's most serious and traditional estates. Their traditionally made, serious Gigondas have been consistently excellent over recent vintages.

2005 Gigondas Cuvée Tradition	88	now–2015
2004 Gigondas Cuvée Tradition	87+	now–2016
2005 Gigondas Cuvée Ventabren	89+	now–2020
2004 Gigondas Cuvée Ventabren	87	now–2015

MOULIN-TACUSSEL ★★★
CHÂTEAUNEUF-DU-PAPE $26.00–$30.00

Relatively light, herbal, soft, sensual Châteauneuf-du-Papes are produced at this property. Not built for long aging, they are best consumed during their first decade of life.

2006 Châteauneuf-du-Pape	89	now–2019
2005 Châteauneuf-du-Pape	87	now–2013
2004 Châteauneuf-du-Pape	84	now–2010
2003 Châteauneuf-du-Pape	88	now–2010
2001 Châteauneuf-du-Pape	88	now–2011
2000 Châteauneuf-du-Pape	87	now
1999 Châteauneuf-du-Pape	87	now
2006 Châteauneuf-du-Pape Hommage à Henry Tacussel	91	now–2022+

DOMAINE DE MOURCHON ★★★★
CÔTES DU RHÔNE $11.50–$22.00

I can't say enough about these cuvées, which have performed consistently well since I began tasting them several years ago. Much of the credit goes to proprietor Walter McKinlay, who is working in one of the most idyllic, photogenic villages of southern France. His debut vintage, 1998, was a good beginning and the estate continues to turn out one superlative performance after another.

2005 Côtes du Rhône-Villages Séguret Grande Réserve	89	now–2015
2004 Côtes du Rhône-Villages Séguret Grande Réserve	85	now–2012
2003 Côtes du Rhône-Villages Séguret Grande Réserve	90	now–2013
2001 Côtes du Rhône-Villages Séguret Grande Réserve	90	now–2012
2000 Côtes du Rhône-Villages Séguret Grande Réserve	90	now–2012
2005 Côtes du Rhône-Villages Séguret Tradition	88+	now–2015
2004 Côtes du Rhône-Villages Séguret Tradition	83	now–2012
2003 Côtes du Rhône-Villages Séguret Tradition	88	now–2010

2001 Côtes du Rhône-Villages Séguret Tradition	89	now–2012
2000 Côtes du Rhône-Villages Séguret Tradition	87	now

CHÂTEAU MOURGUES DU GRÈS ✱ ✱ ✱ ✱
COSTIÈRES DE NÎMES $10.00–$18.00

One of my favorite estates in the Costières de Nîmes, Mourgues du Grès fashions beautiful red, white, and rosé wines that sell for a song. The red wine cuvées tend to be made from Grenache and Syrah, the whites from Roussanne, Grenache Blanc, and a few other white varieties. The overall quality level is very high.

2003 Costières de Nîmes Capitelles des Mourgues	92	now–2018
2005 Costières de Nîmes Les Galets Rouge	89	now–2011
2003 Costières de Nîmes Les Galets Rouge	89	now

MOURRE DU TENDRE (J. PAUMEL) ✱ ✱ ✱/✱ ✱ ✱ ✱
CHÂTEAUNEUF-DU-PAPE $20.00–$55.00

This is one of the bastions of traditional, full-throttle, powerful, muscular Châteauneuf-du-Papes made in the image of Henri Bonneau's Réserve des Célestins. Proprietor Jacques Paumel fashions uncompromising wines with formidable aging potential. Even after release, these wines generally require a few more years of cellaring given their massive extract, high levels of tannin, and robust styles.

2003 Châteauneuf-du-Pape	88+?	2010–2025+
2001 Châteauneuf-du-Pape	89+	now–2020
2000 Châteauneuf-du-Pape	90	now–2030
1999 Châteauneuf-du-Pape	90	now–2020

DOMAINE MICHELAS-ST. JEMMS ✱ ✱
CORNAS $40.00–$50.00

Robert Michelas turns out correct, chunky, frequently rustic wines from his vineyards located between Pont de l'Isère in the south and Mercurol in the north. Much of his harvest is done by machines, and in tasting the wines I have the impression that little selection is made in the cellars. Don't get me wrong; these are not bad wines, just indifferent and blatantly commercial.

2005 Cornas Les Murettes	86?	now–2016
2003 Cornas Les Murettes	83–86	now–2013

DOMAINE DE NALYS ✱ ✱ ✱
CHÂTEAUNEUF-DU-PAPE $28.00–$45.00

The Domaine de Nalys is one of the proponents of carbonic maceration for red wines. These are always impeccably clean, correct, fresh, lively, fruit-driven wines that, for the most part, lack the concentration and intensity of the top estates of the region. Nevertheless, they are well-made and undeniably charming. Their white Châteauneuf-du-Pape is a winner.

2005 Châteauneuf-du-Pape	89	now–2014
2004 Châteauneuf-du-Pape	88	now–2012
2003 Châteauneuf-du-Pape	88	now–2011
2001 Châteauneuf-du-Pape	90	now–2014

CHÂTEAU LA NERTHE ★★★★★
CHÂTEAUNEUF-DU-PAPE $32.00–$95.00

One of the most historic names of Châteauneuf-du-Pape, with a history going back several hundred years, La Nerthe may be the only true Château in Châteauneuf-du-Pape. They produce an assortment of top-quality wines, including their brilliant white Châteauneuf-du-Papes and two cuvées of red Châteauneuf. As does Beaucastel, they include a high percentage of Mourvèdre in their blends, which gives the wines considerable longevity. Cuvée des Cadettes is the only Châteauneuf-du-Pape that is aged in 100% small oak barrels.

2005 Châteauneuf-du-Pape Blanc	89	now–2012
2005 Châteauneuf-du-Pape Clos de Beauvenir Blanc	93	now–2015
2006 Châteauneuf-du-Pape Cuvée des Cadettes	93	2011–2020+
2005 Châteauneuf-du-Pape Cuvée des Cadettes	95	2012–2037+
2004 Châteauneuf-du-Pape Cuvée des Cadettes	93	2011–2030
2003 Châteauneuf-du-Pape Cuvée des Cadettes	91	now
2001 Châteauneuf-du-Pape Cuvée des Cadettes	95	now–2021
2000 Châteauneuf-du-Pape Cuvée des Cadettes	93	now–2016
2006 Châteauneuf-du-Pape Tradition	90	now–2019
2005 Châteauneuf-du-Pape Tradition	90	2009–2020+
2004 Châteauneuf-du-Pape Tradition	89	now–2017
2003 Châteauneuf-du-Pape Tradition	89	now–2017
2002 Châteauneuf-du-Pape Tradition	86	now
2001 Châteauneuf-du-Pape Tradition	90	now–2018
2000 Châteauneuf-du-Pape Tradition	89	now–2015+

ROBERT NIERO ★★★
CONDRIEU $50.00–$55.00

Robert Niero practices cautious vinification, *élevage,* and bottling, with considerable manipulation and filtration. In spite of that, he has produced some very fine wines.

2006 Condrieu Côteau du Chéry	90	now

MICHEL OGIER ★★★★★
CÔTE RÔTIE $15.00–$180.00

Michel Ogier, capably assisted by his son Stéphane, remains an unheralded source of profound Côte Rôtie. He currently estate-bottles the entire production of Côte Rôtie, as well as 8,000 bottles of a 100% Syrah made from 12-year-old vines planted just outside the southern borders of Côte Rôtie, where the Côte Blonde ends, called La Rosine. In addition to making one of the finest values in Côte Rôtie and one of the village's most elegant, stylish wines, this producer also fashions a cuvée dedicated to his wife, Hélène. La Belle Hélène is an impressive 100% new-oak offering from 45-year-old vines on the Côte Rozier, next to La Landonne. It rivals Guigal's three single-vineyard cuvées. A new offering from Côte Rôtie, Lancement, is also a brilliant success. This is one of the most exciting young estates in the Rhône Valley.

2006 Côte Rôtie	90	2009–2016
2005 Côte Rôtie	89+	2012–2020
2004 Côte Rôtie	90+	now–2018
2003 Côte Rôtie	89	now–2016
2001 Côte Rôtie	93	now–2018
2000 Côte Rôtie	89	now–2013
1999 Côte Rôtie	95	now–2018
2006 Côte Rôtie La Belle Hélène	94	2015–2025

2005 Côte Rôtie La Belle Hélène	94+	2012–2025
2004 Côte Rôtie La Belle Hélène	91	2011–2020
2003 Côte Rôtie La Belle Hélène	91+?	2011–2022
2001 Côte Rôtie La Belle Hélène	94	now–2018+
2000 Côte Rôtie La Belle Hélène	93	now–2015
1999 Côte Rôtie La Belle Hélène	100	now–2030
2003 Côte Rôtie Cuvée Embruns	90	now–2016
2001 Côte Rôtie Cuvée Embruns	90	now–2013
2006 Côte Rôtie Lancement	94	2009–2018
2005 Côte Rôtie Lancement	92+	2012–2020
2004 Côte Rôtie Lancement	92	now–2020
2003 Côte Rôtie Lancement	93	now–2015
2005 Côte Rôtie Réserve du Domaine	91	2011–2020
2004 Côte Rôtie Réserve du Domaine	90	now–2019
2005 Syrah l'Ame Soeur	88	now–2012
2004 Syrah l'Ame Soeur	89	now–2010
2005 Syrah La Rosine Vin de Pays	87	now–2010

DOMAINE DE L'ORATOIRE ST.-MARTIN ★ ★ ★
CAIRANNE $24.00–$28.00

One of Cairanne's finest estates, Domaine de l'Oratoire St.-Martin is run by Frédéric and François Alary. Multiple cuvées of high-class Cairanne are produced. All of the wines are bottled unfined and unfiltered.

2005 Côtes du Rhône-Villages Cairanne Cuvée Haut-Coustias	90	now–2012
2004 Côtes du Rhône-Villages Cairanne Cuvée Haut-Coustias	88	now–2010
2005 Côtes du Rhône-Villages Cairanne Cuvée Prestige	89	now–2012
2004 Côtes du Rhône-Villages Cairanne Cuvée Prestige	89+	now–2013
2003 Côtes du Rhône-Villages Cairanne Cuvée Prestige	89	now–2011
2001 Côtes du Rhône-Villages Cairanne Cuvée Prestige	89	now–2010
2005 Côtes du Rhône-Villages Cairanne Réserve des Seigneurs	90	now–2011
2004 Côtes du Rhône-Villages Cairanne Réserve des Seigneurs	87	now–2010
2003 Côtes du Rhône-Villages Cairanne Réserve des Seigneurs	85	now–2010

L'OUSTAU-FAUQUET ★ ★ ★
GIGONDAS $25.00–$30.00

Roger Combe, whose cellars lie midway between the ancient village of Gigondas and the drab town of Vacqueyras, produces only red wine from both appellations. This is a good source for reliable, rarely exciting, but soundly made very reasonably priced Gigondas.

2005 Gigondas Secret de la Barrique	90	2010–2022
2004 Gigondas Secret de la Barrique	88	now–2011

DOMAINE LES PALLIÈRES ★ ★ ★
GIGONDAS $25.00–$28.00

This famous estate is now jointly owned by Vieux Télégraphe's Daniel Brunier and the well-known importer Kermit Lynch. Cool-climate, Burgundian-styled Gigondas are produced at this large property. The domaine is somewhat complicated because of its many different parcels and microclimates. However, the wines appear to be going from strength to strength and promise a return to the hallowed Les Pallières of the '60s and '70s.

2005 Gigondas	90	2009–2034
2004 Gigondas	88	now–2017
2003 Gigondas	90	now–2018
2001 Gigondas	90+	now–2019
2000 Gigondas	89+	now–2021
1999 Gigondas	90	now–2013

DOMAINE DE PANISSE * * *
CHÂTEAUNEUF-DU-PAPE $32.00–$66.00

A young vigneron, Jean-Marie Olivier, revealed tremendous potential when he broke through with some fabulous efforts in 2000, but since then quality has been distressingly irregular. I am perplexed by what is going on here. However, it is a name to watch, as it obviously has superb potential.

2006 Châteauneuf-du-Pape Confidence Vigneronne	89	2010–2025+
2005 Châteauneuf-du-Pape Confidence Vigneronne	90	now–2015
2004 Châteauneuf-du-Pape Confidence Vigneronne	87	now–2011
2003 Châteauneuf-du-Pape Confidence Vigneronne	88	now–2010
2006 Châteauneuf-du-Pape Noble Révélation	93	now–2023
2005 Châteauneuf-du-Pape Noble Révélation	93	2010–2025
2004 Châteauneuf-du-Pape Noble Révélation	88	now–2015
2003 Châteauneuf-du-Pape Noble Révélation	90	now–2014
2006 Châteauneuf-du-Pape Tradition	89	now–2019
2005 Châteauneuf-du-Pape Tradition	86	now–2011
2004 Châteauneuf-du-Pape Tradition	85	now–2010
2005 Côtes du Rhône	86	now
2005 Côtes du Rhône Murmure des Vignes	85	now–2011

DOMAINE VINCENT PARIS * * * *
CORNAS $55.00

A small but promising estate, this domaine produces Cornas cuvées from the appellation's steep granite terraces. It is definitely an estate readers should be closely following.

2005 Cornas Granit 30 Vieilles Vignes	89+	2010–2020
2004 Cornas Granit 30 Vieilles Vignes	87	now–2016
2005 Cornas Granit 60 Vieilles Vignes	92	2011–2022
2004 Cornas Granit 60 Vieilles Vignes	89	now–2016
2003 Cornas Granit 60 Vieilles Vignes	93	now–2021

DOMAINE DES PASQUIERS * * *
GIGONDAS $35.00–$40.00

Recent vintages were impressive efforts from this Sablet proprietor. These tank-aged Gigondas are blends of equal parts Syrah and Grenache.

2005 Gigondas	90	2010–2018
2004 Gigondas	89	now–2016
2003 Gigondas	91	now–2016

DOMAINE DU PÉGAÜ ★ ★ ★ ★ ★
CHÂTEAUNEUF-DU-PAPE $16.00–$300.00

The Domaine du Pégaü has had an impressive track record for more than twenty years. Paul Féraud and his charismatic daughter, Laurence, produce blockbuster, chewy, old-style Châteauneuf-du-Papes in much the same manner as those of Féraud's mentor, Henri Bonneau. Féraud's offerings are uncompromising, high-alcohol, massive wines that hit the heights in the great vintages yet do surprisingly well in the lighter years. No doubt due to the influence of Laurence, the bottling happens much earlier than practiced by Bonneau, within two years, except for the limited production Cuvée Laurence, which is bottled after five to six years of barrel aging. Laurence also introduced the blockbuster Cuvée da Capo, in 1998. It is made only in the top vintages (i.e., 1998, 2000, 2003, and, most recently, 2007).

The irrepressible Laurence Féraud and her animated father also produce a delicious Vin de Pays d'Oc, called either La Plume Bleu or Pegovino, depending on the market.

2003 Châteauneuf-du-Pape Cuvée da Capo	100	2010–2035+
2000 Châteauneuf-du-Pape Cuvée da Capo	100	2010–2030+
1998 Châteauneuf-du-Pape Cuvée da Capo	100	now–2030
2004 Châteauneuf-du-Pape Cuvée Laurence	93	2010–2020
2000 Châteauneuf-du-Pape Cuvée Laurence	92	now–2020
1998 Châteauneuf-du-Pape Cuvée Laurence	96	now–2025
2006 Châteauneuf-du-Pape Cuvée Réservée	92	2012–2032
2005 Châteauneuf-du-Pape Cuvée Réservée	93+	2015–2035+
2004 Châteauneuf-du-Pape Cuvée Réservée	94+	2010–2026+
2003 Châteauneuf-du-Pape Cuvée Réservée	98	now–2026+
2001 Châteauneuf-du-Pape Cuvée Réservée	95+	now–2020
2000 Châteauneuf-du-Pape Cuvée Réservée	95	now–2023
1999 Châteauneuf-du-Pape Cuvée Réservée	92	now–2014
1998 Châteauneuf-du-Pape Cuvée Réservée	94	now–2020
2003 Châteauneuf-du-Pape Inspiration (magnum)	98	now–2025

DOMAINE DU PÈRE CABOCHE ★ ★ ★
CHÂTEAUNEUF-DU-PAPE $22.00–$46.00

Jean-Pierre Boisson, the charismatic mayor of Châteauneuf-du-Pape, continues to turn out wines that mirror his exuberant, generous, affable personality. Fruit-forward, full-bodied, lush, and hedonistic, they will not make old bones, but for drinking during their first decade of life they are undeniably sexy efforts. The basic cuvée is delicious, but the Vieilles Vignes offering called Elisabeth Chambellan offers a gorgeous concoction of black cherries, raspberries, and Provençal herbs in a full-bodied, supple style. This is Châteauneuf-du-Pape at its most seductive and precocious.

2006 Châteauneuf-du-Pape	89	now–2013
2005 Châteauneuf-du-Pape	89	now–2013
2003 Châteauneuf-du-Pape	87	now–2010
2001 Châteauneuf-du-Pape	88	now–2010
2000 Châteauneuf-du-Pape	89	now–2010
2006 Châteauneuf-du-Pape Cuvée Elisabeth Chambellan Vieilles Vignes	90	now–2019
2005 Châteauneuf-du-Pape Cuvée Elisabeth Chambellan Vieilles Vignes	90	now–2015
2003 Châteauneuf-du-Pape Cuvée Elisabeth Chambellan Vieilles Vignes	89	now–2013

2001 Châteauneuf-du-Pape Cuvée Elisabeth		
Chambellan Vieilles Vignes	90	now–2016
2000 Châteauneuf-du-Pape Cuvée Elisabeth		
Chambellan Vieilles Vignes	90	now–2013

DOMAINE DU PÈRE PAPE ★★★★
CHÂTEAUNEUF-DU-PAPE $28.00–$44.00

These are consistently open-knit, seductive, fruit-driven, hedonistically styled Châteauneuf-du-Papes characterized by ripe fruit, good body, and plenty of Provençal typicity. They are meant to be consumed during their first decade of life.

2006 Châteauneuf-du-Pape	88	now–2014
2005 Châteauneuf-du-Pape	87	now–2013
2004 Châteauneuf-du-Pape	88	now–2013
2003 Châteauneuf-du-Pape	90	now–2012+
2001 Châteauneuf-du-Pape	88	now–2012
2006 Châteauneuf-du-Pape Clos du Calvaire	90	now–2017
2005 Châteauneuf-du-Pape Clos du Calvaire	89	now–2015
2004 Châteauneuf-du-Pape Clos du Calvaire	87	now–2012
2003 Châteauneuf-du-Pape Clos du Calvaire	90	now–2016
2001 Châteauneuf-du-Pape Clos du Calvaire	89	now–2014
2000 Châteauneuf-du-Pape Clos du Calvaire	88	now–2012
1999 Châteauneuf-du-Pape Clos du Calvaire	89	now–2013
2006 Châteauneuf-du-Pape La Crau de Ma Mère	90	now–2022
2005 Châteauneuf-du-Pape La Crau de Ma Mère	91	2009–2019
2004 Châteauneuf-du-Pape La Crau de Ma Mère	90	now–2014
2003 Châteauneuf-du-Pape La Crau de Ma Mère	92	now–2016
2001 Châteauneuf-du-Pape La Crau de Ma Mère	89	now–2011
2000 Châteauneuf-du-Pape La Crau de Ma Mère	89	now–2015
1999 Châteauneuf-du-Pape La Crau de Ma Mère	89	now

ANDRÉ PERRET ★★★★★
CONDRIEU/ST.-JOSEPH $18.00–$47.00

One of the great names of Condrieu, Perret produces two spectacular whites that are pure nectar. Both are dry, full-bodied, and powerful as well as elegant and exceptionally perfumed. His red wines have also increased in quality.

2006 Condrieu Clos Chanson	90	now
2005 Condrieu Clos Chanson	92+	now
2006 Condrieu Côteau du Chéry	91	now
2005 Condrieu Côteau du Chéry	94	now

DOMAINE ROGER PERRIN ★★★★
CHÂTEAUNEUF-DU-PAPE $12.00–$60.00

Another of the young turks of Châteauneuf-du-Pape, Luc Perrin (son of Roger Perrin) is also one of the biggest vignerons (physically speaking) of the village. He produces a bevy of delicious, bargain-priced Côtes du Rhônes as well as a basic Châteauneuf-du-Pape and a spectacular Châteauneuf-du-Pape Réserve des Vieilles Vignes. In top years, the latter two cuvées can last 15 or more years.

2005 Châteauneuf-du-Pape	90	2009–2020
2004 Châteauneuf-du-Pape	88	now–2015

2003 Châteauneuf-du-Pape	88	now–2012
2001 Châteauneuf-du-Pape	89	now–2015
2000 Châteauneuf-du-Pape	88	now–2012
2005 Châteauneuf-du-Pape Réserve des Vieilles Vignes	92+	2009–2022+
2004 Châteauneuf-du-Pape Réserve des Vieilles Vignes	90	now–2022
2003 Châteauneuf-du-Pape Réserve des Vieilles Vignes	93+	now–2024
2000 Châteauneuf-du-Pape Réserve des Vieilles Vignes	96	now–2016
2005 Côtes du Rhône	86	now
2005 Côtes du Rhône Cuvée Prestige	88	now–2013

CHÂTEAU PESQUIÉ ★ ★ ★ ★
CÔTES DU VENTOUX $11.00–$40.00

One of the top estates in the Côtes du Ventoux, Pesquié has been a project for importer Eric Solomon, who creates these custom cuvées for the U.S. marketplace. All three of the red wine offerings are superb efforts.

2004 Côtes du Ventoux Cuvée Artemia	91+	now–2017
2005 Côtes du Ventoux La Quintessence	91	now–2012
2004 Côtes du Ventoux La Quintessence	91	now–2012
2005 Côtes du Ventoux Les Terrasses	90	now–2012
2003 Côtes du Ventoux Les Terrasses	89	now

DOMAINE DU PESQUIER ★ ★ ★ ★
GIGONDAS $35.00–$45.00

These are full-blown, rich, spicy Gigondas that, like so many wines in this village, can be irregular, but when they get everything right, they are riveting examples of old winemaking and big, muscular, chewy wines for those with 19th-century palates.

2005 Gigondas	89+	now–2019
2003 Gigondas	88	now–2015
2005 Vacqueyras	90	2009–2020
2004 Vacqueyras	88	now–2013
2003 Vacqueyras	87	now

DOMAINE DE PIAUGIER ★ ★ ★
GIGONDAS $13.50–$24.00

Praise for this small but consistently high-quality producer of both Côtes du Rhone and Gigondas is the result of the intelligence and capable efforts of proprietor Jean-Marc Autran. The Autrans have a modern approach to making wines, resulting in impressive, rich, authoritatively flavored, elegantly styled Gigondas capable of lasting a decade. Unfortunately, the Gigondas estate is small, but the Autrans also produce high-quality wines from their Côtes du Rhône holdings, particularly in Sablet, the village where their cellars are located.

DOMAINE PICHAT ★ ★ ★
CÔTE RÔTIE $60.00–$88.00

This young but serious Côte Rôtie producer is fashioning two excellent single-vineyard cuvées. Le Champon is a pleasant, solidly constructed wine, and Les Grandes Places is a fabulous example of this terrific vineyard.

2005 Côte Rôtie Le Champon	88	now–2018
2004 Côte Rôtie Le Champon	87	now–2015

2005 Côte Rôtie Les Grandes Places	90	2009–2017
2004 Côte Rôtie Les Grandes Places	86?	now–2014

CHRISTOPHE PICHON * * *
CÔTE RÔTIE $45.00–$62.00

Pichon is well known for its excellent Condrieu. The estate also produces two Côte Rôties, the finest of which is La Comtesse en Côte Blonde.

2006 Condrieu	89	now
2005 Côte Rôtie	85	now–2015
2003 Côte Rôtie	85	now
2005 Côte Rôtie La Comtesse en Côte Blonde	91	now–2019

LA PINÈDE * * *
CHÂTEAUNEUF-DU-PAPE $30.00–$35.00

La Pinède's proprietor, Pierre-Georges Coulon, produces leathery, earthy Châteauneuf-du-Papes that display a certain barnyard/animalistic character combined with kirsch and raspberry fruit. These wines are best consumed during their first 10 to 12 years of life.

2005 Châteauneuf-du-Pape	88	2010–2022
2004 Châteauneuf-du-Pape	87	now–2014
2003 Châteauneuf-du-Pape	87	now–2015
2001 Châteauneuf-du-Pape	90	now–2014
2000 Châteauneuf-du-Pape	89	now–2012

DOMAINE PONTIFICAL * * *
CHÂTEAUNEUF-DU-PAPE $30.00–$35.00

This estate, which has been in the Laget-Royer family since the early 1920s, is typical of Châteauneuf-du-Pape, with 30 separate parcels spread throughout all sectors of the appellation—a nightmare at harvest. There are vineyards planted on sandy soil, limestone, clay, and on stony carpets.

2005 Châteauneuf-du-Pape	89	now–2016
2003 Châteauneuf-du-Pape	89	now–2013
2001 Châteauneuf-du-Pape	88	now–2015
2000 Châteauneuf-du-Pape	90	now–2015
1999 Châteauneuf-du-Pape	89	now–2011

DOMAINE DU POURRA * * *
GIGONDAS $30.00–$32.00

This well-run estate's wines are generally blends of 70% Grenache, 20% Syrah, and 10% Mourvèdre and Cinsault, all aged in small barrels and *foudres*.

2004 Gigondas	89	now–2016
2003 Gigondas	90	now–2010
2000 Gigondas Cuvée Prestige	90+	now–2018

DOMAINE DE LA PRÉSIDENTE * * * *
CAIRANNE $22.00–$45.00

This is a relatively large, ambitious firm with reasonably good quality and a few gems in the portfolio. Much of their emphasis is on Châteauneuf-du-Pape, Côtes du Rhône, and Côtes du Rhône-Villages, especially Cairanne, where they are based. These are all well-made efforts that continue to fly under the radar of most Rhône wine enthusiasts.

2006 Châteauneuf-du-Pape Grands Classiques	91	now–2022+
2005 Châteauneuf-du-Pape Grands Classiques	92	now–2017
2004 Châteauneuf-du-Pape Grands Classiques	89	now–2015
2003 Châteauneuf-du-Pape Grands Classiques	91	now–2017
2001 Châteauneuf-du-Pape Grands Classiques	85?	now
2001 Châteauneuf-du-Pape Hommage à Max Aubert	90+	now–2020
2005 Châteauneuf-du-Pape Hommage à Max Aubert Blanc	90	now–2010
2004 Châteauneuf-du-Pape Le Nonce	85	now–2013
2003 Châteauneuf-du-Pape Le Nonce	90	now–2016
2005 Châteauneuf-du-Pape Le Nonce Blanc	91	now–2010
2005 Châteauneuf-du-Pape La Nonciature	92	now–2019
2004 Châteauneuf-du-Pape La Nonciature	89	now–2016
2003 Châteauneuf-du-Pape La Nonciature	89	now–2016
2001 Châteauneuf-du-Pape La Nonciature	90	now–2018
2005 Côtes du Rhône Grands Classiques	88	now
2005 Côtes du Rhône-Villages Cairanne Galifay	89	now–2017
2005 Côtes du Rhône-Villages Cairanne Grands Classiques	88	now–2012
2005 Côtes du Rhône-Villages Cairanne Partides	89	2009–2020

RABASSE CHARAVIN ★★★
CAIRANNE $15.00

The proprietor of Rabasse Charavin is Corinne Coutourier, who apprenticed with her father until 1985, at which time she took over the making of the wines. Like many large Côtes du Rhône estates, they produce a bevy of wines, including an excellent, rich, stylish, peppery, black cherry–flavored Côtes du Rhône-Villages Cairanne.

2005 Côtes du Rhône-Villages Cairanne	87	now

CHÂTEAU RASPAIL ★★★
GIGONDAS $14.00–$30.00

Château Raspail is owned by the Meffre family, whose empire was built by the late Gabriel Meffre. In the post–World War II period, Meffre forged the largest holding of appellation contrôlée vineyards in France. At present, there are 2,222 acres of AOC vines, with estates such as Château Raspail, Domaine des Bosquets, and Domaine La Chapelle.

2005 Gigondas	87	now–2015
2004 Gigondas	89+	now–2014

DOMAINE RASPAIL-AY ★★★★
GIGONDAS $28.00–$35.00

One of the most elegantly styled Gigondas is produced at Domaine Raspail-Ay. Having more in common with a top-notch red Burgundy than with most Gigondas, it is usually medium-bodied, with a forest-floor-like character revealing hints of flowers and sweet kirsch fruit. It ages beautifully in top vintages.

2005 Gigondas	90	now–2020
2004 Gigondas	88	now–2015
2003 Gigondas	88	now–2013
2001 Gigondas	88	now–2012
2000 Gigondas	88	now–2013

CHÂTEAU RAYAS ★★★★★
CHÂTEAUNEUF-DU-PAPE $18.00–$200.00

This is one of the mythical names of France, largely because of the efforts of the late Jacques Reynaud, who made many spectacular wines between 1978 and 1995. In addition to numerous cuvées of Châteauneuf-du-Pape, Rayas produces top-notch Côtes du Rhônes from its sister estate, Fonsalette. These are cool-climate Châteauneufs from a relatively hot region. The vineyards are planted in north-facing sandy soils, which is somewhat rare in Châteauneuf-du-Pape. These wines have an uncanny ability to age longer than their light colors and delicate frameworks would suggest. Truly legendary wines have emerged from Rayas, including those of 1978, 1979, 1981, 1985, 1990, 1995, and 2005. Moreover, consumers should not dismiss the Fonsalette Côtes du Rhônes, which are as ageworthy as the Rayas offerings.

FONSALETTE

2005 Côtes du Rhône	90	now–2017
2004 Côtes du Rhône	89	now–2017
2003 Côtes du Rhône	89	now–2021
2001 Côtes du Rhône	87	now–2019
2000 Côtes du Rhône	89	now–2011
2005 Côtes du Rhône Cuvée Syrah	93	2012–2021
2004 Côtes du Rhône Cuvée Syrah	88+?	2011–2020
2003 Côtes du Rhône Cuvée Syrah	90	2010–2026
2001 Côtes du Rhône Cuvée Syrah	91+	2010–2020
2000 Côtes du Rhône Cuvée Syrah	91	now–2018

PIGNAN

2006 Châteauneuf-du-Pape	92	now–2018
2005 Châteauneuf-du-Pape	91	now–2019
2004 Châteauneuf-du-Pape	90	now–2020
2003 Châteauneuf-du-Pape	91	now–2020

RAYAS

2006 Châteauneuf-du-Pape	93	now–2028
2005 Châteauneuf-du-Pape	98	2013–2030
2004 Châteauneuf-du-Pape	92	2010–2025
2003 Châteauneuf-du-Pape	95	2010–2030+
2001 Châteauneuf-du-Pape	92	now–2022
2000 Châteauneuf-du-Pape	93	now–2016
1999 Châteauneuf-du-Pape	92	now–2015
1998 Châteauneuf-du-Pape	89	now–2017

REDORTIER ★★★
GIGONDAS $28.00–$32.00

Étienne de Menthon is undoubtedly an outsider in Gigondas. A native of the lovely French alpine city of Annecy, in the early 1980s Menthon moved south, building a Provençal farmhouse and carving out a vineyard in the Beaumes de Venise region. His predilection for vineyard planting continued with the acquisition of what has become 12.4 acres of high-altitude terraced vineyards in Gigondas. From his small Gigondas estate, Menthon, an intelligent, articulate man, produces one of the most impressive wines of the appellation.

2005 Gigondas	88+	2010–2018
2003 Gigondas	87	now–2015

| 2001 Gigondas | 87 | now–2011 |
| 2000 Gigondas | 86 | now |

DOMAINE DES RÉLAGNES ★ ★ ★
CHÂTEAUNEUF-DU-PAPE $25.00–$70.00

These Grenache-dominated efforts exhibit all the Provençal characteristics of seaweed, pepper, underbrush, and black cherries. For some reason, the Châteauneufs of Rélagnes remain underpriced.

2005 Châteauneuf-du-Pape	87	now–2014
2004 Châteauneuf-du-Pape	87	now–2014
2003 Châteauneuf-du-Pape	88	now–2013
2001 Châteauneuf-du-Pape	88	now–2011
2000 Châteauneuf-du-Pape	88	now–2015
2005 Châteauneuf-du-Pape Cuvée Vigneronne	90	now–2019
2004 Châteauneuf-du-Pape Cuvée Vigneronne	91	now–2019
2003 Châteauneuf-du-Pape Cuvée Vigneronne	90	now–2018
2001 Châteauneuf-du-Pape Cuvée Vigneronne	90	now–2014
2000 Châteauneuf-du-Pape Cuvée Vigneronne	90	now–2016

DOMAINE LA RÉMÉJEANNE ★ ★ ★ ★
CÔTES DU RHÔNE $11.00–$38.00

This is a consistently top-notch source for impeccably well-made Côtes du Rhône and Côtes du Rhône-Villages that sell for a song. The wines are all well made, loaded with fruit, and best drunk during their first three to four years of life. This is one of the best bargain estates in the southern Rhône.

2005 Côtes du Rhône Les Arbousiers	87	now
2004 Côtes du Rhône Les Arbousiers	87	now
2003 Côtes du Rhône Les Arbousiers	88	now
2001 Côtes du Rhône Les Arbousiers	88	now
2003 Côtes du Rhône Les Arbousiers Rosé	89	now
2005 Côtes du Rhône Les Chevrefeuilles	86	now
2004 Côtes du Rhône Les Chevrefeuilles	85	now
2003 Côtes du Rhône Les Chevrefeuilles	86	now
2001 Côtes du Rhône Les Chevrefeuilles	87	now
2004 Côtes du Rhône-Villages Les Eglantiers	89	now
2003 Côtes du Rhône-Villages Les Eglantiers	90	now–2010
2001 Côtes du Rhône-Villages Les Eglantiers	90	now–2010
2000 Côtes du Rhône-Villages Les Eglantiers	89	now
2004 Côtes du Rhône-Villages Les Genèvriers	86	now
2003 Côtes du Rhône-Villages Les Genèvriers	90	now
2001 Côtes du Rhône-Villages Les Genèvriers	88	now
2000 Côtes du Rhône-Villages Les Genèvriers	90	now

DOMAINE DES REMIZIÈRES ★ ★ ★ ★ ★
HERMITAGE $65.00–$85.00

Philippe Desmeures fashions these cuvées in consultation with the French wine broker Patrick Lesec. Consequently, they are different cuvées than sold elsewhere. Lesec's name appears on the strip label along with his importer information. They are made in mostly new oak, with minimal racking, limited sulfur, and are bottled without fining or filtration. They are superb efforts, and it would be terrific if Desmeures would decide to treat all the wine in his cellars in this manner, as this estate appears to have unlimited potential. Fabulous red and white Hermitage as well as superb Crozes-Hermitage are fashioned by this dedicated producer in the village of Mercurol.

2005 Crozes-Hermitage Autrement	88+	2009–2018
2004 Crozes-Hermitage Cuvée Christophe	89+	now–2014
2003 Crozes-Hermitage Cuvée Christophe	90?	now–2018
2001 Crozes-Hermitage Cuvée Christophe	91	now–2011
2005 Crozes-Hermitage Cuvée Christophe Blanc	88	now–2011
2003 Crozes-Hermitage Cuvée l'Essentiel	93	now–2021
2004 Crozes-Hermitage Cuvée Particulière	88	now–2013
2003 Crozes-Hermitage Cuvée Particulière	88	now–2010
2005 Crozes-Hermitage Cuvée Particulière Blanc	89	now–2012
2004 Croze-Hermitage Patience	90	2010–2018
2005 Hermitage Autrement	91	2012–2025
2005 Hermitage Cuvée Emilie	90	now–2022
2004 Hermitage Cuvée Emilie	89+	now–2021
2003 Hermitage Cuvée Emilie	95	2009–2035+
2001 Hermitage Cuvée Emilie	90+	now–2018+
2005 Hermitage Cuvée Emilie Blanc	90+	now–2020
2003 Hermitage Cuvée l'Essentiel	98	2009–2036+

DOMAINE DE LA RENJARDE ★ ★ ★
CÔTES DU RHÔNE $15.00–$18.00

Produced by Château La Nerthe's administrator, Alain Dugas, these wines are gulpable, soft, fruity Côtes du Rhônes. Made in an uncomplicated manner, they offer pleasure, accessibility, and value.

2005 Côtes du Rhône	87	now
2004 Côtes du Rhône	86	now

DOMAINE LA ROQUETTE ★ ★ ★ ★
CHÂTEAUNEUF-DU-PAPE $45.00–$75.00

Domaine La Roquette, which was acquired by the Bruniers in 1986, produces a modern-style, impressively made Châteauneuf-du-Pape that is often overlooked by many Rhône enthusiasts. Although the wines were good in the past, quality under the Bruniers has improved immensely.

2006 L'Accent de la Roquette	93	now–2022
2005 L'Accent de la Roquette	93	now–2022
2004 L'Accent de la Roquette	93	now–2022
2006 Châteauneuf-du-Pape	90	now–2022
2005 Châteauneuf-du-Pape	89	now–2022
2004 Châteauneuf-du-Pape	89	now–2017
2003 Châteauneuf-du-Pape	89	now–2022
2001 Châteauneuf-du-Pape	89+	now–2014
2000 Châteauneuf-du-Pape	88	now–2013

RENÉ ROSTAING ★ ★ ★ ★ ★
AMPUIS $20.00–$225.00

René Rostaing continues to exhibit considerable winemaking skills, displaying more confidence with each vintage. He has benefited from observing the winemaking of his father-in-law, Albert Dervieux, as well as his uncle, Marius Gentaz. Both men were traditionalist winemakers from Côte Rôtie and possessed some of the finest vines, with parcels of La Fongent (La Garde) and La Viallière. Rostaing decided that beginning in 1998 he would no longer make a separate Viallière, but would include it as part of the blend of his Cuvée Classique. Yields usually average 30 hectoliters per hectare (320 gallons per acre), which is quite low by modern-day standards. The wines are bottled unfiltered after spending 16 to 18 months in a combination of barrels and larger *demimuids*. Depending on the vintage, this producer does not use more than 10 to 20% new oak, a slight decrease over recent vintages, from a high of 30% in the early 1990s.

2006 Condrieu La Bonnette	93	now
2006 Côte Rôtie	89	now–2020
2005 Côte Rôtie	90	2010–2020
2004 Côte Rôtie Cuvée Classique	88	now–2014
2003 Côte Rôtie Cuvée Classique	93	now–2014
2001 Côte Rôtie Cuvée Classique	90	now–2012
2000 Côte Rôtie Cuvée Classique	89	now–2010
2006 Côte Rôtie Côte Blonde	93	2011–2020
2005 Côte Rôtie Côte Blonde	93+	2012–2022
2004 Côte Rôtie Côte Blonde	91	now–2014
2003 Côte Rôtie Côte Blonde	97	now–2018
2001 Côte Rôtie Côte Blonde	92	now–2014
2005 Côte Rôtie La Landonne	92+	2013–2025
2004 Côte Rôtie La Landonne	89+	now–2021
2003 Côte Rôtie La Landonne	97	now–2021
2001 Côte Rôtie La Landonne	91	now–2014

ROUCAS DE ST.-PIERRE ★★★
GIGONDAS $35.00–$40.00

This small property of 12.5 acres is planted primarily with Grenache and a small quantity of Syrah.

2003 Gigondas	88	now–2017
2000 Gigondas	90	now–2011

PAUL ROUMANILLE ★★★
CÔTES DU RHÔNE $15.00–$20.00

A pleasant discovery on my tour of the southern Rhône, this small Sablet producer has made impressive wines in both 2005 and 2004.

2005 Côtes du Rhône-Villages Sablet	89	now–2012
2004 Côtes du Rhône-Villages Sablet	87	now–2010

VIGNOBLES JEAN-MARIE ROYER ★★★★
CHÂTEAUNEUF-DU-PAPE $50.00–$90.00

Two high-class offerings emerge from this producer. Production is relatively small, but these wines represent the essence of concentrated kirsch, raspberries, and Provençal herbs.

2005 Châteauneuf-du-Pape Cuvée Prestige	92	2009–2020
2004 Châteauneuf-du-Pape Cuvée Prestige	90	now–2019
2003 Châteauneuf-du-Pape Cuvée Prestige	90	now–2018
2001 Châteauneuf-du-Pape Cuvée Prestige	90	now–2016
2001 Châteauneuf-du-Pape Hommage à Mon Père	92	now–2018

2004 Châteauneuf-du-Pape Tradition	88	now–2019
2003 Châteauneuf-du-Pape Tradition	89	now–2015
2001 Châteauneuf-du-Pape Tradition	89	now–2015

DOMAINE ROGER SABON * * * * *
CHÂTEAUNEUF-DU-PAPE $28.00–$275.00

One of the irrefutable reference-point estates for traditionally made Châteauneuf-du-Pape, Domaine Roger Sabon is run by the gentlemanly but serious Jean-Jacques Sabon. There are four cuvées of Châteauneuf-du-Pape produced, although the 150 or so cases of the Secret des Sabon are virtually impossible to find, which is rather sad, given that it is one of the greatest wines produced on the planet.

2006 Châteauneuf-du-Pape Cuvée Prestige	93	now–2022
2005 Châteauneuf-du-Pape Cuvée Prestige	93+	2011–2020
2004 Châteauneuf-du-Pape Cuvée Prestige	91	now–2022
2003 Châteauneuf-du-Pape Cuvée Prestige	92	now–2021
2001 Châteauneuf-du-Pape Cuvée Prestige	94	now–2022
2006 Châteauneuf-du-Pape Cuvée Réserve	90	2010–2025+
2005 Châteauneuf-du-Pape Cuvée Réserve	90	now–2020
2004 Châteauneuf-du-Pape Cuvée Réserve	89	now–2015
2003 Châteauneuf-du-Pape Cuvée Réserve	89	now–2015
2001 Châteauneuf-du-Pape Cuvée Réserve	90	now–2016
2006 Châteauneuf-du-Pape Les Olivets	90	now–2017
2005 Châteauneuf-du-Pape Les Olivets	89	now–2015
2004 Châteauneuf-du-Pape Les Olivets	86	now–2014
2003 Châteauneuf-du-Pape Les Olivets	88	now–2013
2001 Châteauneuf-du-Pape Les Olivets	89	now–2012
2006 Châteauneuf-du-Pape Secret des Sabon	95	2012–2037
2005 Châteauneuf-du-Pape Secret des Sabon	96	2014–2034
2004 Châteauneuf-du-Pape Secret des Sabon	95	now–2027
2003 Châteauneuf-du-Pape Secret des Sabon	96	now–2021+
2001 Châteauneuf-du-Pape Secret des Sabon	100	now–2025
2000 Châteauneuf-du-Pape Secret des Sabon	94	now–2020
1998 Châteauneuf-du-Pape Secret des Sabon	100	now–2036

DOMAINE ST.-BENOÎT * * *
CHÂTEAUNEUF-DU-PAPE $25.00–$50.00

This estate offers five cuvées, the lightest, most straightforward being Soleil et Festins, the most concentrated, ageworthy effort the Grande Garde. This relatively new estate, created in 1989, turns out interesting, high-quality Châteauneuf-du-Pape from nearly four dozen vineyard parcels spread throughout the appellation, but I do wonder if there are not too many cuvées emerging from St.-Benoît.

2004 Châteauneuf-du-Pape Cuvée XIII	83	now–2011
2003 Châteauneuf-du-Pape Cuvée XIII	86	now–2014
2001 Châteauneuf-du-Pape Cuvée XIII	91	now–2018
2005 Châteauneuf-du-Pape Grande Garde	89	2011–2018
2004 Châteauneuf-du-Pape Grande Garde	89	2010–2017
2003 Châteauneuf-du-Pape Grande Garde	86?	now–2016
2001 Châteauneuf-du-Pape Grande Garde	90	now–2020
2000 Châteauneuf-du-Pape Grande Garde	90	now–2015
2004 Châteauneuf-du-Pape Soleil et Festins	85	now–2011

2003 Châteauneuf-du-Pape Soleil et Festins	86	now–2011
2001 Châteauneuf-du-Pape Soleil et Festins	87	now–2011
2004 Châteauneuf-du-Pape La Truffière	88	now–2015
2003 Châteauneuf-du-Pape La Truffière	88	now–2011

ST.-COSME * * * * *
GIGONDAS
CHÂTEAU ST.-COSME $18.00–$45.00; ST.-COSME $10.00–$35.00

St.-Cosme is another example of a young, passionate vigneron, in this case Louis Barruol, not only resurrecting the fortunes of the estate's vineyards in Gigondas but starting a high-quality, limited production *négociant* business that is doing stunning work throughout the Rhône Valley. The *négociant* wines are sold under the St.-Cosme label and the estate wines are called Château St.-Cosme.

CHÂTEAU ST.-COSME

2005 Gigondas	91	2010–2022
2004 Gigondas	89	now–2015
2003 Gigondas	89	now–2014
2002 Gigondas	88	now–2010
2001 Gigondas	91	now–2014
2000 Gigondas	90	now–2013
2005 Gigondas Hominis Fides	96	2010–2026
2004 Gigondas Hominis Fides	94	2009–2022
2003 Gigondas Hominis Fides	95	now–2021+
2005 Gigondas Valbelle	93	now–2018
2004 Gigondas Valbelle	92	now–2017
2003 Gigondas Valbelle	95	now–2018
2001 Gigondas Valbelle	93	now–2016

ST.-COSME—*NÉGOCIANT* WINES

2005 Châteauneuf-du-Pape	92	now–2022
2004 Châteauneuf-du-Pape	90	now–2017
2003 Châteauneuf-du-Pape	91	now–2018
2001 Châteauneuf-du-Pape	94	now–2015
2005 Côte Rôtie	90+	2011–2018
2003 Côte Rôtie	93	now–2020
2005 Côtes du Rhône Les Deux Albions	88	now
2004 Côtes du Rhône Les Deux Albions	89	now
2006 Côtes du Rhône Le Poste Blanc	88	now
2005 Côtes du Ventoux Domaine de la Crillonne	88	now

DOMAINE ST.-DAMIEN * * *
GIGONDAS $20.00–$31.00

Joël Saurel, the up-and-coming young Gigondas producer at this estate, has changed things here, moving from rustic, old-style Gigondas to traditionally made offerings that process more purity, texture, and intensity. These unfined, unfiltered offerings all merit attention.

2005 Gigondas Cuvée Spéciale La Louisiane	90+	2011–2018
2004 Gigondas Cuvée Spéciale La Louisiane	91	now–2022
2000 Gigondas Cuvée Spéciale La Louisiane	87	now
2005 Gigondas Les Souteyrades	90	2010–2018
2004 Gigondas Les Souteyrades	89	now–2019

2003 Gigondas Les Souteyrades	90	now–2013
2001 Gigondas Les Souteyrades	88+	now–2014
2005 Gigondas Vieilles Vignes	87	now–2016
2004 Gigondas Vieilles Vignes	87	now–2015
2003 Gigondas Vieilles Vignes	89	now–2011
2001 Gigondas Vieilles Vignes	88	now–2012

ST.-DÉSIRAT CAVES COOPERATIVE ✱ ✱ ✱
NORTHERN RHÔNE $25.00–$30.00

Out of one of the best-run cooperatives in the Rhône Valley, the wines from St.-Désirat should never be overlooked. In addition to being fairly priced, their finest cuvées of St.-Joseph (which includes the Cuvée Côte Diane) are impeccably well made.

DOMAINE ST.-GAYAN ✱ ✱ ✱
GIGONDAS $28.00–$38.00

One of the archconservative, traditional estates, St.-Gayan has modernized ever so slightly. I am glad to see they are bottling earlier than in the past, thus permitting the wines to hold their fruit and reveal more charm and density in their youth. This is a reliable source of good wine.

2003 Châteauneuf-du-Pape	86	now–2010
2005 Gigondas	89	now–2019
2004 Gigondas	87	now–2011
2003 Gigondas	87	now–2011
2001 Gigondas	86	now–2012
2000 Gigondas	89	now–2010
2005 Gigondas Font Maria	89	2010–2020
2004 Gigondas Font Maria	89	now–2015
2003 Gigondas Font Maria	88	now–2013
2001 Gigondas Font Maria	88	now–2014
2000 Gigondas Font Maria	89+	now–2015

DOMAINE DE ST.-PAUL ✱ ✱ ✱
CHÂTEAUNEUF-DU-PAPE $28.00–$34.00

This estate, owned by Eli Jeune of Grand Tinel, produces solidly robust Châteauneuf-du-Papes.

2005 Châteauneuf-du-Pape	87	row–2017
2004 Châteauneuf-du-Pape	87	row–2012
2003 Châteauneuf-du-Pape	85	row–2013
2001 Châteauneuf-du-Pape	88	row–2013
2004 Châteauneuf-du-Pape Cuvée Jumille	88	row–2016
2003 Châteauneuf-du-Pape Cuvée Jumille	90	row–2016

DOMAINE DE ST.-PRÉFERT ✱ ✱ ✱ ✱/✱ ✱ ✱ ✱ ✱
CHÂTEAUNEUF-DU-PAPE $45.00–$60.00

One can't speak highly enough of the efforts by proprietress Isabel Ferrando, who has resurrected this unheralded estate in Châteauneuf-du-Pape. Since 2003 these have been beautifully made wines that merit serious attention. The Domaine de St.-Préfert is clearly one of the up-and-coming superstars of the Côtes du Rhône.

2004 Châteauneuf-du-Pape	90	now–2016
2006 Châteauneuf-du-Pape Collection Charles Giraud	93	2011–2022
2005 Châteauneuf-du-Pape Collection Charles Giraud	93+	2010–2025
2004 Châteauneuf-du-Pape Collection Charles Giraud	90	now–2018
2003 Châteauneuf-du-Pape Collection Charles Giraud	96	now–2018
2006 Châteauneuf-du-Pape Réserve Auguste Favier	92	now–2022
2005 Châteauneuf-du-Pape Réserve Auguste Favier	92+	2010–2025
2004 Châteauneuf-du-Pape Réserve Auguste Favier	92	now–2021
2003 Châteauneuf-du-Pape Réserve Auguste Favier	95	now–2018

DOMAINE DE ST.-SIFFREIN * * *
CHÂTEAUNEUF-DU-PAPE $30.00

Very good, but rarely superb, Châteauneuf-du-Pape emerges from this estate. I like the consistency, fair pricing, and the fact that it is always Provençal in character.

2006 Châteauneuf-du-Pape	89	now–2019
2005 Châteauneuf-du-Pape	90	now–2022+
2004 Châteauneuf-du-Pape	87	now–2013
2003 Châteauneuf-du-Pape	89	now–2013
2001 Châteauneuf-du-Pape	89	now–2012
2000 Châteauneuf-du-Pape	87	now–2010
1999 Châteauneuf-du-Pape	89	now–2012
2003 Côtes du Rhône-Villages	85	now

LE SANG DES CAILLOUX * * * *
VACQUEYRAS $16.00–$42.00

Over the last several years this estate has emerged as a superstar in Vacqueyras. They produce unfined, unfiltered, full-bodied Vacqueyras that is a consistent reference point for the appellation. The wines are named after the proprietor's daughters. The Cuvée Lopy is frequently named the Vacqueyras of the vintage.

2003 Vacqueyras Cuvée Azalaïs	85?	now
2000 Vacqueyras Cuvée Azalaïs	90	now–2011
2005 Vacqueyras Cuvée Doucinello	92	now–2017
2000 Vacqueyras Cuvée Doucinello	90	now
1999 Vacqueyras Cuvée Doucinello	90	now
2004 Vacqueyras Cuvée Floureto	88?	now–2014
2001 Vacqueyras Cuvée Floureto	91	now–2014
2005 Vacqueyras Cuvée Lopy	92	now–2022
2004 Vacqueyras Cuvée Lopy	91	now–2015
2003 Vacqueyras Cuvée Lopy	87?	now–2010
2001 Vacqueyras Cuvée Lopy	93	now–2015
2000 Vacqueyras Cuvée Lopy	93	now–2013
1999 Vacqueyras Cuvée Lopy	92	now–2012

DOMAINE SANTA DUC * * * * *
GIGONDAS $10.00–$48.00

One of the stars of Gigondas, proprietor Yves Gras turns out some of the most complete, concentrated, long-lived, potentially complex wines of the southern Rhône. Other than his standard Gigondas, he also produces a Cuvée Les Hautes Garrigues. Gras also offers a line of *négociant* wines under the label Santa Duc Séléctions.

DOMAINE SANTA DUC

2005 Gigondas	91	2010–2025
2004 Gigondas	90	now–2015
2003 Gigondas	90	now–2021
2002 Gigondas	86	now–2012
2001 Gigondas	90+	now–2019
2000 Gigondas	90	now–2015
1999 Gigondas	89	now–2011
2005 Gigondas Les Hautes Garrigues Cuvée Prestige	94+	2012–2032
2004 Gigondas Les Hautes Garrigues Cuvée Prestige	93	now–2022
2003 Gigondas Les Hautes Garrigues Cuvée Prestige	92	now–2024
2001 Gigondas Les Hautes Garrigues Cuvée Prestige	93+	now–2017
2000 Gigondas Les Hautes Garrigues Cuvée Prestige	94	now–2020
1999 Gigondas Les Hautes Garrigues Cuvée Prestige	92	now–2016

SANTA DUC SELECTIONS

2006 Côtes du Rhône Sablet Blanc	88	now
2005 Côtes du Rhône Vieilles Vignes	88	now

CHÂTEAU DE SÉGRIÈS ✶✶✶
CÔTES DU RHÔNE $10.00–$27.00

This has been an up-and-coming estate over the last six to seven years. The proprietor, Henri de Lanzac, has made significant improvements to this well-known but often underachieving estate. With the help of his cousin, Christian Delorme, of the superbly run Domaine de la Mordorée (which produces top-notch Châteauneuf-du-Pape and Lirac), Lanzac continues to produce better, cleaner, more complete and concentrated wines and has made the Château de Ségriès a property to follow. While the 2004s are not as strong as previous vintages, they are well made, and the regular Côtes du Rhônes represent good value.

2005 Côtes du Rhône	87	now
2005 Côtes du Rhône Clos de l'Hermitage	90	now–2016
2004 Côtes du Rhône Clos de l'Hermitage	87	now–2014
2003 Côtes du Rhône Clos de l'Hermitage	90+	now–2015+
2005 Lirac Cuvée Réservée	86	now–2011
2004 Lirac Cuvée Réservée	86	now–2010

DOMAINE DES SÉNÉCHAUX ✶✶✶✶
CHÂTEAUNEUF-DU-PAPE $30.00–$35.00

This relatively large estate was recently sold to a syndicate headed by the proprietor of the well-known Château Lynch-Bages in Pauillac, Jean-Michel Cazes. This can only be good news for this estate, which always made good wine but now has the potential to push things to the upper echelons of Châteauneuf-du-Pape.

2006 Châteauneuf-du-Pape	92	now–2022
2005 Châteauneuf-du-Pape	90	now–2018
2004 Châteauneuf-du-Pape	90	now–2018
2003 Châteauneuf-du-Pape	90	now–2016
2001 Châteauneuf-du-Pape	89	now–2014
2000 Châteauneuf-du-Pape	88	now–2011
1999 Châteauneuf-du-Pape	89	now–2013

CHÂTEAU SIGNAC ★★★★
CHUSCLAN $14.00–$16.00

Château Signac is a noteworthy estate in the somewhat forgotten Côtes du Rhône village of Chusclan fashioning high-quality blends of Syrah, Grenache, Mourvèdre, and Cinsault.

2003 Côtes du Rhône Le Secret	88	now–2010
2005 Côtes du Rhône-Villages Chusclan Combe d'Enfer	89	now–2013
2005 Côtes du Rhône-Villages Chusclan Cuvée Tradition	87	now–2010
2003 Côtes du Rhône-Villages Chusclan Mélodie d'Amour	86	now
2001 Côtes du Rhône-Villages Chusclan Mélodie d'Amour	89	now
2003 Côtes du Rhône-Villages Chusclan Signac Le Secret	91	now–2015
2005 Côtes du Rhône-Villages Chusclan Terre Amata	89+	now–2012
2004 Côtes du Rhône-Villages Chusclan Terre Amata	89	now–2011
2003 Côtes du Rhône-Villages Chusclan Terre Amata	90	now
2001 Côtes du Rhône-Villages Chusclan Terre Amata	90	now

CHÂTEAU SIMIAN ★★★
CHÂTEAUNEUF-DU-PAPE $10.00–$32.00

This tiny estate of 10 acres, owned by Yves and Jean-Pierre Serguier, is beautifully situated on the plateau behind the village, between the stony vineyards of Château Cabrières and Château Mont Redon.

2005 Châteauneuf-du-Pape	88	now–2017
2004 Châteauneuf-du-Pape	87	now

DOMAINE DE LA SOLITUDE ★★★★
CHÂTEAUNEUF-DU-PAPE $28.00–$250.00

One of the great names of the '60s, Solitude began producing somewhat commercial and insipid wines in the '70s and '80s. However, they have returned to form, producing a stunning array of Châteauneuf-du-Papes as well as some very good Côtes du Rhônes. Given the fact that it is a large estate (over 100 acres) with many old-vine parcels, Solitude is an important producer of top Châteauneuf-du Papes.

2005 Châteauneuf-du-Pape	90	now–2022
2004 Châteauneuf-du-Pape	89	now–2017
2003 Châteauneuf-du-Pape	89	now–2013
2001 Châteauneuf-du-Pape	88	now–2012
2000 Châteauneuf-du-Pape	89	now–2013
2003 Châteauneuf-du-Pape Blanc	88	now
2001 Châteauneuf-du-Pape Blanc	88	now
2005 Châteauneuf-du-Pape Cuvée Barberini	90	2010–2025+
2004 Châteauneuf-du-Pape Cuvée Barberini	92	now–2022
2001 Châteauneuf-du-Pape Cuvée Barberini	93	now–2017
2003 Châteauneuf-du-Pape Cuvée Barberini Blanc	90	now
2005 Châteauneuf-du-Pape Réserve Secrète	92+	2012–2042
2004 Châteauneuf-du-Pape Réserve Secrète	93+	2010–2030
2001 Châteauneuf-du-Pape Réserve Secrète	96	now–2020
2000 Châteauneuf-du-Pape Réserve Secrète	94	now–2020

MARC SORREL ★★★★
HERMITAGE $18.00–$250.00

This small estate, making artisanal-styled wines, usually hits the high notes with their single-vineyard offerings of Les Rocoules white Hermitage and Le Gréal red Hermitage (actually a blend of Méal and Greffieux). Marc Sorrel has also been increasing his production of both red and white Crozes-Hermitage, wines meant for easy, quick consumption.

2005 Crozes-Hermitage	85	now–2011
2004 Crozes-Hermitage	81	now
2003 Crozes-Hermitage	89	now–2013
2004 Crozes-Hermitage Blanc	83	now
2003 Crozes-Hermitage Blanc	87	now
2005 Hermitage	89+	2012–2022
2004 Hermitage	86	now–2015
2003 Hermitage	91	now–2021
2001 Hermitage	88	now–2018
2000 Hermitage	88	now–2010
2005 Hermitage Blanc	89	now–2017
2004 Hermitage Blanc	87	now–2016
2003 Hermitage Blanc	92	now–2014
2005 Hermitage Le Gréal	91+	2014–2030
2004 Hermitage Le Gréal	90	now–2016
2003 Hermitage Le Gréal	96+	now–2034
2005 Hermitage Les Rocoules Blanc	93	now–2025
2004 Hermitage Les Rocoules Blanc	91	now–2021
2003 Hermitage Les Rocoules Blanc	94	now–2011
2001 Hermitage Les Rocoules Blanc	93	now–2018

DOMAINE LA SOUMADE ★★★★★
RASTEAU $12.00–$55.00

Domaine La Soumade's charismatic proprietor, André Romero, is best known for his full-throttle offerings from Rasteau, his home base. In many ways, Romero is a smaller, more extroverted version of Châteauneuf-du-Pape's reclusive Henri Bonneau. He fashions concentrated, exuberant wines that mirror his over-the-top personality. Additionally, he produces two of the Rhône's finest values, the Côtes du Rhône Les Violettes and the straightforward Rasteau Cuvée Prestige. Romero has also recently branched out into Gigondas.

2004 Cabernet Sauvignon Vin de Pays de la Principaute d'Orange	89	now–2012
2003 Cabernet Sauvignon Vin de Pays de la Principaute d'Orange	87?	now–2012
2005 Châteauneuf-du-Pape	88	now–2015
2005 Côtes du Rhône Les Violettes	90	2009–2019
2003 Côtes du Rhône Les Violettes	90	now–2010
2005 Côtes du Rhône-Villages Rasteau Cuvée Confiance	90	2013–2028
2004 Côtes du Rhône-Villages Rasteau Cuvée Confiance	90	now–2019
2003 Côtes du Rhône-Villages Rasteau Cuvée Confiance	92	now–2020

2001 Côtes du Rhône-Villages Rasteau Cuvée Confiance	90	now–2016
2004 Côtes du Rhône-Villages Rasteau Cuvée Prestige	89	now–2017
2003 Côtes du Rhône-Villages Rasteau Cuvée Prestige	88	now–2013
2005 Côtes du Rhône-Villages Rasteau Fleur de Confiance	93+	2015–2035
2004 Côtes du Rhône-Villages Rasteau Fleur de Confiance	91+	2010–2025
2003 Côtes du Rhône-Villages Rasteau Fleur de Confiance	95	now–2021
2001 Côtes du Rhône-Villages Rasteau Fleur de Confiance	92+	now–2019

JEAN-MICHEL STEPHAN ★★★★
CÔTE RÔTIE $40.00–$75.00

A young grower who has quickly emerged as someone to watch, Jean-Michel Stephan utilizes all *barriques,* of which approximately 50% are new. Moreover, he completely destems the grapes. His wines, which are all produced from fruit grown in the southern half of Côte Rôtie, primarily from the Côte Blonde, tend to be low-tech, artisanal Côte Rôties.

2004 Côte Rôtie	87	now–2012
2003 Côte Rôtie	91	now–2016
2001 Côte Rôtie	78	now
2000 Côte Rôtie	83	now
2005 Côte Rôtie Côteau de Tupin	89	2011–2017
2004 Côte Rôtie Côteau de Tupin	88	now–2013
2003 Côte Rôtie Côteau de Tupin	95	now–2018
2001 Côte Rôtie Côteau de Tupin	88	now–2011
2005 Côte Rôtie Vieilles Vignes en Côteau	91	2011–2021
2004 Côte Rôtie Vieilles Vignes en Côteau	86?	now–2012
2003 Côte Rôtie Vieilles Vignes en Côteau	94	now–2018
2001 Côte Rôtie Vieilles Vignes en Côteau	87	now–2011

TARDIEU-LAURENT ★★★★
NORTHERN AND SOUTHERN RHÔNE $16.00–$120.00

Michel Tardieu, in partnership with Burgundian Dominique Laurent, formed this *négociant* company and employed the services of the renowned southern Rhône Valley oenologist Philippe Cambie. A variety of cuvées are produced, from nearly every northern and southern Rhône appellation. Most of these wines are meant for long-term aging, with my personal preferences tending to lean toward the southern Rhône selections. Buyers will need to be patient, even with the softer Grenache-based cuvées.

2005 Châteauneuf-du-Pape	89	2010–2025
2004 Châteauneuf-du-Pape	87	now–2016
2003 Châteauneuf-du-Pape	89	now–2015
2001 Châteauneuf-du-Pape	91	now–2017
2000 Châteauneuf-du-Pape	90	now–2013
2006 Châteauneuf-du-Pape Cuvée Spéciale	93	now–2025
2005 Châteauneuf-du-Pape Cuvée Spéciale	93	2015–2030
2004 Châteauneuf-du-Pape Cuvée Spéciale	91	now–2024
2003 Châteauneuf-du-Pape Cuvée Spéciale	92	now–2021+
2006 Châteauneuf-du-Pape Vieilles Vignes	93	now–2032

2005 Châteauneuf-du-Pape Vieilles Vignes	91	2010–2025
2004 Châteauneuf-du-Pape Vieilles Vignes	91	2010–2021+
2003 Châteauneuf-du-Pape Vieilles Vignes	92	2009–2025
2001 Châteauneuf-du-Pape Vieilles Vignes	93	now–2018
2000 Châteauneuf-du-Pape Vieilles Vignes	94	now–2020
1999 Châteauneuf-du-Pape Vieilles Vignes	92	now–2020
1998 Châteauneuf-du-Pape Vieilles Vignes	94	now–2019
2003 Châteauneuf-du-Pape Vieilles Vignes Cuvée Spéciale	94	now–2020
2001 Châteauneuf-du-Pape Vieilles Vignes Cuvée Spéciale	95+	now–2023
2004 Cornas Côteaux	89	now–2018
2001 Cornas Côteaux	90	now–2018+
2004 Cornas Vieilles Vignes	89	now–2015
2003 Cornas Vieilles Vignes	94	now–2026+
2001 Cornas Vieilles Vignes	90	now–2018
2000 Cornas Vieilles Vignes	91	now–2016
2004 Côte Rôtie	88	now–2018
2003 Côte Rôtie	91	now–2021
2005 Côtes du Rhône Guy Louis	90	now–2018
2004 Côtes du Rhône Guy Louis	88	now–2012
2003 Côtes du Rhône Guy Louis	90	now–2012
2005 Gigondas Vieilles Vignes	90	now–2017
2004 Gigondas Vieilles Vignes	89	now–2016
2004 Hermitage	88	2012–2020
2003 Hermitage	95+	now–2056
2001 Hermitage	90	now–2018
2005 Rasteau Vieilles Vignes	91	2010–2025
2003 Rasteau Vieilles Vignes	90	now–2014
2001 Rasteau Vieilles Vignes	89	now–2018
2005 Vacqueyras Vieilles Vignes	91	now–2019
2004 Vacqueyras Vieilles Vignes	89	now–2016

ÉRIC TEXIER * * *
SOUTHERN AND NORTHERN RHÔNE $16.00–$65.00

Burgundian Eric Texier produces stylish, graceful, surprisingly elegant Rhône Valley reds. Consumers should be aware that Texier is a *négociant* operating in the Beaujolais area from extremely cold cellars. He is also fashioning impressive efforts, especially an old-vine cuvée of Syrah, from the forgotten Côtes du Rhône appellation of Brèzeme. Additionally, he has made some remarkable selections in Côtes du Rhône-Villages, particularly Vaison La Romaine, Séguret, and St.-Gervais.

DOMAINE DE LA TOURADE * * *
GIGONDAS $26.00–$32.00

Proprietor André Richard ages his Cuvée Morgan in barrel, while the Font des Aïeux spends time in *foudre*.

2000 Gigondas Cuvée Morgan	90	now–2014
2003 Gigondas Font des Aïeux	88	now–2012
2000 Gigondas Font des Aïeux	91	now–2015

CHÂTEAU DES TOURS ★★★★
CÔTES DU RHÔNE $15.00–$30.00

This is the home estate of Emmanuel Reynaud, the winemaker at Rayas. These are some-times idiosyncratic wines that often have a deceptively light color but rather powerful, intense flavors. The top wine tends to be the Vacqueyras, followed by the Côtes du Rhône.

2004 Côtes du Rhône	86	now–2012
2003 Côtes du Rhône	89	now
2001 Côtes du Rhône	86	now
2000 Côtes du Rhône	86	now
2004 Vacqueyras	86	now–2015
2003 Vacqueyras	91	now–2017
2001 Vacqueyras	88	now
2000 Vacqueyras	87	now–2010

DOMAINE DU TRAPADIS ★★★
RASTEAU $20.00–$28.00

The Domaine du Trapadis is another excellent underrated, unknown source of top-quality Rasteau.

CHÂTEAU DU TRIGNON ★★/★★★
GIGONDAS $14.00–$25.00

The Château du Trignon has done some serious empire building since the late 1980s. Under the leadership of Pascal Roux the wine quality, which seemed to have slipped badly in 1991 and 1992, has rebounded, with good efforts in 1994 and 1995. Moreover, the wines have taken on greater richness, more natural texture, and are bottled with less trauma.

Fining and filtration appear to have been reduced considerably, in favor of putting in the bottle essentially the same wine that was made in the vineyard. Given the increased intensity of Trignon wines, these wines, usually best drunk within their first four to five years, give every indication in top vintages since 1995 of lasting for a decade or more.

DOMAINE TRINTIGNANT ★★★
CHÂTEAUNEUF-DU-PAPE $30.00–$35.00

This estate rarely participates in any tastings, but it seems to do well selling its wines without reviews from the wine press. They tend to be straightforward, fleshy, fat, fruity, well-made Châteauneuf-du-Papes that are best drunk early in life.

DOMAINE DU TUNNEL ★★★/★★★★
CORNAS $35.00–$65.00

A young producer fashioning an elegantly styled Cornas in a quasimodern style, Stéphane Robert believes in complete destemming as well as barrel aging.

2004 Cornas	88	now–2013
2003 Cornas	88	now–2013
2001 Cornas	88	now–2015
2000 Cornas Cuvée Prestige	90+	now–2014
2005 St.-Joseph	88	now–2015

PIERRE USSEGLIO ★ ★ ★ ★ ★
CHÂTEAUNEUF-DU-PAPE $16.00–$225.00

This estate has always made good wines, but with the ascendancy of brothers Jean-Pierre and Thierry Usseglio it has become one of Châteauneuf-du-Pape's superstars. All of the offerings are noteworthy, including their traditional cuvée of Châteauneuf-du-Pape, the old-vine effort called Cuvée de Mon Aïeul, and the top-of-the-line Réserve des Deux Frères (essentially the same wine as Mon Aïeul, but with more press wine and aged in small and medium-sized *barriques*). One of this estate's sleeper selections is their delicious Côtes du Rhône.

2006 Châteauneuf-du-Pape Tradition	92	now–2019
2005 Châteauneuf-du-Pape Tradition	89	2010–2025
2004 Châteauneuf-du-Pape Tradition	89	now–2017
2003 Châteauneuf-du-Pape Tradition	92	now–2018
1999 Châteauneuf-du-Pape Cuvée de Cinquantenaire	96	now–2023
2006 Châteauneuf-du-Pape Cuvée de Mon Aïeul	97	now–2022
2005 Châteauneuf-du-Pape Cuvée de Mon Aïeul	94+	2012–2023
2004 Châteauneuf-du-Pape Cuvée de Mon Aïeul	92	now–2022
2003 Châteauneuf-du-Pape Cuvée de Mon Aïeul	99	now–2020+
2001 Châteauneuf-du-Pape Cuvée de Mon Aïeul	97+	now–2026
2000 Châteauneuf-du-Pape Cuvée de Mon Aïeul	95	now–2020
1999 Châteauneuf-du-Pape Cuvée de Mon Aïeul	90	now–2021
1998 Châteauneuf-du-Pape Cuvée de Mon Aïeul	95	now–2031
2006 Châteauneuf-du-Pape Réserve des Deux Frères	99	2010–2035
2005 Châteauneuf-du-Pape Réserve des Deux Frères	95+	2014–2034
2003 Châteauneuf-du-Pape Réserve des Deux Frères	98+	now–2026+
2001 Châteauneuf-du-Pape Réserve des Deux Frères	99	now–2022+
2000 Châteauneuf-du-Pape Réserve des Deux Frères	98	now–2030

RAYMOND USSEGLIO ★ ★ ★ ★
CHÂTEAUNEUF-DU-PAPE $30.00–$65.00

Another member of the Usseglio family, Raymond turns out two beautiful Châteauneuf-du-Pape cuvées. The basic bottling is redolent with Provençal aromatics of *garrigue*, lavender, pepper, and spice. The old-vine effort, the Cuvée Impériale, is made from Grenache vines planted in the early 1900s. Usseglio's Châteauneuf-du-Pape Cuvée Girard is a 400-case lot selected by importer Peter Weygandt and bottled unfiltered. It is distinguished by the fact that it has the words "Cuvée Girard" in the upper part of the label.

2006 Châteauneuf-du-Pape	89	now–2022
2005 Châteauneuf-du-Pape	89	2010–2020
2004 Châteauneuf-du-Pape	87	now–2015
2003 Châteauneuf-du-Pape	88	now–2015
2001 Châteauneuf-du-Pape	90	now–2020
2000 Châteauneuf-du-Pape	90	now–2017
2006 Châteauneuf-du-Pape Cuvée Girard	91	now–2022
2005 Châteauneuf-du-Pape Cuvée Girard	90	2010–2025
2004 Châteauneuf-du-Pape Cuvée Girard	90	now–2015
2003 Châteauneuf-du-Pape Cuvée Girard	89	now–2018
2001 Châteauneuf-du-Pape Cuvée Girard	90	now–2016
2000 Châteauneuf-du-Pape Cuvée Girard	90	now–2016
2006 Châteauneuf-du-Pape Cuvée Impériale	93	now–2022+
2005 Châteauneuf-du-Pape Cuvée Impériale	92	2010–2026

2004 Châteauneuf-du-Pape Cuvée Impériale	90	now–2021+
2003 Châteauneuf-du-Pape Cuvée Impériale	92	now–2021
2001 Châteauneuf-du-Pape Cuvée Impériale	92+	now–2016
2000 Châteauneuf-du-Pape Cuvée Impériale	91+	now–2020

CHÂTEAU VALCOMBE ✶✶✶
CÔTES DU VENTOUX $22.00–$25.00

The Château Valcombe is a serious estate in an area I predict will be producing more and more wines of significant quality.

CUVÉE DU VATICAN ✶✶✶✶
CHÂTEAUNEUF-DU-PAPE $12.00–$65.00

A renaissance in quality has occurred at this estate under the young Jean-Marc Diffonty, who took over the reins from his father a number of years ago. Only a few concessions have been made to modern oenology at this 55-acre estate. The basic cuvée is a traditional Châteauneuf-du-Pape made from primarily Grenache with some Syrah and Mourvèdre. Jean-Marc has also introduced a special cuvée called Réserve Sixtine, which is meant to be a modernist approach to winemaking, as it is a blend of 50% Grenache and the rest Syrah and Mourvèdre (the latter two varietals spend time in small new oak). Cuvée du Vatican also makes a very good white wine.

2006 Châteauneuf-du-Pape	88	now–2022
2005 Châteauneuf-du-Pape	89+	2013–2030
2004 Châteauneuf-du-Pape	86	now–2014
2003 Châteauneuf-du-Pape	88	now–2014
2001 Châteauneuf-du-Pape	91	now–2016
2000 Châteauneuf-du-Pape	90	now–2015
2006 Châteauneuf-du-Pape Réserve Sixtine	90	2012–2025
2005 Châteauneuf-du-Pape Réserve Sixtine	92+	2012–2032
2004 Châteauneuf-du-Pape Réserve Sixtine	91	2010–2025
2003 Châteauneuf-du-Pape Réserve Sixtine	95	2009–2030
2001 Châteauneuf-du-Pape Réserve Sixtine	95	now–2020+
2000 Châteauneuf-du-Pape Réserve Sixtine	93+	now–2020

CHÂTEAU VAUDIEU ✶✶✶
CHÂTEAUNEUF-DU-PAPE $32.00–$45.00

A huge estate located south of Rayas, Vaudieu, which has consistently been an underperformer, possesses top-flight vineyards that include an impressive percentage of old vines. The estate appears to have gotten more serious over the last few vintages with both their regular Châteauneuf-du-Pape and their blend of 50% Grenache and 50% Syrah and Mourvèdre called Val de Dieu.

2006 Châteauneuf-du-Pape	88	now–2013
2005 Châteauneuf-du-Pape	89	now–2015
2004 Châteauneuf-du-Pape	87	now–2013
2003 Châteauneuf-du-Pape	88	now–2015
2001 Châteauneuf-du-Pape	84	now–2011
2000 Châteauneuf-du-Pape	87	now–2011
2006 Châteauneuf-du-Pape Cuvée Val de Dieu	90	now–2022
2005 Châteauneuf-du-Pape Cuvée Val de Dieu	90	now–2020
2004 Châteauneuf-du-Pape Cuvée Val de Dieu	90	now–2018
2003 Châteauneuf-du-Pape Cuvée Val de Dieu	90	now–2019+

GEORGES VERNAY ★★★★
CONDRIEU $14.00–$102.00

The lovely Christine Vernay is in charge of the estate made famous by her father, Georges. She continues to produce the reference-point wine for Condrieu, the famed Côteaux du Vernon, from a four-acre parcel of old vines planted on a steep hillside. Other top cuvées include Les Chaillées de l'Enfer.

RED WINES

2003 Côte Rôtie Blonde du Seigneur	88	now–2010
2000 Côte Rôtie Blonde du Seigneur	86	now
2003 Côte Rôtie Maison Rouge	90	now–2012
1999 Côte Rôtie Maison Rouge	92	now–2018

WHITE WINES

2006 Condrieu Les Chaillées de l'Enfer	91	now
2005 Condrieu Les Chaillées de l'Enfer	90	now
2005 Condrieu Côteaux de Vernon	94	now
2004 Condrieu Côteaux de Vernon	94	now
2005 Condrieu Les Terrasses de l'Empire	91	now–2010
2004 Condrieu Les Terrasses de l'Empire	89	now

NOËL VERSET ★★★★
CORNAS $45.00

Now that Verset has retired, these wines are of academic interest only. In the '70s, '80s, and '90s, Noël Verset's Cornas was as good as any producer's, including that of August Clape.

VIDAL-FLEURY ★★★
NORTHERN RHÔNE $10.00–$25.00

Founded in 1781, this firm continues to evolve, with major investments taking place in the cellar. No one should assume that Vidal-Fleury represents the second label of its famous proprietor, Marcel Guigal. This house has a separate identity, having been admirably managed by Jean-Pierre Rochias since Guigal acquired it in the mid-1980s. The release of Vidal-Fleury's wines is somewhat unusual, with some of the red wine cuvées held back for a number of years (e.g., the 1996 Cornas). Nevertheless, this is an undeniable source of top-notch values, particularly their southern Rhône reds from the Côtes du Ventoux, Côtes du Rhône-Villages, Vacqueyras, and Côtes du Rhône.

DOMAINE DE LA VIEILLE JULIENNE ★★★★★
CHÂTEAUNEUF-DU-PAPE $16.00–$250.00

This is a superb estate producing traditional Châteauneuf-du-Papes made from spectacularly old vines and noninterventionistic winemaking. Beginning with the 1998 vintage, proprietor Jean-Paul Daumen has been making wines that are among the most glorious and longest-lived Châteauneuf-du-Papes of the village. He also fashions noteworthy Côtes du Rhônes as well as an amazing *vin de pays* made from Cabernet Sauvignon, Merlot, and Grenache. The latter wine has to be tasted to be believed.

2006 Châteauneuf-du-Pape Tradition	94	now–2027
2005 Châteauneuf-du-Pape Tradition	95+	2010–2030
2004 Châteauneuf-du-Pape Tradition	92	now–2029
2003 Châteauneuf-du-Pape Tradition	92	now–2022
2002 Châteauneuf-du-Pape Tradition	86	now
2001 Châteauneuf-du-Pape Tradition	90+	now–2018

2000 Châteauneuf-du-Pape Tradition	91	now–2018
2006 Châteauneuf-du-Pape Réserve	98	now–2037
2005 Châteauneuf-du-Pape Réserve	100	2012–2040
2003 Châteauneuf-du-Pape Réserve	100	2012–2035
2001 Châteauneuf-du-Pape Réserve	100	2010–2025
2000 Châteauneuf-du-Pape Réserve	99	now–2025
2001 Châteauneuf-du-Pape Vieilles Vignes	96+	now–2022+
2000 Châteauneuf-du-Pape Vieilles Vignes	97+	now–2025
1998 Châteauneuf-du-Pape Vieilles Vignes	96+	now–2031
2005 Côtes du Rhône	90	now–2017
2005 Côtes du Rhône La Bosse	94	now–2025

LE VIEUX DONJON * * * *
CHÂTEAUNEUF-DU-PAPE $27.00–$65.00

One of the most traditionally run estates of Châteauneuf-du-Pape, Le Vieux Donjon is a consistent source for superb wines, thanks to the diligent efforts of proprietors Lucien and Marie-Joseph Michel. Their old-style Châteauneufs will age magnificently for 15 to 20 years. The newest offering, a white Châteauneuf-du-Pape, has gotten stronger with each vintage.

2006 Châteauneuf-du-Pape	91	2012–2032
2005 Châteauneuf-du-Pape	92+	2011–2026
2004 Châteauneuf-du-Pape	90	now–2022
2003 Châteauneuf-du-Pape	94	now–2021
2001 Châteauneuf-du-Pape	93+	now–2019
2000 Châteauneuf-du-Pape	91	now–2016
1999 Châteauneuf-du-Pape	91	now–2020
1998 Châteauneuf-du-Pape	96	now–2026
2005 Châteauneuf-du-Pape Blanc	90	now
2004 Châteauneuf-du-Pape Blanc	89	now
2003 Châteauneuf-du-Pape Blanc	92	now

DOMAINE DU VIEUX LAZARET * * * *
CHÂTEAUNEUF-DU-PAPE $22.00–$45.00

Jérôme Quiot, one of Châteauneuf-du-Pape's most influential residents, has been fashioning serious, concentrated wines over the last few years. These fruit-driven, interesting, savory Châteauneuf-du-Papes include a basic cuvée and an old-vine offering called Cuvée Exceptionnelle. Prices remain very reasonable.

2006 Châteauneuf-du-Pape	88	now–2015
2005 Châteauneuf-du-Pape	89	now–2013
2004 Châteauneuf-du-Pape	87	now–2012
2003 Châteauneuf-du-Pape	88	now–2013
2001 Châteauneuf-du-Pape	87	now–2011
2000 Châteauneuf-du-Pape	88	now–2015
1999 Châteauneuf-du-Pape	86	now
2006 Châteauneuf-du-Pape Cuvée Exceptionnelle	92	now–2022
2005 Châteauneuf-du-Pape Cuvée Exceptionnelle	94	now–2017
2004 Châteauneuf-du-Pape Cuvée Exceptionnelle	89	now–2015
2003 Châteauneuf-du-Pape Cuvée Exceptionnelle	92	now–2020
2001 Châteauneuf-du-Pape Cuvée Exceptionnelle	90	now–2018+
2000 Châteauneuf-du-Pape Cuvée Exceptionnelle	91+	now–2016
1999 Châteauneuf-du-Pape Cuvée Exceptionnelle	90	now–2013

DOMAINE DU VIEUX TÉLÉGRAPHE ✶✶✶✶✶
CHÂTEAUNEUF-DU-PAPE $55.00–$65.00

This enormous vineyard in the eastern area of Châteauneuf-du-Pape owns significant old-vine sites located in one of the appellation's most favored sectors, La Crau. One of the benchmark producers of Châteauneuf-du-Pape, they produce a traditionally made wine dominated by Grenache (70%) with Syrah, Mourvèdre, and a few other varieties added to the blend. The introduction of a second wine, Vieux Mas des Papes, has allowed the proprietors to cull out the finest fruit for Vieux Télégraphe. In top vintages, it requires four to five years of bottle age and can easily last for two decades or more. For bargain hunters, their *vin de pays,* Le Pigoulet, is a noteworthy example.

LE PIGOULET

2005 Le Pigoulet Vin de Pays de Vaucluse	85	now

VIEUX-TÉLÉGRAPHE

2006 Châteauneuf-du-Pape	92	2011–2026+
2005 Châteauneuf-du-Pape	95+	2009–2030
2004 Châteauneuf-du-Pape	92	now–2022
2003 Châteauneuf-du-Pape	92+	now–2018
2001 Châteauneuf-du-Pape	93+	now–2020
2000 Châteauneuf-du-Pape	91	now–2025
1999 Châteauneuf-du-Pape	88	now–2018
1998 Châteauneuf-du-Pape	93	now–2026
2005 Châteauneuf-du-Pape Blanc		now–2011

VIEUX MAS DES PAPES

2005 Télégramme Châteauneuf-du-Pape	88	now–2015
2004 Télégramme Châteauneuf-du-Pape	89	now–2012
2004 Châteauneuf-du-Pape	87	now–2010
2003 Châteauneuf-du-Pape	87	now
2001 Châteauneuf-du-Pape	87	now–2012
1999 Châteauneuf-du-Pape	87	now–2011

DOMAINE FRANÇOIS VILLARD ✶✶✶✶
CONDRIEU $15.00–$55.00

One of the most talented young producers to emerge from the northern Rhône during the 1990s, François Villard has quickly developed a reputation for fine Condrieu and increasingly good reds from both St.-Joseph and Côte Rôtie.

2005 Condrieu Le Grand Vallon	93	now
2004 Condrieu Le Grand Vallon	92	now
2005 Condrieu de Poncins	90	now
2004 Condrieu de Poncins	90	now
2005 Condrieu Les Terrasses du Palat	91	now
2004 Condrieu Les Terrasses du Palat	90	now

DOMAINE VILLENEUVE ✶✶✶✶
CHÂTEAUNEUF-DU-PAPE $32.00–$55.00

From a vineyard planted in 1904, these are mostly Grenache-based, traditionally made, concentrated, long-lived Châteauneuf-du-Papes.

2006 Châteauneuf-du-Pape Vieilles Vignes	90	2009–2020
2005 Châteauneuf-du-Pape Vieilles Vignes	91+	2010–2025
2004 Châteauneuf-du-Pape Vieilles Vignes	89	now–2015
2003 Châteauneuf-du-Pape Vieilles Vignes	91	now–2021
2001 Châteauneuf-du-Pape Vieilles Vignes	89	now–2019
2000 Châteauneuf-du-Pape Vieilles Vignes	90	now–2018

ALAIN VOGE ★ ★ ★ ★
CORNAS $35.00–$100.00

The brilliant oenologist Albéric Mazoyers, who was Michel Chapoutier's technical director for many years, has recently been employed as the winemaker for Alain Voge, one of the benchmark cellars of Cornas. This has resulted in even more spectacular quality from the two Cornas cuvées for which Voge is renowned. An excellent Chablis-like white wine made from 100% Marsanne, the St.-Péray Fleur de Crusoll, was introduced several years ago.

2005 Cornas Les Vieilles Fontaines	95	now–2022
2004 Cornas Vieilles Fontaines	90	now–2021
2003 Cornas Vieilles Fontaines	93	2009–2025+
1999 Cornas Vieilles Fontaines	91	now–2015
2005 Cornas Vieilles Vignes	92	now–2022
2004 Cornas Vieilles Vignes	89+	now–2018
2003 Cornas Vieilles Vignes	92+	now–2018
2001 Cornas Vieilles Vignes	90	now–2014
2005 St.-Péray Fleur de Crussol	91	now
2004 St.-Péray Fleur de Crussol	87	now

A

Baptiste-Boutes, Domaine, 449
Bara, Paul, 410
Barbaresco (town), 795
Barbaresco (wine/region), 786, 787–90
　　aging potential of, 797
　　buying strategy for, 805
　　closer look at winemaking towns and
　　　　vineyards of, 794–96
　　flavors of, 791
　　guide to best multicommune wines
　　　　of, 802–3
　　guide to top vineyards and wines of,
　　　　798, 799, 801–2
　　important information about, 798
　　older vintages of, 808–9
　　overall quality level of, 798
　　ratings of best wines, 809–15
　　recent vintages of, 805–8
　　some thoughts on traditional and
　　　　modern styles of, 796–97
　　tasting commentaries for, 815–61
Barben, Mas de la, 449
Barbera, in California, 1103
Barbera, in Piedmont, 790, 798
　　aging potential of, 797
　　best single-vineyard wines, 803–4
　　flavors of, 791
Barbi, Fattoria dei Barbi, 891
Barca Velha, 957, 960
Barde-Haut, 124
Baret, 124
Barge, Gilles, 560
Barkan, 1443
Barmès-Buecher, 56–57
Barnaut, Edmond, 410
Barnett Vineyards, 1120
Barolo (village), 792, 793
Barolo (wine/region), 786, 787–90, 795
　　aging potential of, 797
　　blended wines of, 798, 802–3
　　buying strategy for, 805
　　closer look at winemaking towns and
　　　　vineyards of, 792–94
　　flavors of, 791
　　guide to best multicommune wines
　　　　of, 802–3
　　guide to top vineyards and wines of,
　　　　798–801
　　important information about, 798
　　older vintages of, 808–9
　　overall quality level of, 798

　　ratings of best wines, 809–15
　　recent vintages of, 805–8
　　some thoughts on traditional and
　　　　modern styles of, 796–97
　　tasting commentaries for, 815–61
Baronia del Monsant, 1037
Barossa Valley, 1358
Barrabaque, 124
Barral, Léon, 450
Barraud, Daniel, 298–99
barrels, 255–56
Barroche, La, 560
Barros, Almeida, 965
Barrot, Lucien, 560
Barry, Jim, 1378
Barsac, 87, 115
　　aging potential of recent top vintages
　　　　for finest wines of, 93
　　general flavor characteristics of, 92
　　rating best producers of, 110–11
　　vintage summaries for, 94–106
　　see also specific growers and producers
Barth, Andreas (Lubentiushof), 758
Barthod, Ghislaine, 299–300
Barville, Domaine, 561
Bas, Francesc Sanchez, 1037
Bassermann–Jordan, Dr. von, 729
Bastardo, 1016
Bastianich, 925
Bastide St.-Dominique, La, 561
Bastide St.-Vincent, 561
Batailley, 124
Batard, Serge, 489
Bâtard-Montrachet, 277
Batoca, 999
bâtonnage, 256, 1467
Battely, 1378
Baubiac, Domaine de, 450
Baudoin, Raymond, 249
Baudry, Bernard, 489
Bäuerl, 672
Baumard, Domaine des, 489–90
Bayer, Heribert—In Signo Leonis, 672
Béarn, 422
Beau Mistral, 561–62
Beau-Séjour Bécot, 125
Beau-Site, 125
Beau Soleil, 126
Beaucastel, Château de, 562–63
Beaujolais, 247, 255, 287–91
　　aging potential of, 288–89, 290

Boscq, Le, 131
Bosquet des Papes, 618
Bosquets, Domaine des, 619
Botrytis cinerea (noble rot) 91, 93, 1467
Bott-Geyl, 59–60
bottling, xx, 257
    fraudulent bottles of fine wine and,
        29
    to specification, 117–18
bottling date, 33
Bouchard, Cédric, 411
Bouchard Père et Fils, Maison, 307–09
Boudreaux Cellars, 1325
Bouissière, Domaine La, 569
Boulay, Gérard, 491
Bourboulenc:
    in Languedoc and Roussillon, 436
    in Provence, 517
    in Rhône Valley, 521
Bourgneuf-Vayron, 131–32
Bourgogne (appellation), 258, 259, 262
Bourgogne Aligoté, 248, 258
Bourgogne Chitry, 283
Bourgogne Côtes d'Auxerre, 283
Bourgogne Hautes–Côtes de Beaune, 258
Bourgogne Hautes–Côtes de Nuits, 258
Bourgogne Passetoutgrains, 248, 258
Bourgueil, 480–81, 482
Bouscat, 132
Bouscaut, 132
Bousquet, Jean, Domaine, 1348
Boutisse, 132
Bouvachon-Nomine, 569
Bouvier, 666
Bouzy, 400, 408
Bovio, Gianfranco, 819
Boxler, Albert, 60–61
Boyd-Cantenac, 183
Braccesca, La, 880
Brachetto, 790
Bradford Mountain, 1128
Braida, 819–20
Branaire-Ducru, 133
Brancaia, 880
Brand, 52
Branda, 133
branded Port, 1010
Brander Vineyard, 1129
Brandl, Günther, 672
Brane-Cantenac, 153–54
Branger, Claude, 491

Branon, 134
Branson Coach House, 1379
Brda, 1424
breathing, 12, 13
Brégeon, André-Michel, 491
Breggo Cellars, 1129
Bremerton, 1380
Bressades, Mas de, 451
Bressia, Bodegas, 1348
Bressy-Masson, 569–570
Bret Brothers/La Soufrandière, 309
Bréton, Cathérine et Pierre, 491–92
Breuer, Georg, 731
Brewer-Clifton, 1129–30
Brezza, 820
Brick House Vineyards, 1306
Bridlewood Winery, 1130
Brillette, 134
Brissac, 476
Brisson, 134
British Columbia, 1285, 1289
Broadbent, Michael, 36
Brocard, Jean-Marc, 309
Brochon, 264
Brokenwood, 1380
Brook, Stephen, 36
Brotte, 570
Brouilly, 290
Brovia, 820
Brown, 134
Bruce, David, 1130
Bründlmayer, Willi, 672–73
Bruneley, La, 570
Brunello di Montalcino, 786, 787, 862, 868
    aging potential of, 867
    buying strategy for, 871
    closer look at, 865–66
    flavors of, 863
Brusset, Domaine, 570
Bryant Family Vineyard, 1130
Bual, 1016
Buccella, 1131
Bugey, 428
Buhl, Reichsrat von, 731
Buisson-Charles, Domaine—Michel
        Buisson, 309
Bulgaria, 1423
Buller, R. L., & Son, 1380
Bunnell Family Cellar, 1325
Buoncristiani, 1131
Burgans, 1037

Cantonella, Celler de, 1039–40
Cap de Faugères, 137
Cap de Mourlin, 138
Capannelle, 882
Caparzo, 882
Capçanes, Celler de, 1040
Cape Barren, 1382
Cape d'Estaing, 1382
Capiaux Cellars, 1133
Capichera, 945
Cappellano, 822
Caprai, 945–46
Caramany, 453
carbonic maceration, 288, 1468
Carbonnieux, 138
Cardinale, 1133
Carema, 790, 792, 797
Carignan:
        in California, 1077, 1080
        in Languedoc and Roussillon,
            435–36, 437, 438, 441, 442, 444
        in Provence, 516
        in Spain (Cariñena), 1019, 1022
Carignan Blanc, 442
Carillon, Louis, Domaine, 310
Carina Cellars, 1133–34
Carinae, 1349
Cariñena (Carignan), 1019
Carlisle Winery and Vineyards, 1134–35
Carlot, Mas, 452
Carm, 966
Carmel Winery, 1443, 1447
Carménère:
        in Argentina, 1345
        in Chile, 1432
Carmes Haut-Brion, Les, 138
Carmignano, 862, 864, 867
Carnasciale, Podere Il, 902–3
Carnuntum, 664
Caro, Bodegas, 1349
Carodorum, 1040
Carr Vineyard and Winery, 1135
Carré, Le, 188
Carriere, J. K., Wines, 1307
Carroy, Jacques, 542
Carruades de Lafite, 192
Carsin, 139
Carter, Brian, Cellars, 1326
Cartlidge and Browne, 1135–36
Carver-Sutro, 1136
Casa Barranca, 1136

Casa de Cello, 1001
Casa Ferreirinha (Sogrape), 982–83
Casa Lapostolle, 1436
Casa Marin, 1436
Casa de Santa Vitória, 988
Casa Silva, 1436
Casa de Vila Verde, 1002
Casablanca Valley, 1432
Casajás, J. A. Calvo, Bodegas, 1040
Casanova di Neri, 883
Casanuova delle Cerbaie, 883
Casas del Bosque, 1436
Cascabel, 1382
Case Basse (Soldera), 912
Casenove, Domaine La, 452–3
Cassagne Haut-Canon, 189
Cassan, Domaine de, 573
Cassis, 513
Castel, Domaine du, 1448
Castelão, 985, 998
Castelgiocondo, 883
Castellada, La, 927
Castellare, 883–84
Castell'in Villa, 884
Castello di Ama, 885–86
Castello Banfi, 884–85
Castello di Bossi, 886
Castello di Neive, 822
Castello di Monsanto, 886
Castello di Nipozzano, 886–87
Castello di Querceto, 887
Castello dei Rampolla, 885
Castello del Terriccio, 885
Castello di Volpaia, 887
Castelnau, Guillaume de, 288
Castiglione Falletto, 792, 793
Castillo de Cuzcurrita, 1041
Castillo Labastida, 1041
Castoro Cellars, 1136
Cat Amongst the Pigeons, 1382–83
Cataldi Madonna, 946
Catena Zapata, 1349
Cathiard, Sylvain, 310
Cattier, 411
Cauze, du, 139
Cavallotto, 823
Cave St.-Pierre, 623
Caves Aliança, 966, 988, 1002
Caves Messias, 967
Caves do Salgueiral, 967
Caves Transmontanas, 967

in Champagne, 400, 401–02, 404, 407, 408

in Chile, 1432

food and wine matchups and, 14

in Germany, 721, 724

in Israel, 1445

in Italy, 787, 790, 804, 863

in Jura, 426

in Languedoc and Roussillon, 436, 441

in Loire Valley, 475, 476, 481, 482

in New York State, 1288

in New Zealand, 1455, 1456, 1457

in Oregon, 1297, 1300

in Portugal, 985, 998

in Provence, 517

in Savoie, 427

in South Africa, 1462, 1463

in Spain, 1019

in Washington State, 1320, 1321

Charlopin, Philippe—Charlopin-Parizot, 310–11

Charmail, 140–41

Charmes-Godard, Les, 141

Chartogne-Taillet, 411

Charvin, G.A.E.C., Domaine, 578

Chassagne-Montrachet, 258, 268, 277

Chasselas, 97

in Germany (Gutedel), 725

in Savoie, 427, 428

Chasse-Spleen, 141

Chasseur, 1138

Château-Chalon, 426, 427

Chateau Ste. Michelle, 1327–28

Châteauneuf-du-Pape, 525, 526, 538–42

aging potential of, 526

at a glance, 538–39

most profound wines of, 539–40

ratings of producers of red wine in, 540–42

ratings of producers of white wine in, 542

Chatter Creek, 1328

Chaumées, Les, 277

Chauvenet–Chopin, Hubert, 311

Chauvet, Jules, 288

Chauvin, 141

Chave, Bernard and Yann, 579

Chave, J. L., 579

Chehalem, 1307

Chénas, 289

Chêne, Domaine du, 579–80

Chenevottes, 277

Chenin Blanc:

in California, 1077, 1082, 1083, 1085

in Languedoc and Roussillon, 441

in Loire Valley, 474, 476, 478–80, 481

in South Africa, 1462, 1463, 1464

in Washington State, 1320

Chenin Rouge (Pineau d'Aunis), 476, 478, 478, 482

Cherasco, 742

Chéreau-Carré, 493

Cherisey, Comtesse Bernard de—Martelet de Cherisey, Domaine, 311

Cheval Blanc, 142

Cheval des Andes, 1349

Chevalier, Château, 1139

Chevalier, Domaine de, 142–43

Chevalier-Montrachet, 277

Cheverny, 481, 482

Chevillon, Robert, 311–12

Chèze, Louis, 580

Chianti, 786, 862

Chianti Classico, 786, 787, 862, 863

aging potential of, 867

buying strategy for, 871

closer look at, 864–65

flavors of, 863

Chiarello Family Vineyards, 1139

Chiarlo, Michele, 824–25

Chidaine, François, 544

Chignin, 478

Chile, Chilean wines, 1432–42

"icon" wines of, 1434

map of, 1433

ratings of best wines of, 1434–35

tasting commentaries for, 1435–42

see also specific growers and producers

Chillag, 1447

Chimney Rock, 1139

Chinon, 480–81, 482

Chionetti, 825

Chiquet, Gaston, 411

Chiroubles, 290

Chocalan, Viña, 1437

Chon, Gilbert, 494

Chorey, Château de (Domaine Germain Père et Fils), 330

Chorey-les-Beaune, 262

Chotard, Daniel, 494

Christmann, A., 732

Farnese, 947–48
Fattoria dei Barbi, 891
Fattoria del Cerro, 891
Fattoria di Felsina, 891–92
Fattoria di Magliano, 892
Fattoria di Petrolo, 892
Fattoria di Piazzano, 893
Faugères, 165, 440
Faurie, Bernard, 593
Faurie de Souchard, 165–66
Faurmarie, Domaine, 457
Faury, Philippe, 593–94
Federspiel, 655, 658
Feiler-Artinger, 673
feinherb Riesling, 706
Felsina, Fattoria di, 891–92
Fer Servadou, 421, 422
Feraud, Eddie, 594
Féraud-Brunel, 594
Feret-Lambert, 166
fermentation, xix, 254–56
    carbonic maceration and, 278
    sugar added to, 17
    three basic strategies for, 255
    yeasts and, 254–55
    yeasts for, 17
Fernão Pires, 985, 998
Ferrand, Domaine de, 594
Ferrand-Lartigue, 166
Ferrando, Isabel, Domaine, 594–95
Ferrari, 929
Ferraton Père et Fils, 595
Ferreira, 957, 960, 1013
Ferrière, 166
Fessardière, Château de la, 499
Feteasca Alba, 1423
Feudi di San Gregorio, 948
Feuduccio, Il, 948
Fèvre, William, Domaine, 326–27
Fèvre, William, Viña, 1439
Feytit-Clinet, 166
Fichet, Jean-Philippe, Domaine, 327
Fiefs Vendéens, 475
Fieuzal, de, 166–67
Figeac, 167
Filles Durma, Domaine des, 595
filtration, xx, 18–20, 30, 33, 256–57
Finca Sandoval, 1047
Fines Roches, Château des, 595
Finger Lakes, Finger Lake wines,
    1287–88

tasting commentaries for, 1291–93,
    1295–96
fining, xx, 18–20, 30, 33, 306
    clarification agents for, 16
Firestone Vineyard, 1161
Firriato, 948–49
First Drop, 1389
Fisher Vineyards, 1161
Fita, Maria, 457
Fitapreta, 990
Fitou, 441
Five Star Cellars, 1330
five-star system, for ratings of producers
    and growers, 2–3
Fixin, 264
Flam, 1448–49
Fleur, La, 167–68
Fleur d'Arthus, La, 168
Fleur de Barbeyron, 168
Fleur de Boüard, La, 168
Fleur-Cardinale, 169
Fleur du Château Bouqueyran, La, 169
Fleur du Rose Ste.-Croix, 169
Fleur de Gay, La, 169
Fleur de Jaugue, La, 169–20
Fleur Mongiron, La, 170
Fleur Morange, La, 170
Fleur de Plince, La, 194
Fleurie, 289–90
Fleur-Pétrus, La, 170–71
Fleury Père et Fils, 412
Flora Springs Wine Co., 1162
Flowers Vineyard and Winery, 1162–63
Fog, Adrian, 1163
Fogarty, Thomas, 1163
Foley Estates, 1163–64
Foley, Robert, 1164
Folie à Deux, 1164
Folle Blanche (Gros Plant), 475
Fombrauge, 171
Fonbadet, 171
Fonbel, 171
Fondrèche, Domaine de, 596
Fonné, Michel, 65
Fonplégade, 171–72
Fonroque, 172
Fonseca, 957, 1011, 1013
Fonseca, José Maria da, 969–70, 1004
Font du Loup, Château de la, 596
Font de Michelle, 596–97
Font-Sane, Domaine de, 597

Gravner, 930

gray market, 27–28

Grayson Cellars, 1170

Great Southern, 1359

Great Vintage Wine Book, The (Broadbent), 36

great wines, characteristics of, 30–32

Grée-Laroque, 182

Green and Red, 1171

Greenock Creek, 1391–92

Grenache:

 in Australia, 1367–72

 in California, 1077, 1080, 1083

 in Languedoc and Roussillon, 435, 436, 439, 441, 442, 444

 in Oregon, 1297

 in Provence, 516

 in Rhône Valley, 520

 in Spain (Garnacha), 1019

Grenache Blanc:

 in Languedoc and Roussillon, 436

 in Rhône Valley, 521

Grenache Gris, 442, 443

Greppi, I, 896

Greppo, Il (Franco Biondi Santi), 879–80

Grès de Montpellier, 439

Grey Wolf Cellars, 1171

Greysac, 182

Grgich, Mike, 1422

Grgich Hills, 1171

Grignolino, 790

Grillet, Château, 526, 528, 606

Grimaldi, Giacomo, 837

Gringet, 428

Grinzane Cavour, 792

Gripa, Bernard, 606

Grippat, J. L., 606

Grivault, Albert, Domaine, 334

Grivot, Jean, Domaine, 334–35

Grochau Cellars, 1309

Groffier, Robert, 335–36

Grolleau, 476, 482

Gros, Anne, 336

Gros Manseng, 422, 423

Gros Plant, 475

Gross, 675

Grosses Gewächs wines, 706, 721

Grosset, 1392

Grosslage, 704

Grossot, Corinne et Jean-Pierre, 336

Groth, 1171

Gruaud-Larose, 183

Grüner Veltliner, 649, 651, 653, 654, 655–66, 658, 659, 660, 661, 662, 663, 664, 665, 666

 in Central Europe, 1422

Gualdo del Re, 896

Gué, Jean de, 183

Guérard, Michel, 15

Guffens-Heynen, Domaine, 336–37

Guibot La Fourvieille, 233

Guigal, 606–07

Guillemot-Michel, Domaine, 337

Guimarães, José Mesquita, 970

Guindon, Jacques, 500

Guiot, Château, 607–08

Guitian, 1048

Gulfi, 949

Gunderloch, 739–40

Gundlach Bundschu, 1172

Gurgue, La, 183–84

Gutedel, 725

Gypsy Dancer Estates, 1310

H

Haag, Fritz, 740–41

Haag, Willi, 741–42

Haan Wines, 1392

Haart, Reinhold, 742

Hacienda Monasterio, 1049

Hagafen Cellars, 1172

Hahn, J. J., 1393

Hahnenhof (Toni Jost), 746

Haider, Martin, 675

halbtrocken:

 on Austrian labels, 655

 on German labels, 703, 705, 706

Halbturn, Schloss, 675

Halleck Vineyard, 1172

Hallgarten, 718

Halliday, James, 20, 36

Halter Ranch, 1172

Hamacher Wines, 1310

Hammerschlag, Benjamin, 1365

Handley Cellars, 1172

Hanna Winery, 1173

Hansel, Walter, Winery, 1173

Hanzell Vineyards, 1174

Happy Canyon Vineyard, 1174

Hardy, Andrew, Wines, 1393

Harlan Estate, 1174

Harris Estate Vineyards, 1174–75

Rousseau, Armand, 384–85
Roussette de Savoie, 426, 427, 428
Roussillon. *See* Languedoc and Roussillon
Roux, Jean-Claude, 508
Roy Estate, 1243–44
Royer, Jean-Marie, Vignobles, 632–33
Rozès, 1015
ruby Port, 1010
Rudd Estate, 1244
Rudderless, 1412
Rüdesheim, 717, 718
Rueda, 1018, 1022
Rufete, 998
Ruffino, 908
Rui Reguinga Enologia, 997
Ruinart, 418
Rully, 269, 277
Ruppertsberg, 722
Rusack Vineyards, 1244
Rusden, 1412
Rust, 665–66
Rusten Family Vineyards, 1245
Rutherford Hill, 1245
Rutherglen, 1362
Ruwer. *See* Mosel, Saar, and Ruwer region
Rycke, Bénédicte de, 508

S

Saale-Unstrut, 725
Saar. *See* Mosel, Saar, and Ruwer region
Saarstein, Schloss, 771
Sablet, 525
Sabon, Roger, Domaine, 633
Sachsen (Saxony), 725
Saddleback Cellars, 1245–46
Saffirio, Josetta, 853
Sage, 1246
Sagrantino, 786
St.-Amour, 289
St.-Antonin, Domaine, 468
St.-Aubin, 277
St.-Benoît, Domaine, 683–84
St.-Bris, 283
St.-Chinian, 440
St. Clement, 1246–47
St.-Cosme, 634
St.-Damien, Domaine, 634–35
St.-Désirat Caves Cooperative, 635
St.-Domingue, 234
St.-Émilion, 87, 115

aging potential of recent top vintages
 for finest wines of, 93
futures in limited-production wines
 from, 117
general flavor characteristics of,
 91–92
vintage summaries for, 94–106
St.-Estèphe, 87
 aging potential of recent top vintages
  for finest wines of, 93
 best wine values in, 115
 general flavor characteristics of, 91
 vintage summaries for, 94–106
St. Francis Winery and Vineyards, 1247
St.-Gayan, 635
St.-Georges–St.-Émilion, 115
St.-Gervais, 525
St. Innocent Winery, 1312
St. Jean, Château, 1247–48
St.-Joseph, 525, 532–34
 aging potential of, 526
 at a glance, 532–33
 most profound wines of, 533
 ratings of producers of, 534
St.-Julien, 87
 aging potential of recent top vintages
  for finest wines of, 93
 best wine values in, 115
 general flavor characteristics of, 91
 vintage summaries for, 94–106
St. Laurent, 652, 653, 661, 663, 666
St.-Laurent:
 in Central Europe, 1422
St. Magdalena, 936
St. Martin de la Garrigue, Domaine, 418
St.-Nicolas-de-Bourgueil, 480
St.-Paul, Domaine de, 635
St.-Péray, 525, 535–536
 at a glance, 535–36
 ratings of producers of, 536
St.-Pierre, 234
St.-Préfert, Domaine de, 635–36
St.-Romain, 262
St.-Saturnin, 439
St.-Siffrein, Domaine de, 636
St. Supéry, 1248
St. Urbans-Hof, 768–69
Saint-Véran, 289
Ste.-Croix-de-Mont, 93
Saintsbury, 1248
Salcheto, 908

appellation system of, 428
ratings of best producers of, 429–30
Saxum Vineyards, 1249
Sbragia Family Vineyards, 1249–50
Scansano, 862
Scarecrow, 1250
Scavino, Paolo, 854–55
Schaefer, Willi, 769–70
Schaetzel, Martin, 75
Schäfer-Fröhlich, 770–71
Scharzhof (Egon Müller), 761–62
Schein, Erna (Behrens and Hitchcock), 1121–22
Scherrer Winery, 1250
Scheurebe:
in Austria, 666
in Germany, 720, 721, 722, 724
Schiava, 725
Schiefer, Uwe, 693
Schild Estate, 1412
Schiopetto, 936
Schleret, Charles, 75–76
Schlossberg, 103
Schmelz, 693
Schmid, Josef, 693
Schmitges, Andreas, 771
Schmitt-Wagner, Carl, 772
Schneider Vineyards, 1295
Schoffit, Bernard, 126–27
School House Vineyard, 1250–51
Schoonmaker, Frank, 249
Schrader Cellars, 1251
Schramsberg, 1252
Schröck, Heidi, 694
Schubert, von—Maximin Grünhaus, 772–74
Schubert Estate, 1413
Schulz, 1413
Schwarz, 695
Schwarzriesling, 725
Scopetone, 911
Screaming Eagle, 1252
Scubla, 936
Sea Smoke Cellars, 1252
Seavey Vineyard, 1252–53
Sebastiani, 1253
secondary labels, in Bordeaux, 111–15
Secondé, François, 418
sediment, 8
decanting and, 12–13
fraudulent bottles of fine wine and, 29

seepage (legs), 23
Seghesio, 855, 1253
Ségriès, Château de, 637
Seguin, Hervé, 509
Séguret, 525
Selbach-Oster, 774–76
sélection de grains nobles wines, 93, 96, 99
Selene, 1253
Selosse, Jacques, 418–19
Selvapiana, 911
Sémillon:
in Australia, 1363–64, 1365, 1374
in Bordeaux, 91
in California, 1077, 1083, 1103–5
in Provence, 517
in South Africa, 1462
in southwest of France, 421
in Washington State, 1321
Seña, Viña, 1441
Sénéchaux, Domaine des, 637
Sénéjac, 235
Sequoia Grove, 1253–54
Serafin, Christian, 386–87
Sercial, 1016
Serena, La (Tuscan wine producer), 911
Sérénite (Poumey) Cuvée d'Exception, La, 235
Sergue, La, 235–36
Serralunga d'Alba, 792, 794
Servin, Domaine, 387
serving wine, 12–13
Servitude Volontaire Cuvée d'Exception, La, 236
Sesta di Sopra, 912
Setzer, 694
Seven Hills Winery, 1337
Seyssel, 428
Shadow Canyon Cellars, 1254
Shafer Vineyards, 1254–55
Shalestone Vineyards, 1295
Sharp, Andrew, 37
Shea Wine Cellars, 1313
Sheldrake Point Vineyard, 1295
Shinn Estate Vineyards, 1295
shipping wine, 9, 311
Shiraz, in Australia, 1358, 1363, 1364, 1367–72
Shirvington, 1413
Shomron, 1443
Sibon, 1424
Sicily, 786–87

NOTES

NOTES

NOTES

NOTES

NOTES

NOTES

NOTES

NOTES

NOTES

NOTES

NOTES

NOTES

NOTES

NOTES

NOTES

NOTES

NOTES

NOTES

NOTES

NOTES

NOTES

NOTES

NOTES

NOTES

NOTES

*The Complete,
Easy-to-Use
Reference
on Recent Vintages,
Prices, and Ratings
for More than 8,000
Wines from All the
Major Wine Regions*

ROBERT M. PARKER, JR.

PARKER'S WINE BUYER'S GUIDE

Seventh Edition

VOLUME 2 THE REST OF THE WORLD

A Dorling Kindersley Book

Dorling Kindersley
LONDON, NEW YORK, MUNICH, MELBOURNE, and DELHI

Seventh edition published in Great Britain in 2008 by
Dorling Kindersley Limited
80 Strand, London WC2R 0RL

A Penguin Company

Designed by Suet Y. Chong

Manufactured in the United States of America

A complete CIP catalogue record for this book is available from the British Library.

Parker, Robert M.
  [Wine buyer's guide]
  Parker's wine buyer's guide.—7th ed. / Robert M. Parker, Jr.
    p. cm.
  Includes bibliographical references and index.
  1. Wine and winemaking.   I. Title.

ISBN-13: 978-1-4053-2639-1

Printed and bound in China by CTPS Ltd

Portions of this book were previously published in Robert Parker's bimonthly newsletter
The Wine Advocate.

Portions of the preface were originally published in the September 2008 issue of *Food & Wine.*

Discover more at **www.dk.com**

CONTENTS

CONTENTS

THE WINES OF WESTERN EUROPE PART II

[austria]

A NEW WINE CONSTELLATION IN THE "OLD WORLD" SKY

A quarter of a century ago, no one would have predicted the emergence of Austria into the footlights of the world's wine stage which took place at the millennium. In mid-1985, dessert wines from the Burgenland region were found to have been laced with ethylene glycol, added by unscrupulous vintners or middlemen to boost (or merely mimic) the unctuous textured and honeyed sweetness associated with botrytis. No one was ever found to have been poisoned by these wines, but the market for Austrian wine most certainly was. "It is the worst disaster to hit this region since World War II," Rust's mayor and vintner Heribert Artinger told *The New York Times* that August. "The job," said Austria's then Chancellor Sinowatz, himself a *Burgenländer,* "is to pick up the pieces, to start anew." And that is just what Austria did. Decisive action instituted stringent quality controls, laying the groundwork for future bragging rights and effective marketing. At the same time, ever wine-thirsty Austrians set out in search of small estate bottlers, since *négociants,* middlemen, and export agents had been wiped out almost overnight. Pulling together, growers along the Danube in the Wachau set benchmarks for quality that, within a decade, would catapult them to fame. The star of South Styria, whose wines from along the Slovenian border had been almost forgotten for a century, began to rise. And back in Burgenland, a young man named Alois Kracher left his job in Vienna as a pharmacist, determined to rescue that region's reputation by crafting at his family's estate nobly sweet wines second to none.

Today the Wachau influences the way that Riesling is perceived both at home and abroad; thence arose the impetus that turned Grüner Veltliner—once merely the name of a humble native grape—into a buzzword known to wine lovers worldwide. South Styria's hilly acreage today struggles just to keep up with domestic demand, as the projects of its vintners spill over into Slovenia. The late Alois Kracher lived to see his wines compared with those of d'Yquem and to consult—as "Mr. Botrytis"—on sweet-wine projects around the globe. Under the influence of new laws and new quality benchmarks, a generation of Austrian growers for whom the wine scandal of 1985 is ancient history has helped give birth to one of the world's great

Austria

CZECH REPUBLIC

KAMPTAL
KREMSTAL
WACHAU
• Langenlois
• Krems
WEINVIERTEL
WAGRAM
• Bisamberg
Danube
TRAISENTAL
SLOVAKIA
Danube

VIENNA
• Vienna
CARNUNTUM

Gumpoldskirchen •
Traiskirchen •
Göttlesbrunn •
Schützen
am Gebirge •
NEUSIEDLERSEE
• Jois
• Gols

Eisenstadt •
Grosshöflein •
Rust •
Frauenkirchen
• Apetlon

THERMENREGION

NEUSIEDLERSEE-
HÜGELLAND
Illmitz •
Neckenmarkt • Deutschkreutz
Horitschon •
MITTELBURGENLAND
Lutzmannsburg

Vienna •
AUSTRIA
Map
area

SÜDBURGENLAND
Eisenberg ▲

SÜDOSTSTEIERMARK
• Graz
WESTSTEIERMARK
HUNGARY

SÜDSTEIERMARK

Wine Regions

SLOVENIA

N
W   E
S

WACHAU
Weissenkirchen •
Joching •
Wösendorf •
Viessling •
Spitz •
Dürnstein
Danube
Oberloiben •
Stein
• Krems
• Mautern
Unterloiben

0   25 miles
0   25 kilometers

0   2 miles
0   3 kilometers

wine constellations, full of fascinating stars, and incorporating a range of grapes, soils, micro-climates, and traditions at times downright exotic, and surely unprecedented for such a small country. Austria accounts for a mere 1.3% of the European Community's wine volume, yet—without even remote competition from other member states—Austria accounts for more than twice as high a percentage of the total *value* of EU wine. Success abroad has been accompanied by an intensification of what was already arguably Europe's most enthusiastic, if not down-right frenetic, wine culture. The hoopla accorded every new vintage is enormous. It is not at all unusual for wines to be sold out on subscription before they have finished fermenting, let alone been bottled. And top vintners are celebrated as national heroes.

Roughly two-thirds of Austrian wine is white. The vast majority of that is dry, but out-standing sweet wines are also crafted in most of Austria's growing regions, particularly in parts of Burgenland, which have reestablished a reputation for the botrytis wines that had al-ready put "German West Hungary" on the world's wine map more than three centuries ago. Most Austrian white wines were still blends much later in the 20th century than was the case in Alsace or California; insofar as they were from Grüner Veltliner, they bore no such indica-tion on the label. Now wines from a single grape and labeled with its name are the norm. Acreage of red grapes, as well as serious quality aspirations and achievements with them, are surging. Increasingly many of the best reds, too, are *monocépage*, although some are blends.

AUSTRIA'S GRAPES: A REAL CAST OF CHARACTERS

Given the huge number of grapes Austria grows, the number of these that are propagated across many or most of her regions, and how many were until recently little known abroad, it will be useful to survey the principal vinous actors in the Austrian wine drama at this point. Further details, with notes on local or infrequently encountered grapes, will follow in the course of regional profiles. (The list that follows is not driven by acreage, so two grapes of great statistical but much less gustatory significance—Müller-Thurgau and Blauer Portugieser—will not be covered here.)

Grüner Veltliner The number one protagonist of the Austrian wine stage is Grüner Veltliner (pronounced "GREWN-air FELT-LEAN-air"). Somehow, largely over the course of the 20th century, this one variety, among the many grapes grown and blended as typical wine of Lower Austria, asserted its dominance; today it accounts for approximately one-third of Austria's total acreage. "Veltliner" traditionally referred to more than one variety; even today, the Roter Veltliner (about whose relatively localized significance, more later) should not in any way be confused with Grüner Veltliner, to which (despite long-standing beliefs to the contrary) it bears scant resemblance and few, if any, family ties. The range of aromas and fla-vors of which Grüner Veltliner is capable is striking and includes those of lentils, green beans, snap peas, cress, beetroot, rhubarb, roasted red peppers, tobacco, white and black pepper, cit-rus zest, iris, nutmeg, caramel, and peach. There are two other notable gustatory features of this grape variety. One is its tactile, signature "bite," a pleasant astringency that often segues into faintly sizzling notes of pepper (its *Pfefferl,* as Austrians say). The other is its ability to achieve satisfying ripeness of flavor and harmonious completeness at extremes in alcohol lev-els. Deliciously refreshing examples abound in the 10.5% to 12% range, yet magnificent, opu-lent, powerful, but still well-balanced Grüner Veltliners frequently approach and occasionally exceed 15% alcohol. There is enormous variation in berry-size, vigor, color of ripe fruit, and ultimately flavor from one population or genetic subgroup of Grüner Veltliner to another. Had it not been for the nearly 40-year work of selection carried out by Franz Pichler in the middle of the last century, this variety might never have achieved its current cachet.

Riesling The next big white wine star of Austria is certainly Riesling. But that statement is deceptive. Riesling takes up less than 4% of Austria's vine acreage and is scarcely grown at all east or south of Vienna. As in Germany, here too this great grape reveals its uncanny ability to channel and reflect specific places and soils, and to be satisfying over a considerable range of finished alcohol. But there is nothing like the under-10% alcohol Kabinett or Spätlese here that one encounters in Germany (although those terms are still sometimes employed in Austria, as we shall see). With rare, late, or selectively harvested exceptions, virtually all Austrian Riesling tastes dry, whereas only by leaving behind a lot of residual sugar can certain German Riesling satisfy with a mere 7% to 10% alcohol. At the other end of the alcohol scale, it is undeniable that dry Austrian Riesling more often manage to taste harmonious at levels of alcohol higher than 13.5% than is the case with their *trocken* German counterparts. The best Austrian Riesling is typically less effusive in aroma and lower in acidity than its German relation, leaner and less oily in texture than its Alsace counterpart, but not quite as long-lived as either of these. It is capable of detonating in the mouth with an explosion of herbs, flowers, spices, pit fruits, stones, and salt, whose finishing flavors are the tail that wags the taster.

Welschriesling Never should Riesling be confused with Welschriesling, a grape that dominates large tracts of Central Europe under many names but seldom brings much good news in the glass. Portions of Austria may be the exception, because this grape is critical to the balance and personality of many a fine botrytis wine from Burgenland. In other regions of Austria, notably Styria, it generally takes uncomplicated, refreshing form; it is so widespread that the national acreage stands at nearly 9%.

Pinot Blanc—or, as it's called here, Weissburgunder—is scarcely ever listed as a major Austrian grape, but that is a mistake. First, its acreage nationwide is probably close to that of Riesling. (Accurate statistics are hard to come by, as it is so often lumped in with Chardonnay when vines are counted.) Second, this is the only variety with which at least one talented grower in nearly every one of Austria's major growing regions is achieving delicious, distinctive, and ageworthy results. (The top practitioners are duly noted in the following section.)

Gelber Muskateller (the Muscat à Petit Grains of southern France) is grown sporadically in Austria, just as it is in such far-flung former portions of the Hapsburg Empire as Tokaj. This variety's pungently herbal, citrus zest, and dried pit-fruit character is much beloved of Austrians in its brisk and dry Styrian renditions. In part as a result of their success, acreage—still well under half a percent of Austria's total—is on the increase outside Styria, too. Muscat Ottonel (discussed in the chapter devoted to Alsace) is much more widely grown, but with the exception of its role in nobly sweet wines from Burgenland, proves less distinctive and less desirable.

Other White Grapes Among internationally familiar white varieties, the two most widely planted are Chardonnay and Sauvignon Blanc, both (but particularly the latter) of special significance in Styria. Results with Sauvignon Blanc among those growers along the Danube and in Burgenland who have taken it seriously to heart strongly suggest that there is much more potential for this grape in Austria than even its current modest acreage, manifest quality, or high reputation in Styria would suggest.

Zweigelt holds a place among Austria's red grapes not unlike that of Grüner Veltliner among the whites. This crossing of Blaufränkisch and St. Laurent dates only to 1922, but Dr. Zweigelt's foundling has received a friendly reception throughout Austria and now covers close to 10% of total acreage. Deep, sweet cherry fruit and a soft texture that by no means precludes lively, lip-smacking juiciness make cleanly crafted and well-concentrated Zweigelt almost irresistible for guzzling, in a way not yet reflected in its low international profile. A few growers are attempting, with some success, to showcase the more serious side of this grape, and it also figures in a number of Austria's most interesting blends.

Blaufränkisch The next most widely planted black grape in Austria (at about 6% of total acreage) is, by local consensus, the candidate most capable of achieving international red wine stardom, Blaufränkisch. This is the same grape known as Lemberger in Germany and the U.S.—although one might not guess that to taste the wines— and as Kékfrankos in its native Hungary. In Austria, it is confined almost entirely to Burgenland, an area that was tradition-ally part of Hungary. Intense black fruits, tobacco, pepper, resinous herbs and spices at times remind one of a Cabernet or Syrah. But though wines from this variety are capable of formi-dable richness and tannic structure, some of the most striking recent examples have displayed subtleties of aroma and texture and sensitivity to soil and microclimate worthy of a great Burgundian Pinot Noir or Piedmontese Nebbiolo.

St. Laurent (pronounced here as "sahnkt-LORE-ent") is another crossing, but its origins are a mystery. Pinot Noir—from which it takes its sweet fruit, raw meat notes, and potentially silken texture—is definitely one parent; the other is unknown. It probably came to Austria from France, but when or how long ago it first appeared in France, none can tell. Not a few growers opine that it is foolish to cultivate a grape that shares its finicky temperament and fragility with Pinot Noir, when one could with the same efforts grow Pinot Noir, and have a name recognized the world over. Enough think otherwise to plant nearly 1% of Austrian acreage in St. Laurent. Proponents of unblended bottlings argue that its sheer richness of fruit and potential for even plusher texture than Pinot justify the effort to grow it.

Pinot Noir itself hovers below 1% of Austrian acreage, but Madame Pinot—as in so many other countries—has seduced dozens of ambitious young Austrian vintners, and their wines will audition increasingly and successfully on an international stage. The combined surface area Austrians devote to Merlot and the much more plentiful Cabernet Sauvignon is not much greater than that devoted to St. Laurent, and there are indications that this acreage may have peaked, as many growers in parts of Burgenland (where Bordeaux grapes figure most prominently) are reducing their presence or eliminating them from Blaufränkisch-based blends. While Syrah is not of statistical significance—yet, anyway—a lot is being written in-side Austria about the numerous Burgenland experiments that are under way. (Come to think of it, where does one nowadays *not* hear growers saying, "Who knows, perhaps tomorrow our region will be known for Syrah"?)

A TOUR OF AUSTRIA'S GROWING REGIONS

Geographically, the Austrian wine constellation can be seen as two great arms with Vienna as a viticultural hub—yes, the city itself is an important growing region. To the north and west of that metropolis—all part of the large political entity or *Land* known as Lower Austria—the dominant grape is Grüner Veltliner. But virtually all of Austria's Riesling is planted west of Vienna, too. One could refer to this as the Danubian arm of Austrian viticulture. Its most important regions are along, near, or influenced by the Danube and its tributaries, but it ex-tends as far as the Czech and Slovak borders. Zweigelt dominates among reds, which are a small minority in this area that is strongly affected by cool air from the mountains and forests farther to the west that funnel down the Danube overnight. During the day, though, the flow reverses: warm air from the Hungarian plain (the steppe, or *Puszta*) flows upstream. Wide diurnal (day-night) temperature variation is among the features influencing the character of wine from these Danubian regions.

Vienna itself reflects a viticultural transition as one moves south from the Danube. Vine-yards in the northern and western hills of the city favor white grapes, including Riesling and, of course, Grüner Veltliner. In the city's warmer southern suburbs, well back from the river, blocks of Pinot, Cabernet, Merlot, and Zweigelt share the hillsides with white wine varieties. Along the south shore of the Danube to the Slovak frontier, just opposite Bratislava, a similar mixture predominates, whereas directly south of Vienna, in the so-called Thermal Region— once far more famous than it is today—two unusual local grapes hold sway

The great southern arm of the Austrian winegrowing constellation hugs the frontiers of Hungary and Slovenia. The strip along Hungary's border, known as Burgenland, only became a *Land* of Austria by plebiscite in 1921. Most of its vineyards are centered on a long and shallow steppe lake known as the Neusiedlersee. (The "new settlers" to which this name refers were Bavarian and Croatian peasants whom Empress Maria Theresa invited to fill the vacuum of a land laid waste by two tumultuous centuries of Ottoman incursions. The local Princes Esterházy offered protection to Jews throughout the Hapsburg Empire, completing this area's unique and polyglot mix of peoples.) White grapes (notably for sweet wine) share acreage with diverse reds. As one moves south through narrow Burgenland, Blaufränkisch becomes the dominant grape.

Austria's southeast corner is the *Land* of Styria (Steiermark). Time was when present-day Styria was recognized as the northern portion of a vast winegrowing region characterized by seemingly endless undulating hills, steep, breezy vineyards, and awesome vistas covering much of the eastern half of present-day Slovenia. The greatest concentration of vine acreage in this area today is in South Styria, right along the frontier, where Sauvignon Blanc has received the greatest recognition but shares acreage with numerous other whites—including the far more plentiful Welschriesling—and a modest amount of Zweigelt.

Armed with this overview, we can now take a closer look at Austria's major growing regions, beginning in the west with her best-known and most prestigious, then moving east and south.

THE WACHAU: AUSTRIA'S TINY ENGINE OF EXCELLENCE

MAJOR GRAPES AND PLACES

The Wachau extends for little more than 20 winding miles along the Danube west of Krems, making up a mere 2% of Austria's vineyard surface. But the quality, prestige, and, above all, influence of this region is totally out of proportion to its size. The principal grapes from both a quality-conscious and international perspective are Grüner Veltliner and Riesling, but a traditional variety known as Neuburger is still widely grown and can yield subtly floral, discreetly flavored, flatteringly silken-textured, and versatile whites, which seldom leave the local market. The Gelber Muskateller, Pinot Blanc, Pinot Gris, and Zweigelt make periodic appearances to supplement a given grower's range, and F. X. Pichler has demonstrated that Sauvignon Blanc can be truly exciting here.

The dramatically steep, terraced sites that dominate the Wachau landscape are collectively known as *Urgestein* ("primordial stone"), being ancient and of volcanic origin. Variations on schist, granite, and gneiss, including their erosion into gravel- or sandlike consistency (especially along the river's edge), as well as the recompression and metamorphosis of such river sediments, largely account for the gamut of conditions that Wachau vine roots encounter while trying to gain a foothold and sustain a crop. Here and there, sites may include an overlay of loess, compacted fine, yellowish glacial dust from the last Ice Age (even more important as a growing medium in several nearby regions).

The rebuilding and maintenance of the Wachau's ancient stone terraces is a colossal task, without which the quality of today's wine could not have been achieved. More than 50 miles of stone walls remained slated for reconstruction in the summer of 2002, when the most catastrophic flood in modern history in this region triggered widespread further collapse of terraces. Most of the Wachau's major vineyards have received drip lines over the past two decades, permitting them to be irrigated with Danube water. Prior to that time—long before anyone had yet uttered the words "global warming"—vines in these exposed, fast-draining terraces would routinely "shut down" and fail to ripen in years of drought. Most growers maintain that the success of today's Wachau wines is unthinkable without irrigation. But drip lines are not problem free—water must be applied judiciously, with insight and foresight, lest the results include superficial roots, vine dependency, and flavor dilution.

WHAT TO EXPECT

In 1986 the Wachau growers, led by such visionaries as Franz Hirtzberger, Sr., Josef Jamek, Franz Prager, and Willi Schwengler (of the region's illustrious Freie Weingärtner cooperative), unveiled a new conception of Wachau wine, codifying their increasingly influential preference for dry, unchaptalized wines and dividing these into three categories based on alcoholic volume and thus, by implication, weight. Named for the feathery grasses that grow at the foot of the Wachau terraces, the so-called Steinfeder could not exceed 11% alcohol. Wines of this category reflect a strong local tradition but have generally not been exported. In some recent years nature has rendered it nearly impossible to produce Steinfeder, much less to satisfy local thirsts that include the hordes of tourists who regularly descend on this spectacularly scenic region. The Wachau's middleweight category is known as Federspiel (a medieval term from falconry) and ranges from 11% to 12.5% in alcohol. At the top end of the scale are the Smaragd wines. (Referring to the iridescent lizards that sun themselves on the Wachau terraces, "Smaragd" is also the word for emerald.) It is on wines in this last category (which, for a brief period after 1986, went by the name Honivogl) that the vintners of the Wachau have staked their international claim. But well-made Federspiel wines can also be excellent examples of their grapes and sites, displaying delicate balance and versatility with cuisine. Expect the best Riesling Smaragd to benefit from 8 to 12 years in the bottle, depending on the vintage, and the Grüner Veltliner from 10 to 15 years. Federspiel bottlings can sometimes develop beautifully for nearly as long; however, generally these are not crafted with cellar expectations and should be enjoyed within 4 to 6 years.

Although the vast majority of white Wachau wine is labeled Steinfeder, Federspiel, or Smaragd, there are sufficient exceptions to demand notice. These terms are exclusively applicable to members of the Vinea Wachau growers' association. Producers of Wachau wine who also purchase fruit from the next-door Kremstal region (such as Rainer Wess) or whose primary holdings are in that region (such as Gerard Malat) are not Vinea Wachau members, so cannot use that organization's terminology. Wines that stop fermenting with levels of residual sugar in excess of 9 grams (and at times, with very sugar-rich juice, a grower may choose to inhibit a wine from fermenting that far, lest it suffer ill effects from too-high alcohol) can still taste virtually dry, but forfeit the right to one of these three special designations. In such instances, the word "*halbtrocken*" ("half dry") will usually be buried in fine print somewhere on the label. Wines that meet a certain level of sugar in the grapes at harvest may be labeled Auslese, although (outside of Burgenland) Austrian wines so labeled are seldom more than discreetly sweet. Finally, while genuinely sweet wines remain relatively rare in the Wachau, some exceptions are crafted from botrytized and/or desiccated fruit and labeled Beerenauslese or Trockenbeerenauslese.

Though Wachau Riesling is typically much lower in acidity than its German counterpart, and Grüner Veltliner lower still, the best Wachau wines do not lack invigorating qualities—quite the contrary, thanks to their often sharply delineated flavors, pungency, and tactile grip. These characteristics can be said to fall under the description "phenolics," pertaining to the grapes' skins. No doubt two characteristics of Wachau's climate contribute to its wines' pronounced phenolics. The first (already mentioned in connection with the Danube area as a whole) is wide diurnal variation in temperature, which accentuates flavors and ensures what acidity is present in the grapes is efficacious in the wine. The second is the length of ripening season. Californians may have coined the term "hang time," but growers in the Wachau could write a book about it. Harvest rarely begins in earnest here before October, and grapes for Smaragd wines are often still being picked well into November, if not December. This generally gives ample opportunity for flavors to ripen, and for temperatures to have dropped by harvest time, locking in freshness and remaining acidity until the grapes can be pressed. The skins are often macerated and permitted to soak overnight or even longer in the press, in order to capture a wider range of flavorful phenols.

The character of Wachau wines as one moves downstream (other factors being equal) becomes subtly riper and richer, reflecting increased access to warm Pannonian breezes by day, and greater distance from the interior forests that are a source of cool air at night. More important differences result from vineyard and cellar practices, location of vines relative to the river, their elevation, exposure, and soils. Generally, wines from the *Urgestein* terraces of the Wachau display a complexity and pungency that gentler, more fruit-dominated examples of the same grapes grown in deeper soils and flatter sites along the river lack. Tasters routinely feel compelled to reach for the word "mineral" in trying to describe the flavors and textures they experience in tasting Wachau wine. Whether the flavors tasters describe in this way can actually be ascribed to rocks and soil, remains a large and open question. Tasters who persevere typically end up both concurring with locals that the site and its soil are extremely important to the personality of Wachau wine and recognizing certain sites by taste, whether the grape is Grüner Veltliner or Riesling. Virtually every estate segregates its best wines by site (or *Ried*), and comparisons within a winery are endlessly fascinating, as are those of a single site in the hands of several growers, a few notable examples of which we shall now consider.

SOME IMPORTANT WACHAU VINEYARDS WITH MULTIPLE HIGH-PERFORMANCE OWNERS

The Singerriedel in Spitz, at the relatively cool western edge of the Wachau, consists of finely eroded gneiss and typically renders Riesling redolent of apricot and spice, as can be observed in the most celebrated of Singerreidel Riesling Smaragd bottlings—those of Franz Hirtzberger—but also in wines from the excellent Freie Weingärtner cooperative.

Two dramatically steep and neighboring vineyards in Weissenkirchen, the Achleiten and the Klaus, typically produce dramatically different wines. A geologist will distinguish between paragneiss and orthogneiss, and the presence or absence of amphibolite. Toni Bodenstein of Weingut Prager grows Riesling on both sites (and Grüner Veltliner as well, in the Achleiten) and offers a theory as to the specific influence of each on plant metabolism and hence flavor. Comparisons can be made with the Achleiten Riesling (always Smaragd) of Rudi Pichler or those of the Freie Weingärtner. The Josef Jamek winery typically bottles Grüner Veltliner from the Achleiten as both Federspiel and Smaragd, and is also, along with Prager, the classic source for Riesling from the Klaus.

The Kellerberg in Dürnstein is another of the Wachau's most renowned sites, supporting both Riesling and Grüner Veltliner. Its eroded—in places sandlike—quartz- and feldspar-rich gneiss and schist seem to promote a signature Szechuan peppery pungency even in Riesling. Compare the celebrated renditions of F. X. Pichler with those of the Freie Weingärtner or Emmerich Knoll.

Around a bend in the river from the Kellerberg is the Loibenberg (sometimes spelled "Loibnerberg") which ranges up to 1,300 feet in elevation and features a dusting of loess over its complex mix of *Urgestein*. Three of the top vintners in Austria are residents of Loiben and bottle both Riesling and Grüner Veltliner Smaragd from this site: Leo Alzinger, Emmerich Knoll, and F. X. Pichler.

[recent vintages]

The relatively cool late summer, September rain, and moderate autumn of 2007 have resulted in wines of relatively high acidity and modest levels of alcohol, circumstances that have favored those who were patient. However, if there was one vintage in which it did *not* pay to harvest later here than did your colleagues elsewhere in Europe, that vintage was 2006. Some wines suffer from too little acidity and too much alcohol, but a balmy autumn certainly permitted one to pick Smaragd at leisure. Federspiel was another matter. Some growers picked before the fruit really tasted ripe just to fill this category at all—forget Steinfeder. Others picked as soon as they felt that the right flavors were there, and had to leave "Federspiel" off the label when they ended up with wines of 12.5% to 13% alcohol, which was still "light" for 2006. But there are plenty of exciting Smaragd wines, make no mistake. The vintage is generally said to have favored Grüner Veltliner, but in the Wachau, specifically, a good case can be made for the interplay of flavors and sharper definition of the best Riesling.

2005 was a nail-biter. A picture-perfect October capped a generally cool and rainy year—stress free for the vine, but not for the vintner! Pressure from botrytis led to growers reversing the normal procedure and harvesting Riesling before Grüner Veltliner. The latter was generally more successful. The extract-rich 2005s can be brusque, but the best of them are lean, sharply focused, bright, and minerally intense. A frustrating, intermittently rainy growing season in 2004 meant that growers needed low yields if the fruit were to ripen properly, patience until it got to that point, and considerable luck. The successful wines retained quite high acidity, but not alcohol, so that many a Grüner Veltliner comes off rather like a Riesling, and many Riesling somewhat resemble their German cousins. As the wines have evolved in bottle, they are quite variable (some, in particular, betraying background botrytis now more than in their youth) and they seem prone to mood swings. Anyone interested in Austrian Riesling and Grüner Veltliner should experience this distinctive—one could even say "extreme"—vintage.

The Wachau harvests that followed both the extraordinary heat and drought of Europe's summer of 2003, and the torrential rains and flood of August 2002, point to the enormous importance for this region of late picking. By the time the grapes were gathered in both of these years, extreme conditions had stabilized. The best 2003s reflect fruit resuscitated by the return of cooler temperatures, and a period of stress-free plant metabolism. In 2002—along with repairing flood-ravaged walls, domiciles, and wineries, or retreating to temporary quarters—Wachau vintners took advantage of green foliage into November to permit their grapes to ripen. Undoubtedly there are some 2003s that betray heaviness; the character and success of wines varied widely as a result of the summer's vine stress and the dubious decision of some vintners to add acid to compensate for high pH. The best wines are imposingly concentrated and surprisingly elegant, though. (Certainly the benefits of drip irrigation should not be overlooked.) From 2002, the Riesling in particular possess plenty of charm, the best of them worth revisiting.

September 2001 was plagued by rain, but an exceptionally warm October largely compensated. The wines retained unusually high acidity, and many a Grüner Veltliner of this year, too, displays Riesling-like brightness. Botrytis was not always benign, and Riesling from this vintage will probably (in a departure from the norm) outlive the Grüner Veltliner. The wines of 2000 are generally rich and full—this vintage did not favor Federspiel—and the best of them avoid bitterness and heat from botrytis or high alcohol. Those who pruned, selected, and picked late to avoid negative consequences from high yields were able to capture outstanding flavors in 1999 as well, when a long, balmy autumn followed an unusually cool, rainy August. The best wines are rich, yet retain invigorating acidity; they will remain enjoyable well into the second decade of the new century.

The Wachau wines of 1998 were surprisingly successful, considering that there was nearly steady rain from mid-August into October. Then, a warm, dry wind—along with some not always welcome help from botrytis—concentrated the fruit very quickly. The resultant wines are often practically off the charts in alcohol, phenolics, and acidity. Eventually, though, bitterness or heat have caught up with most of them, so they must be approached cautiously now.

Conditions and wines in 1997, on the other hand, were virtually picture-perfect. Fruit was exceptionally healthy; the wines—at times somewhat aloof in their youth—boast a tremendously complex interplay of flavors. The best will drink well as they approach the human age of majority, and even beyond. Among earlier vintages, 1990 and 1986 proved particularly successful and ageworthy. In fact, along with 1997, these are generally considered to have been the finest vintages in the Wachau and the greater Krems area for the past quarter-century. Both 1995 and 1985 were also well above average.

[important information]

A frequent limitation on the quality of Federspiel, especially of late, is that, in order to pick for dry wine of less than 12.5% in alcohol, the grapes are sometimes not permitted to ripen fully in flavor. Wachau Smaragd wines have displayed an often uncanny ability to balance high levels of alcohol, but given the recent prevalence of warm or botrytis-tinged vintages, one sometimes comes upon heat or bitterness. (To avoid wines of over 14% on principle, though, would to be miss out on much excitement.) Balancing high alcohol is definitely a talent, if not an art, which points to a more general caution. The reputation of the Wachau and the quality of its best wines is such that prices are almost uniformly high (those from the Freie Weingärtner excepted). Once one leaves behind the upper echelons of producers, though, quality is not nearly as uniform, a circumstance familiar in other regions that experience high demand as well as a regular influx of wealthy tourists.

THE KREMSTAL

The city of Krems was traditionally considered to be part of the Wachau, indeed, one could almost say the "capital" of the Wachau. That its name became attached to a different viticultural region is still a source of unhappiness for many local vintners. When the growers of the Wachau were forming the Vinea Wachau, they were wary of the degree to which the powerful presence of merchant interests in Krems, as well as the dramatic difference in soil and exposure on the far side of that city, might detract from the focus they were determined to place on their *Urgestein* riverside terraces. They lobbied successfully to keep Krems out. In truth, the Kremstal is really four distinctive sectors with a misleading name in common. The tiny Krems runs into the Danube at the edge of the city, and boasts some exceptionally steep terraces that rival those of the Wachau. But the entirety of this genuine Kremstal (i.e., "Krems Valley") acreage stretches sporadically for only about three miles along that winding stream.

Between Krems and the present-day limit of the Wachau lies the town of Stein—long since absorbed into its urban neighbor—whose steep *Urgestein* terraces are capable of sustaining wine as profound as that of next-door Loiben. They seem still to belong to the Wachau in all but name. Northeast of the city, as one moves away from the Danube, one finds a remarkable set of terraces of a very different sort. Huge, broad, fortress-like mounds that can be planted a dozen or more vine rows deep are the product of pure loess, a soil consisting of yellowish dust ground up by the receding glaciers of the last Ice Age and deposited in massive quantities throughout present-day Europe and beyond. Vine roots can sink to amazing depths in this fast-draining medium, which supports highly distinctive Grüner Veltliner that tends to be gentler and less incisive than that grown on *Urgestein* and to emphasize notes of lentil, lime, and cress. Along the south shore of the Danube, opposite Krems, there is considerable diversity of soils including sand, gravel, loess, conglomerate, and clay, with a correspondingly diverse viticultural potential.

Along the banks of the Krems itself, Riesling and Grüner Veltliner are dominant, although Nigl is one of those to have proven the high quality potential of Austrian Sauvignon Blanc. The *Urgestein* vineyards of Stein at the edge of the Wachau are dominated by Riesling and include several of the most renowned sites in Austria for this grape, notably the Steiner Pfaffenberg and Steiner Hund. Ironically, the best examples come from Emmerich Knoll and the Nikolaihof, respectively, both of them Wachau estates, although Pfaffenberg Riesling from the Salomon-Undhof estate can be impressive, as is their Riesling from the Kögl, a site higher up and closer to the city center. The Salomons craft outstanding Grüner Veltliner in this vicinity, too, and (along with Knoll, whom they supplied with cuttings) fashion fascinating dry and sweet wine from the rare Gelber Traminer, a grape that combines scintillating floral perfume with an almost Riesling-like litheness and brightness. The truth is that these steep terraces above Stein and Krems are capable of delivering a far greater number of outstanding wines, provided additional hardy idealists can be found to farm them. Under the dynamic direction of Fritz Miesbauer, the Weingut der Stadt Krems—a municipal institution—has recently made great strides, including the repair of terraces and replanting in their impressively situated Grillenpartz vineyard.

The vast stretch of loess terraces to the north and east of Krems are dominated by Grüner Veltliner, although there is still significant acreage of Riesling, along with, among others, Chardonnay and Zweigelt. Josef Mantler makes something of a specialty of Roter Veltliner (for more on this grape, see under The Wagram). Grüner Veltliner dominates as well on the right bank of the Danube opposite Krems. But the picture there can be more diverse, as befits a multiplicity of soils, and as demonstrated by Gerard Malat, who scores notable successes not only with Riesling and Grüner Veltliner, but also with Muskateller, the full family of Pinots, and the Bordelais reds. A sizeable percentage of the Kremstal's production comes from one gargantuan cooperative, the Winzer Krems, who have been making significant strides in recent years to supplement and improve their basic offerings.

The terms "Kabinett" and "Spätlese" are holdovers from a time when Austrian wine law took its lead from that of Germany and are still occasionally utilized (in tiny print) on bottles of dry white wine from the Kremstal, Kamptal, and surrounding regions. When they appear, the difference in style is roughly comparable to that between Federspiel and Smaragd in the neighboring Wachau. More often nowadays in Austria, the difference between lighter- and fuller-bodied dry whites is indicated by the use of the word "Reserve" for the latter, a term the Kremstal growers recently enshrined into law. Admittedly, "Reserve" is vague and internationally overused, but growers are understandably loath to court confusion, either by perpetuating terminology associated with often sweet German wines, or by inventing some alternative peculiar to the region. In any case, a look at the alcohol level registered on the label will offer a general guide to a wine's body, just as it would in the Wachau—even if that region's growers had not been clever, prescient, and skillful enough to come up with and establish their colorful trio of terms. Wines that exceed 9 grams of sugar will be labeled *halbtrocken*, but that too is buried in tiny print, as is the term *trocken* (dry) on the vast majority of labels. It is simply understood that the principal aim of growers in Austria's Danube regions is to craft dry-tasting wine. Only if a wine is labeled Auslese is it apt to taste discreetly sweet and overtly so if labeled Beerenauslese or Trockenbeerenauslese.

Vintages and wine longevity west of the city of Krems track with those of the Wachau, while vintages along the Krems, and in the loess soils to the northeast of the city, correspond more with the Kamptal and Wagram. One night in June 2007, a wide swath of vineyards east of Krems and across the Danube was shredded by hail so deep it shut down the nearby highway. But the prevalence of hail in all of Austria's growing regions will seldom be reflected in any vintage generalizations, since its sometimes savage effects are usually capricious and localized.

THE TRAISENTAL: A WINDOW ON THE FUTURE

Traveling downstream, the first sizeable or important concentration of viticulture on the south shore of the Danube appears at the eastern edge of the Wachau and in the adjacent portion of the Kremstal, across the river from the city of Krems itself. Follow the river Trais upstream from here and a significant viticultural vista opens, including a range of granulitic, gravelly, and conglomerate hills with diurnal temperature gradients, terraces, and geological complexity reminiscent of the Wachau. It's safe to state that when the Traisental was officially registered as an Austrian winegrowing region in 1995, its name was unfamiliar even to the locals and furthermore that up to now only a single estate—that of Ludwig and Karl Neumayer—has demonstrated this region's potential for world-class performance. But a host of younger vintners, including the Neumayers' cousin Markus Huber, are now stepping up to the plate. Grüner Veltliner dominates here, but Riesling is promising, and Neumayer is one of Austria's most successful pioneers with Pinot Blanc and Sauvignon. Few who visit the Traisental depart unconvinced that its wine potential is about to be unlocked and discovered.

THE WAGRAM: MAKING THE MOST OF LOESS

The loess escarpments to the northeast of Krems are a prelude to the landscape several miles in from the Danube as one continues toward Vienna. Hillsides and broad terraces of loess (interspersed with gravel) dominate the scene, and roads and pathways in places become so-called *Höhlgraben*—literally "cave-trenches"—as they burrow through deep layers of yellow glacial dust. This soil is so root-friendly for vines that pale, ephemeral leaves have been known to sprout from the ceilings of deep cellars where a disoriented vine broke through. Grüner Veltliner dominates here (and Bernhard Ott has shown that it can be world-class), but the leading grape up until the mid-20th century was Roter Veltliner, a distant or nonrelative capable of fascinating aromas of musk, citrus, and rhubarb, a rich texture, and considerable longevity. Rudi Pichler in the Wachau and Josef Mantler in the Kremstal keep this ancient variety alive in their respective regions, while Franz Leth remains the foremost champion of Roter Veltliner in the Wagram. Interest in this former regional specialty is reviving at other addresses.

The local growers have for more than a dozen years promoted their district as the Wagram. (The name, of disputed derivation, is utilized elsewhere in Austria too, always associated with the frontier or *Limes* that once existed between Roman civilization and a "barbarian" north.) It was only in 2007 that this area—at the time (along with Klosterneuburg, west of Vienna) all that remained of a once huge growing region known as Donauland, from which the Kremstal, Kamptal, Carnuntum, and Taisental had spun off—officially became a self-standing region. Beyond the "two colors" of Veltliner, promising results have been achieved with Riesling, Pinot Blanc, Sauvignon, red and yellow variants of Traminer, Pinot Noir, Zweigelt, and, improbably, particularly on the part of Fritsch and Salomon-Oberstockstall, with Cabernet Sauvignon. This is another Austrian region rich in possibility and offering excellent value, as well as one taking on increasing prominence in North American markets.

THE KAMPTAL: CONCENTRATION OF EXCELLENCE

MAJOR GRAPES AND PLACES

The diversity and excellence of wines from no fewer than five different growing regions all within a 20-mile radius of Krems is remarkable. But the concentration of excellence and diversity on display in the Kamptal might be unprecedented anywhere else. This region's leading vintners have long since stepped out from the shadow of their famous Wachau neighbors: The depth of young talent around Langenlois and a few neighboring villages, all tightly clustered along the river Kamp north of Krems, is extraordinary. Approaching Langenlois from any direction, one is overwhelmed by a sea of vines. Half of these are Grüner Veltliner; only around 7% are Riesling, but the latter grape is no less emblematic of the Kamptal, thanks to two of the best sites for it in all of Austria. Pinot Blanc, Sauvignon, Chardonnay, and Muskateller cannot lay claim to major acreage, but they can to major successes at the hands of local vintners. Red wine varieties also claim only a small percentage of the Kamptal's total acreage (15%, to be exact, more than half that of Zweigelt). Nevertheless, some of the most fascinatingly delicious and ageworthy examples of Pinot Noir, St. Laurent, Cabernet Sauvignon and Merlot (not to mention lip-smackingly delicious Zweigelt) in Austria are being grown here. While there is no strong sparkling wine tradition here, in recent years both Bründlmayer and Schloss Gobelsburg have demonstrated world-class results using Champagne methods and their own distinctive mixes of grapes.

The litany of geological structures and soil types in the small but densely planted confines of the Kamptal is a long one, including gneiss, granite, mica-schist, amphibolite, sandstone, loess, limestone, gravel, and clay. West of Langenlois, along the banks of the Loisbach, are the loess Thal; geologically diverse Kittmannsberg; the loess Loiserberg; the steep, schistic, former quarry Steinmassel and its neighbor Steinhaus; and, leveling out above them, the Ladner, Schenkenbichl and Dechant. These vineyards have demonstrated excellence with varieties as diverse as Chardonnay, Pinot Blanc, Sauvignon Blanc, St. Laurent, and Pinot Noir, as well as Grüner Veltliner and Riesling. Along the little river Kamp itself, across from Langenlois, lie the region's three best-known vineyards. The massive Heiligenstein rises like a flight of broad Permean sandstone stairs. Along with its lower, broader neighbor the Gaisberg (with its own distinct mélange of weathered rock), this is the preeminent Kamptal site for Riesling. But the nature preserve that is the Heiligenstein, with its often Mediterranean flora and fauna, is also where Willi Bründlmayer—having long expressed a fear that this region could become too warm for Riesling within the 21st century—has demonstrated amazing results with Cabernet and Merlot. In between these heights lie the Grub and the deeper, loess-bedecked soils of the Lamn; in these sites Bründlmayer, Schloss Gobelsburg, and others grow some of the region's most formidable Grüner Veltliner.

WHAT TO EXPECT IN STYLE AND RECENT VINTAGES

One may expect the finest Kamptal Riesling to resemble, along broad lines, those of the Wachau. With Grüner Veltliner, the character of the wines varies enormously depending on the site, not to mention the style of vinification. The denizens of the Kamptal have proven somewhat more experimental in their winemaking than those of the Wachauer. Some of the most refined use of small oak barrels in Austria can be witnessed with Grüner Veltliner from the Kamptal, and the revival of larger casks made from acacia (once traditional) began in this region as well. In the high-acid vintage of 2004, Kamptal growers (not wedded to sharply defined terms like "Federspiel" or "Smaragd") were more inclined than those of the Wachau to leave atypical residual sugar behind, confident that the wines would balance and still always taste dry. A propos of terminology: "Kabinett" and "Spätlese" are seldom seen anymore on Kamptal labels, nor has the use of "Reserve" become widespread. Rather, one can expect single-site wines to range from 12.5% to 15% alcohol, each winery also offering certain lighter cuvées with proprietary names that, weather permitting, range from 11% to 12.5%. Bründlmayer and Gobelsburg, along with Hiedler, have taken the lead in crafting outstanding, nobly sweet Beerenauslese, Trockenbeerenauslese, and Eiswein, but even at those establishments and in botrytis-prone vintages like 1995 and 1998, the percentage of such wines remains tiny.

The growers of the Kamptal and Kremstal have developed a vineyard classification as a result of which one will often see wines labeled Erste Lage, or E.L., and Klassifizierte Lage. Little attention, frankly, has been or need be paid to these designations even among local vintners. The top sites reveal themselves as such in the hands of the best vintners, as is the case anywhere in the world. At the same time, many a site simply awaits its champion—or is perhaps lucky enough to have found a single champion. Examples are Fred Loimer's Riesling from the Seeberg vineyard and Michael Moosbrugger's Grüner Veltliner from the Steinsetz at Schloss Gobelsburg, which often move this region's most exciting wines, on the strength of which one feels confident in concluding that the sites themselves are inherently top-class. But one will have to search to find another vintner who is even working with these sites, much less one who achieves similar excellence.

Generally, one can expect vintages for white wine in the Kamptal to track relatively closely with those described earlier for the Wachau. As befits the relative warmth of many of the Kamptal's vineyards compared with those of the Wachau, this region has been marginally more successful in certain higher-acid vintages, such as 2004. In the tricky, intermittently rainy harvests of 2002 and 2001, the Wachau had a slight edge. Despite its small overall dimensions, the diversity of soils, exposures, and elevations of vineyards in the Kamptal make it no less difficult—and perhaps more so—to generalize about the quality of a vintage here than in the Wachau or Kremstal. The number of occasions when any given vintner appears to have completely beaten the odds seems blessedly high among Kamptal growers, as witness the superb collections of Gobelsburg in 2002 or Hirsch in 1998. When it comes to reds, so far the general rule applying to the Kamptal would seem to be "the warmer the better." Some of the all-time best were grown in 2003, and 2005 has also proven highly promising for reds.

THE WEINVIERTEL: MORE AND LESS THAN A QUARTER

"Weinviertel" is the name that has for more than two centuries referred to a vast arc of viticulture north of the Danube, extending along the borders of the present-day Czech Republic, east to the Slovak frontier. Its western reaches abut the Kamptal and Wagram, while its eastern territory encroaches on Vienna's northern winegrowing suburbs. The name "wine quarter" fits because vines were grown—sporadically, and in some places densely—over the entire expanse of this poor and rural region; they supplied the bulk of the table wines not just in Vienna, but in Prague and Bruno as well. Sparkling wine has long been associated with Austria's celebrated sense of *Gemütlichkeit* and pageantry, and this region was traditionally the source as well of base wine for a veritable industry of bubbly. Just as Grüner Veltliner makes up one-third of Austria's acreage, so does the Weinviertel, roughly two-thirds of which is planted with that variety. This region is a sleeping giant. Although its international significance is as yet modest, both Austrians and Americans are increasingly falling under the spell of its growing number of enthusiastic estate-bottlers and the price-quality rapport that their wines represent.

Two features of Austria's wine landscape and culture are especially prominent in the Weinviertel. The *Kellergassen* at the edge of a town and adjacent to its vineyards are a feature that follows the former boundaries of the Hapsburg Empire deep into Eastern Europe. These are rows of tiny buildings that served as combined press houses and taverns, which brings us to the second prominent feature—in fact, an institution dating from the early 19th century— the *Heurigen* operated by most bottling Weinviertel growers, taverns licensed to sell simple foods and dispense directly to the consumer solely the wines grown by their proprietors. This legal dispensation and the two-centuries-old tradition of traveling to the countryside to enjoy on weekends and holidays the hospitality of the *Heurigen* and their new wine (from which the name derives), was the economic salvation of small wine growers. However, from the standpoint of the high-quality aspirations that have been emerging in the Weinviertel over the past decade, the labor-intensive *Heurigen* can be a drag on families who remain economically wedded to them. Significantly, the first Weinviertel estate to cast off the shackles of the hospitality business and fearlessly subsist on sales of bottled wine—that of Roman and Adelaide Pfaffl—has become a beacon for Weinviertel quality as well as one of the most successful family wine businesses in all of Austria. (Granted, an incredible amount of ambition, determination, and talent, as well as a prime location on the fringes of Vienna, have all played major roles in that success.)

As Austrians and Americans alike search for value, and as more growers dedicate all of their working energies to estate-bottled wines, the Weinviertel will gain in prominence. (Already, it is not uncommon to see as yet underpriced wines from emerging stars sold out almost immediately upon release.) As Pfaffl, Setzer, and a few others have shown, a wide range of white and red grapes have outstanding potential in this region—one too vast to generalize about soils, sites, vintages, or the sources of future stars in Austria's wine constellation. For all of the newly aroused dreams and ambitions of the Weinviertel, neither vintners nor its consumers are apt to forsake the crisp, infectiously drinkable style of Grüner Veltliner with which it is today primarily associated. In warmer years to come, the diverse microclimates of this enormous region may offer Austria's best locations for perpetuating low-alcohol, refreshing white wines of a sort that will be diligently sought the world over.

VIENNA: WINEGROWING METROPOLIS

Already as a Roman military outpost, Austria's future capital was known for its wine, hence the name "Vindobona." While the city limits can lay claim to only about one-tenth of 1% of Austria's total acreage, this still dwarfs the share of Bordeaux vineyards located within the city's limits. And while no one will ever confuse Viennese crus with the likes of Pape Clément or Haut-Brion, the vineyards of Vienna are not only a beloved part of that city's image, they represent sites of great historical significance and future potential. In fact, one could view the present era as an opportunity for Vienna's vineyards to regain their pre-1900 reputations after the serial calamities of the 20th century: phylloxera, world war, dissolution of empire, revolution, economic depression, *Anschluss* to the Nazi Reich, genocide, Allied bombing, and Soviet occupation. These were followed by an era in which Vienna's vintners were happy just to be able to reopen their *Heurigen* and serve local residents and tourists in peace. (Would that all of Austria's cultural losses in the 20th century could have been reclaimed so easily.)

The urban distribution of grape varieties in itself tells a story. One-third of the acreage is Grüner Veltliner. Riesling and Pinot Blanc (including Chardonnay) account for 15% each. Zweigelt lays claim to 6%, Pinot Noir to 2%, and St. Laurent and Cabernet Sauvignon each to slightly less. So, it is clear that relatively demanding grapes with high quality potential have the upper hand vis-à-vis easily ripening but inherently uninteresting varieties such as Müller-Thurgau, Welschriesling, and Blauer Portugieser. Of the roughly one-quarter of Vienna's acreage not accounted for in the figures just cited, half is planted in *Gemischter Satz*, field blends of many different varieties. The areas of greatest potential shown by the more ambitious Viennese wineries in recent years precisely parallel our survey of grapes: outstanding Grüner Veltliner (from places like the foot of the Bisamberg, shared with the Weinviertel, at the city's northern edge); remarkably full-bodied dry Riesling (above all from the once renowned, steep hills of the Nussberg area, in the hilly northwestern suburb of Grinzing); Pinot Blanc and Chardonnay; serious reds (especially from the southern suburb of Mauer); and *Gemischter Satz*. Those mixed plantings of old vines may owe their survival solely to growers' indifference and lack of incentive to rip them up and replant with single, "superior" varieties as happened in most of the country. Lately, Vienna's vintners have come to realize that this piece of history is a treasure in itself, and they are banding together to promote as a unique, food-friendly category called Wiener Gemischter Satz, with the advantage that each producer's cast of vines—not to mention his or her site and style of vinification—is distinctive. The prospects are so delicious and marketable that new mixed plantings are still going into the ground.

CARNUNTUM: ROMAN CAPITAL WITH MODERN PRETENTIONS

At a time when Vienna was merely a garrison (and where one winter Marcus Aurelius composed his *Meditations*), nearby Carnuntum was Pannonia's capital. That former city is now only a picturesque ruin on the southern shore of the Danube (and on wine labels), but the sea of vines extending from Vienna eastward to a bend in the river opposite Slovakia's capital, Bratislava, has been an official growing region since 1993. The name of a formidable Merlot, Cabernet, and Zweigelt cuvée from Hans Pitnauer—Quo Vadis—unabashedly and appropriately poses the question for Carnuntum. It's really too soon to tell, because ambitious experiments are under way here with a wide range of Austria's native grapes, as well as a full (perhaps too full) range of international varieties. Modestly priced Grüner Veltliner and rich, often powerful and pricey reds have sustained Carnuntum on the Austrian wine market; more and more of these wines are turning up abroad as well. Portuguese and international winemaking superstar Dirk Niepoort is married to a Carnuntum native, Dorli Muhl: their new wine ("Spitzerberg" made from Blaufränkisch) will probably ratchet up the level of attention paid to this region.

THE THERMENREGION: REINVENTING ITSELF

The roughly 30-mile stretch south from Vienna's famous woods through such spa and gambling resorts as Baden, to the city of Wiener Neustadt, was long known as the Südbahn, after the railway first forged here in the mid-19th century to connect the southern outposts of the empire with its capital. Trains and tourism brought this area prosperity and its wines celebrity and a place not just on Austrian but on international tables. As a center for both some of the earliest serious research into the typing and propagation of individual grape varieties and for mercantile activity, the town of Gumpoldskirchen (less than a dozen miles south of Vienna) became practically synonymous the world over with Austrian wine. But wines so labeled seldom displayed much distinction. In the U.S. in the 1960s or 1970s, Gumpoldskirchner signified a slightly sweet and uninspiring blend. Given its former dominance by sweet wines and by merchants and *négociants*, this area has been one of the last to recover from the wine scandal of 1985; and that has happened not because of the rechristening of the Südbahn as the "Thermal [Spa] Region"—most Austrians still call it the Südbahn—but thanks to a few determined growers or former merchants reinventing themselves as serious wine producers.

This region is best known for and achieves some of its finest bottled results with grapes unfamiliar elsewhere. One is Neuburger, which we already met in the Wachau. The two more important are Rotgipfler and Zierfandler. (Despite the root "red" in the one, and the probably historic accident by which the name of the other became affixed to a black grape of Croatian origin that went on to enjoy a stellar career in California, both Rotgipfler and Zierfandler are white grapes. It's the tip—*Gipfel*—of the former's vine shoot that is red). Rotgipfler produces wines with considerable body yet citric brightness. Zierfandler is more alluring, Chenin-like, both in its combination of opulence with refreshing brightness and in its spiced quince, apple, and orange flavors. When blended, as they often are, the resultant wine is traditionally, if curiously, known as Spätrot-Rotgipfler. (There is even a very fine winery that calls itself Spaetrot.) Thanks to the exceptional results of Johann Stadlmann with Zierfandler, as well as the recent acquisition and promotion of the Schellmann winery by quality-conscious and commercially ambitious Kamptal vintner Fred Loimer, it is safe to predict that the wines of this region are slated for a return to wider recognition. A number of Thermenregion growers—sniffing in the direction of their successful neighbors to the east in Burgenland—have also demonstrated serious aspirations with Pinot Noir and other black grapes.

BURGENLAND: AROUND THE NEUSIEDLERSEE

Between them, the two official wine regions that almost surround the narrow, shallow, 20-mile long Neusiedlersee account for more than one-third of Austrian wine. (The southern reaches of this steppe lake are part of a western appendage of Hungary.) Nobody understands just how this "sea" sustains itself, or what caused its return after it dried up completely for nearly a decade in 1865. There is more interest today than ever in answering those questions, since the water level has dropped steadily and alarmingly of late. The relatively small Neusiedlersee-Hügelland region incorporates, as its name suggests, an array of winegrowing hills west of the lake, all part of the Leitha range (traditionally, until 1921, the Austro-Hungarian border), where white grapes dominate, but more of the exciting wines are red. Near the lake shore at Rust, fog promotes botrytis and nobly sweet wine that three centuries ago earned this small town status as a "free city" in the Kingdom of Hungary.

The official region of Neusiedlersee—more than twice the size of the Neusiedlersee-Hügelland—commences near the northern rim of the lake and extends down its eastern edge into the mosaic of sand and small lakes known as the Seewinkel, a "corner" (*Winkel*) of Austria long impoverished by its isolation on the edge of the Hungarian Plain and later by the Iron Curtain at its doorstep. Vinous excitement in the Neusiedlersee region is largely divided between reds and nobly sweet whites, but there is a much higher percentage of the latter than is true of the opposite shore.

MAJOR GRAPES, PLACES, AND STYLES

Grüner Veltliner and Welschriesling account for nearly a third of the acreage of the Neusiedlersee-Hügelland, but wines from these varieties (other than a few Grüner Veltliners from the coolest, breeziest hillside locations, such as those around Donnerskirchen) are undistinguished. Rich, complex reds are rendered from the Blaufränkisch that makes up roughly one-third of the region's acreage, along with sizeable amounts of Zweigelt, Pinot Noir, and Cabernet Sauvignon. A small but increasing number of distinguished dry whites emanate from Pinot Blanc, Chardonnay, and Sauvignon Blanc, particularly in the hands of a few growers such as Kolwentz, Prieler, and Schröck.

Most of the Hügelland hillsides look out on the lake, and their iron, quartzite, and mica-rich schist and gneiss ranges from slab-like to sandy. The Goldberg and Seeberg—between Schützen am Gebirge and Rust—have demonstrated their outstanding potential in the hands of the Prieler family. In hills close to the shore at Rust—sites such as Mariental and Umriss, memorably reflected in the wines of Ernst Triebaumer and Feiler-Artinger—chalk with mussel and coral appear. In all these hills, small undulations or differences in inclination can play a major role in the choice of grape and character of wine. Wind is a constant factor. There is also a significant concentration of vine-bearing hills further inland around Burgenland's capital, Eisenstadt, where one finds complex variations on chalky soil with a wide range of exposures, many with historical significance or geological rarity and just waiting to be rediscovered.

The sweet wines for which Rust (together with its population of storks) is renowned were long known as Ausbruch (in Magyar, *Aszú*, a term still in use in Tokai). Today a wine labeled Ausbruch is effectively a top-quality Beerenauslese or Trockenbeerenauslese, and sweet wines from less ripe or ennobled grapes are bottled as Auslese. Rust's growers were unable to protect the term "Ausbruch" for their exclusive use; however, none of the sweet wine producers of quality or integrity in other areas of Austria utilize that term on their labels. An Ausbruch is generally the product of more than one grape variety, and if there are only two or three of these, growers may list them as part of the wine's name. Grapes featured most often include Welschriesling, Muscat Ottonel, Pinot Blanc, Chardonnay, and Traminer. But many of the most interesting examples involve Sauvignon Blanc, Muskateller, or Pinot Gris, and several magnificent recent examples, from Schandl, Schröck, and Wenzel, have resulted from the reestablishment in Rust of the once traditional Furmint grape (familiar from Tokaj). The crossings Bouvier and Scheurebe (discussed below) are represented here as well. Feiler Artinger and a few others occasionally record striking, nobly sweet success with such red varieties as Zweigelt, Pinot Noir, and even Cabernet Franc.

On the eastern side of the lake, in the official region of Neusiedlersee, Grüner Veltliner still occupies significant acreage, which is a shame, since local renditions tend to be coarse, flabby, and uninteresting. The excitement here is in the realm of rich, full reds and the nobly sweet elixirs, of which those of Kracher have become world-famous. At the border with the Neusiedlersee-Hügelland, one of the most noteworthy locations was originally planted by monks and long the property of the Hungarian crown. The terraces at Jois, unique in the region, and among the few top red-wine vineyards bordering the lake. Josef Umathum has reconstructed a large section of these ancient terraces, achieving exciting results there with Blaufränkisch and young vines of Pinot Noir. Continuing around the top of the lake, we come to three of the region's most important red wine villages: Gols, Mönchhof, and Frauenkirchen. Gentle slopes and undulations featuring sand, gravel, and loess support generally powerful renditions of Zweigelt, Blaufränkisch, St. Laurent, Pinot Noir, Cabernet, and even Syrah from the area's remarkably dense concentration of ambitious—at times, in their extraction of tannins, too ambitious—vintners, to which the astonishing number of strikingly designed and seemingly no-expenses-spared wineries in this sector testify. Typically, the less-expensive reds will be vinified in tank or large oval barrels known as *Fuder* that impart little or no flavor of oak. The upper echelons (sometimes labeled with proprietary names, sometimes with those of vineyards) are more typically raised in small, new *barriques,* although in the past several years vintners have displayed increasing imagination in the size of barrels and how they are employed, sometimes reacting to the excessive woodiness that can be found in many ambitious Burgenland reds. Growers here are increasingly concerned to achieve elegance and distinctiveness in their wines as well as concentration and international image.

Along the shore, as one continues south into the Seewinkel with its patchwork of tiny lakes and marshes, sweet wines dominate. These gently undulating, sandy, gravelly, nutrient-poor soils, under alternating autumn fog and sun, support a rich harvest of Auslesen, Beerenauslesen, and Trockenbeerenauslesen, although it is safe to state that until Alois Kracher came along, no one recognized how rich and complex wines from this corner of Europe could be. The advent of sophisticated plastic films for draping the vines in autumn has also been critical to today's rate of vinous successes, as most of this area, including its vineyards, is a national park known above all for its abundant species of birds. The best wines combine some of the opulence, viscosity, and caramelization of Sauternes with a delicacy and fresh fruit core more reminiscent of the Loire, or even of Germany. Kracher's approach—one series of wines vinified in tank or large ovals, the other in new *barriques*—points to the traditions of this region but also toward the great wines of Sauternes. Today, a variety of vessels are used to ferment and mature nobly sweet Neusiedlersee wines, from most of the same grapes one encounters in Rust (minus Furmint). The two crossings Bouvier (which tends inherently toward oiliness, opulence, and butterscotch flavors) and Scheurebe (often known here as Sämling, and valued for its acid retention and outrageously intense black currant, grapefruit, and mint aromas) play more significant roles here than around Rust, and there is also a flourishing tradition for harvesting Eiswein.

RECENT VINTAGES

For red wines, the Neusiedlersee area was blessed with generally felicitous conditions in both 2007 and 2006, with periods of cool and rain preserving the vines from shutdown or stress, and pushing back the date of harvest which, early on in 2007, looked likely to set a record. In the two preceding years, circumstances were dramatically different. Rain and rot forced growers' hands in 2005, and there are relatively few successes—those generally being with later-ripening and thicker-skinned Blaufränkisch. In 2004, growers with low yields employing impeccable practices were in a position to harvest ripe, flavorful fruit—if they made foresighted or just plain lucky choices. Once rain arrived in October, it stayed for most of the month. Outstanding results were scored with Pinot Noir and Zweigelt, and under the best circumstances Blaufränkisch displayed lovely aromatics and "cool climate' brightness and lift, without entirely sacrificing richness. The notoriously sweltering 2003 vintage brought a record early harvest and record high must weights to the red grapes of the Neusiedlersee. The usual pitfalls can be observed—notably jammy, cooked-fruit flavors, heat, and excess tannins. But those vintners who kept yields low on their stressed-out vines, did not shear away too much foliage, and exercised analogous caution in the cellar with extraction and new wood, could boast some extraordinary successes. Two other outstanding recent red wine vintages around the Neusiedlersee were 2000 and 1997.

Since botrytis is the enemy of red wine but a definitive ingredient for nobly sweet, it is not surprising that great vintages for both seldom coincide; still, given the wide range of grapes in play and the microclimatic differences in effect around the Neusiedlersee, such a coincidence cannot be ruled out. In the outstanding vintages for dry red wine of 1997, 2000, and 2003, relatively little sweet wine above the level of Auslese was even essayed (Kracher being the huge exception in 2000), and the few successful examples from 2003 taste of dried fruit without the complexities of botrytis, and with precariously low acid. But the region has been exceptionally fortunate in recent years, and was blessed with abundant, high-quality botrytis in 2005 and 2006. With the proper selectivity and luck, some outstanding sweet wines were made in 2004 and 2002, with unusually bright acidity and delicacy. The greatest botrytis vintage in modern memory for this region was 1995; there was also a high rate of success in 1998 and 1999.

MIDDLE AND SOUTHERN BURGENLAND: BLAUFRÄNKISCHLAND

Growers southwest of the Neusiedlersee call their region (officially known as Mittelburgenland) Blaufränkischland, and that variety accounts for just over half of the total acreage. In the long, sparsely cultivated tail of Südburgenland, Blaufränkisch, while less dominant, is still the most widely cultivated grape and is the basis for the region's most interesting wines. The three most important of a cluster of villages in northern Mittelburgenland—Neckenmarkt, Horitschon, and Deutschkreuz—feature variations on limestones and weathered schist, being richer in stones or clay according to the situation and elevation, which in Neckenmarkt can reach 1,200 feet, thus offering a cooler, longer growing season. Blaufränkisch from these towns have consistently numbered among the most impressive reds in Austria. Zweigelt, Pinot Noir, and the Bordelais red varieties are widely planted in these villages as well, though generally with less interesting results. In the south of Mittelburgenland, at Lutzmannsburg, clay-rich volcanic soil shows considerable promise with Blaufränkisch as well. In Südburgenland, one spot has stood out historically, as well as among the results of contemporary vintners—the Eisenberg, with iron-rich schist slopes bisected by the Hungarian frontier, is memorably reflected in wines from Krutzler and Schiefer.

STYRIA: HILLS ALIVE WITH THE SMELL OF SUCCESS

Styria is officially made up of three growing regions. Weststeiermark, curiously, is dominated by production of generally tart pink and sparkling wines from a local grape known as Blauer Wildbacher, or Schilcher, which seldom travel beyond the region's, much less Austria's, boundaries. Südoststeiermark represents a large but relatively sparsely planted region whose potential for diverse grape varieties is only gradually being discovered, thanks in large part to the exceptional winegrowing and promotional efforts of Neumeister. Südsteiermark, along the Slovenian border, has much narrower boundaries, but incorporates more than half of Styria's total vine acreage. In its reputation and success inside Austria, this region is rivaled only by the Wachau. Indeed, the problem here will soon be growers running out of vineyards to reclaim or new sites to plant. On these windy, steep pre-Alpine hillsides, the number of sites that are well exposed and not excessively frost-prone is limited. Several of the region's top estates now farm property across the border in Slovenia as well which, under certain circumstances or for a limited period, may actually be bottled under the name "Südsteiermark."

The wines of South Styria fall into two major classes. The vast majority are typically labeled Steierische Klassik. These are harvested at modest levels of sugar to keep alcohol around 12% or less and are vinified bone dry in tank or large, older casks (without malolactic fermentation) to capture freshness. Wines bottled from and labeled with the names of individual vineyards are always much riper, are generally vinified in smaller barrels—often, but not always the classic French 225-liter *barrique*; often, but not always new—and typically go through malolactic transformation. There has been a welcome tendency lately to experiment more with larger and older barrels for ostensibly top wines to reduce overt woodiness and bring into focus the differences among sites. So to some extent, there has been a blurring of the stylistic distinction between Klassik and Lagen (site-specific) wines. Essentially, the growers of this region offer two very different styles at very different price points.

Welschriesling is the most common local grape; grapes with the most cachet are Sauvignon Blanc and Muskateller, the latter almost always vinified in the Klassik style. Other important white grapes are Chardonnay, Traminer (usually the so-called "red" variant), Pinot Gris, and Pinot Blanc. Some 2% of acreage is planted with Riesling, but that normally celebrated grape is accorded little importance and no prestige in southern Styria. Zweigelt completely dominates the modest acreage of reds in Styria; in fact, few other reds will ripen properly in these vineyards, although here too several growers are devotees of that "heartbreak grape," Madame Pinot.

Pronounced phenolic "kick," briskness, and pungency are all classic characteristics of Styrian wine. The region's simpler Sauvignon Blancs can be compared with those of New Zealand for their tendency to evoke gooseberry, passion fruit, and hay, while the Muskateller can be practically, but pleasantly, sneeze-inducing in their pungency. Chardonnay in the Klassik style seldom seems more interesting than the refreshing, modestly endowed Welschriesling of the region. The more ambitious single-vineyard wines of South Styria—particularly from Sauvignon Blanc and Pinot Blanc—can be marvelous in their intricate expressions of citrus, herbs, nut oils, and what most tasters will, for lack of any better word, call "minerals." But there are also many examples where new wood and/or overtly lactic notes create a bifurcated personality. Nobly sweet wines are few and far between in these parts, but Tement and (in Southeast Styria) Neumeister bottle some notable exceptions.

Vintage character can alter the balance of Styrian wine rather radically. In 2003, for instance—besides being plagued by a sheer shortage of juice in an Austrian market that is crazy for their wines—South Styria's growers weren't really capable of delivering the Klassik character at all, as the wines had too much alcohol and too little acidity. At the upper end of that vintage's sugar and price scale, many wines were ponderous and top-heavy. Then came 2004 with cool, rainy weather that caused many Klassik bottlings to take a screeching 180-

degree turn from 2003; Attempts to stick to the barrel-aging and malolactic formula with single-vineyard wines frequently yielded grotesquely oaky or milky results. (The grapes possessed abundant malic and precious little ripe tartaric acid at harvest.) 2005 brought noticeable improvement, while 2006 and 2007 have turned out very well. Klassik wines are generally best consumed within two or three years of bottling. The single-vineyard wines can be fascinating to follow for a decade or more; however, given the wide range of grapes, sites, meteorological vicissitudes, and rapidly evolving, personal winemaking styles that characterize Styria, it is difficult to generalize about this.

—DAVID SCHILDKNECHT

[the ratings]

AUSTRIA'S BEST PRODUCERS

★ ★ ★ ★ ★ (OUTSTANDING)

Willi Bründlmayer (Kamptal)
Schloss Gobelsburg (Kamptal)
Franz Hirtzberger (Wachau)
Emmerich Knoll (Wachau, Kremstal)
Alois Kracher—Weinlaubenhof
  (Neusiedlersee)

Moric—Roland Velich (Mittelburgenland,
  Neusiedlersee-Hügelland)
Nigl—Martin Nigl (Kremstal)
Nikolaihof (Wachau, Kremstal)
F. X. Pichler (Wachau)
Prager—Toni Bodenstein (Wachau)

★ ★ ★ ★ (EXCELLENT)

Leo Alzinger (Wachau)
Heribert Bayer—In Signo Leonis
  (Mittelburgenland)
Gernot Heinrich (Neusiedlersee)
Hiedler (Kamptal)
Hirsch (Kamptal)
Fred Loimer (Kamptal)
Muhr—Niepoort (Carnuntum)
Neumayer (Traisental)
Neumeister (Südoststeiermark)
Ott (Wagram)
Rudi Pichler (Wachau)

Engelbert Prieler (Neusiedlersee-
  Hügelland)
Uwe Schiefer (Südburgenland)
Heidi Schröck (Neusiedlersee-Hügelland)
Strablegg-Leitner (Südsteiermark)
Manfred Tement (Südsteiermark)
Ernst Triebaumer (Neusiedlersee-
  Hügelland)
Tschida—Angerhof (Neusiedlersee)
Umathum (Neusiedlersee)
Velich—Heinz Velich (Neusiedlersee)

★ ★ ★ (VERY GOOD)

Paul Achs (Neusiedlersee)
Kurt Angerer (Kamptal)
Johann Bäuerl (Wachau)
Günther Brandl (Kamptal)
Marion Ebner—Mesuline
  (Carnuntum, Kamptal)
Feiler-Artinger (Neusiedlersee-Hügelland)
Freie Weingärtner (Wachau)
Albert Gesellmann (Mittelburgenland)
Gross (Südsteiermark)
Haider (Neusiedlersee)
Schloss Halbtrun (Neusiedlersee)

Högl (Wachau)
Josef Jamek (Wachau)
Jurtschitsch—Sonnhof (Kamptal)
Kollwentz—Römerhof
  (Neusiedlersee-Hügelland)
Krutzler (Südburgenland)
Lackner-Tinnacher (Südsteiermark)
Karl Lagler (Wachau)
Paul Lehrner (Mittelburgenland)
Josef Lentsch—Gastmifus zur Dankbarkeit
  (Neusiedlersee)
Malat (Kremstal, Wachau)

Mantlerhof—Josef Mantler (Kremstal)
Sepp and Maria Muster (Südsteiermark)
Anita and Hans Nittnaus (Neusiedlersee)
R. & A. Pfaffl (Weinviertel and Vienna)
Pöckl (Neusiedlersee)
Pollerhof (Weinviertel)
Pittnauer (Neusiedlersee)
Polz (Südsteiermark)
Claus Preisinger (Neusiedlersee)
Franz Proidl (Kremstal)
Salomon—Undhof (Kremstal)
Sattlerhof (Südsteiermark)

Schmelz (Wachau)
Josef Schmid (Kremstal)
Schwarz (Neusiedlersee)
Setzer (Weinviertel)
Stadlmann (Thermenregion)
Tinhof (Neusiedlersee-Hügelland)
Weingut der Stadt Krems (Kremstal)
Franz Weninger (Mittelburgenland)
Wenzel (Neusiedlersee-Hügelland)
Rainer Wess (Wachau, Kremstal)
Fritz Wieninger (Vienna)

* * (GOOD)

K. Alphart (Thermenregion)
Arachon—T.FX.T. (Mittelburgenland)
Anton Bauer (Wagram)
Judith Beck (Neusiedlersee)
Berger (Kremstal)
Birgit Braunstein (Neusiedlersee-
   Hügelland)
Buchegger (Kremstal)
Johann Donabaum (Wachau)
Sieghardt Donabaum (Wachau)
Ludwig Ehn (Kamptal)
Josef Ehnmoser (Wagram)
Birgit Eichinger (Kamptal)
Karl Fritsch (Wagram)
Rainer Gerhold (Wagram)
Glatzer (Carnuntum)
Stift Göttweig (Kremstal)
Gritsch—Mauritiushof (Wachau)
Hannes Harkamp (Südsteiermark)
J. Heinrich (Mittelburgenland)
Hillinger (Neusiedlersee)
H. & M. Hofer (Weinviertel)
Holzapfel (Wachau)
Huber (Traisental)
Iby—Lehrner (Mittelburgenland)
Igler (Mittelburgenland)
Jäger (Wachau)
Juris—Axel Stiegelmayer (Neusiedlersee)
Kerschbaum (Mittelburgenland)
Irene Langes (Vienna)
Leth (Wagram)

Mariell (Neusiedlersee-Hügelland)
Gerhard Markowitsch (Carnuntum)
Mayr—Vorspannhof (Kremstal)
Sepp Moser (Kremstal, Neusiedlersee)
Nastl (Kamptal)
Pitnauer (Carnuntum)
Reinisch—Johanneshof (Thermenregion)
Rotes Haus (Vienna)
Erwin Sabathi (Südsteiermark)
Salomon—Falkenstein (Weinviertel)
Fritz Salomon—Oberstockstall (Wagram)
Schandl (Neusiedlersee-Hügelland)
Schellmann—Fred Loimer
   (Thermenregion)
Rosi Schuster (Neusiedlersee-Hügelland)
Schwarzböck (Weinviertel)
Skoff (Südsteiermark)
Söllner (Wagram)
Sommer (Neusiedlersee-Hügelland)
Spätrot—Gebeshuber (Thermenregion)
Taubenschuss (Weinviertel)
Tegernseerhof—Franz & Martin Mittelbach
   (Wachau)
Johann Topf (Kamptal)
Andreas Tscheppe (Südsteiermark)
Wimmer-Czerny (Wagram)
Wohlmuth (Südsteiermark,
   Mittelburgenland)
Zahel (Vienna)
Zantho (Neusiedlersee)
Zull (Weinviertel)

[tasting commentaries]

PAUL ACHS ✶✶✶
NEUSIEDLERSEE $25.00–$75.00

Paul Achs was much influenced by time spent in California and crafts wines with great concentration, often unabashedly marked by new wood, but in recent years increasingly layered and, even in searing 2003, refined. He works with Chardonnay, the Bordeaux varieties, and traditional Austrian reds, but takes greatest pride is his Pinot Noir and in a fascinating series of single-site explorations with Blaufränkisch.

2003 Blaufränkisch Ungerberg	91	now–2014
2003 Blaufränkisch Altenberg	88	now–2010+?

LEO ALZINGER ✶✶✶
WACHAU $30.00–$70.00

The Leo Alzingers, father and son, fashion Riesling and Grüner Veltliner of great refinement and clarity, often understated in their youth compared with the renditions of Loiben *terroir* from Knoll or F. X. Pichler, but capable of formidable bottle evolution. Leo Junior has international experience, but is unlikely to alter the style significantly here, which is itself practically a national treasure.

2005 Grüner Veltliner Federspiel Mühlpoint	87	now
2004 Grüner Veltliner Federspiel Mühlpoint	90	now–2010
2004 Grüner Veltliner Smaragd Mühlpoint	88	now–2014
2004 Grüner Veltliner Smaragd Liebenberg	87	now–2012+?
2000 Grüner Veltliner Smaragd Liebenberg	88	now
2005 Grüner Veltliner Smaragd Loibenberg	89	now–2015
2004 Grüner Veltliner Smaragd Loibenberg	89	now–2014
2005 Grüner Veltliner Smaragd Steinertal	91	now–2018
2004 Grüner Veltliner Smaragd Steinertal	88	now–2012+?
2000 Grüner Veltliner Smaragd Steinertal	89	now
2005 Grüner Veltliner Reserve	89	2009–2012+?
2005 Riesling Smaragd Loibenberg	90	now–2012
2004 Riesling Smaragd Loibenberg	87	now–2010
2000 Riesling Smaragd Loibenberg	89	now
1999 Riesling Smaragd Loibenberg	90	now
2005 Riesling Smaragd Steinertal	91	2009–2014
2004 Riesling Smaragd Steinertal	87	now–2010
2000 Riesling Smaragd Steinertal	88	now
2000 Riesling Smaragd Höhereck	89	now
1997 Riesling Steinertal Reserve	91	now

KURT ANGERER ✶✶✶
KAMPTAL $15.00–$35.00

Voluminous, occasionally somewhat rough-hewn and alcoholically warm Angerer's wines may be, but they make emphatic statements, especially his single-vineyard Grüner Veltliners, each from a distinct *terroir*. Coarse red gravel, loam, chalk-clay, or granite are among the geological variations around Legenfeld, at the eastern edge of the Kamptal.

2005 Grüner Veltliner Kies	87	now
2005 Riesling Donatus	87	now–2010
2005 Riesling Ametsberg	87	now–2010

BÄUERL ★ ★ ★
WACHAU $20.00–$35.00

Johann Bäuerl of Dürnstein (not to be confused with a Wolfgang Bäuerl in Oberloiben, whose label likewise sports only a last name) bottles wines as fascinating as are his excellent sites, and sells them at remarkably modest prices. They may not be the last word in refinement, but his Grüner Veltliner, in particular, displays intense fruit, spice, and the all-important tactile dimension of grip.

HERIBERT BAYER—IN SIGNO LEONIS ★ ★ ★ ★
MITTELBURGENLAND $N/A

Bayer got his start as a collector, but the wine bug bit hard and he set out to establish new standards of excellence and sophistication in Austrian red, while building one of the country's many new vinificatory palaces in the process. Bayer—whose signature cuvée of Blaufränkisch, Zweigelt, and Cabernet, like the winery itself, takes its name from his sign in the Zodiac—is delivering results that live up to his impressive public relations, facilities, and packaging. Hopefully his wines—which also include attractive whites from his home Thermenregion, under the brand name Sails—will soon debut in U.S. markets.

GÜNTHER BRANDL ★ ★ ★
KAMPTAL $20.00–$40.00

Günther Brandl has small but excellent holdings, including a share of the great Heiligenstein, from which he generally bottles the fruits of a November picking.

| 2005 Riesling Novemberlese | 88 | now–2012 |

WILLI BRÜNDLMAYER ★ ★ ★ ★ ★
KAMPTAL $15.00–$100.00

There are few sorts of wine with which the soft-spoken, articulate Willi Bründlmayer does not succeed and where his influence cannot be felt across Austria. Naturally, dry Riesling and Grüner Veltliner are crafted in a range of weight and richness from some of the Kamptal's best sites. From the terraced Heiligenstein, Bründlmayer typically bottles no fewer than three Riesling, including one from especially old vines and one from vines whose canopy is V-shaped (hence, Lyra). Imposingly rich, voluminous old vines and single-vineyard Grüner Veltliner are vinified in cask. To his Pinot Noir, St. Laurent, and Zweigelt, Bründlmayer has added Merlot and the Cabernets as a hedge against climate change long before that topic was on many lips and his reds are typically understated but complex and ageworthy. Impressive barrel-fermented late-harvest elixirs and two ravishing sparkling renditions of the Pinot family help complete Bründlmayer's roster. In order to be fully appreciated, most of his wines should be savored with bottle age.

2005 Grüner Veltliner Loiser Berg	87	now
2004 Grüner Veltliner Vogelsang	90	now–2010
2004 Grüner Veltliner Alte Reben	89	now–2016
2002 Grüner Veltliner Alte Reben	90	now–2013
2000 Grüner Veltliner Alte Reben	89	now
2000 Grüner Veltliner Käferberg	92	now–2010
2005 Grüner Veltliner Lamm	89–91	2009–2012+?
2004 Grüner Veltliner Lamm	88	now–2015

2000 Grüner Veltliner Lamm	91	now–2010
2004 Grüner Veltliner Auslese Loiser Berg	89	now–2018
2000 Grüner Veltliner Trockenbeerenauslese	90	now–2020+?
2001 Riesling Steinmassel	91	now–2012
2005 Riesling Heiligenstein	88	now–2014
2004 Riesling Heiligenstein	87	now–2011
2002 Riesling Heiligenstein	89	now–2012
1999 Riesling Heiligenstein	88	now
2005 Riesling Heiligenstein Lyra	87	now–2012
2004 Riesling Heiligenstein Lyra	90	now–2010
2005 Riesling Heiligenstein Alte Reben	88–90	now–2014
2000 Riesling Heiligenstein Alte Reben	93	now–2012
2000 Riesling Heiligenstein Beerenauslese	91	now–2018
2001 St. Laurent Ladner	87	now
2004 Pinot Noir Cecile	89	now–2012
2002 Pinot Noir Cecile	87	now–2010

MARION EBNER—MESULINE ⋆ ⋆ ⋆
CARNUNTUM, KAMPTAL $60.00–$80.00

Marion Ebner is one of those wine merchants who cannot resist getting their hands full of grapes and *terroir*—although she does not grow but purchases fruit. Her barrel-fermented Grüner Veltliner Lyra (from Kamptal vines) and red blend (from Carnuntum, including some Syrah) are among the more flamboyant and powerful statements to be found in Austrian bottles, and they do not lack depth.

FEILER-ARTINGER ⋆ ⋆ ⋆
NEUSIEDLERSEE-HÜGELLAND $20.00–$150.00

Hans and Kurt Feiler's whites are considerably outnumbered by their reds, including a great many full-bodied, oaky exemplars. But it is the quality of their nobly sweet whites that created Feiler-Artinger's international reputation, as it did the reputation of Rust itself.

2004 Beerenauslese Cuvée [Welschriesling-Chardonnay]	87	now–2012
2004 Ausbruch Pinot Cuvée	91–93	now–2018
2002 Ausbruch Welschriesling-Chardonnay	86	now–2010
2004 Ausbruch Welschriesling-Weissburgunder	88–90	now–2014

FREIE WEINGÄRTNER-DOMÄNE WACHAU ⋆ ⋆ ⋆
WACHAU $13.00–$40.00

In the late 1990s and the first two years of the new century, the Wachau's dominant coop set extraordinary standards of quality and value. After the members parted company with the team that had orchestrated this quality surge, there were a couple of very difficult years. Thankfully, beginning with the 2005 vintage, new director Roman Horvath and Wachauer and Geisenheim-trained cellarmaster Heinz Frischengruber are reestablishing a reputation for delivering some of Austria's best values from some of the Wachau's best sites. All of the premium wines (and those that come to the U.S.) are now labeled "Domäne Wachau."

2005 Grüner Veltliner Federspiel Loibenberg	89	now
2005 Grüner Veltliner Smaragd Achleiten	89	now–2015
2005 Riesling Smaragd Singerriedl	87	now–2010
1999 Riesling Smaragd Singerriedl	90	now–2012
1997 Riesling Smaragd Achleiten	90	now–2012

ALBERT GESELLMANN ✶✶✶
MITTELBURGENLAND $25.00–$100.00

Albert Gesellmann is responsible for some of the most flamboyant, rich reds in Austria, although some may find them disappointingly international in style. The top wine is an age-worthy Blaufränkisch from the Hochacker vineyard (spelled without the umlaut on his labels, which proclaim "Gessellmann" without a given name, although there is more than one wine family in the region with this name.) Beginning in 2006, Gesellmann has been experimented with larger barrels for some of his wines.

SCHLOSS GOBELSBURG ✶✶✶✶✶
KAMPTAL $15.00–$100.00

Former Alpine hotelier Michael Moosbrugger took over the huge acreage, cellar, and palatial headquarters of Schloss Gobelsburg from the Monastery of Zwettl in 1996, and ran them with the assistance of Willi Bründlmayer for several years. To say that that he has succeeded brilliantly would be an understatement. Furthermore, like his mentor, the thoughtful and experimental Moosbrugger excels not just with Riesling and Grüner Veltliner from old vines in some of the Kamptal's top sites but with reds, sweet wines, and sparkling wines as well. His revival of large wooden *Fuder* has been a great success with many whites as well as reds. Furthermore, his inexpensive "Gobelsburger" Grüner Veltliner, Riesling, and Zweigelt—which should be enjoyed two to three years from the harvest—represent exceptional values.

2005 Grüner Veltliner Gobelsburger	89	now
2005 Grüner Veltliner Steinsetz	90	now–2014
2004 Grüner Veltliner Steinsetz	90	now–2014
2005 Grüner Veltliner Renner	90	now–2016
2004 Grüner Veltliner Renner	88	now–2012+?
2005 Grüner Veltliner Grub	88	now–2012
2004 Grüner Veltliner Grub	89	now–2010
2005 Grüner Veltliner Lamm	92	now–2018
2004 Grüner Veltliner Lamm	91	now–2018
2004 Grüner Veltliner Tradition	89–92	now–2014+?
2005 Grüner Veltliner Eiswein	93	now–2015+?
2004 Grüner Veltliner Beerenauslese	89	now–2020+?
2004 Riesling Urgestein	88	now–2010
2005 Riesling Gaisberg	89	2009–2014
2004 Riesling Gaisberg	90	2010–2014
2005 Riesling Heiligenstein	91	now–2015
2004 Riesling Heiligenstein	88–90	now–2014
2005 Riesling Alte Reben	90	2009–2016
2004 Riesling Alte Reben	91–93	now–2016
2005 Riesling Trockenbeerenauslese	91	now–2018+?
2005 St. Laurent Haidegrund	88–90	2009–2013
2004 St. Laurent Haidegrund	90–92	now–2015
2003 St. Laurent Haidegrund	90	now–2010
2003 St. Laurent Reserve	89–91	now–2012
2004 Pinot Noir Alte Haide	89–91	now–2012
2003 Pinot Noir Privatkeller	91	2009–2012+?
2003 Zweigelt	90	now

MARTIN HAIDER ★★★
NEUSIEDLERSEE $25.00–$50.00/375 ml

One of the many sweet-wine vintners in Illmitz, Martin Haider modestly distinguishes himself with Trockenbeerenauslese of considerable refinement and, at times, even delicacy. His results with Sauvignon are especially striking, although he is also a master of locally more familiar varieties.

SCHLOSS HALBTURN ★★★
NEUSIEDLERSEE $15.00–$150.00

The Baroque palace of Halbturn itself (located practically on the Hungarian border) is better known than its wines. The owners were persuaded in 2001 to hire Francois-Xavier Gaboriaud as cellarmaster and to develop an ambitious program that encompasses a range of *négociant* bottlings and international varieties, but also some increasingly distinguished (albeit expensive) estate reds, and minuscule volumes of superb, Sauternes-like nobly sweet blends.

GERNOT HEINRICH ★★★★
NEUSIEDLERSEE $18.00–$100.00

Gernot Heinrich is one of Austria's most celebrated red wine vintners, and his winemaking facility is nothing short of magnificent. Like a number of the best local growers, Heinrich has come to realize that sparing no expense, stringently reducing yields, and selecting bunches are to no avail if fruit and finesse are suffocated by overly aggressive extraction or barrel work. The least expensive, tank-rendered wines here have been consistently brilliant in their straightforward, generous way, while Heinrich's Pinot Noir and his many sophisticated blends seem increasingly nuanced and comfortable in their own skins.

2004 Blaufränkisch	90	now
2003 Salzberg	89	2009–2015

GROSS ★★★
SÜDSTEIERMARK $25.00–$70.00

Alois Gross commands an impressive facility, and view, including nearly six acres of vines, as well as some across the border in Slovenia that he has recently reclaimed for his family. The style runs toward the soft and understated, even when it comes to such usually brisk Styrian specialties as Muskateller and Welschriesling. Some of the wines are allowed or encouraged to go through malolactic transformation, particularly those in Gross's extensive array of single-vineyard bottlings.

2004 Gewürztraminer Gamitzberg	89	now–2011+?
2004 Grauburgunder Rothüttl	88	now–2012
2003 Sauvignon Blanc Nussberg	90	now–2014
2000 Sauvignon Blanc Nussberg	90	now
1999 Sauvignon Blanc Nussberg	91	now
2000 Sauvignon Blanc Sultz	89	now
1999 Sauvignon Blanc Sultz	90	now
2002 Gewürztraminer Trockenbeerenauslese	89	now–2014+?
2000 Gewürztraminer Trockenbeerenauslese	88	now–2011

LUDWIG HIEDLER ★★★★
KAMPTAL $15.00–$75.00

Ludwig Hiedler, now that he has a spacious new cellar, is working to see how many chemical and mechanical accretions of modernity he can strip away. Spontaneous fermentation, no supplemental enzymes, and no sulfur added to the must will, he believes, make for expressive and distinctive wines, even if they are slower to open in the spring and mature a bit ("but only a bit") sooner. This approach is a reaction to what Hiedler sees as creeping standardization of wine; an attempt to bring cellar practices into harmony with his herbicide- and pesticide-free ideals in the vineyard; and a search for excitement. Excitement is what his fans have come to expect in the glass.

2005 Grüner Veltliner Loess	88	now
2005 Grüner Veltliner Vier Weinberge	87	now
2004 Grüner Veltliner Vier Weinberge	89	now
2005 Grüner Veltliner Thal	89	now–2012
2004 Grüner Veltliner Thal	87	now–2010
2005 Grüner Veltliner Thal Novemberlese	92–94	2009–2018
2004 Grüner Veltliner Thal Novemberlese	88	now–2012+?
2005 Grüner Veltliner Maximum	89–91	2009–2016
2004 Grüner Veltliner Maximum	88–90	now–2014
2000 Grüner Veltliner Maximum	90	now
1999 Grüner Veltliner Maximum	91	now
2004 Riesling Loiserberg	89	now–2011
2005 Riesling Steinhaus	87	now–2010
2005 Riesling Gaisberg	90	now–2015
2004 Riesling Gaisberg	91	now–2014
2005 Riesling Heiligenstein	87–89	now–2013
2004 Riesling Heiligenstein	91	now–2014
2000 Riesling Heiligenstein	89	now
1999 Riesling Heiligenstein	91	now–2010
2004 Riesling Maximum	92	now–2014
2000 Riesling Maximum	91	now
1999 Riesling Maximum	92	now–2010
2004 Sauvignon Blanc Steinhaus	90	now–2010
2004 Weißburgunder Maximum	89	now–2012
2003 Weißburgunder Maximum	92	now–2015
2003 Chardonnay Beerenauslese	91	now–2018

HIRSCH ★ ★ ★ ★
KAMPTAL $17.00–$45.00

Johannes Hirsch is young and fearless. He was the first in Austria to convert from cork to screw caps, cold turkey. He was never afraid to leave a little residual sugar in his Riesling if he thought it made the wine more expressive, balanced, and longer-lived. He faced howls of protest from customers when he switched from spring to autumn bottling, because experience showed it was better for the top wines. He is now in the process of converting to a biodynamic regimen. Hirsch's Riesling has excelled and stood the text of bottle age even in a cruel vintage like 1998. Like the man, his wines are infectious. Hirsch's "intro-level" wine—known in the U.S. as "Grüner Veltliner #1"—offers fine value to be enjoyed within a year and a half of harvest.

2005 Grüner Veltliner Heiligenstein	90	now–2010
2005 Grüner Veltliner Lamm	88–90	now–2012
2000 Grüner Veltliner Lamm Alte Reben	90	now
1999 Grüner Veltliner Lamm Alte Reben	90	now–2010
2004 Riesling Zöbing	88	now
2005 Riesling Gaisberg	91–93	now–2017

2004 Riesling Gaisberg	88–91	now–2014
2000 Riesling Gaisberg	91	now–2012
1999 Riesling Gaisberg	92	now–2012
1997 Riesling Gaisberg Reserve	92	now–2014
2005 Riesling Heiligenstein	88–91	2010–2016
2004 Riesling Heiligenstein	88–91	2009–2014
2000 Riesling Heiligenstein	92	now–2012
1999 Riesling Heiligenstein	90	now

FRANZ HIRTZBERGER * * * * *
WACHAU $25.00–$150.00

Franz Hirtzberger is longtime chairman of the Vinea Wachau growers' association, and his wines possess cult status. Even with two sons now helping out, he and his wife, Irmgard, are still two of the busiest growers in Austria. For all the richness and depth of the Riesling and Grüner Veltliner Smaragd here, wine lovers sometimes overlook the amazing quality achieved with Pinot Blanc, as well as at Federspiel level. Nobly sweet wines are generally made in pitiable quantities and sell at very high prices, but they can be extraordinary. Even if botrytized bunches and berries are selected out, Hirtzberger is happy for a few of them to contribute spice and opulence to his dry Smaragd, typically harvested very late.

2005 Grüner Veltliner Federspiel Rotes Tor	93	now–2015
2004 Grüner Veltliner Federspiel Rotes Tor	92	now–2012
2005 Grüner Veltliner Smaragd Rotes Tor	94	now–2018
2004 Grüner Veltliner Smaragd Rotes Tor	90	now–2016
2000 Grüner Veltliner Smaragd Rotes Tor	89	now–2010
1999 Grüner Veltliner Smaragd Rotes Tor	90	now–2010
2005 Grüner Veltliner Axpoint	90	now–2016
2004 Grüner Veltliner Axpoint	91	now–2016
2005 Grüner Veltliner Honivogl	93	now–2018
2004 Grüner Veltliner Honivogl	93	now–2016
2000 Grüner Veltliner Honivogl	92	now–2012
1999 Grüner Veltliner Honivogl	92	now–2012
2005 Riesling Federspiel Steinterrassen	87	now
2005 Riesling Smaragd Setzberg	92	now–2014
2004 Riesling Smaragd Setzberg	88	now–2012
2005 Riesling Smaragd Hochrain	96	now–2016
2004 Riesling Smaragd Hochrain	94	now–2014
2000 Riesling Smaragd Hochrain	92	now–2012
1999 Riesling Smaragd Hochrain	91	now–2012
2005 Riesling Smaragd Singerriedel	95	now–2015
2004 Riesling Smaragd Singerriedel	93	now–2013
2000 Riesling Smaragd Singerriedel	94	now–2011
1999 Riesling Smaragd Singerriedel	94	now–2012
2005 Weissburgunder Smaragd Steinporz	93	now–2018
2004 Weissburgunder Smaragd Steinporz	93	now–2016
2005 Grauburgunder Smaragd Pluris	87	now–2010
2004 Grauburgunder Smaragd Pluris	88	now
2005 Chardonnay Smaragd Schloßgarten	88	now
2005 Neuburger Smaragd	89	now–2012
2005 Riesling Beerenauslese	96–98	now–2020

2005 Weißburgunder Beerenauslese	90–92	now–2016+?
2005 Riesling Trockenbeerenauslese	91–94	2010–2020

HÖGL ★★★
WACHAU $35.00–$65.00

Josef Högl—who honed his craft in part by working with F. X. Pichler—specializes in very pure-fruited renditions of Riesling and Grüner Veltliner from the cool western fringe of the Wachau.

JOSEF JAMEK ★★★
WACHAU $30.00–$150.00

Josef Jamek is the last of the old guard responsible for the modern conception of Wachau wine and its categories. Son-in-law Hans Altmann and his team craft a very broad range of wines, which are showcased in the family's renowned restaurant on the shore of the Danube. Their holdings in the Achleiten (Grüner Veltliner) and Klaus (Riesling) are so extensive they permit the luxury of picking both Federspiel and Smaragd in these steeply terraced, "grand cru" sites. Wines from other varieties and vineyards can also be lovely but are more variable in terms of clarity. When Jamek's lighter-weight versions of Muskateller or Weissburgunder (Pinot Blanc) "click," they can be infectious.

2004 Grüner Veltliner Federspiel Achleiten	90	now–2011
2005 Grüner Veltliner Smaragd Liebenberg	87	now
2005 Grüner Veltliner Smaragd Achleiten	88	now–2010
2004 Grüner Veltliner Smaragd Achleiten	88	now–2014
2005 Riesling Federspiel Jochinger Berg	88	now–2010
2004 Riesling Federspiel Jochinger Berg	89	now
2005 Riesling Federspiel Jochinger Pichl	87	now–2010
2004 Riesling Federspiel Jochinger Pichl	90	now–2010
2005 Riesling Federspiel Klaus	91	now–2012
2004 Riesling Federspiel Klaus	92	now–2012
2005 Riesling Smaragd Freiheit	90	now–2013
2004 Riesling Smaragd Freiheit	88	now–2012
2005 Riesling Smaragd Klaus	93	now–2015+?
2004 Riesling Smaragd Klaus	94	now–2015
2000 Riesling Smaragd Klaus	89	now–2012
2005 Gelber Muskateller Kollmitz	89	now

JURTSCHITSCH—SONNHOF ★★★
KAMPTAL $15.00–$150.00

The three Jurtschitsch brothers were their region's pioneers in organic viticulture. Lately, talk has been of tight vine spacing and old selections, recent cellar upgrading, and their sorting table, as well as of the younger generation who have joined them. All this bespeaks continuous striving for quality. Nobly sweet wines here can be sensationally refined.

2005 Grüner Veltliner Spiegel Reserve	86–88	now–2012

EMMERICH KNOLL ★★★★★
WACHAU $28.00–$150.00

Emmerich Knoll was still maturing most of his best wines in large oaken ovals until September, even when virtually all the rest of Austria had left such practices behind. But as the results in bottle consistently showed, the rest needed to consider falling back in line with Knoll—which is just what many have done over the past half dozen years. The combination in Knoll's wines, of richness with refinement and elegance and of generosity with age-worthiness, is unbeatable. In addition to his superb holdings in the Wachau, Knoll is the foremost landholder in the Pfaffenberg in neighboring Stein (part of the Kremstal). His Vinothek cuvées represent blends from more than one site that he believes will improve particularly well. Knoll and his son, also Emmerich, tend to make nobly sweet wines more frequently and in larger volume than do their neighbors.

2005 Grüner Veltliner Federspiel Kreutles	88	now
2005 Grüner Veltliner Smaragd Kreutles	88–90	now–2016
2004 Grüner Veltliner Smaragd Kreutles	87–89	now–2012
2005 Grüner Veltliner Smaragd Schütt	90–93	now–2022
2004 Grüner Veltliner Smaragd Schütt	86–88	now–2016
2000 Grüner Veltliner Smaragd Schütt	90	now–2012
2005 Grüner Veltliner Smaragd Loibenberg	92–95	now–2022
2004 Grüner Veltliner Smaragd Loibenberg	90–92	now–2016
1999 Grüner Veltliner Smaragd Loibenberg	92	now–2014
2005 Grüner Veltliner Smaragd Vinothekfüllung	90–92	now–2018+?
2004 Grüner Veltliner Smaragd Vinothekfüllung	90–92	now–2016
2000 Grüner Veltliner Smaragd Vinothekfüllung	91	now–2012
1999 Grüner Veltliner Smaragd Vinothekfüllung	93	now–2014
2005 Grüner Veltliner Auslese	87–89	now–2015
2005 Riesling Federspiel Loibenberg	87	now
2005 Riesling Smaragd Kellerberg	86–88	now–2012+?
2004 Riesling Smaragd Kellerberg	86–88	now–2010
2005 Riesling Smaragd Lobenberg	90–92	now–2015
2004 Riesling Smaragd Lobenberg	88–90	now–2012
1999 Riesling Smaragd Lobenberg	91	now–2010
2005 Riesling Smaragd Schütt	92–94	now–2018
2004 Riesling Smaragd Schütt	87–89	now–2012
2000 Riesling Smaragd Schütt	92	now–2010
1999 Riesling Smaragd Schütt	93	now–2012
1997 Riesling Smaragd Schütt	95	now–2014
2005 Riesling Smaragd Vinothekfüllung	87–90	now–2013+?
2000 Riesling Smaragd Vinothekfüllung	94	now–2016
2005 Riesling Pfaffenberg Selektion	87–89	now–2013
2005 Riesling Auslese	88–90	now–2015
2004 Riesling Auslese	91–93	now–2017
2004 Riesling Beerenauslese Pfaffenberg	91–93	now–2020
2005 Riesling Trockenbeerenauslese	91–93	now–2022
2004 Chardonnay Smaragd	88–90	now–2010
2005 Traminer Smaragd	87–89	now–2012
2004 Traminer Auslese	87–89	now–2013
2005 Traminer Beeerenauslese	90–92	now–2018
2004 Muskateller Auslese	91–93	now–2016
2005 Muskateller Trockenbeerenauslese	94–96	now–2020

KOLLWENTZ—RÖMERHOF * * *
NEUSIEDLERSEE-HÜGELLAND $25.00–$150.00

Anton Kollwentz was one of the pioneers of serious red wine in Burgenland and the powerful, tannic Cabernet- as well as Blaufränkisch-based bottlings that he and his son Andi fashion from sites near Eisenstadt enjoy great prestige in Austria. One of the most serious and successful Sauvignons in Austria, a range of single-vineyard Chardonnays, and occasional and intriguing nobly sweet wines complete the Kollwentz lineup.

ALOIS KRACHER—WEINLAUBENHOF * * * * *
NEUSIEDLERSEE $30.00–$175.00/375 ml

Alois "Luis" Kracher, collaborating with and building on the work of his father (also Alois), set out to demonstrate that the eastern shores of the Neusiedlersee could bring forth nobly sweet wine second to none. At the time of his tragically early death in December 2007, he was Austrian wine's foremost ambassador and a "sweet wine guru" to the world. Kracher's father and his son Gerhard will continue his work. The portions of each year's collection designated Zwischen den Seen are vinified in tank or in larger, mature oak casks, while those called Nouvelle Vague are vinified in new barriques, and in consequence tend toward more opulence, caramelization, and Sauternes-like character. But like Luis Kracher himself, for all of their enveloping richness and sheer intensity, his Trockenbeerenauslesen retain playful, engaging, intriguing, and invigorating complexity.

2004 Beerenauslese	89–91	now–2010
2003 Eiswein Cuvée	87	now
2003 #1 Trockenbeerenauslese	92	now–2020+?
2002 #1 Zweigelt Trockenbeerenauslese Nouvelle Vague	88	now–2014
2002 #2 Chardonnay Trockenbeerenauslese Nouvelle Vague	89	now–2015
2002 #3 Welschriesling Trockenbeerenauslese Zwischen den Seen	91	now–2018
2002 #4 Muskat Ottonel Trockenbeerenauslese Zwischen den Seen	87	now–2014
2002 #5 Scheurebe Trockenbeerenauslese Zwischen den Seen	97	now–2030+?
2002 #6 Scheurebe Trockenbeerenauslese Zwischen den Seen	95	now–2030+?
2002 #7 Grande Cuvée Trockenbeerenauslese Nouvelle Vague	96	now–2030+?
2002 #8 Welschriesling Trockenbeerenauslese Zwischen den Seen	91	now–2020
2002 #9 Chardonnay Trockenbeerenauslese Nouvelle Vague	92	now–2020
2002 #10 Scheurebe Trockenbeerenauslese Zwischen den Seen	98	now–2040+?
2002 #11 Welschriesling Trockenbeerenauslese Nouvelle Vague	99	now–2040+?
2002 #12 Trockenbeerenauslese	98	now–2040+?
2000 #1 Traminer Trockenbeerenauslese Nouvelle Vague	92	now–2018
2000 #2 Muskat Ottonel Trockenbeerenauslese Zwischen den Seen	96	now–2030
2000 #3 Chardonnay Trockenbeerenauslese Nouvelle Vague	94	now–2023
2000 #4 Welschriesling Trockenbeerenauslese Zwischen den Seen	95	now–2030

2000 #5 Scheurebe Trockenbeerenauslese Zwischen den Seen	96	now–2030
2000 #6 Grande Cuvée Trockenbeerenauslese Nouvelle Vague	96	now–2030
2000 #7 Chardonnay Trockenbeerenauslese Nouvelle Vague	94	now–2022
2000 #8 Welschriesling Trockenbeerenauslese Zwischen den Seen	98	now–2040+?
2000 #9 Scheurebe Trockenbeerenauslese Zwischen den Seen	97	now–2040+?
2000 #10 Welschriesling Trockenbeerenauslese Zwischen den Seen	99	now–2040+?
1999 #1 Pinot Noir-Zweigelt Trockenbeerenauslese Nouvelle Vague	88	now–2010
1999 #2 Traminer Trockenbeerenauslese Nouvelle Vague	93	now–2020
1999 #3 Chardonnay-Welschriesling Trockenbeerenauslese Nouvelle Vague	90	now–2015
1999 #4 Muskat Ottonel Trockenbeerenauslese Zwischen den Seen	95	now–2020
1999 #5 Scheurebe Trockenbeerenauslese Zwischen den Seen	95	now–2030
1999 #6 Grande Cuvée Trockenbeerenauslese Nouvelle Vague	96	now–2030
1999 #7 Chardonnay Trockenbeerenauslese Nouvelle Vague	96	now–2030
1999 #8 Welschriesling Trockenbeerenauslese Zwischen den Seen	96	now–2035
1999 #9 Scheurebe Trockenbeerenauslese Zwischen den Seen	98	now–2040
1999 #10 Welschriesling Trockenbeerenauslese Nouvelle Vague	98	now–2040
1998 #1 Zweigelt Trockenbeerenauslese Nouvelle Vague	92	now–2012
1998 #2 Chardonnay Trockenbeerenauslese Nouvelle Vague	93	now–2012
1998 #3 Scheurebe Trockenbeerenauslese Zwischen den Seen	95	now–2020
1998 #4 Welschriesling Trockenbeerenauslese Nouvelle Vague	95	now–2025
1998 #5 Muskat Ottonel Trockenbeerenauslese Zwischen den Seen	96	now–2020
1998 #6 Welschriesling Trockenbeerenauslese Zwischen den Seen	92	now–2020
1998 #7 Chardonnay-Welschriesling Trockenbeerenauslese Nouvelle Vague	94	now–2025
1998 #8 Traminer Trockenbeerenauslese Nouvelle Vague	93	now–2025
1998 #9 Chardonnay Trockenbeerenauslese Nouvelle Vague	96	now–2030

1998 #10 Grande Cuvée Trockenbeerenauslese Nouvelle Vague	94	now–2030
1998 #11 Welschriesling Trockenbeerenauslese Zwischen den Seen	96	now–2030
1998 #12 Scheurebe Trockenbeerenauslese Zwischen den Seen	93	now–2030
1998 #13 Chardonnay Trockenbeerenauslese Nouvelle Vague	98	now–2040+?
1997 #1 Muskat Ottonel Beerenauslese Zwischen den Seen	92	now–2010
1997 #2 Bouvier Beerenauslese Zwischen den Seen	91	now
1997 #3 Scheurebe Beerenauslese Zwischen den Seen	92	now–2012
1997 #4 Zweigelt Rosé Beerenauslese Nouvelle Vague	91	now
1997 #5 Muskat Ottonel Beerenauslese Zwischen den Seen	94	now–2010
1997 #6 Chardonnay Beerenauslese Nouvelle Vague	91	now
1997 #7 Welschriesling Trockenbeerenauslese Zwischen den Seen	94	now–2012
1996 #1 Traminer Beerenauslese Nouvelle Vague	89	now
1996 #2 Bouvier-Muskat Ottonel Trockenbeerenauslese Zwischen den Seen	90	now–2015
1996 #3 Scheurebe Trockenbeerenauslese Zwischen den Seen	92	now–2020
1996 #4 Chardonnay-Welschriesling Trockenbeerenauslese Nouvelle Vague	94	now–2020
1996 #7 Grande Cuvée Trockenbeerenauslese Nouvelle Vague	90	now–2020
1996 #8 Chardonnay Trockenbeerenauslese Nouvelle Vague	95	now–2015
1996 #9 Welschriesling Trockenbeerenauslese Zwischen den Seen	97	now–2025
1995 #1 Welschriesling Trockenbeerenauslese Zwischen den Seen	93	now–2015
1995 #2 Welschriesling Trockenbeerenauslese Zwischen den Seen	95	now–2020
1995 #3 Scheurebe Trockenbeerenauslese Zwischen den Seen	94	now–2018
1995 #4 Scheurebe Trockenbeerenauslese Zwischen den Seen	96	now–2040+?
1995 #5 Muskat Ottonel Trockenbeerenauslese Zwischen den Seen	92	now–2020
1995 #6 Scheurebe Trockenbeerenauslese Zwischen den Seen	94–96	now–2020
1995 #7 Chardonnay-Welschriesling Trockenbeerenauslese Nouvelle Vague	94	now–2025
1995 #8 Traminer Trockenbeerenauslese Nouvelle Vague	93	now–2020
1995 #9 Zweigelt Rosé Trockenbeerenauslese Nouvelle Vague	93	now–2025
1995 #10 Zweigelt Rosé Trockenbeerenauslese Nouvelle Vague	95	now–2025

1995 #11 Muskat Ottonel Trockenbeerenauslese		
Zwischen den Seen	98	now–2025
1995 #12 Grande Cuvée Trockenbeerenauslese		
Nouvelle Vague	96–98	now–2025
1995 #13 Chardonnay Trockenbeerenauslese		
Nouvelle Vague	96	now–2030
1995 #14 Scheurebe Trockenbeerenauslese		
Zwischen den Seen	96	now–2040+?
1995 #15 Welschriesling Trockenbeerenauslese		
Zwischen den Seen	95	now–2030

KRUTZLER ★★★
SÜDBURGENLAND $25.00–$125.00

Of the relatively small number of full-time vintners in the often dramatically steep clay-, schist-, and iron-rich vineyards of southern Burgenland, Krutzler is the one who has achieved renown and attained among the highest red wine prices in Austria. To take advantage of his diverse parcels of Blaufränkisch (many with old vines) and because any reputation that accrued to individual sites in Deutsch-Schützen and neighboring Eisenberg is now a distant memory, Reinhold Krutzler elected to curtail the bottling of single-vineyard wines. Instead, his three Blaufränkish cuvées differ in age of vine, style, and ageworthiness, culminating in Perwolf.

2004 Blaufränkisch	88	now
2003 Blaufränkisch	87	now
2003 Perwolf	90	now–2011+?
2002 Perwolf	90	now–2012

LACKNER–TINNACHER ★★★
SÜDSTEIERMARK $20.00–$50.00

Fritz Tinnacher crafts wines of considerable refinement, often including memorable Weissburgunder (Pinot Blanc), and his is one of the few South Styrian estates to devote serious attention to Riesling. Despite the challenges to this region posed in 2003 and 2004, this domain scored some significant successes.

2004 Grauburgunder [Pinot Gris] Steinbach	86	now–2010
2004 Riesling Eiswein	87–89	now–2014
2003 Morillon [Chardonnay] Steinbach	87	now
2003 Weissburgunder Steinbach	88	now–2011
2002 Grauburgunder Trockenbeerenauslese	90	now–2015

KARL LAGLER ★★★
WACHAU $30.00–$70.00

Karl Lagler grows and cellars practically next to Franz Hirtzberger, and fashions Riesling and Grüner Veltliner that reflect the superb locations and distinctiveness of Spitz's best sites in a relatively broad, supple style.

PAUL LEHRNER ★★★
MITTELBURGENLAND $18.00–$45.00

The droll Herr Lehrner takes a skeptical view of wine fashion, particularly that "bigger is better" mind-set, which—it has only just begun to dawn on many Mittelburgenland vintners—is a dead end. Lehrner has gone his own way in search of elegance and drinkability. Here is that rare vintner who, concerned about one or another aspect of wine can be heard asking a taster, "You don't find that exaggerated, do you?" These stylish, subtle reds will grow on you.

2003 Blaufräkisch Gefanger	88	now–2010
2003 Blaufränkisch Hochäcker	89	now–2012
2003 Blaufränkisch Steineiche	90	now–2014+?

JOSEF LENTSCH—GASTMIFUS ZUR DANKBARKEIT ★ ★ ★
NEUSIEDLERSEE $N/A

Restaurateur-vintner Josef Lentsch deserves to be better known in Austria—to say nothing of the U.S., where his wines have yet to appear. His Pinot Noirs are some of the most intriguing and satisfying as well as best values from this variety, while his dry white and nobly sweet wines (from Pinot Gris, Pinot Blanc, and Welschriesling) are fascinating, the latter higher in alcohol and correspondingly lower in residual sugar than is the norm in Burgenland today.

FRED LOIMER ★ ★ ★ ★
KAMPTAL $15.00–$60.00

Fred Loimer's wines have undergone a gradual stylistic transformation over the past decade toward sharper relief and greater intricacy of flavor, with a corresponding concentration of interest in Riesling from diverse sites. Nevertheless, it is for the green cases and labels of his "intro-level" Grüner Veltliner Lois (a wine to relish within a year of bottling), that he is best known around the world. Loimer is very serious about Grüner Veltliner, as well as Pinot Noir.

2005 Grüner Veltliner Terrassen	87	now
2004 Grüner Veltliner Käferberg	87–89	now–2012
2004 Grüner Veltliner Spiegel	86–88	now–2010
2000 Grüner Veltliner Spiegel	89	now
2005 Riesling Terrassen	88	now
2004 Riesling Loiserberg	86–88	now–2010
2005 Riesling Seeberg	90–92	now–2014+?
2004 Riesling Seeberg	87–89	now–2012
2000 Riesling Seeberg	89	now
2005 Riesling Steinmassl	87–89	2009–2012
2004 Riesling Steinmassl	90–92	now–2014
2000 Riesling Steinmassl	90	now–2012

MALAT ★ ★ ★
KREMSTAL, WACHAU $15.00–$100.00

Gerard Malat is one of Austria's most versatile vintners. In addition to his impressive Riesling and Grüner Veltliner, he crafts a wonderful sparkling cuvée, often superb Muskateller, occasionally nobly sweet wines. He is serious about the entire Pinot family, plus all of the grapes of Bordeaux save for Sémillon. Not only that, Malat has adopted and adapted distinctive styles for each of them. He is not afraid to harvest very ripe—Malat's "Das Beste" batch of Grüner Veltliner, for instance, is legally Auslese, yet he can deliver a tightly focused Riesling of only 12.5% alcohol. There are always surprises at this address, most of them pleasant.

2005 Grüner Veltliner Dreigärten	89	now–2010
2004 Grüner Veltliner Dreigärten	87	now
2005 Das Beste vom Grüner Veltliner	90	now–2014
2004 Das Beste vom Grüner Veltliner	89	now–2012
2005 Riesling Steinbühel	89	now–2012

2005 Riesling Silberbühel	87	2009–2012+?
2004 Riesling Silberbühel	89	now–2011
2004 Pinot Blanc Am Zaun	88	now
2004 Pinot Noir Reserve	87–89	now–2012
2003 Cabernet Sauvignon	87	now–2010

MORIC ✶✶✶✶✶
MITTELBURGENLAND, NEUSIEDLERSEE-HÜGELLAND $28.00–$90.00

Roland Velich calls his Moric (Magyar for Moritz) project "Blaufränkisch Unplugged." A better expression might be "in a new key." From old vines and upper-elevation sites in Lutzmannsburg and Neckenmark, Velich handles Blaufränkisch as if it were grand cru Burgundy. His inaugural, Chablis-like 2006 Grüner Veltliner from chalky soils near Eisenstadt is equally groundbreaking in style, and two Blaufränkisch projects from the same neighborhood will follow. Velich is in a world, if not a class, of his own. As his first wines (from 2002) begin to mature and his latest vintages reveal the push toward more refinement with undiminished richness, it becomes evident that our perspective on Austrian red wine has once again (as happened with the wines of Prieler, Triebaumer, and Umathum a decade ago) been profoundly altered.

2004 Blaufränkisch Burgenland	89	now+?
2003 Blaufränkisch Lutzmannsburg Alte Reben	90	2009–2014+?
2002 Blaufränkisch Lutzmannsburg Alte Reben	90	now–2015+?
2003 Blaufränkisch Neckenmarkter	91	now–2012+?
2002 Blaufränkisch Neckenmarkter Alte Reben	92	now–2015+?

MANTLERHOF ✶✶✶
KREMSTAL $25.00–$70.00

Sepp Mantler crafts a fascinating range of Grüner Veltliner with different styles adapted to different sites. He is also a champion of Roter Veltliner and renders excellent Riesling. Never one to seek the easy road, Mantler has recently converted his estate to a biodynamic regimen. He is also famous for generously demonstrating the ageworthiness of his wines, even from difficult vintages.

MUHR—NIEPOORT ✶✶✶✶
CARNUNTUM $30.00–$50.00

Dorli Muhr and husband, Dirk Niepoort, of Port fame are farming one of Carnuntum's few traditional sites for Blaufränkisch, the Spitzerberg, and the early results display a combination of richness, elegance, and clarity that already places them in the upper echelons of Austrian red wine growers.

SEPP AND MARIA MUSTER ✶✶✶
SÜDSTEIERMARK $N/A

Sepp and Maria Muster are among Austria's most maverick vintners; they wear the authorities' habitual refusal of even the Südsteiermark appellation as a badge of honor and a sign that they must be doing something right! Their style tends toward high phenolics, lots of lees, and subtle oxidation, but the entire range of results achieved with this region's classic grapes, organically grown, is fascinating; the best Muster wines are deeply satisfying.

TRAISENTAL $18.00–$50.00

With the aid of his brother Karl, a Vienna banker, the almost obsessively detail-conscious Ludwig Neumayer has practically single-handedly brought to the little Traisental what little international attention it has managed to garner. His boldly aromatic, incisive, yet often intricate whites from conglomerate terraces have distinctive and instantly winning personalities as well as an excellent track record for cellaring.

2005 Grüner Veltliner Engelgarten	87	now
2005 Grüner Veltliner Rafezetzen	89	now–2012
2004 Grüner Veltliner Rafezetzen	89	now–2012
2005 Grüner Veltliner Zwirch	89	now–2012
2004 Grüner Veltliner Zwirch	90	now–2012
2005 Grüner Veltliner Der Wein vom Stein	91	now–2018
2004 Grüner Veltliner Der Wein vom Stein	90	now–2015
2005 Riesling Rothenbart	90	now–2011
2004 Riesling Rothenbart	90	now–2010
2005 Riesling Der Wein vom Stein	87	now+?
2004 Riesling Der Wein vom Stein	90	now–2012
2005 Weißburgunder Der Wein vom Stein	88	now–2014
2005 Sauvignon Blanc Gieß	87	now
2004 Sauvignon Blanc Gieß	88	now
2005 Sauvignon Blanc Der Wein vom Stein	90	now–2012
2004 Sauvignon Blanc Der Wein vom Stein	90	now–2011

NEUMEISTER ★ ★ ★ ★
SÜDOSTSTEIERMARK $18.00–$80.00

Even in a land nowadays liberally sprinkled with multimillion-dollar palaces of vinification, to descend from their modest crush pad down into Albert and Christoph Neumeister's cellar, hidden in one of obscure Straden's steep hillsides, confronts visitors with breathtaking architectural drama, behind which lies a control freak's technological sophistication. Albert built his estate up over three decades from a small mixed agricultural family operation; he also has contracts with neighboring vintners. Neumeister wines blaze a path with effective use of skin, lees, and new wood. The superb nobly sweet wines are in a soft and ingratiating style all their own.

2004 Gelber Muskateller Steierische Klassik	89	now
2004 Grauburgunder Steierische Klassik	87	now
2004 Sauvignon Blanc Steierische Klassik	88	now
2004 Sauvignon Blanc Klausen Selektion	90	now–2011
2004 Sauvignon Blanc Moarfeitl Selektion	89–91	now–2012
2003 Sauvignon Blanc Beerenauslese Klausen	93	now–2015+?
2002 Welschriesling Trockenbeerenauslese Sazianni	88	now–2013+?
2002 Welschriesling Beerenauslese Sazianni	91	now–2015+?

NIGL ★ ★ ★ ★ ★
KREMSTAL $20.00–$70.00

From loess vineyards around Krems—but most of all from steep, volcanic terraces along the little winding Krems at Senftenberg—Martin Nigl crafts some of the most intricately complex and ageworthy wines in Austria. His least expensive Grüner Veltliner bottlings can already be masterpieces. What he must guard against in recent, warm vintages is too precipitant a rise in grape sugars (and thus eventual alcohol), as happened with his ostensibly top Riesling in 2006. The wines labeled "Privat" are from the best portions of the Piri vineyard.

2005 Grüner Veltliner Gärtling	91	now
2005 Grüner Veltliner Kremser Freiheit	90	now–2010
2005 Grüner Veltliner Senftenberger Piri	89	now–2014+?
2004 Grüner Veltliner Senftenberger Piri	90	now–2014
2005 Grüner Veltliner Alte Reben	92	now–2018
2005 Grüner Veltliner Privat	94	2009–2020
2004 Grüner Veltliner Privat	94	now–2018
2000 Grüner Veltliner Privat	90	now
2005 Riesling Dornleiten	90	now
2005 Riesling Kremsleiten	91	now–2014
2004 Riesling Kremsleiten	91	now–2013
2000 Riesling Kremsleiten	92	now–2012
2005 Riesling Hochäcker	92–94	now–2017
2001 Riesling Hochäcker	91–93	now–2014
2000 Riesling Hochäcker	93	now–2015
2005 Riesling Senftenberger Piri	88	now–2012+?
2004 Riesling Senftenberger Piri	88	now–2011
2001 Riesling Senftenberger Piri	90	now–2010
2005 Riesling Privat	93	now–2016
2001 Riesling Privat	92–94	now–2016
2000 Riesling Privat	93	now–2015
1997 Riesling Privat	94	now–2014
2004 Gelber Muskateller	89	now
2005 Sauvignon Blanc	89	now–2010
2004 Sauvignon Blanc	89	now
2003 Zweigelt Eichberg	87	now–2010

NIKOLAIHOF ✶ ✶ ✶ ✶ ✶
WACHAU $25.00–$150.00

At Austria's most ancient winery, things are done differently. Until recently, a 17th-century press was still in use. On occasion, the harvest is finished here before anyone else in the Wachau has begun, a circumstance the proprietors attribute to a scrupulously biodynamic approach, which has suddenly become the new fashion in Austria, as elsewhere in Europe. These wines are never showy and are often reticent in their youth, but they can age magnifcently—even in cask, where selected Vinotek Riesling (and, recently, the first Grüner Veltliner) are held for a decade or more. A 1990 Riesling was held for 162 months, and a sweet 1977 blend for two decades, resulting in riveting glimpses of an earlier era in winemaking.

2005 Grüner Veltliner Hefeabzug	87	now
2004 Grüner Veltliner Hefeabzug	90	now
2005 Grüner Veltliner Federspiel Im Weingebirge	89	now–2014
2004 Grüner Veltliner Federspiel Im Weingebirge	89	now–2014
2000 Grüner Veltliner Smaragd Im Weingebirge	90	now–2012
2004 Grüner Veltliner Schlossberg Jungfernlese	87	2009–2012+?
1991 Grüner Veltliner Vinothek	94	now–2012+?
2004 Riesling Federspiel vom Stein	88	now–2012
2004 Riesling Smaragd vom Stein	92	2009–2018
2000 Riesling Smaragd vom Stein	90	now–2012
2000 Riesling Steiner Hund	89	now–2012

1999 Riesling Spätlese [dry] Steiner Hund	91	now–2012
1990 Riesling Vinotek	95	now–2010+?
2004 Neuburger Burggarten	87	now–2010
2004 Frühroter Veltliner	88	now
2001 Nikolauswein Trockenbeerenauslese	96	now–2045+?
1977 Nikolauswein [Vinotek]	93	now–2040+?

ANITA AND HANS NITTNAUS ★ ★ ★
NEUSIEDLERSEE $25.00–$50.00

There are a number of Nittnaus estates in Gols. That of Anita and Hans Nittnaus renders some of Burgenland's more restrained yet ultimately rewarding reds. The portfolio here is sprawling, all the way from Grüner Veltliner to dessert wines, but reds—including variations on Pinot, on traditional Austrian, and on Bordeaux varieties—are where these talented and enthusiastic folk need to focus their manifest talents.

2003 Pannobile	89	now–2013

OTT ★ ★ ★ ★
WAGRAM $25.00–$50.00

Bernhard Ott has long been the leading vintner in the Wagram and one of Austria's leading practitioners of Grüner Veltliner. Lately he has declared his allegiance to screw-cap closure; to pursuing an ever stricter organic, near-biodynamic regimen in his vineyards; and to crafting wines of greater clarity and refinement. His basic Am Berg bottling represents good value for immediate enjoyment. He also has become more interested in Riesling, planted on the red gravel near the crest of some of Feuersbrunn's loess embankments, which he renders in both dry and (in consultation with Rüdesheim's Johannes Leitz) sweet versions.

2005 Grüner Veltliner Fass 4	87	now
2004 Grüner Veltliner Fass 4	88	now
2005 Grüner Veltliner Der Ott	90	now–2015
2004 Grüner Veltliner Rosenberg	88	now–2014
2005 Grüner Veltliner Rosenberg Reserve	91	now–2018
2004 Grüner Veltliner Rosenberg Reserve	91	now–2017
2003 Grüner Veltliner Tausend Rosen	90	now–2014+?
2005 Riesling vom Roten Schotter	89	now–2012
2005 Rheinriesling Auslese	90	now–2014+?

PFAFFL ★ ★ ★
WEINVIERTEL, VIENNA $18.00–$70.00

The large and technically sophisticated estate of Roman and Adelheid Pfaffl is a hands-on family operation run with passion, ambition, and skill that have taken it in little more than a decade from one of the hundreds of small winery-taverns of the Weinviertel to the standard-bearer of the region. Pfaffl's range of grape varieties is matched by diverse modes of vinification, from light and refreshing white (and a red grown within the Vienna city limits) to richly tannic Zweigelt-Bordeaux blends.

2005 Wien.1 [white]	86	now
2005 Grüner Veltliner Haidviertel	87	2009–2014
2005 Grüner Veltliner Hundsleiten	88	2009–2016
2004 Grüner Veltliner Hundsleiten—Sandtal	89	2009–2014
2005 Riesling Am Berg	90	now–2012+?
2004 Riesling Privat	89–91	now–2011

2004 Sauvignon Blanc	87	now
2004 Weissburgunder	87	now
2004 Wien.2 [red]	88	now
2003 Excellent [red]	88	2009–2014
2003 Heidrom [red]	87–89	2010–2015

F. X. PICHLER ★ ★ ★ ★ ★
WACHAU $30.00–$200.00

"Effix" is an Austrian wine institution. He was also—along with his father, who meticulously pursued a program of vine selection for more than four decades—the single biggest factor in the emergence of Grüner Veltliner from humble obscurity to international stardom. Federspiel (what few the winery still bottles) and Smaragd alike are brilliantly rendered. Pichler is sometimes faulted for high alcohol and almost overwhelmingly voluminous wines. But the truth is, his wines can carry 15% or more alcohol without overheating. Furthermore, he is only too happy (when Nature indulges him) to bottle wines with the same superb concentration and longevity but at 13%, as happened with spectacular results in 1999. M bottlings vary in vineyard makeup and represent the most powerful wines of certain vintages; Unendlich ("Endless") the most sublime. Son Lucas runs the cellar now, and also sees to it that the estates' promising Sauvignon Blanc program advances.

2005 Grüner Veltliner Frauenweingarten	90	now–2012
2004 Grüner Veltliner Frauenweingarten	89	now–2010
2005 Grüner Veltliner Klostersatz	91	now–2014
2004 Grüner Veltliner Klostersatz	90	now–2012
2005 Grüner Veltliner Smaragd Von den Terrassen	91	now–2018
2004 Grüner Veltliner Smaragd Von den Terrassen	87	now–2014?
2005 Grüner Veltliner Smaragd Loibnerberg	93	now–2022
2004 Grüner Veltliner Smaragd Loibnerberg	93	now–2018
2000 Grüner Veltliner Smaragd Loibnerberg	90	now
2005 Grüner Veltliner Smaragd Kellerberg	94–96	now–2022
2004 Grüner Veltliner Smaragd Kellerberg	97	now–2020
2000 Grüner Veltliner Smaragd Kellerberg	92	now–2014
1999 Grüner Veltliner Smaragd Kellerberg	92	now–2016
2005 Grüner Veltliner Smaragd M	89–90	now–2015+?
2004 Grüner Veltliner Smaragd M	89–91	now–2014+?
1999 Grüner Veltliner Smaragd M	93	now–2012
1997 Grüner Veltliner Smaragd M	92	now
2004 Riesling Von den Terrassen	87	now
2005 Riesling Smaragd Oberhauser	91	now–2015
2004 Riesling Smaragd Oberhauser	90	2009–2015
2005 Riesling Smaragd Hollerin	90	now–2014+?
2005 Riesling Smaragd Steinertal	89	2009–2018
2004 Riesling Smaragd Steinertal	90–92	now–2016
2005 Riesling Smaragd Loibnerberg	93	now–2020
2004 Riesling Smaragd Loibnerberg	90	now–2020
2005 Riesling Smaragd Kellerberg	91–93	2009–2020
2004 Riesling Smaragd Kellerberg	93–95	now–2020
2000 Riesling Smaragd Kellerberg	92	now–2012
1999 Riesling Smaragd Kellerberg	92	now–2014
1997 Riesling Smaragd Kellerberg	96	now–2016
2005 Riesling Unendlich	94	now–2022

2000 Riesling Unendlich	97	now–2020
1999 Riesling Unendlich	94	now–2011
2005 Sauvignon Blanc Smaragd	90	now–2012+?
2004 Sauvignon Blanc Smaragd	90–92	now–2012

RUDI PICHLER ★ ★ ★ ★
WACHAU $35.00–$75.00

With his sociability, intense determination, methodical craftsmanship, and splendid vinous results, Rudi Pichler did not have to languish all that long as merely "the other Pichler." After taking extraordinary precautions in the vineyards and in selecting fruit, Pichler most years fearlessly gives his grapes up to 30 hours of prefermentative skin contact, with imposingly piquant and tactile results.

2005 Grüner Veltliner Smaragd Terrassen	89	now–2014
2004 Grüner Veltliner Smaragd Terrassen	90	now–2013
2005 Grüner Veltliner Smaragd Kollmütz	88	2009–2014+?
2004 Grüner Veltliner Smaragd Kollmütz	87	now–2012+?
2005 Grüner Veltliner Smaragd Hochrain	92	now–2018
2004 Grüner Veltliner Smaragd Hochrain	89	now–2014+?
2001 Grüner Veltliner Smaragd Hochrain	90–91	now–2012
2004 Riesling Steinriegl	88	now
2005 Riesling Smaragd Terrassen	89	now–2012
2004 Riesling Smaragd Terrassen	87	now–2010
2004 Riesling Smaragd Steinriegl	90	now–2014
2005 Riesling Smaragd Kirchweg	90	2009–2016
2004 Riesling Smaragd Kirchweg	87	now–2010+?
2005 Riesling Smaragd Achleiten	93	now–2018
2004 Riesling Smaragd Achleiten	90	2009–2014
2000 Riesling Smaragd Achleiten	89	now–2010
1999 Riesling Smaragd Achleiten	92	now–2014
1997 Riesling Smaragd Achleiten	91	now–2014
2005 Weißburgunder Smaragd Kollmütz	90	now–2016
2005 Roter Veltliner	91	now–2015+?
2000 Roter Veltliner	89	now

PITTNAUER ★ ★ ★
NEUSIEDLERSEE $25.00–$60.00

Gerhard Pittnauer is crafting some of the most interesting reds in his region. He is particularly serious about Pinot Noir, and bottles one of the best St. Laurents in Austria from some of the oldest vines in Austria of that variety. (This winery is not to be confused with another red-wine specialist, Pitnauer, with one "t," in Carnuntum.)

PÖCKL ★ ★ ★
NEUSIEDLERSEE $30.00–$150.00

Josef Pöckl pushed the limits of the possible and inspired a generation of vintners with his first Admiral (a Zweigelt-Bordeaux blend) of 1989. Now that he and son René have settled into their spacious, modern facility, they can perhaps also settle down to accepting as routine the many accolades they receive in the Austrian press and take the opportunity to relax—not to take time off from their diligence but to achieve less clenched, hyperconcentrated, or superficially woody results.

| 2004 Rosso e Nero | 86–88 | now–2012 |
| 2003 Admiral | 88 | 2010–2014+? |

POLLERHOF ★ ★ ★
WEINVIERTEL $12.00–$25.00

Some of the most distinctively delicious and affordable Grüner Veltliner in Austria—and certainly in the Weinviertel—is fashioned by Erwin Poller in the out-of-the-way village of Röschnitz.

POLZ ★ ★ ★
SÜDSTEIERMARK $25.00–$75.00

Eric and Walter Polz are among the largest vineyard holders in South Styria, incorporating two other estates under their corporate umbrella. At their best, the single-vineyard wines here—above all from Sauvignon, but from Pinot Blanc and Pinot Gris as well—can be striking. Vintages 2003–2005 were on the whole disappointing, but 2006 shows signs of a welcome bounce.

2004 Sauvignon Blanc Grassnitzberg	85–87	now
2004 Sauvignon Blanc Terese	87	now–2010
2001 Sauvignon Blanc Terese	90	now–2010
2000 Sauvignon Blanc Obegg	88	now–2010
1998 Sauvignon Blanc Hochgrassnitzberg	88	now
1997 Sauvignon Blanc Hochgrassnitzberg	91	now

PRAGER ★ ★ ★ ★ ★
WACHAU $22.00–$75.00

Toni Bodenstein has taken the winery of his father-in-law, Franz Prager, to the outer limits of complexity achievable in dry Riesling. Only the most hardened skeptic could come away from Bodenstein's scientifically informed commentary and dazzling range unconvinced of the influence of *terroir*. Lately, Bodenstein has become increasingly serious about and successful with Grüner Veltliner. His reclamation projects with ancient Grüner Veltliner vines and with terraces above the supposed limits of Riesling's ripening potential have already borne profound fruit. On rare occasions when he turns out noncommercial quantities of Riesling Trockenbeerenauslese, these have proven among the world's finest.

2005 Grüner Veltliner Federspiel Hinter der Burg	89	now–2011
2005 Grüner Veltliner Smaragd Weitenberg	87	now–2011
2004 Grüner Veltliner Smaragd Weitenberg	89	now–2012
2000 Grüner Veltliner Smaragd Weitenberg	89	now
2004 Grüner Veltliner Zwerithaler	90	now–2014
2005 Grüner Veltliner Smaragd Achleiten	90	now–2017
2004 Grüner Veltliner Smaragd Achleiten	90	now–2016
2000 Grüner Veltliner Smaragd Achleiten	91	now–2011
2005 Grüner Veltliner Achleiten Stockkultur	95	now–2018+?
2005 Riesling Federspiel Steinriegel	91	now–2010
2005 Riesling Smaragd Steinriegl	87	now–2012
2004 Riesling Smaragd Steinriegl	91	2009–2015
2000 Riesling Smaragd Steinriegl	91	now–2010
1999 Riesling Smaragd Steinriegl	90	now
2004 Riesling Smaragd Kaiserberg	89	now–2012
2000 Riesling Smaragd Kaiserberg	92	now
1999 Riesling Smaragd Kaiserberg	92	now

2005 Riesling Smaragd Hollerin	87	now–2012
2004 Riesling Smaragd Hollerin	88	now–2011
2000 Riesling Smaragd Hollerin	90	now
2005 Riesling Smaragd Achleiten	92	2009–2016
2004 Riesling Smaragd Achleiten	94	now–2016
2000 Riesling Smaragd Achleiten	95	now–2014
1999 Riesling Smaragd Achleiten	92	now–2012
1993 Riesling Smaragd Achleiten	91	now
2005 Riesling Klaus	91	2010–2017
2004 Riesling Smaragd Klaus	92	2010–2017
2000 Riesling Smaragd Klaus	94	now–2015
1999 Riesling Smaragd Klaus	94	now–2012
1993 Riesling Smaragd Klaus	97	now
2005 Riesling Smaragd Wachstum Toni Bodenstein	90	2009–2014
2004 Riesling Smaragd Wachstum Toni Bodenstein	94	now–2014+?
1999 Riesling Smaragd Wachstum Toni Bodenstein	94	now–2012

CLAUS PREISINGER ★ ★ ★
NEUSIEDLERSEE $30.00–$60.00

Claus Preisinger is one of the young, eager, and talented red-wine vinters of Gols; his experimental bent encourages one to imagine a prestigious future for his at times uncannily successful blends and his ambitious Pinot Noir.

PRIELER ★ ★ ★ ★
NEUSIEDLERSEE-HÜGELLAND $25.00–$175.00

Engelbert and daughter Silvia Prieler harvest some of Austria's most fascinating and ageworthy Blaufränkisch from the windswept, schistic Goldberg with its unique ecological perch overlooking the Neusiedlersee. Their Pinot Blanc is infectiously delicious yet profoundly age-worthy. Silvia Prieler devoted both a doctoral dissertation and now hard labor to Madame Pinot (Noir).

2005 Pinot Blanc Seeberg	88	now–2012
2004 Pinot Blanc Seeberg	91	now–2016
2004 Blaufränkisch Schützner Stein	89–91	2010–2016
2003 Blaufränkisch Schützner Stein	89–91	now–2015
2003 Blaufränkisch Goldberg	91–93	2009–2020
2003 Cabernet Sauvignon Ungerbergen	87–89	now–2013

FRANZ PROIDL ★ ★ ★
KREMSTAL $30.00–$70.00

Franz Proidl and his Riesling and Grüner Veltliner from the stony terraces of Senftenberg are always good for some chuckles, often delighted ones. He is happy to let his wines make a statement, even when residual sugar, botrytis, high alcohol, extremely long fermentation, or human factors may lead to idiosyncrasy.

2004 Grüner Veltliner Ehrenfels	87	now–2014
2005 Riesling Ehrenfels	87	2009–2013
2004 Riesling Pfenningberg	88	now–2010
2004 Riesling Hochäcker	88	2009–2012+?
2004 Riesling Auslese	88–91	2010–2015+?
2004 Riesling Beerenauslese	85–88	2010–2018+?

SALOMON—UNDHOF ✶✶✶
KREMSTAL $20.00–$45.00

Erich Solomon—who died in 2007, and whose father was an Austrian pioneer in Riesling and in export—did much to further the understanding and distribution of Austrian wine abroad. Brother and current proprietor Berthold Salomon left his influential position as director of Austrian Wine Marketing to collaborate with Erich for five years during which quality at this estate beneath the terraces of Krems-Stein advanced, especially with Grüner Veltliner.

2005 Grüner Veltliner Wieden Tradition	88	now–2010
2004 Grüner Veltliner Wieden Tradition	89	now–2010
2005 Grüner Veltliner Wachtberg	88	now–2012
2005 Grüner Veltliner Lindberg Reserve	92	now–2014+?
2004 Grüner Veltliner Lindberg Reserve	87	now–2010+?
2005 Grüner Veltliner von Stein Reserve	93	now–2018+?
2004 Grüner Veltliner von Stein Reserve	90	now–2016
2005 Riesling Kögl	90	now–2012
2000 Riesling Kögl	89	now
2000 Riesling Kögl Reserve	92	now
1999 Riesling Kögl Reserve	87	now–2010
1997 Riesling Kögl Reserve	91	now–2012
2005 Riesling Pfaffenberg	88	now–2010
2005 Riesling Pfaffenberg Reserve Metternich		
& Salomon	87	now+?
2004 Traminer Reserve	88–90	now–2012
2005 Gelber Traminer Noble Selection	87	now–2014+?

SATTLERHOF ✶✶✶
SÜDSTEIERMARK $25.00–$50.00

Willi Sattler renders some of the most pristine reflections of South Styria's grapes and sites. No fewer than three different vineyards are showcased in separate Sattlerhof bottlings of Sauvignon Blanc.

UWE SCHIEFER ✶✶✶✶
SÜDBURGENLAND $20.00–$60.00

Young Uwe Schiefer is showcasing Blaufränkisch from the Eisenberg on the Hungarian border (in fact, he has vinified Magyar Kékfrankos as well) in a refined, relatively "cool"-fruited but formidably concentrated and minerally intense style reminiscent of his friend Roland Velich's (see under Moric). The early results here are not to be missed!

SCHMELZ ✶✶✶
WACHAU $25.00–$60.00

Johann Schmelz bottles satisfying rich yet clear and mineral-inflected representations of Wachau Riesling and Grüner Veltliner. In a throwback to previous, cooler decades, he continues to offer at least as wide a range of Federspiel as Smaragd, and the former seldom evince any deficiency in ripeness of flavor.

JOSEF SCHMID ✶✶✶
KREMSTAL $20.00–$50.00

Josef Schmid is an emerging talent farming both loess and *Urgestein* sites and rendering Grüner Veltliner of exceptional clarity, pure fruit, and mineral expression, at very reasonable prices.

HEIDI SCHRÖCK   ★ ★ ★ ★
NEUSIEDLERSEE-HÜGELLAND $25.00–$125.00

Although from a young age the always affable and inquisitive Heidi Schröck played a leading role in the restoration of Rust's tradition of nobly sweet Ausbruch, it is for rendering the most diverse and delightful dry white wines in Burgenland that she became internationally known. Recent years have seen the revival of Furmint; Schröck's refinement of her techniques with nobly sweet wines bear profound fruit; and her reds (representing a volume unusually small for a Rust vintner) are also distinctive. Schröck now, vintage permitting, bottles two examples of Ausbruch, one from a blend of grapes and one, from the Turner vineyard, 100% Furmint.

2005 Furmint	90	now–2012
2004 Furmint	90	now–2010
2005 Muscat	87	now
2004 Muscat	91	now
2005 Weissburgunder	88	now–2012
2004 Weissburgunder	92	now–2014
2005 Ried Vogelsang	91	now–2010
2004 Ried Vogelsang	88–90	now
2004 Zweigelt Kräften	88	now–2013
2005 Beerenauslese	92	now–2015
2005 Ruster Ausbruch on the Wings of Dawn	93	now–2020
2005 Ruster Ausbruch Turner	94	now–2035
2001 Ruster Ausbruch Furmint-Sauvignon	90–92	now–?
2000 Ruster Ausbruch Furmint-Weissburgunder	87–89	now–?
1999 Ruster Ausbruch Weissburgunder-Grauburgunder	92–93	now–?
1999 Ruster Ausbruch Elysium I Welschriesling	93	now–2035
1999 Ruster Ausbruch Elysium II Muskateller	94	now–2035
1999 Ruster Ausbruch Elysium III Weissburgunder	98	now–2040

SETZER   ★ ★ ★
WEINVIERTEL $20.00–$50.00

Uli and Hans Setzer are an animated and ambitious couple farming sandy, gravelly soils, north of the Wagram and not very far east from the edge of the Kamptal, but quite a bit cooler than either of those regions. Their Grüner Veltliner and Roter Veltliner offer excellent value and have in the past several years achieved a level of refinement and complexity that easily stand comparison with the elite of Austria's more renowned regions.

STADT KREMS   ★ ★ ★
KREMSTAL $15.00–$35.00

Former Freie Weingärtner Wachau winemaker Fritz Miesbauer and his idealistic young team are getting the feel for their outstanding *terroirs* and new cellar. This winery owned by the city of Krems has already become a source of excellent values, and reclamation of vineyards will bear further fruit. (Miesbauer and this facility are now also responsible for the wines of the Göttweig monastery.)

2005 Grüner Veltliner Sandgrube	87	now
2004 Grüner Veltliner Weinzierlberg	89	now
2005 Grüner Veltliner Wachtberg	86	now+?
2004 Grüner Veltliner Wachtberg	87	now+?
2005 Riesling Steinterrassen	87	now–2010
2004 Riesling Kögl	88	now–2010

| 2005 Riesling Grillenparz | 90 | now–2012+? |
| 2004 Riesling Grillenparz | 87 | now+? |

STRABLEGG-LEITNER ✶✶✶✶
SÜDSTEIERMARK $N/A

That Franz Strablegg's wines have received relatively little recognition even in Austria certainly has nothing to do with their quality! Strablegg never bought into the association of single-vineyard Styrian wines with new wood, but aims to let the character of his diverse and dramatically different plots of Sauvignon emerge without obstruction. He succeeds with a clarity and mineral complexity that would immediately resonate with the élite of the Loire. In addition to his ageworthy Sauvignon bottlings, Strablegg crafts Muskateller with few peers. Hopefully, these wines will soon be better known and reach American shores.

SCHWARZ ✶✶✶
NEUSIEDLERSEE $50.00–$100.00

Johann Schwarz is the talented butcher of Illmitz. But his neighbor and protégé Alois Kracher and friend Manfred Krankl (Austrian proprietor and winemaker extraordinaire of Sine Qua Non in California) persuaded him to make wine from his vineyards, and some very formidable, intense, tactile wines these are. Schwarz's aim is to craft a red that will improve with a dozen or more years of age, so in that sense the jury is still out.

STADLMANN ✶✶✶
THERMENREGION $18.00–$35.00

If there is one indispensable stop in the Thermenregion it is chez Stadlmann. His Rotgipfler are excellent, but the rich, unique complexities of his Zierfandler from the Mandel-Höh must be tasted to be believed.

MANFRED TEMENT ✶✶✶✶
SUDSTEIERMARK $15.00–$100.00

South Styria's most celebrated vintner keeps progressing: occupying a vast and sophisticated facility; fine-tuning his vinification; and acquiring more acreage around the great, steep Zieregg, even crossing the border into Slovenia to do so. A more sparing use of new wood and the employment of larger barrel sizes has afforded opportunities for greater refinement in his single-vineyard Sauvignon bottlings, although even Tement had difficulty overcoming the extremes of the 2003 and 2004 Styrian vintages.

2004 Morillon [Chardonnay] Zieregg	86–88	now
2005 Gelber Muskateller Steinbach	89	now
2004 Gewürztraminer	87–89	now–2010
2004 Roter Traminer	88–90	now–2012+?
2005 Sauvignon Blanc Grassnitzberg	87	now–2010
2004 Sauvignon Blanc Grassnitzberg	87–89	now
2003 Sauvignon Blanc Grassnitzberg	88	now
2005 Sauvignon Blanc Zieregg	92	now–2017
2004 Sauvignon Blanc Zieregg	87–90	now–2012
2005 Weißburgunder Hochkittenberg Toms	87	now–2010

TINHOF ✶✶✶
NEUSIEDLERSEE-HÜGELLAND $N/A

Erwin Tinhof, who farms vineyards in the hills above Burgenland's small capital city of Eisenstadt, believes in the virtues of Austria's traditional varieties and in unhurried cask vinification. His basic Blaufränkisch is a paradigm of that grape and of good value, and he is increasing his acreage of St. Laurent, Muskateller, Weissburgunder, and the generally unjustly denigrated Neuburger; he recently began blending the last two with memorable results. Unfortunately, the wines have yet to appear in the U.S.

ERNST TRIEBAUMER   * * * *
NEUSIEDLERSEE-HÜGELLAND $25.00–$150.00

"E. T." was the man who (with his 1997 Mariental) first brought Austrians to a realization that profound wine was possible from Blaufränkisch. The entire line of reds from Triebaumer and his son Herbert is fascinating, even in a difficult vintage like 2005 (though some years they are youthfully tough), and the small assortment of nobly sweet wines here is superb. Only the dry whites here still disappoint a little; for that one can happily look to their friend Heidi Schröck.

2005 St. Laurent	86–88	now
2005 Blaufränkisch	85–87	now
2005 Blaufränkisch Gmärk	87–89	now–2010
2004 Blaufränkisch Oberer Wald	87	now–2012
2003 Blaufränkisch Mariental	91	2010–2018

TSCHIDA-ANGERHOF   * * * *
NEUSIEDLERSEE $30.00–$60.00/375 ml

Hans Tschida has not worried about living almost literally in the shadow of Alois Kracher. His sweet wines have their own elegant style and class, and he can also lay claim to some of the best Eiswein and Strohwein (from fruit dried on mats) made anywhere in the world. Recently he began shipping to the U.S.

JOSEF UMATHUM   * * * *
NEUSIEDLERSEE $25.00–$125.00

"Pepi" Umathum keeps refining his impressive reds and beginning new projects, the latest and most exciting of which is restoring ancient terraces at Jois, on the northwestern edge of the Neusiedlersee, whence his Pinot Noir and Blaufränkisch have already proven revelatory. With Hallebühl, Umathum broke through the Austrian mind-set that refused to envision profound Zweigelt, just as it once rejected the notion of great *vin de garde* from Blaufränkisch. Umathum's dry whites (especially Traminer) and nobly sweet wines are also often memorable. He also directs winemaking for Zantho, a collaboration with the grower cooperative of Andau on the Hungarian border that has resulted in especially youthful, tasty, and inexpensive reds.

2005 Gelber und Roter Traminer	87	now
2004 Hallebühl	87–89	2010–2016
2004 St. Laurent vom Stein	87–89	now–2012
2004 Pinot Noir Unter den Terrassen zu Jois	90	now–2014+?
2004 Blaufränkisch Joiser Kirchsgarten	91–92	now–2016+?
2003 Blaufränkisch Joiser Kirchsgarten	91–92	now–2016+?

VELICH   * * * *
NEUSIEDLERSEE $25.00–$125.00

Heinz Velich—whose brother Rolland left their family's winery to develop his Moric project—continues to produce Austria's most distinguished Chardonnay, lees-enriched, unfiltered, and from mature vines. He also produces extraordinary nobly sweet wines. Few Austrian vintners have a keener or more critical sense of their own opportunities and limitations, and those of their grapes and *terroirs*, than Velich.

2004 Chardonnay Darscho	88–89	now
2004 Chardonnay Tiglat	89–91	now–2014
2004 Beerenauslese	92–95	now–2018+?
2002 Beerenauslese	94	now–2015
2004 Welschriesling Trockenbeerenauslese	91–94	now–2018+?
2002 Welschriesling Trockenbeerenauslese	95	now–2020+?

FRANZ WENINGER ✴ ✴ ✴
MITTELBURGENLAND $20.00–$60.00

Franz Weninger not only vinifies ambitious reds from the classic Austrian and French varieties growing at top sites around Horitschon, he and his son also make lovely Kékfrankos across the border in Balf, and have enjoyed a longtime collaboration with Atilla Gere in Villány in south-central Hungary.

2003 Zweigelt Ranger	87	now–2010
2003 Blaufränkisch Reserve	88–90	now–2014
2003 Blaufränkisch Dürrau	88–90	now–2016

WENZEL ✴ ✴ ✴
NEUSIEDLERSEE-HÜGELLAND $18.00–$100.00

Robert Wenzel's father was one of the great pioneers of Burgenland wine, a patriotic Magyar who in 1921 renounced his Hungarian citizenship to stay with his vines. Wenzel and his son Michael have been prime movers in the reestablishment of Furmint, and some of their most distinctive and satisfying results in both dry and nobly sweet wine are made with that variety. Robert Wenzel was among the last to cultivate a lightly oxidized style of Ausbruch (as well as to speak Magyar in the cellar) but today's earlier-bottled wines have not sacrificed any personality.

RAINER WESS ✴ ✴ ✴
WACHAU, KREMSTAL $16.00–$40.00

Former Freie Weingärtner Wachau director Rainer Wess operates a highly selective and quality-conscious *négociant* firm which, in addition to offering excellent value, has (beginning in 2005) crafted certain wines that can compete with those of the Wachau's better estates.

2005 Grüner Veltliner Terrassen	87	now
2005 Grüner Veltliner Loibenberg	88–89	now–2012+?
2004 Grüner Veltliner Loibenberg	87	now–2010
2004 Grüner Veltliner Pfaffenberg	87	now–2010
2005 Riesling Wachauer	86	now
2005 Riesling Pfaffenberg	90	now–2013
2004 Riesling Pfaffenberg	89	now–2010

WIENINGER ✴ ✴ ✴
VIENNA $15.00–$100.00

Fritz Wieninger has been the dynamo behind whatever overdue recognition the wines of Vienna have garnered over the past decade. While his line-up of cuvées is still sprawling, he continues to refine their quality. His old vines blend from the Nussberg is Exhibit A in the revival of Wiener Gemischter Satz, and his Riesling from that site can also impress. Many of his wines stemming from internationally well-known varieties are also international in style.

1999 Nussberg Trockenbeerenauslese	90	now–2017

[germany]

IN RIESLING'S REALM

Winegrowing along the Rhine and its tributaries dates back to Roman times, and the medieval monastic orders brought site selection and vineyard management to a fine art. But the vine that was to make Germany's international reputation—and which many would call "the world's greatest white grape"—did not appear by name until the late 15th century. During the late-17th-century replanting that followed the devastation of the Thirty Years' War, Riesling began to play a major role for the first time; before long there were entire districts in which foresighted and quality-conscious ecclesiastical and civil authorities were insisting on the choice of this variety. By the mid-18th century there were also regional decrees mandating or at least favoring wines made from naturally ripe grapes to which no sugar had been added. In the late 19th century, when the reputation and price of German wine attained or surpassed those of first-growth Bordeaux, it was on the basis of outstanding sites, impeccable steep-slope viticulture, and the unadulterated Riesling grape. When German Riesling reemerged on the international stage after the disruption and devastation of phylloxera, economic depression, world wars, and foreign occupation, it had lost considerable luster and brought rock-bottom prices when compared with any of the world's other renowned wines. Riesling's loss of prestige during the era of postwar Germany's "economic miracle" could largely be attributed to the expansion of vine acreage into inferior sites (even former potato fields); high-yield farming and machine harvesting; proliferation of earlier-ripening but superficial-tasting grape crossings; and abundant employment of beet sugar. Still, wines from some great German estates at least—thanks in no small part to importer Frank Schoonmaker—were receiving an enthusiastic reception in the United States.

During the 1980s, though, Americans' interest in Germany's Riesling dwindled to a small core of devotees and citizens with family or personal connections to that country. The eyes, noses, and money of wine collectors were certainly not on this category. What's more, the

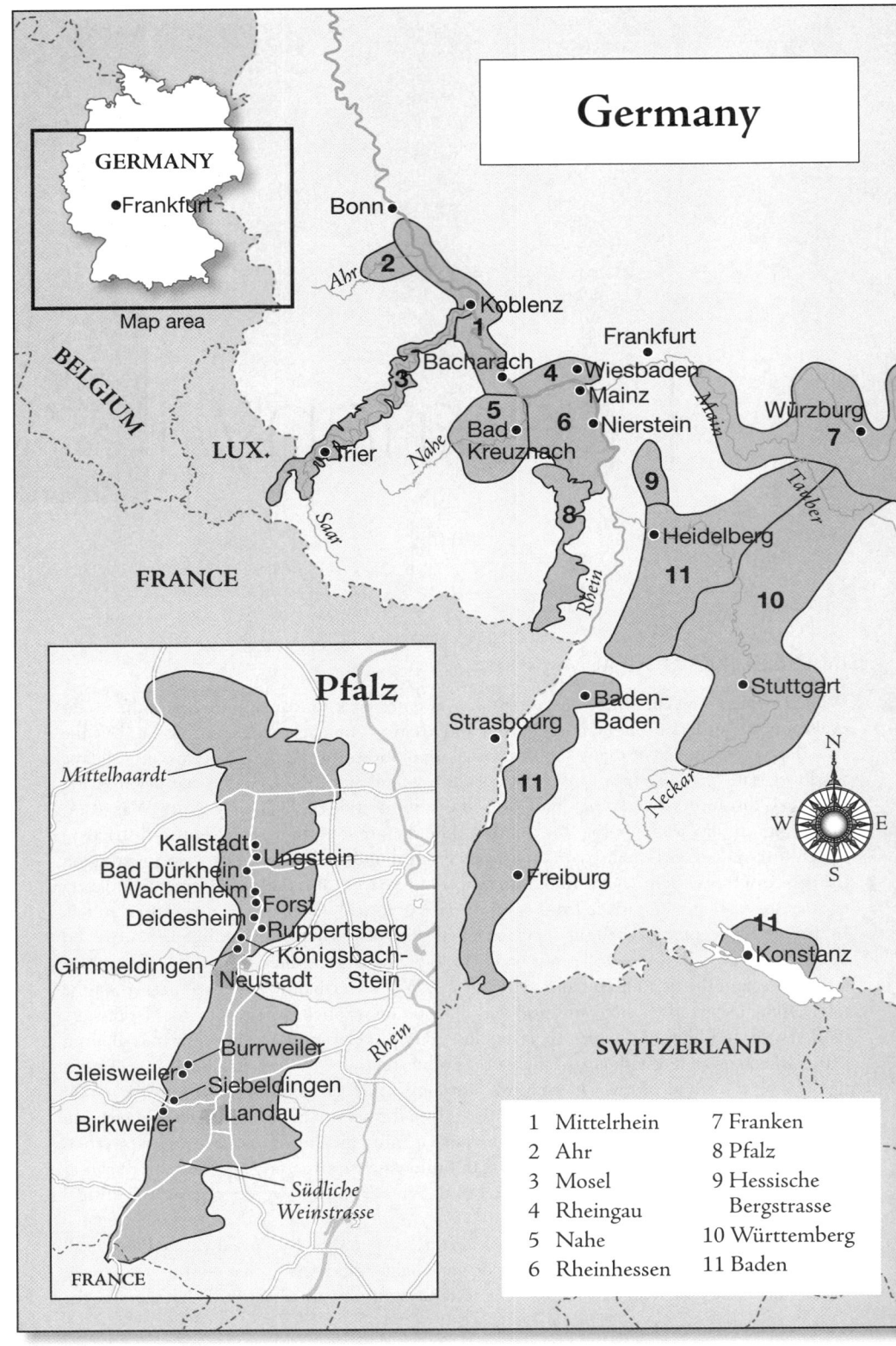

Germany

GERMANY
•Frankfurt

Map area

Bonn •

Ahr 2

Koblenz
1

Bacharach 4 Wiesbaden
5 Mainz
Bad 6 Nierstein
Kreuzhach

BELGIUM

LUX.
Trier

Nahe

Saar

FRANCE

Frankfurt

Würzburg
7

Main

9

Heidelberg

11

10

Stuttgart

Rhein

8

Strasbourg

Baden-
Baden

11

Freiburg

Neckar

N
W   E
S

11
Konstanz

SWITZERLAND

Pfalz

Mittelhaardt

Kallstadt• •Ungstein
Bad Dürkheim•
Wachenheim• •Forst
Deidesheim• •Ruppertsberg
•Königsbach-
Gimmeldingen• Stein
Neustadt

Burrweiler
Gleisweiler• •
•Siebeldingen
Birkweiler• Landau

Rhein

Südliche
Weinstrasse

FRANCE

1 Mittelrhein	7 Franken
2 Ahr	8 Pfalz
3 Mosel	9 Hessische
4 Rheingau	Bergstrasse
5 Nahe	10 Württemberg
6 Rheinhessen	11 Baden

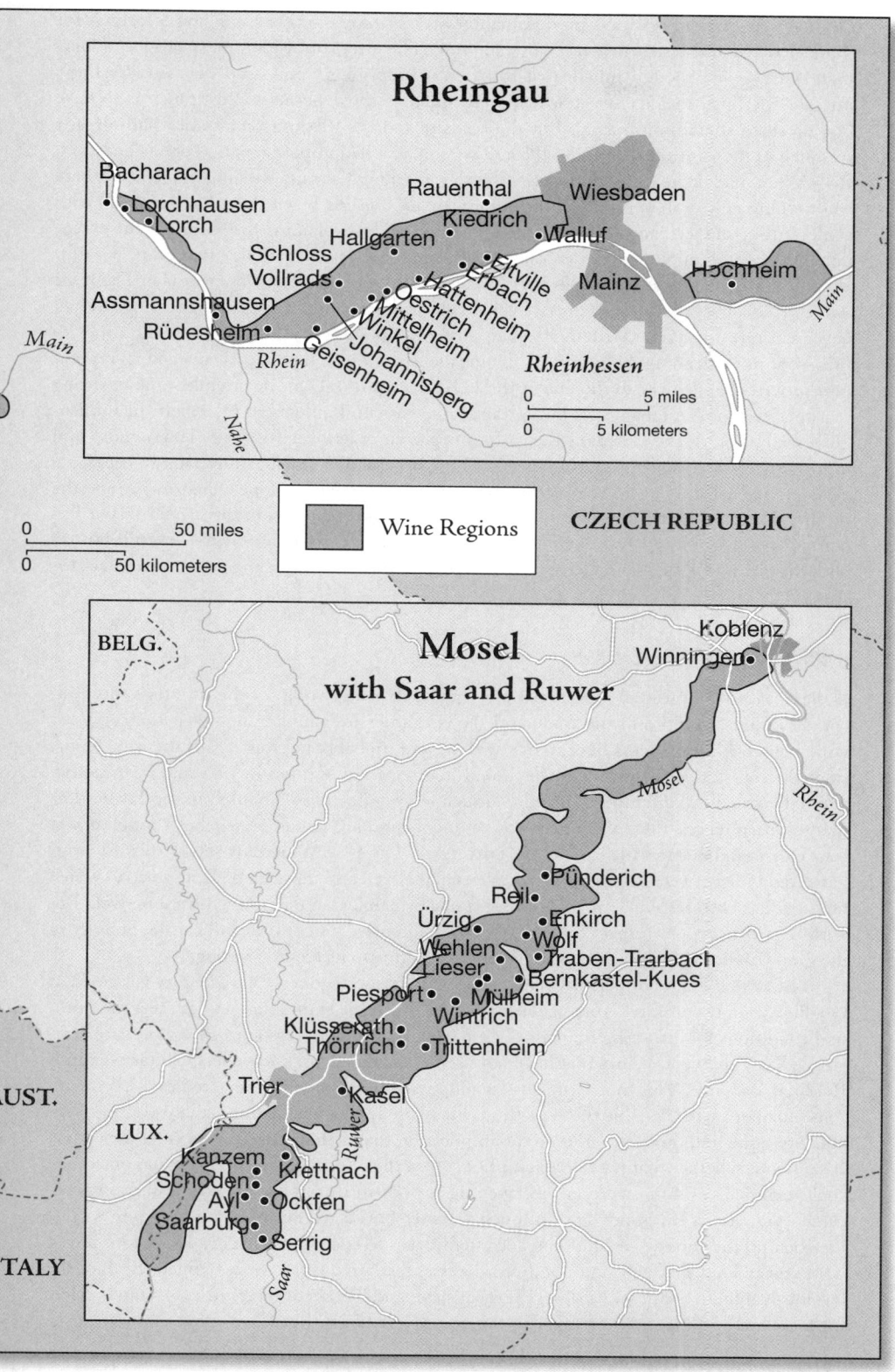

Rheingau

Bacharach
Lorchhausen
Lorch
Assmannshausen
Rüdesheim
Schloss
Vollrads
Hallgarten
Rauenthal
Kiedrich
Wiesbaden
Walluf
Eltville
Erbach
Hattenheim
Oestrich
Mittelheim
Winkel
Johannisberg
Geisenheim
Mainz
Hochheim
Rheinhessen

Main

Rhein

Nahe

Main

0   5 miles
0   5 kilometers

0   50 miles
0   50 kilometers

Wine Regions

CZECH REPUBLIC

Mosel
with Saar and Ruwer

BELG.

Koblenz
Winningen

AUST.

LUX.

ITALY

Pünderich
Reil
Enkirch
Ürzig
Wolf
Wehlen
Traben-Trarbach
Lieser
Bernkastel-Kues
Piesport
Mülheim
Wintrich
Klüsserath
Thörnich
Trittenheim
Trier
Kasel
Kanzem
Krettnach
Schoden
Ayl
Ockfen
Saarburg
Serrig

Mosel

Rhein

Ruwer

Saar

Germans themselves—always predominantly beer drinkers—were following a fashion for things French and Italian when it came to wine. The effect of insipid, mass-produced German wine—even though much of it came from inferior grapes—had debased Riesling's image. "Riesling" meant "sweet white, well suited to those not so sophisticated as to have graduated to something better." But the seeds of today's Riesling renaissance had already sprouted in the wine market of the 1980s. Two impassioned import agents, Terry Theise and Rudi Wiest, had dedicated their lives not merely to selling German Riesling in the U.S. (there was nothing new in that) but to selling Americans *on* Riesling by working hand in hand with a select group of Germany's most talented growers and by explaining to consumers the exceptional labors and unique virtues associated with steep-slope propagation of that grape. Gradually, their message struck home. Robert Parker's enthusiastic early 1990s reports in *The Wine Advocate* encouraged a new degree of consumer curiosity and acceptance. The English had never entirely forsaken German Riesling—its championing by Hugh Johnson testifies to this—but in the waning 20th century, the inexpensive brands that had cheapened its reputation proved even slower to die out in the U.K. than in the U.S. Meanwhile, a new, strong market developed in Japan. Last but certainly not least, and influenced by American and English wine writers, the Germans themselves began to rediscover Riesling. Today more and more growers are aspiring to excellence and to perpetuating small family estates, because a decent living can once again be made by striving for quality. Steep-slope winegrowing and the reclamation or perpetuation of historically renowned sites and traditions is still in peril in many parts of Germany, but the tide has turned. Riesling is once more "in"—even if not yet with the prices of 1900—and Germany has regained its reputation as the preeminent place for that vine.

LIVING WITHIN THE LAW

If there is one thing rotten in the state of German Riesling—most of the country's most talented vintners would join the trade and the consumer in complaining—it is the country's wine laws. Still, consumers have to live with it, and probably not merely for the time being, since the roots of the trouble were anchored in a wine law written in 1971 and have stoutly resisted virtually all attempts at pruning, much less eradication. "Thanks" to this law and its many consequences, there is no easy way to understand a German wine label, though it *is* at least easy to understand the basis of the law: sugar. The 1971 Wine Law starts from an exaggerated divide between wines that have been chaptalized and those made from juice to which no sugar has been added. This is reminiscent of a principle that once served Riesling well. But with regard to proper respect for sites, for labor-intensive viticulture, and for the nobility of the grape itself, the law has wreaked havoc, largely due to its fixation on sugar.

The law envisages or permits chaptalization in two categories. One category is known as Qualitätswein bestimmter Anbaugebiete, "QbA" for short. Wines that do not meet the minimal conditions for assuming the name of a particular growing region (*Anbaugebiet*) are categorized as Tafelwein. Wines that have not been chaptalized are known as Qualitätswein mit Prädikat, or QmP. This merely means "quality wine with some further predicate," i.e., with some further attribute. But the way the term is used, you would think the meaning were "quality wine with *pedigree*," due to the implication that a chaptalized wine is a lesser wine. It's dubious whether that is a fair assumption, given that Germany traditionally has one of the coolest climates and most precarious ripening seasons in Europe, while chaptalization is accepted practice in Burgundy and in much warmer Bordeaux, even for top-class wines. The idea behind the concept of Prädikat, admittedly, was to encourage ripe grapes. And it might have worked out that way, but not given the way the "predicates" were defined. Each of the levels—Kabinett, Spätlese, Auslese, Beerenauslese, and Trockenbeerenauslese—stands solely for a certain minimal level of sugar in the grapes at harvest. But there is a lot more to ripe, tasty grapes and quality wines than mere sugar, and to overlook this is like proposing to rank people by wealth but considering only their bank balances. Furthermore, the minimum levels of sugar set for these "predicates" were lower than those intuitively deemed necessary at the time for Spätlese (literally "late harvest"), Auslese ("selective harvest"), or Beerenauslese ("berry-selective harvest"). "Cabinet," an old and honorable term of approbation borrowed from British usage and meaning in essence "suitable or important enough to reside or take place in a special room," had the sense sucked from it and reemerged with a "K" and two "t's" as a category of wine meeting a very minimal level of sugar indeed. This was like taking the notion "distinguished citizen" and redefining it as "anyone who has managed never to run afoul of the law."

Germany's so-called predicates are not, however, concerned with sugar in the wines, but only in the grapes at harvest (or when added to the juice, i.e., in chaptalization). Of course, grapes harvested for Trockenbeerenauslese in shriveled, botrytized condition and containing an astronomical level of sugar are not going to make a dry wine. Indeed, given the retardant effect of botrytis (an antibiotic fungus) on fermentation and the enormously viscous, sweet medium, you might at times have trouble even getting enough alcohol to officially qualify as "wine" (currently, within the European Community, 5%) before your yeasts give up and die. But the definition of the different predicates says nothing directly about the sweetness of the wine. This contradicted long-standing, pre-1971 practice, when a wine labeled Spätlese or Auslese implied lateness and selectivity of picking, but also at least discreet sweetness. The German Wine Law officially defined the term "dry" (*trocken*) and also created a category as unintelligible in the original as it is untranslatable, namely *halbtrocken*—literally, "half dry." (Some unforeseen consequences of these definitions will be pursued further under the heading Balance.) A wine labeled *trocken*—whether Kabinett, Spätlese, or Auslese—is dry; indeed, if it is a Riesling (given that grape's usually high acidity) it will typically taste austerely dry. But whereas the normal assumption in Germany had been that a wine *not* labeled Spätlese, Auslese, etc., would taste dry, or at most discreetly sweet, in the wake of the 1971 Wine Law, QbA wines—wines heavily sweetened with unfermented or par-fermented grape juice (known as Süssreserve)—were rampant, especially in export markets.

The confusion and damage caused by Germany's new wine law and its so-called predicates went much further. The idea of dressing up as Spätlese, Auslese, Beerenauslese, or Trockenbeerenauslese a wine rendered from nugatory grape varieties, such as crossings generated solely in order to obtain high levels of grape sugar as early in the season as possible, would scarcely have occurred to growers born before 1900, much less become accepted practice. Such terms of approbation as "Cabinet," too, had been confined to wines from the noblest grapes, which meant, in most of Germany's regions, Riesling. With the post-1971 advent of Prädikatsweine one could buy supermarket "Spätlese" or "Auslese" from unspecified grape varieties unworthy of mention. Prädikat became the new pedigree, but at the same time the predicates were cheapened and the importance of certain traditional grapes, above all Riesling, was slighted. This sugar-obsessed law and the planting of inferior grapes reinforced each other. Furthermore, the new law permitted any sort of wine to be sweetened with Süssreserve after its fermentation was finished, and that sweetener could be made from any grapes whatsoever, leading to widespread corruption of Riesling's integrity. (Nowadays, the use of Süssreserve is almost unknown among Germany's elite growers who, if they wish their wine to retain significant residual sugar, arrest the fermentation by chilling, sulfuring, filtering, or some combination thereof.)

If Riesling got a raw deal from the 1971 Wine Law, worse was in store for Germany's great vineyards, not to mention the consumer. Granted, with in excess of 2,500 different vineyard names in use, to become an expert one would have had a lot to learn. No doubt some of these sites never made a really memorable wine, though sometimes that might have been for lack of a champion. But quality-conscious vintners with site-sensitive grapes characteristically wanted to distinguish their wines from different pickings and locations, and most of the names had been in use for generations, or even centuries. True, these growers might—on account of blending or simply as prudent marketing—have chosen to bottle many of their wines without attribution of vineyard, but if a vineyard name was printed on the label, they thereby assured the consumer this referred to a small, discrete area delimited as a result of long experience with its microclimate, geological underpinnings, historical owners, and how these and other factors affected the character of the wine. The 1971 Wine Law stipulated that a site-specific wine would be named according to the formula [town name] + [vineyard name]. It then proceeded to leave only one in ten vineyard names standing, banishing all others from mention on the labels. This meant that, on average, ten different formerly mentioned sites were subsumed under one new name—except that, for the most part, the names were *not* new, they were simply the most marketable, most renowned, and, at times, the least politically unpalatable of the old names.

This was deceptive enough for anyone used to the old names, but then the law took a fateful step in the direction of intentional consumer deception by creating something called a Grosslage. This was a collection of vineyards over a wide area, employed as if naming a single vineyard. And the deception went further, because often wine labeled with the name of a Grosslage did not even come from the town whose name was legally associated with it. A couple of the most egregious examples of this unsavory legal practice will suffice. The town name Piesport had cachet thanks to the Riesling grown, since at least the 17th century, on its great amphitheater of slate. After 1971, the single-vineyard name Goldtröpfchen (referring to "tiny golden tears" of Riesling grapes) applied to numerous formerly distinct sites, all of them at least contiguous and situated on the town's great wall of slate, where nobody was likely to plant anything but Riesling. But the Grosslage "Piesporter Michelsberg," which co-opted another local vineyard name, incorporated eight villages, including wines grown on alluvial soils along the Mosel or far back in the hills above Piesport, where Riesling was unlikely to ripen and the grape of choice was Müller-Thurgau or other crossings. The greatest vineyard on the Saar is the Scharzhofberg in the town of Wiltingen. So a Grosslage named "Wiltinger Scharzberg" was created to capitalize on the name of that great Riesling site and to apply to grapes of all sorts, grown in any of the 18 winegrowing villages of the Saar—anywhere in fact other than in the Scharzhof*berg* itself, whose owner successfully lobbied to be spared the ignominy of inclusion in the Grosslage!

Since 1971, several new wine categories have taken effect, most of them of little usefulness with a period of active employment blessedly short-lived. (They might never die, though, since like other dubious baggage loaded into the original law, they remain officially in effect.) One important change made in 1982 was to recognize the category Eiswein as a separate Prädikat, applying to wine from grapes with sugar levels equivalent to Beerenauslese or higher, harvested from grapes naturally frozen on the vine, and pressed before they begin to thaw. A further change has taken place in recent years, as much in enforcement as in statute, which on the face of it seems positive. Under the 1971 law ("in typically Teutonic fashion," some might say) any information of a sort *not* required on the label was essentially forbidden to appear there. So, for instance, attempts by growers to rank different qualities of Spätlese or Auslese from their vineyards by means of little stars (especially prevalent on the Mosel), let alone through use of traditional terms of approbation such as *fein,* was disallowed. The law had created an unusually large gap for the Mosel between the minimum must weight (measured in Germany in degrees Oechsle) of Spätlese and that required for Beerenauslese, leaving many growers in search of ways to advertise more adequately the degree of richness and concentration of a given wine. The drastic reduction of legally recognized vineyard names greatly increased the likelihood of growers wanting to bottle multiple wines with the same official name (e.g., Erdener Treppchen Riesling Auslese), wines that could otherwise be distinguished from one another only by the penultimate digits of the tiny official registration number (the

Amtliche Prüfnummer, or "A.P.#") that appears on every bottle. The convention arose of calling the richer of two wines "gold capsule," or even "long gold capsule," and of putting a correspondingly impressive capsule on the bottle itself, since capsules were not regulated as part of the label. This practice persists, but in the past several years, stars, asterisks, "R" (as in "reserve"), "Alte Reben" (meaning "old vines" but, as in France, sometimes code for *raize ze price*), and other terms have come to be accepted. Depending on enforcement, even the names of the old, small vineyards or of individual parcels are sneaking their way back onto labels. A change that might seem positive—a loosening of the legal straitjacket—has thus meant yet more confusion, as growers adopt their own winery-internal conventions and terminology, which might be fine for private local cellar-door customers, but are inscrutable to those choosing from a retail or restaurant shelf or list, which means to all foreigners. In another far-reaching development, an increasing number of growers have taken to discarding the so-called predicates for registering, labeling, and selling even their best wine. Legally, then, such wines are "mere" QbA.

Germany's unfortunate wine law and its frequently unforeseen consequences have left the poor consumer grasping for straws with which to choose the Riesling he or she will sip. Without doubt, if the best of these wines were not both so profound and irresistible—indispensable indicators of Riesling's full potential—the effort would hardly justify the aggravation. Which factors are truly significant, and to which aspects of the label should one pay attention? First and foremost—as would be the case anywhere else—one must seek out a quality grower. Among the most fascinating aspects of German Riesling (which will shortly be discussed) is how its flavors vary with the choice of site. However, unless one picks a grower who maintains modest yields and practices scrupulous vinification, there is little hope of being able to smell or taste any differences that might arise from soil and site. The second thing to watch for is the word *"trocken"* or *"halbtrocken"* on the label. You can safely expect a Riesling so labeled to taste dry, if not austerely so. (A 15% alcohol Pinot Gris with 8 or 10 grams of residual sugar is another matter, and might evince a sense of sweetness.) The absence of those terms does not, however, mean that the wine will taste overtly sweet. There is really no way to tell, at least until you become familiar with the preferences and practices of individual growers. But the predicate with which the wine is labeled, as well as its degree of alcohol, will give clues to flavor. Alcohol in itself tells you something of a wine's body, and a Spätlese at 11% alcohol will almost certainly have lower residual sugar than one at 8%, and thus is likely to taste less sweet. If not labeled *"trocken"* or *"halbtrocken,"* an Auslese generally tastes sweeter than a Spätlese, which is generally sweeter than a Kabinett . . . at least among the wines of any given estate. To understand more adequately the perception of sweetness, one must consider balance.

QUESTIONS OF BALANCE AND TRANSPARENCY

German Riesling has a proclivity unprecedented in the world of wine for counterbalancing residual sugar, in fact, for often making it simply disappear on the palate. This talent may be tempered or enhanced depending on region or style. The uncanny balance of sugar with acidity, no doubt aided by the sheer extract of many Riesling and by pristine fruit and winemaking, is what makes possible a Mosel Kabinett of only 7%–8% alcohol that nevertheless tastes complete, mouthwatering, and complex. (Kabinett that merely meets the minimum legal degrees Oechsle will taste thin and weak, if not downright unripe.) It is a trick question to ask about the best Kabinett or Spätlese bottlings, "Is this wine sweet?" German wine import specialist Terry Theise captures this perfectly when he says, "Sweetness should not be what you notice, but neither should you sense its absence." With many a German Riesling labeled *trocken,* one is acutely aware of that absence due to sharpness and astringency. Yet Germans, when they drink German wines, do so almost exclusively from bottles with the imprimatur *trocken.* Numerous sociohistorical factors can be adduced in an attempt to explain what many foreign observers view as a streak of masochism (and Germans for their part often try to account for what they deem Americans' perverse pleasure in "sweet wine"). The simplest explanation is that German consumers, like consumers worldwide, will always ask for "dry wine," believing that "dry wine" best accompanies a meal. Add to this a legal definition of dryness as not exceeding 9 grams of residual sugar—legally *trocken*—and you have a recipe with Riesling for wines that very frequently (often even in the considered opinion of the vintners) would be better for a few more grams of sugar. But many vintners will tell you they "have to" warm them up, blend them out, or call in cultured yeasts to wrestle their misbehaving, fermenting Riesling down to the requisite 9 grams.

Had *halbtrocken* caught on, this frequent imbalance might have been addressed. But Germans loathed that term, not wanting "half" of anything. In fact, while wines with residual sugar are at last creeping back into fashion in certain German circles, there is usually a bipolar insistence that either a Riesling must be legally *trocken,* or else downright sweet—anything else is deemed a "half" measure. As if analyses or ideological slogans, not taste, determined balance! When the VDP—the growers' association to which most of Germany's elite estates belong—set out to assist in reestablishing high prices and renown for wines from the best vineyards, they placed the emphasis on a category they named Grosses Gewächs ("great growth") which must legally be *trocken.* Ironically, the typical dry-tasting Riesling of the early 20th century—of which, thankfully, many still can be savored, in cellars like that of Kloster Eberbach—was often one that would have been *halbtrocken* under current law. (Grosses Gewächs bottlings are not labeled as such, since this is a VDP internal and not a legally sanctioned term, nor do they bear a designation of Prädikat. They do, however, come in tall, heavy bottles embossed with a grape cluster and the numeral "1.") A few vintners, notably along the Saar, are fearlessly taking *trocken* off their labels and educating their customers in the art of balance in wines that *taste* dry, even though they may have more than 9 grams of residual sugar. But one cannot recognize from such labels the style or sweetness of the wine, unless one knows the winery's internal convention. (The term *"feinherb"* is now being allowed on labels, and is used by some vintners for *halbtrocken* wines. But *feinherb* is untranslatable and completely elastic, hence winery-specific in meaning.) One last point cannot be overlooked in a discussion of dry German wine. German Riesling has no more proclivity for buffering the effects of alcohol than do wines of any other sort—possibly less. More and more, among legally *trocken* Riesling, one stumbles over alcohol-induced bitterness and heat. (It's not a matter of measurable degrees of alcohol but of balance.) There are many wonderful *trocken* German Riesling, but be prepared for disappointments, even from very talented growers.

The word "transparency" is often used to describe the virtues of German Riesling and this is profoundly appropriate. No other wine—not even Pinot Noir from Burgundy—is more sensitive to its vineyard of origin, its vintage, or the hand of man. Indeed, if German Riesling does not lead you to believe in the efficacy of *terroir,* no wine on Earth is likely to shake your disbelief. Consider, for instance, Riesling from three nearby Mosel sites: Erdener Treppchen, Ürziger Würzgarten, and Wehlener Sonnenuhr. Again and again, their aromas evince, respectively—even for non-wine-drinkers who merely sniff—citrus (especially tangerine), red berries (especially strawberry), and vanilla-tinged orchard fruits (especially apple). Furthermore, these and other Riesling grown on variants of slate evince a specific character it is hard not to describe as "mineral" or even "wet stone" that those grown in other soils lack. The connection of "stoniness" or "minerality" as flavor descriptors with actual rocks and minerals may be tenuous, or exist only "in our minds." But the taste that evokes these mineral descriptors is on our palates. The character of a specific vintage is often just as strikingly discernible in these wines as are vineyard variations. While the use of new-oak barrels and malolactic fermentation are generally eschewed for German Riesling, stylistic differences—depending on viticultural methods, time and strategy of picking, fermentative regimen, and cellar upbringing—can be dramatic. Nowhere else and with no other grape on Earth can such completely satisfying wines be rendered at little more than 7% alcohol, yet sometimes one finds wonderful dry Riesling with as much as double that amount. There can be balanced German Riesling with only a few grams of residual sugar (although, as noted, this is a challenge), and there can be Eiswein and Trockenbeerenauslese with 200 grams or more that nevertheless do not taste cloying. Taking into account sensitivity to soil, to microclimate, and to the vicissitudes of weather, plus the stylistic latitude exercised by German vintners, there are few if any wines on Earth that can satisfy in so many different ways.

A TOUR OF GERMANY'S GROWING REGIONS

After taking a closer look at the Mosel and its tributaries, the Saar and Ruwer, we'll cross the rugged Hunsrück Hills to survey the Middle Rhine and the Nahe, then travel up the Rhine past the Rheingau and, on the opposite shore, Rheinhessen, finishing our tour of Germany's primary Riesling growing regions in the Pfalz, on the frontier with Alsace. There follow several snapshots of Germany's remaining regions, where grapes other than Riesling play a dominant role, the most important of these being the Ahr (north of the Middle Rhine), Franconia (west up the Main River from the Rheingau), and Baden (across the Rhine from Alsace).

THE MOSEL, SAAR, AND RUWER: RIESLING'S SLATE SIGNATURE

WHAT TO EXPECT

Since 2007, "Mosel" officially stands for the growing region formerly known as Mosel-Saar-Ruwer. Powerful industrial-scale producers and merchants lobbied the government successfully on behalf of this simplification for ease in marketing, but it is a disservice to the Mosel's two tributaries because the Saar and Ruwer enjoy climatic conditions and celebrated wine-growing histories quite distinct from those of the Mosel which, in turn, is for climatic and geological reasons best divided into the Middle Mosel and the less well-known Lower Mosel. The Mosel region is renowned for its ability to engender delicate, refreshing, low-alcohol Riesling with uncanny clarity and balance of sugar against acidity. The classic Mosel Kabinett may soon, however, become an endangered species if growers do not take special pains both to deal with the effects of so many warm, ripe vintages as Germany has enjoyed over the past two decades and to persevere in promoting this category to their customers. Generally, today's wines sold as "Kabinett" exhibit the richness and levels of residual sugar typical of the Spätlese or even Auslese of the 1980s; even with these elevated levels of sugar they are likely to possess an additional percentage point of alcohol as well. In keeping with German wine-drinking fashion (discussed under Balance above), most dry-tasting Mosel Riesling is very dry indeed, in order to stay under the 9-gram threshold for labeling it as *trocken,* but some growers are bucking this trend with wines of 10 to 20 grams of residual sugar, and a few (more on the Saar and Ruwer than in the Middle Mosel) are consistently able to render balanced and expressive legally *trocken* Riesling, particularly with low yields from old vines.

While the classic modern notion of Mosel Riesling implies bright acidity, lightness, lift, and often a slight spritz of CO_2, a number of growers are today experimenting with what they would call a return to the winemaking of their great-grandparents' era, aiming for lower acidity as a result of growing and picking decisions but also longer lees contact and maturation in cask, sometimes with malolactic fermentation. The profiles of growers in this chapter point out instances of such a style being pursued. The range of nobly sweet Auslese, Beerenauslese, Trockenbeerenauslese, and Eiswein from these regions in the past two decades is positively stunning, and totally unprecedented in volume when compared with any previous period in German history. Whereas a Mosel Kabinett, Spätlese, or even a blended proprietary QbA from a top address remains a bargain in today's market, nobly sweet wines are much more expensive. Each year, most of the Mosel-area members of the VDP growers' association offer two or three of their smaller lots, including nobly sweet Riesling, for sale at a Trier auction, where records have frequently been set for the highest prices ever paid for young wines.

The perpetually slim and serpentine Saar runs from the Vosges Mountains of Alsace (not far from the Mosel's own source) through more than 100 miles of heavy industry until, less than a dozen miles from its terminus, smokestacks give way to slate slopes and Riesling vines. Germany's Roman capital Trier lies just below the confluence of the Saar and Mosel. Under ecclesiastical owners and—after Napoleon classified and privatized the Mosel's vineyards—enterprising private proprietors, the vineyards of the Saar long enjoyed notoriety disproportionate to their size, although these great steep slate (and occasionally sandstone or graywacke) sites fell on hard times during much of the 20th century and have only recently been the scene of an inspiring revival. At the northern edge of Trier, the Ruwer—really no more than a brook, but Trier's source of water power and drinking water during Roman times—empties into the Mosel. Its few slate slopes, including those of two of the area's oldest monastic wine estates, enjoy a prestige even more disproportionate to their modest acreage than those of the Saar. Upriver from Trier, along the borders of Luxembourg and France, is the obscure Upper Mosel, known (if at all) for propagating the ancient and inherently tart Elbing grape, but also home to some very satisfying Pinot Blanc from chalky slopes. The long (and, by contrast, renowned) stretch of river known as the Middle Mosel runs from Trier to Zell, featuring many bends and bows, with often precipitous slopes of slate, and incorporating most of the Mosel's best-known villages. The Lower Mosel includes some of the world's steepest vineyards, most ancient terraces, driest microclimates, and most distinctive geological variations on the classic Devonian slate of the greater Mosel. Throughout the Mosel, Saar, and Ruwer, there are many vineyards whose rockiness, incline, and isolation defied even phylloxera; here growers have frequently perpetuated the planting of Riesling on its own roots rather than grafted ones. (A moratorium was placed on this practice in 2007 following a phylloxera scare; time will tell whether that marked the end of an era.) In certain instances, today's ancient vines predate World War I. An excellent argument can be made that, in addition to the quality of the sites themselves, the enterprise and ambition of talented growers and the availability of old, ungrafted vines loom large in accounting for the concentration of so many of Germany's greatest estates along the Mosel, Saar, and Ruwer.

Among the most intriguing and remarkable aspects of Mosel Riesling is its ability to age. You seldom need to worry about holding a really well-made Kabinett for 10 to 15 years. The taste will become drier and the flavors less overtly fruity, but often the CO_2 spritz and the mouthwatering invigoration of ripe acidity still characterize such wines even at 20 years of age. Top-notch examples of Spätlese can age even longer, as do the best of the drier wines, some of which may be labeled without a "predicate." Mosel Auslese, Beerenauslese, and Trockenbeerenauslese from the top sites and producers can easily accumulate further complexity and retain their brilliant fruit even after three-quarters of a century in bottle. As with any German Riesling, however, it is for you the taster or owner of the bottles to decide at what age these wines offer the most appeal. Seldom could it be said that something is "missing" let alone "it's a shame" if one chooses to enjoy them in their youth. Sometimes they will go through awkward or less expressive periods, anywhere from 2 to 10 years after bottling, but this is difficult to predict. (The dates that accompany the ratings of specific wines later in this chapter have intentionally been chosen very conservatively, recognizing the vicissitudes of storage and the proclivity of each wine to "have the last word" and frequently to make a fool of the prognosticator.)

SOME IMPORTANT VINEYARDS AND THEIR OWNERS

The vineyards of Serrig—notably those named for and owned by Schloss Saarstein—form the gateway to the Saar. Not far downstream is Saarburg, the name of its foremost vineyard, Rausch, meaning an intoxicating high—from the vertiginous slope, no doubt, not from its Riesling. This is where the top wines of Hanno Zilliken, and the stylistically very different, mostly dry Riesling of Dr. Heinz Wagner, are grown. Just down and across the river is Ockfen, its Bockstein vineyard a familiar representative of the Saar in America since the days of Frank Schoonmaker. This is a site from which quality varies enormously depending on estate and location on the slope. Zilliken and Wagner craft excellent Riesling here, but the champion is the Sankt Urbans-Hof, based on the Mosel. Wines from Weinhof Herrenberg and their eponymous site in Schoden, and those of Peter Lauer from the well-known Ayler Kupp, should not be missed. Both of these estates, along with the Sankt Urbans-Hof, own a remarkable piece of real estate called the Saarfeilser. At Wiltingen, one set of vineyards overlooks the Saar; the rest turn inland (following the river's former course), inscribing an arc of excellence. Egon Müller's Riesling from the Scharzhofberg and Braune Kupp are second to none, but van Volxem, too, in a dramatically different and dry-tasting style, makes Riesling in the great Scharzhofberg, as well as in the exceptional Braunfels, Kupp, and Gottesfuss. Following the arc away from the Saar, the wines of Oberemmel's Hütte vineyard from von Hövel (also a source for Scharzhofberg Riesling) and of the stylistically distinct Riesling of Falkensteiner Hof (from their Hofberg as well as from lesser-known sites in Krettnach and Niedermennig) are highly rewarding. Around the bend from Wiltingen on the Saar, the Altenberg in Kanzem approaches the Scharzhofberg in excellence, as can be seen above all in the wines of van Volxem and von Othegraven. Saar Riesling sometimes exhibits a rather steely cast in its youth; it is traditionally notorious for wide vintage variation and for achieving true ripeness and excellence only a few years in each decade. But there has been no really "ripeness-deficient" year here since 1987! Notes of cherry, almond, and peach (in nobly sweet instances, of tropical fruits) are common in Saar Riesling, as are notes one can only describe as "mineral."

Two once famous monastic properties stand on either side of the tiny Ruwer on the fringes of Trier. Christoph Tyrell's Karthäuserhof bottles its wines under that name. Across the Ruwer, Carl von Schubert at Maximin Grünhaus segregates Riesling from two principal sites, Abtsberg and Herrenberg, the slate soils and tastes of each being strikingly different. Nearby neighbors von Beulwitz and Karlsmühle render outstanding Ruwer wines as well, particularly from the renowned Nies'chen vineyard in Kasel. A few winding miles upstream is the winery of von Kesselstatt, farming not only Nies'chen, but a who's who of other top Mosel area vineyards (including the Saar's Scharzhofberg) totaling nearly 100 acres. The characteristically long-lived wines of the Ruwer are often marked by red currant, sage, white peach, and citrus (in drier wines sometimes resembling Sauvignon), and they often exhibit a pronounced, smoky pungency and brown spice character. In contrast with the Middle Mosel, the top Ruwer growers regularly demonstrate surprising aptitude in Riesling *trocken* as well as in off-dry and nobly sweet styles.

The principal press house for the monks of St. Maximin was just downstream from Trier, where another Maximiner Herrenberg is today much less celebrated than that of Grünhaus but no less inherently excellent. The highly ageworthy wines of Schmitt-Wagner, from ancient ungrafted vines, will give one an idea of this site's great potential. That winery began in 2008 to operate jointly with the Karl Loewen estate, the foremost recent champion of steep, once famous sites along the Mosel north of Trier, including the Maximiner Klosterlay in Detzem, the Ritsch in Thörnich, and the Laurentiuslay in Leiwen, where Loewen is located. One cannot really call Laurentiuslay neglected any longer, because it is a vineyard with numerous other eager proponents, notably Sankt Urbans-Hof (whom we have met already on the Saar) and Grans-Fassian. Interestingly, all three of these growers bottle Riesling from the Laurentiuslay that is dry-tasting (although not always legally *trocken*). Around another of the

Mosel's many oxbows lies the town of Trittenheim, whose tropical-fruit-prone Altärchen ("little altar") and Apotheke ("apothecary") are well showcased (in dry and off-dry form) by Ansgar-Clüsserath, Grans-Fassian, and Clüsserath-Weiler. Sadly, though, the recent whole-sale restructuring and replanting of Trittenheim's vineyards (a controversial, often economi-cally beneficial practice applied to most of Germany's Riesling sites since the 1960s) has meant the uprooting of many ancient vines. At Dhron, from the Hofberg vineyard, the benchmark is A. J. Adam. The renowned Goldtröpchen in Piesport receives extraordinary treatment at the hands of Sankt Urbans-Hof and the outstanding Reinhold Haart estate, which also farms the excellent, nowadays obscure Ohligsberg, in Wintrich.

Downstream from Piesport, the walls of slate have historically prompted superlatives. At Brauneberg, the Fritz Haag winery sets extraordinary standards with wines from Juffer and Juffer-Sonnenuhr, renderings of which in different styles can be tasted from wineries Willi Haag and Max. Ferd. Richter. The latter's many excellent holdings include unjustly little-known vineyards in Mühlheim and Veldenz, which (uncharacteristically for the Middle Mosel) run perpendicular to the river along two side valleys. Schloss Lieser is the undisputed champion of the Niederberg-Helden vineyard in Lieser but also crafts superb Brauneberg Riesling. Past Lieser we arrive at the world-famous civic and tourist center of this region, Bernkastel. The hugely expensive (but, sadly, too seldom truly memorable) Riesling from its Doctor vineyard is rendered by only five estates, most notably Wegeler and two branches of the family Thanisch. Here is one of the very few places in Germany where quality-oriented growers routinely utilize the name of a Grosslage, because Badstube applies to all and only the best sites on the hillsides above Bernkastel. Seek out especially the renditions of Joh. Jos. Prüm or Selbach-Oster. These two are also among major sources of wines in two neighboring vine-yards known as Sonnenuhr ("sundial") in Wehlen (where Prüm is indisputably number one) and Zeltingen (where Selbach is top dog). Others with excellent Wehlener Sonnenuhr include Dr. Loosen, Weins-Prüm, Markus Molitor (who also renders a wealth of Riesling from Zeltin-gen in a distinctive style), and Heribert Kerpen (where fine wine from Bernkastel is rendered, too). In Graach—just opposite Wehlen, with the sites Domprobst and Himmelreich—the name to look for first is Willi Schaefer, whose wines can subsequently be compared with other excellent Graacher from Joh. Jos. Prüm, Markus Molitor, Max. Ferd. Richter, and von Kes-selstatt (whose *monopole* in Graach is called the Josephshof). Around the bend from Zeltingen come the neighboring vineyards of Erden (the Treppchen and Prälat) and Ürzig (the Würzgar-ten), whose distinctive aromas were commented on above in the discussion of transparency. Nearly all of the principal owners in one town have holdings in the others; among the many names to look for are, above all, Joh. Jos. Christoffel and Dr. Loosen, but also Mönchhof, Markus Molitor, Merkelbach, and (in Erden only) Andreas Schmitges. Swiss-born Daniel Vollenweider is single-handedly restoring the vineyards and reputation of the Goldgrube in the town of Wolf, and the once great but presently underperforming sites of Enkirch are due for revival, which Vollenweider protégé Alexander Weiser (Weiser-Künstler winery) is begin-ning with Riesling from the Ellergrub vineyard.

We now officially enter the Lower Mosel. The champion of Riesling in dry and nobly sweet formats is Clemens Busch, whose holdings are not far downstream from Enkirch in Pünderich's Marienberg. Busch segregates his wines from each of many individual parcels, labeling them with their pre-1971 vineyard names. Along its long, twisted way from here to the Rhine, the Mosel has carved out a large array of steep, well-exposed, and geologically nu-anced vineyards. The ancient, crumbling terraces in these frequently drought-prone locations are generally not (or at least no longer) very well known by name; they await their modern champions. At Winningen, just above the city of Koblenz and the Rhine River, two such cham-pion estates render fantastic wines from what can be called the single most vertiginous and awesome wall of vines in Germany, if not the world. Look for the often hauntingly mineral, herbal, berry-fruited Riesling of Knebel and Heymann-Löwenstein from the Röttgen and

Uhlen vineyards. (Löwenstein is another of those who segregates and has gotten away with labeling his wines according to their old vineyard names, and one taste comparison or glance at a geological map will make clear why.) Bone-rattling, stomach-churning monorails are nowadays used to access these and certain other Lower Mosel sites—the rigors and perils involved in farming any of Germany's steepest vineyards can scarcely be overstated. The number of vintners with hip replacements alone would make a shocking statistic.

[recent vintages]

The Mosel area is unprecedented for its wealth of winemaking talent. That said, just as in any other part of Germany, quality tends to drop steadily once one explores below the top 50 or so addresses; superficial sweetness, lack of clarity, or lack of concentration (due to excessive yields) abound. Even among wines from the best of Mosel growers, superficial or excessively youthful sweetness can occasionally be off-putting for some tasters, as can the slightly cheesy, overtly yeasty, sulfurous notes that occasionally plague young Mosel Riesling. The occurrence of such stinks (which dissipate with time in bottle) is quite capricious but generally associated with slow, ambient (rather than cultured) yeast fermentations that are arrested to leave residual sugar, and with the high levels of fructose that these practices—common to nearly all of the top estates—entail.

In Germany's Riesling regions in general—the Mosel is merely a striking example—the tendency for smaller estates and those with abundant capital to render the best wines has been accentuated by recent social trends. Timely, strategic, and selective picking (by hand, naturally) is essential for excellent quality in most years. Mustering and retaining crews skilled in the necessary hand-eye-palate coordination and mobilizing them at the right time (if not at a moment's notice) are daunting tasks. As in so much of western Europe, temporary workers from central Europe are the norm here. But both Germany (in a spectacularly unsuccessful attempt to match unemployed native German workers with the wineries and to withhold corresponding numbers of permits for guest workers) and the home countries (in an understandable effort to collect taxes) are making this task increasingly difficult for growers. Mother Nature has not helped, either, because precisely the warm (though sometimes rain-plagued) harvest weather Germany has been having frequently leaves grapes vulnerable to rot and often in need of swift yet gentle, selective picking. Riesling picked according to a preestablished calendar by a crew whose makeup changes greatly from one year to the next will almost inevitably lack the clarity and refinement that is the forte of this grape; this is especially true of many large establishments. All of the very best German (and Austrian) Riesling estates either assemble their crews from among family, friends, wine lovers, and local retirees, or else manage somehow to retain the same skilled foreign workers year after year, often from a single village or region and often from one generation to the next.

The greater Mosel has enjoyed incredibly good fortune in recent years. Not only has there been since 1988 but one vintage (1991) when excellent ripeness was not assured (in each decade before then, there were always at least three or four such years), but there has only been one vintage (2000) in which even the top growers rendered many weak wines. In 2007, a cool but clear autumn offered ample opportunity for stringent selection that reflected the record early flowering and warm spring and early summer of that year. August and early September were rainy, but in a pattern often repeated in Germany in recent years, the steep and rocky vineyards around the Mosel could slough off any ill effects, while grapes in other regions with heavier soils and less steep inclinations were more prone to rot. Veteran grower Hans-Leo Christoffel of Ürzig is fond of saying—exaggerating only a little—"With Riesling, it can rain all it wants, provided eventually the sun returns." That said, the rains of late summer 2006 spared nobody; in their aftermath fruit already in an advanced state of ripeness turned lavender or purplish in color, sugar skyrocketed, and rot rapidly set in. Yet this rot did not have to be ignoble: One and the same fungus (*Botrytis cinerea*) can magically concentrate or ruin. Along the Middle and Lower Mosel, occasionally also on the Saar, those who were able to mobilize skilled crews experienced the most stressful and intensive, but also one of the most rewarding, harvests of recent history, with reduced yields but rich, unusually opulent Riesling. The great Middle Mosel wines of 2006 are the best in memory for many of their growers who, despite the wines' relatively low acidity, predict they will be very long keepers.

August and September rains also threatened the harvest of 2005, but then the sun returned for an entire, glorious month in October, resulting in many fine collections along the Mosel and the Ruwer and even more so on the Saar, where warm winds concentrated sugar and flavors with dramatic effects—razor-sharp clarity, brash intensity, mesmerizing complexity, and phenomenal length. 2004 was a year for classic Mosel Riesling virtues: clarity, delicacy, and refinement. This vintage featured one of the few bumper crops in recent years of low-alcohol, high-acid Kabinett and Spätlese (not that Auslese and higher predicates were underrepresented). A certain aura of green herbal flavors in many German Riesling of this vintage seems to be moderated on the Mosel. A spun-out, irregular flowering left gaps in many bunches and many tiny, pipless grapes, good sources of concentration and also of ventilation to ward off rot. But there are still wines (increasingly as one leaves behind the elite estates) that suffer dilution on account of the vines' plethora of bunches. The productive "mind-set" of those vines, which has an evolutionary explanation, was—as in every Western European region—a reaction to the heat and drought that had hammered them in 2003, resulting in one of the smallest crops in recent memory. This was a year in which growers were permitted to acidify their juice, and even on the Mosel many did, although with mixed results. The best German Riesling of 2003—like other wines of this freakish vintage—seem to live by their own set of rules, and that is probably how they will age as well. The longest-lived among them may well prove to be those of the relatively cool Saar (as happened in earlier freakishly hot vintages such as 1959 and 1976).

The Middle Mosel Riesling of 2002 and in particular of 2001 boast outstanding balance between ripe fruit and refreshing acidity; in both those years, this area outperformed most of the rest of Germany's Riesling regions. The Ruwer and Saar performed less consistently in 2001 than the Middle Mosel, whereas in 2002 it was the Saar especially that excelled. The warm and rainy autumn of 2000 made for wines the best of which skirted the dark side of botrytis, and, with few exceptions, should have been drunk within five years. Casting a glance back at some earlier vintages, 1999 was ripe but disappointingly short on personality, whereas by contrast 1998—with its combination of high acidity, sugar, and extract—displays some riveting wines that are beginning to be especially interesting to revisit now that they have had a decade in bottle. There was abundant ripeness and scarcely any rot in 1997, and the best wines of the Middle Mosel are serene but often lacking in energy. Along the Saar and Ruwer, 1997 resembles but is less extreme than 2003; the superbly concentrated Riesling from those subregions—far more riveting than their Mosel cousins—should on no account be missed. The combination of high acids, sugars, and extracts in 1996 led to inscrutably dense wines that most Riesling experts are still trying to figure out. They may still have their day, and certainly it is most instructive to sample such dramatically distinctive wines as these.

Among the most powerfully rich, botrytized Middle Mosel Riesling of the recent past are those of 1994, which for growers who put great store in noble rot are (perhaps together with the 2006s) the best since 1971. The greatness of the 1990 vintage was proclaimed almost immediately. Not long after, many wines nosedived into an angular and ungenerous stage, but nowadays the beauty of these generally sharply focused and only occasionally botrytized wines is on display. The 1989s were 1990's alter ego, with too much noble rot in many instances, superb on both Saar and Ruwer but only selectively excellent elsewhere. 1988 produced very balanced wines that have aged well, and which were held to be outstanding in ripeness at the time—before growers experienced the 20 unprecedented vintages that have followed. The virtues of 1983—another year very welcome at the time, coming on the heels of several uninspiring vintages—ought not to be overlooked. A few great earlier vintages for the Mosel include 1975, 1971, 1959, 1953, 1949, and 1947. Freakishly hot but also rot-prone 1976 produced some opulent German Riesling, almost heavy but in their peculiar way impressive (especially in their youth). Most have long since toppled over, but the very best 1976s from the Saar and Ruwer are not only worth seeking out but taste almost as though frozen in time. From the '60s, 1969, 1966, and 1964 each have distinct and winning personalities and have aged well.

THE MIDDLE RHINE: NOT JUST FOR TOURISTS

The Middle Rhine (*Mittelrhein*) growing area consists of sporadic, steep, and often crenellated slate, graywacke, and quartzite-laced slopes running all the way from the outskirts of Germany's former capital Bonn, upstream past Koblenz, then south until one comes to the Rheingau. Much of this stretch—known for its tourists, the Lorelei, and a host of hulking castles—was far more densely planted a century or more ago, but the rigors of steep-slope vine dressing, an historically daunting climate for ripening Riesling even in heat-trapping corners, and a surplus of wine in other regions, combined to leave many formerly proud sites all but deserted. Still, nature has been smiling lately, and a revived interest in German Riesling possessed of the sort of flavor personality such sites can convey, as well as the youthful eagerness of numerous growers, is leading to a renaissance. All of the Middle Rhine's major vineyards lie upstream from Koblenz, where the Mosel joins the Rhine. The Hamm in Boppard is so huge that its name is joined to that of four separate official vineyards. Florian Weingart and Mathias Müller render the finest and most fascinating Hamm Riesling in both dry and off-dry formats, and August Perll is up-and-coming.

Though there are several historically significant towns and vineyards en route to the Rheingau, those around Bacharach (including the adjoining village of Steeg) hold far and away the greatest interest, as well as being home to the Middle Rhine's two most established and successful wineries, Toni Jost and Jochen Ratzenberger. The Josts, who also own vineyards at the eastern end of the Rheingau, bottle often tropically fruited and sumptuous yet always seemingly mineral-infused Riesling from their *monopole* the Hahn, a site which was given a special legal dispensation decades ago to irrigate with drip lines. The Riesling of Ratzenberger is taut, energetic, and to most tasters' minds overtly mineral. Ripeness has not been really problematic in the Middle Rhine now for more than 20 years. Weingart routinely pulls Spätlese from a site he purchased a decade or more ago with the intention of growing sparkling base wine; the Josts are purchasing vineyards above the Hahn because their generally outstanding Riesling labeled Kabinett has nevertheless for years now had the opulence and must weight of an Auslese, with too much alcohol and residual sugar to justify the Kabinett name; and the Ratzenbergers nowadays render some very serious Pinot Noir. It is difficult to generalize about a small number of growers spread so far apart, but 2002 and 2005 resulted in particularly high rates of success, with 2004 less good than on the Mosel. There have been no real vintage disappointments since the 2000s and 1999s.

THE NAHE: DAZZLING NATURAL RESOURCES

A BIT OF HISTORY, AND WHAT TO EXPECT

Like the Mosel, the Nahe is replete with highly motivated and talented vintners farming exceptional Riesling vineyards, which makes the exploration of its wines a delightful duty for all pleasure- and intrigue-seeking wine lovers. The Nahe growing region is much smaller than that of the Mosel, though. Virtually all of its acreage lies within a dozen miles as the crow flies of the small spa city of Bad Kreuznach. Yet the Nahe is far more diverse, when it comes to vineyard character, than the Mosel, Saar, and Ruwer put together. This mineral-rich region (its historical mining and gem-cutting center of Idar-Oberstein lies not far from the Nahe's westernmost vineyards) boasts a unique degree of dramatic geological diversity. Furthermore, while many of the Nahe's finest vineyards overlook the river itself, a wealth of small tributaries, side valleys, and rugged sites in the region's interior make for a vast array of microclimates and exposures. For all its quality and diversity—not to mention the fact that many of its sites have been planted for more than a thousand years—this region's name is still comparatively little known even inside Germany. "Nahe" did not designate an official growing region until the Wine Law of 1971. Prior to that, these were simply seen as "Rhine wines," and too often the degree of anonymity this conferred meant they were subsumed into uninspiring blends. Despite a lack of recognition as "Nahe," the region's early-20th-century influence was profound. Large landholding and merchant houses in Bad Kreuznach, as well as an enormous State Domaine, set winemaking standards for the entire country. It was here that modern filtration and temperature control were introduced, permitting stable wines at any desired degree of sweetness. Thanks to the wealth of its industry barons and nobility, the Nahe also pioneered in viticultural education. But the grand merchant houses and domaines closed their doors, were sold, or lost much of their influence during the 1980s and early 1990s. At the same time, a new elite and leadership arose from the ranks of family wineries.

Helmut Dönnhoff of Oberhausen built on the wisdom and experience of the last great generation of growers and oenologists associated with the State Domaine and such great private houses as von Plettenberg and August Anheuser. Starting with modest acreage inherited from his father, Hermann, that luckily included holdings in two great sites, Dönnhoff set a stellar example of the degree to which differences of *terroir* may be captured in a glass of Riesling, and of how to work with equal brilliance in dry, off-dry, and nobly sweet formats. He parlayed his increasing celebrity and ambition, despite his personal modesty, into an expansion incorporating portions of most of the greatest sites along the Nahe, all the way downstream to Bad Kreuznach. On the Nahe below Bad Kreuznach, Armin Diel took his inheritance at Schlossgut Diel and built it into another internationally prominent and exemplary estate. But the flamboyance and political savvy of Diel was far removed from the personality of his friend Dönnhoff and, as a journalist and as chairman of the local VDP growers' association, Diel tirelessly and successfully promoted the recognition of Nahe wine outside the region and a culture of excellence within. One should not overlook several others in explaining the recent emergence and discovery of the Nahe. Hugh Johnson's 1983 profile (in his book now known as the *Modern Encyclopedia of Wine*) of veteran grower Hans Crusius offered even many Germans their first inkling of Nahe quality. The talent and determination of Werner Schönleber, and more recently of the family Fröhlich, have borne vinous fruit that only the most optimistic dreamer could have anticipated a quarter century ago, much less from vineyards then practically unknown even to Germany's most enthusiastic partisans. For all its hard-won quality and name recognition, there is a darker side to the history of winegrowing along the Nahe. Many historically important vineyards have been abandoned, and even such great sites as those at Norheim, directly along the Nahe River, might easily have suffered this fate had a benefactor not put prime parcels at Helmut Dönnhoff's disposal. At least, young growers seeking to achieve excellence by arduously working steep slopes of which few wine lovers have ever heard know that on the Nahe, a pathway and precedent for success exist, and that the support of those who have already blazed the trail to stellar quality and international stardom can be counted on.

There are still numerous Nahe vineyards of once proven potential that lack vintners capable of realizing it. But there are fewer such sites of unfulfilled destiny than 20 years ago (or still today in the Rheingau). The character of Nahe Riesling is sometimes—not entirely without justification—described exactly as one can its geographical position: "midway between the Mosel and the Rheingau." The delicacy and refinement, the meeting of citrus, orchard, tropical, and bush fruits with mineral associations, certainly call to mind the Mosel. At the same time, there is a solidity of structure and breadth to many Nahe Riesling, as well as a proclivity for success in dry-tasting as well as off-dry and nobly sweet formats, that set this region apart from the Mosel. The greatest Nahe vineyards have demonstrated a potential second to none.

SOME IMPORTANT VINEYARDS AND THEIR OWNERS

Coming over the rugged, rural Hunsrück Hills from the Mosel, the first Nahe vineyards to appear are those of Monzingen, the Halenberg and Frühlingsplätzchen. Their foremost champion—at an address typical for today's Nahe elite in the vast range of styles, even sparkling, in which its Riesling excels—is Emrich-Schönleber. In the past half dozen years, the Schäfer-Fröhlich winery has also acquired superbly situated, steep parcels in these two predominantly red sandstone but minerally varied vineyards. Across the river lies Meddersheim with its still little-known, iron- and quartzite-rich Rheingrafenberg vineyard, whose potential can be glimpsed thanks to the labors of the family Hexamer. Around a dozen twisting miles downstream one encounters the progression of best-known and foremost Nahe vineyards. At Schlossböckelheim, the former State Domaine of Rheinland-Pfalz was the primary owner; the Kupfergrube vineyard (site of a former copper mine) was terraced by convict labor early in the last century as that vast estate's vineyard showcase. Like so many of this neighborhood's great sites, for modern-day renditions that reflect its quality, one has to turn to (and try to find some bottles from) the Hermann Dönnhoff estate. Under private ownership, large portions of the former State Domaine now function under the mouth-filling title Gutsverwaltung Niederhausen-Schlossböckelheim; quality is variable but sometimes points toward their vineyards' potential. Interpretations of the Felsenberg can be compared from Dönnhoff and Schäfer-Fröhlich, the latter located a dozen miles east in Bockenau and also rendering extraordinary Riesling from their home vineyard, the Felseneck. As reference to rocky cliffs (*Felsen*) suggests, these sites are all defined by extremities of stone and steepness; the resultant Riesling seem to mirror in their diversity of fruit, spice, and pungent minerality the geological complexity that their roots explore. But there is even more dramatic geological and vinous drama to come: No Nahe wines have proven more complex than those of Niederhausen's Hermannshöhle and its neighbor (and Dönnhoff *monopole*) the Brücke, officially part of Oberhausen. Slate, porphyry, sandstone, and other constituents alternate in the soil, and a correspondingly kaleidoscopic whirl of flavors greets the palate. It won't do to experience the Hermannshöhle from a lesser source than Dönnhoff. Around the next bend in Norheim the Dellchen boasts phenomenal quality in the hands of Dönnhoff, whose frequently more immediately seductive Riesling from the slate-dominated Kirchheck can be compared with that of Hans & Peter Crusius. Crusius champions Traisen's vineyards, notably the Rotenfels and Bastei, the latter consisting of volcanic rubble in the lower reaches of a cliff that plummets to the Nahe, supposedly the tallest and sheerest such precipice in western Europe outside the Alps.

Just below Traisen, the Nahe is joined by the Alsenz, some of whose vineyards—at Altenbamberg and Ebernburg in particular—would be more noteworthy if there were growers showcasing their potential. At Bad Kreuznach, the vineyards on the east side of the city resemble those in neighboring Rheinhessen, but on the left bank of the Nahe on the city's western edge, such vineyards as the Kahlenberg and Krötenpfuhl, although having gentler slopes and loamier, deeper soils than those upstream, nevertheless retain slate and quartzite mineral complexities; chez Dönnhoff (beginning with the 2006 vintage) their wines display the sort of qualities that made their reputations in the early 20th century. Along the Gräfenbach northwest of Bad Kreuznach, far from the Nahe, vineyards in Roxheim and Wallhausen are also capable of distinction. Along with the stretch of Nahe below Bad Kreuznach these are collectively known as the Lower Nahe. The most important vineyards are in two places, both close to the mouth of the Nahe at Bingen. The first such place is Burg Layen, where a small side valley west of the Nahe boasts three steep, contiguous sites: the slate-based Pitter-männchen, sandstone Goldloch, and chalk-clay Burgberg. At Schlossgut Diel, these vineyards are brilliantly interpreted in Riesling ranging from dry to nobly sweet. Just above Bingen are the sites of Münster-Sarmsheim, especially Pittersberg and Dautenpflänzer, excellently represented by Göttelmann and Krüger-Rumpf (who also farms in the Burgberg).

[recent vintages]

The Nahe enjoyed shameless good luck in several recent years, having avoided some of the rain that rendered conditions tricky in other Rhine regions in 2006 and 2005. (And 2007 looks highly promising as well.) The best 2004s and 2002s, in their coolly brisk and mineral way, nevertheless do not lack richness. The 2001s are excellent in a slightly richer and less focused way. In 2003, much like the Saar, the vines in this corner of Germany were spared the worst effects of drought and metabolic stress. In the lower echelons of growers, 2000 and 1999 are—as elsewhere in Germany—neither generally noteworthy nor likely to repay a return visit. Yet, particularly in 2000, the wines of Diel, Dönnhoff, and Schönleber were exceptions—indeed, these Riesling enjoy such rude good health that even today they seem to mock the other unfortunate veterans of that tropically warm and rainy campaign. The sharply etched, ripe, and concentrated 1998s are superb here, just as elsewhere in Germany's Riesling regions. 1997 again saw the Nahe teamed with the Saar (and Ruwer) as the most successful of Germany's Riesling regions; in the end, the apparent misfortunes of frost, hail, and poor flowering proved advantageous by limiting the crop to what could really concentrate and ripen. The Nahe's best growers will be a test case for the rather extreme 1996s: If the Riesling of this vintage ever really blossom, they will do so here. In both 1995 and (especially) 1994, the Nahe beat the overall German Riesling batting average. In fact, the best wines from the earlier vintage rival those of the Middle Mosel. The trio 1988–90 is strong here, the Nahe 1989s (and many 1976s, too) typically exhibiting more refinement to accompany their richness than do most Riesling of that vintage. But one must bear in mind that at this time—even more so before 1985 when, among others, the huge State Domaine was crafting liquid gems—the pecking order of producers differed drastically from today's. Outstanding earlier vintages include 1983, 1975, 1971, 1966, 1964, 1959, 1953, 1949, and 1947.

THE RHEINGAU: BETWEEN RENAISSANCE AND RESTING ON ITS LAURELS

WHAT TO EXPECT

From Rüdesheim, for roughly 20 miles upriver until it reaches the city of Wiesbaden, the Rhine flows west to east. Along its right bank lies a continuous carpet of vineyards on diverse soils stretching from the water's edge (including one large island) into the often steep hillsides of the Taunus range. This is the heart of the Rheingau, incorporating the majestic Rüdesheimer Berg; Schloss Johannisberg—planted by Charlemagne and home to the first late-harvest Riesling (if both legends are to be believed); and, next door, Geisenheim's renowned viticultural institute. These were the most expensive German Riesling when Jefferson visited here, as well as in their era of grandeur a century later. That historical image, plus proximity to a cluster of wealthy cities, buoys Rheingau prices today. But as we shall soon see, quality has often not kept pace with reputation; the number of noble addresses that have gone into a slump or been dissolved in the past 20 years is cause for great concern. One is lucky to find at least one grower in any given famous Rheingau village still doing full justice to its vineyards. The Rheingau led the way in rendering German Riesling *trocken* in the late 1970s, but if the truth be told, it was the '90s (when increased know-how coincided with warmer vintages) before truly exemplary instances were crafted with any frequency. Only recently have there been wines one might compare with the great Rheingau Riesling of the early 20th century. (For other observations relevant to this development, consult the earlier discussion under Balance.)

The greatest disadvantage of most large and traditionally well-reputed Rheingau estates is precisely their size and the consequent difficulty in current circumstances of finding adept pickers and scheduling the sorts of surgical strikes across an often wide expanse of vineyards that top quality demands. (This issue, too, was addressed in detail in our discussion of the Mosel under Important Information.) When a Rheingau Riesling vineyard is giving its all, it can generate dry-tasting, off-dry, or nobly sweet wines with complexity and refinement—at times aloof in their youth, yet ultimately sumptuously rich, deftly structured, and spring-loaded for the long, dynamic haul. Time was, when one would not have hesitated to recommend cellaring dry-tasting Rheingau Riesling for 20 or 30 years, and sweet wines even longer. Today, that recommendation can be made at most for just a few. The best approach is this: Pay up in order to experience—and, if possible, to follow in your cellar—the wines of today's elite Rheingau estates. These will prove a profoundly delicious and indispensable part of any wine lover's education, just as they did in Jefferson's day.

SOME IMPORTANT VINEYARDS AND THEIR OWNERS

The Rheingau in fact commences in Lorch and Lorchhausen, whose steep slate southwestern exposures and economically precarious recent past more resemble the Middle Rhine. Regardless, the quality potential here is excellent, as wines from August Kesseler in next-door Assmannshausen prove. Assmannshausen itself is Germany's single best-known town for Pinot Noir. This grape was brought to the Rheingau by Cistercian monks around the same time they were founding Clos Vougeot. The Pinots of Kesseler from the steep slate Höllenberg will silence any doubters about this grape's Germanic potential. Still, the Riesling from Kesseler scales even greater heights—literally the steep slate and quartzite slopes of Rüdesheim: Berg Roseneck, Berg Rottland, and Berg Schlossberg. Rüdesheim has been singularly blessed in recent years among the Rheingau's villages in that no fewer than three outstanding wineries farm its vineyards, the other two being Georg Breuer and Josef Leitz. Breuer concentrates on relatively austere but nowadays usually highly impressive dry Riesling, and in certain vintages exceptionally refined nobly sweet ones. Leitz has proven a master of many styles, including overtly Mosel-like acid-sugar balance achieved on gentler slopes and deeper soils in Rüdesheim that were once deemed uninteresting. Johannes Leitz's reclamation of the elevated ancient terraces of the Berg Kaisersteinfels renders a small amount of stunning Riesling. The famous Schloss Johannisberg has recently shown signs of aiming to fulfill its great potential, but the foremost winery from which to taste the Riesling of Johannisberg has long been the Johannishof of the Eser family, who bottle some excellent Rüdesheimer and the best Rieslings available from Winkel's Jesuitengarten, too. (The best-known Winkel estate, Schloss Vollrads—itself considered an official vineyard and not required to carry "Winkel" on the label—has shown signs of getting back on form of late.) Adjacent to Winkel, Oestrich features soil primarily of that powdery glacial dust called loess. Anyone interested in both the full, exciting potential of these vineyards and an opportunity to contrast two dramatically different styles must taste the Riesling at Peter Jakob Kühn and Josef Spreitzer. Thanks to Spreitzer, we can also sample outstanding dry Riesling from Hattenheim's great Wisselbrunnen vineyard. The best-known estates to own a large share of the outstanding vineyards in Hattenheim and those of Erbach (most famously the Marcobrunn) just upstream, include Baron zu Knyphausen, Schloss Reinhartshausen, Schloss Schönborn, and Langwerth von Simmern. Their wines should be approached with care because prices are high, while quality is still too often merely good, rather than exciting, as befits these vineyards. Admittedly, these gently sloping, relatively deep soils near the river have been handicapped by rain retention and rot in several recent vintages, when sites on steep hillsides could excel. The Hessian State Winery (Staatsweingüter), centered at Kloster Eberbach, is also a vast landholder in Erbach and Hattenheim, not to mention Rüdesheim, and several villages further upstream. (A spectacular new underground winemaking facility and the ambitions of director Dieter Greiner may usher in a return to star status for this mega-estate.)

Set back in the hills from Hattenheim is the town of Hallgarten, whose unusual mélange of soils, including loess, chalk, and slate, are memorably championed, above all in the Schönhell, by Fred Prinz. To the east of Hallgarten on a high hill stands the State Winery's famous *monopole* the Steinberg, the quality of its wines recently improving but still not displaying anywhere near the consistent excellence of the 1960s and before. East of the Steinberg is the town of Kiedrich with its great, chalky Gräfenberg vineyard, most of which has been consolidated in recent years by the winery Robert Weil. Director Wilhelm Weil and his Japanese partner Suntory are one of Germany's greatest late-20th-century success stories; few wineries are doing greater justice to inherently first-class sites than this one. Yet the vineyards of Rauenthal one range of hills to the east possess no less potential than those of Kiedrich— indeed, their vineyard names (the greatest that of Baiken, partly held by the Staatsweingüter) still resonate with any older connoisseurs of German Riesling. Someday, one fervently hopes, the owners of these noble sites will once again be able to do them justice. Meanwhile, the most consistently satisfying wine from Rauenthal—the one worth special note in this brief tour— comes from the Nonnenberg vineyard of Rüdesheim-based Georg Breuer. Curiously, in the Walkenberg vineyard of much less well-known Walluf, J. B. Becker, one of the Rheingau's pioneers in dry wine excellence, and Middle Rhine–based Toni Jost typically offer a pithy concentration and highly distinctive character too often absent from today's Rheingau Riesling. The city of Wiesbaden itself still possesses some vineyard acreage. To its southeast, on the river Main, immediately before it joins the Rhine, lies Hochheim, whose location and chalky soils arguably make it a misfit for inclusion in the Rheingau. But the name "hock," once used by English-speakers for Rhine wine in general, comes from "Hochheim." Many of its vineyards—including the Domdechaney, Hölle, Kirchenstück, and Stielweg—were owned by wineries based along the Rhine. The Künstler estate bottles Riesling from all four of these sites that is well worth exploring (particularly in their dry versions), and they also grow serious Pinot Noir.

[recent vintages]

The greatest problems one encounters in the glass with Rheingau wines are lack of striking personality and clarity of flavors, problems that often have their origin in high yields and less than impeccably picked (or machine-harvested) grapes. This leaves wines, which even at their best can sometimes taste a touch austere, prone in their dry forms to excessive bitterness. As mentioned earlier, recent weather has not favored the Rheingau's riverside vineyards (although it has not deterred either Kühn or Spreitzer, in Oestrich, from their stylistically divergent paths of excellence). Especially given the felt need to make wine legally *trocken,* high alcohol is becoming a problem in some sectors, such as notoriously (normally speaking gloriously) warm Rüdesheim. On the other hand, many Rheingau estates suffer from the bipolar disorder discussed earlier under Balance: When their Riesling are not *trocken* they are too obviously, gratuitously sweet. One senses in the number of marketing schemes pursued here in recent years that growers recognize the need for more excitement, but too seldom look to the place that matters: their great vineyards. There is the bluish green "Rheingau flute," a bottle deeply scored with parallel grooves and flared on top, which has never entirely caught on. A long-standing series of dry-tasting so-called Charta bottlings too often includes Riesling that is severe and lean, although there are certainly exceptions; while ostensibly intended to showcase the Rheingau's great *terroir,* by a curious convention, they omit to mention on their labels their towns or vineyards of origin.

A rating of recent vintages could easily mislead: Not only were hilly locations favored in several recent years with rain near harvest, so that two different ratings would be needed, with Hochheim demanding a third, but the dramatic difference between the meticulous picking and sorting that characterize the very best estates, distinguishing them from all of the others, can make it taste as though these groups experienced different vintages in one and the same year—which, in a way, they did. One should definitely approach 2003–2005 and especially 2006 with caution, although the region's few star vintners often beat the odds. 2001 was more consistently excellent, although one cannot compare the more modest success of this vintage in the Rheingau with that along the Mosel. Again, one should be less concerned with vintage than with the winery of origin, although even the best of them stumbled in 2000. 1999 proved much more interesting at the best Rheingau estates than it did in other German Riesling regions. It would be wonderful to experience again the inherent energy, ripe acids, and concentration of 1998, the recent vintage evincing the most widespread excellence here. While, since 1988, there has not been what would up till then have been considered an average, marginally ripe vintage, in fact the Rheingau Riesling of an earlier era often excelled in just such "minor vintages"—witness the wealth of wines with personality and surprising stamina from the years 1987, 1981, or 1973, most of them, sadly, bottled by establishments that no longer uphold their former standards of excellence. Outstanding, classic Rheingau vintages of yore include 1990, 1971, 1959, 1953, and 1947.

RHEINHESSEN: A WINE LAND OF CONTRASTS

WHAT TO EXPECT

The region known as Rheinhessen (located in the Federal State of Rheinland-Pfalz, not that of Hessen, which can cause some confusion) is enormous, bounded by the city of Worms and the northern edge of the Pfalz to its southeast, the outskirts of Bad Kreuznach and the Lower Nahe to the west, and the city of Mainz to the northeast. Within this area several subregions have their own traditions, but for most of the 20th century a clear class distinction was drawn between the Permian sandstone red slopes overlooking the Rhine south of Mainz—notably at Nackenheim, Nierstein, and Oppenheim—and all the rest. In the past dozen years, the tables have gradually been turned on that traditional pecking order, in part thanks to the rise of talent in the region's interior, but also in part, alas, due to the decline or dissolution of numerous formerly noble establishments in Nierstein. Since World War II, another class distinction has followed a sometimes similar line. Many of the vineyards distant from the Rhine are flat and without long winemaking traditions, but they, along with corresponding areas of the Pfalz, became a reservoir for sweet, inexpensive, machine-harvested wines from crossings. Even at Nierstein, large expanses of uninteresting vineyards distant from the river yielded bumper crops of correspondingly insipid, albeit high-Oechsle wines. As the market for these declined, Rheinhessen fell on hard times. But simultaneously, serious talents emerged in the interior in places (a few of which we shall momentarily tour) that had fine reputations centuries ago. The decline of so many formerly grand, Riesling-dominated estates in Nierstein was not entirely unrelated to the decline in image suffered by this region as a whole. The size of these estates also adversely affected quality, just as in the Rheingau, but they could not fall back on a reputation as strong as the Rheingau's.

Although Riesling is not dominant in Rheinhessen, it is still the most important quality grape. Still, the revival of interest in the region's traditionally dominant variety, Silvaner (since the 20th century, spelled in Germany with an "i" rather than a "y"), has yielded some impressive results at a few estates in diverse locations, including Keller, Wagner-Stempel, and Wittmann. To render Silvaner sleek and long-lined, rather than with a vinous midriff bulge, it's critical to have low yields and nutrient-poor soils. The crossing Scheurebe (see more under The Pfalz) was developed for Rheinhessen soils, and has its lucid latter-day exponents here and there, notably at Wittmann and at Brüder Dr. Becker, where it even informs a deliciously gaudy sparkling wine. Germany's modern-day penchant for Riesling *trocken* has dominated developments here since the 1980s, but excellent off-dry Riesling and a strong current of nobly sweet elixirs have continued to flow.

SOME IMPORTANT VINEYARDS AND THEIR OWNERS, AND RECENT VINTAGES

Picking up where we left off, near the Nahe, Bingen can boast the steep, sandstone Scharlach-berg that sits opposite Rüdesheim, a portion of which is farmed by Krüger-Rumpf (a Nahe vintner). Southeast of Bad Kreuznach, at Siefersheim (in what's known, for its hills, as "Rhine-hessen Switzerland") one of this region's up-and-coming wineries, Wagner-Stempel, is making a name not just for young Daniel Wagner but for the hitherto obscure porphyric Höllberg and Heerkretz vineyards, whose Riesling he renders in a full and impressive range of styles. In the predominantly chalk-clay hills between Alzey and Worms, a remarkable revival of once-renowned sites in Dalsheim and Westhofen—Hubacher, Kirchspiel, and Moorstein—has taken place at the Keller winery, whose rise to fame has been almost without precedent. The nearby Wittmann winery interprets in Riesling the Aulerde vineyard as well as those of Kirchspiel and Moorstein. Worms itself boasts the historical Liebfrauenstift vineyard which, through most of the last century, inadvertently lent its name to an ocean of slightly sweet, nearly always undistinguished wine called Liebfraumilch. That vineyard's principal owner, the merchant house of P. J. Valckenberg, has recently been displaying serious intentions in the vineyard and the glass. Heading north along the Rhine, Oppenheim's well-known Sackträger vineyard may once again be worth investigating thanks to promising wines from Kühling-Gillot. The classic, steep red stone sites of Nierstein include the Hipping, Oelberg, Orbel, and Pettenthal. Two of the most important estates, Freiherr Heyl and Sankt Antony (the latter a bulwark of dry Nierstein Riesling quality since the 1990s), recently changed hands. It is too soon to say how their reorganization will fare. J. & H. A. Strub crafts generous, generally off-dry and sweet Nierstein Riesling from the loamy Paterberg and the "red" slopes, as does Kühling-Gillot from the Oelberg and Pettenthal, as well as from interesting sites in Bodenheim, north of Nackenheim. This neighborhood's one truly shining star, Gunderloch, farms in Nierstein's Pettenthal as well as the adjacent Rothenberg of Nackenheim, with profoundly delicious results in a full range of styles. Floral and pungently smoky or smoked-meat notes, along with tangerine, lemon, and peach, characterize Riesling from many of these sandstone vineyards. In truth, the last really outstanding vintage for climatically and topographically diverse Rheinhessen as a whole was high-acid 1998. But it is futile, and, more important, a disservice for wine lovers to try to generalize. Consult the ratings of producers later in this chapter, please. The stars and overachievers of Rheinhessen will delight and sometimes dazzle you even in a difficult vintage like 2006, although 2000 is a recent year that can now be written off.

THE PFALZ: REPUTATION RESCUED

WHAT TO EXPECT AND WHAT TO BEWARE

Like Rheinhessen, the Pfalz, which represents the northward extension of Alsace's Vosges (here called the Haardt), once suffered from a debased image due to huge volumes of mediocre wine machine-harvested from the flat Rhine plane, as well as to chronic financial, managerial, and quality problems at many of its large, best-known estates. However, beginning in the late '80s, building on the unflagging excellence of a few veterans and the inspiration, ambition, and talent of a new generation, the Pfalz not only restored the reputation of its handful of long-famous villages and vineyards but also created an unprecedented level of excitement inside Germany about growers, towns, and sites all the way from the outskirts of Worms to the French frontier. This restoration was certainly helped by a long-standing local reputation for hospitality and the hordes of German tourists or city-dwellers on weekend excursions who crowd its Weinstrasse. It was also aided by the German penchant for *trocken* Riesling, which from these dry and generally sun-drenched foothills is likely to be not only ripe, but full-bodied.

A long tradition of excellence with off-dry wines has dried up or become marginalized at many establishments, which is a shame. The Pfalz can succeed memorably with nobly sweet wines as well, but nowadays many growers' off-dry wines, if they bottle any such wines at all, come mostly from non-Riesling varieties. Two crossings in particular have experienced unprecedented success here, even though they are statistically minor. Scheurebe has been around for over a century. Its parents are not definitely known, although surely one of them was Riesling. (Dr. Scheu *thought* the other was Silvaner, but DNA analysis casts that claim in doubt.) Scheurebe's exuberant aromas and flavors of grapefruit, cassis, and sage strike some tasters as rudely blatant, while others love them. When vinified dry (as it seldom is nowadays), this grape can resemble a really ripe and opulent Sauvignon. Rieslaner is a crossing, as its name suggests, of Riesling and Silvaner that has a striking ability to resist botrytis yet shrivels spontaneously. Since it is already very high in acidity, its concentration of citrus, tropical fruit, and spice can at times be almost excruciating, hence the tendency to render it with residual sugar. Gewürztraminer (spelled here with an umlaut, unlike in Alsace, where this grape is much more common), Pinot Blanc (here known as Weissburgunder), Pinot Gris (Grauburgunder), Chardonnay, and Pinot Noir (Spätburgunder) are also widely successful in the Pfalz. Interestingly, there is a flourishing business in "traditional-method" sparkling wines here, too, although with few exceptions, notably von Buhl, these do not show up in the U.S. or in most other export markets. But, then, neither, thankfully, do many representatives of the insipid, industrial-scale sparkling wine that abounds in Germany.)

Two dangers to beware of in the Pfalz have already been touched on in discussing Germany in general. An increasing percentage of dry wines (including Riesling) fall in the 13.5% to 15% alcohol range, and some evince heat and bitterness. On the other hand, sweet wines can sometimes be so in-your-face confectionary that one longs for recognition of the golden mean. There are still many excellent values from the Pfalz, but whereas a dozen or 15 years ago one would not have hesitated to cite this region as producing among the world's best values in concentrated, complex, site-specific wines, now one must temper that judgment in light of these wines' enormous success in their home market and consequently steady price increases. Indeed, when the so-called Grosses Gewächs dry wines were introduced by VDP members (see the earlier discussion under Balance) this concept of luxury cuvées caught on so quickly that prices leapt. These intentionally limited-edition bottlings, often sold on subscription and largely to private clients in Germany, are today the primary representatives of many of the Pfalz's best sites, whose owners are predominantly VDP members. There are often no longer any off-dry counterparts from these sites, and to protect the price and reputation of a Grosses Gewächs bottling, a winery cannot bottle any other dry wine under the same site name. The upshot of all this is that one can easily pay the same price for a Riesling representative of great Pfalz *terroir* as one would for a corresponding Rheingauer, and have just as much difficulty locating bottles—not, however, as in the Rheingau, because there are too few top-notch growers with landholdings who own acreage in the best sites, but rather due to high demand inside Germany.

SOME IMPORTANT VINEYARDS AND THEIR OWNERS, AND RECENT VINTAGES

The stretch of Pfalz extending south from Worms to Neustadt is known as the Mittelhaardt. In the low rolling loess, sand, and gravel hills east of the Weinstrasse around Freinsheim, Grosskarlbach, and Weisenheim am Sand, some very interesting and delicious Riesling and

Scheurebe is possible, as has been demonstrated by Rainer Lingenfelder (although several recent vintages have mounted severe challenges to his vines and these sites). But the first really great site one comes to is the concave, chalk-clay Saumagen ("sow's belly") in Kallstadt, from which Koehler-Ruprecht makes exemplary Riesling, in fact consistently among the finest Riesling *trocken* in all Germany. (This exemplary but idiosyncratic estate grows many other varieties—see the thumbnail sketch included with the tasting notes in this chapter.) South of Kallstadt, on the outskirts of the small city of Bad Dürkheim lies Ungstein, whose Herrenberg and Weilberg are expertly exploited by the Pfeffingen estate, where Scheurebe often steals the show from Riesling.

South of Bad Dürkheim one comes to a string of the most famous Pfalz wine villages: Wachenheim, Forst, Deidesheim, and Ruppertsberg. The major share of the best vineyards in these communes is owned by an array of large estates, with common ancestors, that rose to prominence in the mid-19th century. Rather than mention them under each important vineyard, it will suffice to list them here alphabetically (for quality rankings see the ratings of producers that follow) with the proviso that not all of them have a share in all of the top vineyards, and thereafter mention their names only in instances where a vineyard is a *monopole* or particular specialty of the estate. The major wineries in question are: Dr. von Bassermann-Jordan, Josef Biffar, Reichsrat von Buhl, Dr. Bürklin-Wolf, and Dr. Deinhard. To this roll of honor must be added the small family estate of Georg Mosbacher. These top sites are all nestled between the western edge of their respective villages and the lower slopes of the Haardt, on sandstone, chalk-clay, or volcanic soils. Wachenheim's gravel and chalk-clay-dominated Altenburg, Gerümpel, and Goldbächel, as well as the sandstone (Bürklin-Wolf *monopole*) Rechbächel, yield some of the most intricately flavored wines in the Pfalz. They are upstaged in celebrity by the mighty quintet of largely basaltic sites in tiny Forst: Jesuitengarten, Kirchenstück, Pechstein, Ungeheuer, and (at von Buhl and Mosbacher) Freundstück. Each of these vineyards that abut one another displays its distinctive personality; the contrast among the "cool" mineral and herb character of the Jesuitengarten, pungent variations on these themes in Pechstein, and the decadent, musky, peach-and-cherry richness of Kirchenstück are merely among the more dramatic examples. Each of these sites is small save for the Ungeheuer, whose best parcels are under the control of von Buhl; other portions are less consistent in potential. In Deidesheim, further variations on sand, gravel, chalk, and clay are capable of rendering superb Riesling with distinctive fruit characteristics ranging from sweet corn to citrus and tropical fruits, with similarly diverse suggestions of herbs and minerals. Look for the Grainhübel, Kalkofen, Kieselberg, Leinhöhle, Mäushöhle, and (solely at Bürklin-Wolf and the Gimmeldingen-based estate of A. Christmann) Hohenmorgen. Despite many geological similarities with their neighbors immediately to the north, the vineyards of Ruppertsberg—Hoheburg, Nussbien, Reiterpfad, and (a Bürklin-Wolf *monopole*) Gaisböhl—nearly always display pronouncedly peachy fruit and a more robust structure. The best wines from these great Mittelhaardt vineyards have track records for cellar maturation in dry-tasting, off-dry, and nobly sweet versions alike that rival the best Riesling of the Rheingau.

On the northern edge of the city of Neustadt are a cluster of suburbs with excellent vineyards. The Idig in Königsbach is associated with the outstanding work of A. Christmann, who also farm, among other sites, some Reiterpfad in Ruppertsberg and Mandelgarten in Gimmeldingen. This last-named site is also farmed by the renowned Müller-Catoir winery based in Haardt, whose other top vineyards are the Mandelring, Herrenletten, and, above all, Bürgergarten in that village, and the Eselshaut in nearby Mussbach. This estate also has an unrivaled reputation with Muskateller, Rieslaner, and Scheurebe. Longtime Müller-Catoir cellarmaster Hans-Günter Schwarz has exercised unprecedented positive influence on the education of vintners and the evolution of viticultural standards in the Pfalz over the past four decades; without him the Südliche Weinstrasse that runs from south of Neustadt to the French frontier would never have acquired its current cachet. The prevalence of serious dry wines from the Pinot family also no doubt significantly influenced the popularity of the southern Pfalz among German consumers, but today a bevy of world-class Riesling is grown here, too, often on sites considerably steeper than those in the Mittelhaardt. A cluster of villages west of Landau are the most interesting. Theo Minges is demonstrating that the Hölle vineyard in Gleisweiler can support outstanding Riesling in a full range from dry to nobly sweet. The Schäwer in Burrweiler incorporates a measure of slate rare in these parts; the wines it produces are brilliantly rendered in a range of formats by the Herbert Messmer winery. (Wines from that site are also in the Minges estate's future.) Ökonomierat Rebholz—like Minges and Messmer—works with a number of grape varieties, but Riesling from the mussel-chalk vineyard Im Sonnenschein in Siebeldingen and the red sandstone Kastanienbusch in Birkweiler are the star performers. Riesling from the latter site is also superbly showcased at Dr. Wehrheim where, like neighbor Rebholz, they are especially serious about Pinot Blanc and Pinot Noir as well.

A preponderance of precociously ripening, relatively heavy soils has made the Pfalz especially susceptible both to excessive heat and drought and to late-summer or autumn rains. Due to inopportune rain, 2006 and 2005 are less consistent here than elsewhere in Germany; 2000 was a disaster. At the opposite extreme, 2003, too, is more problematic here than in most other German growing regions, for the vines suffered acutely from heat and drought. Excellent results were obtained in 2004, 2002, and 2001, although the last consistently superb vintage in these parts was 1998. Farther back, look out for vintages 1996, 1995, 1990, 1988, and 1986 (a superb come-from-behind finish enjoyed nowhere else in Germany that year). Other historically great harvests include those of 1975, 1971, 1959, 1953, and 1947. As one explores Pfalz wines from decades more "normal" than the two most recent, it is critical to bear in mind that in many years when Riesling failed to ripen properly elsewhere in Germany, it did in the Pfalz. The long-dominant quality trio of Koehler-Ruprecht, Pfeffingen, and Müller-Catoir bottled numerous exciting wines from vintages during the 1970s and 1980s that, on their overall reputation, one would otherwise be inclined to overlook, if not avoid.

THE AHR: NORTH OF RIESLING, PINOT NOIR?

Lying between 50 and 51 degrees north latitude, the valley of the Ahr, which meanders its way east to the Rhine near Bonn, lays claim to being the world's most northerly viticultural region. It comes as a shock, then, to learn that its special claim to fame is not the Riesling that flourishes to the south in protected rocky corners of the Middle Rhine—although some excellent Ahr Riesling exists—but rather the noble, fickle Madame Pinot. Furthermore, Ahr Pinot Noir is by no means a pale imitation of Pinots rendered further south in Germany, nor indeed of those from the Côte d'Or. The best of these wines have excellent color, richness of flavor, and natural alcohol levels typically in the 13% to 14.5% range. How is this possible? In a word, "microclimate," or in three, "steep, rocky slopes." This narrow valley with its terraces of slate, basalt, and graywacke traps heat and shelters its vines from wind. The majority of wine is rendered by local coops, of which the one representing growers in Mayschoss and Altenahr sets exemplary standards. However, increasing numbers of small growers are bottling outstanding wines, a few of which are beginning to find their way to the U.S. The hordes of German tourists who routinely descend on these villages over weekends and holidays, as well as their proximity to Germany's former capital, were long sufficient to sustain a flourishing business, but ambition has caught on like a fever here in the early 21st century. If there is anything to beware of these days, it is the occasionally downright overripe, too ambitiously extracted, or overtly oaky Pinot. There can scarcely have been a better time in the long red wine history of this region for discovering its potential, because after the potent Pinots of 2003, the Ahr also enjoyed outstanding harvests for 2005 through 2007, having escaped the rains that plagued most German regions in 2006.

FRANCONIA: MUSSEL-CHALK AND GOATS' SCROTUMS

The region of Franconia (Franken) along the Main River and centered on the city of Würzburg (also celebrated for its magnificent Baroque buildings) is the best-known of Germany's "non-Riesling" regions. Not that Riesling is neglected here, but it plays second fiddle to Silvaner, which in the local mussel-chalk and related calcareous soils can take on a marvelous combination of breadth and fullness along with firm structure and depth of mineral character. Riesling in these sites tends toward austerity—particularly as most Franconian wine is completely dry—but is capable of considerable diversity, quality, and longevity. Increasingly impressive results are being achieved here with members of the Pinot family as well, although reds account for only a small percentage of production. This is also a region widely planted with various crossings—in surprisingly many instances with impressive results. Rieslaner (which was developed precisely for these soils) and Scheurebe yield highly aromatic, full-bodied wines that preserve refreshing acidity. And here, as in Italy's Alto Adige, the widely planted and much-maligned Müller-Thurgau can be distinctively delicious. Kerner, generally reviled by the cognoscenti for its mawkishly candied black currant aromas, frequently puts in thoughtful and delicious appearances in Franconia as well. Without question, the full-bodied, dry whites from this region—even its Riesling—are big-boned and sometimes brusque; still, the best of them are formidable, complex, and fascinatingly far removed from the flavors of any other wines on Earth. Off-dry Franconian wines can be a delight, but these represent a minority. Even smaller is the amount of nobly sweet wine essayed here—generally from the Silvaner or Rieslaner grape—but anyone who has had a taste of rare and expensive Franconian Beerenauslese, Trockenbeerenauslese, or Eiswein is likely to cherish the memory for life.

Though the great civic and charitable ecclesiastical institutions of Würzburg are still among Franconia's most famous producers, they no longer dominate in quality, and the number of family wineries with ambitious and talented leadership has grown by leaps and bounds in recent years. Representation abroad has not kept pace, largely because of high demand in Germany. The state of Bavaria, renowned for its independence and regional pride, encompasses only this one winegrowing region. (Bavarians also drink more Austrian Riesling and Grüner Veltliner than anyone but the Austrians themselves.) The longtime presence of air force and army bases in Franconia has always ensured a certain level of awareness in the U.S., and at least a steady trickle of these wines in the import pipeline, where they are instantly recognizable by the squat, short-necked oval bottles known locally as *Bocksbeutel*. Literally this means "goat's scrotum," and the derivation is plausible on the face of it; linguists nowadays insist, though, that the origin is more prosaic, referring to a leather book bag. "Goat testicles" would be the preferred translation, frankly, because anything that would do more to attract attention to Franconia's distinctive wines, while it might not be welcomed back home, would enrich the lives of wine drinkers everywhere else. The 2005 and 2007 vintages were quite successful, and the larger volume of wine produced in the latter year especially welcome. The great classic Franconian vintages of recent years have been 2000 and 1997, which dramatically illustrates the fact that vintages here seldom track with those further down the Main in the Rheingau, or elsewhere in Germany.

BADEN: SPOILED BY THE SUN?

Germany's southwestern corner has long advertised having been spoiled by the sun when compared to its northern neighbors. In recent years the question might be posed whether some of its sites are enjoying too much of a good thing. Certainly the Pinot Noir, Pinot Blanc, Pinot Gris, Gewürztraminer, and (particularly in the last two decades) the Riesling and Chardonnay for which Baden is known are becoming increasingly heady libations. The Baden region consists in large part of a nearly continuous string of vineyards, running along the right bank of the Rhine, all the way from the outskirts of Basel, Switzerland (paralleling Alsace and later the German Pfalz), north to Heidelberg and the edges of industrial Mannheim and Ludwigshafen, then turning east and continuing almost to Würzburg and the borders of Franconia (with which this eastern fringe of Baden shares its major grape varieties and squat bottle shape). A smaller, sporadic string of vineyards runs along the Swiss border and the shores of Lake Constance. The Baden vineyards outside Basel and across the Rhine from Mulhouse in Alsace, feature above all the Chasselas grape (here known as Gutedel), which can be quite distinctively refreshing, if unpretentious. As one heads north, the best-known regions of Baden are dramatically visible on a clear day from the vineyards of Alsace, their hilly backdrop of the Black Forest having been cleft from the Vosges in the geologically distant past. The Kaiserstuhl ("Emperor's Throne"), consisting of strikingly steep terraces of loess-covered volcanic stone, rises directly from the Rhine opposite Colmar and is home to Baden's best-known wines from Gewürztraminer, as well as the entire Pinot family, particularly Pinot Gris and Pinot Blanc. Further north in the Ortenau, whose most famous village, Durbach, lies almost directly east of Strasbourg, Riesling takes on significant importance. The majority of Baden's production comes from cooperatives, many of them enormous in size, many bottling consistently good results, and nearly all of them known as models of efficiency. That said, the very best Baden wines, predictably, come from family estates. The German market for the dry, full-bodied wines of Baden is ravenous; as a result of this, very few of them ever travel abroad. The region's already occasionally world-class Pinot Noirs, in particular, will turn heads internationally, given a chance.

OTHER GERMAN WINEGROWING REGIONS

Adjacent to the northern sectors of Baden, the winegrowing region of Württemberg incorporates vineyards on the outskirts of the cities of Tübingen, Stuttgart, and Heilbronn. Two red grapes, either alone or blended, account for most of this region's production. These are Lemberger—none other than the Blaufränkisch or Kékfrankos grape of eastern Austria and Hungary, although it often looks and tastes like a pale shadow—and Trollinger, the uninspiring Schiava or Vernatsch of northern Italy. Pinot Meunier (here known as Schwarzriesling or, in a mutant form, as Samtrot) and Pinot Noir are also widespread. Virtually all of Württemberg's wine is drunk within the region. Although many growers are becoming more quality-conscious and attentive to international red wine trends, the results sometimes call into question the degree to which wines from these grapes and this region can withstand aggressive extraction and new oak. Riesling, Württemberg's most widely planted white grape, can yield interesting results; it dominates in the tiny Hessische Bergstrasse, north of Baden and separated by the wide Rhine plain from Rheinhessen and the Pfalz. The Hessian state–owned domaine (better known for its Rheingau wines and headquarters at Kloster Eberbach) crafts some delicious examples, which are also among the few to travel beyond the bounds of a region that is a magnet for tourists and adjacent to numerous well-to-do bedroom communities. Two tiny growing regions are rebuilding their images after decades of neglect as part of the communist East. The vineyards of Sachsen (Saxony) run along the Elbe River above and below the city of Dresden, and those of the Saale-Unstrut, west of Leipzig, along the two rivers from which the growing region takes its name. Where crossings such as Müller-Thurgau and Kerner once dominated in these eastern German sites, the first signs of serious Riesling and wines of the Pinot family are now appearing.

—DAVID SCHILDKNECHT

[the ratings]

GERMANY'S RIESLING PRODUCERS

Name(s) of the region(s) in which they are working are in parentheses. * = producers who also have ambitious programs with Pinot Noir.

★ ★ ★ ★ ★ (OUTSTANDING)

Joh. Jos. Christoffel (Mosel)
Schlossgut Diel (Nahe)*
Hermann Dönnhoff (Nahe)
Emrich-Schönleber (Nahe)
Gunderloch (Rheinhessen)
Fritz Haag (Mosel)
Reinhold Haart (Mosel)
Keller (Rheinhessen)*
Reinhard & Beate Knebel (Lower Mosel)
Koehler-Ruprecht (Pfalz)*

Dr. Loosen (Mosel)
Egon Müller—Scharzhof / Le Gallais (Saar)
Müller-Catoir (Pfalz)
Joh. Jos. Prüm (Mosel)
Willi Schaefer (Mosel)
Schäfer-Fröhlich (Nahe)
Selbach-Oster (Mosel)
Robert Weil (Rheingau)
Zilliken—Forstmeister Geltz (Saar)

★ ★ ★ ★ (EXCELLENT)

A. J. Adam (Mosel)
Dr. von Bassermann–Jordan (Pfalz)
Georg Breuer (Rheingau)*
Reichsrat von Buhl (Pfalz)*
Bürklin-Wolf (Pfalz)*
A. Christmann (Pfalz)*
Weinhof Herrenberg—Claudia & Manfred
   Loch (Saar)
Heymann-Löwenstein (Lower Mosel)
von Hövel (Saar)
Johannishof—H. H. Eser (Rheingau)
Toni Jost—Hahnenhof
   (Mittelrhein, Rheingau)
Karthäuserhof—Tyrell (Ruwer)
Heribert Kerpen (Mosel)
August Kesseler (Rheingau)*

Peter Jakob Kühn (Rheingau)*
Josef Leitz (Rheingau)
Schloss Lieser (Mosel)
Carl Loewen (Mosel)
Markus Molitor (Mosel, Saar)*
Pfeffingen—Fuhrmann-Eymael (Pfalz)
Fred Prinz (Rheingau)
Ratzenberger (Mittelrhein)*
Sankt Urbans-Hof (Mosel, Saar)
Von Schubert—Maximin Grünhaus
   (Ruwer)
Josef Spreitzer (Rheingau)
Daniel Vollenweider (Mosel)
van Volxem (Saar)
Wagner-Stempel (Rheinhessen)

★ ★ ★ (VERY GOOD)

Acham-Magin (Pfalz)
Ansgar Clüsserath (Mosel)
J. B. Becker (Rheingau)*
C. H. Berres (Mosel)
Erben von Beulwitz (Ruwer)
Josef Biffar (Pfalz)
Clemens Busch (Lower Mosel)
Clüsserath-Weiler (Mosel)
Dr. Crusius (Nahe)
Dr. Deinhard (Pfalz)
Falkensteiner Hof—Erich Weber
   (Saar)*
Göttelmann (Nahe)

Grans-Fassian (Mosel)
Willi Haag (Mosel)
Hexamer (Nahe)
Schloss Johannisberg (Rheingau)
Karlsmühle—Peter Geiben
   (Ruwer)
Reichsgraf von Kesselstatt
   (Mosel, Saar, Ruwer)
Krüger-Rumpf (Nahe)
Künstler (Rheingau)*
Peter Lauer (Saar)
Lubentiushof—Andreas Barth
   (Lower Mosel)

Gebrüder Merkelbach (Mosel)
Herbert Messmer (Pfalz—Südliche
  Weinstrasse)
Theo Minges (Pfalz—Südliche Weinstrasse)
Mönchhof—Robert Eymael (Mosel)
Georg Mosbacher (Pfalz)
Mathias Müller (Mittelrhein)
Villa Niederberger (Pfalz)
von Othegraven (Saar)
Ökonomierat Rebholz
  (Pfalz—Südliche Weinstrasse)*
Max. Ferd. Richter (Mosel)
Schloss Saarstein (Saar)

Andreas Schmitges (Mosel)
Carl Schmitt-Wagner (Mosel)
J. & H. A. Strub (Rheinhessen)
Dr. Thanisch—Erben Thanisch (Mosel)
Dr. Heinz Wagner (Saar)
Ed. Weegmüller (Pfalz)
Wegeler (Mosel, Rheingau)
Dr. Wehrheim
  (Pfalz—Südliche Weinstrasse)*
Florian Weingart (Mittelrhein)
Weins-Prüm (Mosel)
Weiser-Künstler (Mosel)
Wittmann (Rheinhessen)

* * (GOOD)

Paul Anheuser (Nahe)
Bastgen (Mosel)
Friedrich Becker
  (Pfalz—Südliche Weinstrasse)*
Brüder Dr. Becker (Rheinhessen)
Ernst Clüsserath (Mosel)
Darting (Pfalz)
Weingut Deutschherrenhof (Mosel)
Stephan Ehlen—Stefan Justen (Mosel)
Geil (Rheinhessen)
Gies-Düppel (Pfalz–Südliche Weinstrasse)*
Moritz Gogrewe (Saar)
K. F. Grobe (Rheinhessen)
Gysler (Rheinhessen)
Hahnmühle (Nahe)
Kurt Hain (Mosel)
Freiherr von Heddesdorf (Lower Mosel)
Prinz von Hessen (Rheingau)
Dr. Heyden (Rheinhessen)
Freiherr Heyl zu Herrensheim
  (Rheinhessen)
Karp-Schreiber (Mosel)
Knipser (Pfalz)*
Baron zu Knyphausen (Rheingau)
Korrell—Johanneshof (Nahe)
Kühling-Gillot (Rheinhessen)
Sybille Kuntz (Mosel)
Hans Lang (Rheingau)
Langwerth von Simmern (Rheingau)
Lanius-Knab (Mittelrhein)
Jürgen Leiner (Pfalz—Südliche
  Weinstrasse)*
Lingenfelder (Pfalz)*
Lucashof (Pfalz)
Mathern (Nahe)
Merz RDS (Rheinhessen)

Meulenhof—Stefan Justen (Mosel)
Milz—Laurentiushof (Mosel)
Eugen Müller (Pfalz)
Münzberg (Pfalz—Südliche Weinstrasse)*
Gutsverwaltung Niederhausen-
  Schlossböckelheim (Nahe)
Paulinshof (Mosel)
Dr. Pauly-Bergweiler—Peter Nicolay
August Perll (Mittelrhein)
S. A. Prüm (Mosel)
Schloss Reinhartshausen (Rheingau)
Reuscher-Haart (Mosel)
Josef Rosch (Mosel)
St. Antony (Rheinhessen)
Karl Schaefer (Pfalz)
Georg Albrecht Schneider (Rheinhessen)
Jakob Schneider (Nahe)
Schloss Schönborn (Rheingau)
Heinrich Seebrich (Rheinhessen)
Siener (Pfalz—Südliche Weinstrasse)*
Speicher-Schuth (Rheingau)
Heinrich Spindler (Pfalz)
Staatsweingüter Domaine Bergstrasse
  (Hessische Bergstrasse)
Staatsweingüter Kloster Eberbach and
  Domaine Assmannshausen (Rheingau)*
Erbhof Stein (Lower Mosel)*
Günter Steinmetz (Mosel)
Stephan Steinmetz (Upper Mosel)
Weingut Tesch (Nahe)
P. J. Valckenberg—Liebfrauenstift
  (Rheinhessen)
Schloss Vollrads (Rheingau)
Schloss Wallhausen—Prinz Salm (Nahe)*
Domdechant Werner (Rheingau)
J. L. Wolf (Pfalz)

OTHER VERY GOOD TO EXCELLENT GERMAN PRODUCERS FROM REGIONS NOT DOMINATED BY RIESLING

Note: Wines from relatively few of these producers appear in export markets. † = producers for whom Pinot Noir (or Pinot Noir along with other red wines) constitute a significant share of production.

Graf Adelmann (Württemberg)†
J. J. Adeneuer (Ahr)†
Gerhard Aldinger (Württemberg)†
Bürgerspital zum Heiligen Geist (Franken)
Castell—Fürstlich Castellsches Domänenamt (Franken)
Rudolf Fürst (Franken)†
Dr. Heger (Baden)†
Juliusspital (Franken)
Franz Keller—Schwarzer Adler (Baden)†
Andreas Laible (Baden)
Meyer-Näkel (Ahr)†
Grafen Neipperg (Württemberg)†
Johann Ruck (Franken)
Salwey (Baden)†
Horst Sauer (Franken)
Schmitt's Kinder (Franken)
Reinhold and Cornelia Schneider (Baden)†
Schloss Sommerhausen (Franken)
Weingut am Stein—Ludwig Knoll (Franken)
Jean Stodden (Ahr)†
Winzergenossenschaft Mayscohss Altenahr (Ahr)†
Hans Wirsching (Franken)
Wöhrwag (Württemberg)†
Zehnthof—Theo Luckert (Franken)

[tasting commentaries]

ACHAM-MAGIN ★ ★ ★
FORST/PFALZ

Anna-Barbara Acham's dry Riesling long typified traditional Pfalz virtues of sturdy body combined with minerality and refreshment. Recent acquisitions have enhanced the family's holdings in such top Forst sites as Pechstein, Kirchenstück, and Ungeheuer, perhaps preparing the way for some of these wines to at last make their way to the U.S.

A. J. ADAM ★ ★ ★ ★
DHRON/MOSEL $25.00–$250.00

Young Andreas Adams, a protégé of Reinhard Löwenstein of the Lower Mosel's Weingut Heymann-Löwenstein, has been cautiously increasing his holdings in the Dhroner Hofberg, which is good news, considering that his riveting Riesling in their distinctively rich, lees-enriched, plush but consistently convincing style have thus far been bottled in very meager quantities.

2005 Dhronhofberger Riesling feinherb	88–90	ncw–2010
2004 Dhronhofberger Riesling	90	ncw–2010
2002 Dhronhofberger Riesling Tholey	90	ncw–2009
2005 Riesling Kabinett	91	ncw–2012+?
2004 Riesling Kabinett	88	ncw–2010+?
2005 Dhronhofberger Riesling Spätlese	93	ncw–2020+?
2004 Dhronhofberger Riesling Spätlese	90	ncw–2018+?
2003 Dhronhofberger Riesling Spätlese Sängerei	87	ncw–2015+?
2003 Dhronhofberger Riesling Spätlese Tholey	90	ncw–2018
2002 Dhronhofberger Riesling Spätlese Tholey	92	ncw–2019
2005 Dhronhofberger Riesling Auslese	92	ncw–2025+?
2003 Dhronhofberger Riesling Auslese Tholey	93	ncw–2025+?
2005 Dhronhofberger Riesling Beerenauslese	95	ncw–2030+?

ANSGAR CLÜSSERATH ✳ ✳ ✳
TRITTENHEIM/MOSEL $20.00–$175.00

Young Eva Clüsserath has, with her father's support, taken their family estate to a new level of excellence. She has an unusual talent (for the Mosel) with dry Riesling, although the recent reorganization and planting of Trittenheim's vineyards has meant the loss of some of the old vines on which those wines rely; the estate began in 2007 to farm some sites in Dhron and Piesport.

2005 Riesling Trocken Vom Schiefer	87	ncw
2005 Riesling Trocken Steinreich	88	ncw–2010
2005 Trittenheimer Apotheke Riesling Trocken	90	ncw–2012
2004 Trittenheimer Apotheke Riesling Spätlese feinherb	87	ncw
2004 Trittenheimer Apotheke Riesling Spätlese	88	ncw–2018
2005 Trittenheimer Apotheke Riesling Auslese	92	ncw–2025
2004 Trittenheimer Apotheke Riesling Auslese	90	ncw–2022+?
2005 Trittenheimer Apotheke Riesling Beerenauslese	89	ncw–2030

DR. VON BASSERMANN–JORDAN ✳ ✳ ✳ ✳
DEIDESHEIM/PFALZ $20.00–$500.00

At the beginning of entrepreneur Achim Niederberger's era (but with Margit von Bassermann–Jordan still a major shareholder) there has been an impressive remodeling of the facilities here. But in the vineyards and in the bottle, under the continued oversight of vineyard and cellar manager Ulrich Mell, little has changed, nor does much need to. This venerable estate has already pulled itself back to near the forefront of Pfalz viticulture, and Niederberger has the wherewithal to keep it there. It is regrettable that the number of off-dry Riesling bottlings from top sites has been reduced—2005 was the last Forster Jesuitengarten Spätlese—in deference to Grosses Gewächs, which are only very selectively offered in non-German markets.

2004 Riesling auf der Mauer	87	ncw
2004 Forster Pechstein Riesling Grosses Gewächs	89	ncw–2017+?
2004 Deidesheimer Kalkofen Riesling Grosses Gewächs	90	ncw–2017+?
2004 Forster Freundstück Riesling Grosses Gewächs	88	ncw–2015+?
2004 Forster Jesuitengarten Riesling Spätlese	88	ncw–2020
2002 Forster Jesuitengarten Riesling Spätlese	90	ncw–2020
2004 Deidesheimer Leinhöhle Riesling Auslese	93	ncw–2030
2004 Deidesheimer Mäushöhle Riesling Beerenauslese	94	ncw–2035+?
2002 Deidesheimer Leinhöhle Riesling Beerenauslese	95	ncw–2035

J. B. BECKER ★ ★ ★
WALLUF/RHEINGAU $25.00–$400.00

Hans-Josef Becker was one of the pioneers in the revival of dry Rheingau Riesling in the 1970s and early '80s but, unlike most of his neighbors, he already appreciated the importance of low yields, complete ripeness, and cask maturation in achieving a balanced result. (Not that Becker neglected nobly sweet Riesling—on the contrary—and his Pinot Noir was also always among the Rheingau's best.) On account of having long served as sales commissioner for Frank Schoonmaker, Becker and his wines were better known in the United States at one time than they are today, but his tradition of excellence continues.

WEINGUT C. H. BERRES ★ ★ ★
ÜRZIG/MOSEL $20.00–$275.00

In 2004, while only in his early 20s, and following a brief stint in New Zealand, Markus Berres took the reins at this estate, one of several in Ürzig connected with branches of the Berres family. The wines have been consistently clean and exuberantly expressive, giving every indication that they will prove excellent keepers.

2005 Ürziger Würzgarten Riesling Kabinett	87	now–2014
2004 Ürziger Würzgarten Riesling Kabinett A.P. #6	88	now–2014
2004 Ürziger Würzgarten Riesling Spätlese A.P. #8	87	now–2016
2004 Ürziger Goldwingert Riesling Auslese	87	now–2020
2005 Erdener Treppchen Riesling Auslese		
gold capsule A.P. #7	95	now–2028
2005 Ürziger Würzgarten Riesling Trockenbeerenauslese	93	now–2035+?

ERBEN VON BEULWITZ ★ ★ ★
MERTESDORF/RUWER $20.00–$175.00

Hotelier, restaurateur, and winegrower Hubert Weis has had to live in the shadow of more famous neighbors, but he renders some superb examples of classic red, berry-rich, spicy Ruwer Riesling in a full range from dry to nobly sweet.

2005 Kaseler Nies'chen Riesling Spätlese feinherb	88	now–2020
2004 Kaseler Nies'chen Riesling Spätlese feinherb	87	now–2018
2004 Kaseler Nies'chen Riesling Kabinett	90	now–2016
2005 Kaseler Nies'chen Riesling Spätlese "Alte Reben"	91	now–2022
2004 Kaseler Nies'chen Riesling Spätlese		
"Alte Reben" A.P. #6	89	now–2020
2005 Kaseler Nies'chen Riesling Auslese "Alte Reben"	91	now–2028
2004 Kaseler Nies'chen Riesling Auslese ** A.P. #5	91	now–2025
2005 Kaseler Nies'chen Riesling Beerenauslese	93	now–2035
2005 Kaseler Nies'chen Riesling Trockenbeerenauslese	92	now–2040

JOSEF BIFFAR ★ ★ ★
DEIDESHEIM/PFALZ $20.00–$300.00

Following the death in 2004 of Gerhard Biffar, his daughter Lilli returned to take over this estate. Three changes of cellarmaster in four years have contributed to an awkward transition, but the arrival of Tina Herrbruck; Lilli Biffar's prior experience in managing her family's winery; major cleaning and reorganization of their small cellar; and the acquisition of additional acreage all bode well for the immediate future.

2004 Ruppertsberger Nussbien Riesling Kabinett trocken	87	now–2009
2002 Wachenheimer Altenberg Riesling Spätlese trocken	89	now

2004 Deidesheimer Kieselberg Riesling Kabinett	87	now–2012
2001 Deidesheimer Kieselberg Riesling Kabinett	90	now–2012
2002 Deidesheimer Kalkofen Riesling Spätlese	90	now–2020
2001 Wachenheimer Altenberg Riesling Spätlese	92	now–2015

GEORG BREUER ★ ★ ★ ★
RÜDESHEIM/RHEINGAU $20.00–$300.00

The Georg Breuer estate (with holdings in Rauenthal as well as Rüdesheim) and its high quality were long intimately associated with the energy and vision of Bernhard Breuer, who died, at only 57, in 2004. His brother Heinrich and longtime cellarmaster Hermann Schmoranz continue to fashion wines to the same high standards, and in the same uncompromisingly pure, firm, and acid-retentive style, making for impressive but at times almost severe dry wines, as well as nobly sweet elixirs of impeccable purity. The estate also attains quality with its Pinot Noir.

2004 Rüdesheimer Berg Roseneck Riesling trocken	87	now–2015
2004 Rüdesheimer Berg Schlossberg Riesling trocken	88	now–2015
2004 Rheingau Riesling Auslese	91	now–2020
2004 Rüdesheimer Bischofsberg Riesling Auslese	89	now–2018
2004 Rüdesheimer Berg Rottland Riesling Auslese gold capsule	92	now–2025
2004 Rüdesheimer Berg Schlossberg Riesling Auslese gold capsule	94	now–2028
2004 Rüdesheimer Berg Schlossberg Riesling Beerenauslese	94	now–2035
2004 Pinot Noir "GB"	88	now–2010

REICHSRAT VON BUHL ★ ★ ★ ★
DEIDESHEIM/PFALZ $20.00–$300.00

Despite a number of personnel changes, this estate—recently purchased by Achim Niederberger (who also owns the controlling interest in Deidesheim's Bassermann–Jordan and Dr. Deinhard estates)—has rendered high quality under vineyard manager Werner Sebastian and cellarmaster Michael Leibrecht (veterans of Müller-Catoir and former collaborators at Weingut Messmer), who are old hands, even if still relatively young men. A back-to-the-future innovation in place for the 2005 vintage was a collection of new, locally coopered wooden *Fuder,* in a cellar that for nearly two decades operated almost entirely with stainless steel. A longtime specialty of this house has been *méthode champenoise,* including a Riesling from Pechstein and excellent Blanc de [Pinot] Noir.

2004 Deidesheimer Leinhöhle Riesling Kabinett halbtrocken	89	now–2012
2004 Deidesheimer Mäushöhle Riesling Spätlese trocken	89	now–2012
2004 Forster Kirchenstück Riesling Grosses Gewächs	88	now–2016+?
2004 Forster Pechstein Riesling Grosses Gewächs	90	now–2016+?
2004 Forster Jesuitengarten Riesling Spätlese	91	now–2025
2002 Forster Jesuitengarten Riesling Spätlese	89	now–2019
2001 Forster Jesuitengarten Riesling Spätlese	90	now–2020
2004 Forster Ugeheuer Riesling Auslese	92	now–2028+?
2002 Forster Ugeheuer Riesling Auslese gold capsule	91	now–2028
2004 Forster Stift Rieslaner Auslese	89	now–2020

CLEMENS BUSCH ★★★
PÜNDERICH/MOSEL $25.00–$175.00

Clemens Busch farms the steep slopes of the once-famous Pündericher Marienberg on the Lower Mosel entirely organically, which makes him unique in the region and a source of wonder to his fellow vintners. Most of his top wines are labeled with their pre-1971 site names. His Riesling tends toward creaminess of texture and ripe, relatively low acidity (particularly at the dry end of the spectrum), which by no means precludes intricacy of flavor or a wealth of intriguing characteristics one is compelled to call "mineral."

2005 Pündericher Marienberg Riesling Spätlese trocken A.P. #21	89	now–2012
2005 Riesling vom Roten Schiefer	88	now–2010
2005 Pündericher Marienberg Riesling Auslese Falkenlay	92	now–2028
2005 Pündericher Marienberg Riesling Auslese Weissenberg	88	now–2025
2005 Pündericher Marienberg Riesling Auslese Fahrlay	91	now–2028+?
2005 Pündericher Marienberg Riesling Auslese gold capsule	91	now–2028+?
2005 Pündericher Marienberg Riesling Auslese long gold capsule	89	now–2025+?
2005 Pündericher Marienberg Riesling Beerenauslese	87	2012–2025+?

A. CHRISTMANN ★★★★
GIMMELDINGEN/PFALZ $20.00–$300.00

Steffen Christmann, recently named president of the VDP growers' association, and his father, Karl-Friedrich, cultivate an uncompromisingly concentrated, precise, and adamant style of dry Riesling and have long been serious about Pinot Noir as well. This was one of the first estates in Germany (along with Bürklin-Wolf) to conceptualize their acreage (now organically farmed) and wine portfolio as a qualitative pyramid akin to that of Burgundy: from generic, through *villages* and premier cru, to "great growths." This is the view now embraced VDP-wide.

2004 Ruppertsberger Linsenbusch Riesling Kabinett trocken	88	now–2011
2004 Deidesheimer Paradiesgarten Riesling Kabinett trocken	87	now–2011
2004 Gimmeldinger Biengarten Riesling Spätlese trocken	87	now–2011
2004 Deidesheimer Mäushöhle Riesling Spätlese trocken	89	now–2012
2004 Königsbacher Ölberg Riesling Spätlese trocken	90	now–2015
2004 Ruppertsberger Reiterpfad Riesling Grosses Gewächs	89	now–2015
2004 Deidesheimer Langenmorgen Riesling Grosses Gewächs	90	now–2015+?
2004 Deidesheimer Hohenmorgen Riesling Grosses Gewächs	?	2010–2015+?
2004 Königsbacher Idig Riesling Grosses Gewächs	92	now–2018+?
2004 Königsbacher Idig Riesling Auslese	91	now–2020+?
2004 Königsbacher Idig Riesling Beerenauslese	94	now–2025+?

JOH. JOS. CHRISTOFFEL *****
URZIG/MOSEL $25.00-$900.00

Few Mosel growers have produced so many extraordinary and ageworthy Riesling in their careers as has Hans-Leo Christoffel, although he only achieved celebrity at home after attracting the attention of U.S. Riesling lovers through the work of his importer, Terry Theise. In 2001, Christoffel entered into a unique semiretirement, leasing his vineyards to the Mönchhof's Robert Eymael, but consulting on both viticulture and winemaking to ensure that the wines vinified, bottled, and marketed under his name would continue to exhibit both the uncanny marriage of opulence and polish with transparency of flavor and an overall level of excellence that has always characterized Christoffel's estate. Christoffel employs up to four stars (rendered below as asterisks) on certain of his labels to indicate relative quality (and usually corresponding to the wine's place of origin).

2005 Ürziger Würzgarten Riesling Kabinett trocken	88	now
2004 Riesling J. J.	90	now–2010
2005 Erdener Treppchen Riesling Kabinett	89	now–2018
2004 Erdener Treppchen Riesling Kabinett	90	now–2018
2003 Erdener Treppchen Riesling Kabinett	89	now
2001 Erdener Treppchen Riesling Kabinett	93	now–2014
2005 Ürziger Würzgarten Riesling Kabinett	87	now–2015
2004 Ürziger Würzgarten Riesling Kabinett	92	now–2018
2002 Ürziger Würzgarten Riesling Kabinett	89	now–2014
2001 Ürziger Würzgarten Riesling Kabinett	92	now–2014
2005 Erdener Treppchen Riesling Spätlese	91	now–2022
2004 Erdener Treppchen Riesling Spätlese	90	now–2022
2002 Erdener Treppchen Riesling Spätlese	89	now–2019
2001 Erdener Treppchen Riesling Spätlese	93	now–2018
2005 Ürziger Würzgarten Riesling Spätlese	92	now–2025
2004 Ürziger Würzgarten Riesling Spätlese	93	now–2025
2002 Ürziger Würzgarten Riesling Spätlese	89	now–2018
2001 Ürziger Würzgarten Riesling Spätlese	93	now–2020
2005 Ürziger Würzgarten Riesling Spätlese*	90	now–2022+?
2004 Ürziger Würzgarten Riesling Spätlese*	90	now–2022+?
2003 Ürziger Würzgarten Riesling Auslese	89	now–2015+?
2002 Ürziger Würzgarten Riesling Auslese	90	now–2022
2001 Ürziger Würzgarten Riesling Auslese	92	now–2018
2005 Ürziger Würzgarten Riesling Auslese*	93	now–2035
2004 Ürziger Würzgarten Riesling Auslese*	94	now–2035
2003 Ürziger Würzgarten Riesling Auslese*	90	now–2017+?
2002 Ürziger Würzgarten Riesling Auslese*	91	now–2025
2001 Ürziger Würzgarten Riesling Auslese*	94	now–2020
2005 Erdener Treppchen Riesling Auslese**	93	now–2035
2004 Erdener Treppchen Riesling Auslese**	95	now–2035
2003 Erdener Treppchen Riesling Auslese**	93	now–2018
2002 Erdener Treppchen Riesling Auslese**	92	now–2028
2001 Erdener Treppchen Riesling Auslese**	97	now–2025
2005 Ürziger Würzgarten Riesling Auslese**	91	now–2030
2004 Ürziger Würzgarten Riesling Auslese**	92	now–2030
2003 Ürziger Würzgarten Riesling Auslese**	92	now–2017+?
2002 Ürziger Würzgarten Riesling Auslese**	93	now–2030
2001 Ürziger Würzgarten Riesling Auslese**	96	now–2030

2005 Ürziger Würzgarten Riesling Auslese***	95	now–2038+?
2004 Ürziger Würzgarten Riesling Auslese***	96	now–2045
2003 Ürziger Würzgarten Riesling Auslese***	93	now–2020+?
2002 Ürziger Würzgarten Riesling Auslese***	94	now–2035
2001 Ürziger Würzgarten Riesling Auslese***	95	now–2035
2005 Ürziger Würzgarten Riesling Auslese****	96	now–2040+?
2004 Ürziger Würzgarten Riesling Auslese****	95	now–2050
2005 Ürziger Würzgarten Riesling Trockenbeerenauslese	98	now–2045+?
2004 Ürziger Würzgarten Riesling Eiswein	94	now–2030+?
2002 Ürziger Würzgarten Riesling Eiswein	93	now–2040

CLÜSSERATH-WEILER ★ ★ ★
TRITTENHEIM/MOSEL $25.00–$150.00

Helmut Clüsserath and his daughter Verena bottle some of the most satisfying dry though not always legally *trocken* Riesling on the Middle Mosel, of which that from centenarian vines on the Fährfels is consistently extraordinary. Their sweet wines can also be lovely, offering abundant tropical fruit and immediate gratification of the sort associated with Trittenheim Riesling, and their low-toned, unusually soft, mocha-rich Riesling from Mehring are highly distinctive.

2004 Trittenheimer Apotheke Riesling Spätlese trocken A.P. #11	87	now–2010
2005 Trittenheimer Apotheke Riesling Alte Reben	87	now
2004 Trittenheimer Apotheke Riesling Alte Reben	89	now–2012
2005 Mehringer Zellerberg Riesling Alte Reben	89	now–2012
2005 Riesling Fährfels	92	now–2020+?
2004 Riesling Fährfels	93	now–2020+?
2005 Trittenheimer Apotheke Riesling Kabinett	88	now–2015
2005 Trittenheimer Apotheke Riesling Spätlese A.P. #11	89	now–2018
2004 Trittenheimer Apotheke Riesling Spätlese A.P. #12	88	now–2016
2004 Trittenheimer Apotheke Riesling Spätlese* A.P. #9	89	now–2018
2005 Trittenheimer Apotheke Riesling Spätlese**	90	now–2020
2004 Trittenheimer Apotheke Riesling Spätlese** A.P. #14	90	now–2020
2003 Trittenheimer Apotheke Riesling Auslese	87	now–2014+?
2004 Trittenheimer Apotheke Riesling Auslese *	87	now–2020
2005 Trittenheimer Apotheke Riesling Auslese***	89	now–2020+?
2005 Trittenheimer Apotheke Riesling Beerenauslese	90	now–2025+?
2005 Trittenheimer Apotheke Riesling Trockenbeerenauslese	90	now–2028+?
2004 Trittenheimer Apotheke Riesling Eiswein	89	now–2010+?

DR. CRUSIUS ★ ★ ★
TRAISEN/NAHE

Ever since Hans Crusius was profiled by Hugh Johnson in his *Modern Encyclopedia of Wine* this estate has enjoyed a formidable reputation and been the source for many memorable, if generally not exceptionally ageworthy, Riesling from a distinguished collection of sites. Under the direction of Dr. Peter Crusius results have vacillated, but the last several collections have contained some true Nahe gems, leading one to hope that these wines will once again reach American shores.

2004 Traiser Bastei Riesling Spätlese gold capsule A.P. #27	87	now–2014
2004 Traiser Rotenfels Riesling Auslese A.P. #26	88	now–2014
2003 Traiser Rotenfels Riesling Auslese A.P. #27	92	now–2017
2004 Traiser Rotenfels Riesling Auslese gold capsule A.P. #28	90	now–2016
2003 Traiser Rotenfels Riesling Auslese gold capsule A.P. #20	89	now–2015
2003 Norheimer Kirschheck Riesling Beereenauslese	93	now–2022+?
2003 Schlossböckelheimer Felsenberg Riesling Beereenauslese	89	now–2018+?
2004 Traiser Rotenfels Riesling Trockenbeerenauslese A.P. #32	94	now–2025+?

DR. DEINHARD ★ ★ ★
DEIDESHEIM/PFALZ $20.00–$150.00

Longtime cellarmaster Heinz Bauer stuck to the traditional, cask-matured Pfalz wine virtues and, while the quality of this estate's wide range of wines was less consistent than one might wish, the best of them were delicious and frequently included amazing values. This property was purchased in 2007 by Achim Niederberger, who already owns Reichsrat von Buhl and the controlling interest in Dr. von Bassermann–Jordan. It will be most interesting to see whether the future brings them closer together stylistically. Modernization of facilities and high qualitative ideals appear to be inevitable, and a new team has been put in place.

2004 Ruppertsberger Riesling Kabinett trocken	88	now–2010
2001 Deidesheimer Grainhübel Riesling Spätlese trocken	90	now–2010
2004 Deidesheimer Mäushöhle Kabinett halbtrocken	88	now–2012
2002 Ruppertsberger Reiterpfad Riesling Kabinett	89	now–2012
2004 Deidesheimer Kalkofen Riesling Spätlese	87	now–2016
2004 Deidesheimer Kalkofen Riesling Auslese	90	now–2025
2001 Deidesheimer Grainhübel Riesling Auslese	92	now–2019+?
2004 Scheurebe Kabinett	87	now–2013

SCHLOSSGUT DIEL ★ ★ ★ ★ ★ ★
BURG LAYEN/NAHE $25.00–$600.00

Armin Diel (who is also active as a wine journalist and as Nahe VDP chairman) brought his family's property to worldwide notice thanks to his gregarious, flamboyant personality and keen sense for public relations. It was discipline, stylistic vision, and a fabulous trio of vine-yards, however, that brought his estate to the forefront of German viticulture. Skilled Christoph Friedrich is the second cellarmaster here to come from the Mosel, which says a lot about Diel's stylistic paradigm. Eiswein has long been a stunning estate specialty. There are also ambitious programs with Pinot Noir, a white Burgundy blend, and superb sparkling cuvées.

2004 Riesling Eierfels	88	now–2010+?
2004 Dorsheimer Pittermännchen Riesling Grosses Gewächs	87	now–2012+?
2004 Dorsheimer Goldloch Riesling Grosses Gewächs	91	now–2014+?
2004 Dorsheimer Burgberg Riesling Grosses Gewächs	88	now–2012+?
2004 Dorsheimer Goldloch Riesling Kabinett	91	now–2017

2003 Dorsheimer Goldloch Riesling Kabinett	89	now–2009
2004 Dorsheimer Burgberg Riesling Kabinett	87	now–2015
2004 Dorsheimer Pittermännchen Riesling Kabinett	88	now–2015
2004 Dorsheimer Goldloch Riesling Spätlese	93	now–2020
2003 Dorsheimer Goldloch Riesling Spätlese	89	now–2012
2004 Dorsheimer Burgberg Riesling Spätlese	90	now–2018
2004 Dorsheimer Pittermännchen Riesling Spätlese A.P. #13	91	now–2020
2003 Dorsheimer Pittermännchen Riesling Spätlese	91	now–2013
2004 Dorsheimer Pittermännchen Riesling Spätlese gold capsule A.P. #20	95	now–2025
2004 Scheurebe Spätlese	90	now–2015
2004 Dorsheimer Goldloch Riesling Auslese A.P. #14	90	now–2025
2003 Dorsheimer Goldloch Riesling Auslese A.P. #14	89	now–2016
2004 Dorsheimer Pittermännchen Riesling Auslese	92	now–2022
2003 Dorsheimer Pittermännchen Riesling Auslese	91	now–2018
2004 Dorsheimer Goldloch Riesling Auslese gold capsule A.P. #19	91	now–2025
2004 Riesling Eiswein	?	2012–2020+?
2004 Dorsheimer Pittermännchen Riesling Eiswein	96	2010–2030+?

HERMANN DÖNNHOFF ★ ★ ★ ★ ★
OBERHAUSEN/NAHE $25.00–$600.00

Helmut Dönnhoff inherited vineyards in Oberhausen and two choice parcels on the opposite shore of the Nahe, Hermannshöhle and Brücke (the latter formerly considered part of Niederhäuser Hermannsberg). During the 1980s and early '90s, he established a reputation as one of the most conscientious and reflective of Germany's vintners for crafting some of the world's most expressive, pure Riesling in dry, off-dry, and nobly sweet formats. Buoyed by an enormous surge of adulation in the 1990s, Dönnhoff was gradually able, with critical assistance from a benefactor, to achieve his dream of owning parts of each of the top sites between Schlossböckelheim and Bad Kreuznach. There is no better showcase for the concept of *terroir* than a collection of Riesling from this address.

2004 Riesling trocken	87	now–2011
2004 Oberhäuser Felsenberg Riesling Spätlese trocken	88	now–2009
2004 Norheimer Dellchen Riesling Spätlese trocken	90	now–2012
2004 Niederhäuser Hermannshöhle Riesling Grosses Gewächs	94	now–2020
2003 Riesling	89	now–2012
2002 Riesling	89	now–2012
2001 Riesling	90	now
2004 Oberhäuseser Leistenberg Riesling Kabinett	89	now–2016
2003 Oberhäuseser Leistenberg Riesling Kabinett	90	now–2015
2002 Oberhäuseser Leistenberg Riesling Kabinett	92	now–2016
2001 Oberhäuseser Leistenberg Riesling Kabinett	92	now–2010
2002 Norheimer Dellchen Riesling Kabinett	90	now–2013
2004 Norheimer Kirschheck Riesling Spätlese	95	now–2025
2003 Norheimer Kirschheck Riesling Spätlese	92	now–2020
2002 Norheimer Kirschheck Riesling Spätlese	92	now–2022
2001 Norheimer Kirschheck Riesling Spätlese	94	now–2018

2004 Norheimer Dellchen Riesling Spätlese A.P. #11	97	now–2030
2004 Norheimer Dellchen Riesling Spätlese A.P. #14	96	now–2028
2002 Norheimer Dellchen Riesling Spätlese	97	now–2025
2004 Schlossböckelheimer Felsenberg Riesling Spätlese	92	now–2025
2003 Schlossböckelheimer Felsenberg Riesling Spätlese	92	now–2020
2002 Schlossböckelheimer Felsenberg Riesling Spätlese	95	now–2025
2004 Schlossböckelheimer Kupfergrube Riesling Spätlese	92	now–2025
2003 Schlossböckelheimer Kupfergrube Riesling Spätlese	93	now–2020
2002 Schlossböckelheimer Kupfergrube Riesling Spätlese	97	now–2025
2001 Schlossböckelheimer Kupfergrube Riesling Spätlese	95	now–2020
2004 Oberhäuser Brücke Riesling Spätlese	94	now–2030
2003 Oberhäuser Brücke Riesling Spätlese	93	now–2020
2002 Oberhäuser Brücke Riesling Spätlese	97	now–2025+?
2001 Oberhäuser Brücke Riesling Spätlese	94	now–2018
2004 Niederhäuser Hermannshöhle Riesling Spätlese	96	now–2030
2003 Niederhäuser Hermannshöhle Riesling Spätlese	95	now–2020
2002 Niederhäuser Hermannshöhle Riesling Spätlese	96	now–2025+
2001 Niederhäuser Hermannshöhle Riesling Spätlese	98	now–2022+
2003 Norheimer Dellchen Riesling Auslese	98	now–2030
2001 Norheimer Dellchen Riesling Auslese	95	now–2025
2004 Schlossböckelheimer Felsenberg Riesling Auslese	93	now–2032
2003 Oberhäuser Leistenberg Riesling Auslese	93	now–2025
2001 Oberhäuser Leistenberg Riesling Auslese	95	now–2024
2004 Oberhäuser Brücke Riesling Auslese A.P. #16	96	now–2035
2004 Oberhäuser Brücke Riesling Auslese A.P. #21	98	now–2038
2003 Oberhäuser Brücke Riesling Auslese	95	now–2030
2002 Oberhäuser Brücke Riesling Auslese	97	now–2030
2001 Oberhäuser Brücke Riesling Auslese	94	now–2025
2004 Niederhäuser Hermannshöhle Riesling Auslese	95	now–2035
2003 Niederhäuser Hermannshöhle Riesling Auslese	97	now–2035
2002 Niederhäuser Hermannshöhle Riesling Auslese	94	now–2030
2001 Niederhäuser Hermannshöhle Riesling Auslese	92	now–2025
2004 Oberhäuser Brücke Riesling Eiswein A.P. #23	99	now–2035+?
2004 Oberhäuser Brücke Riesling Eiswein A.P. #24	100	now–2040+?
2003 Oberhäuser Brücke Riesling Eiswein A.P. #24	95	now–2020+?
2002 Oberhäuser Brücke Riesling Eiswein A.P. #18	100	now–2035+?
2001 Oberhäuser Brücke Riesling Eiswein A.P. #18	100	now–2030+?

EMRICH-SCHÖNLEBER ✶✶✶✶✶
MONZINGEN/NAHE $20.00–$500.00

For at least two decades, Werner Schönleber has been bottling some of Germany's finest Riesling, ranging from dry to nobly sweet. He is now receiving the recognition he long deserved. With acquisition of additional choice parcels in the Frühlingsplätzchen and Halenberg, his ever more refined approach to viticulture and vinification, and the active participation of son Frank, he has attained new standards of excellence since the 2004 vintage and sent a signal that the Schönlebers are not about to rest on their laurels.

2004 Monzinger Halenberg Riesling Kabinett trocken	87	now–2009
2004 Monzinger Halenberg Riesling Spätlese trocken	88	now–2012+?
2004 Monzinger Halenberg Riesling Grosses Gewächs	88	now–2015+?
2004 Monzinger Halenberg "Lay" Riesling Grosses Gewächs	90	now–2016+?
2004 Monzinger Frühlingsplätzchen Riesling Kabinett halbtrocken	89	now–2012
2004 Monzinger Frühlingsplätzchen Riesling Spätlese	90	now–2018
2004 Monzinger Halenberg Riesling Spätlese	92	now–2018
2004 Monzinger Frühlingsplätzchen Riesling Spätlese "Rutsch"	92	now–2020
2004 Monzinger Frühlingsplätzchen Riesling Auslese	93	now–2025
2002 Monzinger Frühlingsplätzchen Riesling Auslese	89	now–2018
2004 Monzinger Halenberg Riesling Auslese	91	now–2025
2002 Monzinger Halenberg Riesling Auslese	91	now–2025
2002 Monzinger Halenberg Riesling Auslese***	93	2010–2030
2004 Monzinger Halenberg Riesling Eiswein	90	now–2025+?
2002 Monzinger Halenberg Riesling Eiswein	96	2015–2040

FALKENSTEINER HOF—ERICH WEBER ✱ ✱ ✱
NIEDERMENNIG/SAAR $25.00–$75.00

First-generation vintner Erich Weber has gone his maverick winemaking ways for close to two decades, following only procedures that would have been familiar from 50 or 75 years ago, and taking full advantage of the depressed prices that long prevailed even for excellent slate slopes along the Saar. For many years Weber's barrel-fermented, late-bottled Riesling was exclusively *trocken,* but he now embraces discreet residual sugar. The singular, never-chaptalized Falkensteiner Hofberger Pinot Noir (Spätburgunder) is consistently perfumed and nuanced.

2005 Krettnacher Altenberg Riesling Spätlese trocken	90	now–2012
2004 Krettnacher Altenberg Riesling Spätlese trocken A.P. #1	89	now–2010
2005 Niedermenninger Herrenberg Riesling Spätlese	89	now–2015
2004 Niedermenninger Herrenberg Riesling Spätlese	90	now–2018
2005 Niedermenninger Sonnenberg Riesling Auslese A.P. #4	92	now–2020
2005 Krettnacher Euchariusberg Riesling Auslese	87–89	now–2018
2004 Krettnacher Euchariusberg Riesling Auslese	91	now–2020
2004 Falkensteiner Hofberg Riesling Auslese	89	now–2018
2005 Falkensteiner Hofberg Spätburgunder Spätlese trocken	88–90	now–2012
2004 Falkensteiner Hofberg Spätburgunder Spätlese trocken	90	now–2010

GÖTTELMANN ✱ ✱ ✱
MÜNSTER-SARMSHEIM/NAHE $20.00–$100.00

Götz Blessing and his wife, Ruth Göttelmann—like the Rumpfs of Krüger-Rumpf, who live just down the street—have long operated a restaurant to supplement and complement their winery. As part of a conscientious ongoing effort to enhance the already excellent, nuanced quality of their Riesling, the couple recently acquired a large nearby cellar.

GRANS-FASSIAN ★★★
LEIWEN/MOSEL $25.00–$275.00

Gerhard Grans was a leader in restoring prominence to the village of Leiwen, although his wines from sites in Trittenheim and Piesport are better known than his generally dry Riesling from Leiwen's Laurentiuslay. The nobly sweet Riesling and Eiswein here are sometimes stunning.

2005 Leiwener Laurentiuslay Riesling Spätlese trocken S	87	now–2014
2004 Leiwener Laurentiuslay Riesling Spätlese trocken S	88	now–2015
2005 Trittenheimer Riesling Kabinett	86	now–2010
2005 Trittenheimer Apotheke Riesling Spätlese	87	now–2017
2005 Piesporter Goldtröpfchen Riesling Spätlese	88	now–2017+?
2004 Dhronhofberger Riesling Spätlese	87	now–2015
2005 Trittenheimer Apotheke Riesling Auslese "Fass #25," A.P. #13	87	now–2020
2005 Trittenheimer Apotheke Riesling Auslese "Fass #9," A.P. #12	90	now–2025
2004 Trittenheimer Apotheke Riesling Auslese A.P. #12	88	now–2018
2005 Trittenheimer Apotheke Riesling Auslese gold capsule	89	now–2025+?
2004 Trittenheimer Apotheke Riesling Auslese gold capsule A.P. #14	90	now–2025
2004 Trittenheimer Apotheke Riesling Eiswein	93	now–2035

GUNDERLOCH ★★★★★
NACKENHEIM/RHEINHESSEN $22.00–$800.00

During the 1980s, Fritz and Agnes Hasselbach transformed her family's estate into a model of Riesling quality. Today (sadly) this is the sole address to which one can turn to taste the full potential of the famous "Red Slope" of Nierstein and Nackenheim. A decade ago, the Hasselbachs took over the large Nierstein property of Balbach, but at present Pettenthal (which is an extension of the Nackenheimer Rothenberg) is their only Nierstein vineyard subjected to separate bottling. Glacially cold and slow fermentations are the estate norm, with consequent late release. Nobly sweet Riesling is the signature genre for the Hasselbachs (who are nowadays ably assisted by Charlotte Hess), but their dry wines are exemplary and their non-vineyard-designated cuvées often offer mind-boggling value. (Wines here labeled without Prädikat are always dry-tasting, if not *trocken*.)

2004 Riesling trocken	92	now–2012
2004 Niersteiner Pettenthal Riesling	93	now–2014
2004 Nackenheimer Rothenberg Riesling	94–96	now–2018+?
2003 Nackenheimer Rothenberg Riesling	87	now–2011+?
2004 Riesling Spätlese	88	now–2014
2003 Nackenheimer Rothenberg Riesling Spätlese	91	now–2018
2001 Nackenheimer Rothenberg Riesling Spätlese	88	now–2020
2004 Nackenheimer Rothenberg Riesling Auslese	92	now–2022
2001 Nackenheimer Rothenberg Riesling Auslese	92	now–2018+?

2004 Nackenheimer Rothenberg Riesling Auslese gold capsule	92–94	now–2025
2003 Nackenheimer Rothenberg Riesling Auslese gold capsule	90	now–2020
2001 Nackenheimer Rothenberg Riesling Auslese gold capsule	94	now–2022?

FRITZ HAAG * * * * *
BRAUNEBERG/MOSEL $25.00–$1,000.00

Wilhelm Haag, long the chairman of the local chapter of the VDP growers' association, has been singularly influential and a beacon of top quality on the Mosel. Few Rieslings more successfully marry richness with elegance and finesse, and while the best of the wines that Haag sells at the annual Trier auctions often set records, Riesling lovers who can locate his ostensibly simple estate Riesling or impeccably balanced Kabinett will also be able to savor excellent value. Younger son Oliver Haag joined his father here in 2004 after a stint directing the Wegeler estate, and the family's holdings now incorporate a major portion of Brauneberg's best vineyards. (Wilhelm Haag typically arranges for the same registration number to apply to the same parcel each year.)

2005 Riesling trocken	89	now–2013
2004 Riesling trocken	87	now–2011
2005 Brauneberger Juffer-Sonnenuhr Riesling Spätlese trocken	88	now–2015
2004 Brauneberger Juffer-Sonnenuhr Riesling Spätlese trocken	88	now–2015
2005 Brauneberger Juffer Riesling Spätlese trocken	89	now–2015
2005 Brauneberger Juffer Riesling Kabinett feinherb	91	now–2015
2004 Riesling	89	now–2012
2005 Brauneberger Juffer Riesling Kabinett	88	now–2015
2004 Brauneberger Juffer Riesling Kabinett	92	now–2015
2001 Brauneberger Juffer-Sonnenuhr Riesling Kabinett	92	now–2011
2005 Brauneberger Juffer Riesling Spätlese	90	now–2017
2004 Brauneberger Juffer Riesling Spätlese	87	now–2015
2005 Brauneberger Juffer-Sonnenuhr Riesling Spätlese A.P. #7	91	now–2025
2004 Brauneberger Juffer-Sonnenuhr Riesling Spätlese A.P. #7	93	now–2025
2002 Brauneberger Juffer-Sonnenuhr Riesling Spätlese A.P. #7	89	now–2018
2001 Brauneberger Juffer-Sonnenuhr Riesling Spätlese A.P. #7	94	now–2022
2005 Brauneberger Juffer-Sonnenuhr Riesling Spätlese A.P. #14	92	now–2025
2004 Brauneberger Juffer-Sonnenuhr Riesling Spätlese A.P. #14	96	now–2025
2005 Brauneberger Juffer-Sonnenuhr Riesling Auslese A.P. #16	93	now–2025
2004 Brauneberger Juffer-Sonnenuhr Riesling Auslese A.P. #16	94	now–2030

2005 Brauneberger Juffer-Sonnenuhr Riesling		
Auslese A.P. #10	95	now–2030+?
2004 Brauneberger Juffer-Sonnenuhr Riesling		
Auslese A.P. #10	92	now–2030
2002 Brauneberger Juffer-Sonnenuhr Riesling		
Auslese A.P. #6	89	now–2022+?
2001 Brauneberger Juffer-Sonnenuhr Riesling		
Auslese A.P. #6	97	now–2028+?
2005 Brauneberger Juffer-Sonnenuhr Riesling		
Auslese gold capsule A.P. #12	95	now–2030
2002 Brauneberger Juffer-Sonnenuhr Riesling		
Auslese gold capsule A.P. #12	90	now–2024
2005 Brauneberger Juffer-Sonnenuhr Riesling		
Auslese gold capsule A.P. #9	93	now–2025
2004 Brauneberger Juffer-Sonnenuhr Riesling Auslese		
gold capsule A.P. #9	95	now–2035
2005 Brauneberger Juffer-Sonnenuhr Riesling Auslese		
gold capsule A.P. #13	93	now–2030
2004 Brauneberger Juffer-Sonnenuhr Riesling Auslese		
gold capsule A.P. #13	97	now–2040
2002 Brauneberger Juffer-Sonnenuhr Riesling Auslese		
gold capsule A.P. #13	91	now–2025
2005 Brauneberger Juffer-Sonnenuhr Riesling Auslese		
long gold capsule A.P. #15	94	now–2035+
2005 Brauneberger Juffer-Sonnenuhr Riesling		
Beerenauslese	98	now–2045+?

WILLI HAAG ✷ ✷ ✷
BRAUNEBERG/MOSEL $25.00–$175.00

Marcus Haag has never quite reached qualitative heights (albeit largely unheralded) achieved by his late father Dieter in the 1980s and early 1990s. But recently there are increasing signs of excellence from the many outstanding vineyards of this branch of the Haag family, which include the superbly situated Bürgerslay portion of today's Brauneberger Juffer.

2005 Riesling A.P. #12	87	now–2010
2005 Riesling A.P. #17	87	now–2010
2005 Brauneberger Juffer Riesling Spätlese trocken	89	now–2009
2005 Brauneberger Juffer Riesling Spätlese		
halbtrocken	87	now–2011
2005 Brauneberger Juffer Riesling Spätlese A.P. #16	90	now–2020
2004 Brauneberger Juffer Riesling Spätlese A.P. #6	88	now–2018
2005 Brauneberger Juffer Riesling Auslese A.P. #11	88	now–2018
2005 Brauneberger Juffer Riesling Auslese A.P. #6	87	now–2020
2005 Brauneberger Juffer-Sonnenuhr Riesling		
Auslese A.P. #7	88	now–2020
2004 Brauneberger Juffer-Sonnenuhr Riesling		
Auslese A.P. #3	87	now–2020+?
2004 Brauneberger Juffer Riesling Auslese A.P. #8	90	now–2025
2005 Brauneberger Juffer-Sonnenuhr Riesling Auslese		
gold capsule A.P. #9	92	now–2025+?

2005 Brauneberger Juffer-Sonnenuhr Riesling Beerenauslese A.P. #10	93	now–2035+?
2005 Brauneberger Juffer-Sonnenuhr Riesling Beerenauslese A.P. #18	94	now–2035+?
2004 Brauneberger Juffer Riesling Eiswein	87	2012–2030?

REINHOLD HAART ✳ ✳ ✳ ✳ ✳
PIESPORT/MOSEL $20.00–$300.00

Theo Haart has consistently demonstrated why the vineyards of Piesport deserve their historical renown, even if so many other growers' wines from this town disappoint. Haart's championing of the unjustly neglected Ohligsberg in neighboring Wintrich, and more recently his revival of the tiny Piesporter Kreuzwingert have opened up new vistas for lovers of Mosel Riesling. Any wine from this address—including the virtually dry-tasting Haart to Heart Riesling—can be highly recommended.

2005 Piesporter Riesling A.P. #1	87	now
2005 Piesporter Goldtröpfchen Riesling	87	now–2011
2005 Riesling Haart to Heart	88	now–2010
2004 Riesling Haart to Heart	90	now–2010
2005 Piesporter Kreuzwingert Riesling Spätlese feinherb	89	now–2015
2005 Piesporter Riesling Kabinett	89	now–2015
2004 Piesporter Riesling Kabinett	87	now–2012
2005 Piesporter Goldtröpfchen Riesling Kabinett	90	now–2018
2004 Piesporter Goldtröpfchen Riesling Kabinett	92	now–2018
2001 Piesporter Goldtröpfchen Riesling Kabinett	89	now–2012
2005 Piesporter Riesling Spätlese	90	now–2022
2005 Piesporter Domherr Riesling Spätlese	91	now–2025
2004 Piesporter Domherr Riesling Spätlese	90	now–2023
2005 Piesporter Goldtröpfchen Riesling Spätlese	92	now–2025
2004 Piesporter Goldtröpfchen Riesling Spätlese	91	now–2025
2002 Piesporter Goldtröpfchen Riesling Spätlese	89	now–2022
2001 Piesporter Goldtröpfchen Riesling Spätlese	91	now–2022
2005 Piesporter Grafenberg Riesling Spätlese	92	now–2025
2005 Wintricher Ohligsberg Riesling Spätlese	89	now–2011+
2004 Wintricher Ohligsberg Riesling Spätlese	92	now–2025
2002 Wintricher Ohligsberg Riesling Auslese	91	now–2025
2001 Piesporter Domherr Riesling Auslese	91	now–2022
2005 Piesporter Goldtröpfchen Riesling Auslese	93	now–2030+?
2004 Piesporter Goldtröpfchen Riesling Auslese	94	now–2030+?
2001 Piesporter Goldtröpfchen Riesling Auslese	92	now–2025
2005 Piesporter Goldtröpfchen Riesling Auslese gold capsule A.P. #13	93	now–2030+?
2001 Piesporter Goldtröpfchen Riesling Auslese gold capsule	93	now–2025+?
2005 Piesporter Goldtröpfchen Riesling Auslese long gold capsule A.P. #14	95	now–2040+?
2001 Piesporter Goldtröpfchen Riesling Trockenbeerenauslese	93	now–2045+?

WEINHOF HERRENBERG * * * *
SCHODEN/SAAR

Claudia and Manfred Loch began as hobby vintners, but thankfully their early customers and their own curiosity and ambition got the better of them. Meticulous attention to detail results in extraordinarily clear and expressive Riesling from the Herrenberg (which, barring their enterprise, might by now have succumbed largely to scrub) and Saarfeilser, in a range from dry to sweet. This organically farmed estate proclaims itself "150% Riesling," and once you taste their wines you'll know that isn't just a joke! (One hopes that before too long some of these will reach American shores.)

HEXAMER * * *
MEDDERSHEIM/NAHE $22.00–$250.00

Young Harald Hexamer's wines are consistently attention-getting, at times rambunctious or even strident in their acidity and phenolics, but increasingly polished as well as outstanding in the realm of botrytis and Eiswein. Thanks to this estate, the unjustly neglected vineyards of Meddersheim are coming to the attention of the world's Riesling lovers.

2004 Meddersheimer Rheingrafenberg Riesling "Quarzit"	88	now–2012
2003 Meddersheimer Rheingrafenberg Riesling "Quarzit"	90	now–2012
2003 Meddersheimer Rheingrafenberg Riesling Kabinett	88	now–2010+?
2001 Meddersheimer Rheingrafenberg Riesling Kabinett	91	now–2010
2003 Meddersheimer Rheingrafenberg Riesling Spätlese	90	now–2019
2002 Meddersheimer Rheingrafenberg Riesling Spätlese	91	now–2018
2001 Meddersheimer Rheingrafenberg Riesling Spätlese	90	now–2014
2003 Meddersheimer Rheingrafenberg Riesling Spätlese*	90	now–2020
2002 Meddersheimer Rheingrafenberg Riesling Spätlese*	91	now–2018
2001 Meddersheimer Rheingrafenberg Riesling Spätlese*	91	now–2016
2002 Meddersheimer Rheingrafenberg Riesling Spätlese**	93	now–2020
2004 Meddersheimer Rheingrafenberg Riesling Auslese A.P. #16	90	now–2022
2003 Meddersheimer Rheingrafenberg Riesling Auslese	90	now–2020
2001 Meddersheimer Rheingrafenberg Riesling Auslese	92	now–2020
2003 Meddersheimer Rheingrafenberg Riesling Auslese*	92	now–2025
2004 Sobernheimer Marbach Riesling Eiswein	90	now–2022+?
2002 Sobernheimer Marbach Riesling Eiswein	96	now–2030+?
2004 Meddersheimer Rheingrafenberg Riesling Eiswein	92	now–2025+?
2002 Meddersheimer Rheingrafenberg Riesling Eiswein	93	now–2025+?

HEYMANN-LÖWENSTEIN ★ ★ ★ ★
WINNINGEN/LOWER MOSEL $28.00–$200.00

Reinhart Löwenstein patterns his dry wines on a Wachau stylistic model, employing up to two days of skin contact, and tending toward significantly fuller body and lower acidity than are typical for the Mosel. All wines here labeled without Prädikat are dry-tasting but are not labeled *trocken,* because they typically transcend the legal limit on residual sugar for that category. Furthermore, many of these wines are labeled according to pre-1971 vineyard names. Nobly sweet Riesling here can also be strikingly successful.

2004 Riesling Schieferterrassen	87	now–2009
2004 Riesling vom Blauen Schiefer	87	now–2010
2004 Hatzenporter Kirchberg Riesling	88	now–2012+?
2004 Hatzenporter Stolzenberg Riesling	90	now–2014+?
2004 Winninger Röttgen Riesling	91	now–2015+?
2004 Winninger Uhlen Riesling Blaufusser Lay	90	now–2015+?
2004 Winninger Uhlen Riesling Laubach	91	now–2015+?
2004 Winninger Uhlen Riesling Roth Lay	92	now–2018+?
2005 Riesling Auslese Schieferterrassen	91	now–2020
2005 Riesling Auslese gold capsule Schieferterrassen	90	now–2020
2005 Winninger Uhlen Riesling Auslese gold capsule Roth Lay A.P. #5	93	now–2022
2005 Winninger Uhlen Riesling Auslese long gold capsule Roth Lay A.P. #6	90	now–2020+?
2005 Riesling Beerenauslese Schieferterrassen	91	now–2025
2005 Winninger Röttgen Riesling Beerenauslese	92	now–2025
2005 Winninger Uhlen Riesling Beerenauslese Roth Lay	94	now–2030
2005 Riesling Trockenbeerenauslese Schieferterrassen	91	now–2030+?
2005 Winninger Röttgen Riesling Trockenbeerenauslese	95	now–2035

VON HÖVEL ★ ★ ★ ★
OBEREMMEL/SAAR $18.00–$200.00

The Riesling of Eberhard von Kunow—particularly those from his *monopole* Oberemmeler Hütte—were long among the best in Germany and, after a period during which his performance was still high but slightly less exalted, von Kunow is now back up to the best of his old tricks. His wines often carry high residual sugar in their youth but age magnificently. Von Kunow has also long presided with his gavel over the annual Trier auctions of the VDP growers' association.

2005 Oberemmeler Hütte Riesling Spätlese trocken	88	now–2011
2005 Scharzhofberger Riesling Spätlese feinherb	91	now–2011+?
2005 Oberemmeler Hütte Riesling Kabinett	87	now–2015
2005 Scharzhofberger Riesling Kabinett	88	now–2015
2004 Scharzhofberger Riesling Kabinett	87	now–2014
2005 "Balduin von Hövel" Riesling Spätlese	86	now
2005 Oberemmeler Hütte Riesling Spätlese	89	now–2020
2004 Oberemmeler Hütte Riesling Spätlese	90	now–2017
2005 Scharzhofberger Riesling Spätlese	87	now–2018
2005 Oberemmeler Hütte Riesling Auslese	90	now–2022
2004 Oberemmeler Hütte Riesling Auslese A.P. #8	88	now–2018
2005 Oberemmeler Hütte Riesling Auslese*	89	now–2022
2004 Scharzhofberger Riesling Auslese	92	now–2020

2005 Scharzhofberger Riesling Auslese*	92	now–2025
2005 Kanzemer Hörecker Riesling Auslese**	88	now–2020+?
2004 Kanzemer Hörecker Riesling Auslese	88	now–2018+?
2005 Oberemmeler Hütte Riesling Auslese gold capsule**	93	now–2035
2004 Oberemmeler Hütte Riesling Auslese gold capsule** A.P. #11	89	now–2025+?
2005 Oberemmeler Hütte Riesling Auslese long gold capsule***	92	2010–2030
2005 Scharzhofberger Riesling Beerenauslese	96	now–2040
2005 Oberemmeler Hütte Riesling Beerenauslese	91	now–2035
2005 Oberemmeler Hütte Riesling Trockenbeerenauslese	95	now–2040+?
2002 Oberemmeler Hütte Riesling Eiswein	90	now–2025

SCHLOSS JOHANNISBERG ★ ★ ★
JOHANNISBERG/RHEINGAU $30.00–$1,000.00+

Germany's single most famous vineyard site has for several decades seldom rendered any of that country's very best Riesling. Young vines, too-high yields, the sheer extent of acreage . . . various factors have been adduced to account for the underperformance of this almost sacred hill. But under the management of Wolfgang Schleicher, and most recently of his young and energetic successor Christian Witte, quality here has been on the rise and ambitious plans are afoot to promote future excellence. A plethora of nobly sweet Riesling has been essayed from recent vintages, in keeping with this estate's venerable traditions, but it is in the dry wines that the revival of the distinctive Johannisberg personality seems most evident.

2002 Schloss Johannisberger Riesling Auslese "Rosalack" 90		now–2025+?

JOHANNISHOF—H. H. ESER ★ ★ ★ ★
JOHANNISBERG/RHEINGAU $20.00–$300.00

Hans-Hermann Eser's estate was a beacon of Rheingau quality in dark times, without which one would have had difficulty pointing to another cellar where the distinctive characteristics and quality potential of many outstanding Rheingau sites were properly expressed. Son Johannes Eser has presided over an expansion into Rüdesheim, while upholding his family's reputation for honesty and clarity in the glass as well as in the sale of their wines around the world. The cellar track record for these Rieslings is formidable.

2004 Johannisberger Hölle Riesling Erstes Gewächs	91	now–2018
2004 Rüdesheimer Berg Rottland Riesling Erstes Gewächs	88	now–2015
2004 Johannisberger Riesling Kabinett V[ogelsang]	90	now–2025
2004 Johannisberger Riesling Kabinett G[oldatzel]	90	now–2025
2002 Johannisberger Riesling Kabinett G[oldatzel]	89	now–2022
2004 Rüdesheimer Riesling Kabinett B[erg Roseneck and Berg Rottland]	88	now–2015
2004 Johannisberger Klaus Riesling Spätlese	89	now–2025
2004 Rüdesheimer Berg Rottland Riesling Spätlese	89	now–2020+?
2002 Rüdesheimer Berg Rottland Riesling Spätlese	91	now–2018+?
2004 Johannisberger Hölle Riesling Auslese	89	now–2030
2002 Johannisberger Hölle Riesling Auslese	92	now–2035

TONI JOST—HAHNENHOF ★ ★ ★ ★
BACHARACH/MITTELRHEIN $25.00–$600.00

Peter and Linde Jost have achieved greatest recognition for nobly sweet wine from the steep Hahn vineyard (their virtual monopoly) in Bacharach. But their opulent, often powerful dry wines, including those from their holdings in Walluf in the eastern Rheingau, can also be formidable, and their Hahn Kabinett often represents excellent value, given that it displays the richness of an Auslese.

2004 Bacharacher Hahn Riesling Spätlese trocken	88	now–2012
2004 Bacharacher Hahn Riesling Grosses Gewächs	91	now–2015+?
2004 Bacharacher Hahn Riesling Kabinett feinherb	90	now–2015
2003 Bacharacher Hahn Riesling Kabinett feinherb	87	now–2009
2004 Bacharacher Hahn Riesling Spätlese	91	now–2022
2004 Bacharacher Hahn Riesling Auslese A.P. #3	89	now–2020+?
2001 Bacharacher Hahn Riesling Auslese	90	now–2022
2004 Bacharacher Hahn Riesling Auslese gold capsule A.P. #4	90	now–2025
2001 Bacharacher Hahn Riesling Trockenbeerenauslese	94	2015–2035

KARLSMÜHLE—PETER GEIBEN ★ ★ ★
MERTESDORF/RUWER $20.00–$275.00

In the late 1980s, Peter Geiben decided to see how high he could raise the quality at his family's estate (site of a Roman stone-cutting mill), which includes the excellent *monopole* Lorenzhöfer vineyards and holdings in the great Kaseler Nies'chen. He has never looked back, and his wines have often challenged those of his more famous Ruwer neighbors. The acquisition of the Patheiger estate with its outstanding Kasel acreage has further strengthened Geiben's hand, and he is resurrecting the forgotten but once renowned Timpert vineyard (adjacent to Grünhaus). Yet for all of these developments, quality in recent vintages has not been on a par with the best Karlsmühle collections of the 1990s, nor have recent weather conditions permitted the brash, ultraconcentrated Eiswein for which Geiben had become known.

2005 Riesling Trocken "Molaris L."	89	now–2012
2004 Lorenzhöfer Riesling Kabinett trocken	88	now–2010
2005 Lorenzhöfer Riesling Spätlese trocken	88	now–2011
2005 Lorenzhöfer Riesling Selektion Von Quarzitshiefer	89	now–2015
2005 Lorenzhöfer Riesling Selektion Alte Reben	87	now–2012
2004 Lorenzhöfer Riesling Selektion Alte Reben	89	now–2012
2005 Riesling Feinherb "Molaris L."	88	now–2015
2005 Kaseler Timpert Riesling Spätlese feinherb	89	now–2015+?
2005 Kaseler Nies'chen Riesling Kabinett	90	now–2018
2004 Kaseler Nies'chen Riesling Kabinett	87	now–2015
2001 Kaseler Nies'chen Riesling Kabinett	89	now–2011
2005 Kaseler Nies'chen Riesling Spätlese	88	now–2020
2004 Kaseler Nies'chen Riesling Spätlese	90	now–2020
2001 Kaseler Nies'chen Riesling Spätlese	87	now–2016
2005 Kaseler Kehrnagel Riesling Auslese gold capsule	90	now–2020+?
2005 Lorenzhöfer Riesling Auslese gold capsule A.P. #19	89	now–2025
2001 Lorenzhöfer Riesling Auslese gold capsule	92	now–2020
2005 Lorenzhöfer Riesling Auslese long gold capsule	88	2012–2025

2004 Lorenzhöfer Riesling Auslese long gold capsule	94	2010–2035
2003 Lorenzhöfer Riesling Auslese long gold capsule A.P. #14	92	now–2027
2005 Kaseler Nies'chen Riesling Auslese gold capsule A.P. #14	91	2012–2035
2004 Kaseler Nies'chen Riesling Auslese long gold capsule A.P. #14	91	now–2035
2001 Kaseler Nies'chen Riesling Auslese long gold capsule Patheiger	94	now–2035
2003 Lorenzhöfer Riesling Beerenauslese	88	now–2020+?
2004 Lorenzhöfer Riesling Eiswein	93	now–2030+?
2003 Lorenzhöfer Riesling Eiswein	92	now–2020+?

KARTHÄUSERHOF ✶ ✶ ✶ ✶
EITELSBACH/RUWER $25.00–$900.00

During the 1990s, Christoph Tyrell restored the reputation of his family's famous estate. In keeping with his own stylistic preferences, there is a wide range of often impressive Riesling *trocken,* generally culminating in a bottling called "Auslese Trocken 'S' " that can be stunning, but can also at times suffer heat and bitterness due to high alcohol. The classic Ruwer tension of richness and acidity is best displayed in the estate's generally wide range of sweet Auslese, of which that in 2005 was sublime. (As at nearby Grünhaus, nobly sweet wines are often designated with a cask number, separate from the wines' official registration number.)

2005 Eitelsbacher Karthäuserhofberg Weissburgunder Pinot Blanc trocken	88	now
2004 Eitelsbacher Karthäuserhofberg Riesling Kabinett trocken	87	now–2015
2005 Eitelsbacher Karthäuserhofberg Riesling Spätlese trocken	90	now–2012
2004 Eitelsbacher Karthäuserhofberg Riesling Spätlese trocken	89	now–2010
2005 Eitelsbacher Karthäuserhofberg Riesling Auslese trocken	90	now–2012
2004 Eitelsbacher Karthäuserhofberg Riesling Kabinett feinherb	87	now–2012
2004 Eitelsbacher Karthäuserhofberg Riesling Spätlese feinherb	90	now–2025
2005 Eitelsbacher Karthäuserhofberg Riesling Kabinett	88	2010–2018+?
2004 Eitelsbacher Karthäuserhofberg Riesling Kabinett	89	now–2018
2003 Eitelsbacher Karthäuserhofberg Riesling Kabinett	88	now–2011
2001 Eitelsbacher Karthäuserhofberg Riesling Kabinett	88	now
2005 Eitelsbacher Karthäuserhofberg Riesling Spätlese A.P. #9	92	now–2025
2005 Eitelsbacher Karthäuserhofberg Riesling Auslese	89	now–2025
2004 Eitelsbacher Karthäuserhofberg Riesling Auslese	90	now–2030
2001 Eitelsbacher Karthäuserhofberg Riesling Auslese	89	now–2020+?
2005 Eitelsbacher Karthäuserhofberg Riesling Auslese [cask] #30	88	now–2025
2005 Eitelsbacher Karthäuserhofberg Riesling Auslese [cask] #33	91	2010–2028

2005 Eitelsbacher Karthäuserhofberg Riesling Auslese [cask] #18	93	now–2028+?
2005 Eitelsbacher Karthäuserhofberg Riesling Auslese [cask] #31	91	now–2028
2005 Eitelsbacher Karthäuserhofberg Riesling Auslese [cask] #28	92	2012–2035
2004 Eitelsbacher Karthäuserhofberg Riesling Auslese [cask] #55 A.P. #14	91	now–2030
2002 Eitelsbacher Karthäuserhofberg Riesling Auslese [cask] #54	89	now–2025
2005 Eitelsbacher Karthäuserhofberg Riesling Auslese gold capsule [cask] #35	92	now–2035
2005 Eitelsbacher Karthäuserhofberg Riesling Auslese gold capsule [cask] #37	95	now–2045
2003 Eitelsbacher Karthäuserhofberg Riesling Auslese gold capsule [cask] #43	89	now–2025+?
2002 Eitelsbacher Karthäuserhofberg Riesling Auslese long gold capsule [cask] #52	89	now–2025+?
2005 Eitelsbacher Karthäuserhofberg Riesling Beerenauslese [cask] #32	94	2012–2045
2005 Eitelsbacher Karthäuserhofberg Riesling Trockenbeerenauslese [cask] #34	97	now–2045+?
2005 Eitelsbacher Karthäuserhofberg Riesling Trockenbeerenauslese [cask] #20	95	2012–2045+?
2002 Eitelsbacher Karthäuserhofberg Riesling Eiswein [cask] #48	90	2012–2030
2002 Eitelsbacher Karthäuserhofberg Riesling Eiswein [cask] #55	91	2012–2038

KELLER ★ ★ ★ ★ ★
FLÖRSHEIM-DALSHEIM/RHEINHESSEN $20.00–$900.00

Klaus and Hedwig Keller brought their domaine to prominence at a time when the Rhein-hessen "hinterlands" were widely scorned by Riesling aficionados. Over the past decade, son Klaus-Peter has brought the meticulous vineyard and cellar practices and overall ambition here to a fanatic level, all the while retaining his deceptively easygoing personality. The intensity and clarity of dry Keller Riesling from the Hubacker vineyard in Dalsheim and the Kirchspiel and Morstein in neighboring Westhofen are riveting. Even the generic bottlings are impressive. (And the mysteriously sourced "G-Max" dry Riesling has become Germany's foremost cult wine.) An array of powerful, concentrated—at times downright gaudy—nobly sweet wine, and tiny volumes of ambitious Pinot Noir that benefit from Keller's intense study of Burgundy complete the portfolio.

2003 Riesling "G-Max"	90	now–2012+?
2002 Riesling "G-Max"	95	now–2015+?
2002 Dalsheimer Hubacker Riesling Spätlese	89	now–2018
2002 Dalsheimer Hubacker Riesling Spätlese gold capsule	91	now–2020
2002 Dalsheimer Hubacker Riesling Auslese A.P. #23	90	2012–2025
2002 Dalsheimer Hubacker Riesling Auslese A.P. #42	93	2015–2030
2002 Dalsheimer Hubacker Riesling Auslese***	92	2015–2030
2002 Riesling Trockenbeerenauslese	95	2015–2040

2003 Beerenauslese "Pius" [blend]	89	now–2014
2002 Monsheimer Silberberg Rieslaner		
Trockenbeerenauslese	93	now–2020
2002 Scheurebe Trockenbeerenauslese	94	now–2020

HERIBERT KERPEN ★★★★
WEHLEN/MOSEL $20.00–$550.00

In the late 1980s (when only in his mid-20s) Martin Kerpen brought his family's estate to international attention. Over time he has refined his approach and is now routinely crafting outstanding wines in every genre from *trocken* to nobly sweet. Generally opulent and forward (though at times needing to shed some youthful sweetness) these Rieslings mature superbly. The great Wehlener Sonnenuhr is the foundation of Kerpen's line, but his Graachers and his tiny bit of Riesling from Bernkastel represent classic expressions of their sites.

2005 Wehlener Sonnenuhr Riesling Spätlese trocken	92	now–2012
2005 Graacher Domprobst Riesling Auslese trocken	87	now–2010
2004 Graacher Himmelreich Riesling feinherb	87	now–2015
2005 Graacher Domprobst Riesling Spätlese feinherb	90	now–2020
2005 Wehlener Sonnenuhr Riesling Kabinett	90	now–2020
2004 Wehlener Sonnenuhr Riesling Kabinett	87	now–2018
2001 Wehlener Sonnenuhr Riesling Kabinett	90	now
2004 Bernkasteler Bratenhöfchen Riesling Spätlese	90	now–2022
2001 Bernkasteler Bratenhöfchen Riesling Spätlese	90	now–2018
2005 Graacher Himmelreich Riesling Spätlese	92	now–2025
2005 Wehlener Sonnenuhr Riesling Spätlese	92	now–2025
2004 Wehlener Sonnenuhr Riesling Spätlese	90	now–2022
2001 Wehlener Sonnenuhr Riesling Spätlese	88	now–2014
2005 Wehlener Sonnenuhr Riesling Spätlese*	91	2010–2028
2004 Wehlener Sonnenuhr Riesling Spätlese*	90	now–2025
2001 Wehlener Sonnenuhr Riesling Spätlese*	93	now–2020
2005 Wehlener Sonnenuhr Riesling Auslese	91	now–2028
2004 Wehlener Sonnenuhr Riesling Auslese	92	now–2028
2003 Wehlener Sonnenuhr Riesling Auslese	87	now–2018+?
2001 Wehlener Sonnenuhr Riesling Auslese	92	now–2024
2005 Wehlener Sonnenuhr Riesling Auslese*	90	now–2025
2001 Wehlener Sonnenuhr Riesling Auslese*	89	now–2018
2005 Graacher Domprobst Riesling Auslese*	89	now–2025
2005 Wehlener Sonnenuhr Riesling Auslese**	93	now–2030
2003 Wehlener Sonnenuhr Riesling Auslese**	88	now–2020+?
2005 Wehlener Sonnenuhr Riesling Auslese***	94	now–2035
2005 Wehlener Sonnenuhr Riesling Beerenauslese*	91	now–2032
2005 Graacher Domprobst Riesling Beerenauslese*	94	now–2035
2005 Wehlener Sonnenuhr Riesling		
Trockenbeerenauslese	95	2012–2040
2004 Bernkasteler Bratenhöfchen Riesling Eiswein	88	2010–2025+?

AUGUST KESSELER ★★★★
ASSMANNSHAUSEN/RHEINGAU $16.00–$700.00

Not many years ago, August Kesseler was vinifying almost entirely dry Riesling that was seldom seen outside Germany. He was better known abroad for his reputation with Pinot Noir, and as the longtime winemaker for Schloss Reinhartshausen. Nowadays, he is reveling in residual sweetness and is also aggressively marketing wines of incredible value based on fruit he purchases from growers in Lorch. Kesseler and his longtime cellarmaster and vineyard manager Max Himstedt set the bar for German Pinot Noir, and their Riesling in all styles—including Erstes Gewächs (essayed only in top vintages) and nobly sweet (generally sold in tiny lots at auction)—are among the Rheingau's most concentrated and refined.

2004 Riesling R	90	now
2004 Silvaner–Riesling trocken	89	now
2004 Riesling Kabinett trocken	87	now
2004 Riesling Spätlese "530.3"	91	now–2018
2004 Rüdesheimer Berg Schlossberg Riesling Erstes Gewächs	89	now–2016+?
2004 Lorcher Schlossberg Riesling Kabinett	90	now–2015
2003 Lorcher Schlossberg Riesling Kabinett	88	now–2010
2004 Rüdesheimer Berg Roseneck Riesling Spätlese	92	now–2022
2004 Rüdesheimer Bischofsberg Riesling Spätlese gold capsule	90	now–2020+?
2003 Rüdesheimer Berg Schlossberg Riesling Spätlese gold capsule	89	now–2017
2004 Rüdesheimer Berg Roseneck Riesling Auslese	89	now–2022
2003 Rüdesheimer Bischofsberg Riesling Auslese gold capsule	89	now–2020
2003 Rüdesheimer Berg Roseneck Riesling Beerenauslese gold capsule	92	now–2035
2003 Spätburgunder trocken	89	now–2012
2003 Spätburgunder trocken "Cuvée Max"	89	now–2014
2003 Assmannshäuser Höllenberg Spätburgunder trocken	92	now–2018+?
2003 Rüdesheimer Berg Schlossberg Spätburgunder trocken	92	now–2018+?

REICHSGRAF VON KESSELSTATT * * *
MORSCHEID/RUWER $20.00–$900.00

Over the past half-dozen years, director Annegret Reh-Gartner has pared down her estate's surface (although it still represents roughly 100 acres spread across top sites in the Middle Mosel, Saar, and Ruwer) and has ramped up quality to the point that there is always a lot worth tasting and cellaring amid the huge line-up at this address. Arguably, many of the dry Grosses Gewächs bottlings (prior to 2005 labeled as "three-star Spätlese *trocken*") would benefit from a bit more residual sugar and correspondingly less alcohol, but Kesselstatt's share of the German market is much greater than that of most other top Mosel wineries, and for internal consumption the *trocken* imprimatur still carries great weight. The Kesselstatt *monopole* Josephshof is located in Graach.

2005 Kaseler Riesling trocken	87	now–2009
2005 Wiltinger Riesling trocken	89	now–2010
2004 Wiltinger Riesling trocken	88	now–2009
2005 Graacher Riesling trocken	88	now–2010
2004 Graacher Riesling trocken	87	now–2009
2005 Wehlener Sonnenuhr Riesling Grosses Gewächs	87	now–2010+?
2005 Kaseler Nies'chen Riesling Grosses Gewächs	88	now–2014
2005 Josephshöfer Riesling Grosses Gewächs	87	now–2014+?

2004 Piesporter Goldtröpfchen Riesling Spätlese*** trocken	87–89	now–2010+?
2005 Scharzhofberger Riesling Grosses Gewächs	89	now–2015+?
2004 Scharzhofberger Riesling Spätlese*** trocken	88–90	
2004 Wiltinger Gottesfuss Riesling Spätlese*** trocken	91	now–2012+?
2005 Wiltinger Gottesfuss Riesling Kabinett feinherb	87	now–2011
2004 Wiltinger Gottesfuss Riesling Kabinett feinherb	92	now–2014
2004 Scharzhofberger Riesling Kabinett feinherb	88	now–2012
2004 Kaseler Nies'chen Riesling Kabinett feinherb	90	now–2014
2005 Josephshöfer Riesling Kabinett feinherb	88	now–2012
2005 Scharzhofberger Riesling Kabinett	90	now–2013
2005 Josephshöfer Riesling Kabinett	88	now–2012
2004 Josephshöfer Riesling Kabinett	90	now–2013
2004 Wehlener Sonnenuhr Riesling Kabinett	88	now–2012
2004 Piesporter Goldtröpfchen Riesling Kabinett	90	now–2013
2005 Kaseler Nies'chen Riesling Spätlese	88	now–2015
2005 Graacher Domprobst Riesling Spätlese	87	2010–2015
2005 Brauneberger Juffer-Sonnenuhr Riesling Spätlese	90	now–2015
2005 Piesporter Goldtröpfchen Riesling Spätlese	91	now–2015+?
2004 Piesporter Goldtröpfchen Riesling Spätlese	90	now–2015
2004 Josephshöfer Riesling Spätlese	89	now–2015
2005 Scharzhofberger Riesling Spätlese	89	now–2015
2004 Scharzhofberger Riesling Spätlese	93	now–2015+?
2004 Scharzhofberger Riesling Auslese "Fuder #4" A.P. #46	92	now–2025
2004 Scharzhofberger Riesling Auslese gold capsule "Fuder #19" A.P. #47	89	now–2022+?
2005 Scharzhofberger Riesling Auslese long gold capsule "Fuder #10"	94	now–2025+?
2005 Josephshöfer Riesling Auslese long gold capsule "Fuder #3"	88	now–2022
2005 Scharzhofberger Riesling Beerenauslese	92	now–2030
2004 Scharzhofberger Riesling Eiswein	93	now–2028+?

REINHARD & BEATE KNEBEL ★ ★ ★ ★ ★
WINNINGEN/LOWER MOSEL $22.00–$500.00

Beate Knebel and cellarmaster Gernot Kollmann have continued to uphold the extraordinary standards that she and her late husband set for Riesling from Winningen's vertiginous slopes. Here you will find some of the richest yet most elegant and dynamic dry, as well as sweet, Mosel wines, frequently reaching a spectacular level of complexity and sensuality. One wants to believe that, with wines of this caliber joining the distinguished and better-known offerings of neighbor Heymann-Löwenstein, the terraces of the Lower Mosel will at last reclaim the international renown they enjoyed in the late 19th century.

2005 Riesling Trocken von den Terrassen	90	now–2012
2004 Riesling Trocken von den Terrassen	87	now–2009
2005 Winninger Röttgen Riesling Spätlese trocken	93	now–2018
2004 Winninger Röttgen Riesling Spätlese trocken	90	now–2015
2005 Winninger Uhlen Riesling Spätlese trocken	92	now–2018
2004 Winninger Uhlen Riesling Spätlese trocken	87	now–2012

2005 Winninger Hamm Riesling Kabinett feinherb	90	now–2018
2004 Winninger Hamm Riesling Kabinett feinherb	87	now–2014
2005 Winninger Hamm Riesling Spätlese feinherb	89	now–2018
2005 Winninger Brückstück Riesling Spätlese feinherb	89	now–2018
2005 Winninger Brückstück Riesling Spätlese feinherb Alte Reben	91	now–2025
2004 Winninger Brückstück Riesling Spätlese feinherb Alte Reben	89	now–2020
2004 Winninger Brückstück Riesling Spätlese feinherb A.P. #11	89	now–2020
2004 Winninger Röttgen Riesling	89	now–2014
2005 Winninger Röttgen Riesling Kabinett	90	now–2020
2005 Winninger Röttgen Riesling Spätlese	92	now–2025
2004 Winninger Röttgen Riesling Spätlese A.P. #5	91	now–2022
2005 Winninger Röttgen Riesling Spätlese Alte Reben	95	now–2030
2004 Winninger Röttgen Riesling Spätlese Alte Reben A.P. #11	92	now–2022
2005 Winninger Röttgen Riesling Auslese	92	now–2030
2005 Winninger Uhlen Riesling Auslese A.P. #6	93	now–2030
2005 Winninger Uhlen Riesling Auslese A.P. #7	97	now–2035
2004 Winninger Röttgen Riesling Auslese	94	now–2030+?
2005 Winninger Röttgen Riesling Beerenauslese A.P. #8	95	now–2035+?
2005 Winninger Uhlen Riesling Beerenauslese	94	now–2035+?
2004 Winninger Röttgen Riesling Beerenauslese	98	now–2040+?
2004 Winninger Röttgen Riesling Eiswein	94	now–2030+?

KOEHLER-RUPPRECHT ★ ★ ★ ★ ★
KALLSTADT/PFALZ $25.00–$350.00

For more than a quarter century, Bernd Philippi has vinified to the beat of his own heart. On the one hand, it led him to preserve a tradition of dry Riesling with extended cask maturation, and on the other to experiments with a wide range of non-Riesling grapes in new *barriques*. There is no dry Riesling in Germany more complex and ageworthy than the Kallstadter Saumagen bottlings of Koehler-Rupprecht, the best of which are labeled "R" for reserve and released only after several years in bottle. Their off-dry cousins are often also remarkable. As for the experiments, those are an acquired taste but have always helped to sustain the reputation of this estate. (Philippi is also involved in projects in Portugal and South Africa.) Koehler-Rupprecht is about to be sold: The future not just of its superb Riesling but of an entire Riesling style may hang in the balance.

2004 Kallstadter Steinacker Weissburgunder [Pinot Blanc] Kabinett trocken	89	now
2004 Kallstadter Saumagen Riesling Spätlese halbtrocken	91	now–2020
2004 Kallstadter Saumagen Riesling Spätlese	89	now–2020
2004 Kallstadter Saumagen Riesling Auslese	90	now–2025

KRÜGER-RUMPF ★ ★ ★
LIESER/MOSEL $18.00–$500.00

Stefan Rumpf's sprawling collection features nearly every combination and permutation of Prädikat, site, and style, and a range of grape varieties. In recent years, the hits are steadily outpacing the misses; the best Riesling from this address offer clear and distinctive expressions of their Lower Nahe (and, in one instance, Rheinhessen) sites.

2004 Binger Schalachberg Riesling Spätlese trocken	87	now–2010
2004 Münsterer Pittersberg Riesling Grosses Gewächs	87	now–2010+?
2004 Münsterer Dautenpflänzer Riesling Kabinett halbtrocken	87	now–2011
2004 Münsterer Rheinberg Riesling Kabinett	87	now–2012
2001 Münsterer Pittersberg Riesling Kabinett	89	now
2004 Binger Schalachberg Riesling Spätlese	87	now–2013+?
2002 Münsterer Pittersberg Riesling Spätlese	89	now–2020
2004 Münsterer Dautenpflänzer Riesling Spätlese	88	now–2015
2002 Münsterer Dautenpflänzer Riesling Spätlese	91	now–2018
2001 Münsterer Dautenpflänzer Riesling Spätlese	91	now–2014
2004 Münsterer Pittersberg Riesling Auslese	90	now–2022
2003 Münsterer Pittersberg Riesling Auslese	91	now–2025
2004 Münsterer Dautenpflänzer Riesling Auslese A.P. #30	88	now–2018
2001 Münsterer Pittersberg Riesling Eiswein	96	2015–2030
2004 Scheurebe Spätlese	88	now–2011

PETER JAKOB KÜHN ★ ★ ★ ★
OESTRICH/RHEINGAU $25.00–$300.00

Peter Jakob Kühn is one of numerous German vintners who shot from obscurity to fame in the course of the 1990s. In the early years of the new century, he set himself new challenges in the vineyards and cellar, akin to working without a net. Biodynamic viticulture, spontaneous fermentation, long lees contact, and late bottling are among the practices that have led some longtime supporters to criticize Kühn's results as unpredictable. In reality, it is the strikingly distinctive personality of each of Kühn's different but consistently excellent Riesling that surprises and delights.

KÜNSTLER ★ ★ ★
HOCHHEIM/RHEINGAU $25.00–$300.00

In recent years, the weather, his personnel, and the sheer amplitude of his acreage, after purchasing a huge neighboring domaine, have placed obstacles in Gunther Künstler's path. A spacious new cellar and changes in personnel—provided nature cooperates—should pave the way for a return to the outstanding quality, especially in dry wines, that characterized this estate throughout the 1990s. Künstler is also devoted to the cultivation of Pinot Noir; in Hochheim's relatively warm, chalky soils he has achieved some formidable results.

2004 Chardonnay trocken	88	now
2004 Hochheimer Domdechaney Riesling Erstes Gewächs	90	now–2018+?
2004 Hochheimer Hölle Riesling Erstes Gewächs	87	now–2014+?
2003 Hochheimer Kirchenstück Riesling Spätlese	88	now–2013+?
2002 Hochheimer Kirchenstück Riesling Spätlese	89	now–2019
2004 Hochheimer Hölle Riesling Auslese trocken	89	now–2016+?

2003 Hochheimer Reichestal Spätburgunder trocken	89	now–2012
2003 Hochheimer Reichestal Spätburgunder trocken R	90	now–2014
2002 Hochheimer Hölle Riesling Eiswein	93	2010–2040
2001 Hochheimer Hölle Riesling Eiswein	94	2014–2030
2001 Hochheimer Kirchenstück Riesling Eiswein	95	2014–2030

PETER LAUER ✳ ✳ ✳
AYL/SAAR $25.00–$75.00

Peter Lauer was one of, if not the last, vintner on the Saar to perpetuate the practice of spontaneous fermentation and late bottling of each single cask of Riesling, most of which finished dry-tasting, if not technically *trocken*. Son Florian perpetuates numbered identifications of "cask" on each label, but nowadays blends between barrels to manage the size of the family portfolio. These Riesling from the Ayler Kupp and Saarfeilser vineyards are still among the most versatile and distinctive on the Saar, and happily they returned to U.S. markets in late 2007.

JOSEF LEITZ ✳ ✳ ✳ ✳
RÜDESHEIM/RHEINGAU $20.00–$900.00

Due to his father's death, Johannes Leitz became a vintner while still finishing high school. With imagination, tenacity, and self-tutelage, he built one of the Rheingau's strongest estates and has not stopped expanding or experimenting. The range of both full-bodied dry and nobly sweet Riesling on offer here is dramatically diverse. Leitz's Riesling from ostensibly lesser Rüdesheim sites—which form the bulk of his production and are sold almost entirely in the United States—revel in the vivacious acidity and high residual sugar familiar from the Mosel, and offer amazing value. It's safe to say that if Leitz has not already joined the very highest echelon of German growers, he soon will.

2004 Rüdesheimer Bischofsberg Riesling Spätlese trocken	88	now–2012
2004 Rüdesheimer Berg Schlossberg Riesling Spätlese trocken A.P. #20	90	now–2014
2004 Rüdesheimer Berg Schlossberg Riesling Spätlese trocken Alte Reben A.P. #19	93	now–2017+?
2001 Rüdesheimer Berg Schlossberg Riesling Spätlese trocken	89	now–2012
2004 Rüdesheimer Berg Rottland Riesling Spätlese trocken A.P. #18	89	now–2014
2004 Rüdesheimer Berg Rottland Riesling Spätlese trocken Alte Reben A.P. #30	90	2012–2016+?
2001 Rüdesheimer Berg Rottland Riesling Spätlese trocken	90	now–2011
2004 Rüdesheimer Berg Kaisersteinfels Riesling Spätlese	92	now–2020+?
2004 Riesling "Dragonstone" [Rüdesheimer Drachenstein]	89	now–2011
2001 Rüdesheimer Kosterlay Riesling	91	now–2010
2004 Rüdesheimer Kosterlay Riesling Kabinett	90	now–2013
2001 Rüdesheimer Magdalenenkreuz Riesling Kabinett	91	now–2012
2004 Rüdesheimer Magdalenenkreuz Riesling Spätlese	90	now–2015
2003 Rüdesheimer Magdalenenkreuz Riesling Spätlese	89	now–2014
2002 Rüdesheimer Magdalenenkreuz Riesling Spätlese	89	now–2012

2002 Rüdesheimer Berg Roseneck Riesling Spätlese	92	now–2015
2001 Rüdesheimer Berg Roseneck Riesling Spätlese	92	now–2012
2004 Rüdesheimer Berg Schlossberg Riesling Spätlese	90	now–2020
2003 Rüdesheimer Berg Schlossberg Riesling Spätlese	91	now–2018
2002 Rüdesheimer Berg Schlossberg Riesling Spätlese	94	now–2025
2001 Rüdesheimer Berg Schlossberg Riesling Spätlese	93	now–2020
2002 Rüdesheimer Berg Rottland Riesling Auslese	92	2010–2025
2002 Rüdesheimer Kirchenpfad Riesling Beerenauslese	89	2010–2030
2001 Rüdesheimer Drachenstein Riesling Beerenauslese	93	2012–2030
2004 Rüdesheimer Berg Schlossberg Riesling Trockenbeerenauslese	93	now–2030+?
2001 Rüdesheimer Berg Roseneck Riesling Trockenbeerenauslese	97	2014–2040
2001 Rüdesheimer Drachenstein Riesling Eiswein	98	2014–2040

SCHLOSS LIESER ★ ★ ★ ★
LIESER/MOSEL $18.00–$500.00

Thomas Haag, older son of celebrated Brauneberg vintner Wilhelm Haag, acquired the neglected property of Schloss Lieser in 1992 and has already brought it to the threshold of Germany's Riesling elite, in the process gaining recognition for the unjustly forgotten Niederberg Helden vineyard itself. Since the recent acquisition of choice parcels in Brauneberg, one can compare the Schloss Lieser style with that of Thomas Haag's father and brother. One will find that these wines—very much products of a risk-taking mentality in vineyards and cellar—have an opulence all their own, but demand patience, for youthful fermentative and yeasty overtones and unabashed sweetness sometimes mask their outstanding potential. As a "Mosel Riesling 101," incidentally, it is hard to beat Schloss Lieser's consistently fine basic estate Riesling.

2005 Riesling	90	now–2012
2005 Riesling Kabinett	87	now–2014
2005 Brauneberger Juffer Riesling Kabinett	90	now–2016
2004 Brauneberger Juffer Riesling Kabinett	89	now–2014
2005 Lieser Niederberg Helden Riesling Spätlese	89	2009–2020
2004 Lieser Niederberg Helden Riesling Spätlese A.P. #5	90	2009–2020
2004 Lieser Niederberg Helden Riesling Spätlese A.P. #6	93	2009–2022
2005 Brauneberger Juffer-Sonnenuhr Riesling Spätlese	89	2010–2020+?
2004 Lieser Niederberg Helden Riesling Auslese A.P. #7	91	now–2028
2004 Lieser Niederberg Helden Riesling Auslese A.P. #9	93	now–2030
2001 Lieser Niederberg Helden Riesling Auslese	87	now–2010+?
2004 Brauneberger Juffer-Sonnenuhr Riesling Auslese A.P. #12	92	now–2030
2005 Lieser Niederberg Helden Riesling Auslese gold capsule A.P. #7	89	2012–2022+?
2004 Lieser Niederberg Helden Riesling Auslese** gold capsule A.P. #8	94	now–2030

2001 Lieser Niederberg Helden Riesling Auslese**		
[gold capsule]	90	now–2020
2005 Brauneberger Juffer-Sonnenuhr Riesling Auslese		
gold capsule A.P. #9	93	now–2030+?
2004 Brauneberger Juffer-Sonnenuhr Riesling Auslese		
gold capsule A.P. #14	88	2009–2025
2005 Lieser Niederberg Helden Riesling Auslese long		
gold capsule A.P. #8	91	now–2030
2005 Brauneberger Juffer-Sonnenuhr Riesling Auslese		
long gold capsule A.P. #10	93	now–2030+?
2005 Brauneberger Juffer-Sonnenuhr Riesling Auslese		
long gold capsule A.P. #11	95	now–2035+?
2005 Lieser Niederberg Helden Riesling Beerenauslese	96	now–2040
2001 Lieser Niederberg Helden Riesling Beerenauslese	93	now–2030+?

CARL LOEWEN ★ ★ ★ ★
LEIWEN/MOSEL $20.00–$200.00

Iconoclastic experimentalist Carl-Josef Loewen's work in reclaiming old vines and unjustly neglected vineyards along his stretch of the Middle Mosel is of invaluable importance, but would matter less if his finished wines were not so fascinating and delicious. One need no longer consult old maps to imagine what constituted the greatness of Thörnicher Ritsch or Detzemer Maximiner-Herrenberg (and other sites); one can taste for oneself. Loewen is successful in a range of styles with all of his sites, including the great Leiwener Laurentiuslay. He is determined (aided by the location of his Klostergarten) to make Eiswein every year, even, as was the case in 2005, when virtually no other grower managed to do this.

2005 Leiwener Klostergarten Riesling Kabinett feinherb	90	now–2012
2005 Riesling Quant	87	now–2009
2004 Riesling Quant	88	now–2009
2005 Riesling Varidor	90	now–2012
2004 Detzemer Maximinier Klosterlay Riesling		
"Christopher's Wine"	88	now–2010
2005 Leiwener Laurentiuslay Riesling Alte Reben	89	now–2015
2005 Leiwener Klostergarten Riesling Kabinett	88	now–2009
2005 Leiwener Laurentiuslay Riesling Spätlese	89	now–2018
2004 Leiwener Laurentiuslay Riesling Spätlese	90	now–2018
2003 Leiwener Laurentiuslay Riesling Spätlese	89	now–2014
2001 Leiwener Laurentiuslay Riesling Spätlese	88	now–2012
2004 Thörnicher Ritsch Riesling Spätlese	89	now–2015+?
2003 Thörnicher Ritsch Riesling Spätlese	88	now–2014
2001 Thörnicher Ritsch Riesling Spätlese	90	now–2014
2005 Thörnicher Ritsch Riesling Auslese	93	now–2025
2004 Thörnicher Ritsch Riesling Auslese	87	now–2020
2003 Thörnicher Ritsch Riesling Auslese	90	now–2020
2005 Leiwener Laurentiuslay Riesling Auslese		
A.P. #14	88	now–2020
2005 Leiwener Laurentiuslay Riesling Auslese		
Fass #19, A.P. #15	88	now–2022
2004 Leiwener Laurentiuslay Riesling Auslese	92	now–2025
2002 Leiwener Laurentiuslay Riesling Auslese	90	2010–2020
2001 Leiwener Laurentiuslay Riesling Auslese	88	2010–2012+?

2005 Thörnicher Ritsch Riesling Beerenauslese	92	now–2025
2005 Leiwener Klostergarten Riesling Eiswein	91	now–2018+?
2004 Leiwener Klostergarten Riesling Eiswein	88	now–2015+?
2001 Leiwener Klostergarten Riesling Eiswein	92	now–2019

DR. LOOSEN ✦ ✦ ✦ ✦ ✦
BERNKASTEL/MOSEL $15.00–$900.00

When Ernst Loosen, enlisting the help of his pal Bernhard Schug, took over the reins of Dr. Loosen, he had the requisite "Dr." before his name, but neither of them had experience in winemaking. Together, they restored this estate with its exceptional collection of old, ungrafted vines in prime locations to its former glory, remaking it into one of Germany's model estates. Loosen and Schug continue to demonstrate that, for all their wines' celebrity, there are always new heights to scale. The style of their Prälat Riesling, for example, has become more refined and refreshing in recent years, while losing none of its opulence and intensity. Here is an outstanding address for learning to recognize the profound gustatory differences between one great Mosel site and another—in a word, *terroir*. You can also enjoy Kabinett wines scarcely less complex than their nobly sweet counterparts selling for twice as much. (The consistently delicious Riesling "Dr. L." is Loosen's international calling card, rendered from purchased grapes.)

2005 Riesling "Blau Schiefer"	87	now
2005 Bernkasteler Lay Riesling trocken	90	now–2012
2005 Erdener Treppchen Riesling trocken	89	now–2012
2004 Erdener Treppchen Riesling trocken	89	now–2011
2005 Ürziger Würzgarten Riesling trocken Alte Reben	91	now–2015
2004 Ürziger Würzgarten Riesling trocken Alte Reben	88	now–2012
2005 Graacher Himmelreich Riesling Kabinett feinherb	87	now–2014
2004 Graacher Himmelreich Riesling Kabinett feinherb	88	now–2014
2005 Riesling "Dr. L."	89	now
2005 Bernkasteler Lay Riesling Kabinett	92	now–2020
2004 Bernkasteler Lay Riesling Kabinett	90	now–2016
2005 Wehlener Sonnenuhr Riesling Kabinett	92	now–2020
2005 Erdener Treppchen Riesling Kabinett	90	now–2020
2004 Erdener Treppchen Riesling Kabinett	91	now–2018
2001 Erdener Treppchen Riesling Kabinett	89	now
2005 Ürziger Würzgarten Riesling Kabinett	91	now–2020
2005 Wehlener Sonnenuhr Riesling Spätlese	88	now–2022
2004 Wehlener Sonnenuhr Riesling Spätlese	90	now–2022
2005 Erdener Treppchen Riesling Spätlese	92	now–2025+?
2004 Erdener Treppchen Riesling Spätlese	87	now–2016
2005 Ürziger Würzgarten Riesling Spätlese	89	now–2022
2004 Ürziger Würzgarten Riesling Spätlese A.P. #14	89	now–2022
2001 Ürziger Würzgarten Riesling Spätlese	90	now–2018
2005 Ürziger Würzgarten Riesling Spätlese gold capsule	94	now–2030
2004 Ürziger Würzgarten Riesling Spätlese gold capsule A.P. #31	94	now–2030
2004 Graacher Himmelreich Riesling Auslese	88	now–2025
2004 Bernkasteler Lay Riesling Auslese	92	now–2032
2005 Wehlener Sonnenuhr Riesling Auslese	93	2012–2035
2004 Wehlener Sonnenuhr Riesling Auslese	89	now–2025

2001 Wehlener Sonnenuhr Riesling Auslese	92	now–2025
2005 Erdener Treppchen Riesling Auslese	91	now–2030
2004 Erdener Treppchen Riesling Auslese	87	now–2018+?
2005 Ürziger Würzgarten Riesling Auslese	91	now–2030
2004 Ürziger Würzgarten Riesling Auslese	91	now–2030
2005 Erdener Prälat Riesling Auslese	92	2012–2035
2004 Erdener Prälat Riesling Auslese	93	now–2030
2002 Erdener Prälat Riesling Auslese	90	2009–2025
2005 Wehlener Sonnenuhr Riesling Auslese gold capsule	95	now–2035
2005 Ürziger Würzgarten Riesling Auslese gold capsule	93	now–2035
2004 Ürziger Würzgarten Riesling Auslese gold capsule	92	now–2035
2005 Erdener Prälat Riesling Auslese gold capsule	94	now–2035
2004 Erdener Prälat Riesling Auslese gold capsule	95	now–2035
2001 Erdener Prälat Riesling Auslese gold capsule	94	now–2030
2005 Erdener Prälat Riesling Auslese long gold capsule	97	now–2035+?
2005 Ürziger Würzgarten Riesling Beerenauslese	94	2015–2030+?
2004 Erdener Treppchen Riesling Beerenauslese	94	now–2035+?
2004 Wehlener Sonnenuhr Riesling Beerenauslese	91	now–2025
2005 Bernkasteler Lay Riesling Trockenbeerenauslese	92	now–2035+?
2005 Erdener Prälat Riesling Trockenbeerenauslese	95	2015–2040+?
2005 Wehlener Sonnenuhr Riesling Trockenbeerenauslese	94	now–2035+?
2005 Ürziger Würzgarten Riesling Trockenbeerenauslese	97	2015–2040+?
2004 Wehlener Sonnenuhr Riesling Eiswein	90	now–2022+?

LUBENTIUSHOF—ANDREAS BARTH ✳✳✳
NIEDERFELL/LOWER MOSEL $25.00–$300.00

On a large loop of the Lower Mosel upstream from the vineyards of Winningen lies the obscure, 9-acre Gondorfer Gäns with its ancient, ungrafted vines. Long a *monopole,* the site was acquired in 1994 by Andreas Barth, who is also cellarmaster at the von Othegraven estate on the Saar. The first Lubentiushof Riesling are slated to arrive in U.S. markets by 2008.

2005 Gondorfer Gäns Riesling Spätlese	88–90	now–2020
2005 Gondorfer Gäns Riesling Trockenbeerenauslese	92–95	now–2035+?

GEBRÜDER MERKELBACH ✳✳✳
ÜRZIG/MOSEL $20.00–$60.00

The bachelor Merkelbach brothers, now well past normal retirement age, were virtually unknown in Germany until Terry Theise began importing their wines into the U.S. in the mid-1980s. At their best (particularly in botrytis-free vintages) these are clear, beautifully balanced renditions of their respective sites, picked by block (not selectively). And—like their growers—these Rieslings are utterly without artifice or pretension. With rare exceptions, each cask of wine is bottled separately, so unambiguous identification requires reference to its registration number.

2004 Kinheimer Rosenberg Riesling Spätlese	89	now–2020
2002 Kinheimer Rosenberg Riesling Spätlese A.P. #5	89	now–2023

2001 Kinheimer Rosenberg Riesling Spätlese A.P. #7	92	now–2017
2005 Ürziger Würzgarten Riesling Spätlese A.P. #3	87	now–2020
2005 Ürziger Würzgarten Riesling Spätlese A.P. #4	87	now–2020
2004 Ürziger Würzgarten Riesling Spätlese A.P. #19	89	now–2022
2002 Ürziger Würzgarten Riesling Spätlese A.P. #6	89	now–2020
2001 Ürziger Würzgarten Riesling Spätlese A.P. #5	92	now–2017
2001 Ürziger Würzgarten Riesling Spätlese A.P. #12	93	now–2017
2001 Erdener Treppchen Auslese A.P. #10	88	now–2015
2005 Ürziger Würzgarten Riesling Auslese A.P. #14	89	now–2025
2004 Ürziger Würzgarten Riesling Auslese A.P. #18	90	now–2025
2004 Ürziger Würzgarten Riesling Auslese A.P. #15	87	now–2020+?
2003 Ürziger Würzgarten Riesling Auslese A.P. #17	88	now–2014+?
2003 Ürziger Würzgarten Riesling Auslese A.P. #18	87	now–2012+?
2002 Ürziger Würzgarten Riesling Auslese A.P. #19	89	now–2018
2001 Ürziger Würzgarten Riesling Auslese A.P. #20	92	now–2018
2001 Ürziger Würzgarten Riesling Auslese A.P. #15	93	now–2020
2001 Ürziger Würzgarten Riesling Auslese A.P. #16	94	now–2020

HERBERT MESSMER ★★★
BURRWEILER/PFALZ—SÜDLICHE WEINSTRASSE $18.00–$250.00

Gregor Messmer has built on his father's already good work to establish this as one of the foremost estates in the southern Pflaz. In addition to Riesling, the Scheurebe, Muskateller, Gewürztraminer, Pinot Noir, St. Laurent, and sparkling wine at this address are all worthy of wine lovers' attention. The quality of several very recent vintages has been particularly impressive.

2003 Burrweiler Schlossgarten Riesling Kabinett halbtrocken	89	now
2002 Burrweiler Schlossgarten Riesling Kabinett halbtrocken	89	now
2004 Burrweiler Schäwer Riesling Spätlese	92	now–2020
2004 Burrweiler Schäwer Riesling Spätlese trocken	87	now–2012
2004 Weyrerer Michelsberg Riesling Grosses Gewächs	87	now–2011+?
2002 Burrweiler Altenforst Riesling Auslese gold capsule	92	now–2020
2004 Muskateller Kabinett	87	now
2003 Rieslaner Beerenauslese	92	now–2035

THEO MINGES ★★★
FLEMLINGEN/PFALZ—SÜDLICHE WEINSTRASSE $16.00–$100.00

The wines of visionary, experimental-minded Theo Minges have proven consistently recommendable, and often represent outstanding value. Not among the first wave of growers who established the reputation of the southern Pfalz in the 1990s, Minges has recently demonstrated the potential of the Gleisweiler Hölle vineyard for top-class Riesling, thankfully earning him increased attention. His 2006s look to represent a qualitative leap.

2001 Gleisweiler Hölle Riesling Kabinett trocken	89	now
2004 Gleisweiler Hölle Riesling Spätlese trocken A.P. #15	87	now–2011
2004 Gleisweiler Hölle Riesling Spätlese trocken Bundsandstein A.P. #16	87	now–2012
2003 Gleisweiler Hölle Riesling Kabinett	88	now–2009

2002 Gleisweiler Hölle Riesling Kabinett	89	now–2011
2001 Gleisweiler Hölle Riesling Kabinett	88	now–2010
2004 Gleisweiler Hölle Riesling Spätlese	89	now–2016
2003 Gleisweiler Hölle Riesling Spätlese	87	now–2010
2002 Gleisweiler Hölle Riesling Spätlese	90	now–2015
2001 Gleisweiler Hölle Riesling Spätlese	90	now–2012
2002 Gleisweiler Hölle Riesling Auslese	90	now–2018
2001 Gleisweiler Hölle Riesling Auslese	92	now–2019
2003 Gleisweiler Hölle Riesling Auslese gold capsule	91	now–2024
2003 Gleisweiler Hölle Scheurebe Spätlese	89	now–2009+?
2002 Gleisweiler Hölle Scheurebe Spätlese	90	now–2010+?

MARKUS MOLITOR ∗ ∗ ∗ ∗
WEHLEN/MOSEL $20.00–$600.00

Markus Molitor somehow juggles 89 acres across 20 sites, 10 communes, and 2 growing regions, all subdivided into heaven knows how many parcels, resulting in a price list that can run to 200 wines. Very ripe fruit, prefermentative skin contact, and spontaneous fermentation in cask are the norm. Resisting "the tyranny of the new," Molitor seldom bottles before a year in barrel, and generally offers his wines only after they have spent at least six or more months in bottle. The upshot is Riesling with relatively soft acids, leesy richness, and amplitude, yet formidably concentrated and undeniably striking. At times the nobly sweet wines (there are more Trockenbeerenauslesen here some years than a typical grower might render in a lifetime) seem to possess barely sufficient acidity to balance their sweetness and create tension, but Molitor insists that even a Spätlese must have high residual sugar to age gracefully for two or more decades. (Stars on Molitor's labels designate sugar levels in the grapes at harvest—always far in excess of the prescribed minima—completely independent of perceived sweetness.)

2005 Bernkasteler Badstube Riesling Spätlese trocken	88–90	now–2012
2004 Graacher Domprobst Riesling Spätlese trocken	89	now–2012
2005 Riesling Alte Reben	87–89	now–2011
2005 Erdener Treppchen Riesling Auslese∗∗∗	90–92	now–2018+?
2005 Bernkasteler Badstube Riesling Kabinett feinherb	90	now–2014+?
2005 Bernkasteler Badstube Riesling Spätlese feinherb	87–89	now–2016+?
2005 Graacher Himmelreich Riesling Spätlese feinherb	89–90	now–2018+?
2005 Graacher Himmelreich Riesling Auslese∗∗∗ feinherb	86–88	now–2018+?
2005 Erdener Treppchen Riesling Auslese∗∗ feinherb	86–88	now–2018
2005 Zeltinger Schlossberg Riesling Auslese∗∗∗ feinherb	89–91	now–2020
2004 Zeltinger Sonnenuhr Riesling Auslese feinherb A.P. #59	89	now–2020
2004 Zeltinger Sonnenuhr Riesling Auslese∗∗∗	90	now–2020+?
2005 Niedermenniger Herrenberg Riesling Auslese∗∗∗ feinherb	90–92	now–2022+?
2005 Graacher Domprobst Riesling Auslese∗∗∗ feinherb	89–91	now–2020+?
2005 Zeltinger Sonnenuhr Riesling Kabinett	90	now–2015
2004 Zeltinger Sonnenuhr Riesling Kabinett A.P. #69	87	now–2012
2004 Wehlener Sonnenuhr Riesling Kabinett A.P. #11	87	now–2012
2005 Zeltinger Sonnenuhr Riesling Spätlese A.P. #22	89	2010–2018+?
2005 Zeltinger Sonnenuhr Riesling Spätlese A.P. #23	90	now–2018+?
2004 Zeltinger Sonnenuhr Riesling Spätlese A.P. #29	88	now–2016+?
2004 Zeltinger Sonnenuhr Riesling Spätlese A.P. #22	89	now–2016+?

2005 Wehlener Sonnenuhr Riesling Spätlese	88	now–2018
2005 Wehlener Sonnenuhr Riesling Auslese	89	now–2025+?
2005 Zeltinger Deutschherrenberg Riesling Auslese**	90–92	now–2030+?
2005 Zeltinger Sonnenuhr Riesling Auslese**	?	2010–2020+?
2005 Zeltinger Sonnenuhr Riesling Auslese***	87–89	2010–2025+?
2005 Graacher Domprobst Riesling Beerenauslese	92–94	now–2030+?
2005 Zeltinger Himmelreich Riesling Beerenauslese	90–92	now–2030
2005 Wehlener Sonnenuhr Riesling Beerenauslese	87–89	2010–2025+?

MÖNCHHOF–ROBERT EYMAEL ∗ ∗ ∗
URZIG/MOSEL $20.00–$250.00

This may or may not be related to his collaboration with veteran vintner Hans-Leo Christoffel, but Robert Eymael's wines have been creeping steadily upward in quality in recent years, restoring the outstanding reputation that his family's estate enjoyed until the mid-1980s. Eymael by no means attempts to copy the style of the Joh. Jos. Christoffel Riesling that are also vinified in his cellars, but instead renders Mönchhof Riesling with outgoing richness and distinctive, if less refined, appeal. His "Mosel Slate" Spätlese represents a consistently excellent value.

2005 Ürziger Würzgarten Riesling Spätlese feinherb		
Fass #33	89	now–2012
2004 Ürziger Würzgarten Riesling Spätlese feinherb	87	now–2011
2004 Ürziger Würzgarten Riesling Kabinett	89	now–2015
2005 Erdener Treppchen Riesling Spätlese		
"Mosel Slate"	88	now–2012
2002 Erdener Treppchen Riesling Spätlese	89	now–2012
2005 Ürziger Würzgarten Riesling Spätlese	90	now–2018
2004 Ürziger Würzgarten Riesling Spätlese	90	now–2025
2002 Ürziger Würzgarten Riesling Spätlese	89	now–2014
2001 Ürziger Würzgarten Riesling Spätlese	90	now–2015
2005 Ürziger Würzgarten Riesling Auslese	89	now–2020
2004 Ürziger Würzgarten Riesling Auslese	92	now–2032+?
2002 Ürziger Würzgarten Riesling Auslese	89	now–2018
2005 Erdener Treppchen Riesling Auslese	88	now–2020
2004 Erdener Treppchen Riesling Auslese	87	now–2025
2002 Erdener Treppchen Riesling Auslese	89	now–2022
2004 Erdener Prälat Riesling Auslese	90	now–2030
2003 Erdener Prälat Riesling Auslese	90	now–2025
2002 Erdener Prälat Riesling Auslese	90	now–2024
2001 Erdener Prälat Riesling Auslese	92	now–2025

GEORG MOSBACHER ∗ ∗ ∗
FORST/PFALZ $25.00–$500.00

Richard Mosbacher, together with his daughter and son-in-law, Sabine and Jürgen Düringer, has for many years maintained organic viticulture in his vineyards and traditional cask maturation in his cellars, consistently rendering clear, dry Riesling expressions of several top Pfalz sites. On occasion there are striking nobly sweet libations as well.

EGON MÜLLER–SCHARZHOF/LE GALLAIS ∗ ∗ ∗ ∗ ∗
WILTINGEN/SAAR $25.00–$1,000.00+

Egon Müller and his late father (along with previous generations of Egon Müllers) have brought the potential of the great Scharzhofberg (of which they own the lion's share) and the art of selective harvest to a remarkable peak, rendering some of the world's longest-lived, richest, yet most elegant nobly sweet Rieslings. Müller vinifies the fruit of his *monopole* Braune Kupp under the Le Gallais estate label. The best of several bottlings at each Prädikat level and from every site are sold at Trier auctions. Müller bottles a basic "Scharzhof" estate Riesling that nowadays comes primarily from superbly situated vines in Saarburg.

2005 Scharzhofberger Riesling Kabinett A.P. #2	90	now–2018
2004 Scharzhofberger Riesling Kabinett A.P. #8	89	now–2016
2005 Wiltinger Braune Kupp Riesling Spätlese	93	now–2025
2004 Wiltinger Braune Kupp Riesling Spätlese A.P. #19	92	now–2026
2005 Scharzhofberger Riesling Spätlese A.P. #4	91	now–2022
2005 Scharzhofberger Riesling Spätlese A.P. #5	95	now–2030
2004 Scharzhofberger Riesling Spätlese A.P. #15	90	now–2022
2005 Scharzhofberger Riesling Auslese A.P. #6	93	now–2025
2004 Scharzhofberger Riesling Auslese A.P. #14	93	now–2030
2005 Wiltinger Braune Kupp Riesling Auslese gold capsule	97	now–2040
2004 Wiltinger Braune Kupp Riesling Auslese gold capsule A.P. #21	96	now–2035
2005 Scharzhofberger Riesling Auslese gold capsule A.P. #8	92	now–2035
2004 Scharzhofberger Riesling Auslese gold capsule A.P. #22	95	now–2035
2005 Scharzhofberger Riesling Auslese long gold capsule A.P. #9	95	2010–2040+?
2005 Scharzhofberger Riesling Trockenbeerenauslese A.P. #11	98	now–2055+

MATHIAS MÜLLER ★★★
SPAY/MITTELRHEIN $25.00–$200.00

Mathias Müller is crafting luscious and highly site-typical Riesling from the various subsections of the Bopparder Hamm. This estate has of late been both expanding its acreage and enhancing its quality. Happily, too, its wines have begun appearing on the U.S. market.

MÜLLER-CATOIR ★★★★★
HAARDT/PFALZ $25.00–$500.00

Since the arrival here in 2002 (under highly stressful circumstances) of young Mosel-born Martin Franzen, there have been subtle stylistic shifts, but low yields, high selectivity, attention to the minutest details, and exceptional quality have remained constants. This is a tribute both to Franzen's discipline and determination, and to the legacy of longtime cellarmaster Hans-Günter Schwarz—"activism in the vines, minimalism in the cellar"—which has seeped indelibly into the fabric of not just this estate but of nearly every top winery in the Pfalz. Anyone who doubts the potential of Rieslaner or Scheurebe has only to taste samples that have long issued, and continue to issue, from this cellar. The same may be said about the Bürgergarten and other formerly obscure sites.

2004 Riesling Kabinett trocken	89	now–2012
2004 Haardter Bürgergaarten Riesling Kabinett trocken	89	now–2014
2003 Haardter Bürgergaarten Riesling Kabinett trocken	88	now
2003 Hambacher Römerbrunnen Riesling Spätlese trocken	88	now–2010
2004 Haardter Herrenletten Riesling Spätlese trocken	90	now–2016

2004 Haardter Bürgergaarten Riesling Spätlese trocken	88	now–2012
2001 Haardter Bürgergaarten Riesling Spätlese trocken	90	now–2012
2004 Haardter Bürgergaarten Riesling Spätlese trocken im Breumel	91	now–2018+?
2003 Haardter Bürgergaarten Riesling Spätlese trocken im Breumel	90	now–2010+?
2004 Haardter Bürgergaarten Riesling Spätlese trocken Aspen	92	now–2018+?
2003 Haardter Bürgergaarten Riesling Spätlese trocken Aspen	90	now–2010+?
2004 Haardter Bürgergaarten Riesling Spätlese trocken Gehren	90	now–2016+?
2003 Haardter Bürgergaarten Riesling Spätlese trocken Gehren	88	now–2009+?
2004 Haardter Bürgergaarten Riesling Kabinett halbtrocken	89	now–2009
2004 Mussbacher Eselshaut Riesling Kabinett	93	now–2016
2004 Gimmeldinger Mandelgarten Riesling Kabinett	92	now–2015
2003 Gimmeldinger Mandelgarten Riesling Kabinett	90	now–2011
2004 Haardter Bürgergaarten Riesling Spätlese	95	now–2025
2003 Haardter Bürgergaarten Riesling Spätlese	88	now–2016
2001 Haardter Bürgergaarten Riesling Spätlese A.P. #29 ["Lot 2134"]	94	now–2020
2004 Haardter Herrenletten Riesling Spätlese	90	now–2022
2003 Haardter Herrenletten Riesling Spätlese	93	now–2019
2004 Gimmeldinger Mandelgarten Riesling Spätlese	94	now–2025
2004 Mussbacher Eselshaut Riesling Auslese	96	now–2030
2004 Haardter Bürgergaarten Riesling Auslese	97	now–2030
2004 Haardter Bürgergaarten Riesling Eiswein	94	now–2030
2003 Haardter Bürgergaarten Riesling Eiswein	95	now–2025+?
2001 Haardter Bürgergaarten Muskateller Kabinett trocken	89	now
2003 Haardter Bürgergaarten Muskateller Spätlese trocken	90	now–2009
2004 Haardter Mandelring Scheurebe Spätlese	90	now–2015
2003 Haardter Mandelring Scheurebe Spätlese	93	now–2013
2001 Haardter Mandelring Scheurebe Spätlese	94	now–2016
2004 Gimmeldinger Schlössel Rieslaner Spätlese	90	now–2016
2004 Mussbacher Eselshaut Rieslaner Spätlese	91	now–2018
2004 Haardter Herzog Rieslaner Auslese	95	now–2025
2004 Gimmeldinger Schlössel Rieslaner Beerenauslese	98	now–2032
2004 Haardter Bürgergaarten Rieslaner Beerenauslese	99	now–2035
2003 Haardter Bürgergaarten Rieslaner Beerenauslese	92	now–2030
2004 Haardter Herzog Rieslaner Trockenbeerenauslese	95	now–2035+?

VILLA NIEDERBERGER ★★★
HAARDT/PFALZ $N/A

Having entered his self-described *Unruhestand* ("unretirement" or "restlessness"), Müller-Catoir estate manager Hans-Günter Schwarz is now fulfilling his dream of a tiny, immaculately, organically tended vineyard garden. It is that of his friend and multiple estate-owner Achim Niederberger, overlooking the city of Neustadt, a site historically known as the

"Monks' Garden." In these—the fastest-ripening vineyards in the Neustadt area, says Schwarz—he has planted a dozen varieties. The first results from his meticulously appointed mini-cellar adjacent to Niederberger's palatial villa are dramatically distinctive; one hopes some of this wine will trickle into the United States.

2004 Villa Niederberger Riesling trocken	93	now–2011+?
2004 Villa Niederberger Chardonnay trocken	88	2009+?
2004 Villa Niederberger cuvée Cabernet Sauvignon–Merlot–Lemberger	90–93	now–2012+?
2003 Villa Niederberger cuvée Cabernet Sauvignon–Merlot–Lemberger–Pinot Noir–St. Laurent	89	now–2010+?

VON OTHEGRAVEN * * *
KANZEM/SAAR $25.00–$500.00

Dr. Heidi Kegel has restored the reputation that von Othegraven wines enjoyed under her aunt's direction in the 1960s and 1970s. To the family's prime acreage in the great Kanzemer Altenberg, she has added property in Ockfen, and very recently in Wiltingen. With cellarmaster Andreas Barth (himself proprietor of the Lubentiushof on the Lower Mosel), Kegel has established a rather plush, rounded, and relatively soft style. There is a strong emphasis on dry-tasting wines, but the estate's Prädikat wines are unabashedly sweet.

2004 Riesling Maria O.	88	now
2004 Ockfener Bockstein Riesling Spätlese	87	now–2015
2005 Kanzemer Altenberg Riesling Spätlese	88	now–2018
2005 Kanzemer Altenberg Riesling Spätlese Alte Reben	88	now–2020
2005 Kanzemer Altenberg Riesling Auslese Alte Reben	91	now–2025+?
2004 Kanzemer Altenberg Riesling Spätlese A.P. #16	89	now–2020
2004 Kanzemer Altenberg Riesling Auslese A.P. #20	91	now–2025
2005 Wiltinger Kupp Riesling Beerenauslese	91	now–2028+?
2005 Ockfener Bockstein Riesling Trockenbeerenauslese	93	now–2035+?
2005 Kanzemer Altenberg Riesling Trockenbeerenauslese	92	now–2035+?
2004 Kanzemer Altenberg Riesling Eiswein	93	2012–2030

PFEFFINGEN—FUHRMANN EYMAEL * * * *
UNGSTEIN/PFALZ $22.00–$175.00

Throughout a long career, Karl Fuhrmann has produced some of the Pfalz's most consistently excellent Riesling, and his Scheurebe has always vied with that of Müller-Catoir for world champion. Now that Jan Eymael (whose mother, Doris, has long been Pfeffingen's business manager) is in charge, yet still fortunately enjoys his grandfather's wisdom and daily assistance in the vineyards, quality is reaching new heights. Prices remain exceptionally reasonable, even for extraordinary nobly sweet elixirs.

2004 Ungsteiner Herrenberg Riesling Grosses Gewächs	89	now–2012+?
2004 Riesling Kabinett halbtrocken Pfeffo	87	now–2009
2001 Ungsteiner Herrenberg Riesling Spätlese	87	now
2004 Ungsteiner Herrenberg Riesling Auslese	92	now–2025
2004 Ungsteiner Herrenberg Riesling Beerenauslese	94	now–2030
2004 Ungsteiner Herrenberg Scheurebe Spätlese	89	now–2011

2002 Ungsteiner Herrenberg Scheurebe Auslese		
gold capsule	89	now–2020
2001 Ungsteiner Herrenberg Scheurebe Auslese		
gold capsule	94	now–2025
2004 Ungsteiner Herrenberg Scheurebe Beerenauslese	90	now–2025
2002 Ungsteiner Herrenberg Scheurebe Beerenauslese	89	now–2020
2004 Ungsteiner Herrenberg Scheurebe		
Trockenbeerenauslese	94	now–2035

FRED PRINZ ★ ★ ★ ★
HALLGARTEN/RHEINGAU $18.00–$250.00

During his extended career with the Rheingau Staatsweingüter, Fred Prinz was only a part-time vintner, and he still works out of his home. Riesling from his 15 acres goes from strength to strength, reflecting the vinous precision and the wealth of floral and mineral nuances of which Hallgarten's sites are capable. Prinz has balanced his recent acquisitions of old vines in choice parcels with a certain number of more widely spaced younger vineyards that he can cultivate by tractor, enabling him to offer an attractive and inexpensive basic dry Riesling.

2004 Riesling Trocken Tradition	87	now–2009
2004 Hallgartener Jungfer Riesling Kabinett	88	now–2015
2004 Hallgartener Jungfer Riesling Spätlese A.P. #10	91	now–2020
2004 Hallgartener Jungfer Riesling Spätlese gold		
capsule A.P. #14	90	now–2020
2004 Hallgartener Jungfer Riesling Auslese	94	now–2025

JOH. JOS. PRÜM ★ ★ ★ ★ ★
WEHLEN/MOSEL $30.00–$1,000.00

Manfred Prüm has perpetuated and refined the style for which his grandfather made this estate famous in the years after World War I, and which has become an archetype for the Mosel: wines high in residual sugar, acidity, and carbon dioxide, feather-light, and bursting with flavor. He has also perpetuated the tradition of extraordinarily long-lived nobly sweet Riesling. Frankly, it is a shame to open even one of Prüm's exquisite (and, for all of this estate's celebrity, by no means unaffordable) Kabinetts before it has spent six or eight years in bottle. While somewhat less frequently encountered than his flagship Riesling from the Wehlener Sonnenuhr, Prüm's Riesling from the Graacher Himmelreich and Zeltinger Sonnenuhr are on the same exalted level.

2004 Riesling "Dr. M. Prüm" A.P. #4	87	now–2009
2004 Wehlener Sonnenuhr Riesling Kabinett A.P. #9	88	now–2022
2001 Wehlener Sonnenuhr Riesling Kabinett	92	now–2018
2002 Graacher Himmelreich Riesling Kabinett	89	now–2018
2005 Bernkasteler Badstube Riesling Spätlese	91–92	now–2030
2005 Graacher Himmelreich Riesling Spätlese	91–92	now–2030
2004 Graacher Himmelreich Riesling Spätlese A.P. #23	91	now–2028
2001 Graacher Himmelreich Riesling Spätlese	93	now–2025
2005 Wehlener Sonnenuhr Riesling Spätlese	92–93	now–2035
2005 Wehlener Sonnenuhr Riesling Spätlese		
A.P. #21 [auction]	94–95	now–2035
2004 Wehlener Sonnenuhr Riesling Spätlese A.P. #13	92	now–2032
2001 Wehlener Sonnenuhr Riesling Spätlese	94	now–2030
2005 Graacher Himmelreich Riesling Auslese	93–94	now–2035
2004 Graacher Himmelreich Riesling Auslese A.P. #14	92	now–2032

2005 Wehlener Sonnenuhr Riesling Auslese	92–94	now–2035
2005 Wehlener Sonnenuhr Riesling Auslese A.P. #22	94–95	now–2040
2004 Wehlener Sonnenuhr Riesling Auslese A.P. #12	93	now–2035
2002 Wehlener Sonnenuhr Riesling Auslese	89	now–2028
2005 Wehlener Sonnenuhr Riesling Auslese gold capsule A.P. #23	95–96	now–2045
2005 Wehlener Sonnenuhr Riesling Auslese long gold capsule A.P. #24	96–97	now–2045+
2004 Graacher Himmelreich Riesling Auslese long gold capsule	92–95	now–2040

RATZENBERGER ★★★★
STEEG-BACHARACH/MITTELRHEIN $15.00–$800.00

The Jochen Ratzenbergers, father and son, seldom fear letting the acidity of their Rieslings hang out; they craft wines that generally need a couple of years' bottle age to blossom. These are among the most dynamic and ageworthy Riesling in Germany, excelling at the ostensibly simplest level, heaven-storming and at times tooth-jarring in the realm of noble sweetness and Eiswein, for which this estate is renowned. Here is also the source of Germany's finest sparkling Riesling and some increasingly serious and successful Pinot Noir.

2004 Riesling "Kaspar R."	89	now–2015
2004 Bacharacher Riesling Kabinett trocken	87	now–2011
2004 Steeger St. Jost Riesling Spätlese trocken	88	now–2014
2004 Bacharacher Wolfshöhle Riesling Grosses Gewächs	90–92	now–2018+?
2004 Bacharacher Kloster Fürstental Riesling Eiswein	94	now–2035+?

ÖKONOMIERAT REBHOLZ ★★★
SIEBELDINGEN/PFALZ $25.00–$200.00

Ambitious and articulate Hansjörg Rebholz has been the principal mover and shaker among southern Pfalz vintners, virtually all of them protégés of Hans-Günter Schwarz. On top of his formidably concentrated, if at times youthfully severe, dry Riesling and his often explosively aromatic Muskateller and Gewürztraminer, he offers an ambitious range of Pinot Noirs and full-bodied Grosses Gewächs from Pinot Blanc. This is an estate held in extremely high esteem within Germany, whose styles of wine are conceivably underappreciated by some foreign critics, including this author.

2004 Siebeldinger im Sonnenschein Riesling Grosses Gewächs	87	2010–2014+?
2004 Birkweiler Kastanienbusch Riesling Grosses Gewächs	88	now–2016+?

MAX. FERD. RICHTER ★★★
MÜHLHEIM/MOSEL $20.00–$600.00

Among the several Mosel estates officially known by a name with abbreviations, Richter has been recognized for generations for its outstanding, far-flung vineyards (including those in little-recognized Mühlheim and Veldenz, perpendicular to the Mosel) and for its high percentage of exports. The estate is currently under the direction of Dirk Richter, who maintains a regimen of leisurely barrel maturation, characteristically resulting in wines that can make up in their generous personalities and long-term cellar potential for anything they might occasionally lack in youthful polish or refinement.

2005 Brauneberger Juffer-Sonnenuhr Riesling Kabinett trocken	87	now–2010
2005 Mühlheimer Sonnenlay Riesling Kabinett feinherb	87	now–2012
2005 Veldenzer Elisenberg Riesling Kabinett	87	now–2014
2005 Graacher Himmelreich Riesling Kabinett	89	now–2014
2004 Graacher Himmelreich Riesling Kabinett	88	now–2013
2001 Graacher Himmelreich Riesling Kabinett	90	now–2010
2005 Wehlener Sonnenuhr Riesling Kabinett	88	now–2016
2004 Wehlener Sonnenuhr Riesling Kabinett	87	now–2012
2001 Wehlener Sonnenuhr Riesling Kabinett	89	now
2004 Graacher Domprobst Riesling Kabinett	89	now–2014
2004 Mühlheimer Helenenkloster Riesling Kabinett	87	now–2012
2001 Brauneberger Juffer Kabinett	89	now–2009
2005 Veldenzer Elisenberg Riesling Spätlese	90	now–2020
2004 Veldenzer Elisenberg Riesling Spätlese	87	now–2018
2003 Veldenzer Elisenberg Riesling Spätlese	87	now–2012+?
2001 Veldenzer Elisenberg Riesling Spätlese	92	now–2016+?
2005 Graacher Himmelreich Riesling Spätlese	91	now–2025
2005 Brauneberger Juffer-Sonnenuhr Riesling Spätlese	91	now–2022
2004 Brauneberger Juffer-Sonnenuhr Riesling Spätlese	90	now–2020
2003 Brauneberger Juffer-Sonnenuhr Riesling Spätlese	88	now–2012+?
2001 Brauneberger Juffer-Sonnenuhr Riesling Spätlese	93	now–2018
2001 Brauneberger Juffer Riesling Spätlese	91	now–2015
2005 Wehlener Sonnenuhr Riesling Spätlese	91	now–2020
2001 Wehlener Sonnenuhr Riesling Spätlese	90	now–2016
2004 Mühlheimer Helenenkloster Riesling Spätlese	89	now–2016
2001 Mühlheimer Helenenkloster Riesling Spätlese	90	now–2014
2005 Brauneberger Juffer Riesling Auslese	89	2010–2030
2005 Graacher Himmelreich Riesling Auslese	90	now–2030
2005 Veldenzer Elisenberg Riesling Auslese "Fass #77"	92	2010–2030+?
2003 Veldenzer Elisenberg Riesling Auslese "Fass #60"	89	now–2012+?
2001 Veldenzer Elisenberg Riesling Auslese	95	now–2025+?
2005 Brauneberger Juffer-Sonnenuhr Riesling Auslese	90	2010–2030
2004 Brauneberger Juffer-Sonnenuhr Riesling Auslese "Fass 56" A.P. #21	88	now–2030
2003 Brauneberger Juffer-Sonnenuhr Riesling Auslese	90	now–2017+?
2004 Graacher Domprobst Riesling Auslese "Fass 88" A.P. #9	90	now–2028+?
2005 Brauneberger Juffer-Sonnenuhr Riesling Auslese** "Fass #42"	91	2010–2030
2001 Brauneberger Juffer-Sonnenuhr Riesling Auslese**	96	now–2030+?
2005 Mühlheimer Helenenkloster Riesling Beerenauslese	93	2012–2035
2005 Brauneberger Juffer Riesling Beerenauslese	93	now–2035
2001 Graacher Domprobst Riesling Beerenauslese	96	2010–2035+?
2005 Mühlheimer Sonnenlay Riesling Trockenbeerenauslese	94	2015–2055
2005 Graacher Domprobst Riesling Trockenbeerenauslese	95	2015–2050+?

2005 Brauneberger Juffer-Sonnenuhr Riesling		
Trockenbeerenauslese	93	2015–2050+?
2004 Mühlheimer Helenenkloster Riesling Eiswein		
A.P. #22	89	2010–2020+?
2004 Mühlheimer Helenenkloster Riesling Eiswein**		
A.P. #20	92	2010–2025+?
2003 Mühlheimer Helenenkloster Riesling Eiswein	90	now–2018
2001 Mühlheimer Helenenkloster Riesling Eiswein	99	2015–2035

ST. URBANS·HOF ★ ★ ★ ★
LEIWEN/MOSEL $20.00–$350.00

The disciplined and dynamic team here—cellarmaster Rudi Hoffmann, vineyard manager Hermann Jostock, and proprietor Nik Weis—has achieved a highly successful series of harvests lately, turning in outstanding accounts of the well-known Ockfener Bockstein and Piesporter Goldtröpfchen vineyards, as well as of the Leiwener Laurentiuslay and Saarfeilser—two sites whose historically well-documented potential is belatedly being rediscovered in the glass. Single-vineyard Riesling from Mehring and an excellent, bargain-priced *négociant* bottling dubbed "Urban Riesling" were added in the 2006 vintage by Weis, a German vintner unafraid to seek balance at judicious but unfashionable levels of residual sugar, neither legally *trocken* nor downright sweet.

2005 Riesling	88	now
2005 Wiltinger Riesling Kabinett feinherb	90	now–2012
2005 Leiwener Laurentiuslay Riesling Spätlese		
feinherb	92	now–2022+?
2004 Leiwener Laurentiuslay Riesling Spätlese trocken		
A.P. #34	91	now–2016
2004 Leiwener Laurentiuslay Riesling Spätlese		
[halbtrocken] A.P. #36	93	now–2022+?
2004 Leiwener Laurentiuslay Riesling Spätlese		
[feinherb] A.P. #35	89	now–2018
2005 Ockfener Bockstein Riesling Spätlese feinherb	90	now–2020
2005 Piesporter Goldtröpfchen Riesling Kabinett	91	now–2020
2004 Piesporter Goldtröpfchen Riesling Kabinett	88	now–2016
2005 Ockfener Bockstein Riesling Kabinett	89	now–2018
2005 Saarfeilser Riesling Spätlese	90	now–2025
2005 Ockfener Bockstein Riesling Spätlese	90	now–2022
2004 Ockfener Bockstein Riesling Spätlese	88	now–2018
2005 Leiwener Laurentiuslay Riesling Spätlese	93	now–2025
2004 Leiwener Laurentiuslay Riesling Spätlese		
A.P. #29	91	now–2022
2005 Piesporter Goldtröpfchen Riesling Spätlese	91	now–2025
2004 Piesporter Goldtröpfchen Riesling Spätlese	92	now–2025
2005 Ockfener Bockstein Riesling Auslese	89	2010–2022
2004 Ockfener Bockstein Riesling Auslese	92	now–2028
2005 Piesporter Goldtröpfchen Riesling Auslese	94	now–2030+?
2004 Piesporter Goldtröpfchen Riesling Auslese	94	now–2030
2005 Ockfener Bockstein Riesling Auslese gold capsule	92	2010–2032+?
2004 Ockfener Bockstein Riesling Auslese gold capsule		
A.P. #32	90	now–2030

2005 Piesporter Goldtröpfchen Riesling Beerenauslese	95	now–2040+?
2005 Leiwener Laurentiuslay Riesling Trockenbeerenauslese	98	now–2045+?
2004 Ockfener Bockstein Riesling Eiswein	95	now–2030

WILLI SCHAEFER ★ ★ ★ ★ ★
GRAACH/MOSEL $27.00–$400.00

Willi Schaefer has been crafting some of the Mosel's finest and most ageworthy Riesling for more than three decades from his small holdings, particularly in the choicest sections of the Domprobst. Around the turn of the most recent century, the wines briefly seemed to miss the richness, clarity, and consistency of their predecessors, but in the last several years, with the emergence of son Christoph as collaborator, this estate is back at the forefront of Middle Mosel quality. The Schaefers practice meticulous viticulture, vinification, and bottling by parcel, but are keen not to overselect at harvest. Thus, for instance, they ensure that some green-gold healthy berries will inform their Beerenauslese, giving it incredible energy and elegance, and they have chosen never to bottle Trockenbeerenauslese.

2003 Riesling	89	now–2009
2005 Graacher Himmelreich Riesling feinherb	89	now–2012
2005 Graacher Himmelreich Riesling Kabinett	90	now–2018
2003 Graacher Himmelreich Riesling Kabinett	90	now–2018
2002 Graacher Himmelreich Riesling Kabinett	90	now–2019
2001 Graacher Himmelreich Riesling Kabinett	90	now–2012
2002 Wehlener Sonnenuhr Riesling Kabinett	90	now–2015
2001 Wehlener Sonnenuhr Riesling Kabinett	92	now–2016
2005 Graacher Domprobst Riesling Kabinett	90	now–2018
2004 Graacher Domprobst Riesling Kabinett	88	now–2015
2003 Graacher Domprobst Riesling Kabinett A.P. #2	88	now–2010
2003 Graacher Domprobst Riesling Kabinett A.P. #5	91	now–2013
2002 Graacher Domprobst Riesling Kabinett A.P. #7	92	now–2020
2005 Graacher Himmelreich Riesling Spätlese	89	now–2020
2003 Graacher Himmelreich Riesling Spätlese	91	now–2016
2005 Wehlener Sonnenuhr Riesling Spätlese	88	now–2016+?
2003 Wehlener Sonnenuhr Riesling Spätlese	91	now–2015
2005 Graacher Domprobst Riesling Spätlese A.P. #7	92	now–2025
2005 Graacher Domprobst Riesling Spätlese A.P. #8	91	now–2025+?
2005 Graacher Domprobst Riesling Spätlese A.P. #1	94	now–2025+?
2004 Graacher Domprobst Riesling Spätlese A.P. #11	89	now–2020
2004 Graacher Domprobst Riesling Spätlese A.P. #9	90	now–2025
2004 Graacher Domprobst Riesling Spätlese A.P. #10	89	now–2020
2004 Graacher Domprobst Riesling Spätlese A.P. #16	93	now–2028
2004 Graacher Domprobst Riesling Spätlese A.P. #14	91	now–2025
2003 Graacher Domprobst Riesling Spätlese A.P. #9	94	now–2022
2003 Graacher Domprobst Riesling Spätlese A.P. #10	95	now–2025
2003 Graacher Domprobst Riesling Spätlese A.P. #15	94	now–2024
2002 Graacher Domprobst Riesling Spätlese A.P. #9	93	now–2028
2002 Graacher Domprobst Riesling Spätlese A.P. #12	94	now–2030
2001 Graacher Domprobst Riesling Spätlese A.P. #3	94	now–2025
2005 Graacher Himmelreich Riesling Auslese A.P. #14	92	now–2035
2005 Graacher Domprobst Riesling Auslese A.P. #6	89	now–2022

2005 Graacher Himmelreich Riesling Auslese A.P. #9	94	now–2035
2003 Graacher Himmelreich Riesling Auslese A.P. #12	93	now–2030
2003 Graacher Himmelreich Riesling Auslese A.P. #16	92	now–2027
2005 Graacher Domprobst Riesling Auslese A.P. #11	92	now–2030
2005 Graacher Domprobst Riesling Auslese A.P. #10	97	now–2038+?
2005 Graacher Domprobst Riesling Auslese A.P. #2	94	2010–2035
2004 Graacher Domprobst Riesling Auslese A.P. #8	92	now–2030
2004 Graacher Domprobst Riesling Auslese A.P. #17	94	now–2035
2003 Graacher Domprobst Riesling Auslese A.P. #14	95	now–2030
2003 Graacher Domprobst Riesling Auslese A.P. #18	95	now–2030
2002 Graacher Domprobst Riesling Auslese A.P. #10	97	now–2038
2002 Graacher Domprobst Riesling Auslese A.P. #14	98	now–2038
2001 Graacher Domprobst Riesling Auslese A.P. #9	97	now–2032
2001 Graacher Domprobst Riesling Auslese A.P. #11	98	now–2035
2005 Graacher Domprobst Riesling Beerenauslese	98	now–2050
2003 Graacher Domprobst Riesling Beerenauslese	94	now–2035

SCHÄFER-FRÖHLICH ★ ★ ★ ★ ★
BOCKENAU/NAHE $28.00–$300.00

The daring with which young Tim Fröhlich and his parents have approached their work over the past several years and their audacious success in crafting riveting, brilliantly clear Riesling from dry to nobly sweet, that marries intense fruit with distinctive minerality, is not only admirable but downright astonishing. Year after year—seemingly heedless of Mother Nature's performance—the Fröhlichs seem to raise the bar, and they really outdid themselves in vintage 2006. Meanwhile, new acreage in Monzingen and Schlossböckelheim is adding to the excitement at this address in formerly obscure Bockenau.

2004 Riesling	91	now–2014+?
2004 Riesling Kabinett	89	now–2014
2004 Bockenauer Felseneck Riesling Spätlese trocken	90	now–2014+
2004 Bockenauer Felseneck Riesling Grosses Gewächs	91	now–2016+?
2004 Monzinger Halenberg Riesling Grosses Gewächs	89	now–2014+?
2004 Bockenauer Felseneck Riesling Spätlese A.P. #17	94	now–2022
2004 Bockenauer Felseneck Riesling Spätlese A.P. #18	93	now–2022
2004 Monzinger Halenberg Riesling Spätlese	92	now–2020
2003 Monzinger Halenberg Riesling Spätlese	89	now–2014+
2002 Monzinger Halenberg Riesling Spätlese	89	now–2019
2004 Monzinger Frühlingsplätzchen Riesling Spätlese gold capsule	90	2010–2020+?
2003 Bockenauer Felseneck Riesling Spätlese gold capsule	91	now–2020
2002 Bockenauer Felseneck Riesling Spätlese gold capsule	91	now–2023
2004 Bockenauer Felseneck Riesling Auslese A.P. #15	89	now–2022
2003 Bockenauer Felseneck Riesling Auslese	92	now–2022
2004 Bockenauer Felseneck Riesling Auslese gold capsule A.P. #33	95	now–2030
2004 Bockenauer Felseneck Riesling Auslese gold capsule A.P. #18	96	now–2030
2004 Bockenauer Felseneck Riesling Eiswein A.P. #31	90	now–2025+?

2004 Bockenauer Felseneck Riesling Eiswein gold		
capsule A.P. #32	92	now–2030+?
2002 Bockenauer Felseneck Riesling Eiswein gold		
capsule A.P. #19	96	2015–2040

SCHLOSS SAARSTEIN ★★★
SERRIG/SAAR $18.00–$600.00

Andrea and Christian Ebert have built a fine reputation for this steep *monopole* overlooking the Saar that his father, a refugee from eastern Germany, purchased in 1956. Until the streak of warm vintages beginning with 1988, getting Riesling to ripen here was considered a challenge, and a distinctively delicious Pinot Blanc resulted from the need to diversify. But successful Riesling at all Prädikat levels, including superb nobly sweet examples, has since become the norm.

2005 Pinot Blanc	89	now–2009
2004 Pinot Blanc	87	now
2005 Serriger Schloss Saarstein Riesling Kabinett		
A.P. #6	87	now–2015
2005 Serriger Schloss Saarstein Riesling Spätlese	89	now–2020
2004 Serriger Schloss Saarstein Riesling Spätlese		
A.P. #10	88	now–2018
2005 Serriger Schloss Saarstein Riesling Auslese	89	now–2028
2005 Serriger Schloss Saarstein Riesling Auslese gold		
capsule	92	2012–2030
2005 Serriger Schloss Saarstein Riesling		
Trockenbeerenauslese	94	now–2040+?

ANDREAS SCHMITGES ★★★
ERDEN/MOSEL $18.00–$500.00

An ambitious and inspiring young vintner who took over his family's estate in 1990, Andreas Schmitges is gradually expanding his acreage (including his share of old vines—rarities nowadays in Erden), rendering wines of purity and refinement and setting himself up to become a reference point for Erden Riesling and one of the beacons of quality on the Mosel. He is also gradually integrating a number of traditional practices, including spontaneous fermentation in cask.

2005 Riesling Grauschiefer trocken	88	now–2010
2005 Erdener Prälat Riesling Spätlese feinherb	87	now–2015
2005 Riesling feinherb	86	now–2010
2004 Erdener Treppchen Riesling Spätlese feinherb	91	now–2018
2004 Erdener Treppchen Riesling Kabinett	89	now–2015
2004 Erdener Treppchen Riesling Spätlese Fass #14		
A.P. #13	90	now–2020
2004 Erdener Treppchen Riesling Spätlese Selektion		
A.P. #14	92	now–2025
2004 Erdener Prälat Riesling Spätlese	91	now–2028
2005 Erdener Treppchen Riesling Spätlese**	91	now–2028
2005 Erdener Treppchen Riesling Auslese*	92	now–2035
2005 Erdener Prälat Riesling Auslese*** Alte Reben	95	now–2035+?
2005 Erdener Treppchen Riesling		
Trockenbeerenauslese	94	now–2040+?
2004 Erdener Herrenberg Riesling Eiswein	91	now–2020?

CARL SCHMITT-WAGNER ✦ ✦ ✦
LONGUICH/MOSEL $18.00–$200.00

Bruno Schmitt's traditional methods and ancient, ungrafted vines at a site just north of Trier renowned since the Middle Ages are the sources for some of the most ageworthy wines on the Mosel. These are not usually showstoppers in their youth, nor can it be said that success here is entirely consistent; but the best of them offer outstanding value, and with Carl-Josef Loewen of Leiwen's arrival in 2007 (permitting Schmitt to at least semiretire, though he is sure to stay close to his vines and wines), this estate looks poised to enter an exciting period.

2005 Longuicher Maximiner Herrenberg Riesling Spätlese trocken	87	now–2012
2005 Longuicher Maximiner Herrenberg Riesling Spätlese feinherb	88	now–2025
2004 Longuicher Maximiner Herrenberg Riesling A.P. #8	87	now–2025
2004 Longuicher Maximiner Herrenberg Riesling Kabinett A.P. #6	90	now–2025
2003 Longuicher Maximiner Herrenberg Riesling Kabinett	89	now
2002 Longuicher Maximiner Herrenberg Riesling Kabinett	89	now–2020
2005 Longuicher Maximiner Herrenberg Riesling Spätlese A.P. #3	87	now–2030
2004 Longuicher Maximiner Herrenberg Riesling Spätlese A.P. #7	89	now–2030
2003 Longuicher Maximiner Herrenberg Riesling Spätlese	87	now–2012+?
2002 Longuicher Maximiner Herrenberg Riesling Spätlese	89	now–2025
2001 Longuicher Maximiner Herrenberg Riesling Spätlese A.P. #13	89	now–2022
2001 Longuicher Maximiner Herrenberg Riesling Spätlese A.P. #17	88	now–2022
2005 Longuicher Maximiner Herrenberg Riesling Auslese A.P. #7	90	now–2035
2004 Longuicher Maximiner Herrenberg Riesling Auslese A.P. #5	91	now–2035
2003 Longuicher Maximiner Herrenberg Riesling Auslese A.P. #8	90	now–2018+?
2001 Longuicher Maximiner Herrenberg Riesling Auslese A.P. #18	91	now–2025
2001 Longuicher Maximiner Herrenberg Riesling Auslese A.P. #14 [gold capsule]	92	now–2025
2005 Longuicher Maximiner Herrenberg Riesling Beerenauslese	93	now–2040+?

VON SCHUBERT—MAXIMIN GRÜNHAUS ✦ ✦ ✦ ✦
MERTESDORF/RUWER $20.00–$900.00

For most of the last quarter of the 20th century, Carl von Schubert and his father, along with cellar and vineyard manager Alfons Heinrich, crafted from their famed sites on the outskirts of Trier some of the world's most consistently outstanding and ageworthy Riesling, ranging from dry QbA to nobly sweet TBA. After 1998 there was a dip in quality, and then an awkward transition following Heinrich's retirement. With their 2005s, Carl von Schubert and his new young cellar and vineyard manager Stefan Kraml have been able again to showcase the excellence of these vineyards, while bringing subtle stylistic changes to the wines (including a new, nearly dry prestige bottling named "Superior") and embarking on a much needed renovation of the cellars.

Wine	Score	Drink
2005 Maximin Grünhäuser Herrenberg Riesling trocken	88	now–2011
2005 Maximin Grünhäuser Herrenberg Riesling Kabinett trocken	90	now–2012
2005 Maximin Grünhäuser Abtsberg Riesling Kabinett trocken	89	now–2012
2005 Maximin Grünhäuser Herrenberg Riesling Spätlese trocken	90	now–2016
2005 Maximin Grünhäuser Abtsberg Riesling Spätlese trocken	87	now–2015+?
2005 Maximin Grünhäuser Abtsberg Riesling "Superior"	90	now–2018+?
2005 Maximin Grünhäuser Herrenberg Riesling "Superior"	91	now–2018+?
2005 Maximin Grünhäuser Herrenberg Riesling feinherb	87	now–2012
2004 Maximin Grünhäuser Herrenberg Riesling feinherb	88	now–2012
2005 Maximin Grünhäuser Herrenberg Riesling Kabinett feinherb	89	now–2015
2004 Maximin Grünhäuser Abtsberg Riesling Kabinett feinherb A.P. #5	87	now–2012
2005 Maximin Grünhäuser Herrenberg Riesling Spätlese feinherb	89	now–2015
2005 Maximin Grünhäuser Bruderberg Riesling	87	now–2015
2005 Maximin Grünhäuser Herrenberg Riesling Kabinett A.P. #23	91	now–2017
2004 Maximin Grünhäuser Herrenberg Riesling Kabinett	88	now–2015
2005 Maximin Grünhäuser Abtsberg Riesling Kabinett	91	now–2018
2005 Maximin Grünhäuser Herrenberg Riesling Spätlese	91	now–2025
2005 Maximin Grünhäuser Abtsberg Riesling Spätlese A.P. #26	93	now–2028
2005 Maximin Grünhäuser Abtsberg Riesling Spätlese A.P. #27	91	now–2025
2005 Maximin Grünhäuser Abtsberg Riesling Spätlese A.P. #7	92	now–2028
2004 Maximin Grünhäuser Abtsberg Riesling Spätlese	91	now–2025
2005 Maximin Grünhäuser Herrenberg Riesling Auslese	94	2012–2030
2005 Maximin Grünhäuser Abtsberg Riesling Auslese	90	now–2025
2005 Maximin Grünhäuser Herrenberg Riesling Auslese Fuder #30	93	now–2030+?
2005 Maximin Grünhäuser Abtsberg Riesling Auslese Fuder #21	95	now–2032+?

2005 Maximin Grünhäuser Herrenberg Riesling		
Auslese Fuder #44	91	2010–2025+?
2005 Maximin Grünhäuser Herrenberg Riesling		
Beerenauslese	93	2012–2035
2005 Maximin Grünhäuser Abtsberg Riesling		
Trockenbeerenauslese	94	now–2040+?
2005 Maximin Grünhäuser Abtsberg Riesling		
Trockenbeerenauslese gold capsule	97	now–2050+?
2002 Maximin Grünhäuser Abtsberg Riesling Eiswein	92	2010–2035

SELBACH-OSTER ★ ★ ★ ★ ★
ZELTINGEN/MOSEL $22.00–$500.00

After many years spent sharing vineyard and cellar duties with his late father Hans Selbach, Johannes Selbach is nowadays growing, picking, and vinifying Riesling with a sensitivity to nuance, to his sites, and to the voice of the vintage that few German vintners can equal. His dry wines are among the Mosel's most successful and ageworthy; he is waging a convincing campaign to save that endangered species, a genuine, low-alcohol, refreshing Kabinett; his top Spätlesen from Zeltingen's Sonnenuhr and Schlossberg and the Badstube sites of Bernkastel are among the surest values and most complex wines carrying that Prädikat on the Mosel. Finally, the range of nobly sweet wines at this address is extraordinary. Recently, in a throwback to tradition, certain Riesling Auslesen have been picked as a block rather than selectively, in an effort to better capture the character of both site and vintage, as well as to achieve multiple layers of flavor.

2005 Zeltinger Sonnenuhr Riesling Kabinett trocken	89	now–2014
2004 Zeltinger Sonnenuhr Riesling Kabinett trocken	89	now–2015
2005 Zeltinger Schlossberg Riesling trocken	90	now–2016
2005 Zeltinger Sonnenuhr Riesling Spätlese trocken	91	now–2022
2004 Zeltinger Schlossberg Riesling trocken	88	now–2020
2005 Zeltinger Himmelreich Riesling Kabinett		
halbtrocken	91	now–2018
2004 Zeltinger Himmelreich Riesling Kabinett		
halbtrocken	91	now–2016
2001 Zeltinger Himmelreich Riesling Kabinett		
halbtrocken	89	now–2009
2005 Zeltinger Sonnenuhr Riesling Kabinett	91	now–2020
2004 Zeltinger Sonnenuhr Riesling Kabinett	91	now–2020
2003 Zeltinger Sonnenuhr Riesling Kabinett	89	now–2009+?
2001 Zeltinger Sonnenuhr Riesling Kabinett	89	now–2014
2004 Zeltinger Schlossberg Riesling Kabinett	89	now–2018
2003 Zeltinger Schlossberg Riesling Kabinett	88	now–2010+?
2001 Zeltinger Schlossberg Riesling Kabinett	91	now–2012
2005 Bernkasteler Badstube Riesling Kabinett	92	now–2020
2005 Wehlener Sonnenuhr Riesling Kabinett	89	now–2018
2004 Wehlener Sonnenuhr Riesling Kabinett	86–88	now–2015
2002 Wehlener Sonnenuhr Riesling Kabinett	91	now–2015
2005 Riesling Spätlese	90	now–2018
2004 Riesling Spätlese	88–90	now–2018
2001 Riesling Spätlese	89	now–2014
2005 Bernkasteler Badstube Riesling Spätlese	92	now–2025
2005 Wehlener Sonnenuhr Riesling Spätlese	88	now–2016

2005 Zeltinger Schlossberg Riesling Spätlese	92	now–2028
2004 Zeltinger Schlossberg Riesling Spätlese	91	now–2022
2003 Zeltinger Schlossberg Riesling Spätlese	89	now–2014+?
2001 Zeltinger Schlossberg Riesling Spätlese	90	now–2016
2005 Zeltinger Sonnenuhr Riesling Spätlese	93	now–2028
2004 Zeltinger Sonnenuhr Riesling Spätlese A.P. #18	94	now–2025
2003 Zeltinger Sonnenuhr Riesling Spätlese	90	now–2014+?
2002 Zeltinger Sonnenuhr Riesling Spätlese	89	now–2020
2001 Zeltinger Sonnenuhr Riesling Spätlese	91	now–2018
2005 Bernkasteler Badstube Riesling Spätlese*	95	now–2030
2004 Zeltinger Schlossberg Riesling Spätlese*	92	now–2022
2002 Zeltinger Schlossberg Riesling Spätlese*	89	now–2020
2004 Zeltinger Sonnenuhr Riesling Spätlese*	92	now–2028+?
2002 Zeltinger Sonnenuhr Riesling Spätlese*	91	now–2025
2001 Zeltinger Sonnenuhr Riesling Spätlese*	93	now–2018
2005 Zeltinger Schlossberg Riesling Auslese	93	now–2035
2004 Zeltinger Schlossberg Riesling Auslese	91	now–2025
2002 Zeltinger Schlossberg Riesling Auslese	91	now–2025
2001 Zeltinger Schlossberg Riesling Auslese	93	now–2020
2005 Zeltinger Sonnenuhr Riesling Auslese	94	now–2035
2003 Zeltinger Sonnenuhr Riesling Auslese	92	now–2020+?
2002 Zeltinger Sonnenuhr Riesling Auslese	90	now–2030
2005 Graacher Domprost Riesling Auslese	92	now–2032
2005 Wehlener Sonnenuhr Riesling Auslese	90	now–2030
2003 Bernkasteler Badstube Riesling Auslese	93	now–2020
2005 Zeltinger Schlossberg Riesling Auslese*	94	2010–2035
2004 Zeltinger Schlossberg Riesling Auslese*	89	now–2022
2003 Zeltinger Schlossberg Riesling Auslese*	92	now–2019
2002 Zeltinger Schlossberg Riesling Auslese*	90	now–2030
2001 Zeltinger Himmelreich Riesling Auslese*	90	now–2018
2002 Zeltinger Sonnenuhr Riesling Auslese*	92	now–2030
2001 Zeltinger Sonnenuhr Riesling Auslese*	91	now–2025+?
2005 Bernkasteler Badstube Riesling Auslese*	94	now–2035+?
2005 Graacher Domprobst Riesling Auslese*	88	now–2035+?
2005 Zeltinger Schlossberg Riesling Auslese**	96	now–2040
2003 Zeltinger Schlossberg Riesling Auslese**	94	now–2022+?
2002 Bernkasteler Badstube Riesling Auslese**	94	2009–2035
2005 Zeltinger Sonnenuhr Riesling Auslese**	92	now–2035+?
2001 Zeltinger Sonnenuhr Riesling Auslese**	95	now–2030
2005 Zeltinger Sonnenuhr Riesling Auslese "Rotlay"	94	now–2035
2004 Zeltinger Sonnenuhr Riesling Auslese "Rotlay"	95	now–2035+?
2005 Zeltinger Schlossberg Riesling Auslese "Schmitt"	96	now–2040+?
2004 Zeltinger Schlossberg Riesling Auslese "Schmitt"	93	now–2035+?
2003 Zeltinger Schlossberg Riesling Auslese "Schmitt"	92	now–2025+?
2005 Zeltinger Sonnenuhr Riesling Auslese***	97	now–2040+?
2003 Zeltinger Sonnenuhr Riesling Auslese***	93	now–2022+?
2005 Bernkasteler Badstube Riesling Beerenauslese	96	now–2050
2005 Zeltinger Sonnenuhr Riesling Beerenauslese	98	now–2050
2004 Zeltinger Sonnenuhr Riesling Beerenauslese	95	now–2038+?
2003 Zeltinger Sonnenuhr Riesling Beerenauslese	93	now–2035+?
2005 Zeltinger Schlossberg Riesling Beerenauslese*	95	now–2050

2005 Zeltinger Schlossberg Riesling Trockenbeerenauslese	96–98	now–2055
2003 Zeltinger Sonnenuhr Riesling Trockenbeerenauslese	93	now–2040
2004 Zeltinger Himmelreich Riesling Eiswein	94	now–2035+?
2003 Zeltinger Himmelreich Riesling Eiswein	92	now–2018+?
2002 Zeltinger Himmelreich Riesling Eiswein	96	now–2040+?
2001 Zeltinger Himmelreich Riesling Eiswein "Junior"	93	now–2030+?
2004 Bernkasteler Badstube Riesling Eiswein	95	now–2040+?
2002 Bernkasteler Badstube Riesling Eiswein	94	now–2040
2001 Bernkasteler Badstube Riesling Eiswein	99	2015–2040+?

JOSEF SPREITZER ★ ★ ★ ★
OESTRICH/RHEINGAU $25.00–$500.00

Brothers Andreas and Bernd Spreitzer's reductive, fructose-rich style is the perfect antidote to so many less than pristine Rheingau Riesling in today's market, even if purists may consider their wines nontraditional. The loess soils that dominate Oestrich themselves invite Riesling in a different key. Thus far, every indication points to excellent ageability for wines in the striking style that has emerged here over the past decade.

2004 Oestricher Doosberg Riesling Spätlese trocken	87	now–2010
2004 Hattenheimer Wisselbrunnen Riesling Erstes Gewächs Spätlese trocken	90	now–2014+?
2003 Hattenheimer Wisselbrunnen Riesling Spätlese trocken	87	now–2010
2004 Oestricher Lenchen Riesling Kabinett halbtrocken	91	now–2011
2002 Oestricher Doosberg Riesling	89	now
2004 Oestricher Doosberg Riesling Kabinett	89	now–2010
2003 Oestricher Doosberg Riesling Kabinett	88	now–2009
2003 Oestricher Lenchen Riesling Kabinett	88	now–2010
2001 Oestricher Lenchen Riesling Kabinett	89	now–2009
2003 Winkeler Jesuitengarten Riesling Spätlese	90	now–2018
2002 Oestricher Lenchen Riesling Spätlese	89	now–2015
2001 Oestricher Lenchen Riesling Spätlese	89	now–2014
2004 Oestricher Lenchen Riesling Spätlese "303"	92	now–2025
2003 Oestricher Lenchen Riesling Spätlese "303"	89	now–2019
2002 Oestricher Lenchen Riesling Spätlese "303"	93	now–2020
2001 Oestricher Lenchen Riesling Spätlese "303"	92	now–2020
2004 Oestricher Lenchen Riesling Auslese gold capsule	87	now–2025+?
2003 Oestricher Lenchen Riesling Beerenauslese	91	now–2030
2002 Oestricher Lenchen Riesling Beerenauslese	92	now–2035
2002 Oestricher Lenchen Riesling Trockenbeerenauslese	95	2010–2040+?
2004 Hallgartener Jungfer Riesling Eiswein	91	now–2030+?
2003 Mittelheimer St.-Nikolaus Riesling Eiswein	90	now–2030
2002 Mittelheimer St.-Nikolaus Riesling Eiswein	96	now–2040+?

J. & H. A. STRUB ✳✳✳
NIERSTEIN/RHEINHESSEN $15.00–$100.00

Longtime proprietor Walter Strub is one of the most conscientious vintners in Nierstein. Though much of his family acreage is not on the classic red sandstone slopes, his wines from ostensibly "lesser" sites on chalk and loess, notably from Brückchen and Paterberg, have winning personalities all their own. Nearly all of the Riesling here are unabashedly sweet, and all offer unusual value. Grüner Veltiner is a recent curiosity.

2004 Niersteiner Brückchen Riesling Kabinett	87	now–2014
2001 Niersteiner Brückchen Riesling Kabinett	90	now–2010+?
2001 Niersteiner Oelberg Riesling Kabinett	87	now–2014
2001 Niersteiner Pettenthal Riesling Kabinett	90	now–2010
2004 Niersteiner Paterberg Riesling Spätlese	87	now–2018
2003 Niersteiner Paterberg Riesling Spätlese	90	now–2014
2001 Niersteiner Paterberg Riesling Spätlese	92	now–2018
2002 Niersteiner Paterberg Riesling Spätlese**	89	now–2015
2001 Niersteiner Paterberg Riesling Spätlese***	93	now–2018
2003 Niersteiner Oelberg Riesling Spätlese	90	now–2015
2001 Niersteiner Oelberg Riesling Spätlese	91	now–2018
2001 Niersteiner Paterberg Riesling Eiswein	93	now–2015+?

DR. THANISCH-ERBEN THANISCH ✳✳✳
MOSEL $25.00–$800.00

The name Dr. Thanisch is intimately associated with the celebrated and expensive Riesling of the "Doctor" vineyard. The original estate was split in half in 1988 and Sofia Thanisch-Spier continues to operate the portion passed down through the Thanisch family. Most of the crop that does not originate in the Doctor is blended to produce a proprietary Riesling or a wine labeled with the collective vineyard name Bernkasteler Badstube. The Bernkasteler Doctor Riesling needs time in bottle to show its true class, and youthful examples can appear awkwardly plump and superficially sweet. With time, the best examples display nutty, honeyed richness and depth. (The antique label used by Thanisch as well as their price lists utilize the archaic spelling of Berncastel with a "c.")

2001 Bernkasteler Doctor Riesling Kabinett	90	now–2012
2005 Bernkasteler Doctor Riesling Spätlese	87	2010–2018
2002 Bernkasteler Doctor Riesling Spätlese	89	now–2016
2002 Bernkasteler Doctor Riesling Auslese	91	now–2020

DANIEL VOLLENWEIDER ✳✳✳✳
TRABEN-TRARBACH/MOSEL $25.00–$300.00

Swiss Daniel Vollenweider came to wine, and the Mosel, out of sheer infatuation. Face to face with the plight of so many historically distinguished, now neglected Mosel vineyards, he decided to rescue the steep, ancient terraces of the Wolfer Goldgrube. From these, he is crafting unapologetically sweet, highly expressive Riesling whose quality has brought him—in well less than a decade—to the forefront of German viticulture. In top vintages, Vollenweider segregates his individual parcels at the Spätlese level, printing their names on a small neck label.

2005 Wolfer Goldgrube Riesling Spätlese feinherb	87	now–2012+?
2004 Wolfer Goldgrube Riesling Spätlese feinherb	88	now–2012
2005 Wolfer Goldgrube Riesling Kabinett	90	now–2015+?
2004 Wolfer Goldgrube Riesling Kabinett	90	now–2015+?

2004 Wolfer Goldgrube Riesling Spätlese A.P. #4	91	now–2018+?
2004 Wolfer Goldgrube Riesling Spätlese A.P. #5	89	now–2016+?
2005 Wolfer Goldgrube Riesling Spätlese Portz	91	now–2020+?
2004 Wolfer Goldgrube Riesling Spätlese Portz A.P. #7	90	now–2018+?
2005 Wolfer Goldgrube Riesling Spätlese Reiler	93	now–2020+?
2004 Wolfer Goldgrube Riesling Spätlese Padauer A.P. #6	92	now–2020+?
2004 Wolfer Goldgrube Riesling Spätlese gold capsule A.P. #9	91	now–2002+?
2005 Wolfer Goldgrube Riesling Auslese	91	now–2022+?
2005 Wolfer Goldgrube Riesling Auslese gold capsule	95	now–2030+?
2004 Wolfer Goldgrube Riesling Auslese gold capsule	91	now–2025+?
2005 Wolfer Goldgrube Riesling Auslese long gold capsule	94	now–2030+?
2005 Wolfer Goldgrube Riesling Beerenauslese	96	now–2040+?
2003 Wolfer Goldgrube Riesling Trockenbeerenauslese	96	now–2045+?

VAN VOLXEM ★ ★ ★ ★
WILTINGEN/SAAR $30.00–$300.00

Scion of the Bitburger beer dynasty, fanatically quality-conscious Roman Niewodniczanski, together with his young cellarmaster Dominik Völk, is crafting dry-tasting (seldom legally *trocken*) wines with significantly lower (or, as he would prefer to put it, "riper") acidity, fuller body, and more lees-inflected textures than are typical for modern Mosel or Saar Riesling. (Only his few downright sweet bottlings are labeled with a Prädikat.) Since acquiring this estate in 1999, Niewodniczanski has greatly expanded what was already a formidable collection of steep sites and ancient vines, imposing labor-intensive maintenance and draconian yields. His contracts with local growers for fruit from old vines also make possible non-site-specific bottlings of formidable quality, and significantly further the revival of economic fortunes taking place along the Saar. The verdict on how these wines will age long-term remains out, but Niewodniczanksi's intention is to bottle the sort of Saar Riesling crafted a century ago and renowned for its stamina.

2005 Weissburgunder [Pinot Blanc]	88	now–2009+?
2004 Weissburgunder [Pinot Blanc]	87	now
2004 Schiefer Riesling	87	now
2005 Saar Riesling	87	now–2011
2004 Saar Riesling	88	now–2011
2001 Saar Riesling	89	now–2010
2005 Riesling Alte Reben	90	now–2015+?
2004 Riesling Alte Reben	92	now–2018
2004 Wiltinger Braunfels Riesling	89	now–2016
2004 Wiltinger Kupp Riesling	92	now–2018+?
2005 Scharzhofberger Riesling	89	now–2015+?
2004 Scharzhofberger Riesling	91	now–2016+?
2001 Scharzhofberger Riesling	90	now–2014+?
2005 Riesling Volz	91–93	now–2018+?
2004 Riesling Volz	90	now–2015+?
2005 Scharzhofberger Riesling P[ergentsknopp]	89–91	now–2016+?
2004 Scharzhofberger Riesling P[ergentsknopp]	93	now–2018+?
2005 Kanzemer Altenberg Riesling Alte Reben	90–92	now–2018+?
2004 Kanzemer Altenberg Riesling Alte Reben	92	now–2018+?

2005 Wiltinger Gottesfuss Riesling Alte Reben	91–94	now–2020+?
2004 Wiltinger Gottesfuss Riesling Alte Reben	94	now–2020+?
2001 Wiltinger Gottesfuss Riesling Alte Reben	90	now–2015+?
2001 Scharzhofberger Riesling Spätlese	90	now–2020
2004 Kanzemer Altenberg Riesling Auslese	92	now–2022+?
2005 Scharzhofberger Riesling Auslese	91–93	now–2022+?
2005 Scharzhofberger Riesling Auslese long gold capsule	90–93	now–2025+?

DR. HEINZ WAGNER ✳✳✳
SAARBURG/SAAR $20.00–$250.00

Heinz Wagner emphasized dry Riesling for many years, and while his current line-up incorporates an approximately equal volume of off-dry wines, he nowadays eschews Eiswein and Beerenauslese. The approach in the cellar is relatively traditional, including ambient yeast fermentations in small older barrels, and the results are classic Saar Riesling that are not showy in their youth.

2005 Saarburger Kupp Kabinett feinherb	87	now–2015
2005 Saarburger Rausch Spätlese	87	now–2020
2003 Ockfener Bockstein Riesling Kabinett	88	now–2010+?
2003 Ockfener Bockstein Riesling Spätlese	89	now–2012+?
2001 Ockfener Bockstein Riesling Kabinett	88	now
2001 Ockfener Bockstein Riesling Spätlese	89	now–2009+?

WAGNER-STEMPEL ✳✳✳✳
SIEFERSHEIM/RHEINHESSEN $18.00–$200.00

The wines of young, experimental, open-minded Daniel Wagner, in the so-called "Rheinhessen Switzerland" (tucked up against the Nahe), are a revelation. Not only do the best of them demonstrate how greatness can lie dormant in little-known (here well-ventilated porphyric) slopes until a talented visionary unlocks it, but the rest of Wagner's collection demonstrates that less expensive, basic bottlings including his Silvaner can exude refinement and class.

2004 Silvaner trocken	88	now
2004 Siefersheimer Riesling trocken A.P. #2	90	now–2011+?
2004 Siefersheimer Riesling trocken A.P. #5	89	now–2011+?
2004 Siefersheimer Riesling "Vom Porphyr"	93	now–2014
2004 Siefersheimer Höllberg Riesling Grosses Gewächs	88	now–2014+?
2004 Siefersheimer Heerkretz Riesling Grosses Gewächs	92	now–2016+?
2003 Siefersheimer Riesling feinherb	90	now–2010
2004 Siefersheimer Heerkretz Riesling Spätlese	89	now–2018
2003 Siefersheimer Heerkretz Riesling Spätlese	89	now–2015
2002 Siefersheimer Heerkretz Riesling Spätlese	89	now–2014
2004 Siefersheimer Höllberg Riesling Auslese	94	now–2025
2002 Siefersheimer Höllberg Riesling Auslese	91	now–2025

ED. WEEGMÜLLER ✳✳✳
HAARDT/PFALZ $19.00–$150.00

Stefanie Weegmüller's wines are often as delicious as her wit! (Husband Richard Scherr is also actively involved.) This is one of the Pfalz's best sources of Gewürztraminer, and among the few remaining ones for outstanding dry Scheurebe, though there are excellent sweet versions here as well. Outstanding value is delivered throughout the line.

2004 Scheurebe trocken	88	now–2009
2004 Haardter Herrenletten Grauer Burgunder [Pinot Gris] Spätlese Alte Reben	89	now–2011+?
2004 Haardter Bürgergarten Gewürztraminer Spätlese trocken Alte Reben	90	now–2012+?
2004 Haardter Herrenletten Riesling Kabinett trocken	87	now–2010
2004 Haardter Herrenletten Riesling Spätlese trocken Alte Reben	89	now–2012
2003 Haardter Herrenletten Riesling Spätlese trocken Alte Reben	87	now–2010
2004 Haardter Bürgergarten Riesling Kabinett	91	now–2014
2003 Haardter Bürgergarten Riesling Kabinett	89	now–2010
2003 Haardter Bürgergarten Riesling Spätlese	92	now–2016
2002 Haardter Bürgergarten Riesling Spätlese	89	now–2018
2004 Haardter Bürgergarten Riesling Eiswein	94	now–2025+?
2004 Haardter Mandelring Scheurebe Auslese	91	now–2022
2002 Haardter Mandelring Scheurebe Auslese	89	now–2012+?
2003 Rieslaner Auslese	90	now–2015+?

WEGELER * * *
OESTRICH/RHEINGAU; BERNKASTEL/MOSEL $25.00–$800.00

Michael Burgdorf—long affiliated with the Freiherr Heyl zu Herrnsheim estate in Nierstein—has recently taken over as director at the large Rheingau branch of Wegeler from Oliver Haag (who returned to his family's Fritz Haag winery in Brauenberg). Quality here has risen in recent years, although there has been a significant reduction in the total portfolio, with Riesling from only a very limited subset of Wegeler's many outstanding holdings being subjected to single-vineyard bottling. The generic wines (including the branded Geheimrat J Riesling for which Wegeler is best known inside Germany) are merely good. The smaller Mosel branch of Wegeler, under the direction of Norbert Breit, is best known as one of the four principal owners of the Bernkasteler Doctor, a site from which they bottled Riesling of impressive opulence, if excruciatingly high price. At both Wegeler estates, showy nobly sweet wine and Eiswein are regularly essayed.

2003 Bernkasteler Doctor Riesling Spätlese	87	now–2014
2002 Bernkasteler Doctor Riesling Spätlese	89	now–2015
2001 Bernkasteler Doctor Riesling Spätlese	91	now–2014
2002 Wehlener Sonnenuhr Riesling Auslese	90	now–2018
2001 Wehlener Sonnenuhr Riesling Auslese	88	now–2010+?
2003 Bernkasteler Doctor Riesling Auslese	90	now–2022
2002 Bernkasteler Doctor Riesling Auslese	91	now–2025
2001 Bernkasteler Doctor Riesling Auslese	90	now–2017
2003 Geisenheimer Rothenberg Riesling Auslese	88	now–2019
2001 Geisenheimer Rothenberg Riesling Auslese	89	now–2018
2001 Bernkasteler Doctor Riesling Beerenauslese	94	now–2030+?
2002 Bernkasteler Doctor Riesling Eiswein	91	now–2030
2002 Geisenheimer Rothenberg Riesling Eiswein	93	now–2030
2001 Geisenheimer Rothenberg Riesling Eiswein	93	now–2027

DR. WEHRHEIM ✱✱✱
BIRKWEILER/PFALZ—SÜDLICHE WEINSTRASSE $15.00–$150.00

Some would say Dr. Heinz Wehrheim was the father figure of the revival in southern Pfalz viticulture, and some that he was the region's last holdout for a traditional style of dry, cask-conditioned Riesling and Pinot Blanc. Probably he was both. Son Karl-Heinz Wehrheim has refined but not significantly altered the style, rendering dry Riesling of clarity and intensity, full-bodied Pinot Blanc, meaty Gewürztraminer, and serious Pinot Noir. The estate's small acreage of Silvaner informs one of Germany's best wine values.

ROBERT WEIL ✱✱✱✱✱
KIEDRICH/RHEINGAU $28.00–$1,000.00+

When Wilhelm Weil sold the controlling interest in his family's renowned but declining estate to Suntory in 1988, he was probably the only person to envision the remarkable future of the partnership they launched. Weil and his immediate family poured their energy and passion into running an operation that could now afford the best facilities and most labor-intensive methods; the result has been (just as under founder Robert Weil in the late 19th century) some of the world's finest Riesling. Ultralimited, spectacularly noble sweet wine from fanatically selective, and generally very late, harvests—including a nearly two decade-long streak of consecutive Riesling Trockenbeerenauslesen—should not detract from the steady progress and outstanding results Weil exhibits with dry Riesling as well Until recently, only wines from the great Gräfenberg (nearly all of which Weil and Suntory have gradually acquired) were vineyard-designated, but bottlings from the Wasseros and the newly reclassified Turmberg are now appearing, and there may be future surprises in the lineup as well.

2004 Riesling trocken	88	now–2009
2004 Riesling Spätlese trocken	90	now–2014
2004 Kiedricher Gräfenberg Riesling Grosses Gewächs	91	now–2018+?
2004 Riesling Kabinett halbtrocken	89	now–2013
2004 Riesling Spätlese halbtrocken	89	now–2015
2003 Riesling Kabinett	88	now–2011
2001 Riesling Kabinett	92	now–2009
2004 Riesling Spätlese	92	now–2018
2004 Kiedricher Gräfenberg Riesling Spätlese	95	now–2025
2002 Kiedricher Gräfenberg Riesling Spätlese	92	now–2020
2001 Kiedricher Gräfenberg Riesling Spätlese	92	now–2018
2004 Kiedricher Gräfenberg Riesling Auslese	91	now–2028
2002 Kiedricher Gräfenberg Riesling Auslese	95	now–2030
2001 Kiedricher Gräfenberg Riesling Auslese	94	now–2025
2004 Kiedricher Gräfenberg Riesling Auslese gold capsule	96	now–2035
2003 Kiedricher Gräfenberg Riesling Auslese gold capsule	94	now–2030
2001 Kiedricher Gräfenberg Riesling Auslese gold capsule	97	now–2030
2004 Kiedricher Gräfenberg Riesling Beerenauslese	93	now–2035+?
2002 Kiedricher Gräfenberg Riesling Beerenauslese	93	now–2039
2004 Kiedricher Gräfenberg Riesling Beerenauslese gold capsule	95	now–2040
2004 Kiedricher Gräfenberg Riesling Trockenbeerenauslese	99	now–2050+

2002 Kiedricher Gräfenberg Riesling		
Trockenbeerenauslese	99	2015–2045+?
2001 Kiedricher Gräfenberg Riesling		
Trockenbeerenauslese	95	2015–2030+?
2004 Kiedricher Gräfenberg Riesling Eiswein	94	now–2030+?
2002 Kiedricher Gräfenberg Riesling Eiswein	98	2010–2040+?
2001 Kiedricher Gräfenberg Riesling Eiswein	99	2010–2040

FLORIAN WEINGART ✴ ✴ ✴
SPAY/MITTELRHEIN $228.00–$300.00

Florian Weingart's father, Adolf (for whom the estate was still named until recently), was underappreciated as a grower, but the exceptionally conscientious, gracious, and gifted younger Weingart has received plenty of attention from the German press. An enormous lineup of Riesling from each portion of the Bopparder Hamm, and ranging from dry to sweet, lacked a bit of consistency in several recent vintages, but there is no overlooking the distinctive and generous personality, superb potential, and outstanding value offered by a host of wines from this estate.

2004 Schloss Fürstenberg Riesling Spätlese*		
trocken A.P. #17	87	now–2012
2003 Schloss Fürstenberg Riesling Spätlese		
halbtrocken	89	now–2010
2004 Bopparder Hamm-Ohlenberg Riesling Spätlese		
Anarchie A.P. #15	89	now–2015+?
2004 Bopparder Hamm-Ohlenberg Riesling Kabinett	89	now–2014
2001 Bopparder Hamm-Feuerlay Riesling Kabinett	88	now
2003 Schloss Fürstenberg Riesling Spätlese	89	now–2014+?
2001 Schloss Fürstenberg Riesling Spätlese	93	now–2016
2004 Bopparder Hamm-Ohlenberg Riesling Spätlese	90	now–2020
2002 Bopparder Hamm-Feuerlay Riesling Spätlese	89	now–2018
2001 Bopparder Hamm-Feuerlay Riesling Spätlese	89	now–2014
2003 Schloss Fürstenberg Riesling Auslese	90	now–2014+?
2004 Bopparder Hamm-Feuerlay Riesling Auslese		
A.P. #22	91	now–2028
2003 Bopparder Hamm-Feuerlay Riesling Auslese	92	now–2020
2001 Bopparder Hamm-Feuerlay Riesling Auslese	93	now–2018
2003 Bopparder Hamm-Feuerlay Riesling Auslese*	92	now–2022
2004 Bopparder Hamm-Ohlenberg Riesling		
Trockenbeerenauslese	93	now–2030+?
2002 Bopparder Hamm Riesling Trockenbeerenauslese	97	now–2040+?

DR. WEINS-PRÜM ✴ ✴ ✴
WEHLEN/MOSEL $20.00–$275.00

The affable Bert Selbach runs a winery with impeccable standards that has always figuratively, as well as literally, lived in the shadows of neighboring Joh. Jos. Prüm. Selbach's Riesling tends toward exemplary clarity, overt sweetness, and youthful generosity, but it can also age formidably. Gold capsule Auslese, Beerenauslese, and Trockenbeerenauslese are only sparingly essayed. Selbach's basic estate Riesling—generally a good value—comes from holdings along the Ruwer.

2005 Graacher Domprobst Riesling Spätlese feinherb	89	now–2018
2005 Graacher Domprobst Riesling Kabinett	87	2010–2016

2004 Graacher Domprobst Riesling Kabinett	87	now–2015
2005 Wehlener Sonnenuhr Riesling Kabinett	87	now–2015
2005 Graacher Himmelreich Riesling Spätlese	90	now–2025
2004 Graacher Himmelreich Riesling Spätlese	91	now–2025
2003 Graacher Himmelreich Riesling Spätlese	87	now–2013+?
2004 Graacher Domprobst Riesling Spätlese	88	now–2022
2005 Wehlener Sonnenuhr Riesling Spätlese	87	now–2020
2004 Wehlener Sonnenuhr Riesling Spätlese	89	now–2021
2001 Wehlener Sonnenuhr Riesling Spätlese	89	now–2015
2004 Erdener Prälat Riesling Spätlese	90	now–2025
2002 Erdener Prälat Riesling Spätlese	90	now–2020
2005 Graacher Domprobst Riesling Auslese	91	now–2028
2005 Graacher Himmelreich Riesling Auslese	90	now–2025
2003 Graacher Himmelreich Riesling Auslese	90	now–2018+?
2005 Wehlener Sonnenuhr Riesling Auslese	90	now–2025
2003 Wehlener Sonnenuhr Riesling Auslese	89	now–2016+?
2001 Wehlener Sonnenuhr Riesling Auslese	91	now–2015
2005 Erdener Prälat Riesling Auslese	92	now–2030
2003 Erdener Prälat Riesling Auslese	92	now–2020+?
2003 Wehlener Sonnenuhr Riesling long gold capsule	91	now–2025
2005 Wehlener Sonnenuhr Riesling Beerenauslese	93	2010–2032+?
2002 Graacher Himmelreich Riesling Eiswein	91	now–2025+?
2002 Wehlener Sonnenuhr Riesling Eiswein	91	now–2025+?

WEISER-KÜNSTLER * * *
TRABEN-TRARBACH/MOSEL $20.00–$150.00

A lucky tip convinced the widow of Georg Immich (whose Batterieberg estate was until its sale in 1990 among the Mosel's foremost) to ask Konstantin Weiser (then working in New Zealand) to rescue her family's untended remaining five acres of old, ungrafted vines in the Spiegel portion of the Enkircher Ellergrub. Weiser answered the call and vinified his 2005 wine at Daniel Vollenweider's; he and Alexandra Künstler have now officially formed their domaine and are building on Weiser's promising initial success.

2005 Enkircher Ellergrub Riesling feinherb	90	now–2014+?
2005 Enkircher Ellergrub Riesling Spätlese	88	now–2018+?
2005 Enkircher Ellergrub Riesling Auslese	90	now–2022+?

WITTMANN * * *
WESTHOFEN/RHEINHESSEN $25.00–$400.00

The handsome, conscientious, dynamic young Phillip Wittmann (married to Eva Clüsserath of Clüsserath-Weiler on the Mosel) has brought considerable attention to his family domaine for the quality of its wines (already very good in his father Günter's day), as well as for being a pioneer among German growers in conversion to biodynamic practices. Beginning in 2004, the estate reintroduced large ovals (*Fuder*) after several years of working exclusively in stainless steel. It will be interesting to follow how this affects dry Riesling that have tended to be relatively stiff and austere. Nobly sweet wines at this address can, by contrast, be gaudy in their effusive sweetness. Along with Wagner-Stempel, this is the best place to taste delicious evidence of the Silvaner revival in Rheinhessen.

2004 Silvaner trocken S	91	now–2010
2001 Westhofener Aulerde Riesling trocken	91	now–2010
2003 Westhofener Aulerde Riesling Grosses Gewächs	89	now–2009+?

2001 Westhofener Kirchspiel Riesling trocken	90	now–2010
2004 Westhofener Kirchspiel Riesling Grosses Gewächs	87	now–2010
2002 Riesling Spätlese	89	now–2011
2004 Westhofener Moorstein Riesling Spätlese	87	now–2014+?
2002 Westhofener Moorstein Riesling Spätlese	92	now–2016+?
2001 Westhofener Moorstein Riesling Spätlese	91	now–2016
2004 Westhofener Moorstein Riesling Auslese	90	now–2018
2004 Westhofener Moorstein Riesling Auslese S	91	now–2020
2003 Westhofener Moorstein Riesling Auslese S	89	now–2011+
2001 Westhofener Moorstein Riesling Auslese S	91	now–2012
2003 Westhofener Kirchspiel Riesling Auslese S	89	now–2011+
2004 Westhofener Moorstein Riesling Beerenauslese	92	now–2025
2004 Westhofener Moorstein Riesling üTrockenbeerenauslese	92	now–2030
2003 Westhofener Moorstein Riesling Trockenbeerenauslese	93	now–2035
2003 Abalonga Trockenbeerenauslese	93	now–2025+?
2002 Abalonga Trockenbeerenauslese	93	now–2025+?
2001 Abalonga Trockenbeerenauslese	94	now–2020

ZILLIKEN—FORSTMEISTER GELTZ ★★★★★
SAARBURG/SAAR $18.00–$800.00

Though the official name of this estate remains Forstmeister Geltz—Zilliken, its reputation is entirely bound up with that of the Zilliken family. Longtime proprietor Hans-Joachim ("Hanno") Zilliken has slowly brought it to the forefront of German viticulture by bottling spectacularly long-aging Riesling, often incorporating improbably high levels of residual sugar yet always retaining clarity, energy, and lip-smacking balance. In recent years, Zilliken has siphoned a major portion of his production into a brand called "Butterfly," which features more body (at 11.5% to 12% alcohol) than his other wines, and only discreet residual sugar, but no lack of character. Nobly sweet wine and Eiswein are celebrated here: In vintages such as 2002, 2003, and 2005, Zilliken bottled wines in those categories with prodigious potential.

2005 Riesling trocken	87	now
2004 Riesling trocken	89	now
2005 Saarburger Rausch Riesling Kabinett trocken	89	now–2010
2005 Riesling "Butterfly" A.P. #17	88	now–2011+?
2004 Riesling "Butterfly" A.P. #9	88	now–2010+?
2004 Riesling "Butterfly" A.P. #14	87	now–2010+?
2005 Ockfener Bockstein Riesling Kabinett	87	now–2015
2004 Ockfener Bockstein Riesling Kabinett	88	now–2015
2002 Ockfener Bockstein Riesling Kabinett	89	now–2010
2005 Saarburger Rausch Riesling Kabinett	90	now–2020
2004 Saarburger Rausch Riesling Kabinett	90	now–2018
2002 Saarburger Rausch Riesling Kabinett	90	now–2014
2001 Saarburger Rausch Riesling Kabinett	88	now
2002 Ockfener Bockstein Riesling Spätlese	89	now–2017
2005 Saarburger Rausch Riesling Spätlese	92	now–2030
2004 Saarburger Rausch Riesling Spätlese A.P. #4	88	now–2022
2004 Saarburger Rausch Riesling Spätlese A.P. #2	93	now–2025
2002 Saarburger Rausch Riesling Spätlese A.P. #6	90	now–2022

2001 Saarburger Rausch Riesling Spätlese A.P. #3	90	now–2018
2005 Ockfener Bockstein Riesling Auslese	90	now–2028
2005 Saarburger Rausch Riesling Auslese A.P. #11	91	now–2032
2005 Saarburger Rausch Riesling Auslese A.P. #10	92	now–2035
2005 Saarburger Rausch Riesling Auslese A.P. #9	93	2010–2035+?
2004 Saarburger Rausch Riesling Auslese A.P. #3	92	now–2032
2002 Saarburger Rausch Riesling Auslese A.P. #5	92	now–2026
2005 Saarburger Rausch Riesling Auslese gold capsule A.P. #8	95	now–2040
2005 Saarburger Rausch Riesling Auslese gold capsule A.P. #7	94	now–2040
2004 Saarburger Rausch Riesling Auslese gold capsule A.P. #1	91	now–2032
2002 Saarburger Rausch Riesling Auslese gold capsule A.P. #3	93	now–2030
2005 Saarburger Rausch Riesling Auslese long gold capsule A.P. #6	94	now–2042
2005 Saarburger Rausch Riesling Auslese long gold capsule A.P. #5	96	now–2045
2005 Saarburger Rausch Riesling Beerenauslese A.P. #4	94	2012–2055
2005 Saarburger Rausch Riesling Beerenauslese A.P. #3	93	now–2055
2005 Saarburger Rausch Riesling Trockenbeerenauslese A.P. #1	97	2012–2060
2005 Saarburger Rausch Riesling Trockenbeerenauslese A.P. #2	98	now–2060

[piedmont]

[the basics]

A BRIEF INTRODUCTION

Italy is one of the most fascinating countries in the world of wine. The peninsula encompasses a broad range of microclimates, terrains, and grape varieties that yield an almost endless array of wines imbued with notable personality. In Piedmont, hillside vineyards and relatively cool temperatures are perfect conditions for the long-lived wines of Barolo and Barbaresco. Toward the east, Lombardy's Franciacorta is the center of Italy's *méthode champenoise* production, while Valtellina's most famous wines are quirky bottlings made from air-dried Nebbiolo. The Alpine microclimates of Alto Adige yield perfumed, minerally whites that share much in common with France's Alsace and Austria. Friuli too is capable of producing aromatic yet steely whites of notable personality, particularly the multivariety blends that represent the top wines for many estates. Veneto is most known for the jewel city of Venice, but its viticultural gems—Soave, Amarone, and Recioto—are all notable. Moving south, the warmer microclimates of Tuscany give life to some of the most famous Italian wines, including Chianti and Chianti Classico, Brunello di Montalcino, Vino Nobile di Montepulciano, and a number of high-end bottlings made from international grapes. Umbria's Sagrantino, which flourishes in Montefalco, is proving to be a unique variety loaded with personality. Campania is of course famous for its ancient ruins and scenic seaside resort towns, but it also boasts one of the oldest viticultural histories on the planet. These ash- and mineral-rich volcanic soils yield a number of phenomenal whites and reds loaded with character. Montepulciano, an extremely food-friendly and versatile wine, finds many shades of expression in Abruzzo. Not to be outdone, the islands of Sardinia and Sicily have come on the scene with a remarkable range of wines of late. Both islands boast a number of native varieties that are well worth discovering, not to mention newly rediscovered zones, such as the slopes around Mt. Etna in Sicily, that are producing some exciting bottlings sure to provide much enjoyment.

To make matters even more complex, Italy boasts well over 1,000 grape varieties, although some experts place that number much higher. While consumers may be familiar with Nebbiolo and Sangiovese, there is an incredible amount of rewarding drinking that awaits readers who are willing to take a few moments to acquaint themselves with Aglianico, Sagrantino, Lagrein, Corvina, Ribolla Gialla, Arneis, Greco di Tufo, and Fiano di Avellino, to name just a few of Italy's most expressive yet less well known native varieties. Of course, international varieties have a long history of flourishing in Italy as well. Syrah, Cabernet Franc, Cabernet Sauvignon, Merlot, Sauvignon, and Chardonnay have all proven capable of yielding world-class wines. In short, Italy offers a staggering variety of wines that offer something for every palate and budget.

GETTING A HANDLE ON DOCG, DOC, AND IGT

Given the breadth of Italy's wines, the choices can be daunting. Readers new to Italian wines may want to start with the traditional, historically prestigious appellations, which are governed by DOCG (Denominazione de Origine Controllata e Garantita) regulations. The DOCG rules are designed to guarantee that the grapes for a specific wine come from a carefully delimited geographical area and that the wine conforms to predetermined guidelines with regard to a number of criteria, including yields, alcohol, dry extract, color, aromas, taste, and aging. Each wine is tasted by a local tasting commission that certifies—in other words provides the *garantita* (guaranteed) part of the equation—that the wines meet the requirements and therefore quality for DOCG status. Italy currently has 36 DOCG wines, many of which can also qualify for additional designations such as "Riserva" or "Superiore." Some of the most famous DOCGs are Barolo, Barbaresco, Brunello di Montalcino, Chianti Classico, Vino Nobile di Montepulciano, and Taurasi. DOCG wines are easily recognized as they are required to carry a strip across the neck with a serial number that certifies that the wine meets the required criteria.

DOC (Denominazione di Origine Controllata) is similar to DOCG in spirit—that is, minimum quality guidelines are set for the wines—but testing is much less rigorous. DOC in general is used for less prestigious wines. Today there are well over 300 recognized DOCs. One of the most critical aspects to understanding DOC and DOCG is that they typically are used to indicate that fruit must be grown in a very specific, geographically delimited area.

While the DOC and DOCG laws were helpful in elevating the overall reputation of many wines, like any set of government regulations, they have also historically proven excessively restrictive for many of Italy's trailblazing growers and winemakers. The Vino da Tavola and later IGT (Indicazione Geografica Tipica) designations were created for wines made outside of the conventional frameworks. Readers will want to consult the Tuscany chapter for more detail on the historical evolution of these two designations. As a simple example, consider that the Chianti Classico DOCG calls for a minimum of 80% Sangiovese, specifies the source that the fruit must come from, and also sets aging requirements. By contrast, an IGT Toscana wine could be made from fruit grown anywhere in Tuscany, and the types of grapes used and aging are left entirely to the discretion of the winemaker. Upon the creation of IGT, the Vino da Tavola designation became much less widely used, and it appears only rarely these days, as producers are not allowed to specify variety, vintage, or area of origin for IGT wines.

TYPES OF WINE

Piedmont, located in Italy's northwest corner, is home to a number of outstanding wines, including Barolo and Barbaresco, the country's most majestic and ageworthy reds. Barolo and

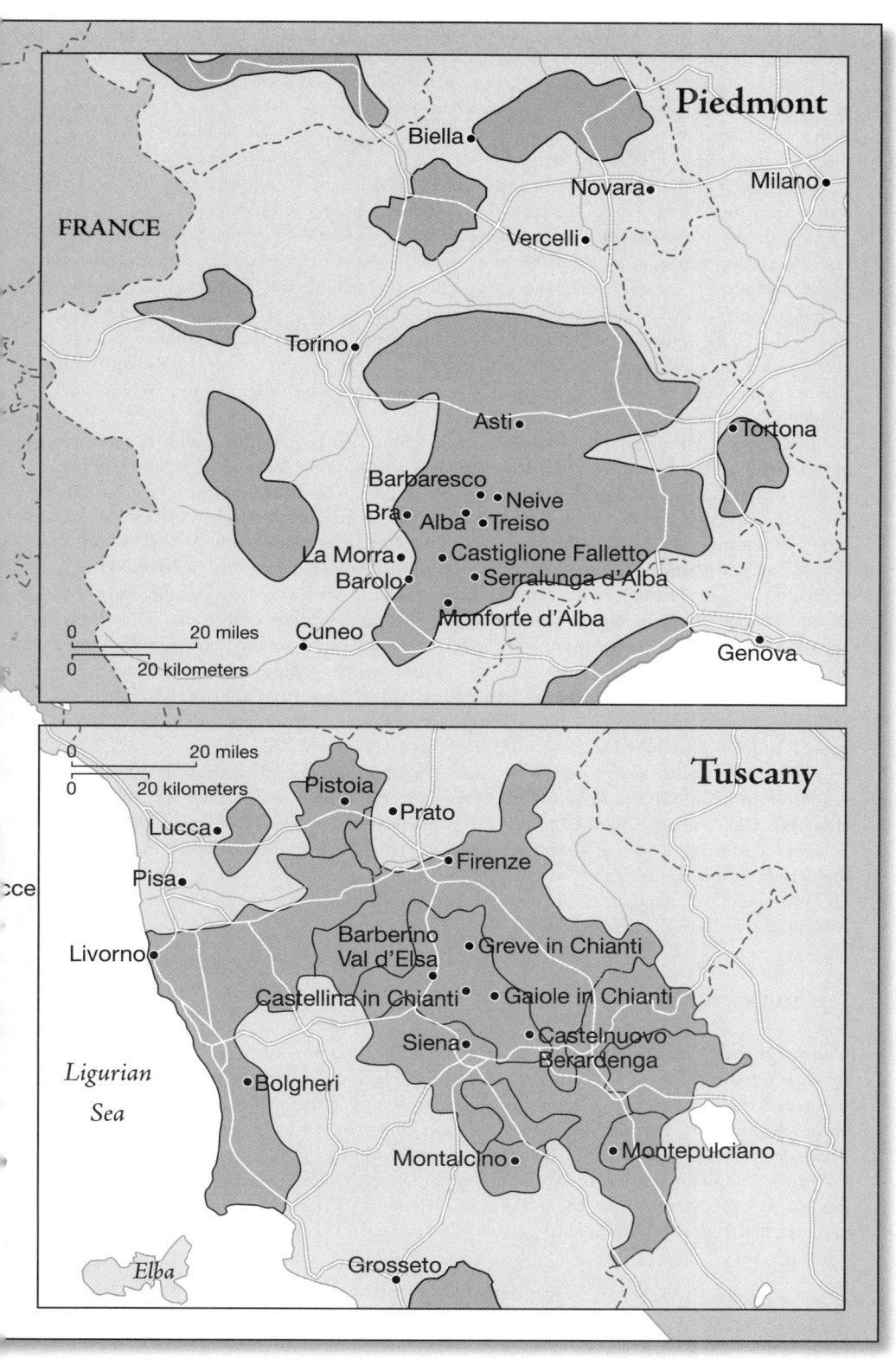

Barbaresco are both produced from the Nebbiolo grape, which finds its most profound expression in the undulating hills outside Alba known as the Langhe. In top vintages Barolos and Barbarescos require a minimum of a few years of cellaring and are capable of developing gracefully in bottle for several decades. Across from Barbaresco in Roero, the newly created Roero designation has stimulated interest in that region's higher-end Nebbiolo-based bottlings (some Arneis is permitted in the blend), but it is still too soon to know what heights Roero can achieve. Langhe Nebbiolo and Nebbiolo d'Alba are two appellations that yield a softer, more immediate style of Nebbiolo that is meant to be enjoyed young.

The lighter Nebbiolo-based wines of the northern districts of Gattinara, Ghemme, and Carema are frequently more accessible at an earlier age yet their relatively higher levels of acidity also allow the wines to drink well to age 20 or 25. In Gattinara, Ghemme, and Carema, Nebbiolo (also known as Spanna) is blended with other indigenous varieties. Nebbiolo is a variety that is naturally lacking in intensity of color, but in an attempt to appeal to modern tastes, producers have often felt the need to give their wines as much color as possible. With the exception of flawed wines, readers should assign no qualitative judgment to a Nebbiolo or Nebbiolo-based wine solely on intensity of color.

Barbera is a fruity wine with naturally high acidity that requires low yields to produce optimal results. The best wines come from the areas surrounding Asti and Alba. Many of the most complex Barberas are made in the province of Asti, where the grape is planted in top sites, unlike in Alba, where Nebbiolo has that privilege. In general, the Barberas from Asti are higher in acidity and more mineral-driven than the softer, lusher Barberas of Alba. The fruity, simple Barberas that can be found the year after the vintage are best consumed two to three years after release. The more important oak-aged bottlings are best enjoyed within their first decade, although there are a few wines capable of further development in bottle. The deeply colored Dolcetto is the everyday wine of Piedmont. Despite its name, Dolcetto is a dry wine. Dolcetto can be made in a variety of styles, from simple quaffing wines to more serious single-vineyard versions. Dolcetto is best enjoyed within two to three years after release. The best Dolcettos, those made from old vines and top sites, will make consumers forget the unfortunate "Beaujolais of Italy" label that has plagued these wines for years.

The top dry white variety in Piedmont is Arneis, a fresh wine best consumed within a year after the harvest. Erbaluce di Caluso, Gavi, and Cortese are simple whites yet can also be enjoyable. Chardonnay is found, but it is rarely interesting, let alone inspiring, in these hills. The sweet Moscato is yet another Piedmontese gem. This light-bodied sparkling wine is the perfect accompaniment to fruit-based desserts and makes a fine conclusion to any meal. Unfortunately, Asti Spumante, Piedmont's other sparkling white, maintains its reputation as a charmless, industrially produced wine.

[grape varieties]

The indigenous Nebbiolo, Barbera, and Dolcetto are the most important red varieties in Piedmont. Interestingly, these varieties have proven capable of making great wines only in Piedmont, and the best examples are imbued with unmistakable regional character. Among the whites the native Arneis and Moscato are the most interesting varieties, although Cortese and Erbaluce can be good as well. Small amounts of international varieties are planted, including Cabernet Sauvignon, Merlot, and Chardonnay, although these have seldom produced satisfying results in Piedmont. Last, the indigenous Grignolino, Freisa, and Brachetto are quirky varieties that appeal mostly to local palates and have found only limited success in international markets.

RED

Barolo, which is made from 100% Nebbiolo, is among the world's most fascinating wines because of its ability to develop a complex array of aromas and flavors over the course of its life. Barolo is also a wine that offers an extraordinary range of expression with regard to vintage, site, and microclimate. When Barolos are young, typical aromas and flavors include roses, violets, dried flowers, baking spices, anise, dried herbs, tar, new leather, cherries, plums, and prunes. With age the wines often gain volume and depth and the flavors turn to more tertiary notes of dried flowers, stewed plums, prunes, pine, menthol, baking spices, tar, and worn-in leather. The finest Barolos develop their tertiary notes while maintaining a core of sweet fruit that accompanies the wines throughout their lives. Differences in site and microclimate also greatly influence the flavor profile of the wines. For example, the Barolos of La Morra are often fragrant and perfumed with prominent notes of small red fruits. At the other extreme of the zone, in Serralunga, the wines tend to feature blacker fruits and a darker set of flavors that can include tar, smoke, iron, and licorice, to name just a few of the nuances that can be found in the wines.

Generally speaking, producers' entry-level Barolos, particularly in warm vintages, can be accessible fairly young, while the top single-vineyard bottlings in cooler vintages will require significant patience. In important, ageworthy vintages, the best wines are capable of lasting 40 years or more.

Barolo must spend a minimum of two years in oak and a third year in bottle prior to being released. The aging regime of any wine and the choice of oak casks and/or smaller French oak barrels will obviously play a role in a wine's flavor profile.

Barbaresco, also made from 100% Nebbiolo, offers an aromatic and flavor profile similar to that of Barolo, but the wines are generally lighter in body and less structured. Like Barolo, Barbaresco is a wine that showcases the unique qualities of vintage, site, and microclimate with notable clarity. Barbaresco is often more accessible than Barolo at a young age and tends to have a shorter aging curve, lasting about 20 years, although a handful of wines will continue to develop into their third decade and beyond. Barbaresco spends a minimum of one year in oak and a second year in bottle prior to being released. As with Barolo, the oak aging regime can play an important role in a given wine's flavor profile.

Barbera has shed its old image as being an overly acidic, rustic wine. Today's Barberas are lush, fruit-driven, and immensely pleasurable. As noted above, the wines of Asti are higher in acidity and minerality, while those of Alba tend to be softer and rounder. Barberas are made in two basic styles. The simpler, fresh Barberas are released a year after the harvest. These fruit-driven wines are often aged in stainless steel and are meant for near-term consumption. The more important Barbera bottlings are usually made from single-vineyard sites that offer notable complexity. These Barberas feature superior concentration of fruit and greater overall structure. The wines typically spend a period of time in oak, which allows them to develop further depth and richness. Barbera is a variety that has proven especially well suited to French oak, which imparts a set of aromas and flavors that marry well with those of the fruit. The traditional cask-aged Barberas are perhaps slightly more transparent with regard to variety and site. At their best, both barrel-aged and cask-aged Barberas offer a thrilling drinking experience. As Barbera ages, it can also develop interesting tertiary nuances, but they usually come at the expense of fruit, which can make the wines' acidity more prominent. There are a few exceptions, but most Barberas, even the finest bottlings, are best consumed within a decade of the vintage.

Dolcetto typically offers a flavor profile of blueberries, blackberries, almonds, chocolate, spices, and minerals. Virtually all Dolcettos are aged in stainless steel and are released the year after the harvest. Dolcetto is a fresh, fruity wine meant to be consumed within two to three years after the vintage. The best wines, those that come from old vines or particularly expressive sites, can offer notable complexity. In particular, the wines of Dogliani and Diano d'Alba are unique.

The Nebbiolo-based wines of northern Piedmont (Gattinara, Ghemme, and Carema) are typically more modest in structure than the bigger Barolos and Barbarescos. Their aromatic and flavor profile tends toward an expression of flowers, mountain herbs, and earthiness. The acidity is more pronounced in these cooler microclimates, and the wines often display distinct mineral notes. Although a lack of ripeness has been a problem in the past, today's trend of warmer growing seasons has been a positive factor for these production zones.

WHITE

ARNEIS Made from a rediscovered indigenous Piedmontese variety, Arneis is a floral, fruity wine with excellent minerality and a medium-bodied profile. In some vintages the fruit can take on a honeyed quality that adds further complexity. Arneis is an excellent aperitif or starter wine. The best versions are delicious and well worth the effort of searching out.

GAVI/CORTESE DI GAVI Gavi tends toward an expression of citrus and minerals with good body but only modest complexity. It is rarely inspiring.

MOSCATO Moscato is the traditional dessert wine of Piedmont. Because Moscato is a sweet sparkling wine that is consumed without much fanfare, it is tempting to think that all Moscatos are essentially the same. Much of what is produced is of a commercial, supermarket level of quality, but there are a small handful of growers who work with low yields and well-positioned vineyards to produce remarkable wines. The best Moscatos are crisp, creamy-textured wines with floral aromatics and peach, apricot, and green apple flavors. Moscato should be purchased and drunk immediately, when it is at the height of its freshness. It is the perfect wine for fruit-based desserts and also a wonderful accompaniment to the hazelnut-based desserts that so often grace the Piedmontese table.

[the region]

A CLOSER LOOK AT THE BAROLO AND BARBARESCO REGIONS

Barolo is produced in eleven villages—Barolo, Castiglione Falletto, Cherasco, Diano d'Alba, Grinzane Cavour, La Morra, Monforte d'Alba, Novello, Roddi, Serralunga d'Alba, and Verduno—but the overwhelming majority of the most important wines come from the five picturesque hillside towns of Barolo, Castiglione Falletto, La Morra, Monforte d'Alba, and Serralunga d'Alba. Although each of these five towns yields wines of distinct character, producers' styles and vintages can often transcend the attributes of any specific site.

The vineyards are rich in marine deposits, a legacy that remains from the period when Piedmont lay under water. The Barolo region can be roughly divided into three main major zones with corresponding soil types. The eastern village of Serralunga contains the oldest and most compact soils. The terrain is composed of gray marls alternating with grayish reddish sandstone, with a heavy presence of calcium carbonate and iron, a mixture also known as *formazione di Lequio,* which gives Serralunga Barolos their famed structure and longevity. In hot vintages this is often the best-performing part of the Barolo zone, as the compact soils have the benefit of being especially water-retentive. Castiglione Falletto and Monforte feature the layers of grayish yellowish sands alternating with gray sandstones known as Diano sandstone. The Barolos of Castiglione Falletto are often very aromatic, yet also ageworthy, while those of Monforte can resemble the bigger, powerful style typical of Serralunga. The towns of La

Morra and Barolo lie in the western part of the zone. The prevailing soil type is the combination of blueish marl, sand, and limestone known as Sant'Agata marl. In general the wines are more aromatic, smaller-scaled Barolos that reach maturity sooner than those of Serralunga and Monforte. Some texts make a further distinction of the Barolo La Morra zone by separating the area into the different soil types. Of course, generalizations are always difficult because each of the vineyards and plots has a personality all its own. For example, Barolo's most famous vineyard, Cannubi, contains layers of both Sant'Agata marls and *formazione di Lequio*.

BAROLO

The town of Barolo is located in the center of the zone geographically and historically, for it is here that Barolo wine as it is known today was first produced. The village courts 405 acres of Barolo-designated vineyards and 90 producers. Barolo is most famous for the Cannubi vineyard, which yields wines of extraordinary perfume and elegance. The best Cannubis are remarkably accessible when young yet also age well. Like so many things in Italy, the boundaries of the vineyard are not particularly well defined, and today the term "Cannubi" seems to be used indiscriminately to speak about not only the vineyard but also the zone covering the adjacent plots. Barolo's other famous vineyards include Brunate and Cerequio, both of which are shared with the town of La Morra. Reference-point Barolos from Barolo range from floral, perfumed wines like Cannubis of Scavino and E. Pira–Chiara Boschis to the very traditional Barolo of Bartolo Mascarello and more powerful classics like Sancrone's Barolo Cannubi Boschis and Giuseppe Rinaldi's Barolo Brunate/Le Coste. Barolo ranks fourth in size among the five most significant winemaking communes of Barolo, with 13% of the total production.

Highly regarded Barolo vineyards: Brunate (shared with La Morra), Cerequio (also shared with La Morra), Sarmassa, Via Nuova, Bricco delle Viole, and Cannubi, which is perhaps the most storied of all Barolo vineyards.

CASTIGLIONE FALLETTO

Castiglione Falletto's 319 acres of vine and 55 growers account for roughly 10% of Barolo production. The Barolos of Castiglione combine elements of both the eastern and western parts of the zones. The wines often show very expressive aromatics, most notably in the Monprivato and Rocche vineyards. The wines from these sites come across as medium in body, especially when young, yet they often fill out with bottle age. Vineyards such as Bricco Fiasco and Bricco Boschis typically yield a massive, powerful style of Barolo that has more in common with the wines of Monforte and Serralunga. The Barolos of Castiglione can be very long-lived. Some examples of representative Castiglione Barolos include Vietti and Brovia's Barolo Rocche, Ceretto's Bricco Rocche, Giuseppe Mascarello's Barolo Monprivato, Scavino's Barolo Bric del Fiasc, and Cavallotto's Barolo Riserva Bricco Boschis Vigna San Giuseppe.

Highly regarded Castiglione Falletto vineyards: Monprivato, Rocche di Castiglione, Bricco Rocche, Bric del Fiasc (also known as Bricco Fiasco), Villero, Vignolo, and Bricco Boschis.

MONFORTE D'ALBA

With its steep vineyards, winding roads, and expansive vistas, Monforte d'Alba is a gorgeous spot. While tourists tend to congregate around La Morra and Barolo, Monforte retains the quiet country air of a small, sleepy town. Monforte has 514 acres of Barolo vineyards under vine, shared by 122 growers, which totals 17% of total production. One of the most profound expressions of Monforte is found in the Ginestra vineyard and Domenico Clerico's Barolo Ciabot Mentin Ginestra. Other representative wines include Conterno Fantino's Barolo Sorì Ginestra, Elio Grasso's Barolo Ginestra Casa Maté, Aldo Conterno's Barolo Cicala, and Rocche dei Manzoni's Barolos Big 'd Big and Vigna d'La Roul. These are big, powerful, and structured wines that are capable of evolving beautifully in bottle for 20-plus years. Aldo Conterno's famed Barolo Riserva Granbussia shows the softer, gentler side of Monforte.

Highly regarded Monforte d'Alba vineyards: Bussia (and its subplots Cicala, Colonello, Romirasco, Dardi, and Pianpolvere), Ginestra, Gavarini, Gramolere, La Villa, Le Coste, Mosconi, and Santo Stefano di Perno.

LA MORRA

La Morra is a beautiful village that offers spectacular views of the surrounding countryside. Its 277 growers and 949 acres of vineyards account for 31% of the Barolo production, making it the largest of the five major towns. The soils here contain a higher percentage of sand and thus yield the most perfumed, delicate Barolos. These are also the most approachable Barolos to enjoy when young. The town remains deeply influenced by its spiritual leader, Elio Altare, who, among his many achievements, inspired an entire generation of small producers to pursue estate-bottling their wines as opposed to selling fruit and wine in bulk. Among the most famous La Morra Barolos are Elio Altare's Barolo Arborina and Barolo Brunate, Roberto Voerzio's Barolo Cerequio and Barolo Brunate, Scavino's Barolo Riserva Rocche dell'Annunziata, Revello's Barolo Conca, Giovanni Corino's Barolo Giachini, and Renato Corino's Barolo Rocche.

Highly regarded La Morra vineyards: Cerequio (shared with Barolo), Rocche dell'Annunziata Brunate (shared with Barolo), Arborina, Giachini, Monfalletto, Conca, Gattera, and La Serra.

SERRALUNGA

Serralunga's 98 producers and 497 acres represent 13% of Barolo production. In many ways Serralunga is the most mysterious of the Barolo villages because its qualities are still being discovered. Although great Barolos have been made here for decades, the village and its reputation have suffered because of the underperforming wines made by Fontanafredda, the town's largest landowner. As a result, Serralunga has been the latest of the five major communes to truly demonstrate the full range of its potential as the town's smaller, artisan growers have been slower to emerge. Serralunga is justly famous for powerful, long-lived wines. Indeed, these are the most complex, structured, and ageworthy Barolos. The top Serralunga Barolos include Bruno Giacosa's Barolos Falletto and Le Rocche del Falletto, Giacomo Conterno's Barolos Cascina Francia and Monfortino, Cappellano's Barolo Gabutti Pie Franco, Azelia's Barolo San Rocco, Brovia's Barolo Ca' Mia, Vietti's Barolo Lazzarito, Pira's Barolos Marenca and Vigna Rionda, and Massolino's Barolo Riserva Vigna Rionda. Bruno Giacosa no longer makes a Barolo from the Vigna Rionda vineyard, but his Collina Riondas from the 1978, 1982, and 1989 vintages are among the greatest wines that have ever been produced anywhere. Angelo Gaja's Sperss contains a small percentage of Barbera, so it falls out of the Barolo designation, but it is packed with Serralunga character.

Highly regarded Serralunga d'Alba vineyards: Vigna Rionda, Falletto, Cascina Francia, Marenca, Margheria, Arione, Lazzarito, Ornato, Parafada, Gabutti, San Rocco, Prapò, Voghera/Brea, and Cerette.

BARBARESCO

In aggregate the Barbaresco zone is about one-third the size of the Barolo-producing area. While the vast majority of Barolo is exported, a far greater percentage of Barbaresco is consumed within Italy. The mentality of producers here is much more closed than that of the Barolo producers, which is remarkable considering that the two areas are separated by just a few kilometers. Barbaresco's image problem is easily demonstrated by Nebbiolo grape prices, which are available at a significant discount when compared to Barolo-designated grapes. Too many wineries have been chronic underachievers, a pity considering the stupendous quality of the vineyards. As the younger generation assumes control of many estates, there is good reason to hope that Barbaresco will soon be able to put its inconsistent past to rest.

Barbaresco is produced in the towns of Barbaresco, Neive, and Treiso. The *terroir* is composed mostly of the Sant'Agata marls found in La Morra and Barolo. At its best Barbaresco is notable for its exquisite aromatics and a more accessible, seductive personality than Barolo. Nebbiolo in Barbaresco typically matures about ten days earlier than in Barolo, and in general the wines possess less structure, concentration, and alcohol than their bigger siblings. The finest Barbarescos also offer silky tannins that make the wines easier to enjoy at a younger age. Although Barbaresco is generally considered a feminine wine, there are a handful of sites that stand out for a decidedly potent, masculine style of wine, including Rabajà, Pajé, Montefico, and Montestefano (all in Barbaresco), Santo Stefano (Neive), and Pajoré and Valeirano (Treiso). In blind tastings these Barbarescos might easily be confused for Barolos.

The town of Barbaresco and its 105 growers share 558 acres of Barbaresco-designated vineyards, which accounts for 47% of total production. Many of Barbaresco's best vineyards are farmed by members of the Produttori del Barbaresco cooperative, whose wines, the Riservas in particular, are benchmarks for traditionally made Barbaresco. The wines also offer terrific value. At the high end of the spectrum, Angelo Gaja has essentially redefined Barbaresco by proving that his wines can be served next to the finest wines from anywhere in the world. With such a famous and successful neighbor, you might think other producers would emulate a proven recipe for success, but the reality is that few producers have had the resources and, perhaps more important, the ambition, to follow in his footsteps. Reference-point Barbarescos from Barbaresco include Bruno Giacosa's Barbarescos Asili and Rabajà (which can be bottled as a Riserva in top vintages), Produttori del Barbaresco's Barbaresco Riservas Asili, Rabajà, Ovello, and Montefico, Bruno Rocca's Barbaresco Rabajà, Cantina del Pino's Barbaresco and Barbaresco Ovello, and Albino Rocca's Bric Ronchi and Sorì Loreto. Gaja's Barbaresco is made from a blend of vineyards across the zone. His Costa Russi, Sorì Tildìn, and Sorì San Lorenzo contain a small percentage of Barbera and are therefore not Barbarescos, but they are consistently among Italy's and the world's finest wines.

Highly regarded Barbaresco vineyards: In late 2007, the Barbaresco vineyard boundaries were updated. The new regulations will go into effect with the 2007 vintage Barbarescos, which will be released beginning in 2010. At that time, some of the vineyard and producer details below will be updated. Rabajà, Asili, Loreto, Martinenga, Moccagatta, Montefico, Montestefano, Ovello, Pajè, Pora, Rio Sordo, Roncagliette (the source of Gaja's Costa Russi and Sorì Tildìn), and Secondine (source of Gaja's Sorì San Lorenzo).

NEIVE

With its 167 estates and 339 acres of Barbaresco vineyards, Neive accounts for 29% of the production of Barbaresco. While Angelo Gaja is the patriarch of Barbaresco, Bruno Giacosa is without question the father figure of Neive. In many ways Giacosa *is* Barbaresco, as no other producer can match the staggering number of monumental Barbarescos he has released over the years. Generally speaking, the Barbarescos from Neive are bigger wines than those of Barbaresco. Textbook examples include Giacosa's Barbaresco Santo Stefano, La Spinetta's Barbaresco Starderi, Sottimano's Barbaresco Cottà, and Vietti's Barbaresco Masseria.

Highly regarded Neive vineyards: Santo Stefano, Basarin, Cottà, Currà, Gallina, Serraboella, and Starderi.

TREISO

Treiso is the smallest of the three Barbaresco communes and accounts for 19% of the total production. Its 232 acres of Barbaresco-designated vineyards are farmed by 88 wineries.

Treiso contains the highest-altitude vineyards in the Barbaresco zone. The wines are often sinewy and powerful, with prominent suggestions of spices, menthol, and minerals. Treiso remains less well known than the other Barbaresco communes because most of its top vineyards are farmed by producers based outside the town. Quintessential expressions of Barbaresco from Treiso include Sottimano's Barbaresco Pajorè, La Spinetta's Barbaresco Valeirano, and Fiorenzo Nada's Barbaresco Rombone. Treiso is also an excellent source of Dolcetto. According to old-timers, Nebbiolo was ripped out of many top sites and replanted with Dolcetto during a period when Barbaresco was a tough sell.

Highly regarded Treiso vineyards: Pajorè, Valeirano, Rombone, Nervo, Marcarini, and Rizzi.

[the wines]

SOME THOUGHTS ON TRADITIONAL AND MODERN STYLES OF BAROLO AND BARBARESCO

Much has been made of traditional and modern styles in Barolo and Barbaresco. At times the debate has reached alarming levels of animosity, but the simple reality is that exceptional wines are being made in both styles. In fact, recent years have seen a convergence of styles that often makes it difficult, if not impossible, to place a producer in a neat little box. The wines have started to speak for themselves.

Of course, the history of Barolo and Barbaresco is rooted in a traditional style of wine-making that harkens back to the region's agrarian past. Grape growing wasn't always a profitable business. It was quite common for land to be planted to mixed agriculture, which is to say vines, grains, and fruit trees in the same plot. Grapes were only one of several crops a farm might produce. In the 1950s, 1960s, and 1970s Piedmont was a poor region, and the prevailing culture was one of producing quantity rather than quality, aided by the abundant use of pesticides and fertilizers. The Nebbiolo harvest occurred in late October and early November, much later than today, in part because the growing season was cooler but also in part because the vines were overloaded with fruit and thus struggled to ripen. An excellent harvest occurred maybe twice a decade, while other years were simply average or worse. Times were challenging, to say the least. Barolo and Barbaresco were hardly the coveted wines they are today. It may seem hard to believe, but as recently as the early 1980s Barolo and Barbaresco were often given away when clients purchased Dolcetto! The wines were left to macerate on the skin for weeks, sometimes until Christmas, while families tended to their other crops. The wines were given an extended period of oak aging, which was needed to smooth out the wines' tannins.

Barrels weren't cleaned properly, nor were they replaced on a regular basis, which left the wines with musty, unclean flavors. Prior to bottling, the wines were often placed in glass demijohns and left to age in attics, where the extreme swing of temperatures from the heat of summer to the bitter cold of winter caused many wines to oxidize prematurely. The wines that did survive this abuse took years, if not decades, to become drinkable. Against this backdrop, it is all the more remarkable that producers like Giacomo Conterno, Aldo Conterno, Bartolo Mascarello, Giuseppe Mascarello, Bruno Giacosa, and Angelo Gaja had the foresight to pursue an unrelenting path of quality that allowed them to succeed in making profound wines that have stood the test of time.

The first early proponents of what can be called the modern school of winemaking in Piedmont were Renato Ratti and Angelo Gaja, both of whom favored shorter periods of skin contact, temperature-controlled alcoholic fermentation, malolactic fermentation that occurred right after the alcoholic fermentation, and shorter periods of oak aging, all of which were innovations in the late 1960s. Gaja, the late Valentino Migliorini of Rocche dei Manzoni, and others began experimenting with small French oak barrels in the late 1970s. In the early 1980s a group of young producers began to radically change the way Barolo was produced. Influenced by their trips to Burgundy, producers such as Elio Altare, Luciano Sandone, Enrico Scavino, and Domenico Clerico took things to another level by aggressively lowering yields, drastically shortening fermentation times, and relying exclusively on French oak barrels to age their wines. The practice of green harvesting, or reducing yields by dropping significant amounts of fruit, looked like heresy to the older generation who had grown up in a period of near famine. Although rarely discussed today, there was more than a little experimenting with adding other varieties to Nebbiolo in an attempt to make wines that were soft, round, and deeply colored and would therefore appeal to international palates.

Attention to the region soared in the mid-1990s, when the superripe, flashy 1990 Barolos and Barbarescos were released. As the 1990s progressed, producers sought to achieve even greater richness and concentration in the wines. As in any reactionary movement, there was an overshooting effect. Many of the wines of the mid- to late 1990s were excessively heavy and laden with new French oak. Toward the end of the decade and into the early 2000s the tide started to change, and producers began backing away from the extreme production methods of the past as they searched for more balance in their wines. Macerations were gradually lengthened, toast levels were reduced, and the use of new oak diminished. The first vintage that hinted at this newfound level of maturity was 2001, but by 2004 the change was evident.

Today there is a convergence of styles that is thankfully making the old, tiresome discussions of traditional versus modern irrelevant. The modernists have largely moved away from the excessively short maceration times of the past. The use of oak is notably more judicious. At the same time, traditionalists have become more attentive to vineyard practices and cleanliness is much improved. The casks may still be large, but some producers have moved toward French oak and virtually all estates are switching out their used casks with greater frequency than before. The trend toward warmer growing seasons has made the wines increasingly user-friendly when young and has also resulted in more consistently excellent to outstanding vintages than was the case in the past.

High-quality winemaking has proven to be style-agnostic. Rather, it is defined by meticulous work in the vineyards and a noninterventionalist approach in the cellar, which calls for handling the wines as little as possible. Fining and filtration are kept to a minimum, as is the use of additives such as sulfur dioxide. The best Piedmont wines reflect a contemporary, updated expression of the region's agrarian heritage. Most high-quality producers are equally fanatic about what they eat, and their wines are made with the same approach to purity that is found in the world's finest artisan meats, vegetables, cheeses, and other high-quality foods. Simply put, the best Piedmontese wines are among the most natural, unadulterated handcrafted wines being made anywhere in the world.

AGING POTENTIAL
Arneis: 1–2 years
Barbera: 5–12 years
Barbaresco: 8–25 years
Barolo: 8–40 years
Carema: 6–12 years
Dolcetto: 2–4 years
Gattinara/Ghemme: 8–20 years
Gavi: 1–2 years
Moscato: 12–18 months

OVERALL QUALITY LEVEL

As a whole, Piedmont delivers outstanding quality. Over the last few years producers have arrived at a new level of maturity reflected in Barolos and Barbarescos that offer notable balance and harmony, as opposed to the overly concentrated and heavily oaked wines that were quite common in the 1990s. The general trend toward low (but not excessively low) yields and noninterventionalist winemaking practiced by top estates is yielding wines of remarkable clarity and expressiveness. I am happy to report that the defective, flawed wines that were once quite common are now very few, although some examples still exist. Broadly speaking, average quality is significantly higher in Barolo than Barbaresco, which means that producers in Barbaresco still have quite a bit of upside to unlock from their vineyards.

The biggest threat to quality in Piedmont is overproduction. For example, in 1990, 6.1 million bottles of Barolo were produced. By 2004, 15 years later, that number had skyrocketed to 10.2 million, an increase of 67%. Barbaresco has seen a similar jump, as producers seek to cash in on the growing value of the Nebbiolo grape and Barolo and Barbaresco as finished wines. Many of the new vines are being planted in sites ill suited to the cultivation of this fickle variety. To be sure, the trend toward warmer growing seasons means that Nebbiolo is ripening in spots that were impractical years ago, but the simple fact remains that many of the new vineyards yield wines of little character, soul, or personality.

IMPORTANT INFORMATION

Getting a handle on Piedmont takes a small investment of time, but the rewards are infinite. A good starting point is to focus on top producers who consistently offer high-quality wines across their entire portfolio. At a minimum, most producers in Piedmont bottle a Dolcetto, a Barbera, and one or more Barolos or Barbarescos. The entry-level wines often allow consumers to gain some understanding of a given producer's style without spending excessive amounts of money. Like Burgundy, Barolo and Barbaresco are divided into many small vineyards, often owned by several growers. Readers who are new to Piedmontese wines will want to spend some time learning about the finest vineyards in the region. Last, vintages offer an extraordinary level of diversity. In the paragraphs below I have outlined a strategy for learning about each of these three elements.

A GUIDE TO THE TOP BAROLO AND BARBARESCO VINEYARDS AND WINES

Barolo and Barbaresco can be loosely compared to Burgundy in that the vineyards are geographically delimited and ownership of plots within any given vineyard is often divided among various families and/or producers. Traditionally Barolo was made from a blend of fruit sourced from various vineyards. The practice of blending fruit from different sites served an important purpose. Some vineyards were known for their aromatics, others for the richness of their fruit, yet others for the structural backbone they gave wines. It is a real treat to taste an impeccably stored bottle from this era, as the wines often show remarkable harmony. Today the blended Barolo is most often (but not always) relegated to an entry-level wine made from an estate's younger or less important sites. These wines are often referred to as Barolo *normale* or Barolo *base,* terms that do an immense disservice to the best of these wines. Personally, I would much rather drink a first-rate producer's Barolo *normale* than an average producer's top wine. Furthermore, these terms are quite harmful to the few producers who still make a blended Barolo the old-fashioned way. For example, taste a great wine from Bartolo Mascarello, a Barolo made from a blend of superb sites, and it is clear there is nothing "normal" about the wine. For those reasons I will dispense with the terms *normale* and *base* in these pages.

The move toward bottling vineyards separately began in the 1960s, even though certain vineyards had long been recognized for yielding remarkably unique wines. Single-vineyard Barolos and Barbarescos naturally allowed for the specific traits of each site to be fully expressed in the wines. Over the years several prominent scholars created hierarchies of sites, but those classifications remained informal, rather than formal, as in Burgundy. While it is clear that the top vineyards merit being bottled on their own, the fashion for single-vineyard Barolos—and their implied prestige—has led to a proliferation of average wines of no real distinction that come from second- or third-class sites. Therefore, consumers can't assume that a single-vineyard bottling is by nature a superior wine.

Following are lists of the best producers of wine from specific vineyards.

BEST BAROLO VINEYARDS, WINES, AND PRODUCERS

VINEYARD	WINE(S)	PRODUCER(S)
Arborina (La Morra)	Barolo, Langhe Nebbiolo	Elio Altare, Mauro Veglio, Bovio, Renato Corino
Arione (Serralunga)	Barolo	Enzo Boglietti
Boscareto (Serralunga)	Barolo	Principiano
Bricco Boschis (Castiglione Falletto)	Barolo	Cavallotto
Bricco delle Viole (Barolo)	Barolo (Barbera d'Alba)	G.D. Vajra, Mario Marengo
Bricco Fiasco (aka Bric del Fiasc) (Castiglione Falletto)	Barolo	Paolo Scavino, Azelia, Brovia (Barolo Garblèt Suè)
Bricco Rocche (Castiglione Falletto)	Barolo	Ceretto
Brunate (La Morra, shared with Barolo)	Barolo	Elio Altare, Roberto Voerzio, Ceretto, Enzo Boglietti, Mario Marengo, Marcarini, Vietti, Giuseppe Rinaldi (Barolo Brunate/ Le Coste)
Bussia (Monforte)	Barolo	Parusso, Prunotto
Cannubi (Barolo)	Barolo	Paolo Scavino, E. Pira–Chiara Boschis, Einaudi, Giuseppe Rinaldi Barolo Cannubi (San Lorenzo/Ravera)
Cannubi Boschis (Barolo)	Barolo	Luciano Sandrone
Capalot (La Morra)	Barolo	Roberto Voerzio (Barolo Riserva Vecchie Viti dei Capalot e delle Brunate)
Cascina Francia (Serralunga)	Barolo	Giacomo Conterno
Case Nere (La Morra)	Barolo	Enzo Boglietti, Roberto Voerzio (Barolo Fossati/Case Nere)
Castelletto (Monforte)	Barolo	Mauro Veglio, Giovanni Manzone
Cerequio (La Morra, shared with Barolo)	Barolo, Langhe Nebbiolo	Roberto Voerzio, Gaja (Conteisa)
Cerretta (Serralunga)	Barolo	Azelia, Ettore Germano, Giovanni Rosso

VINEYARD	WINE(S)	PRODUCER(S)
Cicala (Monforte)	Barolo	Aldo Conterno
Colonello (Monforte)	Barolo	Aldo Conterno
Conca (La Morra)	Barolo	Revello, Mauro Molino, Renato Ratti
Le Coste (Barolo)	Barolo	Giacomo Grimaldi
Dardi (Monforte)	Barolo	Alessandro e Gian Natale Fantino, Poderi Colla
Delizia (Serralunga)	Barolo	Fontanafredda
Fossatti (La Morra)	Barolo	Enzo Boglietti, Roberto Voerzio (Barolo Fossati/ Case Nere)
Gabutti (Serralunga)	Barolo	Cappellano (Barolos Pie Franco and Rupestris)
Gancia/Luciani (La Morra)	Barolo	Silvio Grasso, Mauro Molino
Gattera (La Morra)	Barolo	Revello, Mauro Veglio, Bovio
Gavarini (Monforte)	Barolo	Elio Grasso
Giachini (La Morra)	Barolo	Renato Corino, Giovanni Corino, Revello, Silvio Grasso
Ginestra (Monforte)	Barolo	Domenico Clerico, Conterno-Fantino, Elio Grasso, Paolo Conterno
Gramolere (Monforte)	Barolo	Giovanni Manzone
Lazzarito (Serralunga)	Barolo	Vietti, Fontanafredda, Guido Porro
Liste (Barolo)	Barolo	Borgogno (Barolo Storico)
Manzoni (La Morra)	Barolo	Silvio Grasso
Manzoni Soprani (Monforte)	Barolo	Rocche Manzoni Valentino (Barolo Vigna d'La Roul)
Marcenasco (La Morra)	Barolo	Renato Ratti
Marenca (Serralunga)	Barolo	Luigi Pira, Gaja (Sperss)
Margheria (Serralunga)	Barolo	Massolino, Luigi Pira
Mariondino (Castiglione Falletto)	Barolo	Parusso
Monfalletto (La Morra)	Barolo	Cordero di Montezemolo
Monprivato (Castiglione Falletto)	Barolo	Giuseppe Mascarello
Mosconi (Monforte)	Barolo	Domenico Clerico (Percristina), Parusso, Rocche dei Manzoni Barolo (Big 'd Big), Conterno-Fantino
Ornato (Serralunga)	Barolo	Pio Cesare
Paiagallo (Barolo)	Barolo	Fontanafredda
Pernanno (Castiglione Falletto)	Barolo	Cascina Bongiovanni
Pajana (Manforte d'Alba)	Barolo	Domenico Clerico
Pianpolvere Soprano (Manforte d'Alba)	Barolo	Pianpolvere Soprano
Pira (Castiglione Falletto)	Barolo	Roagna (Barolo La Rocca e La Pira)

VINEYARD	WINE(S)	PRODUCER(S)
Prapò (Serralunga)	Barolo	Ceretto
Ravera (Novello)	Barolo	Giuseppe Rinaldi (Barolo Cannubi (San Lorenzo)/ Ravera), Cogno, Abbona
Rocche di Castiglione (Castiglione Falletto)	Barolo	Vietti, Brovia
Rocche dell'Annunziata (La Morra)	Barolo	Andrea Oberto, Paolo Scavino, Roberto Voerzio, Revello, Renato Corino, Mauro Veglio, Renato Ratti
Rocche di Bussia (Monforte d'Alba)	Barolo	Parusso
Romirasco (Monforte)	Barolo	Aldo Conterno
La Rosa (Serralunga)	Barolo	Fontanafredda
San Rocco (Serralunga)	Barolo	Azelia
Sarmassa (La Morra)	Barolo	Roberto Voerzio
Santo Stefano di Perno (Monforte)	Barolo	Giuseppe Mascarello, Rocche dei Manzoni, Giovanni Manzone
La Serra (La Morra)	Barolo	Roberto Voerzio, Marcarini
Via Nuova (Barolo)	Barolo	E. Pira–Chiara Boschis, Einaudi (Barolo Costa Grimaldi)
Vigna Rionda (Serralunga)	Barolo	Massolino, Luigi Pira, Bruno Giacosa (last produced in 1993), Roagna
Vignolo (Castiglione Falletto)	Barolo	Cavallotto
La Villa (Monforte)	Barolo	Seghesio
Villero (Castiglione Falletto)	Barolo	Giuseppe Mascarello, Vietti (produced only as a Riserva), Cordero di Montezemolo, (Barolo Enrico VI), Brovia, Bruno Giacosa (last produced in 1996)
Voghera/Brea (Serralunga)	Barolo	Azelia, Brovia (Barolo Ca' Mia)

BEST BARBARESCO VINEYARDS, WINES, AND PRODUCERS

Note: A number of new vineyard zoning/mapping regulations in Barbaresco are scheduled to go into effect with the 2007 vintage, which will change how some wines are labeled when they are released, beginning in 2010.

VINEYARD	WINE(S)	PRODUCER(S)
Asili (Barbaresco)	Barbaresco	Bruno Giacosa, Produttori del Barbaresco, Ceretto, Ca' del Baio
Basarin (Neive)	Barbaresco	Moccagatta
Bernardot (Treiso)	Barbaresco	Ceretto
Bordini (Neive)	Barbaresco	Fontanabianca
Bric Balin (Barbaresco)	Barbaresco	Moccagatta

VINEYARD	WINE(S)	PRODUCER(S)
Bricco (Treiso)	Barbaresco	Pio Cesare (Barbaresco Bric Turot)
Cole (Barbaresco)	Barbaresco	Moccagatta
Cottà (Neive)	Barbaresco	Sottimano
Currà (Neive)	Barbaresco	Sottimano
Fausoni (Neive)	Barbaresco	Sottimano
Gallina (Neive)	Barbaresco	La Spinetta
Loreto (Barbaresco)	Barbaresco	Albino Rocca, Varaldo
Marcarini (Treiso)	Barbaresco	Pertinace
Martinenga (Barbaresco)	Barbaresco	Marchesi di Grèsy (Barbaresco Martinenga, Camp Gros, and Gaiun)
Moccagatta (Barbaresco)	Barbaresco	Moccagatta, Produttori del Barbaresco
Montefico (Barbaresco)	Barbaresco	Produttori del Barbaresco
Montestefano (Barbaresco)	Barbaresco	Produttori del Barbaresco, Prunotto
Nervo (Treiso)	Barbaresco	Pertinace
Ovello (Barbaresco)	Barbaresco	Produttori del Barbaresco, Cantina del Pino, Cascina Morassino
Pajè (Barbaresco)	Barbaresco	Roagna, Produttori del Barbaresco
Pajorè (Treiso)	Barbaresco	Sottimano
Pora (Barbaresco)	Barbaresco	Produttori del Barbaresco
Rabajà (Barbaresco)	Barbaresco	Bruno Giacosa, Bruno Rocca, Produttori del Barbaresco, Cortese
Rio Sordo (Barbaresco)	Barbaresco	Produttori del Barbaresco
Rombone (Treiso)	Barbaresco	Fiorenzo Nada
Roncaglie (Barbaresco)	Barbaresco, Langhe	Poderi Colla
Roncagliette (Barbaresco)	Langhe	Angelo Gaja (Costa Russi and Sorì Tildìn)
Ronchi (Barbaresco)	Barbaresco	Albino Rocca
Santo Stefano (Neive)	Barbaresco	Bruno Giacosa, Castello di Neive
Secondine (Barbaresco)	Langhe	Angelo Gaja (Sorì San Lorenzo)
Serraboella (Neive)	Barbaresco	Cigliuti, Paitin, Vietti (Barbaresco Masseria)
Starderi (Neive)	Barbaresco	La Spinetta
Valgrande (Treiso)	Barbaresco	Ca' del Baio

A GUIDE TO THE BEST MULTICOMMUNE WINES

The following wines are made from a blend of several vineyards (often across multiple communes) and are especially notable for their balance, elegance, and class.

BAROLO

Elio Altare Barolo
Aldo Conterno Barolo (beginning with 2004)
Aldo Conterno Barolo Granbussia
Bartolo Mascarello Barolo
Luciano Sandrone Barolo Le Vigne
Vietti Barolo Castiglione

BARBARESCO

Cantina del Pino Barbaresco
Gaja Barbaresco
Bruno Rocca Barbaresco Coparossa

THE BEST SINGLE-VINEYARD BARBERAS

AI SUMA (ROCHETTA TANARO)

Barbera d'Asti
Braida

BIONZO (COSTIGLIOLE D'ASTI)

Barbera d'Asti
La Spinetta

BRICCO DELLA BIGOTTA (ROCHETTA TANARO)

Barbera d'Asti
Braida

BRICCO DELL'UCCELLONE (ROCHETTA TANARO)

Barbera d'Asti
Braida

CASCINA FRANCIA (SERRALUNGA)

Barbera d'Alba
Giacomo Conterno

CODANA (CASTIGLIONE FALLETTO)

Barbera d'Alba
Giuseppe Mascarello

LA CRENA (AGLIANO TERME)

Barbera d'Asti
Vietti

FALLETTO (SERRALUNGA)

Barbera d'Alba Superiore
Bruno Giacosa

GALLINA (NEIVE)

Barbera d'Alba
La Spinetta

LARIGI (LA MORRA)

Barbera d'Alba
Elio Altare

MONGOVONE (ISOLA D'ASTI)

Barbera d'Asti
Elio Perrone

POZZO (LA MORRA)

Barbera d'Alba
Roberto Voerzio, Renato Corino

SCARRONE (CASTIGLIONE FALLETTO)

Vietti
Barbera d'Alba
Barbera d'Alba Scarrone Vigna Vecchia

TOP PRODUCERS OF MOSCATO D'ASTI AND THEIR WINES

Michele Chiarlo Nivole
Massolino
La Morandina
Elio Perrone Clarté
Elio Perrone Sourgal
Paolo Saracco
Paolo Saracco Moscato d'Autunno
La Spinetta Biancospino
La Spinetta Bricco Quaglia

PIEDMONT'S NOTABLE WHITE WINES

The native Arneis remain Piedmont's most interesting dry white wines. In addition, there are a few wines of note made from international varieties that are listed below.

ARNEIS

Bruno Giacosa, Giovanni Almondo (Bricco delle Ciliegie), Val del Prete, Vietti

MÉTHODE CHAMPENOISE SPARKLING WINES

Bruno Giacosa Extra Brut
Rocche dei Manzoni Valentino Brut Zero

CHARDONNAY

Aldo Conterno Bussiador
Gaja Gaia e Rey
Rocche dei Manzoni L'Angelica

CORTESE DI GAVI

Pio Cesare, Albino Rocca

ERBALUCE DI CALUSO

Antoniolo, Ferrando

GAVI

La Scolca

SAUVIGNON

Gaja Alteni di Brassica

ANAS-CËTTA

Elvio Cogno

BUYING STRATEGY

The most important thing to keep in mind is that the top Barolos and Barbarescos are produced in minuscule quantities, so buying the wines early is crucial. The most highly sought
wines average just a few thousand bottles of production, as compared to first-growth Bordeaux, which typically surpass 10,000 cases of production. As prices of collectible Bordeaux
and Burgundy continue to accelerate dramatically, many consumers have turned to Piedmont,
pushing the prices of the most desirable wines to levels never seen before. A weak dollar and
higher prices from the estates have made new releases quite expensive as well. That notwithstanding, the best Barolos and Barbarescos still deliver notable relative value when compared
to the world's most complex and ageworthy wines.

Piedmont witnessed an extraordinary set of strong vintages from 1996 to 2001. Though
most Barolos and Barbarescos of those vintages have long since vanished from retailers'
shelves, readers will want to pick up any remaining well-stored bottles. Of these vintages 1998
is the most open and expressive for current drinking, followed by 1997. The entry-level 2000s
are also good choices for near-term drinking, while the top selections need additional cellaring. The 1996s and 2001s are still quite young, while 1999 remains an underrated vintage, but
only for Barolo. Prices of wines from 1997 and before have gone up considerably, but there are
still some deals to be found on other vintages from 1996 to 2001.

[recent barolo and barbaresco vintages]

Nebbiolo is a unique variety that offers a veritable kaleidoscope of aromas, flavors, and sensations. Each vintage has its own distinct personality, which makes following the wines fascinating. The ideal weather for Nebbiolo consists of high daytime temperatures tempered by
cool evenings, particularly during the last month of the growing season, the most critical time
of the year. Vintages with balanced weather such as 1996, 1999, 2001, and 2004 yielded wines
characterized by complex aromatics, layered fruit, and vibrant color. At their best, the wines
have notable transparency and are highly expressive with regard to site. These Barolos are
often massively structured when young and require significant bottle age before they fully
blossom. In warmer years, such as 1997, 1998, and 2000, the aromatic qualities and delineation
of the wines are diminished, but in exchange, the wines gain body and volume from the additional ripeness of the fruit. These vintages tend to diminish the differences among sites,
robbing the wines of some of their character. The wines also have less color than in cooler
vintages. On the plus side, these wines have historically been more approachable when young,
yet have also proven to age well.

Among recent vintages, readers should focus on 2004, which is extraordinary for both
Barolo and Barbaresco. It is a vintage that happily coincides with the growing maturity and seriousness of producers. The most striking developments taking place in Piedmont are a return
to larger barrels for aging, a reduction in toast levels, and a generally more refined style of winemaking, all of which are very much in evidence in the 2004s. For many estates the 2004s are
without question the finest wines they have ever made. The best 2004 Barolos and Barbarescos
are wonderfully complete, with the sweetness of the 2000s and the greater aromatic complexity,
detail, and finesse of the 2001s. If that sounds particularly appealing, believe me, it is.

The 2004 vintage gave producers picture-perfect conditions, but with some challenges thrown in just to make things interesting. The long, cool growing season unleashed the energy plants had kept in store during the torrid 2003 season. Growers were forced to green harvest more aggressively than normal to keep the plants from overproducing, although lamentably a few estates didn't have the discipline and foresight to do so. The last month of the season, always the most critical period, saw cool evenings bring relief to the daytime heat, precisely the conditions Nebbiolo needs to develop vibrant color, expressive aromatics, layered fruit, and fine tannins. It is a vintage in which specific vineyard characteristics are accentuated to the fullest. The calm weather during the harvest afforded growers the luxury of picking fruit at the optimal level of ripeness rather than being rushed by nature, as was the case in 2003 and 2005. Most producers harvested in mid- to late October, but a few growers in Barolo reported picking into November, something that is pretty much unheard of these days. Stylistically, 2004 is closest to 1996, 1999, and 2001 although the wines in general possess more sweetness, generosity, and finesse than any of those vintages. Simply put, 2004 is a vintage that has the potential to redefine many consumers' views of the heights Nebbiolo can achieve.

As was the case throughout continental Europe, 2003 saw record-setting high temperatures. I can still remember visiting Piedmont in June 2003. The heat was stifling, and the evenings provided no respite whatsoever. Record-breaking temperatures tested the mettle of the most experienced producers. Bruno Giacosa told me it was the hottest vintage since 1947. The scorching heat wreaked havoc, especially in well-exposed plots, where grapes literally burned under the sun. The lack of water caused the vines to shut down, a condition known as hydric stress, which resulted in the seeds not reaching full maturity, yielding many wines characterized by hard, unripe tannins. The hot, dry conditions also resulted in the earliest harvest on record, with the Nebbiolos being picked in early to mid-September, a good two to three weeks earlier than normal. Some of the most successful wines come from cooler microclimates, where the fruit was somewhat protected from the worst of the scorching sun, or specific vineyards where the plants had at least some access to water because of older vines with deeper roots and/or more compact, moisture-retentive soils.

At first producers were not terribly excited with their Barolos and Barbarescos, and some estates weren't sure if they would bottle their top selections. As time passed, many producers told me they were pleasantly surprised with the evolution of the vintage. The wines are very ripe but not cooked, yet also structured. The main question is how and to what extent these wines will develop and age. That is difficult to answer, but my impression is that the hard tannin the wines possess will never entirely melt away. Wines that have the stuffing to provide balance to the tannins should age best. Those that are skimpy on fruit, however, will suffer. As those wines lose their baby fat, the tannins are likely to become more accentuated.

Quality is highly irregular. In general producers in Barolo seem to have been more successful than their colleagues in Barbaresco. Among the surprises of the vintage are a number of very strong entry-level Barolo bottlings. Many of these wines are blends from vineyards in different communes, which is how Barolo was traditionally made in past generations. The ability to blend fruit from sites with different characteristics was a huge advantage in 2003. The best Barolos are those from Serralunga, Monforte, and parts of Castiglione Falletto, in the eastern part of the zone, where the more compact soils were able to provide the plants with access to at least some moisture. Older vines with deeper root systems, and therefore greater access to water, were also favored. The most variable wines come from the western part of the zone, in particular La Morra, where the soils tend to be more loosely packed and contain a higher percentage of sand.

VINTAGE GUIDE

2007

This very dry and unseasonably warm year led to expectations of another very ripe vintage, but a spell of cool weather in September slowed down the maturation of the grapes. The wines are aromatic and nuanced but also concentrated, as yields were quite low. Early tastings suggest a promising vintage.

2006

The vintage yielded powerful, ripe wines loaded with fruit as well as structure. Today they appear to have more stuffing than the 2004s, if less elegance. The Dolcettos give an indication of the ripe, full-bodied style of the vintage.

2005

The growing season was characterized by a slightly early harvest. Producers were forced to pick before a spell of rain toward the end of the season that ended up lasting an entire week or risk significant damage. The wines are on average 1% lower in alcohol and are made in a more slender, smaller-scaled style. The best 2005 Barolos and Barbarescos have lovely balance, harmony, and freshness at this early stage. 2005 looks to be a relatively early-maturing vintage, never a bad thing given the ageworthiness of the surrounding vintages. For Barbera, 2005 is an excellent but not outstanding vintage. The best wines are well balanced and easy to drink, even if they don't have the sheer opulence of the 2003s or the definition, clarity, and freshness of the 2004s. The 2005 Dolcettos are very successful.

2004

Quality is outstanding, particularly among producers who limited yields. Readers will find everything from a number of superb entry-level wines to utterly profound luxury bottlings and everything in between. These are Barolos and Barbarescos of extraordinary elegance and finesse that combine the sweetness of 2000 with the classicism, perfume, and freshness of 2001. The vintage coincides with a growing sense of maturity among growers, especially those of the younger generation. A number of producers made their finest wines yet. The Barberas and Dolcettos offer the same stylistic attributes and overall quality level.

2003

A freakishly hot vintage of highly irregular quality, yet better than initially expected. The best wines are the Barolos of Serralunga, Monforte, and parts of Castiglione Falletto. Quality in Barbaresco is decidedly lower than in Barolo. A few wines will surprise on the upside, but readers should be very discriminating when purchasing the wines. It is a great vintage for Barbera, which thrives in the heat. The Dolcettos are less convincing, as many of the wines are overripe, heavy, and ponderous.

2002

A very damp, cool growing season that produced a disappointing set of wines. There may be a handful of positive surprises, but not more.

2001

A balanced growing season that produced elegant, nuanced Barolos and Barbarescos of remarkable class. Today the wines are shutting down and putting on weight in the bottle, but this is an extraordinary vintage for both Barolo and Barbaresco.

2000

A hot, ripe vintage that yielded a remarkably consistent set of wines at all quality levels. The more modest Barolos and Barbarescos are drinking well, but the top bottlings are structured wines that require patience. It is awfully hard to go wrong with a bottle of 2000 Barolo or Barbaresco even if the wines rarely reach the heights of vintages like 2001 and 2004. It is a modern-day version of 1985.

1999

Less consistent than 2000 or 2001 but profound at the highest levels. A cool vintage with powerful wines that will appeal most to readers who enjoy structured, ageworthy Barolos. The best examples remain fresh, vibrant, and full of promise. Much stronger in Barolo than Barbaresco, where hail was an issue. 1999 is the most overlooked and underrated Barolo vintage since 1986.

1998

A forward vintage with pretty, aromatic wines that are drinking well today. These medium-bodied Barolos and Barbarescos probably won't be terribly long-lived, but they are delicious now. 1998 is still considered one of the great vintages in the 1996–2001 era, but in a decade's time my guess is that it won't be spoken of in the same breath as the best vintages of that period.

1997

A hot vintage that yielded a number of exotic, superripe wines loaded with an unmistakable personality. The wines have aged remarkably well, despite some opinions to the contrary. The most successful wines are the Barolos of Serralunga, Monforte, and parts of Castiglione, where the compact soils helped the wines retain freshness. The Barolos of La Morra and Barolo are as a group further along in their evolution, as are most Barbarescos.

1996

A cold vintage that was poorly regarded at the outset but today is widely recognized as one of the all-time greats. These powerful, tannic wines remain fresh, vibrant, and in many cases incredibly shut down. The weather patterns of the 1970s don't exist today, but 1996 is as close to a modern-day 1978 as we are likely to see.

OLDER VINTAGES

The early 1990s were a mixed bag for Piedmont. The best of these vintages is 1993, which produced a number of good, but not great, wines that have arrived at maturity. Readers should always have space in the cellar for a few bottles from vintages like 1993, which offer plenty of pleasure on a smaller scale, while some of the more important wines from stronger years can be left to age gracefully. 1995 was once a hyped vintage, but that was only because it followed 1991, 1992, and 1994, all of which were very weak. Today the 1995s come across as compact, linear wines that possess hard, rough tannins and offer limited pleasure.

Readers lucky enough to own 1989s and 1990s should count their blessings, as these remain two of the greatest Piedmont vintages of all time. The 1989s are largely still developing and have plenty of life ahead of them. The 1990s show the flashy, ripe quality that made them so attractive when first released. It is a vintage that is drinking beautifully today, yet the best wines will drink well for at least another decade. I have been quite surprised at the fast evolution of the 1988s, especially in recent years. This once hyped vintage has yielded a number of wines that should be consumed sooner rather than later. 1986 is an insider's vintage. Hail limited production considerably, but the wines that were made remain fresh, structured, and full of life. 1985 is a fascinating vintage. At first it was received very enthusiastically, then in recent years a number of revisionist opinions have appeared stating that the vintage is over-rated. Which is it? The secret of understanding vintages is not so much about ranking them hierarchically but rather having a keen understanding of when wines will drink at peak and enjoying the wines precisely at that time. 1985 is not the most profound vintage, but the wines aren't falling apart either, as some have claimed. Today it is, in my opinion, the mature vintage that offers the purest pleasure because the wines have arrived at their peak and continue to offer the fullest splendor of their expressiveness. I have always adored the 1982s for their structure and power. 1978 remains the vintage for readers who love firmly structured, massive Barolos and Barbarescos. Amazingly, the best of those wines continue to convey an impression of youthfulness.

—ANTONIO GALLONI

[the ratings]

PIEDMONT'S BEST WINES

✴ ✴ ✴ ✴ ✴ (OUTSTANDING)

Elio Altare Barbera d'Alba Larigi
Elio Altare Barolo Arborina
Elio Altare Barolo Brunate
Elio Altare Langhe Arborina
Azelia Barolo San Rocco
Cavallotto Barolo Riserva Bricco Boschis
  Vigna San Giuseppe
Domenico Clerico Barolo Ciabot Mentin
  Ginestra
Domenico Clerico Barolo Percristina
Aldo Conterno Barolo Cicala
Aldo Conterno Barolo Riserva Granbussia
Giacomo Conterno Barolo Cascina Francia
Giacomo Conterno Barolo Riserva
  Monfortino
Conterno Fantino Barolo Sorì Ginestra
Gaja Langhe Costa Russi
Gaja Langhe Sorì San Lorenzo
Gaja Langhe Sorì Tildìn
Gaja Langhe Sperss
Bruno Giacosa Barbaresco Asili
Bruno Giacosa Barbaresco Rabajà
Bruno Giacosa Barbaresco Riserva Asili
Bruno Giacosa Barbaresco Riserva Rabajà
Bruno Giacosa Barbaresco Santo Stefano
Bruno Giacosa Barolo Falletto
Bruno Giacosa Barolo Le Rocche del
  Falletto
Bruno Giacosa Barolo Riserva Le Rocche
  del Falletto

Giuseppe Mascarello Barolo Monprivato
Giuseppe Mascarello Barolo Riserva Ca'
  d'Morissio
Massolino Barolo Riserva Vigna Rionda
E. Pira–Chiara Boschis Barolo Cannubi
Luigi Pira Barolo Marenca
Luigi Pira Barolo Vigna Rionda
Bruno Rocca Barbaresco Rabajà
Rocche dei Manzoni Langhe Bricco
  Manzoni
Rocche dei Manzoni Barolo Cappella di
  Santo Stefano
Luciano Sandrone Barolo Cannubi Boschis
Luciano Sandrone Barolo Le Vigne
Paolo Scavino Barolo Cannubi
Paolo Scavino Barolo Bric del Fiasc
Paolo Scavino Barolo Riserva Rocche
  dell'Annunziata
G. D. Vajra Barolo Bricco delle Viole
Vietti Barolo Rocche
Vietti Barolo Riserva Villero
Roberto Voerzio Barolo Brunate
Roberto Voerzio Barolo Cerequio
Roberto Voerzio Barolo Rocche
  dell'Annunziata/Torriglione
Roberto Voerzio Barolo Riserva Vecchie
  Viti dei Capalot e delle Brunate
Roberto Voerzio Barolo Sarmassa

Brovia Barolo Ca' Mia
Cantina del Pino Barbaresco Ovello
Domenico Clerico Barolo Pajana
Aldo Conterno Barolo Romirasco
Giacomo Conterno Barbera d'Alba
  Cascina Francia
Conterno Fantino Barolo Parussi
Giovanni Corino Barolo Vigna Giachini
Renato Corino Barolo Vigneto Rocche
Einaudi Barolo Costa Grimaldi
Einaudi Barolo Nei Cannubi
Gaja Langhe Conteisa
Elio Grasso Barolo Ginestra Vigna
  Casa Maté
Bartolo Mascarello Barolo
Andrea Oberto Barolo Vigneto Rocche
Parusso Barolo Bussia
Pianpolvere Soprano Barolo Bussia
  Riserva 7 Anni
Produttori del Barbaresco Barbaresco
  Riserva Asili
Produttori del Barbaresco Barbaresco
  Riserva Montefico
Produttori del Barbaresco Barbaresco
  Riserva Ovello
Produttori del Barbaresco Barbaresco
  Riserva Pajè

Produttori del Barbaresco Barbaresco
  Riserva Rabajà
Giuseppe Rinaldi Barolo Brunate/
  Le Coste
Giuseppe Rinaldi Barolo Cannubi
  (San Lorenzo)/Ravera
Bruno Rocca Barbaresco Coparossa
Rocche dei Manzoni Barolo Big 'd Big
Rocche dei Manzoni Barolo Vigna
  d'La Roul
Rocche dei Manzoni Valentino Brut Zero
Paolo Scavino Barolo Carobric
Sottimano Barbaresco Pajorè
Sottimano Barbaresco Riserva
La Spinetta Barbaresco Riserva Starderi
La Spinetta Barbaresco Starderi
Vietti Barbaresco Masseria
Vietti Barbera d'Asti La Crena
Vietti Barbera d'Alba Scarrone
  Vigna Vecchia
Vietti Barolo Brunate
Roberto Voerzio Barbera d'Alba Riserva
  Pozzo dell'Annunziata
Roberto Voerzio Barolo La Serra
Roberto Voerzio Langhe Merlot

Claudio Alario Dolcetto di Diano d'Alba
  Montagrillo
Gianfranco Alessandria Barolo San
  Giovanni
Giovanni Almondo Roero Arneis Bricco
  delle Ciliege
Giovanni Almondo Roero Bric Valdiana
Elio Altare Barolo
Elio Altare Langhe La Villa
Azelia Barolo Bricco Fiasco
Azelia Barolo Margheria
Azelia Barolo Riserva Voghera-Brea
Enzo Boglietti Barolo Brunate
Enzo Boglietti Barolo Case Nere
Borgogno Barolo Storico
Brovia Barolo Garblèt Sué
Brovia Barolo Rocche
Brovia Barolo Villero
Cantina del Pino Barbera d'Alba
Cascina Bongiovanni Barolo Pernanno

Castello di Neive Barbaresco Santo
  Stefano Riserva
Cavallotto Barolo Bricco Boschis
Cavallotto Barolo Riserva Vignolo
Cavallotto Dolcetto d'Alba Vigna Scot
Ceretto Bricco Asili Barbaresco Bricco Asili
Domenico Clerico Langhe Arte
Cigliuti Barbaresco Serraboella
Elvio Cogno Barolo Ravera
Elvio Cogno Barolo Vigna Elena
Poderi Colla Barolo Bussia Dardi/Le Rose
Aldo Conterno Barolo
Aldo Conterno Barolo Bussia
Aldo Conterno Barolo Colonnello
Conterno Fantino Barolo Mosconi
Conterno Fantino Barolo Vigna del Gris
Cordero di Montezemolo Barolo Enrico VI
Giovanni Corino Barolo Arborina
Giovanni Corino Barolo Vecchie Vigne
Giovanni Corino Barolo Vigneto Arborina

Giovanni Corino Barolo Vigneto Rocche
Giovanni Corino Barolo Vigneto Roncaglie
Renato Corino Barolo Arborina
Renato Corino Barolo Vecchie Vigne
Matteo Correggia Roero Roche d'Ampsèj
Cortese Barbaresco Rabajà
Cortese Barbaresco Rabajà Riserva
Einaudi Barolo
Einaudi Barolo Costa Grimaldi
Einaudi Barolo Nei Cannubi
Einaudi Dogliani Vigna Tecc
Alessandro e Gian Natale Fantino Barolo
    Vigna dei Dardi
Alessandro e Gian Natale Fantino Barolo
    Vigna dei Dardi Riserva
Fontanafredda Barolo Riserva
Gaja Barbaresco
Bruno Giacosa Arneis
Bruno Giacosa Barbera d'Alba
    Falletto Superiore
Bruno Giacosa Dolcetto d'Alba Basarin
Bruno Giacosa Dolcetto d'Alba Falletto
Bruno Giacosa Nebbiolo
    d'Alba Valmaggiore
Bruno Giacosa Barbera d'Alba Falletto
Elio Grasso Barolo Gavarini Vigna
    Chiniera
Elio Grasso Barolo Rüncot
Giovanni Manzone Barolo Bricat
Giovanni Manzone Barolo Bricat
    Le Gramolere
Giovanni Manzone Barolo Gramolere
Marchesi di Grésy Barbaresco Camp Gros
Marchesi di Grésy Barbaresco Gaiun
Hilberg-Pasquero Barbera d'Alba
    Superiore
Mario Marengo Barolo Brunate
Mario Marengo Barolo Brunate
    Vecchie Vigne
Giuseppe Mascarello Barbera d'Alba
    Superiore Codana
Giuseppe Mascarello Barolo Santo Stefano
    di Perno
Giuseppe Mascarello Barolo Villero
Massolino Barolo Margheria
Massolino Barolo Parafada
Moccagatta Barbaresco Bric Balin
Moccagatta Barbaresco Cole
Mauro Molino Barolo Vigneto Gancia
Fiorenzo Nada Langhe Rosso Seifile
Andrea Oberto Barolo Vigneto Albarella

Paitin Barbaresco Sorì Paitin
Paitin Barbaresco Vecchie Vigne
Parusso Barbera d'Alba Superiore
Parusso Barolo Bussia Rocche
Parusso Barolo Le Coste Mosconi
Parusso Barolo Mariondino
Parusso Barolo Riserva
Pecchenino Barbera d'Asti
    Superiore Mongovone
Pecchenino Dogliani Siri d'Jermu
Pelissero Barbaresco Vanotu
Pio Cesare Barolo Ornato
E. Pira–Chiara Boschis Barolo Via Nuova
Luigi Pira Barolo Margheria
Produttori del Barbaresco Barbaresco
    Riserva Montestefano
Produttori del Barbaresco Barbaresco
    Riserva Rio Sordo
Prunotto Barolo Bussia
Ratti Barolo Marcenasco Conca
Ratti Barolo Marcenasco Rocche
Revello Barolo Giachini
Revello Barolo Rocche dell'Annunziata
Roagna Barbaresco Crichet Pajé
Roagna Barbaresco Pajé
Roagna Barbaresco Riserva Pajé
Roagna Barolo Vigna Rionda
Albino Rocca Barbaresco Sorì Loreto
Albino Rocca Barbera d'Alba Gepin
Bruno Rocca Barbaresco Maria Adelaide
Rocche dei Manzoni Barbera d'Alba
    Sorito Mosconi
Rocche dei Manzoni Langhe Quatr Nas
Rocche dei Manzoni Barolo Rocche
Luciano Sandrone Nebbiolo
    d'Alba Valmaggiore
Paolo Scavino Barbera d'Alba Affinato
    in Carati
Paolo Scavino Barolo
Sottimano Barbaresco Cottà
Sottimano Barbaresco Currà
Sottimano Barbera d'Alba Pairolero
La Spinetta Barbaresco Riserva Valeirano
La Spinetta Barbaresco Valeirano
La Spinetta Barbera d'Asti Bionzo
La Spinetta Barbera d'Asti Superiore
La Spinetta Langhe Pin
La Spinetta Monferrato Rosso Pin
G. D. Vajra Barolo Albe
Val del Prete Roero
Mauro Veglio Barolo Castelletto

Vietti Barbera d'Alba Scarrone
Vietti Barolo Lazzarito
Vietti Langhe Nebbiolo Perbacco

Roberto Voerzio Barbera d'Alba Cerreto
Roberto Voerzio Barolo Riserva Fossati
   Case Nere

★ ★ ★ / ★ ★ ★ ★ (GOOD TO EXCELLENT)

Gianfranco Alessandria Barbera
   d'Alba Vittoria
Elio Altare Dolcetto d'Alba
Enzo Boglietti Barolo Arione
Enzo Boglietti Barolo Fossati
Braida Barbera d'Asti Ai Suma
Braida Barbera d'Asti Bricco della Bigotta
Braida Barbera d'Asti Bricco dell'Uccellone
Ca' del Baio Barbaresco Asili
Ca' del Baio Barbaresco Marcarini
Cantina del Pino Barbaresco
Castello di Neive Barbaresco
Castello di Neive Barbaresco Santo Stefano
Ceretto Barbaresco Bernardot
Ceretto Bricco Rocche Barolo Bricco Rocche
Paolo Conterno Barolo Ginestra
Paolo Conterno Barolo Riserva Ginestra
Matteo Correggia Nebbiolo d'Alba La Val
   dei Preti
Einaudi Barolo
Einaudi Dolcetto di Dogliani
Fontanabianca Barbaresco Sorì Burdin
Fontanafredda Barolo La Rosa
Fontanafredda Barolo Lazzarito
Fontanafredda Barolo Paiagallo Vigna
   la Villa
Ettore Germano Barolo Prapò
Bruno Giacosa Barolo
Silvio Grasso Barolo Ciabot Manzoni
Silvio Grasso Barolo L'Andrè
Giovanni Manzone Barolo S. Stefano
   di Perno
Marcarini Barolo Brunate
Mario Marengo Barolo Bricco delle Viole
Franco M. Martinetti Barolo Marasco

Moccagatta Barbaresco Basarin
Fiorenzo Nada Barbaresco Rombone
Pecchenino Dolcetto di Dogliani San Luigi
Pelissero Barbaresco Tulin
Pio Cesare Barbaresco Il Bricco
Guido Porro Barolo Lazzairasco
Produttori del Barbaresco Barbaresco
   Riserva Moccagatta
Produttori del Barbaresco Barbaresco
   Riserva Pora
Prunotto Barbaresco Bric Turot
Revello Barolo Conca
Revello Barolo Gattera
Roagna Barolo La Rocca e La Pira
Roagna Barolo Riserva La Rocca e La Pira
Bruno Rocca Barbaresco
Giovanni Rosso Barolo Cerretta
Giovanni Rosso Barolo Serralunga
Luciano Sandrone Dolcetto d'Alba
Seghesio Barolo La Villa
Sottimano Dolcetto d'Alba Bric del Salto
La Spinetta Barbera d'Alba Gallina
La Spinetta Barbaresco Gallina
La Spinetta Barbaresco Riserva Gallina
La Spinetta Barolo Campè
La Spinetta Barolo Riserva Campè
Varaldo Barbaresco Sorì Loreto
Mauro Veglio Barolo Arborina
Mauro Veglio Barolo Gattera
Mauro Veglio Barolo Rocche
Mauro Veglio Barolo Rocche
   dell'Annunziata
Vietti Barolo Castiglione
Vietti Barbera d'Alba Tre Vigne
Roberto Voerzio Dolcetto d'Alba Priavino

★ ★ ★ (GOOD)

Marziano Abbona Barolo Pressenda
Marziano Abbona Barolo Terlo Ravera
Orlando Abrigo Barbaresco
   Vigna Montersino
Claudio Alario Barolo Riva
Claudio Alario Barolo Sorano
Fratelli Alessandria Barbera d'Alba Priora
Gianfranco Alessandria Barbera d'Alba
Gianfranco Alessandria Barolo

Giovanni Almondo Barbera
   d'Alba Valbianchéra
Elio Altare Barbera d'Alba
Antoniolo Gattinara
Antoniolo Gattinara Osso San Grato
Antoniolo Gattinara San Francesco
Antoniolo Gattinara Vigneto Castelle
Azelia Barbera d'Alba Vigneto Punta
Azelia Dolcetto d'Alba Bricco dell'Oriolo

Azelia Langhe Nebbiolo
Azelia Barolo
Luigi Baudana Barbera d'Alba
Luigi Baudana Barbera d'Alba Donatella
Luigi Baudana Barolo Baudana
Luigi Baudana Barolo Ceretta
Luigi Baudana Dolcetto d'Alba
Enzo Boglietti Barbera d'Alba
Enzo Boglietti Barbera d'Alba Roscaleto
Enzo Boglietti Dolcetto d'Alba
Enzo Boglietti Dolcetto d'Alba Tiglineri
Bongiovanni Barolo
Borgogno Barolo Classico Riserva
Boroli Barolo
Gianfranco Bovio Barolo Rocchettevino
Gianfranco Bovio Barolo Vigna Arborina
Gianfranco Bovio Barolo Vigna Gattera
Brezza Barolo Bricco Sarmassa
Brezza Barolo Sarmassa
Brovia Barolo
Brovia Dolcetto d'Alba Solatio Brovia
Burlotto Barolo
Piero Busso Barbaresco Borghese
Piero Busso Barbaresco Gallina
Piero Busso Barbaresco Mondino
Piero Busso Barbaresco Santo Stefanetto
Ca' del Baio Barbaresco Valgrande
Ca' Romè Barolo Vigna Cerretta
Ca' Viola Barbera d'Alba Brichet
Ca' Viola Bric du Luv
Ca' Viola Dolcetto d'Alba Barturot
Ca' Viola Dolcetto d'Alba Vilot
Ca' Viola Langhe Nebbiolo
Cascina Bongiovanni Barolo
Cascina Morassino Barbaresco Morassino
Cascina Morassino Barbaresco Ovello
Ceretto Barbaresco Asij
Ceretto Barolo Brunate
Ceretto Barolo Zonchera
Ceretto Bricco Rocche Barolo Brunate
Ceretto Bricco Rocche Barolo Prapo
Michele Chiarlo Barbaresco Reyna
Michele Chiarlo Barbera d'Asti La Court
Michele Chiarlo Barbera d'Asti Le Orme
Michele Chiarlo Barolo Tortoniano
Michele Chiarlo Barolo Brunate
Michele Chiarlo Barolo Cannubi
Michele Chiarlo Barolo Cerequio
Chionetti Dolcetto di Dogliani Briccolero
Ciabot Berton Barolo
Cigliuti Barbaresco Vigna Erte

Cigliuti Barbera d'Alba Serraboella
Cigliuti Langhe Bricco Serra
Domenico Clerico Barbera d'Alba Trevigne
Domenico Clerico Dolcetto d'Alba Visadi
Elvio Cogno Anas-Cëtta
Elvio Cogno Barbera d'Alba Bricco
    dei Merli
Elvio Cogno Barolo
Elvio Cogno Dolcetto d'Alba
Elvio Cogno Langhe Montegrilli
Poderi Colla Bricco Drago
Poderi Colla Dolcetto d'Alba Pian Balbo
Poderi Colla Langhe Nebbiolo
Conterno Fantino Barbera d'Alba Vignota
Conterno Fantino Dolcetto d'Alba
    Bricco Bastia
Paolo Conterno Barolo
Coppo Barbera d'Asti Camp du Rouss
Coppo Barbera d'Asti Pomorosso
Coppo Barolo
Cordero di Montezemolo Barolo
    Bricco Gattera
Cordero di Montezemolo Barolo
    Monfalletto
Giovanni Corino Barolo
Renato Corino Barbera d'Alba
Renato Corino Barbera d'Alba Pozzo
Renato Corino Barolo
Renato Corino Dolcetto d'Alba
Matteo Correggia Barbera d'Alba Marun
Matteo Correggia Le Marne Grigie
Matteo Correggia Roero
Matteo Corregia Roero Arneis
Cortese Barbera d'Alba
Cortese Barbera d'Alba Morassina
Cortese Langhe Nebbiolo
Damilano Barolo Cannubi
Damilano Barolo Lecinquevigne
Damilano Barolo Liste
Dessilani Fara Caramino
Dessilani Fara Lochera
Dessilani Gattinara
Dessilani Ghemme
Einaudi Barbera
Einaudi Dolcetto di Dogliani
Fontanafredda Barolo Serralunga
Gagliasso Barolo Rocche dell' Annunziata
Gagliasso Barolo Torriglione
Gaja Langhe Darmagi
Gaja Langhe Sito Moresco
Ettore Germano Barolo

Ettore Germano Barolo Cerretta
Bruno Giacosa Barbera d'Alba
Bruno Giacosa Barolo Vigna Croera
Bruno Giacosa Dolcetto d'Alba
Silvio Grasso Barolo Bricco Luciani
Silvio Grasso Barolo Giachini
Silvio Grasso Barolo Pi Vigne
Silvio Grasso Barolo Vigna Plicotti
Giacomo Grimaldi Barbera d'Alba Fornaci
Giacomo Grimaldi Barbera d'Alba Pistin
Giacomo Grimaldi Dolcetto d'Alba
Giacomo Grimaldi Barolo Le Coste
Giacomo Grimaldi Barolo Sotto Castello
 di Novello
Giacomo Grimaldi Nebbiolo d'Alba
 Valmaggiore
Hilberg-Pasquero Barbera d'Alba
Hilberg-Pasquero Langhe Nebbiolo
Hilberg-Pasquero Nebbiolo d'Alba
Icardi Barolo Parej
Malvirà Roero Superiore Mombeltramo
Malvirà Roero Superiore Trinità
Giovanni Manzone Barolo
Giovanni Manzone Barolo Castelletto
Giovanni Manzone Barolo Riserva Le
 Gramolere
Marcarini Barolo La Serra
Marchesi di Barolo Barolo Cannubi
Marchesi di Grésy Barbaresco Martinenga
Marchesi di Grésy Dolcetto d'Alba
 Monte Aribaldo
Marchesi di Grésy Langhe Martinenga
Mario Marengo Barolo
Bartolo Mascarello Barbera d'Alba
Bartolo Mascarello Dolcetto d'Alba
Giuseppe Mascarello Barbera d'Alba
 Superiore Santo Stefano di Perno
Giuseppe Mascarello Dolcetto d'Alba Bricco
Giuseppe Mascarello Dolcetto d'Alba Santo
 Stefano di Perno
Massolino Barbera d'Alba Gisep
Massolino Barolo
Massolino Dolcetto d'Alba
Mauro Molino Barolo Conca
Mauro Molino Barolo Gallinotto
Paolo Manzone Barolo Serralunga
Paolo Manzone Barolo Meriame
Fiorenzo Nada Barbaresco
Andrea Oberto Dolcetto d'Alba
Andrea Oberto Barbera d'Alba
Andrea Oberto Langhe Rosso Fabio

Andrea Oberto Barolo
Paitin Barbera d'Alba Superiore
 Campolive
Parusso Dolcetto d'Alba Piani Noce
Parusso Barbera d'Alba Ornati
Parusso Langhe Nebbiolo
Parusso Barolo
Pelissero Dolcetto d'Alba Augenta
Pelissero Dolcetto d'Alba Munfrina
Pelissero Barbera d'Alba I Piani
Pelissero Barbera d'Alba Augenta
Pelissero Barbaresco Nubiola
Elio Perrone Barbera d'Asti Tasmorcan
Pertinace Barbaresco Pertinace
Pertinace Barbaresco Marcarini
Pio Cesare Barbaresco
Pio Cesare Barolo
Luigi Pira Barolo
Guido Porro Barolo Santa Caterina
Ferdinando Principiano Barbera d'Alba
 La Romualda
Ferdinando Principiano Barolo Boscareto
Produttori del Barbaresco Barbaresco
Prunotto Barbera d'Alba Pian Romualdo
Prunotto Barbera d'Asti Costamiole
Prunotto Monferrato Rosso Mompertone
Prunotto Barbaresco
Prunotto Barolo
Ratti Barolo Marcenasco
Revello Dolcetto d'Alba
Revello Barbera d'Alba
Revello Barbera d'Alba Ciabot du Re
Revello Langhe Nebbiolo
Revello Barolo
Francesco Rinaldi Barolo Cannubbio
Francesco Rinaldi Barolo Le Brunate
Roagna Dolcetto d'Alba
Roagna Langhe Rosso
Dante Rivetti Barbaresco Bricco de Neveis
Albino Rocca Barbaresco
Albino Rocca Dolcetto d'Alba Vignalunga
Bruno Rocca Barbera d'Alba
Giovanni Rosso Dolcetto d'Alba Le
 Quattro Vigne
Giovanni Rosso Barbera d'Alba Donna
 Margherita
Luciano Sandrone Barbera d'Alba
Paolo Scavino Dolcetto d'Alba
Paolo Scavino Barbera d'Alba
Paolo Scavino Langhe Nebbiolo
Paolo Scavino Barolo Bricco Ambrogio

Edoardo Sobrino Barolo
  Monvigliero/Pisapola
Sottimano Barbaresco Fausoni
Sottimano Langhe Nebbiolo
San Romano Dolcetto di Dogliani
Seghesio Barbera d'Alba Vigneto
  della Chiesa
La Spinetta Barbaresco Riserva Gallina
La Spinetta Barbera d'Asti Ca' di Pian
La Spinetta Langhe Bianco
La Spinetta Langhe Nebbiolo
La Spinetta Chardonnay Lidia
Travaglini Gattinara Riserva
Travaglini Gattinara Tre Vigne
Val del Prete Roero Arneis Luèt
Val del Prete Barbera d'Alba Serra de' Gatti
Val del Prete Barbera d'Alba Superiore
  Carolina 3.5

Val del Prete Nebbiolo d'Alba Vigna
  di Lino
Varaldo Barbaresco Bricco Libero
Varaldo Barbaresco La Gemma
Varaldo Barolo Vigna di Aldo
Mauro Veglio Dolcetto d'Alba
Mauro Veglio Barbera d'Alba
Mauro Veglio Barbera d'Alba
  Cascina Nuova
Eraldo Viberti Dolcetto d'Alba
  Vigna Vaglio
Eraldo Viberti Barolo
Vietti Barbera d'Alba Tre Vigne
Vietti Barbera d'Asti Tre Vigne
Gianni Voerzio Barolo La Serra
Roberto Voerzio Langhe Nebbiolo
  S. Francesco/Fontanazza

[tasting commentaries]

MARZIANO ABBONA ∗ ∗ ∗
PIEDMONT $55.00–$60.00

Marziano Abbona makes Barolos and Barbarescos in a fairly soft, accessible style. His Dolcetto di Dogliani Papa Celso is also well worth seeking out and is an excellent example of the richer style of Dolcetto that is produced in Dogliani.

2003 Barolo Terlo Ravera	87	now–2013
2001 Barolo Terlo Ravera	89+	now–2018
2003 Barolo Pressenda	89	now–2015

ORLANDO ABRIGO ∗ ∗ ∗
PIEDMONT $42.00–$50.00

This small producer based in Treiso makes a wide range of wines, the best of which is the Barbaresco Vigna Montersino, an earthy, tarry expression of Nebbiolo.

2004 Barbaresco Vigna Montersino	91	now–2018
2003 Barbaresco Vigna Montersino	89	now–2015

CLAUDIO ALARIO ∗ ∗ ∗
PIEDMONT $53.00–$68.00

Alario is based in Diano d'Alba, so he is naturally better known for his Dolcettos, in particular his Costa Fiore, which in most vintages is among the top Dolcettos made in the region. Alario also makes Barolos from his holdings in Verduno (Barolo Riva) and Serralunga (Barolo Sorano), both of which are made in a late-harvest, superripe style.

2004 Barolo Riva	89	now–2018
2001 Barolo Riva	89	2007–2016
2004 Barolo Sorano	88	2008–2016

GIANFRANCO ALESSANDRIA   * * */* * * *
PIEDMONT $53.00–$80.00

Gianfranco Alessandria exemplifies the best of the Piedmontese artisan approach to wine-making. He originally studied for a career in carpentry, but after the unexpected early passing of his father he devoted his energies to the family business, and the wine world has undoubtedly been richer since then. At first Alessandria sold his fruit to other producers, but in 1993 he began bottling his own wines and achieved critical success immediately. Although Alessandria has been making excellent wines for some time, in recent vintages he seems to have arrived at a new level of maturity. His 2004 Barolos are easily the finest and most polished wines he has ever made. In short, these are delicious Barolos made in a contemporary style that are sure to find many admirers. The estate's barrel-aged Barbera d'Alba Vittoria is also well worth seeking out.

2004 Barolo	90	2009–2019
2003 Barolo	89	now–2018
2001 Barolo	89+	now–2015
2004 Barolo San Giovanni	93	2010–2021
2003 Barolo San Giovanni	91	2010–2020
2001 Barolo San Giovanni	92	2009–2021

Past Glories Barolo: 1999 (89); Barolo San Giovanni: 1999 (92)

GIOVANNI ALMONDO   * * */* * * *
PIEDMONT $22.00–$44.00

Giovanni Almondo is one of my favorite producers in the Roero district. In particular, his Arneis Bricco delle Ciliegie and Roero Bric Valdiana are typically among the finest wines in the region and are a great introduction to the unique *terroir* of the Roero, a zone that has begun to emerge in recent years.

2006 Roero Arneis Bricco delle Ciliegie	91	now
2004 Roero Bric Valdiana	91	now–2016
2003 Roero Bric Valdiana	87	now–?
2002 Roero Bric Valdiana	90+	now–?
2004 Barbera d'Alba Valbianchéra	90	now–2010

ELIO ALTARE   * * * * *
PIEDMONT $23.00–$135.00

Elio Altare remains one of the leading figures in the Barolo landscape. Not only has Altare been hugely successful in his own right, he has also served as an inspiration and mentor to a new generation of growers who have been emboldened to pursue the path of quality production and estate-bottled wines. Altare is based in the Annunziata subsection of La Morra. His property sits atop Arborina, a vineyard whose reputation Altare has developed virtually single-handedly. Altare produces three Barolos—a blend made today from parcels in La Morra, Castiglione Falletto, and Serralunga, plus single-vineyard wines from the Arborina and Brunate vineyards. He also makes a superb Langhe Nebbiolo from his holdings in Arborina that is aged for only one year in oak rather than the two years the Barolos see. Altare employs some of the shortest fermentation and maceration times in the zone for his Barolos, which are also aged exclusively in French oak. Critics of this approach said the wines wouldn't age, but they have been amply proven wrong throughout the years. The delicious French oak–aged Larigi (100% Barbera) is made from a plot adjacent to Arborina. The La Villa (60% Barbera and 40% Nebbiolo) and entry-level Dolcetto and Barbera bottlings round out the lineup, which is consistently among Piedmont's very finest from top to bottom.

2006 Dolcetto d'Alba	89	now
2006 Barbera d'Alba	88	now
2005 Langhe La Villa	93	2009–2020
2004 Langhe La Villa	91	2009–2019
2005 Langhe Arborina	93	2010–2022
2004 Langhe Arborina	94	now–2019
2005 Langhe Larigi	92	2009–2020
2004 Langhe d'Alba Larigi	92	now–2016
2004 Barolo	93	2009–2024
2003 Barolo	90	2009–2018
2001 Barolo	91	2011–2019
2004 Barolo Arborina	95	2011–2022
2003 Barolo Arborina	92	2009–2021
2001 Barolo Arborina	93	2011–2021
2004 Barolo Brunate	97	2012–2024
2003 Barolo Brunate	94	2011–2021
2001 Barolo Brunate	95	2009–2021

Past Glories Barolo: 2000 (92), 1999 (90), 1989 (95), 1987 (93), 1982 (94); Barolo Arborina: 1999 (95), 1985 (97); Barolo Brunate: 2000 (94), 1999 (96), 1998 (93)

ANTONIOLO ★★★/★★★★
PIEDMONT $40.00–$55.00

Gattinara is by far the best-known appellation in northern Piedmont, and Antoniolo is its most ambitious, quality-minded producer. Working with low yields and prime vineyard sites, Antoniolo makes wines in a big, structured style that is intended to showcase the full potential of the region as well as compete with the wines of Barolo and Barbaresco. In addition to a range of more modest wines, there is a Gattinara, made from a blend of parcels, as well as three single-vineyard selections.

2003 Gattinara	89	now–2015
2001 Gattinara	88	now–2016
2000 Gattinara	88	now–2012
2003 Gattinara Vigneto Castelle	90	now–2015
2001 Gattinara Vigneto Castelle	89	now–2021
2000 Gattinara Vigneto Castelle	90	now–2016
2003 Gattinara San Francesco	90	now–2018
2001 Gattinara San Francesco	91	2009–2021
2000 Gattinara San Francesco	89	now–2015
2003 Gattinara Osso San Grato	91	now–2018
2000 Gattinara Osso San Grato	91	now–2015

AZELIA ★★★★
PIEDMONT $45.00–$95.00

Luigi Scavino may be less well known than some of his more famous neighbors, but make no mistake, the wines from Scavino's estate, Azelia, can hold their own with the very best of the region. In particular, the Barolo San Rocco, from a vineyard in Serralunga, is often one of the region's top bottlings, as it is in 2001, 2003, and 2004. The Azelia Barolos combine power and elegance with a level of virtuosity matched by few in the region. Although the wines can show much concentration and oak influence when young, there can be no doubt that in top vintages the overall balance and sense of proportion of these wines are outstanding. In addition, Azelia remains a great source of relatively well-priced Barolos.

2004 Barolo	89	2009–2016
2003 Barolo	88	now–2013
2001 Barolo	89	now–2013
2004 Barolo Bricco Fiasco	94	2012–2024
2003 Barolo Bricco Fiasco	89	2009–2019
2001 Barolo Bricco Fiasco	92	2009–2016
2004 Barolo Margheria	92	2012–2024
2003 Barolo Margheria	91	2010–2020
2004 Barolo San Rocco	95	2009–2024
2003 Barolo San Rocco	93	2010–2020
2001 Barolo San Rocco	93	2009–2016
2001 Barolo Riserva Voghera-Brea	91	now–2016
2000 Barolo Riserva Voghera-Brea	90	now–2015

Past Glories Barolo Bricco Fiasco: 1999 (92); Barolo San Rocco: 1999 (94)

ENZO BOGLIETTI ✱ ✱ ✱/✱ ✱ ✱ ✱
PIEDMONT $60.00–$70.00

Enzo Boglietti, a small producer based in La Morra, works with low yields to produce Barolos of notable concentration in a sleek, modern style that emphasizes the ripeness of the fruit. The Case Nere comes across as the most complete among his excellent 2001s and is a wine of uncommon harmony. Boglietti also seems to have gotten the most out of his vines in the challenging 2003 vintage. While these aren't the most complex Barolos on the market, they do offer much pleasure in a soft, rich, and fairly immediate style. His Barolo Arione is a new addition to the lineup beginning with the 2003 vintage.

2003 Barolo Arione	92	2009–2018
2003 Barolo Brunate	91	now–2016
2001 Barolo Brunate	89	now–2016
2003 Barolo Fossati	91	now–2018
2001 Barolo Fossati	87+?	now–2016
2003 Barolo Case Nere	90	now–2015
2001 Barolo Case Nere	90	now–2016

CASCINA BONGIOVANNI ✱ ✱ ✱
PIEDMONT $59.00–$85.00

Proprietor Davide Mozzone is a passionate, energetic man endowed with a charismatic sense of humor. His enthusiasm is reflected in the wines, which seem to improve with every passing vintage.

2004 Barolo	89	2009–2018
2003 Barolo	91	2010–2020
2004 Barolo Pernano	93	2012–2024

BORGOGNO ✱ ✱ ✱
PIEDMONT $60.00–$82.00

Borgogno is one of Barolo's historic firms. Brothers Cesare and Giorgio Boschis have recently sold a 50% stake in the winery to Oscar Farinetti, the entrepreneur behind the Eataly, the chain of high-end gastronomy shops and restaurants. La Spinetta owner Giorgio Rivetti has been brought in to lend a hand in the estate's marketing plans. Farinetti plans to focus on estate wines and vows to keep the signature traditional winemaking style in place. It will be interesting to see what Farinetti and his associates come up with at Borgogno. This is definitely a property that could stand some small improvements and refinements.

At present, Borgogno's top wines include the Barolo Classico, which is made from estate-owned vineyards and is aged exclusively in cask. This wine is offered in both normal and later-release Riserva versions. Despite its name, the Barolo Storico is actually the one wine that does make some concessions to more modern tastes. This selection is made from the Liste vineyard and is aged in smaller French oak barrels. Despite their midweight size, these are deceptively muscular and austere wines that will require significant cellaring to be at their best and that will last for decades. Borgogno also has one of Piedmont's best-stocked collections of older vintages. From time to time the estate rereleases these wines, but the reconditioning process the wines undergo makes them come across as much younger than non-reconditioned original-release bottles.

2000 Barolo Classico	89	20⁻0–2030
1999 Barolo Classico	92	20⁻5–2034
2001 Barolo Classico Riserva	91	2011–2026
2001 Barolo Storico	93	2011–2026
2000 Barolo Storico	90	2012–2025

Past Glories Barolo Classico Riserva: 1997 (90), 1996 (91); Barolo Storico: 1998 (91), 1996 (91)

GIANFRANCO BOVIO ★ ★ ★
PIEDMONT $N/A

This is a lovely set of wines from Gianfranco Bovio, who is based in the Annunziata subzone of La Morra. These midweight Barolos offer notable balance and are excellent choices for near-term consumption.

2003 Barolo Rocchettevino	90	now–2013
2003 Barolo Vigna Arborina	89	2009–2018
2003 Barolo Vigna Gattera	90	now–2015

BRAIDA ★ ★ ★/★ ★ ★ ★
PIEDMONT $64.00–$78.00

In many ways the name Giacomo Bologna is synonymous with Barbera d'Asti. Bologna was among the first, if not the first, producer to believe that Barbera was capable of producing world-class wines by working with low yields and aging the wines in French oak. With his Bricco dell'Uccellone Bologna single-handedly redefined the image of Barbera from a variety that had been seen as giving simple, rustic wines with untamed acidity to one capable of producing modern wines of notable concentration and elegance. Even though Bologna passed away at a young age in 1990, he left an indelible stamp on the world of Piedmontese oenology. Today the estate is run by Giacomo's children Raffaella and Giuseppe, who continue the work of their father. The estate produces a wide range of Barberas, but the most famous are the three selections Bricco dell'Uccellone, Bricco della Bigotta, and Ai Suma. Bricco dell'Uccellone is the estate's flagship Barbera. It is a rich, concentrated wine made from low yields and aged 12 months in *barrique*. Bricco della Bigotta is a more classic wine in some ways. Average yields are a bit higher, and it spends a few additional months in oak. In top vintages Ai Suma is produced from late-harvested superripe grapes. It is the richest and most opulent of the wines. In recent years the estate has introduced a new cask-aged Barbera, Montebruna, intended for nearer-term consumption. Last, there is a simple Barbera called La Monella, made in a traditional *frizzante* style. Readers who enjoy the stylish wines of this estate will find many great choices from the 2001, 2003, and 2004 vintages. Unfortunately, the winery's 2000s are disappointing.

2004 Barbera d'Asti Bricco della Bigotta	89	now–2012
2003 Barbera d'Asti Bricco della Bigotta	91	now–2011

2001 Barbera d'Asti Bricco della Bigotta	90	now–2013
2004 Barbera d'Asti Bricco dell'Uccellone	90	now–2014
2003 Barbera d'Asti Bricco dell'Uccellone	90	now–2011
2001 Barbera d'Asti Bricco dell'Uccellone	91	now–2011
2004 Barbera d'Asti Ai Suma	90	now–2014
2003 Barbera d'Asti Ai Suma	90	now–2013
2001 Barbera d'Asti Ai Suma	90	now–2011

BREZZA ★ ★ ★
PIEDMONT $75.00–$85.00

The Brezza family has turned out two fine 2001 Barolos from its holdings in the Sarmassa vineyard. Vinification remains traditional, and the wines are aged in medium-sized casks of 25 and 30 hectoliters (660 and 792 gallons). Unfortunately, I was not able to taste the estate's 2001 Cannubi and Castellero Barolos.

2001 Barolo Bricco Sarmassa	88	now–2016
2001 Barolo Sarmassa	87	now–2016

BROVIA ★ ★ ★ ★
PIEDMONT $40.00–$70.00

Over the last few years this estate has turned out a number of terrific wines that exemplify the new traditionalism of Barolo, faithfully expressing the distinct qualities of varietal, vintage, and *terroir* in a style that is classic yet accessible at the same time. The estate works with old vines in some of the most prestigious sites in Castiglione Falletto and Serralunga. The average age of the plants is 30 years for Garblèt Sué (also known as Bricco Fiasco), 40 for Villero and Rocche, and 50 for Ca' Mia (also known as Voghera/Brea). Readers seeking fine, traditionally made Barolos would do well to check out these wines, which also happen to be among the most compelling values in the region. The single-vineyard Barolos see roughly 20 days of fermentation and maceration in glass-lined cement tanks. The wines are then racked into 30-hectoliter (792-gallon) French oak casks, where malolactic fermentation takes place naturally. The wines spend about two and a half years in oak prior to being bottled. The estate's Barolo (often one of the best in the region) is made from a blend of the youngest vines in all its vineyards and is aged in a larger Slavonian oak cask. In the best vintages Brovia also makes a unique Dolcetto called Solatio from late-harvested fruit. Readers who want to explore traditionally made Barolos that capture the essence of some of the region's top sites owe it to themselves to check out Brovia.

2004 Dolcetto d'Alba Solatio	88	now–2010
2003 Barolo	88	2009–2015
2001 Barolo	88	now–2016
2003 Barolo Rocche	91	2010–2018
2001 Barolo Rocche	91	2009–2021
2003 Barolo Villero	90	2009–2018
2001 Barolo Villero	92	2011–2021
2003 Barolo Garblèt Sué	91	2010–2020
2001 Barolo Garblèt Sué	92	2011–2026
2003 Barolo Ca' Mia	92	2013–2023
2001 Barolo Ca' Mia	93+	2011–2026

Past Glories Barolo Rocche: 2000 (93), 1999 (93), 1998 (92), 1997 (92), 1996 (92); Barolo Villero: 2000 (91), 1999 (92), 1998 (91), 1997 (93), 1996 (94); Barolo Garblèt Sué: 1999 (92); Barolo Ca' Mia: 2000 (93), 1998 (92), 1997 (94), 1996 (93); Barolo Monprivato: 1985 (97)

BURLOTTO ✶ ✶/✶ ✶ ✶
PIEDMONT $45.00

Burlotto is located in the commune of Verduno, which is known for delicate, aromatic Barolos. Over the years I have had mixed experiences with this producer's wines. Some palates may find the wines excessively green and herbal. These traditionally made wines are often quite feminine and delicate. At their best they faithfully capture the unique qualities that are the hallmark of this part of the Barolo zone.

2003 Barolo	88	now–2015
2003 Barolo Acclivi	90	now–2018
2003 Barolo Monvigliero	89	now–2018

PIERO BUSSO ✶ ✶ ✶
PIEDMONT $25.00–$30.00

This small producer in Neive continues to show improvement. The Barbarescos tend to be medium-bodied wines that are soft, approachable, and easy to understand. They appear to be made in a style intended for near-term consumption rather than extended aging.

2004 Barbaresco Borgese	88	now–2016
2001 Barbaresco Borgese	89	now–2013
2004 Barbaresco Santo Stefanetto	89	2009–2016
2001 Barbaresco Santo Stefanetto	90	now–2015
2001 Barbaresco Gallina	88	now–2013
2001 Barbaresco Mondino	88	now–2013

CA' DEL BAIO ✶ ✶ ✶/✶ ✶ ✶ ✶
PIEDMONT $52.00–$57.00

Ca' del Baio is located in Treiso but has holdings across the Barbaresco zone, including a plot in the prestigious Asili vineyard. The estate favors a soft, fruit-driven style of Barbaresco that seems best suited to midterm drinking. These 2004 Barbarescos are by far the finest wines I have tasted from Ca' del Baio. Hopefully, they represent a level of quality the estate will be able to maintain going forward, because the wines are terrific.

2004 Barbaresco Asili	93	now–2019
2004 Barbaresco Marcarini	92	2009–2018
2004 Barbaresco Valgrande	90	now–2016

CANTINA DEL PINO ✶ ✶ ✶ ✶
PIEDMONT $22.00–$55.00

The humble, down-to-earth, and intensely driven Renato Vacca is making some of the most exciting wines in Barbaresco. Prior to 1997 Vacca sold his fruit to the Produttori del Barbaresco cooperative, run by his cousin Aldo Vacca, but that year he started making wines on his own, a choice that seems to be paying off. Vacca's holdings are concentrated in and around the Ovello vineyard, a site long noted for its combination of cooler microclimate and poor soils that give structured, ageworthy Barbarescos. In addition to his single-vineyard Barbaresco Ovello, Vacca also produces a terrific straight Barbaresco made from a blend of fruit sourced from the Starderi and Albesani vineyards in Neive as well as the less well exposed parts of Ovello. Vacca's 2003s, and the Ovello in particular, are among the most successful Barbarescos of the 2003 vintage. The oldest vines average more than 50 years of age, and there can be no question that that was a huge advantage during the scorching hot 2003. Cantina del Pino's 2004 Barbaresco bodes very well for the release of the Barbaresco Ovello. The estate also produces a juicy Barbera that is sure to provide much pleasure. Not only were the wines from

Cantina del Pino among the standouts in my tastings of that vintage, they also happen to be among the very best values in Barbaresco. In short, I can't say enough good things about the wines of Renato Vacca. Readers owe it to themselves to check out this up-and-coming producer.

2004 Barbera d'Alba	89	now–2014
2004 Barbaresco	92	now–2016
2003 Barbaresco	90	now–2015
2003 Barbaresco Ovello	92	2010–2020
2002 Barbaresco Ovello	89	now–2017
2001 Barbaresco Ovello	92	now–2018

CAPPELLANO * * * *
PIEDMONT $67.00–$103.00

Teobaldo Cappellano prefers that his wines not be formally scored, so I am unable to consider them for Robert Parker's *Wine Advocate* or for this book. That said, a section covering the best wines of Piedmont would be incomplete without at least a few sentences on the gentle giant of Barolo. Cappellano produces two Barolos, both from the Gabutti vineyard in Serralunga. The Pie Franco–Michet is made from a parcel that was planted in the late 1980s with the Michet clone of Nebbiolo on ungrafted vines. Nearly impossible to find even in nearby Alba, it is one of Piedmont's—make that one of Italy's—most unique cult wines. The Pie Rupestris–Per Nebioli is made from vines that are over 40 years old and grafted onto American rootstock. Because of the age of those vines the exact composition of the clones is not known. It is typically a rounder, more fruit-driven Barolo. Both Barolos are produced along traditional lines. Fermentation lasts two to three weeks and is carried out in a mixture of stainless steel and glass-lined cement vats. Only natural yeasts are used. The wines are aged in 25- and 50-hectoliter (660- and 1,320-gallon) casks for a minimum of three years but often more, and the wines are released later than most. These are Barolos that reflect their maker's highly artistic and intimate approach to winemaking. Readers who enjoy traditionally made Barolos should do as well-informed connoisseurs have done for years and seek out these wines whenever possible. Cappellano also makes the finest Barolo Chinato, the aromatic herb-infused drink first invented by his father's uncle.

CASTELLO DI NEIVE * * */* * * *
PIEDMONT $40.00–$63.00

Castello di Neive and proprietor Italo Stupino own the Santo Stefano vineyard in Neive, without question one of the most storied sites in all of Piedmont. It was Bruno Giacosa, with his legendary Barbarescos of the 1960s, 1970s, and 1980s, who first brought the world's attention to these vines. Even today, when he is more focused on making wines from estate-grown fruit, Giacosa speaks of Santo Stefano with reverence and awe and lists it as the top vineyard in Barbaresco. Unfortunately, until recently, Castello di Neive's own wines have lagged considerably, but in recent years Stupino has brought on a new staff to work in the vineyards and in the cellar, and the results are striking. The word is still not out on Castello di Neive. In the U.S. the distribution of these wines has been uneven, and they can be hard to find. Hopefully, that will soon change. As an aside, the castle makes for a fascinating visit. The aristocratic surroundings are somewhat of an anomaly in this winemaking culture defined by an abundance of small, artisan growers.

2004 Barbaresco	89	now–2014
2004 Barbaresco Santo Stefano	93	2009–2019
2001 Barbaresco Santo Stefano Riserva	93	2009–2021
1999 Barbaresco Santo Stefano Riserva	92	2009–2021

CAVALLOTTO ★★★★
PIEDMONT $53.00–$78.00

Cavallotto is one of the hidden gems of Piedmont. Based in Castiglione Falletto, this small family-run estate continues to build on the success of past vintages with a very strong set of wines. The house style here is traditional, with a few concessions to modern-day technology. Although rotary fermentors are used for convenience, maceration time is still on the long side, and the wines, particularly the Riservas, spend a lengthy time in cask. The estate's top wines include the single-vineyard Barolo Bricco Boschis as well as Riservas made from the Vignolo and Bricco Boschis Vigna San Giuseppe vineyards. The Vignolo is the more feminine of the Riservas, while the San Giuseppe is decidedly more masculine in style. I have been fortunate enough to taste a number of older Barolos from Cavallotto, and they have aged exquisitely. As good as past vintages have been, today's wines are even better. Among the more accessible wines, the Dolcetto d'Alba Vigna Scot is often a beautiful glass of wine. Cavallotto is an estate on the rise. Readers will want to give these handcrafted, traditionally made wines careful consideration.

2004 Barolo Bricco Boschis	91–94	now–?
2003 Barolo Bricco Boschis	91	2010–2020
2001 Barolo Bricco Boschis	92	2011–2021
2001 Barolo Riserva Vignolo	92	2011–2021
2000 Barolo Riserva Vignolo	92	now–2020
2001 Barolo Riserva Bricco Boschis Vigna San Giuseppe	95	2013–2026
2000 Barolo Riserva Bricco Boschis Vigna San Giuseppe	93	2012–2022

Past Glories Barolo Riserva Vignolo: 1999 (91), 1998 (92), 1997 (91), 1996 (90); Barolo Riserva Bricco Boschis Vigna San Giuseppe: 1999 (94), 1998 (92), 1997 (93), 1996 (93), 1990 (93), 1989 (94), 1982 (94); Bricco Boschis Vigna San Giuseppe: 1979 (93); Barolo Riserva Bricco Boschis Vigna Colle Sud-Ovest: 1985 (92), 1978 (92)

CA'VIOLA ★★★
PIEDMONT $22.00–$60.00

Although Beppe Caviola is best known for his work consulting for various local estates, he is also an accomplished producer in his own right. Because of his technical background, it is not surprising that in the past Caviola was an ardent advocate of a superclean style of winemaking. While Caviola's wines were always excellent, they often came across as sterile and lacking personality. Today Caviola preaches a much more noninterventionalist philosophy, including the use of natural rather than selected yeasts. The evolution of his thinking is representative of the radical but quiet shift that is taking place at many estates today. Readers are sure to find much pleasure in the approachable, fruit-driven wines of Beppe Caviola.

2006 Dolcetto d'Alba Vilot	88	now
2006 Dolcetto d'Alba Barturot	90	now–2010
2006 Barbera d'Alba Brichet	87	now
2005 Bric du Luv	89	now–2010
2005 Langhe Nebbiolo	90	now–2012

CERETTO ★★★/★★★★
PIEDMONT $40.00–$225.00

Ceretto is one of the older, historic families in Piedmont. Brothers Bruno and Marcello Ceretto brought significant attention to their wines and the region during the 1970s and 1980s with a cutting-edge approach to winemaking and marketing. Today the estate is run by the younger generation, with siblings Roberta, Lisa, Federico, and Alessandro in charge of the family business. Over the last decade Ceretto has been an inconsistent producer. In the meantime, the competition has become much more intense, and though the wines are often outstanding, these days they are rarely among the region's very best. Ceretto owns plots in some of the finest sites, including Asili (in Barbaresco) and Brunate (in Barolo). The house style aims to incorporate aspects of both traditional and modern approaches. Fermentation lasts 12 to 14 days, and aging is done in 300-liter (80-gallon) French oak barrels. While the use of oak remains noticeable, these can be wines of notable overall balance and harmony. Alessandro Ceretto is experimenting with less new oak and giving the wines a more conventional 24 months of oak aging rather than the current 30 months. From what I have tasted in barrel, these changes have the potential to give the wines an additional dimension of expressiveness. As good as some of the single-vineyard wines can be, I remain unimpressed by the entry-level offerings. The 2004 Barbaresco Asij and 2003 Barolo Zonchera are both disappointing relative to the best wines at this level. Ceretto certainly has the resources to do better. As has been the case in recent vintages, I often leave my tastings with the feeling that there is a lot of unrealized potential from the top vineyard sites the family is fortunate enough to own.

2004 Barbaresco Asij	88	now–2014
2001 Barbaresco Asij	90	now–2013
2004 Barbaresco Bernardot	92	2009–2019
2003 Barbaresco Bernardot	90	now–2017
2001 Barbaresco Bernardot	91	now–2016
2004 Barbaresco Bricco Asili	94	2012–2022
2003 Barbaresco Bricco Asili	89	now–2018
2001 Barbaresco Bricco Asili	92	2009–2021
2004 Barolo Zonchera	86–88	now–2014
2003 Barolo Zonchera	87	now–2013
2004 Barolo Brunate	89	now–2016
2003 Barolo Brunate	92	2009–2019
2001 Barolo Brunate	91	now–2021
2004 Barolo Prapò	91	2010–2022
2003 Barolo Prapò	91	2009–2018
2001 Barolo Prapò	92	2011–2023
2004 Barolo Bricco Rocche	92	2012–2024
2001 Barolo Bricco Rocche	90+?	2011–2023

Past Glories Barolo Brunate: 2000 (90), 1999 (91), 1978 (92); Barolo Prapò: 1999 (91), 1978 (93); Barolo Bricco Rocche: 1999 (90), 1985 (93)

MICHELE CHIARLO ★ ★ ★
PIEDMONT $33.00–$90.00

Michele Chiarlo makes Barolos from some of the most prestigious vineyards in the entire appellation. The Chiarlo Barolos are midweight wines made in a classic style. Fermentation and maceration last around 25 days and the wines are aged in 50-hectoliter (1,320-gallon) Allier oak barrels. Unfortunately, I have experienced more bottle variation than should be the case from wines that start with such hallowed *terroirs,* although my most recent bottles suggest that quality may be on the upswing.

2004 Barbaresco Reyna	87	now–2014
2003 Barbaresco	87	now–2013
2003 Barolo Tortoniano	88	now–2015

2001 Barolo Tortoniano	87	now–2016
2003 Barolo Cannubi	90	now–2013
2001 Barolo Cannubi	88	now–2019
2003 Barolo Cerequio	90	now–2018
2001 Barolo Cerequio	90	20˙1–2021
2003 Barolo Brunate	89	now–2018
2001 Barolo Brunate	89	now–2021

CHIONETTI ★★★★
PIEDMONT $16.00–$20.00

Quinto Chionetti makes deeply flavored, intense Dolcettos from his vineyards in Dogliani. The Briccolero tends toward a more aromatic and mineral-driven expression of Dolcetto while the San Luigi is fatter, plumper, and juicier. Both are outstanding, reference-point examples of top-class Dolcetto from Dogliani. The wines are aged in stainless steel.

2006 Dolcetto di Dogliani Briccolero	90	now–2010
2006 Dolcetto di Dogliani San Luigi	90	now–2011

CIGLIUTI ★★★/★★★★
PIEDMONT $50.00–$85.00

This small, family-run estate is located in the Serraboella district of Neive, in the Barbaresco zone. Its top wine is the Barbaresco Serraboella. The Barbaresco Vigna Erte is a relatively recent addition to the lineup. The vines here are still quite young, and the best vintages for this wine clearly belong to the future. Cigliuti also produces the delicious French oak–aged Barbera d'Alba Serraboella.

2007 Barbaresco Serraboella	89	2009–2022
2003 Barbaresco Serraboella	90	now–2018
2001 Barbaresco Serraboella	90	now–2015
2007 Barbaresco Vigna Erte	92	2009–2024
2003 Barbaresco Vigna Erte	89	now–2015
2001 Barbaresco Vigna Erte	88	now–2013

DOMENICO CLERICO ★★★★★
PIEDMONT $18.00–$140.00

Few producers' wines have given me as much pleasure over the years as those of Domenico Clerico. Based in Monforte, Clerico has been turning out spectacular Barolos since the mid-1980s. I find a spirituality and character in these wines that put them in a class with few peers. For this outspoken and intensely passionate vigneron the real work is done in the vineyards, which he tends to with near-fanatical obsession. Yields are among the lowest in the region, averaging around 35 hectoliters per hectare (374 gallons per acre) for the Barolos. Clerico's signature Barolo, Ciabot Mentin Ginestra, comes from vines planted at 400 meters (1,312 feet) with a south-to-southeast exposure, which gives the wine its characteristic explosive aromas. The Pajana comes from a vineyard at 300 meters (984 feet) in altitude, with a due south exposure, and, as would be expected, it is less perfumed on the nose but rounder and lusher on the palate. Clerico's Percristina is produced from old vines planted in the south-facing Mosconi cru. Stylistically I find it more similar to the Pajana, though the older vines give this wine a more concentrated profile along with heady, exotic aromas and flavors. Beginning with the 2006 vintage, Clerico will have a new Barolo from fruit he purchases in Serralunga. The last few years have also seen an evolution in Clerico's philosophy. He has gradually lengthened fermentation times and beginning with his 2005s also backed off the 100% new oak, perhaps the one criticism I have had of some of his wines in the past.

2006 Langhe Dolcetto Visadì	87	now
2005 Barbera d'Alba Trevigne	89	now–2010
2005 Langhe Arte	90	2009–2015
2002 Barolo	88	now–2017
2004 Barolo Pajana	94	2011–2024
2003 Barolo Pajana	92	2009–2018
2001 Barolo Pajana	93	2011–2021
2004 Barolo Ciabot Mentin Ginestra	97	2012–2024
2003 Barolo Ciabot Mentin Ginestra	93	2011–2023
2001 Barolo Ciabot Mentin Ginestra	95	2011–2021
2004 Barolo Percristina	96	2012–2022
2003 Barolo Percristina	91	2011–2018
2001 Barolo Percristina	94	2011–2019
2000 Barolo Percristina	93	now–2016

Past Glories Barolo Pajana: 1999 (95), 1998 (92), 1996 (93), 1990 (93); Barolo Ciabot Mentin Ginestra: 1999 (95), 1998 (93), 1996 (96), 1995 (90), 1990 (96), 1989 (95); Barolo Percristina: 1999 (93), 1998 (92), 1996 (92)

ELVIO COGNO ★★★/★★★★
PIEDMONT $29.00–$90.00

Cogno is one of those properties that always seems to fly below most people's radar screens, which is unfortunate because the wines are consistently excellent to outstanding. Husband and wife Valter Fissore and Nadia Cogno run the small winery, which sits above the Ravera vineyard in Novello. The estate's Barolo Ravera is made in a relatively soft, modern style. It is aged for a year in French oak followed by a year in midsize casks. In top vintages Cogno also produces Vigna Elena, a more classic wine that is aged for three years in large oak casks. These elegant, understated wines offer considerable appeal, yet a fair amount of aeration is necessary to allow the complexity of the wines to come through.

2005 Barbera d'Alba Bricco dei Merli	89	now–2010
2004 Langhe Montegrilli	89	now–2011
2001 Barolo	87	now–2013
2003 Barolo Ravera	92	2009–2018
2001 Barolo Ravera	91	now–2016
2001 Barolo Vigna Elena	91+	2009–2017

PODERI COLLA ★★★★
PIEDMONT $26.00–$74.00

Like so many of his colleagues, Tino Colla is a guardian of the rich history of the Langhe. Spend some time with Colla, and you come away with a deep understanding of the region, its traditions, and what it means to be connected to a territory. The Colla family has been involved in Piedmontese oenology for several generations. Tino's older brother Beppe owned the Prunotto winery, which he managed from 1956 to 1992, before selling the estate to Antinori. Following the sale of Prunotto, the Colla family purchased Cascina Drago, just outside of Alba, which Tino runs today with his niece Federica. The estate owns plots in some of the most prestigious vineyards in the zone, including Bussia and Roncaglie, perhaps best known as being the source of Angelo Gaja's Costa Russi and Sorì Tìldìn.

2004 Langhe Nebbiolo	89	now
2004 Bricco Drago	90	now–2014
2005 Barbaresco Roncaglie	92	2010–2022
2004 Barbaresco Roncaglie	90	2010–2016

2003 Barbaresco Roncaglie	91	now–2015
2001 Barbaresco Roncaglie	91	now–2016
2004 Barolo Bussia Dardi/Le Rose	93	2014–2026
2003 Barolo Bussia Dardi/Le Rose	91	2009–2018
2001 Barolo Bussia Dardi/Le Rose	92	2011–2021

ALDO CONTERNO ★★★★/★★★★★
PIEDMONT $104.00–$290.00

Aldo Conterno is one of Piedmont's historic properties. The estate was founded in 1969, when brothers Giovanni and Aldo Conterno decided to divide their family's winery. Aldo's vision had always been to make a style of Barolo that was more accessible than the sterner style favored by his brother Giovanni. Today the Aldo Conterno winery is run by Aldo's sons, Giacomo, Franco, and Stefano. In normal vintages Conterno releases four Barolos. The single-vineyard selections include the feminine Colonnello and the more structured, masculine Cicala, which is also the most ageworthy of the estate's wines. In top vintages Conterno produces its flagship, Barolo Riserva Granbussia, which is made from a blend of the Romirasco (70%), Colonnello (15%), and Cicala (15%) vineyards. Unlike at many other properties, at Aldo Conterno, the Riserva is not meant to be the most powerful wine but rather the most elegant. The family continues to be extremely stringent in the quality level it seeks to maintain. Aldo Conterno did not release a single bottle of Barolo in the 2002 and 2003 vintages. In 2004 their Cicala vineyard was damaged by hail, so there is no Barolo from this great site, nor is there a Granbussia. Instead the winery bottled its first Romirasco since 1993, and it is a winner.

2003 Langhe Nebbiolo Il Favot	90	now–2015
2004 Barolo	91	now–2019
2001 Barolo Bussia	89	now–2016
2004 Barolo Colonnello	94	2009–2019
2001 Barolo Colonnello	91	2009–2019
2001 Barolo Cicala	92	2011–2021
2004 Barolo Romirasco	95	2009–2024
2001 Barolo Riserva Granbussia	94	2009–2026
2000 Barolo Riserva Granbussia	93	now–2020
1999 Barolo Riserva Granbussia	94	2009–2021

Past Glories Barolo Cicala: 1999 (92), 1978 (94); Barolo Colonnello: 1989 (94); Barolo Riserva Granbussia: 1995 (91), 1990 (95), 1989 (97), 1985 (95), 1978 (96), 1974 (92); Barolo: 1961 (95)

GIACOMO CONTERNO ★★★★★
PIEDMONT $32.00–$335.00

Giacomo Conterno is one of the bastions of traditionally made Barolos. While Conterno's wines have often been profound, in recent vintages the estate has found another level of finesse that was sometimes missing in the wines. It is hard to say if that is because of a general trend toward warmer vintages, the estate's focus on making just three wines, or small improvements in vineyard and cellar work, but the fact remains that over the past few vintages proprietor Roberto Conterno has produced the best and most consistently outstanding wines in his venerable firm's long history. Unlike many of the younger producers who are reactionaries toward the older generation, Roberto Conterno is cut from the same cloth as his father, Giovanni, one of the all-time greats of Barolo. Sadly, Giovanni Conterno passed away in 2002, leaving an unfillable void, but I have a feeling he would be immensely proud to see what his son Roberto Conterno is accomplishing with his wines. The estate produces three wines, all from its Cascina Francia vineyard in Serralunga. This stunningly positioned, high-altitude plot was acquired in 1974. The first wines from Cascina Francia were released in 1978. Prior to 1978 the estate purchased its fruit from a variety of sources, as was the custom during that period. The Barbera is usually one of the top wines in the region. It sees 21 months of aging in medium-sized casks before being released. Conterno is most known for his two Barolos, Cascina Francia and the Monfortino Riserva, which has long been an iconic wine in these parts. The Barolo Cascina Francia is fermented in stainless steel, with temperature control, for three to four weeks. Aging takes place in large Slavonian oak casks for four years. In top vintages, Conterno makes a selection of the very best grapes just before harvest, and this fruit is destined for the Monfortino. Depending on climatic conditions, various parcels within the Cascina Francia vineyard mature differently, so the exact source of the fruit for the Monfortino can vary from year to year. For the Monfortino, the grapes are fermented in a combination of open-top wood vats and stainless-steel tanks without temperature control for four to five weeks. The wine is then aged in a single large Slavonian oak cask for seven years prior to being bottled without fining or filtration.

2005 Barbera d' Alba Cascina Francia	92	now–2015
2004 Barbera d'Alba Cascina Francia	93	now–2014
2003 Barbera d'Alba Cascina Francia	92	now–2013
2004 Barolo Cascina Francia	93–96	???
2003 Barolo Cascina Francia	94	2009–2023
2001 Barolo Cascina Francia	96	2009–2026
2001 Barolo Riserva Monfortino	96–98	???
2000 Barolo Riserva Monfortino	97	2015–2030
1999 Barolo Riserva Monfortino	98	2014–2039
1998 Barolo Riserva Monfortino	97	2012–2023

Past Glories Barolo Cascina Francia: 2000 (92), 1999 (94), 1998 (92), 1997 (94), 1996 (94), 1995 (93), 1994 (90), 1993 (93), 1990 (94), 1989 (95), 1985 (95); Barolo Riserva: 1978 (95), 1958 (94), 1937 (92); Barolo: 1971 (95), 1967 (94), 1964 (96), 1945 (96); Barolo Riserva Monfortino: 1997 (97), 1996 (97), 1995 (94), 1993 (92), 1990 (97), 1987 (94), 1985 (96), 1982 (98), 1979 (94), 1978 (98), 1974 (95), 1971 (97), 1970 (95); Riserva Monfortino: 1988 (93)

PAOLO CONTERNO ⋆ ⋆ ⋆ / ⋆ ⋆ ⋆ ⋆
PIEDMONT $60.00

Proprietor Giorgio Conterno produces sleek, stylish wines from his holdings in the Ginestra subzone in Monforte. I can think of no better estate than this to recommend for readers who want to explore the subtleties of the prestigious Ginestra vineyard. This producer's wide range of bottlings from this famous site offers something for everyone at all price levels. The estate releases three Barolos, all made from Ginestra fruit and representing different levels of quality, with the selection being done first in the vineyards and then in the cellar. The Barolos see a fermentation of around 10 days, and they are aged for two years in 35-hectoliter (924-gallon) French oak barrels which are cleaned and refurbished every few years, while the Riserva bottling sees an additional year of oak.

2003 Barolo	89	now–2013
2001 Barolo	91	now–2014
2003 Barolo Ginestra	91	now–2015
2001 Barolo Ginestra	92	2011–2021
2000 Barolo Riserva Ginestra	92	now–2018

CONTERNO FANTINO ★ ★ ★/★ ★ ★ ★ ★
PIEDMONT $84.00–$117.00

Proprietors Claudio Conterno and Guido Fantino make some of the most stylish wines in Piedmont. Their range is always remarkable in its consistency from top to bottom. The most important holdings are in the Ginestra vineyard in Monforte. The Barolo Vigna del Gris is made from the lower portion of the hillside, while the top bottling, the Barolo Sorì Ginestra, is made from the estate's best-exposed parcels in the vineyard. In most vintages Sorì Ginestra is among the top handful of Barolos. Beginning with the vintage 2004, Conterno Fantino have added a new Barolo from the Mosconi vineyard, also in Monforte. Winemaking remains very much in the modern style. The estate employs rotary fermentors, and fermentations last around a week for the Barolos, which are then aged in 100% new French oak. Readers who want to enjoy the estate's wines at more accessible prices should check out the Dolcetto d'Alba Bastia, Barbera d'Alba Vignota, and Monprà (Nebbiolo, Barbera, and Cabernet Sauvignon). Conterno Fantino also produces small quantities of a Nebbiolo called Ginestrino that is one of the great undiscovered jewels of Piedmont.

2004 Barolo Mosconi	94	20⁻2–2022
2001 Barolo Parussi	93	now–2016
2004 Barolo Vigna del Gris	93	20⁻1–2019
2003 Barolo Vigna del Gris	91	now–2015
2001 Barolo Vigna del Gris	92	now–2018
2004 Barolo Sorì Ginestra	96	2014–2024
2003 Barolo Sorì Ginestra	94	2009–2018
2001 Barolo Sorì Ginestra	95	2008–2021

Past Glories Barolo Mosconi: 2004 (94); Barolo Parussi: 2001 (93), 1999 (89); Barolo Vigna del Gris: 1999 (91); Barolo Sorì Ginestra: 1999 (92)

COPPO ★ ★ ★
PIEDMONT $100.00

Coppo is located in Canelli, a town that is also home to some of the most important cellars in Piedmont. The old cellars of the town's four historic producers—Coppo, Gancia, Bosca, and Contratto—are remarkable treasures of extraordinary beauty, so much so that they are designated as UNESCO World Heritage sites. Canelli is also the center of bustling *négociant* businesses built around Moscato and Asti Spumante, and the large wineries here offer a stark contrast to the more artisan estates seen throughout the region. Today Coppo is best known for its Barberas, but in the past the family also bottled a Barolo, a tradition that has been resumed with the newest addition to the lineup.

2001 Alter Ego	89	now–2011
2001 Barbera d'Asti Pomorosso	87	now
2002 Barbera d'Asti Camp du Rouss	85	now
2003 Barolo	89	now–2015

CORDERO DI MONTEZEMOLO ★ ★ ★
PIEDMONT $40.00–$90.00

The Cordero di Montezemolo property is one of the most picturesque spots in all of Piedmont, as it sits above the spectacular Monfalletto vineyard, which is easily identified by the famous cedar of Lebanon that is planted on the top of the hill. The estate makes two wines from its vineyards in La Morra, the Barolos Monfalletto and Gattera (from a plot within Monfalletto). The house's Barolo Enrico VI is made from the Villero vineyard in Castiglione Falletto. Short fermentations and *barrique* aging give the Cordero di Montezemolo Barolos a distinctly modern feel, and the wines do show a lot of hard new oak tannins in their youth.

2003 Barolo Monfalletto	90	now–2015
2001 Barolo Monfalletto	89	now–2014
2003 Barolo Bricco Gattera	90	now–2015
2001 Barolo Bricco Gattera	87	now–2016
2003 Barolo Enrico VI	92	2009–2019
2001 Barolo Vigna Enrico VI	90	2011–2019

GIOVANNI CORINO ★ ★ ★ ★
PIEDMONT $35.00–$134.00

In 2006 brothers Renato and Giuliano Corino decided to divide their vineyards and work separately. Giuliano Corino kept the family estate name and label. Today he makes an entry-level Barolo, selections from the Giachini and Arborina vineyards in La Morra, and a Vecchie Vigne old-vine cuvée. The 2004s are the first Barolos Giuliano Corino made on his own, and a distinct style is beginning to emerge. He appears to favor a more elegant, restrained approach, while his brother Renato aims for riper, more exuberant wines, very much like their personalities. The wines are made in a modern style deeply influenced by Elio Altare, who mentored so many of La Morra's young producers. Fermentation lasts less than a week, and aging takes place in *barriques* of which 40% to 50% are new for the single-vineyard Barolos, while the Vecchie Vigne sees about 60% to 80% new oak.

2004 Barolo	88	now–2014
2003 Barolo	86	now–2013
2001 Barolo	87	now–2014
2004 Barolo Vigneto Arborina	92	2011–2024
2003 Barolo Vigneto Arborina	89	now–2015
2001 Barolo Vigneto Arborina	91	2009–2019
2004 Barolo Vigna Giachini	95	2009–2024
2003 Barolo Vigna Giachini	90	2009–2018
2001 Barolo Vigna Giachini	92	2009–2019
2001 Barolo Vigneto Roncaglie	89	now–2015
2001 Barolo Vigneto Rocche	93+	2009–2019
2004 Barolo Vecchie Vigne	93	2011–2022

Past Glories Barolo Arborina: 2000 (93), 1999 (90); Barolo Giachini: 2000 (91), 1993 (93); Barolo Rocche: 2000 (92), 1999 (93), 1990 (95); Barolo Vecchie Vigne: 2000 (91), 1999 (91)

RENATO CORINO ★ ★ ★/★ ★ ★ ★
PIEDMONT $35.00–$130.00

Renato Corino is one of the most passionate producers I know. Always generous with his time and his wines, he embodies all of the qualities of La Morra's finest artisan growers. Since dividing the family holdings with his brother Giuliano in 2006, Renato Corino has built a new winery perched atop the Arborina vineyard, just a stone's throw from his neighbors Mauro Veglio and Elio Altare. Renato Corino makes an entry-level Barolo plus single-vineyard wines from his holdings in Arborina and Rocche. Like his brother Giuliano, Renato also produces a Vecchie Vigne old-vine cuvée. As outstanding as Renato Corino's wines can be, the superripe style seems to come at some expense of freshness.

2004 Barolo	89	now–2016
2003 Barolo	87	now–2013
2004 Barolo Arborina	93	2009–2024

2003 Barolo Arborina	88	2009–2015
2004 Barolo Rocche	94	20?4–2024
2003 Barolo Vigneto Rocche	89	2009–2015
2004 Barolo Vecchie Vigne	92	2010–2022
2001 Barolo Vecchie Vigne	90	now–2015

MATTEO CORREGGIA ✱ ✱ ✱
PIEDMONT $18.00–$65.00

The tragic death of Matteo Correggia in 2001 left a huge void in the area that is still felt nearly seven years later. Despite his untimely passing, Correggia remains the spiritual father of the Roero, and judging by the comments of fellow producers, his influence is still widely felt. Today, Matteo's widow, Ornella, runs the estate and continues the work the gifted Matteo started. The wines are made in a modern style that emphasizes low yields and shortish fermentations. This is a very solid set of wines from Correggia. Quality seems to have come back after an understandably difficult series of vintages following the passing of the trailblazing Matteo Correggia.

2005 Barbera d'Alba Marun	89	now–2010
2005 Roero	88	now–2010
2004 Roero	90	now–2010
2005 Nebbiolo d'Alba La Val dei Preti	90	now–2010
2004 Roero Roche d'Ampsèj	90	2009–2016
2003 Roero Roche d'Ampsèj	89	2009–2015
2004 Le Marne Grigie	90	now–2016

CORTESE ✱ ✱ ✱/✱ ✱ ✱ ✱
PIEDMONT $55.00–$95.00

Giuseppe Cortese is a traditionally minded producer operating out of the Rabajà zone in Barbaresco. The Cortese wines are classically styled and structured, as is evident even in the Dolcetto and Barbera bottlings. Overall quality is quite high, and this producer's wines offer good value relative to the other top-notch wines in the area. Pierluigi Cortese told me that in order to keep his 2003 Barbaresco as fresh as possible, he did a shorter fermentation than normal. He also used larger casks than he had in past vintages and reduced the amount of time the wine spent in oak. Those decisions seem to have paid off, as he produced one of the more successful Barbarescos of the vintage.

2003 Barbaresco Rabajà	91	now–2018
2001 Barbaresco Rabajà	92	now–2016
1999 Barbaresco Rabajà Riserva	91	2009–2019

Past Glories Barbaresco Rabajà Riserva: 1996 (92)

DAMILANO ✱ ✱/✱ ✱ ✱
PIEDMONT $39.00–$70.00

Damilano produces three Barolos that include single-vineyard wines from the Cannubi and Liste vineyards as well as Lecinquevigne, a blend made from fruit sourced from a variety of parcels. Made in a simple, accessible style with limited complexity, the wines are best suited for near- or midterm drinking. Damilano recently acquired a long-term lease for a large, choice parcel in the Cannubi vineyard. Let's hope this will be the catalyst for the house to ramp up quality in a meaningful way.

| 2003 Barolo Lecinquevigne | 87 | now–2013 |
| 2003 Barolo Cannubi | 88 | now–2015 |

2001 Barolo Cannubi	90	now–2016
2003 Barolo Liste	89	now–2015
2001 Barolo Liste	89+	2009–2018

DESSILANI ★★/★★★
PIEDMONT $37.00–$52.00

Dessilani makes wines from a variety of the northern Piedmont appellations, where the custom calls for blending Nebbiolo (known here as Spanna) with other indigenous varieties. Winemaking is overseen by Beppe Caviola, who has brought a new level of refinement to the wines, even if that has been achieved at a significant loss of varietal character.

2004 Fara Lochera	88	now–2016
2004 Fara Caramino	89	now–2019
2003 Ghemme	88	now–2013
2003 Gattinara	89	now–2013

EINAUDI ★★★★
PIEDMONT $19.00–$118.00

This historic producer is located in Dogliani, a zone known primarily for its Dolcettos, which tend to be more intensely colored and structured than those made in other appellations. Consulting oenologist Beppe Caviola has been instrumental in ratcheting up the quality of the wines in recent vintages. In fact, I can't think of too many estates that have made such significant strides in a short period of time. Although the estate produces a complete range of wines, emphasis is clearly given to the Dolcetto and Barolo bottlings. The Barolos are made in a very clean, elegant, and contemporary style. Fermentations are carried out with selected yeasts and last 12 to 15 days. The wines are then aged in a mix of 30-hectoliter (792-gallon) barrels and *barriques*. Readers should also consider the estate's Dolcettos, which are among the most unique wines being made in the region. The Vigna Tecc is particularly noteworthy and is now labeled under the new Dogliani designation.

2005 Dolcetto di Dogliani	88	now
2005 Dolcetto di Dogliani Vigna Tecc	90	now–2010
2004 Barolo	91	2009–2019
2003 Barolo	91	now–2015
2001 Barolo	88	now–2014
2004 Barolo Costa Grimaldi	91–94	???
2003 Barolo Costa Grimaldi	92	2009–2018
2001 Barolo Costa Grimaldi	90	2009–2016
2004 Barolo Nei Cannubi	92–95	???
2003 Barolo Nei Cannubi	93	2009–2018
2001 Barolo Nei Cannubi	91	2009–2016

ALESSANDRO E GIAN NATALE FANTINO ★★★★
PIEDMONT $N/A

Brothers Alessandro and Gian Natale Fantino operate out of a tiny cellar in Monforte that gives new meaning to the term "garage wine." The estate produces two Barolos from the prestigious Dardi zone of Bussia, as well as an extraordinary sweet wine made from dried Nebbiolo called Nepas. Alessandro Fantino may be less well known than some of his peers, but he has plenty of experience, most of which he gained during the 18 years he worked with Barolo Mascarello. Fantino is a producer in search of a well-defined style. He is still experimenting with aging regimes, and the various cuvées can be dramatically different. Some of the wines are very classic, while others are made in a more immediate style. Still, Fantino is making some of the most unique wines in Piedmont and is increasingly becoming a producer to watch. These new releases are simply gorgeous.

2003 Barolo Vigna dei Dardi (Chadderdon Cuvée)	90–93	???
2003 Barolo Vigna dei Dardi	89–92	???
2001 Barolo Vigna dei Dardi	91	2009–2021
2001 Barolo Vigna dei Dardi Riserva (Cask-Aged Cuvée)	91–94	???
2001 Barolo Vigna dei Dardi Riserva	90–93	???
2000 Barolo Vigna dei Dardi Riserva	94	2010–2025

FONTANABIANCA * * */* * * *
PIEDMONT $56.00–$68.00

This small Barbaresco producer is located in Neive. Proprietor Aldo Pola's top wine, the Barbaresco Sorì Burdin, is made from the Bordino vineyard, which lies just below the winery. Over the last few vintages it has consistently been an outstanding Barbaresco.

2004 Barbaresco Sorì Burdin	92	2009–2019
2003 Barbaresco Sorì Burdin	89	now–2015
2001 Barbaresco Sorì Burdin	91	now–2016

FONTANAFREDDA * * *
PIEDMONT $48.00–$160.00

Fontanafredda is one of Barolo's most historic and picturesque properties. Unfortunately, the estate has been a huge underperformer for years. Oenologist Danilo Drocco has done much to raise the quality of the wines, particularly at the high end. Although the top Barolo selections are often outstanding, sadly the bulk of the production falls well short of the mark, which is a shame because Fontanafredda owns a large portion of the best vineyards in the entire Barolo zone. The estate has been for sale for some time, and in early 2008 owner Italian bank Monte dei Paschi di Siena announced plans to sell the property to its foundation and a number of smaller investors. It will be fascinating to see if Fontanafredda can finally lift the level of its game.

2003 Barolo Serralunga	90	now–2017
2001 Barolo Serralunga	88	now–2015
2001 Barolo Lazzarito	91	2009–2019
2001 Barolo Paiagallo Vigna La Villa	91	now–2016
2001 Barolo La Rosa	90+?	now–2016
2000 Barolo Riserva	92	now–2017

GAJA * * * * *
PIEDMONT $180.00–$416.00

Angelo Gaja has been the leading light of Piedmont for several decades. He was among the first, if not the first, major Italian producer to believe his wines could equal the finest wines being made in Burgundy, Bordeaux, and California and to market them accordingly. Though now in his mid-sixties, Gaja possesses the raw energy and stamina of someone half his age. In recent years he has expanded his empire with holdings in Tuscany's Maremma and Montalcino. The wines are never inexpensive, but they are consistently outstanding and often profound. Even if the wines can be quite appealing when they are young, they always benefit from at least a few years in the cellar, and they boast an extraordinary track record of aging gracefully. Gaja's Barbaresco is made from a blend of different vineyards throughout the zone. The Costa Russi, Sorì Tildìn, and Sorì San Lorenzo are single-vineyard wines also made from holdings in Barbaresco. Costa Russi is usually the roundest and most accessible of these.

Sorì Tildìn is the most delicate and nuanced, while Sorì San Lorenzo is the most powerful. Conteisa is made from plots in La Morra and Sperss from vineyards in Serralunga, both in the Barolo production zone. With the exception of the Barbaresco, all of the estate's reds carry the broader Langhe designation, which allows Gaja to add 5% to 8% of Barbera to the wines. Fermentation and maceration typically last about 15 to 20 days. The wines are aged for one year in French oak *barriques* to set color and then moved to large casks, where they complete their wood aging. Gaja's 2003s are among the best of that difficult vintage, while the 2004s are some of the very finest wines he and longtime oenologist Guido Rivella (who oversees wine-making at all the family's estates) have ever made.

2004 Barbaresco	93	2009–2024
2003 Barbaresco	93	2009–2021
2001 Barbaresco	93+	now–2021
2004 Langhe Costa Russi	95	2009–2024
2003 Langhe Costa Russi	91	2009–2020
2001 Langhe Costa Russi	94	2009–2021
2004 Langhe Sorì Tildìn	97	2014–2024
2003 Langhe Sorì Tildìn	94+	2013–2025
2001 Langhe Sorì Tildìn	95	2009–2023
2004 Langhe Sorì San Lorenzo	98	2014–2029
2003 Langhe Sorì San Lorenzo	94	2009–2020
2001 Langhe Sorì San Lorenzo	95	2009–2025
2004 Langhe Conteisa	94	2009–2022
2003 Langhe Conteisa	91	2009–2019
2001 Langhe Conteisa	92	2009–2021
2004 Langhe Sperss	96	2014–2029
2003 Langhe Sperss	93	2010–2023
2001 Langhe Sperss	95	2011–2031
2004 Langhe Darmagi	90	2010–2024
2001 Langhe Darmagi	89	2011–2021

Past Glories Barbaresco: 2000 (92), 1999 (91), 1998 (91), 1997 (93), 1982 (93), 1979 (92), 1978 (92), 1958 (92); Barbaresco "Infernot": 1958 (94); Langhe Costa Russi: 2000 (94), 1999 (93), 1998 (93), 1997 (95); Barbaresco Costa Russi: 1985 (93); Langhe Sorì Tildìn: 2000 (95), 1999 (95), 1998 (94), 1997 (97); Barbaresco Sorì Tildìn: 1985 (93), 1982 (95); Langhe Sorì San Lorenzo: 2000 (95), 1999 (94), 1998 (94), 1997 (96); Barbaresco Sorì San Lorenzo: 1971 (97); Langhe Conteisa: 2000 (92), 1999 (92), 1998 (91), 1997 (92); Langhe Sperss: 2000 (94), 1999 (95), 1998 (93), 1997 (98); Barolo Sperss: 1990 (95); Langhe Darmagi: 2000 (92), 1998 (89), 1997 (91)

ETTORE GERMANO ★★★
PIEDMONT $40.00–$52.00

This small estate in Serralunga continues to show improvement under the direction of proprietor Sergio Germano. The winery produces three Barolos, including single-vineyard selections from the Prapò and Cerretta vineyards.

2001 Barolo	85	now–2015
2003 Barolo Cerretta	90	2009–2016
2003 Barolo Prapò	89	2009–2016
2001 Barolo Prapò	90	2009–2018

BRUNO GIACOSA ★★★★★
PIEDMONT $25.00–$320.00

While Angelo Gaja established the importance of his wines globally through sheer willpower and ambition, Bruno Giacosa chose another path. Famously shy and introverted, Giacosa let the wines do the talking, and talk they did, as his majestic Barolos and Barbarescos built a cultish legion of admirers that is equalled by just a small handful of producers around the world. In particular, Giacosa's Red Label Riservas are among the most coveted wines being made anywhere in the world. Even today, at a time in life when many of his colleagues have begun to slow down, Giacosa continues to make stunning wines of the highest level. The wines are still made in a fairly traditional style, with long fermentation/macerations and malolactic fermentations that can go into the following spring. The Barolos and Barbarescos both see around 30 months in large casks, which is longer than average by today's standards. Interestingly, Giacosa prefers French, rather than the more conventional Slavonian, oak for his casks. While the top Barolos and Barbarescos can be monumental, readers should not ignore the entry-level wines. The single-vineyard Dolcettos and Barberas have mostly been excellent to outstanding over the last few years. In addition, Giacosa makes a delicious Arneis and a sparkling Brut that is often among Italy's best *méthode champenoise* wines. In March 2007, longtime oenologist Dante Scaglione, who spent 16 years alongside Giacosa, left the estate to pursue other projects. Although Giacosa's Barolos and Barbarescos had always been of the highest quality, locals credit Scaglione for raising the level of the entry-level wines, which had been quite variable prior to his arrival and which constitute the majority of the house's production. Scaglione has been replaced by Giorgio Lavagana, who previously worked at Batasiolo. According to Giacosa's daughter Bruna, the estate intends to keep making wines in the style die-hard aficionados have come to expect.

2006 Dolcetto d'Alba Basarin	90	now
2006 Dolcetto d'Alba Falletto	90	now–2011
2005 Barbera d'Alba Superiore Falletto	88	now–2012
2004 Barbera d'Alba Superiore Falletto	91	now–2012
2003 Barbera d'Alba Superiore Falletto	92	now–2010
2005 Nebbiolo d'Alba Valmaggiore	89	now–2015
2004 Barbaresco Santo Stefano	95	2010–2022
2001 Barbaresco Santo Stefano	94	2009–2019
2004 Barbaresco Rabajà	97	2014–2029
2001 Barbaresco Riserva Rabajà	98	2011–2026
2004 Barbaresco Riserva Asili	98	2010–2025
2003 Barbaresco Asili	92	now–2018
2001 Barbaresco Asili	95	2009–2021
2001 Barolo	92	2011–2021
2004 Barolo Croera	90	2010–2020
2004 Barolo Falletto	96	2012–2024
2003 Barolo Falletto	91	2009–2019
2001 Barolo Falleto	94	2011–2023
2004 Barolo Riserva Le Rocche del Falletto	99	2014–2034
2003 Barolo Le Rocche del Falletto	94	2010–2023
2001 Barolo Riserva Le Rocche del Falletto	97	2013–2031

Past Glories Barbaresco Santo Stefano: 2000 (93), 1999 (92), 1986 (92), 1970 (38), 1968 (89); Barbaresco Riserva Santo Stefano: 1990 (97), 1989 (97), 1988 (88), 1985 (96), 1982 (97), 1978 (98), 1964 (95); Barbaresco Rabajá: 2000 (95); Barbaresco Asili: 1999 (89), 1998 (92); Barbaresco Riserva Asili: 2000 (97), 1996 (97), 1967 (94); Barbaresco Riserva: 1990 (91); Barbaresco Rio Sordo: 1985 (90); Barbaresco Gallina: 1978 (92); Barbaresco Albesani: 1971 (92); Barbaresco

Riserva Speciale: 1961 (95); Barolo Falleto: 2000 (93), 1999 (94); Barolo Le Rocche del Falletto: 1999 (96), 1998 (95), 1997 (92); Barolo Riserva Le Rocche del Falletto: 2000 (95); Barolo Riserva Falletto: 1996 (97), 1990 (97), 1989 (97), 1986 (97), 1985 (96); Barolo Collina Rionda: 1993 (92), 1985 (96), 1971 (92); Barolo Riserva Collina Rionda: 1990 (96), 1989 (100), 1982 (97); Barolo Riserva Speciale Collina Rionda: 1978 (99); Barolo Villero: 1996 (94), 1989 (95), 1986 (92); Barolo Riserva Speciale Villero: 1978 (97); Barolo Rocche di Castiglione: 1982 (94), 1978 (96); Barolo Riserva Bussia: 1978 (97); Barolo Riserva Speciale: 1964 (92)

ELIO GRASSO ★ ★ ★ ★
PIEDMONT $55.00–$70.00

Elio Grasso's wines are made in a unique, crisply articulated style that highlights balance and harmony over sheer power. For some reason Grasso is not as well known as some of his colleagues, yet in my conversations with other winemakers he is always spoken of with the highest admiration and esteem. The estate's approach is based on rigorous attention to the vineyards, where low yields are the rule. From fruit in the Gavarini and Ginestra crus in Monforte, the estate makes a wide range of excellent wines in a unique style that marries elements of both traditional and modern styles. The Chiniera and Casa Maté Barolos see fermentation of about 12 to 16 days, and the wines are aged in 25-hectoliter (660-gallon) Slavonian oak barrels, while the Rüncot is a more modern-styled wine made from lower yields and aged in *barriques*.

2004 Barolo Gavarini Vigna Chiniera	93	2009–2022
2003 Barolo Gavarini Vigna Chiniera	91	now–2017
2001 Barolo Gavarini Vigna Chiniera	91	now–2018
2004 Barolo Ginestra Vigna Casa Maté	94	2009–2022
2003 Barolo Ginestra Vigna Casa Maté	91	2009–2015
2001 Barolo Ginestra Vigna Casa Maté	93	now–2018
2004 Barolo Rüncot	91–94	2011–2022
2001 Barolo Rüncot	92	now–2016
2000 Barolo Rüncot	89	now–2015
1999 Barolo Rüncot	92	2009–2019
2002 Barolo	89	now–2014

SILVIO GRASSO ★ ★ ★
PIEDMONT $45.00–$100.00

Grasso is a small artisan grower based in La Morra. The estate's Barolos are among my favorite wines for near-term drinking in most vintages, as the wines are generally ready to drink with a minimum of cellaring. The approach here favors soft, supple wines made in an accessible, fruit-forward style. Grasso employs shortish fermentations and *barrique* aging for most of his Barolos with the exception of the more traditional Barolo L'André, which sees a much longer maceration time of a few weeks and is aged in a medium-sized oak cask. The Barolos are undoubtedly clean and well made, but I am not convinced that the relatively minor differences among them warrant six separate bottlings.

2003 Barolo Pi Vigne	88	now–2015
2004 Barolo Bricco Luciani	90	2009–2019
2003 Barolo Bricco Luciani	89	now–2013
2001 Barolo Bricco Luciani	89	now–2016
2003 Barolo Giachini	90	2009–2015
2001 Barolo Giachini	90	now–2016
2003 Barolo Vigna Plicotti	88	now–2013
2001 Barolo Vigna Plicotti	88+?	now–2016

2004 Barolo Ciabot Manzoni	91	2009–2019
2003 Barolo Ciabot Manzoni	90	2009–2016
2001 Barolo Ciabot Manzoni	90	now–2018
2003 Barolo L'André	89	2009–2015
2001 Barolo L'André	91	now–2017

Past Glories Barolo Bricco Luciani: 1999 (89); Barolo Giachini: 1999 (90); Barolo Ciabot Manzoni: 1999 (91)

GIACOMO GRIMALDI ✱ ✱ ✱
PIEDMONT $45.00–$73.00

Ferrucio Grimaldi makes his Barolos in an accessible, forward style that emphasizes very ripe fruit. This young producer has achieved an impressive level of quality even though he has been bottling his own wines only since the 1996 vintage. Grimaldi favors shortish fermentations and *barrique* aging for his Barolos. The estate is somewhat of an anomaly in that the entry-level Dolcetto, Barbera, and Nebbiolo d'Alba Valmaggiore bottlings often show more personality than the Barolos, which I often find excessively sweet.

2004 Barolo	89	now–2014
2004 Barolo Le Coste	93	2009–2019
2003 Barolo Le Coste	89	now–2015
2001 Barolo Le Coste	89	2009–2016
2004 Barolo Sotto Castello di Novello	92	2009–2019
2003 Barolo Sotto Castello di Novello	88	now–2015
2001 Barolo Sotto Castello di Novello	88	now–2015

HILBERG-PASQUERO ✱ ✱ ✱
PIEDMONT $22.00–$46.00

Working out of a tiny cellar in the town of Priocca in Roero, Michele Pasquero and Annette Hilberg make wines with an emphasis on natural farming of the vineyards and a stripped-down, noninterventionalist approach in the cellar. These are very pure wines loaded with personality. In particular, the Barberas are among my favorite wines of the Roero.

2006 Barbera d'Alba	88	now
2005 Barbera d'Alba Superiore	91	now–2010
2005 Nebbiolo d'Alba	88	now–2011
2005 Langhe Nebbiolo	89	now–2012

GIOVANNI MANZONE ✱ ✱ ✱/✱ ✱ ✱ ✱
PIEDMONT $40.00–$85.00

Giovanni Manzone produces some of the most unique Barolos in the zone. Although his hometown of Monforte is best known for structured wines, Manzone's vineyards are among the highest in the region, and as a result his wines show unusually delicate, often ethereal personalities. There are three wines from Gramolere, including a selection from a subplot called Bricat as well as a Riserva. In the past the wines have been very good to excellent, but if the 2004 Barolos are any indication, quality is on the rise. The Barolos are aged in a combination of *tonneaux* and larger oak barrels of 15 to 25 hectoliters (396 to 660 gallons).

2003 Barolo	87	now–2013
2004 Barolo Castelletto	89	2009–2016
2004 Barolo Le Gramolere	94	2012–2024
2003 Barolo Le Gramolere	91	2009–2019
2003 Barolo Bricat Le Gramolere	91+	2010–2020

2001 Barolo Bricat Le Gramolere	87	2009–2019
2004 Barolo Bricat	93+	2014–2024
2001 Barolo S. Stefano di Perno	89+	2009–2019
2001 Barolo Riserva Le Gramolere	92	2010–2020

Past Glories Barolo Le Gramolere: 1999 (91); Barolo Bricat Le Gramolere: 1999 (91); Barolo Riserva Le Gramolere: 1999 (89); Barolo S. Stefano di Perno: 1999 (89)

PAOLO MANZONE ★★★
PIEDMONT $42.00–$62.00

Paolo Manzone is based in Serralunga. Even though Manzone has been bottling his wines for only a few years, he has turned out two very successful 2003s. Manzone favors medium-sized barrels for aging and keeps the percentage of new oak at around 20%.

2003 Barolo Serralunga	88	now–2013
2003 Barolo Meriame	92	2010–2018

MARCARINI ★★★
PIEDMONT $59.00–$63.00

Manuel and Luisa Marchetti make classically built, traditional Barolos from their holdings in Brunate and La Serra, two of La Morra's best-known vineyards. These firm, cask-aged Barolos typically require a few years of bottle age to smooth the tannins, but they have a strong track record of aging well.

2004 Barolo La Serra	91	2011–2022
2003 Barolo La Serra	88	2009–2015
2001 Barolo La Serra	89+	2011–2019
2004 Barolo Brunate	93	2012–2024
2003 Barolo Brunate	90	now–2013
2001 Barolo Brunate	91	2011–2021

Past Glories Barolo Brunate: 2000 (90), 1999 (93), 1998 (92), 1997 (89), 1996 (89)

MARCHESI DI BAROLO ★★/★★★
PIEDMONT $71.00

Marchesi di Barolo is one of the region's historic properties. This gorgeous facility was once the home of the Marchesi Falletti, important figures in the very early history of Barolo wine. Today the estate makes a wide variety of wines from both purchased and estate-grown fruit. The Barolo Cannubi has been the most consistently excellent to outstanding wine, while the other offerings are, sadly, often uninspiring.

2003 Barolo Cannubi	90	2009–2019

MARCHESI DI GRÉSY ★★★/★★★★
PIEDMONT $40.00–$80.00

Marchesi di Grésy is superbly positioned in the prestigious Martinenga cru in Barbaresco, one of the most famous vineyards in the zone. In addition to its Barbaresco Martinenga, the estate produces single-vineyard wines from its Gaiun and Camp Gros, which lie adjacent to two of Barbaresco's most historic sites, Asili and Rabajà, respectively. The Martinenga and Camp Gros are aged in medium-sized casks, while the Gaium is aged in smaller French oak barrels. The wines are made in a very elegant, graceful style.

2004 Barbaresco Martinenga	89	now–2014
2003 Barbaresco Martinenga	88	now–2013

2001 Barbaresco Martinenga	91	now–2013
2001 Barbaresco Gaiun	92	now–2014
2001 Barbaresco Camp Gros	92	now–2016

Past Glories Barbaresco Camp Gros: 2000 (91); Barbaresco Gaiun: 2000 (89)

MARENGO * * */* * * *
PIEDMONT $50.00–$120.00

Marco Marengo is yet another of the small artisanal producers operating out of La Morra. Marengo's wines are made in a soft, fruit-forward style that renders the wines accessible fairly early. Fermentation and maceration typically last 5 to 6 days, and the wines are aged in *barriques*. In top vintages Marengo can give some of his more famous neighbors a run for their money. In recent vintages, Marengo's Barolo Brunate has been especially beautiful and remains one of the undiscovered gems of Piedmont.

2004 Barolo	90	now–2016
2004 Barolo Bricco delle Viole	91	2010–2022
2003 Barolo Bricco delle Viole	88	2009–2015
2001 Barolo Bricco delle Viole	89	now–2018
2004 Barolo Brunate	95	2011–2024
2003 Barolo Brunate	90	2009–2013
2001 Barolo Brunate	91	2009–2019
2004 Barolo Brunate Vecchie Vigne	94	2010–2024

Past Glories Barolo Brunate: 2000 (92)

FRANCO M. MARTINETTI * * *
PIEDMONT $80.00

Franco Martinetti is famous for his extraordinary gastronomical and oenological talent. Although he grew up in a family that produced wine, it wasn't until his advertising business was successful that he set out to make his own high-quality wines. It was, as he says, a way of satisfying a lifelong curiosity and passion. In a region where most of the top wines are made from estate-grown fruit, Martinetti's philosophy is unique, as he does not own any vineyards. Instead he carefully supervises various properties he leases throughout the region. The wines are sleek and refined, much like Martinetti himself.

2001 Barolo Marasco	92	now–2016

BARTOLO MASCARELLO * * * */* * * * *
PIEDMONT $85.00–$125.00

Maria Thérésa Mascarello has just completed a new tasting room that is strikingly modern in design, especially when compared to the rest of this tiny cellar, which is as bare-bones as they come. Mascarello continues to make her wines in the style of her father and grandfather, which is to say traditional in every sense. The estate produces one Barolo, which is made from a blend of some of the best plots in Barolo and La Morra. The vineyards are typically harvested in the following order: San Lorenzo, Cannubi, Torriglione, and Rue, and the grapes are vinified together. The wines are fermented in glass-lined concrete for 15 to 20 days, without the aid of temperature control or selected yeasts. The wine then ages in medium and large casks for three years before being released in the fall of the fourth year after the vintage. Mascarello's Barolos remain some of the most ageworthy wines of the region. They are perhaps a bit less clean and perfect than the modern wines we have become accustomed to, but these highly idiosyncratic wines deserve attention from those who seek to understand what traditional Barolo is all about. Her 2003 Barolo is an unqualified success, and the 2004 is the best young wine I have tasted here in many a year. Readers may also want to check out Mascarello's Dolcetto and Barbera, although I often find them a little lean and austere.

2004 Barolo	95	2014–2029
2003 Barolo	92	2009–2019
2001 Barolo	92	2009–2026

Past Glories Barolo: 2000 (86), 2000 (magnum) (92), 1999 (93), 1998 (93), 1997 (92), 1996 (93), 1990 (94), 1989 (96), 1986 (magnum) (95), 1985 (95), 1982 (94), 1980 (92), 1978 (95), 1971 (1.9-liter magnum) (92), 1964 (1.9-liter magnum) (93), 1958 (1.9-liter magnum) (97); Barolo Riserva Cannubi: 1954 (92)

GIUSEPPE MASCARELLO ★★★★/★★★★★
PIEDMONT $20.00–$275.00

Mauro Mascarello is among the few remaining hard-line traditionalist producers in Barolo. Mascarello owns the lion's share of the superbly positioned Monprivato vineyard that is the source of his two top wines, the Barolo Monprivato and the Barolo Riserva Ca' d'Morissio. When Monprivato is young, its tannins, general lack of color, and unique flavor profile can make it a tough wine to evaluate. But make no mistake, Monprivato is one of the most long-lived, expressive, and profound Barolos around. Because it is such a difficult wine to assess in its youth, Monprivato is a wine that has never caught on to the degree it deserves. Barolo connoisseurs know better, however. I can think of a number of occasions where a perfectly cellared bottle of Monprivato has upstaged better-known and far more expensive collectible wines from around the world. In recent years Mascarello has begun bottling his Barolo Riserva Ca' d'Morissio, which comes from a 1-hectare (2.47-acre) parcel within Monprivato planted to a naturally low-vigor strain of the Michet Nebbiolo clone. Early vintages have been quite promising. Mascarello also makes Barolos from the Villero and Santo Stefano di Perno vineyards. His Villero is typically the most open and feminine of the Barolos, while the Santo Stefano di Perno tends to be a big, chunky wine with firmer and less polished tannins. Winemaking remains very much rooted in tradition. Fermentation and maceration times range from 18 to 20 days for years with less structure to 20 to 25 days in more important vintages. The wines undergo malolactic fermentation in steel and are aged for 36 months in large Slavonian oak casks of various sizes prior to being bottled without clarification or filtration in the summer of the fourth year following the harvest. Mascarello's Riserva Ca' d'Morissio spends anywhere between 48 and 52 months in oak and is released when Mascarello feels the wine is ready. The Barbera Codana has crept up in price recently, yet this compelling Barbera, made from an old-vine plot adjacent to Monprivato, remains the best of Mascarello's more accessible wines. Mauro Mascarello is one of the few producers who prefers his 2003 Barolos to his 2001s, as he finds they have more power and intensity while also maintaining finesse and a sense of classicism. The wines certainly have more power, but I am not sure I would agree that they have more finesse. In any event, his 2003 Barolos, in particular the Santo Stefano di Perno and Monprivato, are among the best of the vintage. Barrel tastings suggest 2004 will be another very strong vintage at this venerable property.

2005 Barbera d'Alba Superiore Codana	91	now–2015
2005 Barbera d'Alba Superiore Santo Stefano di Perno	90	now–2010
2005 Dolcetto d'Alba Bricco	89	now–2010
2005 Dolcetto d'Alba Santo Stefano di Perno	87	now
2004 Barolo Monprivato	92–95	???
2003 Barolo Monprivato	93	now–2023
2001 Barolo Monprivato	95	2009–2026
2004 Barolo Riserva Ca' d'Morissio	93–96	???
2003 Barolo Riserva Ca' d'Morissio	91–93	???

2001 Barolo Riserva Ca' d'Morissio	93–96	???
2004 Barolo Santo Stefano di Perno	91–94	???
2003 Barolo Santo Stefano di Perno	92	now–2018
2001 Barolo Santo Stefano di Perno	93	2011–2021
2004 Barolo Villero	91–94	???
2003 Barolo Villero	90	now–2021
2001 Barolo Villero	91	2009–2019

Past Glories Barolo Villero: 2000 (90), 1999 (92), 1998 (89), 1978 (91); Barolo Santo Stefano di Perno: 2000 (89), 1999 (91); Barolo Monprivato: 2000 (93), 1999 (95+), 1998 (92), 1997 (93), 1996 (94), 1990 (95), 1989 (95), 1988 (91), 1985 (96), 1982 (96), 1979 (93), 1978 (95), 1970 (95); Barolo Riserva Ca' d'Morissio: 1997 (95), 1996 (95+), 1995 (93); Barolo Vigna Rionda: 1979 (94); Barolo: 1967 (96), 1964 (95)

MASSOLINO * * * *
PIEDMONT $39.00–$107.00

Brothers Franco and Roberto Massolino make traditionally styled Barolos from some of the most important vineyards in Serralunga, including Margheria, Parafada, and Vigna Rionda. Their top bottling, the Barolo Riserva Vigna Rionda, is a wine with an exceptional track record of ageability. Fermentation and maceration are done in stainless steel and glass-lined cement, where the wines also undergo malolactic fermentation prior to being racked into cask. Aging times range from to 2 to 2½ years for the Margheria to 3½ to 4 years for the Vigna Rionda. The exception is the Parafada, the estate's more modern Barolo, which sees a much shorter fermentation/maceration time and is aged in smaller French oak barrels. Although the Parafada remains a distinctly contemporary expression of Serralunga Barolo, in recent years the family has made small adjustments to bring it closer to the more classic feel of its other wines. The estate bottled small quantities of all its single-vineyard Barolos in the difficult 2002 vintage, yet opted for a blend of its best fruit in 2003, bucking conventional wisdom, but it's with the top-flight 2004s that the estate shines at its brightest.

2004 Barbera d'Alba Gisep	89	now–2010
2001 Barbera d'Alba Gisep	89	now–2011
2004 Barolo	90	2010–2014
2003 Barolo	92	now–2018
2002 Barolo	85	now–2014
2004 Barolo Parafada	93	2010–2020
2002 Barolo Parafada	87	now–2016
2004 Barolo Margheria	95	2012–2024
2002 Barolo Margheria	89	now–2017
2004 Barolo Riserva Vigna Rionda	92–95	???
2002 Barolo Riserva Vigna Rionda	90+?	2010–2020

Past Glories Barolo: 2001 (89+), 1999 (88); Barolo Parafada: 2001 (90), 1999 (89); Barolo Margheria: 2001 (92), 1999 (91); Barolo Riserva Vigna Rionda: 2001 (95), 2000 (93), 1999 (93), 1998 (92), 1997 (93), 1996 (95), 1995 (90), 1990 (94), 1989 (95), 1988 (92), 1986 (95), 1985 (93), 1984 (88), 1982 (94)

MOCCAGATTA * * */* * * *
PIEDMONT $53.00–$75.00

Brothers Sergio and Franco Minuto make excellent, modern-styled Barbarescos from their vineyards in Barbaresco and Neive. The Moccagatta Barbarescos tend to be intensely perfumed, aromatic wines with generous fruit and engaging personalities. The wines are aged in

French oak, but in recent years the estate has begun to scale back the use of new barrels, which allows the characteristics of the wines to show with greater articulation.

2005 Barbaresco Basarin	88	2010–2020
2004 Barbaresco Basarin	91	2010–2019
2003 Barbaresco Basarin	89	now–2015
2005 Barbaresco Bric Balin	90	2010–2020
2004 Barbaresco Bric Balin	92	2011–2024
2003 Barbaresco Bric Balin	89	now–2018
2005 Barbaresco Cole	92	2012–2025
2004 Barbaresco Cole	94	2011–2024
2003 Barbaresco Cole	91	now–2018

Past Glories Barbaresco Basarin: 2001 (90), 1999 (92); Barbaresco Bric Balin: 2001 (92), 1999 (89); Barbaresco Cole: 2001 (91)

MAURO MOLINO ∗ ∗ ∗
PIEDMONT $38.00–$95.00

Molino is a producer still in search of a well-defined, consistent house style. In recent years the wines have gained in richness and complexity. The oak that dominated the wines' balance in the past has been cut back. It is still too soon to know if these developments signify a long-term commitment to a higher level of quality, but for now Molino certainly seems to be moving in the right direction.

2004 Barolo	87	now–2014
2003 Barolo	87	now–2013
2001 Barolo	88	now–2013
2004 Barolo Gallinotto	89	now–2016
2003 Barolo Gallinotto	88	now–2015
2001 Barolo Gallinotto	89	now–2016
2004 Barolo Vigneto Gancia	90	2009–2016
2003 Barolo Vigneto Gancia	90	2009–2015
2001 Barolo Gancia	90	2009–2016
2004 Barolo Conca	91	2009–2017
2003 Barolo Conca	91	2009–2015
2001 Barolo Conca	89	2009–2016

Past Glories Barolo: 1999 (89); Barolo Gancia: 1999 (91); Barolo Conca: 1990 (90)

LA MORANDINA ∗ ∗ ∗
PIEDMONT $55.00

Readers are more likely to know La Morandina for its excellent Moscatos, but the estate also produces a Barbaresco from holdings in Neive.

2004 Barbaresco Bricco Spessa	88	now–2015

CASCINA MORASSINO ∗ ∗ ∗
PIEDMONT $45.00–$60.00

This small producer, located in the Ovello subzone of Barbaresco, makes pretty, elegant wines that are well worth seeking out.

2004 Barbaresco Morassino	92	now–2019
2004 Barbaresco Ovello	91	2009–2019

FIORENZO NADA　*　*　*/*　*　*　*
PIEDMONT $56.00–$85.00

Bruno Nada has been making excellent wine in Barbaresco for years, yet he remains less well known than he deserves to be. His Barbaresco Rombone is often among the region's top wines, as is his Barbera/Nebbiolo blend, Seifile. Nada favors casks for his entry-level Barbaresco, while the Rombone and Seifile are aged in smaller French oak barrels.

2003 Barbaresco	88	now–2013
2001 Barbaresco	89	now–2013
2004 Barbaresco Rombone	89	2009–2019
2003 Barbaresco Rombone	91	now–2015
2001 Barbaresco Rombone	90	now–2016
2004 Langhe Rosso Seifile	89	now–2016
2003 Langhe Rosso Seifile	91	now–2015
2001 Langhe Rosso Seifile	92	now–2016

ANDREA OBERTO　*　*　*/*　*　*　*
PIEDMONT $20.00–$80.00

In a region full of outspoken, colorful producers, Fabio Oberto comes across as somewhat shy and introverted. Maybe that's one of the reasons this estate remains less well known than it should. However, readers will want to give these wines careful consideration. In most vintages the Barolo Rocche is one of the finest wines from this famous vineyard. The estate produces two single-vineyard Barolos, Albarella (from a vineyard in Barolo), and Rocche (from La Morra), as well as an entry-level wine that is made from less well exposed plots in La Morra. The wines see fermentation of 12 to 15 days and are aged exclusively in *barriques* ranging from 40% to 60% new oak. Oberto's Barbera d'Alba Giada is typically one of the top Barberas in the region.

2006 Dolcetto d'Alba	88	now
2006 Barbera d'Alba	87	now
2003 Langhe Rosso Fabio	88	now
2003 Barolo	90	now–2013
2001 Barolo	88+?	now–2016
2003 Barolo Vigneto Albarella	91	now–2015
2001 Barolo Vigneto Albarella	91	2009–2019
2003 Barolo Vigneto Rocche	92	2009–2018
2001 Barolo Vigneto Rocche	92	now–2018

ODDERO　*
PIEDMONT $75.00

Oddero has been an inconsistent performer in recent vintages, but these are the best Barolos I have tasted from this property in some time. It is a shame the estate can't do better with its holdings in Vigna Rionda, one of the most famous sites in Barolo.

2003 Barolo Mondoca di Bussia Soprana	88	2010–2023
2003 Barolo Rocche di Castiglione	89	2010–2023

PAITIN　*　*　*/*　*　*　*
PIEDMONT $28.00–$68.00

Paitin is based in the Serraboella subsection of Neive, a small corner of the Barbaresco zone known for yielding richly structured wines. The house style favors intense, concentrated wines that at their best offer notable complexity as well as exquisite balance. The Barbaresco

Sorì Paitin, Barbaresco Vecchie Vigne, and Barbera d'Alba Superiore Campolive are consistently strong wines.

2005 Barbera d'Alba Superiore Campolive	89	now–2010
2004 Barbaresco Sorì Paitin	92	2010–2019
2003 Barbaresco Sorì Paitin	89	2009–2015
2001 Barbaresco Sorì Paitin	91	now–2014
2001 Barbaresco Vecchie Vigne	92	now–2016

PARUSSO ★ ★ ★ ★
PIEDMONT $26.00–$122.00

Marco Parusso makes elegant Barolos that emulate much of what he admires among his favorite Burgundy producers. The fruit gets a two- to three-day cold soak to allow the grapes to recover from what Parusso describes as the shock of being harvested. The wines are fermented at a lower temperature than is the norm here in order to preserve freshness. Parusso works with natural yeasts and minimal amounts of sulfur dioxide, leaving the wines on their lees for 16 to 18 months, another practice that is uncommon in these parts.

2005 Langhe Nebbiolo	88	now
2004 Barbera d'Alba Ornati	89	now–2010
2004 Barbera d'Alba Superiore	92	now–2012
2004 Barolo	89	2009–2016
2003 Barolo	87	now–2015
2001 Barolo	90+	now–2015
2004 Barolo Mariondino	91–92	2010–2018
2003 Barolo Mariondino	90	2010–2020
2001 Barolo Mariondino	89	2009–2019
2003 Barolo Bussia Rocche	92	2010–2020
2004 Barolo Bussia	93	2009–2024
2001 Barolo Bussia	93	2011–2021
2004 Barolo Le Coste Mosconi	92	2009–2019
2003 Barolo Le Coste Mosconi	91	2009–2018
1999 Barolo Riserva	92	2009–2019

Past Glories Barolo Bussia Vigna Rocche: 1999 (92)

PECCHENINO ★ ★ ★ ★
PIEDMONT $N/A

Brothers Orlando and Attilio Pecchenino run this small property in Dogliani, where they make some of the most powerful, intense Dolcettos readers are likely to come across. The San Luigi is a fresh, pretty wine. The Sirì d'Jermu, which gets the full treatment of malolactic fermentation and 6 months of aging on its lees, is an especially structured Dolcetto. With the 2005 vintage, it now qualifies for the newly created Dogliani DOCG. 2004 is the first vintage for Pecchenino's Barolo Le Coste from one of Monforte's historic vineyards.

2006 Dolcetto di Dogliani San Luigi	89	now–2010
2006 Dogliani Sirì d'Jermu	90	now–2012
2004 Barolo Le Coste	89	2010–2022

PELISSERO ★★★
PIEDMONT $16.00–$90.00

Giorgio Pelissero crafts beautiful wines made in a supple, modern style. As good as his Barbarescos can be, readers should not overlook the Dolcettos and Barberas, which offer much pleasure at very accessible prices.

2006 Dolcetto d'Alba Munfrina	88	ncw
2005 Barbera d'Alba I Piani	89	ncw–2010
2004 Barbaresco Tulin	89	ncw–2014
2003 Barbaresco Tulin	89	ncw–2016
2001 Barbaresco Tulin	89	now–2013
2004 Barbaresco Nubiola	91	2009–2019
2003 Barbaresco Nubiola	88	now–2013
2001 Barbaresco Nubiola	88	now–2011
2004 Barbaresco Vanotu	92	2009–2019
2003 Barbaresco Vanotu	90	now–2016
2001 Barbaresco Vanotu	91	now–2015

ELIO PERRONE ★★★★
PIEDMONT $17.00–$30.00

Stefano Perrone is perhaps best known for his beautiful Moscatos, but he also makes terrific Barberas from his vineyards near Asti. His Barbera d'Asti Superiore Mogovone comes from vines that are over 70 years old. It is a very representative example of first-rate Barberas from the hills of Asti. His Moscatos, Clarté and Sourgal, are among the very finest being made.

2006 Barbera d'Asti Tasmorcan	88	now–2011
2005 Barbera d'Asti Tasmorcan	88	now–2010
2005 Barbera d'Asti Superiore Mongovone	91	now–2015

PERTINACE ★★★
PIEDMONT $35.00–$45.00

Pertinace, a cooperative based in Treiso, is an excellent source of value-priced Barbarescos made in a style that incorporates elements of both the traditional and modern schools.

2004 Barbaresco Pertinace	90	now–2016
2004 Barbaresco Vigneto Marcarini	93	2009–2019

PIANPOLVERE SOPRANO ★★★★
PIEDMONT $N/A

The late Valentino Migliorini purchased the Pianpolvere Soprano estate after the tragic death of its previous owner, Beppe Fenocchio. Although Migliorini was best known for the wines he made at his estate Rocche dei Manzoni, he chose to leave Pianpolvere Soprano as a separate operation in recognition of the unique properties of this very special vineyard. Speak with old-timers, and they will tell you that Pianpolvere has long been considered one of the very best sites for Nebbiolo production owing to its warm microclimate and the soil s ability to retain water. In fact, when I asked Bruno Giacosa to name the top *terroirs* in Barolo, Pianpolvere was at the top of his list.

2000 Barolo Bussia Riserva	93	now–2020
1999 Barolo Bussia Riserva	93	now–2021
2001 Barolo Bussia Riserva 7 Anni	95	2011–2025

PIO CESARE ★ ★ ★/★ ★ ★ ★
PIEDMONT $57.00–$112.00

Pio Cesare, founded in 1881, is one of the oldest cellars in Piedmont. Tucked away in a corner of the center of Alba, the front door opens to reveal a large, sprawling facility that preserves much of the historic character of the estate. The winery's Barolos and Barbarescos are made in a fairly traditional style while single-vineyard wines are decidedly more contemporary expressions of Nebbiolo.

2003 Barbaresco	90	2009–2018
2001 Barbaresco	90	2009–2016
2003 Barbaresco Il Bricco	89	now–2018
2001 Barbaresco Il Bricco	91	2011–2021
2003 Barolo	91	2010–2023
2001 Barolo	90	2011–2021
2003 Barolo Ornato	92	2011–2023
2001 Barolo Ornato	91	2011–2021

Past Glories Barbaresco: 2000 (89); Barbaresco Il Bricco: 2000 (88); Barolo: 2000 (90); Barolo Ornato: 2000 (92)

E. PIRA–CHIARA BOSCHIS ★ ★ ★ ★
PIEDMONT $69.00–$95.00

Chiara Boschis makes two very elegant Barolos from her holdings in the center of the town of Barolo. Although Boschis prefers to age her Barolos in 100% new oak, the wines are always well balanced. Some of the aromas and flavors may be those of the modern school, but the wines' medium weight and structure are decidedly classic. Her Barolos often require a few years to absorb their oak and express their fullest potential.

2004 Barolo Via Nuova	92	2011–2024
2003 Barolo Via Nuova	92	2010–2018
2004 Barolo Cannubi	95	2009–2022
2003 Barolo Cannubi	90	2009–2015
2001 Barolo Cannubi	93	2009–2019

Past Glories Barolo Cannubi: 2000 (91), 1999 (93), 1998 (92), 1997 (91), 1996 (92); Barolo Via Nuova: 1999 (91)

LUIGI PIRA ★ ★ ★ ★
PIEDMONT $37.00–$123.00

Giampaolo Pira may be quiet and soft spoken, but his wines speak volumes. Pira produces some of the most exciting, modern-styled wines in the region from first-class vineyards in Serralunga. These opulent wines are made from low yields and superripe fruit, and boast great intensity, yet they achieve a level of balance and harmony that is rare among the region's big wines. Fermentations are on the short side, lasting 7 to 10 days, and the wines are aged in an assortment of small and large barrels. I consider Marenca and Vigna Rionda to be this producer's top wines. Readers who prefer a powerful style will gravitate to the former; those who enjoy a more subtle wine will probably prefer the latter.

2004 Barolo	88	2009–2016
2003 Barolo	90	2009–2018
2001 Barolo	87+?	now–2013
2004 Barolo Margheria	93	2012–2024
2003 Barolo Margheria	90	2010–2018
2001 Barolo Margheria	90+?	now–2016

2004 Barolo Marenca	94	2012–2024
2003 Barolo Marenca	91	2011–2018
2001 Barolo Marenca	92	now–2019
2004 Barolo Vigna Rionda	96	2014–2024
2003 Barolo Vigna Rionda	88	2011–2023
2001 Barolo Vigna Rionda	93	2009–2019

Past Glories Barolo Margheria: 1999 (91); Barolo Marenca: 2000 (91), 1999 (93); Barolo Vigna Rionda: 2000 (95), 1999 (93)

GUIDO PORRO ✱ ✱ ✱
PIEDMONT $39.00

I was delighted to discover the wines of Guido Porro, a small artisan producer based in Serralunga. Porro makes two single-vineyard Barolos, both of which are aged in medium-sized casks. The wines are neither filtered nor fined and show a remarkable level of purity and clarity.

2004 Barolo Santa Caterina	88–91	???
2003 Barolo Santa Caterina	90	now–2018
2004 Barolo Lazzairasco	89–92	???
2003 Barolo Lazzairasco	91	2010–2020

PRINCIPIANO ✱ ✱ ✱
PIEDMONT $33.00–$64.00

Ferdinando Principiano is among the young producers whose style is still very much in a phase of discovery. His 2003 Barolo Boscareto is a successful wine, yet beginning with the 2004 vintage Principiano adopted dramatically lower yields and eliminated the use of new French oak. It will be interesting to see how the wines progress over the next few years.

2005 Barbera d'Alba La Romualda	88	now–2010
2003 Barolo Boscareto	91	now–2015
2001 Barolo Boscareto	89	now–2018

PRODUTTORI DEL BARBARESCO ✱ ✱ ✱/✱ ✱ ✱ ✱
PIEDMONT $33.00–$55.00

Managing Director Aldo Vacca oversees this cooperative, whose growers own plots in Barbaresco's most storied vineyards. The approach to vinification and aging is strictly traditional, although in recent years the winery has replaced some of its older casks with slightly smaller barrels. The last few years have also seen a notable increase in both the quality and the consistency of the estate's wines. In particular, readers would do well to seek out the Produttori's Riservas, particularly in top vintages, when the wines are capable of challenging some of the region's most famous (and expensive) bottlings. Even better, the Riservas remain some of the best relative values anywhere in the world of wine.

2004 Barbaresco	90	now–2016
2003 Barbaresco	91	now–2018
2001 Barbaresco	90	now–2016
2001 Barbaresco Riserva Rio Sordo	91	now–2018
2001 Barbaresco Riserva Moccagatta	90	now–2018
2001 Barbaresco Riserva Pora	90	2009–2016
2001 Barbaresco Riserva Asili	92	2011–2021
2001 Barbaresco Riserva Pajè	92	2011–2021
2001 Barbaresco Riserva Montestefano	91	2009–2019

2001 Barbaresco Riserva Montefico	92	2011–2021
2001 Barbaresco Riserva Ovello	92	2011–2021
2001 Barbaresco Riserva Rabajà	94	2011–2021

Past Glories Barbaresco: 2000 (87), 1999 (88); Barbaresco Riserva Moccagatta: 2000 (89), 1999 (88); Barbaresco Riserva Ovello: 2000 (88), 1999 (91), 1997 (89); Barbaresco Riserva Rio Sordo: 2000 (90), 1999 (90); Barbaresco Riserva Asili: 2000 (91), 1999 (91), 1997 (87), 1996 (90), 1990 (89); Barbaresco Riserva Montefico: 2000 (91), 1999 (92); Barbaresco Riserva Montestefano: 2000 (87), 1999 (89), 1978 (92); Barbaresco Riserva Pajè: 2000 (90), 1999 (90), 1996 (92); Barbaresco Riserva Pora: 2000 (87), 1999 (89), 1996 (92); Barbaresco Riserva Rabajà: 2000 (91), 1999 (90), 1997 (91), 1996 (92), 1978 (93)

PRUNOTTO ✱ ✱ ✱
PIEDMONT $48.00–$87.00

Prunotto makes a wide range of wines from their extensive holdings in the region. The entry-level Barolo and Barbaresco are made from purchased fruit, while the single-vineyard wines are made from estate-grown fruit. The wines are aged predominantly in large 50-hectoliter (1,320-gallon) casks, although a small quantity of the wines is aged in smaller barrels as well as used *barriques.* Stylistically, the wines are classic in weight and structure, though the use of French and Austrian oak gives them a more contemporary feel.

2005 Monferrato Rosso Mompertone	89	now–2015
2003 Barbera d'Alba Pian Romualdo	89	now–2013
2004 Barbaresco Classico	91	now–2019
2001 Barbaresco	87	now–2013
2003 Barbaresco Bric Turot	91	now–2018
2001 Barbaresco Bric Turot	89	now–2016
2003 Barolo	90	now–2015
2001 Barolo	89	now–2016
2003 Barolo Bussia	92	2009–2020
2001 Barolo Bussia	90	now–2021

Past Glories Barbaresco Bric Turot: 1999 (90); Barolo Bussia: 1999 (91)

RENATO RATTI ✱ ✱ ✱
PIEDMONT $47.00–$82.00

Twenty years after his passing, it is easy to take the contributions of Renato Ratti for granted. Ratti introduced many innovations to the production of Barolo that today are considered to be standard practice. In the early 1970s Ratti began to experiment with shorter alcoholic fermentations, more controlled malolactic fermentations, and limiting wood aging to two years in order to make softer, fresher wines that could be enjoyed earlier than was the norm. Ratti was also a prolific writer and authored several definitive texts. Perhaps Ratti's greatest contribution in this area is his map classifying the great Barolo vineyards, which is still widely used as a reference tool.

Today Ratti's son Piero runs the estate with his uncle Massimo Martinelli, who is also a highly respected author and scholar in his own right. The Barolos see fermentation and maceration lasting seven to eight days. The wines are then aged for a year in small French oak barrels followed by a year in 25-hectoliter (660-gallon) casks. These are wines of understated elegance that are classic examples of the more fragrant and delicate style of Barolo that is typical of La Morra. I found the 2001s to show a lot of balance and harmony, as the wines show less overt signs of new oak than they did just a few years ago. Unfortunately, the 2003 vintage was especially challenging in La Morra, as is evidenced by the three offerings listed below.

2003 Barolo Marcenasco	87	now–2015
2001 Barolo Marcenasco	88	now–2013
2003 Barolo Marcenasco Rocche	89	2009–2018
2001 Barolo Marcenasco Rocche	89	now–2016
2003 Barolo Marcenasco Conca	88	2010–2020
2001 Barolo Marcenasco Conca	90+	now–2016

Past Glories Barolo Marcenasco: 1995 (90), 1993 (91), 1979 (90); Barolo Marcenasco Rocche: 1990 (92)

REVELLO ★ ★ ★ ★
PIEDMONT $40.00–$105.00

Brothers Enzo and Carlo Revello are part of a new generation of producers in La Morra who are inextricably linked with Elio Altare, the area's father figure. The estate released its first wine in 1992 and began bottling the entire production only in 1997. Yields are kept quite low, at around 5,000 kilos per hectare (4,455 pounds per acre), and the vinification style is decidedly modern. Fermentations last just a few days, and aging is done in *barrique*. The use of oak is still prevalent, but it is increasingly more measured and the wines appear to have gained better balance and poise as the estate has matured.

2004 Barolo	89	now–2014
2003 Barolo	89	now–2013
2001 Barolo	89	now–2013
2004 Barolo Giachini	92	2010–2022
2003 Barolo Giachini	90	2009–2015
2001 Barolo Giachini	90	2009–2016
2004 Barolo Gattera	92	2010–2022
2003 Barolo Gattera	89	now–2013
2001 Barolo Gattera	89+?	2009–2016
2004 Barolo Conca	93	2010–2022
2003 Barolo Conca	89	now–2013
2001 Barolo Conca	92	now–2016
2004 Barolo Rocche dell'Annunziata	94	2010–2022
2003 Barolo Rocche dell'Annunziata	90	2009–2015

Past Glories Barolo Conca: 2000 (89), 1999 (92); Barolo Gattera: 2000 (92), 1999 (91); Barolo Giachini: 1999 (92); Barolo Rocche dell'Annunziata: 1999 (93)

FRANCESCO RINALDI ★ ★ ★
PIEDMONT $56.00–$60.00

Francesco Rinaldi is among the most staunchly traditional Barolo producers. These are austere, structured wines that require considerable patience. I have been fortunate to taste Rinaldi's Barolos back to 1958, and they have a track record of holding up quite well, even if they never develop into especially generous wines. In the past quality has been variable, but the 2003 Barolos represent a big step up in quality. They also happen to be remarkably accessible for this producer.

2003 Barolo Cannubio	89	2010–2020
2003 Barolo Le Brunate	91	2013–2026

Past Glories Barolo: 1971 (90), 1964 (89), 1958 (89), 1945 (93); Barolo Brunata: 1933 (89); Barolo Cannubio: 1985 (91), 1982 (91)

GIUSEPPE RINALDI ★★★★/★★★★★
PIEDMONT $90.00–$94.00

Perhaps because his wines can be austere and hard to understand when young, Beppe Rinaldi remains by far the most underrated producer in Barolo. Even in Italy he has begun to receive recognition from the local press only within the last few years. Unlike other, more outspoken producers, Rinaldi keeps a low profile, adding to the mystique of the man and his wines. Make no mistake, though, these are great wines made in a classic, traditional style that will provide much enjoyment for those who are patient enough to wait. Recent bottles of this producer's 1978, 1985, and 1989 have been nothing short of extraordinary. The Barolos are made in a rigorously traditional fashion. Fermentation and maceration take place in a 100-year-old open-top wood vat for 20 to 30 days, without temperature control or the use of selected yeasts. The Barolos are aged for 3½ years prior to being bottled. Rinaldi also makes small quantities of Dolcetto and Barbera, most of which are consumed locally.

2004 Barolo Cannubi (San Lorenzo)/Ravera	91–94	???
2003 Barolo Cannubi (San Lorenzo)/Ravera	91	now–2019
2001 Barolo Cannubi (San Lorenzo)/Ravera	91	2011–2021
2004 Barolo Brunate/Le Coste	92–95	???
2003 Barolo Brunate/Le Coste	92	2009–2019
2001 Barolo Brunate/Le Coste	93	2013–2031

Past Glories Barolo Brunate/Le Coste: 2000 (92), 1999 (93), 1997 (92); Barolo Brunate Riserva (magnum): 1989 (95), 1985 (96), 1978 (93); Barolo Cannubi (San Lorenzo)/Ravera: 2000 (91), 1999 (91)

ROAGNA ★★★/★★★★
PIEDMONT $15.00–$85.00

Luca Roagna is one of the most promising young winemakers in the Langhe. This small property is a throwback to an earlier time when the pace of life was both much slower and more closely aligned with an agrarian culture. The hallmarks of the house style include late harvests from old-vine plots and an ultratraditional approach in the cellar that calls for macerations on the skins lasting anywhere from a minimum of 50 days for the entry-level Barolos and Barbarescos to an unheard of 75 days for the top bottlings of both wines. Roagna favors French oak barrels, and the wines are aged for extended periods in both barrel and bottle prior to being released. The winery produces three selections of Barbaresco, the Pajé, Pajé Riserva, and Crichet Pajé, as well two selections of the Barolo La Rocca e La Pira, a regular bottling and the Riserva. It is not clear to me that the Riservas represent a quality level that is meaningfully higher than that of the regular bottlings. In fact on some occasions I have found the top selections overextracted and lacking fruit, while the regular bottlings often display better overall balance. These are big, powerful, classically structured wines that will please readers in search of Barolos and Barbarescos made in a rigorously traditional style. Because Roagna has not received a lot of attention from the press the wines remain very reasonably priced considering the quality, something that has become all too rare these days—and you have to love an estate that is only now releasing its wines from the late 1990s.

2006 Dolcetto d'Alba	88	now
2003 Barolo Vigna Rionda	92	2013–2023
2000 Barbaresco Pajé	91	now–2018
1999 Barbaresco Pajé	92	2009–2019
1998 Barbaresco Riserva Pajé	91	2010–2025
1997 Barbaresco Riserva Pajé	91	now–2017

1998 Barbaresco Crichet Pajé	93	2010–2028
2000 Barolo La Rocca e La Pira	92	2010–2025
1999 Barolo La Rocca e La Pira	92	2011–2024
1997 Barolo Riserva La Rocca e La Pira	90	now–2017
1996 Barolo Riserva La Rocca e La Pira	90	2011–2021
1993 Barolo Riserva La Rocca e La Pira	92	now–2017

ALBINO ROCCA ★ ★ ★ ★
PIEDMONT $48.00–$76.00

Like many producers in the region, proprietor Angelo Rocca seems to have reached a new level of maturity in his winemaking in recent years. His wines today are less explosive but offer far more balance and elegance than they have in the past. Rocca increasingly relies on medium-sized 20-hectoliter (528-gallon) casks rather than small French oak barrels to age his Barbarescos. His approach to the vineyards remains the same, however, and these are wines that clearly show this producer's strong commitment to quality through low yields. Unfortunately, Rocca's 2003s show how difficult the vintage proved to be and the wines aren't up to his usual level of quality, but he bounced back with a stellar set of 2004s and 2005s. Readers should also be on the lookout for his more modestly priced wines. The Dolcetto d'Alba Vignalunga, Barbera d'Alba Gepin, and Rosso di Rocca (80% Nebbiolo, 10% Barbera, and 10% Cabernet Franc) are all noteworthy.

2005 Barbaresco	88–91	???
2004 Barbaresco	90	2009–2016
2005 Barbaresco Bric Ronchi	89–92	???
2004 Barbaresco Bric Ronchi	92	2009–2016
2003 Barbaresco Bric Ronchi	88	now–2015
2005 Barbaresco Sorì Loreto	89–92	???
2004 Barbaresco Sorì Loreto	94	2009–2019
2003 Barbaresco Sorì Loreto	89	2009–2015
2002 Barbaresco "Duemiladue"	88	now–2012

Past Glories Barbaresco Bric Ronchi: 2001 (92), 1999 (91); Barbaresco Sorì Loreto: 2001 (91)

BRUNO ROCCA ★ ★ ★ ★
PIEDMONT $63.00–$120.00

Bruno Rocca's small estate is perched above the central portion of the Rabajà vineyard, one of the most legendary sites in Piedmont. Rocca works with low yields to make elegant, modern-styled Barbarescos that at their best achieve a rare combination of power married to weightless elegance. Rocca bottles an entry-level Barbaresco from his younger vines plus the Coparossa (made from vineyards in Neive and Treiso) and the Barbaresco Rabajà. In top vintages Rocca also produces his Barbaresco Maria Adelaide, which is a selection of his best fruit. Among the more accessible wines, the estate's Barbera d'Alba is often a standout. The 2001, 2003, and 2004 vintages are all successful for the forward-thinking Bruno Rocca.

2004 Barbaresco	90	2009–2019
2003 Barbaresco	89	now–2015
2001 Barbaresco	90	now–2011
2004 Barbaresco Coparossa	92	2010–2019
2003 Barbaresco Coparossa	91	now–2015
2001 Barbaresco Coparossa	92	now–2013
2004 Barbaresco Rabajà	93	2011–2024
2003 Barbaresco Rabajà	92	2009–2018

2001 Barbaresco Rabajà	94	now–2016
2001 Barbaresco Maria Adelaide	92	2009–2017

ROCCHE DEI MANZONI ★ ★ ★/★ ★ ★ ★ ★
PIEDMONT $N/A

In a region dominated by small artisan producers, Rocche dei Manzoni stands out for its châteaulike elegance and grandeur. The wines reflect the Francophile passion of the late owner, Valentino Migliorini, and his son Rodolfo. Fermentation and maceration last around three weeks, and the Barolos are aged for 30 to 36 months in 100% new oak, with the wines being racked four times a year. The prolonged wood aging gives these Barolos noticeable new oak tannins that are especially apparent when the wines are young. I have tended to underrate the estate's Barolos when young but then always enjoyed them immensely with bottle age. I have consistently been thrilled with how vintages like 1978, 1982, and 1989 have developed and only wish I had a deeper collection of the wines in my cellar. Migliorini is among the handful of producers who decided not to bottle his single-vineyard selections in 2003, opting instead for a blend, which has turned out to be one of the highlights of the vintage. Migliorini has told me on several occasions, however, that he considers his 2002 Barolo Rocche (also a blend) to have more potential for development over time because it is a fresher wine. Last, readers should not look past the estate's more accessible wines, the best of which are noteworthy and deserving of close consideration. These include the Barbera d'Alba Sorito Mosconi, the Quatr Nas (50% Nebbiolo and 50% Merlot, Cabernet Sauvignon, and Pinot Noir), and the Bricco Manzoni (80% Nebbiolo and 20% Barbera). Rocche dei Manzoni produces one of the best *champenoise*-style wines in Italy, the Valentino Brut Zero.

2000 Valentino Brut Zero	93	now–2020
2003 Barbera d'Alba Sorito Mosconi	91	now–2013
2001 Langhe Quatr Nas	91	now–2016
2001 Langhe Bricco Manzoni	93	now–2018
2003 Barolo Rocche	92	2011–2028
2002 Barolo Rocche	88	now–2014
2001 Barolo Big 'd Big	93	2013–2025
2000 Barolo Big 'd Big	89	2010–2020
2004 Barolo Big 'd Big Red	91–94	???
2004 Barolo Vigna d'la Roul	92–95	???
2001 Barolo Vigna d'la Roul	95	2013–2026
2000 Barolo Vigna d'la Roul	89+?	2012–2022
2004 Barolo Cappella di Santo Stefano	92–95	???
2001 Barolo Cappella di Santo Stefano	94	2013–2022
2000 Barolo Cappella di Santo Stefano	90+	2010–2020

GIOVANNI ROSSO ★ ★ ★
PIEDMONT $50.00–$75.00

Davide Rosso is a young, ambitious producer based in Serralunga whose wines continue to show improvement.

2003 Barolo Serralunga	90	now–2015
2001 Barolo Serralunga	89	now–2016
2003 Barolo Cerretta	91	2009–2018
2001 Barolo Ceretta	91	now–2018

JOSETTA SAFFIRIO ★★★
PIEDMONT $53.00

Josetta Saffirio, a professor at the oenological school at Alba, and her husband, Marchesi di Barolo oenologist Roberto Vezza, made their first Barolo in 1985. The early wines met with critical acclaim, but after a series of disappointing experiences with the U.S. market they stopped producing the wines, preferring to concentrate on their other professional activities instead. In recent years, spurred by the interest of their daughter Sara, the family has begun to once again make wines from their holdings in the Castelletto zone of Monforte. Saffirio's Barolo is made from the Michet Nebbiolo clone, with yields under 2 tons of fruit per acre. It sees a fermentation lasting about ten days, after which it ages in *barriques,* some of which are new, for two years. The wine is then blended in cement tanks prior to bottling.

2004 Barolo	88	2009–2019
2001 Barolo	91	2009–2021
2001 Barolo Persiera	89	2012–2024

LUCIANO SANDRONE ★★★★★
PIEDMONT $23.00–$180.00

No grower manages to reconcile modern and traditional approaches so brilliantly as Luciano Sandrone. The estate's wines are often soft and approachable when young yet also boast a strong track record of aging gracefully. Sandrone spent the early part of his career working at nearby Marchesi di Barolo. By the time he struck out on his own with his first Barolo, the 1982, Sandrone had the benefit of a wealth of experience gained during the years he cut his teeth working at Marchesi. Sandrone was among the first producers in the region to advocate low yields and an enlightened approach in the cellar. Sandrone bottles two Barolos, the single-vineyard Cannubi Boschis and Le Vigne, a blend sourced from four separate vineyards. Both wines are made in a similar fashion. Fermentation takes place in stainless steel, with natural yeasts, and lasts between seven and nine days for the Cannubi Boschis and slightly longer for Le Vigne. Both wines complete malolactic fermentation and aging in 500-liter French oak barrels, of which 20% to 25% are new each year. Sandrone's 2003s are among the finest of the vintage, and his 2004s stand out for their extraordinary elegance. Readers will also want to consider the Dolcetto and Barbera, which are consistently delicious. The Nebbiolo d'Alba Valmaggiore, from one of Roero's top sites, is a benchmark wine for that appellation. As for the 1982 Barolo . . . it is still drinking beautifully today.

2006 Dolcetto d'Alba	90	now
2005 Barbera d'Alba	89	now–2010
2005 Nebbiolo d'Alba Valmaggiore	88	now–2012
2004 Nebbiolo d'Alba Valmaggiore	91	2009–2016
2004 Barolo Le Vigne	96	now–2019
2003 Barolo Le Vigne	93	2009–2015
2002 Barolo Le Vigne	88	now–2012
2001 Barolo Le Vigne	93	2009–2019
2004 Barolo Cannubi Boschis	98	2012–2024
2003 Barolo Cannubi Boschis	92	2009–2019
2001 Barolo Cannubi Boschis	97	2011–2021

Past Glories Barolo Le Vigne: 2000 (93), 1999 (94), 1998 (92), 1997 (92), 1996 (95), 1995 (90); Barolo Cannubi Boschis: 2000 (93), 1999 (96), 1998 (94), 1997 (93), 1996 (97), 1995 (89), 1990 (97), 1989 (98), 1988 (94), 1985 (96); Barolo: 1982 (96)

It is always a challenge to review Moscatos, as the wines come onto the market in the fall and ideally need to be consumed within the following few months. While most Moscatos are boring, uninspiring wines, those of Paolo Saracco merit special attention. Saracco is a fervent believer in low yields and tends to his vines with extraordinary passion, all of which is reflected in the very high quality of his wines. Saracco makes two Moscatos, the regular bottling, which he releases throughout the year, and a special selection, Moscato d'Autunno, which is produced once a year. Both wines should be consumed within a year after the harvest. I can't think of a better way to finish a dinner than with a glass of Saracco Moscato.

PAOLO SCAVINO ★★★★★
PIEDMONT $22.00–$131.00

At an age when some of his colleagues are slowing down, Enrico Scavino, ably assisted by his daughters Enrica and Elisa, continues to push the quality envelope, and it shows in the quality of the wines. Scavino makes a number of single-vineyard Barolos in addition to an entry-level Barolo that is typically among the finest in the region. In top vintages he also releases a Riserva from the Rocche dell'Annunziata vineyard. The wines are aged for one year in French oak (one-third new) after which they are moved to large casks for the second year of aging. The Scavino wines are characterized by superripe fruit, expressive aromatics, and voluptuous textures. The best wines have also proven to age superbly. Because Scavino produces Barolos from so many different sites, including four single-vineyard wines as well as two blends, his Barolos make for a particularly fascinating analysis of the 2003 vintage. Scavino has decided to release his 2003 Rocche dell'Annunziata as a Riserva, so we will have to wait a few years to see that wine. My early tastings of that wine suggested that it is not up to Riserva-level quality, but this is a vintage with many surprises, so it will be interesting to follow its development in bottle. Scavino's 2004 Barolos are among the most powerful, concentrated wines of the vintage. These massively constituted Barolos will require significant patience. Among his other wines, the barrel-aged Barbera d'Alba Affinato in Carati is at the head of the class.

2006 Dolcetto d'Alba	87	now
2004 Barbera d'Alba Affinato in Carati	91	now–2012
2004 Barolo	91	2009–2016
2003 Barolo	88	now–2013
2001 Barolo	89	now–2015
2004 Barolo Cannubi	94	2014–2024
2003 Barolo Cannubi	89	2010–2018
2001 Barolo Cannubi	94+	2009–2019
2004 Barolo Bricco Ambrogio	92	2009–2019
2003 Barolo Bricco Ambrogio	88	2009–2018
2002 Barolo Bricco Ambrogio	89	now–2017
2004 Barolo Carobric	94	2012–2024
2003 Barolo Carobric	90	2010–2018
2001 Barolo Carobric	92	2011–2019
2004 Barolo Bric del Fiasc	96	2014–2022
2003 Barolo Bric del Fiasc	92	2013–2023
2001 Barolo Bric del Fiasc	95	2011–2021
2004 Barolo Riserva Rocche dell'Annunziata	95	2014–2029
2001 Barolo Riserva Rocche dell'Annunziata	96	2009–2021

Past Glories Barolo Carobric: 2000 (92+), 1999 (92), 1998 (91), 1997 (magnum) (90), 1996 (magnum) (92); Barolo Cannubi: 2000 (92), 1999 (93+), 1998 (93), 1997 (91), 1996 (95), 1990

(95), 1989 (95); Barolo Bric del Fiasc: 2000 (95), 1999 (92), 1998 (93), 1997 (92), 1996 (95), 1995 (5-liter) (89), 1993 (5-liter) (91), 1990 (5-liter) (94), 1989 (3-liter) (95), 1985 (magnum) (91); Barolo Riserva Bric del Fiasc: 1978 (92); Barolo Riserva Rocche dell'Annunziata: 2000 (93), 1999 (95), 1998 (94), 1997 (3-liter) (93), 1996 (3-liter) (95), 1990 (magnum) (95)

SEGHESIO ★★★/★★★★
PIEDMONT $30.00–$60.00

Seghesio is another producer who seems to have arrived at a newfound level of elegance in recent vintages. Fermentations have gradually been lengthened and the use of new French oak in the Barolo has been reduced, both of which give the wine a greater sense of harmony and balance. The estate's Barbera d'Alba Vigneto della Chiesa remains one of the more successful French oak–aged Barberas.

2004 Barbera d'Alba Vigneto della Chiesa	90	now–2010
2004 Barolo La Villa	92	2011–2011
2003 Barolo La Villa	90	2009–2019
2001 Barolo Vigneto La Villa	91	2009–2021

SOTTIMANO ★★★★
PIEDMONT $18.00–$73.00

From top to bottom, this is an impressive set of wines from Sottimano, a property that continues its rapid ascent into the top echelon of the region's finest estates. Andrea Sottimano loves Burgundy, and his Barbarescos are clearly informed by the passion he has for those wines. The approach here is strictly noninterventionalist, starting with the use of only natural products in the vineyards. Yields are kept very low, and vinification is fairly traditional. Over the last few vintages the estate has reduced the level of new oak and improved the quality of its cooperage, both of which have given the wines greater transparency. After alcoholic fermentation the wines are racked into French oak barrels (25% new) for the malolactic fermentations, which are kept long, as Sottimano believes this gives the wines greater richness and complexity. Once the malos are finished, the wines are racked into used barrels, where they continue to age prior to being assembled and bottled. As good as the Barbarescos are, readers should not pass up a chance to taste the estate's Dolcetto d'Alba Bric del Salto and Barbera d'Alba Pairolero, two wines that are very representative of the house style and won't break the bank.

2006 Dolcetto d'Alba Bric del Salto	90	now
2004 Barbera d'Alba Pairolero	90	now–2011
2005 Barbaresco Fausoni	89	2010–2017
2004 Barbaresco Fausoni	91	2010–2019
2003 Barbaresco Fausoni	88	now–2015
2005 Barbaresco Currà	92	2010–2019
2004 Barbaresco Currà	93	2010–2019
2003 Barbaresco Currà	90	now–2015
2005 Barbaresco Cottà	91	2010–2020
2004 Barbaresco Cottà	92	2010–2022
2003 Barbaresco Cottà	90	now–2018
2005 Barbaresco Pajorè	92	2013–2023
2004 Barbaresco Pajorè	93	2012–2022
2003 Barbaresco Pajorè	91	2009–2018
2004 Barbaresco Riserva	94	2012–2022

Past Glories Barbaresco Fausoni: 2002 (85), 2001 (90); Barbaresco Currà: 2002 (86), 2001 (91); Barbaresco Cottà: 2002 (86), 2001 (89); Barbaresco Pajorè: 2001 (92), 2002 (97)

This is a very strong set of new releases from La Spinetta and proprietor Giorgio Rivetti. The 2005 Barbarescos are beautiful wines, and the 2004s are easily the best of his career. The estate works with low yields and superripe fruit to craft richly textured modern-style wines that at their best offer tremendous opulence and seamlessness. The wines still see 100% new French oak, but toast levels have been reduced and the Barbarescos now spend 12 months in oak rather than the 18 months they saw in previous vintages. Both changes have had a remarkably positive effect in allowing more site-specific character and Nebbiolo fruit to come through. The 2003 and 2004 Barolo Campè show that Rivetti is making important strides with this wine as well. As if that weren't enough, in recent years Rivetti has begun producing limited quantities of Riserva versions of his Barolos and Barbarescos. The Riservas are made from a portion of the oldest vines in each vineyard, and the wines are offered in magnum only. I admit to having mixed feelings about these Riservas, as I can't help noting that they appear to detract from the overall quality of the regular bottlings, particularly in difficult vintages such as 2003, when those wines could have surely used all the help they would have gotten from the fresher old-vine fruit. Among the more budget-friendly wines, readers will want to consider La Spinetta's Barberas, the Langhe Nebbiolo, Pin (Nebbiolo/Barbera), and of course the Moscatos, the foundation of the estate's early history. In the past La Spinetta was an estate that relied just as much on style as on substance. The 2004 Barbarescos, and especially the Starderi, are the first wines that truly live up to the glamorous image that Giorgio Rivetti has masterfully succeeded in creating.

2005 Barbera d'Asti Ca' di Pian	87	now–2010
2005 Barbera d'Alba Gallina	90	now–2010
2004 Barbera d'Alba Gallina	90	now–2014
2005 Barbera d'Asti Bionzo	88	now–2010
2004 Barbera d'Asti Bionzo	91	now–2014
2005 Monferrato Rosso Pin	91	now–2015
2005 Langhe Nebbiolo	90	now–2015
2005 Barbaresco Gallina	92	2010–2020
2004 Barbaresco Gallina	92	now–2016
2003 Barbaresco Gallina	88	now–2015
2003 Barbaresco Riserva Gallina (magnum)	90	now–2018
2005 Barbaresco Valeirano	93	2012–2022
2004 Barbaresco Valeirano	93	2009–2022
2003 Barbaresco Valeirano	89	now–2015
2003 Barbaresco Riserva Valeirano (magnum)	91	now–2018
2005 Barbaresco Starderi	94	2011–2022
2004 Barbaresco Starderi	95	2009–2022
2003 Barbaresco Starderi	90	2009–2018
2003 Barbaresco Riserva Starderi (magnum)	92	2010–2020
2002 Barbaresco	87	now–2010
2004 Barolo Campè	93	2014–2024
2003 Barolo Campè	92	2009–2018
2001 Barolo Campè	92	2009–2019

Past Glories Barbaresco Gallina: 2001 (88); Barbaresco Riserva Gallina (magnum): 2001 (90); Barbaresco Valeirano: 2001 (90); Barbaresco Riserva Valeirano (magnum): 2001 (91); Barbaresco Starderi: 2001 (93); Barbaresco Riserva Starderi (magnum): 2001 (93); Barolo Campè: 2000 (88); Barolo Riserva Campè (magnum): 2000 (90)

TRAVAGLINI ★★★
PIEDMONT $43.00–$45.00

Travaglini is the largest landowner in the Gattinara appellation in northern Piedmont. Stylistically, the wines bridge traditional and more modern styles, with the Riserva being the most classic wine and the Tre Vigne the most contemporary.

2001 Gattinara Tre Vigne	88	now–2015
2000 Gattinara Tre Vigne	87	now–2015
2001 Gattinara Riserva	89	now–2019

G. D. VAJRA ★★★★
PIEDMONT $32.00–$55.00

For some reason the wines of Aldo Vajra remain less well known than they deserve to be, but this set of new releases may go a long way toward rectifying that situation. It is fairly easy for a producer to make one great wine, and it is also not uncommon to find a large quality gap between an estate's top wine(s) and the more modest wines. Not here. Every wine I tasted was impeccably made and showed this producer's elegant, graceful style at its finest. From top to bottom, this is a thoroughly convincing as well as consistent group of wines that offers something for everyone. Readers should be sure to check out Vajra's Dolcetto d'Alba Coste e Fossati and Barbera d'Alba Superiore, both of which have been outstanding wines of singular character in recent vintages. Last, Vajra's unique interpretation of Freisa, Kyè, elevates this rustic variety to a level that has eluded other growers.

2003 Freisa Kyè	90	now–2017
2001 Barolo Bricco delle Viole	94	now–2021
2000 Barolo Bricco delle Viole	92	2009–2018
1999 Barolo Bricco delle Viole	93	2007–2019
2001 Barolo Albe	90	2009–2018

VAL DEL PRETE ★★★/★★★★
PIEDMONT $20.00–$62.00

This is a very strong set of new releases from Cascina Val del Prete, one of the leading estates in Roero. Working out of his tiny estate in Priocca, proprietor Mario Roagna fashions wines that are remarkable for the sheer pleasure and drinkability they provide.

2006 Roero Arneis Luèt	89	now
2006 Barbera d'Alba Serra de'Gatti	87	now
2005 Barbera d'Alba Superiore Carolina	88	now–2010
2005 Nebbiolo d'Alba Vigna di Lino	88	now–2011
2004 Roero	90	now–2011

VARALDO ★★★/★★★★
PIEDMONT $51.00–$68.00

The Varaldo family was part of the Produttori del Barbaresco cooperative until a few years ago, when they decided to make wines under their own label. The estate is run by gregarious brothers Rino and Michele, who clearly share a huge passion for making highly individualistic wines. Varaldo is another producer who has turned out a series of important 2004s. The best wines here have always been exciting even if they weren't always the models of restraint. Stylistically, these 2004 Barbarescos are on a different level entirely. The wines are more elegant and understated than is normally the case. The overripeness that was the hallmark of so many past wines is nowhere to be found. The use of oak is particularly refined in most of the wines, reflecting the estate's move toward used rather than new oak. The 2004 Barbarescos are the best and most complete wines I have tasted from Varaldo. It will be interesting to see if the estate can maintain this level of quality going forward.

2004 Barbaresco La Gemma	92	now–2018
2003 Barbaresco La Gemma	89	now–2015
2001 Barbaresco La Gemma	90	now–2015
2004 Barbaresco Sorì Loreto	94	2009–2016
2003 Barbaresco Sorì Loreto	91	now–2016
2001 Barbaresco Sorì Loreto	91	now–2013
2004 Barbaresco Bricco Libero	92	now–2016
2003 Barbaresco Bricco Libero	91	now–2018
2001 Barbaresco Bricco Libero	90	now–2013
2003 Barolo Vigna di Aldo	89	now–2013
2001 Barolo Vigna di Aldo	90	now–2016
2000 Barolo Vigna di Aldo	92	now–2016

MAURO VEGLIO ＊＊＊/＊＊＊＊
PIEDMONT $60.00–$86.00

In the last few years Mauro Veglio has doubled the number of days his wines undergo fermentation and maceration from three to four days to seven to eight days. He has also scaled back the new oak considerably. Both of these developments have given his wines more typical Nebbiolo color, aromas, and flavors and less of the astringent new-oak tannins that were found in many of his earlier wines. For now it is too soon to tell if these releases represent a long-lasting stylistic shift, but the joyous 2004 Barolos are easily the finest wines of Mauro Veglio's young career.

2001 Barolo	89	now–2017
2004 Barolo Gattera	92	2010–2019
2003 Barolo Gattera	89	now–2016
2001 Barolo Gattera	92	now–2018
2004 Barolo Arborina	93	2010–2022
2003 Barolo Arborina	90	2009–2018
2001 Barolo Arborina	90	2009–2017
2004 Barolo Castelletto	93	2012–2022
2003 Barolo Castelletto	91	2011–2021
2001 Barolo Castelletto	89+	2009–2017
2004 Barolo Rocche dell'Annunziata	92	2010–2020
2003 Barolo Rocche dell'Annunziata	90	2009–2018

Past Glories Barolo Gattera: 1999 (88); Barolo Arborina: 1999 (90); Barolo Castelletto: 1999 (92); Barolo Rocche dell'Annunziata: 1999 (90)

ERALDO VIBERTI ＊＊＊
PIEDMONT $N/A

Eraldo Viberti is a small producer based in the Santa Maria subzone of La Morra. His 2003 Barolo is a lovely, accessible wine ideal for near-term consumption.

2006 Dolcetto d'Alba Vigna Vaglio	88	now
2003 Barolo	90	now–2013

PIEDMONT $22.00–$160.00

After a period of soul-searching in the 1990s in which the estate's wines lacked a clear sense of direction, Vietti has come back with a vengeance. Today the wines show greater consistency as well as a distinct house style that is more defined than ever, under the direction of brothers-in-law Mario Cordero and Luca Currado. The Vietti wines are made in an updated style that is somewhere between modern and traditional. Yields are kept low, averaging 30 to 35 hecto-liters per hectare (320 to 374 gallons per acre) for the single-vineyard Barolos. The wines are all fermented in stainless steel and do their malolactic fermentations in *barrique,* after which they complete their aging in a combination of larger casks and *barriques*. In general the Castiglione, Rocche, and Villero are aged predominantly in large casks, while the Brunate and Lazzarito show more influence of smaller French oak barrels. As if making great Barolos weren't enough, Vietti also makes some of the very finest Barberas money can buy. In addition to their Scarrone, Scarrone Vigna Vecchia, and La Crena, the estate's entry-level Barbera d'Alba Trevigne and Barbera d'Asti Trevigne offer terrific value for the money. Readers should also make a point to check out the Langhe Nebbiolo Perbacco, which is made from a second selection of wines from Barolo-designated vineyards that the estate has culled from its Castiglione bottling.

2005 Langhe Nebbiolo Perbacco	90	now–2012
2004 Langhe Nebbiolo Perbacco	90	2009–2016
2005 Barbera d'Alba Scarrone	90	now–2012
2004 Barbera d'Alba Scarrone	91	now–2014
2003 Barbera d'Alba Scarrone	91	now–2010
2005 Barbera d'Alba Scarrone Vigna Vecchia	91	now–2015
2004 Barbera d'Alba Scarrone Vigna Vecchia	92	2009–2016
2003 Barbera d'Alba Scarrone Vigna Vecchia	92	now–2010
2004 Barbera d'Asti La Crena	93	now–2014
2003 Barbera d'Asti La Crena	93	now–2012
2005 Barbaresco Masseria	93–95	???
2004 Barbaresco Masseria	93	now–2019
2003 Barbaresco Masseria	93	now–2018
2004 Barolo Castiglione	92	2010–2022
2003 Barolo Castiglione	90	now–2017
2001 Barolo Castiglione	89	now–2016
2004 Barolo Rocche	96	2014–2026
2003 Barolo Rocche	92	2009–2018
2001 Barolo Rocche	92	2011–2021
2004 Barolo Brunate	95	2012–2024
2003 Barolo Brunate	94	2009–2023
2001 Barolo Brunate	90+	2009–2019
2004 Barolo Lazzarito	93	2012–2025
2003 Barolo Lazzarito	91	2009–2019
2001 Barolo Lazzarito	92	2009–2019
2001 Barolo Riserva Villero	95	2011–2021

Past Glories Barolo Castiglione: 2000 (89), 1999 (90); Barolo Rocche: 2000 (93), 1999 (94), 1998 (91), 1997 (94), 1996 (92), 1995 (89), 1988 (93), 1985 (95), 1982 (94), 1979 (91), 1978 (91), 1974 (91); Barolo Brunate: 2000 (91), 1999 (92); Barolo Ravera: 2000 (91), 1999 (91); Barolo Lazzarito: 2000 (90), 1999 (92); Barolo Riserva Villero: 1989 (90), 1982 (91)

GIANNI VOERZIO ★ ★ ★
PIEDMONT $136.00–$140.00

Gianni Voerzio makes wines in a very rich concentrated style that seems to favor opulence over true varietal expression. His Barolo from La Morra's La Serra vineyard is often among the darkest and roundest wines I have encountered.

2003 Barolo La Serra	88	2009–2017
2001 Barolo La Serra	88	now–2015

ROBERTO VOERZIO ★ ★ ★ ★ ★
PIEDMONT $29.00–$650.00

Roberto Voerzio is one of the most fanatical producers I have ever met. He is completely obsessed with quality and has no qualms about not releasing one of his Barolos when he is less than thrilled with the final result, as was the case in 2003, when he chose not to bottle several of his top selections, including the Barolo La Serra and Barolo Rocche dell'Annunziata/Torriglione. Voerzio's philosophy is all about the vineyard, where he maintains what are by far the most dramatically low yields to be seen in the Barolo zone. Although Voerzio prefers small French barrels for his wines, vinification remains fairly traditional, with fermentation lasting 15 days or so. After the alcoholic fermentation is complete, the wines do their malolactic fermentation in stainless steel, which Voerzio prefers for its cleanliness. The cellar is warmed to induce the malolactic fermentation, and the malo is usually completed by the end of the fall. The wines are then moved into *barriques,* where they age prior to being bottled without the aid of fining/filtration. Pure and expressive in a style that is neither modern nor traditional, these are wines that reflect the highly individual style of their maker as well as the profound voice of La Morra's finest sites. Voerzio is one of the very few producers who has always been enthusiastic about his 2003s. His wines are beautiful even if they have shut down considerably since I last tasted them in tank a few months prior to their bottling. 2004 is a rare vintage in which the ultraperfectionist Voerzio produced all seven of his single-vineyard Barolos. I have been following these magnificent wines for three years, and it is a joy to taste them now that they are in bottle. The wines are just as spectacular now as they were in my prior tastings. Voerzio has also proven to be very skilled with Barbera, and his Pozzo dell'Annunziata is one of the very finest Barberas in the region. Unfortunately, it is also by far the most expensive. In recent years Voerzio has introduced the more modestly priced Barbera Cerreto, which faithfully captures his style at a price that won't induce dizziness.

2006 Dolcetto d'Alba Priavino	89	now–2010
2005 Langhe Nebbiolo S. Francesco/Fontanazza	89	now–2015
2004 Langhe Nebbiolo S. Francesco/Fontanazza	90	now–2014
2004 Barbera d'Alba Cerreto	89	now–2012
2003 Barbera d'Alba Cerreto	88	now–2010
2004 Barbera d'Alba Pozzo dell'Annunziata (magnum)	95	2010–2019
2001 Barbera d'Alba Riserva Pozzo dell'Annunziata	93	now–2013
2004 Barolo Riserva Fossati Case Nere	91	2009–2019
2004 Barolo La Serra	93	2009–2022
2001 Barolo La Serra	92	2011–2021
2004 Barolo Riserva Vecchie Viti dei Capalot e delle Brunate	95	2009–2020
2003 Barolo Riserva Vecchie Viti dei Capalot e delle Brunate (Magnum)	93	2013–2023
2001 Barolo Riserva Vecchie Viti dei Capalot e delle Brunate (Magnum)	94+	2011–2021
2004 Barolo Rocche dell'Annunziata/Torriglione	96	2014–2024

2001 Barolo Rocche dell'Annunziata/Torriglione	94	2009–2019
2004 Barolo Cerequio	97	2014–2024
2003 Barolo Cerequio	92	2010–2015
2001 Barolo Cerequio	95	2011–2021
2004 Barolo Sarmassa (Magnum)	98	2014–2024
2003 Barolo Sarmassa (Magnum)	94	2010–2018
2001 Barolo Sarmassa (Magnum)	96	2009–2019
2004 Barolo Brunate	97	20⁻4–2024
2003 Barolo Brunate	94	20⁻0–2018
2001 Barolo Brunate	93	20⁻1–2021
2004 Langhe Merlot	92	2009–2019

Past Glories Barolo Brunate: 2000 (92), 1999 (95), 1993 (magnum) (93); Barolo Cerequio: 2000 (95), 1999 (95), 1991 (90), 1990 (magnum) (94); Barolo La Serra: 2000 (93), 1999 (93); Barolo Rocche dell'Annunziata/Torriglione: 2000 (92); Barolo Riserva Vecchie Viti dei Capalot e delle Brunate (magnum): 2000 (92)

[tuscany]

Tuscany produces an extraordinarily diverse group of wines. Chianti remains Tuscany's, and perhaps Italy's, best-known wine. The finest Chiantis come from the heart of the appellation, the region known as Chianti Classico. Quality, once highly irregular, has improved dramatically under the leadership of a small group of forward-thinking estates. Moving south, Brunello di Montalcino takes advantage of a warmer microclimate to yield a rich, full-bodied expression of Sangiovese. On the Tuscan coast, the number of new wineries has exploded in recent years after early exponents such as Tenuta San Guido and Tenuta dell'Ornellaia amply demonstrated the potential of a *terroir* especially well suited to the cultivation of international varieties. Farther inland, the Scansano appellation is on the rise with a number of food-friendly, midpriced wines that offer terrific value. Lesser-known regions such as Carmigano, Montepulciano, and Cortona also offer a number of wines well worth discovering. Sadly, Tuscany's whites are rarely as exciting as the reds. They are meant mostly for casual drinking and with few exceptions offer little complexity for the reader seeking individualistic, compelling wines. The sweet Vin Santo can be made in a variety of styles and, in the hands of the right producer, can be a very satisfying glass of wine with which to end a meal.

[grape varieties]

Sangiovese is the main indigenous variety in Tuscany. There are many clones of Sangiovese, both ancient and new. To make matters slightly more complicated, Sangiovese is also known by a variety of names according to zone of production. Principal among these are Sangioveto (Chianti Classico), Sangiovese Grosso (Brunello di Montalcino), and Prugnolo Gentile (Vino Nobile di Montepulciano). Growers and agronomists continue to experiment with a variety of newly developed clones that are designed to produce low yields and greater intensity of color, something Sangiovese, like Pinot Noir and Nebbiolo, does not naturally display. The drive to make deeply colored wines has resulted in some extreme examples, but readers should not confuse color intensity with quality. Aside from wines that have obvious technical flaws, there is no relationship whatsoever between color and quality when it comes to Sangiovese, or Nebbiolo for that matter. Colorino and Canaiolo are the other main native Tuscan red varieties, but these days they are used in small percentages as supporting players in Chianti, if at all.

International varieties also play an important role in Tuscan viticulture and oenology. Cabernet Sauvignon, Cabernet Franc, and Merlot are the most widely planted of these. In recent years Syrah has gained in popularity, especially in the warmer microclimates to which it is ideally suited. A few producers are experimenting with Pinot Noir, but this may be the one red variety from which Tuscany has yet to release a truly compelling wine. White varieties include the indigenous Vernaccia, along with Trebbiano, Vermentino, Chardonnay, and Sauvignon, which find more profound expressions in other regions within Italy.

FLAVORS

CHIANTI AND CHIANTI CLASSICO The typical Sangiovese flavor profile tends toward an expression of red cherries, tobacco, underbrush, and grilled herbs. The wines are medium in body and contain a refreshing vein of acidity that makes them great choices for the dinner table. Producers can legally add up to 20% of international varieties such as Merlot and Cabernet Sauvignon to their Chianti Classico, an allowance that was originally intended to make the wines supposedly more appealing to the international (read U.S.) consumer but that has ultimately lead to an enormous amount of confusion in the market (more on that below). Clearly, Chiantis that contain international varieties will offer less Sangiovese character. The aging of wines in small French oak barrels can often yield wines with a darker set of black cherry and plum flavors along with an additional layer of smoke, spice, and vanilla that comes from the oak rather than from the fruit and specific microclimate.

BRUNELLO DI MONTALCINO In general Montalcino is a warmer microclimate than Chianti Classico. The native Sangiovese Grosso clone typically gives wines of great richness, power, and intensity. The vineyards in the higher parts of the Brunello zone have soil composition similar to that of Chianti Classico. As a result, these firm, structured Brunellos often reveal expressive aromatics and a focused, layered quality to their fruit that requires aging to become fully expressive. Brunellos made from lower-altitude vineyards and in the southern part of the zone benefit from a more Mediterranean climate, which gives wines that tend to be softer, riper, and rounder, often with more forward, generous personalities that require a minimum of bottle age. As in Chianti Classico, the use of French oak can impart additional flavors and nuances to the wines. When used well, French oak can be a terrific complement to the wines, but when used poorly, it can dominate the flavor profile. The finest Brunellos are characterized by rich aromatics and generous, ripe fruit, with excellent structure and fine, elegant tannins. Most producers also bottle a Rosso di Montalcino. The majority of Rossos are fruit-driven, fresh wines best enjoyed up to a few years after release, although a handful of wines offer notable complexity.

VINO NOBILE DI MONTEPULCIANO Vino Nobile di Montepulciano combines elements of the more linear Chianti Classicos with some of the riper characteristics of Brunello. The top Vino Nobile bottlings are exciting wines that deliver much pleasure.

BOLGHERI Located in Tuscany's coastal Maremma region, Bolgheri is home to Tuscany's newest generation of supersleek, modern wineries. International varieties have found a welcoming home and flourish in these soils. Cabernet Sauvignon, Cabernet Franc, Syrah, and Merlot are all varietally true here but also offer the unmistakable luminosity, warmth, and generosity of the Tuscan sun. The greatest strides are being made with Cabernet Franc, which offers an exotic array of aromatics to complement its dark fruit, and Syrah, which is proving to be fascinating in certain spots. Where Sangiovese is planted, it yields a richer, weightier style of wine.

MORELLINO DI SCANSANO The Sangiovese-based Morellinos offer some of the best values in Tuscany. The wines are loaded with character, warmth, and richness. This part of Tuscany, once under Spanish rule, also features Alicante (Grenache) and Syrah, often blended with other varieties.

CARMIGNANO Carmignano is another appellation that makes delicious Sangiovese-based wines, with a flavor profile that resembles that of Chianti. Regulations allow for up to 20% Cabernet Sauvignon and Cabernet Franc to be included in the blend.

WHITES Tuscany produces a variety of whites, from floral Vernaccias to the drier Vermentinos, but in general these are simple wines meant for casual drinking. With very few exceptions Tuscany's whites are meant to be drunk one to two years after the vintage.

VIN SANTO The sweet Vin Santo can be a very pleasurable accompaniment to fruit-based desserts, cookies, or a cheese course. Made predominantly from dried Malvasia and Trebbiano, Vin Santo is aged in various wood vessels, sometimes for many years. The wines to look for are those made by small, artisan producers. Quantities are small, but the best Vin Santos can be remarkable wines.

IGT IGT (Indicazione Geografica Tipica) is the designation used for wines that fall outside any of the traditional appellations. IGT is the successor to the Vino da Tavola designation once used for trailblazing Italian reds like Sassicaia and Tignanello. Sometimes referred to as "super-Tuscans," these wines can be made from any variety or combination of varieties and the period of oak aging is at the discretion of the producer. Ironically, there have been so many changes in Italian wine regulations that it often isn't easy to keep track of exact definitions. The 100% Sangiovese IGT (formerly Vino da Tavola) wines that brought so much attention to their producers, such as Le Pergole Torte, Percarlo, and Flaccianello, could now be bottled as Chianti Classico. Paradoxically, there are a number of Chiantis being made with the addition of international varieties that are labeled as Chianti but that are in effect much closer in spirit to IGTs.

CONCLUSION Navigating the wines of Tuscany isn't always easy, but a little effort will pay off. Readers should focus their attention on seeking out the best producers. Formal appellations and designations have historically proven to have little real value to producers obsessed with making the very best wines possible.

[the region]

A CLOSER LOOK AT TUSCANY'S MOST IMPORTANT SUBZONES

CHIANTI CLASSICO

The finest wines of Central Tuscany come from Chianti Classico. The beautiful, picturesque hills outside the art cities of Florence and Siena encompass 70,000 hectares (172,900 acres) under vine. The principal towns in Chianti Classico are Radda, Greve, Gaiole, Castellina, Panzano, and parts of Castelnuovo Berardenga, Baberino Val d'Elsa, and San Casciano in Val di Pesa. Chianti Classico can be released roughly a year after the harvest, while Riservas must be aged a minimum of two years. The main soil types are the porous rock and clay formation known as *galestro* and the more compact *alberese.* Historically, Sangiovese has struggled to ripen in these hills, particularly at some of the higher elevations such as those found in Radda. Even within Chianti Classico microclimates can vary, so while Radda is one of the cooler areas, Castelnuovo Berardenga, which lies in the southern part of the region, is noticeably warmer. The desire of large estates to produce in quantity, along with the generally cool microclimate, led to the ocean of thin, diluted, and highly acidic wines that gave Chianti the poor image it is still trying to shake with some consumers. In the 1970s and 1980s a small group of quality-minded producers recognized that Chianti made from 100% Sangiovese could attain a higher level of quality, but in classic Italian bureaucratic fashion, those wines were rejected by tasting commissions because they didn't contain the blend of varieties required at the time, some of which were white grapes. These producers went ahead anyway and bottled their high-end 100% pure Sangiovese under the designation Vino da Tavola, ironically the lowest designation at the time. These high-quality wines were very well received, and other producers followed suit. Today there are a number of superb 100% Sangioveses, the majority of which carry the IGT (Indicazione Geografica Tipica) designation that is the successor to the older Vino da Tavola. In the meantime, Chianti Classico struggled commercially, so regulations were relaxed to allow producers to blend in international varieties, which, it was believed, would make the wines more appealing to consumers. The requirement to use white varieties was eliminated, and more recently the producers' consortium, the Consorzio Vino Chianti Classico, finally allowed 100% Sangioveses to be labeled Chianti Classico.

All of these machinations put Chianti Classico in the difficult spot it is in today. Top estates that fought to promote their 100% Sangioveses have been recognized by consumers, and today their wines justly command prices that are on average much higher than what is accepted for Chianti Classico, which means that those estates are unlikely to ever return to the Chianti Classico designation, even though today their wines fully qualify. Readers may very well find an internationally styled Chianti Classico that is 80% Sangiovese and 20% Cabernet Sauvignon and Merlot next to a 100% Sangiovese IGT. Sound confusing? It is, but there is another chapter to the story. A parallel development was the craze for international varieties, not as a minor complement to Sangiovese but rather as a central player in the wines. Early wines like Sassicaia, Tignanello, and Solaia proved that international varieties could flourish in Tuscany. Freed from the burden of antiquated, restrictive designations, these wines quickly attained the praise of consumers and critics around the world. Demand soared and high prices soon followed, vaulting these estates into worldwide prominence and spawning a large number of similar new wines. The term "super-Tuscan" was coined to refer to wines like Tignanello and Solaia, in which indigenous and international varieties were blended. Consumers then had yet another difficulty to consider: What was the difference between a modern Chianti Classico and a super-Tuscan? In terms of what was in the bottle, sometimes not very much at all. Today "super-Tuscan" is used more widely for just about any wine that falls outside the traditional designations, but, given that the term is so broad, I won't use it in this book, as I prefer to be more specific. At the end of the day, readers will be best served by focusing on top estates and their wines, rather than spending too much time on formal designations, which are becoming less relevant by the day.

MONTALCINO

Brunello di Montalcino is made from 100% Sangiovese. The wines spend a minimum of two years in oak and can legally be sold in January of the fourth year following the harvest. The Riservas spend at least an additional year in oak and are released a year later than the non-Riservas. Most producers also bottle a Rosso di Montalcino, which can be made from vineyards outside the Brunello designation (but still in Montalcino), from younger vines, or from a selection of barrels that aren't deemed good enough to go into the top wines. Rossos are usually more affordable, and the best versions can offer valuable insights into a given producer's particular style. Montalcino has not escaped the fashion for planting international varieties. There are a number of wines that use those varieties either on their own or blended with Sangiovese. Much of the fame of Brunello di Montalcino can be attributed to the superb organization of the producers' consortium, the Consorzio del Vino Brunello di Montalcino, which has elevated the reputation of the wines to a high level that is deserved by only a handful of exemplary Brunellos. Despite featuring some truly phenomenal wines, Montalcino is unfortunately also responsible for producing large quantities of expensive, sterile, undistinguished wines that continue to proliferate with no end in sight.

Although the Consorzio has done many things right, it has also failed in one major area, and that has been to educate consumers on the notable variety of *terroirs* and microclimates within Montalcino. The region is roughly square-shaped and encompasses 24,000 hectares (59,300 acres) of land. The area can be thought of as a pyramid, with its highest altitude in the center and four descending slopes radiating outward. Its borders are defined by the Asso, Ombrone, and Orcia rivers. The climate is influenced by the warm breezes of the nearby Maremma, and the region is sheltered from inclement weather by the Monte Amiata mountain range, which lies to the southeast. Although the town of Montalcino is surrounded by several hamlets, including Torrenieri, Camigliano, Sant'Angelo in Colle, and Castelnuovo dell'Abate, there is no formal system in place to make it easy for consumers to understand the attributes of the various subzones. In addition, producers' styles clearly vary quite a bit, as do clonal selection, vineyard altitudes, and a host of other factors. In recent years, Brunello producers have expanded to the newly created Sant'Antimo appellation, which lies just over the southern boundary of the Brunello di Montalcino zone. Sant'Antimo has mostly been planted with international varieties. So far, it seems like a region best suited to simple, easygoing wines.

The differences between the microclimates in Montalcino can be quite surprising, with the harvest time in the northern zones taking place anywhere from a few weeks to as much as a month later than in the southern regions. Higher-altitude vineyards benefit from cooler temperatures, more rainfall, and a greater presence of marl and limestone in the soils, all of which combine to produce structured, ageworthy wines. The lower-lying areas contain a higher percentage of alluvial deposits originating from the period in which these areas were under water. In the southern parts of the zone the combination of lower-altitude vineyards, a greater presence of clay in the soils, and warmer temperatures often results in softer, riper wines that can be enjoyed sooner.

Much has also been made of the use of small oak barrels in Montalcino and the desire of some producers to make wines that are more accessible. Ironically, the tannins of inexpertly used *barriques* are much more intrusive and bothersome than those of the fruit itself, but as with all such discussions it is ultimately the skill of the winemaker that counts rather than any specific tool used in the cellar.

News surfaced in April 2008 that several prominent producers were under investigation for allegedly blending international varieties with Sangiovese in their Brunellos. Reports out of Italy seem to change on a day-by-day basis, so it is probably best to allow for the facts to emerge before rushing to judgment, as these are serious allegations that threaten to destabilize the entire appellation. Let's hope the Consorzio and the Chamber of Commerce, Industry and Trades (the group whose tasting committee grants the use of the DOCG label for specific wines) take advantage of this opportunity to finally get serious about guaranteeing consumers an honest product. If they don't, over time consumers will gravitate toward wines of greater regional identity, and Italy is a country that has no lack of fascinating grape varieties and *terroirs,* many of which yield wines with plenty of personality that also happen to be more affordable.

MAREMMA

With its many seaside resorts and state-of-the-art wineries, it is hard to believe that up until the 1930s Maremma was a disease-infested swampland. The noble families preferred to live in the hills, which were set back from the coastline, while their servants lived closer to the sea. In fact, the emergence of Maremma as one of the world's leading wine production zones has been somewhat of an accident. The region owes its prominence to Mario Incisa della Rocchetta. Inspired by the wines of Bordeaux, Incisa wanted to make a similar wine on his own property. In 1944 he planted his first Cabernet vines and subsequently began producing the wine known today as Sassicaia. Incredibly, Incisa originally conceived of his wine for domestic consumption, so the early vintages were drunk exclusively at the estate. The first commercial release, the 1968, was greeted with loud critical acclaim. Despite the early success of Sassicaia, it would take another 20 years and the arrival of other producers such as Grattamacco and Tenuta dell'Ornellaia for the region to establish itself as a source of world-class wines. The rest, as they say, is history, and today the region's top wines are among the most coveted and expensive wines being made in Italy.

Even with all the recent developments and construction that have taken place, Maremma retains some of its Wild West aura. Compared to the hillier landscapes of Chianti Classico and Montalcino, what strikes a first-time visitor is likely to be the vast expanses of land that meet the eye. The climate of Maremma is also unique. Weather conditions are especially hot and dry, yet the heat is tempered by the breezes that come in from the Tyrrhenian Sea. Within that context, there are noticeable differences among the many microclimates that are found in the various subzones. Although some disagreement exists as to where the boundaries of the "real" Maremma lie, for the sake of simplicity and ease of discussion I have divided the various districts into upper and lower Maremma.

In the upper Maremma production is concentrated around the coastal areas of Bolgheri and Castagneto Carducci, which are in the province of Livorno. To the south of Bolgheri lies Suvereto and the valley known as the Val di Cornia, a warmer microclimate that often yields wines of greater power with perhaps slightly less elegance. One of the features of the coastal regions is the dominance of international varieties such as Cabernet Sauvignon, Cabernet Franc, Merlot, and Syrah, all of which have proven to thrive, while the climactic conditions are generally considered to be less favorable for Sangiovese.

The lower Maremma is set slightly more inland. It is also hotter and drier than the coastal areas. Sangiovese plays a more central role in the wines of these inland districts than it does on the coast, although Cabernet Sauvignon, Merlot, Syrah, and Alicante (Grenache) are also found, most often in blends with Sangiovese. The most exciting appellation is Morellino di Scansano, which lies in the province of Grosseto. Morellino encompasses a variety of Sangiovese-based wines that range from simpler, fresh versions, to full-bodied, supple wines packed with flavor as well as character. It is one of the best value-priced wines in Italy today. In recent years Montecucco, which lies just across the valley from the southernmost boundary of the Brunello di Montalcino zone, has also emerged as a source of promising value-priced Sangiovese-based wines.

AGING POTENTIAL
Brunello di Montalcino: 5–25 years
Carmignano: 5–8 years
Chianti Classico: 3–15 years
Chianti Classico Riserva: 7–25 years
Rosso di Montalcino: 5–8 years
Tuscan whites: 1–2 years
Vino Nobile di Montepulciano: 5–10 years
IGTs (red wine blends): 5–20 years

[the wines]

OVERALL QUALITY LEVEL

In recent years quality has been on the upswing, broadly speaking. Despite the region's links to the past, in modern-day terms the renaissance of quality in Tuscan vineyard and cellar practices dates only to the early 1980s. The wines made during the 1980s and 1990s must be viewed as part of a learning curve that was necessary to arrive at the current state, which happens to be very exciting. The superconcentrated, heavy, overoaked wines appear to be largely a thing of the past. Today's top wines are phenomenally well balanced, full of character, and unmistakably Tuscan. The region still produces a large quantity of undistinguished wine, but at least the vast majority of today's wines are being made correctly from a technical standpoint. Prices have escalated considerably in recent years. That notwithstanding, Tuscany's world-class wines must be considered a bargain when compared to the top wines of other regions throughout the world. The exception is Montalcino, where Brunello has unexplicably attained a status and corresponding price level that befit just a small number of wines.

I would be remiss if I didn't make a few comments on pricing and availability. Put simply, in a market environment where prices are being bid to the moon on collectible vintages like 2005 Bordeaux and Burgundy, the wines of Tuscany offer an attractive alternative in the relative value they offer, even if the weakening U.S. dollar has eroded some of that pricing benefit for American consumers. The most desirable wines also remain significantly easier to obtain than similar trophy wines from other regions. In conclusion, Tuscany has much to offer readers looking to enjoy some of the world's most delicious and food-friendly wines.

IMPORTANT INFORMATION

As always, readers should pay special attention to the best producers in each appellation. Quality-minded estates have the resources to make the difficult decisions on what to bottle, especially in challenging vintages, meaning that consumers are less likely to be disappointed regardless of the quality of a specific vintage. Moreover, the finest estates generally make respectable wines, even at the lower end of their lineups.

[recent vintages]

2006 AND 2005

The more important 2005s and 2006s are slowly entering the marketplace. 2005 is a smaller-scaled vintage, with pretty, perfumed wines. Rain toward the end of the vintage compromised the quality of some wines, but diligent estates managed to make wines that are worth seeking out. These are not the showy wines of 2004 or 2006, but the best wines offer lovely balance in restrained style. This is a consumer's vintage—in other words, a vintage for wines that consumers intend to drink rather than collect. As 2005 is sandwiched between 2004 and 2006, both stronger vintages, readers should be in the driver's seat when it comes to obtaining favorable pricing. Based on what I have tasted so far, 2006 is an outstanding vintage in all of Tuscany's regions. The wines are very ripe and generous, but considerable tannin and acidity are buried beneath the wines' sheer opulence. The best wines are incredibly appealing at this early stage and look to get even better with further bottle age. I expect demand for these wines will be high, as the flashy, rewarding style of the vintage is sure to find many admirers.

2004

This vintage is the complete opposite of 2003 (see below). The weather was much more balanced throughout the growing season, which caused plants to unleash the large amounts of energy they had held in reserve from the previous year. The naturally higher yields obligated quality-minded producers to green-harvest more aggressively than normal. Like Nebbiolo, Sangiovese responds especially well to the alternation of hot daytime temperatures with cool, moderating evenings that characterized 2004. Alcoholic and phenolic ripeness were reached gradually and simultaneously, which allowed growers to harvest under calm conditions and within a time frame considered normal to late by today's standards. Even though conditions were quite favorable, the vintage also posed a few challenges. Some growers spoke of rain during August, which caused the grapes to bloat a little, while others, especially those in later-ripening areas, had to deal with rain toward the end of the harvest. A strict selection of fruit at the sorting table was critical, and many producers reported making a second selection of finished wines in the cellar. Those challenges of the vintage notwithstanding, the long growing season and relaxed harvest presented growers with the conditions for making great wines. Quality-minded producers turned out a number of exceptional wines at all levels.

The 2004s feature livelier colors, well-articulated aromatics, and finer tannins than the 2003s. The expression of fruit tends to be more layered, nuanced, and delicate than the decidedly opulent 2003s. The acidities were also higher in 2004, which will allow the wines to age longer as well as more gracefully. Readers will find a bountiful number of outstanding 2004s from which to choose. The Chianti Classicos are terrific and full of flavor. It is a great vintage for Tuscany's finest 100% Sangiovese luxury cuvées, including Flaccianello, Percarlo, and Cepparello, all of which are stunning. Unlike Nebbiolo, which shows its aromatic complexity even when young, Sangiovese is a variety that develops its full range of aromas and flavors only with extended bottle age. Readers will be tempted to enjoy these 2004s young, but the wines will show the true extent of their potential only after some years. Not to be left behind, 2004 is also a superb vintage for the high-end blends of indigenous and international varieties. Wines such as Solaia, Tignanello, and Camartina are especially noteworthy. All of them feature extraordinary length and finesse as well as sweet, silky tannins, which make them incredibly appealing even at this early stage. Much the same can be said for the wines of Maremma, which benefited from the same favorable conditions as central Tuscany. Wines such as Ornellaia, Masseto, Tua Rita's new Syrah bottling, and the wines of Le Macchiole are all particularly successful. What I have tasted so far from Montalcino has been equally promising. In short, 2004 is outstanding in all of Tuscany's major regions. Simply put, the best 2004s are reference-point wines for the region and are not to be missed.

2003

A complete analysis of the 2003 vintage is no easy task, as results vary significantly from zone to zone. During 2003 the weather was excessively hot and dry, to the point that in many places plants simply shut down, a condition known as hydric stress, which is accentuated in younger vineyards, which have shorter root systems and therefore less access to water. Because the maturation of sugars was so advanced, growers had no choice but to harvest, and most estates reported picking, on average, at least two to three weeks earlier than normal. Although the grapes achieved ripeness of the sugars, phenolic ripeness (the ripeness of the skins and seeds) was much more elusive. As a result, many of the wines suffer from caustic levels of hard, green tannins. Longtime readers know I am not a huge fan of vintage ratings as they are by nature general. Wines, particularly those of Italy, encompass an enormous range of microclimates, *terroirs,* and varieties, and that is before beginning a discussion of winemaking styles. As always in difficult vintages, it comes down to producer, producer, producer. Almost without exception the top estates found a way to make important wines, notwithstanding the significant difficulties posed by the vintage. Many growers spoke of the lessons learned in previous hot years, such as 2000, as keys in interpreting the unique circumstances nature presented in 2003.

In general, 2003 is most successful in higher-altitude appellations, such as Chianti Classico, where Sangiovese, the main indigenous variety in Tuscany, has traditionally struggled to ripen under normal weather conditions. Many of those wines can be somewhat austere and lean in typical vintages, but the heat of 2003 helped fill them out with an attractive plumpness of fruit. The naturally higher acidity of Sangiovese also helped in preserving at least some freshness in the wines. The finest 100% Sangiovese bottlings, including Flaccianello, Percarlo, Le Pergole Torte, and Cepparello are among the most successful wines of 2003. Another bright spot is Syrah, which thrives in hot, arid weather.

The 2003 Brunellos have turned out better than I expected. For the most part the wines offer very good balance. As was the case throughout continental Europe, Montalcino experienced a brutally hot, dry year. Montalcino is a large area that encompasses a vast range of terrains and microclimates, so generalizations are always tricky. Broadly speaking, the wines from the northern slopes of Montalcino and the higher-altitude vineyards around town preserved more freshness and aromatic complexity. Older vineyards with deeper roots and more access to water reserves were clearly at an advantage. Many growers reported having to discard burnt, sun-charred fruit in the vineyard and at the sorting table. The grapes were small, with relatively little, yet concentrated, juice. Producers did what they could to treat the fruit gently in order to avoid extracting any additional tannins during fermentation. Most producers noted that malolactic fermentations proceeded at a fast pace. Quite a few winemakers I spoke with chose to give their wines less time in oak than normal, while others cut back on the percentage of new barrels, both choices aimed at trying to keep the wines in balance by not adding additional tannins from oak aging. The majority of estates that typically bottle a Riserva plan to do so in 2003 as well.

The simple fact is that for better or worse the 2003 Brunellos show very little 2003 character. That may sound like a puzzling statement, but readers should remember that the vast majority of Brunellos are made by consulting oenologists whose professional training and expertise allows them to make excellent, even outstanding, wines in just about any vintage. Only a small handful of wines show overripe or candied qualities in their fruit. The widespread technique in Montalcino of refreshing wines with younger vintages explains why very few wines come across as obviously overripe or cooked. A more common problem is the green, unripe tannins that are the hallmark of superhot vintages where the plants shut down because of a lack of water and phenolic ripeness is not achieved. On the plus side, overall quality is consistent as the wines are very competently made. On the down side, many wines taste alike, and there are few truly superlative wines. I saw several cases where an estate's regular bottling is more successful and better balanced than the top selection. The heat helped fill out some of the wines from less well exposed sites, but paradoxically left the best-exposed vineyards with superripe fruit and problematic tannins. Readers will note a compression of scores around the 89–92 range, which reflects the fact that a large number of wines in 2003 are the result of polished cellar work as opposed to pure expressions of site, vintage, and individual producer styles.

In short, 2003 in Montalcino looks to be an excellent vintage for drinking over the near term, particularly in restaurants or other last-minute situations that don't lend themselves to the enjoyment of more important, ageworthy wines that might require aeration and/or decanting. In my many tastings of these wines I have found them to show best when served slightly above cellar temperature, which is to say roughly 62°–67°F, as I would recommend for Nebbiolo or Pinot Noir. The cooler temperature helps tame the tannins as well as the ripeness in the wines. I don't expect most of the 2003 Brunellos to be long-lived, but since so many wines have been generously refreshed, it's hard to tell for certain. My best guess is that most wines will offer the finest enjoyment before 15 years of age, give or take.

Stylistically the 2003s are, of course, very ripe, and while the personality of the vintage may or may not appeal to readers based on individual preferences, I found few examples of overripe or cooked wines. The best 2003s have enough fruit to cover the harder tannins that are almost inevitably present. Many of the wines have come together markedly over the last few months, and some may ultimately be deserving of higher scores. That said, the vintage as a whole is highly irregular, so it pays to choose carefully.

2002

A very weak vintage owing to cool summer temperatures and a considerable amount of rain. There are a few surprises, but these are small-scaled, modest wines to be enjoyed over the near term.

2001

An outstanding vintage across the board. A spring frost in some regions lowered yields dramatically but also gave wines of uncommon grace and power. The wines are consistently strong and should be long-lived.

BUYING STRATEGY

As time passes, I find that I increasingly focus first on producer and second on vintage. I believe that consumers will ultimately be best served by doing the same. Today's awareness of viticulture and oenology, along with generally more favorable weather conditions than in the past, means that truly disastrous vintages are few and far between. Top-tier producers have the discipline and financial resources to bottle only their finest lots in vintages that once would have been considered average or even mediocre. As a result, those producers will almost always make very respectable wines. Readers will benefit immensely from exploring the wines of a variety of producers and choosing a handful of estates whose wines are consistently outstanding and in line with their personal tastes. Ultimately, there is no greater reward in wine than a keen understanding of one's own palate.

Readers should stock up on as many of the top 2004s from central and coastal Tuscany as possible. The more important wines won't be ready to drink for at least several years, but the top entry-level wines will give consumers an accurate read on the overall quality of the vintage. The 2003s will offer more immediate pleasure with a limited amount of cellaring. Any well-stored bottles of the top 2001 Tuscan wines from central and coastal Tuscany should be snapped up. Most of these wines are still on the young side, but it is an outstanding vintage that no one who loves Tuscan wines should be without.

2001 is also a superb vintage for Brunello di Montalcino. The best 2001 Brunellos are characterized by rich aromatics and generous, ripe fruit, with excellent structure and fine, elegant tannins. Although many wines are clearly built to age, a handful are drinking beautifully right now. Only a few of the 2001 Riservas justify their steep price tags, but the regular bottlings will form a solid foundation in the cellar at reasonable prices. So far I have tasted only a limited number of 2003 Brunellos, and they have been better than anticipated.

For current consumption readers should explore select 2005 Chianti Classicos as well as the better 2004s and 2003s. The 2006 Chianti Classicos should be exciting wines when they are released in 2008. The 2004 Rosso di Montalcinos and Rosso di Montepulcianos are also excellent choices for near-term consumption.

—ANTONIO GALLONI

[the ratings]

TUSCANY'S BEST WINES

★ ★ ★ ★ ★ (OUTSTANDING)

Antinori (Solaia)
Avignonesi (Vin Santo)
Avignonesi (Vin Santo Occhio di Pernice)
Castello dei Rampolla (D'Alceo)

Cerbaiona (Brunello di Montalcino)
Fattoria di Felsina (Chianti Classico Riserva Rancia)
Fattoria di Petrolo (Galatrona)

Fontodi (Flaccianello della Pieve)
Bibi Graetz (Testamatta)
Le Macchiole (Messorio)
Podere Il Carnasciale (Il Caberlot)
San Giusto a Rentennano
   (Percarlo)
Siro Pacenti (Brunello di
   Montalcino)

Soldera—Case Basse (Brunello di
   Montalcino Riserva)
Tenuta dell'Ornellaia (Masseto and
   Ornellaia)
Tenuta di Trinoro (Tenuta di Trinoro)
Tua Rita (Syrah)
Valdicava (Brunello di Montalcino Riserva
   Madonna del Piano)

★ ★ ★ ★ / ★ ★ ★ ★ ★ (EXCELLENT TO OUTSTANDING)

Antinori (Tignanello)
Argiano (Suolo)
Franco Biondi Santi—Il Greppo
   (Brunello di Montalcino Riserva)
Brancaia (Il Blu)
Campo alla Sughera (Bolgheri Arnione)
Capannelle (Chianti Classico Riserva)
Capannelle (50 & 50)
Capannelle (Solare)
Casanova di Neri (Brunello di
   Montalcino Cerretalto)
Castell'in Villa (Vin Santo)
Castello dei Rampolla (Sammarco)
Castello di Ama (L'Apparita)
Castello di Ama (Chianti Classico
   Vigneto Bellavista)
Castello di Ama (Chianti Classico Vigneto
   La Casuccia)
Castello di Querceto (Cignale)
Ciacci Piccolomini d'Aragona (Brunello di
   Montalcino Pianrosso)
Ciacci Piccolomini d'Aragona (Brunello di
   Montalcino Riserva Santa Caterina d'Oro)
Collosorbo (Brunello di Montalcino Riserva)
Costanti (Brunello di Montalcino)
Costanti (Brunello di Montalcino Riserva)
Fattoria di Petrolo (Vin Santo)
Fontodi (Case Via Nuova Syrah)
Fontodi (Chianti Classico Riserva Vigna
   del Sorbo)
Fuligni (Brunello di Montalcino Riserva)
Gaja—Pieve Santa Restituta (Brunello di
   Montalcino Sugarille)

La Gerla (Brunello di Montalcino Vigna
   gli Angeli)
Bibi Graetz (Colore)
Isole e Olena (Cepparello)
Lisini (Brunello di Montalcino Ugolaia)
La Massa (Giorgio Primo)
Le Macchiole (Paleo Rosso)
Le Macchiole (Scrio)
Montepeloso (Gabbro)
Montevertine (Montevertine)
Podere San Luigi (Fidenzio)
Poggio di Sotto (Brunello di Montalcino)
Poggio Le Scalette (Il Carbonaione)
Il Poggione (Brunello di Montalcino)
Il Poggione (Brunello di Montalcino
   Riserva)
Le Potazzine (Brunello di Montalcino)
Querciabella (Camartina)
Salicutti (Brunello di Montalcino)
Salvioni (Brunello di Montalcino)
San Giusto a Rentennano (La Ricolma)
San Giusto a Rentennano (Vin San
   Giusto)
Livio Sassetti—Pertimali (Brunello di
   Montalcino Riserva)
Talenti (Brunello di Montalcino Pian
   di Conte)
Talenti (Brunello di Montalcino Riserva
   Vigne del Paretaio)
Tua Rita (Giusto di Notri)
Uccelliera (Brunello di Montalcino
   Riserva)
Valdicava (Brunello di Montalcino)

★ ★ ★ ★ (EXCELLENT)

Altesino (Brunello di Montalcino Riserva)
Ambra (Carmignano Santa Cristina in Pilli)
Ambra Carmignano Riserva Elzana and
   Vigne Alte
Antinori (Bolgheri Guado al Tasso)

Antinori (Brunello di Montalcino Pian
   delle Vigne)
Antinori (Cervaro della Sala)
Antinori (Muffato della Sala)
Argiano (Brunello di Montalcino)

Argiano (Solengo)
Avignonesi (50 & 50)
Avignonesi (Cortona Desiderio)
Avignonesi (Vino Nobile di Montepulciano)
Badia a Coltibuono (Chianti Classico
  Cultus Boni)
Badia a Coltibuono (Chianti
  Classico Riserva)
Badia a Coltibuono (Sangioveto)
Badia a Coltibuono (Vin Santo)
Il Borro (Il Borro)
Boscarelli (Boscarelli dei Boscarelli)
Boscarelli (Vino Nobile di Montepulciano)
Boscarelli (Vino Nobile di Montepulciano
  Nocio dei Boscarelli)
La Braccesca (Cortona Syrah Bramasole)
La Braccesca (Vino Nobile di
  Montepulciano)
La Braccesca (Vino Nobile di
  Montepulciano Vigneto Santa Pia)
Ca' Marcanda (Magari)
Camigliano (Brunello di Montalcino)
Camigliano (Brunello di Montalcino
  Riserva Gualto)
Campo alla Sughera (Bolgheri Adeo)
Canalicchio—Franco Pacenti (Brunello di
  Montalcino Riserva)
Canalicchio di Sopra (Brunello di
  Montalcino)
Canalicchio di Sopra (Brunello di
  Montalcino Riserva)
Capannelle (50 & 50)
Capannelle (Chianti Classico Riserva)
Capannelle (Solare)
Caparzo (Brunello di Montalcino)
Caparzo (Brunello di Montalcino La Casa)
Caparzo (Brunello di Montalcino Riserva)
Casanova di Neri (Brunello di Montalcino)
Casanova di Neri (Brunello di Montalcino
  Tenuta Nuova)
Casanuova delle Cerbaie (Brunello di
  Montalcino Riserva)
Castelgiocondo (Brunello di Montalcino
  Riserva Ripe al Convento)
Castellare (Chianti Classico Riserva
  Vigna Il Poggiale)
Castellare (I Sodi di San Niccolò)
Castell'in Villa (Chianti Classico)
Castell'in Villa (Chianti Classico Riserva)
Castell'in Villa (Chianti Classico Riserva
  Poggio delle Rose)

Castell'in Villa (Santacroce)
Castello Banfi (Brunello di Montalcino
  Poggio alle Mura)
Castello del Terriccio (Castello di Terriccio)
Castello del Terriccio (Lupicaia)
Castello di Ama (Vin Santo)
Castello di Bossi (Chianti Classico
  Riserva Berardo)
Castello di Bossi (Corbaia)
Castello di Bossi (Girolamo)
Castello di Monsanto (Chianti
  Classico Riserva)
Castello di Monsanto (Chianti Classico
  Riserva Il Poggio)
Castello di Monsanto (Nemo
  "Vigneto Il Mulino")
Castello di Nipozzano (Chianti
  Rùfina Riserva)
Castello di Nipozzano (Chianti Rùfina
  Vigneto Montesodi)
Castello di Volpaia (Balifico)
Castello di Volpaia (Chianti Classico
  Riserva Coltassala)
Castello di Volpaia (Vin Santo)
Ciacci Piccolomini d'Aragona (Ateo and
  Brunello di Montalcino)
Cima (Vermentino Nero)
Col d'Orcia (Brunello di Montalcino Riserva
  Poggio al Vento)
Collelceto (Brunello di Montalcino)
Collosorbo (Brunello di Montalcino)
La Colombina (Brunello di
  Montalcino Riserva)
Cupano (Brunello di Montalcino)
D'Alessandro (Cortona Syrah Il Bosco)
Dei (Vino Nobile di Montepulciano)
Enrico Santini (Montepergoli)
Enrico Santini (Poggio al Moro)
Fanetti (Vino Nobile di
  Montepulciano Riserva)
Fattoria dei Barbi (Brunello di Montalcino)
Fattoria dei Barbi (Brunello di
  Montalcino Riserva)
Fattoria del Cerro (Vino Nobile di
  Montepulciano)
Fattoria del Cerro (Vino Nobile di
  Montepulciano Vigneto Antica Chiusina)
Fattoria di Felsina (Chianti Classico Riserva)
Fattoria di Felsina (Fontalloro)
Fattoria di Felsina (Vin Santo)
Fattoria di Petrolo (Il Torrione)

Fattoria di Piazzano (Chianti Rio Camerata)

Fattoria di Piazzano (Chianti Riserva
  Rio Camerata)

Fontodi (Vin Santo)

La Fornace (Brunello di
  Montalcino Riserva)

Fossacolle (Brunello di Montalcino)

Fuligni (Brunello di Montalcino)

Gaja—Pieve Santa Restituta (Brunello di
  Montalcino Rennina)

Giacomo Mori (Chianti Castelrotto)

Bibi Graetz (Bugia)

Bibi Graetz (Canaiolo)

Grattamacco (Grattamacco)

I Greppi (Bolgheri Superiore Greppicaia)

Gualdo del Re (Gualdo del Re)

Gualdo del Re (Il Rennero)

Isole e Olena (Cabernet Sauvignon
  Collezione De Marchi)

Isole e Olena (Syrah)

Isole e Olena (Vin Santo)

Lisini (Brunello di Montalcino)

Le Macioche (Brunello di Montalcino)

Le Macioche (Brunello di
  Montalcino Riserva)

Mastrojanni (Brunello di Montalcino)

Mastrojanni (Brunello di Montalcino Vigna
  Schiena d'Asino)

Mocali (Brunello di Montalcino)

Mocali (Brunello di Montalcino Riserva)

Mocali (Brunello di Montalcino Vigna
  delle Raunate)

Mocali (Brunello di Montalcino Riserva
  Vigna delle Raunate)

Montepeloso (Eneo)

Montepeloso (Nardo)

Montevertine (Le Pergole Torte)

Morisfarms (Avvoltore)

Morisfarms (Morellino di Scansano Riserva)

La Mozza (Aragone)

Silvio Nardi (Brunello di Montalcino)

Silvio Nardi (Brunello di
  Montalcino Manachiara)

Siro Pacenti (Rosso di Montalcino)

Piaggia (Carmignano Il Sasso)

Piancornello (Brunello di Montalcino
  Riserva)

Il Palazzino (Chianti Classico
  Grosso Sanese)

Il Palazzino (Chianti Classico La Pieve)

Il Palazzone (Brunello di Montalcino)

Il Palazzone (Brunello di
  Montalcino Riserva)

Agostina Pieri (Brunello di Montalcino)

Agostina Pieri (Rosso di Montalcino)

Podere Il Carnasciale (Carnasciale)

Podere Forte (Petrucci)

La Poderina (Brunello di Montalcino)

Poggio al Tesoro (Sondraia)

Poggio Antico (Brunello di Montalcino)

Poggio Antico (Brunello di
  Montalcino Altero)

Poggio Antico (Brunello di Montalcino
  Riserva)

Poggio Antico (Rosso di Montalcino)

Poliziano (Le Stanze di Poliziano)

Poliziano (Vino Nobile di
  Montepulciano Asinone)

Pratesi (Carmione)

Le Pupille (Morellino di Scansano Riserva
  Poggio Valente)

Le Pupille (Saffredi)

Querciabella (Batar)

Querciabella (Chianti Classico)

Rocca di Castagnoli (Chianti Classico
  Riserva Capraia)

Rocca di Montegrossi (Chianti Classico
  Riserva San Marcellino)

Rocca di Montegrossi (Geremia)

Rocca di Montegrossi (Vin Santo)

Rodano (Chianti Classico Riserva Viacosta)

Rodano (Monna Claudia)

Ruffino (Chianti Classico Riserva Ruffino
  Riserva Ducale Oro)

Ruffino (Romitorio di Santedame)

Salcheto (Vino Nobile di Montepulciano)

Salcheto (Vino Nobile di Montepulciano
  Salco Evoluzione)

Salicutti (Rosso di Montalcino)

San Fabiano (Armaiolo)

San Giusto a Rentennano (Chianti Classico
  Riserva Le Baroncole)

Vasco Sassetti (Brunello di Montalcino)

Livio Sassetti—Pertimali (Brunello
  di Montalcino)

Sassotondo (San Lorenzo)

Michele Satta (I Castagni)

Michele Satta (Cavaliere)

Michele Satta (Piastraia)

Scopetone (Brunello di Montalcino)

Selvapiana (Chianti Rùfina Riserva
  Vigneto Bucerchiale)

La Serena (Brunello di Montalcino)
Sesta di Sopra (Brunello di Montalcino)
Solaria (Brunello di Montalcino 123)
Soldera—Case Basse (Brunello
  di Montalcino)
La Spinetta (Sezzana)
Tenimenti Angelini (Brunello di Montalcino
  Riserva Vigna Spuntali)
Tenimenti Angelini (Brunello di Montalcino
  Val di Suga)
Tenimenti Angelini (Vino Nobile di
  Montepulciano Simposio)
Tenuta dei Sette Cieli (Indaco)
Tenuta dell'Ornellaia (Le Serre Nuove)
Tenuta di Capezzana (Barco Reale
  di Carmignano)
Tenuta di Capezzana (Ghiaie della Furba)
Tenuta di Capezzana (Vin Santo Riserva
  di Carmignano)
Tenuta di Castiglioni (Giramonte)

Tenuta La Fuga (Brunello di Montalcino)
Tenuta Oliveto (Brunello di Montalcino
  Riserva)
Tenuta San Guido (Bolgheri Sassicaia)
Tenuta di Trinoro (Le Cupole di Trinoro)
Terrabianca (Campaccio)
Terrabianca (Piano del Cipresso)
Terrabianca (Villa Il Tesoro)
Tiezzi (Brunello di Montalcino)
Tua Rita (Redigaffi)
Uccelliera (Brunello di Montalcino)
Valdipiatta (Vino Nobile di
  Montepulciano)
Valdipiatta (Vino Nobile di Montepulciano
  Vigna d'Alfiero)
La Velona (Brunello di Montalcino)
I Veroni (Chianti Rùfina Riserva)
Vignamaggio (Vignamaggio)
Villa Cafaggio (Chianti Classico Riserva)
Viticcio (Prunaio)

★ ★ ★ / ★ ★ ★ ★ (GOOD TO EXCELLENT)

Ambra (Carmignano Montefortini)
Ananda (Ananda di Toscana)
Antinori (Chianti Classico Badia
  a Passignano)
Antinori (Chianti Classico
  Marchesi Antinori)
Antinori (Vin Santo)
Argiano (Non Confunditur)
Badia a Coltibuono (Chianti Classico)
Il Borro (Pian di Nova)
Brancaia (Chianti Classico)
Brancaia (Ilatraia)
Ca' Marcanda (Camarcanda)
Ca' Marcanda (Promis)
Campo di Sasso (Insoglio del Cinghiale)
Casanova di Neri (Pietradonice)
Castelgiocondo (Brunello di Montalcino)
Castelgiocondo (Lamaione)
Castello Banfi (Brunello di Montalcino)
Castello Banfi (Excelsus)
Castello Banfi (Summus)
Castello dei Rampolla (Chianti Classico)
Castello di Ama (Chianti Classico Castello
  di Ama)
Castello di Monsanto (Vin Santo
  La Chimera)
Castello di Nipozzano (Mormoreto)
Castello di Volpaia (Chianti
  Classico Riserva)

Ciacci Piccolomini d'Aragona (Fabius)
Ciacci Piccolomini d'Aragona
  (Montecucco Sangiovese)
Col d'Orcia (Brunello di Montalcino)
La Colombina (Brunello di Montalcino)
Costanti (Calbello Brunello di Montalcino)
Fanti (Brunello di Montalcino)
Fanti (Sant'Antimo Rosso)
Fattoria di Felsina (Chianti Classico)
Fattoria di Magliano (Morellino di
  Scansano Heba)
Fattoria di Piazzano (Chianti)
Fonterutoli (Chianti Classico Castello
  di Fonterutoli)
Fonterutoli (Siepi)
Fontodi (Chianti Classico)
Fortediga (Salebro)
Fortediga (Sodamagri)
Bibi Graetz (Soffocone di Vincigliata)
Grattamacco (Bolgheri Rosso)
I Greppi (Bolgheri Greppicante)
Gualdo del Re (Eliseo)
Gualdo del Re (Federico Primo)
Isole e Olena (Chardonnay Collezione
  de Marchi)
Isole e Olena (Chianti Classico)
Le Macchiole (Le Macchiole)
La Massa (La Massa)
Mocali (Morellino di Scansano Suberli)

Montevertine (Pian del Ciampolo)

Giacomo Mori (Chianti)

Morisfarms (Monteregio di Massa Marittima)

Morisfarms (Morellino di Scansano)

Il Palazzino (Chianti Classico Argenina)

Piaggia (Poggio de' Colli)

Podere Forte (Guardiavigna)

La Poderina (Brunello di Montalcino
  Poggio Banale)

Poggio al Tesoro (Dedicato a Walter)

Poggio Argentiera (Finisterre)

Poggio Argentiera (Morellino di
  Scansano Bellamarsiglia)

Poggio Argentiera (Morellino di
  Scansano Capatosta)

Poggio Mandorlo (Poggio Mandorlo)

Poliziano (Vino Nobile di Montepulciano)

Pomino (Pomino Benefizio)

Pomino (Pomino Casafonte)

Pratesi (Carmignano)

Le Pupille (Morellino di Scansano
  Poggio Valente)

Le Pupille (Sol Alto)

La Rasina (Brunello di Montalcino)

Rocca di Castagnoli (Chianti Classico)

Rocca di Castagnoli (Chianti Classico
  Riserva Poggio ai Frati)

Rocca di Montegrossi (Chianti Classico)

Ruffino (Modus)

Salcheto (Rosso di Montepulciano)

San Fabiano (Piocaia)

San Giusto a Rentennano (Chianti Classico)

Enrico Santini (Campo alla Casa)

Sassotondo (Sangiovese Riserva Franz)

Selvapiana (Chianti Rùfina)

Sette Ponti (Crognolo)

Sette Ponti (Oreno)

Sette Ponti (Poggio al Lupo)

Solaria (Brunello di Montalcino)

Tenimenti Angelini (Vino Nobile di
  Montepulciano Tre Rose)

Tenuta Belguardo (Tenuta Belguardo)

Tenuta dei Sette Cieli (Yantra)

Tenuta di Capezzana (Villa di
  Capezzana Carmignano)

Tenuta di Castiglioni (Tenuta di Castiglioni)

Tenuta di Ghizzano (Nambrot)

Tenuta di Sesta (Brunello di
  Montalcino Riserva)

Tenuta La Fuga (Brunello di Montalcino
  Le Due Sorelle)

Tenuta Oliveto (Brunello di Montalcino)

Tenuta San Guido (Guidalberto)

Terrabianca (Campaccio Selezione Riserva)

Toscolo (Chianti Classico)

Toscolo (Chianti Classico Riserva)

Tua Rita (Perlato del Bosco)

Tua Rita (Rosso di Notri)

Uccelliera (Rapace)

Uccelliera (Rosso di Montalcino)

I Veroni (Chianti Rùfina)

Vignamaggio (Chianti Classico)

Vignamaggio (Chianti Classico Riserva
  Castello di Monna Lisa)

Villa Cafaggio (Chianti Classico)

Villa Cafaggio (Cortaccio)

Villa Cafaggio (San Martino)

Viticcio (Chianti Classico Riserva)

Viticcio (Chianti Classico Riserva Lucius)

Viticcio (Monile)

* * * (GOOD)

Altesino (Brunello di Montalcino Montosoli)

Franco Biondi Santi—Il Greppo
  (Brunello di Montalcino Annata)

Brancaia (Tre)

Calbello (Brunello di Montalcino and Rosso
  di Montalcino)

Castello del Terriccio (Tassinaia)

Castello di Volpaia (Chianti Classico)

D'Alessandro (Cortona Syrah)

Dei (Rosso di Montepulciano)

Fattoria del Cerro (Rosso di Montepulciano)

Fonterutoli (Chianti Classico Fonterutoli)

Morisfarms (Vermentino)

La Mozza (Morellino di Scansano I Perazzi)

Piaggia (Carmignano Riserva)

Poliziano (Rosso di Montepulciano)

Le Pupille (Morellino di Scansano)

Rodano (Chianti Classico)

Ruffino (Chianti Classico Santedame)

Salcheto (Casa al Poggio)

San Fabiano (Chianti Putto)

Livio Sassetti—Pertimali (La Querciolina
  Maremma Istriciaia)

Livio Sassetti—Pertimali (La Querciolina
  Montecucco Sangiovese)

Sassotondo (Rosso Ciliegiolo)

La Serena (Brunello di Montalcino Gemini)

La Spinetta (Il Nero di Casanova)

Tenuta Belguardo (Morellino di
  Scansano Bronzone)
Tenuta Belguardo (Serrata)
Tenuta di Capezzana (Conti Contini
  Sangiovese)

Tenuta di Ghizzano (Il Ghizzano)
Tenuta dell'Ornellaia (Le Volte)
Tua Rita (Lodano Bianco)
Viticcio (Chianti Classico)

[tasting commentaries]

ALTESINO ★★★
TUSCANY $100.00

Altesino is located in a spectacular spot that affords views of Montosoli, the hillside from which the estate makes its most famous Brunello. In past years I have enjoyed this producer's wines very much, often purchasing them for my own cellar. Unfortunately, the estate's 2001s have proven to be very inconsistent in my multiple tastings of the wines. I can recommend only the Montosoli, with the caveat that my score refers to Lot #5343 (indicated on U.S. Importer Leonardo LoCascio's back label) and the Riserva. Unfortunately, both the regular bottling and the Montosoli showed a high degree of bottle variation in vintage 2001. The estate's 2003s are much more consistent.

2003 Brunello di Montalcino	89	now–2015
2003 Brunello di Montalcino Montosoli	91	now–2018
2001 Brunello di Montalcino Montosoli	87	2011–2021
2001 Brunello di Montalcino Riserva	90	2011–2019

AMBRA ★★★
TUSCANY $16.00–$18.00

Ambra is an excellent source of Carmignanos that capture the essence of several of the region's top sites.

2004 Carmignano Riserva Elzana	92	2010–2024
2004 Carmignano Riserva Vigne Alte	92	2009–2024
2005 Carmignano Santa Cristina in Pilli	89	now–2020
2004 Carmignano Santa Cristina in Pilli	90	2010–2020
2005 Carmignano Montefortini	90	2010–2020
2004 Carmignano Montefortini	89	now–2016

ANANDA ★★★
TUSCANY $30.00

Wine writer Judy Beardsall and oenologist Alberto Antonini fashion this attractive blend of equal parts Sangiovese and Merlot from vineyards in Maremma.

2003 Ananda di Toscana	89	now–2015

ANTINORI ★★★★
TUSCANY/UMBRIA $31.00–$170.00

Piero Antinori has been one of the leading forces in Italian wines for decades. With estates spread throughout the country, Antinori produces high-quality wines in many appellations. The highlights among these new releases are without question the 2003 and 2004 Tignanello and Solaia, the wines that Antinori is most closely identified with and among the first wines to incorporate native and international varieties. Tignanello is a blend composed of 85% Sangiovese, 10% Cabernet Sauvignon, and 5% Cabernet Franc, while Solaia contains 75% Cabernet

Sauvignon, 20% Sangiovese, and 5% Cabernet Franc. In recent years the estate's wines have shown much more elegance than was the case in the past as oenologist Renzo Cotarella has moved away from the heavy, concentrated style of previous vintages.

2005 Cervaro della Sala	90	now–2015
2004 Cervaro della Sala	91	now–2016
2003 Cervaro della Sala	90	now–2015
2004 Chianti Classico Riserva Badia a Passignano	89	now–2014
2003 Chianti Classico Badia a Passignano	88	now–2012
2004 Chianti Classico Riserva Marchesi Antinori	91	2009–2019
2003 Chianti Classico Riserva Marchesi Antinori	89	now–2018
2005 Bolgheri Guado al Tasso	92	2010–2019
2004 Bolgheri Guado al Tasso	92	2009–2019
2003 Bolgheri Guado al Tasso	91	2009–2019
2005 Tignanello	91	2010–2020
2004 Tignanello	94	2009–2019
2003 Tignanello	92	now–2018
2005 Solaia	93	2012–2023
2004 Solaia	96	2011–2024
2003 Solaia	93	now–2018
2003 Brunello di Montalcino Pian delle Vigne	91	now–2015
2001 Brunello di Montalcino Pian delle Vigne	92	2009–2019
2005 Muffato	89	now–2010
2004 Muffato della Sala	90	now–2017
2004 Vin Santo del Chianti Classico	89	now–2012
2003 Vin Santo del Chianti Classico	88	now–2015

Past Glories Tignanello: 2001 (92), 1999 (94), 1997 (92), 1993 (91); Solaia: 2001 (94), 1999 (93), 1997 (96), 1994 (92)

ARGIANO ★ ★ ★ ★
TUSCANY $22.00–$145.00

Argiano makes a wide range of wines from its 48 hectares (119 acres) of vineyards in the southern part of the Brunello zone. In addition to its Rosso and Brunello, Argiano produces the IGT Solengo, made from a blend of Merlot, Cabernet, and Syrah. The estate's newest wine is its IGT Suolo. This 100% Sangiovese is made from the estate's oldest vines and is aged in new oak for 12 months, as opposed to the Brunello, which sees at least two years of oak aging, the first year in used *barrique* and the second in cask.

2006 Rosso di Montalcino	89	now–2010
2006 Non Confunditur	90	now–2016
2005 Non Confunditur	89	now–2015
2004 Non Confunditur	89	now–2012
2003 Brunello di Montalcino	91	now–2018
2001 Brunello di Montalcino	91	now–2016
2005 Suolo	91	2010–2020
2004 Suolo	93	2010–2024
2003 Suolo	91	now–2018
2004 Solengo	93	2010–2024
2003 Solengo	89	2009–2019

AVIGNONESI ★★★★/★★★★★
TUSCANY $23.00–$210.00

Avignonesi is one of the qualitative leaders in Montepulciano. In particular readers should not pass up an opportunity to taste the estate's exceptional dessert wines. The Vin Santo is a blend of Trebbiano, Grechetto, and Malvasia that spends up to eight years in barrel, while the Occhio di Pernice is 100% Prugnolo Gentile (Sangiovese) that spends up to a decade in barrel. Both Vin Santos earn the epithet *vino da meditazione*.

2005 Vino Nobile di Montepulciano	88	now–2012
2004 Vino Nobile di Montepulciano	90	now–2016
2005 Cortona Desiderio	89	now–2015
2003 Cortona Desiderio	90	now–2017
2001 50 & 50	92	2010–2020
1996 Vin Santo	94	now–2028
1995 Vin Santo	94	now–2027
1996 Vin Santo Occhio di Pernice	93	now–2030
1995 Vin Santo Occhio di Pernice	96	now–2035

BADIA A COLTIBUONO ★★★
TUSCANY $23.00–$36.00

Badia a Coltibuono has been owned by the Stucchi Prinetti family since the mid–19th century. The original estate and its namesake abbey are located in one of the most picturesque corners of Gaiole, in the heart of Chianti Classico. More recently the family has built a state-of-the-art winemaking facility in Monti. The estate produces a wide range of Sangiovese-based wines, all from organically grown fruit. There is also a *négociant* range marketed under the brand name Coltibuono.

2005 Chianti Classico	87	now–2010
2004 Chianti Classico	88	now–2011
2001 Chianti Classico Riserva	90	now–2016
2003 Chianti Classico Cultus Boni	91	now–2018
2000 Sangioveto	90	now–2015
2002 Vin Santo	90	now–2011
2000 Vin Santo	90	now–2017

FRANCO BIONDI SANTI—IL GREPPO ★★★/★★★★
TUSCANY $175.00

The gorgeous, manicured Il Greppo estate gives visitors a window into the Tuscan aristocracy of a time seemingly long gone by. Biondi Santi's Brunello was winning awards and being served at important diplomatic events well before most of the estates we know today existed. It is also here that Brunello di Montalcino was first produced. In the late 1800s Ferruccio Biondi Santi isolated a clonal mutation of Sangiovese unique to Montalcino, today known as Sangiovese Grosso. He replanted his vineyards with this clone and began producing his wine without adding other varieties, giving birth to Brunello. Now in his mid-80s, the genteel and impeccably dressed Franco Biondi Santi, Ferruccio's grandson, still insists on personally showing visitors around the grounds. The highlight of the tour is the extensive collection of older vintages, kept under lock and key at all times. At 450 to 500 meters (1,475 to 1,640 feet) above sea level, the vineyards are among the highest in the zone. The soils are poor, consisting mostly of the rock, limestone, and sand combination known as *galestro*. The estate produces two Brunellos, a base bottling from its younger vines called simply "Annata" and a Riserva that is made from older vines. Along with the wines of Gianfranco Soldera, these are perhaps the most traditionally made wines in the region. The Annata is fermented in glass-lined cement tanks, while the Riserva is fermented in an open-top wood vat. Both wines see an extended period of cask aging. The high-altitude vineyards and traditional approach to wine-making yield wines that are often decidedly austere in style and that are capable of aging for decades.

2003 Brunello di Montalcino Annata	90	2013–2028
2001 Brunello di Montalcino Annata	87	2011–2021
2000 Brunello di Montalcino Annata	91	now–2025
2001 Brunello di Montalcino Riserva	94	2016–2041

IL BORRO ★ ★ ★
TUSCANY $20.00–$36.00

The Ferragamo family has owned this property, located outside Arezzo, since 1993. Wine-making is overseen by consulting oenologist Niccolò d'Afflitto. The estate's top wine, Il Borro, is a French oak-aged cuvée of 50% Merlot, 35% Cabernet Sauvignon, 10% Syrah, and 5% Petit Verdot.

2004 Pian di Nova	89	now–2012
2004 Il Borro	91	2009–2019

BOSCARELLI ★ ★ ★ ★
TUSCANY $38.00–$92.00

Proprietor Paola De Ferrari makes some of the area's reference-point wines at her estate in Montepulciano. Her single-vineyard Nocio dei Boscarelli is typically among the finest expressions of Vino Nobile. Winemaking is overseen by consulting oenologist Maurizio Castelli.

2003 Vino Nobile di Montelpuciano	90	now–2017
2003 Vino Nobile di Montepulciano Nocio dei Boscarelli	92	now–2018
2003 Boscarelli dei Boscarelli	91	now–2017

LA BRACCESCA ★ ★ ★ ★
TUSCANY $26.00–$38.00

La Braccesca is the Montepulciano property of the Antinori family. I was very impressed with the wines I tasted, especially the Syrah Bramasole, which has found a very welcoming home in the vineyards of Cortona. The wines are made in a flashy, supple style, and the estate uses a percentage of American oak to give the wines a little more sweetness and spiciness.

2004 Vino Nobile di Montepulciano	91	2009–2019
2003 Vino Nobile di Montepulciano	90	now–2015
2003 Vino Nobile di Montepulciano Vigneto Santa Pia	91	2009–2018
2003 Cortona Syrah Bramasole	92	now–2018

BRANCAIA ★ ★ ★ ★
TUSCANY $25.00–$90.00

Consulting oenologist Carlo Ferrini oversees winemaking at Brancaia, which owns vineyards in the Chianti Classico and Morellino di Scansano zones. I have been buying the estate's wines for years, and the 2004 Il Blu, a blend of 50% Sangiovese, 45% Merlot, and 5% Cabernet Franc, is the best wine yet from this small property.

2004 Tre	87	now–2016
2004 Chianti Classico	89	now–2014
2004 Ilatraia	88	now–2016
2004 Il Blu	94	2009–2019

CALBELLO ★★★
TUSCANY $41.00–$60.00

This tiny property is owned by Andrea Costanti, who is best known for the wines he produces at his family's estate. The winemaking style and philosophy are similar to those employed at Costanti but so far the Calbello wines have shown a more linear and less generous expression of Sangiovese.

2005 Rosso di Montalcino	87	now–2010
2003 Brunello di Montalcino	88	now–2016
2001 Brunello di Montalcino	89	2010–2018

CA' MARCANDA ★★★
TUSCANY $44.00–$50.00

While Angelo Gaja continues to maintain a breakneck pace, even he can't resist the more calming influence of the warmer Tuscan weather. I have never seen him as relaxed—if that is the right word—as he was when I paid him a visit at Ca' Marcanda. Over the years Maremma has proven to be especially suitable for international varieties, so it is no surprise that Gaja has gone in that direction with his vineyards. The estate's top wine, Camarcanda, is a blend of 50% Merlot, 45% Cabernet Sauvignon, and 5% Cabernet Franc. The vines are still very young, and at this point Ca' Marcanda is best defined as a work in progress.

2004 Promis	89	now–2014
2004 Magari	91	now–2014
2003 Camarcanda	89	now–2015

CAMIGLIANO ★★★/★★★★
TUSCANY $53.00–$86.00

This property is located in the westernmost part of the region, which was already recognized in Etruscan times as a source of high-quality grapes. The soils are composed of sand and clay with the presence of marine deposits. The estate fervently believes in low yields, and it shows in the detail of these two outstanding Brunellos.

2006 Rosso di Montalcino	88	now
2003 Brunello di Montalcino	89	2009–2015
2001 Brunello di Montalcino	90	now–2018
2001 Brunello di Montalcino Riserva Gualto	90	now–2016

CAMPO ALLA SUGHERA ★★★/★★★★
TUSCANY $36.00–$62.00

This small estate located in Bolgheri produces sleek wines with a lot of style and class. Its vineyards, which are all fairly young, are densely planted and the yields per plant are kept low, which gives the wines much of their characteristic richness. These two releases are outstanding, and I can't recommend them highly enough.

2004 Bolgheri Adeo	90	now–2010
2003 Bolgheri Arnione	93	now–2015

CAMPO DI SASSO ★★★
TUSCANY $28.00

Campo di Sasso is the new project being headed by Lodovico and Piero Antinori, with the consulting services of Michel Rolland. So far I have had a chance to taste only the entry-level Insoglio del Cinghiale, which is a promising debut.

2005 Insoglio del Cinghiale	89	now–2010

CANALICCHIO—FRANCO PACENTI ★★★/★★★★
TUSCANY $55.00

Franco Pacenti is a small producer working out of the Canalicchio zone of Montalcino. The estate's Brunello di Montalcino Riserva sees a lengthy period of time on the skins and is aged in cask. The 2001 is a lovely effort.

2003 Brunello di Montalcino	90	2008–2018
2001 Brunello di Montalcino Riserva	92	now–2018

CANALICCHIO DI SOPRA ★★★★
TUSCANY $70.00–$118.00

This family-run estate makes an excellent Brunello from its 15 hectares (37 acres) of vineyards in the Canalicchio zone of Montalcino. The house favors cask aging for its Brunello, and the wines are made in a fairly traditional style. I recently had the opportunity to taste several vintages of the Brunello, which was a great opportunity to assess recent vintages as well as glean some insights into how the wine ages. From vintage to vintage the wine shows its characteristic notes of scorched earth and ripe dark fruit. With bottle age the wine acquires very pretty tertiary aromas and flavors that complement the fruit.

2003 Brunello di Montalcino	92	now–2016
2001 Brunello di Montalcino	91	2011–2021
2001 Brunello di Montalcino Riserva	91	2009–2019

CAPANNELLE ★★★★
TUSCANY $40.00–$131.00

This state-of-the-art winery located in Gaiole turns out beautiful wines in an updated style. The wines are aged in French oak and also see extended bottle aging prior to being released, which helps them acquire balance before they arrive on the market. The 50 & 50 is a cuvée of equal parts Sangiovese and Merlot made in partnership with Avignonesi in Montepulciano, while the Solare is blend of 80% Sangiovese and 20% Malvasia Nera.

2001 Chianti Classico Riserva	92	now–2017
2000 Chianti Classico Riserva	90	now–2015
2001 50 & 50	92	2010–2020
1999 Solare	92	2009–2019

CAPARZO ★★★★
TUSCANY $50.00–$86.00

Caparzo is located in the northern part of Montalcino. The house makes a variety of excellent wines from its 22 acres of Brunello-designated vineyards. The regular bottling is the most classic of the wines. It sees three years of aging in a mix of 30-hectoliter (792-gallon) French and Slavonian oak casks. The estate's La Casa is made from its holdings on the famed Montosoli hillside. It sees 12 months in *barrique* and completes its aging in 30-hectoliter French oak barrels. In the finest vintages a Riserva is also bottled. It spends three years in 30-hectoliter French and Slavonian oak casks.

2003 Brunello di Montalcino	92	2009–2018
2001 Brunello di Montalcino	90	now–2018
2003 Brunello di Montalcino La Casa	93	2010–2018
2001 Brunello di Montalcino La Casa	91	2010–2020
2001 Brunello di Montalcino Riserva	91	2009–2019

CASANOVA DI NERI ★★★★/★★★★★
TUSCANY $45.00–$180.00

Giacomo Neri makes some of the most exciting modern-styled Brunellos in the zone. Neri is a fervent believer in low yields, and while his wines boast notable concentration, they also show remarkable elegance and expressiveness. The estate produces three Brunellos from its extensive holdings throughout the region. The regular bottling is made from the estate's home vineyard, located in the northern part of the zone. It is also aged in cask for three years, making it the most classic of the three wines. The Tenuta Nuova is a decidedly more contemporary Brunello. Made from vines located in the southern part of the zone, it offers a riper, richer expression of Sangiovese. These two microclimates offer significantly different characteristics, and harvest times can vary by as much as two weeks. In outstanding vintages the estate produces its top bottling, the *barrique*-aged Cerretalto, from vineyards located near the winery. Neri's Pietradonice (generally around 90% Cabernet Sauvignon and 10% Sangiovese) can also be an interesting wine in top vintages.

2006 Sant'Antimo Rosso di Casanova di Neri	90	now–2011
2003 Brunello di Montalcino	89	now–2016
2001 Brunello di Montalcino	91	2009–2021
2003 Brunello di Montalcino Tenuta Nuova	92	2009–2019
2001 Brunello di Montalcino Tenuta Nuova	92	2011–2021
2003 Pietradonice	88	now–2019
2003 Brunello di Montalcino Cerretalto	91	2009–2017
2001 Brunello di Montalcino Cerretalto	93	2009–2019
2000 Brunello di Montalcino Cerretalto	91	now–2017

CASANUOVA DELLE CERBAIE ★★★★
TUSCANY $120.00

This small estate is owned by the Morandini family, who farm 45 acres of vineyards in the northern part of the Brunello zone. The Brunellos see a lengthy period of maceration on the skins. The normal bottling is aged in cask, while the Riserva is aged in French oak. Readers looking for a sumptuous, sleek Brunello should check these out.

2003 Brunello di Montalcino	91	2009–2017
2001 Brunello di Montalcino Riserva	93	2009–2019

CASTELGIOCONDO ★★★
TUSCANY $55.00–$110.00

The Castelgiocondo property, which belongs to the Frescobaldi family, is situated in an area west of Montalcino where the dry microclimate is influenced by nearby Maremma. The wines are made in a decidedly international style.

2003 Brunello di Montalcino	88	now–2015
2001 Brunello di Montalcino	88	now–2016
2003 Lamaione	88	2009–2018
2001 Brunello di Montalcino Riserva Ripe al Convento	90	now–2017

CASTELLARE ★★★/★★★★
TUSCANY $50.00–$70.00

Proprietor Paolo Panerai is perhaps best known for the highly visible role he plays in the Italian financial and lifestyle publishing world, where his various newspapers and magazines have entrenched market shares. Whether about finance or wine, Panerai is a man of strong convictions, as was evident when we met recently. He is especially passionate about the wines he produces at Castellare, the Chianti estate his family has owned since 1980. Panerai refers to his Sangiovese by its historical name, Sangioveto, with an almost religious zeal. The estate's flagship wine is I Sodi di San Niccolò, a blend of 85% Sangioveto and 15% Malvasia Nera. A recent tasting of I Sodi di San Niccolò back to 1985 found the wines fresh and very capable of developing additional complexity and nuance through extended cellaring.

2003 Chianti Classico Riserva Vigna Il Poggiale	90	now–2018
2002 I Sodi di San Niccolò	90	now–2018

Past Glories I Sodi di San Niccolò: 2001 (94), 2000 (93), 1999 (92), 1997 (93), 1995 (88), 1993 (90), 1990 (91), 1988 (88), 1986 (91), 1985 (92)

CASTELL'IN VILLA ★ ★ ★ ★
TUSCANY $26.00–$91.00

In today's increasingly rushed world, Castell'in Villa stands apart for its commitment to making traditionally styled, ageworthy Chianti Classicos. Although the proprietor, Princess Coralia Pignatelli della Leonessa, releases her wines only when she feels they are ready, my sense is that if she had her way the wines would spend many more years in her cellar than they do today. Pignatelli refuses to send her wines for comparative tastings, as she knows the wines take many years to show their full potential. When I asked about her 2003s and 2004s, she replied that the 1985s were showing well and then proceeded to open a series of wines, including the superb 1971 and 1977 Riservas, to prove her point. Pignatelli is also extremely selective in whom she sells to. As a result, Castell'in Villa remains known to only a handful of *appassionati*. Make no mistake about it, though, in top vintages, these are extraordinary wines that merit consideration by those who appreciate a more traditional style of Chianti and who have the patience to let the wines mature in the cellar. From time to time the estate rereleases wines from its library, giving consumers the rare opportunity to enjoy aged Chianti of unparalleled provenance. Readers looking for fine, traditionally made Chianti Classico need look no further than Castell'in Villa.

2003 Chianti Classico	90	now–2018
2000 Chianti Classico Riserva	91	now–2022
1998 Chianti Classico Riserva Poggio delle Rose	90	now–2020
1997 Santacroce	91	now–2022
1993 Vin Santo	93	now–2017

Past Glories Chianti Classico Riserva: 1985 (93), 1993 (92), 1977 (91), 1971 (93)

CASTELLO BANFI ★ ★ ★
TUSCANY $66.00–$81.00

If Brunello di Montalcino is viewed today as a prestigious wine, much of the credit must surely go to this estate and its American owners, the Mariani family. The Marianis have worked tirelessly to promote their wines throughout the world and in so doing have created demand for many of the region's smaller producers. Banfi has also been at the forefront in the extensive research it has conducted throughout the zone, the most important of which has been the comprehensive work it has done in experimenting with the numerous clones of Sangiovese. Banfi makes a variety of wines from its holdings in Montalcino, including Rosso and Brunello bottlings as well as several super-Tuscan blends. These richly colored, concentrated wines are made in an unmistakably international style.

2006 Rosso di Montalcino	89	now–2011
2004 Sant'Antimo Cum Laude	90	now–2017
2003 Brunello di Montalcino	88	now–2015
2001 Brunello di Montalcino	89	now–2016

2003 Brunello di Montalcino Poggio Alle Mura	89	now–2016
2001 Brunello di Montalcino Poggio Alle Mura	90	2009–2021
2004 Summus	89	now–2019
2001 Summus	89	now–2018
2003 Excelsus	88	now–2015
2000 Excelsus	88	now–2018

CASTELLO DEI RAMPOLLA ✶ ✶ ✶ ✶ ✶
TUSCANY $30.00–$240.00

High-density vineyards, biodynamic farming, and low yields are the hallmarks of the wines of Castello dei Rampolla, located in the prestigious Conca d'Oro in Panzano. Despite its elegant name, Castello dei Rampolla is a small, family-run property with a decidedly artisanal approach to working in both the vineyards and the cellar. The estate produces big, concentrated wines with imposing tannic structures that have proven to be extremely ageworthy. The Sammarco is a blend of 90% Cabernet Sauvignon, 5% Merlot, and 5% Sangiovese, while the D'Alceo, which is typically made in a lusher, riper style, is 85% Cabernet Sauvignon and 15% Petit Verdot.

2004 Chianti Classico	89	now–2016
2003 Chianti Classico	89	now–2010
2004 Sammarco	93	2014–2029
2003 Sammarco	92	2013–2023
2004 D'Alceo	95	2014–2026
2003 D'Alceo	94	2013–2023

CASTELLO DEL TERRICCIO ✶ ✶ ✶/✶ ✶ ✶ ✶
TUSCANY $36.00–$124.00

Consulting oenologist Carlo Ferrini oversees the winemaking at Castello del Terriccio, which is located in the province of Pisa, in the northern part of Maremma. The Tassinaia is a blend of Cabernet Sauvignon, Sangiovese, and Merlot. The Castello del Terriccio is a more unusual blend of Syrah, Mourvèdre, and Petit Verdot, while the Lupicaia is a cuvée of Cabernet Sauvignon, Merlot, and Petit Verdot. These are fine efforts from Castello del Terriccio, especially considering that 2002 and 2003 are far from ideal vintages. I look forward to tasting the estate's 2004s.

2002 Tassinaia	87	now–2014
2003 Castello di Terriccio	91	now–2015
2003 Lupicaia	92	now–2015

CASTELLO DI AMA ✶ ✶ ✶ ✶ ✶
TUSCANY $35.00–$150.00

No single producer has done more to promote an upscale image for Chianti Classico than Marco Pallanti and Castello di Ama. Though the vast majority of estates market their top selections under the more fashionable IGT designation, Ama continue to label their top bottlings as Chianti Classico. Perhaps for that reason Pallanti was recently elected president of the Consorzio del Chianti Classico. Highly respected as well as admired by his colleagues, Pallanti appears to be the perfect choice to move the consortium forward. Castello di Ama's style could be synthesized as relying on low yields from old vineyards planted at high altitudes. The soil types range from those that are richer in clay to those that have a higher content of gravel and pebbles. The estate releases three Chianti Classicos. The normal bottling is typically one of the best wines in the region. In top vintages the single-vineyard Chianti Classicos Vigneto La Casuccia and Vigneto Bellavista are also produced. When vintages are deemed to be good enough to produce the selections, the fruit from those plots is added to the normal Chianti Classico, as was the case in both 2002 and 2003. La Casuccia is divided into 17 parcels planted at 480 to 526 meters (1,575 to 1,725 feet), with soils that are composed mostly of clay and limestone. The wine is a blend of 80% Sangiovese and 20% Merlot, which gives the wine its characteristic round, supple character. At Bellavista the vines are planted at similar altitudes, ranging from about 1,500 to 1,735 feet, but the soils are a combination of clay and rocks. Ama's Chianti Classico Bellavista contains 20% Malvasia Nera in the blend, which gives the wine much of its structure. Ama also produces the distinctive single-vineyard Merlot L'Apparita from the upper portion of the Bellavista vineyard.

2004 Chianti Classico	90	2009–2019
2003 Chianti Classico	89	now–2015
2004 Chianti Classico Vigneto La Casuccia	92	2009–2019
2004 Chianti Classico Vigneto Bellavista	93	2009–2022
2004 L'Apparita	94	2010–2020
2003 L'Apparita	93	2009–2019
1999 Vin Santo	90	now–2012

CASTELLO DI BOSSI ∗ ∗ ∗ ∗
TUSCANY $45.00–$53.00

Castello di Bossi, located in Castelnuovo Berardenga, makes a number of outstanding wines. In addition to the Chianti Classico Berardo, the Corbaia (70% Sangiovese and 30% Merlot) and Girolamo (100% Merlot) are worth looking for.

2003 Chianti Classico Riserva Berardo	91	now–2015
2003 Corbaia	92	2009–2019
2003 Girolamo	91	now–2015

CASTELLO DI MONSANTO ∗ ∗ ∗ ∗
TUSCANY $20.00–$55.00

This is a lovely set of releases from Castello di Monsanto, one of Chianti Classico's most historically important estates. In the late 1960s the proprietor, Fabrizio Bianchi, was at the forefront of many innovations that later became standard practice. In the early 1960s Monsanto pioneered the concept of single-vineyard wines, and its Il Poggio is credited as being the first such Chianti Classico. In the years that followed Bianchi removed the traditional white varieties from the Chianti blend, years before other producers followed suit. Today Monsanto makes wines in a slightly more updated style that remains very much connected to the past and, most important, to its unique *terroir*. In addition to the Chiantis, Monsanto also makes a terrific Cabernet Sauvignon, Nemo.

2003 Chianti Classico Riserva	91	now–2017
1999 Chianti Classico Riserva Il Poggio	92	2009–2019
1999 Nemo Vigneto Il Mulino	91	2009–2019
1993 Vin Santo La Chimera	89	now–2013

CASTELLO DI NIPOZZANO ∗ ∗ ∗ ∗
TUSCANY $22.00–$54.00

Lamberto Frescobaldi is a man of stark contrasts. Despite his aristocratic lineage, the U.S.-educated Frescobaldi is very much down to earth, equally at ease discussing the simple pleasures of country life in Tuscany as he is his estate's global marketing strategy and financials. That dualism is very much on display in the wines, which reflect a wide range of styles from the supercommercial wines the family makes in Montalcino to the artisanal, small-production bottlings that emerge from its Pomino estate. The wines of Castello di Nipozzano, located in the Chianti Rùfina appellation, are something of a stylistic middle ground. Unlike some of his colleagues of a similar scale who choose to group wines from diverse properties under one brand name, Frescobaldi has chosen to keep his five estates as separate, distinct entities, which is how they will appear in these pages. The Chianti Rùfina Vigneto Montesodi is the estate's flagship wine, although the Mormoreto, a French oak–aged blend of Cabernet Sauvignon, Merlot, and Cabernet Franc, shows promise.

2003 Chianti Rùfina Riserva	90	now–2018
2004 Chianti Rùfina Vigneto Montesodi	92	2009–2019
2004 Mormoreto	89	2009–2019

CASTELLO DI QUERCETO ★ ★ ★/★ ★ ★ ★ ★
TUSCANY $68.00–$72.00

Unfortunately, the only wine I was able to taste from Castello di Querceto was the Cignale Colli della Toscana, but what a wine it is. This blend of 90% Cabernet Sauvignon and 10% Merlot is made in a superripe, full-bodied style. Though it may not appeal to every palate, it is unquestionably a wine that exudes personality and character, something that can't be said very often about Tuscan wines, especially those made from international varieties.

2003 Cignale	93	now–2023
2001 Cignale	93	2009–2021

CASTELLO DI VOLPAIA ★ ★ ★/★ ★ ★ ★
TUSCANY $22.00–$48.00

Proprietor Giovannella Stianti Mascheroni makes elegant, refined wines that reflect the personality of this part of the Chianti Classico zone. Castello di Volpaia is located in Radda, where the high-altitude vineyards yield wines with very distinct personalities. Years ago the estate's location was often a hindrance in achieving optimal ripeness, but it has proven to be a boon in today's ever-warmer growing seasons. In addition to the Chiantis, Volpaia also make Balifico, an attractive blend of Sangiovese and Cabernet Sauvignon.

2005 Chianti Classico	86	now–2012
2004 Chianti Classico Riserva	89	2009–2016
2003 Chianti Classico Riserva	90	now–2018
2004 Chianti Classico Riserva Coltassala	90	2009–2019
2004 Balifico	91	2009–2022
2003 Balifico	90	now–2018
2000 Vin Santo	90	now–2017

CERBAIONA ★ ★ ★ ★ ★
TUSCANY $125.00

Cerbaiona is located near the town of Montalcino. The vineyards reach an altitude of about 350 meters (1,148 feet) above sea level, and the *terroir* is composed mostly of the rock-and-marl mixture known as *galestro*. Proprietor Diego Molinari regularly turns out some of the most inspiring wines in the region. His Brunello is a classically built, structured wine that expresses the very essence of Sangiovese from Montalcino. Fermentation takes place in glass-lined cement, where the wine also undergoes malolactic fermentation. Only natural yeasts are used. The wine is then racked into 20-hectoliter (528-gallon) Slavonian oak casks, where it spends three or more years prior to being bottled without fining or filtration. After having recently tasted several hundred Brunellos, all I can say is that it is a shame there aren't more producers making wines of such great personality and distinction.

2005 Rosso di Montalcino	90	now–2012
2003 Brunello di Montalcino	94	now–2020
2001 Brunello di Montalcino	96	2011–2023

CIACCI PICCOLOMINI D'ARAGONA ★ ★ ★ ★ ★
TUSCANY $30.00–$120.00

Although Ciacci traces its roots back to the late 1800s, its focus on wine is much more recent and dates to the mid-1980s. The estate's vineyards are located in and around Castelnuovo dell'Abate, in the southern part of the Brunello zone, as well as across the valley in the Montecucco appellation, which lies in the province of Grosseto. Recently Ciacci has built a new, modern facility to augment the winery's original home in the beautiful Palazzo Ciacci in the town center of Castelnuovo. Today the property is managed by the dynamic and energetic Paolo Bianchini, who took over after his father's untimely passing in 2004. No estate has managed to bridge the gap between classic and contemporary styles as gracefully as Ciacci, which one could define as the most modern of the traditional producers or the most traditional of the modern producers when it comes to Brunello. In addition to its Brunellos, Ciacci makes the attractive Ateo (Sangiovese, Cabernet and Merlot), and Fabius (Syrah). The estate's wines tend to be midweight and are defined by extraordinary elegance and precision.

2006 Rosso di Montalcino	90	now–2011
2006 Montecucco Sangiovese	88	now–2010
2004 Montecucco Sangiovese	89	now–2010
2005 Ateo	89	2010–2020
2003 Ateo	90	now–2015
2005 Fabius	89	2010–2017
2003 Fabius	89	now–2018
2003 Brunello di Montalcino	91	now–2018
2003 Brunello di Montalcino Vigna Pianrosso	92	???
2001 Brunello di Montalcino Vigna Pianrosso	93	now–2021

CIMA ★ ★ ★
TUSCANY $33.00

This small estate is located in the Colli Apuani near Carrara, a part of Tuscany best known for its marble and *lardo*. The terraced hillside vineyards are planted to a very high density of 10,000 plants per hectare (24,700 per acre). The all-star team of agronomist Federico Curtaz and oenologist Donato Lanati are involved at the property, so it shouldn't be a surprise that the wines are fascinating expressions of this *terroir*.

2003 Vermentino Nero	90	now–2016

COL D'ORCIA ★ ★ ★/★ ★ ★ ★
TUSCANY $46.00–$98.00

Col d'Orcia is owned by Count Francesco Maroni Cinzano, who is also the newly appointed president of the Brunello producers' consortium. The large property is located in Sant'Angelo in Colle, in the southern part of the Brunello zone. Winemaking is overseen by oenologist Pablo Härri. The estate favors lengthy macerations, and the wines are aged in a combination of French and Slavonian casks. The single-vineyard Poggio al Vento is the top bottling.

2006 Rosso di Montalcino	88	now–2010
2003 Brunello di Montalcino	90	now–2015
2001 Brunello di Montalcino	89	now–2016
2002 Brunello di Montalcino Riserva Poggio al Vento	90	2010–2017

| 1999 Brunello di Montalcino Riserva Poggio al Vento | 91 | now–2018 |
| 1998 Brunello di Montalcino Riserva Poggio al Vento | 90 | now–2016 |

COLLELCETO ★★★
TUSCANY $56.00

Collelceto is located on the western part of the Brunello zone. From 15 acres of vines propri-etor Ezio Palazzesi produces an outstanding Brunello that blends elements of traditional and modern styles.

| 2003 Brunello di Montalcino | 90 | 2008–2021 |
| 2001 Brunello di Montalcino | 92 | 2009–2021 |

COLLOSORBO ★★★★
TUSCANY $49.00–$82.00

Collosorbo, located in Castelnuovo dell'Abate in the southern portion of the Brunello zone, is a relatively young estate that was created when the Ciacci family (a common name in these parts) divided its holdings at the adjacent Tenuta di Sesta. Although the warm Mediterranean microclimate of the subzone often yields Brunellos of notable ripeness and power, the Collo-sorbo Brunellos are among the most elegant and refined of this region. The wines are made under the guidance of oenologist Paolo Caciorgna and are typical of an updated style of Brunello that emphasizes clean, focused flavors with a lot of fruit while maintaining a classic sense of proportion.

2006 Rosso di Montalcino	90	now–2010
2003 Brunello di Montalcino	91	2009–2018
2001 Brunello di Montalcino	91	now–2016
2001 Brunello di Montalcino Riserva	93	now–2019
1999 Brunello di Montalcino Riserva	91	2009–2019

LA COLOMBINA ★★★
TUSCANY $47.00–$65.00

La Colombina is another new estate located in Castelnuovo dell'Abate. The wines are made in a rich, ripe style that is typical of the southern part of the appellation. These Brunellos are excellent choices for nearer-term drinking. The plump, generous style is sure to find many admirers.

2006 Rosso di Montalcino	88	now–2010
2003 Brunello di Montalcino	89	now–2015
2001 Brunello di Montalcino	89	now–2016
2001 Brunello di Montalcino Riserva	91	now–2015

COSTANTI ★★★★★
TUSCANY $74.00–$145.00

This small, historic estate located outside the town of Montalcino has turned out an excellent set of 2001 Brunellos. Andrea Costanti works predominantly with fruit sourced from higher-altitude vineyards, which gives his wines gorgeous aromatics, layered fruit, and finessed tan-nins, all of which are typical of the finest wines of this part of Montalcino. The house style captures the best of modern and traditional styles with perhaps a slight leaning toward the clas-sic. The wines will offer their finest drinking with a minimum of a few years of bottle age.

2003 Brunello di Montalcino	93	now–2018
2001 Brunello di Montalcino	93	now–2018
2001 Brunello di Montalcino Riserva	95	2009–2019

CUPANO ★★★★
TUSCANY $147.00–$180.00

In only its second vintage, this small French-owned estate near Camigliano has produced an outstanding 2001 Brunello. Cupano pursue biodynamic farming in their vineyards, which are among the most densely planted in the region. The Brunello is made from minuscule yields. It undergoes malolactic fermentation in *barrique,* where it also ages on its lees prior to being bottled. Unfortunately, there are only 2,000 bottles of this Brunello and it is already priced in the stratosphere.

2003 Brunello di Montalcino	91	now–2016
2001 Brunello di Montalcino	92	now–2018

D'ALESSANDRO ★★★★
TUSCANY $20.00–$55.00

D'Alessandro was a pioneer in discovering the potential of Syrah in Cortona. The estate works with densely planted vineyards cropped to low yields per plant, and the results are clearly evident in its wines, most notably its flagship Syrah Il Bosco. The family has recently sold half of its holdings to a group of investors. The resulting infusion of cash is being used to make improvements in the winemaking facilities. Cesare Turini, the talented young manager who is involved with several properties, has taken on a central role, while Vietti's Luca Currado will oversee work in the vineyards and cellar. It will be fascinating to follow the estate's progress in coming years. Turini and Currado are convinced that the vineyards hold a significant amount of unrealized potential.

2005 Cortona Syrah	87	now–2015
2004 Cortona Syrah Il Bosco	92	2010–2020

DEI ★★★/★★★★
TUSCANY $18.00–$27.00

The Dei family oversees more than 100 acres of vineyards in Montepulciano, the majority planted with the local variety of Sangiovese, called Prugnolo Gentile in this part of Tuscany. Winemaking is overseen by consulting oenologist Niccolò d'Afflitto.

2005 Rosso di Montepulciano	87	now–2010
2003 Vino Nobile di Montepulciano	92	now–2018

FANETTI ★★★/★★★★
TUSCANY $32.00

Fanetti makes a beautiful Vino Nobile Riserva in a very classic style. The Riserva is given a lengthy period of aging in oak and chestnut cask. There is no doubt that the raw materials are outstanding, but my feeling is that the wine would retain more fruit as well as vibrancy with less time in barrel.

2001 Vino Nobile di Montepulciano Riserva	91	2011–2021

FANTI ★★★
TUSCANY $18.00–$85.00

Fanti's vineyards are located in Castelnuovo dell'Abate, toward the southern part of the zone. Admittedly, I find this producer's Brunellos perplexing as they seemingly have little to do with Sangiovese from Montalcino. The estate's Rosso, from the Sant'Antimo appellation, is consistently a delicious entry-level red.

2005 Rosso di Montalcino	88	now
2005 Sant'Antimo Rosso	88	now–2010
2004 Sant'Antimo Rosso	88	now
2003 Brunello di Montalcino	87	now–2015
2001 Brunello di Montalcino	88	now–2018

FATTORIA DEI BARBI * * */* * * *
TUSCANY $100.00

Fattoria dei Barbi is one of Montalcino's historic estates. The property is run by the Cinelli Colombini family, making it the only winery among the ten largest in Montalcino that is owned by one of Montalcino's historic families. The estate retains a link to the past in its pursuit of mixed agriculture, a practice abandoned in these parts once viticulture surpassed other crops in their profitability. Director Stefano Cinelli Colombini has also taken the lead in developing a museum dedicated to Montalcino and, of course, its wines. The wines are made in a fairly traditional manner, with a long fermentation and *élevage* in Slavonian oak casks. However, over the last few years the estate has experimented with more modern techniques for its Brunellos. In 2001 a portion of the fruit saw 48 hours of cold maceration, a technique used to preserve aromatics, softness of texture, and color. My general feeling is that the estate is still in search of a well-defined style. If these wines are missing anything, it is more conviction behind a specific direction, but as the 2001 Brunello di Montalcino shows, Barbi is capable of making outstanding wines.

2006 Rosso di Montalcino	88	now–2011
2003 Brunello di Montalcino	89	now–2016
2001 Brunello di Montalcino	90	2011–2021
2003 Brunello di Montalcino Riserva	90	2009–2018
2001 Brunello di Montalcino Riserva	92	2009–2019

FATTORIA DEL CERRO * * * *
TUSCANY $19.00–$80.00

Fattoria del Cerro is owned by the large SAI Agricola Group, whose other properties include La Poderina in Montalcino and Colpetrone in Montefalco. The estate's Vino Nobile is aged predominantly in large casks, while the Riserva is aged in small French oak barrels. Both are beautiful wines that capture the essence of this corner of Tuscany.

2005 Rosso di Montepulciano	87	now
2004 Rosso di Montepulciano	89	now–2012
2004 Vino Nobile di Montepulciano	91	now–2016
2003 Vino Nobile di Montepulciano Vigneto		
Antica Chiusina	92	now–2018

FATTORIA DI FELSINA * * * * *
TUSCANY $22.00–$47.00

Felsina is located in Castelnuovo Berardenga, a part of the Chianti Classico zone that straddles the border between the Chianti Classico and Chianti Colli Senesi appellations. Proprietor Giuseppe Mazzocolin consistently turns out reference-point wines for the region. His wines are defined by their superb balance and drinkability. In fact, when I taste these wines I often feel as though I could drink an entire bottle by myself. All of the Felsina Chiantis are made with 100% Sangiovese and represent the maximum expression of the variety. The estate's top wine is the Chianti Classico Riserva Rancia, which has consistently been one of the finest wines in Tuscany, although some might argue that that distinction belongs to the estate's Fontalloro, which is also made from 100% Sangiovese but comes from more fertile soils. The

Vin Santo often flies below the radar, but it too is among the very best in its class. Even though Castelnuovo is regarded as the warmest of the Chianti Classico microclimates, the Felsina 2003s are among the freshest wines of the vintage. According to Mazzocolin, the heat of the vintage was less of a shock to his vineyards, as they are already accustomed to warm conditions. Felsina's 2004s are on another level and are superb examples of this important vintage in Tuscany. Even better, the wines are more affordable than ever, as a few years ago Mazzocolin cut out a layer in his distribution chain. Simply put, no cellar should be without at least a few bottles from Felsina. From top to bottom this is a very high-class set of wines.

2005 Chianti Classico	88	now–2011
2004 Chianti Classico	89	now–2012
2004 Chianti Classico Riserva	91	now–2019
2003 Chianti Classico Riserva	91	now–2018
2004 Chianti Classico Riserva Rancia	95	2010–2022
2003 Chianti Classico Riserva Rancia	93	2009–2019
2004 Fontalloro	94	2010–2019
2003 Fontalloro	92	2009–2015
2003 Maestro Raro Cabernet Sauvignon	90	now–2018
1999 Vin Santo	92	now–2014
1998 Vin Santo	92	now–2020

FATTORIA DI MAGLIANO ★ ★ ★
TUSCANY $18.00–$38.00

Fattoria di Magliano cultivates more than 100 acres of high-density vineyards in the province of Grosseto. Proprietor Agostino Lenci makes richly flavored wines of notable character. The estate's top bottling, Poggio Bestiale, is a gorgeous blend of Merlot, Cabernet Sauvignon, and Cabernet Franc.

2005 Morellino di Scansano Heba	89	now–2010
2004 Poggio Bestiale	91	now–2014

FATTORIA DI PETROLO ★ ★ ★ ★ ★
TUSCANY $37.00–$99.00

Fattoria di Petrolo is located in the hills above Montevarchi, just outside the Chianti Classico zone. Proprietor Luca Sanjust embodies a spirit of intellectual curiosity and sensitivity befitting his training as an art historian. He is very ably assisted by oenologist Stefano Guidi, agronomist Carlo Nesterini, and consulting oenologist Carlo Ferrini. Petrolo produces two wines, the Sangiovese Il Torrione and the Merlot Galatrona. While Galatrona can hardly be described as a bargain, in today's market environment it offers stunning value for the money. The estate is experimenting with several new varieties, and it will be fascinating to see what Sanjust and his team come up with in future vintages. Readers visiting the winery owe it to themselves to taste the olive oil and Vin Santo, both of which are made in minuscule quantities and reflect the estate's unwavering commitment to quality. Petrolo is a jewel of an estate, and I can't recommend the wines highly enough.

2004 Il Torrione	91	now–2016
2003 Il Torrione	89	now–2015
2004 Galatrona	96	2009–2019
2003 Galatrona	91	now–2015
1998 Vin Santo	93	now–2018

Past Glories Galatrona: 2002 (90), 2001 (95), 2000 (94); Il Torrione: 2002 (89), 2001 (90), 2000 (90)

FATTORIA DI PIAZZANO ✱ ✱ ✱
TUSCANY $13.00–$22.00

Piazzano is a great source for terrific value-priced reds. The estate farms 80 acres of vineyards in the province of Empoli.

2005 Chianti	88	now–2010
2004 Chianti Rio Camerata	90	2010–2024
2003 Chianti Riserva Rio Camerata	90	2009–2018

FONTERUTOLI ✱ ✱ ✱
TUSCANY $28.00–$99.00

Filippo Mazzei was in the midst of major construction of a new cellar when I visited the estate recently. The property, which has been owned by the Mazzei family since the middle of the 15th century, is actually a hamlet, a little jewel unto itself, nestled in the hills of Chianti Classico. The wines are made under the direction of consulting oenologist Carlo Ferrini and represent a contemporary expression of Chianti Classico. The estate ages its wines exclusively in French oak barrels, with the entry-level Chianti Classico Fonterutoli seeing roughly 50% new oak while the top selections, Castello di Fonterutoli and Siepi, see between 70% and 100% new oak. Although 2004 is a relatively strong vintage, 2003 has proven to be extremely challenging, as the estate's wines all show the presence of the hard, unripe tannins that are typical of the vintage.

2004 Chianti Classico Fonterutoli	88	now–2012
2003 Chianti Classico Fonterutoli	87	now–2012
2004 Chianti Classico Castello di Fonterutoli	89	2009–2019
2003 Chianti Classico Castello di Fonterutoli	88	now–2015
2004 Siepi	91	2012–2024
2003 Siepi	88	2010–2020

FONTODI ✱ ✱ ✱ ✱ ✱
TUSCANY $32.00–$90.00

Giovanni Manetti continues to turn out some of Italy's most compelling wines at Fontodi, which is located in Panzano, in the famous Conca d'Oro subzone. The estate's farms its more than 170 acres of vines organically farmed vineyards. The estate's top wine, the 100% Sangiovese Flaccianello della Pieve, was first produced in 1981. Flaccianello began its history as a single-vineyard wine. Over the last few years Manetti has begun to gradually replant portions of the vineyard. Beginning with the 2001 vintage, Flaccianello is most accurately described as a selection of the estate's best fruit rather than a single-vineyard Sangiovese. As good as Flaccianello can be, readers should not ignore the estate's other wines, which are equally outstanding. Fontodi's Chianti Classico (100% Sangiovese aged in used *barriques*) is typically one of the region's best and the Riserva Vigna del Sorbo is one of the top Chiantis that employ international varieties. My recent visit at Fontodi ended with a tasting of several older vintages of Flaccianello, including the 1982, which was breathtaking for its poise and sheer beauty of expression. Simply put, I can't say enough good things about Giovanni Manetti and the wines of Fontodi.

2005 Chianti Classico	88	now
2004 Chianti Classico	90	now–2014
2003 Chianti Classico Riserva Vigna del Sorbo	90	2009–2018
2001 Chianti Classico Riserva Vigna del Sorbo	93	now–2021
2004 Flaccianello della Pieve	96	2014–2029
2003 Flaccianello della Pieve	93	2010–2023

2003 Case Via Nuova Syrah	93	now–2021
1997 Vin Santo	92	now–2017

LA FORNACE ★ ★ ★
TUSCANY $75.00

Readers who enjoy a big, powerful style of Brunello should check out the wines of La Fornace. The wines see a lengthy period of contact on the skins during fermentation and are aged
in Slavonian oak casks.

2003 Brunello di Montalcino Riserva	89	now–2018
2001 Brunello di Montalcino Riserva	91	2009–2019

FORTEDIGA ★ ★ ★
TUSCANY $N/A

This new estate is owned by oenologist Alberto Antonini, and these are the first releases of the
estate's two top bottlings. The densely planted vineyards are still very young, but as the wines
attest, there is clearly much to look forward to. Both of the estate's top wines see malolactic
fermentation in *barrique*, followed by 16 months in 100% new medium-toast barrels. The
Salebro is a cuvée of 55% Cabernet Sauvignon and 45% Cabernet Franc, while the Sodamagri
is 100% Syrah.

2004 Salebro	89	now–2016
2004 Sodamagri	88	now–2014

FOSSACOLLE ★ ★ ★
TUSCANY $28.00–$63.00

This young estate made its debut just a few years ago with its 1997 Brunello. Fossacolle makes
pretty, contemporary-styled wines from its 4 hectares (10 acres) of vineyards located in the
Tavernelle hamlet toward the southwestern part of the zone.

2006 Rosso di Montalcino	89	now–2011
2004 Rosso di Montalcino	88	now
2003 Brunello di Montalcino	91	now–2015
2001 Brunello di Montalcino	90	now–2016

FULIGNI ★ ★ ★ ★/★ ★ ★ ★ ★
TUSCANY $76.00–$153.00

Proprietors Roberto Guerrini Fuligni and Maria Flora Fuligni make beautifully elegant wines
in an updated style that marries elements of both traditional and modern schools. The estate
farms about 25 acres of vineyards, which are positioned between 380 and 450 meters (1,245 to
1,475 feet) in altitude just a few kilometers away from the town of Montalcino. The wines are
aged in barrels and casks of various sizes. Winemaking is overseen by Paolo Vagaggini.

2006 Rosso di Montalcino Ginestreto	89	now–2016
2003 Brunello di Montalcino	93	now–2015
2001 Brunello di Montalcino	91	2009–2021
2001 Brunello di Montalcino Riserva	93	2011–2021

GAJA—PIEVE SANTA RESTITUTA ★ ★ ★ ★ ★
TUSCANY $100.00–$142.00

Angelo Gaja makes two Brunellos from his property at Santa Restituta, which lies adjacent to
Soldera's Case Basse estate. The Rennina is made from fruit sourced from three separate vineyards, while Sugarille is the single-vineyard selection. In terms of their structure, the two

wines can be roughly compared to Gaja's Conteisa and Sperss, respectively. The Rennina, from relatively fertile soils, is the more accessible of the wines, while the Sugarille offers more body and complexity owing to the greater presence of clay and limestone. Both wines see a fermentation lasting about three weeks, followed by one year of aging in *barrique* and a second year of aging in cask. Like this producer's wines from Piedmont, these releases from Montalcino reflect more of the Gaja house style rather than what could be called a strict interpretation of variety or *terroir*. That said, these are very beautiful Brunellos. The 2001s in particular may be the best wines I have ever tasted from this property. Gaja chose not to bottle his 2003, but the 2004s, which I tasted just after bottling, are shaping up to be gorgeous wines.

2001 Brunello di Montalcino Rennina	92	now–2017
2000 Brunello di Montalcino Rennina	90	now–2016
2001 Brunello di Montalcino Sugarille	94	2009–2021
2000 Brunello di Montalcino Sugarille	92	now–2016

LA GERLA ★★★★
TUSCANY $90.00

La Gerla was founded in 1976, making it one of Montalcino's historic estates. The estate is owned by Sergio Rossi and winemaking is overseen by Vittorio Fiore. The 2001 single-vineyard Riserva Vigna Gli Angeli is one of the finest wines of the vintage.

2003 Brunello di Montalcino	90	2009–2016
2003 Brunello di Montalcino Vigna Gli Angeli	90	now–2015
2001 Brunello di Montalcino Vigna Gli Angeli	95	now–2020

BIBI GRAETZ ★★★★/★★★★★
TUSCANY $30.00–$375.00

Bibi Graetz is a small, artisanal producer based in Fiesole, just outside Florence. Originally trained as an artist, Graetz has brought his creativity and flair for experimentation to the world of wine. Graetz prefers to work with indigenous grapes, and many of the estate's wines prominently feature varieties such as Colorino and Canaiolo that today are typically used as minor parts of Sangiovese-based blends but that Graetz believes hold unrealized potential. According to Graetz, in prephylloxera times it was Canaiolo rather than Sangiovese that was the principal variety used in Chianti. The estate's flagship wine is Testamatta, a compelling blend of 85% Sangiovese and 15% Canaiolo. Graetz is equally fanatical about yields. He keeps only one bunch of fruit (which weighs as little as 500 grams) per plant, although in plots that have a full southern exposure yields can go up to a still small 800 grams per vine in order to avoid extreme concentration of the fruit. The wines are fermented in a combination of open-top *barriques* and stainless-steel tanks. The microvinifications in *barrique* yield wines that have a lightness Graetz is quite fond of, while the wines vinified in stainless steel have more color as well as structure. The malolactic fermentations occur naturally, and for some varieties, especially the Sangiovese, they can last until the following spring or summer. In addition to his top estate wines, Graetz produces a set of more accessibly priced *négociant* bottlings that are blends from finished wines produced by larger cooperatives according to Graetz's specifications. In a region producing an ocean of average wines, those that emerge from Bibi Graetz's tiny estate are nothing short of extraordinary.

2004 Soffocone di Vincigliata	88	now–2014
2004 Canaiolo	90	2009–2019
2004 Colore	93	now–2017
2004 Testamatta	94	2009–2022
2003 Testamatta	92	2009–2018
2004 Bugia	91	now–2014

GRATTAMACCO ★★★/★★★★
TUSCANY $38.00–$110.00

Grattamacco is one of Bolgheri's historic properties. The estate's first vintage was 1978, well before the area became the fashionable spot it is today. The wines are made under the direction of consulting oenologist Maurizio Castelli. Unlike many of its neighbors, Grattamacco has always included a portion of Sangiovese in its wines with the goal of maintaining some regional typicity. The estate's flagship, Grattamacco, is a blend of 65% Cabernet Sauvignon, 20% Merlot, and 15% Sangiovese.

2004 Bolgheri Rosso	89	now–2010
2001 Grattamacco	91	2009–2017

I GREPPI ★★★
TUSCANY $26.00–$50.00

I Greppi is a new project in Bolgheri owned jointly by the Landini family of Fattoria Viticcio in Chianti and the Cancellieri-Scaramuzzi family. Most of the vineyards were planted only recently, but if these two new releases are indicative of what the estate is capable of, we will have much to look forward to over the coming years.

2005 Bolgheri Greppicante	89	now–2015
2004 Bolgheri Superiore Greppicaia	90	2009–2019

GUALDO DEL RE ★★★
TUSCANY $13.00–$49.00

This young estate is located in Suvereto, a warm microclimate known for yielding wines of notable concentration as well as power. Gualdo del Re's top wine is the French oak–aged 100% Merlot Il Rennero.

2004 Eliseo	88	now
2003 Federico Primo	88	now–2013
2001 Gualdo del Re	90	now–2016
2003 Il Rennero	91	now–2013

ISOLE E OLENA ★★★★★
TUSCANY $22.00–$56.00

Isole e Olena and proprietor Paolo De Marchi produce a wide range of outstanding wines, including the superb Cepparello, one of Tuscany's best high-end 100% Sangiovese bottlings. In my multiple tastings I noted that Cepparello has become much more accessible at an early age than in the past. In recent years De Marchi has experimented with higher-density vineyards and new clones of Sangiovese. He believes that Cepparello's newfound level of finesse is directly attributable to the fruit he is sourcing from those parcels. Both the 2003 and 2004 versions are outstanding. Readers should not ignore the Chianti Classico, regularly one of the region's finest, nor the more internationally styled wines, which are differentiated from the rest of the line by the Collezione De Marchi label.

2004 Chardonnay Collezione De Marchi	88	now–2014
2004 Chianti Classico	89	now–2012
2004 Syrah Collezione De Marchi	91	now–2018
2003 Syrah Collezione De Marchi	92	now–2018
2003 Cabernet Sauvignon Collezione De Marchi	90	2009–2018
2004 Cepparello	95	2009–2022
2003 Cepparello	94	now–2018
1999 Vin Santo	91	now–2017

LISINI ★★★★
TUSCANY $69.00–$146.00

Lisini is a beautiful rural estate located close to the hamlet of Sant'Angelo in Colle. The estate produces an excellent range of wines, including its flagship bottling, the Brunello Ugolaia. During a recent visit I had the opportunity to spend some time tasting the recent releases and seeing the vineyards with Filippo Paoletti, who handles the day-to-day winemaking duties. The Brunello is made from the estate's oldest vines, with yields averaging roughly 2 tons per acre. It is aged 36 months in a variety of casks. The estate's top bottling, the Brunello di Montalcino Ugolaia, is made from a small plot located behind the estate's main buildings. It is a beautiful vineyard, with a higher density of 5,400 plants per hectare and an average age of 25 years for the vines. The vineyards are planted with two low-vigor Sangiovese clones that naturally produce wines of notable concentration. The estate's Rosso is also worth searching for.

2006 Rosso di Montalcino	89	now–2011
2003 Brunello di Montalcino	90	2009–2017
2001 Brunello di Montalcino	92	now–2021
2001 Brunello di Montalcino Ugolaia	94	2009–2019
2000 Brunello di Montalcino Ugolaia	90	now–2016

LE MACCHIOLE ★★★★★
TUSCANY $35.00–$315.00

Proprietor Cinzia Merli has done an outstanding job running her family's small winery after the untimely passing of her husband, Eugenio, whose passion and spirit permeate everything about the estate and its vision. Under the direction of brilliant oenologist Luca d'Attoma, Le Macchiole continues to make some of Italy's most inspired wines. The estate's philosophy starts with what can only be defined as a near-obsessive attention to detail in the vineyards. The original vineyards are planted at 5,000 plants per hectare (12,350 plants per acre), but newer plots have been planted at a very dense 10,000 plants per hectare (24,700 plants per acre). Aggressive green harvesting, along with the high density of the vineyards and the naturally poor soils, results in small bunches and low yields per plant. Once in the cellar, the estate's philosophy is minimalist. The wines see fermentation lasting 20 to 25 days followed by malolactic fermentations in *barrique,* where the wines complete their aging for 12 to 18 months. The estate's most famous wine, Messorio, is aged in smaller, 112-liter (30-gallon) barrels. A slightly different approach is taken for the Scrio (100% Syrah), parcels of which see microfermentation in *barrique,* a laborious and time-consuming practice that the estate employs to give the wines more oxygen during fermentation. The entry-level Bolgheri Rosso is a blend of 50% Merlot, 30% Cabernet Franc, 15% Sangiovese, and 5% Syrah.

2005 Bolgheri Rosso	89	now–2012
2003 Le Macchiole	90	now–2014
2004 Paleo Rosso	94	2009–2010
2003 Paleo Rosso	92	now–2015
2002 Paleo Rosso	89	now–2017
2004 Scrio	94	2010–2020
2003 Scrio	93	now–2015
2004 Messorio	96	2011–2022
2003 Messorio	93	now–2015
2002 Messorio	90	now–2017

Past Glories Messorio: 2001 (97), 2000 (97); Paleo: 2001 (94), 2000 (90); Scrio: 2001 (95), 2000 (92)

LE MACHIOCHE ★ ★ ★ ★
TUSCANY $60.00–$130.00

The tiny Le Maciocche estate is located just down the road from Biondi Santi's Il Greppo. The relatively high altitude of the vineyards and the traditional approach to winemaking combine to produce classically structured, ethereal wines of notable elegance. Often unimpressive at first, this producer's wines show much better with a few hours of aeration.

2005 Rosso di Montalcino	89	now–2010
2005 Brunello di Montalcino	91	2009–2018
2001 Brunello di Montalcino	91	now–2019
2001 Brunello di Montalcino Riserva	92	2011–2021

LA MASSA ★ ★ ★ ★
TUSCANY $30.00–$79.00

Proprietor Giampaolo Motta is best described as a free-spirited renegade. Motta's wines reflect a passion for Bordeaux, a region he first discovered when he spent time in France as a student. Those years would prove to be formative for the young Motta, who decided to pursue a career in wine upon his return to Italy. Despite being disowned by a family that had expected him to take over a successful leather business, Motta continued to work toward his dream of owning an estate. His early work experience included a stint at nearby Castello dei Rampolla, where he is proud to say he helped plant the vineyard that is the source of that estate's D'Alceo. In 1992 Motta secured the financial backing to buy a property in Panzano. Today La Massa produces two wines. The estate's top bottling, Giorgio Primo, is a blend of Sangiovese, Merlot, and Cabernet Sauvignon. Motta named the wine after his grandfather, the only person who supported his oenological pursuits. The entry-level La Massa is a second selection of barrels not deemed to be of sufficient quality to be used for Giorgio Primo.

2004 La Massa	89	now–2016
2004 Giorgio Primo	93	now–2019

MASTROJANNI ★ ★ ★ ★
TUSCANY $59.00

This estate, founded in 1975, is located toward the southern edge of the Montalcino zone. Mastrojanni favor medium-sized Allier oak casks for their Brunellos. The single-vineyard Schiena d'Asino is particularly notable.

2003 Brunello di Montalcino	89	now–2018
2001 Brunello di Montalcino	91	now–2016
2001 Brunello di Montalcino Vigna Schiena d'Asino	92	2011–2021

MOCALI ★ ★ ★
TUSCANY $21.00–$78.00

These are the first wines I have tasted from this small producer. From its 15 acres of vines the estate makes a range of wines that includes a Rosso, a Brunello, and the single-vineyard Brunello Vigna delle Raunate. Like many estates in Montalcino, Mocali has sought to expand production outside its home base, recently purchasing a small property in the Morellino appellation.

2004 Morellino di Scansano Suberli	88	now
2006 Rosso di Montalcino	87	now–2010
2004 Rosso di Montalcino	87	now
2003 Brunello di Montalcino	89	now–2018
2001 Brunello di Montalcino	91	now–2019

2003 Brunello di Montalcino Vigna delle Raunate	91	2009–2018
2001 Brunello di Montalcino Vigna delle Raunate	91	now–2021
2001 Brunello di Montalcino Riserva	90	now–2018
2001 Brunello di Montalcino Riserva Vigna delle Raunate	91	2009–2019

MONTEPELOSO ★ ★ ★ ★
TUSCANY $35.00–$120.00

Fabio Chiarelotto is the charismatic proprietor of this small estate located in Suvereto, just up the road from Tua Rita. Chiarelotto's emphasis is clearly in the vineyards, where, in addition to the main varieties he produces, he has also planted a few rows of grapes not native to Tuscany, such as Refosco and Schiopettino, which are typically found in Friuli. The Eneo and Nardo are Sangiovese-based wines, while the Gabbro is Cabernet Sauvignon. Vinification facilities are bare-bones, and the winemaking is as stripped down as possible. These are very pure, unadulterated, textbook expressions of Suvereto *terroir*. Readers won't want to miss this producer's terrific 2004s.

2004 Eneo	91	now–2014
2004 Nardo	92	now–2016
2004 Gabbro	93	now–2016

MONTEVERTINE ★ ★ ★ ★/★ ★ ★ ★ ★
TUSCANY $23.00–$90.00

This small estate is located in Radda, one of the cooler microzones in Chianti Classico owing to the relatively high altitude of its vineyards. The late Sergio Manetti was a pioneer in Chianti Classico. He pushed for the elimination of the white grapes that had traditionally been included Chianti Classico with the goal of elevating the wines to a higher level. Manetti's vision led him to make a 100% Sangiovese, but that wine was rejected by the Chianti Classico Consortium as it did not adhere to the definition of the wine that was required at the time. Frustrated by his efforts and already experiencing considerable success with his wines, Manetti left the consortium in 1981. Today Manetti's son Martino continues his father's work with the same dedication and passion. Ironically, today all of the estate's wines would qualify for the Chianti Classico designation but Manetti prefers to stay the more individualistic course his father first charted decades ago. From his tiny cellar Manetti crafts delicate, understated wines that are among the finest in the region. Like all of the top Sangiovese-based wines, Montevertine and Le Pergole Torte can be enjoyable relatively young but reveal their maximum expression only after a minimum of several years of bottle age. Le Pergole Torte in particular has proven to be especially ageworthy. This is a beautiful set of releases from Montevertine.

2004 Pian del Ciampolo	88	now–2012
2002 Montevertine	90	now–2017
2001 Montevertine	93	2009–2019
2003 Le Pergole Torte	92	2009–2019

GIACOMO MORI ★ ★ ★
TUSCANY $18.00–$30.00

I was delighted to discover the wines of Giacomo Mori, a small producer based in San Casciano dei Bagni, an area best known for its natural springs. The estate farms 25 acres of vineyards, and winemaking is overseen by consulting oenologist Alberto Antonini.

2004 Chianti	89	now–2012
2003 Chianti Castelrotto	90	now–2018

MORISFARMS ★★★/★★★★
TUSCANY $18.00–$55.00

Morisfarms, located in the province of Grosseto, is a superb source of wines that deliver much pleasure and style at reasonable prices. Consulting oenologist Attilio Pagli oversees winemaking at this estate, which has vineyards in the Morellino di Scansano appellation as well as the emerging Monteregio di Massa Marittima district to the north.

2005 Vermentino	87	now–2010
2005 Morellino di Scansano	88	now–2010
2004 Morellino di Scansano	89	now
2003 Morellino di Scansano Riserva	90	now–2013
2004 Monteregio di Massa Marittima	89	now–2014
2004 Avvoltore	92	2010–2022
2003 Avvoltore	90	2009–2018

LA MOZZA ★★★/★★★★
TUSCANY $15.00–$36.00

This new estate is owned by New York restaurateurs Lidia Bastianich, Joe Bastianich, and Mario Batali. The entry-level Morellino is often delicious and a great value. The Aragone (40% Sangiovese, 25% Alicante, 25% Syrah, and 10% Carignan) is very typical of the "super-Med" Maremma wines, which incorporate varieties typical of southern France and Spain.

2005 Morellino di Scansano I Perazzi	87	now–2010
2004 Morellino di Scansano I Perazzi	89	now–2010
2004 Aragone	92	2010–2018

SILVIO NARDI ★★★★
★★★★ TUSCANY $51.00–$84.00

Nardi make Brunellos in a rich, concentrated style. Most of the estate's vineyards are in the northwest corner of Montalcino. However, the Manachiara vineyard, which is the source of Nardi's top wine, is located in the southern part of the region. The Brunellos spend 12 months in French oak prior to being racked into larger Slavonian oak casks to finish their aging.

2006 Rosso di Montalcino	89	now–2011
2003 Brunello di Montalcino	91	now–2018
2001 Brunello di Montalcino	90	now–2018
2003 Brunello di Montalcino Manachiara	91	2009–2016
2001 Brunello di Montalcino Manachiara	92	2009–2019

SIRO PACENTI ★★★★★
TUSCANY $30.00–$100.00

In an area where estates are very well marked, the lack of signage leading to Giancarlo Pacenti's estate is striking, but I have a sense that Pacenti likes it that way. Since my last visit a few years ago, Pacenti has completed an extensive overhaul of his facilities. In the past I have found this producer's wines overly concentrated and heavy, but in recent vintages Pacenti seems to have a found a new level of elegance and finesse. These were among the finest wines I tasted from Montalcino, and I can't recommend them highly enough. Pacenti takes a different approach from most other producers in the area in that he does not bottle any single-vineyard wines. He believes that a combination of parcels gives him the most complete Brunellos. This allows him to marry the aromatic qualities of his vineyards in the north with the fruit and concentration from his vineyards in the southern part of the zone. Pacenti is also a fanatic when it comes to quality, employing as many as nine people on two sorting tables during the harvest. His Rosso has been a favorite of mine for years, going back to the days when I could not afford Brunello. Pacenti has long been a leader in the zone when it comes to aging his wines in *barrique,* and these wines show superb integration and balance. Readers looking for the finest in Rosso and Brunello owe it to themselves to check out the wines of Giancarlo Pacenti.

2006 Rosso di Montalcino	90	now–2011
2004 Rosso di Montalcino	90	now–2010
2003 Brunello di Montalcino	93	now–2018
2001 Brunello di Montalcino	95	now–2019

IL PALAZZINO ★ ★ ★/★ ★ ★ ★
TUSCANY $20.00–$40.00

Owners Alessandro and Andrea Sderci fashion unique wines in their tiny cellar in Monti. Il Palazzino is best known for its top bottling, the single-vineyard Grosso Sanese, which is one of the most idiosyncratic wines in the region. Its dark color and full-bodied, concentrated style almost seem to have more in common with Brunello than Chianti Classico. The wines have also proven to age extremely well. Recent bottles of the 1990 Grosso Sanese were still in perfect shape and full of life. These are sturdy wines that will benefit from some aeration prior to serving.

2004 Chianti Classico Argenina	88	now–2016
2004 Chianti Classico La Pieve	90	2009–2019
2004 Chianti Classico Grosso Sanese	91	2009–2019

IL PALAZZONE ★ ★ ★/★ ★ ★ ★
TUSCANY $90.00–$126.00

This small estate located just outside the town of Montalcino is owned by Time-Warner chairman Richard Parsons. The vineyards here are fairly high for the region, which helps give this Brunello a lot of its finesse. The style is decidedly modern in its interpretation.

2003 Brunello di Montalcino	90	now–2015
2001 Brunello di Montalcino	90	now–2019
2001 Brunello di Montalcino Riserva	92	now–2016

PIAGGIA ★ ★ ★/★ ★ ★ ★
TUSCANY $45.00–$52.00

Proprietor Mauro Vanucci makes richly structured wines from his 37 acres in the Carmignano appellation. He favors late harvests, long macerations lasting several weeks, and small French oak barrels for aging. Vanucci's approach to making superripe, concentrated wines yields its best results in balanced growing seasons such as 2004, but in the scorching hot 2003 he may have pushed the envelope too far.

2004 Carmignano Il Sasso	91	now–2016
2004 Poggio de' Colli	88	2009–2019
2003 Carmignano Riserva	87	now–2016

PIANCORNELLO ★ ★ ★/★ ★ ★ ★
TUSCANY $79.00

Oenologist Maurizio Castelli oversees winemaking at this small estate. The wines are made in a supple, accessible style.

2003 Brunello di Montalcino	90	now–2015
2001 Brunello di Montalcino Riserva	91	now–2017
2003 Brunello di Montalcino Piancornello	89	2009–2016

AGOSTINA PIERI ★★★★
TUSCANY $22.00–$49.00

This small producer is located in Castelnuovo dell'Abate, in the southern part of the Brunello zone. The estate works with low yields, and as a result these wines are packed with well-defined flavors in a style that shows excellent concentration and precision without coming across as heavy. Although the wines show some influence of *barrique* aging in their oak tannins, they are exceptionally well balanced.

2006 Rosso di Montalcino	???	now–2011
2004 Rosso di Montalcino	90	now–2010
2003 Brunello di Montalcino	???	2009–2018
2001 Brunello di Montalcino	92	now–2021

PODERE FORTE ★★★/★★★★
TUSCANY $90.00

Podere Forte is located in the Val d'Orcia, south of Siena. The estate's Guardiavigna is a blend of Sangiovese, Cabernet, Merlot, and Petit Verdot, while the Petrucci is 100% Sangiovese. Both wines are aged in French oak barrels.

2003 Petrucci	91	now–2013
2003 Guardiavigna	89	now–2018

PODERE IL CARNASCIALE ★★★★★
TUSCANY $55.00–$255.00

In recent years Il Carnasciale's Caberlot has emerged as one of Italy's most distinctive and highly sought wines. With its cult status and tiny production of roughly 1,500 to 1,800 magnums, it is a wine many people have heard of but few have actually tasted, and prices are understandably high. The history of Il Caberlot dates back to the 1960s, when the agronomist Remigio Bordini discovered a highly unique clone growing in an old vineyard in the Veneto. The clone appeared to be a genetic mutation of Cabernet but also exhibited some qualities considered more typical of Merlot. It was the perfect choice for Wolf and Bettina Rogosky, who were looking for something different and unique to plant on their small Tuscan property. After enduring a series of setbacks, as well as much bureaucratic red tape, the first Caberlot vines were planted in 1985. To bring them good fortune, the Rogoskys buried a bottle of the legendary 1985 Sassicaia below the vineyard. Sadly, Wolf Rogosky passed away in 1996, but the wine his vision helped create lives on. Today the wines are made under the direction of oenologist Peter Schilling and consulting oenologist Vittorio Fiore. Yields per plant are kept quite low, which is facilitated by the Caberlot clone's naturally low vigor. Fermentation lasts about a week, after which the wine is racked into a combination of stainless steel and *barriques* for the malolactic fermentation. The wine then spends 18 months in 100% new medium-toast *barriques* (50% Allier, 50% Vosges) prior to being bottled exclusively in magnum. Fortunately, in some vintages the estate also produces a more accessible second wine, called simply Carnasciale, which is a selection of finished wines from barrel that aren't deemed to be Caberlot-level quality.

2004 Carnasciale	90	now–2018
2004 Il Caberlot	95	2014–2024
2003 Il Caberlot	94	2011–2023

Past Glories Il Caberlot: 2002 (90), 2001 (94), 2000 (93), 1999 (92+), 1997 (94), 1996 (92), 1993 (92), 1988 (90)

PODERE SAN LUIGI ★★★★/★★★★★
TUSCANY $60.00

This small estate located in the province of Livorno burst onto the scene with its first wines in 1995. The Fidenzio, a blend of Cabernet Sauvignon, Cabernet Franc, and Merlot is loaded with personality and is often among the finest wines in Tuscany. Winemaking is overseen by Alberto Antonini, who is justly proud of this bottling.

2003 Fidenzio	93	2009–2019

LA PODERINA ★★★★
TUSCANY $35.00–$125.00

I was very impressed with the richly colored, stylish wines I tasted from this winery located in the Castelnuovo dell'Abate subzone in the southeastern corner of Montalcino. Despite being owned by corporate parent SAI Agricola, the quality at this estate is quite high. Readers should also be on the lookout for the Rosso, which in top vintages is among the best in the region.

2006 Rosso di Montalcino	90	now–2011
2005 Rosso di Montalcino	89	now–2010
2003 Brunello di Montalcino	91	2009–2018
2001 Brunello di Montalcino	92	now–2016
2001 Brunello di Montalcino Riserva Poggio Banale	89	2009–2019

POGGIO AL TESORO ★★★/★★★★
TUSCANY $40.00–$85.00

Poggio al Tesoro is a new winery in Bolgheri co-owned by importer Leonardo LoCascio and the Allegrini family. Winemaking is overseen by consulting oenologist Alberto Antonini. The estate works with densely planted vineyards and low yields to produce deeply flavored wines. In particular, readers who enjoy Cabernet Franc will not want to miss the superb 2004 Dedicato a Walter. These first releases establish Poggio al Tesoro as a property to keep an eye on.

2004 Dedicato a Walter	92	2009–2019
2003 Dedicato a Walter	88	now–2013
2004 Sondraia	90	2011–2019

POGGIO ANTICO ★★★★
TUSCANY $38.00–$160.00

The good-humored, enthusiastic Paola Gloder runs this estate located in the central part of the zone, right outside the town of Montalcino. The vineyards here face mostly south to south-west and are fairly high for the zone, averaging about 450 meters (1,475 feet) above sea level. The Brunellos, which are produced from low yields, are richly colored, weighty wines made in a contemporary style that nevertheless remains faithful to the region.

2006 Rosso di Montalcino	90	now–2011
2004 Rosso di Montalcino	90	now
2006 Brunello di Montalcino Altero	90	now–2016
2001 Brunello di Montalcino Altero	91	now–2019
2006 Brunello di Montalcino	89	now–2016
2001 Brunello di Montalcino	92	2009–2021

| 2001 Brunello di Montalcino Riserva | 92 | 2009–2019 |
| 2000 Brunello di Montalcino Riserva | 91 | now–2020 |

POGGIO ARGENTIERA ★ ★ ★
TUSCANY $19.00–$59.00

This small producer located in Grosseto hasn't always been consistent, but the best wines are worth searching for and offer excellent value. The estate's Finisterre is an interesting blend of Alicante and Syrah that is aged in small French oak barrels.

2005 Morellino di Scansano Bellamarsiglia	88	now–2010
2004 Morellino di Scansano Capatosta	90	now–2014
2003 Morellino di Scansano Capatosta	89	now–2013
2003 Finisterre	89	now–2015

POGGIO DI SOTTO ★ ★ ★ ★/★ ★ ★ ★ ★
TUSCANY $95.00–$155.00

Elisabeth and Piero Palmucci turn out gorgeous Brunellos from their holdings in Castelnuovo dell'Abate. Working with low yields and a stringent selection of only the best fruit at the sorting table, Poggio di Sotto produces wines of rare elegance and subtlety for this part of the zone. The estate pursues a decidedly noninterventionalist approach in the cellar. Only indigenous yeasts are used during vinification, which takes place in a combination of steel and wood vats. The Brunello is aged nearly four years in 30-hectoliter (7,920-gallon) oak casks prior to being bottled with no fining and/or filtration. Poggio di Sotto's 2003 Brunello di Montalcino is a beautiful wine and one of the best Brunellos of the vintage. When all was said and done, in 2003 the estate bottled only 40% of its potential Brunello production and decided against making a Riserva. Readers will also want to consider the estate's 2001 Il Decennale, a wine Palmucci describes as his version of a 2001 Brunello Riserva. Il Decennale, conceived to celebrate the estate's 10th anniversary, is 100% Sangiovese that spent six years in cask prior to being bottled without any fining or filtration. It is a terrific example of Sangiovese from Montalcino.

2003 Brunello di Montalcino	94	now–2021
2001 Brunello di Montalcino	93	2009–2021
2001 Il Decennale	94	2011–2023

POGGIO MANDORLO ★ ★ ★
TUSCANY $90.00

Consulting oenologist Roberto Cipresso makes the wines at this new property, which is located just outside his home base in Montalcino.

| 2004 Poggio Mandorlo | 89 | now–2014 |

IL POGGIONE ★ ★ ★ ★ ★
TUSCANY $28.00–$160.00

Il Poggione is one of Montalcino's historic wineries. The estate, which is owned by the Franceschi family, traces its lineage back more than 100 years. Leopoldo Franceschi was one of the founders of the Brunello producers' consortium, the Consorzio del Vino Brunello di Montalcino, and also served as its first president. Today Il Poggione is run by Franceschi's grandson, also named Leopoldo. Il Poggione is located in Sant'Angelo in Colle, in a part of Montalcino known for its warm yet well-ventilated microclimate. The wines are made by Fabrizio Bindocci, who cut his teeth working alongside Piero Talenti, one of the most famous figures in the world of Montalcino oenology. Although some small concessions are made to modern tastes, the wines remain quite classic in their expression of Sangiovese. I have had the privilege of tasting all of Il Poggione's Brunellos back to 1967. The wines have an extraordinary track record of developing beautifully with age. The estate's Rosso di Montalcino is also worthy of note. Even better, prices have remained very fair considering the quality of what is in the bottle.

2005 Rosso di Montalcino	89	now–2020
2003 Brunello di Montalcino	92	2009–2023
2001 Brunello di Montalcino	93	2011–2023
2001 Brunello di Montalcino Riserva	95	2011–2026

Past Glories Brunello di Montalcino Riserva: 1999 (95), 1997 (93), 1995 (94), 1990 (95), 1985 (93), 1982 (95); Brunello di Montalcino: 1988 (93), 1975 (94), 1973 (92), 1967 (91)

POGGIO SCALETTE ★★★★/★★★★★
TUSCANY $60.00

Poggio Scalette occupies a beautiful spot in the hills of Greve it shares with its neighbor Querciabella. Proprietor Vittorio Fiore is one of Italy's best-known consulting oenologists, so it is no surprise that he and his son Jurij turn out gorgeous wines at their own property. The estate's flagship wine is Il Carboniaone, a 100% Sangiovese made from the prized Lamole clone. The vines in this parcel date back to 1925. Il Carbonaione has an outstanding track record of aging beautifully in bottle and is one of Tuscany's most unique wines.

2003 Il Carbonaione	92	2009–2021

Past Glories Il Carbonaione: 2001 (94), 1999 (94), 1998 (92), 1996 (89), 1993 (91), 1992 (93)

POLIZIANO ★★★/★★★★
TUSCANY $16.00–$55.00

Poliziano is one of the historic properties in Montepulciano. The estate's wines, in particular the single-vineyard Vino Nobile Asinone, have been among my favorites for years.

2005 Rosso di Montepulciano	87	now–2010
2004 Vino Nobile di Montepulciano	89	now–2016
2003 Vino Nobile di Montepulciano Asinone	92	now–2018
2004 Le Stanze di Poliziano	90	now–2018

POMINO ★★★
TUSCANY $34.00–$42.00

Lamberto Frescobaldi is especially passionate about the wines his family produces at its Pomino estate. The cool microclimate and high-altitude vineyards yield aromatic wines that are light to medium in body yet offer notable elegance.

2005 Pomino Benefizio	89	now–2015
2004 Pomino Casafonte	89	2010–2018

LE POTAZZINE ★★★★
TUSCANY $62.00

My recent visit to this estate was quite an experience as Giuseppe Gorelli proceeded to open every wine he has produced at his small property. Le Potazzine's vineyards are located high in the northwestern corner of the zone. Up until a few years ago this location was thought to be too high in altitude to make important Brunellos, but today the trend toward warmer growing seasons has caused the locals to reconsider conventional wisdom. The estate makes very small quantities of Rosso and Brunello, which are aged in casks. From 1997 to 1999 the family leased a vineyard that had been abandoned by the owners. The vines gave abnormally low yields, and the wines from this period, notably the 1997 Brunello, present an exotic, atypical expression of Sangiovese that is hard to describe fully.

2006 Rosso di Montalcino	89	now–2010
2003 Brunello di Montalcino	92	now–2015
2001 Brunello di Montalcino	93	now–2016

Past Glories Brunello di Montalcino: 2000 (90), 1999 (93), 1997 (94)

PRATESI ★ ★ ★
TUSCANY $31.00–$33.00

This small estate is located in the Carmignano appellation. Oenologist Stefano Chioccioli oversees work in the vineyards and cellar. In addition to its Carmignano, Pratesi also makes the delicious IGT Carmione, a Cabernet-Merlot cuvée.

2004 Carmignano	88	now–2014
2004 Carmione	90	2009–2019

LE PUPILLE ★ ★ ★ ★
TUSCANY $25.00–$120.00

It's hard to believe that proprietor Elisabetta Geppetti has over 20 harvests to her credit. Geppetti took over her family's small estate when she was just a teenager and has gradually increased her holdings from the original 15 acres to more than the current 170. Le Pupille, located in the province of Grosseto, makes a range of excellent wines. The Morellinos in particular offer highly pleasurable drinking at reasonable prices. One of the distinguishing features of Le Pupille is the use of Alicante (Grenache) in the wines, a remnant of the period when this part of Tuscany was under Spanish rule. In the early days the estate had a lot of help from oenologist Giacomo Tachis, who helped conceive many of the wines, including the estate's Saffredi, a blend of Cabernet Sauvignon, Merlot, and Alicante. First produced in 1985, Saffredi was among the first wines to incorporate nonindigenous varieties. From 1997 to 1999 the wines were made by Riccardo Cotarella, while today Christian Le Sommer is at the helm.

2005 Morellino di Scansano	88	now–2010
2004 Morellino di Scansano	88	now
2004 Morellino di Scansano Riserva Poggio Valente	92	2009–2019
2003 Morellino di Scansano Riserva Poggio Valente	90	now–2013
2002 Morellino di Scansano Poggio Valente	89	now–2012
2003 Saffredi	91	now–2015
2002 Saffredi	89	now–2012
2004 Sol Alto	90	now–2014
2003 Sol Alto	89	now–2013

QUERCIABELLA ★ ★ ★ ★ ★
TUSCANY $29.00–$101.00

Querciabella is owned by entrepreneur Sebastiano Castiglioni, who acquired his passion for wine from his father, Giuseppe. The property occupies a stupendous position in the hills above Greve in Chianti. The estate pursues biodynamic farming and low yields in its vineyards. Longtime oenologist Guido De Santi oversees a noninterventionalist approach in the cellar. The Querciabella wines represent the purest expression of fruit in a contemporary style that is all about elegance. The wines are approachable when young but also have the capacity to gain complexity with cellaring. In addition to a superb Chianti Classico, the estate makes Palafreno

(Merlot) and its signature red Camartina, which is a blend of 70% Cabernet Sauvignon and 30% Sangiovese. The Batar, a blend of Chardonnay and Pinot Bianco, is one of the few Tuscan whites that has the ability to age and develop complexity in bottle. The biggest change at Querciabella is a renewed focus on Sangiovese in the Chianti Classico along with a diminished use of international varieties. Sangiovese, which was once 80% of the blend, represents 90% or more of the final blend in vintages 2004 and 2005. The fruit is being sourced from two of the estate's best Sangiovese plots, which in the past was used for Camartina and Palafreno. This new interpretation of Chianti Classico means that overall production of Camartina has been reduced by about 40%, while the Palafreno is now 100% Merlot. The estate has also been gradually making acquisitions, the most recent of which is a 35-acre plot in Radda, near Montevertine. The estate's constant search for a higher level of quality exemplifies a level of ambition that I wish were more common in these parts. Readers who haven't tasted the Querciabella wines in a few vintages owe it to themselves to do so. This is a superb set of new releases.

2005 Batar	90	now–2017
2004 Batar	92	now–2019
2005 Chianti Classico	91	now–2017
2004 Chianti Classico	91	now–2017
2004 Camartina	95	2012–2022
2003 Camartina	93	now–2018

Past Glories Camartina: 2001 (93), 2000 (92), 1999 (92), 1997 (93), 1996 (90), 1995 (93)

LA RASINA ✶✶✶
TUSCANY $56.00–$94.00

This small estate is located just north of Montalcino on the road that leads from the town center to Torrenieri. Proprietor Marco Mantengoli fashions an attractive, modern-style Brunello from his 8.5 hectares (21 acres) of vineyards.

2003 Brunello di Montalcino	90	2009–2017
2001 Brunello di Montalcino	89	2009–2018
2003 Brunello di Montalcino Il Divasco	91	2007–2018

ROCCA DI CASTAGNOLI ✶✶✶
TUSCANY $19.00–$35.00

Rocca di Castagnoli is located in Gaiole, in the heart of Chianti Classico. The estate makes a variety of excellent wines, including several single-vineyard Chiantis aged in French oak. The Poggio ai Frati is made from traditional Chianti varieties, while the Capraia includes a little Cabernet Sauvignon.

2004 Chianti Classico	88	now–2012
2003 Chianti Classico Riserva Poggio ai Frati	89	2010–2020
2000 Chianti Classico Riserva Capraia	91	now–2014

ROCCA DI MONTEGROSSI ✶✶✶✶
TUSCANY $25.00–$95.00

Marco Ricasoli produces highly individualistic wines from his small estate located in Gaiole. This is a very strong set of releases, made all the more notable by his success in the challenging 2003 vintage. His Chianti Classico Riserva Marcellino and Geremia (60% Merlot and 40% Cabernet Sauvignon) are notable. The Vin Santo is often a showstopper. Made from 100% Malvasia rather than the traditional blend of Trebbiano and Malvasia, the wine spends six years in small casks of various woods, including cherry and mulberry, prior to being bottled unfiltered.

2004 Chianti Classico	88	now–2010
2003 Chianti Classico Riserva San Marcellino	91	now–2017
2003 Geremia	90	now–2018
1998 Vin Santo	92	now–2017

RODANO ★★★/★★★★
TUSCANY $20.00–$46.00

Rodano is located in Castellina in Chianti. The estate makes a range of excellent to outstanding wines, including the Riserva Viacosa and the IGT Monna Claudia, a French oak–aged blend of Sangiovese and Cabernet Sauvignon.

2003 Chianti Classico	87	now
2001 Chianti Classico Riserva Viacosta	90	now–2017
1999 Monna Claudia	92	2009–2019

RUFFINO ★★★
TUSCANY $18.00–$70.00

There are probably only a handful of names consumers recognize more than Ruffino, one of Tuscany's largest and most historic estates. Ruffino makes a number of wines from a multitude of appellations, most of which are competent at best. The high-end bottlings are characterized by a style that might be best defined as trying to be all things to all people. Ultimately, the wines suffer from a clear lack of direction, which is a shame considering that the estate could do so much more.

2005 Chianti Classico Santedame	87	now
2004 Ruffino Modus	88	now–2018
2003 Chianti Classico Riserva Ruffino Riserva Ducale Oro	90	now–2019
2003 Romitorio di Santedame	91	now–2019

SALCHETO ★★★
TUSCANY $18.00–$55.00

Salcheto is based in Montepulciano. The house's top Vino Nobile is made from a unique clone of Prugnolo Gentile (Sangiovese) and aged in French oak barrels.

2004 Casa al Poggio	87	now–2011
2003 Rosso di Montepulciano	88	now–2010
2003 Vino Nobile di Montepulciano	90	now–2018
2002 Vino Nobile di Montepulciano	89	now–2012
2001 Vino Nobile di Montepulciano Salco Evoluzione	91	now–2019

SALICUTTI ★★★★★
TUSCANY $35.00–$120.00

Salicutti is another of the young estates that has come onto the scene in recent years with very-high-quality wines. The vineyards range from 420 to 480 meters (1,378 to 1,574 feet) above sea level, which helps give the wines freshness. The estate uses only natural products to farm its vineyards, and yields are kept low, at about half the legally allowed maximum. In the cellar, the approach is similarly noninterventional. Only indigenous yeasts are used, and the Brunello is aged for three years in a combination of smaller 5-hectoliter (132-gallon) Allier oak barrels and larger Slavonian oak barrels ranging from 10 to 40 hectoliters (264 to 1,056 gallons). The wines are neither fined nor filtered prior to being bottled.

2004 Rosso di Montalcino	90	now–2010
2003 Brunello di Montalcino	93	now–2018
2001 Brunello di Montalcino	94	2011–2023

SALVIONI ✶ ✶ ✶ ✶ ✶
TUSCANY $59.00–$192.00

Proprietor Giulio Salvioni is a firm believer in treating his wines like people, which means avoiding stress at all costs. Everything is done strictly by hand, including bottling and labeling. The vineyards reach an elevation of 420 meters (1,378 feet) above sea level, which is relatively high for the region. The soils are principally *galestro,* which yields wines with higher acidities that are capable of extended aging. Although all of Salvioni's vineyards are legally registered to produce Brunello, some years he decides to make a few thousand bottles of Rosso from parcels that don't offer the same potential as the best fruit does. Over the years the estate has experimented with new Sangiovese clones and replanted its vineyards to higher densities. Yields are kept low, around half the legally allowed limit. In the cellar the approach is very traditional. Long macerations lasting about 30 days are followed by several years of aging in 20-hectoliter (528-gallon) Slavonian oak casks, which are changed every 10 years. Production is about 12,000 to 15,000 bottles per year. Salvioni's Brunello remains one of the benchmark wines for the region.

2005 Rosso di Montalcino	89	now–2015
2003 Brunello di Montalcino	92	now–2018
2001 Brunello di Montalcino	95	now–2021

SAN FABIANO ✶ ✶ ✶
TUSCANY $13.00–$40.00

San Fabiano is a collection of three smaller estates, all located in the hills outside Arezzo. While the wines aren't the last word in complexity, they more than make up for that in the sheer drinkability and pleasure they provide.

2005 Chianti Putto	87	now–2010
2003 Piocaia	88	now–2015
2000 Armaiolo	90	now–2014

SAN GIUSTO A RENTENNANO ✶ ✶ ✶ ✶ ✶
TUSCANY $23.00–$68.00

What a pleasure it is to taste these new releases from San Giusto a Rentennano. Soft-spoken proprietor Luca Martini di Cigala is one of the humblest producers in Chianti Classico, yet he routinely turns out deeply expressive reference-point wines. The estate's 77 acres of vineyards are planted on two distinct soil types. The first is composed of a sandy, marly mixture rich with rocks that reaches 4 to 5 meters (13 to 16 feet) in depth before reaching a bed of clay. Most of the fruit for the estate's signature wine, Percarlo, comes from this *terroir.* The second soil type is richer in clay and lies on a shallower foundation. Beginning in 2003 the estate has made some important changes in vineyard management, most notably in the Merlot plots that are used for La Ricolma. Martini favors a gradual approach to ripening that allows him to increase hang time and harvest fairly late. By changing the timing of green harvests and leaving more leaf cover, he aims to keep the vineyards as fresh as possible in order to delay the ripening of the typically precocious Merlot. Of course, much of that work went for naught in the torrid 2003 vintage, but in 2004 he produced a wine that captures the essence of variety wedded to an unmistakably Tuscan character. The estate favors small French oak barrels for its top bottlings, Percarlo and La Ricolma, both of which see about 50% new oak. The wines are made with the services of consulting oenologist Attilio Pagli, whose transparent hand and deft touch place him among the country's elite winemakers. Readers who want to explore the finest Tuscany has to offer should make a note to check out this outstanding set of wines from San Giusto a Rentennano. Though not inexpensive, in today's market these wines offer incredible value for the money.

2005 Chianti Classico	88	now–2010
2004 Chianti Classico	89	now–2012
2004 Chianti Classico Riserva Le Baroncole	92	2010–2024
2003 Chianti Classico Riserva Le Baroncole	91	2009–2019
2004 Percarlo	96	2009–2026
2003 Percarlo	93	2010–2020
2004 La Ricolma	95	2011–2024
2003 La Ricolma	94	2009–2019
1999 Vin San Giusto	94	now–2019

ENRICO SANTINI ★ ★ ★ ★
TUSCANY $24.00–$68.00

In just a few years Enrico Santini has emerged as one of Bolgheri's most promising producers. The wines are made with the assistance of consulting oenologist Attilio Pagli and are likely to get even better as these organically farmed vineyards gain age. The Poggio al Moro, a blend of Sangiovese, Cabernet, Syrah, and Merlot is the house's entry-level red, while the Montepergoli (Merlot, Cabernet Sauvignon, Syrah, and Sangiovese) is the top bottling.

2005 Campo alla Casa	88	now
2004 Poggio al Moro	90	now–2016
2003 Montepergoli	91	now–2015

LIVIO SASSETTI—PERTIMALI ★ ★ ★ ★ ★
TUSCANY $42.00–$120.00

Livio Sassetti is without question one of Montalcino's most entertaining characters, seemingly able to converse freely in phrases that would put a professional poet to shame. The estate makes a variety of wines from Pertimali, its home estate located in the famous Montosoli cru, as well as the newly acquired La Querciolina property in nearby Montecucco. Like many estates, Pertimali lost a significant amount of its 2001 production during the April frost that year. The plants channeled all their energy into the remaining fruit, and the wines have turned out beautifully. Sassetti favors cask aging for his Brunellos, although the Riserva sees roughly 15% *barrique*. The 2005 Brunello di Montalcino is another success from this reference-point producer.

2006 Rosso di Montalcino	90	now–2016
2003 Brunello di Montalcino	92	now–2018
2001 Brunello di Montalcino	92	now–2018
2001 Brunello di Montalcino Riserva	94	2009–2021
1999 Brunello di Montalcino Riserva	93	now–2019

VASCO SASSETTI ★ ★ ★
TUSCANY $N/A

Vasco Sassetti is a small, artisanal producer based in Castelnuovo dell'Abate, which lies on the southern boundary of Montalcino. His wines often have a rustic quality and benefit from several hours of air prior to drinking.

2001 Brunello di Montalcino	90	now–2019

SASSOTONDO ★★★/★★★★
TUSCANY $18.00–$50.00

Sassotondo, located in the inner part of Maremma, is a unique property in the region, as it has chosen to emphasize the native Ciliegiolo over more conventional varieties. The vineyards, which are farmed according to biological principles, sit on poor soils of volcanic origin. Winemaking is overseen by consulting oenologist Attilio Pagli.

2005 Rosso Ciliegiolo	87	now–2010
2003 Sangiovese Riserva Franz	89	now–2015
2003 San Lorenzo	90	now–2015

MICHELE SATTA ★★★/★★★★
TUSCANY $N/A

This is a beautiful set of wines from Michele Satta, one of the pioneers in making high-class wines in Maremma. Satta's vineyards are located in and around Bolgheri and Castagneto Carducci. Unlike many of his colleagues, Satta has chosen to emphasize Sangiovese, which he says remains his favorite variety. The Cavaliere is 100% Sangiovese, the Piastraia is equal parts Cabernet, Merlot, Syrah, and Sangiovese, and the Castagni is 40% Cabernet, 40% Syrah, and 20% Teroldego.

2003 Piastraia	92	now–2017
2001 Cavaliere	92	2009–2021
2003 I Castagni	91	now–2015

SCOPETONE ★★★★
TUSCANY $60.00

Under the direction of oenologist Attilio Pagli this estate produces a Brunello of rare elegance from its tiny 1.5 hectares (3.7 acres) of Brunello vineyards.

2001 Brunello di Montalcino	92	now–2019

SELVAPIANA ★★★
TUSCANY $19.00–$34.00

Selvapiana is located in Chianti's Rùfina appellation. The consulting oenologist is Giacomo Tachis. The estate's top bottling, the single-vineyard Bucerchiale, is made from 100% Sangiovese and aged in a combination of small and medium-sized barrels.

2004 Chianti Rùfina	89	now–2015
2003 Chianti Rùfina Riserva Vigneto Bucerchiale	90	now–2017

LA SERENA ★★★
TUSCANY $75.00–$205.00

La Serena makes rich, sumptuous Brunellos. In 2001 the estate seems to have overdone the Riserva, an issue that sometimes plagues producers in Montalcino.

2003 Brunello di Montalcino	91	2009–2018
2001 Brunello di Montalcino	92	now–2019
2001 Brunello di Montalcino Riserva Gemini	87	now–2016

SESTA DI SOPRA ★★★/★★★★
TUSCANY $50.00

Located in Castelnuovo dell'Abate, Sesta di Sopra pursues a traditional approach to making its Brunello, which was one of the standouts of my tastings of the 2001 vintage. The vines are still young, and there is much to look forward to from this producer in future years.

2003 Brunello di Montalcino	92	2009–2016
2001 Brunello di Montalcino	91	2009–2021

SOLARIA ★★★
TUSCANY $69.00–$95.00

Proprietor Patrizia Cencioni makes Brunellos in a very ripe, forward style. Her Brunello 123 is a single-vineyard selection from poorer soils.

2003 Brunello di Montalcino	91	now–2018
2001 Brunello di Montalcino	88	2009–2016
2001 Brunello di Montalcino 123	91	2009–2019

SOLDERA—CASE BASSE ★★★★★
TUSCANY $325.00–$400.00

Gianfranco Soldera is a man with an incredible wine culture. He is one of the most knowledgeable people I have ever met when it comes to the great, traditionally made Barolos and Barbarescos of Piedmont. These wines are among his greatest passions, and clearly his own wines share some attributes with them. Soldera's approach, though, is unique. He fervently believes that supporting the entire ecosystem of the estate is fundamental to ensuring that the vines have the right conditions in which to flourish. The grounds at the Case Basse estate are impeccably maintained and are home to many species of animals as well as a rich array of flowers and plants, including more than 200 varieties of roses, to give just one example. To say that the estate is worth a visit just to walk through the property would be an understatement. Soldera's meticulous attention to detail in the vineyard is legendary, and these are some of the best-maintained, manicured vines I have ever seen. No pesticides or fungicides are employed, and only natural fertilizers are used. Soldera believes that light rather than heat is the critical element in vineyard exposure, so all of his plots are planted facing southwest. Yields are very low, but Soldera won't reveal precisely how low. Once the fruit is in the cellar, fermentation is carried out with natural yeasts in wood vats without the aid of temperature control. The wines then age in Slavonian oak casks for roughly five years prior to being bottled. The estate produces a Brunello from its younger Case Basse vineyard and a Riserva from the older Intistieti vineyard. In a typical vintage there is just one cask produced of each wine. At their best Soldera's Brunellos have a level of aromatic complexity, sweet fruit, and overall balance I can only define as breathtaking. The wines also have a strong track record of ageworthiness. That said, these wines are made in a quirky style that may not appeal to every palate. Relative to most other Brunellos, these are lightly colored wines with an ethereal, almost weightless texture. Some may find the level of volatile acidity to be extreme in some vintages. At their best, Soldera's Brunellos have few peers.

1999 Brunello di Montalcino	88+?	2011–2021
1998 Brunello di Montalcino	92	now–2018
2001 Brunello di Montalcino Riserva	96	2016–2031
2000 Brunello di Montalcino Riserva	93	2010–2025
1999 Brunello di Montalcino Riserva	95	2011–2024
1998 Brunello di Montalcino Riserva	94	2010–2025

LA SPINETTA ★★★
TUSCANY $24.00–$45.00

Giorgio Rivetti spends about as much time in the U.S. these days as he does in Italy, so it is remarkable that he manages to keep so many projects running at the same time. These two new releases are made from Rivetti's Casanova della Spinetta property near Pisa. The wines are predominantly Sangiovese and are aged in 600-liter (159-gallon) barrels, which Rivetti feels are more suitable to Sangiovese than the smaller 225-liter (59-gallon) barrels he uses for his other wines.

2005 Il Nero di Casanova	87	now–2010
2003 Sezzana	90	now–2018

TALENTI ★★★★
TUSCANY $45.00–$85.00

Pierluigi Talenti, one of the icons of Montalcino, purchased this property in 1980. The estate is in Sant'Angelo in Colle, in the southern part of Montalcino. Consulting oenologist Carlo Ferrini is making beautiful wines in a style that is contemporary and classic at the same time. The wines are aged in a combination of medium-sized barrels of various capacities. While both 2001 Brunellos are outstanding, I found the Pian di Conte to have more clarity and precision than the Riserva.

2003 Brunello di Montalcino	91	now–2018
2001 Brunello di Montalcino	93	now–2021
2001 Brunello di Montalcino Riserva Vigne del Paretaio	93	2009–2019

TENIMENTI ANGELINI ★★★
TUSCANY $22.00–$104.00

Tenimenti Angelini oversees estates in Montepulciano, Montalcino, and Chianti Classico with more than 1,000 acres under vine. The top selections from Montepulciano and Montalcino are well worth seeking out.

2003 Vino Nobile di Montepulciano Tre Rose	89	now–2015
2003 Vino Nobile di Montepulciano Simposio	91	now–2017
2003 Brunello di Montalcino	88	2009–2015
2003 Brunello di Montalcino Val di Suga	88	2009–2015
2001 Brunello di Montalcino Val di Suga	90	2009–2019
2001 Brunello di Montalcino Riserva Vigna Spuntali	91	2009–2019

TENUTA BELGUARDO ★★★
TUSCANY $22.00–$64.00

Tenuta Belguardo is the Maremma property of the Mazzei family, who are best known for the wines they produce at their Fonterutoli estate in Chianti. The vineyards are located near Grosseto, and winemaking is overseen by consulting oenologist Carlo Ferrini, who interprets this *terroir* in a set of richly colored, concentrated wines. The estate's top wine is Tenuta Belguardo, a blend of 70% Cabernet Sauvignon and 30% Sangiovese. A more moderate use of oak might allow for a greater expression of varietal character to come through.

2004 Morellino di Scansano	86	now–2010
2004 Serrata	86	now–2012
2004 Tenuta Belguardo	92	now–2016
2003 Tenuta Belguardo	90	now–2015

TENUTA DEI SETTE CIELI ★★★/★★★★
TUSCANY $N/A

Tenuta dei Sette Cieli is undoubtedly one of my most pleasant recent discoveries. The estate's high-density vineyards are planted at roughly 400 meters (1,312 feet) above sea level, very much the exception rather than the rule in Bolgheri. The higher altitude of the vineyards results in wider swings between daytime and evening temperatures, yielding wines of notable finesse. The terrain also contains a higher amount of *galestro,* the clay-and-stone formation that is more typical of Chianti Classico and parts of Montalcino than Bolgheri. The wines are made under the direction of talented consulting oenologist Attilio Pagli. Although this is only the second vintage for Tenuta dei Sette Cieli, the wines clearly have the potential to turn into something special. This will be a fascinating property to follow over the next several years. Currently the estate does not have a U.S. importer, but hopefully that will change soon.

2005 Yantra	89	now–2010
2004 Indaco	91	now–2016

TENUTA DELL'ORNELLAIA ★★★★★
TUSCANY $28.00–$280.00

Tenuta dell'Ornellaia is one of Italy's blue-chip properties. The gorgeous, sprawling estate is located in Bolgheri in Tuscany's Maremma. General manager-agronomist Leonardo Raspini oversees work in the vineyards, while oenologist Axel Heinz makes the wines. Ornellaia is a Bordeaux-inspired blend consisting principally of Cabernet Sauvignon, Cabernet Franc, and Merlot. In 2003 a small percentage of Petit Verdot was introduced. The use of several varieties gives the winemaking team the luxury of being able to tailor the exact proportion of the blend to the specific strengths of a given vintage. After harvest the varieties are vinified separately. Fermentation and maceration lasts between 25 and 30 days, after which the wines are moved into French oak barrels (70% new), where they age for 12 months. The wines are then racked and assembled into the final blend, which spends an additional six months in barrel prior to being bottled. The Masseto (100% Merlot), on the other hand, has proven to be a wine of greater singularity. Its unique, unmistakable personality always comes through. The Masseto vineyard measures roughly 17 acres. Set on a gently sloping hill, the vineyard is divided into three sections that contain different clay-based soil types. The structure of Masseto comes from the central portion of the vineyard (Masseto Centrale), where the terrain is most compact. Toward the upper part of the hillside (Masseto Alto) the soils contain a higher percentage of rocks and thus yield wines that are more aromatic. The lower stretch of the vineyard, known as Masseto Junior, is also the most recent to be planted. There is also a small amount of fruit that comes from the Vigna Vecchia plot, which is the source of the Merlot that is used for Ornellaia. Each parcel is harvested and vinified separately. Fermentation and maceration typically last around 25 days, give or take, depending on the quality of the fruit, after which the wines are moved into 100% new French oak barrels for the malolactic fermentations. The wines spend 12 months in oak prior to being assembled, after which the final blend spends an additional 12 months in oak prior to being bottled. The Serre Nuove is a second selection of lots that don't make it into Ornellaia, while Le Volte is a blend of purchased Sangiovese that is blended with estate-grown Merlot and Cabernet Sauvignon. 2004 is a benchmark vintage for the estate. The 2005s are smaller-scaled wines that should mature relatively early, while the 2006s are off the charts for their ripe fruit, tannin, and overall structure.

2005 Le Volte	90	now–2011
2004 Le Volte	87	now–2010
2004 Le Serre Nuove	91	now–2014
2004 Ornellaia	95	2011–2019
2003 Ornellaia	93	now–2018

2002 Ornellaia	92	now–2017
2004 Masseto	97	2011–2024
2003 Masseto	93	now–2017
2002 Masseto	90	now–2017

Past Glories Masseto: 2001 (97), 2000 (91), 1999 (95), 1998 (93), 1997 (94); Ornellaia: 2001 (94), 2000 (92), 1999 (95), 1998 (91), 1997 (93)

TENUTA DI BISERNO   * * *
TUSCANY $28.00–$80.00

Tenuta di Biserno is the new project being headed by brothers Lodovico and Piero Antinori. Winemaking is overseen by Helena Lindberg with the consulting services of Michel Rolland. The Insoglio del Cinghiale is a blend of Syrah, Cabernet Franc, Merlot, and Petit Verdot; the Coronato is a blend of Cabernet Sauvignon, Cabernet Franc, Merlot, and Petit Verdot; and Il Pino di Biserno is Cabernet Franc, Cabernet Sauvignon, Merlot, and Petit Verdot. These are beautiful wines from an estate that is on the rise.

2006 Insoglio del Cinghiale	89	now–2012
2005 Insoglio del Cinghiale	89	now–2010
2005 Bolgheri Coronato	90	now–2015
2005 Il Pino di Biserno	92	20⁻0–2025

TENUTA DI CAPEZZANA   * * *
TUSCANY $10.00–$45.00

Capezzana is located in the historic Carmignano appellation, where wine has been produced since Etruscan times. The Contini Bonacossi family can trace its winemaking lineage at the estate to an astonishing 12 centuries ago. The property encompasses more than 1,600 acres, of which approximately 250 are under vine. The microclimate is warm, but evening breezes from the nearby Apennine mountains temper the daytime heat.

2005 Conti Contini Sangiovese	87	now
2004 Barco Reale di Carmignano	90	now–2014
2003 Villa di Capezzana Carmignano	89	now–2014
2000 Ghiaie della Furba	90	now–2014
1999 Vin Santo Riserva di Carmignano	91	2007–2019

TENUTA DI CASTIGLIONI   * * *
TUSCANY $27.00–$84.00

The Frescobaldi family's Tenuta di Castiglioni is located in the Chianti Colli Fiorentini appellation just outside Florence. The entry-level Tenuta di Castiglioni is a blend of Cabernet Sauvignon and Sangiovese, while the top-of-the-line Giramonte is a cuvée of Merlot and Sangiovese.

| 2005 Tenuta di Castiglioni | 89 | now–2010 |
| 2004 Giramonte | 90 | 2009–2019 |

TENUTA DI GHIZZANO   * * *
TUSCANY $20.00–$60.00

The Pesciolini family farms 45 acres of vineyards at its estate located in the hills outside Pisa. The Ghizzano is a blend of 80% Sangiovese and 20% Merlot, while the top-of-the-line Nambrot is 70% Cabernet, 20% Merlot, and 10% Petit Verdot. Consulting oenologist Carlo Ferrini oversees winemaking.

2005 Il Ghizzano	87	now
2004 Nambrot	90	now–2014
2003 Nambrot	89	now–2013

TENUTA DI SESTA ★ ★ ★
TUSCANY $70.00

This estate, located in the southern reaches of Montalcino, is one of the region's historic properties. The regular bottling is often understated while the Riserva tends toward a more powerful and modern expression of Sangiovese.

2003 Brunello di Montalcino	92	now–2018
2001 Brunello di Montalcino Riserva	89	now–2016

TENUTA DI TRINORO ★ ★ ★ ★/★ ★ ★ ★ ★
TUSCANY $33.00–$180.00

Nestled among the soft, undulating hills of the Val d'Orcia, in the province of Siena, Tenuta di Trinoro gives new meaning to the expression "in the middle of nowhere." Andrea Franchetti is the man behind the singular wines of this small estate. Though somewhat of an eccentric, Franchetti is down to earth and unassuming, qualities made all the more remarkable given his aristocratic lineage. Franchetti's career has encompassed many different activities, from importing fine wines into the U.S. to his latest adventure, producing some of the most exciting wines to come out of Sicily's emerging Mount Etna appellation. The vines at Trinoro are planted at altitudes ranging from 500 to 700 meters (1,640 to 2,297 feet) using a high density of approximately 9,000 plants per hectare (22,230 plants per acre), which was very unusual for Tuscany when the first plots were planted in 1992. The soils are quite poor, which, along with the tight spacing of the vines, stresses the plants and encourages them to develop stronger, deeper root systems. Franchetti classifies the soils at Trinoro into two major subdivisions, using the St.-Émilion terms *côtes* and *graves* to differentiate between the soils composed primarily of clay and limestone on the upper ridges and the more gravelly terrain found in the lower portions of the vineyards. Yields are extremely low and often come in under 1 ton of fruit per acre, depending on the vintage. Franchetti remains deeply influenced by the wines of Bordeaux, and many of his cuttings come from some of that region's top estates, such as Vieux Châteaux Certan, which is the source of his Cabernet Franc. Franchetti favors late harvests that push ripeness to the extreme. This is clearly a high-stakes approach to winemaking, as the likelihood of rain and other inclement conditions increases as the harvest season moves into the fall. Franchetti typically picks his Merlot in early October, while the Cabernet Sauvignon and Petit Verdot are usually picked toward the end of the month, although in some years, such as 2004, the harvest can stretch into November. Because of the extended growing season at Trinoro, the quality of the harvested fruit varies quite a bit from year to year, as does the final blend of the wine. In addition to Tenuta di Trinoro there is a second wine, Le Cupole di Trinoro, which is made from the barrels that aren't deemed to be of the exacting quality Franchetti requires for his Grand Vin and which is priced much more accessibly. Although the wines are as eccentric as Franchetti himself, there can be no doubt that Tenuta di Trinoro produces some of the most exciting wines being made anywhere.

2004 Le Cupole di Trinoro	91	now–2014
2005 Tenuta di Trinoro	95	2011–2025
2004 Tenuta di Trinoro	93	2014–2024

Past Glories Tenuta di Trinoro: 2003 (90), 2001 (96), 2000 (95), 1999 (90), 1998 (95), 1997 (93)

TENUTA LA FUGA ★★★/★★★★
TUSCANY $57.00–$68.00

Tenuta La Fuga is one of the many estates owned by the Folonari family. Although the Riserva Due Sorelle is made only in top vintages, it isn't necessarily a better wine than the estate's non-Riserva Brunello bottling.

2003 Brunello di Montalcino	89	now–2015
2001 Brunello di Montalcino	92	2009–2019
2001 Brunello di Montalcino Riserva Le Due Sorelle	88	now–2016

TENUTA OLIVETO ★★★
TUSCANY $70.00–$119.00

This young winery, located in Castelnuovo dell'Abate, released its first Brunello with the 1997 vintage. The wines are made by consulting oenologist Roberto Cipresso. Like so many young estates in the region, Tenuta Oliveto has yet to find a unique voice. As the recently planted vines acquire age, it will be interesting to see what develops at this winery.

2003 Brunello di Montalcino	90	now–2013
2001 Brunello di Montalcino	89	now–2016
2001 Brunello di Montalcino Riserva	90	now–2017

TENUTA SAN GUIDO ★★★★
TUSCANY $45.00–$193.00

When Marchese Mario Incisa della Rocchetta planted Cabernet Sauvignon on his Maremma estate, he could have hardly known that his decision would inspire a new generation of similar wines and revitalize an old, sleepy coastal area that had been marshland up until a few decades prior. Incisa loved the wines of Bordeaux and wanted to make a similar wine for his own consumption. Over the years the wine proved to age quite well, and the first commercially available vintage was released in 1968 to great acclaim. Since then Sassicaia has gone on to become one of the world's icon wines and the archetype for Italian wines made from international varieties and aged in small French oak barrels. The legendary 1985, last tasted two years ago, is still youthful and primary. Today the wines are made by Incisa's son Nicolò and his stepson Sebastiano Rosa. The house style favors a delicate, finessed expression of Maremma as opposed to the heavy, superconcentrated wines that have become the fashion among so many of the area's other producers.

2004 Guidalberto	91	now–2016
2003 Guidalberto	88	now–2013
2004 Bolgheri Sassicaia	93	2010–2022
2003 Bolgheri Sassicaia	93	now–2023

TENUTA SETTE PONTI ★★★/★★★★
TUSCANY $40.00–$104.00

The Moretti family has been making wine since the mid-1950s at Tenuta Sette Ponti, located just outside Arezzo. Under the leadership of Antonio Moretti the estate started to concentrate on bottling its own wines in 1997. The Poggio al Lupo is a blend of predominantly Cabernet Sauvignon with Alicante and Petit Verdot, made at the winery's Maremma property of the same name. The Crognolo is mostly Sangiovese with a little Merlot, while the flagship, Oreno, is a cuvée of Merlot, Cabernet Sauvignon, and Sangiovese. Sette Ponti is still a very young estate. Its wines reflect more of the highly skilled winemaking of consulting oenologist Carlo Ferrini than an expression of *terroir* or variety, but hopefully the latter will come with time.

2004 Crognolo	88	now–2016
2004 Oreno	90	2009–2019
2003 Oreno	90	2009–2019
2004 Poggio al Lupo	88	now–2015

TERRABIANCA ∗ ∗ ∗
TUSCANY $39.00–$72.00

Terrabianca has a number of new releases on the market, but their quality is inconsistent. I found many of the 2003s to have awkward, slightly green notes, which is very much out of character for the vintage. As a whole the 2004s are much more successful. Readers are best off focusing on the estate's top bottlings. Piano del Cipresso is Sangiovese, Villa Il Tesoro is Merlot, and the flagships, Campaccio and Campaccio Riserva, are Sangiovese and Cabernet Sauvignon.

2004 Piano del Cipresso	91	2009–2019
2003 Piano del Cipresso	91	now–2017
2004 Villa il Tesoro	90	now–2022
2003 Villa il Tesoro	90	now–2018
2004 Campaccio	91	2009–2021
2003 Campaccio	90	now–2017
2003 Campaccio Selezione Riserva	88	now–2018
2001 Campaccio Selezione Riserva	91	now–2017

TOSCOLO ∗ ∗ ∗
TUSCANY $18.00–$25.00

Toscolo is is an excellent source for value-priced Chianti Classico. The wines are made by oenologist Franco Bernabei and are selected by importer Neil Empson.

2004 Chianti Classico	88	now–2012
2003 Chianti Classico	88	now–2013
2003 Chianti Classico Riserva	90	now–2014
2001 Chianti Classico Riserva	89	now–2011

TUA RITA ∗ ∗ ∗ ∗ ∗
TUSCANY $22.00–$275.00

Tua Rita is located in Suvereto, one of the warmer microclimates in Tuscany. Co-owner Stefano Frascolla and consulting oenologist Stefano Chioccioli have turned out a beautiful set of 2004s that I tasted with them at the property. The wines were every bit as impressive when I retasted them again in New York. I found the 2003s to be more variable as the estate was forced to deal with the challenges of a scorching hot vintage that caused many plants to shut down. Vintage 2004 offers greater delineation of aromatics and flavors, along with finer tannins and much better overall balance. The estate works with high-density vineyards and low yields per plant. Frascolla aims to find the right balance for each plant, so yields may be higher on one plant and lower on another. Once the fruit is harvested, it is put through a meticulous sorting process, which I witnessed as the last of the Merlot was being brought in on the day of my visit. Fermentations are carried out with selected yeasts in stainless steel, although in recent vintages the new Syrah as well as parts of the Merlot for Redigaffi have been fermented in wood uprights. Frascolla and Chioccioli favor long fermentations lasting several weeks. The wines undergo malolactic fermentation in *barrique,* where they also age prior to undergoing a slight egg-white clarification but no filtration prior to being bottled. In most vintages the percentage of new oak varies from 60% to 70% for the Giusti di Notri (60% Cabernet

Sauvignon, 20% Merlot, 15% Cabernet Franc, and 5% Petit Verdot) to 100% for the Redigaffi (100% Merlot). The estate's newest wine, the superb Syrah, sees 100% new oak in the first year and then another 100% new oak during the second year of aging.

2004 Lodano Bianco	87	now–2010
2005 Rosso di Notri	88	now–2010
2004 Perlato del Bosco	91	now–2014
2003 Perlato del Bosco	87	now–2011
2004 Giusto di Notri	93	now–2016
2003 Giusto di Notri	91	now–2013
2004 Syrah	95	now–2016
2003 Syrah	93	now–2013
2004 Redigaffi	93	2009–2016
2003 Redigaffi	90	now–2013

UCCELLIERA ★★★★/★★★★★
TUSCANY $26.00–$100.00

Andrea Cortonesi honed his craft during the years he spent working at the nearby Ciacci and Mastrojanni wineries. After many years of hard work, he purchased a small property from Ciacci and began making his own Brunellos from holdings in and around Castelnuovo dell'Abate in the southern part of the region. Cortonesi favors richly concentrated wines. Like many producers, he performs a small *salasso* (*saignée*) during the vinification of his Brunellos in which a portion of the juice is run off the skins, allowing for a greater skin-to-wine ratio that gives the wines their characteristic structure and weight. The runoff juice is then added to the Rosso to give it greater complexity. The wines are made in a big, powerful style.

2006 Rosso di Montalcino	90	now–2011
2004 Rosso di Montalcino	89	now
2005 Rapace	91	now–2017
2003 Rapace	88	now–2015
2005 Brunello di Montalcino	92	2009–2016
2001 Brunello di Montalcino	92	now–2018
2001 Brunello di Montalcino Riserva	93	2009–2019
1999 Brunello di Montalcino Riserva	92	now–2016

VALDICAVA ★★★★★
TUSCANY $110.00–$200.00

Proprietor Vincenzo Abruzzese produces some of the most unique wines in the region from his 20 hectares (49 acres) in the Montosoli zone just north of the town of Montalcino. Made in a richly concentrated, opulent style, these Brunellos represent an interpretation that may not be for everyone. That said, I have always found the wines to be enjoyable, especially after a few years of cellaring allow the baby fat to fall off the wines. Valdicava's Brunello is made from some of the lowest yields in the region, typically averaging a measly 25 quintals per hectare (2,225 pounds per acre). In the late 1980s the estate's vineyards were replanted to high densities with Sangiovese clones rich in color. According to oenologist Attilio Pagli, low yields and the new Sangiovese clones combine to give the wines their deep color and concentration. Abruzzese prefers Slavonian oak for the aging of his Brunellos, which achieve a rare combination of power and elegance. The estate's Rosso is often among the very finest versions in the zone.

2006 Rosso di Montalcino	90	now–2011
2003 Brunello di Montalcino	91	2009–2019

| 2001 Brunello di Montalcino | 93 | now–2021 |
| 2001 Brunello di Montalcino Riserva Madonna del Piano | 96 | now–2018 |

VALDIPIATTA ✶ ✶ ✶ ✶
TUSCANY $30.00–$50.00

This small, family-run estate makes beautiful Vino Nobiles from its 30 hectares (12 acres) of vineyards in Montepulciano. The Vino Nobile is aged in cask, while the single-vineyard Vigna d'Alfiero (100% old-vine Prugnolo Gentile) is aged in small French oak barrels.

| 2003 Vino Nobile di Montepulciano | 90 | now–2013 |
| 2001 Vino Nobile di Montepulciano Vigna d'Alfiero | 92 | now–2021 |

LA VELONA ✶ ✶ ✶/✶ ✶ ✶ ✶
TUSCANY $N/A

La Velona is located in Castelnuovo dell'Abate. This southern part of Montalcino benefits from a Mediterranean climate that gives the wines an added dimension of richness. The estate's Brunello is fermented in wood vats. The wine is aged for one year in small French oak barrels before being racked back into the larger oak vats to finish its aging.

| 2001 Brunello di Montalcino | 92 | now–2018 |

I VERONI ✶ ✶ ✶
TUSCANY $11.00–$22.00

These are the first wines I have tasted from this small estate located in Pontassieve, just outside Florence. The wines are fairly traditional, with just a small influence of international varieties and French oak used to give the wines a little additional roundness.

| 2004 Chianti Rùfina | 87 | now–2012 |
| 2003 Chianti Rùfina Riserva | 90 | now–2015 |

VIGNAMAGGIO ✶ ✶ ✶/✶ ✶ ✶ ✶
TUSCANY $23.00–$65.00

Vignamaggio is located in Greve in Chianti. The Chianti Classico is aged in medium-sized casks, while the Riserva Castello di Monna Lisa is aged in small French oak barrels and includes about 10% Cabernet Sauvignon and Merlot. The estate's Vignamaggio is 100% Cabernet Franc aged in French oak. It is a very Tuscan interpretation of Cabernet Franc.

2004 Chianti Classico	88	now–2010
2001 Chianti Classico Riserva Castello di Monna Lisa	89	2009–2019
2003 Vignamaggio	92	now–2018

VILLA CAFAGGIO ✶ ✶ ✶/✶ ✶ ✶ ✶
TUSCANY $24.00–$70.00

Consulting oenologist Stefano Chioccioli oversees the winemaking at Villa Cafaggio, which is located in Panzano, one of the Chianti Classico towns. In addition to its Chiantis, the estate makes San Martino (100% Sangiovese) and Cortaccio (100% Cabernet Sauvignon), both of which see 100% new French oak.

2005 Chianti Classico	88	now–2010
2004 Chianti Classico Riserva	90	2009–2019
2003 San Martino	89	2010–2020
2003 Cortaccio	89	2009–2019

VITICCIO ✸✸✸
TUSCANY $19.00–$45.00

Proprietor Alessandro Landini runs this small estate, which is located in Greve in Chianti. Viticcio's top wine is Prunaio, a selection of the estate's best Sangiovese that is aged in French oak. The Chianti Riserva Lucius is made to appeal to the American palate, whatever that means. It incorporates international varieties and is also aged in French oak, but I prefer the less obvious and more elegant straight Riserva.

2005 Chianti Classico	87	now–2010
2004 Chianti Classico Riserva Lucius	88	now–2019
2004 Chianti Classico Riserva	89	now–2021
2004 Prunaio	91	2010–2022
2004 Monile	88	2009–2019

[the best of
northern italy

[the ratings]

NORTHERN ITALY'S BEST WINES

✶ ✶ ✶ ✶ ✶ (OUTSTANDING)

Bussola (Amarone Classico TB)
Bussola (Amarone Classico TB
    Vigneto Alto)
Bussola (Recioto della Valpolicella
    Classico TB)
Dal Forno (Amarone)
Maculan (Acininobili)
Maculan (Crosara)
Maculan (Madoro)
Marion (Amarone)
Miani (Sauvignon)
Miani (Tocai Friulano Buri)

Miani (Calvari)
Miani (Merlot Buri)
Miani (Merlot Filip)
Moschioni (Rosso Reâl)
Moschioni (Schiopettino)
Niedrist (Lagrein Berger Gei)
Quintarelli (Amarone Riserva)
Quintarelli (Alzero)
Quintarelli (Recioto della Valpolicella)
Quintarelli (Amabile del Cerè)
St. Magdalena (Lagrein
    Riserva Taber)

✶ ✶ ✶ ✶ / ✶ ✶ ✶ ✶ ✶ (EXCELLENT/OUTSTANDING)

Bellavista (Gran Cuvée Pas Opéré)
Borgo del Tiglio (Rosso della Centa)
Bussola (Amarone Classico BG)

Dal Forno (Valpolicella)
Damijan (Ribolla Gialla)
Foradori (Granato)

Lis Neris (Tal Lùc)
Maculan (Torcolato)
Maculan (Fratta)
Marion (Cabernet Sauvignon)
Miani (Ribolla Gialla)
Moschioni (Rosso Celtico)
Quintarelli (Amarone)
Radikon (Oslavje)

Le Salette (Recioto Pergole Vece)
Tentuta Sant'Antonio (Amarone Campo
dei Gigli)
Vie di Romans (Voos dai Ciamps)
Villa Russiz (Sauvignon de La Tour)
Vodopivec (Vitovska Solo MM4)
Zenato (Amarone Classico Riserva
Sergio Zenato)

★ ★ ★ ★ (EXCELLENT)

Allegrini (Amarone Classico)
Allegrini (La Grola)
Allegrini (Palazzo della Torre)
Allegrini (Recioto della Valpolicella
Giovanni Allegrini)
Bastianich (Calabrone)
Bastianich (Vespa Bianco)
Bellavista (Gran Cuvée Rosé)
Bellavista (Gran Cuvée Brut)
Bellavista (Gran Cuvée Saten)
Borgo del Tiglio (Chardonnay)
Borgo del Tiglio (Collio)
Borgo del Tiglio (Ronco della Chiesa)
Borgo del Tiglio (Studio di Bianco)
Borgo del Tiglio (Tocai Friulano)
Bussola (L'Errante)
Bussola (Recioto della Valpolicella Classico)
Bussola (Valpolicella Classico
Superiore TB)
Ca' del Bosco (Cuvée Annamaria Clementi)
Cantina di Terlano (Gewürztraminer
Lunare)
Cantina di Terlano (Lagrein Porphyr)
Cantina di Terlano (Nova Domus)
Cantina di Terlano (Pinot Bianco Vorberg)
Cantina di Terlano (Pinot Grigio)
Cantina di Terlano (Pinot Nero Montigl)
Cantina di Terlano (Sauvignon Quarz)
Cantina di Terlano (Sauvignon Winkl)
La Castellada (Bianco della Castellada)
La Castellada (Rosso della Castellada)
Corte Sant'Alda (Amarone)
Corte Sant'Alda (Recioto della Valpolicella)
Damijan (Kaplja)
Damijan (Rosso Prelit)
Di Poli (Iugum)
Dorigo (Montsclapade)
Dorigo (Tazzelenghe di Buttri)
Ferrari (Giulio Ferrari Riserva del
Fondatore)
Gottardi (Blauburgunder Mazzon)

Gravner (Breg)
Gravner (Ribolla Gialla)
J. Hofstätter (Gewürztraminer Kolbenhof)
J. Hofstätter (Lagrein Steinraffler)
J. Hofstätter (Pinot Nero Barthenau
Vigna S. Urbano)
J. Hofstätter (Pinot Nero Riserva Mazon)
Jermann (Capo Martino in Ruttaris)
Jermann (Red Angel)
Jermann (Vintage Tunina)
Kante (Chardonnay)
Kante (Malvasia)
Kante (Sauvignon)
Köfererhof (Gewürztraminer)
Köfererhof (Müller-Thurgau)
Lis Neris (Confini)
Lis Neris (Lis Neris)
Marion (Passito Bianco)
Marion (Teroldego)
Meroi (Chardonnay)
Meroi (Dominin)
Meroi (Merlot Ros di Buri)
Meroi (Tocai Friulano)
Miani (Chardonnay)
Miani (Tocai Friulano Filip)
Moschioni (Pignolo)
Moschioni (Refosco dal Peduncolo Rosso)
Nusserhof (Lagrein Riserva)
Nusserhof (Tyroldego)
Pieropan (Recioto di Soave Le Colombare)
Pieropan (Soave Classico La Rocca)
Quintarelli (Rosso del Bepi)
Radikon (Ribolla Gialla)
Roccolo Grassi (Amarone)
Roccolo Grassi (Recioto della Valpolicella)
Roccolo Grassi (Recioto di Soave Vigneto
La Broia)
Roccolo Grassi (Soave Superiore Vigneto
La Broia)
Le Salette (Amarone Classico La Marega)
Le Salette (Amarone Pergole Vece)

Le Salette (Valpolicella Ca' Carnocchio)
St. Magdalena (Cabernet Riserva Mumelter)
St. Magdalena (Kellerei Gries Lagrein
 Grieser Riserva)
Schiopetto (Pinot Bianco)
Schiopetto (Sauvignon)
Schiopetto (Tocai Friulano)
Scubla (Rosso Scuro)
Scubla (Sauvignon)
Scubla (Verduzzo Friulano Cràtis)
Speri (Amarone Classico Sant'Urbano)
Speri (Recioto della Valpolicella Classico
 La Roggia)
Stroblhof (Blauburgunder Riserva)
Tenuta San Leonardo (San Leonardo)
Tenuta Sant'Antonio (Amarone Selezione
 Antonio Castegnedi)

Toros (Chardonnay)
Toros (Merlot)
Toros (Pinot Bianco)
Toros (Sauvignon)
Vie di Romans (Chardonnay Vie
 di Romans)
Vie di Romans (Flors di Uis)
Vie di Romans (Malvasia Istriana
 Dis Cumeris)
Villa Russiz (Chardonnay Grafin de
 La Tour)
Villa Russiz (Merlot Graf de La Tour)
Vodopivec (Vitovska)
Zenato (Amarone)
Zenato (Valpolicella Superiore Ripassa)
Zidarich (Malvasia)
Zidarich (Prulke)

* * * / * * * * (GOOD/EXCELLENT)

Abbazia di Novacella (Kerner Praepositus)
Abbazia di Novacella (Lagrein
 Riserva Praepositus)
Allegrini (Villa Giona)
Ca' del Bosco (Maurizio Zanella)
Ca' del Bosco (NV Brut)
La Castellada (Ribolla Gialla)
Corte Sant'Alda (Soave Vigne
 di Mezzane)
Di Poli (Sauvignon Voglar)
Dorigo (Pignolo di Buttrio)
Dorigo (Refosco dal Peduncolo Rosso)
Foradori (Teroldego Rotaliano)
Jermann (Pignacolusse)
Jermann (Were Dreams)
Kante (Vitovska)
Köfererhof (Kerner)
Lis Neris (Lis)

Maculan (Dindarello)
Pieropan (Soave Classico)
Pieropan (Soave Classico Superiore
 Calvarino)
Quintarelli (Valpolicella)
Radikon (Merlot)
Radikon (Oslavje)
Roccolo Grassi (Valpolicella Superiore)
Tenuta Sant'Antonio (Capitel del Monte)
Tenuta Sant'Antonio (Valpolicella
 Superiore Ripasso Monti Garbi)
Vie di Romans (Chardonnay
 Ciampagnis Vieris)
Vie di Romans (Pinot Grigio Dessimis)
Vie di Romans (Sauvignon Piere)
Vie di Romans (Sauvignon Vieris)
Villa Russiz (Pinot Grigio)
Zidarich (Vitovska)

[tasting commentaries]

ABBAZIA DI NOVACELLA   * * *
ALTO ADIGE $32.00–$43.00

Abbazia di Novacella is located in the Valle Isarco, the most northerly viticultural region in Italy. The estate is a great source of value-priced whites. The entry-level wines are aged in stainless steel and bottled with plastic corks, so they are best consumed young. In particular, the wines made from indigenous varieties are well worth seeking out. These wines beautifully express the qualities of their respective varieties and the unique Valle Isarco *terroir*. The Praepositus range encompasses the top selections. Unfortunately, from this group of whites I was able to taste only the Kerner. The red Praepositus wines have never been fully convincing. There are among the heaviest, most overly concentrated wines being made in Alto Adige.

| 2006 Kerner Praepositus | 90 | now |
| 2003 Lagrein Riserva Praepositus | 89 | now–2012 |

ALLEGRINI   ★ ★ ★ ★
VENETO $19.00–$70.00

Allegrini produces a wide range of consistently outstanding wines, many of which offer terrific value as well. The Palazzo della Torre (70% Corvina, 25% Rondinella, and 5% Sangiovese) has long been one of my favorite *ripasso*-style wines. Allegrini employs a unique variation of the *ripasso* technique for their Palazzo della Torre. The traditional method calls for the wine to undergo a second fermentation on the skins that are left over from the vinification of the Amarone. The estate believes that this method leads to oxidized wines. Instead Allegrini dries a portion of the grapes (around 30%) and ferments them separately in the same style as an Amarone, then adds that wine to the larger portion of the wine, which is fermented in the conventional manner. The La Grola (Corvina, Rondinella, Syrah, and Sangiovese) is made from superripe fruit harvested from a modern, densely planted vineyard. It too is a superb value, while the 2004 Villa Giona (Cabernet Sauvignon, Merlot, and Syrah) presents a decidedly more international expression. Other highlights include the Amarone and Recioto.

2004 Palazzo della Torre	90	now–2010
2004 La Grola	90	now–2014
2004 Villa Giona	90	now–2016
2003 Amarone Classico	92	now–2013
2003 Recioto della Valpolicella Giovanni Allegrini	92	now–2016

BASTIANICH   ★ ★ ★/★ ★ ★
FRIULI $32.00–$60.00

New York restaurateurs Joe Bastianich, Lidia Bastianich, and Mario Batali own this property, which is located in Friuli's Colli Orientali appellation, a region known more for its reds than its whites. The winery releases two Tocai selections, a regular bottling made from purchased fruit and their Tocai Plus, which is made from estate-grown fruit but only in vintages that allow for a late harvest. The range also includes Vespa Bianco (Chardonnay and Sauvignon with a small percentage of dried Picolit) and Calabrone, a bold red made from Merlot, Refosco, Cabernet Franc, and Pignolo, some of which is left to dry, Amarone-style, prior to being fermented.

2004 Vespa Blanco	91	now–2010
2003 Calabrone	90	2010–2017
2000 Calabrone	92	now–2017

BELLAVISTA   ★ ★ ★ ★
LOMBARDY $62.00–$69.00

Oenologist Mattia Vezzola and Bellavista set the standard in Franciacorta, Italy's most important zone for the production of high-quality *méthode champenoise* wines. This is a superb set of releases that is sure to find many fans.

2002 Gran Cuvée Brut	90	now–2014
NV Gran Cuvée Satèn	92	now–2014
2002 Gran Cuvée Rosé	92	now–2012
2001 Gran Cuvée Pas Opéré	92	2009–2021
1999 Gran Cuvée Pas Opéré	93	2009–2019

BORGO DEL TIGLIO　★ ★ ★ ★ ★
FRIULI $32.00–$112.00

Proprietor Nicola Manferrari makes some of the region's most elegant wines at his small estate in the Collio. Manferrari is part of the movement that sought to improve quality in the region by focusing on high-quality vineyard practices beginning in the early 1980s. He and his contemporaries wanted to make riper wines, which also required a shift away from the prevailing Schiopetto-influenced school of thought and a look toward Burgundy rather than Germany as a source of inspiration. In the cellar Manferrari is quite content to let the wines express the qualities of the vintage, so there are no hard-and-fast rules when it comes to malolactic fermentation for his whites, among other topics, although all the wines are aged in French oak. The top white is Studio di Bianco, a blend of Tocai, Riesling, and Sauvignon, but readers shouldn't ignore the superb Rosso della Centa, which is 100% old-vine Merlot. This is a beautiful set of wines from Nicola Manferrari and Borgo del Tiglio.

2005 Tocai Friulano	90	now–2010
2005 Collio	91	now–2012
2005 Chardonnay	92	now–2012
2005 Studio di Bianco	92	now–2012
2004 Ronco della Chiesa	90	now–2011
2001 Rosso della Centa	93	now–2016

BUSSOLA　★ ★ ★ ★/★ ★ ★ ★ ★
VENETO $40.00–$150.00

Tommaso Bussola's wines have received a good deal of critical acclaim over the last few years, and with good reason. The estate produces two lines. In theory the BG wines are more traditional in spirit, while the TB wines are meant to be more modern. In reality the main difference comes down to vineyard selection, as the estate's best fruit is reserved for the TB range. In addition to the typical wines of the region, Bussola also make L'Errante, a Merlot, Cabernet Franc, and Cabernet Sauvignon blend made in a style similar to Amarone and aged in 100% new oak. I confess to having a preference for Bussola's Amarones and Reciotos, which are among the finest being made in the region. Readers owe it to themselves to check these wines out.

2003 Valpolicella Classico Superiore TB	90	now–2013
2003 L'Errante	91	2009–2018
2002 Amarone Classico BG	93	now–2012
2001 Amarone Classico TB	94	now–2015
2000 Amarone Classico TB Vigneto Alto	94	now–2015
2005 Recioto della Valpolicella Classico	90	now–2018
2003 Recioto della Valpolicella Classico TB	95	now–2023

CA' DEL BOSCO　★ ★ ★
LOMBARDY $110.00

Ca' del Bosco is one of Franciacorta's most important estates. Proprietor Maurizio Zanella makes a wide range of sleek, internationally styled wines, but his strong suit remains the *méthode champenoise* wines for which Franciacorta is so well known. The NV Brut is a reliable bottling, while the top-of-the-line Anna Maria Clementi offers more richness as well as complexity. The Maurizio Zanella is a Bordeaux-inspired blend of Cabernet Sauvignon, Cabernet Franc, and Merlot aged in new French oak.

NV Brut	88	now–2010
1999 Cuvée Annamaria Clementi	91	now–2017
2001 Maurizio Zanella	90	now–2013

CANTINA DI TERLANO ★ ★ ★ ★ ★
ALTO ADIGE $18.00–$55.00

Cantina di Terlano is one of Italy's top estates, all the more remarkable considering it is a co-operative. The entry-level bottlings have been among my favorite house wines for many years. Fermented and aged in stainless steel, they offer much varietal character at reasonable prices. They are also a great introduction for readers who want to learn more about the unique wines of Alto Adige. In addition, the estate produces a set of single-vineyard whites and reds that are reference-point wines for the region. The single-vineyard wines typically spend longer on their lees and are aged in partly or wholly in casks. The top-of-the-line selections (in fatter bottles) see a percentage of smaller barrels. The Sauvignon Quarz, Gewürztraminer Lunare, and Nova Domus (Pinot Blanc, Chardonnay, and Sauvignon Blanc) in particular represent some of the most intensely flavored, unique, and ageworthy whites to come out of the region. Among the reds, the mineral-driven Lagrein Porphyr is especially notable.

2006 Pinot Grigio	90	now–2010
2005 Pinot Bianco Vorberg	90	now–2016
2004 Pinot Nero Montigl	91	now–2014
2006 Sauvignon Winkl	91	now–2016
2005 Sauvignon Quarz	92	now–2016
2005 Gewürztraminer Lunare	92	now–2016
2004 Nova Domus	91	now–2016
2004 Lagrein Porphyr	92	2010–2020

LA CASTELLADA ★ ★ ★ ★
FRIULI $65.00–$115.00

La Castellada is located in the hills of Oslavia, just outside Gorizia. Working from a tiny, cramped cellar, the outspoken, passionate Niccolò Bensa crafts artisan wines loaded with personality. His Bianco della Castellada (Pinot Grigio, Chardonnay, and Sauvignon) is often among the region's top wines. The whites, which see partial maceration on the skins, are made in a style that may not appeal to every palate, but readers looking to discover a unique expression of Collio *terroir* owe it to themselves to check out this estate. The estate favors French oak barrels for aging, with the exception of the Ribolla, which is aged in medium-size casks. Bensa prefers to release his wines, the Rosso (Merlot and Cabernet Sauvignon) in particular, later than most of his colleagues do, so these are current releases.

2004 Tocai Friulano	91	now–2014
2004 Bianco della Castellada	91	now–2014
2002 Bianco della Castellada	91	now–2012
2003 Ribolla Gialla	90	now–2011
2002 Ribolla Gialla	91	now–2012
2000 Rosso della Castellada	91	2009–2016
1999 Rosso della Castellada	92	now–2017

CORTE SANT'ALDA ★ ★ ★
VENETO $75.00–$100.00

This small property is located in the town of Mezzane. Proprietor Marinella Camerani's wines can be somewhat inconsistent, but when she gets things right these can be beautiful wines made in an understated style.

2005 Soave Vigne di Mezzane	89	2007–2012
2000 Amarone	91	now–2010
2003 Recioto della Valpolicella	90	2010–2020

DAL FORNO ★ ★ ★ ★ ★
VENETO $145.00–$485.00

Romano Dal Forno is humble and down to earth yet extremely passionate. Just a few minutes with Dal Forno is enough to understand his unwavering, some might say obsessive, pursuit of quality. I have never met a producer with such a maniacal approach to cleanliness in the cellar. Nothing is wasted here. The same aesthetic applies to Dal Forno's work in the vineyards. His newest plot is planted with an extremely dense 12,800 vines per hectare (31,616 vines per acre) and can only be described as a work of surgical precision. He uses roughly 60% to 70% Corvina, 10% to 15% Croatina, 10% to 15% Rondinella, and a small amount of Oseleta for the Valpolicella and Amarone. The fruit from the estate's younger vines goes into the Valpolicella, while Amarone is made from vineyards that range from 10 to 30 years of age. Beginning with the 2002 vintage, Dal Forno's Valpolicella is made from 100% dried fruit, whereas in previous vintages the wine was made only partially with dried fruit.

| 2002 Valpolicella | 94 | 2010–2017 |
| 2001 Amarone | 97 | 2011–2021 |

DAMIJAN ★ ★ ★ ★
FRIULI $45.00

Blood, sweat, and tears. That is the phrase that comes to mind when I think of Damijan Podversic. Damijan (who goes by his first name) is a young, humble producer endowed with an outsize passion for his land as well as an unparalleled work ethic. He has overcome family struggles and a host of other significant odds to piece together what are now ten splendidly positioned hectares (about 25 acres), mostly in the Monte Calvario subzone of the Collio. In doing so he has single-handedly brought renewed attention to this site, which had once been under vine but fell into neglect in more recent times because of the difficulties in farming the steep terrain. Despite having achieved significant critical success with his 1999s and 2000s, Damijan was convinced he could make even better wines. In 2001, with great personal conviction and the encouragement of his mentor, Josko Gravner, Damijan changed course and began to produce whites macerated on the skins, gradually increasing the maceration time with each successive vintage. Damijan's philosophy centers on hillside vineyards, dense crop planting, natural farming, and low yields to produce the best fruit possible. The cellar consists of a small rented space outfitted with just the bare essentials. The approach is decidedly non-interventionalist. The 2004s were fermented in conical oak vats without temperature control or selected yeasts. Macerations lasted up to 60 days. The wines were aged in Slavonian oak casks for 23 months and were bottled without fining or filtration. Readers should note that the whites can be cloudy when compared to more conventionally made wines. This lack of clarity should not be taken as a defect; in this case it is the sign of wines that are pure, unmanipulated expressions of fruit. Like all whites macerated on the skins, these wines should be served at cellar temperature in large glasses. Damijan's signature wine is his Ribolla Gialla, but the Kaplja (Chardonnay, Tocai Friulano, and Malvasia Istriana) and the Prelit Rosso (Merlot and Cabernet Sauvignon) also merit consideration.

2004 Kaplja	92	now–2012
2004 Ribolla Gialla	94	2009–2012
2004 Rosso Prelit	92	2009–2014

DI POLI ★★★/★★★★
ALTO ADIGE $N/A

Peter Di Poli is one of the most knowledgeable as well as outspoken producers I have ever met. Di Poli's vast wine culture is informed by frequent trips to the world's top wine-producing regions. His most representative wine is the Sauvignon Voglar, easily one of Italy's finest. It is produced from vines at 600 meters (1,968 feet) of altitude, which allow for the long and gradual maturation Di Poli favors. The wine does not undergo malolactic fermentation and is aged exclusively in cask. With age it has proven to acquire notable complexity. This year Di Poli's top red, Iugum (Cabernet Sauvignon and Merlot), is also not to be missed.

2005 Sauvignon Voglar	89	now–2015
2004 Iugum	92	now–2014

DORIGO ★★★/★★★★
FRIULI $38.00–$82.00

Dorigo is located in Buttrio, in the province of Udine. The estate produces a variety of wines, although it is most famous for its reds. Today Pignolo has become a trendy variety to produce, but it was Dorigo who rescued this once nearly forgotten grape from obscurity years ago. The estate's Bordeaux-inspired Montsclapade (Cabernet Sauvignon and Merlot aged in French oak) is also often among the region's top wines.

2001 Tazzelenghe di Buttrio	91	now–2013
2001 Montsclapade	91	now–2016
2003 Refosco dal Peduncolo Rosso	90	now–2013
2003 Pignolo di Buttrio	90	2009–2015

FERRARI ★★★★
TRENTINO $94.00

It is amazing to consider that this venerable house based in Trento has produced wines for more than a century. Giulio Ferrari was an innovator in bringing Chardonnay and French production methods to Trento. In addition to the top-of-the-line Riserva del Fondatore (100% Chardonnay) the nonvintage Brut is worth seeking out.

NV Brut	89	new–2010
1997 Giulio Ferrari Riserva del Fondatore	92	now–2017

FORADORI ★★★★
TRENTINO $23.00–$60.00

The highway that leads from Verona to Bolzano, with its dramatic views of the Dolomites, is one of Italy's most picturesque roads. Just outside Trento, Elisabetta Foradori makes reference-point wines from the indigenous Teroldego Rotaliano. Granato, her top bottling, is a selection of the estate's top fruit.

2005 Teroldego Rotaliano	88	now–2011
2004 Granato	94	now–2014
2003 Granato	93	now–2013

GOTTARDI ★★★★
TRENTINO $45.00

Mazzon is considered by many to be one of Italy's top spots for Pinot Noir. Gottardi makes lovely, refined wine that captures the essence of this microclimate.

2004 Blauburgunder Mazzon	92	now–2014

ROCCOLO GRASSI ✶✶✶✶
VENETO $24.00–$100.00

Marco Sartori is the young, ambitious proprietor at Roccolo Grassi. Unlike many of his colleagues, Sartori leaves the fruit for his Amarone to dry for a shorter time, as he believes this approach allows him to achieve concentration in the vineyard while allowing the wines to remain fresh in the bottle. The Soave and Valpolicella are made from the estate's younger plants, while the oldest vines are used for the Amarone and the Reciotos. Sartori prefers to age his wines predominantly in French oak. This is a beautiful set of wines from one of Veneto's most promising young producers.

2005 Soave Superiore Vigneto La Broia	90	now
2004 Valpolicella Superiore	89	now–2012
2003 Amarone	91	now–2013
2003 Recioto di Soave Vigneto La Broia	92	now–2018
2003 Recioto della Valpolicella	91	now–2018

GRAVNER ✶✶✶✶
FRIULI $110.00

Josko Gravner continues to be a large presence in the region by pushing the envelope with his wines and influencing the younger generation of producers. In the 1980s his adoption of stainless steel and *barriques* was widely emulated, as was his move to long maceration times on the skins for his whites in the late 1990s. In 2001 Gravner released his first wines fermented in amphora. These wines are the result of the many trips Gravner made to the Caucasus mountains in the republic of Georgia, which he first visited in his quest to learn more about the ancient origins of wine. All work in the vineyards and cellar is done in strict accordance with lunar phases. The wines are fermented in amphoras using only natural yeasts; they are then left on the skins for about seven months prior to being racked into oak casks for aging. The wines are bottled without fining or filtration. Several producers have told me recently that they are convinced about the amphora as a fermentation vessel and plan to make wines in a similar style. I am not convinced, at least not yet. Gravner's 2001s are clearly transitional wines, and while his 2002s are more successful, a longer track record is essential before any informed opinion can be reached. Readers who want to explore this producer's wines might want to start with the Breg, a blend of predominantly international varieties (Sauvignon, Chardonnay, Pinot Grigio, and Riesling Italico) that most palates are likely to find both more accessible as well as more familiar in terms of its aromatic and flavor profile. Gravner's whites typically feature amber-toned colors and can be a little cloudy (less of an issue with the current amphora wines). These are not flaws; rather, they are the inherent characteristics of the wines themselves. Lastly, Gravner's whites behave like red wines. They will be even more expressive a day after opening, so readers may want to open the wines well in advance of serving them. Decanting is not recommended, however, as these wines are extremely delicate and often don't respond well to movement.

2002 Breg	92	now–2012
2001 Breg	90	now–2011
2002 Ribolla Gialla	90	2009–2014
2001 Ribolla Gialla	88	now–2011

J. HOFSTÄTTER ✶✶✶
ALTO ADIGE $38.00–$82.00

Proprietor Martin Foradori Hofstätter makes a wide range of wines from his vineyards, which are spread out among several of Alto Adige's subzones. Hofstätter is among the most ardent ambassadors for his region and is capable of talking for hours about his wines and Alto Adige, which he clearly adores. The estate's top bottlings are all worth seeking out. If there is one criticism to be made, it is that the quality of the entry-level wines could be more consistent.

2005 Gewürztraminer Kolbenhof	91	now–2015
2003 Pinot Nero Riserva Mazon	90	now–2015
2001 Pinot Nero Barthenau Vigna S. Urbano	91	now–2016
2000 Lagrein Steinraffler	90	now–2010

JERMANN ★ ★ ★ ★
FRIULI $36.00–$97.00

Silvio Jermann was among the early leaders in the move toward high-quality wines in Friuli. His Vintage Tunina, a field blend of late-harvested fruit, was a trailblazing wine in the 1980s even if today it is not always as outstanding as it used to be. Jermann has finally finished construction of what can only be described as a massive, cavernous cellar in Ruttars, the source of the fruit for his Capo Martino and Pignolo. The estate makes a set of entry-level varietal wines as well as its top bottlings, most of which are blends. The flagship Vintage Tunina is a cuvée of late-harvested Sauvignon, Chardonnay, Ribolla Gialla, Malvasia Istriana, and Picolit, while the oak-aged Capo Martino is a richer, more full-bodied wine made from Tocai Friuliano, Pinot Bianco, Ribolla, Malvasia, and Picolit. The greater presence of native varieties gives Capo Martino a slightly more Friulian personality. Jermann's Were Dreams is mostly Chardonnay, Red Angel is Pinot Noir, and Pignacolusse is Pignolo.

2005 Vintage Tunina	88	now–2010
2005 Were Dreams	89	now–2010
2004 Capo Martino in Ruttaris	91	now–2012
2005 Red Angel	90	now–2011
2003 Pignacolusse	89	2009–2018

KANTE ★ ★ ★/★ ★ ★
FRIULI $N/A

Edi Kante makes highly singular wines of extraordinary personality from his vineyards located in the Carso mountains above Trieste. These deceptively medium-bodied wines often express more about this unique mineral-rich *terroir* than they do varietal character.

2004 Vitovska	89	now–2012
2004 Malvasia	91	now–2012
2004 Sauvignon	91	now–2012
2004 Chardonnay	92	now–2012

KÖFERERHOF ★ ★ ★ ★
ALTO ADIGE $22.00–$28.00

I was delighted to discover the wines of Köfererhof during a trip to the region last year. The estate is located in the Valle Isarco. Up until a few years ago Köfererhof sold its fruit to the nearby Abbazia di Novacella. The estate manages just under 6 hectares (15 acres) of vineyards, all of which are planted to high densities. Most of the wines are fermented and aged in stainless steel, although a small portion of the Sylvaner and Pinot Grigio is aged in midsized casks. These are richly structured, concentrated wines packed with personality. They also offer outstanding quality for the money.

2005 Gewürztraminer Valle Isarco	92	now
2006 Müller-Thurgau	91	now

| 2006 Kerner | 90 | now |
| 2006 Gewürztraminer | 92 | now–2011 |

LIS NERIS ★★★/★★★★
FRIULI $30.00–$35.00

Lis Neris is located in the small town of San Lorenzo, which straddles the Collio and Isonzo appellations. Proprietor Alvaro Pecorari makes elegant, refined wines from his holdings, which are located around the winery itself. He favors 500-liter (132-gallon) French oak barrels for his single-vineyard whites and the top-of-the-line cuvées, which help give the wines their characteristic roundness. As is common in Friuli, the top wines are blends. Lis is Pinot Grigio, Sauvignon, and Chardonnay; Confini is Gewürztraminer, Pinot Grigio, and Riesling; Lis Neris is Merlot and Cabernet Sauvignon; and the sweet dessert wine Tal Lùc is air-dried Verduzzo and Riesling.

2005 Confini	90	now–2010
2004 Lis	90	now–2010
2003 Lis Neris	90	2009–2015
2004 Tal Lùc	94	now–2014

MACULAN ★★★★★
VENETO $20.00–$98.00

From top to bottom the most impressive lineup I tasted from Veneto was the wines of Fausto Maculan. Readers will find no shortage of compelling wines at all price points. Maculan remains best known for his sweet wines, but readers will also want to check out some of his table wines from the superb 2004 vintage. Quite honestly, I was not prepared for the stunning quality of his Bordeaux-inspired high-end reds. The Crosara is Merlot, while the Fratta is Cabernet Sauvignon and Merlot. The Dindarello (Moscato Fior d'Arancio) is the most accessible of the sweet wines. The Torcolato and Acininobili are made from 85% Vespaiola, Garganega, and Tocai. Maculan's Madoro is a Recioto-style wine made from dried Cabernet Sauvignon and Marzemino.

2004 Crosara	95	now–2019
2004 Fratta	93	2009–2016
2006 Dindarello	90	now
2004 Torcolato	93	now
2003 Acininobili	96	now–2017
2004 Madoro	96	now–2019

MARION ★★★★★
VENETO $36.00–$75.00

What a joy it is to taste these new releases from Marion, a relative newcomer to the scene. Proprietor Stefano Campedelli, along with Celestino Gaspari (who cut his teeth working with Giuseppe Quintarelli), produces sumptuous, richly textured wines that are sure to find many admirers. The estate's approach is rigorously rooted to an expression of *terroir* as well as a search for the best clones possible, many of which come from the vineyards of other high-quality producers rather than nurseries such as the Teroldego cuttings that come from Elisabetta Foradori. Readers need to make sure the wines of Marion are on their radar screens.

2002 Teroldego	90	now–2012
2001 Cabernet Sauvignon	93	now–2017
2003 Amarone	93	2009–2015

2001 Amarone	95	2009–2016
2001 Passito Bianco	90	now–2011

MEROI ★ ★ ★/★ ★ ★ ★
FRIULI $44.00–$149.00

I suppose it is no surprise I first ran into Paolo Meroi at Miani, since he and Enzo Pontoni have a lifelong friendship. Pontoni has also been behind the estate's rise in recent years as Meroi has adopted an intense, quality-minded focus that comes through in the wines. The top wine is the Merlot-based Dominin, which is made in tiny quantities. The Merlot Ros di Buri is a second selection of fruit and finished wine.

2006 Tocai Friulano	90	now–2010
2006 Chardonnay	90	now–2010
2005 Merlot Ros di Buri	91	now–2012
2003 Dominin	92	now–2018

MIANI ★ ★ ★ ★ ★
FRIULI $89.00–$250.00

It took me several years to get an appointment at Miani. Proprietor Enzo Pontoni literally lives in his vineyards, stopping home only for lunch and dinner. Pontoni represents the finest of the artisanal approach to winemaking, and his meticulous, some would say fanatical, devotion to his old-vine plots is legendary. Once the wines are in the cellar, a strict barrel selection takes place prior to bottling, meaning that the estate releases a total of roughly 8,000 bottles. Pontoni's 2006 whites have come together nicely since I first tasted them in barrel in December 2006. Readers fortunate enough to find this producer's superb 2004 whites should not hesitate to get them since they are terrific, although his 2005s, from a much weaker vintage, are less satisfying. Pontoni's reds are equally breathtaking, as his 2003s and 2004s attest. The Calvari is Refosco, the Merlot Buri is from vineyards in Buttrio, and the Merlot Filip is from vineyards in Rosazzo. The only problem will be finding them, as quantities are minuscule. Pontoni told me that as he has gotten older he has moved away from the massive style that characterized some of his earlier wines (like the legendary 1997 Calvari) toward a more finessed, elegant approach. I can't think of too many wines I would rather have on my dinner table than those of Enzo Pontoni and Miani. These are among the finest wines being made anywhere. Those who think Tocai Friulano isn't capable of producing world-class wines need to taste Miani's 2006s.

2006 Tocai Friulano Filip	92	now–2012
2006 Tocai Friulano Buri	94	now–2014
2006 Sauvignon	94	now–2014
2006 Ribolla Gialla	93	now–2014
2006 Chardonnay	91	now–2014
2004 Merlot Filip	94	now–2018
2004 Merlot Buri	96	2009–2019
2003 Calvari	96	now–2018

MOSCHIONI ★ ★ ★ ★ ★
FRIULI $50.00–$100.00

Michele Moschioni's tiny estate is located in Cividale. An afternoon spent in his cellar is a fascinating education in the purity of expression that Friuli's indigenous red varieties are capable of achieving in the hands of a serious, passionate producer. Moschioni credits Romano Dal Forno as an early inspiration for his wines. He is also very close to Gravner, Damijan, and Zidarich, all small artisan producers who craft handmade, natural wines. Most of the wines are monovarietal with the exception of the Rosso Celtico (Cabernet Sauvignon and Merlot) and Rosso Reâl (Tazzelenghe, Cabernet Sauvignon, and Merlot). Moschioni favors late harvests, which can stretch into mid-October or early November. Because fruit often struggles to ripen in this northerly microclimate, in some vintages Moschioni performs a slight drying or *appassimento* on a portion of his grapes, a technique that is felt most in the Schiopettino. Moschioni likes fat wines, and these are powerful, intense offerings with dry extract levels that are off the charts. The wines are fermented using only natural yeasts. For his top bottlings—Pignolo, Schiopettino, and Rosso Reâl—Moschioni uses open-top wood fermentors without temperature control. The wines all do malolactic fermentation in French oak (Allier and Tronçais, roughly 80% new), where they age for about 2½ years. The sulfur dioxide levels are minuscule, and the wines see no fining or filtration prior to being bottled in accordance with the lunar phases. In short, these wines are among the most natural, unmanipulated wines readers will encounter from anywhere in the world. Consumers who want to understand the potential of indigenous varietals like Pignolo and Schiopettino owe it to themselves to check out the stunning wines of Michele Moschioni.

2004 Refosco dal Peduncolo Rosso	91	2009–2019
2004 Rosso Celtico	93	now–2014
2004 Rosso Reâl	94	now–2014
2004 Schiopettino	95	now–2018
2004 Pignolo	92	2009–2019

NIEDRIST ★ ★ ★ ★
ALTO ADIGE $34.00

Ignaz Niedrist is a small producer based outside Bolzano. Niedrist makes one of my favorite Lagreins, the Berger Gei, which in most vintages is a special wine well worth seeking out.

2005 Lagrein Berger Gei	93	now–2015
2004 Lagrein Berger Gei	92	now–2012

NUSSERHOF ★ ★ ★ ★
ALTO ADIGE $27.00–$32.00

The Nusserhof wines were a delightful discovery. The estate, with its 2.5 hectares (6 acres) of vines, is tiny even by Italian standards. These are wonderful, quirky wines made in a big, powerful style loaded with personality. They require some air to open, after which they provide much pleasure.

2004 Lagrein Riserva	90	now–2014
2004 Tyroldego	91	now–2014

PIEROPAN ★ ★ ★ ★
VENETO $16.00–$49.00

Pieropan makes benchmark wines for the appellation from their pristine cellars located in the heart of Soave. While I generally prefer Soave on the younger side, Pieropan's wines have proven to age gracefully. The Soave Classico is a reliable bottling especially in its price range. The Soave Classico Superiore Calvarino (70% Garganega and 30% Trebbiano) and the Soave Classico Superiore La Rocca (100% Garganega aged in oak) are among the most exciting wines being made in the region. Pieropan also excels with dessert wines.

2006 Soave Classico	89	now
2005 Soave Classico Superiore Calvarino	89	now
2005 Soave Classico Superiore La Rocca	90	2007–2011
2003 Recioto di Soave Le Colombare	90	2007–2011

QUINTARELLI ✶✶✶✶✶
VENETO $N/A

One of my regrets is not having spent time with Giuseppe Quintarelli when he was in his prime. His 1983 Recioto remains one of the greatest wines I have ever tasted. Quintarelli releases his wines when he feels they are ready, and the top bottlings are produced only when the wines are of sufficient quality, as is the case with the Amarone. In vintages where Quintarelli feels the wine does not merit the Amarone designation, it is declassified and sold as Rosso del Bepi. Today the estate is run by Quintarelli's numerous children and grandchildren. It's not too hard to observe what can only be called a lack of direction, not to mention a cavalier attitude that is a clear sign of an estate that finds it easier to coast on its reputation rather than continue to strive toward excellence. Though many of the current releases are outstanding, the future appears much less certain. However, the best wines are phenomenal and are likely to remain objects of desire among the world's best-heeled collectors. Pricing is astronomical even at the cellar door. Highlights among these recent releases include the 1997 Alzero (mostly Cabernet Franc), the 1995 Amarone Riserva, the 1995 Recioto, and the 1990 sweet white Amabile del Cerè.

1999 Valpolicella	89	now–2011
1999 Rosso del Bepi	92	now–2014
1998 Amarone	93	now–2013
1997 Amarone	94	now–2012
1995 Amarone Riserva	97	now–2030
1997 Alzero	97	now–2017
1995 Recioto della Valpolicella	97	now–2025
1990 Amabile del Cerè	97	now–2018

RADIKON ✶✶✶/✶✶✶✶
FRIULI $45.00–$140.00

Stanko Radikon's property is located is the hills of Oslavia, right in the heart of the Collio. Radikon is an intensely passionate, driven man who pushes the envelope as far as he can. Beginning with the 2002 vintage his wines are made with no added sulfur dioxide whatsoever, a practice virtually unheard of in today's world and a choice most modern-day oenologists would consider suicide. The wines are aged in medium-sized casks for about three years and are bottled without fining or filtration. When I drink these wines at home, I always open them several hours before drinking them and often find that they improve significantly into the second day. The estate's Oslavje (Chardonnay, Pinot Grigio, and Sauvignon) is generally the more accessible of the whites. In some vintages Oslavje Riserva is produced. This cuvée substitutes Tocai for Pinot Grigio in the blend. The Ribolla has greater structure that allows it to pair well with robust foods. Radikon also makes small quantities of a Tocai he calls Jakot. Like all whites macerated on the skins, these wines should be served at cellar temperature or slightly above, but not chilled. The wines often show amber colors, which may come as a surprise to readers encountering them for the first time. The richness of color—and sometimes cloudiness—should not be interpreted negatively; rather, these are signs of wines that have been made in the purest, most unmanipulated way possible.

2002 Oslavje	89	now–2010
2001 Oslavje	93	now–2011
2002 Ribolla Gialla	90	now–2012
2001 Ribolla Gialla	92	now–2010
1998 Merlot	89	now–2013

LE SALETTE ★ ★ ★ ★
VENETO $45.00–$127.00

The Scamperle family runs the small Le Salette estate in Fumane, right in the heart of the classic Valpolicella zone. The Amarone Classico La Marega is aged in a combination of large casks and smaller French oak barrels while the Amarone Pergole Vece is a selection of the estate's best fruit and is aged for 36 months in French oak.

2003 Valpolicella Ca' Carnocchio	90	now–2011
2003 Amarone Classico La Marega	91	now–2013
2001 Amarone Pergole Vece	92	now–2016
2000 Amarone Pergole Vece	90	now–2010
2004 Recioto Pergole Vece	93	2009–2016
2003 Recioto Pergole Vece	93	now–2017

ST. MAGDALENA ★ ★ ★/★ ★ ★ ★
ALTO ADIGE $29.00–$36.00

The Cantina Produttori Bolzano is a large cooperative that was born in 2001, when the St. Magdalena and Kellerei Gries wineries joined forces. The wines are still labeled under the two separate labels, which is how I have listed them here. Oenologist Stephan Filippi oversees the estate's large production. The highlights among current releases are the top reds, especially the Lagrein Taber, which is a reference-point wine for the zone. If I could have only one Lagrein, it would without question be St. Magdalena's Lagrein Riserva Taber.

2005 Cabernet Riserva Mumelter	91	now–2015
2005 Lagrein Riserva Taber	93	now–2015
2004 Lagrein Riserva Taber	93	now–2014
2005 Kellerei Gries Lagrein Grieser Riserva	90	now–2010

SCHIOPETTO ★ ★ ★/★ ★ ★ ★
FRIULI $37.00

Mario Schiopetto was an early visionary in making high-quality wines in Friuli. Deeply influenced by his travels in France and especially Germany, he adapted much of what he learned to making wines in Friuli, most importantly the use of stainless steel to make crisp, fresh whites. Today the winery is run by Schiopetto's three children, Carlo, Giorgio, and Maria Angela. The estate is located in Capriva, one of the cooler microclimates in Friuli, and therefore particularly favorable to the cultivation of Sauvignon.

2006 Tocai Friulano	90	now
2006 Pinot Bianco	90	now
2006 Sauvignon	90	now

SCUBLA ★ ★ ★/★ ★ ★ ★
FRIULI $23.00–$48.00

This is a lovely set of releases from Roberto Scubla, whose vineyards lie in the Colli Orientali appellation. The Sauvignon, Rosso Scuro (Merlot and Refosco), and Verduzzo Cràtis are especially noteworthy. The varietal whites are fermented and aged in stainless steel, where they also spend several months on their lees, while the top selections see French oak.

2006 Sauvignon	91	now
2003 Rosso Scuro	92	now–2015
2004 Verduzzo Friulano Cràtis	92	now–2012

SPERI ★★★/★★★★
VENETO $64.00–$75.00

Speri is a small, family-owned estate with vineyards in the historical part of the Valpolicella zone. Stylistically the Amarones are made in a somewhat austere style. I find that the wines, especially the Recioto, typically benefit from a few hours of air.

2003 Amarone Classico Sant'Urbano	91	2009–2015
2001 Amarone Classico Sant'Urbano	90	now–2013
2004 Recioto della Valpolicella Classico La Roggia	91	2009–2019
2003 Recioto della Valpolicella Classico La Roggia	91	now–2018

STROBLHOF ★★★★
ALTO ADIGE $64.00

This small estate is part of a hotel complex located just outside San Michele Appiano. The wines are made under the direction of oenologist Hans Terzer. These are very representative Pinot Noirs from Alto Adige.

2004 Blauburgunder Riserva	91	now–2014
2003 Blauburgunder Riserva	91	now–2011

TENUTA SAN LEONARDO ★★★/★★★★
TRENTINO $65.00

Tenuta San Leonardo is one of Trentino's historic estates. The property has been owned by the Guerrieri Gonzaga family since the mid-18th century, and winemaking is overseen by consulting oenologist Carlo Ferrini. The estate's flagship, San Leonardo (Cabernet Sauvignon, Cabernet Franc, and Merlot), is made from low yields of 50 quintals per hectare (about 4,500 pounds per acre). It spends a few months in cask prior to being racked into French oak barrels, where it ages for 24 months.

2001 San Leonardo	92	now–2018

TENUTA SANT'ANTONIO ★★★★
VENETO $26.00–$220.00

I was very impressed with the wines I tasted from Tenuta Sant'Antonio. This small estate, owned by the Castagnedi family, is located in the Illasi valley. The wines are made with the collaboration of well-known consulting oenologist Celestino Gasparini. The family excels in the production of Amarone. The use of French oak gives the wines their characteristic textural richness.

2004 Valpolicella Superiore Ripasso Monti Garbi	88	now
2003 Capitel del Monte	89	now–2011
2003 Amarone Selezione Antonio Castegnedi	91	now–2011
2003 Amarone Campo dei Gigli	93	now–2015

TOROS ★★★★
FRIULI $36.00–$60.00

Toros is a small artisan producer located just outside Cormons, in Friuli's Colio. The Pinot Bianco and Sauvignon in particular are beautiful expressions of this *terroir*.

2006 Pinot Bianco	92	now–2010
2006 Sauvignon	92	now–2010
2006 Chardonnay	90	now–2010
2003 Merlot	90	now–2015

VIE DI ROMANS ★★★★
FRIULI $32.00–$45.00

Proprietor Gianfranco Gallo's wines reflect his enormous passion for California. Stylistically, they stand apart from the vast majority of wines being made in Friuli today for their level of ripeness, structure, and use of oak. Gallo's vineyards are located in the Isonzo plain, an area that historically has not been particularly highly regarded for the production of high-quality wines, but that doesn't appear to have been an obstacle for the inspired Gallo. Vie di Romans' vineyards are planted to high densities and the fruit is picked as late as possible. Gallo works in a reductive manner in his impeccably clean cellar, eliminating the wines' contact with air as much as possible with the goal of making structured wines capable of extended cellaring. Most of the wines undergo malolactic fermentation in French oak, although a few see only stainless steel. In the past I haven't been a huge fan of the estate's wines, as I often found them heavy and overextracted, with bitter, astringent tannins. I saw none of those qualities in the 2005s, which are almost universally outstanding and seem to represent a new level of finesse. That said, in general I prefer the estate's stainless-steel wines, which tend to exhibit greater expression of *terroir* as well as varietal trueness. The top-of-the-line Flors di Uis (Malvasia Istriana, Riesling Renano, and Tocai Friulano) and Voos dai Ciamps (Merlot) are benchmark wines for the region.

2005 Sauvignon Piere	90	now–2010
2005 Sauvignon Vieris	90	now–2012
2005 Chardonnay Ciampagnis Vieris	90	now–2010
2005 Chardonnay Vie di Romans	91	now–2015
2005 Malvasia Istriana Dis Cumeris	91	now–2010
2005 Flors di Uis	92	now–2012
2005 Pinot Grigio Dessimis	90	now–2012
2003 Voos dai Ciamps	93	2009–2015

VILLA RUSSIZ ★★★★
FRIULI $29.00–$76.00

Villa Russiz is a unique property in that it is run as a nonprofit organization whose mission is to improve the lives of children in need. Oenologist Gianni Menotti is one of the leading lights of the Friulian wine scene. His considerable skills are on display in this terrific set of releases, which are among the most consistently outstanding wines I tasted from Friuli this year. The estate makes a set of entry-level wines plus its higher-end de La Tour bottlings, which bear the name of the original, French, owner of the estate, Comte Théodore de La Tour. Menotti told me he was very happy with the 2006 vintage because it gave him the perfect conditions to make the wines he likes most: fat and ripe, with plenty of structure yet balanced by freshness and aromatic complexity. After undergoing fermentation in stainless steel the whites are left on the lees until the spring after the harvest, which gives the wines their open textures. With the exception of the Chardonnay de La Tour (partly aged in oak), Menotti prefers that his whites not undergo malolactic fermentation in order to maintain as much freshness as possible.

2006 Pinot Grigio	90	now–2010
2006 Sauvignon de La Tour	93	now–2012
2005 Chardonnay Grafin de La Tour	90	now–2011
2003 Merlot Graf de La Tour	90	now–2015

VODOPIVEC ★★★★
FRIULI $85.00–$100.00

This small property is located in the rugged Carso mountain range above Trieste. Until fairly recently the Vodopivec brothers focused on horticulture, their main commercial activity. Their vineyards are located in an inhospitable, rocky *terroir* that is home to a small patchwork of plots suitable for the vine. Vodopivec produce only Vitovska, an indigenous variety that shares similar characteristics with Ribolla Gialla. In 2004 they have a new wine, Solo MM4, which is a vineyard selection. The vineyards are planted to an extremely high density of 10,000 plants per hectare (24,700 plants per acre), and yields are kept to a minuscule 500 grams (1.1 pounds) per plant, which is less than the yields of all but the most fanatical red wine producers in Italy's top regions. Winemaking is minimalist, to say the least. In 2004 the harvest took place toward the end of September. Fermentation and maceration were done in wood vats without temperature control and lasted about 15 days, using only natural yeasts. The wines were then racked into 30-hectoliter (792-gallon) barrels, where they spent a minimum of 25 months prior to being bottled without fining or filtration. These are among the most unmanipulated wines being made in Italy today. They are phenomenal wines that will challenge readers' perceptions about what white wines can be about. For those adventurous enough to give these wines a try, an immensely rewarding world of new experiences awaits. As is the case with all whites fermented on the skins, the wines should be served at cellar temperature or slightly above, but not chilled. I generally prefer larger glasses, suitable for Pinot Noir, which will allow for the fullest expression of the wines' aromatics.

2004 Vitovska	92	now–2012
2004 Solo MM4 Vitovska	93	now–2012

ZENATO ★★★★
VENETO $25.00–$85.00

This historic property makes big, bold wines in a very classic style. The cask-aged Amarone Riserva is particularly notable.

2004 Valpolicella Superiore Ripassa	91	now–2010
2003 Amarone	90	now–2013
2001 Amarone Classico Riserva Sergio Zenato	93	now–2011

ZIDARICH ★★★
FRIULI $48.00–$98.00

There is an expressive purity to Beniamino Zidarich's wines that I adore. Zidarich works out of a small cellar carved out of the dramatic rock formations that are the dominant terrain in the Carso mountain range. The vineyards were planted beginning in 1988, with densities ranging from 8,000 to 10,000 plants per hectare (19,760 to 24,700 plants per acre). The wines are fermented with natural yeasts in open-top wood vats, where they see contact with the skins for eight to ten days. Aging takes place in midsized Slavonian oak casks, and the wines are bottled without fining or filtration. Zidarich's wines are cloudy, but that is simply the result of being made with a bare minimum of intervention. Like all whites macerated on the skins, these wines should be served at cellar temperature in large glasses. Even in the weaker 2005 vintage Zidarich has crafted wines that are well worth seeking out.

2005 Vitovska	89	now–2010
2005 Malvasia	91	now–2010
2005 Prulke	91	now–2010

[the best of central and southern italy]

[the ratings]

CENTRAL AND SOUTHERN ITALY'S BEST WINES

* * * * * (OUTSTANDING)

Milziade Antano (Montefalco
   Sagrantino Colleallodole)
Argiolas (Turriga)
Benanti (Passito di Pantelleria
   Coste di Mueggen)
Caprai (Sagrantino di Montefalco 25 Anni)
Dettori (Dettori Rosso)
Dettori (Tenores)

Galardi (Terra di Lavoro)
Molettieri (Taurasi Cinque
   Vigna Querque)
Molettieri (Taurasi Riserva Vigna
   Cinque Querce)
Montevetrano (Montevetrano)
Passopisciaro (Franchetti)
Sportoletti (Villa Fidelia)

* * * * / * * * * * (EXCELLENT/OUTSTANDING)

Milziade Antano (Montefalco Rosso Riserva)
Argiolas (Angialis)
Benanti (Lamorèmio)

Benanti (Serra della Contessa)
Cantina del Taburno (Bue Apis)
Caprai (Sagrantino di Montefalco 25 Anni)

Feudi di San Gregorio (Taurasi Riserva
Piano di Monte Vergine)
Passopisciaro (Passopisciaro)

Tenuta Le Querce (Vigna della Corona)
Terredora (Taurasi Campo Re)

* * * * (EXCELLENT)

Milziade Antano (Sagrantino di
Montefalco Passito)
Argiolas (Is Solinas)
Argiolas (Korem)
Benanti (Il Drappo)
Benanti (Majora)
Benanti (Nerello Mascalese)
Benanti (Pietramarina)
Caggiano (Taurasi Macchia dei Goti)
Cantine del Notaio (Aglianico del Vulture
La Firma)
Cantine Lonardo (Taurasi)
Cantine Lonardo (Taurasi Riserva)
Capichera (Assajè)
Caprai (Sagrantino di
Montefalco Collepiano)
Cataldi Madonna (Montepulciano
d'Abruzzo Toni)
Colpetrone (Sagrantino de Montefalco)
Cusumano (Noà)
Dettori (Tuderi)
Di Majo Norante (Apinae)
Di Majo Norante (Don Luigi)
Donnafugata (Tancredi)
Donnafugata (Mille e Una Notte)
Emidio Pepe (Montepulciano
d'Abruzzo)
Falesco (Montiano)
Farnese (Montepulciano d'Abruzzo
Riserva Opis)
Feudi di San Gregorio (Pàtrimo)
Feudi di San Gregorio (Serpico)
Feudi di San Gregorio (Taurasi)

Firriato (Camelot)
Gulfi (NeroBufaleffj)
Il Feuduccio (Montepulciano d'Abruzzo
Riserva Margae)
Il Feuduccio (Montepulciano d'Abruzzo
Riserva Ursonia)
Lamborghini (Campoleone)
Masciarelli (Montepulciano Rosso
d'Abruzzo Marina Cvetić S. Martino)
Mastroberardino (Taurasi Radici)
Mastroberardino (Taurasi Radici Riserva)
Monti (Montepulciano d'Abruzzo Pignotto)
Morgante (Nero d'Avola Don Antonio)
Oasi degli Angeli (Kurni)
Poggio Bertaio (Crovello)
San Patrignano (Montepirolo)
Sant'Anastasia (Litra)
Santadi (Carignano del Sulcis Terre Brune)
Santadi (Carignano Riserva Rocca Rubia)
Tasca d'Almerita (Cabernet Sauvignon)
Tasca d'Almerita (Rosso del Conte)
Tenuta delle Terre Nere (Feudo di Mezzo)
Le Terrazze (Chaos)
Le Terrazze (Planet Waves)
Le Terrazze (Rosso Conero Sassi Neri)
Le Terrazze (Rosso Conero Visions of J.)
Terredora (Taurasi)
Tormaresca (Agliancio Bocca di Lupa)
Valentini (Montepulciano d'Abruzzo)
Valentini (Trebbiano d'Abruzzo)
Vestini Campagnano (Casavecchia)
Vestini Campagnano (Pallagrello Nero)
Villa Matilde (Camarato)

* * * / * * * * (GOOD/EXCELLENT)

Milziade Antano (Sagrantino di Montefalco)
Argiolas (Costera)
Argiolas (Perdera)
Benanti (Rovitello)
Caggiano (Aglianico dell'Irpinia Tarì)
Caggiano (Salae Domini)
Cantina del Taburno (Aglianico Delius)
Capichera (Vendemmia Tardiva)
Capichera (Vermentino)
Cataldi Madonna (Montepulciano
d'Abruzzo Malandrino)

Colpetrone (Montefalco
Rosso)
Cusumano (Benuara)
Cusumano (Nero d'Avola)
Cusumano (Sàgana)
Dettori (Vermentino)
Di Majo Norante (Aglianico del
Molise Contado)
Di Majo Norante (Cabernet)
Di Majo Norante (Sangiovese Terre
degli Osci)

Donnafugata (Moscato di Pantelleira
  Ben Ben Ryè)
Emidio Pepe (Trebbiano d'Abruzzo)
Falesco (Marciliano)
Falesco (Merlot)
Farnese (Edizione Cinque Autoctoni)
Feudi di San Gregorio (Campanaro)
Feudi di San Gregorio (Fiano di
  Avellino Pietracalda)
Feudi di San Gregorio (Greco di
  Tufo Cutizzi)
Firriato (Harmonium)
Gulfi (NeroMàccarj)
Lungarotti (Rubesco Riserva
  Vigna Monticchio)
Masciarelli (Trebbiano d'Abruzzo
  Marina Cvetić)
Mastroberardino (Naturalis Historia)
Mazzei (Zisola)
Molettieri (Aglianico Cinque Querce)

Monti (Montepulciano d'Abruzzo)
Planeta (Merlot)
Planeta (Santa Cecilia)
Poggio Bertaio (Cimbolo)
San Patrignano (Avi)
Santadi (Monica di Sardegna Antigua)
Sportoletti (Assisi Rosso)
Tasca d'Almerita (Nero d'Avola Lamùri)
Tenuta delle Terre Nere
  (Calderara Sottana)
Tenuta delle Terre Nere (Etna Rosso)
Tenuta delle Terre Nere (Guardiola)
Le Terrazze (Rosso Conero)
Terredora (Lacryma Christi del
  Vesuvio Rosso)
Tormaresca (Negroamaro Maime)
Tormaresca (Primitivo Torcicoda)
Valle Reale (Montepulciano d'Abruzzo
  San Calisto)
Villa Matilde (Aglianico)

★ ★ ★ (GOOD)

A Mano (Prima Mano)
A Mano (Primitivo)
Milziade Antano (Montefalco Rosso)
Benanti (Bianco di Caselle)
Benanti (Rosso di Verzella)
Cantina del Taburno (Aglianico Fidelis)
Cantine del Notaio (Aglianico del
  Vulture Repertorio)
Caprai (Montefalco Rosso)
Cataldi Madonna (Montepulciano
  d'Abruzzo)
Di Majo Norante (Ramitello Terre
  degli Osci)
Falesco (Sangiovese)
Falesco (Vitiano Rosso)
Farnese (Montepulciano d'Abruzzo)
Feudi di San Gregorio (Primitivo di
  Manduria Ognissole)
Firriato (Ribeca)
Gulfi (NeroBaronj)
Il Feuduccio (Montepulciano d'Abruzzo)

Lamborghini (Trescone)
Masciarelli (Chardonnay Marina Cvetić)
Masciarelli (Montepulciano Trebbiano
  d'Abruzzo Villa Gemma)
Planeta (Burdese)
Planeta (Syrah)
Poggio Bertaio (Stucchio)
San Patrignano (Colli di Rimini Noi)
Sant'Anastasia (Contempo Nero d'Avola)
Sant'Anastasia (Montenero)
Santadi (Carignano del Sulcis
  Grotta Rossa)
Tasca d'Almerita (Regaleali Nero d'Avola)
Tenuta Le Querce (Aglianico Il Viole)
Terra dei Re (Aglianico del
  Vulture Divinus)
Terra dei Re (Aglianico del Vulture Vultur)
Valle Reale (Montepulciano d'Abruzzo)
Valle Reale (Montepulciano d'Abruzzo
  Vigne Nuove)
Villa Matilde (Falerno del Massico Rosso)

[tasting commentaries]

A MANO ★★★
PUGLIA $12.00–$28.00

This estate in Puglia is a reliable source for delicious, value-priced reds. Owners Mark Shannon and Elevezia Sbalchiero fashion fruit-driven wines with irresistible appeal. The Prima Mano is a selection of the estate's finest lots and is released only in the best vintages.

2005 Primitivo	88	now
2003 Prima Mano	89	now

MILZIADE ANTANO ★★★★★
UMBRIA $30.00–$71.00

Antano is located in the Montefalco appellation in Umbria. Proprietor Francesco Antano works with low yields to make pure, unadulterated wines loaded with personality that express the inner beauty of this unique region. The wines often see extended periods of aging in cask. The top selections are the single-vineyard Sagrantino Colleallodole and the Montefalco Rosso Riserva (Sagrantino and Sangiovese). The *passito,* made from dried grapes, reveals a profile similar to Recioto but with the tannic backbone of Sagrantino. These big, powerful wines are essential drinking for readers who want to learn what Sagrantino is all about. They will offer their greatest pleasure when served alongside full-flavored dishes that can handle the wines' imposing structures.

2004 Sagrantino di Montefalco	90	2009–2019
2004 Sagrantino di Montefalco Passito	92	now–2019
2003 Sagrantino di Montefalco	89	2009–2018
2004 Montefalco Rosso	88	now–2010
2003 Montefalco Rosso Riserva	93	now–2021
2004 Montefalco Sagrantino Colleallodole	94	2011–2022

ARGIOLAS ★★★★★
SARDINIA $13.00–$85.00

Argiolas is one of my favorite producers in Italy. The estate, located on the island of Sardinia, makes a number of compelling wines that highlight just how intriguing its unique *terroirs* and indigenous varieties can be. Of course, it never hurts to have the consulting services of one of the world's most renowned oenologists, in this case Sardinia native Giacomo Tachis. To make things even better, most of the wines remain reasonably priced as well. The modestly priced wines include Perdera (90% Monica and 10% Carignano and Bovale Sardo) and Costera (90% Cannonau, 5% Carignano, and 5% Bovale Sardo). The Is Solinas is 95% Carignano and 5% Bovale Sardo, while Korem is 55% Bovale Sardo, 35% Carignano, and 10% Cannonau. The top-of-the-line Turriga is a single-vineyard blend 85% Cannonau and 15% Malvasia Nera, Carignano, and Bovale Sardo. In addition to these superb reds, Argiolas also makes several whites. The Vermentino Costamolino is a perennial favorite. The sweet Angialis, made from late-harvested Nasco and Malvasia, rounds out this very strong set of wines. Readers who want to learn more about the unique wines of Sardegna owe it to themselves to check out Argiolas.

2006 Perdera	89	now–2012
2006 Costera	90	2009–2014
2005 Is Solinas	92	2009–2020
2005 Korem	92	now–2020

2003 Turriga	93	2009–2018
2003 Angialis	93	now–2013

BENANTI ★ ★ ★ ★ ★
SICILY $25.00–$65.00

Benanti is making some of the most compelling wines coming out of Sicily's emerging Mount Etna appellation. These dramatic old vines are grown on the slopes of the volcano. Most of the wines are made from indigenous varieties, although international grapes are used in a few of the reds. The whites are made from the native Carricante, which at its best yields intense, mineral-driven wines that recall Chablis. Among the reds, the Rovitello and Serra dell Contessa are Nerello Mascalese and Nerello Capuccio blends from several sites. The Majora is a blend of Nero d'Avola, Syrah, Tannat, and Petit Verdot, while the Drappo is pure Nero d'Avola. The Lamorèmio is an utterly engaging wine that adds Cabernet Sauvignon to Nerello Mascalese and Nero d'Avola. The sweet Coste di Mueggen is made from air-dried Zibibbo grapes grown on the island of Pantelleria. I can't say much more, except to urge readers to discover the extraordinary wines of Benanti.

2006 Bianco di Caselle	88	now–2010
2003 Pietramarina	91	now–2010
2000 Pietramarina	92	now–2010
2004 Rosso di Verzella	87	now–2010
2003 Rovitello	88	now–2013
2000 Rovitello	90	now–2012
2004 Serra della Contessa	93	2009–2016
2001 Nerello Mascalese	91	now–2011
2004 Majora	91	2009–2016
2004 Il Drappo	91	2009–2016
2002 Lamorèmio	92	2009–2020
2002 Passito di Pantelleria Coste di Mueggen	94	now–2012

CAGGIANO ★ ★ ★ ★
CAMPANIA $20.00–$55.00

Proprietor Antonio Caggiano makes his wines in an accessible, refined style. The Tarì is the entry-level Aglianico. The Salae Domini is made from Taurasi-designated vineyards and is aged in new French oak but given a shorter period of aging than is required to qualify as Taurasi. The flagship wine, Taurasi Vigna Macchia dei Goti, is aged in medium-sized casks.

2005 Aglianico dell'Irpinia Tarì	89	2009–2015
2004 Salae Domini	89	now–2012
2004 Taurasi Macchia dei Goti	92	2011–2024
2003 Taurasi Macchia dei Goti	92	2010–2023

CANTINA DEL NOTAIO ★ ★ ★/★ ★ ★ ★
BASILICATA $30.00–$55.00

Cantina del Notaio is an excellent source of the Aglianicos of the Vulture district in Basilicata. The consulting oenologist is Professor Luigi Moio of the University of Naples, who is behind many of the region's up-and-coming estates. The Aglianico del Vulture Il Repertorio is an accessible expression of this variety, while La Firma is a more important, structured wine. Both wines are aged in French oak.

2005 Aglianico del Vulture Il Repertorio	88	now–2011
2005 Aglianico del Vulture La Firma	91	2010–2020
2004 Aglianico del Vulture La Firma	93	2011–2024

CANTINA DEL TABURNO   * * */* * * *
CAMPANIA $15.00–$105.00

Cantina del Taburno is one of Campania's most promising estates. The winery is a cooperative and quality can be variable, but the top wines compete with those being made anywhere. The estate's best wines are these three selections of Aglianico. Fidelis, the entry-level wine, contains a small percentage of Sangiovese. The Delius is 100% Aglianico aged in new French oak. The Bue Apis is made from vines more than 200 years old. It sees fermentation/maceration lasting more than 40 days and 18 months in new French oak. It is a remarkable wine. Filippo Colandrea is the oenologist.

2004 Aglianico Fidelis	88	now–2012
2004 Delius	89	now–2012
2004 Bue Apis	93	2011–2024
2003 Bue Apis	91	2009–2021

CANTINE LONARDO   * * * *
CAMPANIA $45.00–$65.00

I was delighted to discover the pure, bold wines of Cantine Lonardo. This small, family-run estate makes just 10,000 bottles from its 4 hectares (about 10 acres) of vineyards. The Taurasi sees 20 to 25 days of maceration followed by a year of aging in tank and another 12 to 18 months in oak. The Taurasi Riserva undergoes an incredible four months of maceration on the skins followed by a year in tank and 18 months in oak. The estate favors 600-liter (159-gallon) French oak barrels, of which 30% are new. The wines are neither fined nor filtered prior to being bottled.

2001 Taurasi	91	2009–2019
2001 Taurasi Riserva	92	2009–2026
2000 Taurasi Riserva	91	now–2020

CAPICHERA   * * * *
SARDINIA $53.00–$79.00

Capichera is another of the Sardinian estates making wines of superb quality. The top bottling is the remarkable Assajè, 100% Carignan aged 12 to 16 months in steel made from the Sulcis region on the northern part of the island. The French oak–aged, late-picked Vendemmia Tardiva (Vermentino) is another fascinating wine.

2006 Vermentino	90	now–2010
2003 Vendemmia Tardiva	89	now–2013
2005 Assajè	92	now–2020

CAPRAI   * * * * *
UMBRIA $25.00–$110.00

Marco Caprai has led the way in Montefalco for years, first and foremost through conducting and supporting diligent research on Sagrantino clones, rootstocks, training systems, optimal vine densities, and a host of other factors that play an important role in the overall quality of the fruit. Consulting oenologist Attilio Pagli has also made significant contributions in maximizing the potential of these vineyards. Today the wines are made from low yields and aged in French oak, and they offer a very personal expression of this appellation. The estate's top bottling is the Sagrantino di Montefalco 25 Anni. First made to celebrate the property's 25th anniversary, it is a selection of the best fruit and sees 24 months in small French oak barrels.

2005 Montefalco Rosso	87	now–2010
2004 Sagrantino di Montefalco Collepiano	92	2010–2020
2004 Sagrantino di Montefalco 25 Anni	94	2012–2024

CATALDI MADONNA ★★★/★★★★
ABRUZZO $21.00–$70.00

Cataldi Madonna is a family-run property located in Abruzzo. Oenologist Lorenzo Landi makes full-bodied, intense Montepulcianos. The Malandrino is 100% Montepulciano aged in French oak. The Toni is also 100% Montepulciano but is made in a richer, more sumptuous style, with both malolactic fermentation and aging taking place in French oak.

2005 Montepulciano d'Abruzzo	88	now–2010
2005 Montepulciano d'Abruzzo Malandrino	90	now–2015
2004 Montepulciano d'Abruzzo Malandrino	89	now–2014
2004 Montepulciano d'Abruzzo Toni	92	2009–2016
2003 Montepulciano d'Abruzzo Toni	90	2008–2015

CÒLPETRONE ★★★
UMBRIA $30.00–$60.00

Oenologist Lorenzo Landi oversees winemaking at Còlpetrone, one of the properties owned by the Saiagricola group. The estate makes rich, full-bodied wines. The top wine is the Sagrantino, 100% di Montefalco aged 18 months in French oak, which is a modern-style version of this firm, structured wine. The more accessible Montefalco Rosso is a blend of 70% Sangiovese and 15% Sagrantino aged in cask.

2005 Montefalco Rosso	89	now–2010
2004 Sagrantino di Montefalco	92	2009–2019

CUSUMANO ★★★
SICILY $15.00–$45.00

Brothers Alberto and Diego Cusumano make a variety of wines from their holdings across the island. The Benuara is 70% Nero d'Avola and 30% Syrah, while the Sàgana is 100% Nero d'Avola. The estate's flagship wine Noà is 40% Nero d'Avola, 30% Cabernet Sauvignon, and 30% Merlot from various appellations. As good as the reds are, it would be nice to see Cusumano do more with their whites.

2006 Nero d'Avola	89	now–2010
2006 Benuara	89	now–2011
2004 Sàgana	90	now–2014
2005 Noà	92	now–2016

DETTORI ★★★★★
SARDINIA $36.00–$80.00

Alessandro Dettori makes some of the most exciting wines coming out of Sardinia—and Italy, for that matter. The wines are made in a very natural, unmanipulated manner. The top bottlings—Tuderi, Tenores, and Dettori Rosso—are all 100% Cannonau (Grenache) aged exclusively in cement and steel prior to being bottled without fining or filtration. In particular, the Dettori Rosso, which is made from 80-plus-year-old vines, is a prodigious effort. These wines are not to be missed.

2006 Vermentino	90	now–2010
2003 Tuderi	91	now–2018
2003 Tenores	94	now–2023
2004 Dettori Rosso	95	2010–2024

DI MAJO NORANTE ★ ★ ★ ★
MOLISE $12.00–$50.00

Di Majo Norante is located in Molise, one of the least-known regions in Italy. Proprietor Alessio Di Majo and consulting oenologist Riccardo Cotarella make plump, richly flavored wines that offer incredible value for the money. The top-of-the-line Don Luigi is a blend of Montepulciano and Tintilia aged in French oak. The sweet Apinae, from the grape of the same name, is made from fruit that is left to dry on the vine. This is a compelling dessert wine and is loaded with flavor and personality.

2006 Sangiovese Terre degli Osci	89	now
2004 Ramitello Terre degli Osci	88	now
2004 Aglianico del Molise Contado	90	now–2011
2006 Cabernet	89	now
2004 Don Luigi	92	now–2019
2004 Apinae	92	now–2010

DONNAFUGATA ★ ★ ★ ★
SICILY $40.00–$80.00

Donnafugata is one of Sicily's most historic estates. Although I have always enjoyed the wines, these recent releases are particularly successful. The Mille e Una Notte is a Nero d'Avola–based blend aged in French oak, while the Tancredi is a blend of 70% Nero d'Avola and 30% Cabernet Sauvignon, also aged in French oak. The sweet Ben Ryè is made from Zibbibo grown on the volcanic soils of the island of Pantelleria.

2004 Mille e Una Notte	91	now–2016
2004 Tancredi	92	now–2016
2006 Moscato di Pantelleria Ben Ryè	90	now–2012

FALESCO ★ ★ ★
UMBRIA $11.00–$52.00

Falesco is the Umbrian estate of brothers Riccardo and Renzo Cotarella. Riccardo is best known for the numerous important estates he has as clients to his consulting practice, while Renzo oversees winemaking at Antinori. At Falesco the Cotarellas produce a variety of wines made in a fruit-driven, concentrated style. The top bottlings are Montiano (100% Merlot) and Marciliano (70% Cabernet Sauvignon and 30% Cabernet Franc). The entry-level reds can also be excellent, but bottle variation has been an issue in the past.

2006 Sangiovese	86	now
2006 Vitiano Rosso	88	now–2010
2006 Merlot	89	now–2010
2004 Montiano	91	2009–2018
2004 Marciliano	89	2009–2016

FARNESE ★ ★ ★
ABRUZZO $23.00–$32.00

Farnese, located in Abruzzo, makes Montepulcianos of notable personality. The Riserva Opis is made in an opulent, late-harvested style and spends two years in wood, equal parts Slavonian oak cask and smaller French barrels. The Edizione Cinque Autoctoni is a blend of five indigenous varieties: Montepulciano, Sangiovese, Primitivo, Negroamaro, and Malvasia Nera. It is made outside of any formal designation and therefore labeled NV, but the lot number indicates the vintage.

2003 Montepulciano d'Abruzzo	87	now
2001 Montepulciano d'Abruzzo Riserva Opis	91	now–2016
NV Edizione Cinque Autoctoni	90	now–2019

FEUDI DI SAN GREGORIO ★★★★★
CAMPANIA $18.00–$133.00

This relatively young estate in Campania has come along in recent years with a very consistent range of wines focused mostly on indigenous varieties. Quality is especially remarkable considering the large number of bottles produced. Oenologist Riccardo Cotarella oversees winemaking. The reds are made in a full-bodied, concentrated style and are aged in small French oak barrels. The important reds should be tasted immediately upon release or after a few years, as they tend to shut down considerably in bottle. Serpico is the top Aglianico bottling, while Pàtrimo is 100% Merlot. While these two wines have garnered a lot of attention recently, the Taurasi Riserva Piano di Monte Vergine is the hidden gem in this lineup. Among the whites, the Campanaro (Fiano and Greco) and the selections of Fiano and Greco are notable, while the regular bottlings of those wines offer superb value. As is often the case with reds from southern Italy, I wonder if a more enlightened, refined approach in the cellar might not take these wines to another level.

2006 Greco di Tufo Cutizzi	90	now–2011
2006 Fiano di Avellino Pietracalda	90	now–2011
2006 Campanaro	90	now–2011
2006 Primitivo di Manduria Ognissole	88	now–2012
2004 Taurasi	93	2012–2025
2002 Taurasi Riserva Piano di Monte Vergine	91	2009–2020
2001 Taurasi Riserva Piano di Monte Vergine	94	2010–2026
2005 Serpico	90	2011–2023
2004 Serpico	92	2012–2024
2004 Pàtrimo	93	2012–2026

IL FEUDUCCIO ★★★
ABRUZZO $28.00–$49.00

Il Feuduccio is a terrific source for flavorful Montepulcianos. The estate's top wines are the Montepulciano d'Abruzzo Riservas. The Ursonia is made from tiny yields and spends 12 to 14 months in French oak barrels of various sizes, while the Margae is made from less extreme yields but sees a long period of oak aging.

2003 Montepulciano d'Abruzzo	88	now–2013
2001 Montepulciano d'Abruzzo Riserva Ursonia	91	now–2019
2000 Montepulciano d'Abruzzo Riserva Ursonia	89	now–2017
1999 Montepulciano d'Abruzzo Riserva Margae	91	now–2019

FIRRIATO ★★★
SICILY $52.00–$58.00

Firriato is located on the eastern side of Sicily. The estate makes a number of sleek, modern-style wines from both native and international varieties. Quality could be more consistent, especially at the lower end, but the top reds offer notable personality. The Ribeca is a blend of

Nero d'Avola and Perricone, while the Harmonium is 100% Nero d'Avola. The estate's best-known wine, Camelot, is a blend of Cabernet Sauvignon and Merlot. Firriato favors small oak barrels for its high-end bottlings.

2004 Harmonium	89	row–2014
2004 Ribeca	87	2009–2014
2003 Camelot	92	now–2015

GALARDI ★ ★ ★ ★ ★
CAMPANIA $123.00

Galardi is another property that has come along in recent years with a series of stunning wines. Under the guidance of oenologist Riccardo Cotarella, the estate's Terra di Lavoro (80% Aglianico and 20% Piedirosso) has quickly established itself as one of Italy's top cult wines, and with good reason, as it is consistently outstanding and often profound. At its best Terra di Lavoro offers extraordinary expression of these two ancient varieties and the volcanic soils on which they are grown. As outstanding as Terra di Lavoro is, I often feel as though it is an underachiever. Those may seem like harsh words for such a noteworthy wine, but Terra di Lavoro has ample room for improvement.

2005 Terra di Lavoro	93	2012–2025
2004 Terra di Lavoro	95	2014–2029

GULFI ★ ★ ★ ★
SICILY $38.00–$40.00

Gulfi is one of my favorite producers of Nero d'Avola. The estate owns vineyards in several appellations, the most important of which are in the Val di Noto between Pachino and Noto, an area long renowned for its Nero d'Avolas. The vineyards are planted to the free-standing system known here as *alberello*. Gulfi makes three single-vineyard Nero d'Avolas that offer notable complexity as well as personality. The NeroBaronj is the most accessible of the wines, while the 2004 NeroBufaleffj is the most opulent. I imagine most readers will have a tough time pronouncing the names of these wines, so keep in mind that the "j" is pronounced like an "i."

2004 NeroBaronj	88	now–2012
2004 NeroBufaleffj	92	now–2019
2004 NeroMàccarj	90	now–2014

LAMBORGHINI ★ ★ ★
UMBRIA $25.00–$50.00

Patrizia Lamborghini runs her family's small estate in Umbria. Her signature wine is Campoleone, a blend of equal parts Sangiovese and Merlot aged in French oak. Trescone is a blend of 50% Cabernet Sauvignon, 40% Sangiovese, and 10% Montepulciano.

2004 Trescone	88	now–2010
2004 Campoleone	92	2010–2022

LUNGAROTTI ★ ★ ★
UMBRIA $52.00

Lungarotti is one of Umbria's largest and most historic estates. The flagship wine is the Torgiano Rosso Riserva Vigna Monticchio, a blend of Sangiovese and Canaiolo aged in cask and smaller French oak barrels for 12 months. Winemaking has moved toward a more modern style in recent years, yet the wines could use a little more direction, clarity, and focus.

| 2003 Rubesco Riserva Vigna Monticchio | 90 | now–2018 |
| 2001 Rubesco Riserva Vigna Monticchio | 89 | now–2018 |

MASCIARELLI ★★★
ABRUZZO $35.00–$100.00

Masciarelli produces a range of wines in a style that represents the most international expression of Abruzzo's indigenous varieties. The wines are treated to lavish amounts of new oak, which in many cases covers much of the varietal characteristics, but at their best these can be interesting wines.

2004 Trebbiano d'Abruzzo Marina Cvetić	89	now–2014
2003 Chardonnay Marina Cvetić	87	now–2010
2004 Montepulciano d'Abruzzo Marina Cvetić S. Martino Rosso	90	now–2019
2003 Montepulciano d'Abruzzo Marina Cvetić S. Martino Rosso	91	now–2015
2004 Montepulciano d'Abruzzo Villa Gemma	88	2009–2019
2003 Montepulciano d'Abruzzo Villa Gemma	88	2009–2018
2001 Montepulciano d'Abruzzo Riserva Villa Gemma	89	now–2021

MASTROBERARDINO ★★★/★★★★
CAMPANIA $43.00–$79.00

Mastroberardino is one of the most famous properties in Campania. The estate's legendary Taurasi Riservas of the 1960s set an early benchmark for quality in the region. Amazingly, those early wines are still in great shape. The 2008 Naturalis Historia is a single-vineyard Taurasi-Piedirosso blend aged in small French oak barrels for 18 months, although in subsequent vintages the Piedirosso has been dropped in favor of a 100% Aglianico that is now labeled as Taurasi. The Radici and Radici Riserva (both 100% Aglianico) see a longer period of aging in a combination of large and small oak barrels.

2000 Naturalis Historia	90	now–2018
2003 Taurasi Radici	90	now–2020
2000 Taurasi Radici Riserva	91	now–2020

MAZZEI ★★★
SICILY $20.00–$22.00

The Mazzei family is best known for their Tuscan wines, most notably those of Fonterutoli, but in recent years they have begun making wines in Sicily as well. Zisola is Nero d'Avola made in a plump, engaging style. Some vintages (such as 2006) can show the grape's wilder, animalistic side, but it is nevertheless a wine endowed with much personality. Oenologist Carlo Ferrini oversees winemaking.

| 2006 Zisola | 89 | now–2012 |
| 2005 Zisola | 88 | now–2010 |

MOLETTIERI ★★★★★
CAMPANIA $25.00–$90.00

Molettieri is one of the most fascinating producers to come out of Campania in recent years. For years Salvatore Molettieri sold his fruit to the region's larger producers. The estate's first commercial release was 1996, although a small amount of wine was made in 1994. Today Molettieri is assisted by his son Giovanni, a recent graduate of the Avellino oenological school. Molettieri make a variety of wines, the most notable of which are Aglianicos from their

Cinque Querce vineyard. The wines are aged in a combination of large casks with some small French oak barrels as well. The Taurasi sees 30 months in oak, while the Riserva spends 42 months in oak. Despite the extended period of wood aging, the wines come across as incredibly primary. Drinking windows seem superfluous, as in the finest vintages the wines appear to be nearly immortal. These palate-staining, concentrated big boys are not for the timid, but they do offer thrilling drinking in a full-bodied, intense style.

2005 Aglianico Cinque Querce	89	now–2010
2004 Taurasi Vigna Cinque Querque	95	2014–2029
2003 Taurasi Vigna Cinque Querque	94	2011–2021
2003 Taurasi Riserva Vigna Cinque Querce	95	2013–2028

MONTEVETRANO ★ ★ ★ ★ ★
CAMPANIA $90.00–$108.00

Proprietor Silvia Imparato originally set out to make wine as a hobby. Her family owned a small property in the hills in the province of Salerno, and in 1985 she grafted Cabernet Sauvignon, Merlot, and Aglianico onto existing old rootstocks. With the help of oenologist Riccardo Cotarella she fashioned a modern French oak–aged wine that would ultimately have a profound impact on the wine world by demonstrating the true potential of the wines of southern Italy. Today a number of important wines have emerged from the South, but to the credit of Imparato and Cotarella, Montevetrano remains among the finest and most distinctive. In recent vintages the blend has been 70% Cabernet Sauvignon, 20% Merlot, and 10% Aglianico.

2005 Montevetrano	93	2009–2020
2004 Montevetrano	95	2009–2024
2003 Montevetrano	93	2009–2023

MONTI ★ ★ ★ ★
ABRUZZO $18.00–$35.00

This small family-run estate in Abruzzo makes wines loaded with character. Oenologist Riccardo Cotarella has succeeded in giving the wines a little more polish without robbing them of their distinctive personalities. These unfiltered wines strike a very beautiful balance between traditional and modern styles. The Montepulciano is aged in cask, while the single-vineyard Riserva Pignotto is aged in French oak.

2004 Montepulciano d'Abruzzo	90	now
2003 Montepulciano d'Abruzzo Riserva Pignotto	92	now–2015

MORGANTE ★ ★ ★ ★
SICILY $42.00

Morgante is located in the southern part of Sicily near Agrigento. The estate's top wine is the Nero d'Avola Don Antonio, which brothers Carmelo and Giovanni Morgante named in honor of their father, Antonio Morgante. Don Antonio is a selection made from the estate's finest Nero d'Avola and aged for 12 months in French oak. The wines are made under the guidance of consulting oenologist Riccardo Cotarella.

2004 Nero d'Avola Don Antonio	92	2009–2019

OASI DEGLI ANGELI ★ ★ ★ ★
MARCHE $95.00

This small estate has quickly burst onto the scene with the flashy, opulent Kurni, a 100% Montepulciano lavishly aged in French oak that resembles an Amarone for its textural opulence. Proprietors Eleonora Rossi and Marco Casolanetti fashion their wine from minuscule yields, then give the juice 100% new oak for the first year of aging, followed by another 100% new oak for the second year. This compelling wine must be tasted to be believed.

2005 Kurni	90	now–2015
2004 Kurni	93	2010–2024

PASSOPISCIARO ★★★/★★★★
SICILY $45.00–$105.00

Andrea Franchetti of Tenuta di Trinoro is among those who have recognized the unique qualities of the vineyards located on the hills of Mount Etna. These high-altitude vineyards give Franchetti the optimal conditions for gradual ripening and a late harvest that typically stretches to mid-November, sometimes later. The wines Franchetti makes at his estate, Passopisciaro, present a fascinating expression of his style and these *terroirs*. Passopisciaro is made from the indigenous Nerello Mascalese and captures the essence of that variety in a ripe, opulent style. Franchetti is a much darker, richer wine made from Petit Verdot and Cesanese d'Affile planted at an extremely dense 12,000 plants per hectare (29,640 plants per acre).

2005 Passopisciaro	93	now–2015
2005 Franchetti	95	now–2020

EMIDIO PEPE ★★★★
ABRUZZO $52.00–$65.00

Emidio Pepe's approach to winemaking is quite possibly the most unconventional I have yet encountered. Pepe treats his fruit and the resulting wines with the utmost care. All operations are meticulously carried out by hand. The estate farms its 7 hectares (17 acres) following biodynamic principles. The grapes are picked and destemmed by hand. For the Trebbiano the grapes are crushed by foot in a wood vat and the must is fermented for 8 to 10 days in glass-lined cement. After fermentation the wine is racked into 22-hectoliter (581-gallon) glass-lined cement tanks, where it ages for roughly six months prior to being bottled. The Montepulciano is fermented for about 10 to 12 days and subsequently aged for 24 months in glass-lined cement, which Pepe prefers over oak. Both wines are fermented without the aid of selected yeasts or temperature control. The wines are bottled with no sulfur dioxide and laid down to rest for several years in the cellar, which holds extensive stocks of virtually all past vintages. As they age in bottle, the wines undergo malolactic fermentation naturally. Before being released the bottles are opened and decanted one by one into new bottles, after which they are recorked, labeled, and shipped. There is no fining or filtration or sulfur dioxide added during the second bottling. These are among the most unique and ageworthy wines being made in Italy. Unfortunately, the practice of releasing small batches of the wines over the course of many years leads to a higher amount of bottle variation than is normal these days. That notwithstanding, tasting a well-preserved bottle of Emidio Pepe's Montepulciano is a real treat as the wines can be superb.

2004 Trebbiano d'Abruzzo	90	now–2026
2001 Montepulciano d'Abruzzo	92	2011–2031

Past Glories Montepulciano d'Abruzzo: 2000 (90), 1998 (91), 1995 (90), 1993 (91), 1985 (91), 1983 (89), 1979 (92), 1975 (93), 1964 (90)

PLANETA ★★★
SICILY $39.00

Planeta, based in Menfi, has been among the leaders in planting international varieties in Sicily. The wines are made in a fruit-driven, plump style. The Santa Cecilia (Nero d'Avola) and the Merlot are the most expressive of the wines. The Burdese (70% Cabernet Sauvignon, and 30% Cabernet Franc) is also excellent. In addition to its reds, Planeta also makes a barrel-fermented Chardonnay that is one of the finest Sicilian wines of its type.

2005 Santa Cecilia	90	now–2012
2005 Merlot	89	now–2010
2005 Syrah	88	now–2010
2005 Burdese	88	now–2012

POGGIO BERTAIO ★ ★ ★
UMBRIA $20.00–$65.00

Fabrizio Ciufoli makes full-bodied, concentrated wines from his family's 20 hectares (49 acres) of vineyards near Lake Trasimeno in Umbria. The entry-level Stucchio is 100% Sangiovese aged in French oak. Cimbolo is the estate's more important Sangiovese. A sumptuous wine, it sees 18 months of French oak. Crovello, equal parts Cabernet Sauvignon and Merlot, is also aged in French oak

2004 Stucchio	88	now–2014
2003 Cimbolo	90	now–2013
2003 Crovello	91	2011–2021

SAN PATRIGNANO ★ ★ ★
EMILIA-ROMAGNA $36.00–$48.00

San Patrignano is a remarkable property. The estate was founded by the Muccioli family in the late 1970s as a rehabilitation center for young people with drug and alcohol dependencies. San Patrignano produces a wide variety of agricultural products as part of its programs to offer professional training designed for those in need. The wines, made with the assistance of oenologist Riccardo Cotarella, are often outstanding. Avi is the top Sangiovese selection; Noi is Sangiovese, Cabernet Sauvignon, and Merlot; while Montepirolo is Cabernet Sauvignon, Merlot, and Cabernet Franc.

2005 Colli di Rimini Noi	88	now–2010
2004 Avi	90	2009–2019
2004 Montepirolo	91	2009–2022

SANTADI ★ ★ ★ ★
SARDINIA $14.00–$68.00

Santadi is yet another of the Sardinian properties making compelling wines of notable personality. The estate is located in Sulcis, which lies in the southwest corner of the island. Amazingly, many of the vineyards date from prephylloxera times. Winemaking is overseen by Giacomo Tachis. In addition to reds, Santadi make delicious whites from Vermentino. Readers who are unfamiliar with the unique wines of Sardinia owe it to themselves to check them out. These are some of the most fascinating wines being made in Italy.

2006 Monica di Sardegna Antigua	89	now
2005 Carignano del Sulcis Grotta Rossa	88	now
2004 Carignano Riserva Rocca Rubia	91	now–2012
2003 Carignano del Sulcis Terre Brune	92	now–2015

SANT'ANASTASIA ★ ★ ★
SICILY $14.00–$76.00

This Sicilan producer makes a wide range of wines, but I have had most success with the reds. The Montenero is a blend of 60% Nero d'Avola, 20% Cabernet Sauvignon, and 20% Merlot.

The top-of-the-line Litra is a big, full-bodied Cabernet Sauvignon aged in French oak. Riccardo Cotarella is the consulting oenologist.

2004 Contempo Nero d'Avola	87	now
2003 Montenero	88	now–2010
2004 Litra	92	2011–2024

SPORTOLETTI ★ ★ ★ ★
UMBRIA $18.00–$55.00

Brothers Ernesto and Remo Sportoletti run this small estate located in the hills outside Assisi and Spello. Sportoletti's Villa Fidelia is one of the most compelling wines of Umbria. A blend of Merlot, Cabernet Sauvignon, and Cabernet Franc, it spends 12 months in small French oak barrels. The entry-level Assisi Rosso (Sangiovese, Merlot, and Cabernet) is a more accessible yet equally engaging wine. Consulting oenologist Riccardo Cotarella oversees winemaking.

2006 Assisi Rosso	90	now–2010
2004 Villa Fidelia	94	2009–2024

TASCA D'ALMERITA ★ ★ ★ ★
SICILY $14.00–$65.00

Tasca d'Almerita is one of Sicily's leading wineries. The estate's Rosso del Conte was among the first wines that ushered in the era of important reds from the south. The Nero d'Avola–based Rosso del Conte is made from the oldest vines on the property and given 18 months in French oak, of which 80% is new. In addition to its top reds, the estate's signature white, Nozze d'Oro (50% Inzolia and 50% Sauvignon), is one of my favorite Sicilian whites year in, year out.

2005 Regaleali Nero d'Avola	88	now–2010
2005 Nero d'Avola Lamùri	90	now–2015
2004 Rosso del Conte	92	now–2019
2003 Rosso del Conte	91	now–2018
2003 Cabernet Sauvignon	92	now–2019

TERRA DEI RE ★ ★ ★
BASILICATA $22.00–$36.00

This young estate, located in Basilicata, in an excellent source for Aglianico from the Vulture district. The Vultur is the entry-level Aglianico, while the flagship, Divinus, is made from lower yields and aged in French oak. Winemaking is overseen by Sergio Paternoster. This will be a fascinating property to follow over the coming years.

2004 Aglianico del Vulture Vultur	88	now–2012
2003 Aglianico del Vulture Divinus	88	now–2017

LE TERRAZZE ★ ★ ★/★ ★ ★ ★
MARCHE $18.00–$80.00

This small property located in the Marche has been owned by the Terni family since the late 1800s. Antonio Terni is a longtime fan of Bob Dylan, whose music has been the inspiration of many of the wines. Le Terrazze makes several interesting bottlings, including the Sassi Neri and Visions of J. (both 100% Montepulciano), Chaos (50% Montepulciano, 25% Syrah, and 25% Merlot), and Planet Waves (75% Montepulciano and 25% Merlot). Consulting oenologist Attilio Pagli oversees the winemaking.

2005 Rosso Conero	87	now
2004 Rosso Conero	89	now–2012
2004 Rosso Conero Sassi Neri	92	now–2016
2004 Rosso Conero Visions of J.	91	2009–2015
2004 Chaos	92	2009–2019
2004 Planet Waves	91	2009–2019

TERREDORA ★ ★ ★
CAMPANIA $23.00–$80.00

Terredora is a relatively young property founded in 1994 by Walter Mastroberardino and his family. The estate farms more than 150 hectares (370 acres) of vineyards in Campania, making it one of the larger producers in the region. The top reds are rich, flavorful, and loaded with character. The Taurasi sees 20 to 24 months in French oak barrels and casks, while the Taurasi Campo Re spends 30 months in small French oak barrels.

2005 Lacryma Christi del Vesuvio Rosso	90	now–2012
2001 Taurasi	91	now–2013
2001 Taurasi Campo Re	93	now–2019

TENUTA DELLE TERRE NERE ★ ★ ★/★ ★ ★ ★
SICILY $16.00–$40.00

Proprietors Marco and Iano Grazia are best known for the extensive portfolio their importing company represents, but they are also proving to be very talented winemakers. Tenuta delle Terre Nere is located on Sicily's Mount Etna, a recently rediscovered region that is set to challenge readers' expectations of what Sicilian wines can be. These are believed to be the highest vineyards in Italy. The indigenous Nerello Mascalese and Nerello Capuccio yield wines of notable aromatic complexity, with finessed tannins and a weightless quality that recalls Pinot Noir and Nebbiolo. Many of the best sites are still planted to old vines that proved to be resistant to phylloxera, which contributes to the wines' complexity. Terre Nere's top selections are aged in French oak, of which about 25% is new. Mount Etna is one of the most exciting regions in Italy today. It will be fascinating to follow this young estate, which appears to have a very bright future ahead of it.

2006 Etna Rosso	89	now–2011
2005 Calderara Sottana	89	now–2012
2005 Guardiola	90	now–2015
2005 Feudo di Mezzo	92	now–2015

TENUTA LE QUERCE ★ ★ ★
BASILICATA $18.00–$98.00

Tenuta Le Querce, located in Basilicata, is a terrific source for Aglianico. The entry-level Il Viola is a reliable bottling in its price range, while Vigna della Corona is the estate's top selection. It is a rich, sumptuous Aglianico that sees an extended fermentation/maceration lasting 38 to 40 days followed by two years in new French oak.

2004 Aglianico Il Viole	88	now–2010
2003 Vigna della Corona	93	now–2018

TORMARESCA ★ ★ ★
PUGLIA $21.00–$33.00

Tormaresca is the Apulia estate of the Antinori family. In just a few short years the winery has succeeded in making rich, sumptuous wines imbued with personality.

2005 Negroamaro Maime	86	now–2010
2004 Negroamaro Maime	89	now–2012
2004 Primitivo Torcicoda	90	2009–2016
2004 Agliancio Bocca di Lupa	92	2009–2019

VALENTINI ★ ★ ★ ★
ABRUZZO $N/A

Valentini is among the handful of producers who continues to make his wines in a rigorously traditional, artisan fashion. Sadly, Edoardo Valentini passed away in 2006, but his son Francesco continues to run this small property. The estate's wines have attained a cult status among wine lovers and can be hard to find, not to mention very expensive. At their finest, they offer a very personal expression of Trebbiano and Montepulciano from Abruzzo.

| 2004 Trebbiano d'Abruzzo | 90 | now–2014 |
| 2002 Montepulciano d'Abruzzo | 88 | now–2014 |

VALLE REALE ★ ★ ★
ABRUZZO $12.00–$33.00

Valle Reale is one of my favorite producers in Abruzzo. The estate occupies a spectacular position between two national parks. The unique microclimate of these hills and the relatively high altitude of the vineyards means that the grapes mature gradually, as the growing season is long. The single-vineyard Montepulciano d'Abruzzo San Calisto is made from 35-year-old vines and is aged in French oak. Valle Reale's Cerasuolo is one of Italy's most engaging rosés.

2006 Montepulciano d'Abruzzo Vigne Nuove	88	now
2004 Montepulciano d'Abruzzo	88	now
2004 Montepulciano d'Abruzzo San Calisto	90	now–2019

VESTINI CAMPAGNANO ★ ★ ★ ★
CAMPANIA $65.00

Consulting oenologist Paolo Caciorgna has turned out two gems at this small, family-run estate. Vestini Campagnano works exclusively with indigenous varieties that today are nearly forgotten. The Pallagrello Nero is the more powerful and structured of the two top reds, while the Casavecchia is softer and rounder. Both wines are aged in French oak.

| 2004 Pallagrello Nero | 92 | 2009–2022 |
| 2004 Casavecchia | 92 | 2009–2019 |

VILLA MATILDE ★ ★ ★ ★
CAMPANIA $20.00–$68.00

Proprietors Tani and Maria Ida Avallone run this estate located outside Naples, in the province of Caserta, where the history of viticulture spans many centuries. The mineral and ash-rich soils yield wines of uncommon complexity and elegance. The estate works with a selection of ancient clones of the area's indigenous varieties that were rediscovered several decades ago and subsequently replanted throughout the vineyards. Villa Matilde excels with both reds and whites. The top red is Camarato, a blend of 80% Aglianico and 20% Piedirosso. Among the whites the Greco di Tufo and Fiano di Avellino are of particular note. Riccardo Cotarella is the consulting oenologist.

2006 Aglianico	89	now–2010
2003 Falerno del Massico Rosso	87	now
2003 Camarato	91	2009–2018
2001 Camarato	92	2010–2021

[the table wines of portugal]

For most wine lovers, a discussion of Portuguese wines usually began and ended with the famous fortifieds, Port and Madeira. If table wines were mentioned in days gone by, they were typically the ephemeral Vinhos Verdes, or the inexpensive rosés, like Mateus.

In fact, Portugal had a cult table wine of its own more than half a century ago. Ferreira, the Port house now owned by corporate giant Sogrape, produced Barca Velha, Portugal's answer to Penfolds Grange, in the 1950s. Even as early as 1963, wine writer H. Warner Allen, in his book *The Wines of Portugal*, could write about "the emergence of natural table wines" and claim that Portugal's dry wines competed "in price and quality with any other country." Some wines still exist from that era—José Maria da Fonseca was making Periquita even then (and in fact, since the middle of the 19th century). Yet, despite that history, Portugal's table wine revolution did not really begin in earnest until about 1990, and did not hit stride until the mid- to late 1990s. Most would point to Portugal's 1986 entry into the EU as the catalyst to the growth of Portugal's modern table wine industry. In the single generation since then, everything has changed.

[the wines]

Most regions, even Vinho Verde, which is famed for its light and bright white wines, produce both red (*tinto,* pronounced TEEN-too) and white (*branco,* pronounced BRON-koo) wines.

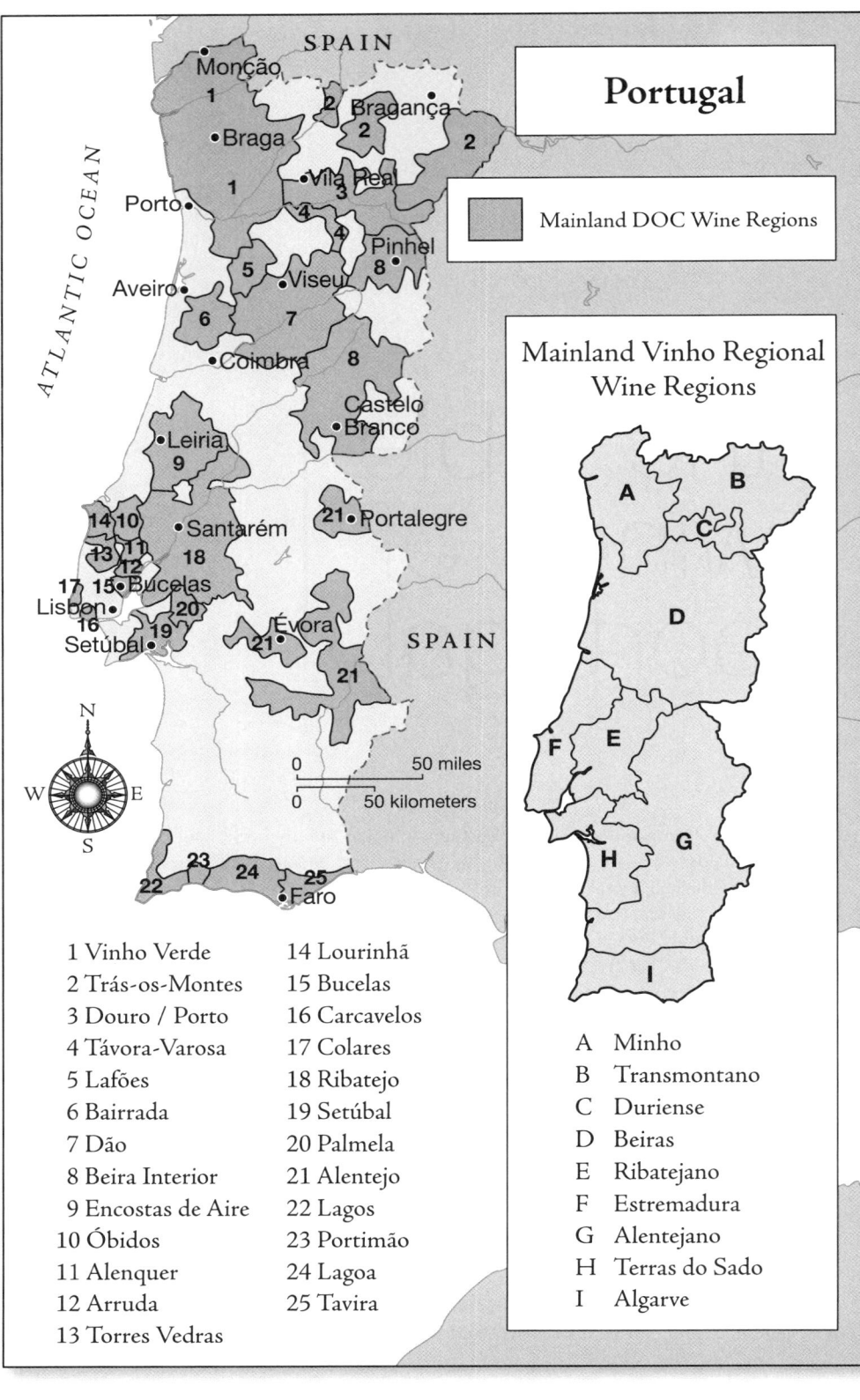

Portugal

SPAIN

Monção
1
Braga
2 Bragança
2
2
Porto
1
Vila Real
3
4
4
Pinhel
8
5
Viseu
Aveiro
6
7
Coimbra
8
Castelo
Branco
Leiria
9
21 Portalegre
14 10
Santarém
13 11
12
18
17 15 Bucelas
Lisbon
16
20
19
Évora
21
SPAIN
Setúbal
21

ATLANTIC OCEAN

Mainland DOC Wine Regions

0   50 miles
0   50 kilometers

N
W   E
S

23
24
22
25
Faro

Mainland Vinho Regional
Wine Regions

A
B
C
D
F   E
H   G
I

1 Vinho Verde
2 Trás-os-Montes
3 Douro / Porto
4 Távora-Varosa
5 Lafões
6 Bairrada
7 Dão
8 Beira Interior
9 Encostas de Aire
10 Óbidos
11 Alenquer
12 Arruda
13 Torres Vedras

14 Lourinhã
15 Bucelas
16 Carcavelos
17 Colares
18 Ribatejo
19 Setúbal
20 Palmela
21 Alentejo
22 Lagos
23 Portimão
24 Lagoa
25 Tavira

A   Minho
B   Transmontano
C   Duriense
D   Beiras
E   Ribatejano
F   Estremadura
G   Alentejano
H   Terras do Sado
I   Algarve

However, Portugal overall and most of its regions are far better known for their reds, with occasional exceptions in places like Vinho Verde and Bucelas.

OVERALL QUALITY

Portugal's table wine reputation rests on the shoulders of a relatively small (but quickly growing) group of top producers, a disproportionate number of which are clustered in the Douro and Alentejo regions. Nonetheless, the country already produces many wines, ranging from interesting to exciting, that should have a place in any cellar. There are already dozens of producers who have made wines rated at 90 points or better. Below the growing number of top producers is a bevy of estates that produce friendly and enjoyable wines at reasonable price points.

Sometimes it is hard to tell what the top wines are called by looking at the label. At many estates, the seemingly simple Tinto is the flagship wine, such as the Tinto from Quinta do Vale Meão. It is the second wine that gets a different name, such as Meandro do Vale Meão (just like Château Latour and Les Forts de Latour). At other wineries, however, the Tinto (Quinta do Vallado, for instance) is indeed a basic red, and the flagship wine is more likely labeled Reserva, or something similar. Then, there are the wineries (like Niepoort) that adopt proprietary names for various levels and styles, such as Batuta and Charme.

Although when people talk about Portugal's dry wine revolution, they are talking mostly about the reds (the tintos), the white wine part of the revolution is well in progress, if several years behind. The whites (brancos) are becoming more and more interesting in regions like Douro, Alentejo, Dão, and Vinho Verde. Producers report increased demand for whites, and they are paying more attention to them as a result. There are neither many top white wine producers nor top white wines yet, but that is changing fast. One caveat: Most Portuguese whites by reputation and in my tastings do not age particularly well. Perhaps that will change in the future, but for the moment, assume that most are best drunk in three to five years and few will be interesting beyond five to seven years.

Portugal is plainly poised to compete with the world's best. The proverbial foot is already in the door, but shoving it wide open and gaining even the recognition already deserved is no easy task. All too often, Portuguese wines I have opened for sophisticated consumers have drawn applause—but no one present had previously heard of a single one. A little exploration will be well rewarded here. Whether you are a Burgundy lover or a Shiraz lover, there is a wine for you, often in a distinctive varietal blend that is hard to find anywhere else.

APPELLATIONS

The basics of Portugal's DOC classification system will be familiar to anyone with some knowledge of France's AOC system or Italy's DOC system. The most important appellations have DOC (Denominação de Origem Controlada) status. Some of the better-known DOC appellations include Douro, Dão, Vinho Verde, Bairrada, Alentejo, and Ribatejo.* If a wine does not qualify for DOC status (*or* the winery chooses to reject the DOC to avoid its regulations), the next level down is Vinho Regional (VR), basically, wines with a geographical indication in a broader region, like a French *vin de pays*. Instead of a Bairrada DOC designation, for instance, you may see instead Vinho Regional Beiras—wine from the Beiras region, in which Bairrada is located. Although in theory the Vinho Regional designation is supposed to

---

*DOC wines are also entitled to the designation VQPRD (Vinho de Qualidade Produzido em Região Demarcada) or QWPSR in English (Quality Wines Produced in Specified Regions). This is EU nomenclature adopted in Portugal after the country's entry into the EU, but you will not see it referred to very often.

be a qualitative step down, many VRs are fully the equal of DOCs in the region. This phenomenon is similar to the "super-Tuscan" wines in Italy. It is more common in some regions than others. For instance, in Alentejo (where the VRs are called Vinho Regional Alentejano), it is par for the course, to the point where some assert that the *best* wines there are in fact the VRs. On the other hand, there are relatively few important Vinho Regional wines in the Douro (Ramos Pinto's Bon Ares is rather good).

The two most important regions for consumers to explore at the moment are Douro and Alentejo, although white wine lovers will want to pay special attention to Vinho Verde as well, and Dão is gaining momentum.

DOURO

The Douro Valley, in northeastern Portugal, is Portugal's best and most famous wine region. In 2006, it celebrated its 250th anniversary as a demarcated and regulated wine region. It has a cachet that is unmatchable by any other region in Portugal—although much of that stems from the Port connection. However, the Douro's connection to an existing, world-famous wine industry—the Port trade—is also a huge advantage for its table wine makers. The Port industry provides human and financial resources, a stable foundation, and a centuries-old tradition for the region. Winemakers here do not wonder if they can compete with the world's best—they know it. There are plenty of role models, even if most of them are fortified wines. It is not surprising that the Douro stirs the blood of rabid enthusiasts with its history and its beautiful and rugged *terroir*.

The Douro has three separate subregions: Baixo Corgo (BAI-shoo CORG-oo) (lower) is the coolest and gets the most precipitation. The heart of the Douro is Cima Corgo (SEE-ma CORG-oo) (middle), which is hot and relatively dry. The final section is the Douro Superior (DOH-roo Su-peh-ree-OR) (highest), the hottest and most arid of the three.

[grape varieties]

DOURO

The hallmark of Douro table wines is blending types of grapes (called *castas*) traditionally used in Port wine. This is what the Port house Ferreira did in making the seminal dry wine Barca Velha in the 1950s. It became standard practice. You won't find many important single-variety wines here, although there are some, and that trend seems to be increasing. You will, on the other hand, often find the polar opposite—"field blends," something from a particular patch of a vineyard where there are numerous different grapes growing together. Sometimes there are literally dozens of different grapes in the field blend. This might be frowned upon elsewhere, but in the Douro even famous and pricey wines can be field blends—for example, *Pintas* from Wine & Soul. Owner Jorge Borges showed me a vineyard that had so many mingled grapes that even he was not sure what they all were. One thing he was sure of, though, was that they were old vines that produced great fruit and he was not ripping them out.

One necessary consumer adjustment is getting used to unfamiliar grapes. Portugal as a whole is said to have some 200 indigenous grapes, and its official wine institute (the Instituto da Vinha e do Vinho, or IVV) lists some 350 grapes of all types in use in the country. In the Douro alone, more than 80 different grapes are permitted in Port.

Most estates rely primarily on native grapes, many of which are obscure to the rest of us, to say the least. It does not help matters that the names of grapes change so often from region to region in Portugal.

RED

The biggest star is Touriga Nacional. Also very common are Tinta Roriz (one of the few familiar grapes to international audiences, known as Tempranillo in parts of Spain and Aragonez or Aragonês in southern Portugal), Touriga Franca (formerly known as Touriga Francesa), Tinta Barroca, and Tinto Cão. Not coincidentally, these are the varieties that were identified as having the highest quality potential for Port wines. When producers begin to pare down the number of varieties in their blends, in practice it seems like Tinta Roriz, Touriga Nacional, and Touriga Franca are first among equals. On any number of wines, you will see other grapes periodically listed, as producers pick and choose from a long list. Tinta Amarela (also known as Trincadeira in the South) is another commonly seen. A handful of important grape varieties. Blending. Sound familiar? You can summarize this Douro model by saying, "Bordeaux." One difference in the Douro, though, is that you can find producers blending together crops from different quintas, the well-known Duas Quintas bottling from Ramos Pinto being a familiar example.

WHITE

The Douro is producing a small number of excellent white wines. Typical brancos are likely to be blends, usually including some combination of Viosinho, Rabigato, Códega do Larinho, Arinto, Malvasia Fina, Donzelinho, and Gouveio (aka Verdelho), among others. It is even rarer to find single-varietal whites than reds. There aren't many fine brancos in the Douro yet, but in varying price ranges try Niepoort's Redoma Branco and Redoma Reserva Branco, Wine & Soul's Douro Guru, Vallado's Branco Reserva, Caves Transmontanas' Branco, Quinta da Sequeira's Vinhas Velhas Branco, and Muxagat's Branco for an idea of the potential that exists here in both trophy wines and value wines.

[recent vintages]

2006

This is a problematic vintage that will likely end the Douro's run of luck for the moment. It is impossible to say just how problematic it is since most top 2006 reds, in particular, have not yet been bottled or released. The year featured a dry winter, then both heavy rain and hailstorms at times, which missed many vineyards but affected others seriously. Some reported a loss of 70% to 80% of the new crop. Quinta de Roriz, for one notable instance, lost half of its crop. Some producers indicated that the crop was smaller but fine. Just to complete the hat trick, however, extended heat also harmed the grapes at times. The summer of 2006 was the fifth hottest on record since 1931.

2005

The trio of vintages 2003–2005 produced many excellent wines, although they are very differently styled. The year 2005 was problematic because it had so little rain—unusual even for the relatively dry Douro—to go with high heat. Some producers said it was difficult to get the grapes to mature, and many feared early on that the grapes would not ripen properly. Many also reported slightly lower alcohol levels. The word "freshness" came up repeatedly in conversations to describe these wines. Charles Symington (Symington Family) probably summed it up most succinctly in calling 2005 "a winemaker's year," because the best wines from a few producers lack little and hold up well, more or less, to their 2004s and 2003s. There are many reasons for this, from some young producers continuing to refine their craft (Pintas, Poeira) to some dedicated producers simply making the most of what nature gave them (Lemos & Van

Zeller, Quinta do Crasto, Quinto do Vale Meão). Wine of the vintage candidates include Vale Meão's flagship Tinto, Lemos & Van Zeller's CV, Crasto's Maria Teresa, Wine & Soul's Pintas, and Quinta do Vallado's Adelaide, the impressive debut release of this old-vine bottling.

Overall, however, the 2005s are less consistently excellent—lighter and less concentrated than the 2004s. Where they do not work, they have the opposite problem of the 2003s: At the lower end, or if they are not fully successful, they can seem routine and foursquare, too elegant for their own good. Many of these will be early maturing. While they match neither the succulence of the 2003s, nor the density and intensity of the 2004s, the best of them are often lovely, impeccably balanced, and seductive.

2004

This is easily the best of this trio of vintages, producing concentrated, ageworthy, and intense wines with excellent fruit that generally still retain their balance and focus. Warm and unusually dry early in the year, the vintage was likely saved by August rain four times normal levels. They are powerful, but they also have some precision, depth, balance, and focus. I believe that they will age well. Many producers indicated it was one of Portugal's best-ever vintages for dry wines—if not the best, considering recent improvements in dry winemaking as well as vintage conditions.

2003

This was the year that shocked most of Europe with scorching heat. In 2003, most producers indicated that it was harder for them to keep the wines in balance than it was in 2004. The 2003 vintage is thus more inconsistent than 2004. The wines that work well—and many do—are ripe, succulent, and sexy. They are more approachable and less dense than the 2004s but often simply delicious. As the wines continue developing, it seems apparent that they are not quite as well structured overall as the 2004s, but at their best, they will give consumers a lot to like.

OLDER VINTAGES 2002 was marred by rain, and most of the wines are light and early maturing. 2001 produced intense and focused wines. Their hallmark is balance. They are very appealing, if not as ripe and sexy as the 2003s and 2004s. After 2004, this is probably the next best vintage in recent times. The 2000s were ripe and big.

—MARK SQUIRES

THE BEST DOURO WINES

All of the following wines are red unless otherwise noted.

Domingos Alves de Sousa Abandonado
Domingos Alves de Sousa Quinta da Gaivosa
Domingos Alves de Sousa Reserva Pessoal
Lavradores de Feitoria Três Bagos Grande Escolha
Lemos & Van Zeller Casa de Casal de Loivos
Lemos & Van Zeller CV
Lemos & Van Zeller Quinta Vale D. Maria
Maria D. P. G. Serôdio de S. Borges Quinta do Fojo
Maria D. P. G. Serôdio de S. Borges Quinta do Manuela
Niepoort Batuta
Niepoort Charme
Niepoort Redoma Branco (white)
Niepoort Redoma Reserva Branco (white)

Poeira Tinto
Prats & Symington Chryseia
Quinta de la Rosa Reserve
Quinta de Roriz Reserva
Ramos Pinto Duas Quintas Reserva
Ramos Pinto Duas Quintas Reserva Especial
Quinta do Crasto Reserva (Old Vines)
Quinta do Crasto Tinta Roriz
Quinta do Crasto Touriga Nacional
Quinta do Crasto Vinha da Ponte
Quinta do Crasto Vinha Maria Teresa
Quinta do Noval Tinto
Quinta do Passadouro Reserva
Quinta do Vale Meão Tinto
Quinta do Vallado Reserva
Quinta do Vallado Branco Reserva (white)
Quinta do Vallado Adelaide Old Vines*
Sogrape—Casa Ferreirinha Barca Velha
Sogrape—Casa Ferreirinha Quinta da Leda
Sogrape—Casa Ferreirinha Reserva
Wine & Soul Guru (white)
Wine & Soul Pintas

[the ratings]

THE DOURO'S BEST PRODUCERS OF DRY WINE

Note: Where a producer has been assigned a range of stars, for example ★ ★ ★/★ ★ ★, the lower rating has been used for placement in this hierarchy. Lack of available data (not all historical data is reprinted here) may affect a winery's ranking. Sometimes a winery is just too new to rank highly. Sometimes data is simply unavailable for one reason or another. For instance, Maria Borges (Fojo) has made stunning wines, but for a variety of reasons, and despite considerable effort in the U.S. and in Portugal, I have not been able to taste any of the top wines beyond the late-released 2000 Tintos.

★ ★ ★ ★ ★ (OUTSTANDING)

Niepoort   Quinta do Vale Meão
Quinta do Crasto

★ ★ ★ ★ (EXCELLENT)

Lemos & Van Zeller   Wine & Soul
Quinta do Vallado

★ ★ ★ (GOOD)

CARM (Casa Agrícola Roboredo Madeira)   Maria D. P. G. Serôdio de S.
Domingos Alves de Sousa ★★★/★★★★   Borges (Fojo) ★★★/★★★★
Lavradores de Feitoria   Poeira

---

*The final name of this new old-vine bottling was not finally registered as of this writing and might change.

Prats & Symington
Quinta do Noval
Quinta do Passadouro
Quinta do Portal
Quinta de Roriz

Quinta de la Rosa
Ramos Pinto ✴✴✴/✴✴✴✴
Roquette e Cazes
Sogrape (Casa Ferreirinha) ✴✴✴/✴✴✴✴

✴ ✴ (AVERAGE)

Aneto
António Alfredo Lamas
Barros, Almeida
Cabanas do Castanheiro Casa Agrícola
   (Gambozinos)
Cálem
Caves Aliança (Quinta dos Quatro Ventos)
Caves Messias
Caves do Salgueiral (Andreza)
Caves Transmontanas
Churchill Graham
   (Churchill Estates) ✴✴/✴✴✴
Companhia das Quintas (Fronteira—Quinta
   da Cova da Barca)
Companhia dos Vinhos do Douro (CVD)
Conceito
Cunha & Prazeres
Jorge Rosas Vinhos Unipessoal

José Maria da Fonseca (Domini)
José Mesquita Guimarães
Lurton, Jacques & François
Muxagat Vinhos
Odisseia
PV
Quanta Terra
Quinta da Padrela
Quinta de São José
Quinta da Sequeira
Quinta do Vale da Perdiz
Quinta de Ventozelo
Real Companhia Velha
Sociedade dos Vinhos Borges
Symington Family Estates
Unicer Vinhos
Vinhos Douro Superior
V. Leite de Faria

THE DOURO'S GREATEST WINE BARGAINS

Note: All of the following wines are red unless otherwise noted.

Aneto Tinto
Barros, Almeida Grande Escolha
Cálem Curva Reserva
CARM (Casa Agrícola Roboredo Madeira) Tinto (Quinta do Côa)
CARM (Casa Agrícola Roboredo Madeira) Tinto
CARM (Casa Agrícola Roboredo Madeira) Reserva Branco (white)
Caves Messias Grande Escolha (Quinta do Cachão)
Caves Transmontanas Branco (Vértice) (white)
Caves Transmontanas Tinto (Vértice)
Caves Transmontanas Vértice Espumante Reserva and Super Reserva (white sparkling)
Lavradores de Feitoria Três Bagos Sauvignon Blanc (white)
Lavradores de Feitoria Três Bagos
Muxagat Vinhos Branco (white)
Poças Novus
Quinta do Portal Reserva
Quinta de Roriz Prazo de Roriz
Quinta da Sequeira Tinto
Quinta da Sequeira Branco Vinhas Velhas (white)
Quinta do Vale Meão Meandro do Vale Meão
Quinta do Vallado Tinto
Quinta de Ventozelo Touriga Nacional

Ramos Pinto Adriano
Ramos Pinto Adriano Branco (white)
Real Companhia Velha Quinta dos Aciprestes Reserva
Symington Family Estates Vale Do Bomfim Reserva (Dow)
Vinhos Douro Superior Reserva Branco (Castello D'Alba) (white)

Note: Although Quinta do Crasto's Old Vines Reserva is priced beyond the $20 cutoff for this section, it would be a shame not to mention it. Year in and year out, this is one of the best wines you can get for modest money (usually upper $20s) in the Douro. It consistently scores 90+ points and is consistently reasonable in price. In many years, it is arguably the best intersection of value and quality in the Douro.

[tasting commentaries]

ANETO ★ ★
DOURO 10 EUROS

This small-production bottling (10,000 bottles) comes from a relatively new winery. These are interesting debuts. The name is taken from a local plant said to have aphrodisiac qualities. The Tintos are tightly wound and focused, the 2004 a bit more dense and tannic, the 2003 more succulent. The wines are a bit brooding and backward, particularly the 2004, which can seem a bit rustic. A mere 10 euros in Portugal, these wines are awfully serious and ageworthy for a pittance. There is no U.S. importer yet, but there likely will be. Aneto is a winery to watch. There will be no 2005, but in 2006 the winery will start making a reserve. The Semillon is delicious, beautifully balanced, and a pleasure to drink.

2004 Tinto	89	2010–2020
2003 Tinto	87	2008–2018
2005 Semillon Colheita Tardia (sweet white)	89	now–2014

ANTÓNIO ALFREDO LAMAS ★ ★
DOURO $19.50

This is an ageworthy wine that takes a couple of hours to come around. The pretty but confusing and obscure label, which makes the name, vintage, and producer hard to read, is not a plus.

2004 Bajancas	87	now–2014

BARROS, ALMEIDA ★ ★
DOURO $9.00–$18.00

This winery provides some good values, although nothing I have seen yet has been truly distinguished. The Grande Escolha held well to significant aeration and is an excellent value.

2003 Tinto	85	now–2009
2001 Grande Escolha	88	now–2012

CABANAS DO CASTANHEIRO CASA AGRÍCOLA ★ ★
DOURO $30.00–$36.00

This winery made well-crafted wines, but absent better deals "on the street," the suggested pricing is a bit high for the results compared to what the Douro has to offer elsewhere. There seems to be promise here, however. The Reserva is nicely structured and less expensive as well.

| 2004 Touriga Nacional (Gambozinos) | 86 | now–2013 |
| 2004 Reserva (Gambozinos) | 87 | now–2013 |

CÁLEM ★ ★
DOURO $16.00

This table wine from Cálem, a well-known Port house, is a nice value and is drinking well.

| 2004 Curva Reserva | 87 | now–2012 |

CARM ★ ★ ★
DOURO $12.00–$50.00

CARM's vineyards are located about 3 kilometers from Spain and right next to Quinta da Leda, the well-known Casa Ferreirinha vineyard. CARM (Casa Agrícola Roboredo Madeira) produced its first vintage in 1999. This fine producer's lineup was particularly impressive for the quality it could deliver for reasonable money. Few estates in the Douro deliver more for less so consistently. The basic Tintos are excellent values, and the Reservas are reasonably priced. The only pricey ($50) wine is the CM. Most of the wines are blends of the Quintas owned by CARM, excepting the Quinta do Côa, a single vineyard bottling. The only remaining thing I would like to see from this producer is some truly exceptional wines, not just exceptional values.

2000 CM	91	now–2015
2003 Grande Escolha	88+	now–2018
2005 Tinto	88	now–2012
2004 Tinto	88	now–2015
2005 Tinto (Quinta do Côa)	89	now–2013
2004 Tinto (Quinta do Côa)	88	now–2015
2003 Reserva	90	now–2016
2004 Grande Reserva	91	now–2017
2004 Reserva (Quinta do Côa)	91	now–2014
2005 Reserva Branco (white)	87	now–2010

CAVES ALIANÇA ★ ★
DOURO $24.00–$49.99

This big company, based in Beiras with holdings throughout several Portuguese wine regions, brought in Michel Rolland and Pascal Chatonnet in 1999 to consult. Chatonnet remains, working with winemaker Francisco Antunes. This relatively new Douro venture comes from Quinta dos Quatro Ventos ("Four Winds") and generally showed well, although the Douro pricing is a little on the high side, it seems. There were also some growing pains evident, with erratic results with the 2001, which makes me hesitant to rank this quinta higher until it is clear that it has hit stride. On the other hand, the 2002 was a very nice off-vintage performance. Ironically, I thought the regular 2004 Tinto, the least expensive wine here, was the best of this bunch, although certainly lighter than the upper-level wines. That may be a good sign that the winery is progressing.

2004 Tinto (Quinta dos Quatro Ventos)	90	now–2015
2002 Reserva (Quinta dos Quatro Ventos)	89	now–2012
2001 Reserva (Quinta dos Quatro Ventos)	86	now–2015

CAVES MESSIAS ★★
DOURO $13.99

This large company provides two pretty good values here. To my mind, the Grande Escolha is a cut above, although those looking to sample a single-varietal Touriga Franca will find this bottling useful and well priced as well, if a bit simple.

2004 Touriga Franca (Quinta do Cachão)	86	now–2012
2004 Grande Escolha (Quinta do Cachão)	88	now–2014

CAVES DO SALGUEIRAL ★★
DOURO $15.00

This has an old-fashioned feel to it in many respects, with lots of tannins. It is also fairly oaky. All things considered, though, there is a lot of wine here for modest money, and it has a chance to age quite well in its price category.

2003 Reserva (Andreza)	86	now–2015

CAVES TRANSMONTANAS ★★
DOURO $11.00–$20.00

This winery was founded in 1988 by Jack Davies of Schramsberg, the noted Napa sparkling wine producer, though Schramsberg is no longer associated with it. The winery focuses on sparkling wine, but began to make dry, still wine in 1999. The whites are perhaps a bit better than the reds. All of these are small-production wines, and the prices are very fair. The sparklers, at $11 and $14 respectively, are very nice deals. The Super Reserva is quite complex for its price range. Call it the winery's "geek wine," likely to satisfy enthusiasts for a very low price.

2003 Grande Reserva (Vértice)	86	now–2012
2004 Tinto (Vértice)	88	now–2014
2004 Branco (Vértice) (white)	89	now–2009
2006 Branco (Vértice) (white)	85	now–2009
2001 Espumante Super Reserva (Vértice)		
(white sparkling)	89	now–2010
2004 Espumante Reserva (Vértice) (white sparkling)	86	now–2011

CHURCHILL GRAHAM ★★/★★★
DOURO $50.00–$60.00

Churchill Graham is owned by personable John Graham, a scion of the Graham family, the former proprietors of Graham's Ports (now owned by the Symington family, with no relationship today to the Graham family). The estate makes relatively restrained and elegant wines. The single-quinta wine from Quinta da Gricha has been my favorite. This estate should certainly earn a higher ranking if it keeps turning out wines like this, but I have not seen enough from them yet.

2005 Quinta da Gricha (Churchill Estates)	91	2009–2016

COMPANHIA DAS QUINTAS ★★
DOURO $13.99

Founded in 1999 and formally registered as Sociedade Agrícola da Quinta da Romeira de Cima, this company trades under the umbrella name Companhia das Quintas (literally, "the Estates Company"), signifying its acquisition and ownership of quintas in various regions. (The latest acquisition is Quinta de Pancas.) As the formal name implies, they are headquartered at Quinta da Romeira, an estate with roots going back centuries. The 2001 Reserva (Fronteira—Quinta da Cova da Barca) is a blend of Touriga Nacional, Tinta Roriz, and Touriga Franca. The label does not indicate Quinta da Cova da Barca, but the winery assures me that this is where this wine is from, and that it "is the last vineyard in the River Douro." It is a nice value, with some age on it.

2001 Reserva (Fronteira—Quinta da Cova da Barca)	87	now–2010

COMPANHIA DOS VINHOS DO DOURO (CVD) ★ ★
DOURO 5–40 EUROS

Owner-winemaker José de Almeida used to be at Quinta do Crasto and the Symington Group, two pretty good résumé points. His first vintage was 2001. Different levels of the wines are named for musical instruments. For example, *fagote* means "bassoon" in English. The Oboé, an upper-level special selection, produced only 5,000 bottles and is the sole pricey bottle here, running around 40 euros in Portugal. Although much more refined and ageworthy than the Fagote, it was a bit burdened with American oak on release, but there are some recent signs that it is integrating well.

2005 Fagote Branco (white)	85	now–2008
2003 Fagote Reserva	88	now–2013
2003 Oboé Grande Escolha	88+	now–2016

CONCEITO ★ ★
DOURO 9–18 EUROS

In truth, there is not much data available to justify ranking this winery, but the debut releases are promising, and I suspect by the time the next edition rolls around, they will be well respected. Consider this a heads-up. *Conceito* means "concept" in Portuguese. This new winery just entered the market in June 2007, releasing a 2005 Port and Tinto, and these two 2006 whites. The whites are very different animals, but both are very interesting debuts in a somewhat difficult year. The Meio-Doce is about 9 euros in Portugal; the regular Branco, about 18. The 2006 Branco Meio-Doce is just a little off-dry, a perfect aperitif. It is a wine that was oddly rich and fat, yet neither unctuous nor thick. It is a "drink me now" wine, the younger the better, I think, but I loved it. The 2006 Branco is another type of wine entirely, serious and structured, from 80-year-old vines. It is largely Rabigato and Códega, with some Viosinho and Gouveio mixed in. There were approximately 292 cases produced.

2006 Branco (white)	88	now–2010
2006 Branco Meio-Doce (white)	88	now–2009

CUNHA & PRAZERES ★ ★
DOURO $50.00–$55.00

João Brito e Cunha also makes wines for Jorge Rosas, as well as his father's estate, Quinta de S. José, and Churchill's. The 2004 Ázeo is a blend of Touriga Nacional (50%), Tinta Roriz (15%), Touriga Franca (10%), plus a field blend of mixed varieties from 60-year-old vines (25%). There were fewer than 600 cases made. Cunha's wines all strike me as good, with potential, if not truly distinguished. There is rarely a failure. At the same time, they seem somewhat similar. There is considerable promise here but also some things to work out. I do see progress; the 2005s are better balanced than the 2004s, if a little lighter, and brighter. They are intense and in need of cellaring.

2005 Ázeo	89	2009–2016
2004 Ázeo	89	now–2014

DOMINGOS ALVES DE SOUSA ✶✶✶/✶✶✶✶
DOURO $27.00–$83.00

This fine and rather underrated estate makes wine from several differen: quintas, including Quinta do Vale da Raposa and Quinta da Gaivosa, which are adjacent to one another. Their first vintage was 1991. This family-owned estate features Domingos and Tiago, father and son, both dedicated and passionate. Tiago is the fourth generation. Esteemed winemaker Anselmo Mendes rounds out the team. Their top wines are always interesting, and some of them are particularly good values, too, like the delicious 2001 Grande Escolha (Quinta do Vale da Raposa), under $30. The wonderful 2004 Abandonado is a limited-production new bottling that comes from a single vineyard, 80 years old, that was almost abandoned, hence the name. The Vinha de Lordelo is another small-production bottling, usually powerful and intense. One fascinating wrinkle here is the difference between Quinta da Gaivosa Tintos (despite using merely a Tinto designation, this is the flagship wine) and the Reserva Pessoal. Both are from Quinta da Gaivosa. They are supposed to be "different expressions" of the same *terroir*. If you want an example of how winemaker decisions and perspectives can completely change a wine and still represent the vineyard, here is an interesting exercise. The Reserva Pessoal is soft and elegant, seductive and early maturing. The flagship Tintos from Quinta da Gaivosa are usually powerfully structured and intense.

2003 Quinta da Gaivosa	90	now–2017
2000 Quinta da Gaivosa	92	now–2013
2003 Reserva Pessoal	90	now–2015
1999 Reserva Pessoal	86	now–2010
2004 Touriga Nacional (Quinta do Vale da Raposa)	87	now–2014
2003 Touriga Nacional (Quinta do Vale da Raposa)	89	now–2013
2001 Grande Escolha (Quinta do Vale da Raposa)	92	now–2013
2001 Tinto Cão (Quinta do Vale da Raposa)	85	now–2010
2004 Abandonado	95	2010–2020
2005 Vinha de Lordelo (Quinta da Gaivosa)	92	2009–2019
2006 Reserva Branco da Gaivosa (white)	88	now–2012

JORGE ROSAS VINHOS UNIPESSONAL ✶ ✶
DOURO $36.00

The winemaker here is João Brito e Cunha, who also makes wines for his own estate, Cunha & Prazeres, separately listed. The 2004 Quinta da Touriga—Chã is 70% Touriga Nacional, 25% Tinta Roriz, and the rest Touriga Franca. It is lush and rather tasty. The 2005 is 85% Touriga Nacional and the rest Tinta Roriz. It is tighter and lighter, but also brighter, with more integrated oak and better balance. Both wines were aged in French oak, never more than 70% new.

2005 Quinta da Touriga—Chã	90	2009–2018
2004 Quinta da Touriga—Chã	88	now–2014

JOSÉ MARIA DA FONSECA ✶ ✶
DOURO $15.99–$40.00

This well-known southern Portuguese winery has holdings in several regions. They are famous for Lancer's Rosé, but there are in fact some nice table wines here, so don't let that Lancer's thing get in your way. The well-known southern table wine Periquita (Fonseca's southern holdings are separately listed in the section dealing with regions other than Douro and Alentejo) is another signature offering, an old Portuguese warhorse whose origins date back to the middle of the 19th century. The Domini wines are a Douro venture made in partnership with Cristiano van Zeller, owner of Quinta do Vale D. Maria, and former co-owner of Quinta do Noval. The Domini Plus is essentially the reserve bottling from this partnership between Fonseca and van Zeller. These have an elegant Bordeaux feel to them.

2004 Domini	86	now–2012
2003 Domini	87	now–2011
2004 Domini Plus	89	now–2014
2001 Domini Plus	89	now–2013

JOSÉ MESQUITA GUIMARÃES   ★ ★
DOURO $13.50–$26.00

This producer, with little profile at the moment, makes wines that have structure and power. They show some ability to age and develop.

2002 Tinto (Quinta dos Poços)	85	now–2011
2003 Escolha (Quinta dos Poços)	87	now–2013

LAVRADORES DE FEITORIA   ★ ★ ★
DOURO $12.00–$65.00

This winery (pronounced, roughly, Lav-ruh-DORSH duh Fay-tor-REE-uh) is a relatively new coop, a collection of 15 growers. Portugal's table wine image has often suffered due to the proliferation of coops, but this one is rather different. It is a very high-quality coop, in large part because a driving force here is Dirk Niepoort, one of the most prestigious names in the Douro for dry table wines. Unlike most coops, they also bottle a single-quinta wine, the Quinta da Costa, often an excellent buy at around $30. The workhorse, blended proprietary line is designated Três Bagos, and these wines are usually good values, too, at around $18 suggested retail. There is also a generic Douro bottling that is less interesting. The Grande Escolha is their Big Boy, and very fine. I had some trouble with burnt match aromas in the 2005 Meruge, normally an excellent bottling.

2006 Três Bagos Sauvignon Blanc (white)	88	now–2010
2005 Três Bagos Sauvignon Blanc (white)	89	now–2009
2005 Três Bagos	88	now–2013
2004 Grande Escolha	92	now–2016
2003 Grande Escolha	91	now–2013
2005 Quinta da Costa das Aguaneiras No. 6	90	2009–2017
2005 Meruge	86	2009–2016
2006 Douro	83	now–2010

LEMOS & VAN ZELLER   ★ ★ ★ ★
DOURO $38.00–$90.00

Cristiano van Zeller's connections are widespread in the Douro, ranging from his former career at Quinta do Noval to various projects with the Roquettes (owners of Quinta do Crasto), PV, and José Maria da Fonseca. Quinta do Vale D. Maria is a single vineyard that was part of his wife's family's holdings. (The "D" stands for "Dona," and is abbreviated on the front label as well, so I have maintained that abbreviation here.) At one point in the past, the vineyard was leased to the Symingtons, where much of its fruit went into Smith Woodhouse Port. Winemaker Sandra Tavares da Silva, also the winemaker for her own Pintas, with her husband, Jorge, and for her family's Estremadura estate Quinta de Chocapalha, does a superb job here, crafting some of the tastiest wines in the Douro.

The wines that Sandra makes tend to be bold and flavorful with lots of everything. The wines are always simply delicious. Some years, they have better balance than others. Some years, they have better structure than others. One constant, however, is that they are, year in, year out, some of the most flavorful wines made in the Douro. I should add, they manage to do this without artificial, candied notes. They always seem like wine, not Kool-Aid. Also, if you are wondering what a typical Douro field blend tastes like, these wines provide good examples. The Vale D. Maria Tinto, for instance, is a field blend of 40-plus varieties. The luxury, small-production CV bottling, from vines facing north and west, tends to be bigger and denser than the Vale D. Maria. The winery says that it is not intended to be in a different qualitative class, but note that its very name, CV, short for Curriculum Vitae, is meant to indicate "the type of wine you would like to have on your résumé," according to Sandra. It is pretty darn good. The substantial price differential (almost double the Vale D. Maria), however, is attributable to scarcity, there being only 125 cases of the 2003 and only 416 of the 2004.

The Casa de Casal de Loivos bottling is sourced from an estate centered around a 1658 manor house owned by another Douro family with whom the van Zellers have worked for generations. It tends to be the most seductive of the offerings. *Note:* On some of the Vale D. Maria wines here, the label will indicate Fonseca and Van Zeller. Cristiano explained it to me this way: "The actual producer is Lemos & Van Zeller. All wines are from my Quinta Vale D. Maria and nowhere else. But, for two harvests (2002 and 2003) . . . the wines were bottled by the joint venture I had with José Maria da Fonseca (a company called José Maria da Fonseca & Van Zeller) to produce Douro wines." To add to the confusion, Cristiano technically owns CV and the Van Zeller brand while Lemos & Van Zeller is the owner of Quinta Vale D. Maria. In that Cristiano is the underlying principal in some fashion, and since all of the wines are still shipped by Lemos & Van Zeller with Sandra as winemaker, I have grouped these under the Lemos & Van Zeller name, with Cristiano's concurrence.

2005 Tinto (Quinta Vale D. Maria)	92	2009–2020
2004 Tinto (Quinta Vale D. Maria)	93	now–2016
2003 Tinto (Quinta Vale D. Maria)	91	now–2015
2001 Tinto (Quinta Vale D. Maria)	90	now–2015
2005 CV (Curriculum Vitae)	94	2009–2020
2004 CV (Curriculum Vitae)	94	now–2022
2003 CV (Curriculum Vitae)	93	now–2018
2004 Casa de Casal de Loivos	91	now–2016
2003 Casa de Casal de Loivos	92	now–2015
2006 VZ (Van Zeller) (white)	89	now–2010
2004 Van Zeller	89	now–2013

JACQUES & FRANÇOIS LURTON   * *
DOURO $11.99–$35.00

The Lurtons make their Douro debut here with wines they made with the cooperation of the well-known co-op Lavradores de Feitoria. The obscure proprietary name "Pilheiros" is the Portuguese name for the holes and cracks in the low walls supporting the Douro's terraces in the vineyards. As explained by the Lurtons, in olden days, this was where grapevines were allowed to grow, while crops deemed to be more important grew on the terrace surface. Some less expensive wines, like the Barco Negro, did not show as well.

2005 Pilheiros	85	now–2013
2004 Pilheiros	87	now–2011
2004 Pilheiros Grande Escolha	88	now–2013
2004 Barco Negro	84	now–2010

MARIA D. P. G. SERÔDIO DE S. BORGES ★★★/★★★★
DOURO $41.00–$80.00

This producer is the sister of co-owner, co-winemaker Jorge Borges of Pintas fame. She has been making some cultish wines of her own for a decade or so. From what I saw here, they walk the walk. As they age, they developed a very Bordeaux-like feel. They are certainly pricey, and to some extent, they have a rather old-fashioned approach to tannins but they deliver. Borges makes wines from different quintas, including Manuela and Fojo. This is one of the many estates that designate flagship wines simply as Tintos, so don't be fooled—those are the upper-level bottlings. Borges is listed as the producer on each label, and the wines are grouped as such here. Based on what I have tasted thus far, this producer would deserve to be higher ranked but her importer had nothing in stock in the United States after 2000, and an attempt to taste at the winery fell through when the owner inadvertently missed the appointment. Note that the 2000 is the current release of the top wine, as the winery tends to release late. I could not justify a higher ranking without having had any recent wines, however. The Vinha da Fojo is the second wine, charming and elegant, interesting in its own right. It has aged very gracefully.

1999 Vinha do Fojo (Quinta do Fojo)	90	now–2012
2000 Tinto (Quinta da Manuela)	94	2010–2020
2000 Fojo (Quinta do Fojo)	95	now–2020
1996 Fojo (Quinta do Fojo)	88	now–2012

MUXAGAT VINHOS ★★
DOURO $11.50–$16.50

This winery began in 2002 as a "garage" winery. It is a project between two partners, Eduardo Lopes and Mateus Nicolau de Almeida. Almeida, 28, studied oenology in Bordeaux and acts as the winemaker. Winemaking runs in the family. His grandfather created the landmark wine Barca Velha, and his father is the winemaker at Ramos Pinto. This winery's attractive labels and presentation will no doubt help with the marketing, but the proof is ultimately in the glass, and the wines show promise. The reds are good values, soft and charming, although not really distinguished. The steal here is the least expensive wine of the group, the 2005 Branco, which is 90% Rabigato, 5% Códega, and 5% Verdelho, raised 50% in new French oak and the rest in stainless steel, on the lees nine months. These are all small-production wines.

2004 Tinto	87	now–2014
2003 Tinto	87	now–2013
2005 Branco (white)	89	now–2009

NIEPOORT ★★★★★
DOURO $25.00–$110.00

Dirk Niepoort is at the helm of this family-owned Port house that has become one of Portugal's leading table wine producers. Niepoort, in fact, is one of the Douro Valley's oldtimers, having plunged into table wines circa 1990. By current standards, that makes him one of the most experienced around. He is one of the folks most responsible for turbocharging the ongoing dry red wine revolution. When he joined the family firm in 1987, he helped arrange the purchase of Quinta de Nápoles, whose roots date back to the 15th century. A year later, Niepoort purchased Quinta do Carril. With those purchases, the Niepoort house finally had its own vineyards. Niepoort's wines tend to be focused and elegant. Those preferring richer, riper wines will have many other choices in the Douro. He has adopted a Burgundian sensibility for the most part, particularly with his Charme, a luxury bottling often mistaken for a Burgundy. As an experienced revolutionary, Niepoort has also paid close attention to Phase

Two of the revolution—his white wines are among the best in Portugal, from the brilliant Redoma Reserva, to the bracing and steely Tiara. Both iconic and iconoclastic (Niepoort can yank some chains with statements averring that he doesn't like fruit), Niepoort is one of the most dedicated people in the Douro, but his importance to the region is almost as great as his importance to his own winery. He is in many respects the Douro's Robert Mondavi. Among recent vintages, in my view, Niepoort's reds are far better in 2004 than 2005. The 2005 whites, however, are stunning, and he achieved a lot with the 2006 whites as well in the context of the vintage. The pick of the red litter for me is usually the Batuta, one of Portugal's most sought-after trophies. I had issues, on the other hand, with the 2005 Charme due to burnt match aromas.

2005 Vertente	87	now–2012
2004 Vertente	89	now–2013
2006 Redoma Branco (white)	89	now–2010
2005 Redoma Branco (white)	92	now–2012
2006 Redoma Branco Reserva (white)	92	now–2012
2005 Redoma Branco Reserva (white)	94	now–2014
2006 Tiara (white)	89	now–2010
2005 Charme	86	now–2015
2004 Charme	93	now–2016
2005 Redoma	89	now–2015
2004 Redoma	92	now–2017
2005 Batuta	92	2009–2020
2004 Batuta	95	now–2021
2003 Batuta	94	now–2018

ODISSEIA ★ ★
DOURO $15.00–$33.00

The Touriga Nacional is the better wine here, better structured, more ageworthy. However, considering that it is more than double the price of the Tinto, many will find the charming Tinto to be an appealing purchase.

2005 Tinto	85	now–2011
2004 Touriga Nacional	88	now–2015

POÇAS ★ ★
DOURO $12.00–$25.00

This old (1918) Portuguese, family-owned Port house (it is said that there are but seven with those attributes) continues the Douro red wine revolution with this interesting, value-priced lineup. The Coroa D'ouro Reserva is a decent value at $12 or under, although it flattens quickly with air. The real pick here is between the Novus ($18) or the regular Reserva ($25). The former is sexier and delicious; the latter, better structured and balanced. They will each have their adherents. The Branco is attractive for those who like them grassy, and at around $12, it is a good deal.

2004 Novus	88	now–2012
2004 Reserva	87	2009–2013
2006 Coroa D'ouro Reserva Branco (white)	87	now–2009
2004 Coroa D'ouro Reserva	85	now–2011

POEIRA ★★★
DOURO $20.00–$45.00

Jorge Moreira's young winery, Poeira (meaning "dust," pronounced Poe-AIR-uh), probably turned the qualitative corner in 2004, a vintage that well exceeds the 2003. I hope to see better and better things as time goes on. Jorge is also the winemaker at Quinta de la Rosa and Quinta do Requeijo. Production totals were approximately 14,000 bottles as of the time this was written. The Poeira résumé is slim at the moment, although Jorge points out that at his young, mid-30s age, he has been making wine for a decade. Poeira is a winery to watch. Poeira's Tinto is another of the Douro's famous field blends, sourced from a 70-year-old vineyard. It tends to be earthy and well structured. With the 2004, this winery went from good to impressive, and with the 2005 perhaps they went a step further, although it is pretty close. The J is Poeira's second wine, a blend of purchased grapes and young Poeira vines. For early to mid-term consumption, it will be quite the crowd-pleaser, as it is utterly charming and delicious, probably around $20. It is not as well structured as the Poeira Tinto, of course, but it tastes too good to ignore. *Note:* On the J, the word "Poeira" is nowhere on the label (because some of the grapes are purchased)—and indeed, you have to look hard and on the back to find anything resembling a producer name (Jorge Moreira, in very, very tiny print). It is sometimes hard to figure out who the actual producer is in Portugal, but since this has been claimed to be a second wine, I have grouped it here.

2005 Tinto	92	2009–2020
2004 Tinto	92	now–2015
2003 Tinto	89	now–2013
2005 J	89	now–2013

PRATS & SYMINGTON ★★★
DOURO $24.00–$66.00

This is one of the famous and increasingly successful partnerships in Portugal with foreign wine interests. Here, the Symingtons, owners of Dow's and Graham's Ports, among others, pair up with Bruno Prats of Cos d'Estournel fame. Chryseia is a relatively new project, the first experimental lots having been made in only 1999. "Chryseia" is the Greek translation of "Douro," literally meaning "of gold." In many respects, you can call this lineup from Prats & Symington one of the more modern faces of the Douro. Old caricatures of Douro wines reference rustic bottlings, with tannins that will never resolve. No one will call these wines rustic. The Post Scriptum is the second wine of Chryseia. It was a bit disappointing considering its price point in 2004, but overachieved, if anything, in 2005. The Chryseia is primarily Touriga Nacional and Touriga Franca with Tinta Roriz and Tinto Cão blended in, raised in new French oak. Fruit is sourced from various quintas of note, such as Perdiz and Bomfim, which lovers of Dow's Ports will know well. Proportions of each varietal used are expected to vary from year to year and are usually unstated as a result. Around 3,000 cases are produced.

2005 Post Scriptum de Chryseia	90	now–2014
2004 Post Scriptum de Chryseia	87	now–2012
2005 Chryseia	92	2009–2020
2004 Chryseia	93	now–2019
2003 Chryseia	92	now–2015
2001 Chryseia	90	now–2013
2000 Chryseia	88	now–2011

DOURO $50.00

There is just one wine made here at the moment, and these are the first releases. The VT is a new joint venture of José Cálem (of the Cálem Port family) and prominent Douro winemakers Jorge Borges/Sandra Tavares da Silva (Pintas, etc.) and Cristiano van Zeller (CV, Quinta Vale D. Maria, etc.). It is admittedly a stretch to include PV in this report at all with just two nice-yet-not-exceptional releases, but considering the star power here, this is an operation that readers should be watching, and it would seem unlikely that PV will remain only a two-star producer. The obscure name arises from the producers being unable to agree on a name—and selecting what was written in chalk on the barrel resting in the cellar "VT'04," meaning Vinho Tinto, 2004. The VT is a blend of Touriga Nacional (50%) and a field blend from 50-year-old vines.

2005 VT'05	88	now–2014
2004 VT'04	89	now–2015

QUANTA TERRA ★★
DOURO $20.00

This is a partnership between two winemakers, Celso Pereira at Caves Transmontanas (Vértice), and Jorge Alves at Quinta do Tedo, owned by Vincent Bouchard of the Burgundy Bouchards. This Tinto has more power and austerity than the wines from Caves Transmontanas. I am told that the wine is a Grande Reserva, although the label I saw did not so indicate. There is a lot of power and structure here for the money. This may be an interesting new venture to watch.

2004 Tinto	88	now–2014

QUINTA DO CRASTO ★★★★★
DOURO $20.00–$125.00

This historic estate, with roots going back to 1615, is owned by the Roquette family. Like most estates in the Douro, the history is somewhat deceptive, as it was only in 1994 that Crasto became active as what it calls an "independent, self-marketing" quinta. It is on most short lists for the designation "best dry wine producer in Portugal," and with good reason. This is one of the estates that turbocharged the dry red revolution in modern Portugal. With winemaker Dominic Morris of Australia at the helm for more than a decade, Crasto (pronounced CRASH-too) goes from strength to strength and its wines are in high demand. Even their off-vintage wines are pretty good, while their upper-level "good vintage" cult wines are some of the most sought after in Portugal, as well as some of the most distinguished the country has to offer. The Roquettes' exciting new joint venture with Jean-Michel and Jean-Charles Cazes (of Château Lynch-Bages) is another feather in their caps. It is separately listed under Roquette e Cazes. If there is a downside, it is the obvious one: The wines are pretty pricey, a function of prestige and, sometimes, scarcity. The luxury cuvées, like the Vinha da Ponte and the Vinha Maria Teresa, are very old vines, small-production bottlings that are not made in every vintage. For example, the 2004 Vinha da Ponte was a field blend from a patch of the vineyard first planted in 1914. Only 250 cases were produced. Adding to the glory, Crasto's single-varietal wines have been among my favorites in a region and country where blending is standard practice. They are in high demand, and relatively small quantities are produced (the 2004 Touriga Nacional produced 750 cases). Crasto's regular Tinto used to be an excellent value, but in 2005 additional vineyard sources were added to it that were not within Crasto's own quinta. In my view, the 2005 and 2006 Tintos were steps back, perhaps as a result of these additions, perhaps because the vintages were not as good for this wine. Time will tell if it rights itself and again becomes an overachiever. The Crasto Reserva Old Vines is the best value point in the lineup, not to mention one of the very best Douro wines you can buy for the least money, usually coming in around the upper $20s on the street. In most years, it is one of the best intersections of value and quality in the Douro—if not the best. It usually contains some juice from whichever luxury bottling (Maria Teresa or Ponte) did not get bottled separately. Crasto also makes an inexpensive, low-end wine called Flor. It is Beaujolais-like, around $10, and not of real interest in comparison to the rest of this impressive lineup.

2006 Tinto	85	now–2011
2005 Tinto	87	now–2012
2003 Tinto	90	now–2013
2005 Reserva Old Vines	91	2009–2019
2004 Reserva Old Vines	94	2009–2019
2003 Reserva Old Vines	93	now–2018
2002 Reserva Old Vines	91	now–2013
2005 Touriga Nacional	91	2009–2020
2004 Touriga Nacional	92	now–2017
2003 Touriga Nacional	89	now–2015
2003 Tinta Roriz	93	now–2017
2004 Vinha da Ponte	95	2010–2024
2000 Vinha da Ponte	93	2010–2020
2005 Vinha Maria Teresa	94	2009–2021
2003 Vinha Maria Teresa	96	2009–2023
2001 Vinha Maria Teresa	95	now–2020

QUINTA DO NOVAL ★★★
DOURO $40.00–$90.00

These two wines are this well-known Port house's entrants into the dry red wine industry. It is a very impressive, if rather pricey, debut. At this house, similar to the practice in Bordeaux (Latour, Les Forts de Latour), the designation Tinto with just the winery's name on the front label is meant to indicate the top-level wine, while the second wine gets a proprietary name, in this case, Cedro. The very fine Tinto is built to last. It is a blend of Touriga Nacional (70%), Tinto Cão (20%), and Touriga Franca (10%) raised exclusively in French oak. The red wine track record here is very slim, but this debut is impressive enough to merit a heads-up. Noval now needs to show some consistency and progress.

2004 Cedro	90	now–2015
2004 Tinto	93	2009–2017

QUINTA DA PADRELA ★★
DOURO $12.00–$21.00

These small-production wines show promise from this producer that is, unfortunately, without a U.S. importer. The basic Tinto produced fewer than 750 cases; the nicely structured Reserva, around 375 cases. Prices are winery estimates.

2004 Tinto	86	now–2012
2004 Reserva	88	now–2015

QUINTA DO PASSADOURO ★★★
DOURO $28.00–$59.00

Jorge Serôdio Borges of Wine & Soul (Pintas) is the winemaker here. He does a fine job, too. The superb 2004 Reserva is mostly an old-vine field blend, the rest being 15% Touriga Franca.

The 2005s are not as interesting, but the basic Tinto has good structure for its status. The 2005 Reserva is a fine wine as well, although lighter and more compact than the 2004, but still with good structure and grip on the finish.

2005 Reserva	90	2009–2017
2004 Reserva	93	now–2016
2005 Tinto	87	now–2013

QUINTA DO PORTAL ★ ★ ★
DOURO $12.00–$70.00

This estate, operating under the supervision of French consultant Pascal Chatonnet, generally produces good but not profound wines at fair prices. The only evidence of hubris comes from the pricey AURU ($70), which is not enough of a step up to justify nearly tripling the price of the Grande Reserva. This proprietary blend was created for the first time in 2001 to celebrate this winery's tenth anniversary. All of the 2003s were tasted in the U.S. but labeled as cask samples.

2003 Tinto	87	now–2011
2005 Reserva	90	2009–2018
2004 Reserva	89	now–2017
2003 Reserva	88	now–2012
2003 Grande Reserva	90	now–2012
2001 Grande Reserva	89	now–2012
2000 Grande Reserva	87	now–2010
2003 Touriga Nacional	89	now–2014
2003 AURU	91	now–2018
2006 Duradero	88	2009–2016
2005 Colheita	87	now–2014

QUINTA DE RORIZ ★ ★ ★
DOURO $14.00–$30.00

This wine was the product of a partnership between João Van Zeller and the Symingtons (see the entries under Prats & Symington and Symington Family Estates). In 2008, however, João Van Zeller and Cristiano van Zeller (his cousin) announced a new partnership to run this old Van Zeller family estate. João is now the full owner. Cristiano's team, including Lemos & Van Zeller winemaker Sandra Tavares da Silva, will oversee operations. This quinta is a particularly historic one, with roots going back to the 18th century. Tempranillo is known as Tinta Roriz in the Douro because of its association with this particular quinta. The elegant Prazo, a second wine, is one of the better bargains in the Douro, around $14, perhaps less on release. It is utterly charming. The Reserva has power and consistency, as a vertical tasting in the Douro in June 2007 proved. The 2002 listed here is an excellent performance in an off year. I expect a lot from this estate, and if it continues to progress, it may move up in ranking. The wines are good values, too.

2005 Prazo de Roriz	88	now–2014
2004 Prazo de Roriz	89	now–2013
2004 Reserva	92+	now–2019
2003 Reserva	91	now–2014
2002 Reserva	90	2009–2017

QUINTA DE LA ROSA ★★★
DOURO $12.00–$45.00

Just a few blocks from the train station in Pinhão, this centrally located estate, owned by the Bergqvists, is also a manor house with guest rooms available for tourists. The winemaker is Jorge Moreira, who also makes wines for his own Poeira. The La Rosa reserve bottling, however, tends to be richer and riper. The basic Tinto is not as interesting as the reasonably priced Reserve, but keep in mind that the basic Tinto is a mere 7 euros or so in Europe. In that context, it performs quite well. Note that the Reserve bottling says "Reserve," not Reserva. The Vale da Clara wines are essentially a second label and usually offer good value. The pink is terrific. The Vale do Inferno and Cerejinha are rare single-vineyard bottlings. They are usually component parts of the Reserve wine.

2005 Tinto	87	now–2012
2004 Tinto	86	now–2012
2005 Vale do Inferno	92	2009–2020
2005 Cerejinha	91	2009–2020
2005 Reserve	89	2009–2018
2004 Reserve	91	now–2019
2003 Reserve	90	now–2016
2001 Reserve	92	now–2016
2006 Rosé (Bergqvist Vinhos—Vale da Clara) (rosé)	89	now–2009
2006 Tinto (Bergqvist Vinhos—Vale da Clara)	84	now–2010

QUINTA DE S. JOSÉ ★★
DOURO $45.00–$50.00

Winemaker João Brito e Cunha makes the wines here for his family's estate, which includes rather attractive bed-and-breakfast accommodations available to tourists, in the heart of the Douro. He also is the winemaker at his own winery (Ázeo) and Jorge Rosas. The 2005 Tinto is smoothly textured but penetrating on the finish. Its tannins are dominating the wine at the moment but should integrate nicely with time, as aeration brought out some delicious, fresh, and juicy fruit. The midpalate is on the lighter side.

2005 Tinto	90	2009–2017

QUINTA DA SEQUEIRA ★★
DOURO $13.00–$45.00

This winery owns some very old vineyards, though it released its first dry wine in only 2001. There are times when I am tasting their wines that I think that this winery should move up in ranking. At other times, the tannins seem hard and rustic, a little too much like the old-fashioned Douro stereotype, and I ponder the wines' balance. There is always structure and power here, as well as value for the money. These can, in fact, seem like really serious wines for the money, but charm is not always their strong suit. Not surprisingly, one favorite red wine of the group came from 2003—a vintage that provided a lot of ripe fruit, and perhaps melds well with the winery's style. The other favorite, the 2004 Grande Reserva, a typical Douro blend, is more overtly fruity, too, elegantly crafted, but retaining its tannic kick. There were 208 cases and some magnums made. It is responsible for the lone price spike here ($45), as everything else is $28 and under. The 2006 Vinhas Velhas ("Old Vines") white wine ($23) is a winner, a blend of Malvasia Fina, Rabigato, Gouveio, and Códega do Larinho from 100-year-old vineyards. The prices are winery estimates as there is no U.S. importer.

2002 Grande Escolha	86	now–2012
2004 Tinto	87	2009–2015

2001 Tinto	88	now–2013
2003 Reserva	89+	2009–2015
2006 Branco Vinhas Velhas (white)	89	now–2010
2006 Rosé (rosé)	85	now–2008
2004 Grande Reserva	90	2009–2019

QUINTA DO VALE MEÃO ★ ★ ★ ★ ★
DOURO $19.00–$62.00

This estate was founded in 1887 by the current owner's famous great-great-grandmother, Dona Antónia Adelaide Ferreira, a dominating force in her time and no doubt one of the most powerful women ever in wine. The Ferreira house, of course, became Portugal's iconic dry red wine producer with Barca Velha. The original Barca Velha vineyard is part of Vale Meão. Since the 1999 vintage, Francisco Javier de Olazabal, the former president of Ferreira, has produced wine from this historic estate with his sons, one of whom (Francisco, Jr.) is the winemaker. (Francisco, Jr., is also the winemaker at the well-regarded Quinta do Vallado, separately listed.) This is one of the Douro's great estates, and between the output here and at Vallado, Olazabal has to rank as one of the Douro's best and most important winemakers. I was treated to a fine vertical at this property in June 2007. Beginning with the 2001, and including the off-vintage 2002, every wine was a 90+ winner and aging gracefully. The Meandro, the estate's second wine, is a good value. In a vintage like 2005, it can be one of the Douro's biggest bargains. The so-called plain Tinto is their equivalent of a reserve bottling. There were few wines I had last year that had more pure charm than the 2004 Tinto. The 2005, unlike most elegant '05s, is very powerful and backward, perhaps even a bit rustic. It is a wine of the vintage candidate, although it still has some things to prove in the cellar.

2005 Meandro do Vale Meão	91	2009–2018
2004 Meandro do Vale Meão	89	now–2012
2005 Tinto	95	2012–2028
2004 Tinto	93	now–2019
2003 Tinto	93	now–2018
2002 Tinto	90	now–2014
2001 Tinto	91	now–2017

QUINTA DO VALE DA PERDIZ ★ ★
DOURO $15.00–$34.00

Some of the wines from this winery are pretty decent values, but others seem to underperform. The hand can be heavy with oak at times. The best wine here is clearly the 2004 Grande Reserva, raised solely in French oak. The 2002 Tinta Roriz is a decent off-vintage performance.

2003 Reserva (Cistus)	85	now–2009
2004 Grande Reserva (Cistus)	88	now–2014
2002 Tinta Roriz	86	now–2010

QUINTA DO VALLADO ★ ★ ★ ★
DOURO $18.00–$60.00

This historic estate has roots dating back to 1716, but its first dry wine was produced in 1997. It was bought in 1818 by the Ferreira family (see notes under Quinta do Vale Meão). Winemaker Francisco Olazabal is also the winemaker at the well-regarded Quinta do Vale Meão. The big modern change here occurred in 1995, when the Ferreira family sold its Port house to corporate giant Sogrape, and the owners of Vallado decided to start marketing their own wines. I was treated to a fine vertical tasting of these wines in the Douro in June 2007. The

Reservas from 2000 on were always above the 90-point barrier, showing both excellence and consistency. The Touriga Nacional is lovely, and the new Adelaide Old Vines is very fine and a future superstar bottling. This cuvée is named after Dona Antónia Adelaide Ferreira, the famous and influential ancestor of the current owners. The Adelaide comes exclusively from the best lots of the west-facing old vines (in excess of 100 years old) and is exclusively a field blend, in contrast to the regular Reserva (a field blend from 70% of west-facing vineyards in excess of 80 years old, plus Touriga Nacional [27%, 15 years old] and a dollop of Sousão). No price has been set as of this writing for the Adelaide bottling. The pricey Branco Reserva ($55) may become one of the Douro's best whites.

2005 Tinto	88	now–2014
2004 Tinto	89	now–2014
2005 Reserva	90	2009–2017
2004 Reserva	93+	2010–2024
2003 Reserva	92	now–2018
2000 Reserva	92	now–2020
2003 Tinta Roriz	89	2010–2020
2004 Sousão	87	2009–2020
2005 Adelaide Old Vines	93	2010–2022
2005 Touriga Nacional	89	now–2017
2006 Branco Reserva (white)	90	now–2011

QUINTA DE VENTOZELO ★ ★
DOURO $9.00–$24.00

This old quinta possesses some very old vineyards. Most of the wines here are fair deals and good values, although the winery sometimes does have a lamentably heavy hand with the oak, and American oak at that. At the upper end, it seems like the winery could and should do better, but considering the price points, there are values to be had here. The small-production Reservas (833 cases) show good structure and absorb the oak, mostly. The single-varietal wines, particularly the 2004s, are quite pleasing at their modest price points ("suggested" retail price of $18, meaning usually available for less). The Cister da Ribeira line of wines can be decent bargains under $10. The entry-level Vinzelo line is usually less interesting and only a couple of dollars less.

2003 Reserva	88	now–2013
2006 Rosé Vinzelo (rosé)	86	now–2008
2006 Vinzelo	84	now–2008
2006 Cister da Ribeira (white)	83	now–2008
2005 Cister da Ribeira	85	now–2009
2003 Cister da Ribeira	86	now–2010
2004 Tinta Roriz	87	now–2010
2004 Touriga Franca	86	now–2010
2004 Touriga Nacional	87	now–2011
2003 Touriga Nacional	86	now–2011
2004 Tinto	85	now–2010

RAMOS PINTO ★ ★ ★/★ ★ ★ ★
DOURO $14.00–$61.00

This well-known, midsize Port producer has been owned by the Roederer Group since 1990. In that time, it has created a long track record of excellence in this region, showing consistency in making well-crafted, ageworthy wines. Winemaker João Nicolau de Almeida has a long history in this region—his father was the creator of Barca Velha, Portugal's seminal, dry cult wine. In June 2007, this winery opened for me more or less every red that they had made, and it was overall an impressive performance. Ramos Pinto also makes a red wine called Bon Ares, a Vinho Regional blend with some Cabernet Sauvignon, not seen in the U.S. It was one of the better I have seen in the Douro. Note that the Adriano entry-level line is marketed as the Duas Quintas regular bottling in Portugal. The first Duas Quintas was made in 1990 and the first Duas Quintas Reserva in 1991, all of which makes this estate one of the Douro's relative old-timers. The best wines here are the Reservas and Reservas Especials, the latter of which produces only about 800 cases when made. The "regular" Reserva is an ageworthy wine that can be cellared for 15 years in good vintage, and still carries a suggested retail price of $32 for current releases. The basic Adriano line can be a nice value in good vintages in the under-$15 price range.

2005 Adriano	85	now–2011
2004 Adriano	86	now–2010
2003 Adriano	85	now–2009
2006 Adriano (white)	86	now–2010
2005 Adriano (white)	87	now–2009
2005 Duas Quintas Reserva	90	2009–2019
2004 Duas Quintas Reserva	90	2009–2019
2003 Duas Quintas Reserva	91	now–2018
2000 Duas Quintas Reserva	87	now–2015
2004 Duas Quintas Reserva Especial	92	2010–2024
2003 Duas Quintas Reserva Especial	94	2009–2020

REAL COMPANHIA VELHA * *
DOURO $20.00–$45.00

These wines were created by Jerry Luper, the well-known American winemaker (formerly of Château Montelena and Château Bouchaine). This is one of the Douro wineries that dabbles in "nonauthorized" DOC grapes, like Cabernet Sauvignon. Those wines, like the Grantom Reserva, get the Vinho Regional designation rather than the DOC. It was the priciest wine here, and also my least favorite, not for any pretentious ideological reason, but simply because of the wine. It is a blend of 80% Cabernet Sauvignon, Touriga Nacional (15%), and the rest Touriga Franca. It spent 18 months in Portuguese oak. It is well structured, actually, but also gives off sour cherry notes up front and green notes on the back end. The Quinta dos Aciprestes Reserva is the best buy here. I liked it about as well as the others, and it is their least expensive wine at $20 (suggested retail).

2003 Evel Grande Escolha	88	now–2013
2003 Reserva (Quinta dos Aciprestes)	88	now–2014
2003 Grantom Reserva	86	now–2014

ROQUETTE E CAZES * * *
DOURO $54.00–$58.00

This is a partnership that has gotten people excited. Jean-Michel and son Jean-Charles Cazes (of Château Lynch-Bages) joined with the Roquette family of Quinta do Crasto, one of the best Douro producers, to produce, under the Roquette e Cazes label, Xisto (SHEES-too), a reference to schist, the nature of the soil in the Douro vineyards. The 2003 debut is 60% Touriga Nacional, 25% Tinta Roriz, and 15% Touriga Franca, raised in French oak for 18 months. The oak really needed some time to integrate, but with lots of air, the Touriga Nacional nuances come through. The track record here is slim, obviously, and for that reason I hesitated to make Roquette e Cazes a three-star producer, but this is a venture that is already doing well, there is a lot of star power, and consumers should be on notice that this is a venture to watch.

2004 Xisto	90	now–2017
2003 Xisto	92	now–2018

SOCIEDADE DOS VINHOS BORGES ★ ★
DOURO $7.43–$21.35

This familiar winery churns out some decent values. If the wines are not exceptional, they are acceptable in the context of their price ranges and sometimes provide a little more. The Lello is the simplest wine, but at $7.50, it's not a bad everyday choice, as long as it is drunk young and fresh.

2004 Lello	85	now–2009
2004 Tinto (Quinta da Soalheira)	87	now–2011
2003 Reserva	88	now–2013

SOGRAPE—CASA FERREIRINHA ★ ★ ★/★ ★ ★ ★
DOURO $13.00–$140.00

Sogrape is Portugal's 800-pound gorilla, a huge company that has holdings throughout the country, from Mateus to Barca Velha, Portugal's equivalent of Penfolds Grange. Their crown jewel for dry wines is the Casa Ferreirinha line, acquired when Sogrape bought Ferreira, probably the Douro's most historic estate for dry red wine, and the creator of Barca Velha. The Casa Ferreirinha line is no longer the best Portugal has to offer, but these wines are still interesting, ageworthy, and sometimes quite impressive. The best of them can still be among the best wines produced in the Douro.

There is change in the air here, however, with a new winemaker at the helm, as well as new styles. A winery that helped create the stereotype of backward, rustic Douro wines that could not be approached for many years produced the 1999 Barca Velha in a more modern style—although it is still powerful and late released. An argument for a higher ranking (or lower one) can be made depending on which factors you weigh the most heavily, but with a new era dawning, new competition to meet, and a new winemaker at the helm, I will straddle the fence and see what comes next.

The better wines are, as a group, rather pricey, and it is sometimes hard to find the value in the upper-level cuvées. The Quinta da Leda bottling is priced around $60; the Reservas run around $70 (suggested retail price); and Barca Velha around $120–$140. The Reservas were arguably the best intersection of price and quality—ageworthy wines that often showed beautifully. It will be interesting to see if newer vintages, when released, will be as good as some of the old beauties such as the 1989 and 1994 (which may still be available in the market or from the importer). The entry-level wines are the Esteva and the Vinha Grande. The latter, particularly, gives a good idea of what a classic Douro blend tastes like, although the structure does not compare to the higher-level bottlings.

Sogrape's output solely under its own name is less impressive. This section applies only to the Casa Ferreirinha wines. Although Sogrape maintained Casa Ferreirinha's own labeling, new releases (albeit in small print) include Sogrape's name on the label, and I actually had a cork from a wine in the Ferreira lineup that said just "Sogrape." Thus, I have listed the Casa Ferreirinha wines under Sogrape.

2001 Esteva (Casa Ferreirinha)	85	now–2009
2001 Vinha Grande (Casa Ferreirinha)	86	now–2010
1999 Callabriga (Casa Ferreirinha)	89	now–2014
2004 Quinta da Leda (Casa Ferreirinha)	90	now–2017

2003 Quinta da Leda (Casa Ferreirinha)	92	2009–2018
2000 Quinta da Leda (Casa Ferreirinha)	91	now–2017
2004 Quinta da Leda Vinha do Pombal (Casa Ferreirinha)	90	now–2014
2004 Quinta da Leda Vinha da Ribeira (Casa Ferreirinha)	89	now–2013
1998 Colheita (Casa Ferreirinha)	90	now–2013
1996 Reserva (Casa Ferreirinha)	89	2010–2021
1994 Reserva (Casa Ferreirinha)	93	now–2015
1989 Reserva (Casa Ferreirinha)	92	now–2011
1999 Barca Velha (Casa Ferreirinha)	94	now–2022
2005 Branco (Casa Ferreirinha) (white)	86	now–2010

SYMINGTON FAMILY ESTATES * *
DOURO $6.00–$18.00

This company owns a major part of the Douro, including famous Port names like Graham's, Warre's, and Dow's. Their red wine ventures at Prats & Symington (Chryseia) and Quinta de Roriz (bought out by their partner as of 2008) have produced both excellent wines and excellent values. On their own, focusing on the Altano label, the wines are less impressive. The basic Altano is a $6 entry-level wine, which at its best tastes like real wine and has some value in the near term, but it does not excel in any way, usually seeming simple and short. The Altano Reservas have more structure and intensity, but are still fairly simple wines with a fair bit of oak and a mass-market feel. If the price is right, they can offer value. I liked the 2003 Altano lineup better than the 2004s. The best deal here, though, is the Vale do Bomfim Reserva, with a suggested retail of only $12. It is quite charming, if light and early maturing.

2004 Altano Reserva	86	now–2012
2003 Altano Reserva	88	now–2013
2005 Vale do Bomfim Reserva (Dow)	87	now–2011
2004 Vale do Bomfim Reserva (Dow)	88	now–2010

UNICER VINHOS * *
DOURO $N/A

Unicer is a substantial company that is involved in everything from water and coffee to wine. Unicer makes wine under several labels in several regions, including Quinta do Minho, Planura, Senhoria, and Quinta da Pedra, as well as the Mazouco reviewed here. I liked what I saw in this vintage, and the Reserva was simply delicious.

2003 Vinha de Mazouco	87	now–2015
2003 Vinha de Mazouco Reserva	90	2009–2018

VINHOS DOURO SUPERIOR * *
DOURO $9.00–$15.00

These are mostly inexpensive wines that are fairly simple but have reasonable values. In this lineup, the white wine, with a suggested retail of $13, is the steal. It is a blend of Códega do Larinho, Rabigato, and Viosinho. Drink it young and well stored for best results.

2003 Colheita Seleccionada (Castello d'Alba)	85	now–2009
2004 Reserva (Castello d'Alba)	85	now–2010
2003 Reserva (Castello d'Alba)	86	now–2012
2006 Reserva Branco (Castello d'Alba) (white)	88	now–2009

V. LEITE DE FARIA (VINHOS) ✦✦
DOURO $13.00–$22.00

These are attractive wines that generally offer good value for the money. There are no block-busters here, but the wines are all precise, sunny, and a pleasure to drink.

2003 Colheita Seleccionada (Gloria)	86	now–2011
2004 Reserva (Gloria)	89	now–2015
2003 Reserva (Gloria)	88	now–2013
2005 Animus	85	now–2011

WINE & SOUL ✦✦✦✦
DOURO $30.00–$70.00

Jorge Serôdio Borges, 34 (also the winemaker at Quinta do Passadouro), makes Pintas in tandem with his winemaker wife, Sandra Tavares da Silva, 35 (Quinta do Vale D. Maria, Chocapalha). They are a pretty impressive, young winemaking team that jointly has an increasingly prestigious reputation. Pintas is relatively new, the first release being 2001. Concerned with the Douro's reputation for hard tannins, this winery focuses on producing wines with refined, ripe tannins. Jorge, in fact, told me that it was his most important issue. The wines overall have a very elegant feel, melding finesse, power, and flavor. The Pintas is a field blend of more than 30 varieties from old vines.

Wine & Soul is still a work in progress. New wines like the Pintas Character (the very fine second wine that debuted in 2005 with a suggested retail of around $30) are appearing, and a surer hand is evident with the flagship Pintas every year. They purchased their vineyard only in May 2003, and now have total control over it. After tasting all of their wines in the Douro in June 2007, I would say that the 2004 vintage marks a new chapter for this young winery. I am going out on a limb a bit, but I think this small winery merits four stars.

The 2004 Pintas (about 458 cases) is superb, and the 2005 may be better. The white Guru has become one of the Douro's hottest brancos. The Guru style has been evolving in its short life (the 2006 vintage is the third; you can tell when you pull the cork, as it has a "3" stamped on top), to make it seem fresher and crisper. The 2006 had no maloactic fermentation. The Guru is a blend of Gouveio, Viosinho, Códega do Larinho, and Rabigato from 40-year-old vines.

Finally, to answer one burning question, note that Pintas, which means "spots" (as in wine splatter), was not named after the owners' frenetic dog, but rather the dog was named after the wine.

2005 Pintas	95	2009–2022
2004 Pintas	94	now–2019
2003 Pintas	92	now–2014
2005 Pintas Character	90	now–2015
2006 Guru (white)	90	now–2013

ALENTEJO

Alentejo is the principal competitor to the Douro at the moment. It is its polar opposite in most respects, the fire to Douro's ice. Geographically, Alentejo (literally, "beyond the Tejo River") is at the other end of the country, a vast region in Portugal's South. There are eight subregions classified within the Alentejo DOC: Borba, Reguengos, Moura, Redondo, Granja-Amareleja, Évora, Portalegre, and Vidigueira.

Circa 1990, Alentejo had a handful of coops and approximately two dozen producers. Today, about 15 years later, official figures as of this writing show 237 producers, an astonishing growth.

Alentejo is sparsely populated, containing only about 7.5% of Portugal's population despite comprising approximately 34% percent of its landmass. Particularly in the southern part of the region, the flat landscape, in sharp contrast to the Douro's steep and beautiful hills, can turn monotonous. People seem few and far between. It is dotted with sprawling farms, olive and cork trees, cattle, sheep, pigs, and, increasingly, vineyards, many of which are springing up out of nowhere. Sectors around Évora and Estremoz are more interesting, but no match for the breathtaking views of the Douro.

Alentejo wines are immensely popular in Portugal, and its table wines are as—if not more—popular there as Douro wines. Stereotypically, Alentejo wines are appreciated for good quality-to-price ratios at the lower end and fruit-forward approachability, in contrast to the opposing Douro caricature of brooding, tannic wines that take years to come around. This Alentejo stereotype is a backhanded compliment, to be sure, and it was never totally true, as structured wines like Quinta do Carmo have proven for decades. It also ignores the increasing number of producers making serious and ageworthy wines today.

Alentejo may mostly lack the Douro's old vineyard sites, but it has certain advantages over the Douro, including ease and cost of harvesting and planting. If its flat landscape lacks the sheer majesty of the Douro's steep hills, it makes vineyard management much easier and cheaper. If Alentejo does not have quite as many exciting wines as the Douro at this time, it has very serious people making substantial investments who obviously intend to change that dynamic.

RED WINES

Alentejo has developed a reputation for making "international" wines. Producers often use internationally familiar grapes such as Syrah to blend into popular local grapes like Aragonez (also known as Tempranillo in Spain and Tinta Roriz in the Douro, and sometimes seen with the alternate spelling of Aragonês), Castelão, and Trincadeira (also known as Tinta Amarela in the Douro). Producers are also increasingly adopting Touriga Nacional (the Douro's signature variety), which seems to be a grape that will do very well in Alentejo. Alicante Bouschet and Cabernet Sauvignon are popular as well. The grape blends in Alentejo (including the Vinho Regional Alentejano) often leave you with an "anything goes" feeling. Some of Alentejo's popular grapes, like Alfrocheiro and Trincadeira, require careful handling. Trincadeira can produce unpleasantly vegetal wines if not handled correctly. I have yet to have an Alfrocheiro that was interesting, let alone compelling. Different grapes may be more common in one subregion than another.

WHITE WINES

Roupeiro (also known as Síria) is frequently seen and very popular. It is "the finest white grape of the Alentejo," according to a pamphlet produced in conjunction with the Portuguese Trade Commission. However, two other particularly important grapes among quality whites in Alentejo are Antão Vaz and Arinto. One producer told me that he considered Antão Vaz his Chardonnay, and expected to get acidity from the Arinto he blended into it. Some producers are obviously counting on Antão Vaz to be a signature variety for quality whites, in blends and on its own. After that—anything goes, from grapes like Verdelho and Chardonnay to Fernão Pires (also known as Maria Gomes). There aren't many top white producers yet, but a rewarding survey would include trying the whites from places like Dona Maria, Herdade do Esporão, Fundação Eugénio de Almeida—Adega de Cartuxa, and Malhadinha Nova, in a variety of price ranges.

[recent vintages]

As in the Douro, the trio of vintages from 2003 to 2005 produced many excellent wines over-all. The best recent vintage is 2004, a warm year that produced focused, concentrated, and intense wines that are nonetheless in good balance. 2003 and 2005 are good, but less consistent than 2004. It was actually surprising to find so many more or less elegant wines—a relative term, to be sure—in such hot years. Although I would rank the vintages in order as 2004, 2005, and 2003, it is dangerous to generalize over a region this large with so many wineries that have different philosophies and, more importantly, different experience levels with their vineyards. Both of these vintages were very hot. Extreme heat and rain at the wrong times badly marred 2006. As David Baverstock, Esporão's winemaker, put it, "2003 and 2005 were very hot, but manageable. 2006 was very hot, but not manageable." Based on my tastings, one saving grace to 2006 is the very good performance of the white wines. From what I saw in Alentejo, good producers often turned out excellent brancos, far exceeding the reputation of the vintage. White wines are going to become a point of pride in Portugal in general and Alentejo in particular. Not many 2006 top reds have been available to taste as yet.

OLDER VINTAGES If you see older vintages on the market, the 2001s are powerful but focused, coming closer to 2004, and the 2000s are succulent and rich. As in the Douro, the weakest older vintage is 2002, problematic in most of Portugal.

—MARK SQUIRES

[the ratings]

THE BEST ALENTEJO WINES

Note: All of the following wines are red unless otherwise noted; this category includes Vinho Regional Alentejano wines.

Cortes de Cima Reserva
Dona Maria Reserva
Dona Maria Branco (white)
Francisco Nunes Garcia Reserva
Fundação Eugénio de Almeida—Adega de Cartuxa Pera-Manca
Herdade de Malhadinha Nova Tinto
Herdade de Malhadinha Nova Pequeno João
Herdade de Malhadinha Nova Marias da Malhadinha
Herdade de Malhadinha Nova Antão Vaz da Pecequina (white)
Herdade de Malhadinha Nova Branco (white)
Herdade do Mouchão Tinto
Herdade do Mouchão Tonel
Herdade do Esporão Garrafeira
Herdade do Esporão Torre do Esporão
Herdade dos Grous Reserva
João Portugal Ramos Reserva (Marquês de Borba)
Quinta do Carmo Reserva
Quinta do Mouro Tinto
Quinta do Zambujeiro Tinto
Quinta do Zambujeiro Terra do Zambujeiro

ALENTEJO'S BEST PRODUCERS OF DRY RED WINE

Note: Where a producer has been assigned a range of stars, for example * * */* * * *, the lower rating has been used for placement in the hierarchy. Lack of available data (not all historical data is reprinted here) may affect a winery's ranking. Sometimes a winery is just too new to rank highly. Sometimes data is unavailable. All of the following wines are red unless otherwise noted.

* * * * (EXCELLENT)

Herdade do Mouchão

Quinta do Zambujeiro

* * * (GOOD)

Cortes de Cima
Dona Maria
Francisco Nunes Garcia
Fundação Eugénio de Almeida—Adega de
   Cartuxa***/****
Herdade do Esporão***/****

Herdade dos Grous
Herdade de Malhadinha Nova***/****
João Portugal Ramos
Quinta do Carmo
Quinta do Mouro

* * (AVERAGE)

Adega Cooperative de Borba
Casa de Santa Vitória
Caves Aliança (Quinta da Terrugem)**/***
Companhia das Quintas (Quinta da Farizoa)
Fitapreta
Herdade da Mingorra (Henrique Uva)
Herdade São Miguel
Monte da Caldeira

Paulo Laureano Vinus
Porta de Santa Catarina (Sociedade Agrícola
   Poeiras & Xarepe)
Roquevale (Sociedade Agrícola de Herdade
   Da Madeira)
Rui Reguinga Enologia
Terras de Alter, CV

ALENTEJO'S GREATEST WINE BARGAINS

Companhia Das Quintas Reserva (Quinta da
   Farizoa)
Cortes de Cima Chaminé
Dona Maria Branco (white)
Dona Maria Tinto
Fundação Eugénio de Almeida—Adega de
   Cartuxa EA Branco (white)
Fundação Eugénio de Almeida—Adega de
   Cartuxa EA Tinto
Fundação Eugénio de Almeida—Adega de
   Cartuxa Foral de Évora
Herdade do Esporão Alicante Bouschet
Herdade do Esporão Monte Velho Branco
   (white)
Herdade do Esporão Monte Velho Tinto
Herdade do Esporão Reserva
Herdade do Esporão Reserva Branco (white)
Herdade do Esporão Touriga Nacional

Herdade do Esporão Verdelho
Herdade do Esporão Vinha da Defesa
   Branco (white)
Herdade da Mingorra (Henrique Uva)
   Branco Reserva (Alfaraz) (white)
Herdade São Miguel Tinto
João Portugal Ramos Tinto (Marquês de
   Borba)
João Portugal Ramos Tinto (Vila Santa)
Monte da Caldeira Tinto
Paulo Laureano Vinus Singularis
Quinta do Mouro Reserva
   (Casa dos Zagalos)
Roquevale (Sociedade Agrícola de Herdade
   da Madeira) Tinto da Talha Grande
   Escolha
Terras de Alter, C.V. Branco Fado (white)
Terras de Alter, C.V. Syrah Fado

[tasting commentaries]

ADEGA COOPERATIVA DE BORBA ✶ ✶
ALENTEJO $5.99–$21.99

This coop provides some bang for the buck. The wines are not particularly distinguished, but most are around $10, the Adegaborba.pt brand even less, and they drink quite well in their price ranges. The pricey wine here is the Garrafeira, at a suggested retail price of $21.99. This upper-level bottling (relatively speaking) is quite seductive, but betrays the off-vintage effort with its "barely there" finish. The rest of the wines are rather good deals, with the Touriga Nacional being a particularly good pick.

2006 Rosé (Adegaborba.pt) (rosé)	85	now
2004 Reserva (Adegaborba.pt)	86	now–2010
2006 Aragonês/Cabernet Sauvignon	85	now–2010
2004 Aragonês/Cabernet Sauvignon (Adegaborba.pt)	85	now
2005 Trincadeira/Alicante Bouschet	78	now–2011
2002 Garrafeira	86	now–2010
2004 Touriga Nacional	87	now–2010

CASA DE SANTA VITÓRIA ✶ ✶
ALENTEJO $12.00–$24.00

The 2004s turned out rather well here. The only 2005 I tried has not been as successful. The Reserva is a nice step up, but it doubles the Tinto price.

2005 Tinto	82	now–2010
2004 Tinto	85	now–2011
2004 Reserva	87	now–2013

CAVES ALIANÇA ✶ ✶/✶ ✶ ✶
ALENTEJO $24.99–$49.99

This big company, with holdings throughout several Portuguese wine regions, brought in Michel Rolland and Pascal Chatonnet in 1999 to consult. The Alentejo fort is held down by Quinta da Terrugem. The upper-level T bottling is a blend of Aragonês, Cabernet Sauvignon, and Trincadeira. There were 1,172 cases produced. The 2002 is a fine effort in a difficult vintage. The 2004 Tinto is a blend of Aragonês and Trincadeira, which saw 12 months in French oak. It is quite charming, if pricey. This winery needs to be able to build on these results, but if they do, they should be entitled to a higher ranking.

2004 Tinto (Quinta da Terrugem)	90	now–2014
2002 T (Quinta da Terrugem)	90	2009–2017

COMPANHIA DAS QUINTAS ✶ ✶
ALENTEJO $9.99–$13.99

Founded in 1999 and formally registered as Sociedade Agrícola da Quinta da Romeira de Cima, this company trades under the umbrella name Companhia das Quintas (literally, "the Estates Company"), signifying its acquisition and ownership of six quintas in various regions, the latest acquisition being Quinta de Pancas. As the formal name implies, they are headquartered at Quinta da Romeira, an estate with roots going back centuries. The Alentejo outpost is Quinta da Farizoa, which produces some simple wines that are decent values. The Tinto is a blend of Trincadeira, Alfrocheiro, and Aragonez. The Reserva is a blend of Trincadeira, Alfrocheiro, Aragonez, Cabernet Sauvignon, and Alicante Bouschet. It is a pretty good performance in a difficult vintage.

2003 Tinto (Quinta da Farizoa)	86	now–2012
2002 Reserva (Quinta da Farizoa)	86	now–2012

CORTES DE CIMA ★ ★ ★
ALENTEJO $10.00–$58.00

Hans and Carrie Jorgensen are the owners here. He is Danish born and Carrie is American (of Portuguese ancestry). Cortes de Cima has become one of Alentejo's signature wineries, popular for Syrah in southern Portugal and the producer of very modern-style wines. The Jorgensens' road to Syrah was a bit rocky—they started using Syrah, ran afoul of the wine regulations, and branded one wine simply Incógnito, which is now their upper-level Syrah bottling. Many of the wines tend to have a considerable bit of flamboyance, certain ones of which may make some tasters think "over-the-top." In other vintages, they may seem more classic, more Old World. Wines like the 2003 Incógnito, 2004 Aragonez, and perhaps the 2003 Syrah as well may remind you of flamboyant Barossa wines, while the 2004 and 2005 Syrahs are more Old World in style. Even those that are not for the shy also have structure—they are not just flabby fruit bombs. I believe there is a trend to more restraint lately with, among other things, the move away from American oak. Given Cortes de Cima's rebellious streak, it is no surprise to find that they generally reject the Alentejo DOC and market their wines as Vinho Regional Alentejano, similar to the super-Tuscan phenomenon. There is no stigma to being a VR in Alentejo. Carrie Jorgensen asserted, "The best wines are VRs in Alentejo." She added, "Alentejo is good for outlaws."

The Reservas (first release, 1996) are superb wines, the best produced here. The 2003 Reserva is a blend of Syrah (42%), Aragonez (39%), and Touriga Nacional. There were about 1,400 cases produced. The Incógnitos can shine, too, as a 2007 vertical tasting at the winery proved. Both can age well. The 1998 Reserva may be my favorite. The Touriga Nacional is making inroads into the upper tier. Of the wines denominated as single varietals, the finest I have tasted is the 2005 Touriga Nacional ($60). It is a serious step up. The Incógnito tends to be the more flamboyant compared to the Reserva, although the 2005 is rather restrained. The 2004 Incógnito will not likely be released in the U.S.

The wines denominated as single varietals are usually midlevel entrants. The Trincadeira is a mixed bag—well structured but funky. Wines like the Chaminé are often nice bargains at around $10, but a better wine at a good price is often the basic Tinto labeled just with "Cortes de Cima" on the front. It retails for under $20 on the street.

2004 Reserva	91	now–2016
2003 Reserva	92	now–2016
2001 Reserva	91	now–2014
1998 Reserva	93	now–2014
1997 Reserva	90	now–2010
2005 Incógnito	89	now–2015
2004 Incógnito	86	now–2014
2003 Incógnito	89	now–2013
2005 Aragonez	89	2009–2015
2004 Aragonez	86	now–2014
2003 Aragonez	86	now–2011
2005 Touriga Nacional	90	now–2015
2003 Touriga Nacional	88	now–2012
2005 Syrah	86	now–2014
2004 Syrah	88	now–2014
2003 Syrah	85	now–2011
2004 Trincadeira	86	now–2014

2006 Chaminé	86	now
2005 Tinto	86	now–2012
2004 Tinto	87	now–2011

DONA MARIA ★ ★ ★
ALENTEJO $15.00–$39.00

In theory, this is a new winery, its first wine issuing in 2003, but the quinta has roots dating back to 1718, and owner Júlio Bastos was the former owner of Quinta do Carmo, one of Alentejo's oldest flagships. The new operation is not firing on all burners quite yet, but the future here is bright, significant resources have been invested, and Bastos is an experienced hand in the region. I predict that this is a winery that people will be talking about a lot in a few years. If it does not become a four-star winery, I'll be surprised. It has "future superstar" written all over it. The Reservas are rich and ageworthy, and the white wine was one of my favorite whites from my Alentejo tastings in June 2007. It is a blend of Antão Vaz, Roupeiro, Arinto, and a field blend of other varieties. The 2004 Reserva is 25% Syrah, 50% Alicante (an Alicante Bouschet hybrid), and the rest divided equally between Cabernet Sauvignon and Aragonês, indicating the winery's willingness to dabble in many different varieties. There were 4,200 cases produced. The Amantis is a midlevel entrant. The 2004 is its very nice debut vintage. Bastos has accomplished quite a lot here in a very short amount of time.

2006 Branco (white)	90	now–2010
2004 Tinto	86	now–2011
2004 Reserva	91	now–2016
2003 Reserva	90	now–2012
2004 Amantis	89	now–2013

FITAPRETA ★ ★
ALENTEJO 7.2–22 EUROS

Fitapreta, meaning "Black Ribbon" in Portuguese, is a new winery featuring viticulturist David Booth, who spent a year at the University of California—Davis, and oenologist António Maçanita, who worked at Merryvale, Rudd, and Lynch-Bages. The Sexy is pretty much an uncomplicated, rather simple party wine with interesting, sort of, marketing. The flagship Preta is another matter, both wines showing good acidity, fine balance, and nice flavors. These wines show promise.

2005 Preta	89	now–2014
2004 Preta	87	now–2011
2005 Sexy	82	now

FRANCISCO NUNES GARCIA ★ ★ ★
ALENTEJO $34.00–$91.00

This winery is run and owned by boisterous Francisco Nunes Garcia. Of the unknown quantities I visited on my last trip to Alentejo, this was probably the biggest pleasant surprise. The wines have structure and age gracefully. Garcia does have an importer, but it is not always clear what wines will be imported in what year. I'd like to see more recent versions of these, as this winery might ultimately merit a higher rating. The pricey wine here is the António Maria ($91), a special bottling that was a tribute to the owner's late brother. It is a blend of Alicante Bouschet and Cabernet Sauvignon. It is not a great wine, but a very good performance in a difficult vintage. The Reservas are running around $34.

2001 Reserva	91	now–2015
2000 Reserva	89	now–2013

| 1999 Reserva | 88 | now–2010 |
| 2002 António Maria | 89 | now–2012 |

FUNDAÇÃO EUGÉNIO DE ALMEIDA—
ADEGA DE CARTUXA ★★★/★★★★
ALENTEJO $9.00–$81.00

The Almeida Foundation has a finger in many pies, including olive oil and cattle, but its biggest operation is its winery, known as Adega de Cartuxa. This is one of Alentejo's stalwarts, most famed for the flagship cult wine, Pera-Manca. If the Douro had Barca Velha, Alentejo answered with Pera-Manca, and it is highly sought after in Portugal. However, Pera-Manca is a wine I have in fact had some problems with over the years. Relying heavily on the difficult Trincadeira grape, it often seems vegetal to me, like a funkier, evil Cabernet Franc, as well as astringent and rustic. Yet this estate has some of Alentejo's older vineyards (60% going back to 1980). There is enormous potential here. From what I saw at the winery in 2007, it is being realized. There is a new winemaker as of 2004 who says that he is rigorous in making sure the Trincadeira does not come in green, and the current vintages look superb. I debated whether to rank this estate with three or four stars. From what I saw in the past, often it was a matter of "the emperor has no clothes" for the priciest wines, both white and red. Yet, from what I saw in mid-2007 at the winery, this estate is ready to fire on all cylinders. Call it 3.5 stars, and let's see if the promise is fulfilled.

The 2005 Pera-Manca will be the ninth Pera-Manca released (first vintage, 1990). It looks to be exceptional, and justifies the wine's reputation as one of Portugal's best. It was tasted just before bottling. The 2003 is excellent, too. The EA Branco is one of Alentejo's fine white wine bargains, $10 and under. It is simply a steal, although '06 is a difficult year. The Foral is a second wine, and this one packs a lot of power for the money. The normal Reserva usually delivers a lot for the money, too.

There is a new winery being completed, and some future wines (not likely the Pera-Manca) will say Adega Cartuxa instead of Adega *de* Cartuxa, to correctly represent the expanded fruit sources. Hopefully, the future will be as bright as it seems.

2006 Branco EA (white)	83	now–2010
2004 Branco EA (white)	88	now
2003 Foral de Évora	86	2009–2018
2005 Pera-Manca	92–95	2010–2023
2003 Pera-Manca	92	2009–2020
1998 Pera-Manca	86	now–2018

HERDADE DO ESPORÃO ★★★/★★★★
ALENTEJO $8.00–$40.00

Esporão is one of Alentejo's iconic producers, with vast vineyards that partly have some age on them (some vines are around 30 years old, which is considerable relative to the many young wineries in the region). It has some of the region's most beautiful and atmospheric cellars. It is one of the big operations in the area. The winemaker here is Australian David Baverstock, a long-time resident in Portugal who has assisted many prominent wineries in the Douro as well.

The lineup tends to be value oriented. The winery is simply terrific at producing nice wines for little money, sometimes to the point where you wonder why you should step up. There are a few specialty wines, like the Garrafeira and the Torre. Only the Garrafeira ($40) exceeds a suggested retail of $24. *Note:* No price has been received for the Torre, but it is likely considerably more expensive. The simple little Monte Velho Branco ($9 suggested retail— meaning it may be available for less) can be great when young. Note that the Reserva is not really positioned as a pricey, upper-level wine, despite the name. It should generally be available under $20. The 2004 Reserva, a blend of 40% Aragonês (Tempranillo), 30% Cabernet Sauvignon, and 30% Trincadeira, is the best I've had here.

I debated whether this should be a three- or four-star winery. If your criteria include providing a slew of great values, reliability, and consistency, this winery is virtually without equal in Alentejo. Everything they make is solid and dependable and usually quite well priced, and they have a track record of excellence in that regard. There is something to be said for that. If I had a quibble, it would be that I would love to see them use their talent and resources to make more distinguished and great wines, not just great values. The Garrafeira and the Torre are steps in that direction. *Wine alert:* I am not publishing a note on the unreleased 2004 Garrafeira at this time because it was totally closed for business when I had it at the winery, but it has the potential to become the best wine I have had from Esporão.

2004 Monte Velho	85	now
2006 Monte Velho Branco (white)	87	now
2004 Reserva	89	now–2014
2003 Reserva	88	now–2012
2001 Reserva	85	now
2006 Reserva Branco (white)	87	now–2011
2004 Reserva Branco (white)	85	now
2006 Reserva Branco Private Selection (white)	90	now–2012
2003 Garrafeira Private Selection	92	now–2015
2001 Garrafeira Private Selection	92	now–2016
2004 Touriga Nacional	87	now–2012
2004 Alicante Bouschet	87	now–2012
2006 Verdelho (white)	88	now
2005 Vinha da Defesa	86	now–2010
2006 Vinha da Defesa Branco (white)	87	now–2009
2004 Torre do Esporão	92	now–2017

HERDADE DOS GROUS ★ ★ ★
ALENTEJO $20.00–$50.00

This winery near Beja includes a beautiful resort facility. It also features, more pertinently, Luis Duarte, the winemaker-consultant who works with Quinta do Mouro and Malhadinha Nova. Although at most wineries the 2004s shine, here the 2005s seem to have the edge. The Reserva is the priciest wine, running around 28–30 euros at the winery and $50 in the U.S. The wines are beautifully crafted, elegant, and well structured. The future here looks bright, although the 2006s—a difficult vintage—are understandably a step back.

2006 Tinto	84	now–2012
2005 Tinto	87	now–2012
2004 Tinto	85	now–2010
2006 23 Barricas	86	now–2014
2005 23 Barricas	89	now–2014
2006 Reserva	87	now–2015
2005 Reserva	91	2009–2019
2004 Reserva	89+	2009–2019
2006 Reserva Branco (white)	88	now–2011

HERDADE DA MALHADINHA NOVA ★★★/★★★★
ALENTEJO $20.00–$89.00

In the middle of nowhere, it seems, this lovely, modern winery has emerged. With wine-maker Luis Duarte, one of the best in the region, and passionate owners João and Rita Soares, who also own a distribution and retail wine business in the Algarve, Malhadinha Nova (as close as I can get, with Rita Soares's help, Ma-lee-uh-DEE-nyuh) seems poised to become one of the superstars of the region. Their vines are still too young, and they certainly are not all the way there yet, but they have accomplished amazing things in a very short while. A small hotel is now on the property, along with cooking classes, giving the property resort status.

The Soares family purchased this estate in 1998. The first planting was just in 2001; and the first wine release in 2003. It is admittedly a stretch to give this young winery four stars, so I have hedged. Still, though there is little track record, nor a superstar wine yet made, these guys are going all the way. They have accomplished astonishing things already. And they have reached an important juncture: I expect their upper-level, good-vintage wines to hit or exceed the 90-point mark routinely. These small-production wines are worth seeking out, al-though the prices are rather high in the U.S. for what they are at the moment. European prices are much more reasonable (for example, the flagship Tinto is under 30 euros in Portu-gal), but they are obviously not translating well here.

This producer is particularly good with the whites, and will be a leading producer for that reason alone. The Branco, the top-of-the-line white, is a blend of 60% Antão Vaz, 20% Char-donnay, and 20% Arinto, raised in 60% French oak and 40% American oak. It was one of the most interesting whites I had in Alentejo during my 2007 visit there. The 2006 Antão Vaz da Peceguina is unoaked. João Soares jokingly refers to it as the winery's Chardonnay, although their top-of-the-line Branco could fill that niche, too. It is just 9 euros at the winery, a value that is hard to translate to the U.S. these days. The lovely Monte da Peceguina Branco is an unoaked blend of Arinto, Antão Vaz, and Roupeiro, but mostly Antão Vaz (60%). Monte da Peceguina (Peh-say-GEEN-uh) is named after the family that once owned the large house on the premises. The 2005 Pequeno Joao (meaning "little João"; note that the label does not include the *til* mark on João) is named after the owners' son, born in 2004, its first vintage. It comes only in a 500 milliliter bottle (it's little!), and is the wild card in the Malhadinha lineup, the winery says, because the varietal blend will likely change every year. In this vintage, it is 40% each Cabernet Sauvignon and Aragonês, and 20% Syrah. The winery considers it to be the same quality level as their flagship wine, the Tinto.

2005 Tinto	90	2009–2016
2004 Tinto	90	now–2016
2006 Branco (white)	90	now–2011
2006 Monte da Peceguina	87	now–2013
2005 Monte da Peceguina	87	now–2014
2006 Monte da Peceguina Branco (white)	88	now–2010
2006 Antão Vaz da Peceguina (white)	89	now–2010
2005 Pequeno Joao	90	2009–2016
2004 Marias da Malhadinha	91	now–2014

HERDADE DA MINGORRA (HENRIQUE UVA) ★★
ALENTEJO 4.25–15 EUROS

This well-known winery makes a number of different cuvées that are often very well priced. The Branco Reserva is a mere 4.25 euros at the winery.

2005 Branco Reserva (Alfaraz) (white)	86	now
2004 Vinhas da Ira	87	2009–2017

HERDADE DO MOUCHÃO ★★★★
ALENTEJO $45.00–$70.00

In a fairly young region, this estate has roots going back a long, long way. If the region has a "grand old man," this estate would be a key candidate for that title. The Reynolds family, who still owns it, first planted vineyards in 1901, although commercial winemaking did not really become a significant matter until the 1950s. The earliest plantings were of Alicante Bouschet, which became the winery's signature grape. Its flagship wine is the Tinto, just called Mouchão, which accounts for approximately 30% of the winery's production. It is dominated by Alicante Bouschet, usually about 70% of the blend (most of the rest is usually Trincadeira), and typically late-released. The winery was kind enough to make available some library wines, included here as reference points. On the whole, it is a very impressive showing of older wines in a region that has hardly any.

The special Tonel ("barrel") bottlings have a reputation for holding very well. The acidity will certainly preserve this 1999 for a long, long time, but it is not as clear whether the wine will remain interesting and pleasing as it gets long in tooth. It did seem a bit better balanced the next day, but that sour cherry nuance heading to rhubarb will not appeal to everyone. For those looking to learn about Alicante Bouschet, beginning with the beautiful, young 2003 Tinto might be the way to go—it is fresh, with good depth, round, ripe, and easy to love and understand, nuanced by lovely cherry notes, with perhaps a hint of kirsch followed by a hint of game after some aeration. It is hardly a fruit bomb, however. Like its siblings reviewed here, it is beautifully structured. At its young age, it packs a bit of a tannic punch, not surprisingly, but it is approachable now. There were some moments when I thought the alcohol was a bit obvious, but it is not a serious issue, and it seemed much better balanced the next day. A couple of hours of air would help. It is simply delicious. The 1997 Tinto was probably my favorite of the older wines. It is simply beautiful and a stunning performance for an Alentejano wine of this age, still seeming fresh, pure, and pristine. It appears to have a long life remaining, but if you want a wine with some fresh fruit yet, while still projecting some notes of maturity, this era will be a good time in which to approach it.

2003 Tinto	93	now–2028
2000 Tinto	90	now–2020
1997 Tinto	95	now–2030
1990 Tinto	92	now–2020
1974 Tinto	88	now–2014
1999 Tinto Tonel No. 3–4	89	now–2030

HERDADE SÃO MIGUEL ★★
ALENTEJO $13.00–$40.00

The consulting oenologist here is the talented Luis Duarte, whose fingerprints are all over a lot of well-known Alentejo wines at the moment, including Malhadinha Nova, Herdade dos Grous, and Quinta do Mouro. I have not seen enough vintages from this winery to justify a higher rating, but it should get one in the future. The Tinto is a blend of Aragonês, Trincadeira, Alicante Bouschet, and Cabernet Sauvignon, which should become quite attractive when it comes together. The Reserva, only 511 cases produced, is a blend of Aragonês, Alicante Bouschet, and Cabernet Sauvignon. It has some potential, some richness and power, but there were times when the alcohol was a bit noticeable.

2004 Reserva	89	now–2014
2005 Tinto	87	now–2013

JOÃO PORTUGAL RAMOS ★★★
ALENTEJO $13.00–$35.00

João Portugal Ramos is one of the best-known names in southern Portugal, making wines under a variety of labels and in several regions. Personable and affable, he is one of Alentejo's best ambassadors. His labels include the familiar Marquês de Borba, as well as Vila Santa. His company also owns Falua in Ribatejo, and he helps out at his father-in-law's estate in the north, Conde Foz de Arouce (listed separately). The wines here are always satisfying and consistent, and the prices are reasonable. The only quibble is that there should be more great wine produced, not just great values. Oh, and just a pet peeve—between Borba, Vila Santa, and Falua, Ramos seems to delight in making the vintage dates tiny and/or indistinct. Bring a magnifying glass.

The Reserva Marquês de Borba is Ramos's flagship wine. It has some intensity, good focus, and an elegantly crafted midpalate of moderate depth. It is a blend of Trincadeira, Aragonês, Alicante Bouschet, and Cabernet Sauvignon. The Branco is a blend of a blend of Arinto, Rabo de Ovelha, and Roupeiro. The Vila Santas, under $20, are utterly charming, if a little on the simple side. They are blends of Aragonês, Trincadeira, Alicante Bouschet, and Cabernet Sauvignon.

2003 Reserva (Marquês de Borba)	90	2009–2018
2005 Syrah	85	now–2013
2005 Branco (Marquês de Borba) (white)	85	now–2008
2005 Tinto (Vila Santa)	88	now–2014
2003 Tinto (Vila Santa)	87	now–2013
2005 Tinto (Marquês de Borba)	86	now–2010
2003 Touriga Nacional/Merlot (Quinta da Viçosa)	90	now–2014

MONTE DA CALDEIRA ★★
ALENTEJO $20.00–$34.00

Both of these wines are blends of Trincadeira and Aragonês. The upper-level 2002, in a difficult vintage, is a very nice performance, although it has some of the funky notes Trincadeira can project.

2004 Tinto	86	now–2013
2002 Casas do Monte Superior	88	now–2012

PAULO LAUREANO VINUS ★★
ALENTEJO $8.00–$24.00

The esteemed winemaker at Herdade do Mouchão, Paulo Laureano, here ventures off on his own. There were many things I liked about these wines, but some, particularly some whites, seemed marred by what appeared to be reductive notes. There is a lot of promise, though, and this is a winery to watch. You may see "Eborae Vitis e Vinus" on some of the labels from Paulo Laureano. That was a prior company, but all of the wines should have Paulo Laureano Vinus as producer eventually. To make things easy, the proprietary names like "Dolium" are what you will see in big letters on the front no matter what. The Dolium represents a midlevel bottling, the Singularis an entry level. Both are pretty nice, and the Singularis is an excellent value at around $10. Both here are blends of Trincadeira and Aragonês. There is also a Vale da Torre that could be an even better value, but the only one I tried again gave some evidence of off aromas, as did the 2005 Dolium Branco Escolha.

2004 Dolium Reserva	88	now–2012
2005 Dolium Branco Escolha (Eborae Vitis e Vinus) (white)	83	now–2010
2006 Dolium Branco Escolha (white)	89	now–2011

2004 Singularis	86	now–2010
2006 Singularis Branco (white)	84	now
2005 Vale da Torre Bin 717	83	now

PORTA DE SANTA CATARINA
(SOCIEDADE AGRÍCOLA POEIRAS & XAREPE) ★★
ALENTEJO $12.00–$34.00

This estate provides some interesting wines, and hopefully future vintages will build on this. The Tinto blends Cabernet Sauvignon with Aragonês and Alicante Bouschet, and is a nice bargain. The Reserva is also a blend of Cabernet Sauvignon with Aragonês and Alicante Bouschet, but with more structure. 885 cases were produced.

2004 Tinto	85	now
2004 Reserva	88	now–2014

QUINTA DO CARMO ★★★
ALENTEJO $54.99

Quinta do Carmo is one of Alentejo's oldest producers, although changes are in the air, with replanted vineyards and the departure of former co-owner Júlio Bastos, who now produces wine under the Dona Maria label. The 2004 Reserva is a very attractive wine, approachable but structured, with ripe and well-integrated tannins. It is focused and appealing, perhaps a bit restrained and reticent at first, but when it finally opens, it is quite delicious, and it drinks brilliantly on day two as well. This old stalwart will likely deserve a higher ranking soon, but given the many changes surrounding the estate at the moment, I would rather be conservative in that regard.

2004 Reserva	92	now–2014

QUINTA DO MOURO ★★★
ALENTEJO $18.00–$37.00

This estate is one of the most esteemed in Alentejo. Run by the personable dentist Miguel Louro, and with winemaker-consultant Luis Duarte (Malhadinha Nova and others), it crafts some of the most serious and structured wines in Alentejo, utterly destroying the stereotype of soft, easy wines. There were times when, if anything, I thought the tannins could be a bit too hard and backward, a comment that rather scared Louro. These are very serious wines, though, as a vertical tasting at the winery showed. When you taste them, your first thought may be Douro rather than Alentejo. There are very few wineries making wines like this in Alentejo. *Wine alert:* They might release a 2005 "gold label," a special bottling—the cask samples I tasted of what might become that bottling were exceptional. The Casa dos Zagalos line is a proprietary brand that is more reasonably priced. Mouro should eventually earn a higher ranking. Although I saw many other wines at the estate in June 2007, promised samples did not arrive in time to be included and could not be sourced in the U.S.

2002 Reserva (Casa dos Zagalos)	85	now
2004 Tinto	92	2011–2022
2003 Tinto	90	now–2018

QUINTA DO ZAMBUJEIRO ★★★★
ALENTEJO $20.00–$100.00

This winery seems poised to make a big splash. Some of the results it posted early on (first vintage, 1999) were erratic. However, from 2003 on, the results here have been exceptional, as good or better than any winery in the region. They seem to have hit stride, as a tasting at the winery in June 2007 demonstrated. The prices are high, but so is the ambition. The owner is Swiss and, not surprisingly, a considerable part of the production is sold in Switzerland (60%). There is a U.S. importer, however. The entry level is the Monte do Castanheiro. The midlevel is the Terra, where you can find some value in the $30s. These can be fine wines in their own right. The top of the line is the Tinto, just labeled Zambujeiro, which produces around 540 cases a year. The 2004s are anticipated to be released in the spring of 2008. They are also dabbling in single-varietal bottlings of Touriga Nacional. If this winery continues on the course it has recently set, it could become Alentejo's biggest star. It is admittedly a bit of a stretch to rate them at four stars at the moment, based largely on two superb vintages, but after tasting through their lineup, I am convinced that a qualitative corner has been turned here, that progress is steady and continuing, and that this is a top-level winery.

2004 Monte do Castanheiro	85	now
2004 Terra do Zambujeiro	91	now–2015
2003 Terra do Zambujeiro	90	now–2014
2002 Terra do Zambujeiro	87	now–2011
2004 Tinto	95	2010–2022
2003 Tinto	95	2009–2020
2002 Tinto	87	now–2012

ROQUEVALE
(SOCIEDADE AGRÍCOLA DE HERDADE DA MADEIRA) * *
ALENTEJO $13.00–$14.00

This winery makes some good value wines. The Tinto da Talha is a blend of Syrah and Touriga Nacional.

2004 Tinto da Talha Grande Escolha	87	now–2012

RUI REGUINGA ENOLOGIA * *
ALENTEJO $25.00

This well-known oenologist (the winemaker at Quinta dos Roques) strikes out on his own here, and it is a very fine debut. Once he gets his feet under him, count on this to be a winery to watch. It is an old-vine blend of Aragonez, Grand Noir, Alicante Bouschet, and others, raised for 14 months in French oak.

2004 Reserva Terrenus	89	now–2104

TERRAS DE ALTER * *
ALENTEJO $10.00–$20.00

This new winery features well-known winemaker Peter Bright. The Syrah is the debut release of that bottling. It looks like a promising start. The Syrah is a bit compact but quite elegant. The 2006 Fado, the third vintage released, is rather simple, but a useful party or picnic wine if drunk young. It is a blend of Trincadeira, Syrah, Touriga Nacional, and Petit Verdot. The Branco, the second vintage released, is a bit more substantial, with rounded edges nonetheless cut by acidity.

2006 Fado	84	now
2006 Branco Fado (white)	87	now–2010
2005 Syrah Fado	87	now–2011

AN INTRODUCTION TO OTHER APPELLATIONS

There are important wines and wineries outside of the Douro and Alentejo, but the stars are for the most part widely scattered rather than clustered. Here is a sampling of Portugal's many other appellations and wineries to keep in mind.

BAIRRADA In northwestern Portugal, Bairrada is one of the DOCs that is hardest to understand. Although there are a number of varieties at issue here, the one that is identified with the region is Baga, the signature red grape traditional in the area. Notoriously difficult, it often produces rather rustic, high-acid red wines. They can be astringent and tart. Despite an ancient history, Bairrada received DOC status only in 1979. Some of the wines from this region, including some of the most famous, will have the Vinho Regional Beiras designation instead of Bairrada. Beiras includes the DOC of Dão, as well as Bairrada. Bairrada is also known for its sparkling wines.

ESTREMADURA This Vinho Regional appellation on Portugal's West Coast, beginning around Lisbon and running north by about an hour by car, uses many familiar Portuguese varieties, including Touriga Nacional and Tinta Roriz, as well as international grapes such as Cabernet Sauvignon in reds. For whites, there is similar variety, from grapes like Síria (Roupeiro) and Fernão Pires (Maria Gomes) to Chardonnay and Gewurztraminer. Estremadura contains within it several classified subregions, such as Óbidos and Alenquer.

DÃO This region, one of the older DOCs in Portugal (1908), is in north-central Portugal. It is surrounded by mountains and said to have a Mediterranean climate. There is great potential here. Known best for its elegant reds, this is a region that should have a bright future. For reds, it would be my pick to join Douro and Alentejo at the top of the heap in the future. Touriga Nacional is a very important variety here, as is Tinta Roriz, both familiar from the Douro. You will also see red varieties like Alfrocheiro, Jaen, and Rufete. Encruzado is the signature white.

RIBATEJO More or less in Portugal's Southwest, not far from Lisbon, this relatively young DOC is a region on the upswing. I sometimes compare it to its southern cousin, Alentejo, because of geographical proximity and because both tend to be liberal in their use of international grape varieties. However, it is well behind Alentejo in prestige and quality. Red varieties include Aragonez, Castelão, Touriga Nacional, Trincadeira, Alfrocheiro, Alicante Bouschet, and Cabernet Sauvignon. White varieties are similarly varied, including Arinto, Fernão Pires (Maria Gomes), and Síria (Roupeiro). The related Vinho Regional classification is Ribatejano.

TERRAS DO SADO This appellation south of Lisbon covers the Setúbal Peninsula and includes the classified subregions of Palmela and Setúbal. The big José Maria da Fonseca company has been based here since the 19th century. Fonseca's Periquita is said to be the oldest brand in continuous existence in Portugal today. A major component (and major red variety in the region) is Castelão, a grape so closely identified with the wine that it is often called Periquita.

VINHO VERDE This region in northwestern Portugal is one of Portugal's best known, largely for its light and bright white wines. Typically inexpensive and ephemeral, they have been viewed as pleasant, low-alcohol summer drinks needing to be consumed quickly. They are referred to as summer wines even on the official (Comissão de Viticultura da Região dos Vinhos Verdes—CVRVV) Vinho Verde website. However, there are producers making serious wines here these days, often from 100% Alvarinho (also called Albariño in Spain). The Alvarinhos and other serious wines are attracting more and more attention, and bust out of the simple, summer-quaffer category. They are generally higher in alcohol and more age-worthy, too.

If you are looking for 100% Alvarinhos, note that such a wine cannot receive the Vinho

Verde DOC label unless the wine is 100% Alvarinho *and* the grapes are sourced from the subregions of Monção or neighboring Melgaço (included in Monção at the moment). The reasons for this are "mostly historical," says Manuel Pinheiro, president of the CVRVV, in that "Alvarinho was traditionally grown in Monção on lower lands. Monção is on the north of the region, bordering the river Minho on the border with Spain exactly where Albariño is produced." There is a push on to give Melgaço more of an identity of its own, Pinheiro reports, because "Monção is a lower land with a milder climate[,] a higher Atlantic influence and a softer soil; Melgaço . . . more a slope vineyard, more granitic, colder in the winter and warmer in the summer." Wines that do not comply with DOC regulations can still be made under the Vinho Regional Minho designation, and many excellent wines carry this designation instead of the more restrictive DOC.

Apart from Alvarinho, the Vinho Verde Commission lists the following as "recommended" white grapes: Avesso, Azal-Branco, Batoca, Loureiro, Pederña (aka Arinto), and Trajadura. Although these are usually blended, there are some single-varietal wines from grapes such as Loureiro as well.

There are red wines here, too, although they are not as well known and rarely as successful as the best whites. Many are often hard to warm up to. In the broader region, VR Minho reds can sometimes be charming. Using any number of grapes, from Touriga Nacional to Cabernet Sauvignon, they remind me a bit of Loire reds in style.

[the ratings]

A SAMPLING OF THE BEST PRODUCERS FROM APPELLATIONS OTHER THAN DOURO AND ALENTEJO

Note: Where a producer has been assigned a range of stars, for example ★★★/★★★★, the lower rating has been used for placement in this hierarchy. Lack of available data (not all historical data is reprinted here) may affect a winery's ranking. Sometimes a winery is just too new to rank highly. Sometimes data is simply unavailable for one reason or another. For instance, well-known producer Álvaro Castro is not represented since promised samples had not arrived as of this writing. Where wineries make a variety of regional and DOC wines, I have usually maintained a primary designation in the specific winery listing (e.g., Vinho Verde rather than Minho/Vinho Verde). Where there are multiple regions (e.g., Dão and Bairrada), that is specified. The following wines are red unless otherwise noted.

★ ★ ★ (GOOD)

Anselmo Mendes—Andreza (Vinho Verde)
Casa de Cello (Dão—Quinta da Vegia)
Casa de Cello (Vinho Verde—Quinta de San Joanne)
Caves Aliança (Bairrada—Quinta das Baceladas)
Conde Foz de Arouce Vinhos (Beiras)
Hotel do Reguengo de Melgaço (Vinho Verde)
Luis Pato (Beiras)

Quinta de Covela (Vinho Verde)
Quinta das Marias (Dão)
Quinta do Ameal (Vinho Verde)
Quinta do Feital (Vinho Verde)
Quinta do Monte d'Oiro (Estremadura)
Quinta dos Roques (Dão)
Quinta do Soalheiro (Vinho Verde)
Quinta do Vale das Escadinhas
Sociedade Agrícola Casa de Santar (Dão)

★ ★ (AVERAGE)

Alto Pina (Terras do Sado)
Campolargo (Bairrada)

Casa de Vila Verde (Vinho Verde)

Caves Aliança (Dão—Quinta
da Garrida)**/***
Colinas de São Lourenço (Silvio Cerveira)
(Bairrada)
Companhia Agrícola do Sanguinhal
(Óbidos)
Companhia das Quintas
(various regions)
Filipa Pato (Beiras)

João Portugal Ramos (Conde de
Vimioso-Falua) (Ribatejo)
José Maria da Fonseca
(Terras do Sado)**/***
Pinhal da Torre (Ribatejo)**/***
Quinta da Alorna (Ribatejo)
Quinta da Aveleda (Vinho Verde/Bairrada)
Quinta do Casal Branco (Ribatejo)
Quinta de Chocapalha (Estremadura)

A SAMPLING OF THE GREATEST PORTUGUESE WINE BARGAINS FROM APPELLATIONS OTHER THAN DOURO AND ALENTEJO

All of the following wines are red unless otherwise noted.

Alto Pina Fernão Pires (Terras do Sado) (white)
Anselmo Mendes Loureiro Escolha (Andreza) (Vinho Verde) (white)
Casa de Cello Branco (Quinta de San Joanne) (Vinho Verde) (white)
Casa de Cello Porta Fronha (Quinta da Vegia) (Dão)
Casa de Vila Verde Alvarinho (Minho) (white)
Caves Aliança Tinto (Quinta das Baceladas) (Bairrada)
Caves Aliança Touriga Nacional (Quinta da Garrida) (Dão)
Colinas de São Lourenço (Silvio Cerveira) Tinto (Bairrada)
Companhia Agrícola do Sanguinhal Tinto (Quinta de S. Francisco) (Óbidos)
Companhia das Quintas Branco Morgado de Sta. Catherina (Quinta da Romeira)
(Bucelas) (white)
Companhia das Quintas Special Selection (Quinta do Cardo) (Beiras Interior)
Companhia das Quintas Tinto (Quinta de Pegos Claros) (Palmela)
Hotel do Reguengo de Melgaço Alvarinho (Vinho Verde) (white)
João Portugal Ramos Conde de Vimioso (Falua—Sociedade de Vinhos) (Ribatejo)
José Maria da Fonseca Periquita (Terras do Sado)
José Maria da Fonseca Periquita Reserva (Terras do Sado)
Pinhal da Torre 2 Worlds Reserva (Quinta do Alqueve) (Ribatejano)
Quinta da Alorna Colheita Seleccionada (Casa da Alorna) (Ribatejo)
Quinta da Alorna Touriga Nacional/Cabernet Sauvignon Reserva (Ribatejano)
Quinta do Ameal Loureiro (Vinho Verde) (white)
Quinta do Casal Branco Branco (Falcoaria) (Ribatejo) (white)
Quinta de Chocapalha Tinto (Estremadura)
Quinta de Covela Escolha Branco (Minho) (white)
Quinta do Feital Auratus (Minho) (white)
Quinta do Vale das Escadinhas Reserva (Quinta da Falorca)

[tasting commentaries]

ALTO PINA **
TERRAS DO SADO $10.00

This winery presents some good values. I particularly liked the white.

2006 Fernão Pires (white)	87	now–2010
2005 Castelão/Alicante Bouschet	86	now–2010

ANSELMO MENDES (ANDREZA) ★★★★
VINHO VERDE $14.00–$21.00

From esteemed winemaker Anselmo Mendes come these two fine whites. These are not simple summer quaffers. Just for your reference, and to avoid as much confusion as possible, the front of the label indicates only the proprietary name Andreza. This Vinho Verde winery is, however, commonly known by its owner's name, Anselmo Mendes, but only the full name, Manuel Anselmo Alfonso Mendes, appears in tiny print on the back. The Loureiro is a single-variety wine, and it is simply delicious, ripe and succulent. The Alvarinho, from the subregion of Monção, is one of those 100% Alvarinhos that is attracting attention and garnering renewed respect for the region. It has 13% alcohol, another change in how you might view Vinho Verde. It is simply remarkable, intense, deep, and penetrating. Most Vinho Verdes are better young—so, too, here, I think—but these will hold better than the old-fashioned wines.

2006 Loureiro Escolha (Andreza) (white)	90	now–2010
2006 Alvarinho (Andreza) (white)	92	now–2011

CAMPOLARGO ★★
BAIRRADA $12.00–$22.00

Campolargo is one of the better-known producers in this region. The inexpensive Os Corvos is a pretty good deal, but fairly high in acid. It is a blend of Tinta Roriz, Syrah, and Merlot. The Termeão blends Cabernet Sauvignon with native varieties. It is better structured than the Os Corvos, but also high in acid and a bit disjointed. It may improve with cellaring.

2004 Os Corvos da Vinha da Costa	85	now–2010
2004 Termeão	86	now–2014

CASA DE CELLO ★★★
VINHO VERDE/DÃO $14.00–$56.00

This winery owns Quinta de San Joanne in Vinho Verde and Quinta da Vegia in Dão. From both places, it produces rather interesting wines, although my favorites were the Vinho Verde (or Vinho Regional Minho) whites from Quinta de San Joanne. The only really expensive wine here is the Reserva from Quinta da Vegia—over $50, and not much of a value. The excellent Escolha Branco from Quinta de San Joanne runs $21, a high price for Vinho Verde but fair for the quality, and not unusual for the better wines these days. It blends in some Chardonnay and technically is a VR Minho. The Porta Fronhas are lighter styled reds from young vines with some charm, around $18. The 2003 Tinto is graceful and elegant, if a little compact. The Reserva is bigger, but not distinguished enough to justify the big price hike from the mid-$20s to the mid-$50s.

2005 Branco (Quinta de San Joanne) (white)	88	now
2003 Escolha Branco (Quinta de San Joanne) (white)	91	now
2005 Porta Fronha (Quinta da Vegia)	85	now–2013
2004 Porta Fronha (Quinta da Vegia)	87	now–2012
2004 Tinto (Quinta da Vegia)	86	now–2015
2003 Tinto (Quinta da Vegia)	88	now–2013
2003 Reserva (Quinta da Vegia)	89	now–2015

CASA DE VILA VERDE ✶✶
VINHO VERDE $8.00–$12.00

These wines are charming and very well priced. The Alvarinho (a Vinho Regional Minho) is particularly nice.

2005 Branco (white)	86	now
2005 Alvarinho (white)	87	now

CAVES ALIANÇA ✶✶/✶✶✶
BAIRRADA/DÃO $19.99

This big company has holdings throughout several Portuguese wine regions. The Quinta das Baceladas is the property in Bairrada. Quinta da Garrida is its property in Dão. Both of these are nice efforts, but I particularly enjoyed the Touriga Nacional from Quinta da Garrida, although the Quinta das Baceladas Tinto is one of the more charming Bairrada reds. At about $20 or under, both are pretty good values.

2003 Tinto (Quinta das Baceladas)	88	now–2013
2003 Touriga Nacional (Quinta da Garrida)	89	now–2015

COLINAS DE SÃO LOURENÇO (SÍLVIO CERVEIRA) ✶✶
BAIRRADA $10.00–$20.00

This producer provides some bang for the buck. The blends include grapes like Cabernet Sauvignon to go with Portuguese varieties like Touriga Nacional and Baga. They tend to have a modern, suave feel, especially for Bairrada. French consultant Pascal Chatonnet is involved.

2004 Private Collection	89	now–2013
2004 Tinto	87	now–2012
2006 Chardonnay/Arinto (white)	86	now–2010

COMPANHIA AGRÍCOLA DO SANGUINHAL ✶✶
ÓBIDOS $10.00

This estate makes some good-value wines. This Tinto is a blend of Castelão, Aragonez, and Touriga Nacional. It is light but charming and inexpensive, a nice value.

2003 Tinto (Quinta de S. Francisco)	86	now–2011

COMPANHIA DAS QUINTAS ✶✶
VARIOUS REGIONS $10.00–$70.00

Founded in 1999 and formally registered as Sociedade Agrícola da Quinta da Romeira de Cima, this company trades under the umbrella name Companhia das Quintas (literally, "the Estates Company"), signifying its acquisition and ownership of six quintas in various regions, the latest acquisition being Quinta de Pancas. As the formal name implies, they are headquartered at Quinta da Romeira, an estate with roots going back to the early 17th century. They make a large number of wines in various regions, which are collected here (other than Douro and Alentejo, which are listed separately). The best-known reds come from Quinta de Pancas, but I have not always been impressed with them or the value that they deliver. The basic Cabernet is only $10.99, but the Premium is responsible for the lone price spike here—$70. Many of the Cabernet Sauvignons seem to have some greenness to them. That said, it would be fun to stick the midlevel Special Selection in a blind tasting and see how many guess Bordeaux. Some of the most impressive wines are the whites, either as values or overall. Note that the Quinta do Cardo Special Selection is 100% Touriga Nacional.

2003 Special Selection (Quinta do Cardo) (red—Beira Interior)	87	now–2013
2004 Cabernet Sauvignon (Quinta de Pancas) (red—Estremadura)	85	now
2003 Cabernet Sauvignon Special Selection (Quinta de Pancas) (red—Estremadura)	86	now–2013
2003 Cabernet Sauvignon Premium (Quinta de Pancas) (red—Estremadura)	88	now–2014
1999 Tinto (Quinta de Pegos Claros) (red—Palmela)	85	now
2005 Branco "Morgado de Sta. Catherina" (Quinta da Romeira) (white—Bucelas)	87	now
2004 Branco "Morgado de Sta. Catherina" (Quinta da Romeira) (white—Bucelas)	87	now
2004 Colheita Tardia (Quinta da Romeira) (white—Bucelas)	88	now–2011

CONDE FOZ DE AROUCE VINHOS ★ ★ ★
BEIRAS $34.99

The consulting winemaker here is the well-known J. Portugal Ramos, who makes a variety of popular wines in southern Portugal under labels including Marquês de Borba. Here in the North, he consults for his father-in-law. This estate produces some interesting old-vine Baga, and has a more modern face than you normally see, with a lot of the rustic edges carved off. It is certainly one of the better producers in the region.

2003 Vinhas Velhas de Santa Maria (Quinta de Foz de Arouce)	88	now–2015

FILIPA PATO ★ ★
BEIRAS $45.00

Filipa Pato is the daughter of the well-known Baga master Luis Pato, one of Portugal's iconic winemakers and a dominant force in his region. I have seen some of Filipa's other wines as well, and I think this winery is going to be a force in its own right in the near future. At the moment, with few data points, it can't be rated any higher, but someday it will be. The elegant Lokal here is all old-vine Baga, which spent 18 months in 500-liter French oak casks. It is surprisingly modern and delicate.

2005 Lokal Calcário	88	now–2013

HOTEL DO REGUENGO DE MELGAÇO ★ ★ ★
VINHO VERDE $N/A

This is a bigger, more concentrated style of Vinho Verde than the fizzy, "barely there" type. It is quite lovely on opening, with substance, some depth, and a reasonably crisp and penetrating finish. It is aromatic, with personality and hints of grass as it airs out. There are not many VVs I would evaluate upward after a year or so, but this was one of them.

2005 Alvarinho (white)	90	now–2010

JOÃO PORTUGAL RAMOS ★ ★
RIBATEJO $11.00–$25.00

This well-known Alentejo winemaker also has a property in Ribatejo. The pick of the litter here is the beautiful and gracefully aging 2001 Reserva. In the unlikely event that you don't like the wine, you'll love the charming bottle.

2003 Conde de Vimioso Reserva	85	now–2015
2001 Conde de Vimioso Reserva	89	now–2012
2004 Conde de Vimioso (Falua—Sociedade de Vinhos)	85	now–2012

JOSÉ MARIA DA FONSECA ★★/★★★
TERRAS DO SADO/VINHO VERDE $8.00–$34.00

This big southern Portuguese winery in Terras do Sado is famous for Lancer's Rosé and the familiar Periquita, which has been made here since the mid-19th century. The most important grape in Periquita is Castelão, so closely identified with Periquita that it was often simply called Periquita. The Periquitas are, by the way, charming. The basic wine, a suggested retail of $9.99, is usually delicious and elegant, a cross between Beaujolais and Burgundy. Admittedly, it should be drunk young for best results. The Clássico is the upper-level Periquita. The Periquita Reserva is the midlevel entrant. Both are very good values, and have more structure than the regular bottlings. Other bottlings here include the FSF (Syrah, Trincadeira, and Tannat) and the Hexagon (Touriga Nacional and Syrah [30% each], Trincadeira [15%], Tinto Cão [13%], Touriga Franca [10%], and Tannat [2%]). The Hexagon is more successful. The only wine here from Vinho Verde is the Twin Vines, which is basic, simple, perhaps fruitier than other entry-level wines, but still retaining some crispness. At its price ($8 suggested retail) and for certain summer events, it has a reasonable place as it is quite friendly and often charming.

2003 Hexagon	89	now–2014
2005 Periquita	84	now
2004 Periquita	85	now
2001 Periquita Clássico	88	now–2010
2004 Periquita Reserva	87	now–2011
2001 FSF	86	now–2010
2007 Twin Vines (white)	83	now
2006 Twin Vines (white)	84	now

LUIS PATO ★★★
BEIRAS $9.99–$110.00

Pato is the standard-bearer in his region (using the Vinho Regional Beiras rather than Bairrada designation), towering over its landscape. He knows too well that he faces significant challenges from his *terroir* and the region's signature variety, Baga. At times, the wines often seem to define the word "rustic," as Baga can produce very acidic, charmless, and astringent wines. Some Baga-based wines can remind one of old-fashioned Nebbiolo. When they do work, though, and often they do, they age effortlessly and gracefully. The 2005s are quite suave here for Baga. Actually, even those that don't work hold for quite a while. Whether there will be much of interest left after long aging is always the question in Bairrada. No one does a better job in the region than Pato, though.

Note: The "plain" Vinhas Velhas is a blend of three old-vine vineyards with an average age of 30 years. This should not be confused with the Barrosa bottling (vines in excess of 80 years). The 2003 Quinta do Ribeirinho Primeira Escolha is an interesting blend of Baga and Touriga Nacional. The sparkling wine is fruity and meant to emphasize fruit flavors rather than lees, toast, etc.

2005 Vinha Pan	86+	2010–2020
2003 Vinha Pan	87	now–2017
2005 Vinha Barrosa Vinha Velha	89+	2010–2025
2003 Vinha Barrosa Vinha Velha	89	now–2020
2005 Vinha Formal (white)	89	now–2012

2005 Vinhas Velhas	88	now–2018
2003 Quinta do Ribeirinho Primeira Escolha	89	now–2018
NV Espumante Bruto Touriga Nacional ($9.99–$11.99)		
(no regional designation) (white sparkling)	84	now
2001 Tinto (Quinta do Ribeirinho)	86	now–2026
1999 Tinto (Quinta do Ribeirinho)	91	now–2021

PINHAL DA TORRE ★★/★★★
RIBATEJO $14.00–$27.00

The wines from this small-production winery seem distinctive and individualistic. Despite the inclusion of international varieties, there was little that was international about them. They could have been from the Douro rather than Ribatejo (or its Vinho Regional designation, Ribatejano), and were among the more interesting wines from Ribatejo that I tasted. That said, on some wines from this winery the American oak is too obvious and gets in the way. Still, these are well-crafted wines, and this is a winery that should move up in rank. The 2 Worlds Reserva, under $14 and a blend of 50% each Cabernet Sauvignon and Touriga Nacional, is the steal here, a beautiful wine and a great bargain. Both of the other wines are likely to age gracefully and they show fine structure. The Touriga Nacional is from prephylloxera vines. The most intense wine is the Touriga Nacional/Syrah blend.

2003 Touriga Nacional/Syrah (Quinta do Alqueve)	90	now–2011
2003 Touriga Nacional (Quinta do Alqueve)	88	now–2012
2003 2 Worlds Reserva (Quinta do Alqueve)	87	now–2012

QUINTA DA ALORNA VINHOS ★★
RIBATEJO $9.00–$18.00

This winery makes attractive wines that are often excellent bargains. Although the oak is sometimes handled well, it is fair to note that it is sometimes too obvious as well. The Touriga Nacional/Cabernet Sauvignon is a beauty, and my favorite in this group. The basic Tinto is the weakest wine, but then, at only $9, as a suggested retail price, it is a pretty fair deal.

2004 Tinto	85	now
2003 Colheita Seleccionada (Casa da Alorna)	87	now–2011
2005 Touriga Nacional/Cabernet Sauvignon Reserva	89	now–2014

QUINTA DO AMEAL ★★★
VINHO VERDE $16.00–$28.00

This well-known and well-regarded producer traces its vineyards back to 1710. It is situated in the lovely Ponte de Lima area, 25 miles south of Galicia, Spain; 12 miles inland from the Atlantic Ocean; and about 200 feet above sea level. It specializes in the Loureiro grape, and owner Pedro Araújo insists on low yields, indicating that he harvests around 6 tons per hectare (15 tons per acre), compared to the average of 15 (37). For Loureiro and for Vinho Verde, the performance of the 2004 Escolha (meaning, in essence, "special selection") is quite remarkable for its age. Not many VVs improve with time.

| 2006 Loureiro (white) | 88 | now |
| 2004 Escolha (white) | 90 | now |

QUINTA DA AVELEDA ★★
VINHO VERDE/BAIRRADA $8.00–$16.00

This iconic Vinho Verde winery has an annual production around 14 million bottles, 60% of which are exported to more than 70 different countries. It is one of Portugal's largest and best-known wineries, with properties in various regions, including Bairrada (Quinta da Aguieira). It is, to be sure, most famous in Vinho Verde, where the family estate is one of the most beautiful. Wines like the basic Branco here are typical of the mass-market entrants that can be churned out in the region, yet this is a wine that has a place on a hot summer evening—light, simple, a hint of fizz, and lots of acidity.

The new (2006) Follies brand represents wines in both Bairrada and Vinho Verde. They are generally well made for their pricing, around $10 to $15. The marketing aim was to describe wines that are unbound to regional traditions and promote experimentation, "letting the final choice to be taken by the consumer and fulfill his/her inner Folly," according to the winery. The Alvarinho is Aveleda's entrant into the Alvarinho craze, and is a nice deal at around $11.99. The Terra d'Aveleda line is comprised of upper-level bottlings. Prices were not set as of this writing. If you are looking for ultimate crispness, try the Trajadura/Loureiro Follies (not yet marketed in the U.S. as of this writing). If you want solidity and more roundness, go for the Follies Chardonnay/Maria Gomes or the Terra d'Aveleda Branco Colheita Seleccionada. The Alvarinho is probably in the middle.

2006 Branco (white)	83	now
2006 Alvarinho (white)	88	now–2010
2006 Follies Chardonnay/Maria Gomes (white)	86	now
2006 Follies Trajadura/Loureiro (white)	85	now
2005 Follies Touriga Nacional/Cabernet Sauvignon	87	2009–2014
2005 Follies Touriga Nacional	86	now–2013
2006 Terra d'Aveleda Branco Colheita Seleccionada (white)	87	now–2011
2003 Terra d'Aveleda Colheita Seleccionada	87	now–2013

QUINTA DO CASAL BRANCO ★★
RIBATEJO $10.00–$20.00

This family-owned estate has been in the same hands for some two centuries. It seems very modern, though, as witnessed by its new Cork Grove line, which will remind people very much of new-world wine. Some of the Cork Grove wines have seemed overoaked and hard to deal with for that reason. On the other hand, the winery does produce some fine values. The white wine, made from Fernão Pires, is a super bargain, usually available on the street well under $10. Drink it young for best results.

2004 Reserva Falcoaria	87	now–2012
2004 Branco Falcoaria (white)	89	now
2004 Castelão/Shiraz The Cork Grove	83	now

QUINTA DE CHOCAPALHA ★★
ESTREMADURA $17.00–$38.00

These wines are made by Sandra Tavares da Silva, also the co-winemaker at Pintas and the winemaker at Vale D. Maria, for her family's estate in Estremadura, a region near Lisbon. The first commercial release was in 2000. My first introduction to Chocapalha was a bit rocky, as the top wines seemed pricey and the Cabernets could seem a bit green. From what I saw at the winery in mid-2007, they can be expected to become a standard-bearer in the region, but they are not all the way there yet.

This estate, owned by Sandra's mom and pop, literally defines a mom-and-pop, garage winery. The total production runs about 90,000 bottles, and at the moment there seems to be no room for more. Space is so tight that Sandra amusingly noted that if they do not have enough of a particular variety to fill the *lagares*, they add an available variety and make a blend. Space can't be wasted. The whites I saw look like they will be excellent. Chocapalha is the reserve wine from this estate, formerly just designated Chocapalha, but with "Reserve" on the label. It is usually a blend of Touriga Nacional and Tinta Roriz that produces a little under 600 cases. The 2005s showed better when tasted at the winery around bottling time. Perhaps they were in an awkward phase when retasted in the U.S. from the bottle.

2005 Tinto	87	now–2014
2004 Tinto	88	now–2014
2003 Chocapalha	87	2009–2015
2005 Chocapalha Reserva	88	2009–2015
2005 Cabernet Sauvignon	85+	2009–2015
2004 Cabernet Sauvignon	84	now–2014

QUINTA DE COVELA ★ ★ ★
VINHO VERDE $19.00–$25.00

This producer actually color-codes its capsules, an interesting and useful idea. Gold capsules indicate wines that saw some oak, while silver capsules indicate unoaked wines. The producer also has an interesting habit of adding in some odd varieties where you'd least expect them, a little Gewurztraminer here, a little Merlot there. The 2005 Escolha Branco, for instance, is a blend of the traditional Avesso grape, with some Chardonnay and Gewurztraminer, the latter giving this an interesting and undefinable nuance I rather liked a lot. The 2001 Colheita Seleccionada is also a blended wine, including Touriga Nacional and Cabernet Sauvignon, among others. These wines carry the VR Minho designation, rather than the Vinho Verde DOC. The owner, Nuno Araújo, is related to the Ramos Pinto family and purchased the property from Ramos Pinto. The wines are elegant, and the whites are excellent. The best of the reds are charming, although they are more of a mixed bag, and at their best, a bit compact. They can, however, be cool, focused, and refreshing. Many reminded me of Loire reds in style.

2005 Escolha Branco (white)	90	now
2003 Escolha Tinto	87	now–2011
2004 Colheita Seleccionada (white)	89	now
2001 Colheita Seleccionada Tinto	88	now–2012

QUINTA DO FEITAL ★ ★ ★
VINHO VERDE $13.00–$24.00

Owner Marcial Dorado, 34, a Spaniard, is engaging and passionate. He chose to make wine in Portugal rather than at his home in nearby Galicia, Spain, because he felt Portugal had older vines and soils that were "less spoiled." The Auratus, a young-vine wine from Quinta do Feital, is a fine value, crisp and lively. The Alvarinho is a single-quinta wine from a 70-year-old vineyard in the subregion of Monção that receives no oak aging. It is one of those wines that is changing the way people think about Vinho Verde.

2005 Auratus (white)	88	now
2005 Alvarinho Superior Dorado (white)	91	now–2010
2004 Alvarinho Superior Dorado (white)	91	now–2010

QUINTA DAS MARIAS ★ ★ ★
DÃO 18–22 EUROS

This small boutique winery is run by Peter Viktor Eckert, a Swiss national who seems to be a hobbyist in his small scale, enthusiasm, and passion, but the results are fully professional. Since retiring from the insurance industry in 2007, he has, with his family, focused even more on running this superb little winery. The winery, named after his wife, Elisabeth, and daughters, who all have Maria in their name somewhere, has developed an enthusiastic following, as well it should considering the reasonable prices and high quality. They purchased the property in 1991 and released what they call their first serious vintage in 1999. There were just 360 cases produced of each of the reds here. They are both nicely structured, elegant, and bursting with flavor. The whites are both beautiful, although I had a slight preference for the surprisingly rich, regular Encruzado rather than the oak-aged Barricas version. Regrettably, this fine estate has no U.S. importer.

2005 Reserva Cuvée TT	91	now–2015
2005 Touriga—Nacional Reserva	91	now–2015
2006 Encruzado (white)	91	now–2010
2006 Encruzado Barricas (white)	90	now–2010

QUINTA DO MONTE D'OIRO   ★ ★ ★
ESTREMADURA $N/A

This estate is rapidly developing a following for its beautifully structured Syrahs. The Reserva is 96% Syrah and the rest Viognier. It is silky and elegant, flavorful and beautifully balanced. The 2004 Reserva is a small step up from the 2003.

2004 Reserva	91	now–2016
2003 Reserva	90	now–2018

QUINTA DO SOALHEIRO   ★ ★ ★
VINHO VERDE $N/A

Quinta do Soalheiro is a familiar name in the Vinho Verde region, having planted their first Alvarinho vines in 1974, and then in 1982 having produced the first Alvarinho wine in Melgaço, according to the winery. *Primeiras Vinhas* means "first vines," signifying in this case a special bottling solely from those first Alvarinho vines planted by the estate in 1974. A joint venture with Dirk Niepoort, the white wine is graceful but mouth coating and crisp.

2006 Alvarinho Primeiras Vinhas (Soalheiro) (white)	90	now–2010

QUINTA DOS ROQUES   ★ ★ ★
DÃO $15.00–$30.00

This historic estate is one of the most prominent in this region. The output is reliable and interesting; the wines are beautifully structured and well crafted by winemaker Rui Reguinga. The prices are fair, too.

2006 Encruzado (white)	89	now–2010
2005 Touriga Nacional	89	now–2016
2005 Tinto	87	now–2013
2005 Reserva	91	now–2017

QUINTA VALE DAS ESCADINHAS   ★ ★
DÃO $20.00–$30.00

This interesting estate in Dão produces beautiful wines. Expect to be impressed by the finesse and elegance, not the power or depth. The prices are quite fair.

2005 T-Nac	89	now–2015
2003 Garrafeira (Quinta da Falorca)	90	now–2013
2003 Reserva (Quinta da Falorca)	91	now–2016

SOCIEDADE AGRÍCOLA CASA DE SANTAR ★ ★ ★
DÃO $13.00–$25.00

This is a very good lineup from this well-known winery. The basic Tinto is a good value at around $13. The Touriga Nacional was charming and elegant, and the Reserva, a blend of 50% Touriga Nacional and the rest evenly divided between Alfrocheiro and Tinta Roriz, is nicely structured and solid.

2003 Tinto (Casa de Santar)	86	now–2011
2001 Touriga Nacional (Casa de Santar)	90	now–2013
2001 Reserva (Casa de Santar)	90	now–2015

[port]

Americans have finally begun to realize the great pleasures of a mature vintage Port after a meal. For years, this sumptuous and mellow fortified red wine was seriously undervalued, as most of it was drunk in the private homes and clubs of the U.K. Prices, which soared in the early and mid-'80s, collapsed in the early '90s. Although there is not much vintage Port produced (there are rarely more than four declared vintages a decade), the international recession and bloated marketplace kept prices stable. In recent years, the weak dollar and a vastly expanding international market for fine wine have caused prices to creep up. Even so, when compared to first-growth Bordeaux, cult Napa Valley Cabernets, and grand cru Burgundy, vintage Port is still a relative value.

BUYING STRATEGY

At the time of writing, it appears that the newest vintage Port declaration for most houses will be 2007. These wines will be available for sale in 2009–2010. Other outstanding vintage years still available at retail are 2003, 2000, and 1997. As with many fine wines, prices for the newest vintages are higher than for older Ports that can be purchased through auction houses. Shrewd consumers should consider buying at auction such vintages as 1995 (if declared), 1991, 1987, 1983, and 1980. These are very fine rather than great years, but the top houses have turned in impeccable efforts, and the wines are closer to full maturity.

An obvious trend has been the explosion of single-quinta offerings, most of which are very good to excellent, although not as compelling as the greatest vintage Ports. Most of the single-quinta Ports are offered in years not declared as vintages.

STYLES OF PORT

CRUSTED PORT

Rarely seen today, crusted Port is usually a blend of several vintages that is bottled early and handled in the same manner as a vintage Port. Significant sediment will form in the bottle and a crusted Port will have to be decanted prior to drinking.

TAWNY PORT

One of the least expensive ways to secure a mature Port is to buy the best shippers' tawny Ports. Tawny Ports are aged in wood by the top houses for 10, 20, 30, 40, or even 50 years. Tawny Port represents a blend of vintages. Tawnys can have exceptional complexity and refinement. I highly recommend some of the best tawnys from firms such as Taylor Fladgate, Fonseca, and Graham's.

RUBY AND BRANDED PORTS

Ruby Ports are relatively straightforward, deeply colored, young Ports that are cherished for their sweet, grapy aromas and supple, exuberant, yet monolithic taste. Most of these Ports are meant to be drunk when released. Each house has its own style. Four of the most popular include Fonseca's Bin No. 27, Taylor's 4XX, Cockburn's Special Reserve, and Graham's Six Grapes. Stylistically, all four of these ruby or branded Ports are different. The richest and fullest is the Fonseca Bin No. 27; the most complex is usually the Taylor's 4XX; the sweetest and fruitiest is the Graham Six Grapes; and the most mature and evolved, as well as least distinguished, the Cockburn Special Reserve.

WHITE PORT

Although the French find white Port appealing, I have never understood the purpose of it, and the market for this eccentricity is dead.

LATE BOTTLED VINTAGE PORT (LBVP)

Certain vintages are held back in cask longer than two years (the time required for vintage Port) and bottled five to seven years following the vintage. These Ports tend to throw less sediment, as much of it has been already deposited in cask. In general, late bottled Ports are ready to drink when released. I typically find them less interesting and complex than the best tawnys and vintage Ports.

SINGLE-QUINTA VINTAGE PORT

This has become an increasingly important area, especially since the late '80s, when a number of vintages, particularly 1987, 1990, 1991, 1992, and 2005, could have been declared vintage years but were not because of the saturated marketplace. Many of the best single quintas, or vineyards, have offered vintage-dated, single-quinta Ports. Most Port authorities, however, feel it is the blending from various vineyards that gives vintage Port its greatest character. Others will argue that in a top year, the finest single-quinta Ports can be as good as a top vintage Port. I tend to believe that a great vintage Port is superior to a single-quinta Port, yet the finest single quintas from 1987, 1990, 1991, 1992, and 2005 are stunning. Star ratings of the different single-quinta Port producers are provided where I have had sufficient tasting experience (more than two vintages) to offer a qualitative ranking.

SINGLE-QUINTA VINTAGE PORTS

Quinta da Agua Alta (Churchill)
Quinta da Boa Vista (Offley)
Quinta do Bomfim (Dow)
Quinta do Cachão (Messias)
Quinta da Cavadinha (Warre)
Quinta do Confradeiro (Sandeman)
Quinta da Corte (Delaforce)
Quinta do Crasto (a consortium)
Quinta da Eira Velha (R. Newman)
Quinta do Fojo (Churchill)

Quinta da Foz (Cálem)
Quinta Guimaraens (Fonseca)
Quinta do Infantado (Roseira)
Quinta Malvedos (Graham's)
Quinta da Roêda (Croft)
Quinta de la Rosa (Bergqvist)
Quinta do Seixo (Ferreira)
Quinta do Tua (Cockburn)
Quinta de Val da Figueira (Cálem)
Quinta de Vargellas (Taylor Fladgate)
Quinta do Vau (Sandeman)
Quinta do Vesuvio (Symington)

VINTAGE PORT

Potentially the finest and most complex, and the subject of most of this chapter, are the vintage Ports. Vintage Ports are declared by the Port shippers the second spring after the harvest. Most of the top Port shippers declared 1991 to be a vintage year. For example, Graham's, Dow's, Quinta do Noval, and Warre had declared it a vintage, but Fonseca and Taylor did not, preferring to declare 1992 instead. Vintage Port, which is a blend of the very best cuvées from various vineyards, is bottled unfiltered two years after the harvest. It can improve and last for 50 or more years. To be a vintage Port, there must be exceptional ripeness, a great deal of tannin, and plenty of rich fruit and body. In fact, the quality of a shipper's vintage Port is the benchmark by which a shipper is evaluated in the international marketplace with each house having its own distinctive style.

These Ports tend to be blends made from various vineyards rather than products of a single vineyard.

—JAY MILLER

[recent vintages]

The greatest Port vintages since 1900 have been 1912, 1927, 1931, 1935, 1945, 1948, 1955, 1963, 1970, 1977, 1983, 1985, 1992, 1994, 1997, 2000, and 2003.

VINTAGE YEARS FOR MAJOR FIRMS

Cockburn 1947, 1950, 1955, 1960, 1963, 1967, 1970, 1975, 1983, 1985, 1991, 1994, 1997, 2003
Croft 1945, 1950, 1955, 1960, 1963, 1966, 1970, 1975, 1977, 1982, 1985, 1991, 2003
Dow's 1945, 1947, 1950, 1955, 1960, 1963, 1966, 1970, 1972, 1975, 1977, 1980, 1983, 1985, 1991, 1994, 1997, 2000, 2003
Fonseca 1945, 1948, 1955, 1960, 1963, 1966, 1970, 1975, 1977, 1980, 1983, 1985, 1992, 1994, 1997, 2000, 2003
Graham's 1945, 1948, 1955, 1960, 1963, 1966, 1970, 1975, 1977, 1980, 1983, 1985, 1991, 1994, 1997, 2000, 2003
Quinta do Noval 1945, 1947, 1950, 1955, 1958, 1960, 1963, 1966, 1967, 1970, 1975, 1978, 1982, 1985, 1991, 1994, 1995, 1997, 2000, 2003
Quinta do Noval Nacional 1931, 1950, 1960, 1962, 1963, 1964, 1966, 1967, 1970, 1975, 1978, 1980, 1982, 1985, 1987, 1994, 2000, 2003
Sandeman 1945, 1947, 1950, 1955, 1957, 1958, 1960, 1962, 1963, 1966, 1967, 1970, 1975, 1977, 1980, 1982, 1985, 2003

Taylor's 1945, 1948, 1955, 1960, 1963, 1966, 1970, 1975, 1977, 1980, 1983, 1985, 1992, 1994, 1997, 2000, 2003

Warre 1945, 1947, 1950, 1955, 1958, 1960, 1963, 1966, 1970, 1975, 1977, 1980, 1983, 1985, 1991, 1994, 1997, 2000, 2003

[the ratings]

PORTUGAL'S BEST PRODUCERS OF PORT

★ ★ ★ ★ ★ (OUTSTANDING)

Dow's

Fonseca

Graham's

Quinta do Noval Nacional

Taylor's

★ ★ ★ ★ (EXCELLENT)

Churchill

Churchill Quinta da Agua Alta

Cockburn

Croft

Dow Quinta do Bomfim

Ferreira Quinta do Seixo

Fonseca Guimaraens

Graham's Malvedos

Quinta do Infantado Touriga Nacional

Quinta do Noval

Symington Quinta do Vesuvio

Taylor Quinta de Vargellas

Warre

★ ★ ★ (GOOD)

Cálem Quinta da Foz

Croft Quinta da Roêda

Delaforce

Delaforce Quinta da Corte

Ferreira

Gould Campbell

Quarles Harris

Martinez

Niepoort

Offley Forrester

Poça Junior

Quinta do Crasto

Quinta do Noval Silval

Quinta do Passadouro

Quinta de la Rosa

Quinta de Roriz

Quinta do Vale D. Maria

Ramos-Pinto

Romariz

Rozès

Sandeman

Sandeman Quinta do Vau

Smith Woodhouse

Warre Quinta da Cavadinha

★ ★ (AVERAGE)

Barros, Almeida

Borges & Irmão

J. W. Burmester

Cálem

H. & C. J. Feist

Feuerheerd

C. N. Kopke

Caves Messias

Osborne

A. Pinto dos Santos

C. da Silva

Quinta do Panascal

Quinta da Romaneira

Vasconcellos

Wiese & Krohn

Van Zeller

[tasting commentaries]

COCKBURN ★ ★ ★ ★
$100.00

2003 Vintage Port	91	2010–2020
2000 Vintage Port	95	2010–2035
1997 Vintage Port	91	now–2020

Past Glories Quinta do Tua 1987 (94); Vintage Port 1991 (88), 1985 (90), 1983 (95), 1955 (92)

CROFT ★ ★ ★ ★
$85.00

2003 Vintage Port	93	2020–2045
2000 Vintage Port	90+	now–2025

Past Glories 1991 (93), 1963 (90)

DOW'S ★ ★ ★ ★ ★
$100.00

2003 Vintage Port	93	2020–2045+
2000 Vintage Port	94	2010–2030
1997 Vintage Port	90	now–2025

Past Glories Quinta do Bomfim 1992 (93), 1990 (95); Vintage Port 1994 (96), 1991 (90), 1983 (93), 1977 (95), 1970 (90), 1966 (91), 1963 (93), 1945 (93)

FERREIRA ★ ★ ★
$60.00

2000 Vintage Port	89+	now–2019
1997 Vintage Port	89	now–2020

FONSECA ★ ★ ★ ★ ★ ★
$125.00

2003 Vintage Port	96+	2035–2060
2000 Vintage Port	95+	now–2025
1997 Vintage Port	93	now–2020

Past Glories Guimaraens 1991 (93); Late Bottled Vintage Port 1988 (88); Twenty Year Old Tawny Port (86); Vintage Port 1994 (97), 1992 (97), 1985 (96), 1983 (92), 1977 (94), 1970 (97), 1966 (92), 1963 (97), 1955 (96), 1948 (100), 1945 (92)

GOULD CAMPBELL ★ ★ ★
$75.00

2003 Vintage Port	87	2010–2025
2000 Vintage Port	92+	2010–2030

GRAHAM'S ★ ★ ★ ★ ★
$125.00

2003 Vintage Port	95	2030–2055
2000 Vintage Port	94	2015–2040
1997 Vintage Port	93	now–2025

Past Glories Malvedos Centenary 1990 (92), 1987 (92), 1986 (92), 1976 (90), 1958 (90); Malvedos Vintage Port 1993 (92); Vintage Port 1994 (96), 1991 (94), 1985 (97), 1983 (94), 1980 (90), 1977 (95), 1970 (95), 1966 (92), 1963 (96), 1955 (95), 1948 (99), 1945 (96)

QUINTA DO INFANTADO ★ ★ ★
$60.00

2003 Vintage Port	88	2015–2030

QUINTA DO NOVAL ★ ★ ★ ★
$110.00

2003 Vintage Port	94	2020–2045+
2000 Vintage Port	92	now–2030
1997 Vintage Port	100	now–2035

Past Glories 1994 (95), 1991 (85)

QUINTA DO NOVAL NACIONAL ★ ★ ★ ★ ★
$1,000.00

2003 Vintage Port	94	2035–2055
2000 Vintage Port	93+	2012–2040
1997 Vintage Port	100	now–2040

Past Glories 1994 (99+), 1987 (92), 1985 (96), 1970 (96), 1966 (92), 1963 (99+), 1962 (98), 1931 (100)

OFFLEY BOA VISTA ★ ★ ★
$65.00

2003 Vintage Port	86	2018–2026
2000 Vintage Port	89+	now–2019

POÇAS ★ ★
$60.00

2003 Vintage Port	86	2025–2040
2000 Vintage Port	88	now–2020
2003 Director's Choice Vintage Port	86	2020–2030

QUINTA DA ROMANEIRA ★ ★
$60.00

2003 Vintage Port	89	2018–2028

ROMARIZ ★ ★ ★
$75.00

2003 Vintage Port	86	2010–2020
2000 Vintage Port	88	now–2020
1997 Vintage Port	92	now–2017

QUINTA DO SILVAL ★ ★ ★
$60.00

2000 Vintage Port	90	2010–2030
1997 Vintage Port	93	now–2020

QUINTA DE RORIZ ★ ★ ★
$65.00

2003 Vintage Port	89+	2020–2030+
2000 Vintage Port	88	now–2020

ROZÈS ★ ★ ★
$90.00

2003 Vintage Port	87	2025–2035
2000 Vintage Port	87	now–2020

SANDEMAN ★ ★ ★
$90.00

2003 Vintage Port	89	2015–2030
2000 Vau Vintage Port	90	now–2020
2000 Vintage Port	88	now–2015

SMITH WOODHOUSE ★ ★ ★
$75.00

2003 Vintage Port	87	2018–2028
2000 Vintage Port	88	now–2018

SYMINGTON QUINTA DO VESUVIO ★ ★ ★
$90.00

2003 Vintage Port	90	2018–2035
2000 Vintage Port	91	now–2020
1997 Vintage Port	90	now–2017

TAYLOR FLADGATE ★ ★ ★ ★ ★
$125.00

2003 Vintage Port	98+	2035–2060
2000 Vintage Port	98+	2010–2040
1997 Vintage Port	96	now–2030

Past Glories Late Bottled Vintage Port 1988 (89); Quinta de Vargellas 1991 (95), 1987 (90); Vintage Ports 1994 (97), 1992 (100), 1985 (90), 1983 (94), 1980 (90), 1977 (96), 1970 (96), 1966

(91), 1963 (96), 1955 (96), 1948 (100), 1945 (96); Ten Year Tawny Port (93); Twenty Year Tawny Port (92); Thirty Year Tawny Port (87)

QUINTA DO VALE D. MARIA ✱ ✱ ✱
$60.00

2000 Vintage Port	88	now–2020
1997 Vintage Port	90	now–2017

WARRE ✱ ✱ ✱ ✱
$110.00

2003 Vintage Port	93	2030–2050
2000 Vintage Port	91	now–2020

[DON'T FORGET THE MADEIRAS]

Sadly, most consumers think of Madeira as a cooking wine. Madeira's glory days were in the 19th century. Today, the bulk of Madeira is a decidedly unnoble fortified wine sold cheaply throughout the world. However, the "real" Madeira is exceedingly rare and very limited in production. Moreover, 80- to 200-year-old Madeiras from reliable producers are indeed remarkable wines, balancing sweetness against high acidity in a distinctive sweet-sour flavor profile, with explosive aromatics. The finest retail source in the U.S. for authentic Madeira is the Rare Wine Company in Sonoma, California; tel. (707) 996-4484 or (800) 999-4342; fax (707) 996-4491 or (800) 893-1501.

STYLES OF VINTAGE MADEIRA

Current laws require that all vintage Madeira be aged at least 20 years in cask prior to being bottled.

BASTARDO
Some ancient Muscatels from the firm of d'Oliveiras are remarkable, as several bottles from 1900 tasted recently have shown. Essentially, Bastardos are fortified Muscats made in very limited quantities. For unknown reasons, they have fallen out of favor, but these rare offerings are generally less expensive than similarly aged Madeiras.

BUAL
Undeniably richer, fuller, and sweeter than Verdelhos or Sercials, Bual Madeira has a deep amber color, and, like its siblings, reveals plenty of roasted, smoky, nutty characteristics.

MALMSEY
This is the sweetest, most unctuously textured Madeira, with caramel, roasted-nut, and espresso notes; thick, succulent flavors; and good acidity. The legal limit of residual sugar is 96–135 grams per liter.

SERCIAL
Sercial is the Portuguese name for the Cerceal grape when grown on the island of Madeira, and Madeiras that bear this name tend to be among the lightest, driest, and palest in color. Most Sercials emerge from Madeira's cooler climates. They have high acidity levels, and no more than 18–65 grams of residual sugar per liter. Their alcohol content is around 17%.

TERRANTEZ

Rarely seen in recent years, the expensive Terrantezes are 80- to 200-year-old, powerful Madeiras with immortal aging potential. Terrantez is more of an historical varietal for Madeira than one of current use, although one would suspect that, given the auction value of ancient Terrantez bottlings, more of it would be planted.

VERDELHO

An amber-colored Madeira, Verdelho is made in a moderately sweet style with good balancing acidity. The finish is full and sweet as the legal limit for residual sugar is 49–78 grams per liter.

TABLE WINES

One other decadent, sumptuous Portuguese wine is the Muscatel de Setúbal made by the José Maria da Fonseca firm. Quality today is not what it used to be, but some of the ancient bottlings I have tasted, particularly the 1900, have been spectacular.

As for Portugal's dry wines, they have more potential than actual quality. Nearly all are produced from indigenous varieties. Though some reveal considerable potential, the whites generally tend to be either oxidized or innocuous, and the reds range from light, fruity wines of little character to powerful, concentrated efforts possessing various degrees of rustic tannin. The chart below provides a simplistic overview of the finest producers. To date, the two best are Luis Pato, who is accomplishing fine things in Bairrada (a well-known Portuguese viticultural region between Lisbon and Porto), and the dynamic oenologist João Portugal Ramos, from Alentejo. Ramos is the locomotive for this viticultural region located south of Lisbon.

—JAY MILLER

VINTAGE GUIDE

Whereas vintages have considerable significance with respect to the Port trade, for white and red Portuguese table wines, it is more a question of who is making them than the actual vintages.

[the ratings]

PORTUGAL'S BEST PRODUCERS OF TABLE WINES

* * * (GOOD)

Quinta do Carmo (Alentejo)
Quinto do Castro (Douro)
Quinta do Côtto (Douro)
Ferreira (Douro)
Quinto do Fojo (Douro)
José Maria da Fonseca (Dão Terras Altas)
José Maria da Fonseca (Garrafeira TE)
José Maria da Fonseca (Morgado do Reguengo-Portalegre)
José Maria da Fonseca (Quinta de Camarate)

José Maria da Fonseca (Rosado Fernandes)
Quinta de Foz de Arouce (Beiras)
Quinta da Gaivosa (Douro)
Quinta da Ponte Pedrinha (Dão)
Luis Pato (Bairrada)
João Portugal Ramos Marqués de Borba (Alentejo)
João Portugal Ramos Trincadeira (Alentejo)
Quinta de la Rosa (Douro)
Vimompor Quinta da Pedra (Vinho Verde)

[spain]

Aside from the glories of Sherry, which is synonymous with Spain, this beautiful sun-drenched country is best known as a treasure trove for red wine values. However, crisp, refreshing white wines have made major inroads over the past several years. The most prominent is the tasty white made from the Albariño grape in Rías Baixas. Two others of note are the Verdejo grape from Rueda and the Godello grape from Valdeorras. And while the booming Spanish sparkling wine business continues to percolate, few makers of sparkling wine actually produce exceptional wine; most of it is reliably pleasant, relatively innocuous, and very cheap— under $20—hence the appeal.

Red wine is king in Spain, with the country increasingly realizing its vast potential. The best red wines predominantly come from northern Spain. The two areas best known for quality are Rioja and Ribera del Duero. Yet these traditional bastions of Spanish wine are being rivaled, and in some cases surpassed by upstart regions. Priorat, Montsant, Bierzo, and Toro are today's overachievers, and Jumilla, Calatayud, and Yecla are beginning to attract attention. There was a time when Spanish consumers wanted their red wines supple, with an aged taste of maturity, as well as a healthy (many would say excessive) dosage of oak, usually the blatant American variety. To achieve this, many Spanish wineries, called bodegas, would age their wines in huge oak or concrete vats for seven or eight years before release. Now tastes are changing, and the Spanish are increasingly desirous of a more international style, wines aged in small barrels, more often of French origin. . . . Some wineries still hold back their best lots for 6 to 10 years or more before releasing them (usually labeled as Reserva or Gran Reserva), enabling the consumer to purchase a mature, fully drinkable wine. However, the international demand for big, dark wines with intense flavors is causing a revolution in winemaking, led by the aforementioned regions.

[grape varieties]

RED

CABERNET SAUVIGNON An important part of Spain's most expensive and prestigious red wine, the Vega-Sicilia, Cabernet Sauvignon has flourished where it has been planted in Spain.

CARIÑENA In English this is the Carignan grape, and in Spain this workhorse grape offers the muscle of Arnold Schwarzenegger. Big and brawny, the tannic, densely colored wine made from this grape is frequently used as a blending agent, particularly with Grenache.

GARNACHA Widely planted in Spain, Garnacha (the Spanish spelling of Grenache) has three types of grapes that are used. The Garnacha Blanc, which produces white wines, is relatively limited, although it is especially noticeable in Tarragona. The Garnacha Tinto, similar to the Grenache known in France, is one of the most widely planted red wine grapes in Spain. There is also the Garnacha Tintorera, which is actually Alicante, the grape that produces black-colored, tannic, dense wines. It is primarily used for blending.

MERLOT This relatively new variety for Spain has performed competently.

MONASTRELL This variety (actually Mourvèdre) primarily produces surprisingly rich, alcoholic wines. Although widely planted, it is most frequently found in hotter microclimates. Some producers from upcoming viticultural regions such as Jumilla and Yecla have done interesting work with Monastrell.

TEMPRANILLO The finest indigenous red wine grape of Spain, Tempranillo travels under a number of names. In Penedès it is called Ull de Llebre and in the Ribera del Duero, Tinto. It provides rich, well-structured wines with good acidity and plenty of tannin and color. The bouquet often exhibits an intense berry/black raspberry character with a floral note. It makes an ideal blending mate with Garnacha, but it is easily complex enough to stand on its own. This is Spain's greatest variety, and a noble one.

WHITE

The white wine grapes parade under names such as Albariño, Chardonnay, Macabeu, Malvasia, Moscatel, Palomina (utilized for sherry), Parellada (the principal component of most sparkling wine cuvées), Pedro-Ximenez, Riesling, Sauvignon, Torrontes, and Xarel-lo. Few of these varieties have proven to be capable of making anything more than neutral-tasting wines, but several appear to have potential, as yields have been kept low and the wines have been impeccably vinified, not eviscerated by food-processor techniques. The best is the Albariño, which, when produced by a top winery in Galicia, has a stunning perfume similar to that of a French Condrieu. However, in the mouth the wine is much lighter, with less body and intensity. At its finest, it is refreshing, fragrant, and an ideal apéritif or seafood wine. Other white wines that have shown potential include Verdejo and Godello; both have a perfumed personality, lovely fruit salad–like flavors, and a pleasant finish. Godello, in particular, seems to have the ability to improve with a year or two of aging and to marry well with oak.

[the wines]

Cabernet Sauvignon is a relatively minor player in the Spanish wine scene. It is used as a blending grape in Priorat and Montsant. In Navarra and La Mancha, it is more prominent but the wines are rarely distinguished (although this is beginning to change).

RIBERA DEL DUERO Three of Spain's greatest red wines are produced in this broad river valley: Pesquera, which comes primarily from the Tempranillo grape; Vega–Sicilia, primar-

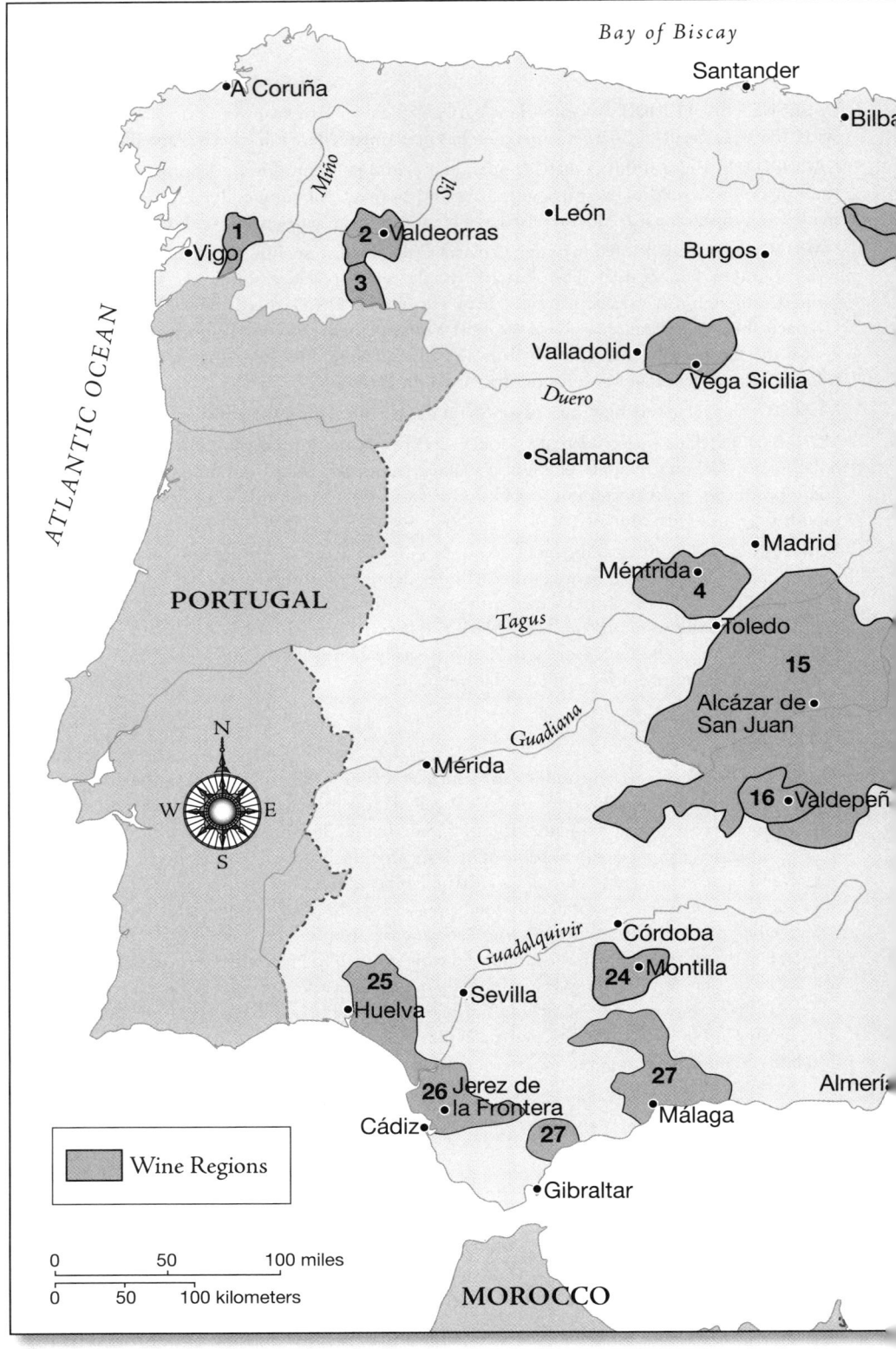

FRANCE

ANDORRA

Spain

Pamplona

5

Ebro

8

9

7

13

Barcelona

14 12 11

Tarragona

18

Valencia

7

20

23

21

19 22 21

Alicante

MEDITERRANEAN SEA

ALGERIA

1 Ribeiro
2 Valdeorras
3 Valle de Monterrei
4 Méntrida
5 Navarra
6 Rioja
7 Cariñena
8 Empordá Costa-Brava
9 Conca de Barberà
10 Alella
11 Tarragona
12 Priorat
13 Penedès
14 Terra Alta
15 La Mancha
16 Valdepeñas
17 Manchuela
18 Utiel-Requena
19 Jumilla
20 Valencia
21 Alicante
22 Yecla
23 Almansa
24 Montilla-Moriles
25 Condado de Huelva
26 Jerez-Xérès-Sherry/
   Manzanilla Sanclúcar
   de Barrameda
27 Málaga

ily a Tempranillo/Cabernet Sauvignon/Merlot/Malbec blend; and Tempranillo-based Pingus. These are world-class wines of considerable majesty. What is noticeable about them is the remarkable purity of berry fruit that can be found in the top vintages. Take superripe fruit and combine it with a minimum of three years (in the case of Vega-Sicilia, 8–12 years) in oak casks, and you have powerfully heady, supple, explosively rich wines that offer a great deal of spicy, sweet, toasty, vanilla-scented oak. The best vintages have been 2005, 2004, 2001, 2000, 1999, 1996, 1995, 1994, 1991, 1990, 1989, 1986, 1983, 1982, 1976, 1975, 1968, and 1962.

RIOJA When made by the finest traditional producers, Rioja is a mature wine having a medium-ruby color often with a touch of orange or brown (normal for an older wine), and a huge, fragrant bouquet of tobacco, cedar, smoky oak, and sweet, ripe fruit. On the palate, there will be no coarseness or astringence because of the long aging of the wine in cask and/or tank prior to bottling. Despite its suppleness, these wines will keep for five to ten years after release. Even a young Rioja, released after just three to four years, will show a ripe, fat, rich, supple fruitiness and a soft, sweet, oaky character. Increasingly, progressive antitraditional winemaking has taken over Rioja, producing wines with more color, riper fruit, and the influence of French rather than American oak. It is a different animal than traditional Rioja. The best vintages include 2005, 2004, 2001, 1996, 1995, 1994, 1991, 1990, 1989, 1987, 1982, 1981, 1978, 1973, 1970, 1968, 1964, and 1958.

TORO Once known for overwhelmingly alcoholic, heavy wines, Toro has adopted modern technology, and the results have been some rich, full-bodied, deeply flavored, southern Rhône–like wines from wineries such as Numanthia-Termes. They taste similar to the big, lush, peppery wines of France's Châteauneuf-du-Pape and Gigondas, and they represent astonishing values. The luxury cuvée of Termanthia, created by cutting-edge Spanish wine importer Jorge Ordoñez, showcases the great potential this region possesses. The best vintages are 2005, 2004, 2001, 1999, and 1998.

AGING POTENTIAL
Albarino (whites): 1–2 years
Alicante: 4–12 years
Almansa: 4–12 years
Bierzo: 4–12 years
Calatayud: 4–15 years
Campo de Borja: 4–12 years
Cariñena: 4–12 years
Costers del Segre: 4–12 years
Jumilla: 4–15 years
La Mancha: 6–15 years
Manchuela: 4–20 years
Montsant: 4–20 years
Navarra: 5–7 years
Penedès: 3–8 years
Priorat: 6–25 years
Ribera del Duero: 6–30 years
Rioja: 6–25 years
Rueda: 1–3 years
Sparkling white wines: 1–4 years
Terra Alta: 4–12 years
Toro: 6–25 years
Valencia: 4–15 years
Yecla: 3–12 years

OVERALL QUALITY LEVEL

Though it may be fashionable to tout the quality and value of all Spanish wines, the only wines with serious merit are the red wines and a handful of the Albariños and Godellos. The finest Spanish reds can hold up to the best international competition. Most of the whites are lively and pleasant, meant for casual quaffing, and, while the sparkling wines are inexpensive, only a few offer value. With the fabulous climate and high percentage of old vines, and the increasing incentives for quality and expanding markets, many of Spain's winemakers are well on the way to realizing their potential, which is formidable.

IMPORTANT INFORMATION

Knowing the names of the best red wine producers and a few top recent vintages (2001, 2004, 2005, and 2006) will get you a long way. Regarding the white wines, keep in mind that most of them, the Albariños, the Verdejos, and the Godellos, should be drunk within their first 1–2 years of life.

BUYING STRATEGY

Spain has become fashionable for both high quality and an ocean of excellent wine values. Thanks to the work of several innovative importers, particularly Jorge Ordóñez, Eric Solomon, Aurelio Cabestrero, Patrick Mata, and Steve Metzler, this country is securing a bigger and bigger share of the fine-wine market, as well as continuing to provide a bevy of exceptional bargains. The increasingly rapid transformation of the Spanish mentality from a cooperative-based, industrial winemaking philosophy, to that based on quality, individuality, and *terroir* has resulted in better and better wines. The principal difficulty for consumers at this moment in time is the increasingly weak dollar. Best buys that sold for $10 in 2007 are selling for $12–$13 in 2008. This is unlikely to change for several years. The good news is that there are abundant quantities of high-quality 2004s, 2005s, and 2006s in the marketplace, as well as others scheduled to be released over the next several years. Given the terrific climate, multitude of fabulous *terroirs*, and incentive to produce world-class wine, look for more and more unknown names to become overnight stars . . . assuming prices do not get out of touch with the realities of the marketplace.

[recent vintages]

2006

A wet harvest in many parts of Spain, especially in Rioja. This will be an irregular year, albeit with some superb wines. Rioja will be more irregular than Ribera del Duero.

2005

It was a sensational harvest in almost every important region of Spain. Rioja and Ribera del Duero performed exceptionally well, as did Priorat, Montsant, and Toro. The wines tend to be a bit more structured than those of 2004 but should be longer-lived.

2004

This was a nearly perfect vintage in Rioja and Ribera del Duero. Priorat and Montsant enjoyed an excellent vintage, nearly as fine as the great 2001. The wines have great perfume, excellent aging potential, and an open, friendly style.

2003

A challenging vintage throughout Spain, due primarily to the record heat wave that affected much of western Europe. However, with its many ancient vineyards and their deep root systems able to handle the heat, there are a surprising number of successful wines in 2003.

2002

This was a wet vintage throughout much of Spain. Given the quality of succeeding vintages, these are best left to gather dust.

2001

In many areas of Spain, this vintage has turned out to be stunning. Everyone from Rioja, Ribera del Duero, and Priorat was thrilled with the ripeness and richness. It appears to be a great vintage for Spain's top producers. Keep an eye out for the Reservas and Gran Reservas from the traditional Rioja producers because they can be special in a vintage such as 2001.

—JAY MILLER

[the ratings]

SPAIN'S BEST DRY RED TABLE WINES

★ ★ ★ ★ ★ (OUTSTANDING)

Bodegas Aalto (Ribera del Duero)
Bodegas Aalto PS (Ribera del Duero)
Bodegas Alion (Ribera del Duero)
Finca Allende Aurus (Rioja)
Allende Calvario (Rioja)
Alto Moncayo Aquilon (Campo de Borja)
Bodegas Ismael Arroyo Valsotillo Reserva (Ribera del Duero)
Bodegas Artadi Pagos Viejos (Rioja)
Bodegas Artadi Viña El Pisón (Rioja)
Bodegas Los Astrales Christina (Ribera del Duero)
Dominio de Atauta Llanos del Almendro (Ribera del Duero)
Francesc Sanchez Bas Blanc de Montsalvat (Priorat)
Bodegas Félix Callejo Family Reserve (Ribera del Duero)
Celler Cal Pla Mas d'En Compte Planots (Priorat)
Clos Erasmus (Priorat)
Clos Figueres (Priorat)
Clos Mogador (Priorat)
J. C. Conde Neo Punta Esencia (Ribera del Duero)
Dos Victorias 2V Premium (Toro)
Espactacle del Montsant (Montsant)
Antonio Izquierdo (Ribera del Duero)

Celler Mas Doix Costers de Viñas Viejas (Priorat)
Bodegas Mauro Terreus (Ribera del Duero)
Bodegas Mauro Vendimia Selecciónada (Ribera del Duero)
Bodegas Emilio Moro Malleolus de Sancho Martin (Ribera del Duero)
Bodegas Emilio Moro Malleolus de Valderramiro (Ribera del Duero)
Bodegas Muga Aro (Rioja)
Bodegas Muga Torre Muga (Rioja)
Bodegas y Viñedos de Murcia Sierra Carche (Jumilla)
Marqués de Murrieta Castillo Ygay Gran Reserva (Rioja)
Bodegas El Nido (Jumilla)
Ester Nin I Llort Nit de Nin (Priorat)
Pago de los Cappellanes Finca el Picón (Ribera del Duero)
Alvaro Palacios L'Ermita (Priorat)
Cellers Pasanau El Vell Coster (Priorat)
Pesquera (Ribera del Duero)
Dominio de Pingus Amelia (Ribera del Duero)
Dominio de Pingus Flor de Pingus (Ribera del Duero)
Dominio de Pingus Pingus (Ribera del Duero)

Bodegas Pintia (Toro)
Fernando Remírez de Ganuza (Rioja)
La Rioja Alta Gran Reserva 890 (Rioja)
Viños de Benjamín Romeo Contador
    (Rioja)
Viños de Benjamín Romeo La Cueva del
    Contador (Rioja)
Viños de Benjamín Romeo La Viña de
    Andres Romeo (Rioja)
Rotllan Torra Tirant (Priorat)

Bodegas Hermanos Sastre—Viña Sastre
    (Ribera del Duero)
Sierra Cantabria Finca El Bosque (Rioja)
Termanthia (Toro)
Vega Sicilia N.V. Gran Reserva Especial
    (Ribera del Duero)
Vega Sicilia Unico Reserva
    (Ribera del Duero)
Finca Villacreces Nebro
    (Ribera del Duero)

* * * * (EXCELLENT)

Abadía de Acón Targum (Ribera del Duero)
Abadía Retuerta Cuvée Palomar (Vino de la
    Tierra de Castilla y León)
Abadía Retuerta Pago Negrolada (Vino de
    la Tierra de Castilla y León)
Aldeasoña (Castilla y León)
Finca Allende (Rioja)
Bodegas Altanza Lealtanza Reserva Spanish
    Artist Collection (Rioja)
Alto Moncayo (Campo de Borja)
Alto Moncayo Veraton (Campo de Borja)
Bodegas Artadi Viñas de Gain Crianza
    (Rioja)
Bodegas Arzuaga Navarro Gran Reserva
    (Ribera del Duero)
Bodegas Los Astrales Astrales
    (Ribera del Duero)
Dominio de Atauta La Mala
    (Ribera del Duero)
Dominio de Atauta Valdegatiles
    (Ribera del Duero)
Bodegas Atteca Armas (Calatayud)
Bodegas Avanthia (Valdeorras)
Bodegas Baigorri Vino de Garage (Rioja)
René Barbier (Priorat)
Baronia del Montsant Englora (Montsant)
Francesc Sanchez Bas Montsalvat (Priorat)
Bodegas Ramón Bilbao Mirto de Ramón
    Bilbao (Rioja)
Celler Cal Pla Mas d'en Compte Tinto
    (Priorat)
Cal Raspallet Nun Vinya dels Taus (Penedès)
Bodegas Félix Callejo Reserva
    (Ribera del Duero)
Cámbrico Rufete (Vino de la Tierra de
    Castilla y León)
Cámbrico Tempranillo (Vino de la Tierra
    de Castilla y León)
Campo Eliseo (Toro)

Celler Can Blau (Montsant)
Celler Can Blau Mas de Can Blau
    (Montsant)
Can Ràfols dels Caus (Penedès)
Celler de Capçanes Cabrida Calissa
    (Montsant)
Carodorum Special Selection (Toro)
Bodegas Julián Chivite 125 Anniversario
    Reserva (Navarra)
Cillar de Silos Altos de Revilla
    (Ribera del Duero)
Cims de Porrera Classic (Priorat)
Clos Dofi (Priorat)
Clos Dominic Vinyes Altes (Priorat)
J. C. Conde Neo Christina
    (Ribera del Duero)
Costers del Siurana Clos de L'Obac (Priorat)
Covento San Francisco (Ribera del Duero)
Covento San Francisco Selección Especial
    (Ribera del Duero)
Descendientes de José Palacios Corullón Las
    Lamas (Bierzo)
Domini de la Cartoixa Clos Galena (Priorat)
Dos Victorias Gran Elias Mora (Toro)
El Escocès Volante 3000 Anos (Bullas)
Exopto Cellars Horizonte de Exopto (Rioja)
Agrícola Falset-Marçà Ètim L'Esparver
    (Montsant)
Finca Sandoval (Manchuela)
Finca Sandoval Cuvée TNS (Manchuela)
Forja del Salnes Goliardo Caiño
    (Rías Baixas)
Forja del Salnes Goliardo Loureiro
    (Rías Baixas)
Forja del Salnes Leirana Barrica (Rías Baixas)
Bodegas y Viñedos Gancedo Bierzo Ucedo
    (Bierzo)
Bodegas y Viñedos Gancedo Bierzo Xestal
    (Bierzo)

Garcia Figuero Noble (Ribera del Duero)
Genium Celler Costers (Priorat)
Hacienda Monasterio Crianza
   (Ribera del Duero)
Hermanos Pérez Pascuas Gran Selección
   (Ribera del Duero)
Vinos Jeromín Manu (Vino de Madrid)
Bodegas Jiménez-Landi Piélago (Mentrida)
Laurel (Priorat)
Celler Laurona 6 Vinyes de Laurona
   (Montsant)
Leda Viñas Viejas (Castilla y León)
La Legua Capricho (Cigales)
Bodega Liberalia 5 Cinco (Toro)
Bodega Viña Mambrilla Alidis Versus Viñas
   Viejas (Ribera del Duero)
Cellers Marc Ripoll Sans 2 Vinyes (Priorat)
Mas de L'Abundància Cuvée Helena del Rio
   (Montsant)
Celler Mas Doix Salanques (Priorat)
Mas d'En Gil Clos Fontà (Priorat)
Mas d'En Gil Coma Vella (Priorat)
Celler Mas Gil Clos d'Agón Blanco
   (Empordà)
Celler Mas Gil Clos d'Agón Tinto
   (Empordà)
Mas Martinet Clos Martinet (Priorat)
Mas Sinen Coster (Priorat)
Bodegas Matarredonda Libranza (Toro)
Bodegas Mauro (Ribera del Duero)
Maurodos San Román (Toro)
Merum Priorati Osmin (Priorat)
Montecastro (Ribera del Duero)
Emilio Moro and Emilio Moro Malleolus
   (Ribera del Duero)
Bodegas Muga (Rioja)
Bodegas Muga Prado Enea Gran Reserva
   (Rioja)
Bodegas Muga Reserva (Rioja)
Bodegas Muga Reserva Selección Especial
   (Rioja)
Bodegas y Viñedos de Murcia Pico Madama
   (Jumilla)
Bodegas El Nido Clio (Jumilla)
Noguerals Abellars (Priorat)
Noguerals Corbatera (Montsant)
Numanthia-Termes Numanthia (Toro)
Numanthia-Termes Termes (Toro)
Bodegas Orben Malpuesto (Rioja)
Jorge Ordonez Old Vines (Málaga)
Jorge Ordonez Victoria (Málaga)

Bodegas Pablo Gran Viu Finca Santiago
   (Cariñena)
Viñedos de Paganos La Nieta (Rioja)
Pago de Carraovejas (Ribera del Duero)
Pago de los Capellanes Parcela el Nogal
   (Ribera del Duero)
Pago de los Capellanes Reserva
   (Ribera del Duero)
Pagos del Moncayo Garnacha
   (Campo de Borja)
Pagos del Moncayo Syrah (Campo
   de Borja)
Paixar (Bierzo)
Alvaro Palacios Finca Dofi (Priorat)
Cellers Pasanau Finca La Planeta (Priorat)
Pazo de Señoráns Albariño (Rías Baixas)
Pazo de Señoráns Selección de Anada
   (Rías Baixas)
Raúl Pérez A Trabe White (Monterrei)
Raúl Pérez Sketch (Rías Baixas)
Raúl Pérez Ultreia St. Jacques (Bierzo)
Celler del Pont Lo Givot (Priorat)
Portal del Montsant Santbru (Montsant)
Bodegas y Viñedos Pujanza Cisma (Rioja)
Bodegas y Viñedos Pujanza Norte (Rioja)
Bodegas Ramiro's (Castilla y León)
Castell de Remei (Costers del Segre)
Bodegas Reyes Teofilo Reyes
   (Ribera del Duero)
La Rioja Alta Reserva 904 (Rioja)
La Rioja Alta Marques de Haro (Rioja)
Bodegas Roda Cirsion (Rioja)
Bodegas Rodero Carmelo Rodero TSM
   (Ribera del Duero)
Telmo Rodríguez (Ribera del Duero)
Señorio de San Vicente (Rioja)
Sierra Cantabria (Rioja)
Tagonius Gran Vino (Vino de Madrid)
Terra de Verema Corelium (Priorat)
Terra de Verema Triumvirat (Priorat)
Finca Torremilanos Cyclo
   (Ribera del Duero)
Finca Torremilanos Cyclo Christina
   (Ribera del Duero)
Bodegas Valcona (Rioja)
Vall Llach (Priorat)
Vega-Sicilia Valbuena (Ribera del Duero)
Villa Creces (Ribera del Duero)
Vizcarra Ramos Celia Vizcarra
   (Ribera del Duero)
La Vinya del Vuit El "8" (Priorat)

Bodega del Abad Carracedo (Bierzo)
Acustic Brao (Montsant)
Albada Calatyud Superior (Calatayud)
Ambos (Bierzo)
Bodegas Arrocal Christina
 (Ribera del Duero)
Bodegas Ismael Arroyo (Ribera del Duero)
Bodegas Artazu Santa Cruz (Navarra)
Bodegas Arzuaga Navarro Reserva
 (Ribera del Duero)
Asenjo & Manso A & M Special Selection
 (Ribera del Duero)
Dominio de Atauta (Ribera del Duero)
Bodegas Baigorri Reserva (Rioja)
Masía Barril (Priorat)
Bellum "El Principio" (Yecla)
Otto Bestue Finca Santa Sabina
 (Somontano)
Bodegas Bienvenida Toro (Toro)
Ramon Bilbao Albarino Mar de Frades
 (Rías Baixas)
Celler La Bollidora Comanda de Vilalba
 (Vi de Tavola)
Marqués de Cáceres (Rioja)
Marqués de Cáceres Reserva (Rioja)
Callejo Crianza (Ribera del Duero)
Campos Góticos Vitis Dea
 (Ribera del Duero)
Celler de Cantonella Cérvoles Tinto
 (Costers del Segre)
Celler de Capçanes Cabrida (Montsant)
Care Finca Bancales (Cariñena)
Care XCLNT (Cariñena)
Carodorum Isos (Toro)
Bodegas J. A. Calvo Casajús Antiguos
 Viñedos (Ribera del Duero)
Bodegas J. A. Calvo Casajús Vendimia
 Selecciónada (Ribera del Duero)
Casar de Burbia Tebaida (Bierzo)
Can Ràfols dels Caus El Rocallis (Penedès)
Can Ràfols dels Caus Xarel-lo Pairal
 (Penedès)
Castillo de Cuzcurrita Cerrado del Castillo
 de Cuzcurrita (Rioja)
Castillo de Cuzcurrita Señorío de
 Cuzcurrita (Rioja)
Castillo Labastida Reserva Especial Manuel
 Quintano (Rioja)
Cava Privat Laetitia (Penedès)

Viñas del Cenit Cenit (Tierra del Vino de
 Zamora)
Viñas del Cenit Triton (Tierra del Vino de
 Zamora)
Bodegas Cepa 21 (Ribera del Duero)
Viñedo Cigarral Santa María Pago del Ama
 Syrah (Vino de la Tierra de Castillo)
Cillar de Silos Torresilos (Ribera del Duero)
Cims de Porrera Solanes (Priorat)
Clos Dominic Vinyes Baixes (Priorat)
Clos Mogador Clos Nelin Blanco (Priorat)
Martin Codax Albarino (Rías Baixas)
Bodegas Comenge (Ribera del Duero)
Bodegas J. C. Conde Neo (Ribera del Duero)
Conde San Cristóbal (Ribera del Duero)
Heras Cordón Reserva (Rioja)
Costers del Siurana Miserere (Priorat)
Descendientes de José Palacios Petalos del
 Bierzo (Bierzo)
Domini de la Cartoixa Galena (Priorat)
Dominio DosTares Leione (Vinos de la
 Tierra de León)
Dos Victorias Elias Mora Crianza (Toro)
Edeteria Via Edetana (Terra Alta)
Edeteria (Terra Alta)
Cellers Els Guiamets Isis (Montsant)
Bodegas Emina Atio (Ribera del Duero)
Enate Crianza (Somontano)
Celler de l'Encastell Marge (Priorat)
Bodegas Estefania Tilenus Crianza
 (Bierzo)
Agrícola Falset-Marçà Castell de Falset
 (Montsant)
Fuentecén Llanum (Ribera del Duero)
Viñyes d'en Gabriel L'Heravi Crianza
 (Montsant)
Bodegas García Burgos Lola García
 (Navarra)
Garcia Figuero Reserva (Ribera del Duero)
Golfo 8 Golfo (Vino de Mesa)
Bodegas Guelbenzu Evo (Vino de la Tierra
 Ribera del Queiles)
Bodegas Guelbenzu Lombana (Vino de la
 Tierra Ribera del Queiles)
Guitian Godello Fermentado en Barrica
 (Valdeorras)
Guitian Godello Sobre Lias (Valdeorras)
Hermanos Pérez Pascuas Viña Pedrosa
 Reserva (Ribera del Duero)

Bodegas Itsas Mendi Itsas No.7 (Bizkaiko Txakolina)

Viñedos del Jalón Claraval (Calatayud)

Bodegas Jiménez-Landi Sotorrondero (Mentrida)

Juve y Camps Gran Juvé (Penedès)

Lan Viña Lanciano Reserva (Rioja)

Celler Laurona (Montsant)

Bodegas Licina (Vino de Madrid)

Lipscomb & Tobella Mosaic (Priorat)

Lopez de Heredia Bosconia Reserva (Rioja)

Lopez de Heredia Tondonia Reserva (Rioja)

Luna Beberide Reserva (Castilla y León)

Luna Beberide Tierras de Luna (Castilla y León)

Luz Divina Amigo Viñademoya Leiros (Bierzo)

Bodegas Viña Magaña Merlot (Navarra)

Bodega Viña Mambrilla Alidis Gran Reserva (Ribera del Duero)

Maria Casanovas Brut Nature Gran Reserva (Penedès)

Marqués de Vargas Reserva Privada (Rioja)

Martinez Bujanda Conde de Valdemar Viño Tinto (Rioja)

Mas de l'Abundància (Montsant)

Mas Alta Artigas (Priorat)

Mas Estela Moscatel (Empordà)

Mas Estela Selva de Mar (Empordà)

Mas Estela Vin Dolç (Empordà)

Mas d'en Gil Coma Blanca (Priorat)

Mas Igneus Costers de Mas Igneus (Priorat)

Mas Martinet Martinet Bru (Priorat)

Mas de les Pereres Nunci Costero (Priorat)

Mas de les Pereres Nunci Negre (Priorat)

Mas Sinen Tradition (Priorat)

Bodegas Matarredonda Juan Rojo (Toro)

Bodegas Matarromera Reserva (Ribera del Duero)

Merum Priorati Ardiles (Priorat)

Abel Mendoza Monge Jarrarte (Rioja)

Montebaco Vendimia Selecciónada (Ribera del Duero)

Heretat Mont-Rubí Durona (Alt Penedès)

Heretat Mont-Rubí Gaintus (Alt Penedès)

Marqués de Murrieta Reserva (Rioja)

Bodegas Mustiguillo Finca Terrerazo (Vino de la Tierra El Terrerazo)

Bodegas Mustiguillo Mestizaje (Vino de la Tierra El Terrerazo)

Caves Naverán Perles Rosé (Penedès)

Nuntia Vini Volvoreta Probus (Toro)

Bodegas Olivares Dulce Monastrell (Jumilla)

Orballo Albariño Fermentado en Barrica (Rías Baixas)

Bodegas Orben (Rioja)

Jorge Ordoñez Selección Especial (Málaga)

Bodega Manuel de la Osa (La Mancha)

Bodegas Pablo Gran Viu Garnacha del Terreno (Cariñena)

Pago de los Capellanes Crianza (Ribera del Duero)

Pagos del Molino Arras de Bobal (Utiel-Requena)

Palacios Remondo Propriedad (Rioja)

Pardevallas Carroleon (Tierras de León)

Cellers Pasanau Ceps Nous (Priorat)

Hermanos Peciña Gran Reserva (Rioja)

Ponce PF (Manchuela)

Puelles Reserva (Rioja)

Hacienda Don Ramón Colección Familiar (Rioja)

Viñas de El Regejal (Vino de Madrid)

La Rioja Alta Viña Alberdi (Rioja)

La Rioja Alta Reserva Viña Arana (Rioja)

La Rioja Alta Reserva Viña Ardanza (Rioja)

Rochal Calixto Nieto (Castilla y León)

Bodegas Rodero Carmelo Rodero Reserva (Ribera del Duero)

Viños de Benjamín Romeo Predicador (Rioja)

Celler del Roure Maduresa (Valencia)

Señorío de San Vicente (Rioja)

Sierra Cantabria Amancio (Rioja)

Sierra Cantabria Colección Privada (Rioja)

Sierra Cantabria Gran Reserva (Rioja)

Sierra Salinas Mira (Alicante)

Sierra Salinas 1237 (Alicante)

Silentium Expresion (Ribera del Duero)

Sitios de Bodega V3 (Rueda)

Finca Sobreño Selección Especial (Toro)

Tagonius Crianza (Vino de Madrid)

Tagonius Reserva (Vino de Madrid)

Bodegas Tardencuba Autor (Toro)

Bodegas Tardencuba Valnuevo (Toro)

Torrederos Crianza (Ribera del Duero)

Torrederos Selección (Ribera del Duero)

Torres Gran Muralles (Coca de Barberà)

Torres Mas La Plana (Penedès)

Torres Salmos (Priorat)

Traslanzas Tinto del Pais (Cigales)

Valderiz (Ribera del Duero)
Valderiz Tomás Esteban (Ribera del Duero)
Vall Llach Embruix (Priorat)
Vall Llach Idus (Priorat)
Valpiculata (Toro)
Valsacro Crianza (Rioja)
Valsacro Dioro (Rioja)
Valtostao Terra Incognita
(Ribera del Duero)
Vallobera Reserva (Rioja)
Bodega Viña Valoria Gran Reserva (Rioja)
Viñas de la Vega del Duero Quinta Sardonia
(Castilla y León)
Veigadares Gran Veigadares (Rías Baixas)
Viñas del Vero Blecua (Somontano)
Terres de Vidalba Tocs (Priorat)

Vila Viniteca Paisajes V (Rioja)
Vila Viniteca Paisajes VII (Rioja)
Vila Vinteca Paisajes VIII (Rioja)
Villaester (Toro)
Vitis Terrarum Cabernet Sauvignon (La
Mancha)
Vitis Terrarum Tempranillo (La Mancha)
Bodegas Vizcarra Ramos Inés Vizcarra
(Ribera del Duero)
Bodegas Vizcarra Ramos J. C. Vizcarra
(Ribera del Duero)
Viñedos Alonso del Yerro (Ribera del
Duero)
Viñedos Alonso del Yerro María (Ribera del
Duero)
Zumaya Reserva (Ribera del Duero)

SPAIN'S BEST SPARKLING WINES

★ ★ ★ ★ ★ (OUTSTANDING)

None

★ ★ ★ ★ (EXCELLENT)

N. V. Carles Andreu Brut
Sabaté I Coca Castell Roig Brut Nature
Reserva

Castell Sant Antoni Gran Reserva
Cava Privat Laietà
Juvé y Camps Gran Juvé

★ ★ ★ (GOOD)

Albet I Noya Cava Brut
Cádiz
Cava Avinyó
Cavas Ferret
Gran Codorníu Brut
Freixenet Cuvée DS
Freixenet Reserva Real

Juvé y Camps Gran Reserva
Juvé y Camps Reserva de la Familia
Mont Marçal Brut
Josep Maria Raventós Blanc Brut
Segura Viudas Aria
Segura Viudas Brut Vintage
Segura Viudas Reserva

SPAIN'S GREATEST WINE BARGAINS

Abadía de Acón Roble (Ribera del Duero)
Abadía Retuerta Primicia (Vino de la Tierra
de Castilla y León)
Abadia Retuerta Rivola (Vino de la Tierra
de Castilla y León)
Acustic (Montsant)
Agapito Rico Altico Syrah (Jumilla)
Viña Alarba Old Vines Grenache
(Calatayud)
Albada Tinto (Calatayud)
Albet I Noya Cava Brut (Penedès)
Adegas d'Altamira Albariño Brandal
(Rías Baixas)

Bodegas Almanseñas La Huella de Adaras
(Almansa)
Alto Almanzora Este (Almería)
Bodegas Altun Albiker (Rioja)
Finca de Arantei Albariño (Rías Baixas)
Atalayas de Golban (Ribera del Duero)
Bodegas Atteca Atteca (Calatayud)
Aventino (Ribera del Duero)
Baronia del Montsant Flor de Englora
(Montsant)
Bodegas Berroa Berroia
(Bizkaiko Txakolina)
Otto Bestué Finca Rableros (Somontano)

Bodegas Borsao Tres Picos Garnacha
   (Campo de Borja)
Bro Valero Syrah (La Mancha)
Burgans Albariño (Rías Baixas)
Campos Reales Gladium Crianza
   (La Mancha)
Celler Can Blau (Montsant)
Canto Petirrojo El Curato (Toro)
Capçanes Mas Donis Barrica (Montsant)
Casa Castillo (Jumilla)
Castaño Hécula (Yecla)
Castaño Monastrell (Yecla)
Castaño Solanera (Yecla)
Castell del Remei Gotim Bru
   (Costers del Segre)
Viñas del Cenit Venta Mazzarron
   (Tierra del Vino de Zamora)
Martin Codax Albarino (Rías Baixas)
La Cova dels Vins Ombra (Montsant)
Cuatro Pasos Mencia (Bierzo)
Bodegas Tomas Cusine El Vilosell
   (Costers del Segre)
Dos Victorias José Pariente Verdejo (Rueda)
Ébano 6 Crianza (Ribera del Duero)
Dominio de Eguren Codice Tinto
   (Castilla y León)
Dominio de Eguren Protocolo Tinto
   (Castilla y León)
El Albar Barricas (Toro)
El Cep Marquis de Gelida (Penedès)
Exopto Cellars Big Bang (Rioja)
Agrícola Falset-Marçà Falset Old Vines
   (Montsant)
Agrícola Falset-Marçà Garnacha Rosé
   (Montsant)
Fescenino Roble (Ribera del Duero)
Flavium Crianza (Bierzo)
Viñyes d'En Gabriel L'Heravi (Montsant)
Bodegas Godeval Viña Godeval
   (Valdeorras)
Celler Gramona Gessami Blanco (Penedès)
Guelbenzu Azul (Navarra)
Guelbenzu Red (Ribera del Queiles)
Guelbenzu Vierlas (Ribera del Queiles)
Jaumandreu Nissu (Plà de Bagés)
Bodegas Juan Gil (Jumilla)
Lezaun Tempranillo Organic (Navarra)
Liberalia Cabeza de Cuba (Toro)
Licia Albariño (Rías Baixas)
Luna Beberibe Mencia (Castilla y León)

Finca Luzon Altos de Luzon (Jumilla)
Bodegas Viña Magaña Barón de Magaña
   (Navarra)
Marqués de Gelida Brut Exclusive (Penedès)
Marqués de Gelida Brut Rosé (Penedès)
Mas Igneus Barranc dels Closos Blanco
   (Priorat)
Mas Que Vinos Ercavio Roble (La Mancha)
Maurodos Prima (Toro)
Hacienda Molleda Garnacha (Cariñena)
Nita (Priorat)
Olivares Altos de la Hoya (Jumilla)
Page de Los Capellanes Joven
   (Ribera del Duero)
Pagos del Moncayo Garnacha-Syrah
   (Campo de Borja)
Rafael Palacios Louro de Bolo (Valdeorras)
Palacios Remondo La Montesa (Rioja)
Pazo de Galegos Albariño (Rías Baixas)
Pazo San Mauro Albariño (Rías Baixas)
Hermanos Peciña Crianza (Rioja)
Bodegas Peique Joven (Bierzo)
Quinta del Cuervo Losada (Bierzo)
Las Rocas Garnacha (Calatayud)
Bodegas Sabor Real (Toro)
Bodegas Sabor Real Viñas Centenarias
   (Toro)
Sierra Cantabria Rioja (Rioja)
Viños Sin-Ley Rosé Series (Various)
Viños Sin-Ley G Series (Various)
Viños Sin-Ley M Series (Various)
Finca Sobreño Crianza (Toro)
Solar de Urbezo Dance del Mar (Cariñena)
Solar de Urbezo Garnacha Vieilles Vignes
   (Cariñena)
Dominio de Tares Baltos (Bierzo)
Bodegas Torremorón Tempranillo
   (Ribera del Duero)
Tria (Ribera del Duero)
Valiente e Hijos Pasamonte (Valencia)
Valmiñor Albariño (Rías Baixas)
Vega Sindoa Cabernet-Tempranillo
   (Navarra)
Vega Sindoa Viura-Chardonnay
   (Navarra)
Bodegas Vizcarra Ramos Vizcarra Roble
   (Ribera del Duero)
Volver Tempranillo (La Mancha)
Bodegas Viñas Zamoranos Los Zorros
   (Castilla y León)

[tasting commentaries]

BODEGAS AALTO ⋆ ⋆ ⋆ ⋆ ⋆
RIBERA DEL DUERO $58.00–$125.00

Aalto is the estate of Mariano Garcia, former longtime winemaker at Vega-Sicilia. The wines, produced from 100% Tempranillo, are structured for extended cellaring. The PS bottling is sourced from vines over 60 years of age.

2005 Aalto PS	98	2018–2040
2004 Aalto PS	98	2020–2045
2003 Aalto PS	93	2015–2030
2005 Aalto	95	2015–2030
2004 Aalto	94	2015–2030
2003 Aalto	92	2012–2027
2002 Aalto	91	now–2018
1999 Aalto	97	now–2019

BODEGA DEL ABAD ⋆ ⋆ ⋆
BIERZO $75.00

Bodega del Abad is a 40-hectare (99-acre) estate planted exclusively to the indigenous varieties Mencia and Godello in the up-and-coming region of Bierzo. The Carracedo cuvée is sourced from vineyards over 80 years of age.

2005 Carracedo	91	now–2020
2003 Carracedo	89	now
2001 Dom Bueno Crianza	87	now–2010

ABADÍA DE ACÓN ⋆ ⋆ ⋆
RIBERA DEL DUERO $20.00–$95.00

Abadía de Acón owns 35 hectares (86 acres) of Tinto Fino planted at high elevation. The quality is excellent from entry level through the top end of the portfolio.

2006 Roble	88	now–2015
2005 Targum	93+	2015–2030
2005 Crianza	89	now–2018
2003 Reserva	91	2012–2025

ABADÍA RETUERTA ⋆ ⋆ ⋆ ⋆
CASTILLA Y LEÓN $17.00–$200.00

This multimillion-dollar showcase winery, located just to the west of the Ribera del Duero demarcation line, is best known for its classic, potentially long-lived reds that sell for moderate to high prices. However, it is also a bargain hunter's dream, with the Rivola and Selección Especial cuvées offering particularly good value.

2004 Cuvée Palomar	90	2010–2020
2001 Cuvée Palomar	91+	2012–2025
2004 Pago la Garduña	91	2012–2025
2003 Pago la Garduña	90	now–2016
2004 Pago Negrolada	92	2012–2025
2003 Pago Negrolada	93	2012–2025
2004 Petit Verdot	92	2015–2030
2002 Petit Verdot	91+	2014–2030

2004 Rivola	88	now–2014
2003 Rivola	87	now–2010
2004 Selección Especial	89	now–2016
2003 Selección Especial	88	now–2012
2000 Selección Especial	91	now–2015

ABELIS CARTHAGO ★ ★ ★
TORO $26.00–$60.00

Abelis Carthago is a 40-acre estate of ungrafted Tinto de Toro vines, many over 100 years of age. The wines are bottled without fining or filtration. The Lui Selection offers excellent value in high-quality Toro.

2004 Fighting Bulls Selection	91	2012–2025
2004 Lui Selection	90	now–2018
2004 William Selection	90	2010–2020

ACUSTIC ★ ★ ★ ★
MONTSANT $20.00–$40.00

Acustic produces wine from 40- to 65-year-old Samso, the local name for Cariñena, and Garnacha. The wines offer the aromas and flavors of Priorat at a far more friendly price.

2006 Acustic	90	now–2020
2005 Acustic	92	2010–2020
2006 Brao	92	2012–2026
2005 Brao	94	2012–2025

ALBADA ★ ★ ★
CALATAYUD $15.00–$75.00

Albada's wines are produced from 100% Garnacha from the up-and-coming region of Calatayud. The Tinto bottling offers sensational value.

2005 Calatayud Superior	93	2012–2025
2005 Tinto	90	now–2015

ADEGA ALGUEIRA ★ ★ ★
RIBEIRA SACRA $35.00

From an obscure D.O. located in Galicia, Adega Algueira's wines are produced entirely from estate-grown Mencia.

2005 Algueira	90	now–2014

ALDEASOÑA ★ ★ ★ ★
CASTILLA Y LEÓN $120.00

This excellent estate is located just outside of the border of Ribera del Duero. It shares the same owners and winemaker as Covento San Francisco. The wine is 100% Tinta del Pais sourced from a vineyard planted in 1912.

2004 Aldeasoña	94+	2014–2035

BODEGAS ALION ★ ★ ★ ★ ★
RIBERA DEL DUERO $75.00

Bodegas Alion was started by the renowned Vega-Sicilia in 1991. Grapes are sourced from vineyards next to the winery and from Vega-Sicilia's own vineyards at Valbuena. Seven hectares (18 acres) of Tinto Fino (Tempranillo) form the actual Alion estate.

2004 Alion	96	2012–2025
2003 Alion	96+	2014–2030
2002 Alion	94	2010–2020
2001 Alion	95	2010–2022
1999 Alion	90	now–2017
1998 Alion	87	now

FINCA ALLENDE ✶ ✶ ✶ ✶ ✶
RIOJA $35.00–$240.00

Finca Allende ranks near the top of producers in Rioja. All of their wines are made in a modern style with a generous use of new French oak and bottling without fining or filtration.

2005 Allende	92	2012–2025
2004 Allende	92	2010–2020
2001 Allende	93	now–2014
1999 Allende	88	now–2014
2005 Calvario	95	2015–2035
2004 Calvario	95	2015–2035
2002 Calvario	93	now–2018
2000 Calvario	93	now–2018
2005 Aurus	98	2015–2040
2004 Aurus	96+	2018–2040
2001 Aurus	95	2010–2025
1999 Aurus	89	now–2016
1998 Aurus	90+	now–2018

BODEGAS ALTANZA ✶ ✶ ✶
RIOJA $22.00–$110.00

Bodegas Altanza has 120 hectares (296 acres) of Tempranillo planted around Fuenmayor in the center of Rioja Alta. All of the wines are 100% Tempranillo fermented with native yeasts. The Altanza bottlings are made in the traditional style of Rioja while the Lealtanza bottlings represent a more progressive style.

2004 Lealtanza Crianza	90	now–2015
2001 Lealtanza Crianza	89	2010–2016
2004 Lealtanza Reserva Spanish Artist Collection	93	2015–2030
2001 Lealtanza Reserva Miro	95	2013–2028
2001 Altanza	90	now–2020
2001 Edulis Crianza	86	now
2001 Altanza Reserva Selección Especial	92	now–2020
2001 Lealtanza Reserva Selección	93	2012–2025
2000 Lealtanza Reserva	89	2010–2016
2000 Lealtanza Reserva	89	2010–2016
2000 Lealtanza Reserva Club	91	2010–2018
1999 Altanza Reserva Especial	90	now–2013
1999 Edulis Reserva Especial	90	now–2010

ALTO MONCAYO ✶ ✶ ✶ ✶ ✶
CAMPO DE BORJA $48.00–$169.00

These brilliant wines, fashioned from 100% Garnacha, are made by the renowned Australian Chris Ringland. They demonstrate what can be achieved in a region thought just a few years ago to be no more than a source for everyday, inexpensive grocery-store wine.

2005 Alto Moncayo Veraton	93	now–2020
2005 Alto Moncayo	95	2010–2020
2002 Alto Moncayo	93	now–2014
2005 Aquilon	97	2015–2030
2002 Aquilon	96	2010–2020

ALZANIA ★ ★ ★
NAVARRA $53.00–$72.00

This winery, founded in 1999, appears to be moving full speed ahead. Most wines from Navarra are budget-priced quaffers, but this winery appears intent on showing what can really be achieved in this region.

2003 Alzania 21 Del 10	90	2012–2020
2002 Alzania Selección	92	2013–2024

AMBOS ★ ★ ★
BIERZO $43.00

Ambos is a biodynamically farmed estate in Bierzo making wine from 40- to 50-year-old Mencia vines.

2005 Ambos	91	now–2015

ANIMA NEGRA ★ ★ ★
VINO DE LA TIERRA ILLES BALEARS $24.00–$110.00

Anima Negra, located on the island of Mallorca, is owned by Pere Obrador and Miguel Ángel Cerdá. They contract with 135 small local vineyards for the indigenous grapes (Callet and Mantonegre-Fogoneu) that range in age from 50 to 85 years. The vines are dry-farmed and not fertilized.

2005 AN	92	now–2020
2005 AN/2	91	now–2015
2005 Son Negre	94	2012–2025

BODEGAS ARROCAL ★ ★ ★
RIBERA DEL DUERO $38.00–$60.00

Bodegas Arrocal is a fine source for moderately priced wine from Ribera del Duero. The wines are 100% Tempranillo, bottled without filtration.

2005 Arrocal Selección	91	now–2018
2004 Arrocal Selección	91	2012–2020
2003 Arrocal Selección	88	now
2005 Arrocal Christina	92	2012–2025
2005 Arrocal	90	now–2013
2004 Arrocal	90	now

BODEGAS ARTADI ★ ★ ★ ★ ★
RIOJA $35.00–$225.00

Bodegas Artadi is on the short list of contenders for finest producer in Rioja. The winery excelled in the difficult 2003 and 2006 vintages and produced extraordinary wines in the great vintages of 2004 and 2005. Their Viñas de Gain cuvée always offers exceptional value in high-class Rioja.

2006 Pagos Viejos	94	2012–2025
2005 Pagos Viejos	95	2020–2040
2004 Pagos Viejos	97	2018–2035
2002 Pagos Viejos	90	now–2017
2001 Pagos Viejos	95	2012–2025
2000 Pagos Viejos	94	2010–2020
1999 Pagos Viejos	90	now–2014
2006 Viña El Pisón	97	2015–2035
2005 Viña El Pisón	98	2020–2050
2004 Viña El Pisón	100	2020–2045
2001 Viña El Pisón	97	2012–2027
2000 Viña El Pisón	96	2010–2022
1999 Viña El Pisón	91	now–2014
2006 Viñas de Gain	92	2010–2020
2005 Viñas de Gain	94	2014–2030
2003 Viñas de Gain	93	now–2015
2000 Viñas de Gain	88	now–2010
2001 Grandes Añadas	98	2016–2040

BODEGAS ARTAZU * * *
NAVARRA $40.00

Navarra, once seen as a source for inexpensive plonk and tasty *rosado* (rosé), is now turning out some high-quality red wine. Artazu's Santa Cruz bottling is sourced from a Garnacha vineyard of the same name with vines ranging from 80 to 100-plus years of age.

2005 Santa Cruz	92	now–2015
2003 Santa Cruz	95	now–2012

BODEGAS ARZUAGA NAVARRO * * *
RIBERA DEL DUERO $35.00–$250.00

Arzuaga is a traditional estate in Ribera del Duero still adhering to the aging regimens specified under the old regulations. The winery produces one white, Fan d'Oro, which is 100% Chardonnay.

2005 Fan d'Oro	89	now–2010
2005 Crianza	90+	2010–2020
2004 Crianza	87	2009–2016
2004 Gran Arzuaga	91	now–2020
2004 La Planta	88	now–2012
2004 Reserva	92	2012–2025
2001 Reserva	91+	2012–2025
2003 Reserva Especial	90	now–2018
2001 Gran Reserva	93	2012–2025

BODEGAS LOS ASTRALES * * * *
RIBERA DEL DUERO $55.00–$75.00

Astrales is a limited-production Ribera del Duero produced from 30- to 85-year-old Tinto Fino (Tempranillo) vines and fermented with native yeasts. The Christina cuvée is sourced from the estate's oldest vines and aged in 100% new French oak.

2005 Astrales	93	2013–2025
2005 Astrales Christina	97	2015–2040
2004 Astrales	92+	2015–2030

DOMINIO DE ATAUTA ★★★★
RIBERA DEL DUERO $45.00–$150.00

Dominio de Atauta was established in 1999 with the first vintage the following year. The vineyards are 100% Tinto Fino, most of them ungrafted vines of 60-plus years of age. The wines at this address are muscular and large scaled, true *vins de garde*, in need of extended cellaring.

2005 Dominio de Atauta	92	2015–2030
2005 La Mala	95	2020–2045
2004 La Mala	93	2016–2030
2005 Llanos de Almendro	96	2018–2040
2004 Llanos del Almendro	96	2015–2030
2005 Valdegatiles	94	2020–2040
2004 Valdegatiles	95	2014–2028
2003 Valdegatiles	96	2010–2022
2004 Atauta	92	now–2015
2003 Atauta	92	now–2017

BODEGAS ATTECA ★★★
CALATAYUD $16.00–$45.00

Bodegas Atteca is a partnership between the Gil family of Jumilla and pioneer importer Jorge Ordoñez. The wines are 100% Garnacha from vines ranging from 80 to 110 years of age. The Atteca cuvée is a sensational red wine value from the up-and-coming D.O. of Calatayud.

2006 Atteca	91	now–2015
2005 Atteca Armas	93	2012–2025

BODEGAS AVANTHIA ★★★★
VALDEORRAS $75.00

Avanthia is 100% old-vine Mencia sourced from two vineyards with 70- and 85-year-old vines respectively. The wine is barrel-fermented and aged in new French oak.

2006 Avanthia	94	2010–2020

BODEGAS BAIGORRI ★★★
RIOJA $30.00–$95.00

Bodegas Baigorri is said to be one of the showplace wineries of Rioja, designed by Basque architect Iñaki Aspiazu Iza. The winery ferments with native yeasts and uses only French oak.

2004 Crianza	90	now–2015
2003 Reserva	91	2010–2020
2003 Vino de Garage	93	2012–2025

HORNILLO BALLESTEROS ★★★
RIBERA DEL DUERO $13.00–$70.00

This is a true "garage" bodega (the winery is in a garage in the town of Roa). These small-production cuvées of 100% Tempranillo are uniformly outstanding.

2005 Mibal Tinto	90	now–2010
2004 Mibal	91+	2012–2020
2003 Mibal	90	now–2012
2004 Mibal Selección	93	2012–2020
2003 Mibal Selección	90+	2010–2017
2003 Perfil de Mibal	94	2012–2025
2003 Valdegatiles	96	2010–2022

BARONIA DEL MONTSANT ★ ★ ★
MONTSANT $16.00–$30.00

Baronia del Montsant is turning out superb values from blends of Garnacha, Cariñena, Syrah, Merlot, and Cabernet Sauvignon. If you want to discover what Priorat is all about without a major investment of capital, check out wines from Montsant and Baronia del Montsant in particular.

2006 Flor d'Englora	92	now–2015
2004 Englora	91	2012–2024
2002 Englora	89+	2009–2016
2001 Clos d'Englora AV 14	93	2010–2018

FRANCESC SANCHEZ BAS ★ ★ ★ ★
PRIORAT $43.00–$70.00

This excellent producer began operations in 1996. The Blanc de Montsalvat, made from Macabeu and Trepat Blanc, is one of the benchmark white wines from Catalunya. The red wine, made entirely from old-vine Garnacha and Cariñena, is first class as well.

2006 Blanc de Montsalvat	96	now–2013
2005 Blanc de Monsalvat	92	now–2011
2004 Montgarnatx	93	2010–2020
2002 Montsalvat	92	now–2020
2001 Monsalvat	95	2012–2025

BODEGAS BORSAO ★ ★ ★ ★
CAMPO DE BORJA $13.00

Bodegas Borsao produces several other wines that offer excellent value. However, their Tres Picos Garnacha is an annual candidate for finest Spanish red wine value. It has been described as cherry pie in a glass.

2006 Tres Picos Garnacha	91	now–2012
2005 Tres Picos Garnacha	91	now–2011
2003 Tres Picos Garnacha	90	now

BURGANS ★ ★ ★
RÍAS BAIXAS $14.00

Burgans is an annual candidate for finest value in Albariño. If the current vintage has already passed through the marketplace, it is a very safe bet to purchase a more recent vintage.

2007 Albariño	90	now–2010
2006 Albariño	89	now–2009

BODEGAS JUAN MANUEL BURGOS ★ ★ ★
RIBERA DEL DUERO $28.00–$100.00

Juan Manuel Burgos is another of the handful of "garage" winemaker-viticulturalists in Ribera del Duero. The Avan wines are all 100% Tempranillo.

2004 Avan Nacimiento	89	now–2013
2003 Avan Nacimiento	90	now–2012
2004 Avan Concentración	91	2009–2017
2003 Avan Concentración	92	now–2018
2004 Avan Cepas Centenarias	95	2012–2025
2003 Avan Cepas Centenarias	96	2010–2022

CELLER CAL PLA ★ ★ ★ ★ ★
PRIORAT $40.00–$110.00

Cal Pla is one of the leading estates of Priorat. The wines are made predominantly from old-vine Cariñena and Garnacha. They are among the more structured wines of the D.O. and will profit from extended cellaring.

2005 Mas d'en Compte Tinto	94	2012–2025
2004 Mas d'en Compte Tinto	95	now–2015
2005 Mas d'en Compte Planots	98	2015–2030
2004 Mas d'en Compte Planots	97	2010–2020
2005 Mas d'en Compte Blanco	91	now–2010

CAL RASPALLET ★ ★ ★ ★
PENEDÈS $65.00

Cal Raspallet's Nun Vinya dels Taus is 100% Xarel-lo from the oldest known surviving Xarel-lo vines in Spain. The vineyard is biodynamically farmed and the wine aged for eight months in French oak. The unique flavors are reminiscent of old-vine Roussanne.

2006 Nun Vinya dels Taus	93	now–2012

BODEGAS FÉLIX CALLEJO ★ ★ ★ ★
RIBERA DEL DUERO $22.00–$134.00

The Callejo family owns 60 hectares (148 acres) of low-yielding Tempranillo vines ranging in age from 25 to 70 years. All of the wines are 100% Tempranillo from estate vines fermented with native yeasts.

2006 Cuatro Meses en Barrica	89	now–2012
2005 Cuatro Meses en Barrica	90	now–2013
2005 Callejo Crianza	91	now–2015
2004 Callejo Crianza	91	2010–2020
2004 Reserva	92	2012–2025
2005 Felix Callejo Family Reserve	97	2015–2030
2004 Felix Callejo Family Reserve	96	2015–2030
2003 Felix Callejo Family Reserve	98	2014–2035
1999 Gran Reserva	90	now–2014

CÁMBRICO ✶✶✶
TIERRA DE CASTILLA Y LEÓN $99.00

Cámbrico's specialty is the obscure indigenous variety Rufete. It was brought to the region by Burgundian settlers 400 years ago. Cambrico biodynamically farms its 60-year-old Rufete vines.

2003 Rufete	92	2010–2020
2003 Tempranillo	93	2012–2025

BODEGAS CAMPILLO ✶✶✶
RIOJA $29.00–$145.00

Bodegas Campillo was built in 1990 by Julio Faustino Martinez, the owner of Bodegas Faustino, for the purpose of creating limited-production, handcrafted wines. The wines come from a 50-hectare (125-acre) vineyard in the Laguardia region of the Rioja Alavesa. These are traditionally styled Riojas in the best sense of that word. The Pago Cuesta Clara Raro is bottled only in large formats.

1998 Reserva	88	now–2014
1998 Pago Cuesta Clara Raro	93	2012–2025
1996 Reserva Especial	91	now–2018
1994 Gran Reserva	92	now–2018

CAMPO ELISEO ✶✶✶✶
TORO $72.00

Campo Eliseo, produced by J. & F. Lurton, is 100% Tinto de Toro sourced from low-yielding vineyards averaging 40 years of age. The wine goes through malolactic fermentation in barrel and is then aged for 18 months in French oak prior to bottling without filtration.

2005 Campo Eliseo	94	2012–2025
2004 Campo Eliseo	94	2012–2025
2003 Campo Eliseo	90	2010–2017

CELLER CAN BLAU ✶✶✶✶
MONTSANT $17.00–$45.00

Celler Can Blau is a partnership between the Gil family and importer Jorge Ordoñez. The estate owns 24 hectares (60 acres) of vineyard with an average age of 35 years. The Can Blau cuvée is one of the finest values in Spanish wine.

2006 Can Blau	92	now–2016
2004 Can Blau	90	now–2014
2005 Mas de Can Blau	95	2013–2025
2004 Mas de Can Blau	92+	2010–2018

CELLER DE CANTONELLA ✶✶✶✶
COSTERS DE SEGRE $30.00–$70.00

The grapes for Celler de Cantonella are sourced from the highest altitude vineyard in the Costers de Segre D.O. (just bordering the Montsant/Priorat D.O.). The Cérvoles Tinto is 40% Tempranillo, 25% Cabernet Sauvignon, 25% Garnacha, and 10% Merlot aged for 12 months in French oak, 50% new. The Estrats is 65% Cabernet Sauvignon, 20% Tempranillo, and 15% Garnacha aged for 15 months in new French oak.

2004 Cérvoles Tinto	92	now–2015
2003 Cérvoles Tinto	94	now–2014
2004 Estrats	93	2012–2025

CELLER DE CAPÇANES ★★★
MONTSANT $14.00–$100.00

Capçanes offers some of the finest values in the emerging D.O. of Montsant. Annually one of the best buys is the Mas Donis Barrica, a custom cuvée made for importer Eric Solomon. These are wines that require little cellaring but have a substantial drinking window.

2005 Cabrida	91	2012–2020
2000 Cabrida	92	now–2016
2006 Cabrida Calissa	93	now–2020
2005 Costers del Gravet	89	2010–2020
2005 Mas Donis Barrica	91	now–2018
2003 Mas Donis Barrica	92	now–2012
2001 Mas Donis Barrica	91	now–2010
2000 Mas Donis Barrica	89	now
2004 Vall de Calàs	90	now–2018
2001 Val de Calàs	93	now–2014

CARODORUM ★★★
TORO $27.00–$66.00

Carodorum is a 16-hectare (40-acre) Toro estate planted on sandy soil where phylloxera never took hold. The Special Selection cuvée was sourced from ungrafted vines over 100 years of age. The wines are 100% Tinto de Toro (Tempranillo).

2005 Isos	91	2010–2020
2005 Special Selection	93	2012–2025
2004 Special Selection	95	2015–2035
2004 Carodorum	89	2010–2018
2004 Crianza	91+	2012–2022

BODEGAS J. A. CALVO CASAJÚS ★★★
RIBERA DEL DUERO $25.00–$40.00

Calvo Casajús is owned and operated by its namesake, José Alberto Calvo Casajús. It is literally a one-man operation, with Casajús also doubling as the village baker. His grandfather planted the estate's Tempranillo vineyards in 1920. Two wines are produced, the Vendimia Selecciónada and Antiguos Viñedos.

2005 Antiguos Viñedos	91	2012–2025
2004 Antiguos Viñedos	93	2015–2030
2001 Antiguos Viñedos	90	now–2018
2006 Vendimia Selecciónada	91	2010–2020
2005 Vendimia Selecciónada	92	2012–2025
2003 Vendimia Selecciónada	89+	now–2010
2003 Tinto	87	now

CAN RÀFOLS DELS CAUS ★★★★
PENEDÈS $24.00–$50.00

Can Ràfols dels Caus is the 450-hectare (1,112-acre) estate of brilliant innovator Carlos Esteva. It is located in the heart of the Garraf Massif, which forms part of the Catalan coastal mountain range. These are among the finest, most ageworthy white wines of Spain, some of them made from indigenous varieties such as Xarel-lo and Incrozzio Manzoni.

2002 El Rocallis	93	now–2012
2005 Gran Caus Blanco	90	now–2012
2004 Xarel-lo Pairal	92	now–2012

CASTILLO DE CUZCURRITA ★ ★ ★ ★
RIOJA $47.00–$80.00

These outstanding Riojas are 100% Tempranillo sourced from single vineyards and aged in French oak.

2004 Cerrado del Castillo de Cuzcurrita	93+	2013–2030
2003 Señorío de Cuzcurrita	92	2012–2025

CASTILLO LABASTIDA ★ ★ ★
RIOJA $59.00

In addition to their top-of-the-line Reserva Especial Manuel Quintano, Castillo Labastida produces several excellent Rioja values worth checking out. The Manuel Quintano cuvée comes from the estate's oldest vineyards and is aged for three years in American oak in the traditional manner.

2001 Reserva Especial Manuel Quintano	92+	2012–2025

VIÑAS DEL CENIT ★ ★ ★
TIERRA DEL VINO DE ZAMORA $17.00–$47.00

The region of Tierra del Vino de Zamora should have been included in the Toro D.O. but was overlooked when the boundaries were drawn. Viñas del Cenit has a total of 44 hectares (109 acres), 15% of it planted in ungrafted 100-year-old vines of Tinto de Toro, used to make Triton. The Venta Mazzarron cuvée is one of Spain's finest red wine values.

2005 Cenit	93	2012–2025
2003 Cenit	90	now–2014
2005 Triton	91	now–2018
2005 Venta Mazzarron	91	now–2015
2003 Venta Mazzaron	90	now–2014

VIÑEDO CIGARRAL SANTA MARÍA ★ ★ ★
VINO DE LA TIERRA DE CASTILLO $95.00

The Pago del Ama Syrah is produced by the chef/owner of one of Spain's best restaurants, Adolfo Munoz of Restaurant Adolfo.

2005 Pago del Ama Syrah	93	2012–2025

CILLAR DE SILOS ★ ★ ★
RIBERA DEL DUERO $30.00–$85.00

Cillar de Silos is a source of reliable and fairly priced old-vine Tempranillo from the prestigious D.O. of Ribera del Duero.

2006 Crianza	90	now–2020
2005 Crianza	90+	2012–2025
2004 Crianza	90+	now–2018
1999 Crianza	88	now
2005 El Quintanal Vendimia Selecciónada	90	2010–2020

2005 Altos de Revilla	94	2010–2035
2004 Altos de Revilla	91	2010–2020
2005 Torresilos	92+	2015–2035
2004 Torresilos	93	2015–2035
2000 Torresilos	90	now–2013
1999 Torresilos	91	now–2014
1998 Torresilos	89	now–2014

CIMS DE PORRERA ★ ★ ★
PRIORAT $28.00–$84.00

The Pérez Overjero family, part of the group of pioneers who rediscovered Priorat in the mid-1980s, began managing Cims de Porrera, the local cooperative, in 1992. The Solanes bottling utilizes all five grapes permitted in Priorat, while the Classic cuvée is produced only in the best years.

2004 Solanes	91	2010–2020
2004 Classic	93	2012–2025
2000 Classic	92+	now–2018
1999 Classic	94	2009–2019
1998 Selección Cariñena	92	now–2016

CLOS DOMINIC ★ ★ ★
PRIORAT $40.00–$70.00

Dominic Baiguret and her husband, Francisco Castillo-Serrano, purchased an old-vine vineyard outside the village of Porrera in 1998, and they continue to manage it with help from only family and friends. The flagship cuvée, Vinyes Altes, is made from vines over 100 years of age.

2004 Vinyes Baixes	92	2010–2020
2004 Vinyes Altes	94	2012–2025

CLOS FIGUERES ★ ★ ★ ★ ★
PRIORAT $36.00–$85.00

Clos Figueres was purchased in 1997 by importer Christopher Cannan upon the advice of Priorat legend René Barbier. The older Cariñena and Garnacha vines, planted for the original Clos Figueres estate, are used for the flagship bottling, while the younger vines, planted in 1998, are used for Font de la Figuera.

2005 Font de la Figuera	90	2010–2020
2004 Font de la Figuera	91	2012–2022
2002 Font de la Figuera	89	now–2013
2000 Font de la Figuera	89	now–2012
2005 Clos Figueres	96	2012–2025
2004 Clos Figueres	93	2013–2038
2003 Clos Figueres	92	2010–2020
2000 Clos Figueres	92	2010–2020

CLOS GALENA ★ ★ ★ ★ ★
PRIORAT $35.00–$50.00

Clos Galena was established recently, in 2001, and is farmed organically. It contains both old vines and new plantings.

| 2004 Galena | 92 | 2010–2020 |
| 2004 Clos Galena | 95 | 2012–2025 |

CLOS I TERRASSES ★ ★ ★ ★ ★
PRIORAT $45.00–$175.00

Clos I Terrasses' second wine, called Laurel, is one of Priorat's finest values. It is the product of a severe triage in both the vineyard and winery. As for the flagship, Clos Erasmus, it is arguably the finest wine of Priorat. The goal is to eventually have it be 100% old-vine Garnacha. Currently it includes 15% Syrah.

2005 Laurel	94	2012–2025
2004 Laurel	94	2012–2025
2003 Laurel	91	2009–2018
2005 Clos Erasmus	100	2015–2035
2004 Clos Erasmus	100	2012–2030
2003 Clos Erasmus	99	2015–2035
2002 Clos Erasmus	93	2010–2022
2000 Clos Erasmus	96	now–2020
1999 Clos Erasmus	93	now–2020

CLOS MANYETES ★ ★ ★ ★
PRIORAT $100.00

Clos Manyetes is owned by René Barbier of Clos Mogador. Manyetes is composed of 70% Cariñena and 30% Garnacha.

| 2004 Manyetes | 93 | 2010–2020 |
| 2003 Manyetes | 91 | now–2017 |

CLOS MOGADOR ★ ★ ★ ★ ★
PRIORAT $49.00–$92.00

Clos Mogador is owned by the renowned René Barbier. The estate produces a superb white wine called Clos Nelin Blanco as well as Clos Mogador itself. The latter is the first wine in Spain entitled to the new classification Vi de Finca Qualificada.

2005 Clos Nelin Blanco	92	now–2014
2005 Clos Mogador	98	2012–2040
2004 Clos Mogador	96+	2017–2035
2003 Clos Mogador	94	2013–2027
2002 Clos Mogador	90	now–2017
2000 Clos Mogador	95	2012–2027
1999 Clos Mogador	95	2010–2020

CONDADO DE HAZA ★ ★ ★ ★
RIBERA DEL DUERO $25.00–$90.00

Condado de Haza is another Alejandro Fernández (of Pesquera fame) property also located in Ribera del Duero. Like all of his estates, the wines are produced from 100% Tempranillo. The first vintage here was in 1993.

| 2004 Condado de Haza | 91+ | now–2018 |
| 1999 Alenza Gran Reserva | 90 | 2010–2020 |

BODEGAS J. C. CONDE ★★★★
RIBERA DEL DUERO $24.00–$90.00

J. C. Conde's wines are 100% Tempranillo, predominantly from old vines. The Neo Christina and Neo Punta Esencia cuvées both receive the so-called 200% new-oak treatment. They are muscular wines with serious aging potential.

2006 Neo Sentido	89	2010–2020
2005 Neo Sentido	91	2010–2017
2004 Neo Sentido	90	now–2015
2005 Neo	92	2012–2025
2004 Neo	94	2014–2032
2003 Neo	92+	2012–2025
2002 Neo	90	now–2013
2005 Neo Christina	93+	2015–2035
2005 Neo Punta Esencia	96+	2017–2040
2004 Neo Punta Esencia	96	2017–2035
2003 Neo Daniel	93	2009–2017

CONDE SAN CRISTÓBAL ★★★
RIBERA DEL DUERO $25.00

The estate-grown Conde San Cristóbal is one of the finest values from Ribera del Duero. The blend is 80% Tinta Fina with the balance Cabernet Sauvignon and Merlot aged for 12 months in French, Russian, and American oak.

2005 Conde San Cristóbal	91+	2012–2025
2004 Conde San Cristóbal	91	now–2020

COSTERS DEL SIURANA ★★★
PRIORAT $82.00–$90.00

Compared to the top wines of Priorat, Costers del Siurana uses a relatively low percentage of old-vine Garnacha and Cariñena. Nevertheless, the wines are almost always outstanding.

2005 Miserere	91	now–2017
2004 Miserere	94	2012–2025
2003 Miserere	92	2010–2020
2002 Miserere	90	now–2018
2005 Clos de L'Obac	93	2013–2025
2004 Clos de L'Obac	95	2012–2025
2003 Clos de L'Obac	86	now–2015
2002 Clos de L'Obac	86	now–2012
2000 Clos de L'Obac	91	2010–2020

COVENTO SAN FRANCISCO ★★★★
RIBERA DEL DUERO $42.00–$90.00

Javier García is owner-winemaker of this small estate. For several years García was Peter Sisseck's right-hand man at Hacienda Monasterio. The estate's two wines are blends of 90% Tempranillo and 10% Merlot.

2005 Covento San Francisco	93	2018–2035
2004 Selección Especial	95	2018–2040
2004 Crianza	93	2012–2022
2003 Crianza	91	2010–2018

DESCENDIENTES DE JOSÉ PALACIOS ★★★★
BIERZO $23.00–$150.00

This estate was started in 1998 by Alvaro Palacios. It has steep hillside vineyards ranging in age from 60 to 100 years planted to 100% Mencia, a grape indigenous to the cool-climate D.O. of Bierzo.

2006 Petalos del Bierzo	91	now–2015
2005 Petalos del Bierzo	90	now–2012
2004 Petalos del Bierzo	91	now–2014
2003 Petalos del Bierzo	92	now–2016
2004 Corullón	91	2010–2018
2003 Corullón	93+	now–2018
2005 Corullón Las Lamas	92	2010–2018
2003 Corullón Las Lamas	94	2013–2027
2003 Corullón "Moncerbal"	92	2010–2018

DOMINI DE LA CARTOIXA ★★★★
PRIORAT $38.00–$58.00

This organically farmed estate's wines are among the better values from Priorat.

2005 Galena	92	now–2020
2005 Clos Galena	95	2012–2025

DOS VICTORIAS ★★★★
TORO $22.00–$135.00

Dos Victorias owns 18 hectares (44 acres) of Tinto de Toro planted at high elevation. The Elias Moro cuvée is own of Toro's best values while the flagship 2V Premium is one of the finest wines of the D.O.

2006 Elias Mora	90	now–2016
2005 Elias Mora	90	2010–2017
2004 Elias Mora	88	now–2013
2003 Elias Mora	90	now–2010
2005 Elias Moro Crianza	92	2012–2020
2004 Elias Mora Crianza	92+	2011–2019
2003 Elias Mora Crianza	91	2010–2017
2001 Elias Mora Crianza	90+	now–2013
2005 Gran Elias Moro	93	2018–2035
2004 Gran Elias Mora	93	2014–2027
2003 Gran Elias Mora	92	2012–2022
2001 Gran Elias Mora	95	2009–2018
2005 2V Premium	96	2018–2040
2004 V2 Premium	95+	2017–2032
2003 Gran Elias Mora Daniel	92	now–2018

EDETERIA ★★★
TERRA ALTA $25.00–$40.00

Edeteria owns 24 hectares (59 acres) of vines in Terra Alta, a D.O. in close proximity to Montsant and Priorat. They offer excellent value in old-vine Garnacha and Cariñena blends.

2005 Via Edetana	91	2010–2020
2004 Edeteria	92	2012–2025

CELLER DE L'ENCASTELL ⋆⋆⋆
PRIORAT $28.00

Marge is a blend of 60% Garnacha, and the balance Syrah, Merlot, and Cabernet Sauvignon. The wine is aged for eight months in French and American oaks. It is an excellent Priorat value. Roquers de Porrera is 40% Garnacha, 40% Carinena, 7% Merlot, 7% Cabernet Sauvignon, and 6% Syrah aged for 16 months in used French oak.

2006 Marge	92	now–2016
2005 Marge	90	now–2015
2004 Roquers de Porrera	94	2010–2020

CELLERS ELS GUIAMETS ⋆⋆⋆
MONTSANT $23.00

Isis is a blend of Syrah, Garnacha, Cariñena, and Cabernet Sauvignon aged for 12 months in French and American oaks, 50% new. It offers superb bang for the buck.

2005 Isis	92	now–2018
2003 Isis	89	2010–2017

EL ESCOCÈS VOLANTE ⋆⋆⋆
BULLAS $90.00

Años is a splendid example of old-vine Monastrell blended with Syrah from the little-known (for the moment) D.O. of Bullas. The wine is aged for 12 months in 500-liter new French oak barrels with *bâtonnage* by rotation of the barrels.

2006 3000 Años	93	2013–2025

ESPECTACLE ⋆⋆⋆⋆⋆
MONTSANT $115.00

This amazing wine is sourced from a single vineyard of Garnacha vines that are over 100 years old located at La Figuera at the northern edge of the Montsant D.O. The vineyard is tended by René Barbier's Clos Mogador team and aged in one special 4,000-liter oak vat at Celler Laurona. It is arguably the greatest wine produced in the Montsant D.O.

2004 Espectacle del Montsant	99	2010–2025

EXOPTO CELLARS ⋆⋆⋆
RIOJA $18.00–$37.00

Exopto Cellars' resident winemaker is the talented David Sampedro. The estate owns 6 hectares (15 acres) of vineyard and their first vintage was in 2003. The Big Bang cuvée is a superb value in Rioja for near-term drinking while the Horizonte merits cellaring.

2006 Big Bang	90	now–2016
2006 Horizonte de Exopto	93+	2014–2030
2005 Horizonte de Exopto	91	2010–2020
2005 Exopto	89	2010–2020

AGRÍCOLA FALSET-MARÇÀ ⋆⋆⋆⋆
MONTSANT $30.00–$60.00

Agrícola Falset-Marçà was founded in 1919 by a consortium of grape growers. Today they own 581 acres in Falset in the D.O. of Montsant.

2005 Ètim L'Esparver	94	2015–2035
2004 Castell de Falset	92	2012–2025
2001 Selection Syrah	89	now–2012

FINCA SANDOVAL ★ ★ ★ ★
MANCHUELA $51.00–$214.00 (1.5L)

Finca Sandoval is the estate of the esteemed journalist Victor de la Serna. This is a true hands-on operation, from the grape growing to the winemaking in the little-known region of Manchuela. The Finca Sandoval is a blend of Syrah, Mourvèdre, and Bobal fermented with native yeasts followed by malolactic fermentation in barrel with lees stirring. The wine is then aged from 11 to 13 months in French and American oak, a mix of new and seasoned 225- and 300-liter barrels. The Cuvée TNS, a blend of 66% Touriga Nacional and 34% Syrah, is bottled only in magnum (without filtration).

2005 Finca Sandoval	94	2012–2025
2003 Finca Sandoval	93	2010–2020
2001 Finca Sandoval	91	now–2014
2005 Cuvée TNS	92	now–2020

FORJA DEL SALNES ★ ★ ★ ★
RÍAS BAIXAS $30.00–$50.00

The following seven wines are made by Raúl Pérez, the most important new name to emerge from the Spanish wine scene in several years. Pérez specializes in the production of tiny lots of indigenous grape varieties from a range of regions (although this set of wines is from Rías Baixas). The Leirana wines are produced from Albariño. Tinto Caiño is indigenous to Galicia, generally producing light, aromatic, tart red wines while Loureiro is also an indigenous red grape with a similar personality to Caiño. They are true "garage" wines bottled without fining or filtration. These small-production wines must be tasted to be believed.

2005 Goliardo Caiño	90	now–2013
2006 Goliardo Caiño	92	2010–2015
2006 Goliardo Loureiro	93	now–2015
2005 Goliardo Loureiro	93	now–2014
2006 Leirana	91	now–2010
2005 Leirana Barrica	92	now–2011
2006 Leirana Barrica	93	now–2012

BODEGAS Y VIÑEDOS GANCEDO BIERZO ★ ★ ★ ★
BIERZO $35.00–$70.00

Bodegas y Viñedos Gancedo is a small family winery consisting of 12 hectares (30 acres) of low-yielding old-vine Mencia and Godello in Quilos, Bierzo. Virtually all of the work is done by hand and by gravity. Both Ucedo and Xestal are 100% Mencia from 60- and 80-year-old vines respectively.

2005 Ucedo	93	2012–2020
2004 Ucedo	94	2010–2017
2003 Xestal	93	now–2018

GARCÍA FIGUERO ★ ★ ★
RIBERA DEL DUERO $20.00–$160.00

José María García and Milagros Figuero own a 45-hectare (111-acre) estate with the oldest vines dating back to the 1930s. The wines are all 100% Tempranillo.

2006 Roble	88	now–2014
2005 Roble	88	now–2015
2004 Crianza	90	2010–2020
2003 Crianza	89	2010–2017
2004 Reserva	92	2013–2025
2004 Noble	95	2013–2025
2003 Noble	94	2014–2027
2003 Vendimia Selecciónada	92	2012–2020

BODEGAS Y VIÑEDOS O. FOURNIER ∗ ∗ ∗
RIBERA DEL DUERO $14.00–$86.00

This is a new estate for importer Jorge Ordoñez. The winery was purchased in 2001 by José Manuel Ortega Gil-Fournier, who also owns a winery of the same name in Mendoza, Argentina.

2004 Urban Ribera	90	now–2011
2004 Spiga	91	2010–2022
2004 AlfaSpiga	90	2012–2025
2004 O. Fournier Syrah	91	2015–2030

GENIUM CELLER ∗ ∗ ∗
PRIORAT $32.00–$65.00

Genium Celler is the joint effort of six families from the municipality of Poboleda in Priorat. The Genium Celler Ecòlogic is sourced from a 3-hectare (7-acre) certified organic vineyard. The wines are blends of Garnacha and Cariñena from old vines as well as Merlot and Syrah.

2005 Genium	89	2012–2025
2004 Genium	91	now–2012
2003 Genium	89	now–2012
2005 Genium Celler Ecòlogic	90+	now–2020
2004 Genium Celler Ecòlogic	92	2009–2016
2003 Genium Celler Ecòlogic	90	now–2014
2005 Genium Celler Costers	93	2013–2030
2004 Genium Celler Costers	93	2010–2018
2003 Genium Celler Costers	91	2010–2020

GUITIAN ∗ ∗ ∗ ∗
VALDEORRAS $23.00–$43.00

The Guitian winery owns 25 acres of Godello vines from which all of their wines are produced. Godello may be Spain's most interesting white grape and it appears to have some affinity for oak. The barrel-fermented cuvée is aged on its lees and has several years of aging potential.

2006 Godello Joven	90	now–2010
2006 Godello Fermentado en Barrica	92	now–2015
2004 Godello Fermentado en Barrica	92	now–2012
2006 Godello Sobre Lias	91	now–2011
2005 Godello Sobre Lias	87	now
2005 Godello	90	now–2012
2004 Godello	93	now–2011

HACIENDA MONASTERIO ✶✶✶✶
RIBERA DEL DUERO $55.00

The wine at Hacienda Monasterio is made by Peter Sisseck of Dominio de Pingus. The vineyards are in the tenderloin of the region between Pesquera del Duero and Valbuena. The Crianza is made up of 80% Tinto Fino, 10% Cabernet Sauvignon, and 10% Merlot.

2005 Crianza	93	2011–2025
2004 Crianza	94	2012–2027
2001 Crianza	92	2010–2020
1999 Crianza	92	now–2017

HERMANOS PÉREZ PASCUAS ✶✶✶
RIBERA DEL DUERO $23.00–$295.00

The three Pérez Pascuas brothers established their bodega in 1980. Today it encompasses 120 hectares (296 acres) planted to 90% Tempranillo and 10% Cabernet Sauvignon. Manuel Pérez, the son of one of the founders, is the estate's oenologist-winemaker.

2005 Viña Pedrosa	90	now–2015
2004 Viña Pedrosa	90	2010–2018
2005 Viña Pedrosa Crianza	89+	2010–2020
2004 Viña Pedrosa Reserva	91	2012–2025
2001 Gran Selección	94	2015–2030

HUERTA DE ALBALÁ ✶✶✶✶
CÁDIZ $30.00–$90.00

These two superb efforts are composed of 100% Syrah. Put these exciting wines in a blind tasting of your favorite northern Rhônes and prepare to be shocked.

2005 Taberner	92	2010–2020
2005 Taberner #1	95	2013–2027

ANTONIO IZQUIERDO ✶✶✶✶✶
RIBERA DEL DUERO $120.00

Antonio Izquierdo's namesake Ribera del Duero is sourced from biodynamically farmed estate Tempranillo vineyards with an average age of 40 years. This is a new name in the important D.O. of Ribera del Duero that merits serious attention. These are opulent, layered wines that merit a decade of cellaring.

2006 Antonio Izquierdo	96	2018–2040
2005 Antonio Izquierdo	95	2018–2040

VIÑEDOS DEL JALÓN ✶✶✶✶
CALATAYUD $32.00–$53.00

These wines demonstrate what can be achieved with old-vine Garnacha in Calatayud.

2006 Las Pizarras	88+	2010–2017
2005 Las Pizarras	91	now–2013
2006 Alto Las Pizarras	90	2012–2025
2005 Alto Las Pizarras	93	2012–2025
2006 Claraval	91	2010–2020
2004 Viña Alarba Pago San Miguel	87	now–2012
2002 Viña Alarba Pago San Miguel	90	now–2010

VINOS JEROMÍN ★★★★
VINO DE MADRID $60.00

In addition to the top-of-the-line Manu cuvée, Vinos Jeromín offers two value-priced wines that merit consideration. The Manu is 40% Syrah, 40% Garnacha, and the balance Tempranillo, Cabernet Sauvignon, and Merlot, aged for 13 months in seasoned oak barrels. It is a forward, pleasurable, lengthy effort that typically has two to three years of aging potential but can be enjoyed near term.

2005 Manu	93	2010–2018
2003 Grego Garnacha Centenaria	90	now–2010

BODEGAS JIMÉNEZ-LANDI ★★★
MÉNTRIDA $24.00–$40.00

Méntrida is a town and wine zone southwest of Madrid. It has been regarded as something of a backwater in the past but the wines of Bodegas Jiménez-Landi, made from Merlot, Tempranillo, and Syrah, may begin to open some eyes.

2006 Sotorrondero	91	now–2014
2006 Piélago	94	2010–2020
2005 Jiménez-Landi	90+	2010–2020
2004 Selección	90	2012–2024

CELLER LAURONA ★★★
MONTSANT $33.00–$54.00

Celler Laurona, founded in 1999, is a joint venture of Bordeaux-based importer Christopher Cannan and René Barbier.

2004 Laurona	91	2012–2020
2003 Laurona	92	2010–2020
2001 Laurona	87	now–2012
2003 6 Vinyes de Laurona	93	2013–2025
2002 6 Vinyes de Laurona	90	now–2015
2001 6 Vinyes de Laurona	92	2009–2017
2000 6 Vinyes de Laurona	90	now–2013

LEDA ★★★
CASTILLA Y LEÓN $25.00–$85.00

Mas de Leda is sourced from 50-plus–year-old Tempranillo vineyards in Toro and Ribera del Duero. The Viñas Viejas is sourced from four D.O.s and 50 to 60 plots in which the Tempranillo vines average over 50 years of age. These wines are testaments to what skilled blending can achieve.

2005 Mas de Leda	90+	now–2020
2004 Mas de Leda	88	now–2014
2004 Viñas Viejas	93	2012–2025
2003 Viñas Viejas	86	now–2015
2003 Bienvenida	91+	2012–2022

LE LEGUA ★★★
CIGALES $14.00–$62.00

Cigales is a D.O. in northern Spain north of Vallodolid in Castilla y León. Tempranillo is the predominant grape, with Garnacha and Cabernet Sauvignon also making an appearance.

The Tempranillo-Garnacha cuvée is a notable value. Only 1,000 bottles are produced of Capricho.

2006 Tempranillo-Garnacha	89	now–2012
2003 Crianza	90	now–2011
2003 Capricho	93	2010–2018

BODEGA LIBERALIA ★ ★ ★
TORO $20.00–$70.00

The Liberalia family winery began in 2000. Its estate vineyards range in age from 30 to 100 years. Both wines are 100% Tinto de Toro—the Cabeza de Cuba (a superb value) from 70-year-old vines, and the 5 Cinco from vines over 100 years of age. Both are aged in new French oak.

2004 Cero	89	now
2004 Tres	90	now
2003 Cabeza de Cuba	91	2012–2020
2002 Cabeza de Cuba	91	now–2011
2003 5 Cinco	94	2015–2025
2001 Cinco Reserva	96	2010–2018
2002 Cuatro Crianza	89	now–2010

LLICORELLA ★ ★ ★
PRIORAT $30.00–$45.00

Llicorella is a blend of Garnacha Negre, Cariñena, Cabernet Sauvignon, Merlot, and Tempranillo aged for 9–10 months in a mixture of French and American oak. The Llicorella Seleccio raises the bar significantly. It is a blend of Garnacha Negra, Cariñena, Cabernet Sauvignon, and Syrah aged for 12–14 months in French and American oak. These are very well-priced Prioratos.

2003 Llicorella	91	now–2017
2002 Llicorella Seleccio	93+	2010–2020

ESTER NIN I LLORT ★ ★ ★ ★ ★
PRIORAT $90.00

The 2004 is the debut vintage of Ester Nin's Nit de Nin. Nin's day job is vineyard manager of Clos Erasmus. A whopping three barrels (about 75 cases) are produced from 80- to 100-year-old vines from the village of Porrera. Nit de Nin is composed of 60% Garnacha, 30% Cariñena, and 10% Syrah aged for 18 months in French oak.

2005 Nit de Nin	98	2012–2022
2004 Nit de Nin	98	now–2020

LUNA BEBERIDE ★ ★ ★ ★
CASTILLA Y LEÓN $27.00–$46.00

The Tierras de Luna cuvée is composed of 75% Mencia, 20% Merlot, and 5% Cabernet Sauvignon aged for 16 months in French and American oaks. The Luna Beberide Reserva is a blend of 55% Mencia, 30% Cabernet Sauvignon, and 15% Merlot aged for 26 months in new oak, 80% French and 20% American.

2005 Luna Beberide Mencia	89	now–2010
2004 Luna Beberide Mencia	89	now–2011
2004 Tierras de Luna	91	2010–2020

2002 Tierras de Luna	88	now–2015
2004 Luna Beberide Reserva	92	2012–2025
2002 Luna Beberide Reserva	85	now
2003 Luna Beberide Merlot	92	2010–2018
2003 Luna Beberide Daniel	92	now–2018
2000 Luna Beberide Tinto	88	now–2017

BODEGAS VIÑA MAGAÑA ★★★★
NAVARRA $20.00–$60.00

Bodegas Viña Magaña was founded in 1970 by Juan Magaña. The estate consists of 247 acres of old-vine French varieties and is located in an unusually warm and dry microclimate in Navarra. The Merlot cuvée is made only in the best vintages.

2004 Dignus	89	2010–2017
2003 Dignus	90	2010–2017
2004 Barón de Magaña	90	2010–2020
2003 Barón de Magaña	91	2009–2018
2005 Magaña Merlot	92	2010–2020
2005 Calchetas	95	2012–2025
2004 Calchetas	93	2010–2020

BODEGA VIÑA MAMBRILLA ★★★★
RIBERA DEL DUERO $70.00–$80.00

Bodega Viña Mambrilla is a small family winery founded by the Arranz family. The wines are 100% Tempranillo, aged in French and American oak.

2004 Alidis Expresión	91	2012–2025
2004 Alidis Versus Viñas Viejas	93	2015–2030
2001 Alidis Gran Reserva	92	2010–2020

CELLERS MARC RIPOLL SANS ★★★
PRIORAT $70.00

The 2 Vinyes is 100% Cariñena sourced from two vineyards with 90-year-old vines.

| 2005 2 Vinyes | 93 | 2012–2025 |

MARQUÉS DE VARGAS ★★★★
RIOJA $30.00–$100.00

Marqués de Vargas owns 65 hectares (161 acres) of estate vineyards. All of their wines are bottled unfined and unfiltered. The wines are blends of Tempranillo, Garnacha, Mazuelo, and other varieties.

2004 Reserva	90	now–2020
2003 Reserva	90	now–2015
2004 Reserva Privada	91	2012–2025
2001 Reserva Privada	93	2010–2020
2004 Hacienda Pradolagar	92	2015–2030
2001 Hacienda Pradolagar	95	2012–2025

MAS DE L'ABUNDÀNCIA ★★★★
MONTSANT $41.00–$65.00

Winemaker and owner Jesús del Rio purchased the Mas de l'Abundància property in the early 1990s and exported to the United States for the first time in 2006. The wines are a blend of Cabernet Sauvignon, Garnacha, and Cariñena.

2004 Mas de l'Abundància	92	now–2020
2003 Cuvée Helena del Rio	93	now–2020

MAS ALTA ★★★
PRIORAT $40.00

Mas Alta is a project of renowned French winemaker-*négoçiant* Michel Tardieu. Artigas is 60% Garnacha, 35% Cariñena, and 5% Cabernet Sauvignon aged for 15 months in new French oak.

2005 Artigas	91	now–2018

CELLER MAS DOIX ★★★★★
PRIORAT $45.00–$130.00

Salanques is the second wine of Celler Mas Doix, a barrel-by-barrel declassification. It is a blend of 65% Garnacha, 20% Cariñena, and the balance Syrah, Merlot, and Cabernet Sauvignon aged in French oak for 14 months. The Costers de Viñas Viejas is aged for 16 months in new French oak. The wine is a blend of 50% Cariñena, 48% Garnacha, and 2% Merlot.

2005 Salanques	93	2015–2030
2004 Salanques	94	now–2018
2003 Salanques	95	2010–2020
2005 Costers de Viñas Viejas	98	2018–2040
2004 Costers de Viñas Viejas	98	2010–2022
2003 Costers de Viñas Viejas	98+	2015–2032
2000 Poboleda	93	now–2017

MAS D'EN GIL ★★★★
PRIORAT $61.00–$115.00

There is very little white wine produced in Priorat but the best examples are among the most compelling in all of Spain. The Coma Blanca is 50% Garnacha Blanca and 50% Macabeo barrel-fermented and aged for six months in French oak. Its flavor and aromatic profile is reminiscent of the famous Château de Beaucastel Vieilles Vignes (as is its price). Coma Vella is a blend of 30% Cariñena, 20% Garnacha Peluda, 20% Garnacha Pais, 20% Cabernet Sauvignon, and 10% Syrah aged for 12 months in French oak. Clos Fonta is composed of 30% Garnacha Peluda, 25% Garnacha Pais, 25% Cabernet Sauvignon, and 20% Cariñena aged for 14 months in French oak.

2005 Coma Blanca	92	now–2013
2004 Coma Blanca	95	now–2014
2003 Coma Vella	92	2010–2020
2001 Coma Vella	94	2010–2018
2000 Coma Vella	87	now–2010
2003 Clos Fonta	94	2012–2025
2001 Clos Fonta	94	2012–2025
2000 Clos Fonta	89	now–2017

CELLER MAS GIL ★★★★
EMPORDA $55.00–$95.00

Celler Mas Gil has been restored by a group of Swiss wine professionals and legendary vigneron Peter Sisseck. The Clos d'Agón Blanco is a blend of 46% Viognier, 36% Roussanne, and 18% Marsanne. The Clos d'Agón Tinto is 30% Cabernet Sauvignon, 30% Syrah, 20% Merlot, and 20% Cabernet Franc, aged for 16 months in new French oak.

2006 Clos d'Agón Blanco	95	now–2012
2004 Clos d'Agón Tinto	93	now–2018

MAS MARTINET ★★★★
PRIORAT $40.00–$82.00

Mas Martinet is owned by José Luis Perez, one of the original Priorat pioneers. He has turned over day-to-day operations to his daughter Sara Perez. The estate owns 10 hectares (25 acres) of vineyard planted in the famous llicorella Catalan soil (alternating layers of slate and quartz). The Clos Martinet cuvée contains a significant percentage of old-vine Cariñena.

2005 Martinet Bru	91+	2012–2025
2004 Martinet Bru	91	2010–2020
2003 Martinet Bru	90	now–2014
2000 Martinet Bru	90	now–2012
1999 Martinet Bru	90	now–2010
2005 Clos Martinet	93+	2015–2030
2004 Clos Martinet	94	2012–2025
2003 Clos Martinet	92	2011–2022
2002 Clos Martinet	90	now–2016
2000 Clos Martinet	94	2010–2020
1999 Clos Martinet	93	now–2016

MAS DE LES PERERES ★★★
PRIORAT $40.00–$80.00

Mas de les Pereres, located in the town of Poboleda, was founded in 2001 by Dirk Hoet and consists of 8 hectares (20 acres) of organically farmed vineyard. Both the whites and reds are bottled without filtration.

2005 Nunci Abocat	91	now–2010
2005 Nunci Blanc	90	now–2010
2004 Nunci Negre	91	now–2016
2004 Nunci Costero	92	2010–2020

MAS ROMANI (MAS ALTA) ★★★★
PRIORAT $85.00–$120.00

La Basseta is 50% old-vine Cariñena, 40% Garnacha, 5% Merlot, and 5% Syrah aged for 15 months in French oak, 50% new. La Creu Alta is 60% old-vine Cariñena and 40% Garnacha from vineyards over 100 years of age.

2004 La Basseta	96	2010–2022
2004 La Creu Alta	97+	2010–2022

MAS SINEN ★★★
PRIORAT $56.00–$70.00

Mas Sinen is located in the Priorat village of Poboleda, where the estate owns 37 acres of vineyard. The Tradition is a blend of 35% Garnacha, 30% Cabernet Sauvignon, 25% Cariñena, and 10% Syrah. The Coster is an old-vine cuvée composed of 50% Garnacha and 50% Cariñena, the two original grapes of Priorat.

2005 Tradition	92	now–2018
2005 Coster	94	2012–2025

BODEGAS MATARREDONDA ★ ★ ★ ★
TORO $22.00–$44.00

Bodegas Matarredonda, with 24 hectares (60 acres) of Tempranillo vines, was founded in 2000 by Alfonso Sanz Rojo. The Libranza bottling is made from prephylloxera 100- to 140-year-old vines while the Juan Rojo uses Tempranillo from vines 80-plus years old.

2004 Juan Rojo	91	2014–2029
2003 Juan Rojo	90	2010–2020
2002 Juan Rojo	88	now
2004 Libranza	94	2015–2035
2003 Libranza	92	2012–2025
2002 Libranza	91	now–2012

BODEGAS MAURO ★ ★ ★ ★
RIBERA DEL DUERO $50.00–$160.00

Because of its geographical location 10 kilometers (6 miles) from the boundary of Ribera del Duero, Bodegas Mauro does not qualify for the more prestigious D.O. Currently it has 35 hectares (86 acres) of vineyard in production. Winemaking is in the hands of Alberto and Eduardo García, sons of renowned Vega Sicilia winemaker Mariano García. The Terreus cuvée is produced only in the best vintages.

2005 Mauro	93	2010–2020
1999 Mauro	91	now–2014
2004 Crianza	92	2012–2022
2002 Crianza	88	now–2015
2003 Vendimia Selecciónada	94+	2012–2030
2002 Vendimia Selecciónada	91+	2010–2018
2001 Vendimia Selecciónada	96	2012–2025
2000 Vendimia Selecciónada	94	2010–2020
1998 Vendimia Selecciónada	95	2013–2025
1997 Vendimia Selecciónada	92	now–2017
2003 Terreus	96	2012–2030
2001 Terreus	96	2012–2032
1999 Terreus	94	2010–2022

MAURODOS ★ ★ ★ ★
TORO $50.00

San Román, 100% Tinto de Toro, is aged for 22 months in French and American oak, mostly new, prior to bottling without filtration.

2004 Prima	90	2010–2017
2003 Prima	90	now–2012
2004 San Román	92	2012–2025
2003 San Román	92+	2012–2022
2002 San Román	89	now–2015

MELIS ★★★
PRIORAT $100.00

From the same team that brings you the Central Coast's superb Sea Smoke Pinot Noirs comes Melis, a splendid example of what can be achieved in Priorat. The 2004 Melis, from an outstanding vintage, is a blend of 63% Grenache, 16% Carignan, 14% Syrah, and 7% Cabernet Sauvignon. It was aged for 15 months in several sizes of 100% new Burgundian oak before being bottled without fining or filtration.

2004 Melis	94	2014–2028

MERUM PRIORATI ★★★
PRIORAT $34.00–$62.00

The Ardiles cuvée is composed of 45% Garnacha, 34% Cariñena, 18% Syrah, and 3% Cabernet Sauvignon. The Osmin bottling is 42% Garnacha, 25% Cariñena, with the balance Syrah, Cabernet Sauvignon, and Merlot aged in new French oak for 12 months.

2005 Ardiles	91	now–2018
2004 Ardiles	93	now–2018
2005 Osmin	93	2010–2020
2004 Osmin	95	2010–2022

MONTECASTRO ★★★
RIBERA DEL DUERO $50.00

Montecastro is a new estate founded in 2001. It is 100% Tempranillo aged in *barrique*.

2005 Montecastro	93	2013–2025
2004 Montecastro	94	2014–2032
2003 Montecastro	92	2010–2022

HERETAT MONT-RUBÍ ★★★★
ALT PENEDÈS $30.00–$70.00

Heretat Mont-Rubí specializes in the indigenous Sumoll grape, a variety which is nearly extinct. The Durona is composed of 30% Sumoll, 20% Garnacha, 20% Cariñena, 20% Shiraz, and 10% Merlot. The Gaintus is 100% Sumoll aged in French oak for 14 months.

2004 Durona	91	now–2015
2004 Gaintus	92	2010–2020

BODEGAS EMILIO MORO ★★★★★
RIBERA DEL DUERO $37.00–$216.00

Bodegas Emilio Moro is a family-owned winery that has been making wine in Ribera del Duero for more than 120 years. The estate owns 105 hectares (260 acres) of vineyard. The wines are all 100% Tempranillo.

2005 Emilio Moro	92	now–2015
2003 Emilio Moro	90	now–2017
2001 Emilio Moro	89	now–2014
2000 Emilio Moro	90+	now–2015
2005 Malleolus	93	2012–2022
2004 Malleolus	95	2012–2025
2001 Malleolus	94	2010–2022
2005 Malleolus de Valderramiro	97	2015–2030
2004 Malleolus de Valderramiro	97	2014–2035

2002 Malleolus de Valderramiro	91	now–2018
2000 Malleolus de Valderramiro	92+	2012–2027
2005 Malleolus de Sancho Martin	98	2016–2040
2004 Malleolus de Sancho Martin	97	2012–2032

BODEGAS MUGA ★ ★ ★ ★ ★
RIOJA $27.00–$212.00

Muga is the only winery left in Spain that uses only oak throughout the entire vinification process. They have their own cooperage and import the oak directly from the U.S. and France.

2004 Muga Reserva	93+	2010–2020
2001 Muga Reserva	92	now–2017
2004 Muga Reserva Selección Especial	94	2014–2030
2000 Muga Reserva Selección Especial	90	now–2013
2004 Torre Muga	96	2014–2027
2003 Torre Muga	92	2010–2020
2001 Torre Muga	95	2012–2030
1998 Torre Muga	91	now–2018
2004 Aro	98	2018–2040
2001 Aro	98	2010–2025
2000 Prado Enea Gran Reserva	92	now–2015
1998 Prado Enea Gran Reserva	91	now–2016
1996 Prado Enea Gran Reserva	92	now–2016
1995 Prado Enea Gran Reserva	89	now–2010

BODEGAS Y VIÑEDOS DE MURCIA ★ ★ ★ ★ ★
JUMILLA $40.00

These superb efforts from Bodegas y Viñedos de Murcia show what can be achieved in the awakening D.O. of Jumilla. The Pico Madama is composed of 50% Monastrell and 50% Petit Verdot. The Sierra Carche contains 50% Monastrell, 25% Malbec, and 25% Petit Verdot aged for 13 months in French and American oak.

2005 Pico Madama	95+	2012–2025
2004 Pico Madama	93	2010–2018
2005 Sierra Carche	96	2012–2025

MARQUÉS DE MURRIETA ★ ★ ★ ★
RIOJA $25.00–110.00

Marqués de Murrieta remains one of the pillars of Rioja tradition, but the winery has not allowed time to pass it by, as the following wines attest.

2001 Dalmau	93	2012–2027
2001 Ygay Reserva	90	now–2014
1998 Castillo Ygay Gran Reserva	87	now–2015

BODEGAS EL NIDO ★ ★ ★ ★ ★
JUMILLA $48.00–$147.00

The winemaking at the El Nido project is overseen by renowned Australian vigneron Chris Ringland. After a meticulous selection process, the grapes are basket-pressed and fermented in oak. Malolactic fermentation occurs in new French and American oak, where the wine remains for 26 months. Clio is composed of 70% old-vine Monastrell and 30% Cabernet Sauvignon, and El Nido is a selection of the best grapes from the same vineyards.

2005 Clio	95	2012–2025
2004 Clio	97	2012–2025
2002 Clio	93+	now–2016
2005 El Nido	98	2015–2030
2004 El Nido	99	2012–2027
2002 El Nido	96	2010–2020

NITA ★ ★ ★
PRIORAT $20.00

Nita was created by young winemaker Meritxell Palleja. It is a rare unoaked Priorat designed to highlight the palette of Priorat minerality and old-vine fruit flavors that can be consumed early on.

2005 Nita	91	now–2014

NOGUERALS ★ ★ ★ ★ ★
PRIORAT AND MONTSANT $50.00–$69.00

The Alzamore family is based in Montsant, where they have owned vineyard for several generations. In 1999 they added a 4-hectare (10-acre) Priorat vineyard to their holdings. The Corbatera Montsant is composed of 70% Garnacha and 30% Cabernet Sauvignon sourced from a 1.5-hectare (4-acre) estate vineyard. The Abellars (Priorat) is a blend of 50% Garnacha, 25% Cariñena, 15% Cabernet Sauvignon, and 10% Syrah.

2004 Corbatera (Montsant)	95	2013–2025
2004 Abellars (Priorat)	96	2013–2025

NUMANTHIA-TERMES ★ ★ ★ ★ ★
TORO $30.00–$234.00

Numanthia-Termes is arguably the finest producer in Toro. The Termes cuvée receives 16 months in seasoned French oak and is a very fine value. Numanthia is a more structured wine that sees 19 months in new French oak. The limited-production Termanthia receives the so-called 200% new oak treatment and remains in *barrique* for 20 months. In February 2008, Numanthia-Termes was sold by the Egueren family to LVMH.

2005 Termes	92	2010–2018
2004 Termes	94	2012–2020
2002 Termes	90	now–2012
2005 Numanthia	92	2012–2025
2004 Numanthia	98	2016–2030
2002 Numanthia	92	2009–2017
2000 Numanthia	93	2010–2020
2005 Termanthia	97	2018–2040
2004 Termanthia	100	2020–2045
2002 Termanthia	94	2010–2020
2000 Termanthia	98	2012–2027

BODEGAS ORBEN ★ ★ ★ ★
RIOJA $45.00–$65.00

The Orben cuvée is sourced from 75 microparcels of old vines of Tempranillo planted between 1945 and 1954. The Malpuesto is sourced from an 80-year-old Tempranillo vineyard of the same name.

2005 Orben	92	2010–2020
2005 Malpuesto	93	2015–2030

BODEGA MANUEL DE LA OSA ★ ★ ★
LA MANCHA $30.00

Manuel de la Osa is a renowned chef with one Michelin star at his restaurant Las Rejas. The 2004 Manuel de la Osa is composed of 40% Syrah, 30% Graciano, 10% Tempranillo, 10% Cabernet Franc, and 10% Merlot. The wine spends 12 months in French oak.

2004 Manuel de la Osa	91	now–2018

BODEGAS PABLO ★ ★ ★
CARIÑENA $60.00–$160.00

Bodegas Pablo farms biodynamically and makes use of indigenous varieties from their estate vineyards. The Finca Gorys Criespiello is from a single vineyard planted to the indigenous Criespiello grape and was sourced from 100-year-old vines. The Gran Viu Garnacha del Terreno is 100% Garnacha from 92-year-old vines while the Gran Viu Finca Santiago is a blend of 60% Garnacha, 20% Vidadillo, and 20% Cariñena sourced from a single 100-year-old vineyard.

2005 Menguante Tempranillo	90	now–2012
2005 Menguante Garnacha	90	now–2012
2004 Menguante Garnacha Selección	91	2010–2016
2004 Finca Gorys Criespiello	88+	2012–2025
2003 Pulchrum Criespiello	88	now–2013
2004 Gran Viu Garnacha del Terreno	92	2010–2020
2002 Gran Viu Garnacha del Terreno	91	2010–2020
2004 Gran Viu Finca Santiago	94	2012–2035
2002 Gran Viu Finca Santiago	94	2012–2025
2001 Gran Viu Selección	92	now–2018

VIÑEDOS DE PAGANOS ★ ★ ★
RIOJA $63.00–$164.00

These excellent wines from Viñedos de Paganos are 100% Tempranillo. The El Puntido cuvée is sourced from its namesake vineyard planted in 1975. The wine is aged in new French oak for 18 months. The La Nieta is also sourced from a namesake vineyard planted in 1975. It too is aged for 18 months in new French oak and bottled without filtration.

2004 El Puntido	90	2010–2020
2003 El Puntido	94	2012–2025
2002 El Puntido	91	now–2018
2005 La Nieta	93	2010–2020
2004 La Nieta	98+	2015–2035

PAGO DE CARRAOVEJAS ★★★
RIBERA DEL DUERO $57.00–$90.00

Pago de Carraovejas is a 60-hectare (148-acre) vineyard planted to 85% Tempranillo, 10% Cabernet Sauvignon, and 5% Merlot.

2005 Crianza	92	2010–2020
2004 Reserva	93	2010–2020
2003 Cuesta de las Liebres	90	2012–2025

PAGO DE LOS CAPELLANES ★★★★
RIBERA DEL DUERO $34.00–$240.00

Pago de los Capellanes is a stellar estate in Ribera del Duero whose portfolio is outstanding from top to bottom.

2006 Joven	90	now–2013
2005 Crianza	91	2010–2015
2004 Reserva	92	2012–2025
2001 Reserva	89	now–2017
2004 Parcela el Nogal	94	2015–2030
2004 Finca el Picón	97	2017–2035

PAGOS DEL MONCAYO ★★★★
CAMPO DE BORJA $17.00–$35.00

Campo de Borja, located in the northwest province of Zaragoza, 200 miles west of Barcelona, has a winemaking tradition dating back to the 12th century. However, the D.O. dates only to 1980. Bodegas Pagos del Moncayo, owned by the Aibar family, has played a significant role in the rebirth of this once forgotten region. Although it is only six years of age, the estate works exclusively with vines in excess of 80 years.

2006 Garnacha-Syrah	91	now–2012
2006 Garnacha	93	now–2018
2006 Syrah	94	now–2018

PAIXAR ★★★★
BIERZO $80.00

The Paixar project began in 2000. The wine is 100% Mencia sourced from 50- to 80-year-old vineyards planted at high elevation in weathered slate. The wine is fermented with native yeasts, aged for 16 months in new French oak, and bottled without filtration.

2005 Paixar	94	2010–2018
2004 Paixar	93	2010–2018
2003 Paixar	92	now–2015
2002 Paixar	90	now–2013

ALVARO PALACIOS ★★★★★
PRIORAT $80.00–$650.00

Finca Dofi is sourced from a single-estate vineyard planted to 60% Garnacha with the balance Cabernet Sauvignon, Merlot, Syrah, and Cariñena aged in 100% new French oak. L'Ermita comes from a parcel of 70-year-old head-pruned vines of which 85% is Garnacha; the balance, Cariñena and Cabernet Sauvignon. It is a benchmark for great Priorat.

2005 Les Terrasses	93	2012–2022
2004 Les Terrasses	93	2010–2018

2003 Les Terrasses	90	now–2012
2005 Finca Dofi	95	2016–2030
2004 Finca Dofi	95	2012–2025
2003 Finca Dofi	93	2010–2020
2005 L'Ermita	98	2020–2045
2004 L'Ermita	98	2015–2035
2003 L'Ermita	95	2012–2030

CELLERS PASANAU ★ ★ ★ ★
PRIORAT $25.00–$73.00

The Pasanaus are growers in the village of La Morera, the highest municipality of Priorat. The Ceps Nous uses fruit from the estate's younger vines aged for three to six months in seasoned French and American oak. The Finca La Planeta is 80% Cabernet Sauvignon and 20% old-vine Garnacha, an unusual blend for Priorat. The wine is aged for 12 months in new French and American oak. The El Vell Coster is 80% old-vine Cariñena and 20% Cabernet Sauvignon from Planeta.

2006 Ceps Nous	92	now–2017
2005 Ceps Nous	91	now–2015
2005 El Vell Coster	97	2012–2023
2004 El Vell Coster	92	2010–2020
2004 Finca La Planeta	95	2015–2030
2003 Finca La Planeta	90+	2012–2025
2003 La Morera de Montsant	88	now–2013

PAZO DE SEÑORÁNS ★ ★ ★ ★ ★
RÍAS BAIXAS $25.00–$70.00

Pazo de Señoráns is always a candidate for Albariño of the vintage. The grapes are sourced from the lowest-yielding, oldest vines in Rías Baixas. The wine is tank-fermented in small vats, and aged on fine lees with *bâtonnage*. The Selección de Anada is aged on lees for three years.

2006 Albariño	92	now–2010
2003 Selección de Anada	93	now–2012

RAÚL PÉREZ ★ ★ ★ ★ ★
MONTERREI, BIERZO, AND RIBERA SACRO $20.00–$80.00

Raúl Pérez is Spain's most intriguing vigneron and a brilliant, outside-the-box winemaker. He produces tiny quantities of outrageously good wine from multiple, obscure wine regions. Sketch may be the finest Albariño I have tasted (as well as the most expensive). The wine is fermented and raised in egg-shaped 1,500-liter barrels with 12 months of *bâtonnage* followed by aging in the bottle for 60 days at 30 meters (100 feet) under the sea. The A Trabe White is made from the indigenous varieties of Verdillo and Torrontes found in Monterrei in southern Galicia. Raúl Pérez's red wines begin with the A Trabe Red, a blend of the indigenous varieties Mencia, Bastardo, and Zammarica. The El Pecado ("The Sin") is 100% Mencia from Ribera Sacra sourced from an insanely steep hillside (which makes Jackass Hill look like a putting green). The least expensive wine in Raúl Pérez's portfolio is the Ultreia St. Jacques, also 100% Mencia from the D.O. of Bierzo. The Ultreia de Valtuille is also 100% Mencia from Bierzo. It is a far more layered and opulent cuvée. These are brilliant, artisanal, handcrafted wines that words simply cannot begin to describe. They must be experienced to be believed.

2006 Sketch (Rías Baixas)	93	now–2011
2005 A Trabe White (Monterrei)	93	now–2011
2006 Ultreia St. Jacques (Bierzo)	93	2010–2020
2005 A Trabe Red	97	2011–2020
2005 El Pecado	98	2014–2028
2005 Ultreia de Valtuille	98+	2012–2025

DOMINIO DE PINGUS ✶ ✶ ✶ ✶ ✶
RIBERA DEL DUERO $75.00–$650.00

Dominio de Pingus is the estate of legendary winemaker Peter Sisseck. The vineyards are farmed biodynamically and the wines are bottled without fining or filtration. The Flor de Pingus comes from rented vineyards planted to 100% Tempranillo. The Amelia is a single-barrel cuvée made from a special parcel of vines 100-plus years old. Pingus spends 18 months in new oak. It is arguably Spain's greatest expression of Tempranillo, always a tour de force.

2005 Flor de Pingus	96	2012–2025
2004 Flor de Pingus	97	2013–2028
2003 Flor de Pingus	94	2009–2020
2005 Amelia	97	2015–2030
2005 Pingus	99	2020–2050
2004 Pingus	100	2017–2045
2003 Pingus	98	2015–2035

BODEGAS PINTIA ✶ ✶ ✶ ✶ ✶
TORO $60.00

Bodegas Pintia is owned by Vega-Sicilia. Pintia is located farther west along the Duero River inside the warmer D.O. of Toro. The estate owns 96 hectares (237 acres) of land. The first vintage released was the 2001.

2005 Pintia	95	2012–2025
2004 Pintia	95+	2012–2025
2003 Pintia	92+	2010–2022
2002 Pintia	94	now–2015

CELLER DEL PONT ✶ ✶ ✶ ✶
PRIORAT $75.00

Celler del Pont is a "garage" wine made by Montse Nadal, a professor of oenology whose specialty is the *terroir* of Priorat. The Lo Givot is 33% Garnacha, 32% Cariñena, 25% Cabernet Sauvignon, and 10% Syrah.

2005 Lo Givot	94	2012–2025

PORTAL DEL MONTSANT ✶ ✶ ✶
MONTSANT $33.00–$40.00

Portal del Montsant is a new estate, started by Barcelona architect Alfredo Arribas in 2001 with his purchase of the Mas de Portal property. He hired the experienced Ricard Rofes as winemaker. The estate is being farmed organically.

2006 Brunus	90+	2010–2020
2006 Santbru	92	2012–2025
2005 Santbru	93	2014–2028

BODEGAS Y VIÑEDOS PUJANZA * * * * *
RIOJA $90.00–$180.00

Bodegas y Viñedos Pujanza is the estate of Carlos San Pedro. The Pujanza Norte is sourced from the 2.2-hectare (5.4-acre) vineyard El Norte that he planted 15 years ago as a teenager. The Pujanza Cisma is also sourced from a single vineyard, named La Valcavada, with over-100-year-old vines at high altitude.

2005 Pujanza Cisma	95+	2015–2035
2004 Pujanza Cisma	90	2017–2035
2005 Pujanza Norte	94	2020–2045
2004 Pujanza Norte	93	2012–2025
2003 Pujanza Norte	87	now
2002 Pujanza Norte	85	now
2001 Pujanza Norte	92	now–2018
2003 Pujanza Daniel	91	now–2018
2004 Pujanza	89+	2010–2020
2003 Pujanza	90	now–2012
2002 Pujanza	87	now
2001 Pujanza	90	now–2012

BODEGAS RAMIRO'S * * * *
CASTILLA Y LEÓN $100.00

Ramiro's was sourced from Toro and Ribera del Duero from 60- to 80-year-old Tempranillo vineyards. The wine is aged in new oak, 80% French and 20% American, for 30 months. This innovative cuvée is produced by Eduardo Garcia and could be likened to the "garage" wines of Bordeaux's St.-Émilion.

2004 Ramiro's	94	2012–2030
2003 Ramiro's	92+	2012–2022

VIÑAS DE EL REGEJAL * * *
VINO DE MADRID $24.00

The El Regejal, from a zone in which increasingly good wine is emerging, is 45% Tempranillo, 25% Cabernet Sauvignon, 20% Syrah, and 10% Merlot.

2006 El Regejal	92	2010–2020

FERNANDO REMÍREZ DE GANUZA * * * * *
RIOJA $84.00

One of the quality leaders in Rioja, Bodegas Fernando Remírez de Ganuza has produced superb wines in the more difficult 2003 vintage and the idyllic 2004 vintage. Both vintages are composed of 85% old-vine Tempranillo, 10% old-vine Graciano, 3% old-vine Garnacha, and 2% other. The wines are estate grown and bottled from 4 parcels with ages ranging from 34 to 97 years. The wine is aged for 2 years in French and American oak prior to being bottled unfined and unfiltered. Fincas de Ganuza is the winery's second label.

2004 Remírez de Ganuza	96	2015–2030
2003 Remírez de Ganuza	93	2015–2025
2001 Remírez de Ganuza	94+	2010–2022
1999 Remírez de Ganuza	92	now–2019
2001 Fincas de Ganuza Reserva	92	2010–2022
2000 Fincas de Ganuza Reserva	90	2010–2018

LA RIOJA ALTA ★★★★
RIOJA $20.00–$140.00

La Rioja Alta continues to be one of the benchmarks for traditionally produced Rioja. What the wines may lack in power, they make up for in finesse and complexity. The winery has just released its first "modern-style" Rioja, called Marqués de Haro, and it is a success.

2005 Marqués de Haro	93	2013–2027
2001 Reserva Viña Alberdi	90	now–2015
2000 Reserva Viña Alberdi	88	now–2012
2001 Reserva Viña Arana	89	now–2012
1998 Reserva Viña Arana	89	now–2012
1997 Reserva Viña Arana	86	now
2000 Reserva Viña Ardanza	90	now–2015
1999 Reserva Viña Ardanza	88	now–2011
1996 Reserva Viña Ardanza	90	now–2010
1995 Gran Reserva 904	92	now–2015
1994 Gran Reserva 904	89	now–2014
1992 Gran Reserva 904	90	now–2012
1995 Gran Reserva 890	95	now–2020
1994 Gran Reserva 890	92	now–2015
1987 Gran Reserva 890	90	now–2012

FRANCESCA VICENT ROBERT ★★★
PRIORAT $80.00

The Francesca Vicent Robert estate has been family owned since the 13th century. The Abat Domenech is 50% Garnacha and 50% Cabernet Sauvignon grown in slate and gravel soils and aged for 12 months in French oak.

2004 Abat Domenech	93+	2011–2020
2002 Abat Domenech	91	2009–2017
2002 Lo Piot	88	now–2010

ROCHAL ★★★★
CASTILLA Y LEÓN $100.00

The Calixto Nieto is 100% Rufete, an indigenous variety, sourced from 105-year-old vines and aged for 14 months in new Allier barrels.

2005 Calixto Nieto	93	2014–2027

BODEGAS RODA ★★★
RIOJA $44.00–$303.00

Roda produces an elegant style of Rioja—the Reserva is designed to have immediate appeal while the Roda I Reserva is sourced from vineyards said to provide more structure and aging potential. One can argue whether the luxury cuvée Cirsion merits the exalted price but it is usually one of the top Riojas of any given vintage.

2005 Cirsion	94	2015–2030
2004 Cirsion	93	2012–2025
2003 Cirsion	91	2009–2017
2003 Roda Reserva	89	now–2015
2002 Roda Reserva	87	now–2013
2001 Roda Reserva	89	now–2012

1998 Roda Reserva	91	now–2013
2003 Roda I Reserva	90	2010–2020
2002 Roda I Reserva	88	now–2015
2001 Roda I Reserva	90	now–2014
1998 Roda I Reserva	91	now–2018

BODEGAS RODERO ★ ★ ★
RIBERA DEL DUERO $20.00–$120.00

Carmelo Rodero sold his grapes to Vega-Sicilia until 1991, when he decided to make his own wine.

2006 Carmelo Rodero Roble	89	now–2013
2005 Carmelo Rodero Crianza	90+	2010–2018
2005 Carmelo Rodero TSM	93	2015–2030
2004 Carmelo Rodero Reserva	91	2012–2025

VIÑOS DE BENJAMÍN ROMEO ★ ★ ★ ★ ★
RIOJA $40.00–$403.00

These Riojas from Benjamín Romeo are among the benchmarks for great wine. Made from 100% Tempranillo, they are the epitome of what can be achieved with this grape. The 2005 Predicador is the new offering priced for the masses with enough quantity (500 cases) to have some distribution.

2005 Predicador	93	2010–2020
2005 La Cueva del Contador	97	2018–2035
2002 La Cueva del Contador	94	2010–2022
2000 La Cueva del Contador	92	2010–2020
2005 La Viña de Andres Romeo	98	2020–2040
2002 La Viña de Andres Romeo	90	2012–2025
2005 Contador	100	2020–2045
2002 Contador	96	2010–2030
2000 Contador	98+	2015–2032

ROTLLAN TORRA ★ ★ ★ ★
PRIORAT $75.00–$100.00

The Reserva is made from 50% Garnacha, 25% Cariñena, and 25% Cabernet Sauvignon aged 24 months in French and American oak. The Balandra cuvée is composed of equal parts Garnacha, Cariñena, and Cabernet Sauvignon and aged for 12 months in American oak. The Amadis is a blend of 30% Garnacha, 35% Cariñena, 20% Syrah, and 15% Cabernet Sauvignon fermented in *foudre* and then aged in new French oak for 12 months. The Tirant is a similar blend as the Amadis. Fermented in *foudre* and aged in French oak for 12 months, it is a more refined version of the Amadis with more complexity and elegance.

2001 Balandra	91	now–2015
1998 Balandra	89	now–2011
2003 Amadis	94	2012–2024
2002 Amadis	92	2009–2018
1999 Amadis	90	now–2014
1998 Amadis	89+	now–2012
2003 Tirant	96	2012–2027
2002 Tirant	93	2010–2020

1999 Tirant	90+	now–2016
2001 Reserva	89	2010–2020

CELLER DEL ROURE ★ ★ ★
VALENCIA $35.00

Maduresa is a blend of the nearly extinct Mando, Monastrell, Syrah, Cabernet Sauvignon, Merlot, and Petit Verdot aged for 12 months in French oak.

2005 Maduresa	91	2012–2020
2003 Maduresa	93	2009–2018
2003 Les Alcusses	92	now–2014

SAN ALEJANDRO ★ ★ ★
CALATAYUD $11.00

Las Rocas Garnacha is one of Spain's best red wine values in almost every vintage. The grapes for Las Rocas are sourced from high-altitude 70- to 100-year-old Garnacha vineyards. This is worth buying by the case.

2006 Las Rocas Garnacha	91	now–2012
2005 Las Rocas Garnacha	90	now–2011
2003 Las Rocas Garnacha	88	now
2005 Las Rocas Garnacha Viñas Viejas	91	now–2012

SEÑORIO DE SAN VICENTE ★ ★ ★
RIOJA $63.00

San Vicente is 100% Tempranillo Peludo sourced from a single vineyard and aged for 20 months in new French and American oak.

2004 San Vicente	91	2015–2025
2003 San Vicente	92	now–2017
2001 San Vicente	93	now–2015

BODEGAS HERMANOS SASTRE—VIÑA SASTRE ★ ★ ★ ★ ★
RIBERA DEL DUERO $40.00–$600.00

Viña Sastre's wines tend to be lavishly oaked, large-scaled, backstrapping wines built for long-term cellaring.

2003 Roble	89	now
2003 Crianza	88	2010–2017
2002 Crianza	88	now
1999 Crianza	88	now–2010
2003 Pesus	98	2015–2035
2001 Pesus	98	2012–2030
1999 Pesus	90+	2010–2024
2001 Pago de Santa Cruz	91+	2010–2020
1999 Pago de Santa Cruz	89	now–2019
1998 Pago de Santa Cruz	88	now–2013
2001 Pago de Santa Cruz Gran Reserva	91	2012–2025
1996 Pago de Santa Cruz Gran Reserva	89	now–2016
2001 Regina Vides	94	2014–2030
1999 Regina Vides	92+	2009–2019

SIERRA CANTABRIA ★ ★ ★ ★
RIOJA $41.00–$167.00

Sierra Cantabria is one of the finest estates in Rioja. It produces a range of wines from entry-level to top-of-the-line single-vineyard limited-production gems. All of Sierra Cantabria's wines are 100% Tempranillo.

2005 Colección Privada	91+	2015–2025
2004 Colección Privada	94	2014–2030
2002 Colección Privada	90	now–2015
2003 Colección Privada	91+	2010–2020
2000 Colección Privada	90	now–2015
2005 Finca El Bosque	96	2018–2040
2004 Finca El Bosque	97	2018–2040
2002 Finca el Bosque	94	2010–2022
2004 Amancio	92	2018–2035
2001 Amancio	96	2012–2025
2002 Amancio	92	now–2018
2003 Cuvée Especial	89+	now–2014
2001 Cuvée Especial	93	2010–2020
2000 Cuvée Especial	88	now–2012
1999 Cuvée Especial	88	now–2012
2003 Crianza	89	now–2013
2001 Crianza	91	now–2013
2000 Crianza	88	now
2002 Reserva	85	now
2000 Reserva	88	now–2010
1999 Reserva	90	now–2013
2001 Gran Reserva	90	now–2015
1998 Gran Reserva	90	now–2013

SIERRA SALINAS ★ ★ ★ ★
ALICANTE $50.00–$115.00

Sierra Salinas is a new winery, a partnership between the Castano family and importer Eric Solomon. These two wines are the debut vintages.

2005 Mira	93	now–2015
2004 1237	95	now–2018

CELLER JOAN SIMO ★ ★ ★
PRIORAT $45.00–$90.00

Les Sentius is a blend of 48% Garnacha, 10% Cariñena, 15% Cabernet Sauvignon, 12% Syrah, and 15% Merlot from vines planted in 1999. Les Eres Viñya Velles is considerably more impressive. It is composed of 55% old-vine Cariñena, 30% old-vine Garnacha, and 15% Cabernet Sauvignon. It is barrel-fermented and aged for 18 months in new French oak.

2004 Les Sentius	89	now–2015
2004 Les Eres Viñya Velles	94	2010–2022

FINCA SOBREÑO ★ ★ ★
TORO $17.00–$39.00

Finca Sobreño's Crianza is 100% Tinto de Toro aged 7 months in American oak. The Selección Especial is 100% Tinto de Toro aged 14 months in American oak.

2005 Crianza	90	now–2016
2004 Crianza	90+	2010–2017
2003 Crianza	88	now–2011
2002 Crianza	87	now–2009
2001 Selección Especial	89	now–2014
2000 Selección Especial	88	now–2010
2003 Selección Especial	92	2013–2025
2003 Reserva Selección de la Familia	89	2009–2018

SOLAR DE URBEZO ★ ★ ★
CARIÑENA $11.00–$37.00

Solar de Urbezo is a 100-hectare (247-acre) estate founded in 1993 by Santiago Gracias.

2006 Garnacha Vieilles Vignes	91	now–2013
2005 Dance del Mar	90	now–2012
2001 Viña de Urbezo Tinto	86	now
1999 Cariñena Reserva	90	now–2015
1999 Solar de Urbezo Reserva	87	now–2010

TAGONIUS ★ ★ ★ ★
MADRID $15.00–$200.00

This is an impressive set of wines from Bodegas Tagonius. They are blends of Cabernet Sauvignon, Merlot, Tempranillo, and Syrah in varying proportions.

2005 Alta Marca	88	now–2012
2004 Alta Marca	87	now–2011
2005 Roble	90	2010–2015
2004 Crianza	91	2012–2025
2003 Crianza	90	now–2014
2003 Reserva	93	2015–2032
2003 Gran Vino	95	2018–2035

BODEGAS TARDENCUBA ★ ★ ★
RIBERA DEL DUERO $24.00–$52.00

Bodegas Tardencuba owns 15 hectares (37 acres) of Tinto de Toro (Tempranillo) in the southwest of Zamora. The top wines are made from ungrafted centennial vines from a sandy region in which phylloxera never took hold. Their wines are fermented with native yeasts and bottled without fining or filtration.

2006 Autor	92+	2012–2025
2004 Crianza	88	now–2015
2004 Valnuevo	93+	2014–2030

DOMINIO DE TARES ★ ★ ★
BIERZO $19.00–$35.00

These are some of the better values in Bierzo, a D.O. that is becoming increasingly fashionable and more expensive. All these wines are 100% Mencia.

2006 Baltos	90	now–2015
2005 Baltos	90	now–2012
2005 Exaltos	90+	2010–2017
2004 Exaltos Cepas Viejas	88+	2010–2017
2004 Bembibre	89	2012–2020
2004 Pagos Tres	91	2010–2020
2003 Pagos Tres	90	2010–2020

TERRA DE VEREMA ★★★★★
PRIORAT $45.00–$80.00

The winemaker for the newly launched Terra de Verema is the talented Ester Nin, the vineyard manager for Clos Erasmus. The vineyard for the Triumvirat is 3.5 hectares (8.6 acres) in size planted to 90% Cariñena, 5% Garnacha, and 5% Syrah. Corelium is 90% Cariñena and 10% Garnacha from a single vineyard with vines ranging from 70 to 100 years of age.

2005 Corelium	95	2012–2025
2006 Triumvirat	95	2012–2025

TORREDEROS ★★★
RIBERA DEL DUERO $18.00–$49.00

This solid portfolio delivers excellent value in Ribera del Duero. The wines are 100% Tempranillo aged in French and American oak.

2005 Barrica Joven Roble	88	now–2012
2004 Crianza	91	2010–2020
2004 Selección	93	2012–2025

FINCA TORREMILANOS ★★★★
RIBERA DEL DUERO $30.00–$50.00

Finca Torremilanos ferments its wines with native yeasts, ages them in French oak, and bottles without fining or filtration. They represent excellent value in quality Ribera del Duero.

2005 Cyclo	94	2014–2030
2004 Cyclo	95	2012–2025
2003 Cyclo	94	2010–2020
2005 Cyclo Christina	94	2015–2032
2004 Crianza	90	2010–2020
2003 Torre Albéniz Reserva	91	2012–2025

TORRES ★★★
VARIOUS $32.00–$105.00

There was a time when *Torres* was virtually synonymous with *Spanish wine* in the U.S. market. Be that as it may, Torres seems to have adapted to changing times, as these wines attest.

2005 Salmos (Priorat)	91	now–2016
2003 Mas La Plana (Penedès)	91	2014–2026
2001 Grans Muralles (Conca de Barbera)	93	2012–2025

VALDERIZ ★★★
RIBERA DEL DUERO $29.00–$135.00

The Valderiz wines are produced from 100% Tinta del País (Tempranillo). The winery also has a value-priced label called Señorío de Valdehermoso, the wines of which merit a try.

2005 Valdehermoso	89	2012–2020
2004 Valderiz	93	2014–2030
2004 Valderiz Tomás Estaban	94+	2016–2035

VALL LLACH ★ ★ ★ ★
PRIORAT $34.00–$85.00

Celler Vall Llach was founded in 1992 by famed Catalan singer Lluís Llach (said to be the Bob Dylan of Catalunya) and his friend Enric Costa. The estate is located in the Priorat village of Porrera.

2005 Embruix	91	now–2016
2004 Embruix	89	2009–2014
2002 Embruix	87	now–2010
2000 Embruix	90	now–2012
2005 Idus	94	2015–2030
2004 Idus	91	2012–2022
2002 Idus	90	now–2013
2005 Vall Llach	96+	2018–2035
2004 Vall Llach	93	2017–2032
2002 Vall Llach	93	2009–2018
2000 Vall Llach	96+	2010–2025

BODEGA VIÑA VALORIA ★ ★ ★
RIOJA $35.00–$40.00

These late releases from Bodega Viña Valoria are blends of 70% Tempranillo, 20% Graciano, and 10% Mazuelo.

1994 Gran Reserva	90	now–2015
1992 Gran Reserva	91	now–2015
1973 Viña Valoria	90	now–2012
1968 Viña Valoria	92	now–2015

VALSACRO ★ ★ ★
RIOJA $35.00–$55.00

Bodegas Valsacro has been amping up the quality in recent vintages. The Crianza is a blend of Garnacha, Tempranillo, and Mazuelo. The Dioro is composed of 40% Tempranillo, 40% Garnacha, 10% Graciano, and—surprise, surprise—10% Macabeo, a white grape.

2004 Vidau	89	2012–2022
2004 Logos I	88	2009–2013
2001 Logos I	87	now–2010
2001 Logos II	85	now
2004 Crianza	91	now–2018
2001 Crianza	90	2010–2017
2004 Dioro	92	now–2016
2003 Dioro	92	2011–2019
2002 Dioro	90	now–2012

VIÑAS DE LA VEGA DEL DUERO ★ ★ ★ ★
CASTILLA Y LEÓN $75.00

This new estate is just beyond the western border of Ribera del Duero. Peter Sisseck is a co-owner and the vineyard is farmed biodynamically.

2005 Quinta Sardonia	94	now–2020
2004 Quinta Sardonia	96	2013–2027

VEGA-SICILIA ✶ ✶ ✶ ✶ ✶
RIBERA DEL DUERO $160.00–$420.00

Still the most prestigious wine estate in Spain (deservedly so), Vega-Sicilia is located 100 miles north of Madrid in the Duero River valley on the high remote plateau of Castilla y León at 700 meters (2,300 feet) of altitude. There are currently 250 hectares (618 acres) under vine. In a good year, 20,000 cases are produced. The Reserva Especial is a selection of the best barrels from the vintages shown on the label.

1990, 1991, and 1996 N. V. Gran Reserva Especial	99	2018–2045
1985, 1991, and 1996 N. V. Gran Reserva Especial	97	2010–2045
1985, 1986, and 1990 N. V. Gran Reserva Especial	96	2010–2040
1998 Unico Reserva	98	2015–2040
1996 Unico Reserva	95	2010–2035
1995 Unico Reserva	97	2018–2050
1994 Unico Reserva	98+	2010–2035
1989 Unico Reserva	94+	2009–2030
1987 Unico Reserva	92	now–2022
2003 Valbuena	94	2012–2025
2002 Valbuena	92	now–2018
2001 Valbuena	93+	2013–2027
2000 Valbuena	92	2010–2020
1998 Valbuena	94	now–2018
1997 Valbuena	91	now–2017

TERRES DE VIDALBA ✶ ✶ ✶ ✶
PRIORAT $65.00

Tocs is sourced from a single vineyard and is composed of 35% Garnacha, 30% Syrah, 30% Cabernet Sauvignon, and 5% Merlot. The wine is aged for 16 months in 80% new French oak.

2004 Tocs	94	2010–2020

VILA VINITECA ✶ ✶ ✶ ✶
RIOJA $40.00–$60.00

Vila Viniteca is a joint venture between Miquel Angel de Gregorio of Finca Allende and Quim Vila, owner of Barcelona's best wine shop, Vila Viniteca.

2001 Paisajes I	95	2010–2020
2005 Paisajes V	94	2013–2025
2004 Paisajes V	91	2012–2027
2005 Paisajes VII	92	2012–2020
2004 Paisajes VII	92	2012–2027
2005 Paisajes VIII	92	now–2018
2004 Paisajes VIII	93	2014–2032
2001 Paisajes VIII	91	now–2015
2004 Paisajes IX	91	now–2018

FINCA VILLACRECES ★★★★★
RIBERA DEL DUERO $45.00–$225.00

The wines of Finca Villacreces have been brilliant in both the 2004 and 2005 vintages. The wines are barrel-fermented and aged in French oak.

2005 Tinto	93	2012–2025
2004 Tinto	95	2012–2027
2005 Nebro	98	2015–2035
2004 Nebro	98	2018–2045
2001 Nebro	98	2010–2022
2001 Reserva	91	now–2017

VITIS TERRARUM ★★★★
LA MANCHA $70.00

Vitis Terrarum is a biodynamically farmed estate that appears to be doing everything right. The wines are all produced from estate-grown fruit, the Tempranillo from ungrafted vines more than 50 years old and the Cabernet Sauvignon from young but also ungrafted vines. The wines are bottled without fining or filtration.

2005 Cabernet Sauvignon	91	2012–2025
2005 Tempranillo	92	2012–2020

BODEGAS VIZCARRA RAMOS ★★★★
RIBERA DEL DUERO $17.00–$155.00

Vizcarra Ramos was founded by Juan Carlos Vizcarra in 1991. The estate owns 26 hectares (64 acres) of Tempranillo vineyard, most of it 30 years of age but with a small number of 80-year-old vines.

2006 Vizcarra Roble	90	now–2016
2005 Vizcarra Roble	89	now–2012
2004 Vizcarra Roble	88	now–2012
2003 Vizcarra Roble	88	now–2012
2006 J. C. Vizcarra	92	2010–2020
2004 J. C. Vizcarra	90	now–2018
2005 Celia Vizcarra	95	2015–2035
2004 Celia Vizcarra	94	2012–2025
2003 Celia Vizcarra	92	2009–2018
2004 Inés Vizcarra	96	2014–2032
2003 Torralvo	90	now–2018

LA VINYA DEL VUIT ★★★★
PRIORAT $100.00

This microcuvée of 2000 bottles takes its name from the eight-member partnership. The wine is 95% Cariñena and 5% Garnacha.

2005 El "8"	94	2012–2025

VIÑEDOS ALONSO DEL YERRO ★★★★
RIBERA DEL DUERO $40.00–$66.00

Viñedos Alonso del Yerro was purchased in 2002 and Stephane Derenoncourt was hired on as consultant. The wines are barrel-fermented and aged *sur-lie* with *bâtonnage,* then in French oak.

2005 Alonso del Yerro	94	2012–2025
2003 Alonso del Yerro	91	now–2018
2005 Alonso del Yerro María	95	2012–2025
2003 Alonso del Yerra María	94	2010–2022

NORTH AMERICA

[california]

Virtually every type of wine seen elsewhere in the wine world is made in California. Fortified Port-style wines, decadently sweet, late-harvest Rieslings, sparkling wines, and major red and white dry table wines from such super grapes as Chardonnay and Cabernet Sauvignon—all are to be found in California.

[grape varieties]

The fine wines of California are dominated by Cabernet Sauvignon, Syrah, Pinot Noir, and Chardonnay, as much of the attention of that state's winemakers is directed at these four grapes. However, California makes interesting red Zinfandel and increasing amounts of very good Sauvignon Blanc and Pinot Gris. Two notable trends started in the late 1980s have proven popular with consumers. These include the proliferation of proprietary red wine blends (usually Cabernet Sauvignon–dominated and superexpensive) and the development of authoritatively flavored, robust, supple red wines made from blends of Syrah, Carignan, Grenache, Mourvèdre, and Alicante, collectively referred to as the "Rhone Rangers." As for the white wines, Sauvignon Blanc and Sémillon, and blends thereof, can be complex and fragrant, and have improved dramatically, but too many remain nondescript. It is a shame that Chenin Blanc has so little sex appeal among consumers, because it can be an inexpensive, delicious drink. Colombard and Muscat suffer from the same image problems as Chenin Blanc, but shrewd consumers know the good ones and seek them out. Gewürztraminer and dry Rieslings have been dismal wines, although a handful of wineries have broken through the wall of mediocrity. For years California has made it simple for the consumer, naming its wines after the varieties from which they are made. By law, any wine called Chardonnay, Cabernet Sauvignon, or any other varietal must contain 75% of that grape.

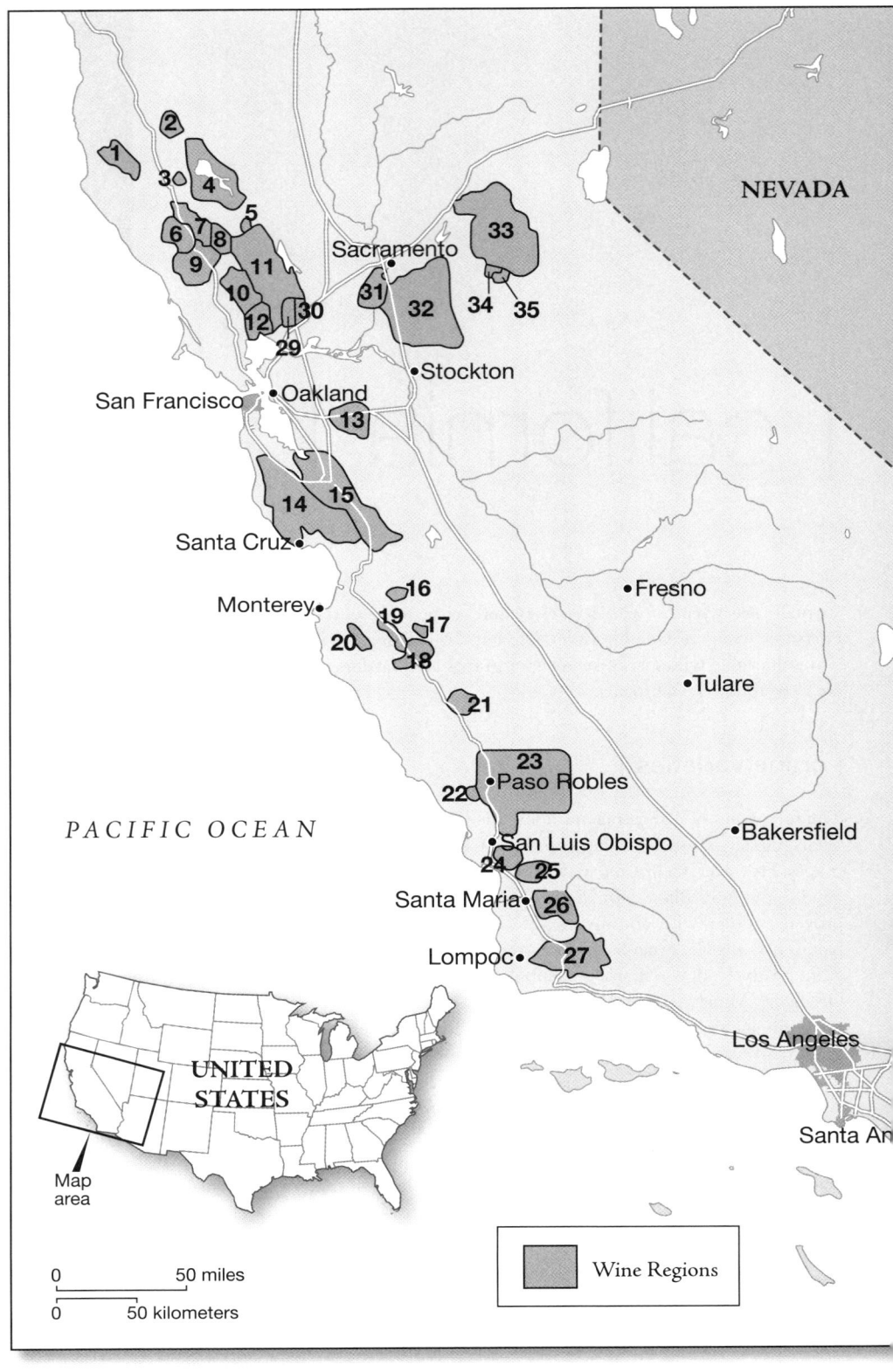

NEVADA

Sacramento

33

31 32 34 35

Stockton

San Francisco Oakland

13

14 15

Santa Cruz

Monterey

16

19 17

20 18

21

23
22 Paso Robles

PACIFIC OCEAN

San Luis Obispo

24 25

Santa Maria 26

Lompoc 27

Fresno

Tulare

Bakersfield

Los Angeles

Santa An

UNITED
STATES

Map
area

0   50 miles

0   50 kilometers

Wine Regions

California

NORTH COAST
1 Anderson Valley
2 Potter Valley
3 McDowell Valley
4 Clear Lake
5 Guenoc Valley
6 Dry Creek Valley
7 Alexander Valley
8 Knights Valley
9 Russian River Valley
10 Sonoma Valley
11 Napa Valley
12 Los Carneros

CENTRAL COAST
13 Livermore Valley
14 Santa Cruz Mountains
15 Santa Clara Valley
16 Mount Harlan
17 Chalone
18 Arroyo Seco
19 Santa Lucia Highlands
20 Carmel Valley
21 San Lucas
22 York Mountains
23 Paso Robles
24 Edna Valley
25 Arroyo Grande
26 Santa Maria Valley
27 Santa Ynez Valley
28 Temecula

INTERIOR
29 Solano County Green Valley
30 Suisun Valley
31 Clarksburg
32 Lodi
33 El Dorado
34 Shenandoah Valley
35 Fiddletown

Death Valley Junction

MOJAVE

•Barstow

DESERT

San Bernardino

•Palm Springs

28

•San Diego

MEXICO

ARIZONA

N
W   E
S

[the wines]

ALICANTE BOUCHET A grape that has fallen out of favor because of its low prestige, Alicante Bouchet remains revered by those who know it well. It yields a black/purple-colored wine with considerable body and richness. It needs time in the bottle to shed its hardness. When mature, the wine offers an array of spicy, earthy flavors, and significant body and alcohol, but be careful—Alicante falls apart quickly after hitting full maturity.

CABERNET FRANC Now being used by more and more wineries to give complexity to a wine's bouquet, Cabernet Franc is a cedary, herbaceous-scented wine that is usually lighter in color and body than either Cabernet Sauvignon or Merlot. It rarely can stand by itself, but used judiciously in a blend, it can provide an extra dimension.

CABERNET SAUVIGNON The king of California's red wine grapes, Cabernet Sauvignon produces densely colored wine with aromas that can include black currants, chocolate, cedar, leather, ground meat, minerals, herbs, tobacco, and tar. Cabernet Sauvignon reaches its pinnacle of success in Napa, Sonoma, and the Santa Cruz Mountains, although a few excellent examples have emanated, infrequently, from Paso Robles and Santa Ynez. The more vegetal side of Cabernet Sauvignon, with intense smells of asparagus and green beans, is found in wines from Monterey or Santa Barbara, two areas that have historically proven too cool for this variety yet where some promising new wineries are now fashioning very fine Bordeaux blends.

CARIGNAN A somewhat lowly regarded grape that deserves more attention, some of California's oldest vineyards are planted with Carignan. Where there are old vines, low yields, and full ripeness, the wines can have surprising intensity and richness in a Rhône-like style. There is a dusty earthiness to most Carignan-based wines that goes along with its big, rich, black fruit and spicy flavors.

GRENACHE A noble grape but even more difficult to farm and produce, Grenache is the equivalent of Pinot Noir's more exuberant and dramatic sibling. It has to be made from very ripe fruit in very low yields, and generally does not like loads of new oak. A few promising Grenaches exist in California, and they deliver unbridled black cherry fruit with scents of licorice, lavender, and pepper. They are usually fuller-bodied and deeper than Pinot Noir, and just as aromatically complex.

MERLOT If Cabernet Sauvignon provides the power, tannin, and structure, Merlot provides opulence, fatness, higher alcohol, and a lush, chewy texture when crop yields are not too high. Telltale aromas of a top Merlot include scents of plums, black cherries, toffee, tea, herbs, sometimes tomatoes, and a touch of orange. Merlot wines will never have the color density of a Cabernet Sauvignon because the Merlot grape's skin is thinner, but they are lower in acidity and less tannic. The higher alcohol and ripeness result in a fleshy, chewy wine that offers early drinking. Wines made primarily from Merlot are here to stay. A few examples can challenge the best of France, but the vast majority (about 90%) remain hollow and frightfully acidified, as well as too vegetal.

MOURVÈDRE/MATARO This variety is making a comeback. It produces a moderately dark-colored wine with a mushroomy-, earthy-, raspberry-scented nose, surprising acidity and tannin, and considerable aging potential. Mourvèdre (often called Mataro) rarely can stand on its own and is often best as part of a blend, usually with Syrah and Grenache.

PETITE SIRAH This varietal, which had fallen from grace, may be making a comeback. Petite Sirah produces almost purple-colored, very tannic, intense wines with peppery, cassis-scented bouquets. The wines age surprisingly well; 15- to 20-year-old examples have shown a consistent ability to hold their fruit. The complexity and bouquet will rarely be that of a Cabernet or Merlot, but these are important wines. The Petite Sirah grape has adapted well to the warmer microclimates of California.

PINOT NOIR The thin-skinned, fickle Pinot Noir is a troublesome grape for everybody. While California continues to produce too many mediocre, washed-out, pruny, vegetal wines from this varietal, no region in the New World has demonstrated more progress with Pinot Noir than California. Major breakthroughs have been made. While good Pinot Noirs are increasingly noticeable from the North Coast areas of Mendocino, Napa, and Sonoma, fine Pinot Noirs also emanate from farther south—the Santa Cruz Mountains, the Monterey area, Arroyo Grande, and Santa Barbara. Yet the areas that have shown the greatest potential are the Sonoma Coast and Santa Barbara's Santa Rita Hills, with their cool maritime climate. A good Pinot Noir will exhibit medium to dark ruby color and an intense explosion of aromatics, including red and black fruits, herbs, earth, and floral aromas. Pinot Noir tends to drop what tannin it possesses quickly, so some acidity is important to give it focus and depth. Most Pinot Noirs are drinkable when released. Few will evolve and improve beyond seven to eight years in the bottle. Consumers should be particularly apprehensive of any Pinot Noir that tastes too tannic or acidic when young.

SANGIOVESE The Italian ancestry of many northern California grape growers and producers is increasingly evident in the number of wineries attempting to produce Sangiovese. The most important red wine grape in the pastoral countryside of Tuscany, Italy, it is the predominant grape of most Chiantis and Vino da Tavolas. In California's fertile soils it achieves mind-boggling crop levels—8 to 12 tons of fruit per acre. Without effective pruning practices or severe crop thinnings, the wines produced are diluted, thin, acidic, and of little interest. However, when the vines are crop-thinned by 50% or more, the result can be fruity, strawberry/cherry/leather-scented and -flavored wines with medium body and penetrating acidity that is ideal for cutting through tomato-based sauces and working with the fusion Mediterranean/Pacific Rim cuisines found in California and elsewhere. To date, few impressive Sangioveses have emerged from California, and many wineries have given up on the grape. Some producers are beginning to add some Cabernet Sauvignon or Merlot to the blend in order to give the wine more color, body, and depth, as the higher crop yields tend to produce a lighter wine than desired. Overall, Sangiovese is largely a failure.

SYRAH Syrah is the great red grape varietal of France's northern Rhône Valley. An increasing number of California wineries have begun to bottle 100% Syrah wines, and some have been exquisite. The style ranges from light, fruity, almost Beaujolais-like wines to black/purple-colored, thick, rich, ageworthy, highly extracted wines bursting with potential. A great Syrah will possess a hickory, smoky, tar, and cassis/blackberry–scented nose, rich, full-bodied, occasionally massive flavors, and considerable tannin. Pepper, tapenade, and beefy smells and tastes are present in many Syrahs. Like Cabernet Sauvignon, a Syrah-based wine is a thoroughbred when it comes to aging, easily lasting for 10 to 20 or more years.

ZINFANDEL Seemingly against all odds, Zinfandel—the red, full-bodied type—has made a modest comeback. Its accessibility, combined with its peppery, berry (cherries, blackberries, and raspberries) nose, spicy fruit, and lush, supple texture, have helped to boost its image. Additionally, Zinfandel's burgeoning popularity might be explained by a growing, and may I say healthy, trend away from excessively priced glamour wines, particularly the chocolate and vanilla flavors of California's Chardonnay and Cabernet Sauvignon. Zinfandel is grown throughout California, but the best clearly comes from relatively old vines grown on hillside vineyards. Selected vineyards (especially head-pruned old vines) from Napa, the Dry Creek Valley, Sonoma, Sierra Foothills, Paso Robles, and Amador have consistently produced the most interesting Zinfandels. While soil certainly plays an important role (gravelly loam is probably the best), low yields, old vines, and harvesting fully mature, physiologically rather than analytically ripe fruit are even more important. Today, most Zinfandels are made in a medium- to full-bodied, spicy, richly fruity style, somewhat in the image of Cabernet Sauvignon. While there is some backbone and structure, it is usually a wine of which consumers can take immediate advantage for its luscious, rich fruit. It must be drunk during the first decade of its life. While many Zinfandels can last longer, my experience suggests the wines rarely improve after four to six years. One lamentable trend to monitor is the increasingly high prices demanded for Zinfandels. Most good Zinfandels fetch $25 to $35 a bottle, with some surpassing $50. This is a dangerous direction.

WHITES

CHARDONNAY The great superstar of the white wines, Chardonnay at its best can produce majestically rich, buttery, honeyed wines with layers of flavors suggesting tropical fruits (pineapples and tangerines), apples, peaches, and even buttered popcorn when the wine has been barrel-fermented. It flourishes in all of California's viticultural districts, with no area having superiority over another. Great examples can be found from Mendocino, Sonoma, Napa, Carneros, Monterey, Santa Cruz, and Santa Barbara. The problem is that of the 600-plus California wineries producing Chardonnay, fewer than 100 make an interesting wine. Crop yields are too high, the wines are manufactured rather than made, are too frequently overoaked, and are excessively acidified, making them technically flawless but lacking in bouquet, flavor intensity, and character, save for their grotesque oakiness. The results are tart, vapid wines of no interest. Moreover, the wines have to be drunk within 12 to 18 months of the vintage. Another popular trend has been to intentionally leave sizable amounts of residual sugar in the wine while trying to hide part of it with additions of acidity. This cosmetically gives the wine a superficial feel of more richness and roundness, but these wines also crack up within a year of the vintage. Most Chardonnays are mediocre and overpriced, with very dubious aging potentials, yet they remain the most popular "dry" white wines produced in California. A positive trend over the last five to six years has been a more balanced approach to the degree of new oak that is utilized.

CHENIN BLANC This maligned, generally misunderstood grape can produce lovely apéritif wines that are both dry and slightly sweet. Most wineries lean toward a fruity, delicate, perfumed, light- to medium-bodied style that pleases increasing numbers of consumers who are looking for delicious wines at reasonable prices. This varietal deserves more attention.

FRENCH COLOMBARD Like Chenin Blanc, Colombard is a varietal that is rarely accorded much respect. Its charm is its aromatic character and crisp, light-bodied style.

GEWÜRZTRAMINER Anyone who has tasted a fine French Gewürztraminer must be appalled by what is sold under this name in California. A handful of wineries have produced some attractive though subdued Gewürztraminers. The bald truth remains that most California Gewürztraminers are made in a slightly sweet, watery, shallow, washed-out style.

MUSCAT There are several Muscat grapes used in California. This is an underrated and underappreciated varietal that produces remarkably fragrant and perfumed wines that are loaded with tropical fruit flavors. They are ideal as an apéritif or with desserts.

PINOT BLANC This grape, a staple of Alsace, France, where it is used to produce richly fruity but generally straightforward, satisfying wines, has had mixed success in California. Some producers have barrel-fermented it, attempting to produce a large-scale, Chardonnay-style wine, with little success. In my opinion, Pinot Blanc is best vinified in a manner that emphasizes its intense fruity characteristics, which range from honeyed tangerines and oranges to a more floral, applelike fruitiness. Pinot Blancs do not typically age well, but they provide immediate appeal and satisfaction in an exuberant yet uncomplicated manner. Most Pinot Blancs should be drunk within two to three years of the vintage.

SAUVIGNON BLANC Until five or six years ago, California winemaking had failed miserably to take advantage of this grape. Overcropping, excessive acidification, and a philosophy of manufacturing the wines have resulted in hundreds of neutral, bland, empty wines with no bouquet or flavor. This is unfortunate, because Sauvignon is one of the most food-friendly and flexible wines produced in the world. It can also adapt itself to many different styles of fermentation and upbringing. At its best, the nonoaked examples of this wine possess vivid, perfumed noses of figs, melons, herbs, and minerals, crisp fruit, wonderful zesty flavors, and a dry finish. More ambitious barrel-fermented styles that often have some Semillon added can have a honeyed, melony character and rich, medium- to full-bodied, grassy, melon- and fig-like flavors that offer considerable authority.

SÉMILLON One of the up-and-coming California varieties, on its own, Sémillon produces wines with considerable body and creamy richness. It can often be left on the vine and has a tendency to develop botrytis, which lends itself to making sweet, honeyed dessert wines. But Sémillon's best use is when it is added to Sauvignon, where the two make the perfect marriage, producing wines with considerable richness and complexity.

WHITE RIESLING OR JOHANNISBERG RIESLING Occasionally some great late-harvest Riesling has been made in California, but attempts at making a dry Kabinett- or *trocken*-style Riesling as produced in Germany most frequently result in dull, lifeless, empty wines with no personality or flavor. Most Riesling is planted in soils that are too rich and in climates that are too hot. This is a shame. Riesling is another varietal that could prove immensely popular to the masses.

AGING POTENTIAL
Cabernet Franc: 5–15 years
Cabernet Sauvignon: 5–30 years
Chardonnay: 2–10 years
Chenin Blanc: 1–2 years
Colombard: 1–2 years
Gamay: 2–4 years
Grenache: 5–15 years
Merlot: 5–15 years
Muscat: 1–3 years
Petite Sirah: 10–30 years
Pinot Blanc: 1–3 years
Pinot Noir: 5–12 years
Riesling (dry): 1–2 years
Riesling (sweet): 2–8 years
Sauvignon Blanc: 1–3 years
Sémillon: 1–4 years
Sparkling Wines: 2–7 years
Syrah: 5–20 years
Zinfandel: 3–10 years

OVERALL QUALITY LEVEL

The top 60 to 70 producers of Cabernet Sauvignon, Merlot, or proprietary red wines, as well as the 35 to 40 or so who produce Chardonnay, make wines that are as fine and as multidimensional as those made anywhere in the world. However, for well over 30 years my tastings have consistently revealed too many California wines that are not made, but manufactured. Excessively acidified by cautious oenologists, and sterile-filtered to the point where there is no perceptible aroma, many wines possess little flavor except for the textural abrasiveness caused by shrill levels of acidity and high alcohol, and in the case of the red wines, excessive levels of green, astringent tannins. Producers have tried to hide their excessive crop yields by leaving residual sugar in the finished wine, hoping to give the impression of more body. This practice is only a quick fix, as the white wines tend to fall apart six to nine months after bottling and the red wines taste cloying.

The time-honored philosophy of California winemaking, which includes an obsession with the vineyard as a manufacturing plant, industrial winemaking in the cellars, and a preoccupation with monolithic, simplistic, squeaky-clean wines that suffer from such strictly controlled technical parameters, is weakening. It is no secret that the principal objective of most California wineries has been to produce sediment-free, spit-polished, stable wines. The means used to attain this goal too frequently eviscerate the wines of their flavor, aromas, personality, and pleasure-giving qualities. But since 1990, significant changes have had dramatic consequences for the better.

Only a fool could ignore the fact that California is now producing many of the greatest wines in the world. While most retailers legitimately carp about the microscopic allocations they receive of the limited-production gems from the most fashionable wineries, it is obvious that California wine quality is surging to greater and greater heights.

Why am I so bullish on California wines? Consider the following:

1. California enjoyed a stunning succession of top-quality vintages in the 1990s. Starting with 1990, every vintage has provided that state's growers with enough high-quality fruit to turn out numerous sensational wines. Only 1998 and 2000, in reality good years, offer less excitement than the other vintages. Truly superb vintages occurred in 1990, 1991, 1992, 1994, 1995, 1997, 2001, 2002, and 2004.

2. Even more important is the shift in mind-set of many top wine producers. Handcrafted wines that reflected the *terroir*, vintage, and varietal, in addition to providing immense pleasure, have had an enormous influence on others. Two decades ago, it was distressing to see the number of wineries that automatically, without any thought whatsoever, compromised and in many cases destroyed a wine by blind faith in the following techniques: (a) harvesting grapes based on analytical rather than physiological ripeness; (b) adding frightfully high levels of tartaric acid to the fermenting juice because it was the "risk-free" thing to do; (c) processing the youthful grape juice utilizing centrifuges and filters that eviscerated and purified the wine before it had a chance to develop any personality; (d) prefiltering wine intensely before it was allowed to go to barrel; and (e) fining and sterile-filtering everything as a rule of thumb so that a wine had no aromatics and nothing but a monolithic personality. The adoption of a less traumatic and less interventionalistic wine philosophy, emphasizing the importance of the vineyard's fruit and preserving its characteristics, is increasingly widespread. The results are increasing quantities of compellingly rich, natural-tasting, unprocessed wines that should be causing French wine producers to shudder. And while many wineries continue to fight this trend toward higher-quality, more natural wines, often with considerable support from a gullible wine press, the fact is that you, the wine consumer, are the beneficiary!

3. As financially devastating as the phylloxera epidemic has been for California viticulture, the silver lining is that the replanting of vineyards over the last decade has addressed important issues that key industry personnel refused to acknowledge as being important prior to this epidemic. Many new vineyards have been planted with tighter spacing, thus making the vines struggle. The result is deeper root systems and vines that produce lower quantities of higher-quality grapes. Additionally, the problem of varietals planted in the wrong soils and/or microclimates can be rectified by these new plantations. Superior rootstocks and less productive clones that produce smaller crops with more individual character are other positive results of the phylloxera epidemic. As time passes, it will become evident that the mistakes made

in the 1940s, 1950s, and 1960s have largely been corrected, ironically because of phylloxera. If the grapes from these new vineyards are markedly superior, as they should be, it takes no genius to realize that wine quality will also improve.

4. The influence of the French, combined with a new generation of well-traveled, open-minded, revisionist California winemakers, must also be given credit for the remarkable progress in quality. California wines are as rich as they have ever been, but they no longer possess the heaviness of those great vintages of the 1960s and 1970s. Do readers realize why the finest French cuisine and French wines are cherished throughout the world as standards of reference? Because France, in both her cooking and her wines, achieves, at the highest level of quality, extraordinary intensity of flavor without weight or heaviness. Call this elegance, harmony, finesse, or whatever, but it is what I now detect in increasing numbers of California's finest wines.

BUYING STRATEGY

Except for the poor 2005 Zinfandels, California has experienced a very good set of vintages to start off the 21st century. Combine that with an unprecedented run of eight consecutive years (1990–1997) in which most of the state's producers turned out wines that were made from ripe fruit. No area of California has had an off vintage since 1998. As long as you know the best producers and the style of wines for which you are looking, it is almost impossible to make a mistake in selecting a California wine. The biggest issue is pricing, as California wine producers have no incentive to lower prices, and in fact, most are raising prices as the weak dollar abroad makes imports so much more expensive.

The most fashionable varietal in the American marketplace is Pinot Noir. Thank the movie *Sideways* for bringing attention to this fascinating grape. However, today's overproduction of Pinot Noir, not only in California but in Oregon as well, has resulted in many Pinot Noirs that are devoid of any charm, texture, or fruit. Because of the aforementioned movie, American culture, quick to become obsessed by fashion, has given Pinot Noir producers—especially those who have no conscience—license to produce mediocre wine and charge ridiculously high prices for their insipid products. There are profound Pinot Noirs being made in California, more than anywhere else in the United States. This varietal experienced enormous progress from the cool-climate sites of the Russian River Valley to the Sonoma Coast, the Anderson Valley in the north, and Santa Rita in the south. While the quality of the best Pinot Noirs remains one of the most exciting developments in the wine world over the last 30 years, the percentage of shabby, largely undrinkable Pinot Noirs sold at high prices is shameful. It is only a matter of time before consumers smarten up and realize what scams these wines represent and the bubble bursts. In short, there is too much production and there are too many mediocre wines. We saw this same phenomenon a decade ago with Merlot, and before that with White Zinfandel.

At the same time, it is distressing to see how many terrific Syrahs are being made throughout California, often at remarkably fair prices, with fabulous personalities and characters, that are largely ignored in the retail marketplace. One hopes that consumers will smarten up and realize how much better a $20-to-$25 Syrah is than a thin, acidic, flavorless $25-to-$50 Pinot Noir. Wine tasting and wine appreciation is always a matter of education and experience, and I am certain that Syrah will attain greater popularity. It's a shame to see so many young men and women accomplishing fabulous things with Syrah and having a difficult time selling world-class wines.

The best California values continue to be the Rhone Ranger blends and Zinfandels for red wines and, when you can find them, the good Chenin Blancs, Sauvignon Blancs, and Colombards for white wines.

[recent vintages]

2007

I had not tasted any of California's North Coast wines at the time of publication, but the wine-makers are generally optimistic about this vintage. Overall, a warm, dry spring yielded a smaller crop than previous vintages. Unlike many years, there were no unusual heat spikes in August and September. Mild weather in September and October allowed those who were patient to harvest at their leisure, although there were some unusual periods of rain. The only negative will be the lower crop levels, and most producers report slightly lower alcohols than in such blockbuster years as 2001, 2002, and 2004.

In the Central Coast, production was also down significantly, but the quality of the wines is very high. Some areas did experience significant heat spikes, but the wines are believed to be fruitier than the 2005s, and not as structured or tannic. They should be very concentrated because of lower yields. Most of the Chardonnay and Pinot Noir producers have reported good levels of natural acidity, which is always a good sign.

2006

This was a much warmer year than 2005, but it was by no means a hot year along the lines of 2004, 2003, 2002, or 2001. For the most part, the wines are relatively fruit-forward and front-end-loaded, which is always a good sign. There were some botrytis and rot problems with low-lying vineyards of Chardonnay and Pinot Noir, but this did not appear to be a problem at the finest wineries. While 2006 is a very good vintage for Chardonnay and Pinot Noir, it is not at the quality level of 2005. The Bordeaux varietals look relatively strong, and Zinfandel was much better in 2006 than 2005.

The Rhone Ranger wines are also promising. In particular, the Central Coast appears to have had a fruit-forward, opulent vintage. It was a cool August and September in the Central Coast, but patient vignerons were rewarded with significant heat in October.

2005

This is an intriguing vintage. Yields were high, the alcohols were lower, and the acidity levels were slightly higher. Consequently the wines are more streamlined and obviously tannic, especially the bigger reds. The bottled Pinot Noirs and Syrahs appear to be strong. Along with 2002, 2005 may be the finest vintage for Chardonnay in the last two decades. The biggest surprise was how much weight the Bordeaux varietals gained in cask prior to bottling. I was blown away by much of the quality of the top 2005 Cabernet Sauvignons and proprietary blends of Cabernet Sauvignon, Merlot, Cabernet Franc, and Petit Verdot. They deserve comparison to another cool year, 1975, which was also highly underrated at conception. In any event, 2005 has turned out to be a very strong vintage. Its one weakness was the challenging conditions for producing high-quality Zinfandel. Some producers succeeded, but overall the wines have turned out to be mediocre. Zinfandel needs abundant heat in order to ripen fully, and that did not occur. It will be a long-lived vintage for the Bordeaux varietals, as well as Chardonnay and Pinot Noir.

As in the north, 2005 was a cool, abundant vintage in the Santa Cruz Mountains and Central Coast. Some of the Central Coast Bordeaux varietals have a tendency to be borderline herbal, but the Chardonnay, Pinot Noir, and Rhone Ranger varietals did very well.

2004

This is a vintage of exceptional charm. A small crop and a hot, ripe growing season resulted in beautifully concentrated wines, neither heavy nor overbearing, with sweet tannins, loads of ripe fruit, and a tremendous consistency across the field of play. From the most conscientious producers, it is easy to find impeccably made, well-balanced Bordeaux varietals such as Cabernet Sauvignon and proprietary reds, delicious, up-front Pinot Noirs, gorgeously fat, fleshy Zinfandels, and plenty of heady Chardonnays and Pinot Blancs. This is a vintage for consumers who are unable to defer their gratification, and the top wines will provide pleasure now and for many years to come.

In the Santa Cruz Mountains, an overall hot year produced impressive, heady wines that are on a faster evolutionary track than their 2005 counterparts. Like their northern brethren, the 2004s are consistently fleshy wines with considerable appeal.

2003

If it were not for two of its immediate predecessors, this vintage would look very strong. It was a year of numerous heat spikes, which gave headaches to winemakers and viticulturists. While 2003 can be irregular, at the top end the vintage has turned out to be very good, with relatively chunky, full-bodied, powerful wines produced from the Bordeaux varietals as well as Syrah and Zinfandel. The Chardonnays are excellent, as are the Pinot Noirs. I tasted hundreds of innocuous, excessively tannic, overly oaked wines that lacked concentration and character, yet when chosen carefully, the 2003s offer consumers many rewards. I believe this is a very good to excellent vintage, and significantly better than such vintages as 2000, 1999, and 1998.

Heat spikes and good yields produced ripe, heady wines with relatively high alcohol and low acids in the Central Coast. Already performing beautifully, they are full-bodied and opulent, in total contrast to the more racy, delineated style of vintages such as 2005.

2002

This is a classic vintage of superripe California wines. Most of the Chardonnays and Zinfandels should be consumed over the next one to three years. The Pinot Noirs are just hitting their full stride and should hold for at least another two to three years, as will the Syrahs. The top Cabernet Sauvignons, Merlots, and proprietary Bordeaux-style blends are magnificent wines of opulence, richness, fruit, and stunning purity as well as texture. It's my favorite vintage for wines that have some accessibility now but will keep for 20 to 30 years. It was also a very consistent vintage for the top producers.

In the Central Coast, this is an exceptional vintage—consistent, abundant, and impressive.

2001

This was a classic, powerful, tannic year in the North Coast, especially for the Bordeaux varietals. Most of the Chardonnays and Zinfandels should have been drunk up by now, but Cabernet Sauvignons, Merlots, and proprietary Bordeaux blends, while superb, are very structured and tannic, and will be among the longest lived of the last two decades. Overall, it is a laidback, austere, and tannic vintage, and not nearly as opulent as 2002, but the top wines possess fabulous concentration and potential for longevity.

It's a more challenging vintage in the Central Coast, where the wines can be austere if picked too early; some wines have turned out to be slightly herbal, but producers with good vineyard sites who waited to pick produced fabulous wines.

2000

Overall, a good but irregular year in northern California, yet with exceptional quality in the Central Coast and Santa Barbara regions.

1999

Following 1998, this was another cool year, with mountain vineyards and cooler *terroirs* challenged to get their fruit fully ripe. It is an excellent vintage for thin-skinned varietals such as

Chardonnay and Pinot Noir. Syrah has also performed well. As in 1998, mountain vineyards had difficulty obtaining fully ripened Cabernet Sauvignon.

1998

This is the first vintage of the 1990s to present irregularities and inconsistencies throughout California's viticultural regions. A cool late spring and abnormally cool summer resulted in one of the latest harvests of the decade. Many Cabernet Sauvignon vineyards on the cooler hillsides were not harvested until late October. Some areas, particularly Santa Barbara and to the north, were touched by rain. The crop size was moderate, and the quality ranged from exceptional to spotty. Overall, 1998 is the least consistent and compelling year of the 1990s.

1997

For California's North Coast, this vintage has the potential to compete with 1994 and 1991 as one of the decade's finest years for Cabernet Sauvignon, Merlot, and Cabernet Franc. The vintage possesses the characteristics that separate great years from merely excellent ones. The finest wines are seamless, with velvety textures, wonderful purity, sweet tannin, and expressive aromatic profiles. Much to the joy of winemakers, the abundant crop produced ripe wines with surprisingly high extract and alcohol. Pinot Noir looks exceptional throughout the North Coast, and the Chardonnays are very good to excellent. In particular, the Chardonnays do not appear to have the intensity of the 1995s, but they are extremely fragrant with the vintage's crisp acidity and high alcohol. However, consumers need to be careful, as yields for many producers were entirely too high to produce quality wines. Hence, 1997, which is undeniably great at the top end, has many deceptions and frustrating irregularity.

In the Santa Cruz Mountains, Central Coast, and Santa Barbara, the vintage becomes trickier, but certainly the potential for high quality exists. My visit to these areas left me with the impression that 1997 is a very good vintage as opposed to a potentially great one. One last caveat—the Zinfandels are far less successful because of enormous yields, and they should have been consumed by 2008.

1996

If this were a vintage from the 1980s, it would stand out as one of the greatest years of that decade. However, sandwiched between 1997, 1994, and 1995, the year 1996, while having no shortcomings, simply does not match up. The products of a hot drought year with a short growing season, the North Coast wines are powerful, concentrated, and weighty, but some lack the sweet tannin and near perfect equilibrium achieved in 1994, 1995, and 1997. Readers will notice more rustic tannin in many Cabernet Sauvignons and certain Pinot Noirs. Brilliant wines were made, but the tannin level can be aggressive. If it were not for 1997, 1995, and 1994, this would be considered a top-flight year. For now, it is unquestionably an excellent year. The Zinfandels and the white wines should have been drunk up.

This does appear to be a great year in the Santa Cruz Mountains, where wines of exceptional ripeness, richness, and balance were achieved.

1995

Like 1994, 1995 enjoyed a long, cool growing season, and while the wines are not as forward, fragrant, and expressive as many 1994s, a bevy of fabulous wines has emerged from Napa and Sonoma's top wineries. This year gets my nod as the finest vintage in the 1990s for Chardonnay, but most readers buying high-quality California Chardonnay should have consumed them by 2001. For Cabernet Sauvignon and Pinot Noir, 1995 is an outstanding vintage that comes close to rivaling the greatness of 1994. In fact, some producers may have turned out Cabernet Sauvignons, Merlots, and proprietary reds that surpass what they achieved in 1994. In short, 1995 is another phenomenal vintage in a decade of top-notch years.

1994

A vintage of great uniformity and prodigious quality, especially for Cabernet Sauvignons, which are approachable, exceptionally aromatic, wonderfully sweet and rich, but neither heavy nor cumbersome. The top producers have made long-lived classics of remarkable symmetry and opulence. It was also a superb year in the Santa Cruz Mountains.

1993

If the 1993s are not as dramatic as the finest 1994s, 1992s, 1991s, and 1990s, they are by no means inferior. This is another rich, velvety-textured vintage for red wines.

1992

An abundant crop was harvested that ranged from very good to superb in quality. When Mother Nature is as generous as she was in most viticultural regions in 1992, the potential high quality can be diluted by excessive crop yields and harvesting grapes that are not physiologically mature. However, the top producers have turned out fat, rich, opulent, low-acid, dramatic wines. The finest Cabernets are flattering and richly fruity, and will keep for another ten years. Virtually all the Syrahs, Pinot Noirs, and Zinfandels should have been drunk up.

1991

A cool, surprisingly long growing season resulted in potentially excessive crop yields. However, those producers who had the patience to wait out the cool weather and harvest fully mature fruit, as well as to keep their yields down, made some superb red wines that will compete with the finest wines of 1997, 1995, 1994, 1993, 1992, 1990, 1987, 1986, 1985, and 1984. For all the red Bordeaux varietals it is a splendid year, with many producers expressing a preference for their 1991s because of the incredibly long hang time on the vine. The 1991 vintage produced an enormous crop of good white wines that should be consumed by the end of 1995.

—ROBERT PARKER

WHERE TO FIND CALIFORNIA'S BEST WINE VALUES

Adelaida Cellars (Syrah Schoolhouse Paso Robles)
Anglim (Syrah Paso Robles)
Arrowood Vineyards & Winery (Côte de Lune Rouge Sonoma)
Beckman Vineyards (Cuvée Le Bec red and white Santa Ynez)
Beringer (Knights Valley Chardonnay, Sauvignon Blanc, Cabernet Sauvignon, Alluvium Blanc, Napa Chardonnay)
Bonny Doon Vineyard (Clos de Gilroy, Ca' Del Solo cuvées, Pacific Rim Riesling)
Breggo Cellars (Pinot Gris, Sauvignon Blanc)
Cartlidge and Browne (Chardonnay, Zinfandel, Cabernet Sauvignon, Sauvignon Blanc Dancing Crow, Rabid Red)
Chesebro Wines (Syrah Cedar Lane Vineyard Carmel Valley)
Concannon (Petite Sirah Central Coast, Syrah Central Coast)
Curtis Winery (Syrah Santa Ynez)
Di Arie (Zinfandel Amador)
Edmeades (Zinfandel Mendocino)
Frei Brothers (Chardonnay)
Gallo Family Vineyards (Pinot Gris, Chardonnay)
Grayson Cellars (Cabernet Sauvignon Paso Robles, Chardonnay Central Coast)
Honig (Sauvignon Blanc Napa)

Husch Vineyards (Chenin Blanc Mendocino, Muscat Canelli Mendocino, Sauvignon Blanc Mendocino)

Jaffurs Wine Cellars (Syrah Santa Barbara)

Kendall-Jackson (Vintner's Reserve Chardonnay, Fumé Blanc, Vintner's Reserve Zinfandel)

Kunin Wines (Pape Star Central Coast)

Marietta Cellars (N.V. Red Lot, Cabernet Sauvignon Alexander Valley)

Michael-David Winery (Syrah Earthquake, Syrah Sixth Sense, Earthquake Zin Lodi, 7 Deadly Zins Lodi, Zinfandel Windmill Old Vine Lodi)

Murphy-Goode (Fumé Blanc)

J. Pedroncelli (Sauvignon Blanc, Zinfandel, Cabernet Sauvignon)

Joseph Phelps Vineyard (Vins du Mistral cuvées)

Qupé (Syrah Central Coast)

Rosenblum Cellars (Petite Sirah Heritage Clones San Francisco Bay, Syrah Santa Barbara, Syrah Abba Vineyard Lodi)

Château St. Jean (Fumé Blanc)

Seventy-Five (Sauvignon Blanc Napa, Cabernet Sauvignon Amber Knolls Red Hills Lake County)

Château Souverain (Cabernet Sauvignon Alexander Valley)

Spencer-Roloson (Palaterra California)

Stratford (the Chardonnay and Canterbury line of wines, particularly Chardonnay and Sauvignon Blanc)

Summers Wines (Chardonnay Alexander Valley, Cabernet Sauvignon Adrianna's Cuvée Napa)

Tablas Creek (Côtes de Tablas Paso Robles red and white)

Domaine de la Terre Rouge (GSM Tête à Tête, Syrah Les Côtes de l'Ouest)

Trentadue Winery (Old Patch Red, Zinfandel, Carignan, Sangiovese, Petite Sirah, Merlot, Salute Proprietary Red Wine)

Zaca Mesa (Z Cuvée Santa Ynez)

[the ratings]

CALIFORNIA'S BEST PRODUCERS OF CABERNET SAUVIGNON, MERLOT, OR BLENDS

★ ★ ★ ★ ★ (OUTSTANDING)

Abreu Vineyards Madrona Ranch (Napa)

Abreu Vineyards Thorevilos (Napa)

Anderson's Conn Valley Eloge Proprietary Red (Napa)

Anderson's Conn Valley Right Bank Proprietary Red (Napa)

Araujo Estate Eisele Vineyard (Napa)

Arrowood Reserve Spéciale (Sonoma)

Beringer Private Reserve (Napa)

Blankiet (Napa)

Bond E Pluribus (Napa)

Bond Melbury (Napa)

Bond St. Eden (Napa)

Bond Vecina (Napa)

Bryant Family Vineyard (Napa)

Cardinale Proprietary Red Wine (Napa)

Caymus Special Selection (Napa)

Colgin Cariad (Napa)

Colgin Lamb Vineyard (Napa)

Colgin IX Proprietary Red (Napa)

Colgin Tychson Hill (Napa)

Dalla Valle Maya Proprietary Red Wine (Napa)

Dominus (Napa)

Forman Special Cuvée (Napa)

Futo (Napa)

Gemstone Proprietary Red Wine (Napa)

Harlan Estate Proprietary Red Wine (Napa)

Paul Hobbs Beckstoffer To-Kalon Vineyard (Napa)

Hundred Acre Ark Vineyard (Napa)
Hundred Acre Deep Time Vineyard (Napa)
Hundred Acre Kayli Morgan Vineyard
 (Napa)
Hundred Acre Previous Vineyard (Napa)
Kapcsándy Family Winery Roberta's
 Reserve State Lane Vineyard (Napa)
Kapcsándy Family Winery State Lane
 Vineyard (Napa)
Tor Kenward Family Beckstoffer To-Kalon
 (Napa)
Lail Vineyards J. Daniel Cuvée (Napa)
Larkmead Solari Reserve (Napa)
Levy and McClellan (Diamond Mountain)
Lokoya Diamond Mountain (Napa)
Lokoya Howell Mountain (Napa)
Lokoya Mount Veeder (Napa)
Lokoya Spring Mountain (Napa)
Merus (Napa)
Metisse Proprietary Red (Napa)
Peter Michael Les Pavots Proprietary Red
 Wine (Knight's Valley)
Château Montelena Estate (Napa)
O'Shaughnessey (Mt. Veeder)
Pahlmeyer Proprietary Red Wine (Napa)
Joseph Phelps Insignia Proprietary Red
 Wine (Napa)
PlumpJack Reserve (Napa)
Pride Mountain Claret (Napa)
Pride Mountain Reserve (Napa)

Ramey Larkmead Vineyard (Napa)
Ramey Pedregal (Oakville)
Ridge Monte Bello (Santa Cruz Mountains)
Rudd Estate (Napa)
St. Clement Progeny (Mt. Veeder)
Sbragia Family Vineyards Monte Rosse
 (Sonoma)
Sbragia Family Vineyards Wall Vineyard
 (Mt. Veeder)
Scarecrow (Rutherford)
Schrader Cellars Beckstoffer George III
 Vineyard (Rutherford)
Schrader Cellars CCS (Oakville)
Schrader Cellars Clone 4 (Oakville)
Schrader Cellars Old Sparky (Oakville)
Schrader Cellars RBS (Oakville)
Schrader Cellars T6 (Oakville)
Screaming Eagle (Napa)
Seavey (Napa)
Shafer Hillside Select (Napa)
Sloan Proprietary Red (Napa)
Spottswoode (Napa)
Switchback Ridge Peterson Family
 Vineyard (Napa)
Philip Togni Estate (Napa)
Vérité Le Désir (Sonoma)
Vérité La Joie (Sonoma)
Vérité La Muse (Sonoma)
Vineyard 29 (Napa)

* * * * (EXCELLENT)

Altamura (Napa)
Amuse Bouche Merlot (Napa)
Anderson's Conn Valley Vineyard (Napa)
Anomaly (Napa)
Araujo Estate Wines Altagracia (Napa)
Arnot-Roberts Bugay Vineyard (Sonoma)
Arnot-Roberts Wild Iris (Chalk Hill)
Arrowood (Sonoma)
David Arthur Elevation 1147 (Napa)
Bacio Divino Proprietary Red Wine
 (California)
Bacio Divino To-Kalon Vineyard (Oakville)
Barnett Spring Mountain Rattlesnake
 Hill (Napa)
Beringer St. Helena Vineyard (Napa)
Beringer State Lane Vineyard (Napa)
Beringer Tre Colline Vineyard (Napa)
Black Coyote Bates Creek Vineyard
 (Stags Leap)

Blackbird Vineyards Paramour Proprietary
 Red (Napa)
Blackbird Vineyards Proprietary Red Wine
 (Napa)
Bond Matriarch (Napa)
Caymus Vineyards (Napa)
Chappellet Winery Donn Chappellet (Napa)
Chappellet Winery Pritchard Hill Estate
 Proprietary Red (Napa)
Clare Luce Abbey Estate (Napa)
Continuum Proprietary Red (Napa)
Corté Riva (Napa/Sonoma)
Corté Riva Cabernet Franc (Napa/Sonoma)
Corté Riva Merlot (Napa)
Covenant (Napa)
Robert Craig Affinity Proprietary Red
 Wine (Napa)
Robert Craig Howell Mountain (Napa)
Robert Craig Mt. Veeder (Napa)

Crane Brothers Brodatious Crane Ranch Vineyard Proprietary Red (Napa)

Crane Brothers Crane Ranch Vineyard Hillside Block (Napa)

Crocker & Starr Stone Place (Napa)

Dalla Valle (Napa)

Dana Estates (Rutherford)

Dehlinger Estate (Russian River)

Del Dotto (Howell Mountain)

Del Dotto (Rutherford)

Del Dotto (St. Helena Mountain)

Del Dotto Cabernet Franc (Rutherford)

Del Dotto Vineyard 887 (St. Helena Mountain)

Diamond Creek Gravelly Meadow (Napa)

Diamond Creek Lake (Napa)

Diamond Creek Red Rock Terrace (Napa)

Diamond Creek Volcanic Hill (Napa)

Duckhorn Vineyards Merlot Three Palms Vineyard (Napa)

Duckhorn Vineyards Rector Creek Vineyard Estate (Napa)

Dunn (Napa)

Dunn Howell Mountain (Napa)

Eagles Trace Latitude 38 (Napa)

Étude (Napa)

Étude (Oakville)

Étude (Rutherford)

Fisher Coach Insignia (Sonoma) (since 1991)

Fisher Wedding Vineyard (Sonoma)

Flanagan Family Vineyards (Bennett Valley)

Flora Springs Hillside Reserve (Napa)

Flora Springs Out of Sight Vineyard (Napa)

Flora Springs Trilogy Proprietary Red Wine (Napa)

Robert Foley Claret (Napa)

Forman (Napa)

Peter Franus (Napa)

Freemark Abbey Bosche Vineyard (Rutherford)

Freemark Abbey Sycamore Vineyards (Rutherford)

Gemstone Facets Proprietary Red Wine (Napa)

Andrew Geoffrey Vineyard Diamond Mountain (Napa)

Grace Family Vineyard (Napa)

Harris Estate Vineyards Jake's Creek Vineyard (Napa)

Harris Estate Vineyards Lakeview Vineyard (Napa)

Harris Estate Vineyards Treva's Vineyard (Napa)

Havens Bourriquot (Napa)

Havens Merlot Reserve (Napa)

Hestan Vineyards (Napa)

Paul Hobbs (Napa)

Paul Hobbs Beckstoffer Dr. Crane Vineyard (Napa)

Paul Hobbs Hyde Vineyard (Sonoma)

Paul Hobbs Stagecoach Vineyard (Napa)

Hourglass (Napa)

Jericho Canyon (Napa)

Jones Family Vineyard (Napa)

Juslyn Perry's Blend (Napa)

Juslyn Spring Mountain Estate (Napa)

Juslyn Vineyard Select (Napa)

Kamen (Sonoma)

Kapcsándy Estate Cuvée State Lane Vineyard (Napa)

Robert Keenan (Napa)

Robert Keenan (Spring Mountain)

Robert Keenan Cabernet Franc (Spring Mountain)

Robert Keenan Merlot (Napa)

Robert Keenan Merlot Reserve Mailbox Vineyard (Spring Mountain)

Robert Keenan Mernet Reserve (Napa)

Robert Keenan Reserve (Spring Mountain)

Kendall-Jackson Grand Reserve (Sonoma)

Kendall-Jackson Merlot Taylor Peak Bennett Valley (Sonoma)

Kendall-Jackson Napa Mountain (Mt. Veeder)

Tor Kenward Family Cimarossa Vineyard (Howell Mountain)

Tor Kenward Family Mast Vineyard (Yountville)

Kobalt (Napa)

La Sirena (Napa)

Lail Vineyards J. Daniel Cuvée Proprietary Red Wine (Napa)

Larkin (Napa)

Larkin Cabernet Franc (Napa)

Jack Larkin (Napa)

Jack Larkin Merlot (Napa)

Larkmead Estate (Napa)

Larkmead Firebelle Proprietary Red (Napa)

Larkmead LMV Salon Proprietary Red (Napa)

Cliff Lede Cinnamon Stardust Stags Leap (Napa)

Cliff Lede Poetry Stags Leap (Napa)
Cliff Lede Songbook (Napa)
Cliff Lede Stags Leap District (Napa)
Lewelling (Napa)
Lewelling Wight Vineyard (Napa)
Jocelyn Lonen (Napa)
Jocelyn Lonen Cabernet Franc
    Reserve (Napa)
Jocelyn Lonen Founder's Reserve (Napa)
Jocelyn Lonen Reserve (Napa)
Marston Family Vineyard (Napa)
Maybach Materium (Napa)
McCauley Beckstoffer To-Kalon Vineyard
    (Oakville)
Philip Melka Metisse Proprietary Red
    Wine (Napa)
Merus (Napa)
Robert Mondavi Reserve (Napa)
Mount Eden Estate (Santa Cruz)
Mount Eden Old Vine Reserve (Santa Cruz)
Newton Cabernet Sauvignon (Napa)
Newton Merlot (Napa)
Neyers Ame Proprietary Red (Conn Valley)
Neyers Merlot Neyers Ranch (Conn Valley)
Neyers, Neyers Ranch (Conn Valley)
On the Edge Cabernet Franc Frediani
    Vineyard (Napa)
Opus One (Napa)
O'Shaughnessy Merlot
    (Howell Mountain)
Pahlmeyer Merlot (Napa)
Palazzo Proprietary Red (Napa)
Paloma Merlot (Spring Mountain)
Paoletti (Napa)
Joseph Phelps Backus Vineyard (Napa)
Pine Ridge (Oakville)
Pine Ridge (Rutherford)
Pine Ridge (Stags Leap District)
Pine Ridge Onyx Proprietary Red
    Wine (Napa)
PlumpJack Estate (Oakville)
PreVail Mountain Winery Back 40
    (Alexander Valley)
PreVail Mountain Winery West Face
    (Alexander Valley)
Pride Mountain Cabernet Franc (Napa)
Pride Mountain Vineyards (Napa)
Ramey (Napa)
Ramey Diamond Mountain (Napa)
Realm The Absurd (Napa)
Realm The Bard (Napa)

Realm Beckstoffer Dr. Crane Vineyard
    (Napa)
Realm Beckstoffer To-Kalon Vineyard
    (Oakville)
Realm Farella Vineyard (Napa)
Realm The Tempest (Napa)
Reverie Diamond Mountain (Napa)
Reverie Special Reserve Proprietary Red
    Wine (Napa)
Roy Estate (Napa)
Roy Estate Proprietary Red (Napa)
Rudd Estate Mt. Veeder Estate (Napa)
Rudd Estate Oakville Estate Proprietary
    Red (Napa)
Rusten Family Vineyards (Napa)
Rusten Family Vineyards La Maestra
    (Napa)
Rusten Family Vineyards Stagecoach
    Vineyard (Napa)
Saddleback Cellars Venge Family Reserve
    Merlot (Napa)
Sage (Napa)
St. Clement (Napa)
St. Clement Armstrong Ranch
    (Diamond Mountain)
St. Clement Oroppas Proprietary Red
    (Napa)
St. Clement Star Vineyard (Rutherford)
St. Clement Steinhauer Ranch
    (Howell Mountain)
Sbragia Family Vineyards Andolsen
    (Dry Creek)
Sbragia Family Vineyards Cimarossa
    Vineyard (Howell Mountain)
Scherrer Winery Scherrer Vineyard Estate
    (Alexander Valley)
Seavey Caravina (Napa)
Selene Chesler Proprietary Red (Napa)
Shafer Merlot (Napa)
Silverado Limited Reserve (Napa)
Silverado Solo (Stags Leap District)
Simi Reserve (Sonoma)
Snowden Reserve (Napa)
Snowden The Ranch (Napa)
Château Souverain Winemaker's Reserve
    (Sonoma)
Staglin Estate (Rutherford)
Staglin Ineo Proprietary Red (Rutherford)
Stag's Leap Wine Cellars The Leap Estate
    Reserve (Stags Leap District)
Stewart (Napa)

Stonefly Cabernet Franc (Napa)
Switchback Ridge Merlot Peterson Family
   Vineyard (Napa)
2480 Hollywood & Vine (Napa)
Jean-Louis Vermeil Frediani
   Vineyard (Napa)
Viader Proprietary Red Wine (Napa)

Vine Cliff Cellars (Napa)
Vineyard 29 Aida Vineyard (Napa)
Vineyard 29 Cru Proprietary Red
   Wine (Napa)
Winter (Napa)
Wolf Family Vineyards Cabernet
   Franc (Napa)

⋆ ⋆ ⋆ (GOOD)

Ahlgren (Santa Cruz)
Ahlgren Bates Ranch (Santa Cruz)
Alexander Valley (Sonoma)
Amizetta Vineyards (Napa)
Arietta (Napa)
Atalon Madrona Ranch (Napa)
Aubert Proprietary Red Lucia Abreu
   Vineyard (Howell Mountain)
Bacio Divino Cloudy's Vineyard (Napa)
Bacio Divino Janzen Vineyard (Napa)
Barnett Spring Mountain (Napa)
Beaulieu Cabernet Sauvignon Georges de
   Latour Private Reserve (Napa)
Benziger (Glen Ellen)
Benziger Tribute (Glen Ellen)
Blackjack Ranch Harmonie (Santa Barbara)
Blackjack Ranch Merlot (Santa Barbara)
Cain Cellars Cain Five Proprietary Red
   Wine (Napa)
Cakebread Cellars Benchland Select (Napa)
Cakebread Cellars Three Sisters (Napa)
Caymus (Napa)
Chalk Hill (Sonoma)
Château Chevalier Spring Mountain (Napa)
Chimney Rock (Napa)
Clark-Claudon (Napa)
B. R. Cohn Olive Hill Vineyard (Sonoma)
Constant Cabernet Franc Diamond
   Mountain (Napa)
Constant Diamond Mountain (Napa)
Corison (Napa)
Cosentino (Napa)
Cuvaison (Napa)
Dry Creek Meritage (Sonoma)
Duckhorn (Napa)
Duckhorn Estate (Napa)
Duckhorn Merlot (Napa)
Duckhorn Merlot Estate (Napa)
Duckhorn Patzimaro Vineyard
   Estate (Napa)
Eagles Trace (Napa)

Eagles Trace Merlot (Napa)
Elyse Morisoli Vineyard (Napa)
Ferrari-Carano (Sonoma)
Ferrari-Carano Reserve Proprietary Red
   Wine (Sonoma)
Fisher Cameron Proprietary Red (Napa)
Fisher Unity (Napa)
Flora Springs (Napa)
Flora Springs Holy Smoke Vineyard
   (Napa)
Flora Springs Wild Boar Pope
   Valley (Napa)
Robert Foley Merlot (Napa)
Foxen (Santa Ynez)
Franciscan Meritage Oakville Estate (Napa)
Franciscan Oakville Estate (Napa)
Frazier (Napa)
Freemark Abbey (Napa)
Grayson Cellars (California)
Grgich Hills Merlot (Napa)
Groth Reserve (Napa)
Hartwell Stags Leap (Napa)
Havens Wine Cellars Merlot (Napa)
Heitz (Napa)
Heitz Bella Oaks (Napa)
Heitz Martha's Vineyard (Napa)
Hess Collection (Napa)
Hess Collection Reserve (Napa)
Honig (Napa)
Honig Bartolucci Vineyard (Napa)
Johnson-Turnbull (Napa)
Johnson-Turnbull Vineyard Selection 67
Jordan (Sonoma)
Judd's Hill (Napa)
Justin Isosceles Proprietary Red Wine
   (Paso Robles)
W. S. Keyes Merlot (Napa)
La Jota (Napa)
La Jota Anniversary Cuvée (Napa)
La Jota Cabernet Franc (Napa)
Laurel Glen (Sonoma)
Mantra (Alexander Valley)

Marietta (Sonoma)
McCauley (Napa)
Merryvale Profile Proprietary Red
  Wine (Napa)
Peter Michael L'Esprit des Pavots
  (Knight's Valley)
Robert Mondavi Napa (Napa)
Robert Mondavi Oakville Unfiltered
  (Napa)
Château Montelena (Napa)
Monticello Cellars Corley Reserve (Napa)
Monticello Cellars Jefferson Cuvée (Napa)
Mount Eden (Santa Clara)
Murphy-Goode Merlot (Sonoma)
Palmaz (Napa)
Pelton House (Knight's Valley)
Pelton House Merlot (Knight's Valley)
Joseph Phelps (Napa)
Pine Ridge Howell Mountain (Napa)
Pine Ridge Merlot (Napa)
Pine Ridge Rutherford Cuvée (Napa)
Pine Ridge Stags Leap District (Napa)
PlumpJack Estate (Napa)
Rubicon Cask Cabernet (Rutherford)
Rubicon Estate (Rutherford)
Rubicon Proprietary Red Wine (Napa)
Rusten Family Cuvée Simone
Rutherford Hill (Napa)
Rutherford Hill Rhiannon Proprietary
  Red (Napa)
Saddleback Cellars (Napa)
St. Francis Merlot Reserve (Sonoma)
St. Francis Reserve (Sonoma)
St. Jean Cinq Cepages Proprietary Red
  Wine (Sonoma)
St. Jean Estate (Sonoma)
St. Jean Merlot Reserve (Sonoma)
Selene Merlot (Napa)
Selene Merlot Frediani Vineyard (Napa)

Silver Oak (Alexander Valley)
Silver Oak (Napa)
Silverado (Napa)
Simi (Sonoma)
Château Souverain (Sonoma)
Château Souverain Merlot (Sonoma)
Spottswoode Lyndenhurst (Napa)
Spring Mountain Estate Miravalle
  Vineyard (Napa)
Stag's Leap Wine Cellars (Napa)
Stag's Leap Wine Cellars Cask 23
  Proprietary Red Wine (Napa)
Stag's Leap Wine Cellars Fay Vineyard
  (Napa)
Stag's Leap Wine Cellars Stag's Leap
  Vineyard (Napa)
Stonestreet Christopher's Vineyard
  (Alexander Valley)
Summers Adrianna's Cuvée (Napa)
Summers Estate (Napa)
Summers Merlot Reserve (Knight's Valley)
Titus (Napa)
Titus Cabernet Franc (Napa)
Titus Reserve (Napa)
Von Strasser Diamond Mountain (Napa)
Von Strasser Diamond Mountain Reserve
  (Napa)
Von Strasser Estate Vineyard Diamond
  Mountain (Napa)
Von Strasser Post Vineyard Diamond
  Mountain (Napa)
Von Strasser Rainin Vineyard Diamond
  Mountain (Napa)
White Rock Claret Proprietary Red
  Wine (Napa)
Whitehall Lane Leonardi Vineyard
  (Napa)
Whitehall Lane Morisoli (Napa)
Whitehall Lane Reserve (Napa)

CALIFORNIA'S BEST PRODUCERS OF CHARDONNAY

★ ★ ★ ★ ★ (OUTSTANDING)

L'Angevin Pierson Meyer (not yet named)
  (Russian River)
Arrowood Reserve Spéciale Michel Beringer
  Private Reserve (Napa)
Aubert Lauren Vineyard (Sonoma Coast)
Aubert Reuling Vineyard (Sonoma Coast)
Aubert Ritchie Vineyard (Sonoma Coast)
Beringer Sbragia Select (Napa)

Brewer-Clifton Marcella's Vineyard
  (Santa Maria)
Brewer-Clifton Sweeney Canyon
  (Santa Maria)
Chasseur Green Acres Hill (Sonoma Coast)
DuMOL Chloe (Russian River)
DuMOL Isobel Green Valley
  (Russian River)

Fisher Whitney's Vineyard (Sonoma)
Walter Hansel Cuvée Alyce (Russian River)
Kalin Cellars Cuvée LD (Sonoma)
Kalin Cellars Cuvée W (Livermore)
Kistler Vineyards Durell Vineyard
  (Sonoma)
Kistler Vineyards Kistler Estate (Sonoma)
Kistler Vineyards Kistler Vineyard Cuvée
  Cathleen (Sonoma)
Kistler Vineyards McCrea Vineyard
  (Sonoma)
Kistler Vineyards Stone Flat Vineyard
  (Sonoma Coast)
Kistler Vineyards Vine Hill Road
  (Russian River)
Kongsgaard (Napa)
Kongsgaard The Judge (Napa)
Marcassin Marcassin Vineyard
  (Sonoma Coast)
Marcassin Three Sisters Vineyard
  (Sonoma Coast)
Peter Michael Belle Côte (Sonoma)
Peter Michael Cuvée Indigène (Sonoma)
Peter Michael Mon Plaisir (Sonoma)

Peter Michael Point Rouge (Sonoma)
Mount Eden Vineyards Santa Cruz Estate
  (Santa Clara)
Newton Unfiltered (Napa)
Pahlmeyer (Napa)
Pahlmeyer (Sonoma Coast)
Ramey Hyde Vineyard (Carneros)
Ramey Ritchie Vineyard (Russian River)
J. Rochioli Allen Vineyard (Sonoma)
J. Rochioli River Block (Sonoma)
J. Rochioli Rochioli Vineyard
  (Russian River)
J. Rochioli South River Vineyard
  (Sonoma)
J. Rochioli Sweetwater Vineyard
  (Russian River)
Talley Vineyards Rincon Vineyard (Arroyo
  Grande)
Talley Vineyards Rosemary's Vineyard
  (Arroyo Grande)
Williams-Selyem Allen Vineyard
  (Russian River)
Williams-Selyem Hawk Hill Vineyard
  (Russian River)

* * * * (EXCELLENT)

Anderson's Conn Valley (Napa)
l'Angevin Charles Heintz Vineyard
  (Sonoma Coast)
l'Angevin Laughlin (Russian River)
Arrowood (Sonoma)
Bjornstad Porter Bass Vineyard
  (Sonoma Coast)
Bjornstad Ritchie Vineyard (Russian River)
Breggo Cellars Savoy Vineyard
  (Anderson Valley)
Calera (Mt. Harlan)
Chalk Hill Chardonnay Founder's
  Block (Sonoma)
Chasseur Durell Vineyard (Sonoma)
Chasseur Lorenzo Vineyard (Russian River)
Del Dotto Cinghiale Vineyard
  (Sonoma Coast)
DuMOL (Russian River)
DuMOL Clare (Carneros)
DuNah Dedee's Estate (Sonoma Coast)
DuNah Tre Cuvée (Sonoma Coast)
El Molino (Rutherford)
Failla (Sonoma Coast)
Failla Keefer Ranch (Russian River)
Ferrari-Carano (Sonoma)

Ferrari-Carano Reserve (Sonoma)
Fisher Vineyards Mountain Estate Vineyard
  (Sonoma)
Fisher Vineyards Whitney's Vineyard Estate
  (Sonoma)
Forman (Napa)
Foxen (Santa Ynez)
Gainey Limited Selection (Santa Ynez)
Walter Hansel Cahill Lane (Russian River)
Walter Hansel North Slope Vineyard
  (Russian River)
Walter Hansel Walter Hansel Vineyard
  (Russian River)
Hanzell Vineyards (Sonoma)
Hartford Family Winery Four Hearts
  (Russian River)
Hartford Family Winery Stone Côte
  (Sonoma Coast)
Paul Hobbs (Russian River)
Paul Hobbs Richard Dinner Vineyard
  Cuvée Agustina (Sonoma)
Paul Hobbs Ritchie Vineyard (Sonoma)
Paul Hobbs Ulises Valdez Vineyard
  (Russian River)
Paul Hobbs Walker Station (Russian River)

Kalin Cellars Cuvée CH (Sonoma)
Kalin Cellars Cuvée DD (Marin)
Kalin Cellars Cuvée LD (Sonoma)
Robert Keenan (Spring Mountain)
Kendall-Jackson Highland Estates Camelot
  Vineyard (Santa Maria)
Tor Kenward Family Cuvée Torchiana
  (Napa)
Tor Kenward Family Molly-Hudson
  Vineyard (Carneros)
Tor Kenward Family Tor Durell Vineyard
  (Sonoma Coast)
Kesner (Napa)
Kistler Dutton Ranch (Russian River)
Kistler Hudson (Carneros)
Landmark Armagh (Sonoma Coast)
Landmark Damaris Reserve Sangiacomo
  Vineyard (Carneros)
Landmark Lorenzo Vineyard
  (Russian River)
Landmark Overlook (California)
Levendi (Carneros)
Littorai Mays Canyon (Sonoma)
Littorai Thieriot Vineyard (Sonoma)
Jocelyn Lonen (Carneros)
Jocelyn Lonen Reserve (Carneros)
Jocelyn Lonen Reserve (Russian River)
Longoria (Santa Barbara)
Martinelli Charles Ranch (Sonoma Coast)
Martinelli Martinelli Road (Sonoma Coast)
Martinelli Three Sisters Vineyard Sea Ridge
  Meadow (Sonoma Coast)
Martinelli Woolsey Road (Sonoma Coast)
Martinelli Zio Tony Ranch (Russian River)
Merryvale Silhouette (Napa)
Robert Mondavi Reserve (Napa)
Château Montelena (Napa)
Newton (Napa)
Neyers (Carneros)
Neyers (Napa)
Neyers El Novillero (Carneros)
Neyers Thieriot (Sonoma Coast)
Ojai Talley Reserve (Arroyo Grande)
Fess Parker Marcella's Vineyard
  (Santa Barbara)

Patz and Hall (Napa)
Patz and Hall Alder Springs (Mendocino)
Patz and Hall Carr Vineyard (Napa)
Patz and Hall Dutton Ranch (Sonoma)
Patz and Hall Hyde Vineyard (Carneros)
Pine Ridge Dijon Clones (Napa)
Pine Ridge Epitome (Napa)
Château Potelle VGS Mount Veeder
  (Napa)
Radio-Coteau Savoy (Anderson Valley)
Ramey Hudson Vineyard (Carneros)
Rancho Sisquoc Estate (Santa Barbara)
J. Rochioli Estate (Russian River)
Rudd Estate Bacigalupi Vineyard
  (Russian River)
Château St. Jean Belle Terre Vineyard
  (Sonoma)
Château St. Jean Reserve (Sonoma)
Château St. Jean Robert Young Vineyard
  (Alexander Valley)
Saintsbury Reserve (Carneros)
Sanford Sanford & Benedict Vineyard
  (Santa Barbara)
Sbragia Family Vineyards Gamble
  Ranch (Napa)
Scherrer Winery Helfer Vineyard
  (Russian River)
Shafer (Napa)
Shafer Red Shoulder Ranch (Napa)
Signorello Vineyards (Napa)
Signorello Vineyards Founder's Reserve
  (Napa)
Silverado Limited Reserve (Napa)
Château Souverain single-vineyard cuvées
  (Sonoma)
Staglin Family Vineyard Estate
  (Rutherford)
Stonestreet Broken Road (Alexander Valley)
Stonestreet Red Point (Alexander Valley)
Stonestreet Upper Barn (Alexander Valley)
Stony Hill (Napa)
2480 Hollywood & Vine (Napa)
Williams-Selyem Heintz Vineyard
  (Russian River)
Robert Young Estate (Alexander Valley)

* * * (GOOD)

Acacia (Napa)
Adler Fels (Sonoma)
Arcadian Bien Nacido (Santa Barbara)
Arcadian Sleepy Hollow (Monterey)

Au Bon Climat (Santa Barbara)
Au Bon Climat Bien Nacido (Santa Barbara)
Au Bon Climat Sanford & Benedict
  Vineyard (Santa Barbara)

Au Bon Climat Talley Vineyard
  (Santa Barbara)
Babcock (Santa Barbara)
Beaulieu Carneros Reserve (Napa)
Belvedere Wine Company (Sonoma)
Benziger (Sonoma)
Beringer (Napa)
Bernardus (Monterey)
Cain Cellars (Napa)
Calera Central Coast (California)
Chalk Hill (Sonoma)
Clos du Bois Barrel-Fermented (Sonoma)
Clos du Bois Calcaire (Sonoma)
Clos du Bois Flintwood (Sonoma)
B. R. Cohn Olive Hill Vineyard (Sonoma)
Cuvaison (Napa)
A Donkey and Goat Brosseau Vineyard
  (Chalone)
Edna Valley (San Luis Obispo)
Far Niente (Napa)
Gary Farrell (Sonoma)
Fetzer Sundial (California)
Franciscan (Napa)
Frog's Leap (Napa)
Gallo Estate (Sonoma)
Grayson Cellars (California)
Grgich Hills (Napa)
Grgich Hills Carneros Selection (Napa)
Handley (Dry Creek)
Hanna (Sonoma)
Hirsch Vineyards (Sonoma Coast)
Husch Vineyards (Mendocino)
Iron Horse Vineyards (Sonoma)
Kendall-Jackson Vintner's Reserve
  (California)
Kistler (Sonoma)
Charles Krug Carneros Reserve (Napa)
La Crema (California)
Lolonis (Mendocino)
Long Vineyards (Napa)

MacRostie (Carneros)
Matanzas Creek (Sonoma)
Merryvale Reserve (Napa)
El Molino (Napa)
Robert Mondavi (Napa)
Morgan (Monterey)
Navarro Vineyards (Mendocino)
Fess Parker (Santa Barbara)
Ridge Santa Cruz Mountain (Santa Cruz)
St. Francis (Sonoma)
St. Francis Reserve (Sonoma)
Saintsbury (Carneros)
Sanford (Santa Barbara)
Santa Barbara (Santa Ynez)
Sausal Winery (Sonoma)
Sebastiani single-vineyard cuvées (Sonoma)
Silverado Vineyards (Napa)
Simi Winery (Sonoma)
Simi Winery Reserve (Sonoma)
Sonoma-Loeb (Sonoma)
Château Souverain (Sonoma)
  (since 1990)
Stonestreet (Alexander Valley)
Rodney Strong Chalk Hill (Sonoma)
Summers (Alexander Valley)
Swanson (Napa)
Robert Talbott Diamond T Estate
  (Monterey)
Robert Talbott Estate (Monterey)
Marimar Torres (Sonoma)
Trefethen (Napa)
Truchard (Carneros/Napa)
Vine Cliff Cellars Proprietress Reserve
  (Napa)
Wente Brothers Reserve (Alameda)
  (since 1988)
Wente Brothers Wente Vineyard (Alameda)
  (since 1988)
Whitehall Lane Reserve (Napa)
ZD (Napa)

CALIFORNIA'S BEST PRODUCERS OF PINOT NOIR

* * * * * (OUTSTANDING)

Aubert UV Vineyard (Sonoma Coast)
Brewer-Clifton (Santa Maria Hills)
Brewer-Clifton Clos Pepe (Santa Rita Hills)
Brewer-Clifton Julia's (Santa Ynez)
Brewer-Clifton Melville (Santa Rita Hills)
DuMol Finn (Russian River)
DuMol Ryan Green Valley (Russian River)

Walter Hansel Cuvée Alyce (Russian River)
Hartford Court Arrendel Vineyard
  (Russian River)
Hartford Court Dutton Ranch/Sanchietti
  Vineyard (Russian River)
Hartford Court Marin Vineyard
  (Marin County)

Hartford Court Sevens Bench Vineyard (Napa/Carneros)

Hartford Court Velvet Sisters Vineyard (Anderson Valley)

Kistler Bodega Headlands Cuvée Elizabeth (Sonoma Coast)

Kistler Kistler Vineyard (Russian River)

Kistler Kistler Vineyard Cuvée Catherine Occidental Station (Sonoma)

Marcassin Blue Slide Ridge (Sonoma Coast)

Marcassin Marcassin Vineyard (Sonoma Coast)

Marcassin Three Sisters–Sea Ridge Meadow Vineyard (Sonoma Coast)

Martinelli Blue Slide Ridge (Sonoma Coast)

J. Rochioli Reserve East Block (Russian River)

J. Rochioli Reserve Estate West Block (Sonoma)

J. Rochioli Reserve Little Hill Vineyard (Russian River)

Talley Vineyards Rincon Estate (Arroyo Grande)

Talley Vineyards Rosemary's Vineyard (Arroyo Grande)

Williams-Selyem Precious Mountain (Sonoma Coast)

* * * * (EXCELLENT)

Ancien Poplar Vineyard (Russian River)

Ancien Steiner Vineyard (Sonoma Mountains)

L'Angevin Stage Vineyard (Sonoma)

Bjornstad Hellenthal Vineyard (Sonoma Coast)

Bjornstad Vandercamp Vineyard (Sonoma Coast)

Black Kite Anderson Valley (Carneros)

Breggo Cellars (Anderson Valley)

Breggo Cellars Donnelly Creek Vineyard (Anderson Valley)

Breggo Cellars Ferrington Creek Vineyard (Anderson Valley)

Breggo Cellars Savoy Vineyard (Anderson Valley)

Calera Jensen Vineyard (San Benito)

Calera Mills Vineyard (San Benito)

Calera Reed Vineyard (San Benito)

Calera Selleck Vineyard (San Benito)

Capiaux Cellars Chimera Vineyard (Sonoma Coast)

Capiaux Cellars Freestone Hill Vineyard (Russian River)

Capiaux Cellars Widdoes Vineyard (Russian River)

Capiaux Cellars Wilson Vineyard (Sonoma Coast)

Chasseur Blank Road Vineyard (Sonoma Coast)

Chasseur Freestone Station (Russian River)

Chasseur Sexton Vineyard (Russian River)

Chasseur Sylvia's (Russian River)

Chasseur Twin Hill (Sonoma Coast)

Dehlinger Estate (Russian River)

Dehlinger Goldridge Vineyard (Russian River)

Del Dotto Cinghiale Vineyard (Sonoma Coast)

DuMOL (Russian River)

DuMOL Aidan Green Valley (Russian River)

DuNah Estate (Russian River)

DuNah Sangiacomo Vineyard (Sonoma Coast)

El Molino (Rutherford)

Étude Heirloom (Carneros)

Étude Temblor (Carneros)

Failla (Sonoma Coast)

Failla Estate (Sonoma Coast)

Failla Hirsch Vineyard (Sonoma Coast)

Failla Keefer Ranch (Russian River)

Failla Occidental Ridge (Sonoma Coast)

Failla Pearl Essence Vineyard (Sonoma Coast)

Failla Peay Vineyard (Sonoma Coast)

Adrian Fog Numbers (Sonoma Coast)

Adrian Fog Oppenlander Vineyard (Mendocino)

Adrian Fog Savoy Vineyard (Anderson Valley)

Adrian Fog Two Sisters Vineyard (Russian River)

Foxen Julia's Vineyard (Santa Ynez)

Goldeneye The Narrows Vineyard (Anderson Valley)

Walter Hansel Winery (Russian River)

Walter Hansel Winery Cahill Lane (Russian River)

Walter Hansel Winery The North Slope
(Russian River)

Walter Hansel Winery The South Slope
(Russian River)

Walter Hansel Winery Three Rows
(Russian River)

Hartford Family Winery Arrendell
Vineyard (Russian River)

Hartford Family Winery Far Coast
Vineyard (Sonoma Coast)

Hartford Family Winery Hailey's Block
Arrendell Vineyard (Green Valley)

Hartford Family Winery Jennifer's–
Marshall Vineyard (Russian River)

Hartford Family Winery Sevens Bench
Vineyard (Carneros)

Hartford Family Winery Velvet Sisters
(Anderson Valley)

Paul Hobbs (Russian River)

Paul Hobbs Hyde Vineyard (Carneros)

Paul Hobbs Lindsay Estate (Russian River)

Paul Hobbs Ulises Valdez Vineyard
(Russian River)

Kalin Cellars Cuvée DD (Sonoma)

Kalin Cellars Cuvée JL (Sonoma)

Kistler Camp Meeting Ridge (Sonoma)

Landmark Kanzler (Sonoma Coast)

Littorai One Acre Vineyard (Anderson
Valley)

Littorai Savoy Vineyard (Anderson Valley)

Martinelli Bondi Home Ranch Water
Trough Vineyard (Russian River)

Martinelli Three Sisters Vineyard Sea Ridge
Meadow (Sonoma Coast)

Martinelli Zio Tony Ranch (Russian River)

Peter Michael Le Moulin Rouge (Santa
Lucia Highlands)

Robert Mondavi Reserve (Napa)

Morlet Family Estate Coteaux Nobles
(Sonoma Coast)

Morlet Family Estate En Famille (Sonoma
Coast)

Morlet Family Estate Joli Coeur (Sonoma
Coast)

Ojai Bien Nacido Vineyard (Santa Barbara)

Ojai Pisoni Vineyard (Santa Lucia)

Patz and Hall Hyde Vineyard (Carneros)

Patz and Hall Pisoni Vineyard (Santa Lucia
Highlands)

Joseph Phelps Freestone (Sonoma Coast)

Radio-Coteau Alberigi (Russian River)

Radio-Coteau La Neblina (Sonoma Coast)

Radio-Coteau Savoy (Anderson Valley)

Radio-Coteau Terra Neuma
(Sonoma Coast)

J. Rochioli Estate (Sonoma)

Scherrer Winery (Russian River)

Talley Vineyards Stone Corral Vineyard
(Arroyo Grande)

Williams-Selyem Allen Vineyard
(Russian River)

Williams-Selyem Coastlands Vineyard
(Sonoma Coast)

Williams-Selyem Cohn Vineyard (Sonoma)

Williams-Selyem Flax Vineyard
(Russian River)

Williams-Selyem Hirsch Vineyard (Sonoma
Coast)

Williams-Selyem Olivet Lane Vineyard
(Russian River)

Williams-Selyem Riverblock Vineyard
(Russian River)

Williams-Selyem Rochioli Vineyard
(Sonoma)

Williams-Selyem Westside Road Neighbors
(Russian River)

★ ★ ★ (GOOD)

Au Bon Climat La Bauge Au Dessus
Bien Nacido Vineyard (Santa
Barbara)

Au Bon Climat Sanford & Benedict
Vineyard (Santa Barbara)

Au Bon Climat Talley Vineyard
(Arroyo Grande)

Dain Wines American Beauty Amber Ridge
(Russian River)

Dain Wines Dandy Brosseau Vineyard
(Chalone)

Dain Wines Rebel Rancho Ontiveros
(Santa Maria Valley)

Dain Wines Savage Juliet (Anderson Valley)

Dehlinger (Sonoma)

Donum (Carneros)

Drew Fog-Eater (Anderson Valley)

Drew Weir Vineyard (Yorkville Highlands)

Eagles Trace Valhalla Vineyard (Napa)

Étude (Carneros)

Étude Deer Camp Vineyard (Carneros)

Foxen (Santa Ynez)

Harrington Brosseau Vineyards (Chalone)
Harrington Gap's Crown Vineyard
(Sonoma Coast)
Harrington Iund Vineyard (Carneros)
Harrington Wild Horse Valley (Napa)
Harrington Wiley Vineyard (Anderson
Valley)
Hirsch Vineyards (Sonoma Coast)
Hirsch Vineyards The Bohan-Dilon Pinot
Noir (Sonoma Coast)
The Hitching Post (Santa Maria)
The Hitching Post Highliner (Santa
Barbara)
The Hitching Post Sanford & Benedict
Vineyard (Santa Barbara)
Ketcham Estate (Russian River)
La Crema (Russian River)
La Crema Ahmen Vineyard (Carneros)
La Crema Falk Vineyard (Anderson Valley)
Landmark Grand Detour (Sonoma Coast)
Landmark Solomon Hills (Santa Barbara)
Meridian Reserve (Santa Barbara)

Robert Mondavi (Napa)
Mount Eden Estate (Santa Cruz)
Morgan (Monterey)
Navarro (Mendocino)
Pahlmeyer (Sonoma Coast)
School House Spring Mountain
(Napa)
W. H. Smith (Sonoma Coast)
W. H. Smith Marimar Estate Vineyard
(Sonoma Coast)
W. H. Smith Maritime (Sonoma Coast)
W. H. Smith Umino Vineyard
(Sonoma Coast)
Talley (Arroyo Grande)
Williams-Selyem Bucher Vineyard
(Russian River)
Williams-Selyem Ferrington Vineyard
(Anderson Valley)
Williams-Selyem Peay Vineyard
(Sonoma Coast)
Williams-Selyem Weir Vineyard
(Yorkville Highlands)

CALIFORNIA'S RHONE RANGERS

* * * * * (OUTSTANDING)

Alban Vineyard Syrah Lorraine
Alban Vineyard Syrah Pandora's
Alban Vineyard Syrah Reserve
Alban Vineyard Syrah Seymour's Vineyard
Araujo Estate Syrah Eisele Vineyard
Carlisle Petite Sirah
Carlisle Syrah (Dry Creek)
Carlisle Syrah (Russian River)
Carlisle Syrah Cardiac Hill
Carlisle Syrah James Berry Vineyard
Carlisle Syrah Papa's Block
Carlisle Two Acres (blend)
Clos Mimi Syrah Shell Creek
Colgin IX Syrah Estate
Copain Syrah Garys' Vineyard
Copain Syrah James Berry Vineyard
DuMOL Syrah Eddie's Patch
JC Cellars Syrah Buffalo Hill Rockpile
Vineyard
JC Cellars Syrah Philary Vineyard
Kongsgaard Roussanne/Viognier
Kongsgaard Syrah Hudson Vineyard
Lagier-Meredith Syrah
Lewis Syrah
Ojai Vineyard Syrah Bien Nacido

Ojai Vineyard Syrah Roll Ranch
Ojai Vineyard Syrah Stolpman Vineyard
Ojai Vineyard Syrah Thompson Vineyard
Pax Cellars Syrah Cuvée Christine
Pax Cellars Syrah Kobler Family Vineyard
Green Valley
Pax Cellars Syrah Obsidian
Pax Cellars Syrah Richards Family
Vineyard
Ridge York Creek Petite Sirah
Rudd Estate Edge Hill Mixed Blacks
Shafer Vineyards Relentless
Sine Qua Non Grenache/Syrah (the name
changes with each vintage)
Sine Qua Non Roussanne and Chardonnay
blends (the name changes with each
vintage)
Sine Qua Non Syrah (the name changes
with each vintage)
Switchback Ridge Petite Sirah Peterson
Family Vineyard
Sean Thackrey Orion (Syrah)
Turley Cellars Petite Sirah Aida Vineyard
Turley Cellars Petite Sirah Hayne
Vineyard

Turley Cellars Petite Sirah Library Vineyard

Turley Cellars Petite Sirah Rattlesnake Ridge

* * * * (EXCELLENT)

Arietta Variation One (Syrah/Merlot)
Arnot-Roberts Syrah Alder Springs
Arnot-Roberts Syrah Griffin's Lair
Arnot-Roberts Hudson Vineyard
Arrowood Syrah Saralee's Vineyard
Arrowood Viognier Saralee's Vineyard
L'Aventure Optimus Syrah/Cabernet Blend
Beckmen Grenache Purisima Mountain
Black Bart Bride Proprietary White Wine
Black Bart Marsanne Stagecoach Vineyard
Black Bart Syrah Stagecoach Vineyard
Carlisle Syrah Pelkan Ranch
Carlisle Two Acres
Carver-Sutro Petite Sirah Palisade Vineyard
Copain Roussanne James Berry Vineyard
Copain Syrah Brosseau Vineyard
Copain Syrah Harrison Clark
Copain Syrah Hawke's Butte
Copain Syrah McDowell Valley Vineyard
Copain Syrah Thompson Vineyard
Corté Riva Petite Sirah
Culler Wines Napa
Culler Wines Syrah Griffin's Lair Vineyard
Culler Wines Syrah Sawi Vineyard
Dehlinger Syrah Estate
Dehlinger Syrah Goldridge Vineyard
A Donkey and Goat Syrah Fenaughty Vineyard
Dry Stack Syrah Marie's Block
DuMOL Syrah
DuMOL Viognier Lia
Failla Syrah Estate
Failla Syrah Phoenix Ranch
Ferrari-Carano Syrah
Fisher Syrah Hidden Terrace
Flanagan Family Vineyards Syrah
Robert Foley Petite Sirah
Foxen Syrah Carhartt
Foxen Syrah Morehouse
Havens Wine Cellars Black and Blue Proprietary Red
Havens Wine Cellars Syrah Hudson Vineyard
Paul Hobbs Syrah Kick Ranch Vineyard
Jaffurs Syrah Bien Nacido Vineyard
Jaffurs Syrah Melville Vineyard
Jaffurs Syrah Stolpman Vineyard

Jaffurs Syrah Thompson Vineyard
JC Cellars Petite Sirah Frediani Vineyard
JC Cellars Syrah Caldwell Vineyard
JC Cellars Syrah Fess Parker Vineyard
JC Cellars Syrah Rodney's Vineyard
JC Cellars Syrah Ventana Vineyard
Kamen Estate Syrah
Tor Kenward Family Vineyards Tor Rock Grenache Judge Family Vineyard Cuvée Cooper
Tor Kenward Family Vineyards Tor Rock Syrah Hudson Vineyard
Kongsgaard Syrah Hudson Vineyard
Kunin Syrah Santa Rita Hills
Martinelli Syrah Chico's Hill
Martinelli Syrah Lolita Ranch
Morlet Family Estate Syrah Bouquet Garni
Neyers Vineyard Syrah Cuvée d'Honneur
Neyers Vineyard Syrah Hudson Vineyard
Neyers Vineyard Syrah Old Lakeville
Pax Cellars Grenache Dry Stack Vineyard
Pax Cellars Pax Nepenthe Proprietary White Alder Springs Vineyard
Pax Cellars Syrah Alder Springs The Terraces
Pax Cellars Syrah Alder Springs Vineyard
Pax Cellars Syrah Griffin's Lair
Pax Cellars Syrah Lauterbach Hill
Pax Cellars Syrah Cuvée Moriah
Pax Cellars Syrah Walker Vine Hill
Plumpjack Syrah
Radio-Coteau Syrah Cherry Camp
Radio-Coteau Syrah Timbervine
Ramey Syrah
Ramey Syrah Rodger's Creek Vineyard
Renard Syrah Timbervine Ranch
Ridge Grenache Lytton Estate
Ridge Mataro Bridgehead
Ridge Mataro Evangelo Vineyard
Ridge Syrah Lytton Estate
Rosenblum Cellars Petite Sirah Rockpile Vineyard
Signorello Syrah Napa Valley Unfiltered
Sean Thackrey Sirius (Petite Sirah)
Sean Thackrey Taurus (Mourvèdre)
Truchard Syrah

Turley Petite Sirah Pesenti Vineyard
Turley Petite Sirah Rattlesnake Ridge

Turley Petite Sirah Turley Estate
Turley Roussanne Rattlesnake Ridge

* * * (GOOD)

Anderson's Conn Valley Syrah Green Valley
Bonny Doon Le Cigare Volant (blend)
Bonny Doon Clos de Gilroy (Grenache)
Bonny Doon Old Telegram (Mourvèdre)
Constant Syrah Diamond Mountain
Copain Syrah Madder Lake
Dain Wines Syrah Abner Las Madres
  Vineyard
Dain Wines Syrah The Smart Set White
  Hawk Vineyard
A Donkey and Goat Syrah Vieilles Vignes

A Donkey and Goat Three Thirteen
Edmunds St. John Syrah Durell Vineyard
Havens Wine Cellars Syrah
La Sirena Syrah (Napa)
La Sirena Syrah (Santa Ynez)
La Sirena Syrah Barrett Vineyard
Andrew Murray Syrah Hillside Reserve
Pax Wine Cellars Syrah Majik
Radio-Coteau Syrah Las Colinas
Ruduis Syrah
Turley Grenache Pesenti Vineyard

CALIFORNIA'S BEST PRODUCERS OF ITALIAN-INSPIRED VARIETALS— SANGIOVESE, BARBERA, NEBBIOLO

* * * * * / * * * * (OUTSTANDING/EXCELLENT)

None

* * * (GOOD)

Luna Pinot Grigio
Luna Sangiovese Reserve
Palmina Barbera Bien Nacido Vineyard
Palmina Sangiovese Stolpman Vineyard
La Pantera L'Uvaggio di Giacomo
  (various cuvées)

Pride Mountain Vineyards
Saddleback Cellars Venge Family Reserve
  Sangiovese Penny Lane

CALIFORNIA'S BEST PRODUCERS OF SAUVIGNON BLANC AND SÉMILLON AND BLENDS THEREOF

* * * * * (OUTSTANDING)

Araujo Estate Eisele Vineyard (Napa)
Arietta The White Keys (Napa)
Breggo Cellars Sauvignon Blanc Ferrington
  Vineyard
Ferrari-Carano Fumé Blanc Reserve
  (Sonoma)
Iron Horse Cuvée R (Alexander Valley)
Kalin Cellars Sauvignon Blanc Reserve
  (Potter Valley)

Lail Georgia Sauvignon Blanc (Napa)
Peter Michael Sauvignon Blanc l'Apres-
  Midi (California)
Rudd Estate Sauvignon Blanc (Napa)
Château St. Jean Fumé Blanc La Petite
  Étoile (Sonoma)
Spottswoode Sauvignon Blanc (Napa)
Vineyard 29 Sauvignon Blanc
  (Napa)

* * * * (EXCELLENT)

Altamura Sauvignon Blanc (Napa)
Babcock Sauvignon Blanc (Santa Barbara)
Babcock Sauvignon Blanc 11 Oaks Ranch
  (Santa Barbara)
Beringer Alluvium Blanc (Knight's Valley)
Brander Cuvée Nicolas (Santa Ynez)

Cain Cellars Sauvignon Musqué (Napa)
Caymus Conundrum Proprietary White
  Wine (Napa)
Chalk Hill Sauvignon Blanc
  (Sonoma)
Chimney Rock Fumé Blanc (Napa)

Clos du Bois Sauvignon Blanc (Alexander Valley)

Dry Creek Fumé Blanc (Sonoma)

Dry Stack Sauvignon Blanc Rosemary's Block (Bennett Valley)

Duckhorn Vineyards Sauvignon Blanc (Napa)

Flora Springs Sauvignon Blanc Soliloquy (Napa)

Gainey Sauvignon Blanc Limited Selection (Santa Ynez)

Grgich Hills Fumé Blanc Estate (Napa)

Grgich Hills Sauvignon Blanc Essence (Napa)

Handley Cellars Sauvignon Blanc (Dry Creek)

Honig Sauvignon Blanc Reserve (Rutherford)

Husch Sauvignon Blanc (Mendocino)

Juslyn Sauvignon Blanc (Napa)

Cliff Lede Sauvignon Blanc (Napa)

Mason Cellars (Napa)

Robert Mondavi Fumé Blanc (Napa)

Robert Mondavi Fumé Blanc Reserve (Napa)

Morlet Family Estate La Proportion Dorée (Sonoma County)

Murphy-Goode Fumé Blanc Reserve (Sonoma)

Navarro Sauvignon Blanc (Mendocino)

Ojai (California)

J. Rochioli Sauvignon Blanc Estate (Russian River)

Sage Sauvignon Blanc (Napa)

St. Clement Sauvignon Blanc Bale Lane Vineyard (Napa)

Château St. Jean Fumé Blanc (Sonoma)

Château St. Jean Fumé Blanc Lyon Vineyard (Alexander Valley)

Selene Sauvignon Blanc (Napa)

Selene Sauvignon Blanc Hyde Vineyards (Carneros)

Signorello Sauvignon Blanc (Napa)

Signorello Sémillon Barrel Fermented (Napa)

Silverado Sauvignon Blanc Miller Ranch (Yountville)

Simi Sendal Proprietary White Wine (Sonoma)

Snowden Sauvignon Blanc (Napa)

Wolf Family Vineyard Sauvignon Blanc (Napa)

★ ★ ★ (GOOD)

Acacia (Napa)

Adler Fels (Sonoma)

Ahlgren Semillon (Santa Cruz)

Alderbrook Sauvignon Blanc (Sonoma)

Babcock Fathom Proprietary White Wine (Santa Barbara)

Beaulieu Fumé Blanc (Napa)

Bel Arbors Sauvignon Blanc (California)

Bellerose Sauvignon Blanc (Sonoma)

Benziger Fumé Blanc (Sonoma)

Beringer Sauvignon Blanc (Napa)

Bernardus Sauvignon Blanc (Monterey)

Brutocao Sauvignon Blanc (Mendocino)

Buena Vista Fumé Blanc (Lake)

Buttonwood Farm Sauvignon Blanc (Santa Ynez)

Carmenet Meritage Proprietary White Wine (Sonoma)

De Loach Fumé Blanc (Sonoma)

De Lorimer Spectrum Estate (Alexander Valley)

Duckhorn Sauvignon Blanc (Napa)

Ferrari-Carano Fumé Blanc (Sonoma)

Fetzer Fumé Blanc (Mendocino)

Fetzer Sauvignon Blanc Barrel Select (Mendocino)

Field Stone Sauvignon Blanc (Sonoma)

Geyser Peak Sauvignon Blanc (Sonoma)

Geyser Peak Semchard (Sonoma)

Grgich Hills Fumé Blanc (Napa)

Guenoc Winery Langtry Meritage (Lake County)

Louis Honig Cellars Sauvignon Blanc (Napa)

Husch Vineyards Sauvignon Blanc (Mendocino)

Kendall-Jackson Vintner's Reserve Sauvignon Blanc (California)

Konocti Fumé Blanc (Lake County)

Larkmead Sauvignon Blanc (Napa)

Lolonis Fumé Blanc (Mendocino)

Monterey Vineyards Classic Sauvignon Blanc (California)

Morgan Sauvignon Blanc (Monterey)

Napa Ridge Sauvignon Blanc (Napa)
Page Mill Sauvignon Blanc (San Luis
  Obispo)
Joseph Phelps Sauvignon Blanc (Napa)
Preston Vineyards Cuvée de Fumé
  (Dry Creek)

Sanford Sauvignon Blanc (Santa Barbara)
Seventy-Five Sauvignon Blanc (Napa)
Stag's Leap Sauvignon Blanc Rancho
  Chimiles (Napa)
Ivan Tamas Fumé Blanc (Livermore)
William Wheeler Fumé Blanc (Sonoma)

CALIFORNIA'S BEST PRODUCERS OF ZINFANDEL

* * * * * (OUTSTANDING)

Robert Bialé Aldo's Vineyard (Napa)
Robert Bialé Monte Rosso (Sonoma)
Robert Bialé Old Crane Ranch (Napa)
Robert Bialé Zappa (Napa)
Carlisle Bacchi Ranch (Dry Creek)
Carlisle Carlisle Vineyard (Russian River)
Carlisle Carlo's Ranch (Russian River)
Carlisle Montafi Ranch (Russian River)
Carlisle Pietro's Ranch (Russian River)
Carlisle Rossi Ranch (Sonoma)
Carlisle Tom Feeney Ranch (Russian River)
Hartford Court Dina's Vineyard
  (Russian River)
Hartford Court Fanucchi-Wood Road
  (Russian River)
Hartford Court Hartford Vineyard
  (Russian River)
Martinelli Jackass Hill (Russian River)

Martinelli Jackass Vineyard
  (Russian River)
Ridge Geyserville Proprietary Red Wine
  (primarily Zinfandel) (Sonoma)
Ridge Lytton Springs (Sonoma)
Storybook Mountain Reserve (Napa)
Turley Cellars Dragon Vineyard
  (Howell Mountain)
Turley Cellars Hayne Vineyard (Napa)
Turley Cellars Moore Vineyard (Napa)
Turley Cellars Vineyard 101 (Alexander
  Valley)
Williams-Selyem Bacigalupi Vineyard
  (Russian River)
Williams-Selyem Feeney Vineyard
  (Russian River)
Williams-Selyem Forchini Vineyard
  (Russian River)

* * * * (EXCELLENT)

Acorn Heritage Alegria Vineyard
  (Russian River)
Robert Biale Aldo's Vineyard (Napa)
Robert Biale Black Chicken (Napa)
Robert Biale Grande Vineyard (Napa)
Robert Biale Napa Ranches (Napa)
Robert Biale Stagecoach Vineyard (Napa)
Robert Biale Valsecchi Vineyard (Sonoma)
Carlisle Gold Mine Ranch (Dry Creek)
Dashe Cellars (Dry Creek)
Dashe Cellars Florence Vineyard
  (Dry Creek)
Dashe Cellars Louvau Vineyard
  (Dry Creek)
Dashe Cellars Todd Brothers Vineyard
  (Alexander Valley)
Edmeades Ciapusci Vineyard (Mendocino)
Edmeades Piffero Vineyard (Redwood
  Valley)
Edmeades Zeni Vineyard (Mendocino)
Franus Brandlin Ranch (Napa)

Franus Pianchon (Contra Costa)
Green and Red Chiles Mill Vineyard (Napa)
Hartford Court Highwire Vineyard
  (Russian River)
JC Cellars Arrowhead Mountain
  (Sonoma)
JC Cellars Iron Hill Vineyard (Sonoma)
Mara Winery Dolinsek (Russian River)
Mara Winery Luvisi Ranch Old Vines
  (Napa)
Marietta Cellars (Sonoma)
Marietta Cellars Angeli Cuvée
  (Alexander Valley)
Martinelli Giuseppe & Luisa (Russian River)
Mauritson Rockpile Cemetery Vineyard
  (Napa)
Mauritson Rockpile Jack's Cabin Vineyard
  (Napa)
Mauritson Rockpile Ridge Vineyard (Napa)
Neyers Vineyards Pato Vineyard
  (Contra Costa)

Neyers Vineyards Tofanelli Vineyard
(Napa)
Château Potelle Mount Veeder (Napa)
Rafanelli (Sonoma)
Ridge Pagani Ranch (Sonoma)
Rosenblum Cellars Annette's Reserve
(Mendocino)
Rosenblum Cellars Harris-Kratka Vineyard
(Alexander Valley)
Rosenblum Cellars Hendry Vineyard
(Napa)
Rosenblum Cellars House Family Vineyard
(Sonoma)
Rosenblum Cellars Lyon's Reserve (Napa)
Rosenblum Cellars Maggie's Reserve
(Sonoma)
Rosenblum Cellars Monte Rosso Vineyard
(Sonoma)
Rosenblum Cellars Planchon Vineyard (San
Francisco Bay)
Rosenblum Cellars Rockpile Road Vineyard
(Dry Creek)
Rosenblum Cellars Snows Lake (Lake
County)
St. Francis Old Vines (Sonoma)
Sausal Winery (Sonoma)
Sausal Winery Private Reserve (Sonoma)
Scherrer Old Vines (Alexander Valley)
Schrader Cellars Vieux-Os Old Vine Hell
Hole Vineyard (Napa)
Seghesio Home Ranch (Alexander Valley)
Seghesio Old Vine (Sonoma)
Seghesio San Lorenzo (Alexander Valley)

Storybook Mountain Eastern Exposure
(Napa)
Storybook Mountain Estate (Napa)
Storybook Mountain Howell Mountain
(Napa)
Joseph Swan cuvées (Sonoma)
Turley Cellars Cedarman Vineyard
(Howell Mountain)
Turley Cellars Dogtown Vineyard
(California)
Turley Cellars Duarte Vineyard
(Contra Costa)
Turley Cellars Dusi Vineyard (Paso Robles)
Turley Cellars Grist Vineyard (Alexander
Valley)
Turley Cellars Mead Ranch Atlas Peak
(Napa)
Turley Cellars Moore Earthquake Vineyard
(Napa)
Turley Cellars Old Vines (California)
Turley Cellars Pesenti Vineyard
(Paso Robles)
Turley Cellars Rattlesnake Ridge
(Howell Mountain)
Turley Cellars Salvador Vineyard
(Contra Costa)
Turley Cellars Tofanelli Vineyard (Napa)
Turley Cellars Ueberroth Vineyard
(Paso Robles)
Turley Cellars Vineyard 101 (Alexander
Valley)
Vineyard 29 Aida Vineyard (Napa)
Zoom (Contra Costa)

★ ★ ★ (GOOD)

Chiarello Felicia Old Vine (Napa)
Chiarello Giana (Napa)
Di Arie (Amador)
Di Arie (Shenandoah)
Di Arie Southern Exposure (Shenandoah)
Edmeades Chase Vineyard (Redwood
Valley)
Edmeades Perli Vineyard (Redwood Valley)
Grgich Hills Miljenko's Old Vines (Napa)
Neyers High Valley (Chiles Valley)
Neyers Pato Vineyard (Contra Costa)

Neyers Tofanelli Vineyard (Napa)
Rosenblum Cellars (North Coast)
Rosenblum Cellars Vintner's Cuvée XXIX
(California)
Scherrer Winery Scherrer Vineyard
(Alexander Valley)
Sequum Kidd Ranch (Napa)
Sequum Sonoma River (Napa)
Turley Cellars Juvenile (California)
Turley Cellars Rancho Burro
(Russian River)

CALIFORNIA'S BEST SPARKLING WINE PRODUCERS

* * * * * (OUTSTANDING)

None

* * * * (EXCELLENT)

Domaine Chandon Blanc de Noir (Napa)
Domaine Chandon Étoile (Napa)
Domaine Chandon Reserve Brut (Napa)
Iron Horse cuvées (Sonoma)
Maison Deutz Blanc de Noir
   (San Luis Obispo)

Mumm Blanc de Noir Rosé (Napa)
Roederer L'Ermitage (Anderson Valley)
Roederer Estate (Anderson Valley)
Schramsberg Vineyard cuvées (Napa)

[tasting commentaries]

ABREU VINEYARDS   * * * * *
NAPA $225.00–$350.00

This is an irrefutable blue-chip superstar, but sadly, the small production is either sold via a mailing list or available only at some of the country's top restaurants. There are approximately 500 cases of the Madrona Ranch Cabernet, and fewer than 300 cases of the Thorevilos. Some of Abreu's new vineyards, especially the Cappella, have come on board, and that will add another 300 to 400 cases of wine. David Abreu is the world-class viticulturist for many of Napa Valley's best-run vineyards, and is an uncompromising perfectionist whose "take no prisoners" policy and demanding formula for producing top-quality fruit does not always sit well with some people. However, for those seeking great wines, Abreu is the real deal. These are as good as Napa Cabernet Sauvignons can be . . . monumental examples of wines that will last 25 to 30 or more years.

2006 Cabernet Sauvignon Madrona Ranch	94–96	2010–2030
2005 Cabernet Sauvignon Madrona Ranch	95–98	2009–2036
2004 Cabernet Sauvignon Madrona Ranch	97	now–2032
2003 Cabernet Sauvignon Madrona Ranch	95	2010–2040
2002 Cabernet Sauvignon Madrona Ranch	98	now–2026+
2001 Cabernet Sauvignon Madrona Ranch	97+	2011–2030+
2006 Cabernet Sauvignon Thorevilos	95–98	2010–2030
2005 Cabernet Sauvignon Thorevilos	96–99	2010–2046+
2004 Cabernet Sauvignon Thorevilos	98	2009–2025+
2003 Cabernet Sauvignon Thorevilos	96–100	2009–2025
2002 Cabernet Sauvignon Thorevilos	100	now–2025+
2001 Cabernet Sauvignon Thorevilos	99	now–2030
2006 Cappella Proprietary Red Wine	94–96	2010–2025

ACACIA WINERY   * * / * * *
CARNEROS $35.00–$55.00

This was one of the original, high-quality producers in the Carneros region, having been founded in 1979. A number of top vineyards were developed, and initially the quality was very good. However, the number of single-vineyard bottlings seemed to get out of hand, quality slipped, and today Acacia seems to be a mere shadow of what it was in its heyday. They have added a sparkling cuvée to the Chardonnays and Pinot Noirs, and the wines are competent rather than exciting.

ACORN WINERY ★★★
RUSSIAN RIVER $30.00–$32.00

Founded in 1994 by owners Betsy and Bill Nachbaur, Acorn produces fewer than 3,000 cases of wine. Their top offering is a Zinfandel from the Alegria Vineyard in Russian River. They also produce small quantities of Dolcetto, Syrah, Cabernet Franc, and Sangiovese, as well as a rosé. These are generally well-made, artisanal, fairly priced offerings.

2003 Syrah Alegria Vineyards Axiom	88	now–2011
2001 Syrah Alegria Vineyards Axiom	86	now
2004 Zinfandel Alegria Vineyards Heritage Vines	88	now–2010
2003 Zinfandel Alegria Vineyards Heritage Vines	89	now
2001 Zinfandel Alegria Vineyards Heritage Vines	90	now

ADELAIDA CELLARS ★★★
PASO ROBLES $18.00–$65.00

Quality has been on the rise at Adelaida Cellars over the last three or four years. This 15,000–case winery originated in 1981 on limestone soils on the west side of Paso Robles. A bevy of wines is produced, but the finest are their Rhône-style efforts.

2005 Grenache Blanc Roussanne Glenrose Vineyard	90	now–2010
2004 Grenache Glenrose Vineyard	89	now–2011
2002 Mourvèdre/Grenache/Syrah/Counoise Glenrose Vineyard	87	now
2003 Rhône Style Red Glenrose Vineyard	86	now–2010
2004 Rhône Style White Glenrose Vineyard	90	now
2004 Roussanne Tablas Creek Vineyard	88	now
2003 Syrah Debro and Viking Vineyards	87	now–2012
2002 Syrah Debro, Glenrose, and Viking Vineyards	90	now
2002 Syrah Debro and Glenrose Vineyards	87	now
2004 Syrah Reserve Chelle Mountain Vineyard	89	now–2010
2004 Syrah Reserve Glenrose Vineyard	89	now–2012
2003 Syrah Reserve Glenrose Vineyard	89+	now–2017
2004 Syrah Reserve Viking Estate Vineyard	90	now–2013
2003 Syrah Reserve Viking Estate Vineyard	89+	now–2016
2002 Syrah Reserve Viking Estate Vineyard	91+	now–2017
2004 Syrah Schoolhouse	87	now–2010
2003 Syrah Slo Debro Vineyard	87	now–2011
2004 Version Proprietary Red Glenrose Vineyard	90	now–2011
2005 Viognier Glenrose Vineyard	89	now–2010

ADLER FELS WINERY ★★
SONOMA $15.00–$25.00

I have never been that impressed with the Gewürztraminers, Fumé Blancs, or red wines from Adler Fels. However, I do enjoy the sense of humor evident on the labels of their Chardonnay, Cabernet, Syrah, and Zinfandel, which are called "Big Ass."

ALBAN VINEYARDS ★★★★★
EDNA VALLEY $32.00–$95.00

The great shining success story of Edna Valley is undoubtedly Alban Vineyards, one of the pioneers in the Rhone Ranger movement and today one of the two or three best practitioners with Grenache, Syrah, Viognier, and more recently, Mourvèdre. Proprietors John and Lorraine Alban have 66 acres under vine with the potential for planting others. The wines are quickly snapped up by the winery's mailing-list customers and select restaurants. This is a stunning source for terrific wines.

2006 Forsythe Mourvèdre	93	2012–2027
2005 Forsythe Mourvèdre	95+	2013–2025
2004 Forsythe Mourvèdre	95	now–2026
2006 Grenache	96	2010–2020
2005 Grenache	96	2009–2019
2004 Grenache	98	now–2016
2003 Grenache	95	now–2016
2002 Grenache	95	now–2016
2001 Grenache	92	now–2014
2005 Pandora Syrah/Grenache	94	now–2020
2004 Pandora Syrah/Grenache	97	now–2021
2003 Pandora Syrah/Grenache	93	now–2018
2002 Pandora Syrah/Grenache	95	now–2019
2001 Pandora Syrah/Grenache	93	now–2014
2004 Roussanne Estate	90	now–2010
2006 Syrah Lorraine Vineyard	97	2010–2025
2005 Syrah Lorraine Vineyard	97	now–2023
2004 Syrah Lorraine Vineyard	99	now–2026
2003 Syrah Lorraine Vineyard	99	now–2020
2002 Syrah Lorraine Vineyard	96	now–2016
2001 Syrah Lorraine Vineyard	94	now–2016
2006 Syrah Reva Vineyard	95	2010–2022
2005 Syrah Reva Vineyard	96	2009–2021
2004 Syrah Reva Vineyard	96	now–2022
2003 Syrah Reva Vineyard	98	now–2021
2002 Syrah Reva Vineyard	95+	now–2019
2001 Syrah Reva Vineyard	93+	now–2020
2005 Syrah Seymour's Vineyard	96	2010–2025
2004 Syrah Seymour's Vineyard	99	2010–2027
2003 Syrah Seymour's Vineyard	96	now–2021
2002 Syrah Seymour's Vineyard	96+	now–2019
2001 Syrah Seymour's Vineyard	95+	now–2019
2006 Viognier	92	now–2010

ALCINA CELLARS * * *
SONOMA $40.00–$50.00

This small (under 2,000 cases) *négociant* Pinot Noir producer buys fruit from four separate sites, all located in the Russian River–Sonoma Coast region. The wines are made in a fruit-forward, soft style meant to be consumed in their first three to four years.

2006 Pinot Noir Ramondo Vineyard	87	now–2010
2006 Pinot Noir Russian River	87	now–2011
2005 Pinot Noir Sangiacomo Vineyard	88	now–2012
2006 Pinot Noir Sonoma Coast	87	now–2011

MARTIN ALFARO ★ ★ ★
SANTA LUCIA HIGHLANDS $40.00

Alfaro is a small Pinot Noir specialist fashioning wines from vineyard sites south of San Francisco, primarily the Santa Cruz Mountains, Monterey County, and the Santa Lucia Highlands. My tastings have been limited, but what I have seen has been impressive.

2005 Pinot Noir Garys' Vineyard	87	now–2011
2004 Pinot Noir Garys' Vineyard	90	now–2012

DOMAINE ALFRED ★ ★
EDNA VALLEY $28.00–$42.00

Domaine Alfred has been producing wines for approximately a decade, but they still appear unsure of which direction they want to take. Their Pinots are styled big and nearly resemble their Syrahs, but recent vintages have gotten stronger as their primary source vineyard, the Chamisal (planted in 1972), has aged.

2003 Pinot Noir Califa Chamisal Vineyards	89	now–2012
2004 Syrah Domaine Alfred Estate Chamisal Vineyard	89	now–2012
2004 Syrah Califa Chamisal Vineyard	87?	now–2012
2003 Syrah Califa Chamisal Vineyard	90	now–2015
2003 Syrah Chamisal Vineyard	87+?	now–2015
2001 Syrah Chamisal Vineyard	90	now–2015
2002 Syrah Edna Valley	84	now

ALMA ROSA ★ ★ ★/★ ★ ★
SANTA RITA HILLS $16.00–$49.00

Alma Rosa was founded in 2005 by one of the pioneers of California's Central Coast, Richard Sanford. When Sanford founded the Sanford & Benedict Vineyard in 1970, he was one of the first producers to plant Pinot Noir in the cool Santa Rita Hills. Alma Rosa's first releases have been impressive, suggesting this is an up-and-coming operation that is worth following.

2005 Chardonnay	90	now
2005 Chardonnay El Jabali Vineyard	90	now
2005 Pinot Blanc	87	now
2005 Pinot Blanc La Encantada Vineyard	89	now
2005 Pinot Noir	89	now–2013
2005 Pinot Noir La Encantada Vineyard	88	now–2013

ALTA MARIA ★ ★ ★ ★
SANTA MARIA $60.00

Well-known Santa Maria personalities James Ontiveros and Paul Wilkins have hit pay dirt with this new estate. Their first offerings suggest this is another promising new operation from California's Central Coast.

2005 Grenache Nielson Vineyard	90	now–2012
2005 Pinot Noir Bien Nacido Vineyard	89	now–2013
2005 Syrah	94	now–2016

AMBULLNEO VINEYARDS ★ ★ ★ ★
SANTA MARIA $59.00–$95.00

This ambitious project is the brainchild of Greg Linn, a Burgundy lover and longtime supporter of Burgundy varieties planted in Santa Barbara. A refreshing and welcome addition to the winemaking scene, he has established himself as a serious player in California's Central Coast, specializing in Pinot Noir, Chardonnay, Syrah, and a few Italian varietals.

2006 Chardonnay Big Paw	87	now–2012
2005 Chardonnay Big Paw	91	now–2011
2004 Chardonnay Big Paw	90	now
2006 Chardonnay Fang Blanc	88	now
2005 Chardonnay Fang Blanc	92	now
2006 Chardonnay Solomon Hills	93	now–2010
2006 Pinot Noir Bulldog Reserve	89	now–2012
2005 Pinot Noir Bulldog Reserve	92	now–2017
2004 Pinot Noir Bulldog Reserve	93	now–2015
2003 Pinot Noir Bulldog Reserve	93	now–2012
2002 Pinot Noir Bulldog Reserve	95	now
2005 Pinot Noir Canis Major	90	now–2012
2004 Pinot Noir Canis Major	88	now
2005 Pinot Noir Mastiff Cuvée	92	now–2012
2004 Pinot Noir Mastiff Cuvée	91	now
2006 Pinot Noir Rancho Ontiveros	93	now–2017
2006 Pinot Noir Rim Rock	90	now–2012
2005 Syrah Howling	93	now–2015
2004 Syrah Howling	90	now–2011

AMPELOS CELLARS ★★★
SANTA BARBARA $16.00–$34.00

Less than a decade old, this small firm produces Syrah, Grenache, and several white wines from their Santa Rita Hills vineyard. It is too early to get a true feel for what direction they are heading, but the wines have been good.

2004 Gamma Ampelos Vineyard	89	now–2012
2003 Syrache	87	now
2004 Syrache Harrison Clarke/Alisos	85?	now–2011
2003 Syrah Evans Ranch	85	now

AMUSE BOUCHE ★★★
NAPA $175.00–$200.00

An artistic label, ambitious pricing, and good rather than inspirational wines are the basis for this boutique operation that promises more than what is delivered in the bottle.

2005 Merlot	89+	2009–2018
2004 Proprietary Red Wine	90	now–2013
2002 Proprietary Red Wine	87	now–2010

ANAKOTA ★★★★
KNIGHT'S VALLEY $40.00–$75.00

Jess Jackson's Anakota is a collection of single-vineyard/single-variety efforts from Sonoma's Mount St. Helena. Made from high-elevation vineyards, these 100% Cabernet Sauvignons are serious wines meant for long-term aging.

2004 Cabernet Sauvignon Helena Dakota	90	now–2020
2003 Cabernet Sauvignon Helena Dakota	93	now–2020
2002 Cabernet Sauvignon Helena Dakota	92	2011–2024
2004 Cabernet Sauvignon Helena Montana	90	now–2015

| 2003 Cabernet Sauvignon Helena Montana | 92 | now–2018+ |
| 2002 Cabernet Sauvignon Helena Montana | 93+ | 2009–2020+ |

ANDERSON'S CONN VALLEY VINEYARDS ★★★★★
NAPA $40.00–$80.00

Founded in 1987 by Gus Anderson, this 40-acre vineyard is now run by Gus's son, Todd, while Gus has begun a new operation called Eagle Trace. Planted predominantly with Cabernet Sauvignon in the Conn Valley (a somewhat forgotten area east of St. Helena), the wines have consistently been excellent to outstanding, seeming to go from strength to strength. Over the years, they have added a Burgundy-style, nonmalolactic Chardonnay, a Lake County Sauvignon Blanc, and a Syrah, but their finest offerings remain their Bordeaux varietals, especially the Cabernet Sauvignon Reserve, the Right Bank Proprietary Red Wine, and the Eloge Proprietary Red, the latter three all superb examples that handsomely repay cellaring.

2006 Cabernet Sauvignon Reserve	90–92+	2012–2025
2005 Cabernet Sauvignon Reserve	94+	now–2026
2004 Cabernet Sauvignon Reserve	95	now–2021
2003 Cabernet Sauvignon Reserve	94	now–2026
2002 Cabernet Sauvignon Reserve	95	now–2020+
2001 Cabernet Sauvignon Reserve	94	now–2028
2006 Chardonnay Fournier Vineyard	87	now
2005 Chardonnay Fournier Vineyard	91	now–2011
2004 Chardonnay Fournier Vineyard	90	now–2010
2004 Chardonnay Green Island	90–93	now–2013
2006 Eloge Proprietary Red Wine	92–95	2010–2023
2005 Eloge Proprietary Red Wine	96	2010–2021
2004 Eloge Proprietary Red Wine	95	now–2026
2003 Eloge Proprietary Red Wine	96	now–2021
2002 Eloge Proprietary Red Wine	96	now–2020
2001 Eloge Proprietary Red Wine	93	now–2020
2006 Right Bank Proprietary Red Wine	94–96	2010–2025
2005 Right Bank Proprietary Red Wine	95	now–2021
2004 Right Bank Proprietary Red Wine	94	now–2021
2003 Right Bank Proprietary Red Wine	93	now–2021
2002 Right Bank Proprietary Red Wine	94	now–2018
2001 Right Bank Proprietary Red Wine	92	now–2015
2006 Sauvignon Blanc	85	now
2005 Sauvignon Blanc	88	now

L'ANGEVIN ★★★★
SONOMA $40.00–$60.00

This is a superb artisanal group of wines from Robbie Meyer and Alan Peirson, both of whom previously worked at the Peter Michael Winery before becoming independent specialists of single-vineyard Chardonnays and Pinot Noirs.

2005 Chardonnay Charles Heintz Vineyard	93	now–2011
2004 Chardonnay Charles Heintz Vineyard	95	now–2010
2005 Chardonnay Laughlin	90	now–2010
2005 Chardonnay Pierson Meyer (not yet named)	94	now–2011
2005 Chardonnay Russian River	91	now
2004 Chardonnay Russian River	91	now
2004 Pinot Noir Hyde SSV	89	now–2010

| 2005 Pinot Noir Russian River | 88 | now–2012 |
| 2005 Pinot Noir Stage Vineyard | 91 | now–2011 |

ANGLIM ★★★
PASO ROBLES $15.00–$40.00

Another small (3,000 to 4,000 cases) operation, Anglim specializes in Rhône varieties, Pinot Noir, and limited amounts of Cabernet Sauvignon. The first releases have been well received. Moreover, the prices are fair.

2003 Grenache Vista Creek Vineyard	85	now
2006 Rosé	87	now
2005 Roussanne	89	now
2004 Syrah	89	now–2010
2003 Syrah Best Barrel Blend	87	now

ANTIQV²S ★★★★
SANTA LUCIA HIGHLANDS $60.00–$65.00

Jeff Pisoni, from the Pisoni family of the Santa Lucia Highlands, is the force behind these high-class Syrahs. Although made in limited quantities, they are striking in their fragrance and velvety richness.

2005 Syrah Garys' Vineyard	92	now–2012
2004 Syrah Garys' Vineyard	90+	now–2016
2004 Syrah Pisoni Vineyard	90	now–2016
2005 Syrah Pisoni Vineyard Susan's Hill	91	now–2012

ARAUJO ESTATE WINES ★★★★★
NAPA $38.00–$185.00

One of the world's most superb wine estates, Araujo continues to demonstrate both remarkable consistency and impeccably high quality. Nothing ever seems to change except for some minor tweaking to viticulture and winemaking. Proprietors Bart and Daphne Araujo own one of the foremost winemaking sites of California, the Eisele Vineyard. They also have employed a fabulous winemaking team, Françoise Peschon and globe-trotting oenologist Michel Rolland. While the Cabernet Sauvignon receives all the glory, readers should not miss out on their brilliant Sauvignon Blanc or Syrah.

2005 Altagracia	92	now–2022
2004 Altagracia	90	now–2021
2003 Altagracia	93	now–2021
2002 Altagracia	91	now–2017
2001 Altagracia	90	now–2011
2006 Cabernet Sauvignon Eisele Vineyard	93–95+	2012–2026
2005 Cabernet Sauvignon Eisele Vineyard	98+	now–2026
2004 Cabernet Sauvignon Eisele Vineyard	94+	now–2026
2003 Cabernet Sauvignon Eisele Vineyard	98	now–2026
2002 Cabernet Sauvignon Eisele Vineyard	99	now–2025
2001 Cabernet Sauvignon Eisele Vineyard	97	now–2025
2006 Sauvignon Blanc	92	now
2005 Sauvignon Blanc	98	now
2006 Syrah Eisele Vineyard	91–93	now–2016
2005 Syrah Eisele Vineyard	93	now–2016
2004 Syrah Eisele Vineyard	92	now–2016

2003 Syrah Eisele Vineyard	94	now–2017
2002 Syrah Eisele Vineyard	95	now–2015
2001 Syrah Eisele Vineyard	95	now

ARCADIAN WINERY ★ ★ ★
SANTA LUCIA HIGHLANDS $50.00–$80.00

Winemaker-proprietor Joe Davis fashions a bevy of cool-climate Pinot Noirs and Chardon-nays as well as an occasional Syrah. They all reflect his attempts to produce wines that emulate French wines. He tries to find that elusive "somewhereness" and "transparent quality of the *terroir*." In large part these are somewhat meaningless marketing concepts, but readers look-ing for lean, sculptured, austere wines will appreciate these efforts.

2002 Pinot Noir Dierberg Vineyard	85?	now–2010
2001 Pinot Noir Fiddlestix Vineyard	89	now
2001 Pinot Noir Francesca	85	now
2001 Pinot Noir Garys' Vineyard	86	now
2001 Pinot Noir Gold Coast Vineyard	87	now
2001 Pinot Noir Jill's Cuvée Bien Nacido Vineyard	90	now–2011
2001 Pinot Noir Lafond Vineyard	87	now
2004 Pinot Noir Pisoni Vineyard	90	now–2012
2003 Pinot Noir Pisoni Vineyard	85	now–2015
2002 Pinot Noir Pisoni Vineyard	85?	now–2012
2001 Pinot Noir Pisoni Vineyard	86	now–2010
2001 Pinot Noir Santa Lucia Highlands	85	now
2001 Pinot Noir Sleepy Hollow Vineyard	87	now
2001 Syrah Garys' Vineyard	88	now–2010
2001 Syrah Garys' Vineyard Robert O. Fleming Cuvée	89	now–2012

ARIETTA ★ ★ ★ ★
NAPA $100.00–$125.00

The project of charismatic auctioneer Fritz Hatton, whose love of music is the basis for the play on words for Arietta, these are serious wines produced from innovative blends, especially the Variation One, a blend of Syrah and Merlot. Recently, an impressive white wine made of 85% Sauvignon Blanc and 15% Semillon, The White Keys, has been added to the portfolio. Although these offerings are expensive, they possess impressive credentials and should age well. The only exception is the white wine, which is meant to be drunk in its youth.

2006 Cabernet Sauvignon	92–94	2009–2022
2005 Cabernet Sauvignon	88?	2010–2025
2004 Cabernet Sauvignon	90	now–2014
2003 Cabernet Sauvignon	90	now–2020
2006 Proprietary Red H Block Hudson Vineyard	92–94	now–2017
2005 Proprietary Red H Block Hudson Vineyard	94	now–2021
2004 Proprietary Red H Block Hudson Vineyard	90	now–2020
2003 Proprietary Red H Block Hudson Vineyard	93+	now–2020+
2002 Proprietary Red H Block Hudson Vineyard	98	now–2020
2001 Proprietary Red H Block Hudson Vineyard	92+	now–2023
2006 Variation One (Syrah/Merlot)	91–93	now–2020
2005 Variation One (Syrah/Merlot)	92	2009–2024
2004 Variation One (Syrah/Merlot)	89	now–2015
2003 Variation One (Syrah/Merlot)	92+	now–2017
2002 Variation One (Syrah/Merlot)	95	now–2020

2001 Variation One (Syrah/Merlot)	93	now–2026
2006 The White Keys	91	now
2005 The White Keys	92	now

ARISTA WINERY ★★★
RUSSIAN RIVER $35.00–$50.00

Founded only in 2002, Arista is dedicated to the production of elegant Russian River Pinot Noirs. Transplanted Texans Al and Janis McWilliams are the proprietors, farming just under 36 acres of Russian River benchlands on the Westside Road south of Healdsburg.

2003 Pinot Noir Ferrington Vineyard	87	now
2003 Pinot Noir Harper's Rest	86	now
2003 Pinot Noir Mononi Vineyard	86	now
2003 Pinot Noir Toboni Vineyard	88	now–2010

ARNOT-ROBERTS ★★★★
CARNEROS $60.00–$75.00

This joint project of Duncan Arnot Meyers and Nathan Lee Roberts is a small boutique operation focusing on fewer than 1,000 cases of impressively endowed, well-made wine.

2004 Cabernet Sauvignon Bugay Vineyard	92	2010–2020
2004 Cabernet Sauvignon Wild Iris	92	now–2027
2005 Syrah Alder Springs	93+	now–2015
2005 Syrah Griffin's Lair	91	now–2015
2005 Syrah Hudson Vineyard	93	now–2014
2004 Syrah Hudson Vineyard	92	now–2012

ARROWOOD VINEYARDS & WINERY ★★★★
SONOMA $20.00–$100.00

Richard Arrowood still produces the wines at this estate in spite of its sale, first to Robert Mondavi, then to Constellation, and recently to Jess Jackson. Things have changed little, which is good news for wine consumers, as this has long been a noteworthy source for beautiful white and red wines. Arrowood has no weak spots in its portfolio. It offers extraordinary sweet wines, Rhone Ranger blends, and glorious Chardonnays and Cabernet Sauvignons.

2004 Cabernet Sauvignon	89	now–2022
2003 Cabernet Sauvignon	89	now–2016
2002 Cabernet Sauvignon	90	now–2015
2001 Cabernet Sauvignon	91	now–2020
2004 Cabernet Sauvignon Monte Rosso Vineyard	95+	2011–2040+
2003 Cabernet Sauvignon Monte Rosso Vineyard	89+	now–2021
2002 Cabernet Sauvignon Monte Rosso Vineyard	93	now–2020
2004 Cabernet Sauvignon Reserve Spéciale	95	now–2027+
2003 Cabernet Sauvignon Reserve Spéciale	92+	2010–2026
2002 Cabernet Sauvignon Reserve Spéciale	93+	now–2025
2001 Cabernet Sauvignon Reserve Spéciale	96	now–2022
2005 Chardonnay	92+	now
2004 Chardonnay	89	now
2004 Chardonnay Alary Vineyards	92	now
2005 Chardonnay Reserve Spéciale	89	now–2011
2004 Chardonnay Reserve Spéciale	92	now–2010
2006 Côte de Lune Blanc Saralee's Vineyard	91	now

2005 Côte de Lune Blanc Saralee's Vineyard	90	now
2004 Côte de Lune Blanc Saralee's Vineyard	91	now
2005 Côte de Lune Rouge	89	now–2010
2006 Gewürztraminer Saralee's Vineyard	86	now
2005 Gewürztraminer Saralee's Vineyard	89	now–2010
2004 Malbec	87	now–2013
2004 Merlot	89	now–2012
2002 Merlot	88	now–2011
2006 Select Late Harvest Riesling Saralee's Vineyard	93	now–2017
2005 Select Late Harvest Riesling Saralee's Vineyard	93	now
2005 Special Select Late Harvest Riesling Hoot Owl Creek Vineyard	95	now
2004 Syrah Le Beau Mélange	89	now–2016
2003 Syrah Le Beau Mélange	89	now–2011
2005 Syrah Kuljian Vineyard	91	now–2014
2004 Syrah Kuljian Vineyard	91	now–2016
2003 Syrah Kuljian Vineyard	86?	now
2002 Syrah Kuljian Vineyard	93	now–2010
2005 Syrah Saralee's Vineyard	94	now–2018
2004 Syrah Saralee's Vineyard	91	now–2016
2003 Syrah Saralee's Vineyard	91	now–2012
2002 Syrah Saralee's Vineyard	94	now–2013
2001 Syrah Saralee's Vineyard	93	now–2011
2006 Viognier Saralee's Vineyard	90	now

DAVID ARTHUR VINEYARDS ★★★★
NAPA $75.00–$125.00

High in the mountains overlooking Lake Hennessy, David Arthur has a 40-plus-acre tract of land from which he produces concentrated, intense Cabernet Sauvignons. I have not seen recent vintages, but those from previous years were generally among the finest wines of Napa.

ATALON ★★★
NAPA $30.00–$60.00

Emerging from an old ghost winery dating back to 1888, Atalon is based on Howell Mountain vineyards, owned by Jess Jackson. At one time, the fruit was utilized by such successful wineries as Duckhorn and La Jota. There are two levels of wines, the Napa Valley Cabernet Sauvignon and Merlot, and the Mountain Estate–designated Cabernet Sauvignon and Merlot.

2004 Cabernet Sauvignon	90	2009–2024
2002 Cabernet Sauvignon	90	now–2016
2004 Merlot Keyes Vineyard	89	now–2016
2004 Merlot Napa	88	now–2011
2002 Merlot Napa	89	now–2011
2001 Merlot Napa	91	now–2010

ATLAS PEAK VINEYARDS ★★
NAPA $20.00–$50.00

High hopes for this mountain site originated from William Hill, who developed the property in the early 1980s, then sold it to a consortium of investors led by Tuscany's Antinori family.

Despite different winemakers and the Antinori involvement, quality has been distressingly mediocre.

AU BON CLIMAT WINERY ***/****
SANTA BARBARA $30.00–$50.00

One of California's most experienced and charismatic wine producers is Jim Clendenen, who has been a pioneer of the Santa Barbara region, focusing on cool-climate Chardonnays and Pinot Noirs, all with a French stylistic flourish. Founded in 1982 (the name means "in a well-positioned or exposed vineyard site"), Au Bon Climat's wines can all stand the test of time, and are often somewhat closed early in life. The winery is located near Solvang, and the estate vineyard in the Santa Maria Valley is certified organic.

2004 Chardonnay Le Bon Climat Vineyard	88+	2009–2017
2003 Chardonnay Le Bon Climat Clendenen Family Vineyards	88+	now–2015
2004 Chardonnay Mt. Carmel Vineyard	85	now
2003 Chardonnay Mt. Carmel Vineyard	91	now–2010
2004 Chardonnay Nuits-Blanches au Bouge	90	now–2012
2004 Chardonnay Sanford & Benedict Vineyard	88	now–2015
2003 Chardonnay Sanford & Benedict Vineyard	89+	now–2011+
2003 Chardonnay Unity Nuits-Blanches au Bouge	91	now–2013
2003 Pinot Noir Barham Mendelsohn Estate	86	now–2014
2005 Pinot Noir La Bauge Au-dessus	88	now–2013
2004 Pinot Noir La Bauge Au-dessus	87	now–2012
2003 Pinot Noir La Bauge Au-dessus	83	now–2011
2005 Pinot Noir Bien Nacido Vineyard	88+	2009–2019
2005 Pinot Noir Le Bon Climat	88	now–2014
2002 Pinot Noir Le Bon Climat	88+	now–2011
2004 Pinot Noir Isabelle Morgan	88	now–2014
2004 Pinot Noir Knox Alexander	89	now–2017
2003 Pinot Noir Knox Alexander	88	now–2012
2004 Pinot Noir Mt. Carmel Sanford & Benedict Le Bon Climat	85	now
2005 Pinot Noir Nielson Vineyard	90	now–2017
2004 Pinot Noir Sanford & Benedict Vineyard	85	now–2013
2003 Pinot Noir Sanford & Benedict Vineyard	88	now–2012

AUBERT *****
SONOMA COAST $65.00–$95.00

Mark Aubert, who previously fashioned wines at Colgin and Peter Michael, is currently the winemaker at Bryant Family Vineyard. Additionally, he has his own operation, where he produces some of the world's top Chardonnays and Pinot Noirs from superb vineyard sites in the Russian River and Sonoma Coast regions. His cuvées rank alongside the world's finest, and there is no question that the man has the Midas touch. Recently he expanded his boutique empire to include a Bordeaux-style red wine from a vineyard on Howell Mountain owned by David Abreu.

2006 Chardonnay Lauren Vineyard	96–98	now–2014
2005 Chardonnay Lauren Vineyard	98	now–2016
2004 Chardonnay Lauren Vineyard	97	now–2012
2005 Chardonnay Quarry Vineyard	97	now–2015
2004 Chardonnay Quarry Vineyard	95	now–2011

2005 Chardonnay Reuling Vineyard	99	now–2016
2004 Chardonnay Reuling Vineyard	95+	now–2016
2006 Chardonnay Ritchie Vineyard	94–96	now–2012
2005 Chardonnay Ritchie Vineyard	96	now–2013
2004 Chardonnay Ritchie Vineyard	96	now–2014
2006 Pinot Noir Reuling Vineyard	90–92	now–2017
2005 Pinot Noir Reuling Vineyard	95	now–2016
2004 Pinot Noir Reuling Vineyard	93	now–2016
2003 Pinot Noir Reuling Vineyard	95	now–2014
2006 Pinot Noir UV Vineyard	94–96	now–2017
2005 Pinot Noir UV Vineyard	95	now–2015
2004 Pinot Noir UV Vineyard	97	now–2016
2006 Proprietary Red Wine Lucia Abreu Vineyard	91–94	2010–2020
2005 Proprietary Red Wine Lucia Abreu Vineyard	89–91	2010–2023

AUDELSSA ESTATE WINERY ✳ ✳ ✳ ✳
SONOMA $35.00–$50.00

A relatively new winery featuring impressively made reds from terraced mountain hillside vineyards, Audelssa's focus has been on Bordeaux blends, Syrah, and a Syrah-Grenache-Mourvèdre blend called Zephyr. Although my experience with this estate is limited, everything I have tasted has been enormously impressive. This tiny property is situated near Glen Ellen, California.

2003 Cabernet Sauvignon Reserve Mountain Terraces	92	2009–2024
2004 Summit Mountain Terraces	90	now–2018
2003 Syrah Tempest Mountain Terraces	93	now–2014
2003 Zephyr Mountain Terraces	90	now–2011

L'AVENTURE WINERY ✳ ✳ ✳ ✳
PASO ROBLES $35.00–$80.00

One of Paso Robles's most impressive producers, former St.-Émilion resident Stephan Asseo continues to turn out a bevy of intriguing and provocative high-quality wines, the finest of which should have excellent aging potential. Other than the Bordeaux-like Cabernet Sauvignon, the L'Aventure wines are generally blends. They include a brilliant white wine made from Roussanne and Viognier; the Optimus, which is a blend of Syrah, Cabernet Sauvignon, and Petit Verdot; the Côte à Côte, a Syrah-Grenache-Mourvèdre combination; and the usually sensational Estate Cuvée, a blend of Syrah, Cabernet Sauvignon, and Petit Verdot. At the top of its game, this winery is doing spectacular work.

2005 Cabernet Sauvignon Estate	94+	2010–2035
2004 Cabernet Sauvignon Estate	95+	2009–2022
2003 Cabernet Sauvignon Estate	92+	now–2022
2002 Cabernet Sauvignon Estate	91+	now–2019
2005 Côte à Côte	91	now–2017
2004 Côte à Côte	97+	now–2016
2003 Côte à Côte	96	now–2018+
2002 Côte à Côte	93	now–2012
2005 Estate Cuvée	94	2010–2022
2004 Estate Cuvée	98	now–2020
2003 Estate Cuvée	94	now–2022
2002 Estate Cuvée	94	now–2014
2005 Optimus Estate	90+	2010–2020

2003 Optimus Estate	93+	now–2021
2002 Optimus Estate	92	now–2015
2006 Roussanne	91	now
2004 Syrah Estate	96+	now–2021
2003 Syrah Estate	91	now–2016
2002 Syrah Estate	88	now–2017
2002 Syrah Paso Robles	89	now–2011
2002 Syrah Stephan Ridge	85	now–2011

BABCOCK VINEYARDS ★★★
SANTA BARBARA $20.00–$30.00

This winery originated when Brian Babcock's restaurateur parents purchased 110 acres and planted nearly 80 of them with Chardonnay, Sauvignon Blanc, Pinot Noir, Syrah, and a few experimental varieties. Currently, they produce 20,000 cases of consistently good to very good reds and whites.

2005 Chardonnay Grand Cuvée	91	now
2005 Chardonnay Rita's Earth Cuvée	90	now
2001 Pinot Noir Cargasacchi	88	now
2004 Pinot Noir Granite's Ghost	89	now–2012
2001 Pinot Noir Mt. Carmel	86	now
2001 Syrah Santa Barbara	87	now

BACIO DIVINO CELLARS ★★★★
NAPA $30.00–$80.00

An independent-spirited, visionary gentleman, Claus Janzen started this project in 1993. Janzen was dedicated to producing a California version of a super-Tuscan, a blend of Cabernet Sauvignon, Merlot, and Sangiovese. Little did he realize what success that wine would have, and he has followed it with a less expensive offering called Pazzo, a terrific bistro red, and more recently, some single-vineyard Cabernet Sauvignons as well as his Syrah–Cabernet Sauvignon blend called Vagabond. These are distinctive, high-class offerings.

2005 Cabernet Sauvignon Cloudy's Vineyard	87–89	2010–2020
2004 Cabernet Sauvignon Cloudy's Vineyard	88–90	now–2016
2005 Cabernet Sauvignon Janzen Vineyard	89	now–2019
2004 Cabernet Sauvignon Janzen Blue Squirrel Vineyard	89	now–2018
2005 Cabernet Sauvignon Janzen To-Kalon Vineyard	89	now–2018
2004 Cabernet Sauvignon Janzen To-Kalon Vineyard	93	now–2020
2005 Cabernet Sauvignon To-Kalon Vineyard	90–93	2009–2024
2004 Cabernet Sauvignon To-Kalon Vineyard	90	now–2019
2005 Pazzo	91	now–2010
2004 Pazzo	90	now–2010
2003 Pazzo	91	now
2002 Pazzo	87	now
2001 Pazzo	89	now
2005 Proprietary Red Wine	92	now–2014
2004 Proprietary Red Wine	90	now–2013
2003 Proprietary Red Wine	93	now–2013
2002 Proprietary Red Wine	89	now–2013
2001 Proprietary Red Wine	93+	now–2018
2005 Vagabond	93	now–2015
2004 Vagabond	91	now–2014

BAILEYANA WINERY ★★/★★★
EDNA VALLEY $30.00–$38.00

With their estate vineyard, Firepeak, and a relatively new winery, Baileyana seems to still be a work in progress. Their finest efforts have traditionally been their Syrahs, but they also do an admirable job with Chardonnay, Pinot Noir, and Sauvignon Blanc. They also have a second label called Tangent, which is screw-cap-finished. It represents good value.

2005 Syrah Firepeak	85	now
2004 Syrah Firepeak	75	now
2004 Syrah Grand Firepeak Cuvée Firepeak Vineyard	86	now–2010
2003 Syrah Grand Firepeak Cuvée Firepeak Vineyard	89	now–2010

BARNETT VINEYARDS ★★★
NAPA $45.00–$100.00

High atop Spring Mountain, Barnett Vineyards has an irregular performance record, but when the wines hit on all cylinders, they are impressive examples of mountain viticulture, especially the Rattlesnake Hill Vineyard Cabernet Sauvignon. Recently they have added wines made from purchased fruit, including a Pinot Noir and Chardonnay from Anderson Valley.

2002 Cabernet Sauvignon Rattlesnake Hill Estate Spring Mountain	93	now–2017
2002 Cabernet Sauvignon Spring Mountain	88	now–2012
2002 Merlot Spring Mountain	90	now–2010

BEAULIEU VINEYARD ★★/★★★
NAPA $15.00–$85.00

One of the legendary names of Napa Valley, BV was founded in 1900 by French immigrant Georges de Latour. After prohibition, it was guided by legendary winemaker André Tchelistcheff. Beaulieu became renowned for the extraordinary Cabernet Sauvignons produced in the 1950s, 1960s, and 1970s. In 1969, the winery was sold to the Heublein company and subsequently to the corporate giant Diageo. Production is over 1,500,000 cases, and the bevy of wines tends to be uninspiring. The finest remain the Georges de Latour Private Reserve Cabernet Sauvignon and, occasionally, the other Cabernet-based offerings. However, the overall quality level is unexciting, as the legends of the past are distant memories.

2003 Cabernet Sauvignon Georges de Latour Private Reserve	86	now–2016
2002 Cabernet Sauvignon Georges de Latour Private Reserve	87	now–2015
2001 Cabernet Sauvignon Georges de Latour Private Reserve	88+	now–2015
2002 Dulcet Reserve	86	now–2010
2003 Tapestry Reserve	85	now–2014
2002 Tapestry Reserve	87	now–2015
2004 Zinfandel Napa	84	now

BECKMAN VINEYARDS ★★★★
SANTA YNEZ VALLEY $16.00–$55.00

Tom Beckman purchased a 365-acre hillside property overlooking the Santa Ynez Valley in 1996. Now known as the Purisima Mountain Vineyard, it is largely dedicated to Rhône varieties. Beckman, which has become one of my favorite Santa Ynez Valley vineyards, deserves praise not only for increasing the quality of their wines, but for their healthy respect for consumers as reflected in their realistic pricing policies. Their portfolio includes high-quality whites as well as reds.

2005 Cuvée Le Bec	88	now–2010
2004 Cuvée Le Bec	85	now
2003 Cuvée Le Bec	88	now
2002 Cuvée Le Bec	87	now
2005 Cuvée Le Bec Blanc	89	now
2004 Cuvée Le Bec Blanc	87	now
2005 Grenache Purisima Mountain	91	now–2011
2004 Grenache Purisima Mountain	85	now–2011
2003 Grenache Purisima Mountain	91	now–2013
2002 Grenache Purisima Mountain	87	now
2005 Marsanne Purisima Mountain	88	now
2001 Mourvèdre Purisima Mountain	88	now–2015
2005 Proprietary Red Wine Purisima Mountain	91+	2009–2024
2005 Syrah Block 6 Purisima Mountain	93	now–2019
2004 Syrah Block 6 Purisima Mountain	93	now–2016
2003 Syrah Block 6 Purisima Mountain	94	now–2017+
2005 Syrah Clone #1 Purisima Mountain	93	now–2017
2004 Syrah Clone #1 Purisima Mountain	92	now–2014
2003 Syrah Clone #1 Purisima Mountain	94	now–2017
2002 Syrah Clone #1 Purisima Mountain	93	now–2014
2005 Syrah Estate	90	now–2013
2004 Syrah Estate	89	now–2012
2003 Syrah Estate	87	now–2009
2005 Syrah Estate Purisima Mountain	91	now–2017
2004 Syrah Estate Purisima Mountain	91	now–2011
2003 Syrah Estate Purisima Mountain	90	now–2013
2002 Syrah Estate Purisima Mountain	88	now

BEHRENS AND HITCHCOCK–ERNA SCHEIN ✶ ✶ ✶/✶ ✶ ✶ ✶
NAPA $40.00–$65.00

Behrens and Hitchcock is now known as Erna Schein, as founding member Bob Hitchcock has left the partnership. This syndicate led by Les Behrens and his wife, Lisa, is all about finding superb vineyards, taking control of the viticulture, and turning out fun-filled, fruit-driven, amazingly delicious wines. The Behrenses have a remarkable knack for accessing top sites and assembling striking blends with innovative names. Production under the Erna Schein label (named for Les Behrens's mother) will be around 3,000 cases.

2003 Alder Springs Cuvée	93	now
2004 B and H Cabernet Sauvignon	92	now–2016
2004 B and H Everything But the Kitchen Sink	92	now–2012
2004 B and H Ode to Picasso Proprietary Red	93	now–2013
2004 B and H Syrah Alder Springs Vineyard	90	now–2012
2003 Cabernet Sauvignon Beckstoffer Vineyard To-Kalon	92	now–2015
2002 Cabernet Sauvignon Beckstoffer Vineyard To-Kalon	96	2010–2030
2003 Cabernet Sauvignon Herrick-Moulds Vineyard	93	now–2017
2002 Cabernet Sauvignon Ink Grade	95	now–2020+
2001 Cabernet Sauvignon Kenefick Ranch	93	now–2020
2002 Cabernet Sauvignon Kenefick Ranch & Herrick Vineyard	96	now–2020+

2001 Cabernet Sauvignon Oakville	96	now–2022
2003 Cemetery	91	now–2017
2003 Chien Lunatique	90	now–2013
2003 The Contender	92	now–2015
2003 Dr. Crane Cuvée	92	now–2020
2002 Dixième Recolte	92	now–2015
2003 The Heavy Weight	93	now–2020
2003 Kenefick Ranch Cuvée	94	now–2015+
2003 Merlot	90	now–2015
2002 Merlot	90	now–2012
2003 Merlot Alder Springs Vineyard	92	now–2015
2002 Merlot Alder Springs Vineyard	92	now–2011
2002 Merlot Las Amigas Vineyard	93	now–2013
2002 Merlot Fortuna Vineyard	93	???
2001 Ode to Picasso	96	now–2018
2003 Old Gravely	95	now–2014
2005 Erna Schein Cabernet Sauvignon Herrick- Moulds Vineyard	94	now–2021
2005 Erna Schein Cemetery	94	now–2022
2005 Erna Schein Family Reserve Proprietary Red	93	now–2015
2005 Erna Schein Fat Boy Proprietary Red	94	now–2016
2005 Erna Schein Jersey Boy	91	now–2011
2005 Erna Schein Petite Sirah	93	2010–2025
2005 Erna Schein Syrah Alder Springs Vyd Homage to Ed Olivera	90	now–2015
2003 Syrah Alder Springs Vineyard 4 Blocks	92+	now–2013
2003 Syrah Alder Springs Vineyard Homage to Ed Olivera	94	now–2015
2002 Syrah Alder Springs Vineyard Homage to Ed Olivera	93	now–2012
2001 Syrah Alder Springs Vineyard Homage to Ed Olivera	94	now–2011
2003 Tenth Anniversary Cuvée	92	now–2013

BELL WINE CELLARS * */* * *
NAPA $26.00

While Bell Wine Cellars is situated in Napa, this small producer seeks grapes from through-out California, ranging from the Santa Cruz Mountains to the Sierra Foothills. The finest of these straightforward wines are the Syrahs, although several of the Cabernet Sauvignons have shown good character.

2005 Syrah Canterbury Vineyard	85	now–2011
2001 Syrah Canterbury Vineyard	86	now

BELLE GLOS * * *
NAPA $36.00–$51.00

Made by Joey Wagner, the son of Caymus Vineyards' Chuck Wagner, Belle Glos emphasizes single-vineyard Pinot Noirs from various sites, particular in Sonoma, the Santa Lucia High-lands, and Santa Maria. Quality is very high.

2005 Pinot Noir Las Alturas Vineyard	92	now–2010
2005 Pinot Noir Clark and Telephone Vineyard	91	now–2010
2005 Pinot Noir Taylor Lane Vineyard	89	now–2010

BENESSERE VINEYARDS ★ ★ ★
ST. HELENA $32.00–$40.00

Although dedicated to Sangiovese, Benessere's finest success to date has been their Zinfandels, which are impressively endowed and full of character with a decidedly Italian influence.

2004 Zinfandel B K Collins Old Vines Vineyard	90	now–2010
2004 Zinfandel Black Glass Estate Vineyard	90	now–2011

BENZIGER FAMILY WINERY ★ ★/★ ★ ★
SONOMA $30.00–$65.00

This beautiful site near Glen Ellen, developed by Bruno Benziger and his children, was sold to Heublein in 1993. The Benzigers have retained some control, but the quality of many of the wines is mediocre at best. The most interesting offerings, which are promoted independently, are under the Imagery Series label. To their credit, the Benzigers have pursued biodynamic farming for their Sonoma Mountain estate vineyards.

2001 Cabernet Sauvignon Reserve	88	now–2012
2004 Sauvignon Blanc Paradiso de Maria	86	now
2002 Tribute Proprietary Red Wine	93	now–2020
2001 Tribute Proprietary Red Wine	94	now–2020

BERINGER ★ ★ ★ ★/★ ★ ★ ★ ★
NAPA $16.00–$80.00

One of the top success stories of California, this historic winery, built in the late 1800s by German-born Frederick Beringer, is now owned by the huge Australian conglomerate the Mildara-Blass Group. Surprisingly, Beringer's success has continued despite a succession of giant corporate owners. Their superb Chardonnay and brilliant single-vineyard reds, led by the outstanding Cabernet Sauvignon Private Reserve, are the envy of many estates with equal resources but without the vision to keep quality high despite the enormous quantity of wine produced and the dangers of corporate globalism. This is an impeccably run winery at all levels.

2006 Alluvium Blanc	90	now
2005 Alluvium Proprietary Red Wine	87	now–2015
2004 Alluvium Proprietary Red Wine	89	now–2014
2005 Cabernet Franc Steinhauer Vineyard	90	now–2017
2004 Cabernet Franc Steinhauer Vineyard	90	now–2021
2004 Cabernet Sauvignon Bancroft Ranch	90+	now–2020
2003 Cabernet Sauvignon Bancroft Ranch	88	now–2016
2004 Cabernet Sauvignon Chabot Vineyard	90	now–2022
2003 Cabernet Sauvignon Chabot Vineyard	87	now–2016
2005 Cabernet Sauvignon Knight's Valley	88	now–2015
2003 Cabernet Sauvignon Knight's Valley	88	now–2011
2004 Cabernet Sauvignon Lampyridae Vineyard	95	2012–2026
2004 Cabernet Sauvignon Marston Vineyard	86	2010–2018
2004 Cabernet Sauvignon Napa	87	now–2015
2005 Cabernet Sauvignon Private Reserve	94–96	2010–2030
2004 Cabernet Sauvignon Private Reserve	95	now–2024
2003 Cabernet Sauvignon Private Reserve	92	now–2026
2002 Cabernet Sauvignon Private Reserve	92	now–2020
2004 Cabernet Sauvignon Quarry Vineyard	91	2009–2020
2003 Cabernet Sauvignon Quarry Vineyard	91	2009–2020

2004 Cabernet Sauvignon Rancho del Oso	93	2011–2025
2003 Cabernet Sauvignon Rancho del Oso	91	2009–2018
2004 Cabernet Sauvignon St. Helena Home Vineyard	92	now–2022
2003 Cabernet Sauvignon St. Helena Home Vineyard	92	now–2018
2004 Cabernet Sauvignon Steinhauer Vineyard	93	now–2020
2003 Cabernet Sauvignon Steinhauer Vineyard	91	now–2018
2006 Chardonnay	87	now–2010
2006 Chardonnay Private Reserve	92	now–2010
2005 Chardonnay Private Reserve	93	now–2011
2006 Chardonnay Sbragia Limited Release	92	now–2011
2005 Chardonnay Sbragia Limited Release	93	now–2010
2006 Chardonnay Stanly Ranch	89	now
2005 Chardonnay Stanly Ranch	87	now
2004 Merlot	87	now–2011
2001 Merlot	87	now–2010
2005 Merlot Bancroft Ranch	90–92	now–2015
2004 Merlot Bancroft Ranch	88+	now–2014
2003 Merlot Bancroft Ranch	89	now–2016
2004 Montagia	91	now–2022+
2003 Montagia	89	now–2016
2001 Montagia	90	now–2023+
2006 Pinot Noir Stanly Ranch	87	now–2011
2005 Pinot Noir Stanly Ranch	89	now–2011
2003 Pinot Noir Stanly Ranch	87	now
2005 Syrah Marston Vineyard	88+	now–2018

ROBERT BIALE VINEYARDS ★★★★/★★★★★
NAPA/SONOMA $27.00–$50.00

One of California's top half dozen or so Zinfandel specialists, Italian immigrant Aldo Biale planted Aldo's Vineyard in 1937. A bevy of striking Zinfandels, buttressed by some amazingly thick, ageworthy Petite Sirahs as well as a few red Italian varietal blends, emerge from this superb estate. Production ranges between 4,000 and 5,000 cases of top-flight wines.

2003 Petite Sirah Old Crane Ranch	91	now–2020
2004 Petite Sirah Royal Punishers	95	now–2027
2003 Petite Sirah Royal Punishers	92+	2009–2029
2004 Petite Sirah Thomann Station	95	now–2027
2003 Petite Sirah Thomann Station	93	now–2028
2002 Spenker Vineyard Proprietary Red Wine	89	now
2004 Syrah Hill Climber Jack and Jill Vineyard	92	now–2015
2004 Syrah Hill Climber Pilgrimage Vineyard	90	now–2015
2005 Zappa Proprietary Red Wine	90	now–2011
2003 Zappa Proprietary Red Wine	90	now
2005 Zinfandel Aldo's Vineyard	87	now
2004 Zinfandel Aldo's Vineyard	94	now–2016
2003 Zinfandel Aldo's Vineyard	91	now–2010
2005 Zinfandel Black Chicken	87	now–2010
2004 Zinfandel Black Chicken	93	now–2013
2005 Zinfandel Grande Vineyard	89	now–2010
2004 Zinfandel Grande Vineyard	90	now–2014
2003 Zinfandel Grande Vineyard	88	now

2005 Zinfandel Monte Rosso	90	now–2010
2004 Zinfandel Monte Rosso	91	now–2016
2002 Zinfandel Monte Rosso	94	now–2015
2005 Zinfandel Napa Ranches	89	now–2010
2004 Zinfandel Napa Ranches	92	now–2013
2003 Zinfandel Napa Ranches	89	now
2004 Zinfandel Old Crane Ranch	89	now
2005 Zinfandel Stagecoach Vineyard	86	now
2004 Zinfandel Stagecoach Vineyard	91	now–2011
2005 Zinfandel Valsecchi Vineyard	85	now–2011

BIG BASIN VINEYARDS ★★★★
SANTA CRUZ MOUNTAINS $45.00–$55.00

This is a top-flight Santa Cruz winery specializing in mountain-style, impeccable, high-quality Syrah. Unfortunately, proprietor Bradley Brown produces limited quantities of these cuvées.

2005 Syrah Fairview Ranch	92	now–2017
2005 Syrah Mandala Rattlesnake Rock	92	now–2022
2004 Syrah Mandala Rattlesnake Rock	90	now–2017
2005 Syrah Rattlesnake Rock	92	now–2019
2004 Syrah Rattlesnake Rock	92	now–2022
2003 Syrah Rattlesnake Rock	93	now–2016
2002 Syrah Rattlesnake Rock	93	now–2012

BISHOP'S PEAK ★★/★★★
EDNA VALLEY $15.00

The inexpensive label of Edna Valley's Talley Vineyards, Bishop's Peak offers good-value wine.

2005 Syrah	86	now

BJORNSTAD CELLARS ★★★★
SONOMA $58.00

This is a small artisanal estate specializing in Pinot Noirs and Chardonnays from Russian River and Sonoma Coast vineyards. Winemaker-proprietor Greg Bjornstad is doing everything right at this Sebastopol winery.

2006 Chardonnay Porter Bass Vineyard	91	now–2010
2005 Chardonnay Porter Bass Vineyard	91	now–2010
2006 Chardonnay Ritchie Vineyard	91	now–2010
2005 Chardonnay Ritchie Vineyard	92	now
2006 Pinot Noir Hellenthal Vineyard	89	now–2011
2005 Pinot Noir Hellenthal Vineyard	92	now–2012
2006 Pinot Noir Vandercamp Vineyard	88+	now–2010
2005 Pinot Noir Vandercamp Vineyard	90	now–2011

BLACK KITE CELLARS ★★★★
CARNEROS $48.00

A small, family-run operation, Black Kite's goal is to produce high-quality, distinctive Pinot Noirs, and their first vintages have been enormously impressive.

2005 Pinot Noir Anderson Valley	92	now–2022

BLACKBIRD VINEYARDS ★★★
NAPA $90.00

The force behind these offerings is former Joseph Phelps winemaker Sarah Gott. (Her husband is also a winemaker, but is probably more renowned for his fabulous St. Helena burger and milkshake joint called Taylor's Refresher.)

2005 Paramour Proprietary Red Wine	89	now–2015
2005 Proprietary Red Wine	91	now–2017

BLACKJACK RANCH ★★★/★★★★
SANTA BARBARA $30.00–$55.00

Proprietor Roger Wisted, a longtime lover of French wines, particularly Bordeaux and Burgundy, planted a vineyard outside Los Olivos in 1996. Wisted has proven to be adept at producing terrific Chardonnays, Pinot Noirs, and Bordeaux blends. His ranch includes some stunningly steep hillside sites, which he has named Billy Goat Hill, Suicide Hill, and Hamburger's Hill. These French-style offerings all age beautifully.

2005 Chardonnay Black Cap Reserve Special Selection	91	now–2011
2005 Chardonnay Reserve	89	now
2005 Chardonnay Twenty-One	90	now–2010
2005 Chardonnay Wilkening Vineyard Reserve	91	now
2003 Harmonie Proprietary Red Wine	94	2009–2029
2002 Harmonie Proprietary Red Wine	92+	now–2027
2001 Harmonie Proprietary Red Wine	91	now–2022
2004 Pinot Noir Alix de Vergy Special Selection	90	now–2014
2002 Pinot Noir Alix de Vergy Special Selection	90	now
2004 Syrah Double-Down	89	now–2016
2002 Syrah Double-Down	88	now
2003 Syrah Maximus	91+	now–2017
2002 Syrah Maximus	90+	now–2022
2001 Syrah Maximus	94	now–2020
2004 Syrah Maximus Hillside Reserve	90	now–2021

BLANKIET ESTATE–PARADISE HILLS ★★★★★
NAPA $150.00–$250.00

Situated behind the Dominus winery and vineyard near Yountville, Blankiet's impressive, rolling hillside vineyard was originally established by Helen Turley and John Wetlaufer. The goal has always been to produce world-class wines, and that has been accomplished under the capable hands of brilliant winemaker Martha McClellan and French oenologist Michel Rolland. Such high quality comes at a high cost, but the Blankiet wines are worth the price of admission. Beginning in 2006, they decided to produce only one wine, a blend of the finest lots of Cabernet Sauvignon and Merlot, as opposed to separate cuvées of each. I thoroughly agree with this decision.

2005 Cabernet Sauvignon Paradise Hills Vineyard	95+	2010–2040
2004 Cabernet Sauvignon Paradise Hills Vineyard	96	now–2026
2003 Cabernet Sauvignon Paradise Hills Vineyard	95+	now–2022
2002 Cabernet Sauvignon Paradise Hills Vineyard	95	now–2025
2005 Merlot Paradise Hills Vineyard	93	now–2021
2004 Merlot Paradise Hills Vineyard	94	now–2021
2003 Merlot Paradise Hills Vineyard	96	now–2017
2002 Merlot Paradise Hills Vineyard	94	now–2018

| 2006 Proprietary Red Wine | 95–98 | 2010–2030 |
| 2005 Rive Droite | 93 | now–2022+ |

BOEGER WINERY ★★/★★★
EL DORADO $16.00

Founded in 1972, production at Boeger is moving toward 30,000-plus cases, with about 90% of the wines made from estate-owned or leased vineyards. Boeger's wines tend to be pleasant, fairly priced efforts.

| 2004 Zinfandel El Dorado | 86 | now |
| 2004 Zinfandel Walker Vineyard | 90 | now |

BONACCORSI ★★★★
SANTA BARBARA $42.00–$60.00

Following the tragic death of former sommelier Mike Bonaccorsi, in 2004, his widow, assisted by several prominent Santa Ynez wine producers, has continued his legacy, remaining faithful to the philosophy of producing high-quality single-vineyard Pinot Noirs and Syrahs.

2005 Pinot Noir	90	now–2013
2004 Pinot Noir	86	now–2010
2003 Pinot Noir Arita Hills Vineyard	87	now–2010
2004 Pinot Noir Cargasacchi Vineyard	92	now–2014
2005 Pinot Noir Fiddlestix Vineyard	90	now–2015
2004 Pinot Noir Fiddlestix Vineyard	93	now–2014
2005 Pinot Noir Melville Vineyard	91	now–2015
2005 Pinot Noir Presidio Vineyard	88	now–2013
2005 Pinot Noir Sanford & Benedict Vineyard	88	now–2015
2003 Pinot Noir Sanford & Benedict Vineyard	89+	now–2010
2003 Syrah Bien Nacido Vineyard	92+	now–2017
2003 Syrah Larner Vineyard	92	now–2013
2002 Syrah Santa Barbara	89	now–2011
2005 Syrah Star Lane Vineyard	88	now–2013

BOND ★★★★★
NAPA $175.00–$250.00

This project of Bill Harlan's utilizes the same winemaking team as his beloved Harlan Estate, Bob Levy and Michel Rolland. Bond spotlights the different microclimates and *terroirs* in Napa Valley. Each of these offerings comes from vineyards on which Harlan has signed 20-year leases that have long been recognized as some of the top Cabernet Sauvignon–growing sites in Napa. Production ranges between 600 and 700 cases. The less successful barrels are culled out for a sensational second wine called Matriarch. The St. Eden cuvée represents a vineyard in the Oakville sector; the Melbury is on the western hillsides of Napa near Lake Hennessy; the Vecina is a hillside vineyard situated next to Harlan, above the Oakville Corridor; and E Pluribus is a Spring Mountain site.

2005 Matriarch Proprietary Red Wine	90–92	now–2019
2004 Matriarch Proprietary Red Wine	93	now–2016
2003 Matriarch Proprietary Red Wine	90	now–2021
2002 Matriarch Proprietary Red Wine	90	now–2020
2005 Melbury Proprietary Red Wine	91–93	now–2025
2004 Melbury Proprietary Red Wine	95	now–2026
2003 Melbury Proprietary Red Wine	92	now–2021

2002 Melbury Proprietary Red Wine	96	now–2020
2005 E Pluribus Proprietary Red Wine	96–98	2011–2026
2004 E Pluribus Proprietary Red Wine	95	now–2026
2003 E Pluribus Proprietary Red Wine	93	now–2021
2005 St. Eden Proprietary Red Wine	92–95	2012–2030
2004 St. Eden Proprietary Red Wine	97	now–2021
2003 St. Eden Proprietary Red Wine	95	now–2026
2002 St. Eden Proprietary Red Wine	96	now–2020
2005 Vecina Proprietary Red Wine	96–98	2012–2030
2004 Vecina Proprietary Red Wine	96+	2010–2036
2003 Vecina Proprietary Red Wine	93	2010–2036
2002 Vecina Proprietary Red Wine	95+	now–2020

BONNY DOON VINEYARD ★★
CALIFORNIA $12.00–$32.00

Contrarian Randall Grahm is one of the most gifted and brilliant wine producers in California. He is a pioneer in the Rhone Ranger movement as well as in producing California wines from Italian varieties. Sadly, he seemingly lost his way by growing too fast and emphasizing quantity over quality. However, he appears to be getting back on track, selling off some of his major cash-cow brands in recent years to focus on what he originally did so well—turning out top-quality wines from Rhône varieties. Let's hope this positive trend continues, as he is far too important to the wine industry to cash it in.

2004 Le Cigare Blanc	88	now
2004 Le Cigare Volant	87	now
2003 Le Cigare Volant	85	now
2004 Clos de Gilroy	85	now
2004 Old Telegram	84	now
2003 Old Telegram	84?	now
2004 Syrah Le Pousseur	78	now
2003 Syrah Le Pousseur	86	now

BOOKER VINEYARD ★★★★
PASO ROBLES $45.00–$48.00

The year 2005 marks the debut vintage of Booker Wines, a 40-acre vineyard just to the west of Highway 101 on a beautiful hillside not far from the L'Aventure winery. The wines are made by Justin Smith at Saxum, and that no doubt explains their impeccable quality out of the gate.

2006 Grenache The Ripper	95	now–2018
2005 Grenache The Ripper	95	now–2017
2006 Syrah Fracture	92	now–2018
2005 Syrah Fracture	93	now–2017
2006 Syrah Vertigo	92	now–2019
2005 Syrah Vertigo	92	now–2019

BRADFORD MOUNTAIN ★★/★★★
DRY CREEK $30.00–$35.00

This small Dry Creek operation produces several decent Zinfandels.

| 2004 Zinfandel Dry Creek Valley | 85 | now |
| 2004 Zinfandel Grist Vineyard | 86 | now |

BRANDER VINEYARD ★★/★★★
SANTA BARBARA $22.00–$25.00

It is hard to believe this winery has been around for more than 30 years. They produce straightforward wines with the exception of their finest offerings, Sauvignon Blanc and Syrah. In 2006, the Sauvignon Blanc cuvée included the 30th Anniversary Cuvée, Mesa Verde, Purisima Mountain, and Au Naturel.

2006 Sauvignon Blanc Santa Ynez	87	now–2011
2005 Syrah Santa Barbara	87	now–2011
2005 Syrah Santa Ynez	87	now–2010

BREGGO CELLARS ★★★★
ANDERSON VALLEY $25.00–$55.00

Anderson Valley is becoming one of the "hot" new cool-climate sources of not only white varietals, but also increasing quantities of high-quality Pinot Noir. Breggo Cellars pays homage to what used to be a robust sheep-farming area. The wines are brilliantly fashioned by winemaker-proprietor Doug Stewart. Readers would be hard pressed to find a better Sauvignon Blanc or Pinot Gris elsewhere in California.

2006 Chardonnay Savoy Vineyard	90	now–2010
2006 Gewürztraminer	91	now
2006 Pinot Gris Wiley Vineyard	93	now
2006 Pinot Noir Anderson Valley	90+	now–2011
2006 Pinot Noir Donnelly Creek Vineyard	89+	now–2012
2006 Pinot Noir Ferrington Vineyard	92	now–2013
2006 Pinto Noir Savoy Vineyard	92	now–2012
2006 Sauvignon Blanc Ferrington Vineyard	93	now–2010

BREWER-CLIFTON ★★★★★
SANTA RITA HILLS $45.00–$75.00

I can't say enough positive things about the complexity and singular nature of Steve Clifton and Greg Brewer's Pinot Noirs and Chardonnays. Philosophically committed to 100% whole-cluster Pinot Noir winemaking techniques, and dealing only with vineyards in the cool Santa Rita Hills, Brewer-Clifton's wines rival the finest Pinot Noirs and Chardonnays made throughout the world, including the top Burgundies. Moreover, they have an impressive track record of aging brilliantly.

2005 Chardonnay Ashley's	94	now–2014
2004 Chardonnay Ashley's	96	now–2014
2004 Chardonnay Clos Pepe Vineyard	90	now–2011
2004 Chardonnay Melville Vineyard	94	now–2014
2005 Chardonnay Mount Carmel	94	now–2013
2004 Chardonnay Mount Carmel	95	now–2014
2005 Chardonnay Rancho Santa Rosa	94	now–2017
2004 Chardonnay Rancho Santa Rosa	92	now–2012
2005 Chardonnay Sea Smoke	92	now–2017
2005 Chardonnay Sweeney Canyon	94	now–2017
2004 Chardonnay Sweeney Canyon	93+	now–2016
2005 Pinot Noir Ashley's	93	2009–2022
2004 Pinot Noir Ashley's	93	now–2014
2005 Pinot Noir Cargasacchi	92+	2009–2022
2004 Pinot Noir Cargasacchi	92	now–2016

2003 Pinot Noir Cargasacchi	89+	now–2015
2002 Pinot Noir Cargasacchi	95	now–2015
2005 Pinot Noir Clos Pepe	91+	2009–2022
2004 Pinot Noir Clos Pepe	91	now–2014
2003 Pinot Noir Clos Pepe	94	now–2016
2005 Pinot Noir Melville	95	now–2017
2004 Pinot Noir Melville	95	now–2016+
2003 Pinot Noir Melville	95	now–2015
2005 Pinot Noir Mount Carmel	94	now–2022
2004 Pinot Noir Mount Carmel	95	now–2016
2005 Pinot Noir Rancho Santa Rosa	94	now–2022
2004 Pinot Noir Rancho Santa Rosa	91	now–2014
2003 Pinot Noir Rancho Santa Rosa	93	now–2012
2005 Pinot Noir Rio Vista	93	now–2017
2004 Pinot Noir Rio Vista	92	now–2014
2003 Pinot Noir Rio Vista	94	now–2014

BRIDLEWOOD WINERY * *
CENTRAL COAST $18.00–$40.00

I have never been impressed with these uninspiring wines that are meant for immediate consumption.

2003 Syrah	81	now
2002 Syrah Estate	85	now
2003 Syrah Reserve	84	now
2003 Syrah Winner's Circle Dusty Trail	86	now

DAVID BRUCE * *
SANTA CRUZ MOUNTAINS $25.00–$50.00

I remember tasting some fascinating old bottles of David Bruce Zinfandel and an occasionally over-the-top Pinot Noir that were powerful and undeniably memorable. The quality has always been irregular at this small estate situated in the Santa Cruz Mountains. Moreover, the vineyards were ravaged by disease, and the cellars were contaminated with bacteria over the years. Today the wines are unquestionably clean and pure, but they lack character. This is just another example of a winery with a historic name that is living off its reputation rather than what is in the bottle.

BRYANT FAMILY VINEYARD * * * * *
NAPA $250.00

Don Bryant is a perfectionist who demands the very best from his brilliantly exposed 15 acres situated near Pritchard Hill and Lake Hennessy. Just over 1,000 cases of profoundly concentrated wine can be produced from this vineyard. Since the first vintage, 1992, there has been only one slight hiccup, when the winemaker was changed after 2001. Bryant produces one of Napa Valley's most profound Cabernet Sauvignons.

2006 Cabernet Sauvignon	92–94	2011–2025
2005 Cabernet Sauvignon	90–92	2010–2025
2004 Cabernet Sauvignon	95	now–2022+
2003 Cabernet Sauvignon	96	now–2025
2002 Cabernet Sauvignon	96	now–2020
2001 Cabernet Sauvignon	91?	now–2023

BUCCELLA ★★★★
NAPA $80.00–$90.00

Fashionable winemaking consultant Mark Herold oversees a production of 500 to 700 cases of Cabernet Sauvignon from a multivineyard blend.

2005 Cabernet Sauvignon	93	now–2021
2004 Cabernet Sauvignon	94	now–2021
2003 Cabernet Sauvignon	95	now–2020+
2002 Cabernet Sauvignon	92	now–2017

BUONCRISTIANI ★★★
NAPA $48.00–$50.00

This family winery owned by four brothers specializes primarily in intensely flavored Cabernet Sauvignon, but also produces a Syrah and Dolcetto. The quality is consistently good, with the Cabernet usually the top wine in the relatively small portfolio.

2002 Cabernet Sauvignon Napa	91	now–2015
2003 Syrah Artistico	87	now–2011
2002 Syrah Artistico	86	now–2010

BURGESS WINERY ★★
NAPA $35.00–$75.00

This ghost winery from the 1880s became a reality in 1972 when Tom Burgess began making wine. I remember cutting my wine-tasting teeth on some fabulous Cabernet Sauvignons and Chardonnays in the early 1970s. As is so often the case, production soared and the initial beautiful quality became increasingly dull and commercial. The wines remain average in quality.

BYRON VINEYARD ★★
SANTA MARIA $25.00–$40.00

Byron was started in 1983, purchased by the Mondavis in 1990, and subsequently sold when that winery was purchased by Constellation. The quality used to be very good, but has slipped significantly with the changes in ownership.

2004 Chardonnay	87	now
2004 Chardonnay Nielson Vineyard	85	now
2005 Pinot Noir	86	now–2011
2003 Pinot Noir	86	now
2002 Pinot Noir	84	now
2004 Pinot Noir Bien Nacido Vineyard	85	now–2011
2003 Pinot Noir Bien Nacido Vineyard	87	now
2002 Pinot Noir Bien Nacido Vineyard	88	now
2001 Pinot Noir Monument Hill	87	now
2004 Pinot Noir Nielson Vineyard	86	now–2011
2003 Pinot Noir Nielson Vineyard	86	now
2002 Pinot Noir Nielson Vineyard	84	now
2001 Pinot Noir Nielson Vineyard	87	now

CALDWELL VINEYARD ★★★★
NAPA $90.00–$150.00

John Caldwell has divided his Proprietary Red Wine into two separate cuvées, a Cabernet Sauvignon/Syrah blend called Silver (500 to 600 cases produced) and a 100% Cabernet Sauvignon called Gold (600 cases). All of the fruit comes from the estate's high-elevation, cool-climate vineyards in the Coombsville area. These are seriously endowed efforts meant for long-term cellaring.

2005 Gold	89?	now–2014
2004 Gold	90?	now–2014
2004 Proprietary Red Wine	93	now–2017
2003 Proprietary Red Wine	93	now–2020
2002 Proprietary Red Wine	90	now–2017
2001 Proprietary Red Wine	91	now–2015+
2005 Silver	90	now–2013
2004 Silver	93	now–2014

CALERA ★ ★ ★ ★/★ ★ ★ ★ ★
MT. HARLAN $16.00–$75.00

This venerable winery, which has over 30 years of history (long by California standards), continues to turn out some of the state's finest Pinot Noirs and Chardonnays from the limestone soils of the Gavilan Mountains. This low-tech operation represents artisanal winemaking at its finest. Production of the single-vineyard offerings is limited, but Calera makes nearly 30,000 cases of basic cuvées of Chardonnay and Pinot Noir.

2006 Aligoté	89	now
2006 Chardonnay	87	now
2004 Chardonnay	87	now
2006 Chardonnay La Petite	89	now–2011
2005 Chardonnay 30th Anniversary	92	now–2012
2004 Pinot Noir	85	now
2004 Pinot Noir Jensen Vineyard	94	2009–2022
2002 Pinot Noir Jensen Vineyard	85	now–2021
2001 Pinot Noir Jensen Vineyard	92	now–2017+
2002 Pinot Noir Mills Vineyard	89	now–2016
2001 Pinot Noir Mills Vineyard	91	now–2013
2004 Pinot Noir Reed Vineyard	90	now–2017
2002 Pinot Noir Reed Vineyard	90+	now–2015
2001 Pinot Noir Reed Vineyard	90	now–2013
2002 Pinot Noir Ryan Vineyard First Harvest	89	now–2011
2003 Pinot Noir Ryan Vineyard Second Harvest	87	now–2010
2004 Pinot Noir Selleck Vineyard	96	2011–2022
2002 Pinot Noir Selleck Vineyard	89+	now–2016
2001 Pinot Noir Selleck Vineyard	90+	now–2015
2005 Pinot Noir 30th Anniversary	87	now–2012
2005 Viognier	87	now
2004 Viognier	91	now

CAMBRIA ★ ★ ★
SANTA MARIA $20.00–$40.00

Cambria has large Chardonnay, Pinot Noir, and Syrah vineyards planted on the Santa Maria Benchlands. Since the mid-1980s it has been owned by Jess Jackson and his wife, Barbara Banke. The flagship wines include Katherine's Chardonnay, Julia's Pinot Noir, and Tepusquet Syrah. The quality is solidly reliable rather than inspiring, but like many of this husband-and-wife team's vineyards, they are always pushing for higher and higher quality. Moreover, the Cambria wines are reasonably priced.

2004 Chardonnay Benchbreak Vineyard	84?	now
2004 Chardonnay Katherine's Vineyard	90	now
2004 Chardonnay Rae's Vineyard	88	now
2005 Pinot Noir	85	now
2005 Pinot Noir Clone 23	84	now
2005 Pinot Noir 115	86	now
2005 Pinot Noir Julia's Vineyard	84?	now

CAPIAUX CELLARS ★ ★ ★ ★
SANTA LUCIA HIGHLANDS $36.00–$55.00

Proprietor-winemaker Sean Capiaux, who also makes the superb wines for Howell Mountain's O'Shaughnessey winery, is dedicated to producing single-vineyard Pinot Noir from Russian River and Sonoma Coast vineyard sites. He does a superb job.

2005 Pinot Noir Chimera Vineyard	90	now–2010
2005 Pinot Noir Freestone Hill Vineyard	88	now–2015
2004 Pinot Noir Freestone Hill Vineyard	91	now–2011
2005 Pinot Noir Garys' Vineyard	93	now–2015
2004 Pinot Noir Garys' Vineyard	94	now–2012
2003 Pinot Noir Garys' Vineyard	88?	now–2012
2005 Pinot Noir Pisoni Vineyard	90+	2009–2017
2004 Pinot Noir Pisoni Vineyard	94+	now–2012
2003 Pinot Noir Pisoni Vineyard	90	now–2012
2005 Pinot Noir Widdoes Vineyard	92	now–2012
2004 Pinot Noir Widdoes Vineyard	89	now–2010
2003 Pinot Noir Widdoes Vineyard	90	now–2012
2005 Pinot Noir Wilson Vineyard	94	now–2012

CARDINALE ★ ★ ★ ★
NAPA $135.00–$175.00

One of the flagship wines of the brilliant California visionary and vineyard owner Jess Jackson, Cardinale is a 1,000-case cuvée fashioned from three separate Napa vineyards, the Veeder Peak site high up on Mt. Veeder, the Keyes Vineyard on Howell Mountain, and the Stags Leap Vineyard on the valley floor. It is generally a Cabernet Sauvignon–dominated wine with 10 to 12% Merlot included in many vintages.

2005 Proprietary Red Wine	95	2010–2025
2004 Proprietary Red Wine	95	now–2021
2003 Proprietary Red Wine	95	now–2020
2002 Proprietary Red Wine	95	now–2020
2001 Proprietary Red Wine	93+	now–2016

CARINA CELLARS ★ ★ ★
SANTA BARBARA $22.00–$28.00

This under-the-radar Santa Barbara estate employs the talented winemaking consultant Joey Tensley to produce the wines for proprietor David Hardee. These are well-made offerings that sell for a song.

2004 Syrah Santa Barbara	90	now–2014
2003 Syrah Santa Barbara	88	now–2012
2002 Syrah Santa Barbara	87	now
2004 Syrah 7 Percent	91	now–2014

2002 Syrah Thompson Vineyard	85?	now
2003 Syrah Westerly Vineyards	90	now–2013
2004 Viognier	86	now

CARLISLE WINERY AND VINEYARDS * * * * *
RUSSIAN RIVER $30.00–$45.00

In a short period of time, Carlisle has become one of California's top producers of Zinfandel, Syrah, and Petite Sirah. Onetime home winemaker Mike Officer started this winery in 1998 in an attempt to produce a few cases as well as save some of California's historic old-vine Zinfandel sites. Production is now up to 5,000 cases, and Officer has a waiting list for his stunningly rich, opulent, intensely flavorful wines. Loaded with soul and personality, these are not to be missed.

2006 Petite Sirah	94–96	2010–2023
2005 Petite Sirah	95+	2012–2035
2004 Petite Sirah	92–94	2010–2020
2003 Petite Sirah	94+	2010–2020
2002 Petite Sirah	95	2010–2030
2001 Petite Sirah	94	now–2020
2005 Syrah Bennett Valley	92	now–2016
2003 Syrah Bennett Valley	95	now–2014
2006 Syrah Cardiac Hill	94–96	2010–2016
2005 Syrah Cardiac Hill	92	now–2016
2006 Syrah Dry Creek	93–95	now–2020
2005 Syrah Dry Creek	93	now–2016
2004 Syrah Dry Creek	91	now–2012
2001 Syrah Dry Creek	92	now–2015
2006 Syrah James Berry Vineyard	93–95	now–2025
2005 Syrah Judge Family Vineyard	92	now–2016
2004 Syrah Judge Family Vineyard	95	now–2016
2006 Syrah Papa's Block	94–96	now–2017
2005 Syrah Papa's Block	93	now–2016
2006 Syrah Pelkan Ranch	92	now–2015
2005 Syrah Pelkan Ranch	93	now–2019
2004 Syrah Pelkan Ranch	90	now–2014
2003 Syrah Pelkan Ranch	93	now–2016
2006 Syrah Russian River	91–93	now–2013
2005 Syrah Russian River	94	now–2015
2006 Syrah Sonoma	90–92	now–2014
2004 Syrah Sonoma	92+	now–2016
2002 Syrah Sonoma	94	now–2015
2001 Syrah Sonoma	90	now–2013
2004 Three Birds	93	now–2011
2002 Three Birds	93	now–2010
2001 Three Birds	88	now
2006 Two Acres	92–94	now–2017
2005 Two Acres	92	now–2016
2004 Two Acres	93	now–2013
2003 Two Acres	94	now–2012
2002 Two Acres	91	now–2015+
2001 Two Acres	89	now

2002 Zinfandel Arrowood Mountain	93	now–2013
2005 Zinfandel Bacchi Ranch	93	now–2012
2006 Zinfandel Carlisle Vineyard	92–94	now–2017
2005 Zinfandel Carlisle Vineyard	93	now
2004 Zinfandel Carlisle Vineyard	93	now–2014
2003 Zinfandel Carlisle Vineyard	93	now–2012
2002 Zinfandel Carlisle Vineyard	94	now–2012
2001 Zinfandel Carlisle Vineyard	95	now–2010
2006 Zinfandel Carlo's Ranch	92–94	now–2017
2005 Zinfandel Carlo's Ranch	91	now–2011
2004 Zinfandel Carlo's Ranch	91	now–2012
2006 Zinfandel Dry Creek	90–92	now
2005 Zinfandel Dry Creek	88	now
2004 Zinfandel Dry Creek	94	now–2016
2003 Zinfandel Dry Creek	91	now–2012
2004 Zinfandel Fava Ranch	91	now–2012
2003 Zinfandel Fava Ranch	92	now–2011
2005 Zinfandel Gold Mine Ranch	91	now–2010
2001 Zinfandel Gum Tree Ranch	93	now
2006 Zinfandel Montafi Ranch	93–95	now–2017+
2006 Zinfandel Pietro's Ranch	95–97	now–2015
2005 Zinfandel Pietro's Ranch	89	now–2012
2004 Zinfandel Pietro's Ranch	93	now–2013
2003 Zinfandel Riebli Ranch	90	now–2012
2001 Zinfandel Riebli Ranch	90	now
2006 Zinfandel Rossi Ranch	92–94	now–2015
2004 Zinfandel Rossi Ranch	92	now–2012
2003 Zinfandel Rossi Ranch	94	now–2012
2006 Zinfandel Sonoma County	91–93	now–2014
2004 Zinfandel Sonoma County	93	now–2011
2005 Zinfandel Tom Feeney Ranch	92	now–2013
2004 Zinfandel Tom Feeney Ranch	94	now–2012
2003 Zinfandel Tom Feeney Ranch	95	now–2011

CARR VINEYARD AND WINERY * * *
SANTA RITA HILLS $30.00–$40.00

This small artisanal producer makes tiny quantities of wine (between 100 and 400 cases) meant for immediate drinking. They are consistently good.

2004 Pinot Noir Ashley's Vineyard	88+	now–2014
2005 Pinot Noir Clos Pepe Vineyard	85?	now
2004 Pinot Noir Clos Pepe Vineyard	88	now–2014
2005 Pinot Noir Three Vineyards	86	now
2005 Pinot Noir Turner Vineyards	87	now
2004 Pinot Noir Turner Vineyard	87	now–2011

CARTLIDGE AND BROWNE * * *
CALIFORNIA $10.00–$15.00

One of the premium purveyors of value-priced California wines, Cartlidge and Browne continues to provide rewarding and surprisingly tasty drinking at price points that are hard to believe. These offerings are meant to display their fruit rather than oak or structure. Most wines are best consumed during their first year.

2005 Cabernet Sauvignon California	85	now–2010
2006 Chardonnay California	87	now
2005 Merlot California	82	now
2006 Pinot Noir California	87	now
2005 Rabid Red California	86	now
2006 Sauvignon Blanc Dancing Crow	89	now

CARVER-SUTRO ★ ★ ★ ★
NAPA $45.00–$48.00

From the northeastern corner of Napa Valley, this Petite Sirah specialist turns out pedal-to-the-metal, powerful, intense wines from this underrated grape. All of their Petite Sirahs possess 20 to 25 years of aging potential.

2005 Petite Sirah Palisade Vineyard	91–93	2012–2037
2004 Petite Sirah Palisade Vineyard	93+	2012–2037+
2003 Petite Sirah Palisade Vineyard	91+	now–2026
2002 Petite Sirah Palisade Vineyard	92+	now–2013
2001 Petite Sirah Palisade Vineyard	94	2012–2037

CASA BARRANCA ★ ★
CENTRAL COAST $15.00–$19.00

One could not ask for a better location than picturesque Ojai, California. Casa Barranca is a certified organic winery producing uninspiring but pleasant, drinkable, as well as realistically priced wines.

2004 Bungalow Red (Syrah/Grenache) Stolpman Vineyard	87	now
2003 Bungalow Red (Syrah/Grenache) Stolpman Vineyard	88	now
2003 Syrah Sunstone Vineyard	83	now
2005 Viognier Wolf Vineyard	87	now

CASTORO CELLARS ★ ★
PASO ROBLES $15.00–$30.00

This somewhat under-the-radar Paso Robles winery produces over 25,000 cases of wine a year. The quality is satisfying rather than exciting.

2004 Oakenshield Wine Works	87	now
2001 Petite Sirah Shell Creek	84	now
2001 Petite Sirah Stone's Throw	87	now
2001 Syrah Paso Robles	86	now
2004 Zinfandel Cobble Creek Vineyard	89	now–2010
2004 Zinfandel Paso Robles	85	now
2004 Zinfandel Whale Rock/Cobble Creek Vineyards	87	now

CAYMUS VINEYARDS ★ ★ ★ ★/★ ★ ★ ★ ★
NAPA $40.00–$150.00

One of the most successful Cabernet Sauvignon–based operations in Napa, Caymus boasts a nearly unequaled record of consistency. Winemaker-proprietor Chuck Wagner produces classic Napa Cabernets, including his top cuvée, the Special Selection, which is an intensely rich, cassis-flavored wine with the oak much less aggressive than it was 15 or so years ago. They also offer two very good Chardonnays from their Monterey County vineyards. While critics of this highly popular Cabernet complain that the wines do not age, the truth is they age quite well despite their deliciousness early in life.

2004 Cabernet Sauvignon	92	now–2016
2005 Cabernet Sauvignon Special Selection	93	now–2021
2004 Cabernet Sauvignon Special Selection	95	now–2021
2003 Cabernet Sauvignon Special Selection	94	now–2018
2002 Cabernet Sauvignon Special Selection	96	now–2020
2004 Mer Soleil Chardonnay Barrel Fermented	89	now–2010
2005 Mer Soleil Chardonnay Silver Unoaked	90	now–2010

CEDARVILLE VINEYARD * * *
EL DORADO $20.00–$25.00

In less than a decade, this winery has managed to produce some very tasty wines offered at intriguing prices. They are well-made, reasonably priced, delicious efforts that never disappoint.

2005 Grenache Estate	87	now–2010
2004 Grenache Estate	84	now
2003 Grenache Estate	87	now
2002 Grenache Estate	87	now
2004 Petite Sirah Naylor Vineyard	87	now–2017
2003 Petite Sirah Naylor Vineyard	86?	now–2015
2002 Petite Sirah Naylor Vineyard	88	2010–2020
2003 Syrah Estate	87	now
2002 Syrah Estate	87	now
2006 Viognier Estate	86	now
2005 Viognier Estate	87	now

CHALK HILL * * */* * * *
SONOMA $30.00–$85.00

This large estate of over 300 acres was founded by lawyer Fred Firth in the early 1970s. Production initially focused on Chardonnay and Sauvignon Blanc as well as some Merlot, but has gradually branched out into more seriously endowed Chardonnays, one of northern California's finest Sauvignons, and some impressive blends of Cabernet Sauvignon, Malbec, and Carménère. Quality has always been good, but it appears to have hit new heights over recent vintages.

2004 Cabernet Sauvignon	88	now–2013
2004 Cabernet Sauvignon/Carménère	91	now–2022
2005 Cabernet Sauvignon/Malbec	92+	now–2022
2005 Chardonnay Clone 76	89	now–2010
2005 Chardonnay Founder's Block	94	now–2013
2006 Sauvignon Blanc	88	now

CHALONE * *
CHALONE $30.00–$35.00

One of California's saddest stories, Chalone provided this critic with some of the greatest Chardonnays I ever tasted in the late 1970s and early 1980s. Their dry Chenin Blanc, from extremely old vines, was also superb. The Pinot Noirs were mixed in quality. This was all during the heyday of the winery's founder, the late Dick Graff, who purchased the property in 1965 and planted this vineyard in the forbidding limestone soils of what is now the Chalone appellation. Interestingly, the first winemaker here was no other than Napa's brilliant Philip Togni. Dick Graff was killed in a plane crash in 1998, but by that time the quality had already begun to seriously slip, with the catalyst a contamination in the winery that caused so many moldy-tasting wines in the mid-1980s. Today, Chalone is part of a larger wine group, and the quality is distressingly average . . . a tragedy given the utterly profound wines that emerged throughout the decade of the 1970s and early 1980s. Today, the Chalone Wine Group is owned by the beverage giant Diageo.

DOMAINE CHANDON * * *
NAPA $20.00–$55.00

The Napa Valley outpost of the great French wine house Moët Hennessy, Domaine Chandon possesses over 1,000 acres of vineyards, from which their Private Cellar Crémant and Étoile, as well as some still wines made from Chardonnay and Pinot Noir, are produced. This has been one of California's most successful sparkling-wine operations, but while the wines are good, they have not yet reached the level of the Champagnes produced by their parent firm in France.

CHAPPELLET WINERY * * * *
NAPA $28.00–$120.00

When Philip Togni was the winemaker at this estate in the late 1960s, Donn Chappellet made some of Napa's finest Cabernet Sauvignons. The wines then went through an irregular period, but they have bounced back over the last decade. As evidenced by recent releases, the full potential of this fabulous site on Pritchard Hill overlooking Lake Hennessey is now being exploited.

2004 Cabernet Sauvignon Donn Chappellet	93	now–2022+
2001 Cabernet Sauvignon Donn Chappellet	90	now–2015
2002 Cabernet Sauvignon Napa	91	now–2023
2002 Cabernet Sauvignon Pritchard Hill Estate	92+	now–2020
2001 Cabernet Sauvignon Pritchard Hill Estate	92	now–2022
2005 Chardonnay Napa	88	now
2004 Merlot	91	now–2019
2004 Pritchard Hill Estate Proprietary Red Wine	94	2010–2030
2003 Pritchard Hill Estate Proprietary Red Wine	92	now–2021

CHASSEUR * * * * *
SONOMA $45.00–$60.00

Winemaker Bill Hunter is the force behind these beautiful Burgundian-style Chardonnays and Pinot Noirs. For some reason, Chasseur has remained under consumers' radar, but it is one of the finest estates for these two varietals in northern California.

2005 Chardonnay Durell Vineyard	94	now–2010
2005 Chardonnay Green Acres Hill	95	now–2011
2005 Chardonnay Lorenzo Vineyard	94	now–2011
2005 Pinot Noir Blank Road Vineyard	91	now–2013
2005 Pinot Noir Freestone Station	94	now–2013
2005 Pinot Noir Sexton Vineyard	91	now–2010
2005 Pinot Noir Sylvia's	94	now–2011
2005 Pinot Noir Twin Hill	93	now–2012

CHÂTEAU CHEVALIER ✱✱✱
NAPA $35.00

A historic name that produced some remarkable Spring Mountain Cabernet Sauvignons in the mid-1970s, Château Chevalier has resurfaced with a very good effort in 2003.

2003 Cabernet Sauvignon Spring Mountain	89	2010–2025

CHIARELLO FAMILY VINEYARDS ✱✱✱
NAPA $35.00–$50.00

Very fine Zinfandels, made by the highly regarded winemaking consultant Thomas Brown, emerge from Chiarello Family Vineyards.

2005 Zinfandel Felicia Old Vine	88	now–2010
2005 Zinfandel Giana	89	now–2010

CHIMNEY ROCK ✱✱✱
NAPA $30.00–$60.00

Elegant, Bordeaux-style reds are made by winemaker Doug Fletcher from vineyards at the southern end of Napa Valley. The Chicago-based Terlato Wine Group has purchased a major interest in this estate, but I have not seen any change in the overall elegance and finesse of these wines.

CLARE LUCE ABBEY ESTATE ✱✱✱
NAPA $115.00

In 1991, this producer (from the famous publishing family) purchased an 8.5-acre mountainside vineyard north of St. Helena. These are 100% Cabernet Sauvignon–based wines that exhibit considerable elegance and freshness.

2006 Cabernet Sauvignon	91–93	2010–2024
2005 Cabernet Sauvignon	91	2009–2022

CLARK-CLAUDON VINEYARDS ✱✱✱
NAPA $90.00

Clark-Claudon began with great promise, and recent vintages have been excellent, although not as exciting as some of the earlier efforts. Nevertheless, this property is well worth following.

2005 Cabernet Sauvignon Estate	89	now–2016
2004 Cabernet Sauvignon Estate	88	now–2015
2003 Cabernet Sauvignon Estate	89	now–2014
2002 Cabernet Sauvignon Estate	87	now–2014
2001 Cabernet Sauvignon Estate	92+	2009–2025

CLAUTIERE VINEYARD ✱✱/✱✱✱
PASO ROBLES $23.00–$33.00

The principals, Claudine Blackwell and Terry Bradley, started this winery in 1999, dedicating themselves to producing Syrah, Mourvèdre, and Cabernet Sauvignon. They have since added Grenache, Viognier, Counoise, and even some Portuguese varietals. The wines are straightforward and pleasant but largely unexciting.

2003 Grand Rouge	86	now
2002 Grand Rouge	86	now
2003 Grenache	82	now

2003 Mon Beau Rouge	85	now
2002 Mon Beau Rouge	88	now
2003 Mon Rouge	86	now
2002 Mon Rouge	85	now
2003 Syrah	83	now
2002 Syrah	87	now

CLAY STATION * *
LODI $13.00–$16.00

A branch of the Delicato family vineyard operation, Clay Station is named after an old California gold rush stagecoach stop. The wines are well made, fruity, fairly priced, and best drunk in their first several years.

2004 Petite Sirah	84	now–2011
2002 Petite Sirah	85?	now
2001 Petite Sirah	85?	now
2002 Shiraz	86	now
2005 Viognier	87	now
2004 Zinfandel Lodi	87	now
2005 Zinfandel Old Vine	87	now

CLINE CELLARS * */* * *
CONTRA COSTA $16.00–$28.00

Production has soared at this winery, but while the wines are value-priced, their quality is decidedly inferior to what it was seven to ten years ago.

CLOS LACHANCE * */* * *
SANTA CRUZ MOUNTAINS $25.00–$35.00

This small Santa Cruz Mountain estate produces around 15,000 cases of Chardonnay, Cabernet Franc, and a few other varietals. The quality is good if never exciting.

CLOS MIMI * * * *
PASO ROBLES $19.00–$90.00

Clos Mimi's proprietor, Tim Spear, is one of California's most idiosyncratic wine producers. His wines range from profound artisanal expressions to ones that are, for lack of a better expression, weird. They all represent Spear's personal vision of wine, and most of the time he hits home runs. However, readers should be forewarned . . . these wines are not for everybody. Fermented with 100% indigenous yeasts, with no acidulation, enzymes, nutrients, or water, they often possess some residual sugar and are rich, thick, and late harvest–like in style. My instincts suggest that with long aging, some of them will turn into magnificent wines.

2003 Hommage à Henri Bonneau	91+	now–2018
2003 Syrah Brave Oak Vineyard	92	now–2021
2001 Syrah Bunny Slope Vineyard	89	now
2004 Syrah The Carlyle Hotel	88	now
2005 Syrah Petite Rousse	89	now–2012
2003 Syrah Petite Rousse	92	now–2011
2003 Syrah Shell Creek Vineyard	90+?	now–2020
2003 Syrah Westerly Vineyard	93	now–2017
2002 Syrah White Hawk Vineyard	94+	now–2026

CLOS PEGASE ★★/★★★
NAPA $25.00–$75.00

This estate has always impressed me as more of an art museum than a winemaking facility. Proprietor Jan Shrem has impeccable credentials, as well as unlimited resources based on his collection of artwork and the fact that he owns significant acreage. The wines have always seemed like a work in progress, with various winemakers trying to sculpt something of interest. The offerings, which include Sauvignon Blanc, Chardonnay, Pinot Noir, Merlot, and Cabernet Sauvignon, are competent but never exciting. Each year one hopes things will dramatically improve, but at present, these are pleasant rather than great wines.

CLOS PEPE ESTATE ★★/★★★
SANTA RITA HILLS $47.00–$53.00

One of the ironies of wine tasting is that I have enjoyed the wines made by other producers from this impressive hillside site in the Santa Rita Hills more than the wines made by the proprietor of the vineyard. Perhaps that will change. Clos Pepe's wines are good, but are high in acidity as well as extremely austere.

2005 Pinot Noir	86?	now
2004 Pinot Noir	88	now
2002 Pinot Noir	88+?	now

CLOS DU VAL ★★★
NAPA $25.00–$75.00

Founded in 1972, Clos du Val has been the inspiration of Frenchman Bernard Portet, who produces Chardonnay, Pinot Noir, Merlot, and Cabernet Sauvignon in an understated, subtle, occasionally innocuous style. The wines were much stronger in the early and mid-1970s, but they became nearly devoid of aromatics, as if the winery were too obsessed with cleanliness and technical perfection. Over recent years the wines have taken on slightly more aromatics, but they remain monolithic and unexciting in character.

B. R. COHN ★★★
SONOMA $50.00

From an old dairy farm in Glen Ellen, the Olive Hill Estate Vineyard emerged in 1974. Ironically, B. R. Cohn's finest wine to date may have been their first, the 1984 Cabernet Sauvignon, which was made by Helen Turley. It is still drinking well. Since then, the wines have been irregular, although recently they have tended to be good to very good. However, recent vintages have not matched the splendor of those early years.

2005 Cabernet Sauvignon Olive Hill Estate Vineyard	88	now–2016
2004 Cabernet Sauvignon Olive Hill Estate Vineyard	90	now–2015

COLGIN ★★★★★
NAPA $150.00–$250.00

Colgin is a stunningly beautiful winery overlooking Lake Hennessy. Ann Colgin, her husband, Joe Wender, French wine consultant Dr. Alain Raynaud, and a bevy of well-known assistants including Mark Aubert, who has since moved on, oversee every detail, from pruning to crop thinning. The results are some of the world's greatest wines—whether from their home vineyard, the IX Red Estate, or their Bordeaux blends such as Cariad, or from their other vineyard, Tychson Hill, just north of St. Helena. Even their Herb Lamb Vineyard wine made from purchased fruit is special. This is a great, great address with splendid wines that will stand the test of time.

2006 Cabernet Sauvignon Herb Lamb Vineyard	92–95+	now–2027
2005 Cabernet Sauvignon Herb Lamb Vineyard	94	now–2021
2004 Cabernet Sauvignon Herb Lamb Vineyard	95	now–2031
2003 Cabernet Sauvignon Herb Lamb Vineyard	94	now–2021
2002 Cabernet Sauvignon Herb Lamb Vineyard	96	now–2020
2001 Cabernet Sauvignon Herb Lamb Vineyard	95+	now–2018
2006 Cabernet Sauvignon Tychson Hill Vineyard	92–94+	now–2027
2005 Cabernet Sauvignon Tychson Hill Vineyard	96+	now–2026
2004 Cabernet Sauvignon Tychson Hill Vineyard	98	now–2025
2003 Cabernet Sauvignon Tychson Hill Vineyard	96	now–2031
2002 Cabernet Sauvignon Tychson Hill Vineyard	100	2009–2028
2001 Cabernet Sauvignon Tychson Hill Vineyard	96+	2010–2040
2006 Cariad Proprietary Red Wine	94–96	2011–2026
2005 Cariad Proprietary Red Wine	96+	now–2026
2004 Cariad Proprietary Red Wine	99	now–2026
2003 Cariad Proprietary Red Wine	96	now–2031
2002 Cariad Proprietary Red Wine	97	now–2025+
2001 Cariad Proprietary Red Wine	98	now–2028
2006 IX Proprietary Red Estate	95–98	now–2037+
2005 IX Proprietary Red Estate	97	now–2031
2004 IX Proprietary Red Estate	98	now–2026
2003 IX Proprietary Red Estate	95	now–2031
2002 IX Proprietary Red Estate	98	2009–2034
2006 IX Syrah Estate	92–94	now–2017+
2005 IX Syrah Estate	95	now–2020
2004 IX Syrah Estate	96	now–2018
2003 IX Syrah Estate	95	now–2014
2002 IX Syrah Estate	95	now–2015

CONCANNON ★★/★★★
CENTRAL COAST $14.00–$30.00

One of the oldest wineries of Livermore Valley (founded in 1883 by Irish immigrant James Concannon), this estate currently emphasizes inexpensive, generally pleasant wines. Fruity as well as reasonably priced, these are cleanly made, pleasurable though one-dimensional offerings with which consumers can't go wrong.

2004 Petite Sirah	87	now–2012
2004 Petite Sirah Limited Release	86	now–2012
2003 Petite Sirah Reserve	87	now–2016
2005 Pinot Gris	84	now
2003 Stampmaker's Red	87	now
2004 Stampmaker's Syrah	84	now
2005 Stampmaker's White	87	now

CONSILIENCE ★★★★
SANTA BARBARA $18.00–$38.00

Founded in 1999, Consilience accesses some of Santa Barbara's top vineyard sites, from the Solomon Hills in the west to the Star Lane Vineyard in the east. Consilience certainly does not cheat the consumer on flavor intensity or power. These are all high-test, high-octane, full-flavored, impressively well-made wines.

2004 Cuvée Mambo	88	now
2004 Grenache Rodney Shull Vineyard	85	now
2004 Petite Sirah	90	now–2027
2003 Petite Sirah	92	now–2026
2005 Pinot Noir	85	now–2011
2002 Pinot Noir	85	now
2001 Pinot Noir	90	now
2005 Pinot Noir Bien Nacido Vineyard	91	now–2012
2005 Pinot Noir Solomon Hills Vineyard	90	now–2013
2004 Syrah	89	now–2010
2003 Syrah	88	now–2011
2004 Syrah Camp Four Vineyard	90	now–2015
2004 Syrah Falcone Vineyard	89	now–2014
2003 Syrah Great Oaks Vineyard	89	now–2011
2004 Syrah Hampton Vineyard	90	now–2014
2003 Syrah Hampton Vineyard	91	now–2016
2004 Syrah La Prusa Vineyard	93	now–2017
2004 Syrah Rodney Shull Vineyard	90+	???
2003 Syrah Rodney Shull Vineyard	92	now–2016
2004 Syrah Star Lane Vineyard	91	now–2017
2003 Syrah Star Lane Vineyard	90	now–2016

CONSTANT WINE ★★★
NAPA $50.00–$85.00

This magnificently situated vineyard high on Diamond Mountain, with striking views in every direction, is still a work in progress. The 42 acres of vineyards look superb, and the winemaking appears to be moving in a positive direction. They feature an excellent Cabernet Sauvignon along with a good Cabernet Franc and increasingly high-quality Syrahs.

2005 Cabernet Franc Diamond Mountain	89	now–2014
2004 Cabernet Franc Diamond Mountain	87	now–2013
2005 Cabernet Sauvignon Diamond Mountain	90	now–2018
2004 Cabernet Sauvignon Diamond Mountain	88	now–2016
2004 Cabernet Sauvignon MF	91	2009–2020+
2005 Syrah Diamond Mountain	89	now–2011
2004 Syrah Diamond Mountain	88	now–2014

CONTINUUM ★★★★
NAPA $100.00

Following the sale of the Robert Mondavi Winery, winemaker Tim Mondavi started his own winery. His debut project is 1,000 cases of a Bordeaux blend of Cabernet Sauvignon, Cabernet Franc, and Petit Verdot called Continuum. It is a brilliant beginning, and one should expect even greater things in the future.

2005 Proprietary Red Wine	95+	now–2022+

COPAIN ★★★★★
CALIFORNIA $28.00–$65.00

Wells Guthrie is one of the new breed of California wine producers who believes in the primary importance of the vineyard. Nothing of quality can be divorced from the intrinsic character of the vineyards, their exposition, soils, and clonal selections. Having worked in the Rhône Valley as well as at Turley Winery in California, Guthrie applies his brilliance to some of the state's top vineyard sites, resulting in one of the bright, shining success stories for vineyard-designated superb wines. They are mostly Syrah, with some diversions into Pinot Noir, Zinfandel, and a handful of exotic whites.

2005 Les Copains James Berry Vineyard	93	now–2011
2003 Grenache Eaglepoint Ranch	93	now–2012
2004 Pinot Noir Cerise	91	now
2003 Pinot Noir Kiser	91	now
2004 Pinot Noir Kiser En Bas	87	now
2004 Pinot Noir Kiser En Haut	88	now
2005 Roussanne James Berry Vineyard	92	now
2004 Roussanne James Berry Vineyard	88	now–2016
2006 Saisons des Vins Pinot Noir l'Automne	87	now
2005 Saisons des Vins Pinot Noir l'Automne	87	now
2005 Saisons des Vins Syrah l'Hiver	90	now–2010
2005 Saisons des Vins Viognier l'Été	85	now
2004 Syrah Broken Leg Vineyard	94	now–2014
2003 Syrah Broken Leg Vineyard	94	now–2020
2006 Syrah Brosseau Vineyard	94	now–2017
2005 Syrah Brosseau Vineyard	94	now–2017
2004 Syrah Cailloux & Coccinelle	95+	now–2016
2003 Syrah Cailloux & Coccinelle	92+	now–2020
2002 Syrah Cailloux & Coccinelle	95	now–2020
2005 Syrah Eaglepoint Ranch	92	now–2016
2004 Syrah Eaglepoint Ranch	92+	now–2016
2003 Syrah Eaglepoint Ranch	92	now–2013
2006 Syrah Garys' Vineyard	93–95	now–2015
2005 Syrah Garys' Vineyard	93	now–2016
2004 Syrah Garys' Vineyard	94	now–2016
2003 Syrah Garys' Vineyard	91	now–2014
2003 Syrah Garys' Vineyard Whole Cluster	92	2009–2024
2006 Syrah Harrison Clark	92–94	now–2014
2005 Syrah Harrison Clark	91	now–2013
2005 Syrah Hawks Butte	92+	2009–2021
2004 Syrah Hawks Butte	92+	now–2016
2003 Syrah Hawks Butte	95+	now–2015
2002 Syrah Hawks Butte	96	now–2021
2006 Syrah James Berry Vineyard	95–97	now–2022+
2005 Syrah James Berry Vineyard	94	now–2022
2004 Syrah James Berry Vineyard	96	now–2018
2006 Syrah Madder Lake	90	now–2012
2004 Syrah Madder Lake	91	now–2012
2005 Syrah McDowell Valley Vineyard	93	now–2014
2006 Syrah Thompson Vineyard	92–94	
2005 Syrah Thompson Vineyard	94	now–2019
2004 Syrah Thompson Vineyard	95	now–2014

CORE ★★★★
SANTA BARBARA $14.00–$47.00

These are all creative, individualistic wines that reveal considerable soul and character. One has to admire the wacky art on the label as well as the nonconformist blends that represent enticing renditions of California versions of Rhône Valley wines. The force behind Core is proprietor-winemaker Dave Corey. Most important from a consumer's perspective, the wines deliver loads of pleasure and possess terrific aromatics.

2005 B. Core	87	now
2004 B. Core	88+?	now
2003 Blend 442 Alta Mesa Vineyard	87	now
2004 Blend 163 Cuyama Valley	90	now–2010
2002 Blend 352	90	now
2005 Core Red	89	now–2011
2005 Coreferment	91	now–2015
2004 Coreferment	90	now
2005 Elevation Sensation Alta Mesa Vineyard	93	now–2015
2004 Elevation Sensation Alta Mesa Vineyard	92	now–2013
2003 Elevation Sensation Alta Mesa Vineyard	90	now
2005 Grenache Alta Mesa Vineyard	90	now–2011
2005 Ground Around	90	now–2011
2005 Hard Core	91	now–2012
2004 Hard Core	92	now–2013
2003 Hard Core Alta Mesa Vineyard	90	now–2010
2005 Mister Moreved Alta Mesa Vineyard	94	now–2013
2004 Mister Moreved Alta Mesa Vineyard	91	now–2013
2005 Rose Cuyama Valley	89	now
2005 Syrah Turchi	84	now–2010
2005 White 613	89	now

CORTÉ RIVA VINEYARDS * * * *
NAPA $50.00–$75.00

Pride Mountain Vineyard's well-known viticulturist, Romel Rivera, produces wines under his own label, Corté Riva. Having worked closely with formidable winemaker Bob Foley, Rivera has learned how to fashion full-flavored, intense wines that should stand the test of time.

2005 Cabernet Franc Napa	92	now–2015
2005 Cabernet Sauvignon Napa	93+	2011–2030
2004 Cabernet Sauvignon Napa	89+	now–2024
2003 Cabernet Sauvignon Napa	89+	now–2020
2002 Cabernet Sauvignon Riva Vineyard	87	now–2015
2005 Merlot Napa	91	now–2015
2004 Merlot Napa	91	now–2014
2003 Merlot Napa	92	now–2012
2005 Petite Sirah Lake County	92+	2012–2032
2004 Petite Sirah Napa	94	2010–2035

COTTONWOOD CANYON VINEYARD * *
SANTA MARIA $20.00–$29.00

Proprietor-winemaker Norman Beko focuses on Pinot Noir, Chardonnay, and Syrah from vineyard sites in the Santa Maria Valley. The quality is good rather than inspirational.

2005 Syrah Bistro Classic	86	now–2010
2005 Syrah Estate	87	now–2010

COTTURI WINERY   * *
SONOMA $25.00–$40.00

I had to stop reviewing these wines because of enormous bottle variation. That's a shame, as I admire the Cotturi family's dedication to organic viticulture and minimalist winemaking. The winery was started by Tony Cotturi, his brother, and father in 1979, and they unquestionably know just about all there is to know about viticulture, but their refusal to use any sulfur during the winemaking process, and bottling barrel by barrel, results in mind-numbing levels of bottle variation. When the wines are stable, they represent some of the more interesting and natural expressions of wine in California. However, it's impossible to know what you are going to get in the bottle, hence the problem.

COVENANT   * * * *
NAPA $15.00–$85.00

Jeff Morgan makes arguably the finest kosher wine in California from the superb Larkmead Vineyard on the valley floor in Napa, just north of St. Helena. He also produces a second label called Red C, which is both kosher and delicious. Readers should look for his bevy of terrific nonkosher dry rosés as well.

2006 Cabernet Sauvignon Napa	90–92	now–2017+
2005 Cabernet Sauvignon Napa	91	now–2021
2004 Cabernet Sauvignon Napa	91	now–2021
2003 Cabernet Sauvignon Napa	93	now–2017+
2002 Cabernet Sauvignon Napa	90	now–2014
2005 Gewürztraminer Z Mor	89	now
2006 Red C	88–90	now–2015

ROBERT CRAIG WINERY   * * */* * * *
NAPA $40.00–$70.00

Small quantities of Cabernet Sauvignon–based wines from mountain sites are the hallmark of Robert Craig Winery. Three Cabernets are produced: the Affinity, Howell Mountain, and Mt. Veeder. Total production is generally around 8,000-plus cases.

2004 Affinity Proprietary Red Wine	89	now–2014
2002 Affinity Proprietary Red Wine	89	now–2020
2001 Affinity Proprietary Red Wine	89	now–2017
2003 Cabernet Sauvignon Howell Mountain	88	now–2014
2002 Cabernet Sauvignon Howell Mountain	88+	now–2020
2001 Cabernet Sauvignon Howell Mountain	88	now–2018
2003 Cabernet Sauvignon Mt. Veeder	91	now–2016
2002 Cabernet Sauvignon Mt. Veeder	90	now–2017
2001 Cabernet Sauvignon Mt. Veeder	90	now–2017

CRANE BROTHERS   * * *
NAPA $36.00–$44.00

This small Napa winery is making surprisingly strong, bold wines, including a Bordeaux blend called Brodatious and some single-vineyard Cabernet Sauvignons and Syrahs. My experience with these wines is limited, but I have been impressed with what I have tasted to date.

2004 Brodatious Crane Ranch Vineyard Proprietary Red Wine	90	now–2015
2004 Cabernet Sauvignon Crane Ranch Vineyard Hillside Block	89	now–2019

2004 Syrah Crane Ranch Vineyard	90	now–2012
2003 Syrah Crane Ranch Vineyard	88	now–2012
2002 Syrah Crane Ranch Vineyard	88	now
2001 Syrah Crane Ranch Vineyard	91	now–2010

LA CREMA ★ ★ ★/★ ★ ★ ★
SONOMA $24.00–$29.00

This is a reliable source of reasonably priced Chardonnays and Pinot Noirs. Both are made with classic Burgundian techniques.

2006 Chardonnay Russian River	90	now–2010
2004 Chardonnay Russian River	89	now
2005 Pinot Noir Ahmen Vineyard	90	now–2010
2004 Pinot Noir Anderson Valley	87	now–2010
2003 Pinot Noir Anderson Valley	87	now
2005 Pinot Noir Falk Vineyard	90	now–2010
2004 Pinot Noir Los Carneros	89	now–2010
2003 Pinot Noir Los Carneros	89	now
2003 Pinot Noir Nine Barrel	89+	now–2010
2005 Pinot Noir Russian River	88	now–2011
2004 Pinot Noir Russian River	87	now–2010
2003 Pinot Noir Russian River	88	now

CROCKER & STARR ★ ★ ★
NAPA $42.00–$90.00

Well-known winemaker Pam Starr is the force behind these efforts, which are made at the huge warehouse in Oakville, the Napa Wine Company. The finest wine is the Stone Place cuvée, a blend of Bordeaux varieties.

2001 Cabernet Frac	89	now–2013
2004 Stone Place	92	now–2022+
2003 Stone Place	92	now–2021
2001 Stone Place	92	now–2020

CULLER WINES ★ ★ ★ ★
NORTHERN CALIFORNIA $35.00–$70.00

Karen Culler, one of the most sure-handed winemakers in California, demonstrates a Midas touch with Syrah. She achieves both richness and elegance in her offerings, which include wines from the Sonoma Coast and Napa Valley.

2004 Cabernet Sauvignon Howell Mountain	91	now–2018
2005 Syrah Napa	94	now–2016
2004 Syrah Napa	90	now–2012
2003 Syrah Napa	90	now–2010
2005 Syrah Griffin's Lair Vineyard	93	now–2015
2004 Syrah Griffin's Lair Vineyard	91	now–2012
2002 Syrah Griffin's Lair Vineyard	92	now–2014
2005 Syrah Sawi Vineyard	92	now–2014
2004 Syrah Sawi Vineyard	91	now–2016

CURTIS WINERY ★★
SANTA YNEZ $18.00–$30.00

Realistic pricing and reasonably good quality characterize the wines from Curtis Winery. They specialize in Rhône-style wines, sourcing their fruit from the Santa Ynez Valley. Their pricing policy is one of humility, and consumers will certainly benefit from that.

2003 The Crossroad	87	now–2014
2005 Heritage Blanc	87	now
2004 Heritage Cuvée	86	now–2010
2003 Heritage Cuvée	89	now
2004 Mourvèdre	86	now
2005 Roussanne	89	now–2010
2003 Syrah Ambassador's Vineyard	90	now–2013
2004 Syrah Crossroads Vineyard	87	now–2011
2003 Syrah Crossroads Vineyard	88+	now–2013
2004 Syrah Vogelzang Vineyard	89	now–2014
2003 Syrah Vogelzang Vineyard	89	now–2012
2006 Viognier	86	now

CUVAISON WINERY ★★★/★★★★
CARNEROS $30.00–$48.00

This winery, founded in 1969, once boasted the great Philip Togni as its winemaker. It is owned by a Swiss family who have more than 400 acres of prime vineyard land in the Carneros region; they also purchased the historic 170-acre Brandlin Ranch on Mt. Veeder in the late 1990s. The wines have always been very good but rarely spectacular. Cuvaison produces over 65,000 cases of wine, the great majority of which is Chardonnay. It is worth keeping an eye on, as the quality is very good and, with a little more effort, it could easily be pushed to the next level.

2004 Pinot Noir	88	now
2004 Pinot Noir Estate Selection	90	now
2003 Syrah	89	now–2010
2004 Syrah Carneros	90	now–2011

DAIN WINES ★★★/★★★★
CALIFORNIA $45.00–$50.00

This is an interesting group of wines sporting distinctive labels of old photographs of family members. Production is extremely small, with an emphasis on small lots of handcrafted single-vineyard Pinot Noirs and Syrahs. They are all worth the effort to find and drink.

2006 Pinot Noir American Beauty Amber Ridge	91	now–2010
2005 Pinot Noir American Beauty Amber Ridge	89	now–2011
2006 Pinot Noir Dandy Brosseau Vineyard	88	now–2011
2005 Pinot Noir Dandy Brosseau Vineyard	92	now–2011
2006 Pinot Noir Rebel Rancho Ontiveros	90	now–2011
2005 Pinot Noir Rebel Rancho Ontiveros	90	now–2013
2006 Pinot Noir Savage Juliette	91	now–2011
2005 Pinot Noir Savage Juliette	90	now–2011
2006 Syrah Abner Las Madres Vineyard	88	now–2012
2006 Syrah The Smart Set White Hawk Vineyard	86?	now–2012
2005 Syrah The Smart Set White Hawk Vineyard	89+	now–2015
2005 Syrah Sojourn Las Madres Vineyard	90	now–2012

DALLA VALLE ★★★★★
OAKVILLE/NAPA $65.00

This 21-acre vineyard planted on the red soils of the eastern side of the Oakville Corridor was founded in 1986 by the late Gustav Dalla Valle and his wife, Naoko, who continues to run the estate. Dalla Valle offers only two wines, a brilliant Cabernet Sauvignon and a blend of Cabernet Sauvignon and Cabernet Franc called Maya (named after the Dalla Valles' daughter). These are full-bodied, powerful reds. Production for the Cabernet Sauvignon is 2,000 cases, and there are a mere 400 cases of the Maya. Rare and expensive, with enormous aging potential, these wines are well worth the effort to find.

2005 Cabernet Sauvignon	94	2009–2029
2004 Cabernet Sauvignon	93	2009–2024
2003 Cabernet Sauvignon	90	now–2018
2002 Cabernet Sauvignon	93	now–2020
2001 Cabernet Sauvignon	88	now–2023
2005 Maya Proprietary Red Wine	95+	2011–2036+
2003 Maya Proprietary Red Wine	90+?	2012–2025
2002 Maya Proprietary Red Wine	92+	2012–2030
2001 Maya Proprietary Red Wine	92	2009–2024

DANA ESTATES ★★★★
RUTHERFORD $75.00–$100.00

Dana Estates is the creation of a Korean businessman who planted 30 acres in the Rutherford appellation and also purchased a vineyard that was once part of the Livingston Estate. There are just under 500 cases of his debut release, a 100% Cabernet Sauvignon made by well-known French winemaking consultant Philippe Melka.

2005 Cabernet Sauvignon	93	now–2022+

DARIOUSH ★★★
NAPA $40.00–$80.00

A supermarket tycoon, Darioush Khaledi, purchased the Altamura property in Stags Leap in the late 1990s. Since then he has been making good wines from such varietals as Chardonnay, Viognier, Cabernet Sauvignon, and Merlot.

DASHE CELLARS ★★★★
DRY CREEK $25.00–$30.00

While they produce a handful of white wines along with some Cabernet Sauvignon and Petite Sirah, Dashe Cellars' finest successes tend to be their small lots of handcrafted, single-vineyard Zinfandels. Readers will also enjoy the unusual label with what appears to be a chimpanzee riding a big fish.

2001 Zinfandel Big River Vineyard	90	now
2005 Zinfandel Dry Creek	90	now–2010
2004 Zinfandel Dry Creek	90	now–2010
2001 Zinfandel Dry Creek	87	now
2005 Zinfandel Florence Vineyard	89	now–2010
2005 Zinfandel Louvau Vineyard	88	now–2011
2001 Zinfandel Louvau Vineyard Old Vines	87	now
2005 Zinfandel Todd Brothers Vineyard	91	now–2010

DE LOACH VINEYARDS ★★
RUSSIAN RIVER $25.00–$40.00

De Loach Vineyards, which was founded in 1976 by former fireman Cecil De Loach, built a substantial following with consistently high-quality Chardonnays and old-vine Zinfandels from heritage sites in Sonoma County. The wines went from strength to strength, and some terrific winemakers, including Bob Cabral, now of Williams-Selyem, worked here. However, in 2003 the winery partnered with the huge Burgundian family of Boisset, and the quality is no longer as high as it was in the 1980s or 1990s. Prices remain fair, but De Loach appears to have abandoned many of the old Zinfandel sites, jumping on the Pinot Noir bandwagon at the expense of their Zinfandel program. Perhaps it is only a temporary hiccup, but this winery is no longer living up to its once impressive reputation.

DEHLINGER WINERY ★★★★
RUSSIAN RIVER $32.00–$60.00

One of the blue-chip wineries of Russian River, Dehlinger was begun by Tom Dehlinger and his wife, Carol, in 1975. It now encompasses over 45 acres, specializing in superb Pinot Noir and Chardonnay. They were also one of the first California estates to make high-quality Syrah from their Russian River site. Perhaps the least well-known great wine Dehlinger makes is a Cabernet Sauvignon, which is comparable to the finest of Napa. Prices have always been among the fairest in northern California, reflecting Tom Dehlinger's intrinsic humility.

2004 Cabernet Sauvignon Estate	93	now–2022
2003 Cabernet Sauvignon Estate	92	now–2021
2002 Cabernet Sauvignon Estate	91	now–2020
2005 Chardonnay Estate	93	now–2012
2004 Claret	90	now–2017
2005 Pinot Noir Estate	91+	now–2017
2004 Pinot Noir Estate	91	now–2016
2003 Pinot Noir Estate	91	now–2014
2002 Pinot Noir Estate	90+	now–2013
2005 Pinot Noir Goldridge Vineyard	91	now–2015
2004 Pinot Noir Goldridge Vineyard	90	now–2014
2003 Pinot Noir Goldridge Vineyard	89	now–2012
2002 Pinot Noir Goldridge Vineyard	90	now–2010
2002 Pinot Noir Octagon Vineyard	91+	now–2013
2002 Pinot Noir Old Vine Reserve	92+	now–2014
2004 Pinot Noir Reserve	94	now–2016
2004 Syrah Estate	93	now–2015
2004 Syrah Goldridge Vineyard	91	now–2013

DEL DOTTO ★★★★
NAPA $55.00–$150.00

Proprietor David Del Dotto's cave tour and lavish new estate winery in St. Helena make even the wealthiest Napa Valley proprietors take notice. In spite of his enormous marketing and telecommunication skills, Del Dotto is deadly serious about wine. Working with well-known consultant Nils Venge, he has acquired more than 400 acres, with 96 under vine, and seems to be on an acquisition trend over recent years, purchasing a vineyard on Howell Mountain in St. Helena, one on Pritchard Hill, and nearly 360 acres on the Sonoma Coast. The wines more than live up to the hype as these are impressive efforts, ranging from their Sangiovese-based cuvées to their Cabernet Sauvignons, Cabernet Francs, and Pinot Noirs.

2005 Cabernet Franc	90	now–2015
2004 Cabernet Franc	90	now–2011
2003 Cabernet Franc	92	now–2016
2002 Cabernet Franc	90	now–2011
2005 Cabernet Sauvignon Howell Mountain	93	now–2027
2004 Cabernet Sauvignon Howell Mountain	90–92	2010–2020
2006 Cabernet Sauvignon Rutherford	94–96	now–2027
2004 Cabernet Sauvignon Rutherford	92	now–2018
2003 Cabernet Sauvignon Rutherford	91	now–2016
2002 Cabernet Sauvignon Rutherford	93	now–2017
2006 Cabernet Sauvignon St. Helena Mountain	94–96	now–2022
2005 Cabernet Sauvignon St. Helena Mountain	94	now–2027
2004 Cabernet Sauvignon St. Helena Mountain	94	now–2021
2006 Cabernet Sauvignon Vineyard 887	93–95	now–2022
2006 Chardonnay Cinghiale Vineyard	94	now
2005 David Proprietary Red Wine	93	now–2015
2004 David Proprietary Red Wine	91	now–2016
2003 David Proprietary Red Wine	90	now–2014
2002 David Proprietary Red Wine	94	now–2013
2004 Giovanni Tuscan Reserve	94	now–2016
2006 Pinot Noir Cinghiale Vineyard	90–92	now–2013
2005 Pinot Noir Cinghiale Vineyard	93	now–2011
2005 Pinot Noir Cinghiale Vineyard Clone 828	94	now–2013

DEMETRIA ESTATE * * *
SANTA RITA HILLS $35.00–$55.00

This is a new estate purchased by Santa Monica real estate developer John Zahoudanis. His intention is to biodynamically farm a vineyard he purchased from Fess Parker (Ashley's Vineyard) and several other sites, and produce a bevy of Pinot Noirs as well as such white wines as Pinot Blanc and a white Rhône varietal blend. The early releases look strong.

2005 Pinot Noir Le Belier	89	now–2012
2005 Pinot Noir Cuvée Sandra	89	now–2012
2005 Pinot Noir Jours De Bonheur	90	now–2013

DENNER VINEYARDS * * * *
PASO ROBLES $29.00–$40.00

Denner Vineyards is still under the radar, but is undoubtedly an up-and-coming source for excellent Rhone Ranger offerings. And why shouldn't it be, with its vineyards situated just across the street from the fabulous grand cru site of Saxum's James Berry Vineyard?

2005 The Ditch Digger Estate	92	row–2015
2004 The Ditch Digger Estate	93	row–2013
2005 Grenache Estate	90	row–2011
2005 Syrah Estate	92	row–2015
2003 Syrah Estate	92	now–2013
2002 Syrah Estate	88	now–2011
2006 Theresa Denner Vineyard	89	now–2010
2005 Theresa Denner Vineyard	88	now
2006 Viognier Estate	91	now

DIAMOND CREEK ★ ★ ★ ★
NAPA $125.00–$175.00

The late Al Brounstein developed this extraordinary grand cru site on Diamond Mountain in the late 1960s. His single-vineyard Cabernet Sauvignons, Volcanic Hill, Red Rock Terraces, Gravelly Meadow, and subsequently a Lake Vineyard, were as great as California Cabernets can be, especially all the vintages in the 1970s and early 1980s. Then came an unexplained, irregular period in which the wines were excessively tannic and austere. However, the Diamond Creek offerings have been back on track over the last few years, and this remains the reference-point estate on Diamond Mountain. Production from the 21 acres of beautiful hillside vineyards is around 3,000 cases. The early vintages from the 1970s are still drinking beautifully, and there is no reason to believe that recent offerings won't last 25 to 30 years or more.

DIATOM ★ ★ ★ ★
SANTA RITA HILLS $42.00–$45.00

This is a tiny but fascinating project producing Chardonnays from the Clos Pepe and Huber vineyards in the Santa Rita Hills by the talented Greg Brewer. There is no malolactic fermentation nor any exposure to wood, resulting in naked expressions of vineyard sites. The early releases have been distinctive as well as superb.

2006 Chardonnay Clos Pepe Vineyard	92	now
2005 Chardonnay Clos Pepe Vineyard	92	now
2006 Chardonnay Huber Vineyard	94	now–2013
2005 Chardonnay Huber Vineyard	90	now
2006 Chardonnay Samurai Vineyard	95	now

DOMINUS ESTATE ★ ★ ★ ★ ★
NAPA $75.00–$125.00

This great vineyard, which formed the basis for the legendary Inglenook Cabernet Sauvignons, is owned by Frenchman Christian Moueix (who has made every vintage of Bordeaux's Pétrus since the late 1960s). The Dominus wines possess a distinctive French character, and the winery itself, designed by the brilliant Swiss architects Hertzog and de Meuron, is a fascinating concoction of caged rock and has been one of the more controversial addresses in Napa. The wines go from strength to strength and are meant to age for 20 to 25 years. They represent profound expressions of Napa Cabernet Sauvignon made in the style of an outstanding Bordeaux.

2006 Dominus	94–96	2010–2025
2005 Dominus	96	2009–2035
2004 Dominus	94	now–2026
2003 Dominus	95	now–2022
2002 Dominus	96	2010–2035
2001 Dominus	95	now–2028
2006 Napanook Proprietary Red Wine	90–92	now–2020+
2005 Napanook Proprietary Red Wine	91	now–2022
2004 Napanook Proprietary Red Wine	91	now–2016
2003 Napanook Proprietary Red Wine	90	now–2016
2002 Napanook Proprietary Red Wine	92	now–2023
2001 Napanook Proprietary Red Wine	88	now–2011

A DONKEY AND GOAT * * *
CALIFORNIA $35.00–$45.00

A relatively new, fun operation dedicated to Rhône varieties along with Chardonnay planted in both central and northern California, this winery produces well-made, fairly priced offerings.

2006 Chardonnay Brosseau Vineyard	88	now
2005 Chardonnay Brosseau Vineyard	88	now
2005 Syrah Broken Leg Vineyard	89	now–2012
2004 Syrah Carson Ridge	89	now
2005 Syrah Fenaughty Vineyard	90	now–2013
2004 Syrah Vidmar Vineyard	90	now–2012
2005 Syrah Vieilles Vignes	89	now
2004 Syrah Vieilles Vignes	88	now
2005 Three Thirteen	87	now

DOVER CANYON * * */* * * *
PASO ROBLES $19.00–$32.00

This small, artisanal winery producing just under 3,000 cases has been in existence for nearly two decades. It specializes in Syrah, Zinfandel, and occasionally some tasty whites usually made from blends of Viognier and Roussanne. A Cabernet Sauvignon complements their Zinfandel and Syrah portfolio. Recently, some Sangiovese, Grenache, Mourvèdre, and Malbec have also been made, although they tend to be somewhat rustic. These are big, classic Paso Robles efforts that lack some finesse and charm but offer plenty of flavor.

2004 Alto Pomar	86	now
2001 Alto Pomar	87?	now–2010
2005 Roussanne Starr Ranch	88	now
2001 Syrah DeBro Vineyard	89	now
2002 Syrah Dove Pond Vineyard	85	now
2003 Syrah Ginny's Vineyard	87	now
2001 Syrah Jimmy's Vineyard	90	now–2011
2005 Syrah Starr Ranch	89	now–2012
2004 Syrah Starr Ranch	88+	now–2016
2001 Syrah/Zinfandel Fralich Vineyard	88	now
2005 Viognier Hansen Vineyard	87	now
2005 White Bone	88	now
2004 Zinfandel Benito Dusi Vineyard Old Vine	89	now–2011
2004 Zinfandel Cujo	89	now
2004 Zinfandel Reserve	91	now–2010

DREW FAMILY CELLARS * * * *
CALIFORNIA $30.00–$40.00

This up-and-coming winery was formed by Jason and Molly Drew, a husband-and-wife team working out of their Anderson Valley location. They access their Pinot Noir and Syrah from primarily coastal vineyard appellations, from the Santa Rita Hills in the south to Mendocino Ridge and the Yorkville Highlands in the north. Quality and pricing are remarkably fair.

2004 Grenache Yin & Yang	85	now
2004 Pinot Noir Arita Hills Vineyard	84	now
2005 Pinot Noir Fog-Eater	90	now–2011
2004 Pinot Noir Gatekeeper	87	now–2010

2003 Pinot Noir Gatekeeper	86	now
2003 Pinot Noir Julia's Vineyard	89	now–2010
2003 Pinot Noir Rio Vista Vineyard	88	now–2011
2004 Pinot Noir Threesome	88	now–2010
2005 Pinot Noir Weir Vineyard	89	now–2011
2002 Syrah Alisos and Thompson Vineyards	87	now
2004 Syrah Hearthstone Vineyard	88	now–2012
2004 Syrah Larner Vineyard	94	now–2016
2004 Syrah Morehouse Vineyard	88	now–2012
2003 Syrah Morehouse Vineyard	88	now–2013
2003 Syrah Old Westy–Alisos Vineyard	92	now–2014
2003 Syrah Rodney's–Larner Vineyard	90+	now–2016
2002 Syrah Rodney's–Larner Vineyards	89	now–2010

DRINKWARD PESCHON ENTRE DEUX MÈRES ★ ★ ★ ★
NAPA $52.00

This is the home project of two mothers, Lisa Behrens of Erna Schein winery and Françoise Peschon, the longtime winemaker for Araujo Estate. Fewer than 500 cases of this beautiful Bordeaux-styled red are made, and the wine sells for a remarkably fair price.

2004 Cabernet Sauvignon Napa	92	now–2020
2003 Cabernet Sauvignon Napa	91	now–2020
2002 Cabernet Sauvignon Napa	92	now–2020

DUCKHORN VINEYARDS ★ ★ ★/★ ★ ★ ★
NAPA $25.00–$95.00

From its debut vintage in 1978 (1,000 cases of Merlot), Duckhorn has grown its production to 75,000-plus cases of top-notch Merlots and seriously endowed, vineyard-designated Cabernet Sauvignons. After going through a series of winemakers over the last decade, they seem to have settled into a very positive style that represents a hypothetical blend of the ripeness of Napa allied with the elegance of a top Bordeaux.

2004 Cabernet Sauvignon Estate	90	now–2013
2002 Cabernet Sauvignon Estate	87	now–2010
2001 Cabernet Sauvignon Estate	89+	now–2014
2002 Cabernet Sauvignon Estate Monitor Ledge Vineyard	88	now–2015
2001 Cabernet Sauvignon Estate Monitor Ledge Vineyard	93	now–2018
2004 Cabernet Sauvignon Napa	87	now–2017
2002 Cabernet Sauvignon Napa	85	now–2011
2001 Cabernet Sauvignon Napa	88	now–2012
2004 Cabernet Sauvignon Patzimaro Vineyard Estate	88+	2009–2024
2001 Cabernet Sauvignon Patzimaro Vineyard Estate	93	now–2020+
2004 Cabernet Sauvignon Rector Creek Vineyard Estate	92	now–2022+
2004 Merlot Estate	86	2009–2019
2002 Merlot Estate	86	now
2001 Merlot Estate	89+	now–2015
2005 Merlot Napa	85	now–2012
2003 Merlot Napa	85	now
2002 Merlot Napa	90	now–2012
2004 Merlot Three Palms Vineyard	89	now–2017

2002 Merlot Three Palms Vineyard	86+?	now–2015
2006 Sauvignon Blanc	90	now
2004 Sauvignon Blanc	88	now

DUMOL ★ ★ ★ ★ ★
RUSSIAN RIVER $48.00–$78.00

A fabulous producer of Chardonnay, Pinot Noir, and more recently Viognier and Syrah, proprietor Kerry Murphy and his winemaker, Andy Smith, do terrific work in the cool-climate Russian River area. Everything produced at this winery is world-class, strikingly intense, complex, and elegant.

2006 Chardonnay Chloe	93–96	now–2015
2005 Chardonnay Chloe	95	now–2016
2004 Chardonnay Chloe	95	now–2010
2006 Chardonnay Clare	93–95	now–2014
2005 Chardonnay Clare	92	now–2015
2004 Chardonnay Clare	95+	now–2015
2006 Chardonnay Isobel Green Valley	95–97	now–2012
2005 Chardonnay Isobel Green Valley	96	now–2016
2004 Chardonnay Isobel Green Valley	94+	now–2012
2006 Chardonnay Russian River	91–93	now–2012
2005 Chardonnay Russian River	93	now
2004 Chardonnay Russian River	91–94	now
2006 Pinot Noir Aidan Green Valley	90–92	now–2013
2005 Pinot Noir Aidan Green Valley	91	now–2016+
2004 Pinot Noir Aidan Green Valley	89	now–2014
2006 Pinot Noir Finn	93–95	now–2015
2005 Pinot Noir Finn	94+	now–2016
2004 Pinot Noir Finn	94	now–2016
2003 Pinot Noir Finn	90	now–2015
2002 Pinot Noir Finn	94	now–2015
2006 Pinot Noir Russian River	88–91	now–2014
2005 Pinot Noir Russian River	91	now–2016
2003 Pinot Noir Russian River	88	now
2002 Pinot Noir Russian River	90	now
2006 Pinot Noir Ryan Green Valley	90–93	now–2013
2005 Pinot Noir Ryan Green Valley	95	now–2016
2004 Pinot Noir Ryan Green Valley	91	now–2014
2003 Pinot Noir Ryan Green Valley	89	now–2010
2002 Pinot Noir Ryan Green Valley	91	now–2015
2006 Syrah Eddie's Patch	94–96	now–2015
2005 Syrah Eddie's Patch	94	now–2016
2004 Syrah Eddie's Patch	93+	now–2018
2003 Syrah Eddie's Patch	95	now–2020
2001 Syrah Eddie's Patch	93	now–2017
2005 Syrah Jack Robert's Run	91	now–2014
2004 Syrah Jack Robert's Run	95	now–2016
2006 Syrah Russian River	88–90	now–2012
2005 Syrah Russian River	92	now–2012
2004 Syrah Russian River	91	now–2013
2003 Syrah Russian River	90	now–2011

2006 Viognier Lia	90	now
2005 Viognier Lia	92	now–2010

DUNAH VINEYARD AND WINERY   ★ ★ ★ ★
SONOMA $38.00–$50.00

DuNah is a boutique winery founded by a couple who retired from the electronic component manufacturing business. The winemaker is the talented Greg La Follette, who fashions Burgundian-styled Chardonnays and Pinot Noirs.

2004 Chardonnay DeDee's Estate	91	now
2004 Chardonnay Tre Cuvée	90	now
2005 Pinot Noir Estate	90	now–2010
2004 Pinot Noir Estate	90	now–2013
2003 Pinot Noir Estate	91	now
2005 Pinot Noir Sangiacomo Vineyard	90	now–2011
2004 Pinot Noir Sangiacomo Vineyard	89+	now–2012
2003 Pinot Noir Sangiacomo Vineyard	90	now
2003 Tre Cuvée Proprietary Red Wine	87	now–2010

DUNN   ★ ★ ★ ★
NAPA $60.00–$85.00

Randy Dunn has an extraordinary track record of producing majestic, long-lived, tannic, monster mountain-style Cabernet Sauvignons from his vineyards on Howell Mountain, and a slightly softer version from Napa. His son is now working with him, and whether it was intentional or not, his 2004s seemed much more opulent and up front than previous vintages. Nevertheless, these are still classic Napa Cabernets meant for 20 to 30 or more years of aging.

2004 Cabernet Sauvignon Howell Mountain	94+	now–2032
2003 Cabernet Sauvignon Howell Mountain	93	2012–2030
2002 Cabernet Sauvignon Howell Mountain	92	2009–2024
2001 Cabernet Sauvignon Howell Mountain	93+	2010–2035
2004 Cabernet Sauvignon Napa	91	now–2022
2003 Cabernet Sauvignon Napa	91	now–2020+
2002 Cabernet Sauvignon Napa	90	now–2024+
2001 Cabernet Sauvignon Napa	88	now–2020

EAGLES TRACE   ★ ★ ★
NAPA $60.00–$75.00

This is Gus Anderson's (father of Todd Anderson of Anderson's Conn Valley Vineyards) new project, which debuted in 2003. The finest efforts appear to be the Pinot Noirs and Bordeaux blends, especially the Latitude 38, and Cabernet Sauvignon. The Merlot has been uninspiring.

2005 Cabernet Sauvignon	90–92	now–2024
2004 Cabernet Sauvignon	90	now–2022
2005 Latitude 38	91	now–2016
2004 Latitude 38	92	now–2015
2005 Merlot	85	now–2011
2004 Merlot	86	now–2010
2005 Pinot Noir Valhalla Vineyard	88	now
2004 Pinot Noir Valhalla Vineyard	90	now

EBERLE WINERY ★★
PASO ROBLES $18.00–$30.00

Rustic, hard-edged, tannic, earthy wines emerge from this winery. They don't lack for concentration, but more charm and elegance would be noteworthy additions.

2002 Syrah Lonesome Oak Vineyard	86	now
2001 Syrah Reid Vineyard	86	now
2002 Syrah Reserve Steinbeck Vineyard	86	now
2002 Syrah Steinbeck Vineyard	86	now
2001 Syrah Steinbeck Vineyard	89	now
2004 Zinfandel Remo Belli Vineyard	88	now–2010
2004 Zinfandel Steinbeck Vineyard	90	now–2011

EDGE HILL ★★★★★
NAPA $28.00–$70.00

A single wine from a five-acre parcel of old vines in St. Helena, across from the Hayne Vineyard, is one of the finest reds of northern California. While dominated by Zinfandel, it includes Grenache, Petite Sirah, Carignan, Cabernet Sauvignon, and Mourvèdre in the blend. It is one of the most compelling wines in existence thanks to its handcrafted nature and the visionary talents of proprietor Leslie Rudd.

2004 St. Helena Estate Mixed Blacks Field Blend	93	now–2014
2003 St. Helena Estate Mixed Blacks Field Blend	94	now–2012

EDMEADES ★★★★
MENDOCINO $18.00–$29.00

This winery has a relatively long history by California standards, having been founded in 1962 by Dr. Donald Edmeades, one of the first to plant vineyards in Anderson Valley. The early winemaker was Jed Steele, but in 1992, Kendall-Jackson purchased the property and it is now part of the luxury portfolio of the Jackson Family Estates. The current winemaker, Van Williamson, continues to turn out impressive Zinfandels, and occasionally a delicious Chardonnay and Pinot Noir. These are low-tech, artisanal wines made from the estate's 60-plus acres of vines. Prices are remarkably low for such quality.

2005 Zinfandel Chase Vineyard	89	now–2012
2005 Zinfandel Ciapusci Vineyard	89	now
2004 Zinfandel Ciapusci Vineyard	87?	now
2003 Zinfandel Ciapusci Vineyard	91	now–2012
2001 Zinfandel Ciapusci Vineyard	91	now–2010
2006 Zinfandel Mendocino	90	now–2011
2005 Zinfandel Mendocino	89	now–2010
2003 Zinfandel Mendocino	89	now
2001 Zinfandel Mendocino	90	now
2005 Zinfandel Perli Vineyard	86	now
2004 Zinfandel Perli Vineyard	90	now–2011
2005 Zinfandel Piffero Vineyard	87	now
2004 Zinfandel Piffero Vineyard	89	now–2011
2003 Zinfandel Piffero Vineyard	89	now–2010
2001 Zinfandel Piffero Vineyard	90	now
2001 Zinfandel Zeni Vineyard	90+?	now

EDMUNDS ST. JOHN ★ ★ ★
CALIFORNIA $18.00–$40.00

One of California's pioneer Rhone Rangers, Steve Edmunds (also a fine musician) began this winery in the mid-1980s. It is now a 4,000-plus case facility emphasizing innovative blends, distinctive Syrahs, and an occasional detour into white wines such as Pinot Grigio. His early releases included some of the great Rhône varietal wines of California, especially his Durell Vineyard Syrahs produced in the early 1990s. Recently the quality has become less exciting, and the wines increasingly austere and lean, perhaps because the fruit sources have changed. Nevertheless, Steve Edmunds is a wine personality worth following given his noteworthy talents.

2002 Gamay Bone-Jolly	86	now
2005 Red Neck 101 Eaglepoint Ranch	86	now
2001 Los Robles Viejos Rozet Vineyard	90	now
2004 Rocks and Gravel	85	now
2005 Shell and Bone	84	now
2005 Syrah Bassetti Vineyard	86	now–2012
2003 Syrah Bassetti Vineyard	87	now–2012
2001 Syrah Bassetti Vineyard	91	now–2012
2005 Syrah Parmelee-Hill	87	now–2011
2001 Syrah Peay Vineyard	91	now–2013
2005 Syrah Wylie Fenaughty	86	now–2014
2001 Syrah Wylie Fenaughty	90	now
2001 Zinfandel Peay Vineyard	87	now–2010

ELYSE ★ ★ ★ ★
NAPA $30.00–$37.00

Producing just under 10,000 cases of high-quality wine, winemaker Ray Coursen is a crusty gentleman who is almost reminiscent of some of the old-vine Zinfandel from which he makes wine. These wines are at least very good, and often outstanding, as Coursen knows how to coax high quality out of Zinfandel, Petite Sirah, and Cabernet Sauvignon, all well worth the effort to seek them out.

2004 Petite Sirah Rutherford	90+	2010–2030
2002 Zinfandel AKA	94	now–2013
2004 Zinfandel Black Sears Vineyard	92	now–2010
2004 Zinfandel Howell Mountain	91	now–2012
2002 Zinfandel Howell Mountain	93	now–2013
2001 Zinfandel Howell Mountain	90	now
2004 Zinfandel Korte Ranch Vineyard	94	now–2011
2002 Zinfandel Korte Ranch Vineyard	93	now–2013
2001 Zinfandel Morisoli Vineyard	90	now

ENKIDU WINE ★ ★ ★ ★
SONOMA $30.00–$32.00

This impressive new producer has turned out some attractive reds that merit serious attention. The focus is on grapes that made Burgundy and the Rhône Valley famous, and are now flourishing in California.

2005 Petite Sirah Diener Ranch	90	now–2013
2005 Petite Sirah Fazekas Vineyard	89	now–2013
2004 Petite Sirah Fazekas Vineyard	92	now–2027

| 2005 Syrah Odyssey Vineyard | 89 | now–2019 |
| 2004 Syrah Odyssey Vineyard | 89 | now–2012 |

EPIPHANY CELLARS ★ ★ ★ ★
SANTA BARBARA $18.00–$45.00

Part of the Fess Parker empire, Epiphany Cellars is run by Parker's son, Eli, who draws from the Fess Parker vineyards, some of the finest sites in the Santa Rita Hills and Santa Maria Valley. The wines are full-flavored, consistently well-made efforts.

2004 Grenache	88	now–2010
2005 Marsanne Rodney's Vineyard	87	now
2003 Petite Sirah Rodney's Vineyard	92	now–2026
2002 Petite Sirah Rodney's Vineyard	90+	now–2025
2001 Petite Sirah Rodney's Vineyard	90+	now–2023
2003 Revelation Proprietary Red Wine	90	now–2012
2001 Revelation Proprietary Red Wine	93	now–2012
2005 Roussanne Camp Four Vineyard	88	now–2010
2004 Syrah Camp Four Vineyard Block Z	88	now–2011
2004 Syrah Hampton Vineyard	90	now–2017
2003 Syrah Hampton Vineyard	89	now–2015
2002 Syrah Hampton Vineyard	91	now–2017
2001 Syrah Hampton Vineyard	90	now–2012
2004 Syrah Paradise Road Vineyard	89	now–2017
2004 Syrah Rodney's Vineyard F Block	92	now–2019
2003 Syrah Starlane Vineyard	89+	now–2014
2001 Syrah Starlane Vineyard	92	now–2014

ÉTUDE ★ ★ ★ ★
NAPA $24.00–$100.00

Founded by Tony Soter, Étude has grown to a 10,000-case producer of high-class Pinot Noir, Pinot Blanc, Pinot Gris, and Cabernet Sauvignon. Since Soter sold the winery in 2001 to the huge Beringer-Blass conglomerate, quality has remained exceptionally high, and little has changed thanks to the wisdom and intelligence of that international company.

2004 Cabernet Sauvignon Napa	94	now–2022
2003 Cabernet Sauvignon Napa	91	now–2020
2002 Cabernet Sauvignon Napa	91	now–2017
2001 Cabernet Sauvignon Napa	90+	now–2023
2004 Cabernet Sauvignon Oakville	95+	now–2027
2004 Cabernet Sauvignon Rutherford	92+	now–2022+
2002 Cabernet Sauvignon Rutherford	90+	now–2020
2001 Cabernet Sauvignon Rutherford	88?	now–2015
2002 Cabernet Sauvignon St. Helena	92	now–2020
2002 Merlot Napa	89	now–2013
2006 Pinot Gris	90	now
2005 Pinot Noir Carneros	88	now–2013
2004 Pinot Noir Carneros	90	now–2013
2005 Pinot Noir Deer Camp Vineyard	87?	2009–2017
2004 Pinot Noir Deer Camp Vineyard	92	now–2013
2005 Pinot Noir Heirloom	90+	2009–2014
2004 Pinot Noir Heirloom	92	now–2016
2002 Pinot Noir Heirloom	88	now

| 2001 Pinot Noir Heirloom | 90 | now–2011 |
| 2005 Pinot Noir Temblor | 90 | now–2013 |

FAILLA ★ ★ ★ ★
NORTHERN CALIFORNIA $35.00–$52.00

Winemaker-proprietor Ehren Jordan, who also makes the wines for the great Zinfandel specialist Turley Cellars, continues to exhibit a French-inspired sensitivity to winemaking, regardless of whether he's turning out Chardonnay, Pinot Noir, or Syrah. Failla is an excellent source of elegant, flavor-filled, complex wines that remain realistically priced.

2006 Chardonnay Estate	92	now–2012
2004 Chardonnay Estate	92	now–2011
2006 Chardonnay Keefer Ranch	90	now–2011
2005 Chardonnay Keefer Ranch	92	now–2010
2004 Chardonnay Keefer Ranch	91	now–2010
2006 Pinot Noir Estate	89+	now–2013
2006 Pinot Noir Hirsch Vineyard	92	???
2005 Pinot Noir Hirsch Vineyard	93	now–2016
2004 Pinot Noir Hirsch Vineyard	92	now–2014
2003 Pinot Noir Hirsch Vineyard	91	now–2011
2002 Pinot Noir Hirsch Vineyard	90	now
2006 Pinot Noir Keefer Ranch	89	now–2011
2005 Pinot Noir Keefer Ranch	90	now–2014
2004 Pinot Noir Keefer Ranch	90	now–2012
2003 Pinot Noir Keefer Ranch	88+	now–2012
2002 Pinot Noir Keefer Ranch	91	now
2006 Pinot Noir Occidental Ridge	90	now–2013
2005 Pinot Noir Occidental Ridge	92+	now–2016
2006 Pinot Noir Pearl Essence Vineyard	88	now–2012
2006 Pinot Noir Peay Vineyard	85+?	now–2013
2005 Pinot Noir Rancho Santa Rosa	89	now–2011
2006 Pinot Noir Sonoma Coast	90	now–2013
2005 Pinot Noir Sonoma Coast	88	now–2011
2003 Pinot Noir Sonoma Coast	91	now
2002 Pinot Noir Sonoma Coast	89	now
2006 Syrah Estate	93	2009–2019
2005 Syrah Estate	91	now–2012
2004 Syrah Estate	93	now–2013
2003 Syrah Estate	92	now–2012
2006 Syrah Phoenix Ranch	91	now–2015
2005 Syrah Phoenix Ranch	89+	now–2012
2004 Syrah Phoenix Ranch	91	now–2013
2003 Syrah Phoenix Ranch	90	now–2012
2002 Syrah Phoenix Ranch	88	now
2006 Viognier Alban Vineyard	89	now
2005 Viognier Alban Vineyard	91	now

FAR NIENTE ★ ★/★ ★ ★
NAPA $65.00–$150.00

The late Gil Nickel, a nurseryman from Oklahoma, built this extraordinarily beautiful winery in the late 1970s. He concentrated on three wines: an oaky Chardonnay and Cabernet

Sauvignon, and a sweet wine called Dolce. From the beginning, the pricing was bold, and the wines never lived up to the promise of such high entry fees. The Nickel family has some sensationally well-placed vineyards, including 100 acres in Oakville called the Martin-Stelling Vineyard, 42 acres in Oakville called the John C. Sullenger Vineyard, and 18 acres in cool Coombsville called the Barrel Lane Vineyard. Two more sites, the John's Creek Vineyard (50 acres) and the Carpenter Vineyard (25 acres), are also in the Coombsville area. Spin-offs of Far Niente are the Nickel and Nickel single-vineyard cuvées, which are generally good but overpriced.

FIRESTONE VINEYARD * *
SANTA YNEZ $25.00

With significant acreage and a wine business established in 1972 by the tire magnate Brooks Firestone, high hopes have never quite been fulfilled at this lovely winery in the Santa Ynez Valley. Considerable quantities of average-quality Sauvignon Blanc, Merlot, Riesling, Chardonnay, Syrah, Gewürztraminer, and Cabernet Sauvignon are produced.

2004 Chardonnay Reserve	87	now

FISHER VINEYARDS * * * *
SONOMA/NAPA $50.00–$60.00

One of the jewels of the Mayacamas Mountains, situated on the Sonoma County side, Fisher Vineyards was founded in 1973 by Fred and Juelle Fisher. Fred appears to be moving toward retirement as his daughter and son-in-law take charge of this beautiful mountain estate whose superb vineyards extend into Napa. Fisher does a superb job with Cabernet Sauvignon, Merlot, and Chardonnay, and they recently added an impressive Syrah to the portfolio. This impeccably well-run winery is at the top of its game.

2005 Cabernet Sauvignon Coach Insignia	91	now–2021
2004 Cabernet Sauvignon Coach Insignia	90	now–2018
2003 Cabernet Sauvignon Coach Insignia	90	now–2018
2002 Cabernet Sauvignon Coach Insignia	90	now–2017
2003 Cabernet Sauvignon Lamb Vineyard	90+	now–2020
2002 Cabernet Sauvignon Lamb Vineyard	92	now–2022
2005 Cabernet Sauvignon Mountain Estate Vineyard	88	2010–2022
2005 Cabernet Sauvignon Unity	90+	2010–2019
2005 Cabernet Sauvignon Wedding Vineyard	90	now–2021
2002 Cabernet Sauvignon Wedding Vineyard	92	now–2020
2005 Cameron Proprietary Red Wine	92	now–2018
2004 Cameron Proprietary Red Wine	89	now–2016
2003 Cameron Proprietary Red Wine	89+	now–2018
2002 Cameron Proprietary Red Wine	90	now–2017
2005 Chardonnay Mountain Estate Vineyard	91	now
2004 Chardonnay Mountain Estate Vineyard	89	now
2005 Chardonnay Whitney's Vineyard Estate	90	now
2004 Chardonnay Whitney's Vineyard Estate	93	now
2002 Merlot RCF Vineyard	88	now–2011
2005 Syrah Hidden Terrace	90	now–2011
2004 Syrah Hidden Terrace	91	now–2011

The ever-reliable Flora Springs continues to turn out a noteworthy and impressive lineup of wines. They were among the first to see the future in high-class Sauvignon Blanc (the Soliloquy), and also recognized the potential for big, back-strapping Cabernet Sauvignons from Napa's Pope Valley. Their Trilogy Proprietary Red was among the first of the so-called Meritage blends, but their real glories are their single-vineyard Cabernet Sauvignons and their Cabernet Sauvignon Hillside Reserve. They are among Napa's most traditional and classic Cabernets.

Wine	Score	Drink
2002 Cabernet Sauvignon Crossroads	92	now–2018
2002 Cabernet Sauvignon Hardman	92	now–2018
2006 Cabernet Sauvignon Holy Smoke Vineyard	88–90+	2009–2020
2005 Cabernet Sauvignon Holy Smoke Vineyard	90	now–2022
2004 Cabernet Sauvignon Holy Smoke Vineyard	90	now–2022
2003 Cabernet Sauvignon Holy Smoke Vineyard	88	now–2022
2002 Cabernet Sauvignon Holy Smoke Vineyard	93	now–2020
2004 Cabernet Sauvignon Napa	87	now–2017
2002 Cabernet Sauvignon Napa	90	now–2015
2006 Cabernet Sauvignon Out of Sight Vineyard	91–93	2010–2023
2005 Cabernet Sauvignon Out of Sight Vineyard	93	now–2027+
2004 Cabernet Sauvignon Out of Sight Vineyard	92	now–2022+
2003 Cabernet Sauvignon Out of Sight Vineyard	89	now–2019
2002 Cabernet Sauvignon Out of Sight Vineyard	90	now–2023
2006 Cabernet Sauvignon Rutherford Hillside Reserve	90–93	2010–2025
2005 Cabernet Sauvignon Rutherford Hillside Reserve	90+	now–2027
2004 Cabernet Sauvignon Rutherford Hillside Reserve	89+	2009–2024+
2003 Cabernet Sauvignon Rutherford Hillside Reserve	92	2010–2025
2002 Cabernet Sauvignon Rutherford Hillside Reserve	94	now–2025
2006 Cabernet Sauvignon St. Helena Reserve	90–92	2010–2022
2005 Cabernet Sauvignon St. Helena Reserve	91+	2009–2019
2006 Cabernet Sauvignon Wild Boar Vineyard	90–92	2010–2019
2005 Cabernet Sauvignon Wild Boar Vineyard	88	2011–2020
2004 Cabernet Sauvignon Wild Boar Vineyard	89	now–2022
2003 Cabernet Sauvignon Wild Boar Vineyard	88	now–2016
2002 Cabernet Sauvignon Wild Boar Vineyard	90	now–2017
2002 Cabernet Sauvignon 25th Anniversary	94+	now–2020
2006 Sauvignon Blanc Soliloquy	90	now
2005 Trilogy Proprietary Red Wine	93	now–2022+
2004 Trilogy Proprietary Red Wine	88	now–2019
2003 Trilogy Proprietary Red Wine	91	now–2016
2002 Trilogy Proprietary Red Wine	91	now–2017

FLOWERS VINEYARD AND WINERY   ★ ★ ★/★ ★ ★ ★
SONOMA $48.00–$60.00

Former nursery owners Walt and Joan Flowers have one of the most gorgeous vineyard sites on the Sonoma Coast. Production is approximately 15,000 cases of Chardonnay and Pinot Noir from their two major estate holdings, the Camp Meeting Ridge Vineyard and the Keefer Ranch. With 300 total acres, 23 planted, the quality of the Flowers wines has generally been very high, although they have gone through a number of different winemakers, which can affect consistency. Nevertheless, the enormous potential of these cool-climate sites is obvious. Made from low yields, the wines possess Burgundy-like personalities.

2003 Pinot Noir Andreen-Gale Cuvée	89	now–2010
2002 Pinot Noir Andreen-Gale Cuvée	90	now
2003 Pinot Noir Camp Meeting Ridge	89	now–2010
2003 Pinot Noir Frances Thompson	91	now–2012
2003 Pinot Noir Grand Bouquet	88	now
2003 Pinot Noir Keefer Ranch	87	now
2002 Pinot Noir Keefer Ranch	87	now
2003 Pinot Noir Moon Select	90+	now–2013
2003 Pinot Noir Sonoma Coast	89	now

ADRIAN FOG ★ ★ ★ ★
NORTHERN CALIFORNIA $75.00

This winery is dedicated to making top-flight, single-vineyard Pinot Noirs from sites in the Russian River, Anderson Valley, Mendocino, and the Sonoma Coast. They are intensely perfumed, but very limited in availability as there are fewer than 350 cases of each cuvée.

2003 Pinot Noir Demuth Vineyard	90	now
2003 Pinot Noir Hunnicutt Vineyard	89	now
2006 Pinot Noir Numbers	89	now–2010
2005 Pinot Noir Numbers	89	now–2011
2006 Pinot Noir Oppenlander Vineyard	90	now–2012
2004 Pinot Noir Oppenlander Vineyard	89	now
2003 Pinot Noir Oppenlander Vineyard	95	now–2013
2006 Pinot Noir Savoy Vineyard	89+	now–2013
2005 Pinot Noir Savoy Vineyard	92	now–2010
2004 Pinot Noir Savoy Vineyard	90	now
2003 Pinot Noir Savoy Vineyard	94	now–2010
2006 Pinot Noir Two Sisters Vineyard	91	now–2011
2004 Pinot Noir Two Sisters Vineyard	88	now–2011
2003 Pinot Noir Two Sisters Vineyard	91	now–2011

THOMAS FOGARTY ★ ★/★ ★ ★
SANTA CRUZ MOUNTAINS $45.00–$68.00

Founded in 1981, this winery has had a mixed track record regarding wine quality. They have fashioned some very fine Pinot Noirs and Chardonnays, an irregular, unusual Gewürztraminer, and mixed offerings of Cabernet Sauvignon, Sangiovese, and Barbera. Some so-so sparkling wines are also produced.

2004 Chardonnay Camel Hill Vineyard	86	now–2010
2004 Chardonnay Damiana Vineyard	86	now
2004 Chardonnay Portola Springs	87	now–2010
2004 Pinot Noir Rapley Trail Vineyard M Block	86	now–2013

FOLEY ESTATES ★ ★ ★/★ ★ ★ ★
SANTA RITA HILLS $30.00–$50.00

Originally founded as Carey Cellars in the late 1970s, this property has experienced a number of ownership changes, but it is now in the competent hands of William Foley. The wines have gotten significantly stronger in quality over recent vintages, and the Pinot Noirs and Chardonnays are now among the finest of Santa Barbara County.

2005 Chardonnay Barrel Select Rancho Santa Rosa	90	now–2012
2004 Chardonnay Barrel Select Rancho Santa Rosa	92	now–2011
2005 Chardonnay Clone 76 Rancho Santa Rosa	90	now–2011
2004 Chardonnay Clone 76 Rancho Santa Rosa	91	now–2011
2005 Chardonnay Clone 96 Rancho Santa Rosa	89	now–2011
2004 Chardonnay Clone 96 Rancho Santa Rosa	90	now–2011
2005 Chardonnay Rancho Santa Rosa	90	now–2011
2004 Chardonnay Rancho Santa Rosa	90	now–2011
2005 Pinot Noir Barrel Select Rancho Santa Rosa	90	now–2017
2004 Pinot Noir Barrel Select Rancho Santa Rosa	92	now–2012
2005 Pinot Noir Clone 2A Rancho Santa Rosa	90	now–2012
2004 Pinot Noir Clone 2A Rancho Santa Rosa	90	now–2013
2005 Pinot Noir 115 Rancho Santa Rosa	90	now–2015
2005 Pinot Noir Dijon Clone 667 Rancho Santa Rosa	91	now–2014
2004 Pinot Noir Dijon Clone 667 Rancho Santa Rosa	89	now–2011
2005 Pinot Noir Pommard Clone Rancho Santa Rosa	88	now–2013
2004 Pinot Noir Pommard Clone Rancho Santa Rosa	89	now–2013
2005 Pinot Noir Rancho Santa Rosa	89	now–2012
2004 Pinot Noir Rancho Santa Rosa	90	now–2012
2005 Syrah Rancho Santa Rosa	87	now–2011
2003 Syrah Rancho Santa Rosa	88+	now–2010

ROBERT FOLEY ★ ★ ★ ★
NAPA $38.00–$125.00

One of California's most talented winemakers, Robert Foley carved out an admirable reputation while working at Pride Mountain Vineyards. He now has his own Howell Mountain vineyard and also serves as a winemaking consultant. These are consistently top-notch efforts with impressive personalities.

2005 Charbono	85?	now
2004 Charbono	90	now
2003 Charbono	87?	now
2002 Charbono	91	now–2011
2005 Claret	94	now–2022
2004 Claret	95	now–2021
2003 Claret	96	now–2020
2002 Claret	95+	now–2018
2001 Claret	99	now–2020
2005 Merlot	89	now–2015
2005 Petite Sirah	93	now–2027
2004 Petite Sirah	95	2009–2025+
2003 Petite Sirah	92	2010–2030
2006 Pinot Blanc	86	now

FOLIE À DEUX ★ ★
NAPA $20.00–$45.00

This winery was sold by its original owners in the mid-1990s, and the wines continue to be made in a monolithic, one-dimensional style emphasizing straightforward fruit flavors and little depth, richness, concentration, or character.

FOPPIANO VINEYARDS ★★
RUSSIAN RIVER $17.50–$23.00

Established by Italian immigrants in the 19th century, Foppiano's rustic Old World–styled wines are often tannic, but never lack personality. Their finest efforts are the Zinfandels and Petite Sirahs.

2003 Petite Sirah Bacigalupe Vineyard	86	now–2012
2003 Petite Sirah Estate	88	now–2016

FORMAN VINEYARD ★★★★
NAPA $35.00–$65.00

Ric Forman, who began his winemaking career at Sterling in 1969, is one of the most experienced and seasoned wine producers in all of California. Although he is often accused of being too stubborn to change gears, he does seem to make cellar improvements almost every year. He also pioneered one of the classic nonmalolactic styles of Chardonnay.

2006 Cabernet Sauvignon	93–95	now–2032
2005 Cabernet Sauvignon	93+	2010–2020+
2004 Cabernet Sauvignon	91	now–2021
2003 Cabernet Sauvignon	90	now–2020
2002 Cabernet Sauvignon	94	now–2020
2001 Cabernet Sauvignon	93	now–2023
2006 Chardonnay	91	now–2012
2005 Chardonnay	93	now–2010
2006 Special Cuvée (not yet named)	94–96	2011–2040

FORT ROSS ★★★
SONOMA $30.00–$60.00

Fort Ross is a small operation on the Sonoma Coast dedicated to handcrafted Chardonnays and Pinot Noirs. My experience with these wines is limited, but their first vintages (they debuted in 2000) have shown good potential.

2002 Pinot Noir Fort Ross Vineyard	88	now
2002 Pinot Noir Fort Ross Vineyard	88?	now
2002 Pinot Noir Symposium	85	now

FOUR VINES WINERY ★★★
PASO ROBLES $25.00–$40.00

This playful partnership appears to show no respect for how wines are traditionally marketed. The results are plenty of fun-filled wines, particularly Zinfandels and intriguing blends from vineyards in Amador County and the estate's home base, Paso Robles. Prices are also refreshingly modest.

2005 Anarchy	89	now–2013
2004 Anarchy	89	now–2010
2001 Anarchy	88	now
2005 Loco Tres Cajones Vineyard	88	now–2010
2004 Loco Tres Cajones Vineyard	85	now–2010
2005 Peasant	88	now–2011
2004 Peasant	87	now–2010
2005 Petite Sirah Heretic	90	now–2019
2004 Petite Sirah Heretic	89	now–2024

2005 Syrah Phoenix Kiler Canyon	88	now–2013
2004 Syrah Phoenix Kiler Canyon	88	now–2015

BLAIR FOX CELLARS ★ ★ ★ ★
SANTA BARBARA $26.00–$48.00

In addition to making wines under his own label, Blair Fox is employed as the head wine-maker at the Fess Parker Winery. At his own operation, he produces small-lot, handcrafted Syrahs that all merit serious attention. Moreover, prices are fair.

2005 Syrah The Dare	89	now–2015
2004 Syrah The Dare	92	now–2016
2001 Syrah Harmon Family Vineyard	87	now–2014
2004 Syrah Paradise Road Vineyard	90	now–2014
2003 Syrah Paradise Road Vineyard	91	now–2015
2002 Syrah Paradise Road Vineyard	91	now–2017
2005 Syrah Purisima Mountain	90	now–2017
2004 Syrah Purisima Mountain	89+	now–2014
2005 Syrah Tierra Alta Vineyard	92	now–2015
2004 Syrah Tierra Alta Vineyard	90+	now–2016

FOXEN ★ ★ ★ ★
SANTA YNEZ $18.00–$75.00

With more than 20 years of experience, owners-winemakers Dick Dore and Bill Wathen con-tinue to fine-tune an already impressive portfolio of Chardonnays, Pinot Noirs, and Syrahs. They also produce small quantities of Merlot and a Merlot–Cabernet Franc blend, as well as a tiny bit of Sangiovese.

2005 Chardonnay Tinaquaic Vineyard	88	now
2004 Chardonnay Tinaquaic Vineyard	90	now
2004 Chenin Blanc Old Vines Ernesto Wickenden Vineyard	89	now
2005 Cuvée Jeanne-Marie Williamson-Doré Vineyard	91	now–2013
2004 Cuvée Jeanne-Marie Williamson-Doré Vineyard	90	now–2012
2005 Pinot Noir Bien Nacido Vineyard Block Eight	89	now–2013
2004 Pinot Noir Bien Nacido Vineyard Block Eight	93	now–2013
2003 Pinot Noir Bien Nacido Vineyard Block Eight	89	now
2005 Pinot Noir Julia's Vineyard	86	now–2012
2004 Pinot Noir Julia's Vineyard	92	now–2010
2003 Pinot Noir Julia's Vineyard	91	now
2005 Pinot Noir Sea Smoke Vineyard	89+	now–2017
2004 Pinot Noir Sea Smoke Vineyard	96	???
2003 Pinot Noir Sea Smoke Vineyard	90	now–2010
2005 Syrah Tinaquaic Vineyard	92	now–2017
2004 Syrah Tinaquaic Vineyard	92	now–2016
2005 Syrah Williamson-Doré Vineyard	90	now–2017
2004 Syrah Williamson-Doré Vineyard	92+	now–2016+

FRANCISCAN OAKVILLE ESTATE ★ ★/★ ★ ★
NAPA $25.00–$50.00

Mixed quality tends to emerge from Franciscan despite their impressive, well-situated vine-yard sites in the heart of Napa Valley. The original proprietors were forced to sell after own-ing this winery for several years, and today Franciscan is directed by Agustin Huneeus, whose personal estate, Quintessa, seems to be trumping the quality of these wines. They are often blatantly woody and overwhelmingly simple.

2003 Cabernet Sauvignon Napa	86	now–2015
2005 Chardonnay Napa	85	now
2002 Magnificat Napa	??	now–2015

PETER FRANUS ★ ★ ★ ★
NAPA $32.00–$45.00

For more than 20 years, Peter Franus has been producing high-quality Zinfandel and Cabernet Sauvignon. He has access to some top-notch sites, and I have always enjoyed the purity and overall balance of his wines. For some reason, this winery continues to fly under most consumers' radar.

2003 Cabernet Sauvignon Napa	89	now–2014
2001 Cabernet Sauvignon Napa	89+	now–2017
2004 Zinfandel Brandlin Vineyard	89	now
2003 Zinfandel Brandlin Vineyard	90	now–2013
2001 Zinfandel Brandlin Vineyard	90	now
2002 Zinfandel Napa	88	now

FRAZIER ★ ★ ★
NAPA $50.00–$55.00

This is a 5,000-case operation dedicated to Bordeaux varietal wines, primarily Cabernet Sauvignon and Merlot. Frazier also makes limited quantities of Petit Verdot and a proprietary blend called Memento.

2003 Cabernet Sauvignon Napa	87	now–2013
2001 Cabernet Sauvignon Napa	88	now–2013

FREEMARK ABBEY ★ ★ ★/★ ★ ★ ★
NAPA $55.00–$65.00

In the 1970s and 1980s, Freemark Abbey was a top-notch winery renowned for their fabulous Cabernet Sauvignon Bosche Vineyard. Sadly, they fell on hard times and went through a long period of mediocrity. Thankfully, the winery is now being resurrected to its former glory by Jess Jackson, who hit pay dirt with his 2004s, the finest Cabernet Sauvignons made at Freemark Abbey in nearly 20 years. This is a winery to watch.

2004 Cabernet Sauvignon Bosche Vineyard	92	now–2027+
2004 Cabernet Sauvignon Napa	90	now–2022
2004 Cabernet Sauvignon Sycamore Vineyards	93	now–2027

FREI BROTHERS ★ ★ ★
RUSSIAN RIVER $20.00–$25.00

Frei Brothers are part of the huge Gallo operation, producing wines with Sonoma appellations such as Chardonnay, Cabernet Sauvignon, Merlot, Pinot Noir, Sauvignon Blanc, and Syrah. The Gallo Brothers purchased grapes from the Frei vineyards for more than 50 years before actually buying the winery in 1978. These are generally well-priced, well-made wines.

2005 Chardonnay Reserve	87	now

FRICK WINERY ★ ★ ★
DRY CREEK $21.00–$25.00

This Dry Creek winery has been in existence for more than 30 years, turning out an idiosyncratic lineup of wines, including a rare Cinsault (and a good one at that) and Carignan, and of course, more conventional wines such as Merlot and Syrah. Prices are reasonable and the wines have a definite artisanal, almost homemade character.

2004 Cinsault	87	now–2010
2004 Syrah Owl Hill	86	now–2012
2005 Viognier Gannon Vineyard	85	now

FROG'S LEAP ★ ★ ★
RUTHERFORD $20.00–$60.00

Frog's Leap has more than 130 acres in Rutherford and a history that dates back nearly 20 years. It has been a pace-setter with regard to Sauvignon Blanc, and occasionally produces very good Zinfandel and Cabernet Sauvignon. The regional partnership between Larry Turley and John Williams broke up in 1994, with Turley setting up his remarkable Zinfandel operation farther north in Napa. Wine production seems to have jumped considerably here, and the wines are always competent and pleasant, if largely uninspiring.

FUTO ★ ★ ★ ★/★ ★ ★ ★ ★
NAPA $200.00

This tiny boutique operation, a stone's throw down the hill from Harlan Estate, has only five acres of vineyards and is just debuting its first wine, from a vineyard formerly known as the Oakford Estate. Superstar consultant Mark Aubert is the winemaker. Owners Tom and Kyle Futo are intent on producing something of world-class quality, and they have no problem charging an arm and a leg for it.

2006 Napa	93–95	2011–2020
2005 Napa	95+	now–2033
2004 Napa	96	now–2028

GAINEY VINEYARDS ★ ★/★ ★ ★
SANTA YNEZ $32.00–$40.00

After a relatively irregular track record from the estate's 120-plus acres of vineyards, when many herbal and dilute wines were the rule of thumb, things have improved dramatically over the last few vintages. The wines are hardly inspirational, but they are certainly much better than in the past.

2004 Chardonnay Limited Selection	90	now–2010
2005 Pinot Noir Limited Selection	87	now–2011
2002 Pinot Noir Limited Selection	87	now
2004 Syrah Limited Selection	86	now–2011
2001 Syrah Limited Selection	88	now–2011
2001 Syrah Santa Rita Hills	90	now–2015

GALLO FAMILY VINEYARDS ★ ★ ★
SONOMA $15.00–$80.00

One needs to distinguish between the Gallo of Sonoma, which produces over a half-million cases of generally sound, high-quality wines, and their huge, nearly 100 million–case production facility in Modesto, California, which produces an enormous line of wines under many different labels, including Carlo Rossi, Turning Leaf, Anapamu Indigo Hills, Zabaco, and many others. Despite the temptation to criticize such a colossal operation, even the low end of quality from E & J Gallo, represented by such wines as Hearty Burgundy and their notorious Chablis Blanc (although no longer called that), are surprisingly competent. The Sonoma end of the range is by far the best, with some very serious wines in the portfolio.

2003 Cabernet Sauvignon Estate	90	now–2012
2004 Cabernet Sauvignon Frei Ranch	89+	now–2016
2003 Cabernet Sauvignon Frei Ranch	89	now–2021
2004 Chardonnay	88	now
2004 Chardonnay Laguna	90	now
2004 Chardonnay Northern Sonoma Estate	90	now
2003 Chardonnay Northern Sonoma Estate	89	now
2004 Chardonnay Two Rock	90	now
2005 Pinot Gris	88	now–2012
2006 Pinot Gris Sonoma Reserve	87	now
2004 Pinot Noir	89	now–2011
2004 Pinot Noir WM Signature Two Rock	91	now–2011
2003 Zinfandel Frei Ranch	90	now–2016
2003 Zinfandel Sonoma	87	now

GARRETSON WINE CO. ★ ★ ★
PASO ROBLES $16.00–$75.00

Matt Garretson, who founded this winery in 2001, makes a dizzying assortment of Rhone Ranger wines, with his less expensive ones bottled with a capital "G" designation and the others all given rather unusual Nordic names. His reds seems to be far superior to his whites, which are hit-or-miss propositions, but the wines are never boring and often exceptionally interesting. Garretson is also the major force behind the successful Hospice du Rhône celebration held every May.

2005 Le Celeidh	89	now
2005 G (white)	88	now
2004 G (red)	89	now
2003 G (red)	86	now
2005 Grenache The Spainneach	85	now–2010
2004 Grenache The Spainneach	90	now–2010
2003 Grenache The Spainneach	86	now
2004 Mourvèdre The Graosta	89+	now–2014
2003 Mourvèdre The Graosta	88	now
2003 The Reliquary (red)	93	now–2015
2005 Roussanne The Limoid Cior	87?	now
2003 Syrah The Aisling	90	now–2013
2002 Syrah The Aisling	91	now–2013
2005 Syrah The Bulladoir	91	now–2017
2004 Syrah The Bulladoir	95	now–2018
2003 Syrah The Bulladoir	93	now–2013
2004 Syrah The Craic	92	now–2014
2003 Syrah The Craic	89	now–2013
2002 Syrah The Craic	91	now–2010
2004 Syrah The Luascain	90+	now–2013
2003 Syrah The Luascain	88	now–2011
2005 Syrah Mon Amie	90	now–2010
2004 Syrah Mon Amie	94	now–2016

2003 Syrah Mon Amie Bassetti Vineyard	90	now–2013
2002 Syrah Mon Amie Bassetti Vineyard	90	now

GEMSTONE VINEYARD ★ ★ ★ ★
NAPA $65.00–$95.00

These are superb wines made by winemaking consultant Philippe Melka for owners Paul Frank and his wife, Suzie. While much of the fruit from their Silverado Trail vineyard in Napa is sold to well-known wineries, they keep enough to produce limited quantities of these top-flight wines. Their flagship wine, the Gemstone Proprietary Red, is one of the finest in Napa.

2005 Chardonnay	88	now
2006 Facets Proprietary Red Wine	92–94	now–2022
2005 Facets Proprietary Red Wine	90	now–2019
2004 Facets of Gemstone	94	2010–2025
2002 Facets One	89	now–2015
2006 Proprietary Red Wine	92–94	now–2022+
2005 Proprietary Red Wine	95	now–2021
2004 Proprietary Red Wine	95	now–2030
2003 Proprietary Red Wine	91	now–2020

ANDREW GEOFFREY VINEYARD ★ ★ ★ ★
NAPA $75.00

This 13-acre vineyard high on Diamond Mountain produces stylish, complex, supple wines that retain the intrinsically high tannins of this mountain site. The former Stag's Leap Wine Cellars winemaker, John Gibson, is the proprietor. His goal is to produce a finesse-styled Bordeaux look-alike from these steep vineyards.

2005 Cabernet Sauvignon Diamond Mountain	92	now–2022
2004 Cabernet Sauvignon Diamond Mountain	89	now–2018
2003 Cabernet Sauvignon Diamond Mountain	91	now–2017

GRACE FAMILY VINEYARDS ★ ★ ★ ★
NAPA $225.00–$900.00

This boutique operation produces just one wine, a pure, concentrated Cabernet Sauvignon meant for 15 to 20 years of aging, made from a tiny, three-acre gem of a vineyard just to the north of St. Helena. Most of this wine is allocated to members of the mailing list and to fashionable restaurants.

GRAYSON CELLARS ★ ★ ★
NAPA $9.00–$13.00

This *négociant* operation has an impressive track record of turning out value-priced wines, especially Cabernet Sauvignons, Chardonnays, and Zinfandels, at incredibly low price points. (I am less impressed by their Merlot and Pinot Noir.) This is a very reliable source for bargain hunters.

2005 Cabernet Sauvignon	87	now–2011
2005 Chardonnay	88	now–2010

GREEN AND RED ★★★/★★★★
NAPA $15.00–$25.00

One of the best producers of elegant, cool-climate Zinfandel at a relatively high elevation of 1,000 to 1,500 feet, this winery never fails to impress me. The production seems to be gobbled up very quickly, even though there are 5,000-plus cases. I am less taken with their Chardonnay.

GREY WOLF CELLARS ★★★
PASO ROBLES $24.00–$50.00

This small family winery was founded in 1994 and is part of the ever-growing group of artisanal, small, yet high-quality wineries emerging on the west side of Highway 101 in Paso Robles. Winemaker-proprietor Joe Barton seems to have a fine touch with Zinfandel as well as Syrah.

2005 Chianti Cuvée Chanticleer Vineyard	91	now–2012
2005 Syrah Predator	90	now–2014
2005 Soulmate	89	now–2012
2004 Zinfandel Estate	89	now–2014
2004 Zinfandel The Jackal	90	now–2012
2004 Zinfandel Reserve	91	now–2013

GRGICH HILLS ★★★
NAPA $30.00–$73.00

One of the well-established names of Napa Valley, Mike Grgich has an impressive résumé, having worked for André Tchelistcheff at Beaulieu and at Château Montelena before starting this winery in 1977. I find his wines somewhat overrated. His best successes tend to be his Fumé Blancs and Zinfandel from old vines, while the Cabernets are often oaky and somewhat monolithic and the Chardonnays good but hardly inspirational.

2005 Chardonnay Carneros Selection	89	now–2010
2003 Chardonnay Paris Tasting Commemorative		
Bottling Estate	87	now
2005 Fumé Blanc Estate	90	now
2004 Fumé Blanc/Dry Sauvignon Blanc Estate	90	now
2006 Sauvignon Blanc Essence	91	now
2004 Zinfandel Miljenko's Old Vines	89	now
2001 Zinfandel Miljenko's Old Vines	89	now
2001 Zinfandel Napa	86	now

GROTH ★★★
NAPA $65.00–$250.00

The first 100-point, perfect score I ever gave to a California wine was to the Groth Cabernet Sauvignon Reserve made by Nils Venge. That level of quality largely continued for a few more years, but then the wines became increasingly herbal and vegetal, and Venge, the brilliant force behind the great successes of Groth in the 1980s, moved down the road to start his own winery. There is still enormous potential here as Groth still owns the 121-acre Oak Cross Vineyard, which was the source of some extraordinary Cabernet Sauvignons from Villa Mt. Eden winery in the 1970s. For now the wines remain pleasant but lacking in complexity and charm, which is hard to explain given the phenomenal location of some of their core vineyards right in Oakville, sandwiched between some of the great Cabernet producers of California.

GUNDLACH BUNDSCHU ★★
SONOMA $35.00

Pleasant, straightforward wines that sell at a reasonable price characterize this charming Sonoma winery, which has quite a history, having been established in the mid-1800s but closed down during prohibition. The president of the company, Jim Bundschu, replanted the vineyards in the late 1960s, and their Chardonnay, Riesling, and occasionally Zinfandel is of sound quality as well as modestly priced.

2004 Zinfandel Rhinefarm Vineyard	89	now–2010

HAGAFEN CELLARS ★★
NAPA $25.00

A rather bland group of wines, including some kosher wines, is the specialty of this operation owned by Ernie Weir. The winery is located in southern Napa, near both the Stags Leap and Oak Knoll districts.

HALLECK VINEYARD ★★★/★★★★
RUSSIAN RIVER $28.00–$58.00

A small but promising Pinot Noir specialist started by Ross and Jennifer Halleck, this winery's initial wines have been very impressive and fairly priced. Their Pinots are named after their three sons.

2004 Pinot Noir Halleck Vineyard	90+	now–2017
2002 Pinot Noir Halleck Vineyard	92	now–2010
2004 Pinot Noir Three Sons Cuvée	90	now–2010
2003 Pinot Noir Three Sons Cuvée	89	now–2011
2004 Sauvignon Blanc Piner Creek Ranch	87	now

HALTER RANCH ★★/★★★
PASO ROBLES $14.00–$28.00

A work-in-progress, this 900-acre ranch is owned by Swiss businessman Hansjörg Wyss and has a wide array of grape varieties planted, including Bordeaux and Rhône varieties as well as Zinfandel. The quality of the wines to date has been good, if unexciting.

2004 Syrah Halter Ranch Vineyard	90	now–2015
2003 Syrah Halter Ranch Vineyard	89	now–2010
2002 Syrah Halter Ranch Vineyard	86	now–2010
2005 Viognier Halter Ranch Vineyard	89	now

HANDLEY CELLARS ★★/★★★
MENDOCINO $20.00–$25.00

These reliable, soundly made Sauvignon Blancs, Chardonnays, Pinot Noirs, and sparkling wines are always fruit-forward and pleasant. Moreover, pricing is very fair.

2004 Syrah Handley Vineyard	83?	now
2004 Syrah Kazmet Vineyard	85	now–2012
2001 Syrah Mendocino	87	now
2005 Viognier Handley Vineyard	86	now
2004 Zinfandel Gianoli Ranch Vineyard	86	now

HANNA WINERY * *
SONOMA $19.00–$49.00

Hard-edged, chunky wines are produced at Hanna. I have never been impressed with the Bordeaux varietal wines; their strong suits seem to be Zinfandel and Syrah. Prices are reasonable.

2003 Syrah Bismarck Mountain Vineyard	89+	now–2017
2001 Syrah Bismarck Mountain Vineyard	86	now
2001 Zinfandel Bismarck Ranch	90	now

WALTER HANSEL WINERY * * * */* * * * *
RUSSIAN RIVER $30.00–$45.00

This is a terrific source for sensational Pinot Noirs and Chardonnays, made very much in the style of wines proprietor Stephen Hansel loves the most, white and red Burgundies. The wines emerge from an 80-acre estate that has built a brilliant track record over the past five to six years. Moreover, prices are remarkably low for such a level of quality.

2006 Chardonnay Cahill Lane	94	now–2013
2005 Chardonnay Cahill Lane	93	now–2013
2004 Chardonnay Cahill Lane	91	now–2010
2006 Chardonnay Cuvée Alyce	96	now–2016
2005 Chardonnay Cuvée Alyce	94	now–2016
2004 Chardonnay Cuvée Alyce	92	now–2011
2005 Chardonnay Estate	91	now–2011
2004 Chardonnay Estate	91	now
2006 Chardonnay North Slope Vineyard	93	now–2013
2005 Chardonnay North Slope Vineyard	93	now–2013
2004 Chardonnay North Slope Vineyard	93	now–2012
2006 Chardonnay Walter Hansel Vineyard	92	now–2013
2006 Pinot Noir Cahill Lane	92–94	now–2014
2005 Pinot Noir Cahill Lane	91	now–2016
2004 Pinot Noir Cahill Lane	93	now–2016
2003 Pinot Noir Cahill Lane	91	now–2012
2006 Pinot Noir Cuvée Alyce	92–95	now–2015
2005 Pinot Noir Cuvée Alyce	91	now–2014
2004 Pinot Noir Cuvée Alyce	92+	now–2016
2003 Pinot Noir Cuvée Alyce	92+	now–2013
2006 Pinot Noir Russian River	90–92	now–2012
2006 Pinot Noir The North Slope	91–93	now–2013
2005 Pinot Noir The North Slope	92	now–2015
2004 Pinot Noir The North Slope	94	now–2015
2003 Pinot Noir The North Slope	90+	now–2013
2006 Pinot Noir The South Slope	90–92	now–2015
2004 Pinot Noir The South Slope	91	now–2016
2003 Pinot Noir The South Slope	88?	now–2012
2006 Pinot Noir Three Rows	91–94	now–2015
2004 Pinot Noir Three Rows	90+	now–2015
2003 Pinot Noir Three Rows	88?	now–2013

HANZELL VINEYARDS ★ ★ ★ ★
SONOMA $65.00–$75.00

Founded by Burgundy enthusiast James Zellerbach in 1957, this property was owned by the De Brye family for many years. The winemaker, Bob Sessions, was backed up by former Acacia whiz kid Michael Terrien. The original six-acre vineyard has grown to 42 acres, and the production is around 6,000 cases of what can be stunningly rich, ageworthy Chardonnay as well as very good Pinot Noir. Overall, these wines can be very special.

2005 Chardonnay Sonoma	92	now–2012
2003 Pinot Noir Ambassador's 1953 Vineyard	92	2011–2020
2004 Pinot Noir Sonoma	90	now–2015

HAPPY CANYON VINEYARD ★ ★/★ ★ ★
SANTA YNEZ $30.00–$60.00

This is an unusual Santa Barbara vineyard, since the entire site is planted with Bordeaux varieties (Cabernet Sauvignon, Merlot, and Cabernet Franc). Historically, these grapes have struggled in Santa Barbara. The winemaker is Doug Margerum, who ran the successful Wine Cask program.

2004 Barrack Brand Happy Canyon Vineyard	90+	now–2019
2004 Barrack Ten Goal Happy Canyon Vineyard	91	now–2023
2004 Piocho Happy Canyon Vineyard	92+	now–2018

HARLAN ESTATE ★ ★ ★ ★ ★
OAKVILLE $125.00–$450.00

Not yet 20 years old, this estate was founded by Bill Harlan, a visionary real-estate entrepreneur and proprietor of the luxurious Meadowood Country Club and Resort. Harlan Estate, a beautifully manicured and situated 40-acre hillside vineyard overlooking the Oakville Corridor, produces 1,500 cases of utterly profound wines, regardless of vintage conditions. Along with the rest of his team, Bob Levy and Michel Rolland, Bill Harlan represents winemaking. These are legendary wines representing the finest Napa, or any other viticultural region, can achieve. For some reason, the Harlan wines remind me of a hypothetical blend of a top Pauillac and a great Graves, with more ripeness because of the California climate. If you can afford them, you won't be disappointed.

2005 Harlan Estate	96+	2014–2035
2004 Harlan Estate	98	now–2031
2003 Harlan Estate	95	now–2026
2002 Harlan Estate	100	now–2035
2001 Harlan Estate	100	2009–2028+
2005 The Maiden	92	now–2022
2004 The Maiden	95	now–2021
2003 The Maiden	91	now–2021
2002 The Maiden	94	now–2020
2001 The Maiden	93	now–2020

HARRIS ESTATE VINEYARDS ★ ★ ★ ★
NAPA $75.00–$95.00

Located on the north slope of the Diamond Mountain appellation, near Calistoga, this 28-acre estate was purchased by Mike and Treva Harris in 1997. The wines are all single-vineyard, 100% Cabernet Sauvignons aged in Taransaud barrels and made under the guidance of the brilliant consultant Mark Herold.

2006 Cabernet Sauvignon Jake's Creek Vineyard	91–94	2010–2025
2005 Cabernet Sauvignon Jake's Creek Vineyard	90+?	2014–2028
2004 Cabernet Sauvignon Jake's Creek Vineyard	90+	now–2018
2003 Cabernet Sauvignon Jake's Creek Vineyard	90+	2009–2029
2006 Cabernet Sauvignon Lakeview Vineyard	92–94	now–2022+
2005 Cabernet Sauvignon Lakeview Vineyard	94	now–2022
2004 Cabernet Sauvignon Lakeview Vineyard	90	2009–2018
2003 Cabernet Sauvignon Lakeview Vineyard	90	now–2017
2006 Cabernet Sauvignon Treva's Vineyard VSR	92–94	2011–2025+
2005 Cabernet Sauvignon Treva's Vineyard VSR	92+	2010–2030
2004 Cabernet Sauvignon Treva's Vineyard VSR	94	now–2022
2003 Cabernet Sauvignon Treva's Vineyard VSR	92	now–2020
2002 Cabernet Sauvignon Treva's Vineyard VSR	94	now–2018

HARTFORD FAMILY WINERY ⋆ ⋆ ⋆ ⋆ ⋆
RUSSIAN RIVER $30.00–$75.00

One of the superstar estates in the portfolio of boutique wineries owned by Jess Jackson and his wife, Barbara Banke, Hartford Family Winery specializes in cool-climate Chardonnays, Pinot Noirs, and Zinfandels. These are thrilling, single-vineyard efforts that possess extraordinary character, personality, and pleasure-giving characteristics. Moreover, prices are realistic for such excellent quality.

2006 Chardonnay Four Hearts	91	now–2010
2005 Chardonnay Four Hearts	91	now–2010
2004 Chardonnay Seascape	93	now–2011
2006 Chardonnay Stone Côte	96	now–2010
2005 Chardonnay Stone Côte	93	now–2012
2004 Chardonnay Stone Côte	89	now–2012
2005 Pinot Noir Arrendell Vineyard	93	now–2013
2004 Pinot Noir Arrendell Vineyard	91	now–2012
2003 Pinot Noir Arrendell Vineyard	91	now–2012
2002 Pinot Noir Arrendell Vineyard	96	now–2011
2005 Pinot Noir Far Coast	93	now–2013
2005 Pinot Noir Hailey's Block	90	now–2012
2004 Pinot Noir Hailey's Block	88	now–2010
2005 Pinot Noir Jennifer's–Marshall Vineyard	90	now–2015
2004 Pinot Noir Seascape	88	now–2010
2003 Pinot Noir Seascape	90	now–2012
2002 Pinot Noir Seascape	87	now–2011
2005 Pinot Noir Sevens Bench Vineyard	91	now–2013
2004 Pinot Noir Sevens Bench Vineyard	88	now–2010
2002 Pinot Noir Sevens Bench Vineyard	94	now–2011
2005 Pinot Noir Velvet Sisters	92	now–2012
2004 Pinot Noir Velvet Sisters	88	now–2011
2002 Pinot Noir Velvet Sisters	93	now–2014
2006 Zinfandel Dina's Vineyard (Hartford)	94	now–2014
2004 Zinfandel Dina's Vineyard (Hartford)	90?	now–2013
2003 Zinfandel Dina's Vineyard (Hartford)	93	now–2015
2006 Zinfandel Fanucchi-Wood Road Vineyard (Hartford)	94	now–2013
2005 Zinfandel Fanucchi-Wood Road Vineyard (Hartford)	90	now

2004 Zinfandel Fanucchi-Wood Road		
Vineyard (Hartford)	94	now–2013
2003 Zinfandel Fanucchi-Wood Road		
Vineyard (Hartford)	93	now–2014
2001 Zinfandel Fanucchi-Wood Road		
Vineyard (Hartford)	90	now–2011
2006 Zinfandel Hartford Vineyard (Hartford)	90	now–2011
2005 Zinfandel Hartford Vineyard (Hartford)	89	now–2010
2004 Zinfandel Hartford Vineyard (Hartford)	94	now–2015
2003 Zinfandel Hartford Vineyard (Hartford)	91	now–2012
2004 Zinfandel Highwire Vineyard (Hartford)	91	now–2013
2003 Zinfandel Highwire Vineyard (Hartford)	93	now–2012
2004 Zinfandel Russian River (Hartford)	93	now–2015
2003 Zinfandel Russian River (Hartford)	93	now–2015

HARTLEY-OSTINI HITCHING POST ★★★/★★★★
SANTA BARBARA $24.00–$50.00

Hitching Post, a well-known steak house in Buellton, became famous when the movie *Sideways* filmed several scenes there. The restaurant's proprietors, Frank Ostini and his partner, Gray Hartley, made their first wine in 1979, and launched their first Pinot Noirs in the early 1980s. The production is now more than 5,000 cases of generally reliable single-vineyard Pinots as well as some Syrahs. Their winemaking philosophy is one of hands-off, noninterventionalistically made wines possessing plenty of soul. And they are sold at realistic prices.

2004 Pinot Noir	87	now
2002 Pinot Noir	88	now
2005 Pinot Noir Bien Nacido Vineyard	86?	now–2014
2004 Pinot Noir Bien Nacido Vineyard	90	now–2016
2002 Pinot Noir Bien Nacido Vineyard	88	now–2011
2005 Pinot Noir Cargasacchi Vineyard	88	now–2015
2004 Pinot Noir Cargasacchi Vineyard	90	now–2012
2003 Pinot Noir Cargasacchi Vineyard	85?	now
2002 Pinot Noir Cargasacchi Vineyard	87	now
2004 Pinot Noir Cork Dancer	89	now–2010
2005 Pinot Noir Fiddlestix Vineyard	86?	now–2015
2004 Pinot Noir Fiddlestix Vineyard	88	now–2012
2003 Pinot Noir Fiddlestix Vineyard	83	now
2002 Pinot Noir Fiddlestix Vineyard	90	now–2011
2005 Pinot Noir Highliner	89	now–2015
2004 Pinot Noir Highliner	91	now–2016
2003 Pinot Noir Highliner	86	now
2002 Pinot Noir Highliner	90	now–2010
2005 Pinot Noir Julia's Vineyard	87	now–2012
2004 Pinot Noir Julia's Vineyard	87	now–2010
2003 Pinot Noir Julia's Vineyard	87	now
2002 Pinot Noir Julia's Vineyard	91	now–2011
2005 Pinot Noir Rio Vista Vineyard	84	now
2004 Pinot Noir Rio Vista Vineyard	92	now–2013
2003 Pinot Noir Rio Vista Vineyard	87?	now–2013
2005 Pinot Noir Santa Barbara	88	now–2012
2005 Pinot Noir Santa Maria	90	now–2015

2005 Pinot Noir Saint Rita's Earth	88	now–2014
2004 Pinot Noir Saint Rita's Earth	89+	now–2011
2002 Pinot Noir Saint Rita's Earth	88	now
2005 Pinot Noir Sanford & Benedict Vineyard	84	now
2004 Pinot Noir Sanford & Benedict Vineyard	90	now–2011
2003 Pinot Noir Sanford & Benedict Vineyard	86	now
2003 Pinot Noir Santa Barbara	86	now
2005 Syrah Big Circle	89	now–2012
2004 Syrah Big Circle	88	now
2002 Syrah Hitching Post	88	now
2001 Syrah Hitching Post Bien Nacido Vineyard	88+	now–2012
2005 Syrah Purisima Mountain Vineyard	89	now–2012
2004 Syrah Purisima Mountain Vineyard	89+	now–2014
2003 Syrah Purisima Mountain Vineyard	87	now–2011
2002 Syrah Purisima Mountain Vineyard	89+	now–2011

HAVENS WINE CELLARS ★ ★ ★ ★
NAPA $24.00–$50.00

Michael and Kathryn Havens founded this winery in 1984, largely to pursue two areas they loved, Bordeaux and Rhône Valley wines. The results are consistently well-made wines with a European elegance. Michael Havens, who has been producing wines for over two decades, continues to turn out fine Merlots, a complex Bordeaux proprietary blend that tastes like a Napa version of the famed Cheval Blanc called Bourriquot, a Syrah from the Hudson Vineyard, and a Cabernet Sauvignon–Syrah blend called Black and Blue. Prices are among the most realistic in northern California.

2006 Albarino	87	now
2005 Black and Blue Proprietary Red Wine	93	now–2017+
2004 Black and Blue Proprietary Red Wine	91	now–2015
2002 Black and Blue Proprietary Red Wine	90	now
2005 Bourriquot Proprietary Red Wine	92+	2011–2026+
2004 Bourriquot Proprietary Red Wine	90	now–2022
2002 Bourriquot Proprietary Red Wine	90	now–2015
2001 Bourriquot Proprietary Red Wine	90+	now–2021
2005 Merlot Carneros	90	now–2017
2004 Merlot Carneros	90	now–2015
2002 Merlot Carneros	90	now–2011
2005 Merlot Napa	89	now–2014
2004 Merlot Napa	88	now–2015
2002 Merlot Napa	86	now
2001 Merlot Napa	89	now
2001 Merlot Reserve	90	now–2012
2002 Syrah Havens/Hudson/Kate's Vineyards	87	now
2005 Syrah Hudson Vineyard	90	now–2017+
2004 Syrah Hudson Vineyard	91	now–2015
2001 Syrah Hudson Vineyard	91	now–2015
2002 Syrah Hudson T Block	91	now–2012
2005 Syrah Napa	90	now–2017+
2004 Syrah Napa	89	now–2012
2001 Syrah Napa	88	now

HEINTZ ★★★
SONOMA $45.00

This small vineyard is used by a lot of top Chardonnay and Pinot Noir specialists because of its excellent viticulture. They also estate-bottle a small portion of the production, but it is not easy to find.

2005 Chardonnay Sonoma Coast	89	now
2005 Pinot Noir Sonoma Coast	87	now–2010

HEITZ CELLARS ★★/★★★
NAPA $50.00–$125.00

Founded in 1961 by the late Joe Heitz and his wife, Alice, Heitz's Cabernet Sauvignons, especially those from Oakville's Martha's Vineyard, became legendary in the mid- to late 1960s. Their reputation for phenomenal wine quality continued through the early 1980s. The winery also made a bevy of other wines that were generally uninteresting, but the Cabernet Sauvignons were as good as any made in California. By the mid- to late 1980s, there were major bacterial problems in the winery and the wines began to suffer, as did the estate's reputation. Since Joe Heitz's death in 2000, the family has tried to resurrect the winery's reputation, with little success. Heitz Cellars is still a great name, but today it is primarily recognized for some of the monumental Cabernet Sauvignon Martha's Vineyard cuvées made between the mid-1960s and early 1980s, which are still in great shape.

HENDRY WINES ★★★
NAPA $30.00

There are more than 50 different blocks of grapes in this 117–acre estate, which is situated in the southwestern sector of Napa Valley. Most of the fruit is sold to other wine producers, but some tasty Pinot Noir, Chardonnay, Primitivo, Zinfandel, Albarino, and Pinot Gris also emerge from this well-run winery.

2004 Primitivo	89	now–2011
2001 Primativo Hendry Block 24	87	now
2004 Zinfandel Block 7	88	now–2010
2001 Zinfandel Block 7	88	now
2001 Zinfandel Block 28	90	now

HERRERA–MI SUEÑO WINERY ★★★
NAPA $125.00

It is still hard to determine in what direction these wines are going. A former dishwasher at Auberge du Soleil and line cook at Mustard's Grill learned to make wine at Stag's Leap Wine Cellars, Château Potelle, and Paul Hobbs. This estate's debut efforts have been impressive.

2003 Cabernet Sauvignon Selección Rebecca Carpignano Vineyard	90	now–2016
2004 Cabernet Sauvignon Rolando Jr. Frog Tree Vineyard	89	now–2018

HESS ★★
NAPA $15.00–$75.00

Mega-millionaire Swiss businessman Donald Hess purchased this Mt. Veeder property in the late 1970s. Some top-notch wines emerged in the early to mid-1980s. After a second label, Hess Select, was introduced, production soared, and the overall quality fell dramatically. Today, the inexpensive line offers some value, but the more expensive wines are monolithic, charmless, and mediocre.

HESTAN VINEYARDS ★★★★
NAPA $75.00–$90.00

Hong Kong–born Stanley Cheng purchased 127 acres in Napa Valley, and with the assistance of winemaking consultant Mark Herold, he produces fewer than 500 cases of a 100% Cabernet Sauvignon that is aged 19 to 20 months in Taransaud barrels. A Chardonnay will be added to the portfolio in the future. The first several vintages have been immensely impressive.

2006 Cabernet Sauvignon Napa	92–95	now–2022+
2005 Cabernet Sauvignon Napa	94	2011–2025
2004 Cabernet Sauvignon Napa	91	now–2018
2003 Cabernet Sauvignon Napa	93	now–2025
2002 Cabernet Sauvignon	95	now–2018

TERRY HOAGE VINEYARDS ★★★/★★★★
PASO ROBLES $20.00–$45.00

An impressive, relatively new, artisanal, family-owned and -operated vineyard on the western side of Paso Robles, Terry Hoage is dedicated to Rhône varietals. Production is under 2,000 cases, and the early releases have been impressive.

2006 Grenache Bam Bam Estate	88	now–2010
2005 Proprietary Red Wine The Pick Estate	91	now–2013
2005 Proprietary Red Wine The 46 Estate	90	now–2013
2004 The 46 Terry Hoage Vineyard	90	now–2010
2005 Syrah The Hedge Estate	91	now–2013
2004 Syrah The Hedge Estate	89	now–2016

PAUL HOBBS ★★★★★
NORTHERN CALIFORNIA $55.00–$300.00

Paul Hobbs is one of the great names in winemaking. Moreover, he remains remarkably youthful and surprisingly humble. He has had decades of experience working with some of the finest vineyards in Argentina and California. When the history of high-quality Argentinean wines is written, Hobbs will certainly play an important role. In California he has moved aggressively, purchasing a 177-acre Russian River vineyard called Hillick Hill, most of which is located in the relatively cool Green Valley sector. Until that site comes into production, he has shown the Midas touch in accessing some of the finest Pinot Noir, Merlot, Chardonnay, and Cabernet Sauvignon vineyards in northern California, signing viticultural contracts that allow him to control the acreage and viticulture. The results are full-throttle, intense wines made with classical European methods, with minimal clarification and intense flavors as well as personalities. Hobbs's greatest efforts are his Cabernet Sauvignons, Chardonnays, and Malbecs from Argentina, but the strength of his Merlots and Pinot Noirs is surprising.

2006 Cabernet Sauvignon Beckstoffer Dr. Crane Vineyard	93–95	now–2021
2005 Cabernet Sauvignon Beckstoffer Dr. Crane Vineyard	95	now–2021
2004 Cabernet Sauvignon Beckstoffer Dr. Crane Vineyard	92+	now–2021
2003 Cabernet Sauvignon Beckstoffer Dr. Crane Vineyard	95	now–2020
2006 Cabernet Sauvignon Beckstoffer To-Kalon Vineyard	96–98	2011–2041

2005 Cabernet Sauvignon Beckstoffer		
To-Kalon Vineyard	95+	2009–2026+
2004 Cabernet Sauvignon Beckstoffer		
To-Kalon Vineyard	95+	now–2031
2003 Cabernet Sauvignon Beckstoffer		
To-Kalon Vineyard	97	now–2022
2002 Cabernet Sauvignon Beckstoffer		
To-Kalon Vineyard	99	2010–2030
2004 Cabernet Sauvignon Cross Barn	87	now–2018
2003 Cabernet Sauvignon Cross Barn	87	now–2012
2006 Cabernet Sauvignon Hyde Vineyard	92–94	now–2022
2005 Cabernet Sauvignon Hyde Vineyard	93	now–2018
2004 Cabernet Sauvignon Hyde Vineyard	91+	now–2021
2003 Cabernet Sauvignon Hyde Vineyard	93	now–2016
2002 Cabernet Sauvignon Hyde Vineyard	90+	now–2022
2006 Cabernet Sauvignon Napa	90–92	now–2022
2005 Cabernet Sauvignon Napa	92	now–2021
2004 Cabernet Sauvignon Napa	90	now–2018
2003 Cabernet Sauvignon Napa	93	now–2016
2006 Cabernet Sauvignon Stagecoach Vineyard	92–94	2012–2025+
2005 Cabernet Sauvignon Stagecoach Vineyard	93	now–2021
2004 Cabernet Sauvignon Stagecoach Vineyard	94	now–2026
2003 Cabernet Sauvignon Stagecoach Vineyard	94+	now–2022
2005 Chardonnay Richard Dinner Vineyard	92	now–2011
2004 Chardonnay Richard Dinner Vineyard	93	now–2010
2006 Chardonnay Richard Dinner Vineyard		
Cuvée Agustina	94	now–2011
2005 Chardonnay Richard Dinner Vineyard		
Cuvée Agustina	94	now–2012
2004 Chardonnay Richard Dinner Vineyard		
Cuvée Agustina	93	now–2012
2006 Chardonnay Ritchie Vineyard	92	now–2012
2005 Chardonnay Ritchie Vineyard	93	now–2011
2006 Chardonnay Russian River	91	now–2010
2004 Chardonnay Russian River	90	now
2006 Chardonnay Ulises Valdez Vineyard	90	now–2010
2005 Chardonnay Ulises Valdez Vineyard	95	now–2013
2004 Chardonnay Ulises Valdez Vineyard	95	now–2012
2006 Chardonnay Walker Station	92	now–2010
2005 Chardonnay Walker Station	94	now–2012
2004 Chardonnay Walker Station	94	now
2003 Merlot Michael Black Vineyard	93	now–2022
2002 Merlot Michael Black Vineyard	93	now–2017
2006 Pinot Noir Hyde Vineyard	87–90	now–2012
2005 Pinot Noir Hyde Vineyard	94	now–2012
2003 Pinot Noir Hyde Vineyard	91	now–2013
2002 Pinot Noir Hyde Vineyard Cuvée Agustina	94	now–2015
2006 Pinot Noir Lindsay Estate	91–93	now–2012
2005 Pinot Noir Lindsay Estate	94	now–2016
2006 Pinot Noir Russian River	87–88	now–2010
2005 Pinot Noir Russian River	90	now–2012

2004 Pinot Noir Russian River	86–88	now–2012
2006 Pinot Noir Ulises Valdez Estate	90–92	now–2010
2005 Pinot Noir Ulises Valdez Estate	92+	now–2016+
2006 Syrah Kick Ranch Vineyard	91–93	now–2013
2005 Syrah Kick Ranch Vineyard	92	now–2012

HOLUS BOLUS ★★★★
SANTA YNEZ $25.00–$28.00

Holus Bolus is a cooperative effort led by one of the most talented winemakers in southern California, Sashi Moorman. His partners include Jim Knight, the winemaker at Jelly Roll; Chad Melville, the owner and winemaker of Samsara; and Peter Hunken, who owns the Piedrasassi label. These are Syrah fruit bombs.

2006 Syrah	89	now–2012
2005 Syrah	85	now–2013
2004 Syrah	93	now–2013
2003 Syrah	93	now–2012

HONIG ★★★
NAPA $15.00–$75.00

Honig's success story dates back to 1964, when Louis Honig purchased a 68-acre ranch in the heart of Rutherford. The wines are consistently reliable, if never spectacular. Honig's most noteworthy success is their crisp, mineral-laced, lively Sauvignon Blancs, but their Cabernet Sauvignons are also well worth trying. Moreover, prices are fair.

2004 Cabernet Sauvignon Bartolucci Vineyard	90	2009–2024
2001 Cabernet Sauvignon Bartolucci Vineyard	90	now–2022
2005 Cabernet Sauvignon Napa	86	now–2015
2001 Cabernet Sauvignon Napa	89	now–2015
2001 Cabernet Sauvignon Stagecoach Vineyard	90	now–2020
2006 Sauvignon Blanc Napa	87	now
2004 Sauvignon Blanc Napa	87	now
2006 Sauvignon Blanc Reserve	89	now
2004 Sauvignon Blanc Rutherford	88	now

AUSTIN HOPE ★★★/★★★★
PASO ROBLES $42.00

This is an emerging source of high-quality Rhône-styled Syrah, Mourvèdre, and Grenache from vineyards on the west side of Paso Robles. Early efforts have been very promising.

2005 Grenache Hope Family Vineyard	87	now
2004 Syrah Hope Family Vineyard	91	now–2017
2001 Syrah Hope Family Vineyard	87	now
2002 Westside Red	88	now
2001 Westside Red	87	now

HOURGLASS ★★★★
NAPA $90.00–$110.00

A tiny four-acre site located near St. Helena, Hourglass is owned by Jeff and Carolyn Smith. Their frequently brilliant Cabernet Sauvignons are produced under the guidance of wine consultant Bob Foley. Production averages 500 to 600 cases, and these offerings are well worth the effort to track down.

2005 Cabernet Sauvignon Napa	93	2010–2030
2004 Cabernet Sauvignon Napa	94	now–2021
2003 Cabernet Sauvignon Napa	87	now–2010
2002 Cabernet Sauvignon	98	now–2020
2001 Cabernet Sauvignon	95	now–2020+

HUG CELLARS ★★★★
PASO ROBLES $16.00–$48.00

This is another high-quality operation in the Paso Robles area dedicated to Rhône varietals. Hug produces impressive Syrahs as well as Pinot Noirs.

2005 Casa Mireles Romanze Syrah Rose	85	now
2005 Pinot Noir Cedar Lane Vineyard	85	now–2011
2005 Pinot Noir Orchid Hill Vineyard	89	now–2013
2005 Pinot Noir Rancho Ontiveros	88	now–2013
2005 Syrah	87	now
2002 Syrah Bassetti Vineyard	92	now
2005 Syrah Bassetti Vineyard Rena Block	86?	now–2014
2004 Syrah Bassetti Vineyard Rena Block	87	now
2003 Syrah Bassetti Vineyard Rena Block	87+?	now–2011
2005 Syrah Cedar Lane Vineyard	88	now–2012
2004 Syrah Central Coast	87	now

HUNDRED ACRE ★★★★★
NAPA $225.00

One of California's most ambitious proprietors is Napa's Jayson Woodbridge, the owner of this estate. His first vintage was a blockbuster effort in the challenging year 2000, and he has gone from strength to strength. These are 100% Cabernet Sauvignons made with the assistance of French guru Philippe Melka. The obsessive attention to detail is noticeable in both the viticulture and wines, which come from the 10-acre Kayli Morgan Vineyard or the 15-acre Ark Vineyard on Howell Mountain. These handmade, personality-filled, original wines are about as good as anything Napa can offer.

2006 Cabernet Sauvignon Ark	94–96	now–2022
2005 Cabernet Sauvignon Ark	94–96	2010–2030
2005 Cabernet Sauvignon Deep Time	96–98	now–2022+
2001 Cabernet Sauvignon Deep Time	96	now–2018
2006 Cabernet Sauvignon Kayli Morgan Vineyard	94–96	2009–2029
2005 Cabernet Sauvignon Kayli Morgan Vineyard	96–99	now–2027+
2004 Cabernet Sauvignon Kayli Morgan Vineyard	94	now–2027
2003 Cabernet Sauvignon Kayli Morgan Vineyard	95	now–2021
2002 Cabernet Sauvignon Kayli Morgan Vineyard	98	now–2020+
2001 Cabernet Sauvignon Kayli Morgan Vineyard	95	now–2020
2006 Cabernet Sauvignon Previous	96–98+	2010–2022
2005 Cabernet Sauvignon Previous	96–100	2010–2025
2004 Port	97	now–2026

HUSCH VINEYARDS ★★★
ANDERSON VALLEY $15.00–$31.00

Husch owns over 250 acres, from which they produce 35,000-plus cases of wine. There is a lot to like about the 18 different cuvées they produce. These are fruit-forward, delicious, pure, somewhat underrated offerings. Their most pleasing wines include those listed below. Perhaps their more ambitious efforts, such as Cabernet Sauvignon and Reserve Cabernet Sauvignon, do not benefit as much as the whites from the estate's lighter style. Prices are very fair.

2006 Chenin Blanc	89	now
2006 Muscat Canelli	86	now
2003 Pinot Noir Anderson Valley	88	now
2001 Pinot Noir Reserve	89	now–2011
2006 Sauvignon Blanc	89	now

IRON HORSE ★ ★ ★ ★
SONOMA $30.00–$60.00

Founded in 1976 by the Sterling family, this family-owned 300-acre estate focuses on producing California's finest sparkling wines, backed up by some surprisingly strong Chardonnays, Viogniers, and such wines as Petit Verdot, Cabernet Franc, Sangiovese, and Pinot Noir. In the past an underrated Cabernet Sauvignon was made, but that has been discontinued. All seven of their sparkling wine cuvées are well worth a search of the marketplace. In some blind tastings, the Iron Horse sparklers frequently score higher than the domestic sparklers made by French companies. My favorite efforts include the Blanc de Blancs, Brut Rosé, Wedding cuvée, and the wine named after Joy Sterling called Joy!

2001 Cabernet Sauvignon Proprietor Grown	90	now–2021
2005 Chardonnay Estate	89	now
2005 Pinot Noir Green Valley	89	now
2005 Pinot Noir Q	91	now–2014
2004 Wedding Cuvée Sparkling Wine	90	now

J. WINE CO. ★ ★
SONOMA $30.00–$45.00

This sparkling wine offshoot of the huge Jordan Winery produces a standard-quality blend of Pinot Noir and Chardonnay. These are pleasant sparkling wines.

JADE MOUNTAIN ★ ★ ★
NAPA $18.00–$28.00

When the winery was started in 1988, and dedicated to Rhône varieties primarily grown on Mt. Veeder, the quality of these wines was excellent, and prices were fair. Having quickly developed a reputation for high quality, especially for their proprietary southern Rhône varietal blend called La Provençale and their single-vineyard Syrahs, Jade Mountain was sold to the Chalone group in 2000, and quality began a dramatic downturn. The wines are still good, but not at the level they were under their original ownership.

2004 Mourvèdre Evangelho Vineyard	88	now–2014
2003 Mourvèdre Evangelho Vineyard	84	now
2002 Mourvèdre Evangelho Vineyard	88	now–2011
2004 La Provençale	87	now
2003 La Provençale	86	now
2002 La Provençale	87	now
2003 Syrah Monterey	84	now
2003 Syrah Napa	85	now
2002 Syrah Napa	88	now
2001 Syrah Paras Vineyard	89+	now–2011
2004 Syrah Snows Lake Vineyard	84	now
2004 Viognier Paras Vineyard	87	now

JAFFURS WINE CELLARS ★★★★
SANTA BARBARA $23.00–$43.00

Jaffurs's wines continue to go from strength to strength, and recent vintages have been the finest I have yet tasted from this producer. With production under 3,000 cases, this small Santa Barbara estate produces fine-quality Rhone Ranger cuvées from some of the area's finest vineyards. All the fruit is purchased from these sites. Prices are very fair.

2003 Grenache Stolpman Vineyard	86	now
2002 Grenache Stolpman Vineyard	85	now
2005 Syrah Ampelos Vineyard	90	now–2019
2004 Syrah Ampelos Vineyard	91	now–2014
2004 Syrah Bien Nacido Vineyard	93	now–2022
2003 Syrah Bien Nacido Vineyard	93	now–2014
2002 Syrah Bien Nacido Vineyard	89	now–2010
2003 Syrah Larner Vineyard	88	now–2010
2003 Syrah Melville Vineyard	94	now–2016
2002 Syrah Melville Vineyard	90	now–2016+
2005 Syrah Santa Barbara	90	now–2011
2004 Syrah Santa Barbara	90	now–2010
2003 Syrah Santa Barbara	87	now
2002 Syrah Santa Barbara	88	now
2002 Syrah Stolpman Vineyard	89	now–2011
2004 Syrah Thompson Vineyard	90+	now–2019
2003 Syrah Thompson Vineyard	91	now–2014
2002 Syrah Thompson Vineyard	88	now–2014
2004 Syrah Verna's Vineyard	93	now–2019

TOBIN JAMES CELLARS ★★
PASO ROBLES $38.00–$55.00

This winery is situated on Highway 46 in Paso Robles. They produce rustic but attractive country-style wines that sell at reasonable prices and are meant to be consumed in their exuberant youth.

2002 Syrah Blue Moon Reserve	86+?	now
2004 Zinfandel Blue Moon Reserve	87	now
2004 Zinfandel Dusi Vineyard	85	now
2004 Zinfandel Silver Reserve	86?	now

JC CELLARS ★★★★
PASO ROBLES $27.00–$55.00

Proprietor Jeff Cohn, who fashioned many excellent wines at Rosenblum Cellars, continues to demonstrate a superb hand with his own impressive portfolio of full-throttle, all-American, intensely flavored wines primarily based on Rhône varieties. He also produces some terrific Zinfandels. These brilliant efforts all deserve considerable attention, including his rare white made from Marsanne and Roussanne.

2003 Cuvée Isabelle Rhodes Vineyard	92	now
2005 The First Date	90	now–2011
2004 The First Date	88	now
2005 The Imposter	90	now–2010
2005 Marsanne Preston Vineyard	86	now–2010
2005 Petite Syrah Frediani Vineyard	92+	2012–2040

2004 Petite Syrah Frediani Vineyard	93	now–2026+
2003 Petite Syrah Frediani Vineyard	92+	now–2022
2002 Petite Syrah Frediani Vineyard	94+	now–2020+
2005 Syrah à La Cave	88	now–2011
2004 Syrah à La Cave	90	now–2011
2005 Syrah Buffalo Hill Rockpile Vineyard	96	now–2017
2005 Syrah Caldwell Vineyard	88?	???
2004 Syrah Caldwell Vineyard	91	now–2016
2003 Syrah Caldwell Vineyard	91	now–2016
2002 Syrah Caldwell Vineyard	92	now–2012
2005 Syrah California Cuvée	89	now–2011
2004 Syrah California Cuvée	89	now–2010
2003 Syrah California Cuvée	89	now
2002 Syrah California Cuvée	89	now–2011
2005 Syrah Fess Parker Vineyard	93	now–2015
2004 Syrah Fess Parker Vineyard	92	now–2012
2003 Syrah Fess Parker Vineyard	90	now–2013
2002 Syrah Fess Parker Vineyard	90	now–2010
2001 Syrah Fess Parker Vineyard	90+	now–2017
2005 Syrah Philary Vineyard	95	2009–2024
2004 Syrah Philary Vineyard	96	now–2018
2003 Syrah Philary Vineyard	90+	now–2016
2002 Syrah Philary Vineyard	93	now–2018+
2004 Syrah Rockpile Vineyard Haley's Reserve	93+	now–2016
2003 Syrah Rockpile Vineyard Haley's Reserve	93+	now–2020
2002 Syrah Rockpile Vineyard Haley's Reserve	94	now–2016
2005 Syrah Ventana Vineyard	89	now–2011
2004 Syrah Ventana Vineyard	89	now–2012
2002 Syrah Ventana Vineyard	89	now–2010
2005 Zinfandel Arrowhead Mountain Vineyard	91	now
2004 Zinfandel Arrowhead Mountain Vineyard	87	now–2011
2003 Zinfandel Arrowhead Mountain Vineyard	92	now
2005 Zinfandel Iron Hill Vineyard	87	now–2012
2004 Zinfandel Iron Hill Vineyard	89	now–2010
2003 Zinfandel Iron Hill Vineyard	94	now–2011

JELLY ROLL ★ ★ ★ ★
SANTA YNEZ $34.00–$40.00

This is the brainchild of Jim Knight, who, along with Sashi Moorman, fashions these Syrahs at a warehouse in Lompac. These are artisanal, exceptionally well-made efforts.

2005 Syrah	90	now–2012
2004 Syrah	90+	now–2012
2003 Syrah	91	now–2012

JONATA ★ ★ ★ ⋆/★ ★ ★ ★ ★
SANTA YNEZ $85.00–$125.00

With 81 acres (out of 600) currently under vine, Jonata could turn out to be one of the most promising newcomers to emerge from Santa Ynez in decades. The owner, Charles Banks, is also the proprietor of Napa's Screaming Eagle, and the winemaker, Matt Dees, is assisted by Screaming Eagle's winemaker, Andy Erickson, as well as the roving oenologist-consultant,

Bordeaux's Michel Rolland. Although this is still a work in progress, these debut 2004s and 2005s are spectacular wines. Furthermore, a look at the unfinished 2006s suggested that they will be among the most exciting wines produced in Santa Ynez. When you consider that they are made primarily from Bordeaux varieties (as well as a remarkable Sangiovese), this is big, big news. All the wines are aged in French oak.

2005 El Alma de Jonata	95	now–2017
2005 El Corazón de Jonata	94	now–2022
2004 El Corazón de Jonata	91	now–2017
2005 El Desafío de Jonata	95	now–2015
2004 El Desafío de Jonata	91	now–2022
2005 La Flor de Jonata	91	now–2011
2005 La Fuerza de Jonata	91	now–2017
2005 La Sangre de Jonata	95	now–2019
2004 La Sangre de Jonata	94	now–2017+
2005 La Tierra de Jonata	93+	now–2013
2004 La Tierra de Jonata	93	now–2015

JONES FAMILY VINEYARD ★ ★ ★ ★
NAPA $45.00–$85.00

This tiny boutique winery employs superstar viticultural manager David Abreu and winemaker Heidi Barrett. Their wines have been consistently well made since the first vintage was released in 1996. A second label, The Sisters, a proprietary Bordeaux blend, was added to the portfolio.

2003 Cabernet Sauvignon Napa	90+	now–2018
2002 Cabernet Sauvignon Napa	92	now–2020+
2001 Cabernet Sauvignon Napa	95	now–2015+
2003 The Sisters Proprietary Red Wine	89	now–2011
2002 The Sisters Proprietary Red Wine	89	now–2010

JORDAN ★ ★ ★
SONOMA $55.00–$60.00

Founded in the early 1970s, Jordan's first vintages of Cabernet Sauvignon met with considerable praise and aged better than many critics suggested they would. The winery continues to turn out around 100,000 cases of Cabernet Sauvignon and Chardonnay. The Cabernets emphasize elegant, soft tannins as well as easygoing fruit. The wines, while never exciting, are well balanced and pleasant.

LA JOTA ★ ★
NAPA $50.00–$185.00

This was a terrific source of fabulous Cabernet Sauvignon and Cabernet Franc between 1991 and 1999, but in 2001, La Jota was sold to the huge Markham group, and the quality plummeted. That's a shame, as the La Jota Cabernet Sauvignon Anniversary Selections from 1991, 1992, 1993, 1994, 1995, and 1996 are aging magnificently, and are testaments to great winemaking and fabulous fruit.

JUDD'S HILL ★ ★ ★
NAPA $42.00

After having enjoyed great success at Whitehall Lane winery, proprietor Art Finkelstein sold that winery and moved to the more remote Conn Valley, where he began producing flavorful Cabernet Sauvignons from Conn Valley vineyards.

2004 Cabernet Sauvignon Napa	88	now–2017
2003 Cabernet Sauvignon Napa	89	now–2015
2003 Petite Sirah Old Vine Lodi	86	now–2015

JUSLYN VINEYARDS ★★★★
NAPA $25.00–$95.00

Proprietors Carolyn and Perry Butler quickly made Juslyn one of the top sources of high-quality wine on Spring Mountain. After sourcing grapes from several of Andy Beckstoffer's top Napa Valley vineyards, they planted their estate vineyard in 1997, and are moving to full estate production in the future. The Juslyn wines emphasize elegance, balance, and excellent longevity. Don't miss the super Sauvignon Blanc made here.

2005 Cabernet Sauvignon Spring Mountain Estate	91–93	2010–2025
2004 Cabernet Sauvignon Spring Mountain Estate	93	now–2027
2003 Cabernet Sauvignon Spring Mountain Estate	93	now–2021
2002 Cabernet Sauvignon Spring Mountain Estate	93	2009–2026
2001 Cabernet Sauvignon Spring Mountain Estate	92	now–2020
2004 Cabernet Sauvignon Vineyard Select	92+	now–2021
2003 Cabernet Sauvignon Vineyard Select	91	now–2021
2002 Cabernet Sauvignon Vineyard Select	93	now–2021
2001 Cabernet Sauvignon Vineyard Select	91+	now–2022
2002 Napa Blend Proprietary Red Wine	89	now–2013
2001 Napa Blend Proprietary Red Wine	88	now–2011
2005 Perry's Blend	90–92	2010–2030
2004 Perry's Blend	94	now–2022
2003 Perry's Blend	92	now–2018
2002 Perry's Blend	93	now–2021
2001 Proprietary Red Wine	90	now–2017
2006 Sauvignon Blanc	88	now
2005 Sauvignon Blanc	89	now
2004 Sauvignon Blanc	88	now

JUSTIN VINEYARDS & WINERY ★★★★
PASO ROBLES $25.00–$44.00

An impressive 160-acre estate planted with major Bordeaux varieties, Justin has been making wines in Paso Robles for nearly 30 years. Their finest offerings tend to be their Bordeaux blends named Isosceles and Justification, but they also do increasingly good work with Syrah. I have been less impressed by their white wine offerings.

2002 Cabernet Sauvignon Paso Robles	89	now–2015
2002 Isosceles Reserve Proprietary Red Wine	95	now–2015
2001 Isosceles Reserve Proprietary Red Wine	93	now–2020
2002 Justification	90	now–2014
2004 Savant Proprietary Red Wine	90	now–2015
2004 Syrah Paso Robles	87	now–2011
2003 Syrah Reserve	90	now–2012
2002 Syrah Reserve	90	now–2011

KAENA WINE COMPANY ★★★
SANTA YNEZ $25.00–$42.00

A potential name to watch closely, Hawaiian native Mikael Sigouin has demonstrated a fine touch in producing open-knit Grenache and Syrah from selected microclimates in Santa Barbara.

2002 Grenache	87	now
2004 Syrah	90	now–2014
2002 Syrah	88	now

KALEIDOS ★★★
PASO ROBLES $28.00–$38.00

The enormous potential for high-quality wines from vineyards west of Paso Robles, not far from the Pacific Ocean, is evident with the numerous top-notch offerings emerging from this family-owned winery. Established in 2004, Kaleidos is nestled in the Templeton Gap. Owner Steve Martel's interests lie with Rhône varietal wines, producing both Grenache- and Syrah-dominated blends. Early releases have been impressive.

2005 Morpheus	91	now–2014
2004 Morpheus	90	now–2014
2005 Osiris	88	now–2015
2005 Syrah	90	now–2014
2004 Syrah	90	now–2013
2005 Syrah Reserve	89+	2009–2014

KALIN CELLARS ★★★★
SONOMA $29.00–$42.00

The idiosyncratic Terry Leighton, who has produced some magnificent wines that have stood the test of time for nearly two decades, releases his wines five to ten years later than most producers. I have always loved them, but they are difficult to find given the reluctance of many consumers and retailers to purchase wines that appear to be too old. In fact, most of them are just beginning their lives. This is one of California's most distinctive and singular wine producers.

1997 Sémillon	93	now–2017
1994 Chardonnay Cuvée LD	92	now–2017
1997 Pinot Noir Cuvée DD	91	now–2017

KAMEN ESTATE WINES ★★★★
SONOMA $50.00–$55.00

Robert Kamen, who was the screenwriter for a number of top movies, purchased 280 acres on the southwestern slopes of the Sonoma side of the Mayacamas Mountains. This small artisanal estate produces a just over 1,000 cases, with the vineyards organically farmed by Philip Coturri. Winemaking consultant Mark Herold is the wizard behind the wines, which seem to be going from strength to strength. It would be hard to argue against the fact that Kamen is now producing one of the top four or five Cabernet Sauvignons from Sonoma as well as some top-notch Syrahs.

2006 Cabernet Sauvignon	93–95	2011–2027
2005 Cabernet Sauvignon	95	2011–2025
2004 Cabernet Sauvignon	93	2009–2024
2001 Cabernet Sauvignon	89	now–2015
2006 Syrah	91–94	now–2017

2005 Syrah	89–91	now–2015
2004 Syrah	92	now–2015

KAPCSÁNDY FAMILY WINERY ✶ ✶ ✶ ✶ ✶
NAPA $65.00–$150.00

What a great success story Kapcsándy Family Winery is! I first met Lou Kapcsándy when he was the owner of a construction company in Seattle. A Hungarian immigrant (he fled the country during the 1956 revolution), he gave up his business to follow the grapevine—so to speak—with his son, Louis, and wife, Bobbie. The family moved to Napa, purchased Beringer's old State Lane Vineyard (often a component of that winery's Private Reserve bottling), completely replanted it, and brought in well-known Bordelais Denis Malbec to work with Californian Rob Lawson to craft undeniably Bordeaux-styled blends of elegance and longevity. The rate at which they have achieved success is shocking. From their tightly spaced vineyard (2,700 vines per acre), new state-of-the-art winery, and draconian selection process, they are producing three outstanding cuvées.

2006 Cabernet Sauvignon State Lane Vineyard	92–94	now–2028+
2005 Cabernet Sauvignon State Lane Vineyard	95+	2012–2030
2006 Estate Cuvée State Lane Vineyard	91–93	now–2022
2005 Estate Cuvée State Lane Vineyard	91	now–2022+
2004 Proprietary Red Wine State Lane Vineyard	95	now–2027
2003 Proprietary Red Wine State Lane Vineyard	90	now–2022
2006 Roberta's Reserve State Lane Vineyard	92–94	now–2022
2005 Roberta's Reserve State Lane Vineyard	95	2010–2032

ROBERT KEENAN WINERY ✶ ✶ ✶ ✶
NAPA $27.00–$100.00

This old ghost winery from 1904 closed during prohibition, only to be resurrected in 1974 when Robert Keenan purchased 180 acres of forest and the defunct winery site. The initial vineyard was wiped out by Pierce's disease and replanted in the mid-1990s. Robert's son, Michael Keenan, continues to take this estate to new quality levels. His laserlike focus is on three varietals: Chardonnay, Cabernet Sauvignon, and Merlot. These are textbook Spring Mountain offerings that possess good freshness, tremendous fruit purity, and impressive quality.

2005 Cabernet Franc	93	now–2022
2004 Cabernet Franc	94	now–2017
2003 Cabernet Franc	91	now–2014
2002 Cabernet Franc	94	now–2017
2005 Cabernet Sauvignon	90	now–2022
2004 Cabernet Sauvignon	92	now–2022
2003 Cabernet Sauvignon	89	now–2011
2002 Cabernet Sauvignon	92+	now–2020
2005 Cabernet Sauvignon Reserve	92	now–2022+
2004 Cabernet Sauvignon Reserve	94+	now–2022
2003 Cabernet Sauvignon Reserve	95	now–2021
2002 Cabernet Sauvignon Reserve	93+	now–2025
2001 Cabernet Sauvignon Reserve	93+	now–2027
2006 Chardonnay	89	now–2011
2005 Chardonnay	89	now–2010
2004 Chardonnay	90	now
2005 Merlot	89	now–2015
2004 Merlot	90	now–2017

2003 Merlot	87	now–2013
2002 Merlot Reserve	94	now–2015
2005 Mernet Reserve	94	now–2022
2004 Mernet Reserve	95	now–2027
2003 Mernet Reserve	94	now–2021+
2002 Mernet Reserve	95	now–2020+
2005 Merlot Reserve Mailbox Vineyard	92	now–2019
2004 Merlot Reserve Mailbox Vineyard	91	now–2022
2003 Merlot Reserve Mailbox Vineyard	93	now–2021

KENDALL-JACKSON ✳✳✳
CALIFORNIA $12.00–$120.00

This is the colossal empire of Jess Jackson and his wife, Barbara Banke. Despite the size of some of the cuvées produced at Kendall-Jackson (2.3 million bottles of the Vintner's Reserve Chardonnay and 300,000 bottles of Sauvignon Blanc), winemaker Randy Ullom is at the top of his game. The quality hierarchy begins with the Vintner's Reserve cuvées, followed by the Grand Reserves and the single-vineyard offerings, with the top-of-the-line wine called Stature Proprietary Red. All of these wines are made from estate vineyards. This is certainly an example of bigger being better.

2002 Cabernet Sauvignon Knight's Bridge Estate	90	now–2016
2005 Cabernet Sauvignon Napa Mountain Estate	94+	2010–2040
2002 Cabernet Sauvignon Napa Mountain Estate	92	now–2028
2005 Grand Reserve Cabernet Sauvignon Jackson Estates	88	2010–2021
2004 Grand Reserve Cabernet Sauvignon Jackson Estates	89	now–2021
2003 Grand Reserve Cabernet Sauvignon Jackson Estates	88	now–2016
2002 Grand Reserve Cabernet Sauvignon	87	now–2015
2006 Grand Reserve Chardonnay	90	now–2010
2005 Grand Reserve Chardonnay	90	now–2010
2004 Grand Reserve Chardonnay	91	now
2005 Grand Reserve Meritage	89	now–2016
2004 Grand Reserve Meritage	88+	now–2019
2004 Grand Reserve Merlot	88	now–2013
2003 Grand Reserve Merlot	88	now–2014
2005 Grand Reserve Pinot Noir	87	now–2010
2004 Highland Estates Cabernet Sauvignon Hawkeye Mountain	89+	now–2022
2003 Highland Estates Cabernet Sauvignon Hawkeye Mountain	89?	2009–2023
2002 Highland Estates Cabernet Sauvignon Hawkeye Mountain	91	now–2020
2003 Highland Estates Cabernet Sauvignon Napa Mountain Estate	92	2009–2024+
2005 Highland Estates Cabernet Sauvignon Trace Ridge Estate	89+	now–2017+
2004 Highland Estates Cabernet Sauvignon Trace Ridge Estate	90+	2009–2020+

2003 Highland Estates Cabernet Sauvignon Trace Ridge Estate	91	now–2021+
2006 Highland Estates Chardonnay Camelot Vineyard	92	now–2010
2005 Highland Estates Chardonnay Camelot Vineyard	92	now–2010
2004 Highland Estates Chardonnay Camelot Vineyard	91+	now–2010
2006 Highland Estates Chardonnay Seco	87	now–2010
2005 Highland Estates Chardonnay Seco	87	now–2011
2003 Highland Estates Merlot Taylor Peak	91	now–2018
2004 Highland Estates Pinot Noir Arroyo Seco	87	now–2012
2003 Highland Estates Pinot Noir Arroyo Seco	89	now–2010
2004 Stature Meritage	90	2009–2027
2003 Stature Meritage	92	now–2021+
2002 Stature Meritage	93	2010–2020
2001 Stature Meritage	91	now–2020+
2004 Stature Proprietary Red	92	2012–2028
2005 Syrah Alisos Hills	90	now–2015
2005 Taylor Peak Merlot Bennett Valley	90	2009–2024+
2004 Vintner's Reserve Cabernet Sauvignon	87	now–2012
2003 Vintner's Reserve Cabernet Sauvignon	87	now–2011
2006 Vintner's Reserve Chardonnay	87	now
2005 Vintner's Reserve Chardonnay Jackson Estates	89	now
2004 Vintner's Reserve Meritage	87	now–2012
2006 Vintner's Reserve Sauvignon Blanc	87	now

KENNETH-CRAWFORD WINES ★★★★
SANTA BARBARA $32.00–$40.00

Kenneth-Crawford is a small boutique partnership dedicated to producing high-quality, single-vineyard Pinot Noir, Grenache, and Syrah from Santa Rita Hills and Santa Ynez Valley vineyards. The first releases have been impressive across the board. This is a winery to watch.

2005 Grenache Larner Vineyard	88	now–2011
2005 Pinot Noir Babcock Vineyard	88	now–2012
2005 Pinot Noir Turner Vineyard	87	now–2011
2004 Syrah Blue Fin	89	now–2013
2005 Syrah Four Play	89	now–2013
2005 Syrah Purisima Mountain Vineyard	89	now–2013
2004 Syrah Purisima Mountain Vineyard	90	now–2015
2005 Syrah Turner Vineyard	88	now–2014

TOR KENWARD FAMILY VINEYARDS ★★★★
NAPA $40.00–$62.00

One of Beringer's top executives, Tor Kenward has his own *garagiste* operation from which he produces interesting handcrafted reds and whites.

2006 Cabernet Sauvignon Beckstoffer To-Kalon	96–100	now–2028+
2005 Cabernet Sauvignon Beckstoffer To-Kalon	96	now–2028+
2006 Cabernet Sauvignon Cimarossa Vineyard	94–96	2010–2025
2004 Cabernet Sauvignon Cimarossa Vineyard	90	now–2016
2003 Cabernet Sauvignon Cimarossa Vineyard	93+	2009–2034
2005 Cabernet Sauvignon Cimarossa Block 10	93	2010–2028
2006 Cabernet Sauvignon Mast Vineyard	92–94	2010–2030

2004 Cabernet Sauvignon Mast Vineyard	94	now–2022
2003 Cabernet Sauvignon Mast Vineyard	93	now–2020
2005 Cabernet Sauvignon Mast-Cimarossa	93	now–2020
2003 Cabernet Sauvignon Oak Knoll Mast Vineyard	92	now–2014
2002 Cabernet Sauvignon Oakville Heritage Clones	92	now–2022
2004 Cabernet Sauvignon Rock Vineyard	93	now–2022
2005 Chardonnay Cuvée Torchiana	94–96	now–2011
2004 Chardonnay Durell Vineyard (Dijon Clone)	89	now–2010
2005 Chardonnay Durell Vineyard (Wente Clone)	92	now–2014
2004 Chardonnay Durell Vineyard (Wente Clone)	93	now–2012
2006 Chardonnay Molly Hudson Vineyard	92–95	now–2011
2005 Chardonnay Two Rivers Ranch	92	now–2014
2004 Chardonnay Two Rivers Ranch	92	now–2011
2005 Syrah Hudson Vineyard (Alban Clone)	91	2011–2026
2005 Syrah Hudson Vineyard (Noir Clone)	92	now–2019
2004 Syrah Los Carneros	89	now
2004 Syrah Mt. Veeder	90	now–2014
2004 Syrah Napa	91	now–2012
2005 Syrah Rock Vineyard	90	now–2014
2004 Syrah Rock Vineyard	88	now–2012
2006 Tor Chardonnay Durell Vineyard	92–94	now–2011
2006 Tor Rock Grenache Judge Family Vineyard Cuvée Cooper	89–91	now–2013
2006 Tor Rock Homage Allen Judge Family Vineyard	91–93	now–2014
2006 Tor Rock Syrah Hudson Vineyard	92–94	now–2015
2005 Tor Rock Syrah Hudson Vineyard (Alban Clone)	92	now–2018+
2005 Tor Rock Syrah Hudson Vineyard (Noir Clone)	93	now–2016
2006 Tor Rock Syrah Judge Family Vineyard	92–94	???
2005 Tor Rock Syrah Los Madres Vineyard	91	now–2015

KENWOOD ✶ ✶
SONOMA $20.00–$50.00

This winery, founded in 1970, has enjoyed tremendous commercial success, but to me, the wines have never been impressive. They are somewhat monolithic, commercial, and lacking in character. In fact, mediocrity appears to be the rule of thumb at Kenwood, regardless of whether it's the Reserve line, Jack London cuvées, or their single-vineyard series. This large estate produces more than 350,000 cases of wine, which they seemingly sell with ease.

KESNER ✶ ✶ ✶
NAPA $60.00

Kesner produces a very small amount of wine (around 300 cases) made by Jason Kesner, who is the manager of Hudson Vineyards.

2005 Chardonnay	92	now–2011
2004 Chardonnay	88	now–2010

KETCHAM ESTATE ✶ ✶ ✶
RUSSIAN RIVER $52.00

Ketcham specializes in well-made Pinot Noir from the renowned winemaker Michael Browne.

2005 Pinot Noir	88	now–2012

Steve Kistler and his assistant, Mark Bixler, have been one of California's bright, shining success stories ever since they launched their wines in 1979. Going from strength to strength, they now have at least ten single-vineyard Chardonnays as well as some single-vineyard Pinot Noirs, all representing the pinnacle of quality that these Burgundian varietals can reach. Low-tech winemaking, along with purity, cleanliness, temperature control, and a respect for vineyard sites and what each vintage provides, has resulted in a range of provocative as well as profound wines that is largely unequaled in its consistency and breadth of flavors and aromas. This is one of the world's great wineries.

2006 Chardonnay Durell Vineyard	94–96	now–2015
2005 Chardonnay Durell Vineyard	95	now–2015
2004 Chardonnay Durell Vineyard	92	now–2013
2006 Chardonnay Dutton Ranch	92–94	now–2012
2005 Chardonnay Dutton Ranch	95	now–2015
2004 Chardonnay Dutton Ranch	94	now–2010
2005 Chardonnay Hirsch Vineyard	92	now–2017
2006 Chardonnay Hudson	93–95	now–2014
2005 Chardonnay Hudson	93	now–2013
2004 Chardonnay Hudson	93	now–2012
2006 Chardonnay Hyde Vineyard	93–95	now–2015
2005 Chardonnay Hyde Vineyard	95	now–2017
2004 Chardonnay Hyde Vineyard	95	now–2014
2006 Chardonnay Kistler Vineyard	96–98	now–2018
2005 Chardonnay Kistler Vineyard	97	now–2015
2004 Chardonnay Kistler Vineyard	95+	now–2016
2006 Chardonnay Kistler Vineyard Cuvée Cathleen	96–98	now–2018
2005 Chardonnay Kistler Vineyard Cuvée Cathleen	98	now–2015
2004 Chardonnay Kistler Vineyard Cuvée Cathleen	96	now–2014
2006 Chardonnay McCrea Vineyard	93–94	now–2015
2005 Chardonnay McCrea Vineyard	94	now–2017
2004 Chardonnay McCrea Vineyard	93	now–2013
2006 Chardonnay Stone Flat Vineyard	95–96	now–2016
2005 Chardonnay Stone Flat Vineyard	95	now–2015
2006 Chardonnay Vine Hill Vineyard	93–96	now–2016
2005 Chardonnay Vine Hill Vineyard	95	now–2014
2004 Chardonnay Vine Hill Vineyard	95	now–2014
2006 Pinot Noir Bodega Headlands Cuvée Elizabeth	96–98	now–2018+
2005 Pinot Noir Bodega Headlands Cuvée Elizabeth	99	now–2020
2004 Pinot Noir Bodega Headlands Cuvée Elizabeth	97	now–2018
2006 Pinot Noir (not yet named)	94–96	now–2018
2006 Pinot Noir Cuvée Catherine Occidental Station	94–96	now–2017
2005 Pinot Noir Cuvée Catherine Occidental Station	96	now–2020
2004 Pinot Noir Cuvée Catherine Occidental Station	94	now–2018
2006 Pinot Noir Kistler Vineyard	90–92	now–2017
2005 Pinot Noir Kistler Vineyard	94	provocative–2016
2004 Pinot Noir Kistler Vineyard	93	now–2016
2003 Pinot Noir Kistler Vineyard	91	now–2015
2003 Pinot Noir Kistler Vineyard Cuvée Catherine	95	now–2016
2002 Pinot Noir Kistler Vineyard Cuvée Catherine	95	now–2017

2003 Pinot Noir Occidental Vineyard Cuvée Elizabeth	94	now–2017
2002 Pinot Noir Occidental Vineyard Cuvée Elizabeth	95	now–2020

KOBALT ★ ★ ★ ★
NAPA $90.00

Kobalt is owned by Kevin Carriker, who works with vineyards in some of Napa Valley's cooler sectors, including Coombsville and Stags Leap. The wines are full-throttle, intense, and very rich and ageworthy.

2006 Cabernet Sauvignon	92–94+	2010–2033+
2005 Cabernet Sauvignon	94	now–2033
2004 Cabernet Sauvignon	92	now–2028
2003 Cabernet Sauvignon	91	now–2020
2002 Cabernet Sauvignon	94	now–2017

KONGSGAARD ★ ★ ★ ★ ★
NAPA $75.00–$175.00

Winemaker John Kongsgaard fashions low-tech, artisanal wines that see no commercial yeasts, bacterial strains, or enzymes. The results are reds and whites that represent the essence of their varietal, vintage, and vineyard. In short, these are artisanal wines at their finest.

2006 Chardonnay	92–94	now–2014
2005 Chardonnay	95	now–2018
2004 Chardonnay	94	now–2017
2006 Chardonnay The Judge	96–98	now–2015
2005 Chardonnay The Judge	98	now–2018
2004 Chardonnay The Judge	98	now–2013
2006 Roussanne/Viognier	95	now–2010
2005 Roussanne/Viognier	96	now
2004 Roussanne/Viognier	89	now
2006 Syrah Hudson Vineyard	95–97	now–2018
2005 Syrah Hudson Vineyard	98	now–2023+
2004 Syrah Hudson Vineyard	90	now–2018
2003 Syrah Hudson Vineyard	94+	now–2015
2002 Syrah Hudson Vineyard	95	now–2020
2001 Syrah Hudson Vineyard	96+	now–2020

KOSTA BROWNE ★ ★ ★
SANTA LUCIA HIGHLANDS $75.00–$85.00

This hugely popular Pinot Noir producer is the brainchild of Dan Kosta and Michael Browne, who previously worked at a fashionable Sonoma restaurant. They began accessing some of the better Pinot Noir sites in California because of their love for that varietal. I am not nearly as enamored of these wines as many writers are—I find them somewhat superficial and overripe—but there is no doubting their popularity and appeal.

2005 Pinot Noir Garys' Vineyard	86	now
2005 Pinot Noir Rosella's Vineyard	85?	now

KRUPP BROTHERS ESTATES ★ ★ ★ ★
NAPA $45.00–$50.00

Jan Krupp, the owner of Stagecoach Vineyard, the largest vineyard on Atlas Peak, produces a remarkable Syrah as well as some fascinating white wine blends. Occasionally, a Cabernet

Sauvignon is also released, but it is usually far less interesting than its siblings. Krupp also produces a less expensive line of unexciting wines sold under the Veraizon label.

2006 Bride Proprietary White Wine	92	now
2005 Marsanne Stagecoach Vineyard	87	now
2005 Syrah Stagecoach Vineyard	94	now–2017
2003 Syrah Stagecoach Vineyard	91	now–2012
2002 Syrah Stagecoach Vineyard	90	now–2012

KULETO ESTATE ★ ★ ★ ★
NAPA $45.00–$50.00

Pat Kuleto, a well-known restaurateur, produces these full-flavored, savory wines, made from various northern California sites that are meant to be drunk in their first four to five years. I have enjoyed everything they have produced.

2001 Cabernet Sauvignon	90	now–2015
2004 Syrah Kuleto Estate	92	now–2013
2001 Zinfandel Napa	90	now

KUNDE ESTATE ★ ★ ★
SONOMA $20.00–$55.00

With more than 800 acres of vines, producing 150,000-plus cases of wine, Kunde, which has been in business since 1990, offers a bevy of Chardonnays, Zinfandels, Syrahs, Viogniers, and Bordeaux varietals. The wines tend to be made in an up-front, superficial, fruit-driven, pleasant style that has many followers. There is enormous potential here, but I think they could do better.

KUNIN WINES ★ ★ ★ ★
SANTA BARBARA $18.00–$36.00

One of the Central Coast's finest Rhone Ranger wine producers, Seth Kunin founded this winery in 1988, and he currently produces over 3,000 cases of high-class, French-inspired wines from Syrah, Zinfandel, Viognier, and Rhone Ranger blends. These elegant, flavorful offerings reveal very natural textures.

2004 Pape Star Larner Vineyard	91	now–2010
2005 Pape Star Proprietary Red Wine	89	now–2011
2005 Syrah	90	now–2014
2004 Syrah	89	now–2012
2002 Syrah	92	now–2013
2001 Syrah	89	now
2005 Syrah Alisos Vineyard	90	now–2015
2004 Syrah Alisos Vineyard	90	now–2014
2002 Syrah Alisos Vineyard	91	now–2015
2001 Syrah Alisos Vineyard	92	now–2011
2006 Viognier Stolpman Vineyard	90	now–2010
2005 Viognier Stolpman Vineyard	90	now
2001 Zinfandel Paso Robles	89	now

KYNSI WINERY ★ ★ ★/★ ★ ★ ★
SANTA BARBARA $32.00–$48.00

Kynsi produces well-made Pinot Noirs and Syrahs that are worth a search of the marketplace.

2004 Pinot Noir Bien Nacido Vineyard	90	now–2012
2003 Pinot Noir Bien Nacido Vineyard	88	now
2003 Syrah Bien Nacido Vineyard	89+	now
2003 Syrah Edna Ranch	90	now
2003 Syrah Kalanna	92	now–2016

LADERA ★ ★ ★
NAPA $68.00

This good winery has been dedicated to producing one wine, a 100% Cabernet Sauvignon from a single vineyard on the hillsides of Mt. Veeder. More recently, a Syrah as well as a Howell Mountain Cabernet Sauvignon have been added to the portfolio. Ladera is a large estate of 400 acres, of which 75 are planted with vines.

2004 Cabernet Sauvignon Lone Canyon Vineyard	89	now–2011
2002 Cabernet Sauvignon Lone Canyon Vineyard	92	now–2022

LAETITIA VINEYARD & WINERY ★ ★/★ ★ ★
ARROYO GRANDE $25.00–$60.00

The products of a huge operation with 620 acres currently under vine, with Pinot Noir representing 450 acres, these wines have been mixed in quality, with most being deep and woody but lacking charm and finesse.

2003 Pinot Noir Estate	85	now
2002 Pinot Noir Estate	87	now
2003 Pinot Noir Estate La Colline	86+?	now–2012
2002 Pinot Noir Estate La Colline	90	now–2014
2001 Pinot Noir Estate La Colline	88	now
2003 Pinot Noir Les Galets	87	now–2010
2002 Pinot Noir Les Galets	90	now–2014
2003 Pinot Noir Reserve	87?	now–2012
2002 Pinot Noir Reserve	88	now
2004 Syrah Clone 383 Laetitia Vineyard	85?	now–2012
2004 Syrah Clos Galets Laetitia Vineyard	84	now–2012
2004 Syrah Laetitia Vineyard	85	now–2012

LAFOND WINERY ★ ★ ★
SANTA RITA HILLS $18.00–$38.00

A reliable but uninspiring selection emerges from Lafond. In 1972, they were among the first vineyards to recognize the potential in what is now regarded as a premium viticultural area, the Santa Rita Hills.

2004 Chardonnay Lafond Vineyard	89	now
2004 Chardonnay SRH	87	now
2003 Pinot Noir Arita Hills Vineyard	87	now
2003 Pinot Noir Lafond Vineyard	88	now–2011
2002 Pinot Noir Lafond Vineyard	86	now
2002 Pinot Noir Santa Rita Hills	89	now
2001 Syrah Joughin Vineyard	90	now–2013
2004 Syrah Lafond Vineyard	87	now
2003 Syrah Lafond Vineyard	87	now
2001 Syrah Lafond Vineyard	85	now
2004 Syrah SRH	88	now

| 2003 Syrah SRH | 88 | now |
| 2001 Syrah SRH | 87 | now–2010 |

LAGIER-MEREDITH ★★★★
NAPA $50.00–$55.00

Since their debut release in 2000, I have enjoyed the elegant, French-style Syrahs from this small cult winery on Mt. Veeder. Carole Meredith is the winemaker-proprietor. These are beautiful wines.

2005 Syrah	95	now–2016
2004 Syrah	92	now–2014
2003 Syrah	93	now–2011
2001 Syrah	90+	now–2020

LAIL VINEYARDS ★★★★
NAPA $80.00

Robin Lail is one of the grand dames of Napa Valley. Her father is the legendary John Daniel, who made many of the great Inglenook Reserve Cabernets, and she once partnered with Frenchman Christian Moueix to produce wines at Dominus. She now concentrates on her own Howell Mountain Estate vineyard, and also buys fruit from the Vine Hill Vineyard in Yountville. In addition to her J. Daniel Cuvée, she produces super French-styled Sauvignon Blanc with the help of French winemaking consultant Phillipe Melka. These are impressive, long-lived efforts made in relatively limited quantities.

2006 J. Daniel Cuvée	94–96	2012–2030+
2005 J. Daniel Cuvée	94+	2012–2030
2004 J. Daniel Cuvée	92+	2009–2027
2003 J. Daniel Cuvée	94	now–2021+
2002 J. Daniel Cuvée	95	now–2020+
2001 J. Daniel Cuvée	93	now–2015
2006 Georgia Sauvignon Blanc	89–91	now–2012
2004 Georgia Sauvignon Blanc	91	now–2013

LANDMARK ★★★★
SONOMA $20.00–$65.00

Elegant Chardonnays and Pinot Noirs as well as a Syrah (still a work in progress) are made at this impeccably well-run Sonoma winery. Longtime winemaker Eric Stern and proprietors Mike and Mary Calhoun received some valuable pointers from the great Helen Turley when they first started, and have never deviated from that path. They continue to make one of the best values in high-class Chardonnay with their Overlook cuvée.

2005 Chardonnay Armagh	92	now–2012+
2004 Chardonnay Damaris Reserve	91	now–2011
2005 Chardonnay Damaris Reserve Sangiacomo Vineyard	93	now–2011
2005 Chardonnay Lorenzo	91	now–2012
2004 Chardonnay Lorenzo	93	now–2014
2006 Chardonnay Overlook	90	now–2011
2005 Chardonnay Overlook	90	now–2010
2006 Pinot Noir Grand Detour	89	now–2011
2005 Pinot Noir Grand Detour	90	now–2013
2003 Pinot Noir Grand Detour	91	now–2011

2006 Pinot Noir Kanzler	90	now–2012
2005 Pinot Noir Kanzler	91	now–2013
2002 Pinot Noir Kastania Vineyard	94	now–2013
2006 Pinot Noir Solomon Hills	89+	now–2016
2003 Syrah Steel Plow El Farolito Vineyard	87	now–2011

LARKIN * * * *
NAPA $60.00–$65.00

Larkin is a small artisanal producer making fewer than 1,000 cases of high-octane, flavorful Cabernet Sauvignon and Cabernet Franc.

2005 Cabernet Franc	92	now–2018
2004 Cabernet Franc	92	now–2018
2003 Cabernet Franc	90	now–2012
2002 Cabernet Franc	91	now–2015
2001 Cabernet Franc	92	now–2018
2005 Cabernet Sauvignon	91+	2010–2030
2003 Cabernet Sauvignon	94	now–2017

JACK LARKIN * * * *
NAPA $75.00

The son of Sean Larkin, who runs Larkin winery, Jack Larkin produces super wines from a vineyard on Pritchard Hill overlooking Lake Hennessy. He turns out tiny quantities of a beautiful Merlot as well as superb Cabernet Sauvignon.

2005 Cabernet Sauvignon	92+	2010–2028
2004 Cabernet Sauvignon	90+	2009–2024
2005 Merlot	93	now–2018

LARKMEAD VINEYARDS * * * */* * * * *
NAPA $45.00–$70.00

This historic vineyard north of St. Helena continues to prove that proprietor Cam Baker has a super site, with 120 acres under vine in a 150-acre parcel flat on the valley floor. Recent vintages have been exceptional thanks to the brilliant young winemaker, Andy Smith. This spectacular *terroir* has long been regarded as one of the great sites of Napa Valley.

2005 Cabernet Sauvignon Estate	90	2010–2020+
2004 Cabernet Sauvignon Estate	93	now–2021+
2003 Cabernet Sauvignon Estate	93	now–2021
2002 Cabernet Sauvignon Estate	93	now–2020
2005 Cabernet Sauvignon Solari Reserve	94	2012–2030
2004 Cabernet Sauvignon Solari Reserve	95	now–2022
2003 Cabernet Sauvignon Solari Reserve	94	now–2018
2002 Cabernet Sauvignon Solari Reserve	95	now–2020
2005 Firebelle Proprietary Red Wine	91	now–2023
2004 Firebelle Proprietary Red Wine	91	now–2022
2003 Firebelle Proprietary Red Wine	92	now–2016
2002 Firebelle Proprietary Red Wine	93	now–2017
2005 LMV Salon Proprietary Red Wine	91	2011–2025
2004 LMV Salon Proprietary Red Wine	94	now–2022
2003 LMV Salon Proprietary Red Wine	90	now–2018
2006 Sauvignon Blanc	90	now–2010

PAUL LATO ★★★★
SANTA MARIA $40.00–$75.00

Paul Lato, a Polish immigrant working out of a Santa Maria warehouse, is making a name for himself with both Syrah and Pinot Noir. His passion and impeccable attention to detail have resulted in some outstanding wines.

2006 Pinot Noir Fiddlestix Vineyard	92	now–2014
2006 Pinot Noir Goldcoast Vineyard Duende	93	now–2015
2005 Pinot Noir Goldcoast Vineyard Duende	94	now–2017
2004 Pinot Noir Goldcoast Vineyard Duende	92	now–2014
2003 Pinot Noir Goldcoast Vineyard Duende	90	now–2012
2005 Pinot Noir Solomon Hills Vineyard Clone 115	92	now–2015
2005 Pinot Noir Solomon Hills Vineyard Suerte	94	now–2017
2003 Syrah Bien Nacido Vineyard	89	now–2015
2005 Syrah Bien Nacido Vineyard Skywatcher	92+	now–2014
2005 Syrah Larner Vineyard Cinematique	95	now–2017

LAUREL GLEN ★★★
SONOMA $55.00–$65.00

Patrick Campbell was a pioneer in Sonoma Mountain Cabernet Sauvignon, planting a 20-plus-acre vineyard from which he produced some high-quality wines in the early to mid-1980s. He has supplemented his production by making a *négociant* line called Terra Rossa, a simple, bistro-style, dry red. For unknown reasons, the quality of Laurel Glen's Cabernet Sauvignons has fallen since the early days. Recent vintages possess less character and lower quality than was exhibited in the brilliant early offerings.

KARL LAWRENCE ★★★
NAPA $60.00–$75.00

This small, high-quality producer's wines are difficult to find, but they are well thought of by insiders.

2003 Cabernet Sauvignon	90	now–2019
2002 Cabernet Sauvignon	91	now–2021
2001 Cabernet Sauvignon	88	now–2017
2001 Cabernet Sauvignon Reserve Gary Morisoli Vineyard	92+	now–2023
2001 Cabernet Sauvignon Reserve Herb Lamb Vineyard	93	now–2022

CLIFF LEDE VINEYARDS ★★★★
NAPA $18.00–$125.00

Canadian businessman Cliff Lede has Michelle Edwards as his winemaker, David Abreu as his viticulturalist, and none other than Michel Rolland as his winemaking consultant, so big things are expected. If 2005 is any indication, they are already well on their way to making world-class wines. This 60-acre property with vineyards and winery in the Stags Leap area made their first vintages in 2002, but I think the 2005s transport the winery to even higher ground.

2005 Cabernet Sauvignon Stags Leap District	92	now–2023
2005 Cinnamon Stardust Cabernet Sauvignon Stags Leap	94	now–2028
2005 Poetry Cabernet Sauvignon Stags Leap	95	2011–2041
2006 Sauvignon Blanc	89	now
2005 Songbook Cabernet Sauvignon	94	???

LEDSON * *
SONOMA $20.00–$45.00

Mediocre wines with little character emanate from this haunted house–looking property in Sonoma.

LEGACY * * *
ALEXANDER VALLEY $70.00

This 1,500-case blend of Cabernet Sauvignon with some Merlot, Cabernet Franc, and Petit Verdot comes from two vineyards on Jess Jackson's Alexander Mountain estate.

2005 Proprietary Red Wine	91+	2011–2028+
2004 Proprietary Red Wine	92	now–2022
2003 Proprietary Red Wine	88+	now–2020

LEVY AND MCCLELLAN * * * * *
DIAMOND MOUNTAIN $250.00–$300.00

Martha McClellan-Levy, the wine consultant for Blankiet and Sloan, and Bob Levy, longtime winemaker at Harlan, make up the husband-and-wife team behind this extraordinary vineyard designed to produce about 400 cases of a blend of 90% Cabernet Sauvignon and the rest Cabernet Franc and Petit Verdot. Planted on the steep volcanic soils of Diamond Mountain at 500- to 600-foot elevation, with 2,900 vines per acre, this vineyard is planted as tightly as one is likely to find in Napa Valley. If you can find and afford these wines, they're gems.

2006 Cabernet Sauvignon	93–95+	2010–2025
2005 Cabernet Sauvignon	94–98	now–2033+
2004 Cabernet Sauvignon	96	now–2028+

LEWELLING VINEYARDS * * * */* * * * *
NAPA $35.00–$65.00

This underrated source of top-flight Napa Cabernet Sauvignon from proprietor Dave Wight suggests a good Trivial Pursuit question: It is the oldest continuously owned family vineyard in Napa Valley (133 years). The wines represent Napa's version of a great Pauillac. Pure crème de cassis, licorice, and a subtle note of toast are found in these brilliant efforts.

2005 Cabernet Sauvignon	92	now–2023+
2004 Cabernet Sauvignon	90	now–2021+
2003 Cabernet Sauvignon	91	now–2023
2002 Cabernet Sauvignon	88	now–2015
2001 Cabernet Sauvignon	93	now–2015
2005 Cabernet Sauvignon Wight Vineyard	96+	now–2033
2004 Cabernet Sauvignon Wight Vineyard	96+	now–2021
2003 Cabernet Sauvignon Wight Vineyard	94	now–2020
2002 Cabernet Sauvignon Wight Vineyard	93+	now–2028
2001 Cabernet Sauvignon Wight Vineyard	95	now–2024

LEWIS CELLARS * * * *
NAPA $48.00–$175.00

High-quality Syrahs and Cabernet Sauvignons from selected vineyards in Oakville, Rutherford, and Pritchard Hill emerge from Lewis Cellars. Although they can be oaky, they possess enough concentration and fruit to back up the wood.

2005 Alec's Blend Proprietary Red Wine	91	now–2016
2002 Alec's Blend Proprietary Red Wine	86	now
2005 Cabernet Sauvignon	90	2010–2025
2002 Cabernet Sauvignon	90	now–2015
2006 Chardonnay	88	now
2004 Cuvée L	94	now–2025
2002 Merlot	88	now–2011
2005 Syrah	90	now–2015
2002 Syrah	91	now–2016
2005 Syrah Hudson Vineyard	92	now–2016

LINCOURT ★ ★ ★
SANTA MARIA $18.00–$30.00

The wines at Lincourt, a ten-year-old Santa Barbara winery founded by Bill Foley, have gotten significantly better over the last several years.

2004 Chardonnay	89	now
2005 Chardonnay Bien Nacido Vineyard	87	now–2010
2004 Chardonnay Bien Nacido Vineyard	90	now
2004 Pinot Noir Santa Barbara	88	now–2011
2004 Pinot Noir Santa Rita Hills	89	now–2011
2004 Syrah	89	now–2010
2003 Syrah Bien Nacido Vineyard	90	now–2012

LINNE CALODO ★ ★ ★ ★
PASO ROBLES $36.00–$95.00

One of the more innovative winemakers in California, proprietor Matt Trevisan continues to base his impressive portfolio on blended wines. All these cuvées possess singular names as well as personalities. The reds tend to be based on Rhône Valley varietal blends, with the exception of a handful of wines such as the Problem Child, Outsider, and Cherry Red, which are primarily Zinfandel-based cuvées. The only white wine produced is a brilliant Roussanne-Viognier blend called The Contrarian.

2005 Cherry Red	92	now–2014
2006 The Contrarian	93	now
2005 The Contrarian	91	now
2005 Leone's	93	now–2011
2005 Martyr	93	now–2019
2005 Nemesis	95	now–2017
2004 Nemesis	95+	now–2016+
2003 Nemesis	94	now–2017
2001 Nemesis	95	now–2010
2005 The Outsider	94	now–2014
2004 The Outsider	92	now–2014
2005 Problem Child	92	now–2013
2005 Rising Tides	93	now–2014
2004 Rising Tides	95+	now–2020
2001 Rising Tides	90	now–2011
2005 Sticks and Stones	94	now–2014
2004 Sticks and Stones	95	now–2016
2003 Sticks and Stones	95	now–2015
2001 Sticks and Stones	96	now

| 2003 Zinfandel Barley Vineyard | 93 | now |
| 2003 Zinfandel Cherry Vineyard | 91 | now–2011 |

LITTORAI ★ ★ ★ ★
NORTHERN CALIFORNIA $50.00–$55.00

One of northern California's most impressive producers is Ted Lemon, who worked for many years at Burgundy's Domaine Roulot, then returned to America to work for the now defunct Château Woltner. Lemon is a *terroiriste* making crisp, fresh, subtle Chardonnays and Pinot Noirs from cool-climate sites in northern California. Production is around 2,000 to 3,000 cases of elegant, restrained, understated wines, all from purchased fruit.

2003 Pinot Noir Cerise Vineyard	88	now
2002 Pinot Noir Cerise Vineyard	89	now–2010
2003 Pinot Noir Hirsch Vineyard	88	now–2013
2002 Pinot Noir Hirsch Vineyard	90	now–2010
2002 Pinot Noir One Acre Vineyard	91	now–2010
2003 Pinot Noir Savoy Vineyard	86	now
2002 Pinot Noir Savoy Vineyard	89	now–2010
2003 Pinot Noir Summa Vineyard	88	now–2010
2002 Pinot Noir Summa Vineyard	88	now–2011
2003 Pinot Noir Thieriot Vineyard	89	now–2012
2002 Pinot Noir Thieriot Vineyard	91	now–2012

LOKOYA ★ ★ ★ ★ ★
NAPA $175.00–$225.00

One of the gems of the Jess Jackson portfolio, Lokoya produces four limited-production 100% Cabernet Sauvignons from mountain vineyard sites, all unfined and unfiltered, and all irrefutably of great quality.

2005 Cabernet Sauvignon Diamond Mountain	94+	now–2028
2004 Cabernet Sauvignon Diamond Mountain	92	now–2021+
2003 Cabernet Sauvignon Diamond Mountain	92	now–2021+
2002 Cabernet Sauvignon Diamond Mountain	94	now–2020
2001 Cabernet Sauvignon Diamond Mountain	96	now–2028
2005 Cabernet Sauvignon Howell Mountain	94+	2013–2038
2004 Cabernet Sauvignon Howell Mountain	92+	now–2021+
2003 Cabernet Sauvignon Howell Mountain	96	now–2021+
2002 Cabernet Sauvignon Howell Mountain	95	???
2001 Cabernet Sauvignon Howell Mountain	95	2010–2040
2005 Cabernet Sauvignon Mount Veeder	96	2013–2035
2004 Cabernet Sauvignon Mount Veeder	96	2009–2029
2003 Cabernet Sauvignon Mount Veeder	94+	2009–2020+
2002 Cabernet Sauvignon Mount Veeder	96	2010–2030
2001 Cabernet Sauvignon Mount Veeder	97+	now–2023
2005 Cabernet Sauvignon Spring Mountain	96	now–2033

LONDER VINEYARDS ★ ★ ★
MENDOCINO $30.00–$60.00

This tiny 15-acre Mendocino County vineyard is planted with Pinot Noir as well as small amounts of Gewürztraminer and Chardonnay. The Pinots are impressive efforts fashioned by winemaking consultant Greg La Folette.

2003 Pinot Noir Anderson Valley	86	now
2001 Pinot Noir Anderson Valley	87	now
2003 Pinot Noir Keefer Ranch	89	now
2003 Pinot Noir Paraboll Vineyard	90	now
2001 Pinot Noir Paraboll Vineyard	92	now
2001 Pinot Noir Vanderkamp Vineyard	88	now

JOCELYN LONEN ★ ★ ★
NAPA $30.00–$65.00

This 44-acre estate is located in the Atlas Peak sector of Napa, a high-elevation site with a cool climate as well as porous, volcanic soils. My first look at these wines was very promising.

2005 Cabernet Franc Reserve	90	now–2018
2005 Cabernet Sauvignon	86	now–2020
2005 Cabernet Sauvignon Reserve	89	now–2018
2006 Chardonnay Carneros	88	now–2010
2006 Chardonnay Reserve Carneros	89	now–2010
2006 Chardonnay Reserve Russian River	91	now–2011
2005 Founder's Reserve	89+	2010–2025+

LONGORIA ★ ★ ★/★ ★ ★
SANTA RITA HILLS $22.00–$42.00

One of the pioneers of the Santa Barbara wine industry, Rick Longoria arrived in 1976 and began his career by making wines for other wineries. He started his own operation in 1997. These are all handcrafted, very good, limited-quantity efforts. My favorites tend to be the single-vineyard Pinot Noirs.

2003 Pinot Noir Bien Nacido Vineyard	87	now
2002 Pinot Noir Bien Nacido Vineyard	92	now–2011
2003 Pinot Noir Fe Ciega Vineyard	88	now–2011
2002 Pinot Noir Fe Ciega Vineyard	89	now
2001 Pinot Noir Fe Ciega Vineyard	86	now
2002 Pinot Noir Mt. Carmel Vineyard	91	now
2002 Pinot Noir Sanford & Benedict Vineyard	90	now–2011
2001 Syrah Santa Barbara	88	now

LORING WINE CO. ★ ★ ★
CENTRAL COAST $46.00–$48.00

Pinot Noir specialist Brian Loring accesses some special sites from which he fashions intensely fruity, soft, consumer-friendly Pinots that are meant to be drunk in their first four to five years. Production is limited to 3,000 cases per vintage.

2005 Pinot Noir Brosseau Vineyard	87	now–2010
2005 Pinot Noir Cargasacchi Vineyard	87	now–2010
2005 Pinot Noir Clos Pepe Vineyard	86	now–2010
2005 Pinot Noir Garys' Vineyard	86	now–2010
2003 Pinot Noir Garys' Vineyard	90	now–2011
2002 Pinot Noir Garys' Vineyard	91	now–2011
2005 Pinot Noir Rosella's Vineyard	84	now–2010
2003 Pinot Noir Rosella's Vineyard	89+	now–2012
2002 Pinot Noir Rosella's Vineyard	90	now–2010
2005 Pinot Noir Russell Family Vineyard	87	now–2010

LOST CANYON WINERY ★★/★★★
NORTHERN CALIFORNIA $35.00

This *négociant* operation specializes in small lots of single-vineyard Pinot Noir and Syrah from the Russian River, Sonoma Coast, and Los Carneros. The wines are fruity, soft, somewhat superficial, and pleasant.

2005 Syrah Alegria Vineyard	83	now–2010
2004 Syrah Alegria Vineyard	87	now–2010
2005 Syrah Stage Gulch Vineyard	84	now
2004 Syrah Stage Gulch Vineyard	86	now
2005 Syrah Trenton Station Vineyard	85	now
2004 Syrah Trenton Station Vineyard	82	now

LUCIA VINEYARDS AND WINERY ★★★★
SANTA LUCIA HIGHLANDS $32.00–$45.00

A project of the Pisoni family, Lucia produces wines from two major vineyards, the Pisoni and Garys' vineyards, both of which were planted with Syrah and Pinot Noir in the mid-1990s. The Pisoni family consists of Gary Pisoni and his sons, Mark and Jeff, the latter being the winemaker at Lucia. They produce superb wines with considerable character.

2004 Chardonnay	92	now
2005 Pinot Noir	91	now–2013
2004 Pinot Noir	91	now–2012
2003 Pinot Noir	90	now–2012
2005 Pinot Noir Garys' Vineyard	92	now–2014
2004 Pinot Noir Garys' Vineyard	92+	now–2012
2003 Pinot Noir Garys' Vineyard	90	now–2011
2005 Syrah Garys' Vineyard	93	now–2017
2004 Syrah Garys' Vineyard	93	now–2016
2005 Syrah Pisoni Vineyard	94	now–2017
2004 Syrah Susan's Hill	94	now–2016

LUNA VINEYARDS ★★★/★★★★
NAPA $18.00–$100.00

Of all the Italian varietal ventures in California, Luna has done the most to beat the trend of mediocre wines, specializing in top-notch Pinot Grigio- and Sangiovese-based wines that are sometimes blended with other grapes. Much of the credit for their success goes to the estate's founders, George Vare and Mike Moone, who had the foresight to bring in the brilliant winemaker John Kongsgaard. Although Kongsgaard has moved on, the Luna wines remain among the finest of the Italian-inspired offerings made in northern California.

2004 Cabernet Sauvignon	88	now–2013
2002 Canto Proprietary Red Wine	87	now
2004 Freakout Reserve	88	now
2004 Merlot	86	now–2011
2002 Merlot	84	now
2006 Pinot Grigio Barrel Fermented	88	now
2005 Sangiovese	90	now–2011
2003 Sangiovese	86	now

MacMURRAY RANCH * * *
SONOMA $20.00–$60.00

Originally owned by the family of well-known Hollywood actor Fred MacMurray, this estate was purchased by Gallo in 1999 and is dedicated to producing around 70,000 cases from the Sonoma Coast and smaller quantities from the Russian River. One of California's finest Pinot Gris as well as some very good Pinot Noirs emerge from this winery. Moreover, prices are realistic.

2005 Pinot Gris	90	now–2010
2004 Pinot Noir Santa Rita Hills	88	now–2011
2004 Pinot Noir Sonoma Coast	87	now–2012
2004 Pinot Noir WM Block Russian River	90	now–2012

MacPHAIL FAMILY WINES * * *
DRY CREEK $40.00–$56.00

This small, high-quality Pinot Noir specialist fashions tasty wines from different sites in northern California.

2005 Pinot Noir Ferrington Vineyard	89	now–2014
2005 Pinot Noir Pratt Vineyard	88+	now–2015
2005 Pinot Noir Sangiacomo Vineyard	89	now–2012
2005 Pinot Noir Toulouse Vineyard	90	now–2015

MacROSTIE WINERY * * *
SONOMA $19.00–$39.00

Founded in 1987 by Steve MacRostie, this estate produces fruit-forward, well-made, consumer-friendly wines from their Wildcat Mountain Vineyard. The focus appears to be on Chardonnay, Pinot Noir, and Syrah, although a small amount of Merlot is also released.

2001 Syrah Blueoaks Vineyard	86	now
2001 Syrah Wildcat Mountain	89	now–2011

BERNARD MAGREZ * * * *
NAPA $45.00

The Bordeaux visionary and proprietor of Pape Clément as well as many other Bordeaux estates, Bernard Magrez set up shop in Napa, making a wine at Quintessa along with oenologist Michel Rolland. His debut vintage was 2004, which was a decidedly rich, concentrated, impressive wine.

2004 Cabernet Sauvignon	92	now–2022

MANTRA * * *
ALEXANDER VALLEY $27.00–$40.00

This *négociant* operation features high-elevation Alexander and Dry Creek Valley vineyards. The wines are both well made and realistically priced.

2005 Cabernet Sauvignon Alexander Valley	89	now–2018
2004 Cabernet Sauvignon Alexander Valley	98+	now–2022
2003 Cabernet Sauvignon Reserve Revelations	91	now–2022
2005 Cabernet Sauvignon Sonoma	89	now–2018
2004 Cabernet Sauvignon Sonoma	89	now–2017
2001 Proprietary Red Wine	90	now–2011
2001 Revelations Reserve Proprietary Red wine	91	now–2015

| 2002 Zinfandel | 88 | now |
| 2002 Zinfandel Reserve | 90 | now |

MARA WINERY ★★★★
NORTHERN CALIFORNIA $40.00–$45.00

Charles Mara, a well-known wine retailer, has been making top-flight Zinfandels from the Dolinsek Ranch in the Russian River and the Luvisi Ranch in Napa Valley. Production for these full-throttle, rich, savory wines is limited.

| 2005 Zinfandel Dolinsek | 91 | now–2012 |
| 2005 Zinfandel Luvisi Ranch Old Vines | 88 | now–2011 |

MARCASSIN ★★★★★
SONOMA $40.00–$125.00

One of the world's finest producers, the husband-and-wife team of Helen Turley and John Wetlaufer offers wines of the highest quality level. An unwavering, uncompromising wine-making philosophy is reflected in their meticulous work in the vineyard as well as in their highly detailed winemaking, which consistently succeeds in producing some of the finest Chardonnays and Pinot Noirs in the world. Helen Turley has also been a consultant for a number of great start-up operations such as Colgin, Bryant Family Vineyard, Blankiet, Pahl-meyer, and a handful of others. She has created an extraordinary legacy of greatness that is largely unequaled by any other wine consultant in North America. These are wines of true genius.

2005 Chardonnay Marcassin Vineyard	96+	2011–2023+
2004 Chardonnay Marcassin Vineyard	97	2011–2023
2005 Chardonnay Three Sisters Vineyard	94+	now–2018+
2004 Chardonnay Three Sisters Vineyard	95	now–2023
2004 Chardonnay Zio Tony Ranch	93	now–2016
2004 Pinot Noir Blue Slide Ridge	96	now–2018
2003 Pinot Noir Blue Slide Ridge	98	now–2016
2002 Pinot Noir Blue Slide Ridge	95+	now–2013
2003 Pinot Noir Bondi Home Ranch	90	now–2012
2002 Pinot Noir Bondi Home Ranch	94	now–2015
2004 Pinot Noir Marcassin Estate	96	2010–2028+
2003 Pinot Noir Marcassin Estate	99	now–2021
2002 Pinot Noir Marcassin Estate	98	now–2015+
2001 Pinot Noir Marcassin Estate	93	now–2015
2004 Pinot Noir Three Sisters	91	2010–2018+
2003 Pinot Noir Three Sisters	95	now–2016
2002 Pinot Noir Three Sisters	96	now–2015

MARGERUM WINE CO. ★★★
SANTA BARBARA $15.00–$45.00

Proprietor Doug Margerum ran Santa Barbara's highly renowned Wine Cask until it was sold. He now produces wines in a warehouse in Los Olivos. This is a good source of interesting vineyard-designated cuvées from a multitude of varieties planted in some of Santa Barbara's finest vineyards.

2006 M5	85	now–2010
2005 M5	90	now–2010
2005 Pinot Gris Alisos Vineyard	85?	now

2005 Pinot Gris Margerum Ranch Vineyard	89	now
2005 Riesling	89	now
2005 Rosé	89	now
2005 Sauvignon Blanc Vogelzang Vineyard	90	now
2005 Sauvignon Blanc Westerly Vineyard	92	now
2005 Syrah Alondra de Los Prados Vineyard	87	now–2011
2004 Syrah Alondra de Los Prados Vineyard	92	now–2016
2004 Syrah Black Oak Vineyard	91	now–2013
2005 Syrah Colson Canyon Vineyard	89	now–2017
2004 Syrah Colson Canyon Vineyard	90	now–2013
2002 Syrah Colson Canyon Vineyard	91	now–2013
2005 Syrah Great Oaks Vineyard	89	now–2015
2005 Syrah Purisima Mountain Vineyard	88	now–2014
2004 Syrah Purisima Mountain Vineyard	91	now–2018
2002 Syrah Purisima Mountain Vineyard	91	now–2015
2005 Syrah Uber Vineyard	89+	now–2015
2004 Syrah Vogelzang Vineyard	87	now–2014
2002 Syrah Vogelzang Vineyard	92	now–2013+

MARIETTA CELLARS * * */* * * *
SONOMA $13.00–$30.00

The Bilbro family produces around 35,000 cases of wine, including one of California's great bargains in dry red wines, their sensational nonvintage blend of Petite Sirah, Alicante, Zinfandel, Carignan, and who knows what else. The lot number is now in the upper 40s, and this wine sells out quickly as Chris Bilbro and his son, Jake, know how to deliver plenty of quality for a song. Marietta also produces the full-flavored Angeli cuvée, a blend of Zinfandel, Petite Sirah, and Carignan, as well as the Emilia's Cuvée, which includes numerous Italian varietals, and a tasty Zinfandel and Cabernet Sauvignon. This is a bargain hunter's treasure trove.

2003 Angeli Cuvée	92	now–2012
2001 Angeli Cuvée	89	now–2010
2004 Cabernet Sauvignon	86	now–2015
2004 Emilia's Cuvée Proprietary Red Wine	88	now–2011
2003 Emilia's Cuvée Proprietary Red Wine	87	now
N.V. Old Vine Red Lot 37	87	now
N.V. Old Vine Red Lot 44	86	now

MARKHAM * *
NAPA $20.00–$65.00

Founded in 1978 by Bruce Markham, and sold to a Japanese company in 1988, this estate currently releases in excess of 200,000 cases. The present owners continue to build up their holdings, having recently acquired the La Jota estate on Howell Mountain. However, the quality of the wines is decidedly mediocre and uninteresting.

MARSTON FAMILY VINEYARD * * */* * * *
NAPA $85.00

This winery on Spring Mountain owned by Michael and Alexandra Marston has been around for well over three decades, with the fruit sold primarily to Beringer. They are now estate-bottling some of their wines, which are made by the highly regarded French consultant Philippe Melka.

2006 Cabernet Sauvignon	92–95	now–2023+
2005 Cabernet Sauvignon	94	now–2023+
2004 Cabernet Sauvignon	87?	2010–2030
2003 Cabernet Sauvignon	90+?	???
2002 Cabernet Sauvignon	89?	now–2020

MARTIN AND WYRICH ★ ★
PASO ROBLES $18.00–$35.00

There has always been an Italian slant to the wines made at this winery, founded in 1981 on the site of an old dairy farm. Their attempts at Nebbiolo, Sangiovese, Primitivo, Pinot Grigio, Chardonnay, and Cabernet Sauvignon were largely failures. However, prices are low, which gives them some attraction in the marketplace.

MARTINELLI ★ ★ ★ ★/★ ★ ★ ★ ★
SONOMA $32.00–$100.00

One of the great family names of northern California agriculture (apples and grapes), the Martinellis have shown an astute, nearly uncontested ability to spot terrific vineyard sites and coax them into producing impressive wines. They were among the first to recognize the potential on the Sonoma Coast, and have produced some superb Chardonnays from their Three Sisters and Charles Ranch vineyards as well as some fabulous Pinot Noirs from the Blue Slide Ridge Vineyard. They also do stunning work in the Russian River region. In the background is the brilliant winemaking consultant Helen Turley.

2006 Chardonnay Charles Ranch	93	now–2012
2005 Chardonnay Charles Ranch	93	now–2012
2004 Chardonnay Charles Ranch	91	now–2010
2006 Chardonnay Martinelli Road	93	now–2012
2005 Chardonnay Martinelli Road	93	now–2013
2004 Chardonnay Martinelli Road	94	now–2012
2005 Chardonnay Three Sisters Vineyard Sea Ridge Meadow	94	now–2015
2004 Chardonnay Three Sisters Vineyard Sea Ridge Meadow	94	now–2014
2003 Chardonnay Three Sisters Vineyard Sea Ridge Meadow	92	now–2011
2006 Chardonnay Woolsey Road	90	now–2011
2005 Chardonnay Woolsey Road	94	now–2011
2004 Chardonnay Woolsey Road	92	now
2006 Chardonnay Zio Tony Ranch	93	now–2012
2004 Chardonnay Zio Tony Ranch	89?	now–2013
2005 Pinot Noir Blue Slide Ridge	95	now–2016
2004 Pinot Noir Blue Slide Ridge	92	now–2014
2003 Pinot Noir Blue Slide Ridge	92	now–2015
2002 Pinot Noir Blue Slide Ridge	95	now–2015
2006 Pinot Noir Bondi Home Ranch Water Trough Vineyard	91	now–2012
2005 Pinot Noir Bondi Home Ranch Water Trough Vineyard	90	now–2014
2004 Pinot Noir Bondi Home Ranch Water Trough Vineyard	89	now–2011

2003 Pinot Noir Bondi Home Ranch Water Trough Vineyard	93	now–2012
2002 Pinot Noir Bondi Home Ranch Water Trough Vineyard	90+	now–2012
2005 Pinot Noir Lolita Ranch	92	now–2012
2005 Pinot Noir Moonshine Ranch	89+	now–2013
2004 Pinot Noir Moonshine Ranch	92	now–2015
2003 Pinot Noir Reserve	93	now–2013
2002 Pinot Noir Reserve	91	now–2011
2006 Pinot Noir Three Sisters Vineyard Sea Ridge Meadow	93	now–2013
2004 Pinot Noir Three Sisters Vineyard Sea Ridge Meadow	93	now–2016
2006 Pinot Noir Zio Tony Ranch	94	now–2014
2005 Pinot Noir Zio Tony Ranch	91	now–2016
2004 Pinot Noir Zio Tony Ranch	90	now–2014
2003 Pinot Noir Zio Tony Ranch	94	now–2015
2003 Pinot Noir 7 Mules	89	now–2010
2005 Syrah Chico's Hill	95	now–2016
2005 Syrah Hop Barn Hill	95+	now–2016
2002 Syrah Hop Barn Hill	96	now–2017
2001 Syrah Hop Barn Hill	95+	now–2015
2005 Syrah Lolita Ranch	94	now–2014
2006 Zinfandel Giuseppe & Luisa	94	now–2015
2005 Zinfandel Giuseppe & Luisa	94	now–2013
2004 Zinfandel Giuseppe & Luisa	93	now–2012
2003 Zinfandel Giuseppe & Luisa	90?	now
2002 Zinfandel Giuseppe & Luisa	94	now–2011
2005 Zinfandel Jackass Hill Vineyard	96	now–2014
2004 Zinfandel Jackass Hill Vineyard	95	now–2020
2001 Zinfandel Jackass Hill Vineyard	94	now–2013
2006 Zinfandel Jackass Vineyard	94	now–2015
2005 Zinfandel Jackass Vineyard	95	now
2004 Zinfandel Jackass Vineyard	93	now–2015
2003 Zinfandel Jackass Vineyard	95	now–2013

LOUIS M. MARTINI ★ ★ ★/★ ★ ★ ★
NAPA $17.00–$100.00

With more than 600 acres of vines, Louis Martini winery is one of the historic sites of northern California. Louis Martini emigrated from Genoa, Italy, in 1899, founded a winery in the San Joaquin Valley in 1922, and moved to Napa in 1933. Building up sensational vineyards, Martini quickly developed a top-notch reputation for a charming, bubbly Moscato and some superb Private Reserve Cabernet Sauvignons, especially those made in the 1950s and 1960s, which aged remarkably well. In 2002, the Gallo winemaking family purchased this estate but kept the Martinis in control, and quality seems to be even higher over recent vintages. They still own some superb vineyard sites, including the 10-acre Home Vineyard near the winery and the sensational Monte Rosso Vineyard, originally planted in the 1880s. Their top wines remain their cuvées of Cabernet Sauvignon.

2004 Cabernet Sauvignon Barrelli Creek	88	now–2014
2003 Cabernet Sauvignon Barrelli Creek	89	now–2016

2004 Cabernet Sauvignon Lot 1 Mike Martini		
Barrel Select	91	now–2022
2003 Cabernet Sauvignon Lot 1 Mike Martini		
Barrel Select	91+	2010–2035
2004 Cabernet Sauvignon Monte Rosso Vineyard	90	now–2022
2003 Cabernet Sauvignon Monte Rosso Vineyard	93	2012–2032
2001 Cabernet Sauvignon Monte Rosso Vineyard	91+	2009–2024+
2004 Cabernet Sauvignon Napa	87	now–2015
2003 Cabernet Sauvignon Napa	89	now–2017
2001 Cabernet Sauvignon Napa	88+	now–2020
2001 Cabernet Sauvignon Reserve	88	now–2015
2003 Cabernet Sauvignon Sonoma	88	now–2017
2002 Cabernet Sauvignon Sonoma	87	now–2013
2003 Zinfandel Monte Rosso Gnarly Vine	90	now–2015

MASON CELLARS * * *
NAPA $17.00–$28.00

This winery, which was founded in 1993, does a very good job with Sauvignon Blanc, but I am less impressed by their Merlot and Cabernet Sauvignon.

2006 Sauvignon Blanc	89	now–2010
2005 Sauvignon Blanc	89	now
2005 Sauvignon Blanc Reserve	88	now–2010

MATANZAS CREEK * */* * *
SONOMA $20.00–$35.00

Since acquiring this estate, Jess Jackson has been attempting to return Matanzas Creek to its glory days of the early 1990s. The quality has risen to a satisfactory level, but this is still a work in progress.

2003 Cabernet Sauvignon	83?	now–2014
2001 Cabernet Sauvignon	85	now
2005 Chardonnay	90	now
2004 Chardonnay	87	now
2002 Journey	89	now–2011
2004 Merlot Bennett Valley	83	now
2002 Merlot Bennett Valley	88+	now–2019
2002 Merlot Jackson Park	90	now–2015
2004 Syrah	85	now

MAURITSON FAMILY WINERY * */* * * *
NAPA $35.00–$39.00

The 2005 vintage is my first experience with the Healdsburg-based Mauritson Family Winery, which merits high marks for producing three brilliant Zinfandels in such a difficult vintage. It helped that they were working with one of the finest Zinfandel sites in northern California, the Rockpile appellation.

2005 Zinfandel Rockpile Cemetery Vineyard	90	now
2005 Zinfandel Rockpile Jack's Cabin Vineyard	88	now–2012
2005 Zinfandel Rockpile Ridge Vineyard	91	now–2012

MAYACAMAS VINEYARDS ★★
NAPA $50.00–$75.00

About 5,000 cases of Chardonnay, Pinot Noir, Sauvignon Blanc, and Cabernet Sauvignon are made at this estate. In the 1960s and 1970s, there was no greater or longer-lived Cabernet Sauvignon than that made high in the Mayacamas Hills by Bob Travers, a San Francisco banker who bought this historic mountain property in 1968. His 1968, 1970, 1973, and 1974 Cabernet Sauvignons remain etched in my memory as wines of first-growth quality. For unknown reasons, the current offerings have nothing in common with those early vintages.

MAYBACH ★★★★
NAPA $110.00

Named after the famed luxury car, Maybach has Thomas Brown as its winemaker. The 2004 debut vintage of 340 cases of 100% Cabernet Sauvignon is from a single parcel on the Silverado Trail in Napa. This is a serious wine.

2004 Materium	95	now–2033

MAYO FAMILY WINERY ★★★
SONOMA $15.00–$45.00

Until a few years ago, this winery demonstrated a nice touch with just about everything they made. The winemaker is Michel Berthoud, who did such excellent work for Dick Arrowood. However, a number of cork issues arose with recent releases, and I have not retasted the wines. One hopes the problem was just the misfortune of getting a bad batch of corks, which can happen with any winery.

2001 Cabernet Sauvignon Los Chamizal Vineyard Premier Block	88	now–2013
2001 Cabernet Sauvignon Napa River Ranch Julia's Block	89	now–2015
2002 Chris' Cuvée The Libertine	87	now
2001 Meritage	89	now–2011
2001 Merlot Laurent Vineyard	88	now–2010
2001 Syrah Page-Nord Vineyard	90	now
2001 Zinfandel Ricci Vineyard Old Vine	90	now
2001 Zinfandel Ricci Vineyard Old Vine Reserve	91	now–2010

McCAULEY ★★★
NAPA $58.00–$100.00

A small operation making very good Cabernet Sauvignon from purchased fruit, this producer should be followed closely over the upcoming years.

2005 Cabernet Sauvignon	88–90	now–2018+
2004 Cabernet Sauvignon	89	now–2020
2005 Cabernet Sauvignon Beckstoffer To-Kalon Vineyard	90–93	2009–2020+
2004 Cabernet Sauvignon Beckstoffer To-Kalon Vineyard	93	now–2023+

McDOWELL VINEYARDS * *
MENDOCINO $25.00–$40.00

Straightforward, pleasant, commercially styled wines are made at this large Mendocino estate. McDowell was one of the first wineries to produce Rhone Ranger cuvées, but virtually everything I have tasted has been innocuous and simple.

2001 Grenache	85	now
2004 Syrah	85	now
2001 Syrah Potato Patch Vineyard	88	now–2012

McMANIS FAMILY VINEYARDS * * *
CALIFORNIA $10.00–$12.00

One of California's finest purveyors of inexpensive Chardonnays, Cabernet Sauvignons, Petite Sirahs, and Syrahs, these are fruit-forward, medium-bodied efforts that are meant to be drunk during their first two to three years. They represent excellent value.

2003 Cabernet Sauvignon	85	now
2005 Chardonnay	87	now
2003 Petite Sirah	86	now
2003 Syrah	86	now

McPRICE MYERS WINE CO. * * * *
SANTA BARBARA $24.00–$45.00

This impressive small boutique winery is turning out innovative blends from top-notch vineyards in the Edna and Santa Ynez Valleys.

2005 Alta Mesa Proprietary Red Wine	90	now–2011
2005 Beautiful Earth Proprietary Red Wine	92	now–2014
2005 Cuvée Kristina Proprietary Red Wine	93	now–2013
2004 Grenache	89	now–2010
2005 Grenache L'Ange Rouge	90	now–2011
2005 Syrah Larner Vineyard	91	now–2015
2004 Syrah Larner Vineyard	89	now–2014
2002 Syrah Larner Vineyard	90+	now–2012
2005 Syrah Les Galets Vineyard	89	now–2011
2004 Syrah Les Galets Vineyard	91	now–2014
2005 Viognier Larner Vineyard	92	now–2010

PHILIPPE MELKA * * * *
NAPA $75.00–$100.00

Philippe Melka's name is best associated with some of the top wineries of California, including Lail, Vineyard 29, Gemstone, Hundred Acre, and the Roy Estate. However, in 1995, Philippe Melka and his wife, Cherie, began producing a top-notch Bordeaux-style red that is usually dominated by Cabernet Sauvignon but includes small portions of Cabernet Franc, Merlot, and Petit Verdot. The 500-case production is fashioned from several sources, including the Gamble Ranch and one of David Abreu's vineyards. This is a beautiful, high-quality wine meant for long-term aging.

2006 Metisse Proprietary Red	93–95	now–2023+
2005 Metisse Proprietary Red	95	now–2028+
2004 Metisse Proprietary Red Wine	92+	now–2022
2003 Metisse Proprietary Red Wine	93+	now–2020
2001 Metisse Proprietary Red Wine	94	now–2020

MELVILLE ★★★★
SANTA RITA HILLS $20.00–$52.00

The Melvilles have been visionaries, developing 82 acres in the Lompac area of the Santa Rita Hills planted with 14 different clones of Pinot Noir and four separate clones of Chardonnay, as well as smaller plantings of Syrah and Viognier. They also possess a site in Cat Canyon, Verna's Vineyard, which is two miles north of Los Alamos. These top-notch efforts are made by the brilliant Greg Brewer of the Brewer-Clifton Winery.

2006 Chardonnay Clone 76 Inox	90	now–2010
2005 Chardonnay Clone 76 Inox	92	now
2004 Chardonnay Clone 76 Inox	91	now
2004 Chardonnay Estate	92	now
2005 Chardonnay Estate Verna's	93	now
2004 Chardonnay Estate Verna's	90	now
2005 Pinot Noir Carrie's	92	now–2017
2004 Pinot Noir Carrie's	95	now–2012
2003 Pinot Noir Carrie's	91	now–2013
2002 Pinot Noir Carrie's	92+	now–2014
2005 Pinot Noir Clone 115 Indigène	90	now–2015
2004 Pinot Noir Clone 115 Indigène	95	now–2012
2003 Pinot Noir Clone 115 Indigène	89	now–2011
2005 Pinot Noir Estate	90	now–2013
2004 Pinot Noir Estate	92	now–2011
2003 Pinot Noir Estate	88	now
2005 Pinot Noir Estate Verna's Vineyard	89	now–2011
2004 Pinot Noir Estate Verna's Vineyard	91	now–2013
2005 Pinot Noir High Density	93	now–2014
2004 Pinot Noir High Density	93	now–2013
2003 Pinot Noir High Density	89	now
2005 Pinot Noir Terraces	91	now–2013
2004 Pinot Noir Terraces	96	now–2014
2003 Pinot Noir Terraces	90+	now–2013
2005 Syrah Donna's	92	now–2014
2004 Syrah Donna's	90	now–2016
2005 Syrah High Density	92	now–2014
2004 Syrah High Density	94	now–2016
2005 Syrah Verna's	90	now–2011
2004 Syrah Verna's	91	now–2014
2005 Viognier Estate	94	now–2010
2005 Viognier Estate Verna's	90	now–2010

MERRYVALE ★★/★★★
NAPA $45.00–$55.00

This large St. Helena estate is located adjacent to the fashionable Tra Vigne restaurant. It was founded in 1983 by Bill Harlan and several partners who had the foresight to bring in Bob Levy. When Harlan sold his interest, Levy was replaced by other winemakers. At times the wines have been very good, but recently they have been pleasant rather than exciting. Both the regular cuvées and Reserves tend to be very oaky and underfruited.

MERUS ★★★★/★★★★★
NAPA $125.00

Sold in late 2007 to the Foley family but still being run by the husband-and-wife team of Mark Herold and Erika Gottl, this winery's objective is to produce full-throttle, brilliantly etched, ageworthy Cabernet Sauvignons. It appears they have succeeded admirably at this small, "seat of the pants" operation run out of a garage on the back streets of Napa. Mark Herold is also a consultant for some of Napa Valley's artisanal high-quality producers. At the end of 2007, Merus was sold to the Foley Wine Group.

2006 Cabernet Sauvignon	91–94	2012–2025
2005 Cabernet Sauvignon	95	2012–2026
2004 Cabernet Sauvignon	94	2010–2030
2003 Cabernet Sauvignon	95	now–2028
2002 Cabernet Sauvignon	95	now–2020
2001 Cabernet Sauvignon	95	now–2027

PETER MICHAEL WINERY ★★★★★
KNIGHT'S VALLEY $42.00–$175.00

Sir Peter Michael, an incredibly successful electronics businessman from England, purchased 112 acres in Knight's Valley in 1981 and produced his first wines in 1987 under the guidance of winemaker Helen Turley. A succession of "who's who" winemakers have followed Turley, including Mark Aubert, Luc Morlet, and Morlet's brother. This is an irrefutable source of handcrafted, naturally made wines of extraordinary purity and quality, whether they be their single-vineyard Chardonnays or their Bordeaux-style red wine called Les Pavots. They also make a sensational Sauvignon Blanc called L'Après-Midi. This is California fruit wedded to a European philosophy of winemaking. The results from these high-elevation Knight's Valley sites are profound.

2006 Chardonnay La Carrière	92–94	now–2016
2005 Chardonnay La Carrière	95	now–2015
2004 Chardonnay La Carrière	95	now–2012
2006 Chardonnay Belle Côte	92–94	now–2014
2005 Chardonnay Belle Côte	95	now–2018
2004 Chardonnay Belle Côte	95	now–2015
2006 Chardonnay Cuvée Indigène	92–94	now–2013
2005 Chardonnay Cuvée Indigène	96	now–2018
2004 Chardonnay Cuvée Indigène	97	now–2014
2006 Chardonnay Ma Belle Fille	94–96	now–2014
2005 Chardonnay Ma Belle Fille	94+	now–2014
2004 Chardonnay Ma Belle Fille	94	now–2013
2006 Chardonnay Mon Plaisir	90–93	now–2012
2005 Chardonnay Mon Plaisir	94	now–2016
2004 Chardonnay Mon Plaisir	94	now–2011
2006 Chardonay Point Rouge	94–96	now–2018
2005 Chardonnay Point Rouge	97	now–2018+
2004 Chardonnay Point Rouge	95+	now–2016
2005 L'Esprit des Pavots	90–92	now–2019
2004 L'Esprit des Pavots	95	now–2018
2005 Les Pavots Proprietary Red Wine	95	2010–2023+
2004 Les Pavots Proprietary Red Wine	93	2010–2023+
2003 Les Pavots Proprietary Red Wine	94	now–2020

2002 Les Pavots Proprietary Red Wine	98	now–2027
2006 Pinot Noir Le Moulin Rouge	91–93	now–2015
2005 Pinot Noir Le Moulin Rouge	91	2009–2020+
2004 Pinot Noir Le Moulin Rouge	95	now–2016
2003 Pinot Noir Le Moulin Rouge	93	now–2013
2006 Sauvignon Blanc L'Après-Midi	90	now–2010

MICHAEL-DAVID WINERY ★★★
LODI $12.00–$49.00

Onetime vegetable farmers Michael and David Phillips represent the fifth generation of Lodi growers. Instead of vegetables, they now own 350 acres of premium wine grapes, from which they produce fruit-driven, well-made, value-priced wines that are ideal for drinking during their exuberant youth.

2005 Earthquake Zin	88	now–2011
2004 Incognito	87	now
2004 Syrah Earthquake	85	now
2004 Syrah Sixth Sense	86	now–2010
2003 Syrah Windmill	85	now
2006 Viognier Incognito	85	now
2005 Viognier Incognito	86	now
2005 Zinfandel Lust	90	now–2012
2005 Zinfandel Windmill Old Vine	88	now–2010
2006 7 Deadly Zins	86	now–2010
2005 7 Deadly Zins	87	now–2010

MILLER WINE WORKS ★★★★
NAPA $30.00–$42.00

This *négociant* operation in Napa is owned by Gary Miller, a graduate of the Culinary Institute of America, who is pursuing his passion to make wines that he enjoys. Miller has accessed some fine vineyards, and in a few short years has produced excellent to outstanding wines that merit serious attention.

2004 Grenache Sage Canyon Vineyard	89	now–2012
2003 Grenache Sage Canyon Vineyard	88	now
2004 Syrah Brookside Vineyard	89+	now–2014
2003 Syrah Brookside Vineyard	88	now–2016+
2004 Syrah Castle Rock Vineyard	91	now–2019
2003 Syrah Castle Rock Vineyard	92+	now–2018
2004 Syrah Sage Canyon Vineyard	91	now–2015
2003 Syrah Sage Canyon Vineyard	91	now–2016+

MINER FAMILY VINEYARDS ★★/★★★
NAPA $48.00–$60.00

A flamboyant winery along the Silverado trail built by a family that made its fortune in the software business, Miner's wine quality is good, but the overall impression left by many of the offerings is one of distinctive oakiness. The two most impressive efforts to date have been their Syrah from the Stagecoach Vineyard and the Bordeaux blend called Oracle. The latter wine is a blend of Cabernet Sauvignon, Merlot, Cabernet Franc, and Malbec.

| 2004 The Oracle | 90 | now–2018 |
| 2004 Pinot Noir Garys' Vineyard | 89 | now–2012 |

2005 Pinot Noir Rosella's Vineyard	85	now–2010
2004 Pinot Noir Rosella's Vineyard	88	now–2010
2003 Pinot Noir Rosella's Vineyard (777 Clone)	84	now
2003 Pinot Noir Rosella's Vineyard (Pisoni Clone)	87	now
2005 Syrah La Diligence Stagecoach Vineyard	90	now–2018

MIURA VINEYARDS ★★★★
CENTRAL COAST $53.00–$60.00

Miura, the Spanish name of the breed of bulls used in bullfighting, is the small artisanal winery of winemaker Emmanuel Kemiji, who was previously a sommelier in San Francisco as well as part-owner of the famous restaurant of Gary Danko. The wines I have tasted to date have all been outstanding, suggesting this is a serious Pinot Noir specialist.

2005 Pinot Noir Garys' Vineyard	91+	2009–2017
2004 Pinot Noir Garys' Vineyard	90+	now–2016
2005 Pinot Noir Pisoni Vineyard	90	2009–2019
2004 Pinot Noir Pisoni Vineyard	94	now–2014
2003 Pinot Noir Pisoni Vineyard	92	now–2013

EL MOLINO WINERY ★★★★
RUTHERFORD $45.00–$50.00

Founded in 1871, this is one of the most historic wineries in Napa Valley. It was restored in 1981 and produces only two wines, a Pinot Noir and a Chardonnay, both from the Star Vineyard in Rutherford.

2005 Chardonnay	90	now
2004 Pinot Noir	91	now–2011

ROBERT MONDAVI ★★★/★★★★★
NAPA $27.00–$125.00

Sadly, one of the most important chapters in the history of quality wine in the United States as well as North American civilization closed with the sale of the Robert Mondavi Corporation to Constellation Brand in 2005. Robert Mondavi's spirit, soul, and creativity will continue to live through other wineries, and through his own winery, even though it is now under new ownership. His contribution to the qualitative wine movement in America and importance to wine in this country is impossible to properly measure. In terms of wine quality and the promotion of fine wine, no one will ever equal what Robert Mondavi accomplished. The Mondavi wines are currently a work in progress, as his chief winemaker, his son, Tim, is following his own project called Continuum. Quality at Mondavi remains very good, and the top Reserve offerings are still among the finest made in California. Let's hope that does not change.

2002 Cabernet Sauvignon Moffet Vineyard M-Bar	93	now–2022
2001 Cabernet Sauvignon Moffet Vineyard M-Bar	94+	now–2020+
2003 Cabernet Sauvignon Napa	90	now–2017
2002 Cabernet Sauvignon Napa	90	now–2017
2004 Cabernet Sauvignon Oakville	88	now–2021
2003 Cabernet Sauvignon Oakville	93+	now–2020
2002 Cabernet Sauvignon Oakville	91	now–2020
2002 Cabernet Sauvignon Private Reserve	92	now–2020+
2001 Cabernet Sauvignon Private Reserve	94+	now–2020+
2004 Cabernet Sauvignon Reserve	92+	now–2022
2003 Cabernet Sauvignon Reserve	94	now–2025

2004 Cabernet Sauvignon Stags Leap District	89	now–2021
2002 Cabernet Sauvignon Stags Leap District	93	now–2020
2001 Cabernet Sauvignon Stags Leap District	92	now–2018
2001 Cabernet Sauvignon To-Kalon Reserve	95	2009–2034
2002 Cabernet Sauvignon Vine Hill Ranch	96	now–2028
2004 Chardonnay Reserve Carneros	88	now
2005 Fumé Blanc I Block	92	now–2010
2005 Fumé Blanc Reserve To-Kalon Vineyard	91	now–2009

CHÂTEAU MONTELENA * * * * *
NAPA $45.00–$100.00

The Barrett family is only the second owner of this estate since it was founded in 1882. After prohibition, Montelena became a Napa ghost winery, which it remained until 1972, when Jim Barrett formed a partnership and resurrected this once great name. From relatively old vineyards in northern Napa, surrounding the town of Calistoga, they produce a bevy of wines, the finest being their estate Cabernet Sauvignon. Purchasing one of these offerings is the equivalent of buying a blue-chip stock. They get better and better with age, and as vertical tastings prove, they improve and last for 20 to 25 years. While modern-day society seems to always be in search of new stars, this winery has been a Cabernet Sauvignon superhero for more than 30 years. Perhaps their most underrated wines are their delicious, dry Riesling and their excellent, nonmalolactic Chardonnay.

2005 Cabernet Sauvignon	90	now–2016
2004 Cabernet Sauvignon	89	now–2016
2003 Cabernet Sauvignon	90	now–2015
2002 Cabernet Sauvignon	91	now–2017
2001 Cabernet Sauvignon	87	now–2015
2005 Cabernet Sauvignon Estate	91+	2012–2030
2004 Cabernet Sauvignon Estate	94+	2010–2035
2003 Cabernet Sauvignon Estate	93+	2009–2034
2002 Cabernet Sauvignon Estate	95+	2014–2040
2001 Cabernet Sauvignon Estate	95+	2010–2025
2006 Chardonnay	91	now–2018+
2005 Chardonnay	91	now–2018+
2006 Johannisberg Riesling Potter Valley	88	now
2005 Johannisberg Riesling Potter Valley	89	now
2005 Zinfandel Estate	87	now
2004 Zinfandel Estate	90	now–2013
2003 Zinfandel Estate	90	now

MONTICELLO CELLARS * */* * *
NAPA $35.00–$65.00

The Corley family has been working in Napa Valley since the early 1970s. At Monticello, also known as Corley Family Winery, they produce 15,000 cases of wines that are generally sound but frequently uninspiring. The finest efforts tend to be their Corley Reserve Cabernet Sauvignon–based wines.

2004 Cabernet Sauvignon State Lane Vineyard	88	now–2018
2004 Corley Reserve Cabernet Sauvignon	87	now–2016
2005 Corley Reserve Chardonnay Estate	86	now–2010
2004 Proprietary Red Wine	86	now–2017

MORAGA ★★★★
SOUTHERN CALIFORNIA $150.00–$200.00

One of the most distinctive vineyards located on some of the world's most expensive real estate, this 15-acre site is situated in a deep canyon in Bel Air. Former aviation executive Tom Jones brought in the well-known Bordeaux consultant Dr. Alain Raynaud to assist in making these impressive Bordeaux blends that possess excellent aging potential. This is a serious boutique winery located a stone's throw from Beverly Hills.

MORGAN ★★★
MONTEREY $18.00–$55.00

Founded in 1992 by Dan Lee, the original winemaker at the now defunct Jekel winery, Morgan's wines are always attractive, fruit-forward efforts, easy to understand and consume. Unquestionably satisfying and savory, their only downside is that they are not terribly complex.

2004 Chardonnay Hat Trick Double L Vineyard	89	now
2006 Chardonnay Metallico	89	now–2010
2005 Chardonnay Metallico	88	now
2004 Chardonnay Metallico	90	now
2004 Chardonnay Rosella's Vineyard	90	now
2005 Côtes du Crow's	86	now
2004 Côtes du Crow's	87	now
2006 Pinot Gris R and D Franscioni Vineyard	87	now
2004 Pinot Noir Double L Vineyard	87	now–2010
2001 Pinot Noir Double L Vineyard	87	now
2005 Pinot Noir Garys' Vineyard	90	now–2011
2004 Pinot Noir Garys' Vineyard	91	now–2012
2003 Pinot Noir Garys' Vineyard	86	now
2001 Pinot Noir Garys' Vineyard	88	now
2005 Pinot Noir Rosella's Vineyard	90	now–2011
2003 Pinot Noir Rosella's Vineyard	89	now
2001 Pinot Noir Rosella's Vineyard	88	now
2003 Syrah Tierra Mar	89	now–2011

MORLET FAMILY ESTATE ★★★★/★★★★★
NORTHERN CALIFORNIA $60.00–$100.00

Luc Morlet, who was the highly renowned winemaker at both Peter Michael and Staglin Family Vineyards, has his own portfolio of enormously impressive wines. He knows how to make great wine, which is evident in his debut releases listed below. As one might expect, this high quality comes at an equally high price.

2006 Pinot Noir Coteaux Nobles	93	now–2018
2006 Pinot Noir En Famille	93	now–2015
2006 Pinot Noir Joli Coeur	94+	2009–2018
2006 La Proportion Dorée	94	now–2014
2006 Syrah Bouquet Garni	92	now–2014

MOUNT EDEN VINEYARDS ★★★★
SANTA CRUZ $25.00–$75.00

A historic as well as spectacularly beautiful estate high atop Mount Eden, this property was established by one of the pioneers of modern California winedom, Martin Ray. He lost the estate in the 1970s, and it is now owned by Jeff and Eleanor Patterson. While their sensational

Chardonnay can be long-lived, the quality is somewhat irregular. They also produce potentially superb Pinot Noir and Cabernet Sauvignon. The Cabernets Mount Eden made in the mid-1970s are among the all-time greatest of California, but that level of quality has not been reached in many years. However, the Chardonnays are still among the finest in the state.

2004 Cabernet Sauvignon Estate	93+	2016–2043
2003 Cabernet Sauvignon Estate	90+	2013–2033
2004 Chardonnay Estate	95	now–2018
2004 Chardonnay Saratoga Cuvée	92	now
2004 Chardonnay Wolff Vineyard	89	now
2005 Pinot Noir Estate	87?	now–2014
2004 Pinot Noir Estate	92	2010–2023
2003 Pinot Noir Estate	90	now–2018
2002 Pinot Noir Estate	89	now–2015

MUMM ★★★
NAPA $30.00–$65.00

Owned by the huge firm Diageo, Mumm specializes in sparkling wines, of which their top-selling cuvée is the Cuvée Napa. Their flagship offering is the DVX. Quality is good, but never reminiscent of the finest French Champagnes.

MURPHY-GOODE ★★★
ALEXANDER VALLEY $24.00–$45.00

Since this Alexander Valley winery was founded in 1988, it has produced fruit-driven, attractively priced reds and whites. Their finest cuvées tend to be their Sauvignon Blanc, Zinfandel, and Chardonnay. The winery and its 350-plus acres were recently sold to Jess Jackson, so quality should get even better.

2004 Cabernet Sauvignon Terra a Lago Vineyards	89	now
2005 Zinfandel Liar's Dice	83	now
2005 Zinfandel Snake Eyes Ellis Vineyards	87	now

ANDREW MURRAY VINEYARDS ★★★/★★★★
SANTA YNEZ $16.00–$45.00

One of the stars of Santa Ynez, Andrew Murray produces flavorful yet elegant, consistently fine reds and whites reminiscent of France's Rhône Valley offerings. The estate is located near Los Olivos, north of Santa Barbara.

2003 Espérance	87	now
2002 Espérance	87	now
2002 Syrah Bien Nacido Vineyard	88	now–2011
2003 Syrah Estate	88	now–2011
2002 Syrah Gainey Vineyard	89	now–2012
2003 Syrah Hillside Reserve	91	now–2014
2003 Syrah Roasted Slope Vineyard	90	now–2013
2003 Syrah Tous Les Jours	89	now

NALLE ★★★/★★★★
SONOMA $25.00–$35.00

A reliable, tiny producer, Nalle produces just over 2,000 cases of primarily old-vine Zinfandel that reveals as much elegance and finesse as this varietal can produce. Small amounts of fairly priced, good-quality Pinot Noir, Sauvignon Blanc, and Chardonnay are also made. For some reason, this winery continues to fly well below most consumers' radar.

NATIVE 9 ★ ★ ★ ★
SANTA MARIA $40.00–$55.00

A new, small but promising operation from James Ontiveros, who owns an eight-acre vineyard in the Santa Maria Valley, the name relates to the nine generations of Ontiveroses who have farmed and run cattle in California.

2005 Pinot Noir Rancho Ontiveros Vineyard	89	now–2011
2004 Pinot Noir Rancho Ontiveros Vineyard	90	now–2011
2004 Pinot Noir Solomon Hills Vineyard	85	now

NAVARRO ★ ★ ★/★ ★ ★ ★
MENDOCINO $16.00–$35.00

Navarro is one of my favorite wineries for value-priced, delicious, crisp whites, especially their Riesling, Chardonnay, Pinot Gris, and Gewürztraminer, as well as—surprisingly—a light but solidly made Pinot Noir. Just about everything that emerges from this high-quality winery is noteworthy. Moreover, prices are exceptionally fair.

NEWTON VINEYARD ★ ★ ★ ★
NAPA $21.00–$75.00

Owner Su Hua Newton, a believer in low yields, along with her French winemaking staff, produces wines that appeal to those with European sensitivities. There is nothing wimpy about any of the reds or whites that emerge from this winery, but they do not possess the unfettered power and explosive fruit found in many California wines.

2005 Cabernet Sauvignon Unfiltered	92	2010–2033
2003 Cabernet Sauvignon Unfiltered	93	now–2020+
2002 Cabernet Sauvignon Unfiltered	91+	now–2018
2001 Cabernet Sauvignon Unfiltered	90	now–2020
2005 Chardonnay Unfiltered	96	now–2018
2003 Claret	87	now–2011
2002 Claret	88	now–2013
2002 Epic	93	now–2024
2005 Merlot Unfiltered	91	now–2023
2003 Merlot Unfiltered	90	now–2015
2002 Merlot Unfiltered	88	now–2013
2001 Merlot Unfiltered	88	now–2015
2002 Pinot Noir Unfiltered	87	now–2010
2005 The Puzzle Unfiltered	92–94+	2012–2028+
2004 The Puzzle Unfiltered	94–96	2011–2033
2002 The Puzzle Unfiltered	93+	2009–2030

NEYERS VINEYARDS ★ ★ ★ ★
NAPA $26.00–$60.00

Former research chemist Bruce Neyers, who founded this Conn Valley winery in 1980, fashions impressive reds and whites with the assistance of his talented winemaker, Ehren Jordan.

2006 Ame Proprietary Red Wine	91	now–2028
2005 Ame Proprietary Red Wine	92	2009–2018
2006 Cabernet Sauvignon Neyers Ranch	89+	2010–2022

2005 Cabernet Sauvignon Neyers Ranch	89	now–2019
2004 Cabernet Sauvignon Neyers Ranch	88	now–2017
2003 Cabernet Sauvignon Neyers Ranch	90	now–2017
2002 Cabernet Sauvignon Neyers Ranch	89	now–2013
2006 Chardonnay Carneros	90	now
2005 Chardonnay Carneros	91	now–2011
2004 Chardonnay Carneros	91	now
2006 Chardonnay Napa	89	now–2010
2005 Chardonnay Napa	89	now–2010
2006 Chardonnay El Novillero Vineyard	92	now–2012
2005 Chardonnay El Novillero Vineyard	91	now–2012
2004 Chardonnay El Novillero Vineyard	90+	now–2010
2006 Chardonnay Thieriot Vineyard	93	now–2012
2005 Chardonnay Thieriot Vineyard	89	now–2013
2004 Chardonnay Thieriot Vineyard	90?	now–2012
2006 Merlot Neyers Ranch	90	2010–2023
2005 Merlot Neyers Ranch	88	now–2014
2003 Merlot Neyers Ranch	87	now
2006 Mourvèdre Pato Vineyard	90	now–2014
2006 Syrah Cuvée d'Honneur	91	now–2016
2005 Syrah Cuvée d'Honneur	91	now–2015
2003 Syrah Cuvée d'Honneur	90	now–2012
2006 Syrah Hudson Vineyard	90	now–2014
2005 Syrah Hudson Vineyard	89	now–2012
2004 Syrah Hudson Vineyard	87	now–2011
2002 Syrah Hudson Vineyard	91	now–2011
2006 Syrah Old Lakeville	90+	2010–2018
2005 Syrah Old Lakeville Highway	91	now–2012
2006 Zinfandel High Valley	91	now–2012
2005 Zinfandel High Valley	91	now–2014
2006 Zinfandel Pato Vineyard	90	now–2011
2005 Zinfandel Pato Vineyard	88	now–2012
2006 Zinfandel Tofanelli Vineyard	88	now–2010
2005 Zinfandel Tofanelli Vineyard	87	now–2011

NIEBAUM-COPPOLA ∗∗∗
RUTHERFORD $100.00–$150.00

Purchased by Francis Ford Coppola in 1975, this historic vineyard and mansion, which once belonged to Gustav Niebaum, produced the Cabernet Sauvignon grapes that went into the majestic Beaulieu Private Reserves during their glory years of the 1950s, 1960s, and early 1970s. Coppola's flagship wine is Rubicon, a Bordeaux blend that remains somewhat rustic and underachieving. He also fashions a pleasant white wine blend called Blancaneaux. Additionally, wines are released under the Edizione Pennio label, which include a competent but unexciting Zinfandel, and a new Cask Cabernet Sauvignon, another underachiever. For all Coppola's talents as a film director, he has not made the transition to making top wines despite owning over 200 acres of fabulous vineyards that offer unlimited potential.

2003 Cask Cabernet Sauvignon	87	2009–?
2004 Rubicon	89	now–2023
2002 Rubicon	86	now–2015
2001 Rubicon	90	now–2020

NOVY FAMILY WINERY   * * *
CALIFORNIA $22.00–$40.00

A spin-off of Adam and Diana Lee's Siduri Winery, this *négociant* operation specializes in Syrah and a handful of other varietals from different vineyard sites. The overall quality is very good, and prices are realistic.

2005 Chardonnay	88	now
2004 Syrah Christensen Family Vineyard	88	now–2013
2005 Syrah Garys' Vineyard	89	now–2013
2004 Syrah Garys' Vineyard	92	now–2014
2004 Syrah Judge Vineyard	89+	now–2016
2003 Syrah Judge Vineyard	90	now–2010
2005 Syrah Napa	85	now
2004 Syrah Napa	88	now
2005 Syrah Page-Nord Vineyard	88	now–2011
2002 Syrah Page-Nord Vineyard	90	now–2013
2001 Syrah Page-Nord Vineyard	91+	now–2015
2005 Syrah Parson's Vineyard	87	now–2011
2005 Syrah Pisoni Vineyard Susan's Hill	89	now–2016
2005 Syrah Rosella's Vineyard	89	now–2014
2004 Syrah Rosella's Vineyard	92	now–2013
2005 Syrah Russian River	87	now
2005 Syrah Santa Lucia Highlands	89	now
2004 Syrah Sonoma	89	now–2011
2004 Syrah Susan's Vineyard	94	now–2013
2005 Syrah Unti Vineyard	86	now

OJAI VINEYARD   * * * *
SANTA BARBARA $26.00–$58.00

It is hard to believe, but Adam and Helen Tolmach have been making wines for nearly 25 years. A Rhone Ranger pioneer, Adam Tolmach remains one of the most reclusive wine producers in California, and only a handful of wineries have matched his brilliant performance record from vineyards spread out through Santa Barbara and Ventura counties. Just about any Ojai wine is well worth checking out, including their crisp, fresh Chardonnays, brilliant Pinot Noirs and Syrahs, and, more recently, a tasty Grenache. Perhaps Tolmach's least-known superb offering is his Sauvignon Blanc from the Westerly Vineyard.

2005 Chardonnay Bien Nacido Vineyard	91	now–2011
2004 Chardonnay Bien Nacido Vineyard	88	now
2005 Chardonnay Clos Pepe Vineyard	93	now–2011
2004 Chardonnay Clos Pepe Vineyard	89	now
2005 Grenache	90	now–2011
2003 Grenache Purisima Mountain Vineyard	91	now–2015
2004 Grenache Thompson Vineyard	91	now–2014
2005 Pinot Noir Bien Nacido Vineyard	92	now–2017
2004 Pinot Noir Bien Nacido Vineyard	91	now–2014
2003 Pinot Noir Bien Nacido Vineyard	91	now–2013
2002 Pinot Noir Bien Nacido Vineyard	92	now
2001 Pinot Noir Bien Nacido Vineyard	88	now–2010
2005 Pinot Noir Clos Pepe Vineyard	88	now–2013
2004 Pinot Noir Clos Pepe Vineyard	89+	now–2014

2003 Pinot Noir Clos Pepe Vineyard	89+	now–2012
2001 Pinot Noir Clos Pepe Vineyard	92	now–2013
2005 Pinot Noir Fe Ciega	91	now–2017
2004 Pinot Noir Fe Ciega	91	now–2015
2003 Pinot Noir Fe Ciega	93	now–2012
2005 Pinot Noir Solomon Hills	91	now–2017
2004 Pinot Noir Solomon Hills	90	now–2012
2005 Sauvignon Blanc Westerly	92	now–2010
2005 Syrah	89	now–2012
2005 Syrah Bien Nacido Vineyard	95	now–2022
2004 Syrah Bien Nacido Vineyard	93	now–2019
2003 Syrah Bien Nacido Vineyard	92+	now–2021
2005 Syrah Melville Vineyard	93	now–2022
2004 Syrah Melville Vineyard	94	now–2022
2003 Syrah Melville Vineyard	90+	now–2015
2005 Syrah Presidio Vineyard	88	now–2017
2005 Syrah Roll Ranch	91	now–2015
2004 Syrah Roll Ranch	94	now–2017
2003 Syrah Roll Ranch	92	now–2014
2004 Syrah Stolpman Vineyard	94	now–2014
2003 Syrah Stolpman Vineyard	93	now–2016
2005 Syrah Thompson Vineyard	91	2009–2020
2004 Syrah Thompson Vineyard	94	now–2022
2003 Syrah Thompson Vineyard	93	now–2017
2005 Syrah Verna's Vineyard	92	now–2022
2004 Syrah Verna's Vineyard	88	now–2012
2003 Syrah Verna's Vineyard	89	now–2011
2003 Syrah Vogelzang Vineyard	90	now–2014
2005 Syrah White Hawk Vineyard	92	now–2022
2004 Syrah White Hawk Vineyard	93	now–2013
2003 Syrah White Hawk Vineyard	95	???

MALOY O'NEILL VINEYARD * * *
PASO ROBLES $20.00–$50.00

This family-owned winery is dedicated to producing Cabernet Sauvignon, Petite Sirah, and Syrah. The wines I have tasted are high-octane, high-quality, high-alcohol efforts meant to be drunk in their first decade.

2005 Petite Sirah O'Neill Vineyards	90	now–2022
2004 Petite Sirah O'Neill Vineyards	90	now–2017
2004 Syrah Hillside O'Neill Vineyards	89	now–2012
2004 Syrah "Katie O" O'Neill Vineyards	90	now–2013
2005 Syrah O'Neill Vineyards	88	now–2013
2004 Syrah O'Neill Vineyards	87?	now–2011
2004 Syrah Private Reserve O'Neill Vineyards	88	now–2013
2004 Syrah Windy Hill O'Neill Vineyards	90	now–2013

OPUS ONE * * */* * * *
NAPA $165.00

The two principals who founded this historic partnership and vineyard, the late Baron Philippe de Rothschild and the now fully retired Robert Mondavi, are no longer the guiding lights for this visionary project, originally meant to be a Napa interpretation of a great Bordeaux. The Mondavis sold their interest and Opus One is now in the hands of the Philippe de Rothschild's daughter, Philippine. The wine has rarely lived up to its potential and extraordinary pedigree, but things seem to be moving in the right direction now that the Rothschilds have full control over the operation. The high-tech Oakville winery is an aesthetic tour de force.

2004 Proprietary Red Wine	92	now–2020
2003 Proprietary Red Wine	91	now–2015
2002 Proprietary Red Wine	89	now–2020
2001 Proprietary Red Wine	87	now–2015

O'SHAUGHNESSY ESTATE WINERY * * * *
NAPA $65.00–$75.00

For years, the O'Shaughnessy family sold much of their fruit to Beringer, but they are now making some estate-bottled wines. This relatively new operation appears to be off to a flying start. Winemaker Sean Capiaux (who has his own Pinot Noir operation) is doing some stunning work with this 35-acre mountain vineyard, planted with 29 acres of Cabernet and the rest other Bordeaux varieties. There is also a small cuvée (under 1,000 cases) of fabulous Cabernet Sauvignon from Mt. Veeder.

2006 Cabernet Sauvignon Howell Mountain	91–93	2010–2023
2005 Cabernet Sauvignon Howell Mountain	95	2011–2026+
2004 Cabernet Sauvignon Howell Mountain	94	now–2028+
2003 Cabernet Sauvignon Howell Mountain	93	now–2022
2002 Cabernet Sauvignon Howell Mountain	91	2009–2025
2001 Cabernet Sauvignon Howell Mountain	88+	now–2023
2006 Cabernet Sauvignon Mt. Veeder	92–94	now–2033
2005 Cabernet Sauvignon Mt. Veeder	95	2012–2025
2004 Cabernet Sauvignon Mt. Veeder	95	now–2028
2003 Cabernet Sauvignon Mt. Veeder	96	now–2027+
2002 Cabernet Sauvignon Mt. Veeder	95	now–2020
2006 Merlot Howell Mountain	89–92	now–2020
2005 Merlot Howell Mountain	92	now–2018
2004 Merlot Howell Mountain	92	now–2017
2006 Syrah Howell Mountain	88–89	now–2020

PAHLMEYER * * * * *
NAPA $70.00–$120.00

The charismatic Jayson Pahlmeyer and his exuberant winemaker, Erin Green, who apprenticed for Helen Turley for many years, are turning out some fabulous wines. Without question, Green has more than adequately filled the enormous shoes of Turley. Pahlmeyer has long been one of California's most consistently reliable producers of brilliant Chardonnay, Merlot, and Proprietary Bordeaux blends. A Sonoma Coast Chardonnay was recently added to the portfolio, and there should be significantly more estate-bottled wines from the Home Vineyard on Atlas Peak (a 220-acre ranch with 88 acres under vine). These are brilliant efforts on all levels.

2006 Chardonnay Napa	95	now–2015
2005 Chardonnay Napa	92	now–2012
2004 Chardonnay Napa	91	now
2006 Chardonnay Sonoma Coast	95	now–2015

2005 Chardonnay Sonoma Coast	93	now–2014
2004 Chardonnay Sonoma Coast	93	now–2011
2006 Merlot	92–94	now–2023+
2005 Merlot	94	now–2023+
2004 Merlot	90	now–2014
2003 Merlot	92	now–2013
2002 Merlot	91	now–2015
2006 Pinot Noir	88	now–2013
2005 Pinot Noir	92	now–2015
2006 Proprietary Red Wine	93–95	now–2028+
2005 Proprietary Red Wine	96	now–2038+
2004 Proprietary Red Wine	91	now–2021
2003 Proprietary Red Wine	94	now–2020+
2002 Proprietary Red Wine	94	now–2020

PALAZZO WINE * * * *
NAPA $45.00–$55.00

Scott Palazzo runs this small boutique operation, producing around 1,000 cases of unfined, unfiltered wine that represents a Napa version of a top-notch Pomerol. It is usually a blend of 70% Merlot and the rest Cabernet Franc as well as a touch of Cabernet Sauvignon. It is a sexy, full-bodied red.

2005 Proprietary Red Wine	93	now–2020
2004 Proprietary Red Wine	90	now–2017
2003 Proprietary Red Wine	91	now–2015

PALMAZ VINEYARDS * *
NAPA $75.00

This old ghost winery was resurrected with great fanfare. An amazing high-tech winery with large underground caves and top-notch winemaking consultant Mia Klein suggested great things. However, to date, everything is still a work in progress, and the wines have not yet lived up to their early promise.

2004 Cabernet Sauvignon	85?	now–2016

PALMINA * * * *
SANTA BARBARA $16.00–$50.00

In the capable hands of Steve Clifton (part of the brilliant Brewer-Clifton duo), Palmina is one of the few California wineries that is able to translate the fragile yet ethereal character of Nebbiolo, Sangiovese, and white grapes such as Malvasia, Pinot Gris, and Tocai Friulano into wines of considerable class and interest. Consumers seeking Italian varietals made in California should definitely check out the wines of Palmina.

2004 Alisos	90	now–2010
2002 Alisos	89	now
2005 Arneis Honea Vineyard	89	now
2004 Dolcetto Zotovich Vineyard	86	now
2005 Malvasia Bianca Larner Vineyard	91	now
2003 Nebbiolo Sisquoc Vineyard	90	now
2002 Nebbiolo Sisquoc Vineyard	90+	now–2014
2003 Nebbiolo Stolpman Vineyard	87	now–2012
2002 Nebbiolo Stolpman Vineyard	89+	now–2010

2001 Nebbiolo Stolpman Vineyard	89	now
2005 Pinot Grigio	87	now
2005 Pinot Grigio Alisos Vineyard	89	now
2005 Pinot Grigio Honea Vineyard	90	now
2003 Savoia	90	now–2010
2002 Savoia	91	now
2005 Tocai Friulano Honea Vineyard	90	now
2005 Traminer Alisos Vineyard	87	now
2004 Undici Eleven Oaks Vineyard	92	now

PALOMA ★ ★ ★ ★
NAPA $50.00–$55.00

This 15-acre site at the top of Spring Mountain consistently produces one of California's finest Merlots. It achieved heroic status when one vintage was named *The Wine Spectator*'s Wine of the Year. It is all that a Merlot should be—plump, fleshy, and seductive.

2005 Merlot	92	now–2016
2004 Merlot	92	now–2018
2003 Merlot	89	now–2011
2002 Merlot	90	now–2013
2001 Merlot	94	now–2011
2002 Syrah	92	now–2012

PARAISO VINEYARDS ★ ★
MONTEREY $20.00–$45.00

Proprietor Rick Smith has around 3,000 acres of grapes in Monterey County, but he bottles his wines at selected sites in the Santa Lucia Highlands. They tend to be straightforward, fruity, pleasant, realistically priced but superficial offerings.

2003 Syrah Estate	87	now–2010
2004 Syrah Wedding Hill Vineyard	84	now
2003 Syrah Wedding Hill Vineyard	88	now

FESS PARKER WINERY ★ ★ ★ ★
SANTA BARBARA $18.00–$58.00

A bundle of energy and creativity, real estate developer and winery owner Fess Parker, now in his early 80s, recently opened a new luxury spa and resort across from his beachfront hotel in Santa Barbara. He also owns the Wine Country Inn in Los Olivos. Even more important, he has developed some of the finest vineyard sites in Santa Ynez. With the assistance of his son, Eli, and a capable team, he has fashioned a portfolio of very impressive reds and whites, especially Syrahs, Pinot Noirs, and Chardonnays. The best value offering is his nonvintage Frontier Red, a very good Santa Barbara take on a French Côtes du Rhône.

2005 Chardonnay	88	now
2004 Chardonnay	87	now
2005 Chardonnay Ashley's Vineyard	90	now–2010
2004 Chardonnay Ashley's Vineyard	91	now–2010
N.V. Frontier Red Lot 61	88	now
2005 Pinot Noir	85	now–2011
2004 Pinot Noir American Tradition Reserve	88	now–2012
2005 Pinot Noir Ashley's Vineyard	90	now–2015
2004 Pinot Noir Ashley's Vineyard	90	now–2014

2003 Pinot Noir Ashley's Vineyard	91	now
2002 Pinot Noir Ashley's Vineyard	89+	now–2016
2005 Pinot Noir Bien Nacido Vineyard	92	now–2019
2004 Pinot Noir Bien Nacido Vineyard	89	now–2013
2003 Pinot Noir Bien Nacido Vineyard	90	now
2005 Pinot Noir Clone 115	88	now–2013
2002 Pinot Noir Marcella's Vineyard	90	now–2014
2004 Syrah	86	now–2010
2003 Syrah	89	now–2011
2004 Syrah The Big Easy	91	now–2015
2003 Syrah The Big Easy	90	now–2016
2004 Syrah Rodney's Vineyard	90	now–2015
2003 Syrah Rodney's Vineyard	93	now–2018
2005 Viognier Rodney's Vineyard	90	now–2010

RICHARD PARTRIDGE ★ ★ ★
NAPA $55.00–$65.00

Since 1998, Richard Partridge has produced a Cabernet Sauvignon from the Sacrashe Vineyard, which is beautifully situated above the Auberge du Soleil in the Rutherford appellation. The wine is often blended with fruit from an Oakville site. The wines have been very good, but given their *terroir,* they could be even better.

2003 Cabernet Sauvignon	89	now–2015
2002 Cabernet Sauvignon	89	now–2015
2001 Cabernet Sauvignon	90	now–2017

PATZ AND HALL ★ ★ ★ ★
SANTA LUCIA HIGHLANDS $36.00–$60.00

Perhaps California's finest *négociant* firm for Burgundy varietals, Patz and Hall is run much like a similar operation in France. A talented quartet of wine lovers—Anne Moses, her husband, James Hall, and the Patzes—have a knack for finding and contracting with some of California's top Chardonnay and Pinot Noir vineyards. Classic Burgundian techniques are utilized with California fruit, resulting in this firm's well-deserved reputation for distinctive, impeccably well-made offerings.

2003 Pinot Noir Alder Springs Vineyard	89	now–2012
2002 Pinot Noir Alder Springs Vineyard	90	now–2010
2001 Pinot Noir Alder Springs Vineyard	92	now
2003 Pinot Noir Burnside Vineyard	92	now–2013
2002 Pinot Noir Burnside Vineyard	90	now
2003 Pinot Noir Hyde Vineyard	89	now–2012
2002 Pinot Noir Hyde Vineyard	87	now–2012
2001 Pinot Noir Hyde Vineyard	86	now
2005 Pinot Noir Pisoni Vineyard	90	now–2012
2003 Pinot Noir Pisoni Vineyard	92	now–2017
2002 Pinot Noir Pisoni Vineyard	88	now
2001 Pinot Noir Pisoni Vineyard	92	now–2010
2001 Pinot Noir Russian River	87	now
2003 Pinot Noir Sonoma Coast	88	now–2010
2002 Pinot Noir Sonoma Coast	90	now

PAX WINE CELLARS ★★★★★
CALIFORNIA $43.00–$90.00

A rising star in California's Rhone Ranger firmament, Pax Wine Cellars is run by its young, talented winemaker, Pax Mahle, who is essentially self-trained after working as a wine consultant at St. Helena's gourmet Dean & DeLuca store. Mahle has the carte blanche backing of wine connoisseur and proprietor Joe Donelan. Exciting wines seem to emerge annually from this estate. Mahle has accessed some top-notch, cool-climate hillside sites throughout northern California. The results are exceptional wines from one of the youngest, most talented new breed of California wine babies.

2004 Cuvée Moriah	93	now–2012
2003 Cuvée Moriah	93	now–2010
2006 Grenache Dry Stack Vineyard	93–95	now
2004 Grenache Dry Stack Vineyard	91	now–2011
2006 Pax Nepenthe Proprietary White Alder		
Springs Vineyard	94	now–2010
2005 Roussanne Venus	92	now
2006 Syrah Alder Springs Vineyard	91–93	now–2016
2003 Syrah Alder Springs Vineyard	95	now–2013
2004 Syrah Alder Springs Vineyard The Emerald Pool	95	now–2020
2005 Syrah Alder Springs Vineyard The Knob	93	now–2014
2006 Syrah Alder Springs Vineyard The Terraces	92–94	now–2016
2005 Syrah Alder Springs Vineyard The Terraces	92	now–2016
2004 Syrah Alder Springs Vineyard The Terraces	93	now–2014
2003 Syrah Alder Springs Vineyard The Terraces	96	now–2015
2002 Syrah Alder Springs Vineyard The Terraces	96	now–2013
2005 Syrah Castelli-Knight Ranch	94	2010–2030
2004 Syrah Castelli-Knight Ranch	96	now–2013
2003 Syrah Castelli-Knight Ranch	96	now–2017
2002 Syrah Castelli-Knight Ranch	94+	now–2020
2005 Syrah Cuvée Christine	95	now–2015
2004 Syrah Cuvée Christine	90	now–2011
2003 Syrah Cuvée Christine	91	now–2010
2004 Syrah Cuvée Keltie	96	now–2020
2003 Syrah Cuvée Keltie	94+	now–2020
2002 Syrah Cuvée Keltie	95+	2011–2031
2006 Syrah Griffin's Lair	94–96	now–2018
2005 Syrah Griffin's Lair	94	now–2016
2004 Syrah Griffin's Lair	95	now–2030
2003 Syrah Griffin's Lair	95	now–2013
2002 Syrah Griffin's Lair	92+	now–2017
2005 Syrah Kobler Family Vineyard	95	now–2023
2004 Syrah Kobler Family Vineyard	90+	now–2014
2003 Syrah Kobler Family Vineyard	92	now–2014
2005 Syrah Lauterbach Hill	91	now–2016
2004 Syrah Lauterbach Hill	94	now–2013
2003 Syrah Lauterbach Hill	93	now–2015+
2005 Syrah Majik	88	now–2012
2005 Syrah Obsidian	96+	2010–2023
2003 Syrah Obsidian	96	now–2020
2003 Syrah Pangea	96	now–2021+

2006 Syrah Richards Family Vineyard	96–98	now–2017
2004 Syrah Richards Family Vineyard	96	now–2016
2005 Syrah Walker Vine Hill	94	now–2018+
2004 Syrah Walker Vine Hill	94	now–2023
2003 Syrah Walker Vine Hill	94	now–2017
2005 Viognier Aphrodite	88	now

PEACHY CANYON WINERY ★★/★★★
PASO ROBLES $20.00–$45.00

Production is more than 30,000 cases at Peachy Canyon, most of it an assortment of competent but rarely exciting Zinfandels. The wines tend to be rustic, with jagged tannins as well as acid levels, but every once in a while an impressive Zinfandel emerges, so this estate can never be discounted.

J. PEDRONCELLI ★★
SONOMA $15.00–$25.00

One of the great old Italian families that settled in northern California more than a century ago, Pedroncelli produces pleasant, simple wines reminiscent of a jug Chianti of yesteryear. They are meant to be drunk immediately upon release.

PELTON HOUSE ★★★
KNIGHT'S VALLEY $40.00

This is a promising Knight's Valley operation owned by Jess Jackson.

| 2005 Cabernet Sauvignon | 90 | now–2018 |
| 2005 Merlot | 87 | now–2014 |

RICHARD PERRY WINES ★★★★
NAPA $35.00–$55.00

Previously having sold most of the production from their 15-acre, cool-climate hillside vineyard in Coombsville, the Perrys jumped into the commercial end of winemaking with a very fine Syrah as well as a good Cabernet Sauvignon, both realistically priced.

2003 Cabernet Sauvignon Napa	89	now–2018
2001 Syrah	91	now–2011
2004 Syrah Perry Vineyards	92	now–2012
2003 Syrah Perry Vineyards	89+	now–2016

JOSEPH PHELPS VINEYARD ★★★★/★★★★★
NAPA $25.00–$175.00

One of the historic standard bearers of high-quality California wine, Joseph Phelps was a pioneer in several respects. He was one of the first to recognize the potential for Rhône Valley varietals in California, as well as one of the first to produce a Bordeaux varietal blend, his famous flagship cuvée, Insignia. First made in 1974, it remains one of the most majestic and complex Cabernet Sauvignon–based blends made in California. There has also been remarkable consistency in this estate's winemaking, with Craig Williams at the helm since the early 1980s (having replaced the original winemaker, Walter Shug). Phelps has expanded significantly, now owning holdings in Napa and Monterey County (where all the Rhone Ranger fruit is grown). Having eliminated Merlot and Chardonnay from the portfolio, they are now concentrating on Pinot Noir from a large vineyard planted on the Sonoma Coast called Freestone. Their two greatest wines remain the Insignia Proprietary Red and the spectacular single-vineyard Cabernet Sauvignon from Oakville's Backus Vineyard.

2006 Cabernet Sauvignon Backus Vineyard	91–93+	2014–2038
2005 Cabernet Sauvignon Backus Vineyard	94+	2013–2038
2004 Cabernet Sauvignon Backus Vineyard	95	now–2028
2003 Cabernet Sauvignon Backus Vineyard	96	2009–2030
2002 Cabernet Sauvignon Backus Vineyard	96+	now–2030+
2001 Cabernet Sauvignon Backus Vineyard	93+	2010–2025
2006 Cabernet Sauvignon Napa	88–90	now–2018
2005 Cabernet Sauvignon Napa	88	now–2018
2004 Cabernet Sauvignon Napa	90	now–2016
2003 Cabernet Sauvignon Napa	88	now
2002 Cabernet Sauvignon Napa	90	now–2017
2001 Cabernet Sauvignon Napa	88	now–2013
2005 Icerebe	91	now
2006 Insignia Proprietary Red Wine	92–94	2011–2038
2005 Insignia Proprietary Red Wine	93–96	2012–2038
2004 Insignia Proprietary Red Wine	95	now–2028+
2003 Insignia Proprietary Red Wine	94	now–2026
2002 Insignia Proprietary Red Wine	95	now–2035
2006 Le Mistral	87–89	now–2015
2005 Le Mistral	90	now–2013
2006 Pinot Noir Freestone	89–91	now–2018
2005 Pinot Noir Freestone	91	now–2012
2006 Sauvignon Blanc	86	now–2010
2005 Sauvignon Blanc	89	now
2005 Syrah	90	now–2012
2004 Syrah	89	now–2010

PIEDRASASSI ★ ★ ★ ★
SANTA YNEZ $50.00

The project of Sashi Moorman, who is better known as the major winemaker at Stolpman Vineyards, this is a 400-case cuvée of impressive 100% Syrah from the limestone soils of the Harrison Clarke Vineyard.

2006 Syrah	92	now–2016
2005 Syrah	92	now–2017
2004 Syrah	91	now–2018
2003 Syrah	95	now–2014

PINE RIDGE ★ ★ ★/★ ★ ★ ★
NAPA $12.00–$120.00

With nearly 250 acres of vines and a production of over 100,000 cases, Pine Ridge was founded in 1978 by Gary Andrus, a charismatic wine connoisseur. While the first decade or so of wines were mixed in quality, over the last five to six years, with Stacy Clark in charge of the wine-making, quality has become remarkably consistent, and Pine Ridge is now fashioning top-flight wines, especially their single-appellation Cabernet Sauvignons, their excellent Chardonnays, and one of the better Chenin Blancs produced in California. Prices are high, but this is Napa Valley.

2003 Cabernet Sauvignon Howell Mountain	90	now–2019
2001 Cabernet Sauvignon Howell Mountain	88	now–2015
2004 Cabernet Sauvignon Oakville	91	now–2023
2003 Cabernet Sauvignon Oakville	89+	now–2017

2001 Cabernet Sauvignon Oakville	90	now–2013
2004 Cabernet Sauvignon Rutherford	89	now–2018
2002 Cabernet Sauvignon Rutherford	88	now–2012
2003 Cabernet Sauvignon Stags Leap District	89	now–2018
2002 Cabernet Sauvignon Stags Leap District	91	now–2022
2001 Cabernet Sauvignon Stags Leap District	93	now–2018
2003 Chardonnay Dijon Clones	87	now
2005 Chardonnay Epitome	90	now–2012
2004 Merlot Crimson Creek	86	now–2011
2001 Merlot Crimson Creek	85	now
2004 Onyx Proprietary Red Wine	91	now–2018
2002 Onyx Proprietary Red Wine	89	now–2015

PISONI VINEYARDS * * * * *
SANTA LUCIA HIGHLANDS $60.00–$65.00

A hippie, a visionary, and a great winemaker, Gary Pisoni first planted five acres of Pinot Noir in the Santa Lucia Mountains in Monterey County in 1982. Today, Pisoni Vineyards consists of 45 acres of small vineyard blocks with primarily Pinot Noir as well as a small amount of Chardonnay planted. Gary Pisoni became one of the country's finest winemakers, and his Pinot Noirs are superb. The clonal material, which came from one of Burgundy's most renowned vineyards, has flourished in the Santa Lucia Highlands' decomposed granite soils. Gary's son Jeff, whose philosophy is the same as his father's, has now taken over the winemaking.

2005 Pinot Noir Pisoni Vineyard	93+	2010–2025
2004 Pinot Noir Pisoni Vineyard	95	now–2013
2003 Pinot Noir Pisoni Vineyard	94	now–2012
2002 Pinot Noir Pisoni Vineyard	89	now
2001 Pinot Noir Pisoni Vineyard	93+	now–2012

PLUMPJACK WINERY * * * */* * * * *
OAKVILLE/NAPA $40.00–$180.00

Founded in 1996 by San Francisco's prominent Getty family, along with major investor and current San Francisco mayor Gavin Newsom, PlumpJack has 48 prime acres in the Oakville Corridor. Their vineyards previously were the basis for the fabulous Villa Mt. Eden Cabernet Sauvignons made in the 1970s. They produce two Cabernet Sauvignons, an Estate and a Reserve, and recently a Syrah has been added to the portfolio. All are fabulous, thanks to the brilliant efforts of winemaker Tony Biagi and consultant Nils Venge.

2006 Cabernet Sauvignon Estate	91–93	now–2023
2005 Cabernet Sauvignon Estate	92	now–2028+
2004 Cabernet Sauvignon Estate	94	now–2021+
2003 Cabernet Sauvignon Estate	93	now–2020+
2002 Cabernet Sauvignon Estate	94	now–2020
2001 Cabernet Sauvignon Estate	91	now–2021
2006 Cabernet Sauvignon Reserve Estate	94–97	2012–2042
2005 Cabernet Sauvignon Reserve Estate	94+	2010–2038
2004 Cabernet Sauvignon Reserve Estate	96	now–2026+
2003 Cabernet Sauvignon Reserve Estate	95	2010–2035+
2002 Cabernet Sauvignon Reserve Estate	96	now–2025
2001 Cabernet Sauvignon Reserve Estate	95	now–2022+
2006 Syrah	92–95	now–2016

| 2005 Syrah | 94 | now–2018 |
| 2004 Syrah | 92 | now–2013 |

PREVAIL MOUNTAIN WINERY ESTATE * * */* * * *
ALEXANDER VALLEY $55.00–$95.00

Ferrari-Carano's proprietor, Don Carano, planted these mountainside vineyards in 1996 with a vision of trying to produce the finest Cabernet Sauvignon this area of Sonoma could turn out. There are about 4,000 cases of the West Face and about 1,000 cases of the Back 40, all made by Frenchman Philippe Melka. The West Face is usually a blend of 70% Cabernet Sauvignon and 30% Syrah, and the Back 40 is 90 to 100% Cabernet Sauvignon, although occasionally there is a small dose of Syrah.

2006 Back 40	90–93	now–2020
2005 Back 40	91	2009–2024+
2004 Back 40	90+	2009–2021+
2003 Back 40	91	now–2015
2006 West Face	91–94	now–2020
2005 West Face	90	now–2020+
2004 West Face	91	now–2017
2003 West Face	90	now–2015

PRIDE MOUNTAIN VINEYARDS * * * */* * * * *
NAPA/SONOMA $40.00–$125.00

This 220-acre estate (80 planted in vines) cloaks the summit of the Mayacamas Ridge and undulates down both sides of the Napa county lines. Situated at a high elevation (2,000-plus feet), Pride Mountain was the vision of the late Jim Pride, who had the foresight to bring in the brilliant Robert Foley as winemaker. Although Foley has moved on, this remains one of northern California's benchmark estates for Cabernet Sauvignon and a Bordeaux blend called Reserve Claret.

2005 Cabernet Franc	91	now–2018
2004 Cabernet Franc	88	now–2013
2003 Cabernet Franc	90	now–2013
2002 Cabernet Franc	93	now–2020
2005 Cabernet Sauvignon	92	now–2018
2004 Cabernet Sauvignon	87	now–2013
2003 Cabernet Sauvignon	88+	now–2017
2002 Cabernet Sauvignon	92	now–2015
2005 Cabernet Sauvignon Reserve	96–98	now–2021
2003 Cabernet Sauvignon Reserve	93+	now–2021
2002 Cabernet Sauvignon Reserve	96+	now–2020+
2005 Cabernet Sauvignon Vintner's Select	94	now–2023+
2006 Chardonnay Vintner's Select	89	now–2011
2005 Chardonnay Vintner's Select Mountaintop Vineyard	91	now–2010
2005 Merlot	91	now–2016
2004 Merlot	87	now–2010
2003 Merlot	88	now–2013
2004 Merlot Mountaintop Vineyard	88	now–2013
2005 Merlot Vintner's Select	94	now–2018
2003 Merlot Vintner's Select Mountaintop Vineyard	91	now–2014
2002 Merlot Vintner's Select Mountaintop Vineyard	93	now–2015

2005 Reserve Claret	93–96	now–2023+
2004 Reserve Claret	90	now–2018
2003 Reserve Claret	94	now–2021
2002 Reserve Claret	97+	now–2020
2005 Sangiovese	88	now–2011
2004 Sangiovese	91	now–2011
2005 Syrah	91–93	now–2016
2004 Syrah	88	now–2011
2003 Syrah	90	now–2010
2006 Viognier	89	now–2010
2005 Viognier	89	now
2004 Viognier	89	now

PROVENANCE VINEYARDS ★ ★ ★
NAPA $19.00–$45.00

This Rutherford estate produces Merlot, Cabernet Sauvignon, and Sauvignon Blanc. To date, quality has been good but rarely exciting.

2001 Cabernet Sauvignon Napa	87?	now–2018
2001 Cabernet Sauvignon Oakville	87	now–2013
2001 Merlot	86	now
2002 Merlot Paras Vineyard	91	now–2013
2001 Merlot Paras Vineyard	90	now–2013

PROVISO VINEYARDS ★ ★ ★
DRY CREEK $30.00–$42.00

A tiny boutique operation in Healdsburg, Proviso specializes in small lots of Syrah.

2003 Syrah Estate	88	now–2010
2002 Syrah Estate	89	now–2012

QUINTESSA ★ ★ ★
RUTHERFORD $110.00

Originally, Quintessa was the luxury flagship vineyard of Franciscan winery, but it is now the personal estate of Agustin Huneeus. Both owners have utilized French winemaking consultants, starting with Philippe Melka and now, Michel Rolland. While the wines are excellent, sometimes even outstanding, they have never lived up to the fabulous potential of this Napa Valley site—280 acres in prime Rutherford Dust territory.

2004 Proprietary Red Wine	91	now–2020
2003 Proprietary Red Wine	89	now–2018
2002 Proprietary Red Wine	90	now–2014
2001 Proprietary Red Wine	88	now–2012

QUIVIRA ★ ★ ★
DRY CREEK $18.00–$35.00

This small Dry Creek operation specializes in small lots of Rhône-style blends, Petite Sirahs, Syrahs, Sauvignon Blanc, and an excellent, elegant Zinfandel. Recently they have increased the number of Zinfandel offerings and added a Grenache to the portfolio.

2005 Grenache Wine Creek Ranch	87	now
2006 Sauvignon Blanc Fig Tree Vineyard	87	now

2004 Zinfandel Dry Creek Valley	89	now
2004 Zinfandel Wine Creek Ranch	88	now

QUPÉ ★★★/★★★★
SANTA BARBARA $16.00–$45.00

Proprietor Bob Lindquist is one of the pioneers in producing Rhône-style wines that emphasize the elegance of European-based wines more than the exuberant richness and intensity of most California offerings. Production averages around 20,000 cases from Lindquist's small vineyard as well as purchased grapes.

2005 Bien Nacido Cuvée	90	now
2005 Chardonnay Bien Nacido Reserve Block Eleven	87	now–2012
2004 Grenache Purisima Mountain	85	now
2005 Los Olivos Cuvée	90	now–2012
2004 Los Olivos Cuvée	86	now
2006 Marsanne	88	now
2005 Roussanne Bien Nacido Vineyard	92	now–2010
2005 Syrah	88	now–2012
2004 Syrah	84	now
2003 Syrah Alisos Vineyard	89	now
2005 Syrah Bien Nacido Vineyard	90	now–2018
2004 Syrah Bien Nacido Vineyard	92	2009–2024
2003 Syrah Bien Nacido Vineyard Hillside Estate	92	now–2016
2002 Syrah Bien Nacido Vineyard Hillside Estate	90+	now–2021
2004 Syrah Colson Canyon Vineyard	91	now–2018
2005 Syrah Nielson Vineyard	90	now–2017
2005 Syrah Purisima Mountain Vineyard	89	now–2013
2004 Syrah Purisima Mountain Vineyard	???	now–2016
2005 Syrah Stolpman Vineyard	91	now–2019
2004 Syrah Stolpman Vineyard	90	now–2014
2006 Viognier Ibarra Young Vineyard	90	now

RADIO-COTEAU ★★★★
SONOMA $38.00–$60.00

Proprietor-winemaker Eric Sussman, who apprenticed with Tom Dehlinger, has quickly established himself as an up-and-coming specialist of single-vineyard Chardonnay, Pinot Noir, Syrah, and Zinfandel. As with most cutting-edge winemakers, Sussman believes in a natural approach to winemaking, including indigenous yeast fermentation, extended aging on lees, little or no racking, and no fining or filtration. It is hard to pick a favorite, as everything in this portfolio is well worth trying.

2006 Chardonnay Savoy	88–90	now–2011
2005 Chardonnay Savoy	94	now–2011
2006 Pinot Noir Alberigi	88–90	now–2014
2005 Pinot Noir Alberigi	90	now–2014
2004 Pinot Noir Alberigi	89+	now–2010
2006 Pinot Noir La Neblina	89–91	now–2012
2005 Pinot Noir La Neblina	89	now–2012
2004 Pinot Noir La Neblina	88	now–2010
2003 Pinot Noir La Neblina	88	now
2006 Pinot Noir Savoy	90–92	now–2013
2005 Pinot Noir Savoy	92	now–2014

2004 Pinot Noir Savoy	91	now–2013
2003 Pinot Noir Savoy	87	now–2011
2006 Pinot Noir Terra Neuma	88–90	???
2005 Pinot Noir Terra Neuma	92	now–2014
2004 Pinot Noir Terra Neuma	90	now–2014
2006 Syrah Cherry Camp	94–96	now–2018
2005 Syrah Cherry Camp	94	now–2018
2004 Syrah Cherry Camp	93+	now–2016
2006 Syrah Las Colinas	91–94	now–2016
2005 Syrah Las Colinas	91	now–2012
2004 Syrah Las Colinas	88	now–2010
2006 Syrah Timbervine	91–93	???
2005 Syrah Timbervine	93	now–2016
2004 Syrah Timbervine	95	now–2013
2005 Zinfandel Von Weidlich	88	now–2010
2004 Zinfandel Von Weidlich	90	now–2011
2003 Zinfandel Von Weidlich	90	now–2010

RAFANELLI ★★★★
SONOMA $25.00–$40.00

Onetime grape growers, the Rafanelli family has built a strong following for their beautifully rich, but never over-the-top, nicely balanced Zinfandels. A Cabernet Sauvignon is also produced, but it is generally monolithic and less interesting. The top-notch Zins age nicely for five to seven years.

2004 Zinfandel Dry Creek	90	now–2012

RAMEY ★★★★
NORTHERN CALIFORNIA $36.00–$140.00

One of northern California's most successful winemakers-consultants, David Ramey's personal winery continues to go from strength to strength. Ramey has had the best of both worlds, working in Bordeaux for the Moueix family and in California at Dominus, Chalk Hill, and Rudd Estate. His specialty is Chardonnay, but consumers should not discount his brilliant Cabernet Sauvignon and Syrah. Ramey's classical winemaking training is evident, as his offerings represent an intelligent compromise between European, *terroir*-based, more austere styles and the opulent, ripe fruit of California.

2006 Cabernet Sauvignon Diamond Mountain	92–95	now–2028
2005 Cabernet Sauvignon Jericho Canyon	94	now–2028
2004 Cabernet Sauvignon Jericho Canyon	94	now–2025
2006 Cabernet Sauvignon Larkmead Vineyard	92–94	now–2023+
2005 Cabernet Sauvignon Larkmead Vineyard	91	now–2028
2004 Cabernet Sauvignon Larkmead Vineyard	95	now–2024
2006 Cabernet Sauvignon Napa	91–94	now–2023
2005 Cabernet Sauvignon Napa	91	now–2023
2006 Cabernet Sauvignon Pedregal	96–100	2013–2033+
2005 Cabernet Sauvignon Pedregal	96	2012–2033+
2004 Cabernet Sauvignon Pedregal	95+	2010–2040+
2005 Chardonnay Carneros	91	now–2011
2004 Chardonnay Carneros	89	now
2005 Chardonnay Hudson Vineyard	94	now–2011
2004 Chardonnay Hudson Vineyard	91	now–2010

2005 Chardonnay Hyde Vineyard	95	now–2013
2004 Chardonnay Hyde Vineyard	94	now–2014
2005 Chardonnay Ritchie Vineyard	95	now–2013
2004 Chardonnay Ritchie Vineyard	93	now–2010
2005 Chardonnay Russian River	92	now–2011
2004 Chardonnay Russian River	91	now
2005 Chardonnay Sonoma Coast	90	now–2011
2004 Chardonnay Sonoma Coast	90	now–2011
2006 Claret	89	now–2018
2005 Claret	89	now–2015
2003 Diamond Mountain Proprietary Red Wine	91+	now–2023
2002 Diamond Mountain Proprietary Red Wine	95	now–2019
2003 Jericho Canyon Proprietary Red Wine	93	now–2028
2002 Jericho Canyon Proprietary Red Wine	96	now–2020+
2006 Syrah	90–92	now–2018
2005 Syrah	93	now–2011
2004 Syrah	90	now–2014
2006 Syrah Rodger's Creek Vineyard	90–93	now–2020
2005 Syrah Rodger's Creek Vineyard	94	now–2020

RANCHO SISQUOC ★ ★ ★
SANTA BARBARA $18.00–$38.00

This winery has been in existence for a considerable amount of time, but their portfolio continues to be a mixed bag, with good Pinot Noirs, Chardonnays, and occasionally Syrahs mixed in with weird efforts made from Marsanne and Sylvaner. It is hard to know just what their vision is.

2004 Chardonnay Flood Family Vineyard	90	now
2001 Pinot Noir	88	now
2005 Pinot Noir Flood Family Vineyard	82?	now–2011
2003 Syrah	88	now–2012
2001 Syrah	90	now–2013

RANCHO ZABACO ★ ★ ★/★ ★ ★ ★
SONOMA $12.00–$60.00

While small amounts of a very good Sauvignon Blanc are produced here, this estate is essentially the Gallo specialist in high-quality, spicy, exuberant, realistically priced Zinfandels. The quality is very consistent, and at the top level, especially the single-vineyard Monte Rosso cuvée, the wines are brilliant.

2005 Dancing Bull Sauvignon Blanc California	87	now
2004 Dancing Bull Zinfandel California	89	now–2010
2001 Dancing Bull Zinfandel California	86	now
2005 Sauvignon Blanc Reserve Russian River	88	now
2001 Zinfandel Chiotti Vineyard	88	now
2004 Zinfandel Dry Creek	88	now
2001 Zinfandel Heritage Vines	87	now
2004 Zinfandel Monte Rosso Sonoma Valley	93	now–2015
2003 Zinfandel Monte Rosso Sonoma Valley	92	now–2015
2004 Zinfandel Monte Rosso Toreador Sonoma	94	now–2017
2003 Zinfandel Monte Rosso Toreador Sonoma	93	now
2004 Zinfandel Russian River	90	now–2011

RAVENSWOOD　★★/★★★
NORTHERN CALIFORNIA　$45.00–$55.00

This is a sad story. Ravenswood, along with Ridge, was my benchmark Zinfandel producer in the late 1970s and much of the 1980s, when winemaker-proprietor Joel Peterson fashioned one great Zinfandel after another. Even his inexpensive Vintner's Blend was one of the finest bargains in Zinfandel. However, in 2001 the temptation to cash out was too great, and Ravenswood was purchased by Constellation. Since then, the quality has plummeted. The wines are still competent, but the superb single-vineyard Zins are a shadow of past quality. Today the wines are much more monochromatic and dramatically less interesting. Peterson remains at Ravenswood, so there is still hope that this onetime great estate may return to form.

2001 Zinfandel Barricia	88	now
2001 Zinfandel Belloni Vineyard	91	now–2011
2001 Zinfandel Big River	86?	now
2001 Zinfandel Cooke Vineyard	90	now–2010
2001 Zinfandel Dickerson Vineyard	85?	now
2001 Zinfandel Monte Rosso Vineyard	85?	now–2010
2001 Zinfandel Old Hill Ranch	90	now–2010
2001 Zinfandel Teldeschi Vineyard	87+	now

RAYMOND　★★
NAPA　$20.00–$45.00

This winery has gone through a number of changes, and perhaps that is why the wine quality is shockingly irregular. The basic offerings, sold under a California appellation, are dull and uninteresting. The next level, the Raymond Estate wines, are slightly better although still mediocre. The top Reserve offerings are overpriced, excessively oaky, and distressingly insipid. Production is nearly a half million cases, so there must be a market for these wines.

REALM CELLARS　★★★★
NAPA　$75.00–$100.00

A small boutique winery dedicated to very high-quality wines, Realm was started in 2002 by Juan Marcado, formerly of Pax Winery, and Wendell Laidley. Their winemaker is Mike Hirby, who worked at Behrens and Hitchcock. This is hands-off winemaking at its best, with long macerations, minimal rackings, and innovative blends. The top efforts tend to be Bordeaux blends with names such as The Tempest and The Bard, as well as their single-vineyard Cabernet Sauvignons.

2005 The Absurd Proprietary Red Wine	91	now–2023
2005 The Bard Proprietary Red Wine	93	???
2004 The Bard Proprietary Red Wine	94	now–2022
2003 The Bard Proprietary Red Wine	94	now–2015+
2005 Cabernet Sauvignon Beckstoffer Dr. Crane Vineyard	94	now–2023+
2005 Cabernet Sauvignon Beckstoffer To-Kalon Vineyard	95	now–2028+
2004 Cabernet Sauvignon Beckstoffer To-Kalon Vineyard	94	now–2022+
2003 Cabernet Sauvignon Beckstoffer To-Kalon Vineyard	93	now–2020+

2002 Cabernet Sauvignon Beckstoffer To-Kalon Vineyard	92	now–2020
2005 Cabernet Sauvignon Farella Vineyard	92	now–2023+
2004 Cabernet Sauvignon Farella Vineyard	91	now–2022
2003 Cabernet Sauvignon Farella Vineyard	91	now–2017
2005 The Tempest	94	now–2023
2004 The Tempest	91	now–2019
2003 The Tempest	91+	now–2017
2002 The Tempest	91	now–2015

RED CAR WINE CO. * * * *
SANTA BARBARA $30.00–$60.00

This is a serious *négociant* operation dedicated to producing innovatively named and blended wines from purchased fruit.

2004 Amour Fou	87	now–2010
2001 The Dreaming Detective Thompson Vineyard	91+	now–2015
2002 The Fight	92+	now–2016
2005 Pinot Noir Bartolomei Vineyard The Aphorist	90	now–2015
2005 Pinot Noir Chapter Four	89	now–2011
2002 Some Like It Red	90	now
2004 Syrah The Fight Round 3	92	now–2016
2005 Syrah The Fight Round 3 Continues	90	now–2015
2004 Syrah Red Wind	89	now–2013
2005 Syrah Shake, Rattle, Roll	93	now–2017
2001 Syrah The Stranger	93	now–2013
2002 Syrah Sugar Daddy	94	now–2012
2005 Syrah Twenty-Two	92	now–2017
2002 The Table	93	now–2016

RELIC * * * *
MENDOCINO/NAPA $45.00

Run by the husband-and-wife team of Mike Hirby and Shatzi Throckmorton, the Relic wines are made at the Behrens and Hitchcock facility, now renamed Erna Schein. To date, they have specialized in high-quality Syrahs from Mendocino and Napa vineyards.

2004 Syrah Alder Springs Vineyard	90	now–2013
2003 Syrah Alder Springs Vineyard	90	now–2011
2005 Syrah Richard Perry Vineyard	92	now–2013

RENARD * * */* * * *
REGION $12.00–$55.00

Proprietor Bayard Fox got his first taste of winemaking while working for a Pinot Noir producer in Oregon. But, as he says, he needed to find the tomboy of Pinot Noirs, which he did with Syrah. I have always enjoyed the diversity and character of the Renard wines. While they are occasionally rustic, they are always loaded with soul and personality, and are undeniably intriguing.

2005 Grenache Unti Vineyard	89	now
2004 Grenache Unti Vineyard	87	now
2006 Rosé	89	now
2005 Roussanne Westerly Vineyard	88	now–2010

2005 Syrah California	85	now
2003 Syrah California	87	now
2005 Syrah Kick Ranch	91	now–2013
2003 Syrah Peay Vineyard	90	now–2014
2004 Syrah Purisima Mountain Vineyard	92	now–2015
2003 Syrah Santa Rita Hills	90	now–2012
2005 Syrah Sonoma	84	now–2010
2003 Syrah Sonoma	86	now–2013
2003 Syrah Truchard Vineyard	89	now–2011
2003 Syrah Unti Vineyard	87	now–2011
2004 Tres Niños Proprietary Red Wine	94	now–2022
2005 Viognier	88	now

REVANA FAMILY VINEYARD ★ ★ ★/★ ★ ★ ★
NAPA $90.00–$95.00

Stylish, elegant Cabernet Sauvignons are produced by proprietor Dr. Madaiah Revana. The wines combine the best of European elegance with the exuberant ripeness of California.

2004 Cabernet Sauvignon	90	now–2017
2003 Cabernet Sauvignon	89	now–2019
2002 Cabernet Sauvignon	91	now–2019
2001 Cabernet Sauvignon	88	now–2015

REVERIE ★ ★ ★/★ ★ ★ ★
NAPA $42.00–$85.00

This Diamond Mountain estate boasts 40 acres and has built a fine reputation for their Bordeaux varietal wines, including an excellent proprietary red, a Cabernet Sauvignon, and a strong Cabernet Franc. Owned by Norm and Evelyn Kiken, Reverie may not be the best-known winery on Diamond Mountain, but it is certainly one of the finest.

2004 Cabernet Franc Diamond Mountain	90	now–2014
2003 Cabernet Franc Diamond Mountain	91	now–2015
2002 Cabernet Franc Diamond Mountain	90	now–2015
2001 Cabernet Franc Diamond Mountain	90	now–2020
2004 Cabernet Sauvignon Diamond Mountain	88	???
2003 Cabernet Sauvignon Diamond Mountain	89	now–2015
2002 Cabernet Sauvignon Diamond Mountain	90+	now–2017
2001 Cabernet Sauvignon Diamond Mountain	90+	now–2015
2004 Cabernet Sauvignon Special Reserve Diamond Mountain	90	now–2023
2003 Special Reserve Proprietary Red Wine Diamond Mountain	92	now–2019
2002 Special Reserve Proprietary Red Wine Diamond Mountain	92	now–2018
2001 Special Reserve Proprietary Red Wine Diamond Mountain	92	now–2020+

RHYS VINEYARDS ★ ★ ★ ★
SANTA CRUZ MOUNTAINS $49.00

Kevin Harvey is the brain trust behind this relatively new Santa Cruz operation dedicated to handcrafted wines. I have tasted only a handful of offerings from their 13-acre Alpine Vineyard and quarter-acre Home Vineyard, and nothing from their 17.5-acre Horseshoe Ranch or

6.2-acre Family Home Vineyard sites. The vineyards are cultivated organically if not biody-namically, and the nonestate cuvées are bottled under the name Alesia, which allows Harvey to purchase fruit from other proprietors. Early returns on these wines are exceptionally prom-ising.

2005 Chardonnay Alpine Vineyard	91+	now–2013
2004 Pinot Noir Alpine Vineyard	94	now–2019
2004 Pinot Noir Home Vineyard	92	now–2017

RIDEAU VINEYARDS ★★★
SANTA YNEZ $42.00–$65.00

Founded in 1997 by New Orleans native Iris Rideau, this winery's goal is to produce Rhône varietals, although some Pinot Noir and Chardonnay are also offered. Initially the wine qual-ity was shaky, but it seems to have dramatically improved over the last few years.

2005 Chardonnay Reserve	88	now–2010
2004 Chardonnay Reserve	89	now
2004 Château Duplantier Cuvée	90	now
2005 Pinot Noir	89	now–2013
2005 Pinot Noir Bien Nacido Vineyard	89	now–2012
2005 Pinot Noir Clone 115 Rancho Santa Rosa Vineyard	85	???
2004 Pinot Noir Sanford & Benedict Vineyard	90	now–2010
2004 Syrah Bon Temp Vineyard	88	now–2011
2003 Syrah Bon Temp Vineyard	88	now–2011
2004 Syrah Iris Bon Temp Vineyard	90	now–2012

RIDGE VINEYARDS ★★★★★
SANTA CRUZ MOUNTAINS $20.00–$125.00

Ridge has been a reference-point winery for so many years, one would think they have been around for centuries. In fact, their history began in 1886, when an Italian doctor purchased over 180 acres on top of Monte Bello Ridge in the Santa Cruz Mountains. Prohibition put an end to that period of history, but in 1959, some of the original vineyard was purchased by the founders of the modern-day Ridge Vineyards. The first commercial vintage was 1962, and the current winemaker, Paul Draper, arrived in 1968. Ridge boasts an almost unbroken record of 40 years of fabulous Cabernet Sauvignon as well as a bevy of terrific Zinfandels. The Char-donnay program has gone from strength to strength, producing better and better wines. This is undeniably one of California's top wineries. Ridge now controls over 500 acres of vines, from which they produce just under 100,000 cases of wine. Despite the winery's sale to the Japanese Suntory Company, the quality is unchanged. The wines are as profound as ever.

2004 Cabernet Sauvignon	93	2014–2030
2002 Carignan Buchignani Ranch	87	now
2005 Chardonnay Estate	92	now–2015
2004 Chardonnay Estate	90	now–2012
2002 Geyserville Proprietary Red Wine	92	now–2013
2002 Lytton Springs Proprietary Red Wine	93	now–2011
2002 Mataro Pato Vineyard	91	now–2012
2003 Monte Bello Proprietary Red Wine	91+	2011–2025
2002 Monte Bello Proprietary Red Wine	94	2012–2037
2001 Monte Bello Proprietary Red Wine	95+	now–2035
2003 Syrah/Viognier Lytton West	91	now–2012

2002 Zinfandel Dusi Ranch (ATP)	92	now–2012
2002 Zinfandel Ponzo Vineyards	89	now–2011
2002 Zinfandel Spring Mountain	88	now–2011

ROAR ★ ★ ★ ★/★ ★ ★ ★ ★
SANTA LUCIA HIGHLANDS $38.00–$50.00

This small family-owned winery has quickly developed a sensational reputation for extraordinary Pinot Noirs and Syrahs. Owned by Gary and Rosella Franscioni, who first planted grapes in 1996 and work closely with the Pisoni family for vineyard development and winemaking, Roar's first wines were launched in 2003, and they haven't looked back since. I expect one will only hear more and more great things from this up-and-coming superstar.

2005 Pinot Noir	92	now–2015
2004 Pinot Noir	90	now–2011
2003 Pinot Noir	90	now
2005 Pinot Noir Garys' Vineyard	94	now–2017
2004 Pinot Noir Garys' Vineyard	94	???
2003 Pinot Noir Garys' Vineyard	88	now–2010
2005 Pinot Noir Pisoni Vineyard	95	now–2017
2004 Pinot Noir Pisoni Vineyard	96	now–2014
2003 Pinot Noir Pisoni Vineyard	91	now
2005 Pinot Noir Rosella's Vineyard	93	now–2015
2004 Pinot Noir Rosella's Vineyard	95	now–2012
2003 Pinot Noir Rosella's Vineyard	92	now–2011
2005 Syrah	94	now–2015
2004 Syrah	92	now–2016
2005 Syrah Garys' Vineyard	94	now–2015
2005 Syrah Rosella's Vineyard	92	now–2015
2004 Syrah Rosella's Vineyard	93	now–2016
2003 Syrah Rosella's Vineyard	92	now–2011

J. ROCHIOLI VINEYARD ★ ★ ★ ★ ★
RUSSIAN RIVER $25.00–$90.00

The 161-acre J. Rochioli Vineyard is run by one of the outstanding grape-growing and winemaking families of Sonoma, Tom and Joe Rochioli. Everything here is of terrific quality, and it would be hard to find better Chardonnays and Pinot Noirs than the single-vineyard offerings from this estate. They are unfined, unfiltered wines made from low yields and with meticulous attention to detail. Amazingly, Rochioli still sells the majority of their grapes to other growers, despite the fact that their 10,000-case production cannot fill the demand for these cuvées.

2006 Chardonnay Estate	89	now–2011
2005 Chardonnay Estate	92	now–2012
2004 Chardonnay Estate	91	now
2005 Chardonnay Rachel's Vineyard	96	now–2016
2004 Chardonnay Rachel's Vineyard	95	???
2006 Chardonnay River Block	95	now–2016
2005 Chardonnay River Block	95	now–2014
2004 Chardonnay River Block	95	now–2010
2006 Chardonnay Rochioli Vineyard	95	now–2016
2006 Chardonnay South River Vineyard	93	now–2014
2005 Chardonnay South River Vineyard	94	now–2013

2004 Chardonnay South River Vineyard	96	now–2011
2006 Chardonnay Sweetwater Vineyard	92	now–2018
2006 Pinot Noir East Block	92–95	???
2005 Pinot Noir East Block	94	now–2016+
2004 Pinot Noir East Block	96	now–2017
2003 Pinot Noir East Block	96	now–2015
2006 Pinot Noir Estate	89–91	now–2011
2005 Pinot Noir Estate	91	now–2016
2004 Pinot Noir Estate	92	now–2010
2003 Pinot Noir Estate	92	now–2011
2006 Pinot Noir Little Hill Vineyard	90–92	now–2020
2005 Pinot Noir Little Hill Vineyard	94	???
2004 Pinot Noir Little Hill Vineyard	96	now–2015
2003 Pinot Noir Little Hill Vineyard	95	now–2016
2002 Pinot Noir Little Hill Vineyard	92	???
2004 Pinot Noir River Block	95	now–2015
2003 Pinot Noir River Block	93	now–2015
2002 Pinot Noir River Block	92	now–2010
2005 Pinot Noir Three Corner Vineyard	93	now–2016+
2003 Pinot Noir Three Corner Vineyard	94	now–2014
2002 Pinot Noir Three Corner Vineyard	93	???
2006 Pinot Noir West Block	91–94	now–2016
2005 Pinot Noir West Block	99	now–2016
2004 Pinot Noir West Block	97	now–2015
2003 Pinot Noir West Block	95	now–2017
2002 Pinot Noir West Block	93	now–2012
2001 Pinot Noir West Block	93+	now–2015
2006 Sauvignon Blanc Estate	88	now–2011
2005 Sauvignon Blanc Estate	89	???
2004 Sauvignon Blanc Estate	90	now

ROEDERER ESTATE   * * *
MENDOCINO $25.00–$45.00

The California outpost of France's Rouzaud family that runs that country's Roederer firm, this is one of California's finest sparkling wine producers. Their estate brut is delicious, but their top cuvée, called L'Ermitage, may be one of the two or three finest sparklers made in California. A small amount of dry rosé sparkling wine is also made. It is not to be missed.

ROESSLER CELLARS   * * */* * * *
SONOMA $36.00–$60.00

Roessler Cellars began with a 250-case production in 2000 and is now making nearly 5,000 cases, primarily focused on single-vineyard Pinot Noirs as well as a few small lots of Chardonnay. They have a knack for selecting some of California's finest vineyard sites, and the quality of their wines is very impressive.

2004 Pinot Noir La Brisa Kanzler Vineyard	91	now–2011
2003 Pinot Noir La Brisa Peay Vineyard	90	now–2010
2004 Pinot Noir Clos Pepe Vineyard	90	now–2013
2003 Pinot Noir Conmemorativo Pisoni Vineyard	90	now–2012
2004 Pinot Noir Griffin's Lair	88	now–???
2004 Pinot Noir Sanford & Benedict Vineyard	92	now–2015

| 2003 Pinot Noir Sangiacomo Vineyard | 89+? | now |
| 2003 Pinot Noir Savoy Vineyard | 87 | now |

ROSENBLUM CELLARS ＊＊＊＊
CALIFORNIA $12.00–$55.00

One of the most staggering arrays of wines produced in California emerges from Rosenblum Cellars under the guidance of winemaker-veterinarian Kent Rosenblum, one of the most reliable producers of high-quality as well as attractively priced wines. The major focus is on Zinfandel, Petite Sirah, and Syrah. Their less expensive blends are also well worth pursuing. While they do not own any vineyards, this exceptional winery definitely knows how to make tasty wines.

2001 Château La Paws Côte du Bone Roan	86	now
2001 Mourvèdre Continente Vineyard	88	now
2005 Petite Sirah Heritage Clones	90	now–2015
2004 Petite Sirah Heritage Clones	92	now–2026
2005 Petite Sirah Pickett Road Vineyard	92	now–2022
2004 Petite Sirah Pickett Road Vineyard	93	now–2026
2002 Petite Sirah Pickett Road Vineyard	90	now–2014
2004 Petite Sirah Reserve Rockpile Road Vineyard	90	2010–2030
2004 Petite Sirah Rhodes Vineyard	88	???
2003 Petite Sirah Rockpile Road Vineyard	92+	now–2021
2002 Petite Sirah Rockpile Road Vineyard	93	now–2024
2004 Syrah	89	now–2010
2004 Syrah Abba Vineyard	90	now–2013
2002 Syrah Abba Vineyard	87	now
2002 Syrah England-Shaw Vineyard	90	now–2014
2004 Syrah Reserve Fran's Vineyard	91	now–2014
2003 Syrah Reserve Rockpile Road Fran's Vineyard	93+	now–2021+
2005 Syrah Rominger Vineyard	87	now–2012
2004 Syrah Rominger Vineyard	89	now–2013
2005 Vintner's Cuvée XXIX	86	now–2010
2005 Zinfandel	87	now–2011
2005 Zinfandel Annette's Reserve	90	now–2015
2005 Zinfandel Harris-Kratka Vineyard	90	now–2015
2005 Zinfandel Hendry Vineyard	90	now–2012
2005 Zinfandel House Family Vineyard	91	now–2014
2005 Zinfandel Lyon's Reserve	91+	now–2016
2005 Zinfandel Maggie's Reserve	88	now–2014
2005 Zinfandel Monte Rosso Vineyard	90	now–2012
2005 Zinfandel Planchon Vineyard	87	now–2011
2005 Zinfandel Rockpile Road Vineyard	92	now–2016
2005 Zinfandel Snows Lake	91	now–2015

ROY ESTATE ＊＊＊＊
NAPA $75.00–$95.00

This 17-acre vineyard on the eastern side of Napa is owned by Charles and Shirley Roy. Located in the Soda Canyon area, the vineyard was planted under the direction of Helen Turley, and today's winemaker is Philippe Melka. The Cabernet-dominated wines are of very high quality, and there is considerable promise at this new facility.

2006 Cabernet Sauvignon	91–93	???
2005 Cabernet Sauvignon	92–94	2010–2025
2004 Cabernet Sauvignon	94	2010–2025
2006 Proprietary Red	92–95	now–2023
2005 Proprietary Red	95	2010–2025

RUDD ESTATE ★ ★ ★ ★
NAPA $35.00–$70.00

Leslie Rudd, the affable proprietor of Rudd Estate, as well as the owner of the gourmet Dean & DeLuca stores and one of Napa's hottest bistros, Press, continues to ratchet up the quality level at this winery. From their estate vineyards in the Oakville Corridor, just across the street from Screaming Eagle, Rudd produces an outstanding Cabernet Sauvignon as well as an excellent blend called Edge Hill Mixed Blacks, fashioned from a parcel of St. Helena vines. A stunning Sauvignon Blanc is also produced from a vineyard on Mt. Veeder.

2004 Cabernet Sauvignon Estate Grown	89	now–2020
2003 Cabernet Sauvignon Estate Grown	91+	now–2020
2002 Cabernet Sauvignon Estate Grown	95	now–2022
2006 Cabernet Sauvignon Mt. Veeder Estate	93–95	2012–2033
2006 Chardonnay Bacigalupi Vineyard	91–93	now–2012
2005 Chardonnay Bacigalupi Vineyard	90	now–2012
2004 Chardonnay Bacigalupi Vineyard	91	now–2011
2006 Edge Hill Mixed Blacks	94–96	now–2015
2004 Edge Hill Mixed Blacks	95	now–2015
2006 Oakville Estate Proprietary Red Wine	93–95	now–2033
2005 Oakville Estate Proprietary Red Wine	94	now–2028+
2004 Oakville Estate Proprietary Red Wine	94	now–2021
2003 Oakville Estate Proprietary Red Wine	93+	now–2020
2002 Oakville Estate Proprietary Red Wine	95	2010–2025
2006 Sauvignon Blanc	93	now–2013

RUSACK VINEYARDS ★ ★ ★
SANTA BARBARA $30.00–$45.00

Started in the mid-1990s, Rusack came of age a few years ago as some new vineyard plantings reached maturity. Chardonnay, Pinot Noir, and Syrah seem to be the most successful offerings, although there are also small quantities of Bordeaux varietals as well as a so-so Sangiovese. Production from the estate vineyards is supplemented by fruit purchased from some of the region's better vineyards.

2005 Chardonnay	90	now–2013
2004 Chardonnay	89	now
2005 Chardonnay Reserve	91	now–2013
2004 Chardonnay Reserve	90	now
2005 Pinot Noir Rancho Santa Rosa	90	now–2014
2005 Pinot Noir Reserve	87	now–2014
2004 Pinot Noir Reserve	88?	???
2003 Pinot Noir Reserve	89+	now–2014
2004 Pinot Noir Solomon Hills Vineyard	90	now–2010
2005 Syrah	89	now–2014
2004 Syrah	91	now–2014
2005 Syrah Ballard Canyon Estate	89+	now–2017
2004 Syrah Ballard Canyon Reserve	92+	now–2016

RUSTEN FAMILY VINEYARDS * * */* * * *
NAPA $35.00–$75.00

This family, which has grown grapes since 1941, only recently began producing estate-bottled wines.

2002 Cabernet Franc	88	now–2012
2002 Cabernet Franc Stagecoach Vineyard	89+	now–2012
2004 Cabernet Sauvignon	89	now–2020
2004 Cabernet Sauvignon Stagecoach Vineyard	92	now–2028
2002 Cabernet Sauvignon Stagecoach Vineyard	90	now–2015
2004 Cuvée Simone	89	???
2002 Cuvée Simone	90	now–2017
2004 La Maestra	90	2010–2025
2002 La Maestra	90+	now–2018
2001 La Maestra	89+	now–2016
2002 Merlot	87	now–2011

RUTHERFORD HILL * *
NAPA $12.00–$25.00

Acquired by Chicago's Terlato Wine Group in the late 1990s, much of Rutherford Hill's huge production is mediocre, but they do fashion some noteworthy values in Cabernet Sauvignon and, occasionally, Chardonnay.

2005 Cabernet Sauvignon	87	now–2011
2005 Chardonnay	88	now–2010
2004 Rhiannon Proprietary Red	88	now–2011

SADDLEBACK CELLARS * * * *
NAPA $25.00–$100.00

The father-and-son team of Nils and Kirk Venge farms 15 acres to produce the Saddleback Cellars wines, and an additional six acres that are used for their Venge Family Reserve offerings. The style of white wines made at this estate is nonmalolatic, aiming for crispness, freshness, and immediate drinkability. Nils Venge's expertise is with red wines; he made some of Napa's finest Cabernets when he was in charge at Villa Mt. Eden in the mid-1970s and at Groth in the mid-1980s. His powerful, tannic reds handsomely repay aging.

2005 Cabernet Franc	86?	now–2011
2005 Cabernet Sauvignon	89–91	now–2017
2004 Cabernet Sauvignon	86	now–2015
2003 Cabernet Sauvignon	89	now–2014
2002 Cabernet Sauvignon	91	now–2020
2001 Cabernet Sauvignon	92	now–2023
2004 Charbono	90	now–2011
2006 Chardonnay	85	now
2005 Chardonnay	87	now
2004 Chardonnay	88	now
2006 Marsanne	85	now
2006 Merlot	87	now–2011
2005 Merlot	84	now–2013
2003 Merlot	89	now–2015
2006 Pinot Blanc	89	now
2006 Pinot Grigio	84	now

2006 Venge Family Reserve Bianco Spettro	90	now
2005 Venge Family Reserve Bianco Spettro	89	now
2006 Venge Family Reserve Cabernet Sauvignon	91–93	now–2027
2005 Venge Family Reserve Cabernet Sauvignon	90–92	now–2022
2004 Venge Family Reserve Cabernet Sauvignon	93	now–2022
2003 Venge Family Reserve Cabernet Sauvignon	93	2009–2029
2002 Venge Family Reserve Cabernet Sauvignon	97	now–2030
2006 Venge Family Reserve Merlot	90–93	???
2005 Venge Family Reserve Merlot	89	now–2017
2004 Venge Family Reserve Merlot	90	now–2016
2005 Venge Family Reserve Sangiovese Penny Lane Vineyard	89	now
2004 Venge Family Reserve Sangiovese Penny Lane Vineyard	90	now–2010
2005 Venge Family Reserve Scouts Honor Proprietary Red	88	now–2011
2004 Venge Family Reserve Scouts Honor Proprietary Red	89	now–2011
2005 Venge Family Reserve Syrah Glady's Vineyard	89+	now–2013
2005 Venge Family Reserve Syrah The Muhler Steps	90	now–2014
2006 Viognier	87	now

SAGE ★★★★
NAPA $25.00–$65.00

The first releases from winemaker-proprietor Robbie Meyer, these are both top-notch efforts.

2004 Cabernet Sauvignon	91	now–2022+
2006 Sauvignon Blanc	93	now

ST. CLEMENT ★★★★
NAPA $17.00–$80.00

Purchased by the Beringer Wine Group just before the new century began, these wines have gotten considerably stronger under the new owners. They produce a bevy of impressive Cabernet Sauvignons from different Napa appellations. Their realistically priced wines from some of Napa's top sites are well worth seeking out.

2005 Cabernet Sauvignon Armstrong Ranch	89+	now–2022
2004 Cabernet Sauvignon Armstrong Ranch	90	2010–2025
2003 Cabernet Sauvignon Armstrong Ranch	92+	now–2022+
2002 Cabernet Sauvignon Howell Mountain	94	???
2005 Cabernet Sauvignon Napa	89	now–2018
2003 Cabernet Sauvignon Napa	87	now–2013
2002 Cabernet Sauvignon Napa	86	now–2015
2005 Cabernet Sauvignon Progeny	95	2010–2020
2003 Cabernet Sauvignon Progeny	95	now–2026
2002 Cabernet Sauvignon Progeny	90?	2010–2020?
2005 Cabernet Sauvignon Star Vineyard	92	now–2022
2004 Cabernet Sauvignon Star Vineyard	91+	now–2022
2003 Cabernet Sauvignon Star Vineyard	92	now–2020
2002 Cabernet Sauvignon Star Vineyard	93+	2010–2025
2001 Cabernet Sauvignon Star Vineyard	96	now–2020

2005 Cabernet Sauvignon Steinhauer Ranch	92	2010–2030
2004 Cabernet Sauvignon Steinhauer Ranch	93	2010–2025
2003 Cabernet Sauvignon Steinhauer Ranch	92	now–2021
2006 Chardonnay	82	now
2005 Chardonnay	87	now
2005 Oroppas Proprietary Red Wine	91	now–2022
2004 Oroppas Proprietary Red Wine	91	now–2022
2003 Oroppas Proprietary Red Wine	91	now–2017
2006 Sauvignon Blanc Bale Lane Vineyard	88	now
2005 Sauvignon Blanc Bale Lane Vineyard	87	now

ST. FRANCIS WINERY AND VINEYARDS * * *
SONOMA $26.00–$45.00

With production of around one-half million cases, Tom Mackey has run the show here since 1983. St. Francis has always enjoyed a strong following for their oaky Zinfandels, Merlots, and Cabernet Sauvignons. The wines are powerful, but often lack charm as well as harmony. Recent vintages have been dominated more by wood than fruit.

2001 Zinfandel Old Vine	89	now
2001 Zinfandel Old Vine Bacchi Vineyard	87	now
2001 Zinfandel Pagani Reserve	90	now
2001 Zinfandel Rowe Vineyard	87	now
2001 Zinfandel Zichichi Vineyard	89	now

CHÂTEAU ST. JEAN * * * *
SONOMA $13.00–$90.00

Château St. Jean is an excellent source for value-priced, high-quality wines. They are often considered primarily a white wine–producing estate because of the brilliant quality of their Fumé Blancs and Chardonnays, but they also fashion very fine Cabernet Sauvignons as well as an excellent Bordeaux blend called Cinq Cépages. Their Pinot Noirs, Malbecs, and Syrahs have been uneven in quality.

2003 Cabernet Franc St. Jean Estate	91	now–2017
2001 Cabernet Franc St. Jean Estate	88	now–2011
2005 Cabernet Sauvignon	87	now–2012
2004 Cabernet Sauvignon	87	now–2015
2003 Cabernet Sauvignon	90	now–2013
2003 Cabernet Sauvignon Reserve	92	now–2022
2002 Cabernet Sauvignon Reserve	90	now–2022
2005 Chardonnay Belle Terre Vineyard	93	now–2011
2004 Chardonnay Belle Terre Vineyard	91	now–2010
2005 Chardonnay Reserve	90	now–2011
2004 Chardonnay Reserve	92	now–2012
2005 Chardonnay Robert Young Vineyard	89	now–2014
2004 Chardonnay Robert Young Vineyard	90	now–2012
2004 Chardonnay Robert Young Vineyard Reserve	89	???
2004 Cinq Cépages Proprietary Red Wine	90	now–2015
2003 Cinq Cépages Proprietary Red Wine	89	now–2017
2006 Fumé Blanc	89	now
2006 Fumé Blanc Lyon Vineyard	91	now
2006 Fumé Blanc La Petite Étoile	91	now
2004 Malbec Reserve	86	now

2003 Malbec Reserve	89	now
2005 Pinot Noir Durell Vineyard	???	now
2004 Pinot Noir Durell Vineyard	90	now–2011
2005 Pinot Noir Reserve	89	now–2010
2004 Pinot Noir Reserve	91	now–2012
2004 Syrah Benoist Ranch	85?	now–2011
2004 Syrah Durell Vineyard	90	now–2013

ST. SUPÉRY ★★
NAPA $20.00–$50.00

This historic Napa estate has been reinvigorated by the Skally family from southern France. However, despite the involvement of globe-trotting oenologist Michel Rolland, the wines have been mediocre at best.

SAINTSBURY ★★★
CARNEROS $17.00–$75.00

Proprietors David Graves and Richard Ward founded this winery, one of the pioneers of high-quality Pinot Noir, in 1983. Since then, they have produced fragrant, fruit-forward Pinots as well as some tasty Chardonnays. While the wines can lack concentration and are rarely profound, they are consistently enjoyable. Production is nearly 100,000 cases.

2001 Pinot Noir	88	now
2002 Pinot Noir Garnet	88	now

SAMSARA ★★★★
SANTA RITA HILLS $40.00–$45.00

This is a small *garagiste* operation owned by Chad Melville of Melville Vineyard, with no other than Sashi Moorman as the winemaker. The first vintages have been enormously impressive.

2005 Pinot Noir Ampelos Vineyard	89	now–2012
2005 Pinot Noir Melville Vineyard	90	now–2013
2004 Pinot Noir Melville Vineyard	89	now–2011
2005 Syrah Ampelos Vineyard	91	now–2013
2004 Syrah Ampelos Vineyard	90	now–2013
2005 Syrah Melville Vineyard	94	now–2013
2004 Syrah Melville Vineyard	92	now–2011
2005 Syrah Purisima Mountain Vineyard	89	now–2013
2004 Syrah Purisima Mountain Vineyard	90	now–2014
2005 Syrah Verna's Vineyard	90	now–2011
2004 Syrah Verna's Vineyard	92	now–2011

SANS PERMIS ★★★★
SANTA BARBARA $28.00–$43.00

This new Chardonnay specialist made its debut in 2004 with three stunning wines.

2004 Chardonnay La Chanson Argentée de Cuillère	92	now–2011
2004 Chardonnay Cuvée Juliet	92+	now–2015
2004 Chardonnay La Séléction de Wayfarer	93	now–2017

V. SATTUI ★★
NAPA $30.00–$65.00

One of the most popular venues in Napa for picnicking day-trippers, this winery turns out significant quantities of Cabernet Sauvignon, Zinfandel, Chardonnay, and Riesling, all average in quality.

SAUSAL ★★★
NAPA $30.00–$35.00

Powerful, rustic, earthy Zinfandels are the rule of thumb from the Demostene family's Sausal winery.

SAXUM VINEYARDS ★★★★★
PASO ROBLES $36.00–$70.00

From one of California's top estates, Justin Smith's 3,000 cases of superb wine are hard to find. Like some of the other top producers in the Paso Robles area, he believes that blends represent the best potential for complex, high-quality wines from these limestone soils. Smith possesses one of the most renowned vineyards of California, the James Berry Vineyard, from which most of these offerings emerge.

2006 James Berry Vineyard Proprietary Red Wine	93	now–2017
2005 James Berry Vineyard Proprietary Red Wine	95	2010–2030
2004 James Berry Vineyard Proprietary Red Wine	91	now–2014
2006 Bone Rock James Berry Vineyard	95	now–2016
2005 Bone Rock James Berry Vineyard	98	now–2020
2004 Bone Rock James Berry Vineyard	93	now–2018
2002 Bone Rock James Berry Vineyard	95+	now–2016
2006 Booker Vineyard	94	now–2020
2005 Booker Vineyard	93	2010–2030
2006 Broken Stones	94	now–2016
2005 Broken Stones	94+	now–2017
2004 Broken Stones	92	now–2016+
2006 Heart Stone Vineyard	93	now–2014
2005 Heart Stone Vineyard	95	2010–2025
2004 Heart Stone Vineyard	92	now–2018+
2006 Rocket Block James Berry Vineyard	91?	now–2013
2005 Rocket Block James Berry Vineyard	97	now–2022
2002 Syrah Broken Stones	96	now–2016

SBRAGIA FAMILY VINEYARDS ★★★★
DRY CREEK $25.00–$75.00

Ed Sbragia departed from Beringer in 2008 to concentrate on his own vines. He has built his family operation up to approximately 4,500 to 5,500 cases of wine, featuring top-notch Chardonnay and single-vineyard Cabernet Sauvignon. I have been less impressed with his Merlot and Zinfandel.

2005 Cabernet Sauvignon Andolsen	91	now–2022
2004 Cabernet Sauvignon Andolsen	87	now–2020
2003 Cabernet Sauvignon Andolsen	90	now–2015
2005 Cabernet Sauvignon Cimarossa Vineyard	92–94	2011–2022
2004 Cabernet Sauvignon Cimarossa Vineyard	90+	2011–2025
2005 Cabernet Sauvignon Monte Rosso	90–92	2011–2022

2004 Cabernet Sauvignon Monte Rosso	94	now–2022+
2003 Cabernet Sauvignon Monte Rosso	91	now–2022
2002 Cabernet Sauvignon Monte Rosso	89	now–2017
2005 Cabernet Sauvignon Rancho del Oso	90–93+	2012–2025
2004 Cabernet Sauvignon Rancho del Oso	89+	2010–2020
2003 Cabernet Sauvignon Rancho del Oso	91	now–2022
2002 Cabernet Sauvignon Rancho del Oso	92	now–2022
2001 Cabernet Sauvignon Rancho del Oso	92	2009–2016
2005 Cabernet Sauvignon Wall Vineyard	94–96	???
2004 Cabernet Sauvignon Wall Vineyard	95	2010–2025
2006 Chardonnay Dry Creek	90	now
2005 Chardonnay Dry Creek	90	now–2012
2006 Chardonnay Gamble Ranch	92–94	now–2010
2005 Chardonnay Gamble Ranch	91	now–2011

SCARECROW ✶ ✶ ✶ ✶ ✶
RUTHERFORD $100.00

Scarecrow (Bret Lopez, proprietor) is one of the oldest vineyards in Napa Valley. The Cabernet Sauvignon—produced by talented winemaker Celia Masyczek from vines 60-plus years old—has complexity, richness, and potential longevity. If there is a Lafite-Rothschild style in Napa Valley, this might be it. Sadly, production is usually fewer than 500 cases per vintage.

2006 Cabernet Sauvignon	93–96	now–2030
2005 Cabernet Sauvignon	94–97	now–2030
2004 Cabernet Sauvignon	95	now–2027
2003 Cabernet Sauvignon	98	now–2027

SCHERRER WINERY ✶ ✶ ✶ ✶
SONOMA $35.00–$50.00

Fred Scherrer, a longtime winemaking veteran who apprenticed for nearly a decade at Dehlinger, has been making wines at his family estate since 1991. These artisanally made wines include very fine Chardonnays, Zinfandels, Pinot Noirs, and a somewhat under-the-radar but superb Cabernet Sauvignon from Alexander Valley. Scherrer offers consumers very fine wines at realistic prices.

2003 Cabernet Sauvignon	88	now–2017
2002 Cabernet Sauvignon Scherrer Vineyard	90	now–2022
2001 Cabernet Sauvignon Scherrer Vineyard	90	now–2022
2005 Chardonnay Helfer Vineyard	89+	now
2004 Chardonnay Helfer Vineyard	87	now–2011
2005 Chardonnay Scherrer Vineyard	91	now–2012
2004 Pinot Noir	90	now–2010
2003 Pinot Noir	89	now–2013
2003 Pinot Noir Scherrer Vineyard High Slopes	90	now–2015
2003 Zinfandel Scherrer Vineyard	85	now

SCHOOL HOUSE VINEYARD ✶ ✶ ✶
NAPA $40.00–$90.00

Made by Pride Mountain's Bob Foley, these offerings emerge from a vineyard at the base of Spring Mountain.

2004 Mescolanza	93	now–2014
2002 Mescolanza	90	now
2004 Pinot Noir Spring Mountain	87	now–2010
2002 Pinot Noir Spring Mountain	90	now
2001 Pinot Noir Spring Mountain	90	now

SCHRADER CELLARS ★★★★
NAPA/OAKVILLE $35.00–$95.00

This is a fascinating portfolio of 100% Cabernet Sauvignon wines, all but one from one of Napa Valley's most renowned sites, the Beckstoffer To-Kalon Vineyard in Oakville. The twist here is that Fred Schrader and his winemaker, Thomas Brown, tend to present their different bottlings based on specific blocks or clones of Cabernet Sauvignon from the Beckstoffer site. The wines are all aged in 100% new Darnajou barrels and are full-throttle, spectacular Cabernets with great richness, texture, and intensity. They should last for 15 to 20 years. Some old-vine Zinfandel from head-pruned vineyards near Calistoga are also produced under the Vieux Os label.

2005 Cabernet Sauvignon	92+	2010–2030
2004 Cabernet Sauvignon	96+	2012–2037
2003 Cabernet Sauvignon	95	now–2020+
2006 Cabernet Sauvignon Beckstoffer George III Vineyard	94–96	2010–2025
2001 Cabernet Sauvignon Beckstoffer Vineyard	93+	now–2026
2006 Cabernet Sauvignon CCS	95–97	2010–2020
2005 Cabernet Sauvignon CCS	95	2011–2036
2004 Cabernet Sauvignon CCS	94	now–2022+
2006 Cabernet Sauvignon Clone 4	96–98	2010–2020
2005 Cabernet Sauvignon Old Sparky	96	now–2027
2004 Cabernet Sauvignon Old Sparky	95+	now–2028
2003 Cabernet Sauvignon Old Sparky	94+	now–2028
2006 Cabernet Sauvignon RBS	95–97	2010–2025
2005 Cabernet Sauvignon RBS	93	now–2022+
2004 Cabernet Sauvignon RBS	93+	2012–2037
2003 Cabernet Sauvignon RBS	94	now–2020
2002 Cabernet Sauvignon RBS	93	now–2020
2001 Cabernet Sauvignon RBS	94	now–2018
2006 Cabernet Sauvignon T6	94–96	now–2025
2005 Cabernet Sauvignon T6	95	now–2027+
2004 Cabernet Sauvignon T6	91	now–2020
2003 Cabernet Sauvignon T6	92+	now–2028
2002 Cabernet Sauvignon To-Kalon Vineyard	95	now–2017
2001 MX	96	now–2020
2005 Vieux-Os Zinfandel Old Vine Hell Hole Vineyard	88	now–2010
2004 Vieux-Os Zinfandel Old Vine Hell Hole Vineyard	92	now–2014
2003 Vieux-Os Zinfandel Old Vine Hell Hole Vineyard	92	now–2011
2004 Vieux-Os Zinfandel Old Vine Ira Carter Vineyard	92	now–2012
2003 Vieux-Os Zinfandel Old Vine Ira Carter Vineyard	90	now
2002 Vieux-Os Zinfandel Old Vine Ira Carter Vineyard	87	now–2010
2005 Vieux-Os Zinfandel Old Vine Tofanelli Vineyard	91	now–2013
2004 Vieux-Os Zinfandel Old Vine Tofanelli Vineyard	89	now–2012
2003 Vieux-Os Zinfandel Old Vine Tofanelli Vineyard	88	now

SCHRAMSBERG ＊＊＊＊
NAPA $50.00–$95.00

Although this is one of California's two or three finest sparkling wine producers, that does not mean it competes favorably with high-quality French Champagne. However, some very good efforts, including their Prestige Cuvée called J. Schram as well as their Blanc de Blancs, emerge from Schramsberg.

SCREAMING EAGLE ＊＊＊＊＊
NAPA $150.00–$500.00

Napa's most expensive wine was the brainchild of Jean Phillips, who sold her beautiful Oakville estate to Charles Banks several years ago. Banks is also the proprietor of the promising Jonata winery in the Santa Ynez Valley. Screaming Eagle's 54-acre vineyard is being torn up and replanted. By 2011, today's limited production of 500 to 700 cases should have grown dramatically. What has always stood out about this wine is its extraordinary pure black currant liqueur fruit character, stunning texture, and power allied to elegance. In most vintages, it is a blend of 90% Cabernet Sauvignon and tiny percentages of Cabernet Franc and Merlot.

2006 Cabernet Sauvignon	94–97	2012–2037+
2005 Cabernet Sauvignon	97	2012–2032+
2004 Cabernet Sauvignon	95	now–2027+
2003 Cabernet Sauvignon	95	2009–2020+
2002 Cabernet Sauvignon	99	now–2030
2001 Cabernet Sauvignon	98	2010–2025+

SEA SMOKE CELLARS ＊＊＊＊
SANTA RITA HILLS $25.00–$70.00

In the Santa Rita Hills, proprietor Bob Davis created the Sea Smoke vineyard with 23 distinct vineyard blocks. The wines have been tremendously impressive since their inception and continue to go from strength to strength. They all reveal intense Pinot Noir characteristics, fragrant, rich, full-bodied personalities, and abundant charm as well as power.

2004 Pinot Noir Botella	92	now–2016
2003 Pinot Noir Botella	90+?	now–2012
2002 Pinot Noir Botella	91+	now–2012
2004 Pinot Noir Southing	90+	now–2016
2003 Pinot Noir Southing	92	now–2012
2002 Pinot Noir Southing	92	now–2011
2004 Pinot Noir Ten	94+	now–2016+
2003 Pinot Noir Ten	96	now–2015
2002 Pinot Noir Ten	93	now–2012

SEAVEY VINEYARD ＊＊＊＊/＊＊＊＊＊
NAPA $38.00–$78.00

My vote as the most underrated Cabernet Sauvignon in Napa Valley goes to Mary and Bill Seavey's wine from the dry-farmed hillside vineyards of Conn Valley. These offerings possess 25 to 30 years of aging potential. For example, the 1990 and 1991 are still cruising along in great shape. The well-known French winemaking consultant Philippe Melka is the guru behind these beauties.

2006 Cabernet Sauvignon	92–94	2011–2025
2005 Cabernet Sauvignon	95+	2013–2032
2004 Cabernet Sauvignon	94	now–2027

2003 Cabernet Sauvignon	96	now–2032
2002 Cabernet Sauvignon	94	2010–2025
2001 Cabernet Sauvignon	93+	2012–2028
2006 Caravina	89–91	now–2020
2005 Caravina	91	now–2015
2004 Caravina	91	now–2019
2003 Caravina	91	now–2022
2002 Caravina	90	now–2019

SEBASTIANI ∗∗∗
SONOMA $17.00–$75.00

With considerable high-quality vineyard acreage as well as a relatively large production facility, this winery has never lived up to its potential. Family quarrels over the years explain part of the irregularity. However, over recent years it appears Sebastiani has gotten its act together and the wines have become increasingly better, while prices have remained generally fair. This historic old name in California may be making a serious comeback.

SEGHESIO ∗∗∗∗
SONOMA $18.00–$35.00

Serious single-vineyard, realistically priced Zinfandels are made by the Seghesio family along with a few other varietals. The winery was founded by the Seghesios in the late 1800s, and for much of their history they sold fruit to other producers. They began estate-bottling their wines in 1983.

2002 Zinfandel Cortina	93	now–2012
2002 Zinfandel Home Ranch	92	now–2012
2002 Zinfandel Old Vine	92	now
2002 Zinfandel San Lorenzo	93	now–2010

SELENE ∗∗∗/∗∗∗∗
NAPA $26.00–$70.00

The owner-winemaker for Selene is the well-known Mia Klein. These are all made from purchased fruit.

2004 Cabernet Sauvignon	86	now–2014
2003 Cabernet Sauvignon	88	now–2015
2002 Cabernet Sauvignon	88	now–2015
2004 Cabernet Sauvignon Dead Fred Vineyard	89	now–2017
2004 Chesler Proprietary Red Wine	92	now–2020
2003 Chesler Proprietary Red Wine	89	now–2018
2002 Chesler Proprietary Red Wine	88	now–2015
2005 Merlot Frediani Vineyard	89	now–2013
2006 Sauvignon Blanc Hyde Vineyards	90	now
2005 Sauvignon Blanc Hyde Vineyards	88	now

SEQUOIA GROVE ∗∗∗
NAPA $30.00–$65.00

Situated in central Napa, this estate, founded by the Allen family in 1978, was sold to the Kopf family in the 1990s. The new owners brought in Mike Trujillo as the winemaker, and although the wines are very good, they lack that extra excitement offered by Napa's finest producers.

2004 Cabernet Sauvignon Napa	86	now–2015
2003 Cabernet Sauvignon Rutherford Reserve	88	now–2020
2005 Chardonnay Carneros	86	now
2004 Syrah Stagecoach Vineyard	87	now–2012

SHADOW CANYON CELLARS ★ ★ ★ ★
SAN LUIS OBISPO $25.00–$65.00

This up-and-coming estate is owned by winemaker Gary Gibson. The vineyard on York Mountain is planted with different clones of Syrah, and that production is supplemented by purchased fruit from other sources, especially the highly regarded Larner Vineyard. In addition to an impressive red wine portfolio, Shadow Canyon produces one of California's finest rosés.

2004 Amila Syrah/Grenache	92	now–2018
2006 Grenache Larner Vineyard	88	now–2012
2005 Grenache Larner Vineyard	91	now–2017
2004 Grenache Larner Vineyard	91	now–2016
2003 Grenache Larner Vineyard	91	now–2012+
2005 D. Salvador Shadow Canyon/Larner Vineyards	89+	now–2014
2003 Syrah Larner & Dominion Vineyards	89	now–2016
2006 Syrah Shadow Canyon Vineyard	89	now–2016
2005 Syrah Shadow Canyon Vineyard	90	now–2015
2004 Syrah Shadow Canyon Vineyard	92+	now–2021+
2003 Syrah Shadow Canyon Vineyard	90	now–2014
2002 Syrah Shadow Canyon Vineyard	88	now–2012
2001 Syrah York Mountain	87	now

SHAFER VINEYARDS ★ ★ ★ ★ ★
NAPA $36.00–$175.00

Shafer Vineyards, run impeccably well by the father-and-son team of John and Doug Shafer with assistance from their brilliant winemaker and vineyard manager, Elias Fernandez, now boasts 210 acres of estate holdings, with 55 at the home estate in Stags Leap. This is an irrefutable reference point for world-class wines.

2006 Cabernet Sauvignon Hillside Select Stags Leap	94–97	2010–2025
2005 Cabernet Sauvignon Hillside Select Stags Leap	95–97	2011–2030
2004 Cabernet Sauvignon Hillside Select Stags Leap	97	now–2022+
2003 Cabernet Sauvignon Hillside Select Stags Leap	95	now–2032
2002 Cabernet Sauvignon Hillside Select Stags Leap	100	now–2037
2001 Cabernet Sauvignon Hillside Select Stags Leap	99	2009–2034
2004 Cabernet Sauvignon Napa	90	now–2014
2003 Cabernet Sauvignon Napa	91	now–2022
2002 Cabernet Sauvignon Napa	90	now–2015
2006 Cabernet Sauvignon One Point Five Stags Leap	85–87	2009–2015
2005 Cabernet Sauvignon One Point Five Stags Leap	90	2010–2020
2004 Cabernet Sauvignon One Point Five Stags Leap	90	now–2019
2006 Chardonnay Red Shoulder Ranch	90–92	now–2012
2005 Chardonnay Red Shoulder Ranch	91	now–2012
2006 Merlot	86	now–2015
2005 Merlot	88	now–2017
2004 Merlot	88	now–2013
2006 Relentless	90–94	now–2025

2005 Relentless	92–94	now–2022
2004 Relentless	91	now–2022
2003 Relentless	93	now–2022+

SIDURI * * * *
CALIFORNIA $28.00–$48.00

This high-class *négociant* operation owns no vineyards, but from purchased fruit they produce a considerable number of single-vineyard Pinot Noirs, all of which merit attention. Founder Adam Lee has a knack for accessing top-notch spots on the Sonoma Coast, Santa Lucia Highlands, and even Oregon, from which he turns out unfined, unfiltered, naturally made wines. Their Syrahs are sold under a different label, Novy.

2004 Pinot Noir	91	now
2004 Pinot Noir Arbre Vert Vineyard (Oregon)	87	now
2005 Pinot Noir Cargasacchi Vineyard	89	now–2011
2004 Pinot Noir Cargasacchi Vineyard	85	now
2005 Pinot Noir Clos Pepe Vineyard	91	now–2016
2004 Pinot Noir Clos Pepe Vineyard	89	now–2012
2003 Pinot Noir Clos Pepe Vineyard	91	now–2013
2005 Pinot Noir Ewald Vineyard	89	now–2012
2004 Pinot Noir Ewald Vineyard	90	now–2011
2005 Pinot Noir Garys' Vineyard	92	now–2013
2004 Pinot Noir Garys' Vineyard	91	now–2012
2004 Pinot Noir Hirsch Vineyard	88+	now–2015
2003 Pinot Noir Keefer Ranch Vineyard	89	now–2012
2005 Pinot Noir Muirfield Vineyard	85	now–2010
2004 Pinot Noir Muirfield Vineyard	89+	now–2013
2005 Pinot Noir Pisoni Vineyard	93	now–2014
2004 Pinot Noir Pisoni Vineyard	94	now–2012
2003 Pinot Noir Pisoni Vineyard	92	now–2012
2005 Pinot Noir Rosella's Vineyard	91	now–2012
2004 Pinot Noir Rosella's Vineyard	90	now–2012
2003 Pinot Noir Rosella's Vineyard	90	now–2010
2005 Pinot Noir Russian River	88	now
2004 Pinot Noir Russian River	88	now–2012
2005 Pinot Noir Santa Lucia Highlands	88	now–2011
2003 Pinot Noir Santa Lucia Highlands	87	now
2005 Pinot Noir Santa Rita Hills	89	now–2013
2004 Pinot Noir Santa Rita Hills	88	now
2005 Pinot Noir Sonatera Vineyard	91	now–2012
2004 Pinot Noir Sonatera Vineyard	91	now–2015
2005 Pinot Noir Terra di Promissio Vineyard	90	now–2011
2005 Pinot Noir Vanderkamp Vineyard	87	now–2011

SIGNORELLO VINEYARDS * * *
NAPA $36.00–$95.00

Wine lover Ray Signorello, Jr., splits his time between Vancouver, Canada, and San Francisco. He purchased a 100-acre estate on the Silverado trail in the mid-1970s, and currently he has 42 acres planted in different varietals. This winery tends to produce European-styled wines, as Ray Signorello's love of white and red Burgundy as well as Bordeaux has no doubt influenced his winemaking philosophy. While this estate still seems to be somewhat of a work in progress, I have high hopes that some superb wines will emerge from Signorello Vineyards.

2004 Cabernet Sauvignon Estate	88+	now–2018
2005 Chardonnay Estate	88	now–2011
2006 Chardonnay Hope Cuvée	90	now–2012
2006 Chardonnay Vieilles Vignes	91	now–2013
2004 Padrone Proprietary Red Wine	90	2011–2025
2002 Padrone Proprietary Red Wine	90	now–2020
2001 Padrone Proprietary Red Wine	90+	now–2020
2005 Syrah	86	now–2012
2004 Syrah	86	now–2011
2001 Syrah	85	now
2005 Syrah Napa Valley Unfiltered	90	now–2012
2002 Zinfandel	89	now
2005 Zinfandel Luvisi Vineyard	87	now

SILVER OAK CELLARS ★★/★★★
ALEXANDER VALLEY/NAPA $60.00–$100.00

Founded in 1972, Silver Oak became one of the hottest, most fashionable Cabernet Sauvignon producers under the leadership of its late co-founder, Justin Meyer. The emphasis was on ripe Cabernets, made from their 338 acres of vines (in both the Alexander and Napa valleys) and aged nearly three years in 100% new American oak. The wines hit their zenith in quality in the 1980s through the mid-1990s, then production soared, and with the passing of Justin Meyer, quality became increasingly irregular. The wines now seem like a caricature of their former style. They remain incredibly oaky, but the dense, concentrated fruit that used to back up all the wood is missing. Production has jumped from 35,000 to over 100,000 cases, which may explain part of the current problem.

2004 Cabernet Sauvignon Alexander Valley	88	now–2015
2003 Cabernet Sauvignon Alexander Valley	88	now–2014
2002 Cabernet Sauvignon Alexander Valley	90	now–2015
2001 Cabernet Sauvignon Alexander Valley	90	now–2015
2004 Cabernet Sauvignon Napa Valley	88	now
2003 Cabernet Sauvignon Napa Valley	89	now–2013
2002 Cabernet Sauvignon Napa Valley	91	now–2017
2001 Cabernet Sauvignon Napa Valley	92	now–2017

SILVERADO VINEYARDS ★★★/★★★★
NAPA $20.00–$75.00

This winery was founded in the early 1980s by Walt Disney's widow, Lillian. Production from the 300-plus acres of vines is over 100,000 cases. The primary vineyards are in the Stags Leap District of the southern Napa Valley, Yountville, and Soda Creek. After a period of lean, austere efforts, the wines have become richer and more complex. The top wines include their Cabernet Sauvignon Solo.

2004 Cabernet Sauvignon Napa	89	now–2014
2004 Cabernet Sauvignon Solo	92	now–2022
2001 Cabernet Sauvignon Reserve	92+	now–2020
2006 Sauvignon Blanc Miller Ranch	88	now

SIMI WINERY ★ ★ ★
ALEXANDER VALLEY $40.00–$65.00

This winery was founded in the 1800s, closed during prohibition, then resurrected in the 1950s. It became part of the huge Constellation group of wineries in 1999. Veteran winemaker Zelma Long moved on and for a time, the quality of Simi's wines became blatantly commercial. However, after Steve Reeder, who did such great work at Château St. Jean, became the winemaker, there was noticeable improvement. There is enormous potential, as Simi owns more than 600 acres and produces in excess of a quarter of a million cases. Bigger and better things from Simi are anticipated by this critic.

2005 Cabernet Sauvignon Sonoma	89+	2011–2020
2004 Cabernet Sauvignon Sonoma	87	now–2016
2002 Cabernet Sauvignon Reserve	88	now–2017
2006 Chardonnay Sonoma	87	now
2004 Merlot Sonoma	84	now–2011
2006 Sauvignon Blanc Sonoma	88	now
2001 Shiraz Landslide Vineyard	85	now
2005 Zinfandel Sonoma	81	now

SINE QUA NON ★ ★ ★ ★ ★
SANTA BARBARA $75.00–$150.00

Restaurateur Manfred Krankl and his wife, Elaine, made their first wine at Sine Qua Non in 1994 in an attempt to produce something to sell at their restaurant. However, the wine bug proved too compelling, and the part-time restaurateur and former owner of La Brea Bakery in Los Angeles went into winemaking full-time, and the wine world has been all the better for it. At first purchasing grapes from some of the finest vineyards in Edna Valley as well as Santa Ynez Valley, Krankl moved to all-estate fruit from his 30 acres of vines planted in Ventura and Santa Barbara counties. In an ocean of mediocre wines, the SQN offerings are totally profound. They inspire and energize anyone who tastes them. This is all due to the Krankls' uncompromising vision and their courage to push the envelope and challenge themselves to go beyond anything that has been achieved. They produce California's finest Grenache, one of the two or three best Syrahs, and some of the top white varietal blends in addition to some utterly profound dessert wines. This is one of the world's great wineries, and it continues to go from strength to strength.

2005 Atlantis Fe 203-1a (Syrah)	96	now–2020
2005 Atlantis Fe 203-2a (Grenache)	97	now–2022
2003 Boots, Pasties, Scanty Panties & A Ten Gallon Hat	96	now–2014
2004 Covert Fingers Arita Hills Vineyard (Pinot Noir)	95	now–2016+
2002 Heart Chorea (Syrah)	99	2010–2025
2002 Hollerin' M Shea Vineyard (Pinot Noir)	96	now–2014
2003 The Inaugural (Grenache)	99	now–2017
2003 The Inaugural (Syrah)	100	now–2022
2004 Into the Dark (Grenache)	96	2010–2005
2002 Just for the Love of It (Syrah)	100	2010–2028
2003 Li'l E (Grenache)	96	now–2016
2001 Midnight Oil (Syrah)	96	now–2018
2006 Mr. K. The Iceman (Viognier)	96	now–2027
2002 Mr. K. The Iceman (Gewürztraminer)	96	now–2025
2003 Mr. K. The Nobleman (Chardonnay)	94	now–2025
2001 Mr. K. The Nobleman (Chardonnay)	97	now–2025

2004 Mr. K. The Strawman (Sémillon)	100	now–2027
2003 Mr. K. The Strawman (Sémillon)	97	now–2025
2001 Mr. K. The Strawman (Sémillon)	97	now–2025
2001 Not Yet Named (Syrah)	96	now–2016
2004 Ode to E (Grenache)	99	now–2022
2004 Ode to E (Syrah)	97	now–2022
2003 Omega Shea Vineyard (Pinot Noir)	92	now–2013
2005 Over and Out Arita Hills Vineyard (Pinot Noir)	92	now–2014
2003 Papa (Syrah)	98	now–2021
2005 The Petition	95	now–2012
2004 Poker Face (Syrah)	100	now–2022
2004 The Rejuvenators	96	now–2011
2003 SQN (Grenache/Syrah)	96+	now–2018
2000 Suey Trockenbeerenauslese (Roussanne)	100	now–2025
2001 Ventriloquist (Grenache/Syrah)	92	now–2020

ROBERT SINSKEY ★ ★ ★
CARNEROS $30.00–$40.00

Surgeon Robert Sinskey, who first planted vineyards in the early 1980, is best known as the producer of attractive, elegant albeit superficial, pleasant Pinot Noirs with loads of underbrush and cherrylike fruit flavors. His selections all come from Carneros vineyard sites, and in most vintages, four different Pinots are produced.

2004 Pinot Noir Four Vineyards Los Carneros	87	now–2012
2005 Pinot Noir Los Carneros	86	now–2010
2004 Pinot Noir Three Amigos Vineyard Los Carneros	88	now–2013
2002 Pinot Noir Vandel Vineyard	87?	now–2010

LA SIRENA ★ ★ ★ ★
NAPA $20.00–$150.00

The home-based project of renowned wine consultant Heidi Barrett, La Sirena consistently produces high-quality Cabernet Sauvignon and, more recently, Syrah, and a delightfully fresh Moscato.

2005 Cabernet Sauvignon	91+	2010–2023+
2004 Cabernet Sauvignon	93	now–2023+
2003 Cabernet Sauvignon	93	now–2022
2001 Cabernet Sauvignon	91	now–2021
2006 Moscato Azul	90	now
2005 Moscato Azul	90	now
2004 Moscato Azul	89	now
2005 Syrah Barrett Vineyard	90+	now–2018
2004 Syrah Barrett Vineyard	89+	now–2014
2005 Syrah Napa	90	now–2015
2004 Syrah Napa	90	now–2014
2003 Syrah Napa	93	now–2012
2002 Syrah Napa	92	now–2013
2001 Syrah Napa	87	now–2010
2005 Syrah Santa Ynez	89	now–2013
2004 Syrah Santa Ynez	89	now–2012
2003 Syrah Santa Ynez	90	now–2012
2002 Syrah Santa Ynez	90	now–2011

SLOAN   ★ ★ ★ ★ ★
NAPA $165.00

Stuart Sloan, a successful Seattle businessman, is the hands-on owner of this high-end, luxury, 13-acre vineyard planted on a 60-acre tract planted high on the hillsides above the Auberge de Soleil. Sloan has a superstar team in place, including viticulturist David Abreu, winemaker Martha McClellan, and French oenologist Michel Rolland. Only 500 cases of extraordinary red wine are produced from this grand cru site.

2006 Proprietary Red	93–95+	now–2025
2005 Proprietary Red	98–100	2010–2015+
2004 Proprietary Red	96	now–2037+
2003 Proprietary Red	96	now–2032+
2002 Proprietary Red	100	now–2030
2001 Proprietary Red	98	now–2025+

W. H. SMITH   ★ ★ ★
SONOMA COAST $52.00

Pinot Noir specialists with vineyards on the Sonoma Coast, proprietors Joan and Bill Smith became well known for their top-notch La Jota wines produced during the 1990s. They sold that operation and are now focused on Pinot Noir, about which I have had somewhat mixed reactions.

2006 Pinot Noir Marimar Estate Vineyard	88	now–2010
2006 Pinot Noir Maritime	85?	now
2006 Pinot Noir Sonoma Coast	83	now
2006 Pinot Noir Umino Vineyard	85?	now–2010

SNOWDEN   ★ ★ ★ ★
NAPA $20.00–$65.00

Scott Snowden, a former judge, has instituted a complete makeover of the wines from his 23 acres of vineyards, most of which are superbly situated on the hillsides near Sloan Vineyards, above Auberge du Soleil. The vineyard is planted primarily with Bordeaux varities, and the production of 2,000 cases includes gorgeous Cabernet Sauvignons as well as an attractive Sauvignon Blanc. Snowden's consultant is the highly renowned David Ramey. This operation deserves serious attention.

2006 Cabernet Sauvignon The Ranch	90–92	2010–2020
2005 Cabernet Sauvignon The Ranch	90	now–2022
2006 Cabernet Sauvignon Reserve	94–96	2010–2025
2005 Cabernet Sauvignon Reserve	94	2011–2025
2006 Sauvignon Blanc	88	now

SONOMA COAST VINEYARDS   ★ ★ ★/★ ★ ★ ★
SONOMA COAST $50.00–$60.00

This is a relatively recent operation on the Sonoma Coast, a burgeoning area for extraordinary Pinot Noir, Chardonnay, and Syrah.

2005 Chardonnay	90	now–2012
2002 Chardonnay	91	now
2002 Pinot Noir	85	now
2004 Pinot Noir Balistreri Family Vineyard	90	now–2013
2006 Sauvignon Blanc Hummingbird Hill Vineyard	88	now
2004 Syrah	87	now–2013

SONOMA-CUTRER ★★
SONOMA $35.00–$55.00

Begun in 1973 by Brice Jones to turn out world-class Chardonnay and Pinot Noir, Sonoma-Cutrer originally produced three Chardonnays: a Russian River Ranches, a Cutrer Vineyard, and a Les Pierres Vineyard. The wines merited the acclaim they received, as they were superb Chardonnays offering both elegance and flavor. Production grew from the winery's 450-acre estate, but the quality declined and the wines became pleasant but boring. Thirty-five years later the great acclaim and promise of the early years has dissipated, leaving a highly successful commercial enterprise producing around 150,000 cases of pleasant, simple Chardonnay.

CHÂTEAU SOUVERAIN ★★★/★★★★
ALEXANDER VALLEY $14.00–$60.00

One of the historic names of Sonoma, this estate produced some fabulous Cabernet Sauvignons in the late 1960s and early to mid-1970s. It was purchased by Beringer in 1996, and became part of the Mildara-Blass empire when that company bought Beringer in 2000. To their credit, Mildara-Blass kept winemaker Ed Killian in charge, and the Souverain wines continue to represent excellent value. They are stylish and well made, especially the Cabernet Sauvignons and Chardonnays.

2005 Cabernet Sauvignon Asti Estate Vineyard	90–92	now–2022
2005 Cabernet Sauvignon Estate	87–89	now–2017
2004 Cabernet Sauvignon Estate	87	now–2017
2003 Cabernet Sauvignon Estate	89	now–2017
2002 Cabernet Sauvignon Estate	90	now–2020
2004 Cabernet Sauvignon Stuhlmuller Vineyard	90	now–2022+
2004 Cabernet Sauvignon Winemaker's Reserve	89	now–2022
2002 Cabernet Sauvignon Winemaker's Reserve	92	now–2017
2005 Chardonnay Winemaker's Reserve	90	now
2004 Chardonnay Winemaker's Reserve	89	now
2004 Merlot Winemaker's Reserve	86	now–2010
2002 Merlot Winemaker's Reserve	87	now–2010
2005 Sauvignon Blanc	82	now

SPENCER-ROLOSON ★★★/★★★★
CALIFORNIA $20.00–$40.00

Sam Spencer is the winemaker and Wendy Roloson is the marketing force behind this *négociant* operation making intriguing, delicious wines from Zinfandel, Viognier, Grenache, Syrah, and Tempranillo, and a fine bistro blend called Palaterra. I like the wines, and I like their good-value prices even more.

2004 Palaterra	87	now–2010
2003 Palaterra	89	now–2010
2001 Palaterra	87	now
2004 Syrah La Herradura Vineyard	92	now–2012
2003 Syrah La Herradura Vineyard	90	now–2014
2001 Syrah La Herradura Vineyard	89	now–2012
2004 Syrah Madder Lake Vineyard	90	now–2013
2001 Syrah Sueño Vineyard	87	now–2012
2005 Viognier Noble Vineyard	90	now
2004 Viognier Noble Vineyard	89	now

SPOTTSWOODE ★ ★ ★ ★ ★
NAPA $32.00–$120.00

A historic estate founded in 1882, and resurrected by the late Dr. Jack Novak in 1972, this beautiful St. Helena vineyard produces the Château Margaux of Napa. Since Dr. Novak's death, his wife, Mary, and daughter, Beth, have run this estate with great precision and grace. They produce three wines: a brilliant Sauvignon Blanc; a fabulous, elegant, long-lived Cabernet Sauvignon that has become compelling over the last decade; and a second Cabernet Sauvignon called Lyndenhurst. This winery is at the top of its game.

2005 Cabernet Sauvignon Estate	96	2011–2030
2004 Cabernet Sauvignon Estate	91	now–2022+
2003 Cabernet Sauvignon Estate	94	now–2022+
2002 Cabernet Sauvignon Estate	97	now–2025
2001 Cabernet Sauvignon Estate	95	now–2020
2005 Lyndenhurst Cabernet Sauvignon	89	???
2004 Lyndenhurst Cabernet Sauvignon	90	now–2019
2003 Lyndenhurst Cabernet Sauvignon	90	now–2015
2002 Lyndenhurst Cabernet Sauvignon	89	now–2015
2006 Sauvignon Blanc	90	now
2005 Sauvignon Blanc	91	now
2004 Sauvignon Blanc	91	now

SPRING MOUNTAIN VINEYARD ★ ★/★ ★ ★
NAPA $50.00–$90.00

Sadly, this estate's enormous potential has largely gone unrealized. The original estate dates back to the late 1800s, and part of that old winery still remains. A huge operation, covering three large ranches—Miravalle (257 acres), Château Chevalier (120 acres), and Draper Vineyards–La Perla (435 acres)—the winery became famous thanks to the television show *Falcon Crest*. Today, the wines consist of Sauvignon Blanc, Cabernet Sauvignon Estate, and a Bordeaux blend of Cabernet Sauvignon, Merlot, and Cabernet Franc called Elivette. Recently a Syrah was added to the portfolio. The wines are good but never exciting. Given the *terroirs* available, one hopes better things will emerge.

2003 Cabernet Sauvignon	88	now–2015
2002 Elivette Proprietary Red Wine	89	now–2017
2001 Proprietary Red Wine	89	now–2017
2004 Syrah	86	now–2013

STAGLIN FAMILY VINEYARD ★ ★ ★ ★
RUTHERFORD $55.00–$135.00

This beautiful Rutherford estate produces gorgeous, nonmalolactic Chardonnays and one of Rutherford's finest Cabernet Sauvignons from their estate vineyard. Recently, they added a proprietary red wine called Ineo. These are serious efforts meant for long-term aging.

2006 Cabernet Sauvignon Estate	94–96	2011–2025
2005 Cabernet Sauvignon Estate	93	2013–2038
2004 Cabernet Sauvignon Estate	92	2010–2030
2003 Cabernet Sauvignon Estate	94	now–2022+
2002 Cabernet Sauvignon Estate	93	now–2020
2001 Cabernet Sauvignon Estate	94	now–2020+
2002 Cabernet Sauvignon Salus	89+	now–2014
2002 Cabernet Sauvignon 20th Anniversary	93+	2010–2028

2006 Chardonnay Estate	92	now–2011
2005 Chardonnay Estate	94	now–2013
2004 Chardonnay Estate	94	now–2010
2006 Chardonnay Salus	89	now
2006 Ineo Proprietary Red	92–95	2011–2025

STAG'S LEAP WINE CELLARS ★ ★ ★
NAPA $75.00–$150.00

The brilliance of Warren Winarski brought worldwide fame to Stag's Leap Wine Cellars, particularly for their Cabernet Sauvignon and their luxury cuvée, a Reserve Cabernet called Cask 23. These were wines of extraordinary richness, elegance, and longevity that were remarkably consistent through the 1970s and 1980s. In the 1990s the style became increasingly austere, and smaller, more narrowly constructed wines emerged. For whatever reason, this winery has never returned to its earlier greatness, yet their reputation remains largely intact. The recent sale to a Piero Antinori–led syndicate will hopefully infuse new energy with this once famous producer.

2005 Cabernet Sauvignon Artemis	88?	2011–2019
2004 Cabernet Sauvignon Fay Vineyard	89	now–2020
2001 Cabernet Sauvignon Fay Vineyard	89	now–2018
2005 Cabernet Sauvignon The Leap Estate Reserve	91–93	now–2025
2004 Cabernet Sauvignon The Leap Estate Reserve	93	now–2022+
2004 Cabernet Sauvignon SLV	87	now–2016
2001 Cabernet Sauvignon SLV	88?	now–2020
2004 Cask 23 Proprietary Red Wine	90	now–2020
2001 Cask 23 Proprietary Red Wine	87+?	now–2016
2005 Merlot Napa	86	now–2015
2006 Sauvignon Blanc Rancho Chimiles	86	now

STAGS' LEAP WINERY ★ ★ ★
NAPA $20.00–$85.00

Not to be confused with its more illustrious neighbor, Stag's Leap Wine Cellars, Stags' Leap Winery was purchased by Beringer and absorbed into the Blass-Midara group. Their reputation is based on their tannic, tough-textured Petite Sirah, but for me, their finest wine is the Cabernet Sauvignon Estate Reserve, which actually surpasses that of its more famous neighbor but sells for a much lower price.

| 2006 Petite Syrah Ne Cede Malis | 88+ | 2010–2020 |
| 2004 Petite Syrah Ne Cede Malis | 86? | 2010–2020 |

STERLING ★ ★
NAPA $20.00–$75.00

With more than 1,000 acres of vineyards, and a production inching up toward a half million cases of Cabernet Sauvignon, Merlot, Chardonnay, Sauvignon Blanc, and Pinot Noir, this winery continues to disappoint. Sterling was floundering in quality long before it was purchased by the huge Diageo group in 2000. When the estate was founded in 1969, with the talented Ric Forman as winemaker, they produced a bevy of extraordinary Cabernet Sauvignons and Merlots. Nothing over the last 15 years has remotely resembled the wines produced in the 1970s and 1980s.

STEWART CELLARS ★★★★
NAPA $44.00–$62.00

A small, under-the-rader Napa producer, Stewart turns out high-quality Pinot Noir and Cabernet Sauvignon. Production remains under 2,500 cases per year. This is a true insider's wine.

2005 Cabernet Sauvignon	91	2009–2024
2004 Cabernet Sauvignon	93	now–2020
2003 Cabernet Sauvignon	93	now–2022
2002 Cabernet Sauvignon	89+	now–2015
2004 Pinot Noir	91	now–2011
2003 Pinot Noir	89	now–2010

STOLPMAN VINEYARDS ★★★★
SANTA YNEZ $25.00–$50.00

Winemaker Sashi Moorman has built a strong portfolio of wines from Stolpman Vineyards, one of the up-and-coming estates in the Santa Ynez Valley. With more than 220 acres that include some superb vineyard sites, Stolpman should be a name to reckon with for many decades to come.

2005 Angeli	94	now–2017
2004 Angeli	95	now–2015
2002 Angeli	90	now–2011
2005 Angeli Blanc	90	now–2011
2004 L'Avion	95	now
2005 La Croce Proprietary Red Wine	90	now–2012
2004 La Croce Proprietary Red Wine	94	now–2011
2002 La Croce Proprietary Red Wine	87	now
2005 Syrah Estate	93	now–2014
2004 Syrah Estate	93	now–2012
2005 Syrah Hilltops Estate	93	now–2015
2004 Syrah Hilltops Estate	95	now–2014

STONESTREET ★★★/★★★★
ALEXANDER VALLEY $25.00–$100.00

Some top-notch Chardonnays as well as tannic Cabernet Sauvignons emerge from this Jess Jackson–owned winery. Its Alexander Valley mountain vineyard is the primary source for the fruit used in these wines. While the Chardonnays are impressive, the Cabernets are somewhat austere and tannic.

2003 Cabernet Sauvignon	86	now–2013
2002 Cabernet Sauvignon	89	now–2013
2003 Cabernet Sauvignon Black Cougar Ridge	90	2011–2024
2002 Cabernet Sauvignon Black Cougar Ridge	93	now–2020
2004 Cabernet Sauvignon Christopher's Vineyard	88+?	2009–2025
2006 Chardonnay Alexander Valley	92	now–2011
2005 Chardonnay Alexander Valley	87	now–2011
2004 Chardonnay Block 26	92	now
2004 Chardonnay Block 66	90	now
2006 Chardonnay Broken Road	91	now–2012
2005 Chardonnay Broken Road	93	now–2012
2006 Chardonnay Red Point	91	now–2012

2005 Chardonnay Red Point	92	now–2011
2006 Chardonnay Upper Barn	94	now–2015
2005 Chardonnay Upper Barn	92	now–2012
2004 Chardonnay Upper Barn	93	now–2013
2003 Legacy Proprietary Red Wine	91	now–2017
2002 Legacy Proprietary Red Wine	92	now–2017
2003 Meritage	89	now–2015

STONY HILL VINEYARD ⋆ ⋆ ⋆ ⋆
NAPA $50.00–$55.00

Founded by Fred and Eleanor McCrea in 1943, this is one of California's oldest continuously operating vineyards in the valley. Wine production began a decade later with their renowned nonmalolactic, minimally oaked Chardonnay, a style to which they have remained faithful. The vineyards were replanted after being wiped out by disease. This is one of the more discreet, Chablis-style Chardonnays made in California. The rest of the portfolio, made by the McCreas' son, Peter, is much less impressive.

2005 Chardonnay	90	now–2015
2006 Chardonnay SHV	87	now

HERMAN STORY WINES ⋆ ⋆ ⋆ ⋆
SAN LUIS OBISPO $28.00–$35.00

This newcomer debuted in 2001, and the releases to date have been very impressive as well as exceptional bargains. Herman Story produces high-quality Rhone Ranger wines from California's Central Coast.

2005 Grenache Larner Vineyard	93	now–2013
2004 Grenache Larner Vineyard	88	now
2005 Syrah	91	now–2014
2004 Syrah	89	now–2013
2005 Syrah Larner Vineyard	93	now–2015
2004 Syrah Larner Vineyard	91	now–2014
2002 Syrah Larner Vineyard	88	now–2011
2005 Syrah White Hawk Vineyard	94	now–2015

STORYBOOK MOUNTAIN VINEYARDS ⋆ ⋆ ⋆ ⋆
NAPA $25.00–$45.00

Another old ghost winery, having been founded by a German immigrant in the late 1880s, Storybook Mountain was closed during prohibition and resurrected by Jerry and Sigrid Seps in 1976, when they began replanting the hillside vineyards with Zinfandel. Seps believes in an elegant, ageworthy style rather than the big, backstrapping Zins produced by many of his peers. The finest offerings are the Estate Reserve, Eastern Exposure, and Mayacamas Range Zinfandels. A terrific rosé is also produced. I have had less positive experience with their Bordeaux varietal and Zinfandel blend called Antaeus.

2003 Zinfandel Atlas Peak	88	now–2010
2002 Zinfandel Atlas Peak	90	now–2013
2001 Zinfandel Atlas Peak	89	now
2003 Zinfandel Eastern Exposure	91	now–2010
2002 Zinfandel Eastern Exposure	93	now–2015
2001 Zinfandel Eastern Exposure	90	now–2011
2003 Zinfandel Estate Reserve	92	now–2020

2002 Zinfandel Estate Reserve	94	now–2015+
2001 Zinfandel Estate Reserve	92	now–2015
2003 Zinfandel Mayacamas Range	89	now–2012
2002 Zinfandel Mayacamas Range	91	now–2015
2001 Zinfandel Mayacamas Range	88+	now–2010

RODNEY STRONG * * *
SONOMA $20.00–$45.00

Before Rodney Strong passed away, he had built a fine reputation for producing consistently good-value wines as well as some top-end, impressive Cabernet Sauvignons, especially from the Alexander's Crown Vineyard. Since the winery was sold to Klein Foods, there appear to have been some major changes in the winemaking philosophy, with the potential for an increase in quality.

SUMMERLAND WINERY * * *
SANTA MARIA $25.00–$38.00

This *négociant* operation is dedicated to generic Central Coast offerings as well as some single-vineyard wines, the latter of which are well made and worthy of attention.

2004 Chardonnay Bien Nacido Vineyard Block U	87	now–2011
2003 Pinot Noir Bien Nacido Vineyard	90	now–2011
2002 Pinot Noir Bien Nacido Vineyard	93	now–2011
2004 Syrah Bien Nacido Vineyard Block X	87	now–2012
2004 Syrah Paradise Road Vineyard	90	now–2018

SUMMERS WINES * * *
NAPA $15.00–$30.00

One of the top value names in California, Jim Summers, who began as a grape grower in Knight's Valley, knows his vineyards and his wines. He fashions delicious, up-front, fruit-driven offerings that sell for a song.

2006 Chardonnay Alexander Valley	90	now
2005 Merlot Reserve	88	now–2011
2005 Cabernet Sauvignon Adrianna's Cuvée	88	now–2014
2004 Cabernet Sauvignon Estate	90	now–2014

SUMMERWOOD WINERY * * */* * * *
PASO ROBLES $35.00–$85.00

These impressive offerings emerge from the Denner and Lock vineyards, situated on the west side of Paso Robles in the Templeton Gap. Summerwood doubles as a luxury inn.

2005 Diosa Proprietary Red Wine	88	now–2012
2004 Diosa Proprietary Red Wine	92	now–2016
2002 Diosa Proprietary Red Wine	90	now–2010
2001 Diosa Proprietary Red Wine	88	now
2005 GSM	90	now–2013
2004 GSM	91	now–2014
2005 Private Reserve Proprietary Red Wine	88	now–2016
2004 Private Reserve Proprietary Red Wine	90	now–2015
2006 Roussanne/Viognier	87	now–2010
2005 Syrah	88+	now–2015
2001 Syrah	87	now

2004 Syrah James Berry Vineyard	93	now–2018
2004 Syrah Denner Vineyard	89+	now–2013
2002 SZG	90	now

SURH LUCHTEL ★ ★ ★
NAPA $40.00–$48.00

The debut vintage at Surh Luchtel was 1999. They produce around 3,000 cases of small-lot, often single-vineyard wines that deserve considerable attention.

2005 Cabernet Sauvignon Sacrashe Vineyard	91	2010–2020
2001 Cabernet Sauvignon Sacrashe Vineyard	90	now–2011
2005 Mosaique Proprietary Red Wine	90	now–2016
2005 Pinot Noir Garys' Vineyard	89	now–2011
2004 Pinot Noir Garys' Vineyard	92	now–2011

SUTTER HOME ★ ★
NAPA $10.00–$25.00

Purchased by the Trinchero family in 1947, this ghost winery, which was in existence in the late 1800s, became a national success with the birth of the cloyingly sweet White Zinfandel. For the most part, that craze has, fortunately, died, but White Zinfandel is still available from Sutter Home, and if one is going to try it, this is the place to do it. The rest of the portfolio, which includes just about all the varieties planted in California, is distressingly commercial but enormously popular. The McDonald's of wine?

JOSEPH SWAN VINEYARDS ★ ★ ★
DRY CREEK $45.00–$60.00

The late Joseph Swan, one of Dry Creek's pioneers, made one of the region's finest Zinfandels from a small farm on Laguna Road, near Forestville, that he purchased in 1967. He also produced a good Pinot Noir. The first Ravenswood wines were born in Joseph Swan's cellars because of his friendship with Joel Peterson. Swan's son-in-law, Rod Berglund, has run the property since Swan's death, and he still focuses on small quantities of Zinfandels and Pinot Noirs. I have not tasted recent vintages of these wines, but until 2002 quality was somewhat unpredictable, with some splendid efforts offered alongside earthy, overripe, disjointed cuvées.

SWANSON VINEYARDS ★ ★ ★
NAPA $25.00–$75.00

Multimillionaire businessman Clark Swanson started this winery by purchasing some superb vineyards, particularly in Oakville and Carneros. Although there is nothing wrong with them, the wines have not lived up to their early promise. Their finest efforts continue to be a delicious rosé, a stylish Pinot Grigio, a very fine Merlot, and their flagship proprietary red, called Alexis, a Cabernet Sauvignon–based blend from the Oakville vineyards.

2004 Alexis	88	now–2020
2004 Merlot Oakville	85	now–2013

SWITCHBACK RIDGE ★ ★ ★ ★/★ ★ ★ ★ ★
NAPA $60.00–$85.00

Pride Mountain's Robert Foley, the winemaker at this estate, consistently produces teeth-staining, spectacular, immensely concentrated, ageworthy offerings from the Peterson Family Vineyard, located directly across from the Three Palm Vineyard made famous by the Duckhorn Winery. These superb wines are limited in availability as, despite the 100 acres of vineyards, only 20 are in vine.

2005 Cabernet Sauvignon Peterson Family Vineyard	95	now–2022+
2004 Cabernet Sauvignon Peterson Family Vineyard	92	now–2022
2003 Cabernet Sauvignon Peterson Family Vineyard	94	now–2020+
2002 Cabernet Sauvignon Peterson Family Vineyard	96	now–2020
2001 Cabernet Sauvignon Peterson Family Vineyard	98	now–2023
2005 Merlot Peterson Family Vineyard	93	now–2015
2004 Merlot Peterson Family Vineyard	92+	now–2017
2003 Merlot Peterson Family Vineyard	91	now–2013
2002 Merlot Peterson Family Vineyard	92	now–2013
2001 Merlot Peterson Family Vineyard	95	now–2018
2005 Petite Sirah Peterson Family Vineyard	95+	now–2027
2004 Petite Sirah Peterson Family Vineyard	95	now–2027
2003 Petite Sirah Peterson Family Vineyard	92	???
2002 Petite Sirah Peterson Family Vineyard	96	now–2020
2001 Petite Sirah Peterson Family Vineyard	96	now–2020

TABLAS CREEK VINEYARD ★★★★/★★★★★
PASO ROBLES $22.00–$95.00

In partnership with the renowned importer Robert Haas of Vineyard Brands, Tablas Creek is the California outpost of France's Perrin family (of Château Beaucastel fame). They were among the first owners to plant on the steep limestone hillsides west of Highway 101, at elevations that approach 1,600 feet. Much like their French counterparts, these wines possess a distinctive minerality. While Tablas Creek makes some varietal cuvées, their finest wines are their blends, whether white or red.

2006 Antithesis	92	now–2013
2005 Antithesis	91	now–2012
2004 Antithesis	89	now
2005 Côtes de Tablas	90	now
2004 Côtes de Tablas	89	now
2006 Côtes de Tablas Blanc	88	now
2005 Esprit de Beaucastel	93	now–2022
2004 Esprit de Beaucastel	92	now–2020
2002 Esprit de Beaucastel	92+	now–2014+
2006 Esprit de Beaucastel Blanc	94	now–2012
2005 Esprit de Beaucastel Blanc	93	now–2012
2006 Grenache Blanc	89	now
2005 Mourvèdre	87	now
2005 Panoplie	95	now–2022
2004 Panoplie	95	now–2022
2002 Panoplie	95	now–2020
2006 Rosé	90	now
2006 Roussanne	91	now
2005 Syrah	90	now–2015
2006 Vermentino	89	now
2005 Vin de Paille	90	now–2028
2005 Vin de Paille Quintessence	94	now–2028
2006 Viognier	91	now–2010

TALBOTT VINEYARDS ★★★
MONTEREY $18.00–$75.00

After making their fortune in the necktie business, the Talbott family founded this vineyard in 1982. Talbott produces approximately 30,000 cases of Chardonnay as well as small quantities of Pinot Noir. The estate's early cuvées of Chardonnay were among the finest in California, but while the current offerings are good, quality has never reached the level of the early vintages.

2002 Chardonnay Cuvée Cynthia	89	now
2002 Chardonnay Diamond T Estate Cuvée Audrey Unfiltered	90	now
2002 Chardonnay Sleepy Hollow Vineyard	87	now
2004 Logan Chardonnay Sleepy Hollow Vineyard	86	now

TALLEY VINEYARDS ★★★★/★★★★★
EDNA VALLEY $16.00–$75.00

Better known as vegetable farmers in Arroyo Grande than as grape growers, the Talley family, especially Brian Talley, has built a fabulous reputation for their brilliant, Burgundy-style Chardonnays and Pinot Noirs. They essentially transcend anything made from these varieties in this area. Their second label, Bishop's Peak, offers terrific value.

2003 Bishop's Peak Pinot Noir	85	now
2004 Chardonnay Estate	88	now
2004 Chardonnay Oliver's Vineyard	88	now
2004 Chardonnay Rincon Vineyard	91	now–2010
2004 Chardonnay Rosemary's Vineyard	90	now–2010
2005 Pinot Noir Estate	85+?	now–2014
2004 Pinot Noir Estate	89	now–2010
2003 Pinot Noir Estate	90	now–2011
2002 Pinot Noir Estate	89	now
2005 Pinot Noir Rincon Vineyard	90+	???
2004 Pinot Noir Rincon Vineyard	91+	now–2018
2003 Pinot Noir Rincon Vineyard	94	now–2013
2005 Pinot Noir Rosemary's Vineyard	89+	2010–2020
2004 Pinot Noir Rosemary's Vineyard	92+	now–2016
2003 Pinot Noir Rosemary's Vineyard	93	now–2012
2002 Pinot Noir Rosemary's Vineyard	94	now–2014
2005 Pinot Noir Stone Corral	90+	2009–???
2004 Pinot Noir Stone Corral	91+	now–2014
2004 Syrah Bishop's Peak	86	now–2010

TALLULAH ★★★/★★★★
CALIFORNIA $25.00–$40.00

Former wine retailer Ben Davis and his wife, Diane, have partnered with a number of growers, both in California and in Oregon, to produce a bevy of beautiful wines from Rhône varietals, particularly Syrah. Their first releases have been impressive.

2004 Grenache Del Rio Vineyard	89	now
2004 Syrah	90	now–2013
2004 Syrah Bald Mountain Ranch	91	now–2016
2004 Syrah Del Rio Vineyard	91	now–2016

TANDEM ★★★/★★★★
NORTHERN CALIFORNIA $40.00–$60.00

This *négociant* winery boasts the highly regarded Greg La Follette as their winemaker. Tandem focuses on cool-climate sites for Chardonnay and Pinot Noir, with an occasional Zinfandel added to the portfolio. The first releases have all been very good efforts made in a pure, up-front style with an undeniable Burgundian personality allied with the beautiful, ripe fruit of California.

2003 Chardonnay Porter Bass Vineyard	87	now
2004 Chardonnay Kent Ritchie Vineyard	89	now–2010
2004 Chardonnay Sangiacomo Vineyard	87	now–2010
2004 Pinot Noir Auction Block	90+	now–2012
2002 Pinot Noir Auction Block	87+?	now–2011
2004 Pinot Noir Keefer Ranch	89	now–2011
2003 Pinot Noir Keefer Ranch	90	now–2012
2003 Pinot Noir Sangiacomo Vineyard	86?	now–2010
2004 Pinot Noir Silver Pines Vineyard	90	now–2012
2003 Pinot Noir Vanderkamp Vineyard	87	now–2011

LANE TANNER ★★/★★★
SANTA MARIA $25.00–$30.00

The feisty Lane Tanner began making wine in 1984, primarily for the local Hitching Post restaurant in Buellton. Today, she produces nearly 2,000 cases of competent Pinot Noir and Syrah.

2005 Pinot Noir Bien Nacido Vineyard	88	now–2013
2005 Pinot Noir Julia's Vineyard	89	now–2013
2003 Pinot Noir Julia's Vineyard	85	now

TANTARA WINERY ★★★★
SANTA MARIA $30.00–$80.00

With production close to 8,000 cases, this winery, which has been in existence for more than a decade, has built a stunning reputation for beautiful single-vineyard Pinot Noirs, Chardonnays, and Syrahs. Quality is consistently high, and the prices are realistic thanks to the meticulous attention of winemaker-owner Jeff Fink and his partner, Bill Cates.

2005 Chardonnay Bien Nacido Vineyard	88	now
2004 Chardonnay Bien Nacido Vineyard	88	now
2005 Chardonnay Brosseau Vineyard	87	now–2010
2005 Chardonnay Dierberg Vineyard	85?	now
2004 Chardonnay Dierberg Vineyard	90	now
2005 Chardonnay Talley-Rincon Vineyard	89	now–2011
2004 Pinot Noir Bien Nacido–Adobe Vineyard	90	now–2013
2003 Pinot Noir Bien Nacido–Adobe Vineyard	90	now–2011
2002 Pinot Noir Bien Nacido–Adobe Vineyard	90	now–2010
2005 Pinot Noir Bien Nacido Vineyard Old Vine	90	now–2015
2004 Pinot Noir Bien Nacido Vineyard Old Vine	91	now–2012
2005 Pinot Noir Brosseau Vineyard	90	now–2012
2004 Pinot Noir Brosseau Vineyard	90	now–2016
2005 Pinot Noir La Colline Vineyard	89	now–2015
2004 Pinot Noir La Colline Vineyard	88	now
2005 Pinot Noir Dierberg Vineyard	87	now–2013

2004 Pinot Noir Dierberg Vineyard	89	now–2013
2003 Pinot Noir Dierberg Vineyard	89	now–2013
2005 Pinot Noir Evelyn Vineyard	90	now–2015
2004 Pinot Noir Evelyn Vineyard	91	now–2014
2003 Pinot Noir Evelyn Vineyard	91	now–2017
2005 Pinot Noir Gaia Vineyard	89	now–2011
2005 Pinot Noir Garys' Vineyard	91	now–2014
2004 Pinot Noir Garys' Vineyard	90	now–2011
2005 Pinot Noir Pisoni Vineyard	91	now–2013
2004 Pinot Noir Pisoni Vineyard	93	now–2012
2003 Pinot Noir Pisoni Vineyard	91	now–2013
2005 Pinot Noir Rio Vista Vineyard	90	now–2014
2004 Pinot Noir Rio Vista Vineyard	91	now–2012
2003 Pinot Noir Rio Vista Vineyard	91	now
2005 Pinot Noir Sanford & Benedict Vineyard	88	now–2012
2004 Pinot Noir Santa Maria	86	now
2005 Pinot Noir Silacci Vineyard	89	now–2011
2004 Pinot Noir Silacci Vineyard	90	now–2014
2005 Pinot Noir Solomon Hills Vineyard	87	now–2011
2004 Pinot Noir Solomon Hills Vineyard	90	now–2011
2004 Syrah Bien Nacido Vineyard	89+	now–2015

TENSLEY ★ ★ ★ ★
SANTA BARBARA $28.00–$72.00

Proprietor Joe Tensley's stunning Syrahs have quickly propelled this small winery to the fore-front of the Santa Barbara wine scene. Tensley, a former hockey player, made 100 cases of wine in 1998, a production that has grown to over 3,000 cases today. His portfolio consists of single-vineyard Syrahs as well as a few intriguing dry whites. Tensley is among the most promising of the new breed of Rhone Ranger producers in the Santa Barbara area.

2006 Blanc Camp 4 Vineyard	90	now
2005 Blanc Camp 4 Vineyard	90	now
2005 Syrah BMT	95	now–2017
2005 Syrah Colson Canyon Vineyard	94	2009–2021
2004 Syrah Colson Canyon Vineyard	93	now–2016+
2005 Syrah OGT	93	now–2027
2005 Syrah Thompson Vineyard	91+	2009–2024
2004 Syrah Thompson Vineyard	91+	now–2016+
2005 Syrah Three Creek Vineyard	92+	2009–2022
2005 Syrah Tierra Alta Vineyard	91+	2009–2020
2004 Syrah Tierra Alta Vineyard	90+	now–2016
2005 Syrah Turner Vineyard	92	2009–2021

DOMAINE DE LA TERRE ROUGE ★ ★ ★
SIERRA FOOTHILLS $24.00–$75.00

This reliable winery was founded in 1987 by William Easton, who remains the proprietor. The focus is on Rhône-style wines from Sierra Foothills and Amador fruit sources. While they are rarely profound, they are consistently delicious, well made, and fairly priced.

2005 Enigma Proprietary White Wine	87	now
2004 GSM Tête à Tête	86	now–2010
2003 Mourvèdre	86	now

2004 Syrah Ascent	89+	now–2018
2004 Syrah Les Côtes de l'Ouest	86	now–2010
2003 Syrah Les Côtes de l'Ouest	87	now
2004 Syrah High Slopes	86	now–2012
2004 Syrah Sentinel Oak Vineyard Pyramid Block	88	now–2012
2003 Syrah Sentinel Oak Vineyard Pyramid Block	86	now–2011
2003 Tête à Tête	86	now

TESTAROSSA VINEYARDS ***
CENTRAL COAST $36.00–$75.00

This large *négociant* operation started by Rob and Diana Jensen in 1994 focuses on single-vineyard Chardonnays and Pinot Noirs as well as a handful of Syrahs from Chalone, Santa Lucia Highlands, and Santa Maria sites. The wines are all very good, but more similar than dissimilar given the diverse vineyards from which they emerge; my only complaint is that there is not enough differentiation between the various cuvées. The prices are realistic, and the wines are made in an up-front, fruity, moderately oaky style meant for consumption in their first four to six years.

2005 Chardonnay Bien Nacido Vineyard Elder Series	90	now
2005 Chardonnay Brosseau Vineyard	90	now–2010
2004 Chardonnay Brosseau Vineyard	89	now
2005 Chardonnay Castello Vineyard	85	now
2005 Chardonnay Diana's Reserve	89	now–2011
2004 Chardonnay Diana's Reserve	90	now–2010
2005 Chardonnay Rosella's Vineyard	86	now
2005 Chardonnay Sanford & Benedict Vineyard	90	now
2005 Pinot Noir Bien Nacido Vineyard Elder Series	86	now–2010
2003 Pinot Noir Bien Nacido Vineyard Elder Series	89	now
2005 Pinot Noir Brosseau Vineyard	88	now–2011
2004 Pinot Noir Brosseau Vineyard	86	now–2010
2004 Pinot Noir La Cruz Vineyard	85+	now–2011
2004 Pinot Noir Cuvée Niclaire	88	now–2011
2004 Pinot Noir Fritschen Vineyard	86	now
2004 Pinot Noir Garys' Vineyard	86	now–2010
2003 Pinot Noir Garys' Vineyard	89	now
2005 Pinot Noir Graham Family Vineyard	85	now
2005 Pinot Noir Pisoni Vineyard	85	now–2010
2004 Pinot Noir Pisoni Vineyard	88	now–2011
2005 Pinot Noir Rosella's Vineyard	88	now–2012
2005 Pinot Noir Sanford & Benedict Vineyard	88	now–2010
2004 Pinot Noir Schultze Family Vineyard	87+	now–2012
2005 Pinot Noir Sleepy Hollow Vineyard	86	now–2010
2005 Syrah Garys' Vineyard	89	now–2013
2005 Syrah Thompson Vineyard	88	now–2013

SEAN THACKREY ****/*****
NORTHERN CALIFORNIA $24.00–$115.00

This idiosyncratic wine producer has been making wine for as long as I have been writing about it. He does everything with a flair, and the results are some of the more original wines of California. Now in his mid-60s, former San Francisco art dealer Thackrey is best known for his extraordinary Syrah called Orion but also produces some wacky yet delicious blends, such as the nonvintage Pleiades, and a brilliant Petite Sirah called Sirius. These are extraordinarily pure, natural expressions of winemaking . . . primitive in the best sense of the word. Sadly, they are made in limited quantities.

2003 Orion Syrah	95	now–2016?
2002 Orion Syrah	98	now–2020
2001 Orion Syrah	94+	now–2020
N.V. Pleiades XIV	90	now
N.V. Pleiades XIII	90	now
N.V. Pleiades XII	89	now
2001 Sirius Petite Sirah	96	now–2028
2003 Sirius Petite Sirah Eaglepoint Ranch	93	2010–2025+

TITUS VINEYARDS * * */* * * *
NAPA $34.00–$60.00

I have always enjoyed these offerings from a vineyard first acquired in 1967 by Lee and Ruth Titus, who for much of their life grew grapes for such wineries as Charles Krug, Beaulieu, and Pine Ridge. Their sons, Peter and Paul, now make these noteworthy, character-filled efforts, which are fairly priced. One would be hard-pressed to find a better Cabernet Franc from California than the offering from Titus Vineyards.

2005 Cabernet Franc	88	now–2015
2004 Cabernet Franc	90	now–2015
2002 Cabernet Franc	89	now–2012
2005 Cabernet Sauvignon	89	now–2017
2004 Cabernet Sauvignon	90	now–2017
2004 Cabernet Sauvignon Reserve	90	now–2017
2003 Lot 1 Proprietary Red Wine	92	2011–2026
2001 Lot 1 Proprietary Red Wine	90	now–2013
2004 Petite Sirah	91+	2009–2020

PHILIP TOGNI * * * * *
NAPA $90.00–$160.00

This artisanal producer tucked away on the steep hillsides of Spring Mountain continues to fashion some of the most concentrated, inky Cabernet Sauvignons in California. Togni, assisted by his daughter, Lisa, boasts an extraordinary résumé, having produced outstanding wines at Chalone in the mid-1960s and Chappellet in 1969. The first vintages of his estate wines from the early 1980s remain extraordinary, and this may be the Château Latour of Napa Valley. A little-known treasure at this estate is the sweet dessert wine made from Black Muscat called Ca Togni.

2002 Ca Togni	94	now–2015
2001 Ca Togni	96	now–2017+
2006 Cabernet Sauvignon Estate	94–96	now–2035
2005 Cabernet Sauvignon Estate	92+	now–2027+
2004 Cabernet Sauvignon Estate	95	2012–2040
2003 Cabernet Sauvignon Estate	95	2013–2043
2002 Cabernet Sauvignon Estate	89	now–2015
2001 Cabernet Sauvignon Estate	96	now–2028
2002 Cabernet Sauvignon Tanbark Hill	89	now–2019
2001 Cabernet Sauvignon Tanbark Hill	91	2010–2025

MARIMAR TORRES ✷✷✷
SONOMA $35.00–$50.00

The dynamic daughter of Spain's well-known Torres family, Marimar planted 80 acres of vines in Sonoma's Sebastopol area, focusing on Chardonnay and Pinot Noir. Some acreage from the Sonoma Coast has been added, and the vineyards are farmed organically. Quality is very good but rarely exceptional.

2006 Chardonnay Acero	86	now
2005 Chardonnay Don Miguel Vineyard	87	now
2004 Pinot Noir Donna Margarita	88	now–2012
2005 Pinot Noir Earthquake Block	90	now–2013

TREFETHEN ✷✷
NAPA $30.00–$50.00

The Trefethens have owned one of the largest vineyards in southern Napa Valley since the late 1960s, a 650-acre tract producing over 100,000 cases of Chardonnay, Riesling, and Cabernet Sauvignon. The wines are straightforward, somewhat austere, and, for lack of a better descriptor, dull.

TRENTADUE WINERY ✷✷✷
SONOMA $14.00–$48.00

This winery consistently delivers excellent value and good wines at prices that reflect a certain humility and respect for consumers. One of their finest bargains is their proprietary blend called Old Patch Red.

2004 Merlot	87	now–2015
2003 Merlot	89	now–2010
2005 Old Patch Proprietary Red Wine	87	now
2003 Old Patch Proprietary Red Wine	89	now–2010
2004 Petite Sirah	88	now–2017
2002 Petite Sirah	90	now–2019
2001 Petite Sirah	90	now–2015
2002 La Storia Meritage	89	now–2015
2003 La Storia Petite Sirah	90+	now–2022
2003 La Storia Zinfandel	88	now
2002 La Storia Zinfandel	90	now
2001 La Storia Zinfandel	90	now

TRESPASS VINEYARD ✷✷✷
NAPA $38.00–$54.00

A ghost winery from the 1800s has been resurrected and now features tasty Cabernet Franc and Cabernet Sauvignon made by Kirk Venge, the son of Nils Venge. Production from this vineyard located on the back streets of St. Helena is limited to fewer than 1,000 cases of wine per year. These are very promising efforts.

2004 Cabernet Franc	89	now–2015
2003 Cabernet Franc	88	now–2011
2002 Cabernet Franc	89	now–2014
2004 Cabernet Sauvignon	90	now–2016
2003 Cabernet Sauvignon	88+	now–2017
2002 Cabernet Sauvignon	90	now–2015

TRUCHARD VINEYARDS ★ ★ ★
CARNEROS $25.00–$28.00

Two of the pioneers in the Carneros region, Tony and Joanne Truchard were successful grape growers who started their own estate winery in 1989. The Truchard offerings are fruit-forward, somewhat superficial but tasty wines that are ideal for near-term consumption.

2001 Pinot Noir	88	now
2003 Roussanne Estate	88	now
2003 Syrah Estate	88	now–2011
2001 Syrah Estate	90	now
2001 Zinfandel	88	now

TURLEY WINE CELLARS ★ ★ ★ ★ ★
CALIFORNIA $28.00–$45.00

California's, and hence the world's, premier Zinfandel specialist, Larry Turley put Zinfandel back on center stage with his emphasis on accessing and exploiting old vine, often forgotten parcels of Zinfandel planted throughout central and northern California. Combined with minimalist winemaking, he built Turley Wine Cellars into a showcase for the fruit, power, and intensity of Zinfandel made from low yields and historic sites. Production runs about 15,000 cases of brilliant wines that are as good as Zinfandel can be. They also make a few curiosities, including some incredibly long-lived (20 to 30 years) Petite Syrahs, and more recently, a Charbono, Grenache, and Roussanne. This is winemaking at its finest.

2006 Charbono Tofanelli Vineyard	88–90	now–2010
2005 Charbono Tofanelli Vineyard	87	now
2004 Charbono Tofanelli Vineyard	90	now–2010
2003 Charbono Tofanelli Vineyard	90	now
2006 Grenache Pesenti Vineyard	87–88	now–2012
2005 Grenache Pesenti Vineyard	87	now–2010
2005 Petite Syrah	90	2010–2020
2002 Petite Syrah	93	2011–2030+
2006 Petite Syrah Hayne Vineyard	93–96	2015–2030
2005 Petite Syrah Hayne Vineyard	93	2012–2037
2004 Petite Syrah Hayne Vineyard	97	2014–2038
2003 Petite Syrah Hayne Vineyard	94	2015–2040
2002 Petite Syrah Hayne Vineyard	94	2012–2032
2006 Petite Syrah Library Vineyard	91–94	2010–2030
2005 Petite Syrah Library Vineyard	92	2012–2038
2004 Petite Syrah Library Vineyard	97	2012–2035
2003 Petite Syrah Library Vineyard	93	now–2025
2006 Petite Syrah Pesenti Vineyard	93–95	2011–2035
2006 Petite Syrah Rattlesnake Ridge	90–92	2015–2040
2005 Petite Syrah Rattlesnake Ridge	92?	2017–2035
2004 Petite Syrah Rattlesnake Ridge	97	2012–2030
2003 Petite Syrah Rattlesnake Ridge	93?	2015–2050
2006 Petite Syrah Turley Estate	89–91	2015–2030
2005 Petite Syrah Turley Estate	89?	2011–2025
2004 Petite Syrah Turley Estate	94	2012–2025
2003 Petite Syrah Turley Estate	92	now–2020
2006 Roussanne Rattlesnake Ridge	90	now
2006 Zinfandel Cedarman Vineyard	90–92	now–2013

2005 Zinfandel Cedarman Vineyard	91	now
2006 Zinfandel Dogtown Vineyard	87–89	now–2011
2005 Zinfandel Dogtown Vineyard	87	now–2012
2004 Zinfandel Dogtown Vineyard	88	now–2012
2003 Zinfandel Dogtown Vineyard	92	now–2010
2006 Zinfandel Dragon Vineyard	91–93	now–2015
2005 Zinfandel Dragon Vineyard	91	now
2004 Zinfandel Dragon Vineyard	94	now–2013
2003 Zinfandel Dragon Vineyard	94	now–2013
2005 Zinfandel Duarte Vineyard	90	now
2004 Zinfandel Duarte Vineyard	92	now–2012
2003 Zinfandel Duarte Vineyard	87	now–2010
2006 Zinfandel Dusi Vineyard	91–93	now–2013
2005 Zinfandel Dusi Vineyard	89	now
2004 Zinfandel Dusi Vineyard	90	now–2013
2003 Zinfandel Dusi Vineyard	90	now–2012
2006 Zinfandel Grist Vineyard	90–92	now–2013
2005 Zinfandel Grist Vineyard	90	now–2012
2004 Zinfandel Grist Vineyard	94	now–2012
2003 Zinfandel Grist Vineyard	91	now–2010
2006 Zinfandel Hayne Vineyard	90–93	now–2014
2005 Zinfandel Hayne Vineyard	91	now–2013
2004 Zinfandel Hayne Vineyard	95	now–2015
2003 Zinfandel Hayne Vineyard	95	now–2015+
2006 Zinfandel Juvenile	88–89	now–2010
2005 Zinfandel Juvenile	84	now
2004 Zinfandel Juvenile	89	now–2011
2006 Zinfandel Mead Ranch Atlas Peak	88–91	now–2012
2005 Zinfandel Mead Ranch Atlas Peak	89	now–2012
2004 Zinfandel Mead Ranch Atlas Peak	89	now
2003 Zinfandel Mead Ranch Atlas Peak	91	now–2011
2006 Zinfandel Moore Earthquake Vineyard	88–90	now–2013
2005 Zinfandel Moore Earthquake Vineyard	92	now–2015
2004 Zinfandel Moore Earthquake Vineyard	92	now–2015
2003 Zinfandel Moore Earthquake Vineyard	94	now–2015
2006 Zinfandel Old Vines	88–90	now–2011
2005 Zinfandel Old Vines	91	now–2012
2004 Zinfandel Old Vines	91	now
2006 Zinfandel Pesenti Vineyard	91–94	now–2015
2005 Zinfandel Pesenti Vineyard	92	now
2004 Zinfandel Pesenti Vineyard	92	now–2015
2003 Zinfandel Pesenti Vineyard	90	now–2011
2006 Zinfandel Rancho Burro	87–89?	now
2004 Zinfandel Rancho Burro	93	now–2012
2003 Zinfandel Rancho Burro	91	now–2011
2004 Zinfandel Rancho Escondido	89	now–2010
2006 Zinfandel Rattlesnake Ridge	89–91+	now–2012
2005 Zinfandel Rattlesnake Ridge	90	now–2013
2004 Zinfandel Rattlesnake Ridge	92	now–2012
2003 Zinfandel Rattlesnake Ridge	93	now–2011
2006 Zinfandel Salvador Vineyard	90–92	now–2014

2006 Zinfandel Tofanelli Vineyard	90–93	now–2013
2005 Zinfandel Tofanelli Vineyard	88	now–2011
2004 Zinfandel Tofanelli Vineyard	89	now–2010
2003 Zinfandel Tofanelli Vineyard	94	now–2012
2005 Zinfandel Turley Estate	86	now
2004 Zinfandel Turley Estate	91	now–2010
2003 Zinfandel Turley Estate	92	now–2010
2006 Zinfandel Ueberroth Vineyard	92–95	now–2014
2005 Zinfandel Ueberroth Vineyard	92	now–2017
2004 Zinfandel Ueberroth Vineyard	92	now–2014
2003 Zinfandel Ueberroth Vineyard	89	now–2013
2002 Zinfandel Ueberroth Vineyard	93	now–2010
2006 Zinfandel Vineyard 101	91–93	now–2012
2005 Zinfandel Vineyard 101	90	now–2011
2004 Zinfandel Vineyard 101	95	now–2013
2003 Zinfandel Vineyard 101	92	now–2011

2480 HOLLYWOOD & VINE * * * *
NAPA $45.00–$100.00

This luxury-priced *négociant* operation boasts a brilliant Chardonnay and superb Cabernet Sauvignon, both made in limited quantities. The gifted winemaking consultant Celia Masy-czek is in charge of these cuvées.

TWOMEY CELLARS * * *
NAPA $65.00

The Duncan family, which has a large interest in the Silver Oak Cellars, also runs this winery dedicated to making Merlot. From a vineyard in Soda Canyon, in southeastern Napa Valley, they produce a classic Napa Merlot as well as a Pinot Noir from a small Russian River site. The first several vintages of the latter wine were uninteresting. A Sauvignon Blanc has recently been added to the portfolio. For the most part, the high prices asked are not justified by what is in the bottle.

2004 Merlot	87?	now–2011
2003 Merlot	87	now–2011
2002 Merlot	94	now–2020
2001 Merlot	90	now–2012

UNTI VINEYARDS * * *
DRY CREEK $19.00–$35.00

In 1990, this 25-acre vineyard was planted with Zinfandel, Syrah, Sangiovese, Petite Sirah, and Grenache. The winery was founded in 1997, and there is also an estate vineyard of 35 acres planted with similar varieties as well as Mourvèdre, Barbera, Montepulciano, Picpoul, and Vermentino. Production is just under 7,000 cases. These are competent, pleasant, reasonably priced offerings lacking only dimension and depth.

2004 Grenache Estate	86	now
2003 Grenache Estate	85	now
2002 Petite Sirah Estate	88	now–2014
2003 Syrah Estate	85	now
2003 Syrah Estate Benchland Reserve	88	now–2013
2002 Syrah Estate Benchland Reserve	86	now
2002 Syrah Estate Petit Frères	86	now

VARNER ★ ★ ★ ★ ★
SANTA CRUZ MOUNTAINS $45.00–$55.00

One of the most impressive wineries situated in the cool, high elevations of the Santa Cruz Mountains, Varner makes low-tech wines from small yields, which are bottled with neither fining nor filtration.

2005 Chardonnay Amphitheater Block	94	now–2013
2004 Chardonnay Amphitheater Block	93	now–2012
2003 Chardonnay Amphitheater Block	90	now–2011
2005 Chardonnay B Block	94	now–2015
2004 Chardonnay B Block	91	now–2014
2003 Chardonnay B Block	94	now–2013
2006 Chardonnay Fox Glove	90	now
2005 Chardonnay Home Vineyard	95	now–2017
2004 Chardonnay Home Vineyard	95	now–2014
2003 Chardonnay Home Vineyard	92	now–2012
2004 Chardonnay Neely	95	now–2012
2003 Chardonnay Neeley	90	now–2012
2005 Chardonnay Neely Holly's Cuvée	92	now–2017
2005 Foxglove	90	now–2010
2004 Pinot Noir Hidden Blocks	89	now–2013
2003 Pinot Noir Hidden Blocks	90	now–2013
2002 Pinot Noir Hidden Blocks	88	now

VÉRITÉ ★ ★ ★ ★ ★
SONOMA $150.00

One of the shining stars in Jess Jackson's firmament, Vérité produces three distinctively different wines from top vineyards. The talented Bordelais winemaker Pierre Seillan fashions the Pomerol-styled La Muse, Pauillac-styled La Joie, and St.-Émilion-style Le Désir, which are undeniably three of the finest wines being made in California.

2005 Le Désir	94–96+	2015–2030
2004 Le Désir	94+	2010–2030
2003 Le Désir	94+	2009–2040
2002 Le Désir	97	now–2020
2001 Le Désir	95	now–2025
2005 La Joie	96–98	2015–2045
2004 La Joie	93+	2011–2026+
2003 La Joie	95+	2010–2035
2002 La Joie	98	now–2025
2001 La Joie	96	now–2020+
2005 La Muse	89–91+	2015–2028
2004 La Muse	93	now–2022+
2003 La Muse	93	now–2025
2002 La Muse	94	now–2020+
2001 La Muse	94	now–2020+

JEAN-LOUIS VERMEIL ★ ★ ★ ★
NAPA $85.00

This is the personal wine project of Super Bowl–winning, renowned NFL coach Dick Vermeil. His family has French origins, having moved to San Francisco in late 1800s, and Vermeil was raised in Napa Valley. His initial dive into the wine world is impressive, which goes against the rule of thumb that celebrities rarely achieve anything special in the world of wine.

2003 Cabernet Sauvignon Frediani Vineyard	90	now–2018
2002 Cabernet Sauvignon Frediani Vineyard	93	now–2020

VICE VERSA ★★★★
NAPA $35.00–$90.00

This small boutique operation is the result of proprietor Patrice Breton, a former software entrepreneur, following his dream. After getting good advice from Paul Hobbs, his first few vintages have been impressive.

2004 Cabernet Sauvignon Le Petit Vice	90	now–2015
2004 Cabernet Sauvignon Vice Versa	93	now–2022
2003 Cabernet Sauvignon Vice Versa	90	2010–2025

VILLA CREEK CELLARS ★★★★
PASO ROBLES $12.00–$55.00

Cris and JoAnn Cherry, established restaurateurs in Paso Robles, have also developed some remarkable vineyard contracts. They fashion some of the most interesting and beautifully made wines of the region. These wines are realistically priced, creative blends that satisfy the most demanding connoisseur.

2005 Avenger	93	now–2015
2004 Avenger	89	now–2014
2002 Avenger	94	now–2011
2005 Bête Noire	92	now–2015
2002 Garnacha James Berry Vineyard	91	now–2010
2005 Garnacha Denner Vineyard	91	now–2011
2004 Garnacha Denner Vineyard	91	now–2011
2005 High Road James Berry Vineyard	92	now–2014
2004 High Road James Berry Vineyard	93	now–2013
2002 High Road James Berry Vineyard	94	now–2011
2005 Mas de Maha	93	now–2012
2004 Mas de Maha	91	now–2011
2006 Proprietary White	86	now
2005 Willow Creek Cuvée	90	now–2011
2004 Willow Creek Cuvée	92	now–2014
2002 Willow Creek Cuvée	90	now

VINEYARD 29 ★★★★/★★★★★
NAPA $50.00–$175.00

The impressive talents of viticulturist David Abreu and winemaker-consultant Philippe Melka have turned Vineyard 29, owned by Chuck and Anne McMinn, into a bright new star of Napa. There are essentially two levels of wine: the estate cuvées, which come from the Aida and Vineyard 29 sites, and the *négociant* line of wines, which are represented by 3,000 or so cases of their Napa Cabernet Sauvignon called Cru. The least-well-known offering is their brilliant Sauvignon Blanc.

2006 Aida Proprietary Red Wine	92–94	2009–2024+
2005 Aida Proprietary Red Wine	91+	now–2022
2003 Aida Proprietary Red Wine	96	now–2020+
2002 Aida Proprietary Red Wine	95	now–2020

2001 Aida Proprietary Red Wine	91+	now–2016
2006 Cru Proprietary Red Wine	90–92	now–2017+
2005 Cru Proprietary Red Wine	92	now–2022
2004 Cru Proprietary Red Wine	91	now–2018
2006 Sauvignon Blanc	90–92	now–2012
2005 Sauvignon Blanc	94	now–2014
2004 Sauvignon Blanc	92	now–2013
2006 Vineyard 29 Cabernet Sauvignon	93–95	now–2022+
2005 Vineyard 29 Cabernet Sauvignon	95	now–2022
2004 Vineyard 29 Cabernet Sauvignon	95	now–2022
2003 Vineyard 29 Cabernet Sauvignon	95	now–2020+
2002 Vineyard 29 Cabernet Sauvignon	94	now–2017
2006 Zinfandel Aida	91–93	now–2014
2005 Zinfandel Aida	90	now–2014
2004 Zinfandel Aida	94	now–2013
2002 Zinfandel Aida	93	now–2010

VISION CELLARS ★★★/★★★★
CALIFORNIA $28.00–$50.00

Even though winemaker Mac McDonald's operation is north of Windsor, his emphasis is clearly on single-vineyard Pinot Noirs from Central Coast vineyard sites. However, things may be changing with his wine from Marin County. He also turns out a very fine white wine, and appears to be adding more single-vineyard Pinots to his portfolio each year.

2006 Pinot Noir Las Alturas Vineyard	89+	now–2013
2006 Pinot Noir Garys' Vineyard	90	now–2013
2004 Pinot Noir Garys' Vineyard	90	now–2011
2003 Pinot Noir Garys' Vineyard	85	now
2004 Pinot Noir Rosella's Vineyard	89	now–2013
2003 Pinot Noir Rosella's Vineyard	87	now
2004 Pinot Noir Santa Rita Hills	89	now–2010
2006 Pinot Noir Sonoma	88	now–2012
2006 Proprietary White Wine (Sauvignon Blanc and Pinot Gris)	88	now

KENNETH VOLK VINEYARDS ★★★
SANTA BARBARA $24.00–$48.00

After selling Wild Horse Winery, Ken Volk began his personal project dedicated to wines primarily from the Santa Maria Valley. The excellent debut releases have all been significantly more interesting than what he produced at Wild Horse.

2004 Chardonnay Bien Nacido Vineyard	87	now
2004 Chardonnay Sierra Madre Vineyard	88	now
2004 Pinot Noir Garey Vineyard	85	now
2004 Pinot Noir Santa Barbara	90	now–2013
2004 Pinot Noir Sierra Madre Vineyard	91	now–2011

VOLKER EISELE FAMILY ESTATE ★★★
NAPA $25.00–$50.00

The "other" Eisele, not to be confused with the Eisele Vineyard, owned by Araujo, this family owns 60 acres of vines in the cool-climate Chiles Valley. They produce three wines: an interesting blend of Sémillon and Sauvignon Blanc called Gemini, an equal-part blend of Cabernet Sauvignon, Cabernet Franc, and Merlot called Terzetto, and an estate Cabernet Sauvignon.

2004 Cabernet Sauvignon Estate	89+	now–2020
2002 Cabernet Sauvignon Estate	89	now–2017
2006 Gemini Proprietary White Wine	89	now
2004 Gemini Proprietary White Wine	87	now
2003 Terzetto Proprietary Red Wine	90	now–2017
2002 Terzetto Proprietary Red Wine	90	now–2022

VON STRASSER * * *
NAPA $50.00–$100.00

A dizzying array of single-vineyard Cabernet Sauvignons emerge from this vineyard on Diamond Mountain that was purchased by Rudy Von Strasser in 1990. The wines tend to be very tannic, bordering on rustic. Nevertheless, there is good potential if the tannin levels can be managed.

2004 Cabernet Franc Marcellini Vineyard	88	now–2015
2004 Cabernet Sauvignon Diamond Mountain	88	now–2015
2004 Cabernet Sauvignon Estate	89	now–2016
2004 Cabernet Sauvignon Post Vineyard	89+	2010–2025
2004 Cabernet Sauvignon Rainin Vineyard	89	2010–2023
2004 Proprietary Red Reserve Diamond Mountain	89+	2011–1026+
2004 Proprietary Red Sori Bricco Vineyard	88?	now–2019

WESTERLY VINEYARDS * * * *
SANTA YNEZ $22.00–$30.00

This 85-acre vineyard, located in the southeastern corner of Santa Ynez Valley, is beginning to make some serious wines under the guidance of winemaker Seth Kunin (who has also produced impressive efforts under his own name).

2003 Syrah	88	now–2014
2003 Syrah Estate Reserve Côte Blonde	95+	now–2017
2006 Viognier Estate	89	now
2005 Viognier Estate	91	now
2005 W Blanc Estate	88	now–2010
2004 W Blanc Estate	90+	now–2011

WHITCRAFT WINERY * * *
SANTA MARIA $45.00

Longtime Santa Barbara resident Chris Whitcraft produces handcrafted, earthy Pinot Noirs from some of the renowned Bien Nacido Vineyard's finest blocks. Quality is somewhat irregular, but at their finest, the wines are very good.

2005 Pinot Noir	87	now
2005 Pinot Noir Bien Nacido Vineyard N Block	88	now–2013
2004 Pinot Noir Bien Nacido Vineyard N Block	88	now–2013
2002 Pinot Noir Bien Nacido Vineyard N Block	84?	now
2005 Pinot Noir Bien Nacido Vineyard Q Block	90	now–2015
2004 Pinot Noir Bien Nacido Vineyard Q Block	89+	now–2016+
2002 Pinot Noir Bien Nacido Vineyard Q Block	86	now
2005 Pinot Noir Melville Vineyard	83?	now

WHITE ROCK VINEYARDS ★ ★ ★/★ ★ ★ ★
NAPA $44.00

This ghost winery was established in the late 1800s and resurrected in 1977, with a 36-acre vineyard planted in 1979. White Rock Vineyards turns out elegant, Bordeaux-style reds as well as a Burgundy-style Chardonnay. The wines are relatively restrained by the standards of northern California, but they are impeccably well made and pure.

2003 Cabernet Sauvignon Napa	90	now–2018
2005 Chardonnay Napa	89	now–2012
2002 Claret	88	now–2015

WHITEHALL LANE WINERY ★ ★ ★
NAPA $30.00–$65.00

Owned since 1993 by San Francisco's Leonardini family, Whitehall Lane turns out oaky but solidly constructed, fleshy Cabernet Sauvignon as well as Chardonnay, Pinot Noir, and Sauvignon Blanc.

2004 Cabernet Sauvignon Napa	86	now–2015
2004 Cabernet Sauvignon Reserve Silver Anniversary	88	now–2016
2005 Chardonnay Carneros	87	now
2004 Merlot Napa	84	now

WILD HORSE WINERY ★ ★
CENTRAL COAST $15.00–$25.00

Sold by its founder, Ken Volk, to Peak Wines International in 2003, production at this estate has jumped to 150,000-plus cases. While the wines have been enormously successful commercially, they are essentially superficial, gently fruity, and overall rather innocuous.

J. WILKES ★ ★ ★
SANTA BARBARA $38.00

This small artisanal operation is dedicated to single-vineyard Pinot Noirs, primarily from the Bien Nacido Vineyard. They also produce a small amount of Pinot Blanc. Wilkes previously worked for 18 years at Bien Nacido, marketing the vineyard and the grapes, so he should have an insider's knowledge of the finest plots of that enormous life.

2005 Pinot Noir Bien Nacido Vineyard Block Q	90	now–2015
2005 Pinot Noir Bien Nacido Vineyard Hillside	89	now–2013
2003 Pinot Noir Solomon Hills Vineyard	87	now
2005 Pinot Noir Solomon Hills Vineyard Block 8	88	now–2011

WILLIAMS-SELYEM ★ ★ ★ ★
NORTHERN CALIFORNIA $35.00–$85.00

Among the first cult Pinot Noir producers in California, partners Bert Williams and Ed Selyem made a series of distinctive, artisanal, unfined, and unfiltered Pinot Noirs in the 1980s and built a huge following for their wines, only to sell the winery in 1998 to John Dyson. Since then, Bob Cabral, who has a nearly identical winemaking philosophy, has been making the wines, and little has changed in either their style or consistently high quality. There is a dizzying array of Pinot Noirs with relatively small productions, ranging from 100 cases for some of the single-vineyard cuvées to 700 cases for others. Their biggest-production Pinot Noir is the Westside Road Neighbors. The best-kept secret emerging from this winery may be the exquisite Chardonnays and Zinfandels being fashioned by Cabral. The overall style of the Williams-

Selyem Pinots remains one of elegant, high-acid wines that can age for 10 to 15 or more years.

2006 Chardonnay Allen Vineyard	88–90	now–2011
2005 Chardonnay Allen Vineyard	92	now–2014
2004 Chardonnay Allen Vineyard	92	now–2013
2006 Chardonnay Hawk Hill Vineyard	87–89	now–2011
2005 Chardonnay Hawk Hill Vineyard	95	now–2014
2004 Chardonnay Hawk Hill Vineyard	92	now–2013
2006 Chardonnay Heintz Vineyard	85–87	now
2005 Chardonnay Heintz Vineyard	94	now–2014
2004 Chardonnay Heintz Vineyard	93	now–2011
2006 Chardonnay Russian River (possibly Drake Vineyard)	91–94	now–2010
2005 Chardonnay Russian River	93	now–2011
2004 Chardonnay Russian River	91	now–2010
2006 Pinot Noir Allen Vineyard	88–90	now–2015
2005 Pinot Noir Allen Vineyard	89+	now–2013
2004 Pinot Noir Allen Vineyard	89	now–2018
2003 Pinot Noir Allen Vineyard	92	now–2013
2002 Pinot Noir Allen Vineyard	93	now–2015
2001 Pinot Noir Allen Vineyard	91	now–2015
2006 Pinot Noir Bucher Vineyard	87–89	now–2014
2005 Pinot Noir Bucher Vineyard	88	now–2012
2004 Pinot Noir Bucher Vineyard	88	now–2018
2003 Pinot Noir Bucher Vineyard	87	now–2013
2006 Pinot Noir Coastlands Vineyard	92–94	now–2017
2005 Pinot Noir Coastlands Vineyard	90+	now–2011
2004 Pinot Noir Coastlands Vineyard	91	now–2018
2006 Pinot Noir Ferrington Vineyard	90–93	now–2013
2005 Pinot Noir Ferrington Vineyard	90	now–2012
2004 Pinot Noir Ferrington Vineyard	89	now–2018
2006 Pinot Noir Flax Vineyard	90–92	now–2017
2005 Pinot Noir Flax Vineyard	93	now–2016
2004 Pinot Noir Flax Vineyard	90	now–2018
2006 Pinot Noir Hirsch Vineyard	90–92	now–2017
2005 Pinot Noir Hirsch Vineyard	93	2011–2026
2004 Pinot Noir Hirsch Vineyard	92	now–2016
2006 Pinot Noir Peay Vineyard	86–89	now–2017
2005 Pinot Noir Peay Vineyard	90	now–2022
2004 Pinot Noir Peay Vineyard	88	now–2018
2006 Pinot Noir Precious Mountain	91–94	now–2017
2005 Pinot Noir Precious Mountain	90+	now–2018
2004 Pinot Noir Precious Mountain	89+	now–2018
2006 Pinot Noir Rochioli Riverblock Vineyard	90–92	now–2015
2005 Pinot Noir Rochioli Riverblock Vineyard	90	now–2013
2004 Pinot Noir Rochioli Riverblock Vineyard	89	now–2018
2006 Pinot Noir Weir Vineyard	86–88	now–2012
2005 Pinot Noir Weir Vineyard	89	now–2015
2004 Pinot Noir Weir Vineyard	88	now–2018
2006 Pinot Noir Westside Road Neighbors	91–93	now–2013

2005 Pinot Noir Westside Road Neighbors	91	now–2012
2004 Pinot Noir Westside Road Neighbors	87	now–2012
2003 Pinot Noir Westside Road Neighbors	91	now–2013
2006 Zinfandel Bacigalupi Vineyard	91–93	now–2013
2005 Zinfandel Bacigalupi Vineyard	92	now
2004 Zinfandel Bacigalupi Vineyard	93	now
2006 Zinfandel Feeney Vineyard	92–94	now–2013
2005 Zinfandel Feeney Vineyard	92	now
2004 Zinfandel Feeney Vineyard	87	now–2014
2006 Zinfandel Forchini Vineyard	92–94	now–2014
2005 Zinfandel Forchini Vineyard	91	now
2004 Zinfandel Forchini Vineyard	90	now–2010
2003 Zinfandel Forchini Vineyard	92	now–2013

WINTER * * * *
NAPA $100.00

There are approximately 650 cases per year of these 100% Cabernet Sauvignon offerings from proprietors Rob and Tamara Winter. Produced from David Abreu's famed Madrona Ranch vineyard located at the base of Spring Mountain, they are impressive efforts meant to age for 15 or more years.

2006 Cabernet Sauvignon	90–93	now–2022
2005 Cabernet Sauvignon	95+	now–2027
2004 Cabernet Sauvignon	95	2010–2025

WOLF FAMILY VINEYARDS * * *
NAPA $32.00–$78.00

Karen Culler is the force behind these tasty, Bordeaux-style offerings as well as an excellent Sauvignon Blanc.

2004 Cabernet Franc	93	now–2020
2004 Cabernet Sauvignon	92	2010–2030
2003 Cabernet Sauvignon	94	now–2022
2002 Cabernet Sauvignon	96	now–2020
2003 Cabernet Sauvignon Phaedrus	89	now–2017
2003 Meritage	91	now–2019
2002 Meritage	92	now–2015
2006 Sauvignon Blanc	89	now

ZACA MESA WINERY AND VINEYARDS * */* * *
SANTA BARBARA $17.00–$50.00

Occasionally, excellent values emerge from this Santa Barbara winery, especially their Z Cuvée, which is Santa Barbara's take on a good French Côtes du Rhône. Prices are very fair.

2004 Syrah Black Bear Block Estate	86?	now
2003 Syrah Black Bear Block Estate	90	now–2015
2002 Syrah Black Bear Block Estate	90	now–2014
2001 Syrah Black Bear Block Estate	87	now
2004 Syrah Estate	85	now–2010
2003 Syrah Estate	88	now–2012
2002 Syrah Estate	85	now

2001 Syrah Estate	84	now
2001 Syrah The Mesa O & N	90	now–2012
2003 Z Cuvée Estate	88	now
2003 Z Three Estate	90	now–2013

ZD ★★★
NAPA $45.00–$50.00

This winery was founded in 1969 by two aircraft engineers whose initials were Z and D, Gino Zepponi and Norman de Leuze. ZD was a hot commodity for Chardonnay, as it was one of the first estates to realize the potential of the Winery Lake Vineyard in Carneros. Their full-throttle, oaky Chardonnays became enormously popular. While the style has not changed, one wonders whether the wine is as good as it was 10 or 15 years ago. The estate now produces a Reserve Chardonnay as well as some Pinot Noir, Merlot, and Cabernet Sauvignon, all attractive rather than inspiring.

[east of the
west coast]

A CONTINENT'S WORTH OF LARGELY OVERLOOKED WINES

The growth in acreage and fame of California, Oregon, and Washington State since the 1970s is one of the major worldwide wine stories. And in the past two decades, there has been phenomenal growth in acreage and in the number of wineries across the rest of the U.S. and Canada. In many instances, this boom involved a revival of long-dormant winegrowing traditions. The banks of the Ohio River were home to the earliest manifestation of viticulture in the United States that could in any way be called an "industry," until savage outbreaks of mildew and fungus destroyed it in the mid-19th century. By the end of that century, a flourishing wine culture had emerged on the shores and islands of Lake Erie, only to be wiped out (as was most U.S. viticulture) by the grand experiment of prohibition. Grape growing along the shores of Lake Michigan fared better, thanks to the teetotaling Dr. Welch and the "unfermented wine" that brought fame and considerable fortune to him and to the Concord grape. Today, Ohio and Michigan are home to active wine revivals. Winegrowing in the American Southwest began in Spanish colonial times—wine having been an essential part of the Eucharist—and only really died out with the Eighteenth Amendment to the U.S. Constitution. Today, the remarkably successful sparkling wine producer Gruet in New Mexico comes upon vestiges of ancient vineyards as they expand, and Texas vies with Virginia as the fifth-largest U.S. wine producer. Two decades ago—after having sustained roughly a century of sporadic viticulture—the Okanagan Valley was home to 13 wineries but virtually unknown outside of British Columbia. Today, the number is more than ten times that, and few who have tasted even a small sampling from the better among them will doubt this region's importance and potential. But not every burgeoning North American wine region represents a revival of ancient roots; some appear to have come from nowhere. Two decades ago there was one winery

[1285]

in Colorado. Today there are more than 50 such high-altitude outposts of viticultural exploration. The number of wineries in North Carolina has more than tripled since the turn of the most recent century, and the former tobacco-growing Yadkin Valley has become an official American Viticultural Area (AVA).

The explosive growth of interest in wine across America, of wine tourism, and in the number of American wineries to beyond what even the most fervent partisans of a generation ago could have imagined, are all trends that may or may not continue. We cannot assume that a wine industry will be sustainable long-term in all of the many places where grapes are today replacing other unprofitable (or, in the case of tobacco, discredited) crops. Nor will by any means all of these wines merit the attention of consumers accustomed to excellent offerings from Europe, Australia, or the U.S. West Coast.

The economic challenges to wineries and growing regions east of the West Coast are daunting—indeed, the most obvious challenge is the one just mentioned: steep competition from around the world. Tourists and local partisans alone are unlikely to keep a fledgling regional wine industry in the black, much less permit the sorts of investment necessary if the aim is to grow wines of genuinely high quality, an endeavor notoriously labor intensive and subject to nature's whims. Support of state and local government, too, is critical. And, in the end, there has to be some "there" there: a synergy of vine and microclimate to render excellence possible, a few intrepid pioneers to show the way, and a vinous message that can reach a wide enough consumer base. All of these factors explain, for instance, the amazing degree of success experienced by the State of Virginia. Its tourist industry is truly immense, and wherever there is a historic site, some vineyards seem to be nearby. The nation's capital sits on its periphery, supplying a major market as well as venues and occasions to showcase Virginia wines. There is active government promotion and assistance. And no less renowned a pioneer than Thomas Jefferson started it all—never mind the fact that this most famous of U.S. wine geeks failed to establish a successful vineyard, despite repeated tries.

Jefferson's travails two centuries ago foreshadowed some of the viticultural problems that have beset American growers ever since. Cold winters and high summer humidity have always presented enormous challenges for European *Vitis vinifera* vines in much of eastern and middle North America. Native grape vines had demonstrated their capability to render palatable but not fine wines. America's early wine "industry"—to the extent that certain regions justified that name—was based on these indigenous varieties, but Jefferson's dream of cultivating vinifera lived on, only to find its first large-scale realization in the more temperate and drier climes of California. After the devastation wrought almost worldwide by phylloxera (a root louse native to North America) in the 19th century, the grafting of vinifera vines to the phylloxera-resistant roots of America's *V. labrusca* proved to be the salvation for Europe's (and California's) vineyards—but not until a great many other remedies had been tried. And one of the more influential alternative "cures" for phylloxera was the hybridization of the vinifera and labrusca grapes, carried out with great intensity by the French, who deployed a host of newly minted grape varieties to replant their country's devastated vineyards. The problem was that these hybrid grapes, at their best, produced results scarcely reminiscent of what had been before. They gradually disappeared in all but a few corners of Europe. Back in North America, though, the so-called French hybrids became the basis of early-20th-century viticulture outside of California. Two decades after the repeal of prohibition, vinifera finally secured a toehold in the east—in upper New York State—from which eventually these European vines and their stubborn advocates would disprove the common wisdom that northeastern, mid-Atlantic, and midwestern winters were too severe for their survival. Today, vinifera vines are still the minority in eastern and midwestern North America, but, with a very few exceptions, the most interesting wines come from the grape varieties with which Americans are familiar from Europe or California. Nonetheless, the problems of frost and humidity have not gone away, and it is only in certain favorable microclimates—when well matched to certain strains of vine—that vinifera grapes in North America east of the Rockies can achieve consistent ripeness, much less distinctive character.

The challenges to success with vinifera ought not deter American wine lovers from seriously exploring what is grown east of their West Coast. Indeed, the challenge of discovering those places where there is a synergy between vine and site make the gems one finds all the more savory and intriguing. And many of us, often without knowing it, pass near these vineyards in our business and tourist travels. The number of vinous gems in New York State has reached proportions that justify serious international consideration, as well as separate treatment in this guide, which follows below. Still, for all the new vineyards and facilities that cover the North American landscape, it is sobering to consider the formidable commercial and climatic obstacles wine-growers face. The litany of wineries that have failed is also long, and sadly this was not always for want of growing truly excellent wines. In Maryland in the 1980s, for instance, Byrd Winery with their berry-intense Cabernet Sauvignon and Montbray with their Cabernet Sauvignon and long-aging Seyve Villard (a hybrid) drew praise not just from Robert Parker's *Wine Advocate* but even from journalists abroad. Yet neither of these ventures outlived their founding generation. For excellence and excitement to flourish in the glass requires not just pioneering growers and favorable micro- and business climates, but inquisitive and intrepid wine consumers as well.

NEW YORK STATE'S GREAT PROMISE

New York State includes one long-established region that has been revived (the Finger Lakes), and one place (Long Island) of explosive growth where no vines existed a quarter century ago. Both regions highlight small family wineries, but the Finger Lakes were once dominated by several of America's largest, industrial-scale wineries. Many of today's Finger Lakes vintners are veteran growers or their descendants, getting by in part thanks to the region's flocks of tourists. On Long Island, intrepid and wealthy Americans and adventurous foreigners— often with no previous wine experience—tend to dominate the scene. With Manhattan 80 miles away, Long Island enjoys an incredible marketing advantage. Growers frequently complain that not enough respect is paid them, but in truth even a toehold on the wine lists of New York City represents both publicity and a volume of sales for which most other emerging viticultural regions of North America would kill. All of New York's growing regions, however, including the less celebrated Hudson River Valley, enjoy promotional and tax support from state and local governments, a critical factor wherever young American wine regions are managing to flourish. (Without the Peconic Land Trust of Suffolk County, for example, some of the highest residential land values in North America would have nipped Long Island's vines and industry in the bud.) And New York's growers have yet another powerful force in their favor: the viticultural research and outreach programs of Cornell University, without which the recent history of two of the most important winegrowing regions east of the Rocky Mountains is unthinkable.

When Alex and Louisa Hargrave established their Long Island vineyards in the early 1970s, it had been only 20 years since Konstantin Frank and Charles Fournier of the Finger Lakes region collaborated to introduce European vinifera into New York State. These, then, are relatively young viticultural areas, and over the past decade they have become rapidly proliferating ones as well. The number of start-ups and new facilities here (and in New York's other emerging growing regions along the Hudson and Lake Erie) is impressive . . . or perhaps a bit frightening, depending on how one views the market. New York's two principal growing regions also represent unique microclimates that are unusually dependent on their attendant bodies of water: the ocean surrounding Long Island with its regular breezes and temperate influence and the deep Finger Lakes with their thermal retention and reflective light. Given the overall climatic conditions prevailing in North America at these latitudes, spring frost is an ever-present danger in the Finger Lakes and fierce storms or early onset of winter can plague the harvest season in either district. Furthermore, whether it is the shale rock sloping down to the lakes or the gently undulating loam, gravel, and sand of Long Island (both of these underlaid here and there with seams of clay), one must be prepared to accept significant differences in microclimate and fruit maturation over distances as short as a few hundred yards. Incidentally, the terrific drainage afforded by these soils can be a two-edged sword, and in hot summers many vines depend on drip irrigation (itself a two-sided tool) as a lifeline.

At their best, the wines of both Long Island and the Finger Lakes are charting their own distinctive and gradually recognized ways. For Long Island, that means reds with the forward fruit of the New World allied to the lower alcohol, marginally lighter frame, and mineral expression that are traditionally associated with Bordeaux. In the Finger Lakes a softer, more loosely structured Riesling than that associated with the Old World offers a unique charm. But beyond the by now established associations of Riesling with the Finger Lakes and Merlot with Long Island lies a host of exciting explorations with a wide range of grapes. Not surprisingly, Chardonnay is still ubiquitous in both regions—and occasionally distinguishes itself—although interest appears to be waning. In the Finger Lakes, some outstanding Gewürztraminer is grown that no one would confuse with its Alsace or German kin. Rigorous projects with Pinot Noir and Cabernet Franc are bearing fascinatingly satisfying fruit, and Millbrook in New York's Hudson River Valley has also scored particular success with those two red varieties. In Long Island's Hamptons, Channing Daughters is rendering a fascinatingly delicious array of whites from northern Italian grape varieties. Cabernet Franc, Cabernet Sauvignon, and other Bordelais varieties are increasingly joining Merlot on Long Island's North Fork, and in the warmest, westernmost stretches—just before farmland completely gives way to suburban sprawl—Schneider Vineyards has demonstrated the remarkable local potential for Syrah. Long Island and the Finger Lakes—both places where wine lovers will encounter outstanding values—are regions in the process of rapid transformation and discoveries in the vineyard and the cellar. Asked to defend his eight-variety roster, Charles Massoud of Paumanok echoed the sentiments of many New York growers in replying: "I am torn in two directions [but] ours is a young region, and we have not yet fully explored what will shine here. I would not know today which variety to discontinue."

—DAVID SCHILDKNECHT

[the ratings]

NEW YORK'S BEST PRODUCERS

✶ ✶ ✶ ✶ (EXCELLENT)

The Grapes of Roth (Long Island)	Hermann J. Wiemer Vineyard
Paumanok (Long Island)	(Finger Lakes)✶

✶ ✶ ✶ (VERY GOOD)

Anthony Road Wine Company (Finger Lakes)	Dr. Konstantin Frank Vinifera Wine Cellars (Finger Lakes)
Bedell Cellars / Corey Creek (Long Island)	Heron Hill Winery (Finger Lakes)
Channing Daughters (Long Island)	Jamesport Vineyards (Long Island)

*Producers whose range includes deliciously distinguished sparkling wines.

Lamoreaux Landing Wine Cellars
   (Finger Lakes)
The Lenz Winery (Long Island)★
Millbrook Vineyards (Hudson River Valley)
Pellegrini Vineyards (Long Island)

Shinn Estate Vineyards (Long Island)
Schneider Vineyards (Long Island)
Silver Thread Vineyard (Finger Lakes)
Wölffer Estate Vineyard (Long Island)

★ ★ (GOOD)

Atwater Estate Vineyards (Finger Lakes)
Castello di Borghese (Long Island)
Chateau LaFayette Reneau (Finger Lakes)
The Old Field Vineyards (Long Island)★
Fox Run Vineyards (Finger Lakes)
Lieb Family Cellars (Long Island)★
Palmer Vineyards (Long Island)
Peconic Bay Winery (Long Island)

Raphael (Long Island)
Red Newt Cellars (Finger Lakes)
Roanoke Vineyards (Long Island)
Shalestone Vineyards (Finger Lakes)
Sheldrake Point Vineyard (Finger Lakes)
Standing Stone Vineyards (Finger Lakes)
Waters Crest Winery (Long Island)

WINERIES WORTH DISCOVERING IN CANADA AND THE "OTHER 46" STATES

ARIZONA

Callaghan Vineyards

BRITISH COLUMBIA

Black Hills Estate Winery
Burrowing Owl Estate Winery
Mission Hill Family Estate
Osoyoos Larose
Quails' Gate Estate Winery

Sandhill Estate Vineyard
Sumac Ridge Estate Winery
Tantalus Vineyards
Wild Goose Vineyards

COLORADO

Carlson Vineyards
Holy Cross Abbey

S. Rhodes Vineyards

CONNECTICUT

Jonathan Edwards Winery

Stonington Vineyards

GEORGIA

Persimmon Creek Vineyards

IOWA

Jasper Winery

KENTUCKY

Equus Run Vineyards

Smith-Berry Vineyard and Winery

MARYLAND

Basignani Winery
Black Ankle Vineyards

Boordy Vineyards
Elk Run Vineyards

MASSACHUSETTS

The Neighborhood Cellar

MICHIGAN

Brys Estate Vineyard and Winery
Chateau Grand Traverse
Left Foot Charley

L. Mawbry
Shady Lane Cellars

NEW JERSEY

Unionville Vineyards

NEW MEXICO

Gruet Winery

OHIO

Harpersfield Winery
Kinkead Ridge
Maple Ridge Vineyard

Markko Vineyard
St. Joseph Vineyard

ONTARIO

Cave Spring Cellars
Château des Charmes
Le Clos Jordanne
Closson Chase Vineyards
Creekside Estate Winery

Flat Rock Cellars
Norman Hardie Winery
Inniskillin
Daniel Lenko Estate Winery
Vineland Estates Winery

PENNSYLVANIA

Allegro Vineyards
Chaddsford Winery

Manatawny Creek Winery
Pinnacle Ridge Winery

RHODE ISLAND

Sakonnet Vineyards

TEXAS

Alamosa Wine Cellars
Becker Vineyards
Cap Rock Winery

Inwood Estates Vineyards
McPherson Cellars
Sandstone Cellars

VERMONT

Snow Farm Vineyard

VIRGINIA

Barboursville Vineyards
The Boxwood Winery
Horton Vineyards
Keswick Vineyards
Kluge Estate Winery and Vineyard

Linden Vineyards
Naked Mountain Vineyard and Winery
Rockbridge Vineyard
White Hall Vineyards
Willowcroft Farm Vineyards

[tasting commentaries]

ANTHONY ROAD WINE COMPANY
*** FINGER LAKES $9.00–$40.00

German-born Johannes Reinhardt (who arrived here in 2000) and owners Ann and John Martini are on an ambitious curve with this winery on the west side of Seneca Lake.

2005 Pinot Gris	87–89	now
2005 Pinot Noir	87–89	now–2010

ATWATER ESTATE VINEYARDS **
** FINGER LAKES $10.00–$30.00

Katie and Ted Marks, along with winemaker Vincent Aliperti, farm a relatively warm stretch of eastern Seneca Lake shoreline and the sold-out status of most of their wines testifies to the reputation they have been building within the state. They bottle many ambitious wines from vinifera, but their entry-level wine from the hybrid Vidal Blanc represents an amazing, irresistibly lip-smacking value.

2005 Vidal Blanc	88	now

BEDELL CELLARS/COREY CREEK ***
NORTH FORK, LONG ISLAND $20.00–$100.00

John Irving Levenberg, an enthusiastic new winemaker, has recently taken charge at this winery founded nearly a quarter of a century ago by Kip Bedell (who, along with oenologist Pascal Marty, continues to consult here), and numerous cellar and vineyard improvements are in train. Purchased in 2000 by *Lord of the Rings* movie producer Michael Lynne, Bedell incorporates three vineyards and two labels; the Corey Creek label is utilized mainly for white wines. Their flagship red, Cupola, is a promising Bordeaux blend.

2005 Gewürztraminer A-Block	87–89	now

CHANNING DAUGHTERS ***
THE HAMPTONS, LONG ISLAND $20.00–$40.00

Channing Daughters, under the direction of co-owner and Long Island viticultural veteran Larry Perrine and husband-wife winemaking team Christopher Tracy and Allison Dubin, is bottling some of the most intriguing and delightful wines in Long Island, utilizing fruit from closely affiliated North Fork growers, as well as from Walter and Molly Channing's South Fork home farm. Production of the whites here so far rarely exceeds 200 cases per bottling, so interested parties should get on the winery's mailing list.

2004 Sylvanus	87	now
2005 Pinot Grigio	89–90	now–2009
2004 Tocai Friulano	90	now–2009
2004 Meditazione	87	now–2011+

DR. KONSTANTIN FRANK VINIFERA WINE CELLARS ***
FINGER LAKES $10.00–$30.00

The Dr. Frank winery high above the shores of Keuka Lake was the child of the Finger Lakes' father figure, the man whose vision of vinifera on the American East Coast—unlike Thomas Jefferson's—actually bore fruit. Dr. Frank's son Willy—who died in 2006—and his grandson Fred have been the stewards of his legacy.

| 2005 Riesling Dry | 90 | now–2015 |
| 2005 Riesling Reserve | 89 | now–2015+? |

THE GRAPES OF ROTH ★★★★
NORTH FORK, LONG ISLAND $50.00–$60.00

Roman Roth—winemaker for Wölffer Estate and Roanoke Vineyards (and formerly for Shinn Estate)—has attempted to pull out all the stops in crafting a couple hundred cases of his own brand, the first of which have only recently been released. The results are of a sort guaranteed to bring down the house at blind tastings, but it would be a shame not to set some aside in one's cellar to await the verdict of time. Consumers who fail to order these wines in advance of release should recall that they were warned.

| 2002 Merlot | 92 | now–2012+? |
| 2001 Merlot | 91 | now–2015+? |

HERON HILL WINERY ★★★
FINGER LAKES $10.00–$200.00

Canadian-Hungarian Thomas Laszlo, formerly cellarmaster at Pajzos-Megyer in Tokaj, has directed this winery since 2002, working with fruit from the home vineyards that were first planted in 1968 on shale ridges high above Keuka Lake, as well as the vineyard of Heron Hill owners John and Josephine Ingle along Canandaigua Lake. Riesling takes pride of place.

2005 Riesling Ingle Vineyard	87–89	now–2012
2004 Riesling Ingle Vineyard	87	now–2009
2005 Riesling Estate Reserve	86–88	now–2011
2004 Riesling Late Harvest	90	now–2018+?
2003 Riesling Ice Wine	89	now–2016

JAMESPORT VINEYARDS ★★★
NORTH FORK, LONG ISLAND $13.00–$50.00

Proprietor Ron Goerler, Jr., and winemaker and native Long Islander Les Howard turn out around 5,000 cases annually, including many outstanding values that typify the unique potential of Long Island wine to feature generous ripe fruit at relatively low levels of alcohol. Their inexpensive East End Chardonnay is surprisingly vivacious, and a portion of its proceeds benefits a Cornell University project for restoring the shellfish banks off Long Island. Their Merlot will embarrass most of the (many too many) others of this variety in the marketplace, and at a reasonable price.

2005 Sauvignon Blanc	86–88	now–2009
2004 Riesling Late Harvest	90	now–2016+?
2002 Merlot Estate	88	now–2012
2001 Merlot Reserve	89	now–2012
1998 Merlot Reserve	91	now–2010
2002 Cabernet Franc	87	now–2012
1998 Cabernet Franc	89	now–2009
2002 Mélange de Trois	90	now–2014

LAMOREAUX LANDING WINE CELLARS ★★★
FINGER LAKES $10.00–$70.00

Lifetime local and long-time viticulturalist Mark Wagner's impressive facility on the eastern shore of Seneca Lake offers one of the more colorful and promising arrays of wine in a region full of both color and promise. Most of the fruit comes from his own 100 acres.

2005 Gewürztraminer	88	now–2011
2002 Cabernet Franc T 23	89	now
2002 Cabernet Franc	89	now–2012

THE LENZ WINERY ★★★
NORTH FORK, LONG ISLAND $20.00–$55.00

Microbiologist Eric Fry went to the Dr. Konstantin Frank winery from California two decades ago on the recommendation of André Tchelistcheff and a few years later went to Long Island and Lenz. Nowadays, he is one of the region's veteran winemakers, and is much in demand as a consultant. Fry's devotion to Gewürztraminer (and to the estate's oldest vines, planted in 1979); to Pinot Noir–based, late-disgorged sparkling wine; and to Bordeaux blends is evident in his enthusiasm and profound success.

2003 Gewürztraminer	87	now–2010
1999 Cuvée Brut	89	now
2001 Cabernet Sauvignon	88	now–2011
2001 Merlot Estate Selection	89	now–2014
1997 Merlot Old Vines	90	now–2010

LIEB FAMILY CELLARS ★★
NORTH FORK, LONG ISLAND $14.00–$25.00

Mark and Kathy Lieb founded their winery in 1992 and eight years later opened Long Island's (indeed, the East Coast's) only custom crush facility, Premium Wine Group, which has since become an exceedingly bustling incubator for numerous talented vintners and their wines. Their Pinot Blanc–based sparkler and understated, attractive Bordeaux blend are distinctively delicious.

2004 Pinot Blanc	87	now

MILLBROOK VINEYARDS ★★★
HUDSON VALLEY $15.00–$65.00

One of the best-known wineries in New York is Millbrook, since its proprietors, John and Kathe Dyson, also own Williams Selyem in Sonoma. There is a significant jump in ripeness, richness, and complexity when one comes to the special, late-released reserve wines of this estate.

2002 Pinot Noir Proprietor's Special Reserve	89	now–2011
2002 Cabernet Franc Proprietor's Special Reserve	88	now–2012

THE OLD FIELD VINEYARDS ★★
NORTH FORK, LONG ISLAND $11.00–$40.00

With the advice and assistance of Lenz Winery's Eric Fry, husband-wife team Christian Baiz and Rosamond Phelps Baiz may have found the key to success with their small production of Pinot Noir–based sparkling wine. The family's property was first planted with vines in 1974 and has a cool, exposed bay-side location at the narrow eastern end of the North Fork.

2000 Blanc de Noir Brut	90	now

PALMER VINEYARDS ★★
NORTH FORK, LONG ISLAND $13.00–$22.00

Sourcing from the extensive acreage of the Palmer family farm and one additional vineyard, recently departed winemaker Tom Drozd has crafted some, at times, quite distinctive wines.

2005 Sauvignon Blanc	87–89	now
2004 Pinot Blanc	88	now

PAUMANOK ★★★★
NORTH FORK, LONG ISLAND $15.00–$45.00

Lebanese-born Charles Massoud and his wife, Ursula (from a wine-growing family in Germany's southern Pfalz), began working these soils in 1983. Any who meet Massoud will quickly recognize that his is still a labor of love. Joined in the cellar now by his oldest son, Kareem, Massoud displays success with a wide range of wines, but especially with some of the most elegant, profound, ageworthy, and best-value red wines grown anywhere in North America east of the Rockies.

2003 Sauvignon Blanc Late Harvest	88	now–2011+?
2003 Riesling Late Harvest	90	now–2015+?
2004 Cabernet Franc	89–91	now–2014
2004 Cabernet Sauvignon	87–89	now–2012
2002 Cabernet Sauvignon Grand Vintage	90	now–2014
2000 Cabernet Sauvignon Grand Vintage	90	now–2014
2004 Merlot	88–90	now–2013
2002 Merlot	88	now–2010
2004 Merlot Grand Vintage	90–92	2010–2017+?
2002 Merlot Grand Vintage	89	now–2012
2004 Assemblage	88–91	2009–2014+?
2002 Assemblage	90	now–2014
2000 Assemblage	89	now–2014

PECONIC BAY WINERY ★★
NORTH FORK, LONG ISLAND $15.00–$90.00

One of the earliest wineries on Long Island, Peconic Bay is owned by founders Ursula and Paul Lowerre. Winemaker Greg Gove is also a local veteran. His basic bottling of Merlot offers excellent value and a lovely example of Long Island sweetness of fruit allied to moderate alcohol.

2001 Merlot	88	now–2010

PELLEGRINI VINEYARDS ★★★
NORTH FORK, LONG ISLAND $15.00–$40.00

Australian Russell Hearn is responsible for some terrific wine values at the estate of Joyce and Robert Pellegrini. Even their basic bottlings are interesting as well as delicious, and their special reserve reds (released late) can offer not just alluring richness and complexity, but excellent value.

2004 Chardonnay	88	now
2001 Cabernet Franc	88	now–2010
1997 Cabernet Franc	90	now–2009
2001 Cabernet Sauvignon	87	now–2009
1997 Encore—Vintner's Pride	90	now–2009

RAPHAEL ★★
NORTH FORK, LONG ISLAND $15.00–$30.00

Owner John Petrocelli and veteran winemaker Richard Olsen-Harbich have called on no less a luminary than Château Margaux's Paul Pontallier for ongoing, on-site advice, and their nine-year-old vines and sophisticated cellar—devoted entirely to the Bordeaux varieties—are rendering wines of considerable promise. They emphasize Merlot but their Cabernet Franc is a charmer.

2001 Cabernet Franc	87	now–2009+?

SCHNEIDER VINEYARDS ★ ★ ★
NORTH FORK, LONG ISLAND $25.00–$40.00

Bruce Schneider regularly commutes between his job in public relations in Manhattan and his Roanoke Point vineyards. He dedicated himself to Cabernet Franc since his first harvest of 1994, rendering wines of floral, fruit, and mineral nuance. In 2002 Schneider planted Syrah in a new site in Mattituck. Any who think this act must have been quixotic have obviously not tasted the early results! Following Schneider's progress in the bottle will reward the most jaded wine lover.

2004 Cabernet Franc Le Breton	88	now
2004 Cabernet Franc Roanoke Point	87–89	now–2012+?
2004 Syrah Hermitage Clones	88	now–2012+?

SHALESTONE VINEYARDS
★ ★ FINGER LAKES $14.00–$24.00

Shalestone is the 1,000-case and—unique for their region—entirely red wine establishment of Rob and Kate Thomas. Their Cabernet Franc is among the most convincing in the Finger Lakes area.

2003 Cabernet Franc	88	now–2010+

SHELDRAKE POINT VINEYARD ★ ★
FINGER LAKES $15.00–$150.00

His "2004" Riesling ice wine—actually from the 2003 vintage, but harvested in January 2004, which by U.S. law misleadingly makes it a 2004—put the wine world on notice of Ontario-born Bob Madill's ambitious plans for this estate on the western shore of Cayuga Lake.

2004 Riesling Ice Wine	90	now–2011+

SHINN ESTATE VINEYARDS ★ ★ ★
NORTH FORK, LONG ISLAND $15.00–$60.00

Husband-wife team David Page and Barbara Shinn—who also run the Manhattan restaurant Home—began planting here in 2000. In a remarkably short period of time, and with the initial consultation of Roman Roth, they have clearly become intimate with their vines, bottling promising wines of proportion and finesse. The emphasis on sustainable agriculture here is admirable and will certainly continue to pay gustatory as well as environmental dividends. Production is small, quality is rapidly advancing, and wine lovers would be well advised to add their names to the Shinn mailing list before it becomes a waiting list.

2004 Merlot Nine Barrels Reserve	89–91	now–2016+?
2002 Merlot Six Barrels Reserve	87	now–2011+?
2004 Cabernet Franc	88–90	now–2014+?

SILVER THREAD VINEYARD ★ ★ ★
FINGER LAKES $15.00–$30.00

Richard Figiel planted his first vineyard on the east side of Seneca Lake more than a quarter of a century ago and he shifted to an herbicide- and pesticide-free, sustainable regimen in the late 1980s. Even the Chardonnay here is polished, juicy, and satisfying, and Riesling, Pinot Noir, and the Cabernet Franc–based Blackbird are elegant and fascinating.

2002 Riesling	88	now
2002 Blackbird	87	now–2010+

STANDING STONE VINEYARDS * * *
FINGER LAKES $10.00–$50.00

Marti and Tom Machinski farm a site on the southeast shore of Seneca Lake that was singled out by Gold Seal for planting Riesling back in 1972, vines the Machinskis still harvest with excellent results. There are a lot of ice wines from hybrid grapes in Canada and the northern U.S. and there are also a lot of ice*box* wines (in which the freezing is not left to nature), but Standing Stone's is one of the few to have proven entirely satisfying.

2005 Riesling	88	now
2004 Vidal Ice	87	now–2010+?

HERMANN J. WIEMER VINEYARD * * * *
FINGER LAKES $15.00–$80.00

Since his arrival in the Finger Lakes three decades ago, Mosel-born Hermann Wiemer has worked tirelessly as a vintner and nurseryman to preach the gospel of vinifera and show the way to new standards of wine quality. For much of that time, he was virtually a lone voice crying in the wilderness, but in recent years Wiemer was only too happy to have serious competition and rose to the occasion. Ownership and day-to-day control of the winery was turned over in 2007 to Wiemer's long-time assistant Fred Merwarth. Their sparkling cuvées and Pinot Noir should not be overlooked.

2005 Gewürztraminer Dry	87–89	now
2005 Riesling Dry	87–89	now–2012
2004 Riesling Dry	90	now–2012
2003 Riesling Late Harvest	89	now–2011+?
2003 Riesling Select Late Harvest Ice Wine	90	now–2015+?

WÖLFFER ESTATE VINEYARD * * *
THE HAMPTONS, LONG ISLAND $12.00–$130.00

Hamburg-born Christian Wölffer traveled the world for decades before settling down to realize his horticultural dreams in the Hamptons, and now he has become one of the most influential wine practitioners and spokespersons on Long Island. Cellarmaster Roman Roth (who has his own impressive fledgling label) and vineyard manager Richard Pisacano (whose own Roanoke Vineyards is among the North Fork's most important sources of fruit) complete the enthusiastic team here. The extensive Wölffer portfolio ranges into pricing territory that is far from bashful, but the best wines are undeniably impressive in an elegant, understated, and at times quite intricate way.

2005 Chardonnay Estate Selection	85–87	now–2010
2002 Pinot Noir	88	now–2011
2001 Merlot Estate Selection	87	now–2012

[oregon]

Oregon makes wine from most of the same grapes used in California, although the cooler, more marginal climate in Oregon's best viticultural area, the Willamette Valley, has meant more success with cool-climate varietals such as Pinot Noir than with hotter-climate varietals such as Cabernet Sauvignon, Merlot, Syrah, and Grenache. Chardonnay and Riesling have done well in Oregon, but the "great white hope" here is Pinot Gris, which has shown fine potential and is the perfect partner for the salmon of the Pacific Northwest. Pinot Blanc has made a significant appearance in recent years, but has not produced wines meriting serious consumer attention, most probably due to severe overcropping. High-quality sparkling wines can be found, particularly under the Argyle label. Oregon's wines are distinctive, with a kinship to European wines. The higher natural acidities, lower alcohol content, and more subtle nature of Oregon's wines bode well for the area's future.

[grape varieties]

CHARDONNAY Oregon can make some wonderful Chardonnays, but far too many winemakers let it spend too much time in oak and have not chosen the best clones for their vineyards. The Chardonnay grape in Oregon is naturally high in acidity, and that is the principal difference between California's and Oregon's Chardonnay. In California, most Chardonnays must have tartaric acid added to them for balance. In Oregon, the wines must be put through a secondary or malolactic fermentation, à la Burgundy, in order to lower their perceptible acidity. The high quality of Chardonnays produced from recent plantings of Dijon clones indicates that Oregon may have found the answer to its clonal problems with this varietal.

PINOT GRIS This is the hardest wine to find, as virtually all of it is snapped up before it has a chance to leave Oregon. Fruitier and more floral than Chardonnay, Pinot Gris, from the world's most underrated great white wine grape, can be a delicious, opulent, smoky wine with every bit as much character and even more aging potential than Chardonnay. Though a specialty of Oregon, much of it is mediocre and diluted due to overcropping.

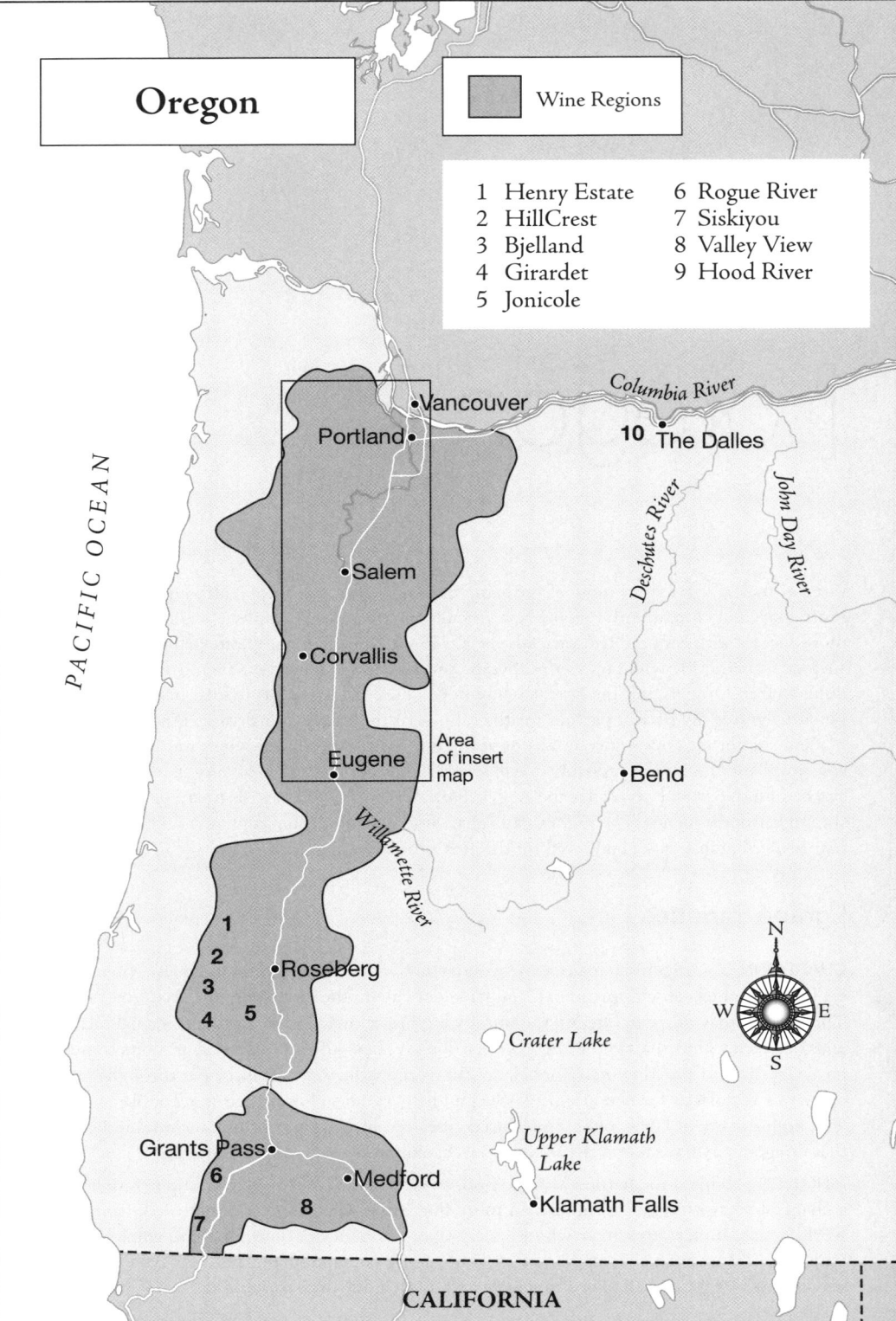

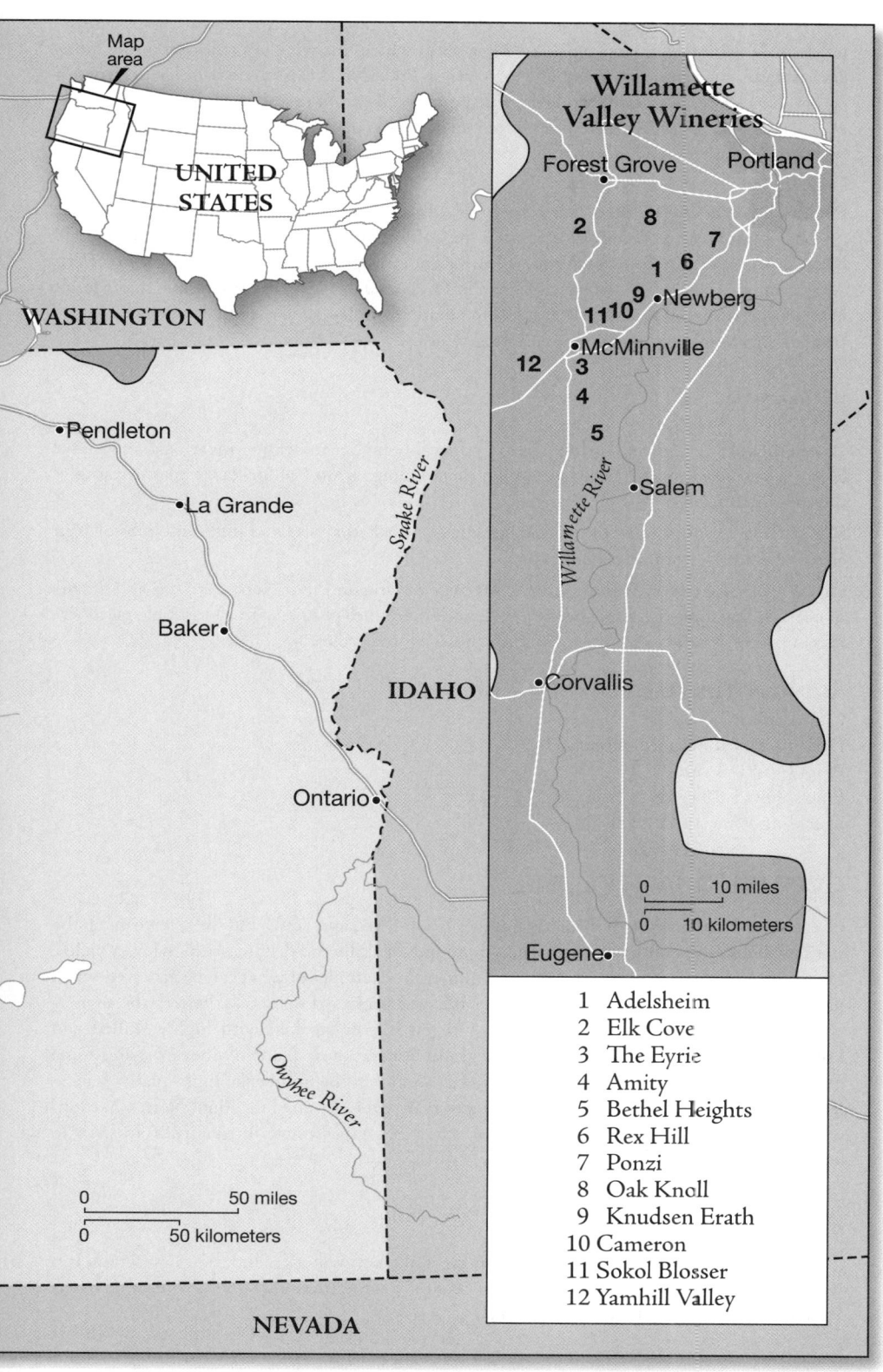

Willamette
Valley Wineries

Map
area

UNITED
STATES

WASHINGTON

Pendleton

La Grande

Baker

IDAHO

Ontario

Snake River

Owyhee River

NEVADA

0   50 miles
0   50 kilometers

Forest Grove   Portland

2   8
                7
        6
    1
11 10 9 Newberg
    McMinnville
12
    3
    4
    5
            Salem

Willamette River

Corvallis

0   10 miles
0   10 kilometers

Eugene

1 Adelsheim
2 Elk Cove
3 The Eyrie
4 Amity
5 Bethel Heights
6 Rex Hill
7 Ponzi
8 Oak Knoll
9 Knudsen Erath
10 Cameron
11 Sokol Blosser
12 Yamhill Valley

PINOT NOIR As in Burgundy, the soil, yield per acre, choice of fermentation yeasts, competence of the winemaker, and type of oak barrel in which this wine is aged profoundly influence its taste, style, and character. The top Oregon Pinot Noirs can have a wonderful purity of cherry, loganberry, and raspberry fruit. Furthermore, they can reveal an expansive, seductive, broad, lush palate, as well as crisp acids for balance. Yet far too many are washed out and hollow because of the tendency to harvest less than fully mature fruit and to permit crop yields to exceed three tons per acre.

OTHER GRAPE VARIETIES With respect to white wines, Gewürztraminer has generally proven no more successful in Oregon than in California. Oregon, however, can make good Riesling, especially in the drier Alsace style. Recent tastings of delicious sparkling wines from Argyle show promise for this style of wine in Oregon. The Cabernet Sauvignon and Merlot have not been special to date, although some made from the state's southern vineyards have resulted in several good though not exciting wines.

FLAVORS

CHARDONNAY Oregon Chardonnays are noticeably higher in acidity, more oaky, and have less of a processed, manipulated taste than their siblings from California. In many examples the oak is excessive.

PINOT GRIS A whiff of smoke, the creamy taste of baked apples and nuts, and gobs of fruit characterize this promising white wine.

PINOT NOIR Red berry fruits dominate the taste of Oregon Pinot Noirs. Aromas and flavors of cherries, loganberries, blackberries, cola, and sometimes plums, with a streak of spicy, herbaceous scents characterize these medium ruby–colored wines.

AGING POTENTIAL
Chardonnay: 2–5 years
Dry/Off-Dry Riesling: 2–4 years
Pinot Gris: 1–3 years
Pinot Noir: 3–10 years
Sparkling Wines: 1–4 years

OVERALL QUALITY LEVEL

Oregon has faced a string of difficult vintages (2005, 2004, and 2001), but these have given the state's winemakers enormous experience, honing their skills and driving them to lower yields. On the other hand, 2006 and 2002 provide numerous examples of what can be achieved when nature cooperates. Once a region of underfinanced backyard operations where the owner-winemakers learned as they went along, Oregon is now stocked with highly skilled and knowledgeable winemakers. Low-quality grape clones, poorly planted vineyards, and some questionable winemaking decisions can still be found, but the number of high-quality wineries is growing. While they are just beginning to realize the potential for Pinot Noir, Chardonnay, and Pinot Gris, their future is bright. Oregon's wines range in quality from poor to outstanding.

IMPORTANT INFORMATION

To purchase good wine, know the finest vintages, the best wineries, and their best wines. It is worth knowing that the finest Pinot Noirs generally come from a stretch of vineyards in the Willamette Valley, southwest of Portland.

[recent vintages]

2007

A relatively large crop and normal growing conditions set the stage for a bountiful vintage. Heavy rains just after the start of harvest complicated matters, but early reports indicate that many growers are pleasantly surprised that the wines are not as diluted as many outside observers expected. Certainly the early style of the vintage looks to be one of charm, finesse, and pretty fruit, but not the concentration and power of the most ageworthy years.

2006

A warm and abundant crop yielded powerful, rich, concentrated wines (assuming yields were managed by growers who crop-thinned). 2006 produced almost atypically fleshy, succulent, California-style Pinot Noirs in nearly every sector of Oregon's viticultural landscape. This is an exciting vintage, but the jury is still out as to how well the wines will age given their precociousness, gorgeous up-front fruit, and seductiveness.

2005

Textbook growing conditions and a reasonably good crop size resulted in very good wines, with only moderate rainfall complicating the harvest conditions in Oregon Tastings from the bottle have shown very good Chardonnays, very good to excellent Pinot Noirs, and tasty but fruit-forward other wines. This is certainly a fine vintage for Pinot Noir, but not an exceptional one.

2004

An early harvest of rich, sugar-filled grapes caused alcohols to be slightly higher than normal, crop size very small, and the wines, at the top level, stunningly concentrated, fleshy, rich, and impressive. Ageworthiness may be somewhat suspect given the naturally low acidities and precociousness of the wines.

2003

A hotter than normal year, a relatively large crop, and heady alcoholic, high-octane Pinot Noirs and Chardonnays seemed to be the rule of thumb for most Oregon growers. The wines are undeniably impressive, but chunkier and fleshier than normal.

2002

Perhaps the finest vintage in the last decade for Oregon Pinot Noir as well as other varietals. After a textbook growing season, the harvest took place under surprisingly dry conditions for Oregon, and the resulting wines were structured, rich, pure, medium- to full-bodied, and very layered and nuanced. This is also a vintage that should age very well for the best producers.

2001

A huge crop (even for those growers who crop-thinned), heavy rains at harvest, and very diluted wines for the most part emerged from this mediocre vintage in Oregon.

2000

An excellent vintage that is now fully mature.

[older vintages]

Among the older years, 1999, 1994, 1993, and 1992 stand out in that decade. In the 1980s, 1985 was a winner.

As a general rule, most Oregon Pinot Noirs must be consumed within 7 to 8 years of the vintage. There are always a few exceptions, as anyone who has tasted the 1975 Eyrie or 1975 Knudsen Erath Pinot Noirs can attest. But in general, aging Oregon Pinot Noir for longer than 7 to 8 years (10 to 12 for the absolute finest) is a dangerous gamble.

Oregon's white wines should be drunk within several years of the vintage, even though they tend to have better natural acidity than their California counterparts. Yields are frequently too high, and the extract levels questionable, so whether it is Pinot Gris, Chardonnay, or dry Riesling, if you are not drinking these wines within three to four years of the vintage you are more likely to be disappointed than pleasantly surprised.

Note: Robert M. Parker, Jr., has a one-third interest in an Oregon vineyard that was commercially bonded in 1992 and began selling wine in 1993. Due to an obvious conflict of interest, this wine has not been reviewed.

— JAY MILLER

[the ratings]

OREGON'S BEST PRODUCERS OF PINOT NOIR

Note: Where a producer has been assigned a range of stars (***/****), the lower rating has been used for placement in this hierarchy.

* * * * * (OUTSTANDING)

Argyle Winery (sparkling wines)
Bergström Winery
Brick House Vineyards
Domaine Drouhin

St. Innocent Winery
Soter Vineyards
Ken Wright Cellars

* * * * (EXCELLENT)

Adelsheim Vineyard
ArborBrook Vineyards
Argyle Winery
Ayoub Vineyard
Bethel Heights Vineyard
Le Cadeau Vineyard
J. K. Carriere Wines
Chehalem
Cristom Vineyards

Domaine Coteau
Domaine Serene
Evesham Wood Vineyard
Hamacher Wines
Penner-Ash Wine Cellars
Ponzi Vineyards
ROCO Wines
Shea Wine Cellars
WillaKenzie Estate

* * * (GOOD)

Anne Amie Vineyards
Aramenta Cellars
Archery Summit
Boedecker Cellars
Cana's Feast (formerly Cuneo Cellars)
Carlton Cellars

Coelho Winery
Daedalus Cellars
De Lancellotti Family Vineyards
Dobbes Family Estate
Elk Cove Vineyards
Erath Winery

Grochau Cellars
Gypsy Dancer Estates
Lachini Vineyards
Lemelson Vineyards
Maysara Winery
Nysa Vineyard
Owen Roe
Panther Creek Cellars

Patton Valley Vineyard
Rex Hill Vineyards and Winery
Sokol Blosser Winery
Stoller Vineyards
Stony Mountain Vineyard
Torii Mor Winery
White Rose Wines

* * (AVERAGE)

Adea Wine Company
Airlie Winery
Alloro Vineyard
Amalie Robert Estate
Amity Vineyards
Anam Cara Cellars
Apolloni Vineyards
Ayres Vineyard
Bella Vida Vineyard
Benton-Lane Winery
Bishop Creek Cellars
Broadley Vineyards
Cancilla Cellars
Cherry Hill Winery

Coleman Vineyard
Cooper Mountain Vineyards
Duck Pond Cellars
Matello
Methven Family Vineyard
Seufert Winery
Stangeland Vineyards and Winery
Tyee Wine Cellars
Vercingetorix
Whistling Ridge Vineyards
Willamette Valley Vineyards
Yamhill Valley Vineyards
Youngberg Hill Vineyards

[tasting commentaries]

ADELSHEIM VINEYARD
* * * * WILLAMETTE VALLEY $30.00–$50.00

Adelsheim Vineyard was founded in 1971 and the winery's first vintage was in 1978. David Adelsheim remains in charge as the winery has expanded and planted more vineyards in the Chehalem Mountain AVA. In addition to Pinot Noir, the winery produces a bevy of quality white wines worthy of consumer attention.

2005 Pinot Noir	83	now–2011
2004 Pinot Noir	89	now–2012
2003 Pinot Noir	88	now–2010
2005 Pinot Noir Bryan Creek Vineyard	87	2010–2015
2004 Pinot Noir Bryan Creek Vineyard	89	now–2010
2003 Pinot Noir Bryan Creek Vineyard	92	now–2015
2005 Pinot Noir Calkins Lane Vineyard	90+	now–2012
2004 Pinot Noir Calkins Lane Vineyard	91	now–2014
2003 Pinot Noir Calkins Lane Vineyard	91	now–2015
2002 Pinot Noir Calkins Lane Vineyard	90+	now–2012
2002 Pinot Noir Dundee Hills Vineyard	93	now–2012
2005 Pinot Noir Elizabeth's Reserve	90	now–2015
2004 Pinot Noir Elizabeth's Reserve	91	now–2014
2003 Pinot Noir Elizabeth's Reserve	87	now–2011
2002 Pinot Noir Elizabeth's Reserve	93	now–2012
2004 Pinot Noir Goldschmidt Vineyard	91	now–2014

2003 Pinot Noir Goldschmidt Vineyard	90	now–2013
2005 Pinot Noir Quarter Mile Lane	89	now–2012
2003 Pinot Noir Quarter Mile Lane	90	now–2013
2005 Pinot Noir Ribbon Springs Vineyard	91	now–2015
2002 Pinot Noir Ribbon Springs Vineyard	92	now–2014

ANNE AMIE VINEYARDS ★ ★ ★
WILLAMETTE VALLEY $35.00

| 2004 Pinot Noir Winemaker's Selection | 89+ | 2010–2018 |

ARAMENTA CELLARS ★ ★ ★
WILLAMETTE VALLEY $25.00–$38.00

| 2005 Pinot Noir | 87 | now–2015 |
| 2005 Pinot Noir Reserve | 88 | now–2015 |

ARBORBROOK VINEYARDS ★ ★ ★ ★
CHEHALEM MOUNTAIN $35.00–$55.00

| 2005 Pinot Noir Estate 777 Block | 91 | now–2015 |
| 2005 Pinot Noir Vintner's Select | 93 | 2012–2025 |

ARCHERY SUMMIT ★ ★ ★
DUNDEE HILLS $45.00–$85.00

2004 Pinot Noir Arcus Estate	88	2010–2017
2004 Pinot Noir Premier Cuvée	85	now–2012
2004 Pinot Noir Red Hills Estate	90	now–2014
2004 Pinot Noir Renegade Ridge Estate	86	now–2012

ARGYLE WINERY ★ ★ ★ ★ ★
WILLAMETTE VALLEY $35.00–$70.00

Argyle Winery, under the leadership of longtime winemaker Rollin Soles, produces 50,000 cases including 12,000 cases of some of the best sparkling wine made in the U.S. (The five-star part of their rating is for the sparkling wines.) Argyle's first vintage was 1987 and they currently offer Riesling and Chardonnay in addition to sparkling wine and, of course, Pinot Noir.

2002 Argyle Brut	90	now–2012
1996 Extended Tirage	93	now–2010
1999 Julia Lee's Block Blanc de Blancs	91	now–2012
1999 Knudsen Vineyard Brut	92	now–2012
2004 Pinot Noir Nuthouse	91	now–2016
2003 Pinot Noir Nuthouse	90	now–2013
2002 Pinot Noir Nuthouse	90	now–2012
2005 Pinot Noir Spirithouse	92	2012–2022
2003 Pinot Noir Spirithouse	89+	now–2013
2002 Pinot Noir Spirithouse	92+	now–2014
2005 Pinot Noir Reserve	92	2010–2017

AYOUB VINEYARD ★★★★
DUNDEE HILLS $45.00

Mo Ayoub planted a four-acre vineyard in the Dundee Hills in 2001 and is now reaping the fruits of his labor. He also has the good sense to allow the talented Josh Bergström (see Bergström Winery) to make the wine.

2004 Pinot Noir	92	2009–2017
2005 Pinot Noir	87	now–2012

BERGSTRÖM WINERY ★★★★★
VARIOUS $35.00–$75.00

In a remarkably brief time (the first vintage was 1999), Bergström, under the leadership of winemaker Josh Bergström, has become one of the quality leaders of the Willamette Valley. All of the estate vineyards are biodynamically farmed and Demeter certified.

2005 Chardonnay The Eyrie Vineyard	93	now–2017
2004 Pinot Noir	89	now–2014
2003 Pinot Noir Arcus Vineyard	88	now–2015
2005 Pinot Noir Bergström Vineyard	94	2012–2025
2004 Pinot Noir Bergström Vineyard	88	now–2014
2003 Pinot Noir Bergström Vineyard	88	now–2014
2005 Pinot Noir Bergström Winery Estate	80	now–2010
2004 Pinot Noir Broadley Vineyard	90	now–2012
2005 Pinot Noir Cumberland Reserve	91	2012–2022
2004 Pinot Noir Cumberland Reserve	88+	now–2014
2005 Pinot Noir de Lancellotti Vineyard	93	2012–2025
2004 Pinot Noir de Lancellotti Vineyard	91	now–2012
2005 Pinot Noir Nysa Vineyard	90	now–2017
2004 Pinot Noir Nysa Vineyard	88	now–2012
2005 Pinot Noir Shea Vineyard	94	2012–2025
2004 Pinot Noir Shea Vineyard	92	now–2014

BETHEL HEIGHTS VINEYARD ★★★★
EOLA-AMITY HILLS $25.00–$50.00

Bethel Heights Vineyard is one of Oregon's pioneer producers. The winery was founded in 1977 and the first vintage was in 1984. Currently, 70% of the wine comes from estate-grown fruit, and production stands at 13,000 cases. In addition to Pinot Noir, Bethel Heights also makes excellent Pinot Gris, Pinot Blanc, and Chardonnay.

2005 Pinot Noir Eola-Amity Hills Cuvée	88	now–2012
2005 Pinot Noir Estate Grown	89	2010–2020
2004 Pinot Noir Estate Grown	87	now–2012
2003 Pinot Noir Estate Grown	89	now–2015
2002 Pinot Noir Estate Grown	87	now–2012
2005 Pinot Noir Casteel Reserve	92	2012–2025
2003 Pinot Noir Casteel Reserve	93	now–2015
2002 Pinot Noir Casteel Reserve	93	now–2014
2005 Pinot Noir Flat Block Reserve	89+	now–2013
2002 Pinot Noir Flat Block Reserve	91	now–2012
2004 Pinot Noir Freedom Hill Vineyard	87	now–2016
2003 Pinot Noir Freedom Hill Vineyard	87	now–2015
2002 Pinot Noir Freedom Hill Vineyard	92	now–2012

2005 Pinot Noir Seven Springs Vineyard	90	2009–2017
2004 Pinot Noir Seven Springs Vineyard	91	now–2014
2003 Pinot Noir Seven Springs Vineyard	89	now–2013
2002 Pinot Noir Seven Springs Vineyard	91+	now–2012
2005 Pinot Noir Justice Vineyard	89+	now–2013
2005 Pinot Noir Southeast Block Reserve	91	2012–2025
2003 Pinot Noir Southeast Block Reserve	91+	now–2015
2005 Pinot Noir West Block Reserve	91	2012–2025
2004 Pinot Noir West Block Reserve	90	now–2014
2003 Pinot Noir West Block Reserve	89	now–2013

BOEDECKER CELLARS ★ ★ ★
WILLAMETTE VALLEY $18.00–$40.00

2004 Pinot Noir Athena	89	now–2012
2005 Pinot Noir Pappas Wine Co.	88	now–2011
2004 Pinot Noir Shea Vineyard	87	now–2012
2003 Pinot Noir Stewart	88	now–2012

BRICK HOUSE VINEYARDS ★ ★ ★ ★ ★
WILLAMETTE VALLEY $22.00–$50.00

Doug Tunnell, a hands-on viticulturalist if ever there was one, received biodynamic certification for his vineyards in 2005. He is also a champion of the Gamay Noir grape, and crafts arguably the finest version made outside of Beaujolais.

2005 Chardonnay	90	now–2013
2005 Gamay Noir	87	now–2011
2004 Gamay Noir	88	now–2012
2003 Gamay Noir	90	now–2011
2002 Gamay Noir	89	now–2009
2002 Pinot Noir Clos Ladybug	87	now–2010
2004 Pinot Noir Cuvée du Tonnelier	87	now–2010
2003 Pinot Noir Cuvée du Tonnelier	92	now–2015
2002 Pinot Noir Cuvée du Tonnelier	91	now–2014
2003 Pinot Noir Estate	91	now–2014
2002 Pinot Noir Estate	91	now–2012
2005 Pinot Noir Evelyn's	92+	2013–2027
2003 Pinot Noir Evelyn's	92+	now–2015
2002 Pinot Noir Evelyn's	93+	now–2014
2005 Pinot Noir Les Dijonnais	91+	2010–2020
2003 Pinot Noir Les Dijonnais	91	now–2015
2002 Pinot Noir Les Dijonnais	94	now–2014
2005 Pinot Noir Select	90	2013–2021

LE CADEAU VINEYARD ★ ★ ★ ★
WILLAMETTE VALLEY $50.00

Le Cadeau is a 28-acre microestate owned by Tom and Deb Mortimer. Previously flying under Robert Parker's *Wine Advocate* radar screen, if the wines continue to perform as they did in 2005, Pinot fans everywhere will be jumping on this winery's mailing list. The three wines are all estate grown and bottled.

2005 Pinot Noir Côte Est	90+	2010–2020
2005 Pinot Noir Diversité	91	2012–2022
2005 Pinot Noir Rocheux	93	2010–2020

CANA'S FEAST (FORMERLY CUNEO CELLARS) * * *
VARIOUS $40.00–$50.00

2005 Cana's Feast Pinot Noir	88	now–2013
2005 Cana's Feast Pinot Noir Elton Vineyard	91	2010–2020
2005 Cana's Feast Pinot Noir Meredith Mitchell Vineyard	89	now–2017

J. K. CARRIERE WINES * * * *
WILLAMETTE VALLEY $24.00–$65.00

Jim Prosser is owner-winemaker of the 3,500-case J. K. Carriere winery. He began in 1995 after several apprenticeships in Oregon, New Zealand, and Burgundy (with Roumier). His goal is to make "Pinot with high acids, smooth tannins, meant to age."

2004 Pinot Noir	90	now–2014
2004 Pinot Noir Anderson Family	92	2012–2024
2004 Pinot Noir Antoinette	88	now–2014
2003 Pinot Noir Antoinette	90	now–2015
2005 Pinot Noir Provocateur	89	2009–2017

CHEHALEM * * * *
VARIOUS $27.00–$60.00

Chehalem is led by co-owner and winemaker Harry Peterson-Nedry. He planted the estate's Ridgecrest Vineyard in 1980 and founded the winery in 1990. Chehalem is unusual for Willamette Valley in that over 50% of its production is white wine from Riesling, Pinot Blanc, Pinot Gris, and Chardonnay. Readers who see Chehalem's whites should try these uniformly excellent wines.

2005 Pinot Noir Corral Creek	91	2010–2020
2004 Pinot Noir Corral Creek	87	now–2011
2003 Pinot Noir Corral Creek	92	now–2015
2002 Pinot Noir Corral Creek	90	now–2012
2005 Pinot Noir Reserve	92	2012–2027
2004 Pinot Noir Reserve	89	now–2014
2003 Pinot Noir Reserve	92	2009–2017
2002 Pinot Noir Reserve	93	now–2014
2005 Pinot Noir Ridgecrest	89+	now–2013
2004 Pinot Noir Ridgecrest	88	now–2014
2003 Pinot Noir Ridgecrest	86+	now–2010
2002 Pinot Noir Ridgecrest	92	now–2012
2005 Pinot Noir RR	89	2015–2027
2005 Pinot Noir Stoller	90	2012–2025
2004 Pinot Noir Stoller	87	now–2011
2003 Pinot Noir Stoller	89	now–2013
2002 Pinot Noir Stoller	91+	now–2012
2005 Pinot Noir 3 Vineyard	89	now–2013
2004 Pinot Noir 3 Vineyard	87	now–2012
2002 Pinot Noir 3 Vineyard	88	now–2010

2005 Pinot Noir Paciência Estate	90	2009–2017

CRISTOM VINEYARDS ★ ★ ★ ★
WILLAMETTE VALLEY $30.00–$100.00

Cristom Vineyards is a 65-acre estate owned by Paul Gerrie. Winemaking is in the skilled hands of Steve Doerner, who has been present from the beginning (after a stint in California putting Calera on the map during the mid- to late '80s). Aside from Pinot Noir, the winery makes excellent Pinot Gris, Viognier, Chardonnay, and Syrah, all from estate-grown fruit.

2005 Pinot Noir Eileen Vineyard	91+	2012–2022
2004 Pinot Noir Eileen Vineyard	90	now–2014
2002 Pinot Noir Eileen Vineyard	93	now–2014
2005 Pinot Noir Jessie Vineyard	92+	2013–2025
2002 Pinot Noir Jessie Vineyard	92	now–2014
2004 Pinot Noir Louise Vineyard	90	2010–2020
2002 Pinot Noir Louise Vineyard	92+	now–2012
2005 Pinot Noir Marjorie Vineyard	92+	2012–2022
2004 Pinot Noir Marjorie Vineyard	91	now–2018
2003 Pinot Noir Marjorie Vineyard	90	now–2015
2002 Pinot Noir Marjorie Vineyard	89	now–2012
2005 Pinot Noir Mt. Jefferson Cuvée	88+	now–2017
2002 Pinot Noir Reserve	88	now–2010
2004 Pinot Noir Signature Cuvée	94	2010–2020
2004 Pinot Noir Sommers Reserve	89+	2009–2020
2005 Pinot Noir Sommers Reserve	93+	2012–2025

DOBBES FAMILY ESTATE ★ ★ ★
WILLAMETTE VALLEY $24.00–$50.00

2005 Pinot Noir Cuvée Noir	86	now–2011
2005 Pinot Noir Grand Assemblage Cuvée	90	now–2011
2005 Pinot Noir Griffin's Cuvée	88	now–2011

DOMAINE COTEAU ★ ★ ★ ★
EOLA-AMITY HILLS $30.00

2005 Pinot Noir Reserve	92+	2011–2022

DOMAINE DROUHIN ★ ★ ★ ★ ★
DUNDEE HILLS $45.00–$90.00

Domaine Drouhin has been on a roll since the 2002 vintage. Dare I say the winery seems to be making better wine in Oregon than they are in France?

2005 Chardonnay	91	now–2011
2005 Pinot Noir	90	now–2015
2005 Pinot Noir Laurène	93	2012–2027
2004 Pinot Noir Laurène	83	now–2014
2002 Pinot Noir Laurène	89	now–2013
2005 Pinot Noir Louise Drouhin	95	2014–2030
2004 Pinot Noir Louise Drouhin	93	2012–2025

DOMAINE SERENE ★★★★
WILLAMETTE VALLEY $52.00–$90.00

At Domaine Serene no expense is spared in the pursuit of quality. The winery turns out some of Oregon's finest Chardonnays and Pinot Noirs. That said, on occasion a vintage presents problems that are difficult to overcome, as with Domaine Serene's 2004 Pinot Noirs. They range from very good to excellent but are not at the level normally associated with this estate. The good news is that the 2005 Pinot Noirs are among the finest of that challenging year.

2004 Pinot Noir Evenstad Reserve	86	now–2012
2003 Pinot Noir Evenstad Reserve	89+	now–2013
2002 Pinot Noir Evenstad Reserve	89	now–2012
2001 Pinot Noir Evenstad Reserve	86	now–2009
2000 Pinot Noir Evenstad Reserve	88	now–2010
2004 Pinot Noir Grace Vineyard	90	now–2014
2003 Pinot Noir Grace Vineyard	92	now–2014
2002 Pinot Noir Grace Vineyard	90	now–2015
2000 Pinot Noir Grace Vineyard	90	now–2012
2004 Pinot Noir Jerusalem Hill Vineyard	83	now–2012
2003 Pinot Noir Jerusalem Hill Vineyard	91	now–2015
2002 Pinot Noir Jerusalem Hill Vineyard	92	now–2012
2004 Pinot Noir Mark Bradford Vineyard	89	now–2014
2003 Pinot Noir Mark Bradford Vineyard	91+	2009–2017
2002 Pinot Noir Mark Bradford Vineyard	90	now–2014
2003 Pinot Noir Winery Hill Vineyard	92	now–2013
2002 Pinot Noir Yamhill Cuvée	89	now–2011

ELK COVE VINEYARDS ★★★
WILLAMETTE VALLEY $24.00–$55.00

Elk Cove started to produce wine in 1977, making them one of Oregon's pioneers.

2005 Pinot Noir	88	now–2013
2004 Pinot Noir	88	now–2011
2002 Pinot Noir Reserve	87	now–2010
2004 Pinot Noir La Bohème	89	2009–2017
2004 Pinot Noir Mount Richmond	91	now–2014
2004 Pinot Noir Roosevelt	90+	2010–2020
2002 Pinot Noir Roosevelt	87	now–2010

EVESHAM WOOD VINEYARD ★★★★
WILLAMETTE VALLEY $40.00–$50.00

2003 Pinot Noir Cuvée J	90	now–2013
2003 Pinot Noir Le Puits Sec	90	now–2013

GROCHAU CELLARS ★★★
WILLAMETTE VALLEY $24.00–$35.00

Grochau Cellars is owned and operated by John Grochau, who doubles as winemaker at Aramenta Cellars. He uses the winery facilities at Aramenta to make his wine, the first vintage of which was 2002.

2005 GC Pinot Noir	87	now–2013
2005 Pinot Noir Cuvée des Amis	88	now–2015

GYPSY DANCER ESTATES ★★★
VARIOUS $43.00–$60.00

2005 Pinot Noir A & G Estate Vineyard	87+	now–2015
2005 Pinot Noir Broadley Vineyard	89	now–2015
2005 Pinot Noir Gary & Christine's Vineyard	88	now–2015

HAMACHER WINES ★★★★
WILLAMETTE VALLEY $30.00–$45.00

Eric Hamacher is one of the few producers of Pinot Noir who will not admit to being a *ter-roirist*. On his web page he states that Oregon's vineyards are mostly too young and too inconsistent to get locked into specific sites. He feels that better wine can be made by careful selection across a number of the Willamette Valley's districts and by judicious blending.

2004 Chardonnay Cuvée Forêts Diverses	90	now–2011
2004 Pinot Noir	89	now–2014
2003 Pinot Noir	94+	now–2015
2002 Pinot Noir	90+	now–2015
2001 Pinot Noir	90	now–2010

LACHINI VINEYARDS ★★★
DUNDEE HILLS $60.00

2005 Pinot Noir Ana Vineyard	90	2009–2017
2004 Pinot Noir Cuvée Giselle	89	now–2012

LEMELSON VINEYARDS ★★★
WILLAMETTE VALLEY $38.00–$40.00

2004 Pinot Noir Meyer Vineyard	88	now–2012
2004 Pinot Noir Thea's Selection	89	now–2014
2002 Pinot Noir Jerome Reserve	90	now–2012
2002 Pinot Noir Resonance Vineyard	89	now–2010

NYSA VINEYARD ★★★
DUNDEE HILLS $45.00

Nysa Vineyard, owned by Michael Mega, is a densely planted vineyard (2,400 vines per acre) dating to 1990 and has been the source of vineyard-designated Pinot Noirs by a number of notable wineries. These are the first estate bottlings.

2004 Pinot Noir	90	now–2016
2005 Pinot Noir	88	now–2015

OWEN ROE ★★★
VARIOUS $42.00

2005 Pinot Noir	87	now–2011
2005 Pinot Noir The Kilmore	91	now–2011

PANTHER CREEK CELLARS ★★★
VARIOUS $40.00

2002 Pinot Noir Anden Vineyard	86	now–2010
2002 Pinot Noir Bednarik Vineyard	88	now–2012

2003 Pinot Noir Freedom Hill	88+	now–2013
2002 Pinot Noir Freedom Hill	89	now–2012
2002 Pinot Noir Nysa Vineyard	88	now–2012
2004 Pinot Noir Shea Vineyard	87	now–2014
2003 Pinot Noir Shea Vineyard	91	now–2015
2002 Pinot Noir Shea Vineyard	87	now–2009
2003 Pinot Noir Temperance Hill	90+	now–2015
2002 Pinot Noir Temperance Hill	88	now–2012
2002 Pinot Noir White Rose Vineyard	88	now–2012

PENNER-ASH WINE CELLARS ★★★★
VARIOUS $45.00–$60.00

Lynn Penner-Ash had a long, successful career at Rex Hill before starting her namesake winery with her husband, Ron, in 1998. They are now ensconced in a new gravity-flow winery of their own design. 2005 was their first vintage in the new facility.

2005 Pinot Noir	90	now–2015
2004 Pinot Noir	89	now–2014
2002 Pinot Noir	88	now–2012
2002 Pinot Noir Bethel Heights Vineyard	88	now–2012
2005 Pinot Noir Dussin Vineyard	93	2011–2021
2005 Pinot Noir Goldschmidt Vineyard	91	2010–2020
2004 Pinot Noir Goldschmidt Vineyard	90	now–2014
2002 Pinot Noir Goldschmidt Vineyard	92	now–2014
2005 Pinot Noir Seven Springs Vineyard	80?	now–2010
2004 Pinot Noir Seven Springs Vineyard	90	now–2014
2002 Pinot Noir Seven Springs Vineyard	88	now–2102
2005 Pinot Noir Shea Vineyard	91	2012–2025
2004 Pinot Noir Shea Vineyard	89	now–2014
2003 Oregon Syrah	91	now–2013
2002 Oregon Syrah	89	now–2012

PONZI VINEYARDS ★★★★
WILLAMETTE VALLEY $17.00–$60.00

Ponzi Vineyards began in 1970, making them one of Oregon's pioneers. Dick and Nancy Ponzi, the founders, remain very much involved although winemaking duties were turned over to daughter Luisa in 1993. In addition to remaining a reference point for Oregon Pinot Noir, the winery fashions excellent wines from Italian varietals, including Arneis and Dolcetto, in honor of their heritage.

2005 Pinot Noir	89	now–2013
2005 Pinot Noir Il Luce	91	2010–2020
2005 Pinot Noir Abetina	92	2010–2020

REX HILL VINEYARDS AND WINERY ★★★
WILLAMETTE VALLEY $25.00–$50.00

2004 Pinot Noir	86	now–2012
2004 Pinot Noir Seven Springs Vineyard	90	now–2014

ROCKBLOCK ★ ★ ★ ★
VARIOUS $30.00–$45.00

Rockblock is Domaine Serene's Rhone Ranger winery.

2004 Syrah Del Rio Vineyard	90	2009–2017
2003 Syrah Del Rio Vineyard	88	now–2012
2001 Syrah Del Rio Vineyard	89	now–2009
2001 Syrah Seven Hills Vineyard	88	now–2010
2004 Syrah Seven Hills Vineyard	91	2010–2020
2003 Syrah Seven Hills Vineyard	86	now–2012
2002 Syrah Seven Hills Vineyard	86	now–2011
2001 Syrah Seven Hills Vineyard	88	now–2010
2005 Del Rio Vineyard Viognier	89	now–2009

ROCO WINES ★ ★ ★ ★
VARIOUS $40.00–$70.00

ROCO wines are owned and operated by Rollin and Corby Soles and include their seven-acre Wits' End Vineyard. Rollin Soles has been the winemaker at Argyle Winery since 1987.

2005 Pinot Noir	92	2012–2025
2005 Pinot Noir Private Stash	91	2009–2017

ST. INNOCENT WINERY ★ ★ ★ ★ ★
WILLAMETTE VALLEY $22.00–$45.00

Owner-winemaker Mark Vlossak operates his winery out of an industrial park in Salem. He sources from some of the finest sites in the Willamette Valley, turning out flavorful Pinot Gris, Pinot Blanc, Chardonnay, and Pinot Noir, selling them at remarkably fair prices. Check out St. Innocent's website for Vlossak's harvest reports to get the lowdown on recent vintages and to see how a skilled winemaker adapts to the varied conditions presented by the region's fickle weather.

2002 Pinot Noir	90	now–2012
2004 Pinot Noir Anden Vineyard	85	now–2011
2003 Pinot Noir Anden Vineyard	93	2009–2017
2002 Pinot Noir Freedom Hill Vineyard	94	now–2016
2005 Pinot Noir Justice Vineyard	92+	2013–2023
2004 Pinot Noir Seven Springs Vineyard	85	now–2011
2003 Pinot Noir Seven Springs Vineyard	91+	2009–2017
2002 Pinot Noir Seven Springs Vineyard	94+	now–2016
2005 Pinot Noir Shea Vineyard	91+	2011–2023
2004 Pinot Noir Shea Vineyard	90	now–2014
2003 Pinot Noir Shea Vineyard	93	now–2015
2002 Pinot Noir Shea Vineyard	94	now–2014
2003 Pinot Noir Temperance Hill	86	now–2011
2002 Pinot Noir Temperance Hill	85	now–2009
2003 Pinot Noir Villages Cuvée	87	now–2011
2004 Pinot Noir Villages Cuvée	89	now–2014
2003 Pinot Noir White Rose Vineyard	94	now–2015
2002 Pinot Noir White Rose Vineyard	91+	now–2014

SHEA WINE CELLARS ★ ★ ★ ★
WILLAMETTE VALLEY $40.00–$75.00

Dick and Deirdre Shea began planting their 200-acre site in 1989 (140 acres are now planted) and started the winery in 1996. Over the years, some of the most renowned wineries in the region, including Manfred Krankl at California's Sine Qua Non, have made Shea Vineyard–designated Pinot Noirs, a testament to the quality of the fruit. As one might expect with a vineyard of this size, there are numerous exposures and microclimates, and the vineyard is planted with a wide variety of clones.

2005 Pinot Noir East Hill	90	2013–2027
2005 Pinot Noir Estate	90+	2012–2025
2002 Pinot Noir Estate	85	now–2012
2005 Pinot Noir Pommard Clones	92	2012–2024
2002 Pinot Noir Pommard Clone	86	now–2012
2005 Pinot Noir Wadenswil Clone	92+	2012–2024
2005 Pinot Noir Homer	93	2012–2024

SOKOL BLOSSER WINERY ★ ★ ★
DUNDEE HILLS $40.00–$60.00

2002 Pinot Noir	85	now–2009
2002 Pinot Noir Estate Cuvée	89	now–2012
2002 Pinot Noir Watershed Block	88	now–2010

SOTER VINEYARDS ★ ★ ★ ★ ★
YAMHILL-CARLTON $35.00–$48.00

Renowned Napa Valley winemaker Tony Soter (Étude, Spottswoode, among others) has made a full-time commitment to Willamette Valley, moving his family, building a winery, and planting a vineyard. In addition to Pinot Noir, Soter also produces superb sparkling wine.

2001 Beacon Hill Brut Rosé	92	now–2011
2005 Pinot Noir Beacon Hill	91	2011–2021
2003 Pinot Noir Beacon Hill	93	2009–2017
2002 Pinot Noir Beacon Hill	91	now–2012
2005 Pinot Noir Mineral Springs	92	2012–2022
2005 Pinot Noir North Valley	90	now–2015

STOLLER VINEYARDS ★ ★ ★
DUNDEE HILLS $28.00–$65.00

Stoller Vineyards is a 373-acre estate in the Dundee Hills AVA. Planting began in 1995 and there are now 130 acres under vine. The winery's first vintage was 2001.

2005 Chardonnay Estate	88	now–2011
2004 Pinot Noir	90	now–2014
2003 Pinot Noir	89	now–2013
2004 Pinot Noir JV	87	now–2010
2005 Pinot Noir Estate	87	2011–2020
2004 Pinot Noir Estate	88	now–2014
2002 Pinot Noir Estate Grown	91	now–2012
2005 Pinot Noir Estate Kathy's	90	2011–2020
2004 Pinot Noir Estate Kathy's	89	now–2014

STONY MOUNTAIN VINEYARD ★★★
McMINNVILLE $27.00

2004 Pinot Noir	87	now–2014

TORII MOR WINERY ★★★
DUNDEE HILLS $55.00

2005 Pinot Noir La Colina Vineyard	86	now–2011

WHITE ROSE WINES ★★★
DUNDEE HILLS $45.00–$50.00

2005 Pinot Noir Quiotee's Lair	89	now–2015
2004 Pinot Noir Quiotee's Lair	88	now–2014

WILLAKENZIE ESTATE ★★★★
WILLAMETTE VALLEY $23.00–$55.00

Over the past 15 years Willakenzie Estate (named for the soil type on which the winery sits) has been a consistently excellent source for Pinot Blanc, Pinot Gris, and particularly, Pinot Noir. The quality has been solid and the prices have been fair.

2005 Pinot Noir	88	now–2013
2004 Pinot Noir Aliette	90	now–2012
2004 Pinot Noir Emery	90	2009–2017
2002 Pinot Noir Emery	89	now–2012
2004 Pinot Noir Kiana	82	now–2010
2004 Pinot Noir Pierre Léon	87	now–2012
2002 Pinot Noir Pierre Léon	88	now–2012
2004 Pinot Noir Terres Basses	90	2010–2018
2002 Pinot Noir Terres Basses	89+	now–2016
2004 Pinot Noir Triple Black Slopes	88	now–2014
2002 Pinot Noir Triple Black Slopes	90	now–2015

KEN WRIGHT CELLARS ★★★★★
VARIOUS $45.00

Ken Wright Cellars has long been one of the reference points for Pinot Noir fanatics. Ken Wright is the ultimate *terroirist*, stating on his website (which I highly recommend reading) that Pinot Noir is the perfect vehicle for expressing the characteristics of the site in which it is grown. He says that the secret to making great Pinot Noir is ". . . learning how to farm. Every vineyard has its own issues."

2005 Pinot Noir Abbott Claim Vineyard	92+	2013–2026
2005 Pinot Noir Canary Hill Vineyard	89	now–2015
2003 Pinot Noir Canary Hill Vineyard	86	now–2011
2002 Pinot Noir Canary Hill Vineyard	91	now–2012
2005 Pinot Noir Carter Vineyard	93+	2014–2030
2004 Pinot Noir Carter Vineyard	90	now–2014
2003 Pinot Noir Carter Vineyard	89	now–2013
2002 Pinot Noir Carter Vineyard	90	now–2012
2005 Pinot Noir Elton Vineyard	92+	2012–2025
2002 Pinot Noir Elton Vineyard	89	now–2010
2005 Pinot Noir Freedom Hill Vineyard	87	now–2011

2005 Pinot Noir Guadalupe Vineyard	92	now–2017
2003 Pinot Noir Guadalupe Vineyard	86	now–2013
2005 Pinot Noir McCrone Vineyard	92	
2004 Pinot Noir McCrone Vineyard	90	now–2012
2003 Pinot Noir McCrone Vineyard	91	now–2013
2005 Pinot Noir Meredith Mitchell Vineyard	90	now–2015
2003 Pinot Noir Meredith Mitchell Vineyard	87	now–2011
2005 Pinot Noir Nysa Vineyard	92	2012–2025
2004 Pinot Noir Nysa Vineyard	93	2009–2017
2005 Pinot Noir Savoya Vineyard	91	now–2017
2004 Pinot Noir Savoya Vineyard	88+	now–2014
2003 Pinot Noir Savoya Vineyard	88+	now–2011
2005 Pinot Noir Shea Vineyard	94	2012–2025
2004 Pinot Noir Shea Vineyard	91	now–2011
2003 Pinot Noir Shea Vineyard	90+	now–2015
2002 Pinot Noir Wahle Vineyard	90	now–2012

[washington] [state]

In 1990 I traveled to Washington to do research for a review published in Robert Parker's *Wine Advocate*, issue 69. There were 42 working wineries in total, 4 in Walla Walla, all of which I was able to visit in just a few days. Today there are more than 500 wineries and 100 in the Walla Walla AVA (American Viticultural Area). In the early days Riesling was king, accounting for more than 50% of vineyard acreage, and Merlot was a major player among the red wines. Today Riesling has fallen below 20% and Merlot is primarily a blending grape. In 1990 I was not offered a single Syrah to taste! Today Washington is one of the leaders in the production of world-class Syrah, much of it coming out of the Walla Walla AVA. Also, we are beginning to see more and more Cabernet Franc and Petit Verdot, both of which seem to thrive in the Columbia Valley. In the future, I would expect to see some of these bottled as varietal wines—that is how good they can be. In 1990 the city of Walla Walla appeared to be dying; now it is in the midst of a renaissance thanks to the booming wine industry, and it is well established that great Bordeaux-style wines can be produced in eastern Washington. With vineyard property in Napa Valley at a premium, when it can be found, and with plenty of land still available in Washington at relatively inexpensive prices, wealthy winery-owner wannabees are just beginning to descend on eastern Washington, Walla Walla in particular.

As has been noted in these pages previously, Washington weather is ideal for grape growing. There is plenty of sunshine, a long growing season, virtually no chance of harvest rainfall, and control of the water supply through drip irrigation. The main challenges are winter freezes—such as occurred in 1996 and 2004. While growers are better equipped than ever to deal with this problem, in Walla Walla Valley in 2004 nearly the entire crop was ruined during these freezes. Only the tiny handful of vineyards whose owners buried their vines prior to winter and those vineyards at the highest elevations were spared total loss. One of the nicer stories is that large producers such as Chateau Ste. Michelle sold fruit to wineries who would otherwise have had no wine in 2004. As a result, there is not much Walla Walla AVA wine in the 2004 vintage but plenty of Columbia Valley wine.

A GEOGRAPHY PRIMER

Virtually all of the wines described here are from the Columbia Valley appellation, which includes the Yakima and Walla Walla Valleys. Primarily a desert, it is located in southeastern Washington and overlaps into Oregon. As Pacific Ocean depressions approach the Washington coastline, they are often trapped by the coastal Olympic Mountains, dropping much of their precipitation on the rain forests located on the range's western slopes. When a weather front is powerful enough to remain intact after traversing the Olympic Mountains, it then faces the even higher elevations of the Cascades. Very few depressions are capable of clearing both these ranges and, as a consequence, eastern Washington experiences desertlike conditions (in fact, the U.S. Army stages desert training exercises in Yakima).

As one flies from Seattle to Walla Walla, it is amazing to see the contrast between the lush green western slopes of the Cascades and the barren eastern side. From the tips of the Cascades all the way to Walla Walla, the only signs of vegetation are the trees bordering rivers and irrigated farms. One statistic clearly demonstrates this weather pattern: Within the town of Walla Walla, on the eastern edge of the Columbia Valley appellation, annual rainfall increases by one inch per mile as one travels eastward. On the parched western edge of Walla Walla, abutting the L'Ecole Nº 41 and Woodward Canyon wineries, are dusty asparagus fields. On the eastern edge, where Walla Walla Vintners' and Leonetti Cellar's new vineyards are located, the rolling hills are lush and green.

Rain, the bane of wine producers the world over, is rarely a nuisance for Washington's main grape-growing region. Because Washington State vineyards are irrigated, viticulturalists can control the quantity of water each row of vines gets.

Readers should not assume that because Washington State borders Canada it has a cold climate. Once spring arrives, the Columbia Valley enjoys a grape-growing season that winemakers the world over would envy. Sun and heat are plentiful and evenings are cool— excellent for maintaining natural acidity levels.

This is not, however, a viticultural paradise. The winters and early springs can be a grape grower's nightmare. Why? The region is prone to "killer freezes" (as they are known in these parts) on average once every six years, the last of which descended from the Arctic in late January and early February 1996 and devastated the vineyards. A less severe freeze in 2004 decimated much of the crop, except at the highest elevations.

THE WINEMAKERS AND GRAPE GROWERS

Unlike those in California, Oregon, Bordeaux, and Burgundy, the majority of Washington State wineries do not own vineyards. With the exception of large producers such as Chateau Ste. Michelle, Columbia Winery, and some others, winemakers in this state are dependent upon grapes purchased from growers. For the most part, Washington State's producers are converted home winemakers. Prior to going into wine full-time, Gary Figgins (Leonetti) was a machinist at the local Walla Walla cannery; Alex Golitzin (Quilceda Creek) was an engineer for Scott Paper; Chris Camarda (Andrew Will) was a waiter, as was Matthew Loso (Matthews Cellars); and so on. It's the same story—they fell in love with wine, decided to try their hand at it, acquired grapes, and the rest is history.

Increasingly, the top wineries contract with their growers to buy grapes by the acre rather than by the ton. This allows growers the freedom to lower yields without sacrificing earnings. Even better, a number of the top wineries are increasingly reinvesting profits into purchasing vineyards and planting new ones. The results from these new, winery-owned vineyards are

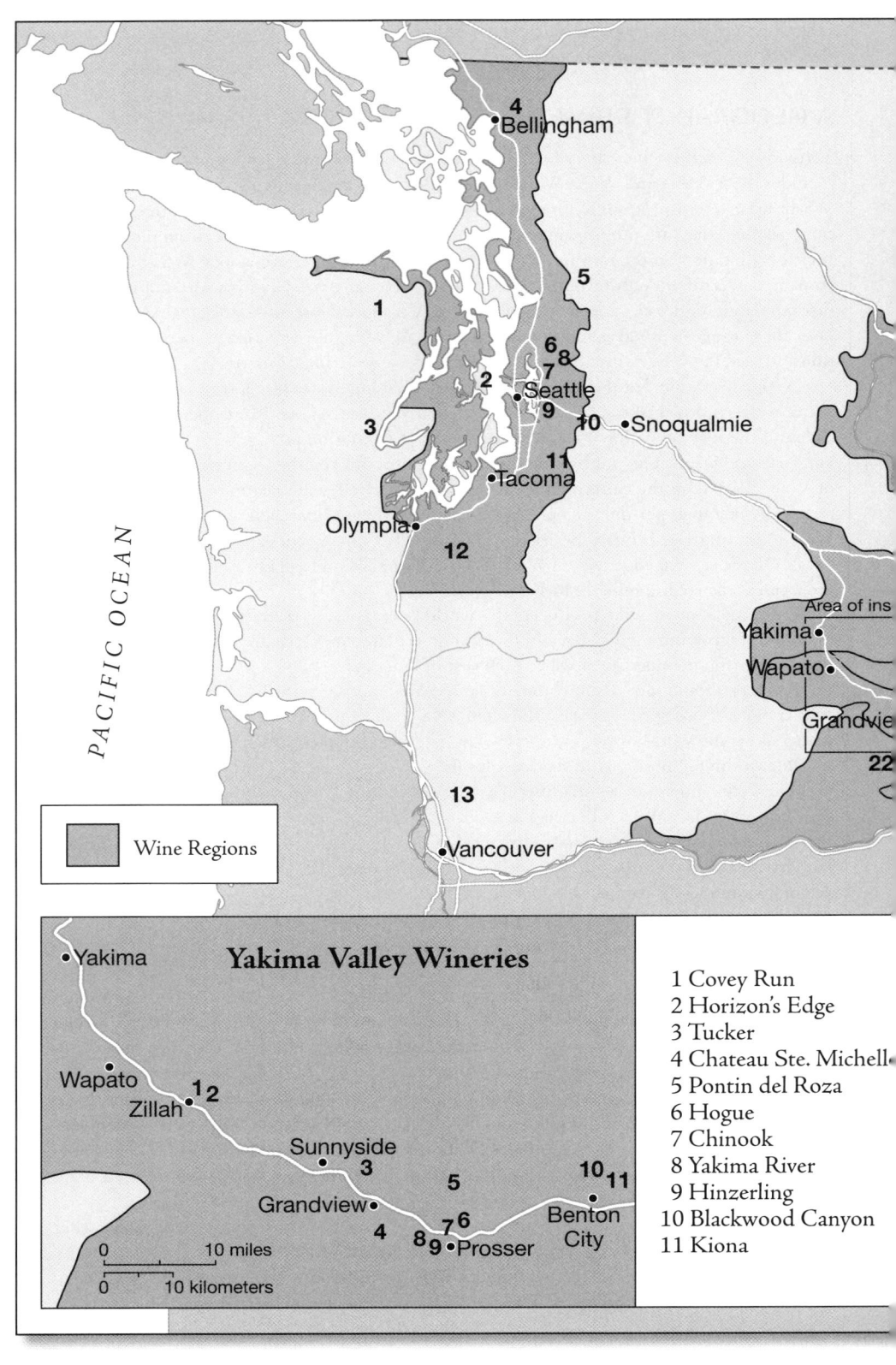

PACIFIC OCEAN

4 •Bellingham

5

1

6 8
7
2 •Seattle
9
3 10 •Snoqualmie

11
•Tacoma

Olympia•

12

Area of ins

Yakima•

Wapato•

Grandvie

22

13

•Vancouver

Wine Regions

Yakima Valley Wineries

•Yakima

Wapato•
1 2
Zillah•

Sunnyside•
3

Grandview•
4
8 7 6
9 •Prosser

10 11

Benton
City

5

0   10 miles
0   10 kilometers

1 Covey Run
2 Horizon's Edge
3 Tucker
4 Chateau Ste. Michell
5 Pontin del Roza
6 Hogue
7 Chinook
8 Yakima River
9 Hinzerling
10 Blackwood Canyon
11 Kiona

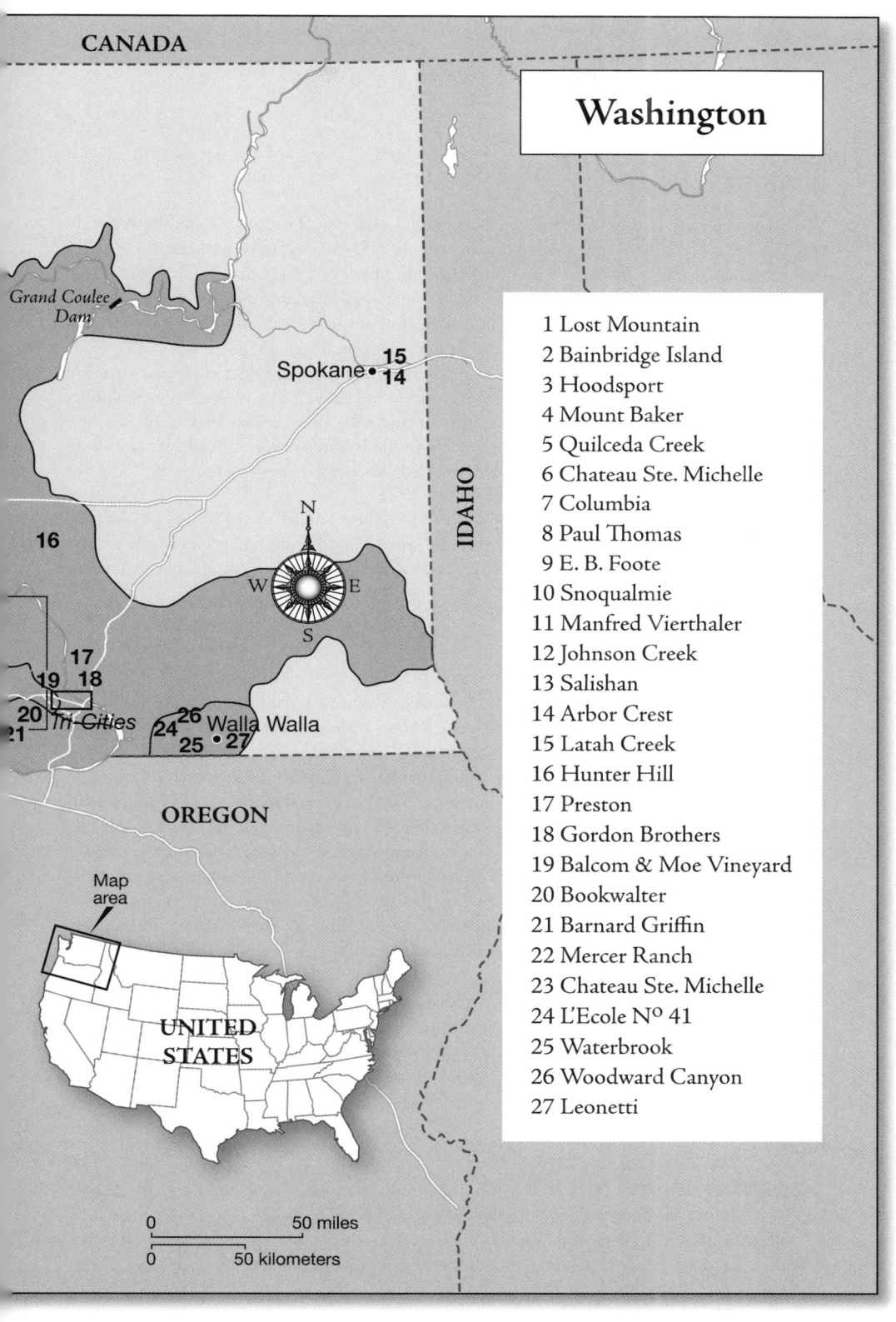

Washington

CANADA

Grand Coulee Dam

Spokane • 15
14

IDAHO

N
W E
S

16

17
19 18
20 Tri-Cities 26 Walla Walla
21 24 25 • 27

OREGON

Map area

UNITED STATES

0   50 miles
0   50 kilometers

1 Lost Mountain
2 Bainbridge Island
3 Hoodsport
4 Mount Baker
5 Quilceda Creek
6 Chateau Ste. Michelle
7 Columbia
8 Paul Thomas
9 E. B. Foote
10 Snoqualmie
11 Manfred Vierthaler
12 Johnson Creek
13 Salishan
14 Arbor Crest
15 Latah Creek
16 Hunter Hill
17 Preston
18 Gordon Brothers
19 Balcom & Moe Vineyard
20 Bookwalter
21 Barnard Griffin
22 Mercer Ranch
23 Chateau Ste. Michelle
24 L'Ecole Nº 41
25 Waterbrook
26 Woodward Canyon
27 Leonetti

just beginning to be reflected in the quality of the wines, but it is clear that the state's top estates have an exceedingly bright future.

[the wines]

WINE STYLES

We all have notions of what a Bordeaux, Burgundy, California, Tuscan, or Piedmontese wine tastes like. Granted, there are exceptions to every rule, and even the most sophisticated palates in the world can easily be tricked in a blind tasting. However, there are certain basic flavor profiles and styles that characterize all of the great wine-producing regions of the world— except Washington State. I have tasted hundreds of wines from the Columbia, Yakima, and Walla Walla Valleys and I was incapable of finding a regional signature.

Thankfully, winemakers such as those just named are crafting wines each year that one hopes will serve as a reference point for others in the industry. Many producers craft subtle, elegant, and focused wines (DeLille, for example), and still others have achieved an amazing combination of power and finesse (Quilceda Creek) that is reminiscent of Bordeaux at its very best. Their polar opposites—dense, hyperextracted, alcoholic wines—can also be found in Washington but increasingly less frequently.

Washington State as a wine region is still in its infancy, and that's the beauty of it. These converted home winemakers are defining the future of Washington wines before our eyes— and palates. There are no traditions and no parameters. Any style is acceptable. Anything goes. It truly is a frontier.

TYPES OF WINE

Virtually all the varieties seen in California are also grown in Washington. Recently, Rhone Rangers (wines produced from the traditional Rhône varieties) have come very much into vogue, and a few (particularly Cayuse) show immense promise. However, Washington's wineries are still banking on Chardonnay and Cabernet Sauvignon. Merlot has been relegated to the status of blending grape. A relatively large percentage of the state's vineyards are planted with Riesling, but this is diminishing as newly planted vineyards rarely include this variety. Fortunately, Washington's consumers appear to enjoy Riesling, which is usually bargain priced. The producers continue to crank it out because it is easy and inexpensive to make— the perfect cash-flow wine. For Riesling aficionados, these wines represent fine values. Washington also produces this country's best Chenin Blanc and Muscat. Their crisp natural acidity, easily obtained due to Washington's northern latitude, makes these wines, finished in an off-dry to slightly sweet style, ideal summer sipping and picnic wines. Sadly, the market for these wines is limited. For better or worse, the state's future rests with the superstar grapes—Cabernet Sauvignon, Syrah, and Chardonnay. The good news is that these are the wines the marketing people claim consumers desire, and Washington State's main rival, California, is pricing itself out of the competition.

RED

CABERNET SAUVIGNON This is Washington's most successful grape variety. In capable hands, it renders an almost opaque, purple wine. Cabernet Sauvignon usually ripens fully in eastern Washington, resulting in wines with aromas of currants, spices, plums, and cedar, as well as excellent extract, medium to full body, and good depth and concentration. Overwhelming aromas and flavors of herbs and vegetables are rarely as intrusive in Washington Cabernet Sauvignons as they can be in California.

MERLOT It was already happening prior to the film *Sideways*. Merlot has fallen from favor and has been relegated to blending-grape status. Washington is capable of growing outstanding Merlot (better than in Napa Valley), but no one wants to buy it.

SYRAH Washington producers are hoping that Syrah will bring the state fame. Some wineries (Cayuse, Betz Family, and Amavi, for example) are crafting some of the finest Syrahs made in the U.S. They have proved that Washington State can compete on the world stage with this varietal.

PETIT VERDOT Still primarily a blending grape but the enormous potential for this nearly forgotten Bordeaux variety is readily apparent. Expect to see some sensational varietally labeled Petit Verdot over the next 8 to 10 years.

WHITE

CHARDONNAY Washington Chardonnay occupies more than 15% of vineyard acreage and can ripen fully while retaining excellent natural acidity. This has caused increasing numbers of producers to barrel-ferment it, and to encourage their Chardonnay to complete malolactic fermentation. Extended lees contact, in vogue in California, is also favored by many Washington producers. A number of wineries have invested heavily in new French oak barrels and are trying to make a wine in the Côte de Beaune style. Others are going after a fruitier style (à la Fetzer's Sundial), and still others are aiming for something in between. In short, there is a wide range of styles, but the potential for making outstanding Washington State Chardonnay exists, although much of it remains unrealized. The state's finest Chardonnays are produced by Chateau Ste. Michelle and Woodward Canyon.

SAUVIGNON BLANC When vinified in Washington, the potentially extroverted, herbal, grassy qualities of this grape are held in check. Many wineries also give the wines some exposure to oak barrels. As in California, most wineries strive for a safe, middle-of-the-road style that too often results in bland, insipid wines. Washington State Sauvignons are, however, priced to sell in the $12 to $20 range, which makes them attractive to consumers.

SÉMILLON This grape has excellent potential in Washington. It yields a wine with plenty of body and richness combined with the lively acidity typically found in Washington grapes.

WHITE (JOHANNISBERG) RIESLING Washington's Rieslings are good but often simple and one-dimensional when compared to the slaty, mineral-scented aromatic complexity and the incredible lightness and zestiness attainable in the best German Rieslings. However, Washington's abundant quantities of Rieslings are practically given away, usually selling for less than $12.

—JAY MILLER

[the ratings]

WASHINGTON'S BEST PRODUCERS

Note: Where a producer has been assigned a range of stars (***/****), the lower rating has been used for placement in this hierarchy.

★ ★ ★ ★ ★ (OUTSTANDING)

Andrew Will Winery
Betz Family Winery
Cayuse Vineyards
Col Solare
DeLille Cellars
Doyenne

Januik Winery
Leonetti Cellar
Long Shadows Vintners
Pepper Bridge Winery
Quilceda Creek Vintners
Woodward Canyon Winery

★ ★ ★ ★ (EXCELLENT)

Amavi Cellars
Animale
Bergevin Lane Vineyards
Boudreaux Cellars
Buty Winery
Cadence
Brian Carter Cellars
Chateau Ste. Michelle
Cullin Hills Winery
Dunham Cellars
L'Ecole Nº 41
Forgeron Cellars
Gorman Winery
Hence Cellars
Isenhower Cellars

JM Cellars
K Vintners
Latitude 46° N
Mark Ryan Winery
Matthews Estate
Nicholas Cole Cellars
Northstar Winery
Novelty Hill
Reininger Winery
Seven Hills Winery
Spring Valley Vineyard
Tamarack Cellars
Tertulia Cellars
Three Rivers Winery

★ ★ ★ (GOOD)

Abeja
Apex Cellars
Balsamroot Winery and Vineyard
Bunnell Family Cellar
Chatter Creek
Columbia Crest Winery
DiStefano Winery
Dumas Station Wines
Ensemble Cellars
Fall Line Winery
Five Star Cellars
Fort Walla Walla Cellars
Gifford Hirlinger Winery
Gordon Brothers Family Vineyards

James Leigh Cellars
Maryhill Winery
Merry Cellars
Morrison Lane
O-S Winery
Snoqualmie Winery
Soos Creek Wine Cellars
Sparkman Cellars
Stevens Winery
Syzygy
Va Piano Vineyards
Whitman Cellars
Zerba Cellars

★ ★ (AVERAGE)

Bookwalter Winery
Canoe Ridge Vineyard
Columbia Winery

Gamache Vintners
Walter Dacon Wines

[tasting commentaries]

ABEJA ✦ ✦ ✦
VARIOUS $30.00–$38.00

2004 Cabernet Sauvignon	88	2009–2017
2002 Cabernet Sauvignon Reserve One	89	now–2012
2005 Chardonnay	92	now–2011
2005 Merlot	89	2009–2017
2005 Syrah	88	now–2018

AMAVI CELLARS ✦ ✦ ✦ ✦ ✦
WALLA WALLA $25.00

Amavi Cellars is the sister winery to the better known Pepper Bridge Winery. It shares the same winemaker, Jean-François Pellet, and the same estate vineyards (Seven Hills, Pepper Bridge, and Les Collines) but from different vineyard blocks. Prices are about half of those of Pepper Bridge with virtually the same level of quality but made in a more forward style— immediate gratification is the name of Amavi's game.

2005 Sémillon	90	now–2010
2004 Syrah	92	2010–2022
2004 Syrah Les Collines Vineyard	91	now–2018
2004 Syrah Seven Hills Vineyard	93	2010–2022

ANDREW WILL WINERY ✦ ✦ ✦ ✦ ✦
VARIOUS $60.00–$65.00

Chris Camarda's Andrew Will Winery began in 1989 and currently produces 4,300 cases of predominantly Bordeaux-style blends. They reflect Carmada's interpretation of each vineyard's *terroir*.

2003 Annie Camarda Syrah	88	2010–2020
2002 Annie Camarda Syrah	89	now–2012
2002 Cabernet Sauvignon Klipsun Vineyard	89+	2011–2021
2001 Cabernet Sauvignon Klipsun Vineyard	92	2009–2018
2004 Champoux Vineyard	93	2012–2027
2003 Champoux Vineyard	93+	2009–2022
2002 Champoux Vineyard	93	2012–2024
2001 Champoux Vineyard	95	now–2018
2004 Ciel du Cheval Vineyard	89	now–2018
2003 Ciel du Cheval Vineyard	94+	2009–2022
2002 Ciel du Cheval Vineyard	94	2010–2019
2001 Ciel du Cheval Vineyard	94	2009–2017
2003 Klipsun Vineyard	88	2010–2020
2002 Merlot Klipsun Vineyard	91	now–2017
2004 Merlot Cuvée Lucia	89	2009–2017
2002 Seven Hills Vineyard	90	2009–2018
2004 Sheridan Vineyard	89	now–2018
2002 Sheridan Vineyard	91	2009–2018
2004 Sorella	92	2012–2027
2003 Sorella	93	2010–2022
2002 Sorella	93	2009–2018

| 2001 Sorella | 93 | now–2018 |
| 2004 Two Blondes Vineyard | 91 | now–2018 |

ANIMALE ★ ★ ★ ★
YAKIMA VALLEY $24.00–$26.00

Animale is a tiny, 150-case winery that began operations in 2001. Their website proudly proclaims it to be a no-holds-barred winery where power and flavor are paramount.

2005 Maria Carmela	90	now–2015
2001 Maria Carmela	87	now–2011
2005 Syrah	89	now–2013

APEX CELLARS ★ ★ ★
YAKIMA VALLEY $17.00–$30.00

Apex Cellars began operations in 1988. The veteran winemaker is Brian Carter, who recently began his own namesake winery in Woodinville.

2003 Cabernet Sauvignon	85	now–2010
1999 Cabernet Sauvignon Klipsun Vineyard	89+	now–2015
2005 Chardonnay	89	now–2009
2006 Dry Riesling	87	now–2009
2004 Gewürztraminer Ice Wine	90	now–2011
2000 Merlot	86	now–2010
2003 Syrah	89+	2009–2017

BERESAN WINERY ★ ★ ★
WALLA WALLA $35.00

Named after the region in the Ukraine where owner Tom Waliser's forebears established themselves in the early 19th century, Beresan Winery is located near the Oregon state line, south of Walla Walla.

2003 Cabernet Sauvignon	89	now–2013
2003 Merlot	89	now–2011
2003 Stone River	89	now–2011
2003 Syrah	89+	now–2013

BERGEVIN LANE VINEYARDS ★ ★ ★ ★
COLUMBIA VALLEY $25.00–$45.00

Bergevin Lane, located in Walla Walla, is owned and operated by Annette Bergevin and Amber Lane. Based on what is in the bottle and in the barrel, these young women are off to a flying start.

2004 Cabernet Sauvignon Alder Ridge Vineyard	90	2011–2022
2003 Cabernet Sauvignon	89	now–2013
2004 Intuition Reserve	92	2012–2027
2003 Intuition	91	2009–2017
2004 Syrah	90	now–2014
2003 Syrah	90	now–2013
2004 Syrah Barrel Select	92+	2012–2027

BETZ FAMILY WINERY ✴ ✴ ✴ ✴ ✴
COLUMBIA VALLEY $40.00–$65.00

Bob Betz, formerly a longtime executive at Chateau Ste. Michelle, started his winery in 1997 and has recently opened a new facility in Woodinville. He makes some of Washington's best Syrah, which typically spends 12 months in 50% new French oak, as well as Bordeaux-style blends, which see 17 months in varying proportions of new oak, depending on the type of grape.

2005 Clos de Betz	92	2010–2022
2002 Clos de Betz	88	now–2012
2001 Clos de Betz	90	now–2011
2005 Le Parrain	96	2015–2035
2005 Cabernet Sauvignon Père de Famille	90	2010–2020
2003 Cabernet Sauvignon Père de Famille	92	2010–2022
2002 Cabernet Sauvignon Père de Famille	92	2009–2017
2001 Cabernet Sauvignon Père de Famille	92	2009–2018
2004 Bésoleil	89	now–2014
2003 Bésoleil	88	now–2011
2005 Syrah Chapitre 3	94	2009–2017
2005 Syrah La Côte Rousse	93	2012–2027
2004 Syrah La Côte Rousse	90	now–2015
2003 Syrah La Côte Rousse	88	now–2014
2002 Syrah La Côte Rousse	90	now–2012
2001 Syrah La Côte Rousse	91	now–2011
2005 Syrah La Serenne	93	2011–2024
2004 Syrah La Serenne	91	now–2014
2003 Syrah La Serenne	89	now–2012
2002 Syrah La Serenne	88	now–2012
2001 Syrah La Serenne	90	now–2011

BOUDREAUX CELLARS ✴ ✴ ✴ ✴
VARIOUS $40.00–$80.00

Rob Newsom is the winemaker behind this impressive set of wines from Boudreaux Cellars. The winery purchases and blends grapes from some of the finest vineyards in Washington.

2004 Cabernet Sauvignon	91+	2013–2027
2003 Cabernet Sauvignon Champoux Vineyard	90+	2011–2022
2004 Merlot Bacchus and Desert Hills Vineyards	91	2010–2022
2002 Merlot Pepper Bridge and Seven Hills Vineyards	89	now–2012
2001 Merlot Pepper Bridge Vineyard	87	now–2011

BUNNELL FAMILY CELLAR ✴ ✴ ✴
VARIOUS $28.00–$38.00

Bunnell Family Cellar is a specialist in Rhône-style wines located in the foothills of the Horse Heaven Hills AVA.

2005 Syrah Boushey-McPherson Vineyards	86	now–2011
2005 Syrah Clifton Hill Vineyard	87	2009–2017
2005 VIF	88	now–2011

BUTY WINERY ★ ★ ★ ★
VARIOUS $21.00–$45.00

Caleb Foster, owner-winemaker of the 2,400-case Buty (pronounced "beauty") Winery, worked as assistant winemaker to Rick Small at Woodward Canyon for eight years prior to starting his own venture, beginning with the 2000 vintage.

2004 Beast	90	2010–2020
2005 Chardonnay Connor Lee Vineyard	90	now–2010
2002 Merlot	88	now–2011
2005 Merlot-Cabernet Franc	90	2011–2022
2004 Rediviva	90	2011–2022
2004 Rediviva of the Stones	91	2012–2025
2005 Sémillon-Sauvignon Blanc	89	now–2011

CADENCE ★ ★ ★ ★
RED MOUNTAIN $40.00–$55.00

Cadence Winery takes all of its fruit from the Red Mountain AVA, some of it from a recently planted estate vineyard.

2001 Camerata	88	now–2015
2001 Red Wine Ciel du Cheval Vineyard	87	now–2011
2004 Red Wine Bel Canto	90	2013–2027
2004 Red Wine Tapteil Vineyard	86	2011–2022
2001 Red Wine Tapteil Vineyard	87	now–2011

BRIAN CARTER CELLARS ★ ★ ★ ★
COLUMBIA VALLEY $20.00–$62.00

Brian Carter, longtime winemaker at Apex, is a big believer in the art of blending. In each vintage he produces one white blend and four red blends, each with its own proprietary name. There is also a sixth wine, Abracadabra, for declassified fruit. In all, the winery produces 4,000 cases in a given vintage.

2003 Abracadabra	87	now–2011
2004 Byzance	89	2011–2022
2003 L'Etalon	91+	2013–2027
2005 Oriana	90	now–2009
2001 Solesce	91+	2013–2027
2003 Tuttorosso	90	2009–2017

CAYUSE VINEYARDS ★ ★ ★ ★ ★
WALLA WALLA $45.00–$65.00

Cayuse Vineyards is the domain of transplanted Frenchman Christophe Baron. While searching for a place to start a vineyard in the mid-1990s, he stumbled upon this spot just on the Oregon side of the Walla Walla Valley where the stones sitting on the topsoil reminded him of Châteauneuf-du-Pape. The estate consists of five small but distinct vineyards (41 acres in total) planted predominantly to Syrah, but the Bordeaux varietals are well represented, as is possibly the finest patch of Tempranillo outside Ribera del Duero. The vineyards are farmed biodynamically and the vines are buried during the winter to protect against freezes (which allowed Baron to be one of a very few in Walla Walla to produce a full supply of grapes in 2004). The vines are also planted on rootstock because Baron believes that phylloxera will inevitably work its way through the Walla Walla AVA. The wines are all fermented with indigenous yeasts and are bottled unfined and unfiltered.

2004 Syrah Bionic Frog Coccinella Vineyard	99	2014–2039
2003 Syrah Bionic Frog	92	now–2015
2002 Syrah Bionic Frog	90+	now–2014
2001 Syrah Bionic Frog	90	now–2013
2004 Camaspelo	92	2012–2022
2003 Camaspelo	91	now–2015
2004 Flying Pig	94	2014–2030
2004 Impulsivo En Chamberlin Vineyard	98	2015–2035
2003 Impulsivo	89	now–2013
2003 Syrah Armada Vineyard	99	2018–2040
2004 Syrah Cailloux Vineyard	93	2012–2025
2003 Syrah Cailloux Vineyard	87	now–2013
2002 Syrah Cailloux Vineyard	86	now–2009
2001 Syrah Cailloux Vineyard	89	now–2011
2003 Syrah Coccinelle Vineyard	87	now–2013
2002 Syrah Coccinelle Vineyard	89	now–2012
2001 Syrah Coccinelle Vineyard	89	now–2011
2004 Syrah En Cerise Vineyard	96	2013–2030
2003 Syrah En Cerise Vineyard	90	now–2013
2002 Syrah En Cerise Vineyard	89	now–2012
2004 Syrah En Chamberlin Vineyard	97	2015–2035
2003 Syrah En Chamberlin Vineyard	92	now–2015
2002 Syrah En Chamberlin Vineyard	88	now–2012
2004 Cabernet Sauvignon The Widowmaker En Chamberlin Vineyard	97	2010–2024
2003 The Widowmaker	90	now–2018
2005 Viognier Cailloux Vineyard	94	now–2010

CHATEAU STE. MICHELLE ★ ★ ★ ★
VARIOUS $18.00–$48.00

In Issue 154, Pierre Rovani reported that numerous personnel changes at Chateau Ste. Michelle might be having an impact on wine quality. Three years later the ship appears to be sailing smoothly under the leadership of CEO Ted Baseler and, if anything, the wines are better than they have ever been.

2003 Artist Series Meritage	90	now–2015
2001 Artist Series Meritage	91	2009–2017
2003 Cabernet Sauvignon Cold Creek Vineyard	89	now–2014
2004 Cabernet Sauvignon Ethos	89+	2011–2021
2003 Cabernet Sauvignon Ethos	91+	2010–2020
2004 Cabernet Sauvignon Indian Wells	89	2009–2017
2003 Cabernet Sauvignon Indian Wells	91	now–2015
2005 Chardonnay Cold Creek Vineyard	90	now–2010
2005 Chardonnay Ethos	91	now–2011
2005 Chardonnay Indian Wells	90	now–2010
2006 Riesling Eroica	91	now–2012
2004 Riesling Eroica	91	now–2014
2003 Riesling Eroica	91	now–2013
2004 Meritage Artist Series	92	2012–2025
2004 Merlot Canoe Ridge Estate	86	now–2011
2003 Merlot Ethos	89	now–2013

2004 Red Blend Orphelin	88	now–2014
2004 Syrah Ethos	91+	2011–2024
2003 Syrah Ethos	88	now–2011
2001 Syrah Reserve	87	now–2011

CHATTER CREEK ★ ★ ★
VARIOUS $14.00–$42.00

Chatter Creek is a 2,000-case winery founded in 1996.

2005 Cabernet Franc Alder Ridge Vineyard	90	2009–2017
2004 Syrah Clifton Hill Vineyard	85	now–2011
2005 Syrah Lonesome Spring Ranch	90	2010–2020

COL SOLARE ★ ★ ★ ★ ★
COLUMBIA VALLEY $70.00

Col Solare is a partnership between Tuscany's Marchesi Piero Antinori and Chateau Ste. Michelle.

2003 Red Table Wine	94	2013–2028
2002 Red Table Wine	94	now–2012
2001 Red Table Wine	90	2009–2017

COLUMBIA CREST WINERY ★ ★ ★
COLUMBIA VALLEY $11.00–$44.00

2003 Cabernet Sauvignon Reserve	91	2009–2017
2002 Cabernet Sauvignon Reserve	89	now–2015
2001 Cabernet Sauvignon Reserve	88	now–2014
2004 Merlot Grand Estates	87	now–2009
2003 Merlot Reserve	89	now–2013
2002 Merlot Reserve	89	now–2012
2001 Merlot Reserve	87	now–2015
2004 Syrah Reserve	89	now–2014
2003 Syrah Reserve	87	now–2010
2003 Walter Clore Private Reserve	93	2012–2025
2002 Walter Clore Private Reserve	91+	now–2016

CULLIN HILLS WINERY ★ ★ ★ ★
VARIOUS $27.00–$32.00

2005 Syrah	90	2012–2022
2005 Syrah The Dungeon	91	2010–2020

DELILLE CELLARS ★ ★ ★ ★ ★
COLUMBIA VALLEY $34.00–$69.00

Located in Woodinville, DeLille Cellars' first vintage was in 1992.

2005 Chaleur Estate Blanc	91	now–2011
2004 Chaleur Estate Blanc	90	now–2010
2002 Chaleur Estate Dixième Anniversaire Blanc	89	now–2009
2004 Chaleur Estate	93	2010–2020
2003 Chaleur Estate	95	2012–2027

2002 Chaleur Estate	95+	2012–2025
2001 Chaleur Estate Dixième Anniversaire	94	now–2013
2000 Chaleur Estate	92	now–2015
2004 D2	91	2009–2017
2003 D2	90	now–2015
2002 D2	92	2009–2017
2001 D2 Dixième Anniversaire	90	now–2013
2000 D2	89	now–2010
2004 Harrison Hill	94	2012–2024
2003 Harrison Hill	94	2011–2022
2002 Harrison Hill	93+	2010–2020
2001 Harrison Hill Dixième Anniversaire	93+	now–2016
2000 Harrison Hill	92	now–2015

DISTEFANO WINERY ★★★
COLUMBIA VALLEY $22.00–$36.00

2003 Cabernet Sauvignon	90	2010–2020
2003 Syrah R	87	now–2011

DOYENNE ★★★★★
VARIOUS $32.00–$49.00

Doyenne is a sister label to DeLille Cellars. Doyenne focuses on Rhône- and Provençal-style wines, whereas DeLille produces Bordeaux-style wines.

2004 Aix	92	2010–2020
2003 Aix	88	now–2013
2001 Doyenne Dixième Anniversaire	91	now–2011
2005 Métier Blanc	91	now–2009
2005 Roussanne	92	now–2010
2004 Roussanne	89	now–2009
2004 Syrah	93	2009–2017
2003 Syrah	92	now–2015
2002 Syrah	92+	now–2014

DUMAS STATION WINES ★★★
WALLA WALLA $25.00

This is the first release for Dumas Station, a winery located in the Walla Walla Valley AVA.

2003 Cabernet Sauvignon Estate	89	2009–2017

DUNHAM CELLARS ★★★★
COLUMBIA VALLEY $45.00–$75.00

Dunham produces two tiers of red wines, the Columbia Valley varietals and the Artist Series from the Lewis Vineyard.

2003 Cabernet Sauvignon	87	now–2015
2004 Cabernet Sauvignon Artist Series Lewis Vineyard	93	2014–2030
2004 Merlot Artist Series Lewis Vineyard	92+	2012–2027
2004 Syrah	89	2009–2017
2004 Syrah Artist Series Lewis Vineyard	92	2012–2025

L'ECOLE N° 41 ★ ★ ★ ★
WALLA WALLA $12.00–$45.00

L'Ecole N° 41 is one of Walla Walla's pioneer wineries. When I visited for the first time in 1990, it was one of four wineries and was operating out of the schoolhouse for which it is named. The school now houses the winery's offices and tasting room. Martin Clubb, owner-winemaker, has been there from the beginning. What sets L'Ecole N° 41 apart from the masses is their barrel-fermented Sémillons, produced from several different sites.

2003 Apogee Pepper Bridge Vineyard	91	2011–2022
2004 Cabernet Sauvignon	90	now–2016
2003 Cabernet Sauvignon	89	2011–2022
2002 Cabernet Sauvignon	88	now–2012
2004 Ferguson Commemorative Reserve	90	2010–2020
2004 Merlot	88	now–2014
2005 Merlot Seven Hills Vineyard Estate	89	2009–2017
2003 Merlot Seven Hills Vineyard Estate	87	now–2011
2003 Perigee Seven Hills Vineyard Estate	92+	2013–2028
2005 Sémillon Columbia Valley	89	now–2009
2005 Sémillon Fries Vineyard	90	now–2015
2004 Sémillon Fries Vineyard	90	now–2010
2005 Sémillon Seven Hills Estate	91	now–2010
2005 Sémillon Ice Wine Seven Hills Vineyard Estate	89	now–2009
2004 Syrah	89	2009–2017
2005 Syrah Seven Hills Estate Vineyard	90	2011–2023
2003 Syrah Seven Hills Estate Vineyard	87	now–2011

ENSEMBLE CELLARS ★ ★ ★
WALLA WALLA $48.00

Ensemble Cellars, a new Walla Walla start-up whose first vintage was 2003, is dedicated to blending vintages, vineyards, and Bordeaux grape varieties to make the best wine.

N.V. Release Number One	86	now–2012
N.V. Release Number Two	87	now–2013

FALL LINE WINERY ★ ★ ★
HORSE HEAVEN HILLS $30.00

2004 Red Blend	90	2012–2022

FIVE STAR CELLARS ★ ★ ★
WALLA WALLA $28.00–$30.00

Five Star Cellars is another recent addition to the Walla Walla wine scene with the first vintage dating to 2000.

2004 Cabernet Sauvignon	89	2010–2020
2005 Malbec	90	2011–2022
2005 Sangiovese	88	now–2015
2005 Syrah	85	now–2013

FORGERON CELLARS ★ ★ ★ ★
VARIOUS $25.00–$46.00

2001 Cabernet Sauvignon	87	now–2012
2005 Chardonnay	90	now–2010
2004 Merlot Boushey Vineyard	90	2010–2020

FORT WALLA WALLA CELLARS ★ ★ ★
COLUMBIA VALLEY $18.00–$35.00

2004 Trapper Red	87	now–2012
2004 Treaty	90	2010–2020

GIFFORD HIRLINGER WINERY ★ ★ ★
WALLA WALLA $22.00–$25.00

Another Walla Walla start-up whose first vintage was 2003, Gifford Hirlinger's focus will be on estate-bottled wine.

2004 18 Below Canoe Ridge Vineyard	88	now–2016
2003 Stateline Red	87	now–2013

GORDON BROTHERS FAMILY VINEYARDS ★ ★ ★
COLUMBIA VALLEY $18.00–$45.00

It would appear that little has changed since I first visited the Gordon Brothers Family Vineyards in 1990 when they were one of 42 wineries in Washington. Their estate-bottled wines were friendly and well priced and they still are today.

2005 Cabernet Sauvignon	88	now–2015
2005 Merlot	87	now–2013
2003 Syrah	85	now–2013
2001 Tradition	87	now–2013

GORMAN WINERY ★ ★ ★ ★
VARIOUS $25.00–$50.00

Owner-winemaker Chris Gorman produces 600 to 700 cases of full-throttle wines from some of Washington's top vineyards.

2004 Cabernet Sauvignon The Bully	91	2010–2020
2004 The Evil Twin	87	now–2014
2004 Syrah The Pixie	92+	2011–2022
2004 Zachary's Ladder	91	2010–2020

HENCE CELLARS ★ ★ ★ ★
WALLA WALLA $20.00–$45.00

These are the first offerings for Hence Cellars, a new Walla Walla start-up.

2005 Cabernet Sauvignon	91	2012–2025
2005 Cabernet Sauvignon-Merlot-Syrah	90	2010–2020
2005 Malbec	91	2010–2020
2005 Syrah	91	2012–2025

ISENHOWER CELLARS ★ ★ ★ ★
WALLA WALLA $28.00–$32.00

Isenhower Cellars, a 3,300-case Walla Walla winery, started in 1999. The winery purchases and blends grapes from a variety of AVAs.

2004 Cabernet Sauvignon Bachelor's Button	91+	2011–2022
2004 Syrah River Beauty	90	2010–2020

JAMES LEIGH CELLARS ★ ★ ★
WALLA WALLA $28.00–$32.00

2003 Cabernet Sauvignon	86	now–2013
2003 Merlot Estate Spofford Station	87	now–2013

JANUIK WINERY ★ ★ ★ ★ ★
COLUMBIA VALLEY $25.00–$50.00

Mike Januik was winemaker at Chateau Ste. Michelle for many years until starting his namesake winery in 1999. He was moving to a new winemaking facility on the day of my tasting. The portfolio is sourced primarily from the Columbia Valley AVA, including some of its finest *terroirs*.

2004 Cabernet Sauvignon	91	2011–2022
2003 Cabernet Sauvignon	94	2009–2017
2002 Cabernet Sauvignon	92	2010–2020
2001 Cabernet Sauvignon	92	now–2015
2004 Cabernet Sauvignon Champoux Vineyard	93	2013–2028
2003 Cabernet Sauvignon Champoux Vineyard	94	2010–2020
2002 Cabernet Sauvignon Champoux Vineyard	91+	2009–2020
2001 Cabernet Sauvignon Champoux Vineyard	95	now–2016
2004 Cabernet Sauvignon Ciel du Cheval Vineyard	94	2014–2032
2003 Cabernet Sauvignon Seven Hills Vineyard	91	2009–2017
2002 Cabernet Sauvignon Seven Hills Vineyard	88+	now–2013
2005 Chardonnay Cold Creek Vineyard	89	now–2011
2005 Chardonnay Elerding Vineyard	90	now–2011
2004 Merlot	90	now–2014
2003 Merlot	90	now–2015
2002 Merlot	89	2009–2015
2001 Merlot	92	now–2011
2004 Merlot Klipsun Vineyard	90+	2009–2019
2003 Merlot Klipsun Vineyard	94	2010–2020
2002 Merlot Klipsun Vineyard	93	now–2012
2004 Petit Verdot Ciel du Cheval Vineyard	91	2010–2020
2003 Petit Verdot Ciel du Cheval Vineyard	92+	2011–2022
2004 Reserve Red	92+	2014–2030
2003 Syrah	88	now–2011
2002 Syrah	87	now–2012
2001 Syrah	87	now–2011

JM CELLARS ★ ★ ★ ★
COLUMBIA VALLEY $18.00–$35.00

JM Cellars is worth a visit just to see the exquisite landscaping. As a bonus, the wines are pretty darn good, as these scores attest. Total production is only 3,000 cases so potential customers would be well advised to get on the mailing list.

2004 Columbia Valley Cuvée	90+	2010–2020
2006 Sauvignon Blanc Klipsun Vineyard	90	now–2009
2004 Syrah	91	2009–2017
2004 Tre Fanciulli	90	2011–2022

K VINTNERS ★ ★ ★ ★
WALLA WALLA $35.00–$70.00

2003 The Boy	87	now–2010
2003 The Creator	88+	now–2013
2003 Ovide En Cerise	90	now–2016
2003 Roma En Chamberlin	90	now–2013
2003 Syrah Cougar Hills	93	now–2015
2003 Syrah Morrison Lane	93	now–2015
2003 Syrah Phil Lane	90	now–2013

LATITUDE 46°N ★ ★ ★ ★
VARIOUS $28.00

The winery is named for the geographical line that runs just south of the town of Walla Walla and through the entire AVA. Latitude 46°N, the winery, purchases and blends fruit from a number of vineyards.

2005 Syrah Destiny Ridge Vineyard	90+	2011–2022
2005 Syrah The Power and the Glory	91	2010–2020

LEONETTI CELLAR ★ ★ ★ ★ ★
WALLA WALLA $55.00–$110.00

When I first visited this reference-point winery in 1990, it consisted of owner-winemaker Gary Figgins's house and a *chai*. Now Monsieur Figgins, ably assisted by his 20-something son, presides over a resplendent château while turning out the best wines of his lengthy career, all from estate-grown fruit. These are limited-production wines sold predominantly by mailing list but also available in a few select markets.

2004 Cabernet Sauvignon	95	2014–2034
2003 Cabernet Sauvignon	96	2011–2025
2002 Cabernet Sauvignon	95	2010–2019
2000 Cabernet Sauvignon	89	now–2010
2005 Merlot	94	2012–2027
2004 Merlot	94	2009–2017
2003 Merlot	95	now–2016
2001 Merlot	90	now–2011
2004 Reserve	97	2018–2040
2003 Reserve	97	2013–2030
2002 Reserve	91+	2010–2019
2001 Reserve	96	2010–2022
2000 Reserve	92	now–2016
2005 Sangiovese	93	now–2022

| 2004 Sangiovese | 90 | now–2014 |
| 2003 Sangiovese | 92 | now–2013 |

LONG SHADOWS VINTNERS ★ ★ ★ ★ ★
COLUMBIA VALLEY $20.00–$55.00

Long Shadows is a winery begun by Alan Shoup, longtime CEO of Stimson Lane and Chateau Ste. Michelle. It is a consortium of seven different labels, each with its own star winemaker who has a 25% share in the brand. The concept is that each "is dedicated to producing a single Columbia Valley wine representing a 'best of type' that reflects the winemaker's signature style."

2004 Cabernet Sauvignon Feather	91	2014–2028
2004 Merlot Pedestal	94	2014–2032
2003 Red Wine Chester-Kidder	91	2014–2033
2004 Red Wine Pirouette	93	2014–2032
2004 Red Wine Saggi	91	2014–2024
2005 Riesling Poet's Leap	91	now–2015
2004 Syrah Sequel	93	2012–2024

MARK RYAN WINERY ★ ★ ★ ★
VARIOUS $28.00–$40.00

Mark Ryan Winery was founded in 1999 by Mark Ryan McNeilly and is located in Woodinville. The five wines below range from excellent to outstanding—this is a winery to watch closely.

2005 Chardonnay	89	now–2010
2005 Dead Horse Ciel du Cheval Vineyard	90+	2012–2025
2005 The Dissident	89	now–2013
2005 Long Haul Ciel du Cheval Vineyard	91+	2014–2030
2005 Syrah Wild Eyed	88	2010–2020

MATTHEWS ESTATE ★ ★ ★ ★
COLUMBIA VALLEY $30.00–$110.00

Matthew Loso began operations at Matthews Estate in 1993. He purchases and blends lots from some of the more highly regarded vineyards in eastern Washington.

2003 Cabernet Franc Reserve Conner Lee Vineyard	96	2013–2033
2004 Claret	89	2010–2020
2003 Red Wine	90+	2009–2017

MARYHILL WINERY ★ ★ ★
COLUMBIA VALLEY $16.00–$36.00

Maryhill Winery's first vintage was 1999 and since then production has risen to 55,000 cases, placing it in the top 20 of Washington's largest wineries.

2004 Cabernet Sauvignon Proprietor's Reserve	89	2010–2020
2004 Sangiovese Proprietor's Reserve	88	now–2014
2004 Syrah Proprietor's Reserve	89	2009–2017

MERRY CELLARS ✶✶✶
WALLA WALLA $30.00–$35.00

2005 Carménère	87	now–2013
2005 Merlot	87	2009–2017
2005 Twilight Hills Red	86	2009–2017

MORRISON LANE ✶✶✶
WALLA WALLA $29.00

Morrison Lane produces wine entirely from estate-grown fruit in the Walla Walla Valley AVA from a vineyard the family began planting in 1994.

2003 Syrah Estate	88	2009–2018

NICHOLAS COLE CELLARS ✶✶✶✶
WALLA WALLA $48.00

Mike Neuffer is the owner-winemaker of this new winery located in the Walla Walla AVA. The good news is that the best is yet to come at Nicholas Cole. I tasted from barrel three 2005 Bordeaux-style blends, one from 100% estate fruit, which were all exhibiting outstanding potential, and a scintillating 2005 estate Syrah that should ultimately be in the 94- to 96-point range.

2004 Camille	92	2014–2032
2003 Camille	90	2013–2025
2002 Camille	90	now–2016

NORTHSTAR WINERY ✶✶✶✶
COLUMBIA VALLEY $29.00–$41.00

Northstar is a Walla Walla Merlot specialist founded in the early 1990s under the Stimson Lane umbrella with Jed Steele as consulting winemaker. The winery now has estate vineyards, which have not yet come online.

2004 Merlot	90	2009–2017
2003 Merlot Columbia Valley	88	now–2013
2001 Merlot Columbia Valley	92+	2009–2017
2003 Merlot Walla Walla	92	now–2014
2001 Merlot Walla Walla Valley	90	2009–2017
2003 Syrah	89	now–2011
2004 Stella Maris	88	now–2016
2001 Stella Maris	88	now–2011

NOVELTY HILL ✶✶✶✶
COLUMBIA VALLEY $20.00–$28.00

Mike Januik makes the wines for Woodinville-based Novelty Hill. Fruit is sourced from the Columbia Valley AVA and their estate-owned Stillwater Creek Vineyard.

2004 Cabernet Sauvignon	86	now–2014
2003 Cabernet Sauvignon	89	now–2013
2001 Cabernet Sauvignon	89	now–2013
2004 Cabernet Sauvignon Stillwater Creek Vineyard	87	now–2012
2004 Merlot	86	now–2014
2003 Merlot	89	now–2013
2001 Merlot	90	now–2011

2004 Merlot Stillwater Creek Vineyard	91	2009–2017
2004 Syrah	90	now–2014
2003 Syrah	87+	now–2012
2002 Syrah	88	now–2010
2004 Syrah Stillwater Creek Vineyard	91	2009–2017

O-S WINERY ✶ ✶ ✶
VARIOUS $20.00–$50.00

2006 Riesling Champoux Vineyard	90	now–2012
2004 Ulysses Sheridan Vineyard	91+	2010–2020

PEPPER BRIDGE WINERY ✶ ✶ ✶ ✶ ✶
WALLA WALLA $55.00–$65.00

Pepper Bridge managing partner, Norm McKibben, one of the Washington wine industry's pioneers, planted the Pepper Bridge Vineyard in 1991 and purchased the Seven Hills Vineyard (in partnership with Leonetti Cellar and L'Ecole Nº 41) in the late 1990s. These two vineyards, planted to Cabernet Sauvignon and Merlot, form the core of the Pepper Bridge Winery.

2004 Cabernet Sauvignon	93	2012–2025
2003 Cabernet Sauvignon	91	2011–2023
2002 Cabernet Sauvignon	86	now–2011
2004 Merlot	92	now–2019
2003 Merlot	90	now–2015
2003 Pepper Bridge Vineyard Reserve	94	2015–2035
2003 Reserve	93	2015–2035
2003 Seven Hills Vineyard Reserve	91	2009–2018

QUILCEDA CREEK VINTNERS ✶ ✶ ✶ ✶ ✶
COLUMBIA VALLEY $40.00–$125.00

The more things change, the more they remain the same. When I visited Quilceda Creek Vintners for the first time in 1990, I wrote in Robert Parker's *Wine Advocate* (issue 69), "Owner-winemaker Alex Golitzin, the nephew of Andre Tchelistcheff, makes only one wine, Washington's finest Cabernet Sauvignon." Since then, the portfolio has expanded to include a Merlot, a red wine (for declassified lots), and a Cabernet Sauvignon from the winery's new Galitzine Vineyard, located near the superb Champoux Vineyard, where much of the fruit is sourced for the renowned Cabernet Sauvignon. And Quilceda Creek continues to make Washington's (and arguably, America's) finest Cabernet Sauvignon.

2004 Cabernet Sauvignon	99	2018–2040
2003 Cabernet Sauvignon	100	2010–2024
2002 Cabernet Sauvignon	100	2010–2022
2001 Cabernet Sauvignon	98+	2011–2026
2004 Cabernet Sauvignon Galitzine Vineyard	97	2014–2030
2004 Merlot	94	2012–2025
2003 Merlot	94	2010–2020
2002 Merlot	92	2011–2022
2004 Red Wine	92	2010–2020
2003 Red Wine	92	2010–2020
2002 Red Wine	89	2009–2018
2001 Red Wine	89	now–2013

REININGER WINERY ★★★★
WALLA WALLA $18.00–$45.00

Reininger Winery, located in the Walla Walla AVA, began operations in 1997. In addition to the Walla Walla bottlings under the Reininger label, the winery produces a series of lower priced wines from Columbia Valley under the Helix label.

2003 Cabernet Sauvignon	90	2010–2020
2002 Cabernet Sauvignon	90	now–2014
2003 Carménère Seven Hills Vineyard	91	now–2015
2001 Cima	92	now–2011
2004 Helix Merlot	89	2009–2017
2004 Helix Sangiovese	89	now–2012
2005 Helix So-Rho	88	now–2010
2004 Helix Syrah	86	now–2011
2003 Merlot	89	now–2015
2002 Merlot	89	now–2012
2003 Syrah	92	now–2013

SEVEN HILLS WINERY ★★★★
WALLA WALLA $28.00–$50.00

Seven Hills Winery was a partner in the planting and cultivation of the well-known Seven Hills Vineyard but sold their interest in 1995. However, they have a long-term contract on the original blocks of the vineyard that they have used since 1988.

2004 Cabernet Sauvignon	90	2010–2020
2004 Cabernet Sauvignon Klipsun Vineyard	91	2012–2025
2004 Ciel du Cheval Vineyard	93	2014–2030
2005 Malbec	92+	2010–2020
2003 Merlot Seven Hills Vineyard	92	2010–2020
2003 Pentad	92+	2013–2028
2005 Tempranillo	89	now–2017

SNOQUALMIE WINERY ★★★
COLUMBIA VALLEY $23.00

2003 Cabernet Sauvignon Reserve	90	2009–2017
2003 Merlot Reserve	88	now–2015

SOOS CREEK WINE CELLARS ★★★
COLUMBIA VALLEY $30.00–$40.00

This small (1,500 cases) family-owned winery was established in 1989 by David and Cecile Larsen. Dave, who retired from Boeing in 2004, is responsible for the winemaking and sources his fruit from two of the state's finest vineyards.

2003 Cabernet Sauvignon Ciel du Cheval Vineyard	91+	2010–2020
2002 Cabernet Sauvignon Ciel du Cheval Vineyard	91+	2010–2020
2002 Champoux Vineyard	90+	2010–2020

SPARKMAN CELLARS ★★★
RED MOUNTAIN $40.00–$50.00

Sparkman Cellars, founded in 2004 and located in Woodinville, employs the talented Mark Ryan McNeilly as winemaker.

2004 The Outlaw Merlot	90	2011–2022
2004 Ruby Leigh Bordeaux Blend	88	2010–2020
2004 Stella Mae Syrah	87	now–2014

SPRING VALLEY VINEYARD ★ ★ ★ ★
WALLA WALLA $50.00

This 40-acre Walla Walla estate is planted primarily to Bordeaux varieties (with 4 acres devoted to Syrah). The winery's first vintage was 1999 and all of the wines are now estate-bottled.

2004 Frederick	94	2014–2030
2003 Frederick	94	2011–2023
2004 Uriah	93	2012–2024
2003 Uriah	91	now–2016
2004 Syrah Nina Lee	89	now–2014

STEVENS WINERY ★ ★ ★
YAKIMA VALLEY $28.00–$42.00

2005 Red Wine 424	87	2009–2017
2004 Merlot	85	now–2012
2005 Syrah Black Tongue	86	now–2013
2004 Cabernet Sauvignon XY Reserve	89	2009–2017

SYZYGY ★ ★ ★
COLUMBIA VALLEY $32.00

Syzygy is a small Walla Walla winery that purchases fruit by the acre (rather than by the ton) from prestigious vineyards.

| 2004 Cabernet Sauvignon | 89 | 2010–2020 |

TAMARACK CELLARS ★ ★ ★ ★
COLUMBIA VALLEY $20.00–$40.00

Tamarack Cellars, located on the former Air Force base complex in Walla Walla (where a substantial number of wineries have taken up residence), is producing some of the best values in Washington.

2005 Cabernet Franc	92	2010–2020
2004 Cabernet Sauvignon	90	2011–2022
2004 DuBrul Vineyard Reserve	93	2014–2032
2005 Firehouse Red	90	now–2015
2005 Merlot	89	now–2017
2004 Syrah	91	2012–2025

TERTULIA CELLARS ★ ★ ★ ★
WALLA WALLA $29.00

| 2005 Syrah Les Collines | 90 | now–2017 |

THREE RIVERS WINERY ★ ★ ★ ★
VARIOUS $19.00–$50.00

Three Rivers Winery, located in metropolitan Walla Walla, produces 15,000 cases of wine sourced from as many as 25 vineyards. Three Rivers offers many solid wines at fair prices.

2003 Cabernet Sauvignon	86	2009–2016
2004 Cabernet Sauvignon Champoux Vineyard	92	2012–2025
2005 Malbec	90	2010–2020
2005 Malbec-Merlot	89	2009–2017
2005 Merlot Champoux Vineyard	91	2010–2022
2003 Syrah	85	now–2011
2004 Syrah Boushey Vineyards	90	2010–2020

VA PIANO VINEYARDS ★ ★ ★
WALLA WALLA $38.00

Va Piano Vineyards, located in the Walla Walla AVA, began production in 1999. The winery's 20-acre estate vineyard is supplemented by purchased fruit.

2005 Syrah	89	now–2015

WHITMAN CELLARS ★ ★ ★
WALLA WALLA $24.00–$32.00

Whitman Cellars is a 5,000-case winery located in the Walla Walla AVA. The winery sources and blends from multiple vineyards within the AVA.

2003 Merlot	87	now–2013
2003 Narcissa Red	88	now–2013

WOODWARD CANYON WINERY ★ ★ ★ ★ ★
WALLA WALLA $44.00–$75.00

Rick Small, founder, proprietor, and winemaker of Woodward Canyon, remains as enthusiastic as when I first met him in 1990 when his winery was one of four in Walla Walla (there are now over 100 bonded wineries). What's even better is that he appears to be making the finest wines of his career. The winery is producing about 15,000 cases, 25% to 33% of which are sold directly to consumers.

2004 Cabernet Sauvignon Artist Series	93	2013–2030
2003 Cabernet Sauvignon Artist Series	91	2009–2017
2004 Cabernet Sauvignon Old Vines	94	2015–2035
2003 Cabernet Sauvignon Old Vines	91	2009–2017
2003 Estate Red Wine	92	2013–2030
2003 Merlot	87	now–2013

ZERBA CELLARS ★ ★ ★
WALLA WALLA $19.00–$40.00

Zerba Cellars, located in the Walla Walla AVA, is just on the Oregon side of the border. The winery makes use of both estate-grown and purchased fruit.

2005 Cabernet Sauvignon	89	now–2017
2005 Malbec	83	now–2009
2004 Merlot	85	now–2011
2004 Sangiovese	86	now–2009
2004 Syrah	89	now–2014
2005 Syrah Ice Wine	90	now–2011
2005 Wild Z	85	now–2010

ARGENTINA

AUSTRALIA

CENTRAL EUROPE

CHILE

ISRAEL

NEW ZEALAND

SOUTH AFRICA

THE BEST OF
THE REST

[argentina]

Argentina has broken out of the value category in wine, as has Chile, and now produces wines that can be recommended across the spectrum, from below $10 to luxury wines that fetch more than $100. While many wineries have remained faithful to their price points, preferring to fashion large quantities of inexpensive wines, some, like Bodega Catena Zapata, are presently offering wines that can compete with the finest in the world. Led by Nicolás Catena and others, those wineries wanting to better the quality of their wines have abandoned the Mendoza's highly fertile valley floor for its less productive hillsides.

Argentina is the world's fifth-largest wine producer (behind France, Italy, Spain, and the U.S.) and a major consumer of their own product (annual per capita consumption is 35 liters vs. 7 liters in the U.S.). Until recently there was relatively little pressure to export, but that figure of 35 liters per capita in 2000 represents a drop from 92 liters in 1970. As a result, the more insightful Argentina wine producers came to realize that if they wanted to export (to make up for decreased domestic consumption) and to sell abroad and make a profit, they had to raise quality. Consequently, there has been an increased focus on lowering yields, discovering new vineyard sites, and experimenting with clones.

Though Mendoza is not Argentina's only wine-producing region, it is far and away the most significant. It features a high desert climate with most vineyards planted at elevations of 2,500 to 4,500 feet (some even higher), resulting in intense sunshine but cooler air temperatures. This results in physiologically ripe grapes in almost every vintage, with alcohol levels rarely topping 14.5%. There is very little rainfall, but no shortage of water thanks to proximity to the Andes mountains (which can be seen from every vineyard, and appear to be next door because of their immense size). Irrigation is the rule. Phylloxera is not an issue, so most vines are planted on their own roots. Because soils at these high elevations are poor in organic material, the vines must develop deep roots, thus intensifying flavors. Pesticides and herbicides in this climate are rarely used, and hand harvesting is the rule. The only significant weather risk is hail (13% of the annual crop is typically lost to this problem) and most vineyards are netted for protection.

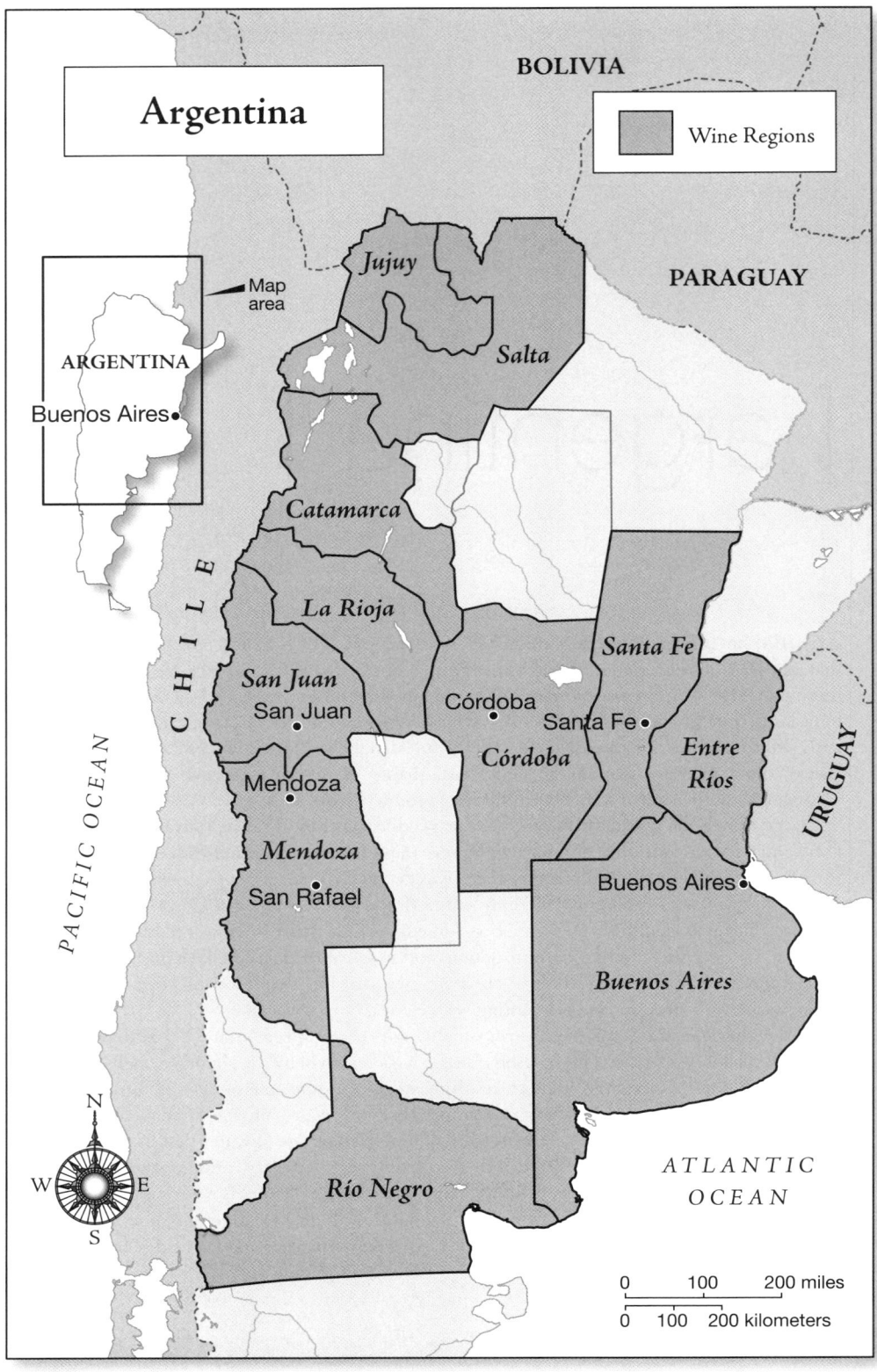

BOLIVIA

Argentina

Wine Regions

PARAGUAY

Jujuy

Salta

Map area

ARGENTINA

Buenos Aires

Catamarca

La Rioja

Santa Fe

CHILE

San Juan

San Juan

Córdoba

Santa Fe

Entre Ríos

PACIFIC OCEAN

Mendoza

Córdoba

URUGUAY

Mendoza

San Rafael

Buenos Aires

Buenos Aires

N

W   E

S

Río Negro

ATLANTIC OCEAN

0   100   200 miles

0   100   200 kilometers

IMPORTANT INFORMATION

Argentina is on the rise. Recent vintages, particularly 2006 and 2005, have been superb, and this country's improved viticultural and winemaking practices as well as the arrival on the scene of quality-conscious boutique wineries (such as Luca, Tikal, and Paul Hobbs's Cobos) foreshadow an extremely bright future.

[grape varieties]

Delicious and thirst-quenching whites, primarily Chardonnays and Sauvignon Blancs, are produced in Argentina. In recent years, a few outstanding Chardonnays, from wineries such as Catena and Luca, have displayed the depth of fruit, complexity, and concentration found in the world's best examples of this ubiquitous variety. Malbec, a French grape that has had limited success in the Old World, can produce magnificent reds in Argentina. Characterized by its spicy dark fruit character, Argentinian Malbec flourishes at a level of quality unparalleled anywhere else in the world. Cabernet Sauvignon is also important and frequently blended with Malbec. The other Bordeaux varieties (Cabernet Franc, Petit Verdot, even Carménère) exist, but are used almost exclusively for blending. Pinot Noir is just beginning to make an appearance and appears to have some potential. Syrah and Tempranillo can be found, but they play subsidiary roles.

There are two other grapes that are virtually indigenous to Argentina. The red grape is Bonarda, originally from Lombardy in Italy, where ripening is typically an issue. In Mendoza it makes juicy, flavorful, vibrant wine. Moreover, it rarely sells for over $15 a bottle. There are a number of them recommended below. The white grape is Torrontés, most of it grown in Cafayate in northern Argentina. Research has shown that it is a cross of Muscat Alexandria and the Mission grape once planted widely in California. When grown well, it is remarkably fragrant, with the fruit nicely buttressed by zesty acidity. For those looking for Chardonnay alternatives, this is a variety worth exploring. Even better, they rarely sell for more than $15 a bottle and there are a number of fine examples listed below. As for other white varieties, Chardonnay does well, but there is not much of it. The top examples (Catena Zapata and Luca, to name a couple) tend to taste like a hypothetical cross between high-quality white Burgundy and a California Chardonnay. There is also some Sauvignon Blanc and other international varieties, but they are all minor players.

—JAY MILLER

[the ratings]

ARGENTINA'S BEST WINES

***** (OUTSTANDING)

Achaval-Ferrer	Viña Cobos
Alta Vista	Luca
Catena Zapata	

**** (EXCELLENT)

Altos Las Hormigas	Bodegas Caro
Susana Balbo	Cheval des Andes
Benmarco	Clos de los Siete

Crios de Susana Balbo	Monteviejo
Cuvelier Los Andes	Noemia de Patagonia
Enrique Foster	Poesia
Mariflor	Tikal
Mendel	Trapiche

★ ★ ★ (GOOD)

Alamos	Melipal
Altocedro	Finca Las Moras
Finca La Anita	Navarro Correas
Añoro	Nieto Senetiner
Belasco de Baquedano	Norton
Benegas	Peñiwen
Bodegas Bressia	El Porvenir de los Andes
Luigi Bosca	La Posta
Domaine Jean Bousquet	Quara
Budini	Reginato
CarinaE	Alfredo Roca
Cicchitti	Finca Sophenia
Finca La Chamiza	Sur de los Andes
Colomé	Tempus Alba
Doña Paula	Terrazas de Los Andes
Durigutti	Tittarelli
Eral Bravo	Tiza
Fabre Montmayou	Michel Torino
Huarpe	Pascual Toso
Jaure Winery	Val de Flores
Kaiken	Valentin Bianchi
Mapema	Viejo Isaias
Marguery	Zolo
Masi Tupungato	Zuccardi

★ ★ (AVERAGE)

Aleph	Felipe Rutini
Alto3	Tapiz
Calathus	Viñas de Vila
Finca Las Nubes	

ACHAVAL-FERRER ★ ★ ★ ★ ★
MENDOZA $26.00–$112.00

Founded only in 1998, Achaval-Ferrer is already established as one of Argentina's benchmark wineries. They specialize in single-vineyard Malbecs from prime Mendoza sites. Finca Altamira is located in La Consulta in the Uco Valley, 60 miles to the south of Mendoza at an elevation of 3,400 feet, and contains 10 acres of densely planted old-vine Malbec. Finca Bella Vista is located in the Pedriel district of Lujan de Cuyo, 15 miles south of the city of Mendoza, at an elevation of 3,100 feet, with 18 acres of Malbec planted in 1910, as well as a bit of Merlot and Syrah. Finca Mirador is located in Medrano, 34 miles southeast of Mendoza, at 2,400 feet above sea level, with 12 acres of densely planted Malbec vines averaging 40-plus years of age. The winery uses predominantly French oak and bottles without fining or filtration. The winemaker is Roberto Cipresso.

2005 Malbec	91	now–2017
2006 Malbec	92	2010–2020
2004 Malbec Finca Altamira	98	2015–2035
2005 Malbec Finca Altamira	95	2015–2035
2004 Malbec Finca Bella Vista	97	2014–2032
2004 Malbec Finca Mirador	96	2014–2030
2005 Malbec Finca Mirador	94	2015–2032
2004 Quimera	93	2010–2022
2005 Quimera	92+	2012–2025

ALTA VISTA ★ ★ ★ ★ ★
MENDOZA $30.00–$70.00

Alta Vista is owned by the d'Aulan family. The estate is located in Chacras de Coria, just south of Mendoza City, and consists of 397 acres. In addition to the single-vineyard wines and Alto, they also produce two excellent value wines, a Malbec and a Torrontés.

2003 Alto	93	2013–2030
2004 Malbec Alizarine	92	2012–2025
2004 Malbec Serenade	93	2012–2025
2004 Malbec Temis	91	2010–2020
2004 Malbec Terroir Selection	92	2010–2020

ALTOCEDRO ★ ★ ★
MENDOZA $80.00

Desnudos is 100% Tempranillo (a rarity in Mendoza) sourced from a densely planted vineyard 70-plus years old located in Consulta, a subregion of Mendoza. The wine is fermented with native yeasts and aged for 30 months in French oak before being bottled unfiltered.

2003 Desnudos	92+	2012–2025

ALTOS LAS HORMIGAS ★ ★ ★ ★
MENDOZA $11.00–$25.00

The wines of Altos Las Hormigas offer some of the best values coming out of Argentina.

2006 Malbec	90	now–2012
2005 Malbec Reserva	91	2009–2018

FINCA LA ANITA ★ ★ ★
MENDOZA $39.00

2004 Malbec	90	2010–2020
2005 Petit Verdot	91	2012–2025

AÑORO ★ ★ ★
MENDOZA $25.00

2005 Malbec	90	2009–2017

SUSANA BALBO ★ ★ ★ ★
MENDOZA $27.00–$88.00

The pioneering Susana Balbo was the first female graduate of Mendoza's top school of oenology in 1981. All of her wines are bottled without fining or filtration.

2005 Brioso	92+	2013–2028
2004 Cabernet Sauvignon	91	2010–2020
2006 Malbec	91	2010–2020
2005 Nosotros	93	2012–2025
2006 Virtuoso	90	now–2016

BELASCO DE BAQUEDANO ★ ★ ★
MENDOZA $20.00–$30.00

2004 Malbec Ar Guentata	87	now–2015
2005 Malbec Swinto	90	2010–2020

BENEGAS ★ ★ ★
MENDOZA $21.00–$48.00

The Benegas estate vineyards are located in the Maipu region of Mendoza. The Benegas family has been involved in the Argentine wine business since 1883 and was a pioneer in introducing French varieties to Argentina.

2003 Finca Libertad	90+	2010–2023
2003 Lynch Meritage	91	2013–2028
2005 Syrah Estate	90	now–2015

BENMARCO ★ ★ ★ ★
MENDOZA $20.00–$35.00

Owner Pedro Marchevsky, the husband of Susana Balbo, is a renowned viticulturist in Mendoza.

2005 Cabernet Sauvignon	90	now–2015
2005 Expresivo	90	2010–2020
2006 Malbec	91+	2010–2020

LUIGI BOSCA ★ ★ ★
MENDOZA $18.00–$35.00

Gala 2	90+	2010–2020
2004 Malbec	88	now–2012
2005 Pinot Noir	87	now–2011
2006 Pinot Noir Reserva	89	now–2013

DOMAINE JEAN BOUSQUET ★ ★ ★
MENDOZA $18.00

2006 Malbec Reserva	90	now–2016

BODEGAS BRESSIA ★ ★ ★
MENDOZA $24.00–$110.00

Bodegas Bressia is a 20-hectare (50-acre) estate owned by Walter Bressia, a veteran winemaker of 30 years.

2004 Conjuro	94	2014–2035
2005 Malbec Monteagrelo	91	now–2015
2004 Profundo	92	2010–2020

CARINAE ★★★
MENDOZA $15.00–$32.00

2004 Prestige	91+	2010–2020
2004 Malbec Reserva	90	now–2014

BODEGAS CARO ★★★★
MENDOZA $19.00–$40.00

Bodegas Caro is a joint project of Domaines Barons de Rothschild (Lafite) and Nicolás Catena.

2006 Amancaya	91	now–2016
2004 Caro	93	2012–2025

CATENA ZAPATA ★★★★★
MENDOZA $20.00–$120.00

When all is said and done, Catena Zapata is the Argentina winery of reference—the standard of excellence for comparing all others. The brilliant, forward-thinking Nicolás Catena remains in charge, with his daughter, Laura, playing an increasingly large role. The Catena Zapata winery is an essential destination for fans of both architecture and wine in Mendoza. It is hard to believe, given the surge in popularity of Malbec in recent years, that Catena Zapata only began exporting Malbec to the U.S. in 1994.

2004 Cabernet Sauvignon	90	now–2018
2004 Cabernet Sauvignon Alta	93	2014–2030
2005 Chardonnay Alta	92	now–2015
2005 Malbec	91	now–2017
2004 Malbec Alta	94	2012–2025
2004 Malbec Catena Zapata Adrianna Vineyard	97	2010–2024
2004 Malbec Catena Zapata Argentino Vineyard	98+	2014–2034
2004 Malbec Catena Zapata Nicasia Vineyard	96	2012–2025
2004 Nicolás Catena Zapata	98+	2020–2050

FINCA LA CHAMIZA ★★★
MENDOZA $39.00

2004 Martin Alsima Malbec	90+	2012–2025

CHEVAL DES ANDES ★★★★
MENDOZA $70.00

Cheval des Andes is owned by Château Cheval Blanc, legendary St.-Émilion producer. The wine is sourced from their 50-hectare (124-acre) estate vineyard planted on its own roots in 1929. The first vintage was 1999 and the 2004 was the first in which there was more Malbec than Cabernet Sauvignon in the blend. New oak is utilized for the Cabernet and one-year-old barrels for the Malbec.

2004 Cheval des Andes	93	2014–2030
2002 Cheval des Andes	93	2012–2025
1999 Cheval des Andes	92	2010–2020

BODEGA CICCHITTI ★★★
MENDOZA $15.00–$19.00

Bodega Cicchitti was founded in 1882 by Jose Antonio Cicchitti. All the wines are produced from the estate's 240 acres of vines, undergo fermentation with native yeasts, are bottled unfined and unfiltered, and offer superb value.

2004 Cabernet Sauvignon Gran Reserva	90	2009–2017
2004 Malbec Gran Reserva	92	2010–2022
2005 Malbec-Cabernet Sauvignon	89	now–2012
2006 Sangiovese	88	now–2011

CLOS DE LOS SIETE ★★★★
CANTON DE TUNUYAN $16.00

Clos de los Siete is a project of Michel Rolland. The vineyard, located about 60 miles south of Mendoza at about 3,000 feet of elevation, has 300 acres in production with another 875 planted.

2005 Clos de los Siete	90	now–2015
2006 Clos de los Siete	92	now–2016

VIÑA COBOS ★★★★★
MENDOZA $17.00–$150.00

Viña Cobos is the Argentina winery of the renowned Paul Hobbs, best known for his namesake wines from California's North Coast. Hobbs began consulting in South America in 1988 and, early on, became involved with Nicolás Catena in the startup of that winery's Chardonnay program. In 1998 he temporarily left his consulting projects to start Viña Cobos with the first vintage coming in 1999. In 2005 Viña Cobos constructed its own winery.

2005 Cabernet Sauvignon Bramare	92	2009–2017
2005 Cabernet Sauvignon Bramare Marchiori Vineyard	94	2012–2025
2006 Cabernet Sauvignon Cocodrilo	91	now–2014
2005 Malbec Bramare	93	2010–2018
2005 Malbec Bramare Marchiori Vineyard	96	2012–2025
2006 Malbec Bramare Marchiori Vineyard	96–99	2016–2035
2005 Malbec Cobos Marchiori Vineyard	98	2015–2035
2006 Malbec Cobos Marchiori Vineyard	98–100	2016–2036
2006 Malbec El Felino	92	now–2012
2006 Merlot La Garto	90	now–2012
2005 uNico Marchiori Vineyard	98+	2015–2032

COLOMÉ ★★★
SALTA $25.00–$90.00

Bodega y Estancia Colomé is located in the northern province of Salta at high elevation (5,500–9,850 feet), possibly the highest vineyards in the world. The vineyards are biodynamically and sustainably farmed.

2004 Estate	87	now–2014
2005 Malbec Estate	88	2010–2020
2003 Reserva	93	2013–2028

CRIOS DE SUSANA BALBO ★ ★ ★ ★
MENDOZA $15.00

Although Susana Balbo's Crios offerings are the declassified lots from her more expensive "signature" wines, they need make no apologies. They rank among the best values coming out of Argentina.

2006 Cabernet Sauvignon	90	now–2012
2006 Malbec	90	now–2012
2005 Syrah-Bonarda	89	now–2012

CUVELIER LOS ANDES ★ ★ ★ ★
MENDOZA $35.00–$50.00

Bodega Cuvelier Los Andes, owned by Bertrand and Jean-Guy Cuvelier, is another consulting client of the peripatetic Michel Rolland. The estate encompasses 46 hectares (115 acres) of young vines (four years of age for the 2005 vintage).

2005 Grand Malbec	94	2010–2020
2005 Grand Vin	94	2013–2028

DOÑA PAULA ★ ★ ★
MENDOZA $16.00–$35.00

2006 Malbec Estate	87	now–2016
2004 Malbec Selección de Bodega	90+	2010–2020
2006 Shiraz-Malbec	88	now–2016

DURIGUTTI ★ ★ ★
MENDOZA $25.00

2004 Malbec Familia Reserva	91	2012–2025

ERAL BRAVO ★ ★ ★
MENDOZA $25.00–$40.00

2005 Cabernet Sauvignon Erales	89	2010–2020
2005 Malbec Erales	90	now–2015
2005 YBS Eral Bravo	91	2009–2018

FABRE MONTMAYOU ★ ★ ★
MENDOZA $30.00

The 2005 Malbec Gran Reserva was sourced from a vineyard 60-plus years old in Vistalba, Lujan de Cuyo. It was fermented with native yeasts and aged in French oak for 12 months.

2005 Malbec Gran Reserva	89	now–2017

ENRIQUE FOSTER ★ ★ ★ ★
MENDOZA $50.00–$100.00

2004 Firmado	96	2012–2025
2003 Malbec Limited Edition	92	2010–2020
2003 Malbec Reserva	92	2009–2018

HUARPE ★★★
MENDOZA $25.00

Huarpe was started in 2003 by two fourth-generation members of the Toso family.

2003 Selection	89	now–2013

JAURE WINERY ★★★
MENDOZA $80.00

2003 JJ Jacinto Jaure Gran Reserva	92+	2012–2025

KAIKEN ★★★
MENDOZA $14.00–$23.00

2005 Cabernet Sauvignon	87	now–2015
2006 Cabernet Sauvignon Ultra	90	2010–2020
2005 Malbec	88	now–2013
2006 Malbec Ultra	91	2010–2020

LUCA ★★★★★
ALTOS DE MENDOZA $33.00–$125.00

Luca is the personal project of Laura Catena, daughter of Nicolás Catena. The winery takes its name from Laura's oldest son.

2005 Beso de Dante	89	now–2015
2006 Chardonnay	92	now–2010
2006 Malbec	93	2014–2028
2004 Nico by Luca Malbec	95	2014–2034
2006 Pinot Noir	93	2011–2019
2005 Syrah	87	now–2015

MAPEMA ★★★
MENDOZA $20.00–$31.00

Mapema is run jointly by longtime winemakers Pepe Galante and Mariano di Paoloa.

2005 Malbec	90	2010–2020
2002 Primera Zona	90	2012–2025

MARGUERY ★★★
MENDOZA $15.00–$26.00

2004 Malbec Casa Marguery	88	2009–2017
2004 Malbec Familia Marguery	89	now–2014

MARIFLOR ★★★★
MENDOZA $35.00

The Mariflor winemakers are Marcelo Pelleriti and Michel Rolland. The Pinot Noir grapes were sourced from a 10-acre parcel in Vista Flores in Mendoza. The wine is aged 14 months in new French oak.

2005 Pinot Noir	90	now–2015
2006 Pinot Noir	90	2012–2022

MASI TUPUNGATO ★★★
MENDOZA $17.00

The well-known Masi winery, located in Italy's Veneto, is now making wine in Mendoza's Tupungato region. Their slogan is "Argentinian soul, Venetian style." The 2005 Passo Doble is a 65% Malbec, 30% Corvina, 5% Merlot blend made using the ripasso method—this involves double fermentation of the Malbec grapes with lightly dried, whole Corvina grapes. The wine then spends nine months in French oak.

2005 Passo Doble	88	now–2015

MELIPAL ★★★
MENDOZA $20.00–$45.00

Given that 2005 is one of Mendoza's finest vintages in recent memory, it is not surprising that Melipal's "regular" bottling of Malbec considerably surpasses the 2004 Reserva from a solid but not great year.

2005 Malbec	91	2010–2020
2004 Malbec Reserva	86	now–2014

MENDEL ★★★★
MENDOZA $47.00–$65.00

The head winemaker and a partner at Mendel is Roberto de la Mota, who formerly held the same position at Cheval des Andes.

2005 Malbec	93	2012–2025
2005 Unus	94	2014–2030

MONTEVIEJO ★★★★
MENDOZA $14.00–$65.00

Bodega Monteviejo, owned by Catherine Péré-Vergé (also the proprietor of Pomerol's Le Gay), is located at the foothills of the Andes, next to Vista Flores, south of Mendoza. Globe-trotting Michel Rolland is in charge of winemaking.

2004 Festivo	91	now–2014
2006 Lindaflor Chardonnay	91	now–2011
2005 Lindaflor Malbec	94	2013–2028
2005 Monteviejo	90+	2009–2017
2003 Petite Fleur	91	2010–2020

FINCA LAS MORAS ★★★
TULUM VALLEY $39.00

Finca Las Moras is a Trapiche-owned winery.

2004 Mora Negra	91+	2012–2025

NAVARRO CORREAS
MENDOZA $20.00–$40.00★ ★ ★

2004 Malbec Alegoria Gran Reserva	90	now–2014
2004 Ultra	91+	2012–2025

NIETO SENETINER ★★★
MENDOZA $22.00

2004 Bonarda	90	now–2014

NOEMIA DE PATAGONIA
PATAGONIA $27.00–$117.00* ★★★

2006 A Lisa	90	now–2016
2006 J. Alberto	91	2009–2017
2004 Malbec	93	2012–2028

NORTON ★★★
MENDOZA $20.00–$28.00

2005 Cabernet Sauvignon Reserva	87	now–2015
2004 Privada	90	2009–2017

PEŃIWEN ★★★
MENDOZA $25.00

2005 Cabernet Sauvignon Paso de Piedra	90	2010–2020
2005 Malbec Paso de Piedra	90	now–2015

BODEGAS POESIA ★★★★
MENDOZA $15.00–$80.00

Bodegas Poesia is owned by Bordeaux proprietors Hélène Garcin and Patrice Lévêque, with Lévêque doubling as winemaker with consultation from Dr. Alain Raynaud.

2005 Clos des Andes	91	2012–2025
2005 Pasodoble	90	now–2015
2005 Poesia	93	2015–2030

EL PORVENIR DE LOS ANDES ★★★
MENDOZA $25.00–$50.00

2005 Amauta	90	2010–2020
2004 Malbec Laborum	91+	2012–2025

LA POSTA ★★★
MENDOZA $15.00–$18.00

2006 Bonarda	89	now–2014
2006 Cocina Blend	90	now–2014
2006 Malbec Paulucci Vineyard	90	now–2016
2006 Malbec Pizzella Vineyard	90+	2010–2020

ALFREDO ROCA ★★★
MENDOZA $25.00

Bodega Alfredo Roca is a family-owned, 282-acre estate in the San Rafael region of Mendoza.

2005 Malbec Family Reserva	89+	2009–2017
2005 Pinot Noir Family Reserva	85	now–2011
2005 Tempranillo Family Reserva	90	2010–2020

FINCA SOPHENIA ★ ★ ★
MENDOZA $17.00

Finca Sophenia is owned and operated by Roberto Luka, formerly president of Wines of Argentina. The winemaking consultant is Michel Rolland. The estate's vineyard is located in the Tupungato district at an elevation of 4,000 feet.

2005 Synthesis Malbec	90	now–2015

TEMPUS ALBA ★ ★ ★
MENDOZA $17.00–$45.00

2003 Acorde #1 Reserva	88	2009–2017
2004 Syrah Preludio	87	now–2014
2005 Tempranillo Preludio	90	now–2015

TERRAZAS DE LOS ANDES ★ ★ ★
MENDOZA $16.00–$45.00

2003 Malbec Afincado	90	2010–2020
2004 Malbec Reserva Estate	87	now–2014

TIKAL ★ ★ ★ ★
MENDOZA $25.00–$50.00

Tikal is owned by Ernesto Catena of the renowned Argentine wine family.

2006 Amorio	92	2010–2020
2005 Jubilo	92	2012–2025
2005 Patriota	90	2009–2018
2006 Patriota	92	2010–2020

TITTARELLI ★ ★ ★
MENDOZA $18.00–$47.00

2004 Malbec Reserva de Familia	89	now–2014
2004 Red Wine	91+	2012–2025

BODEGAS TIZA ★ ★ ★
MENDOZA $17.00

2005 Malbec	90	now–2015

MICHEL TORINO ★ ★ ★
CAFAYATE $16.00–$45.00

Michel Torino was founded in 1892. Located in the Cafayate Valley in northern Argentina, the estate owns 700 hectares of vines, most of it farmed organically.

2004 Altimus MMIV	91+	2012–2025
2005 Cabernet Sauvignon Don David	89	now–2015
2005 Malbec Don David	90	2010–2020

PASCUAL TOSO ✷✷✷
MENDOZA $20.00–$100.00

These Pascual Toso wines are single-vineyard offerings from the Las Barrancas Vineyard located in the Maipu District of Mendoza. The winery also produces a bevy of excellent red and white wine values.

2006 Cabernet Sauvignon Reserva	89	2009–2017
2002 Magdalena Toso	92	2012–2025
2006 Malbec Reserva	90	2010–2020

TRAPICHE ✷✷✷✷
MENDOZA $15.00–$55.00

Trapiche is best known for its value-priced wines. However, the mid-range and upper end of the Trapiche portfolio offer some super wines that should not be missed.

2005 Cabernet Sauvignon Broquel	89	now–2015
2004 Iscay	90	now–2016
2005 Malbec Broquel	89	now–2015
2003 Malbec Tributo Viña Felipe Villafane	95	2015–2035
2004 Malbec Viña Carlos Gei Berra	93	2014–2030
2004 Malbec Viña Victorio Coletto	94	2014–2030
2004 Malbec Viña Pedro Gonzalez	94	2015–2035

VAL DE FLORES ✷✷✷
MENDOZA $50.00

Val de Flores Malbec is made in consultation with Michel Rolland. The grapes are sourced from a vineyard 50-plus years old in the Vista Flores region of Mendoza.

2004 Malbec	92	2014–2030

VALENTIN BIANCHI ✷✷✷
MENDOZA $18.00–$30.00

2005 Malbec Famiglia Bianchi	87	now–2012
2004 Malbec Particular	89	now–2014

VIEJO ISAIAS
✷✷✷ MENDOZA $20.00

2006 Malbec Reserva	89	now–2016

ZOLO ✷✷✷
MENDOZA $20.00–$55.00

2004 Premium Malbec San Pablo Vineyard	92+	2014–2030
2005 Reserva Malbec	89	now–2015

ZUCCARDI ✷✷✷
MENDOZA $15.00–$50.00

Familia Zuccardi is a family-owned winery started in 1963 when they planted the first vineyard in Maipu, then a desert region, followed in 1973 by a second vineyard in Santa Rosa, another desert. Familia Zuccardi has also been a pioneer in the introduction of nonindigenous varieties into Argentina. These are bottled under the Textual label.

2006 Ancellota Textual	88+	now–2016
2004 Malbec Q	90+	now–2017
2006 Marselan Textual	88	now–2012
2006 Tannat Textual	88+	2009–2017
2004 Tempranillo Q	88	now–2014
2003 Zeta	92	2012–2022

[australia]

You name it and the Australians no doubt grow it, make it into wine, blend it with something else, and give it an unusual name. Australian wines have been hot—and not just in America. The combination of quality and value that many of them offer is the biggest thing in town from London to New York. Australia, like California in the U.S. and Alsace in France, labels its wines after the grape (or grapes) from which they are made. All of the major grapes are used here. While great wines are produced from most varieties, Syrah (called Shiraz in Australia) triumphs over all of the others. The major viticultural districts are listed alphabetically below.

[wine regions]

ADELAIDE HILLS (South Australia) Located in southern Australia, this is a high-altitude, cooler-climate region. Petaluma was the pioneer winery here. Other names of note include Ashton Hills, Nepenthe, Shaw & Smith, and Geoff Weaver. Chardonnay and Pinot Noir appear to be the varieties with the greatest promise.

BAROSSA VALLEY (South Australia) In southern Australia, this huge, well-known viticultural area north of Adelaide is the home of some of the quantitative titans of Australia's wine industry (i.e., Penfolds, Henschke, Seppelt, Wolf Blass, Orlando, and Yalumba). It is the source for Australia's finest wines, including spectacular old-vine Shiraz cuvées produced by Rolf Binder, Burge Family Winemakers, Elderton, Glaetzer, Greenock Creek, Ringland Vintners, Rockford, Torbreck, and Yalumba. Lastly, Australia's most renowned wine, Penfolds Grange, is largely a blend from selected Barossa vineyards.

BENDIGO (Victoria) Bendigo is an up-and-coming area, although it has a long history as a wine-producing region. Balgownie, Jasper Hill, and Wild Duck Creek are the finest wineries.

VICTORIA (Victoria) The best-known subregions of Victoria are Goulburn Valley, Bendigo, Geelong, Yarra Valley, and Rutherglen, all within a day's drive of Melbourne.

CLARE VALLEY (South Australia) Located north of Adelaide and the Barossa Valley, this beautiful area is better known for its whites than for its red wines. A number of high-quality wineries call Clare Valley their home, including Jim Barry, Clos Clare, Grosset, Pikes, Kilikanoon, Tim Adams, and Knappstein. Some surprisingly fine Riesling emerges from this area.

COONAWARRA (South Australia) Situated in South Australia, west of the Goulburn Valley, Coonawarra is among the most respected red wine–growing areas of Australia. Top wineries such as Penley, Parker, Highbank, Majella, Katnook, and Lindemans (their Limestone Ridge and St. George vineyards are there) pull their grapes from Coonawarra.

GEELONG (Victoria) Southwest of Melbourne near the coast is the small area of Geelong. The best-known wineries are Bannockburn, Clyde Park, and Mount Anakie.

GLENROWAN (Victoria) Located in northeastern Victoria, this hot area is famous for its inky, rich, chewy red wines, especially the full-throttle Shiraz from one of Australia's historic producers, Baileys. A more commercial Cabernet and a Shiraz are made by Wynns. Brown Brothers, one of the most successful high-quality Australian wineries, makes its home at nearby Milawa.

GRAMPTANS (Victoria) Situated between Ararat and Stawell, to the northwest of Melbourne and Geelong, is an area known for its sparkling wines (primarily from the huge producer Seppelt) and for its smooth, fat, low-acid but tasty red wines. The top red-wine producers are Mount Langi Ghiran and Cathcart Ridge.

GREAT SOUTHERN (Western Australia) In the remote southwestern tip of Australia, approximately 150 miles south of Perth, is a vast, burgeoning viticultural area called Great Southern. Apple orchards thrive more than vineyards, but wineries such as Howard Park, Mount Barker, Frankland Estate, and Alkoomi have well-deserved good reputations.

HUNTER VALLEY (New South Wales) Less than a three-hour drive from Sydney is Australia's famed Hunter Valley. It is to Sydney what the Napa Valley is to San Francisco and the Médoc is to Bordeaux—a major tourist attraction and source for some of Australia's most desired wines. Originally this area was known for its rich, exotic, full-bodied red wines from the Shiraz (produced by the legendary Maurice O'Shea) and Cabernet Sauvignon grapes, but more recently Chardonnay and Sémillon have proven successful as well. No doubt because of the region's size and the intense competitive spirit here, this area's wineries are well represented in the export market. In spite of this region's renown, considerable quantities of mediocre, industrial swill emerge from both the "lower" and "upper" Hunter Valley. Familiar names from the Hunter Valley include Tyrell's, Rothbury Estate, Lindemans, Rosemount, Arrowfield, Hungerford Hill, and Brokenwood.

MARGARET RIVER (Western Australia) In the very southwestern tip of this country is the Margaret River viticultural zone. Australian wine experts claim that Australia's most French-like Cabernet Sauvignons and Chardonnays come from this area, which produces wines with higher natural acidities. There are many fine producers located here, including Vasse Felix, Moss Wood, Leeuwin Estate, Cullen, Abbey Vale, Devil's Lair, Pierro, and Woody Nook.

MCLAREN VALE (South Australia) The traditional fare of this hot area south of Adelaide was high-alcohol, thick, rich Grenache wines. This has all changed in the last 15 years with the advent of cold fermentations and the perception that the public yearns for lighter, fruitier wines. Some of the giants of the Australian wine business are in McLaren Vale, including Hardys and its higher-quality sibling, Reynella. Smaller wineries, producing some of Australia's most exciting wines, include Kay Brothers, Clarendon Hills, Noon, d'Arenberg, Coriole, Maxwell, and Mitolo.

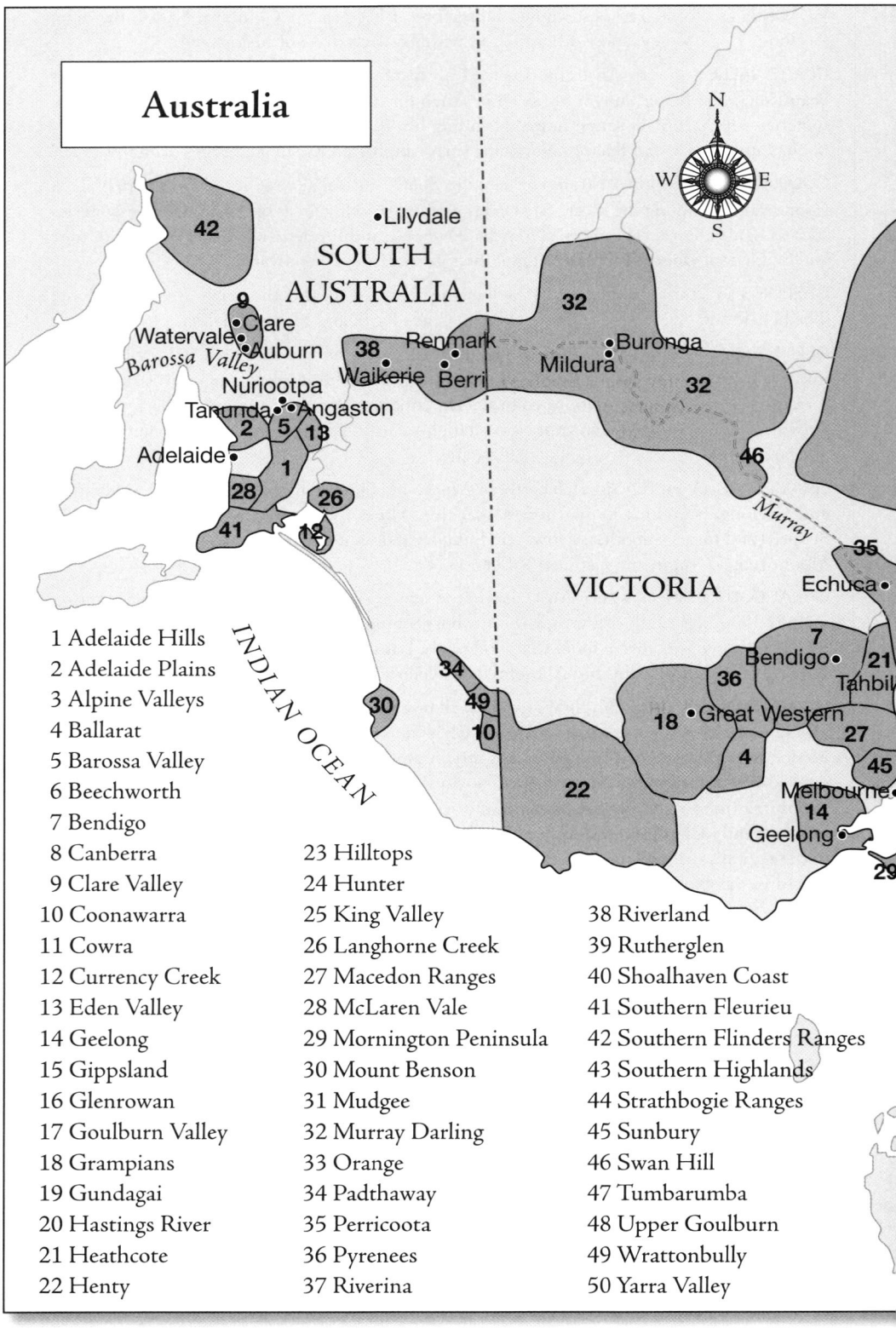

Australia

SOUTH AUSTRALIA

VICTORIA

INDIAN OCEAN

•Lilydale

42

9
Clare
Watervale•
Barossa Valley •Auburn
Nuriootpa
Tanunda• •Angaston
Adelaide•
2 5 13
1
28
26
41
12

38
Waikerie Berri

Renmark

32

Buronga
Mildura•

32

46

Murray

35

Echuca•

7
Bendigo• 21
36 Tahbilk
18 •Great Western
4
27
45
Melbourne•
14
Geelong•
29

34
30
49
10

22

18

1 Adelaide Hills
2 Adelaide Plains
3 Alpine Valleys
4 Ballarat
5 Barossa Valley
6 Beechworth
7 Bendigo
8 Canberra
9 Clare Valley
10 Coonawarra
11 Cowra
12 Currency Creek
13 Eden Valley
14 Geelong
15 Gippsland
16 Glenrowan
17 Goulburn Valley
18 Grampians
19 Gundagai
20 Hastings River
21 Heathcote
22 Henty

23 Hilltops
24 Hunter
25 King Valley
26 Langhorne Creek
27 Macedon Ranges
28 McLaren Vale
29 Mornington Peninsula
30 Mount Benson
31 Mudgee
32 Murray Darling
33 Orange
34 Padthaway
35 Perricoota
36 Pyrenees
37 Riverina

38 Riverland
39 Rutherglen
40 Shoalhaven Coast
41 Southern Fleurieu
42 Southern Flinders Ranges
43 Southern Highlands
44 Strathbogie Ranges
45 Sunbury
46 Swan Hill
47 Tumbarumba
48 Upper Goulburn
49 Wrattonbully
50 Yarra Valley

NEW SOUTH WALES

20

24

31
•Mudgee

Hunter Valley

•Muswellbrook

Pokolbin• •Rothbury
Cessnock

•Forbes

33

11• Cowra

Rooty Hill• •Sydney
Cobbitty•

•Yenda
Griffith

•Young

23

43

19
•Wagga Wagga

8

40

37

•Canberra

The Riverland

47

Barooga
•Corowa

39

17

16

6

Australian Alps

Glenrowan •Milawa

44

25

3

48

Yarra Valley

50

VICTORIA

15

Wine Regions

PACIFIC OCEAN

AUSTRALIA

Map area

•Melbourne

BASS STRAIT

TASMANIA

0   100 miles

0   100 kilometers

MUDGEE (New South Wales) Located in New South Wales, west of the famed Hunter Valley, is Mudgee (an aboriginal name meaning "nest in the hills"). With its cool nights and hot days, Mudgee has proven to be not only a fine red wine area but also a consistent source for tropical fruit-scented, luxuriously rich Chardonnays. For whatever reason, the wines of Mudgee also tend to be less expensive than those from other top areas. Reliable producers include Craigmoor, Montrose, Miramar, and Huntington Estate.

PADTHAWAY (South Australia) This southern Australian viticultural area has developed a following for its value-priced white wines, especially the Chardonnay and Sauvignon Blanc. Sadly, Padthaway vineyards have proven how easy it is to produce industrial quantities of uninspiring white and red wines. Among the brightest lights are the wines produced at Henry's Drive and Pillar Box.

PYRENEES (Victoria) The attractive, rolling-hill countryside of the Pyrenees, northwest of Melbourne, forms a triangle between Redbank, Moonambel, and Avoca. The top wines are the reds from the Cabernet Sauvignon and Shiraz grapes. Wineries of note include Redbank, Taltarni, Mount Avoca, and Dalwhinnie.

RIVERLAND (South Australia) Located in South Australia, Riverland is to Australia what the San Joaquin Valley is to California. This vast source of grapes of mediocre quality is dominated by huge cooperatives and producers who turn out Australia's jug wines and bag-in-the-box generic wines. Some big enterprises have their jug-wine business centered here, including Penfolds, Kaiser Stuhl, Angove's, Berri, and Renmano. While most of the wines from this area are decidedly insipid, some good-value, fresh whites at bargain-basement prices can be found.

RUTHERGLEN (Victoria) Rutherglen is synonymous with Australia's fortified sweet wines, many of which are extraordinary. The famous sweet, nectarlike, ageless Ports and fortified Muscats and Tokays of R. L. Buller, Chambers Rosewood, Campbells, Stanton and Killeen, as well as Seppelt are made from Rutherglen grapes.

SWAN VALLEY (Western Australia) This hot, arid area in Western Australia, just northeast of the coastal city of Perth, produces large-framed, muscular red wines and increasingly better white wines. Houghton is the area's most famous winery, but good wines are made by Moondah Brook and Sandalford.

YARRA VALLEY (Victoria) This is Australia's most fashionable viticultural area, and its proponents (the provincial Australian wine press) argue that the climate and resulting wines come closest in spirit to those of Bordeaux and Burgundy in France. I am not convinced. Located in Victoria, this is a cool-climate area outside Melbourne, where every major red and white glamour variety is planted, from Cabernet Sauvignon, Merlot, and Pinot Noir to Chardonnay, Riesling, and Gewurztraminer. The best wineries are Lillydale, Yarra Yering, Coldstream Hills, and St. Huberts, but beware, there is much more "sizzle" than substance for most wines from Yarra Valley.

[grape varieties]

REDS

CABERNET SAUVIGNON This variety can excel in Australia and generally produces a very fruity, often jammy, intensely curranty, fat wine, sometimes low in acidity but round, generous, and surprisingly ageworthy. Despite complaints from palates trained on European wines, vignerons have been learning year by year how to produce better-balanced wines.

PINOT NOIR There are those who claim to have made successful wines from this infinitely fickle variety, but the majority of Australian Pinot Noirs to date have either been raisiny, unusual, and repugnant, or watery, pale, innocuous, and excessively acidified. One prominent exception is Bass Phillip, which produces the country's most profound Pinot Noir from the cool microclimate of South Gippsland in Victoria. In the last few years, Tasmania has become increasingly important for Pinot Noir, although viticulture here is still in its early stages of development.

SHIRAZ Despite the Aussies' present-day infatuation with such international grapes as Cabernet Sauvignon, Merlot, and Pinot Noir, it is Shiraz that produces their greatest wines. The problem is that there is an enormous amount of it, and only a handful of producers treat Shiraz (Syrah) with the respect and care that is accorded Cabernet. It can produce Australia's greatest red wine when left to stand on its own, as Penfolds Grange has convincingly proven for over 50 years. Additionally, it can provide more dimension and character to a red wine when blended with Cabernet Sauvignon, as Penfolds and Petaluma have proven time and time again. The greatest examples emerge from only two regions, Barossa and McLaren Vale. Elsewhere, Shiraz usually produces one-dimensional, heavy wines.

WHITES

CHARDONNAY The shrewd Aussies, taking full advantage of wine consumers' thirst for Chardonnay wines, have consistently offered plump, fat wines filled with the flavors of apples, pears, oranges, and ripe melons. Although the wines still tend to be overoaked or, worse, artificially oaked as well as excessively acidified, more and more Australian Chardonnays are fresh and exuberant and bottled early to preserve their youthful grapy qualities. With the advent of centrifuges and micropore filters, many Chardonnays have no bouquet or flavor. The one major disappointment is the aging potential of these naturally low-acid wines, but most consumers are drinking them within several months of purchase, so this is probably a moot issue. One positive trend has been the increasing quantities of delicious "nonoaked" or so-called "virgin" Chardonnays.

GEWURZTRAMINER Contrary to the local salespeople, who hype the quality of Gewurztraminer, this grape produces insipid, pale, watery wines that are a far cry from what Gewurztraminer does in France.

MARSANNE Château Tahbilk and Mitchelton are proponents of this grape, which tends to turn out one-dimensional, bland wines.

MUSCAT This hot-climate grape excels in Australia and is at its best in the decadently rich, sweet, fortified Muscats that can age for decades. It is also made into a medium-sweet table wine with which Brown Brothers does a particularly admirable job.

RIESLING Australia has proven to be the New World's best alternative to German and Alsace Riesling. This grape has done extremely well with Kabinett-and Spätlese-style drier Riesling in the Barossa Valley, Adelaide Hills, and Clare Valley. Wineries such as Petaluma, Pewsey Vale, Pikes, Grosset, Leeuwin, and Mount Horrocks have turned out some remarkable wines. Overall, this grape gets good marks.

SAUVIGNON BLANC The results have been mixed, as the hot climate causes this grape to overripen and to take on a grotesque, vegetal, oily, thick fruitiness. There are some fresh, tasty, dry Sauvignons coming from Australia, but for now, New Zealand consistently beats Australia when it comes to quality Sauvignon-based wines.

SÉMILLON Sémillon can be delicious, whether it is blended with Chardonnay or Sauvignon or allowed to stand by itself. It produces big, creamy, rich wines loaded with flavor. Wineries such as Rothbury, Rosemount, Montrose, Peter Lehmann, and Henschke have done better with Sémillon than anyone. Some great sweet wines have been made from Sémillon affected by the botrytis fungus. Look for those from Rothbury, Rosemount, and Peter Lehmann, which are world-class.

FLAVORS

REDS

CABERNET SAUVIGNON These wines can be very ripe, often overripe, with sweet, intense black currant flavors; supple, fat textures; and oodles of fruit. When poorly made or overly acidified, the wines are musty, dirty, and tart.

PINOT NOIR Raisiny, pruny fruit flavors with no finesse or complexity represent appallingly bad examples of Pinot Noir. Recent examples from Tasmania and Adelaide Hills are much truer to type with Burgundy as the role model.

SHIRAZ Intense aromas of blackberry liqueur, cassis, leather, licorice, cedar, tar, and pepper are found in wines that have a healthy dose of Shiraz. Quite full-bodied and rich, with softer tannins than Cabernet Sauvignon, these wines are drinkable young but usually age better than the more glamorous Cabernet Sauvignons. The finest examples almost always emerge from Barossa and McLaren Vale.

WHITES

CHARDONNAY Tropical fruit flavors predominate in this creamy-textured, voluptuous wine. Oak is sometimes too noticeable, but better-balanced wines with the fruit in the forefront have been the rule in recent vintages. Unoaked Chardonnays are seen more frequently with most of them selling at value prices.

GEWURZTRAMINER Where's the spice and exotic lychee nut character found in the great Gewurztraminers of Alsace? These are generally watery, thin wines that are usually disappointing.

MARSANNE Marsanne can be described as usually neutral or, as Jancis Robinson says, "reminiscent of glue." It typically tastes much better old than young, but because it tastes so uninteresting young, no one ages it.

MUSCAT Huge aromas of brown sugar, fruitcake, crème brûlée, buttered and baked apricots, and oranges with honey and nuts give this varietal its appeal.

RIESLING The classic Riesling aromas of spring flowers, green apples, and wet stones are present in the drier versions of this wine. As the wines get sweeter, aromas and flavors of oranges, peaches, apricots, butter, baked apples, and honeyed nuts arise.

SAUVIGNON BLANC Unfortunately, these wines seem to be either feeble, bland, and tasteless or oily, vegetal, and grotesque.

SÉMILLON In the drier versions, lemon-lime aromas intertwined with honey and toasty oak are often the most interesting. With the sweet versions, buttery nuts and honey-coated-raisin flavors take over.

AGING POTENTIAL
Cabernet Sauvignon: 5–20 years
Shiraz: 5–30 years
Chardonnay: 1–2 years
Gewurztraminer: 1–2 years
Marsanne: 4–12 years

Muscat (dry): 1–3 years; (fortified): 5–50+ years
Pinot Noir: 4–6 years
Riesling (dry): 1–4 years; (sweet): 4–10 years
Sauvignon Blanc: 1–3 years
Sémillon (dry): 2–8 years; (sweet): 4–12 years

[the wines]

OVERALL QUALITY LEVEL

At the top level, wines such as the Penfolds Grange or Penfolds Bin 707 Cabernet Sauvignon, in addition to some of the old-vine Shiraz cuvées from relatively small producers, such as Torbreck, Rolf Binder, Greenock Creek, Kay Brothers, Chris Ringland, and Clarendon Hills, are as fine as any red wine made in the world. Sadly, most of Australia's greatest wines are made in minuscule quantities, but readers lucky enough to latch onto any of the production of my five-star wineries are sure to be impressed. Australia's overall wine quality is average, with oceans of mediocre and poorly made wines. There are, however, plenty of good, agreeable wines at attractive prices, and therein lies the reason for the success of Australia's wines. Australia is the world's leader in offering industrial quantities of tasty, user-friendly wines at low prices. In that area, Australia has little competition.

IMPORTANT INFORMATION

Given the remarkable diversity of wines, the best thing for a consumer to do is to memorize the names of some of the better producers, and restrict your initial purchases to the surefire successes from that particular winery—usually Chardonnay, Cabernet, and Shiraz. Use the producers' chart for each varietal as a guideline until you have decided which wines and producers you prefer.

BUYING STRATEGY

For 95% of Australia's wines, buy only what you intend to drink over the next 12 to 16 months. The white wines have a particularly short shelf life, and the great majority of the reds are meant to be consumed within two to four years of the vintage. Thus, for dry white wines, only the 2007s, 2006s, and 2005s should be purchased. For inexpensive red wines, readers can safely purchase vintages back to 2002 without worrying about the wine's senility. Australia does produce sensational world-class red wines, but they are often produced in minute quantities and are just as expensive as a grand cru from France or a California cult wine. Readers should try to buy their Australian wines from some of the most creative American importers, who have done a fabulous job in ferreting out some of the limited-production, spectacularly high-quality estates reviewed on the following pages. In particular, readers should look for Australian wines carrying the import label of Dan Philips, The Grateful Palate, Oxnard, California; John Larchet, The Australian Premium Wine Collection, whose importer is USA Wine West, San Rafael, California; Gavin Speight, Old Bridge Cellars, Napa, California; Benjamin Hammerschlag, Epicurean Wines, Seattle, Washington; Ken Onish and John Gorman, Southern Starz, Huntington Beach, California; and Ronnie Sanders, Vine Street Imports, Philadelphia, Pennsylvania. These importers do not have an exclusive on every great wine from Australia, but they are dealing with some of the smaller estates whose approach to winemaking is artisanal and oriented to the true connoisseur. Readers should also remember that Australia produces spectacular late-harvested fortified wines at a fraction of the price one pays for vintage Ports and the sweet wines of France and Germany. These decadently rich wines are well worth seeking out.

[recent vintages]

As in California, constant sunny weather virtually guarantees at least good-quality wines in Australia, but each year is different as a result of drought as well as heat or cold waves. However, the extremes in quality that one often sees in Europe do not exist in Australia.

2007
It was a year of extreme drought, and production was at about 25% of normal, but it is too soon to make any statements about quality.

2006
A solid year, the 2006s are very good to excellent but lack the majesty and multiple dimensions found in southern Australia's finest vintages. In Western Australia, quality is excellent, particularly in Margaret River, Great Southern, and Pemberton.

2005
In Barossa and McLaren Vale, this is an excellent to outstanding vintage, as well as superb in Clare Valley. The red wines have structure and richness, and the top wines should have lengthy drinking windows. It is also a first-class vintage throughout most of Western Australia.

2004
This is an exciting vintage for Barossa, Clare, and McLaren Vale. The wines are ripe, fleshy, and relatively forward but with enough structure to age for at least a decade for the icon wines. It is also a fine vintage in Western Australia for both red and white wines.

2003
The 2003 vintage is a moderately challenging one in the top regions of South Australia. The wines tend to be a bit compressed and firm, lacking generosity. However, it is a superb vintage for Clare and Eden Valley Rieslings, wines capable of aging like top Mosel Kabinetts. It is a difficult vintage in Western Australia for both red and white wines.

2002
There are those who believe that 2002 is the finest vintage to date in the 21st century for Barossa, McLaren Vale, and Clare red wines with the wines having splendid balance, layers of fruit, and serious aging potential. The Rieslings of Clare and Eden valleys are concentrated and potentially long-lived. Throughout Western Australia, it is a good but uninspiring vintage with the white wines faring a bit better than the reds.

OTHER VINTAGES

The 2001 vintage was a very hot one in South Australia, but the wines of Barossa and McLaren Vale have turned out well. The top wines continue to evolve and should turn out to be 20-year wines at the least. 1998 was a great vintage in which the top wines are aging gracefully, while 1996 was a fine year in which the wines are beginning to peak.

—JAY MILLER

[the ratings]

AUSTRALIA'S BEST PRODUCERS OF CABERNET SAUVIGNON, SHIRAZ, MERLOT, AND GRENACHE

* * * * * (OUTSTANDING)

Australian Domaine Wines/Pikes Shiraz
  Gaelic Cemetery (Clare Valley)
d'Arenberg The Dead Arm Shiraz
  (McLaren Vale)
Jim Barry Shiraz The Armagh
  (Clare Valley)
Rolf Binder Shiraz Hanisch (Barossa)
Rolf Binder Shiraz Heysen (Barossa)
Branson Coach House Cabernet Sauvignon
  (Barossa)
Clarendon Hills Cabernet Sauvignon
  Hickinbotham Vineyard (Clarendon)
Clarendon Hills Grenache Old Vines Romas
  Vineyard (Clarendon)
Clarendon Hills Grenache Onkaparinga
  (Clarendon)
Clarendon Hills Syrah Astralis Vineyard
  (Clarendon)
Clarendon Hills Syrah Brookman Vineyard
  (Clarendon)
Clarendon Hills Syrah Hickinbotham
  Vineyard (Clarendon)
Clarendon Hills Syrah Moritz Vineyard
  (Clarendon)
Clarendon Hills Syrah Piggott Range
  (Clarendon)
Elderton Shiraz Command (Barossa)
Gibson Shiraz Old Vine Collection (Barossa)
Glaetzer Shiraz Amon-Ra (Barossa)
Glaetzer Shiraz-Cabernet Sauvignon
  Anaperenna (Barossa)
Glaymond Shiraz The Distinction
  (Barossa)
Greenock Creek Cabernet Sauvignon
  Roennfeldt Road (Barossa)
Greenock Creek Shiraz Alice's (Barossa)
Greenock Creek Shiraz Apricot Block
  (Barossa)
Greenock Creek Shiraz Creek Block
  (Barossa)
Greenock Creek Shiraz Roennfeldt Road
  (Barossa)
Greenock Creek Shiraz Seven Acre
  (Barossa)

Andrew Hardy Shiraz The Ox
  (McLaren Vale)
Hazyblur Shiraz Invictus (Barossa)
Henschke Shiraz Hill of Grace
  (Eden Valley)
Hobbs Shiraz (Barossa)
Peter Howland Shiraz Parsons Vineyard
  (Frankland River)
Kaesler Shiraz Old Bastard (Barossa)
Kalleske Shiraz Johann Georg
  (Barossa)
Kay Brothers Shiraz Amery Vineyard
  Block 6 (McLaren Vale)
Kilikanoon Shiraz Attunga 1865
  (Clare Valley)
Magpie Estate Shiraz The Malcolm
  (Barossa)
Mollydooker Shiraz Carnival of Love
  (McLaren Vale)
Mollydooker Shiraz The Velvet Glove
  (McLaren Vale)
Noon Cabernet Sauvignon Reserve
  (Langhorne Creek)
Noon Eclipse Proprietary Red
  (Grenache-Shiraz) (McLaren Vale-
  Langhorne Creek)
Noon Shiraz Reserve (Langhorne Creek)
Penfolds Cabernet Sauvignon Bin 707
  (South Australia)
Penfolds Cabernet Sauvignon Cellar
  Reserve (Barossa)
Penfolds Grange (South Australia)
R Winery Anamorphosis Shiraz
  (Barossa Valley-Kalimna)
R Winery Chateau Chateau Columns
  Grenache (Barossa Valley-Greenock)
R Winery Chateau Chateau Island
  Grenache (Barossa Valley-Ebenezer)
R Winery Chateau Chateau Magic Window
  Grenache (Barossa Valley-Marananga)
R Winery Longitude Shiraz
  (Barossa Valley-Ebenezer)
R Winery Marquis Philips Shiraz Integrity
  (McLaren Vale)

R Winery 3 Rings Shiraz Reserve
(Barossa Valley-Kalimna)

R Winery The Wine Shiraz
(Barossa Valley-Ebenezer)

Corrina Rayment Shiraz Expatriate
(McLaren Vale)

Ringland Vinters Shiraz Chris Ringland
(Barossa)

Rusden Shiraz Black Guts (Barossa)

Torbeck Les Amis (Grenache) (Barossa)

Torbreck Descendant (Shiraz-Viognier)
(Barossa)

Torbreck RunRig (Shiraz/Viognier)
(Barossa)

Two Hands Cabernet Sauvignon Aphrodite
(Barossa)

Two Hands Shiraz Roennfeldt
Road Zippy's Block (Barossa)

Wild Duck Creek Estate Cabernet
Sauvignon Reserve (Heathcote)

Yalumba The Octavius (Old-Vine Shiraz)
(Barossa)

Yalumba The Reserve (Cabernet-Shiraz)
(Barossa)

Yarra Yering Dry Red No. 2
(Shiraz-Viognier-Roussanne)
(Yarra Valley)

★ ★ ★ ★ (EXCELLENT)

d'Arenberg The Coppermine Road
Cabernet Sauvignon (McLaren Vale)

d'Arenberg Ironstone Pressings Grenache-
Shiraz-Mourvèdre (McLaren Vale)

d'Arenberg The Twentyeight Road
Mourvèdre (Fleurieu)

Barossa Old Vine Company Shiraz (Barossa)

Jim Barry Cabernet Sauvignon The
Benbournie (Clare Valley)

Jim Barry Shiraz-Cabernet The James
Brazill (Clare Valley)

Battely Syrah (Beechworth)

Berrys Bridge Shiraz (Pyrenees)

Rolf Binder Shiraz-Mataro Hubris (Barossa)

Branson Coach House Shiraz House
Block-Rare (Barossa)

Brokenwood Shiraz Graveyard (Hunter
Valley)

Grant Burge Shiraz Meshach (Barossa)

Burge Family Garnacha (Barossa)

Burge Family Shiraz Draycott (Barossa)

Cape Barren Shiraz Old Vine
(McLaren Vale)

Cape d'Estaing Shiraz Admiral's Reserve
(Kangaroo Island)

Cascabel Monastrell (McLaren Vale)

Cascabel Shiraz (Fleurieu Peninsula)

Charles Cimicky Petite Sirah (Barossa)

Charles Cimicky Shiraz Autograph
(Barossa)

Charles Cimicky Shiraz Reserve (Barossa)

Clarendon Hills Cabernet Sauvignon
Brookman Vineyard (Clarendon)

Clarendon Hills Cabernet Sauvignon
Sandown Vineyard (Clarendon)

Clarendon Hills Grenache Old Vines
Hickinbotham Vineyard (Clarendon)

Clarendon Hills Grenache Old Vines
Kangarilla Vineyard (Clarendon)

Clarendon Hills Merlot Brookman
Vineyard (Clarendon)

Clarendon Hills Syrah Liandra Vineyard
(Clarendon)

Clarendon Hills Syrah Moritz Vineyard
(McLaren Vale)

Clarendon Hills Syrah Onkaparinga
(Clarendon)

Clonakilla Shiraz-Viognier
(Canberra District)

The Colonial Estate Émigré (Barossa)

The Colonial Estate Exile (Barossa)

The Colonial Estate John Speke Grenache-
Shiraz-Mourvèdre Single Vineyard
(Barossa)

Coriole Shiraz Lloyd Reserve
(McLaren Vale)

Deisen Shiraz (Barossa)

The Don Shiraz Crystal Hill (Victoria)

Dutschke Oscar Semmler Shiraz (Barossa)

Dutschke Shiraz Single Barrel (Barossa)

John Duval Wines Entity (Barossa)

John Duval Wines Plexus (Barossa)

Elderton Cabernet Sauvignon Ashmead
(Barossa)

Elderton Shiraz Nurioopta (Barossa)

Famille Chapoutier and Famille Laughton
Shiraz La Pleiade (Heathcote)

Gibson Wines Shiraz Old Vine Collection
(Eden Valley)

Glaetzer Bishop (Shiraz) (Barossa)

Glaetzer Wallace (Shiraz-Grenache)
(Barossa)

Glaymond Grenache Gerhard (Barossa)

Glaymond Shiraz Glen's Selection (Barossa)

Glaymond Shiraz The Distance (Barossa)

Glen Eldon Dry Bore Shiraz Reserve
(Barossa and Eden Valley)

Gralyn Estate Cabernet Sauvignon
(Margaret River)

Greenock Creek Cabernet Sauvignon
(Barossa)

Greenock Creek Grenache Cornerstone
(Barossa)

Grosset Gaia Proprietary Red
(Clare Valley)

J. J. Hahn Shiraz 1914 (Barossa)

Hazyblur Shiraz Baroota

Hazyblur Shiraz Barossa Valley

Hazyblur Shiraz McLaren Vale

Henry's Drive Shiraz Reserve (Padthaway)

Henschke Shiraz Mount Edelstone (Barossa)

Hobbs Shiraz Gregor (Barossa)

Steve Hoff Wines Cabernet Sauvignon
(Barossa)

Steve Hoff Wines Shiraz Rossco's Vineyard
(Barossa)

Peter Howland Shiraz Langley Vineyard
(Donnybrook)

J. P. Belle Terroir Shiraz (Barossa)

Jasper Hill Grenache Cornelia Vineyard
(Heathcote)

Jasper Hill Shiraz Cambria (Heathcote)

Jasper Hill Shiraz Emily's Paddock
(Heathcote)

Jasper Hill Shiraz Georgia's Paddock
(Victoria)

Kaesler Shiraz The Bogan (Barossa)

Kalleske Shiraz Greenock (Barossa)

Kangarilla Road Shiraz-Viognier
(McLaren Vale)

Kay Brothers Shiraz Amery Vineyard
Hillside (McLaren Vale)

Kilikanoon Grenache The Duke
(Clare Valley)

Kilikanoon Shiraz Green's Vineyard
(Barossa)

Kilikanoon Shiraz Oracle (Clare Valley)

Kilikanoon Shiraz R Reserve (Barossa)

Kilikanoon Shiraz Testament (Barossa)

Killibinbin Cabernet Sauvignon (Langhorne
Creek)

Killibinbin Shiraz Old Chestnut
(Paracombe)

Koltz Shiraz Pagan (McLaren Vale)

Langmeil Shiraz 1843 Freedom (Barossa)

Peter Lehmann Shiraz Stonewell (Barossa)

Lengs & Cooter Shiraz Clarendon
(Clarendon)

Loan Shiraz (Barossa)

Longview Shiraz Block 3 (Adelaide Hills)

Lunar Shiraz (Barossa)

Magpie Estate Shiraz The Election
(Barossa)

Massena Moonlight Run (Blend) (Barossa)

Maxwell Wines Cabernet Sauvignon Lime
Cave (McLaren Vale)

Maxwell Wines Shiraz Ellen Street
(McLaren Vale)

Maxwell Wines Shiraz Minatour
(McLaren Vale)

Mr. Riggs Shiraz (McLaren Vale)

Mitolo Cabernet Sauvignon Serpico
(McLaren Vale)

Mitolo Shiraz GAM (McLaren Vale)

Mitolo Shiraz The Reiver (Barossa)

Mitolo Shiraz Savitar (McLaren Vale)

Mollydooker Cabernet Sauvignon Gigglepot
(McLaren Vale)

Mollydooker Shiraz Blue-Eyed Boy
(McLaren Vale)

Mollydooker Shiraz-Cabernet Sauvignon
Enchanted Path (McLaren Vale)

Oliver's Taranga Shiraz H. J. Reserve
(McLaren Vale)

Oliverhill Shiraz Jimmy Section
(McLaren Vale)

Parson's Flat Cabernet-Shiraz (Padthaway)

Penfolds Cabernet Sauvignon-Shiraz Cellar
Reserve (Coonawarra)

Penfolds Shiraz Magill Estate
(South Australia)

Penfolds Shiraz RWT (Barossa)

Penley Estate Cabernet Sauvignon Reserve
(Coonawarra)

Penny's Hill Shiraz Footprint (McLaren
Vale)

Piombo Shiraz (McLaren Vale)

Poonawatta Shiraz Estate (Eden Valley)

R Winery Boarding Pass Shiraz First Class
(South Australia)

R Winery Chateau Chateau Grenache
(Barossa)

R Winery Chateau Chateau My Sun Is Your
Sun Grenache (Barossa Valley-Stonewell)
R Winery Chateau Chateau Triumphal Arc
Grenache (Barossa Valley-Light Pass)
R Winery Evil Incarnate Shiraz (Barossa)
R Winery Marquis Philips Shiraz 9
(McLaren Vale)
R Winery Re: Serve Cabernet Sauvignon
(Barossa)
Reschke Cabernet Sauvignon Empyrean
(Coonawarra)
Rockford Shiraz Basket Pressed (Barossa)
Rusden Cabernet Sauvignon Boundaries
(Barossa)
Rusden Cabernet Sauvignon-Shiraz Ripper
Creek (Barossa)
Rusden Zinfandel Chookshed (Barossa)
Schild Estate Shiraz Moorooroo Limited
Release (Barossa)
Schubert Estate Shiraz Goose-Yard Block
(Roennfeldt Road)
Schulz Shiraz Marcus Old Vine (Barossa)
Schwarz Wine Co. Grenache Thiele Road
(Barossa)
Schwarz Wine Co. Shiraz Nitschke Block
(Barossa)
Shirvington Shiraz (McLaren Vale)
Solitary Vineyards Grenache Greenock
Creek (Barossa)
Solitary Vineyards Shiraz Greenock Creek
(Barossa)
Solitary Vineyards Shiraz Solitary Block
(Barossa)
Spinifex Shiraz-Viognier (Barossa)
Standish Shiraz (Barossa)
Standish Shiraz-Viognier The Relic
(Barossa)
Tait Shiraz Basket Pressed (Barossa)

Tatiarra Shiraz Cambrian (Heathcote)
Tatiarra Shiraz Pressings Caravan of
Dreams (Heathcote)
Teusner Shiraz Albert (Barossa)
Teusner Shiraz The Riebke (Barossa)
Torbreck Shiraz The Struie (Barossa)
Torbreck The Steading (Grenache-Shiraz-
Mourvèdre) (Barossa)
Torzi Matthews Shiraz-Roussanne Lost
Highway (Barossa)
Troll Creek Cabernet Sauvignon (Barossa)
Troll Creek Shiraz (Barossa)
Turkey Flat Cabernet Sauvignon (Barossa)
Turkey Flat Shiraz (Barossa)
Two Hands Shiraz Ares (Barossa)
Two Hands Shiraz Bella's Garden (Barossa)
Two Hands Shiraz Lily's Garden
(McLaren Vale)
Two Hands Shiraz Samantha's Garden
(Clare Valley)
Vasse Felix Cabernet Sauvignon Heytesbury
(Margaret River and Great Southern)
Whip-Hand Cabernet Sauvignon
(McLaren Vale)
Wild Duck Creek Estate Alan's Cabernet
Sauvignon Vat 1 (Heathcote)
Wild Duck Creek Estate Shiraz Springflat
(Heathcote)
Wild Duck Creek Estate Shiraz Springflat
Pressings (Heathcote)
Wynns Cabernet Sauvignon John Riddoch
(Coonawarra)
Yalumba The Signature (Cabernet
Sauvignon-Shiraz) (Barossa)
Yangarra Estate Grenache High Sands
(McLaren Vale)
Yarra Yering Cabernet Sauvignon Dry Red
No. 1 (Yarra Valley)

★ ★ ★ (GOOD)

Alkoomi Blackbutt (Cabernet Sauvignon-
Malbec) (Frankland River)
Angus Wines Shiraz A3 (Hindmarsh
Island)
Aramis Syrah The Governor
(McLaren Vale)
d'Arenberg Grenache The Derelict
Vineyard (McLaren Vale)
d'Arenberg Shiraz-Viognier The Laughing
Magpie (McLaren Vale)
AusVetia Shiraz (South Australia)

Balgownie Estate Cabernet Sauvignon
(Bendigo)
Jim Barry Cabernet Sauvignon
The First XI (Clare Valley)
Jim Barry Shiraz The McRae Wood
(Clare Valley)
Rolf Binder Shiraz-Grenache Halliwell
(Barossa)
Binder-Mitchell Shiraz Gunslingers (Barossa)
Bremerton Shiraz-Cabernet Sauvignon
BOV (Langhorne Creek)

Brokenwood Shiraz Rayner Vineyard
(McLaren Vale)

Buckshot Vineyard Shiraz (Heathcote)

Grant Burge Cabernet Sauvignon Shadrach
(Barossa and Coonawarra)

Grant Burge The Holy Trinity (Barossa)

Cape Barren Shiraz Native Goose
(McLaren Vale)

Cape d'Estaing Shiraz (Kangaroo Island)

Cascabel Tempranillo (McLaren Vale)

Cascabel Tipico (McLaren Vale)

Chapel Hill Bush Vine Grenache Abbott
(McLaren Vale)

The Colonial Estate Grenache Alexander
Laing Old Vines (Barossa)

The Colonial Estate Grenache-Shiraz-
Mourvèdre Envoy (Barossa)

The Colonial Estate Shiraz Mungo Park
(Barossa)

Connor Park Shiraz The Honour (Bendigo)

Coriole Shiraz-Mourvèdre The Dancing Fig
(McLaren Vale)

Craneford Cabernet Sauvignon John Zilm
(Barossa and Adelaide Hills)

Craneford Shiraz John Zilm (Barossa)

De Lisio Grenache (McLaren Vale)

De Lisio Shiraz-Grenache The Catalyst
(McLaren Vale)

William Downie Pinot Noir (Mornington
Peninsula)

Dutschke Shiraz St. Jakobi (Barossa)

Dutschke Willow Bend (Barossa)

Eden Hall Shiraz-Viognier (Eden Valley)

Eppalock Ridge Shiraz (Heathcote)

First Drop Shiraz The Cream (Barossa)

First Drop Shiraz Fat of the Land
(Barossa-Ebenezer)

First Drop Shiraz Fat of the Land
(Barossa-Seppeltsfield)

Fox Gordon Shiraz Hannah's Swing
(Barossa)

Frankland Estate Shiraz Isolation Ridge
(Frankland River)

Giaconda Shiraz Warner Vineyard
(Beechworth)

Giant Steps Pinot Noir Sexton Vineyard
(Yarra Valley)

Glaymond Cabernet Sauvignon Asif
(Barossa)

Glen Eldon Shiraz Dry Bore
(Barossa and Eden Valley)

Haan Shiraz Prestige (Barossa)

J. J. Hahn Shiraz 1928 (Barossa)

Hardy's E & E Black Pepper Shiraz
(Barossa)

Hattrick The Hattrick (Shiraz-Grenache-
Cabernet Sauvignon) (McLaren Vale)

Hazyblur Shiraz Kangaroo Island

Heathcote II Shiraz (Heathcote)

Heathcote II Shiraz Reserve HD
(Heathcote)

Henry's Drive Shiraz (Padthaway)

Henschke Cabernet Sauvignon Cyril
Henschke (Eden Valley)

Henschke Keyneton Estate Shiraz
Euphonium (Barossa)

Henschke Mount Edelstone Shiraz
(Eden Valley)

Hewitson Mourvèdre Old Garden (Barossa)

Hewitson Shiraz The Mad Hatter (McLaren
Vale)

Howard Park Cabernet Sauvignon
Scotsdale (Great Southern)

Robert Johnson Vineyards Shiraz
(Eden Valley)

Trevor Jones Shiraz Wild Witch (Barossa)

Journey's End Shiraz Arrival (McLaren
Vale)

Juniper Estate Shiraz (Margaret River)

Kaesler Shiraz Old Vine (Barossa)

Kilikanoon Cabernet Sauvignon Reserve
(Clare Valley)

Kilikanoon Grenache Prodigal
(Clare Valley)

Kilikanoon Shiraz Parable (McLaren Vale)

K1 Tzimmukin (Cabernet Sauvignon-
Shiraz) (Adelaide Hills)

Koonowla Shiraz (Clare Valley)

Kurtz Family Vineyards Boundary Row
Shiraz (Barossa)

Lawson Wines Shiraz (Barossa)

Lawson Wines Shiraz Vintage Reserve
(Barossa)

Lunar Shiraz (Barossa)

Magpie Estate Mourvèdre The Black Sock
(Barossa)

Maxwell Wines Cabernet Sauvignon Lime
Cave (McLaren Vale)

Maxwell Wines Shiraz Ellen Street
(McLaren Vale)

Mollydooker Shiraz The Boxer
(South Australia)

Mollydooker Shiraz-Merlot-Cabernet
Sauvignon Two Left Feet
(South Australia)
Moss Wood Cabernet Sauvignon Estate
(Margaret River)
Mt. Billy Shiraz Antiquity (Barossa)
The Old Faithful Shiraz Top of the Hill
(McLaren Vale)
Oliverhill Petite Sirah (McLaren Vale)
S. C. Pannell Grenache (McLaren Vale)
S. C. Pannell Shiraz-Grenache
(McLaren Vale)
Passing Clouds Reserve Shiraz (Bendigo)
Penfolds Cabernet Sauvignon-Shiraz Bin
389 (South Australia)
Penfolds Shiraz Magill Estate
(South Australia)
Penfolds Shiraz St. Henri (South Australia)
Penny's Hill Shiraz (McLaren Vale)
Pertaringa Shiraz Over the Top
(McLaren Vale)
Pikes Shiraz Eastside (Clare Valley)
Pillar Box Shiraz Reserve (Padthaway)
Piombo Shiraz Valletta (McLaren Vale)
Pirie Tasmania Pinot Noir (Tasmania)
Pirie Tasmania Pinot Noir Estate
(Tasmania)
Pirie Tasmania Pinot Noir Estate Sigma
(Tasmania)
R Winery (big) R Cabernet Sauvignon
(Barossa)
R Winery Marquis Philips Shiraz
(McLaren Vale)
R Winery Marquis Philips Shiraz Tabla
(South Australia)
R Winery Chris Ringland CR Shiraz
(Barossa Valley-Ebenezer)
Red Edge Shiraz (Heathcote)

Reilly's Shiraz Stolen Block (Clare Valley)
Ross Estate Shiraz Reserve (Barossa)
Rudderless Grenache (McLaren Vale)
Rusden Shiraz Stockade (Barossa)
Samuel's Gorge Shiraz (McLaren Vale)
Shirvington Cabernet Sauvignon
(McLaren Vale)
Small Gully Wines Shiraz Black Magic
(Barossa)
Spinifex Indigene (Mataro-Shiraz) (Barossa)
Tait Cabernet Sauvignon Basket Pressed
(Barossa)
Tait Shiraz Basket Pressed (Barossa)
Teusner Avatar (Grenache-Shiraz-Mataro)
(Barossa)
Wayne Thomas Petit Verdot (McLaren
Vale)
Torbreck Cuvée Juveniles (Grenache-
Mataro-Shiraz) (Barossa)
Torbreck The Pict Mataro (Barossa)
Torbreck Woodcutter's Shiraz (Barossa)
Turkey Flat Mourvèdre (Barossa)
Turkey Flat Shiraz (Barossa)
Two Hands Shiraz Angel's Share
(McLaren Vale)
Two Hands Shiraz Deer in the Headlights
(Barossa and Eden Valley)
Wild Duck Creek Estate Shiraz-Malbec
Yellow Hammer Hill (Heathcote)
The Willows Vineyard Shiraz Bonesetter
(Barossa)
Wilson Gunn Shiraz (McLaren Vale)
Winner's Tank Shiraz Velvet
Sledgehammer (Langhorne Creek)
Yangarra Estate Vineyard Shiraz
(McLaren Vale)
Yarra Yering Pinot Noir
(Yarra Valley)

AUSTRALIA'S BEST PRODUCERS OF CHARDONNAY

★ ★ ★ ★ ★ (OUTSTANDING)

Cullen (Margaret River)
Giaconda Estate (Beechworth)

Leeuwin Art Series (Margaret River)

★ ★ ★ ★ (EXCELLENT)

Bannockburn (Geelong)
The Colonial Estate Evangéliste Reserve
(Adelaide Hills)
Dromana Estate Reserve (Mornington
Peninsula)

Frankland Estate Isolation Ridge
(Frankland River)
Giaconda Nantua (Beechworth)
Grosset Piccadilly (Adelaide Hills)
Heggies (Eden Valley)

Heggies Reserve (Eden Valley)
Henschke Lenswood Croft (Lenswood)
Howard Park (Western Australia)
Peter Howland Maxwell Vineyard
   (Hunter Valley)
Trevor Jones Virgin (South Australia)
Juniper Estate Juniper Crossing
   (Geographe)
Leeuwin Estate Prelude Vineyards
   (Margaret River)
Moorooduc Estate (Mornington Peninsula)
Mountadam (Adelaide Hills)
Nicholson River (Gippsland)
Nugan Estate Frasca's Lane Vineyard
   (King Valley)
Paringa Estate (Mornington Peninsula)

Penfolds Bin 05A (Adelaide Hills)
Penfolds Yattarna (Drumborg/Adelaide
   Hills)
Petaluma (Piccadilly Valley)
Petaluma Tiers (Piccadilly Valley)
Pierro (Margaret River)
Rosemount Roxburgh (Hunter Valley)
Rosemount Show Reserve (Coonawarra)
Rothbury Estate Broken Back Vineyard
   (Hunter Valley)
Salitage (Pemberton)
Shaw & Smith M3 Vineyard (Adelaide Hills)
Tapanappa Tiers Vineyard (Wratonbully)
Vasse Felix Heytesbury (Margaret River)
Geoff Weaver (Lenswood)
Yeringberg (Yarra Valley)

★ ★ ★ (GOOD)

Alkoomi (Frankland River)
d'Arenberg The Lucky Lizard
   (Adelaide Hills)
Grant Burge Summers (Eden Valley)
Cassegrain (New South Wales)
Coldstream Hills (Yarra Valley)
The Colonial Estate Piccadilly Valley
   (Adelaide Hills)
Craigmoor (Mudgee)
Dalwhinnie (Victoria)
Hungerford Hill (Hunter Valley)
Innocent Bystander (Yarra Valley)
Kangarilla Road (McLaren Vale)
Katherine Hills (Southeastern Australia)
Katnook Estate (Coonawarra)
K1 (Adelaide Hills)
Krondorf (Barossa)
Maverick Trial Hill (Eden Valley)
Maxwell Wines (McLaren Vale)

Miramar (Mudgee)
Mitchelton (Goulburn)
Moss Wood (Western Australia)
Nugan Estate (Riverina)
Penfolds Bin 311 (Tumbarumba)
Penley Estate (Coonawarra)
Petaluma (South Australia)
RockBare (McLaren Vale and Adelaide
   Hills)
Rothbury Estate Broken Back Vineyard
   Reserve (Hunter Valley)
Tapanappa (Piccadilly Valley)
TarraWarra Estate (Victoria)
Thorn-Clarke Shotfire (Eden Valley)
Tyrell's Vat 47 (New South Wales)
Wynns (Coonawarra)
Yangarra Estate Vineyard (McLaren Vale)
Yarra Yering (Yarra Valley)
Yeringberg (Yarra Valley)

AUSTRALIA'S BEST PRODUCERS OF RIESLING

★ ★ ★ ★ ★ (OUTSTANDING)

Rolf Binder Highness (Eden Valley)
Frankland Estate Isolation Ridge
   (Frankland River)

Frankland Estate Poison Hill Vineyard
   (Frankland River)
Pewsey Vale Contours (Eden Valley)

★ ★ ★ ★ (EXCELLENT)

Tim Adams (Clare Valley)
Ashton Hills (Adelaide Hills)
Jim Barry The Lodge Hill (Clare Valley)
Grant Burge Thorn (Eden Valley)

Clos Clare (Clare Valley)
Eden Hall (Eden Valley)
Glen Eldon (Eden Valley)
Grosset Polish Hill (Clare Valley)

Grosset Watervale (Clare Valley)
Henschke Julius (Eden Valley)
Kanta (Adelaide Hills)
Kilikanoon Mort's Reserve (Clare Valley)
Kilikanoon Mort's Block (Clare Valley)
Lalla Gully Vineyard (Tasmania)
Leeuwin Estate Art Series (Margaret River)
Maverick Trial Hill (Eden Valley)

Mesh Riesling (Eden Valley)
Mount Horrocks (Clare Valley)
Penfolds Riesling Bin 51 (Adelaide Hills)
Petaluma (South Australia)
Pikes (Clare Valley)
Pirie Tasmania (Tasmania)
Tamar Ridge Nine Degrees (Tasmania)
Viking Wines (Barossa)

AUSTRALIA'S BEST PRODUCERS OF DRY SAUVIGNON BLANC, VERDELHO, VIOGNIER, ROUSSANNE, AND SÉMILLON

* * * * * (OUTSTANDING)

None

* * * * (EXCELLENT)

Brokenwood Sémillon (Hunter Valley)
Burge Family Sémillon Olive Hill (Barossa)
Chapel Hill Angelico Verdelho (Fleurieu)
Clonakilla Viognier (Canberra District)
The Colonial Estate Expatrié Reserve
    Sémillon (Barossa)
Cullen Sauvignon/Sémillon
    (Margaret River)
Giaconda Roussanne Aeolia (Beechworth)
Grosset Sémillon-Sauvignon Blanc
    (Clare Valley)
Heggies Viognier (Eden Valley)
Kangarilla Road Viognier (McLaren Vale)
Katnook Estate Sauvignon (Coonawarra)
Kilikanoon Sémillon Barrel-Fermented
    (Watervale)
Loan Sémillon (Barossa)
Lost Valley Winery Sauvignon Blanc
    (Upper Goulburn)
Margan Sémillon (Hunter Valley)
Maxwell Wines Sémillon Old Vines
    (McLaren Vale)
Mollydooker Verdelho The Violinist
    (South Australia)

Moss Wood Sémillon-Sauvignon Blanc
    Ribbon Vale Vineyard (Margaret River)
Nepenthe Sauvignon Blanc
    (Adelaide Hills)
Nepenthe Sémillon (Adelaide Hills)
Nicholson River Sémillon (Gippsland)
Pertaringa Sauvignon Blanc Scarecrow
    (McLaren Vale)
Pierro Sémillon-Sauvignon Blanc
    (Margaret River)
Corrina Rayment Viognier Revolution
    (McLaren Vale)
Reilly's Watervale (Clare Valley)
Reschke Fumé Sauvignon Blanc
    (Limestone Coast)
Rothbury Estate (Hunter Valley)
Shaw & Smith Sauvignon Blanc
    (Adelaide Hills)
Torbreck Woodcutter's Sémillon (Barossa)
Geoff Weaver Sauvignon Blanc
    (Lenswood)
The Willows Vineyard Sémillon (Barossa)
Wrattonbully Vineyard Marsanne-Viognier
    (Wrattonbully)

* * * (GOOD)

Evans and Tate (Margaret River)
Henschke Sauvignon Blanc Lenswood
    Coralinga (Adelaide Hills)
Henschke Sémillon Louis (Eden Valley)
Tim Knappstein (Clare Valley)
K1 Sauvignon Blanc (Adelaide Hills)

Krondorf (Barossa)
Penfolds Sauvignon Blanc Cellar Reserve
    (Adelaide Hills)
Rosabrook Estate Sauvignon Blanc
    (Margaret River)
Rosemount (Hunter Valley)

AUSTRALIA'S BEST PRODUCERS OF FORTIFIED WINES

★ ★ ★ ★ ★ (OUTSTANDING)

d'Arenberg Nostalgia Rare Tawny
  (McLaren Vale)
R. L. Buller Calliope Rare Muscat
  (Rutherglen)
R. L. Buller Calliope Rare Tokay
  (Rutherglen)
Burge Family Winemakers Wilsford
  (various cuvées) (Barossa)
Campbell's Merchant Prince Rare Muscat
  (Rutherglen)
Campbell's Isabella Rare Tokay
  (Rutherglen)

Chambers Rosewood Muscadelle and
  Muscat (various cuvées) (Rutherglen)
Dutschke Tawny (Barossa)
Ralph Fowler Old and Rare Muscat
  (Limestone Coast)
Trevor Jones (various cuvées) (Barossa)
Penfolds Grandfather Port (Barossa)
Seppelt Para Port (Barossa)
Seppelt Show Wines (Barossa)
Yalumba Port (Barossa)
Yarra Yering Potsorts
  (Yarra Valley)

AUSTRALIA'S GREATEST WINE BARGAINS FOR $17 OR LESS

d'Arenberg The Stump Jump Grenache-
  Shiraz-Mourvèdre
d'Arenberg The Stump Jump White
Bleasdale Vineyards Shiraz-Cabernet
  Sauvignon (Langhorne Creek)
Bleasdale Vineyards Shiraz-Cabernet
  Sauvignon Langhorne Crossing
  (Langhorne Creek)
Buckeley's Chardonnay
Buckeley's Cabernet-Shiraz
Buckeley's Chardonnay-Sémillon
Cat Amongst the Pigeons Cabernet
  Sauvignon (Barossa)
Cat Amongst the Pigeons Shiraz
  (Barossa)
Cat Amongst the Pigeons Shiraz-Cabernet
  Sauvignon (Barossa)
Cat Amongst the Pigeons Shiraz-Grenache
  (Barossa)
Earthworks Cabernet Sauvignon (Barossa)
Earthworks Shiraz (Barossa)
Fonty's Pool Sauvignon Blanc-Sémillon
  (Pemberton)
Fonty's Pool Viognier (Pemberton)
The Gatekeeper Shiraz (South Australia)
Haan Hanenhof Shiraz (Barossa)
Andrew Hardy Shiraz Little Ox
  (McLaren Vale)
Heartland Stickleback Red (South
  Australia)
Jip Jip Rocks Shiraz (Limestone Coast)

Jip Jip Rocks Shiraz-Cabernet
  (Limestone Coast)
Trevor Jones Boots Grenache (Barossa)
Trevor Jones Boots Shiraz (Barossa)
Kangarilla Road Zinfandel (McLaren Vale)
Killibinbin Cabernet-Shiraz
  (Langhorne Creek)
Kurtz Family Vineyards Seven Sleepers
  (Barossa)
Lalla Gully Vineyard Riesling (Tasmania)
Lindemans Chardonnay Bin 65
Margan Sémillon (Hunter Valley)
Margan Shiraz (Hunter Valley)
Margan Verdelho (Hunter Valley)
Milton Park Shiraz (South East Australia)
Mitchelton Sémillon-Chardonnay
Nepenthe Unwooded Chardonnay
  (Adelaide Hills)
Nugan Estate Cabernet Sauvignon
  (Riverina)
Nugan Estate Chardonnay (Riverina)
Nugan Estate Shiraz (Riverina)
Oxford Landing Cabernet Sauvignon
Oxford Landing Chardonnay
Paringa Cabernet Sauvignon
Paringa Merlot
Paringa Shiraz
Penfolds Shiraz-Cabernet Sauvignon
  Koonunga Hill
Pertaringa Sauvignon Blanc Scarecrow
  (McLaren Vale)

Pewsey Vale Riesling (Eden Valley)

Pillar Box Red (Padthaway)

Prima Estate La Biondina (Colombard) (Adelaide Hills)

R Winery Bon-Bon Rosé (Riverland)

R Winery (Little) r Cabernet Sauvignon (Barossa)

R Winery Evil Cabernet Sauvignon (South East Australia)

R Winery Pure Evil Chardonnay (South East Australia)

R Winery Bitch Grenache (Barossa)

R Winery Luchador Shiraz (Barossa and McLaren Vale)

R Winery Marquis Philips Cabernet Sauvignon (McLaren Vale)

R Winery Marquis Philips Holly's Blend (McLaren Vale)

R Winery Marquis Philips Sarah's Blend (McLaren Vale)

R Winery Marquis Philips Shiraz (McLaren Vale)

R Winery Chris Ringland CR Shiraz (Barossa-Ebenezer)

R Winery Roogle Red (South East Australia)

R Winery Roogle Riesling (Western Australia)

R Winery Roogle Rosé (Riverland)

R Winery Roogle Shiraz (South East Australia)

Redbank Chardonnay Long Paddock (Victoria)

Reilly's Barking Mad Cabernet Sauvignon (Clare Valley)

Reilly's Barking Mad Riesling (Clare Valley)

Reilly's Barking Mad Shiraz (Clare Valley)

Reilly's Old Bush Vine Grenache (Clare Valley)

Ringbolt Cabernet Sauvignon (Margaret River)

RockBare Chardonnay (McLaren Vale and Adelaide Hills)

Small Gully Wines Cabernet Sauvignon-Shiraz (Barossa)

Small Gully Wines Robert's Shiraz The Formula (Adelaide Plains)

Step Rd Shiraz Black Wing (South Australia)

Tait The Ball Buster (Barossa)

Tamar Ridge Riesling Nine Degrees (Tasmania)

Thorn-Clarke Chardonnay Terra Barossa (Eden Valley)

Thorn-Clarke Shiraz Terra Barossa (Barossa)

Torbreck Woodcutter's Sémillon (Barossa)

Tscharke Girl Talk (Albariño) (Barossa)

Turkey Flat The Turk Red (Barossa)

Turkey Flat The Turk White (Barossa)

Water Wheel Cabernet Sauvignon (Bendigo)

Water Wheel Memsie Red (Bendigo)

Water Wheel Memsie White (Bendigo)

Water Wheel Shiraz (Bendigo)

Winner's Tank Shiraz (Langhorne Creek)

Woop Woop Cabernet Sauvignon (South Australia)

Woop Woop Shiraz (South Australia)

Yalumba Barossa Shiraz-Viognier (Barossa)

Yalumba Y Series Shiraz-Viognier (South Australia)

Yalumba Clocktower Port

Zonte's Footstep Shiraz-Viognier (Langhorne Creek)

Zonte's Footstep Viognier (Langhorne Creek)

[tasting commentaries]

D'ARENBERG ★ ★ ★ ★
MCLAREN VALE $10.00–$75.00

D'Arenberg has been owned and operated by the Osborn family since its inception in 1912. The portfolio, with a focus on Rhône-grape varietals, is wide ranging and value oriented from top to bottom.

2005 d'Arry's Original Shiraz-Mourvèdre	88	now–2015
2004 d'Arry's Original Shiraz-Grenache	91	now–2013
2002 d'Arry's Original Shiraz-Grenache	90	now

2005 The Cadenzia Grenache-Shiraz-Mourvèdre	91	now–2015
2004 The Cadenzia Grenache-Shiraz-Mourvèdre	90	now–2014
2005 The Coppermine Road Cabernet Sauvignon	93	2012–2025
2004 The Coppermine Road Cabernet Sauvignon	92+	2013–2027
2002 The Coppermine Road Cabernet Sauvignon	93+	now–2020
2004 The Custodian Grenache	89	now–2014
2005 The Dead Arm Shiraz	95	2015–2030
2004 The Dead Arm Shiraz	95+	2014–2035
2002 The Dead Arm Shiraz	92+	2010–2022
2005 The Derelict Vineyard Grenache	92	2009–2019
2004 The Derelict Vineyard Grenache	92	now–2014
2002 The Derelict Vineyard Grenache	90	now–2012
2005 The Footbolt Shiraz	89	now–2015
2004 The Footbolt Shiraz	87+	2009–2017
2002 The Footbolt Shiraz	88	now–2010
2004 The Galvo Garage Proprietary Red	90+	2012–2025
2002 The Galvo Garage Proprietary Red	91	2010–2020
2005 The High Trellis Cabernet Sauvignon	91	now–2015
2004 The High Trellis Cabernet Sauvignon	89+	now–2015
2002 The High Trellis Cabernet Sauvignon	88	now–2012
2005 The Ironstone Pressings Grenache-Shiraz-Mourvèdre	94	2012–2028
2004 The Ironstone Pressings Grenache-Shiraz-Mourvèdre	94	2012–2025
2002 The Ironstone Pressings Grenache-Shiraz-Mourvèdre	93+	now–2017
2006 The Laughing Magpie Shiraz-Viognier	92	2010–2020
2005 The Laughing Magpie Shiraz-Viognier	93	now–2017
2003 The Laughing Magpie Shiraz-Viognier	90	now–2015
2006 The Lucky Lizard Chardonnay	90	now–2010
2004 The Sticks & Stones Tempranillo-Grenache-Souzao	90	now–2018
2002 The Sticks & Stones Tempranillo-Grenache-Souzao	93	2010–2020
2006 The Stump Jump Grenache-Shiraz-Mourvèdre	89	now–2011
2005 The Stump Jump Grenache-Shiraz-Mourvèdre	88	now–2012
2003 The Stump Jump Grenache-Shiraz-Mourvèdre	87	now–2009
2005 The Twentyeight Road Mourvèdre	93	2010–2020
2004 The Twentyeight Road Mourvèdre	89+	now–2018
2002 The Twentyeight Road Mourvèdre	93	2010–2020

AUSVETIA ★ ★ ★
SOUTH AUSTRALIA $75.00

AusVetia is produced by Kym Tolley, proprietor of Penley Estate, and a Swiss partner, hence the "Aus" and the "Vetia" (from "Helvetia," an ancient name for Switzerland). The fruit is sourced from several geographical indications (GIs) and blended to produce the type of style that the partners have in mind.

2004 Shiraz	92	now–2020
2002 Shiraz	90	2012–2025

BALGOWNIE ESTATE ★ ★ ★
BENDIGO $30.00

Balgownie Estate was established in 1968 with the first vintage in 1972. The estate consists of 30.4 hectares (75 acres) located in Bendigo in cool-climate central Victoria.

2005 Cabernet Sauvignon	90	2011–2020
2004 Cabernet Sauvignon	89	2010–2020
2002 Cabernet Sauvignon	92	2010–2022
2005 Shiraz	89+	2009–2015
2004 Shiraz	87	2009–2017
2002 Shiraz	91+	2009–2020

JIM BARRY ✶ ✶ ✶ ✶ ✶
CLARE VALLEY $19.00–$175.00

A case can be made that Jim Barry is the finest estate in the Clare Valley. By Australia standards, it is quite ancient, having been founded in 1959. Their Shiraz The Armagh is one of the iconic wines of Australia.

2004 Cabernet Sauvignon The Benbournie	93+	2014–2032
2002 Cabernet Sauvignon The Benbournie	96	2014–2032
2005 Cabernet Sauvignon The Cover Drive	88	now–2013
2004 Cabernet Sauvignon The Cover Drive	88	now–2012
2002 Cabernet Sauvignon The Cover Drive	90	now–2010
2005 Cabernet Sauvignon The First XI	93	2012–2025
2007 Riesling The Lodge Hill	89	now–2015
2005 Riesling The Lodge Hill	89	now–2015
2005 Shiraz The Armagh	96	2015–2035
2004 Shiraz The Armagh	98	2013–2030
2002 Shiraz The Armagh	99	2014–2032
2001 Shiraz The Armagh	96	2012–2027
2005 Shiraz The Lodge Hill	90+	now–2015
2004 Shiraz The Lodge Hill	89	now–2013
2002 Shiraz The Lodge Hill	90	now–2012
2004 Shiraz The McRae Wood	91	2010–2020
2003 Shiraz The McRae Wood	90	now–2017
2002 Shiraz The McRae Wood	93	2009–2017
2002 Shiraz-Cabernet The James Brazill	96	2010–2020

BATTELY ✶ ✶ ✶ ✶
BEECHWORTH $70.00

Russell Bourne is the owner-winemaker of Battely, located in Beechworth, a four-hour drive north of Melbourne. His winemaking role model is the northern Rhône Valley, hence "Syrah" rather than "Shiraz."

2005 Syrah	94	2012–2025
2004 Syrah	92	2010–2020
2002 Syrah	91	now–2016

BEER BROTHERS ✶ ✶ ✶
BAROSSA $40.00–$45.00

These wines are made by the irrepressible David Powell of Torbreck.

2003 Shiraz Pheasant Farm Home Block	92	now–2015
2003 Shiraz Pheasant Farm Old Vine	95	2011–2022

BERRYS BRIDGE ★★★★
PYRENEES $65.00

A fabulous offering from Berrys Bridge, this 100% Shiraz, cropped at a tiny 1.83 tons of fruit per acre and aged 18 months in a combination of French and American oak, was fashioned with the help of consulting winemaker Dan Standish.

2004 Shiraz	95	2010–2022
2003 Shiraz	91	now–2015

ROLF BINDER WINES ★★★★★
BAROSSA AND EDEN VALLEY $18.00–$125.00

The whites at Rolf Binder Wines are made by Christa Deana, Rolf Binder's sister. Binder's Hanisch and Heysen Shiraz cuvées rank among the finest produced in Australia. The 2002s and 2003s listed here were bottled under the Veritas label, now defunct.

2002 Grenache-Mataro-Shiraz Heinrich	92	now–2017
2005 Grenache-Mourvèdre-Shiraz Heinrich	93	now–2017
2007 Riesling Highness	92	now–2015
2006 Riesling Highness	88	now–2014
2002 Shiraz Christa Rolf	90	now–2012
2006 Shiraz Hales	90	2009–2016
2005 Shiraz Hales	91	now–2015
2005 Shiraz Hanisch	98	2013–2027
2004 Shiraz Hanisch	95	2018–2040
2002 Shiraz Hanisch	98	2012–2027
2005 Shiraz Heysen	96	2013–2027
2004 Shiraz Heysen	93+	2013–2030
2002 Shiraz Heysen	93+	2012–2027
2003 Shiraz-Cabernet Hoary	91	now–2013
2003 Shiraz-Grenache Christa Rolf	90	now–2013
2002 Shiraz-Grenache Christa Rolf	91	now–2012
2006 Shiraz-Grenache Halliwell	91+	2009–2016
2005 Shiraz-Grenache Halliwell	92	now–2014
2005 Shiraz-Mataro Hubris	94	2012–2025
2004 Shiraz-Mataro Hubris	95	2010–2020
2002 Shiraz-Mataro Pressings	92+	now–2017
2006 Shiraz-Mataro-Grenache Heinrich	92	2012–2025

BRANSON COACH HOUSE ★★★★★
BAROSSA $65.00–$125.00

Say what you will about a Cabernet Sauvignon with 18% alcohol, ultimately it is balance that counts. The fruit is sourced from the Greenock region of the Barossa, one of the Valley's premier *terroirs,* and is 100% Cabernet Sauvignon. Those in the know call it a "seat belt" wine.

2005 Cabernet Sauvignon Coach House Block	98	2015–2032
2004 Cabernet Sauvignon Coach House Block	98	2018–2040
2005 Shiraz Greenock Block	90	2010–2020
2004 Shiraz Greenock Block	90	2010–2020
2002 Shiraz Greenock Block	92	now–2017
2005 Shiraz Coach House Block-Rare	96+	now–2018
2004 Shiraz Coach House Block	93	2010–2020
2002 Shiraz Coach House Block	97	2010–2022

BREMERTON ★★★
LANGHORNE CREEK $25.00–$75.00

Several generations of the Willson family have run this 100-hectare (247-acre) estate. The signature wine is the Old Adam Shiraz.

2004 Cabernet Sauvignon Reserve	89	2010–2018
2003 Cabernet Sauvignon Reserve	91	2010–2020
2000 Cabernet Sauvignon Walters	89	now–2013
2004 Malbec	90	now–2012
2005 Shiraz Old Adam	91	2012–2025
2001 Shiraz Old Adam	90	now–2013
2004 Shiraz Reserve Old Adam	89	now–2015
2005 Shiraz Selkirk	90	now–2015
2004 Shiraz Selkirk	89	now–2014
2003 Shiraz Selkirk	90	now–2013
2001 Shiraz Selkirk	88	now–2011
2005 Shiraz-Cabernet Sauvignon BOV	92+	2012–2025
2004 Shiraz-Cabernet Sauvignon BOV	89+	now–2013
2005 Tamblyn	85	now
2004 Tamblyn	90+	now–2014
2003 Tamblyn	90	now–2013
2001 Tamblyn	89	now–2011
2007 Verdelho	89	now–2010

BROKENWOOD ★★★
HUNTER VALLEY $28.00–$87.00

Brokenwood has established a reputation as one of Hunter Valley's most respected estates. However, the winery practices multidistrict blending with an apparent focus on McLaren Vale.

2003 Cricket Pitch Red	88	now–2010
2003 Shiraz Area Blend	89+	2010–2020
2005 Shiraz Graveyard	92+	2012–2025
2004 Shiraz Graveyard	88+	2012–2025
2005 Shiraz Rayner Vineyard	91	now–2017
2004 Shiraz Rayner Vineyard	91	2010–2020
2005 Shiraz Wade Block 2	85	now–2010
2004 Shiraz Wade Block 2	90	2010–2020

R. L. BULLER & SON ★★★★★
RUTHERGLEN $13.00–$90.00

R. L. Buller & Son was started in 1921 by the grandfather of Andrew Buller, the current wine-maker. The winery remains one of the quality leaders in the production of sweet wines from the warm *terroir* of Rutherglen. These are the types of wines that cannot be duplicated anywhere else in the world. The product of a *solera* system, they require no further cellaring.

NV Calliope Rare Muscat	99	now
NV Calliope Rare Tokay	98	now
NV Fine Muscat	96	now
NV Fine Tawny	94	now
NV Fine Tokay	95	now
NV Victoria Tawny	91	now

GRANT BURGE ✷✷✷
BAROSSA $20.00–$95.00

Grant Burge and Burge Family Winemakers have a familial but not philosophical connection. The former is big, while the latter is an artisanal, hands-on operation. Not that big is bad, as this Grant Burge lineup demonstrates.

2001 Cabernet Sauvignon Shadrach	91	now–2015
2003 The Holy Trinity	91	now–2018
2006 Riesling Thorn	89	now–2015
2005 Shiraz Filsell	91	2010–2020
2004 Shiraz Filsell	90	2009–2018
2002 Shiraz Meshach	93	now–2020
2005 Shiraz Miamba	89	now–2013
2002 Shiraz Grenache-Mourvèdre Abednego	92	2010–2020

BURGE FAMILY WINEMAKERS ✷✷✷✷
BAROSSA $33.00–$60.00

The owner-winemaker of Burge Family Winemakers is Rick Burge. The wines are all produced from estate fruit, much of it from old vines. Only French oak *barriques* are used for maturation of the Burge Family wines.

2005 Clochemerle	89	now–2014
2004 Clochemerle	93	now–2014
2002 Clochemerle	93	now–2015
2005 D & OH	91	2009–2018
2004 D & OH	89	now–2014
2002 D & OH	94	2009–2017
2005 Garnacha	92	now–2017
2004 Garnacha	94	now–2018
2002 G3	96	2012–2027
2005 Olive Hill Red Blend	90	2010–2020
2004 Olive Hill Red Blend	92	now–2016
2002 Olive Hill Red Blend	93+	2010–2020
2002 La Renoux	88	now–2012
2005 Sémillon	91	now–2014
2005 Shiraz Draycott	93	2013–2028
2004 Shiraz Draycott	95	2012–2025

CAMPBELLS ✷✷✷
RUTHERGLEN $19.00–$85.00

Campbells began producing dessert and fortified wines in Rutherglen, 93 miles northeast of Melbourne, in the 1870s. These wines are essentially identical from year to year as they emerge from the same *soleras*.

NV Isabella Rare Tokay	96	now
NV Merchant Prince Rare Muscat	98	now
NV Rutherglen Muscat	92	now
NV Rutherglen Tokay	93	now

CAPE BARREN ★ ★ ★
McLAREN VALE $24.00–$32.00

Cape Barren, whose first vintage was in 1998, produces wine from the Blewitt Springs region of McLaren Vale.

2005 Grenache-Shiraz-Mourvèdre	91	now–2013
2005 Shiraz Native Goose	92	2010–2020
2004 Shiraz Wild Goose	89	now–2015
2005 Shiraz Old Vine	94	2012–2025
2004 Shiraz Old Vine	93	now–2017
2002 Shiraz Old Vine	90	now–2015

CAPE D'ESTAING ★ ★ ★ ★
KANGAROO ISLAND $45.00–$125.00

Cape d'Estaing rates 100 points for its breathtaking location on Kangaroo Island south of Adelaide. The fruit is entirely sourced from a 25-acre estate vineyard located on the north coast of the island.

2003 Cabernet Sauvignon	90	2010–2020
2004 Cabernet Sauvignon Admiral's Reserve	91+	2012–2025
2004 Shiraz	92	2013–2024
2003 Shiraz	91	now–2015
2005 Shiraz Admiral's Reserve	93	2011–2026
2004 Shiraz Admiral's Reserve	93	2013–2024

CASCABEL ★ ★ ★ ★
McLAREN VALE $23.00–$32.00

Cascabel is a five-hectare (12.35-acre) estate, four of which are planted to nine varieties. It is the project of Duncan Ferguson and Susana Fernandez, a native of Madrid. The goal is to put a Spanish face on McLaren Vale wines.

2005 Monastrell	93	2012–2025
2004 Monastrell Viña Cascabel	89	2010–2020
2005 Shiraz	94	2009–2018
2004 Shiraz	94	2012–2022
2002 Shiraz Fleurieu	93	now–2015
2005 Tempranillo-Graciano	92	now–2015
2004 Tempranillo-Graciano	89	now–2013
2005 Tipico	92	now–2015
2004 Tipico	90	now–2013

CAT AMONGST THE PIGEONS ★ ★ ★ ★
BAROSSA $15.00

Cat Amongst the Pigeons is a new label owned by Rosedale Wines, a subsidiary of Barossa Vines Ltd. The fruit is 100% estate grown from a single vineyard in Rosedale, a small village in the center of Barossa. It is surrounded by Torbreck, Two Hands, Greenock Creek, Rolf Binder, and Kalleske, hence the name "cat amongst the pigeons." The wines offer a serious challenge to the Marquis Philips and Mollydooker The Lefty Series in the less than $20 category.

2006 Cabernet Sauvignon	91	now–2012
2006 Shiraz	92	now–2012

| 2006 Shiraz-Cabernet Sauvignon | 91 | now–2012 |
| 2006 Shiraz-Grenache | 91 | now–2012 |

CHAMBERS ROSEWOOD VINEYARDS ★ ★ ★ ★ ★
RUTHERGLEN $15.00–$300.00

Chambers Rosewood Vineyards makes Robert Parker's *Wine Advocate*'s short list of greatest fortified-wine producers. The winery was started in 1858 and continues to be owned by the Chambers family. Some of the material for these blends is more than 100 years old. These wines are the product of *solera* systems, so there is very little, if any, difference from release to release.

NV Grand Muscadelle	96	now
NV Grand Muscat	96	now
NV Muscadelle	92	now
NV Muscat	93	now
NV Rare Muscadelle	100	now
NV Rare Muscat	100	now

CHAPEL HILL ★ ★ ★
McLAREN VALE $19.00–$30.00

Chapel Hill Winery, located in McLaren Vale, produces 50,000 cases of wine. Michael Fragos is chief winemaker.

2006 Bush Vine Grenache Abbott	92	now–2016
2005 Cabernet Sauvignon Estate	88	now–2013
2005 Cabernet Sauvignon Reserve	90	2010–2020
2006 Shiraz	90	now–2014
2005 Shiraz	90	now–2014
2005 Shiraz The Prophet	91	now–2015
2006 Shiraz-Grenache	89	now–2012

CHARLES CIMICKY ★ ★ ★ ★
BAROSSA $20.00–$60.00

Founded in 1973, the winery is now run by Charles Cimicky, who succeeded his father at the helm. Charles Cimicky has established a reputation for both high quality and excellent values.

2006 Grenache-Shiraz Trumps	90	now–2015
2005 Grenache-Shiraz Trumps	89	now–2012
2002 Grenache-Shiraz Trumps	91	now–2010
2005 Petite Sirah	94	2015–2035
2005 Shiraz Autograph	93	2012–2025
2003 Shiraz Autograph	93	2010–2020
2005 Shiraz Reserve	95	2012–2025
2006 Shiraz Trumps	90	now–2014
2005 Shiraz Trumps	91	now–2012
2003 Shiraz Trumps	92	now–2013

CLARENDON HILLS ★ ★ ★ ★ ★
CLARENDON $70.00–$350.00

Roman Bratasiuk's Clarendon Hills is one of the world's benchmark wineries. I can think of only two other cellars, Domaine Zind-Humbrecht in Alsace and Domaine Leroy in Burgundy, where the entry-level wines begin at such a superb level of quality, and the portfolio ascends from there to otherworldly at the top of the hierarchy. Clarendon Hills produces wine from Grenache, Merlot, Cabernet Sauvignon, and Syrah, all 100% varietals with no blending. The vineyards are all ungrafted, planted on their own roots, with most of them having very old vines. Only French oak is utilized; seasoned barrels are used for the Grenaches, 100% new for the Merlots and Cabernets, and 50%–100% new oak for the Syrahs, depending upon the vineyard. The wines typically spend 18 months in oak before being bottled unfined and unfiltered.

2006 Cabernet Sauvignon Brookman Vineyard	91–94	2010–2020
2005 Cabernet Sauvignon Brookman Vineyard	94	2010–2020
2004 Cabernet Sauvignon Brookman Vineyard	92	2010–2020
2003 Cabernet Sauvignon Brookman Vineyard	90	2009–2021
2006 Cabernet Sauvignon Hickinbotham Vineyard	94–97	2012–2030
2005 Cabernet Sauvignon Hickinbotham Vineyard	97	2015–2035
2004 Cabernet Sauvignon Hickinbotham Vineyard	94	2015–2035
2003 Cabernet Sauvignon Hickinbotham Vineyard	93+	2012–2027
2002 Cabernet Sauvignon Hickinbotham Vineyard	95	2010–2025
2006 Cabernet Sauvignon Sandown Vineyard	90–93	2012–2025
2005 Cabernet Sauvignon Sandown Vineyard	93	2014–2030
2004 Cabernet Sauvignon Sandown Vineyard	94	2010–2020
2003 Cabernet Sauvignon Sandown Vineyard	90	2010–2022
2002 Cabernet Sauvignon Sandown Vineyard	90	2012–2025
2006 Grenache Old Vines Clarendon Vineyard	90–92	2009–2018
2005 Grenache Old Vines Clarendon Vineyard	92	2010–2020
2004 Grenache Old Vines Clarendon Vineyard	90	now–2015
2003 Grenache Old Vines Clarendon Vineyard	92	now–2015
2002 Grenache Old Vines Clarendon Vineyard	94	2009–2020
2006 Grenache Old Vines Blewitt Springs Vineyard	91–94	2012–2025
2005 Grenache Old Vines Blewitt Springs Vineyard	91	2010–2020
2004 Grenache Old Vines Blewitt Springs Vineyard	93	now–2015
2003 Grenache Old Vines Blewitt Springs Vineyard	93	2009–2020
2002 Grenache Old Vines Blewitt Springs Vineyard	93	2009–2020
2006 Grenache Old Vines Hickinbotham Vineyard	91–94	2010–2020
2005 Grenache Old Vines Hickinbotham Vineyard	93	2012–2025
2004 Grenache Old Vines Hickinbotham Vineyard	92	now–2015
2003 Grenache Old Vines Hickinbotham Vineyard	92	now–2017
2002 Grenache Old Vines Hickinbotham Vineyard	92	2010–2020
2006 Grenache Old Vines Kangarilla Vineyard	91–94	now–2016
2005 Grenache Old Vines Kangarilla Vineyard	94	2010–2020
2004 Grenache Old Vines Kangarilla Vineyard	92	now–2018
2003 Grenache Old Vines Kangarilla Vineyard	94	2010–2022
2002 Grenache Old Vines Kangarilla Vineyard	94	2010–2022
2006 Grenache Old Vines Romas Vineyard	93–96	2014–2030
2005 Grenache Old Vines Romas Vineyard	95	2012–2025
2004 Grenache Old Vines Romas Vineyard	94+	2012–2026
2003 Grenache Old Vines Romas Vineyard	96	2012–2025
2002 Grenache Old Vines Romas Vineyard	96	2012–2025
2006 Grenache Onkaparinga	92–95	2012–2025
2005 Grenache Onkaparinga	95	2010–2018
2006 Merlot Brookman Vineyard	91–93	2010–2020

2005 Merlot Brookman Vineyard	93	2012–2022
2004 Merlot Brookman Vineyard	93	now–2016
2003 Merlot Brookman Vineyard	88	now–2013
2002 Merlot Brookman Vineyard	91	2010–2020
2006 Syrah Astralis Vineyard	96–99	2016–2035
2005 Syrah Astralis Vineyard	99	2017–2045
2004 Syrah Astralis Vineyard	98	2020–2050
2003 Syrah Astralis Vineyard	98	2012–2030
2002 Syrah Astralis Vineyard	99	2012–2030
2006 Syrah Bakers Gully	90–93	2010–2020
2005 Syrah Bakers Gully	92	2010–2020
2004 Syrah Bakers Gully	90	now–2014
2003 Syrah Bakers Gully	89	now–2013
2006 Syrah Brookman Vineyard	94–97	2014–2032
2005 Syrah Brookman Vineyard	96	2013–2030
2004 Syrah Brookman Vineyard	95	2012–2026
2003 Syrah Brookman Vineyard	95	2012–2027
2002 Syrah Brookman Vineyard	96	2013–2030
2006 Syrah Hickinbotham Vineyard	95–98	2012–2026
2005 Syrah Hickinbotham Vineyard	97	2013–2030
2004 Syrah Hickinbotham Vineyard	95	2015–2035
2003 Syrah Hickinbotham Vineyard	95	2010–2030
2002 Syrah Hickinbotham Vineyard	97	2012–2033
2006 Syrah Liandra Vineyard	92–95	2009–2018
2005 Syrah Liandra Vineyard	94	2010–2020
2004 Syrah Liandra Vineyard	92	2010–2020
2003 Syrah Liandra Vineyard	94	2010–2022
2002 Syrah Liandra Vineyard	93	2010–2022
2006 Syrah Moritz Vineyard	94–97	2014–2030
2005 Syrah Moritz Vineyard	96	2012–2025
2004 Syrah Moritz Vineyard	95	2012–2026
2003 Syrah Moritz Vineyard	94	2014–2028
2002 Syrah Moritz Vineyard	95	2014–2028
2006 Syrah Onkaparinga	92–95	2012–2026
2005 Syrah Onkaparinga	95	2014–2030
2006 Syrah Piggott Range	94–98	2012–2026
2005 Syrah Piggott Range	97	2015–2035
2004 Syrah Piggott Range	95+	2020–2045
2003 Syrah Piggott Range	92	2012–2027
2002 Syrah Piggott Range	97	2015–2035

CLONAKILLA ★ ★ ★ ★
CANBERRA DISTRICT $26.00–$64.00

Clonakilla was established in 1971 by Dr. John Kirk and is now run by his son, Tim Kirk. The flagship wine is the Shiraz-Viognier.

2003 Shiraz	89	now–2011
2006 Shiraz Hilltops	90	now–2013
2005 Shiraz Hilltops	88	now–2013
2006 Shiraz-Viognier	95	2016–2036
2005 Shiraz-Viognier	91	2009–2018

2006 Viognier	90	now–2010
2005 Viognier	93	now–2011

THE COLONIAL ESTATE ★ ★ ★ ★
BAROSSA $30.00–$80.00

The Colonial Estate is the Australian project of Englishman and Bordeaux château owner Jonathan Maltus. His 45 hectares (111 acres) in St.-Émilion encompass Le Dôme, Château Laforge, Clos Nardian, and Château Teyssier. His first vintage in Australia was 2002. Current production is up to 25,000 cases.

2005 Alexander Laing Old Vines Grenache	93	2012–2025
2005 Chardonnay Piccadilly Valley	89	now–2010
2005 Émigré	94	2013–2028
2004 Émigré	94+	2012–2026
2002 Émigré	95	2010–2022
2005 Envoy Grenache-Shiraz-Mourvèdre	91	now–2018
2004 Envoy Grenache-Shiraz-Mourvèdre	91	now–2014
2005 Etranger Cabernet Sauvignon	91	2010–2020
2003 Etranger Cabernet Sauvignon	90	2010–2020
2006 Evangéliste Reserve Chardonnay	90	now–2010
2005 Exile	95	2014–2030
2004 Exile	96	2013–2030
2002 Exile	98	2012–2027
2006 Expatrié Reserve Sémillon	90	now–2010
2005 Explorateur Old Vines Shiraz	90	2010–2020
2003 Explorateur Old Vines Shiraz	91	now–2013
2005 Grenache-Shiraz-Mourvèdre John Speke	96	2010–2020
2005 Shiraz Mungo Park	92+	2015–2035

CORIOLE ★ ★ ★
McLAREN VALE $21.00–$70.00

Coriole Vineyards was founded by the Lloyd family in 1967. The estate has 33 hectares (81.5 acres) of vines with some plantings dating back to 1919 and the rest from the late 1960s and early 1990s.

2005 Shiraz Estate Grown	89	now–2014
2005 Shiraz Lloyd Reserve	93	2014–2030
2005 Shiraz Redstone	86	now–2010
2004 Shiraz The Soloist	91	2012–2024
2004 Shiraz-Mourvèdre The Dancing Fig	92	2012–2020

CRANEFORD ★ ★ ★
BAROSSA $30.00–$40.00

Craneford has no estate vineyards, so they purchase fruit from selected Barossa Valley grape growers. The wines generally offer very good value.

2006 Cabernet Sauvignon	90	now–2016
2003 Cabernet Sauvignon	91	now–2013
2005 Cabernet Sauvignon John Zilm	93	2010–2020
2005 Grenache-Shiraz-Mourvèdre	90	now–2012
2005 Merlot John Zilm	89+	2009–2018
2005 Quartet Proprietary Red	91	2010–2020

2006 Shiraz	91	2010–2020
2003 Shiraz	92	now–2015
2002 Shiraz	92	now–2015
2005 Shiraz John Zilm	94	2010–2020

CULLEN ★ ★ ★ ★
MARGARET RIVER $30.00–$75.00

Cullen's vineyards are certified biodynamic. In Margaret River's cool climate, their white wines are the stars.

2005 Chardonnay	94	now–2014
2005 Diana Madeline	89+	2010–2020
2006 Sauvignon Blanc-Sémillon Cullen Vineyard	90	now–2010

DE LISIO ★ ★ ★
McLAREN VALE $24.00–$56.00

De Lisio produces a solid range of wines offering good value for the money.

2006 Grenache	93	now–2018
2005 Grenache	92	now–2013
2006 Quarterback	91	now–2012
2005 Quarterback	91	2010–2020
2006 Shiraz	89	now–2018
2006 Shiraz Krystina	90	now–2018
2005 Shiraz Krystina	93	2012–2025
2005 Shiraz-Grenache The Catalyst	92	2010–2020
2004 Shiraz-Grenache The Catalyst	96	2012–2025

DEISEN ★ ★ ★
BAROSSA $65.00

This tiny, artisanal Barossa Valley winery has turned out superb Shiraz in every vintage since 2001. The Grenache and Mataro are good but appear to be works in progress.

2004 Shiraz	93	2014–2030
2003 Shiraz	95	2015–2032

WILLIAM DOWNIE ★ ★ ★
YARRA VALLEY $75.00

William Downie, owner-winemaker, is a Pinot Noir specialist with extensive experience in Burgundy's Côte d'Or. He is also senior winemaker at De Bortoli.

2006 Pinot Noir Mornington Peninsula	91+	2010–2020
2005 Pinot Noir Yarra Valley	90+	2010–2020

DUTSCHKE ★ ★ ★ ★
BAROSSA $20.00–$100.00

Wayne Dutschke produces consistently excellent wines from the Barossa Valley. His Shiraz offerings are top-class, but the secret here is just how good his fortified wines can be.

2005 Cabernet Sauvignon	91	2010–2020
2005 Cabernet Sauvignon Sami	88	now–2018
2005 Shiraz Gods Hill Road	90	2009–2018
2005 Shiraz Oscar Semmler	93	2012–2025

2004 Shiraz Oscar Semmler	93	2010–2022
2002 Shiraz Oscar Semmler	94	2010–2022
2005 Shiraz St. Jakobi	91	2010–2020
2004 Shiraz St. Jakobi	92	now–2017
2002 Shiraz St. Jakobi	92	now–2018
2005 Shiraz Single Barrel	95	2014–2030
2004 Shiraz Single Barrel	94	2012–2027
2002 Shiraz Single Barrel	96	2012–2027
NV Shiraz Sun Raisined Fortified	95	now
2005 Willow Bend	91	2010–2020
2004 Willow Bend	90	now–2016
2002 Willow Bend	88	now–2012

JOHN DUVAL WINES ★★★★
BAROSSA $40.00–$50.00

John Duval was the chief winemaker of Penfolds Grange from 1986 to 2002.

2005 Entity	93	2010–2020
2004 Entity	95	2012–2025
2005 Plexus	92	now–2018
2004 Plexus	93	2010–2020

EDEN HALL ★★★
EDEN VALLEY $24.00–$38.00

Eden Hall Wines are sourced from the 120-hectare (296-acre) Avon Brae vineyard owned by David and Mardi Hall.

2004 Cabernet Sauvignon	90	2012–2024
2004 Cabernet-Shiraz-Viognier	90	now–2018
2007 Riesling	90	now–2015
2005 Shiraz	91	2010–2020
2004 Shiraz-Viognier	92	now–2018

ELDERTON ★★★★★
BAROSSA $17.00–$83.00

The Elderton lineup is impressive as usual, which is not surprising given the high quality of recent vintages in Barossa Valley. Elderton was jump-started when their 1992 Cabernet Sauvignon Ashmead won the Jimmy Watson Trophy, Australia's most prestigious award. The flagship wine continues to be the Command Shiraz.

2005 Cabernet Sauvignon Ashmead	96	2015–2035
2004 Cabernet Sauvignon Ashmead	91+	2014–2032
2002 Cabernet Sauvignon Ashmead	92	2012–2026
2000 Cabernet Sauvignon Ashmead	88	now–2015
2005 Cabernet Sauvignon Nurioopta	93	2012–2022
2000 Cabernet-Shiraz-Merlot Proprietary Red	90	now–2012
2004 Ode to Lorraine	90	2010–2020
2002 Ode to Lorraine	92	now–2017
2004 Shiraz	90	now–2016
2002 Shiraz	92	now–2012
2004 Shiraz Command	98	2018–2040
2003 Shiraz Command	94	2010–2022

2002 Shiraz Command	95	2012–2027
2000 Shiraz Command	92+	2010–2024
2005 Shiraz Nurioopta	94	2010–2020

EPPALOCK RIDGE ★ ★ ★
HEATHCOTE $35.00

Eppalock Ridge began in 1978 and since 1985 has been producing 1,500 cases annually from their estate vineyards in Heathcote.

2004 Cabernet Sauvignon-Merlot	91+	2010–2020
2003 Cabernet Sauvignon-Merlot	90	2009–2018
2002 Cabernet Sauvignon-Merlot	88	now–2012
2004 Shiraz	92	2012–2024
2003 Shiraz	88	now–2017
2002 Shiraz	91	now–2012

FIRST DROP ★ ★ ★
BAROSSA $50.00–$75.00

First Drop's top-of-the-line Shiraz portfolio is uniformly outstanding. The lower-level wines remain a work in progress.

2005 Shiraz The Cream	93+	2012–2025
2005 Shiraz Fat of the Land Ebenezer	92	2014–2030
2005 Shiraz Fat of the Land Seppeltsfield	93	2012–2025

FRANKLAND ESTATE ★ ★ ★ ★
FRANKLAND RIVER $25.00–$35.00

Frankland Estate is considered by many to be the leading estate from the Frankland River GI. As the scores below attest, all of their wines in my recent tastings have been outstanding.

2005 Chardonnay Isolation Ridge	90	now–2012
2004 Chardonnay Isolation Ridge	90	now–2010
2006 Dry Riesling Cooladerah Vineyard	90	now–2012
2006 Dry Riesling Isolation Ridge	92	2010–2020
2005 Dry Riesling Isolation Ridge	90	now–2015
2006 Dry Riesling Poison Hill Vineyard	91	2010–2020
2003 Olmo's Reward	90+	2012–2025
2002 Olmo's Reward	91	2009–2018
2000 Olmo's Reward	90	now–2013
2004 Shiraz Isolation Ridge	91+	2010–2020
2003 Shiraz Isolation Ridge	88	now–2013
2001 Shiraz Isolation Ridge	90	now–2011
2003 Shiraz-Viognier Rocky Gully	87	now–2010

GIACONDA ★ ★ ★ ★ ★
*BEECHWORTH $60.00–$100.00

Giaconda, founded by Rick Kinzbrunner, released its first wines in 1987. The winery and vineyards are located in Beechworth in northeastern Victoria. The flagship Chardonnay Estate is on the short list of Australia's best Chardonnays.

2005 Chardonnay Estate	95	2010–2020
2004 Chardonnay Estate	96	now–2014
2002 Chardonnay Estate	92	now–2010

2005 Chardonnay Nantua	94	now–2017
2003 Chardonnay Nantua	90	now–2009
2006 Roussanne Aeolia	91	now–2013
2005 Roussanne Aeolia	93	now–2011
2003 Roussanne Aeolia	93	now–2009
2005 Shiraz Warner Vineyard	91	now–2018
2004 Shiraz Warner Vineyard	93+	2010–2020
2002 Shiraz Warner Vineyard	94	now–2017

GIBSON WINES ★★★★
BAROSSA $120.00

The owner-winemaker of Gibson Wines is Rob Gibson, who left Penfolds to start his own winery. The showstoppers in the portfolio are the Old Vine Collection Shiraz.

2004 Grenache Old Vine Collection	93	2010–2020
2004 Shiraz	92	now–2015
2002 Shiraz	95	2010–2020
2005 Shiraz Old Vine Collection Barossa	96	2015–2035
2004 Shiraz Old Vine Collection Barossa	95	2010–2022
2002 Shiraz Old Vine Collection Barossa	96+	2012–2027
2005 Shiraz Old Vine Collection Eden Valley	92	2012–2025
2004 Wilfreda Blend	92	now–2013

GLAETZER WINES ★★★★★
BAROSSA $30.00–$100.00

The renowned winemaker Ben Glaetzer sources all of his fruit for this label from the Ebenezer district in the northern Barossa. Many knowledgeable experts cite this subregion as the finest in the Valley.

2006 Bishop	93	2016–2034
2005 Bishop	92	2010–2020
2002 Bishop	93+	now–2017
2002 Shiraz	95	2010–2022
2006 Shiraz Amon-Ra	98	2020–2050
2005 Shiraz Amon-Ra	98	2018–2040
2003 Shiraz Amon-Ra	98	2010–2025
2006 Shiraz-Cabernet Anaperenna	95	2014–2030
2005 Shiraz-Cabernet Godolphin	93	2012–2026
2006 Wallace	92	2010–2020
2005 Wallace	92	now–2018
2004 Wallace	93	now–2015
2002 Wallace	89	now–2012

GLAYMOND ★★★★
BAROSSA $60.00–$70.00

Glaymond's owner-winemaker is Damien Tscharke, who receives winemaking consultation from superstar Chris Ringland. The vineyards are owned by the Tscharke family, which had previously sold the fruit to larger producers. The vines are in a tenderloin portion of the Barossa for growing top-class Shiraz.

2002 Cabernet Sauvignon	92	2009–2017
2005 Cabernet Sauvignon Asif	92	2012–2025

2004 Cabernet Sauvignon Asif	88	2012–2025
2005 Grenache Gerhard	93	now–2017
2004 Grenache Gerhard	89	now–2014
2005 Shiraz The Distance	94	2014–2030
2004 Shiraz The Distance	90	2009–2018
2002 Shiraz The Distance	92	2010–2020
2005 Shiraz The Distinction	97	2016–2035
2002 Shiraz The Distinction	95+	2012–2030
2005 Shiraz Glen's Selection	96+	2010–2022
2005 Shiraz-Mataro Landrace	86	now–2013
2004 Shiraz-Mataro Landrace	93	2010–2022
2002 Shiraz-Mataro Landrace	96	2010–2020

GLEN ELDON * * *
BAROSSA AND EDEN VALLEY $35.00–$60.00

Glen Eldon is run by Richard Sheedy, formerly the winemaker at Elderton. The star of the show is the Dry Bore Reserve Shiraz.

2002 Cabernet Sauvignon	90	now–2014
2001 Cabernet Sauvignon	88	now–2011
2005 Shiraz Dry Bore	91	2010–2020
2004 Shiraz Dry Bore	92	now–2014
2002 Shiraz Dry Bore	92	2009–2017
2004 Shiraz Dry Bore Reserve	95	2014–2030

GRALYN ESTATE * * * *
MARGARET RIVER $70.00

This small Margaret River boutique operation is run by Merilyn Hutton, who restricts yields to 1.5 to 3 tons of fruit per acre and ages the wines in 100% new French and American oak. These are serious efforts that should age for 15 or more years.

2003 Cabernet Sauvignon	89+	2009–2018
2001 Cabernet Sauvignon	94	2011–2026
2003 Select Barrel Reserve	92	2010–2022
2001 Select Barrel Reserve	91	2009–2018

GREENOCK CREEK * * * * *
BAROSSA $70.00–$400.00

Greenock Creek Vineyard and Cellars, owned by Michael and Annabelle Waugh, is one of the Barossa's benchmark wineries. Start with a great *terroir,* add in old-vine material and meticulous winemaking, and the results are usually extraordinary.

2004 Cabernet Sauvignon	94	2012–2025
2003 Cabernet Sauvignon	93	2010–2020
2001 Cabernet Sauvignon	93	2009–2018
2001 Cabernet Sauvignon Roennfeldt Road	96	2012–2025
2000 Cabernet Sauvignon Roennfeldt Road	91	2010–2020
1998 Cabernet Sauvignon Roennfeldt Road	100	2013–2033
2005 Grenache Cornerstone	93	now–2018
2004 Grenache Cornerstone	91	now–2014
2002 Grenache Cornerstone	95	now–2012
2004 Shiraz Alice's	98	2014–2030

2003 Shiraz Alice's	97	2010–2022
2001 Shiraz Alice's	98	2011–2026
2004 Shiraz Apricot Block	95	2010–2025
2003 Shiraz Apricot Block	95	2010–2022
2001 Shiraz Apricot Block	99+	now–2021
2004 Shiraz Creek Block	99	2010–2030
2003 Shiraz Creek Block	100	2013–2035
2001 Shiraz Creek Block	100	2011–2026
2001 Shiraz Roennfeldt Road	99+	2016–2036
2000 Shiraz Roennfeldt Road	93	2010–2020
1998 Shiraz Roennfeldt Road	100	2013–2033
2004 Shiraz Seven Acre	95	now–2020
2003 Shiraz Seven Acre	98	2013–2030
2001 Shiraz Seven Acre	98	2011–2021

GROSSET ★★★★
CLARE VALLEY $31.00–$60.00

As the scores below attest, Grosset Wines remains a consistently outstanding producer of red and white wines. The house specialty is ageworthy dry Riesling.

2005 Chardonnay Piccadilly	90	now–2012
2004 Chardonnay Piccadilly	89	now
2006 Dry Riesling Polish Hill	89	2010–2016
2005 Dry Riesling Polish Hill	89	now–2015
2003 Dry Riesling Polish Hill	91	now–2010
2006 Dry Riesling Watervale	90	2010–2016
2005 Dry Riesling Watervale	90	now–2015
2003 Dry Riesling Watervale	90	now–2010
2004 Gaia	92	2012–2025
2002 Gaia	88	2010–2022
2001 Gaia Proprietary Red	90	now–2013
2005 Pinot Noir	89	now–2015
2002 Pinot Noir	88	now–2009
2006 Sémillon-Sauvignon Blanc	90	now–2010

HAAN WINES ★★★
BAROSSA $16.00–$50.00

Hans and Fransien Haan began operations in 1993 after purchasing a 45-acre Barossa vineyard located between Tununda and Angston. The wines are made by Mark Jamieson.

2005 Cabernet Franc Hanenhof	92	2012–2026
2005 Hanenhof Proprietary Red	90	now–2013
2006 Hanenhof Shiraz	90	now–2016
2005 Merlot Prestige	91	now–2014
2004 Merlot Prestige	90	2009–2017
2002 Merlot Prestige	91	now–2015
2005 Shiraz Prestige	92	2010–2020
2004 Shiraz Prestige	90	2010–2020
2002 Shiraz Prestige	94	now–2015
2005 Wilhelmus	91	2010–2020
2004 Wilhelmus	91+	2012–2026
2002 Wilhelmus	92	now–2017

J. J. HAHN ★ ★ ★
BAROSSA $50.00–$60.00

The J. J. Hahn wines are made by Rolf Binder from two vineyards separated by 50 yards, one planted in 1914 and the other in 1928. They are aged in American oak of which 30% are new.

2005 Shiraz 1914	93	2012–2025
2004 Shiraz 1914	94	2012–2025
2001 Shiraz 1914	95	2010–2020
2005 Shiraz 1928	92	2010–2020
2004 Shiraz 1928	91	2009–2018
2002 Shiraz-Cabernet Reginald	92	now–2017

ANDREW HARDY WINES ★ ★ ★ ★ ★
McLAREN VALE $20.00–$110.00

Andrew Hardy is the winemaker for Petaluma. His family holdings include an amazing Upper Tintara vineyard planted to Shiraz in 1891 that has been producing ever since. The Shiraz The Ox comes from that 117-year-old vineyard with microscopic yields of 0.25 to 0.50 tons per acre. It spends 24 months in old French oak and is bottled unfined and unfiltered. The Ox is one of the greatest Shiraz produced in South Australia, while the Little Ox is one of the finest values.

2005 Shiraz Little Ox	93	2010–2020
2003 Shiraz The Ox	99	2014–2032

HAZYBLUR ★ ★ ★ ★
VARIOUS $33.00–$175.00

Owner-winemaker Ross Trimboli produces full-throttle Shiraz from a number of South Australia regions with his most recent project focused on Kangaroo Island. These Shiraz prove convincingly that *terroir* makes a difference in South Australia.

2005 Shiraz Adelaide Plains	91	2012–2025
2004 Shiraz Adelaide Plains	91	now–2017
2002 Shiraz Adelaide Plains	91	now–2015
2005 Shiraz Baroota	93	now–2018
2004 Shiraz Baroota	92+	2010–2020
2002 Shiraz Baroota	93	now–2015
2005 Shiraz Barossa Valley	95+	2012–2025
2004 Shiraz Barossa Valley	89	2012–2022
2002 Shiraz Barossa Valley	94+	2009–2018
2004 Shiraz Invictus	90+	2012–2022
2005 Shiraz Invictus Barossa Valley	97	2015–2035
2005 Shiraz Kangaroo Island	91	2010–2020
2004 Shiraz Kangaroo Island	88	now–2014
2005 Shiraz McLaren Vale	93	2012–2025
2004 Shiraz McLaren Vale	93	2010–2022
2002 Shiraz McLaren Vale	92	2009–2018

HENRY'S DRIVE ✶✶✶
PADTHAWAY $30.00–$55.00

Henry's Drive is owned by Kim and Mark Longbottom with Kim Jackson as winemaker. This task was previously handled by Sparky and Sarah Marquis but since their departure, Henry's Drive has not missed a beat.

2005 Cabernet Sauvignon	90	now–2018
2002 Cabernet Sauvignon	92	now–2012
2005 Shiraz Dead Letter Office	90	now–2015
2004 Shiraz Dead Letter Office	93	now–2014
2005 Shiraz	91	now–2018
2004 Shiraz	91	now–2014
2002 Shiraz	93	2009–2017
2005 Shiraz Reserve	93	2012–2025
2004 Shiraz Reserve	93	2009–2018
2002 Shiraz Reserve	97	now–2015

HENSCHKE ✶✶✶✶✶
EDEN VALLEY $35.00–$550.00

Henschke, one of Australia's oldest and most renowned wineries, continues to perform at a high level. The Hill of Grace Shiraz remains one of Australia's icon wines.

2003 Cabernet Sauvignon Cyril Henschke	92+	2012–2025
2002 Cabernet Sauvignon Cyril Henschke	94+	2012–2027
2000 Cabernet Sauvignon Cyril Henschke	88	now–2012
2005 Grenache-Shiraz-Mourvèdre Johann's Garden	90	now–2013
2004 Grenache-Shiraz-Mourvèdre Johann's Garden	87	now–2011
2002 Grenache-Shiraz-Mourvèdre Johann's Garden	89	now–2010
2005 Henry's Seven	90	now–2013
2004 Henry's Seven	90	now–2014
2002 Henry's Seven	89	now–2012
2003 Hill of Grace	98	2015–2035
2002 Hill of Grace	98	2018–2040
1999 Hill of Grace	98	2012–2027
2005 Keyneton Estate	89	now–2011
2003 Keyneton Estate	89+	2010–2020
2001 Keyneton Estate	91	now–2017
2004 Keyneton Estate Shiraz Euphonium	92+	2012–2025
2004 Lenswood Abbotts Prayer	91+	2010–2020
2003 Lenswood Abbotts Prayer	89	2009–2017
2001 Lenswood Abbotts Prayer	87	now–2011
2004 Mount Edelstone	93	2014–2030
2003 Mount Edelstone	94	2010–2022
2001 Mount Edelstone	95+	2010–2020

HEWITSON ✶✶✶
BAROSSA $25.00–$48.00

Hewitson remains a reliable source for prototypical Barossa Valley big red wines at consumer-friendly prices.

2005 Mourvèdre Old Garden	92	2010–2020
2004 Mourvèdre Old Garden	90	2010–2020

2002 Mourvèdre Old Garden	92	now–2014
2005 Shiraz The Mad Hatter	92	2014–2030
2004 Shiraz The Mad Hatter	90	2012–2025
2003 Shiraz The Mad Hatter	93	2010–2020
2005 Grenache-Shiraz-Mourvèdre Miss Harry	90	now–2015
2004 Grenache-Shiraz-Mourvèdre Miss Harry	87	now–2012
2003 Grenache-Shiraz-Mourvèdre Miss Harry	91	now–2013
2005 Shiraz Ned & Henry's	92	2009–2018
2004 Shiraz Ned & Henry's	90	now–2015
2002 Shiraz Ned & Henry's	92	now–2012
2005 Shiraz-Tempranillo Two Big Men	91	now–2015
2001 Shiraz L'Oizeau	93	now–2017

HOBBS * * * * *
BAROSSA $140.00

Greg and Allison Hobbs's vineyards are contiguous with Chris Ringland's Three Rivers vine-yards; furthermore, Ringland is a consultant to Hobbs winemaker Peter Schell. The Hobbs wines are made with minimal intervention and are bottled unfined and unfiltered.

2004 Shiraz	97	2014–2030
2003 Shiraz	97	2013–2028
2001 Shiraz	96	2009–2018
2004 Shiraz Gregor	95	2014–2030
2003 Shiraz Gregor	96	2011–2026
2004 Shiraz-Viognier	90	2010–2022

STEVE HOFF WINES * * *
BAROSSA $28.00–$47.00

Steve Hoff, the burly owner-winemaker of Steve Hoff Wines, hit the wicket in Barossa's recent string of outstanding vintages. The winery is composed of 20 acres of estate vineyards, and Hoff purchases some fruit from neighbors. His first vintage was in 1984. Total produc-tion stands at 5,000 to 5,500 cases annually.

2005 Cabernet Sauvignon	94	2015–2030
2004 Cabernet Sauvignon	91	2009–2020
2005 Shiraz	89	2010–2020
2004 Shiraz	89	now–2014
2005 Shiraz Rossco's Vineyard	93	2015–2030
2004 Shiraz Rossco's Vineyard	91	now–2016

HOWARD PARK * * * *
MARGARET RIVER $23.00–$30.00

Howard Park is an excellent source for elegant red and white wines from Western Australia. Even better, they offer an outstanding price-to-quality ratio.

2003 Cabernet Sauvignon	90+	2010–2020
2005 Cabernet Sauvignon Leston	90	2010–2020
2004 Cabernet Sauvignon Leston	90	2012–2025
2005 Cabernet Sauvignon Scotsdale	91	2011–2022
2005 Chardonnay	90	now–2011
2004 Chardonnay	88	now–2010
2005 Shiraz Leston	88	now–2012

2004 Shiraz Leston	91	2009–2018
2005 Shiraz Scotsdale	90	2010–2020
2004 Shiraz Scotsdale	89+	now–2014

PETER HOWLAND ★ ★ ★ ★
VARIOUS $30.00–$35.00

Peter Howland is a *terroir* guy who specializes in the production of vineyard-designated wines. His three Shiraz vineyards are in various Western Australia GIs, but his winery is in Newcastle, New South Wales. Consequently, the grapes are crushed and chilled in a refrigerated container, then transported by train in a seven-day agitated cold soak across the country. This process is fundamental to the style of Peter Howland's Shiraz.

2004 Shiraz Langley Vineyard Donnybrook	92	2010–2020
2004 Shiraz Parsons Vineyard Frankland River	95	2014–2030
2004 Shiraz Pine Lodge Vineyard Mt. Barker	90+	2012–2025

J. P. BELLE TERROIR ★ ★ ★ ★
BAROSSA $100.00

This is a new project between winemakers Chris Ringland and Trevor Jones and innovative importer Dan Philips. There are 350 cases of this 100% Shiraz produced from a single vineyard planted in 1960 and aged completely in new French oak for 30 months.

| 2003 Shiraz | 94 | 2010–2022 |
| 2002 Shiraz | 96 | 2012–2027 |

JASPER HILL ★ ★ ★ ★ ★
HEATHCOTE $55.00–$125.00

Jasper Hill is one of the top guns in Heathcote. The winery practices organic viticulture, dry farming, and has recently entered into a joint venture with Michel Chapoutier to develop a vineyard adjacent to the existing property.

2005 Grenache Cornelia Vineyard	93	now–2018
2004 Shiraz Cambria	95	2012–2025
2005 Shiraz Emily's Paddock	93+	2012–2025
2004 Shiraz-Cabernet Franc Emily's Paddock	92	2012–2027
2005 Shiraz Georgia's Paddock	92	2010–2020
2004 Shiraz Georgia's Paddock	90	2010–2020
2002 Shiraz Georgia's Paddock	90+	now–2017

ROBERT JOHNSON VINEYARDS
EDEN VALLEY $35.00* ★ ★

Robert Johnson Vineyards is a 30-acre estate with 400-meter elevation in the cool-climate Eden Valley region of Barossa Valley. All the wines are made from estate-grown fruit.

| 2005 Shiraz | 92 | 2014–2030 |
| 2004 Shiraz-Viognier | 90 | 2010–2020 |

JOURNEY'S END ★ ★ ★
MCLAREN VALE $30.00–$50.00

The Journey's End wines are made by the ubiquitous Ben Riggs.

| 2004 Shiraz Arrival | 93 | 2010–2020 |
| 2003 Shiraz Arrival | 91 | now–2015 |

2004 Shiraz Ascent	91	now–2016
2003 Shiraz Ascent	90	now–2015
2005 Shiraz The Embarkment	88	now–2014
2004 Shiraz Beginning	88	now–2011

KAESLER ★ ★ ★ ★ ★
BAROSSA $25.00–$140.00

Although these vineyards were established in the late 19th century, the Kaesler winery didn't begin until the 1990s and did not hit full stride until 1997, when young Reid Bosward took over the winemaking responsibilities. One of the most exciting portfolios in South Australia, these are exuberant, full-throttle, classic wines that are the antithesis of restrained European offerings. There is nothing here with less than 15% alcohol, and the old-vine Grenache pushes 16%+. Nevertheless, they all possess extraordinary balance even though they are big, fruit-forward efforts, and they appear capable of a decade or more of aging.

2006 Cabernet	90	2011–2021
2005 Cabernet Old Vine	93	2010–2020
2002 Cabernet Old Vine	88+	2010–2020
2006 Grenache The Fave	91	2010–2022
2005 Grenache The Fave	89	now–2012
2003 Grenache The Fave	95	2009–2017
2006 Grenache-Shiraz-Mourvèdre Avignon	91	2011–2021
2005 Grenache-Shiraz-Mourvèdre Avignon	90	now–2015
2003 Grenache-Shiraz-Mourvèdre Avignon	93	now–2015
2006 Grenache-Shiraz-Mourvèdre Stonehorse	90	now–2016
2005 Grenache-Shiraz-Mourvèdre Stonehorse	92	now–2015
2003 Grenache-Shiraz-Mourvèdre Stonehorse	89	now–2013
2006 Shiraz The Bogan	95	2013–2026
2005 Shiraz The Bogan	96	2013–2028
2002 Shiraz The Bogan	96	2012–2027
2005 Shiraz Old Bastard	98	2015–2035
2004 Shiraz Old Bastard	95	2014–2032
2002 Shiraz Old Bastard	96+	2012–2032
2006 Shiraz Old Vine	92	2010–2020
2005 Shiraz Old Vine	94	2010–2020
2002 Shiraz Old Vine The Hammer	93	2012–2027
2006 Shiraz Stonehorse	91	2010–2020
2005 Shiraz Stonehorse	92	now–2015
2003 Shiraz Stonehorse	93	now–2013
2006 Shiraz-Cabernet WOMS	89	now–2016
2004 Shiraz-Cabernet WOMS	95	2013–2028

KALLESKE ★ ★ ★ ★
BAROSSA $55.00–$135.00

Owner-winemaker Troy Kalleske owns a remarkable 400 acres in the Greenock region of the Barossa Valley, of which about 200 acres are cultivated with vines. From the northern section of the Barossa, where conditions are much more extreme and the vines are incredibly stressed, he appears to have a talent for turning out magnificently concentrated, full-throttle reds that are indigenous to the top echelon of South Australia producers.

2005 Shiraz Greenock	93	2014–2030
2004 Shiraz Greenock	94	2010–2022

2003 Shiraz Greenock	98	2012–2027
2002 Shiraz Greenock	96	2010–2022
2005 Shiraz Johann Georg	96	2016–2035
2004 Shiraz Johann Georg	96	2020–2045
2003 Shiraz Johann Georg	98	2014–2032
2003 Shiraz Red Nectar	95	now–2013
2005 Grenache Old Vine	93	2009–2017
2004 Grenache Old Vine	92	now–2014
2003 Grenache Old Vine	97	2010–2020
2002 Grenache Old Vine	97	2010–2020

KANGARILLA ROAD ★ ★ ★ ★
MCLAREN VALE $18.00–$33.00

Over the past several vintages, Kangarilla Road has established a track record of turning out high-quality South Australia wines at consumer-friendly prices. Founded in 1997 by Kevin and Helen O'Brien and located 22 miles south of Adelaide, the estate consists of 30 acres. Kevin O'Brien is winemaker.

2005 Cabernet Sauvignon	90+	2010–2020
2004 Cabernet Sauvignon	91	now–2016
2002 Cabernet Sauvignon	91	now–2015
2005 Shiraz	90	now–2018
2004 Shiraz	92	now–2016
2002 Shiraz	93	now–2012
2006 Shiraz-Viognier	93	2011–2021
2005 Shiraz-Viognier	91	now–2016
2003 Shiraz-Viognier	95	now–2015
2006 Zinfandel	90	now–2016
2004 Zinfandel	89	now–2012
2003 Zinfandel	88	now–2013
2002 Zinfandel	92	now–2015

KANTA ★ ★ ★ ★ ★
ADELAIDE HILLS $40.00

Kanta is produced by renowned German winemaker Egon Müller, who spends ten days each vintage selecting and crushing the grapes. Indigenous yeasts are used, and there is no added acidity.

2006 Riesling	91	2012–2022

KAY BROTHERS ★ ★ ★ ★ ★
MCLAREN VALE $40.00–$100.00

The Kay Brothers Amery Winery and Vineyards was founded in 1890 and continues to be 100% owned by the Kay family. For wine tourists looking for an out-of-the-ordinary visit, the winery is a veritable museum of how things were done back in the "ol' days."

2005 Amery Cabernet	85	now–2012
2004 Amery Cabernet	89	2009–2018
2002 Amery Cabernet	91	now–2015
2005 Amery Shiraz	88	now–2012
2004 Amery Shiraz	90+	2010–2020
2002 Amery Shiraz	92	now–2015

2005 The Cuthbert	89	2011–2021
2005 Shiraz Block 6	97	2014–2030
2004 Shiraz Block 6	98	2014–2032
2002 Shiraz Block 6	95+	2014–2032
2005 Shiraz Hillside	93	2012–2025
2004 Shiraz Hillside	93	2012–2027
2002 Shiraz Hillside	95	2012–2027

KILIKANOON * * * * *
CLARE VALLEY $15.00–$200.00

Kilikanoon's winemaker is the talented Kevin Mitchell. The house specialty is Shiraz, but Mitchell does equally well with Riesling, Cabernet Sauvignon, and Grenache.

2004 Cabernet Sauvignon Blocks Road	94+	2010–2020
2002 Cabernet Sauvignon Blocks Road	91	2010–2020
2006 Cabernet Sauvignon Killerman's Run	90	now–2018
2004 Cabernet Sauvignon Killerman's Run	92	2009–2018
2002 Cabernet Sauvignon Killerman's Run	87	now–2012
2005 Cabernet Sauvignon Reserve	92+	2012–2025
2004 Grenache The Duke	92+	2009–2018
2005 Grenache Prodigal	91	now–2018
2004 Grenache Prodigal	92	now–2014
2002 Grenache Prodigal	92	2009–2017
2005 Grenache-Shiraz-Mourvèdre The Medley	91	now–2018
2004 Grenache-Shiraz-Mourvèdre The Medley	93	now–2016
2002 Grenache-Shiraz-Mourvèdre The Medley	90	now–2012
2007 Riesling Mort's Reserve	91	now–2017
2006 Riesling Mort's Reserve	91	now–2016
2004 Riesling Mort's Reserve	90	now–2011
2005 Shiraz Attunga 1865	97	2015–2035
2004 Shiraz Attunga 1865	98	2018–2040
2004 Shiraz Baroota Reserve	90	now–2019
2005 Shiraz Covenant	92	2010–2020
2004 Shiraz Covenant	94	2009–2018
2002 Shiraz Covenant	95	2010–2020
2005 Shiraz Green's Vineyard	94	2012–2025
2004 Shiraz Green's Vineyard	98	2018–2040
2002 Shiraz Reserve Green's Vineyard	93	2010–2022
2006 Shiraz Killerman's Run	91	now–2016
2005 Shiraz Killerman's Run	92	now–2015
2004 Shiraz Killerman's Run	90	now–2014
2002 Shiraz Killerman's Run	90	now–2012
2006 Shiraz The Lackey	89	now–2016
2005 Shiraz The Lackey	90	now–2011
2005 Shiraz M Reserve	92+	2012–2025
2004 Shiraz M Reserve	98	2012–2027
2005 Shiraz Oracle	92	2012–2025
2004 Shiraz Oracle	97	2014–2035
2003 Shiraz Oracle	97	2013–2035
2002 Shiraz Oracle	96	2012–2027
2001 Shiraz Oracle	95	2010–2024

2004 Shiraz Parable	96	2014–2035
2002 Shiraz Parable	89+	2009–2017
2005 Shiraz R Reserve	94	2014–2030
2004 Shiraz R Reserve	96+	2014–2032
2002 Shiraz Secret Places	89	now–2015
2005 Shiraz Testament	94	2012–2025
2004 Shiraz Testament	95	2014–2032
2006 Shiraz-Grenache Killerman's Run	90+	now–2016
2004 Shiraz-Grenache Killerman's Run	92	now–2014
2002 Shiraz-Grenache Sybarites	90	now–2012

KILLIBINBIN ★ ★ ★ ★
LANGHORNE CREEK $15.00–$35.00

Killibinbin is establishing a consistent track record for producing high-quality, consumer-friendly wines at fair prices from the underrated GI of Langhorne Creek.

2003 Blend	89	now–2013
2006 Cabernet Sauvignon	93	2010–2020
2002 Cabernet Sauvignon	90	now–2015
2005 Cabernet-Malbec Scaredy Cat	91	now–2017
2006 Cabernet-Shiraz	90	now–2012
2004 Cabernet-Shiraz Cellar Reserve	90	now–2014
2005 Malbec Barking Mad	90	2010–2020
2006 Shiraz	90+	now–2016
2002 Shiraz	91	now–2014
2005 Shiraz Old Chestnut	93	2010–2020

KOLTZ ★ ★ ★ ★ ★
MCLAREN VALE $59.00

Koltz began as a small wine label in 1995 and now has a winery under construction located near a vineyard in the Blewitt Springs region of McLaren Vale.

2005 Pagan Shiraz	97	2015–2045

K1 ★ ★ ★ ★
ADELAIDE HILLS $20.00–$70.00

K1 winery was founded by Geoff Hardy in 1987 when he began planting a 75-acre vineyard in the Adelaide Hills, now known as Kuitpo Vineyard. The wines are all produced from 100% estate fruit, organically grown, in the southernmost vineyard in Adelaide Hills. The winemaker is the renowned Ben Riggs.

2005 Cabernet Sauvignon	91+	2010–2020
2005 Chardonnay	89	now
2005 Merlot	91	now–2013
2007 Sauvignon Blanc	89	now
2005 Shiraz	90	2010–2020
2005 Tzimmukin	92	2015–2035

KURTZ FAMILY VINEYARDS ★ ★ ★
BAROSSA $17.00–$20.00

Kurtz Family Vineyards produces some of the best value-priced wines in South Australia. They can easily compete with most wines costing twice the price.

2005 Boundary Row Grenache-Shiraz-Mataro	89	now–2018
2005 Boundary Row Shiraz	92	2010–2020
2004 Boundary Row Shiraz	87	now–2014
2002 Boundary Row Shiraz	92	now–2012
2005 Seven Sleepers	91	now–2015

LANGMEIL ★ ★ ★
BAROSSA $22.00–$100.00

Langmeil's flagship Shiraz 1843 Freedom comes from a dry-grown vineyard planted in 1843 that is believed to have the oldest surviving prephylloxera Shiraz vines in Australia. The wine is aged for 24 months in 70% new French oak and bottled unfined and unfiltered.

2005 Cabernet Sauvignon The Blacksmith	89	2010–2020
2002 Cabernet Sauvignon The Blacksmith	88	now–2012
2005 Grenache The Fifth Wave	91	now–2018
2001 Grenache The Fifth Wave	86	now–2011
2005 Shiraz 1843 Freedom	94	2012–2025
2004 Shiraz The Freedom	91+	2012–2025
2002 Shiraz The Freedom	92	2010–2020
2005 Shiraz Orphan Bank	91	2010–2020
2006 Shiraz Valley Floor	87	now–2012
2005 Shiraz Valley Floor	90	now–2015
2002 Shiraz Valley Floor	88	now–2012
2006 Shiraz-Grenache-Mourvèdre Three Gardens	90	now–2016
2005 Shiraz-Grenache-Mourvèdre Three Gardens	90	now–2013
2006 Shiraz-Viognier Hangin' Snakes	87	now–2012
2005 Shiraz-Viognier Hangin' Snakes	90	now–2015

LEEUWIN ESTATE ★ ★ ★ ★ ★
MARGARET RIVER $22.00–$79.00

Leeuwin Estate is one of the benchmark wineries of Western Australia. Both reds and whites exhibit cool-climate character and European elegance.

2003 Cabernet Sauvignon Art Series	88	2012–2025
2000 Cabernet Sauvignon Art Series	89+	now–2012
2004 Chardonnay Art Series	93	now–2014
2003 Chardonnay Art Series	93+	now–2013
2001 Chardonnay Art Series	91	now–2011
2005 Chardonnay Prelude Vineyards	90	now–2011
2006 Riesling Art Series	90	now–2016
2005 Riesling Art Series	87	now–2010
2006 Sauvignon Blanc-Sémillon Siblings	89	now–2010
2004 Shiraz Art Series	90	2010–2020
2003 Shiraz Art Series	89+	now–2017
2001 Shiraz Art Series	87	now–2011
2004 Shiraz Siblings	89	now–2015
2003 Shiraz Siblings	88	now–2010

PETER LEHMANN ★★★
BAROSSA $38.00–$95.00

The venerable Peter Lehmann winery has turned out three outstanding late-release efforts in the superb 2002 Barossa vintage.

2002 Mentor	91	now–2018
2002 Shiraz Eight Songs	91+	now–2018
2002 Shiraz Stonewell	92+	2013–2027

LOAN ★★★★
BAROSSA $20.00–$30.00

Loan was the second farm planted in the history of the Barossa. Today, the Loan property is the Barossa's only certified organic vineyard. The current owners are Richard and Jessie Loan; the winemaker is the renowned Chris Ringland.

2005 Sémillon	89	now–2010
2004 Sémillon	87	now–2010
2002 Sémillon	90	now–2010
2003 Shiraz	94	2012–2015
2002 Shiraz Front Block	95	2009–2018
2001 Shiraz Front Block	91	now–2016

LONGVIEW ★★★
ADELAIDE HILLS $50.00

Made by none other than the talented Christian Canute of Rusden, the Shiraz Block 3 is aged for 22 months in large French oak and bottled unfined and unfiltered.

2005 Shiraz Block 3	94	2010–2020

LUNAR ★★★
BAROSSA $45.00

Lunar's owner-winemaker is Corey Chaplin. He worked at Rockford under Chris Ringland and is currently producing his wines at Rusden.

2005 Cabernet Sauvignon	91	2010–2020
2004 Cabernet Sauvignon	91	2010–2020
2005 Shiraz	93	2012–2025
2004 Shiraz	91	now–2016

MAGPIE ESTATE ★★★★
BAROSSA $22.00–$125.00

The Magpie Estate wines are made by Rolf Binder, who is famous for his large-scaled Shiraz. The flagship of the winery is the Shiraz The Malcolm. The wine is sourced from a single, dry-grown vineyard, with vine age ranging from 20 to 120 years. It is barrel-fermented and receives the "200% new oak" treatment, spending the first 12 months in new French oak before being transferred to new American oak for another 12 months. It is bottled unfined and unfiltered.

2005 Grenache The Fakir	90	now–2012
2004 Grenache The Fakir	90	now–2012
2002 Grenache The Fakir	89	now–2010
2004 Grenache The Gomersal	92	now–2014
2002 Grenache The Gomersal	92+	now–2015

2005 Mourvèdre The Black Sock	92	2009–2018
2004 Mourvèdre The Black Sock	93	now–2016
2005 Mourvèdre-Grenache The Call Bag	91	now–2015
2005 Shiraz The Election	95	2013–2030
2004 Shiraz The Election	92+	2012–2027
2002 Shiraz The Election	93	2012–2022
2006 Shiraz The Malcolm	98	2015–2035
2005 Shiraz The Malcolm	95	2020–2045
2005 Shiraz The Sack	91	now–2017
2004 Shiraz The Sack	91	now–2016
2002 Shiraz The Sack	90+	2009–2017
2006 Shiraz-Grenache The Schnell	89	now–2016
2005 Shiraz-Grenache The Schnell	90	now–2013
2004 Shiraz-Grenache The Schnell	89	now–2012

MARIUS ★★★
McLAREN VALE $50.00

This small McLaren Vale grower produces only three wines, one of which is a single-vineyard Shiraz that is aged in a combination of 70% French and 30% American oak. Both vintages acquit themselves exceptionally well.

2003 Shiraz Single Vineyard	91	now–2017
2002 Shiraz Single Vineyard	93	2010–2020

MASSENA ★★★★
BAROSSA $32.00–$50.00

Massena is one of the new stars in Barossa. The winery produces no-holds-barred, full-throttle Shiraz from old vines.

2005 Barbera Dolcetto	87	now–2010
2005 Durif The Howling Dog	93	2012–2027
2002 Durif The Howling Dog	92+	2009–2030
2005 Moonlight Run	93	2010–2020
2004 Moonlight Run	91+	2012–2027
2002 Moonlight Run	91	now–2012
2006 Shiraz The Eleventh Hour	91	2010–2020
2005 Shiraz The Eleventh Hour	96	2012–2032
2003 Shiraz The Eleventh Hour	95	now–2018
2005 Shiraz Epsilon	94	now–2017

MAXWELL WINES ★★★★
McLAREN VALE $17.00–$70.00

Maxwell Wines is a 40-acre, family-owned estate that began operations in 1979. The winery has a well-established reputation for producing elegant, concentrated, stylish red wines.

2006 Cabernet Sauvignon Lime Cave	92	2012–2026
2004 Cabernet Sauvignon Lime Cave	90+	2010–2022
2003 Cabernet Sauvignon Lime Cave	92	2009–2018
2002 Cabernet Sauvignon Lime Cave	91	now–2016
2005 Cabernet Sauvignon-Merlot Little Demon	88	now–2012
2005 Four Roads	90	now–2014
2004 Four Roads	91	now–2012

2005 Shiraz Ellen Street	92	2010–2020
2004 Shiraz Ellen Street	92	now–2016
2003 Shiraz Ellen Street	92	now–2016
2002 Shiraz Ellen Street	92	now–2015
2004 Shiraz Kangaroo Island	90	now–2017
2004 Shiraz Meracus 53	93+	2012–2027
2005 Shiraz Minatour	95	2015–2035
2005 Shiraz Silver Hammer	91	now–2016

MR. RIGGS ★ ★ ★ ★
McLAREN VALE $21.00–$55.00

These outstanding efforts come from talented winemaker Ben Riggs. Mr. Riggs is Ben's tribute to his great-grandfather, who converted the previously sober-minded family into wine imbibers. His great-grandfather is pictured on the label.

2006 Riesling Watervale	89	now–2012
2006 Shiraz	93	2014–2030
2005 Shiraz	92	2010–2020
2003 Shiraz	92	now–2015
2006 Shiraz The Gaffer	90	now–2016
2005 Shiraz The Gaffer	90	now–2015
2006 Shiraz-Viognier	91	2010–2020
2005 Shiraz-Viognier	91	now–2017
2003 Shiraz-Viognier	90	now–2013

MITOLO ★ ★ ★ ★
McLAREN VALE $20.00–$65.00

Mitolo, which began operations in 1999, is a partnership of the Mitolo family and winemaker Ben Glaetzer. The focus is on McLaren Vale fruit from Willunga, the southernmost part of the district.

2006 Cabernet Sauvignon Jester	92	2010–2022
2005 Cabernet Sauvignon Jester	91	now–2015
2005 Cabernet Sauvignon Serpico	94	2014–2032
2003 Cabernet Sauvignon Serpico	92	2010–2023
2006 Shiraz GAM	95	2018–2040
2005 Shiraz GAM	95	2012–2025
2003 Shiraz GAM	98	2015–2035
2006 Shiraz Jester	91	now–2018
2005 Shiraz Jester	92	now–2015
2002 Shiraz Jester	90	now–2010
2006 Shiraz Reiver	94	2010–2020
2005 Shiraz Reiver	94	2010–2020
2003 Shiraz Reiver	97	2013–2028
2006 Shiraz Savitar	94+	2013–2026
2005 Shiraz Savitar	96	2010–2020
2003 Shiraz Savitar	95	2013–2028

MOLLYDOOKER ★ ★ ★ ★ ★
McLAREN VALE $20.00–$175.00

Mollydooker is the label of the renowned winemaking team of Sparky and Sarah Marquis. ("Mollydooker" is the Australian equivalent of "southpaw." Both Sparky and Sarah are left-handed.) This is their second vintage following the schism with The Grateful Palate and the end of their involvement in the hugely successful Marquis Philips project. Total case production is 72,000, down from the 120,000 cases produced under the Marquis Philips label. They have also set up their own importing company in the United States.

2006 Cabernet Sauvignon Gigglepot	95	2013–2027
2006 Cabernet Sauvignon The Maître D'	91	now–2014
2006 Merlot The Scooter	91	now–2012
2006 Shiraz Blue-Eyed Boy	96	2013–2027
2006 Shiraz The Boxer	94	2010–2018
2006 Shiraz Carnival of Love	97	2014–2032
2005 Shiraz Carnival of Love	99	2010–2020
2006 Shiraz The Velvet Glove	99	2018–2040
2006 Shiraz-Cabernet Sauvignon Enchanted Path	94	2015–2036
2005 Shiraz-Cabernet Sauvignon Enchanted Path	96	2015–2035
2006 Shiraz-Merlot-Cabernet Sauvignon Two Left Feet	93	2009–2017

NICHOLSON RIVER ★★★★
GIPPSLAND $60.00

Nicholson River is located in Gippsland, four hours east of Melbourne, in a mild, coastal climate. The owner-winemaker is Ken Eckersley, a self-described flavor fanatic. The Nicholson River Chardonnay is sourced from vines 25-plus years old with modest yields of two tons per acre. It is aged in 40% new François Frères barrels and 60% one-year-old French oak.

2005 Nicholson River Chardonnay	91	now–2011

NOON WINERY ★★★★★
MCLAREN VALE/LANGHORNE CREEK $75.00

Noon Winery is owned and operated by Drew and Rae Noon. It continues to be one of Australia's benchmarks.

2005 Cabernet Sauvignon Reserve	97	2010–2030
2004 Cabernet Sauvignon Reserve	96	2012–2027
2002 Cabernet Sauvignon Reserve	96	2012–2030
2005 Eclipse	95	2010–2025
2004 Eclipse	94	2010–2022
2002 Eclipse	97	now–2017
2005 Shiraz Reserve	99	2015–2035
2004 Shiraz Reserve	98	2014–2032
2002 Shiraz Reserve	99	2010–2020

OCCAM'S RAZOR ★★★
HEATHCOTE $38.00

Occam's Razor is produced by Emily Laughton, a member of the family that owns Jasper Hill winery.

2005 Shiraz	91	now–2015
2004 Shiraz	89+	2010–2020

THE OLD FAITHFUL ★★★
MCLAREN VALE $37.00

The Old Faithful is a brand 50% owned by importer John Larchet, designed to express the quality of McLaren Vale fruit. Each cuvée is made in 300-case lots.

2005 Grenache Northern Exposure	90	2012–2022
2005 Mourvèdre Almond Grove	90	2010–2020
2005 Shiraz Cafe Block	91	2015–2030
2005 Shiraz Top of the Hill	92	2012–2025

OLIVER'S TARANGA ★★★★
McLAREN VALE $46.00–$65.00

The Oliver family is the sixth generation of grape growers on the same property. They retain a small portion of the best fruit to bottle under their own label. The wine is made by a family member, the talented Corrina Rayment, who also produces wine under her own label.

2002 Blend	93	now–2012
2005 Shiraz	88	now–2015
2004 Shiraz	87	now–2016
2002 Shiraz	93	now–2014
2004 Shiraz H. J. Reserve	95	2014–2028
2002 Shiraz H. J. Reserve	91+	2012–2027
2001 Shiraz H. J. Reserve	89	now–2013

OLIVERHILL ★★★★
McLAREN VALE $25.00–$35.00

The big red wines of Oliverhill consistently deliver a major bang for the buck. The flagship Jimmy Section Shiraz has been one of South Australia's Best Buys in high-quality Shiraz for several vintages.

2002 Cabernet Sauvignon	89	now–2015
2006 Petite Sirah	91	2020–2046
2005 Petite Sirah	92+	2012–2035
2006 Shiraz Clarendon	90+	2012–2025
2005 Shiraz Clarendon	94	2012–2025
2006 Shiraz Jimmy Section	93	2013–2027
2005 Shiraz Jimmy Section	96	2012–2025
2003 Shiraz Jimmy Section	94	now–2015

PEARSON ★★★★
CLARE VALLEY $35.00–$40.00

An artisanal winemaker dedicated to producing small lots from 50-year-old Cabernet Franc and Cabernet Sauvignon vines, Jim Pearson established this operation in 1993. He appears to be content to fashion two wines that have the potential to be very long-lived.

2004 Cabernet Franc	92	2012–2025
2002 Cabernet Franc	90	now–2015
2004 Cabernet Sauvignon	92+	2012–2025
2002 Cabernet Sauvignon	90+	now–2015

PENFOLDS ★★★★★
SOUTH AUSTRALIA $20.00–$300.00

Penfolds, arguably Australia's most famous winery, continues to perform at a high level under the leadership of head winemaker Peter Gago.

2004 Cabernet Sauvignon Bin 407	88	now–2014
2004 Cabernet Sauvignon Bin 707	95	2020–2040
2001 Cabernet Sauvignon Bin 707	87	now–2011

2004 Cabernet Sauvignon Block 42 Kalimna	96+	2018–2040
2005 Cabernet Sauvignon Cellar Reserve	96	2013–2030
2004 Cabernet Sauvignon-Shiraz Bin 60A Kalimna	98	2020–2050
2004 Cabernet Sauvignon-Shiraz Bin 389	91	2010–2020
2003 Cabernet Sauvignon-Shiraz Bin 389	91	now–2015
2005 Cabernet Sauvignon-Shiraz Cellar Reserve	93+	2018–2035
2006 Chardonnay Bin 311	90	now–2011
2005 Chardonnay Reserve Bin 05A	92	now–2014
2004 Chardonnay Yattarna	91	now–2012
2003 Chardonnay Yattarna	91	now–2010
2002 Grange	98	2022–2050
2001 Grange	98+	2011–2035
1999 Grange	92	2009–2021
2004 Grenache-Shiraz-Mourvèdre Bin 138	91	now–2014
2005 Grenache-Shiraz-Mourvèdre Bin 138 Old Vine	91+	2010–2020
2006 Pinot Noir Cellar Reserve	90	2010–2020
2004 Shiraz Bin 28 Kalimna	90	now–2014
2003 Shiraz Bin 28 Kalimna	89	now–2013
2004 Shiraz Magill Estate	93	2011–2024
2003 Shiraz Magill Estate	94	2010–2020
2001 Shiraz Magill Estate	87	now–2011
2004 Shiraz RWT	95	2016–2032
2003 Shiraz RWT	96	2010–2020
2001 Shiraz RWT	87	now–2011
2003 Shiraz St. Henri	90	2011–2023
2002 Shiraz St. Henri	92	2009–2017
2006 Shiraz-Cabernet Sauvignon Koonunga Hill	91	2012–2022
2004 Shiraz-Cabernet Sauvignon Koonunga Hill	91	2009–2018

PENLEY ESTATE ★ ★ ★ ★
COONAWARRA $20.00–$50.00

Penley Estate, established in 1988, is one of Coonawarra's leading producers. Both the reds and whites are uniformly excellent and well priced.

2005 Cabernet Sauvignon Phoenix	89	now–2015
2004 Cabernet Sauvignon Phoenix	91+	2012–2027
2002 Cabernet Sauvignon Phoenix	88	now–2012
2004 Cabernet Sauvignon Reserve	92	2012–2024
2005 Chardonnay	88	now–2010
2004 Chardonnay	89	now–2010
2004 Chertsey	90	2010–2020
2002 Merlot	87	now–2010
2005 Merlot Gryphon	87	now–2014
2005 Shiraz Hyland	87	now–2013
2004 Shiraz Hyland	91	2009–2018
2002 Shiraz Hyland	89	now–2012
2001 Shiraz-Cabernet	87	now–2009
2004 Shiraz-Cabernet Condor	90	2010–2020

PENNY'S HILL ★★★
McLAREN VALE $35.00–$65.00

Penny's Hill is another Ben Riggs winery. The flagship Footprint Shiraz is a barrel selection of the best estate Shiraz produced only in top vintages. It is aged for 24 months in a mix of new and used French and American oak.

2006 Shiraz	91	2010–2020
2005 Shiraz	90+	2010–2020
2002 Shiraz	92	now–2012
2005 Shiraz Footprint	94	2013–2030
2005 Shiraz Red Dot	91	now–2015

PERTARINGA ★★★
McLAREN VALE $18.00–$30.00

The Pertaringa Vineyard was planted in 1970 and subsequently purchased and expanded by Geoff Hardy and Ian Leask beginning in 1980. The vineyard now covers 77 acres, planted primarily to Shiraz with small plots of seven other varieties.

2005 Cabernet Sauvignon Rifle & Hunt	91	2012–2025
2005 Cabernet-Petit Verdot Understudy	88	now–2015
2004 Grenache Two Gentlemens [per label]	87	now–2010
2005 Shiraz Over the Top	92	2010–2020
2004 Shiraz Over the Top	92	2009–2017
2005 Shiraz Undercover	91	now–2015
2004 Shiraz Undercover	90	now–2016

PEWSEY VALE ★★★★
EDEN VALLEY $16.00–$25.00

Pewsey Vale was the first Australian wine to be sealed with a Stelvin screw cap in 1976. Aside from that factoid, the winery specializes in Riesling from their high-elevation estate vineyard in the cool Eden Valley.

2007 Riesling	88	now–2014
2005 Riesling	89	now–2011
2002 Riesling Contours	91	now–2015
2001 Riesling Contours	91	now–2011

PIKES ★★★
CLARE VALLEY $14.00–$25.00

Pikes is one of the top producers of the Clare Valley, known for their elegant style of wine-making.

2004 The Assemblage	90	now–2015
2003 The Assemblage	89	now–2012
2001 Cabernet Sauvignon	89	now–2011
1999 Cabernet Sauvignon Reserve	90	now–2014
2006 Dry Riesling	88	now–2016
2005 Dry Riesling	87	now–2011
2001 Grenache-Shiraz-Mourvèdre	89	now–2011
2005 Luccio	88	now–2014
2001 Merlot	86	now–2011
2005 The Red Mullet	87	now–2012

2004 Riesling The Merle Reserve	90	now–2010
2002 Shiraz	89	now–2015
2001 Shiraz	86	now–2011
2004 Shiraz Eastside	91+	2012–2025
2003 Shiraz Eastside	90	2009–2018
2002 Shiraz The EWP Reserve	92	2010–2020

PILLAR BOX ★ ★ ★
PADTHAWAY $12.00–$20.00

Pillar Box has had a powerful pedigree: fruit sourced from Henry's Drive and winemaking consultation from the renowned Chris Ringland. Following the 2006 vintage, Ringland and Pillar Box parted ways, so it remains to be seen if the high level of quality will be maintained in the future.

2006 Pillar Box Red	91	now–2012
2005 Pillar Box Red	91	now–2012
2006 Shiraz Reserve	92	2009–2016

PIOMBO ★ ★ ★
McLAREN VALE $35.00–$60.00

The proprietor, Modestino Piombo, passed away in March 2007, so the work is now being carried on by his winemaker, Paul Petanga. This is my first experience with these unique and impressive wines.

2005 Shiraz	94	2014–2032
2005 Shiraz Petanga Diavolo	92	2020–2050
2005 Shiraz Valletta	93	2010–2020

R WINERY ★ ★ ★ ★ ★
BAROSSA $10.00–$1,000.00

R Winery is a new company founded by importer and marketing genius Dan Philips and re-nowned winemaker Chris Ringland. Winemakers for R Winery are Ringland, Lisa Wether-ell, Andrew Hercock, and John Hughes. The winery encompasses the familiar labels Marquis Philips, 3 Rings, Roogle, and Bitch, along with 13 others created especially for R Winery. Needless to say, the packaging of these wines is amazingly creative, but, more important, what is in the bottle consistently overdelivers from low end to high end.

2006 Cabernet Sauvignon Evil	90	now–2014
2005 Cabernet Sauvignon (Big) R	92	2010–2020
2005 Cabernet Sauvignon (Little) r	89	now–2014
2005 Cabernet Sauvignon Re: Serve	93	2014–2032
2006 Cabernet Sauvignon Marquis Philips	90+	now–2016
2006 Cabernet Sauvignon Marquis Philips S2	89	now–2014
2003 Cabernet Sauvignon Marquis Philips S2	91	now–2015
2006 Grenache Chateau Chateau Chateau	93	2010–2020
2006 Grenache Chateau Chateau Columns	96	2013–2026
2006 Grenache Chateau Chateau Island	98	2014–2032
2006 Grenache Chateau Chateau Magic Window	96	2013–2026
2006 Grenache Chateau Chateau My Sun Is Your Sun	94+	2012–2025
2006 Grenache Chateau Chateau Triumphal Arc	94	2009–2021
2006 Sarah's Blend Marquis Philips	91	now–2016
2006 Shiraz Anamorphosis	98	2016–2040

2005 Shiraz Boarding Pass	92	now–2015
2005 Shiraz Boarding Pass First Class	94	now–2018
2004 Shiraz Evil Incarnate	94	2012–2025
2005 Shiraz Longitude	100	2020–2050
2006 Shiraz Luchador	92	now–2016
2006 Shiraz Marquis Philips	92	now–2016
2006 Shiraz Marquis Philips Integrity	96	2013–2026
2003 Shiraz Marquis Philips Integrity	94	2009–2918
2006 Shiraz Marquis Philips 9	94	2011–2022
2003 Shiraz Marquis Philips 9	93	now–2015
2005 Shiraz Marquis Philips Tabla	93	now–2015
2006 Shiraz Chris Ringland CR	93	2011–2022
2006 Shiraz Roogle	90	now–2012
2006 Shiraz Strong Arms	91	now–2013
2006 Shiraz Suxx	91	2010–2018
2006 Shiraz 3 Rings	91	now–2014
2004 Shiraz 3 Rings Reserve	96	2014–2030
2004 Shiraz The Wine	99	2016–2040

CORRINA RAYMENT ★★★★
McLAREN VALE $21.00–$56.00

These are full-bodied, voluptuous wines from rising star Corrina Rayment. They can be enjoyed near term or cellared for a decade and more.

2006 Shiraz Expatriate	96	2015–2036
2005 Shiraz Expatriate	93	2012–2025
2006 Shiraz Revolution	91	now–2016

RED EDGE ★★★
HEATHCOTE $35.00–$63.00

Peter Dredge is the owner-winemaker of Red Edge. The vineyard was planted in 1971 in ancient Cambrian red volcanic soil and is not irrigated. The wines are estate-bottled, all fruit sourced from this single parcel of mature vines with small yields of 1.0 to 1.5 tons of fruit per acre.

2005 Cabernet Sauvignon	90	2012–2025
2004 Cabernet Sauvignon	92+	2010–2022
2002 Cabernet Sauvignon	92	2009–2018
2005 Degree	91	2010–2020
2004 Degree	90+	now–2014
2005 Shiraz	92	2014–2030
2004 Shiraz	91	2012–2025
2002 Shiraz	92	2010–2020

REILLY'S ★★★
CLARE VALLEY $17.00–$35.00

Reilly's is one of South Australia's leaders when it comes to delivering great value throughout their portfolio.

2004 Cabernet Sauvignon Dry Land	91	2012–2024
2002 Cabernet Sauvignon Dry Land	89	now–2014
2005 Grenache Old Bush Vine	90	now–2015

2003 Grenache-Shiraz Old Bush Vine	88	now–2010
2007 Riesling Watervale	91	now–2017
2005 Riesling Watervale	90	now–2012
2004 Shiraz Dry Land	91+	2010–2020
2003 Shiraz Dry Land	91	2009–2020
2002 Shiraz Dry Land	89	now–2012
2004 Shiraz Stolen Block	92	2012–2024
2002 Shiraz Stolen Block	91	now–2015

RESCHKE ★★★★
COONAWARRA $18.00–$115.00

Reschke, whose first vintage in 1998 was well received in Robert Parker's *Wine Advocate,* has emerged as the rising star of Coonawarra, a region in need of an infusion of new blood. The winery specializes in Cabernet Sauvignon but makes one white wine from the Limestone Coast.

2004 Cabernet Sauvignon Bos	90	now–2016
2003 Cabernet Sauvignon Bos	92	2011–2023
2004 Cabernet Sauvignon Empyrean	95	2018–2024
2004 Cabernet Sauvignon Vitulus	89	2010–2020
2003 Cabernet Sauvignon Vitulus	90+	2012–2025
2006 Fumé Sauvignon Blanc	90	now

RINGLAND VINTNERS ★★★★★
BAROSSA $300.00

It is difficult to say that Chris Ringland's latest Shiraz is his best to date because he has set the bar so high. Ringland stands with Chave, Chapoutier, Guigal, Bratasiuk, Powell, and Krankl on the short list of world's greatest Syrah producers.

2002 Shiraz Chris Ringland	100	2012–2040
2001 Shiraz Chris Ringland	100	2020–2050
2000 Shiraz Chris Ringland	96	2014–2032
1999 Shiraz Chris Ringland	98+	2009–2039
1998 Shiraz Chris Ringland	100	2015–2050

ROSS ESTATE ★★★
BAROSSA $22.00–$37.00

Ross Estate has established a track record for producing outstanding Barossa Valley red wines at consumer-friendly prices. The most recent releases continue in that vein.

2005 Cabernet Sauvignon	89	now–2015
2002 Cabernet Sauvignon	90	2010–2022
2006 Grenache	90	now–2016
2003 Grenache Old Vine	90	now–2013
2005 Lynedoch	90	2009–2018
2002 Lynedoch	93	2010–2020
2005 Shiraz	91	2010–2020
2002 Shiraz	91	now–2012
2005 Shiraz Lights Out	89	now–2015
2005 Shiraz Reserve	92	2012–2025
2002 Shiraz Reserve	92	2010–2022

RUDDERLESS ★★★
MCLAREN VALE $40.00

Rudderless is the conception of Doug Govan, owner of the Victory Hotel, which importer Dan Philips claims is the finest pub in South Australia. It also houses a "bottle shop" with some rarities seldom seen in the U.S. for sale. Govan decided to plant the hillsides around his pub and hired Justin McNamee to make the wines. There are only 100 cases of each cuvée.

2005 Grenache	92	2010–2020
2004 Grenache	94	now–2014
2005 Grenache-Shiraz-Mataro	91	2010–2020
2004 Grenache-Shiraz-Mataro	95	2009–2018
2005 Mataro	91	2012–2025
2004 Mataro	90	2010–2020

RUSDEN ★★★★★
BAROSSA $20.00–$100.00

Rusden is owned by Dennis and Christian Canute with the talented Christian serving as winemaker. The vines were planted in the early 1970s in the tenderloin of the Barossa. Christian Canute has a unique ability to produce wines of great finesse combined with the intensity and power obtained from Barossa Valley fruit.

2006 Cabernet Sauvignon Bakery Hill	92	now–2018
2005 Cabernet Sauvignon Bakery Hill	91	2009–2018
2004 Cabernet Sauvignon Boundaries	94	2010–2020
2003 Cabernet Sauvignon Boundaries	94	2014–2032
2001 Cabernet Sauvignon Boundaries	95	2009–2021
2005 Cabernet Sauvignon-Shiraz Ripper Creek	94	2010–2020
2004 Cabernet Sauvignon-Shiraz Ripper Creek	94	2010–2022
2002 Cabernet Sauvignon-Shiraz Ripper Creek	94	2009–2017
2005 Driftsand Red Blend	90	now–2016
2004 Driftsand Red Blend	90	now–2011
2002 Driftsand	89	now–2010
2005 Grenache Christine's Vineyard	91	now–2018
2004 Grenache Christine's Vineyard	90	now–2014
2002 Grenache Christine's Vineyard	93	now–2012
2004 Shiraz Black Guts	97	2012–2025
2003 Shiraz Black Guts	96	2015–2040
2001 Shiraz Black Guts	97	2011–2026
2006 Shiraz Stockade	92	now–2016
2005 Shiraz Stockade	92	now–2015
2005 Zinfandel Chookshed	93	now–2015
2004 Zinfandel Chookshed	93	now–2014
2002 Zinfandel Chookshed	92	now–2012

SCHILD ESTATE ★★★
BAROSSA $80.00

The family-owned Schild Estate dates back to the early 1950s. Their vineyard holdings now encompass 380 acres. The first Schild Estate wines were produced in 1998.

2003 Shiraz Moorooroo Limited Release	94	2015–2035
2002 Shiraz Moorooroo Limited Release	90	2009–2018

SCHUBERT ESTATE ✳✳✳
BAROSSA $85.00

Schubert Estate is situated in one of the prime spots in the Barossa Valley, Roennfeldt Road, which was made famous by the Greenock Creek winery.

2005 Shiraz Goose-Yard Block Roennfeldt Road	95	2014–2030
2004 Shiraz Goose-Yard Block	92	2010–2022

SCHULZ ✳✳✳✳
BAROSSA $25.00–$90.00

Marcus Schulz, a grower of German descent, is a good friend of David Powell and sells Powell some fruit for his Torbreck label. These cuvées are serious wines made by Powell for Schulz.

2003 Shiraz Benjamin	92	2009–2018
2002 Shiraz Benjamin	91	now–2012
2004 Shiraz Marcus Old Vine	97	2012–2027
2002 Shiraz Marcus Old Vine	92	2009–2016
2004 Zinfandel Johanne	91	now–2014
2001 Zinfandel Johanne	91	now–2011

SHIRVINGTON ✳✳✳✳
MCLAREN VALE $65.00–$75.00

Shirvington's proprietors are Paul and Lynn Shirvington and the winemaker is Kim Jackson. Two wines, a Cabernet and a Shiraz, are produced annually from estate vineyards that are now 20 years of age.

2006 Cabernet Sauvignon	92	2014–2032
2005 Cabernet Sauvignon	95	2012–2027
2003 Cabernet Sauvignon	94	now–2015
2006 Shiraz	95	2012–2026
2005 Shiraz	93	2012–2022
2003 Shiraz	96	2010–2020

SOLITARY VINEYARDS ✳✳✳✳✳
BAROSSA $60.00

Solitary Vineyards is a joint venture of ADW and a group of Barossa Valley wine aficionados to make small-lot, single-varietal wines from the finest Barossa sites. The wines are made at the outstanding Pikes Winery in Clare Valley under the direction of Neil Pike.

2005 Grenache Greenock Creek	94	2012–2025
2005 Shiraz Greenock Creek	97	2014–2030
2005 Shiraz Solitary Block	95	2014–2030

SPINIFEX ✳✳✳✳
BAROSSA $33.00–$49.00

It should come as no surprise that one of the partners in this venture has a family history of wine growing in Montpellier, France, spanning more than ten generations. These wines show a clear French influence, with Châteauneuf-du-Pape, Bandol, and Côte Rôtie coming to mind.

2005 Esprit	90+	2012–2025
2004 Esprit	89	now–2012

2001 Esprit	94	now–2011
2004 Grenache	92	now–2014
2005 Indigene	92	2014–2030
2004 Indigene	93	now–2016
2002 Indigene	96	2009–2017
2005 Papillon	89	now–2012
2005 Shiraz-Viognier	94	2014–2030
2004 Shiraz-Viognier	94	2010–2020

STANDISH ★ ★ ★ ★
BAROSSA $25.00–$95.00

Dan Standish, who started his namesake winery in 1999, was once a winemaker at Torbreck and, like David Powell, is a fan of Rhône wines.

2004 Shiraz	92+	2015–2035
2003 Shiraz	99	2018–2040
2001 Shiraz Second Release	95	2011–2021
2005 Shiraz Epsilon	90	2010–2017
2005 Shiraz-Viognier The Relic	93+	2018–2040
2004 Shiraz-Viognier The Relic	99	2014–2032
2002 Shiraz-Viognier The Relic	91	now–2012

TAIT ★ ★ ★ ★
BAROSSA $17.00–$40.00

There is no holding the brakes on these offerings from proprietor Bruno Tait, who likes his wines packed and stacked. Consumers looking for European-styled, restrained, delicate reds will have their sensitivities offended by these boisterous, exuberant, full-throttle, palate-coating reds. However, they are to be admired for their singularity, purity, and extraordinary amount of fruit.

2006 The Ball Buster	92	now–2014
2005 The Ball Buster	92	now–2015
2003 The Ball Buster	91	now–2013
2005 Cabernet Sauvignon Basket Pressed	92	2013–2030
2004 Cabernet Sauvignon Basket Pressed	90	now–2016
2002 Cabernet Sauvignon Basket Pressed	91	2010–2022
2005 Shiraz Basket Pressed	93	2012–2025
2004 Shiraz Basket Pressed	93+	2009–2018
2002 Shiraz Basket Pressed	95	2010–2022

TAPANAPPA ★ ★ ★
WRATTONBULLY $50.00–$70.00

Tapanappa is a joint venture of the Cazes family of Bordeaux, the Bollinger family of Champagne, and winemaker Brian Croser of Australia.

2005 Cabernet Sauvignon-Shiraz Whalebone Vineyard	89+	2012–2025
2005 Chardonnay Piccadilly	89	now–2013
2005 Chardonnay Tiers Vineyard	90	now–2012
2006 Chardonnay Tiers Vineyard	89	now–2012

TATIARRA ★ ★ ★ ★ ★
HEATHCOTE $65.00–$78.00

Tatiarra is a collaboration of noted winemaker Ben Riggs and Melbourne retailer Nick Chleb-nikowski to make Shiraz from Heathcote's famous Cambrian soils.

2006 Shiraz Cambrian	94	2013–2026
2005 Shiraz Cambrian	94+	2010–2025
2004 Shiraz Cambrian	93+	2009–2025
2003 Shiraz Cambrian	92	2010–2020
2002 Shiraz Cambrian First Release	91	2010–2022
2003 Shiraz Pressings	95	now–2015
2002 Shiraz Pressings	91+	now–2012
2006 Shiraz Pressings Caravan of Dreams	95	2013–2026
2005 Shiraz Pressings Caravan of Dreams	95	2012–2027

TEUSNER ★ ★ ★ ★ ★
BAROSSA $25.00–$60.00

Teusner produces rich, structured red wines from old vines. The Shiraz cuvées have excellent aging potential.

2005 Avatar	92	2010–2020
2004 Avatar	88	now–2014
2002 Avatar	89	now–2012
2006 Joshua	91	now–2013
2005 Joshua	89	now–2011
2003 Joshua	91	now–2013
2005 Shiraz Albert	94	2012–2025
2004 Shiraz Albert	92	2010–2022
2003 Shiraz Albert	93	2009–2017
2006 Shiraz The Riebke	93	2012–2025
2005 Shiraz The Riebke	91	2009–2018

TORBRECK VINTNERS ★ ★ ★ ★ ★
BAROSSA $20.00–$225.00

An exceptional turnaround success, Torbreck Vintners was founded by David Powell in 1994 and suffered a period of financial difficulties. However, Torbreck has reemerged from that debacle to produce even finer wines over the last several vintages. Powell, who first worked under Chris Ringland at Rockford, has an impressive résumé, but it is his ability to source ancient vineyards and, as he says, behave like a maverick by paying the highest prices for the highest-quality grapes from the oldest vines that allows him to fashion such extraordinary of-ferings, all distinctively named. His Scottish heritage is reflected in the name Torbreck, which is a forest in Scotland where Powell once worked as a lumberjack.

2005 Les Amis	98	2014–2030
2004 Les Amis	98	2018–2032
2002 Les Amis	99	2012–2027
2005 Descendant	97	2015–2035
2004 Descendant	98	2012–2027
2002 Descendant	96	2010–2027
2005 The Factor	97	2014–2032
2004 The Factor	97	2010–2024
2002 The Factor	99	2012–2030

2001 The Factor	98	2011–2026
2006 Cuvée Juveniles	91	now–2013
2005 Cuvée Juveniles	91	now–2013
2003 Cuvée Juveniles	90	now–2011
2005 The Pict	92	now–2018
2004 The Pict	95+	2012–2027
2004 RunRig	99+	2020–2050
2003 RunRig	99	2018–2040
2001 RunRig	99+	2011–2031
2005 The Steading	93	now–2018
2004 The Steading	93	2009–2016
2002 The Steading	93	now–2015
2005 The Struie	94	2013–2027
2004 The Struie	96	2012–2027
2002 The Struie	95	2009–2017
2006 Woodcutter's Shiraz	92	now–2013
2005 Woodcutter's Shiraz	93	now–2017
2003 Woodcutter's Shiraz	92	now–2011

TROLL CREEK * * * *
BAROSSA $85.00

Troll Creek is a collaboration between winemaker Christian Canute (of Rusden fame) and his uncle, grape grower James Hage.

2004 Cabernet Sauvignon	93	2010–2020
2003 Cabernet Sauvignon	88	now–2015
2005 Shiraz	95	2012–2024
2003 Shiraz	93	2010–2018
2001 Shiraz Hage Family Vineyards	96	2011–2021

TURKEY FLAT VINEYARDS * * *
BAROSSA $29.00–$46.00

Turkey Flat Vineyards has been owned by the Schulz family since 1865. The winery has established a consistent track record over the years and has a fine portfolio from top to bottom.

2006 Butchers Block Red	92	2010–2020
2004 Butchers Block Red	93	2009–2016
2002 Butchers Block Red	92	now–2012
2006 Cabernet Sauvignon	93	2015–2030
2005 Cabernet Sauvignon	93	2009–2018
2004 Cabernet Sauvignon	93	2009–2018
2002 Cabernet Sauvignon	90	2009–2017
2006 Grenache	90	2010–2020
2005 Grenache	91	now–2015
2004 Grenache	89	now–2014
2002 Grenache Noir	92	now–2012
2006 Mourvèdre	92	2010–2020
2005 Mourvèdre	92	2009–2017
2006 Shiraz	93	2012–2026
2005 Shiraz	95	2012–2025
2004 Shiraz	94	2009–2018
2002 Shiraz	94	2009–2017

2004 The Turk	90	now–2012
2002 The Turk	88	now–2010

TWO HANDS ★ ★ ★ ★ ★
VARIOUS $32.00–$150.00

Two Hands is a *négociant* operation run impeccably by Michael Twelftree. It reflects the best that can be sourced from all over South Australia. The packaging provides some serious design competition to Dan Philips's Grateful Palate and R Winery portfolio.

2005 Cabernet Sauvignon Aphrodite	98	2015–2035
2004 Cabernet Sauvignon Aphrodite	98	2014–2040
2003 Cabernet Sauvignon Aphrodite	95	2013–2028
2005 Grenache Aerope	92	2012–2025
2004 Grenache Aerope	90	2010–2020
2006 Grenache Yesterday's Hero	90	now–2012
2005 Grenache Yesterday's Hero	89	now–2011
2003 Grenache Yesterday's Hero	93	now–2015
2003 Merlot-Cabernet Franc Shovel Blanc	87	now–2013
2006 Shiraz Angel's Share	93	now–2016
2005 Shiraz Angel's Share	92	2009–2018
2003 Shiraz Angel's Share	91	now–2013
2005 Shiraz Ares	95	2012–2025
2004 Shiraz Ares	96+	2014–2032
2002 Shiraz Ares	98	2012–2027
2005 Shiraz Bad Impersonator	90	now–2015
2004 Shiraz Bad Impersonator	90	now–2014
2002 Shiraz Bad Impersonator	95	2009–2017
2005 Shiraz Bella's Garden	93	2010–2020
2004 Shiraz Bella's Garden	94	2012–2027
2002 Shiraz Bella's Garden	95	2009–2017
2005 Shiraz Deer in the Headlights	92+	now–2015
2002 Shiraz Deer in the Headlights	95	2010–2022
2005 Shiraz Gnarly Dudes	91	now–2014
2004 Shiraz Gnarly Dudes	90	now–2014
2005 Shiraz Harry & Edward's Garden	91	2010–2020
2004 Shiraz Harry & Edward's Garden	92	2010–2020
2005 Shiraz Lily's Garden	94	2012–2025
2004 Shiraz Lily's Garden	95	2012–2027
2002 Shiraz Lily's Garden	96	2009–2017
2004 Shiraz Max's Garden	90+	2009–2018
2005 Shiraz Roennfeldt Road Zippy's Block	99	2020–2045
2004 Shiraz Roennfeldt Road Zippy's Block	97	2020–2045
2005 Shiraz Samantha's Garden	94+	2010–2020
2004 Shiraz Samantha's Garden	93	2010–2020
2002 Shiraz Samantha's Garden	95	2009–2017
2005 Shiraz Sophie's Garden	91	2014–2032
2004 Shiraz Sophie's Garden	95+	2014–2032
2005 Shiraz-Cabernet Sauvignon The Bull and the Bear	90	now–2015
2004 Shiraz-Cabernet Sauvignon The Bull and the Bear	93	2009–2018

2002 Shiraz-Cabernet Sauvignon The Bull and		
the Bear	94	now–2015
2005 Shiraz-Grenache Brave Faces	94	2009–2018

VASSE FELIX ★ ★ ★ ★ ★
MARGARET RIVER $40.00–$60.00

Vasse Felix is one of Margaret River's pioneer wineries, founded in 1987. The fruit is all estate grown.

2004 Cabernet Sauvignon	90	2010–2020
2002 Cabernet Sauvignon	90+	2010–2020
2004 Cabernet Sauvignon Heytesbury	92	2012–2025
2005 Chardonnay Heytesbury	91	now–2013
2004 Chardonnay Heytesbury	92	now–2012
2003 Heytesbury Red Blend	95+	2010–2020
2002 Heytesbury Red Blend	91+	2009–2017
2004 Shiraz	89	now–2016
2002 Shiraz	89	now–2012
2004 Shiraz Adams Road	89	now–2014

WATER WHEEL ★ ★ ★ ★
BENDIGO $14.00–$17.00

Water Wheel consistently produces wines of exceptional value.

2005 Cabernet Sauvignon	90	now–2015
2004 Cabernet Sauvignon	89	now–2012
2006 Memsie Red	90	now–2012
2005 Memsie Red	90	now–2011
2005 Shiraz	91	now–2018
2004 Shiraz	89	now–2012

WHIP-HAND ★ ★ ★ ★
McLAREN VALE $40.00

Whip-Hand is made by Justin Lane and Hamish Maguire from the Red Heads Studio in McLaren Vale.

| 2005 Cabernet Sauvignon | 97 | 2017–2040 |

WHISTLING EAGLE ★ ★ ★
HEATHCOTE $63.00

Ian Rathjen is the owner-winemaker of Whistling Eagle. His mentor was David "Duck" Anderson of the renowned Wild Duck Creek Estate (below).

2005 Shiraz Eagles Blood	91	2010–2020
2004 Shiraz Eagles Blood	92	2012–2027
2005 Shiraz-Viognier	92+	2010–2022

WILD DUCK CREEK ESTATE ★ ★ ★ ★ ★
HEATHCOTE $30.00–$300.00

David "Duck" Anderson is the resident guru here. Most would agree that these are the finest and most distinctive wines coming out of Heathcote.

2005 Alan's Cabernet Sauvignon Vat 1	94	2012–2025
2004 Alan's Cabernet Sauvignon Vat 1	92	2012–2025
2005 The Blend	91	2010–2020
2004 The Blend	88	now–2016
2004 Shiraz Duck Muck	96+	2015–2038
2002 Shiraz Duck Muck	95	2012–2030
2005 Shiraz Springflat	94	2012–2025
2004 Shiraz Springflat	94	2010–2022
2002 Shiraz Springflat	91	now–2015
2005 Shiraz Springflat Pressings	95	2014–2032
2005 Shiraz Reserve	97	2015–2035
2004 Shiraz Reserve	95	2014–2032
2005 Shiraz-Malbec Yellow Hammer Hill	91	2010–2020

THE WILLOWS VINEYARD ★ ★ ★
BAROSSA $35.00–$63.00

The owner-winemaker of The Willows Vineyard is Peter Scholz, whose grandfather began planting the vineyard in 1936 with subsequent expansions in the '60s, '70s, and '90s. The wines are all produced from the estate's vineyards.

2004 Shiraz	90	2010–2020
2003 Shiraz	92	now–2016
1999 Shiraz	91	now–2014
2004 Shiraz Bonesetter	92+	2012–2024
2003 Shiraz Bonesetter	94	2010–2022
2001 Shiraz Bonesetter	95	2010–2020

WINNER'S TANK ★ ★ ★ ★
LANGHORNE CREEK $16.00–$22.00

The Winner's Tank Shiraz is a perennial Best Buy. It spends nine months in tank with French oak staves. The Shiraz Velvet Sledgehammer, the 2006 being the first vintage of this wine, comes from the same vineyard but from a higher-elevated, lower-yielding section. The winemakers, David Knight and Reid Bosward, decided to harvest this section one week later, keep it separate, and age it in French oak *barriques,* 35% new, for 16 months.

2006 Shiraz	91	now–2012
2005 Shiraz	91	now–2012
2006 Shiraz Velvet Sledgehammer	92	2009–2018

YALUMBA ★ ★ ★ ★
VARIOUS $18.00–$125.00

At Yalumba, size has not been an impediment to high quality from the bottom to the top of their product line. The following wines represent the top tier.

2004 Cabernet Sauvignon The Menzies	90+	now–2016
2003 Cabernet Sauvignon The Menzies	94	2014–2032
NV Museum Reserve Antique Tawny	92	now
NV Museum Reserve Muscat	93	now
NV Museum Reserve 21 Years Old Antique Tawny	95	now
2002 The Reserve	94+	2018–2040
2001 The Reserve	95+	2018–2040
2000 The Reserve	91	now–2016

2004 Shiraz The Octavius	96	2015–2035
2003 Shiraz The Octavius	97	2014–2032
2001 Shiraz The Octavius	98	2011–2031
2000 Shiraz The Octavius	90	now–2012
2002 Shiraz-Viognier	93	now–2015
2004 The Signature	94	2014–2030
2003 The Signature	92	2010–2020
2002 The Signature	96+	2012–2027
2001 The Signature	94	2011–2026
2000 The Signature	90	now–2012

YANGARRA ESTATE VINEYARD * * *
MCLAREN VALE $25.00–$60.00

Yangarra Estate Vineyard, whose first vintage was in 2000, was purchased by Jess Jackson in 2001. It is located in the Foothills/Blewitt Springs region of McLaren Vale. Grenache and Shiraz are the two principal varieties planted on the estate. The winery uses all wild ferments and 100% French oak, predominantly new for the Shiraz and two to three years old for the Grenache. The Grenache is all grown on bush vines.

2005 Grenache	91+	2010–2020
2005 Grenache High Sands	93	2012–2025
2005 Grenache-Shiraz-Mourvèdre Cadenzia	87	2012–2022
2005 Shiraz	92	now–2017

YARRA YERING * * * * *
YARRA VALLEY $75.00

Ancient by Australian standards, this artisanal winery was started in 1969 by Dr. Bailey Carrodus. It now encompasses 78 dry-farmed acres. All of the wines are produced from estate fruit.

2005 Dry Red Wine No. 1	93+	2015–2035
2004 Dry Red Wine No. 1	95+	2015–2035
2001 Dry Red Wine No. 1	88+	2009–2018
2005 Dry Red Wine No. 2	95	2014–2032
2004 Dry Red Wine No. 2	94+	2014–2032
2001 Dry Red Wine No. 2	93	2011–2026
2005 Pinot Noir	91	2012–2022
2004 Pinot Noir	87	now–2012
2001 Pinot Noir	90	now–2016
2004 Potsorts Fortified	94+	now–2025
2000 Potsorts Fortified	92	2010–2025
2005 Shiraz Underhill	89	now–2017
2004 Shiraz Underhill	96	2012–2027
2001 Shiraz Underhill	90+	2010–2020

ZONTE'S FOOTSTEP * * *
LANGHORNE CREEK $17.00

Zonte's Footstep is the creation of Geoff Hardy and John Pargeter. Over the last several years, they have produced a number of notable values from their Langhorne Creek vineyards.

2006 Shiraz-Viognier	90	now–2013

[central
europe]

A SLEEPING GIANT?

Central Europe encompasses a vast range of viticultural regions, nearly all of which slipped from international attention during an extended 20th-century period of war and economic deprivation, and languished for 40 or more years under Soviet-style controlled economies utterly inimical to quality. Prior to World War I, most of these regions were associated with the Austro-Hungarian Empire, and a considerable number of important Central European wine-growing countries—as the account that follows will reveal—straddle borders with Austria, Germany, Italy, or one another, in what was once practically a sea of vines running from the Alps and the foothills of the Carpathians to the Black Sea.

Hungary and Slovenia have witnessed the most dramatic postcommunist evolution, and their wines are the most promising and most prominently exported of those produced in recent times in this vast area of Europe (excepting Austria, to which a separate chapter of this guide has been devoted). That evolution owes much to their proximity to two major wine-growing regions of the capitalist world—Austria and Italy—and to the relatively loose restrictions on private ownership in Tito's Yugoslavia and under János Kádár during his more than three decades as the leader of Hungary's Communist Party. Both countries also harbor several of the historically most celebrated growing regions of Central Europe. All of these factors have helped them attract investment of foreign capital and the participation of internationally known winemakers in many projects. Before considering Slovenia and Hungary in more detail, let's take a swift-moving tour of the rest of Central Europe, beginning in the north.

Vine acreage in Slovakia and the Czech Republic is largely proximate to better-known growing regions in neighboring countries. For example, the northern fringe of the area traditionally considered Tokaj laps into Slovakia, growing the same grapes with the intention of producing a similar wine. (See the account of Hungarian wine below for details on Tokaji.) But while Slovakia's total wine production remains small, hillsides are planted with vines near the shores of the Danube for its entire journey along the southwestern and western edges of the country. A few miles north of the river and of the ancient Hungarian capital of Esztergom, in the Sturovo growing region, star Saar vintner Egon Müller (at Kastiel Béla, a palatial property of his wife's family) has demonstrated the potential for crafting highly expressive, distinctively delicious dry Riesling. And this startling quality has been achieved almost overnight, working with what Müller and his veteran vineyard manager, Miroslav Petrech, readily acknowledge are inferior Riesling clones that were planted and trained for cultivation by Soviet-era tractors and machine harvesting. With time and new vines, some truly profound wines are likely to emerge. Nearer the border with Austria's Carnuntum and Weinviertel regions, significant importance is placed on Grüner Veltliner, St.-Laurent, and Zweigelt, which may all have considerable promise. (For more about these varieties and their principal growing regions, consult the chapter devoted to Austria.) Despite the example of Béla's early success in export markets, however, nearly all Slovakian wine is consumed at home. This is true too of the Czech Republic, where small amounts of Müller-Thurgau, Gewürztraminer, and other grapes are cultivated along the river Elbe, just upstream from Germany's almost equally obscure Sachsen vineyards. And in Moravia, north of Austria's vast Weinviertel, the same Grüner Veltliner, Silvaner, Riesling, St.-Laurent, and Zweigelt (all but the last bottled under Czech versions of their names) are grown, to sometimes more than merely decent effect. Interestingly, at least one vintner from this once largely German-speaking southern fringe of Moravia is famous: Franz Künstler of the eponymous Rheingau winery (now run by his son Günter and profiled in the chapter devoted to Germany), who settled in Germany as a postwar refugee.

All of the former Yugoslav states and provinces—even tiny, long-contested Kosovo—can boast significant vine acreage, and several are clearly poised for a revival of viticulture, if not in fact a future as important wine-producing states. Slovenia is clearly in the vanguard of post-Yugoslav renewal. Curiously *n*-shaped Croatia is best known to many wine-loving Americans for having been revealed as the original home of the grape we call Zinfandel (there known as Crljenak, and one of the most obscure of an already obscure local bunch). But most of Croatia's wine is in fact white, its vineyards having counted as important sources to the Hapsburg Empire. The second well-known fact about Croatian wine involves another California connection: Iconic Napa grower Mike Grgich is Croatian-born, and he returned in 1996 to start a winery, Grgić Vina, where he grows Plavac Mali, a "child" of Crljenak. (In fact, without Grgich's notoriety and encouragement, it's doubtful that the search for Zinfandel's DNA on the Dalmatian Coast would ever have been so thorough, and ultimately successful.) Coastal Croatia's host of vinous characters includes Malvasia and Muscat; Chardonnay and the three Pinots; plus Plavac Mali and such indigenous black grapes as Babič, Debejan, Lasin, Plavina, and Sansigot. Eastern Croatia follows the river Drava from Slovenia southeast along the border with Hungary and shares many varieties with those neighbors, notably Sauvignon, Riesling, and Furmint (called "Moslavac"), not to mention Central Europe's ubiquitous but generally uninspiring Laški Riesling (aka Welschriesling, aka Riesling Italico, and in Croatia, aka Graševina—but under no name in the least like genuine Riesling!). Some intriguing estate-bottled Croatian wines are beginning to trickle into the U.S. market, but these are very early days in their revival. Macedonia has been mounting an export drive. Its several dozen wineries grow a range of internationally well-known varieties, as well as the indigenous (white) Smederevka and (black) Vranec, which are also favored in neighboring Montenegro.

Romania's vineyards are significantly reduced from pre–World War II levels, but still cover a half million acres, a number whose enlargement the EU—which Romania joined in 2007—has authorized. Given that the existing vines are responsible for more than twice as much wine as those of Austria, yet with only half the market worth, it might be wise for Romania's growers to focus on the quality of existing acreage. The obscure Fetească Alba variety is the country's most widely planted, along with Riesling Italico (which until Romania's accession to the EU was simply labeled "Riesling"). But these two account for only about 10% of total acreage, so colorful is the entire Romanian cast (on which accurate figures are hard to get). Players include Sauvignon, Chardonnay, Pinot Noir, Merlot, and Cabernet—all apt to become increasingly important as part of an effort to boost exports; a range of local varieties including a black variant on Fetească; a host of other grapes more familiar from France or from elsewhere in Central Europe; and a considerable contingent of hybrids. (There is even a little genuine "Rhine" Riesling.) Vineyard areas are spread the length and breadth of the country, including clusters along the Danube and virtually the entire Black Sea coast. The best-known Romanian growing region is Transylvania, with its often steep slopes. During the 1980s, a large volume of wine from Romania's cooperatives was marketed by the State in the U.S. In the post-Ceaușescu era, exports—which are largely to Germany, the U.K., neighboring Moldova, and the U.S.—have fluctuated, and most wine is still shipped in bulk, to be bottled at the export destination or in a third country. Wines from fledgling private estates have thus far been slow to reach American markets. There is clearly the potential for a new wave of nondescript Romanian wine to wash over foreign grocery store shelves, but also perhaps, with time, for the emergence of wines offering quality, distinctiveness, and still-modest prices.

Wine is grown almost throughout Bulgaria as well, although during the first half of the 20th century, table grapes were more important for export. Like Romania (with its more than 50% larger vine acreage), Bulgaria has an ancient winegrowing tradition, but it is largely associated among English-speaking drinkers with inexpensive libations from the best-known French varieties, which were planted in the 1970s and bore prominent fruits on American (and British) retail shelves in the 1980s. Since the advent of privatization, the situation in Bulgaria has been in some disarray, with a protracted period of claims settlements for precommunist ownership and repeated rounds of dissolution, consolidation, and liquidation of former cooperatives. But gradually, investment from outside is stimulating some worthy estate-bottled projects, including the German-backed venture Enira, which involves no less a wine luminary than Stephan von Neipperg of St.-Émilion's Château Canon-La Gaffelière. (The nearly omnipresent Michel Roland is already consulting on another Bulgarian project, Telish.) Germany and the U.K. are the prime export markets for Bulgarian wine, just as they are for the wine of Romania, but Americans can expect to see some interesting values emerging in their markets, with one California-based company now devoted entirely to Bulgarian winemakers and representing more than a dozen estates and assorted projects. One can expect, too, a continued emphasis on familiar French grape varieties, as well as (in the would-be premium sector) the common Central European overindulgence in small new barrels, which the Hungarian cooperages were only too happy to sell inexpensively—at least until recent surges in worldwide demand for wood and recognition of Hungarian quality led to steep price increases. Hopefully, increasing emphasis will be placed on quality of *fruit*. Given Bulgaria's wide range of microclimates and relatively neglected indigenous grapes, as well as its disjointed viticultural history, it is intriguing to ask just how many fascinating permutations are possible. But hopefully, tasty answers will be increasingly forthcoming.

The impoverished former Soviet state of Moldova has more than half the vine acreage of its many times larger western neighbor, Romania. Yet, curiously, Romania exports wine to its diminutive neighbor, in bulk and destined for Moldova's major markets, Russia and other former Soviet republics. (A 2006 political spat that led to Russia boycotting Moldovan and Georgian wines has had a devastating effect on their industries. The next year, drought reduced Moldova's crop by half.) Moldova is distinguished by its dominance of French grape varieties—going back to the aftermath of phylloxera in the late 19th century. Well into its second decade of independence, this small, politically uneasy nation is seeing some outside investment in ventures oriented toward wine for export. The U.K. is already Moldova's primary Western market, whereas for Georgia it is the U.S., but so far quantities exported from either of these countries are small, and we may be a long way from seeing significant consumer values emerging in the American market.

SLOVENIA: ON THE CUSP OF RECLAIMING FAME?

The first of the former Yugoslav states to join the EU, without question Slovenia—despite its diminutive size, and a wine production only one-third that of Austria—is turning out the most interesting wines and has advanced farthest in the direction of sophisticated methods of growing, vinification, and marketing. Not that the wine industry here is entirely free of the burdensome legacy of political turbulence and four decades of controlled, socialist economy. But Slovenia's viticultural windows onto Italy and Austria both encouraged cross-border collaboration and investment, and offered at least limited exposure to markets in the West. Furthermore, the nearly casualty-free ten-day war of Slovenian independence in 1991 was all that this young nation had to endure of the bloody, protracted, sometimes devastating Balkan conflicts of the 1990s.

The growing area known as Primorje follows the rugged limestone Karst (a name appropriated by geologists for all similar places), which rims the northeastern Adriatic. The Brda subregion is named for its hills, just as is Italian Friuli's neighboring Collio. Both sides of this stretch of the former Iron Curtain speak a common dialect and grow common grapes. Collaboration has grown since Slovenian independence, to the point where cross-border ownership of vineyards is commonplace. Pinot Blanc, Pinot Gris, Friuliano (until 2008 known in Italy as Toccai Friuliano), Ribolla Giala, Refosco, and Malvasia are all grown here (under the local Slavic variants of their names), along with Sauvignon, Chardonnay, the black Bordelais grapes, and such indigenous varieties as Pika and Glera. The most distinguished estate in Brda—and the oldest privately owned estate in the former Yugoslavia—is Movia, where Aleš Kristančič (also much in demand as a consultant) crafts a truly impressive range of reds as well as whites, to a highly original as well as biodynamic beat. Marjan Simčič and his eponymous winery represent another well-established source of Brda excellence, his white winemaking characterized by skin contact, low sulfur, and barrel maturation, as is that of so many of his better-known Friulian neighbors. Risk-taking in the cellar in Brda goes hand in hand with an increasing, encouragingly large number of small growers willing to assume the financial risk of estate-bottling, and wine enthusiasts will be hearing much more about them in the years to come. South of Brda, along the Adriatic in the Istrian Peninsula, the Santomas winery is making major investments in quality and achieving local celebrity for their reds from Cabernet Sauvignon and the local variant of Refosco.

The winegrowing regions in southeast and central Slovenia collectively known as Posavje are the country's least well known or distinguished, dominated by Central Europe's ubiquitous Laški Rizling, but here and there featuring more interesting grapes such as Furmint (known locally as Sibon, a name by legend derived from the approbation of Napoleon's occupying troops: *"C'est si bon!"*). The entire northeastern neck of Slovenia is known as the Podravje growing region, and is quite intensively planted with vines. On dramatic and seemingly endlessly undulating hills running along the Austrian border—from north of Maribor to the Hungarian frontier, as well as south along the Croatian line—grow many of Slovenia's most promising wines. This extensive area was once loosely known as Lower Styria. Archduke Johann of Hapsburg seized upon its winegrowing potential, and from his estate (founded in 1822) a vast array of viticultural improvements and incentives emanated for nearly four decades, without which neither the Podravje nor the neighboring Styrian growing regions of Austria would ever have acquired their historical importance. The same wide temperature swings, breezes, and steep slopes dominate the microclimates on both sides of the border, offering ideal conditions for a wide range of white grapes including Riesling, Traminer, Sauvignon Blanc, Pinot Blanc, Pinot Gris, Furmint, and Chardonnay. Near Maribor, Janez and Mirč Valdhuber are crafting a promising range of these. A number of the most prominent South Stryian wineries have vineyards across the border in Slovenia (in some instances, property lost after 1945 and now reclaimed), and vintner Erich Krutzler (who hails from the southern tip of Austria's Burgenland) planted both feet in Slovenia for a time, farming vineyards belonging to the Benedictine Order and making wine at the eight-century-old Jarighof in Jarenina, under the winery name Dveri-Pax. Krutzler scored impressive early results with several white varietals, but most notably Riesling (from vines in theory suffering under similar handicaps to those at Béla in Slovakia—see above). Danilo Flakus has now taken the reins from Krutzler, who is directing a promising new project called Marhof, at the former summer residence of Hungarian nobility on the northeastern fringe of Slovenia.

Within the Podravje, the tiny eastern subregion known as Ljutomer-Ormož—between the Mura and Drava rivers—long enjoyed the highest-quality reputation. The hilltop hamlet of Jeruzalem (said to have been named by crusaders and today consisting of scarcely more than its prominent church) was considered the qualitative epicenter and lent its name to wines grown on the steep hillsides of numerous nearby villages. In Hapsburg days, this was a name to conjure with, almost as much as Tokaji or Rust. Estates with wines worth seeking here nowadays include Kogl, where Franci Cvetko is bottling fascinating Riesling and Sipon, as well as strikingly serious reds from Pinot and Syrah; MiroVino, where Miro Munda excels with Sauvignon and Sipon in a collaborative project with Austrian South Styria's Erich and Walter Polz; and Joze Kupljen (very near Jeruzalem itself, although his portfolio is less focused and his wines are slightly less refined). New vineyards planted here in a joint project between Gerhart Conrad Fürst (whose family recently reclaimed the property) and Austrian-Styrian vintner Alois Gross will bear their first crop in 2010. If history, geology, and today's isolated successes are any guide, a decade hence, wine lovers will be reading about this place—with its stunning vistas of a hundred hills in all directions—as if the clock had been turned back to Hapsburg time.

HUNGARY'S HARD REBIRTH

Hungary seems to be moving in two directions at once. Set aside the fact that vine acreage in the pre–World War I Hungarian monarchy was nearly twice that of the 1960s; after all, the monarchy included much of the vineyard land of present-day Romania, Croatia, Slovenia, and Slovakia, as well as what is now Austrian Burgenland. Since 1965, Hungary's acreage has dropped by roughly half again. Yet even if one could revisit the era of empire, one would be unlikely to find a time when there were remotely as many different outstanding Hungarian wines as exist today. Add to this the paradox that while there is talk of a "renaissance" and of rediscovering this country's great winemaking roots, in some important regions the grapes—and in virtually all regions the style of wine—are not those of an earlier era in Magyar history. Rebirth and rediscovery will be prominent themes in our consideration of Tokaj, Hungary's (indeed Central Europe's) most famous wine. First, though, let's take a cursory tour of the entire country, beginning in the northwest, and emphasizing the promise of reds from Hungary's deep south.

Along the Austrian border in northwestern Hungary, the city of Sopron is central to a small winegrowing region that has demonstrated excellent potential with the traditional Kékfrankos. (See the chapter devoted to Austria for further details on this variety, there known as Blaufränkisch.) Weninger, a noted Austrian vintner, has vineyards and a cellar in the town of Balf, just outside Sopron, and on the southern edge of the shallow, reedy Lake Fertöd (in German, Neusiedlersee, further described—along with this area's history—in the coverage of

Austria's Burgenland). Weninger has also achieved promising results with young Syrah vines on these stony soils. Some 30 miles south along the border, one arrives at vineyards of considerable historical significance and potential even though the nearest town—Vaskeresztes—is so tiny it doesn't appear on many road maps, much less form the nucleus of any official Hungarian wine region. The adjacent iron-rich, mica-schist hillside—much of it in Austria—is the Eisenberg, a site whose fabulous potential with Kékfrankos has been reexplored by the Krutzler family and by Austrian vintner Uwe Schiefer, who works both sides of the border. (For further details, again consult the chapter on Austria.)

West-central Hungary is dominated by Europe's largest lake—and by white wine grapes. On the basaltic shores of Lake Balaton, Pinot Gris (here called Szürkebarát) is the best known of many white grapes. The indigenous and once endangered Jufark is staging a comeback, particularly 20 miles northwest of the lake at Somló, whose warm volcanic terraces were once a site of renown. The aromatic varieties Hárslevelű (more familiar from Tokaj) and Gewürztraminer also ripen to considerable opulence here, and Hungarian, Austrian, and German pioneers are probing the opportunities to reestablish Somló's reputation (although increasingly warmer vintages might render it more suitable for red wines in the future).

South-central Hungary is dominated by red wine production, although this was not always so. The loess, sand, and gravel hills of Szekszárd have a long tradition with the indigenous Kadarka grape, but nowadays that variety has largely given way to the black Bordelais varieties and to Kékfrankos. Numerous growers here (see Hungary's Red Wine Producers, page 1430) are rendering concentrated, rich cuvées. The challenge is to craft something distinctive of the region, rather than permitting an international cast of grapes and methods to result in wine that is rich but less than intriguing. Given the strong demand in Hungary and elsewhere in Central and Eastern Europe for the top wines of Szekszárd, one should not expect any outright bargains here, much less from farther south, in Villány. The village of Villány, along with its neighbor Siklós, has a long viticultural history. Just as in the region long known as German West Hungary (today's Austrian Burgenland), the wine growers in this southernmost portion of Hungary arrived in the wake of the 17th-century Turkish wars and were of Slavic—in this case Serbian—and German origin. These hills of dolomitic limestone, with intermittent sand and loess overlays, enjoy warm but breezy microclimates that traditionally favored white wines and sparkling wines (internationally known and already exported to the U.S. by the late 19th century) as well as reds from Kadarka and Kékoportó (aka Portugieser, a variety conspicuously disassociated with quality). But the modern excitement—and no other word will do—surrounding Villány arises from the success of its Merlot and Cabernets and to a lesser extent Kékfrankos and Pinot Noir. In few if any places in the world can one taste a more richly berry-fruited, florally aromatic, or downright seductive Cabernet Franc, for instance, than in the cellars of Attila Gere, and his blends—culminating in one called Kopar—are world class, yet taste distinctively of their origins. A host of other growers (including, once again, Weninger, who is a partner with Gere in one of Villány's outstanding ventures) are benefiting from the better clonal selections, more labor-intensive farming, and improved cellar installations that increasingly high demand and high prices for the best Villány wines afford them. (For a list of recommended producers, see below.) Paul Hobbs—famous for his work in Sonoma and Mendoza—has joined with Hungarian Christian Sauske, and beginning with the first impressive Sauske wines (due to debut late 2008, although the vintage is 2005), this team will have already neared their aspiration of resetting the qualitative bar in Villány.

The hills running northeast from Budapest and paralleling the Slovakian border were Hungary's best-known red wine–growing region during most of the 20th century. The most important town is Eger, and the so-called Bull's Blood of Eger (Egri Bikavér) became a regular feature in export markets, albeit as a co-op–rendered wine of at best simple, rustic pleasure and low price. Today, the face of Eger is no longer the bull. Tibor Gál (who died in a car crash in 2005 while developing a project in South Africa) made his reputation as a consultant at Tenuta dell'Ornellaia in Tuscany and then came home to establish an estate in his own name, to show the way to a new level of quality in Eger and to inspire local growers to estate-bottle and to strive for excellence. (His family and team carry on there today, with the owners of Sassicaia and the U.S. importer Kobrand as partners.) Kadarka may simply await the kiss of its vintner-prince, but meanwhile its acreage is on the wane in Eger just as elsewhere, with the leading edge of quality relying on Kékfrankos and a wide range of the most famous and fashionable French varieties (including Syrah). Some 60 miles farther east, in the northeastern corner of Hungary near the Slovakian and Ukrainian borders, come the most famous hills in Hungary, home to this country's best-known wine.

TOKAJI

Like a 50-mile-long check mark or a *J*, the Zemplín Hills of the Tokaj region are shadowed by the rivers Tisza and Bodrog, which come together at the crook. Here the landmark Mt. Tokaj rises, frequently from the mists that prime this place to give birth to *Botrytis cinerea*, the fungus that in exceptional places and cases in the world of wine makes possible "noble" concentration and sweetness. Beyond its physical structure, though—including its slopes, reminiscent of Burgundy's Côte d'Or in their subtle complexities of microclimate, with rhyolite and loess soils formed over eons of volcanic eruption and accumulation of glacial dust—the shape of Tokaj is more of a question mark. Few wines in the world have been more celebrated than Tokaji. We know that its reputation as the "wine of kings, and king of wines" developed rapidly after the first production—around the year 1600—of wine from shriveled, nobly rotten fruit. By the early 18th century, its vineyards had been classified officially and in detail, well ahead of Bordeaux's. Few wines were more written about in the 19th century, so there are meticulous records of at least certain aspects of viticulture and cellar technique. And yet Tokaji remains a mystery today, even to the best of this region's growers and winemakers. We have some truly glorious wines to savor, but their styles and their components differ widely. Tiny details can make an enormous difference in the taste of any wine, and with Tokaji, there are a myriad of branching alternatives, a wealth of contingencies, and no shortage of controversy regarding what makes for tradition, much less for quality.

On certain points, nearly all growers and historians would agree. Few regions or styles of wine were more severely impacted by the phylloxera, wars, economic depression, revolution, and recession of nobility that were the lot of nearly all of Europe and its vineyards in the first half of the 20th century. On top of this, Hitler's "Final Solution" decimated the ranks of local vintners and wine merchants and their customers across the continent. Second, the culture that evolved thereafter under the communist system was hostile to quality, from its industrial mentality, through winemaking almost literally by recipe, to the degradation of the soil itself and the squandering of the vines' genetic heritage. It is almost a miracle that a few idealistic souls and old vines—trapped, as it were, in The Machine—kept Tokaji's flame alive and lived to play their parts in its late 20th–century reemergence. The leading roles in privatizing Tokaj's estates during the 1990s were played by wealthy outside investors. And given the cost of making nobly sweet elixirs from shriveled fruit—a great vintage coming only every half dozen or more years—and the labor- and time-intensive methods in the cellar as well as the vineyards, capitalization was critical. Each of the new companies that purchased former noble estates began its own traditions and built up a cellar designed to reflect its own conception of Tokaji. Among the most important and influential voices were those of András Básco, the former oenologist for the State who answered a call from the Alvarez family of Spain's Vega Sicilia to direct Oremus; Hugh Johnson, who helped put together investors in Royal Tokaji and whose vision helped guide its evolution; and István Szepsy, who prior to privatization worked for the State but made his own wine on the side, and after a short stint with Royal

Tokaji went off to set extraordinary standards at his small estate. The influence of Bordeaux was also strong, at Disznókő (owned by A.X.A. insurance and originally overseen by Daniel Llose and Lynch-Bages's Jean-Michel Cazes); at Pajzos-Megyer (begun by star Bordeaux winemakers Jean-Louis Laborde and Jean-Michel Arcaute); and at the former Hapsburg gem of Hétszőlő (on the Tokaj mountain itself and purchased by Bordeaux traders Grands Millésimes de France).

Tokaji today is vinified with just a few exceptions (over which we won't linger) from three grapes, although a century ago there were many more. Furmint makes up half the surface area and is the grape whose botrytization forms the traditional foundation for the region's sweet wines. However, for the rotting of these grapes to be truly "noble," the fungus must arrive only when the fruit is already ripe. And Furmint is a stubbornly tardy ripener, which means—since it retains high acid and has pronouncedly tart, thick skin—that in a "normal" year, when much of the crop must be pressed in healthy condition for dry wine, one needs to take great care in both the vineyard and the cellar to get a good result. It may be that in the age of royalty, it was enough to make Tokaji as a sweet elixir (Tokaji Aszú) several times each decade, unconcerned about the fate of lesser fruit. But trying to grow, vinify, and market a satisfying dry Furmint or blend is one of the major challenges for today's producers. Visionaries like András Básco, István Szepsy, and young Judit Bott are showing the way toward distinctively delicious dry Tokaji. And at Királyudvar—owned by American Anthony Hwang—Zoltán Demeter is taking inspiration and advice from Noel Pinguet of Vouvray's Domaine Huet (which Hwang also owns), with encouraging results. All of these efforts are worthy, not only to subsidize the production of nobly sweet Tokaji Aszú, but because the mysteriously musky pungency, the bittersweet nuttiness and spice, and the combination of textural density with bracing citricity that characterize dry (or dryish) Furmint are well worth capturing in a bottle. (A genuinely dry Tokaji will normally be labeled as such—in Magyar, *száraz*.) The number two grape—Hárslevelű—is Furmint's alter ego. It lives to flatter, from its hauntingly sweet floral aromas to its oily richness. The minority partner is Sarga Muskotály (aka Muscat Lunel, aka Gelber Muskateller), pungently redolent of apricot, resinous green herbs, and citrus zest. Any of these grapes or their blends can make dry, as well as late-harvested sweet, wine (the latter frequently labeled as such in English, but officially *késői szüretelésu*). And a traditional category known as *szamorodni*—literally "as it grew"—represents dry wine resulting from picking and pressing healthy and shriveled fruit together. But the usual concept of "blend," and even of "vineyard designate," is stretched when one contemplates Tokaji Aszú.

The principle behind Aszú is that a healthy wine, or grape juice, or actively fermenting juice is used to extract the essence of flavor from the darkened, shriveled, nobly rotten berries. Traditionally, the medium of extraction might be wine from the previous year—calling the very notion of vineyard designation into question, the year on the label being that of the Aszú berries—but under the 21st-century rules of Tokaji, that is no longer permitted. One may employ grape must, fermenting must, or fully fermented wine of the current vintage, and very different results will be obtained, depending on the chosen extractive medium (particularly its level of alcohol). As a base wine or must, Muscat plays a role disproportionate to its acreage, frequently chosen because its grapes so often ripen early and rot-free. But this is a variety with an intense aromatic signature, just like Hárslevelű, so its use as a base wine makes an enormous difference to the taste. When it comes to the shriveled Aszú berries, there are extractive options, too. Traditionally they are "pasted" before macerating, but to what degree determines much of the character of the eventual wine, and a few vintners now favor leaving the raisins virtually intact. The ripeness and richness of Tokaji Aszú is measured in *puttonyos*. This refers to the number of small tubs of pasted berries that were traditionally added to a standard-sized barrel of base wine, although in practice the standard today—typically running from three to six *puttonyos*—is determined by levels of sugar and dry extract in the finished wine. Since picking botrytis berries is arduous and selective work, harvesters often range over a large area. In the early years postprivatization, the top estates typically purchased Aszú berries from small growers in order to have enough, so the base wine might be from the estate and perhaps as well from the vineyard named on the label; yet at least some of the botrytized berries might be of unknown origin, having traded as commodities. Nevertheless, even in the mid-1990s—and especially in 1999, the first truly classic "Aszú vintage" after privatization—sensational successes went to bottle at many addresses.

As with any wine, whether Tokaji is fermented in stainless steel or barrels and how long it ages have great significance for its ultimate flavor. But with Tokaji, the differences in method and flavor are accentuated and also fought over to an unusual degree. The standard Tokaji barrel (the Zemplín Hills are Hungary's most celebrated source for oak and barrels) is small and squat, promoting relatively rapid oxidation. And in this region, for much of the 20th century, if not in centuries before, oxidation was thought a virtue. The French influence in the 1990s brought maturation in *barrique* and avoidance of more than very subtle oxidation. Until accommodations were gradually made among the law, the practice of tasting commit-tees that authorized the labeling of wine as Tokaji Aszú, and the new wave of owners, many a wonderful sweet libation languished in legal limbo, or was bottled as "late harvest" but not "Aszú." Today, the minimum stay in barrel for Tokaji Aszú is 24 months, which some wine-makers think is too long for all but the most concentrated examples, preferring to bottle many potential Aszú earlier as "late harvest." The majority of Tokaji is nowadays bottled by the cooperatives—and one huge co-op in particular—that are the successors of the old State mo-nopoly. Tokaji Aszú from these establishments generally exhibits pronounced oxidation. But most of the region's top growers are sensitive to nuance and degree. Some of the signature smokiness that accrues to Tokaji in the glass may come from the mix of grapes or their envi-ronment (and that could include the heavy layers of fungus that hang from this region's count-less miles of cellar walls and quickly envelop barrels). But there is no question that the more exposure the wine has to air, and in particular the more time it spends in barrels (and the smaller their size), the more pronouncedly smoky, toasty, or nutty it becomes, and the more flavors of citrus marmalade, pit fruit preserves, flowers, herbal essences, or honey (among others) recede.

Tasting Tokaji Aszú from a top practitioner is a pleasure that no wine lover should forgo. You should expect to pay $50 or more for 500 milliliters (the size of Tokaji's traditional bottle) from a top-flight estate (consult the list of recommended producers that follows). But if mea-sured by the sheer intensity of each sip, the number of seconds the flavor lingers on the palate, the number of days it takes an open bottle to decay, or the number of years the memory will stay with you, the price is reasonable. Like any nobly sweet wines, these demand time to savor and careful matching at table. But of all the world's great sweet wines, Tokaji Aszú is the most versatile. Its firm, keen blade of citricity and phenolic bite balance its oily lushness and opulence, leaving a surprisingly modest impression of sweetness considering its high residual sugar. It surprises tasters, too, to discover that alcohol levels in Tokaji—while they vary widely, due to the very nature of the Aszú genre—are generally in a modest 9% to 12% range. (Dry Tokaji wines are another matter, and often exceed 14%.)

There is one vinous specialty of the Tokaj region, though, that does not lend itself to food. Neither was it ever really intended to be drunk on its own, save perhaps by royalty or those bedridden and in desperate need of its corpse-quickening intensity. That is the legendary Eszencia. It is fermented from whatever small amount of viscous juice drops of its own accord from a tub of shriveled Aszú berries (without being pressed, save by the weight of the berries themselves). This juice of super-high density and sugar barely ferments at all, and even after several years may have achieved only a low percent of alcohol. When Hungary joined the EU, the nation lobbied for—and eventually won—a special dispensation for this sweet essence to be legally considered wine, despite its never reaching the otherwise requisite threshold of

4.5% alcohol. Eszencia—whose ethereal, implosively concentrated peach, apricot, and honey; gelatinous thickness yet sense of palate lightness; amazingly restrained sweetness; and endless aftertaste are unforgettable—is only occasionally bottled. Its principal use is to fine-tune an Aszú wine by blending. "Aszú-Eszencia" refers to Tokaji wines of exceptional richness, frequently with a significant measure of Eszencia included in the blend. (Such wines are in effect Aszú of seven *puttonyos*.)

The most important and quality-conscious estates of Tokaji have banded together under the banner "Tokaj Renaissance," struggling to regain world markets and recrown their vinous king. In fact, theirs is a work of rediscovery, reinterpretation, and reinvention, but they should fight too stringent a restriction of the vintner's methods or vision. The term *renaissance* implies the flowering of a range of styles. If one may be permitted to revisit a communist metaphor, after the agony and mediocrity that preceded it, the revolutionary decade of the 1990s represented Tokaj's Great Leap Forward. But that revolution will have failed—today's estates will lose their qualitative edge and the owners their enthusiasm—unless this former wine of royalty is rediscovered and its diversity relished by wine lovers the world over.

—DAVID SCHILDKNECHT

[the ratings]

HUNGARY'S TOKAJI PRODUCERS

✶ ✶ ✶ ✶ ✶ (OUTSTANDING)

István Szepsy   Üri Borok Pincészete—Vince Gergely
Royal Tokaji

✶ ✶ ✶ ✶ (EXCELLENT)

Füleky Pincészet—Judit Bott   Királyudvar
Hétszőlő   Tokaj Oremus

✶ ✶ ✶ (VERY GOOD)

Disznókő   Château Pajzos
Homonna Szőlőbirtok

✶ ✶ (GOOD)

Alana-Tokaj—Atilla Nemeth   Château Megyer
Béres Szőlőbirtok és Pincészet   Patricius Borház
Gróf Degenfeld   Tokaj Pendits—Márta Wille-Baumkauff
Dobogó Pincészet—Zwack   Árvay Pincészet
Hímesudvar

HUNGARY'S RED WINE PRODUCERS

✶ ✶ ✶ ✶ ✶ (OUTSTANDING)

Attila Gere (Villány)

✶ ✶ ✶ ✶ (EXCELLENT)

Bock Pincészet—József Bock (Villány)   Ede & Zsolt Tiffán (Villány)
Márton Mayer (Villány)   Weninger & Gere (Villány)
Sauska (Villány)

Tibor Gál (Eger)

Thummerer (Eger)

Tamás & Zsolt Gere (Villány)

Ferenc Vesztergombi (Szekszárd)

Csaba Sebestyén (Szekszárd)

Weninger Borászat (Sopron)

* * (GOOD)

Heimann Pince (Szekszárd)

Landmann (Villány)

Hummel Pincészet (Villány)

Vylvan (Villány)

CHILE

[chile]

Like Argentina, its Andean neighbor, Chile has made enormous progress in recent years. At present, this South American country produces wines that can satisfy any consumer's desires, from cheap quaffing wines to world-class ageworthy reds.

What my tastings and two visits to Chile in the past several years reveal is that much progress has been made and much remains to be done. One encouraging sign is the amount of foreign investment, especially European, that has been taking place. Another positive sign is the exploration of new regions where high-quality Pinot Noir, Carménère, and Syrah can be grown successfully. Some names worthy of attention are the San Antonio Valley (which includes Leyda), the Aconcagua Valley, where much organic and biodynamic farming is being done, the Casablanca Valley for cool-climate varieties, and the Colchagua Valley for top-quality red wines.

Chile produces many of the standard grape varieties grown everywhere. Sauvignon Blanc and Chardonnay are ubiquitous. Among the reds, Merlot, Cabernet Sauvignon, Cabernet Franc, and Syrah are widely planted. Chile's unique grape is Carménère, a Bordeaux variety and close relative of Merlot that is nearly extinct in France. Some producers are hopeful that Carménère will become for them what Malbec has become for Argentina, something that will set them apart from everyone else. My tastings indicate that Carménère grown in the right microclimates can produce unique, unforgettable wines, the primary example being Concha y Toro's Terrunyo Carménère. However, most Carménère, especially those priced in the bargain category, turn out horribly green and vegetal. But when it's done right, this is remarkably exotic, hedonistic wine.

A couple of other cautionary notes. Most Chardonnay from Chile is overly oak-flavored and unbalanced. However, Chile has a knack for producing some amazing values in Sauvignon Blanc from a variety of regions, mostly in a Loire Valley style, and these wines sell for a song. Among red wines, much of the production is overly acidified or picked underripe from huge yields, causing the wines to have gritty tannins in the finish. That said, wineries such as Montes, Cono Sur, Cousiño-Macul, and Casa Silva, among others, have figured out how to produce terrific red wines at bargain prices.

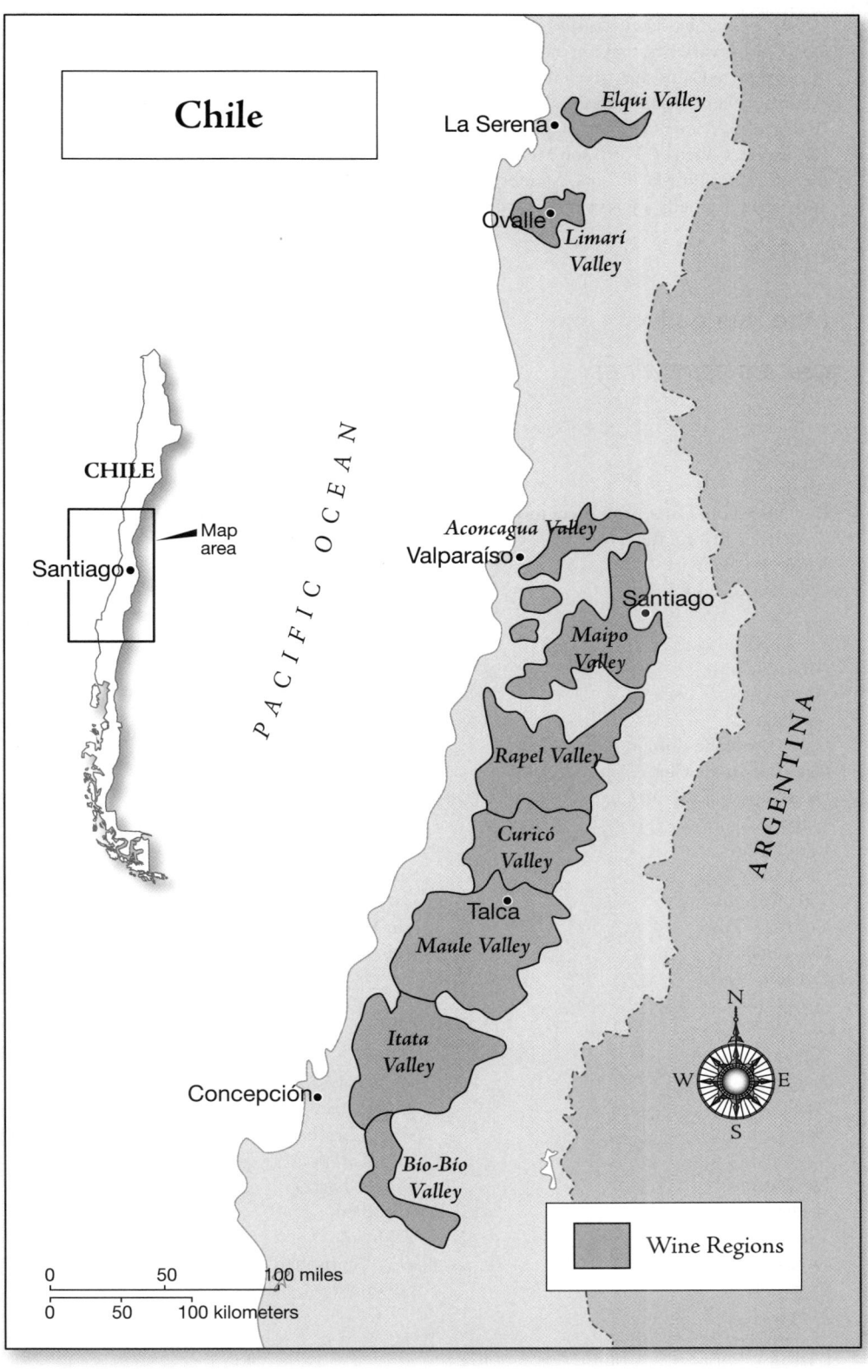

Chile

Elqui Valley

La Serena

Ovalle

Limarí
Valley

CHILE

Santiago

Map
area

PACIFIC OCEAN

Aconcagua Valley

Valparaíso

Santiago

Maipo
Valley

Rapel Valley

Curicó
Valley

Talca

Maule Valley

ARGENTINA

Itata
Valley

Concepción

Bío-Bío
Valley

N
W   E
S

0   50   100 miles

0   50   100 kilometers

Wine Regions

And Chile has begun turning out what they refer to as "icon" wines, mostly from Bordeaux grape varieties, that are increasingly world-class. These wines owe much more to Bordeaux than to California, given that the best are made in an elegant style meant for long-term cellaring. Names to keep in mind are Almaviva (made in conjunction with Château Mouton-Rothschild), Altair (a French-Chilean joint venture), Casa Lapostolle Clos Apalta, Viñedo Chadwick, Concha y Toro Don Melchor Cabernet Sauvignon, Concha y Toro Terrunyo Carménère, Cousiño-Macul Lota, Montes Alpha M, Santa Rita Casa Real Cabernet Sauvignon, and Seña (originally a joint venture with Robert Mondavi).

—JAY MILLER

[the ratings]

CHILE'S BEST WINES

✷ ✷ ✷ ✷ ✷ (OUTSTANDING)

Almaviva

Altair

Concho y Toro Cabernet Sauvignon Don
  Melchor Private Reserve

Vinñedo Chadwick

Cousiño-Macul Lota

Montes Alpha M

Viña Seña

Concha y Toro Terrunyo Carménère
  Peumo Vineyard

Concha y Toro Terrunyo Carménère
  Carmin de Peumo

✷ ✷ ✷ ✷ (EXCELLENT)

Altair Sideral

Antiyal

Apaltagua

Casa Lapostolle Borobo

Casa Lapostolle Clos Apalta

Casa Lapostolle Syrah Cuvée Alexandre Las
  Kuras Vineyard

Casa Marin

Casa Silva

Viña Chocalan

Concha y Toro

Cono Sur

Cousiño-Macul

Emiliana

Erasmo

Errazuriz

J & F Lurton

Montes Blue Angel

Montes Folly

Neyen del Apalta

Santa Ema

Santa Rita

Garces Silva

Viu Manent

Von Siebenthal

✷ ✷ ✷ (GOOD)

Apaltagua Grial

Anakena

Azul

Casa Lapostolle

Casas del Bosque

De Martino

Echeverria

Viña William Fèvre

Leyda

Loma Larga

Matetic

Montes

MontGras

San Esteban

Santa Carolina

Viña Tarapacá

Miguel Torres

2 Brothers

Valdivieso

Viña Ventisquero

Veramonte

Casa Rivas
El Toqui
Estampa
Gillmore
Kingston Family Vineyards
La Playa
Lauca

Maquis
Misiones de Rengo
Viña Penalolen
Perez Cruz
Porta
Tabali

[tasting commentaries]

VIÑA ALMAVIVA ★ ★ ★ ★ ★
ALTO MAIPO $85.00

Almaviva is a partnership of Bordeaux first-growth Château Mouton-Rothschild and Concha y Toro. Made in the style of top-of-the-line Pauillac, the blend is typically 73% Cabernet Sauvignon, 22% to 23% Carménère, and 4% to 5% Cabernet Franc. It spends 18 months in new French oak and is bottled unfined and unfiltered.

2005 Almaviva	94	2012–2028
2004 Almaviva	93	2010–2025
2003 Almaviva	95	2015–2035
2001 Almaviva	92	2009–2022

ALTAIR SIDERAL ★ ★ ★ ★
RAPEL VALLEY $30.00

ALTAIR ★ ★ ★ ★ ★
CACHAPOAL VALLEY $65.00

Altair, one of Chile's foremost wine estates, is owned by the Dassault family, proprietors of Château Dassault in St.-Émilion in partnership with Viña San Pedro. The first vintage was produced in 2002.

2004 Sideral	92	2012–2025
2003 Sideral	91	2010–2020
2004 Altair	94	2014–2030
2003 Altair	93	2012–2025

ANAKENA ★ ★ ★
RAPEL VALLEY $20.00

2006 Ona White Blend	88	now–2010
2005 Ona Syrah	89	2010–2020

ANTIYAL ★ ★ ★ ★
MAIPO VALLEY $50.00

2004 Antiyal	91	2010–2020

APALTAGUA ★★★★
COLCHAGUA VALLEY $40.00

2003 Grial Carménère	92	2010–2022

AZUL ★★★
VARIOUS $18.00

2005 Pinot Noir Profundo	88	now–2011
2005 Syrah Profundo	86	now–2012

CASA LAPOSTOLLE ★★★★
VARIOUS $18.00–$70.00

Casa Lapostolle is French-owned by the proprietors of Grand Marnier.

2005 Cabernet Sauvignon Cuvée Alexandre—Apalta Vineyard	87	2010–2018
2005 Chardonnay Cuvée Alexandre—Atalayas Vineyard	89	now–2009
2004 Clos Apalta	91+	2012–2027
2005 Merlot Cuvée Alexandre—Apalta Vineyard	88	2009–2016
2004 Syrah Cuvée Alexandre—Las Kuras Vineyard	90	2010–2020

CASA MARIN ★★★★
SAN ANTONIO VALLEY $36.00–$62.00

Casa Marin's portfolio is most impressive. The San Antonio Valley is a cool climate region particularly suited to the production of Pinot Noir. However, the white wines from Casa Marin are every bit as good.

2005 Gewürztraminer—Casona Vineyard	89	now–2009
2004 Pinot Noir—Litoral Vineyard	90	now–2014
2004 Pinot Noir—Lo Abarca Hills	92	2010–2018
2006 Sauvignon Blanc—Cypress Vineyard	92	now–2010
2005 Sauvignon Blanc—Laurel Vineyard	91	now–2011

CASA SILVA ★★★★
COLCHAGUA VALLEY $17.00–$25.00

2001 Altura	90	2011–2021
2005 Cabernet Sauvignon Los Lingues Estate	88	now–2015
2005 Carménère Los Lingues Estate	91	2009–2018
2005 Carménère Micro-terroir	93	2012–2027
2005 Merlot Angostura Estate	89	now–2015
2004 Quinta Generación	89	now–2014

CASAS DEL BOSQUE ★★★
CASABLANCA VALLEY $16.00–$60.00

2004 Estate Selection Family Reserve	91+	2012–2022
2006 Pinot Noir Casa del Bosque	87	now–2011

VIÑEDO CHADWICK ★ ★ ★ ★
MAIPO VALLEY $100.00

Viñedo Chadwick, whose first vintage was 1999, is quickly gaining recognition as one of Chile's icon wines. The 32-acre vineyard is located in Puente Alto along the northern bank of the Maipo River at the foothills of the Andes. To date, every vintage has been composed of 100% Cabernet Sauvignon and is typically aged for 18 months in new French oak.

2003 Viñedo Chadwick	91	2010–2020
2004 Viñedo Chadwick	93	2012–2027

VINA CHOCALAN ★ ★ ★ ★
MAIPO VALLEY $18.00

2004 Gran Reserva	91+	2010–2020

CONCHA Y TORO ★ ★ ★ ★
VARIOUS $19.00–$35.00

2005 Cabernet Sauvignon Marques de Casa Concha	88	2009–2017
2005 Chardonnay Amelia	90	now–2011
2005 Chardonnay Marques de Casa Concha	92	now–2012
2005 Syrah Marques de Casa Concha	91+	2012–2022

CONCHA Y TORO TERRUNYO
MAIPO AND RAPEL $27.00–$68.00* ★ ★ ★

Concha y Toro's Terrunyo Carménère gets my vote as the finest Carménère produced in Chile. (*Terruño* is the Spanish equivalent of *terroir*.) The Carménère Carmin de Peumo, the flagship Carménère, is a blend of the best parcels in the Peumo Vineyard. It spends 20 months in new French oak and is bottled unfined and unfiltered.

2004 Cabernet Sauvignon Old Pirque Vineyard	91	2012–2025
2004 Carménère Peumo Vineyard	95	now–2024
2003 Carmin de Peumo Carménère Peumo Vineyard	97	2013–2035

CONO SUR ★ ★ ★ ★
VARIOUS $13.00–$50.00

2004 Cabernet Sauvignon 20 Barrels	87	now–2014
2005 Cabernet Sauvignon Vision	90	now–2015
2005 Carménère	89	now–2013
2005 Chardonnay 20 Barrels	90	now–2010
2004 Merlot 20 Barrels	91	now–2016
2005 Pinot Noir Ocio	92	now–2017
2005 Pinot Noir 20 Barrels	91	now–2017
2005 Sauvignon Blanc 20 Barrels	88	now–2009

COUSIÑO-MACUL LOTA ★ ★ ★ ★ ★
MAIPO VALLEY $65.00

COUSIÑO-MACUL ★ ★ ★ ★
MAIPO VALLEY $10.00–$20.00

Cousiño-Macul was one of the first wineries from Chile to make an impression on the U.S. market in the mid-1980s. The winery continues to make wines offering superior bang for the buck. Lota is Cousiño-Macul's new entry into the high-end sweepstakes. If this first vintage is any indicator, the winery is off to a great start. It is 85% Cabernet Sauvignon and 15% Merlot from two vineyard sources. It spent 13 months in new French oak and was bottled unfined and unfiltered.

2006 Cabernet Sauvignon	87	now–2011
2005 Cabernet Sauvignon Antiguas Reserva	90	2009–2017
2006 Chardonnay Antiguas Reserva	90	now–2010
2004 Finis Terrae	88	2009–2017
2004 Lota	93	2014–2030
2006 Merlot	85	now–2010

DE MARTINO ★ ★ ★
LIMARI VALLEY $21.00

2005 Chardonnay Single Vineyard	90	now–2011

DON MELCHOR (CONCHA Y TORO) ★ ★ ★ ★ ★
PUENTE ALTO $60.00

Don Melchor has been considered one of Chile's icon wines from the time of its inception in 1987.

2004 Cabernet Sauvignon	94+	2014–2032
2003 Cabernet Sauvignon	93	2013–2028
2002 Cabernet Sauvignon	90	now–2012
2001 Cabernet Sauvignon	93	2012–2027
1997 Cabernet Sauvignon	94	now–2015

ECHEVERRIA ★ ★ ★
VARIOUS $20.00–$40.00

2004 Cabernet Sauvignon Family Reserva	87	now–2014
2004 Cabernet Sauvignon Limited Edition	88	now–2014
2003 Perfecto	89+	2010–2020

EMILIANA ★ ★ ★ ★
COLCHAGUA VALLEY $30.00–$89.00

2005 Coyam	90	2012–2025
2003 G	92+	2013–2028

ERASMO ★ ★ ★ ★
MAULE VALLEY $27.00

Erasmo is owned and operated by Count Francesco Marone Cinzano, who also owns Col d'Orcia, an excellent producer of Brunello di Montalcino in Tuscany. As the vines acquire some age, it seems likely that Erasmo will gain recognition as one of Chile's "icon" wines.

2004 Reserva De Caliboro	91	2010–2020

ERRAZURIZ ★ ★ ★ ★
ACONCAGUA VALLEY $21.00–$50.00

2005 Cabernet Sauvignon Max Reserva	87	now–2015
2005 Carménère Single Vineyard	90	2010–2020

2003 Founder's Reserve—Don Maximiano Series	92	2012–2025
2004 Founder's Reserve—Don Maximiano Series	91	2010–2020
2004 Shiraz La Cumbra	91	2012–2025
2005 Shiraz Max Reserva	88	2009–2017

VIÑA WILLIAM FÈVRE ★ ★ ★
MAIPO VALLEY $14.00–$38.00

William Fèvre is a well-respected producer of Chablis in Burgundy. Their efforts in Chile so far are a mixed bag.

2004 Antis	90	2010–2020
2005 Cabernet Sauvignon Gran Cuvée	87	2009–2017
2005 Cabernet Sauvignon La Mision	85	now–2012

LEYDA ★ ★ ★
LEYDA VALLEY $17.00–$36.00

2005 Chardonnay Single Vineyard	86	now–2009
2005 Pinot Noir Lot 21	87	now–2012
2006 Pinot Noir Single Vineyard	86	now–2011
2006 Sauvignon Blanc Single Vineyard	87	now–2009

LOMA LARGA ★ ★ ★
CASABLANCA VALLEY $21.00–$30.00

2005 Cabernet Franc Bl	88	now–2015
2005 Syrah BK-BL	87	now–2015

J & F LURTON ★ ★ ★ ★
COLCHAGUA VALLEY $22.00–$50.00

2003 Alka	90	2009–2017
2003 Clos de Lolol	87	now–2011
2002 Gran Araucano	88	now–2014

MATETIC ★ ★ ★
SAN ANTONIO VALLEY $27.00–$30.00

2005 Pinot Noir EQ	86	now–2011
2005 Syrah EQ	90	2012–2022

MONTES ALPHA M ★ ★ ★ ★ ★
COLCHAGUA VALLEY $93.00

MONTES FOLLY ★ ★ ★ ★
APALTA VALLEY $80.00

MONTES PURPLE ANGEL ★ ★ ★ ★
COLCHAGUA VALLEY $65.00

MONTES ★★★
COLCHAGUA VALLEY $16.00–$25.00

Over recent years, Montes has been one of the standard-bearers of quality wines from Chile under the leadership of Aurelio Montes. The entire lineup is top-notch, from entry level to the top of the line.

2005 Alpha Cabernet Sauvignon	89	now–2015
2005 Alpha Merlot	87	now–2012
2005 Alpha Syrah	89	2009–2017
1999 Alpha M	94	2012–2025
2001 Alpha M	92	2010–2020
2003 Alpha M	90	now–2015
2004 Montes Folly (Syrah)	92	2013–2027
2006 Pinot Noir Limited Selection	88	now–2016
2004 Purple Angel Carménère	91	2010–2020

MONTGRAS ★★★
COLCHAGUA VALLEY $20.00

The Antu Ninquén wines come from a single vineyard atop the plateau of Ninquén Mountain in the Colchagua Valley. The well-known Paul Hobbs serves as a consultant to the project.

2005 Antu Ninquén Cabernet Sauvignon-Carménère	88	2009–2017
2005 Antu Ninquén Syrah	88	2010–2020

NEYEN DE APALTA ★★★★
COLCHAGUA VALLEY $65.00

2004 Espiritu de Apalta	92+	2012–2027

SAN ESTEBAN ★★★
ACONCAGUA VALLEY $35.00

2005 Laguna del Inca In Situ	88	2010–2020

SANTA CAROLINA ★★★
MAIPO VALLEY $17.00

2005 Cabernet Sauvignon Reserva de Familia	87	now–2012
2005 Carménère Reserva de Familia	87	now–2012

SANTA EMA ★★★★
VARIOUS $22.00–$80.00

2004 Amplus Cabernet Sauvignon	90	2013–2027
2004 Amplus One	91+	2012–2025
2003 Rivalta	90	2013–2028

SANTA RITA ★★★★
VARIOUS $19.00–$60.00

2002 Cabernet Sauvignon Casa Real	94	2012–2032
2002 Cabernet Sauvignon Floresta Apalta	90	now–2017

| 2003 Cabernet Sauvignon Medalla Real | 88 | 2009–2017 |
| 2004 Triple C | 93+ | 2014–2030 |

VIÑA SEÑA * * * * *
ACONCAGUA VALLEY $70.00

Seña was originally a joint venture between Robert Mondavi and Eduardo Chadwick. The first vintage was in 1995, and in 1999 the Seña Hillside Vineyard was purchased. Currently, all the grapes going into Seña come from this biodynamically farmed vineyard. It is planted with Cabernet Sauvignon, Merlot, Carménère, and Cabernet Franc.

2004 Seña	94	2015–2035
2003 Seña	93	2013–2030
2002 Seña	88	now–2012
2001 Seña	90	now–2013
2000 Seña	91	now–2015

VIÑA GARCES SILVA * * * *
LEYDA VALLEY $17.00–$27.00

2005 Amayna Chardonnay	90	now–2010
2005 Amayna Pinot Noir	90	now–2013
2006 Amayna Sauvignon Blanc	92	now–2009

VIÑA TARAPACÁ
* * * MAIPO VALLEY $19.00–$30.00

2004 Cabernet Sauvignon Gran Reserva	89+	2009–2017
2005 Carménère Gran Reserva	85	now–2011
2005 Zavala	90+	2012–2025

MIGUEL TORRES * * *
CURICO VALLEY $34.00–$53.00

| 2003 Conde de Superunda | 92+ | 2015–2030 |
| 2004 Manso de Velasco Cabernet Sauvignon Old Vines | 88 | 2009–2017 |

VALDIVIESO * * *
COLCHAGUA VALLEY $17.00

| 2004 Cabernet Franc Single Vineyard Reserva | 90 | 2009–2017 |
| 2004 Cabernet Sauvignon Single Vineyard Reserva | 89+ | 2010–2020 |

VIÑA VENTISQUERO * * *
MAIPO VALLEY $19.00–$27.00

Ventisquero is one of the larger Chilean wine producers. Their focus on quality is attested to by the fact that Aurelio Montes and John Duval (former head winemaker for Penfolds Grange) are consultants.

| 2005 Cabernet Sauvignon Grey | 87 | now–2015 |
| 2005 Cabernet Sauvignon Quelat Gran Reserva | 87 | now–2013 |

VERAMONTE ★★★
CASABLANCA VALLEY $17.00

2004 Primus	88	now–2012

VIU MANENT ★★★★
COLCHAGUA VALLEY $14.00–$26.00

2005 Cabernet Sauvignon La Capilla Estate	88+	2009–2017
2006 Carménère Secreto	88	now–2012
2005 Carménère Reserva	90	now–2015
2005 Malbec San Carlos Estate	91	2012–2025
2004 Viu 1	92+	2013–2027

VON SIEBENTHAL ★★★★
ACONCAGUA VALLEY $30.00–$60.00

2003 Montelig	90	2012–2025
2004 Montelig	92	2014–2030
2003 Syrah Carabantes	91	now–2018
2004 Syrah Carabantes	92	2010–2020

[israel]

Quietly and without attracting much consumer attention, Israel has developed a wine industry that will confound preconceptions. A country whose wine industry once was largely considered insipid and mostly aimed at satisfying religious needs today has dozens of wineries and a serious enough industry to have a few trophies. That, to be sure, does not mean Israeli wine production is new. Aside from biblical times, Israel has been producing wine since long before it was actually a state. Carmel, Israel's largest winery, was founded by Baron Edmond de Rothschild, the owner of Château Lafite-Rothschild. Carmel traces its roots back to 1882, and it dominated Israel's wine scene for a century.

It is only recently, however, that more than an occasional Israeli wine has attracted serious interest. Even prestigious Golan Heights, an old stalwart familiar for its Yarden label in the U.S., did not begin operating until 1983. Its founding was one of the important landmarks in modern Israeli wine history.

In the generation since Golan Heights' debut, the industry has undergone massive change. While giant Carmel still has a dominating market share, and Carmel, Golan Heights, and Barkan together control about 75% of the marketplace, much of the attention has shifted to Israel's boutique wineries, a relatively new phenomenon. Tiny Margalit, for instance, calls itself Israel's first boutique winery. Its debut vintage, the 1989 Cabernet Sauvignon, was released in 1991. This shouldn't be taken to mean that the larger wineries are bad. Incidentally, Golan Heights is on every short list for Best of Israel, and Carmel is producing small-production, high-quality wines, too, both under its own label and Yatir.

Israel's major wine regions are the Galilee in the north, including the Upper and Lower Galilee and the Golan Heights; Samson; Shomron; the Judean Hills; and the Negev. The Galilee is generally considered the best of Israel's regions, although there are many fine wines from other regions as well, particularly the Judean Hills.

The first issue in dealing with Israeli wines is invariably whether they are kosher. The large wineries generally produce kosher wines, but most of the boutique wineries do not. Importer Haim Hassin of SolStars asserted that there "are close to 200 wineries in Israel and about 150 of them are nonkosher boutique wineries." The total output for the boutique win-

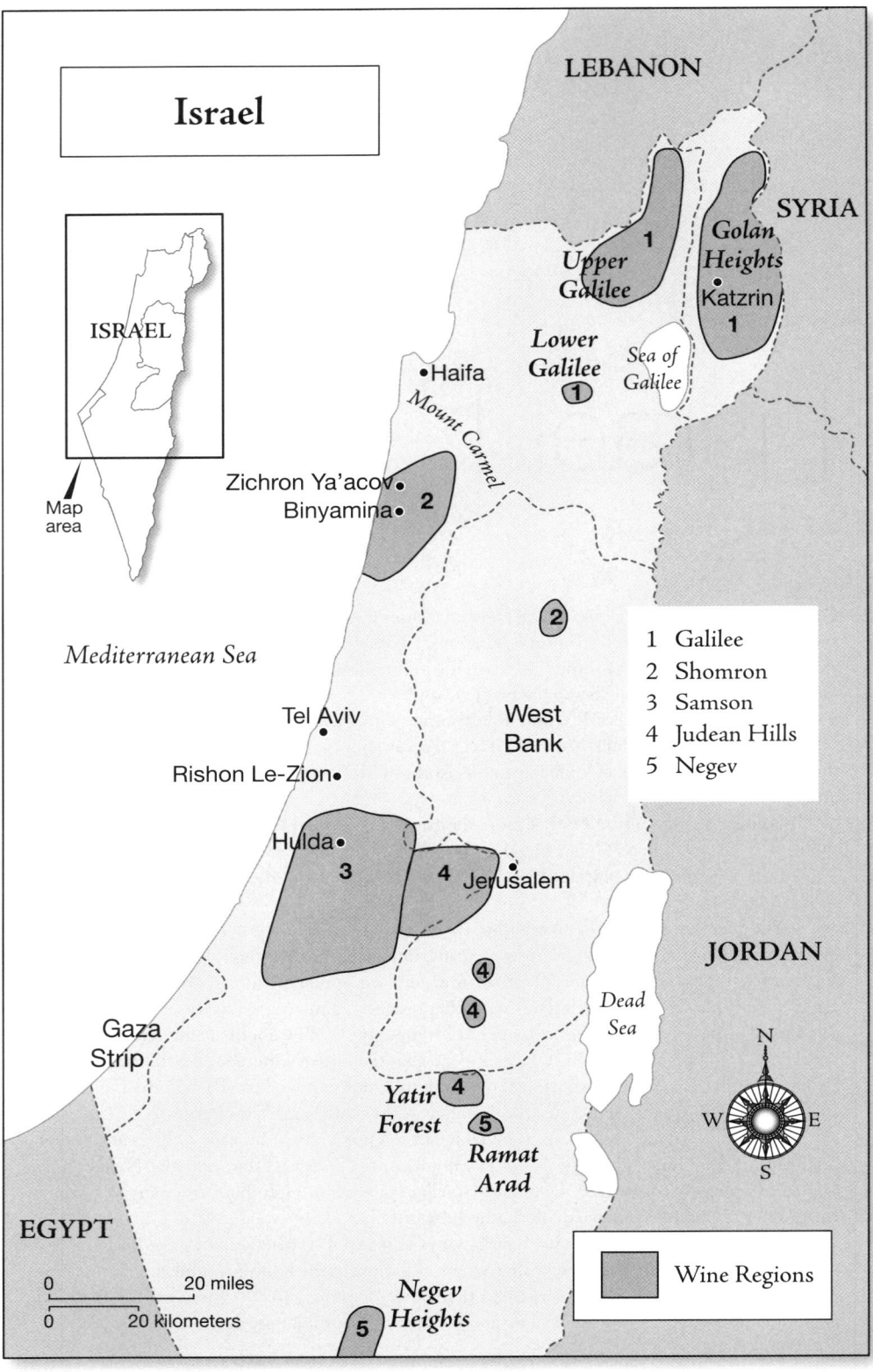

Israel

ISRAEL

Map area

LEBANON

SYRIA

Upper Galilee ①

Golan Heights ①

Katzrin

Lower Galilee ①

Sea of Galilee

Haifa

Mount Carmel

Zichron Ya'acov ②
Binyamina

②

Mediterranean Sea

Tel Aviv

West Bank

1 Galilee
2 Shomron
3 Samson
4 Judean Hills
5 Negev

Rishon Le-Zion

Hulda ③

④

Jerusalem

JORDAN

Gaza Strip

④

④

Dead Sea

N

W   E

S

Yatir Forest ④
⑤
Ramat Arad

EGYPT

0   20 miles
0   20 kilometers

Negev Heights ⑤

Wine Regions

eries is, however, small. It is fair to say that if you are going to be drinking Israeli wines regularly, you will regularly encounter kosher wines. The second and therefore more important issue is what significance a kosher certification has for the nonkosher consumer to whom such wines must be marketed if they are to be considered mainstream products. The simple answer is that no one should avoid wines simply because they have kosher certifications. Based on my tastings, in fact, kosher wines are among the best in this report, such as those from Domaine du Castel and Yatir. Kosher designation seems irrelevant, as long as the wines are not also Mevushal.*

The most important thing to understand is that those sickly sweet Passover wines Americans are used to have nothing to do with the types of wine Israel is bragging about these days. Today, the mainstream wines are more likely to be bottlings of Bordeaux varietals, Chardonnay, or Syrah that have typicity and will seem familiar to sophisticated consumers. The wines can be big and bold, as at Yatir, or graceful and old-world, as at Domaine du Castel. You can put a bag over a Bustan Syrah and watch your friends argue about whether it is a Languedoc or a Rhône. Israeli wine isn't an oddity anymore, and it is certainly not just for those who keep kosher.

[grape varieties]

Many international grapes are grown in Israel, but red Bordeaux varieties (Cabernet Sauvignon, Cabernet Franc, Merlot, and Petit Verdot) are probably the leading grapes for high-end wines. Syrah and Syrah-based blends are popular as well.

For whites, Chardonnay is very popular. You can also find other international grapes such as Viognier and Sauvignon Blanc. Late-harvest wines are often made from Gewürztraminer.

[the wines]

OVERALL QUALITY LEVEL

Clearly, the corner has been turned qualitatively. Israel has a real wine industry that deserves consumer attention. The best are attractive wines with typicity and some distinction. Do some blind tastings and see. Many are classic and charming, and the best will impress anyone.

Bordeaux varietals show great typicity and are usually successful. In terms of quality, these comprise the leading wine category. There are also many popular Shiraz/Syrah-based wines, some of which are quite beautiful. They are more erratic as a group, however, from a typicity standpoint.

---

*Mevushal, a subset of kosher intended to meet additional religious requirements, is controversial. Not all kosher wines are mevushal. A wine listed as mevushal, the so-called "boiled wine," is pasteurized. The mevushal debate includes issues such as how high the heat becomes, at what stage of the winemaking process the heat is applied, whether it affects the taste and ageworthiness of the wine, and so on. For the record, I did one blind taste test with a high-end wine made in both mevushal and nonmevushal fashion. I opened it for a group of professionals. While opinions differed—at least for *drinking on that day*—as to which wine people preferred, there was no question that the wines were different. In particular, the nonmevushal wine was more backward and tannic. In my view, it was also far more likely to develop with cellaring into something more interesting. This controversy is beyond the scope of this article, as it is not a major issue for those seeking out the top Israeli wines, the ones attracting international attention, because even those that are kosher are rarely, if ever, also mevushal. Wines that are mevushal should be clearly indicated as such on the back label. Many kosher wines will also specifically indicate "not mevushal."

Many of the popular Bordeaux blends have green streaks, sometimes subtle, usually tolerable but occasionally off-putting. It is not always a big issue, but there is a pattern of herbaceousness. In some wines, it very much mars the performance.

Most of these wines have a ceiling for a simple reason: Most have little prospect of aging for very long or developing considerable complexity in the cellar. The 2003s were generally drinking beautifully. The 2004s, at three years of age, seemed largely to be drinking well. Even most of the 2005s were quite approachable. Not every good wine has to be a *vin de garde,* but the greatest wines tend to be those that can age a reasonable time, improve, and become more complex in the cellar. However, older Cabernet Sauvignons and Bordeaux blends I had in tastings at wineries like Golan Heights, Castel, and Margalit were superb. They prove not only that Israel can present quality wines but that they have some that can age gracefully for 10 to 15 years. These, to be sure, are not typical. Israel has only a tiny number of wineries that have track records of producing ageworthy wines.

The degree of progress in Israeli wine is impressive, but it is overrated on the home front. When a country's wine industry comes from nowhere, getting to somewhere understandably leads to enthusiasm, but the number of superb wines remains small. Moreover, the boutique wines are often high priced for what they are. At $15 to $30 (U.S.), they would be quite nice and a pleasure to drink. At $50 to $60, few distinguish themselves. There are, of course, some exceptions.

[the best wines from some of israel's best wineries]

Israel already has some wineries well deserving of attention and support. Its best wineries, in no particular order, are Domaine du Castel and Golan Heights (aka Yarden). Yatir (wholly owned by Carmel), and Margalit are contenders. Three of the four (all but Golan Heights) are small-production wineries. Three (all but Yatir) have significant track records. There are many other interesting wineries, some quite small. These include Vitkin, Pelter, Flam, Tulip, Chillag, Galil Mountain, Ella Valley, and Clos de Gat. Recanati is also making big strides and may be a winery to be reckoned with in the future. These producers are committed and passionate, and deliver excellent results. They, along with several others, demonstrate that the next group is about to arrive, if they haven't already.

Note: Some of the small wineries do not have importers. In the following list, some wineries, such as Tulip, estimated prices that the wines might sell for in the U.S., just to provide a guideline. Also, many wines are blended with grapes from different regions, and many wineries have important vineyards in more than one region. Hence, regional designations are frequently omitted.

—MARK SQUIRES

[tasting commentaries]

ALEXANDER
GALILEE PRICE UNKNOWN

Alexander makes wines with fine structure that can age and develop. The 2003 Cabernet Sauvignon is charming and classic, with an old-world feel to it. The 2004 Gaston is a blend of Grenache (12%), Merlot (76%), and Syrah (12%) from different appellations. The Rhône components have a modest percentage here but seem to dominate the wine's flavor profile.

2003 Cabernet Sauvignon (red)	88	now–2012
2004 Gaston (red)	87	now–2012

BEN HANNA WINERY
JUDEAN HILLS $25.00

This winery usually uses Petit Verdot as a blending grape (as some do in Bordeaux), but in this year they decided to bottle it as a single varietal because of its perceived quality. There were only 49 cases produced according to the label, although a fact sheet noted 75. Either way, this microcuvée will be hard to come by. It spent 12 months in French oak, and all the grapes came from Mata Vineyard, first planted in 1996 with other varietals.

2005 Petit Verdot La Mariée (red)	88	now–2013

BUSTAN FAMILY WINERY
JUDEAN HILLS $60.00

This classic Syrah is as varietally true as any Syrah I saw from Israel. It deserves a lot of credit for style, and there is a lot to like here, but the substance could be better. It is also the perfect wine to stick in a blind tasting of French Syrahs. Unfortunately, it is pricey in the U.S. for what it is. This wine is kosher.

2003 Syrah (red)	88	now–2010

CARMEL WINERY
ISRAEL $18.00–$55.00

This familiar winery dating back to 1882 is Israel's largest, once having controlled almost the entire Israeli wine market. Carmel started modern winemaking in Israel and helped stake out the path to serious wine, although it has a bit of a checkered past. One spokesperson described it as the Gallo of Israel. It sells a wide range of products, including sweet kiddush wines. For a long while, Carmel and Israeli wine were more or less synonymous. Carmel still has a huge market share (harvesting about 35% of Israel's grapes), although it has declined over the decades with the founding of many competitors, from Golan Heights to the boutiques. Not surprisingly, Carmel has been reshaping itself, establishing a boutique called Yatir (listed separately here) to turn out high-quality wines and making small-production wines under its own label as well. Its single-vineyard and Limited Edition wines have production runs of only about 1,083 cases each. Carmel is making some fine wines at the high end, and its attention to small-production wines seems to be paying off. These are all kosher.

2004 Cabernet Sauvignon Kayoumi Vineyard (red)	89	now–2014
2005 Gewürztraminer Sha'al Vineyard (white dessert)	90	now–2011
2004 Limited Edition (red)	90	now–2014
2004 Shiraz Kayoumi Vineyard (red)	88	now–2013

CHILLAG
ISRAEL PRICE UNKNOWN

Chillag is a small winery that has a reputation for value in Israel. Owner-winemaker Orna Chillag studied oenology in Milan. Like a lot of the Bordeaux blends from little Israeli wineries, this Merlot Riserva shows typicity. There are notes of tobacco, game, and earth, and I suspect many will be astounded to find that this is Israeli. It opens rather harshly, but it comes around. It feels very much like an old-world Merlot, structured and restrained.

2004 Merlot Riserva Primo (red)	88	now–2013

CLOS DE GAT
JUDEAN HILLS $35.00–$65.00

From the Judean Hills, an appellation generally surrounding Jerusalem, come these wines from Clos de Gat, one of Israel's finer boutique wineries. ("Gat" is an ancient winepress.) The

Chardonnay was one of the nicer ones I tasted, while their top-of-the-line brand, the Syrah Sycra (Aramaic for bright red), was one of the best in that varietal. The proprietary Bordeaux blend, Ayalon, was lovely as well.

2005 Chardonnay (white)	89	now–2010
2003 Red Wine Ayalon Valley	89	now–2013
2005 Syrah Har'el Vineyard (red)	88	now–2013
2004 Syrah Sycra (red)	90	now–2013

DOMAINE DU CASTEL
JERUSALEM-JUDEAN HILLS $40.00–65.00

Domaine du Castel is one of Israel's most prestigious wineries, invariably on most short lists in the "best winery in Israel" debate. Founded in 1988, it produced its first wine in 1992. The winery is a little bigger than some of the microboutiques but still produces only around 8,300 cases a year. There is a French sensibility on the labels, from the winery's name to the identification of the appellation (Judean Hills, near Jerusalem) as Haute Judée. This is not surprising, perhaps, given that Castel is a family-run business, and son Ariel trained in Burgundy, then worked at Domaine Emile Voarick. The Chardonnay is probably the best of that varietal I saw from Israel. The Petit Castel is their second wine—and it is a fine wine in its own right. The Grand Vin is a Bordeaux blend that is a short-list contender for Israel's best such wine. In 2005, the charming Petit Castel may actually be preferred by many over the Grand Vin. However, with time, the gap between them will widen as the Petit Castel declines and the Grand Vin evolves. These are all kosher.

2005 Chardonnay Blanc Du Castel (white)	91	now–2011
2003 Grand Vin (red)	90	now–2013
2004 Grand Vin (red)	92	now–2015
2005 Petit Castel (red)	89	now–2013
2005 Grand Vin (red)	90	now–2016

ELLA VALLEY VINEYARDS
ISRAEL $29.00–$36.00

Ella Valley, started in 1998, has become one of Israel's more prestigious wineries. Winemaker Dron Rav-Hon studied oenology in Burgundy and apprenticed at Domaine Jacques Prieur. Ella Valley currently produces a bit less than 17,000 cases a year, although production is expected to more than double by 2008. The powerful Merlot is gripping. Its intensity is quite remarkable for an Israeli Merlot that is already a few years old, but its development in the decanter is not nearly as impressive. These are kosher.

2005 Chardonnay Vineyard's Choice (white)	87	now–2010
2003 Merlot Vineyard's Choice (red)	88	2009–2015

FLAM
JERUSALEM HILLS $29.00–$49.00

Brothers Golan and Gilad Flam established Flam, one of Israel's well-regarded boutiques, in 1998 in the Jerusalem Hills. Their father studied winemaking in South Africa and then at the University of California at Davis. Golan, the winemaker, studied in Italy, worked for Carpineto in Tuscany, and then worked in Australia. The winery has vineyards in the Upper Galilee and Judean Hills regions. Production runs around 7,000 cases. The Classico is a Bordeaux blend that is lighter and less expensive than the Reserve but quite charming. The Reserve is better structured and impeccably balanced.

| 2004 Cabernet Sauvignon Reserve (red) | 89 | now–2013 |
| 2005 Classico (red) | 87 | now–2012 |

GALIL MOUNTAIN
GALILEE PRICES UNKNOWN

Owned by prestigious Golan Heights Winery in a joint venture with Kibbutz Yiron, Galil Mountain has been attracting some attention on its own. The Yiron is a lovely Bordeaux blend with great typicity, and the Pinot Noir is a very interesting Pinot, along the lines of southern California style. These are kosher.

| 2005 Pinot Noir (red) | 87 | now–2013 |
| 2003 Yiron (red) | 90 | now–2013 |

GOLAN HEIGHTS WINERY
GALILEE $23.00–$121.00

Golan Heights is on most short lists for the title "best winery in Israel." It is one of Israel's larger wineries, with about 20% of the local market share. Some of its vineyards were first planted in 1976, and the winery's 1983 founding was a landmark and turning point in Israel's development into a country that produces wines that can compete in the world marketplace. It is not one of the trendy boutiques, obviously, but the quality level is high and few have as much prestige. Golan Heights is perhaps best known for its flagship subsidiary Yarden with the familiar ancient oil lamp design on the label. (*Yarden* is Hebrew for Jordan, as in the Jordan River.) In addition to Yarden, it also owns Galil Mountain Winery and the Gamla and Golan brands. The wines from Yarden seem generally restrained and elegant in terms of tannins and depth, although not always in terms of oak treatment. The tannins are usually refined and well integrated. The upper-level wines can be pricey for what they are. The El Rom is $59.99, the Katzrin is $120.99, and the Gewürztraminer is $22.99 for 375ml. The Katzrin is beautifully balanced and harmonious, drinking well through day 2. The Gewürztraminer is succulent and hedonistic, unctuous and ripe. The El Rom is seriously structured but perhaps not entirely in balance. These are kosher.

2003 Cabernet Sauvignon El Rom Vineyard		
(Yarden) (red)	88	now–2012
2005 Gewürztraminer Heights Wine Harvest (Yarden)		
(white dessert)	93	now–2011
2003 Katzrin (Yarden) (red)	91	now–2015

MARGALIT
ISRAEL $50.00–$60.00

Margalit, located between Tel Aviv and Haifa in the Mediterranean Coast area, produced its first vintage in 1989, releasing 80 cases of a Cabernet Sauvignon in 1991. Margalit calls itself the first boutique winery in Israel. Annual production today is still only about 1,500 cases. Owners Yatir Margalit and son Assaf emphasize Bordeaux varietals. The Cabernet Franc has an old-world feel, along with streaks of green. The Cabernet Sauvignon is light and bright, friendly and appealing. The Enigma is a Bordeaux blend, harmonious and utterly charming. The best wines are the Special Reserves, which can be quite exotic.

2005 Cabernet Franc Binyamina Vineyard (red)	88	now–2013
2005 Cabernet Sauvignon Kadita Vineyard (red)	87	now–2013
2005 Enigma (red)	89	now–2014
2002 Cabernet Sauvignon Special Reserve (red)	90	now–2017

PELTER
ISRAEL $50.00

Tal Pelter is the owner winemaker here. He started Pelter in 2002. Previously, he worked at Evans & Tate in Australia, among other places. Production should shortly reach 2,500 to 3,333 cases. The T-Selection brand is Pelter's top of the line. Grapes come from a variety of regions and vineyards. This Shiraz has charm, flavor, and structure. It is a promising offering.

2004 Shiraz T-Selection (red)	90	now–2013

SASLOVE WINERY
GALILEE $35.00

Saslove was founded in 1998 by Canadian immigrant Barry Saslove, who eventually became an Israeli wine educator. Saslove's wines all come with synthetic corks. All of its vineyards are from the Upper Galilee, about 800 meters above sea level. The 2003 Cabernet Sauvignon Reserved (yes, the label says "Reserved," not "Reserve") is elegant and already drinking quite well. There is not much complexity here, but it is a pleasure to drink in many respects and usually exceptionally charming. There were approximately 229 cases made.

2003 Cabernet Sauvignon Reserved (red)	88	now–2013

TABOR
GALILEE $37.00

Mes'ha is the name of the Tabor village established in 1901 in the region. This is a blend of Cabernet Sauvignon (82%), Merlot (10%), and Shiraz (8%). At this point in its evolution, it is quite approachable, although it is youthful and lively and packs a punch. Its juicy fruit is delicious. This is kosher.

2003 Mes'ha (red)	89	now–2012

TULIP
UPPER GALILEE $23.00–$27.00

Tulip is a small, family-owned winery, with a total production of about 60,000 bottles at the moment, although some expansion is contemplated. The Mostly Shiraz showed far better after an hour or so and actually becomes rather pleasant, with some succulence on the finish and some grip. It is a pretty good value that has a bit more class than seems apparent from a quick taste. The Syrah Reserve is from Israel's northernmost vineyard, Kfar Yuval. It also contains 10% Cabernet Sauvignon from a Judean Hills vineyard. It is a wine that has the structure that the Mostly Shiraz needs. It has a bright finish, typicity, and more of a French style. These are some of the best values in Israel.

2005 Mostly Shiraz (red)	88	now–2012
2005 Syrah Reserve (red)	90	now–2014

TZORA VINEYARDS
UPPER GALILEE $27.00

Tzora's 2006 Or Dessert Wine is one of the most pleasing late-harvest wines I saw from Israel. It is a Gewürztraminer that is just denominated as Or Dessert Wine on the front. This is youthful, exuberant, and sweet, as you might expect, but it is not just a thick fruit bomb. For one thing, it isn't that thick, relatively speaking. For another, there is rather good acidity here, and the wine has some crispness after it airs out a little. It also has a lingering, succulent finish. This wine is kosher.

2006 Or Dessert Wine (white dessert)	92	now–2011

VITKIN WINERY
JUDEAN HILLS $30.00

This is another of Israel's tiny boutiques and one of the newer ones. The team is wife Sharona, an architect, who designed the winery; husband Doron, who calls himself an autodidact, came late to winemaking, and says he fell in love with wine in Italy; and brother-in-law Assaf, who studied in Bordeaux and has worked for several wineries. Their home, they say, is situated between a small vineyard and a cowshed in the Sharon region of Israel. Production began in 2001, with just 200 bottles of Cabernet Sauvignon. They currently produce around 2,500 cases. The future looks bright for this innovative winery. This was about the best use of Petite Sirah that I saw in Israeli wine, and the Riesling was charming.

2004 Petite Syrah (red)	89	now–2014
2006 Riesling (white)	87	now–2009

YATIR
JUDEAN HILLS $28.00–$60.00

Yatir is a winery situated in the Yatir Forest in the southern Judean Hills region. Founded in 2000, it is now wholly owned by Carmel Winery. Winemaker Eran Goldwasser studied wine-making in Australia, and yes, these wines have a certain Barossa feel to them. The wines are bold and ripe but also well balanced and structured. Yatir has a sense of history, reporting that artifacts in the area allow scientists to trace wine production in the region back some 2,500 years. The wines here are very modern, though, and this winery looks to be a future short-list contender for "best winery in Israel" and producer of "Israel's best Bordeaux blend." The proprietary red wine is a Bordeaux blend from the Yatir Forest area, and the Cabernet-Merlot-Shiraz is one of the best values I saw in Israeli wine. These wines are kosher.

2003 Cabernet-Merlot-Shiraz (red)	90	now–2013
2003 Red Wine Yatir Forest (red)	93	now–2015

OTHER WINERIES

Israel has a large number of other wineries whose wines are worth trying. These include, in no particular order, Avidan, Barkan and its sister winery Segal, Karmei Yosef (Bravdo), Dalton, Binyamina, Sea Horse, Amphorae (known as Marvah in the U.S.), Benhaim, Agur, Gustavo & Jo, Chateau Golan, Meishar, Recanati, and Tanya.

[new zealand]

Over the last five or six years, New Zealand's wine industry has witnessed a remarkable rise in productivity as well as in quality and regional diversification, a trend that seems to accelerate with each passing year. Producers have learned the subtleties of their *terroir,* planted appropriate clones and varieties, and have shared intellectual knowledge, all of which has helped eradicate much of the underripeness that afflicted too many of New Zealand's wines. Now wines tend to be riper and more complex, while characteristics between subregions have become more recognized. As increasing numbers of vineyards reach maturity, their vines are finally able to fully exploit the long, cool, maritime-influenced growing season. Meanwhile, growers themselves are broadening their horizons by experimenting with new techniques and grape varieties. Both the North Island and South Island are home to world-famous wine regions, their differences in latitude engendering diverse styles of wine.

[wine regions]

NORTH ISLAND

AUCKLAND Just 3% of New Zealand's vineyards lie in Auckland. Improvements in vineyard techniques have bettered the quality of wines in subregions such as Waiheke Island, Clevedon, and Matakana. The region is producing some fine Bordeaux-style blends.

GISBORNE Lying on the east coast, this region was severely affected by phylloxera. But the silver lining is that vast tracts of Müller-Thurgau were replaced by Chardonnay, whose wines veer toward a more tropical style. Perhaps it is no surprise to find Gewurztraminer is also suc-

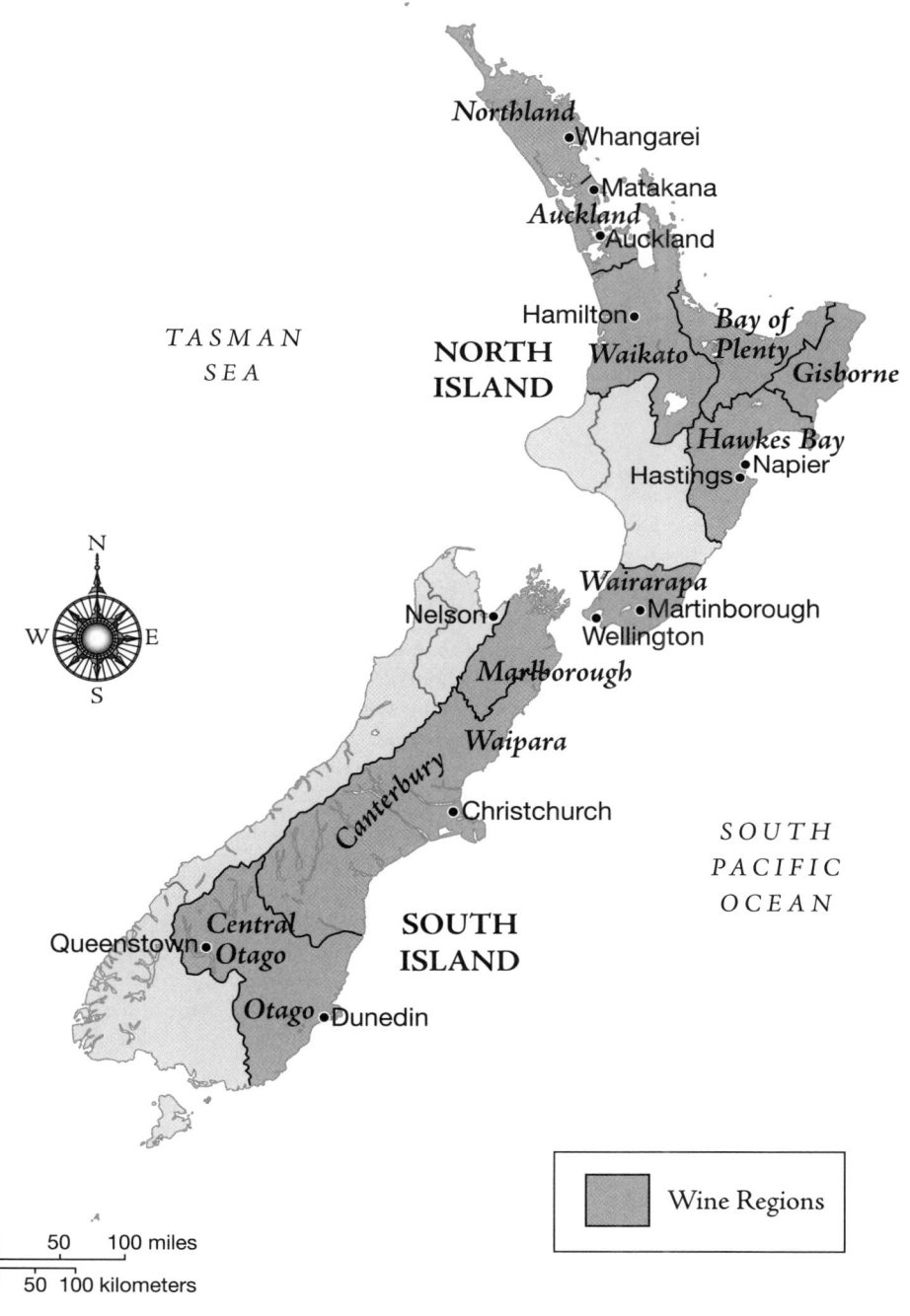

New Zealand

Northland
•Whangarei

•Matakana

Auckland
•Auckland

Hamilton•

Bay of Plenty

TASMAN SEA

NORTH ISLAND

Waikato

Gisborne

Hawkes Bay
•Napier

Hastings•

Wairarapa
•Martinborough

Nelson•

Wellington

Marlborough

Waipara

Canterbury

•Christchurch

SOUTH PACIFIC OCEAN

Central Otago
Queenstown•

SOUTH ISLAND

Otago
•Dunedin

N
W • E
S

| | Wine Regions |

0   50   100 miles

0   50   100 kilometers

cessfully cultivated here. The region has a tradition of contract growers selling their crops to the Auckland wineries, but more boutique operations are beginning to prosper.

HAWKE'S BAY An esoteric array of wines are produced in Hawke's Bay, thanks to a complex mosaic of soil and mesoclimates and a topography that ranges from vast fertile plains to well-drained gravelly soils able to nurture high-quality fruit (for example, the Gimblett Gravels district). Chardonnay and Merlot are grown in large quantities. The cool climate of the region engenders a slightly herbaceous quality to some of the Bordeaux blends. The Sauvignon Blancs tend to have less pungency on the nose and lower acidity than their Marlborough counterparts.

NORTHLAND After decades of declining production, the region has recently begun to see an increase. Being the most northerly region, Northland suffers from high levels of rain and humidity, making crops more prone to fungal diseases. Currently, there are fewer than a dozen wineries, most of which specialize in later-ripening varieties that are less prone to rot, such as Cabernet Sauvignon.

WAIRARAPA Situated at the southern extreme of the North Island, Wairarapa is home to the well-known region of Martinborough and a plethora of boutique wineries striving for low yields and high quality. The climate is a little cooler than in Marlborough with greater diurnal temperature variation. Here one finds some of the best Pinot Noirs and high-performing, relatively tannic Cabernet Sauvignons that often impart meaty, sometimes chocolate-tinged flavors.

SOUTH ISLAND

CANTERBURY Centered around the town of Christchurch, Canterbury is a cool, dry region that is susceptible to early- and late-season frost. It is most widely known for its subregion Waipara, whose cool climate is suitable for growing Chardonnay and Pinot Noir. Small parcels produce Riesling and Pinot Gris.

CENTRAL OTAGO The most southerly of vineyards, the region is the only one influenced by a continental climate, marked by many hours of sunshine and high diurnal temperature variations. Its hillsides are home to Pinot Noir, which constitutes around three-quarters of plantings. The wines tend toward the more intense, fruit-driven style, especially in the Bannockburn and Lowburn areas. There is immense variation in microclimate between subregions; for example, Bendigo is the warmest, Gibbston the coolest.

MARLBOROUGH The largest wine region in New Zealand, Marlborough found international fame thanks to Cloudy Bay in the mid-1980s. Most of the Wairau Valley is now under vine, while the more southerly Awatere Valley is rapidly filling up. Home to a large number of contracted grape producers, the region is known for its intense gooseberry, lime, and tropical fruit–infused Sauvignon Blanc, with Pinot Noir now more widely cultivated than Chardonnay. The Pinots tend toward raspberry and plum flavors, with well-defined structures and tannic backbone. There are also expanding plantations of Riesling. Some of the Chardonnay and Pinot Noir are used to make sparkling wine.

NELSON The most northerly wine region of the South Island, Nelson is the warmest in New Zealand with the surrounding mountains creating a mild, sunny climate. Nelson is home to Sauvignon Blanc, augmented by Pinot Noir, Chardonnay, and a little Riesling. Wines tend to be fragrant and supple with signature flavors of cherry, wild strawberry, and plum.

[grape varieties]

Two grape varieties have become synonymous with New Zealand. The first is Sauvignon Blanc, for which the country has carved out a niche in many international markets, serving as a viable alternative to the ubiquitous Chardonnay. The second is Pinot Noir, which has become a serious challenger to the supremacy of Burgundy. Waiting in the wings are Riesling, Pinot Gris, Syrah, and, of course, Cabernet Sauvignon, which are sure to expand over the next decade. Few countries rival New Zealand in terms of experimenting with new varieties, evaluating their success in rigorous blind tastings, and exchanging information between growers.

WHITES

SAUVIGNON BLANC This grape has become synonymous with New Zealand, a key player in the country's international success. Presently, it comprises 40% of plantings in New Zealand, which equates to 8,860 hectares (21,884 acres), 87% of which is in Marlborough. The cool climate allows it to ripen slowly, especially in Marlborough, where subregions have their own typicity: ripe, passion fruit flavors from the Rapaura District and more herbaceous flavors from Awatere Valley. Nelson tends to produce the more minerally, gooseberry-infused Sauvignon Blanc, while the flavors are more acidic in Canterbury and tropical in Hawke's Bay, Wairarapa, and Central Otago.

CHARDONNAY There has been a radical increase in Chardonnay plantings in recent years, primarily in Hawke's Bay, Gisborne, and Marlborough, with a total of 3,779 hectares (9,334 acres) planted. New Zealand's cooler climate and longer growing season often allow Chardonnay to develop more complexity and nuance than in other new-world countries. The more judicious use of new oak and the willingness to experiment with wild ferments has led to some outstanding Chardonnays that tend toward lush and peachy in the North Island and more zesty in the south.

RIESLING This remains a rather peripheral grape in New Zealand with just 853 hectares (2,107 acres) under vine, mainly in Marlborough and Canterbury. The majority of wines are fermented to leave just a little residual sugar. They tend to have more acidity and definition than their Australian counterparts, although they rarely develop a petrol character that defines German Rieslings. Rieslings from Waipara tend to be citrusy, while those from Marlborough are spicier.

GEWURZTRAMINER Although Gewurztraminer is a minority white grape variety with 284 hectares (701 acres) under vine, there are some exciting ones being produced by a small cluster of growers who know how to avoid its tendency to become blowsy. Wines tend to be pungent and spicy with a prevalent lychee character.

PINOT GRIS Like Gewurztraminer, a small number of growers are producing some fine Italian-style Pinot Gris aimed for early drinking. The wines tend toward flavors of apple, honeysuckle, apricot, and apple. Presently, there are 762 hectares (1,882 acres) under vine, the majority in Marlborough.

REDS

PINOT NOIR Where practically every wine region outside Burgundy has tried and failed to harness this capricious grape, New Zealand has almost staked its reputation on it with presently 4,063 hectares (10,036 acres) under vine (37% in Marlborough and 24% in Central Otago). Central Otago has attracted the most attention with a proliferation of boutique wineries over the last decade. Their Pinots tend to have darker-fruit characters rather than the cherry-infused styles from Marlborough.

CABERNET SAUVIGNON The underripe, green Cabernet Sauvignons have become a thing of the past as growers have gotten a grip on this noble grape variety, although there are still only 531 hectares (1,312 acres) planted, three-quarters of which are in Hawke's Bay. The top boutique wineries produce wines that deserve international acclaim, although they tend to veer away from the more hedonistic, fruit-driven style. Their wines are leafier with higher acidity and definition. Like Bordeaux, Cabernet Sauvignon is often blended with Merlot, Cabernet Franc, or Malbec.

MERLOT Although Merlot is often used to complement and soften other Bordeaux varietals, there are some fine Merlot-dominated wines produced in regions such as Hawke's Bay. Planting is wider than Cabernet Sauvignon with 1,420 hectares (3,507 acres) under vine.

SYRAH In New Zealand, there is enormous potential for Syrah, which would have become extinct but for Dr. Alan Limmer (now of Stonecroft Wines), who saved some cuttings from a condemned vineyard. Some exceptional full-bodied, peppery styles are emerging from the best producers. It is still comparatively small in production with just 214 hectares (529 acres) under vine, mainly in Hawke's Bay.

[the wines]

With New Zealand being a relative newcomer, the country is yet to establish a global reputation for wines that can not only age but also evolve into something unique with the passing of time. But it soon will.

With respect to white grape varieties and Sauvignon Blanc in particular, shelf life is limited to one or two years. Dry Sauvignon Blanc can age, but I find little reason why one would wish to forgo its virtue of primal pungency, freshness, and zest. In terms of longevity, perhaps Chardonnay or some of the aromatic varieties have more potential, since growers are finally handling the variety with more care and prudence.

Naturally, red grape varieties are what hold the most promise in terms of aging, and those wineries beginning to establish a track record show immense promise. Mature wines from the likes of Felton Road and Te Mata's Coleraine suggest that the top New Zealand wines can age well, but for a majority, whether the nuances and secondary flavors are worth waiting for is something that will be revealed with time.

But with such improvement in quality, I believe recent vintages will merit cellaring. Two factors are worth considering: First, the longevity of New Zealand wines will surely be enhanced by both the maturing of vines and current advances in viticultural techniques. Second, a tasting of 20-year-old Pinot Noirs and Cabernets will be a true test of the wines' ability to age under screw cap rather than cork, since 90%–95% of bottlings now use this closure. A summary of grapes' drinking plateaus is presented below.

AGING POTENTIAL
Cabernet Sauvignon: 4–15 years
Chardonnay: 2–8 years
Gewurztraminer: 1–3 years
Merlot: 3–8 years
Pinot Gris: 1–2 years
Pinot Noir: 3–15 years
Riesling: 2–8 years

Sauvignon Blanc: 1–3 years
Syrah: 3–10 years

OVERALL QUALITY LEVEL

There is little doubt that the quality of New Zealand wines has increased dramatically in a short time: This is a wine industry focused on quality rather than quantity. Some accuse New Zealand of producing masses of cleanly made, technically correct wines but few complex, profound wines. I agree with this to an extent: Certainly the country has built its success on dependable, consistent Sauvignon Blancs and Merlots that satisfy demand, but each year more wineries are being feted as world-class producers. As in Burgundy, the name of the producer is crucial, perhaps more so than region or vintage. There are many New Zealand Pinot Noirs equivalent to premier cru Burgundy, but it takes time to create a truly profound wine equivalent to a top grand cru. However, in terms of quality-to-price ratio, New Zealand would win hands down, and given the acceleration of quality, it would give me no surprise to find a cluster of top growers inching closer to profound greatness.

IMPORTANT INFORMATION

With few international brands (Montana and Villa Maria being the most conspicuous), New Zealand is a treasure trove of small boutique, hands-on wineries. Therefore, consumers should spend time familiarizing themselves with the styles of the regions and then narrow their buying decision toward individual producers. This is such a dynamic country that there are always new names being promulgated by the media, eager to thrust their new discovery into the limelight. It sometimes gives an impression that any bottle bearing the New Zealand label will be outstanding, but one must always remember that this is a marginal climate. The weather is a constant threat to quality, and some of the more peripheral vineyards are still in their infancy. To put it prosaically, things go wrong, and some commentators believe that the almost insatiable drive to establish new vineyards is leading to plantings on land unsuitable for sustainable production.

The small nature of many wineries means that many seek to maintain sustainable viticulture, and a program was implemented as early as 1993 to establish this across the industry. At the time of this writing, only one producer has been certified biodynamic (Millton Vineyard), although I am certain this will increase, with others such as Seresin, Pyramid Valley, and Felton Road applying a complete regime of biodynamic techniques.

BUYING STRATEGY

While Sauvignon Blanc has been phenomenally successful in the U.K., figures show that the U.S. market is embracing these wines in similar fashion, so expect a proliferation of these wines over the next five years with regional variations becoming more entrenched. Chardonnay has improved dramatically as growers' use of new oak becomes commensurate with the wine. Some are eschewing new oak entirely and experimenting more with wild ferments that often lead to more individuality. Many are excited by the prospects of aromatic varieties. Plantings of Riesling, Gewurztraminer, and Pinot Gris have increased by 369% since 1999, the latter to the delight of consumers seeking innocuous wines and to the chagrin of some critics who regard it as a second-rate variety.

Pinot Noir will continue its rapid elevation in consumers' minds as a source of outstanding wines that rival established names from the Old World. Already producers such as Mt Difficulty, Felton Road, Neudorf, Rippon Vineyard, Ata Rangi, and Martinborough Vineyard are creating outstanding wines that deserve global recognition. Perhaps a more exciting prospect is the quality of Syrah: Examples from Craggy Range and Te Mata have demonstrated that New Zealand can produce cool, very northern Rhône–like wines with a softer, more silky textured palate in a similar vein to Côte de Rhône.

[recent vintages]

2007
Despite a depleted crop for growers, especially in terms of Marlborough Sauvignon Blanc, the rapid expansion of vineyard acreage could mean that the overall quantity is higher than ever. Early indications are for a good-quality vintage in Hawke's Bay and Gisborne.

2006
Early flowering and new plantings coming onstream produced a large vintage. The growing season was excellent, but in late March, the threat of cyclone Wati coerced some growers to harvest their red grapes early (most of the whites were already picked). Wati never hit land, so those who took the risk and waited were rewarded with clement harvest conditions. Overall this is a high-quality vintage.

2005
The harvest yielded a slight reduction in quantity compared with 2004, but it is high in quality thanks to prolonged, dry late-summer weather. Reds tend to be superior to whites; they are deep in color with relatively higher levels of alcohol. Some regions such as Hawke's Bay and Martinborough suffered from rain, while frost afflicted Canterbury. Central Otago is patchier than usual.

2004
This year marked New Zealand's largest crop ever, but February rain compromised quality. It was generally a cool growing season redeemed by warmer temperatures toward harvest, leading to wines that are variable. Some Sauvignon Blancs are excessively high in acidity, while some reds, especially Cabernet Sauvignon, were unable to obtain full ripeness.

2003
A small vintage was the result of severe frost damage, particularly in Hawke's Bay, but less so in areas such as Central Otago. It was a better vintage for the South Island, which suffered less rain than did the North. The South Island produced some outstanding Sauvignon Blancs from a depleted crop.

2002
This great vintage was marked by a long spell of hot, dry weather. It was especially fine in Central Otago and Gisborne.

2001
A terrible vintage resulted for the North Island, who found salvation only with the later-ripening varieties that benefited from late warm summer weather.

2000
This was generally a variable vintage, better on the South Island than on the North.

Inconsistent quality marked the vintage, with wines slightly better on the South Island.

Some great red wines were produced thanks to the long, hot, dry summer, although many are now past their best.

—NEAL MARTIN

[the ratings]

NEW ZEALAND'S BEST PRODUCERS

★ ★ ★ ★ ★ (OUTSTANDING)

Ata Rangi
Felton Road Wines
Pegasus Bay (whites)

Rippon Vineyard & Winery
Te Mata Estate (Coleraine)

★ ★ ★ ★ ★ (EXCELLENT)

Bell Hill Vineyard
Bilancia
Craggy Range Winery ★★★★/★★★★★
Dog Point Vineyards
Dry River Wines
Esk Valley Estate
Kumeu River Winery ★★★★/★★★★★
Martinborough Vineyard ★★★★/★★★★★
Millton Vineyard ★★★★/★★★★★
Mt Difficulty Wines
Neudorf Vineyards

Palliser Estate ★★★★
Pyramid Valley Vineyards
Sacred Hill Wines
Seresin Estate
Te Awa Winery
Terravin
Trinity Hill ★★★★/★★★★★
Vidal Wines
Vinoptima Estate
Unison Vineyard

★ ★ ★ (GOOD)

Akarua Winery
Alan McCorkindale
Alan Scott Wines ★★★/★★★★
Alana Estate
Alpha Domus ★★★/★★★★
Amisfield Wine Company
Anthem Wine Company ★★★/★★★★
Aurum Wines
Babich Wines ★★★/★★★★
Benfield & Delamare ★★★/★★★★
Bridge Pa Vineyard
Burnt Spur
Bushmere Estate
Cable Bay Vineyards
Carrick Wines
Chard Farm ★★★/★★★★
Church Road Winery ★★★/★★★★
CJ Pask Winery ★★★/★★★★
Cloudy Bay Vineyards ★★★/★★★★

Coopers Creek
Corbans Wines
Crossroads Winery
Daniel Schuster Wines
Delta Vineyard
Eradus ★★★
Escarpment Vineyard ★★★/★★★★
Framingham Wine Company
Fromm Winery ★★★/★★★★
Gibbston Valley Wines
Goldwater Estate
Grasshopper Rock
Greenhough Vineyard & Winery
Hatton Estate ★★★
Hawkshead Vineyard ★★★/★★★★
Clos Henri ★★★
Herzog
Highfield Estate
Hunter's ★★★

Judge Rock
Julicher Estate
Kahurangi Estate
Kawarau Estate ***/****
Kemblefield Estate Winery
Kim Crawford Wines
Lamont Wines
Lawson's Dry Hills
Lowburn Ferry Vineyard
Mahi Wines ***/****
Man O'War Vineyards
Matakana Estate ***
Matariki Wines ***/****
Mills Reef Winery
Montana Wines
Mount Dottrel
Mount Edward Winery
Mountford Estate ***/****
Mudbrick Vineyard
Muddy Water ***/****
Murdoch James
Nautilus Estate
Ngatawara Wines
Passage Rock Wines ***/****
Pegasus Bay (reds)
Peninsula Estate
Peregrine Wines ***/****
Pisa Range Estate

Quartz Reef ***/****
Rockburn Wines
Saint Clair Estate Wines
Clos de Ste. Anne ***/****
Seifried ***
Sherwood ***
Sileni Estates
Spy Valley Wines
Staete Landt Vineyards
Steve Bird Winery ***/****
Stonecroft Wines
Stonyridge Vineyard ***/****
Te Hera Estate
Te Whau Vineyard
Tohu Wines
Two Paddocks
Valli Vineyards ***/****
Villa Maria ***/****
Waimea Estates
Waipara Springs ***/****
Wairau River Wines
Weeping Sands
Wild Earth Wines
William Thomas Wines
Wither Hills Vineyards ***/****
Wooing Tree Vineyard
Woollaston Estates

[south africa]

Since the abolition of apartheid and the first democratic elections in 1994, the South African wine industry has strived to become one of the eminent new-world wine producers. Echoing the country's political rebirth, the South African renaissance has not been unproblematic. The epidemic of leafroll virus, accusations of flavorants such as pyrazine within Sauvignon Blanc, and divisive opinions on the Pinotage grape are but three factors that have hampered (but not thwarted) the immense progress that has been made. There is no doubt that there is a move toward quality rather than quantity, and while there is still some way to go, there are fewer instances of innocuous whites or reds that are paradoxically sweet and alcoholic but undeniably green. There is a cluster of wineries that have justifiably attained global recognition, and their success is inspiring others, in particular young, dynamic winemakers, in a similar direction.

[wine regions]

The W.O. (Wine of Origin) is the equivalent of the French AOC system. South Africa consists of three tiers with W.O. regions split into districts, which can be split into specific wards. Below are listed the most common W.O.s that are synonymous with quality wine (mostly within the Coastal Region W.O.). W.O.-labeled wines must be sourced 100% from the named region, while stated grape varieties must constitute 85% of the final blend (until 2006 it was 75%).

CONSTANTIA A historic region, Constantia is the site of the wine estate whose Muscat-based dessert wines were as revered as first growths in the early 19th century. Located on a peninsula just outside Cape Town, this region benefits from summers that are cooled by sea breezes from two directions. Of the five producers located in Constantia, the most famous is Klein Constantia, which entered a new and hopefully more fruitful era with the appointment of Adam Mason since the 2004 vintage. Expect more wineries to appear in the next few years.

[1461]

STELLENBOSCH Home of the famous Stellenbosch University, this region includes five wards, each with its own characteristics in terms of soils and mesoclimates: Devon Valley, Bottelary, Simonsberg-Stellenbosch, Papegaaiberg, and Jonkershoek Valley. Generally the region is cooled by Atlantic breezes, so that summer temperatures average just over 20°C (68°F). Red varieties, including Bordeaux blends and Shiraz, thrive upon the eastern granite-based soils, while superb Chardonnay and some Sauvignon Blanc–based wines are cultivated in cooler areas on western sandstone.

PAARL This well-known region is situated northeast of Stellenbosch and home to numerous wineries as well as KWV. The best vineyards are located at altitude since the climate is warm, with an emphasis toward Shiraz and Merlot. Some cooler mesoclimates are home to Sauvignon Blanc and Sémillon. Franschhoek is the widely known ward with some high-quality wines from the likes of Graham Beck Wine, Boekenhoutskloof, and Chamonix.

SWARTLAND Located northwest of Paarl, this region has great potential with its cooling maritime breeze, granite soils, and tracts of old dry vines. It is home to Spice Route Company and Sadie Family Wines.

ROBERTSON Located west of Worcester within the Breede River Valley, most of the vineyards flank the river for irrigation, for this is a dry, warm region well known for its Chardonnays and Muscat.

WALKER BAY A cooler region, thanks to the more maritime-influenced climate—with some commendable Burgundy-inspired wines made from Chardonnay and Pinot Noir—Walker Bay is most notable for being home to Hamilton Russell Vineyards and Bouchard Finlayson.

ELGIN A relative newcomer located east of Cape Town, Elgin's high-altitude vineyards produce some fine Sauvignon Blanc, with increasing emphasis upon Pinot Noir.

WORCESTER The mainly fertile soils located within the Breede River Valley region produce around one-quarter of South Africa's crop, which are dominated by cooperatives, with most wine used for fortification or distillation. Despite extensive planting of Colombard and Chenin Blanc, Worcester is more noteworthy for some award-winning fortified wines.

Other notable W.O.s include Tulbagh, Overberg, Elim, Durbanville, and Darling.

[grape varieties]

CHENIN BLANC According to recent statistics, Chenin Blanc covers only 18.7% of vine plantings, where it once stood at approximately one-third. They were predominantly sweet and rather unmemorable, but some progress has been made toward drier, more complex wines cultivated in cooler mesoclimates.

CHARDONNAY Once subject to excessive oak aging, especially in the 1990s, South African Chardonnays have certainly come on leaps and bounds in the last five or six years as more appropriate sites have been found. Presently around 8% of vineyards are planted with Chardonnay, still less than Colombard (11.4%).

SAUVIGNON BLANC Although covering 8.2% of vineyard area, South Africa's Sauvignon Blancs have veered toward the more herbaceous style. Whether they can export the grape globally as well as New Zealand remains to be seen.

SÉMILLON Despite occupying 1.1% of vineyard area, Sémillons have shown great promise among a small cluster of growers, such as Boekenhoutskloof and Steenberg.

PINOT NOIR Only 0.6% of South African vineyards dare to cultivate capricious Pinot Noir, and so far the results have been unimpressive, with the exception of Hamilton Russell.

PINOTAGE Synonymous with South Africa, Pinotage covers only 6.2% of vineyard plantings. A cross between Cinsault and Pinot Noir, it is a grape that you either love or hate. Personally, this writer is not enamored, although, to be fair, some recent Pinotage has shown less tendency to reek of bubblegum, acetate, or Wellington boots. Perhaps if it can be cultivated in cooler areas, the wines will continue to improve, and it can be a useful blending component.

CABERNET SAUVIGNON Many South African premium wines are Cabernet or Cabernet-based. Around 13.1% of vines are dedicated to this noble grape, although the best results are usually found when blended with Bordeaux varieties such as Merlot, Cabernet Franc, or Malbec. They tend to be very structured, ripe, and tannic, but, thanks to the warm climate, can be endowed with immense fruit concentration.

MERLOT With 6.7% under vine, South African Merlot has tended to be very patchy in terms of ripeness, although producers such as Thelema have demonstrated that with a little care and application, they can create supple, lithe Merlot-based wines.

SYRAH Although less than 10% of vineyards are planted with Syrah, in recent years, as in New Zealand, there has been a rapid expansion of planting. There is great potential when Syrah is planted in the right areas and tended by conscientious winemakers, for example at the Vergelegen and Rust en Vrede estates.

[the wines]

AGING POTENTIAL

White wines should be consumed immediately after bottling, or at least within 12 months, with the exception of a few barrel-fermented Chardonnays, some of the premium Chenin Blancs, or perhaps some of the lots auctioned by the Cape Winemakers Guild. The general rule for South African red wines is to drink them sooner rather than later, ideally between one and four years after bottling. As with other new-world countries, their wines can excel in terms of their youthful fruitiness and vibrancy, virtues that should be reluctantly forsaken. However, certainly the top Cabernets and Syrahs have the potential to last up to a decade and evolve secondary nuances that make cellaring worthwhile, and their number will increase for the reasons mentioned below.

OVERALL QUALITY LEVEL

Much like that other southern-hemisphere wine country, New Zealand, there has been a phenomenal expansion in just the last ten years, although one could argue that South Africa's has been a greater struggle given its starting position. Leafroll virus continues to be an issue, though experienced, conscientious growers have been successful at identifying affected vines and eradicating them from the fermentation vat. The problem is that more commercial, volume-oriented brands are not so picky, and consequently lower-priced brands are often made with fruit that has not reached phenolic ripeness, lending the final wine an unsavory greenness.

On the other hand, there are many positives to consider. First, one must consider that many of the vines are still young: At present only 17% of vines are more than 20 years of age, but as they mature, the quality of their fruit will inevitably improve. The second factor is knowledge. South African winemakers have been "feeling their way," learning about their own *terroir* and cultivating appropriate grape varieties and clones that will maximize potential. In this respect, improvements in clonal material are proving to be crucial. Winemakers are honing their craft both in the vineyard and in the winery, especially regarding the art of using American and French oaks through both the intrawinery exchange of information and by working overseas. All these factors have raised the quality of South African wine and are sure to have a greater influence.

There is a growing emphasis toward establishing deluxe premium brands, such as Vilafonté's Series C and Rustenberg's Peter Barlow Cabernet. These tend toward full-bodied, sinewy, assertive wines that can be a revelation in terms of embracing finesse and delineation, though I would caution that most (not all) need to establish a track record to prove their longevity. Pinot Noirs tend to be very patchy in quality, with the notable exception from Hamilton Russell.

Certainly South African white wines have improved immensely in recent years, particularly Loire-inspired Chenin Blancs and Sauvignon Blancs, which impart fewer herbaceous aromas and display greater purity on the palate. Rieslings have not been overly convincing since the climate is too warm, although the Viognier may hold greater prospects. There are some fine Ports being produced by the likes of Axe Hill and Boplaas.

[recent vintages]

2008
At the time of writing, the vintage is imminent. There was a cold, wet winter followed by an exceptionally cool growing season that has resulted in a late but healthy crop with lower potential alcohol than average.

2007
Mild temperatures were followed by a January heat wave. Some rain in early March precipitated some fungal problems, although it benefited botrytis-affected wines. Good potential.

2006
An uneven flowering due to high winds affected Syrah more than other grape varieties, but generally this should be an outstanding vintage, particularly for the white wines.

2005
A smaller crop than 2004, growers faced problems with mildew due to rain early in the growing season. A difficult growing season that tends to favor reds more than whites.

2004
Uneven fruit set did not prevent this from becoming one of South Africa's largest crops thanks to a long, unproblematic harvest.

2003
A healthy crop of outstanding quality.

2002
This very difficult vintage was hampered by the spread of fungal diseases and winter rains. The year is notable for many of the famous wineries declassifying their prestige labels.

—NEAL MARTIN

[the ratings]

SOUTH AFRICA'S BEST PRODUCERS

⋆ ⋆ ⋆ ⋆ ⋆ (OUTSTANDING)

Boekenhoutskloof

⋆ ⋆ ⋆ ⋆ (EXCELLENT)

Anwilka

Ataraxia Mountain Vineyards

Bouchard Finlayson

Capia

Hamilton Russell Vineyards

Jack & Knox Winecraft

Jean Daneel Wines

Meerlust Estate (Rubicon)

De Morgenzon

Neil Ellis Wines

Rustenberg (Peter Barlow)

Sadie Family Wines

Thelema Mountain Vineyards

Tulbagh Mountain Vineyards ⋆⋆⋆⋆/⋆⋆⋆⋆⋆

Vergelegen

⋆ ⋆ ⋆ (GOOD)

L'Avenir ⋆⋆⋆/⋆⋆⋆⋆

Beyerskloof

Bon Cap

Boschendal

Cape Chamonix

Cederberg ⋆⋆⋆/⋆⋆⋆⋆

Cloof Estate

De Trafford

Ernie Els Wines ⋆⋆⋆/⋆⋆⋆⋆

Fairview

The Foundry

Glen Carlou Vineyards

Hartenberg Estate

Iona Vineyards

Kanonkop

Klein Constantia

Lammershoek Winery

Luddite

Meerlust Estate

Mont du Toit

Morgenhof Estate

Morgenster Estate

Mulderbosch Vineyards

Nitida Cellars

Quoin Rock

Raka

Rustenberg

Sanctum

Saxenberg Wine Farm

Steenberg Vineyards

Veenwouden Private Cellar

Vilafonté

Warwick Estate

A quick glance at the following glossary will reveal that it does not contain all the wine-making terms that appear in the text. Nor does it contain terms that are specific to a region and are explained under the relevant geographic section. There are some terms, however, that are used throughout the text but without always being explained in context, and that are not commonly in dictionaries or whose dictionary definition might not be terribly helpful. This short glossary attempts to address those gaps. For basic, traditional French winemaking processes, much useful information is contained in the introduction and in the chapters on Bordeaux and Burgundy.

assemblage (n) French term for the process of assembling and judging the different lots of separately fermented wines from a single year's harvest or, in the case of nonvintage Champagne, from wines of numerous years, in order to decide which wines are of sufficient quality or desired flavor profile to be blended into the final wine.

ban de vendange (n) The official starting date of the harvest *(vendange)* in France, which is determined separately for each growing district. See also *vendange.*

bâtonnage (n) French term for the process of stirring usually white wine held in a barrel, vat, or other container after fermentation in order to disrupt the layer of yeast cells which has settled to the bottom. This has a number of effects, including the promotion of lees flavor in the wine, and an improved mouthfeel. See also *lees.*

biodynamic (adj) A method of organic agriculture, considered radical by some, which is based on the early-20th-century philosophy of Rudolf Steiner. Biodynamics treats the land as a living organism and sustains it based on conditions created by cosmic cycles.

Botrytis cinerea; "noble rot" (n) A grape mold that forms under favorable environmental conditions and causes desiccation of the berries, concentrating the grape sugars and lending a distinctive honeyed aroma to the resulting wine. Botrytis is essential to many of the world's renowned sweet white wines, including Sauternes, Tokaj aszú, and the *beerenauslese* and *trockenbeerenauslese* Rieslings of Germany. There is also an undesirable form, called gray rot.

Brettanomyces; "brett" (n) A natural yeast found on grapes and in the winery that can affect the flavor of wine to varying degrees. It is generally undesirable and its aroma in wine, often called "barnyard" or "horse," is considered a fault, although some tasters find that in small amounts it adds an appealing note to red wines.

cap (n) The grape solids, including skins, pulp, seeds, and any stems, that rise to the surface of the tank or vat during the fermentation process. Because contact between the juice and these solids contributes desirable flavor elements, color, and tannin to the wine, it is necessary to remix the solids into the juice below by one of various processes. See punching down / *pigeage; remuage* / pumping over.

carbonic maceration / *macération carbonique* (n) A process most widely used in Beaujolais. Whole grape clusters are placed in a vat or tank in which oxygen has been replaced by carbon dioxide gas, and fermentation is begun inside each berry, converting a small amount of grape sugar to alcohol. Wines made using this method are usually light-bodied, brightly colored, highly fruity, and low in tannin.

Cask and barrel sizes:

barrique French name for the small, 225-liter barrel used in Bordeaux; also used somewhat casually in Italy and elsewhere as a term to describe any small barrel.

demi-muid French name for the large, 600-liter barrel used in Australia, Châteauneuf-du-Pape, and Burgundy but growing in popularity.

foudre French name for the oval, large-capacity barrel used principally in Alsace, Germany, southern Rhône, and Italy.

Fuder German name for the large, 1000-liter barrel used in the Mosel.

tonneau French unit of wine volume equal to 900 liters (four *barriques*), the size of a large barrel of the same name that is no longer in use.

cépage (n) French word for "vine variety."

chaptalize (v) To add sugar to grape must before fermentation in order to increase the alcoholic strength of the finished wine. Chaptalization is a form of must enrichment, a term which also includes the use of concentrated grape juice and other nonsugar sweeteners. Chaptalization is regulated by winegrowing region, and is generally permitted only in cooler regions where the natural sugars of grapes may not reach sufficient levels during ripening.

chai, maître de chai (n) French term, used particularly in Bordeaux but often in California as well, for a building or hall used for maturing and storing wine. The *maître de chai* is the master responsible for the development of this wine. See *élevage.*

coulure (n) A condition shortly after flowering in which grape berries fail to develop and instead fall off the vine. It is often caused by cold, wet, or cloudy weather during flowering, and in severe instances can adversely affect crop size and grape and wine prices. Certain grape varieties are particularly susceptible.

délestage / rack and return (n) A method of aerating wine and extracting flavor from grape skins during fermentation, in which the fermenting juice is siphoned from beneath the cap and into a separate tank, then gently sprayed back over the top of the cap to trickle through to the bottom again.

dosage (n) A mixture of sugar and wine (called *liqueur d'expédition*) added to Champagne and sparkling wine after disgorgement or before bottling whose strength determines the final sweetness level of the wine, as described by the terms brut natur, extra-brut, brut, extra-dry, sec, and so forth on the bottle label.

dry-grown / dry-farmed (adj) Grown without use of irrigation, depending only on rainfall for water. Dry farming is taken for granted in areas (such as much of Europe) where irrigation is forbidden, but the term is used as an indicator of quality in areas where the practice is adopted by choice, as grapes grown without irrigation are often perceived as superior to irrigated fruit, despite the lack of evidence that irrigated vineyards cannot produce great wine when properly managed.

élevage (n) French term for "raising" or "rearing," used to describe collectively the processes of winemaking between the end of fermentation and bottling. In Bordeaux, much of the *élevage* is overseen by the *maître de chai*.

en primeur (adj) Sold in advance, as a future. Common in Bordeaux, *en primeur* sales begin in the spring following harvest, when barrels of young wine are available for sampling, and involve an early assessment of the quality of harvest and wine in order to weigh the potential future value of the wine against monies paid for it now. *En primeur* sales are a way for châteaux to have immediate income on wines not yet ready for release, and a way for brokers or, increasingly, consumers to pre-purchase a potentially valuable commodity at a lower initial price.

extract (n) The solid components of wine, including sugars, phenolics, some acids, minerals, glycerol, and proteins. Wines with high extract are often, but not always, perceived as full-bodied and full-flavored; these wines are sometimes described during tasting as "highly extracted."

fining (n) A process used before bottling to clarify and stabilize wine by adding an agent to cause certain elements, such as proteins, to cluster together for easy removal from the liquid by racking or filtering. Common fining agents include activated charcoal or carbon, bentonite clay, casein, egg whites, and gelatin.

fortified wines (n) A class of wines to which grape spirit is added during or after fermentation, resulting in a higher final alcoholic strength and, in some cases, residual sugar. Port, Sherry, Madeira, and *vins doux naturels* are fortified wines.

glycerine / glycerol (n) A by-product of fermentation that is slightly sweet but without color or aroma. It is commonly thought to contribute to the body or viscosity of wine, but in fact has little impact on all but the sweetest wines, in which its concentration is highest.

lees / *sur-lie* / on the lees Lees are the sediment resulting from fermentation, consisting mostly of dead yeast cells. Most red wines are separated from the lees immediately after fermentation, but for certain white wines and for Champagne or sparkling wine, it is desirable that the lees impart flavor to the wine. In this case, the wine is left to rest *sur-lie,* or on the lees, for a length of time determined by the winemaker. See also *bâtonnage; sur lattes.*

malolactic fermentation ("malo") (n) A bacterial (nonalcoholic) fermentation that is often encouraged after the initial, alcoholic fermentation to convert harsh malic acid in the wine into softer lactic acid. It is widely used for red wines, and can be encouraged or prevented in whites depending on the quality of the wine's existing acidity and fruit character, and whether the soft, sometimes buttery flavors that result from malolactic fermentation are desired.

méthode champenoise (n) Winemaking method used in the Champagne region of France which is distinguished by the second fermentation occurring in the wine's final bottle, trapping carbon dioxide inside to produce bubbles in the wine and necessitating a relatively laborious process of removing the yeast from the bottle which includes the practice of riddling. The less labor-intensive Charmat, *cuve close,* tank, or bulk method induces second fermentation in a pressurized tank before bottling. Many wines outside the Champagne region are made by *méthode champenoise,* but they must be labeled "traditional method," or "classic method" because of the regional exclusivity of the word *champenoise.* Within France, these wines are called *crémant,* such as Crémant de Bourgogne; outside France they include Spain's Cava, Italy's Franciacorta, and many other sparkling wines of the world. See also riddling.

microbullage / micro-oxygenation (n) A technique, originally used in Madiran in France, to introduce oxygen to red wine in a controlled fashion during or after fermentation, often for the purpose of softening tannins while stabilizing color.

millerandage (n) A condition caused by poor pollination that results in variation in the size of grape berries, with smaller, seedless berries forming in the same bunch as full-size berries. Severe millerandage can result in loss of yield, but some grape growers welcome limited millerandage as it is believed that small grapes yield better-quality wine.

must (n) The mixture of crushed grapes, including pulp, skins, seeds, and juice, that undergoes fermentation to make wine.

négociant (n) French term for an individual or firm that buys the grapes or wine of a number of growers and then vinifies or blends and bottles the wine for sale under separate label. It can also be a firm that buys a percentage of the production of an estate in bottle and then markets the wine to importers.

phenols / phenolics (n) A group of hundreds of chemical compounds present particularly in the skins, seeds, and stems of grapes, but also in oak barrels, which are responsible for color, tannins, and certain flavors in wine. During tasting, wines that are bitter or astringent are sometimes said to be phenolic.

punching down / *pigeage* (n) The process, during fermentation, of pushing the floating cap of grape solids down into the juice beneath to allow the juice controlled contact with oxygen and increase extraction of flavor, color, and tannin from the skins. Often used in conjunction with *remontage* / pumping over.

remontage / pumping over (n) The process, during fermentation, of circulating juice from beneath the floating cap of grape solids up and over the top, to allow controlled contact with oxygen and increase extraction of flavor, color, and tannin from the skins as the juice flows through the cap. Often used in conjunction with punching down / *pigeage*.

residual sugar / RS (n) Sugar that remains unfermented in the finished wine, measured as a percent or in g/l. Dry wines contain little or no residual sugar, the yeast having converted it to alcohol during fermentation. Semisweet or sweet wines can contain up to 30 percent RS due to the yeast being overcome by alcohol before converting all the sugar in a sweet must, or due to the addition of alcohol to stop the fermentation, as with fortified wines.

riddling / *remuage* (n) In the making of Champagne and sparkling wine using *méthode champenoise,* the process of twisting and tilting inverted wine bottles after second fermentation to slowly coax the dead yeast cells in the bottles to collect in the neck for disgorgement. Traditionally, the process takes place over six to eight weeks in tilted racks called *pupitres,* and is carried out by a skilled *remuer,* but it can also be accomplished in a matter of days by machine.

ripasso (adj) An Italian term meaning "repassed," for a method of making certain Valpolicella wines by fermenting them a second time on the skins of grapes left from the fermentation of Amarone. In theory, the remnants of the dried grapes used to make Amarone add complexity to the Valpolicella wine.

saignée (n) French term for a method of releasing a portion of free-run juice from crushed red wine grapes before fermentation, usually to increase the skin-to-juice ratio in the remaining must and thereby concentrate the color, flavor, and tannin of the resulting wine.

sélection massale (n) French term for mass selection, a method of vine propagation in which cuttings are taken from a number of different vines, as opposed to clonal selection, in which cuttings are taken from only a single, ideal vine. Done carefully, mass selection can promote variety in a vineyard without sacrificing vine performance.

solera method (n) A method of maturing wine, traditionally used for Sherry, that involves blending younger wines into older wines over time to increase complexity and maintain style consistency. The *solera* consists of groups of barrels, each containing progressively younger wine. When a percentage of wine is drawn from the oldest level of the *solera* for bottling, it is replaced with the next oldest wine from the next group of barrels, which is replaced with the next oldest wine, and so forth. The oldest wine in a *solera* may be more than 50 years old, depending on when the *solera* was started, and a fraction of wine from every year of the *solera* remains in the oldest level, increasing the complexity of the final wine over the life of the *solera*.

sur lattes A method used particularly in Champagne in which the bottles are stored on their sides in stacks, traditionally separated by laths or *lattes,* after second fermentation and before riddling and disgorgement, to allow complex flavors to develop in the wine due to its contact with the lees.

tannins (n) A group of substances most evident in red wine as an astringency or drying of the mouth, derived from the skins, seeds, and stems of grapes, as well as from the walls of oak barrels. Certain varieties of grapes have higher natural tannins, and certain winemaking processes can promote or inhibit strong tannins in wine. As wine ages in the bottle, tannins cluster together with proteins in the wine and fall to the bottom of the bottle as sediment, decreasing the astringency of the wine.

vendange (n) French term for "harvest." *Vendange tardive* is a term used in Alsace, meaning "late harvest," and refers to wine made from grapes picked later than usual with higher sugars and more-intense flavor. *Vendange entière* is a process whereby entire bunches of unbroken grapes, including stems, are put into the fermenting vessel. See also *ban de vendange.*

vieilles vignes (French) / *viñas viejas* (Spanish) / *vinhos viejos* (Portuguese) / *alte Rebe* (German) / *vecchie vigne* (Italian) (n, adj) French term meaning "old vines." Primarily in Europe, it is commonly believed that old vines produce superior wine of concentrated flavor, and for this reason the term is sometimes used as a marketing point on the bottle label. Vines may survive to 100 years of age or more, but there are no legal guidelines in any country as to the meaning of the term.

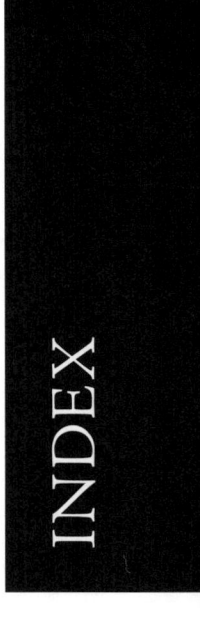

INDEX

Blanchet, Francis, 491
Blanck, Paul, 58
Blankiet Estate—Paradise Hills, 1126–27
Blauer Portugieser, 663
Blaufränkisch:
    in Austria, 652–53, 654, 665, 666, 667
    in Germany (Lemberger), 653, 725
    in Hungary (Kékfrankos), 653, 1425,
        1426, 1427
Blaufränkischland, 667
Blaye, 93
Bocquenet, Daniel, 302
Boede, Domaine de, 451
Boedecker Cellars, 1306
Boeger Winery, 1127
Boesch, Léon, 58
Boglietti, Enzo, 818
Boillot, Henri, Maison—Jean Boillot,
    302–03
Boillot, Jean, 304
Boillot, Jean-Marc, 304–05
Boillot, Louis, et Fils, 305
Boillot, Lucien, et Fils, 306
Bois de Boursan, Domaine, 565
Bois Dauphin, Domaine de, 565
Bois des Mèges, Domaine du, 566
Bois de St.-Jean, Domaine du, 566
Boisdauphin, Cuvée de, 566
Boisseyt-Chol, de, 566
Boisson, Domaine, 566
Bolaire, 130
Bolghieri, 863
Bollinger, 411
Bon Pasteur, Le, 130–31
Bonaccorsi, 1127
Bonalgue, 131
Bonarda, 1345
Bond, 1127–28
Bongiovanni, Cascina, 818
Bongran, Domaine de—Jean Thévenet,
    306
Bonneau, Henri, 566–67
Bonneau du Martray, Domaine, 306–07
Bonnefond, Patrick et Christophe, 567
Bonnet, 131
Bonnezeaux, 476
Bonny Doon Vineyard, 1128
Bonserine, Domaine de, 567–68
Booker Vineyard, 1128
books on wine, recommended, 35–37
Borba, 984

Bordeaux, 87–244
    aging potential of recent top vintages
        for finest wines of, 93
    best producers of Barsac/Sauternes
        in, 110–11
    best producers of dry red wine in
        (ratings), 106–09
    best producers of dry white wines in
        (ratings), 109
    best wine values in, 115
    best wines of 2001, 105–06
    best wines of 2002, 104
    best wines of 2003, 102
    best wines of 2004, 100
    best wines of 2005, 98–99
    best wines of 2006, 96
    buying wine futures for, 116–18
    food and wine matchups and, 15
    fraudulent bottles of, 26–29
    general flavor characteristics of
        major appellations in, 91–92
    map of, 138–39
    most important information to learn
        about, 93–94
    most important satellite appellations
        in, 92–93
    overall quality level of, 93
    recommended books on, 36–37
    red grape varieties in, 87–90
    rest of France's southwest in relation
        to, 420, 421
    secondary labels in, 111–15
    tasting commentaries for, 118–244
    vintage summaries for, 94–106
    white grape varieties in, 90–91
    see also specific appellations, growers,
        and producers
Bordeaux (Parker), 36–37
Bordeaux (generic), best wine values in,
    115
Bordeaux, The People, Power, and Politics
    (Brook), 36
Bordeaux Premières Côtes, 115
Borgo del Tiglio, 926
Borgogno, 818–19
Borie La Vitarelle, 451
Borro, Il, 880
Borsao, Bodegas, 1037
Bosca, Luigi, 1348
Boscarelli, 880
Boschis, Chiara, 846

Malvasia:
    in Central Europe, 1422, 1424
    in Spain, 1019
    in Tuscany, 864
Malvasia Fina, 961
Mambourg, 53
Mambrilla, Bodega Viña, 1052
Manchuela, 1022
Mann, Albert, 69–70
Mantlerhof, 685
Mantra, 1205–6
Manzone, Giovanni, 837–38
Manzone, Paolo, 838
Mapema, 1352
Mara Winery, 1206
Marbuzet, 208
Marc Ripoll Sans, Cellers, 1052
Marcarini, 838
Marcassin, 1206
Marchand, Jean, 612
Marchesi di Barolo, 838
Marchesi di Grésy, 838–39
Marcoux, Domaine de, 612–13
Mardon, Domaine, 503
Maremma, 866–67
Marengo, 839
Marestal, 428
Margaine, A., 415
Margalit, 1443, 1449
Margaret River, 1359
Margaux (appellation), 87
    aging potential of recent top vintages
        for finest wines of, 93
    best wine values in, 105
    general flavor characteristics of, 91
    vintage summaries for, 94–106
Margaux, Château, 27, 208–09
Margerum Wine Co., 1206–7
Marguery, 1352
Maria D. P. G. Serôdio de S. Borges, 972
Maria Gomes, 985, 998
Marietta Cellars, 1207
Mariflor, 1352
Marion, 932–33
Marionnet, Henry, 503
Maris, Domaine, 462
Marius, 1403
Marjosse, 209
Mark Ryan Winery, 1334
Markham, 1207
Marlborough, 1454

Marojallia, 209–10
Marqués de Vargas, 1052
Marquis d'Alesme Becker, 250
Marquis de Terme, 250
Marsannay, 262, 264, 275
Marsanne:
    in Australia, 1363, 1364
    in Languedoc and Roussillon, 436
    in Provence, 517
    in Rhône Valley, 524
Marsau, 210
Marston Family Vineyard, 1207–8
Martin and Wyrich, 1208
Martinelli, 1208–9
Martinens, 210
Martinetti, Franco M., 839
Martini, Louis M., 1209–10
Maryhill Winery, 1334
Maryland, 1287, 1289
Mas de l'Abundància, 1053
Mas Alta, 1053, 1054
Mas Amiel, Domaine, 448
Mas d'Auzières, 449
Mas de la Barben, 449
Mas Blanc, Domaine du, 450–51
Mas de Boislauzon, 613
Mas de Bressades, 451
Mas des Bressades, 613
Mas Carlot, 502, 613–14
Mas Champart, 453
Mas de la Deveze, 456
Mas Doix, Celler, 1053
Mas d'En Gil, 1053
Mas Gil, Celler, 1054
Mas Janeil, 460
Mas Jullien, 460–61
Mas Lumen, 462
Mas Martinet, 1054
Mas Morties, 463
Mas Neuf, Château, 614
Mas de les Pereres, 1054
Mas Romani (Mas Alta), 1054
Mas Sinen, 1054–55
Mascarello, Bartolo, 839–40
Mascarello, Giuseppe, 840–41
Masciarelli, 950
Masi Tupungato, 1353
Mason Cellars, 1210
Massa, La, 898
Massachusetts, 1290
Massamier la Mignarde, Domaine, 462–63

Sales, de, 234
Salette, Le, 936
Salicutti, 908–9
Salomon—Undhof, 693
Salon, 468
Salvioni, 909
Sämling, 666
Samsara, 1248
Samson, 1443
Samtrot, 725
San Alejandro, 1066
San Antonio Valley, 1432
San Esteban, 1440
San Fabiano, 909
San Giusto a Rentennano, 909–10
San Luigi, Podere, 903
San Patrignano, 953
San Vicente, Señorio de, 1066
Sancerre, 474, 483–84
Sanctus, 235
Sandeman, 1011, 1015
Sanders, Ronnie, 1365
Sandoval, Finca, 1047
Sandrone, Luciano, 853
Sang des Cailloux, Le, 636
Sangiovese:
    in California, 1081, 1103
    in Tuscany, 787, 862–63, 864–65, 866,
        867
Sangiovese Grosso, 862, 863
Sangioveto, 862
sanitary conditions, xix, 33
Sans Permis, 1248
Sansigot, 1422
Sansonnet, 235
Sant'Anastasia, 953–54
Sant'Antimo, 866
Santa Carolina, 1440
Santa Duc, Domaine, 636–37
Santa Ema, 1440
Santa Rita, 1440–41
Santadi, 953
Santenay, 263, 268–69, 277
Santenots, 268, 276
Santini, Enrico, 910
Saracco, 854
Sarda-Malet, Domaine, 469
Sardinia, 786–87
Sarga Muskotály, 1428
Saslove Winery, 1450
Sassetti, Livio—Pertimali, 910

Sassetti, Vasco, 910
Sassicaia, 865, 867
Sassotondo, 911
Sastre, Hermanos, Bodegas—Viña Sastre,
    1066
Satta, Michele, 911
Sattlerhof, 693
Sattui, V., 1249
Saumagen, 722
Saumur, 474, 476–78
    important information about, 478
    recent vintages of, 477–78
    what to expect from wines of, 526–27
Sausal, 1249
Saussignac, 421
Sauternes, 87, 115
    aging potential of recent top vintages
        for finest wines of, 93
    food and wine matchups and, 14–15
    general flavor characteristics of, 52
    rating best producers of, 110–11
    vintage summaries for, 94–106
    see also specific growers and producers
Sauvageonne, Domaine La, 469
Sauvignon Blanc:
    in Argentina, 1345
    in Australia, 1363, 1364, 1365, 1374
    in Austria, 652, 654, 659, 660, 661,
        665, 666, 668
    in Bordeaux, 90–91
    in California, 1077, 1083, 1085,
        1103–5
    in Central Europe, 1422, 1423, 1424,
        1425
    in Chile, 1432
    in Israel, 1445
    in Italy, 787, 805, 863
    in Languedoc and Roussillon, 436
    in Loire Valley, 474, 476, 481, 482,
        483–84
    in New Zealand, 1455, 1456, 1457
    in Provence, 517
    in South Africa, 1462, 1464
    in southwest of France, 421, 422
    in Spain, 1019
    in Washington State, 1321
Sauzet, Étienne, 385–86
Savennières, 476, 477
Savignin, 426, 428
Savigny-les-Beaune, 262
Savoie, 425, 426, 427–28

NOTES

NOTES

NOTES

NOTES

NOTES

NOTES

NOTES

NOTES

NOTES

NOTES

NOTES